W9-AVJ-341

RANDOM HOUSE
WEBSTER'S

Crossword
Puzzle
Dictionary

Third Edition

RANDOM HOUSE WEBSTER'S

Crossword Puzzle Dictionary

Third Edition

Random House
New York

Library of Congress Catalog Card Number: 98-67266

Visit the Random House Reference Web site at www.randomwords.com

Typeset and printed in the United States of America.

Third Edition
0 9 8 7 6 5 4
October 2001

ISBN 0-679-45856-5 (HC)
ISBN 0-375-70624-0 (PB)

New York Toronto London Sydney Auckland

Preface

Although various word games and puzzles have existed almost since the beginnings of language, the modern crossword puzzle is a 20th-century innovation. The first newspaper crossword appeared on December 21, 1913, in the *New York World,* and this new type of word puzzle quickly captured the public's fancy. Within a decade, crossword puzzles were featured in most American newspapers, and they soon became the rage in England as well. Since the 1920s, crossword puzzles have been a standard feature of daily newspapers and have proved enormously popular when collected in book form.

Now found in almost every language and in variations ranging from theme puzzles to diagramless puzzles, crosswords are available for almost any age and vocabulary level. Those who solve crossword puzzles invariably relish the challenge of completing a puzzle, of "getting it right." When faced with a clue they cannot answer, they resist "cheating"—looking at the puzzle's solution. One way out of this difficulty is to consult a reference work—just as the puzzle's creator may have done in finding words or crafting clues. Yet neither a dictionary nor an encyclopedia nor an almanac contains the necessary information in a useful, quick-reference format. A standard dictionary might give a few synonyms for a word, an encyclopedia would give information about countries or historical figures, and an almanac usually has information about sports figures or the Academy Awards, but only a crossword puzzle dictionary combines in one handy volume the information that might be found in all three. Equally important, it does so without extraneous information and with the convenience of an arrangement by the number of letters in each word, and it includes the many words that are common in crossword puzzles but too obscure to be in other references.

Random House Webster's Crossword Puzzle Dictionary, drawing on the resources of the Random House dictionaries and thesauruses, with research into a host of other topics, answers the need of crossword puzzlers for one single-purpose reference work. In addition to general vocabulary and synonyms, there are entries covering history; the natural and physical sciences; literature; music, painting, and other arts; religion; mythology; sports; popular culture; and current affairs, among others. Longer items provide easy-to-find detailed information on the continents and countries of the world, states of the United States, U.S. presidents, the months of the year, and other facts of special interest. This Third Edition has been fully updated, with special emphasis placed on the pop cultural questions that are now such an important part of puzzledom—sports teams, TV characters, even sneaker manufacturers.

While *Random House Webster's Crossword Puzzle Dictionary*'s primary purpose is to meet the needs of the growing numbers of people who find crosswords both relaxing and challenging, even a cursory glance will demonstrate the book's usefulness as a reference for trivia buffs. From who won the Academy Award for best actress in 1970 (Glenda Jackson) to the name of a coffee grown in Jamaica (Blue Mountain), it's all here.

Staff

Editor of Third Edition: Nancy Schuster
Project Editor: Jesse Sheidlower
Editor of First and Second Editions: Stephen P. Elliott/Sachem Publishing
  Associates
Editorial Staff: Jessica Erace, Michael Lewis
Contributors to Previous Editions: Julianne Arbo, Suzanne Stone Burke,
  Francine Esposito, Gretchen Ferrante, Jan Jamilkowski, Elizabeth Jewell,
  Rebecca Lyon, Julie E. Marsh, Blaine Merritt, Laurie Romanik, Christine
  Lindberg Stevens, and Diane Bell Surprenant
Database Manager: Constance A. Baboukis
Database Associate: Diane M. João
Managing Editor: Andrew Ambraziejus
Director of Production: Patricia W. Ehresmann
Editorial Director: Wendalyn Nichols
Associate Publisher: Page Edmunds
Publisher: Charles M. Levine

How To Use This Book

The main entries in *Random House Webster's Crossword Puzzle Dictionary* are words or phrases likely to appear as crossword puzzle clues. Each entry consists of a clue word or phrase and a list of answer words, arranged first by the number of letters in each word and then alphabetically. For example, if the main entry—**banal**—is the clue for a five-letter answer, the answer—"trite"—will be found alphabetically listed under the five-letter answer words. For phrases, such as **contracted form,** the answer could be "digest," "summary," or "synopsis." Entries may also contain indented subheads and secondary subheads. If, for instance, the clue is a phrase, like **cotton fabric,** the word **cotton** will be found as a main entry in the dictionary, and **fabric** will be found as a subhead under it, with such possible answer words as "terry," "poplin," and "gingham." In some cases, the answer can be found in more than one place. For example, if the clue is **Mexican coin,** the answer could be found by looking under the main entry **Mexico** and the subhead **monetary unit,** or by looking under the main entry **coin/currency** and the subhead **of Mexico.**

There are also cross references for alternate spellings and very closely related items. Many terms that do not have explicit cross references may still have valuable additional answers at related entries. The reader is encouraged to look up synonyms even when there is no explicit cross reference. To take one example, the clue **canine** has a short entry in this book, but **dog** has a much longer list that could be examined as well.

The main entries, subheads, secondary subheads, and numbers all appear in boldface type; the answer words are in regular roman type. Most punctuation and accent marks have been omitted, since they are not used in puzzle answers; occasionally, apostrophes and other marks have been included in answers to make them more readable.

RANDOM HOUSE WEBSTER'S

Crossword Puzzle Dictionary

Third Edition

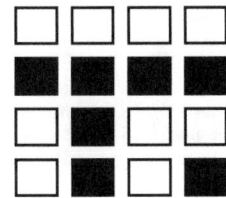

aardvark
also: 7 ant bear 8 anteater
native to: 6 Africa
food: 4 ants 8 termites
name comes from: 9 Africaans
    meaning: 8 earth hog, earth pig

Aaron
brother: 5 Moses
father: 5 Amram
mother: 8 Jochebed
sister: 6 Miriam
son: 5 Abihu, Nadab 7 Eleazar, Ithamar
wife: 8 Elisheba
successor: 7 Eleazar
Aaron's Rod 21 miraculously blossomed
    yielded: 7 almonds
deathplace: 3 Hor 8 Mount Hor
priestly descendant of: 8 Aaronite
set up: 10 golden calf

Aaron, Henry (Hank)
sport: 8 baseball
position: 10 outfielder
record: 8 homeruns
team: 13 Atlanta Braves 15 Milwaukee Braves 16 Milwaukee Brewers

Aaron's Rod 21 miraculously blossomed
    yielded: 7 almonds

Aatam see 4 Pima

Ab 16 fifth Hebrew month

Abaddon 4 hell 9 Appolyon

abaft 6 behind 11 to the rear of 12 to the stern of

Abagtha 6 eunuch
    served: 9 Ahasuerus

abandon 4 dash, drop, elan, jilt, junk, quit, stop 5 ardor, cease, forgo, gusto, leave, let go, scrap, verve, waive 6 desert, give up, spirit 7 discard, forfeit, forsake, freedom 8 abdicate, evacuate, forswear, get rid of, renounce, run out on 9 animation, cast aside, repudiate, surrender 10 depart from, enthusiasm, exuberance, relinquish, wantonness 11 discontinue, impetuosity, leave behind, spontaneity, unrestraint 12 immoderation, intemperance, recklessness, withdraw from 13 impulsiveness

abandoned 4 lewd, wild 5 loose 6 impure, jilted, sinful, vacant, wanton, wicked 7 debased, immoral 8 cast away, degraded, deserted, desolate, forsaken, marooned, rejected, un-

chaste 9 cast aside, debauched, discarded, dissolute, neglected, reprobate, shameless 10 dissipated, left behind, licentious, profligate, unoccupied 11 unrepentant 12 disreputable, incorrigible, irreformable, relinquished, unprincipled 13 irreclaimable

abandon oneself to 7 yield to 8 give in to, give up to 9 indulge in

Abaris
origin: 5 Greek
form: 4 sage

Abas
mentioned in: 5 Iliad
king of: 7 Argolis
father: 6 Celeus 7 Lynceus 9 Eurydamas
mother: 8 Metanira 12 Hypermnestra
wife: 6 Aglaia
son: 7 Proetus 8 Acrisius
daughter: 7 Idomene
changed into: 4 bird 6 lizard
mocked: 7 Demeter
protected by: 11 magic shield
companion: 8 Diomedes
killed by: 8 Diomedes

a bas 8 down with 11 to the bottom

abase 4 mock 5 shame 6 debase, defame, demean, humble, malign, vilify 7 cheapen, degrade, mortify, put down, vitiate 8 badmouth, belittle, besmirch, bring low, cast down, disgrace, dishonor 9 denigrate, devaluate, discredit, downgrade, humiliate 13 bring down a peg, cut down to size

abash 3 awe, cow 4 dash, faze 5 daunt 6 deject, dismay 7 depress 8 dispirit 9 discomfit, embarrass 10 discompose, disconcert, discourage, dishearten

abashed 3 shy 5 cowed, fazed 7 ashamed, bashful, crushed, daunted, humbled, subdued 8 confused, dismayed, overawed 9 chagrined, mortified 10 bewildered, confounded, humiliated, nonplussed, taken aback 11 dumbfounded, embarrassed, intimidated 12 disconcerted, disheartened 13 self-conscious

abate 3 ebb 4 cool, dull, ease, fade, slow, wane 5 allay, blunt, lower, quell, quiet, slack 6 dampen, go down, lessen, pacify, recede, reduce, soften, soothe, temper, weaken 7 assuage, curtail, decline, dwindle, fall

off, lighten, mollify, relieve, slacken, subside 8 decrease, diminish, fade away, fall away, mitigate, moderate, palliate, restrain, restrict, slack off, slow down, taper off 9 alleviate

Abba
means: 6 father
statesman: 4 Eban

abbey 6 cenoby, chapel, church, friary, priory 7 convent, nunnery 8 cloister, seminary 9 cathedral, hermitage, monastery

Abbott, Bud
real name: 14 William A Abbott
partner: 11 Lou Costello
born: 12 Asbury Park NJ
roles: 11 Who's on First 12 Buck Privates 13 Hold that Ghost 33 Abbott and Costello Meet Frankenstein

abbreviate 3 cut 4 clip, trim 6 reduce 7 abridge, curtail, cut down, shorten 8 boil down, compress, condense, contract, cut short, diminish, truncate 9 summarize, synopsize

abbreviated 5 brief, short 7 limited, summary 8 abridged 9 condensed, curtailed, shortened 10 compressed, summarized

abbreviation 5 brief 6 digest 7 cutting, pruning, summary 8 abstract, clipping, synopsis, trimming 9 lessening, reduction, short form 10 abridgment, diminution, shortening 11 abstraction, compression, contraction, curtailment, cut-down form, reduced form 12 condensation 13 condensed form, shortened form 14 compressed form, contracted form

abdicate 4 cede, quit 5 forgo, waive, yield 6 abjure, give up, resign 7 abandon 8 abnegate, renounce 9 surrender 10 relinquish 15 vacate the throne

abdomen 3 gut, pot 5 belly, tummy 6 paunch, venter 7 stomach 8 pot belly 9 bay window 11 breadbasket

abduct 5 seize, steal 6 kidnap 7 bear off 8 carry off, take away 10 run off with 11 make off with

Abduction from the Seraglio, The
also: 25 Die Entfuhrung aus dem Serail
opera by: 6 Mozart
character: 5 Osmin 6 Blonde 8 Belmonte, Pedrillo 9 Constanze 10 Pasha Selim

Abdul-Jabbar, Kareem
  formerly: **11** Lew Alcindor
  sport: **10** basketball
  position: **6** center
  team: **8** LA Lakers **10** UCLA Bruins
    14 Milwaukee Bucks **16** Los Angeles
    Lakers
  shot: **7** sky hook
Abednego
  companion: **6** Daniel
  friend: **8** Meschach, Shadrach
  former name: **7** Azariah
Abel
  father: **4** Adam
  mother: **3** Eve
  brother: **4** Cain, Seth
  killer: **4** Cain
Abel, Walter
  field: **9** film actor
Abe Lincoln in Illinois
  author: **14** Robert Sherwood
  director: **12** John Cromwell
  cast: **10** Alan Baxter, Mary Howard,
    Ruth Gordon (Mary Todd Lincoln)
    11 Dorothy Tree, Minor Watson **12**
    Gene Lockhart **13** Howard da Silva,
    Raymond Massey (Abraham Lincoln)
aberrant 3 odd **7** unusual **8** abnormal,
  atypical, peculiar, uncommon **9**
  anomalous, eccentric, irregular
aberration 5 lapse, quirk **6** lunacy,
  oddity **7** anomaly, madness **8** delusion, illusion, insanity, mutation, rambling, straying **9** aberrance, aberrancy,
  curiosity, departure, deviation, exception, wandering **10** digression, distortion, divergence **11** abnormality, derangement, incongruity, mental lapse,
  peculiarity, singularity, strangeness
abet 3 aid **4** back, goad, help, spur,
  urge **5** egg on **6** assist, incite, lead on,
  second, uphold, urge on **7** advance,
  endorse, promote, support, sustain **8**
  advocate, join with, sanction **9** encourage, instigate
abettor 4 ally **6** cohort **7** partner **9** accessory, associate, colleague **10** accomplice **11** confederate **12** collaborator
abeyance 5 delay, on ice, pause **6** hiatus, recess **7** latency **8** deferral, dormancy, inaction **9** cessation, remission **10** quiescence, suspension **11**
  adjournment **12** intermission, postponement **13** in cold storage, on a
  back burner, waiting period **14** discontinuance
abhor 4 hate, shun **5** scorn **6** detest,
  eschew, loathe **7** despise, disdain, dislike **8** execrate, recoil at **9** abominate,
  can't stand, shudder at **10** shrink
  from **11** can't stomach **12** be revolted
  by **13** be nauseated by, find repulsive
abhorrence 4 hate **5** odium, scorn **6**
  hatred **7** disdain, disgust, dislike **8**
  aversion, contempt, distaste, loathing

9 antipathy, revulsion **10** repugnance
  11 abomination
abhorrent 4 foul, vile **6** odious **7**
  hateful **8** accursed **9** execrable, loathsome, repellent, repugnant, repulsive,
  revolting **10** abominable, despicable,
  disgusting, nauseating
abide 3 sit **4** bear, last, live, stay, stop
  5 brook, dwell, stand, tarry, visit **6**
  accept, endure, linger, remain, reside,
  suffer **7** sojourn, stomach **8** stand for,
  submit to, tolerate
abide by 4 obey **6** follow **8** accede to,
  adhere to, submit to **9** conform to **10**
  comply with **11** go along with
abiding 4 fast, firm **6** steady **7** durable, eternal, lasting **8** constant, enduring, unending **9** immutable, permanent, steadfast **10** changeless,
  continuing, unchanging, unshakable
  11 everlasting **12** indissoluble, wholehearted **13** unquestioning
Abidjan
  capital of: **10** Ivory Coast
Abigail
  husband: **5** David, Nabal
  brother: **5** David
Abihu
  father: **5** Aaron
  mother: **8** Elisheba
  brother: **5** Nadab **7** Eleazar, Ithamar
  killed with: **5** Nadab
  accompanied to Mt Sinai: **5** Moses
Abijah
  father: **8** Rehoboam
  grandfather: **7** Solomon
  grandmother: **6** Naamah
ability 4 bent, gift **5** flair, knack,
  power, skill **6** acumen, genius, talent
  7 faculty, knowhow, mind for **8** aptitude, capacity, facility **9** adeptness,
  expertise, potential **10** adroitness, capability, competence **11** proficiency
  12 potentiality **13** qualification
Abimelech
  king of: **5** Gerar
  means: **15** the father is king
  father: **6** Gideon **8** Abiathar
  brother: **6** Jotham
  army commander: **7** Phichol
Abinoam
  father: **4** Saul
  son: **5** Barak
abject 3 low **4** base, mean, vile **6** sordid **7** ignoble **8** complete, cringing,
  hopeless, horrible, terrible, thorough,
  wretched **9** groveling, miserable **10**
  deplorable, despicable, spiritless **11**
  inescapable **12** contemptible
abjure 6 desert, give up, recant, reject
  7 abandon, disavow **8** disallow, disclaim, forswear, renounce **9** repudiate
  10 relinquish
ablaze 5 afire, eager, fiery **6** aflame,
  alight, ardent, fervid, on fire, red-hot
  7 blazing, burning, excited, fervent,
  flaming, flushed, glowing, ignited,

zealous **8** feverish, hopped-up, in
  flames, turned-on **10** passionate,
  switched-on **11** conflagrant, impassioned, intoxicated
able 3 apt, fit **4** good **5** adept **6** adroit,
  expert, fitted **7** capable, equal to,
  learned **8** adequate, skillful, talented
  9 competent, effective, efficient, masterful, practiced, qualified **10** proficient **11** experienced **12** accomplished
able-bodied 5 beefy, hardy, husky,
  lusty, thewy **6** brawny, hearty, robust,
  rugged, strong, sturdy **8** athletic, muscular, powerful, stalwart, vigorous **9**
  herculean, strapping, well-built **15**
  broad-shouldered
ablution 4 bath, wash **7** bathing,
  washing **8** cleaning, lavation **9** cleansing **12** purification **13** ritual washing
Abnaki (Wabanaki)
  language family: **9** Algonkian **10** Al-
    gonquian
  tribe: **6** Micmac **8** Malecite **9** Penob-
    scot **13** Norridegewock, Passama-
    quoddy
  location: **5** Maine **6** Canada, Quebec
    7 Old Town **9** Norumbega **10** New
    England **12** New Brunswick
abnegate 5 forgo, waive **6** abjure, eschew, give up, refuse **7** abstain, forbear **8** renounce **9** repudiate **10** relinquish **11** deny oneself
abnegation 7 refusal **8** eschewal, giving up **9** rejection, sacrifice, surrender
  10 abstinence, continence, forbearing,
  self-denial, temperance **11** forbearance, resignation **12** renunciation **14**
  relinquishment
Abner
  commanded: **9** Saul's army
  father: **3** Ner
  cousin: **4** Saul
abnormal 3 odd **4** rare **5** queer, weird
  7 bizarre, curious, deviant, strange,
  unusual **8** aberrant, atypical, deformed, freakish, peculiar, uncommon
  9 anomalous, eccentric, grotesque, irregular, monstrous, unheard of, unnatural **10** inordinate, outlandish, unexpected **11** exceptional **12**
  unaccustomed **13** extraordinary **14**
  unconventional
abnormality 6 oddity **7** anomaly **9**
  aberrance, curiosity, deformity, deviation **10** aberration, perversion **11** peculiarity **12** eccentricity, idiosyncrasy,
  irregularity, malformation, unconformity
abode 3 pad **4** home, nest **5** house **7**
  address, habitat, lodging **8** domicile,
  dwelling **9** residence **10** habitation **13**
  dwelling place **14** living quarters
abolish 3 end **5** annul, erase, quash **6**
  cancel, repeal, revoke **7** blot out, nullify, rescind, squelch, vitiate, wipe out
  8 abrogate, set aside, stamp out **9**
  eliminate, eradicate, extirpate, repudi-

ate, terminate **10** annihilate, do away with, extinguish, invalidate, obliterate, put an end to **11** exterminate **18** declare null and void

abolition 6 ending, repeal **9** annulment, vitiation **10** abrogation, extinction, rescinding, retraction, revocation **11** abolishment, dissolution, elimination, eradication, recantation, repudiation, termination **12** cancellation, invalidation **13** nullification

abominable 4 base, evil, foul, vile **5** awful, lousy **6** cursed, horrid, odious **7** hateful, heinous, hellish **8** accursed, damnable, horrible, infamous, terrible, wretched **9** abhorrent, atrocious, execrable, loathsome, miserable, repellent, repugnant, repulsive, revolting **10** deplorable, despicable, detestable, disgusting, unsuitable, villainous **11** ignominious **12** contemptible, disagreeable **13** reprehensible

abominate 4 hate **5** abhor, scorn **6** detest, loathe **7** despise **8** execrate **9** can't stand **10** recoil from, shrink from **11** can't stomach **12** be revolted by **13** find repugnant, find repulsive

abomination 4 evil, hate **6** hatred, horror, plague **7** bugbear, disgust, torment **8** anathema, aversion, disgrace, loathing **9** annoyance, antipathy, bete noire, obscenity, revulsion **10** abhorrence, affliction, defilement, repugnance **11** detestation

aboriginal 5 first, prime **6** native **7** ancient, endemic, primary **8** earliest, original, primeval **9** primitive **10** indigenous, primordial **13** autochthonous

aborigine 6 native **16** indigenous person **18** original inhabitant **19** primitive inhabitant

abort 3 end **4** fail, halt, stop **7** call off **8** miscarry **9** terminate

abortion 6 ending, fiasco **7** failure, halting **8** disaster **10** calling off **11** miscarriage, termination **16** fruitless attempt **19** unsuccessful attempt

abortive 4 vain **6** futile **7** sterile, useless **8** bootless **9** fruitless, nonviable, worthless **10** profitless, unavailing, unfruitful **11** ineffective, ineffectual, unrewarding **12** unproductive, unprofitable, unsuccessful **13** inefficacious

abound 4 gush, teem **5** swarm **6** thrive **7** run wild **8** be filled, be rich in, flourish, overflow **9** be flooded, luxuriate, spill over **10** be numerous **11** be plentiful, superabound, proliferate

abounding 4 rich, rife **5** ample **6** lavish, plenty **7** profuse, replete, teeming **8** abundant, brimming, swarming **9** bounteous, bountiful **11** overflowing, running over **14** more than enough

about 2 in, of, on **4** inre, near **5** astir, circa **6** abroad, almost, around, cir-

cum, nearby, nearly **7** close to **9** proximate, regarding **10** concerning, in regard to **13** approximately

about-face 5 shift **6** switch **7** reverse **8** reversal **9** disavowal, turnabout, volte-face **10** retraction, rightabout, turnaround **11** recantation **13** change of heart **14** tergiversation

above 4 atop, over **5** aloft, north, supra **6** before, beyond, dorsal, excess, heaven, higher **7** earlier **8** in heaven, overhead, superior, upstairs **9** exceeding **10** surpassing

aboveboard 4 just, open **5** blunt, frank, legal, legit, licit, moral, overt, plain **6** candid, direct, honest, public, square **7** artless, ethical, sincere, upright **8** revealed, straight, truthful, virtuous **9** disclosed, guileless, ingenuous, righteous **10** forthright, foursquare **11** unconcealed **12** on the up and up, plain-dealing, out in the open **13** square-dealing, undissembling **15** straightforward **16** straight-shooting

ab ovo 10 from the egg **16** from the beginning

abracadabra 5 charm, magic, spell **6** voodoo **7** sorcery **8** exorcism **10** hocus-pocus, invocation, magic spell, mumbo-jumbo, open sesame, witchcraft **11** incantation

abrade 3 rub **4** file, fray, sand **5** chafe, erode, grate, scour, scuff **6** scrape **7** scratch

Abraham
   former name: **5** Abram
   founded: **12** Hebrew nation
   father: **5** Terah
   wife: **5** Sarah, Sarai **7** Keturah
   brother: **5** Haran, Nahor
   son: **5** Isaac **6** Midian **7** Ishmael
   nephew: **3** Lot
   birthplace: **15** Ur of the Chaldees
   received: **17** law of circumcision
   sacrificed Isaac at: **6** Moriah
   burial place: **6** Hebron
   tomb in: **9** Machpelah

Abraham Lincoln
   author: **12** Carl Sandburg

Abraham's bosom 6 heaven

Abram see **7** Abraham

Abrams, Creighton
   served in: **4** WWII **10** Vietnam War
   rank: **16** army chief of staff

abrasive 4 harsh, nasty, rough, sharp **6** biting, coarse **7** caustic, chafing, cutting, galling, grating, hurtful, rasping **8** annoying **10** irritating **11** excoriating **16** grinding material, scouring material, scraping material

abreast 6 in rank **7** aligned **8** arm in arm **10** side by side **11** in alignment

abridge 3 cut **4** trim **5** limit **6** digest, lessen, reduce **7** curtail, cut down, shorten **8** compress, condense, decrease, diminish, pare down, restrict,

take away, truncate **9** scale down, telescope **10** abbreviate

abridgment 6 digest **8** decrease **9** lessening, reduction, restraint **10** diminution, limitation, truncation **11** curtailment, diminishing, restriction **12** abbreviation, condensation

abroad 3 out **4** rife **5** astir, forth **7** at large, outside **8** overseas **9** all around **10** out of doors **13** in circulation, out of the house, round and about **15** making the rounds, out in the open air, out of the country

abrogate 3 end **4** junk, undo, void **5** annul, quash **6** abjure, cancel, negate, recall, repeal, revoke **7** abolish, nullify, rescind, retract, reverse, vitiate **8** dissolve, override, renounce, set aside, throw out, withdraw **9** repudiate, terminate **10** do away with, invalidate, put an end to **11** countermand

abrupt 4 curt, rude **5** blunt, brisk, crisp, gruff, hasty, quick, rapid, rough, sharp, sheer, short, steep, swift **6** sudden, brusque, uncivil **8** impolite **9** impulsive **10** unexpected, unforeseen, ungracious **11** precipitate, precipitous, unannounced, unlooked for **12** discourteous **13** instantaneous, unanticipated, unceremonious

Absalom
   father: **5** David
   mother: **6** Maacah
   half-sister: **5** Tamar
   brother: **7** Solomon **8** Adonijah
   half-brother: **5** Amnon
   defeated at: **6** Gilead
   killed by: **4** Joab

Absalom, Absalom!
   author: **15** William Faulkner
   character: **5** Henry **6** Judith **10** Charles Bon **13** Rosa Coldfield **14** Quentin Compson, Shreve McCannon **16** Goodhue Coldfield **19** Colonel Thomas Sutpen **20** Ellen Coldfield Sutpen

Absalom and Achitophel
   author: **10** John Dryden

abscond 3 fly **4** flee, skip **5** split **6** escape, run off, vanish **7** make off, run away, take off **8** steal off **9** disappear, steal away **10** take flight

absence 3 cut **4** lack, want **6** dearth **7** truancy **8** scarcity **10** deficiency, scantiness **11** absenteeism, nonpresence

absent 3 cut, out **4** away, AWOL, gone **5** blank, empty, vague **6** dreamy, musing, truant, vacant **7** faraway, missing, out of it, removed, unaware **8** heedless, keep away, stay away, tuned out **9** not appear, not show up, oblivious **10** distracted, nonpresent, not present, out to lunch, play truant, unthinking **11** inattentive, preoccupied, unconscious **12** nonattendant

absentee 6 no show, truant **10** nonpresent **11** nonattendee, nonpresence **12** nonattendant **13** nonattendance

absenteeism 5 hooky **7** truancy **11** nonpresence **13** nonappearance **19** absence without cause

absent-minded 5 blank, vague **6** dreamy **9** oblivious **10** abstracted, distracted **11** preoccupied **14** out in left field **17** out of it

Absent Without Leave
author: **12** Heinrich Boll

absinthe
ingredient: **8** licorice, wormwood **9** aromatics, star anise
color: **11** yellow green
substitute: **4** Ouzo **6** Pastis, Pernod **8** Anisette

absolute 4 full, pure, real, sure **5** sheer, total, utter **7** certain, genuine, perfect, supreme **8** complete, decisive, definite, outright, positive, reliable, thorough **9** confirmed, out-and-out, unbounded, unlimited **10** conclusive, consummate, infallible, undeniable

Absolute, Sir Anthony
character in: **9** The Rivals
author: **8** Sheridan

absolutely 3 yes **4** sure **5** truly **6** indeed, really, wholly **7** utterly **8** entirely **9** certainly, decidedly **10** completely, definitely, positively, thoroughly **11** indubitably, undoubtedly

absolution 5 mercy **6** pardon **7** amnesty, release **9** acquittal, clearance, quittance, remission **10** indulgence, liberation **11** deliverance, exculpation, exoneration, forgiveness, vindication **12** dispensation

absolve 4 free **5** clear, loose **6** acquit, exempt, pardon, shrive **7** deliver, forgive, release, set free **9** discharge, exculpate, exonerate, vindicate **10** excuse from **13** find not guilty, judge innocent

absolved 5 freed **6** exempt, spared **7** cleared, excused **8** forgiven, innocent, not guilty, pardoned, released, relieved **9** acquitted **10** discharged, exonerated, vindicated **13** found innocent

absorb 3 fix, get **5** grasp, rivet, sop up **6** arrest, digest, engage, enwrap, ingest, occupy, soak up, suck up, take up **7** consume, drink in, engross, immerse **8** sponge up **9** fascinate, preoccupy, swallow up **10** assimilate, understand **11** incorporate

absorbed 4 deep, rapt **8** immersed, involved, soaked up, sucked up **9** blotted up, engrossed

absorbent 6 porous, spongy **7** osmotic, thirsty **8** bibulous, pervious **9** permeable **10** absorptive, penetrable **12** assimilative

absorbing 8 engaging, exciting **9**

thrilling **10** engrossing, intriguing **11** captivating, fascinating, interesting

abstain 5 avoid, forgo **6** desist, eschew, refuse, resist **7** decline, forbear, refrain

abstainer 3 dry **7** ascetic **10** nondrinker, self-denier, teetotaler

abstemious 3 dry **5** sober **7** ascetic, austere, sparing, spartan **8** teetotal **9** abstinent, continent, temperate **10** forbearing **11** abstentious, self-denying, straitlaced, teetotaling **12** nonindulgent **15** self-disciplined

abstention 7 refusal **8** eschewal **9** avoidance, desisting, eschewing **10** abstaining, refraining, resistance **11** forbearance, holding back **13** nonindulgence **14** denying oneself **16** nonparticipation

abstinence 8 chastity, sobriety **10** abstention, continence, discipline, self-denial, temperance **11** forbearance, self-control **13** nonindulgence, self-restraint

abstinent 3 dry **5** sober **6** chaste **8** celibate, virginal **9** continent **10** abstemious, forbearing

abstract 4 take **5** brief **6** arcane, digest, precis, remote, remove, resume, subtle **7** abridge, extract, general, isolate, obscure, outline, summary, take out **8** abstruse, compress, condense, esoteric, profound, separate, synopsis, withdraw **9** imaginary, recondite, summarize, synopsize, theoretic, unapplied, visionary **10** abridgment, conceptual, dissociate, indefinite, intangible **11** generalized, impractical, nonspecific, theoretical **12** condensation, hypothetical, intellectual **14** recapitulation

abstruse 4 deep **6** arcane, remote, subtle **7** complex, obscure **8** abstract, esoteric, profound, puzzling **9** enigmatic, recondite **10** perplexing **11** complicated **12** unfathomable **16** incomprehensible

absurd 4 wild **5** crazy, funny, inane, kooky, silly **6** screwy, stupid **7** asinine, comical, foolish, idiotic **8** farcical **9** illogical, laughable, ludicrous, senseless **10** irrational, ridiculous **11** nonsensical **12** preposterous, unreasonable

absurdity 6 drivel, idiocy **7** fallacy, inanity **8** delusion, nonsense **9** asininity, falsehood, silliness **10** buffoonery **11** comicalness, foolishness **13** irrationality **14** ridiculousness **15** unbelievability **16** unreasonableness

Absyrtus see **8** Apsyrtus

Abu Dhabi
capital of: **18** United Arab Emirates

Abuja
capital of: **7** Nigeria

abundance 4 glut, heap **5** flood **6** bounty, excess, plenty, wealth **7** sur-

feit, surplus **8** plethora, richness **9** plenitude, profusion, repletion **10** cornucopia **11** copiousness, full measure, sufficiency

abundant 4 rich, rife **5** ample **6** enough, galore, lavish, plenty **7** copious, profuse, replete, teeming **8** brimming, prolific **9** abounding, bounteous, bountiful, luxuriant **10** sufficient

ab urbe condita 24 from the founding of the city

abuse 4 harm, hurt, slur **5** curse, scold **6** berate, carp at, defame, deride, illuse, injure, injury, insult, malign, misuse, rail at, revile, tirade, vilify **7** assault, bawl out, beating, carping, censure, cruelty, cursing, exploit, harming, insults, railing, slander, torment, upbraid **8** badmouth, belittle, berating, denounce, derision, diatribe, ill-treat, maltreat, mistreat, reproach, ridicule, scolding, sneering, torments **9** castigate, criticism, criticize, denigrate, disparage, excoriate, invective **10** belittling, defamation, impose upon, imposition, oppression, speak ill of, upbraiding **11** castigation **12** exploitation, maltreatment, mistreatment, vilification **13** disparagement, misemployment, tongue-lashing **14** inveigh against, misapplication **15** take advantage of

abusive 4 rude, vile **5** cruel, gross, harsh **7** harmful, hurtful, obscene **8** critical, improper, reviling, scornful **9** injurious, insulting, maligning, offensive, vilifying **10** censorious, defamatory, derogatory, scurrilous, slanderous **11** acrimonious, castigating, deprecatory, disparaging, foulmouthed **12** vituperative

abusive word 5 curse **6** insult **7** epithet **9** blasphemy, expletive, invective, obscenity

abut 4 join, meet **5** touch **6** adjoin, border

abutment 4 prop, stay **5** brace, union **7** contact, meeting, support **8** buttress, junction, shoulder, touching **9** adjacency

abutting 6 next to **7** joining, meeting **8** adjacent, touching **9** bordering **10** contiguous, juxtaposed **12** conterminous

abysmal 4 deep, vast **7** endless, extreme, immense **8** complete, enormous, profound, thorough, unending **9** boundless **10** bottomless, incredible, stupendous **12** unfathomable, unbelievable, unimaginable

abyss 4 gulf, void **5** depth, gorge, gully, nadir **7** fissure **8** crevasse **9** vast chasm **13** bottomless pit

Abyssinia see **8** Ethiopia

Acacallis
father: **5** Minos

mother: 8 Pasiphae
son: 11 Amphithemis
acacia 9 gum arabic
also called: 5 thorn **6** mimosa, wattle
academic 4 moot **6** remote, school **7**
bookish, erudite, general, learned **8**
abstract, educated, pedantic, studious
9 scholarly **10** collegiate, scholastic,
university **11** conjectural, educational,
liberal-arts, presumptive, speculative,
theoretical **12** hypothetical, ivory-
towered, nontechnical, not practical
13 nonvocational, suppositional **14**
nonspecialized **18** college-preparatory
Academus
origin: 8 Arcadian
owned: 6 estate
located in: 6 Athens
served as meeting place for: 12
philosophers
Academy Award
also called: 5 Oscar
1927-28:
actor: 12 Emil Jannings
actress: 11 Janet Gaynor
director: 12 Frank Borzage **14**
Lewis Milestone
picture: 5 Wings
1928-29:
actor: 12 Warner Baxter
actress: 12 Mary Pickford
director: 10 Frank Lloyd
picture: 14 Broadway Melody
1929-30:
actor: 12 George Arliss
actress: 12 Norma Shearer
director: 14 Lewis Milestone
picture: 25 All Quiet on the Western Front
1930-31:
actor: 15 Lionel Barrymore
actress: 13 Marie Dressler
director: 12 Norman Taurog
picture: 8 Cimarron
1931-32:
actor: 12 Fredric March
actress: 10 Helen Hayes
director: 12 Frank Borzage
picture: 10 Grand Hotel
1932-33:
actor: 15 Charles Laughton
actress: 16 Katharine Hepburn
director: 10 Frank Lloyd
picture: 9 Cavalcade
1934:
actor: 10 Clark Gable
actress: 16 Claudette Colbert
director: 10 Frank Capra
picture: 18 It Happened One Night
1935:
actor: 14 Victor McLaglen
actress: 10 Bette Davis
director: 8 John Ford
picture: 17 Mutiny on the Bounty
1936:
actor: 8 Paul Muni
actress: 11 Luise Rainer
director: 10 Frank Capra

picture: 16 The Great Ziegfeld
1937:
actor: 12 Spencer Tracy
actress: 11 Luise Rainer
director: 10 Leo McCarey
picture: 15 Life of Emile Zola
1938:
actor: 12 Spencer Tracy
actress: 10 Bette Davis
director: 10 Frank Capra
picture: 20 You Can't Take It with
You
1939:
actor: 11 Robert Donat
actress: 11 Vivien Leigh
director: 13 Victor Fleming
picture: 15 Gone with the Wind
1940:
actor: 12 James Stewart
actress: 12 Ginger Rogers
director: 8 John Ford
picture: 7 Rebecca
1941:
actor: 10 Gary Cooper
actress: 12 Joan Fontaine
director: 8 John Ford
picture: 19 How Green Was My
Valley
1942:
actor: 11 James Cagney
actress: 11 Greer Garson
director: 12 William Wyler
picture: 10 Mrs Miniver
1943:
actor: 9 Paul Lukas
actress: 13 Jennifer Jones
director: 13 Michael Curtiz
picture: 10 Casablanca
1944:
actor: 10 Bing Crosby
actress: 13 Ingrid Bergman
director: 10 Leo McCarey
picture: 10 Going My Way
1945:
actor: 10 Ray Milland
actress: 12 Joan Crawford
director: 11 Billy Wilder
picture: 14 The Lost Weekend
1946:
actor: 12 Fredric March
actress: 17 Olivia de Havilland
director: 10 William Wyler
picture: 22 The Best Years of Our
Lives
1947:
actor: 12 Ronald Colman
actress: 12 Loretta Young
director: 9 Elia Kazan
picture: 19 Gentleman's Agreement
1948:
actor: 15 Laurence Olivier
actress: 9 Jane Wyman
director: 10 John Huston
picture: 6 Hamlet
1949:
actor: 17 Broderick Crawford
actress: 17 Olivia de Havilland
director: 17 Joseph L Mankiewicz

picture: 14 All the King's Men
1950:
actor: 10 Jose Ferrer
actress: 12 Judy Holliday
director: 17 Joseph L Mankiewicz
picture: 11 All About Eve
1951:
actor: 14 Humphrey Bogart
actress: 11 Vivien Leigh
director: 13 George Stevens
picture: 17 An American in Paris
1952:
actor: 10 Gary Cooper
actress: 12 Shirley Booth
director: 8 John Ford
picture: 19 Greatest Show on Earth
1953:
actor: 13 William Holden
actress: 13 Audrey Hepburn
director: 13 Fred Zinnemann
picture: 18 From Here to Eternity
1954:
actor: 12 Marlon Brando
actress: 10 Grace Kelly
director: 9 Elia Kazan
picture: 15 On the Waterfront
1955:
actor: 14 Ernest Borgnine
actress: 11 Anna Magnani
director: 11 Delbert Mann
picture: 5 Marty
1956:
actor: 10 Yul Brynner
actress: 13 Ingrid Bergman
director: 13 George Stevens
picture: 26 Around the World in
Eighty Days
1957:
actor: 12 Alec Guinness
actress: 14 Joanne Woodward
director: 9 David Lean
picture: 23 The Bridge on the River
Kwai
1958:
actor: 10 David Niven
actress: 12 Susan Hayward
director: 16 Vincente Minnelli
picture: 4 Gigi
1959:
actor: 14 Charlton Heston
actress: 14 Simone Signoret
director: 12 William Wyler
picture: 6 Ben-Hur
1960:
actor: 13 Burt Lancaster
actress: 15 Elizabeth Taylor
director: 11 Billy Wilder
picture: 12 The Apartment
1961:
actor: 16 Maximilian Schell
actress: 11 Sophia Loren
director: 10 Robert Wise **13** Jerome
Robbins
picture: 13 West Side Story
1962:
actor: 11 Gregory Peck
actress: 12 Anne Bancroft
director: 9 David Lean

picture: 16 Lawrence of Arabia
1963:
  actor: 13 Sidney Poitier
  actress: 12 Patricia Neal
  director: 14 Tony Richardson
  picture: 8 Tom Jones
1964:
  actor: 11 Rex Harrison
  actress: 12 Julie Andrews
  director: 11 George Cukor
  picture: 10 My Fair Lady
1965:
  actor: 9 Lee Marvin
  actress: 13 Julie Christie
  director: 10 Robert Wise
  picture: 15 The Sound of Music
1966:
  actor: 12 Paul Scofield
  actress: 15 Elizabeth Taylor
  director: 13 Fred Zinnemann
  picture: 17 A Man for All Seasons
1967:
  actor: 10 Rod Steiger
  actress: 16 Katharine Hepburn
  director: 11 Mike Nichols
  picture: 19 In the Heat of the Night
1968:
  actor: 14 Cliff Robertson
  actress: 15 Barbra Streisand 16
  Katharine Hepburn
  director: 12 Sir Carol Reed
  picture: 6 Oliver!
1969:
  actor: 9 John Wayne
  actress: 11 Maggie Smith
  director: 15 John Schlesinger
  picture: 14 Midnight Cowboy
1970:
  actor: 12 George C Scott
  actress: 13 Glenda Jackson
  director: 17 Franklin Schaffner
  picture: 6 Patton
1971:
  actor: 11 Gene Hackman
  actress: 9 Jane Fonda
  director: 15 William Friedkin
  picture: 19 The French Connection
1972:
  actor: 12 Marlon Brando
  actress: 11 Liza Minnelli
  director: 8 Bob Fosse
  picture: 12 The Godfather
1973:
  actor: 10 Jack Lemmon
  actress: 13 Glenda Jackson
  director: 13 George Roy Hill
  picture: 8 The Sting
1974:
  actor: 9 Art Carney
  actress: 12 Ellen Burstyn
  director: 18 Francis Ford Coppola
  picture: 12 The Godfather (Part II)
1975:
  actor: 13 Jack Nicholson
  actress: 14 Louise Fletcher
  director: 11 Milos Forman
  picture: 25 One Flew Over the
  Cuckoo's Nest

1976:
  actor: 10 Peter Finch
  actress: 11 Faye Dunaway
  director: 13 John G Avildsen
  picture: 5 Rocky
1977:
  actor: 15 Richard Dreyfuss
  actress: 11 Diane Keaton
  director: 10 Woody Allen
  picture: 9 Annie Hall
1978:
  actor: 9 Jon Voight
  actress: 9 Jane Fonda
  director: 13 Michael Cimino
  picture: 13 The Deer Hunter
1979:
  actor: 13 Dustin Hoffman
  actress: 10 Sally Field
  director: 12 Robert Benton
  picture: 14 Kramer vs Kramer
1980:
  actor: 12 Robert De Niro
  actress: 11 Sissy Spacek
  director: 13 Robert Redford
  picture: 14 Ordinary People
1981:
  actor: 10 Henry Fonda
  actress: 16 Katharine Hepburn
  director: 12 Warren Beatty
  picture: 14 Chariots of Fire
1982:
  actor: 11 Ben Kingsley
  actress: 11 Meryl Streep
  director: 19 Richard Attenborough
  picture: 6 Gandhi
1983:
  actor: 12 Robert Duvall
  actress: 15 Shirley MacLaine
  director: 12 James L Brooks
  picture: 17 Terms of Endearment
1984:
  actor: 14 F Murray Abraham
  actress: 10 Sally Field
  director: 11 Milos Forman
  picture: 7 Amadeus
1985:
  actor: 11 William Hurt
  actress: 13 Geraldine Page
  director: 13 Sydney Pollack
  picture: 11 Out of Africa
1986:
  actor: 10 Paul Newman
  actress: 12 Marlee Matlin
  director: 11 Oliver Stone
  picture: 7 Platoon
1987:
  actor: 14 Michael Douglas
  actress: 4 Cher
  director: 18 Bernardo Bertolucci
  picture: 14 The Last Emperor
1988:
  actor: 13 Dustin Hoffman
  actress: 11 Jodie Foster
  director: 13 Barry Levinson
  picture: 7 Rain Man
1989:
  actor: 14 Daniel Day-Lewis
  actress: 12 Jessica Tandy

  director: 11 Oliver Stone
  picture: 16 Driving Miss Daisy
1990:
  actor: 11 Jeremy Irons
  actress: 10 Kathy Bates
  director: 12 Kevin Costner
  picture: 16 Dances With Wolves
1991:
  actor: 14 Anthony Hopkins
  actress: 11 Jodie Foster
  director: 13 Jonathan Demme
  picture: 20 The Silence of the
  Lambs
1992:
  actor: 8 Al Pacino
  actress: 12 Emma Thompson
  director: 13 Clint Eastwood
  picture: 10 Unforgiven
1993:
  actor: 8 Tom Hanks
  actress: 11 Holly Hunter
  director: 15 Steven Spielberg
  picture: 14 Schindler's List
1994:
  actor: 8 Tom Hanks
  actress: 12 Jessica Lange
  director: 14 Robert Zemeckis
  picture: 11 Forrest Gump
1995:
  actor: 11 Nicolas Cage
  actress: 13 Susan Sarandon
  director: 9 Mel Gibson
  picture: 10 Braveheart
1996:
  actor: 12 Geoffrey Rush
  actress: 16 Frances McDormand
  director: 16 Anthony Minghella
  picture: 17 The English Patient
1997:
  actor: 12 Jack Nicholson
  actress: 9 Helen Hunt
  director: James Cameron
  picture: 7 Titanic

Accad
  kingdom of: 6 Nimrod
  location: 13 Plain of Shinar
  captured by: 6 Sargon (I)

Acca Larentia
  form: 7 goddess
  corresponds to: 6 Dea Dia

accede 5 admit, grant 6 accept, permit 7 abide by, agree to, approve, concede, defer to, endorse, inherit, yield to 8 assent to, submit to 9 acquiesce, conform to, consent to, succeed to 10 comply with, concur with 11 acknowledge, subscribe to, surrender to

accede to the throne 4 keep 5 claim, usurp 6 ascend 7 possess, succeed 8 take over 9 be crowned 15 ascend the throne

accelerando
  music: 15 becoming quicker

accelerate 4 rush, spur 5 hurry, impel 6 hasten, step up 7 advance, augment, further, promote, quicken, speed up 8 expedite 9 intensify 10 facilitate, to go faster **11** pick up speed, precipitate

accelerator 3 gas **4** goad, prod, spur **8** gas pedal **13** encouragement

accent 4 hint, tone **5** drawl, touch, twang **6** detail, stress **7** feature **8** emphasis, ornament, tonality, trimming **9** adornment, emphasize, highlight, punctuate, spotlight, underline **10** accentuate, inflection, intonation, modulation, underscore **11** enunciation **12** articulation **13** embellishment, primary stress, pronunciation

accentuate 6 accent, stress **7** feature, point up **9** emphasize, punctuate, underline **10** underscore

accentuation 6 accent, stress **8** emphasis

accept 3 buy **4** avow, bear **5** admit **6** assume **7** agree to, fall for, swallow **8** accede to, assent to **9** consent to, undertake **11** acknowledge, go along with

acceptable 4 fair, good, so-so **6** proper, worthy **8** adequate, passable, suitable **9** agreeable, allowable, tolerable **10** admissible **12** satisfactory

acceptable person
Latin: **12** persona grata

acceptance 6 belief, taking **7** consent, receipt **8** approval, sanction **9** accepting, agreement, receiving, reception **10** concession, permission **11** affirmation, approbation, endorsement, recognition **12** acquiescence, confirmation **14** acknowledgment **15** stamp of approval

accepted 5 usual **6** common, normal **7** regular **8** approved, standard **9** confirmed, customary, universal **10** acceptable, agreed upon **11** established, time-honored **12** acknowledged, conventional

access 3 way **4** door, gate, path, road **5** entry **6** avenue, course, entree **7** gateway, passage **8** entrance **10** admittance

accessible 5 handy, on tap, ready **6** at hand, nearby, on hand **8** possible **9** available, reachable **10** attainable, obtainable **11** within reach **12** approachable

accession 7 seizure **9** induction **10** arrogation, assumption, investment, taking over, usurpation **11** inheritance **12** inauguration, installation

accessory 4 plus **6** accent, cohort, detail **7** adjunct, partner **8** addition **9** adornment, assistant, associate, auxiliary, colleague, component, extension **10** accomplice, attachment, complement, decoration, supplement **11** confederate, contributor **13** accompaniment

accident 4 fate, luck **5** crash, fluke, wreck **6** chance, mishap **7** smashup **8** fortuity **9** collision, mischance **10** mis-

fortune **11** good fortune, serendipity **12** happenstance, misadventure

accidental 6 chance, random **9** haphazard, unplanned, unwitting **10** fortuitous, incidental, unexpected, unforeseen

acclaim 4 hail, laud **5** cheer, exalt, extol, honor, kudos **6** bravos, praise, salute **7** applaud, commend, ovation **8** applause, cheering, eulogize, plaudits **9** celebrate, rejoicing **10** compliment, enthusiasm **11** acclamation, endorsement

acclamation 6 cheers, homage **7** acclaim, hurrahs, ovation, tribute **8** cheering, hosannas, plaudits **9** adulation **10** salutation **11** approbation

acclimate 5 adapt, enure, inure **6** adjust, orient **8** accustom **9** get used to, habituate, reconcile **11** accommodate **16** become seasoned to

acclimation 9 seasoning **10** adaptation, adjustment **11** habituation

acclivity 4 hill, ramp, rise **5** slope **6** ascent **9** elevation **11** upward slope

accolade 5 award, honor, prize **6** praise, trophy **7** acclaim, tribute **8** applause, citation **10** admiration, compliment, decoration **11** recognition, testimonial **12** commendation

accommodate 3 aid, fit **4** help, hold **5** adapt, board, house, lodge, put up **6** adjust, assist, billet, modify, oblige, supply **7** bed down, conform, contain, furnish, provide, quarter, shelter **8** accustom **9** acclimate, entertain, get used to, harmonize, lend a hand, reconcile

accommodating 4 kind **6** polite **7** helpful **8** friendly, gracious, obliging, yielding **9** courteous **10** hospitable, neighborly **11** considerate **12** conciliatory

accommodation 5 rooms **7** concord, housing **8** lodgings, quarters **9** agreement **10** adjustment, compromise, settlement **12** arrangements **14** reconciliation

accompaniment 6 escort **7** support **8** ornament **9** accessory, adornment **10** incidental

accompany 5 guard, usher **6** attend, back up, convoy, escort, follow **7** conduct, support **8** chaperon

accomplice 4 aide, ally **5** crony **6** cohort, helper, stooge **7** abettor, comrade, partner **8** henchman, sidekick **9** accessory, assistant, associate, colleague, supporter **11** confederate, participant, subordinate **12** collaborator **13** co-conspirator **14** partner-in-crime

accomplish 2 do **6** attain, finish **7** achieve, execute, fulfill, get done, perform, produce, realize **8** carry out, complete, expedite, knock off **9** succeed at **10** bring about

accomplished 3 apt **4** able, deft, fine **6** adroit, expert, gifted, proved, proven **7** capable, eminent, skilled **8** accepted, effected, existing, finished, masterly, polished, realized, seasoned, skillful, talented **9** brilliant, completed, concluded, practiced, qualified **10** cultivated, proficient **11** consummated, established, experienced, well-trained

accomplishment 3 act **4** deed, feat, gest, gift **5** skill, geste **6** talent **7** exploit, success, triumph, victory **9** execution **10** attainment, capability **11** achievement, carrying out, culmination, fulfillment, proficiency, realization, tour de force **12** consummation

accord 4 cede, give, jibe **5** agree, allow, award, grant, match, tally **6** bestow, concur, render, square, tender, unison **7** concede, concert, conform, entente, harmony, present, rapport **8** be in tune, bequeath, sympathy **9** agreement, harmonize, unanimity, vouchsafe **10** accordance, be in unison, comply with, conformity, consonance, correspond, uniformity **11** concurrence, go along with **19** mutual understanding

accordant 4 like **7** similar **8** parallel **10** consistent **11** homogeneous

accordingly 2 so **4** ergo, then, thus **5** hence **6** thence, whence **8** suitably **9** as a result, therefore, wherefore, whereupon **11** conformably, in due course, in which case **12** consequently **15** correspondingly

accost 3 nab **4** hail, halt, stop **5** greet **6** call to, salute, waylay **7** address, solicit **8** approach, confront **10** buttonhole **11** proposition

accouchement 10 childbirth **11** confinement

accoucheur 12 obstetrician **25** assistant during childbirth

accoucheuse 7 midwife **25** assistant during childbirth

account 3 IRA, use **4** deem, hold, note, rank, rate, sake, tale **5** basis, books, cause, count, gauge, honor, judge, merit, score, story, think, value, weigh, worth **6** esteem, import, reason, reckon, record, regard, report, repute, view as **7** believe, clarify, dignity, explain, grounds, history, justify, recital, version **8** appraise, consider, estimate, megillah, standing **9** calculate, chronicle, narration, narrative, statement **10** accounting, commentary, illuminate, importance

accountable 6 guilty, liable **7** at fault, to blame **8** beholden, culpable **9** obligated **10** answerable, chargeable **11** blameworthy, responsible

accountant 3 CPA **7** actuary, auditor **10** bookkeeper **25** certified public accountant

account for 6 excuse 7 explain, justify 9 answer for

accounting 5 cause 6 answer, motive, reason 7 warrant 10 motivation 11 explanation

account rendered
   French: 11 compte rendu

accoutrements 4 gear 7 apparel 8 supplies 9 equipment, trappings 11 accessories, furnishings 13 paraphernalia

Accra, Akkra
   capital of: 5 Ghana

accredit 6 assign, credit 7 ascribe, certify, empower, endorse, license 8 sanction 9 attribute, authorize, guarantee 10 commission 19 officially recognize 22 furnish with credentials

accredited 8 ascribed, assigned, endorsed, licensed 9 authentic, certified, empowered 10 attributed, authorized, recognized, sanctioned 12 commissioned 20 officially recognized

accretion 4 rise 6 growth 7 accrual 8 addition, increase 9 expansion, extension, increment 10 supplement 11 enlargement 12 accumulation, augmentation 13 amplification

accrue 4 grow 5 add up, amass 6 pile up 7 build up, collect 8 increase 10 accumulate

accumulate 4 grow 5 amass, hoard 6 accrue, garner, gather, heap up, pile up, save up 7 collect, store up 8 assemble, cumulate 9 aggregate 10 congregate 14 gather together

accumulation 4 heap, mass, pile 5 hoard, stack, stock, store 6 pile-up, supply 7 accrual 8 amassing, hoarding 9 acquiring, gathering, stockpile 10 assemblage, collecting, collection 11 aggregation 13 agglomerating 14 conglomeration

accuracy 5 truth 6 verity 8 fidelity 9 exactness, precision 10 exactitude 11 correctness 12 accurateness, faithfulness

accurate 4 true 5 exact, right 7 careful, correct, perfect, precise 8 faithful, truthful, unerring 9 authentic, faultless 10 meticulous, scrupulous 11 punctilious 12 without error

accursed 4 base, foul, vile 6 cussed, horrid, odious 7 hellish 8 damnable, horrible, infamous 9 abhorrent, atrocious, execrable, loathsome, revolting 10 abominable, despicable, detestable, disgusting 12 contemptible

accusation 6 charge 8 citation 9 complaint 10 allegation, imputation, indictment 11 insinuation 13 incrimination

accuse 4 cite 5 blame 6 charge, indict 7 arraign, upbraid 8 reproach 10 take to task 13 call to account 22 lodge a complaint against

accuser 8 attacker 11 complainant 13 finger pointer

accustomed 3 set 5 fixed, prone, trite, usual 6 cliche, common, inured, normal, used to, wonted 7 general, given to, regular, routine 8 everyday, expected, familiar, habitual, hardened, ordinary, seasoned 9 customary, hackneyed, ingrained, prevalent, well-known 10 acclimated, habituated, prevailing 11 commonplace, established 12 conventional, familiarized

ace 2 A-1 3 top, one 4 A-one, star, tops 5 crack, pilot, super 6 expert, master, tip-top, victor, winner 7 one-spot 8 champion, medalist, terrific, top-notch, top-rated, 9 excellent, first-rate, headliner 10 first-class 11 crackerjack, outstanding 12 front-ranking

Aceldama
   means: 12 field of blood
   purchased by: 5 Judas

Acerbas see 8 Sychaeus

acerbity 7 acidity, sarcasm 8 acidity, acrimony, pungency, sourness, tartness 9 nastiness, sharpness 10 bitterness 11 astringency, brusqueness 12 irascibility

aces 2 A-1 4 fine, tops 5 great, prime, super 6 grade-A, superb, tip-top 8 peerless, superior, terrific, top-notch 9 excellent, first-rate, marvelous, matchless, superfine, wonderful 10 first-class, tremendous 11 outstanding, superlative 13 extraordinary

Acesius
   epithet of: 6 Apollo
   means: 6 healer

Achaeus
   founder of: 6 Achaea
   father: 6 Xuthus
   mother: 6 Creusa
   brother: 3 Ion

Achan
   punishment: 13 stoned to death

ache 4 hurt, need, pain, pang, want 5 covet, crave, mourn, smart, throb, yearn 6 be sore, desire, grieve, hanker, hunger, lament, sorrow, suffer, twinge 7 agonize, long for 8 soreness 10 discomfort

Achech
   origin: 8 Egyptian
   form: 8 creature
   body of: 4 lion
   wings of: 4 bird

Achelous
   form: 3 god
   habitat: 5 river
   father: 7 Oceanus
   mother: 6 Tethys
   daughter: 6 Sirens 8 Castalia 10 Callirrhoe
   defeated by: 8 Hercules
   struggled over: 8 Deianira

Acheron
   river in: 5 Hades
   ferryman: 6 Charon
   carries: 4 dead

Acheson, Dean
   Secy. of State 6 Truman
   author of: 20 Present at the Creation

a cheval 7 by horse 11 on horseback

achieve 2 do 3 get, win 4 earn, gain 5 reach 6 attain, effect, finish, obtain 7 acquire, fulfill, procure, realize 8 arrive at, carry out, complete, dispatch 9 succeed in 10 accomplish, bring about, effectuate 11 bring to pass

achievement 3 act 4 coup, deed, fear 5 skill 6 effort 7 command, exploit, mastery 9 expertise 10 attainment 11 acquirement, fulfillment, realization, tour de force 14 accomplishment

achieve recognition 6 arrive, make it 7 succeed 8 make good 10 be somebody 11 reach the top

Achilles
   mentioned in: 5 Iliad
   father: 6 Peleus
   mother: 6 Thetis
   foster father: 7 Phoenix
   grandfather: 6 Aeacus
   teacher: 6 Chiron
   charioteer: 9 Automedon
   friend: 9 Patroclus
   warrior in: 9 Trojan War
   vulnerability: 4 heel
   killed: 6 Hector
   killed by: 5 Paris

acid 4 sour, tart 5 acrid, harsh, nasty, sharp 6 biting, bitter, ironic 7 acerbic, caustic, crabbed, cutting, pungent 8 scalding, scathing, stinging, vinegary 9 acidulous, irascible, sarcastic, satirical, vitriolic 10 astringent, vinegarish 11 acrimonious

acidity 8 acerbity, pungency, sourness, tartness 9 sharpness 10 bitterness 11 astringency 13 nonalkalinity

Acis
   lover: 7 Galatea
   killed by: 10 Polyphemus

Acis and Galatea
   opera by: 6 Handel

Acis et Galatee
   opera by: 5 Lully

acknowledge 3 own 5 admit, allow, grant, yield 6 accede, accept, answer, assent, concur 7 concede, confess, own up to, reply to 8 call upon, thank for 9 recognize, respond to

acknowledgment 5 reply 6 answer, credit, thanks 8 response 9 admission, gratitude 10 concession, confession 11 affirmation, recognition 12 appreciation, recognizance

acme 3 top 4 apex, peak 5 crest, crown 6 apogee, climax, height, heyday, summit, zenith 8 pinnacle 9 flowering, high point 11 culmination 12 highest point
   Latin: 11 ne plus ultra

Acmon
companion: **8** Diomedes
changed into: **4** bird
defied: **9** Aphrodite

acolyte 3 fan **6** helper, novice **7** admirer, devotee, groupie **8** adherent, altar boy, follower **9** assistant, attendant

Acoma
language family: **6** Pueblo
location: **3** Ako **4** Acus **8** Valencia **9** New Mexico
noted for: **7** pottery

acorn
from: **3** oak
shape: **8** balanoid

a couvert 9 sheltered **10** under cover

acquaint 4 meet, tell **6** advise, inform, notify, reveal **7** apprise **8** disclose **9** divulge to, enlighten, introduce, make aware **11** familiarize

acquaintance 8 dealings **9** awareness, knowledge **10** cognizance, friendship **11** association, conversance, familiarity **12** relationship

acquiesce 5 admit, agree, allow, bow to, grant, yield **6** accede, assent, comply, concur, give in, submit **7** concede, conform, consent **10** capitulate, fall in with **13** resign oneself **16** reconcile oneself

acquiescence 5 leave **7** consent **8** approval, giving in, sanction **10** permission, submission **11** concurrence

acquiescent 7 willing **8** amenable, yielding **9** agreeable **10** submissive

acquire 3 get, win **4** earn, gain **6** attain, obtain, pick up, secure **7** achieve, capture, procure, realize **9** cultivate

acquisition 4 gain **5** prize **8** property, purchase **10** attainment, obtainment, possession **11** achievement, acquirement, procurement

acquisitive 6 greedy **7** selfish **8** covetous, grasping **10** avaricious, possessive **13** materialistic

acquit 3 act **5** clear **6** behave, excuse, exempt, let off, pardon **7** absolve, comport, conduct, deliver, release, relieve, set free **8** liberate, reprieve **9** discharge, exculpate, exonerate, vindicate

Acraea
epithet of: **9** Aphrodite
means: **6** height

acre
one-fourth: **4** rood
one-half: **3** erf **5** erven
two-thirds: **5** cover
ten: **6** decare **7** furlong
one hundred: **7** hectare
one hundred twenty: **4** hide

Acres, Bob
character in: **9** The Rivals
author: **8** Sheridan

acrid 4 acid **5** harsh, nasty, sharp **6** biting, bitter, ironic, smelly **7** burning, caustic, pungent **8** stinging **9** sarcastic, satirical, vitriolic **10** irritating, malodorous **11** acrimonious **12** foul-smelling

acrimonious 4 sour **5** nasty, testy **6** biting, bitter **7** caustic, cutting, peevish **8** venomous, spiteful **9** corrosive, irascible, rancorous, sarcastic, splenetic, vitriolic **10** ill-natured

acrimony 5 anger, scorn, spite **6** animus, malice, rancor, spleen **7** ill will **8** asperity, derision **9** animosity, hostility, malignity **10** antagonism, bitterness, malignancy **12** hard feelings, spitefulness

Acrisius
king of: **5** Argos
father: **4** Abas
mother: **6** Aglaia
twin brother: **7** Proetus
daughter: **5** Danae
grandson: **7** Perseus
killed by: **7** Perseus

acrophobia
fear of: **7** heights

acrostic 6 cipher, puzzle **7** acronym

act 2 do **3** bit, gig, law **4** bill, deed, do it, fake, feat, move, play, pose, show, skit, step, work **5** edict, enact, feign, front, order, put-on **6** action, affect, behave, decree, stance **7** execute, exploit, go about, mandate, measure, operate, perform, portray, posture, press on, routine, statute **8** carry out, function, pretense, put forth, simulate **9** enactment, ordinance, represent **10** pretension, resolution **11** achievement, affectation, counterfeit, impersonate, legislation, performance, pretend to be **14** accomplishment

Actaeon
form: **6** hunter
father: **9** Aristaeus
mother: **7** Autonoe
changed into: **4** stag
transformed by: **5** Diana
killed by: **6** hounds
killed at: **9** Gargaphia

acting 5 drama **6** deputy, ersatz, pro tem **7** interim, theater **8** the stage **9** dramatics, simulated, surrogate, temporary **10** dramaturgy, stagecraft, substitute, the theater **11** dramatic art, officiating, provisional, thespianism **12** stage playing

actinium *see* **8** elements

action 3 act **4** deed, feat, move, step, suit, work **5** force, power **6** battle, combat, effect, effort, motion **7** exploit, process, warfare **8** activity, conflict, endeavor, exertion, fighting, movement, progress **9** adventure, execution, influence, operation **10** enterprise, excitement, performing, production **11** achievement, functioning,

performance, prosecution **14** accomplishment

Actis
father: **6** Helius
mother: **5** Rhoda
crime: **10** fratricide
taught: **9** astrology
fled to: **5** Egypt
memorial: **16** Colossus of Rhodes

activate 4 stir **5** drive, impel, start **6** prompt, propel, turn on **7** actuate **8** energize, mobilize, motivate, vitalize **9** stimulate

activated 5 began **7** started **8** impelled, in action, in effect, turned on **9** effective, energized, mobilized, operative, vitalized **10** stimulated **11** in operation

active 4 busy, spry **5** agile, alert, alive, peppy, quick **6** acting, at work, frisky, lively, nimble **7** engaged, in force, on the go, working, zealous **8** animated, diligent, forceful, occupied, spirited, vigorous **9** ambitious, assertive, effectual, energetic, go-getting, operative, sprightly, strenuous **10** aggressive, productive **11** functioning, imaginative, industrious **12** enterprising **13** indefatigable

active person 4 doer **6** beaver, dynamo **7** hustler **8** activist, go-getter

activist 4 doer **6** zealot **7** apostle **8** advocate, exponent **9** proponent, supporter

activity 4 fuss, stir, to-do **6** action, bustle, flurry, hustle, tumult **7** project, pursuit, venture **8** endeavor, exercise, exertion, function, goings on, movement, vivacity **9** agitation, animation, avocation, commotion **10** assignment, enterprise, hurly-burly, liveliness, occupation **11** undertaking **13** sprightliness

act of the faith
Spanish: **8** auto da fe, auto de fe

act of war 4 raid **6** attack, strike **7** assault, offense **8** invasion **10** aggression, hostile act

actor 3 ham **4** doer, star **6** player, walk on **7** starlet, trouper **8** thespian **9** bit player, performer **11** functionary, participant, perpetrator **14** dramatic artist **15** supporting actor
type: **4** hero **5** cameo **7** feature, leading **9** character **10** supporting
hint: **3** cue

Actor
king of: **6** Phthia
father: **8** Myrmidon
mother: **8** Pasidice
brother: **6** Augeas
son: **7** Cteatus, Eurytus

actual 4 real, sure, true **7** certain, current, factual, genuine, present **8** bona fide, concrete, existent, existing, physical, tangible **9** authentic, confirmed, corporeal **10** legitimate, prevailing, true-to-life, verifiable

actual being 4 esse

actuality 4 fact, life **5** being, truth **6** effect, living, verity **7** reality **8** existing **9** existence, plain fact, substance **10** brutal fact **11** point of fact

actually 5 truly **6** indeed, in fact, really, verily **9** genuinely, literally
Latin: **7** ex facto

actually existing
Latin: **6** in esse **7** de facto

actuary 5 clerk **9** tabulator **12** statistician

actuate 4 move, stir **5** cause, drive, impel, rouse **6** arouse, excite, incite, induce, prompt **7** animate, inspire, trigger **8** activate, motivate **9** influence, instigate, stimulate **10** bring about

acumen 6 wisdom **7** insight **8** keenness, sagacity **9** acuteness, ingenuity, smartness **10** astuteness, cleverness, perception, shrewdness **11** discernment **12** intelligence, perspicacity **13** sound judgment **15** clearheadedness

acute 4 keen **5** sharp **6** clever, fierce, peaked, severe **7** intense, very bad **8** critical, piercing, powerful **9** agonizing, ingenious, intuitive, sensitive, very great **10** discerning, perceptive **11** distressing, penetrating **12** excruciating, needle-shaped **14** discriminating

acute suffering 5 agony **7** anguish, torment, torture **8** distress

A.D. *see* **10** anno Domini

adage 3 saw **4** quip, wise **5** axiom, maxim, motto **6** cliche, dictum, old saw, saying, truism **7** epigram, precept, proverb **8** aphorism **9** platitude **11** observation

adagio
music: **4** slow

Adah
also: **9** Bashemath
husband: **4** Esau **6** Lamech
son: **5** Jabal, Jubal **7** Eliphaz

Adam
wife: **3** Eve
son: **4** Abel, Cain, Seth
home: **4** Eden
grandson: **4** Enas **5** Enoch

adamant 3 set **4** firm **5** fixed, rigid, tough **7** uptight **8** obdurate, resolute, stubborn **9** immovable, insistent, unbending **10** determined, hard as rock, inexorable, inflexible, unyielding **12** intransigent **14** uncompromising

Adam Bede
author: **11** George Eliot
character: **8** Seth Bede **11** Dinah Morris, Hetty Sorrel **12** Martin Poyser **17** Arthur Donnithorne

Adams, Henry
author of: **6** Esther **9** Democracy **14** Chapters of Erie **24** History of the

United States (Under the Jefferson and Adams Administration), The Education of Henry Adams **26** Mont-Saint Michel and Chartres **34** The Degradation of the Democratic Dogma

Adams, John
nickname: **19** Atlas of Independence
presidential rank: **6** second
party: **10** Federalist
state represented: **2** MA
defeated: **9** Jefferson
vice president: **9** Jefferson
cabinet:
    state: **8** (John) Marshall **9** (Timothy) Pickering
    treasury: **6** (Samuel) Dexter **7** (Oliver) Wolcott
    war: **6** (Samuel) Dexter **7** (James) McHenry
    attorney general: **3** (Charles) Lee
    navy: **8** (Benjamin) Stoddert
born: **2** MA **9** Braintree
    town now called: **6** Quincy
died/buried: **6** Quincy
education: **7** Harvard
religion: **9** Unitarian
author: **18** Discourses on Davila **20** Thoughts on Government
political career: **13** vice president **24** First Continental Congress **25** Second Continental Congress
    minister: **11** Netherlands **12** Great Britain
civilian career: **6** lawyer
notable events of lifetime/term: **9** XYZ Affair
    act: **9** Judiciary **16** Alien and Sedition
father: **4** John
mother: **7** Susanna (Boylston)
siblings: **5** Elihu **13** Peter Boylston
wife: **7** Abigail (Smith)
children: **7** Charles, Susanna **10** John Quincy (6th president) **13** Abigail Amelia **14** Thomas Boylston

Adams, John Quincy
nickname: **14** Old Man Eloquent
presidential rank: **5** sixth
party: **4** Whig **10** Federalist **20** Democratic-Republican
state represented: **2** MA
defeated: **4** (Henry) Clay **7** (Andrew) Jackson **8** (William H) Crawford
vice president: **7** (John C) Calhoun
cabinet:
    state: **4** (Henry) Clay
    treasury: **7** (Richard) Rush
    war: **6** (Peter Buell) Porter **7** (James) Barbour
    attorney general: **4** (William) Wirt
    navy: **8** (Samuel Lewis) Southard
born: **2** MA **9** Braintree
    town now called: **6** Quincy
died: **2** DC **10** Washington
buried: **2** MA **6** Quincy
education:
    studied in: **5** Paris **9** Amsterdam

    11 Latin School
University of: **6** Leyden
College: **7** Harvard
religion: **9** Unitarian
author: **7** Memoirs **14** Eulogy to Monroe, The Adams Papers **17** Eulogy to Lafayette **18** Letters from Silesia
political career: **8** US Senate **19** Massachusetts Senate **24** US House of Representatives
    secretary of: **5** state
    minister: **6** Russia **7** Prussia **8** Portugal **11** Netherlands **12** Great Britain
civilian career: **6** lawyer
notable events of lifetime/term: **19** Pan-American Congress **20** Tariff of Abominations
father: **4** John
mother: **7** Abigail (Smith)
siblings: **7** Abigail, Charles, Susanna **14** Thomas Boylston
wife: **6** Louisa (Catherine Johnson)
children: **4** John **14** Charles Francis **15** Louisa Catherine **16** George Washington

Adams, Parson
character in: **13** Joseph Andrews
author: **8** Fielding

Adams, Richard
author of: **4** Maia **7** Shardik **12** Girl in a Swing **13** The Plague Dogs, Watership Down

Adam's Rib
director: **11** George Cukor
script by: **10** Ruth Gordon **11** Garson Kanin
cast: **8** Tom Ewell **9** Jean Hagen **10** David Wayne **12** Judy Holliday, Spencer Tracy **16** Katharine Hepburn

adapt 3 fit **4** suit **5** alter, frame, shape **6** adjust, change, modify, rework **7** conform, convert, fashion, make fit, remodel, reshape **8** attune to **9** acclimate, harmonize, recompose, reconcile, transform **10** assimilate, coordinate **11** accommodate, acculturate **12** make suitable

adaptable 6 pliant, usable **7** unrigid **8** amenable, flexible, obliging **9** alterable, compliant, easygoing, malleable, tractable **10** adjustable, applicable, changeable, open- minded **11** conformable, serviceable **13** accommodating, accommodative

adaptation 5 shift **6** change **8** revision **9** refitting, reshaping, reworking **10** adjustment, alteration, conversion, remodeling **12** modification **13** metamorphosis

Adar 18 twelfth Hebrew month

add 4 join **5** affix, sum up, total **6** append, attach, join on, reckon, tack on **7** combine, compute, count up, enlarge, include **8** figure up, increase **9**

calculate, enlarge by **10** increase by, supplement

Addams, Frankie
character in: 19 A Member of the Wedding
author: 15 Carson McCullers

Addams Family, The
character: 5 Gomez, Lurch **7** Pugsley **8** Morticia **9** Cousin Itt, Grandmama, Wednesday **11** Uncle Fester
cast: 9 John Astin **10** Lisa Loring, Ted Cassidy **11** Blossom Rock **12** Carolyn Jones, Jackie Coogan **13** Ken Weatherwax

add details 6 expand **7** clarify **9** elaborate, embellish **13** particularize

added 5 bonus, extra **6** joined **7** totaled **8** appended, attached, computed, included, joined on, reckoned, summed up, tacked on **9** counted up **10** additional, enlarged by, enumerated **11** increased by **13** supplementary

addendum 7 codicil **8** addition **9** appendage **10** attachment, postscript, supplement **12** afterthought

addict 3 fan, nut **4** buff, head, hook, user **5** freak, hound **6** junkie, submit, turn on, votary **7** acolyte, devotee, druggie, habitue **8** adherent **9** dope fiend, indulge in, surrender

addiction 5 craze, mania, quirk **6** fetish, hangup **8** fixation **9** cocainism, obsession **10** alcoholism, compulsion, dipsomania, morphinism **11** barbiturism, enslavement **12** addictedness, enthrallment **13** preoccupation

adding machine
invented by: 6 Pascal **9** Burroughs

Addis Ababa
capital of: 8 Ethiopia

Addison, Joseph
author of: 4 Cato **9** The Tatler **12** The Spectator **13** The Freeholder
co-author: 13 Richard Steele

addition 4 wing **5** annex, extra **6** adding **7** adjunct, joining **8** addendum, additive, annexing, increase, totaling **9** adjoining, appendage, appending, attaching, embracing, expansion, extending, extension, including, increment, reckoning, summation, summing up **10** counting up, increasing **11** enlargement, enumeration **12** appurtenance, augmentation, encompassing

additional 5 added, extra, spare **7** added on **8** appended **12** over-and-above **13** supplementary

additional feature 5 extra **7** adjunct **10** attachment, complement, supplement **12** appurtenance **13** accompaniment

additive 5 extra **8** addition **10** adulterant, supplement **12** augmentation, preservative

addle 5 mix up **6** muddle **7** confuse, nonplus, stupefy **8** befuddle

addled 5 silly **7** foolish, mixed-up, muddled **8** confused **9** befuddled, nonplused **10** nonplussed

add on 5 affix **6** append, attach, tack on **7** include **10** increase by

address 4 talk **5** greet, orate **6** salute, speech, talk to **7** lecture, oration, speak to, write to **8** dwelling, locality, location **9** discourse, statement

Address to the Deil
author: 11 Robert Burns

add to 6 expand, extend, pad out **7** amplify, augment, bolster, enlarge **8** compound, increase, lengthen **10** strengthen, stretch out, supplement

Ade, George
author of: 13 Fables in Slang **15** The College Widow **17** The County Chairman

Aden
seaport of: 5 Yemen
Gulf in: Arabian Sea

adept 3 apt **4** able, good **6** adroit, expert, gifted, master **7** skilled **8** skillful **9** dexterous, ingenious, masterful, practiced **10** proficient **12** accomplished

adequacy 7 fitness **11** sufficiency **16** satisfactoriness

adequate 3 fit **4** so-so **5** ample **6** enough **7** fitting **8** passable, suitable **9** tolerable **10** sufficient **12** satisfactory

a deux 6 for two **10** two at a time

ad extremum 6 at last **7** finally **12** to the extreme

ad fin 8 at the end **12** toward the end

adhere 3 fix **4** glue, hold, keep **5** cling, paste, stick **6** be true, cement, cleave, fasten, glue on, keep to **7** abide by, be loyal, stand by **8** maintain **9** stick fast **10** be constant, be faithful

adherence 6 fealty **7** loyalty **8** adhesion, devotion, fidelity **9** constancy, keeping to, obedience **10** allegiance, attachment, observance, stickiness **12** adhesiveness, faithfulness

adherent 3 fan **4** ally **5** gummy, pupil **6** sticky, viscid **7** acolyte, devotee, viscous **8** adhering, adhesive, advocate, champion, clinging, disciple, follower, partisan, sticking, upholder **9** supporter

adhesion 9 adherence **10** attachment, sticking to

adhesive 4 glue **5** epoxy, gummy, paste **6** cement, gummed, mortar, solder, sticky **7** stickum **8** adherent, adhering, clinging, sticking **12** mucilaginous, rubber cement

ad hoc 17 with respect to this **18** for this purpose only

ad hominem 8 to the man **17** against an opponent **20** appealing to prejudice

adieu 4 by-by, ciao, ta-ta **5** adios,

aloha **6** bye-bye, goodby, so long **7** a demain, cheerio, goodbye, good day **8** a bientot, au revoir, farewell, godspeed, toodle-oo **10** take it easy **11** leavetaking, see you later, valediction **14** Auf Wiedersehen

ad infinitum 9 endlessly **10** infinitely, to infinity, unendingly **11** boundlessly, ceaselessly, limitlessly, unceasingly **12** continuously, interminably, without limit

ad initium 14 at the beginning

ad interim 13 in the meantime

adios 4 by-by, ciao, ta-ta **5** adieu, aloha **6** bye-bye, goodby, so long **7** a demain, cheerio, goodbye, good day **8** a bientot, au revoir, farewell, godspeed, toodle-oo **10** take it easy **11** leavetaking, see you later, valediction **14** Auf Wiedersehen

adjacent 6 beside, next to **8** abutting, touching **9** bordering, proximate **10** contiguous, juxtaposed, next door to, tangential **12** conterminous

adjoining 6 joined **7** joining **8** nextdoor, touching **9** connected **10** contiguous **14** interconnected

adjourn 3 end **4** move **5** close **6** put off, recess, remove, repair **7** dismiss, suspend **8** break off, dissolve, postpone, withdraw **9** depart for, interrupt **11** discontinue

adjournment 6 recess **7** removal **8** abeyance **9** dismissal **10** suspension **12** postponement

adjudge 4 deem, rule **5** judge **6** decide, decree, ordain, rule on, settle, umpire **7** referee **8** consider **9** arbitrate, determine, pronounce **10** adjudicate

adjudicate 4 rule **5** judge **6** settle **7** adjudge **9** arbitrate

adjunct 9 accessory, auxiliary, secondary **10** complement, incidental, subsidiary, supplement **12** appurtenance

adjuration 4 oath, plea, suit **6** appeal **8** advising, entreaty **12** supplication

adjure 3 beg **5** plead **6** charge, enjoin, exhort **7** beseech, command, entreat, implore, solicit **8** appeal to, petition **9** importune **10** supplicate

adjust 3 fix, set **4** move **5** adapt, alter, order, reset **6** attune, change, modify **7** conform **8** accustom, regulate **9** acclimate, reconcile **11** accommodate

adjustable 7 movable **9** adaptable, alterable **11** rectifiable, regulatable **12** controllable

adjusting 8 adapting, altering **9** modifying **10** regulating **11** acclimating, controlling

adjusting device 5 lever, tuner, valve **6** handle **7** adapter **8** governor **9** modulator, regulator **11** control knob

adjustment 6 fixing **7** control, setting **8** adapting, focusing **9** adjusting, alignment, regulator **10** alteration, regulating, regulation, settlement, settling in **11** acclimation, orientation **12** modification **13** justification, rectification, straightening **14** reconciliation

adjutant 3 ADC **4** aide **9** assistant, right hand **10** aide-de-camp **12** right-hand man

ad-lib 6 make up **9** improvise **11** extemporize **13** improvisation **14** speak impromptu **15** speak off the cuff **21** speak extemporaneously **23** extemporaneous wisecrack

ad loc, ad locum 10 at the place, to the place

ad majorem Dei gloriam 23 for the greater glory of God

Admete
father: **10** Eurystheus
received: **12** golden girdle
belonged to: **4** Ares
received from: **8** Hercules
stolen from: **9** Hippolyte

Admeto, Re di Tessaglia
also: **21** Admetus King of Thessaly
opera by: **6** Handel

Admetus
king of: **8** Thessaly
member of: **9** Argonauts
father: **6** Pheres
wife: **8** Alcestis

administer 3 run **4** boss, give **5** apply **6** direct, govern, manage, tender **7** oversee **8** dispense **9** supervise **11** preside over, superintend **12** administrate

administering 7 bossing, running, tending **8** managing **9** directing, executing **10** dispensing, governance, overseeing **11** carrying out, supervising, supervision **14** administration, superintending

administration 5 brass **8** officers **9** execution, governing, tendering **10** executives, government, leadership, management, overseeing **11** application **12** dispensation, distribution **13** administering, governing body **15** superintendence

administrative 9 executive **10** management, managerial **11** supervisory **14** organizational

administrative head 3 CEO **7** manager **8** chairman, director **9** executive, president **10** supervisor **13** administrator **14** superintendent

admirable 6 worthy **8** laudable **9** estimable, venerable **11** commendable **12** praiseworthy

Admirable Crichton, The
author: **12** James M Barrie

admiration 5 honor **6** esteem, praise **7** respect **8** approval **10** high regard, veneration **11** high opinion **12** commendation

admire 5 prize, value **6** esteem, praise **7** respect

admirer 3 fan **5** swain **6** suitor, votary **7** acolyte, devotee, groupie **8** adherent, advocate, champion, disciple, follower, partisan **9** attendant **10** aficionado

admissible 7 allowed **8** passable **9** allowable, permitted, tolerable, tolerated **10** acceptable, admittable, legitimate **11** permissible

admission 3 fee **5** entry **6** access, assent, charge, entree, tariff, ticket **8** entrance **10** admittance, concession, confession, profession **11** affirmation, declaration, entrance fee **14** acknowledgment

admit 3 let **5** allow, grant, let in, own up **6** induct, invest, permit **7** appoint, concede, confess, declare, profess, receive, welcome **8** let enter **11** acknowledge

admittable 7 allowed **9** allowable, permitted, tolerable, tolerated **10** acceptable, admissible **11** permissible

admittance 5 entry **6** access, entree **7** ingress **8** entrance **9** admission

admixture 4 mess, olio **5** blend **6** jumble, medley **7** amalgam, melange, mixture **8** compound, mishmash **9** composite, confusion, potpourri **10** commixture, hodgepodge, salmagundi **11** combination, commingling, gallimaufry **12** amalgamation, intermixture **13** intermingling **14** conglomeration

admonish 4 warn **5** chide, scold **6** advise, enjoin, rebuke, tip off **7** caution, censure, chasten, counsel, reprove, upbraid **8** reproach **9** criticize, reprimand **10** put on guard, take to task **11** remonstrate **13** call to account **16** rap on the knuckles

admonition 6 advice, rebuke **7** chiding, warning **8** reproach, scolding **9** reprimand **11** mild reproof **12** remonstrance **16** rap on the knuckles

Adnah
deserted from: **4** Saul
deserted to: **5** David
fought against: **10** Amalekites
commander for: **10** Jehosaphat

ado 4 fuss, stir, to-do **5** furor **6** bother, bustle, flurry, fracas, furore, hubbub, pother, racket, tumult, uproar **7** flutter, trouble, turmoil **9** agitation, commotion, confusion **10** hurlyburly

adobe 3 mud **4** clay, silt, tile **5** brick, marly **6** earthy **7** clayish **13** sun-dried brick

adolescence 5 teens, youth **7** puberty **10** pubescence

adolescent 3 lad **4** lass, teen **5** minor, youth **6** boyish, callow, lassie **7** babyish, girlish, puerile **8** childish, immature, juvenile, teenager, young man, youthful **9** fledgling, pubescent, schoolboy, stripling, young teen **10** schoolgirl, sophomoric, young woman **11** undeveloped

Adolf Hitler 9 der Fuhrer **10** der Fuehrer

Adonai 3 God **6** my Lord

Adonijah
father: **5** David
mother: **7** Haggith
brother: **5** Amnon **7** Absalom, Chileab
executed by: **7** Solomon
conspired to overthrow: **5** David

Adonis
represents: **15** vegetation cycle
father: **7** Cinyras
mother: **6** Myrrha, Smyrna
favorite of: **9** Aphrodite
killed by: **4** boar
festival in honor of: **6** Adonia

adopt 3 use **4** take **6** accept, affect, assume, choose, employ, follow, take up **7** approve, embrace, espouse, utilize **9** conform to **11** acknowledge, appropriate

adorable 4 cute **6** divine **7** darling, likable, lovable, winsome **8** charming, engaging, fetching, pleasing, precious **9** appealing **10** delightful **11** captivating **12** irresistible

adoration 5 honor **7** worship **8** devotion **9** adulation, reverence **10** exaltation, veneration, worshiping **11** idolization **13** glorification, magnification

adore 4 like, love **5** exalt, fancy, prize **6** admire, dote on, revere **7** cherish, glorify, idolize, worship **8** hold dear, venerate

adorer 3 fan **5** lover **7** admirer **8** follower **9** worshiper

adorn 5 array **6** bedeck **7** bejewel, deck out, furbish **8** beautify, decorate, ornament **9** embellish

adornment 6 attire, finery **7** jewelry **8** ornament **10** decoration **13** embellishment, ornamentation

ad patres 4 dead

Adrammelech 13 Sepharvite god
father: **11** Sennacherib
killed: **11** Sennacherib

Adrastea
also: **7** Nemesis
origin: **5** Greek
goddess of: **17** divine retribution
father: **9** Melisseus
reared: **4** Zeus
entrusted by: **4** Rhea

Adrastus
also: **8** Adrastos
king of: **5** Argos
son: **8** Aegialus
leader of: **18** Seven against Thebes
companions: **6** Tydeus **8** Capaneus **9** Polynices **10** Amphiaraus, Hippomedon **13** Parthenopaeus
horse: **5** Arion

ad rem 9 pertinent **15** straightforward **17** without digression

Adrian, Edgar Douglas
field: **8** medicine **10** physiology
nationality: **7** British
discovered function of: **10** nerve cells
awarded: **10** Nobel Prize

Adriana
character in: **17** The Comedy of Errors
author: **11** Shakespeare

adrift 4 lost **5** at sea **6** afloat, aweigh **8** confused, drifting, unmoored, unstable **9** perplexed, uncertain, unsettled **10** bewildered, irresolute, unanchored

adroit 3 apt **4** deft **5** slick **6** artful, clever, expert, facile, nimble **7** cunning, skilled **8** skillful **9** dexterous, masterful **10** proficient

adroitness 7 aptness **8** deftness, facility **9** dexterity, handiness **10** cleverness **11** proficiency **12** skillfulness
French: **11** savoir-faire

adulation 7 fawning **8** flattery **9** adoration **11** fulsomeness **13** fulsome praise

adulatory 7 fulsome **8** admiring **10** flattering **13** complimentary

adult 3 big, man **5** elder, of age, woman **6** father, granny, mature, mother, parent, senior, x-rated **7** grandma, grandpa, grownup, oldster **8** seasoned **9** developed, full-grown **11** experienced, grandfather, grandmother **13** senior citizen

adulterate 3 cut **4** thin **5** water **6** dilute **9** water down **10** depreciate **11** contaminate

adulterated 3 cut **6** impure, watery **7** debased, diluted, thinned, watered **8** doctored, weakened **11** watered down

adultery 3 sin **9** carnality, cuckoldry **10** unchastity **11** fornication, promiscuity **14** unfaithfulness **17** marital infidelity **18** illicit intercourse **21** extramarital relations

adulthood 8 maturity, ripeness **10** full growth **11** age of reason

adumbrate 3 dim **6** darken, sketch **7** obscure, outline **8** intimate **9** prefigure **10** foreshadow, overshadow

adumbrated 3 dim **5** murky **7** shadowy **8** darkened **9** intimated **10** indistinct, prefigured **12** foreshadowed, overshadowed

advance 3 pre **4** gain, lend, loan, pass, step **5** add to, offer, prior **6** assign, binder, growth, move up, pay now, propel, send up **7** bring up, forward, further, improve, in front, lay down, press on, proffer, promote, upgrade, up front **8** foremost, increase, multiply, overture, previous, progress **9** go forward, promotion **10** furthering, move onward, prepayment, put up

front **11** advancement, down payment, improvement, preliminary, proposition **12** breakthrough, bring forward, pay on account

advanced 7 extreme, far gone, radical **10** avant-garde **12** farther along, further along **14** industrialized

advanced in years 3 old **4** aged **5** hoary, older **7** ancient, antique, elderly **8** outmoded **9** senescent, venerable **10** antiquated, gray-haired

advancement 4 rise **5** boost **9** bettering, elevation, promotion **10** betterment, forwarding **11** improvement, progression

Advancement of Learning
author: **12** Francis Bacon

advance slowly 4 inch **5** crawl, creep

advantage 3 aid **4** boon, edge, help **5** asset, clout **6** profit **7** benefit, comfort, service, success, support **8** blessing **9** dominance, upper hand **10** precedence **11** convenience, superiority

advantageous 6 useful **7** helpful **8** enviable, superior, valuable **9** favorable, fortunate **10** auspicious, beneficial, dominating, profitable

advent 5 onset, start **6** coming **7** arrival **9** appearing, beginning, emergence, opening up **10** appearance, occurrence **12** commencement

adventitious 5 alien **6** exotic **7** foreign, strange **9** adventive, extrinsic **10** accidental

adventure 5 geste, quest **7** emprise, venture **8** escapade **10** enterprise **11** undertaking

adventurer 4 hero **7** heroine, upstart **8** romantic, vagabond **9** buccaneer, daredevil **11** giant-killer **12** dragonslayer, swashbuckler **16** soldier of fortune

Adventures of Robin Hood, The
director: **13** Michael Curtiz **15** William Keighley
cast: **8** Alan Hale (Little John) **10** Errol Flynn (Robin Hood) **11** Claude Rains (Prince John) **13** Basil Rathbone **17** Olivia de Havilland (Lady Marion)
Oscar for: **5** score (Erich Wolfgang Korngold)

Adventures of Sherlock Holmes
author: **16** (Sir) Arthur Conan Doyle
character: **9** Mrs Hudson **10** Irene Adler **12** Dr John Watson **13** Mycroft Holmes **14** Sherlock Holmes **17** Inspector Lestrade, Professor Moriarty **21** Baker Street Irregulars

adventuresome 4 bold **6** daring **9** audacious, daredevil **11** adventurous

adventurous 4 bold **5** brave, risky **6** daring **7** valiant **8** intrepid, perilous **9** audacious, dangerous, hazardous **10**

courageous **11** challenging, venturesome

ad verbum 8 verbatim **9** to the word

adversary 3 foe **5** enemy, rival **8** opponent **10** antagonist, competitor

adverse 3 ill **4** evil **7** harmful, hostile **8** contrary, inimical, negative, opposing **9** difficult, injurious **10** pernicious, unfriendly **11** detrimental, unfavorable **12** antagonistic, unpropitious

adversity 3 woe **4** ills **5** trial **6** mishap **7** bad luck, trouble **8** calamity, disaster, distress, hardship **9** suffering **10** affliction, ill-fortune, misfortune **11** catastrophe, tribulation

advertise 4 show, tout **5** vaunt **6** reveal **7** display **8** proclaim **9** broadcast, publicize **11** noise abroad

advertisement 4 spot **5** blurb, flier, pitch, promo **6** notice, poster, want ad **7** leaflet, placard, trailer **8** circular, handbill **9** billboard, broadside, throwaway **10** commercial **12** announcement, classified ad, public notice

advice 4 news, view, word **6** report **7** account, counsel, message, opinion, tidings **8** guidance **10** advisement, suggestion **11** information **12** intelligence, notification **13** communication **14** recommendation

advisable 3 fit **4** best, wise **5** smart, sound **6** proper, seemly **7** fitting, prudent **8** a good bet, suitable **9** expedient, judicious **13** recommendable

advise 4 tell, urge, warn **6** enjoin, exhort, inform, notify, report **7** apprise, caution, commend, counsel, suggest **8** admonish **9** encourage, make known, recommend, suggest to **10** give notice **11** communicate

advise against 5 deter **8** dissuade **10** discourage, disincline

advisement 5 study **7** thought **12** deliberation **13** consideration

adviser, advisor 4 aide **5** coach, guide, tutor **6** egeria, mentor, nestor **7** monitor, teacher **8** Dear Abby, director **9** admonitor, assistant, counselor, preceptor, surrogate **10** Ann Landers, consultant, idea person, instructor

advisory 7 caution, guiding, warning **10** admonitory, cautionary, counseling **11** informative, instructive **12** consultative, consultatory **13** informational

advisory board 7 cabinet, council **8** ministry

advocaat
type: **7** liqueur
origin: **7** Holland

advocacy 4 egis **5** aegis **7** backing, defense, support **8** auspices, espousal **9** patronage, promotion **10** furthering, supporting **11** advancement, endorsement, pressing for, propagation, spon-

advocate 4 back, urge 5 favor 6 advise, backer, lawyer, patron 7 advance, apostle, counsel, endorse, espouse, further, pleader, promote, propose, push for, support 8 argue for, attorney, believer, champion, defender, press for, promoter, upholder 9 apologist, barrister, counselor, encourage, prescribe, propagate, proponent, recommend, solicitor, spokesman, supporter 10 mouthpiece, stand up for 11 campaign for, speak out for 12 legal adviser, propagandist, spokesperson 13 attorney-at-law

advocatus diaboli 14 devil's advocate

adz or **adze** 2 ax 3 axe 5 addis 7 hatchet

Aeacus
  descendants of: 8 Aeacides
  form: 5 judge
  habitat: 5 Hades
  father: 4 Zeus
  mother: 6 Aegina
  brother: 12 Rhadamanthys
  wife: 6 Endeis
  son: 6 Peleus, Phocus 7 Telamon
  grandson: 8 Achilles

Aeetes
  king of: 7 Colchis
  custodian of: 12 Golden Fleece
  father: 6 Helios
  mother: 5 Perse
  sister: 5 Circe 8 Pasiphae
  wife: 5 Idyia 9 Asterodea
  son: 8 Absyrtus, Apsyrtus
  daughter: 5 Medea 9 Chalciope

Aegaeon *see* 8 Briareus

Aegean Sea
  branch of: 13 Mediterranean
  islands: 5 Chios, Crete, Samos 6 Euboea, Lesbos, Rhodes 8 Cyclades 10 Dodecanese 16 Northern Sporades
  rivers into: 6 Struma, Vardar 7 Maritsa 8 Menderes
  surrounding countries: 6 Greece, Turkey

Aegeon
  character in: 17 The Comedy of Errors
  author: 11 Shakespeare

Aegeria *see* 6 Egeria

Aegesta *see* 6 Egesta

Aegeus
  king of: 6 Athens
  son: 6 Medeus 7 Theseus

Aegimius
  king of: 5 Doris 7 Dorians
  father: 5 Dorus
  son: 5 Dymas 9 Pamphylus

Aeginaea
  epithet of: 7 Artemis
  means: 11 goat goddess

Aegir
  origin: 6 Nordic

form: 5 giant
  god of: 3 sea
  wife: 3 Ran

aegis 4 wing 5 favor, guard 6 surety 7 backing, shelter, support 8 advocacy, auspices, guaranty 9 patronage 10 protection 11 sponsorship 12 championship, guardianship

Aegis
  form: 6 shield
  shield of: 4 Zeus 6 Athena

Aegisthus
  father: 8 Thyestes
  mother: 7 Pelopia
  cousin: 9 Agamemnon
  daughter: 7 Erigone
  seduced: 12 Clytemnestra
  killed by: 7 Orestes

Aegle
  member of: 8 Heliades 10 Hesperides
  mother of: 6 Graces

Aegyptus
  king of: 5 Egypt
  father: 5 Belus
  twin brother: 6 Danaus
  number of sons: 5 fifty

Aella
  form: 6 Amazon
  gift: 9 swiftness
  killed by: 8 Hercules

Aello
  member of: 7 Harpies

aelurophobia
  fear of: 4 cats

Aemilia
  character in: 17 The Comedy of Errors
  author: 11 Shakespeare

Aeneas
  hero of: 4 Troy
  father: 8 Anchises
  mother: 5 Venus
  grandfather: 5 Capys
  son: 5 Iulus 7 Silvius 8 Ascanius
  ancestor of: 6 Romans

Aeneas Silvius
  king of: 9 Alba Longa

Aeneid
  author: 6 Virgil
  character: 4 Gyas 5 Amata, Dares, Nisus 6 Arruns, Iarbas, Lausus, Pallas, Salius, Turnus 7 Acestes, Allecto, Camilla, Celaeno, Drances, Evander, Harpies, Helenus, Juturna, Latinus, Lavinia, Tarchon, Trojans, Venulus, Virbius 8 Ascanius, Entellus, Euryalus, Messapus 9 Cloanthus, Mezentius, Mnestheus, Palinurus, Sergestus 10 Andromache 12 Cumaean Sibyl
    gods: 4 Juno 5 Diana, Venus 6 Vulcan 7 Jupiter, Neptune
    Queen of Carthage: 4 Dido
    Aeneas' father: 8 Anchises
    Aeneas' mother: 9 Aphrodite
    Aeneas' wife: 6 Creusa
    Aeneas' son: 5 Iulus

Aeneas meets in underworld: 6 Charon 8 Cerberus 9 Palinurus
  parts of the underworld: 7 Elysium 8 Tartarus 9 Ivory Gate
    river: 4 Styx 5 Lethe
  Aeneas plucks: 11 Golden Bough
  Aeneas visits: 5 Crete, Delos 6 Latium, Sicily, Thrace 8 Carthage

Aeolus
  other name: 5 Eolis
  ruler of: 5 winds
  founder of: 8 Aeolians
  father: 6 Hellen
  mother: 6 Orseis
  brother: 5 Dorus 6 Xuthus
  wife: 7 Enarete
  son: 5 Deion 6 Magnes 7 Athamas, Misenus 8 Cretheus, Macareus, Perieres, Sisyphus 9 Salmoneus
  daughter: 6 Calyce, Canace 7 Alcyone 8 Cleobule, Perimede, Pisidice

aerate 3 air 9 ventilate 10 mix with air 11 expose to air

aerial 3 air 4 airy 5 by air, lofty 6 dreamy, flying, unreal 7 antenna, elusive, soaring, tenuous 8 airborne, ethereal, fanciful, in the air 9 ephemeral, imaginary, visionary 10 by aircraft, from the air, of aircraft 11 atmospheric, impractical, wind-created 13 unsubstantial 15 capable of flight

aerobatic group 10 Blue Angels

aeronautics 6 flight, flying 8 aviation

Aerope
  father: 7 Catreus, Cerheus
  husband: 6 Atreus 10 Plisthenes
  sister: 9 Clymene
  son: 8 Menelaus 9 Agamemnon

aerophobia
  fear of: 6 flying

aeroplane 5 plane 8 aircraft, airplane

Aeschylus
  author of: 8 Oresteia 9 Agamemnon, Choephori (The Libation-bearers), Eumenides 11 The Persians 13 The Suppliants 15 Prometheus Bound 16 The House of Atreus 18 Seven Against Thebes

Aesculapius
  origin: 5 Roman
  god of: 7 healing 8 medicine
  corresponds to: 9 Asclepius

Aesir
  also: 4 Asar
  means: 9 chief gods
  origin: 12 Scandinavian
  leader: 4 Odin 5 Othin
  home: 6 Asgard
  conflicting with: 5 Vanir

aesthetic *see* 8 Esthetic

Aethalides
  member of: 9 Argonauts
  father: 6 Hermes
  trait: 6 memory

Aether
  origin: 5 Greek
  personifies: 3 air, sky

Aethra
  father: **8** Pittheus
  son: **7** Theseus

Aethylla
  brother: **5** Priam

Afars and the Issas *see* **8** Djibouti

affability 9 geniality **10** amiability, cordiality **11** sociability **12** friendliness, pleasantness **13** compatibility

affable 4 open, warm **5** civil **6** genial **7** amiable, cordial **8** friendly, gracious, mannerly, pleasant, sociable **9** agreeable, congenial, courteous, easygoing **10** compatible **11** goodhumored, good-natured

affair 5 amour, event, party **6** effort, matter **7** concern, episode, liaison, pursuit, romance, shindig **8** activity, business, function, incident, interest, intrigue, occasion **9** adventure, festivity, happening, operation **10** love affair, occurrence, proceeding **11** celebration, transaction, undertaking **12** circumstance, relationship **14** social function **15** social gathering

affaire d'honneur 4 duel **13** affair of honor

affect 4 fake, move, stir **5** act on, adopt, alter, fancy, feign, put on, touch **6** assume, change, modify, regard **7** embrace, concern, imitate, impress **8** interest, relate to, simulate **9** impinge on, influence, pertain to, pretend to **10** tend toward **11** counterfeit

affectation 4 airs, sham **5** put-on **6** facade **8** false air, pretense **10** pretension **11** insincerity **13** artificiality, false mannerism

affected 4 vain **5** moved, phony, sorry, upset **6** harmed, la-di-da, unreal **7** assumed, changed, grieved, injured, pompous, stirred, studied, touched **8** impaired, mannered, troubled **9** acted upon, afflicted, concerned, conceited, contrived, impressed, pertinent, sorrowful, unnatural **10** artificial, distressed, influenced, interested, not genuine **11** pretentious **12** vainglorious

affectedness 4 airs **7** hauteur, tension **9** formality **10** constraint **11** haughtiness, pretensions **12** affectations **15** pretentiousness

affection 4 love **6** liking, malady, warmth **7** ailment, disease, illness **8** disorder, fondness, sickness **10** proclivity, tenderness

affectionate 4 fond, warm **6** ardent, caring, doting, loving, tender **10** lovey-dovey **11** warmhearted **13** demonstrative, tenderhearted

affectionate term 3 hon **4** dear **5** cheri, honey, sugar **7** pet name, sweetie, darling, dearest **8** nickname **9** sobriquet **10** endearment

Affery

character in: **12** Little Dorrit
author: **7** Dickens

affettuoso
  music: **8** tenderly

affiance 6 engage, pledge **7** betroth **13** engage to marry **15** solemnly promise

affiancing 5 troth **8** pledging **9** betrothal **10** engagement

affiche 6 poster **12** public notice

affidavit 4 oath **8** document **11** affirmation **14** sworn statement

affiliate 3 arm **4** ally, join, part **5** merge, unite **6** branch **7** chapter, connect, consort **8** division **9** associate, colleague **10** amalgamate, fraternize **11** incorporate, subdivision **12** band together

affiliated 6 allied, joined, united **9** connected **10** associated **12** incorporated

affiliation 5 union **8** alliance **10** connection **11** association **12** relationship

affinity 4 bent **5** fancy **6** liking **7** leaning, rapport **8** fondness, homology, likeness, penchant, relation, sympathy, tendency **10** connection, partiality, proclivity, propensity, similarity **11** inclination, parallelism **13** compatibility

affirm 4 aver, avow, hold **5** claim **6** allege, assert, ratify, uphold **7** approve, confirm, contend, declare, endorse, profess, support, sustain, warrant **8** maintain, proclaim, validate

affirmation 6 avowal **7** consent **8** approval **11** declaration, endorsement **12** confirmation, ratification **13** certification

affirmative 3 yes **8** emphatic, positive **9** affirming, approving, assenting, ratifying **10** conclusive, concurring, confirming **11** affirmatory, categorical **12** confirmatory **13** corroborative

affix 3 fix, tag **4** glue, seal **5** add on, paste, put on, set to, stick **6** attach, fasten, tack on

afflict 5 beset **6** plague **7** oppress, torment **8** distress

afflicted 6 cursed **7** plagued **8** affected, troubled **9** tormented **10** distressed

affliction 4 pain **5** curse, trial **6** misery, ordeal **7** anguish, torment, trouble **8** calamity, distress, hardship **9** adversity **10** misfortune, oppression **11** tribulation **12** wretchedness

affluence 5 money **6** plenty, riches, wealth **7** success **10** prosperity **14** prosperousness, successfulness

affluent 4 rich **6** loaded **7** moneyed, wealthy, well-off **8** well-to-do **9** well-fixed **10** prosperous, well-heeled

afford 4 bear, give, lend, risk **5** grant, offer, yield **6** chance, impart, manage, supply **7** command, furnish, provide, support, sustain

affray 4 fray **5** brawl, melee **6** fracas **7** contest, scuffle **8** conflict **9** encounter **11** altercation

affright 4 fear **5** alarm, dread, panic, scare **6** dismay, fright, horror, terror **8** frighten

affront 4 slur **5** abuse, wrong **6** injury, insult, offend, slight **7** offense, outrage, provoke, put-down **8** disgrace, dishonor, ignominy, rudeness **9** indignity, insolence **11** discourtesy, humiliation **12** ill-treatment, impertinence **13** mortification **16** contemptuousness

afghan 5 shawl, throw **7** blanket **8** covering, coverlet

Afghanistan
  other name: **6** Ariana, Aryana
  capital/largest city: **5** Kabul
  others: **3** Rui **4** Jurm, Nani, Wama **5** Asmar, Balkh, Doshi, Farah, Herat, Kunar, Makur, Maruf, Matun, Pahra, Tagab, Tulak, Urgan **6** Chaman, Gardez, Ghazni, Haibak, Kunduz, Nauzad, Panjao, Rustak, Sangan, Sarobi, Tukzar, Washir **7** Andkhui, Baghlan, Bamiyan, Dilaram, Ghurian, Girishk **8** Charikar, Faizabad, Kandahar **9** Jalalabad **10** Daulatabad, Pul-i-Khumri, Shibarghan **12** Mazar-i-Sharif
  government:
    parliament: **10** Loya-Jirgah
    radical group: **7** Taliban
  leader: **4** amir, emir **5** ameer, emeer **6** sharif, sherif
  measure: **3** paw, sir **5** jerib, karoh **6** khurds **7** kharwar
  monetary unit: **3** pul **5** abaze, riyal, rupee **6** abbasi, amania **7** afghani
  weight: **3** pau, paw, ser, sir
  lake: **13** Hamud-i-Helmand
  mountain: **3** Koh **5** Safeo **6** Chagai, Pamirs **7** Nowshak **8** Koh-i-Baba, Safed Koh, Sulaiman **9** Himalayas, Hindu Kush **11** Khwaja Amran, Paropamisus
  highest point: **9** Istoro Nal
  river: **4** Lora, Oxus **5** Cabul, Indus, Kabul, Kunar **6** Kokcha, Kunduz **7** Hari Rud, Helmand, Helmund, Murghab, Taleqan **8** Amu Darya, Farah Rud, Harut Rud, Khash Rud **9** Arghandab
  sea: **5** Darya
  physical feature:
    desert: **8** Registan
    panhandle: **6** Wakhan
    pass: **6** Khyber
    wind: **9** Afghanets
  people: **5** Aimak, Aymak, Kafir, Nuris **6** Baloch, Baluch, Chahar, Durani, Hasara, Hazara, Kaffir, Kirgiz, Pathan, Tajiks, Uzbeks **7** Beluchi, Belucki, Ghilzai, Pakhton, Pakhtun, Pashtun, Pukhtun, Pushtun, Sistani, Taimani, Taimuri **8** Jamshidi, Siah Push **9** Firuzkuhi, Safed Push, Safid Push

dynasty: 8 Barakzai
leader: 5 Najib **7** Mohmand **10** Najibullah **12** Babrak Karmal **14** Hafizullah Amin **17** Mohammad Zahir Shah, Mohammed Daoud Khan **18** Burhanuddin Rabbani Noor Mohammed Taraki
language: 4 Dari **5** Farsi **6** Afghan, Pashto, Pushtu **7** Balochi, Baluchi, Persian
religion: 5 Islam
place:
  dam: 6 Boghra **7** Kajakai **9** Arghandab
feature:
  clothing: 7 chaderi
  coat: 6 chapan
  dance: 5 attan
  game: 8 buz-kashi
  guest room: 5 hujra
  hat: 7 karakul
  head-cloth: 7 chawdar
  house with tower: 4 qala
  medicinal plant: 9 asafetida
  wrestling: 6 ghosai
food:
  potluck meal: 6 sohbat

aficionado 3 fan, nut **5** freak, pupil **7** devotee, pursuer, student **8** disciple

afield 5 amiss **6** abroad, astray **10** off the mark **11** out of the way **16** off the right track

afire 5 fiery **6** ablaze, aflame, alight, ardent, fervid, fuming, on fire **7** blazing, burning, fervent, flaming, flaring, glowing, ignited, smoking, zealous **8** aflicker, in flames, inspired **10** flickering, smoldering

afloat 5 at sea **6** adrift, wafted **7** sailing, wafting **8** drifting, floating

afoot 5 astir **8** underway **10** in the works

a fortiori 10 all the more

afraid 5 sorry **6** scared **7** alarmed, anxious, chicken, fearful, panicky, unhappy **8** cowardly, timorous **9** regretful, terrified **10** apologetic, frightened **11** lily-livered **12** apprehensive, disappointed, fainthearted **13** anxiety-ridden, panic-stricken **14** chicken-hearted, chicken-livered, terror-stricken

Afreet
  also: 5 Afrit
  origin: 7 Arabian
  form: 5 demon

afresh 4 anew **5** again **11** from scratch **16** from the beginning
  Latin: 6 de novo

Africa
  country: 4 Chad, Mali, Togo **5** Benin, Congo, Egypt, Gabon, Ghana, Kenya, Libya, Niger, Sudan, Zaire **6** Angola, Gambia, Guinea, Malawi, Rwanda, Uganda, Zambia **7** Algeria, Burundi, Comoros, Eritrea, Lesotho, Liberia, Morocco, Namibia, Nigeria, Reunion, Senegal, Somalia, Tunisia **8** Botswana, Cameroon, Djibouti, Ethiopia, Tanzania, Zimbabwe **9** Cape Verde, The Gambia, Mauritius, Swaziland **10** Ivory Coast, Madagascar, Mauritania, Mozambique, Seychelles **11** Burkina Faso, Sierra Leone, South Africa **12** Guinea-Bissau **13** Canary Islands, Western Sahara **15** South-West Africa **16** Equatorial Guinea **18** Sao Tome and Principe **22** Central African Republic

  people: 2 Ga **3** Ibo, Kru, Luo, San, Tiv, Yao **4** Arab, Beja, Bobo, Boer, Fang, Hutu, Kota, Kuba, Luba, Nuba, Nuer, Nupe, Teda, Tibu, Zulu **5** Bemba, Dinka, Galla, Hausa, Kamba, Makua, Masai, Mende, Mongo, Negro, Pygmy, Rundi, Serer, Shona, Sotho, Swazi, Temne, Tigre, Tutsi, Wolof, Xhosa **6** Bateke, Berber, Fulani, Herero, Ibibjo, Kikuyu, Mau Mau, Nubian, Ovambo, Rwanda, Senufo, Sidamo, Somali, Tswana, Tuareg, Yoruba, Watusi **7** Ashanti, Baganda, Bambara, Bushmen, Chaamba, Makonde, Mashoma, Ndebele, Nilotic, Oshogbo, Songhai, Turkana **8** Khoikhoi, Mangbetu, Matabele **9** Africaner, Afrikaner, Hottentot

  desert: 5 Namib **6** Sahara **8** Kalahari

  island: 5 Bioko, Pemba **6** Canary **7** Comoros, Madeira, Mayotte, Reunion **8** St Helena, Zanzibar **9** Ascension, Cape Verde, Mauritius **10** Madagascar, Seychelles

  ancient people/empire: 3 Oyo **4** Kush, Mali, Toro **5** Aksum, Benin, Ghana, Kongo, Mossi, Nubia, Wadai **6** Ankole, Tekrur **7** Ashanti, Buganda, Bunyoro, Dahomey, Songhai **8** Baguirmi, Carthage **10** Kanem-Bornu, Monomotapa **11** Ife and Benin

  ancient city: 5 Kilwa, Meroe **8** Timbuktu

  language: 4 Afar, Peul, Teda **5** Bantu, Bemba, Click, Hausa, Masai, Wolof **6** Arabic, Berber, French, Kanuri, Tsonga **7** Amharic, Khoisan, Lingala, Nilotic, Songhai, Swahili, Turkana **8** Cushitic, Mandingo **9** Afrikaans

  river: 4 Juba, Nile, Sudd **5** Congo, Kasai, Niger **6** Kwango, Orange, Ubangi **7** Senegal, Zambezi **8** Blue Nile **9** White Nile

  lake: 4 Chad, Kivu, Tana **5** Assal, Nyasa **6** Albert, Edward, Kariba, Malawi, Nassar, Red Sea, Rudolf **8** Victoria **10** Tanganyika **12** Chott Melrhir

  falls: 8 Victoria

  mountain/mountain range: 3 Air **4** Bihu, Meru **5** Atlas, Elgon, Kenya **6** Hoggar **7** Ahaggar, Crystal, Tibesti, Toubkal **8** Cameroon **9** Emi Koussi, Munchinga, Ruwenzori **10** Futa Jal-lon **11** Drakensberg, Kilimanjaro **13** Tibesti Massif

  lowest point: 17 Qattari Depression

  mineral/natural resource: 3 oil, tin **4** gold **5** ivory **6** cloves, copper, rubber **7** diamond, palm oil, uranium

  disease: 4 AIDS **5** Ebola **7** malaria **9** bilharzia **11** yellow fever **16** sleeping sickness

  homeland: 5 Venda **6** Ciskei **8** Transkei **14** Bophuthatswana

  game reserve: 5 Tsavo **6** Kruger **8** Amboseli **9** Serengeti

  tree: 4 cork, teak **5** cedar, ebony, olive **6** acacia, baobab, okoume, rubber **7** juniper, oil palm **8** date palm, mahogany, tamarisk **10** silk-cotton

  animal: 4 lion **5** bongo, hippo, hyena, zebra **6** jackal, monkey **7** buffalo, cheetah, giraffe, gorilla, leopard, wild pig **8** aardvark, antelope, elephant **9** crocodile **10** chimpanzee, rhinoceros **11** wildebeeste **12** hippopotamus

  bird: 5 heron, stork **6** falcon **7** bustard, ostrich, pelican **8** flamingo, hornbill **10** kingfisher

  fly: 6 tsetse

  snake: 5 cobra, mamba **6** python

Africaine, L'
  also: 14 The African Girl
  opera by: 9 Meyerbeer

African Queen, The
  director: 10 John Huston
  cast: 12 Robert Morley **14** Humphrey Bogart **16** Katharine Hepburn
  setting: 5 Congo
  Oscar for: 5 actor (Bogart)

Afrit see **6** Afreet

after 4 next, post **5** later **6** behind **9** afterward, following **10** conclusion, subsequent, succeeding

aftereffect 6 result **11** consequence

After Hours
  director: 14 Martin Scorsese
  cast: 12 Griffin Dunne **15** Rosanna Arquette

Afterlife
  god of: 4 Gwyn

aftermath 6 payoff, result, sequel, upshot **7** outcome **8** follow-up, offshoot **9** byproduct **11** consequence

afterpart 4 back, tail **5** stern **6** far end **7** back end, rear end, tail end **8** backside, hind part **9** posterior

after the fact 4 late **5** tardy **7** belated, delayed, too late **10** behindhand, behind time

After the Fall
  author: 12 Arthur Miller

after this, therefore because of it
  Latin: 21 post hoc ergo propter hoc
  describes: 14 logical fallacy

afterword 4 coda **8** addendum, epilogue **10** conclusion

Agacles
  king of: 9 Myrmidons

Agag
  king of: **10** Amalekites
  captured by: **4** Saul
  killed by: **6** Samuel

again 3 bis **4** also, anew, more **6** encore **7** besides **8** moreover, once more **10** in addition, repetition **11** another time, duplication, furthermore **12** additionally
  Latin: **6** de novo

against 7 adverse, opposed **8** conflict, contrary, opposite **10** opposition **11** unfavorable

against an opponent
  Latin: **9** ad hominem

Against Our Will
  author: **16** Susan Brownmiller

against the property
  Latin: **5** in rem
  describes: **15** legal proceeding

against the thing
  Latin: **5** in rem

Agamemnon
  author: **9** Aeschylus
  mentioned in: **5** Iliad
  king of: **7** Mycenae
  leader of: **6** Greeks
  fought in: **9** Trojan War
  father: **6** Atreus
  brother: **8** Menelaus
  sister: **8** Anaxibia
  wife: **12** Clytemnestra
  daughter: **7** Electra **9** Iphigenia **12** Chrysothemis
  son: **7** Orestes
  cousin: **9** Aegisthus
  captive: **9** Cassandra
  Clytemnestra's lover: **9** Aegisthus
  killed by: **12** Clytemnestra

Aganippe 8 fountain
  location: **6** Greece **7** Helicon
  sacred to: **5** Muses

Aganus
  father: **5** Paris
  mother: **5** Helen

agape 4 agog **6** amazed, gaping **8** wide open **9** awestruck, stupefied **10** astonished, dumbstruck, spellbound **11** dumbfounded **12** wonderstruck **13** flabbergasted

Agassiz, Jean Louis Rodolphe
  field: **7** zoology
  worked on: **7** fossils **8** glaciers **14** classification

agate
  species: **6** quartz
  variety of: **10** chalcedony
  type: **3** eye **4** moss, onyx, ring **9** landscape **13** fortification
  source: **4** Ider **6** Brazil **7** Uruguay **9** Oberstein **14** Rio Grande de Sul

Agathon
  father: **5** Priam

Agathyrsus
  father: **8** Hercules

Agave

  father: **6** Cadmus
  mother: **8** Harmonia
  sister: **3** Ino **6** Semele **7** Autonoe
  husband: **6** Echion
  son: **8** Pentheus

age 3 eon, era **4** date **5** epoch, phase, ripen **6** mature, mellow, period, season **7** develop, forever, make old **8** life span, lifetime **9** adulthood, a long time, grow older, seniority **10** generation, millennium **11** stage of life, stage of time
  French: **6** siecle

aged 3 old **4** ripe **6** mature, mellow **7** ancient, as old as, elderly, ripened **8** enduring, grown old **9** developed, full- grown, long-lived

Agee, James
  author of: **10** Agee on Film **17** A Death in the Family **23** Let Us Now Praise Famous Men
  screenwriter for: **15** The African Queen **19** The Night of the Hunter

Agelaus
  mentioned in: **5** Iliad **7** Odyssey
  occupation: **8** herdsman
  father: **8** Hercules, Phradmon
  mother: **7** Omphale
  courted: **8** Penelope
  raised: **5** Paris
  employer: **5** Priam

ageless 7 classic, eternal **8** enduring, timeless

agency 5 force, means, power **6** action, bureau, charge **8** activity **9** influence, mediation, operation **10** department, instrument **12** intervention **15** instrumentality

agenda 6 docket **7** program **8** schedule **9** timetable

agent 4 doer **5** cause, envoy, force, means, mover, power **6** agency, author, deputy, worker **7** vehicle **8** advocate, emissary, executor, operator **9** go-between, performer **10** instrument, negotiator **11** perpetrator **12** intermediary, practitioner **14** representative

Age of Innocence, The
  author: **12** Edith Wharton
  character: **10** May Welland **12** Ellen Olenska **13** Newland Archer

age-old 4 aged **7** ancient, antique, very old **9** venerable

agglomerate 4 clot, mass **5** amass, bunch, clump, rally **6** gather, heap up, muster, pile up **7** cluster, collect **8** assemble, condense, mobilize **10** accumulate, collection **12** accumulation, conglomerate, heap together, lump together **14** conglomeration **15** gather into a mass

agglomeration 4 heap, mass, pile **5** bunch, clump **7** cluster **10** collection **12** accumulation **14** conglomeration

aggrandize 5 bloat, exalt, widen **6** beef up, blow up, dilate, expand, extend, puff up, step up **7** amplify,

broaden, build up, distend, enhance, enlarge, inflate, magnify, stretch **8** escalate, increase **9** intensify **10** strengthen

aggrandizement 8 increase, widening **9** expansion, extension **10** broadening, escalation, exaltation, stepping up **11** enhancement, enlargement **13** amplification, magnification **15** intensification

aggravate 3 vex **4** rile **5** anger, annoy **6** nettle, worsen **7** affront, inflame **8** heighten, increase, irritate **9** intensify, make worse **10** exacerbate, exasperate

aggravating 7 irksome **9** inflaming, vexatious, worsening **10** irritating **11** heightening **12** exacerbating, exasperating, intensifying

aggregate 3 mix **4** mass **5** blend, union **7** mixture **8** amassing, compound **9** composite, gathering, summation **10** collection **11** combination **12** accumulation, conglomerate **14** conglomeration

aggregation 3 mob **4** army, band, bevy, crew, gang, host, mass, pack **5** crowd, horde, swarm **6** throng **7** cluster **9** multitude **10** collection

aggression 4 raid **7** assault, offense **8** act of war, invasion **9** hostility, pugnacity **11** viciousness **12** belligerence **13** combativeness

aggressive 4 bold **5** harsh, pushy **7** dynamic, hostile, intense, vicious, warlike, warring, zealous **8** forceful, militant **9** ambitious, assailant, assertive, attacking, combative, energetic **10** pugnacious **11** belligerent, competitive, contentious, quarrelsome **12** antagonistic, enterprising **13** self-assertive **15** tending to attack

aggressiveness 9 hostility, pugnacity **10** antagonism **12** belligerence **13** combativeness

aggressor 7 invader **8** attacker **9** assailant **11** belligerent **12** antagonistic

aggrieved 3 sad **4** hurt **5** stung **6** abused, pained **7** injured, put upon, tearful, wounded, wronged **8** grieving, mournful, offended, saddened, troubled **9** affronted, disturbed, sorrowful **10** distressed, ill-treated, maltreated, persecuted **11** imposed upon **13** grief-stricken

aghast 6 amazed **7** shocked, stunned **8** appalled **9** astounded, horrified, terrified **10** astonished, fear-struck, frightened **12** horror-struck **13** thunderstruck

agile 4 keen, spry **5** alert, fleet, lithe, quick, swift **6** active, clever, limber, nimble, supple **8** athletic, graceful **9** dexterous

agility 8 alacrity, spryness **9** dexterity, quickness, swiftness **10** limberness, nimbleness **12** gracefulness

agitate 3 jar, mix **4** beat, goad, rock,

stir **5** alarm, churn, shake, upset **6** excite, foment, stir up, work up **7** disturb, provoke, shake up, trouble **8** disquiet

agitated 5 tense **6** uneasy **7** anxious, frantic, nervous, uptight **8** confused, seething **9** disturbed, perturbed, unsettled **10** disquieted, distracted, distraught **11** discomfited, discomposed **12** disconcerted

agitation 7 anxiety **9** confusion **10** discomfort, uneasiness **11** disquietude, distraction, nervousness **12** discomfiture, discomposure, perturbation

agitato
   music: 8 agitated

agitator 7 inciter **8** fomentor, inflamer, provoker **9** firebrand **10** incendiary, instigator **11** provocateur **12** rabblerouser, troublemaker **13** mischiefmaker, revolutionary **16** agent provocateur

Aglaia
   member of: 6 Graces
   father: 7 Jupiter
   mother: 8 Eurynome
   sister: 6 Thalia **10** Euphrosyne
   husband: 4 Abas
   son: 7 Proteus **8** Acrisius
   daughter: 7 Idomene

aglow 4 warm **5** fiery **6** ablaze, redhot **7** blazing, glowing, radiant, shining

Agnes Grey
   author: 10 Anne Bronte
   character: 8 Mr Weston **13** Rosalie Murray

agnostic 5 pagan **7** atheist, doubter, heathen, heretic, infidel, skeptic **10** empiricist, free spirit, secularist, unbeliever **11** disbeliever, freethinker, nonbeliever **14** doubting Thomas

ago 4 gone, over, past **5** since **6** gone by **7** earlier **8** backward **15** retrospectively

agog 5 astir **7** excited **8** thrilled, worked up **9** awestruck **10** enthralled **11** openmouthed

Agon
   ballet by: 10 Stravinsky

agonize 5 labor, sweat, worry **6** strain, suffer **7** anguish, wrestle **8** struggle

agonizing 6 severe **7** painful, racking **8** grievous, worrying **9** suffering, torturous **10** tormenting, unbearable **11** distressing, intolerable, unendurable **12** excruciating, insufferable

agony 3 woe **4** pain **5** trial **6** effort, misery, sorrow, strain, throes **7** anguish, anxiety, torment, torture **8** distress, striving, struggle **9** suffering **10** affliction **11** tribulation

Agony and the Ecstasy, The
   author: 11 Irving Stone
   about: 12 Michelangelo

Agoraea

epithet of: 6 Athena
   means: 16 of the marketplace

agoraphobia
   fear of: 10 open spaces

Agraeus
   epithet of: 6 Apollo
   means: 6 hunter

agrarian 5 rural **7** farming **8** pastoral **11** agronomical, crop-raising **12** agricultural

agree 4 jibe **5** admit, allow, chime, grant, match, tally **6** accede, accept, accord, assent, concur, settle, square **7** concede, conform, consent, support **8** coincide, side with **9** harmonize, subscribe **10** correspond, think alike

agreeable 4 nice **7** fitting **8** amenable, amicable, in accord, pleasant, pleasing, suitable **9** approving, complying, congenial **10** acceptable, concurring, consenting, gratifying **11** appropriate
   German: 9 gemutlich

agreeableness 7 amenity **9** geniality **10** amiability **11** sociability **12** pleasantness

agreed
   French: 7 d'accord

agreed upon 6 common, normal **8** accepted, approved **9** confirmed, customary **10** acceptable **11** established **12** acknowledged

agreement 4 deal, pact **6** accord **7** analogy, bargain, compact, concert, concord, harmony, promise **8** affinity, alliance, contract, covenant **10** accordance, compliance, conformity, settlement, similarity **11** arrangement, concordance, conformance **13** compatibility **14** correspondence

agricultural 4 farm **5** rural **7** farming **8** agrarian **9** gardening **11** agronomical, crop-raising **13** nonindustrial

agriculture 7 farming, tillage **8** agronomy **9** geoponics, husbandry **10** agronomics **11** crop-raising, cultivation **15** market gardening

Agriculture
   god of: 4 Dago **5** Dagan, Dagon, Picus **6** Saturn **12** Bonus Eventus
   goddess of: 5 Ceres **6** Brigit, Dea Dia, Vacuna **7** Demeter

Agriope see **8** Eurydice

Agrius
   member of: 8 Gigantes
   form: 7 centaur
   mother: 5 Circe
   father: 8 Odysseus
   son: 9 Thersites
   attacked: 8 Hercules

agronomics 7 farming, tillage **8** agronomy **9** geoponics **11** agriculture, crop-raising

agronomy 7 farming **9** gardening, husbandry **11** agriculture, cultivation

aground 5 stuck **6** ashore **7** beached **8** grounded, stranded **9** foundered

ague 5 chill, fever **7** malaria, shivers **12** sweating fits

Aguecheek, Sir Andrew
   character in: 12 Twelfth Night
   author: 11 Shakespeare

Agyius
   epithet of: 6 Apollo
   means: 15 god of the streets

Ah, But Your Land Is Beautiful
   author: 9 Alan Paton

Ah! Wilderness
   author: 12 Eugene O'Neill

Ahab
   character in: 8 Moby Dick
   author: 8 Melville
   rank: 7 captain
   feature: 6 pegleg

Ahab
   father: 4 Omri
   wife: 7 Jezebel
   son: 7 Ahaziah
   daughter: 8 Athaliah
   opposed: 6 Elijah
   killed by: 4 Aram

Ahasuerus
   known as: 6 Xerxes **8** Cyaxares
   wife: 6 Esther
   divorced: 6 Vashti
   son: 6 Darius
   eunuchs: 6 Biztha, Carcas, Zethar **7** Abagtha, Harbona, Mehuman
   servant: 7 Abagtha
   courtier: 5 Haman
   conqueror of: 7 Nineveh

ahead of time 5 early **6** before, in time, sooner **7** betimes, earlier **9** before now, in advance **10** beforehand, in good time **13** before the fact

Ahib 16 first Hebrew month

Ahithophel
   counseled: 5 David
   rebelled with: 7 Absalom
   granddaughter: 9 Bathsheba

aid 4 abet, alms, dole, help **5** serve **6** assist, foster, relief **7** advance, charity, further, promote, subsidy, support, sustain **8** donation, minister **9** allowance **10** assistance, contribute, facilitate **11** accommodate, helping hand **12** contribution

Aida 17 Ethiopian princess
   opera by: 5 Verdi
   character: 4 Aida **6** Ramfis **7** Amneris, Radames **8** Amonasro, Rhadames
   set in: 5 Egypt

aide 5 gofer **6** deputy, helper **7** abettor, acolyte **8** adherent, adjutant, follower, retainer, sidekick **9** assistant, associate, auxiliary, man Friday **10** aide-de-camp, apprentice, girl Friday, lieutenant **11** helping hand, subordinate **12** right-hand man

aide-de-camp 3 ADC **4** aide **6** helper **8** adjutant **9** assistant, man Friday, right hand **12** right-hand man

aide memoire 4 memo, note 10 memorandum

aider 4 aide 6 helper 7 abettor 9 assistant 11 helping hand

Aiken, Conrad Potter
author of: 6 Ushant 10 Blue Voyage 12 Reviewer's ABC 14 The Charnel Rose 15 Earth Triumphant

Aiken, Howard H
field: 11 mathematics
designed: 15 digital computer

ail 4 pain 5 annoy, be ill, upset, worry 6 be sick, bother, sicken 7 afflict, make ill, trouble 8 be infirm, be unwell, distress 12 be indisposed, fail in health

ailing 3 ill 4 sick 6 infirm, sickly, unwell 8 delicate

ailment 6 malady 7 disease, illness 8 disorder, sickness, weakness 9 complaint, infection, infirmity 10 affliction, disability, discomfort 13 indisposition

ailurophobia
fear of: 4 cats

aim 3 end, try 4 beam, goal, mean, plan, seek, want, wish 5 essay, focus, level, point, sight, slant 6 aiming, design, desire, direct, intend, intent, object, scheme, strive, target 7 attempt, be after, purpose, take aim, train on 8 ambition, aspire to, endeavor 9 intention 10 aspiration, have in mind, have in view, work toward 11 have an eye to, line of sight 12 marksmanship

aim at 4 seek 6 pursue, target 8 aspire to, shoot for

aimless 6 chance, random 7 erratic, wayward 8 unguided 9 frivolous, haphazard, hit-or-miss, pointless, unfocus(s)ed 10 accidental, rudderless, undirected 11 purposeless, unorganized 12 inconsistent, unsystematic 13 directionless, unpredictable 14 indiscriminate

aine 5 elder 6 eldest

Ainsworth, William Harrison
author of: 8 Boscobel, Crichton, Rookwood 9 Guy Fawkes 10 Old St Paul's 12 Jack Sheppard 13 Windsor Castle 16 The Flitch of Bacon, The Tower of London 17 The Miser's Daughter, The South Sea Bubble 20 The Lancashire Witches

Ainu
language spoken in: 8 Hokkaido, Sakhalin
native of: 5 Japan

air, airs 3 lay, sky 4 aura, look, mood, puff, song, tell, tone, tune, vent, waft, wind 5 blast, carol, ditty, draft, ozone, style, swank, utter, voice, whiff 6 aerate, ballad, breath, breeze, expose, manner, melody, reveal, spirit, strain, zephyr 7 declare, display, divulge, exhibit, express, feeling, hauteur, quality 8 ambience, disclose,

pretense, proclaim 9 arrogance, publicize, ventilate 10 appearance, atmosphere, make public 11 haughtiness, pretensions 12 affectations, affectedness, stratosphere 16 superciliousness
god of: 5 Enlil
goddess of: 6 Ninlil

airborne 5 aloft 6 aerial, Eolian 8 in flight 12 off the ground

aircraft 3 jet, SST 4 bird 5 blimp, crate, plane 6 copter, glider 7 balloon, chopper, prop-jet 8 airplane, jumbo jet, zeppelin 10 helicopter, whirlybird

air current 4 puff, wind 5 blast, draft, whiff 6 breeze, zephyr 11 breath of air

airdrome, aerodrome 7 airbase, airport, jet base 8 airfield 11 flying field 12 landing field

airfield 7 air base, airport, jet base 8 airstrip 11 flying field 12 landing field, landing strip

airfoil
insect: 4 wing

airless 8 stifling 10 overheated, sweltering 16 poorly ventilated

airlines, American 3 TWA 4 Reno, Mesa 5 Aloha, Delta, Pan Am, USAir 6 United, Alaska 7 Eastern, Simmons, ValuJet 8 American, Hawaiian, Carnival, TowerAir 9 Southwest, Northwest 10 Transworld, Horizon Air 11 Continental, America West, Trans States 12 Air Wisconsin 14 Western Pacific 16 American Trans Air 17 Atlantic Southeast 18 Continental Express 21 Continental Micronesia

airplane 3 jet 4 bird 5 crate, plane 7 airship, prop-jet 8 aircraft 9 aeroplane 11 flying jenny 19 heavier-than-air craft 20 propeller-driven plane
invented by:
automatic pilot: 6 Sperry
jet engine: 5 Ohain
with motor: 12 Wilbur Wright 13 Orville Wright 14 Wright Brothers
hydro: 7 Curtiss
first: 5 Flyer
part: 3 fin 4 flap, nose, tail, wing 5 cabin, cargo, pylon 6 rudder 7 aileron, cockpit, turbine 8 elevator, fuel tank, fuselage, throttle, turbofan, turbojet 9 empennage, propeller, turboprop 10 flight deck, power plant, stabilizer 11 landing gear 13 undercarriage
kind: 3 MIG 4 Zero 5 Eagle, Gotha, Piper, Sabre 6 Boeing, Cessna, Fokker, Mirage 7 Concorde, Piper Cub 10 Beechcraft, Dornier Do-X 11 Piper Navajo 12 Lockheed Vega, Sopwith Camel 13 Boeing Clipper, Messerschmitt, Piper Cherokee, Super Fortress 14 Cessna Citation, Flying Fortress, Grumman Hellcat, Stratofortress 15 Hawker Hurrican 16 De Havilland Comet

variation: 3 SST 4 STOL, VTOL 5 blimp, drone, VSTOL 6 bomber, glider 7 airship, fighter 8 zeppelin 10 hang glider, helicopter, supersonic
battle: 8 dog fight

airport 5 field 7 air base, jet base 8 airdrome, airfield, airstrip 9 aerodrome 11 flying field 12 landing field, landing strip
Paris: 4 Orly
Chicago: 5 O'Hare
New York: 3 JFK
London: 8 Heathrow
Boston: 5 Logan
Airport Abbreviations:
Atlanta: 3 ATL (Hartsfield International)
Boston: 3 BOS (Logan International)
Chicago: 3 ORD (O'Hare)
Dallas/Ft. Worth: 3 DFW
Denver: 3 DEN
Detroit: 3 DTW
Honolulu: 3 HNL
Houston: 3 IAH
Las Vegas: 3 LAS (McCarren International)
Los Angeles: 3 LAX
Miami: 3 MIA
Minneapolis/St. Paul: 3 MSP
Newark: 3 EWR
New York: 3 JFK, LGA (John F. Kennedy International, LaGuardia)
Orlando: 3 MCO
Phoenix: 3 PHX (Sky Harbor International)
St. Louis: 3 STL (Lambert St. Louis International)
San Francisco: 3 SFO
Seattle/Tacoma 3 SEA

airship 5 blimp 7 balloon 9 dirigible 19 lighter-than-air craft

airship, rigid dirigible
invented by: 8 Zeppelin

airstrip 6 runway 12 landing field, landing strip

air weapon
German: 9 Luftwaffe

airy 5 light, merry, sunny, windy 6 breezy, cheery, drafty, dreamy, jaunty, lively 8 cheerful, ethereal, fanciful, gossamer, illusory, spacious 9 idealized, imaginary, sprightly 10 frolicsome, immaterial 11 unrealistic 12 lighthearted, light-of-heart 13 unsubstantial 14 well-ventilated

aisle 3 way 4 lane, path, walk 5 alley 6 avenue 7 passage, walkway 8 cloister, corridor 10 ambulatory, passageway

Aius Locutius
form: 5 voice
warned: 6 Romans
warned of: 14 Gallic invasion

ajar 4 open 5 agape 6 gaping 8 unclosed 10 partly open

Ajax
  also: 4 Aias
  called: 9 Great Ajax 10 Oilean Ajax
    11 Locrian Ajax 13 Ajax the Lesser
    14 Telamonian Ajax
  king of: 7 Locrius
  father: 6 Oileus 7 Telamon
  mother: 8 Periboea
  brother: 6 Teucer
  author: 9 Sophocles
  character: 8 Achilles, Odysseus
    9 Agamemnon
    son: 9 Eurysaces
    slave: 8 Tecmessa
    seer: 7 Calchas
  rescued body of: 8 Achilles
  violated shrine of: 6 Athena
  killed in: 9 shipwreck
Akela
  character in: 14 The Jungle Books
  author: 7 Kipling
Akh
  origin: 8 Egyptian
  transfiguration of: 4 dead
Akihito
  position: 7 emperor 11 crown prince
  reign name: 6 Heisei 17 Establishing
    Peace
  family:
    father: 5 Showa 8 Hirohito
    mother: 6 Nagako
    wife: 7 Michiko
    children: 4 Hito 8 Narahito
    schools: 6 Oxford 9 Gakushuin
akin 3 kin 4 like 5 alike 6 allied 7 kindred, related, similar, uniform 8
  agreeing, parallel 9 analogous, congenial, connected, identical 10 affiliated, comparable, resembling 11 correlative 13 corresponding 14
  consanguineous
Akkad *see* 5 Accad
Akutagawa, Ryunosuke
  author of: 5 Kappa 8 Rashomon 13
    The Hell Screen
a la 9 in honor of 13 in the manner of
Alabama
  abbreviation: 2 AL 3 Ala
  nickname: 6 Cotton 12 Heart of
    Dixie, Yellowhammer
  capital: 10 Montgomery
  largest city: 10 Birmingham
  others: 5 Selma 6 Athens, Dothan,
    Marion, Mobile 7 Decatur, Gadsden
    8 Anniston 10 Huntsville, Tuscaloosa
  colleges: 5 Miles 6 Auburn 7 Ala-
    bama 8 Tuskegee 9 Talladega 10
    Huntingdon
  explorer: 12 Herman DeSoto
  feature:
    festival: 11 Azalea Trail
    statue: 6 Vulcan
  tribe: 5 Creek 6 Tohome 7 Alabamu,
    Alibamu, Koasati 8 Tuskegee
  people: 8 Joe Louis 9 Hank Aaron,
    Hugo Black 10 Willie Mays 11 Helen
    Keller, Nat King Cole 13 George

Wallace, William C Handy, William
Gorgas
  lake: 12 Guntersville
  land rank: 11 twenty-ninth
  physical feature:
    gulf: 6 Mexico
    highest point: 6 Cheaha
    highlands: 11 Appalachian
  river: 3 Pea 5 Coosa 6 Mobile 7 Ala-
    bama 9 Tombigbee, Tennessee 10
    Tallapoosa 13 Chattahoochee
  state admission: 12 twenty-second
  state bird: 7 flicker 12 yellowhammer
  state fish: 6 tarpon
  state flower: 8 camellia 9 goldenrod
  state motto: 21 We Dare Defend Our
    Rights
  state song: 7 Alabama
  state tree: 20 southern longleaf pine
Alabama, Alibamu
  language family: 9 Muskogean
  location: 5 Texas 9 Louisiana 10 Polk
    County 12 Alabama River
  related to: 7 Koasati
alacrity 4 zeal 5 speed 6 fervor 7 agility, avidity 8 dispatch 9 alertness,
  briskness, eagerness, readiness 10 enthusiasm, liveliness, nimbleness,
  promptness 11 willingness 13 sprightliness
Aladdin
  character in: 27 Arabian Nights' En-
    tertainments
  character: 13 Chinese sailor
Al Aiun, El Aaiun
  capital of: 13 Western Sahara
a la mode 12 in the fashion, in the
  style of 13 in the manner of
Alarcon, Pedro Antonio de
  author: 10 The Scandal 12 Captain
    Venom 14 El Nino de la Bola 19 The
    Three-Cornered Hat
alarm 4 fear 5 alert, panic, scare 6 appall, dismay, fright, terror, war cry 7
  agitate, disturb, terrify, trouble, unnerve, warning 8 affright, distress,
  frighten 9 agitation, hue and cry, misgiving 11 trepidation 12 apprehension, perturbation 13 consternation
alarmed 6 afraid, scared 7 anxious,
  fearful, panicky, worried 8 dismayed
  9 concerned, terrified 10 frightened
  12 apprehensive 13 panic-stricken 14
  terror-stricken
alarming 5 awful, dread, scary 7 fearful 8 dreadful 10 horrifying, terrifying
  11 frightening, hair-raising
alas
  expresses: 4 pity 5 grief 6 sorrow 7
    concern 9 weariness 11 unhappiness
    12 wretchedness
  phrase: 7 woe is me
Alaska
  abbreviation: 2 AK 4 Alas
  nickname: 9 Great Land, Sourdough
    12 Last Frontier 20 Land of the Mid-
    night Sun

  capital: 6 Juneau
  largest city: 9 Anchorage
  others: 4 Nome 5 Sitka 6 Barrow,
    Kodiak 7 Cordova, Douglas, Skag-
    way 9 Fairbanks, Ketchikan
  feature: 5 Alcan 13 Alaska Highway
    national park: 13 Mount McKinley
  tribe: 3 Han 5 Aleut, Haida, Inuit 6
    Ahtena, Akkhas, Eskimo, Karluk,
    Tetlin 7 Amerind, Ingalik, Kayukon,
    Khotana, Kutchin, Tanaina, Tlingit,
    Tlinkit, Venetie 9 Tsimshian, Unaka-
    lett
  island: 4 Adak, Atka 5 Aleut 6 Ko-
    diak, Unimak 7 Diomede, Nunivak 8
    Aleutian, Pribilof 9 Alexander
  lake: 6 Naknek 7 Iliamna 8 Becharof
    9 Teshekpuk
  land rank: 5 first
  mountain: 3 Ada 4 Muir 5 Coast 6
    Alaska, Brooks 7 Foraker, St Elias 8
    Aleutian, Wrangell 9 Blackburn
    highest point: 8 McKinley
  physical feature:
    bay: 7 Glacier, Prudhoe
    channel: 9 Gastineau
    glacier: 9 Malaspina
    pass: 8 Chilkoot
    peninsula: 5 Kenai 6 Alaska, Sew-
      ard
    rapids: 10 Whitehorse
    sea: 6 Arctic 8 Beaufort
    strait: 6 Bering
  river: 5 Kobuk, Yukon 6 Copper,
    Noatak, Tanana 7 Koyukuk, Susitna
    8 Colville 9 Kuskokwim, Matanuska,
    Porcupine
  sled race: 8 Iditarod
  state admission: 10 forty-ninth
  state bird: 15 willow ptarmigan
  state fish: 10 king salmon
  state flower: 11 forget-me-not
  state motto: 16 North to the Future
  state song: 11 Alaska's Flag
  state symbol: 9 bald eagle
  state tree: 11 sitka spruce
Alaskan Adventures
  author: 8 Rex Beach
Albania
  other name: 8 Shqiperi 9 Shqiprija,
    Shqyptare
  capital/largest city: 6 Tirana, Tirane
  others: 3 Opp 4 Fier, Klos, Puka,
    Puke 5 Berat, Dukat, Korce, Kruje,
    Pecin, Peqin, Qukes, Rubic, Spash,
    Vlore 6 Avlona, Bitsan, Dardhe, Dur-
    res, Karaje, Preshe, Valona 7 Chi-
    mara, Coritza, Durazzo, Elbasan,
    Koritsa, Preyesa, Scutari, Shkoder 8
    Tepeleni 11 Gjirokaster
  monetary unit: 3 lek 5 franc 6 qintar
    7 quintar
  island: 6 Saseno
  lake: 4 Ulze 5 Matia, Ohrid 6 Prespa
    7 Ochrida, Scutari, Shkoder 8 Ohrid-
    sko
  mountain: 5 Shala 6 Pindus 8 Korit-
    njk 12 Albanian Alps

highest point: 10 Mount Korab
river: 3 Mat **4** Arta, Drin **5** Byene, Erzen, Seman **6** Bojana, Bojane, Vijosa, Vijosa, Vijose **7** Drin-i-ci, Shkumbi
sea: 6 Ionian **8** Adriatic
physical feature:
  bay: 5 Vlore
  cape: 6 Glossa
  gulf: 4 Drin
  lagoon: 10 Kara Vastas
  peninsula: 6 Balkan
  promontory: 13 acroceraunium
  strait: 7 Otranto
  wind: 4 bora
people: 3 Geg **4** Cham, Gheg, Gueg, Tosk **6** Arnaut, Arnout **8** Illyrian, Skipetar
  king: 3 Zog **9** Ahmet Zogu
  leader: 4 Alia **5** Hoxha **7** Berisha **10** Scanderbeg, Skenderbeg **13** Bishop Fan Noli
language: 3 Geg **4** Cham, Gheg, Hish, Tosk **5** Greek **8** Albanian
religion: 5 Islam **7** Bektash **13** Roman Catholic **15** Eastern Orthodox
place:
  square: 10 Skenderbeg
feature:
  lute: 6 luhata
  soldier: 7 palikar
  stone house: 4 kula
food:
  cheese: 8 kackaval

Albanian
  language family: 12 Indo-European
  spoken in: 7 Balkans

Albee, Edward
  author of: 3 Box **7** All Over **8** Seascape, Zoo Story **9** Tiny Alice **10** The Sandbox **16** A Delicate Balance, The American Dream **18** The Lady from Dubuque **21** The Ballad of the Sad Cafe, The Death of Bessie Smith **25** Who's Afraid of Virginia Woolf?
  identified with: 18 theater of the absurd

Albeniz, Isaac
  born: 5 Spain **9** Camprodon
  composer of: 6 Iberia **12** The Magic Opal **13** Henry Clifford

Alberich
  origin: 8 Teutonic
  king of: 6 dwarfs
  possessed treasure of: 8 Niblungs **9** Nibelungs
  also possessed: 9 Tarnkappe

Albert, Eddie
  real name: 21 Eddie Albert Heimberger
  wife: 5 Margo
  born: 12 Rock Island IL
  roles: 8 Oklahoma **10** Brother Rat, Green Acres **11** Room Service **12** Roman Holiday **13** The Longest Day **16** The Heartbreak Kid **19** The Boys from Syracuse

Alberta
  abbreviation: 4 Alta

capital/largest city: 8 Edmonton
others: 7 Calgary, Reddeer **10** Lethbridge **11** Medicine Hat
lakes: 5 Banff, Claire **6** Jasper **8** Waterton **9** Athabasca **11** Lesser Slave
rivers: 3 Bow **4** Milk **6** Oldman, Wapiti **9** Athabasca **12** Saskatchewan
religion: 13 Roman Catholic **20** United Church of Canada **22** Anglican Church of Canada
people: 5 Dutch **6** French, German **7** British, English **9** Ukrainian **12** Scandinavian

Albert Herring
  opera by: 7 Britten

Alberti, Leon Battista
  architect of: 15 Palazzo Rucellai **18** Church of Sant' Andrea, Temple Malatestiano **20** Church of San Sebastian **25** Church of Santa Maria Novello

Albertson, Jack
  born: 8 Malden MA
  roles: 14 Chico and the Man **15** The Sunshine Boys **18** Days of Wine and Roses, The Subject Was Roses

album 2 LP **4** book **6** record **8** register **9** portfolio, scrapbook

Alceste
  opera by: 5 Gluck

Alcestis
  author: 9 Euripides
  character: 6 Apollo **7** Admetus **8** Heracles, Thanatos

Alcestis
  father: 6 Pelias
  mother: 8 Anaxibia **10** Phylomache
  husband: 7 Admetus
  son: 7 Eumelus **8** Hippasus
  returned from: 5 Hades
  returned by: 8 Hercules

Alchemist, The
  author: 9 Ben Jonson
  character: 4 Face **5** Surly **6** Dapper, Subtle **7** Ananias, Drugger, Kastril, Love-wit **9** Dol Common **10** Dame Pliant **16** Sir Epicure Mammon **20** Tribulation Wholesome

alchemy 5 magic **7** sorcery **8** wizardry **10** conversion, witchcraft **11** magic appeal **13** transmutation **17** medieval chemistry
  god of: 6 Hermes
  purpose: 12 lead into gold

Alcimede
  father: 8 Phylacus
  mother: 7 Clymene
  husband: 8 Aeson
  son: 5 Jason

Alcimedon
  origin: 8 Arkadian
  mentioned in: 5 Iliad
  father: 7 Laerces
  daughter: 6 Philao
  captain of: 9 Myrmidons

Alcina

opera by: 6 Handel
character: 6 Alcina **8** Ruggiero

Alcindor, Lew
  former name of: 17 Kareem Abdul-Jabbar

Alcmaeon
  father: 10 Amphiaraus
  mother: 8 Eriphyle
  brother: 11 Amphilochus
  wife: 10 Callirrhoe
  son: 7 Acarnan **10** Amphoterus
  daughter: 9 Tisiphone
  commanded: 7 Thebans

Alcmene
  father: 9 Electryon
  mother: 5 Anaxo
  husband: 10 Amphitryon **12** Rhadamanthys
  twin sons: 8 Hercules, Iphicles

alcohol 3 ale **4** beer, wine **5** drink **6** liquor **7** whiskey **9** the bottle
  Latin: 9 aqua vitae

alcoholic 3 sot **4** hard, lush, soak **5** drunk, rummy, souse, toper **6** barfly, boozer, strong **7** guzzler, imbiber, tippler **8** drunkard **9** distilled, fermented, inebriate **10** spirituous **11** dipsomaniac, hard drinker, inebriating, inebriative, whiskey head **12** intoxicating

alcoholism 3 DT's **9** oenomania **10** dipsomania **12** intemperance **15** delirium tremens

Alcon
  form: 6 archer, Trojan **7** warrior
  aided: 8 Hercules
  wounded: 8 Odysseus
  abducted: 13 Geryons cattle
  killed by: 8 Odysseus

Alcott, Louisa May
  author of: 7 Jo's Boys **9** Little Men **11** Little Women **12** Eight Cousins, Flower Fables **15** Aunt Jo's Scrap-Bag **18** An Old-Fashioned Girl

alcove 3 bay **4** nook **5** niche **6** corner, recess **7** cubicle, opening **11** compartment

Alcyoneus
  form: 5 giant
  hurled: 5 stone
  killed by: 8 Hercules

Alda, Alan
  born: 9 New York NY
  father: 10 Robert Alda
    real name: 15 Alfonso D'Abruzzo
  roles: 4 MASH **8** A New Life **9** Paper Lion, Playmates, White Nile **12** Sweet Liberty **13** Betsy's Wedding, Hawkeye Pierce, The Glass House **14** The Four Seasons **16** Same Time Next Year, The Mephisto Waltz

Alden, Roberta
  character in: 17 An American Tragedy
  author: 7 Dreiser

al dente 10 to the tooth

alder 5 Alnus
  varieties: 3 Red **5** Black, Hazel,

White, Witch **6** Oregon, Smooth, Yellow **7** Italian, Seaside **8** Japanese, Mountain, Speckled **9** Caucasian **10** Manchurian **13** American green, European green

Aldiss, Brian W
author of: **7** Non-Stop **9** Greybeard **13** The Saliva Tree **19** Frankenstein Unbound, The Billion Year Spree, The Eighty Minute Hour **20** The Trillion Year Spree

ale 4 beer, brew **5** stout **12** malt beverage **15** English festival

Alea
epithet of: **6** Athena
means: **9** sanctuary

Alecto
member of: **6** Furies

alehouse 3 pub **6** saloon, tavern **7** taproom **11** public house

Aleichem, Sholom
author of: **12** The Great Fair **14** Tevye's Daughter

Alembert, Jean le Rond d'
field: **11** mathematics
nationality: **6** French
studied: **13** fluid dynamics **18** celestial mechanics **28** partial differential equations

Aleph and Other Stories
author: **15** Jorge Luis Borges

alert 4 warn, wary **5** alarm, aware, quick, siren **6** active, inform, lively, nimble, notify, signal **7** careful, heedful, on guard, warning **8** diligent, forewarn, keen-eyed, vigilant, watchful **9** attentive, observant, sprightly, wideawake **10** perceptive **11** intelligent

alertness 8 alacrity, dispatch **9** awareness, readiness, vigilance **10** liveliness **12** watchfulness

Aleut
language family: **6** Eskimo
tribe: **4** Atka **8** Unalaska
location: **6** Alaska **15** Shumagin Islands **17** Aleutian Peninsula
noted for: **7** hunting

Aleutians
islands: **3** Fox, Rat **4** Attu, Near **5** Kiska **9** Andreanof **25** Islands of the Four Mountains
state: **6** Alaska
people: **6** Aleuts
language: **5** Atkan **9** Unalaskan

Alexander, Jane
real name: **11** Jane Quigley
born: **8** Boston MA
roles: **9** Testament **17** The Great White Hope **18** Eleanor and Franklin **19** All the President's Men

Alexander's Feast
author: **10** John Dryden

Alexander the Great
battle: **5** Issus **9** Gaugamela
birthplace: **5** Pella

conquered: **6** Darius, Persia
father: **8** Philip II
founded: **10** Alexandria
friend: **11** Hephaestion
general: **7** Cleitus **8** Philotas **9** Parmenion
horse: **10** Bucephalus
mother: **8** Olympias
nationality: **10** Macedonian
tutor: **9** Aristotle
wife: **6** Roxana

alexandrite
species: **11** chrysoberyl
source: **8** Sri Lanka
color: **3** red **5** green

Alfheim
origin: **12** Scandinavian
dwelling place of: **5** elves
location: **11** above ground

Alfie
director: **12** Lewis Gilbert
based on play by: **12** Bill Naughton
cast: **12** Michael Caine **14** Shelley Winters

alga, algae 6 fungus **8** pond scum
contains: **4** agar **5** algin **11** carrageenan, chlorophyll
type: **3** red **7** brown, green **9** blue-green, euglenids **11** golden-brown, yellow-green **15** dinoflagellates
forms: **4** kelp **5** dulse **7** diatoms, seaweed **8** plankton, rockweed **9** Irish moss, stonewort

Alger, Horatio
author of: **10** Ragged Dick **11** Tattered Tom **12** Luck and Pluck

Algeria
other name: **7** Algerie, Numidia, Pomaria **9** al-Djazair
capital/largest city: **7** Algiers
others: **4** Bona, Bone, Oran **5** Aflou, Arzew, Batna, Blida, Medea, Saida, Setif, Tenes **6** Abadla, Annaba, Aumale, Barika, Bechar, Bejaia, Benoud, Biskra, Bougie, Dellys, Djanet, Djelfa, Dzioua, Eloued, Frenda, Guelma, Skikda **7** Boghari, Mascara, Miliana, Negrine, Nemours, Ouargla, Tebessa, Tlemcen **8** Ghardaia, Laghouat **9** Touggourt **11** Constantine **12** Sidi-bel-abbes
division: **4** Oran **6** Annaba **7** Algiers **11** Constantine
leader: **3** bey, dey **6** disawa **9** beylerbey
measure: **3** pik **5** rebis, tarri **6** termin
monetary unit: **5** dinar **7** centime
weight: **4** rotl
lake: **5** Hodna **6** Sabkha **7** Cherqui, Fedjadj, Meirhir **10** Azzel Matti, Mekerrhane
mountain: **5** Aissa, Atlas, Aures, Dahra **6** Chelia **7** Ahaggar, Kabylia, Mouydir **8** Djurjura **9** Djurdjura, Tell Atlas **12** Saharan Atlas
highest point: **5** Tahat
river: **6** Shelif **7** Cheliff **8** Medjerda **15** Cheliffmedjerda

sea: **13** Mediterranean
physical feature: **14** Tropic of Cancer
desert: **6** Sahara
giant sand dune: **3** erg
grass: **4** diss **7** esparto
hill: **4** tell
oasis: **4** Mzab
oil field: **7** Edjeleh, El Gassi **10** Zarzaitine **13** Hassi Messaoud (happy spring), Tiguentourine
plain: **7** Cheliff, Mitidja
rocky plateau: **7** hammada
salt basin: **5** chott, shatt
wind: **7** sirocco
people: **4** Arab **6** Berber, Kabyle, Shawia, Tuareg **7** Haratin
author: **3** Dib **5** Camus, Fanon **6** Yacine
leader: **9** Bendjedid **10** Abd al-Qadir, Abd-al-Kadir, Abd- el-Kader **11** Boumedienne **13** Ahmed Ben Bella
ruler: **8** Jugurtha **9** Masinissa
language: **6** Arabic, Berber, French, Zenata **7** Senhaja
religion: **5** Islam
place:
monastery: **5** Ribat
ruins: **7** Djemila
feature:
camel: **6** mehari
cavalry man: **5** spahi **6** spahee
commune: **5** setif
dwelling: **6** gourbi
French settler/landowner: **5** colon **8** piednoir
holy man: **8** marabout
kingdom: **7** Numidia
native quarter: **6** casbah, kasbah
pirate: **7** corsair
ship: **5** xebec, zebec
slum: **10** bidonville
food:
dish: **8** couscous
fruit drink: **5** syrop
seasoning: **4** mint **5** anise, cumin **6** cloves, fennel, ginger, pepper **7** parsley, pimento **8** cinnamon **9** coriander

Algiers
Arabic: **8** al-Jazair
building: **11** Great Mosque
capital of: **7** Algeria
center of city: **6** Casbah
French: **5** Alger
hills: **5** Sahel
Roman: **7** Icosium
ruled by: **5** Turks **6** French **7** Berbers **10** Free French **14** Barbary Pirates
sea: **13** Mediterranean

Algonkian-Ritwan
language family: **14** Algonkian-Mosan
subgroup: **3** Fox **4** Cree, Sauk **5** Wiyot, Yurok **6** Ojibwa **7** Abenaki, Arapaho, Mohican **8** Cheyenne, Delaware, Menomini **9** Blackfoot

Algonkin, Algonquin

language family: 9 Algonkian **10** Algonquian
tribe: 7 Abitibi **8** Algonkin **9** Nipissing **11** Temiscaming
location: 6 Canada **11** Ottawa River
spirit of nature: 7 Manitou

Algonquian, Algonkian
tribe: 3 Fox, Sac **4** Cree, Innu, Sauk **5** Miami **6** Abnaki, Atsina, Micmac, Ojibwa, Ottawa, Pequot **7** Arapaho, Mahican, Mohegan, Mohican, Ojibway, Shawnee **8** Algonkin, Cheyenne, Chippawa, Delaware, Haaninin, Iliniwek, Illinois, Kickapoo, Menomini, Merrimac, Powhatan, Puyallop **9** Algonquin, Blackfeet, Blackfoot, Massasoit, Menominee, Menomonie, Mesquakie, Pennacook, Penobscot, Pokanoket, Twightwee, Wampanoag **10** Leni-Lenape, Potawatomi **11** Gros Ventres **12** Narragansett **17** Montagnais-Naskapi

algophobia
fear of: 4 pain

Algum 13 red sandalwood

Ali, Muhammad
formerly: 11 Cassius Clay
sport: 6 boxing
class: 11 heavyweight
won: 8 Olympics **16** heavyweight title

alias 9 pseudonym **11** assumed name, nom de guerre

Ali Baba
character in: 27 Arabian Nights' Entertainments

alibi 3 out **6** excuse **7** pretext **11** explanation **13** justification

Alice Adams
author: 15 Booth Tarkington
character: 6 Mr Lamb **11** Virgil Adams, Walter Adams **13** Arthur Russell, Mildred Palmer

Alice's Adventures in Wonderland
author: 12 Lewis Carroll **22** Charles Lutwidge Dodgson
character: 5 Alice **7** Duchess **9** Mad Hatter, March Hare **10** Mock Turtle **11** Cheshire Cat, White Rabbit **13** Knave of Hearts, Queen of Hearts

Alice Sit-by-the-Fire
author: 12 James M Barrie

alien 6 exotic, remote, unlike **7** distant, foreign, opposed, strange **8** contrary, newcomer, outsider, stranger **9** different, estranged, foreigner, immigrant, not native, outlander, separated, unrelated **10** dissimilar, outlandish **11** conflicting, incongruous, unconnected **12** incompatible, inconsistent **13** contradictory
German: 9 Auslander

alienate 7 divorce **8** estrange, separate, turn away

alienation 5 exile **7** divorce **9** isolation **10** separation, withdrawal **13** repulsiveness

alight 4 land **6** get off **7** deplane, de-

scend, detrain, get down **8** come down, dismount **9** climb down, disembark, thump down, touch down

align 4 ally, even, join, side **6** even up, line up **9** affiliate, associate **10** straighten

alignment 7 allying, evening **9** evening up **13** straightening

alike 4 akin, even, same **5** equal **6** evenly **7** equally, kindred, uniform **8** of a piece, parallel **9** analogous, identical, similarly, uniformly **10** equivalent, synonymous **11** homogeneous, identically **13** corresponding

Alisande (Sandy)
character in: 36 A Connecticut Yankee in King Arthur's Court
author: 5 Twain

alive 4 spry **5** alert, aware, eager, quick, vital **6** active, extant, lively, living, viable **7** animate, in force, not dead **8** animated, possible, spirited, vigorous **9** breathing, energetic, operative, vivacious **10** subsisting, unquenched **11** above ground, in existence, in operation **14** unextinguished

alive to 5 alert, awake, aware **7** heedful, mindful **8** watchful **9** attentive, conscious, wide-awake

alkaline 3 lye **5** salty **7** antacid **9** non-acidic

alkaloid 7 alkaline, codeine, guinine **8** morphine, nicotine **16** colorless complex

all 4 each, full, very **5** any of, every, fully, total, utter, whole **6** each of, entire, to a man, utmost, wholly **7** highest, perfect, totally, utterly **8** any one of, complete, entirely, everyone, greatest, the sum of, the total, the whole **9** every item **10** altogether, completely, every one of, everything, the total of, the whole of **11** every member, every part of, exceedingly, the entirety

All About Eve
director: 17 Joseph L Mankiewicz
cast: 10 Anne Baxter, Bette Davis **11** Celeste Holm, Gary Merrill **12** Thelma Ritter **13** George Sanders, Marilyn Monroe
Oscar for: 7 picture **8** director **10** screenplay **15** supporting actor (George Sanders)

Allan-a-Dale, Alan-a-Dale
character in: 9 Robin Hood

allargando
music: 13 getting slower

all around 6 abroad **7** all over **10** everywhere, far and wide **15** making the rounds

all-around 5 broad **6** adroit, gifted **8** flexible **9** adaptable, many-sided, versatile **11** well-rounded **12** ambidextrous, multifaceted **13** comprehensive

allay 4 calm, dull, ease, hush **5** blunt, check, quell, quiet, slake **6** lessen,

pacify, quench, reduce, smooth, soften, soothe, subdue **7** appease, assuage, lighten, mollify, relieve, slacken **8** diminish, mitigate, moderate **9** alleviate, put to rest **14** cause to subside

all but 6 almost, nearly **7** close to **8** not quite **10** not far from, very nearly **14** except everyone, within an inch of **16** everything except

all by oneself 5 alone **7** unaided **9** on one's own **10** unassisted **13** unaccompanied

all-consuming 3 hot **5** fiery **6** ardent, fervid, raging, red-hot **7** burning, fanatic, fervent, frantic, glowing, intense, zealous **8** frenzied **10** passionate **11** impassioned

allegation 5 claim **6** avowal, charge **9** assertion, statement **10** accusation, contention, indictment, profession **11** declaration

allege 3 say **4** aver, avow **5** claim, state **6** accuse, affirm, assert, charge, impugn, impute **7** contend, declare, profess **8** maintain

allegiance 6 fealty, homage **7** loyalty **8** devotion, fidelity **9** adherence, constancy, deference, obedience **12** faithfulness

allegory 5 fable **7** parable

allegro
music: 4 fast

all-embracing 5 broad **6** all-out **7** general, overall **8** complete, sweeping, thorough **9** expansive, extensive, universal, unlimited **10** exhaustive, widespread **11** far-reaching, wide-ranging **12** all-inclusive, encyclopedic **13** comprehensive

Allen, Arabella
character in: 14 Pickwick Papers
author: 7 Dickens

Allen, Ethan
served in: 16 Revolutionary War
commander of: 17 Green Mountain Boys
captured: 15 Fort Ticonderoga
state: 7 Vermont

Allen, Fred
real name: 20 John Florence Sullivan
born: 11 Cambridge MA
roles: 11 What's My Line **16** The Fred Allen Show

Allen, Steve
real name: 12 Stephen Allen
wife: 12 Jayne Meadows
nickname: 10 Mr Midnight
born: 9 New York NY
roles: 13 I've Got a Secret **14** The Tonight Show

Allen, William Hervey
author of: 7 Israfel **14** Anthony Adverse

Allen, Woody
author of: 11 Getting Even, Side Ef-

fects **15** Without Feathers
real name: 22 Allen Stewart Konigsberg
wife: 12 Louise Lasser, Soon-Yi Previn
born: 10 Brooklyn NY
films: 5 Alice, Zelig **7** Bananas, Sleeper **9** Annie Hall, Interiors, Manhattan, Radio Days **12** Casino Royale, Love and Death **14** New York Stories **15** Mighty Aphrodite, Scenes from a Mall **16** Husbands and Wives, Stardust Memories **17** Broadway Danny Rose **19** Bullets over Broadway, Hannah and Her Sisters **20** The Purple Rose of Cairo **21** Crimes and Misdemeanors **22** Manhattan Murder Mystery

alleviate 4 dull, ease, quit **5** abate, allay, blunt, check, slake **6** lessen, quench, reduce, soften, subdue, temper **7** assuage, lighten, mollify, relieve, slacken **8** diminish, mitigate, moderate

alleviation 6 easing, relief **9** lessening **10** palliation

alley 4 lane **5** byway **7** passage, pathway **10** passageway **16** narrow back street

Alley Oop
  creator: 14 Vincent T Hamlin
  character:
    girlfriend: 5 Ooola
    dinosaur: 5 Dinny
    king: 6 Guzzle
    scientist: 8 Dr Wonmug
  place:
    kingdom of: 3 Moo

All for Love
  author: 10 John Dryden
  character: 6 Antony, Caesar **7** Octavia **9** Cleopatra, Dolabella, Ventidius

All God's Chillun Got Wings
  author: 12 Eugene O'Neill
  character: 6 Mickey **9** Jim Harris **10** Ella Downey

alliance 4 pact **5** union **6** league, treaty **7** compact, company **9** agreement, coalition, concordat **10** federation **11** affiliation, association, confederacy, partnership **13** confederation **15** entente cordiale

allied 4 akin, like **5** alike, joint **6** united **7** cognate, kindred, related, similar **8** combined **9** corporate, federated **10** affiliated, associated, resembling **11** amalgamated **12** incorporated

all in 4 beat **5** spent, tired, weary **6** bushed, done in, pooped **7** drained, wearied, worn out **8** dog tired, fatigued, tired out **9** bone weary, dead tired, exhausted, played out

all in all 5 in sum **10** on the whole **20** when all is said and done

all-inclusive 5 broad **6** all-out, entire **7** general, overall **8** absolute, complete, sweeping, thorough **9** expansive, extensive, universal, unlimited **10** altogether, exhaustive, widespread **11** far-reaching, wide-ranging **12** all-embracing **13** comprehensive

All in the Family
  character: 10 Joey Stivic, Mike Stivic (Meathead) **11** Edith Bunker (Dingbat) **12** Archie Bunker **18** Gloria Bunker Stivic
  cast: 9 Rob Reiner **13** Jean Stapleton **14** Carroll O'Connor, Sally Struthers
  spinoffs: 5 Maude **12** Archie's Place **13** The Jeffersons

allocate 5 allot, allow **6** assign, budget **7** earmark **8** set aside **9** apportion, designate **11** appropriate

allocation 5 quota, share **7** measure, portion **8** division **9** allotment, meting out **10** dealing out **11** consignment, designation **12** apportioning, dispensation, distribution **13** apportionment

allot 4 dole, mete **5** allow, grant **6** assign **7** appoint, consign, dole out, earmark, give out, mete out, provide **8** allocate, dispense, divide up **9** apportion, parcel out **10** distribute, portion out

allotment 5 grant, quota, share **6** ration **7** measure, portion **9** allowance **10** allocation **11** consignment **12** dispensation **13** apportionment, appropriation

all-out 5 broad, total **7** full-out, maximum **8** complete, sweeping, thorough **9** extensive, full-scale **11** unqualified, unremitting **12** all-embracing, all-inclusive **13** comprehensive, thoroughgoing

all over 4 done **5** ended, kaput **8** finished **9** concluded **10** everywhere **11** universally

All Over
  author: 11 Edward Albee

allow 3 let **4** give **5** allot, grant **6** assign, permit **7** agree to, approve, concede, provide **8** allocate, sanction **9** authorize

allowable 7 allowed **8** accepted **9** permitted, tolerable, tolerated **10** acceptable, admissible, admittable, authorized, sanctioned **11** permissible

allowance 5 grant **6** bounty, income, ration **7** annuity, payment, pension, stipend, subsidy **8** discount **9** allotment, deduction, reduction **10** concession **11** subtraction

allow to go 4 free **5** let go **6** excuse, parole **7** dismiss, release, set free **8** liberate **9** discharge

allow to pass
  French: 13 laissez passer

alloy 3 mix **5** admix, blend **6** commix, dilute, fusion, impair **7** amalgam, combine, mixture **8** compound, intermix **9** admixture, composite, synthesis **10** adulterate, commixture, interblend **12** conglomerate

alloyed 5 mixed **6** impure **7** debased

All Quiet on the Western Front
  author: 18 Erich Maria Remarque
  character: 6 Muller, Tjaden **10** Paul Baumer **11** Albert Kropp, Haie Westhus **20** Stanislaus Katczinsky (Kat)
  director: 14 Lewis Milestone
  cast: 8 Lew Ayres **12** Louis Wolheim **14** Russell Gleason
  setting: 3 WWI
  Oscar for: 7 picture

all right 2 OK **3** yes **4** fair, hale, safe, sure, well **6** hearty **7** healthy **8** properly, unharmed **9** certainly, correctly, uninjured **10** absolutely, acceptably, unimpaired **14** satisfactorily
  Spanish: 5 bueno

All Said and Done
  author: 16 Simone de Beauvoir

allspice
  botanical name: 7 pimenta, p dioica **12** p officinalis
  also called: 7 pimento
  origin: 7 Jamaica **16** Caribbean Islands
  flavor: 5 clove **6** nutmeg **8** cinnamon
  use: 6 baking

Allston, Washington
  born: 10 Waccamaw SC
  artwork: 9 The Deluge **13** Uriel in the Sun **16** Belshazzar's Feast, Moonlit Landscape **20** Spanish Girl in Reverie

All's Well That Ends Well
  author: 18 William Shakespeare
  character: 5 Diana **6** Helena **7** Bertram **8** Parolles **12** King of France **14** Duke of Florence **19** Countess of Rousillon

All That Jazz
  director: 8 Bob Fosse
  cast: 9 Ben Vereen **11** Ann Reinking, Cliff Gorman, Roy Scheider **12** Jessica Lange, Leland Palmer

All the King's Men
  author: 16 Robert Penn Warren
  character: 10 Jack Burden, Judge Irwin, Sadie Burke **11** Adam Stanton, Willie Stark **12** Annie Stanton
  director: 12 Robert Rossen
  cast: 9 Joanne Dru, John Derek **11** John Ireland **17** Broderick Crawford **19** Mercedes McCambridge
  Oscar for: 5 actor (Crawford) **7** picture **17** supporting actress (McCambridge)

all the more
  Latin: 9 a fortiori

All the President's Men
  author: 11 Bob Woodward **13** Carl Bernstein
  subject: 16 Watergate scandal
  newspaper: 14 Washington Post
  director: 11 Alan J Pakula

cast: 10 Jack Warden **11** Hal Holbrook **12** Jason Robards, Martin Balsam **13** Dustin Hoffman (Carl Bernstein), Jane Alexander, Robert Redford (Bob Woodward)
Oscar for: 12 screenwriter **15** supporting actor (Robards)

all the same 5 alike **7** however, uniform **8** unvaried **9** identical **11** homogeneous

all together 7 en masse, in a body **8** as a group, in a group, in unison
French: 12 tout ensemble

all told 5 in sum, total **6** in toto **7** totally **8** as a whole **10** altogether

allude 4 hint **5** refer **7** mention, speak of, suggest **8** intimate **9** touch upon

allure 4 bait, lure **5** charm, tempt **6** entice, lead on, seduce **7** attract, beguile, enchant, glamour **8** intrigue **9** captivate, fascinate **10** attraction, enticement, temptation **11** enchantment, fascination

allurement 4 draw, lure **5** charm **9** magnetism **10** attraction **11** fascination

alluring 4 sexy **8** charming, enticing, magnetic **10** attractive **11** fascinating

allusion 4 hint **7** mention **9** reference **10** suggestion

Allworthy, Squire
　character in: 8 Tom Jones
　author: 8 Fielding

ally 5 unite **6** league **7** combine, partner **8** confrere **9** accessory, affiliate, associate, colleague **10** accomplice, join forces **11** confederate **12** band together, bind together, collaborator, join together

Ally McBeal
　creator/writer: 11 David E Kelly
　actor (role): 16 Calista Flockhart (**10** Ally McBeal) **19** Courtney Thorne-Smith (**7** Georgia) **11** Greg Germann (**11** Richard Fish) **16** Lisa Nicole Carson (**11** Renee Radick) **13** Jane Krakowski (**12** Elaine Vassal) Peter MacNicol (**8** John Cage) **10** Gil Bellows (**15** Billy Alan Thomas)
　music: 13 Vonda Sheppard
　setting: 6 Boston

Allyson, June
　real name: 11 Ella Geisman
　husband: 10 Dick Powell
　born: 9 New York NY
　roles: 8 Good News **9** Interlude, The Shrike **11** Little Women **12** My Man Godfrey **16** The Stratton Story **19** The Glenn Miller Story

Almagest
　author: 7 Ptolemy
　title means: 11 the greatest
　subject: 9 astronomy

Al Maghrib see **7** Morocco

almandite

species: 6 garnet
color: 3 red

Almaviva, Count and Countess
　author: 12 Beaumarchais
　characters in: 18 The Barber of Seville **19** The Marriage of Figaro

Almayer's Folly
　author: 12 Joseph Conrad

almighty 7 supreme **8** absolute, infinite **9** sovereign, unlimited **10** invincible, omnipotent **11** all-powerful **12** transcendent

Almira
　opera by: 6 Handel

almond 12 Prunus dulcis
　varieties: 4 Wild **5** Earth, Green, Sweet **6** Bitter, Desert, Indian **8** Tropical **9** Flowering **12** Dwarf Russian
　candy: 8 marzipan
　liqueur: 6 orgeat **7** ratafia

almost 5 about **6** all but, nearly **7** close to **8** not quite, well-nigh **9** just about **10** not far from, very nearly **11** practically, on the verge of **13** approximately **14** within an inch of

almost alike 5 close **7** similar **10** resembling **11** approaching, much the same **15** nearly identical

alms 3 aid **4** dole, gift **5** mercy **6** relief **7** charity, handout, largess, present, subsidy, tribute **8** donation, gratuity, offering, pittance **9** baksheesh **10** assistance **11** benefaction, beneficence **12** contribution

almshouse 6 asylum **9** poorhouse, workhouse

almsman 5 tramp **6** beggar **9** mendicant **10** panhandler

Almug 13 red sandalwood

aloe 4 balm **9** succulent
　full name: 8: aloe vera
　in: 6 lotion **7** shampoo

aloft 2 up **5** above, way up **6** high up, on high **7** skyward **8** in the air, in the sky, overhead **10** heavenward

Aloha State
　nickname of: 6 Hawaii

alone 4 only, sole **6** lonely, single, singly, solely, unique **7** forlorn, unaided **8** deserted, desolate, forsaken, isolated, lonesome, peerless, singular, solitary, uniquely **9** abandoned, matchless, nonpareil, separated, unmatched, unrivaled **10** friendless, separately, singularly, solitarily, unassisted, unattended, unequalled, unescorted **11** unsurpassed, without help **12** incomparable, unchaperoned, unparalleled, without peers **13** unaccompanied, without others **14** singlehandedly
　Latin: 4 sola **5** solus
　French: 4 seul

along 2 on **4** over **6** beside, during, onward **7** abreast, forward, through

alongside 2 at, by **6** beside, next to **7** abreast, close by **9** at the side **10** parallel to **12** collaterally, parallelwise **13** equidistantly

aloof 3 icy **4** cold, cool **5** above, apart **6** chilly, formal, remote **7** distant, haughty, high-hat **8** detached, reserved **10** unsociable **11** at a distance, indifferent, standoffish, unconcerned **12** uninterested, unresponsive **14** unsympathetic **14** unapproachable

aloofness 7 reserve **8** coldness, coolness **9** formality **10** detachment, remoteness **11** haughtiness **12** indifference **13** unsociability **15** standoffishness

aloud 7 audibly

alphabet 4 ABCs **6** schema **7** grammar, letters **8** elements **9** rudiments, tablature **10** characters, principles **13** writing system

Alphesiboea
　also: 7 Arsinoe
　form: 5 nymph
　father: 4 Bias **7** Phegeus **9** Leucippus
　mother: 9 Philodice
　husband: 8 Alcmaeon
　son: 6 Adonis
　rejected: 8 Dionysus
　nurse for: 7 Orestes

Alpheus
　father: 7 Oceanus
　mother: 6 Tethys
　loved: 8 Arethusa
　changed into: 5 river

Alphonse and Gaston
　creator: 14 Frederick Opper
　saying: 22 After you my dear Alphonse, No after you my dear Gaston

alpine 5 alpen, lofty **6** aerial **8** elevated, snow-clad, towering **9** subalpine **10** alpestrine, sky-kissing, snow-capped **11** cloud-capped, mountainous **13** cloud- piercing, cloud-touching **14** heaven-touching

Alps, Alpine
　country: 5 Italy **6** France **7** Austria, Germany **10** Yugoslavia **11** Switzerland **13** Liechtenstein
　range: 6 Carnic, Graian, Julian, Otztal **7** Bernese, Cottian, Pennine **8** Bavarian, Ligurian, Maritime, Rhaetian **9** Dolomites, Lepontine **10** Hohe Tauern
　peak: 4 Rosa **5** Eiger, Monch **8** Jungfrau **10** Karawanken, Matterhorn, Piz Bernina **13** Grossglockner
　highest point: 5 Blanc
　pass: 7 Brenner, Simplon, Splugen, Stelvio **9** Semmering **10** St Gotthard **14** Great St Bernard
　lake: 4 Como **6** Alpine, Geneva **7** Lucerne **8** Maggiore **9** Constance
　phenomenon: 4 echo
　resort: 7 Zermatt **8** Chamonix, Salzburg, St Moritz **9** Innsbruck **13**

Berchtesgaden
singing: 5 yodel
wind: 5 foehn

already 5 early, so far 6 before 8 formerly, hitherto, until now 10 heretofore, previously

already seen
French: 6 deja vu

also 3 and, too 4 more, plus 5 extra 6 as well 7 besides 8 moreover 9 including 10 in addition 12 additionally

Altaic
language branches: 6 Turkic 8 Tungusic 9 Mongolian

altar 5 bomos 6 hestia, scribis 7 eschara 8 credence 9 holy table, prothesis 10 Lord's table

Altar
constellation of: 3 Ara

Altdorfer, Albrecht
born: 7 Germany 10 Regensburg
artwork: 16 Susanna at the Bath 20 St George and the Dragon, Susannah and the Elders 24 Landscape with a Footbridge 39 The Battle of Alexander and Darius on the Issus

alter 4 vary 5 amend 6 change, modify, recast, revise 7 convert, remodel 9 transform 13 make different

alterable 7 unfixed 8 variable 9 adaptable 10 adjustable, changeable, modifiable 11 convertible

alteration 6 change 10 adjustment, conversion, remodeling 12 modification 13 transmutation 14 transformation

altercation 3 row 4 spat, tiff 5 brawl, broil, fight, melee, scene 6 affray, fracas, rumpus, scrape 7 discord, dispute, quarrel, scuffle 8 argument 9 bickering, wrangling 10 falling-out 11 controversy 12 disagreement

alter ego 4 twin 5 match 6 double 9 duplicate, other self, semblable 10 complement, other image, second self, simulacrum 11 counterpart 12 Doppelganger

alternate 3 sub 4 vary 5 alter, proxy 6 backup, change, deputy, rotate, second 7 another, standby, stand-in 9 surrogate, take turns 10 every other, reciprocal, substitute, successive, understudy 11 alternating, consecutive, every second, interchange, intersperse, pinch hitter

alternative 6 choice, option, way out 8 recourse 9 selection 10 substitute 11 other choice

although 3 but, yet 4 even 5 still 7 however 11 nonetheless 12 nevertheless 15 notwithstanding

altitude 4 apex 6 height, vertex, zenith 8 eminence, tallness 9 elevation, loftiness, sublimity 10 prominence

Altman, Robert
director of: 4 Aria, MASH 6 Popeye 8 A Wedding 9 Short Cuts, The Player, Streamers, Nashville 10 Kansas City 11 Ready to Wear 14 The Long Goodbye 17 The James Dean Story

altogether 5 fully, in all, in sum, quite 6 in toto, wholly 7 all told, totally, utterly 8 all in all, as a whole, entirely 9 in general, out and out, perfectly 10 absolutely, completely, in sum total, on the whole, thoroughly 12 all inclusive, collectively

altruism 7 charity 10 generosity 11 benevolence 12 philanthropy, public spirit 13 unselfishness 14 bigheartedness, charitableness 15 humanitarianism

altruistic 8 generous 9 unselfish 10 benevolent, charitable 12 humanitarian, largehearted 13 philanthropic 14 public-spirited

aluminum
chemical symbol: 2 Al

alumni 5 grads

alumnus, alumna 4 grad 8 graduate 13 former student

Alverio, Rosita Dolores
real name of: 10 Rita Moreno

always 7 forever 8 evermore 9 eternally, every time, regularly 10 for all time, invariably 11 continually, incessantly, perpetually, unceasingly 12 consistently 13 everlastingly, unremittingly 14 forever and ever

Amadan
origin: 5 Irish
form: 5 fairy

Amadeus
director: 11 Milos Forman
cast: 8 Tom Hulce (Wolfgang Amadeus Mozart) 14 F Murray Abraham (Antonio Salieri)
choreography: 10 Twyla Tharp
Oscar for: 5 actor (Abraham) 7 picture 8 director

Amadis of Gaul
author: 16 Garcia de Montalvo
character: 6 Oriana, Perion 7 Elisena 8 Garinter, Lisuarte

Amado, Jorge
author of: 14 Tent of Miracles 15 Home Is the Sailor 19 Shepherds of the Night 24 Gabriela Clove and Cinnamon 25 Dona Flor and Her Two Husbands 30 The Two Deaths of Quincas Wateryell

Amahl and the Night Visitors
opera by: 7 Menotti

Amalek
father: 7 Eliphaz
mother: 6 Timnah
grandfather: 4 Esau
descendant of: 9 Amalekite

amalgam 5 alloy, blend, combo, union 6 fusion, league, merger 7 joining, mixture 8 alliance, compound, mash 9 admixture, composite 10 assemblage, commixture 11 combination 12 amalgamation, intermixture

amalgamate 3 mix 4 fuse 5 blend, merge, unify, unite 7 combine 8 coalesce, federate 9 commingle, integrate 10 synthesize 11 consolidate, incorporate 12 join together

Amarcord
director: 15 Federico Fellini
cast: 10 Bruno Zanin, Magali Noel 13 Pupella Maggio

amaretto
type: 7 liqueur
origin: 5 Italy
flavor: 6 almond
with vodka: 9 Godmother

Amaryllis
character in: 9 Ecologues
author: 6 Virgil
represented: 11 shepherdess

amass 6 gather, heap up, pile up 7 acquire, collect, compile, round up 8 assemble 10 accumulate

amateur 4 tyro 6 novice, non-pro 7 dabbler 8 beginner, hobbyist, inexpert, neophyte 9 greenhorn, unskilled 10 dilettante, unpolished 13 inexperienced 14 unprofessional 15 nonprofessional

amateurish 5 inept 6 clumsy 7 awkward 8 inexpert, mediocre 9 unskilled, untrained 10 unskillful 11 incompetent, ineffective, unpracticed 13 inexperienced 14 unaccomplished, unprofessional

amatory 3 hot 4 fond, sexy 6 ardent, doting, erotic, loving, sexual, steamy, tender 7 adoring, amorous, devoted, fervent, sensual, sexed-up 8 lovesick, romantic, yearning 9 libidinal, loverlike, rapturous 10 infatuated, lascivious, passionate 11 impassioned, languishing

amaxophobia
fear of: 7 driving 8 vehicles

amaze 3 awe 4 daze, stun 5 shock 7 astound, stagger, stupefy 8 astonish, surprise 9 dumbfound 11 flabbergast

amazement 3 awe 5 shock 6 wonder 8 surprise 9 disbelief 11 incredulity 12 astonishment, bewilderment, stupefaction

Amazon
occupation: 7 warrior
sex: 6 female
queen: 9 Hippolyta
river: 6 Brazil

amazonite
species: 8 feldspar

Amazonomachia
battle between: 6 Greeks 7 Amazons

ambassador 5 agent, envoy 6 consul, deputy, legate, nuncio 7 attache, courier 8 diplomat, emissary, minister 9 go-between 11 diplomatist 12 intermediary **13** consul general **14** representative

Ambassadors, The
author: **10** Henry James
character: **8** Strether, Waymarsh **10** Mrs Newsome **11** Mamie Pocock, Sarah Pocock **12** Maria Gostrey **15** Chadwick Newsome **17** Comtesse de Vionnet

amber
formed from: **5** resin
color: **6** yellow
Greek: **8** elektron

ambiance 3 air **4** aura, mood, tone **5** tenor **6** spirit, flavor, milieu, temper **7** climate, setting **9** character **10** atmosphere **11** environment **12** surroundings

ambiguity 9 vagueness **11** uncertainty **12** abstruseness, doubtfulness, equivocation **14** indefiniteness
French: **13** double entente

ambiguous 5 vague **7** cryptic, unclear **8** doubtful, puzzling **9** enigmatic, equivocal, uncertain **10** indefinite, misleading

ambition 3 aim **4** goal, hope, plan, push, zeal **5** dream, drive **6** design, desire, intent **7** longing, purpose **8** striving, yearning **9** objective **10** aspiration

ambitious 4 avid **5** eager **6** ardent, intent **7** arduous, zealous **8** aspiring, desirous **9** difficult, energetic, grandiose, strenuous **10** determined **11** industrious **12** enterprising

ambivalent 7 mixed **7** warring **8** clashing, confused, opposing, wavering **9** equivocal, undecided, unfocused **10** wishy-washy **11** conflicting, fluctuating, vacillating **13** contradictory

amble 6 ramble, stroll **7** meander, saunter **15** wander aimlessly

Ambler, Eric
author of: **11** The Levanter **12** A Kind of Auger **13** The Care of Time **14** The Night-Comers, Uncommon Danger **15** Journey Into Fear, The Dark Frontier **16** The Light of the Day **19** A Coffin for Dimitrios **22** The Siege of the Villa Lipp

Ambling Alp, The
nickname of: **12** Primo Carnera

ambrosial 5 balmy **8** fragrant, luscious, perfumed **9** delicious **13** sweet-smelling

ambrosia of the gods 4 food **5** drink **6** nectar **7** perfume

ambulance chaser 4 beak **6** lawyer **8** attorney **9** counselor **10** mouthpiece **12** legal advisor

ambulatory 6 mobile, moving **7** walking **10** up and about **11** peripatetic

ambush 4 trap **5** blind, cover **6** attack, entrap, hiding, lay for, waylay **7** assault **8** hideaway, surprise **9** ambus-

cade **11** concealment, hiding place **13** stalking-horse

Ameche, Don
real name: **17** Dominic Felix Amici
born: **9** Kenosha WI
roles: **4** Pais **5** Folks (Oscar) **6** Cocoon (Oscar) **12** Things Change **13** Heaven Can Wait, Moon Over Miami, Silk Stockings, Trading Places **14** That Night in Rio **16** Down Argentine Way **18** The Three Musketeers **21** Harry and the Hendersons **29** The Story of Alexander Graham Bell

Amelia
author: **13** Henry Fielding
character: **10** Dr Harrison **11** Mrs Atkinson **12** Miss Matthews **19** Captain William Booth

ameliorate 4 heal, help, mend **5** amend, fix up **6** better, perk up, pick up, reform, remedy, revise **7** advance, correct, improve, patch up, promote, rectify **8** palliate, progress **9** come along, get better **10** grow better **11** improve upon

ameliorative 8 remedial **9** improving **10** corrective, palliative **11** therapeutic **12** compensatory

amen 5 truly **6** it is so, so be it, verily **8** hear hear **9** let it be so, yes indeed **11** so shall it be **17** would that it were so

Amen
also: **4** Amon **5** Ammon
origin: **8** Egyptian
king of: **4** gods
worshiped at: **6** Thebes
personifies: **3** air **6** breath
represented by: **3** ram **5** goose
patron of: **6** Thebes
corresponds to: **4** Jove, Zeus **6** Amen Ra, Amon Ra **7** Jupiter

amenable 4 open **7** cordial, willing **8** obliging, yielding **9** agreeable, tractable **10** open-minded, responsive, submissive **11** acquiescent, complaisant, cooperative, persuadable, sympathetic **17** favorably disposed

amend 3 fix **4** mend **5** alter, emend **6** better, change, modify, polish, reform, remedy, revise **7** correct, develop, enhance, improve, perfect, rectify

amendment 6 change, reform **7** adjunct **8** addition, revision **10** alteration, correction, emendation **11** improvement **12** modification **13** rectification

amends 7 apology, defense, payment, redress **8** requital **9** atonement, expiation **10** recompense, reparation **11** explanation, restitution, restoration, retribution, vindication **12** compensation, satisfaction **13** justification, peace offering **14** acknowledgment **15** indemnification

amenity, amenities 8 civility, mild-

ness, niceties **9** geniality, gentility **10** affability, amiability, courtesies, gentleness, politeness, refinement **11** gallantries, good manners **12** friendliness, graciousness, pleasantness **13** agreeableness

Amen Ra
also: **6** Amon Ra, Amen Re
origin: **8** Egyptian
god of: **8** universe
corresponds to: **4** Amen, Amon, Jove, Zeus **5** Ammon **7** Jupiter

America
author: **19** Stephen Vincent Benet

America, North
country: **4** Cuba **5** Haiti **6** Belize, Canada, Mexico, Panama **8** Honduras **9** Costa Rica, Guatemala, Nicaragua **10** El Salvador **12** United States **17** Dominican Republic
island: **5** Banks **6** Baffin, Kodiak **7** Bahamas, Bermuda **8** Victoria **9** Alexander, Anticosti, Ellesmere, Greenland, Vancouver **10** Aleutians, Cape Breton, Long Island, West Indies **11** Southampton **12** Newfoundland, Prince Edward **13** Prince of Wales **14** Queen Charlotte
mountain: **5** Coast, Rocky **6** Brooks **7** Cascade **9** Mackenzie **10** Bitterroot **11** Appalachian **12** Sierra Nevada
highest point: **8** McKinley
lowest point: **11** Death Valley
river: **3** Red **4** Ohio **5** Yukon **6** Copper, Fraser, Hudson, Nelson **8** Arkansas, Colorado, Columbia, Delaware, Missouri **9** Mackenzie **10** Coppermine, Sacramento, San Joaquin, St Lawrence **11** Connecticut, Mississippi
lake: **4** Erie **5** Huron **6** Carson, Walker **7** Nipigon, Ontario **8** Manitoba, Michigan, Reindeer, Superior, Winnipeg **9** Athabasca, Champlain, Great Bear, Great Salt **10** Great Slave **11** Yellowstone
animal: **3** bat, rat **4** bear, lynx, puma, wolf **5** bison, moose, skunk **6** beaver, musk ox **7** bighorn, caribou **8** sewellel **9** pronghorn, white goat
bird: **4** hawk **5** eagle, snipe **8** bobwhite, woodcock, wood ibis **9** blue heron, ptarmigan
sea: **6** Bering **7** Chukchi, Lincoln **8** Beaufort **9** Caribbean
religion: **7** Judaism **10** Protestant **13** Roman Catholic **27** Eastern Orthodox Christianity
people: **6** Eskimo **8** European **12** African Negro **14** American Indian
language: **6** French **7** English, Spanish

America, South
country: **4** Peru **5** Chile **6** Brazil, Guyana **7** Bolivia, Ecuador, Uruguay **8** Colombia, Paraguay, Suriname **9** Argentina, Venezuela
city: **4** Lima **5** Quito **6** Bogota, Recife

7 Caracas **8** Salvador, Santiago, Sao Paulo **10** Montevideo **11** Buenos Aires, Porto Alegre **12** Rio de Janeiro **13** Belo Horizonte
island: 6 Chiloe, Chonos, Marajo **9** Galapagos **10** Wellington **11** Madre de Dios **13** Juan Fernandez, Reina Adelaida **14** Tierra del Fuego
sea: 9 Caribbean
lake: 5 Patos, Poopo, Mirim **6** Viedma **8** Titicaca **9** Maracaibo, San Martin **10** Concepcion
mountain: 6 Andes **9** Pakaraima **12** Monte Fitz Roy **14** Cerro Aconcagua, Monte Sarmiento **15** Serra dos Parecis **16** Monte San Valentin, Serra do Espinhaco
highest point: 9 Aconcagua
lowest point: 15 Peninsula Valdes
river: 3 Ica **4** Beni, Iaco, Jari, Meta, Napo **5** Abuna, Cauca, Chico, Iriri, Ituxi, Jurua, Jutai, Negro, Palma, Pardo, Purus, Tiete, Tigre, Xingu **6** Amazon, Arauca, Branco, Chubut, Cumina, Curaco, Cuyuni, Grande, Gurupi, Iguacu, Japura, Javari, Mamore, Maroni, Mortes, Parana, Salado, Vaupes **7** Bermejo, Caqueta, Deseado, Guapore, Jamunda, Juruena, Madeira, Mapuera, Maranon, Orinoco, Oyapock, Ucayali, Vichada **8** Amazonas, Araguaia, Colorado, Guaviare, Jamachim, Paraguay, Parnaiba, Putumayo, Tapajoz, Urubamba, Uruguay **9** Essequibo, Jaguaribe, Paranaiba, Saladillo, Sao Manuel, Tocantins **10** Courantyne **12** Sao Francisco
animal: 3 bat **4** bear, deer **5** llama, sloth, tapir **6** alpaca, monkey, ocelot, weasel **7** opossum, peccary, raccoon **8** capybara, javelina **9** armadillo
bird: 3 owl **4** hawk, rhea **5** eagle **6** condor, falcon, jabiru **7** hoatzin **8** flamingo **11** hummingbird
people: 6 Indian **7** African, Chibcha, Mestizo, Mulatto, Spanish **10** Araucanian, Portuguese
religion: 7 Judaism **10** Protestant **13** Roman Catholic
language: 5 Dutch **7** English, Spanish **10** Portuguese

American, The
author: 10 Henry James
character: 8 Mrs Bread **10** Mr Tristram **11** Mrs Tristram **12** Noemie Nioche **13** Count Valentin **14** Claire de Cintre **17** Christopher Newman **25** Marquis Urbain de Bellegarde
setting: 5 Paris

American Caesar
author: 17 William Manchester

American Claimant, The
author: 9 Mark Twain

American Dreams
author: 11 Studs Terkel

American Graffiti
director: 11 George Lucas

cast: 9 Paul Le Mat, Ron Howard **10** Candy Clark **11** Wolfman Jack **12** Harrison Ford **13** Cindy Williams **15** Richard Dreyfuss **17** MacKenzie Phillips

American Indian *see under* **14** Native American

American in Paris, An
director: 16 Vincente Minnelli
cast: 8 Nina Foch **9** Gene Kelly **11** Leslie Caron, Oscar Levant **14** Georges Guetary
score: 14 George Gershwin
Oscar for: 7 picture

Americanization of Emily
director: 12 Arthur Hiller
script by: 14 Paddy Chayefsky
cast: 11 James Coburn, James Garner **12** Julie Andrews **13** Melvyn Douglas

American Tragedy, An
author: 15 Theodore Dreiser
character: 12 Roberta Alden **14** Clyde Griffiths, Sondra Finchley **15** Samuel Griffiths
movie: 14 A Place in the Sun

America's Sweetheart
nickname of: 12 Mary Pickford

amethyst
species: 6 quartz
color: 6 purple
month: 8 February

Amfortas
leader of: 7 knights
in search of: 9 holy grail

ami, amie 6 friend

amiability 10 good nature, kindliness **12** agreeability, friendliness, pleasantness

amiable 6 genial, kindly, polite **7** affable, cordial, winning **8** amicable, charming, engaging, friendly, gracious, obliging, pleasant, pleasing, sociable **9** agreeable, congenial **10** attractive **11** good-natured

amicability 5 amity **7** concord **8** good will **9** affection **10** cordiality, friendship **12** friendliness **14** neighborliness

amicable 4 kind **5** civil **6** kindly, polite **7** amiable, cordial **8** amenable, friendly, sociable **9** agreeable, courteous, peaceable **10** benevolent, harmonious, neighborly **11** kindhearted

Amici, Dominic Felix
real name of: 9 Don Ameche

amicus curiae 17 a friend of the court

amigo, amiga 6 friend

Amis, Kingsley
author of: 8 Ending Up, Lucky Jim **10** Colonel Sun, Jake's Thing **11** I Like It Here, The Green Man **16** One Fat Englishman, Take A Girl Like You **18** Russian Hide-and-Seek, The Anti-Death League **20** That Uncertain Feeling
father of: 10 Martin Amis

amiss 4 awry **5** askew, false, wrong **6**

astray, faulty **7** falsely, mixed-up, off base, wrongly **8** faultily, improper, mistaken, untoward **9** erroneous, incorrect, out of line **10** fallacious, improperly, mistakenly, out of order, unsuitable, unsuitably, untowardly **11** erroneously, incorrectly **12** inaccurately **13** inappropriate **15** inappropriately

Amittai
son: 5 Jonah

amity 6 accord **7** concord, harmony **8** good will, sympathy **9** agreement **10** cordiality, fellowship, fraternity, friendship **11** brotherhood, cooperation **13** understanding

Ammishaddai
son: 7 Ahiezer

Ammon
father: 3 Lot
descendants: 9 Ammonites

Ammonite god 6 Molech, Moloch

ammunition 4 ammo, arms **5** shell **6** bullet, rocket **7** missile, torpedo **9** artillery, cartridge, small arms **11** iron rations **13** powder and shot

ammunition dump 7 arsenal **8** magazine **18** military storehouse, munitions warehouse

amnesia 4 daze **5** fugue **6** stupor **7** agnosia **8** blackout **9** memory gap **11** anterograde, trance state

amnesty 6 pardon **8** immunity, reprieve **10** absolution **11** forgiveness **14** reconciliation

amoeba, ameba 4 dyad, germ, mold **5** spore, virus **6** fungus **7** ciliate, microbe **8** bacteria, reovirus **9** bacterium, echovirus **13** microorganism
part: 7 nucleus **8** membrane **9** pseudopod **10** protoplasm **11** food vacuole **18** contractile vacuole
reproduction by: 7 fission

amok *see* **5** amuck

Amon *see* **4** Amen

among 2 at **3** mid **4** amid, with **6** amidst **7** amongst, between, betwixt **12** in the midst of

among other persons
Latin: 10 inter alios

among others 8 attended, escorted, in a crowd, in a group, together **11** accompanied

among other things
Latin: 9 inter alia

among themselves
Latin: 7 inter se

Amon Ra *see* **6** Amen Ra

Amor *see* **5** Cupid

Amore dei Tre Re, L'
opera by: 10 Montemezzi

Amoretti
author: 13 Edmund Spenser

amoretto
art figure: 5 Cupid

amorous 4 fond **6** ardent, doting, loving, tender **8** enamored, lovesick **10** passionate **11** impassioned **12** affectionate

amorousness 4 love **5** ardor **6** warmth **7** passion

amor patriae 10 patriotism **13** love of country

amorphous 5 vague **8** formless, unshapen **9** anomalous, shapeless, undefined **11** nondescript **12** undelineated **13** characterless, indeterminate

Amos
　father: 4 Naum

Amos 'n' Andy
　character: 8 Lightnin' **9** Amos Jones, Andy Brown **13** George (the King Fish) Stevens **15** Sapphire Stevens
　cast: 8 Tim Moore **13** Ernestine Wade, Horace Stewart **14** Alvin Childress **15** Spencer Williams

amount 3 sum **4** bulk, mass **5** total **6** extent, volume **7** measure **8** quantity, sum total **9** aggregate, magnitude

amour 6 affair **7** liaison, romance **8** intrigue **10** love affair

amour propre 8 self-love **10** self-esteem **11** self-respect

Ampelos
　form: 5 satyr

Ampere, Andre-Marie
　field: 7 physics **11** mathematics
　nationality: 6 French
　founded: 15 electrodynamics **16** electromagnetism

amphibian 8 seaplane **10** hydroplane, vertebrate **14** aerohydroplane
　kind: 4 frog, newt, toad **9** caecilian **10** salamander
　young: 6 larvae **7** tadpole **8** polliwog

Amphisbaena
　form: 7 serpent
　number of heads: 3 two

amphitheater 4 bowl **5** arena **7** gallery, stadium **8** coliseum **10** auditorium
　Roman: 9 Colosseum

Amphitrite
　origin: 5 Greek
　goddess of: 3 sea
　father: 6 Nereus
　mother: 5 Doris
　husband: 8 Poseidon

Amphitruo (Amphitryon)
　author: 7 Plautus
　character: 4 Zeus **7** Alcmena, Jupiter, Mercury **10** Amphitryon

Amphitryon
　father: 7 Alcaeus
　grandfather: 7 Perseus
　uncle: 9 Electryon, Sthenelus
　wife: 7 Alcmene
　son: 8 Iphicles
　daughter: 8 Perimede

Amphitryon 38
　author: 13 Jean Giraudoux

amphora 3 jar, jug, urn **4** vase

ample 3 big **4** huge, vast, wide **5** broad, large, roomy **6** enough, plenty **7** copious, immense, liberal, profuse **8** abundant, adequate, extended, generous, spacious **9** bountiful, capacious, expansive, extensive, outspread, plentiful **10** commodious, sufficient, voluminous **11** substantial **12** satisfactory **14** more than enough

amplification 7 raising **8** increase, widening **9** expansion, extension **10** developing, filling out, increasing **11** added detail, development, elaboration, enlargement, expatiation, fleshing out, heightening, lengthening, rounding out **12** augmentation **13** magnification **14** aggrandizement **15** supplementation

amplify 5 add to, raise, widen **6** deepen, expand, extend **7** augment, broaden, develop, enlarge, fill out **8** complete, heighten, increase, lengthen **9** elaborate (on), expatiate, intensify **10** illustrate, strengthen, supplement

amplitude 4 bulk, mass, size **5** range, reach, scope, sweep, width **6** extent, volume **7** bigness, breadth, compass, expanse **8** fullness, plethora, richness, vastness **9** abundance, dimension, largeness, magnitude, plenitude, profusion **11** copiousness **12** completeness, spaciousness **13** capaciousness

amply 5 fully **6** richly **8** lavishly **9** copiously, liberally, profusely **10** abundantly, adequately, completely, generously, thoroughly **11** bountifully, plentifully **12** sufficiently, unstintingly **14** satisfactorily

amputate 5 sever **6** cut off, excise, lop off, remove **9** dismember

Amram
　father: 4 Bani **6** Dishon
　son: 5 Aaron, Moses
　daughter: 6 Miriam

Amsterdam
　airport: 8 Schiphol
　canal: 11 Herengracht **13** Keizersgracht, Prinsengracht
　capital of: 7 Holland **11** Netherlands
　landmark: 8 Oude Kerk **10** Nieuwe Kerk
　museum: 7 Van Gogh **9** Stedelijk **11** Rijksmuseum
　nickname: 16 Venice of the North
　waters: 6 Amstel **7** Ij River **9** Zuiderzee **10** Ijsselmeer **13** North Sea

amuck 4 amok, nuts **6** wildly **7** berserk, bonkers **8** crackers, insanely **9** in a frenzy **10** frenziedly, maniacally **11** ferociously, murderously **14** uncontrollably

amulet 5 charm **6** fetish **8** talisman **10** lucky piece

amuse 5 cheer **6** absorb, divert, oc-

cupy, please **7** beguile, engross, enliven, gladden **8** interest **9** entertain

amusement 3 fun **4** game, play **5** hobby, revel **7** delight, pastime **8** pleasure **9** avocation, diversion, enjoyment, merriment **10** recreation **11** distraction **13** entertainment

amusing 5 droll, funny, witty **7** comical, waggish **8** cheering, farcical, humorous, pleasant, pleasing **9** absorbing, beguiling, diverting **10** delightful, engrossing **11** interesting, pleasurable **12** entertaining

Amy, Gilbert
　composer of: 9 Alpha-Beth **10** Epigrammes, Mouvements **11** Antiphonies **12** Trajectories

anagram 4 code **6** cipher

Anakim 11 giant people

analects 8 extracts **9** gleanings **10** miscellany, selections **11** collectanea, miscellanea

Analects of Confucius, The
　author: 9 Confucius

analeptic 9 stimulant **11** restorative

analgesic 4 drug **6** opiate **7** anodyne **8** narcotic **10** anesthetic, painkiller

analogous 4 akin, like **7** similar **8** parallel **10** comparable, equivalent **11** correlative **13** corresponding

analogy 6 simile **8** likeness, metaphor **10** comparison, similarity, similitude **11** correlation, equivalence, parallelism, resemblance **14** correspondence

analysis 4 test **5** assay, brief, study **6** digest, precis, review, search **7** breakup, inquiry, outline, summary, therapy **8** abstract, judgment, synopsis, thinking **9** appraisal, breakdown, diagnosis, partition, reasoning, reduction **10** dissection, estimation, evaluation, resolution, separation **11** examination, observation, speculation **12** dissociation **13** investigation, psychotherapy **14** interpretation, psychoanalysis

analyst 5 judge **6** shrink, tester **8** examiner, observer **9** appraiser, estimator, evaluator **12** headshrinker, investigator **13** psychoanalyst

analytic, analytical 7 logical, testing **8** rational, studious **9** inquiring, organized, searching **10** diagnostic, systematic **14** problem-solving

analyze 5 assay, judge, study **6** search **7** examine **8** appraise, consider, diagnose, evaluate, question **9** reason out **11** investigate **12** think through

Ananais
　father: 8 Nebedeus
　wife: 8 Sapphira
　sent to: 4 Paul, Saul
　lied to: 5 Peter
　same as: 4 liar

anarchist 5 rebel **8** mutineer, nihilist **9**

insurgent, terrorist **11** syndicalist **13** revolutionary

anarchy 5 chaos **6** utopia **8** disorder **11** lawlessness **13** the millennium **19** absence of government

Anastasia
director: **13** Anatole Litvak
cast: **10** Helen Hayes, Yul Brynner **12** Akim Tamiroff **13** Ingrid Bergman (Oscar)

anathema 3 ban **5** curse, taboo **7** censure **11** abomination, malediction **12** condemnation, denunciation, proscription **13** unmentionable **15** excommunication

Anathema
author: **14** Leonid Andreyev

anathematize 4 damn **7** accurse, condemn **8** execrate, maledict **9** abominate **13** excommunicate **17** hold in abomination

Anatolia see **7** Armenia

Anatolian
language family: **12** Indo-European
includes: **6** Luwian Lycian Lydian **7** Hittite
spoken in: **9** Asia Minor
spoken by: **8** Hittites

anatomist 12 morphologist
American: **5** Allen, Evans **7** Herrick **8** Stockard
Arabian: **8** Avicenna
British: **4** Owen **5** Hooke **6** Harvey
Dutch: **10** Swammerdam
French: **6** Buffon, Cuvier
German: **5** Wolff **7** Schwann
Greek: **5** Galen **9** Aristotle **10** Herophilus **12** Erasistratus
Italian: **8** Malpighi
Scottish: **5** Brown

anatomize 7 analyze, dissect **18** separate into pieces

anatomy 4 body **8** analysis **9** structure **10** dissection **11** examination

Anatomy Lesson, The
author: **10** Philip Roth

Anatomy of a Murder
director: **13** Otto Preminger
cast: **8** Eve Arden **9** Lee Remick **10** Ben Gazzara **12** George C Scott, James Stewart, Kathryn Grant **14** Arthur O'Connell
score: **13** Duke Ellington

Anatomy of Melancholy, The
author: **12** Robert Burton

Anatosaurus
type: **8** dinosaur **10** ornithopod
period: **10** Cretaceous
characteristic: **10** duck-billed
location: **12** North America

Anaxibia
father: **6** Atreus
mother: **6** Aerope
brother: **8** Menelaus **9** Agamemnon
husband: **6** Nestor **9** Strophius
son: **7** Pylades

Anaximander
field: **11** mathematics
nationality: **5** Greek
doctrine: **11** single-world
first: **22** geometric universe model

ancestor 8 begetter, forebear **9** precursor, prototype **10** antecedent, forefather, forerunner, procreator, progenitor **11** predecessor

ancestry 4 line, race **5** house, stock **6** family, origin **7** descent, lineage **8** heredity, pedigree **9** ancestors, blood line, genealogy, parentage **10** derivation, extraction, family tree **11** progenitors

Anchisaurus
type: **8** dinosaur
location: **17** Connecticut Valley

Anchises
prince of: **4** Troy
father: **5** Capys
mother: **8** Themiste
grandfather: **9** Assaracus
uncle: **8** Laomedon
brother: **7** Laocoon
son: **5** Lyrus **6** Aeneas

anchor 3 fix **4** hook, moor **5** affix, basis **6** fasten, secure **7** bulwark, defense, mooring, support **8** mainstay, security **9** safeguard **10** foundation **12** ground tackle

anchorage 3 key **4** bund, dock, pier, port, quay, slip **5** berth, haven, jetty, wharf **6** harbor, marina **7** dockage, mooring, seaport **9** harborage, roadstead

ancient 3 old **4** aged **5** early, hoary, Greek, olden, passe, Roman **6** age-old, bygone, old hat, remote **7** antique, archaic, classic, very old **8** long past, obsolete, outmoded, primeval, timeworn **9** classical, out-of-date, primitive **10** antiquated, fossilized, Greco-Roman **11** obsolescent, prehistoric **12** old-fashioned, out-of-fashion

ancientness 8 great age **9** antiquity **11** advanced age

ancient times 9 antiquity **10** days of yore **12** the Golden Age

ancillary 5 minor **7** adjunct **8** inferior **9** accessory, auxiliary, dependent, secondary **10** additional, subsidiary **11** subordinate, subservient **12** contributory **13** supplementary

Ancius
form: **7** centaur

Ancus Marcius
king of: **4** Rome

and 3 too **4** also, more, plus **8** as well as **10** in addition **11** furthermore

andante
music: **4** even **14** moderately slow

Andean
language family: **16** Andean-Equatorial

group: **3** Ona **6** Aymara, Yahgan, Zaparo **7** Quechua **10** Araucanian

Andean-Equatorial
language branch: **6** Andean **10** Equatorial

and elsewhere 4 et al **7** et alibi

Andersen, Hans Christian
known for: **10** fairy tales
born: **7** Denmark
author of: **10** Thumbelina **11** The Red Shoes **12** The Snow Queen, The Swineherd, The Tinder Box **14** The Nightingale **15** The Ugly Duckling **16** The Little Mermaid **18** The Little Match Girl **20** The Princess and the Pea **21** The Emperor's New Clothes **22** The Steadfast Tin Soldier **25** The Shepherdess and the Sweep
played by: **9** Danny Kaye

Anderson, Frances Margaret
real name of: **14** Judith Anderson

Anderson, Judith
real name: **23** Frances Margaret Anderson
born: **8** Adelaide **9** Australia
roles: **5** Medea **6** Hamlet, Salome **7** Macbeth, Rebecca **8** Kings Row **16** Cat on a Hot Tin Roof

Anderson, Maxwell
author of: **7** High Tor **8** Key Largo **9** Winterset **11** Valley Forge **14** Both Your Houses, Lost in the Stars, Mary of Scotland, What Price Glory? **17** Elizabeth the Queen **20** Knickerbocker Holiday

Anderson, Sherwood
author of: **9** Poor White **12** Beyond Desire, Dark Laughter, Horses and Men **13** Many Marriages, Winesburg Ohio **15** Death in the Woods **18** The Triumph of the Egg

Anderson, Sparky (George Lee)
sport: **8** baseball
position: **7** manager
team: **9** Minnesota **14** Cincinnati Reds

Andersonville
author: **15** MacKinlay Kantor

Andersson, Bibi
born: **6** Sweden **9** Stockholm
roles: **14** The Seventh Seal **16** Wild Strawberries **19** Scenes from a Marriage **20** Smiles of a Summer Night

Andes
Spanish: **20** Cordillera de los Andes
peak: **6** Pissis, Sajama, Sorata **7** Illampu **8** Cotopaxi, Illimani **9** Huascaran **10** Chimborazo **14** Cristobal Colon
highest point: **9** Aconcagua
volcano: **6** Sangay, Tolima **8** Cotopaxi **10** Tungurahua
country: **4** Peru **5** Chile **6** Panama **7** Bolivia, Ecuador **8** Colombia **9** Argentina, Venezuela
river: **5** Cauca **6** Amazon, Parana **7** Orinoco, Ucayali **9** Magdalena

lake: 5 Poopo **8** Titicaca
animal: 5 llama **6** alpaca, condor,
huemul **10** chinchilla
**And I Worked at the Writer's
Trade**
author: **13** Malcolm Cowley
Andorra
other name: 13 Valls d'Andorra **16**
Valleys of Andorra
capital/largest city: 14 Andorra-la-
Vella
others: 3 Pal **5** Ramio **6** Ordino,
Soldeu **7** Canillo, Certers **9** La Massana **11** Les Escaldes **16** San Julian
de Loria
division: 6 Encamp, Ordino **7** Andorra, Camillo **9** La Massana, Sant
Julia
heads of state: 13 Bishop of Urgel
(Spain) **17** President of France
head of government: 11 First Syndic
monetary unit: 5 franc **6** peseta
lake: 11 Engolasters
location: 8 Pyrenees
mountain: 6 d'Etats **8** l'Estanyo, Pyrenees **10** Cataperdis
highest point: 11 Como Pedrosa
neighbors: 5 Spain **6** France
river: 6 Ariege, Valira
people: 7 Catalan **8** Andosian
language: 6 French **7** Catalan, Spanish
religion: 13 Roman Catholic
place: 12 Casa de la Vall
  Moorish ruin: 4 Ceca, Meka
feature:
  co-princes' representative: 7
  vigueer, viguier
  fiesta: 13 Bal de Morratxa
  food payment to bishop: 9 la
  quistia
Andorra-la-Vella
capital of: 7 Andorra
and others 3 etc **4** et al **6** et alii **7**
and so on **8** et cetera **10** and so forth,
and the rest
And Quiet Flows the Don
author: **15** Mikhail Sholokov
character: 6 Piotra **7** Bunchuk, Natalia **14** Gregor Melekhov **16** Aksinia
Astakhova
Andrea del Sarto
real name: 32 Andrea Domenico
d'Agnolo di Francesco
born: 5 Italy **8** Florence
artwork: 7 Caritas **9** A Young Man
16 Birth of the Virgin, Journey of the
Magi **19** Madonna of the Harpies,
Portrait of a Sculptor
Andrea del Sarto
author: **14** Robert Browning
Andress, Ursula
husband: 9 John Derek
born: 5 Bern **11** Switzerland
roles: 3 She **4** Dr No **12** Casino Royale, Four for Texas

Andrew 7 apostle
brother: 5 Peter, Simon
Andrews, Dana
real name: 17 Carver Dana Andrews
brother: 12 Steve Forrest
born: 9 Collins MS
roles: 5 Laura **9** State Fair **12** Elephant Walk **13** A Walk in the Sun,
Ox-Bow Incident **15** Two for the Seesaw **22** The Best Years of Our Lives
Andrews, Julie
real name: 19 Julia Elizabeth Wells
husband: 12 Blake Edwards
born: 7 England **14** Walton-on-
Thames
roles: 10 My Fair Lady **11** Mary Poppins (Oscar) **14** Victor Victoria **15**
The Sound of Music
Andreyev, Leonid Nikolaevich
author of: 3 S O S **5** Savva **7** Lazarus, Silence **8** Anathema **10** To the
Stars **11** The Red Laugh **12** The Life
of Man **16** He Who Gets Slapped **18**
Love of One's Neighbor **19** Seven
That Were Hanged
Andria
author: **7** Terence
Androcles
origin: 5 Roman
position: 5 slave
Androcles and the Lion
author: **17** George Bernard Shaw
removed: 5 thorn
androgenous 8 bisexual **14** hermaph-
roditic
Andromache
father: 6 Eetion
husband: 6 Hector
son: 6 Pielus **8** Astyanax, Molossus,
Pergamus **9** Cestrinus
author: 9 Euripides
character: 6 Peleus, Thetis **7** Orestes
8 Menelaus
  mistress of: 11 Neoptolemus
  rival: 8 Hermione
  son: 8 Molossus
setting: 8 Thessaly
Andromaque
author: **18** Jean Baptiste Racine
character:
  son: 8 Astyanax
  king: 7 Pyrrhus
setting: 8 Epirus
Andromeda
astronomy: 13 constellation
father: 7 Cepheus
mother: 10 Cassiopeia
husband: 7 Perseus
son: 6 Mestor, Perses **7** Alcaeus,
Heleius **9** Electryon, Sthenelus
daughter: 10 Gorgophone
rescued from: 10 sea monster
rescued by: 7 Perseus
Andromeda Strain, The
author: **15** Michael Crichton
androphobia
fear of: 3 men

Androsphinx
form: 6 sphinx
head of: 3 man
and so forth 3 etc **7** and so on **8** et
cetera **9** and others **10** and the rest
and so on 3 etc **8** et cetera **9** and
others **10** and so forth, and the rest
And Then There Were None
director: **9** Rene Clair
based on novel by: 14 Agatha Christie
cast: 11 Roland Young **12** Louis Hayward, Walter Huston **15** Barry Fitzgerald
remade as: 16 Ten Little Indians
and thou, Brutus
Latin: 9 et tu Brute
spoken by: 12 Julius Caesar
Andvari
origin: 6 Nordic
form: 5 dwarf
Andy Capp
creator: 14 Reginald Smythe
character: 5 Vicar
  wife: 3 Flo
plays: 7 snooker
Andy Griffith Show, The
character: 10 Andy Taylor, Barney
Fife, Goober Pyle, Helen Crump,
Opie Taylor **11** Floyd Lawson **12**
Otis Campbell **13** Aunt Bee Taylor,
Howard Sprague
cast: 8 Hal Smith **9** Don Knotts, Ron
(Ronny) Howard **10** Jack Dodson **12**
Andy Griffith, Anita Corsaut, Howard
McNear **13** Frances Bavier, George
Lindsey
setting: 8 Mayberry
Andy's job: 7 sheriff
anecdote 4 tale, yarn **5** story **6** sketch
12 brief account, reminiscence
collection: 3 ana
anemic, anaemic 3 wan **4** dull, pale,
weak **5** quiet **6** feeble, pallid **7** subdued **9** colorless **11** thin-blooded **13**
characterless
anemone 4 lily **5** plant **6** flower
**anesthesia, anaesthesia, anesthe-
sis 6** stupor **8** numbness **11** insentience **13** loss of feeling **15** unconsciousness
anesthetic, anaesthetic 4 drug **5**
ether, local **6** caudal, opiate, spinal **7**
general **8** narcotic, procaine **9** analgesic, enflurane, halothane, lidocaine,
peridural **10** chloroform, isoflurane,
painkiller, tetracaine, thiopental **11**
acupuncture, laughing gas **12** nitrous
oxide **15** sodium pentothal
anesthetize 4 dope, drug, numb **6**
deaden, sedate
anew 5 again, newly **6** afresh **8** once
more **9** over again **11** from scratch
Latin: 6 de novo
a new order of the ages is born
Latin: 17 novus ordo seclorum

author: 6 Virgil
work: 8 Eclogues
motto of: 11 US great seal

angel 3 gem **4** doll **5** jewel, power, saint **6** cherub, patron, seraph, throne, virtue **7** sponsor **8** cherabim, seraphim, treasure **9** archangel **10** benefactor, domination **11** underwriter **12** principality **14** celestial being, heavenly spirit, messenger of God **15** financial backer

Angel, fallen 5 Satan **6** Azazel **7** Lucifer

angelic 4 good, pure **5** ideal **6** divine, lovely **7** saintly **8** adorable, beatific, cherubic, ethereal, heavenly, innocent, seraphic **9** angel-like, beautiful, celestial, rapturous, spiritual **10** entrancing **11** enrapturing

Angelic Doctor
nickname of: 15 St Thomas Aquinas

Angelico, Fra
real name: 13 Guido di Pietro
born: 7 Vicchio **14** Castell Vecchio
artwork: 12 Annunciation **15** Madonna Annalena **19** Descent from the Cross **21** Coronation of the Virgin **29** Madonna of the Linen Drapers' Guild

Angelo
character in: 17 Measure for Measure
author: 11 Shakespeare

Angel of Fire, The
also: 13 The Fiery Angel
opera by: 9 Prokofiev

anger 3 ire, vex **4** bile, fury, gall, rage, rile **5** annoy, chafe, pique, wrath **6** choler, dander, enmity, enrage, hatred, madden, nettle, rankle, ruffle, spleen, temper **7** incense, inflame, outrage, provoke, umbrage **8** acrimony, embitter, irritate, vexation **9** animosity, annoyance, displease, hostility, hot temper, ill temper, infuriate, petulance **10** antagonism, antagonize, exacerbate, exasperate, irritation, resentment **11** displeasure, indignation **12** exasperation, make bad blood **14** disapprobation **15** get one's dander up **16** cause ill feelings **18** ruffle one's feathers

Anger
author: 9 May Sarton

Angerboda
also: 9 Angrbodha, Angurboda
origin: 12 Scandinavian
form: 8 giantess
children: 3 Hel **6** Fenrir, Fenris **11** Iormungandr, Jormungandr **14** Midgard Serpent

angle 4 bend, cusp, edge, side, turn **5** focus, slant **6** aspect, corner **7** outlook **8** position **9** viewpoint **10** divergence, standpoint **11** perspective, point of view
kind: 5 acute, right **6** obtuse **8** straight

point: 6 vertex
measure: 7 degrees

angled 4 bent **6** fished **7** crooked, slanted **8** diverged

Anglo-Frisian
language family: 12 Indo-European
branch: 8 Germanic
group: 15 Western Germanic
language: 7 English, Frisian

Angola
other name: 7 Bakongo **20** Portuguese West Africa
capital/largest city: 6 Luanda
others: 5 Dundo **6** Ambriz, Huambo, Lobito **7** Cabinda, Kampala, Malange, Malanje, Salazar **8** Benguela, Cassinga, Vila Luso **9** Ambrizete, Mocamedes **10** Mossamedes, Nova Lisboa, Silva Porto
division: 3 Bie **4** Uige **5** Huila, Lunda, Zaire **6** Cunene, Huambo, Luanda, Moxico **7** Cabinda, Malanje **8** Benguela **9** Cuanza Sul, Mocamedes **11** Cuanza Norte **13** Cuando Cubango
monetary unit: 6 escudo, macuta, macute **7** angolar, centavo
mountain: 5 Chela **6** Loviti **16** Humpata Highlands
highest point: 4 Moco
river: 4 Cuvo **5** Congo, Cuito, Longa **6** Cassai, Coanza, Cuando, Cuanza, Cunene, Kunene, Kwango, Kwanza, Luando **7** Chiumbe, Cubango, Zambezi **11** Lungue- Bungo
sea: 6 Indian **8** Atlantic
physical feature:
basin: 8 Okavango
desert: 9 Mocamedes
falls: 15 Catarata Ruacana, Duque de Braganca
plain: 8 Planalto
plateau: 4 Rand **5** Huila **11** Benguela Bie, Lunda Divide
people: 5 Bantu, Kongo, Lundu **6** Chokwe, Herero, Mbundu, Ovambo **7** Bakongo, Kangela, Kikongo **8** Kimbundu, Kwangare **9** Ovinbundu **12** Nyaneka-Humbi
leader: 13 Agostinho Neto **20** Jose Eduardo dos Santos
language: 5 Bantu **8** Kimbundu, Oumbundu **9** Ovimbundu **10** Portuguese
religion: 7 animism **10** Protestant **13** Roman Catholic
place:
fortress: 9 Sao Miguel
feature:
mahogany: 5 khaya
weed: 6 archil

angry 3 mad **5** huffy, irate, riled, vexed **6** fuming, galled, piqued, raging **7** annoyed, boiling, burnt up, enraged, furious, hateful, hostile, nettled **8** incensed, inflamed, offended, outraged, petulant, provoked **9** affronted, indignant, irascible, irritated, resent-

ful, splenetic, turbulent **10** displeased, embittered, infuriated **11** acrimonious, exasperated, ill-tempered **12** antagonistic

angst 5 dread **6** unease **7** anxiety **10** foreboding, uneasiness **12** apprehension

angstrom
abbreviation: 1 A

Angstrom, Anders Jon
field: 7 physics **9** astronomy
founded: 12 spectroscopy
mapped: 11 solar system
angstrom unit: 17 wavelength of light

Angstrom, Harry see **6** Updike

anguish 3 woe **4** pain **5** agony, grief **6** misery, sorrow **7** anxiety, despair, remorse, torment **8** distress **9** heartache, suffering

Anguish
goddess of: 8 Angerona

anguished 6 pained **7** anxious, fearful **9** tormented **10** distressed **11** heartbroken

angular 4 bent, bony, lank, lean **5** gaunt, lanky, spare **6** jagged **7** crooked, scrawny **8** rawboned **13** sharp- cornered

Angus Og
origin: 5 Irish
god of: 4 love **5** youth **6** beauty

animadversion 4 flak **7** nagging, quibble **9** aspersion, criticism, pestering **12** faultfinding **14** censoriousness

animal 3 pet **5** beast, brute **6** mammal **8** creature, nonhuman, organism **9** quadruped
group: 4 bird, fish, worm **6** insect, mammal, sponge **7** primate, reptile, rotifer **8** ruminant **9** amphibian **10** vertebrate **12** invertebrate

Animal Crackers
director: 13 Victor Heerman
cast: 5 Chico, Harpo, Zeppo **7** Groucho **11** Lillian Roth **12** Marx Brothers **14** Margaret Dumont
song: 25 Hooray for Captain Spaulding

Animal Farm
author: 12 George Orwell
character: 5 Boxer **7** Mr Jones **8** Napoleon, Snowball

Animals in That Country, The
author: 14 Margaret Atwood

animate 4 fire, goad, move, stir, urge, warm **5** alive, impel, liven, set on **6** arouse, excite, fire up, incite, moving, prompt, spur on, vivify, work up **7** actuate, enliven, inspire, provoke, quicken **8** activate, energize, vitalize **9** instigate, make alive, stimulate **10** invigorate, make lively **11** add spirit to **12** give energy to

animated 3 gay, hot **4** airy **5** brisk, quick, vivid **6** active, ardent, blithe, breezy, bright, elated, lively **7** buoyant, dynamic, fervent, glowing, vibrant, zealous, zestful **8** exciting, spirited, sportive, vigorous **9** ebullient, energetic, sprightly, vivacious **10** passionate **12** invigorating

animation 3 vim **4** fire, glow, life, zest **5** ardor, verve, vigor **6** action, gaiety, spirit **7** elation **8** activity, alacrity, buoyancy, vibrancy, vitality, vivacity **9** alertness, briskness, eagerness, good cheer **10** brightness, ebullience, enthusiasm, excitement, liveliness **12** exhilaration, sportiveness **13** sprightliness

animosity 4 hate **5** anger **6** enmity, hatred, malice, rancor, strife **7** dislike, ill will **8** acrimony **9** antipathy, hostility, malignity **10** antagonism, bitterness, resentment **11** malevolence **14** unfriendliness

animus 5 anger, spite, venom **6** enmity, hatred, malice, rancor **7** disdain, dislike, ill will **8** acrimony, bad blood **9** animosity, antipathy, hostility **10** antagonism, bitterness, ill feeling, resentment **12** hard feelings

anise
  botanical name: 16 Pimpinella Anisum
  origin: 5 Egypt, India **13** Mediterranean
  flavor: 8 licorice
  use: 5 cakes, fruit, rolls **7** cookies
  plant with similar flavor: 9 star anise
  legend:
    safeguards against: 7 evil eye **10** nightmares **11** indigestion
    antidote to: 12 scorpion bite

anisette
  type: 7 liqueur
  origin: 6 France
  flavor: 5 anise
  drink: 17 Suissesse cocktail
  with gin: 8 Snowball **11** Bachio Punch
  substitute for: 8 Absinthe

Ankylosaurus
  type: 8 dinosaur **10** ornithopod
  location: 12 North America
  period: 10 Cretaceous
  characteristic: 7 armored

Anna
  husband: 5 Tobit
  daughter: 4 Mary
  sister: 4 Dido
  corresponds to: 11 Anna Perenna
  died by: 8 drowning

Annabel Lee
  author: 13 Edgar Allan Poe

Anna Christie
  author: 12 Eugene O'Neill
  character: 6 Marthy **8** Mat Burke **19** Chris Christopherson
  ship: 14 Simeon Winthrop

Anna Karenina
  author: 10 Leo Tolstoy
  character: 12 Count Vronsky **13** Alexei Karenin **15** Konstantin Levin **19** Kitty Shcherbatskaya **20** Prince Stepan Oblonsky
  setting: 6 Moscow, Russia **12** St Petersburg
  director: 13 Clarence Brown
  cast: 9 May Robson **10** Greta Garbo (Anna Karenina) **13** Basil Rathbone (Karenin), Frederic March (Vronsky) **16** Maureen O'Sullivan **18** Freddie Bartholomew
  earlier film version: 4 Love

annals 7 history, minutes, records **8** archives **9** registers **10** chronicles, chronology **13** yearly records **15** historical rolls **20** chronological records

Annam *see* **7** Vietnam

Anna Marie
  character in: 16 Giants of the Earth
  author: 7 Rolvaag

Anna of the Five Towns
  author: 13 Arnold Bennett

anneal 6 harden, temper **7** toughen

Anne of Geierstein (or, The Maiden of the Mist)
  author: 14 Sir Walter Scott

annex 3 add **4** grab, join **5** affix, merge, seize **6** adjoin, append, attach, tack on **7** acquire, connect, subjoin **8** addition **9** appendage **10** attachment **11** appropriate, expropriate, incorporate

Annfwn
  also: 5 Annwn
  origin: 5 Welsh
  means: 8 paradise

Annie Hall
  director: 10 Woody Allen
  cast: 9 Carol Kane, Paul Simon **10** Woody Allen **11** Diane Keaton, Tony Roberts **13** Shelley Duvall **15** Colleen Dewhurst
  Oscar for: 7 actress (Keaton), picture **8** director (Allen) **10** screenplay

annihilate 3 end **5** erase, waste **7** abolish, destroy, wipe out **8** decimate, demolish, lay waste **9** eradicate, extirpate, liquidate **10** extinguish, obliterate **11** exterminate

annihilation 9 abolition, wiping out **11** destruction, extirpation, laying waste, liquidation **12** obliteration **13** extermination

anniversary 4 fete **7** holiday, name day **8** birthday, feast day **9** centenary **10** centennial **11** bicentenary, celebration **12** bicentennial **13** commemoration, golden jubilee **16** sesquicentennial

Ann-Margret
  real name: 16 Ann-Margret Olsson
  husband: 10 Roger Smith
  born: 6 Sweden **9** Valsjobyn
  roles: 5 Tommy **8** Scarlett **12** Bye-Bye Birdie **15** Carnal Knowledge, Grumpy

Old Men **21** A Streetcar Named Desire

anno Domini 18 in the year of our Lord
  abbreviation: 2 AD
  alternative: 2 CE Common Era

anno mundi 19 in the year of the world

anno regni 19 in the year of the reign

annotate 5 gloss **6** remark **7** comment, explain, expound **8** construe, footnote **9** elucidate, explicate, interpret **10** commentate

annotation 4 note **5** gloss **6** remark **7** comment **8** exegesis, footnote **10** commentary, marginalia **11** elucidation, explication, observation

announce 5 augur **6** herald, reveal, signal **7** betoken, declare, divulge, give out, portend, presage, publish, signify, trumpet **8** disclose, foretell, proclaim **9** advertise, broadcast, harbinger **10** promulgate **11** disseminate

announcement 9 broadcast, statement **11** declaration **12** proclamation

annoy 3 irk, nag, tax, vex **4** gall, rile **5** harry, tease, worry **6** badger, bother, harass, heckle, hector, nettle, pester, plague, ruffle **7** disturb, provoke, torment, trouble **8** distract, irritate **10** exasperate **13** inconvenience

annoyance 6 bother **8** irritant, nuisance, vexation **10** irritation **11** distraction, disturbance

annoyed 5 irked, upset, vexed **9** disturbed, irritated, perturbed **11** discomposed **12** disconcerted

annual 4 weed **5** plant **6** flower, serial **7** gazette, journal, reports **8** bulletin, magazine, notebook, periodic **9** vegetable **10** periodical, record book

annuity 6 income **7** pension, stipend **9** allowance

annul 4 undo, void **6** cancel, negate, recall, repeal, revoke **7** abolish, nullify, rescind, retract, reverse **8** abrogate, dissolve **10** invalidate

annulment 6 recall, repeal **7** undoing, voiding **8** reversal **9** abolition **10** abrogation, retraction, revocation **11** dissolution, repudiation **12** cancellation, invalidation **13** nullification

annus mirabilis 13 year of wonders

anodyne 4 balm **6** solace **7** comfort **9** comforter **10** palliative

anoint 3 oil **5** crown **6** ordain **8** put oil on **9** pour oil on

Anointed One 5 Jesus **7** Messiah

anomalous 3 odd **7** bizarre, strange **8** abnormal, atypical, peculiar **9** irregular, monstrous **11** incongruous **12** out of keeping

anomaly 6 oddity, rarity **9** deviation **10** aberration **11** abnormality, incongruity, peculiarity **12** eccentricity, irregularity **18** exception to the rule

anon 4 soon, then **5** again, later **7** by and by, shortly **8** tomorrow **9** afterward, presently **10** before long **11** immediately, in the future

anonymous 7 unnamed **8** nameless, unsigned **12** unidentified **13** bearing no name **14** unacknowledged **19** of unknown authorship

another 4 else, more **5** extra, other **7** further, renewed **9** accessory, otherwise **10** additional **12** supplemental **13** something else, supplementary **14** different thing

Anouilh, Jean
  author of: **6** Becket **8** Antigone, Eurydice, Leocadia, L'hermine **11** Dear Antoine **14** Time Remembered **15** Le Bal des Voleurs, Thieves' Carnival **16** Point of Departure, Ring Round the Moon **19** Waltz of the Toreadors **20** L'Invitation au Chateau **23** Traveller Without Luggage

ansate 7 handled

anser 5 goose **6** stupid **7** foolish **8** anserine

answer 3 say **4** fill, meet, suit **5** reply, serve, solve, write **6** be like, rejoin, retort **7** conform, fulfill, react to, resolve, respond **8** be enough, response, solution **9** be similar, rejoinder **10** be adequate, correspond, pass muster, resolution **11** acknowledge, explanation **12** be correlated, be equivalent, be sufficient, do well enough **14** acknowledgment, be satisfactory

answerable 6 liable **8** beholden **10** chargeable **11** accountable, responsible

Answer as a Man
  author: **14** Taylor Caldwell

ant
  caste: **4** male **5** queen **6** worker **7** soldier
  kind: **3** red **4** army, fire **5** dairy, thief **6** beggar, farmer, velvet, weaver **7** formica, janitor, pharaoh **8** honeypot, mushroom **9** Argentine, carpenter, cornfield, harvester, legionary **10** leaf cutter **11** little black **12** fungus grower, odorous house, southern fire **13** mound building **14** Texas harvester
  group of: **6** colony

antagonism 5 spite **6** animus, enmity, hatred, rancor, strife **7** discord, dislike, rivalry **8** aversion, clashing, conflict, friction **9** animosity, antipathy, hostility **10** bitterness, dissension, opposition, resentment **11** detestation

antagonist 3 foe **5** enemy, rival **7** opposer **8** attacker, opponent **9** adversary, assailant, disputant **10** competitor, contestant

antagonistic 7 hostile **8** contrary, inimical **9** rancorous **10** antisocial, unfriendly **11** belligerent **12** antipathetic, disputatious

antagonize 5 repel **6** offend **8** alienate, estrange

Antananarivo, Tananarive
  capital of: **10** Madagascar

Antarctica
  division: **10** Wilkes Land **13** Marie Byrd Land, Queen Maud Land **14** Edith Ronne Land **17** Ellsworth Highland
  island: **4** Ross **5** Peter, Scott **6** Biscoe, Hearst **7** Ballery, Charcot **8** Adelaide, Elephant **9** Alexander, Joinville, Roosevelt **10** Coronation, King George **11** South Orkney **13** South Shetland
  mountain: **8** Sentinel **9** Pensacola **14** Transantarctic **23** Executive Committee Range
  valley: **6** Wright
  river: **4** Onyx
  natural resource/mineral: **4** coal
  plant life: **4** moss **5** algae, fungi **6** lichen, pollen **8** bacteria
  animal: **4** lice, mite, tick **5** whale **7** fur seal **8** ross seal **9** crabeater **11** weddell seal, wingless fly
  bird: **4** skua **6** fulmar, petrel **7** penguin **10** cape pigeon
  sea: **4** Ross **5** Davis **6** Scotia **7** Weddell **8** Amundsen **14** Bellingshausen

ante 3 bet, pot **5** stake, wager **12** beginning bet

anteater 5 sloth **7** echidna **8** aardvark **9** armadillo

antecede 7 precede, predate **8** go before, preexist **10** anticipate

ante Christum 12 before Christ
  abbreviation: **2** AC

antedate 7 precede, predate **8** antecede, go before **9** come first **10** anticipate **12** happen before

Antediluvian 14 before the flood

antediluvian 7 antique, archaic **8** obsolete **10** antiquated

antelope 8 ruminant
  family: **7** Bovidae
  kind: **3** doe, gnu **4** buck, deer, fawn, kudu, oryx, roan **5** bongo, eland, moose, sable **6** dik-dik, duiker, impala, lechwe, nilgai **7** gazelle, gemsbok, gerenuk **8** bluebuck, bontebok, steinbok **9** blackbuck, sitatunga, springbok, waterbuck **10** four-horned **12** Klipspringer
  habitat: **4** Asia **6** Africa

Antelope State
  nickname of: **8** Nebraska

antenna 6 aerial, feeler

anterior 5 front, prior **7** forward, in front **8** previous **9** precedent **10** antecedent **12** placed before

Anteros
  brother: **4** Eros
  avenger of: **14** unrequited love

Anthea
  epithet of: **4** Hera
  means: **7** flowery

Antheil, George
  born: **9** Trenton NJ
  autobiography: **13** Bad Boy of Music
  composer of: **7** Volpone **12** Helen Retires, Jazz Symphony **13** Sonata Sauvage, Transatlantic **14** Airplane Sonata **15** Ballet Mecanique

anthem 4 hymn, song **5** carol, ditty, music, paean, psalm **6** ballad, sacred **7** cantata **8** doxology **11** church music

Anthesteria
  origin: **5** Greek
  festival of: **4** wine **6** spring **7** flowers

anthology 6 choice, digest **7** garland **8** analects, chapbook, extracts, treasury **9** gleanings, scrapbook **10** collection, compendium, miscellany, selections **11** collectanea, compilation, florilegium, miscellanea **15** commonplace book

Anthony, Susan B.
  leader in: **14** women's suffrage

Anthony Adverse
  author: **18** William Hervey Allen

anthophobia
  fear of: **7** flowers

anthropologist
  American: **4** Boas, Mead **5** Lowie, Sapir **6** Geertz, Linton, Morgan **7** Kroeber **8** Benedict
  British: **5** Leach, Tylor **6** Fortes, Leakey, Rivers **14** Evans-Pritchard, Radcliffe-Brown
  French: **5** Mauss **8** Durkheim **11** Levi-Strauss
  Polish: **10** Malinowski

anthropology
  term: **4** myth **6** custom, ritual **7** culture, kinship **8** artifact **9** ethnology, evolution, field work **11** ethnography **16** natural selection
  type/related study: **5** legal, urban **6** social **7** applied, medical **8** cultural, economic, physical **9** political **11** linguistics **12** human ecology **13** psychological **19** structural-symbolist
  famous study: **3** San **4** Kung **7** Eskimos, Samoans, Tasaday **10** Aborigines **16** Pacific Islanders

anthropophobia
  fear of: **6** people

antibiotic 4 drug **5** venom **6** poison **8** curative **9** antidotal, antitoxic, pesticide **10** wonder drug **11** insecticide, miracle drug
  kind: **8** neomycin, subtilin **9** mycomycin **10** ampicillin, penicillin **12** erythromycin

antic, antics 5 larks, sport **6** pranks, tricks **9** escapades **10** buffoonery, skylarking, tomfoolery **11** shenanigans **12** clownishness, monkeyshines **14** practical jokes

anticipate 5 await **6** expect **7** count on, foresee, long for, look for, predict **8** envision, forecast, foretell **9** pin hope on **10** look toward **13** look forward to

anticipation 4 hope **10** expectancy **11** expectation, preparation

anticlimax 7 letdown **8** comedown **14** disappointment

antidote 4 cure **6** remedy **9** antitoxin **10** antipoison, corrective **12** counteragent, countervenom **13** counterpoison **14** countermeasure

Antigone
  author: 9 Sophocles **11** Jean Anouilh
  character: 6 Ismene **8** Tiresias
    father: 7 Oedipus
    mother: 7 Jocasta
    brother: 8 Eteocles **9** Polynices
    sister: 6 Ismene
    uncle: 5 Creon
    cousin/lover: 6 Haemon
    defied: 5 Creon

Antigua and Barbuda
  capital/largest city: 7 St John's
  government:
    member of: 26 West Indies Associated States
  head of state: 14 British monarch **15** governor-general
  island: 4 Long **5** Guana **7** Antigua, Barbuda, Redonda
  highest point: 9 Boggy Peak
  sea: 9 Caribbean
  physical feature:
    cove: 5 Royal
    harbor/harbour: 7 English
  people: 7 African, British **8** Lebanese **10** Portuguese
  language: 7 English
  religion: 8 Anglican, Moravian **13** Roman Catholic
  feature: 15 Nelson's Dockyard

anti-intellectual 5 yahoo **7** lowbrow **9** ignoramus, vulgarian **10** illiterate, philistine

antimony
  chemical symbol: 2 Sb

Antinous
  suitor of: 8 Penelope
  killed by: 8 Odysseus

antipathetic 6 averse **7** hostile **8** inimical **9** rancorous **11** ill-disposed

antipathy 6 enmity, rancor **7** disgust, dislike, ill will **8** aversion, distaste, loathing **9** animosity, hostility, repulsion **10** abhorrence, antagonism, repugnance **14** unfriendliness

Antiphas
  father: 7 Laocoon

Antipholus
  character in: 17 The Comedy of Errors
  author: 11 Shakespeare

antiphony 6 chorus **7** refrain **8** response

antipode 8 contrary, opposite **10** antithesis

Antiquary, The
  author: 14 Sir Walter Scott

antiquated 5 dated, passe **7** antique, archaic **8** obsolete, outdated, outmoded **9** out-of-date **11** obsolescent **12** old-fashioned

antique 3 old **5** curio, relic **6** rarity **7** bibelot, trinket **9** objet d'art **10** antiquated, memorabile **11** memorabilia

antiquities 6 relics **8** artifact **9** monuments

antiquity 7 oldness **8** great age **11** ancientness **12** ancient times

antiseptic 6 iodine **7** aseptic, sterile **8** germ-free **9** germicide **10** germ killer **11** bactericide **12** disinfectant, prophylactic

antisocial 7 asocial, hostile **8** menacing, retiring, unsocial **9** alienated **10** disruptive, rebellious, unfriendly, unsociable **11** belligerent, sociopathic **12** antagonistic, misanthropic

antithesis 7 inverse, reverse **8** antipode, contrary, contrast, converse, opposite

antithetical 8 contrary, opposing, opposite **10** discrepant, refutatory **11** conflicting, disagreeing **13** contradictory **14** countervailing, irreconcilable

antitoxin 5 serum **8** antidote **9** antivenom **12** counteragent **13** counterpoison

antler 4 horn, knob, rack **5** spike **6** shovel **8** deerhorn, troching
  part: 3 bay **4** brow **5** crown, royal

ant lion
  also: 8 lacewing **9** doodlebug
  kind: 6 owlfly **9** dusty wing, mantidfly **12** spongillafly **13** brown lacewing, giant lacewing, green lacewing **14** beaded lacewing **15** ithonid lacewing **16** pleasing lacewing

Antonello da Messina
  born: 5 Italy **7** Messina
  artwork: 8 Ecce Homo **11** Three Angels **13** Il Condottiere (Portrait of a Man), Salvador Mundi **21** Saint Jerome in his Study

Antonio
  character in: 12 Twelfth Night **19** The Merchant of Venice
  author: 11 Shakespeare

Antonioni, Michelangelo
  director of: 6 Blowup **8** The Night **10** The Eclipse **12** The Adventure, The Passenger **14** Zabriskie Point

Antony, Mark
  also: 14 Marcus Antonius
  member of: 11 triumvirate
  other triumvirs: 7 Lepidus **8** Octavian (Caesar Augustus)
  lover: 9 Cleopatra
  cousin: 12 Julius Caesar
  wife: 7 Octavia
  battle: 6 Actium **8** Philippi **9** Pharsalus
  invaded: 7 Parthia
  died by: 7 suicide

Antony and Cleopatra
  author: 18 William Shakespeare
  character: 7 Octavia **9** Cleopatra **10** Mark Antony **14** Octavius Caesar
  setting: 5 Egypt
  Cleopatra bitten by: 3 asp

antonym 8 opposite **10** antithesis
  abbreviation: 3 ant

Antrodemus
  type: 8 dinosaur, therapod
  also called: 10 Allosaurus
  period: 8 Jurassic **10** Cretaceous

Anu
  origin: 8 Akkadian
  god of: 6 heaven
  corresponds to: 2 An

Anubis
  origin: 8 Egyptian
  god of: 5 tombs **9** embalming
  weigher of: 15 hearts of the dead
  represented by head of: 6 jackal

anvil 5 block, incus **9** converter **11** transformer

anxiety 4 fear **5** alarm, angst, dread, worry **6** unease **7** anguish, concern, tension **8** disquiet, distress, suspense **9** misgiving **10** foreboding, solicitude, uneasiness **11** disquietude, fretfulness **12** apprehension

anxiety-ridden 7 anxious, fearful, nervous **10** distraught **11** worried sick **12** apprehensive

anxious 4 avid, keen **5** eager, tense **6** ardent, intent, uneasy **7** alarmed, earnest, fearful, fervent, fretful, itching, uptight, wanting, worried, zealous **8** desirous, troubled, yearning **9** anguished, concerned, disturbed, expectant, impatient **10** disquieted, distressed **11** overwrought **12** apprehensive

any 3 all, one **4** each, lone, sole, some **5** every **6** single, unique **8** anything, singular, solitary **9** something **10** individual, quantifier

anybody 3 any **6** anyone **8** anything

anyhow see **6** anyway

anything 3 any **4** some **5** aught **6** anyone **7** anybody

anyway 6 anyhow **8** sloppily **9** at any rate, in any case **10** carelessly, in any event, regardless **11** haphazardly, just the same, nonetheless **12** nevertheless **13** indifferently **14** without concern

anywhere 8 anyplace, wherever **11** wheresoever

A-1 3 ace **4** aces, fine, tops **5** great, prime, super **6** choice, grade-A, superb, tip-top **7** capital **8** sterling, superior, top-notch **9** excellent, first-rate, superfine **10** first-class, tremendous **11** crackerjack, outstanding, superlative

Aornis
tributary of: **4** Styx

Aornum
entrance to: **5** Hades
used by: **7** Orpheus

apace 4 fast **7** flat-out, hastily, quickly, rapidly, swiftly **8** speedily **9** posthaste **10** at top speed **11** double-quick, on the double **12** lickety-split **13** expeditiously, precipitately **18** hell bent for leather

Apache
language family: **10** Athabascan, Athapaskan
band: **9** Jacarilla, Mescalero, San Carlos **13** White Mountain
location: **7** Arizona **8** Oklahoma **9** New Mexico
leader: **7** Cochise **8** Geronimo
noted for: **8** basketry

apart 4 afar **5** alone, aloof, aside **6** cut off **7** asunder, distant **8** by itself, divorced, isolated, separate **9** by oneself, into parts, to one side **10** into pieces, separately

apartment 3 pad **4** flat **5** rooms, suite

Apartment, The
director: **11** Billy Wilder
cast: **10** Jack Lemmon, Ray Walston **13** Fred MacMurray **15** Shirley MacLaine
Oscar for: **7** picture

apathetic 4 cold **7** unmoved **9** impassive, unfeeling **10** disengaged, impossible, phlegmatic, spiritless **11** emotionless, indifferent, passionless, uncommitted, unconcerned, unemotional **12** uninterested, unresponsive

apathy 8 coolness, lethargy, numbness **9** lassitude, unconcern **11** impassivity, inattention, passiveness **12** indifference **13** impassibility, lack of feeling **14** lack of interest **15** emotionlessness **16** unresponsiveness

apatite
source: **5** Burma, Mogok

Apatosaurus *see* **12** Brontosaurus

ape 4 copy, echo, mock **5** mimic **6** follow, mirror, monkey, parody, parrot **7** emulate, imitate, primate **8** travesty **9** burlesque **10** caricature
family: **8** Pongidae
combining form: **8** pithecus
study of: **11** pithecology
kind: **6** gibbon **7** gorilla, siamang **9** orangutan **10** chimpanzee
famous: **8** Godzilla, King Kong

apercu 6 glance **7** glimpse, insight, outline, summary

aperture 3 gap **4** hole, rent, rift, slit, slot **5** chink, cleft, space **6** breach **7** fissure, opening, orifice **10** interstice

apex 3 cap, tip **4** acme, peak **5** crest, crown **6** apogee, climax, height, summit, vertex, zenith **8** pinnacle **11** culmination **12** consummation, highest point **13** crowning point

aphasic 4 dumb, mute **12** inarticulate **17** incapable of speech

aphid
variety: **3** pea **4** pine, rose **5** apple, grape, peach, tulip **6** cereal, cotton, potato, spruce **7** adelgid, cabbage **8** pear root **9** elm woolly, plant lice, water lily **10** gall-making, phylloxera

aphorism 3 saw **5** adage, axiom, maxim **6** dictum, old saw, saying, slogan, truism **7** epigram, proverb **8** apothegm

aphrodisiac 4 sexy **6** carnal, erotic, turn-on **7** fleshly, philter, raunchy **8** prurient **9** cantharis **10** love potion **11** cantharides, magic potion, stimulating

Aphrodite
also: **6** Urania **7** Cyprian, Paphian **8** Cytherea **10** Anadyomene
origin: **5** Greek
goddess of: **4** love **6** beauty
husband: **10** Hephaestus
lover: **4** Ares
son: **5** Lyrus **6** Deimos, Phobus, Rhodus **7** Priapus
daughter: **8** Harmonia
corresponds to: **5** Venus
epithet: **6** Acraea, Scotia **7** Doritis, Erycina, Limenia **8** Melaenis, Nymphaea, Pandemos **9** Migonitis **11** Aphrogeneia, Apostrophia

Apia
capital of: **12** Western Samoa

apiary 4 hive **7** beehive

apiece 4 each **9** severally **12** individually, respectively

a pied 6 on foot **7** walking

Apis
origin: **8** Egyptian
also: **3** Hap **4** Hapi
form: **4** bull
from: **7** Memphis
father: **6** Apollo **9** Phoroneus
mother: **8** Teledice
sister: **5** Niobe
nephew: **5** Argus
rid Argos of: **8** serpents
killed by: **7** Aetolus
worshipped at: **7** Memphis

aplomb 5 poise **7** balance **8** calmness, coolness **9** composure, sang-froid, stability **10** confidence, equanimity **11** intrepidity, savoir faire **13** self-assurance, self- composure **14** self-confidence, self-possession **15** level-headedness **16** imperturbability

Apocalypse Now
director: **18** Francis Ford Coppola
based on: **15** Heart of Darkness
novel by: **12** Joseph Conrad
cast: **11** Martin Sheen **12** Marlon Brando, Robert Duvall **16** Frederick Forrest
setting: **7** Vietnam

apocalyptic 4 dire **7** ominous **8** oracular **9** far-seeing, ill- boding, ill-omened, prescient, prophetic, reveal-ing **10** disclosing, eye-opening, foreboding, portentous, predictive, revelatory **11** prophetical **12** inauspicious, revelational **15** prognosticative

apocryphal 7 dubious **8** disputed, doubtful, mythical, spurious **10** fabricated, fictitious, unofficial, unverified **11** unauthentic, uncanonical **12** questionable, unauthorized **14** probably untrue **15** unauthenticated, unsubstantiated

apogee 3 top **4** acme, apex, peak **5** crest, crown **6** climax, summit, vertex, zenith **8** meridian, pinnacle **9** high point **11** culmination **12** highest point

Apollo
also: **7** Phoebus, Pythius **9** Musagetes
origin: **5** Greek, Roman
god of: **5** light, music **6** beauty, poetry **7** healing **8** prophecy
father: **4** Zeus
mother: **4** Leto
twin sister: **7** Artemis
sons: **3** Ion **5** Iamus **8** Laodocus **9** Aristaeus, Asclepius, Philammon **10** Polypoetes
corresponds to: **5** Paeon **8** Hyperion
epithet: **6** Loxias **7** Acesius, Agraeus, Agyieus, Carneus, Phyteus, Spodius **8** Grynaeus **9** Parnopius, Smintheus **10** Alexicacus, Archegetes, Boedromius, Delphinius **11** Argyrotoxus, Epibaterius **12** Platanistius

Apollyon 4 hell **7** Abaddon

apologetic 5 sorry **8** contrite, penitent **9** defensive, regretful **10** excusatory, mitigatory, remorseful **11** exonerative, extenuatory, vindicatory **12** apologetical **13** justificatory, making excuses **15** self-reproachful

Apologia pro Vita Sua
author: **15** John Henry Newman (Cardinal)

Apologie for Poetrie (Defense for Poetry)
author: **15** Sir Philip Sidney

apologist 7 pleader **8** advocate, defender **9** supporter

apologize 9 beg pardon **11** make apology **13** express regret

apology 6 excuse **7** defense **11** explanation, vindication **13** begging pardon, justification

Apophis
also: **5** Apepi
form: **7** serpent
habitat: **8** darkness
destroyed daily by: **4** Dawn

Apophthegms New and Old
author: **12** Francis Bacon

apostasy 7 atheism, perfidy **8** unbelief **9** defection, disbelief, recreancy **10** disloyalty, infidelity, irreligion **11** godlessness **13** double-dealing

apostate 6 bolter **7** heretic, seceder, traitor **8** defector, deserter, recanter, recusant, renegade, turncoat **9** dissenter, dissident, turnabout **10** backslider **13** nonconformist, tergiversator

apostle 5 envoy **6** zealot **7** pioneer, witness **8** activist, advocate, disciple, emissary, exponent, preacher **9** messenger, proponent, supporter **10** evangelist, missionary, propagator **12** propagandist, proselytizer, spokesperson

Apostle, The
author: 10 Sholem Asch
film by: 12 Robert Duvall

Apostles 4 John, Jude, Levi, Paul **5** Jacob, James, Peter, Simon **6** Andrew, Philip, Thomas **7** Matthew **8** Barnabas, Matthais **9** Nathanael, Thaddaeus **11** Bartholomew **12** James the Less **13** Judas Iscariot
apostle to the Gentiles: 4 Paul
apostle to the English: 9 Augustine
apostle to the Irish: 7 Patrick
apostle to the Goths: 7 Ulfilas
apostle to the Germans: 8 Boniface
apostle to the French: 5 Denis
apostle to the American Indians: 9 John Eliot

apothegm 3 saw **5** adage, axiom, maxim, motto **6** dictum, slogan **7** epigram, proverb **8** aphorism **9** catchword, watchword

apotheosis 7 epitome, essence **9** elevation **10** embodiment, exaltation **11** deification **12** canonization, consecration, enshrinement, idealization, quintessence **13** dignification, glorification, magnification **15** immortalization

Appalachian Spring
ballet by: 7 Copland

appall 4 stun **5** abash, alarm, repel, shock **6** dismay, offend, revolt, sicken **7** disgust, horrify, outrage, terrify, unnerve **8** frighten, nauseate **10** dishearten

appalled 6 aghast **7** alarmed, shocked **8** dismayed, outraged, repelled, revolted **9** disgusted, horrified, nauseated

appalling 4 dire, grim **5** awful **6** horrid **7** fearful, ghastly **8** alarming, dreadful, horrible, horrific, shocking, terrible **9** dismaying, frightful, repellent, repulsive, revolting, sickening **10** abominable, disgusting, horrifying, nauseating, outrageous, terrifying **11** frightening, intolerable **12** insufferable **13** disheartening

apparatus 4 gear **5** gismo, setup, tools **6** device, gadget, outfit, system, tackle **7** machine **8** material, utensils **9** appliance, equipment, machinery, materials, mechanism **10** implements **11** contraption, contrivance, instruments **12** organization **13** paraphernalia

apparel 4 duds, garb, gear, togs **5** array, dress, habit, robes **6** attire **7** clothes, costume, raiment, threads, vesture **8** clothing, garments **9** equipment, trappings, vestments **13** accoutrements

appareled 4 clad **5** robed **6** garbed, suited **7** attired, clothed, covered, dressed

apparent 4 open **5** clear, overt, plain **6** likely, marked, patent **7** blatant, evident, obvious, seeming, visible **8** clear-cut, distinct, manifest, probable **10** clear as day, ostensible, presumable **11** conspicuous, discernible, perceivable, perceptible, self-evident, unequivocal **12** unmistakable **14** understandable

apparently
Latin: 7 ex facie

apparition 5 ghost, shade, spook **6** spirit, wraith **7** phantom, specter **8** phantasm, presence, revenant **10** phenomenon **13** manifestation **15** materialization

appeal 3 beg, SOS **4** plea, pull, suit **5** apply, charm, plead, sue to, tempt **6** adjure, allure, engage, entice, excite, invite, invoke **7** attract, beseech, entreat, implore, request, solicit **8** call upon, charisma, entreaty, interest, petition **9** fascinate **10** adjuration, attraction, supplicate **11** fascination **12** solicitation, supplication

appealing 7 likable, lovable **8** adjuring, charming, engaging, enticing, fetching, inviting, pleading, pleasing, tempting **10** attractive, entreating, requesting, soliciting **11** charismatic, petitioning **12** irresistible, supplicating

appear 4 look, seem, show **5** arise **6** crop up, emerge, loom up, show up, turn up **7** be clear, be plain, come out, perform, surface **8** be patent **9** be evident, be obvious **10** be apparent, be manifest **11** be published, come to light, materialize

appearance 4 look **5** guise, image **6** advent, aspect, coming **7** arrival, pretext **8** pretense **9** appearing, emergence, showing up, turning up **10** impression **11** outward show **13** manifestation **15** materialization

appear at 6 attend, show up **9** perform at

appease 4 calm, dull, ease, lull **5** abate, allay, blunt, quell, quiet, slake, still **6** pacify, quench, solace, soothe, temper **7** assuage, compose, mollify, placate, relieve, satisfy **8** mitigate **9** alleviate **10** conciliate, propitiate **11** accommodate

appeasement 6 easing **7** abating, dulling **8** allaying, blunting, giving in **9** abatement, assuasion, quenching **10** mitigation, submission **11** alleviation, assuagement **12** conciliation, pacification, propitiation, satisfaction **13** accommodation, gratification, mollification

appellation 3 tag **4** name **5** title **6** handle **7** epithet, moniker **8** cognomen **9** sobriquet **11** designation, nom de guerre

append 3 add **4** join **5** affix **6** attach, hang on, tack on **7** subjoin, suspend **10** supplement

appendage 3 arm, leg **4** limb, tail **6** branch, feeler, member **7** adjunct **8** addition, offshoot, tentacle **9** accessory, auxiliary, extension, extremity **10** attachment, supplement

appendix 7 codicil **8** addendum, addition **10** back matter, postscript, supplement

appertain 7 apply to, concern, refer to **8** bear upon, be part of, belong to, inhere in, relate to **9** touch upon

appetite 4 zest **5** gusto **6** desire, hunger, liking, relish, thirst **7** craving, passion, stomach **8** fondness, penchant, yearning **10** proclivity **11** inclination

appetizer 6 canape, dainty, savory, tidbit **8** aperitif, cocktail, delicacy **9** antipasto **11** bonne bouche, hors d'oeuvre

appetizing 6 savory **8** alluring, enticing, inviting, tempting **9** appealing, palatable, succulent **10** attractive **11** tantalizing **13** mouth-watering

applaud 4 clap, hail, laud **5** extol **6** praise **7** acclaim, commend **8** eulogize **10** compliment **12** congratulate

applaudable 8 laudable **9** admirable, desirable, excellent **11** commendable, meritorious, outstanding **12** praiseworthy

applause 5 kudos **6** praise **7** acclaim, ovation **8** approval, clapping, plaudits **9** accolades **11** compliments

apple 5 Malus **15** Malus Sylvestris
varieties/fruit: 4 Crab, Lodi **6** Pippin **7** Baldwin, Stayman, Winesap **8** Ben Davis, Cortland, Jonathan, McIntosh **9** Delicious **10** Rome Beauty **11** Granny Smith, Gravenstein, Northern Spy, Summer Rambo **12** Grimes Golden, York Imperial **13** Yellow Newtown **14** Stayman Winesap **15** Yellow Delicious **17** Esopus Spitzenberg, Yellow Transparent **19** Rhode Island Greening
varieties/tree: 2 Wi **3** Kai, Kau, Sea, Wax **4** Cane, Java, Jew's, Pond, Rose, Star **5** Adam's, Baked, Belle, Blade, Chess, Conch, Malay, Melon, Thorn **6** Balsam, Indian, Mammee, Possum **7** Chinese, Custard, Dead Sea, Mexican **8** Elephant, Kangaroo, Otaheite, Paradise, Peruvian **11** Soulard crab, Toringo crab **12** Siberian crab
beverage: 5 cider **8** Calvados **9** Applejack

apple brandy
  drink: **8** Jack Rose **12** Jack-in-the-Box
  with rum: **6** Bolero **8** Apple Pie
applejack
  type: **6** brandy
  origin: **6** Canada **10** New England
  flavor: **10** apple cider
  drink: **11** Frozen Apple **13** Harvard
    Cooler
Apple of discord
  color: **6** golden
  thrown by: **4** Eris
  awarded to: **9** Aphrodite
  awarded by: **5** Paris
  inscription: **13** for the fairest
apple of one's eye 11 pride and joy
  15 light of one's life
applesauce 3 rot **4** bull, bunk **5** hokum, hooey **6** bunkum **7** baloney,
  hogwash, spinach **8** tommyrot **9** poppycock **12** fiddlesticks **13** horsefeathers **16** stuff and nonsense
Apples of the Hesperides
  color: **6** golden
  given to: **4** Hera
  kept by: **5** Ladon **10** Hesperides
appliance 4 gear **6** device **7** fixture,
  machine **9** apparatus, equipment, implement, mechanism **11** contraption,
  contrivance
applicable 3 apt, fit **6** useful **7** apropos, fitting, germane **8** relevant, suitable **9** adaptable, befitting, pertinent
applicant 7 hopeful **8** aspirant, claimant **9** candidate, job seeker, suppliant
  10 petitioner
application 4 balm, form, suit, wash
  5 claim, salve **6** appeal, lotion **7** request, unguent **8** dressing, entreaty,
  industry, ointment, petition, poultice,
  solution **9** assiduity, attention, diligence, emollient, putting on, relevance **10** commitment, dedication,
  pertinence **11** germaneness, persistence, requisition, suitability **12** appositeness, perseverance, solicitation **13**
  attentiveness
Appling, Luke (Lucius Benjamin)
  nickname: **16** Old Aches and Pains
  sport: **8** baseball
  position: **9** shortstop
  team: **15** Chicago White Sox
apply 3 fit, use **4** suit **5** adapt, lay on,
  put on, refer **6** devote, direct, employ,
  relate **7** address, pertain, request, utilize **8** dedicate, exercise, petition,
  practice, spread on **9** implement
apply oneself 6 attend **10** buckle
  down **13** give oneself to **15** give it all
  one has **16** put one's heart into
appoint 3 fix, set **4** name **5** equip **6**
  assign, choose, engage, fit out, select,
  settle, supply **7** arrange, furnish, provide **8** decide on, delegate, deputize,
  nominate **9** designate, determine, establish, prescribe **10** commission
appointment 3 job **4** date, post, spot

5 berth, place **6** naming, office **7**
  meeting, station **8** choosing, position
  9 placement, selection, situation **10**
  assignment, engagement, nomination,
  rendezvous **11** designation, meeting
  time **13** commissioning
Appointment in Samarra
  author: **9** John O'Hara
  character: **8** Al Grecco, Caroline **11**
    Harry Reilly **13** Julian English
appointments 4 gear **6** outfit **8** equipage **9** equipment, furniture **11**
  furnishings **13** accoutrements
apportion 5 allot, share **6** divide, ration **7** consign, deal out, dole out,
  mete out, prorate **8** allocate, disperse
  9 parcel out, partition **10** measure out
apportioning 8 alloting, dividing **9**
  doling out, meting out **10** allocating,
  consigning, dealing out, dispensing **12**
  distributing
apportionment 5 quota **6** ration **7**
  measure, portion **8** division **9** allotment **10** allocation **11** consignment
  12 distribution, pro rata share
apposite 3 apt **7** apropos, fitting, germane **8** material, relevant, suitable **9**
  pertinent **10** applicable **11** appropriate
appositeness 9 relevance **10** pertinence **11** germaneness **15** appropriateness
appraisal 8 estimate, judgment **9** valuation **10** assessment, evaluation **14**
  estimated value
appraise 5 assay, judge, value **6** assess, review, size up **7** examine, inspect **8** evaluate
appreciable 7 evident, obvious **8**
  clear-cut, definite **10** detectable, noticeable, pronounced **11** discernible,
  perceivable, perceptible, significant,
  substantial **12** recognizable **13** ascertainable
appreciate 4 like **5** prize, savor, value
  6 admire, esteem, relish **7** cherish, enhance, improve, inflate, realize, respect **8** perceive, treasure **9** recognize
  10 comprehend, sympathize, understand **11** acknowledge
appreciation 4 rise **6** growth, liking,
  regard, relish, thanks **7** advance **8**
  sympathy **9** awareness, elevation,
  gratitude **10** admiration, cognizance
  12 gratefulness, thankfulness **13** comprehension, understanding
apprehend 3 bag, nab, see **4** know **5**
  catch, grasp, seize, sense **6** arrest, collar **7** capture, discern, realize **8** perceive **9** recognize **10** comprehend, understand **12** take prisoner **15** take into
  custody
apprehension 4 fear **5** alarm, dread,
  worry **6** arrest, dismay **7** anxiety, capture, concern, seizure **8** disquiet, distress, mistrust **9** misgiving, suspicion
  10 foreboding, perception, uneasiness
  11 premonition **12** presentiment **13**

comprehension, understanding **16** apprehensiveness
apprehensive 6 afraid, scared, uneasy
  7 alarmed, anxious, fearful, jittery,
  nervous, worried **9** concerned, misgiving **10** disquieted, distressed, suspicious **11** distrustful
apprehensiveness 5 dread, worry **6**
  dismay **7** anxiety **9** misgiving **10** foreboding, uneasiness **12** apprehension
apprentice 4 tyro **5** pupil **6** novice **7**
  learner, student **8** beginner, neophyte
  19 indentured assistant
apprise 4 tell **6** advise, inform, notify
  8 disclose **9** enlighten, make aware
approach 3 way **4** come, near, road **5**
  begin, equal, match **6** access, avenue,
  be like, method, system **7** advance,
  compare, passage, solicit **8** attitude,
  come near, draw near, embark on,
  gain upon, initiate, resemble, set
  about, sound out **9** come close, enter
  upon, procedure, technique, undertake **10** move toward, passageway **11**
  approximate
approachable 9 available, reachable
  10 accessible
approbation 6 praise **7** acclaim, support **8** applause, approval, sanction **9**
  laudation **10** acceptance, compliment
  11 endorsement **12** commendation,
  ratification **14** congratulation
appropriate 3 apt **4** take **5** allot, seize
  6 assign, proper, seemly **7** apropos,
  correct, earmark, fitting, germane **8**
  allocate, relevant, set apart, suitable **9**
  apportion, befitting, belonging, congruous, opportune, pertinent **10** confiscate, to the point, well-chosen,
  well-suited **11** expropriate **12** to the
  purpose **14** characteristic
appropriateness 7 aptness, fitness **9**
  congruity, propriety, relevance **10** pertinence **11** correctness, suitability
appropriation 6 taking **9** allotment
  10 allocation, arrogation, usurpation
  12 confiscation **13** expropriation,
  money set aside **16** misappropriation
approval 5 favor, leave **6** esteem, liking, regard **7** acclaim, consent, license, mandate, respect **8** sanction **9**
  agreement **10** acceptance, admiration,
  compliance, permission **11** approbation, concurrence, countenance, endorsement, good opinion **12** acquiescence, appreciation, confirmation **13**
  authorization **14** acknowledgment
approve 4 like, pass **5** allow **6** accept,
  affirm, defend, esteem, permit, praise,
  ratify, second, uphold **7** condone,
  confirm, endorse, respect, sustain **8**
  accede to, advocate, assent to, concur
  in, sanction **9** authorize, consent to
  10 appreciate **11** countenance, go
  along with, rubber-stamp, subscribe to
approved 8 official **9** canonical **10** authorized, sanctioned

approving 9 endorsing, favorable **10** concurring **11** affirmative, sanctioning **12** appreciative

approximate 5 guess, rough **6** reckon **7** inexact, verge on **8** approach, border on, estimate, look like, relative, very near **9** estimated

approximately 5 circa **6** almost, around **7** close to **9** generally, just about **10** more or less, not far from, very nearly

appurtenance 4 wing **5** annex, extra **7** adjunct **8** addendum, addition **9** accessory, appendage, extension **10** attachment

APR
  abbreviation for: 14 above prime rate **20** annual percentage rate

Apres-midi d'un Faune, L' (The Afternoon of a Faun)
  author: 16 Stephane Mallarme
  (prelude) ballet music: 7 Debussy

April
  event: 11 Black Monday (13)
  flower: 5 daisy **8** sweet pea
  French: 5 Avril
  gem: 7 diamond
  German: 5 April
  holiday: 6 Easter **11** All Fool's Day (1) **13** April Fool's Day (1)
  Italian: 6 Aprile
  Latin: 7 Aprilis
  number of days: 6 thirty
  origin of name: 4 aper (wild boar) **6** aparas (following) **7** aperire (to open) **9** Aphrodite
  place in year:
    Gregorian: 6 fourth
    Roman: 6 second
  saying: 24 April is the cruellest month **27** April showers bring May flowers
  Spanish: 5 Abril
  zodiac signs: 5 Aries **6** Taurus

April Fool's Day
  French: 9 April Fish

a priori 6 theory **7** opinion **11** of reasoning

apron 3 bib **5** smock **8** covering **10** stagefront

apropos 3 apt **6** seemly **7** correct, fitting, germane, related **8** relevant, suitable **9** befitting, congruous, opportune, pertinent **10** applicable, to the point, well-suited **11** appropriate **12** just the thing

apry
  type: 7 liqueur
  origin: 6 France
  flavor: 7 apricot

Apsyrtus
  also: 8 Absyrtus
  father: 6 Aeetes
  sister: 5 Medea
  killed by: 5 Medea

apt 5 prone **6** bright, clever, gifted, liable, likely, proper, seemly **7** apropos, fitting, germane, given to **8** inclined, relevant, suitable **9** befitting, congruous, opportune, pertinent **10** disposed to, well-suited **11** appropriate, intelligent, predisposed

aptitude 4 bent, gift, turn **5** flair, knack, skill **6** genius, talent **7** ability, faculty, leaning **8** capacity, facility, penchant, tendency **9** endowment, proneness, quickness **10** capability, cleverness, proclivity, propensity **11** inclination, proficiency **12** predilection **14** predisposition

aptness 4 bent, gift **5** flair, knack **6** talent **7** ability, faculty **8** aptitude, facility **11** suitability **15** appropriateness

Apuleius
  author of: 12 The Golden Ass **13** Metamorphoses

aqua 4 blue **5** water **6** bluish **9** turquoise **10** aquamarine **12** greenish-blue

aquamarine 4 aqua, blue **5** beryl **9** turquoise **12** greenish-blue
  color: 9 blue-green

aquaphobia
  fear of: 5 water

aquarelle 10 watercolor

Aquarius
  symbol: 11 water bearer **12** water-carrier
  planet: 6 Saturn, Uranus
  rules: 5 hopes **7** friends
  born: 7 January **8** February

aquatic 6 marine **7** abyssal, fluvial, neritic, oceanic, pelagic **8** littoral **9** thalassic **10** fluviatile, lacustrine

aquavit
  type: 6 spirit
  origin: 11 Scandinavia
  flavor: 4 dill **7** caraway **9** coriander
  drink: 5 Glogg

aqua vitae 7 alcohol **11** water of life

aqueduct 4 duct, race **7** channel, conduit **11** watercourse **18** artificial waterway

aqueous 4 damp **5** moist **6** liquid, serous, watery **7** hydrous **8** waterish **9** lymphatic

Aquinas, St Thomas
  nickname: 13 Angelic Doctor
  followers: 8 Thomists
  author of: 15 Summa Theologica **21** Summa Totius Theologiae **34** Summa Catholicae Fidei contra Gentiles

Arab
  clothing: 3 fez **4** veil
  country: 4 Iraq, Oman **5** Egypt, Libya, Qatar, Sudan, Syria, Yemen **6** Jordan, Kuwait **7** Algeria, Bahrain, Lebanon, Morocco, Tunisia **11** Saudi Arabia **18** United Arab Emirates
  demon: 5 afrit **6** afreet
  habitat: 6 desert
  Holy City: 5 Mecca **6** Medina
  language: 6 Arabic
  people: 7 Semitic
  religion: 6 Muslim **7** Islamic
  tribe: 4 Kurd **6** Berber, Nubian, Tuareg

Arabella
  opera by: 7 (Richard) Strauss

Arabia
  ancient name: 14 Jazirat al-Arab
  ancient people: 6 Sabean **8** Egyptian **10** Babylonian
  bounded by: 5 Syria **6** Jordan, Red Sea **10** Gulf of Aden, Gulf of Oman **11** Indian Ocean, Persian Gulf
  country: 4 Oman **5** Qatar, Yemen **6** Kuwait **11** Saudi Arabia **18** United Arab Emirates
  highest peak: 11 Jabal Shayib
  holy book: 5 Koran
  Holy City: 5 Mecca **6** Medina
  island: 7 Bahrain, Socotra **9** Laccadive
  language: 6 Arabic
  mineral/natural resource: 3 oil **4** goat **5** sheep, wheat **6** barley, millet **7** iron ore, granite **8** porphyry **9** manganese, petroleum
  nomadic tribe: 5 Maaza **6** Ababda
  prophet: 8 Muhammad
  religion: 6 Muslim **7** Islamic
  river: 4 Nile, Oxus **5** Indus **6** Tigris **9** Euphrates
  sea: 3 Red **7** Arabian **11** Persian Gulf **13** Mediterranean

Arabian Nights
  director: 17 Pier Paolo Pasolini
  based on: 20 Thousand and One Nights
  cast: 11 Franco Citti **13** Ninetto Davoli **14** Ines Pellegrina

Arabian Nights' Entertainments, The (The Thousand and One Nights)
  author: 7 unknown
  storyteller: 12 Scheherazade
  character: 3 Roc **5** Ahmed **6** Fatima, Sinbad **7** Aladdin, Ali Baba, Sindbad **9** Abu Hassan

Arabic
  national language in: 4 Iraq **5** Syria **6** Jordan **7** Lebanon **11** North Africa **16** Arabian Peninsula
  also spoken in: 6 Israel **12** North America, South America **17** Soviet Central Asia, Sub-Saharan Africa
  language of: 5 Koran

arable 6 fecund **7** fertile **8** farmable, fruitful, plowable, tillable **10** cultivable, productive

Arachne
  origin: 6 Lydian
  challenged: 6 Athena
  contest: 7 weaving
  changed into: 6 spider

arachnid
  class: 4 mite, tick **6** spider **8** scorpion **13** daddy-long-legs

phylum: 9 Arthropod
pairs of legs: 4 four
respiratory organ: 12 pulmonary sac, tracheal tube
dwelling: 4 land **5** water
body part: 15 anterior prosoma **20** posterior opisthosoma
way of feeding: 8 parasite, predator **9** scavenger

arachnophobia
fear of: **7** spiders

Aram see **5** Syria

Aramis
character in: **18** The Three Musketeers
author: **5** Dumas (pere)

Arapaho
language family: **9** Algonkian **10** Algonquian
tribe: **6** Atsine **11** Gros Ventres **15** Northern Arapaho, Southern Arapaho
location: **6** Plains **8** Colorado, Red River
related to: **8** Cheyenne
ceremony: **8** sun dance

Arawak
language family: **8** Arawakan
tribe: **5** Taino **6** Igneri, Lucayo
location: **4** Cuba **5** Haiti **6** Guyana **8** Antilles, Colombia **9** Venezuela **12** South America

Arawakan
tribe: **6** Arawak **8** Boriquen **9** Borinquen

arbiter 5 judge **6** pundit, umpire **7** referee **9** authority **10** arbitrator **11** connoisseur

arbitrary 6 chance, random **7** summary, willful **8** absolute, despotic, fanciful, personal **9** frivolous, imperious, unlimited, whimsical **10** autocratic, capricious, peremptory, subjective **12** inconsistent, uncontrolled, unrestrained

arbitrate 5 judge **6** decide, settle, umpire **7** adjudge, mediate, referee **9** reconcile **10** adjudicate **12** bring to terms **13** sit in judgment

Arbitration, The
author: **8** Menander

arbitrator 5 judge **6** umpire **7** arbiter, referee **8** mediator **9** go-between, moderator **10** negotiator **11** adjudicator **12** intermediary

arbor 5 bower, folly, kiosk **6** gazebo, grotto **7** pergola **8** pavilion **9** belvedere **10** shaded walk **11** summerhouse

arc 3 bow **4** arch **5** curve **8** crescent, half-moon **10** semicircle

arcade 6 loggia, piazza **7** archway, area-way, gallery, skywalk **8** cloister, overpass **9** breezeway, colonnade, peristyle, underpass

Arcadia, The
author: **15** Sir Philip Sidney
character: **5** Mopsa **6** Pamela **7** Dametas, Gynecia, Zelmane **8** Basilius, Cecropia, Pyrocles **9** Amphialus, Musidorus, Philoclea, Plexistus

Arcadian stag see **8** Ceryneam

Arcanan
father: **8** Alcmaeon
mother: **10** Callirrhoe
brother: **10** Amphoterus

arcane 6 mystic, occult **7** obscure **8** abstruse, esoteric, hermetic, mystical **9** enigmatic, recondite **10** mysterious

arch 3 arc, bow, sly **4** bend, dome, main, span, wily **5** chief, curve, major, saucy, vault **7** cunning, primary, roguish **8** bow shape **9** curvature, designing, principal **10** curved span **11** mischievous

archaeologist
American: **7** Bingham **8** Douglass, Stephens
British: **5** Evans **6** Carter, Childe, Layard, Leakey, Petrie, Wooley **7** Lubbock, Ventris, Wheeler **9** Rawlinson **10** Pitt-Rivers **13** Caton-Thompson
Danish: **7** Thomsen, Worsaae
French: **5** Botta **8** Cousteau **11** Champollion
German: **5** Conze **7** Curtius **8** Dorpfeld, Koldewey **9** Grotefend **10** Schliemann **11** Winckelmann
Italian: **8** Fiorelli
Swedish: **4** Geer **9** Montelius

archaic 5 passe **6** bygone **7** ancient, antique **8** obsolete **9** out-of-date **10** antiquated **11** obsolescent **12** old-fashioned

archangel 5 Satan, Uriel **7** Gabriel, Michael, Raphael

arched 4 bent **5** bowed **6** curved

archenemy 3 foe **7** archfoe, bugbear, nemesis, scourge **8** opponent **9** adversary, assailant, bete noire, combatant, disputant **10** antagonist

archeology
term: **3** dig **6** midden **9** earthwork **11** burial mound **17** aerial photography
type: **7** salvage **8** American, medieval **9** classical, text- aided **10** Egyptology, industrial, underwater **11** Assyriology, prehistoric **12** Mesopotamian
ages: **4** Iron **6** Bronze
Old Stone Age: **11** Paleolithic
Middle Stone Age: **10** Mesolithic
New Stone Age: **9** Neolithic
dating method: **5** cross **8** absolute, carbon-14 **13** geochronology **16** dendrochronology **18** thermoluminescence **28** potassium-argon varved deposits
site/artifact: **2** Ur **4** Giza, Troy **5** Copan, Crete, Delos, Minos **6** Amarna, Carnac, Nimrud, Nippur, Tiryns **7** Alalakh, Babylon, Ephesus, Knossos, Mycenae, Nineveh, Olympia, Pom-
peii, Rio Azul **8** Behistun, Kuyunjik, Pergamum, pyramids **9** Arikamedu, Hissarlik, Khorsabad, New Grange, Tarquinia, Woodhenge **10** Carchemish, Persepolis, Samothrace, Stonehenge **11** Herculaneum, Machu Picchu, Mohenjodaro **12** Easter Island, Hadrian's Wall, Olduvai Gorge, Rosetta Stone **13** Avebury Circle, Zimbabwe Ruins **14** Dead Sea Scrolls, Laocoon statues **15** temple of Artemis **16** Valley of the Kings **18** Ostrava-Petrokovice, Royal Palace of Minos
tomb: **11** Tutankhamen **15** Ch'in Shih Huang Ti

archer 6 bowman **8** spearman
famous: **5** Cupid **9** Robin Hood **11** William Tell

Archer
constellation of: **11** Sagittarius

Archer, Isabel
character in: **18** The Portrait of a Lady
author: **5** James

Archer, Lew
created by: **13** Ross Macdonald
role: **10** private eye
played by: **10** Paul Newman (as Harper)
on TV: **10** Brian Keith

Archer, Miles
character in: **16** The Maltese Falcon
author: **7** Hammett

Archer, Newland
character in: **17** The Age of Innocence
author: **7** Wharton

Archer in Jeopardy
author: **13** Ross MacDonald

archery
athlete: **10** Linda Myers, Luanne Ryon **11** Darrell Pace

archetypal 5 model **7** classic **8** original **9** classical, exemplary **10** definitive, prototypal, protypical

archetype 5 model **7** classic **8** exemplar, original **9** prototype **12** prime example

Archias
founder of: **8** Syracuse
location: **6** Sicily
descendant of: **8** Hercules

Archie
creator: **10** Bob Montana **13** John Goldwater
character: **5** Betty, Moose **6** Reggie **7** Sabrina **8** Big Ethel, Veronica **11** Mr Weatherby **12** Jughead Jones
place: **9** Riverdale

Archimago
character in: **15** The Faerie Queene
author: **7** Spenser

Archipenko, Alexsandr
born: **4** Kiev **6** Russia
artwork: **8** Medranos **9** Gondolier, Medrano II, Pregnancy, The Bather

11 Boxing Match **12** Archipentura, Walking Woman **15** Geometric Statue **18** Wilhelm Furtwangler **19** Woman Combing Her Hair

architect 6 author, shaper **7** creator, deviser, founder, planner **8** designer, engineer **9** artificer, contriver, draftsman, innovator **10** instigator, originator, prime mover **13** master builder **16** building designer
  name 3 Pei **4** Hunt, Mead, Pope, Root, Wren **5** Hoban, IM Pei, Jones, Le Vau, McKim, Mills, Roche, Stone, Tange, White, Wyatt **6** Breuer, Fuller, Owings, Smirke, Wright **7** Bernini, Burnham, Gilbert, Gropius, Johnson, Latrobe, Mansart, Merrill, Renwick **8** Bramante, Harrison, Palladio, Saarinen, Skidmore, Sullivan, Yamasaki **9** Jefferson **10** Richardson **11** Le Corbusier **12** Brunelleschi, Michelangelo **14** Mies van der Rohe **15** Hardouin-Mansart
  legendary first: 8 Daedalus
    designed: 18 Minotaur's Labyrinth
  Roman: 9 Vitruvius

architecture 5 style **6** design **11** structuring **12** construction **14** architectonics **16** structural design

archives 6 annals, museum, papers **7** library, records **9** documents **10** chronicles, depository **11** memorabilia

arctic 3 icy **5** gelid, polar **6** bitter, frigid, frozen **7** glacial, ice-cold **8** freezing, icebound **9** North Pole **10** frostbound **11** far-northern, hyperborean **13** septentrional

Arden, Eve
  real name: 13 Eunice Quedens
  born: 12 Mill Valley CA
  roles: 13 Mildred Pierce, Our Miss Brooks

ardent 4 keen **5** eager, fiery, lusty **6** fierce **7** earnest, fervent, intense, zealous **8** feverish, spirited, vehement **10** passionate **11** impassioned, tempestuous **12** enthusiastic

ardor 4 love, zeal **5** gusto, verve, vigor **6** fervor, spirit **7** feeling, passion, rapture **8** devotion **9** eagerness, intensity, vehemence **10** enthusiasm, excitement, fierceness **11** amorousness **12** feverishness

Ardrey, Robert
  author of: 17 The Social Contract

arduous 4 hard **5** heavy, tough **6** severe, tiring, trying **7** onerous **8** toilsome, vigorous **9** difficult, energetic, fatiguing, Herculean, laborious, strenuous, wearisome **10** burdensome, exhausting, formidable **11** troublesome

arduousness 5 trial **8** tough job **10** difficulty, rough going, uphill work **12** hard sledding, toilsomeness **13** laboriousness, wearisomeness

area 4 turf, zone **5** arena, field, range, realm, scope, space, tract **6** domain, extent, region, sphere **7** expanse, portion, section, stretch, terrain **8** district, locality, precinct, province **9** territory

Areithous
  origin: 5 Greek
  mentioned in: 5 Iliad
  king of: 7 Arcadia
  son: 10 Menesthius
  nickname: 7 maceman
  weapon: 8 iron mace
  killed by: 8 Lycurgus

Areius *see* **5** Areus

arena 4 area, bowl, ring **5** field, lists, realm, scene, stage **6** circus, domain, sector, sphere **7** stadium, theater **8** coliseum, platform, province **9** gymnasium, territory **10** hippodrome **11** battlefield, marketplace **12** amphitheater, underground, playing field

Arendt, Hannah
  author of: 10 On Violence **12** On Revolution **13** Life of the Mind **17** The Human Condition **19** Crises of the Republic, Eichmann in Jerusalem **27** The Origins of Totalitarianism

Arene
  son: 4 Idas **7** Lynceus

Arensky, Anton Stepanovich (Antony)
  born: 6 Russia **8** Novgorod
  composer of: 7 Tempest **13** Egyptian Night **18** Variations on Legend

Areopagitica
  author: 10 John Milton

Ares
  also: 8 Theritas
  origin: 5 Greek
  god of: 3 war
  father: 4 Zeus
  mother: 4 Hera
  sister: 4 Hebe
  son: 5 Molus **6** Cycnus, Deimos, Phobos, Tereus **8** Diomedes, Eurytion, Meleager, Oenomaus, Phlegyas, Thestius **10** Ascalaphus
  daughter: 7 Alcippe **8** Harmonia **9** Melanippe **11** Penthesilea
  nurse: 5 Thero
  corresponds to: 4 Mars
  epithet: 8 Enyalius **14** Gynaecothoenas

Arete
  father: 8 Rhexenor
  husband: 8 Alcinous
  daughter: 8 Nausicaa
  personifies: 7 courage

Arethusa
  form: 5 nymph
  changed into: 6 spring
  saved from: 7 Alpheus

Aretus
  father: 5 Priam
  killed by: 9 Automedon

Areus
  also: 6 Areius
  father: 4 Bias
  mother: 4 Pero
  brother: 6 Talaus **8** Leodocus
  member of: 9 Argonauts
  epithet of: 4 Zeus
  means: 7 warlike

Are You There, God? It's Me, Margaret
  author: 9 Judy Blume

Argades
  father: 3 Ion

Argeiphontes
  also: 11 Argiphontes
  epithet of: 6 Hermes
  means: 13 slayer of Argus

argent 5 white **6** silver **7** shining, silvery

Argentina
  name means: 6 silver
  capital/largest city: 11 Buenos Aires
  others: 4 Acha, Azul, Goya, Oran, Puan, Rosa **5** Jujuy, Junin, Lanus, Lujan, Metan, Monte, Salta, Tigre **6** Parana, Rufino, Zarate **7** Bolivar, Caseros, Cordoba, Dolores, Formosa, LaBanda, LaPlata, LaRioja, Mendoza, Neuquen, Posadas, Quilmes, Rafaela, Rosario, San Juan, Santa Fe, Tucuman **9** Catamarca, Rio Cuerto **10** Avellaneda, Corrientes **11** Bahai Blanca, Mar del Plata, Resistencia **17** Santiago del Estero **20** San Carlos de Bariloche
  division: 5 Andes, Chaco, Pampa **9** Patagonia **11** Mesopotamia **14** Tierra del Fuego
  measure: 4 sino **5** legua **6** cuadra, lastre **7** manzana
  monetary unit: 4 peso **7** centavo **9** argentino
  weight: 4 last **5** libra **7** quintal **8** tonelada
  island: 14 Tierra del Fuego
  lake: 6 Viedma **7** Cardiel, Fagnano, Musters **11** Buenos Aires, Mar Chiquita, Nahuel Huapi
  mountain: 4 Toro **5** Andes, Chato, Laudo, Potro **6** Bonete, Conico, Pissis, Rincon **8** Famatina, Murallon, Olivares, Tronador, Zapaleri **9** Aconcagua, Tupungato **10** Cordillera **13** Ojos del Salado **15** Cerro Mercedario, Sierra de Cordoba
  highest point: 9 Aconcagua
  river: 4 Sali **5** Atuel, Chico, Coyle, Dulce, Limay, Negro, Plata, Teuco **6** Blanco, Chubut, Cuarto, Flores, Grande, Iguazu, Parana, Quinto, Salado **7** Bermejo, Deseado, Iguassu, Mendoza, Tercero, Tunuyan, Uruguay **8** Colorado, Paraguay, Picomayo, Senguerr **9** Pilcomayo
  sea: 8 Atlantic
  physical feature:
    falls: 6 Grande, Iguazu **7** Iguassu
    lowland: 5 chaco
    plains: 6 pampas
    plateau: 4 Puna **6** Parana
    salt flat: 14 Salinas Grandes
    volcano: 5 Lanin, Maipo **6** Domuyo

7 Peteroa
wind: 5 Zonda **7** Pampero
people: 3 Api **4** Lule **5** Vejoz **6**
Abipon, Vilela **7** Guarani, Puelche,
Ranquel, Taluhet **8** Querandi,
Querendy
  artist: 6 Borges
  author: 4 Wast **6** Banchs, Borges **7**
Lugones **9** Guiraldes, Hernandez
10 Echeverria
  leader: 4 Roca **5** Illia, Menem, Mitre, Peron, Rosas **6** Videla **7** Urqu-
iza **8** Aramburu, Belgrano, Eva Peron (Evita), Frondici, Galtieri **9**
San Martin, Sarmiento **11** Isabel
Peron
language: 7 Spanish
religion: 13 Roman Catholic
place:
  opera house: 11 Teatro Colon
  world's southernmost town: 7
Ushuaia
feature:
  bird: 6 chunga
  cowboy: 6 gaucho **7** vaquero
  dance: 5 samba, tango, zamba **6**
cuando, gaucho **7** milonga **9** cha-
carera
  farm: 6 quinta
  knife: 5 facon
  metal straw: 8 bombilla
  ranch: 8 estancia
  school smock: 9 delantale
  shawl: 6 poncho
  trousers: 9 bombachas
  weapon: 4 bola
food:
  cocktail: 7 clarito
  dish: 4 luna **7** criollo, puchero **8**
chivitos, empanada **10** parrillada

Arges
  member of: 8 Cyclopes
Argia
  also: 5 Aegia
  father: 7 Oceanus
  mother: 6 Tethys
  husband: 7 Polybus
  son: 5 Argus
Argiope
  form: 5 nymph
  father: 8 Teuthras
  husband: 6 Agenor **8** Telephus
  son: 6 Cadmus
  daughter: 6 Europa
Argiphontes *see* **12** Argeiphontes
Argive
  pertaining to: 5 Argos
Argo
  built by: 5 Argus
  ship of: 4 Argo
argon
  chemical symbol: 2 Ar
Argonauts
  crew: 6 Castor, Mopsus, Peleus, Pollux **7** Acastus, Orpheus, Telamon **8**
Atalanta, Heracles, Hercules, Melam-
pus, Meleager **10** Polydeuces

searchers for: 12 Golden Fleece
leader: 5 Jason
ship: 4 Argo
sailed to: 7 Colchis
pilot: 6 Tiphys
argot 4 cant **5** idiom, lingo, slang **6**
jargon, patois **10** vernacular
arguable 7 at issue **9** debatable **10**
disputable **12** questionable **13** controversial, problematical
argue 4 hold, show **5** claim, imply,
plead **6** assert, bicker, debate, denote,
evince, reason **7** contend, display, dispute, exhibit, express, point to, quarrel, quibble, wrangle **8** indicate, maintain, manifest **11** demonstrate,
expostulate, remonstrate
argument 3 row **4** case, gist, plot,
spat, tiff **5** clash, fight, story **6** debate,
reason **7** dispute, outline, quarrel,
summary **8** abstract, contents, squabble, synopsis **9** bickering, imbroglio
10 war of words **11** altercation, central idea, controversy, embroilment **12**
disagreement
argumentation 6 debate **7** dispute **8**
argument **10** discussion
argumentative 5 testy **7** peevish,
scrappy **8** contrary, petulant, snappish
9 combative, fractious, litigious, querulous **11** belligerent, contentious,
quarrelsome **12** cantankerous, disputatious
aria 3 air **4** solo, song, tune **6** melody,
number **7** arietta, excerpt, section **9**
selection **10** canzonetta **13** aria cantabile
Ariadne
  also: 7 Ariadna
  father: 5 Minos
  mother: 8 Pasiphae
  husband: 8 Dionysus
  son: 8 Oenopion
  gave thread to: 7 Theseus
  deserted by: 7 Theseus
Ariadne auf Naxos
  also: 14 Ariadne on Naxos
  opera by: 7 (Richard) Strauss
  character: 7 Bacchus, Theseus **8**
Composer **10** Zerbinetta
Ariana *see* **11** Afghanistan
Ariane et Barbe-Bleu
  also: 19 Ariadne and Bluebeard
  opera by: 5 Dukas
  character: 7 Ariadne **9** Bluebeard
Arianrhod
  origin: 5 Welsh
  form: 7 goddess
  brother: 7 Gwydion
  mistress of: 7 Gwydion
  son: 14 Llew Llaw Gyffes
  cursed: 14 Llew Llaw Gyffes
arid 3 dry **4** dull **5** vapid **6** barren,
dreary, jejune **7** dried-up, parched, tedious **8** lifeless, pedantic **9** colorless,
dry as dust, waterless **10** desertlike,

uninspired **13** unimaginative, uninteresting **15** drought-scourged
aridity 6 dearth **7** drought, dryness **8**
aridness, dullness **10** barrenness **12**
lifelessness, rainlessness **17** unimaginativeness
aridness 6 dearth **7** aridity, drought,
dryness **8** dullness **10** barrenness **12**
lifelessness, rainlessness **17** unimaginativeness
arid region 6 desert **9** wasteland **16**
barren wilderness
Ariel
  author: 11 Shakespeare, Sylvia Plath
  character in: 10 The Tempest
Aries
  symbol: 3 ram
  planet: 4 Mars
  rules: 11 personality
  born: 5 April, March
Arimaspians
  member of: 9 Scythians
  number of eyes: 3 one
Arion
  form: 11 winged horse
  father: 8 Poseidon
  mother: 7 Demeter
Ariosto, Ludovico
  author of: 14 Orlando Furioso
arise 4 dawn, go up, rise, wake **5**
awake, begin, climb, ensue, get up,
mount, occur, set in, start **6** appear,
ascend, crop up, emerge, result, wake
up **7** emanate, stand up **8** commence,
spring up, stem from **9** originate **11**
come to light
arista 3 awn **7** bristle
aristocracy 5 elite **6** gentry **7** peerage,
society **8** nobility **9** beau monde **10**
patricians, upper class, upper crust **11**
high society
aristocrat 4 duke, earl, lady, lord, peer
5 noble **7** Brahmin, duchess, grandee,
marquis **8** countess, marquess, nobleman **9** blue blood, gentleman, patrician **10** noblewoman **11** gentlewoman
12 silk stocking
aristocratic 5 noble, regal, royal **6**
lordly, titled **7** courtly, genteel, refined **8** highborn, highbred, wellborn
9 dignified, patrician **10** of high rank,
upper-class **11** blue- blooded, gentlemanly **12** silk-stocking **13** of gentle
blood
Aristophanes
  author of: 6 Plutus **8** The Birds, The
Frogs, The Peace, The Wasps **9** The
Clouds **10** Lysistrata, The Knights **13**
Ecclesiazusae, The Acharnians
Aristotle
  author of: 7 Physics, Poetics **8** On
Plants, Politics, Rhetoric, Sophisms **9**
On the Soul **10** Generation **11** Metaphysics **12** On the Heavens **14** Parts
of Animals, Prior Analytics **17** Ni-

comachean Ethics **18** Posterior Analytics **23** On Beginning and Perishing
Arizona
  abbreviation: 2 AZ **4** Ariz
  nickname: 11 Grand Canyon
  capital/largest city: 7 Phoenix
  others: 3 Ajo **4** Eloy, Mesa, Naco,
  Yuma **5** Globe, Leupp, Tempe **6** Bis-
  bee, McNary, Salome, Toltec, Tucson
  7 Cortaro **8** Chandler, Glendale,
  Prescott **9** Flagstaff **10** Scottsdale
  college: 11 Grand Canyon **12** Southwestern
  explorer: 8 Coronado **12** Marcos de
  Niza
  feature:
    dam: 6 Hoover **8** Coolidge **9** Roose-
    velt
    national park: 11 Grand Canyon
    15 Petrified Forest
  tribe: 4 Hano, Hopi, Pima **6** Apache,
  Navaho, Navajo, Papago
  people: 7 Cochise **8** Geronimo **14**
  Barry Goldwater
  lake: 4 Mead **6** Havasu, Mohave,
  Mormon, Powell **9** Roosevelt
  land rank: 5 sixth
  mountain: 5 White **6** Lemmon **7**
  Hualpai **8** Mazatzal **9** Baldy Peak **13**
  Santa Catalina
    highest point: 13 Humphreys Peak
  physical feature:
    canyon: 5 Grand
    desert: 6 Sonora **7** Painted
    forest: 9 Petrified
  river: 4 Gila, Salt, Zuni **5** Verde **6**
  Puerco **8** Colorado **12** Bill Williams
  14 Little Colorado
  state admission: 11 forty-eighth
  state bird: 10 cactus wren
  state flower: 13 saguaro cactus
  state motto: 11 God Enriches
  state song: 7 Arizona
  state tree: 9 palo verde
ark 3 box **4** ship **5** barge, chest **8** flatboat **9** houseboat **10** Noah's boat
Ark
  built by: 4 Noah
  landing place: 6 Ararat
  groups: 5 pairs
Arkansas
  abbreviation: 2 AR **3** Ark
  nickname: 4 Bear **9** Bowie Land **17**
  Land of Opportunity
  capital/largest city: 10 Little Rock
  others: 3 Coy, Cuy, Keo, Ola, Roe,
  Ulm **4** Alma, Bono, Casa, Dell, Diaz,
  Moro **5** Enola, Perla, Rondo **6** Alicia,
  Camden **8** El Dorado **9** Fort Smith,
  Jonesboro, Pine Bluff, Texarkana **10**
  Hot Springs **11** Blytheville **12** Fayetteville
  feature:
    national park: 10 Hot Springs
  tribe: 5 Caddo, Osage **6** Quapaw **7**
  Choctaw, Wichita **8** Cherokee
  people: 8 Alan Ladd **10** Dick Powell
  11 Bill Clinton **16** Douglas Mac-

Arthur
  lake: 6 Beaver, Chicot, Conway, Nimrod **7** Greeson, Norfork **8** Maumelle,
  Ouachita **10** Bull Shoals **11** Greers
  Ferry **12** Blue Mountain
  land rank: 13 twenty-seventh
  mountain: 4 Blue **5** Ozark **6** Boston,
  Gaylor **7** Fourche **8** Magazine,
  Ouachita
    highest point: 8 Magazine
  river: 3 Red **5** Black, White **6** Saline
  7 Buffalo, Current **8** Arkansas, Cos-
  satot, Ouachita **9** St Francis **11** Mississippi
  state admission: 11 twenty-fifth
  state bird: 11 mockingbird
  state flower: 12 apple blossom
  state motto: 13 (Let) The People
  Rule
  state song: 8 Arkansas
  state tree: 13 shortleaf pine
Arkin, Alan
  born: 9 New York NY
  roles: 5 Simon **6** Havana **7** Catch-22
  9 The In-Laws, Rocketeer **12** Indian
  Summer, The **13** Wait Until Dark **16**
  Grosse Point Blank **17** Glengarry
  Glen Ross **21** Last of the Red-Hot
  Lovers **23** The Heart Is a Lonely
  Hunter **40** The Russians Are Coming
  The Russians Are Coming
Ark of the Covenant
  gold covering: 9 mercy seat **12** pro-
  pitiatory
arm, arms 4 guns **5** brace, crest,
equip, prime **6** branch, outfit, sector **7**
forearm, fortify, prepare, protect, section, weapons **8** armament, blazonry,
division, firearms, insignia, materiel,
offshoot, ordnance, weaponry **9** appendage, make ready, upper limb **10**
coat of arms, department, detachment,
obtain arms, projection, strengthen,
take up arms **12** anterior limb **13** prepare for war **14** heraldic emblem **18**
furnish with weapons
armada 4 navy **5** fleet **8** flotilla,
squadron **10** escadrille
armadillo 4 a par
  family: 11 Dasypodidae
  order: 8 Edentata
  body: 5 armor **6** plates
  habitat: 12 South America, United
  States **14** Central America
  habit: 9 nocturnal
Armageddon 8 doomsday **11** final
battle **13** great conflict
  author: 8 Leon Uris
armagnac
  type: 6 brandy **7** liqueur
  origin: 6 France **7** Gascony
armament 4 arms, guns **7** weapons **8**
ordnance, weaponry **9** equipment,
munitions **10** outfitting **13** military
might **16** war-making machine
Armenia
  other name: 5 Minni **6** Urartu **8** Ana-

tolia
  former name: 31 Armenian Soviet
  Socialist Republic
  capital/largest city: 6 Erivan **7** Yerevan
  ancient capital: 3 Ani **8** Artashat, Ar-
  taxata
  others: 3 Van **5** Sivas **7** Trabzon **9**
  Kirovakan, Leninakan, Trabizond **13**
  Bitlisarzurum
  head of state: 9 President
  monetary unit: 5 ruble
  lake: 3 Van **5** Sevan, Urmia **8** Urumiyah
  mountain: 6 Ararat, Taurus **7** Aladagh **8** Karabakh
  highest peak: 12 Mount Aragats
  river: 3 Ara **4** Aras, Kura **5** Araks,
  Cyrus, Halys, Zanga **6** Araxes, Raz-
  dan, Tigris **9** Euphrates **10** Kizil-
  Irmak
  physical feature:
    volcano: 7 Aragats
  people: 5 Armen, Ermyn, Gomer,
  Hadji
    apostle: 7 Gregory
    gypsy: 5 bosha
    hero: 4 haik **6** vartan
    leader: 26 Levon Akopovich Ter
    Petrosyan
    me: 3 ara
    saint: 5 Sahak **6** Mesrop
  language: 7 Russian **8** Armenian
  religion: 16 Armenian Orthodox
  feature:
    cap: 6 calpac
    fortress: 7 erebuni
    game: 7 barbout
    kingdom: 6 Urartu, Vannic **7** Cili-
    cia, Sophene **8** Ardsruni
  food:
    bread: 4 peda
    cucumber: 4 guta
    dish: 7 lahvosh **9** paraghatz, sou-
    beoreg
Armenian
  language family: 12 Indo-European
  spoken in: 4 USSR **6** Russia **7** Armenia
Armida
  opera by: 5 Gluck, Haydn, Lully **6**
  Dvorak **7** Rossini **10** Eszterhazy
Armies 7 Sabaoth
Armies of the Night
  author: 12 Norman Mailer
armistice 5 peace, truce **9** cease-fire
23 suspension of hostilities
armlet 6 bangle **8** bracelet, ornament
arm of the sea 5 bight, firth, fjord
(fiord), inlet **6** strait **7** channel, estuary, narrows
armoire 8 cupboard, wardrobe **12**
clothespress
armor 4 mail **5** chain **6** shield **7** bulwark **10** coat of mail, protection **11**
suit of armor **18** protective covering

armorial bearings 4 arms **5** crest **10** coat of arms, escutcheon

armory 7 arsenal **9** arms depot **13** ordnance depot

Arms and the Man
  author: **17** George Bernard Shaw

arms depot 6 armory **7** arsenal **13** ordnance depot **18** military storehouse

Armstrong, Henry
  sport: **6** boxing
  class: **11** lightweight **12** welterweight

army 3 mob **4** band, bevy, crew, gang, host, mass, pack **5** crowd, force, horde, swarm **6** legion, throng, troops **7** legions, militia **8** military, soldiers, soldiery **9** land force, multitude **10** land forces **11** aggregation, fighting men **12** congregation **13** military force **15** military machine

Arnaeus
  also: **4** Irus
  origin: **5** Greek
  mentioned in: **7** Odyssey
  form: **6** beggar **9** errandboy
  errandboy for: **16** Penelopes suitors

Arne
  author: **20** Bjornstjerne Bjornson

Arne
  son: **6** Aeolus **7** Boeotus
  foster father: **9** Desmontes

Arne, Thomas Augustine
  born: **6** London **7** England
  composer of: **6** Alfred, Judith **8** Rosamond, Tom Thumb **10** Artaxerxes **13** Rule, Britannia **14** Love in a Village, Thomas and Sally

Arness, James
  real name: **12** James Aurness
  brother: **11** Peter Graves
  born: **13** Minneapolis MN
  roles: **8** Gunsmoke **10** Matt Dillon

Arnold, Matthew
  author of: **7** Thyrsis **10** Dover Beach **15** Sohrab and Rustum, The Scholar-Gypsy **16** Empedocles on Etna **17** Culture and Anarchy, Essays in Criticism **18** On Translating Homer

aroma 4 odor **5** savor, scent, smell **7** bouquet **9** fragrance, redolence

aromatic 5 spicy **7** odorous, piquant, pungent, scented **8** fragrant, perfumed, redolent **11** odoriferous

around 4 near **5** about, circa **10** encircling, on all sides, roundabout **11** surrounding

Around the World in Eighty Days
  author: **10** Jules Verne
  director: **15** Michael Anderson
  character: **11** Phileas Fogg **12** Passepartout
  cast: **10** Cantinflas, David Niven **12** Robert Newton **15** Marlene Dietrich, Shirley MacLaine
  score: **11** Victor Young
  Oscar for: **5** score **7** picture

arouse 3 fan **4** goad, move, spur, warm, whet **5** pique, rouse, waken **6** awaken, bestir, excite, foment, foster, heat up, incite, kindle, stir up, wake up **7** provoke, quicken, sharpen **8** summon up **9** stimulate

Arowhena
  character in: **7** Erewhon
  author: **6** Butler

arpeggio 5 chord, scale **8** flourish **13** musical device

arraign 6 accuse, charge, impute, indict **7** censure **8** denounce **9** criticize

arrange 4 file, plan, plot, pose, rank, sort **5** adapt, array, fix up, group, order, range, score **6** assort, design, devise, lay out, line up, map out, set out, settle **7** agree to, marshal, prepare, provide **8** classify, contrive, organize, schedule **9** methodize **11** orchestrate, systematize

arrangement 5 order **8** arraying, disposal, grouping, ordering **10** assortment **12** distribution, organization **13** methodization **14** categorization, classification **15** systematization
  German: **9** Ausgleich
  flower: **7** ikebana

arrangements 5 plans, score, terms **7** compact **8** measures **9** agreement **10** adaptation, provisions, settlement **12** preparations **13** orchestration

arrant 4 rank **5** utter **7** extreme **8** flagrant, outright, thorough **9** confirmed, downright, egregious, notorious, out-and-out **11** undisguised, unmitigated **13** thoroughgoing

array 4 deck, garb, pose, rank, robe, show, wrap **5** adorn, align, dress, group, order, place, range **6** attire, bedeck, clothe, deploy, finery, fit out, outfit, parade, set out, supply **7** apparel, arrange, display, marshal, raiment **8** clothing, garments, organize **9** pageantry **10** assortment, collection, exhibition, marshaling **11** arrangement, disposition

arrears 5 debit **9** liability **10** balance due, obligation, unpaid debt **11** overdue debt **12** indebtedness **15** outstanding debt

arrest 3 end, fix, nab **4** bust, halt, hold, slow, stay, stop **5** block, catch, check, delay, pinch, rivet, roust, seize, stall **6** absorb, collar, detain, engage, hinder, occupy, retard, secure **7** attract, capture, engross, inhibit, seizure, slowing, staying **8** blocking, checking, hold back, restrain, stoppage, stopping, suppress **9** apprehend, interrupt, retention **10** inhibiting **11** holding back **12** apprehension, take prisoner

Arrhenius, Svante August
  field: **7** physics **9** chemistry
  nationality: **7** Swedish
  theory of: **24** electrolytic dissociation

arriere pensee 12 hidden motive **17** mental reservation

arrival 5 comer **6** advent, coming **7** entrant, visitor **8** approach, arriving, entrance, newcomer, visitant **10** appearance

arrive 4 come, near **5** get to, occur, reach **6** appear, befall, happen, show up, turn up **7** succeed **8** approach, make good

arrivederci, a rivederci 7 goodbye **8** farewell **16** until we meet again

arrogance 5 scorn **6** egoism, vanity **7** bluster, conceit, disdain, swagger **8** contempt **9** assurance, insolence, loftiness, vainglory **10** lordliness, pretension **11** braggadocio, haughtiness, presumption **13** imperiousness **14** self-importance

arrogant 4 vain **6** lordly **7** haughty, pompous **8** insolent, scornful **9** conceited, imperious **10** disdainful, egoistical, swaggering **11** egotistical, overbearing, overweening, pretentious **12** contemptuous, presumptuous, self-assuming, supercilious, vainglorious **13** high-and- mighty, self-important

arrogate 5 adopt, claim, seize, usurp **6** assume **7** preempt **8** take over **10** commandeer **11** appropriate

arrogation 6 taking **7** seizure **10** assumption, usurpation **12** confiscation **13** appropriation, expropriation

arrow 3 bow **4** bolt, dart, nock **5** shaft **7** pointer **9** direction **12** pointed shaft

Arrow
  constellation of: **7** Sagitta

Arrowsmith
  author: **13** Sinclair Lewis
  character: **10** Leora Tozer **11** Max Gottlieb **12** Terry Wickett **14** Capitola McGurk **15** Gustaf Sondelius **16** Martin Arrowsmith **18** Dr Almus Pickerbaugh

arroyo 4 wadi **5** gorge, gully **6** ravine, trench

arsenal 6 armory **7** weapons **8** magazine **9** arms depot **11** arms factory **13** ordnance depot **14** ammunition dump

arsenic
  chemical symbol: **2** As

Arsenic and Old Lace
  director: **10** Frank Capra
  cast: **9** Cary Grant **10** Jack Carson, Peter Lorre **13** Josephine Hull, Priscilla Lane, Raymond Massey

Arsinoe see **11** Alphesiboea

Arsinous
  son: **8** Aecamede

Arsippe
  father: **6** Minyas
  mocked: **8** Dionysus

ars longa, vita brevis 18 art is long, life short

Ars Poetica
  author: **5** Homer

art, arts 5 craft, knack, skill **6** genius **7** finesse, mastery, methods **8** artistry, facility, strategy **9** dexterity, expertise, technique **10** fine points, humanities, principles, subtleties, virtuosity
   goddess of: 6 Athena, Athene, Pallas, Saitis **7** Minerva **11** Tritogeneia **12** Pallas Athena **18** Alalcomenean Athena

Artegall
   character in: 15 The Faerie Queene
   author: 7 Spenser

Artemis
   also: 7 Cynthia **9** Astrateia
   origin: 5 Greek
   form: 6 virgin **7** goddess **8** huntress
   habitat: 4 moon
   mother: 4 Leto
   twin brother: 6 Apollo
   companion: 4 Opis **5** Oread
   corresponds to: 5 Diana **6** Phoebe, Selene **11** Britomartis
   epithet: 6 Orthia **7** Eurippa, Laphria, Limnaea, Pyronia **8** Aeginaea, Agrotera, Calliste, Caryatis, Daphnaea **9** Hemerasia, Lygodesma **10** Polymastus **11** Leucophryne

artery 3 way **4** path, road, vein **5** aorta **6** street **7** channel, highway **11** blood vessel

artful 3 apt, sly **4** able, deft, foxy, wily **5** adept, quick, sharp, smart **6** adroit, astute, clever, crafty, gifted, shifty, shrewd, subtle, tricky **7** cunning, knowing, politic **8** masterly, scheming, skillful, talented **9** deceitful, deceptive, designing, dexterous, ingenious, inventive, strategic, underhand **10** contriving, diplomatic, proficient **11** imaginative, machinating, maneuvering, resourceful **12** disingenuous

artfulness 5 guile **6** deceit **7** cunning, slyness **8** artifice, foxiness, scheming, subtlety, trickery, wiliness **10** craftiness **11** machination

Arthur
   director: 11 Steve Gordon
   cast: 11 Dudley Moore, John Gielgud **12** Liza Minnelli **19** Geraldine Fitzgerald
   Oscar for: 15 supporting actor (Gielgud)

Arthur
   began: 10 Round Table
   buried: 6 Avalon
   chronicler: 4 Wace **6** Malory **8** Chretien
   father: 14 Uther Pendragon
   half-sister: 11 Morgan le Fay
   home: 7 Camelot
   island: 6 Avalon
   knights: 3 Kay **6** Gareth, Gawain **7** Geraint **8** Bedivere, Lancelot, Percival, Tristram **9** Launcelot
   knights sought: 9 Holy Grail
   mother: 7 Igraine, Ygaerne
   nephew: 6 Modred **7** Mordred

sword: 9 Excalibur
   given by: 13 Lady of the Lake
   wife: 9 Guinevere
   wizard: 6 Merlin
   women, Arthurian: 4 Anna, Enid **5** Nimue **6** Elaine, Gyneth, Iseult, Isolde **7** Igraine, Ygaerne **9** Bellicent, Guinivere **11** Morgan le Fay

Arthur, Chester Alan
   nickname: 4 Chet **16** The Gentleman Boss
   presidential rank: 11 twenty-first
   party: 10 Republican
   state represented: 2 NY
   defeated: 5 no-one
      succeeded upon death of: 8 Garfield
   vice president: 4 none
   cabinet:
      state: 6 (James Gillespie) Blaine **13** (Frederick Theodore) Frelinghuysen
      treasury: 6 (Charles James) Folger, (William) Windom **7** (Walter Quintin) Gresham **9** (Hugh) McCulloch
      war: 7 (Robert Todd) Lincoln
      attorney general: 8 (Benjamin Harris) Brewster, (Isaac Wayne) MacVeagh
      navy: 4 (William Henry) Hunt **8** (William Eaton) Chandler
      postmaster general: 4 (Timothy Otis) Howe **5** (Thomas Lemuel) James **6** (Frank) Hatton **7** (Walter Quinton) Gresham
      interior: 6 (Henry Moore) Teller **8** (Samuel Jordan) Kirkwood
   born: 2 VT (or Canada) **9** Fairfield
   died: 2 NY **11** New York City
   buried: 2 NY **6** Albany
   education:
      college: 5 Union
      studied: 3 law
   religion: 12 Episcopalian
   interests: 8 good food (an epicure) **13** salmon fishing
   political career: 13 vice president **26** customs collector for New York
   civilian career: 6 lawyer **7** teacher
   military service: 8 Civil War
      quartermaster general of: 12 state militia (New York)
   notable events of lifetime/term: 5 Panic (of 1883)
      Act: 9 Pendleton **16** Chinese Exclusion **19** Edmunds Anti-Polygamy
   father: 7 William
   mother: 7 Malvina (Stone)
   siblings: 4 Jane, Mary **6** Almeda, George, Regina **7** Malvina, William **8** Ann Eliza
   wife: 5 Ellen (Lewis Herndon)
      nickname: 4 Nell
   children: 11 Chester Alan **12** Ellen Herndon **19** William Lewis Herndon

artichoke 14 Cynara Scolymus
   varieties: 5 Globe **7** Chinese **8** Japa-

nese **9** Jerusalem **14** White Jerusalem

article 4 item, part, term **5** count, essay, paper, piece, point, story, theme, thing **6** clause, detail, matter, object, review, sketch **7** portion, product, proviso, write-up **8** division **9** commodity, condition, paragraph, provision, substance **10** commentary, particular **11** proposition, stipulation

articulate 4 join **5** hinge, state, utter, voice **6** convey, facile, fluent, hook up **7** connect, enounce, express **8** eloquent, organize **9** enunciate, formulate, pronounce **10** enunciated, expressive, meaningful, speechlike **12** intelligible

articulation 5 hinge, joint **7** diction **8** juncture **9** elocution, utterance **10** connection **11** enunciation **13** pronunciation

artifact 4 tool **7** manmade **9** arrowhead

artifice 4 hoax, ruse, trap, wile **5** blind, dodge, feint, guile, trick **6** deceit, device, tactic **7** cunning, slyness **8** foxiness, intrigue, maneuver, scheming, trickery, wiliness **9** deception, duplicity, falsehood, imposture, ingenuity, invention, stratagem **10** artfulness, cleverness, craftiness, subterfuge **11** contrivance, machination **13** inventiveness

artificer 7 artisan, deviser **9** contriver, craftsman

artificial 4 fake, mock, sham **5** bogus, false, phony, stagy **6** ersatz, forced **7** feigned, labored, manmade, stilted **8** affected, mannered, specious, spurious **9** imitation, insincere, pretended, simulated, synthetic, unnatural **10** factitious, non-natural, theatrical **11** counterfeit **12** manufactured

artillery 6 cannon **7** big guns **8** ordnance **11** mounted guns

artisan 6 master **9** craftsman **10** technician **14** handicraftsman

art is long, life short
   Latin: 18 ars longa vita brevis

artist 6 expert, master **8** virtuoso

artistic 7 elegant, stylish **8** graceful, handsome, tasteful **9** aesthetic, exquisite **10** attractive

artistic ability 6 talent **7** mastery **8** artistry **10** virtuosity

artistry 5 taste, touch **6** talent **7** mastery **10** virtuosity **11** proficiency, sensibility **14** accomplishment

artless 4 naif, open, pure, true **5** crude, frank, naive, plain **6** candid, honest, humble, simple **7** natural, sincere **8** innocent, trusting **9** guileless, ingenuous, primitive, unadorned **10** inartistic, lacking art, unaffected, untalented **11** open-hearted, undesigning

13 unpretentious **15** straightforward, unselfconscious, unsophisticated

artlessness 6 candor **7** honesty, naivete **8** openness **9** frankness, sincerity **10** simplicity **11** naturalness **13** guilelessness, ingenuousness **14** unaffectedness

art object
  French: **9** objet d'art

Art of Living, The
  author: **11** John Gardner

Art of Love, The (Ars Amatoria)
  author: **4** Ovid

arty 6 dainty **7** foppish **8** affected, high- brow, overnice, precious **9** dandified, overblown **10** effeminate **11** overrefined, pretentious **12** artsycraftsy, bluestocking, high-sounding

Aryan
  modern name: **13** Indo-European
  origin: **10** North India **11** Central Asia
  family of languages: **5** Hindi **7** Bengali, Panjabi **9** Sinhalese
  religion: **8** Hinduism
  originated in: **11** caste system

Aryana *see* **11** Afghanistan

as 4 that, when **5** while **7** because, equally

Asa
  father: **6** Abijah
  grandfather: **8** Rehoboam
  grandmother: **6** Maacah
  deposed: **6** Maacah
  defeated: **6** Baasha

as above
  Latin: **7** ut supra

as a group 7 en masse, in a body **8** as a whole, together **11** all together

as a matter of form
  Latin: **8** pro forma

Asar *see* **5** Aesir

as a result 2 so **5** due to **7** because **9** therefore, wherefore, whereupon **11** accordingly **12** consequently **13** in consequence

as a whole 6 in toto **8** all in all **10** altogether **19** all things considered
  French: **6** en bloc

as below
  Latin: **7** ut infra

Ascalaphus
  occupation: **6** sentry **8** gardener
  location: **10** underworld
  father: **4** Ares
  brother: **8** Ialmenus
  member of: **9** Argonauts
  killed by: **9** Deiphobus
  changed into: **3** owl
  changed by: **7** Demeter

Ascanius
  also: **5** Iulus
  father: **6** Aeneas
  mother: **6** Creusa
  founder of: **9** Alba Longa

ascend 4 rise **5** climb, mount, scale **7** inherit **9** succeed to

ascendancy, ascendance 4 edge, rule, sway **5** power, reign **7** command, control, mastery **8** whip hand **9** advantage, authority, dominance, influence, supremacy, upper hand **10** domination, leadership **11** preeminence, sovereignty, superiority **12** predominance

ascension 6 ascent, rising **7** scaling **8** climbing, mounting **10** ascendancy

ascent 4 rise **5** climb, grade, slope **6** rising **7** advance, incline, scaling, upgrade **8** climbing, gradient, mounting, progress **9** ascension **11** advancement, progression

ascertain 5 learn **6** detect, verify **7** certify, find out, unearth **8** discover **9** determine, establish, ferret out

ascertainable 10 detectable **11** discernible, perceivable, perceptible

ascetic 3 nun **4** monk, yogi **5** fakir, stern **6** essene, hermit, strict **7** austere, dervish, eremite, recluse, Spartan **8** celibate, cenobite, rigorous, solitary **9** abstainer, anchorite, religious **10** abstemious, flagellant, self-denier **11** self- denying **13** self-mortifier **14** self-mortifying

Asch, Sholem
  author of: **4** Mary **5** Moses **8** A Village **10** The Apostle, The Prophet **11** The Nazarene, Three Cities **15** Song of the Valley **17** The God of Vengeance

Asclepius
  origin: **5** Greek
  god of: **7** healing **8** medicine
  father: **6** Apollo
  mother: **7** Coronis
  wife: **6** Epione
  son: **7** Machaon **10** Podalirius
  daughter: **4** Iaso **6** Hygeia
  nurse: **6** Trygon
  corresponds to: **11** Aesculapius
  epithet: **8** Cotyleus

ascribe 6 assign, credit, impute, relate **7** trace to **8** accredit, charge to **9** attribute

asea 4 lost **6** addled, adrift **7** puzzled **8** confused **10** bewildered

Asgard
  home of: **4** Asar **5** Aesir
  origin: **12** Scandinavian
  connected to earth by: **7** bifrost **13** rainbow bridge
  location of: **8** Valhalla

ash 4 dust **6** cinder **7** residue **12** powdered lava
  family: **5** olive
  genus: **8** Fraxinus
  climatic zone: **17** northern temperate
  varieties: **3** Pop, Red, Sea **4** Blue **5** Black, Green, Manna, Texas, Wafer, Water, White **6** Alpine, Ground, Shamel, Syrian, Velvet **7** Arizona,

Modesto, Prickly **8** Carolina, Stinking **9** Evergreen, Flowering **10** Manchurian, Montebello **18** Yellow-topped mallee
  use: **4** fuel **6** timber **7** barrels **8** landscape **9** furniture **10** motor parts, sport goods
  most common species: **8** white ash

ashamed 3 shy **7** abashed, bashful, prudish **9** chagrined, mortified, squeamish **10** chapfallen, distressed, humiliated, shamefaced **11** crestfallen, discomfited, embarrassed **12** disconcerted **13** guilt-stricken **18** conscience-stricken

Ashby, Hal
  director of: **10** Being There, Coming Home

ashen 3 wan **4** gray, pale **5** livid, pasty **6** anemic, leaden, pallid **8** blanched

Asher
  father: **5** Jacob
  mother: **6** Zilpah
  brother: **3** Dan, Gad **4** Levi **5** Judah **6** Joseph, Reuben, Simeon **7** Zebulun **8** Benjamin, Issachar, Nephtali
  sister: **5** Dinah
  city in: **8** Manasseh
  descendant of: **8** Asherite

Ashkenaz
  father: **6** Japhet
  mother: **5** Gomer

Ashley, Lady Brett
  character in: **15** The Sun Also Rises
  author: **9** Hemingway

ashore 6 on land **7** aground **9** on dry land

Ashton-Warner, Sylvia
  author of: **5** Three **6** Myself **7** Teacher **8** Spinster **10** Greenstone

Ashtoreth
  origin: **7** Semitic
  corresponds to: **6** Inanna, Ishtar **7** Astarte, Mylitta

Ash Wednesday
  author: **7** T S Eliot

ashy 3 wan **4** pale **5** ashen, pasty, white **6** pallid, sallow **7** ghastly, ghostly **8** blanched **9** colorless

Asia
  country: **4** Iran, Iraq, Laos, Oman **5** Burma, China, India, Japan, Macao, Nepal, Qatar, Syria, Tibet, Yemen **6** Bhutan, Brunei, Cyprus, Israel, Jordan, Russia, Sikkim, Taiwan, Turkey **7** Armenia, Bahrain, Georgia, Kashmir, Lebanon, Myanmar, Vietnam **8** Cambodia, Hong Kong, Malaysia, Maldives, Mongolia, Pakistan, Sri Lanka, Thailand **9** East Timor, Indonesia, Kirghizia, Singapore **10** Azerbaijan, Bangladesh, Kazakhstan, Kyrgyzstan, North Korea, South Korea, Tajikistan, Uzbekistan **11** Afghanistan, Saudi Arabia **12** North Vietnam, South Vietnam, Turkmenistan **13** Inner Mongolia **14** Papua New

Guinea **15** Sinkiang-Uighur **18** United Arab Emirates
desert: 4 Gobi, Thar **6** Syrian **7** Arabian, Karakum **8** Kyzylkum **10** Takla Makan
island: 5 Kuril, Japan **6** Taiwan **7** Hai-nan **8** Sri Lanka **9** Indonesia: **3** Aru **4** Java, Sulu **5** Ceram, Sumba, Timor **6** Borneo, Flores **7** Celebes, Sumatra **8** Moluccas, Tanimbar **9** Halmahera, New Guinea **11** Philippines
ancient people/empire: 4 Elam, Thai **5** Akkad, Aryan, Indus, Khmer, Media, Shang **6** Mongol, Ohoman, Semite **7** Amorite, Assyria, Hwang Ho, Parthia, Persian **8** Sumerian **9** Babylonia, Dravidian, Sassanian **11** Hephthalite, Mesopotamia
ancient city: 2 Ur **5** Pagan, Sumer **6** Anyang **7** Ayuthia, Harappa **8** Mandalay **12** Mohenjo-daro
ancient leader: 5 Asoka, Kassi **6** Darius **9** Anawratha, Zoroaster **13** Cyrus the Great **17** Alexander the Great
religion: 5 Islam **6** Muslim, Shinto, Taoism **7** Jainism, Judaism **8** Buddhism, Hinduism **12** Christianity, Confucianism **13** Protestantism **16** Roman Catholicism
language: 5 Hindi, Malay **6** Arabic, French, Korean **7** Chinese, English, Russian, Spanish **8** Japanese **10**Indonesian, Portuguese
   Chinese dialects: 2 Wu **3** Min **5** Hakka **8** Mandarin **9** Cantonese
river: 2 Ob **3** Amu, Hsi, Syr **4** Amur, Lena **5** Indus **6** Ganges, Mekong, Tigris **7** Hwang Ho, Salween, Yangtze, Yenisei **9** Euphrates, Irrawaddy **11** Brahmaputra **16** Tigris-Euphrates
lake: 6 Baikal **7** Aral Sea **8** Balkhash **10** Caspian Sea
mountain/mountain range: 5 Altai, Urals **6** Kunlon, Pamirs, Taurus, Zagros **8** Caucasus, Sulaiman, Tien Shan **9** Himalayas, Hindu Kush, Karakoram **10** Arakan Yoma
highest point: 12 Mount Everest
lowest point: 7 Dead Sea
mineral/natural resources: 3 oil, tin **4** coal, mica, talc, zinc **7** bauxite, iron ore, mercury **8** chromium, graphite, selenium, tungsten **9** manganese **10** natural gas
largest city: 8 Shanghai
vegetation: 3 fir, sal **4** moss, pine, teak **5** larch **6** bamboo, lichen, spruce **8** ironwood
animal: 3 elk, yak **4** bear, wolf **5** camel, panda, sable, takin, tiger **6** ermine, kuland **7** markhor **8** antelope, elephant, reindeer **9** arctic fox, polar bear
people: 4 Huis, Kurd, Thai, Turk **5** Aryan, Khmer, Malay, Tungu **6** Buryat, Chuang, Kalmyk, Mongol, Semite, Vighor **7** Baluchi, Burmese, Chinese, Chukchi, Persian, Russian, Tadzhik, Tibetan **8** Armenian, Filipino, Japanese **9** Dravidian **10** Han Chinese, Indonesian, Vietnamese

aside 4 away **5** apart **6** aslant, beside **7** whisper

As I Lay Dying
  author: 15 William Faulkner
  character:
    Bundren family: 4 Anse, Cash, Darl **5** Addie, Jewel **9** Dewey Dell

Asimov, Isaac
  author of: 6 I Robot **10** Foundation (trilogy) **12** Caves of Steel, Robots of Dawn **17** The Gods Themselves
  character: 12 Elijah Bailey **13** R Daneel Olivaw

asinine 5 silly **6** absurd, insane, stupid **7** foolish, idiotic, moronic, witless **9** brainless, imbecilic, senseless **10** half-witted, irrational, muddleheaded, ridiculous **11** lamebrained, thickheaded, thick-witted **12** dunderheaded, feebleminded, simpleminded, thick-skulled

asininity 5 folly **8** dumbness **9** silliness, stupidity **10** imbecility **11** doltishness, foolishness **16** simplemindedness

as it should be
  French: 11 comme il faut

Asius
  origin: 5 Greek
  mentioned in: 5 Iliad
  king of: 7 Percote
  father: 8 Hyrtacus
  killed by: 9 Idomeneus

ask 3 beg, bid, sue **4** call, pump, quiz, seek, urge **5** apply, claim, grill, plead, press, query **6** appeal, charge, demand, desire, expect, invite, summon **7** beseech, entreat, implore, inquire, request, solicit **8** petition, question, sound out **10** supplicate **11** interrogate

askance 11 skeptically **12** disdainfully, suspiciously **13** distrustfully, mistrustfully **14** disapprovingly

askew 4 awry **6** aslant **7** crooked **8** cockeyed, lopsided, sleeping **9** crookedly

Askkimey see **6** Eskimo

aslant 4 awry **5** askew **7** crooked **8** cockeyed, lopsided **9** crookedly, obliquely, slantwise

asleep 6 dozing **7** napping **10** slumbering **13** taking a siesta **14** dead to the world

as much as this
  Latin: 8 quoad hoc

Asner, Ed
  born: 12 Kansas City KS
  roles: 5 Roots **6** Daniel **8** El Dorado, Lou Grant **12** A Case of Libel, The Gathering, Silent Motive **14** Rich Man Poor Man **18** Mary Tyler Moore Show

asocial 8 unsocial **9** nonsocial, reclusive **10** antisocial **12** misanthropic

Asopus
  form: 3 god
  habitat: 5 river
  father: 7 Oceanus
  mother: 6 Tethys
  wife: 6 Metope
  son: 7 Ismenus, Pelagon
  number of daughters: 6 twenty

asparagus
  varieties: 4 Cape **6** Common, Garden, Smilax **7** Cossack **8** Prussian, Sprenger

aspect 3 air **4** look, side **5** angle, facet, point **7** feature **10** appearance **13** consideration

aspen 7 Populus
  varieties: 7 Chinese, Quaking **8** European, Japanese **9** Trembling **12** Large-toothed

asperity 5 rigor **6** rancor **8** acrimony, hardship, severity **9** harshness, hostility, roughness **10** difficulty

Aspern Papers, The
  author: 10 Henry James

aspersion 4 slur **5** abuse, smear **7** calumny, censure, obloquy, railing, slander **8** reproach, reviling **10** defamation, detraction **11** deprecation **12** vilification **13** disparagement

Asphodel Fields
  meadow of: 10 dead heroes

asphyxiate 5 choke **6** stifle **7** smother **9** suffocate **11** strangulate

aspirant 7 hopeful, nominee **9** applicant, candidate **10** competitor, contestant

aspiration 3 end **4** hope, mark, wish **6** design, desire, intent, object **7** craving, longing, purpose **8** ambition, daydream, endeavor, yearning **9** hankering, intention, objective

aspire 4 seek **5** aim at, covet, crave **6** desire, pursue **7** hope for, long for, pine for, wish for **8** yearn for **9** pant after **10** hunger over **11** hanker after, thirst after

ass 3 oaf **4** dolt, fool, jerk **5** booby, burro, dunce, idiot, moron, ninny **6** donkey, dum-dum, nitwit **7** half-wit, jackass **8** bonehead, imbecile, lunkhead, numskull **9** blockhead, lamebrain **10** dunderhead, nincompoop

assail 5 fly at **6** attack **7** assault, lunge at, set upon **9** pitch into **11** descend upon

assailant 6 mugger **8** assailer, attacker, molester **9** aggressor, assaulter

assailer 8 attacker **9** aggressor, assailant, assaulter

Assamese
  language family: 12 Indo-European
  branch: 11 Indo-Iranian
  group: 5 Indic
  spoken in: 5 (northern) India

Assaracus
origin: **5** Greek
mentioned in: **5** Iliad
father: **4** Tros
son: **5** Capys
founder of: **10** royal house

assassin 6 hit man, killer, slayer **8** murderer **11** executioner

assassinate 4 kill, slay **6** murder, rub out **7** bump off **9** do to death, liquidate **10** put to death **11** exterminate

assault 4 push, raid **5** drive, fly at, foray, lunge, sally, siege, storm **6** assail, attack, charge, invade, strike, thrust **7** besiege, bombard, lunge at, offense, set upon **8** fall upon, invasion, storming, strike at, thrust at **9** assailing, lash out at, onslaught **10** aggression **11** bombardment

assaulter 6 mugger **8** assailer, attacker **9** aggressor, assailant

assay 3 try **4** rate, test **5** essay, prove **6** assess **7** analyze, attempt **8** appraise, endeavor, estimate, evaluate **9** undertake

assemblage 4 body, heap, herd, mass, pack, pile **5** batch, bunch, clump, flock, group, stock, store **6** throng **7** cluster, company **8** assembly, conclave **9** aggregate, amassment, gathering **10** collection **11** aggregation **12** accumulation, congregation

assemble 4 join, meet **5** amass, flock, rally **6** gather, heap up, muster, pile up, summon **7** collect, compile, connect, convene, convoke, marshal, round up **9** construct, fabricate **10** accumulate, congregate **11** fit together, put together **12** call together, come together **13** bring together, group together

assembly 4 body, herd, mass, pack **5** crowd, flock, group, troop **6** throng **7** cluster, company, council **8** conclave, congress **9** aggregate, gathering **10** assemblage, collection **11** aggregation, convocation, legislature **12** congregation

assembly hall 8 auditory **10** auditorium **11** concert hall, lecture hall, meeting hall

assent 5 agree, allow, grant, yield **6** accept, accord, comply, concur, permit **7** approve, concede, consent, defer to **8** approval, sanction **9** acquiesce, admission, agreement **10** acceptance, compliance, concession, fall in with **11** affirmation, approbation, concurrence, endorsement, recognition, subscribe to **12** acquiescence, confirmation, ratification, verification **13** corroboration **14** acknowledgment

assent to 4 okay **5** allow **6** accept, permit **7** approve **8** sanction, say yes to **9** agree with, authorize **11** acquiesce to, go along with

assert 4 aver, avow **5** argue, claim, state, swear **6** accent, affirm, avouch, insist, stress, uphold **7** advance, contend, declare, profess **8** advocate, maintain, propound, set forth **9** emphasize **10** put forward

assertion 5 claim **6** avowal, dictum **8** argument, averment **9** statement, upholding **10** allegation, contention **11** declaration, maintaining **12** protestation

assertive 5 pushy **8** cocksure, decisive, emphatic, forceful, positive **9** confident, insistent, outspoken **10** aggressive **11** domineering, self-assured **12** strong-willed

assertiveness 10 insistence **11** forwardness **12** cocksureness, forcefulness, positiveness **13** agressiveness, outspokenness **14** self-confidence

assess 3 tax **4** levy **5** judge, value **6** charge **8** appraise, consider, estimate, evaluate, look over

assessment 3 fee, tax **4** dues, fine, rate, toll **6** charge, impost, tariff **8** judgment **9** appraisal **10** estimation, evaluation

asset 3 aid **4** boon, help, plus **7** benefit, service **9** advantage

assets 4 cash **5** goods, means, money **6** wealth **7** capital, effects **8** property, reserves **9** resources **10** belongings **11** possessions

asseverate 4 aver, avow **5** state, swear **6** affirm, assert, attest, avouch, insist **7** certify, contend, declare, protect **8** maintain, proclaim **9** emphasize, pronounce

as shown below
Latin: **7** ut infra

assiduity 8 industry, tenacity **9** diligence **10** dedication, doggedness **11** application, persistence **13** determination

assiduous 6 dogged **7** earnest **8** constant, diligent, sedulous, tireless, untiring **9** laborious, steadfast, tenacious **10** determined, persistent, unflagging **11** hardworking, industrious, persevering, unremitting **13** indefatigable

assign 3 fix, set **4** give, name **5** allot, grant **6** charge, choose, invest **7** appoint, consign, entrust, mete out, specify **8** allocate, delegate, dispense, set apart **9** apportion, designate, determine, prescribe, stipulate **10** commission, distribute

assignation 4 date **5** tryst **7** meeting **10** rendezvous **11** appointment

assignment 3 job **4** duty, post, task **5** chore **6** lesson **8** exercise, homework **9** allotment **10** allocation, commission **11** appointment, designation **12** distribution **13** apportionment

assimilate 6 absorb, digest, imbibe, in-gest, take in **9** integrate **10** metabolize **11** incorporate

Assiniboine, Assiniboin
language family: **6** Siouan
location: **9** Minnesota **12** Lake Winnipeg, Saskatchewan
related to: **7** Dakotas

assist 3 aid **4** abet, hand, help **5** boost, serve **6** back up, uphold, wait on **7** benefit, support, sustain **9** cooperate, lend a hand, reinforce **11** accommodate, collaborate, helping hand

assistance 3 aid **4** alms, help **6** relief **7** charity, service, stipend, subsidy, support **10** sustenance **11** cooperation, helping hand **12** contribution **13** collaboration, reinforcement **16** financial support

assistant 3 aid **4** aide, ally **5** aider **6** helper **7** partner **8** adjutant, coworker, sidekick **9** accessory, associate, auxiliary, colleague, subaltern, supporter **10** accomplice, apprentice, cooperator, lieutenant **11** confederate, helping hand, subordinate **12** collaborator **15** second-in-command

associate 3 mix, pal, tie **4** ally, bind, chum, club, join, link, mate, pair, peer, yoke **5** buddy, crony, merge, unite **6** allied, couple, fellow, friend, hobnob, league, mingle, relate **7** combine, comrade, connect, consort, hang out, partner, related **8** confrere, coworker, identify, intimate, sidekick **9** affiliate, colleague, companion, confidant, correlate, pal around, rub elbows, run around **10** accomplice, affiliated, fraternize **11** confederate, subordinate **12** collaborator

associated 6 allied, joined, united **9** connected **10** affiliated **11** amalgamated

association 3 tie **4** body, bond, club, meld **5** blend, group, union **6** clique, league **7** combine, company, linkage, mixture, society **8** alliance, intimacy, mingling, relation **9** coalition, community, relations, syndicate **10** assemblage, connection, federation, fellowship, fraternity, friendship, membership **11** affiliation, camaraderie, combination, confederacy, corporation, correlation, familiarity, partnership **12** acquaintance, friendliness, organization, relationship **13** collaboration, companionship, confederation, participation **14** fraternization, identification

assorted 5 mixed **6** motley, sundry, varied **7** diverse, various **9** different **11** diversified **13** heterogeneous, miscellaneous

assortment 5 array, stock, store **6** medley, motley **7** melange, mixture, sorting, variety **8** grouping, quantity **9** arranging, assorting, diversity, potpourri, selection **10** collection, hodgepodge, miscellany **11** arrangement, classifying, disposition **14** classification, conglomeration

assuage 4 calm, ease **5** allay, quiet, still **6** lessen, pacify, soften, soothe, temper **7** appease, lighten, mollify, relieve **8** mitigate, tone down **9** alleviate **14** take the edge off

assuagement 6 easing, relief, solace **7** comfort **8** blunting, easement **9** abatement, lessening, tempering **10** mitigation **11** appeasement **13** mollification

assume 4 take **5** fancy, guess, infer, judge, seize, think, usurp **6** accept, deduce, gather, take on, take up **7** believe, imagine, presume, suppose, surmise, suspect **8** arrogate, shoulder, take over, theorize **9** postulate, speculate, undertake **10** commandeer, conjecture, understand **11** appropriate, expropriate, hypothesize **14** take for granted

assumed 4 fake **5** bogus, false, phony **6** made-up **8** presumed, supposed **9** falsified **10** fictitious **11** make-believe, presupposed, pseudonymic **12** pseudonymous

assumed name 5 alias **7** pen name **9** pseudonym **13** false identity
  French: 10 nom de plume **11** nom de guerre

assuming 4 bold **5** nervy, pushy **6** brazen, cheeky **7** forward, haughty **8** arrogant, insolent **9** audacious, presuming **11** overbearing **12** presumptuous **13** self-assertive

assumption 6 belief, taking, theory **7** premise, seizure **8** assuming, taking on, taking up **9** accepting, postulate **10** acceptance, arrogation, hypothesis, usurpation **11** postulation, presumption, shouldering, supposition, undertaking **13** appropriating **14** presupposition

assurance 3 vow **4** oath **5** poise **6** binder, pledge **7** promise **8** averment, boldness, coolness, sureness, warranty **9** certainty, certitude, guarantee **10** confidence, profession **11** affirmation, assuredness, word of honor **12** self-reliance **14** aggressiveness, self-confidence, self-possession

assure 5 vow to **6** clinch, ensure, secure **7** confirm, promise **8** pledge to **9** guarantee **11** make certain **14** give one's word to

assured 4 sure **5** fixed **6** poised, secure **7** certain, settled **8** positive **9** confident, undoubted **10** dependable, guaranteed **11** indubitable, irrefutable **12** indisputable **13** self-confident, self-possessed **14** unquestionable

Astaire, Fred
  real name: 19 Frederick Austerlitz
  partner: 12 Ginger Rogers
  born: 7 Omaha NE
  roles: 6 Top Hat **9** Funny Face, Let's

Dance, Swing Time **10** Holiday Inn **12** Easter Parade, Royal Wedding, Shall We Dance **14** The Gay Divorcee

Astarte
  origin: 7 Semitic
  goddess of: 9 fertility **12** reproduction
  habitat: 4 moon
  corresponds to: 6 Inanna, Ishtar **7** Mylitta **9** Ashtoreth

aster 12 Callistephus
  varieties: 4 Tree **5** Black, China, Heath **6** Annual, Golden, Mojave, Stoke's **7** Italian **8** Blue-wood **9** Tartarian, White wood **10** New England **11** White upland

Asteria
  form: 8 Titaness
  father: 5 Coeus
  mother: 6 Phoebe
  sister: 4 Leto
  husband: 6 Perses
  son: 8 Paropeus
  daughter: 6 Hecate
  changed into: 5 Delos **6** island

Asterius
  also: 8 Asterion
  form: 5 giant **8** minotaur
  king of: 5 Crete
  father: 4 Anax **8** Tectamus **10** Cretan Bull, Hyperasius
  mother: 8 Pasiphae
  wife: 6 Europa
  adopted sons: 5 Minos **8** Sarpedon **12** Rhadamanthys
  daughter: 5 Crete
  member of: 9 Argonauts

astern 3 aft **5** abaft **6** behind

asteroid 6 debris **9** planetoid

Asteropaeus
  origin: 5 Greek
  mentioned in: 5 Iliad
  father: 7 Pelegon
  ally of: 4 Troy
  killed by: 8 Achilles

Asterope *see* **7** Sterope

astir 2 up **5** afoot, awake **6** active, roused **8** in motion, out of bed **10** up and about

astonish 4 daze, stun **5** amaze, shock **6** dazzle **7** astound, confuse, perplex, stagger, startle, stupefy **8** bewilder, confound, dumfound, surprise **9** electrify, overwhelm, take aback **10** strike dumb **11** flabbergast **15** make one's eyes pop **18** take one's breath away

astonishing 7 amazing **8** dazzling, shocking, striking **9** confusing, startling **10** astounding, impressive, perplexing, staggering, stupefying, surprising **11** bewildering, confounding **12** breathtaking, electrifying, overpowering, overwhelming

astonishment 3 awe **5** shock **6** wonder **8** surprise **9** amazement, confu-

sion **10** perplexity, wonderment **12** bewilderment, stupefaction

Astor, Mary
  real name: 28 Lucille Vasconcellos Langhanke
  born: 8 Quincy IL
  roles: 6 Marmee **11** Little Women, The Great Lie **15** Meet Me in St Louis **16** The Maltese Falcon **17** The Palm Beach Story **18** The Prisoner of Zenda

astound 4 daze, stun **5** amaze, shock **6** dazzle **7** stagger, startle, stupefy **8** astonish, dumfound, surprise, take back **9** electrify, overwhelm **10** strike dumb **11** flabbergast **15** make one's eyes pop **18** take one's breath away

Astrabacus
  origin: 5 Greek **7** Spartan
  form: 6 prince
  found: 11 wooden image
    hidden by: 7 Orestes
    co-finder: 8 Alopecus

Astraea
  also: 6 Astrea
  goddess of: 7 justice
  father: 4 Zeus
  mother: 6 Themis

Astraeus
  form: 5 Titan
  consort of: 3 Eos
  father of: 4 wind **5** stars

astral 6 starry **9** celestial **12** astronomical

Astrateia *see* **7** Artemis

astray 3 off **5** amiss **6** afield **10** off the mark **12** off the course **16** off the right track

Astrea *see* **7** Astraea

astringent 4 acid, keen, sour, tart **5** brisk, sharp, stern, tonic **6** biting, severe **7** acerbic, austere, bracing, puckery, styptic **8** curative, incisive, piercing, salutary, stabbing, vinegary **10** antiseptic, salubrious **11** contracting, penetrating, restorative **12** invigorating

astrology 6 Zodiac **9** horoscopy, starcraft **10** astromancy, astrometry, stargazing **11** genethliacs **13** mathematicals **14** astrodiagnosis
  belief in: 8 siderism
  term: 4 sign **5** house, trine **6** alnath, apheta, aspect **7** almuten, anareta, mansion, mundane, sextile **8** alkahest, nativity, quartile, synastry **9** planetary **10** opposition **11** conjunction

astronomer 4 Bode, Bopp, Gold, Hale **5** Adams, Baade, Bayer, Bethe, Gould, Hoyle, Royer **6** Bessel, Halley, Hubble, Jansky, Kepler, Newton, Piazzi **7** Bradley, Celcius, Galileo, Huggins, Huygens, Kapteyn, Laplace, Ptolemy, Russell, Shapley, Slipher **8** Angstrom, Einstein, Herschel, Hevelius, Lacaille, Lemaitre, Mercator **9** Eddington, Leverrier **10** Copernicus, Hipparchus, Tycho Brahe **11** Aristarchus, Hertzsprung **13** Petrus Apianus

astronomy
    term: 5 comet, orbit **6** apogee, meteor, nebula, parsec, quasar **7** azimuth, eclipse, equinox, perigee, transit **8** aphelion, asteroid, ecliptic, meridian, solstice **9** meteorite, satellite **10** perihelion, precession **11** declination, occultation **12** perturbation, spectroscopy **16** celestial equator
    type/related study: 9 cosmogony, cosmology **10** astrometry, photometry **12** astrophysics **18** celestial mechanics
    see also **4** star

Astrophel and Stella
    author: 15 Sir Philip Sidney

astute 3 sly **4** able, foxy, keen, wily **5** acute, sharp, smart **6** adroit, artful, bright, clever, crafty, shrewd, subtle **7** cunning, knowing, politic **9** designing, sagacious **10** discerning, keen-minded, perceptive **11** calculating, intelligent, penetrating **13** Machiavellian, perspicacious

astuteness 6 acumen **8** keenness **9** acuteness, smartness **10** cleverness, shrewdness **12** perspicacity

Astyanax
    also: 11 Scamandrius
    father: 6 Hector **9** Strophius
    mother: 10 Andromache
    thrown from: 11 Trojan walls
        thrown by: 6 Greeks
    slain by: 8 Menelaus

Asuncion
    capital of: 8 Paraguay

asunder 4 rent **5** apart **8** in pieces, to shreds **9** torn apart **11** broken apart

asylum 4 home **5** haven **6** harbor, refuge **7** retreat, shelter **8** madhouse, preserve **9** almshouse, orphanage, poorhouse, sanctuary **10** sanatorium, sanitarium **11** institution **13** children's home, state hospital **14** mental hospital **15** place of immunity **17** mental institution **23** eleemosynary institution

Asynjur
    origin: 12 Scandinavian
    goddesses of: 4 Asar **5** Aesir
    leader: 3 Fri **5** Frigg, Frija **6** Frigga

As You Like It
    author: 18 William Shakespeare
    character: 5 Celia (Aliena) **6** Audrey, Jaques, Oliver **7** Orlando **8** Rosalind (Ganymede) **9** Frederick **10** Touchstone

Atabyrian *see* **4** Zeus

at a distance 4 afar, away **5** above, aloof, apart **6** far off **9** separated

Atala
    author: 21 Francois Chateaubriand

Atalanta
    also: 8 Atalante
    form: 6 virgin **8** huntress

    father: 5 Iasus
    mother: 7 Clymene
    son: 13 Parthenopaeus
    wounded: 14 Calydonian boar
    lost race to: 10 Hippomenes

Atalanta in Calydon
    author: 24 Algernon Charles Swinburne

at any rate 6 anyhow, anyway **9** in any case **10** in any event

at cross purposes 7 counter, opposed **8** contrary, converse, inimical, opposite **9** disparate **10** at variance, discordant **11** conflicting **12** antithetical, incompatible **13** contradictory

Ate
    origin: 5 Greek
    form: 7 goddess
    personifies: 12 recklessness **16** divine punishment

at ease 4 calm, cool **6** at rest, serene **7** content, relaxed, unmoved **8** composed **9** at leisure, confident, unruffled **10** complacent, nonchalant, unbothered, untroubled **11** comfortable, unconcerned

a tergo 9 at the back **10** from behind

at fault 6 guilty **8** culpable **10** implicated **11** blameworthy, responsible

at full length
    Latin: 9 in extenso

Athabascan, Athapascan (Slave Indians)
    language family: 10 Athabascan, Athapaskan
    location: 6 Canada **14** Great Slave Lake
    dominated by: 4 Cree
    related to: 9 Chipewyan
    tribe: 4 Dine **5** Slave **6** Apache, Navaho, Navajo **9** Mescalero **10** Athabascan

Athalie
    author: 18 Jean Baptiste Racine

Athamas
    king of: 6 Thebes
    father: 6 Aeolus
    wife: 3 Ino **7** Nephele
    son: 5 Ptous **6** Leucon **7** Phrixus **8** Learchus **10** Melicertes
    daughter: 5 Helle

at hand 4 near, nigh **5** close, handy, on tap, ready **6** nearby **7** close by **8** imminent **9** available, impending **10** accessible, convenient **11** at one's elbow, forthcoming **14** at one's disposal **15** within arm's reach

atheism 8 apostasy, unbelief **9** disbelief **10** irreligion **11** godlessness

atheist 7 infidel **10** unbeliever **11** disbeliever, nonbeliever

Athena
    also: 6 Athene, Pallas, Saitis **11** Tritogeneia **12** Pallas Athena **18** Alalcomenean Athena
    origin: 5 Greek

    goddess of: 4 arts **6** wisdom **7** warfare **9** fertility
    father: 4 Zeus **6** Triton
    mother: 5 Metis
    sprang from head of: 4 Zeus
    raised by: 12 Alalcomeneus
    symbol: 3 owl
    corresponds to: 7 Minerva
    epithet: 4 Alea **5** Meter, Xenia **6** Ergane, Itonia, Polias **7** Agoraea, Cissaea, Paeonia, Pronaus, Pronoea **8** Anemotis, Poliates, Zosteria **9** Oxyderces, Parthenia, Poliuchus, Promachus **10** Axiopoenus, Chalinitis, Cyparissia **11** Promachorma

Athens
    capital of: 6 Greece
    Greek: 7 Athinai
    hills: 9 Acropolis **14** Hagios Georgios
    landmark: 4 Stoa **9** Areopagus, Parthenon **10** Erechtheum, Propylaeum **17** Theater of Dionysus
    marketplace: 5 Agora
    mountain: 6 Parnes **8** Aigaleos, Hymettus **10** Pentelikon
    named for: 6 Athena
    port: 7 Piraeus
    river: 7 Ilissus
    sea: 6 Aegean **11** Saronic Gulf
    square: 8 Syntagma (Constitution)

Athens Graces 4 Auxe **8** Hegemone

athirst 4 avid, keen **5** eager **6** raring **7** longing, panting **8** yearning

athlete 4 jock **8** champion **9** contender, sportsman **10** contestant, game player

athletic 5 burly, hardy, husky, manly **6** brawny, robust, strong, sturdy, virile **8** muscular, powerful, stalwart, vigorous **9** masculine, strapping **10** able-bodied

athletics 5 games **6** sports **8** exercise **9** exercises **10** gymnastics

at home 6 at ease, inside, shut in **7** indoors **8** confined **10** in the house **11** comfortable
    French: 4 chez

Athos
    character in: 18 The Three Musketeers
    author: 5 Dumas (pere)

athwart 6 across **7** astride **8** sideways, sidewise **9** crossways, crosswise **12** transversely

Atlanta
    baseball team: 6 Braves
    basketball team: 5 Hawks
    football team: 7 Falcons
    hockey team: 9 Thrashers

Atlantean
    pertaining to: 5 Atlas

Atlantic City
    director: 10 Louis Malle
    cast: 8 Kate Reid **13** Burt Lancaster, Michel Piccoli, Susan Sarandon

at large 5 astir, loose **6** abroad **8** as a whole, at length **9** at liberty, in general **10** on the loose, unconfined **11** out and about **13** in circulation **14** around and about **15** making the rounds

Atlas
form: **5** Titan
father: **7** Iapetus
mother: **7** Clymene
brother: **9** Menoetius **10** Epimetheus, Prometheus
wife: **7** Pleione
daughters: **6** Hyades **7** Calypso **8** Pleiades **10** Hesperides
supported: **3** sky
identified with: **14** Atlas Mountains

Atlas Shrugged
author: **7** Ayn Rand
character: **8** John Galt **11** Hank Reardon **12** Dagny Taggart, James Taggart

at last
Latin: **10** ad extremum

at leisure 4 idle **7** off duty **8** inactive **9** at liberty **10** unemployed, unoccupied

Atli
origin: **12** Scandinavian
sister: **8** Brynhild
wife: **6** Gudrun, Kudrun **7** Guthrun
killed by: **6** Gudrun, Kudrun **7** Guthrun
represents: **6** Atilla

atmosphere 3 air **4** aura, feel, mood, tone **5** color **6** spirit **7** feeling, quality **8** ambience **11** environment **12** surroundings

atmospheric 3 air **4** airy **8** ethereal

at odds 6 unlike **8** contrary **9** different **10** at variance, discordant, discrepant, dissimilar **11** contrasting

at odds with 9 counter to **10** contrary to **14** at variance with

atoll 6 island
made of: **5** coral
pool: **6** lagoon
famous: **6** Bikini **8** Eniwetok

atom 3 bit, dot, jot **4** iota, mite, mote, whit **5** crumb, grain, scrap, shred, speck, trace **6** morsel, tittle **7** smidgen **8** fragment, particle **9** scintilla **10** smithereen

atomic 6 cobalt **7** fission, neutron, nuclear, uranium **8** hydrogen **9** molecular, plutonium, subatomic, unseeable **10** impalpable **11** fissionable, microcosmic, microscopic, superatomic **13** imperceptible, indiscernible, infinitesimal, thermonuclear

atom part 6 proton **7** neutron **8** electron

at once
French: **11** tout de suite

atone 6 pay for, redeem, repent, shrive **7** expiate **9** make up for **10** compensate, recompense, remunerate **12** do

penance for **13** make amends for **17** make reparation for

atonement 6 amends, shrift **7** penance, redress **9** expiation **10** recompense, redemption, reparation, repentance **12** compensation, satisfaction **14** penitential act

at one's disposal 5 handy **6** at hand, on hand **9** available **10** accessible, convenient **11** at one's elbow, ready for use **13** at one's service

at one's elbow 5 handy **6** at hand, nearby **9** available **10** accessible, convenient

at rest 5 quiet, still **6** asleep, at ease, serene **7** at peace, content **8** in repose **9** quiescent **10** motionless

Atreus
father: **6** Pelops
mother: **10** Hippodamia
sister: **7** Nicippe
wife: **6** Aerope
son: **8** Menelaus **9** Agamemnon **10** Plisthenes
daughter: **8** Anaxibia
killed: **6** Aglaus

Atridae
descendants of: **6** Atreus
family name of: **8** Anaxibia, Menelaus **9** Agamemnon **10** Plisthenes

atrium 4 hall **6** cavity **7** auricle **8** entrance **13** Roman entrance

atrocious 3 bad, low **4** dark, evil, rude, vile **5** black, cruel **6** brutal, savage, tawdry, vulgar **7** heinous, hellish, inhuman, uncouth, vicious **8** dreadful, enormous, fiendish, flagrant, grievous, horrible, infamous, infernal, pitiless, ruthless, terrible **9** barbarous, execrable, merciless, monstrous, nefarious, tasteless **10** diabolical, outrageous, villainous

atrociousness 6 infamy **7** cruelty **8** enormity, vileness **9** barbarity, brutality, depravity **11** heinousness, viciousness **13** monstrousness, offensiveness **14** outrageousness

atrocity 6 horror **7** outrage **8** enormity, savagery, villainy **9** barbarism, barbarity, brutality **10** inhumanity **11** heinousness

atrophy 7 decline **8** decaying, drying up **9** lack of use, withering **10** emaciation, shriveling **11** wasting away **12** degeneration **13** deterioration

Atropos
member of: **5** Fates
cuts thread of: **4** life

Atsina (Gros Ventres, Haaninin)
language family: **9** Algonkian **10** Algonquian
location: **6** Canada **7** Montana **9** Milk River **12** Saskatchewan **13** Missouri River
related to: **7** Arapaho

attach 3 fix **4** join **5** affix, allot, annex **6** append, assign, couple, detail, se-

cure **7** connect, destine, earmark **8** allocate, be fond of, fasten to, make fast **9** affiliate, associate, designate

attache 4 aide **5** envoy **6** consul **8** adjutant, diplomat, emissary, minister **9** assistant **10** ambassador, vice consul **11** diplomatist, subordinate **12** ambassadress **13** consul general

attachment 4 bond, love **6** fixing, liking, regard **7** adjunct, fixture, respect **8** addendum, addition, affinity, affixing, appendix, coupling, devotion, fondness, securing **9** accessory, affection, appendage, attaching, fastening **10** connection, friendship, supplement, tenderness **12** predilection

attack 3 fit **4** damn, go at **5** abuse, blame, fault, fly at, onset, spasm, spell **6** assail, charge, impugn, strike, stroke, tackle **7** assault, censure, lunge at, offense, seizure **8** denounce, fall upon, invasion, paroxysm **9** criticism, criticize, denigrate, disparage, incursion, offensive, onslaught, pitch into, undertake **10** aggression, impugnment **11** denigration **13** disparagement

attacker 6 mugger **7** accuser **8** assailer, opponent **9** adversary, aggressor, assailant **10** antagonist **11** belligerent

attain 3 win **4** earn, gain, reap **5** reach **6** effect, obtain, secure **7** achieve, acquire, procure, realize **10** accomplish

attainable 6 at hand **9** available, reachable **10** accessible, achievable, realizable **11** within reach

attainment 5 skill **6** talent **7** earning, gaining, getting, mastery, success, winning **8** securing **9** acquiring, attaining, obtaining, procuring **10** competence **11** achievement, acquirement, acquisition, fulfillment, procurement, proficiency, realization **14** accomplishment

attempt 3 aim, try **4** seek **5** essay **6** attack, effort, hazard, strive, tackle, work at **7** assault, venture **8** endeavor **9** have a go at, onslaught, undertake **11** undertaking **12** make an effort, take a crack at, take a whack at

Attenborough, Richard
director of: **6** Gandhi (Oscar) **7** Chaplin **10** Cry Freedom **11** A Chorus Line, Shadowlands **12** In Love and War, Young Winston **13** A Bridge Too Far
roles: **10** Wavelength **12** Jurassic Park **14** The Great Escape **15** Doctor Doolittle **16** Ten Little Indians

attend 4 go to, heed, mark, mind, note **5** serve, usher, visit **6** convoy, escort, follow, show up, squire, tend to **7** care for, conduct, observe, oversee, service **8** appear at, consider, frequent, harken to, listen to, wait upon **9** accompany **11** superintend

French: **4** oyez
cry used by: **10** court crier
preceded: **12** proclamation

attendance 4 gate **5** crowd, house **8** audience, presence **10** appearance, assemblage, being there

attendant 3 aid **6** escort, flunky, helper, lackey, menial **7** related, servant **8** adherent, chaperon, follower **9** accessory, assistant, companion, underling **10** associated, consequent **12** accompanying

attention 4 care, heed, mind, note, suit **5** court **6** homage, notice, regard, wooing **7** concern, respect, service, thought **8** civility, courtesy, devotion, wariness **9** alertness, deference, diligence, vigilance **10** observance, politeness **11** assiduities, compliments, gallantries **12** deliberation **13** concentration, consideration, contemplation **14** thoughtfulness

attentive 5 alert, awake **6** intent, polite **7** devoted, heedful, mindful, zealous **8** diligent, obliging **9** courteous, dedicated, listening, observant, wide awake **10** respectful, thoughtful **11** considerate, deferential, painstaking **13** accommodating

attentiveness 7 concern **8** devotion, industry **9** alertness, attention, diligence **10** commitment, dedication **11** application, devotedness, heedfulness, mindfulness **14** thoughtfulness

attenuate 6 dilute, impair, lessen, reduce, weaken **7** draw out, spin out **8** decrease, diminish, enervate, enfeeble **9** water down **10** adulterate

attest 4 show **5** prove **6** affirm, assert, assure, evince, verify **7** bear out, certify, confirm, declare, display, exhibit, support, swear to, testify, warrant **8** vouch for **11** bear witness, corroborate, demonstrate **12** substantiate

attestation 9 testimony **10** deposition **11** declaration

at the back
Latin: **6** a tergo

at the beginning
Latin: **9** ad initium

at the bottom
French: **6** au fond

at the end
Latin: **5** ad fin

at the place
Latin: **5** ad loc **7** ad locum

At the Sign of the Reine Pedauque
author: **13** Anatole France

attic 4 loft **6** garret **7** mansard **8** cockloft **10** clerestory
French: **7** grenier
German: **9** Dachboden
Spanish: **9** guardilla

attire 3 don **4** duds, garb, gown, robe, togs **5** array, dress **6** bedeck, clothe,

finery, fit out, invest, outfit, rig out **7** apparel, clothes, costume, deck out, raiment, turn out **8** clothing, garments, glad rags, wardrobe **9** vestments **11** habiliments

Attis
also: **4** Atys
form: **5** youth
home: **7** Phrygia
loved: **6** Cybele
driven mad by: **6** Cybele

attitude 3 air **4** pose **6** manner, stance **7** outlook, posture **8** demeanor, position **11** disposition, frame of mind, perspective, point of view

attorney 4 beak **6** lawyer **7** counsel **8** advocate **9** barrister, counselor, solicitor **10** mouthpiece **12** legal adviser **14** member of the bar **15** ambulance chaser

attract 4 draw, lure, pull **5** cause, charm, evoke **6** allure, beckon, entice, induce, invite **7** bewitch, enchant, provoke **8** appeal to, interest **9** captivate, fascinate **11** precipitate

attraction 4 lure, pull **5** charm **6** allure, appeal **7** glamour **8** affinity, charisma, tendency **9** magnetism **10** enticement, inducement, temptation **11** captivation, enchantment, fascination **12** drawing power

attractive 4 chic, fair, foxy, sexy **6** lovely, pretty **7** elegant, likable, sightly, winning **8** alluring, becoming, charming, engaging, enticing, fetching, handsome, inviting, pleasant, pleasing, tasteful, tempting **9** agreeable, appealing, beautiful, seductive **10** bewitching, delightful, enchanting **11** captivating, charismatic, fascinating

attractiveness 5 charm **6** beauty **9** good looks **11** pulchritude **12** handsomeness

attribute 4 gift **5** facet, grace, lay to, trait **6** aspect, assign, credit, impute, talent, virtue **7** ability, ascribe, blame on, cause by, faculty, feature, quality, trace to **8** charge to, property **9** character, endowment, set down to **10** account for, attainment, derive from, saddle with **11** acquirement, bring home to, distinction **14** accomplishment, characteristic

attrition 4 loss **7** erosion **8** abrasion, decrease, friction, grinding, scraping **9** reduction **10** decimation **11** wearing away, wearing down **14** disintegration

attune 5 adapt **6** adjust, tailor **8** accustom **9** acclimate **11** acclimatize

attune to 3 fit **5** adapt **6** adjust **7** conform **9** harmonize **11** accommodate

at variance 7 counter, opposed **8** contrary, converse, inimical, opposite **9** disparate **10** discordant **11** conflicting **12** antithetical, incompatible **13** contradictory **15** at cross purposes

Atwood, Margaret

author of: **7** Cat's Eye **8** Survival **9** Surfacing **10** Alias Grace, Bodily Harm, Lady Oracle **11** Second Words **13** Bluebeard's Egg, Life Before Man, Power Politics, The Circle Game **14** The Robber Bride **16** The Handmaid's Tale

at work 4 busy **5** in use **6** active **7** engaged, working **8** occupied

Atymnius
mentioned in: **5** Iliad
companion of: **8** Sarpedon
killed by: **10** Antilochus

atypical 7 unusual **8** abnormal, contrary, uncommon **9** anomalous, irregular, unnatural, untypical **10** nontypical **11** uncustomary, unlooked for **12** out of keeping **16** unrepresentative

Atys see **5** Attis

Auber, Daniel Francois Esprit
born: **4** Caen **6** France
composer of: **6** Haydee **7** La Macon **10** Fra Diavolo **12** Le Domino Noir **14** The Bronze Horse **16** Le Cheval de Bronze, The Crown Diamonds **17** La Muette de Portici **19** La Bergere Chatelaine **20** The Dumb Girl of Portici **22** Le Premier Jour de Bonheur

auberge 3 inn **6** tavern

auburn 5 henna, tawny **6** russet **8** cinnamon, nutbrown **11** golden-brown, rust-colored **12** reddish-brown **13** copper-colored **15** chestnut-colored

Aucassin and Nicolette
author: **7** unknown

Auchincloss, Louis
author of: **10** Watchfires **11** The Dark Lady, The Partners **12** Second Chance, The Embezzler **14** A World of Profit **16** Powers of Attorney, Tales of Manhattan, The Country Cousin **17** The Rector of Justin **19** The Winthrop Covenant **20** Portrait in Brownstone

au contraire 13 on the contrary

au courant 8 up-to-date

auction 3 sale **7** bidding **8** offering

Auction Block, The
author: **8** Rex Beach

audacious 4 bold, pert, rash, rude, wild **5** bossy, brave, fresh, gutsy, risky, saucy **6** brazen, cheeky, daring, plucky **7** defiant, forward, valiant **8** assuming, fearless, heedless, impudent, insolent, intrepid, reckless, stalwart, unafraid, valorous **9** breakneck, daredevil, dauntless, desperate, foolhardy, hotheaded, imprudent, shameless, unabashed **10** courageous, outrageous, self-willed **11** adventurous, impertinent, injudicious, lionhearted, venturesome **12** death-defying, devil-may-care, discourteous, enterprising, presumptuous, stouthearted **13** disrespectful

audaciousness 6 daring **8** audacity,

boldness **11** forwardness **13** assertiveness **14** aggressiveness **15** adventurousness

audacity 4 gall, grit, guts **5** brass, cheek, nerve, pluck, spunk, valor **6** daring, mettle **7** bravery, courage **8** backbone, boldness, chutzpah, rashness, temerity **9** brashness, derring-do, impudence, insolence **10** brazenness, effrontery **11** forwardness, presumption **12** fearlessness, impertinence, recklessness **13** bumptiousness, foolhardiness, shamelessness **15** venturesomeness

Auden, W H
  author of: **11** Another Time, Thank You Fog **12** Homage to Clio, The Dyer's Hand **13** About the House, Journey to a War **15** For the Time Being, The Age of Anxiety **16** City Without Walls, Epistle to a Godson **17** In Memory of W B Yeats, Musee des Beaux Arts **20** The Dog Beneath the Skin **22** Forewords and Afterwords

Audhumbla
  also: **8** Audhumla
  origin: **12** Scandinavian
  form: **3** cow
  owner: **4** Ymir
  birth from: **3** ice
  uncovered: **4** Buri

audible 5 clear, heard **8** distinct **11** discernible, perceptible

audience 4 talk **5** house **6** market, parley, public **7** hearing, meeting **8** assembly, audition **9** following, interview, listeners, onlookers, reception **10** conference, discussion, readership, spectators **12** congregation, constituency, consultation

audit 5 check **6** go over, review, verify **7** balance, examine, inspect **10** inspection, scrutinize **11** examination, investigate, take stock of **12** scrutinizing, verification **13** investigation

audition 6 tryout **7** hearing **15** test performance

auditor 8 listener **10** accountant, bookkeeper **11** comptroller **17** financial examiner

auditorium 4 hall **5** arena **7** theater **8** auditory, coliseum **11** concert hall, lecture hall, meeting hall **12** assembly hall

Audrey
  character in: **11** As You Like It
  author: **11** Shakespeare

Audubon, John James
  born: **8** Les Cayes **12** Santo Domingo
  artwork: **14** Birds of America **34** Viviparous Quadrupeds of North America

Auel, Jean M
  author of: **15** Plains of Passage **17** The Mammoth Hunters, The Valley

of Horses **20** The Clan of the Cave Bear

Auerbach, Arnold (Red)
  sport: **10** basketball
  position: **5** coach
  team: **13** Boston Celtics

au fait 6 expert, versed **11** experienced **13** knowledgeable

Aufklarung 13 enlightenment **16** the Enlightenment

au fond 9 basically, in reality **11** at the bottom

auf Wiedersehen 7 goodbye **8** farewell **16** until we meet again

Auge
  priestess of: **6** Athena
  father: **9** King Aleus
  mother: **6** Neaera
  son: **8** Telephus
  assaulted by: **8** Hercules

Augean stables
  owned by: **10** King Augeas
  number of oxen: **13** three thousand
  cleaned by: **8** Hercules
  river running through: **7** Alpheus

auger 4 bore **5** drill **6** pierce **10** boring tool

aught 3 all, zip **4** love, nada, null, zero **6** naught **7** a cipher, nothing **8** goose egg **11** horse collar

augment 5 add to, boost, raise, swell, widen **6** deepen, expand, extend **7** amplify, build up, enlarge, inflate, magnify **8** flesh out, heighten, increase, lengthen **9** intensify

augmentation 5 boost, extra, raise **8** addition, increase, swelling, widening **9** deepening, expansion, extension, inflation **10** supplement **11** elaboration, enlargement, heightening, lengthening **13** amplification, magnification **15** intensification

augur 4 bode, seer **6** herald, oracle **7** diviner, portend, predict, presage, promise, prophet, signify **8** forecast, foretell, forewarn, intimate, prophesy **9** be a sign of **10** be an omen of, foreshadow, soothsayer **13** prognosticate **14** prognosticator

augury 4 omen, sign **5** token **6** herald **7** auspice, portent, promise, warning **8** prophecy **9** harbinger, precursor, sortilege **10** divination, forerunner, indication **11** forewarning, soothsaying **14** fortunetelling **15** prognostication

august 5 grand, lofty, noble, regal **6** solemn, superb **7** eminent, exalted, stately, sublime, supreme **8** glorious, imposing, majestic **9** dignified, estimable, grandiose, venerable **10** impressive, monumental **11** high-ranking, illustrious, magnificent **12** awe-inspiring **13** distinguished

August
  Anglo-Saxon: **10** Weod-Monath
  characteristic: **7** dog days

  flower: **5** poppy
  French: **4** Aout
  gem: **7** peridot **8** sardonyx **9** carnelian
  German: **6** August
  holiday:
    England/Scotland: **11** Harvest Home (1)
  Italian: **6** Agosto
  number of days: **9** thirty-one
  original name: **8** Sextilis **12** Metageitnion
  origin of name: **6** Augere (Latin to open) **8** Augustus (Roman emperor)
  place in year:
    Roman: **5** sixth
    Gregorian: **6** eighth
  Spanish: **6** Agosto
  zodiac sign: **3** Leo **5** Virgo

Augustine, St (of Hippo)
  author of: **10** Civitas Dei **11** Confessions, Enchiridion **12** The City of God

augustness 7 dignity, majesty **8** eminence, nobility **9** loftiness **11** distinction **13** monumentality **15** illustriousness

August 1914
  author: **23** Aleksandr Solzhenitsyn Jr

au naturel 4 nude **8** uncooked **15** in a natural state

Auntie Mame
  author: **13** Patrick Dennis

Aunt Jo's Scrap-Bag
  author: **15** Louisa May Alcott

Aunt Julia and the Scriptwriter
  author: **16** Mario Vargas Llosa

au pair 4 maid **9** nanny **9** governess **13** mother's helper

aura 3 air **4** feel, mood **5** aroma **7** essence, feeling, quality **8** ambience **9** character, emanation **10** atmosphere, suggestion

Aura
  companion of: **7** Artemis
  bore: **5** twins
    fathered by: **9** Dionysius
  changed into: **6** spring
    changed by: **4** Zeus

au revoir 7 goodbye **8** farewell **16** until we meet again

Aurora
  origin: **5** Roman
  goddess of: **4** dawn
  corresponds to: **3** Eos

Aurora Leigh
  author: **24** Elizabeth Barrett Browning

Ausgleich 10 compromise **11** arrangement **12** equalization

Auslander 5 alien **9** foreigner, outlander

auspice 4 omen, sign **6** augury **7** portent, warning **10** indication **15** prognostication

auspices 4 care, egis **5** aegis **6** charge **7** control, support **8** advocacy, guid-

ance 9 authority, influence, patronage **10** protection **11** countenance, sponsorship **12** championship

auspicious 4 good **5** happy, lucky **6** benign, timely **7** hopeful **9** favorable, fortunate, opportune, promising, red-letter **10** felicitous, heartening, propitious, reassuring, successful **11** encouraging

Austen, Jane
  author of: 4 Emma **10** Persuasion **13** Mansfield Park **15** Northanger Abbey **17** Pride and Prejudice **19** Sense and Sensibility

austere 5 rigid, spare, stark, stern **6** chaste, severe, simple, strict **7** ascetic, Spartan **8** rigorous **10** abstemious, forbidding **11** self-denying, strait-laced

Austerlitz, Frederick
  real name of: 11 Fred Astaire

Australia
  other name: 9 Down Under
  name means: 19 unknown southern land
  capital: 8 Canberra
  largest city: 6 Sydney
  others: 3 Ayr **4** Yass **5** Dubbo, Perth **6** Albury, Cairns, Casino, Coburg, Darwin, Hobart **7** Bendigo, Geelong, Kogarah, Mildura, Mitcham, Whyalla **8** Adelaide, Ballarat, Bathurst, Brighton, Brisbane, Essendon, Randwick, Ringwood **9** Melbourne, Newcastle, Port Pirie, Toowoomba **10** Broken Hill, Kalgoorlie, Waggawagga, Wollongong **11** Collingwood, Rockhampton **12** Alice Springs
  division: 8 Tasmania, Victoria **10** Queensland **13** New South Wales **14** South Australia **16** Western Australia **17** Northern Territory **26** Australian Capital Territory
  head of state: 14 British monarch **15** governor general
  measure: 4 arna, naut, saum
  monetary unit: 4 dump, tray, zack **5** pound **6** dollar **8** shilling
  island: 4 Cato, King **5** Cocos, Green, Timor **6** Barrow, Koolan **7** Coringa, Keeling, Neptune, Norfolk **8** Flinders, Kangaroo, Lacepede, Melville, Rottnest, Tasmania, Thursday **9** Admiralty
  lake: 4 Eyre **5** Carey, Cowan, Frome, Moore, Wells **6** Austin, Barlee, Bulloo, Dundas, Harris, Mackay **7** Amadeus, Blanche, Everard, Torrens **8** Carnegie, Gairdner **9** MacDonald **10** Yammayamma **14** Disappointment
  mountain: 3 Ise **4** Blue, Olga, Ossa, Zeil **5** Bruce, Snowy **6** Cradle, Doreen, Garnet, Gawler, Magnet, Morgan **7** Bongong, Gregory, Herbert **8** Augustus, Brockman, Cuthbert, Jusgrave, Mulligan, Surprise **9** Murchison, Woodroffe **14** Australian Alps

15 New England Range **18** Great Dividing Range
  highest point: 9 Kosciusko
  river: 3 Hay **4** Avon, Daly, Swan, Yule **5** Bullo, Comet, Drava, Naomi, Paroo, Roper, Yarra **6** Barcoo, Barwon, Bulloo, Culgoa, Degrey, Hunter, Isaacs, Murray, Norman **7** Darling, Derwent, Fitzroy, Georges, Gilbert, Lachlan, Staaten, Warrego **8** Belyando, Brisbane, Burdekin, Clarence, Drysdale, Flinders, Gascoyne, Georgina, Mitchell, Thompson, Victoria, Weeribee, Wooramel **9** Ashburton, Fortescue, Hawksbury, MacKenzie, Macquarie, Murchison, Saltwater **10** Diamantina, Shoalhaven **12** Murrambidgee
  sea: 5 Coral, Timor **6** Indian, Tasman **7** Arafura, Pacific
  physical feature:
    bay: 5 Bight, Shark **6** Botany **7** Moreton **11** Port Phillip
    cape: 4 Howe, York **5** Byron **9** Southeast
    channel: 5 Cowal **9** Anabranch, Billabong
    desert: 6 Arunta, Gibson, Stuart, Tanami **7** Simpson **10** Great Sandy **13** Great Victoria
    gulf: 8 Spencers **9** Van Dieman **11** Carpentaria **15** Joseph Bonaparte **20** Great Australian Bight
    peninsula: 4 Eyre
    reef: 12 Great Barrier
    strait: 4 Bass
  people: 3 Abo **4** Koko, Mara, Wong **5** Anzac, Binge, Dieri, Maori, Myall **6** Aranda, Arunta, Aussie, Binghi, Digger, Kipper, Papuan **7** Arawong, Ilpirra **8** Antipode, Barkinji, Billijim, Euahlayi, Warragal, Warrigal **9** Aborigine **10** Australoid, Melanesian, Sandgroper
    actor: 9 Judy Davis, Mel Gibson, Paul Hogan **10** Bryan Brown
    author: 4 West **5** White **7** Russell **10** Richardson
    explorer: 4 Bass, Cook **6** Mawson, Tasman **7** Wilkins
    leader: 4 Holt **5** Hawke **7** Keating, Menzies, Whitlam
    nurse: 11 Sister Kenny
  language: 7 English
  religion: 7 Judaism **8** Anglican **10** Protestant **13** Roman Catholic
  place: 7 outback **9** billabong **11** back country
    aborigine area: 9 Arhemland
    beach: 5 Manly
    dam: 4 Hume
  possession: 12 Cocos Islands **13** Norfolk Island **16** Christmas Islands
  feature:
    animal: 5 dingo **6** kelpie **7** wallaby **8** anteater, kangaroo **9** koala bear **18** duckbilled platypus
    bird: 3 emu **10** kookaburra

    cowboy: 6 waddie **8** jackaroo
    dance: 6 dreher
    flower: 7 boronia, fuchsia, waratah **9** coachwood **12** kangaroo paws
    game: 3 sye **10** tambaroora
    tree: 3 gum **10** eucalyptus
    weapon: 5 kiley, kyley **7** wommera **9** boomerang
  food: 3 kai **6** tucker
    cake: 6 damper **7** brownie
    dish: 8 coolamon
    drink: 9 arkaloola
    fruit: 5 nonda **7** kumquat **11** desert-lemon

Austria
  other name: 10 Osterreich
  name means: 12 eastern state
  capital/largest city: 6 Vienna
  others: 4 Enns, Graz, Lech, Linz, Ried, Wels **5** Krems, Steyr, Traun **6** Leoben **7** Bregenz, Modling, Spittal, Villach **8** Bad Ischl, Dornbirn, Salzburg **9** Innsbruck, Semmering **10** Kapfenberg, Klagenfurt **11** Sankt Polten **14** Wiener Neustadt
  division: 5 Tirol, Tyrol **6** Istria, Styria, Triest **7** Bohemia, Galicia, Moravia, Silesia **8** Bukowina, Dalmatia, Earniola, Gradisca **9** Earinthia **10** Burgenland, Vorarlberg **12** Lower Austria, Upper Austria
    Roman province: 6 Raetia **7** Noricum **8** Pannonia
  government:
    legislature: 9 Bundesrat, Reichsrat **10** Herrenhaus, Reichsrath
  head of government: 10 Chancellor
  other leader: 7 emperor **12** burgomeister
  measure: 4 fass, fuss, joch, mass, muth, yoke **5** halbe, linie, meile, metze, pfiff, punkt **6** achtel, becher, leipoa, seidel **7** dlafter, viertel **8** dreiling **12** futtermassel
  monetary unit: 4 lira **5** crown, ducat, krone **6** florin, gulden, heller, zehner **8** albertin, groschen, kreutzer **9** schilling
  weight: 4 marc, unze **5** denat, karch, stein **6** centner, pfennig **8** vierling **9** quantchen
  lake: 6 Almsee **7** Fertoto, Mondsee **8** Bodensee, Traunsee **9** Constance **10** Neusiedler
  mountain: 4 Alps **6** Stubai, Tirols, Tyrols **8** Eisenerz, Rhatikon **9** Dolomites, Kitzbuhel **10** Hohe Tauern **14** Silvretta Group
  highest point: 13 Grossglockner
  river: 3 Inn, Mur **4** Drau, Elbe, Enns, Iser, Kamp, Lech, Murz, Raab **5** Donau, Drava, Drave, March, Salza, Thaya, Traun **6** Danube, Moldau
  physical feature:
    basin: 7 Styrian
    canal: 6 Danube
    mountain pass: 7 Brenner
    wind: 6 Foehen

woods: 6 Vienna
people: 5 Poles **6** Croats, Czechs **7** Germans, Gypsies **8** Slovenes **10** Hungarians
  botanist: 6 Mendel
  composer: 5 Haydn **6** Czerny, Mahler, Mozart, Webern **7** Amadeus, Strauss **8** Bruckner, Schubert **9** Beethoven **10** Schoenberg
  emperor: 7 Charles, Francis **9** Ferdinand, Habsburgs, Hapsburgs **10** Franz Josef
  philosopher: 12 Wittgenstein
  psychiatrist: 5 Adler, Freud, Reich
  statesman: 10 Metternich **12** Kurt Waldheim
language: 5 Czech **6** German, Magyar **8** Croatian **9** Slovenian
religion: 7 Judaism **10** Protestant **13** Roman Catholic
place:
  boulevard: 3 Kai **11** Ringstrasse
  cathedral: 9 St Stephen
  city hall: 7 Rathaus
  fortress: 13 Hochosterwitz, Hohensalzburg
  imperial palace: 7 Hofburg
  monastery: 4 Melk **8** Gottweig **14** Klosterneuburg
  museum: 6 Mozart **9** Johanneum
  people's garden: 11 Volksgarten
  resort: 5 Baden **7** Bregenz **8** Bad Ischl **9** Innsbruck, Semmering
feature: 8 yodelers **11** ice grottoes
  clothing: 5 loden **10** lederhosen
  dance: 5 waltz **6** dreher **7** landler **13** schuhplattler **14** grand polonaise
  festival: 8 Salzburg
  horse: 10 Lippizaner
  pastry shop: 12 konditoreien
food:
  breaded veal cutlet: 15 Wiener schnitzel
  cake: 11 linzer torte, sacher torte
  cookie: 7 kipferl
  roll: 10 golatschen
Austroasiatic
  language subfamily: 5 Khasi, Munda **8** Annamite, Mon-Khmer **9** Palaung-Wa **10** Nicobarese **11** Semang-Sakai **13** Annamite-Muong
  spoken in: 5 Burma, India **7** Nicobar, Vietnam **8** Cambodia, Malaysia **9** Kampuchea
authentic 4 pure, real, true **5** valid **6** actual **7** factual, genuine **8** accurate, attested, bona fide, faithful, original, reliable, verified **9** veritable **10** accredited, dependable, legitimate **11** trustworthy **12** unquestioned **13** authoritative, unadulterated
authenticate 6 attest, avouch, verify **7** certify, confirm, endorse, warrant **8** document, validate, vouch for **9** guarantee **11** corroborate **12** substantiate
authenticated 7 genuine **8** attested,

verified **9** validated **10** accredited, vouched for **13** substantiated
authentication 7 voucher **10** validation **11** certificate **12** verification **13** authorization, certification
author 4 poet **5** maker **6** father, framer, writer **7** creator, founder, planner **8** essayist, inventor, novelist, producer **9** initiator, innovator, organizer **10** originator, playwright, prime mover **16** short-story writer
  see author under each country
authoritarian 5 harsh **6** severe, strict, tyrant **7** austere, fascist **8** autocrat, dogmatic, martinet **9** by the book, by the rule **10** inflexible, tyrannical, unyielding **11** dictatorial, doctrinaire **12** disciplinary, rule follower **14** disciplinarian, little dictator, uncompromising
authoritative 5 sound, valid **6** lordly, ruling **7** factual, learned **8** arrogant, decisive, dogmatic, imposing, official, reliable **9** authentic, masterful, scholarly, sovereign **10** autocratic, commanding, definitive, dependable, imperative, impressive, peremptory, sanctioned, tyrannical **11** dictatorial, trustworthy **14** administrative
authoritativeness 6 belief **9** authority **10** conviction **11** credibility **14** conclusiveness
authorities 6 expert, police, pundit **7** scholar **10** mastermind, specialist **11** connoisseur, officialdom **12** powers that be
authority 4 rule, sway **5** clout, force, might, power **6** esteem, weight **7** command, control, respect **8** dominion, prestige, strength **9** influence, supremacy **10** domination, importance **12** jurisdiction **14** administration
authorization 7 license **8** approval, sanction **10** commission, imprimatur, permission **11** entitlement **12** confirmation, legalization **13** accreditation, certification
authorize 5 allow **6** enable, invest, permit **7** approve, certify, charter, confirm, empower, entitle, license, warrant **8** accredit, sanction, vouch for **9** give leave **10** commission
authorized 8 approved, official **9** canonical **10** sanctioned
Autobiography of Alice B Toklas
  author: 13 Gertrude Stein
Autobiography of Miss Jane Pittman, The
  author: 13 Ernest J Gaines
autochthonous 5 first **6** native, primal **7** ancient **8** earliest, original, primeval **10** aboriginal, indigenous, primordial
autocracy 7 czarism, tyranny **8** autarchy, monarchy **9** Caesarism, despotism, Hitlerism, kaiserism, monocracy, Stalinism **10** absolutism **11** Bonapart-

ism **12** dictatorship **14** tyrannical rule **15** totalitarianism
autocrat 5 ruler **6** despot, tyrant **7** monarch **8** dictator, overlord **13** absolute ruler
autocratic 8 despotic **9** czaristic, imperious, tyrannous **10** iron-handed, oppressive, repressive, tyrannical **11** dictatorial, monarchical **13** authoritarian
auto da fe, auto de fe 13 act of the faith **17** burning of heretics
  from: 18 Spanish Inquisition
autograph 4 mark, sign **5** x-mark **9** John Henry, signature **11** endorsement, handwriting, inscription, John Hancock **16** countersignature
Autolycus
  character in: 14 The Winter's Tale
  author: 11 Shakespeare
Autolycus
  form: 5 thief
  father: 6 Hermes
  mother: 6 Chione
  half-brother: 9 Philammon
  wife: 9 Amphithea
  daughter: 8 Anticlea
  grandson: 8 Odysseus
  gift: 12 invisibility **13** shape changing
automated 9 automatic **10** mechanical, mechanized **15** machine-operated
automatic 6 reflex **7** natural, routine **8** electric, habitual, inherent, unwilled **9** automated **10** mechanical, push-button, self-acting, self-moving **11** instinctive, involuntary, spontaneous, unconscious **12** uncontrolled **13** nonvolitional, self-operating **14** self-propelling
automaton 4 pawn, tool **5** golem, patsy, robot **6** puppet, stooge **7** android, cat's-paw, fall guy, machine **10** fantoccino, marionette
automobile
  invented by:
    differential gear: 4 Benz
    electric: 8 Morrison
    gasoline: 6 Duryea **7** Daimler
    muffler: 5 Maxim
    self-starter: 9 Kettering
  see also **3** car
automobiles
  Buick: 7 LeSabre
  Chevrolet: 6 Lumina **7** Beretta, Corsica
  Chrysler-Plymouth: 7 LeBaron
  Dodge: 4 Neon **8** Intrepid
  Ford: 5 Tempo **6** Escort, Taurus **7** Mustang
  Honda: 5 Civic **6** Accord
  Lexus
  Mercury: 5 Sable
  Nissan: 6 Altima, Maxima, Sentra
  Oldsmobile: 5 Ciera **7** Achieva **11** Ninety-Eight
  Pontiac: 7 Grand Am, Trans Am **8** Firebird

Saturn
Toyota: 5 Camry **7** Corolla

Autonoe
father: 6 Cadmus
mother: 8 Harmonia
sister: 3 Ino **5** Agave **6** Semele
husband: 9 Aristaeus
son: 7 Actaeon
daughter: 6 Macris

autonomous 4 free **9** sovereign **11** independent, self-reliant **13** self-governing **14** self-determined, self-sufficient

autonomy 7 freedom **8** home rule, self-rule **10** liberation **11** sovereignty **12** independence **14** self-government **17** self-determination

auto racing
driver: 6 A J Foyt **7** Al Unser **8** Tom Sneva **9** Niki Lauda **10** Bobby Unser, Jeff Gordon, Juan Fangio **11** Jack Brabham **12** Bobby Allison, Janet Guthrie, Richard Petty **13** Jackie Stewart, Mario Andretti **14** Barney Oldfield, Cale Yarborough, Craig Breedlove **16** Johnny Rutherford

Autry, Gene
horse: 8 Champion
born: 7 Tioga TX
roles: 11 Melody Ranch **16** The Singing Cowboy **19** Tumbling Tumbleweeds **22** Springtime in the Rockies

autumn 4 fall **11** harvest time **12** Indian summer **15** autumnal equinox

auxiliary 6 backup, helper **7** partner, reserve **9** accessory, ancillary, assistant, associate, companion, emergency, secondary **10** accomplice, subsidiary, supplement **11** subordinate **13** supplementary

avail 3 aid, use **4** help **5** serve **6** assist, profit **7** benefit, purpose, service, success, utilize **9** advantage

available 4 free, open **5** handy, on tap **6** at hand, on hand **9** in reserve **10** accessible, convenient, obtainable

avalanche 4 heap, mass, pile **5** flood **6** deluge **7** barrage, cascade, torrent **8** blizzard **9** cataclysm, rockslide, snowslide **10** earthslide, inundation **11** bombardment

Avalon
island of: 8 Paradise
burial place for: 6 heroes **10** King Arthur

avant-garde 7 leaders **8** pioneers, vanguard **10** innovators **11** forerunners, originators, tastemakers **12** advance guard, trailblazers, trendsetters

avarice 5 greed **6** penury **8** rapacity, venality **9** parsimony **10** greediness, stinginess **11** miserliness **12** covetousness, graspingness **13** money-grubbing, niggardliness, penny-pinching **15** close-fistedness

Ave Maria 8 Hail Mary

avenge 5 repay **6** injure, punish **7** revenge **9** retaliate

Avengers, The
character: 8 Emma Peel, Tara King **9** John (Jonathan) Steed
cast: 9 Diana Rigg **12** Linda Thorson **13** Patrick Macnee
movie cast: 10 Uma Thurman **12** Ralph Fiennes

avenue 3 way **4** gate, path, road **5** means, route **6** access, chance, course, outlet **7** gateway, parkway, passage, pathway **8** approach **9** boulevard, concourse, direction, esplanade **10** passageway **11** opportunity **12** thoroughfare

aver 4 avow **5** state, swear **6** affirm, assert, avouch, insist, verify **7** certify, contend, declare, profess, protest **8** maintain, proclaim **9** emphasize, guarantee, pronounce, represent **10** asseverate

average 3 par **4** fair, mean, norm, so-so **5** ratio, usual **6** common, medial, median, medium, normal, not bad **7** the rule, typical **8** mediocre, midpoint, moderate, ordinary, passable, standard, standing, the usual **9** tolerable **10** mean amount **11** indifferent, rank and file **12** run-of-the-mill

averment 5 claim **6** avowal **8** argument **9** assertion, assurance **10** allegation, contention, profession **11** affirmation

averse 5 loath **7** opposed **8** inimical **9** reluctant, unwilling **10** indisposed, unamenable **11** disinclined, ill-disposed, unfavorable **12** antipathetic, recalcitrant

aversion 6 hatred, horror **7** disgust, dislike **8** distaste, loathing **9** animosity, antipathy, hostility, prejudice, repulsion, revulsion **10** abhorrence, opposition, reluctance, repugnance **11** detestation **13** unwillingness **14** disinclination

avert 4 turn **5** avoid, deter, shift **7** beat off, deflect, fend off, keep off, prevent, ward off **8** preclude, stave off, turn away **10** forestall, frustrate, keep at bay, sidetrack **11** nip in the bud

aviary 4 cage **9** birdhouse, enclosure

aviation 6 flight, flying **11** aeronautics **12** aerodynamics

aviator, aviatrix 4 bird **5** flyer, pilot **6** airman, fly-boy **7** birdman

avid 4 keen **5** eager, rabid **6** ardent, greedy, hungry **7** anxious, devoted, fanatic, intense, zealous **8** covetous, desirous, grasping **9** rapacious, voracious **10** avaricious, insatiable **11** acquisitive **12** enthusiastic

avidity 4 zeal **5** greed **6** fervor, hunger **8** rapacity, voracity **9** eagerness **10** enthusiasm, fanaticism, greediness **12** covetousness **15** acquisitiveness

Avignon Papacy 15 Babylonian Exile **19** Babylonian Captivity

avocado 9 dark green **13** alligator pear, tropical fruit
origin: 6 Mexico **12** South America **14** Central America
family: 9 Lauraceae
used to make: 9 guacamole

avocation 5 hobby **7** pastime **8** sideline **9** diversion **10** recreation **11** distraction **13** entertainment

Avogadro, Amedeo
field: 7 physics **9** chemistry
nationality: 7 Italian
formulated: 19 molecular hypothesis

avoid 4 shun **5** avert, dodge, elude, evade, skirt **6** escape, eschew **7** boycott, forbear, forsake **8** sidestep **10** fight shy of **11** refrain from **12** steer clear of

avoidance 7 eluding, evasion **8** shirking, shunning, skirting

avoid the issue 4 duck **5** dodge, evade, hedge, stall **10** equivocate **17** beat around the bush

a votre sante 5 toast **12** to your health

avouch 5 argue, swear **6** affirm **7** declare **8** advocate, maintain

avow 3 own **4** aver **5** admit, state, swear **6** affirm, assert, reveal **7** confess, declare, profess **8** announce, disclose, proclaim **11** acknowledge

avowal 4 word **8** averment **9** admission, assertion, assurance, statement **10** confession, profession **11** affirmation, declaration **12** proclamation, protestation **14** acknowledgment

avowed 5 sworn **8** admitted, declared **9** confessed, professed **12** acknowledged, self-declared **14** self-proclaimed

await 6 attend, expect **7** look for **10** anticipate

awake 5 alert, aware, spark **6** arouse, awaken, bestir, excite, incite **7** alive to, heedful, inspire, mindful, provoke **8** open-eyed, vigilant, watchful **9** attentive, conscious, stimulate

Awake and Sing!
author: 13 Clifford Odets

awaken 3 fan **4** fire **6** arouse, excite, kindle, revive, stir up **9** stimulate

awakening 7 arising, arousal **8** sparking, stirring **11** stimulation

award 4 give **5** allot, allow, grant, honor, medal, prize **6** accord, assign, bestow, decree, trophy **7** appoint, concede, laurels, tribute **8** citation, confer on **10** decoration

aware 6 with it **7** alert to, alive to, awake to, mindful **8** apprised, informed, sensible, sentient **9** cognizant, conscious, tuned in to **10** conversant **11** enlightened **12** familiar with **13** knowledgeable

awareness 9 acuteness, alertness, appraisal, knowledge 10 cognizance, perception 11 familiarity, information, mindfulness, realization, recognition, sensibility 12 acquaintance 13 consciousness, understanding

away 3 far 4 gone 6 absent, at once, way off 8 distance 9 elsewhere

awe 3 cow 4 fear 5 abash, alarm, amaze, dread, panic, shock 6 dismay, fright, horror, terror, wonder 7 perturb, quaking, respect, terrify 8 astonish, disquiet, frighten 9 abashment, adoration, amazement, quivering, reverence, solemnity, trembling 10 exaltation, intimidate, veneration 11 disquietude, trepidation 12 apprehension, astonishment, perturbation 13 consternation

awe-inspiring 5 giant, grand, great, noble 6 august, mighty 7 eminent, exalted, mammoth, sublime, supreme, titanic 8 colossal, enormous, gigantic, glorious, imposing, majestic, wondrous 9 excessive 10 impressive, incredible, monumental, prodigious, stupendous, tremendous 11 astonishing, extravagant, illustrious, magnificent, spectacular 12 breathtaking, overwhelming

awesome 6 solemn 7 amazing, fearful 8 alarming, dreadful, fearsome, majestic, wondrous 9 inspiring 10 formidable, perturbing, stupefying, terrifying 11 astonishing, disquieting, frightening, magnificent 12 breathtaking, intimidating, overwhelming

awestruck 6 humble 8 overcome 11 reverential

awful 3 bad, low 4 base, dire, mean, ugly 5 lousy 6 solemn 7 amazing, awesome, fearful, ghastly, heinous, hideous 8 alarming, dreadful, fearsome, gruesome, horrible, majestic, shocking, terrible, wondrous 9 appalling, frightful, monstrous, revolting 10 deplorable, despicable, formidable, horrendous, horrifying, stupefying, terrifying, unpleasant 11 displeasing, disquieting, distressing, redoubtable 12 awe-inspiring, contemptible, disagreeable 13 reprehensible

awfully 4 very 5 quite 8 horribly, terribly 9 extremely, immensely 10 dreadfully 11 excessively 13 exceptionally

awkward 5 inept 6 clumsy, touchy, trying 7 unhandy 8 bungling, delicate, inexpert, ticklish, ungainly, unwieldy 9 difficult, graceless, maladroit 10 blundering, cumbersome, unpleasant, unskillful 11 troublesome 12 embarrassing, inconvenient, unmanageable 13 disconcerting, uncomfortable, uncoordinated
  French: 6 gauche

Awkward Age, The
  author: 10 Henry James

awkwardness 9 gaucherie 10 clumsiness, difficulty, ineptitude 12 ungainliness, unwieldiness 13 embarrassment, inconvenience

awl 4 nail 6 gimlet 11 leather tool, sharp device

awning 4 hood 6 canopy 7 marquee 8 covering, sunshade

awry 5 amiss, askew, wrong 6 astray, uneven 7 crooked, twisted 8 unevenly 9 crookedly, obliquely 11 out of kilter

axe, ax 3 can 4 chop, fire, oust, sack 5 let go, split 6 bounce, cut out, delete, remove 7 cut down, dismiss 8 get rid of, tomahawk 9 discharge, terminate 11 send packing
  type: 4 pick 6 poleax 7 hatchet 8 tomahawk

Axelrod, Julius
  field: 9 chemistry
  studied: 24 nerve-impulse transmission
  awarded: 10 Nobel Prize

axiom 3 law 5 basic 7 precept 9 postulate, principle 10 assumption 14 fundamental law

axiomatic 5 banal, given 6 cliche 7 assumed 8 accepted, manifest 9 apodictic 11 self-evident 12 demonstrable, epigrammatic, indisputable, unquestioned 13 incontestable, platitudinous

axis 4 stem 5 pivot, shaft 7 compact, entente, spindle 8 alliance 9 alignment, coalition 10 center line 11 affiliation 12 pivotal point 13 confederation 14 line of rotation, line of symmetry

axle 3 bar, pin 5 shaft, wheel 7 spindle 8 crossbar 10 turning bar

ayah 4 maid 5 nurse

aye 3 yea, yes 11 affirmative

Aykroyd, Dan
  born: 6 Canada, Ottawa 7 Ontario
  roles: 6 My Girl 7 Dragnet 8 Sgt. Bilko 9 Coneheads 11 Spies Like Us 12 Ghostbusters 13 Doctor Detroit, Trading Places 16 The Blues Brothers, Driving Miss Daisy, The Great Outdoors, Grosse Point Blank 17 Saturday Night Live

Aymara
  location: 4 Peru 7 Bolivia 12 South America

Ayres, Lew
  wife: 8 Lola Lane 12 Ginger Rogers
  born: 13 Minneapolis MN
  roles: 7 Holiday, The Kiss 9 Dr Kildare 25 All Quiet on the Western Front

azalea 12 Rhododendron
  varieties: 4 Cork, Mock, Snow 5 Coast, Dwarf, Early, Flame, Hiryu, Hoary, Luchu, Royal, Sims's, Swamp, Sweet, Torch 6 Alpine, Balsam, Clammy, Indian, Korean, Kurume, Kyushu, Oconee, Pontic, Smooth, Spider, Summer, Yellow 7 Alabama, Chinese, Maries's, Mt Amagi, Oldham's, Western 8 Five-leaf, Japanese, Piedmont, Rusticum, Yodogawa 9 Kirishima, Mayflower, Pink-shell, Rose-shell, Wild-thyme 10 Cumberland, Macranthum, Plum-leaved, White swamp 11 Gable hybrid, Ghent hybrid, Molle hybrid 12 Arnold hybrid, Florida flame, Sander hybrid 13 Indicum hybrid 15 Glenn Dale hybrid, Kaempferi hybrid, Knapp Hill hybrid 16 Rutherford hybrid 24 Rusticum Flore Pleno hybrid

Azan
  father: 5 Arcas
  mother: 5 Erato

Azariah
  also: 6 Uzziah
  father: 4 Jehu 5 Ethan 6 Nathan 7 Hilkiah, Jehoram, Johanan 11 Jehoshaphat
  son: 4 Joel
  known as: 8 Abednego
  companion: 6 Daniel
  friend: 7 Meshach 8 Shadrach
  succeeded: 5 Zadok

Azazel 9 scapegoat 11 fallen angel

Azerbaijan
  capital/largest city: 4 Baku
  others 9 Kirovabad
  division 24 Nagorno-Karabakh Territory 29 Nakhichevan Autonomous Republic
  head of state: 9 president
  government: 8 republic
  monetary unit: 5 manat
  mountain: 8 Caucasus
  sea: 7 Caspian
  people: 5 Azeri 11 Azerbaijani
  language: 6 Turkic
  religion: 6 Muslim

Aziz, Dr
  character in: 15 A Passage to India
  author: 7 Forster

Aztec (Nahua, Mexica)
  language family: 7 Nahuatl 10 Uto-Aztecan
  location: 6 Mexico, Puebla 8 Guerrero, Veracruz 9 Guatemala, Michoacan 11 Lake Texcoco 14 Central America
  leader: 9 Montezuma
  worshipped: 12 Quetzalcoatl
  capital: 12 Tenochtitlan
  conquerer: 6 Cortes, Cortez

Azuela, Mariano
  author of: 8 The Flies 9 The Bosses 12 The Underdogs 26 Trials of a Respectable Family

azure 4 blue 5 lapis 6 cobalt 7 sky blue 8 cerulean 9 clear blue, cloudless 11 lapis lazuli

Baade, Walter
  field: **9** astronomy
  discovered: **15** Hidalgo asteroid
Baal 3 god **5** deity
Baal Merodach *see* **6** Marduk
Babbage, Charles
  field: **11** mathematics
  nationality: **7** British, English
  first: **15** actuarial tables
  inventor of: **13** adding machine **18** calculating machine
  invented forerunner of: **15** digital computer
  planned: **10** calculator
Babbitt 9 bourgeois **10** conformist, middlebrow, philistine
Babbitt
  author: **13** Sinclair Lewis
  character: **11** Myra Babbitt, Seneca Deane **12** Paul Riesling **15** Mrs Tanis Judique **22** George Folansbee Babbitt
babble 3 coo, din, gab, hum **4** blab, talk **5** prate **6** burble, clamor, drivel, gabble, gibber, gurgle, hubbub, jabber, murmur **7** blabber, blather, chatter, prattle, twaddle **8** chitchat, rattle on **9** jabbering, murmuring **14** chitter-chatter
babbling 6 drivel, hubbub **7** blabber, twaddle **8** burbling, gabbling, gurgling, nonsense **9** clamoring, gibberish, jabbering, murmuring
babe 3 tot **4** baby **5** child **6** infant
babe in arms 4 baby **6** infant **7** neonate, newborn
babe in the woods 8 innocent **9** fledgling, greenhorn **10** tenderfoot
babel, Babel 3 din **6** bedlam, clamor, hubbub, tumult, uproar **7** turmoil **9** confusion **10** hullabaloo **11** pandemonium
Babel, Isaac
  author of: **9** Benia Krik **11** Odessa Tales **13** The Red Cavalry
Babe Ruth
  nickname of: **16** George Herman Ruth
Babe the Blue Ox
  character in: **10** Paul Bunyan
baboon 6 monkey
  breeding: **9** year round
  characteristic: **4** mane, pads **6** muzzle
  diet: **6** plants **8** scorpion **12** small animals
  dwelling: **5** Egypt, Sudan **6** Africa, Arabia **7** Somalia **8** Ethiopia
  family: **15** cercopithecidae
  habitat: **5** hills **6** plains
  largest genus: **6** Chacma
  most sacred: **6** Anobis
  smallest genus: **7** Western
babushka 4 baba, veil **5** scarf, stole **8** kerchief **11** grandmother
baby 3 wee **4** babe, tiny **5** dwarf, humor, pygmy, small, spoil, young **6** bantam, coddle, coward, infant, little, midget, minute, pamper, petite **7** crybaby, indulge, neonate **8** dwarfish, sniveler **9** miniature, youngster **10** babe in arms, diminutive **11** mollycoddle, overindulge, pocket-sized
Baby
  nickname of: **12** Lauren Bacall
baby carriage 4 cart, pram **6** cradle **12** perambulator
babyish 7 puerile **8** childish, immature, juvenile **9** infantile
babylike 3 wee **4** tiny **5** small **9** infantile **10** diminutive
Babylonian Captivity 13 Avignon Papacy **15** Babylonian Exile
Babylonian god 3 Bel **6** Marduk
Babylonian Mythology
  chief of gods: **6** Marduk **8** Merodach **12** Baal Merodach
  demon: **6** Namtar
  goddess of air: **6** Ninlil
  goddess of death: **10** Ereshkigal
  goddess of love/war/ fertility: **6** Ananna, Inanna, Ishtar **7** Astarte, Mylitta **9** Ashtoreth
  god of air: **5** Enlil
  god of dead: **6** Nergal
  god of fire: **5** Ishum
  god of heaven: **2** An **3** Anu
  god of moon: **3** Sin
  god of pastures/vegetation: **6** Dumuzi
  god of pestilence: **4** Irra
  god of shepherds: **6** Tammuz
  god of sun: **3** Utu **7** Shamash
  god of wisdom: **4** Enki
  hero: **5** Ninib **7** Ninurta
  king: **9** Gilgamesh
  king of gods: **5** Enlil
  mother of gods: **5** Nammu
  queen of heaven: **6** Ishtar
  world of dead: **3** Kur
Baby Roo
  character in: **13** Winnie-the-Pooh
  author: **5** Milne
  mother: **5** Kanga
Baby Snooks 10 Fanny Brice
Baby Snookums
  character in: **12** The Newlyweds
Bacall, Lauren
  real name: **15** Betty Joan Perske
  husband: **12** Jason Robards **14** Humphrey Bogart
  nickname: **4** Baby
  born: **9** New York NY
  roles: **8** Applause, Key Largo **11** Dark Passage, The Big Sleep **12** Cactus Flower **16** To Have and Have Not **22** How to Marry a Millionaire
Bacchae
  form: **11** priestesses
  attendants of: **7** Bacchus
  participants in: **11** Bacchanalia
Bacchae, The
  author: **9** Euripides
  character: **4** Zeus **5** Agave **6** Cadmus, Semele **8** Dionysus, Pentheus, Tiresias
bacchanal 4 orgy **5** feast, revel, spree **6** frolic **7** carouse, debauch, revelry, wassail **8** carnival, carousal, festival **10** debauchery, Saturnalia **11** merrymaking
Bacchanalia
  festival honoring: **7** Bacchus
Bacchant
  priest who worships: **7** Bacchus
Bacchante
  also: **6** Thyiad
  priestess who worships: **7** Bacchus
Bacchus
  also: **5** Evius **8** Dionysus
  god of: **4** wine **5** drama **9** fertility
  father: **4** Zeus
  mother: **6** Semele
  son: **6** Phlias **7** Narcaus, Priapus **8** Oenopion
  epithet: **6** Lyaeus **7** Bromius, Cresius **8** Thyoneus, Triambus **9** Pyrigenes **11** Dithyrambus, Mitrephorus
Bach, Carl (Karl) Philipp Emanuel
  born: **6** Weimar Germany
  father: **19** Johann Sebastian Bach
  composer of: **14** Prussian Sonata **19** Wurtembergian Sonata
Bach, Johann Sebastian
  born: **7** Germany **8** Eisenach
  composer of: **8** Chaconne **10** Giant Fugue, Inventions, Magnificat,

Wedge Fugue **11** Dorian Fugue, Fiddle Fugue, Little Fugue **12** Corelli Fugue, French Suites, Fuga alla Giga, German Suites, St Anne's Fugue **13** Coffee Cantata, English Suites, St John Passion **14** Alla Breve Fugue, Easter Oratorio, Peasant Cantata, Wedding Cantata **15** Jesu Meine Freude, Musical Offering **16** St Matthew Passion, The Art of the Fugue **17** Christmas Oratorio **18** Goldberg Variations **20** Brandenburg Concertos **22** The Well-Tempered Clavier **24** The Wise and Foolish Virgins **30** The Dispute Between Phoebus and Pan

Bach, Richard
author of: **25** Jonathan Livingston Seagull

bachelor 6 single **9** single man, unmarried **12** unmarried man

Bachelor Father
character: **9** Peter Tong **10** Kelly Gregg **12** Bentley Gregg **13** Ginger Farrell
cast: **10** Sammee Tong **12** John Forsythe **14** Noreen Corcoran **17** Bernadette Withers

bachelorhood 8 celibacy **13** baccalaureate **14** unmarried state

bacillus 3 bug **4** germ **7** microbe **8** pathogen **9** bacterium **13** microorganism

back 3 aid, ebb **4** abet, gone, help, hind, late, past, rear, tail **5** after, guard, minor, rural, spine, tardy **6** affirm, assist, attest, behind, bygone, caudal, dorsal, dorsum, far end, former, hinder, hold up, praise, recede, recoil, remote, retire, return, revert, second, succor, tergal, uphold, verify **7** belated, bolster, certify, confirm, delayed, distant, earlier, elapsed, endorse, expired, far side, finance, not paid, overdue, promote, protect, rear end, rebound, retract, retreat, reverse, sponsor, support, sustain, tail end, warrant **8** advocate, backbone, hind part, hindmost, maintain, move away, obsolete, previous, sanction, secluded, turn tail, validate, vouch for, withdraw **9** afterpart, encourage, in arrears, out-of-date, patronize, posterior, reinforce, subsidize **10** retrogress, testify for, underwrite, untraveled **11** bear witness, corroborate, countenance, countrified, countryside, farthermost, furthermost, reverse side, undeveloped, unimportant, unpopulated **12** beat a retreat, hindquarters, spinal column, substantiate **13** take sides with

back away from 7 back off **11** retreat from **12** draw back from, withdraw from

backbiter 5 scold **6** carper, critic **7** reviler **8** vilifier **9** slanderer

backbiting 5 abuse, catty **6** gossip,

malice **7** abusive, calumny, gossipy, hurtful, obloquy, slander **8** libeling, reviling **9** aspersion, cattiness, censuring, contumely, injurious, invective, malicious, maligning, vilifying **10** belittling, bitchiness, calumnious, defamation, defamatory, derogating, detracting, detraction, scandalous, scurrility, slanderous, traduction **11** badmouthing, denigrating, deprecating, disparaging, traducement **12** backstabbing, calumniation, vilification, vituperation **13** disparagement, maliciousness **16** scandal-mongering

backbone 4 grit, guts, sand **5** basis, chine, nerve, pluck, spine, spunk **6** dorsum, mettle, spirit **7** bravery, courage, resolve **8** firmness, mainstay, strength, tenacity **9** character, fortitude, manliness, vertebrae **10** foundation, resolution **11** intrepidity **12** resoluteness, spinal column **13** dauntlessness, steadfastness **15** vertebral column **19** strength of character

back-country 4 farm **5** rural **6** rustic **7** farming **10** provincial

back down 7 back off **8** draw back, move away **9** withdrawn

backdrop 4 flat **7** curtain, scenery **10** background

backer 4 ally **5** angel **6** patron **7** sponsor **8** adherent, advocate, champion, follower, investor, promoter **9** financier, guarantor, supporter **10** wellwisher **11** underwriter

backfire 4 flop, miss **5** crash **6** fizzle, go awry **8** backlash, lay an egg, miscarry, ricochet **9** boomerang **10** bounce back, disappoint **11** come to grief, fall through **12** come to naught **13** come to nothing

background 3 set **4** past, rear **5** flats **6** milieu **7** context, history, rearing, setting **8** backdrop, breeding, distance, heritage, training **9** education, grounding, landscape, life story **10** experience, upbringing **11** antecedents, credentials, environment, mise-enscene, preparation **13** circumstances

backhanded 7 awkward **8** reversed **9** insincere

backing 3 aid **4** core, help **5** aegis **6** succor **7** support **8** advocacy, interior, sanction **9** patronage, prompting **10** assistance, inner layer, sustenance **11** championing, cooperation, endorsement, helping hand, sponsorship **13** encouragement

backlash 4 flop, snag **5** crash, ravel **6** fizzle, go away, recoil **7** rebound **8** backfire, kick back, miscarry, ricochet, snap back **9** animosity, boomerang, hostility, reversion **10** antagonism, bounce back, opposition, resistance **11** come to grief, fall through **12** come to naught **13** come to nothing, counteraction, recalcitrance

backlog 5 hoard, stock, store **6** assets, excess, supply **7** nest egg, reserve, savings **9** abundance, amassment, inventory, reservoir, stockpile **12** accumulation **13** reserve supply **14** superabundance

back matter 5 index **8** addendum, appendix **10** supplement **12** bibliography

back off 7 retreat **8** back down, pull back, withdraw

backpack 4 hike, load **5** pouch **6** bundle **8** knapsack

backside 3 can **4** buns, butt, duff, prat, rear, rump, seat, tail **5** fanny **6** behind, bottom, settee, setter, sitter **7** keister, rear end **8** buttocks, derriere **9** fundament, posterior

backslide 5 lapse **6** revert **7** relapse **10** recurrence, regression **11** deteriorate **14** slip from virtue

back street 5 alley, byway **8** alleyway **13** secondary road

Back Street
director:
    1941 version: 15 Robert Stevenson
    1961 version: 11 David Miller
based on story by: **11** Fannie Hurst
cast:
    1932 version: 9 John Boles **10** Irene Dunne
    1941 version: 12 Charles Boyer **16** Margaret Sullavan
    1961 version: 9 John Gavin, Vera Miles **12** Susan Hayward

back talk 3 jaw, lip **4** gall, guff, rude, sass **5** cheek **8** pertness, rudeness **9** impudence, insolence, sassiness, sauciness **12** impertinence

Back to the Future
director: **14** Robert Zemeckis
cast: **11** Lea Thompson, Michael J Fox **16** Christopher Lloyd

backup 6 second **7** reserve, standby, stand-in **9** alternate, auxiliary, emergency, secondary **10** substitute, understudy **11** pinch-hitter **13** supplementary

back up 4 abet **6** assist, uphold **9** reinforce **11** corroborate

backward, backwards 3 shy **4** dull, slow **5** dense, tardy, timid, wrong **6** behind, ebbing, remiss, toward **7** bashful, impeded, laggard, messily, reverse, the rear **8** inverted, rearward, receding, reserved, retarded, reticent, reversed, sluggish **9** in retreat, in reverse, inside out, returning, slowpaced, to the past, to the rear, withdrawn **10** disorderly, improperly, regressive, retreating, retrograde, slowwitted, topsy-turvy, upside down **11** chaotically, undeveloped, withdrawing **12** wrong side out **13** retrogressive **15** uncommunicative
French: **9** en arriere

backwash 4 burg, wake **6** result,

sticks, upshot **7** boonies, outcome **8** frontier, tank town **9** aftermath, backwater, boondocks, provinces, upcountry **10** hinterland **11** aftereffect, backcountry, consequence

backwater 3 ebb **5** slack **7** retreat, reverse **8** holdback, stagnant, withdraw

backwoods 5 rural, wilds **6** rustic, simple, sticks **7** boonies, country **8** woodland **9** boondocks, rural area **10** hinterland, provincial **11** backcountry, countryside, hinterlands **15** unsophisticated

bacon 3 pig **4** pork **6** gammon **8** porkslab **10** smoked pork **11** porkbellies
measure: **6** rasher

Bacon, Francis
author of: **6** Essays **11** New Atlantis **12** Novum Organum **14** Maxims of the Law **16** Instauratio Magna **17** History of Henry VII **18** De Sapientia Veterum **20** Apophthegms New and Old **21** Advancement of Learning **25** Reading on the Statute of Uses

Bacon, Francis
born: **6** Dublin **7** Ireland
artwork: **15** Henrietta Moraes **35** Three Studies at the Base of a Crucifixion **44** Studies After Velazquez' Portrait of Pope Innocent X

Bacon, Henry
architect of: **15** Lincoln Memorial

bactericide 9 germicide **10** antiseptic, germ killer **12** disinfectant

bacteriologist
American: **4** Reed
British: **7** Fleming
German: **4** Koch **7** Behring, Ehrlich **10** Wassermann
Japanese: **7** Noguchi **8** Kitasato

bacterium 3 bug **4** germ **5** virus **7** microbe **8** bacillus, pathogen **13** microorganism

bad 3 ill, sad, sin **4** base, dire, evil, foul, glum, grim, mean, poor, rank, sick, sour, vile **5** acrid, acute, angry, awful, cross, false, fetid, grave, harsh, lousy, moldy, nasty, risky, sorry, unfit, wrong **6** ailing, bitter, crimes, faulty, gloomy, guilty, infirm, odious, putrid, rancid, rotten, severe, sickly, sinful, touchy, tragic, turned, unwell, wicked, wrongs **7** baneful, beastly, corrupt, decayed, harmful, hurtful, immoral, joyless, lacking, naughty, not good, noxious, painful, searing, serious, spoiled, tainted, unsound, useless **8** below par, contrite, criminal, dreadful, grievous, inferior, menacing, mildewed, offenses, polluted, terrible, troubled, villainy, wretched **9** agonizing, dangerous, defective, deficient, erroneous, frightful, hazardous, imperfect, incorrect, injurious, irascible, irritable, loathsome, miserable, nefarious, obnoxious, offensive, regretful, repugnant, repulsive, revolting, sad events,

sickening, troubling, unethical, unhealthy, unnerving, unwelcome, valueless **10** calamitous, decomposed, deplorable, detestable, disastrous, disgusting, distressed, disturbing, fallacious, immorality, inadequate, indisposed, melancholy, misfortune, nauseating, not correct, perfidious, putrescent, remorseful, second-rate, unpleasant, villainous, wickedness **11** detrimental, discouraged, distasteful, distractive, distressing, ineffective, inefficient, opprobrious, regrettable, substandard, troublesome, unpalatable **12** contaminated, disagreeable, discouraging, disreputable, excruciating, questionable, unprincipled, unproductive **13** below standard, disappointing, disheartening, harmful things, nonproductive, reprehensible, short-tempered **14** disappointment **15** disadvantageous, under the weather **18** conscience-stricken

bad faith 7 perfidy, treason **8** betrayal **9** falseness, treachery, two timing **10** disloyalty **11** double-cross **13** breach of faith, double-dealing **14** unfaithfulness

badge 4 mark, seal, sign, star **5** brand, stamp, token **6** device, emblem, ensign, shield, symbol **7** earmark **8** hallmark, insignia **9** medallion

badger 3 nag, vex **4** bait, goad **5** annoy, beset, bully, chafe, harry, hound, tease **6** coerce, harass, hector, nettle, pester, plague **7** provoke, torment, trouble **8** irritate **9** persecute
group of: **4** cete

Badger State
nickname of: **9** Wisconsin

badinage 5 chaff **6** banter, joking **7** jesting, joshing, kidding, ragging, ribbing, waggery **8** chaffing, raillery, repartee, word play

bad judgment 5 folly **10** imprudence **11** foolishness **12** carelessness **13** senselessness **15** thoughtlessness **16** shortsightedness, unperceptiveness

bad luck 6 mishap **7** ill wind **8** bad break **9** adversity, mischance **10** ill fortune, misfortune

badly 3 ill **5** wrong **6** basely, poorly, sorely, vilely **7** acutely, greatly, ineptly, not well, wrongly **8** faultily, horribly, severely, shoddily, sinfully, sloppily, terribly, very much, wickedly **9** corruptly, extremely, immorally, intensely, unsoundly **10** carelessly, criminally, dreadfully, improperly, wretchedly **11** defectively, deficiently, desperately, erroneously, exceedingly, frightfully, imperfectly, incorrectly, nefariously, offensively, unethically **12** disreputably, inadequately, villainously **13** incompetently, in the worst way **16** unsatisfactorily

bad manners 8 rudeness **9** surliness

10 incivility **11** boorishness, discourtesy **12** impoliteness

bad mark 4 blot **7** demerit **9** poor grade

badminton
racket: **10** battledore
racket used to hit: **4** bird **7** shuttle **11** shuttlecock
Indian version: **5** poona
stroke: **4** drop **5** clear, smash **7** service **13** backhand drive, forehand drive

badmouthing 5 barbs **7** dissing, insults, slander **9** criticism, insulting **10** slandering **11** criticizing

bad taste 9 crudeness, vulgarity **10** coarseness, garishness, tawdryness

bad tasting 4 sour **5** nasty **6** bitter **7** spoiled **9** medicinal, revolting **10** disgusting **11** unpalatable

bad-tempered 5 cross, testy **6** grumpy **7** grouchy **8** choleric, churlish **9** difficult, irascible, irritable **10** ill-natured **11** acrimonious **12** disagreeable

bad times 4 bust **5** slump **9** hard times, recession **10** depression

bad turn 4 harm, hurt **5** wrong **6** injury **7** ill turn **8** disfavor **9** injustice **10** disservice **11** discourtesy

Baekleland, Leo Hendrik
field: **9** chemistry
invented: **8** Bakelite **32** artificial light photographic paper

Baer, Max (Maximillian Adalbert)
nickname: **17** Livermore Larruper
sport: **6** boxing
class: **11** heavyweight

Baeyer, Johann Friedrich Wilhelm Adolph von
field: **9** chemistry
nationality: **6** German
synthesized: **6** indigo
discovered: **13** phthalein dyes
awarded: **10** Nobel Prize

baffle 3 bar **4** daze, dull, foil, stop **5** amaze, check, stump **6** deaden, muddle, puz- zle, reduce, thwart **7** astound, confuse, inhibit, mystify, nonplus, perplex **8** astonish, befuddle, bewilder, confound, dumfound, minimize, restrain, surprise **10** disconcert

baffling 7 elusive **8** puzzling **9** confusing, enigmatic **10** mysterious, mystifying, perplexing **11** confounding **16** incomprehensible

bag 3 get, sag **4** hunt, kill, sack, take, trap **5** bulge, catch, droop, pouch, purse, shoot, snare **6** bundle, entrap, obtain, packet **7** acquire, capture, collect, ensnare **8** paper bag, protrude, suitcase **10** receptacle

bagatelle 6 trifle **7** nothing, trinket **10** knickknack, light music **11** unimportant

baggage 4 bags, gear **5** grips **6** trunks

7 bundles, effects, luggage, valises **8** movables, packages **9** apparatus, equipment, suitcases, trappings **10** belongings **11** impedimenta **13** accoutrements, paraphernalia

baggy 4 limp **5** loose, slack **6** droopy, flabby, puffed **7** bloated, bulbous, flac- cid, paunchy, sagging, swollen **9** unpressed, unshapely **12** loose-fitting

Baghdad
    capital of: 4 Iraq
    founder: 8 (Caliph) al-Mansur
    landmark:
        minaret: 10 Suq al-Ghazi
        mosque: 8 Madrasah **14** al-Mustansiriya
    means: 8 God-given
    river: 6 Tigris

Bagheera
    character in: 14 The Jungle Books
    author: 7 Kipling

bagnio 4 bath, stew **5** house **6** bordel, prison **7** brothel **8** bordello, cathouse **10** bawdy house, fancy house, whorehouse **13** sporting house **14** house of ill fame **16** house of ill repute **19** house of prostitution

Bagnold, Enid
    author of: 14 National Velvet, The Chalk Garden **23** The Chinese Prime Minister

Bagstock, Joe
    character in: 12 Dombey and Son
    author: 7 Dickens

Bahamas
    capital/largest city: 6 Nassau
    others: 8 Freeport **9** Rock Sound **10** George Town **11** Mastic Point **12** Spanish Wells
    head of state: 14 British monarch **15** governor general
    island: 3 Cat **4** Long **5** Berry, Exuma **6** Andros, Bimini, Caicos, Rum Cay **7** Crooked, Harbour, Watling **9** Eleuthera, Mayaguana **10** Great Abaco **11** Grand Bahama, Great Inagua, Great Ragged, San Salvador **13** New Providence
    sea: 8 Atlantic **9** Caribbean
    physical feature:
        strait: 7 Florida
        swamp: 8 mangrove
    people: 5 black **7** Haitian
    language: 6 Creole **7** English
    religion: 12 Christianity
    place:
        harbor: 9 Governors
        naval base: 9 Mayaguana
    feature:
        key: 3 cay
        native: 5 conch

Bahrain
    capital/largest city: 6 Manama
    others: 5 Rifaa **7** Jidhafs **8** Muharraq
    head of state/government: 4 emir
    monetary unit: 4 fils **5** dinar
    island: 5 Hawar, Jidda **6** Sitrah **7**

Bahrain **9** Umm Nassan **10** al-Muharraq **11** An Nabi Salih
    physical feature:
        gulf: 7 Bahrain, Persian
    people: 4 Arab **6** Indian **7** Persian **8** American, European **9** Pakistani
        ruling family: 9 al-Khalifa
    language: 4 Urdu **5** Farsi **6** Arabic **7** English, Persian
    religion: 5 Islam

bail 3 dip **4** bond, lade **5** ladle, scoop, spoon **6** surety **9** guarantee **11** post bond for

bailiff 6 deputy **8** marshall, overseer **9** assistant, constable **12** court officer

bailiwick 4 area, beat, turf **5** arena, orbit, place, realm **6** domain, sphere **7** compass **8** dominion, province **9** territory **10** department **12** neighborhood

Baird, Spencer Fullerton
    field: 7 zoology
    authority on: 5 birds **7** mammals
    established: 30 US Commission of Fish and Fisheries
    laboratory at: 11 Woods Hole MA

bait 3 vex **4** lure, ride, worm **5** annoy, bribe, harry, hound, tease, worry **6** allure, bad- ger, come-on, harass, heckle, hector, magnet, needle **7** provoke, torment **9** put bait on, tantalize **10** allurement, antagonize, attraction, enticement, inducement, temptation

bake 3 fry **4** boil, burn, cook, sear, stew **5** grill, roast, saute, toast **6** braise, pan-fry, scorch, simmer **7** parboil, swelter

Baked Bean State
    nickname of: 13 Massachusetts

Baker, Norma Jean Mortenson
    real name of: 13 Marilyn Monroe

Balaam
    father: 4 Beor
    brother: 4 Bela
    lived at: 4 Aram **6** Pethor
    commanded by: 5 Balak
    killed by: 6 Israel
    rebuked by: 3 ass

Balak
    father: 6 Zippor
    commanded: 6 Balaam

Balakiref, Mily
    born: 6 Russia **13** Nijni-Novgorod
    member of: 7 Kutchka, The Five
    composer of: 6 Russia, Tamara, Thamar **7** Islamey **8** King Lear (overture)

balance, balances 3 pay **4** cool, mean, rest **5** poise, ratio, scale, sum up, tally, total, tot up, weigh **6** aplomb, equate, offset, parity, ponder, reckon, scales, set off, square, steady, weight **7** compare, compute, harmony, opinion, reflect, remnant, residue **8** cogitate, consider, contrast, coolness, equality, estimate, evaluate, judgment, leftover, level off, parallel, presence, symmetry **9** appraisal,

calculate, composure, equipoise, juxtapose, make level, remainder, stability, stabilize **10** amount owed, comparison, counteract, deliberate, equanimity, evaluation, keep steady, neutralize, proportion, steadiness **11** equilibrium **12** counterpoise, equalization, middle ground **13** compensate for, consideration, judiciousness **14** amount credited, self-possession, unflappability **15** level-headedness **16** imperturbability
    constellation of: 5 Libra

balanced 4 fair, just **9** equitable, impartial **12** unprejudiced **13** disinterested

balance out 6 cancel, offset **9** make up for **10** neutralize **13** compensate for **14** counterbalance

Balanchine, George
    choreographer of: 4 Agon **6** Jewels **8** Episodes, Ivesiana, Serenade **15** Concerto Barocco **16** Allegro Brillante

balcony 4 deck **5** boxes, foyer, loges **6** loggia **7** portico, terrace, veranda **9** mezzanine

bald 4 bare, flat, open **5** blunt, naked, plain, stark, utter **6** barren, simple, smooth **7** denuded, obvious **8** flagrant, glabrous, hairless, outright, treeless **9** depilated, out- and-out, unadorned **11** categorical, undisguised, unqualified, unvarnished **12** without cover **13** unembellished, unequivocable **15** straightforward

Balder
    also: 5 Baldr **6** Baldur
    origin: 6 Nordic
    god of: 6 beauty **8** radiance
    father: 4 Odin **5** Othin
    mother: 3 Fri **5** Frigg, Frija **6** Frigga
    twin brother: 5 Hoder, Hodur
    killed by: 5 Hoder, Hodur

balderdash 3 rot **4** bosh, bull, bunk **5** crock, trash **6** bunkum, drivel, hot air **7** twaddle **8** buncombe, claptrap, flummery, nonsense, tommyrot **9** gibberish, poppycock **10** double-talk, tomfoolery **11** obfuscation **16** stuff and nonsense

baldheaded 8 hairless **9** baldpated, depilated **10** skin- headed **11** chrome-domed

Baldr
    see: 6 Balder

Baldung Grien, Hans
    born: 6 Alsace **10** Weyersheim
    artwork: 9 Todentanz **17** Death and the Maiden **19** Death Kissing a Maiden **21** The Bewitched Stable Boy **24** Rest on the Flight into Egypt

Baldur
    see: 6 Balder

Baldwin, James
    author of: 13 Giovanni's Room, The Amen Corner **14** Another Country **15**

Just Above My Head, The Fire Next Time **17** Going to Meet the Man, Nobody Knows My Name, No Name in the Street **21** Blues for Mister Charlie, Go Tell It on the Mountain

bale 4 case, load, pack **6** bundle, packet, parcel **7** package **11** bound bundle

balefire 6 beacon **9** watchfire **10** signal fire

baleful 3 icy **4** cold, dire, evil **6** deadly, malign **7** baneful, furious, harmful, hurtful, ominous **8** sinister, spiteful, venomous **9** malicious, malignant **10** malevolent **11** coldhearted, threatening

Balfe, Michael William
born: **6** Dublin **7** Ireland
composer of: **15** The Bohemian Girl, The Maid of Artois **17** I rivali di se stessi **18** The Siege of Rochelle

Balfour, David
character in: **9** Kidnapped
author: **9** Stevenson

Bali
province of: **9** Indonesia
capital: **8** Denpasar
city: **10** Singaraja
island: **11** Lesser Sunda
highest peak: **6** Agoeng
climate: **3** dry **7** monsoon
tree: **8** waringin
animal: **4** deer **5** tiger
people: **7** Malayan
religion: **8** Hinduism
agriculture: **3** pig **4** corn, rice **6** cattle, coffee **7** tobacco

Balius
horse of: **8** Achilles
gift: **11** immortality

balk 3 bar **4** foil, shun **5** block, check, demur, evade, shirk, spike, stall **6** baffle, defeat, derail, eschew, hinder, impede, recoil, refuse, resist, stymie, thwart **7** inhibit, prevent **8** draw back, hang back, hesitate, obstruct **9** forestall, frustrate **10** shrink from

Balkan 16 Forested mountain
agriculture: **5** grain **6** cotton, grapes, olives **7** tobacco
ancient people: **4** Slav **5** Greek, Roman **8** Illyrian, Thracian
language: **9** Slovenian **10** Macedonian **14** Serbo-Croatian
mountain: **6** Balkan, Massif **7** Rhodope **10** Carpathian **11** Dinaric Alps **13** Transylvanian
religion: **5** Islam **8** Orthodox **13** Roman Catholic
river: **6** Danube, Morava, Vardar
sea boundary: **5** Black **6** Aegean, Ionian **8** Adriatic **13** Mediterranean
state: **6** Greece, Turkey **7** Albania, Romania **8** Bulgaria **10** Yugoslavia

balky 6 mulish, ornery, unruly **7** restive, wayward, willful **8** contrary, perverse, stubborn **9** fractious, obstinate,

pigheaded **10** rebellious, refractory **11** disobedient, intractable **12** recalcitrant, unmanageable

ball 3 hop, orb **4** prom, shot **5** dance, globe **6** pellet, soiree, sphere **7** bullets, globule **8** spheroid **9** cotillion, promenade **11** projectiles

Ball, Lucille
husband: **9** Desi Arnaz
children: **4** Desi **5** Lucie
born: **11** Jamestown NY
roles: **9** Here's Lucy, I Love Lucy **11** The Lucy Show

Balla, Giacomo
born: **5** Italy, Turin
artwork: **8** The Sewer **11** The Mad Woman **18** Speeding Automobile **20** Rhythm of the Violinist **22** Dynamism of a Dog on a Leash **26** The Street Light Study of Light **29** Mercury Passing in Front of the Sun **40** Swifts Paths of Movement and Dynamic Sequences

ballad 3 lay **4** song **5** carol, ditty **6** chanty **8** folk song **12** rhyming story **13** narrative poem **14** narrative verse

Ballad of Reading Gaol, The
author: **10** Oscar Wilde

Ballads and Poems
author: **19** Stephen Vincent Benet

ballast 6 weight **7** balance, control **9** equipoise **10** ballasting, dead weight, makeweight, stabilizer **12** counterpoise **13** counterweight **14** counterbalance **19** stabilizing material

Ballesteros, Severiano
nickname: **4** Seve
sport: **4** golf
nationality: **7** Spanish

ballet 4 Agon **5** Manon, Rodeo **6** Apollo, Parade **7** Giselle, Orpheus **8** Coppelia, Episodes, Ivesiana, Les Noces, Serenade, Swan Lake, The Doves **9** Anastasia, Fancy Free, Interplay, Petrushka, The Jewels **10** La Sylphide, Petrouchka **11** Billy the Kid, Lilac Garden, Soccer Dance, Symphony in C, The Firebird **12** Pillar of Fire, Sailor's Dance, Spring Waters, The Partisans **13** The Nutcracker **14** Romeo and Juliet **15** Concerto Barocco, Fall River Legend, The Rite of Spring **16** Allegro Brillante, La Fille Mal Gardee, Specter of the Rose **17** The Sleeping Beauty **18** Raymonda Variations **19** The Afternoon of a Faun, The Four Temperaments **24** Stravinsky Violin Concerto
ballet company: **5** Kirov, Royal **7** Bolshoi, Joffrey **9** Mariinsky, Maryinsky **11** New York City **13** Ballets Russes **20** Dance Theater of Harlem **21** American Ballet Theater **22** National Ballet of Canada
choreographer: **9** Hanya Holm, Lev Ivanov **10** John Weaver **11** Jules Perrot **12** Agnes de Mille, Igor Moi-

seyev, Marius Petipa, Michel Fokine **13** Jean Dauberval, Jerome Robbins, Leonid Massine **15** Arthur Saint-Leon **16** George Balanchine, Kenneth Mac-Millan **18** August Bournonville, Bronislava Nijinska, Jean Georges Noverre, Sir Frederick Ashton
chorus: **8** ensemble **13** corps de ballet
dancer: **9** Karen Kain **10** Anton Dolin, Marie Lieta, Serge Lifar **11** Allegra Kent, Anna Pavlova, Anthony Blum, Lucile Grahn, Lynn Seymour, Nadia Nerina **12** Fanny Cerrito, Marie Camargo, Peter Martins **13** Alicia Markova, Andre Eglevsky, Anthony Dowell, Carlotta Grisi, Frank Augustyn, Galina Ulanova, Margot Fonteyn, Marie Taglioni, Melissa Hayden, Patricia Neary, Rudolf Nureyev **14** Arthur Mitchell, Cynthia Gregory, Edward Villella, Gelsey Kirkland, Leonide Massine, Maria Tallchief, Suzanne Farrell, Vaslav Nijinsky **15** Jacques D'Amboise, Martine Van Hamel, Maya Plisetskaya, Natalia Makarova, Patricia McBride, Tamara Karsavina **16** Antoinette Sibley, Olga Spessivtseva **17** Alexandra Danilova, Marina Kondratieva **18** Mikhail Baryshnikov
fast movement: **7** allegro
first ballet: **22** Ballet Comique de la Reine
impresario: **12** Marie Rambert **15** Ninette de Valois, Sergei Diaghilev
kick: **9** battement
modern dancer/choreographer: **8** Ted Shawn **9** Eliot Feld **10** Mary Wigman, Paul Draper, Twyla Tharp **11** Anna Sokolow, Antony Tudor, Eric Hawkins, Ruth St Denis **12** Martha Graham **13** Alwin Nikolais, Doris Humphrey, Isadora Duncan **14** Charles Weidman **15** Merce Cunningham
position/step: **4** jete, plie, tour **5** saute **6** releve **7** en avant, fouette, on point, pas seul, turnout **8** batterie, cabriole, en dedans, en dehors, glissade **9** arabesque, developpe, en arriere, entrechat, pas de chat, pas-de- deux, pirouette **10** demipointe, port de bras, tour en l'air **11** rond de jambe, terre-a-terre **12** pas de bourree, saut de basque **17** changement de pieds
principal female dancer: **6** etoile **9** ballerina **14** prima ballerina
principal male dancer: **12** danseur noble
skirt: **4** tutu
slow movement: **6** adagio
term: **4** coda **5** barre **6** ballon **14** divertissement

Ball of Fat
author: **15** Guy de Maupassant

balloon 4 grow **5** belly, bloat **6** billow, blow up, dilate, expand **7** distend, enlarge, fill out, inflate, puff out **8** increase, swell out

ballot 4 poll, vote **5** slate **6** ticket, voting **7** polling **13** round of voting **16** list of candidates

ballyhoo 4 hype, puff, push, tout **6** herald, hoopla **7** buildup, promote, puffery, trumpet **8** proclaim **9** advertise, promotion, publicity, publicize **10** hullabaloo, propaganda **11** advertising **15** public relations

balm 5 cream, salve **6** balsam, lotion, solace **7** anodyne, comfort, unguent **8** curative, narcotic, ointment, sedative **9** comforter, emollient **10** palliative **11** restorative **12** tranquilizer

balmy 3 odd **4** calm, fair, mild, soft, warm **5** bland, kooky, weird **6** easing, gentle **7** calming, clement, summery **8** aromatic, fragrant, perfumed, pleasant, redolent, soothing **9** agreeable, ambrosial, eccentric, temperate **10** refreshing, salubrious

Balnibari
    fictional land in: 16 Gulliver's Travels
    author: 5 Swift

baloney 3 rot **4** bull, bunk **5** hokum, hooey, stuff **6** bunkum, hot air, humbug **7** hogwash, sausage, spinach **8** claptrap, nonsense, tommyrot **9** poppycock **10** applesauce **11** foolishness

Baloo
    character in: 14 The Jungle Books
    author: 7 Kipling

balsam 3 fir **4** balm **5** cream, salve **7** unguent **8** ointment **9** Impatiens
    varieties: 2 He **3** Fir, She **4** Rose, Wild **6** Garden **8** Zanzibar

Balsam, Martin
    born: 9 New York NY
    roles: 6 Psycho **7** Catch-22 **15** A Thousand Clowns, On the Waterfront

Baltic
    language family: 12 Indo-European
    group: 11 Balto-Slavic
    subgroup: 7 Latvian **10** Lithuanian
    canal: 4 Kiel
    port: 4 Kiel, Riga **6** Danzig, Gdansk **7** Tallinn

Baltimore
    baseball team: 7 Orioles
    football team: 5 Stars **6** Ravens

Baltimore, David
    field: 12 microbiology
    studied: 11 animal cells **13** viral genetics
    awarded: 10 Nobel Prize

Balto-Slavic
    language family: 12 Indo-European
    branch: 6 Baltic, Slavic

baluster 4 post, rail **6** column, pillar **7** support, upright **8** pilaster

balustrade 7 railing **8** baluster, banister, handrail

Balzac, Honore de

author of: 7 Gobseck **10** La Vendetta **11** Cousin(e) Bette **12** Father Goriot, Le Cousin Pons, Le Pere Goriot **13** Lost Illusions **14** Eugenie Grandet, The Human Comedy **15** The Wild Ass's Skin **16** La Comedie Humaine **23** The Physiology of Marriage

Bamako
    capital of: 4 Mali

Bambi
    author: 11 Felix Salten
    character: 3 Ena **6** Faline, Flower **7** Thumper
    film made by: 6 Disney
    directed by: 9 David Hand

bamboo 4 Sasa **7** Bambusa **9** Shibataea **10** Pseudosasa **11** Arundinaria **13** Phyllostachys **14** Chimonobambusa **15** Semiarundinaria
    varieties: 4 Moso **5** Arrow, Black, Dwarf, Giant, Hardy, Hedge, Henon, Meyer, Pygmy, Simon, Stake **6** Buddha, Common, Forage, Oldham, Sacred, Sickle, Square, Tonkin **7** All-gold, Beechey, Mexican **8** Calcutta, Feathery, Heavenly, Narihira **9** Canebrake, Castillon **10** Red- berried, Square-stem **11** Punting-pole **12** Alphonse Karr, Yellow-groove **13** Dwarf fern-leaf, Fern-leaf hedge, Oriental hedge **14** Chinese-goddess **16** Dwarf white-stripe **17** Silver-stripe hedge **18** Stripe-stem fern- leaf

bamboozle 3 con, gyp **4** coax, dupe, fool, gull, hoax, lure, rook, take **5** cheat, coz- en, trick **6** delude **7** beguile, deceive, defraud, mislead, swindle **8** hoodwink **9** victimize

ban 3 bar **5** debar, taboo **6** banish, enjoin, forbid **7** barring, embargo, exclude **8** disallow, prohibit, stoppage, suppress **9** exclusion, interdict, proscribe, restraint **10** banishment, censorship **11** forbiddance, prohibition, restriction **12** interdiction, proscription

banal 4 dull **5** corny, stale, stock, tired, trite, vapid **6** jejune **7** humdrum, insipid, prosaic **8** bromidic, everyday, ordinary, shopworn **9** hackneyed **10** pedestrian, threadbare, unexciting, unoriginal **11** commonplace, stereotyped **12** cliche-ridden, conventional **13** platitudinous, unimaginative, uninteresting

banality 6 cliche **7** bromide **9** platitude, staleness, triteness **10** insipidity

banana 4 Musa
    varieties: 3 Fe'i **4** Fehi, Koae **5** Dwarf **6** Edible **7** Chinese **9** Flowering **10** Abyssinian, Ladyfinger **12** Canary Island, Chinese dwarf
    similar to: 8 plantain

Bananas
    director: 10 Woody Allen
    cast: 10 Woody Allen **12** Howard Cosell, Louise Lasser **15** Carlos Montalban

Bancroft, Anne
    real name: 23 Anna Maria Louise Italiano
    husband: 9 Mel Brooks
    born: 7 Bronx NY
    roles: 11 Mrs Robinson, The Graduate **15** The Pumpkin Eater, The Turning Point, Two for the Seesaw **16** The Miracle Worker (Oscar)

band 3 set **4** belt, body, club, crew, gang, hoop, join, pack, ring, sash **5** bunch, crowd, group, junta, party, strap, strip, swath, thong, troop, unite **6** caucus, circle, clique, collar, fillet, gather, girdle, league, ribbon, streak, stripe, throng **7** bandeau, binding, circlet, company, society **8** assembly, cincture, ensemble **9** multitude, orchestra, surcingle **10** fellowship, sisterhood **11** association, brotherhood, confederacy, consolidate **13** confederation

bandage 4 bind **5** dress **7** binding, plaster **8** compress, dressing

bandanna, bandana 5 scarf **8** kerchief **10** silk square **11** neckerchief **12** handkerchief

Bandar Seri Begawan
    capital of: 6 Brunei

bandeau 3 bra **4** band **6** fillet **7** binding, circlet **9** brassiere

bandit 4 thug **5** crook, thief **6** badman, outlaw, robber **7** brigand, burglar, footpad, ladrone **8** blackleg **9** desperado, road agent **10** highwayman

bandleader 6 master **7** maestro **8** director **9** conductor
    famous: 11 Glenn Miller, Tommy Dorsey **12** Lawrence Welk

Band of Merry Men
    followers of: 9 Robin Hood

band together 5 unify, unite **6** league **7** combine **10** join forces **11** consolidate

bandy 4 swap **5** trade **6** barter **7** shuffle **8** exchange **9** toss about **11** interchange **16** toss back and forth

bandying 4 swap **5** trade **8** exchange **9** tit for tat **10** quid pro quo **11** give and take

bane 3 woe **4** ruin **5** curse, toxin, venom **6** blight, burden, canker, plague, poison **7** scourge, torment, tragedy **8** calamity, disaster, downfall, nuisance **9** destroyer, detriment, ruination **10** affliction **13** pain in the neck **14** thorn in the side **16** fly in the ointment

baneful 4 evil **6** deadly, malign, woeful **7** harmful, noxious **8** venomous **9** injurious, malignant, poisonous **10** malevolent **11** destructive

bang 3 box, hit, pop, rap, tap **4** beat, blow, boom, clap, cuff, kick, lick, slam, slap, sock **5** burst, clout, crash, knock, smack, thump, whack **6** buffet, charge, report, thrill, thwack, wallop **7** delight **8** good time, headlong, pleasure, suddenly **9** enjoyment, explosion **10** crashingly, excitement

Bangkok
  also: 9 Krung Thep
  capital of: 8 Thailand
  landmark: 5 Wat Po **11** Grand Palace **16** Wat Emerald Buddha
  means: 12 City of Angels
  nickname: 15 Venice of the East
  port: 8 Klongtoi
  river: 10 Chao Phraya

Bangladesh
  other name: 10 East Bengal **12** East Pakistan
  capital/largest city: 5 Dacca
  others: 6 Khulna, Sylhet **7** Comilla, Jessore, Rangpur, Saidpur **8** Jamalpur, Rajshahi **9** Madaripur **10** Chittagong **11** Narayanganj **12** Brahmanbaria
  monetary unit: 4 taka **5** paisa
  island: 10 Sundarbans
  mountain: 15 Chittagong Hills
  highest point: 10 Keokradong
  river: 5 Padna **6** Ganges, Meghna **10** Burhi Ganga, Karnaphuli **11** Brahmaputra
  physical feature:
    bay: 6 Bengal
  people: 7 Bengali
    guerrillas: 11 muktibahini
    leader: 6 Ershad **11** Ziaur Rahman **19** Sheikh Mujibur Rahman
  language: 6 Bihari **7** Bengali, English
  religion: 5 Hindu, Islam
  feature:
    clothing: 4 sari **5** lungi

bangle 3 fob **5** chain, charm **6** armlet, bauble, gewgaw, tinsel **7** bibelot, fribble, trinket **8** bracelet, gimcrack, ornament, wristlet **10** knickknack **11** junk jewelry **14** costume jewelry

Bangui
  capital of: 22 Central African Republic

banish 3 ban, bar **4** drop, oust **5** eject, erase, evict, exile, expel **6** deport, dispel, outlaw, reject, remove **7** cast out, discard, dismiss, exclude, put away, shut out, turn out **8** cast away, dislodge, drive out, get rid of, send away, shake off **9** discharge, eliminate, eradicate, extradite **13** excommunicate **14** send to Coventry

banished person 5 exile **6** emigre, pariah **7** outcast **8** deportee, expellee **10** expatriate **14** deported person **15** displaced person

banishment 3 ban **5** exile **6** ouster **7** removal **8** eviction **9** dismissal, exclusion, expulsion **11** deportation **12** expatriation **14** transportation **15** excommunication

Banjo Eyes
  nickname of: 11 Eddie Cantor

Banjul, Bathurst
  capital of: 6 Gambia

bank 3 bar, row, tip **4** dike, dune, edge, file, flat, fund, heap, hill, keep, line, mass, pile, rank, reef, rise, save, side, tier, tilt **5** amass, array, brink, chain, knoll, mound, ridge, shelf, shoal, shore, slant, slope, stack, store, train **6** barrow, line up, margin, pile up, series, strand, string, supply **7** deposit, parapet, reserve, savings, shallow, terrace **8** keyboard, sandbank **9** exchequer, reservoir, stockpile **10** depository, embankment, repository, storehouse, succession **12** accumulation, trust company **14** savings and loan

Bank Dick, The
  director: 10 Eddie Cline
  cast: 8 W C Fields **9** Una Merkel **15** Cora Witherspoon

Bankhead, Tallulah
  father: 16 William B Bankhead
  born: 12 Huntsville AL
  roles: 8 Lifeboat **14** The Little Foxes **17** The Skin of Our Teeth

banknote 4 bill **9** greenback **11** certificate, legal tender **12** currency note, treasury note **17** silver certificate

bank of pity
  French: 11 mont-de-piete
  literal name for: 10 pawnbroker

bankrupt 5 broke **6** busted, failed, ruined **8** depleted, indigent, in the red, wiped out **9** destitute, exhausted, insolvent, penniless **12** impoverished, without funds

Bankruptcy, A
  author: 20 Bjornstjerne Bjornson

Banks, Ernie
  nickname: 5 Mr Cub
  sport: 8 baseball
  noted for: 7 hitting
  team: 11 Chicago Cubs

banner 4 flag **6** burgee, colors, ensign, record **7** leading, notable, pendant, pennant, winning **8** standard, streamer **9** red-letter **10** profitable **11** outstanding **14** most successful

Bannock
  language family: 10 Shoshonean
  location: 5 Idaho

banquet 4 dine **5** feast, revel **6** dinner, repast **9** symposium

Banquo
  character in: 7 Macbeth
  author: 11 Shakespeare

bantam 3 hen, wee **4** cock, fowl, tiny **5** dwarf, pygmy, runt, small, teeny, weeny **6** little, midget, minute, petite **7** chicken, dwarfed, rooster, stunted **9** miniature **10** diminutive, pocket-size, teeny-weeny **11** Lilliputian, pocket-sized

banter 3 kid, rib **4** dish, josh, mock, ride, twit **5** chaff, jolly, taunt, tease **6** joking, needle **7** jesting, joshing, kid-

ding, rag- ging, ribbing, teasing, waggery **8** badinage, chaffing, raillery, repartee, word play

Banting, Frederick Grant
  field: 8 medicine
  nationality: 8 Canadian
  extracted: 7 insulin
  awarded: 10 Nobel Prize

Bantu
  means: 9 the people
  dwelling: 6 Africa
  tribe: 5 Xosas, Zulus **6** Swazis **7** Basutos, Kalanga

baptism 9 beginning, immersion, sacrament **10** initiation, sprinkling **11** christening **12** introduction, purification **13** rite of passage **16** spiritual rebirth

baptize 3 dub **4** name **8** christen

bar 3 ban, pub, rib, rod **4** band, bank, beam, belt, bolt, cake, curb, flat, line, lock, oust, pale, pole, rail, reef, snag, spar, spit, stay, stop **5** block, catch, check, court, debar, eject, evict, exile, expel, forum, ingot, jimmy, lever, limit, shelf, shoal, slice, sprit, stake, stick, strip, taboo **6** banish, enjoin, fasten, forbid, impede, lounge, paling, ribbon, saloon, secure, streak, stripe, stroke, tavern **7** barrier, block up, canteen, cast out, close up, crowbar, exclude, grating, lock out, measure, prevent, sandbar, shallow, shut out, taproom **8** alehouse, crossbar, disallow, judgment, obstacle, obstruct, preclude, prohibit, restrain, restrict, tribunal **9** barricade, blackball, blacklist, hindrance, long table, lunchroom, restraint, speakeasy **10** constraint, crosspiece, impediment, injunction, limitation **11** obstruction, public house, restriction **14** cocktail lounge, serving counter, stumbling block **15** legal profession

Bara, Theda
  real name: 16 Theodosia Goodman
  nickname: 7 The Vamp
  born: 12 Cincinnati OH
  roles: 6 Carmen, Salome **7** Camille **8** The Vixen **9** Cleopatra **13** A Fool There Was, Madame Du Barry

Barabbas 6 robber **8** murderer

Barak
  father: 7 Abinoam
  summoned by: 7 Deborah
  defeated: 6 Sisera

barb 3 cut, dig, nib **4** cusp, jibe, snag, spur, tine **5** point, prong, spike **6** insult **7** affront, barbule, bristle, prickle, putdown, sarcasm, spicule **9** complaint, criticism **11** badmouthing

Barbados
  capital/largest city: 10 Bridgetown
  others: 7 Oistins **8** Boscabel, Crab Hill, Hastings, Holetown, Portland, Worthing **9** Bathsheba **10** Martin's Bay **11** Belleplaine **12** Speightstown

school: 10 Codrington
head of state: 14 British monarch **15** governor general
mountain: 6 Chalky
highest point: 7 Hillaby
river: 12 Constitution
sea: 8 Atlantic **9** Caribbean
physical feature:
　bay: 4 Foul, Long **8** Carlisle
　beach: 5 Crane
　gully: 12 Welchman Hall
　hill: 10 Cherry Tree
　point: 5 North, South **6** Ragged **8** Harrison, Kitridge
people: 5 Bajan **9** Barbadian
　leader: 5 Adams
language: 7 English
religion: 8 Anglican
place:
　airport: 7 Seawell
　castle: 8 Sam Lords
　church: 7 St Johns
feature:
　sea crab: 7 shagger
barbarian 4 boor, hood, lout, punk **5** alien, bully, crude, rowdy, tough, yahoo **6** savage, vandal **7** boorish, hoodlum, lowbrow, peasant, ruffian, uncouth **8** hooligan **9** ignoramus, outlander, roughneck, vulgarian **10** delinquent, illiterate, philistine, provincial, troglodyte, uncultured **11** know-nothing **12** uncultivated **15** unsophisticated **16** anti-intellectual
barbaric 4 rude, wild **5** crude **6** coarse, savage, vulgar **7** boorish, uncouth, untamed **9** barbarian, barbarous **10** unpolished **11** ill-mannered, uncivilized
barbarism 7 cruelty **8** savagery **9** brutality **10** inhumanity **11** viciousness
barbarity 7 cruelty **9** brutality **10** savageness **12** ruthlessness
barbarous 4 mean **5** crass, crude, cruel, harsh, rough **6** brutal, coarse, vulgar **7** inhuman, vicious **8** barbaric, impolite **10** outrageous
barber 3 cut **4** trim **5** dress, shave, style **6** Figaro **7** arrange, stylist, tonsure **10** haircutter **11** hairdresser
Barber, Samuel
　born: 13 West Chester PA
　composer of: 7 Vanessa **10** Dover Beach **16** Adagio for Strings **17** Capricorn Concerto **19** Anthony and Cleopatra, The School for Scandal
Barber of Seville, The
　author: 12 Beaumarchais
　opera by: 7 Rossini
　character: 6 Bazile, Figaro, Rosine, Rosina **8** Almaviva, Bartholo **9** Dr Bartolo **13** Count Almaviva
barbette 5 mound **7** bastion, rampart **8** platform **9** earthwork **10** breastwork
barbiturate 8 euphoria, hypnotic, sedative **10** depressive **13** anesthesiatic **14** barbituric acid

kind: 7 seconal **10** thiopental **11** amobarbital **12** secobarbital **13** phenobarbital
barbule 4 barb **11** feather part
Barchester Towers
　author: 15 Anthony Trollope
　sequel to: 9 The Warden
　character: 7 Mr Slope, Mrs Bold **8** Mr Arabin **9** Dr Proudie, Mr Harding **10** Mrs Proudie **11** Mr Quiverful **13** Canon Stanhope **17** Archdeacon Grantly **18** Signora Vesey-Neroni
bard 4 poet **6** rhymer, writer **8** epic poet, minstrel, poetizer **9** poetaster, rhymester, troubador, versifier **10** poet-singer **13** narrative poet
Bardell, Mrs
　character in: 14 Pickwick Papers
　author: 7 Dickens
Bardot, Brigitte
　husband: 10 Roger Vadim
　born: 5 Paris **6** France
　roles: 18 And God Created Woman
bare 4 bald, mere, nude, open, show, thin, void, worn **5** basic, blank, empty, naked, offer, plain, scant, stark, strip **6** denude, divest, expose, meager, peeled, reveal, simple, unclad, unmask, unveil, vacant **7** austere, exposed, hapless, uncover, undrape, undress, unrobed **8** disrobed, in the raw, marginal, stripped **9** endurable, essential, unadorned, unclothed, uncolored, uncovered, undressed, unsheathe **10** elementary, just enough, threadbare **11** fundamental, supportable, undecorated, undisguised, unvarnished **12** unelaborated, unornamented **13** unembellished **15** straightforward
barefaced 4 bald, bold, flip **5** brash, fresh, sassy **6** brazen, cheeky, snotty **7** forward **8** flippant, impudent, insolent, palpable **9** shameless, unabashed **11** transparent
barefoot 6 unshod **8** shoeless **9** discalced **10** unsandaled **11** discalceate
Barefoot Boy
　author: 21 John Greenleaf Whittier
Barefoot in the Park
　director: 8 Gene Saks
　based on play by: 9 Neil Simon
　cast: 9 Jane Fonda **12** Charles Boyer **13** Robert Redford
barely 4 just **6** almost, hardly **7** faintly, scantly **8** meagerly, only just, scarcely, slightly **9** almost not, just about, sparingly **10** no more than **20** by the skin of one's teeth
bareness 6 nudity **9** bleakness, emptiness, nakedness **10** barrenness
Baresark
　origin: 12 Scandinavian
　form: 7 warrior
　trait: 7 courage
Baretta
　character: 7 Rooster **11** Billy Truman,

(Det) Tony Baretta, (Lt) Hal Brubaker
　cast: 8 Tom Ewell **11** Robert Blake **12** Edward Grover **15** Michael D Roberts
Tony's pet: 8 cockatoo
　named: 4 Fred
barfly 3 sot **4** lush, soak **5** drunk, rummy, souse, toper **7** tippler **8** drunkard **9** alcoholic **11** dipsomaniac
bargain 4 deal, pact **5** steal **6** accord, barter, dicker, haggle, higgle, pledge, treaty **7** compact, entente, good buy, promise **8** contract, covenant, good deal **9** agreement, negotiate **10** settlement **11** arrangement, transaction **13** understanding
　French: 9 bon marche
bargain for 6 expect **7** foresee **8** envision, reckon on **11** contemplate
barge 4 bust, scow, ship **6** launch, vessel **7** freight, intrude
barium
　chemical symbol: 2 Ba
bark 3 bay, cry, rub, yap, yip **4** flay, hide, howl, hull, husk, peel, rind, roar, skin, woof, yell, yelp **5** crust, scale, shout, strip **6** abrade, arf-arf, bellow, bow-wow, casing, cry out, holler, scrape **7** howling **8** covering, periderm **9** sheathing
Barker, Lex
　real name: 25 Alexander Crichlow Barker Jr
　wife: 10 Arlene Dahl, Lana Turner
　born: 5 Rye NY
　roles: 6 Tarzan **11** La Dolce Vita
Barkis
　character in: 16 David Copperfield
　author: 7 Dickens
Barkley, Catherine
　character in: 15 A Farewell to Arms
　author: 9 Hemingway
Barlach, Ernst
　born: 5 Wedel **7** Germany **8** Holstein
　artwork: 9 Expellees **10** Seated Girl, Singing Man **11** Man in a Stock **13** Mater Dolorosa **14** Crippled Beggar, The Hovering One **16** Man Drawing a Sword **25** The Community of the Holy Ones
barn 4 mews **6** corral, stable
Barnabas
　companion: 4 Paul
Barnaby Jones
　character: 7 J R (Jedediah Romano) Jones **8** Lt Biddle **10** Betty Jones
　cast: 9 Mark Shera **10** Buddy Ebsen, John Carter **13** Lee Meriwether
Barnaby Rudge
　author: 14 Charles Dickens
　character: 8 Mrs Rudge **9** Miss Miggs **10** John Willet **11** Dolly Varden **12** Emma Haredale **13** Edward Chester, Gabriel Varden **14** Reuben Haredale, Simon Tappertit, Sir John Chester **16** Dennis the Hangman, Geoffrey

Haredale
subject: **11** Gordon riots

Barnard, Christiaan
field: **7** surgery **8** medicine
nationality: **12** South African
performed first: **15** heart transplant

Barnard, Edward Emerson
field: **9** astronomy
named for him: **12** red dwarf star

Barnes, Jake
character in: **15** The Sun Also Rises
author: **9** Hemingway

Barney Google
creator: **11** Billy DeBeck
character: **11** Snuffy Smith
baby: **5** Bunky
horse: **9** Spark Plug

Barney Miller
character: **8** (Det) Phil Fish **9** (Det)
Ron Harris **10** (Det Wojo) Wojo-
howicz, (Det) Nick Yamana, (Officer)
Carl Levitt **14** Inspector Luger, (Det)
Arthur Dietrich
cast: **7** Jack Soo **8** Ron Carey, Ron
Glass **9** Abe Vigoda, Hal Linden **11**
Maxwell Gail **12** James Gregory **15**
Steve Landesberg

Barnstock *see* **9** Branstock

Baroja y Nessi, Pio
author of: **15** Caesar or Nothing **23**
The Struggle for Existence **26** Mem-
orias de un Hombre de Accion

barometer
invented by: **10** Torricelli

baroque 6 florid, ornate **10** flamboyant
11 extravagant

Barrack-Room Ballads
author: **14** Rudyard Kipling

barracks 3 BOQ **4** base, camp **7** lodging **8** garrison

barrage 5 blast, burst, salvo, spray **6**
ack-ack, deluge, shower, stream, vol-
ley **7** battery, torrent **8** shelling **9** cannonade, fusillade **10** outpouring **11**
bombardment

barrel 3 keg, tub, tun, vat **4** butt, cask,
drum, tube **8** hogshead
abbreviation: **3** bar, bbl

barren 3 dry **4** arid, dull **5** stale, waste
6 farrow, futile **7** austere, prosaic,
sterile, useless **8** depleted, desolate,
infecund **9** fruitless, infertile **10** lackluster, unfruitful **11** ineffectual, uninspiring, unrewarding **12** unproductive
13 uninformative, uninstructive, uninteresting

barrenness 8 bareness **9** bleakness,
emptiness **10** desolation

barren wilderness 6 desert **9** wasteland

barricade 5 block, fence **7** barrier, bulwark, rampart **8** blockade, obstacle,
obstruct **10** impediment **11** obstruction

Barrie, Sir James M
author of: **7** The Will **8** Mary Rose,

Peter Pan **10** Dear Brutus **13** Quality
Street **15** Margaret Ogilvie, The Wedding Guest **17** Alice Sit-By-the-Fire,
The Little Minister **18** A Kiss for Cinderella, The Twelve- Pound Look **19**
What Every Woman Knows **20** Shall
We Join the Ladies?, The Admirable
Crichton
character: **8** Peter Pan **10** Tinkerbell
11 Captain Hook
Darling children: **4** John **5** Wendy
7 Michael
nurse/Newfoundland dog: **4** Nana
setting: **14** Never-Never Land

barrier 3 bar **4** moat, wall **5** ditch,
fence, hedge **6** hurdle, trench **7** rampart **8** blockade, handicap, obstacle **9**
barricade, hindrance **10** difficulty, impediment, limitation **11** obstruction,
restriction **13** fortification **14** stumbling block

Barrier, The
author: **8** Rex Beach

barring 3 but **4** save **6** except, saving
7 besides **9** excepting, excluding,
other than **11** exclusive of

barrister 6 lawyer **7** counsel **8** advocate, attorney **9** counselor **10** mouthpiece **13** attorney-at-law

barroom 3 bar, pub, **6** bistro, lounge,
saloon, tavern **7** taproom

barrow 4 heap, pile **5** mound **7** tumu-
lus **8** handcart, pushcart **11** wheelbarrow

Barrow, Joe Louis
real name of: **8** Joe Louis

Barry, Gene
real name: **11** Eugene Klass
born: **9** New York NY
roles: **9** Burke's Law **11** Thunder
Road **12** Bat Masterson **16** The
Name of the Game **17** The War of
the Worlds

Barry, John
served in: **16** Revolutionary War
commander of ship: **7** Raleigh **8** Alliance **9** Effingham, Lexington
ship captured: **6** Edward

Barry, Redmond
character in: **11** Barry Lyndon
author: **9** Thackeray

Barry, Sir Charles
architect of: **8** Cliveden **14** City Art
Gallery (Manchester) **18** Houses of
Parliament (London)

Barry Lyndon
author: **25** William Makepeace
Thackeray
character: **12** Redmond Barry **14** Lord
Bullingdon **17** Lady Honoria Lyndon
(Countess of Lyndon) **19** Chevalier
de Balibari
director: **14** Stanley Kubrick
cast: **9** Ryan O'Neal **11** Hardy Kruger
12 Patrick Magee **14** Marisa Berenson

Barrymore, Ethel

real name: **14** Ethel Mae Blythe
brother: **4** John **6** Lionel
born: **14** Philadelphia PA
roles: **11** A Doll's House **14** The Corn
Is Green **16** Portrait of Jennie **19**
Trelawney of the Wells **21** None But
the Lonely Heart, Rasputin and the
Empress

Barrymore, John
real name: **10** John Blythe
brother: **6** Lionel
sister: **5** Ethel
son: **17** John Drew Barrymore
daughter: **4** Diana Barrymore
granddaughter: **4** Drew
nickname: **12** Great Profile
born: **14** Philadelphia PA
roles: **6** Hamlet **7** Don Juan **8** Moby
Dick, Svengali **9** Richard IV **10**
Grand Hotel **11** Beau Brummel **13**
Dinner at Eight **17** Dr Jekyll and Mr
Hyde **21** Rasputin and the Empress

Barrymore, Lionel
real name: **12** Lionel Blythe
brother: **4** John
sister: **5** Ethel
born: **14** Philadelphia PA
roles: **7** The Jest **9** A Free Soul (Oscar), (friend of) Dr Kildare **11** Dr Gillespie **13** Peter Ibbitson, The Copperhead **21** Rasputin and the Empress

Barsabbas *see* **6** Joseph

Barstad, John
character in: **16** A Tale of Two Cities
author: **7** Dickens

Bart, Lily
character in: **15** The House of Mirth
author: **7** Wharton

barter 4 swap **5** trade **8** exchange **11**
interchange

Bartered Bride, The
opera by: **7** Smetana
character: **5** Jenik, Kecal, Micha,
Vasek **7** Marenka

Barth, John
author of: **7** Chimera **12** Giles Goat-
Boy **15** The End of the Road **16** The
Floating Opera, The Sot-Weed Factor
17 Lost in the Funhouse

Barthelme, Donald
author of: **7** Sadness **8** City Life **9**
Great Days, Snow White **12** Sixty
Stories **13** The Dead Father **15** Guilty
Pleasures **18** Come Back Dr Caligari
33 Unspeakable Practices Unnatural
Acts

Bartholdi, Frederic-Auguste
born: **6** Alsace, Colmar
artwork: **13** Lion of Belfort **26** Liberty
Enlightening the World (Statue of
Liberty)

Bartholo, Dr
character in: **18** The Barber of Seville
19 The Marriage of Figaro
author: **12** Beaumarchais

Bartholomew 7 apostle
also called: **9** Nathanael

Bartholomew Fair
    author: 9 Ben Jonson
Bartok, Bela
    born: 7 Hungary 15 Nagyszentmiklos
    composer of: 9 Wrestling 11
    Mikrokosmos 12 Divertimento 14
    Cantata Profana 15 The Wooden
    Prince 20 Duke Bluebeard's Castle
    21 The Miraculous Mandarin
Bartolommeo, Fra
    born: 5 Italy 8 Florence
    real name: 31 Bartolommeo di Pagolo
    del Fattorino
    artwork: 5 Jonah 6 Isaiah 13 Salva-
    tor Mundi 15 The Last Judgment 17
    Vision of St Bernard 24 Madonna
    della Misericordia 30 The Mystic
    Marriage of St Catherine
Barton, Benjamin Smith
    field: 6 botany
    noted for first American: 14 botany
    textbook
Bartram, John
    field: 6 botany
    noted for first American: 12 hybrid
    plants
Baruch
    father: 5 Judah 6 Neriah
    friend and scribe of: 8 Jeremiah
Baruch, Bernard 9 statesman, finan-
    cier
basal 3 key 4 easy 5 basic, vital 6 sim-
    ple 7 initial, minimal, primary 8 car-
    dinal 9 beginning, essential, intrinsic,
    necessary 10 elementary, lower-level,
    simplified 11 fundamental, rudimen-
    tary 12 prerequisite 13 indispensable
bas bleu 12 bluestocking
base 3 bad, bed, key, low 4 camp,
    core, foul, mean, post, root, vile 5 ba-
    sis, dirty, gross, heart, petty, place,
    stand 6 abject, billet, bottom, craven,
    ground, impure, locate, scurvy, sinful,
    sneaky, sordid, source, vulgar, wicked
    7 alloyed, corrupt, debased, essence,
    found on, ignoble, immoral, install,
    model on, scrubby, situate, station,
    support 8 backbone, cowardly, de-
    graded, depraved, garrison, infamous,
    inferior, pedestal, rudiment, shameful,
    spurious, unworthy 9 dastardly, disso-
    lute, establish, faithless, insidious, ne-
    farious, principle 10 degenerate, de-
    rive from, despicable, detestable, evil-
    minded, foundation, groundwork,
    iniquitious, villainous 11 adulterated,
    disgraceful, ignominious, poor quality,
    scoundrelly 12 black-hearted, con-
    temptible, dishonorable, disreputable,
    installation, substructure, underpin-
    ning, unprincipled 13 discreditable,
    reprehensible
baseball
    term: 3 bag, ERA, fan, RBI, run 4
    balk, base, bunt, bush 5 choke,
    curve, error, fungo, liner, pop-up,
    slide 6 assist, bat- ter, cellar, double,

dugout, duster, inning, on deck, relief (pitcher), rookie, single, slider,
triple, umpire, windup 7 blooper,
bullpen, catcher, cleanup, fly ball,
home run, infield, pickoff, pitcher,
rhubarb, rundown, shutout, slugger
8 bean ball, changeup, grounder,
keystone, no hitter, outfield, pitch-
out, southpaw, spitball 9 bleachers,
brushback, grand slam, hot corner,
infielder, line drive, sacrifice, shortstop 10 bush league, gopher ball, infield fly, outfielder, passed ball 11
bases loaded, knuckleball, pinch hitter, triple crown, World Series 12
Texas leaguer 16 designated hitter,
earned run average
Hall of Fame:
    1936: 4 Cobb (Ty), Ruth (Babe) 6
    Wagner (Honus) 7 Johnson (Wal-
    ter) 9 Mathewson (Christy)
    1937: 4 Mack (Connie) 5 Young
    (Cy) 6 Lajoie (Nap), McGraw
    (John), Wright (George) 7 John-
    son (Ban), Speaker (Tris) 8 Bulke-
    ley (Morgan)
    1938: 8 Chadwick (Henry) 9 Alex-
    ander (Grover) 10 Cartwright (Al-
    exander)
    1939: 5 Anson (Cap), Ewing (Buck)
    6 Gehrig (Lou), Keeler (Willie),
    Sisler (George) 7 Collins (Eddie) 8
    Comiskey (Charlie), Cummings
    (Candy), Spalding (Albert) 9 Rad-
    bourne (Old Hoss)
    1942: 7 Hornsby (Rogers)
    1944: 7 Kenesaw (M. Landis)
    1945: 5 Duffy (Hugh), Kelly (King)
    6 Clarke (Fred) 7 Collins (Jimmy),
    O'Rourke (Jim) 8 Jennings
    (Hughey), Robinson (Wilbert) 9
    Bresnahan (Roger), Brouthers
    (Dan), Delahanty (Ed)
    1946: 5 Evers (Johnny), Plank (Ed-
    die), Walsh (Ed) 6 Chance
    (Frank), Tinker (Joe) 7 Burkett
    (Jesse), Chesbro (Jack), Waddell
    (Rube) 8 Griffith (Clark),
    McCarthy (Tommy) 9 McGinnity
    (Joe)
    1947: 5 Grove (Lefty) 6 Frisch
    (Frankie) 7 Hubbell (Carl) 8 Coch-
    rane (Mickey)
    1948: 7 Pennock (Herb), Traynor
    (Pie)
    1949: 5 Brown (Mordecai) 7
    Nichols (Kid) 9 Gehringer (Char-
    lie)
    1951: 3 Ott (Mel) 4 Foxx (Jimmie)
    1952: 5 Waner (Paul) 8 Heilmann
    (Harry)
    1953: 4 Dean (Dizzy), Klem (Bill) 6
    Barrow (Ed), Bender (Chief),
    Wright (Harry) 7 Simmons (Al),
    Wallace (Bobby) 8 Connolly
    (Tom)
    1954: 5 Terry (Bill) 6 Dickey (Bill)
    1955: 5 Baker (Frank), Lyons

(Ted), Vance (Dazzy) 6 Schalk
(Ray) 8 DiMaggio (Joe), Hartnett
(Gabby) 10 Maranville (Rabbit)
    1956: 6 Cronin (Joe) 9 Greenberg
    (Hank)
    1957: 8 Crawford (Sam), McCarthy
    (Joe)
    1959: 5 Wheat (Zach)
    1961: 5 Carey (Max) 8 Hamilton
    (Billy)
    1962: 5 Roush (Edd) 6 Feller (Bob)
    8 Robinson (Jackie) 9 McKechnie
    (Bill)
    1963: 4 Rice (Sam), Eppa (Rixey) 5
    Flick (Elmer) 8 Clarkson (John)
    1964: 4 Ward (Monte) 5 Faber
    (Red), Keefe (Tim) 6 Grimes (Bur-
    leigh), Manush (Heinie) 7 Appling
    (Luke), Huggins (Miller)
    1965: 6 Galvin (Pud)
    1966: 7 Stengel (Casey) 8 Williams
    (Ted)
    1967: 5 Waner (Lloyd) 6 Rickey
    (Branch) 7 Ruffing (Red)
    1968: 6 Cuyler (Kiki), Goslin
    (Goose) 7 Medwick (Joe)
    1969: 4 Hoyt (Waite) 6 Musial
    (Stan) 9 Coveleski (Stan) 10 Cam-
    panella (Roy)
    1970: 5 Combs (Earle), Frick (Ford)
    6 Haines (Jesse) 8 Boudreau (Lou)
    1971: 5 Paige (Satchel), Hafey
    (Chick), Weiss (George) 6 Hooper
    (Harry), Kelley (Joe) 7 Beckley
    (Jake) 8 Bancroft (Dave), Marq-
    uard (Rube)
    1972: 4 Wynn (Early) 5 Berra
    (Yogi), Gomez (Lefty) 6 Gibson
    (Josh), Koufax (Sandy), Youngs
    (Ross) 7 Leonard (Buck) 8 Har-
    ridge (Will)
    1973: 5 Evans (Billy), Irvin
    (Monte), Kelly (George), Spahn
    (Warren), Welch (Mickey) 8 Cle-
    mente (Roberto)
    1974: 4 Bell (Cool Papa), Ford
    (Whitey) 6 Conlan (Jocko), Mantle
    (Mickey) 8 Thompson (Sam) 9
    Bottomley (Jim)
    1975 5 Kiner (Ralph) 6 Harris
    (Bucky), Herman (Billy) 7 Averill
    (Earl), Johnson (Judy)
    1976: 5 Lemon (Bob) 6 Connor
    (Roger) 7 Hubbard (Cal), Roberts
    (Robin) 9 Lindstrom (Fred) 10
    Charleston (Oscar)
    1977: 5 Banks (Ernie), Lloyd (Pop),
    Lopez (Al), Rusie (Arnos) 6 Di-
    higo (Martin), Sewell (Joe)
    1978: 4 Joss (Addie) 7 Mathews
    (Eddie) 8 MacPhail (Larry)
    1979: 4 Mays (Willie) 5 Giles
    (Warren) 6 Wilson (Hack)
    1980: 5 Klein (Chuck) 6 Kaline
    (Al), Snider (Duke), Yawkey
    (Tom)
    1981: 4 Mize (Johnny) 6 Foster
    (Rube), Gibson (Bob)

1982: 5 Aaron (Hank) **7** Jackson (Travis) **8** Chandler (Happy), Robinson (Frank)

1983: 4 Kell (George) **6** Alston (Walter) **8** Marichal (Juan), Robinson (Brooks)

1984: 5 Reese (Pee Wee) **7** Ferrell (Rick) **8** Aparicio (Luis), Drysdale (Don) **9** Killebrew (Harmon)

1985: 5 Brock (Lou) **7** Vaughan (Arky), Wilhelm (Hoyt) **9** Slaughter (Enos)

1986: 5 Doerr (Bobby) **7** McCovey (Willie) **8** Lombardi (Ernie)

1987: 6 Hunter (Jim "Catfish") **8** Williams (Billy) **9** Dandridge (Ray)

1988: 8 Stargell (Willie)

1989: 7 Bench (Johnny) **7** Barlick (Al) **11** Yastrzemski (Carl) **12** Schoendienst (Red)

1990: 6 Morgan (Joe), Palmer (Jim)

1991: 5 Carew (Rod), Perry (Gaylord), Veeck (Bill) **7** Jenkins (Ferguson), Lazzeri (Tony)

1992: 6 Seaver (Tom) **7** Fingers (Rollie), McGowan (Bill) **9** Newhouser (Hal)

1993: 7 Jackson (Reggie)

1994: 7 Carlton (Steve), Rizzuto (Phil "Scooter") **8** Durocher (Leo)

other player/coach: 7 Jim Rice **8** Pete Rose, Vida Blue **9** Alvin Dark, Bowie Kuhn, Gil Hodges, Hank Bauer, Luis Tiant, Nellie Fox, Nolan Ryan, Ralph Houk, Ron Guidry, Ted Turner, Tommy John **10** Boog Powell, Earl Weaver, Maury Wills, Roger Maris, Sparky Lyle **11** Billy Martin, Dave Kingman, Frank Thomas, George Brett, Mark Fidrych, Mike Schmidt, Rich Gossage **12** Graig Nettles, Dave Winfield, Dennis McLain, Dick Williams, Elston Howard, Ken Griffey Jr, Tommy Lasorda **13** Rocky Colavito, Thurman Munson, Walter O'Malley **14** Keith Hernandez, Peter Ueberroth, Sparky Anderson **15** Rickey Henderson **16** Darryl Strawberry **18** Fernando Valenzuela, George Steinbrenner

baseball leagues
National: 11 Chicago Cubs, New York Mets **13** Atlanta Braves, Houston Astros, Montreal Expos **14** Cincinnati Reds, Florida Marlins, San Diego Padres **15** Colorado Rockies **16** Milwaukee Brewers, St Louis Cardinals **17** Los Angeles Dodgers, Pittsburgh Pirates **18** San Francisco Giants **19** Arizona Diamondbacks **20** Philadelphia Phillies
American: 9 Oakland A's **12** Boston Red Sox, Texas Rangers **13** Anaheim Angels, Detroit Tigers **14** Minnesota Twins, New York Yankees **15** Chicago White Sox, Seattle Mariners,

Toronto Blue Jays **16** Baltimore Orioles, Cleveland Indians, Kansas City Royals, Oakland Athletics **17** Tampa Bay Devil Rays

baseball team
Anaheim: 6 Angels
  stadium: 11 Edison Field **7** Anaheim
Atlanta: 6 Braves
  stadium: 11 Turner Field
Arizona 12 Diamondbacks
  stadium 15 Bank One Ballpark
Baltimore: 7 Orioles
  stadium: 11 Camden Yards
Boston: 6 Red Sox
  stadium: 10 Fenway Park
Chicago: 4 Cubs
  stadium: 12 Wrigley Field
Chicago: 8 White Sox
  stadium: 12 Comiskey Park
Cleveland: 7 Indians
  stadium: 11 Jacobs Field
Cincinnati: 4 Reds
  stadium: 10 Riverfront **12** Cinergy Field
Colorado: 7 Rockies
  stadium: 8 Mile High **10** Coors Field
Detroit: 6 Tigers
  stadium: 5 Tiger
Florida: 7 Marlins
  stadium: 9 Joe Robbie, Pro Player
Houston: 6 Astros
  stadium: 9 Astrodome
Kansas City: 6 Royals
  stadium: 8 Kauffman
Los Angeles: 7 Dodgers
  stadium: 6 Dodger **18** Los Angeles Coliseum
Milwaukee: 7 Brewers
  stadium: 6 County
Minnesota: 5 Twins
  stadium: 12 Metropolitan **24** Hubert H Humphrey Metrodome
Montreal: 5 Expos
  stadium: 7 Olympic
New York: 4 Mets
  stadium: 4 Shea
New York: 7 Yankees
  stadium: 6 Yankee
Oakland: 2 A's
  stadium: 7 Oakland **8** Coliseum
Philadelphia: 8 Phillies
  stadium: 9 Veterans
Pittsburgh: 7 Pirates
  stadium: 11 Three Rivers
St Louis: 9 Cardinals
  stadium: 13 Busch Memorial
San Diego: 6 Padres
  stadium: 8 Qualcomm **10** Jack Murphy
San Francisco: 6 Giants
  stadium: 7 3Com Park **15** Candlestick Park
Seattle: 8 Mariners
  stadium: 8 Kingdome
Tampa bay: 9 Devil Rays
  stadium: 14 Tropicana Field

Texas: 7 Rangers
  stadium: 11 The Ballpark
Toronto: 8 Blue Jays
  stadium: 7 Sky Dome

baseless 7 unsound **9** unfactual, unfounded **10** groundless, ungrounded **11** unjustified, unsupported **12** without basis **13** unjustifiable **14** uncorroborated **15** unsubstantiated

basement 5 below **6** bottom, cellar **15** underground room

baseness 7 lowness **8** meanness, vileness **9** depravity **11** ignobleness **14** iniquitousness **16** contemptibleness

base of operations
  Greek: 6 pou sto

bash 4 blow **5** blast, clout, crack, knock, party, whack **7** clopper **8** wingding **9** bacchanal

Bashemath see **4** Adah

bashful 3 shy **5** timid **6** demure, modest **8** blushing, reserved, reticent, retiring, sheepish, skittish, timorous **9** diffident, shrinking, uncertain **10** shamefaced **11** constrained, unconfident

bashfulness 7 shyness **10** diffidence **12** sheepishness **14** self-effacement **15** unassertiveness

basic 3 key **4** base, core **5** prime, vital **7** bedrock, primary **8** rudiment **9** essential, intrinsic **10** elementary, foundation **11** fundamental, rudimentary **12** foundational, prerequisite, underpinning

basically
  French: 6 au fond

basic ideas 6 basics **7** essence, factors, origins **8** elements, features **9** rudiments **10** principles **11** foundations

basic need 9 essential, necessity, requisite, vital part **10** key element, sine qua non

basic part 4 unit **7** element **9** component **10** ingredient **11** constituent **13** building block

basic quality 6 nature **7** essence **9** principle, substance **12** quintessence

basics 4 ABCs **8** elements **9** rudiments **10** principles **11** nitty-gritty **12** fundamentals

basil
  also called: 6 tulasi
  botanical name: 6 Ocimum **8** O minimum **10** O basilicum
  means: 5 royal **6** kingly, lizard (basilisk)
  nickname: 14 kiss-me-Nicholas
  origin: 5 India
  sacred to: 6 Vishnu **7** Krishna, Lakshmi
  symbol of: 4 hate, love
  use: 5 pasta, pesto, sauce **10** vegetables

basilica **6** church **10** house of God **14** house of worship

Basilisk
   form: 6 dragon

basin 3 pan, tub, vat **4** bowl, dale, dell, font, glen, sink **5** gulch, gully, stoup **6** crater, hollow, lavabo, ravine, tureen, valley **7** dishpan, washtub **8** lavatory, sinkhole, washbowl **9** porringer, washbasin, washstand **10** depression, finger bowl

basis, bases 4 base, root **6** ground **7** bedrock **9** essential, principle **10** foundation, touchstone **11** cornerstone, fundamental **12** underpinning **13** starting point

bask 5 revel, savor **6** relish, wallow **7** delight **8** sunbathe **9** luxuriate **11** warm oneself **12** soak up warmth, toast oneself

basket 5 cesta, crate **6** barrel, hamper **7** carrier, pannier **8** bassinet, canister

basketball
   term: 3 key **4** dunk, hoop, pick, post, trap, zone **5** court, guard, lay-up, pivot, point, press, steal **6** assist, basket, center **7** dribble, forward, palming, rebound, referee **8** charging, hook shot, jump shot, sixth man, turnover **9** backboard, backcourt, fast break, field goal, free throw, give-and-go, traveling **11** goal tending, pick-and-roll **12** three-pointer

   Hall of Fame:
     1959: 5 Allen (Phog; Forrest Clare), Hyatt (Charles), Mikan (George), Olsen (Harold), Stagg (Amos Alonzo), Tower (Oswald) **6** Gulick (Luther), Hickox (Edward), Morgan (Ralph) **7** Carlson (Henry), Kennedy (Matthew) **8** Luisetti (Hank), Meanwell (Walter E), Naismith (James), Schommer (John) **15** Original Celtics
     1960: 5 Blood (Ernest) **6** Hanson (Victor), Keaney (Frank), Murphy (Charles), Porter (Henry), Wooden (John) **7** Hepbron (George), Lambert (Ward) **8** Macauley (Ed) **9** McCracken (Branch)
     1961: 4 Hoyt (George) **5** Sachs (Leonard), Tobey (David), Walsh (David) **6** Keogan (George), O'Brien (John), Roosma (John) **7** Kurland (Bob), Phillip (Andy), Quigley (Ernest), Trester (Arthur), Wachter (Edward) **8** Borgmann (Bernhard) **9** Steinmetz (Christian) **10** DeBernardi (Forrest), Schabinger (Arthur) **14** Buffalo Germans
     1962: 4 Page (Harlan) **6** Sedran (Barney), St John (Lynn) **8** Thompson (John) **9** McCracken (Jack) **10** Morgenweck (Frank)
     1963: 4 Reid (William) **7** Gruenig (Robert) **11** New York Rens
     1964: 4 Bunn (John) **5** Irish (Ned),

Jones (R William) **6** Foster (Harold), Holman (Nat) **7** Russell (John) **8** Loeffler (Kenneth)
1965: 5 Brown (Walter) **6** Hinkle (Paul), Hobson (Howard), Mokray (William)
1966: 4 Dean (Everett) **8** Lapchick (Joe)
1967: 3 Bee (Clair) **4** Cann (Howard), Gill (Amory) **6** Julian (Alvin)
1968: 3 Iba (Hank; Henry P) **4** Rupp (Adolph F) **6** Taylor (Charles H) **7** Denhart (Henry G) **8** Auerbach (Red; Arnold J)
1969: 6 Davies (Bob) **9** Carnevale (Bernard L)
1970: 5 Cousy (Bob) **6** Pettit (Bob) **10** Saperstein (Abe)
1971: 5 Wells (W R Clifford) **6** Diddle (Edgar A) **7** Douglas (Robert L) **8** Endacott (Paul), Friedman (Max), Gottlieb (Edward)
1972: 5 Drake (Bruce) **6** Ripley (Elmer H), Wooden (John) **7** Beckman (John), Lonborg (Arthur C), Schayes (Dolph)
1973: 6 Fisher (Harry A) **7** Schmidt (Ernest) **8** Podoloff (Maurice)
1974: 6 Liston (Emil) **7** Brennan (Joseph), Russell (Bill) **9** Vandivier (Robert)
1975 4 Gola (Tom) **6** Krause (Edward W) **7** Litwack (Harry), Sharman (Bill)
1976: 4 Gale (Lauren) **6** Baylor (Elgin), Cooper (Charles T) **7** Johnson (Wiliam C), McGuire (Frank)
1977: 5 Fulks (Joe), Hagan (Cliff) **6** Arizin (Paul) **7** Pollard (Jim) **8** Nucatola (John P)
1978: 5 Barry (Sam; Justin M), Meyer (Raymond J) **6** Hickey (Edgar S), Newell (Peter F) **7** Enright (James E) **8** McLendon (John B) **11** Chamberlain (Wilt)
1979: 4 West (Jerry) **5** Lucas (Jerry) **7** Shelton (Everett), Shirley (J Dallas) **8** Harrison (Lester) **9** Robertson (Oscar)
1980: 4 Hepp (Ferenc) **6** Barlow (Thomas B) **7** Kennedy (J Walter) **9** McCutchan (Arad A)
1981: 4 Case (Everett N), Duer (Alva O), Reed (Willis) **5** Greer (Hal) **6** Gaines (Clarence E), Martin (Slater), Ramsey (Frank)
1982: 5 Leith (Lloyd R), Smith (Dean E), Wilke (Louis G) **6** Twyman (Jack) **7** Bradley (Bill) **11** DeBusschere (Dave)
1983: 5 Fagan (Clifford B), Jones (Sam) **6** Steitz (Edward S) **7** Gardner (Jack) **8** Havlicek (John)
1984: 4 Wade (L Margaret) **5** Cervi (Al) **6** Abbott (Senda Berenson), Teague (Bertha F) **8** Anderson (W Harold), Harshman (Marv K), Thurmond (Nate)

1985--1986: 5 Watts (Stanley H) **6** Taylor (Fred R) **7** Holzman (Red), Mihalik (Red) **8** Heinsohn (Tom) **10** Cunningham (Billy)
1986--1987: 5 Barry (Rick) **6** Wanzer (Bobby) **7** Frazier (Walt) **8** Houbregs (Robert J), Maravich (Pete)
1987--1988: 6 Miller (Ralph H), Unseld (Wes) **9** McDermott (Robert), Lovelette (Clyde)
1988--1989: 5 Gates (William "Pop"), Jones (K C) **7** Wilkens (Lenny)
1989--1990 4 Bing (Dave) **5** Hayes (Elvin) **6** Monroe (Earl) **8** Johnston (Neil)
1990--1991: 6 Cowens (Dave), Knight (Bobby), O'Brien (Lawrence F) **8** Fleisher (Lawrence), Gallatin (Harry) **9** Archibald (Nate), Stankovic (Borislav)
1991--1992: 5 Belov (Sergei), White (Nera) **6** Lanier (Bob), Ramsay (Jack) **7** Hawkins (Connie), McGuire (Al) **8** Woolpert (Phillip) **10** Carnesecca (Louie) **13** Harris-Stewart (Lusia)
1992--1993: 5 Issel (Dan) **6** Erving (Julius), Meyers (Ann), Murphy (Calvin), Walton (Bill) **7** Bellamy (Walter), McGuire (Dick) **9** Semjonova (Uljana)
1994: 4 Crum (Denny), Daly (Charles J) **6** Rubini (Cesare) **9** Jeannette (Buddy) **11** Blazejowski (Carol)

other player/coach: 8 Pat Riley **9** Bob McAdoo, Larry Bird **10** Danny Ainge, Kobe Bryant **11** Alex English, Bernard King, Bill Lambeer, Dick Barnett, James Worthy, Kevin McHale, Lew Alcindor, Moses Malone **12** Clyde Drexler, George Gervin, Isaiah Thomas, Larry Johnson, Patrick Ewing, Robert Parish **13** David Robinson, Earvin (Magic) Johnson, Michael Jordan, Scottie Pippen, Terry Cummings **14** Charles Barkley, Hakeem Olajuwon, Shaquille O'Neal **17** Kareem Abdul-Jabbar

basketball team
   league: 3 NBA **29** National Basketball Association
   Atlanta: 5 Hawks
   Boston: 7 Celtics
   Charlotte: 7 Hornets
   Chicago: 5 Bulls
   Cleveland: 9 Cavaliers
   Dallas: 9 Mavericks
   Denver: 7 Nuggets
   Detroit: 7 Pistons
   Golden State: 8 Warriors
   Houston: 7 Rockets
   Indiana: 6 Pacers
   Los Angeles: 6 Lakers **8** Clippers
   Miami: 4 Heat

Milwaukee: **5** Bucks
Minnesota: **12** Timberwolves
New Jersey: **4** Nets
New York: **14** Knickerbockers
Orlando: **5** Magic
Philadelphia: **5** 76ers **13** Seventy-Sixers
Phoenix: **4** Suns
Portland: **12** Trail Blazers
Sacramento: **5** Kings
San Antonio: **5** Spurs
Seattle: **11** SuperSonics
Toronto: **7** Raptors
Utah: **4** Jazz
Vancouver: **9** Grizzlies
Washington: **7** Wizards
WNBA
Charlotte: **5** Sting
Cleveland: **7** Rockers
Detroit: **5** Shock
Houston: **6** Comets
Los Angeles: **6** Sparks
New York: **7** Liberty
Phoenix: **7** Mercury
Sacramento: **8** Monarchs
Utah: **6** Starzz
Washington: **7** Mystics

Basque
language spoken in: **5** Italy, Spain **6** France

bas-relief
Italian: **12** basso-rilievo

bass 3 low **4** alto **5** basso **7** harmony **8** baritone, bass clef

bass
types: **3** sea **4** rock **5** black **6** calico **7** striped, sunfish **10** largemouth, smallmouth
characteristic: **10** forked-tail **12** spiny-finned

Bassanio
character in: **19** The Merchant of Venice
author: **11** Shakespeare

basso-rilievo 9 bas-relief

Bast, Jacky and Leonard
characters in: **10** Howards End
author: **9** E M Forster

bastard 6 impure **8** inferior, spurious **9** imperfect, irregular, love child **12** natural child **17** illegitimate child

bastardize 6 debase, weaken **7** degrade **9** downgrade

baste 3 sew **4** drip **5** roast **6** cudgel, flavor, stitch, thrash **7** moisten **15** temporary stitch

bastinado 4 beat, blow, cane, drub **5** whale **7** beating **8** drubbing

bastion 4 fort **5** tower **6** pillar **7** bulwark, citadel, rampart **8** barbette, fortress **10** breastwork, stronghold

bat 3 hit, rod **4** cane, clip, club, cuff, mace, slug, sock **5** baton, billy, knock, smack, staff, stick, whack **6** buffet, cudgel, mallet, strike, thwack, wallop **7** clobber **8** bludgeon **9** blackjack, truncheon **10** shillelagh

batch 3 lot **5** bunch, crowd, group, stock **6** amount, number **8** quantity **9** aggregate **10** collection

Bates, Alan
born: **7** England **9** Allestree **10** Derbyshire
roles: **6** Hamlet **8** The Fixer **10** Duet for One, Georgy Girl **12** King of Hearts **13** A Kind of Loving, The Collection, Zorba the Greek **16** An Unmarried Woman **18** An Englishman Abroad, A Prayer for the Dying **22** Far From the Madding Crowd

Bates, Kathy
born: **7** Memphis
roles: **6** Misery **7** Titanic **10** Diabolique, Used People **12** The Late Shift, Men Don't Leave **18** Fried Green Tomatoes

Bates, Miss
character in: **4** Emma
author: **6** Austen

Bateson, William
field: **7** biology
nationality: **7** British
founded: **8** genetics

bath 3 dip, tub **4** wash **5** sauna **6** douche, shower **7** washing **8** ablution, lavement **9** cleansing, immersion, steam bath **10** irrigation
type: **3** hip, mud **4** sitz **5** steam **6** shower, sponge **7** Turkish bath

bathe 3 dip, tub, wet **4** lave, soak, wash **5** douse **6** douche, shower, sponge **7** cleanse **8** irrigate

bathing 3 dip, tub **6** laving, plunge **7** washing **8** swimming **9** ablutions, immersion

bathos 4 corn, mush **5** slush **8** schmaltz **9** mushiness, soppiness **10** maudlinism, slushiness **11** false pathos, mawkishness **14** sentimentalism, sentimentality

bathroom 2 W C **3** can, loo **4** head, john **5** biffy **6** toilet **7** commode, latrine **8** facility, lavatory, men's room, restroom, washroom **10** ladies' room, powder room **11** water closet **14** little boys' room **15** little girls' room

Bathsheba
also: **8** Bathshua
father: **5** Eliam
husband: **5** David, Uriah
son: **7** Solomon
grandfather: **10** Ahithophel

Batman
character: **6** Alfred **7** Egghead, King Tut **8** Catwoman, The Joker **10** Bruce Wayne (Batman), Chief O'Hara, The Penguin, The Riddler **11** Dick Grayson (Robin) **13** Barbara Gordon (Batgirl) **17** Aunt Harriet Cooper **24** Police Commissioner Gordon
cast: **8** Adam West, Burt Ward **9** John Astin **10** Alan Napier, Eartha Kitt, Madge Blake **11** Cesar Romero, Julie Newmar, Victor Buono, Yvonne

Craig **12** Frank Gorshin, Neil Hamilton, Stafford Repp, Vincent Price **13** Lee Meriwether **15** Burgess Meredith
city: **10** Gotham City
nickname: **9** Boy Wonder **10** Dynamic Duo **13** Caped Crusader
gimmick: **6** Batlab **8** Batphone **9** Batmobile, Batsignal

Bat Masterson
cast: **9** Gene Barry

baton 3 bat, rod **4** club, mace, wand **5** billy, crook, staff, stick **6** cudgel, fasces **7** crosier, scepter, war club **8** bludgeon, caduceus **9** billy club, truncheon **10** nightstick, shillelagh

batter 4 beat, lash, maul **5** break, crush, pound, smash, smite **6** beat up, buffet, mangle, pummel **7** clobber, shatter

battercake 6 waffle **7** biscuit, pancake

battered 4 shot **6** beat-up, ruined, shabby **8** decrepit **11** dilapidated **12** disreputable

battery 3 set **4** army, band, pack, team **5** block, cadre, force, group, suite, troop **6** caning, cannon, convoy, legion, lineup, outfit, series **7** beating, brigade, company, hitting, hurting, maiming, phalanx, section **8** armament, cannonry, clubbing, division, drubbing, flogging, ordnance, squadron, whipping, wounding **9** cudgeling, spearhead, strapping, thrashing

battle 3 war **4** bout, duel, feud, fray, meet **5** argue, brawl, clash, fight, siege **6** action, affray, combat, debate, engage, tussle **7** contend, contest, crusade, dispute, quarrel, warfare **8** campaign, conflict, skirmish, struggle **9** agitation, encounter, firefight **10** engagement **11** altercation, controversy **13** confrontation

Battle, final
place: **10** Armageddon

battle cry 6 war cry **8** Geronimo, war whoop **9** Rebel yell

Battle Cry
author: **8** Leon Uris

battlefield 5 arena, lists **8** the front, war arena **9** front line **10** battle line, no man's land **11** battlefront **12** battleground

battleground 5 arena, lists **11** battlefield, battlefront

Battle of the Books
author: **13** Jonathan Swift

battle-ready 5 armed **7** arrayed **8** prepared **9** fortified

battleship 4 Iowa **5** Maine **6** Oregon **7** carrier, warship **8** Missouri **9** Ironsides, New Jersey, Wisconsin **10** bluish-gray **11** Dreadnought **12** Constitution
first: **7** Gloire
largest: **6** Yamato
German: **8** Graf Spee

Battus
 ruler of: 5 Libya
 form: 7 peasant
 witness to: 11 cattle theft
 thief: 6 Hermes
 turned to: 5 stone
 cured of: 16 speech impediment

batty 4 nuts **5** crazy, loony, queer, wacko, wacky **6** cuckoo, crazed **7** bat-like, cracked

bauble 3 toy **4** bead **6** geegaw, trifle **7** trinket **8** gimcrack, ornament

Baucis
 form: 7 peasant
 home: 7 Phrygia
 husband: 8 Philemon
 offered hospitality to: 4 Zeus **6** Hermes

Baudelaire, Charles
 author of: 13 Flowers of Evil **14** Les Fleurs du Mal

Baugh, Sammy
 nickname: 13 Slinging Sammy
 sport: 8 football
 position: 11 quarterback
 team: 18 Washington Redskins

Baum, Lyman Frank
 author of: 13 The (Wonderful) Wizard of Oz **18** Father Goose His Book, Mother Goose in Prose

Baum, Vicki
 author of: 8 Shanghai **10** Grand Hotel, Grand Opera **12** Men Never Know **13** A Tale from Bali, And Life Goes On

Baumer, Paul
 character in: 25 All Quiet on the Western Front
 author: 8 Remarque

Baumgarner, James
 real name of: 11 James Garner

bawdy 4 blue, lewd, sexy **5** dirty, gross, lusty **6** coarse, earthy, ribald, risque, sexual, vulgar **7** raunchy **8** immodest, improper, indecent, off-color **10** indecorous, indelicate, licentious, suggestive

bawdy house 7 brothel **8** bordello, cathouse **10** fancy house, whorehouse **13** sporting house **14** house of ill fame **16** house of ill repute **19** house of prostitution

bawl 3 cry **4** call, howl, roar, wail, weep, yell, yowl **5** shout **6** bellow, clamor, cry out, squall **7** blubber, call out

bawling out 6 rebuke **7** censure, chiding, reproof **8** reproach, scolding **9** reprimand **10** chewing out, upbraiding **11** castigation, reprobation **12** dressing-down, remonstrance **13** tongue-lashing

bawl out 5 scold **6** berate, rail at, rebuke, yell at **7** censure, chew out, reprove, upbraid **8** admonish, reproach **9** castigate, dress down, reprimand **10** take to task, tongue-lash **14** read the riot act

Bax, Arnold Edward Trevor
 born: 6 London **7** England
 composer of: 8 Tintagel **13** November Woods **14** Mater Ora Filium **15** The Garden of Fand **27** Overture to a Picaresque Comedy

Baxter, Anne
 grandfather: 16 Frank Lloyd Wright
 born: 14 Michigan City IN
 roles: 8 Applause **11** All About Eve **13** The Razor's Edge

Baxter, Jody
 character in: 11 The Yearling
 author: 8 Rawlings

Baxter, William Sylvanus
 character in: 9 Seventeen
 author: 10 Tarkington

bay 3 cry, yap **4** bank, bark, cove, gulf, howl, nook, road, yelp **5** basin, bayou, bight, fiord, firth, inlet, niche, sound **6** alcove, bellow, clamor, lagoon, recess, strait **7** barking, estuary, howling, narrows, yapping, yelling, yelping **9** bellowing **11** compartment **13** natural harbor

bay (at bay) 7 trapped **8** cornered

bay leaf
 botanical name: 12 Pimenta acris
 expression: 16 to win one's laurels
 from tree: 9 bay laurel
  transformation of: 6 Daphne
  tree sacred to: 6 Apollo
  laurel berries called: 10 bacca lauri
  source of: 13 baccalaureate
 gives gift of: 8 prophecy
 helps girls win back: 12 errant lovers
 origin: 5 Italy
 protects against: 5 death **6** poison **7** sorcery **11** evil spirits
 symbol of: 7 victory (laurel wreath)
 use: 4 fish, fowl, meat, soup, stew

bayou 4 slew **5** creek, inlet, marsh, river, swamp **6** outlet, slough, stream **9** backwater **13** stagnant marsh

Bayou State
 nickname of: 9 Louisiana **11** Mississippi

Bay Psalm Book
 author: 9 John Eliot

Bay State
 nickname of: 13 Massachusetts

bazaar 4 fair, mart **6** market **8** carnival, exchange **11** charity fair, charity sale, marketplace

Bazile
 character in: 18 The Barber of Seville
 author: 12 Beaumarchais

Bazzard, Deputy
 character in: 22 The Mystery of Edwin Drood
 author: 7 Dickens

BC *see* **12** before Christ

B C

creator: 10 Johnny Hart
 character: 3 Tor **4** Grog **5** Peter **8** anteater **10** Clumsy Carp **11** the Fat Broad
 poet: 5 Wiley
 era: 11 Neanderthal, prehistoric

BCE 15 before Common Era

be 4 last, live, stay **5** exist, occur **6** befall, endure, happen, remain **7** persist, subsist **8** continue **9** be present, take place **10** come to pass

be absent 4 miss **12** fail to attend

beach 4 coast, shore **6** strand **8** littoral, seashore **10** water's edge

Beach, Rex
 author of: 6 The Net **7** Oh Shoot **8** Pardners **9** Going Some **10** Jungle Gold, The Barrier **11** Don Careless, The Spoilers **12** Son of the Gods The Goose Woman, The Ne'er-do-well **15** The Auction Block **17** Alaskan Adventures

beached 7 aground **8** grounded, stranded **11** shipwrecked **12** washed ashore

beacon 4 beam **5** light **6** pharos, signal **7** seamark **8** bale-fire, landmark **9** watch fire **10** lighthouse, watchtower **11** lighted buoy

bead 3 dot **4** blob, drop, pill **5** speck **6** bubble, pellet **7** droplet, globule **8** particle, spherule

be adequate 2 do **6** answer **8** be enough **10** pass muster **12** be sufficient, do well enough **14** be satisfactory

be afraid of 4 fear **5** dread **7** cower at **8** cringe at **10** shrink from

beak 3 neb, tip **4** bill, nose, pike, prow **5** lorum, snout, spout **7** process, rostrum, snozzle **8** hooknose **9** headmaster, proboscis **10** magistrate

beaker 3 cup **5** glass **6** vessel **9** container

beam 3 ray **4** emit, glow, prop, spar, stud **5** brace, glare, gleam, glint, joist, shine, width **6** girder, rafter, streak, stream, timber **7** breadth, expanse, glimmer, glitter, radiate, trestle **8** transmit **9** broadcast, radiation

bean 9 Phaseolus
 varieties: 3 goa, pea, soy, wax, yam **4** fava, jack, lima, moth, mung, rice, seim, snap, soja, soya, tick, wild **5** azuki, black, broad, civet, coral, field, green, horse, lubia, pinto, salad, screw, sewee, sieva, snail, sword, tonka **6** butter, castor, common, French, Indian, kaffir, kidney, lablab, locust, manila, mescal, nicker, potato, romano, runner, sacred, string, tepary, velvet, winged, wonder **7** cluster, English, sarawak, Windsor **8** Bovanist, Bush lima, Carolina, Cherokee, European, Egyptian, hyacinth, yard-long **9** algarroba, asparagus, bonavista, dwarf lima, Java

glory **10** dwarf sieva, giant stock, Hottentot's **12** Italian queen, scarlet flame **13** African locust, Florida velvet, Scarlet runner **14** Dutch caseknife **16** white Dutch runner
bean curd: 4 tofu
be a party to 3 aid **4** abet **7** support **9** connive in **11** cooperate in **13** be accessory to, participate in
be apparent 6 appear **7** be clear, be plain **8** be patent **9** be evident, be obvious **10** be manifest
bear 4 bend, drop, give, haul, have, lead, push, show, take, tend, tote, turn, wear **5** abide, admit, allow, apply, brace, brave, bring, brook, carry, curve, drive, force, hatch, press, refer, spawn, stand, whelp, yield **6** affect, aim for, convey, convoy, create, endure, escort, go with, harbor, invite, permit, relate, render, suffer, take on, uphold **7** bolster, cherish, concern, conduct, contain, deliver, develop, deviate, display, diverge, exhibit, pertain, possess, produce, stomach, support, sustain, undergo, warrant **8** bear down, engender, generate, maintain, manifest, shoulder, submit to, tolerate, transfer, underpin **9** accompany, appertain, encourage, germinate, hold close, propagate, put up with, reproduce, touch upon, transport **10** bring forth, keep in mind **11** give birth to, hold up under

bear
combining form: 4 arct, ursi **5** arcto
constellation: 4 ursa **9** ursa major, ursa minor
family: 7 Ursidae
group of: 6 sleuth
kind: 3 sun **5** black, brown, koala, malay, panda, polar, sloth **6** kodiak, wombat **7** grizzly **9** roachback, silvertip **10** spectacled, thalarctos
male: 4 boar
mythological: 8 Callisto
order: 9 carnivora
young: 3 cub
famous: 6 Smokey
beard 4 dare, defy, face, trap **5** brave **6** corner **7** stubble **8** bristles, confront, whiskers **10** bring to bay **16** five- o'clock shadow
bearded 5 bushy, hairy **6** shaggy **7** bristly, hirsute **8** unshaven **9** whiskered **11** bewhiskered
bear down 4 push **5** press **13** apply pressure
bear down upon 6 assail, attack, come at **7** assault **11** descend upon
Beardsley, Aubrey Vincent
born: 7 England **8** Brighton
artwork: 6 Salome **10** Lysistrata **12** Morte d'Arthur
Beard's Roman Women
author: 14 Anthony Burgess
bearer 5 Atlas **6** holder, porter **7** car-

rier **8** conveyer, producer **9** messenger **13** beast of burden **16** one holding a check
Spanish: 8 escudero, portador
bear fruit 4 bear **6** mature **7** develop, prosper **8** fructify
bearing 3 air **4** mien, port **5** sense **6** import, manner **7** concern, meaning **8** attitude, behavior, breeding, carriage, demeanor, presence, relation **9** producing, reference, relevance **10** conception, connection, deportment, importance, pertinence **11** application, association, comportment, germination, giving birth, procreation, propagation, reproducing **12** relationship, reproduction, significance **13** applicability
bearing no name 7 unnamed **8** unsigned **9** anonymous
bearings 3 way **6** course **8** position **9** direction **11** orientation **16** sense of direction
bearish 5 cross, gruff, surly, testy **6** crusty, sullen **7** brusque, crabbed, grouchy **8** churlish **9** crotchety, irascible **10** ill-humored, out of sorts **11** ill-tempered, pessimistic **12** cantankerous
bear off 5 seize, steal **6** abduct, convey, kidnap
bear out 5 prove **6** verify **7** confirm **11** corroborate **12** substantiate
Bear State
nickname of: 8 Arkansas
bear up under 4 bear, take **5** abide, brave, brook, stand **6** endure, suffer **7** stomach, undergo, weather **9** go through, withstand
bear witness 4 back **6** attest **7** confirm, testify **11** corroborate, demonstrate **12** give evidence, substantiate
beast 3 cad, cur, pig, rat **4** ogre **5** brute, swine **6** animal, mammal, savage **8** creature **9** barbarian, quadruped
beastly 3 bad **4** vile **5** awful, cruel, gross, lousy, nasty **6** brutal, coarse, savage **7** bestial, brutish, inhuman, swinish **8** degraded, dreadful, terrible **9** barbarous, loathsome, monstrous **10** abominable, deplorable, disgusting, unpleasant **12** contemptible, disagreeable
beat 3 bat, hit, mix, rap, tap, way **4** area, bang, best, blow, cane, club, drub, flap, flog, flop, lick, maul, path, rout, slap, time, whip, zone **5** clout, count, crush, flail, knock, meter, outdo, pound, pulse, quake, quell, realm, repel, route, shake, smack, smite, strap, throb, whack **6** accent, batter, course, defeat, domain, hammer, master, pummel, quiver, rhythm, rounds, stress, strike, stroke, subdue, switch, thrash, thwack, twitch, wallop **7** cadence, circuit, clobber, conquer, destroy, eclipse,

flutter, pulsate, put down, repulse, scourge, shellac, surpass, trounce, vibrate, win over **8** overcome, vanquish **9** excel over, fluctuate, go pit-a-pat, overpower, palpitate, pulsation, territory **10** win out over **11** predominate, prevail over, triumph over **14** stir vigorously
beat a retreat 6 beat it **7** back off **8** turn tail, withdraw **10** high tail it
beat around the bush 5 dodge, evade, hedge, stall **10** equivocate, mince words
beatific 4 rapt **6** divine, serene **7** angelic, exalted, saintly, sublime **8** blissful, ecstatic, glorious, heavenly **9** rapturous **10** enraptured **14** transcendental
beat it 2 go **3** out **4** away, scat, shoo **5** be off, leave, scram **6** cut out, depart, get out, go away **7** get lost, vamoose **10** hit the road, make tracks
beatitude 5 bliss **7** ecstasy, rapture **8** euphoria, felicity **10** exaltation **11** blessedness, exaltedness, saintliness **13** transcendence **15** transfiguration
Beatles 10 John Lennon, Ringo Starr **13** Paul McCartney **14** George Harrison
Songs: 6 Taxman **7** Hey Jude, Get Back **10** Nowhere Man, Drive My Car, Revolution **12** Come Together, Dear Prudence, Eleanor Rigby, Rocky Raccoon **13** Twist and Shout **14** A Hard Day's Night, Eight Days A Week **23** Strawberry Fields Forever **24** Lucy in the Sky with Diamonds
albums: 4 Help **7** Hey Jude, Let It Be **8** Revolver **9** Abbey Road **10** Rubber Soul, White Album **14** A Hard Day's Night, Meet the Beatles **15** Yellow Submarine **17** Yesterday...and Today **18** Magical Mystery Tour **30** Sgt. Pepper's Lonely Hearts Club Band
be at loggerheads 5 clash **7** quarrel **8** disagree
be at odds 6 differ **7** dispute, diverge **8** conflict, disagree
beat rhythmically 3 rap, tap **4** drum **6** tattoo **7** pulsate
Beatrice
character in: 12 Divine Comedy
author: 5 Dante
Beatrice
character in: 19 Much Ado About Nothing
author: 11 Shakespeare
Beatrice et Benedict
opera by: 7 Berlioz
Beat the Clock
host: 10 Bud Collyer
Beattie, Ann
author of: 11 Distortions **14** Falling in Place **15** The Burning House **19** Secrets and Surprises **20** Chilly Scenes of Winter

Beatty, Ned
  born: **10** Louisville
  roles: **3** Spy **4** Rudy **9** The Affair **10** The Big Easy, Black Water, Hear My Song **11** Deliverance **14** Prelude to a Kiss

Beatty, Warren
  real name: **11** Warren Beaty
  sister: **15** Shirley MacLaine
  born: **10** Richmond VA
  wife: **13** Annette Bening
  roles: **4** Reds **5** Bugsy **6** Ishtar **8** Bulworth **9** Dick Tracy **10** Love Affair **11** All Fall Down **13** Heaven Can Wait **14** Bonnie and Clyde **18** Splendor in the Grass **24** The Roman Spring of Mrs Stone
  director of: **4** Reds (Oscar) **8** Bulworth

beat up 3 mug **4** lick, maul, whip **6** batter, pummel **7** assault, clobber

beat-up 4 shot **6** shabby **7** worn-out **8** battered **10** broken-down **11** dilapidated

Beaty, Shirley MacLean
  real name of: **15** Shirley MacLaine

Beaty, Warren
  real name of: **12** Warren Beatty

beau, beaux 3 fop, guy, nob **4** buck, dude, love, stud, toff **5** blade, dandy, flame, lover, Romeo, spark, swain, swell, wooer **6** adorer, escort, fellow, fiance, garcon, squire, steady, suitor **7** admirer, beloved, courter, coxcomb, cupidon, Don Juan, gallant, playboy **8** cavalier, courtier, gay blade, Lothario, paramour, popinjay, true love, young man **9** betrothed, boyfriend, courtesan, gentleman, inamorato, ladies' man **10** sweetheart, young blood **15** gentleman caller, gentleman friend
  nickname of: **14** George Brummell

Beauchamp's Career
  author: **14** George Meredith

Beau Geste
  author: **6** P C Wren **15** Christopher Wren
  director: **14** William Wellman
  cast: **10** Gary Cooper, Ray Milland **12** Brian Donlevy, Susan Hayward **13** Robert Preston
    silent version starred: **12** Ronald Colman
  setting: **19** French Foreign Legion

Beaumarchais, Pierre Augustin Caron de
  author of: **18** The Barber of Seville **19** The Marriage of Figaro

beau monde 5 elite **6** gentry **7** society **10** upper class, upper crust **11** aristocracy, high society **15** beautiful people

Beaumont, Ned
  character in: **11** The Glass Key
  author: **7** Hammett

Beauregard, P G T (Pierre Gustave Toutant)
  served in: **8** Civil War
  side: **11** Confederate
  rank: **7** general
  ordered firing on: **8** Ft Sumter
  battle: **7** Bull Run

beaut 4 lulu, oner **5** daisy, dandy **6** beauty **7** stunner **8** knockout **10** good-looker

beautification 9 adornment **10** decoration **13** embellishment, ornamentation

beautiful 4 fair, fine **5** bonny, great **6** comely, lovely, pretty, seemly, superb, worthy **7** radiant **8** alluring, gorgeous, handsome, pleasing, splendid, very good **9** admirable, beauteous, enjoyable, estimable, excellent, exquisite, first-rate, ravishing, wonderful **10** attractive, stupendous **11** captivating, commendable, fine-looking, good-looking, resplendent **15** pulchritudinous

beautify 4 do up **5** adorn, grace **7** dress up, enhance, gussy up, improve **8** ornament **9** embellish, glamorize

beauty 4 boon, doll **5** asset, beaut, belle, grace, Venus **6** eyeful, looker **7** benefit, feature, goddess, stunner **8** knockout, radiance, splendor **9** advantage, good looks, good thing **10** attraction, excellence, good-looker, loveliness **11** pulchritude **12** handsomeness, magnificence, resplendence **14** attractiveness
  goddess of: **6** Graces **7** Gratiae **9** Aphrodite, Charities
  god of: **5** Baldr **6** Apollo, Balder, Baldur **7** Angus Og, Phoebus, Pythias **9** Musagetes

Beauvoir, Simone de
  author of: **12** The Mandarins, The Second Sex **14** A Very Easy Death, All Said and Done, The Coming of Age, The Prime of Life **17** Ethics of Ambiguity **22** The Force of Circumstance **25** Memoirs of a Dutiful Daughter **34** Brigitte Bardot and the Lolita Syndrome

beaver
  young: **3** kit

Beaver State
  nickname of: **6** Oregon

be blessed with 3 own **4** have **5** enjoy **7** possess **16** have the benefit of

because 2 so **3** for **4** that, then, thus **5** cause, hence, since **6** whence **7** whereas **8** inasmuch **9** therefore **10** seeing that **11** considering

Bechuanaland
  now called: **8** Botswana

Bechuanland see **8** Botswana

beck 3 bid **4** call **7** bidding, summons **9** summoning

Becket
  author: **11** Jean Anouilh **18** Alfred Lord Tennyson
  director: **14** Peter Glenville
  cast: **11** John Gielgud, Peter O'Toole (King Henry II) **13** Richard Burton (Becket)

Beckett, Samuel
  author of: **4** Not I, Play, Watt **6** Embers, Molloy **7** Endgame **8** That Time **9** Footfalls, Happy Days **10** Malone Dies **11** All that Fall, The Lost Ones **13** The Unnameable **15** Waiting for Godot **16** Mercier and Camier **20** Murphy Krapp's Last Tape **25** Stories and Texts for Nothing

Beckmann, Max
  born: **7** Germany, Leipzig
  artwork: **6** Kasbek **7** Perseus **8** Acrobats, The Night **9** The Actors **11** View of Genoa **12** Charnel House, The Argonauts, The Departure **13** Blindman's Buff, Family Picture **14** Double Portrait **17** David and Bathsheba **18** Odysseus and Calypso **19** Sinking of the Titanic **20** Destruction of Messina **22** The Descent from the Cross

beckon 4 call, coax, draw, lure, pull **6** allure, entice, invite, motion, signal, summon, wave at, wave on **7** attract, gesture **11** gesticulate **14** crook a finger at

be clear 6 appear **7** be plain **8** be patent **9** be evident, be obvious **10** be apparent, be manifest

becloud 3 fog **4** blur, hide, veil **5** befog, cloud **6** muddle, screen, shroud **7** confuse, cover up, eclipse, obscure **8** confound, make hazy, overcast **9** obfuscate **10** camouflage, overshadow **14** make indistinct

become 3 get **4** grow, suit, turn **6** go with **7** enhance, flatter, get to be **8** come to be **9** agree with, begin to be **10** complement **11** be reduced to, turn out to be

become apparent 4 dawn, loom **5** arise **6** appear, crop up, emerge, turn up **7** develop, surface

become bigger 4 grow **5** swell **6** expand **7** develop, enlarge, inflate **8** increase

become irrational 5 break, crack **7** crack up **9** break down, fall apart, go berserk **10** go to pieces **11** lose control **12** lose one's mind

become one 3 wed **4** fuse **5** blend, marry, merge, unite **7** combine **8** coalesce **10** amalgamate **11** consolidate

become seasoned to 5 adapt, inure **6** adjust **8** accustom **9** acclimate, get used to, habituate **15** learn to live with

become smaller 6 lessen, shrink **7** decline, dwindle, shrivel **8** decrease, diminish

become visible 4 loom, show **6** appear, crop up, emerge, show up, turn up **7** surface **11** come to light **12** come into view

becoming 3 apt, fit **4** meet **6** pretty, proper, seemly, worthy **7** fitting **8** suitable **9** befitting, congenial, congruous, enhancing, in keeping **10** attractive, compatible, consistent, flattering, harmonious **11** appropriate, good-looking

Becquerel, Antoine Henri
  field: 7 physics
  nationality: 6 French
  discovered: 13 radioactivity
  awarded: 10 Nobel Prize

bed 3 cot, hay **4** band, bank, base, belt, bunk, crib, lode, plot, sack, seam, zone **5** berth, floor, layer, patch **6** bottom, cradle, pallet **7** deposit, stratum **8** bedstead **10** foundation

bedazzle 4 daze **6** dazzle **7** astound, confuse, enchant, fluster, nonplus, stagger, stupefy **8** befuddle, bewilder, confound, dumfound **9** captivate, overpower, overwhelm **10** disconcert **11** flabbergast **19** sweep one off one's feet

bed chamber 7 bedroom, boudoir

bed down 5 sleep **7** lie down, sack out **8** doss down **10** hit the hay, settle down **11** accommodate, hit the sack

bedeck 4 deck, trim **5** adorn, array **7** garnish **8** decorate, ornament **9** embellish

be deficient in 4 fail, lack, want **7** be scant **9** be short of **10** have too few

be deprived of 4 lack, lose, want

be deserving of 4 earn, rate **5** merit **7** deserve **10** be worthy of **12** be entitled to

bedevil 3 dog **5** annoy, hound, worry **6** badger, harass, pester, plague **9** beleaguer

be devoted to 4 love **5** adore **6** dote on **7** cherish **8** be fond of

bedim 4 blur **6** darken **7** obscure

Bedivere
  character in: 16 Arthurian romance

bedizen 5 adorn, array **6** bedeck, rig out **7** bejewel, costume

bedlam 5 chaos **6** tumult, uproar **7** turmoil **8** madhouse **11** pandemonium

bed of justice
  French: 12 lit de justice

Bedouin, Beduin
  also: 4 Absi, Arab **5** nomad **7** bedawee
  Arabic: 6 badawi
    means: 13 desert dweller
  found in: 5 Egypt, Syria **6** Arabia **11** North Africa
  religion: 5 Islam

bedraggled 4 limp **5** dirty, dowdy, messy, seedy, soggy, tacky, tatty **6** blowsy, frowsy, frumpy, matted, ragtag, sloppy, soiled, untidy **7** unkempt **8** frumpish, sluttish, tattered **10** disarrayed, disordered, disheveled, slatternly, threadbare **11** disarranged **13**

draggletailed 14 down-at-the-heels, out-at-the-elbows

bedridden 7 invalid **8** disabled, immobile **13** incapacitated

bedroom 7 boudoir, chamber **10** bedchamber

bedspread 5 quilt **8** bedcover, coverlet **9** comforter

bedstead 3 bed **8** bed frame **10** four poster

bee
  caste: 5 drone, queen **6** worker
  classification: 6 social **8** solitary
  communication: 13 dance language
  family: 6 Apidae **7** Apoidea **8** Bombidae **10** Andrenidae, Halictidae **11** Meliponidae, Xylocopidae **12** Megachilidae
  group of: 5 grist, swarm
  order: 11 Hymenoptera
  scent: 10 pheromones
  variety: 5 mason, miner **6** alkali, cuckoo **8** burrower, honeybee **9** bumblebee, carpenter, plasterer **10** leaf-cutter **11** yellow-faced

beech 5 Fagus
  varieties: 4 Blue **5** Water **6** Copper, Purple **7** Cut-leaf, Weeping **8** American, European, Fern-leaf, Japanese

Beedle, William Franklin, Jr,
  real name of: 13 William Holden

beef 4 heft, kick, meat **5** brawn, gripe, steer **6** cattle, grouch, grouse **7** grumble **8** complain **9** bellyache, complaint, criticize, find fault

Beef State
  nickname of: 8 Nebraska

beefy 5 bulky, burly, hefty **6** brawny, robust **8** thickset **9** strapping

beehive 4 hive **6** apiary **9** busy place **10** powerhouse

Beehive State
  nickname of: 4 Utah

Beekeeping
  god of: 9 Aristaeus

Beelzebub
  character in: 12 Paradise Lost
  author: 6 Milton

be enough 2 do **6** answer **7** suffice

be entitled to 4 rate **5** merit **7** deserve **10** be worthy of **13** be deserving of

beer 3 ale, keg, mum **4** bier, bock, brew, dark, faro, flip, gail, grog, gyle, hops, kvas, malt, mild, quas, scud, suds **5** chang, chica, draft, grout, kvass, lager, light, quass, scuds, stout, weiss **6** bitter, chicha, double, gatter, porter, spruce, stingo, swanky, swipes, wallop, zythum **7** bottled, cerveza, pangasi, pharaoh, Pilsner, tankard, taplash, tapwort **8** bock beer, cervisia, near beer, pilsener **9** microbrew **10** malt liquor
  add to beer: 7 krausen
  bad/inferior beer: 4 tack **5** belch **6**

swanky **7** taplash
  brand: 3 Bud **5** Beck's, Coors, Pabst, Piels **6** Corona, Miller, Molson, Stroh's **7** Schlitz **8** Bud Light, Michelob **9** Budweiser, Lowenbrau **10** Miller Lite, Molson Gold **11** Samuel Adams **13** Guinness Stout **14** Pete's Wicked Ale **15** Pabst Blue Ribbon
  cask: 4 butt
  cup: 3 mug **4** toby **5** glass, stein **6** flagon, seidel **7** tankard **8** schooner **9** blackjack
  hot beer and gin: 4 purl
  ingredient: 4 hops, malt **5** yeast **6** barley
  maker: 6 brewer **8** brewster, maltster
  mythological inventor: 9 Gambrinus
  quantity of: 3 keg **4** case **7** six-pack
  small beer: 4 tiff **5** grout
  sour beer: 4 kuas, kvas **5** quash, quass **8** beeregar
  thin beer: 6 pritch, swipes
  Tibetan beer: 5 chang
  warm beer and oatmeal: 6 storry
  with whiskey: 11 Boilermaker

beer-bust 4 toot **5** binge, drunk, spree **6** bender **8** carousal **9** bacchanal

Beery, Noah
  brother: 7 Wallace
  son: 6 Noah Jr
  born: 12 Kansas City MO
  roles: 7 Lord Jim, The Dove **9** Beau Geste **10** The Sea Wolf **14** The Mark of Zorro

Beery, Wallace
  brother: 4 Noah
  nephew: 6 Noah Jr
  wife: 13 Gloria Swanson
  born: 12 Kansas City MO
  roles: 8 The Champ (Oscar) **9** The Bowery, Viva Villa **10** Grand Hotel **11** The Big House **13** Dinner at Eight **14** Treasure Island **15** The Mighty Barnum **16** A Message to Garcia

beet 12 Beta vulgaris
  varieties: 3 Red, Sea **4** Leaf, Wild **5** Sugar **6** Garden, Yellow **7** Spinach
  base for: 6 borsch **7** borscht

Beethoven, Ludwig van
  born: 4 Bonn **7** Germany
  composer of: 5 Laube (sonata) **6** Egmont, Eroica (symphony no 3), Spring (sonata) **7** Fidelio, Leonore **8** Coriolan, Dramatic (sonata), Kreutzer (sonata), Pastoral (symphony no 6), The Storm **9** Moonlight (sonata), Pastorale (sonata), Waldstein (sonata) **10** Bagatellen, Great Fugue (no 133), Pathetique (sonata), Spirit Trio **11** Grosse Fugue (no 133), Harp Quartet (no 74), Namensfeier **12** Appassionata (sonata), Archduke Trio, Konig Stephan **13** Hammerklavier (sonata), Missa Solemnis **15** Emperor Concerto (No 5) **16** Christus am Olberg, The Mount of Olives, The Ruins of Athens **17** Die Ruinen von Athen, Die Weihe des Hauses **18** An

die ferne Geliebte, Rage over a Lost Penny **20** Rasoumoffsky Quartets (no 59) **24** The Creatures of Prometheus **25** Die Geschopfe des Prometheus

beetle
variety: 3 bog, may, sap **4** bark, bean, flea, leaf, mold, moss, pill, rove, sand, stag **5** cedar, click, flour, grain, marsh, penny, tiger, water **6** beaver, diving, flower, fungus, ground, hister, lizard, scarab, spider, weevil **7** bessbug, blister, burying, carrion, firefly, goldbug, goliath, lady- bug, soldier **8** elephant, glow-worm, hercules, Japanese, ladybird, tortoise **9** ant loving, bombadier, burrowing, checkered, fruitworm, goldsmith, grassroot, scavenger, tumblebug, whirligig **10** deathwatch, false clown, longhorned, mammal nest, shiptimber **11** reticulated, trout stream **12** antlike stone, lightning bug **13** feather winged, horseshoe crab

Beetle Bailey
creator/artist: 9 Dik Browne **10** Mort Walker **12** Bob Gustafson
character: 5 Cosmo, Plato **6** Killer, Lt Flap, Lt Fuzz **10** Miss Buxley **12** Gen Halftrack **17** Sgt Orville Snorkel
chef: 6 Cookie
place: 10 Camp Swampy

be evident 6 appear **7** be clear, be plain **8** be patent **9** be obvious **10** be apparent, be manifest

befall 5 ensue, occur **6** betide, chance, follow, happen **10** come to pass **11** materialize

befitting 3 apt, fit **5** right **6** decent, proper, seemly **8** becoming, relevant, suitable **11** appropriate

be fond of 6 dote on **11** be devoted to **12** be in love with

before 3 ere, yet **5** afore, ahead, prior **6** rather, sooner **7** already, earlier, vis-a-vis **8** erewhile, until now **9** in advance, in front of, in sight of **10** face-to-face, previously

before Christ
abbreviation: 2 BC
alternative: 3 BCE **15** before Common Era
Latin: 2 AC **12** ante Christum

beforehand 6 in time, sooner **7** earlier **9** in advance **11** ahead of time

before now 6 in time, sooner **7** earlier **9** in advance

before the fact 6 in time **9** in advance **10** beforehand **11** ahead of time

before the public
Latin: 11 coram populo

befoul 4 soil **5** dirty, smear, stain, sully, taint **6** defile, poison **7** blacken, corrupt, pollute, tarnish **8** besmirch **9** desecrate **11** contaminate

befriend 4 help **6** assist, defend, suc-

cor, uphold **7** comfort, embrace, help out, protect, stand by, stick by, support, sustain, welcome **8** side with **9** give aid to, look after **10** minister to **11** consort with **13** associate with **14** fraternize with, sympathize with **17** take under one's wing

be friends 7 consort **9** associate, pal around **10** fraternize

befringe 3 hem **4** bind, edge, trim **6** border **7** festoon **8** decorate

befuddle 4 daze **5** addle, mix up **6** baffle, muddle, puzzle, rattle **7** confuse, fluster, perplex, stupefy **8** bewilder, confound, unsettle **9** disorient, inebriate, make drunk, make tipsy **10** intoxicate, make groggy **11** disorganize

beg 3 bum, sue **4** pray, shun **5** avert, avoid, cadge, dodge, evade, mooch, parry, plead, shirk **6** escape, eschew, hustle, sponge **7** beseech, entreat, fend off, implore, solicit **8** appeal to, petition, sidestep **9** importune, panhandle **10** supplicate

beg, bey 4 lord **6** prince **8** governor

beget 3 get **4** sire **5** breed, cause, spawn **6** effect, father, lead to **7** produce **8** engender, generate, occasion, result in **9** call forth, procreate, propagate **10** bring about, give rise to

begetter 4 sire **6** father **7** creator **9** generator **10** progenitor

beggar 3 bum, guy **4** chap **5** devil, tramp **6** baffle, fellow **7** almsman, moocher, sponger, surpass **8** be beyond **9** challenge, mendicant **10** panhandler

Beggar 7 Lazarus

Beggar's Opera, The
author: 7 John Gay
form: 11 ballad opera
character: 6 Lockit **10** Lucy Lockit **12** Polly Peachum **15** Captain Macheath

begin 5 arise, found, start **6** be born, crop up, emerge, launch, set out **8** break out, commence, embark on, initiate **9** establish, institute, introduce, originate, undertake **10** burst forth, inaugurate **11** set in motion **16** take the first step

beginner 4 babe, tyro **6** author, father, novice, rookie **7** creator, founder, learner, starter, student **8** freshman, neophyte **9** fledgling, greenhorn, initiator, organizer **10** apprentice, originator, prime mover, tenderfoot **11** inaugurator **14** babe in the woods

beginning 3 new **4** germ, seed **5** birth, onset, start **6** embryo, novice, origin, outset, source, spring **7** kickoff, student, untried **8** neophyte, zero hour **9** embryonic, inception, incipient, launching **10** foundation, wellspring **11** preliminary, springboard **12** commencement, fountainhead, inauguration, introduction **13** inexperi-

enced, starting point
Latin: 12 terminus a quo

Beginning of Wisdom, The
author: 19 Stephen Vincent Benet

Beginnings
god of: 5 Janus

begone 3 out **4** away, scat, shoo **5** be off, leave, scram **6** beat it, depart, get out, go away **7** get lost, vamoose

begonia
varieties: 3 Rex, Wax **4** Fern, King, Star, Wild **5** Hardy, Trout **6** Bamboo, Kidney, Shrimp, Winter, Zigzag **7** Bedding, Dewdrop, Elm-leaf, Eyelash, Fuchsia, Leopard, Lily-pad, Swedish **8** Climbing, Fern-leaf, Fire-king, Lorraine, Palm-leaf, Pond-lily, Star-leaf, Trailing **9** Alder- leaf, Angel-wing, Beefsteak, Calla-lily, Christmas, Crazy-leaf, Grape-leaf, Grape-vine, Hollyhock, Holly- leaf, Honeybear, Iron-cross, Maple-leaf, Miniature, Pennywort, Trout-leaf, Whirlpool **10** Bronze-leaf, Castorbean, Finger-leaf, Guinea-wing, Seersucker, Strawberry **11** Fairy-carpet, Lettuce-leaf, Painted-leaf **12** Blooming-fool, Elephant's Ear, Metallic-leaf **13** Peanut-brittle **14** Hybrid tuberous, Nasturtium-leaf, Youth-and-old-age **15** Winter-flowering **16** Manda's woolly-bear, Philodendron-leaf **17** Miniature pond-lily **18** Trailing watermelon

beg pardon 6 excuse **9** apologize **13** express regret, say one is sorry

be grateful 9 be obliged **10** appreciate, be beholden, be thankful **11** be obligated

begrime 4 soil **5** dirty, muddy, smear, stain, sully **6** smudge, soot up **7** besmear, tarnish

begrimed 5 dirty, grimy, muddy **6** filthy, grubby, soiled **7** unclean **8** unwashed **9** tarnished

begrudge 4 envy **5** covet **6** grudge, resent **11** be jealous of, hold against

beguile 4 dupe, hoax, lull, lure **5** amuse, charm, cheat, cheer, trick **6** delude, divert, occupy, please **7** bewitch, deceive, enchant, ensnare **8** distract, hoodwink **9** bamboozle, captivate, entertain **10** lead astray

beguiling 7 winning, winsome **8** charming, magnetic **9** appealing, disarming **10** bewitching, entrancing **11** captivating **12** ingratiating, irresistible

behalf 3 aid, for **4** part, side **5** favor **7** benefit, by proxy, defense, in aid of, support **8** interest

Behan, Brendan
author of: 10 Borstal Boy, The Hostage **12** The Scarperer **14** The Quare Fellow **25** Confessions of an Irish Rebel

be handed down 4 pass **7** descend **11** be inherited

behave 3 act 13 acquit oneself, deport oneself 14 comport oneself, conduct oneself, control oneself

behavior 4 acts 5 deeds 6 action, habits, manner 7 actions, bearing, conduct, control 8 activity, attitude, demeanor, practice, reaction, response 9 operation 10 deportment 11 comportment, functioning, performance, self-control

behead 9 decollate 10 decapitate, guillotine 15 bring to the block

behest 4 fiat 5 edict, order, say-so 6 charge, decree, ruling 7 bidding, command, dictate, mandate 9 direction, ultimatum 10 injunction 11 instruction

behind 4 rump, seat, slow 5 abaft, after, fanny 8 backward, buttocks, in back of 9 fundament, in arrears 11 to the rear of 12 hindquarters

behind closed doors 7 sub rosa 8 in secret, secretly 9 in private, privately

behindhand 4 late, slow 5 tardy 7 belated 8 backward 10 unpunctual

behind the times 5 passe 7 archaic 9 out-of-date 10 antiquated 12 old-fashioned

behind time 4 late, slow 5 tardy 7 belated, delayed 12 after the fact

behold 3 see 4 heed, look, mark, note, scan, view 5 watch 6 attend, gaze at, look at, notice, regard, survey 7 discern, examine, inspect, observe, stare at, witness 8 look upon 10 scrutinize 11 contemplate 12 pay attention

beholden 5 bound 6 liable 7 obliged 8 indebted 9 obligated 10 answerable, in one's debt 11 accountable, responsible 15 under obligation

behold the man
Latin: 8 ecce homo
said by: 13 Pontius Pilate
spoken of: 6 Christ

behoove 4 suit 5 be apt, befit 6 become, be wise 7 benefit 8 be proper 9 be fitting 11 be advisable, be necessary 13 be appropriate 14 be advantageous

Behring, Emil Adolph von
field: 12 bacteriology
nationality: 6 German
developed: 19 diphtheria antitoxin
awarded: 10 Nobel Prize

beige 3 tan 4 ecru, fawn 6 greige 8 brownish

be ill 3 ail 6 be sick 8 be unwell 12 be indisposed 13 be in ill health

be in a class with 5 equal, match 6 be up to 7 compare 8 approach 10 be as good as 11 compete with 12 be comparable, be on a par with 13 hold a candle to 14 bear comparison

being 4 core, life, soul 5 human 6 living, mortal, nature, person, psyche, spirit 7 essence, persona, reality 8 creature, existing 9 actuality, existence 10 individual, occurrence 11 subsistence

be inherited 4 pass 7 descend 12 be handed down

be in short supply 4 lack, want 8 be scanty, be scarce 9 fall short

be intemperate 7 carouse, debauch 9 dissipate 11 overindulge

be in tune 4 jibe 5 agree, match, tally 6 accord, square 7 conform 9 harmonize

Beirut, Beyrouth
capital of: 7 Lebanon
Phoenician name: 7 Berytus
sea: 13 Mediterranean
settled by: 11 Phoenicians
square: 15 Place des Martyrs

be jealous of 4 envy 6 resent 8 begrudge

Bekesy, Georg von
field: 7 physics
researched: 3 ear 7 cochlea, hearing
awarded: 10 Nobel Prize

Bel 3 god 5 deity

belabor 6 rehash, repeat 7 dwell on 9 reiterate 11 pound away at 12 hammer away at, recapitulate 14 beat a dead horse, go on and on about

Bel-Ami
author: 15 Guy de Maupassant

Belarus
other name: 10 Belorussia 11 Byelorussia, White Russia
capital/largest city: 5 Minsk
head of state: 9 president
government: 8 republic
monetary unit: 5 ruble
river: 5 Dvina 7 Dnieper
physical feature: 13 Pripet Marshes
people: 12 Byelorussian

Belasco, David
author of: 7 DuBarry 15 Madame Butterfly 21 The Return of Peter Grimm 22 The Girl of the Golden West

belated 4 late, slow 5 tardy 6 behind 7 delayed, overdue, past due 8 deferred 10 behindhand, behind time, unpunctual 12 after the fact

belch 4 burp, emit, gush, spew, vent 5 eject, eruct, erupt, expel, issue, spout, spurt, vomit 7 cough up, issuing 8 disgorge, ejection, emission, eruption 9 discharge, roar forth, send forth 10 eructation

Belch, Sir Toby
character in: 12 Twelfth Night
author: 11 Shakespeare

beleaguer 3 vex 5 annoy 6 assail, badger, bother, harass, hector, pester, plague 7 besiege, bombard 8 blockade, surround

bel-esprit 3 wit 12 intellectual

belfry 4 dome 5 spire 7 steeple 9 bell tower, campanile

Belgian Congo see 5 Congo

Belgium
other name: 13 Gallia Belgica 15 Cockpit of Europe 16 Koninkrijk Belgie 17 Royaume de Belgique
capital/largest city: 8 Brussels 9 Bruxelles
others: 2 As 3 Aat, Ans, Ath, Hal, Huy, Mol, Spa 4 Aath, Amay, Asse, Boom, Bree, Doel, Gaud, Geel, Genk, Gent, Hoei, Lier, Looz, Mons, Vise, Waha, Zele 5 Aalst, Alost, Arlon, Ciney, Ecklo, Essen, Eupen, Evere, Genck, Ghent, Heist, Ieper, Jette, Jumet, Liege, Namur, Ronse, Tielt, Uccle, Vorst, Wezet, Ynoir, Ypres 6 Aarlen, Anvers, Bergen, Bilzen, Bruges, Deurne, Izegem, Leuven, Lierre, Merxem, Opwijk, Ostend 7 Antwerp, Ardooie, Berchem, Brabant, Hainaut, Herstal, Hoboken, Ixelles, Leliven, Limburg, Louvain, Malmedy, Mechlin, Roulers, Seraing, Tournai 8 Bastogne, Courtrai, Doorwick, Flanders, Kortrijk, Mouscron, Turnhout, Verviers, Waterloo 9 Antwerpen, Charleroi 10 Anderlecht, Borgerhout, Luxembourg, Quatrebras, Schaerbeek
school: 7 Louvain
division: 5 Liege, Namur 7 Antwerp, Brabant, Hainaut, Limburg 8 Flanders, Wallonia
head of state: 4 king
measure: 3 vat 4 aune, pied 5 carat 6 perche 8 boisseau
monetary unit: 5 belga, franc 7 brabant, centime, crocard
weight: 4 last 5 carat, livre 6 charge 7 chariot 8 esterlin
mountain: 8 Ardennes
highest point: 16 Signal de Botrange
river: 3 Lys 4 Dyle, Leie, Maas, Mark, Yser 5 Boucq, Demer, Lesse, Meuse, Nethe, Rupel, Senne 6 Dender, Escaut, Manjel, Ourthe, Sambre, Semois, Vesdre, Warche 7 Ambleve, Schelde, Scheldt
sea: 5 North
physical feature:
canal: 4 Yser 5 Union 6 Albert 7 Campine
cave: 7 Furfooz 8 Grenelle
forest: 8 Ardennes
plateau: 8 Hohevenn
people: 4 Remi 6 Nervii 7 Belgian, Fleming, Flemish 8 Walloons 9 Bellovaci
artist: 5 Ensor 6 Rubens 7 Delvaux, Van Dyke, Van Eyck 8 Brueghal, Magritte
author: 6 Coster 7 Simenon 9 Verhaeren 10 Conscience, Ghelderode 11 Maeterlinck
composer: 6 Franck
king: 6 Albert 7 Leopold 8 Baudouin
leader: 5 Spaak 9 Tindemans
language: 5 Dutch 6 French, German

7 Flemish
religion: 13 Roman Catholic
place:
  battleground: 5 Bulge **8** Waterloo
  breadhouse: 9 Broodhuis
  castle: 5 Steen
  cathedral: 5 Ghent **13** Saint Rombauts
  city hall: 12 Hotel de Ville
  home for elderly women: 9 Beguinage
  museum: 9 Beaux Arts
  palace: 10 Gruuthuuse
features:
  horse: 9 Brabancon
  lace: 5 fichu **6** Bruges **7** Malines, Mechlin **8** Brussels
  lawn bowling: 6 boules
  linen: 7 brabant
  musical instrument: 8 carillon
  religious procession: 9 Holy Blood
  tapestry: 9 oudenarde
food:
  cheese: 9 Limburger
  gingerbread: 12 pain d'espices
  raisin bread: 8 cramique
  soup: 9 Waterzooi
Belgrade, Beograd
  capital of: 10 Yugoslavia
  landmark:
    fortress: 10 Kalemegdan
    parliament house: 9 Skupstina
  name means: 11 white forest
  river: 4 Sava **6** Danube
  Roman fort: 10 Singidinum
  Serbian: 7 Beograd
Belial
  character in: 12 Paradise Lost
  author: 6 Milton
belie 4 defy, deny, mask **5** cloak **6** betray, negate, refute **7** conceal, falsify, gainsay **8** disguise, disprove **9** repudiate **10** camouflage, contradict, controvert, invalidate **12** misrepresent
belief 4 view **5** faith, guess, trust **6** theory **7** feeling, opinion **8** judgment, reliance **9** assurance, certitude, deduction, inference **10** assumption, conclusion, confidence, conviction, firm notion, hypothesis, impression, persuasion **11** expectation, presumption, supposition
beliefs 5 canon, creed, dogma, faith, tenet **6** ethics, gospel, morals **8** doctrine, morality **9** principle, teachings **10** conviction, persuasion
believable 8 credible, knowable, possible **9** plausible, thinkable **10** acceptable, convincing, imaginable, supposable **11** conceivable, perceivable
believe 4 hold **5** guess, infer, judge, think, trust **6** assume, credit, deduce, rely on **7** count on, fall for, imagine, presume, suppose, surmise, suspect, swallow, swear by **8** be sure of, consider, depend on, maintain, theorize **9**

speculate **10** conjecture, presuppose, put faith in **11** hypothesize
believe in 5 trust **6** accept, esteem **7** approve, go in for, respect **11** have faith in **16** have confidence in
Believe It or Not
  author: 13 Robert L Ripley
believer 7 admirer **8** advocate, disciple, partisan **9** supporter **16** faithful adherent
be like 5 equal, match **8** approach, resemble
Bel-Imperia
  character in: 17 The Spanish Tragedy
  author: 3 Kyd
Belinda
  character in: 16 The Rape of the Lock
  author: 4 Pope
belittle 5 knock, scorn **6** deride, malign **7** disdain, put down, run down, sneer at **8** minimize, mitigate, play down, pooh-pooh **9** deprecate, disparage, underrate **10** depreciate, undervalue **11** make light of **13** underestimate **16** cast aspersions on
belittling 5 snide **10** derogatory **11** deprecating, disparaging, unfavorable **12** depreciating **15** uncomplimentary
Belize
  other name: 15 British Honduras
  capital: 8 Belmopan
  largest city/former capital: 10 Belize City
  head of state: 13 prime minister **14** British monarch **15** governor-general
  monetary unit: 6 dollar
  island: 8 Turneffe
  mountain range: 4 Maya
  highest point: 12 Victoria Peak
  river: 3 New **4** Moho **6** Belize, Monkey
  sea: 9 Caribbean
  physical feature:
    gulf: 8 Honduras
    peninsula: 7 Yucatan
    swamp: 8 mangrove
  people: 5 Mayan **6** Indian, Syrian **7** African, Chinese **15** Spanish-American
  language: 7 English, Spanish
bell 4 gong, peal **5** chime **6** tocsin **7** ringing **8** carillon **16** tintinnabulation
Bell, Alexander Graham
  born: 8 Scotland
  inventor of: 9 telephone **14** record cylinder
  saying: 24 Mr Watson come here I want you
Bellamann, Henry
  author of: 8 King's Row
Bellamy, Edward
  author of: 8 Equality **15** Looking Backward
Bellamy, Ralph
  born: 9 Chicago IL
  roles: 11 Ellery Queen, Mike Barnett **13** The Awful Truth **14** Detective

Story **15** Man Against Crime, State of the Union **19** Sunrise at Campobello
Bellarius
  character in: 9 Cymbeline
  author: 11 Shakespeare
Bellaston, Lady
  character in: 8 Tom Jones
  author: 8 Fielding
bell buoy 5 float **6** signal **13** channel marker
belle 4 star **5** queen **6** beauty **7** charmer **12** heart-stopper
Belle Dame Sans Merci, La
  author: 9 John Keats
Bellefleur
  author: 15 Joyce Carol Oates
Belle Helene, La
  also: 14 Beautiful Helen
  operetta by: 9 Offenbach
Bellerophon
  form: 4 hero
  brother: 8 Deliades
  son: 11 Hippolochus
  home: 7 Corinth
  rode: 7 Pegasus
  killed: 7 Chimera
Bell for Adano, A
  author: 10 John Hersey
  director: 9 Henry King
  cast: 10 John Hodiak **11** Gene Tierney **13** William Bendix
bellicose see **11** belligerent
belligerence, belligerency 9 animosity, hostility, pugnacity **10** aggression, antagonism **11** bellicosity **12** warmongering **13** combativeness **14** aggressiveness, unfriendliness
belligerent 7 fighter, hostile, martial, warlike, warring **8** attacker, inimical **9** adversary, aggressor, bellicose, combatant, combative, irascible, irritable, truculent **10** aggressive, antagonist, pugnacious, unfriendly **11** bad-tempered, contentious, quarrelsome **12** antagonistic, cantankerous
belligerent state 3 foe **5** enemy **9** aggressor **13** hostile nation
Bellini, Gentile
  born: 5 Italy **6** Venice
  father: 6 Jacopo
  brother: 8 Giovanni
  artwork: 24 The Miracle of the True Cross **26** A Procession in St Mark's Square, The Miracle at Ponte di Lorenzo **27** St Mark Preaching in Alexandria **38** A Procession of Relics in the Piazza San Marco
Bellini, Giovanni (Giambellino)
  born: 5 Italy **6** Venice
  father: 6 Jacopo
  brother: 7 Gentile
  artwork: 8 St Jerome **16** Venus with a Mirror **18** St Francis in Ecstasy, The Madonna and Child **19** Allegory of Purgatory, The Agony in the Garden, The Barberini Madonna

Bellini, Jacopo
born: 5 Italy 6 Venice
son: 7 Gentile 8 Giovanni
artwork: 11 Crucifixion 16 Christ on
the Cross 35 The Madonna and
Child with Lionello d'Este

Bellini, Vincenzo
born: 5 Italy 7 Catania
composer of: 5 Norma, Zaira 8 Il
Pirata 9 I Puritani 11 La Straniera 12
La Sonnambula 15 Bianca e Fernando

Bell Jar, The
author: 11 Sylvia Plath

bellow 4 bawl, roar, yell 5 shout,
whoop 6 holler, scream, shriek

Bellow, Saul
author of: 6 Herzog 13 Dean's December, Humboldt's Gift, Mosby's
Memoirs 15 The Last Analysis 16 Mr
Sammler's Planet 18 To Jerusalem
and Back 25 The Adventures of Au-
gie March

Bellows, George Wesley
born: 10 Columbus OH
artwork: 8 Lady Jean 11 Billy Sunday, Edith Cavell, Floating Ice, Up
the Hudson 12 Forty-Two Kids 13
Men of the Docks 14 Rain on the
River, Stag at Sharkey's 16 The Cliff
Dwellers 18 Emma and her Children
21 Both Members of This Club

Bells Are Ringing
music: 5 Styne
lyric: 5 Green 6 Comden
director: 16 Vincente Minnelli
cast: 9 Fred Clark 10 Dean Martin 12
Judy Holliday
song: 10 Just in Time 13 The Party's
Over

Bells in Winter
author: 13 Czeslaw Milosz

Bells of St Mary's, The
director: 10 Leo McCarey
cast: 10 Bing Crosby (Father
O'Malley) 12 Henry Travers 13 Ingrid Bergman
sequel to: 10 Going My Way
song: 20 Aren't You Glad You're You

bell tower 5 spire 6 belfry 7 steeple 9
campanile

Belluschi, Pietro
architect of: 21 Bank of America
Building (San Francisco) 22 Juilliard
School of Music (NYC) 31 Pan
American World Airways Building
(NYC, with Gropius)

bellwether 4 lead 5 doyen, guide, pilot 6 leader 8 director, shepherd 9
conductor, guidepost, precursor 10
forerunner, pacesetter 14 standard-
bearer

belly 3 abs, gut, yen 4 guts 5 taste,
tummy 6 bowels, depths, desire, hunger, liking, paunch, vitals 7 abdomen,
insides, midriff, stomach 8 appetite,
interior, recesses 11 breadbasket

bellyache 4 beef, kick 5 gripe 6
grouch, grouse, squawk 7 grumble 8
complain 9 tummy ache 11 stomach
ache 12 upset stomach

belong 6 go with 7 concern 8 attach
to, be held by, be part of 9 be owned
by, pertain to 10 be allied to 11 be a
member of 12 be included in 15 be
connected with, be the property of

belongings 4 gear, junk 5 goods, stuff
6 things 7 effects 8 movables 11
possessions 13 accoutrements, paraphernalia 16 personal property

Beloved
author: 12 Toni Morrison

beloved 4 beau, dear, love, wife 5
loved, lover 6 adored, fiance, spouse,
steady 7 admired, darling, dearest, fiancee, husband, revered 8 endeared,
esteemed, loved one, precious 9 betrothed, boyfriend, cherished, respected, treasured 10 girlfriend,
sweetheart

below 4 less 5 lower, under 6 in hell
7 beneath, on earth, short of 8 inferior, unworthy 9 at a low ebb, down-
wards 10 downstairs, downstream,
second-rate, underneath 11 at a discount, at the foot of, indifferent, subordinate, underground

below par 3 bad 4 poor 8 inferior 9
imperfect 10 second-rate 12 below average, not up to snuff

below standard 3 bad 4 poor 5 lousy
6 faulty, shoddy 8 below par, inferior,
slipshod, terrible 9 imperfect 10 second-rate 12 not up to snuff

belt 4 area, band, land, sash, zone 5
cinch, layer, strip 6 circle, girdle, region, stripe 7 country 8 district, encircle 9 waistband 10 cummerbund

Belushi, James
born: 7 Chicago
roles: 8 Curly Sue 9 Mr. Destiny 13
Working Stiffs 14 About Last Night
15 Jumpin' Jack Flash 19 Little Shop
of Horrors

Belushi, John
born: 9 Chicago IL
roles: 9 Neighbors 11 Animal House
16 The Blues Brothers 17 Saturday
Night Live

be manifest 6 appear 7 be clear, be
plain 8 be patent 9 be evident, be obvious 10 be apparent

bemoan 3 rue 5 mourn 6 bewail, lament, regret 7 cry over 8 weep over
9 whine over 10 grieve over

bemused 5 dazed, fuzzy 7 muddled,
stunned 8 confused 9 engrossed, stupefied 10 bewildered, dull- witted,
thoughtful 11 preoccupied 12 absent-
minded

be nauseated by 4 hate 5 abhor 6
detest, loathe 7 despise 8 execrate 9
abominate 11 can't stomach 13 be

disgusted by, find repulsive, find revolting, find sickening

Benbow, Horace
character in: 9 Sanctuary
author: 8 Faulkner

Ben Casey
character: 12 Dr David Zorba, Dr Ted
Hoffman 13 Nick Kanavaras 14 Dr
Maggie Graham
cast: 8 Sam Jaffe 10 Nick Dennis 12
Harry Landers, Vince Edwards 14
Bettye Ackerman

bench 3 pew 4 banc, seat 5 board,
court, stool, table 6 settee 7 counter,
take out, trestle 8 sideline, tribunal 9
judiciary, workbench, worktable 10
second team 11 judge's chair, substitutes 12 second string

Benchley, Peter
author of: 4 Jaws 7 The Deep

Benchley, Robert
author of: 14 From Bed to Worse 21
Benchley Beside Himself, My Ten
Years in a Quandary

benchmark 4 norm 5 gauge, guide,
model 7 example, measure 8 exemplar, paradigm, standard 9 criterion,
principle, prototype, reference, yardstick 10 touchstone

bend 3 arc, bow 4 flex, hook, lean,
loop, mold, sway, turn, warp, wind 5
crook, curve, defer, force, shape,
stoop, twist, yield 6 accede, attend,
buckle, coerce, compel, crouch, give
in, relent, submit 7 bow down, contort, control, succumb 9 genuflect, influence, surrender 10 buckle down,
capitulate 11 make crooked

Bend in the River, The
author: 9 V S Naipaul

Bendix, William
born: 9 New York NY
roles: 8 Hostages, Lifeboat 11 The
Hairy Ape 13 A Bell for Adano 14
The Life of Riley 16 Guadalcanal Diary, The Babe Ruth Story

bend to one's own will 4 tame 5
break, train 6 master, subdue 8 overcome 10 discipline 12 show who's
boss 18 have under one's thumb

beneath 5 below, lower, under 9 covered by 10 inferior to, underneath,
unworthy of 11 subordinate, underground 16 below one's dignity

Benedick
character in: 19 Much Ado About
Nothing
author: 11 Shakespeare

Benedict 5 groom 8 newlywed

benedictine
type: 6 brandy, cognac 7 liqueur
flavor: 4 herb
with brandy: 5 B and B
with bourbon: 9 Twin Hills 13
Brighton Punch
with whiskey: 10 Frisco Sour

benediction 6 prayer **7** benison **8** blessing **10** invocation **12** consecration **13** closing prayer

benefaction 4 alms, gift **5** grant **7** charity **8** bestowal, donation, offering **9** endowment **10** almsgiving **12** contribution, dispensation, philanthropy

benefactor 5 angel, donor **6** backer, friend, helper, patron **7** sponsor **8** upholder **9** supporter **11** contributor **14** fairy godmother

beneficent 6 benign, kindly **7** liberal **8** generous, salutary **10** beneficial, benevolent, charitable **11** magnanimous **13** philanthropic

beneficial 6 useful **7** good for, healing, helpful **8** valuable **9** favorable, healthful **10** productive, profitable, propitious **12** advantageous, contributive

beneficiary 4 heir **7** grantee, heiress, legatee **8** receiver **9** inheritor, recipient

benefit 3 aid, use **4** gain, good, help **5** asset, avail, serve, value, worth **6** assist, behalf, better, profit **7** advance, be aided, service **8** be helped, be served, blessing, interest **9** advantage, do good for **10** be useful to, betterment, profit from **13** charity affair **18** charity performance

Benet, Stephen Vincent
author of: **7** America **8** Tiger Joy **11** Western Star **14** John Brown's Body, Thirteen O'Clock, Young Adventure **16** Five Men and Pompey **19** Tales Before Midnight, The Headless Horseman **20** The Beginning of Wisdom **24** The Devil and Daniel Webster

benevolence 7 charity **8** good will, kindness **9** benignity **10** compassion, generosity, kindliness, liberality **13** bountifulness **14** charitableness **15** humanitarianism, kindheartedness

benevolent 3 kin **6** benign, humane, tender **7** liberal **8** generous **9** benignant, bounteous, bountiful, unselfish **10** bighearted, charitable **11** considerate, kindhearted, warmhearted **12** humanitarian **13** compassionate, philanthropic

Bengali
language family: **12** Indo-European
branch: **11** Indo-Iranian
group: **5** Indic
spoken in: **5** (northern) India

Ben-Hur
author: **10** Lew Wallace
character: **4** Iras, Isas **5** Jesus **6** Esther **7** Messala **9** Balthasar, Simonides **11** Judah Ben-Hur
director: **12** William Wyler
cast: **11** Jack Hawkins, Stephen Boyd **12** Hugh Griffith **14** Charlton Heston (Judah Ben-Hur)
setting: **9** Palestine

Oscar for: **5** actor (Heston) **7** picture **8** director **14** cinematography **15** supporting actor (Griffith)

benighted 4 dumb **5** crude, unhip **8** backward, ignorant, untaught **9** primitive, untutored **10** illiterate, uncultured, uneducated, uninformed, unlettered, unschooled **11** empty-headed, know-nothing, uncivilized **12** uncultivated **13** unenlightened

benign 4 good, kind, mild, nice, soft **5** balmy, lucky **6** genial, gentle, humane, kindly, tender **7** affable **8** gracious, harmless, pleasant, salutary **9** favorable, healthful, innocuous, temperate **10** auspicious, benevolent, propitious **11** encouraging, kindhearted, soft-hearted **13** tender-hearted

benignant 4 kind **6** benign, humane, kindly, tender **9** forgiving **10** benevolent **11** kindhearted **13** compassionate, tenderhearted

benignity 8 good will, kindness **10** compassion, kindliness **11** benevolence **15** kindheartedness

Benin
other name: **17** Republic of Dahomey
capital: **9** Porto-Novo
largest city: **7** Cotonou
others: **4** Pobe **5** Kandi, Kerou, Ketou, Porga **6** Abomey, Ouidah **7** Parakou, Savalou **8** Aplahoue
government: **30** Military Council of the Revolution
monetary unit: **5** franc **7** centime
lake: **5** Aheme **6** Nokoue
mountain: **7** Atakora
river: **4** Mono **5** Niger, Oueme **6** Couffo
sea: **8** Atlantic
physical feature:
  gulf: **6** Guinea
  plains: **6** Borgou
people: **3** Fon, Pla **4** Adja, Aizo, Mina, Peul **5** Pedah, Peuhl, Somba **6** Bariba, Fulani, Yoruba **8** Pilapila **9** Dahomeyan
language: **3** Fon **5** Dendi **6** Bariba, French, Fulani, Yoruba
religion: **5** Islam **6** tribal **7** animism **13** Roman Catholic
food:
  tapioca: **4** gari

Benito Cereno
author: **14** Herman Melville

Benjamin
father: **5** Jacob
mother: **6** Rachel
also known as: **6** Benoni
brother: **3** Dan, Gad **4** Levi **5** Asher, Judah **6** Joseph, Reuben, Simeon **7** Zebulun **8** Issachar, Naphtali
sister: **5** Dinah
descendant of: **11** Benjaminite

Bennet family
characters in: **17** Pride and Prejudice
members: **4** Jane, Mary **5** Kitty, Lydia

9 Elizabeth
author: **6** Austen

Bennett, Arnold
author of: **8** Accident **10** Clayhanger, Lord Raingo, Milestones, These Twain **11** Buried Alive **13** Hilda Lessways, Riceyman Steps **15** The Old Wives' Tale **18** Anna of the Five Towns

Benny, Jack
real name: **16** Benjamin Kubelsky
born: **10** Waukegan IL
roles: **12** Charley's Aunt **13** Jack Benny Show, To Be or Not To Be **16** Artists and Models

Benoni see **8** Benjamin

Benson
character: **5** Kraus **12** (Lt Gov) Benson DuBois **13** (Gov) Eugene Gatling
cast: **10** James Noble **11** Inga Swenson **15** Robert Guillaume

bent 4 bias, gift, mind **5** bowed, flair, knack **6** angled, arched, curved, genius, liking, talent **7** ability, aptness, crooked, faculty, hunched, leaning, stooped, twisted **8** aptitude, capacity, facility, fondness, penchant, tendency **9** contorted, endowment **10** attraction, partiality, proclivity, propensity **11** disposition, inclination **12** predilection **14** predisposition

bent into folds 6 fluted, ridged **7** creased, grooved, pleated **8** crinkled, furrowed, puckered, wrinkled **10** corrugated

Benton, Robert
director of: **14** Kramer vs Kramer (Oscar) **16** Places in the Heart

Benton, Thomas Hart
born: **8** Neosho MO
artwork: **7** Bubbles **8** Boomtown **9** Homestead **12** American Life **13** Arts of the West, Cotton Pickers **14** Threshing Wheat **19** Louisiana Rice Fields, The Lord Is My Shepherd

Benue-Congo
language family: **16** Niger-Kordofanian
group: **10** Niger-Congo
includes: **3** Tiv **4** Zulu **5** Bantu, Jukun **6** Chwana, Nyanja **7** Kikongo, Luganda, Swahili

benumb 4 daze, dull **5** blunt **6** deaden **7** stupefy **15** make insensitive

Benvolio
character in: **14** Romeo and Juliet
author: **11** Shakespeare

Benz, Karl
nationality: **6** German
inventor of: **22** electric ignition engine **26** differential gear automobile
built first practical: **10** automobile

be obvious 6 appear **7** be clear, be plain **8** be patent **9** be evident **10** be apparent, be manifest

be off 2 go **5** leave, scram **6** beat it, begone, cut out, depart, go away, set out **8** set forth, withdraw **10** make tracks

be of one mind 5 agree **6** accord, concur **10** think alike **11** see eye to eye

be of use 3 aid **4** help **5** serve **6** assist **7** benefit

be on a par with 5 equal **6** be up to **7** compare **10** be as good as **12** be comparable **14** be in a class with

be on the sick list 3 ail **5** be ill **6** be sick **8** be unwell **12** be indisposed **13** be in ill health **17** be under the weather

Beor
son: **4** Bela **6** Balaam

Beothuk (Red Indians)
location: **6** Canada **12** Newfoundland
intermixed with: **7** Naskapi

Beowulf
author: **7** unknown
character: **4** Finn **5** Breca, Hnaef, Oslaf, Scyld **6** Wiglaf **7** Guthlaf, Hengest, Higelac, Hrethel, Unferth **8** Aeschere, Heardred, Hondscio, Hrothgar **9** Hildeburh
great hall: **6** Heorot
monster: **7** Grendel **14** Grendel's mother
tribe: **5** Danes, Geats **8** Frisians
Beowulf tears from Grendel: **3** arm

be part of 4 form **6** make up **8** belong to **9** appertain, pertain to **10** constitute

be patent 6 appear **7** be clear, be plain **9** be evident, be obvious **10** be apparent, be manifest

be pertinent to 4 bear **5** apply, refer **6** affect, relate **7** concern, pertain **9** appertain, touch upon

be plain 6 appear **7** be clear **8** be patent **9** be evident, be obvious **10** be apparent, be manifest

be pleased with 4 like **5** favor **7** approve

bequeath 4 will **5** endow, leave **6** impart **7** consign **8** hand down

bequest 6 legacy **8** bestowal **9** endowment **10** settlement **11** inheritance

berate 5 scold **6** rail at, rebuke **7** bawl out, chew out, reprove, upbraid **8** reproach **9** castigate, criticize, reprimand **10** take to task, tongue-lash

Berber
language family: **11** Afro-asiatic **13** Hamito-Semitic
spoken in: **6** Sahara **11** North Africa

bereave 3 rob **5** strip **6** divest **7** deprive **10** dispossess

Berenice's Hair
constellation of: **13** Coma Berenices

be resigned to 6 accept **8** tolerate

Beret
character in: **16** Giants of the Earth
author: **7** Rolvaag

be revolted by 4 hate **5** abhor **6** de-

test, loathe **7** despise **8** execrate **9** abominate **10** recoil from, shrink from **11** can't stomach **13** find repulsive

berg 4 floe **7** glacier, iceberg, icefloe
South African: **8** mountain
French: **4** neve **5** serac

Berg, Alban
born: **6** Vienna **7** Austria
composer of: **4** Lulu **7** Wozzeck

Bergen, Candace
father: **11** Edgar Bergen
born: **14** Beverly Hills CA
roles: **8** The Group **11** Murphy Brown **15** Carnal Knowledge
husband: **10** Louis Malle

Berger, Thomas
author of: **7** The Feud **9** Neighbors **10** Vital Parts **11** Killing Time **12** Little Big Man, Sneaky People **15** Regiment of Women

Bergman, Ingmar
director of: **14** The Seventh Seal **16** Cries and Whispers, Wild Strawberries **17** Fanny and Alexander **19** Scenes from a Marriage **20** Smiles of a Summer Night

Bergman, Ingrid
born: **6** Sweden **9** Stockholm
children: **12** Pia Lindstrom **18** Isabella Rossellini
roles: **8** Gaslight (Oscar) **9** Anastasia (Oscar), Golda Meir, Joan of Arc, Notorious **10** Casablanca, Intermezzo, Spellbound **17** A Woman Called Golda, The Bells of St Mary's **19** For Whom the Bell Tolls **24** Murder on the Orient Express **25** The Inn of the Sixth Happiness

Berith, Berit, Bris, Brith, Brit 8 covenant **12** circumcision

Berle, Milton
real name: **15** Milton Berlinger
nickname: **11** Uncle Miltie **12** Mr Television
born: **9** New York NY
roles: **17** The Texaco Star Hour **18** Who's Minding the Mint **23** Always Leave Them Laughing

Berlin (East, West)
landmark: **14** Humboldt Castle **15** Gruenwald Castle **16** Berlin Opera House, Markisches Museum **21** Scharlottenburg Castle **29** Kaiser-Wilhelm-Gedachtniskirche
river: **5** Spree
square: **14** Alexander-Platz

Berlin, Elaine
real name of: **9** Elaine May

Berlinger, Milton
real name of: **11** Milton Berle

Berlioz, (Louis) Hector
born: **6** France **13** La Cote St Andre
composer of: **6** Rob Roy, Te Deum **7** Requiem, **8** Herminie, King Lear, Waverley **9** Cleopatra, Nuits d'Ete **10** Le Corsaire, Les Troyens, The Trojans **11** Sardanapale **13** Harold in It-

aly **14** Les Francs Juges, Romeo and Juliet **16** Benvenuto Cellini, Damnation of Faust, Le Carnaval Romain, L'Enfance du Christ **18** Beatrice et Benedict **20** Symphonie Fantastique **28** Symphonie Funebre et Triomphale

Bermuda
other name: **13** Somers Islands
capital/largest city: **8** Hamilton
others: **8** St George
head of state: **14** British monarch **15** governor general
island: **4** Boaz **5** Coney **7** Bermuda, Ireland, Watford **8** Somerset, St Davids **9** St Georges
highest point: **8** Town Hill
sea: **8** Atlantic
physical feature:
harbor: **6** Castle
hill: **5** Gibbs
people:
discoverer: **14** Juan de Bermudez
language: **7** English
religion: **8** Anglican **10** Protestant **15** Church of England
feature:
dancers: **6** Gombey

Bermuda Triangle
bounded by: **7** Bermuda, Florida **9** Melbourne **10** Puerto Rico
site of: **24** mysterious disappearances of: **5** ships **9** airplanes

Bern, Berne
capital of: **11** Switzerland
landmark: **10** Clock Tower **12** Nydegg Church
river: **3** Aar **4** Aare

Bernard, Henriette-Rosine
real name of: **14** Sarah Bernhardt

Bernhardt, Sarah
real name: **22** Henriette-Rosine Bernard
nickname: **11** Divine Sarah
born: **5** Paris **6** France
roles: **6** Phedre **7** Hernani, Ruy Blas **8** King Lear **14** Queen Elizabeth **17** La Dame aux Camelias

Bernini, Gianlorenzo (Giovanni Lorenzo)
born: **5** Italy **6** Naples
father: **6** Pietro
artwork: **7** Montoya **8** Louis XIV, Vigevano **10** Bellarmine, St Longinus **13** Cathedra Petri, Francis I d'Este, The Assumption **15** Apollo and Daphne **18** Costanza Buonarelli **19** The Rape of Proserpina **21** Saints Andrew and Thomas, The Ecstasy of St Theresa **24** Blessed Lodovica Albertoni **25** Aeneas Anchises and Ascanius
architect of: **12** Santa Bibiana **16** Piazza of St Peter's (Rome) **19** Palazzo Montecitorio **21** Sant' Andrea al Quirinale **22** Palazzo Chigi-Odescalchi **23** Fountain of the Four

Rivers **24** Santa Maria dell' Assunzione

Bernoulli, Daniel
field: **11** mathematics
nationality: **5** Swiss
theory of: **5** gases **6** fluids **18** Bernoulli's Equation

Bernstein, Carl
author of: **12** The Final Days (with Bob Woodward) **19** All the President's Men (with Bob Woodward)
newspaper reporter for: **14** Washington Post
ex: **10** Nora Ephron

Bernstein, Leonard
born: **10** Lawrence MA
composer of: **4** Mass **7** Candide, Kaddish **8** Jeremiah **9** Facsimile, Fancy Free, On the Town **13** West Side Story, Wonderful Town **15** The Age of Anxiety, Trouble in Tahiti **16** Chichester Psalms

Beroe
father: **6** Adonis
mother: **9** Aphrodite
nurse of: **6** Semele

Berowne
character in: **16** Love's Labour's Lost
author: **11** Shakespeare

Berra, Yogi (Lawrence Peter Berra)
sport: **8** baseball
position: **5** coach **7** catcher
team: **14** New York Yankees

berry 3 egg **4** seed **5** fruit, grain, grape **6** dollar, kernel, tomato, banana **7** currant **8** allspice, bayberry, mulberry **9** blueberry, cranberry, raspberry **10** blackberry, gooseberry, peppercorn, strawberry **11** boysenberry, huckleberry, pomegranate **12** checkerberry
poisonous: **9** baneberry

Berryman, John
author of: **8** Recovery **9** Delusions **11** Love and Fame **12** 77 Dream Songs **13** The Dream Songs **16** Berryman's Sonnets **19** The Freedom of the Poet **21** His Toy His Dream His Rest **26** Homage to Mistress Bradstreet

berserk 4 amok, wild **5** crazy **6** insane **7** frantic, violent **8** demented, deranged, frenzied, maniacal, wild-eyed **9** desperate **10** distracted, distraught **12** out of control

Berserker
origin: **6** Nordic
form: **7** warrior

berth 3 bed, job **4** bunk, dock, pier, post, quay, slip, spot **5** haven, niche, place, wharf **6** billet, employ, office **8** position **9** anchorage, situation **11** appointment **12** resting place **13** sleeping place

Berthollet, Claude Louis
field: **9** chemistry
nationality: **6** French
researched: **7** ammonia **8** chlorine

Bertram
character in: **20** All's Well That Ends Well
author: **11** Shakespeare

Bertram family
characters in: **13** Mansfield Park
members: **3** Tom **5** Julia, Maria **6** Edmund **9** Sir Thomas
author: **6** Austen

beryl
color: **5** green **6** yellow

Berzelius, Jons Jakob
field: **9** chemistry
nationality: **7** Swedish
developed: **15** chemical symbols
discovered: **6** cerium **7** silicon, thorium **8** selenium, titanium **9** zirconium
founded: **15** modern chemistry

be satisfactory 2 do **6** answer **7** suffice **8** be enough **10** be adequate, pass muster **12** be sufficient, do well enough

be scant 4 lack, want **8** be skimpy **9** fall short **14** be insufficient **15** be in short supply

beseech 3 beg **4** pray **6** adjure **7** entreat, implore **9** plead with **10** supplicate

beset 3 dog, set **4** bead, deck, stud **5** annoy, array, hem in, hound, worry **6** assail, badger, harass, pester, plague **7** bedevil, besiege, set upon **8** surround **9** beleaguer, embellish

be sick 3 ail **5** be ill **8** be unwell **12** be indisposed **13** be in ill health

beside 2 by **4** near **5** saved **6** except, nearby, unless **7** abreast, barring, without **8** let alone **9** adjoining, alongside, aside from, other than **10** on a par with, side by side **12** compared with, in addition to

beside oneself 4 wild **6** elated, joyful, joyous, raging **7** berserk, exalted, frantic, furious, ranting **8** agitated, blissful, distrait, ecstatic, frenetic, frenzied **9** delirious, in a frenzy, overjoyed, rapturous **10** distracted, distraught, distressed, enraptured **11** carried away, overwrought, transported **13** out of one's wits

besides 3 but **4** also, save **6** as well, except, saving **7** barring **8** moreover **9** excepting, excluding, other than **11** exclusive of, furthermore

besiege 3 dog **5** annoy, beset, hound **6** assail, badger, harass, pester, plague **7** assault, bedevil **9** beleaguer **10** lay siege to

besmear 4 soil **5** dirty, muddy, smear, stain, sully **6** mess up, slop up, smudge **7** begrime, tarnish **8** besmirch

besmeared 5 dirty, grimy, messy **6** grubby, smudgy **7** muddied, sullied **8** begrimed **10** besmirched

besmirch 4 soil **5** smear, stain, sully,

taint **6** defame, defile **7** blacken, corrupt, debauch, degrade, slander, tarnish **8** discolor, disgrace, dishonor **9** discredit

besotted 5 drunk **6** sodden, soused, wasted, zapped, zonked **7** smashed **9** plastered **10** inebriated, infatuated **11** intoxicated **17** under the influence **20** three sheets to the wind

bespangle 3 dot **4** gild, star, stud **5** adorn, jewel **6** bedeck **7** dress up, festoon, garnish **8** decorate, ornament **9** embellish **10** illuminate

bespatter 4 blot, soil, spot **5** decry, dirty, libel, smear, stain, sully, taint **6** debase, defame, defile, smudge, splash **7** condemn, slander, smotter, tarnish **8** denounce, reproach **9** deprecate, fling dirt **10** calumniate, disapprove

Bessemer, Sir Henry
nationality: **7** English
inventor of manufacturing process for: **5** steel

best 3 top **4** most, pick **5** cream, elite **6** choice, finest, nicest, utmost **7** hardest, largest **8** foremost, greatest, superior, topnotch **9** greetings, loveliest, most fully, most of all, unequaled, unrivaled **10** unexcelled **11** compliments, unsurpassed **13** most competent, most desirable, most excellent **14** highest quality, kindest regards

Best, Charles Herbert
field: **10** physiology
nationality: **8** Canadian
discovered: **7** insulin

best group 3 top **5** cream, elite **6** choice **9** chosen few **10** select body **14** cream of the crop, creme de la creme

bestial 5 cruel **6** brutal, savage **7** beastly **8** barbaric, depraved, inhumane, ruthless **9** barbarous, merciless

bestir 4 goad, spur, stir, urge **5** rouse, speed **6** arouse, excite, hasten **7** quicken **8** activate **9** get moving

bestir oneself 5 rouse **8** be active **9** make haste **10** get up early, lose no time **11** keep moving **15** make short work of **19** seize the opportunity

bestow 3 use **4** give, mete **5** apply, award, grant, lay on, spend **6** accord, confer, devote, donate, employ, expend, impart, occupy, render **7** consign, consume, deal out, deliver, hand out, present, utilize **8** dispense, give away **9** apportion **10** settle upon, turn over to

bestowal 4 alms, gift **5** bonus, favor, grant **6** reward **7** charity, present, tribute **8** donation, gratuity, offering **9** endowment **10** conferment, recompense **11** benefaction **12** contribution, dispensation

best society
  French: **10** grand monde
Best Years of Our Lives, The
  director: **12** William Wyler
  based on story by: **15** MacKinlay Kantor
  script: **14** Robert Sherwood
  cast: **8** Myrna Loy **11** Dana Andrews **12** Teresa Wright, Virginia Mayo **13** Frederic March, Harold Russell **15** Hoagy Carmichael
  Oscar for: **5** actor (March) **7** picture **8** director

be sufficient 6 answer **7** suffice **8** be enough **10** be adequate, pass muster **12** do well enough **14** be satisfactory

bet 4 ante, risk **5** stake, wager **6** chance, gamble, hazard, plunge **7** venture **8** make a bet **9** speculate **11** speculation

bete noir 5 bogey **6** plague **7** bugaboo, bugbear **8** anathema, bogeyman **9** annoyance **10** black beast

be thankful 8 thank God **10** appreciate **11** thank heaven **19** thank one's lucky stars

Bethe, Hans Albrecht
  field: **7** physics
  developed: **8** atom bomb
  awarded: **10** Nobel Prize

be the same 5 agree, equal, match **6** equate **7** balance **11** be identical

betide 4 fall **5** occur **6** befall, chance, happen **10** come to pass

betimes 5 early **10** in good time

betoken 4 show **5** augur **6** attest, denote **7** portend, presage, signify **8** foretell

betray 4 dupe, fink, jilt, show, tell **5** rat on, trick **6** expose, reveal, squeal, tell on, unmask **7** abandon, deceive, divulge, lay bare, let down, let slip, sell out, two-time, uncover, violate **8** blurt out, disclose, give away **9** play Judas **10** be disloyal **11** double-cross **12** be unfaithful **13** inform against, play false with **14** break faith with

betrayal 7 perfidy, telling, treason **8** bad faith, sedition, trickery **9** chicanery, deception, duplicity, falseness, treachery, two-timing, violation **10** disclosure, disloyalty, divulgence, revelation **11** double-cross **13** breach of faith, double-dealing **14** unfaithfulness

betrayal of trust 7 falsity, perfidy **8** apostasy, cheating **9** falseness, recreancy **10** disloyalty, infidelity **11** inconstancy **13** deceitfulness, double-dealing, faithlessness **14** unfaithfulness

Betrayer 13 Judas Iscariot

betroth 6 commit, engage, pledge **7** espouse, promise **8** affiance, contract

betrothal 5 troth **8** espousal **10** affiancing, betrothing, engagement

betrothed 6 fiance **7** engaged, fiancee **8** promised **9** affianced

Bettelheim, Bruno
  author of: **15** Love Is Not Enough **16** The Informed Heart **20** The Uses of Enchantment

better 3 top **4** more **5** finer, outdo, raise **6** bigger, enrich, exceed, fitter, larger, longer, refine, uplift **7** advance, elevate, enhance, farther, forward, further, greater, improve, mending, promote, surpass, upgrade **8** heighten, improved, increase, outstrip, stronger, superior **9** cultivate, healthier, improving **10** preferable, recovering, strengthen **11** more healthy, progressing

bettering 9 elevation **10** betterment **11** advancement, improvement

betterment 4 good **6** reform **7** benefit **8** revision **9** advantage, amendment, promotion **10** correction, enrichment **11** advancement, improvement **12** amelioration, regeneration **13** rectification **14** reconstruction

better than average 2 A-1 **3** A-OK **4** aces, a-one, fine, good, tops **5** great, prime, super **6** choice, grade-A, superb **7** capital, special **8** peerless, sterling, superior, terrific, top-notch **9** excellent, first-rate, marvelous, matchless, wonderful **10** first-class, inimitable, preeminent, remarkable, tremendous **11** exceptional, outstanding, superlative **12** incomparable **13** extraordinary

between 4 amid **5** among, entre **6** amidst, atwixt, shared **7** betwixt, joining **9** in the midst **10** connecting

between ourselves
  French: **9** entre nous
  Latin: **8** inter nos

Between the Battles
  author: **20** Bjornstjerne Bjornson

between themselves
  Latin: **7** inter se

between us 9 entre nous, privately **14** confidentially **15** between you and me **16** between me and thee, between ourselves

betwixt and between 4 so-so **7** average **8** confused **9** in between, undecided **14** halfway between **21** neither one nor the other

Beulah, Land of
  place in: **16** Pilgrim's Progress
  author: **6** Bunyan

be unlike 4 vary **6** differ **7** deviate, diverge **8** conflict, disagree **12** be at variance, be discordant, be dissimilar

be unwell 3 ail **5** be ill **6** be sick **12** be indisposed **13** be in ill health

be unwilling to pursue
  Latin: **13** nolle prosequi

bevel 4 blow, cant, ream, tool **5** angle, bezel, miter, mitre, slant, slope, snape, splay **6** aslant **7** incline, oblique **8** slanting

beverage 3 ade, ale, cup, nog, pop, tea **4** beer, brew, cafe, dram, grog, milk, soda, soup, wine **5** broth, caffe, cider, cocoa, draft, drink, juice, julep, lager, latte, leban, punch, toddy, water **6** bishop, coffee, cordial, eggnog, liquor, potion **7** limeade, seltzer, spirits, wassail **8** aperitif, cocktail, espresso, expresso, highball, lemonade, libation, potation **9** champagne, chocolate, orangeade **10** cappuccino

Beverley, Constance de
  character in: **7** Marmion
  author: **5** Scott

Beverly Hillbillies, The
  character: **11** Jed Clampett **12** Jane Hathaway, Jethro Bodine **14** Granny Clampett, Milton Drysdale **16** Ellie May Clampett
  cast: **9** Irene Ryan, Max Baer Jr, Nancy Kulp **10** Buddy Ebsen **12** Donna Douglas **13** Raymond Bailey

Beverly Hills Cop
  director: **11** Martin Brest
  cast: **11** Eddie Murphy **13** Judge Reinhold, Lisa Eilbacher

bevy 4 band, body, herd, host, pack **5** brood, covey, crowd, drove, flock, group, horde, party, shoal, swarm **6** clutch, flight, gaggle, school, throng **7** company, coterie **9** gathering, multitude **10** assemblage, collection

bewail 3 rue **5** mourn **6** bemoan, lament, regret **7** cry over, deplore **8** moan over, weep over **10** grieve over

beware 4 mind **6** be wary **7** look out **8** take care, take heed **9** be careful **11** take warning, watch out for **12** be on the alert, guard against **15** take precautions

beware of the dog
  Latin: **9** cave canem

bewhiskered 5 bushy, hairy **6** shaggy **7** bearded, bristly, hirsute **8** unshaven **11** mustachioed

bewilder 5 addle, mix up **6** baffle, bemuse, muddle, puzzle **7** confuse, fluster, mystify, nonplus, perplex, stupefy **8** befuddle **10** disconcert

bewildered 7 at a loss, up a tree **8** all at sea, confused **9** perplexed **10** confounded, nonplussed **12** disconcerted

bewilderment 9 confusion **10** perplexity, puzzlement **11** frustration **13** mystification

bewitch 4 jinx **5** charm, spook **6** turn on **7** bedevil, beguile, delight, enchant **8** entrance **9** captivate, enrapture, fascinate **12** cast a spell on **14** put under a spell

bewitched 7 charmed, seduced **8** beguiled **9** bedeviled, enchanted, entranced **10** captivated, enraptured, fascinated, spellbound **11** under a spell

Bewitched
  character: 6 Endora, Serena **7** Maurice **9** Aunt Clara, Esmerelda, Larry Tate **11** Uncle Arthur **12** Abner Kravitz **13** Gladys Kravitz **14** Darrin Stephens **15** Tabitha Stephens **16** Samantha Stephens
  cast: 8 Dick York **9** Paul Lynde **10** David White **11** Dick Sargent, Marion Lorne, Sandra Gould **12** George Tobias, Maurice Evans **13** Alice Ghostley **14** Agnes Moorehead **19** Elizabeth Montgomery

bewitching 8 alluring, charming, enticing, fetching, tempting **9** appealing, beguiling, disarming, seductive **10** enchanting, entrancing **11** captivating, fascinating **12** irresistible

be worthy of 4 earn, rate **5** merit **7** deserve

bey, beg 4 lord **6** prince **8** governor

beyond 2 by **4** over, past **5** above, later, ultra **6** abroad, except, yonder **7** beneath, besides, farther, further, outside, passing **8** superior **9** exceeding, hereafter **10** out of range, out of reach **11** at a distance, in addition to

Beyond Desire
  author: 15 Maxwell Anderson

beyond hope 8 hopeless **9** desperate **10** despairing

Beyond Human Power
  author: 20 Bjornstjerne Bjornson

beyond one's means 10 immoderate **11** extravagant **15** too high on the hog

beyond question 4 sure **6** surely **7** certain, decided, settled **9** certainly, decidedly **10** absolutely, positively **12** without doubt

Bharat (Varsha) *see* **5** India

Bhot *see* **5** Tibet

Bhutan
  other name: 7 Druk-Yul **15** Kingdom of Bhutan, Land of the Dragon
  capital/largest city: 6 Thimbu **7** Thimphu
  others: 4 Paro **12** Phuntsholing **14** Wangdu Phedrang
  government:
    assembly: 7 Tsongdu
  head of state/ government:
    hereditary king: 10 dragon king, druk gyalpo
  other leader:
    spiritual leader: 10 dharma raja
    temporal ruler: 7 deb raja
  monetary unit: 5 paisa, rupee **8** chetrums, ngultrum
  mountain: 5 Black **9** Himalayas **10** Chomo Lhari
  highest point: 10 Kula Kangri
  river: 4 Kuru, Paro **5** Machu, Manas, Pachu, Torsa **6** Amochu, Raidak, Tongsa **7** Sankosh, Thinchu
  physical feature:
    plain: 5 Duars

people: 5 Monpa **6** Bhutia **7** Tibetan **8** Assamese, Nepalese
  dragon people: 7 Drukpas
language: 5 Hindi, Lhoke **7** Tibetan **8** Dzongkha, Nepalese
religion: 15 Tibetan Buddhism
place:
  fortress (dzong): 4 Paro **6** Bya Kar, Tongsa **8** Tashi Cho
feature:
  pony: 6 Tangun

Bianca
  character in: 10 Kiss Me Kate **19** The Taming of the Shrew
  author: 11 Shakespeare

Bianchi, Mose
  born: 5 Italy, Milan
  artwork: 11 Snow in Milan **21** Return from the Festival

bias 4 bent, sway **5** angle, slant **7** bigotry, feeling, leaning **8** tendency **9** fixed idea, prejudice, proneness **10** narrow view, partiality, predispose, proclivity, propensity, unfairness **11** inclination, intolerance **12** diagonal line, one-sidedness, predilection **13** preconception **16** narrow-mindedness, preconceived idea

biased 6 unfair, unjust **7** bigoted, slanted **8** inclined **9** arbitrary **10** intolerant, prejudiced **11** close-minded, opinionated **12** narrow-minded

bibelot 5 curio **7** trinket **8** ornament **9** objet d'art

bible 5 guide **6** manual **8** handbook **9** authority, guidebook **13** reference book

Bible 6 Gospel **7** the Book **8** good book, Holy Writ **10** Scriptures **11** bibliotheca, the Good Book **13** holy scripture **14** Holy Scriptures, sacred writings

Bible, books of
  Old Testament: 3 Job **4** Amos, Ezra, Joel, Osee, Ruth **5** Hosea, Jonah, Jonas, Josue, Kings, Micah, Nahum, Tobit **6** Abdias, Aggeus, Baruch, Daniel, Es- dras, Esther, Exodus, Haggai, Isaiah, Isaias, Joshua, Judges, Judith, Psalms, Samuel, Sirach, Tobias, Wisdom **7** Ezekiel, Genesis, Habacuc, Malachi, Micheas, Numbers, Obadiah **8** Ezechiel, Habakkuk, Jeremiah, Jeremias, Nehemiah, Proverbs **9** Leviticus, Maccabees, Machabees, Malachias, Sophonias, Zacharias, Zechariah, Zephaniah **10** Chronicles **11** Deuteronomy, Song of Songs **12** Ecclesiastes, Lamentations **13** Paralipomenon, Song of Solomon **14** Ecclesiasticus **19** Canticle of Canticles
  New Testament: 4 Acts, John, Jude, Luke, Mark **5** James, Peter **6** Romans **7** Hebrews, Matthew, Timothy **9** Ephesians, Galatians **10** Colossians, Revelation **11** Corinthians,

Philippians **13** Thessalonians, Titus Philemon
  first five books called: 3 Law **5** Torah **10** Pentateuch
  first seven books called: 10 Heptateuch

Bible scholar 7 biblist **9** biblicist

Bible version 5 Douay **6** The Way **7** Vulgate **8** Peshitta **9** Gutenberg, Jerusalem, King James **10** Authorized, New English **11** New American, Rheims-Douay **14** The Living Bible **15** American revised, revised standard

Biblical animal 7 unicorn

Biblical gemstone 6 ligure **7** sardius **8** sardonyx

Biblical instrument 7 sackbut

Biblical length
  reed: 9 six cubits

Biblical measure 3 cab, cor **4** epah, omet, reed, seah **5** cubit, epheh, homer **6** shekel **9** half homer

Biblical personage 9 patriarch

Biblical plant 6 hyssop **12** Rose of Sharon

Biblical precept
  Hebrew: 7 mitsvah, mitzvah

Biblical tree 5 algum, almug **6** storax **7** juniper **8** sycamire **10** gopherwood **11** shittim wood **12** opobalsammum **13** red sandalwood

Biblical weed 4 tare **6** darnel

Biblical weight 6 talent

Biblicist 12 Bible scholar

Bibliotheca 5 Bible **14** sacred writings

Biblist 12 Bible scholar

Bickel, Ernest Frederick McIntyre
  real name of: 13 Frederic March

bicker 4 spar, spat **5** argue, fight **6** haggle **7** dispute, quarrel, wrangle **8** disagree, squabble

bickering 4 spat **5** fight **7** arguing, dispute, quarrel **8** argument, fighting **9** wrangling **10** quarreling, squabbling **12** disagreement

Bickford, Charles
  born: 11 Cambridge MA
  roles: 12 Anna Christie **13** Johnny Belinda **16** Song of Bernadette **18** The Farmer's Daughter

bicycle 4 bike, ride **5** cycle, moped **10** two-wheeler
  invented by: 7 Starley

Bicycle Thief, The
  director: 14 Vittorio De Sica
  cast: 14 Lianella Carell **18** Lamberto Maggiorani

bid 3 ask, say, try **4** call, tell, wish **5** greet, offer, order **6** beckon, charge, demand, direct, effort, enjoin, insist, invite, ordain, summon, tender **7** attempt, command, proffer, propose, request, require **8** call upon, endeavor, instruct, offering, proposal **10** invitation

bidding 4 beck, call **5** offer, order **6** behest, charge, demand, offers **7** command, dictate, mandate, request, summons **8** offering, proposal **9** direction, summoning, tendering **10** injunction, invitation, proffering **11** instruction

bide 4 stay, wait **5** abide, dwell, stand, tarry **6** endure, linger, remain, suffer **8** tolerate **9** put up with

Bierce, Ambrose
author of: **15** Can Such Things Be? **16** In the Midst of Life **19** The Devil's Dictionary

Bierstadt, Albert
born: **7** Germany **8** Solingen
artwork: **11** Laramie Park **13** Mount Corcoran **17** The Rocky Mountains **20** Discovery of the Hudson, Storm on the Matterhorn **21** Sunrise Yosemite Valley **22** Settlement of California **31** Thunderstorm in the Rocky Mountains

bifocal lenses
invented by: **8** Franklin

Bifrost
origin: **12** Scandinavian
form: **6** bridge
bridge of: **4** gods
made of: **7** rainbow
from: **6** Asgard
to: **5** earth

bifurcate 4 fork **5** split **6** branch, divide **7** diverge **8** separate

big 3 top **4** head, high, huge, just, kind, main, vast **5** adult, ample, bulky, chief, great, grown, heavy, husky, large, major, noble, prime, vital **6** heroic, humane, mature **7** eminent, grown-up, haughty, hulking, immense, leading, liberal, mammoth, massive, notable, pompous, sizable, weighty **8** abundant, arrogant, boastful, bragging, colossal, enormous, generous, gigantic, gracious, princely **9** conceited, grandiose, honorable, important, momentous, prominent, strapping **10** benevolent, chivalrous, high-minded, monumental, prodigious **11** magnanimous, pretentious, significant, substantial **12** considerable **13** consequential

Big Apple
nickname of: **11** New York City

Big Bend State
nickname of: **9** Tennessee

Big Chill, The
director: **14** Lawrence Kasdan
cast: **8** Meg Tilly **10** Glenn Close, Kevin Kline **11** Tom Beringer, William Hurt **12** Jeff Goldblum

Big Daddy
character in: **16** Cat on a Hot Tin Roof
author: **8** Williams
played by: **8** Burl Ives

Big E
nickname of: **10** Elvin Hayes

Bigfoot 4 Yeti **9** Sasquatch **17** Abominable Snowman

big guns 4 VIPs **5** brass **6** cannon **7** bigwigs, top dogs **8** big shots, ordnance **9** artillery **14** heavy artillery, high mucky-mucks **15** important people

bighearted 6 lavish **7** liberal **8** generous, handsome, princely, prodigal **9** bounteous, bountiful, unselfish **10** beneficent, benevolent, charitable, free-handed, open- handed, unstinting **11** magnanimous, open-hearted **12** humanitarian

bight 3 bay **4** bend, cave, road

Biglow Papers
author: **18** James Russell Lowell

Big Money, The
author: **13** John Dos Passos

bigness 4 bulk **8** enormity, hugeness **9** amplitude, great size, greatness, largeness, magnitude **11** massiveness

Big O, The
nickname of: **14** Oscar Robertson

bigoted 6 biased **10** intolerant, prejudiced **12** closed- minded, narrow-minded

bigotry 4 bias **6** racism **9** prejudice **10** unfairness **11** intolerance **14** discrimination **16** closed-mindedness, narrow-mindedness

Big Parade, The
director: **9** King Vidor
cast: **11** John Gilbert, Renee Adoree **14** Hobart Bosworth

big shot 3 VIP **4** name **5** mogul, nabob, wheel **6** big gun, bigwig, fat cat, tycoon **7** big deal, magnate, notable **8** somebody **9** big cheese, dignitary, personage **13** high-muck-a-muck, wheeler-dealer

Big Six
nickname of: **16** Christy Mathewson

Big Sky, The
author: **11** A B Guthrie Jr

Big Sky State
nickname of: **7** Montana

Big Sleep, The
author: **15** Raymond Chandler
hero: **13** Philip Marlowe
director: **11** Howard Hawks
cast: **12** Elisha Cook Jr, Lauren Bacall **13** Dorothy Malone, Martha Vickers **14** Humphrey Bogart (Philip Marlowe)
setting: **10** Los Angeles

Big Train
nickname of: **13** Walter Johnson

Big Valley, The
character: **11** Nick Barkley **12** Audra Barkley, Heath Barkley **13** Jarrod Barkley **15** Victoria Barkley
cast: **9** Lee Majors **10** Linda Evans, Peter Breck **11** Richard Long **15** Barbara Stanwyck

bigwig 3 VIP **7** big shot, notable **9** dignitary, personage

bikini 8 two-piece **11** bathing suit
top: **3** bra
bottom **5** thong
topless: **8** monokini
type: **6** string

Bikini 5 atoll **9** Namu islet **10** West Pacific **15** Marshall Islands

bile 4 gall, rage **5** anger, venom, wrath **6** choler, spleen

bilge 3 rot **4** bosh, bull, bunk, tosh **5** hooey, tripe **6** drivel, humbug, jabber, piffle **7** baloney, hogwash, rubbish, twaddle **8** malarkey, nonsense **9** gibberish **10** balderdash **11** foolishness, jabberwocky **13** horsefeathers **16** stuff and nonsense

bilious 4 sick **5** angry, cross, huffy, nasty, testy **6** crabby, cranky, grumpy, queasy, sickly, touchy **7** grouchy, peevish **8** bile- like, greenish, nauseous, petulant, snappish **9** irritable, sickening **10** ill-humored, out of sorts **11** ill-tempered **12** cantankerous **13** short-tempered **15** green at the gills

bilk 3 gyp **4** dupe, gull, rook, take **5** cheat, cozen, trick **6** fleece, rip off **7** deceive, defraud, swindle **8** hoodwink **9** bamboozle, victimize

bill 3 act, fee, law **4** card, chit, list **5** tally **6** agenda, charge, decree, docket, poster, roster, ticket **7** account, catalog, charges, invoice, leaflet, measure, placard, program, statute **8** banknote, brochure, bulletin, calendar, circular, handbill, proposal, register, schedule **9** greenback, inventory, ordinance, reckoning, statement **10** regulation **12** treasury note **13** advertisement **17** silver certificate

billet 3 job **4** base, bunk, camp, digs, note, post **5** berth, house, lodge, place, put up **6** letter, office **7** bed down, lodging, quarter, shelter **8** domicile, dwelling, lodgment, position, quarters **9** residence, situation **11** accommodate, appointment **13** accommodation

billfold *see* **6** wallet

billiards
player: **11** Willie Hoppe **13** Minnesota Fats, Willie Mosconi

Bill of Divorcement, A
director: **11** George Cukor
cast: **11** Billie Burke **13** John Barrymore **16** Katharine Hepburn

billow 4 roll, wave **5** belly, cloud, crest, surge, swell **6** puff up **7** balloon, breaker

Billy Budd
author: **14** Herman Melville
character: **8** Claggart **11** Captain Vere
opera by: **7** Britten

billyclub 3 bat **5** billy, stick **8** bludgeon **9** truncheon

bin 3 box 4 cart, crib, silo 5 crate, frame, hatch 6 barrel, basket, bunker, hamper, holder, trough, vessel 9 container, inclosure 10 receptacle

binate 4 dual 6 double 7 coupled, two fold 14 growing in pairs

bind 3 rim, tie 4 edge, gird, glue, join, lash, rope, trim, wrap 5 affix, chafe, cover, cramp, force, frame, hitch, paste, stick, strap, tie up, truss 6 attach, border, coerce, compel, encase, fasten, fringe, oblige, secure, swathe 7 bandage, confine, require 8 encumber, obligate 9 prescribe 11 necessitate

binder 4 glue, roux 5 paste 6 cement 8 notebook 9 assurance, guarantee 11 down payment 12 earnest money 17 looseleaf notebook

binding 4 band, face, tape 5 valid 6 edging, ribbon 7 styptic 8 fastener, ligative 9 stringent 10 compulsory, obligatory, peremptory 12 constricting

binge 3 jag 4 bust, orgy, tear, toot 5 blast, drunk, fling, revel, spree 6 bender 7 carouse 8 beer-bust, carousal 11 bacchanalia 12 drunken spree

Bingham, George Caleb
born: 15 Augusta County VA
artwork: 13 Stump Speaking 17 The Trapper's Return 18 Verdict of the People 19 The Jolly Flatboatman 20 Raftsmen Playing Cards 31 Fur Traders Descending the Missouri

Bingley, Mr
character in: 17 Pride and Prejudice
author: 6 Austen

biochemist 17 biological chemist
American: 4 Cori 5 Bloch, Moore, Ochoa 7 Axelrod, Lipmann 8 Kornberg
English: 5 Krebs 6 Porter, Sanger 8 Mitchell
French: 5 Monod 7 Duclaux
German: 5 Lynen

biogenesis
discoverer: 12 Louis Pasteur

biography 3 bio 4 life, vita 6 memoir 7 account, history 9 life story

biologist
American: 6 Carson, Yerkes 7 Burbank 8 Delbruck
British: 6 Darwin, Huxley 7 Bateson, Medawar
French: 5 Jacob, Monod 7 Lamarck
German: 7 Schwann
Swiss: 6 Haller

biology
branch: 6 botany 7 zoology
classification: 15 Carolus Linnaeus

birch 6 Betula
varieties: 3 Low, Red 4 Fire, Gray 5 Black, Canoe, Dwarf, Paper, River, Swamp, Sweet, Water, White 6 Cherry, Yellow 7 Monarch 8 Mahogany, Old-field 10 West Indian 13 European white, Japanese white, Young's weeping 14 Japanese cherry

Birches
author: 11 Robert Frost

bird
anatomy: 3 bec, neb, nib 4 beak, bill, cere, crop, lora, lore, mala, nape, rump, tail, tuft, wing 5 alula, crest, crown, flank, larum, lorum, pilea, rosta 6 breast, gullet, pecten, pileum, pinion, syrinx, tarsus 7 ambiens, crissum, gizzard, rostrum 8 gigerium, pectines, scapular 9 auchenium, gastraeum 10 cordylanus
aquatic/water: 3 auk, cob, ern, mew 4 cobb, coot, duck, erne, gony, gull, ibis, loon, rail, shag, skua, sora, swan, teal, tern 5 booby, cahow, crane, diver, goose, grebe, heron, murre, ousel, rotch, snipe, solan, stilt, stork 6 avocet, curlew, cygnet, dipper, fulmar, gannet, godwit, hagdon, jabiru, jacana, osprey, petrel, plover, puffin, rotche, scoter, wigeon 7 anhinga, bidcock, bittern, bustard, dovekey, dovekie, finfoot, mallard, moorhen, pelican, penguin, seriema, skimmer, widgeon 8 alcatras, baldpate, dabchick, flamingo, murrelet, umbrette 9 albatross, baptornis, cormorant, gallinule, guillemot, kittiwake, phalarope, snakebird, spoonbill 10 gaviformes, kingfisher, shearwater, sheathbill, yellowlegs 13 whooping crane
bird cage/home: 4 cote, mews, nest 5 roost 6 aviary, volary, volery 7 rookery
bird of freedom: 9 bald eagle
bird of ill-omen: 5 raven
bird of Jove: 5 eagle
bird of June: 7 peacock
bird of Minerva: 3 owl
bird of peace: 4 dove
bird of prey: 3 owl 4 gled, hawk, kite 5 buteo, eagle, glead, glede, harpy, saker 6 condor, elanet, elenet, falcon, musket, osprey, raptor 7 buzzard, goshawk, harrier, kestrel, stooper, vulture 8 caracara 9 accipiter, gyrfalcon, peregrine 11 accipitrine, lammergeier
bird of wonder/rebirth: 7 phoenix
carrion-eater: 4 aura 5 urubu 6 condor 7 buzzard, vulture
class: 4 Aves
combining form: 3 avi 4 orni 5 ornis 6 ornith 7 ornitho 8 ornithes
crow family: 3 daw, jay, kae 4 crow, rook 5 crake, raven 6 chough, corbie, magpie 7 corvine, jackdaw
duck family: 4 clee, coot, lory, smew, teal, wood 5 eider, goose 6 scoter 7 gadwall, mallard, Muscovy, pintail, pochard 8 baldpate, redshank, shoveler 9 merganser 10 bufflehead, canvasback
extinct: 3 auk, jib, moa 4 dodo, jibi,

mamo 5 didus 8 Diatryma 9 aepyornis, apatornis, gastornis, hespornis, solitaire 11 archaeornis
flightless: 3 emu, ihi, moa 4 dodo, gorb, kagu, kiwi, rhea, weka 5 nandu 6 callow, kakapo, moorup, ratite, takahe 7 apteryx, horling, ostrich, peacock, penguin, roatelo 8 notornis 9 cassowary
game: 4 duck, guan, rail, sora, teal 5 brant, goose, quail, snipe 6 chukar, colima, grouse, pigeon, plover, turkey 7 bustard, chicken, flapper, gadwall, mallard, pintail, prairie, widgeon 8 baldpate, bobwhite, moorfowl, pheasant, shoveler, tragopan, wildfowl, woodcock 9 merganser, partridge, ptarmigan 10 canvasback
group of birds: 3 nye 4 bank, bevy, cast, nide, sord 5 aerie, brood, covey, drove, flock, plump 6 covert, flight, gaggle, litter, spring
largest: 7 ostrich 11 lammergeier
legendary: 3 roc 6 simurg 7 phoenix, simurgh 9 feng- huang, feng-hwang
loss of feathers: 7 molting
smallest: 11 hummingbird
nocturnal: 3 owl 5 cahow, owlet, potoo 7 bullbat, dorhawk 8 guacharo, nightjar 9 nighthawk, thickknee 10 goatsucker 11 nightingale
pet: 4 myna 5 mynah 6 canary, parrot, pigeon 8 cockatoo, lovebird, parakeet
plumage: 8 ptilosis
poultry: 3 hen 4 duck 5 goose 6 pigeon, turkey 7 chicken, rooster 8 pheasant 14 Cornish game hen
talking: 4 myna 5 mynah 6 parrot
wingless: 4 kiwi, weka 7 apteryx
young: 4 eyas, gull 5 chick, piper, poult, squab 6 gorlin, pullus 7 flapper, nestler 8 birdikin, nestling 9 fledgling
of Africa: 4 coly, fink, taha, tock 5 crane, paauw 6 barbet, bulbul, cuckoo, jabiru, quelea, whidah 7 courser, finfoot, marabou, ostrich, touraco 8 hornbill, oxpecker, parakeet, umbrette 9 beefeater, broadbill, francolin, napecrest, trochilus 10 hammerhead, weaverbird
of Antarctic/Arctic: 3 auk 4 gull, knot, skua, xema 5 brant, murre, rotch 6 dunlin, fulmar, jaeger, rotche 7 dovekey, dovekie, penguin 8 grayling 9 guillemot, gyrfalcon, ptarmigan 10 sheathbill
of Asia: 4 kora, myna, ruff, smew 5 mynah, pewit, pitta 6 bulbul, chukar, drongo, dunlin, hoopoe, linnet 7 boobook, courser, hill tit, lapwing, peacock, sirgang 8 accentor, dotterel, hornbill, leaf bird, parakeet, tragopan, wheatear 9 brambling, francolin, muted swan
of Australia: 3 emu 4 kahu, kiwi, koel, koil, lory 5 arara, galah, lowan,

pitta **6** drongo, leipoa **7** boobook, bustard, figbird, grinder, waybung **8** bellbird, bushlark, cockatoo, gang-gang, lorikeet, lyrebird, megapode, manucode, morepork, parakeet, platypus **9** bowerbird, cassowary, coachwhip, cockatiel, frogmouth, pardalote, thornbird **10** kookaburra

of Central America: 4 guan, ibis **5** booby, macaw **6** barbet, jabiru, quezal, toucan **7** bittern, cotinga, jacamar, quetzal, tinamou **8** curassow, puffbird, troupial

of Cuba: 6 trogon **8** tocororo **14** bee hummingbird

of England: 4 kite, rook **9** cormorant **11** carrion crow

of Europe: 3 dar, mag, mew, nun **4** clee, gled, mall, merl, pope, rook, ruff, shag, smew, wren **5** amsel, crake, egret, glede, merle, ousel, ouzel, pewit, pipit, stilt, stork, swift, tarin, terek, whaup **6** cuckoo, dunlin, godwit, grouse, hoopoe, linnet, martin, merlin, missel, redleg, roller, siskin, thrush **7** bittern, bustard, jackdaw, kestrel, lapwing, martlet, ortolan, redwing, ruddock, skylark, sparrow, starnel, wagtail, wryneck **8** bee eater, blackcap, brantail, daychick, dotterel, garganey, nightjar, nuthatch, peesweep, redstart, reedling, starling, throstle, wheatear, whimbrel, whinchat, whinshat, woodcock **9** brambling, chaffinch, crossbill, field fare, gallinule, sheldrake, stonechat **10** chiffchaff, goatsucker, kingfisher, lammergeier, turtledove **11** lammergeier, nightingale, wallcreeper **12** capercaillie

of Hawaii: 2 io **3** ava, ioa, iwa, poe **4** nene, iiwi, koae, mamo, moho, omao **6** parson **7** frigate

of India: 4 baya, kala, koel, koil **5** sarus, shama **6** argala, bulbul, homrai, luggar **7** peacock **8** adjutant, amadavat, pheasant, tragopan **11** red hornbill

of Jamaica: 7 vervain

of Java: 7 sparrow **8** rice bird **9** fruit dove

of Madagascar: 6 drongo **7** anhinga, kirombo, roatelo

of Mexico: 6 jacana

of New Guinea: 9 cassowary **14** bird of paradise

of New Zealand: 3 ihi, kea, moa, poe, tui **4** huia, kaka, kaki, kiwi, koko, kuku, ruru, titi, weka **6** kakapo **7** apteryx **8** morepork, notornis

of North America: 3 ani, auk, tit **4** coot, crow, dove, ibis, lark, loon, pape, rook, sora, stib, swan, tern, wamp, wren **5** booby, brant, colin, crane, egret, finch, grebe, junco, murre, quail, robin, snipe, swift, veery, vireo **6** chebec, cuckoo, cur-

lew, darter, dunlin, fulmar, grouse, hagdon, magpie, martin, oriole, phoebe, plover, shrike, thrush, towhee, turkey, verdin, willet **7** anhinga, bittern, blue jay, catbird, flicker, goshawk, grackle, lapwing, pelican, sparrow, swallow, tanager, warbler **8** bluebird, bobolink, bobwhite, cardinal, grosbeak, killdeer, nuthatch, poorwill, starling, thrasher, titmouse, wheatear **9** blackbird, chickadee, crossbill, goldfinch, gyrfalcon, nighthawk, partridge, sandpiper, snakebird **10** bufflehead, kingfisher, meadowlark, woodpecker **11** hummingbird, mockingbird **12** whippoorwill

of South America: 3 ara, hia **4** anna, guan, jacu, loro, mitu, rhea, soco, toco, yeni **5** egret, macaw, potoo, sylph **6** barbet, chatja, chunga, cracid, jabiru, motmot, sappho, toucan **7** cariama, cotinga, hoatzin, jacamar, limpkin, manakin, seriema, tinamou, warrior **8** boatbill, caracara, curassow, guacharo, hoactzin, screamer, tapacolo, tapaculo, terutero, troupial **9** campanero, trumpeter **11** scarlet ibis

of West India: 3 ani **4** tody

Bird, Larry
sport: 10 basketball
position: 5 coach **7** forward
team: 13 Boston Celtics
from: 7 Indiana

Birdman of Alcatraz
director: 17 John Frankenheimer
cast: 10 Karl Malden **12** Edmond O'Brien, Neville Brand, Thelma Ritter **13** Burt Lancaster (Robert Stroud)

Bird of Paradise
constellation of: 4 Apus

Birds, The
author: 12 Aristophanes
character: 4 Iris **5** Meton **8** Basileia, Cinesias **9** Euelpides **10** King Tereus, Prometheus **12** Peithetairos

Birds, The
director: 15 Alfred Hitchcock
based on story by: 15 Daphne du Maurier
cast: 9 Rod Taylor **11** Tippi Hedren **12** Jessica Tandy **16** Suzanne Pleshette
setting: 10 California

Birds Fall Down, The
author: 15 Dame Rebecca West

Birkin, Rupert
character in: 11 Women in Love
author: 8 Lawrence

Birmingham
football team: 9 Stallions

Birmingham, Stephen
author of: 8 Our Crowd **11** The Grandees **14** The Right People **15** Life at the Dakota

Birnbaum, Nathan
real name of: 11 George Burns

birth 5 blood, start, stock **6** family, origin, source, strain **7** bearing, descent, genesis, lineage **8** ancestry, breeding, delivery **9** beginning, being born, emergence, genealogy, inception, parentage **10** background, beginnings, childbirth, derivation, extraction **11** confinement, parturition **12** commencement

Birth of a Nation, The
director: 10 D W Griffith
cast: 8 Mae Marsh **11** Lillian Gish **14** Henry B Walthall

Birth of Tragedy, The
author: 18 Friedrich Nietzsche

birthstones
January: 6 garnet
February: 8 amethyst
March: 6 jasper **10** aquamarine, bloodstone
April: 7 diamond **8** sapphire
May: 5 agate **7** emerald
June: 5 pearl **7** emerald **9** moonstone **11** alexandrite
July: 4 onyx, ruby **8** star ruby
August: 7 peridot **8** sardonyx **9** carnelian
September: 8 sapphire **10** chrysolite **12** star sapphire
October: 4 opal **5** beryl **10** aquamarine, tourmaline
November: 5 topaz
December: 4 ruby **6** zircon **9** turquoise

biscuit 3 bun **4** cake, roll **5** cooky, scone, wafer **6** bisque, cookie, muffin, parking, simnel **7** cracker, dogbone **8** hardtack, zwieback **9** pale-brown **10** crisp bread, quick bread **15** unglazed pottery

bisect 5 cross, split **8** cut in two **9** cut in half, intersect

bishop 4 abba, pope **5** punch **6** cleric, despot, priest **7** pontiff, prelate, primate **8** overseer **9** clergyman, patriarch **10** chesspiece, high priest
of Rome: 4 pope
Greek: 9 episkopos
means: 8 overseer
district: 7 diocese
headdress: 5 miter, mitre

Bismarck, Otto von
nickname: 14 Iron Chancellor
unified: 7 Germany
chancellor/minister for: 15 Emperor William I
policy: 12 "iron and blood"

bison 4 urus **6** wild ox, wisent **7** aurochs, buffalo
native to: 6 Europe **12** North America

Bissau
capital of: 12 Guinea-Bissau

Bisset, Jacqueline
real name: 22 Jacqueline Fraser Bis-

set

born: 7 England **9** Weybridge

roles: 5 Class **7** Airport, The Deep **11** Day for Night **12** Anna Karenina **16** The Mephisto Waltz **24** Murder on the Orient Express

bistro 3 bar **4** cafe **6** tavern **7** cabaret **9** nightclub **10** supper club
French: 9 estaminet

bit 3 dab **4** chip, drop, iota, mite, snip, whit **5** crumb, grain, pinch, scrap, shred, speck, spell, trace **6** dollop, moment, morsel, paring, trifle **7** droplet, granule, shaving, smidgen **8** fragment, particle **9** short time **10** short while, small piece, smithereen, sprinkling

type: 5 auger, drill **6** gimlet, wimble **7** bradawl **11** brace and bit

bitch 3 nag **5** botch, brood, cheat, fault, shrew, spoil, witch, whine **6** kvetch, virago **7** blunder, bungle, grouse **8** complain, harridan **9** complaint, female dog, termagant

bitchy 4 mean **5** catty, cruel, nasty **6** wicked **7** hateful, vicious **8** spiteful **9** heartless, malicious **10** backbiting, malevolent, vindictive

bite 3 bit, dab, dig, nip **4** gnaw, grip, snip **5** champ, crumb, gnash, prick, scrap, shred, smart, speck, sting, taste **6** morsel, nibble, pierce **7** eat into **8** mouthful, stinging, take hold **10** small piece, tooth wound **12** small portion

biting 5 harsh, sharp **6** bitter **7** caustic, cutting, mordant, nipping **8** piercing, scathing, smarting, stinging **9** sarcastic, trenchant, withering **12** sharp-tongued

bit player 5 extra **6** walk on **14** minor character

bitte 6 please **12** you're welcome **14** I beg your pardon

bitter 4 acid, mean, sour, tart **5** acrid, angry, cruel, harsh, sharp **6** biting, morose, severe, sullen **7** acerbic, caustic, crabbed, painful **8** grievous, piercing, scornful, smarting, spiteful, stinging, wretched **9** rancorous, resentful **10** astringent **11** distressing

bitterness 5 anger, scorn, spite **6** animus, rancor, spleen **7** ill will **8** acerbity, acrimony, sourness **9** animosity, harshness, hostility, malignity, sharpness **10** antagonism, malignancy **11** astringency **12** hard feelings, spitefulness **14** unpleasantness

bitters
type: 6 spirit
flavor: 6 orange **7** gentian
brand: 9 Angostura, Peychaud's

bivalve 4 clam **5** pinna **6** cockle, mussel, mollusk, scallop **8** mollusca **9** pelecypod **13** lamellibranch

bivouac 4 camp **5** tents **10** campground, encampment

bizarre 3 odd **5** kinky, kooky, queer,

weird **7** strange, unusual **8** freakish **9** fantastic, grotesque **10** outlandish

Bizet, Georges
real name: 26 Alexandre Cesar Leopold Bizet
born: 5 Paris **6** France
composer of: 4 Roma (suite) **6** Carmen, Patrie **8** Djamileh **11** Don Procopio, L'Arlesienne **12** Jeux d'enfants, Pearl Fishers **14** Children's Games **15** Ivan the Terrible **16** Le Docteur Miracle **18** The Fair Maid of Perth

Bjornson, Bjornstjerne
author of: 4 Arne **7** The King **8** Magnhild **9** A Happy Boy, In God's Way, Lame Hulda, The Editor **10** King Sverre **11** A Bankruptcy, The Bankrupt **12** Sigurd Slembe **14** Arnljot Gelline, Beyond Our Power **15** The Fisher Maiden, The Newly Married **16** Beyond Human Might, Sigurd the Bastard **17** Between the Battles **20** Mary Stuart in Scotland **24** Paul Lange and Tora Parsberg **27** Flags Are Flying in Town and Port

blab 3 rat **6** babble, tattle **7** blabber, prattle **9** tell tales **13** spill the beans **20** let the cat out of the bag

blabber 3 gab, gas, yak **4** blab, bull **5** prate **6** babble, drivel, gabble, gibber, gossip, jabber **7** blather, chatter, palaver, prattle, twaddle **8** blah-blah, chitchat, idle talk **9** jabbering **10** mumbo-jumbo **12** gobbledegook **14** chitter-chatter

blabbermouth 6 gabber, gossip, prater **7** blabber **8** bigmouth, busybody, gossiper, informer, jabberer, liverlip, prattler, quidnunc **9** chatterer **10** chatterbox, talebearer, tattletale **11** rumormonger **12** gossipmonger **13** scandalmonger

black, Black 3 bad, dim, jet **4** dark, evil, grim, inky **5** angry, ebony, murky, Negro, raven, sable **6** dismal, gloomy, som- ber, sullen, wicked **7** colored, furious, hostile, stygian, sunless, swarthy **8** moonless **9** coal-black, lightless, nefarious, unlighted **10** calamitous **11** dark-skinned, threatening **12** Afro-American **13** unilluminated

Black Arrow, The
author: 20 Robert Louis Stevenson

blackball 3 ban, bar, cut **4** snub **5** debar **6** banish, outlaw, reject **7** boycott, exclude, keep out, shut out **8** pass over, turndown **9** blacklist, ostracize, proscribe **11** vote against **12** cold-shoulder **14** send to Coventry

black beast
French: 9 bete noire

blackberry 5 Rubus
variety: 4 Sand **5** Swamp **7** Cut-leaf, Pacific, Running, Sow-teat **9** Evergreen **13** Parsley-leaved **18** Evergreen thornless

Blackberry Winter
author: 12 Margaret Mead

blackbird 3 ani **4** crow, rook **5** raven, slave **6** thrush **7** cowbird, grackle, redwing **8** song bird **9** slave ship **11** slave trader **17** kidnapped islander, plantation laborer
kind: 9 red-winged **12** yellow-headed
family: 8 Turdidae **8** Icteridae

Blackboard Jungle, The
director: 13 Richard Brooks
based on novel by: 10 Evan Hunter
cast: 9 Glenn Ford, Vic Morrow **11** Anne Francis **12** Louis Calhern, Paul Mazursky, Richard Kiley **13** Sidney Poitier **14** Warner Anderson

Black Boy
author: 13 Richard Wright

blacken 5 libel, smear, stain, sully **6** befoul, darken, defame, defile, revile, vilify **7** slander, tarnish **8** besmirch, disgrace, dishonor **9** denigrate, discredit **10** stigmatize

Blackfoot, Blackfeet
language family: 9 Algonkian **10** Algonquian
tribe: 6 Bloods, Kainah, Piegan, Pikuni **7** Siksika
location: 6 Canada **7** Alberta, Montana **12** Saskatchewan

blackguard 3 cad, rat, SOB **5** knave, louse, rogue, scamp **6** rascal **7** bastard, villain **9** miscreant, scoundrel

blackhearted 4 base, vile **6** sinful, wicked **7** ignoble **10** despicable, evil-minded, villainous **11** scoundrelly **12** unprincipled **13** reprehensible

blackjack
also known as: 9 twenty-one
French: 9 vingt-et-un
play against: 6 dealer
additional card: 3 hit

Black Lamb and Grey Falcon
author: 15 Dame Rebecca West

Black Land, The *see* **5** Egypt

blackleg 7 cheater **8** swindler **9** trickster

blacklist 3 ban, bar **4** shun **5** debar **6** reject **7** exclude, lock out, shut out **8** preclude **9** blackball, ostracize

blacklisting 7 boycott **8** spurning **9** exclusion, ostracism, rejection **12** blackballing

black magic 7 sorcery **10** witchcraft

blackmail 5 force **6** coerce, extort, payoff **7** squeeze, tribute **8** threaten **9** extortion, hush money, shakedown

black mark 4 blot **5** stain **6** bruise **7** blemish, demerit **9** contusion

Blackmore, Richard Doddridge
author of: 10 Lorna Doone **11** Springhaven **13** The Maid of Sker

black mountain *see* **10** Montenegro

Black Narcissus
author: 11 Rumer Godden
director: 13 Michael Powell **17**

Emeric Pressburger
cast: 4 Sabu **11** David Farrar, Deborah Kerr, Jean Simmons
setting: 9 Himalayas
blackness 4 dark **5** gloom, shade **7** dimness **8** darkness
Blackpool, Stephen
character in: 9 Hard Times
author: 7 Dickens
Black Prince, The
author: 11 Iris Murdoch
Blackstone, Sir William
author of: 12 Commentaries (on the Laws of England)
Black Uhlan
nickname of: 12 Max Schmeling
Blackwater State
nickname of: 8 Nebraska
Blackwell, Elizabeth
first American: 11 woman doctor
bladder 3 bag, sac **4** cyst **5** pouch **7** blister, pustule, saccule, utricle **10** receptacle
blade 4 epee, leaf **5** frond, knife, razor, saber, sword **6** cutter, needle, switch **7** scalpel **10** sled runner **11** cutting edge, skate runner
blah 4 bosh, dull, flat, guff, so-so **5** bland, ho-hum, hooey, vapid **6** boring, bunkum, dreary, hot air, humbug **7** blather, eyewash, humdrum, nothing, tedious, twaddle **8** claptrap, lifeless, listless, nonsense **9** gibberish **10** balderdash, monotonous, pedestrian **11** uninspiring **13** characterless, unimaginative, uninteresting, unstimulating
Blaik, Earl H
sport: 8 football
position: 5 coach
team: 4 Army **9** Dartmouth
military rank: 7 colonel
Blair, Eric Arthur
real name of: 12 George Orwell
Blake, Robert
real name: 28 Michael James Vijencio Gubitosi
born: 8 Nutley NJ
roles: 7 Baretta, Our Gang **8** Red Ryder **11** In Cold Blood **12** Little Beaver **23** Tell Them Willie Boy Is Here **24** The Treasure of Sierra Madre
Blake, William
born: 6 London **7** England
author of: 6 Milton, Tiriel **9** Jerusalem **13** The Book of Thel **14** Prophetic Books **15** The Book of Urigen **16** Songs of Innocence **17** Songs of Experience **21** Little Lamb Who Made Thee **23** Marriage of Heaven and Hell, Tiger Tiger Burning Bright
artwork: 6 Milton **9** Book of Job, Jerusalem **11** The Four Zoas **12** Book of Urizen, Divine Comedy **16** Songs of Innocence **17** Songs of Experience **23** Marriage of Heaven and Hell

blamable 10 censurable, deplorable, punishable, reprovable **11** blameworthy **12** reproachable **13** reprehensible
Blamauer, Karoline
real name of: 10 Lotte Lenya
blame 4 onus **5** fault, guilt **6** accuse, burden, charge, rebuke **7** censure, condemn, reproof, reprove **8** reproach **9** castigate, criticism, criticize, liability **10** accusa- tion, disapprove **11** castigation, culpability **12** condemnation, denunciation, remonstrance **13** find fault with, recrimination **14** accountability, responsibility **15** hold responsible
blameless 5 clear **8** innocent, spotless **9** guiltless, not guilty, unspotted, unstained, unsullied, untainted **10** inculpable, not at fault, unblamable **11** unblemished, uncorrupted **13** unimpeachable **14** irreproachable, not responsible
blameless in life
Latin: 12 integer vitae
blame on 7 trace to **8** charge to **9** set down to **11** attribute to **14** lay at the door of
blameworthy 8 blamable **10** censurable, deplorable, punishable, reprovable **12** reproachable **13** reprehensible
blanch 4 fade **6** bleach, whiten **7** lighten **8** turn pale
blanched 3 wan **4** pale **5** ashen, faded **6** chalky, pallid **8** bleached **9** bloodless
bland 4 blah, calm, dull, even, flat, mild **5** balmy, quiet, vapid **6** benign, smooth **7** calming, humdrum, nothing, prosaic, tedious **8** moderate, peaceful, soothing, tiresome, tranquil **9** peaceable, temperate, unruffled **10** monotonous, unexciting, untroubled **11** uninspiring **13** nonirritating, uninteresting, unstimulating
blandish 4 coax, lure, urge **5** charm, tempt **6** cajole, entice, prompt **7** blarney, flatter, wheedle **8** inveigle, persuade
blandishment, blandishments 7 blarney, coaxing **8** cajolery, flattery **9** sweet talk, wheedling **12** ingratiation, inveiglement
Blandois, Monsieur
character in: 12 Little Dorrit
author: 7 Dickens
blank 3 gap **4** dull, idle, void **5** clean, clear, empty, inane, plain, space **6** futile, hollow, unused, vacant, vacuum, wasted **7** useless, vacancy, vacuous **8** unmarked **9** emptiness, fruitless, valueless, worthless **10** empty space, hollowness, profitless **11** meaningless, thoughtless, unrewarding **12** inexpressive **14** expressionless
blanket 4 coat, film **5** cloak, cover, quilt, throw **6** afghan, carpet, mantle,

veneer **7** coating, overlay **8** covering, coverlet **9** comforter
blare 4 honk, peal, roar **5** blast **6** bellow, scream **7** resound, trumpet
blarney 4 fibs, line **5** pitch, spiel **6** hot air **7** coaxing, fawning, snow job, stories **8** cajolery, flattery **9** hyperbole, wheedling **10** inveigling, overpraise, sweet words **12** exaggeration, honeyed words **13** blandishments, overstatement
blase 4 full **5** bored, jaded **6** gorged **7** glutted **9** apathetic, satisfied, saturated, surfeited, unexcited, unmovable **10** insouciant, nonchalant, spiritless, world-weary **11** indifferent, unconcerned **12** uninterested **14** unenthusiastic
Blasko, Bela
real name of: 10 Bela Lugosi
blaspheme 5 curse, swear **6** revile **7** profane **10** take in vain
blasphemous 7 godless, impious, profane, ungodly **10** irreverent **11** irreligious **12** sacrilegious
blasphemy 7 cursing, impiety **8** swearing **9** profanity, sacrilege **11** impiousness, irreverence, profanation
blast 4 bomb, boom, bore, gale, gust, honk, peal, roar, rush, toot **5** blare, bleat, burst, level, shell, surge **6** bellow, blow up, report, scream, shriek **7** explode, resound, torpedo **8** dynamite, eruption **9** discharge, explosion, loud noise **10** detonation **11** sound loudly
blasting material 3 TNT **8** dynamite **9** explosive
blatant 4 loud **5** cheap, clear, crass, crude, gross, harsh, noisy, overt **6** brazen, coarse, tawdry, vulgar **7** blaring, glar- ing, obvious, uncouth **8** flagrant, piercing, unsubtle **9** clamorous, deafening, obtrusive, offensive, prominent, tasteless, ungenteel, unrefined **10** indelicate, unpolished **11** conspicuous, ill-mannered, undignified **12** earsplitting, unmistakable
blather 4 stir **7** chatter, prattle **8** nonsense **9** commotion
Blatty, William P
author of: 11 The Exorcist
Blaue Reiter 10 Blue Riders
group of: 13 German artists
blaze 3 ray **4** beam, burn, fire, glow, rush **5** blast, burst, flame, flare, flash, glare, gleam, shine **6** flames **7** glisten, glitter, shimmer, torrent **8** eruption, outbreak, outburst, radiance **9** explosion **10** brightness, brilliance, effulgence **12** resplendence **13** conflagration
blazer 4 coat **6** jacket **12** sports jacket
blazing 3 hot **5** fiery, afire **6** firing, on fire **7** burning, flaming, flaring, glaring, glowing, intense, shining **8** burst-

ing, bleaming, shooting, shouting **9** brilliant

Blazing Saddles
director: **9** Mel Brooks
cast: **9** Mel Brooks **10** Alex Karras, Dom DeLuise, Gene Wilder **11** Slim Pickens **12** Harvey Korman, Madeline Kahn **13** Cleavon Little, John Hillerman **15** David Huddleston

blazon 5 blare, boast **7** trumpet **8** proclaim **10** coat of arms, make public **16** armorial bearings

blazonry 4 arms **5** crest **6** blazon **8** insignia **10** coat of arms **14** heraldic emblem **16** heraldic bearings

bleach 4 fade **6** blanch, whiten **7** lighten, wash out **8** make pale

bleak 3 icy, raw **4** bare, cold, grim **5** chill **6** barren, biting, bitter, dismal, dreary, frosty, gloomy, somber, wintry **7** nipping **8** desolate, piercing **9** cheerless, windswept **10** depressing, forbidding **11** distressing, unpromising **13** weather-beaten

Bleak House
author: **14** Charles Dickens
character: **2** Jo (the crossing sweeper) **4** Nemo **5** Guppy, Krook **6** Bucket, Guster **7** Snagsby **8** Ada Clare, Chadband **9** Miss Flite **10** Mrs Jellyby, Turveydrop **11** Dr Woodcourt, Lady Dedlock, Tulkinghorn **12** John Jarndyce **13** Captain Rawdon **14** Harold Skimpole **15** Esther Summerson, Richard Carstone **19** Sir Leicester Dedlock
satire of: **3** law **6** courts **8** chancery
case: **19** Jarndyce and Jarndyce

bleakness 8 bareness, grimness **10** barrenness, desolation, dreariness, gloominess **13** cheerlessness

bleat 3 baa, cry, maa **5** whine **7** whimper

bleb 6 bubble **7** blister

bleed 3 run, tap **4** leak, soak **5** drain, valve **6** fleece, suffer **7** diffuse, extract, let blood **9** draw blood, sacrifice **10** hemorrhage, overcharge **12** phlebotomize

Blefuscu
fictional land in: **16** Gulliver's Travels
author: **5** Swift

blemish 3 mar, zit **4** blot, blur, flaw, mark, spot **5** spoil, stain, sully, taint **6** blotch, defect, smirch, smudge **7** tarnish **9** disfigure **12** imperfection **13** disfigurement

blend 3 mix **4** fuse **5** merge, unite **6** fusion, go well, merger, mingle **7** amalgam, combine, mixture **8** coalesce, compound, mergence, mingling **9** harmonize **10** amalgamate, complement, concoction **11** combination, incorporate, intermingle

bless 4 give **5** endow, favor, grace, guard, honor **6** anoint, bestow, hal-

low, oblige, ordain **7** baptize, benefit, protect, support **8** dedicate, sanctify **9** watch over **10** consecrate

blessed 4 holy **5** happy, lucky **6** adored, graced, joyful, joyous, sacred **7** endowed, favored, revered **8** blissful, hallowed **9** fortunate, venerated, wonderful **10** felicitous, sanctified **11** consecrated

Blessed Damozel, The
author: **20** Dante Gabriel Rossetti

blessedness 5 bliss **8** felicity **9** beatitude **11** saintliness

blessing 4 boon, gain, gift, good **5** favor, grace, leave **6** bounty, profit, regard **7** backing, benefit, consent, support **8** approval, sanction **9** advantage, hallowing **10** dedication, good wishes, invocation, permission **11** benediction, concurrence, good fortune **12** consecration, thanksgiving **14** sanctification

blessings 4 joys **5** gifts **6** favors **7** success **8** benefits, delights **10** advantages **11** good fortune

Blifil, Master
character in: **8** Tom Jones
author: **8** Fielding

Bligh, Captain William
character in: **17** Mutiny on the Bounty
authors: **4** Hall **8** Nordhoff

blight 3 pox, rot **4** harm, kill, ruin, rust **5** blast, crush, curse, decay, smash, spoil, wreck **6** cancer, canker, dry rot, fungus, injure, mildew, plague, thwart, wither **7** cripple, destroy, scourge, shrivel **8** demolish **9** frustrate **10** affliction, corruption, pestilence **12** plant disease **13** contamination

Blimber, Dr
character in: **12** Dombey and Son
author: **7** Dickens

blind 4 dull, ruse **5** cover, dodge, front, shade **6** hidden, insane, obtuse, screen **7** obscure, pretext, unaware **8** disguise, heedless, ignorant, mindless, unseeing **9** concealed, deception, senseless, sightless, sun shield, unfeeling, unknowing, unmindful, unnoticed **10** camouflage, insouciant, irrational, masquerade, neglectful, subterfuge, unthinking **11** inattentive, incognizant, indifferent, insensitive, smoke screen, unconcerned, unconscious, unobservant, unobserving **12** imperceptive, uncontrolled, undiscerning, uninterested, unnoticeable, unperceptive, unreasonable **13** unenlightened **14** uncontrollable **15** uncomprehending

blind alley 7 closure, dead-end, impasse **8** blockade, cul-de-sac, dead lock, no escape **9** hindrance, stone wall **10** impassable, standstill **11** obstruction

blinder 4 hood **5** blind, shade **6** screen **7** blinker **9** blindfold

blindfold 6 darken **7** bandage, blinder, obscure **8** covering heedless, reckless **11** strike blind

blind seer 8 Tiresias

blink 4 wink **5** flash, shine, waver **6** fal- ter, flinch, squint **7** flicker, glimmer, shimmer, sparkle, twinkle **9** nictitate, vacillate

blinker(s) 3 eye **6** peeper **7** blinder, flasher, goggles **8** black eye **13** warning signal

blintz, blintze 4 blin **5** crepe **6** blints **7** pancake

blip 3 dot, tap **4** spot **5** bleep, image **6** censor **7** replace

bliss 3 joy **4** glee **6** heaven, luxury **7** delight, ecstasy, rapture **8** gladness, paradise **9** cloud nine, happiness **10** exaltation, jubilation **12** exhilaration

blissful 5 happy **6** divine, joyful, joyous **7** blessed, sublime **8** beatific, ecstatic, glorious, heavenly **9** rapturous

blithe 3 gay **4** airy, glad **5** blind, happy, jolly, merry, sunny **6** casual, cheery, jaunty, jovial, joyous, lively **7** gleeful, radiant **8** carefree, careless, cheerful, debonair, exaltant, heedless, mirthful, uncaring **9** ebullient, sprightly, unfeeling, unmindful **10** blithesome, frolicking **11** indifferent, insensitive, thoughtless, unconcerned, unconscious **12** light-hearted **13** inconsiderate

Blithedale Romance, The
author: **18** Nathaniel Hawthorne

blithesome 3 gay **5** light, merry, sunny **6** breezy, jaunty, lively **7** buoyant **8** animated, carefree, cheerful **11** free and easy

Blixen-Finecke, Karen
real name of: **11** Isak Dinesen

blizzard 4 blow, gale **5** blast **6** flurry, squall **7** tempest **8** snowfall **9** snowstorm **11** winter storm

Blizzard State
nickname of: **11** South Dakota

bloat 5 swell **6** blow up, dilate, expand, puff up **7** balloon, distend, enlarge, inflate

blob 3 dab **4** daub, drop, glob, mass **7** globule, splotch

bloc 4 body, ring, wing **5** cabal, group, union **6** clique **7** combine, faction **8** alliance **9** coalition **11** combination

Bloch, Ernest
born: **6** Geneva **11** Switzerland
composer of: **7** Macbeth, Solomon **8** Baal Shem, Schelomo **13** Sacred Service **14** Avodath Hakdesh, Israel Symphony **16** American Symphony **19** Concerto Symphonique **20** Voice in the Wilderness

block 3 bar, jam **4** cube, form, halt, mold **5** brick, check, choke, shape **6**

hinder, impede, re-form, square, stop up, thwart **7** barrier, prevent, reshape **8** blockade, blockage, obstacle, obstruct **9** hindrance **10** impediment **11** obstruction **12** interference

blockade 3 bar, dam **4** dike **5** block, check, levee **6** hurdle **7** barrier, parapet, rampart **8** blockage, obstacle, obstruct, stockade, stoppage **9** barricade, hindrance, roadblock **10** checkpoint, earthworks, impediment **11** obstruction, restriction **13** fortification

blockage 3 jam **8** obstacle **9** hindrance **10** impediment **11** obstruction

blockhead 3 ass, oaf **4** clod, dolt, dope, fool, yutz **5** booby, dummy, dunce, idiot, klutz, moron, ninny **6** dum-dum, nitwit **7** fathead, half-wit, jackass **8** bonehead, dumb-dumb, dummkopf, imbecile, lunkhead, mushhead, numskull **9** harebrain, lamebrain, simpleton **10** chowerhead, dunderhead, nincompoop, noodlehead **12** featherbrain

block out 3 hew **5** carve **6** chisel, devise, map out, sculpt, sketch **7** outline **8** indicate **9** formulate

block up 3 bar **4** clog **6** stop up **7** brick up **9** barricade

blond, blonde 4 fair, gold, pale **5** light **6** flaxen, golden, yellow **8** light tan **9** yellowish **10** fair-haired **11** fair-skinned **12** light-colored

Blonde Bombshell
 nickname of: **10** Jean Harlow

Blondell, Joan
 husband: **8** Mike Todd **10** Dick Powell
 born: **9** New York NY
 roles: **8** The Champ **11** Blonde Crazy, Gold Diggers, The Blue Veil **14** Blondie Johnson, The Public Enemy **20** A Tree Grows in Brooklyn

Blondie
 creator: **9** Chic Young
 character:
  husband: **15** Dagwood Bumstead
  children: **6** Cookie **9** Alexander **12** Baby Dumpling
  boss: **6** Julius **9** Mr Dithers
  boss's wife: **4** Cora
  neighbor: **11** Herb Woodley **14** Tootsie Woodley
  dog: **5** Daisy

blood 4 gore **5** birth, stock **6** family, source, spirit, temper **7** descent, lineage, passion **8** ancestry, heritage, vitality **9** lifeblood **10** extraction, family line, vital fluid, vital force **11** temperament **13** consanguinity **14** vital principle

Blood, field of 8 Aceldama

bloodless 4 pale **5** ashen **6** anemic, pallid **7** insipid **8** blanched, lifeless, peaceful **9** colorless, deathlike, washed out

bloodline 6 family **8** ancestry, pedigree **9** genealogy **10** family tree

Bloodline
 author: **13** Sidney Sheldon

bloodshed 4 gore **6** murder, pogrom **7** carnage, killing, slaying **8** butchery, massacre **9** blood bath, blood feud, slaughter **10** mass murder **12** bloodletting, manslaughter **15** spilling of blood

Bloodsmoor Romance, A
 author: **15** Joyce Carol Oates

bloodstone
 month: **5** March

Blood, Sweat and Tears
 author: **17** Winston S Churchill

blood system
 part: **5** blood, liver **6** spleen **9** lymph node **10** bone marrow

bloodthirsty 5 cruel **6** bloody, brutal, fierce, savage **7** bestial, demonic, inhuman, vicious **8** barbaric, demoniac, fiendish, pitiless, ruthless **9** atrocious, barbarous, cutthroat, heartless, homicidal, merciless, murdering, murderous **10** demoniacal, sanguinary **11** sanguineous

blood vessel 4 vein **5** aorta **6** artery **7** carotid **9** capillary
 prefix: **5** angio

Blood Wedding
 author: **19** Federico Garcia Lorca

bloody 3 red **4** gory, rude, vevy **5** cruel, lurid **6** cursed, damned **7** crimson, scarlet **8** bleeding **9** merciless, murderous **10** sanguinary

Bloody Shame see **10** Virgin Mary (drink)

bloom 3 bud **4** glow, grow, zest **5** flare, flush, prime, shine, vigor **6** beauty, flow- er, heyday, luster, sprout, thrive **7** blossom, burgeon, develop, prosper, succeed **8** fare well, flourish, fructify, radiance, rosiness, strength **9** bear fruit, flowerage, flowering, germinate **10** blossoming **11** florescence, flourishing

Bloom, Claire
 real name: **11** Claire Blume
 husband: **10** Rod Steiger
 born: **6** London **7** England
 roles: **6** Charly **9** Limelight **10** Richard III **15** Look Back in Anger **26** The Spy Who Came in from the Cold

Bloom, Leopold and Molly
 characters in: **7** Ulysses
 author: **5** Joyce

bloomers 8 knickers, trousers **9** plus fours, underwear **10** underpants **15** knickerbockers

blooming 3 fit **4** pert, rosy **5** utter **6** abloom, robust, strong **7** healthy **8** vigorous **9** healthful **10** blossoming **11** flourishing **12** efflorescent, fit as a fiddle **15** picture of health

blooper 4 goof, slip **5** boner, botch, er-

ror, fluff, gaffe, lapse **6** bobble, boo-boo, slip-up **7** blunder, mistake, screwup

blossom 4 grow **5** bloom **6** flower, thrive **7** burgeon, develop **8** flourish, progress

Blossomed miraculously 9 Aaron's rod

blossoming 5 bloom **8** blooming, thriving **9** flowering **10** burgeoning, developing **11** florescence, flourishing

blot 3 dry **4** flaw, mark, spot **5** smear, stain, taint **6** absorb, blotch, remove, smirch, smudge, soak up, stigma, take up **7** bad mark, blemish, splotch **8** besmirch **13** discoloration

blotch 4 blot, mark, spot **7** splotch

Blot on the 'Scutcheon, The
 author: **14** Robert Browning

blot out 5 erase **6** remove, rub out **7** abolish, eclipse, expunge **9** eliminate, eradicate **10** obliterate

blotting out 7 eclipse, erasing **9** expunging, wiping out **11** eradicating, eradication **12** annihilation, obliterating, obliteration **13** overshadowing

blouse 4 coat **5** drape, tunic, shirt, smock **6** camise, billow **7** blouson **8** casaquin

blow 3 box, hit, jab, pop **4** bang, bash, belt, cuff, gale, gust, honk, jolt, play, puff, sock, toot, wind **5** blast, burst, clout, crack, knock, punch, shock, smack, sound, storm, thump, upset, whack **6** exhale, rebuff, squall, wallop **7** breathe, explode, tempest, tragedy, whistle **8** calamity, disaster, expel air, reversal **9** detriment, windstorm **10** affliction, misfortune **11** catastrophe **14** disappointment

blow from the hand
 French: **10** coup de main

blowhard 6 gascon **7** boaster, bragger, egotist **8** braggart **9** big talker **11** braggadocio

blow of mercy
 French: **11** coup de grace

blow out 5 burst **7** rupture **10** extinguish

blowsy, blowzy 5 messy **6** frowzy, mussed, sloppy, untidy **7** unkempt **10** disarrayed, disheveled, disordered, disorderly, in disorder **11** disarranged

blow up 5 bloat, burst **6** billow, dilate, expand **7** balloon, distend, enlarge, explode, inflate, puff out **8** dynamite, swell out **12** lose one's cool **14** lose one's temper

Blowup
 director: **21** Michelangelo Antonioni
 cast: **8** Verushka **10** Sarah Miles **13** David Hemmings **15** Vanessa Redgrave

blowy 5 gusty, windy **6** breezy **7** squally **8** blustery

blubber 3 cry, fat, sob 4 bawl, flab, wail, weep 6 boohoo

Blubber
author: 9 Judy Blume

bludgeon 3 bat, hit 4 club 5 billy, clout, stick 6 cudgel 7 clobber 9 billy-club, truncheon

blue 3 low, sad 4 aqua, down, navy 5 azure 6 bluish, cobalt, gloomy, indigo, morose 7 doleful 8 cerulean, dejected, downcast, sapphire 9 depressed, turquoise 10 aquamarine, despondent, melancholy 11 downhearted, lapis lazuli, ultra-marine 12 disconsolate 14 down in the dumps, down in the mouth

Blue Angel, The
director: 17 Josef von Sternberg
based on novel by: 12 Heinrich Mann
cast: 10 Kurt Gerron 12 Emil Jannings 15 Marlene Dietrich (Lola-Lola)
song: 18 Falling in Love Again

Bluebeard
characteristic: 9 many wives

bluebell 9 Mertensia 18 Mertensia Virginica 21 Campanula rotundifolia
variety: 7 English, Spanish 8 Virginia 10 Australian, California 11 Clanwilliam

blueberry 9 Vaccinium
variety: 3 Low 4 Male 5 Swamp 7 Lowbush, Sourtop, Western 8 Creeping, Elliott's, Highbush, Low sweet 9 Late sweet, Rabbit-eye 10 Velvet-leaf 13 Black highbush

blueblood 4 peer 5 noble 8 nobleman 9 patrician, socialite 10 aristocrat, noblewoman 14 peer of the realm

blue-blooded 5 noble, regal, royal 6 titled 7 courtly 8 highbred, wellborn 9 patrician 10 upper-class 12 aristocratic, of royal blood

blue bloods 5 elite, toffs 8 nobility 9 haut monde 10 patricians 11 aristocracy, high society 14 creme de la creme

bluegrass 3 Poa
varieties: 3 Big 4 Wood 5 Rough, Texas 6 Annual, Canada 7 Bulbous, English 8 Kentucky, Sandberg 10 Rough-stalk

Bluegrass State
nickname of: 8 Kentucky

Blue Hen State
nickname of: 8 Delaware

Blue Knight, The
author: 14 Joseph Wambaugh

Blue Law State
nickname of: 11 Connecticut

blue-pencil 3 cut 4 edit, trim 6 censor, cut out, delete, digest, reduce 7 abridge, shorten 8 boil down, condense, pare down 9 expurgate 10 abbreviate

blueprint 4 plan 5 chart 6 design, scheme 7 diagram 9 schematic

Blue Riders
German: 11 Blaue Reiter
group of: 7 artists

blues 5 dumps 8 doldrums 10 depression, low spirits, melancholy 11 despondency

bluestocking
French: 7 bas bleu

bluff 3 lie 4 bank, bold, crag, curt, dupe, fake, fool, hoax, liar, open, peak, sham 5 blunt, boast, cliff, faker, frank, fraud, ridge, rough 6 abrupt, candid, crusty, delude, direct, humbug 7 bluffer, boaster, brusque, deceive, fake out, mislead, pretend 8 bragging, headland, headlong, palisade, pretense 9 bamboozle, deception, idle boast, outspoken, precipice, pretender 10 escarpment, forthright, promontory, subterfuge 11 braggadocio, counterfeit, plainspoken 13 unceremonious, straightforward

bluffer 5 bluff, faker, fraud, phony 6 humbug 9 pretender

bluish 7 off-blue 12 somewhat blue

Blume, Claire
real name of: 11 Claire Bloom

Blume, Judy
author of: 5 Wifey 6 Deenie 7 Blubber, Forever 19 Then Again Maybe I Won't 22 It's Not the End of the World 26 Tales of a Fourth Grade Nothing 27 Are You There God? It's Me Margaret

Blumenbach, Johann Friedrich
field: 7 anatomy 10 physiology
nationality: 6 German
father of: 20 physical anthropology

blunder 4 goof, slip 5 boner, error, gaffe 6 booboo, bumble, bungle, slip up 7 faux pas, mistake, stagger, stumble 8 flounder 9 gaucherie 11 impropriety, make a booboo 12 indiscretion

blunt 4 curt, dull, numb, open 5 frank, rough, thick 6 abrupt, benumb, candid, deaden, dulled, soften, weaken 7 brusque, lighten, stupefy 8 edgeless, explicit, mitigate, moderate, tactless 9 outspoken, unpointed 10 to the point 11 insensitive, unsharpened 15 straightforward

bluntness 6 candor 10 directness 14 forthrightness 15 plainspokenness

blur 3 dim, fog, run 4 blot, haze, veil 5 bedim, befog, cloud, smear 6 blotch, darken, smudge, spread 7 becloud, obscure, splotch 9 confusion, obscurity

blurb 2 ad 4 rave, spot 5 brief 10 commercial 13 advertisement

blurred 3 dim 5 vague 6 blurry 7 smeared 10 ill-defined, indefinite, indistinct

blurt out 4 blab, sing 7 confess, divulge, let slip 8 give away 9 come clean

blush 5 color, flush 6 redden 7 grow red, turn red 8 rosy tint 9 reddening

blushing 3 coy, red 4 rosy 5 fresh, timid 6 demure, modest 7 colored, bashful, flushed, glowing 8 blooming, sheepish 9 rosaceous 10 embarrassed 11 flourishing

bluster 4 brag, crow, rant 5 bluff, boast, bully, gloat, noise, storm 7 bombast, bravado, crowing, protest, ranting, swagger 8 boasting, gloating, threaten 9 noisy talk 10 swaggering 14 boisterousness

blustery 5 blowy, gusty, windy 6 breezy 7 squally

Blythe, Ethel Mae
real name of: 14 Ethel Barrymore

Blythe, John
real name of: 13 John Barrymore

Blythe, Lionel
real name of: 15 Lionel Barrymore

Boadicea
Latin name: 8 Boudicca
queen of: 5 Iceni
husband: 10 Prasutagus
ruled: 7 Norfolk (England)
fought: 6 Romans
died: 7 suicide

Boanerges
means: 13 sons of thunder
name given to: 4 John 5 James

boar
group of: 7 sounder

board 3 bed 4 deal, feed, food, slat 5 enter, get on, house, lodge, meals, panel, plank, put up 6 batten, billet, embark, go onto 7 council, quarter 8 tribunal 9 clapboard, directors 10 daily meals

board game 4 Clue, Life, ludo 5 chess 7 Othello 8 checkers, cribbage, dominoes, draughts, fanorona, Monopoly, Scrabble 9 Alquerque 10 backgammon 14 Trivial Pursuit 15 Chinese checkers
Egyptian: 5 Senat
Korean: 5 Nyout, Pa-tok
Indian: 7 pachisi 8 parchesi, shatranj 9 ashtapada 10 shaturanga
Japanese: 2 Go 3 I-go 5 Sho-gi
Chinese: 6 Ma-jong, wei-ch'i 7 Mahjong, Ma-jongg 8 Mah-jongg
Swedish: 6 tablut

boast 4 brag, crow, have 5 vaunt 6 flaunt 7 contain, exhibit, possess, show off, talk big 15 blow one's own horn

boaster 6 gascon 7 bragger, egotist 8 blowhard, braggart 9 big talker 11 braggadocio

boastful 5 cocky 7 crowing, pompous, swollen 8 bragging, cocksure, inflated, puffed up, vaunting 9 conceited 11 braggadocio, exaggerated, pretentious **12** vainglorious

boastfulness 7 conceit, egotism **8** bragging **9** cockiness, immodesty, pomposity, vainglory **10** self-praise **11** braggadocio **12** cocksureness

boastful soldier
   Latin: **14** miles gloriosus

boat 4 ship **5** craft **6** vessel

Boaz
   father: **5** Salma **6** Salmon
   wife: **4** Ruth
   son: **4** Obed
   kinsman of: **5** Naomi **9** Elimelech

bob 3 cut, hop, nod **4** clip, crop, dock, duck, leap, trim **5** dance, shear **6** bounce **7** shorten

Bobadill
   character in: **19** Every Man in His Humour
   author: **6** Jonson

bobbin 3 pin **4** coil, cord, reel **5** quill, spool **6** piping **7** ratchet, spindle, torchon **8** cylinder

bobcat 3 cat **4** lynx **7** wildcat

Bob Cummings Show, The
   later name: **11** Love That Bob
   character: **10** Bob Collins **14** Chuck MacDonald **15** Charmaine (Shultzy) Shultz **17** Margaret MacDonald
   cast: **9** Ann B Davis **11** Bob Cummings **13** Dwayne Hickman **14** Rosemary DeCamp

Bob Newhart Show, The
   character: **12** Elliot Carlin, Emily Hartley, Howard Borden **13** Jerry Robinson, Robert (Bob) Hartley **20** Carol Kester Bondurant
   cast: **9** Bill Daily, Jack Riley **11** Peter Bonerz **13** Marcia Wallace **16** Suzanne Pleshette

Boccaccio, Giovanni
   author of: **10** Filostrato, Filocopo **11** Life of Dante **12** The Decameron

Boccherini, Luigi
   born: **5** Italy, Lucca
   composer of: **8** La Divina **9** The Aviary **10** Clementina **11** L'Uccelliera

Boccioni, Umberto
   born: **5** Italy **12** Reggio Emilia **16** Reggio di Calabria
   artwork: **10** Elasticity **12** The City Rises **15** Charge of Lancers **18** Dynamism of a Cyclist, The Forces of a Street **21** Fusion of Head and Window **30** Unique Forms of Continuity in Space

Bock, Hier
   field: **6** botany
   nationality: **6** German
   founded: **12** modern botany
   classified: **6** plants
   author of: **15** Neu Kreutterbuch

Bocklin, Arnold
   born: **5** Basel **7** Germany

artwork: **13** Pan in the Reeds **16** The Isle of the Dead

Bod see **5** Tibet

bode 4 omen **5** augur **6** herald **7** betoken, ominate, point to, portend, predict, presage, signify **8** forecast, foretell, precurse **9** foreshadow, prefigure

bodega 9 warehouse **12** grocery store

bodice 3 top **5** stays, waist **6** bolero, corset, girdle **7** corsage **8** camisole, corselet **9** stomacher **10** underwaist

bodily 8 corporal, physical

Bodily Harm
   author: **14** Margaret Atwood

bodkin 3 awl **4** pick, tool **5** auger, borer, drill, point, probe **6** dagger, lancet, needle, reamer **7** hair pin, piercer **8** puncheon, stiletto

body 3 mob **4** bloc, bulk, form, mass **5** being, build, force, frame, group, shape, stiff, thing, torso, trunk **6** corpse, corpus, figure, league, person, throng **7** cadaver, carcass, combine, council, faction, remains, society **8** assembly, cohesion, congress, deceased, main part, majority, physique, quantity **9** coalition, multitude, stiffness, thickness **10** federation **11** brotherhood, consistency **13** confederation

Body and Soul
   director: **12** Robert Rossen
   cast: **10** Anne Revere **11** Hazel Brooks, Lilli Palmer **12** John Garfield **13** William Conrad

bodybuilder 12 Charles Atlas **20** Arnold Schwarzenegger

Boeotus
   father: **8** Poseidon
   mother: **4** Arne

Boer, Boor 6 farmer **9** Afrikaner
   language: **9** Afrikaans
   ancestry: **5** Dutch
   inhabitants of: **9** Transvaal **11** South Africa **15** Orange Free State

Boffin
   character in: **15** Our Mutual Friend
   author: **7** Dickens

bog 3 fen **4** mire, sink **5** marsh, swamp **6** morass **7** be stuck **8** quagmire, wetlands **9** marshland, swampland

Bogaerde, Derek Van den
   real name of: **11** Dirk Bogarde

Bogarde, Dirk
   real name: **19** Derek Van den Bogaerde
   born: **6** London **7** England **9** Hampstead
   roles: **6** Victim **7** Darling **10** The Servant **13** Death in Venice **14** Song Without End, The Night Porter **16** A Tale of Two Cities

Bogart, Humphrey
   nickname: **5** Bogie
   wife: **12** Lauren Bacall
   born: **9** New York NY

roles: **8** Key Largo **10** Casablanca, High Sierra **11** The Big Sleep **14** The Caine Mutiny **15** The African Queen (Oscar) **16** The Maltese Falcon, To Have and Have Not **18** The Petrified Forest **27** The Treasure of the Sierra Madre

Bogdanovich, Peter
   director of: **4** Mask **7** Targets, The Trip **9** Paper Moon, Saint Jack **10** Texasville **18** They all Laughed, Picture Windows **18** The Last Picture Show
   roles: **7** Targets, The Trip **9** Saint Jack

bogey
   term in: **4** golf
   song: **18** Colonel Bogey's March

boggle 3 shy **4** balk, muff **5** botch, demure, hover, waver **6** bungle, shrink, wobble **7** blunder, stumble **8** flounder, frighten, hesitate, hold back **9** overwhelm **11** make a mess of

boggy 3 wet **4** soft **5** foggy, mossy, soggy **6** marshy, spongy, swampy **7** squashy

Bogie
   nickname of: **14** Humphrey Bogart

Bogota
   capital of: **8** Colombia

bogus 4 fake, sham **5** dummy, false, phony **6** ersatz, forged, pseudo **7** feigned, pretend **8** spurious **9** imitation, simulated, synthetic **10** artificial, fraudulent **11** counterfeit, make-believe

Boheme, La
   also: **12** Bohemian Life
   opera by: **7** Puccini
   character: **4** Mimi **7** Colline, Musetta, Rodolfo **8** Marcello **9** Schaunard

bohemian, Bohemian 6 hippie **7** beatnik **10** unorthodox **13** nonconformist **14** unconventional

Bohr, Niels
   field: **7** physics
   nationality: **6** Danish
   developed: **8** atom bomb **13** quantum theory, uranium theory

Boiardo, Matteo Maria
   author of: **17** Orlando Innamorato

boil 4 brew, burn, foam, fume, rage, rant, rave, sore, stew, toss **5** chafe, churn, froth, storm **6** bubble, fester, quiver, seethe, simmer, sizzle, well up **7** abscess, bristle, parboil, pustule, smolder **8** furuncle **9** carbuncle, fulminate

boil down 3 cut **6** reduce **7** abridge, cut down, shorten **8** condense, contract **10** abbreviate

boiler 6 copper, geyser, heater, kettle **7** alembic, caldron, furnace

Boilermaker, the
   nickname of: **20** James Jackson Jeffries

boisterous 4 loud, wild **5** noisy, rowdy **6** unruly **9** clamorous, out-of-hand **10** disorderly, uproarious **12** obstreperous, uncontrolled, unrestrained

boite, boite de nuit 7 cabaret **9** nightclub

Bojer, Johan
    author of: 12 Folk by the Sea, The Emigrants **14** The Great Hunger, The Power of a Lie **16** Last of the Vikings

bold 3 hot **4** loud, rude **5** brash, brave, fiery, fresh, saucy, vivid **6** brazen, cheeky, daring, flashy, heroic **7** defiant, forward, valiant **8** colorful, creative, fearless, impudent, insolent, intrepid, spirited, stalwart, striking, unafraid, valorous **9** audacious, daredevil, dauntless **10** courageous **11** eye-catching, imaginative, impertinent, indomitable, lionhearted, unshrinking **12** stouthearted **13** adventuresome

boldfaced 5 brash, saucy **6** brassy, brazen **7** forward **8** immodest, impudent, insolent **9** audacious, barefaced, shameless, unabashed

boldness 4 grit **5** nerve, pluck, spunk **6** daring, mettle **7** bravery, courage **8** audacity **9** brashness, hardihood **10** brazenness **13** audaciousness, determination, self-assurance **14** courageousness **15** adventurousness

Bolger, Ray
    born: 12 Dorchester MA
    roles: 9 Scarecrow **10** On Your Toes **13** The Wizard of Oz, Where's Charley

Bolivia
    named for: 12 Simon Bolivar
    capital:
        administrative: 5 La Paz
        legal: 5 Sucre
    largest city: 5 La Paz
    others: 3 Ivo **4** Icla, Itau, Mojo, Saya, Yaco, Yato, Yura **5** Cliza, Llica, Oruro, Quime, Uyuni, Zongo **6** Guaqui, Potosi, Tiraja, Tupiza **8** Pulacayo **9** Santa Cruz **10** Chuquisaca, Cochabamba **11** Vallegrande, Villa Montes
    school: 6 Xavier **8** St Andrew **12** San Francisco
    division: 6 Valles **7** Oriente, Valleys **8** Montanas **9** Altiplano
    measure: 6 league **7** celemin
    monetary unit: 7 centavo **13** peso boliviano
    weight: 5 libra, marco
    lake: 5 Poopo **7** Allagas, Coipasa, Rogagua **8** Titicaca **10** Desaguader
    mountain: 4 Jara **5** Andes, Cusco, Cuzco **6** Pupuya, Sajama, Sorata, Sunsas **7** Illampu **8** Illimani, Mururata, Sansimon, Santiago, Zapaleri **12** Eastern Range, Western Range **18** Cordillera Oriental **20** Cordillera Occidental

    highest point: 8 Ancohuma
    river: 4 Beni, Yata **5** Abuna, Lauca, Orton **6** Blanco, Ichilo, Itenez, Madidi, Mamore, Mizque, Yacuma **7** Guapore, Machupo **8** Inambari, Itonamas **9** Pilcomayo, Rio Grande, San Miguel **11** Desaguadero, Madre de Dios
    physical features:
        lowlands: 6 Llanos
        plateau: 9 Altiplano
        swamp: 6 Izozog
        valley: 5 Yunga
        volcano: 7 Ollague
    people: 6 Aymara **7** mestizo, Quechua
        author: 7 Mendoza **8** Arguedas **11** Costa du Rels
        leader: 5 Busch, Sucre **6** Candia, Ortuno, Zamora **7** Bolivar **9** Melgarejo, Paz Zamora, Santa Cruz **10** Barrientos, Estenssoro
    language: 6 Aymara **7** Quechua, Spanish
    religion: 13 Roman Catholic
    place:
        church: 9 St Francis, St Michael **10** San Lorenzo
        monument: 11 La Coronilla
        ruins: 10 Tiahuanaco
        tower: 6 Chulpa
    feature:
        animal: 5 llama **6** alpaca, vicuna
        bar/club: 7 boliche
        boat: 5 balsa
        dance/song: 5 cueca **7** huainos, pasillo **8** morenada **9** taquirari **10** palla-palla **11** cacharpayas, wakatokonis
        devil dance: 8 Diablado
        guitar: 8 charango
        skirt: 7 pollera
        wind instrument: 4 kena, sicu **5** erque, quena, tarka **6** pututu **9** pinquillo
    food:
        chicken dish: 14 picante de pollo
        corn: 4 mote
        corn drink: 3 api **14** chicha taratena
        dish: 11 plato paceno **14** sajta de gallina
        dried meat: 7 charque
        pancakes: 7 bunulos
        potato: 5 chuno

Bolkonsky, Andrei
    character in: 11 War and Peace
    author: 7 Tolstoy

Boll, Heinrich
    author of: 8 The Clown **12** The Safety Net **18** Absent Without Leave **21** Group Portrait With Lady **27** The Lost Honor of Katharina Blum **28** Missing Persons and Other Essays

bolster 3 aid **4** help **5** add to, brace **6** assist, cradle, hold up, pillow, prop up, uphold **7** cushion, shore up, support, sustain **8** buttress, maintain, shoulder **9** reinforce **10** strengthen

bolster one's spirits 5 cheer **7** cheer up, comfort, hearten **8** inspirit **9** buoy one up, encourage

bolt 3 bar, fly, peg, pin, rod, run **4** dart, dash, flee, gulp, jump, leap, lock, roll, rush, tear, wolf **5** bound, brand, catch, dowel, flash, hurry, latch, rivet, scoot, shaft, speed **6** fasten, gobble, hasten, hurtle, length, secure, spring, sprint, stroke **8** fastener **12** swallow whole

bolt down 4 wolf **5** scarf **6** devour, gobble **8** gulp down

bomb 3 dud, egg **4** bust, fail, flop, mine **5** lemon **6** fiasco, fizzle, turkey **7** bombard, grenade, failure, washout

bombard 5 beset, hound, shell, worry **6** assail, attack, batter, harass, pepper, pester, strafe **7** assault, barrage, besiege **8** fire upon **9** cannonade

bombardment 5 blitz, siege **7** air raid, assault, barrage, bombing **10** blitzkrieg

bombast 3 pad **4** puff, rant **6** cotton **7** bluster, fustian, palaver **8** boasting, flummery, rhapsody, tall talk, verbiage **9** bavardage **10** balderdash **12** braggadocio, exaggeration **13** magniloquence, overstatement **14** grandiloquence **17** sesquipedalianism

bombastic 5 tumid, windy, wordy **6** padded, turgid **7** pompous, verbose **8** inflated **12** magniloquent **13** grandiloquent

Bombay
    area: 7 Trombay **8** Salsette **12** Bombay Island
    called: 14 Gateway to India
    creek: 7 Bassein
    landmark: 9 High Court **13** Taj Mahal Hotel **14** Gateway of India **16** Victoria Terminus **17** Rajabai Clock Tower
    rock formation: 10 Deccan Trap
    sea: 7 Arabian

Bona Dea
    also: 5 Fauna
    origin: 5 Roman
    goddess of: 8 chastity **9** fertility
    worshipped by: 5 women
    father: 6 Faunus
    brother: 6 Faunus
    husband: 6 Faunus

bona fide 4 real, true **5** legal **6** actual, honest, lawful **7** genuine, sincere **9** authentic, honorable **10** legitimate **11** in good faith

bon ami 5 lover **8** cleanser. **10** good friend

bonanza 8 gold mine, windfall

Bonanza
    character: 3 Ben **4** Adam, Hoss **5** Candy **7** Hop Sing **9** Little Joe
    family: 10 Cartwright
    cast: 10 Dan Blocker **11** David Ca-

nary, Lorne Greene **13** Michael Landon, Victor Sen Yung **14** Pernell Roberts
ranch: 9 Ponderosa

Bonanza State
nickname of: 7 Montana

bon appetit 14 hearty appetite

Bonario
character in: 7 Volpone
author: 6 Jonson

bonbon 5 candy, sweet **7** fondant **9** sweetmeat **10** confection, sugar candy **13** confectionery **14** chocolate cream

bond, bonds 3 tie **4** cord, knot, link, rope **5** irons, scrip, union **6** chains, pledge **7** compact, fetters, promise **8** affinity, bindings, manacles, security, shackles **9** agreement, guarantee, handcuffs **10** allegiance, attachment, connection, fastenings, obligation **11** certificate, stipulation

Bond, James
actor: 10 Roger Moore **11** Sean Connery **12** Peter Sellers **13** George Lazenby, Pierce Brosnan, Timothy Dalton
appears in: 4 Dr No **9** Golden Eye, Moonraker, Octopussy **10** Goldfinger **11** Thunderball **12** A View To A Kill **13** Licence to Kill, Live and Let Die **15** For Your Eyes Only **16** The Spy Who Loved Me, You Only Live Twice **17** Tomorrow Never Dies **18** Diamonds Are Forever, From Russia with Love, Never Say Never Again, The Living Daylights **22** The Man with the Golden Gun **26** On Her Majesty's Secret Service
author: 10 Ian Fleming
drink: 12 vodka martini **16** shaken not stirred
employer: 3 MI-6 **20** British Secret Service
foe: 7 Blofeld, SPECTRE
office staff: 1 M, Q **14** Miss Moneypenny
university: 6 Oxford
wife: 5 Tracy

bondage 4 yoke **6** chains **7** fetters, serfdom, slavery **8** shackles **9** captivity, servitude, vassalage **11** enslavement

bone
comprise: 8 skeleton
contain: 6 marrow **9** cartilage **11** blood vessel
fitted together by: 5 joint
held by: 8 ligament
pulled by: 6 muscle
specific: 3 rib **4** ulna **5** femur, skull, tibia **6** carpal, fibula, pelvis, radius, sacrum, tarsal **7** humerus, patella, scapula, sternum **8** clavicle, vertebra **9** vertebrae

bone chilling 3 icy **4** cold **5** harsh, sharp **6** arctic, biting, bitter, frigid **7**

cutting, glacial **8** piercing, stinging **11** penetrating **15** teeth-chattering

bonehead 3 ass **4** clod, dolt, fool **5** booby, dunce, idiot, moron, ninny **6** dimwit, nitwit **7** fathead, half-wit **8** dumb- dumb, imbecile, lunkhead **9** blockhead, lamebrain, numbskull **10** dunderhead, nincompoop **11** chowderhead

boner 4 goof, slip **5** error **6** boo-boo, slip-up **7** blooper, blunder, mistake

boneyard 4 dump **7** ossuary **8** Boot Hill, cemetery, junkyard **9** graveyard **10** churchyard **12** burial ground **13** burying ground

Bonheur, Rosa
real name: 19 Marie Rosalie Bonheur
born: 6 France **8** Bordeaux
artwork: 12 The Horse Fair **23** Ploughing in the Nivernais

bonjour 5 hello **7** good day

Bonjour Tristesse
author: 14 Francoise Sagan

bon marche 7 bargain

bon mot 4 quip **7** epigram **9** witticism

Bonn
former capital of: 11 West Germany
landmark: 10 Bundeshaus **11** Munsterkerk
museum: 18 Ludwig van Beethoven
river: 5 Rhine
Roman fort: 15 Castra Bonnensia

Bonnard, Pierre
born: 6 France **16** Fontenay-aux-Roses
artwork: 8 Intimist, Luncheon **9** The Review **10** Nude in the Bath, The Open Window, Women with a Dog **14** After the Shower, Farm at Le Cannet **16** The Breakfast Room **17** The Terrasse Family **22** Figure Before a Fireplace

bonne amie 5 lover **6** friend **10** good friend

bonne nuit 9 good night

bonnet 3 cap, hat **4** cowl, hood, sail **5** cover, toque **7** chapeau, commode **8** headgear **9** headdress

Bonnie and Clyde
director: 10 Arthur Penn
cast: 11 Faye Dunaway (Bonnie Parker), Gene Hackman **12** Warren Beatty (Clyde Barrow) **15** Michael J Pollard

bonny 4 fair **6** comely, lovely, pretty, seemly **7** winning, winsome **8** engaging, fetching, handsome, pleasing **9** beautiful, exquisite, ravishing **10** attractive

bon soir 9 good night **11** good evening

bonus 4 gift **5** prize **6** bounty, reward **7** benefit, premium **8** dividend, gratuity **10** honorarium

Bonus Eventus
also: 7 Eventus
origin: 5 Roman

god of: 4 luck **10** prosperity **11** agriculture

bon vivant 7 epicure, gourmet **8** gourmand, sybarite **10** gastronome

bony 4 lean **5** gaunt, lanky, spare **6** skinny **7** angular, scrawny **11** full of bones **12** skin-and-bones

boo 3 pan **4** hiss **5** taunt **6** deride, heckle, revile **7** catcall **8** ridicule **9** criticize, shout down **11** give the bird **16** give the raspberry

boo-boo 4 goof, slip **5** boner, error **6** slip-up **7** blunder, mistake

boobtube 2 TV **3** box **5** telly **8** idiot box **13** television set

booby 4 bird, dope, fool **5** dummy, dunce, idiot, moron, ninny **6** dimwit, gannet, nitwit **7** fathead, halfwit **8** bonehead, dumb-dumb, imbecile, lunkhead, numskull **9** blockhead, lamebrain, simpleton **10** nincompoop **11** chowderhead

Booby, Lady
character in: 13 Joseph Andrews
author: 8 Fielding

boodle 4 loot, swag **5** booty, bribe, crowd, graft, group **7** plunder **10** collection **11** stolen goods

Boog
nickname of: 10 John Powell

boohoo 3 cry, sob **4** bawl, weep **7** blubber **9** shed tears

book 4 bill, file, list, note, opus, post, tome **5** album, enter, index, slate **6** accuse, charge, engage, enroll, indict, insert, line up, record, tablet, volume **7** catalog, procure, program, put down, reserve **8** mark down, notebook, register, schedule, treatise **9** bound work, write down **10** arrange for **11** publication, written work **16** make reservations

bookish 7 erudite, learned, stilted **8** academic, educated, informed, literary, pedantic, studious, well-read **9** scholarly **11** pedagogical, impractical **12** intellectual

bookkeeper 5 clerk **7** auditor **10** accountant **11** comptroller

booklet 5 folio **7** leaflet, program **8** brochure, circular, pamphlet

Book of Common Prayer
author: 10 Joan Didion

Book of Lights, The
author: 10 Chaim Potok

Book of Manuel
author: 13 Julio Cortazar

Book of Odes
author: 9 Confucius

Book of psalms 12 psalter

Book of Sand, The
author: 15 Jorge Luis Borges

Book of the Duchess, The
author: 15 Geoffrey Chaucer

boom 3 bar **4** bang, beam, gain, grow,

push, roar, spar **5** blast, boost, shaft, spurt **6** growth, rumble, thrive, thrust, upturn **7** advance, develop, prosper, thunder, upsurge **8** flourish, increase **9** expansion, good times

Boom Boom
nickname of: **15** Bernie Geoffrion

boomerang 5 kalie, kiley, kylie, wango **6** atlatl, recoil **7** rebound, womerah, woomera **8** backfire, ricochet, trombush **9** bound back, solitaire **10** projectile

Boomer State
nickname of: **8** Oklahoma

boon 3 fun, gay **4** gift **5** favor, jolly, merry **6** kindly **7** benefit, bequest **8** blessing, donation, offering, pleasant **9** advantage, congenial, convivial, endowment **11** full of cheer, good-natured

boon companion 3 pal **4** chum **5** buddy, crony **6** friend **7** comrade **8** confrere, intimate **9** confidant **10** bosom buddy

boondocks 4 bush, veld **6** Podunk, sticks **7** boonies, country, outback **8** frontier **9** backwater, backwoods, provinces **10** hinterland **11** backcountry, countryside **12** squaresville **13** nowheresville **14** wide open spaces

Boone, Richard
born: **12** Los Angeles CA
roles: **5** Medic **6** Hombre **7** Paladin **8** The Alamo **11** The Shootist **12** Ten Wanted Men, The Desert Fox **17** Have Gun Will Travel

boonies 6 sticks **7** country **9** backwoods, boondocks, provinces **10** hinterland **11** countryside

boor 3 oaf **4** hick, lout, rube **5** brute, churl, yokel **6** rustic **7** bumpkin, hayseed, peasant **9** vulgarian **10** clodhopper, philistine **11** guttersnipe

boorish 4 rude **5** crude **6** coarse, gauche, oafish, rustic, vulgar **7** loutish, uncouth **9** unrefined **10** unpolished **11** peasantlike

boorishness 8 rudeness **9** surliness, vulgarity **10** bad manners, coarseness, incivility, oafishness **12** churlishness, impoliteness

boost 4 hike, laud, lift, plug, push, rise **5** add to, extol, heave, hoist, pitch, raise, shove, steal, swipe **6** expand, foster, free ad, growth, pickup, praise, upturn, urge on **7** acclaim, advance, develop, elevate, enlarge, forward, further, improve, nurture, promote, root for, support, sustain, upsurge, upswing **8** addition, applause, good word, increase, propound, shoplift **9** expansion, incre- ment, promotion **10** compliment, give a leg up, stick up for **11** development, enlargement, improvement, speak well of

boot
French: **9** chaussure

booth 3 pen **4** coop, nook, tent **5** hutch, stall, stand, table **7** counter **9** cubbyhole, enclosure **11** compartment

Booth, Shirley
real name: **15** Thelma Booth Ford
born: **9** New York NY
roles: **5** Hazel **13** The Matchmaker **19** Come Back Little Sheba (Oscar)

bootleg 5 hooch **7** illegal, illicit **8** unlawful **9** moonshine **12** football play

bootless 6 futile **7** useless **11** ineffective, ineffectual **12** unproductive, unprofitable

bootlick 4 fawn **5** toady **6** cringe, grovel **7** flatter, truckle

bootmaker 7 cobbler **9** shoemaker

booty 4 gain, loot **5** prize **6** boodle, spoils **7** pillage, plunder, takings **8** pickings, winnings

booze 4 bout, soak **5** drink, hooch, spree **6** guzzle, liquor, tipple **7** alcohol, spirits, swizzle **8** cocktail **10** intoxicant **14** drink like a fish
type: **3** gin, rum, rye **4** beer, wine **5** vodka **6** scotch **7** bourbon, whiskey

boozer 3 sot **4** lush **5** drunk, souse, toper **7** tippler **8** drunkard **9** alcoholic, inebriate **11** hard drinker

bordello, bordel 4 stew **5** house **6** bagnio **7** brothel **8** cathouse **10** bawdy house, fancy house, whorehouse **13** sporting house **14** house of ill fame **16** house of ill repute **19** house of prostitution

border 3 hem, rim **4** abut, bind, brim, curb, edge, join, line, pale, trim **5** brink, flank, frame, limit, skirt, touch, verge **6** adjoin, fringe, margin **8** befringe, be next to, boundary, frontier, outskirt **9** extremity, perimeter, periphery **13** circumference

borderline 4 open **5** vague **7** halfway, inexact, obscure, unclear **8** marginal **9** ambiguous, equivocal, uncertain, undecided, unsettled **10** ambivalent, indefinite **11** indefinable, problematic **13** indeterminate

bore 4 drag, drip, sink, tire **5** drill, drive, weary **6** burrow, pierce, tunnel **7** caliber, exhaust, fatigue, wear out **8** gouge out **9** hollow out **10** wet blanket **14** inside diameter

Boreal
pertaining to: **6** Boreas

Boreas
origin: **5** Greek
personifies: **9** north wind
father: **8** Astraeus
mother: **3** Eos
twin sons: **5** Zetes **6** Calais
daughter: **6** Chione **9** Cleopatra

bored 5 jaded **7** wearied **12** discontented, uninterested

boredom 5 ennui **6** tedium **8** doldrums, dullness, monotony **9** weariness **11** tediousness

Borges, Jorge Luis
author of: **8** The Aleph **10** Labyrinths **11** Dreamtigers **13** The Book of Sand **18** A Personal Anthology, In Praise of Darkness **19** Doctor Brodie's Report, Fervor of Buenos Aires **25** A Universal History of Infamy
nationality: **9** Argentina

Borghild
origin: **12** Scandinavian
mentioned in: **8** Volsunga
husband: **7** Sigmund

Borgia, Alfonso de 16 Pope Callistus III

Borgia, Rodrigo de 15 Pope Alexander VI

Borglum, (John) Gutzon
born: **10** Bear Lake ID
artwork: **7** Lincoln **18** Mt Rushmore Memorial, The Mares of Diomedes

Borgnine, Ernest
real name: **18** Ermes Effron Borgnine
wife: **11** Ethel Merman
born: **8** Hamden CT
roles: **5** Marty (Oscar) **8** Barabbas **11** McHale's Navy **12** The Wild Bunch **13** The Dirty Dozen **17** Bad Day at Black Rock **18** From Here to Eternity **20** The Poseidon Adventure

boring 4 dull, flat **5** stale **6** tiring **7** humdrum, insipid, tedious **8** tiresome **9** wearisome **10** monotonous, unexciting **11** repetitious **13** uninteresting

boring tool 3 bit **5** auger, drill **11** brace and bit

Borinquen *see* **10** Puerto Rico

Boriquen, Borinquen
language family: **8** Arawakan
location: **10** Puerto Rico
related to: **5** Taino

Boris Godunov
author: **16** Alexander Pushkin
opera by: **10** Mussorgsky **12** Shostakovich **14** Rimsky- Korsakov
role: **4** czar, tsar
character: **6** Dmitri, Feodor, Maryna **7** Gregory, Grigory **8** Basmanov, Otrepyev

born 6 innate **7** natural **9** delivered, intuitive **12** brought forth

Born, Max
field: **7** physics
nationality: **7** British
worked on: **13** quantum theory
awarded: **10** Nobel Prize

borne 6 afloat, braved **7** carried, endured **9** put up with, tolerated **11** gone through, went through **12** given birth to

Borneo
other name: **10** Kalimantan
largest city: **12** Bandjermasin
others: **5** Kumai **6** Sambas, Sampit **7** Malinau, Pagatan, Sanggau, Sintang, Tarakan **8** Ketapang **9** Pontianak **10** Balikpapan
division of island:

independent: 6 Brunei
Malaysian state: 5 Sabah **7** Sarawak
part of Indonesia: 10 Kalimantan
measure: 7 gantang
weight: 4 para **6** chapah
mountain: 4 Iran, Raja **5** Saran **6** Kapuas, Muller, Nijaan, Tebang **8** Kinibalu, Schwaner
highest point: 8 Kinibalu
river: 4 Arut, Iwan **5** Bahau, Berau, Kajan, Padas, Pawan **6** Barito, Kapuas, Rajang, Sebuku **7** Kahajan, Mahakam, Mendawi **8** Pembuang
sea: 4 Java, Sulu **7** Celebes **10** South China
physical feature:
  bay: 5 Adang, Kumai **6** Sampit
  cape: 3 Aru **4** Datu **5** Lojar **6** Puting, Sambar **7** Selatan
  port: 4 Miri **5** Balik, Papan **6** Brunei **9** Pontianak **12** Bandjermasin
  strait: 8 Macassar
people: 4 Iban **5** Bukat, Dajak, Dayak, Dusan, Malay, Punan **6** Illano **7** Bakatan, Chinese, Illanum
language: 5 Malay **6** tribal **7** Chinese, English
religion: 5 Islam **7** animism **12** Christianity
feature:
  tree: 5 kapor, kapur **7** billian

Born Yesterday
director: 11 George Cukor
cast: 12 Judy Holliday **13** William Holden **17** Broderick Crawford
Oscar for: 7 actress (Holliday)

Borodin, Alexander
born: 6 Russia **12** St Petersburg
member of: 7 The Five
composer of: 8 Bogatyri **10** Prince Igor **25** In the Steppes of Central Asia

boron
chemical symbol: 1 B
compound: 5 borax

borough 4 burg, town **5** borgo, shire **6** county, parish **7** village **8** district, precinct, province, township **12** municipality
of New York City: 5 Kings, Bronx **6** Queens **8** Brooklyn, Richmond **9** Manhattan **12** Staten Island

Borromini, Francesco
architect of: 10 San Carlino **17** Palazzo Falconieri **20** Sant' Ivo della Sapienza **23** Oratory of San Filippo Neri **24** Collegio di Propaganda Fide **26** San Carlo alle Quattro Fontane (Rome)

borrow 3 get, use **4** copy, take **5** filch, steal, usurp **6** obtain, pilfer, pirate **7** acquire **10** commandeer, plagiarize, take on loan **11** appropriate

Borrow, George Henry
author of: 8 Lavengro **9** Romany Rye, Wild Wales **10** The Zincali **15** The Bible in Spain

Bors, Sir
character in: 16 Arthurian romance

Bosch, Hieronymus
real name: 13 Jerome van Aken **14** Jerome van Aeken **17** Jeroen Anthoiszoon
artwork: 7 Hay-Wain **11** Ship of Fools **14** The Crucifixion **19** Adoration of the Kings **21** The Crowning with Thorns **26** The Garden of Earthly Delights

bosh 3 rot **4** bunk **6** bunkum, drivel **7** twaddle **8** claptrap, nonsense, tommyrot **10** balderdash, tomfoolery **11** foolishness **16** stuff and nonsense

bosky 5 bushy, drunk, shaded, tipsy, treed **6** wooded

Bosnia-Herzegovina
capital/largest city: 8 Sarajevo
others: 4 Neum **5** Tuzlal **6** Citluk, Kupres, Lenica, Mostar **8** Prijedor **9** Banja Luka, Bijeljina **10** Srebrenica **12** Bosanski Brod, Siroki Brijeg
head of state: 9 president
monetary unit: 5 dinar
mountain: 11 Dinaric Alps
river: 3 Una **4** Sava **5** Bosna, Drina, Vrbas **7** Neretva
sea: 8 Adriatic
people: 4 Serb **5** Croat **6** Muslim **8** Yugoslav
language: 13 Serbo Croatian
religion: 11 Sunni Muslim **15** Serbian Orthodox

bosom 4 bust, core, dear, soul **5** chest, close, heart, midst **6** breast, center, spirit **7** beloved, nucleus **8** intimate **9** cherished **11** inner circle

bosom buddy 4 chum **5** crony **6** cohort **7** best pal, comrade **8** alter ego, intimate, sidekick **9** companion, confidant **10** best friend

bosomy 5 busty, buxom **6** zaftig **11** full-figured **13** large- breasted

boss 4 head, push **5** chief, order **6** leader, master **7** command, foreman, kingpin, manager **8** employer **9** big cheese, executive **10** supervisor **13** administrator **14** superintendent

bossy 3 cow **9** imperious **10** commanding, tyrannical **11** dictatorial, domineering

Boston
airport: 5 Logan
area: 7 Back Bay **10** Bunker Hill, Fenway Park **11** Faneuil Hall **14** Kennedy Library, Old North Church
baseball team: 6 Red Sox
basketball team: 7 Celtics
dish: 10 baked beans
hockey team: 6 Bruins
landmark: 10 Beacon Hill
leader: 7 Brahmin
nickname: 8 Bean town
river: 7 Charles

Bostonians, The
author: 10 Henry James

Boston Strong Boy
nickname of: 13 John L Sullivan

Boswell, James
author of: 22 The Life of Samuel Johnson

botanist
American: 6 Barton, Carver, Torrey **7** Bartram
Austrian: 6 Mendel
Dutch: 7 DeVries
German: 4 Bock, Cohn
Scottish: 5 Brown
Swedish: 8 Linnaeus
Swiss: 6 Bauhin

botch 3 err, mar **4** blow, fail, flop, flub, goof, hash, mess, muff, ruin **5** spoil **6** bungle, foul up, fumble **7** blunder, butcher, failure, louse up **8** butchery **9** mismanage **11** make a mess of

bother 3 ado, irk, nag, tax, try, vex **4** care, drag, fret, fuss, load, onus, stir **5** annoy, harry, trial, upset, worry **6** dismay, flurry, harass, pester, racket, rumpus, strain, stress, tumult **7** attempt, disturb, problem, trouble **8** disquiet, distress, hardship, headache, irritate, nuisance, vexation **9** aggravate, commotion, hindrance **10** affliction, difficulty, impediment, irritation **11** aggravation, disturbance, encumbrance **12** make an effort **13** inconvenience, pain in the neck **14** responsibility

bothersome 6 taxing, vexing **8** annoying **9** worrisome **10** disturbing **11** aggravating, disquieting, distressing, troublesome **12** inconvenient

Botswana
other name: 12 Bechuanaland
capital/largest city: 8 Gaborone **9** Gaberones
others: 5 Kanye, Orapa, Tsane **6** Serowe **7** Lobatse, Lobotsi, Mochudi, Palapye, Thamaga **10** Molepolole **11** Francistown, Selebi-Pikwe
monetary unit: 4 pula, rand
lake: 3 Dow, Xau **5** Ngami
highest point: 11 Tsodilo Hill
river: 4 Nata, Okwa **5** Chobe, Nosob **6** Cuando, Molopo, Shashi **7** Cubango, Limpopo **8** Botletle, Okovango **9** Okovanggo
physical feature:
  desert: 8 Kalahari
  salt pans: 10 Makarikari
  swamp: 8 Okavango
people: 5 Bantu **6** Tswana **7** Bakatla, Bakwena, Bushman **8** Bamalete, Baralong, Batawana, Batlokwa, Botswana **10** Bamangwato **11** Bangwaketse
language: 5 Bantu, Click **6** Tswana **7** English, Khoisan **8** Setswana

religion: 7 animism **10** Protestant **12** Christianity

Botticelli, Sandro
 real name: 30 Alessandro di Mariano dei Filipepi
 born: 5 Italy **8** Florence
 artwork: 12 Birth of Venus **14** Mystic Nativity **16** Calumny of Apelles **18** Adoration of the Magi **22** Pallas Subduing a Centaur **25** The Madonna of the Magnificat

bottle 3 jar **4** vial **5** flask, phial **6** carafe, flagon, vessel **7** canteen

bottleneck 3 bar, jam **4** clog, stop **5** block **6** detour **7** barrier, embolus **8** blockage, embolism, gridlock, obstacle, stoppage, thrombus **10** congestion, impediment, infarction **11** costiveness, obstruction

bottom 3 can **4** base, core, foot, gist, root, rump, seat, sole **5** basis, belly, cause, fanny, heart, lower **6** center, deeper, depths, ground, lowest, origin, source, spring **7** deepest, essence **8** backside, buttocks, pedestal, riverbed **9** beginning, fundament, principle, rudiments, substance, underpart, underside **10** foundation, mainspring, wellspring **12** quintessence

Bottom
 character in: 21 A Midsummer Night's Dream
 author: 11 Shakespeare
 turned into: 3 ass

bottomless 4 deep **7** abysmal **8** profound **11** measureless **12** immeasurable, unfathomable

Boucher, Francois
 born: 5 Paris **6** France
 artwork: 9 The Rising **13** Madame Boucher, Reclining Girl **16** Evening Landscape, Rinaldo and Armida, The Toilet of Venus **17** Chinese Tapestries, The Triumph of Venus **18** The Setting of the Sun

boudoir 7 bedroom **10** bedchamber **12** dressing room

bough 4 limb **6** branch

bougie 3 dip, wax **5** light, taper **6** candle, cierge, tallow

boulder, bowlder 3 nob **4** crag, knob, rock **5** block, stone **6** gibber **7** dornick **8** megalith

boulevard 6 avenue **7** parkway **9** concourse

bouleversement 7 turmoil **9** confusion, upsetting **11** overturning

bounce 3 bob, hop, pep **4** bump, life **5** bound, thump, verve, vigor **6** energy, jounce, recoil, spirit **7** rebound **8** dynamism, ricochet, vitality, vivacity **9** animation **10** liveliness

bouncing 3 big **4** full **5** jolly, large, lusty, plump **6** chubby, lively, robust, strong **7** healthy **8** animated, vigorous **12** in good health

bound 3 bob, orb, rim **4** area, edge, jump, leap, line, mark, pale, romp, sure, tied **5** dance, fated, hedge, limit, orbit, range, realm, vault **6** border, bounce, define, domain, doomed, forced, fringe, gambol, liable, prance, region, spring, tied up **7** certain, compass, confine, covered, encased, enclosed, flounce, going to, in bonds, limited, obliged, rebound, secured, trussed, wrapped **8** beholden, boundary, confined, destined, district, encircle, fastened, province, required, resolute, resolved, surround, tethered **9** bailiwick, committed, demarcate, extremity, periphery, territory **10** determined, restrained **11** demarcation **12** circumscribe

boundary 3 rim **4** edge, line, pale **6** border, margin **7** barrier **8** frontier, landmark **9** extremity, periphery **11** demarcation **12** dividing line

boundary line 4 edge **5** bound **6** border **8** sideline

bounder 3 cad, rat **4** heel **5** knave, louse, rogue **6** rascal, rotter **7** caitiff, dastard, villain **9** scoundrel **10** blackguard

Bounderby, Mr
 character in: 9 Hard Times
 author: 7 Dickens

boundless 4 vast **7** endless, immense **8** infinite, unending **9** limitless, perpetual, unbounded, unlimited **10** without end **11** everlasting, measureless **12** immeasurable, incalculable, unrestricted **13** inexhaustible

bounteous, bountiful 4 free, full, rich **5** ample, large **6** lavish **7** copious, liberal, profuse, teeming **8** abundant, generous, prolific **9** abounding, plenteous, plentiful, unsparing **10** beneficent, benevolent, charitable, munificent, unstinting **11** magnanimous, overflowing

Bountiful, Lady
 character in: 17 The Beaux Stratagem
 author: 8 Farquhar

bountifulness 10 liberality, generosity **11** benevolence, magnanimity, munificence **14** charitableness **15** humanitarianism

bounty 3 aid **4** gift, help **5** bonus, favor, grant **6** giving, reward **7** charity, present, tribute **8** bestowal, donation, gratuity **9** endowment **10** almsgiving, assistance, generosity, liberality, recompense **11** benefaction, benevolence, munificence **12** contribution, philanthropy **14** charitableness, openhandedness

bouquet 4 odor **5** aroma, scent, spray **7** essence, garland, nosegay, perfume **9** fragrance **11** boutonniere

bouquet garni
 ingredient: 5 basil, thyme **6** celery,

savory **7** bay leaf, chervil, parsley **8** rosemary, tarragon

bourbon
 variety of: 7 whiskey
 origin: 7 America
 ingredient: 4 corn
 type: 7 blended **8** straight
 drink: 9 Mint Julep **10** Boston Sour **11** John Collins **12** Old Fashioned
 with Benedictine: 9 Twin Hills
 with brandy and Benedictine: 13 Brighton Punch
 with Cointreau: 10 Temptation
 with rum: 14 Artillery Punch
 with sloe gin: 9 Black Hawk
 with Southern Comfort: 14 Blended Comfort
 with triple sec: 10 Chapel Hill
 with vermouth: 9 Allegheny

bourgeois 6 square **7** Babbitt, burgher **8** commoner, ordinary **11** middle-class **12** conventional **13** unimaginative

Bourgeois Gentleman, The
 author: 7 Moliere
 character: 6 Lucile, Nicole **7** Cleonte, Dorante **8** Covielle, Dorimene **14** Madame Jourdain **16** Monsieur Jourdain

Bourget, Charles Joseph Paul
 author of: 11 The Disciple **12** A Cruel Enigma **14** The Night Cometh

Bourgh, Lady Catherine de
 character in: 17 Pride and Prejudice
 author: 6 Austen

Bourjaily, Vance
 author of: 11 The Violated **14** The End of My Life **18** Brill Among the Ruins **22** Now Playing at Canterbury

Bourne Identity, The
 author: 12 Robert Ludlum

bout 4 fray, term, tilt, turn **5** brush, clash, cycle, fight, match, set-to, siege, spell, spree **6** affair, battle, course, period, series **7** contest, go-round, scuffle, session, tourney **8** conflict, interval, skirmish, struggle **9** encounter **10** contention, engagement **11** boxing match, embroilment

boutonniere 4 posy **7** nosegay **16** buttonhole flower

bow 3 arc **4** bend, knot, prow, stem **5** agree, curve, defer, front, stoop, yield **6** archer, comply, curtsy, give in, kowtow, relent, salaam, submit, weapon **7** concede, succumb, crescent **9** acquiesce, genuflect, surrender **10** capitulate, forward end **12** genuflection, knuckle under

Bow, Clara
 nickname: 6 It Girl
 born: 10 Brooklyn NY
 roles: 2 It **7** Mantrap **12** The Wild Party

bowdlerize 6 censor **9** expurgate **10** blue-pencil

bow down 5 yield **6** give in, submit **9**

surrender 10 capitulate **12** knuckle under

bowed 4 bent **6** arched, curved, nodded **7** hunched, stooped

bowels 3 gut, pit **4** core, guts, womb **5** abyss, belly, bosom, heart, midst **6** depths, hollow, vitals **7** innards, insides, stomach, viscera **8** entrails, interior, recesses **10** intestines **11** vital organs **13** innermost part

Bowen, Elizabeth
author of: **8** Eva Trout, The Hotel **10** To the North **11** Bowen's Court, Little Girls, The Cat Jumps **12** A World of Love **15** The Heat of the Day, The House in Paris **18** The Death of the Heart

Bowen's Court
author: **14** Elizabeth Bowen

bower 4 jack, joker, nook **5** arbor **6** alcove, anchor, pandal **7** bedroom, chamber, cottage, enclose, retreat, sanctum, shelter **8** dwelling, snuggery

Bowie, David
real name: **16** David Robert Jones
born: **6** London **7** England
roles: **9** Cat People, Labyrinth, The Hunger **20** The Man Who Fell to Earth **24** Merry Christmas Mr Lawrence
wife: **4** Iman
Personae: **11** Aladdin Sane **13** Ziggy Stardust

Bowie Land, Bowie State
nickname of: **8** Arkansas

bowl 4 boat **5** arena, basin **6** cavity, hollow, tureen, valley, vessel **7** dishful, helping, portion, stadium **8** coliseum, deep dish **9** container, porringer **10** depression, receptacle **12** amphitheater

bowler 11 Earl Anthony

bowling
variation: **7** tenpins **8** duckpins, fivepins **10** candlepins
term: **4** miss **5** frame, spare, split **6** strike **10** gutterball
perfect score: **12** three hundred

bow-shape 3 arc **4** arch, bend **5** curve **9** curvature

bow to 5 yield **6** give in, give up, submit **9** acquiesce

box 3 bat, hit, rap **4** belt, cuff, slap, spar **5** booth, caddy, chest, crate, fight, punch, stall, whack **6** buffet, carton, coffer, strike, thwack **8** thumping **9** container **10** receptacle **11** compartment **13** exchange blows

boxer 7 Max Baer **8** Joe Louis **9** Mike Tyson **10** Barney Ross, Gene Tunney, Joe Frazier, Joe Walcott, Leon Spinks **11** Archie Moore, Jack Dempsey, Jack Johnson, Jake LaMotta, Larry Holmes, Muhammad Ali, Sonny Liston **12** Benny Leonard, James Corbett, John Sullivan, Johnny Dundee, Max Schmeling, Mickey Walker, Primo Carnera, Roberto Duran, Thomas Hearns **13** Carmen Basilio, Ezzard Charles, George Foreman, Hector Camacho, James Jeffries, Rocky Graziano, Rocky Marciano **14** Bob Fitzsimmons, Floyd Patterson, Henry Armstrong **15** Maxie Rosenbloom, Sugar Ray Leonard **16** Evander Holyfield, Sugar Ray Robinson

boy 3 lad **5** youth **8** man child **9** male child, stripling, youngster
French: **6** garcon

Boy
character in: **6** Tarzan
author: **9** Burroughs

boycott 5 spurn **6** reject **7** exclude **8** spurning **9** blackball, blacklist, exclusion, ostracism, ostracize, rejection **12** blackballing, blacklisting

Boyd, James
author of: **5** Drums **8** Long Hunt **9** Roll River **10** Marching On

Boyd, William
born: **13** Hendrysburg OH
roles: **15** Hopalong Cassidy

Boyer, Charles
born: **6** Figeac, France
roles: **7** Algiers **8** Conquest, Gaslight **10** Back Street **11** Lost Horizon **16** The Garden of Allah **19** All This and Heaven Too

boyfriend 3 man **4** beau, date **5** flame, lover, swain, wooer **6** escort, fellow, old man, squire, steady, suitor **7** admirer, beloved, Don Juan **8** cavalier, Lothario, paramour, truelove, young man **9** companion, inamorato **10** sweetheart **15** gentleman caller

boyish 5 boyey, fresh **6** callow, tender **7** boylike, puerile **8** childish, immature, innocent, juvenile, youthful **9** childlike **10** sophomoric

Boylan, Blazes
character in: **7** Ulysses
author: **5** Joyce

Boyle, Robert
field: **9** chemistry
nationality: **7** British
father of: **9** chemistry
advocated: **20** experimental approach
established: **9** Boyle's Law

boylike 5 fresh, young **6** boyish, callow **7** puerile **8** childish, immature, innocent, juvenile, youthful **9** childlike

Boys Town
director: **12** Norman Taurog
cast: **9** Henry Hull **12** Mickey Rooney, Spencer Tracy (Father Flanagan)
Oscar for: **5** actor (Tracy)
sequel: **13** Men of Boys Town
near: **5** Omaha

Boy Wonder
nickname of: **5** Robin **6** Mel Ott

brace 3 duo **4** pair, prop, stay **5** shore, strut, truss **6** bracer, couple, hold up, prop up, steady **7** bolster, bracket, fortify, prepare, shore up, support, sustain, twosome **8** buttress **9** reinforce, stanchion **10** strengthen **13** reinforcement

bracelet 6 armlet, bangle

bracer 10 stiff drink, stimulator, wristguard **11** invigorator **12** strengthener, strong drink

Brachiosaurus
type: **8** dinosaur, sauropod
location: **10** East Africa **12** United States
period: **8** Jurassic

bracing 8 arousing, reviving **10** energizing, fortifying, refreshing **11** restorative, stimulating **12** exhilarating, invigorating **13** strengthening

Brack, Judge
character in: **11** Hedda Gabler
author: **5** Ibsen

bracken 4 fern **5** brake, brush, ferns **10** underbrush **11** undergrowth

bracket 4 prop, rank, stay **5** brace, class, group, range, shore, strut, truss **6** prop up, status **7** shore up, support **8** category, classify, division, grouping **9** designate, stanchion **10** categorize **11** designation **14** classification

brackish 4 salt **5** briny, salty **6** saline

Bracknell, Lady Augusta
character in: **27** The Importance of Being Earnest
author: **5** Wilde

bract 4 leaf

Bradbury, Ray
author of: **13** Dandelion Wine, Fahrenheit 451 **17** The Illustrated Man **20** The Martian Chronicles **27** Something Wicked This Way Comes

Bradford, Barbara Taylor
author of: **17** A Woman of Substance

Bradford, Richard
author of: **15** Red Sky at Morning

Bradley, Bill (William Warren)
nickname: **10** Dollar Bill
sport: **10** basketball
team: **13** New York Knicks
elected: **7** Senator
from: **9** New Jersey

Bradstreet, Anne
author of: **35** The Tenth Muse Lately Sprung Up in America

Brady Bunch, The
character: **3** Jan **4** Greg **5** Alice, Bobby, Cindy, Peter **6** Marcia **9** Mike Brady **10** Carol Brady
cast: **8** Eve Plumb **9** Ann B Davis **10** Robert Reed, Susan Olsen **13** Barry Williams **14** Mike Lookinland **16** Maureen McCormick **17** Christopher Knight, Florence Henderson

brag 4 crow **5** boast, vaunt **7** big talk, crowing, talk big **8** boasting, bragging **10** exaggerate, self-praise **12** boastfulness, exaggeration **15** blow one's own horn **19** pat oneself on the back

Brage *see* 5 Bragi

Bragg, William Henry and William Lawrence
field: 7 physics
nationality: 7 British
determined: 16 crystal structure
by: 15 X-ray diffraction
established: 9 Bragg's Law
awarded: 10 Nobel Prize

braggadocio 5 pride 6 egoism, vanity 7 bluster, conceit, swagger 9 cockiness, vainglory 10 pretension 14 self-importance

braggart 7 boaster, bragger 8 blowhard 9 big talker

Bragi
also: 5 Brage
origin: 6 Nordic
god of: 5 music 6 poetry
father: 4 Odin 5 Othin
wife: 4 Idun 5 Iduna, Ithun 6 Ithunn
mother: 3 Fri 5 Frigg, Frija 6 Frigga

Brahe, Tycho
field: 9 astronomy
nationality: 6 Danish
built: 11 observatory

Brahman
country: 5 India
religion: 8 Hinduism
system: 5 caste
rank: 7 highest
function: 6 leader, priest 7 teacher

Brahms, Johannes
born: 7 Germany, Hamburg
composer of: 7 Rinaldo 10 Rain Sonata 11 Triumphlied, Volkslieder 12 Thuner-Sonate 13 German Requiem, Song of Destiny, Song of Triumph 14 Schicksalslied, Song of the Fates, Tragic Overture 15 Gesang der Parzen, Hungarian Dances 19 Liebeslieder Waltzes, Meistersinger Sonata 24 Academic Festival Overture 31 Variations on the St Anthony Chorale

braid 4 knit, lace 5 plait, ravel, twine, twist, weave 7 entwine, wreathe 9 interlace 10 intertwine

brain
part: 7 medulla 8 cerebrum 9 pituitary 10 cerebellum

brainchild 8 creation 9 invention 12 original work 15 imaginative work

braininess 6 genius 9 smartness 10 brightness, brilliance, cleverness 12 intelligence

brainless 4 dumb 6 stupid 7 asinine, foolish, idiotic, moronic, witless 8 mindless 9 imbecilic 10 half-witted 11 lamebrained 12 feeble-minded, simple-minded

brain power 4 mind 9 intellect 12 intelligence 14 mental capacity

Brainworm
character in: 19 Every Man in His Humour
author: 6 Jonson

brainy 5 smart 6 bright, clever 9 brilliant 11 intelligent

brainy group 5 mensa

brake 4 curb, drag, halt, rein, slow, stay, stop 5 check 6 arrest 7 control 9 restraint 10 constraint 11 reduce speed

Bramante, Donato
architect of: 9 Tempietto 14 Belvedere Court (the Vatican), Palazzo Caprini 19 Santa Maria della Pace 21 Santa Maria della Grazie

bramble 4 bush, vine 5 rough, shrub 7 thicket 8 prickers 13 raspberry bush 14 blackberry bush

Bramble, Matthew
character in: 14 Humphry Clinker
author: 8 Smollett

Bran
origin: 5 Welsh
giant king of: 7 Britain
habitat: 3 sea
saint in: 12 Christianity
brother: 9 Evnissyen 10 Manawyddan
sister: 7 Branwen
head buried in: 6 London

branch 3 arm, leg 4 fork, limb, part, wing 5 bough, prong, spray 6 agency, bureau, divide, feeder, member, office, ramify 7 channel, chapter, diverge, radiate, section, segment 8 division, offshoot, separate, shoot off 9 bifurcate, component, extension, tributary 10 department 11 subdivision 12 ramification

branched 6 forked, parted 7 divided 8 extended 9 spread out

Brancusi, Constantin
born: 7 Romania 13 Pestisani Gorj
artwork: 4 Fish 7 Chimera, The Kiss, The Seal 9 Sorceress 10 Adam and Eve, Prometheus 11 Bird in Space, Prodigal Son 12 Flying Turtle, Sleeping Muse 13 Endless Column 20 Sculpture for the Blind

brand 4 blot, kind, make, mark, sear, sign, slur, sort, spot, type 5 class, grade, label, smear, stain, stamp, taint 6 burn in, emblem, smirch, stigma 7 blemish, quality, variety 8 besmirch, disgrace 9 discredit, trademark 10 imputation, stigmatize 11 manufacture

brandish 4 wave 5 shake, swing, wield 6 flaunt, waggle 7 display, exhibit, show off 8 flourish

brand new 4 mint 5 fresh, young 6 unused

Brando, Marlon
born: 7 Omaha NE
roles: 8 Sayonara 10 The Wild One, Viva Zapata 12 Julius Caesar, The Godfather (Oscar refused) 13 Apocalypse Now 15 On the Waterfront (Oscar) 16 Last Tango in Paris 17 Mutiny on the Bounty 21 A Streetcar Named Desire

brandy 6 cognac, grappa, kahlua, kirsch, metaxa 8 Armagnac, Calvados, Tia Maria 9 applejack, Slivovitz 12 Grand Marnier, Peter Heering 14 forbidden fruit
French: 8 eau de vie

Brangwen, Ursula and Gudrun
characters in: 11 Women in Love
author: 8 Lawrence

Branstock
also: 9 Barnstock
origin: 12 Scandinavian
mentioned in: 8 Volsunga
form: 3 oak 4 tree
location: 7 Volsung
house of: 7 Volsung
Odin (Othin) thrusts: 4 Gram 5 sword

Brant, Captain Adam
character in: 22 Mourning Becomes Electra
author: 6 O'Neill

Branwen
origin: 5 Welsh
brother: 4 Bran
husband: 10 Matholwych
son killed by: 9 Evnissyen

Braque, Georges
born: 6 France 18 Argenteuil sur Seine
artwork: 7 Atelier, Grand Nu (Great Nude), The Echo 8 The Table 13 The Portuguese 14 Man with a Guitar 16 Violin and Palette, Violin and Pitcher 18 Woman with a Mandolin

brash 4 bold, rash, rude 5 fresh, hasty, sassy 6 brazen, cheeky, madcap 7 forward 8 careless, heedless, impudent, reckless 9 foolhardy, impetuous, imprudent, know-it-all 10 incautious 11 impertinent, precipitous, smart-alecky 12 unconsidered 13 overconfident

brashness 4 gall 5 brass, cheek, nerve 8 audacity, boldness, chutzpah, temerity 10 brazenness, effrontery 11 forwardness, presumption

Brasilia
capital of: 6 Brazil

brass 4 gall, sand, VIPs 5 cheek, nerve 8 audacity, boldness, chutzpah, officers, temerity 9 impudence 10 brazenness, effrontery 11 forwardness, presumption

Brass, Sampson
character in: 19 The Old Curiosity Shop
author: 7 Dickens

brass instrument 4 tuba 5 bugle 6 cornet 7 trumpet 8 trombone 9 euphonium 10 French horn, sousaphone
ancient: 3 lur 7 Alphorn, buisine, serpent 10 ophicleide

brass tacks 4 crux, meat 7 details 9 realities, substance 10 essentials 11 nitty-gritty 15 sum and substance

brassy 4 bold, loud 5 brash, cheap, cocky, sassy, saucy, showy 6 brazen

7 blaring, forward **8** arrogant, impudent, insolent, overbold **9** barefaced, outspoken, shameless, unabashed **10** unblushing **11** impertinent

brat 3 imp **4** chit **5** whelp **6** hoyden, rascal **9** rude child **10** holy terror **12** spoiled child

Brauhaus 6 tavern **7** brewery

Brautigan, Richard
  author of: 15 Sombrero Fallout **18** The Hawkline Monster **21** Trout Fishing in America **38** The Pill Versus the Springhill Mine Disaster

bravado 7 big talk, blowing, bluster, bombast, bravura, crowing, puffery, swagger **8** boasting, bragging **9** cockiness **10** swaggering **11** braggadocio **12** boastfulness **13** show of courage

brave 4 bear, dare, defy, face, game, take **5** abide, brook, gutsy, stand **6** breast, endure, gritty, heroic, plucky, spunky, suffer **7** doughty, stomach, sustain, undergo, valiant, weather **8** confront, fearless, intrepid, stalwart, tolerate, unafraid, valorous **9** challenge, dauntless, outbrazen, put up with, stand up to, undaunted, withstand **10** courageous **11** lionhearted, unflinching, unshrinking **12** stouthearted

brave deed 4 feat, gest **5** geste **7** exploit **9** heroic act **11** achievement

Brave New World
  author: 12 Aldous Huxley
  character: 4 John **11** Bernard Marx **12** Lenina Crowne, Mustapha Mond

bravery 4 grit **5** pluck, spunk, valor **6** daring, mettle, spirit **7** courage, heroism **8** audacity, boldness **11** intrepidity **12** fearlessness **13** dauntlessness

Bravo, The
  author: 19 James Fenimore Cooper

brawl 3 row **4** fray, tiff **5** broil, clash, fight, melee, scrap, set-to **6** battle, fracas, ruckus, rumpus, uproar **7** dispute, quar- rel, scuffle, wrangle **8** squabble **9** imbroglio **11** altercation, embroilment

brawn 5 might, power **7** muscles, stamina **8** strength **9** beefiness, huskiness **10** robustness, ruggedness, sturdiness **12** muscular development

brawny 5 burly, husky **6** mighty, robust, rugged, strong, sturdy **8** muscular, powerful **9** strapping

Bray, Madeline
  character in: 16 Nicholas Nickleby
  author: 7 Dickens

brazen 4 bold, open **5** brash, saucy **6** brassy, cheeky **7** forward **8** arrogant, immodest, impudent, insolent **9** audacious, barefaced, boldfaced, shameless, unabashed

brazenness 4 gall **5** brass, cheek, nerve **8** audacity, boldness, chutzpah

9 impudence **10** effrontery, fowardness **11** presumption

Brazil
  capital: 8 Brasilia
  former capital: 12 Rio de Janeiro
  largest city: 8 Sao Paulo
  others: 5 Bahia, Belem **6** Recife, Sabara, Santos **7** Vitoria **8** Salvador **9** Ouro Preto, Paranagua **10** Diamantina **11** Porto Alegre **13** Belo Horizonte, Cruzeiro do Sul
  school:
    junior high: 7 ginasio
    senior high: 7 colegio
  measure: 2 pe **4** moio, sack, vara **5** braca, legoa, milha, tonel **6** canada, cuarto, quarto, tarefa **7** garrafa **8** alqueire
  monetary unit: 3 joe **4** reis **5** dobra **7** centara, halfjoe, milreis **8** cruzeiro
  weight: 3 bag **4** onca **5** libra **6** arroba, oitava **7** quilate, quintal **8** tonelada
  island: 6 Maraca, Marajo **7** Bananal, Cardoso, Caviana, Mexiana **8** Comprida
  lake: 4 Aima, Feia **5** Mirim **13** Logo dos Platos
  mountain: 3 Mar **5** Geral, Organ, Piaui **6** Acarai, Gurupi, Parima, Urucum **7** Amambai, Carajas, Gradaus, Oragaos, Roraima **8** Bandeira, Itatiaja, Roncador, Tombador **9** Pacaraima, Sugar Loaf **10** Tumuc-Humac
  highest point: 7 Neblina
  river: 3 Apa, Ica **4** Doce, Geio, Ivai, Jari, Para, Paru, Sono, Tefe **5** Abuna, Anaua, Apore, Capim, Claro, Corua, Icana, Iriri, Itapi, Jurua, Jutai, Manso, Negro, Pardo, Piaui, Preto, Tiete, Turvo, Urubu, Verde, Xingu **6** Ajuana, Amazon, Arinos, Balsas, Branco, Canuma, Contas, Cuiaba, Demini, Grajau, Grande, Gurupi, Ibicui, Iguacu, Japura, Javari, Mearim, Mortes, Mucuri, Parana, Purpus, Ronuro, Sangue, Tacutu, Tibagi, Uatuma, Uaupes **7** Corumba, Iguassu, Madeira, Madiera, Orinoco, Paraiba, Sucuriu, Tapajos, Taquari, Teodoro, Uruguai, Uruguay, Velhass **8** Araguaia, Padauiri, Paracatu, Paraguay, Parnaiba, Solimoes, Tarauaca **9** Tocantins **12** Sao Francisco
  sea: 8 Atlantic
  physical feature:
    bay: 9 All Saints
    cape: 4 Frio **6** Blanco, Buzios, Gurupy, Orange **7** Saotome **8** Saoroque
    dam: 6 Furnas **7** Peixoto
    estuary: 4 Para
    rain forest: 5 selva
    waterfall: 6 Guaira, Iguacu **7** Iguassu **11** Paulo Afonso
  people: 2 Ge **4** Anta **5** Acroa, Arara, Araua, Bravo, Carib, Guana, Negro **6**

Arawak, Caraja **7** Carayan, Javahai, Tariana **8** Botocudo, Chambioa **9** Caucasian, mamelucos, mulattoes **10** Portuguese **11** Tupi-Guarani
  architect: 8 Niemeyer
  artist: 6 Segall **9** Portinari **10** Cavalcenti
  author: 5 Amado, Bilac, Ramos **6** Freyre
  composer: 10 Villalobos
  discoverer: 6 Cabral
  leader: 6 Aranha, Branco, Collor, Franco, Geisel, Medici, Vargas **7** Goulart
  sculptor: 11 Aleijadinho
  language: 10 Portuguese
  religion: 10 Protestant **13** Roman Catholic
  place:
    beach: 7 Ipanema **9** Boa Viagem **10** Copacabana
  feature:
    bird: 4 mitu **5** mitua
    dance: 5 frevo, samba **6** maxixe **9** bossa nova
    fish: 7 piranha
    gourd: 4 cuia
    plantation: 7 fazenda
    slums: 7 favelas
    tree: 5 icica **6** ucuuba **7** arariba
  food:
    dish: 6 vatapa **8** feijoada
    dried salted beef: 7 charque
    drink: 4 acai **9** cafezinho
    tea: 4 mate
    turtle soup: 16 cas quinho de mucua

Brazil
  director: 12 Terry Gilliam
  cast: 8 Ida Lowry **9** Kim Greist **12** Robert De Niro **13** Jonathan Pryce

Brazilian Bombshell
  nickname of: 13 Carmen Miranda

Brazzaville
  capital of: 5 Congo

breach 3 gap **4** gash, hole, rent, rift, slit **5** break, chink, cleft, crack, split **7** crevice, failure, fissure, neglect, opening, rupture **8** defiance, trespass **9** disregard, violation **10** infraction **11** dereliction **12** disobedience, infringement **13** noncompliance, nonobservance, transgression

breach of faith 7 perfidy **8** bad faith, betrayal **9** falseness, treachery, two-timing **10** disloyalty **11** double-cross **13** double-dealing

breach of order 4 riot **6** fracas, mutiny, ruckus, uproar **7** turmoil **8** uprising **9** commotion, rebellion **10** dissension **11** disturbance, pandemonium **18** disturbance of peace

breach of trust 7 falsity, perfidy **9** falseness, treachery **10** disloyalty, infidelity **13** deceitfulness, double-dealing

bread 3 rye **4** food, pita **5** bucks, dough, money, wheat, white **6** staple

9 sourdough **10** livelihood, sustenance **11** staff of life **12** pumpernickel

bread and butter 3 job **6** career, living **7** calling **8** business, vocation **9** life's work **10** livelihood **14** means of support

Bread and Wine
author: **13** Ignazio Silone

breadbasket 3 gut **5** belly, tummy **6** paunch **7** abdomen, labonza, midriff, Midwest, stomach **11** solar plexus

breadth 4 area, size, span **5** range, reach, scope, width **6** extent, spread **7** compass, expanse, measure, stretch **8** latitude, wideness **9** broadness **10** dimensions **13** extensiveness

break 3 cap, end, fly, gap, off, run, top **4** beat, bust, chip, dash, defy, flee, gash, halt, hole, rend, rent, rest, rift, rive, ruin, snap, stop, tame, tear, tell **5** burst, cease, cleft, crack, crush, erupt, excel, lapse, occur, outdo, pause, sever, shirk, smash, split, train **6** appear, better, breach, chance, cleave, detach, divide, escape, exceed, happen, hiatus, ignore, inform, lessen, master, powder, recess, reveal, soften, subdue, sunder, weaken **7** control, cushion, destroy, disobey, divulge, eclipse, fissure, fortune, give out, lighten, neglect, opening, pull off, respite, run away, rupture, shatter, surpass, suspend, tear off, violate, wipe out **8** announce, bankrupt, burst out, cracking, demolish, diminish, disclose, disjoint, division, fracture, fragment, go beyond, interval, outstrip, overcome, proclaim, renege on, separate, shut down, slip away, splinter **9** dismember, disregard, granulate, interlude, interrupt, make a dash, pulverize, splitting, transcend **10** discipline, disconnect, fall back on, fly the coop, fracturing, impoverish, infringe on, make public, overshadow, separation, shattering, take flight, wrench away **11** discontinue, get away from, opportunity, pay no heed to **12** be derelict in, disintegrate, intermission, interruption, make a getaway, stroke of luck **13** strap for funds **14** bend to one's will, take the force of **15** take to one's heels

breakable 5 frail, shaky **6** flimsy **7** brittle, crumbly, fragile **8** delicate

break apart 7 crumble, shatter **8** collapse **9** fall apart **12** disintegrate, fall to pieces

breakdown 6 mishap **7** crackup, decline, failure **8** analysis, collapse, disorder, division **12** detailed list **13** deterioration **14** categorization

break down 6 divide **7** dissect **8** collapse, separate **9** decompose **11** deteriorate

breaker 4 cask, wave **6** comber **7** crusher **8** boat cask **9** destroyer

break faith with 6 betray **7** do wrong **9** play false **11** double-cross **12** be unfaithful **13** be treacherous **16** sell down the river

Breakfast at Tiffany's
author: **12** Truman Capote
director: **12** Blake Edwards
cast: **10** Buddy Ebsen **12** Mickey Rooney, Patricia Neal **13** Audrey Hepburn (Holly Golightly), George Peppard
score: **12** Henry Mancini
song: **9** Moon River

Breakfast Club, The
director: **10** John Hughes
cast: **10** Ally Sheedy, Judd Nelson **13** Emilio Estevez, Molly Ringwald **18** Anthony Michael Hall

Breakfast of Champions
author: **12** Kurt Vonnegut

break free 4 bolt, flee, skip **6** escape **7** get away, make off, run away **9** cut and run **10** fly the coop **12** make a getaway

breakfront 5 hutch **7** cabinet **8** bookcase, cupboard **12** china cabinet

break in 5 train **7** intrude **8** accustom, initiate **9** acclimate, interrupt **10** burglarize **12** indoctrinate

break-in 5 theft **7** robbery **8** burglary, stealing **12** burglarizing **13** housebreaking **19** breaking and entering

Breaking Away
director: **10** Peter Yates
screenplay: **11** Steve Tesich
cast: **10** Paul Dooley **11** Daniel Stern, Dennis Quaid **13** Barbara Barrie **16** Jackie Earle Haley **17** Dennis Christopher
setting: **7** Indiana **11** Bloomington

break loose 4 bolt, flee, skip **6** escape **7** get away, make off **9** cut and run **10** fly the coop **12** make a getaway

breakneck 4 rash **5** risky **8** reckless, very fast **9** dangerous, daredevil **12** death-defying

break of day 4 dawn **5** sunup **7** dawning, sunrise **8** daybreak **11** crack of dawn

break off 3 end **4** halt **5** cease **6** recess **7** adjourn, snap off, suspend **8** conclude, shut down **11** discontinue

breakout 6 escape, flight **7** getaway **10** decampment

break out 4 bolt, skip **5** begin, erupt **6** escape **7** bust out, get away **10** burst forth, fly the coop **12** make a getaway

Break the Bank
host: **9** Bert Parks **10** Bud Collyer

break the habit 4 kick, quit, stop **6** eschew, give up **8** renounce, withdraw **14** quit cold turkey

breakthrough 7 advance **11** advancement, improvement, penetration, step forward

breakup 5 split **7** crackup **9** dispersal,

splitting **10** separation **14** disintegration

break with 5 leave **8** be untrue, part from **10** be disloyal **11** divorce from **12** fall away from, separate from

breast 4 bust, core **5** bosom, chest, heart **10** very marrow
Italian: **5** petto

breastwork 7 bastion, rampart **8** barbette **9** earthwork **13** fortification

breath 4 wind **6** spirit **9** animation, breathing, lifeblood, life force **10** exhalation, inhalation, vital spark **11** divine spark, respiration, vital spirit **12** vitalization

breathe 4 gasp, huff, pant, puff **5** utter **6** impart, murmur **7** respire, whisper **9** draw in air **10** draw breath **15** inhale and exhale

breathe in 6 inhale **7** inspire, respire

breathe out 4 huff, pant, puff **6** exhale, expire **7** respire

breathing 4 live **5** alive **6** living **7** animate **11** respiratory **13** drawing breath

Breathless
director: **14** Jean-Luc Goddard
written by: **16** Francois Truffaut
cast: **10** Jean Seberg **16** Jean-Paul Belmondo
setting: **5** Paris

breathtaking 7 amazing, awesome **8** exciting **9** startling **10** surprising **11** astonishing

Brecht, Bertolt
author, of: **13** Mother Courage **15** Drums in the Night **18** The Threepenny Opera **21** St Joan of the Stockyards **23** The Caucasian Chalk Circle **27** The Resistable Rise of Arturo Ui **29** The Private Life of the Master Race

Breck, Alan
character in: **9** Kidnapped
author: **9** Stevenson

breech 4 rump, seat **6** behind **8** buttocks, haunches, hind part **9** fundament, posterior **12** hindquarters

breeches 5 pants **8** trousers

breed 4 bear, grow, kind, race, sire, sort, type **5** beget, cause, order, raise, spawn, stock **6** family, father, foster, lead to, mother, strain **7** develop, nurture, pro- duce, promote, species, variety **8** generate, multiply, occasion **9** cultivate, give forth, procreate, propagate, reproduce **10** bring forth, give rise to **11** proliferate **16** produce offspring

breeding 4 line **5** grace **6** mating, polish **7** bearing, descent, growing, lineage, manners, raising, rearing **8** ancestry, courtesy, hatching, heredity, pedigree, spawn- ing, training **9** begetting, bloodline, genealogy, gentility, parentage, producing **10** background, extraction, family tree, generation, politeness, production, refinement, upbringing **11** cultivation, germination, multiplying, procreation, propagation **12** reproduction

breeze 4 flit, pass, sail, snap, waft **5** coast, float, glide, sweep **6** zephyr **9** light gust, light wind **10** gentle wind, puff of wind

breezy 3 gay **4** airy, pert, spry **5** blowy, brisk, fresh, gusty, light, merry, pep- py, sunny, windy **6** bouncy, casual, frisky, jaunty, lively **7** buoyant, squally **8** animated, blustery, carefree, cheerful, debonair, spirited **9** energetic, resilient, sprightly, vivacious, windswept **10** blithesome **11** free and easy

Brennan, Walter
  born: 12 Swampscott MA
  roles: 8 Kentucky **12** Come and Get It, The Westerner **13** The Real McCoys **16** To Have and Have Not

Brent, George
  real name: 18 George Brendan Nolan
  wife: 11 Ann Sheridan **14** Ruth Chatterton
  born: 7 Ireland **14** Shannonsbridge
  roles: 7 Jezebel **11** Dark Victory, The Great Lie **17** Forty- Second Street

Bres
  origin: 5 Irish
  king of: 7 Ireland

Breton, Andre
  author of: 5 Nadja **21** Manifesto of Surrealism

Breuer, Marcel
  architect of: 17 IBM Research Center (La Gaude France) **18** UNESCO headquarters (Paris) **25** St John's Abbey and University (Collegeville MN) **26** Whitney Museum of American Art (NYC)
  designed: 5 chair

brevity 9 briefness, pithiness, quickness, shortness, terseness **10** transience **11** conciseness **12** ephemerality, impermanence, succinctness

brew 3 ale **4** beer, boil, cook, form, make, plan, plot, soak, suds **5** begin, drink, hatch, ripen, start, steep, stout **6** cook up, devise, foment, gather, porter, scheme, seethe **7** arrange, brewski, concoct, ferment, mixture, prepare, produce, think up **8** beverage, contrive, initiate **9** formulate, germinate, originate **10** concoction, malt liquor

brewery
  German: 8 Brauhaus

Brian de Bois, Sir
  character in: 7 Ivanhoe
  author: 5 Scott

bribe 3 sop **5** graft **6** buy off, grease, pay off, payola, suborn **9** hush money **10** inducement **11** illegal gift **15**

grease the hand of, grease the palm of
  French: 7 douceur

bric-a-brac 7 baubles, gewgaws **8** bibelots, trinkets **9** gimcracks, kickshaws, ornaments **11** knickknacks

Brick
  character in: 16 Cat on a Hot Tin Roof
  author: 8 Williams

Bricks
  god of: 5 Kulla

bridal 7 nuptial, wedding **8** marriage **11** matrimonial

Bridehead, Sue
  character in: 14 Jude the Obscure
  author: 5 Hardy

Bride of Lammermoor, The
  author: 14 Sir Walter Scott
  character: 10 Lady Ashton, Lucy Ashton, Ravenswood **14** Laird of Bucklaw **16** Sir William Ashton

Brideshead Revisited
  author: 11 Evelyn Waugh
  character: 5 Celia, Julia **8** Cordelia **9** Sebastian **10** Brideshead (Bridey), Rex Mottram **12** Boy Mulcaster, Charles Ryder **13** Lady Marchmain, Lord Marchmain **14** Anthony Blanche

bridge 3 tie **4** band, bind, bond, link, span **5** cross, unify, union **6** go over **7** catwalk, connect, liaison, viaduct **8** alliance, overpass, traverse **9** cross over **10** connection, passageway **11** association, reach across **12** extend across

bridge
  derived from: 5 whist
  type: 7 auction **8** contract
  partnership: 9 East/West **11** North/South
  cards/hand: 8 thirteen
  no cards of a suit: 4 void
  one card of a suit: 9 singleton
  two cards of a suit: 9 doubleton
  rule book by: 5 Goren
  position: 4 east
  action: 3 bid **4** pass
  term: 4 slam **5** trump **6** double, renege, tenace

Bridge of San Luis Rey, The
  author: 14 Thornton Wilder
  character: 5 Clara, Jaime **6** Manuel, Pepita **7** Esteban, Viceroy **8** Uncle Pio **11** La Perichole **14** Brother Juniper **20** Marquesa de Montemayor

Bridge on the River Kwai, The
  director: 9 David Lean
  based on story by: 12 Pierre Boulle
  cast: 11 Jack Hawkins **12** Alec Guinness **13** William Holden **14** Sessue Hayakawa
  Oscar for: 5 actor (Guinness) **7** picture

Bridges, Beau
  real name: 21 Lloyd Vernet Bridges III

father: 5 Lloyd
brother: 4 Jeff
born: 12 Los Angeles CA
roles: 5 Space **8** Norma Rae **11** Signs of Life, The Landlord, The Wild Pair **17** The Fifth Musketeer **20** The Fabulous Baker Boys **25** The Other Side of the Mountain

Bridges, Jeff
  father: 5 Lloyd
  brother: 4 Beau
  born: 12 Los Angeles CA
  roles: 4 Tron **7** Starman **8** King Kong **10** Jagged Edge **12** The Vanishing **13** Kiss Me Goodbye, The Fisher King **14** Against All Odds **18** The Last Picture Show **20** The Fabulous Baker Boys

Bridges, Lloyd
  sons: 4 Beau, Jeff
  born: 12 San Leandro CA
  roles: 7 Sea Hunt **8** Airplane, High Noon

Bridges at Toko-ri, The
  author: 13 James Michener

Bridget
  character in: 19 Every Man in His Humour
  author: 6 Jonson

Bridge Too Far, A
  author: 13 Cornelius Ryan

Bridgetown
  capital of: 8 Barbados

bridle 3 gag **4** curb, rule **5** check **6** arrest, direct, draw up, flinch, hinder, manage, master, muzzle, rear up, recoil **7** con- trol, harness, inhibit, repress **8** draw back, restrain, restrict, suppress **9** constrain, restraint **11** bit and brace, head harness

brief 4 case **5** hasty, pithy, quick, short, swift, terse **6** advise, inform, precis, resume **7** capsule, compact, concise, defense, limited, prepare, summary **8** abridged, abstract, argument, fill in on, fleeting, instruct, succinct **9** condensed, curtailed, momentary, shortened, temporary, thumbnail, transient **10** abridgment, compressed, contention, describe to, short-lived, summarized, transitory **11** abbreviated **12** legal summary

brief account 6 precis, sketch **7** outline, summary **8** anecdote

brier, briar 4 Rosa **5** Rubus, thorn **6** Smilax **7** bramble
  varieties: 3 Cat, Dog, Hag, Saw **4** Bull **5** Green, Horse, Sweet **7** Jackson **8** Austrian **9** Sensitive **14** Austrian copper

brigade 4 crew, team, unit **5** corps, force, group, squad **6** legion, outfit **7** company **9** regiments, squadrons **10** army groups, battalions, contingent, detachment

Brigadoon
  director: 16 Vincente Minnelli

based on Broadway hit by: 14 Lerner and Loewe
cast: 9 Gene Kelly **10** Van Johnson **11** Cyd Charisse
setting: 8 Scotland

brigand 5 thief **6** bandit, gunman, looter, outlaw, pirate, robber, vandal **7** corsair, hoodlum, ruffian, rustler, spoiler **8** marauder, pilferer, pillager **9** buccaneer, cutthroat, desperado, despoiler, plunderer, privateer **10** highwayman

bright 3 gay **4** glad, good, keen, rosy, sage, warm, wise **5** acute, alert, aware, grand, great, happy, jolly, merry, quick, sharp, smart, sunny, vivid **6** astute, blithe, brainy, clever, gifted, joyful, joyous, lively, shrewd **7** beaming, blazing, capable, glowing, healthy, hopeful, intense, lambent, radiant, shining **8** cheerful, dazzling, exciting, gleaming, luminous, lustrous, profound, splendid, talented **9** brilliant, competent, effulgent, excellent, favorable, ingenious, inventive, masterful, promising, sagacious, sparkling, wide-awake **10** auspicious, discerning, glittering, optimistic, perceptive, proficient, propitious, prosperous, remarkable, shimmering, successful **11** clearheaded, illuminated, illustrious, intelligent, light-filled, magnificent, outstanding, quick- witted, resourceful, resplendent **12** exhilarating

brighten 4 lift **5** boost, cheer, light **6** buoy up, lift up, perk up **7** animate, enliven, gladden, lighten **9** make happy, stimulate **10** illuminate

bright-eyed 5 alert, awake **9** wide-awake **12** on the qui vive

Bright Flows the River
   author: 14 Taylor Caldwell

brightness 4 glow **5** glare, gleam, shine **6** dazzle, luster **7** glitter, sparkle **8** radiance **9** lightness **10** brilliance, luminosity **12** intelligence

bright spot 3 joy **6** solace **7** comfort **8** pleasure **13** consolation

Brigit
   origin: 5 Welsh
   goddess of: 4 fire **6** wisdom **9** fertility, household **11** agriculture

Brigitte Bardot & the Lolita Syndrome
   author: 16 Simone de Beauvoir

Brill Among the Ruins
   author: 14 Vance Bourjaily

brilliance, brilliancy 4 gift, glow **5** blaze, eclat, gleam, sheen, shine **6** acuity, dazzle, genius, luster, talent, wisdom **7** glitter, shimmer, sparkle **8** grandeur, keenness, radiance, sagacity, splendor **9** alertness, awareness, greatness, ingenuity, intensity, quickness, sharpness, smartness, vividness **10** braininess, brightness, capability, cleverness, competence, effulgence,

excellence, luminosity, perception, profundity, shrewdness **11** discernment, distinction, proficiency **12** intelligence, magnificence, resplendence **13** inventiveness, masterfulness **15** clearheadedness, illustriousness, resourcefulness

brilliant *see* **6** bright

brim 3 fill, lip, rim **5** brink, flood, ledge, verge **6** border, fill up, margin, well up **8** overflow

brimless hat 3 cap **5** beret **6** beanie **11** stocking cap, tam o'shanter

brimming 4 full **7** flooded, teeming **8** overfull, swarming **11** overflowing

Brimo
   origin: 5 Greek
   form: 7 goddess
   corresponds to: 6 Hecate **7** Demeter **10** Persephone

brine 6 the sea **8** sea water **9** salt water **12** salt solution **14** saline solution **16** pickling solution

bring 4 bear, make, take, tote **5** begin, carry, cause, fetch, force, start **6** compel, convey, create, effect, induce **7** deliver, produce, sell for, usher in **8** convince, engender, generate, initiate, persuade, result in **9** accompany, institute, originate, transport **10** bring about

bring about 2 do **4** form, open **5** begin, cause, found, set up, start **6** attain, create, effect, lead to **7** achieve, execute, produce **8** carry out, generate, initiate, organize **9** establish, institute, succeed at **10** accomplish, effectuate, inaugurate **11** bring to pass, precipitate **18** bring into existence

bring back 6 return **7** restore **8** recreate **9** surrender **10** return with

bring down a peg 5 abase **6** humble **7** mortify **9** humiliate **13** cut down to size

bring down to earth 10 disenchant **11** disenthrall, disillusion, open the eyes **13** break the spell **14** burst the bubble **20** shatter one's illusions

bring forth 4 bear **5** breed, elicit, evoke, hatch, spawn, whelp **7** deliver, produce **9** reproduce **10** make appear **11** give birth to

bring home to 7 blame on, clarify **11** attribute to **15** place emphasis on

bringing together 7 joining, wedding **8** amassing **9** combining, gathering, including **10** assembling, collecting **12** accumulating **13** incorporating

Bringing Up Baby
   director: 11 Howard Hawks
   cast: 9 Cary Grant **14** Charlie Ruggles **16** Katharine Hepburn
   "Baby": 7 leopard

Bringing Up Father
   creator: 13 George McManus
   character: 5 Jiggs **6** Maggie

   daughter: 5 Rosie
   brother-in-law: 5 Bimmy
   place: 11 Dinty Moore's
   favorite dish: 20 corned beef and cabbage

bring into being 4 bear, form, make **5** erect, hatch, spawn, whelp **6** create, design, devise, invent, render **7** concoct, deliver, develop, fashion, produce **8** contrive, generate **9** construct, fabricate, formulate, originate **10** bring forth **11** give birth to

bring into existence 4 form **5** begin, set up, start **6** create **8** organize **9** establish, institute **10** bring about, inaugurate

bring into line 5 adapt **6** adjust **7** conform, shape up **9** harmonize, reconcile **10** discipline **11** accommodate **13** whip into shape

bring into question 11 cast doubt on **18** throw suspicion upon

bring into relief 6 accent, stress **7** dwell on, feature, point up **9** emphasize, press home, underline **10** accentuate, underscore

bring low 5 abase, shame **6** humble **8** cast down **9** denigrate, humiliate

bring off 4 gain **6** attain, effect, secure **7** achieve **10** accomplish

bring to an end 5 cease **6** finish **8** break off, conclude **9** call a halt, terminate **11** discontinue

bring to a standstill 3 end **4** halt, stay, stop **5** block, check **6** arrest **12** bring to a halt

bring to bay 4 trap, tree **6** corner **8** confront, hunt down

bring to bear 5 apply **6** employ **7** utilize **9** implement

bring together 5 amass **6** gather, muster **7** collect, marshal, round up **8** assemble **10** accumulate

bring to light 6 expose, reveal, unveil **7** clarify, divulge, explain, uncover **8** disclose **9** explicate, make known, make plain **10** illuminate, make public

bring to one's senses 3 jar **5** alarm, alert, shock **9** make aware

bring to pass 5 cause **6** create, effect **8** carry out **10** bring about, effectuate

bring to terms 6 settle **7** mediate **9** arbitrate, reconcile

bring to view 5 dig up **6** reveal **7** exhibit, uncover, unearth **8** disclose, retrieve **10** come up with

bring word 4 tell **6** advise, convey, inform, notify, relate, reveal **7** divulge, publish **8** announce, disclose, proclaim **9** apprise of, broadcast, make known, publicize **11** communicate

brink 3 rim **4** bank, brim, edge **5** point, shore, skirt, verge **6** border, margin **9** threshold

briny 4 salt **5** salty **6** saline

brio, con
music: **9** with vigor **10** with spirit

Briseis
origin: **5** Greek
mentioned in: **5** Iliad
father: **18** Briseus of Lyrnessus
husband: **5** Mynes
captured by: **8** Achilles
caused: **7** quarrel
between: **8** Achilles **9** Agamemnon

Briseus
origin: **5** Greek
mentioned in: **5** Iliad
daughter: **7** Briseis
death by: **7** suicide

Brisingamen 8 necklace
origin: **12** Scandinavian
trait: **5** magic
owned by: **5** Freia, Freya

brisk 4 busy, spry **5** alert, fresh, peppy, quick, swift **6** active, breezy, lively, snappy **7** bracing, chipper, dynamic, rousing **8** animated, bustling, spirited, stirring, vigorous **9** energetic, sprightly, vivacious, vivifying **10** refreshing **11** stimulating **12** exhilarating, invigorating

briskness 3 pep **5** vigor **6** energy **8** alac- rity, spryness **9** quickness, swiftness **13** sprightliness

bristle 4 hair, seta **5** quill **7** stiffen, whisker

bristles 5 barbs, setae **6** quills **7** stubble **8** prickles, whiskers

bristletail
variety: **7** jumping **8** firebrat **9** primitive **10** nicoletiid, silverfish

bristly 5 rough **6** barbed, coarse **7** prickly, stubbly **8** unshaven **9** whiskered **11** bewhiskered

Britannia *see* **7** England

British 6 Breton, Briton **7** English **8** Brittany

British Columbia
bordered by: **5** Idaho, Yukon **6** Alaska **7** Montana **10** Washington **12** Pacific Ocean, United States **20** Northwest Territories
country: **6** Canada
Indian: **5** Haida **6** Nootka, Salish **8** Kwakiutl **9** Tsimshian **10** Bella Coola
island: **9** Vancouver **14** Queen Charlotte
mountain: **5** Coast, Rocky **7** Cascade **8** Columbia **11** Cordilleran **14** Cassiar Omineca
nickname: **2** BC
park: **7** Glacier
rank in size: **5** sixth
river: **6** Fraser
section: **8** province

British Guiana *see* **6** Guyana

British Honduras *see* **6** Belize

British Mythology
god of rebirth/afterlife: **4** Gwyn

chief of gods: **5** Woden
island of paradise: **6** Avalon

Britomart
character in: **15** The Faerie Queene
author: **7** Spenser

Britomartis
origin: **6** Cretan
goddess of: **7** hunters, sailors **9** fishermen
father: **4** Zeus
mother: **5** Carme
corresponds to: **7** Artemis **8** Dictynna

Briton 4 Celt **6** Celtic **7** British

Brittany
coast: **5** Armor
country: **6** France
inhabitant: **5** Celts **6** French, Romans
interior: **6** Argoat
land form: **9** peninsula
language: **6** Breton
other name: **5** Breiz **6** Breton **8** Bretagne

Britten, (Edward) Benjamin
born: **7** England **9** Lowestoft
composer of: **8** Gloriana **9** Billy Budd **10** Paul Bunyan, War Requiem **11** Curlew River, Peter Grimes, Winter Words **12** Owen Wingrave, The Poet's Echo **13** Albert Herring, Death in Venice **14** The Prodigal Son, Turn of the Screw **15** Phantasy Quartet **17** A Ceremony of Carols, A Charm of Lullabies, Sinfonia da Requiem, The Rape of Lucretia **18** Holderlin Fragments **20** Cantata Misericordium **21** A Midsummer Night's Dream, Sonnets of Michelangelo **22** The Burning Fiery Furnace

brittle 7 crumbly, fragile, friable **9** breakable, frangible

broach 4 pose **6** launch, open up, submit **7** advance, bring up, mention, propose, suggest, touch on **9** institute, introduce

broad 4 full, open, wide **5** ample, clear, large, plain, rangy, roomy, thick **7** general, immense, obvious, sizable **8** extended, spacious, sweeping **9** capacious, expansive, extensive, inclusive, outspread, universal, unlimited **10** undetailed **11** far-reaching, nonspecific, wide-ranging **12** all-embracing, encyclopedic **13** comprehensive

broadcast 4 beam, show, talk **5** cable, radio, relay **7** program, send out **8** televise, transmit **9** statement **10** distribute **11** disseminate, put on the air **12** announcement

broaden 5 boost, raise, swell, widen **6** dilate, expand, extend **7** advance, amplify, augment, build up, develop, distend, enlarge, improve, stretch **8** increase **9** intensify, reinforce, spread out **10** strengthen, supplement

broadened 7 dilated, swelled, swollen,

widened **8** enlarged, expanded, extended **9** distended, spread out

broad-minded 7 liberal **8** amenable, catholic, flexible, tolerant, unbiased **9** receptive, unbigoted **10** charitable, open-minded, undogmatic **11** magnanimous **12** unprejudiced, unprovincial

Broadway Joe
nickname of: **9** Joe Namath

Brobdingnag
fictional land in: **16** Gulliver's Travels
author: **5** Swift

Brobdingnagian 4 huge **5** giant **7** immense, mammoth **8** colossal, enormous, gigantic **10** gargantuan, tremendous **11** elephantine

broccoli 9 vegetable **12** Brassica rapa **16** Brassica oleracea (Botyris Group) **17** Brassica septiceps
variety: **6** Turnip **7** Italian **9** Asparagus, Sprouting

brochure 5 flier **6** folder **7** booklet, leaflet **8** circular, handbill, pamphlet **9** throwaway

Brockton Blockbuster
nickname of: **13** Rocky Marciano

Broglie, Louis Victor de
field: **7** physics
nationality: **6** French
developed: **13** wave mechanics
awarded: **10** Nobel Prize

broil 3 fry **4** bake, burn, cook, sear **5** parch, roast, toast **6** scorch **7** blister

broiler 3 hot, pan **4** rack **5** grill **6** cooker **8** scorcher **12** young chicken

broke 8 bankrupt, strapped, wiped out **9** insolvent, penniless **10** down and out **12** impoverished, on one's uppers, without funds **16** strapped for funds

broken 4 torn **5** rough, split, tamed **6** ruined, uneven **7** crushed, damaged **8** bankrupt, in pieces, ruptured **9** fractured, separated, shattered **10** incomplete **11** fragmentary, interrupted

Broken Commandment, The
author: **14** Toson Shimazaki

broken-down 6 beat-up, ruined **7** rickety, worn-out **8** battered, decrepit **10** ramshackle **11** dilapidated **12** deteriorated

broken-hearted 3 sad **6** gloomy, woeful **7** crushed, doleful, forlorn, unhappy **8** dejected, desolate, downcast, mournful, wretched **9** depressed, long-faced, miserable, sorrowful, woebegone **10** despairing, despondent, melancholy **11** heartbroken **12** disconsolate, inconsolable

Brom Bones
also: **12** Brom Van Brunt
character in: **23** The Legend of Sleepy Hollow
author: **6** Irving

Bromfield, Louis

author of: 11 Early Autumn, Malabar Farm **12** The Rains Came **13** Mrs Parkington, Night in Bombay **14** Wild Is the River **15** The Green Bay Tree **31** The Strange Case of Miss Annie Spragg

bromide 6 cliche **8** banality **9** platitude **10** stereotype **11** trite phrase **19** hackneyed expression

bromidic 4 dull **5** banal, corny, stale, tired, trite, vapid **6** jejune **7** humdrum, insipid **8** ordinary **9** hackneyed **10** pedestrian, unexciting, unoriginal **13** platitudinous, unimaginative

bromine
chemical symbol: **2** Br

Bromius
epithet of: **8** Dionysus
means: **7** thunder

Bronson, Charles
real name: **16** Charles Buchinsky
wife: **11** Jill Ireland
born: **11** Ehrenfeld PA
roles: **9** Death Wish **13** The Dirty Dozen **14** The Great Escape **16** Battle of the Bulge, The Valachi Papers **19** The Magnificent Seven

Bronte, Anne
author of: **9** Agnes Grey **23** The Tenant of Wildfell Hall
pseudonym: **9** Acton Bell

Bronte, Charlotte
author of: **7** Shirley **8** Jane Eyre, Villette **12** The Professor
pseudonym: **10** Currer Bell

Bronte, Emily
author of: **16** Wuthering Heights
pseudonym: **9** Ellis Bell

Brontes
member of: **8** Cyclopes

brontophobia
fear of: **7** thunder

Brontosaurus
also: **11** Apatosaurus
type: **8** dinosaur, sauropod
period: **8** Jurassic

Bronx Bull
nickname of: **11** Jake La Motta

bronze 3 tan **5** metal **8** brownish, chestnut **10** reddish- tan **12** reddish-brown **13** copper-colored

brooch 3 pin **5** clasp

brood 4 chew, fret, mope, mull, sulk **5** cover, dwell, hatch, spawn, worry, young **6** chicks, family, litter **7** agonize, sit upon **8** children, incubate **9** offspring **10** hatchlings

brook 3 run **4** bear, rill, take **5** abide, allow, creek, stand **6** accept, endure, stream, suffer **7** rivulet, stomach **8** tolerate **9** put up with, streamlet

Brooks, Gwendolyn
author of: **4** Riot **10** Annie Allen **14** Family Pictures

Brooks, James L

director of: **13** Broadcast News **17** Terms of Endearment (Oscar)

Brooks, Mel
real name: **14** Melvin Kaminsky
wife: **12** Anne Bancroft
born: **10** Brooklyn NY
director of/roles: **10** Life Stinks, Spaceballs **11** High Anxiety, Silent Movie **12** The Producers **14** Blazing Saddles **17** Young Frankenstein **20** The History of the World

Brooks, Richard
director of: **10** Fever Pitch **11** Elmer Gantry, In Cold Blood **16** Cat on a Hot Tin Roof, Sweet Bird of Youth **19** Looking for Mr. Goodbar, The Blackboard Jungle **20** The Brothers Karamazov, The Last Time I Saw Paris

broom 4 bush **5** besom, brush, whisk **7** sweeper

broth 5 stock **8** bouillon, consomme **9** clear soup

brothel 4 stew **5** house **6** bagnio, bordel **8** bordello, cathouse **10** bawdy house, fancy house, whorehouse **11** maison close **13** maison de passe, sporting house **14** house of ill fame **16** house of ill repute **19** house of prostitution

brother 3 pal **4** chum, monk, peer **5** buddy, friar **6** cleric **7** comrade, kinsman, part- ner, sibling **8** confrere, landsman, monastic, relative, relation **9** associate, colleague, companion, fellowman **10** countryman **11** male sibling **12** fellow member **13** fellow citizen
French: **5** frere

brotherhood 4 club **5** amity, lodge **10** fellowship, fraternity, friendship **11** association

Brother Juniper
character in: **21** The Bridge of San Luis Rey
author of: **6** Wilder

Brothers Karamazov, The
author of: **10** Dostoevsky **17** Fyodor Dostoyevsky
character: **4** Ivan **6** Dmitri **7** Alyosha (Alexey), Zossima **8** Katerina **9** Grushenka **10** Smerdyakov **15** Fyodor Karamazov

brougham 3 car **8** carriage **10** automobile

brought 6 caused **7** carried, fetched, sold for **8** conveyed **9** conducted, convinced, persuaded

brow 3 rim **4** brim, edge, side **5** brink, verge **6** border, margin **8** boundary, forehead **9** periphery

browbeat 3 cow **5** abash, bully, cower **6** badger, harass, hector **7** henpeck **8** bulldoze, domineer, frighten, threaten **9** terrorize, tyrannize **10** intimidate

browbeater 5 bully **6** despot **7** co-

ercer **9** oppressor, tormenter, tormentor **11** intimidator, petty tyrant

browbeating 8 bullying **11** threatening, tyrannizing **12** intimidation

brown 3 bay, dun, fry, tan **4** buff, cook, drab, fawn, puce, roan, rust **5** beige, camel, cocoa, hazel, khaki, saute, taw- ny, toast, umber **6** auburn, bronze, brunet, coffee, copper, ginger, russet, sorrel, walnut **8** brunette, chestnut, cinnamon, mahogany **9** chocolate, olive drab **10** terra- cotta **11** dirt-colored, sand-colored **12** liver-colored

Brown, Angeline
real name of: **14** Angie Dickinson

Brown, Berenice Sadie
character in: **19** A Member of the Wedding
author: **9** McCullers

Brown, Charles Brockden
author of: **6** Ormond **7** Wieland **11** Edgar Huntly **12** Arthur Mervyn

Brown, Claude
author of: **16** The Children of Ham **25** Manchild in the Promised Land

Brown, Dee
author of: **15** Creek Mary's Blood **24** Bury My Heart at Wounded Knee

Brown, Helen Gurley
author of: **19** Sex and the Single Girl
editor of: **12** Cosmopolitan

Brown, Helen Hayes
real name of: **10** Helen Hayes

Brown, Jim (Jimmy)
sport: **8** football
position: **8** fullback
team: **15** Cleveland Browns
actor in: **10** Dirty Dozen

Brown, Robert
field: **6** botany
nationality: **8** Scottish
established: **16** Brownian movement

Brown Bomber
nickname of: **8** Joe Louis

Browne, Dik
creator/artist of: **9** Hi and Lois **12** Beetle Bailey **16** Hagar the Horrible

Browne, Sir Thomas
author of: **9** Urn Burial **12** Hydriotaphia **13** Religio Medici **16** The Garden of Cyrus

brownie 3 elf **4** cake, puck **5** fairy, pixie **6** sprite **9** girl scout **10** leprechaun

Browning, Elizabeth Barrett
author of: **11** Aurora Leigh **14** How Do I Love Thee **16** Casa Guidi Windows **24** Sonnets from the Portuguese

Browning, Robert
author of: **8** Sordello **10** Paracelsus **11** Pippa Passes **13** Fra Lippo Lippi, My Last Duchess **14** Andrea del Sarto **17** The Ring and the Book **20** The Pied Piper of Hamlin **29** Solilo-

quy of the Spanish Cloister **30** Childe Roland to the Dark Tower Came

brownish 3 tan **5** taupe **6** bronze **8** chestnut **13** copper- colored

Brownlow, Mr
  character in: 11 Oliver Twist
  author: 7 Dickens

Brownmiller, Susan
  author of: 14 Against Our Will

Brown's Descent
  author: 11 Robert Frost

browse 3 eat **4** feed, scan, skim, surf **5** graze **6** nibble, peruse, survey **7** dip into, pasture **8** look over **9** check over **11** look through **13** glance through

Bruckner, Anton
  born: 7 Austria **9** Ansfelden
  composer of: 6 Te Deum **7** Psalm CL **11** Grosse Messe **16** Romantic Symphony **26** Intermezzo for String Quartet

Brueghel, Pieter (the Elder)
  born: 5 Breda **8** Flanders
  nickname: 14 Peasant Bruegel
  sons: 3 Jan **6** Pieter
  artwork: 9 Blue Cloak, The Months **10** Dulle Griet (Mad Meg) **12** Fall of Icarus, Peasant Dance, Tower of Babel **14** Children's Games, The Misanthrope **15** Return of the Herd **16** Hunters in the Snow **17** The Triumph of Death **19** Peasant Wedding Dance **21** Peasant Wedding Banquet, The Magpie on the Gallows **22** Massacre of the Innocents **23** The Blind Leading the Blind, The Fall of the Rebel Angels

Brueghel, Jan
  born: 8 Brussels, Flanders
  nickname: 6 Velvet
  father: 13 Pieter Bruegel
  artwork: 12 Four Elements **13** Village Street **15** The Garden of Eden (with Rubens) **17** The Battle of Arbela

Brueghel, Pieter (the Younger)
  born: 8 Brussels, Flanders
  nickname: 12 Hell Brueghel **19** The Infernal Brueghel
  father: 13 Pieter Bruegel (the Elder)
  artwork: 11 Village Fair **14** The Crucifixion **16** The Burning of Troy

Brugh, Spangler Arlington
  real name of: 12 Robert Taylor

bruise 3 mar **4** hurt, mark **5** abuse, wound **6** damage, injure, injury, offend **7** blacken, blemish **8** discolor **9** black mark, contusion **13** discoloration

bruit 3 din **5** noise, rumor **6** clamor, hubbub, racket, report, uproar **7** clangor **10** clattering, noise about **11** voice abroad

Brunei
  capital/largest city: 17 Bandar Seri Begawan
  others: 4 Labi **5** Badas, Danau, Muara, Seria **6** Bangar, Tutong **7**

Kampong **10** Kuala Abang, Kuala Balai **11** Kuala Belait
  head of state/government: 6 sultan
  island: 6 Borneo **8** Sipitang
  mountain: 6 Teraja **9** Ulu Tutong
  highest point: 10 Pagon Priok
  river: 6 Belait, Brunei, Tutong **9** Temburong
  sea: 10 South China
  physical feature:
    bay: 6 Brunei
  people: 4 Iban **5** Dayak, Malay **7** Chinese, Kadazan
  language: 4 Iban **5** Malay **7** Chinese, English
  religion: 5 Islam **6** Taoism **7** animism **8** Buddhism **12** Christianity
  feature: 3 oil

Brunelleschi, Filippo
  architect of: 10 San Lorenzo **11** Pazzi Chapel (Santa Croce), Pitti Palace **12** Santo Spirito **14** Badia Fiesolana **15** Duomo of Florence **16** Palazzo Quaratesi **21** Santa Maria degli Angeli **22** Ospedale degli Innocenti **23** Dome of Florence Cathedral

brunet, brunette 4 dark **5** black **9** brown-eyed, dark brown **10** dark-haired **11** brown-haired, dark-skinned **12** olive-skinned **16** dark-complexioned

Brunhild
  origin: 8 Germanic
  Scandinavian: 8 Brynhild
  character in: 14 Nibelungenlied
  queen of: 8 Isenland
  husband: 7 Gunther
  won by: 9 Siegfried

brunt 5 force **6** impact, stress, thrust **8** violence **9** full force, main shock

brush 4 bush, dust, fern, wash **5** clean, copse, flick, graze, groom, paint, run-in, scrub, sedge, set-to, shine, sweep, touch, whisk **6** battle, bushes, caress, duster, forest, fracas, polish, shrubs, stroke **7** bracken, cleanse, dusting, grazing, meeting, scuffle, thicket, varnish **8** skirmish, woodland **9** encounter, shrubbery, woodlands **10** engagement, underbrush, whisk-broom **11** bush country, undergrowth **12** bristled tool **13** confrontation
  type: 4 hair, nail, shoe, wash **5** paint, scrub, tooth **7** clothes

brush aside 6 slight **7** neglect **8** pass over **9** disregard

brush-off 3 cut **4** snub **5** brush **6** rebuff, slight **7** put-down, squelch **9** disregard, rejection **11** repudiation **12** cold shoulder

brusque 4 curt, rude, tart **5** bluff, blunt, gruff, harsh, rough, short **6** abrupt, crusty **7** bearish **8** impolite, ungentle **10** ungracious **12** discourteous **13** unceremonious

Brussels
  canal: 9 Charleroi **10** Willebroek

  capital of: 7 Belgium
  cathedral: 26 Saint Michel and Sainte Gudule
  early name: 10 Bruoc-sella
    means: 16 marshy settlement
  Flemish: 7 Brussel
  French: 9 Bruxelles
  headquarters of: 3 EEC **4** NATO **12** Common Market **25** European Economic Community
  landmark: 11 Royal Palace **15** Palace of Justice **17** Palace of the Nation
  province: 7 Brabant
  river: 5 Senne, Zenne
  square: 11 Grande Place

brutal 5 crude, cruel, harsh **6** bloody, coarse, fierce, savage **7** brutish, hellish, inhuman, vicious **8** barbaric, pitiless, ruthless **9** atrocious, barbarous, heartless, merciless, unfeeling **10** demoniacal **11** hardhearted, remorseless **12** bloodthirsty

brutality 7 cruelty **8** ferocity, savagery **9** barbarity, harshness **10** inhumanity, savageness **11** brutishness, viciousness **12** ruthlessness

brute 5 beast, demon, devil, fiend, swine **6** animal, savage **7** monster **9** barbarian **10** wild animal **11** cruel person **12** dumb creature

brutish 5 cruel, feral **6** bloody, brutal, fierce, savage **7** inhuman **8** barbaric **9** barbarous, ferocious, unfeeling **11** remorseless

brutishness 8 ferocity, savagery **9** barbarity, brutality **10** bestiality, coarseness, inhumanity, savageness **11** viciousness **15** remorselessness

Brutus
  also: 12 Marcus Brutus
  character in: 12 Julius Caesar
  author: 11 Shakespeare

Bruxelles *see* **8** Brussels

Bryan, C D B
  author of: 12 Friendly Fire **24** Ugly Scenes Beautiful Women

Bryant, Bear (Paul)
  sport: 8 football
  position: 5 coach
  team: 7 Alabama **11** Crimson Tide

Brynhild
  origin: 12 Scandinavian
  Germanic: 8 Brunhild
  husband: 6 Gunnar
  won by: 6 Sigurd
  position: 8 Valkyrie

Brynhildr Sigrdrifa *see* **9** Sigrdrifa

Brynner, Yul
  real name: 10 Taidje Khan
  born: 14 Sakhalin Island
  roles: 9 Anastasia, West World **11** The King and I (Oscar) **18** The Ten Commandments **19** The Magnificent Seven **20** The Brothers Karamazov **23** Invitation to a Gunfighter

Brythonic
  language family: 12 Indo-European

group: 5 Welsh **6** Breton **7** Cornish, Pictish

Bschliessmayer, Oskar Josef
   real name of: 11 Oskar Werner

Bubba Smith
   nickname of: 17 Charles Aaron Smith

bubble, bubbles 4 bleb, boil, fizz, foam **5** froth **6** burble, fizzle, gurgle, seethe **7** air ball, blister, droplet, globule, sparkle **9** percolate **10** effervesce **13** effervescence

bubbliness 9 fizziness, foaminess **10** ebullience, enthusiasm, frothiness, liveliness **11** high spirits **13** effervescence

bubbling 5 fizzy, foamy **6** frothy **7** fizzing, foaming **9** sparkling **12** effervescent

bubbly 5 fizzy, foamy **6** frothy, lively **7** fizzing, foaming **9** champagne, sparkling **12** effervescent, high-spirited

buccaneer 6 pirate **7** corsair **9** privateer **10** freebooter

Buchan, John (Baron Tweedsmuir)
   author of: 10 John Macnab **11** Greenmantle, Pilgrim's Way **17** John Burnet of Barns **18** The Thirty-Nine Steps

Buchanan, Daisy
   character in: 14 The Great Gatsby
   author: 10 Fitzgerald

Buchanan, Edgar
   born: 13 Humansville MO
   roles: 5 Shane, Texas **7** Arizona **8** Cimarron **9** McLintock **13** Penny Serenade **17** Petticoat Junction **18** Ride the High Country

Buchanan, James
   nickname: 7 Old Buck
   presidential rank: 9 fifteenth
   party: 8 Democrat
   state represented: 2 PA
   defeated: 7 (John Charles) Fremont **8** (Millard) Fillmore
   vice president: 12 (John Cabell) Breckinridge
   cabinet:
      state: 4 (Lewis) Cass **5** (Jeremiah Sullivan) Black
      treasury: 3 (John Adams) Dix **4** (Howell) Cobb **6** (Philip Francis) Thomas
      war: 4 (Joseph) Holt **5** (John Buchanan) Floyd
      attorney general: 5 (Jeremiah Sullivan) Black **7** (Edwin McMasters) Stanton
      navy: 6 (Isaac) Toucey
      postmaster general: 4 (Horatio) King, (Joseph) Holt **5** (Aaron Venable) Brown
      interior: 8 (Jacob) Thompson
   born: 11 Cove Gap PA (near Mercersburg)
   died/buried: 11 Lancaster PA
   education:
      Academy: 8 Old Stone

   College: 9 Dickinson
   studied: 3 law
   religion: 12 Presbyterian
   political career: 13 state assembly **24** US House of Representatives
   secretary of: 5 State
   minister: 6 Russia **12** Great Britain
   civilian career: 6 lawyer
   notable events of lifetime/term: 5 Panic (of 1857) **11** English Bill, Pony Express
      raid by: 9 John Brown
      raid on: 12 Harper's Ferry
      Supreme Court case: 9 Dred Scott
   father: 5 James
   mother: 9 Elizabeth (Speer)
   siblings: 4 Jane, John, Mary **5** Maria, Sarah **7** Harriet **9** Elizabeth **11** Edward Young **12** William Speer **16** George Washington
   wife: 4 none
   children: 4 none

Bucharest
   capital of: 7 Romania, Rumania
   founder: 5 Bucur
   landmark: 8 Scinteia **13** Village Museum
   river: 9 Dimbovita
   Rumanian: 9 Bucuresti

Buchinsky, Charles
   real name of: 14 Charles Bronson

buck 3 man **4** beau, deer, dude, kick, male **5** dandy **6** dollar, oppose **7** coxcomb **8** cavalier, gay blade **9** go against **10** young blood

Buck
   character in: 16 The Call of the Wild
   author: 6 London

Buck, Pearl S
   author of: 8 The Exile **9** Other Gods **10** Dragon Seed **12** The Good Earth **13** A House Divided

bucket 3 can, hod, tub **4** cask, pail **5** scoop **6** vessel **7** pailful, pitcher, scuttle **9** container **10** receptacle

Buckeye State
   nickname of: 4 Ohio

buckle 3 sag **4** bend, clip, curl, hasp, hook, warp **5** bulge, catch, clasp **6** cave in, couple, fasten, secure **7** contort, crinkle, crumple, distort, wrinkle **8** belly out, collapse, fastener

buckle down 6 attend **12** apply oneself

Buckley, William F Jr
   author of: 11 Who's on First? **15** God and Man at Yale, God Save the Queen
   editor of: 14 National Review
   wife: 3 Pat
   son: 11 Christopher

Buck Rogers
   creator: 14 Richard Calkins
   character: 5 Alura, Buddy, Dercu, Kayla, Wilma **6** Ardala **10** Killer Kane

bucolic 4 idyl, poem **5** idyll, rural **6** poetic, rustic **7** eclogue, idyllic, peasant **8** pastoral, shepherd

bud 4 open **5** shoot **6** flower, sprout **7** blossom, burgeon, develop

Bud, Rosa
   character in: 22 The Mystery of Edwin Drood
   author: 7 Dickens

Budapest
   area: 4 Buda, Pest **5** Obuda
   capital of: 7 Hungary
   cathedral: 13 Saint Matthias
   hill: 10 Castle Hill
   island: 6 Csepel
   river: 6 Danube
   Roman town: 8 Aquincum

Buddenbrooks
   author: 10 Thomas Mann

Buddha
   also called: 5 Butsu
   born: 11 Kapilavastu
   father: 11 Suddhodhana
   founded: 8 Buddhism
   means: 15 enlightened one
   message: 6 dharma
   name for: 17 Siddhartha Gautama
   son: 6 Rahula
   tree: 2 bo **5** bodhi
   wife: 9 Yasodhara

Buddhism
   action: 5 karma
   branch: 3 Zen **8** Mahayana **9** Theravada **12** Great Vehicle **14** way of the elders
   doctrine: 6 duhkha **7** nirvana **9** suffering **13** eightfold path **15** four noble truths **17** pratityasamutpada
   founded by: 6 Buddha **17** Siddhartha Gautama
   monk: 7 bhikshu
   nun: 9 bhikshuni
   rebirth: 7 samsara
   religious community: 6 sangha

buddy 3 pal **4** chum, mate **5** amigo, crony **6** cohort, fellow, friend **7** brother, comrade, partner **8** confrere, intimate, playmate, sidekick **9** associate, colleague, companion, confidant **10** playfellow **11** confederate

buddy-buddy 5 close, palsy **6** chummy **8** friendly, intimate **10** palsy-walsy

budge 4 move, push, roll, stir, sway **5** shift, slide **6** change **8** convince, dislodge, persuade **9** dislocate, influence

budget 4 cost, plan **5** funds, means **6** moneys, ration **7** arrange **8** allocate, schedule **9** allotment, allowance, apportion, resources **10** allocation, portion out **12** spending plan **13** financial plan

budgetary 6 fiscal **8** economic, monetary **9** financial, pecuniary

buenas noches 9 good night

bueno 4 good

Buenos Aires
   capital of: 9 Argentina

landmark: 11 Teatro Colon **16** Saavedra Monument, San Martin Theater **17** Wildestein Gallery, Witcomb Art Gallery **18** Church of El Salvador **27** Christopher Columbus Monument
park: 7 Palermo
people: 8 portenos
   means: 15 people of the port
river: 12 Rio de la Plata
buff 3 bug, fan, nut, rub, tan **4** swab **5** freak, hound, maven, mavin, sandy, straw, tawny **6** addict, dauber, polish, smooth, the raw **7** admirer, burnish, devotee, leather **8** bare skin, follower, polisher **9** nakedness, yellowish **10** aficionado, enthusiast **11** buffalo hide, connoisseur **14** yellowish-brown
buffalo 5 bison **6** puzzle **7** mystify **10** intimidate
kind: 7 African **10** Asian water
African: 14 syncerus caffer
Asian water: 14 bubalus bubalis
Buffalo
football team: 5 Bills
hockey team: 6 Sabres
buffer 6 bumper, fender, shield **7** cushion **9** protector
buffet 3 box, hit, jab, rap **4** bang, beat, bump, cuff, meal, push, slap **5** baste, knock, pound, shove, thump **6** pum- mel, strike, supper, thrash, thwack, wallop **7** cabinet, counter **8** credenza **9** cafeteria, sideboard **11** smorgasbord
Buffone, Carlo
character in: 22 Every Man out of His Humour
author: 6 Jonson
buffoon 3 wag **4** fool, zany **5** clown, comic, joker, mimic, Punch **6** jester, madcap **7** Pierrot **8** comedian, funnyman **9** harlequin, pantaloon, prankster, trickster **10** Scaramouch, sillybilly **11** merry-andrew, punchinello, Scaramouche
buffoonery 6 antics, comedy **7** foolery, inanity **8** zaniness **9** asininity, horseplay, silliness, slapstick **10** tomfoolery **11** foolishness, loutishness **12** clownishness, monkeyshines, prankishness **14** clowning around, playing the fool
bug 3 nag **4** flaw, germ **5** annoy, fault, virus **6** badger, bother, defect, insect, pester **7** wiretap **8** drawback, listen in, weakness **9** eavesdrop, Hemiptera **11** Heteroptera
variety: 3 bat, bed, red **4** gnat, lace, leaf, seed, toad **5** negro, plant, shore, stilt, stink, water **6** ambush, damsel, fungus, pirate, ripple **7** boatman, stainer **8** assassin, burrower, creeping **9** royal palm **10** leaf footed **11** ashgray leaf, backswimmer, broadheaded, jumping tree, velvet water **12** velvety shore, water strider, water treader **13** jumping

ground, water measurer, water scorpion **14** scentless plant **17** terrestrial turtle
bugaboo 4 ogre **5** scare **6** fright **7** anxiety
bugbear 4 ogre **5** bogey **6** goblin **7** bugaboo **8** bogeyman **9** bete noire
buggy 4 cart **5** wagon **7** vehicle **8** carriage **10** conveyance
bugle 4 horn **10** instrument
Bugs Bunny
creator: 15 Leon Schlesinger
character: 9 Elmer Fudd
voice of: 8 Mel Blanc
saying: 10 what's up doc
build 4 body, form, make, mold, open **5** begin, brace, erect, forge, found, put up, raise, renew, set up, shape, start, steel **6** create, extend, figure, harden, launch **7** amplify, augment, develop, enhance, enlarge, fashion, greaten, improve, produce **8** embark on, increase, initiate, multiply, physique **9** construct, establish, fabri- cate, institute, intensify, originate, reinforce, structure, undertake **10** inaugurate, strengthen, supplement **11** manufacture, put together **12** construction
building 7 edifice **9** structure **12** construction
building front 6 facade **8** frontage
build up 5 amass **7** develop, promote **8** increase **10** accumulate
Bujold, Genevieve
born: 6 Canada **8** Montreal
roles: 4 Coma **9** Monsignor, Obsession **12** King of Hearts **21** Anne of the Thousand Days
Bujumbura
capital of: 7 Burundi
Bul 17 eighth Hebrew month
bulb 3 bud **4** corm, seed **5** plant, tuber **8** swelling
Bulfinch, Charles
architect of: 7 Capitol (Washington DC) **16** Hartford City Hall (CT) **23** Massachusetts State House (Boston)
style: 7 Federal
Bulgakov, Mikhail
author of: 9 Black Snow **13** The White Guard **14** The Heart of a Dog **19** The Days of the Turbins **21** The Master and Margarita
Bulgaria
capital/largest city: 5 Sofia
others: 3 Lom **4** Rila, Ruse **5** Aytos, Butan, Byclu, Elena, Iskra, Stara, Varna **6** Bleven, Burgas, Devnia, Dulovo, Levsky, Pernik, Pleuna, Pleven, Plevna, Shumen, Shumla, Sliven, Slivno, Widden, Yambol, Zagora **7** Gabrovo, Karlovo, Plovdiv, Sistova, Tirnova **8** Khaskovo, Rustchuk, Svishtov **9** Ruse Vidin, Silistria **11** Kolorovgrad **12** Dimitrovgrad

school: 5 Sofia **7** Plovdiv **13** Veliko Turnovo
measure: 3 oka, oke **5** krine, lekhe, likhe
monetary unit: 3 lev **8** stotinki
weight: 3 oka, oke **5** tovar
mountain: 3 Kom **5** Botev, Pirin, Sapka **6** Balkan, Sredna **7** Vikhren **11** Rila-Rhodope
highest point: 6 Musala **8** Musallah
river: 3 Lom, Vit **4** Arda, Osma **5** Isker, Iskur, Mesta **6** Danube, Marica, Ogosta, Struma, Yantra **7** Maritsa, Stryama, Tundzha
sea: 5 Black
physical feature:
cape: 5 Emine, Sabla **7** Kuratan
gulf: 5 Burga
plateau: 6 Danube
resort: 9 Pyassatzi **13** Slunchev Bryay
valley: 7 Maritsa
people: 4 Slav, Turk **5** Gypsy, Pomak, Tatar **6** Bulgar, Slavic **7** Chuvash **9** Cheremiss **10** Macedonian
language: 9 Bulgarian
religion: 5 Islam **24** Bulgarian Eastern Orthodox
place:
church: 9 St Nedelja
monastery: 4 Rila **6** Rilski
monument: 7 Red Army
mosque: 10 Banya Bashi
museum: 21 Revolutionary Movement
square: 5 Lenin
valley of roses: 8 Kazanluk
feature:
dance: 4 horo
holiday: 12 St Georges Day
newspaper: 17 Rabot Nichesko Delo
food:
stew: 8 giuvetch
bulge 3 bag, sag **4** bump, lump **5** curve, swell **6** excess **7** distend, project, puff out, sagging **8** protrude, stand out, stick out, swelling, swell out **9** bagginess **10** projection, prominence, protrusion **12** protuberance
bulk 4 body, mass, most, size **6** extent, volume, weight **7** bigness, measure **8** enormity, hugeness, main part, majority, quantity **9** amplitude, greatness, largeness, magnitude, major part, plurality, substance **10** better part, dimensions, lion's share **11** greater part, massiveness, proportions **13** preponderance
bulky 3 big **4** huge **5** large **6** clumsy **7** awkward, hulking, immense, lumpish, massive, sizable, unhandy **8** enormous, ungainly, unwieldy **9** capacious, extensive **10** cumbersome, voluminous **12** unmanageable
bull 2 ox **4** male
male of the: 3 elk **4** seal **5** moose, whale **6** bovine **8** elephant

constellation of: 6 Taurus
Spanish: 4 toro

bulldoze 3 cow **4** bump, fell, push, rage, raze **5** abash, bully, drive, force, level, press, shove **6** coerce, hector, jostle, propel, subdue, thrust **7** buffalo, dragoon, flatten **8** bludgeon, browbeat, domineer, shoulder **9** push about, tyrannize **10** intimidate

Bullen, Frank T
author of: 19 Told in the Dry Watches **22** The Cruise of the Cachalot

bullet 4 ball, lead, shot, slug **7** missile **8** buckshot

bulletin 4 note **6** report **7** account, message, release **8** dispatch **9** statement **10** communique, news report **12** notification **13** communication

Bullet Park
author: 11 John Cheever

bullfighter 6 torero **7** matador, picador **8** Manolete, toreador **9** Escamillo **10** El Cordobes (Manuel Benitez Perez) **15** Miguel Dominguin

Bullion State
nickname of: 8 Missouri

Bullitt
director: 10 Peter Yates
cast: 9 Don Gordon **12** Robert Duvall, Robert Vaughn, Steve McQueen **16** Jacqueline Bisset
setting: 12 San Francisco

bullock 2 ox **4** beef, bull **5** steer

bullocks 4 kine, oxen **5** beefs, bulls **6** beeves, cattle, steers

bull session 3 rap **4** talk **7** gabfest, palaver **8** dialogue **9** discourse **10** discussion **12** conversation **13** confabulation

bull's-eye 5 black **6** center **7** exactly **8** on target **9** dead center, precisely

bully 3 cow **4** good **5** annoy, swell, tough **6** cheers, coerce, despot, harass, hurrah, hurray **7** coercer, right on, ruffian, tread on **8** browbeat, bulldoze, domineer, frighten, ride over, well done **9** oppressor, terrorize, tormentor, tyrannize **10** browbeater, intimidate **11** intimidator

bullying 7 torment **8** coercion **9** despotism **10** harassment, tormenting **11** browbeating, domineering, tyrannizing **12** intimidation

bulrush 5 plant, sedge **7** cattail, papyrus

bulwark 5 guard **7** barrier, parapet, rampart, support, defense **8** mainstay **9** earthwork **10** embankment

Bulwer-Lytton, Edward
author of: 6 Harold, Pelham, Rienzi **9** Richelieu **13** The Coming Race **16** Kenelm Chillingly **18** The Last of the Barons **20** The Last Days of Pompeii

bum 3 beg **4** grub, hobo **5** cadge, idler, mooch, tramp **6** borrow, loafer,

sponge **7** drifter, vagrant **8** derelict, vagabond

bumble 6 bungle **7** blunder, stagger, stumble **8** flounder

Bumble
character in: 11 Oliver Twist
author: 7 Dickens

bumcombe, bunkum 3 rot **4** bosh, bunk **6** drivel **7** twaddle **8** nonsense, tommyrot **10** balderdash **16** stuff-and-nonsense

bump 3 hit, jar, rap **4** bang, blow, butt, hump, jolt, knob, knot, lump, node, poke, slam, slap, sock **5** bulge, clash, crack, crash, gnarl, knock, punch, shake, smack, smash, thump, whack **6** bounce, buf- fet, impact, jostle, jounce, nodule, rattle, strike, wallop **7** collide, run into **8** swelling **9** collision, crash into, smash into **11** excrescence **12** protuberance

bump into 4 meet **7** collide, run into **9** encounter

bumpkin 3 oaf **4** boor, lout **5** churl, yokel **8** ship beam **10** clodhopper

bump off 4 do in, kill, slay **6** murder, rub out **7** execute, gun down **8** dispatch **11** assassinate **12** take for a ride

bumptious 4 bold **5** cocky, pushy **6** brazen **7** forward, haughty **8** arrogant, boastful, cocksure, impudent, insolent **9** bodacious, conceited, obtrusive **10** aggressive, swaggering **11** impertinent, overbearing **12** presumptuous **13** overconfident, self-assertive

bumptiousness 4 gall **5** cheek **8** audacity, boldness **9** impudence **11** forwardness, presumption **12** impertinence **13** obtrusiveness **17** self-assertiveness

bumpy 5 lumpy, rocky, rough **6** uneven **10** undulating

bun 4 coil, knot, roll **8** soft roll **9** sweet roll

Bunaea
epithet of: 4 Hera
refers to: 6 temple

bunch 3 lot, mob **4** band, bevy, gang, heap, herd, host, knot, mass, pack, pile, team **5** array, batch, clump, crowd, flock, group, shock, stack, tribe, troop **6** amount, bundle, gather, huddle, number, string **7** cluster, collect, company **8** assemble, assembly, quantity **9** gathering, multitude **10** assortment, collection, congregate **12** accumulation

bundle 3 lot **4** bale, bind, heap, mass, pack, pile, wrap **5** array, batch, bunch, group, sheaf, stack, truss **6** amount, packet, parcel **7** package **8** quantity **9** multitude **10** assortment, collection **11** tie together **12** accumulation

Bundren family

characters in: 11 As I Lay Dying
member: 4 Anse, Cash, Darl **5** Addie, Jewel **9** Dewey Dell
author: 8 Faulkner

bungalow 5 cabin, house, lodge **7** cottage

bungle 3 mar **4** flub, goof, miff, ruin **5** botch, spoil **6** foul up, mess up, muddle **7** blunder, butcher, do badly, louse up, screw up **8** misjudge **9** mismanage, misreckon **10** miscompute **11** make a mess of, misestimate **12** miscalculate

Bunin, Ivan Alekseyevich
author of: 10 The Village **15** The Elagin Affair **17** The Life of Arseniev **28** The Gentleman from San Francisco

bunk 3 bed, cot, rot **4** bull **5** berth, hokum, hooey, stuff **6** bunkum, hot air, humbug, pallet **7** baloney, blather, bombast, hogwash, inanity, malarky, spinach **8** claptrap, nonsense, tommyrot **9** poppycock **10** applesauce, balderdash **11** foolishness **16** stuff and nonsense

Bunsen, Robert Wilhelm
nationality: 6 German
inventor of: 9 gas burner **10** photo meter **12** Bunsen burner, spectroscope **24** electromechanical battery

Bunshaft, Gordon
architect of: 10 Lever House (NY) **23** Beinecke Rare Book Library (Yale) **33** Hirshhorn Museum and Sculpture Garden (Washington DC) **34** Lyndon Baines Johnson Memorial Library (Austin TX)

Bunyan, John
author of: 10 The Holy War **16** Pilgrim's Progress **25** The Life and Death of Mr Badman **33** Grace Abounding to the Chief of Sinners

buona notte 9 good night

buona sera 11 good evening

buon giorno 7 good day **11** good morning

Buono, Victor
born: 10 San Diego CA
roles: 11 The Stranger **12** Four for Texas **22** Hush Hush Sweet Charlotte **26** Whatever Happened to Baby Jane

buoy 4 bell, lift **5** boost, cheer, float, raise **6** beacon, uplift **7** cheer up, elevate, gladden, lighten **8** brighten **10** keep afloat **14** floating marker

buoyancy, buoyance 4 glee **6** gaiety **7** jollity **8** gladness, vivacity **9** animation, good humor, joviality, lightness, sunniness **10** brightness, cheeriness, enthusiasm, floatiness, joyousness **11** good spirits **12** cheerfulness, exhilaration, floatability **14** weightlessness **16** lightheartedness

buoyant 3 gay **4** glad **5** happy, jolly, light, merry, peppy, sunny **6** afloat, breezy, bright, elated, joyful, joyous, lively **7** hopeful **8** animated, carefree, cheerful, floating, sportive **9** energetic, floatable, sprightly, vivacious **10** blithesome, optimistic, weightless **11** exhilarated, free and easy **12** enthusiastic, lighthearted

buoyed 6 elated **7** exalted, pleased **8** elevated **9** confident, heartened, reassured **10** inspirited

buoy up 4 warm **6** assure, uplift **7** comfort, hearten, inspire **8** inspirit, reassure **9** encourage

Burbank, Luther
    field: **7** biology
    developed: **13** plant breeding

burble 6 babble, bubble, gurgle, murmur **8** babbling

Burce, Suzanne
    real name of: **10** Jane Powell

Burchill, Mr
    character in: **19** The Vicar of Wakefield
    author: **9** Goldsmith

burden 3 tax, try, vex **4** care, load, onus, pack **5** cargo **6** hamper, hinder, strain, stress, weight **7** afflict, anxiety, freight, oppress, trouble **8** encumber, handicap, hardship, load with, obligate, overload **9** press down, weigh down **10** saddle with **11** encumbrance **14** responsibility

Burden, Jack
    character in: **14** All the King's Men
    author: **6** Warren

burden of proof
    Latin: **12** onus probandi

burdensome 4 hard **5** heavy **6** tiring **7** arduous, onerous **8** wearying **9** Herculean, laborious **10** exhausting

bureau 6 agency, branch, office **7** cabinet, commode, dresser, service, station **8** division **10** chiffonier, department **14** administration, chest of drawers

bureaucrat 8 mandarin, official, politico **9** penpusher **10** politician **11** apparatchik, functionary, rubber stamp **12** civil servant, officeholder **13** public servant

burgee 4 flag **6** banner, colors, ensign **7** pennant

burgeon 3 wax **4** blow, grow, open **5** bloom **6** expand, flower, spread, thrive **7** augment, blossom, develop, enlarge, prosper, shoot up, succeed **8** escalate, flourish, fructify, increase, mushroom, spring up **9** bear fruit **10** effloresce **11** proliferate

Burgess, Anthony
    author of: **2** MF **13** Man of Nazareth, Time for a Tiger **14** Enderby Outside, The Wanting Seed **16** A Clockwork Orange, Beard's Roman Women **17** Nothing Like the Sun **20** The End of the World News

burgher 7 citizen **9** bourgeois **11** townsperson

burglar 3 cat **4** yegg **5** thief **6** robber **7** prowler **8** pilferer **9** cracksman, purloiner **12** housebreaker **14** second-story man

burglary 5 theft **6** felony **7** break-in, larceny, robbery **8** filching, stealing **9** pilfering **10** purloining **13** housebreaking **19** breaking and entering

burgundy 3 red **4** wine **5** color **13** reddish-purple

Burgundy
    ancient city: **5** Autun
    city: **5** Dijon
    district: **5** Youne **6** Nievre **7** Cote d' Or **12** Saone-et-Loire
    French: **9** Bourgogne
    location: **6** France
    river: **5** Rhone, Saone
    tribe: **9** Burgundii

Buri
    origin: **12** Scandinavian
    first: **3** god
    revealed by: **8** Audhumla **9** Audhumbla

burial 5 rites **7** funeral **9** interment, obsequies **10** entombment, inhumation

burial ground 7 ossuary **8** boneyard, Boot Hill, catacomb, cemetery **9** graveyard **10** churchyard, necropolis **12** potter's field

buried 4 laid, sunk **6** hidden **7** covered, inhumed, immured **9** concealed, deep sixed **10** laid to rest **11** underground

Burke, Francis
    character in: **21** The Master of Ballantrae
    author: **9** Stevenson

Burkina Faso see **10** Upper Volta

burlap 3 bag **4** hemp, jute **5** cloth **6** fabric **8** material

burlesque 5 farce, spoof **6** comedy, parody, satire **7** mockery, takeoff **8** ridicule, travesty **10** buffoonery, caricature **15** slapstick comedy

burly 3 big **5** beefy, bulky, hefty, large **6** brawny, stocky, strong, sturdy **7** hulking, sizable **8** thickset **9** ponderous, strapping

Burma see **7** Myanmar

burn 3 nip, tan **4** bite, char, fire, glow, hurt, pain, sear, skin **5** be hot, blaze, brown, chafe, flame, flare, flash, parch, prick, scald, singe, smart, smoke, sting **6** abrade, bronze, flames, ignite, kindle, nettle, scorch, scrape, suntan, tingle, wither **7** blister, consume, cremate, flicker, oxidize, prickle, shrivel, smolder, sunburn, swelter **8** abrasion, be ablaze, be on fire, charring, irritate, kindling **9** be flushed, reddening, set fire to, set on fire, use as fuel **10** be feverish,

be in flames, blistering, incandesce, incinerate, irritation, smoldering **12** incineration **13** reduce to ashes

burnable 9 flammable, ignitable **10** combustive **11** combustible, inflammable **13** conflagrative

Burne-Jones, Sir Edward Coley
    born: **7** England **10** Birmingham
    artwork: **11** Laus Veneris **15** The Golden Stairs **16** The Mirror of Venus **18** The Star of Bethlehem **28** King Cophetua and the Beggar Maid

burner, gas
    invented by: **6** Bunsen

Burnett, Carol
    born: **12** San Antonio TX
    roles: **14** The Four Seasons **19** The Carol Burnett Show

Burnett, Frances H
    author of: **20** Little Lord Fauntleroy

Burney, Fanny
    author of: **7** Camilla, Diaries, Evelina

Burnham, Daniel Hudson
    partner: **16** John Wellborn Root
    architect of: **7** Rookery **12** Union Station (Washington DC) **15** Calumet Building **16** Flatiron Building (NYC), Reliance Building **17** Monadnock Building **25** World's Columbian Exposition

burning 3 hot **5** acrid, afire, aglow, eager, fiery, sharp **6** aflame, ardent, biting, fervid, heated, raging, red-hot **7** blazing, boiling, caustic, earnest, fanatic, fervent, flaming, flaring, frantic, glowing, ignited, intense, kindled, painful, pungent, sincere, smoking, zealous **8** flashing, frenzied, piercing, resolute, sizzling, smarting, stinging, tingling **9** corroding, prickling **10** astringent, compelling, flickering, irritating, passionate, smoldering **11** impassioned **12** all-consuming

burnish 3 wax **4** buff **5** rub up, shine **6** polish, smooth

burnished 5 shiny **6** bright, buffed, shined **8** lustrous, polished, smoothed

burnoose 4 cape, robe **5** cloak **6** mantle **7** pelisse

burn out 3 pop **4** blow **7** exhaust **10** exhaustion, extinguish

Burns, George
    real name: **14** Nathan Birnbaum
    wife: **11** Gracie Allen
    born: **9** New York NY
    roles: **5** Oh God **12** Going in Style **15** The Sunshine Boys **17** Burns and Allen Show

Burns, Robert
    author of: **8** To a Louse, To a Mouse **11** A Red Red Rose, Tam O'Shanter **12** Auld Lang Syne **16** Address to the Deil, Coming Thro the Rye **17** Holy Willie's Prayer **20** Flow Gently Sweet Afton **22** My Heart's in the Highlands **23** The Cotter's Saturday

Night **32** Poems Chiefly in the Scottish Dialect

Burnt Norton
author: **7** T S Eliot

burp 5 belch, eruct **10** eructation

burr 4 buhr, rock **5** notch, stone **9** whetstone **13** pronunciation

Burr
author: **9** Gore Vidal

Burr, Aaron 13 vice president
event: **4** duel
victim: **17** Alexander Hamilton

Burr, Raymond
born: **6** Canada **14** New Westminster **15** British Columbia
roles: **8** Ironside **10** Perry Mason, Rear Window

burro 3 ass **4** mule **6** donkey, onager **7** jackass

Burroughs, Edgar Rice
author of: **15** Tarzan of the Apes

Burroughs, William S
author of: **5** Junky, Queer **6** Junkie **13** The Naked Lunch
member of: **14** Beat Generation

Burroughs, William Seward
nationality: **8** American
inventor of: **13** adding machine
grandson: **17** William S Burroughs (author)

burrow 3 den, dig **4** cave, hole, lair **6** covert, dugout, furrow, tunnel **8** excavate, scoop out **9** hollow out

Burrows, Abe
author of: **41** How to Succeed in Business without Really Trying

bursa 3 bag, sac **5** pouch, purse **6** cavity

bursar 6 purser **7** cashier **9** paymaster, treasurer **10** cashkeeper

burst 3 fly, pop, run **4** bang, bust, rend, rush **5** barge, blast, break, crack, erupt, split, spout **6** blow up, detach, divide, sunder **7** disjoin, explode, rupture, shatter, torrent **8** breaking, break out, cracking, crashing, detonate, eruption, fly apart, fracture, fragment, outbreak, separate, splinter **9** break open, discharge, explosion, gush forth, pull apart, splitting, tear apart **10** detonation, disconnect, outpouring, shattering **11** spring forth **12** disintegrate

burst forth 5 arise, begin, erupt, start **6** arrive, emerge **8** break out, commence

Burstyn, Ellen
real name: **14** Edna Rae Gillooly
born: **9** Detroit MI
roles: **11** The Exorcist **16** Same Time Next Year **18** The Last Picture Show **26** Alice Doesn't Live Here Anymore (Oscar)

Burton, Richard
real name: **22** Richard Walter Jenkins Jr

wife: **15** Elizabeth Taylor
born: **5** Wales **11** Pontrhydfen Wales
roles: **6** Becket, Hamlet **7** Camelot, The Robe **9** Cleopatra **14** My Cousin Rachel **19** The Night of the Iguana, The Taming of the Shrew **21** Anne of the Thousand Days **25** Who's Afraid of Virginia Woolf **26** The Spy Who Came in from the Cold

Burton, Robert
author of: **22** The Anatomy of Melancholy

Burundi
capital/largest city: **9** Bujumbura
others: **5** Ngozi **6** Bururi, Gitega, Kitega, Rutana, Ruyigi **7** Kibumbu, Muyinga
monetary unit: **5** franc **7** centime
lake: **7** Rugwero **8** Tshohoha **10** Tanganyika
mountain: **9** Nyamisana
highest point: **8** Nyarwana
river: **6** Akanya, Ruvuvu, Ruzizi **8** Rukagera **10** Malagarasi
people: **3** Twa **4** Hutu **5** Bantu, Batwa, Pygmy, Tutsi **6** Bahutu, Watusi **7** Barundi
language: **6** French **7** Kirundi, Swahili
religion: **5** Islam **7** animism **10** Protestant **13** Roman Catholic
feature:
  king: **4** mwam
food:
  coffee: **7** Arabica

Burushaski
language spoken in: **7** Kashmir

bury 4 hide **5** cache, cover, inter **6** encase, engulf, entomb, inhume **7** conceal, cover up, enclose, immerse, secrete **8** submerge, submerse **13** lay in the grave **17** consign to the grave

Bury My Heart at Wounded Knee
author: **8** Dee Brown

bush 4 veld **5** brush, hedge, plant, shrub, woods **6** forest, jungle **8** barrens **9** shrubbery, woodlands

Bush, George Herbert Walker
presidential rank: **10** forty-first
party: **10** Republican
state represented: **2** TX **5** Texas
defeated: **7** (Michael) Dukakis
defeated by: **7** (Bill) Clinton
vice president: **6** (James Danforth) Quayle
born: **8** Milton MA
education: **4** Yale **7** Andover
religion: **12** Episcopalian
vacation spot: **5** Maine **13** Kennebunkport
political career: **13** vice president **14** representative **21** Ways and Means Committee
  ambassador to: **2** UN **13** United Nations
  chairman of: **27** Republican National Committee

head of: **3** CIA
liaison with: **5** China
civilian career: **3** oil **14** Zapata Offshore
military career: **5** pilot **6** US Navy
vice president under: **12** Ronald Reagan
notable events of lifetime/term: **7** Gulf War **14** Persian Gulf War **20** Operation Desert Storm
  Supreme Court appointments: **11** David Souter **14** Clarence Thomas
  invasion of: **6** Panama
father: **15** Prescott Sheldon
mother: **13** Dorothy Walker
wife: **13** Barbara Pierce
children: **4** John, Neil **5** Robin (died 1953) **6** George, Marvin **7** Dorothy

bush country 5 scrub, wilds **7** outback **10** wilderness

bushed 4 beat **5** all in, spent, tired, weary **6** done it, pooped **7** drained, wearied, worn out **8** dog tired, fatigued, tired out **9** dead tired, exhausted, played out

bushel
abbreviation: **2** bu **4** bush

bushes 5 brush **6** shrubs **9** brushwood, shrubbery **10** underbrush **11** undergrowth

bushy 5 hairy **6** fluffy, shaggy **7** hirsute **9** overgrown

business 3 job **4** case, duty, firm, line, shop, task, work **5** chore, field, place, point, store, topic, trade **6** affair, career, living, matter, office, racket **7** affairs, calling, company, concern, dealing, factory, mission, problem, pursuit, subject, venture **8** activity, commerce, function, industry, position, province, question, vocation **9** procedure, situation, specialty **10** assignment, bargaining, employment, enterprise, livelihood, occupation, profession, walk of life **11** corporation, negotiation, partnership, transaction, undertaking **13** establishment, manufacturing, merchandising **14** bread and butter, responsibility

businesslike 7 careful, correct, orderly, regular, serious **8** diligent, sedulous, thorough **9** assiduous, efficient, organized, practical **10** methodical, systematic **11** industrious, painstaking **12** professional

Busiris
king of: **5** Egypt
father: **8** Poseidon
mother: **10** Lysianassa

Busoni, Ferruccio
born: **5** Italy **6** Empoli
composer of: **8** Turandot **10** Arlecchino **11** Doctor Faust, Doktor Faust **12** Die Brautwahl **14** Comedy Overture **25** Fantasia Contrappuntistica

bus station 5 depot **8** terminal, terminus

Bus Stop
director: 11 Joshua Logan
cast: 9 Don Murray **10** Betty Field **13** Eileen Heckart, Marilyn Monroe **14** Arthur O'Connell

bust 3 nab **4** head, raid **5** bosom, chest, seize **6** arrest, breast, collar **7** capture **9** apprehend, sculpture **12** take prisoner **15** take into custody

Buster Brown
creator: 10 RF Outcault
bulldog: 4 Tige
trademark: 9 sailor hat **10** wide collar

bustle 3 ado, fly **4** dash, flit, fuss, rush, stir, tear, to-do **5** hurry **6** bestir, flurry, hustle, pother, scurry, tumult **7** be quick, fluster, flutter, press on, scamper, scuttle **8** activity, be active, scramble **9** agitation, commotion, make haste **10** excitement, hurlyburly

busy 4 full **6** active, employ, engage, intent, occupy, on duty, work at **7** engaged, labor at, slaving, toiling, working **8** absorbed, bustling, employed, laboring, occupied **9** engrossed, in harness, strenuous **10** hard at work **11** industrious **12** be absorbed in, keep occupied **13** be engrossed in

busybody 3 pry **5** snoop **6** gossip **7** blabber, meddler, Paul Pry **8** telltale **10** chatterbox, newsmonger, talebearer, tattletale **12** blabbermouth **13** scandalmonger

busy place 4 hive **6** warren **7** anthill, beehive

but 3 yet **4** save, than that **5** if not, still **6** except, saving, unless **7** however, outside, that not **9** excepting, other than, otherwise **10** except that **14** on the other hand

Butch Cassidy and the Sundance Kid
director: 13 George Roy Hill
cast: 10 Paul Newman (Butch) **13** Katharine Ross (Etta Place), Robert Redford (The Kid)
score: 13 Burt Bacharach
Oscar for: 5 score
song: 27 Raindrops Keep Fallin' on My Head

butcher 4 goof, kill, muff, ruin, slay **5** botch, purge, spoil **6** boggle, bungle, fumble, hack up, hit man, killer, mess up, murder **7** louse up, screw up **8** assassin, decimate, homicide, massacre, murderer **9** liquidate, manhandle, mishandle, slaughter **10** annihilate, hatchet man, liquidator **11** assassinate, exterminate, make a mess of, slaughterer **12** exterminator, massmurderer **15** homicidal maniac

butchery 4 flop, mess **5** botch **8** massacre **9** slaughter

Butes
father: 6 Boreas **7** Pandion
mother: 8 Zeuxippe
brother: 8 Lycurgus **10** Erechtheus
sister: 6 Procne **9** Philomela
son: 4 Eryx
priest of: 6 Athena **8** Poseidon
member of: 9 Argonauts
stricken with: 8 insanity
enticed by: 6 Sirens
leaped into: 3 sea
rescued by: 9 Aphrodite

Butkus, Dick (Richard Marvin)
sport: 8 football
position: 10 linebacker
team: 12 Chicago Bears

Butler, Rhett
character in: 15 Gone With the Wind
author: 8 Mitchell

Butler, Samuel
author of: 7 Erewhon **8** Hudibras **16** The Way of All Flesh **20** The Elephant in the Moon

butt 3 end, hit, jab, ram, rap **4** buck, bump, bunt, dupe, goat, mark, push, slap, stub **5** knock, shank, shove, smack, stump, thump **6** bottom, buffet, jostle, object, strike, target, thrust, thwack, victim **8** blunt end **13** laughingstock

buttercup 10 Ranunculus
variety: 4 Tall **5** Early **6** Common **7** Bermuda, Bulbous, Persian **8** Colombia, Creeping **11** Yellow water

butterfingered 5 inept **6** clumsy **7** awkward **8** bungling **9** maladroit **10** ungraceful

butterfly
pupa: 9 chrysalis **10** chrysalids **11** chrysalides
variety: 4 blue **5** giant, nymph, satyr, snout, tiger, zebra **6** alpine, apollo, arctic, kalima **7** alfalfa, budwing, dogface, monarch, peacock, viceroy **9** Baltimore, bathwhite, brimstone, christmas, metalmark, orange tip, wood nymph **10** Parnassian **11** painted lady, spring azure **12** blue mountain, cabbage white, clouded white, silver stripe, white admiral **13** chalkhill blue, mourning cloak, pearl crescent **14** American copper, gulf fritillary, tailed birdwing **15** longtail skipper, regal fritillary **16** black swallowtail, black veined white, camberwell beauty, green veined white, Leonardus skipper, red-spotted purple **18** orchard swallowtail **19** European swallowtail **20** spicebush swallowtail, variegated fritillary **21** great purple hairstreak, questionmark anglewing, white admiral wood nymph

butter up 4 coax **6** cajole **7** flatter, wheedle **8** soft-soap

buttocks 4 buns, butt, rear, rump, seat **5** fanny, nates **6** behind, bottom **7** keister, rear end **8** backside, derriere, haunches **9** fundament, posterior **12** hindquarters

buttonhole 4 halt, slit, stop **6** accost, waylay **7** solicit **8** approach, confront

button one's lip 7 keep mum **10** keep silent **16** keep one's trap shut **18** keep one's lips sealed

Buttons, Red
real name: 11 Aaron Chwatt
born: 9 New York NY
roles: 8 Sayonara **13** The Longest Day **20** The Poseidon Adventure **23** They Shoot Horses Don't They

buttress 4 arch, prop, stay **5** boost, brace, shore, steel **6** prop up **7** bolster, shore up, support **8** abutment, shoulder **9** reinforce, stanchion **10** strengthen

buxom 5 plump **6** bosomy, chesty, robust, zaftig **9** strapping **10** voluptuous **13** large-breasted, well-developed

buy 3 get **4** deal, gain **5** bribe **6** buy off, obtain, pay for, suborn **7** acquire, bargain, corrupt, procure **8** invest in, purchase **9** influence

buy and sell 4 deal **5** trade **6** market

buy off 5 bribe **6** pay off **13** grease the palm

Buzi
son: 7 Ezekiel

Buz Sawyer
creator: 8 Roy Crane
sidekick: 7 Sweeney

Buzuhov, Pierre
character in: 11 War and Peace
author: 7 Tolstoy

buzz 3 hum **4** whir **5** drone **6** murmur **7** whisper

by 4 near, over, past **5** along **6** beside, beyond, during, toward **7** through **9** alongside **10** concerning, on or before **11** according to, no later than

by air
French: 8 par avion

Byam, Roger
character in: 17 Mutiny on the Bounty
authors: 4 Hall **8** Nordhoff

Byblis
father: 7 Miletus
mother: 6 Cyanea
twin brother: 6 Caunus
loved: 6 Caunus
changed into: 8 fountain

by few words
Latin: 12 paucis verbis

bygone 4 past **5** olden **6** former, gone by, of yore **7** ancient, earlier **8** departed, obsolete, previous **10** antiquated

by horse
French: 7 a cheval

Byington, Spring
born: 17 Colorado Springs CO
roles: 7 Jezebel **11** Little Women **13** December Bride, Heaven Can Wait **17** Mutiny on the Bounty **20** The Devil and Miss Jones, You Can't

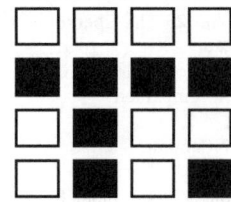

Caan, James
   born: **9** New York NY
   roles: **6** Misery **9** Dick Tracy, Funny Lady **10** Brian's Song, For the Boys, Rollerball **11** Bulletproof, The Gamblers **12** Brian Piccolo, The Godfather **13** Sonny Corleone **17** Cinderella Liberty

cab 4 hack, taxi **7** taxi cab

Cab 15 Biblical measure

cabal 4 band, plan, plot, ring **5** junta **6** design, league, scheme **7** faction **8** intrigue **10** connivance, conspiracy **11** combination, machination

cabalistic 6 arcane, mystic, occult, secret **7** cryptic, obscure, strange **8** abstruse, esoteric, mystical **10** mysterious, unknowable **11** inscrutable **12** impenetrable, supernatural, unfathomable **16** incomprehensible

cabaret 4 cafe, club **6** bistro **9** nightclub **10** supper club
   French: **5** boite **11** boite de nuit

Cabaret
   director: **8** Bob Fosse
   based on stories by: **20** Christopher Isherwood
   cast: **8** Joel Grey **11** Fritz Wepper, Helmut Griem, Michael York **12** Liza Minnelli (Sally Bowles) **14** Marisa Berenson
   Oscar for: **7** actress (Minnelli) **8** director **15** supporting actor (Grey)
   song: **12** The Money Song

cabbage 16 Brassica oleracea (Capitata Group)
   varieties: **3** Cow **4** Deer, Head, Wild **5** John's, Savoy, Skunk **6** Celery **7** Chinese **9** Flowering, Tronchuda **10** Portuguese **11** Yellow skunk **12** Western skunk

Cabecar
   language family: **10** Talamancan
   location: **9** Costa Rica **12** Sixaola River **14** Central America, Talamanca Plain
   intermixed with: **6** Bribri

Cabell, James Branch
   author of: **6** Jurgen **12** The High Place **14** Figures of Earth **17** The Cream of the Jest

cabin 3 hut **4** room **5** hutch, lodge, shack **6** shanty **7** cottage **8** bungalow, log cabin, quarters **9** stateroom **11** compartment

cabinet 3 box **4** case, file **5** chest **6** bureau **7** council **8** advisors, cupboard, ministry **10** breakfront, counselors, receptacle **11** china closet **13** advisory board **14** chest of drawers

cable 4 cord, line, rope, wire **5** chain, wires **6** hawser **7** mooring **8** wire line, wire rope **12** electric wire **16** overseas telegram

Cable, George W
   author of: **8** Dr Sevier **13** Old Creole Days **15** The Grandissimes

cablegram 4 wire **5** cable **7** message **8** wireless **16** overseas telegram

Cabot, Ephraim
   character in: **18** Desire Under the Elms
   author: **6** O'Neill

Caca
   origin: **5** Roman
   goddess of: **6** hearth
   corresponds to: **5** Vesta

Cacambo
   character in: **7** Candide
   author: **8** Voltaire

cache 4 heap **5** hoard, stock, store **8** hideaway **9** stockpile **11** hiding place, secret place

cachet 4 mark, seal **5** stamp, wafer **6** design, slogan **7** capsule

cackle 7 chatter **10** harsh laugh **11** shrill laugh
   sound made by: **3** hen **4** chicken

cacophonous 5 harsh **6** off-key **7** grating, jarring, raucous **8** off-pitch, screechy, strident **9** dissonant, out of tune, unmusical **10** discordant **11** unmelodious **12** inharmonious, nonmelodious **13** disharmonious

cacophony 3 din **5** noise **7** discord **9** harshness **10** disharmony, dissonance

cactus
   varieties: **3** Cob, Sun **4** Ball, Cane, Chin, Claw, Club, Comb, Crab, Hook, Lace, Leaf, Moon, Rose, Star, Toad, Vine, Yoke **5** Agave, Apple, Brain, Chain, Coral, Crown, Devil, False, Giant, Leafy, Melon, Paper, Plain, Prism, Snake, Spice, Torch **6** Barrel, Button, Cholla, Dagger, Dollar, Easter, Hatpin, Hot-dog, Myrtle, Nipple, Old-man, Orchid, Peanut, Pencil, Ribbon, Spider **7** Cushion, Eve's pin, Feather, Hatchet, Hat-rack, Jumping, Old-lady, Popcorn, Rain-

bow, Rattail, Redbird, Serpent, Thimble, Whisker **8** Cinnamon, Dumpling, Fishbone, Fishhook, Flapjack, Gold lace, Golf-ball, Hedgehog, Oldwoman, Polka-dot, Pond-lily, Snowball, Snowdrop, Starfish, Tortoise, Turk's-cap **9** Bird's nest, Chain-link, Christmas, Cow-tongue, Electrode, Fire-crown, Hairbrush, Lamb's-tail, Mistletoe, New old-man, Organ-pipe, Porcupine, Red orchid, Sea-urchin, Spineless, Teddy-bear, Toothpick, Totem-pole, Turk's-head, White chin **10** Bluebarrel, Candelabra, Cottonpole, Easter-lily, Golden ball, Goldenstar, Living-rock, Powder-puff, Silver ball, Strawberry, Unguentine, White torch, Wickerware **11** Frilled lace, Grizzlybear, Joseph's coat, Large barrel, Scarlet ball, Woolly torch **12** Dancing-bones, Golden barrel, Mulecrippler, Scarlet crown, Thanksgiving **13** Colombian ball, Creeping-devil, Dutchman's pipe, Peruvian apple, Peruvian torch, Silver cluster **15** Golden bird's nest **16** Mexican dwarf tree **17** Burbank's spineless **18** Fishhook pincushion

Cacus
   form: **5** giant
   father: **6** Vulcan
   eats: **3** men
   killed by: **8** Hercules

cad 3 cur, rat **4** heel, lout **5** churl, knave, louse, rogue **6** rascal, rotter **7** bounder, caitiff, dastard, villain **9** scoundrel

cadaver 4 body **5** stiff **6** corpse **7** remains **8** dead body, deceased

cadaverous 4 pale **5** ashen, gaunt **6** chalky, pallid **7** deathly, ghastly **8** blanched **9** bloodless, deathlike **10** corpselike

caddisfly
   variety: **5** micro **8** northern **9** fingernet, primitive, snailcase **10** longhorned, trumpetnet, tubemaking **11** netspinning

Caddoan
   tribe: **6** Pawnee **14** Chahiksichhiks

caddy 3 box, can, tin **5** chest **6** coffer

cadence 4 beat, lilt **5** meter, pulse, swing, tempo, throb **6** accent, rhythm **7** measure

Caderousse
   character in: **21** The Count of Monte

Cristo
author: 5 Dumas (pere)

cadet 5 plebe **7** recruit, student **11** youngest son **14** military student

cadge 3 beg, bum **5** mooch **6** hustle, peddle, sponge **7** solicit, scrounge **9** panhandle

cadmium
chemical symbol: 2 Cd

Cadmus
form: 6 prince
realm: 9 Phoenicia
father: 6 Agenor
mother: 10 Telephassa
brother: 5 Cilix **7** Phoenix
sister: 6 Europa
wife: 8 Harmonia
son: 8 Illyrius **9** Polydorus
daughter: 3 Ino **5** Agave **6** Semele **7** Autonoe
introduced to the Greeks: 7 writing
founded: 6 Thebes
planted: 12 dragons teeth

Caduceus
staff of: 7 Mercury

Caeneus
also: 6 Caenis
member of: 9 Argonauts
gift: 15 invulnerability
former identity: 6 Caenis

Caenis
also: 7 Caeneus
father: 6 Elatus
violated by: 8 Poseidon
changed into: 3 man
subsequent identity: 7 Caeneus

caesar, Caesar 5 ruler **6** despot, kaiser, tyrant **7** emperor **8** autocrat, dictator

Caesar, Julius
adopted son: 8 Octavian **14** Caesar Augustus
author of: 13 On the Civil War **14** On the Gallic War
battle: 4 Zela **5** Munda **7** Durazzo, Thapsus **8** Mytilene **9** Pharsalus **11** Dyrrhachium
conquered: 4 Gaul
crossed: 7 Rubicon (river)
defeated: 6 Pompey
lover: 9 Cleopatra
member of: 16 First Triumvirate
murdered by: 5 Casca **6** Brutus **7** Cassius
murdered on: 11 Ides of March
other triumvirs: 6 Pompey **7** Crassus
saying: 9 Et tu Brute? (Even you Brutus?) **12** Veni vidi vici (I came I saw I conquered)
wife: 7 Pompeia **8** Cornelia **9** Calpurnia

Caesar, Sid
partner: 11 Imogene Coca
born: 9 Yonkers NY
roles: 15 Your Show of Shows

Caesar and Cleopatra
author: 17 George Bernard Shaw

Caesar or Nothing
author: 9 Pio Baroja

caesura 5 break, pause **6** hiatus **12** interruption

cafe 3 bar, inn **5** diner **6** bistro, eatery, nitery, tavern **7** automat, beanery, cabaret **9** cafeteria, chophouse, hash house, lunchroom, nightclub **10** restaurant, supper club **11** bar and grill, coffeehouse, discotheque **12** luncheonette
French: 9 estaminet

cafe au lait 10 light brown **14** coffee with milk

cafe noir 11 black coffee

cage 3 pen **4** coop **5** pen in **6** coop up, encage, lock up, shut in **7** confine, impound **8** imprison, restrain, restrict **9** enclosure

cagey 3 sly **4** foxy, keen, wary, wily **5** alert, chary, leery, sharp **6** artful, crafty, shifty, shrewd **7** careful, cunning, heedful, prudent **8** cautious, discreet, watchful

Cagliari
capital of: 8 Sardinia

Cagney, James
nickname: 5 Jimmy
born: 9 New York NY
roles: 7 Ragtime **14** The Public Enemy **17** Yankee Doodle Dandy (Oscar) **19** Man of a Thousand Faces

Cagney and Lacey
cast: 8 Tyne Daly **11** Sharon Gless

Cain
father: 4 Adam
mother: 3 Eve
brother: 4 Abel, Seth
home: 4 Eden
son: 5 Enoch
killed: 4 Abel
traveled to: 3 Nod

Caine, Michael
real name: 24 Maurice Joseph Micklewhite
born: 6 London **7** England
roles: 4 Zulu **5** Alfie **6** Sleuth **9** Deathtrap **13** Educating Rita, Jekyll and Hyde **14** The Ipcress File **17** A Shock to the System **19** Hannah and Her Sisters **20** The Man who would be King **21** Dirty Rotten Scoundrels

Caine Mutiny, The
author: 10 Herman Wouk
director: 13 Edward Dmytryk
cast: 7 May Wynn **9** Lee Marvin **10** E G Marshall, Jose Ferrer, Van Johnson **13** Fred MacMurray, Robert Francis **14** Humphrey Bogart (Captain Queeg)

Caingua see **7** Guarani

Cairo
Arab camp: 8 al-Fustat
Arabic: 9 al-Qahirah
capital of: 5 Egypt
island: 5 Rodah **7** Zamalik
landmark:

mosque: 7 al-Azhar **11** Muhammed Ali
statue: 8 Ramses II
museum: 8 Egyptian
river: 4 Nile
Roman fortress: 7 Babylon
rulers: 5 Turks **7** British, Saladin **8** Fatimids **9** Mamelukes **11** Ismail Pasha, Muhammed Ali **12** Ottoman Turks
university: 7 Al-Azhar **8** Ain Shams, American

Cairo, Joel
character in: 16 The Maltese Falcon
author: 7 Hammett
played by: 10 Peter Lorre

caitiff 3 cad, cur, rat **4** heel **5** churl, knave, louse, rogue **6** rascal, rotter **7** bounder, dastard, villain **9** scoundrel **10** blackguard

cajole 4 coax **7** beguile, deceive, flatter, wheedle **8** blandish, inveigle, persuade

cajolery 7 blarney, coaxing, fawning **8** flattery, promises, soft soap **9** adulation, sweet talk, wheedling **10** enticement, inveigling, persuasion **11** beguilement **12** blandishment

cake 3 bar, bun, dry **4** lump, mass **5** block, crust, tort **6** cookie, eclair, gateau, harden, pastry, **7** congeal, cupcake, thicken **8** compress, solidify **9** coagulate, sweet roll **11** consolidate

Cakes and Ale
author: 16 W Somerset Maugham

cakewalk 5 cinch, dance **9** promenade **12** dance contest

calaboose 3 pen **4** jail, stir **6** prison **7** slammer **8** hoosegow

Calah
founder: 6 Nimrod

Calais
origin: 5 Greek
member of: 9 Argonauts
father: 6 Boreas
mother: 8 Orithyia
twin brother: 5 Zetes

calamitous 5 fatal **6** tragic, woeful **7** adverse, baleful, harmful, ruinous, unlucky **8** dreadful **9** blighting **10** disastrous, pernicious **11** cataclysmic, deleterious, destructive, detrimental, distressful, unfortunate **12** catastrophic

calamity 3 ill, woe **4** blow, ruin **5** trial **6** misery, mishap **7** bad luck, failure, ill wind, reverse, scourge, tragedy, trouble, undoing **8** disaster, distress, downfall, hardship **9** adversity, cataclysm, mischance **10** affliction, ill fortune, misfortune **11** catastrophe, tribulation **13** sea of troubles **15** stroke of ill luck

calando
music: 22 getting weaker and slower

calcium
chemical symbol: 2 Ca

calculate 4 mean, plan 5 add up, aim at, count, judge, sum up 6 design, devise, figure, intend, reckon 7 compute, measure, predict, project, surmise, work out 8 estimate 9 ascertain, determine 10 conjecture

calculated 7 planned 10 deliberate, purposeful, thought out 11 intentional, prearranged 12 premeditated

calculating 3 sly 4 foxy, wily 6 artful, crafty, shrewd, tricky 7 cunning, devious 8 plotting, scheming 9 designing 10 contriving, intriguing 12 manipulative 13 Machiavellian

calculating machine
  invented by: 7 Babbage

calculation 6 answer, result 8 figuring, judgment 9 reckoning 10 estimation 11 computation

calculator 6 abacus 7 counter, thinker 8 computer, reckoner

Calcutta
  captured by: 5 Clive
  founded by: 23 British East India Company
  landmark: 10 Jain Temple 12 Howrah Bridge, Indian Museum 16 Botanical Gardens, Victoria Memorial 17 Zoological Gardens 18 Dakshineswar Temple
  opposite city: 6 Howrah
  river: 7 Hooghly
  state: 10 West Bengal

Calder, Alexander
  born: 14 Philadelphia PA
  sculptures also called: 7 mobiles 8 stabiles
  artwork: 3 Man 5 Whale 6 Spiral 10 Teodelapio 12 Ticket Window 13 La Grande Voile 14 The Brass Family 23 Lobster Traps and Fish Tail

Calderon de la Barca, Pedro
  author of: 12 Life Is a Dream

caldron, cauldron 3 pot 6 boiler, kettle

Caldwell, Erskine
  author of: 10 Georgia Boy 11 Tobacco Road 14 God's Little Acre

Caldwell, Taylor
  author of: 12 Answer as a Man 13 A Pillar of Iron 14 Great Lion of God 17 Testimony of Two Men, The Devil's Advocate 19 Bright Flows the River 20 Glory and the Lightning 22 The Captains and the Kings 24 Dear and Glorious Physician

Caleb Williams
  author: 13 William Godwin

Caledonia see 8 Scotland

calendar 4 list 5 chart, diary, table 6 agenda, docket 7 day book, program 8 register, schedule

calf 4 veal 5 dogie 6 weaner 7 leg part
  young of: 3 cow 4 bull, seal 5 whale 8 elephant

Calgary
  hockey team: 6 Flames

Calhern, Louis
  real name: 13 Carl Henry Vogt
  born: 10 Brooklyn NY
  roles: 8 King Lear 12 Julius Caesar 15 Annie Get Your Gun 16 The Asphalt Jungle 20 The Magnificent Yankee

Calhoun, Rory
  real name: 20 Francis Timothy Durgin
  born: 12 Los Angeles CA
  roles: 8 The Texan 21 Treasure of Pancho Villa 22 How to Marry a Millionaire, Requiem for a Heavyweight

Caliban
  character in: 10 The Tempest
  author: 11 Shakespeare

caliber 4 bore, rank 5 gifts, merit, place, power, scope, skill, worth 6 repute, talent 7 ability, quality, stature 8 capacity, diameter, eminence, position, prestige 10 capability, competence, estimation, excellence, importance, prominence, reputation 11 achievement, distinction

California
  abbreviation: 2 CA 3 Cal 5 Calif
  nickname: 6 Golden 8 Eldorado 12 Promised Land
  capital: 10 Sacramento
  largest city: 10 Los Angeles
  others: 4 Lodi 5 Azusa, Chico, Chino, Indio 6 Blythe, Carmel, Covina, Eureka, Fresno, Lompoc, Merced, Oxnard, Pomona, Sonoma, Tulare 7 Alameda, Anaheim, Burbank, Gardena, Needles, Oakland, Salinas, Vallejo, Visalia 8 Altadena, Berkeley, Palo Alto, Pasadena, Redlands, San Diego, Stockton 9 Cucamonga, Long Beach 11 Palm Springs, Santa Monica 12 Beverly Hills, San Francisco, Santa Barbara
  college: 3 USC 4 UCLA 5 Mills 6 Pitzer, Pomona 7 Caltech, Chapman, Scripps 8 Stanford, Whittier 10 Occidental, Pepperdine
  explorer: 6 Cortez
  feature:
    amusement park: 10 Disneyland 15 Knotts Berry Farm
    area: 9 Hollywood 15 Fishermans Wharf
    dam: 6 Hoover, Shasta 7 Boulder
    island prison: 8 Alcatraz
    mill: 7 Sutters
    national park: 7 Redwood, Sequoia 8 Yosemite 11 Kings Canyon 14 Channel Islands, Lassen Volcanic
    parade: 4 Rose
    prison: 6 Folsom 10 San Quentin
  tribe: 4 Hupa, Pomo, Yana, Yuki 5 Karok, Maidu, Miwok, Wappo, Wiyot, Yurok 6 Patwin, Shasta, Tolowa, Yokuts 7 Chumash, Luiseno, Salinan, Serrano 8 Dieguено

  people: 6 Sutter 10 Earl Warren 11 Robert Frost 13 George S Patton, John Steinbeck 14 William Saroyan
  island: 4 Goat, Mare 7 Anacapo, Channel 8 Alcatraz, Catalina, Coronado 9 Farallone
  lake: 4 Mono, Soda 5 Clear, Eagle, Owens, Tahoe 6 Salton, Tulare 7 Almanor 8 Elsinore 9 Berryessa
  land rank: 5 third
  mountain: 4 Muir 5 Coast 6 Lassen, Shasta, Wilson 7 Cascade, Klamath, Palomar, Whitney 10 Peninsular, Transverse 12 Sierra Nevada
    highest point: 7 Whitney
  physical feature:
    bay: 8 Monterey, San Diego 12 San Francisco
    cape: 9 Mendocino
    desert: 6 Mohave, Mojave 8 Colorado
    fault: 10 San Andreas
    glacier: 8 Palisade
    sea: 6 Cortez 7 Pacific
    tree: 7 redwood
    valley: 5 Death
    volcano: 6 Lassen
    wind: 7 Collada 8 Santa Ana
  president: 13 Richard M Nixon, Ronald W Reagan
  river: 3 Eel, Mad, Pit 4 Kern 5 Kings, Owens, Putah, Smith, Stony 6 Little, Merced, Salmon 7 Feather, Klamath, Rubicon, Russian, Salinas, Trinity, Truckee 10 Sacramento, San Jacinto, San Joaquin, Stanislaus
  state admission: 11 thirty-first
  state bird: 21 California Valley quail
  state fish: 21 California golden trout
  state flower: 11 golden poppy
  state motto: 6 Eureka (I have found it)
  state song: 18 I Love You California
  state symbol: 11 grizzly bear
  state tree: 17 California redwood
  baseball team: 6 Angels, Giants, Padres 7 Dodgers 9 Athletics
  basketball team: 6 Lakers 8 Clippers 19 Golden State Warriors
  football team: 7 Raiders 8 Chargers 11 Forty-Niners

Calinieff, Martin
  real name of: 13 Michael Callan

Calinky State
  nickname of: 13 South Carolina

calisay
  type: 7 liqueur
  origin: 5 Spain 9 Catalonia
  flavor: 5 herbs 7 quinine

Calkins, Richard
  creator/artist of: 10 Buck Rogers

call 3 ask, bid, cry, dub, tag 4 bawl, buzz, hail, name, need, plea, ring, roar, stop, term, yell 5 cause, claim, label, order, phone, rally, right, shout, style, title, visit 6 appeal, ask for, bellow, charge, clamor, cry out, decree, demand, direct, drop in, excuse, gather, halloo, holler, invite, invoke, know as, muster, notice, outcry, pray to, reason, scream, stop by, summon **7** collect, command, contact, convene, convoke, declare, entitle, entreat, grounds, refer to, request, require, specify, stop off, summons, warrant **8** announce, appeal to, assemble, christen, entreaty, identify, instruct, look in on, occasion, petition, proclaim **9** crying out, designate, direction, pay a visit, telephone **10** describe as, invitation, supplicate **11** declaration, instruction **12** announcement, call together, characterize, proclamation, supplication **13** justification

Callan, Michael
   real name: 15 Martin Calinieff
   born: 14 Philadelphia PA
   roles: 9 Cat Ballou **10** The Interns **18** Gidget Goes Hawaiian, The Flying Fontaines **23** The Magnificent Seven Ride

call for 4 need **6** demand, pick up **7** request, require

call forth 4 spur **5** evoke, raise **6** arouse, awaken, excite, incite, invoke, kindle, stir up **7** command, conjure, provoke **8** summon up **9** make aware, stimulate **10** make appear

calling 3 job **4** line, work **5** craft, field, forte, trade **6** career, crying, living, metier, outcry **7** hailing, mission, passion, yelling **8** activity, business, devotion, function, province, shouting, vocation **9** bellowing, crying out, first love, hallooing, life's work, screaming, specialty **10** assignment, attachment, dedication, employment, enthusiasm, livelihood, occupation, profession, walk of life **14** bread and butter, means of support, specialization

calling off 6 ending **7** halting **8** giving up **11** termination **12** backing out of, cancellation

calling oneself thus
   French: 9 soi-disant

Calliope
   member of: 5 Muses
   presided over: 10 epic poetry
   father: 4 Zeus
   mother: 9 Mnemosyne
   son: 7 Orpheus

Callisto
   form: 5 nymph
   attended: 7 Artemis
   loved: 4 Zeus
   changed into: 4 bear
   killed by: 7 Artemis

call off 3 end **4** halt **5** abort **6** cancel, give up **8** postpone **9** back out of, terminate **10** summon away **12** dispense with

Call of the Wild, The
   author: 10 Jack London
   dog: 4 Buck
   master: 12 John Thornton

callous 4 cold, hard **5** cruel, horny, tough **6** inured **8** hardened, uncaring **9** apathetic, heartless, unfeeling **11** hard-hearted, indifferent, insensitive **12** thick-skinned, unresponsive **13** dispassionate, unsympathetic **14** pachydermatous

call out 3 cry **4** bawl, hail, yell **5** shout **6** bellow, cry out, holler, summon **9** challenge

callow 3 raw **5** crude, green, naive **7** artless, awkward, puerile, shallow, untried **8** childish, ignorant, immature, juvenile **9** infantile **10** sophomoric, uninformed, unschooled, unseasoned **11** uninitiated **13** inexperienced **15** unsophisticated

call to 4 hail **5** greet **6** accost, salute **7** address, shout at

call to account 5 chide, scold **6** accuse, charge, rebuke **7** arraign, bawl out, censure, chasten, reprove, upbraid **8** admonish, denounce, reproach **9** criticize, dress down, reprimand **10** take to task **11** remonstrate

call to arms 6 war cry **9** battle cry **11** rallying cry

call to order 4 open **6** muster **7** convene, convoke

call upon 3 ask, bid **4** urge **5** visit **6** charge, enjoin, exhort, invite, invoke **7** beseech, entreat, request, require **8** appeal to, petition, summon up **9** encourage **11** acknowledge

callused 4 hard **5** horny, tough **8** hardened **12** thick- skinned **14** pachydermatous

calm 4 cool, ease, mild **5** allay, balmy, bland, quell, quiet, still **6** becalm, gentle, lessen, pacify, placid, reduce, repose, sedate, serene, smooth, soothe, subdue **7** assuage, collect, compose, cool off, halcyon, mollify, pacific, placate, relaxed, relieve **8** composed, coolness, diminish, mitigate, moderate, peaceful, serenity, tranquil, unshaken **9** alleviate, collected, composure, impassive, placidity, quietness, stillness, unexcited, unruffled **10** cool-headed, motionless, simmer down, smoothness, unagitated, untroubled **11** impassivity, passionless, restfulness, self-control, tranquility, tranquilize, undisturbed, unflappable, unperturbed **12** peacefulness, tranquillity, windlessness **13** imperturbable, self-possessed, stormlessness **14** self- possession **16** imperturbability

calmness 5 poise **6** aplomb **8** coolness, serenity **9** composure, placidity, sangfroid, stillness **10** equanimity, steadiness **11** self-control, tranquility **12** peacefulness, tranquillity **14** presence of mind, self-possession **16** imperturbability

Calpurnia

character in: 12 Julius Caesar
   author: 11 Shakespeare

calumnious 8 libelous **9** maligning, vilifying **10** defamatory, derogatory, slanderous **11** disparaging

calumny 4 barb, slur **5** libel, smear **6** malice **7** slander **8** innuendo **9** aspersion **10** backbiting, defamation, derogation, revilement **11** denigration, deprecation, insinuation **12** backstabbing, calumniation, depreciation, vilification **13** animadversion, disparagement, malicious lies

calvados
   type: 6 brandy
   origin: 6 France **8** Normandy
   flavor: 5 apple
   aged in: 3 oak

Calvary 8 Golgotha
   means: 10 skull place

Calydonian boar
   sent by: 5 Diana
   killed by: 8 Meleager

Calydonian hunt
   pursuit of: 4 boar

Calypso
   form: 5 nymph
   home: 6 Ogygia
   father: 10 Titan Atlas
   detained: 8 Odysseus
      for: 10 seven years

calyx 4 husk **5** sepal

cam 3 cog **4** disk **8** cylinder **10** projection
   located on: 5 shaft, wheel
   motion: 7 rocking **8** circular **12** back and forth

camaraderie 7 jollity **8** bonhomie, good will **10** affability, clubbiness, fellowship, friendship **11** brotherhood, comradeship, sociability **12** congeniality, conviviality, friendliness **13** companionship, esprit de corps **14** goodfellowship

Camarasaurus
   type: 8 dinosaur, sauropod
   location: 12 United States
   period: 8 Jurassic

Cambodia
   other name: 7 Camboja **8** Cambodge **9** Kampuchea
   capital/largest city: 8 Pnom-Penh
   others: 3 Som **4** Ream **5** Takeo **6** Kampot, Kratie, Pursat **7** Kohnieh, Kompong, Kracheh, Rovieng, Samrong **8** Siem Reap, Sisophon **10** Battambang, Stung Treng **11** Kompong Cham **12** Krungkoh Kong **13** Sihanoukville
   head of state: 4 King
   monetary unit: 3 sen **4** quan, riel **6** puttan **7** piaster
   weight: 4 mace, tael
   island: 4 Kong, Rong
   lake: 8 Tonle Sap
   mountain: 3 Pan **7** Dangrek, Dong Rek **8** Cardamom, Elephant

highest point: 10 Phnom Aoral, Phnom Aural

river: 3 San, Sen **5** Sreng **6** Bassac, Chinit, Mekong, Porong, Pursat, Srepok **7** Kamlong, Sekhong **8** Tonle Sap

physical feature:
  bay: 10 Kompongsom
  cape: 5 Samit
  gulf: 4 Siam **8** Thailand
people: 4 Cham, Thai **5** Khmer **7** Chinese **10** Vietnamese
  leader: 6 Pol Pot **8** Sihanouk
language: 5 Khmer **6** French **9** Cambodian **10** Vietnamese
religion: 7 animism **8** Buddhism **12** Christianity
places:
  ruins/temple: 6 Angkor **9** Angkor Wat
feature:
  Communist group: 10 Khmer Rouge

Cambria *see* **5** Wales

cambric 5 cloth, linen **6** cotton, fabric **8** material

camel
  called: 13 beast of burden **15** ship of the desert
  chews: 3 cud
  group: 4 herd
  habitat: 4 Asia **6** Africa, desert
  kind: 7 Arabian **8** Bactrian **9** dromedary
  number of humps: 3 one, two
  species: 6 mammal
  type of: 8 ruminant
  young: 4 calf

camellia
  varieties: 5 Silky **6** Common **8** Mountain, Sasanqua

Camenae
  means: 11 foretellers
  form: 6 nymphs **7** deities
  gift: 8 prophecy
  names: 6 Egeria **8** Carmenta **9** Antevorta, Postvorta
  habitat: 8 fountain
  correspond to: 5 Muses

camera 3 APS, SLR **4** 35mm, view **6** manuel **8** plastic **8** panorama, Polaroid, twin lens **9** automatic **11** large format, range finder **12** medium format **13** point-and-shoot
  brand: 4 Fuji **5** Canon, Kodak, Leica, Nikon, Ricoh **6** Konica, Pentax, Rollei **7** Bronica, Minolta, Olympus **8** Polaroid **10** Hasselblad
  invented by:
    Kodak: 6 Walker **7** Eastman
    Polaroid: 4 Land
    photography: 6 Niepce, Talbot **8** Daguerre
    film, celluloid: 6 Edison **11** Reichenbach
    film, transparent: 7 Eastman, Goodwin
    color photo: 4 Ives

Cameroon
  capital: 7 Yaounde
  largest city: 6 Douala
  others: 3 Wum **4** Bali, Buea, Edea, Tiko **5** Kumba, Lomie, Mamfe **6** Garona, Maroua **7** Batouri, Dschang, Ebolowa, Foumban **8** Victoria **10** N'Gaoundere, N'Kongsamba
  monetary unit: 5 franc **7** centime
  island: 5 Nanny **8** Fernando
  lake: 4 Chad
  mountain: 5 Mbabo **7** Bambuto, Kapsiki, Mandara **8** Batandji **9** Atlantika
  highest point: 8 Cameroon
  river: 3 Dja, Lom **4** Faro, Mbam, Vina **5** Benue, Campo, Cross, Kadei, Mbere, Nyong, N'Goko, Sanga, Shari **6** Djerem, Ivindo, Logone, Sanaga
  sea: 8 Atlantic
  physical feature:
    cape: 10 Debundscha
    gulf: 6 Guinea
    plateau: 7 Adamawa **8** Mambilla
  people: 3 Abo, Edo, Ibo **4** Beti, Bulu, Ekoi, Ijaw, Sara **5** Bantu, Bassa, Kirdi, Pygmy, Tikar **6** Bamoun, Donala, Ewondo, Fulani, Ibibio **7** Bakweri **8** Bamileke
    Fulani chief: 7 Lamidos
  language: 4 Bulu **5** Bantu, Bassa, Hausa **6** Douala, Ewondo, French, Fulani **7** English **8** Bamileke, Fulfulde
  religion: 5 Islam **7** animism **12** Christianity
  places:
    home of prime minister: 7 Schloss

Camille
  also: 17 La Dame aux camelias
  author: 14 Alexander Dumas (fils)
  character: 6 Nanine **11** Armand Duval **17** Marguerite Gautier (Camille)
  director: 11 George Cukor
  cast: 10 Greta Garbo (Camille) **12** Henry Daniell, Robert Taylor (Armand) **14** Elizabeth Allan, Laura Hope Crews **15** Lionel Barrymore

Camillo
  character in: 14 The Winter's Tale
  author: 11 Shakespeare

Camirus
  origin: 5 Greek
  grandfather: 6 Helios, Helius

camisole 3 top **4** slip **6** jacket **10** underwaist

camouflage 4 hide, mask, veil **5** blind, cloak, cover, front **6** screen, shroud **7** conceal, cover up **8** disguise **10** masquerade, subterfuge **11** concealment

camouflaged 6 hidden, masked **7** cloaked **8** shrouded **9** concealed, disguised

camp 4 tent **5** tents **7** bivouac, lodging, rough it **8** army base, barracks, quarters **10** pitch a tent

campaign 3 run **4** push **5** drive, stump **6** action, effort **7** crusade **8** endeavor, movement **9** offensive, operation **11** electioneer, whistle-stop **12** battle series, beat the drums, solicit votes

campanile 6 belfry **9** bell tower

campari
  type: 7 bitters **8** aperitif
  origin: 5 Italy

campground 7 bivouac **8** tent city **16** temporary shelter

Campin, Robert
  born: 8 Flanders
  also known as/identified with: 14 Master of Merode **16** Master of Flemalle
  artwork: 10 St Veronica, The Trinity **13** The Entombment **16** Merode Altarpiece (Merode Triptych) **17** The Virgin and Child **18** The Thief on the Cross

Camptosaurus
  type: 8 dinosaur **10** ornithopod
  location: 12 North America
  period: 8 Jurassic
  characteristic: 10 duck-billed

Camus, Albert
  author of: 4 L'ete **6** Summer **7** The Fall **8** Caligula, The Rebel **9** The Plague **11** A Happy Death, The Stranger **12** Cross Purpose **17** The Myth of Sisyphus

can 3 tin **4** buns, fire, rump, seat **5** fanny, put up **6** bottom **8** backside, buttocks, preserve **9** container, fundament, give the ax

Canaan
  father: 3 Ham
  brother: 4 Cush
  grandfather: 4 Noah
  known as: 12 promised land
  see also **6** Israel

Canada
  capital: 6 Ottawa
  largest city: 8 Montreal
  others: 4 Hull **5** Banff, Laval **6** Dawson, Guelph, London, Oshawa, Quebec, Regina, Sarnia, Val d'or **7** Calgary, Halifax, Moncton, Nanaimo, Sudbury, Toronto, Welland, Windsor **8** Edmonton, Hamilton, Kingston, Moose Jaw, Victoria, Winnipeg **9** Saskatoon, Vancouver **10** Port Arthur, Sherbrooke **11** Fredericton **12** Niagara Falls, Peterborough, Prince Albert, Prince George **13** Charlottetown **21** St Catherines Stratford
  school: 3 UBC **5** Laval **6** McGill, Queens **7** Toronto **8** McMaster, Montreal **9** Concordia, Dalhousie **11** Simon Fraser
  division: 5 Yukon **6** Quebec **7** Alberta, Ontario **8** Manitoba **10** Nova Scotia **12** Newfoundland, New Brunswick, Saskatchewan **15** British Columbia **18** Prince Edward Island **20** Northwest Territories

New division: 7 Nunavut
head of state: 14 British monarch **15** governor general
measure: 3 ton **5** minot, perch, point **6** arpent **7** chainon
island: 4 Read **5** Banks, Bylot, Coats, Devon, Grand, Manan, Parry, Sable **6** Baffin, Breton, Mansel, Middle **7** Belcher **8** Bathurst, Magdalen, Victoria **9** Anticosti, Ellesmere, Vancouver **10** Campobello, Manitoulin **11** Southampton **14** Queen Charlotte
lake: 4 Cree, Erie, Gras, Seul **5** Garry, Huron, Rainy **6** Louise, St John **7** Abitibi, Dubawnt, Nipigon, Ontario, Testlin **8** Kootenay, Manitoba, Okanagan, Reindeer, Superior, Winnipeg **9** Athabaska, Great Bear, Nipissing **10** Great Slave, Mistassini **12** Winnipegosis
mountain: 5 Coast, Royal **6** Robson, Skeena **7** Cariboo, Cascade, Purcell, Rockies, Selkirk, St Elias **8** Columbia, Hazelton, Monashee **9** Mackenzie, Notre Dame, Tremblant **10** Laurentian, Richardson, Shickshock **14** Jacques Cartier
highest point: 5 Logan
river: 3 Hay, Red **4** Peel **5** Liard, Peace, Slave, Yukon **6** Albany, Fraser, Nelson, Nicola, Ottawa, Skeena, St John, Thames, Thelon **7** St Marys **8** Columbia, Gatineau, Kootenay, Petawawa, Saguenay **9** Athabasca, Athapaska, Churchill, Mackenzie, Richelieu **10** Coppermine, St Lawrence **11** Assiniboine, **12** Saskatchewan
sea: 6 Arctic **7** Pacific **8** Atlantic, Labrador
physical features:
  bay: 5 Basin, Fundy, Hecla, James, Minas **6** Baffin, Griper, Hudson, Ungava **8** Georgian
  canal: 3 Soo **7** Welland **10** Wellington
  cape: 5 Canso
  falls: 7 Niagara **9** Horseshoe
  gulf: 10 St Lawrence
  pass: 8 Chilkoot
  peninsula: 5 Gaspe **7** Boothia **8** Labrador, Melville
  plain: 11 Barren lands
  port: 6 Quebec **7** St Johns **8** Hamilton, Victoria **9** Churchill
  strait: 5 Cabot, Davis, Dease **6** Hecate, Hudson **7** Georgia **9** Belle Isle **10** Juan de Fuca
people: 5 Inuit **6** Canuck, Eskimo, French **7** English
  explorer: 5 Cabot **6** Fraser, Joliet **7** Cartier, LaSalle, Selkirk **8** Thompson **9** Champlain, MacKenzie, Marquette
  leader: 4 King, Riel **5** Clark **6** Borden **7** Laurier, Trudeau **8** Campbell, Chretien, Mulroney **9** Macdonald, St Laurent **11** Diefenbaker

language: 6 Eskimo, French **7** English
religion: 8 Anglican **13** Roman Catholic **20** United Church of Canada
places:
  battlefield: 15 Plains of Abraham
  national park: 4 Yoho **5** Banff **6** Jasper **7** Glacier **8** Kootenay **9** Elk Island **10** La Mauricie, Revelstoke **11** Wood Buffalo **12** Prince Albert **13** Waterton Lakes
  resort: 5 Banff **10** Lake Louise
feature:
  airport: 6 Gander
  emblem: 9 maple leaf
  fish: 5 charr, trout
  flower: 10 Juneflower
  police: 8 Mounties **12** Royal Mounted
food:
  soup: 7 rubaboo
canaille 6 proles, rabble **8** riffraff **9** commoners, hoi polloi **11** proletariat **13** great unwashed
canal 4 duct, Erie, Kiel, Suez, tube **5** Grand **6** Panama **7** channel, conduit, passage **8** aqueduct
Canaletto
  real name: 20 Giovanni Antonio Canal
  born: 5 Italy **6** Venice
  artwork: 18 The Stonemason's Yard
canard 4 hoax **5** rumor **7** slander **9** falsehood **12** exaggeration
Canary Islands
  other name: 14 Fortunate Isles **15** Isles of the Blest
  named for: 3 dog **5** canis **6** canine
  capital: 9 Las Palmas **19** Santa Cruz de Tenerife
  largest city: 9 Las Palmas
  others: 4 Icod **6** Laguna **7** Orotava **8** Arrecife, Valverde **12** San Sebastian
  government: 16 overseas province of: **5** Spain
  measure: 8 fanegada
  monetary unit: 6 peseta
  island: 4 Roca **5** Clara, Ferro, Lobos, Rocca **6** Gomera, Hierro **7** Inferno, La Palma **8** Graciosa, Tenerife **9** Lanzarote **10** Lanzarotte **11** Gran Canaria **13** Fuerteventura
  mountain: 6 La Cruz **8** El Cumbre, Tenerife
  highest point: 5 Teide, Teyde
  sea: 8 Atlantic
  people: 7 Spanish
  language: 7 Spanish
  religion: 13 Roman Catholic
canasta
  number of players: 4 four
  cards/hand: 6 eleven
  meld: 12 three of a kind
  wild card: 5 deuce, joker
Canberra
  capital of: 9 Australia
  territory: 13 New South Wales **26**

Australian Capital Territory
  lake: 13 Burley Griffin
cancel 4 undo, void **5** abort, annul, erase, quash, scrub **6** delete, offset, recall, recant, repeal, revoke **7** abolish, call off, nullify, rescind, retract, vitiate **8** abrogate, call back, set aside **9** repudiate **10** balance out, bluepencil, do away with, invalidate, neutralize **11** countermand **12** dispense with **13** compensate for **14** counterbalance **18** declare null and void
cancellation 6 repeal **9** abolition **10** abrogation, effacement, rescinding, revocation **11** abolishment, eradication, repudiation, termination
cancer 3 rot **4** crab **6** plague **7** sarcoma, scourge **8** neoplasm, sickness **9** carcinoma **10** malignancy **14** malignant tumor **15** malignant growth
Cancer
  symbol: 4 crab
  planet: 4 Moon
  rules: 4 home **6** family
  born: 4 July, June
Cancer Ward, The
  author: 21 Aleksandr Solzhenitsyn
candelabrum 7 menorah **8** dikerion **9** girandole, trikerion **11** candlestick **12** candleholder
Candia see **5** Crete
candid 4 fair, free, just, open **5** blunt, frank, plain **6** direct, honest **7** genuine, natural, relaxed, sincere, unposed **8** informal, outright, truthful **9** downright, impromptu, outspoken **10** forthright **11** plain spoken, spontaneous, unvarnished **14** extemporaneous **15** straightforward
Candida
  author: 17 George Bernard Shaw
candidate 7 hopeful, nominee **8** aspirant, eligible **9** applicant, contender, job seeker **10** competitor, contestant **11** possibility **12** office seeker
Candid Camera
  host: 9 Allen Funt
  co-host: 11 Bess Myerson **12** Durward Kirby **13** Arthur Godfrey
  tag: 5 smile
Candide
  author: 8 Voltaire
  character: 6 Martin **7** Cacambo **8** Pangloss **9** Cunegonde **11** Admiral Byng **17** Thunder-ten-Tronckh
candidness 6 candor **7** honesty, openess **9** frankness, sincerity **10** directness **12** truthfulness **13** guilelessness
candle 3 dip, wax **5** light, taper **6** bougie, cierge, tallow **9** rush light
candleholder, candlestick 6 sconce **7** menorah **8** dikerion **9** girandole, trikerion **10** chandelier **11** candelabrum
candor 7 honesty **8** fairness, justness, openness **9** bluntness, frankness, sin-

cerity 10 directness **11** artlessness **12** impartiality, truthfulness **14** forthrightness **15** plainspokenness **19** straightforwardness

candy 3 bar **4** kiss **5** cream, fudge, jelly, sweet, taffy **6** bonbon, comfit, dainty, nougat, sweets, toffee **7** brittle, caramel, fondant, gumdrop, praline **8** lollipop **9** chocolate, jellybean, sweetmeat **10** confection **12** all-day sucker **13** confectionery, peanut brittle

cane 3 hit, rap, rod, tan **4** beat, drub, flog, lash, whip **5** baste, flail, smite, staff, stick, whack **6** strike, switch, thrash, wallop **7** trounce **12** walking stick

cane 11 Arundinaria
  varieties: 4 Dumb, Wild **5** Arrow, Sugar **6** Rattan, Switch, Tobago, Tonkin **7** Tsingli **8** Southern **11** Spotted dumb **12** Chinese sweet **14** Yellow-leaf dumb

Canea
  capital of: 5 Crete

Canetti, Elias
  author of: 8 Auto da Fe **12** Tower of Babel **14** Crowds and Power **15** The Torch in My Ear **16** Kafka's Other Trial, The Tongue Set Free

Caniff, Milton
  creator/artist of: 10 Dickie Dare **11** Steve Canyon **14** The Gay Thirties **18** Terry and the Pirates

canine 3 cur, dog, fox, pup **4** mutt, wolf **5** hound, hyena, puppy, tooth **6** coyote, cuspid, jackal **7** mongrel **8** eyetooth

canker 4 sore **5** ulcer **6** blight, cancer, lesion **9** mouth sore **12** inflammation

Cannibal Galaxy, The
  author: 12 Cynthia Ozick

cannon 3 bit, gun **4** bone **5** carom **6** mortar **7** battery **8** field gun, howitzer, ordnance **9** artillery **10** field piece, mounted gun, pickpocket

Cannon
  character: 11 Frank Cannon
  cast: 13 William Conrad

Cannon, Dyan
  real name: 19 Samille Diane Friesen
  husband: 9 Cary Grant
  born: 8 Tacoma WA
  roles: 6 Shamus **9** Deathtrap **10** Ally McBeal **13** Heaven Can Wait **15** Such Good Friends **19** Bob & Carol & Ted & Alice **23** Revenge of the Pink Panther

cannonade 5 burst, salvo **6** volley **7** barrage, battery **8** shelling **9** fusillade **11** bombardment

canny 4 foxy, wary, wily, wise **5** cagey, sharp **6** artful, astute, clever, crafty, shrewd, subtle **7** careful, cunning, knowing **8** skillful **9** judicious, sagacious **10** convincing **11** circumspect, intelligent **13** perspicacious

Cano, Alonso
  born: 5 Spain **7** Granada
  artwork: 16 Granada Cathedral (facade) **18** Madonna of the Rosary **20** Immaculate Conception **23** The Seven Joys of the Virgin

canoe 4 boat **5** bungo, kayak **6** dugout **7** pirogue

canoeing
  athlete: 11 Marcia Smoke

canon 3 law **4** code, rule **5** dogma, edict, model, order **6** decree **7** pattern, precept, statute **8** doctrine, standard **9** bench mark, criterion, ordinance, principle, yardstick **10** regulation, touchstone

canonical 6 proper **8** accepted, approved, official orthodox **9** authentic, customary **10** authorized, legitimate, recognized, sanctioned **12** conventional **13** authoritative

Canonization, The
  author: 9 John Donne

canopy 4 hood **5** cover **6** awning, tester **8** covering

Canova, Antonio
  born: 5 Italy **8** Possagno
  artwork: 7 Perseus **12** Venus Victrix (Pauline Bonaparte Borghese) **14** Cupid and Psyche **16** Letizia Bonaparte **17** Daedalus and Icarus

Cansino, Margarita Carmen
  real name of: 12 Rita Hayworth

cant 4 sham, talk **5** argot, lingo, slang **6** humbug, jargon **8** parlance, pretense **9** hypocrisy **10** lip service, vernacular **11** insincerity **15** pretentiousness **16** sanctimoniousness

cantabile
  music: 7 flowing, singing **8** songlike

cantaloupe 5 fruit, melon **9** muskmelon

cantankerous 4 mean **5** cross, huffy, short, sulky, surly, testy **6** crabby, cranky, crusty, grumpy, morose, ornery, sullen, touchy **7** bearish, crabbed, fretful, grouchy, peevish, waspish **8** choleric, churlish, contrary, snappish **9** irascible, irritable, splenetic **10** ill-humored, ill-natured **11** contentious, ill-tempered, quarrelsome **12** disagreeable **13** argumentative

cantatrice 6 singer **9** chanteuse **10** songstress **18** professional singer

canteen 2 PX **4** club **5** flask **6** bottle **10** commissary **11** pocket flask **12** post exchange

canter 4 gait, lope, pace, trot **6** gallop, singer, whiner

Canterbury Tales, The
  author: 15 Geoffrey Chaucer
  starting point: 9 Southwark, Tabard Inn
  goal:
    tomb of: 6 Becket
  character/tale: 3 Nun **4** Cook, Dyer,

Monk **5** Canon, Friar, Reeve, Webbe **6** Knight, Miller, Parson, Squire, Yeoman **7** Shipman, Tapicer **8** Franklin, Manciple, Merchant, Pardoner, Prioress, Summoner **9** Carpenter, Ploughman **10** Wife of Bath **11** Haberdasher **13** Clerk of Oxford, Sergeant of Law **14** Doctor of Physic

Cantor, Eddie
  real name: 21 B Edward Israel Iskowitz
  nickname: 9 Banjo Eyes
  wife: 9 Ida Tobias
  born: 9 New York NY
  roles: 7 Whoopee **8** Kid Boots **9** Banjo Eyes

cantor of a synagogue
  Hebrew: 5 hazan **6** chazan

Cantos
  author: 9 Ezra Pound

can't stand 4 hate **5** abhor **6** detest, eschew, loathe **7** despise **8** execrate **9** abominate, can't abide **11** can't stomach **14** hate the sight of

canvas 4 duck **7** painting **8** painting **9** sailcloth, tarpaulin, tent cloth

canvass 4 poll, scan, sift **5** study, tally **6** survey **7** analyze, discuss, examine, explore, inquiry, inquire, inspect, solicit **8** analysis, campaign, scrutiny **10** evaluation, scrutinize **11** enumeration, exploration, inquire into, investigate, take stock of **13** give thought to, investigation

canyon 3 col, cut, gap **4** draw, pass, wadi, wash **5** break, chasm, cleft, crack, gorge, gulch, gully, notch **6** arroyo, coulee, defile, divide, ravine, valley **7** fissure, opening **8** corridor, crevasse, water gap

cap 3 fez, lid, tam, top **4** acme, seal **5** beret, cover, limit, outdo **6** better, exceed, top off **7** surpass **8** headgear, out-strip **9** headdress **10** visored hat

capability 3 art **4** gift **5** flair, knack, power, skill **6** talent **7** ability, faculty, know-how **8** capacity, efficacy, facility **9** potential **10** attainment, competence, competency **11** proficiency **12** potentiality **13** qualification

capable 3 apt **4** able, deft **5** adept **6** adroit, artful, clever, expert, gifted **7** skilled **8** masterly, skillful, talented **9** competent, effective, ingenious **10** proficient **11** efficacious, intelligent **12** accomplished

capable of assuming legal responsibility
  Latin: 8 sui juris

Capable of Honor
  author: 10 Allan Drury

capable of managing one's own affairs
  Latin: 8 sui juris

capacious 3 big **4** huge, vast, wide **5** ample, broad, large, roomy **7** mammoth, massive **8** gigantic, spacious **9**

expansive, extensive **10** commodious, expandable, tremendous, voluminous **13** amplitudinous

capaciousness 9 amplitude, roominess **12** spaciousness **14** commodiousness

capacitate 5 allow **6** enable, permit **7** empower, qualify **8** make able

capacity 4 mind, role, room, size **5** gifts, limit, might, power, range, scope, space **6** extent, talent, volume **7** ability, faculty **8** aptitude, facility, function, judgment, position, sagacity, strength **9** amplitude, endowment, intellect, potential **10** brain power, capability **11** discernment **12** intelligence, perspicacity **15** maximum contents

caparison 5 adorn, equip **6** bedeck **9** equipment, trappings

cape 4 spit **5** cloak, manta, point, shawl **6** mantle, poncho, serape, tabard, tongue **7** pelisse **8** headland **9** peninsula **10** promontory

Capek, Karel
     author of: 3 R U R **8** Hordubal, Krakatit **9** The Mother **13** Power and Glory **18** The War with the Newts

caper 3 hop **4** jape, jump, lark, leap, romp, skip **5** antic, bound, fling, frisk, prank, spree, stunt, trick **6** bounce, cavort, frolic, gambol, prance **7** caprice **8** escapade **9** adventure, high jinks **10** carrying on **11** shenanigans **14** monkey business

capital 4 cash, fine **5** great, money, super **6** center, riches, superb, wealth **7** supreme **9** excellent, financing, firstrate, majuscule, matchless, principal, resources **10** cash on hand, first-class **11** large letter, wherewithal **12** headquarters **13** working assets **14** available means **15** investment funds, upper-case letter

capital city (of countries)
     of Afghanistan: 5 Kabul
     of Albania: 6 Tirana, Tirane
     of Algeria: 7 Algiers
     of Andorra: 14 Andorra-la-Vella
     of Angola: 6 Luanda
     of Antigua and Barbuda: 7 St John's
     of Argentina: 11 Buenos Aires
     of Armenia: 6 Erivan **7** Yerevan
     of Australia: 8 Canberra
     of Austria: 6 Vienna
     of Azerbaijan: 4 Baku
     of the Bahamas: 6 Nassau
     of Bahrain: 6 Manama
     of Bangladesh: 5 Dacca
     of Barbados: 10 Bridgetown
     of Belarus: 5 Minsk
     of Belgium: 8 Brussels **9** Bruxelles
     of Belize: 8 Belmopan
     of Benin: 9 Porto-Novo
     of Bermuda: 8 Hamilton
     of Bhutan: 6 Thimbu **7** Thimphu
     of Bolivia: 5 La Paz, Sucre
     of Bosnia-Herzegovina: 8 Sarajevo

     of Botswana: 8 Gaborone **9** Gaberones
     of Brazil: 8 Brasilia
     of Brunei: 17 Bandar Seri Begawan
     of Bulgaria: 5 Sofia
     of Burkina Faso: 11 Ouagadougou
     of Burundi: 9 Bujumbura
     of Cambodia: 8 Pnom-Penh
     of Cameroon: 7 Yaounde
     of Canada: 6 Ottawa
     of the Canary Islands: 9 Las Palmas **19** Santa Cruz de Tenerife
     of Cape Verde: 5 Praia
     of the Central African Republic: 6 Bangui
     of Chad: 8 Fort-Lamy, N'Djamena
     of Chile: 8 Santiago
     of China: 6 Peking
     of Colombia: 6 Bogota
     of Comoros: 6 Moroni
     of the Congo: 11 Brazzaville
     of Costa Rica: 7 San Jose
     of Crete: 5 Canea **8** Iraklion
     of Croatia: 6 Zagreb
     of Cuba: 6 Havana **8** La Habana
     of Cyprus: 7 Nicosia
     of Czechoslovakia/ Czech Republic: 6 Prague
     of Denmark: 10 Copenhagen
     of Djibouti: 8 Djibouti
     of the Dominican Republic: 12 Santo Domingo **14** Ciudad Trujillo
     of Ecuador: 5 Quito
     of Egypt: 5 Cairo
     of El Salvador: 11 San Salvador
     of England: 6 London
     of Equatorial Guinea: 6 Malabo
     of Eritrea: 6 Asmara
     of Estonia: 7 Tallinn
     of Ethiopia: 10 Addis Ababa
     of Fiji: 4 Suva
     of Finland: 8 Helsinki **11** Helsingfors
     of France: 5 Paris
     of the Gabon Republic: 10 Libreville
     of The Gambia: 6 Banjul **8** Bathurst
     of Georgia: 7 Tbilisi
     of Germany (East): 10 East Berlin
     of Germany (West): 4 Bonn
     of Germany (reunited): 5 Berlin
     of Ghana: 5 Accra, Akkra
     of Greece: 6 Athens
     of Greenland: 3 Nuk **8** Godthaab, The Point
     of Grenada: 9 St Georges
     of Guatemala: 13 Guatemala City
     of Guinea: 7 Conakry
     of Guinea-Bissau: 6 Bissau
     of Guyana: 10 Georgetown
     of Haiti: 12 Port-au-Prince
     of Honduras: 11 Tegucigalpa
     of Hong Kong: 8 Victoria
     of Hungary: 8 Budapest
     of Iceland: 9 Reykjavik
     of India: 8 New Delhi
     of Indonesia: 7 Jakarta **8** Djakarta
     of Iran: 6 Tehran **7** Teheran
     of Iraq: 7 Baghdad
     of Ireland: 6 Dublin

     of Israel: 9 Jerusalem
     of Italy: 4 Roma, Rome
     of the Ivory Coast: 7 Abidjan
     of Jamaica: 8 Kingston
     of Japan: 3 Edo **5** Tokyo
     of Java: 7 Jakarta **8** Djakarta
     of Jordan: 5 Amman
     of Kazakhstan: 7 Alma-Ata
     of Kenya: 7 Nairobi
     of Kiribati: 6 Tarawa
     of Korea (North): 9 Pyongyang
     of Korea (South): 5 Seoul
     of Kuwait: 10 Kuwait City
     of Kyrgyzstan: 7 Bishkek (Frunze)
     of Laos: 9 Viengchan, Vientiane
     of Latvia: 4 Riga
     of Lebanon: 6 Beirut **8** Beyrouth
     of Lesotho: 6 Maseru
     of Liberia: 8 Monrovia
     of Libya: 7 Tripoli
     of Liechtenstein: 5 Vaduz
     of Lithuania: 5 Vilna **6** Kausas **7** Vilnius
     of Luxembourg: 10 Luxembourg
     of Macedonia: 6 Skopje
     of Madagascar: 10 Tananarive **12** Antananarivo
     of Malawi: 8 Lilongwe
     of Malaysia: 11 Kuala Lumpur
     of Maldives: 4 Male
     of Mali: 6 Bamako
     of Malta: 8 Valletta
     of Mauritania: 10 Nouakchott
     of Mauritius: 9 Port Louis
     of Mexico: 10 Mexico City
     of Moldova: 16 Chisinau, Kishinev
     of Monaco: 11 Monaco-Ville
     of Mongolia: 9 Ulan Bator
     of Montenegro: 7 Cetinje **8** Titograd **9** Podgorica
     of Morocco: 5 Rabat **6** Rabbat
     of Mozambique: 6 Maputo **15** Lourenco Marques
     of Myanmar: 6 Yangon **7** Rangoon
     of Namibia: 8 Windhoek
     of Nauru: 13 Yaren District
     of Nepal: 8 Katmandu **9** Kathmandu
     of Netherlands: 8 The Hague **9** Amsterdam
     of New Guinea: 11 Port Moresby
     of New Zealand: 10 Wellington
     of Nicaragua: 7 Managua
     of Niger: 6 Niamey
     of Nigeria: 5 Abuja, Lagos
     of Northern Ireland: 7 Belfast
     of Norway: 4 Oslo **11** Christiania
     of Oman: 6 Masqat, Muscat
     of Pakistan: 9 Islamabad
     of Panama: 10 Panama City
     of Paraguay: 8 Asuncion
     of Peru: 4 Lima
     of the Philippines: 6 Manila
     of Poland: 6 Warsaw
     of Portugal: 6 Lisbon
     of Puerto Rico: 7 San Juan
     of Qatar: 4 Doha **7** al-Dawha
     of Romania: 9 Bucharest
     of Russia: 6 Moscow

of **Rwanda: 6** Kigali
of **Samoa (American): 8** Pago Pago
of **Samoa (Western): 4** Apia
of **San Marino: 9** San Marino
of **Sao Tome and Principe: 7** Sao Tome
of **Sardinia: 8** Cagliari
of **Saudi Arabia: 6** Riyadh
of **Scotland: 9** Edinburgh
of **Senegal: 5** Dakar
of **Seychelles: 8** Victoria
of **Sicily: 7** Palermo
of **Sierra Leone: 8** Freetown
of **Sikkim: 7** Gangtok
of **Singapore: 9** Singapore
of **Slovakia: 10** Bratislava
of **Slovenia: 9** Ljubljana
of **the Solomon Islands: 7** Honiara
of **Somalia: 9** Mogadishu **10** Mogadiscio
of **South Africa: 8** Cape Town, Pretoria **12** Bloemfontein
of **Spain: 6** Madrid
of **Sri Lanka: 7** Colombo
of **the Sudan: 8** Khartoum
of **Suriname: 10** Paramaribo
of **Swaziland: 7** Mbabane
of **Sweden: 9** Stockholm
of **Switzerland: 4** Bern
of **Syria: 8** Damascus
of **Taiwan: 6** Taipei
of **Tajikistan: 8** Dushanbe
of **Tanzania: 11** Dar es Salaam
of **Thailand: 6** Bankok **7** Bangkok **8** Thonburi **9** Ayutthaya
of **Tibet: 5** Lassa, Lhasa
of **Togo: 4** Lome
of **Tongo: 9** Nukualofa
of **Trinidad and Tobago: 11** Port of Spain
of **Tunisia: 5** Tunis
of **Turkey: 6** Ankara
of **Turkmenistan: 9** Ashkhabad
of **Tuvalu: 8** Funafuti
of **Uganda: 7** Kampala
of **Ukraine: 4** Kiev
of **United Arab Emirates: 8** Abu Dhabi
of **United States: 12** Washington DC
of **Uruguay: 10** Montevideo
of **Uzbekistan: 8** Tashkent
of **Vanuatu: 4** Vila
of **Venezuela: 7** Caracas
of **Vietnam: 5** Hanoi **6** Saigon
of **Wales: 7** Cardiff
of **Western Sahara: 6** Al Aiun **7** El Aaiun
of **Western Samoa: 4** Apia
of **Yemen: 4** Sana, Aden **5** Sanaa
of **Yugoslavia: 7** Beograd **8** Belgrade
of **Zaire: 8** Kinshasa
of **Zambia: 6** Lusaka
of **Zimbabwe: 6** Harare **9** Salisbury
capital city (of states) *see state capitals*
capitalism 14 free enterprise
capitalist 5 mogul **6** tycoon **8** investor **9** financier, plutocrat **14** businessperson

capitalize 4 back, fund **5** stake **7** exploit, finance, support, trade on, utilize **8** bankroll, cash in on, profit by **9** subsidize **11** foot the bill **13** make the most of **17** turn an honest penny **23** strike while the iron is hot **24** make hay while the sun shines
capitalize on 7 exploit, utilize **8** profit by **13** turn to account **14** use to advantage
capitol 10 statehouse **11** legislature **15** government house
capitulate 5 yield **6** accede, give in, give up, relent, submit **7** succumb **8** cry quits **9** acquiesce, surrender **11** come to terms, sue for peace **15** lay down one's arms **17** acknowledge defeat, hoist the white flag
capitulation 8 giving in, giving up, quitting, yielding **9** surrender **10** submission

Capote, Truman
  author of: **11** In Cold Blood **12** A Tree of Night **19** Breakfast at Tiffany's **21** other voices other rooms
  character: **14** Holly Golightly

Capp, Al
  real name: **18** Alfred George Caplin
  creator/artist of: **13** Li'l Abner Yokum

Cappotas
  epithet of: **4** Zeus
  means: **8** reliever

Capra, Frank
  director of: **11** Lady for a Day, Lost Horizon **15** State of the Union **17** Arsenic and Old Lace, It's a Wonderful Life, Mr Deeds Goes to Town (Oscar) **18** It Happened One Night (Oscar) **20** You Can't Take It with You (Oscar) **23** Mr Smith Goes to Washington

caprice 3 fad **4** lark, whim **5** antic, caper, craze, fancy, fling, prank, quirk, spree, stunt **6** notion, oddity, vagary **7** impulse **8** crotchet, escapade **10** erraticism **11** peculiarity **12** eccentricity, idiosyncrasy
capricious 6 fickle, fitful, quirky, uneven **7** erratic, faddish, flighty **8** fanciful, skittish, unstable, unsteady, variable, wavering **9** eccentric, impulsive, mercurial, uncertain, undecided **10** changeable, indecisive, irresolute **11** vacillating **12** inconsistent **13** irresponsible **15** shilly-shallying
capriciousness 7 caprice **10** fickleness **11** instability **12** irresolution **13** impulsiveness, inconsistency **15** shilly-shallying

Capricorn
  symbol: **4** goat
  planet: **6** Saturn
  rules: **6** career
  born: **7** January **8** December

capsicum peppers
  origin: **15** tropical America
  color: **3** red **5** green, white **6** violet, yellow
  variety: **5** ancho, chile **7** cayenne, paprika, serrano **8** chipotle, habanero, jalapeno **9** red pepper **11** chili pepper, chili powder, curry powder, sweet pepper
  flavor: **3** hot
  use: **5** chili, curry, pizza **8** barbecue **9** paprikash
capsize 5 upset **6** invert **7** tip over **8** flip over, keel over, overturn, turn over **10** turn turtle
capsule 4 case, pill **6** ampule **7** cockpit **8** covering **9** spore case **12** condensation
captain 4 boss, head **5** chief, pilot **6** leader, master, old man **7** headman, skipper **9** chieftain, commander **10** commandant **12** chief officer **16** company commander **17** commanding officer
  famous: **4** Ahab, Andy, Hook, Kirk, Nemo

Captain Blood
  director: **13** Michael Curtiz
  cast: **10** Errol Flynn **12** Lionel Atwill **13** Basil Rathbone **17** Olivia de Havilland

Captain Carpenter
  author: **15** John Crowe Ransom

Captain Craig
  author: **22** Edwin Arlington Robinson

Captain Hook
  character in: **8** Peter Pan
  author: **6** Barrie
  henchman: Smee

Captain Horatio Hornblower
  author: **10** C S Forester

Captains Courageous
  author: **14** Rudyard Kipling
  director: **13** Victor Fleming
  cast: **12** Mickey Rooney, Spencer Tracy **13** John Carradine, Melvyn Douglas **15** Lionel Barrymore **18** Freddie Bartholomew
  Oscar for: **5** actor (Tracy)

Captain's Daughter, The
  author: **16** Alexander Pushkin

Captain Video and His Video Rangers
  character: **7** Dr Pauli **9** The Ranger **12** Captain Video
  cast: **7** Al Hodge **10** Hal Conklin **11** Don Hastings **13** Richard Coogan
  slogan: **29** Guardian of the Safety of the World
  villain: **4** Atar **7** Nargola **8** Dahoumie, Kul of Eos **9** Dr Clysmok **12** Heng Foo Seeng **14** Mook the Moon Man
  gimmick: **5** Tobor **9** Discatron **11** Atomic Rifle **16** Barrier of Silence, Radio Scillograph **17** Cosmic Ray Vibrator **18** Opticon Scillometer **19** Cloak of Invisibility, Trisonic Com-

pensator

spaceship: 6 Galaxy

caption 5 title **6** legend **7** heading, subhead **8** headline, subtitle **11** explanation

captious 4 mean **5** picky, testy **6** ornery **7** carping, cutting, peevish **8** caviling, contrary, niggling, perverse, petulant, picayune, snappish **9** fractious, querulous **10** belittling, censorious, nitpicking **11** deprecating **12** cantankerous, faultfinding **13** hypercritical

captivate 4 lure **5** charm **6** dazzle, enamor, seduce **7** attract, bewitch, delight, enchant, win over **8** enthrall **9** carry away, enrapture, fascinate, hypnotize, infatuate, mesmerize, transport **13** turn the head of **14** take the fancy of

captivated 7 charmed, pleased **9** delighted, enchanted **10** enraptured, enthralled, spellbound

captivating 7 winning, winsome **8** adorable, charming, dazzling, engaging, fetching, magnetic **9** appealing, beguiling, disarming **10** attractive, bewitching, delightful, enchanting, entrancing **11** enthralling, fascinating, mesmerizing **12** ingratiating, irresistible

captive 3 POW **5** caged **6** penned **7** hostage **8** confined, enslaved, interned, locked up, prisoner **9** oppressed **10** imprisoned, subjugated **12** incarcerated

captivity 7 bondage, holding, slavery **9** servitude **10** detainment **12** imprisonment

capture 3 bag, nab **4** bust, grab, snag, take, trap **5** catch, grasp, pinch, seize, snare **6** arrest, collar, taking **7** bagging, ensnare, procure, seizure, snaring **8** catching, trapping **9** apprehend, collaring, ensnaring, lay hold of **12** apprehension, laying hold of, take prisoner **14** taking prisoner **15** take into custody

Capulet family

characters in: 14 Romeo and Juliet

author: 11 Shakespeare

Capys

father: 9 Assaracus

son: 7 Laocoon **8** Anchises

grandson: 6 Aeneas

founded: 5 Capua

warned against: 11 Trojan horse

car 4 auto, heap **5** buggy, coach, diner, motor **6** boxcar, hot rod, jalopy, wheels **7** flivver, machine, sleeper, vehicle **8** carriage **9** tin lizzie **10** automobile **12** motor vehicle

kind: 4 coal **5** cable, horse, motor **6** cattle, dining, parlor, street **7** baggage, freight, Pullman, railway **8** sleeping

carabiniere 9 policeman

Caracas

birthplace of: 12 Simon Bolivar

capital of: 9 Venezuela

founder: 13 Diego de Losada

museum: 7 Bolivar **8** Criolan **11** Colonial Art, Raul Santana

river: 6 Guaire

carafe 5 flask **6** bottle, vessel **9** container

carapace 4 case **5** shell **6** lorica, shield **7** carapax **8** calipash, covering **11** turtle shell

Caravaggio, Michelangelo Merisi da

born: 5 Italy **10** Caravaggio

artwork: 12 Young Bacchus **14** Burial of St Lucy **16** Raising of Lazarus **17** The Supper at Emmaus **18** Calling of St Matthew, The Life of St Matthew **20** St Matthew and the Angel **21** The Conversion of St Paul **23** The Crucifixion of St Peter **30** The Beheading of St John the Baptist

caravan 4 band, file, line **5** queue, train, troop **6** coffle, column, convoy, parade, string **7** company, cortege, retinue, trailer **9** cavalcade, chain gang, entourage, motorcade **10** procession, wagon train

caravansary 3 inn **5** hotel **8** hostelry

caraway

botanical name: 10 Carum carvi

origin: 6 Europe **9** Asia Minor **14** the Netherlands

liqueur: 6 Kummel

candy-covered caraway seeds: 6 comfit **12** whisky-killer

use: 4 pork, soup, stew **8** rye bread

carbohydrate

consists of: 5 water **6** carbon, oxygen **8** hydrogen **13** carbon dioxide

kinds: 5 sugar **6** simple, starch, xylose **7** complex, glucose, lactose, maltose, sucrose **8** dextrose, fructose **9** cellulose

carbon 4 coal, coke, copy **8** charcoal **9** lampblack

chemical symbol: 1 C

carbon copy 5 clone **7** replica **9** duplicate, facsimile **12** reproduction

carbonize 4 burn, char, sear **5** singe **6** scorch **10** incinerate

carbuncle 4 boil, sore **11** excrescence **12** inflammation

carcass 4 body, bouk, husk, wall **5** shell, stiff, trunk **6** corpse **7** cadaver, carrion, remains **8** dead body, fireball, skeleton **9** framework

carcinoma 5 tumor **6** cancer **8** neoplasm **10** malignancy **15** malignant growth

card 4 bill **6** ticket **7** program **8** postcard

kind: 7 calling, get-well, playing **8** birthday, business, greeting **9** Christmas, Valentine

cardamon

botanical name: 19 Elettaria cardamomum

origin: 4 Asia **5** India **13** southeast Asia

related to: 6 ginger

color: 5 black

use: 5 curry **7** dessert **12** Danish pastry

Cardew, Cecily

character in: 27 The Importance of Being Earnest

author: 5 Wilde

card game 3 loo, war **4** brag, faro, fish, skat, vint **5** ombre, poker, rummy, whist **6** boston, bridge, casino, chemmy, ecarte, euchre, go fish, hearts, memory, piquet, pocher **7** bezique, canasta, cooncan, Old Maid, plafond, primero **8** baccarat, conquian, cribbage, gin rummy, napoleon, patience, pinochle, slapjack **9** blackjack, pelmanism, solitaire, spoil five, twenty-one, vingt-et-un **11** chemin de fer, crazy eights **13** concentration **14** contract bridge **16** beggar-my-neighbor, trente et quarante

card names: 3 ace **4** fool, jack, king, trey **5** deuce, joker, queen

combination of cards: 4 meld

one hand or round: 5 trick

rulebook by: 5 Hoyle

suits: 4 club **5** heart, spade **7** diamond

French: 5 coeur, pique **6** trefle **7** carreau

German: 4 grun, herz, piks **5** karos, treff **6** eichel **7** schelle

Italian: 5 coppa, cuori, fiori, spada **6** denaro, picchi, quadri **7** bastone

Spanish: 3 oro **4** copa **5** basto **6** espada

Cardiff

capital of: 5 Wales

Cardiff Giant 4 hoax **5** relic

cardigan 5 corgi **6** jacket, wampus **7** sweater **10** Welsh corgi

cardinal 3 key, top **4** head, main **5** basic, chief, first, prime, vital **6** cherry, claret, red hat **7** carmine, central, deep-red, highest, leading, primary, scarlet **8** blood-red, dominant, foremost, greatest **9** essential, intrinsic, necessary, paramount, principal, uppermost **10** elementary, preeminent, underlying **11** fundamental, outstanding, predominant, wine-colored **13** indispensable, most important

number suffix: 3 eth

care 3 TLC **4** heed, load, mind, want, wish **5** grief, pains, worry **6** bother, charge, desire, effort, misery, regard, sorrow, strain, stress **7** anguish, anxiety, caution, concern, control, custody, keeping, sadness, thought, trouble **8** distress, give a rap, hardship, nuisance, pressure, vexation **9** annoyance, attention, be worried, diligence, exactness, give a hoot, heartache, vigilance **10** affliction, management, precaution, protection, solicitude **11** application, be concerned, bother about, carefulness, supervision, tribulation, unhappiness **12** ministration, trouble about, watchfulness **13** attentiveness, consideration **14** be interested in, circumspection, discrimination, fastidiousness, meticulousness, responsibility, scrupulousness **17** conscientiousness

Careas 6 eunuch

careen 3 tip, yaw **4** lean, list, sway, tilt, veer **5** heave, slant, slope **7** capsize **8** lean over, overturn

career 3 job **4** line, work **7** calling, pursuit **8** activity, business, lifework, vocation **10** employment, livelihood, occupation, profession, walk of life

care for 4 like, mind, tend **5** fancy **7** oversee **8** attend to, wait upon **9** look after, watch over **10** minister to, provide for

carefree 3 gay **4** glad **5** happy, jolly, sunny **6** breezy, elated, jaunty, joyous **7** buoyant, gleeful, radiant, relaxed, smiling **8** careless, cheerful, jubilant, laughing **9** easygoing **10** full of life, optimistic, untroubled **11** free-and-easy **12** happy-go-lucky, light-hearted, without worry **13** in high spirits **23** without a worry in the world
French: 9 sans souci

careful 4 fine, nice, wary **5** alert, chary, exact, fussy **7** correct, guarded, heedful, mindful, on guard, precise, prudent, tactful **8** accurate, cautious, diligent, discreet, vigilant, watchful **9** attentive, concerned, judicious, observant, regardful **10** fastidious, meticulous, particular, scrupulous, solicitous, thoughtful **11** circumspect, painstaking, punctilious **13** conscientious

carefulness 7 caution **10** steadiness **12** deliberation **14** circumspection

careless 3 lax **4** rash **5** messy, slack **6** casual, sloppy, untidy **7** inexact, offhand **8** heedless, mindless, slapdash, slipshod, slovenly **9** forgetful, imprecise, incorrect, negligent, unmindful **10** disorderly, inaccurate, neglectful, nonchalant, unthinking, untroubled **11** indifferent, thoughtless, unconcerned **12** absent-minded, devilmay-care **13** inconsiderate, lackadaisical

carelessness 6 laxity **7** neglect **9** messiness, slackness **10** inaccuracy, negligence, sloppiness, untidiness **11** imprecision, inexactness **12** heedlessness, indiscretion, slovenliness **13** unmindfulness **14** disorderliness **15** thoughtlessness **16** absentmindedness, irresponsibility

Care of Time, The
author: **10** Eric Ambler

caress 3 hug, pat, pet **5** clasp, touch **6** cuddle, fondle, stroke **7** embrace, petting, toy with **8** fondling, stroking **11** gentle touch

caretaker 6 keeper, porter, warden **7** curator, janitor, steward **8** overseer, watchman **9** concierge, custodian **10** gatekeeper **14** superintendent

careworn 7 haggard, worried **8** fatigued, troubled **11** pessimistic

cargo 4 load **5** goods **6** burden, lading **7** freight **8** shipment **11** consignment, merchandise

Carib
language family: **7** Cariban
location: **7** Guianas **9** Caribbean, Venezuela **12** South America
alleged custom: **11** cannibalism

Cariban
tribe: **5** Carib **6** Acawai, Akawai

Caribbean 3 sea
channel: **7** Yucatan
city: **6** Havana **7** San Juan **8** Santiago **10** Guantanamo **12** Port au Prince **13** Santo Domingo **15** Charlotte Amalie
Indian: **5** Carib **6** Arawak
island: **4** Cuba **5** Aruba, Haiti, Nevis **6** Cayman, Nassau, Tobago, Virgin **7** Antigua, Bahamas, Barbuda, Curacao, Grenada, Jamaica, Leeward **8** Anguilla, Dominica, Trinidad, Windward **9** Saint John **10** Guadeloupe, Hispaniola, Martinique, Montserrat, Puerto Rico, Saint Kitts, Saint Lucia **11** Saint Thomas **12** Saint Vincent **14** Lesser Antilles **15** Greater Antilles **19** Dominican Republic, Netherlands Antilles
language: **6** gullah **10** papiamento
product: **3** rum **5** fruit, spice, sugar **6** coffee

caricature 4 mock **6** parody, satire **7** lampoon, mockery, takeoff **8** satirize, travesty **9** absurdity, burlesque **10** distortion **12** exaggeration

Carker
character in: **12** Dombey and Son
author: **7** Dickens

Carlisle, Kitty
real name: **13** Katherine Conn
husband: **8** Moss Hart
born: **12** New Orleans LA
roles: **13** She Loves Me Not **14** To Tell the Truth **16** A Night at the Opera **19** Murder at the Vanities

Carlton, Steve (Steven Norman)
nickname: **5** Lefty
sport: **8** baseball
position: **7** pitcher
team: **20** Philadelphia Phillies

Carlyle, Thomas
author of: **8** Cromwell **14** Sartor Resartus **17** Frederick the Great **19** The

French Revolution **20** Heroes and Hero-Worship

Carmen
author: **14** Prosper Merimee
opera by: **5** Bizet
setting: **7** Seville
character: **7** Don Jose **9** Escamillo, Frasquita
song: **8** Habanera

Carmen Jones
director: **13** Otto Preminger
based on opera by: **5** Bizet (Carmen)
adaptation by: **18** Oscar Hammerstein II
cast: **11** Pearl Bailey **14** Harry Belafonte **16** Dorothy Dandridge

carmine 3 red **6** cherry **7** crimson, deep red, scarlet **8** blood red **9** bright red

carnage 8 butchery, massacre **9** blood bath, slaughter

carnal 4 lewd **6** erotic, impure, sexual, sinful, wanton **7** fleshly, immoral, lustful, sensual **8** prurient, sensuous, unchaste, venereal **9** lecherous, salacious **10** lascivious, libidinous, voluptuous

Carnegie, Dale
author of: **33** How To Win Friends and Influence People

carnelian
species: **6** quartz

Carnera, Primo
nickname: **13** the Ambling Alp
sport: **6** boxing
class: **11** heavyweight

Carney, Art
real name: **26** Arthur William Matthew Carney
partner: **13** Jackie Gleason
born: **13** Mount Vernon NY
roles: **8** Ed Norton **13** Harry and Tonto (Oscar) **15** The Honeymooners

carnival 4 fair, fete, gala **6** circus **7** holiday, jubilee **8** festival, jamboree, sideshow **9** Mardi Gras **11** celebration

carnivore 3 cat, dog, fox **4** bear, lion, lynx, mink, puma, wolf **5** civet, dingo, fossa, hyena, otter, panda, skunk, tayra, tiger **6** badger, bobcat, coyote, ferret, grison, hyaena, jackal, jaguar, marten, olingo, weasel **7** polecat, raccoon, suricat **8** aardwolf, kinkajou, mongoose **9** meat eater, wolverine **10** cacomistle, coatimundi, flesh eater

carnivorous 9 predatory **10** meateating, predaceous **11** flesh-eating

carol 4 hymn, noel, sing **5** paean **6** warble **8** canticle **9** song of joy **12** song of praise

Caroline Islands
district: **3** Yap **4** Truk **5** Palau **6** Ponape
inhabitant: **10** Polynesian **11** Micronesian
island: **3** Yap **6** Ponape, Ulithi **8**

Nukuroro **10** Babelthuap **14** Kapina-
marangi
language: 7 English **10** Polynesian
11 Micronesian
ocean: 7 Pacific

carom 6 bounce, strike **7** collide, rebound, **8** billiard, ricochet **9** bounce
off

Caron, Leslie
born: 6 France **19** Boulogne-
Billancourt
roles: 4 Gaby, Gigi, Lili **5** Fanny **11**
Father Goose **13** Daddy Longlegs **14**
The L-Shaped Room **17** An American
in Paris

Carothers, Wallace Hume
field: 9 chemistry
discovered: 5 nylon

carousal 4 orgy **5** binge, drunk, spree
7 debauch **9** bacchanal **10** debauchery, saturnalia

carouse 5 drink, party, quaff, revel **6**
guzzle, imbibe, tipple **7** roister, wassail **8** live it up **9** make merry **10** go
on a binge **11** make whoopee

Carousel (film)
director: 9 Henry King
based on: 6 Liliom
  adaptation by: 21 Rodgers and
  Hammerstein
cast: 12 Gordon MacRae (Billy Bigelow), Shirley Jones **15** Cameron
Mitchell
song: 9 Soliloquy **11** If I Loved You
19 You'll Never Walk Alone

carp 3 nag **5** cavil, chide, decry, knock
6 deride, impugn, jibe at, pick on **7**
censure, condemn **8** belittle, complain, reproach **9** criticize, deprecate,
disparage, fault-find, find fault **10** disapprove

Carpaccio, Vittore
born: 5 Italy **6** Venice
artwork: 13 Two Courtesans **18** The
Dream of St Ursula **19** The Legend
of St Ursula **21** St Augustine in his
Study **24** St George Killing the
Dragon **28** St Augustine's Vision of
St Jerome **29** The Arrival of St Ursula at Cologne

carpal
bone of: 5 wrist

carpe diem 11 seize the day **15** enjoy
the present

carpenter 6 fitter, joiner **7** builder **8**
repairer **10** woodworker **12** cabinet-
maker
ant: 10 camponotus
bee: 8 xylocopa
bird: 10 woodpecker
fish: 10 hammerhead
moth: 10 prinoxysus

Carpenter, Harlean
real name of: 10 Jean Harlow

carper 6 critic **7** caviler **9** nit-picker **11**
fault-finder

carpet 3 mat, rug **4** shag **5** cover,
layer, sheet **7** blanket, matting **8** covering

Carpetbaggers, The
author: 13 Harold Robbins

Carr, Emily
born: 6 Canada **8** Victoria **15** British
Columbia
artwork: 3 Sky **8** Big Raven **14** Blun-
den Harbour, Kispiax Village **15**
Woods and Blue Sky **17** Forest Landscape II **36** Cape Mudge An Indian
Family with Totem Pole

Carra, Carlo
born: 5 Italy **9** Quargneto
artwork: 13 Lot's Daughters **16** Metaphysical Muse **20** Patriotic Celebration **29** The Funeral of the Anarchist
Galli

Carradine, David
father: 4 John
half-brothers: 5 Keith **6** Robert
born: 11 Hollywood CA
roles: 6 Kung Fu **13** Bound for Glory
14 The Serpent's Egg

Carradine, John
real name: 21 Richmond Reed Carradine
son: 5 David, Keith **6** Robert
born: 18 Greenwich Village NY
roles: 9 Cleopatra, Kidnapped **10**
Stagecoach **12** Count Dracula **15** The
Invisible Man **18** Captains Courageous, The Three Musketeers

Carradine, Keith
father: 4 John
brother: 6 Robert
half-brother: 5 David
born: 10 San Mateo CA
roles: 9 Nashville **10** Pretty Baby

Carraway, Nick
character in: 14 The Great Gatsby
author: 10 Fitzgerald

Carrere, John Merven
partner: 14 Thomas Hastings
architect of: 19 House Office Building
(Washington DC) **20** New York Public Library, Senate Office Building
(Washington DC) **21** Henry Clay
Frick mansion (now Frick Collection
NYC)
style: 18 French neo-classical, Spanish Renaissance

carriage 3 air, rig **4** mien **5** buggy,
coach, poise, wagon **6** aspect, manner
7 bearing, posture, vehicle **8** attitude,
behavior, demeanor, presence **10** appearance, conveyance, deportment **11**
comportment

Carrie
author: 11 Stephen King

carried away 7 excited, frantic, seduced **8** ecstatic, frenzied, overcome
9 delirious **10** fascinated, infatuated
11 transported

carrier 3 bus, car **4** rack, wave **5**
agent, barge, plane, coach, drain,
ferry, train, truck, wagon **6** bearer,
boxcar, pigeon, porter **7** airline, channel, mailman, postman, trucker, vehicle **8** airplane, aircraft, carriage, catalyst, railroad **9** messenger **11**
transmitter, wheelbarrow

carrion 5 bones, offal, waste **6** corpse,
refuse **7** cadaver, carcass, garbage,
remains, wastage **8** crowbait, dead
body, leavings

Carroll, Leo G
born: 6 Weedon **7** England
roles: 6 Topper **7** Rebecca **9** Suspicion **10** Spellbound **11** Cosmo Topper **15** A Christmas Carol, The Man
from UNCLE, The Paradine Case **16**
Father of the Bride, North by Northwest

Carroll, Lewis
real name: 22 Charles Lutwidge
Dodgson
author of: 11 Jabberwocky **20** The
Hunting of the Shark **22** Through the
Looking Glass **28** Alice's Adventures
in Wonderland

carrousel 4 ride, tray **8** conveyor **9**
quadrille, whirligig **10** tournament **12**
merry-go-round

carry 3 lug, run **4** bear, cart, haul, lift,
move, prop, ship, take, tote **5** brace,
bring, fetch, offer, print, shift, stock **6**
convey, hold up, supply, uphold **7**
conduct, deliver, display, publish, release, support, sustain **8** displace,
maintain, shoulder, transfer, transmit
9 broadcast, transport **10** keep on
hand **11** communicate, disseminate

carry away 4 lure **6** abduct, kidnap,
seduce **7** attract **9** captivate, fascinate,
infatuate, transport

carry off 5 seize, steal **6** abduct, kidnap **7** bear off **9** succeed at **11** get
away with

carry out 2 do **6** effect, wind up **7**
achieve, execute, fulfill, perform, realize **8** complete, conclude, dispatch **9**
discharge, dispose of, succeed at **10**
accomplish, bring about **11** bring to
pass

carry through 6 effect, finish **7**
achieve, develop, execute, fulfill, perform, realize **8** complete, conclude **9**
discharge **10** accomplish, consummate, effectuate, perpetuate **13** put
into effect

Carson, Rachel Louise
field: 7 biology
studied: 9 pollution
author of: 12 Silent Spring **14** The
Sea Around Us **15** The Edge of the
Sea

Carstone, Richard
character in: 10 Bleak House
author: 7 Dickens

cart 3 gig, lug **4** bear, dray, haul,
move, take, tote, trap **5** bring, carry,
fetch, truck, wagon **6** barrow, convey
7 schlepp, trundle, tumbrel **8** curricle,

transfer, transmit **9** transport **10** handbarrow, transplant, two-wheeler **11** wheelbarrow

kind: 2 go **3** dog, tip **4** dump, hand, push

carte blanche 7 license **9** a free hand, free reign **10** blank check **12** open sanction **13** full authority **18** unconditional power

cartel 4 OPEC, pool **5** chain, trust **7** combine **8** monopoly **9** syndicate **10** consortium, federation **11** corporation

Carter, Charles
   real name of: 14 Charlton Heston

Carter, James Earl, Jr
   nickname: 3 Hot **5** Jimmy **7** Hotshot
   presidential rank: 11 thirty-ninth
   party: 10 Democratic
   state represented: 2 GA **7** Georgia
   defeated: 4 (Gerald R) Ford **8** (Eugene) McCarthy
   vice president: 7 (Walter Frederick "Fritz") Mondale
   cabinet:
      state: 5 (Cyrus R) Vance **6** (Edmund S) Muskie
      treasury: 6 (G William) Miller **10** (W Michael) Blumenthal
      defense: 5 (Harold) Brown
      attorney general: 4 (Griffin B) Bell **9** (Benjamin R) Civiletti
      interior: 6 (Cecil D) Andrus
      agriculture: 8 (Robert S) Bergland
      commerce: 5 (Juanita Morris) Kreps **9** (Philip M) Klutznick
      labor: 8 (F Ray) Marshall
      HEW: 6 (Patricia Roberts) Harris **8** (Joseph A) Califano (Jr)
      HUD: 6 (Patricia Roberts) Harris **8** (Moon) Landrieu
      transportation: 5 (Brockman) Adams **11** (Neil E) Goldschmidt
      education: 10 (Shirley) Hufstedler
   born: 2 GA **6** Plains
   education: 14 US Naval Academy **26** Georgia Southwestern College **28** Georgia Institute of Technology
   religion: 15 Southern Baptist
   interests: 5 track **6** tennis **7** fishing, hunting **8** football, softball **10** basketball **12** cross country **13** square dancing **17** collecting bottles
      music: 8 folk rock **9** classical
   author: 11 Living Faith **12** Keeping Faith **13** Why Not the Best? **16** Everything to Gain **17** The Blood of Abraham
   political career: 12 state senator
      governor of: 7 Georgia
   civilian career: 12 peanut farmer
   military service: 6 US Navy
   notable events of lifetime/term: 6 SALT II **9** Love Canal, recession **18** Habitat for Humanity
      deaths at: 9 Jonestown
      eruption of: 13 Mount St Helens
      first baby from: 8 test tube
      hostages taken in: 4 Iran

nuclear accident: 15 Three Mile Island
   pipeline: 5 Alcan
   scandal/investigation: 6 Abscam **9** Bert Lance, Koreagate **11** Billy Carter
   Supreme Court case: 5 Bakke
   treaty: 11 Panama Canal **16** Camp David Accords
   father: 11 James Earl Sr
   mother: 7 Lillian (Gordy)
      nickname: 11 Miss Lillian
   siblings: 6 Gloria **17** William "Billy" Alton **19** Ruth Carter Stapleton
   wife: 8 Rosalynn (Smith)
   children: 7 Amy Lynn **11** John William (Jack) **12** James Earl III (Chip) **13** Donnel Jeffrey (Jeff)
   first lady: 36 Presidential Commission on Mental Health
      author: 19 First Lady from Plains

Carthage see **7** Tunisia

carton 3 box **4** case **5** crate **9** container **11** packing case **12** cardboard box, packing crate **18** cardboard container

Carton, Sydney
   character in: 16 A Tale of Two Cities
   author: 7 Dickens

cartoon 5 comic **6** design, satire, sketch **7** drawing, funnies, picture **8** animated **10** caricature, comic strip

cartoonist 6 artist, drawer **7** gagster **12** caricaturist
   famous: 6 Al Capp, C C Beck, Ted Key **7** Bob Kane, Stan Lee **8** Herblock (Herbert L. Block), Jim Davis, Roy Crane **9** Bud Fisher, Chic Young, Dik Browne, Frank King, Hal Foster, Ham Fisher, Walt Kelly **10** Bob Montana, Gary Larson, Harold Gray, Jimmy Hatlo, Johnny Hart, Joe Shuster, Mort Walker, Paul Conrad, Thomas Nast, Walt Disney **11** Alex Raymond, Bill Mauldin, Dale Messick, David Levine, Ding Darling, Elzie C. Segar, Hank Ketcham, Max Beerbohm, Rollin Kirby **12** Al Hirschfeld, Brad Anderson, Chester Gould, Garry Trudeau, James Thurber, Jeff MacNelly, Jules Feiffer, Milton Caniff, Rube Goldberg, Rudolph Dirks, Virgil Partch **13** Bill Watterson, Charles Addams, Charles Schulz, George McManus, Honore Daumier, Joseph Keppler, Saul Steinberg **14** Homer Davenport, William Hogarth **15** Ernie Bushmiller, Patrick Oliphant, Richard Outcault **16** Benjamin Franklin, George Cruikshank

cartridge 3 dud **4** case, tape **5** blank, shell **6** holder **7** capsule, package **8** cassette, cylinder **9** container

Cartwright, Edmund
   nationality: 7 English
   inventor of: 9 power loom **18** woolcombing machine

carve 3 hew, saw **4** etch, form, hack, mold, rend, turn, work **5** allot, cleve, cut up, model, shape, slash, slice, split **6** chisel, divide, incise, sculpt **7** engrave, fashion, pattern, quarter **8** block out, dissever **9** apportion, sculpture

Carver, George Washington
   field: 9 chemistry
   worked in: 11 agriculture
   studied: 6 peanut **7** soybean **11** sweet potato

carving 5 cameo **8** intaglio, triptych **9** sculpture

caryatid 6 column
   shape of: 12 female figure

Casablanca
   director: 13 Michael Curtiz
   cast: 10 Peter Lorre **11** Claude Rains (Louis), Conrad Veidt, Paul Henreid (Victor Laslo) **12** Dooley Wilson (Sam), **13** Ingrid Bergman (Ilsa Lund) **14** Humphrey Bogart (Rick) **17** Sydney Greenstreet
   Oscar for: 7 picture
   song: 12 As Time Goes By

Casanova 3 cad, rip **4** beau, lech, roue, wolf **5** lover, Romeo, swain, wooer **6** chaser, lecher, suitor **7** admirer, bounder, Don Juan, gallant, rounder **8** cavalier, Lothario, lover boy, paramour **9** ladies' man, libertine, womanizer **10** lady-killer, profligate **11** philanderer

Casby
   character in: 12 Little Dorrit
   author: 7 Dickens

cascade 4 fall, gush, pour, rush **5** chute, falls, surge **6** plunge, rapids, tumble **7** Niagara **8** cataract **9** waterfall

Cascade Range
   location: 9 northwest
   highest peak: 9 Mt. Rainier

case 3 bin, box **4** plea, suit, tray **5** cause, chest, cover, crate, event **6** action, affair, appeal, carton, debate, injury, jacket, matter, sheath, victim **7** cabinet, concern, disease, dispute, episode, example, hearing, housing, inquiry, invalid, lawsuit, overlay, patient, wrapper **8** argument, business, covering, envelope, incident, instance, sufferer **9** condition, container, happening, incidence, sheathing, situation **10** litigation, occurrence, proceeding, protection, receptacle, sick person **11** controversy **12** circumstance, illustration

case in point 7 example **8** instance **12** illustration

Case of Sergeant Grischa, The
   author: 11 Arnold Zweig

Casey
   nickname of: 20 Charles Dillon Stengel

team: 7 Yankees
role: 7 manager

Casey at the Bat
author: 6 Thayer
town: 8 Mudville

Casey Jones 8 engineer, folksong, railroad

cash 5 bills, bread, coins, dough, money **6** change, redeem **8** currency, exchange **9** bank notes **10** paper money **11** legal tender **13** turn into money **14** coin of the realm

cashier 6 banker, bursar, purser, teller **9** treasurer **10** bank teller

cash register
invented by: 4 till **5** Ritty
sign: 6 no sale

casing 4 skin **5** frame **9** sheathing

Casino Royale
author: 10 Ian Fleming

cask 3 keg, tub, tun, vat **4** butt, pipe **6** barrel **8** hogshead

casket 4 case, pall **5** chest **6** coffer, coffin **8** jewel box **11** sarcophagus

Cask of Amontillado, The
author: 13 Edgar Allan Poe
character: 9 Fortunato, Montresor

Cassandra 7 seeress
also: 9 Alexandra
father: 5 Priam
mother: 6 Hecuba
brother: 5 Paris
concubine of: 9 Agamemnon
son: 6 Pelops **9** Teledamus
cursed by: 6 Apollo
violated by: 4 Ajax
killed by: 12 Clytemnestra

Cassatt, Mary
born: 15 Allegheny City PA
artwork: 6 La Loge **7** The Bath **11** The Cup of Tea **12** After the Bath, Woman Bathing **14** Gathering Fruit **15** Reading Le Figaro **20** Girl Arranging Her Hair, Woman and Child Drawing

Cassavetes, John
wife: 12 Gena Rowlands
born: 9 New York NY
roles/films: 8 Husbands **10** The Tempest **13** Rosemary's Baby, The Dirty Dozen **23** A Woman Under the Influence

casserole 4 dish, food, mold **6** tureen, vessel **8** saucepan

Cassio
character in: 7 Othello
author: 11 Shakespeare

Cassiopeia 13 constellation
husband: 7 Cepheus
daughter: 9 Andromeda
offended: 7 Nereids

Cassius
also: 12 Caius Cassius
character in: 12 Julius Caesar
author: 11 Shakespeare

Cass Timberlane

author: 13 Sinclair Lewis
character: 11 Bradd Criley **24** Jinny Marshland Timberlane

cast 3 set, sow **4** fire, form, hurl, look, mien, mint, mold, pick, shed, toss **5** fling, heave, model, pitch, shape, shoot, sling, stamp, throw **6** actors, assign, casing, choose, direct, launch, let fly, propel, sculpt, spread, troupe **7** appoint, company, deposit, diffuse, pattern, players, project, scatter **8** catapult, disperse **9** broadcast, circulate, discharge, launching, semblance **10** appearance, distribute, impression, performers, propulsion **11** disseminate, give parts to **16** dramatis personae

Castalia
origin: 5 Greek
sacred: 6 spring
location: 14 Mount Parnassus
sacred to: 5 Muses **6** Apollo
source of: 11 inspiration

cast aside 4 junk, shed **6** desert, reject **7** abandon, discard, forsake, neglect **8** get rid of, renounce, throw out **9** repudiate, throw away **11** discontinue

cast a spell on 3 hex **4** jinx **5** charm **7** bewitch, conjure, enchant **8** entrance **11** work magic on

cast aspersions on 5 knock, scorn **6** deride, malign **7** disdain, put down, run down, sneer at **8** belittle, poohpooh **9** criticize, disparage **13** find fault with

castaway 3 bum **4** hobo, waif **5** exile, leper, nomad, rover, stray **6** outlaw, pariah **7** Ishmael, outcast, vagrant **8** deportee, derelict, renegade, unperson, vagabond, wanderer **9** foundling, nonperson **10** expatriate **11** beachcomber, offscouring, untouchable **12** down-and-outer **15** knight-of-the-road

cast away 4 junk **6** launch, propel, reject **7** abandon, discard, toss out **8** get rid of, pitch out, throw out **9** throw away

cast down 5 abase, droop, lower **6** abased, deject, droopy, humble, sadden **7** depress, humbled, lowered **8** bring low, dejected, disgrace, saddened **9** depressed, disgraced, humiliate **10** brought low, dishearten, humiliated **11** crestfallen **12** disheartened

caste 4 rank **6** status **7** lineage, station **8** position **9** condition
Hindu: 5 sudra, varna **6** vaisya **7** brahman **9** kshatriya

castigate 5 chide, scold **6** berate, punish, rebuke **7** bawl out, censure, chasten, chew out, correct, reprove, upbraid **8** admonish, chastise, penalize, reproach **9** criticize, dress down, reprimand **10** discipline, take to task **15** call on the carpet **16** haul over the coals

castigation 9 reprimand **10** chastening, correction, discipline, penalizing, punishment **12** chastisement

Castiglione, Baldassare
author of: 20 The Book of the Courtier

castle 4 hall, keep, rook **5** manor, tower, villa **6** palace **7** chateau, citadel, mansion **8** fortress **10** stronghold

Castle, Vernon[1]
wife: 5 Irene **15** ballroom dancers
invented: 10 Castle Walk

Castle, The[2]
author: 10 Franz Kafka
character: 1 K

Castle of Otranto, The
author: 13 Horace Walpole
character: 6 Conrad **7** Alfonso, Manfred, Matilda **8** Isabella, Theodore **12** Father Jerome

Castle Rackrent
author: 14 Maria Edgeworth

cast off 4 shed **6** reject **7** discard, set sail, toss out **8** throw off, throw out **9** repudiate, throw away **11** weigh anchor

Castor and Pollux
also: 6 Gemini **8** Dioscuri **10** Polydeuces, Tyndaridae
form: 8 twin sons
mother: 4 Leda
father: 4 Zeus
sister: 5 Helen **12** Clytemnestra
members of: 9 Argonauts
protectors of: 6 seamen

cast out 4 oust **5** eject, evict, exile, expel **6** banish, reject **7** discard, dismiss, turn out **8** drive out, send away, throw out

cast up 4 spew **5** eject, expel, vomit **6** spew up **7** cough up, throw up **8** disgorge

casual 4 cool, so-so **5** blase, vague **6** chance, random, sporty **7** offhand, passing, relaxed **8** informal **9** easygoing, haphazard, non-dressy, unplanned **10** accidental, fortuitous, incidental, nonchalant, unarranged, undesigned, undirected, unexpected, unforeseen **11** half-hearted, indifferent, unlooked for **13** lackadaisical, serendipitous, unintentional **14** indiscriminate, unpremeditated

Casuals of the Sea
author: 12 William McFee

casualty 4 loss **6** injury, victim **7** injured **8** fatality

casuistry 5 guile **6** deceit **7** fallacy, sophism **8** subtlety **9** Jesuitism, quibbling, sophistry **10** nitpicking **12** equivocation, pettifoggery, speciousness **13** deceptiveness, hair-splitting **14** sophistication

casus belli 10 cause of war

Casy, Jim

character in: 16 The Grapes of Wrath
author: 9 Steinbeck

cat 3 pet **4** puss, whip **5** kitty, pussy, tabby **6** feline, kitten, mouser, tomcat
anatomy: 3 paw **4** loin, nape, rump, tail **5** break, flank, shank **6** feeler **7** dewclaw, leather, whisker **8** vibrissa **10** metatarsus
breed/kind: 3 tom **4** coon, Eyra, lion, lynx, Manx, puma **5** alley, civet, hyena, kitty, Korat, tabby, tiger **6** Angola, angora, bobcat, cougar, jaguar, ocelot, serval **7** Burmese, caracal, cheetah, leopard, linsang, Maltese, panther, Persian, polecat, Siamese, Turkish, wildcat **8** Balinese, Cheshire, Egyptian, ringtail **9** Himalayan, shorthair **10** Abyssinian, chinchilla **11** Russian blue **13** tortoise-shell
combining form: 5 aelur, ailur, felin **6** aeluro, ailuro, felino
Egyptian goddess of: 4 Bast
extinct: 10 saber-tooth
family: 7 Felidae
famous: 6 Morris **8** Cheshire, Garfield, Kilkenny **9** Mehitabel **10** Heathcliff
fastest: 7 cheetah
fear of: 12 aelurophobia, ailurophobia
female: 5 queen **7** lioness, tigress **8** wheencat **9** grimalkin
genus: 5 Felis
grinning: 8 Cheshire
group: 7 clowder, clutter
group of kittens: 6 kendle, kindle
lover: 11 aelurophile, ailurophile
male: 3 gib, tom **6** tomcat
ring-tailed: 6 serval **10** cacomistle
tailless: 4 Manx
young: 6 kitten

cataclysm 4 blow **7** debacle **8** calamity, disaster, upheaval **11** catastrophe, devastation
cataclysmic 4 dire **6** tragic **7** ruinous **10** calamitous, disastrous **12** catastrophic, earth-shaking
catacomb 4 tomb **7** ossuary **8** cemetery **10** passageway **12** burial ground
catafalque 3 box **4** pall **6** casket, coffin
catalog, catalogue 4 file, list, post, roll **5** index **6** record, roster **7** listing **8** classify, register, syllabus, tabulate **9** directory, enumerate, inventory, mail order
Catamitus see **8** Ganymede
Cat and Mouse
  author: 11 Gunter Grass
catapult 4 cast, hurl, toss **5** fling, heave, pitch, shoot, sling, throw **6** hurtle, onager, propel **9** slingshot **13** hurling engine
cataract 5 falls, flood **6** deluge, rapids **7** cascade, torrent **8** downpour **9** lens cover, waterfall **10** inundation
catastrophe 4 blow **5** havoc **6** mis-

hap, ravage **7** debacle, scourge, tragedy **8** calamity, disaster **9** cataclysm **10** affliction, misfortune **11** devastation
catastrophic 6 tragic **7** ruinous **10** calamitous, disastrous **11** cataclysmic
catcall 3 boo **4** gibe, hiss, hoot, jeer, razz **7** whistle **8** heckling **9** raspberry **10** Bronx cheer
catch 3 bag, bat, get, hit, nab **4** bait, bang, belt, bump, bust, dupe, feel, find, fool, grab, hasp, haul, hoax, hook, lock, lure, make, snag, snap, spot, take, trap **5** booty, break, charm, clasp, crack, get to, grasp, hitch, latch, prize, reach, seize, sense, smack, smite, snare, trick, whack, yield **6** allure, arrest, betray, buffet, collar, corner, corral, dazzle, deceit, delude, descry, detect, expose, fasten, fathom, kicker, snatch, strike, take in, turn on, unmask **7** attract, bewitch, capture, closure, deceive, delight, discern, enchant, ensnare, find out, gimmick, mislead, rasping, seizure **8** catching, come upon, contract, coupling, discover, drawback, enthrall, hoodwink, overtake, perceive, pickings, surprise **9** apprehend, bamboozle, captivate, carry away, enrapture, fastening, intercept, lay hold of, play false, recognize, transport **10** comprehend, understand **11** take captive **12** break out with, come down with, disadvantage, seize and hold, take off guard **14** stumbling block **15** take into custody **18** become infected with
catch-as-catch-can 7 cursory **9** haphazard, hit-or-miss, unplanned **10** disorderly, incomplete **11** superficial, unorganized **12** disorganized, unsystematic
Catcher in the Rye, The
  author: 10 J D Salinger
  character: 15 Holden Caulfield
    Phoebe Caulfield
catching 10 contagious, infectious **12** communicable **13** transmittable
catch on to 3 get **5** grasp, savvy **6** absorb, digest, fathom, pick up **10** assimilate, comprehend, get the idea, understand
catch sight of 3 see **4** espy **6** behold, descry, detect, notice **7** discern, make out, observe, pick out **8** perceive
Catch-22
  author: 12 Joseph Heller
  character: 9 Yossarian
  means: 7 paradox
catchword 4 motto **6** byword, cliche, slogan, war cry **8** password **9** battle cry, guide word, pet phrase, watchword **10** shibboleth
categorical 4 flat, sure **7** certain, express **8** absolute, definite, emphatic, explicit **10** pronounced, unreserved

11 unequivocal, unqualified **12** unmistakable **13** unconditional
categorically 10 absolutely, definitely, positively **12** conclusively
categorization 5 order **11** arrangement **14** classification
category 5 class, group **8** division, grouping **14** classification
cater 5 humor **6** pamper, pander, please **7** gratify, indulge, satisfy
caterpillar 4 moth, worm **5** larva **7** cutworm, tractor, webworm **8** hangworm, silkworm, wortworm **9** butterfly, woolybear **10** astragalus
caterwaul 3 cry **4** bawl, howl, wail, yelp **5** whine **6** clamor, scream, shriek, squawk, squeal **7** screech **10** rend the air
catfish 4 barb **5** banjo **6** dorado, madtom, mudcat, sucker **7** ariidae, bluecat **8** bagridae, bullhead, claridae, electric, flathead **9** siluridae **10** channel cat, cuttlefish, mochocidae, plotosidae, spotted cat **11** ictaluridae, pimelodidae, schilbeidae **12** aspredinidae, ostariophysi **14** malapteruridae **16** trichomycteridae
Catfish
  nickname of: 9 Jim Hunter
Catfish Row
  setting of: 12 Porgy and Bess
catharsis 7 purging, release, venting **9** cleansing **12** purification
Catharsius
  epithet of: 4 Zeus
  means: 8 purifier
cathartic 5 purge **6** physic **8** aperient, evacuant, laxative **9** castor oil, purgative, purifying
cathedral 3 see **6** church, temple **7** lateran **8** basilica, official **9** authority **10** pontifical
  Italian: 5 duomo
Cather, Willa
  author of: 9 A Lost Lady, My Antonia, One of Ours, O Pioneers! **13** My Mortal Enemy **16** Shadows on the Rock, The Song of the Lark **18** The Professor's House **23** Sapphira and the Slave Girl **26** Death Comes for the Archbishop
cathode ray tube
  abbreviation: 3 CRT
  invented by: 7 Crookes
catholic, Catholic 5 broad **7** liberal **9** universal, worldwide **12** all-embracing, all-inclusive **13** comprehensive
cathouse 4 stew **5** house **6** bagnio, bordel **7** brothel **8** bordello **10** bawdy house, fancy house, whorehouse **13** sporting house **14** house of ill fame **16** house of ill repute **19** house of prostitution
Cat Jumps, The
  author: 14 Elizabeth Bowen

catlike 5 catty, lithe **7** sinuous **8** stealthy **14** light on the feet

Catlin, George
born: **13** Wilkes-Barre PA
artwork: **16** Gallery of Indians

catnap 3 nap **4** doze **6** siesta, snooze **10** forty winks, light sleep

Cato 5 Roman
Elder: **6** Censor
younger (grandson): **5** Stoic

Cato
author: **13** Joseph Addison

Cat on a Hot Tin Roof
author: **17** Tennessee Williams
director: **13** Richard Brooks
cast: **8** Burl Ives (Big Daddy) **10** Jack Carson, Paul Newman (Brick) **14** Judith Anderson **15** Elizabeth Taylor (Maggie)

cats-eye
species: **11** chrysoberyl
source: **8** Sri Lanka

cat's paw 4 dupe, pawn, tool **5** patsy **7** fall guy

cattle 4 cows, kine, oxen **5** beefs, bulls, stock **6** beeves, calves, dogies, steers **8** bullocks, milk cows **9** livestock
family: **7** Bovidae
group of: **5** drove
kind: **2** ox **3** yak **4** Zebu **5** Angus **6** Ankole, Jersey **7** Brahman **8** Ayrshire, Guernsey, Hereford, Highland, Holstein **9** Charolais **12** water buffalo **13** Texas Longhorn **16** English Shorthorn, Holstein-Friesian
young: **4** calf **6** heifer **8** yearling

Catton, Bruce
author of: **22** A Stillness at Appomattox

catty 4 mean **7** catlike **8** spiteful **9** malicious, malignant **10** malevolent

catwalk 6 bridge **7** walkway **10** passageway

Caucasian
language branch: **5** Ubykh **9** Daghestan **10** Circassian **11** Khartvelian

Caucon
brought mysteries to: **8** Messenia

caucus 6 parley, powwow **7** council, meeting, session **8** assembly, conclave **10** conference

caudal 4 back, tail **7** tail-end

cauldron see **7** caldron

Caulfield, Holden
character in: **18** The Catcher in the Rye
author: **8** Salinger

Caulfield, Joan
real name: **21** Beatrice Joan Caulfield
born: **8** Orange NJ
roles: **8** Dear Ruth **17** My Favorite Husband

causation 4 root **5** cause **6** author, origin, reason, source **7** creator, genesis **8** etiology, inventor, stimulus **9** gener-

ator, invention **10** antecedent, conception, mainspring, originator **11** determinant, inspiration, origination

cause 4 goal, make, root, side **5** ideal, impel, tenet **6** belief, create, effect, incite, lead to, motive, object, origin, reason, source, spring, stir up **7** genesis, grounds, incline, inspire, produce, provoke, purpose **8** etiology, generate, motivate, occasion, stimulus **9** incentive, principle, stimulate **10** aspiration, bring about, conviction, foundation, give rise to, inducement, initiation, mainspring, motivation, persuasion, prime mover **11** bring to pass, inspiration, instigation, precipitate, provocation

cause of war
Latin: **10** casus belli

cause to appear 6 expose, reveal **7** uncover **8** disclose **12** bring to light **13** bring into view

caustic 3 lye **4** tart **5** acrid, harsh, sharp **6** biting, bitter **7** burning, cutting, erosive, gnawing **8** scathing, stinging **9** corroding, corrosive, sarcastic **10** astringent **11** acrimonious

caution 4 care, heed, warn **5** alarm, alert **6** advise, caveat, exhort, notify, regard, tip-off **7** concern, thought, warning **8** admonish, forewarn, prudence, wariness **9** alertness, restraint, vigilance **10** admonition, discretion, precaution **11** carefulness, forewarning, guardedness, heedfulness, mindfulness **12** deliberation, watchfulness **14** circumspection, put on one's guard

cautionary 7 warning **8** advisory **10** admonitory **11** admonishing

cautious 4 wary **5** alert, cagey **7** careful, guarded, prudent **8** discreet, vigilant, watchful **9** attentive, judicious **11** circumspect

cavalcade 5 troop **6** column, parade **7** caravan, retinue **10** procession

Cavalcade
director: **10** Frank Lloyd
based on play by: **10** Noel Coward
cast: **10** Clive Brook **11** Ursula Jeans **12** Diana Wynyard **13** Herbert Mundin **15** Margaret Lindsay
Oscar for: **7** picture

cavalier 3 fop **4** beau **5** blade, cocky, dandy, swell **6** hussar, lancer **7** cursory, dragoon, gallant, haughty, offhand, playboy **8** arrogant, courtier, gay blade, horseman, uncaring **9** easygoing **10** cavalryman, disdainful, nonchalant **11** indifferent, thoughtless

cavalry 7 hussars, lancers **8** dragoons **10** mounted men **11** horse troops **13** horse soldiers, mounted troops

cavalryman 6 hussar, lancer **7** dragoon **8** cavalier, horseman **12** horse soldier, horse trooper **14** mounted soldier

cave 3 den **4** lair, sink **6** burrow, cav-

ern, cavity, dugout, grotto, hollow
growth: **10** stalactite, stalagmite
explorer: **9** spelunker

caveat 5 alarm, alert, aviso **6** tip-off **7** caution, red flag, warning **8** high sign, red light **10** admonition, danger sign, yellow jack **11** forewarning **12** admonishment, flea in the ear **13** word to the wise **20** handwriting on the wall

caveat emptor 17 let the buyer beware

cave canem 14 beware of the dog

cave in 6 buckle, fall in, give up, submit **7** crumple, give way, implode **8** collapse **10** capitulate **12** fall to pieces

Cavendish, Henry
field: **7** physics **9** chemistry
nationality: **7** British
discovered: **8** hydrogen
determined composition of: **3** air **5** water **10** nitric acid
method: **19** Cavendish experiment

cavernous 4 huge, vast **5** roomy **6** gaping **7** chasmal, immense, yawning **8** cavelike, enormous, spacious **10** tremendous

cavil 6 deride **7** nitpick, quibble **8** belittle, complain **9** criticize, deprecate, discredit, disparage, faultfind, find fault **12** pick to pieces

cavity 3 dip, pit **4** bore, dent, hole, sink **5** basin, niche **6** burrow, crater, hollow, pocket, tunnel **7** opening, orifice, vacuity **8** aperture **9** concavity **10** depression, excavation

cavort 4 play, romp **5** bound, caper, frisk **6** frolic, gambol, prance

Cawdor
author: **15** Robinson Jeffers

Caxtons, The
author: **12** Bulwer Lytton

Cayuga
language family: **9** Iroquoian
location: **4** Ohio **6** Canada **7** New York **8** Oklahoma **9** Wisconsin
branch of: **10** Six Nations **19** Iroquois Confederacy, League of the Iroquois

CE 9 Common Era

cease 3 end **4** halt, pass, quit, stop **5** abate, pause **6** desist, finish **7** adjourn, die away, forbear, suspend **8** break off, conclude, leave off **9** terminate **11** abstain from, discontinue, refrain from **12** bring to an end

cease-fire 5 truce **9** armistice

ceaseless 7 endless, eternal **8** constant, enduring, unending **9** continual, incessant, permanent, perpetual, unceasing **10** continuous, protracted **11** everlasting, never-ending, unremitting **12** interminable **13** uninterrupted

cease to be 3 die, end **6** die out, expire, vanish **9** disappear, evaporate **13** become extinct

Cecilia (Memoirs of an Heiress)
author: **11** Fanny Burney

Cecrops
also: **8** Cecropia
form: **3** man **6** dragon
founder of: **6** Attica
king of: **6** Attica
father: **14** King Erechtheus
brother: **6** Metion, Orneus
wife: **8** Aglaurus
son: **11** Erysichthon
daughter: **5** Herse **8** Aglaurus **9** Pandrasos
renamed Attica: **8** Cecropia

cedar 6 Cedrus
varieties: **3** red **4** pink, salt **5** Atlas, giant, white **6** Alaska, Cyprus, ground, Mlanje **7** Bermuda, incense, Russian, Spanish **8** Barbados, cigarbox, creeping, Japanese, stinking **10** Ozark white, Port Orford, swamp white, western red, West Indian, Willowmore **11** Clanwilliam, Colorado red, southern red **13** Atlantic white, southern white **14** Chilean incense, Formosa incense **17** California incense

cede 4 give **5** grant, leave, yield **6** tender **7** abandon, deliver, release **8** hand over, transfer **9** deliver up, surrender **10** relinquish

cedez
music: **8** slow down

Cedric the Saxon
character in: **7** Ivanhoe
author: **5** Scott

ceiling 3 top **4** roof **5** cover, limit **6** canopy, cupola, lining **7** maximum **8** altitude **10** upperlimit

Celebes
also: **8** Sulawesi
bordered by: **6** Borneo **8** Moluccas **10** Celebes Sea, Kalimantan **12** Flores Strait **14** Makassar Strait
city: **4** Poso **6** Manado **7** Kendari, Madjene **8** Bonthain, Donggala, Makassar **9** Gorontalo
location: **9** Indonesia
people: **4** Bugi, Laki, Mori, Muna, Napu, Palu, Peso, Seko, Wana **5** Besoa, Buton, Toala **6** Bungku, Butung, Parigi, Sadang, Sangir, Toland **7** Banggai, Bolaang, Kabaena, Loinang, Toradja **8** Balantak, Buginese, Mongondu, Rongkong, Sanghike **9** Gorontalo **11** Makassarese
province: **13** North Sulawesi, South Sulawesi **15** Central Sulawesi **17** Southeast Sulawesi

Celebes ox 4 anoa

celebrate 4 laud **5** bless, cheer, exalt, extol, honor **6** hallow, praise, revere **7** acclaim, applaud, commend, glorify, observe **8** proclaim, sanctify, venerate **9** broadcast, ritualize, solemnize **10** consecrate **11** commemorate **13** ceremonialize

celebrated 5 famed, feted, noted **6** famous, prized **7** eminent, honored, notable, revered **8** lionized, renowned **9** acclaimed, important, prominent, respected, treasured, venerable, wellknown **11** illustrious, outstanding **13** distinguished

Celebrated Jumping Frog of Calaveras County, The
author: **9** Mark Twain

celebration 4 fete, gala **5** feast, party **6** ritual **7** jubilee, revelry **8** carnival, ceremony, festival **9** festivity, hallowing **10** ceremonial, observance **13** commemoration, solemnization **14** sanctification **15** memorialization

celebrity 3 VIP **4** fame, name, note, star **5** glory, wheel **6** bigwig, renown **7** big shot, notable, stardom **8** eminence, luminary **9** dignitary, notoriety, personage **10** notability, popularity, prominence **11** distinction, personality **12** famous person, person of note

celerity 5 haste, hurry, speed **6** hustle **8** alacrity, dispatch, fast clip, fastness, legerity, rapidity **9** briskness, quickness, swiftness **10** expedition, snappiness, speediness **12** precipitance **14** lightning speed **15** expeditiousness

celery seed
also called: **8** smallage
origin: **13** Mediterranean
use: **4** soup **5** salad, sauce **6** pickle **10** vegetables

celestial 3 sky **5** solar **6** astral, divine **7** angelic, elysian, stellar, sublime **8** beatific, blissful, empyrean, ethereal, hallowed, heavenly, seraphic **9** planetary, unearthly **12** astronomical, otherworldly, paradisiacal

celestial being 3 god **5** angel, deity **7** goddess, divinity **11** divine being

Celestial City
place in: **16** Pilgrim's Progress
author: **6** Bunyan

Celia (Aliena)
character in: **11** As You Like It
author: **11** Shakespeare

celibacy 6 purity **8** chastity **9** virginity **10** abstinence, continence **12** bachelorhood, spinsterhood

celibate 4 pure **5** unwed **6** chaste, single **8** bachelor, spinster, virginal **9** abstinent, continent, unmarried

Celine, Louis-Ferdinand
author: **12** Guignol's Band **25** Death on the Installment Plan, Journey to the End of the Night

cell
part: **7** nucleus **8** membrane **9** cytoplasm
made of: **3** fat **4** salt **5** water **7** protein **12** compounds **13** carbohydrate
theory of: **7** (Rudolf) Virchow, (Theodor) Schwann

cellar 3 den **4** cave **6** dugout **8** base-

ment **10** downstairs **14** wine collection

Cellini, Benvenuto
born: **5** Italy **8** Florence
artwork: **7** Cosimo I, Perseus **13** Bindo Altoviti **18** The Crucified Christ **20** Nymph of Fontainebleau
autobiography: **22** Life of Benvenuto Cellini

Celsius
abbreviation of: **1** C

Celt 4 Gaul, Kelt, Manx, Pict, Scot **5** Irish, Welsh **6** Breton, Briton, chisel **8** Scottish **10** Highlander

Celtic 4 Erse
language group: **6** Gaelic **9** Brythonic
family: **12** Indo-European
language of: **5** Gauls

cement 3 fix, set **4** bind, fuse, glue, join, seal, weld **5** paste, stick, unite **6** mortar, secure **8** concrete

cemetery 7 ossuary **8** boneyard, Boot Hill, catacomb **9** graveyard **10** churchyard, necropolis **12** burial ground, memorial park, potter's field **13** burying ground

Cenci, The
author: **18** Percy Bysshe Shelley

cenobite 4 monk **7** ascetic **8** celibate **9** religious

censor 4 blip, edit **5** amend, bleep, judge, purge **6** critic, delete, excise **7** amender, Bowdler, clean up **8** black out, examiner, reviewer, suppress **9** expurgate, inspector **10** blue-pencil, bowdlerize, expurgator, suppressor **11** bowdlerizer, faultfinder, scrutinizer **12** investigator **17** custodian of morals **25** guardian of the public morals

censorious 5 picky **7** abusive, carping **8** critical **10** defamatory **12** faultfinding

censurable 8 blamable **10** deplorable, punishable, reprovable **11** blameworthy **12** reproachable **13** reprehensible

censure 3 pan, rap **5** chide, scold **6** berate, rebuke **7** bawl out, chew out, chiding, condemn, reproof, reprove, upbraid **8** admonish, denounce, reproach, scolding **9** castigate, complaint, criticism, criticize, reprehend, reprimand **10** admonition, bawling-out, chewing-out, disapprove, upbraiding **11** castigation, disapproval, reprobation **12** condemnation, dressing-down, remonstrance **13** tonguelashing **14** disapprobation **15** rap on the knuckles, take over the coals
god of: **5** Momos, Momus

census 3 tax **4** data, list, poll **5** count **6** amount, number **11** enumeration **12** registration

Centaur
form: **3** man **5** horse **7** monster **16** half-man half-horse
constellation of: **9** Centaurus

famous: 6 Chiron
represents: 11 Sagittarius
Centennial
    author: 13 James Michener
Centennial State
    nickname of: 8 Colorado
center, centre 3 fix, hub, mid **4** axis, core, crux **5** focus, heart, pivot, point **6** direct, gather, middle **7** address, essence, nucleus **8** converge, interior **9** middle **10** focal point **11** concentrate
centered 4 even, true **5** right **7** focused **8** straight **10** pinpointed **12** concentrated
centigrade 5 scale **6** degree **7** celcius **11** thermometer
centigram
    abbreviation of: 2 cg
centiliter
    abbreviation of: 2 cl
centimeter
    abbreviation of: 2 cm
centipede 4 boat **5** shrub **6** earwig, insect **8** chilopod, multiped **9** arthropod **13** muehlenbeckia
central 3 key **4** core, main **5** basic, chief, focal, inner, major, prime **6** inmost, middle **7** leading, midmost, pivotal, primary **8** dominant, foremost, interior **9** essential, paramount, principal **10** middlemost **11** fundamental, predominant **13** most important
Central African Republic
    other name: 11 Ubangi-Chari **20** Central African Empire
    capital/largest city: 6 Bangui
    others: 3 Obo **4** Bria, Ippy **5** Birao, Bouar, Kembe, Ndele, Ngoto, Paoua, Rafai, Zemio **6** Baboua, Bakala, Bozoum, Mbaiki **7** Bambari, Grimari, Zemongo **9** Bangassou, Berberati, Bossangoa, Fort-Sibut
    monetary unit: 5 franc **7** centime
    lake: 4 Chad
    mountain: 5 Karre, Tinga **6** Mongos **9** Dar Challa
    highest point: 11 Kayagangiri
    river: 4 Bomu, Nana **5** Chari, Kotto, Mbari, Mpoko, Ouaka **6** Chinko, Lobaye, Mbomou, Ubangi **11** Upper Sangha
    people: 4 Baya, Sara **5** Banda, Bwaka, Sango **6** Azande, Yakoma **7** Banziri, Mandjia, Nzakara
    language: 5 Sango, Zande **6** French
    religion: 5 Islam **7** animism **12** Christianity **13** Roman Catholic
    place:
        plaza: 13 Edouard Renard
    food:
        tapioca: 6 manioc **7** cassava
Central America
    land form: 7 isthmus
    countries: 6 Belize, Panama **8** Honduras **9** Costa Rica, Guatemala, Nicaragua **10** El Salvador
    bordered by: 6 Mexico, **8** Colombia

12 Caribbean Sea, North America, Pacific Ocean, South America
    capital city: 7 Managua, San Jose **8** Belmopan **10** Panama City **11** San Salvador, Tegucigalpa **13** Guatemala City
    river: 3 New **4** Axul, Coco, Sico, Tuma, Ulua, Wawa **5** Aguan, Chepo, Hondo, Lempa, Wauks **6** Chixoy, Grande, Pasion, Patuca, Sulaco, Waspuk **7** Motagua, Paulaya, San Juan, Sarstun, Segovia **8** Kukalaya **9** Choluteca, Escondido **10** Chucunague **11** Prinzapolca
    lake: 5 Gatun, Guija, Yojoa **7** Atitlan, Managua **9** Nicaragua, Peten Itza
    mountain: 4 Maya, Pija **5** Colon, Huapi, Minas, Pando **6** Blanco **7** Dipilto, Gongora, San Blas **8** Brewster, Dariense, Isabelia, San Pablo, Santa Ana **9** Esperanza **14** Chirripo Grande
    people: 3 Mam **5** Zambo **6** Indian, Ladino, Quiche **7** mestizo **8** Miskitas **10** Black Carib, Cakchiquel
    animal: 5 tapir **6** agouti **7** opossum, peccary **8** anteater, kinkajou, marmoset **9** armadillo, porcupine, tree sloth **12** howler monkey, spider monkey **14** capuchin monkey
Central Amerind
    language branch: 9 Oto-Mangue **10** Uto-Aztecan **11** Kiowa-Tanoan
central city 8 core city, downtown **9** inner city, urban area **10** metropolis **16** business district, metropolitan area
central idea 3 nut **4** core, crux, gist, meat **5** heart, theme **6** kernel **7** essence **9** main point
centralization 5 focus **11** convergence **13** concentration, consolidation
centralize 5 focus, unify **6** center, gather **7** collect, compact **8** center on, coalesce, converge, pinpoint **9** integrate **10** congregate **11** concentrate, consolidate
central part 4 core, crux, gist, pith **5** heart **6** center, kernel **7** nucleus
century
    abbreviation of: 4 cent
    French: 6 siecle
cephalopod 5 squid **7** mollusk, octopus **8** nautilus **10** cuttlefish
ceramic ware 5 china, glass **7** pottery **8** crockery **9** chinaware, glassware, porcelain, stoneware **10** enamelware **11** earthenware
ceratopsid
    type of: 8 dinosaur
    member: 10 Torosaurus **11** Monoclonius, Triceratops **13** Protoceratops, Styracosaurus **14** Psittacosaurus
Ceratosaurus
    type: 8 dinosaur
    period: 8 Jurassic
Cerberus
    form: 3 dog

    father: 6 Typhon
    mother: 7 Echidna
    sibling: 5 Hydra **7** Orthrus **8** Chimaera **10** Nemean lion **12** Theban Sphinx
    number of heads: 5 three
    guarded: 10 Underworld
Cercopes
    race of: 6 Gnomes
cereal 4 bran, corn, oats, rice, seed **5** grain, grass, gruel, plant, wheat **6** barley, pablum **7** oatmeal, pabulum **8** porridge
cerebellum
    part of: 5 brain
    controls: 7 balance **8** movement
cerebrum
    part of: 5 brain
    controls: 6 seeing **7** hearing, tasting **8** deciding, feelings, learning, smelling, thinking, touching **9** awareness **11** remembering
ceremonial 4 rite **6** formal, ritual **7** liturgy, service **8** ceremony **9** formality, sacrament **10** liturgical, observance **11** celebration, ritualistic
ceremonialize 7 observe **9** celebrate, ritualize **11** commemorate
ceremonious 5 exact, fussy, rigid, stiff **6** formal, proper, solemn **7** careful, correct, pompous, precise **8** starched **9** dignified **10** methodical, meticulous **11** punctilious
ceremony 4 rite **6** custom, nicety, ritual **7** amenity, decorum, pageant, service **8** function, protocol **9** etiquette, formality, propriety **10** observance, politeness **11** celebration, formalities **13** commemoration
Cerenkov, Pavel Alekseevich
    field: 7 physics
    nationality: 7 Russian
    discovered: 12 cause of light **14** Cerenkov effect
Ceres
    origin: 5 Roman
    goddess of: 11 agriculture
    corresponds to: 7 Demeter
certain 4 sure **5** valid **6** secure **7** assured, express, settled, special **8** absolute, cocksure, definite, positive, reliable, specific **9** confident, convinced, satisfied **10** conclusive, individual, inevitable, particular, undeniable, undisputed, undoubtful, undoubting, unshakable **11** indubitable, inescapable, irrefutable, unalterable, unequivocal, unqualified **12** indisputable, unchangeable, unmistakable, wellgrounded **13** bound to happen, incontestable **14** unquestionable **16** incontrovertible
certainly 5 truly **6** indeed, surely **7** for sure **8** of course **9** decidedly **10** absolutely, definitely, positively **11** indubitably, undoubtedly **13** unequivocally,

without a doubt **14** unquestionably
21 beyond a shadow of a doubt

Certain Smile, A
author: **14** Francoise Sagan

certainty 4 fact **5** faith, trust **6** belief,
surety **7** reality, sure bet **8** sureness **9**
actuality, assurance, certitude, sure
thing **10** confidence, conviction **11**
presumption **12** positiveness **13** inevitability **14** conclusiveness, inescapability **17** authoritativeness

certificate 4 deed **6** permit **7** diploma,
license, voucher **8** document, warranty **9** affidavit **10** credential **11** testimonial **13** authorization **14** authentication

certification 7 voucher **8** approval **10**
validation **11** endorsement **12** confirmation, ratification, verification
13 authorization, corroboration **14** authentication, substantiation

certify 4 aver **5** swear, vouch **6** assure,
attest, ratify, second, verify **7** confirm,
declare, endorse, support, warrant,
witness **8** notarize, sanction, validate
9 authorize, guarantee, testify to **10**
underwrite **11** corroborate **12** authenticate, give one's word, substantiate

certitude 5 faith, trust **6** belief, surety
8 reliance, sureness **9** assurance, certainty **10** confidence **12** positiveness
14 conclusiveness

cerulean 4 blue **5** azure **6** cobalt **7** sky
blue **9** clear blue

Cervantes Saavedra, Miguel de
author of: **20** Don Quixote de la
Mancha

Cesar Birotteau
author: **14** Honore de Balzac

cessation 3 end **4** halt, stay, stop **5**
pause **6** ending, recess **7** ceasing,
halting, respite **8** quitting, stopping,
surcease **9** desisting **10** concluding,
leaving off, suspension **11** adjournment, breaking off, termination **12** interruption **13** coming to a halt, dis-
continuing **14** discontinuance

c'est la vie 9 that's life **10** such is life

Cestus
girdle of: **5** Venus

cetacean 4 apod, orca **5** whale **6** beluga, mammal **7** cetacea, dolphin,
dowfish, grampus, narwhal **8** porpoise, sturgeon **9** blue whale **11** baleen whale, killer whale

Cetinje
capital of: **10** Montenegro

Ceylon see **8** Sri Lanka

Cezanne, Paul
born: **6** France **13** Aix-en-Provence
artwork: **7** Bathers **11** Card Players
13 The Black Clock, The Railway
Out **14** Uncle Dominique **15** La Maison du Pendu **16** The Suicide's
House **17** Grandes Baigneuses **19**

Woman with a Coffee Pot **36** Mont-
Sainte-Victoire with Large Pine Trees

Chabrier, (Alexis) Emmanuel
born: **6** Ambert, France
composer of: **6** Espana **7** L'Etoile **10**
Gwendoline **13** Marche Joyeuse **14**
Le Roi Malgre Lui **18** King Despite
Himself **19** Une Education Manquee

Chad
other name: **5** Tchad
capital/largest city: **8** Fort-Lamy,
N'Djamena
others: **3** Ati, Bol, Lai, Mao **4** Fada,
Faya, Sarh **5** Mongo **6** Abeche, Bon-
gor **7** Largeau, Moundou **8** Moussoro
monetary unit: **5** franc **7** centime
lake: **4** Chad
mountain: **7** Tibesti, Touside
highest point: **9** Emi Koussi
river: **5** Chari **6** Logone **8** Bahraouk
physical feature:
plateau: **6** Ennedi
people: **4** Arab, Daza, Maba, Sara,
Teda, Tubu **5** Barma, Hakka, Kreda,
Massa **6** Fulani, Kotoko, Toubou,
Wadaii **7** Kamadja, Kanembu, Moun-
dan
language: **4** Sara **5** Turku **6** Arabic,
French
religion: **5** Islam **7** animism **12** Christianity

Chadband
character in: **10** Bleak House
author: **7** Dickens

Chadic
language family: **11** Afroasiatic **13**
Hamito-Semitic
includes: **5** Hausa
spoken in: **6** Africa **8** Lake Chad

Chadwick, James
field: **7** physics
nationality: **7** British
discovered: **7** neutron
awarded: **10** Nobel Prize

chafe 3 rub **4** boil, burn, foam, fume,
rage, rasp **6** abrade, rankle, scrape,
seethe **7** scratch **9** be annoyed **11** be
irritated

chaff 3 bug, kid, rag, rib **4** josh, junk,
pods, razz, ride, slag, twit **5** dross,
hulls, husks, jolly, trash, waste **6** banter, debris, litter, refuse, rubble,
shells, shoddy, shucks **7** kidding, ragging, remnant, residue, ribbing, rubbish, waggery **8** badinage, chaffing,
leavings, raillery, ridicule **9** sweepings
9 give and take

chaffing 6 banter **7** jesting, joshing,
kidding, ragging, ribbing, waggery **8**
badinage, raillery

chafing 5 harsh **6** fuming **7** rasping,
rubbing **8** abrading, abrasive **10** irritating

Chagall, Marc
born: **6** Liosno, Liozno, Russia
artwork: **8** Birthday, Cockcrow **9** The
Circus, The Red Sun **10** The Juggler

11 Over Vitebsk **12** The Violinist **14**
Double Portrait, I and the Village **16**
The Jewish Wedding **17** Lovers with
Rooster **20** Paris Through My Win-
dow

chagrin 5 shame **6** dismay **8** distress
11 humiliation **13** embarrassment,
mortification

chagrined 7 abashed, ashamed **9** mortified **10** humiliated **11** embarrassed

Chahiksichhiks see **6** Pawnee

chain 3 fob **5** cable, links **7** shackle **8**
necklace **10** metal links **11** linked cable
abbreviation: **2** ch

Chain, Ernst Boris
field: **12** biochemistry
nationality: **7** British
discovered: **10** penicillin
worked with: **6** Florey **7** Fleming
awarded: **10** Nobel Prize

Chained Lady
constellation of: **9** Andromeda

chains 3 tie **4** bind, lash, moor **5**
bonds, irons, tie up, train **6** fasten,
fetter, secure, series, string, tether **7**
bondage, fetters, manacle, serfdom,
shackle, slavery **8** leg irons, manacles,
sequence, shackles **9** handcuffs, servitude, thralldom **10** put in irons, succession **11** enslavement, subjugation

chair 4 seat **5** bench, couch, sedan
stool **6** chaise, lounge, rocker, settee,
throne **7** conduct, ottoman **11** preside
over **16** presiding officer

chairman 4 head **5** chair, emcee **6**
leader **7** manager, preside, speaker **8**
director **9** chairlady, executive, moderator **10** chairwoman, supervisor **11**
chairperson, toastmaster **13** administrator **16** presiding officer **18** master
of ceremonies

Chair of Forgetfulness
form: **4** seat
made of: **5** stone
location: **10** Underworld

chaise 3 gig **4** shay **5** chair **6** daybed,
longue, lounge **7** calesin **8** carriage,
duchesse

chalcedony 3 gem **4** onyx, opal, sard
5 agate, prase **6** jasper, plasma,
quartz, silica **7** catseye, mineral, opal-
ine, sardius **8** hematite, sardonyx **9**
carnelian **10** bloodstone, heliotrope
11 chrysoprase **12** semiprecious **14**
silicon dioxide

Chaldean 4 seer **5** magic **6** Syriac **7**
Aramaic, semitic **8** magician **9** astrology, enchanter, Nabonidus **10** astrologer, Babylonian, soothsayer **12** Nabopolassar **14** Nebuchadnezzar

chalice 3 cup **5** grail **6** goblet, vessel

chalk 4 draw **6** crayon, pastel, sketch **9**
limestone

chalk up 4 earn **5** score **6** attain,
charge, credit **7** achieve, ascribe

chalky 3 wan 4 pale 5 ashen, white 6 pallid 7 powdery 8 blanched 9 bloodless

challenge 3 bid, tax, try 4 dare, defy, gage, test 5 doubt, trial 6 demand, impute, summon 7 defiant, dispute, summons 8 question 15 take exception to 20 fling down the gauntlet

chamber 4 diet, hall, room 5 board, court, house, salon 6 office, parlor 7 bedroom, boudoir, council 8 assembly, congress 9 apartment

Chamberlain, Owen
field: 7 physics
developed: 8 atom bomb
awarded: 10 Nobel Prize

Chamberlain, Richard
real name: 24 George Richard Chamberlain
born: 12 Los Angeles CA
roles: 6 Shogun 9 Dr Kildare 10 Wallenberg 13 The Thorn Birds 17 The Bourne Identity 21 The Count of Monte Cristo

Chamberlain, Wilt (Wilton Norman)
nickname: 6 Dipper 12 Wilt the Stilt
sport: 10 basketball
position: 5 coach 6 center
team: 16 Los Angeles Lakers 17 Philadelphia 76ers 20 Philadelphia Warriors, San Francisco Warriors 21 San Diego Conquistadors

chambermaid
French: 14 femme de chambre

chambord
type: 7 liqueur
origin: 6 France
flavor: 14 black raspberry

chameleon 4 newt 6 lizard 8 renegade, turncoat 10 fickleness 14 changeableness

champ 4 bite, chew, gnaw 5 chomp, crush, grind, munch 6 crunch 8 champion

champagne 4 fizz 6 bubbly
type: 4 wine
drink: 7 the Pope
with white wine: 8 Cold Duck
with orange juice: 6 Mimosa
measure: 4 magnum 8 jeroboam, rehoboam 9 balthazar 10 methuselah, salmanazar 14 Nebuchadnezzar

Champaigne, Philippe de
born: 7 Belgium 8 Brussels
artwork: 6 Ex Voto 17 Cardinal Richelieu 26 The Adoration of the Shepherds

champion 3 aid 4 abet, back 6 backer, defend, master, uphold, victor, winner 7 espouse, paladin, paragon, promote, support 8 advocate, defender, fight for, laureate, promoter, speak for, upholder 9 battle for, conqueror, protector, supporter 10 stand up for, vanquisher 11 protagonist, title holder

Champion
constellation of: 7 Perseus

championship 3 cup 5 crown, title 7 backing, defense, support, winning 8 advocacy, espousal

Chan, Charlie
creator: 15 Earl Derr Biggers
actors: 7 E. L. Parks 10 George Kuwa 11 Warner Oland, Sidney Toler 13 Roland Winters, Kamiyama Sojin
films: 7 The Trap 8 Jade Mask 11 Dead Men Tell 13 Shanghai Cobra, The Chinese Cat, The Black Camel 16 House Without a Key 17 Castle in the Desert, Behind that Curtain

chance 3 try 4 fall, fate, luck, risk 5 lucky, occur 6 befall, danger, gamble, happen, hazard, random 7 attempt, destiny, fortune, turn out, venture 8 accident, jeopardy, occasion 9 come about, fortunate, unplanned 10 accidental, fortuitous, likelihood, likeliness, providence, undesigned, unexpected, unforeseen 11 opportunity, possibility, probability, speculation, unlooked for 12 happenstance 13 unintentional 14 unpremeditated

chance upon 4 find, meet 7 learn of, run into 8 come upon, discover 9 encounter, light upon 10 happen upon 11 stumble upon

chancy 4 iffy 5 dicey, risky 6 touchy, tricky 7 dubious, erratic, unsound 8 doubtful 9 hazardous, uncertain, whimsical 10 capricious, precarious 11 speculative, venturesome 13 problematical, unpredictable

chandelier 11 hanging lamp 12 candleholder 15 lighting fixture

Chandler, Jeff
real name: 10 Ira Grossel
born: 10 Brooklyn NY
roles: 7 Cochise 11 Broken Arrow 17 Merrill's Marauders

Chandler, Raymond
author of: 11 The Big Sleep 14 The Long Goodbye 16 Farewell My Lovely
born: 7 England
character: 13 Philip Marlowe
screenplay: 13 The Blue Dahlia 15 Double Indemnity 17 Strangers on a Train

Chaney, Lon
real name: 12 Alonso Chaney
son: 9 Creighton (Lon Chaney Jr)
nickname: 19 Man of a Thousand Faces
born: 17 Colorado Springs CO
roles: 14 The Unholy Three 18 Tell It to the Marines 20 Hunchback of Notre Dame, The Phantom of the Opera

Chaney, Lon Jr
real name: 9 Creighton
father: 3 Lon
born: 14 Oklahoma City OK

roles: 6 Lennie 8 The Mummy 10 The Wolf Man 12 Of Mice and Men, Son of Dracula 20 Frankenstein's Monster

change 4 swap, turn, vary 5 alter, coins, shift, trade 6 modify, mutate, recast, reform, silver, switch 7 convert, novelty, remodel, replace, restyle, shuffle, variety, veering 8 pin money, swapping, transfer 9 deviation, diversion, exception, restyling, transform, transmute, turn about, variation 10 alteration, conversion, difference, remodeling, reorganize, revolution, small coins, substitute 11 fluctuation, pocket money, reformation 12 metamorphose, modification, substitution, transmogrify 13 make different, metamorphosis, revolutionize, transmutation, transposition 14 reorganization, transformation 15 transfiguration

changeable 6 fickle, fitful 7 erratic, flighty, mutable, varying 8 unstable, unsteady, variable, volatile 9 deviating, irregular, mercurial, uncertain 10 capricious, inconstant, modifiable, reversible 11 alternating, convertible, fluctuating, vacillating 13 transformable

change in plan
French: 8 demarche

changeless 4 fast 5 fixed 6 stable 7 abiding, certain, durable, eternal, lasting 8 constant, enduring 9 immutable, steadfast, unvarying 10 unshakable 11 everlasting, unalterable 12 indissoluble

changelessness 9 certainty, constancy, stability 10 durability, permanence 12 immutability 13 steadfastness

change of heart 10 conversion 16 change of attitude

changeover 10 conversion

channel 3 cut 4 gash, lead, send 5 guide, route, steer 6 convey, course, direct, furrow, groove, gutter, strait, trough 7 narrows, passage 11 watercourse 21 avenue of communication

Channing, Carol
born: 9 Seattle WA
roles: 10 Hello Dolly 22 Gentlemen Prefer Blondes, Thoroughly Modern Millie

chanson 4 song

Chanson de Roland
also: 12 Song of Roland
author: 7 unknown
character: 4 Aude 6 Turpin 7 Ganelon, Marsile, Olivier 11 Charlemagne, Twelve Peers
foe: 8 Saracens
knight: 7 paladin

chant 2 om 3 ode 4 hymn, lied, sing, song 5 carol, croon, dirge, elegy, psalm, theme, trill, troll 6 chorus, intone, melody, monody, strain **7** chanson, chorale, descant **8** canticle, doxology, threnody, vocalize **9** homophony, monophony, offertory, plainsong **11** Gloria Patri **14** Gregorian chant

chanteuse 6 singer (female)

Chants de Maldoror, Les
  author: 18 Comte de Lautreamont

chaos 4 mess **5** furor **6** bedlam, jumble, muddle, tumult, uproar **7** turmoil **8** disarray, disorder, upheaval **9** agitation, commotion, confusion **10** turbulence **11** pandemonium **12** discomposure **14** disarrangement **15** disorganization

Chaos
  origin: 5 Greek
  personifies: 9 confusion

chaotic 7 jumbled, mixed-up, muddled, tangled **8** confused **9** confusing, illogical, turbulent **10** disjointed, incoherent, in disarray **11** unorganized **12** disorganized **13** disharmonious

chap 3 boy, dry, guy, jaw, lad, man, rap **4** chop, gent **5** bloke, buyer, crack, knock, split **6** fellow, redden, split, stroke **7** fissure, roughen **8** customer **9** purchaser

chapbook 7 garland **8** treasury **9** anthology **10** collection **11** florilegium

chapeau 3 hat

chapel 6 church, shrine **7** oratory **9** sanctuary **10** house of God, tabernacle **14** place of worship

chaperon, chaperone 5 guard, watch **6** duenna, escort **7** oversee **8** guardian, shepherd **9** accompany, attendant, custodian, protector, safeguard **11** keep an eye on

chaperoned 7 oversaw **8** attended, escorted **10** supervised **11** accompanied

chapfallen 6 droopy **8** cast down, dejected **9** depressed

chaplain 4 abbe **5** padre, rabbi, vicar **6** cleric, curate, father, parson, pastor, priest, rector **7** Holy Joe **8** minister, preacher, reverend, sky pilot **9** churchman, clergyman **12** ecclesiastic

chaplet 4 band **6** fillet, wreath **7** circlet, coronet

Chaplin, Charlie
  real name: 24 Sir Charles Spencer Chaplin
  nickname: 14 the Little Tramp
  wife: 10 Oona O'Neill **15** Paulette Goddard
  daughter: 9 Geraldine
  born: 6 London **7** England
  director of/roles: 6 The Kid **8** The Tramp **9** Limelight **10** City Lights **11** Modern Times, The Gold Rush **15** Monsieur Verdoux **16** The Great Dictator

Chaplin, Geraldine
  father: 14 Charlie Chaplin

  mother: 17 Oona O'Neill Chaplin
  born: 13 Santa Monica CA
  roles: 12 The Hawaiians **13** Doctor Zhivago

chapter 3 era **4** body, part, span, unit **5** group, phase **6** branch, clause, period **7** episode, portion, section **8** division **9** affiliate **11** subdivision

Chapters of Erie
  author: 10 Henry Adams

char 4 burn, sear **5** singe **6** scorch **9** carbonize **10** incinerate

character 4 part, role, self **5** being, honor **6** makeup, nature, person, traits, weirdo **7** honesty, oddball, persona **8** goodness, morality, original, specimen **9** eccentric, integrity, odd person, qualities, rectitude **10** attributes, individual, one-of-a-kind **11** personality, uprightness **13** individuality, moral strength **15** distinctiveness **16** dramatis personae

characteristic 4 mark **5** trait **6** aspect **7** earmark, feature, quality, typical **8** property, symbolic **9** attribute, mannerism, specialty, trademark **10** emblematic, indicative **11** distinctive, peculiarity **14** distinguishing, representative

characterization 8 portrait **9** depiction, picturing, portrayal **11** delineation, description **12** representing **14** representation

characterize 4 mark **5** class **6** define, depict, typify **7** earmark, portray **8** classify, describe, indicate **9** designate, represent **11** distinguish

characterless 4 weak **5** vague **6** anemic **11** nondescript **13** indeterminate **14** expressionless

Characters of Shakespeare's Plays, The
  author: 14 William Hazlitt

Charcot, Jean Martin
  nationality: 6 French
  father of: 9 neurology

Chardin, Jean Baptiste Simeon
  born: 5 Paris **6** France
  artwork: 7 The Kiss **8** The Grace **14** Young Governess **16** The Copper Cistern **17** Attributes of Music **19** Attributes of the Arts **28** Rayfish Cat and Kitchen Utensils

charge 3 ask, bid, fee **4** care, cost, duty, fill, heap, lade, levy, load, pack, pile, rate, rush, toll **5** beset, blame, debit, exact, onset, order, price, stack, storm, stuff **6** accuse, advice, amount, assail, assess, assign, attack, come at, demand, direct, enjoin, impute, indict, sortie, summon **7** ascribe, assault, bidding, command, control, custody, dictate, expense, keeping, payment, require **8** call upon, instruct, storming **9** attribute, complaint, direction, enjoining, onslaught **10** accusation, allegation, assessment, indictment, in-

junction, management, protection **11** arraignment, incriminate, instruction, safekeeping, supervision **12** delay payment, guardianship, jurisdiction **14** administration, lay the blame for, request payment **15** superintendence **16** put on one's account

chargeable 6 liable **10** answerable **11** responsible

charged 5 taxed, tense **6** blamed, filled, levied, loaded, priced **7** accused, ordered, uptight **8** assessed, attacked, exhorted, mandated, prepared **9** commanded, entrusted **10** accusation, allegation, indictment

Charge of the Light Brigade, The
  author: 18 Alfred Lord Tennyson
  director: 13 Michael Curtiz
  cast: 10 David Niven, Errol Flynn, Nigel Bruce **11** Donald Crisp **13** Patric Knowles **15** Henry Stephenson **17** Olivia de Havilland
  setting: 6 Russia

charger 5 horse, mount, steed **6** vessel **7** accuser, platter **8** warhorse

charge with 5 trust **6** assign, commit **7** consign, entrust **8** delegate, hand over, turn over **9** authorize

chariot 3 car **5** buggy **7** phaeton, vehicle **8** carriage

Charioteer
  constellation of: 6 Auriga

Chariots of Fire
  director: 10 Hugh Hudson
  cast: 7 Ian Holm **8** Ben Cross (Harold Abrahams) **11** John Gielgud, Nigel Havers **12** Ian Charleson (Eric Liddell)
  Oscar for: 5 score (Vangelis) **6** script **7** picture

charisma 5 charm **6** allure, appeal **7** glamour **8** presence, witchery **9** magnetism, sex appeal **10** bewitchery **11** enchantment, fascination **14** attractiveness

charitable 4 kind **6** giving, kindly **7** lenient, liberal **8** generous, gracious, tolerant **9** bounteous, bountiful, forgiving, indulgent **10** almsgiving, benevolent, munificent, open-handed **11** considerate, kindhearted, magnanimous, sympathetic, warmhearted **12** eleemosynary, sympathizing **13** philanthropic, understanding

charitableness 10 liberality **11** benevolence, generousity **12** philanthropy **13** bountifulness **14** openhandedness **15** humanitarianism

Charites see **6** Graces

charity 3 aid **4** alms, fund, gift, help, love **6** bounty, giving **7** handout **8** altruism, donating, good will, goodness, humanity, kindness, offering, sympathy **9** benignity, donations, endowment, tolerance **10** alms-giving, assistance, compassion, generosity **11** benefaction, benevolence, fundraising, munificence **12** graciousness, philanthropy **13** contributions, financial help, love of mankind **14** openhandedness

charlatan 4 fake **5** cheat, fraud, quack **7** cozener **8** deceiver, imposter, impostor, swindler **9** trickster **10** mountebank **16** confidence artist

Charles, Nick and Nora
　characters in: 10 The Thin Man
　author: 7 Hammett
　pet dog 4 Asta

Charles O'Malley
　author: 12 Charles Lever

Charleston 5 dance **13** ballroom dance
　capital of: 9 W Virginia

Charlie's Angels
　character: 10 Jill Monroe, John Bosley, Kris Munroe **12** Kelly Garrett **13** Sabrina Duncan **15** Charlie Townsend
　cast: 10 Cheryl Ladd, David Doyle **11** Jaclyn Smith, Kate Jackson **18** Farah Fawcett-Majors
　voice of Charlie: 12 John Forsythe

Charlotte's Web
　author: 7 E B White
　Charlotte: 6 spider
　saved: 6 Wilbur (piglet)

Charly
　director: 11 Ralph Nelson
　based on story by: 11 Daniel Keyes (Flowers for Algernon)
　cast: 10 Leon Janney, Lilia Skala **11** Claire Bloom **13** Dick van Patten **14** Cliff Robertson
　Oscar for: 5 actor (Robertson)

charm 4 draw, grip, lure, take **5** magic, spell **6** allure, amulet, bauble, cajole, engage, please, seduce, turn on **7** attract, beguile, bewitch, conjure, delight, enchant, gratify, sorcery, trinket, win over **8** charisma, enthrall, entrance, ornament, talisman **9** captivate, enrapture, fascinate, magnetism **10** allurement, attraction, cast a spell, lucky piece **11** conjuration, enchantment, fascination, incantation, work magic on

charmer 4 vamp **5** belle, siren **9** enchanter, temptress **11** enchantress, femme fatale, spellbinder

charming 6 lovely **7** likable, winning, winsome **8** alluring, engaging, enticing, fetching, graceful, magnetic, pleasing **9** agreeable **10** attractive, bewitching, delightful, enchanting, entrancing **11** captivating, charismatic, enthralling, fascinating **12** irresistible

charmless 4 dull **5** blunt **6** dreary **9** repulsive, unlikable, unlovable **10** unpleasant **12** disagreeable, unattractive

Charon
　father: 6 Erebus
　mother: 3 Nyx
　occupation: 8 ferryman
　river: 4 Styx

Charops
　epithet of: 8 Hercules
　means: 14 with bright eyes

Charpentier, Gustave
　born: 6 Dieuze, France
　composer of: 6 Julien, Louise **18** Impressions of Italy

chart 3 map, plan **4** plan, plot **5** draft, graph, table **6** design, draw up, lay out, map out, scheme, sketch **7** diagram, outline **8** tabulate **9** blueprint, delineate **10** tabulation

charter 3 let **4** deed, hire, rent **5** grant, lease **6** employ, engage, permit **7** compact, license **8** contract, covenant, sanction **9** agreement, authority, authorize, franchise **10** commission, concession

Charterhouse of Parma, The
　author: 23 Marie Henri Beyle Stendhal
　character: 8 Marietta **10** Count Mosca **11** Clelia Conti **14** Gina Pietranera **16** Fabrizio del Dongo

chartreuse
　type: 7 liqueur
　origin: 6 France **15** Carthusian monks
　flavor: 4 herb
　color: 5 green **6** yellow
　with apricot brandy: 13 Golden Slipper
　with gin: 5 Bijou **9** Green Lady

chary 3 shy **4** wary **5** alert, cagey, leery **7** careful, guarded, heedful, prudent, sparing **8** cautious, hesitant, vigilant, watchful **10** economical, suspicious **11** circumspect, distrustful

Charybdis
　form: 7 monster
　father: 8 Poseidon
　mother: 4 Gaea
　identified with: 9 whirlpool

chase 3 dog **4** hunt, oust, rout, shoo, tail **5** drive, evict, hound, quest, stalk, track, trail **6** dispel, follow, pursue, shadow **7** cast out, go after, hunting, pursuit, repulse, scatter **8** pursuing, run after, send away, stalking, tracking **9** drive away, following **11** put to flight, send packing

Chase, Chevy
　real name: 19 Cornelius Crane Chase
　born: 9 New York NY
　roles: 4 Hero **6** Fletch **8** Foul Play, Vacation **10** Caddyshack **11** Spies Like Us, Three Amigos **17** Saturday Night Live

chasm 3 gap, pit **4** gulf, hold, rift **5** abyss, break, cleft, crack, gorge, gulch, split **6** breach, cavity, crater, divide, ravine **7** fissure **8** crevasse

chasseur 6 hunter

chaste 4 pure **5** clean **6** decent, modest, severe, strict **7** austere, classic, precise, sinless **8** virginal, virtuous **9** continent, righteous, unadorned, unsullied, untainted, wholesome **10** im-

maculate, restrained **11** clean-living, uncorrupted **12** unornamented **13** unembellished

chasten 5 chide, scold **6** berate, punish, rebuke **7** censure, reprove, upbraid **8** admonish, chastise, reproach **9** reprimand **10** discipline, take to task

chastened 7 humbled **8** contrite, penitent **9** repentant **10** remorseful **18** conscience-stricken

chastise 4 beat, flog, whip **5** chide, roast, scold, spank, strap **6** berate, punish, rebuke, thrash **7** censure, chasten, correct, reprove, scourge, upbraid **8** admonish, call down, penalize, reproach **9** castigate, criticize, reprimand **10** discipline, take to task, tongue-lash **15** call on the carpet **16** fulminate against, haul over the coals

chastisement 10 correction, discipline, punishment **11** castigation **12** reprimanding

chastity 6 purity **8** celibacy **9** innocence, virginity **10** abstinence, continence, singleness **12** bachelorhood, spinsterhood **14** abstemiousness
　goddess of: 5 Diana, Fauna **7** Artemis, Bona Dea

chasuble 6 casual **7** garment **8** vestment

Chasuble, Reverend Canon
　character in: 27 The Importance of Being Earnest
　author: 5 Wilde

chat 3 gab, rap **4** talk **5** prate **7** chatter, palaver, prattle **8** chitchat, converse **10** chew the fat, chew the rag, rap session **11** talk session **12** conversation **13** confabulation **16** heart-to-heart talk

chateau 4 wine **6** castle, estate **7** mansion **8** chatelet **12** country house

Chateaubriand, Francois Rene
　author of: 4 Rene **5** Atala **10** Los Natchez, The Martyrs **19** Memoires d'Outre-tombe **24** Memoirs from Beyond the Tomb

Chateau d'If
　prison in: 21 The Count of Monte Cristo
　author: 5 Dumas (pere)

Chateaupers, Phoebus de
　character in: 23 The Hunchback of Notre Dame
　author: 4 Hugo

chattel 4 gear **6** things **7** effects **8** movables **9** trappings **10** belongings **13** accoutrements, paraphernalia **15** personal effects **19** personal possessions

chatter 3 gas **4** blab, talk **5** clank, click, prate **6** babble, gabble, gibber, gossip, jabber, patter **7** blabber, blather, clatter, palaver, prattle, talking, twaddle **8** blabbing, chitchat, idle talk, talk idly **11** confabulate **14** chitterchatter

chatterbox 6 gabber, gasbag, gossip, talker **7** babbler, tattler, windbag **8** jabberer, prattler, tell tale **9** chatterer **10** talebearer, tattle tale **12** blabbermouth, blatherskite, hot-air artist **13** chatterbasket

chatty 5 gabby, gassy, gushy, talky, windy **7** gossipy, gushing, prating, verbose, voluble **8** babbling, chatting, effusive **9** garrulous, jabbering, talkative **10** blabbering, long-winded, loquacious **11** loose-lipped **12** loose-tongued **13** tongue-wagging

Chaucer, Geoffrey
author of: 18 The Canterbury Tales, Troilus and Criseyde **19** The Book of the Duchess **20** The Legend of Good Women, The Parlement of Fowles

Chauchoin, Claudette Lily
real name of: 16 Claudette Colbert

chauffeur 6 driver

chaussure 4 boot, shoe **8** footwear

chauvinism 8 jingoism **10** flag-waving, militarism, patriotism **11** nationalism **15** ethnocentricity, superpatriotism

cheap 4 base, easy, mean, poor **5** close, gaudy, petty, tacky, tight **6** common, flashy, meager, paltry, shabby, shoddy, sordid, stingy, tawdry, trashy, two-bit, vulgar **7** ignoble, immoral, miserly **8** costless, gimcrack, indecent, inferior, wretched **9** inelegant, low-priced, penurious, worthless **10** despicable, economical, effortless, in bad taste, reasonable, second-rate **11** inexpensive, tightfisted **12** contemptible

Cheaper by the Dozen
author: 14 Frank B Gilbreth (with Ernestine Gilbreth Carey)

cheat 3 con, gyp **4** bilk, dupe, fake, foil, fool, gull, hoax, rook, take **5** cozen, crook, fraud, quack, shark, trick **6** baffle, betray, defeat, delude, dodger, escape, fleece, humbug, outwit, thwart **7** deceive, defraud, mislead, swindle **8** chiseler, deceiver, hoodwink, imposter, impostor, swindler **9** bamboozle, charlatan, con artist, frustrate, trickster, victimize **10** circumvent, mountebank **11** shortchange **13** break the rules, doublecrosser

check 3 bar, end, fit, gag, tab **4** curb, halt, hold, jibe, mesh, rein, slow, stay, stop, test **5** agree, block, brake, chime, choke, limit, probe, stall, study, tally **6** arrest, bridle, impede, look at, muzzle, peruse, rein in, retard, review, search, survey, thwart **7** barrier, conform, control, examine, explore, harness, inhibit, inspect, perusal, prevent, smother **8** hold back, look into, look over, obstacle, obstruct, restrain, scrutiny, stoppage,

suppress **9** cessation, constrain, frustrate, harmonize, hindrance, restraint **10** circumvent, constraint, correspond, impediment, inspection, limitation, prevention, repression, scrutinize **11** examination, exploration, investigate, obstruction, prohibition, restriction, take stock of **13** investigation **18** bring to a standstill

checkered 4 pied **6** fitful, motley, seesaw, uneven, varied **7** checked, dappled, mottled, piebald **9** irregular, up-and-down **10** inconstant, variegated **11** fluctuating, vacillating **12** particolored

checkmate 4 rout, stop **6** corner, defeat, outwit, stymie, thwart **8** chess win, deadlock **9** frustrate, overthrow **11** countermove

cheder, heder 12 Jewish school

cheek 4 jowl **5** brass, nerve **8** audacity, boldness, temerity **9** arrogance, brashness, impudence, insolence **10** brazenness, effrontery **11** forwardness **12** impertinence

cheep 4 peep **5** chirp, tweet **7** chirrup, chitter, twitter

cheer 3 cry, fun, joy, ole, rah **4** glee, hail, hope, root, warm, yell **5** bravo, shout **6** assure, buoy up, gaiety, hooray, hurrah, huzzah, shriek, uplift **7** acclaim, animate, comfort, delight, enliven, fortify, gladden, hearten, inspire, revelry **8** brighten, buoyance, buoyancy, gladness, optimism, pleasure, reassure, vivacity **9** animation, assurance, encourage, festivity, geniality, joviality, merriment, rejoicing **10** joyfulness, jubilation, liveliness **11** acclamation, high spirits, hopefulness, merrymaking, reassurance **13** encouragement

cheerful 3 gay **4** airy, glad **5** happy, jolly, merry, sunny **6** blithe, breezy, bright, cheery, elated, jaunty, jovial, joyful, joyous, lively **7** buoyant, gleeful **8** gladsome, pleasant **9** agreeable, sparkling, sprightly **10** optimistic **11** in high humor **12** high-spirited, lighthearted

cheerfulness 5 gaity **7** jollity **8** buoyancy, optimism **9** joviality, merriment **10** brightness, cheeriness **11** high spirits **16** lightheartedness

cheerless 3 sad **4** dull, glum, gray, grim **5** bleak **6** dismal, dreary, gloomy, morose, rueful, solemn, somber, sullen, woeful **7** austere, doleful, forlorn, joyless, sunless, unhappy **8** dejected, desolate, dolorous, downcast, funereal, mournful **9** miserable, saturnine, woebegone **10** depressing, despondent, dispirited, lugubrious, melancholy, spiritless, uninviting **11** comfortless, downhearted **12** disconsolate, heavy-hearted

Cheers

location: 3 bar **6** Boston
character: 4 Norm **5** Cliff, Coach, Woody **5** Lilith **7** Rebecca **9** Sam Malone **13** Carla Tortelli, Diane Chambers
cast: 9 Ted Danson **11** George Wendt, Rhea Perlman, Shelley Long **12** Kirstie Alley **13** Kelsey Grammer **14** Woody Harrelson **16** John Ratzenberger

cheer up 5 elate, pep up **6** buoy up **7** comfort, enliven, hearten **8** brighten, inspirit **9** bolster up, encourage **18** bolster one's spirits

cheery 3 gay **5** happy, jolly, merry, sunny **6** bright, joyful **9** sprightly **12** lighthearted

Cheeryble Brothers
nephew: 5 Frank
characters in: 16 Nicholas Nickleby
author: 7 Dickens

cheese
French: 7 fromage
kind: 4 bleu, blue, brie, edam, feta, jack **5** brick, colby, cream, gouda, Swiss **6** romano, samsoe **7** cheddar, cottage, fontina, gjetost, gruyere, limburg, munster, ricotta, sapsago, stilton **8** American, bel paese, cheshire, emmental, muenster, parmesan, port wine, raclette **9** camembert, jarlsberg, limburger, port salut, provolone, roquefort **10** caerphilly, Danish blue, Gloucester, gorgonzola, mozzarella, neufchatel **11** emmenthaler, liederkranz, petit suisse, port du salut, wensleydale **12** monterey jack

Cheever, John
author of: 8 Falconer **10** Bullet Park **16** The Enormous Radio, The World of Apples **17** The Wapshot Scandal **19** The Wapshot Chronicle **20** The Way Some People Live **22** Oh What a Paradise It Seems

Chekhov, Anton
author of: 6 Ivanov **10** The Sea Gull, Uncle Vanya **15** The Three Sisters **16** The Cherry Orchard

chemical compound 4 acid, base, enol **5** amide, amine, ester, imide **6** isomar, ketone **8** aldehyde

chemical symbols
actinium: 2 Ac
aluminum: 2 Al
antimony: 2 Sb
argon: 2 Ar
arsenic: 2 As
barium: 2 Ba
boron: 1 B
bromine: 2 Br
cadmium: 2 Cd
calcium: 2 Ca
carbon: 1 C
chlorine: 2 Cl
chromium: 2 Cr
cobalt: 2 Co
columbium: 2 Cb

copper: 2 Cu
fluorine: 1 F
gold: 2 Au
hafnium: 2 Hf
helium: 2 He
hydrogen: 1 H
iodine: 1 I
iron: 2 Fe
krypton: 2 Kr
lead: 2 Pb
lithium: 2 Li
magnesium: 2 Mg
manganese: 2 Mn
mercury: 2 Hg
molybdenum: 2 Mo
neon: 2 Ne
nickel: 2 Ni
nitrogen: 1 N
oxygen: 1 O
phosphorus: 1 P
platinum: 2 Pt
plutonium: 2 Pu
potassium: 1 K
radium: 2 Ra
radon: 2 Rn
rhodium: 2 Rh
rubidium: 2 Rb
silicon: 2 Si
silver: 2 Ag
sodium: 2 Na
sulfur: 1 S
thorium: 2 Th
tin: 2 Sn
titanium: 2 Ti
tungsten: 1 W
uranium: 1 U
xenon: 2 Xe
zinc: 2 Zn
zirconium: 2 Zr

chemise 4 slip **5** dress, shift, shirt, smock **6** blouse **7** garment **8** camisole, lingerie, unbelted **12** undergarment

chemist
American: 4 Urey **5** Tatum **6** Carver **7** Axelrod, Lipmann, Pauling **8** Kornberg, Langmuir, McMillan **9** Carothers **10** Baekeland
British: 4 Davy **5** Boyle, Chain, Soddy **6** Dalton, Ramsay **7** Faraday **8** Smithson **9** Cavendish, Priestley, Wollaston
Dutch: 4 Hoff
French: 5 Curie, Le Bel **6** Cuvier, Dulong **7** Pasteur **9** Gay-Lussac, Lavoisier **10** Berthollet **11** Joliot-Curie
German: 4 Hahn **5** Krebs **6** Baeyer, Wohler **7** Glauber, Ostwald
Italian: 8 Avogadro
Russian: 9 Mendeleev **10** Mendeleyev
Scottish: 5 Dewar
Swedish: 7 Scheele **9** Arrhenius, Berzelius
Swiss: 6 Muller

Chemosh 10 Moabite god
Chennault, Claire L
served in: 4 WWII **15** Sino-Japanese War

commander of: 12 Flying Tigers
general in: 12 Army Air Force
air advisor to: 13 Chiang Kai-shek
cherchez la femme 15 look for the woman
cheri, cherie 4 dear **10** sweetheart
cherish 4 love **5** honor, nurse, prize, value **6** dote on, esteem, revere, succor **7** care for, idolize, nourish, nurture, shelter, sustain **8** hold dear, treasure, venerate **10** appreciate, take care of
cherished 4 dear **5** loved **7** beloved, darling, dearest **8** favorite, held dear, precious **9** treasured
Cherokee
language family: 9 Iroquoian
location: 7 Alabama, Georgia **8** Oklahoma, Virginia **9** Tennessee **13** North Carolina, South Carolina
associated with: 12 Trail of Tears
scholar: 7 Sequoya
cherry
varieties: 3 pie, pin, rum **4** bing, bird, duke, fire, sand, sour, wild **5** black, brush, choke, dwarf, Higan, Naden, sweet **6** bitter, Brazil, ground, Indian, Madden, Oregon, Taiwan, winter **7** bastard, Cayenne, Morello, Nanking, Potomac, prairie, rosebud, sargent, Spanish, St Lucie, wild red, Windsor, Yoshino **8** Barbados, Catalina, oriental, perfumed, Suriname **9** christmas, cornelian, evergreen, Jerusalem, wild black **10** west indian **11** downy ground, Hansen's bush, holly-leaved, western sand **12** clammy ground, European bird, Japanese bush, purple ground **13** European dwarf **14** European ground, false Jerusalem, purple-leaf sand **15** Australian brush **17** Japanese cornelian, Japanese flowering, north Japanese hill
drink: 6 kirsch
cherry brandy 6 kirsch **12** Peter Heering
Cherry Orchard, The
author: 12 Anton Chekhov
character: 4 Anya, Gaev **5** Fiers, Varya, Yasha **7** Pischin **8** Dunyasha, Lopakhin, Trofimov **9** Charlotta **16** Madame Ranevskaya
cherub 4 amor **5** angel, child, cupid, youth **6** moppet **8** amoretto, cherubim **13** heavenly being
cherubic 7 angelic **8** innocent **9** spiritual
Cherubin
character in: 19 The Marriage of Figaro
author: 12 Beaumarchais
chervil
botanical name: 20 Anthriscus cerefolium
origin: 6 Europe, Russia

use: 4 soup **5** salad **11** fines herbes, potato salad
Chesapeake
author: 13 James Michener
Cheshire Cat
character in: 28 Alice's Adventures in Wonderland
author: 7 Carroll
chess
also called: 9 Royal Game
chess champion: 3 Tal **4** Euwe, Fine **6** Karpov, Lasker, Morphy **7** Fischer, Kashdan, Smyslov, Spassky **8** Alekhine, Kasparov, Philador, Steinitz **9** Anderssen, Botvinnik, Petrosian, Reshevsky **10** Capablanca
French: 6 echecs
German: 11 schachspiel
horizontal rows: 4 rank
international chess federation: 4 FIDE
patron goddess/muse: 6 Caissa
piece: 4 king, pawn, rook **5** queen **6** bishop, castle, knight **8** chessman, material
Russian: 8 shakhmat
Spanish: 7 Ajedrez
term: 3 pin **4** fork, hole **5** check, tempo **6** center **7** isolani, outpost **8** castling, majority, open file, queening, zugzwang **9** checkmate, en passant, promotion **10** fianchetto **11** zwischenzug
tied game: 4 draw **9** stalemate
vertical rows: 4 file
chest
Italian: 5 petto
Chester, Edward
character in: 12 Barnaby Rudge
author: 7 Dickens
chesterfield 4 coat, sofa **5** couch **8** overcoat **9** davenport
Chesterton, G K (Gilbert Keith)
author of: 20 The Man Who Was Thursday **24** The Napoleon of Notting Hill **25** The Innocence of Father Brown
chestnut 8 Castanea
varieties: 4 Cape, Wild **5** Horse, Water **6** Guiana, Marron **7** Chinese, Spanish **8** American, Eurasian, European, Japanese, Red horse **10** Dwarf horse, Moreton Bay **11** Common horse **12** Chinese water **13** European horse, Japanese horse **15** California horse
chestnut-colored 6 auburn, russet, sienna **8** cinnamon, nut-brown **11** golden-brown, rust-colored **12** reddish-brown
chest of drawers 5 chest **6** bureau, lowboy **7** cabinet, commode, dresser, highboy, tallboy **10** chiffonier
cheval 5 horse
chevalier 4 lord **5** cadet, noble **6** knight **7** gallant **8** cavalier
Chevalier, Maurice

born: 5 Paris **6** France
roles: 4 Gigi **5** Fanny **6** Can-Can **13** The Love Parade, The Merry Widow **18** Love in the Afternoon

chew 4 gnaw **5** champ, crush, grind, munch **6** crunch, nibble **8** ruminate **9** masticate

Chew
character in: 21 The Master of Ballantrae
author: 9 Stevenson

chewing-out 6 rebuke **7** censure, chiding, reproof **8** reproach, scolding **9** reprimand **10** bawling-out, upbraiding **11** castigation, reprobation **12** dressing-down, remonstrance **13** tongue-lashing

chew noisily 4 gnaw **5** chomp, gnash, grind, munch **6** crunch

chew out 5 scold **6** berate, rail at, rebuke **7** bawl out, reprove, upbraid **8** reproach **9** castigate, reprimand **10** take to task, tongue-lash **14** read the riot act

chew the fat 3 gab, gas, jaw, rap, yak **4** blab, chat, chin, talk **5** prate **6** gossip, patter **7** blather, chatter, palaver, prattle, twaddle **8** chitchat, converse, talk idly **10** chew the rag **11** confabulate **14** chitterchatter

chew the rag 4 talk

Cheyenne
language family: 9 Algonkian **10** Algonquian
location: 6 Platte **7** Montana, Wyoming **8** Oklahoma, Red River **9** Minnesota **11** South Dakota
allied with: 7 Arapaho

Cheyenne
character: 6 Smitty **13** Cheyenne Bodie
cast: 7 L Q Jones **11** Clint Walker

chez 4 with **11** at the home of

Chiang Kai-shek
leader of: 5 China **6** Taiwan
ally: 9 Sun Yat-sen
party: 10 Kuomintang **11** Nationalist
defeated by: 10 Communists
wife: 12 Soong Mei-ling

Chibcha (Muisca)
location: 6 Bogota, Panama **8** Colombia **12** South America
associated with: 8 El Dorado

Chibchan
language family: 13 Macro-Chibchan
group: 4 Cuna, Paya, Rama **5** Lenca, Xinca **7** Chibcha

chic 4 tony **5** natty, ritzy, smart, swank **6** classy, modish, snazzy, swanky **7** elegant, stylish, voguish **11** fashionable

Chicago
author: 12 Carl Sandburg

Chicago
airport: 5 O'Hare **6** Midway
baseball team: 4 Cubs **8** White Sox

basketball team: 5 Bulls
downtown area: 4 Loop
football team: 5 Bears
fort: 8 Dearborn
hockey team: 10 Black Hawks
lake: 4 Wolf **7** Calumet **8** Michigan
landmark: 10 Meigs Field, Sears Tower **12** Board of Trade, Comiskey Park, Humboldt Park, Soldier Field, Wrigley Field **13** Shedd Aquarium **15** Lincoln Monument, Merchandise Mart, Newberry Library, Wrigley Building **16** Adler Planetarium **17** Holy Name Cathedral, John Hancock Center **18** Mercantile Exchange, Prudential Building **20** Midwest Stock Exchange **21** Art Institute of Chicago **23** Museum of Contemporary Art **26** Museum of Science and Industry **27** Field Museum of Natural History
mayor: 5 Byrne, Daley **10** Washington
nickname: 9 Windy City
river: 7 Chicago **10** Des Plaines
street: 11 Wacker Drive **13** Chicago Skyway **14** Lake Shore Drive
university: 6 DePaul, Loyola **9** Roosevelt **12** Northwestern **19** University of Chicago **29** Illinois Institute of Technology

chicanery 4 ruse, wile **5** craft, fraud, guile **6** deceit, duping **7** cunning, gulling, knavery, roguery **8** artifice, cozenage, trickery, villainy **9** deception, duplicity, rascality, sophistry **10** craftiness, hocus-pocus, humbuggery, subterfuge **11** hoodwinking **12** pettifoggery **13** double-dealing

chichi 4 arty **5** fussy, showy **6** flashy, frilly, garish, prissy, vulgar **7** finical, pompous, splashy **8** affected, gimcrack, overnice, precious, sissyish **9** arty-tarty, grandiose, nasty-nice **10** flamboyant **11** overrefined, pretentious **12** artsy-craftsy, ostentatious

chick
group of: 5 brood **6** clutch

Chickasaw
language family: 10 Muskhogean
location: 8 Oklahoma **9** Tennessee **11** Mississippi
related to: 7 Choctaw
member of: 19 Five Civilized Tribes

chicken, chickenhearted 3 hen **4** cock, fowl **5** layer, timid **6** afraid, coward, craven, pullet, scared, yellow **7** caitiff, dastard, fearful, gutless, rooster **8** cowardly, poltroon, timorous **9** flinching, fraidy-cat, shrinking **11** lily-livered, yellow-belly **12** fainthearted **13** pusillanimous, yellowbellied **22** showing the white feather

chickenheartedness 8 timidity **9** cowardice **10** yellowness **11** fearfulness, poltroonery **12** timorousness **13** pusillanimity **16** faintheartedness

chide 5 scold **6** berate, rebuke **7** cen-

sure, chasten, reprove, upbraid **8** admonish, denounce, reproach **9** criticize, find fault, reprimand **10** take to task

chief 3 key **4** boss, head, lord, main **5** first, major, prime, ruler **6** leader, master, ruling **7** captain, highest, leading, monarch, primary, supreme **8** cardinal, chairman, crowning, director, dominant, foremost, greatest, overlord, overseer **9** chieftain, commander, governing, number-one, paramount, potentate, principal, sovereign, uppermost **10** prevailing, ringleader, supervisor **11** outstanding, predominant **12** preponderant **13** administrator

chief good
Latin: 11 summum bonum

chiefly 5 first **6** mainly, mostly **8** above all expressly, in the main, most of all, primarily **10** especially **11** principally **12** particularly **13** predominantly

chieftan 4 boss, head **6** leader **7** captain, head man

chiffonier 6 bureau **7** dresser **8** cupboard **14** chest of drawers

chignon 3 bun **4** knot, roll **6** hairdo **9** hairpiece, hairstyle

child 3 boy, kid, lad, son, tad, tot **4** baby, girl, lass, tyke **5** youth **6** infant, moppet, rug rat **7** toddler **8** daughter, juvenile **9** little one, offspring, youngster

childbearing 5 birth **11** parturition
childbirth 8 delivery **11** confinement, parturition
French: 12 accouchement
goddess of: 4 Upis **5** Parca **6** Lucina, Matuta **7** Artemis **8** Ilithyia **10** Eileithyia

Childe Harold's Pilgrimage
author: 21 George Gordon Lord Byron

Childe Roland to the Dark Tower Came
author: 14 Robert Browning

childhood 5 youth **7** boyhood **8** girlhood **10** school days **11** adolescence, nursery days

childish 5 naive, silly **6** callow, simple **7** asinine, babyish, foolish, puerile **8** immature, juvenile **9** infantile **10** adolescent

childlike 8 childish, immature, innocent **9** ingenuous

child prodigy 7 quiz kid, whiz kid
German: 10 Wunderkind

children 4 boys, kids, sons, tads, tots **5** girls, issue, young **6** babies, result, youth **7** infants, product, progeny **9** daughters, juveniles **11** descendants

Children of God
author: 12 Vardis Fisher

Children of Paradise

director: 11 Marcel Carne
cast: 7 Arletty **11** Albert Remay **14** Pierre Brasseur **17** Jean-Louis Barrault

Child's Garden of Verses, A
author: 20 Robert Louis Stevenson

Chile
other name: 6 Tchile
name means: 21 deepest part of the Earth
capital/largest city: 8 Santiago
others: 4 Boco, Cuya, Lebu, Lota, Ocoa, Tome **5** Angol, Arica, Cobya, Talca **6** Arauco, Calama, Curico, Gatico, Osorno, Ovalle, Serena, Temuco, Vicuna, Yumbel, Yungay **7** Caldera, Chillan, Copiapo, Iquique, Valdiva **8** Coquimbo, Rancagua, Santiago, Vallenar **9** Cauquenes **10** Concepcion, Coquembana, Valparaiso, Vina del Mar **11** Antofagasta, Puerto Montt, Punta Arenas, San Bernardo
measure: 4 vara **5** legua, linea **6** cuadra, fanega
monetary unit: 4 peso **5** libra **6** condor, escudo
weight: 5 grano, libra **7** quintal
island: 3 Luz **4** Prat **5** Byron, Guafo, Hoste, Mocha, Nueva, Nunez, Vidal **6** Chiloe, Chonos, Dawson, Easter, Lennox, Piazzi, Picton, Quilan, Riesco, Stosch, Talcan **7** Angamos, Campana, Hanover, Hermite, Pajaros, Refugio, Tranqui **8** Chauques, Clarence, Huamblin, Nalcayec, Navarino, Traiguen **13** Juan Fernandez **14** Tierra del Fuego
lake: 5 Ranco **6** Yelcho **7** Puyehue, Rupanco **8** Cochrane **10** General Paz, Llanquihue **11** Buenos Aires
mountain: 4 Maca, Toro **5** Chato, Maipo, Maipu, Paine, Potro, Pular, Torre, Yogan **6** Apiwan, Burney, Conico, Jervis, Poquis, Rincon **7** Chaltel, Copiapo, Fitzroy, Palpana, Velluda **8** Cochrane, Tronador, Yanteles **9** Tupungato
highest point: 13 Ojos del Salado
river: 3 Loa **4** Laja, Yali **5** Alhue, Azapa, Bravo, Bueno, Elqui, Lauca, Lluta, Maipo, Maule, Puelo, Rahue, Rapel, Stata, Vitor **6** Biobio, Camina, Choapa, Choros, Cisnes, Colina, Huasco, Limari, Morado, Palena, Poscua, Tolten **7** Copiapo **8** Valdivia
sea: 7 Pacific
physical features:
  bay: 4 Cook, Eyre, Nena, Tarn **5** Lomas, Otway, Sarco **6** Darwin, Inutil, Moreno, Stokes, Tongoy **7** Dyneley, Inglesa, Skyring **8** Desolate
  cape: 4 Dyer, Horn **6** Choros, Falsos, Hornos, Quilan, Tablas **7** Deseado **10** Tres Montes
  channel: 5 Ancho, Cheap **6** Beagle **8** Cockburn, Moraleda
  desert: 7 Atacama

  gulf: 5 Ancud, Guafo, Penas **6** Arauco
  isthmus: 5 Ofqui
  peninsula: 5 Hardy, Lacuy **6** Taitao, Tumbes
  point: 4 Toro **5** Gallo, Liles, Lobos, Loros, Morro, Talca, Tetas, Vieja **6** Cachos, Galera, Molles **7** Angamos, Lavapie
  strait: 6 Nelson **8** Magellan
  volcano: 5 Lanin, Maipo **6** Antuco, Llaima, Oyahue, Tacora **7** Peteroa, Socomap
people: 3 Ona **4** Auca, Inca, Onan **6** Arauca, Chango, Yahgan **7** Mapuche, mestizo, Moluche, Pampean, Patagon, Puegian, Ranquel **8** Alikuluf, Picunche, Tsonecan
  author: 5 Bello **6** Donoso, Neruda **7** Mistral
  conqueror: 7 Valdiva
  explorer: 8 Magellan
  leader: 7 Allende **8** O'Higgins, Pinochet **9** San Martin **10** Alessandri
language: 7 Spanish
religion: 13 Roman Catholic
places:
  copper mine: 12 Chuquicamata
  resort: 8 Portillo **10** Vina del Mar
possession: 12 Easter Island **20** Juan Fernandez Islands
feature:
  cowboy: 5 huaso
  dance: 5 cueca **6** pequen **9** resbalosa
  shrub: 5 litre
  slum: 9 callempas
  tree: 5 rauli
  wind instrument: 4 sicu
food:
  drink: 5 pisco **6** chicha
  hot red pepper: 3 aji
  meat pie: 8 empanada
  soup: 7 cazuela **8** caldillo

chile peppers *see* **15** capsicum peppers

chill, chilly 3 icy, nip, raw **4** bite, cold, cool, keen **5** aloof, brisk, crisp, fever, harsh, nippy, sharp, stiff, stony **6** arctic, biting, bitter, frigid, frosty, frozen, wintry **7** callous, coolish, cutting, glacial, hostile, iciness, rawness, shivery **8** coolness, uncaring **9** crispness, frigidity, sharpness, unfeeling **10** forbidding, frostiness, unfriendly **11** indifferent, passionless, penetrating **12** unresponsive

chilled 4 cold, iced **6** cooled, frozen **7** frosted **8** hardened **10** dispirited **11** discouraged **12** refrigerated

chilling 3 icy, raw **5** nippy, on ice **6** frigid **7** bracing, cooling **10** unfriendly

Chillingworth, Roger
character in: 16 The Scarlet Letter
author: 9 Hawthorne

chime 4 gong, peal, ring, toll **5** knell, sound **6** jingle, tinkle **7** pealing, ring-

ing **8** carillon, ding-dong, tinkling, tollings **10** set of bells **14** tintinnabulate **16** tintinnabulation

Chimene
character in: 6 The Cid
author: 9 Corneille

chimera 5 dream, fancy **6** bubble, mirage **7** fantasy, monster, phantom **8** daydream, delusion, idle whim, illusion **9** pipe dream **10** self-deceit, shemonster **12** will-o'-the-wisp **13** castle in Spain, fool's paradise, hallucination, self-deception **14** castle in the air **24** figment of one's imagination

Chimera
form: 7 monster
father: 6 Typhon
mother: 7 Echidna
breathes: 4 fire

Chimera
author: 9 John Barth

chimerical 6 absurd, unreal **7** utopian **8** delusive, ethereal, fabulous, fanciful, illusory, mythical quixotic **9** fantastic, imaginary, visionary **10** impossible, phantasmal, **11** nonexistent

chimney 4 flue, tube, vent **5** cleft, gully, spout, stack **6** funnel, hearth **7** opening **9** stovepipe **10** smokestack

chimpanzee 3 ape **6** animal, baboon, monkey

chin 3 gab, jaw, rap **4** chat, talk **7** chatter, palaver **8** chitchat, converse **10** chew the fat, chew the rag **11** confabulate

china 6 dishes, plates **7** pottery **8** crockery **9** chinaware, porcelain, stoneware, tableware **11** ceramicware, earthenware **14** cups and saucers

China
other name: 3 PRC **13** Middle Kingdom **14** Flowery Kingdom **22** People's Republic of China
capital: 6 Peking **7** Beijing
largest city: 8 Shanghai
others: 3 Bai, Noh **4** Ahpa, Amoy, Fuyu, Guma, Hami, Huma, Ipin, Kian, Kisi, Lini, Loho, Luta, Moho, Moyu, Niya, Noho, Omin, Rima, Saka, Sian, Taku, Tali, Tayu, Wuhu, Yaan **5** Chiai, Fusin, Kirin, Koklu, Linyu, Macao, Penki, Shasi, Soche, Taian, Talai, Tihwa, Tuyun, Wuhan, Wusih, Yenan, Yenki, Yulin, Yumen **6** Anshan, Antung, Canton, Dairen, Fuchau, Fuchow, Fushun, Hankow, Harbin, Ilhasa, Kalgan, Loyang, Lushun, Mukden, Nanhai, Ningpo, Singan, Sining, Taipei, Tsinan, Yangku, Yunnan **7** Fuskhih, Hanyang, Kunming, Lanchow, Lioyang, Mengtze, Nanking, Nanning, Paoshan, Peiping, Soochow, Taiyuan, Tatshan, Urumchi, Urumsti, Waichow, Wuchang, Yenping **8** Chinchow, Fengkiek, Fengtien, Hangchow, Kingchow, Nanchang,

Shanghai, Shenyang, Siangtan, Tientsin, Tungchow, Wanchuan, Wanhsien **9** Chungking, Kiangling, Tsingyuan **10** Chiangling, Port Arthur

school: 5 Futan **6** Peking **7** Nanking **8** Hangchow **9** Sun Yat-sen **16** Cheng-tu Technical

division:

  province: 5 Honan, Hunan, Hupei, Kansu **6** Anhwei, Fukien, Shansi, Shensi, Yunnan **7** Kiangsi, Kiangsu **8** Chekiang, Kweichow, Shantung, Szechwan, Tientsin, Tsinghai **9** Kwangtung, Manchuria

measure: 3 cho, fan, fen, pau, tou, tun, yan, yin **4** chek, chih, fang, kish, papa, quei, shih, teke, tsan, tsun **5** catty, chang, ching, sheng, shing **6** chupak, gungli, kungho, kungmu, tching **7** kungfen, kungyin **8** kungchih, kungshih, **9** kungching

monetary unit: 4 cash, cent, fyng, mace, tael, tiao, yuan **5** sycee **12** jen nin piao pu

weight: 3 fan, fen, hao, kin, ssu, tan, yin **4** chee, chin, dong, shih, tael, tsin **5** catty, chien, picul, tchin, tsien **6** kungli **7** haikwan, kungfen, kungssu, kungtun **8** kungchin **9** candareen **10** kupingtael

island: 4 Amoy **5** Macao, Matsu, Namki, Taipa **6** Chusan, Hainan, Pratas, Quemoy, Taiwan, Tinian, Yuhwan **7** Coloane, Formosa, Hungtow, Tungsha **8** Ching Hai, Chouchan, Kulangsu

lake: 3 Tai **4** Chao, Na-mu **5** Kaoyu, Oling, Telli **6** Bamtso, Bornor, Ebinor, Erhhai, Khanka, Lopnor, Namtso, Poyang **7** Chaling, Hungtse, Karanor, Kokonor **8** Hulunnor, Montcalm, Taroktso, Tellinor, Tienchih, Tsinghai, Tungting

sea: 6 Yellow **9** East China **10** South China

physical features:

  bay: 7 Laichow **8** Hangchow
  cape: 7 Olwanpi
  channel: 5 Bashi
  desert: 4 Gobi **5** Ordos, Shamo **7** Alashan **10** Takla Makan
  dry lake: 6 Lopnor
  gulf: 5 Pohai **6** Chihli, Tonkin **7** Pechili **9** Liaotung
  peninsula: 6 Leichu **7** Luichow **8** Liaotung
  plateau: 5 Loess **7** Tibetan
  port: 4 Amoy, Wuhu **5** Aigun, Shasi **6** Antung, Canton, Chefoo, Dairen, Ichang, Ningpo, Pakhoi, Swatow, Wuchow **7** Foochow, Hunchun, Luichow, Nanking, Samshui, Santuao, Soochow, Wenchow, Yinkkow, Yungkia **8** Changsha, Hangchow, Kiukiang, Kongmoon, Shanghai, Tengyueh, Tientsin, Tsingtao, Wanhsien **9** Kwangchow, Weihaiwei **10** Tsing-

kiang
  strait: 6 Hainan, Taiwan **7** Formosa

people: 3 Han, Yis **4** Huis, Lolo, Miao, Pu-is **5** Hakka, Hoklo, Seres, Sinic **6** Cataia, Chuang, Johnny, Korean, Manchu, Mongol, Serian, Uighun **7** Sinaean, Tibetan

  leader: 9 Sun Yat-sen, Zhou Enlai **10** Kublai Khan, Mao Tse-tung **11** Genghis Khan **12** Deng Xiaoping **13** Chiang Kai-shek

  philosopher: 6 Lao-tzu **9** Confucius

language: 7 Chinese **8** Mandarin, Shanghai **9** Cantonese

religion: 5 Islam **6** Taoism **8** Buddhism **12** Christianity, Confucianism

place:

  palace: 6 Summer **8** Imperial **13** Forbidden City
  ruins: 9 Ming Tombs
  square: 9 Tiananmen
  wonder: 9 Great Wall

feature:

  boat: 4 junk
  conspirators: 10 Gang of Four
  dynasty: 3 Han, Sui **4** Chou, Ch'in, Ming, Sung, T'ang **5** Ch'ing, Shang **6** Manchu
  military academy: 7 whompoa
  watercolor: 8 shan shiu

China Syndrome, The
  director: 12 James Bridges
  cast: 9 Jane Fonda **10** Jack Lemmon, Scott Brady **14** Michael Douglas
  setting: 17 nuclear power plant

Chinatown
  director: 13 Roman Polanski
  cast: 10 John Huston **11** Faye Dunaway **13** Jack Nicholson
  Oscar for: 10 screenplay

chinaware 6 dishes, plates **7** pottery **8** crockery **9** porcelain, stoneware, tableware **11** ceramicware, earthenware **14** cups and saucers

chine 5 spine **6** dorsum **8** backbone

Chinese book of divination 6 I Ching

Chingachgook
  character in: 13 The Pathfinder **20** The Last of the Mohicans
  author: 6 Cooper

chink 3 cut, gap **4** gash, hole, rent, rift, ring, slit **5** break, clank, cleft, clink, crack, fault, split **6** breach, jangle, jingle, rattle, tinkle **7** crevice, fissure, opening **8** aperture

Chinook (Flathead)
  language family: 9 Chinookan
  location: 7 Pacific **10** Washington
  ritual: 15 head deformation

Chinookan
  tribe: 7 Chinook **8** Flathead

chintzy 5 cheap, close, dowdy, tacky, tatty, tight **6** frowzy, frumpy, shabby, sleazy, stingy **7** miserly **8** grudging, schlocky, stinting **9** niggardly, penuri-

ous **11** closefisted **12** parsimonious **13** penny-pinching

chip 3 bit, cut, hew **4** chop, gash, hack, nick **5** chunk, crumb, flake, scrap, shred, slice, split, wafer **6** chisel, morsel, paring, sliver **7** cutting, shaving, whittle **8** fragment, splinter

chipmunk 4 Chip, Dale **6** chippy, gopher, rodent **8** chipmuck, squirrel **14** ground squirrel **16** chipping squirrel

chipper 3 gay **4** pert, spry **5** alive, brisk, peppy **6** frisky, jaunty, lively **8** animated, carefree, cheerful, spirited **9** easygoing, energetic, sprightly, vivacious **12** high- spirited, light-hearted

Chippewa (Ojibwa, Ojibway)
  language family: 9 Algonkian **10** Algonquian
  tribe: 4 Cree **6** Ottawa **8** Chippewa **10** Missisauga
  location: 6 Canada **9** Lake Huron **11** North Dakota **12** Lake Superior, Niagara Falls
  leader: 7 Pontiac

CHiPS
  character: 8 (Officer) Jon Baker **10** (Sgt) Joe Getraer **16** (Officer) Frank (Ponch) Poncherello
  cast: 10 Robert Pine **11** Erik Estrada, Larry Wilcox

Chirico, Giorgio de
  born: 5 Volos **6** Greece
  artwork: 15 Enigma of the Hour **19** Enigma of an Afternoon **21** Enigma of an Autumn Night **22** Nostalgia of the Infinite **32** The Melancholy and Mystery of a Street

Chiron
  also: 7 Cheiron
  form: 7 centaur
  father: 6 Cronos, Cronus, Kronos
  mother: 7 Philyra
  wife: 8 Chariclo
  daughter: 6 Endeis
  grandson: 6 Peleus
  occupation: 7 teacher

chirp 4 peep, sing **5** cheep, chirr, tweet **7** chirrup, chitter, peeping, twitter **8** cheeping

chirrup 4 peep **5** cheep, chirp, tweet **7** chitter, twitter

chisel 3 cut, gyp **4** gull, hoax, rook, tool **5** blade, cheat, slice **6** incise
  type: 4 cape, cold, wood **7** v-shaped

Chisel
  constellation of: 6 Caelum

chiseler 4 fake **5** cheat, fraud, quack **7** cheater **8** swindler

Chislev 16 ninth Hebrew month

chit 3 IOU, tab **4** note **5** check **7** voucher

chitchat 3 gab **4** chat **5** prate **6** drivel, gossip **7** chatter, palaver, prattle **8** converse **9** small talk **10** chew the fat, chew the rag **11** confabulate **13** confabulation

Chitimacha
  language family: 6 Tunica
  location: 9 Louisiana
  noted for: 8 basketry

chitter 4 peep **5** cheep, chirp, tweet **7** chatter, chirrup, twitter

chitter-chatter 3 gab **4** blab **6** babble, drivel, gabble, jabber **7** blabber, prattle, twaddle **8** chitchat **9** jabbering **16** idle conversation

chivalrous 6 polite **7** courtly, gallant **8** mannerly

chivalry 8 courtesy **9** gallantry **10** knighthood, politeness **11** courtliness

Chivery, Young John
  character in: 12 Little Dorrit
  author: 7 Dickens

chivy 3 nag **4** hunt, race **5** annoy, chase, chevy, hound, trail, worry **6** badger, bother, harass, pursue **7** scamper, torment

Chlidanope
  form: 5 Naiad

Chloe
  epithet of: 7 Demeter
  means: 5 green

chloride 7 muriate **8** chemical, compound

chlorine
  chemical symbol: 2 Cl

chocolate 5 brown, candy, cacao, cocoa, drink **6** bon bon **10** confection

Choctaw
  language family: 10 Muskhogean
  location: 7 Alabama **11** Mississippi
  related to: 9 Chickasaw

Choephoroe
  author: 9 Aeschylus
  character: 6 Furies **7** Electra, Orestes, Pylades **9** Aegisthus **12** Clytemnestra

choice 3 say **4** A-one, best, fine, pick, vote **5** array, elite, prime, prize, stock, store, voice **6** better, opting, option, select, supply, tip-top **7** display, special, variety **8** choosing, deciding, decision, superior **9** excellent, exclusive, first-rate, preferred, selection, top drawer **10** assemblage, assortment, collection, consummate, discretion, first-class, preferable, preference, well-chosen **11** alternative, appointment, exceptional, superlative **13** determination, extraordinary

choice food 5 treat **8** delicacy

choicest part
  French: 14 creme de la creme

choir 4 band **5** quire **6** angels, chorus **7** chorale, singers **10** choristers

Choirboys, The
  author: 14 Joseph Wambaugh

choke 3 dam, gag **4** clog, plug **5** block, check, dam up, stuff **6** arrest, bridle, hamper, hinder, impede, plug up, retard, stifle, stop up **7** congest, garrote, inhibit, repress, smother **8** blockade, hold back, obstruct, restrain, strangle,

suppress, throttle **9** constrain, constrict, suffocate **10** asphyxiate

choler 3 ire **4** fury, rage **5** anger, wrath **6** spleen, temper

choleric 3 mad **5** angry, irate, testy, vexed **6** cranky, grumpy, shirty, touchy **7** enraged, furious, grouchy, peevish, waspish **8** snappish, wrathful **9** dyspeptic, indignant, irritable, irascible, splenetic **10** infuriated, short-fused **11** contentious, hot-tempered, ill-tempered, thin-skinned **12** cantankerous, sour-tempered **13** quick-tempered, short-tempered

choose 3 opt **4** like, pick, take, wish **5** adopt, elect **6** decide, desire, intend, opt for, prefer, see fit, select **7** call out, embrace, espouse, extract, fix upon, pick out, resolve **8** decide on, settle on **9** determine, single out **10** be inclined **13** commit oneself **14** make up one's mind

choosy 5 fussy, picky **7** finicky **9** selective **10** fastidious, particular **14** discriminating

chop 3 cut, hew, hit, lop **4** blow, chip, crop, cube, dice, fell, gash, hack **5** cut up, mince, slash, slice, split, swipe, whack **6** cleave, cutlet, stroke, sunder **8** fragment, rib slice **9** cotelette, pulverize

Chopin, Frederic Francois
  born: 6 Poland **12** Zelazowawola
  companion: 10 George Sand
  composer of: 5 Etude **7** Ballade **8** Berceuse, Cat Valse, Dog Valse, Fantasie **9** Ecossaise **10** Barcarolle **11** Minute Valse **15** Andante Spianato, Heroic Polonaise (No 6), Raindrop Prelude, Winter Wind Etude **16** Shepherd Boy Etude **17** Impromptu Fantasie, Rondo a la Krakowiak **18** Revolutionary Etude **20** Butterfly's Wings Etude

choral ode
  Greek: 7 parodos **8** stasimon

chord 4 cord, line, note, tone **5** music, triad **6** accord, string, tendon **7** cadence, emotion, feeling, harmony **9** harmonize

chore 3 job **4** duty, task, work **5** stint **6** burden, errand, strain **8** farm task, small job **10** assignment **13** household task **14** responsibility

choreography 5 dance **12** stage dancing **16** dance composition

chorister 6 singer **7** changer **8** choirboy

chortle 5 laugh **7** chuckle

chorus 5 choir, unity **6** accord, unison **7** concert, concord, refrain **8** glee club, one voice, response **9** antiphony, consensus, unanimity **11** concordance **12** singing group

chosen 5 elite **6** picked, sorted **7** elected **8** selected **9** picked out

Chosen, The
  author: 10 Chaim Potok

Chosen *see* **5** Korea

Chouans, The
  author: 14 Honore de Balzac

chough
  group of: 10 chattering

Chowbok
  character in: 7 Erewhon
  author: 6 Butler

Christ, the *see* **5** Jesus

christen 3 dip, dub **4** name **6** launch **7** baptize, immerse **8** dedicate, sprinkle **9** designate

Christian
  character in: 16 Pilgrim's Progress
  author: 6 Bunyan

Christian, Fletcher
  character in: 17 Mutiny on the Bounty
  authors: 4 Hall **8** Nordhoff

Christian, Linda
  real name: 16 Blanca Rosa Welter
  husband: 11 Tyrone Power **12** Edmund Purdom
  born: 6 Mexico **7** Tampico
  roles: 6 Athena **15** Slaves of Babylon **18** Green Dolphin Street

Christiania
  capital of: 6 Norway
  now called: 4 Oslo

Christie, (Dame) Agatha
  author of: 7 Curtain **11** The Mousetrap **14** Death on the Nile **15** The Mirror Crack'd **16** Ten Little Indians **19** Murder at the Vicarage **20** And Then There Were None **22** What Mrs McGillicuddy Saw! **23** The Murder of Roger Ackroyd **24** Murder on the Orient Express, Witness for the Prosecution **27** The Mysterious Affair at Styles
  character: 6 Mr. Pine **10** Jane Marple **13** Hercule Poirot

Christie, Julie
  born: 5 Assam, India **6** Chukua
  roles: 7 Darling (Oscar), Shampoo **9** Billy Liar **11** Heat and Dust **13** Doctor Zhivago, Fahrenheit 451, Heaven Can Wait **18** McCabe and Mrs Miller **22** Far From the Madding Crowd

Christine
  author: 11 Stephen King

Christmas
  also: 4 Noel, Yule **8** Yuletide
  feature/symbol: 4 bell, star, tree **5** angel, gifts, holly **6** candle, carols, creche, manger, sleigh, wreath **7** Yule log **8** presents **9** evergreen, mistletoe, snowflake, stockings **10** Santa Claus

Christmas, Joe
  character in: 13 Light in August
  author: 8 Faulkner

Christmas Carol, A
  author: 14 Charles Dickens

character: 7 Tiny Tim **8** Fezziwig **11** Bob Cratchit **12** Marley's Ghost **15** Ebenezer Scrooge
   ghosts of: 13 Christmas Past **15** Christmas Future **16** Christmas Present
director: 17 Brian Desmond Hurst
cast: 10 Jack Warner **11** Alastair Sim (Ebenezer Scrooge), Mervyn Johns **14** Michael Hordern **16** Kathleen Harrison

Christopher Robin
   character in: 13 Winnie-the-Pooh
   author: 5 Milne

chromium
   chemical symbol: 2 Cr

chronic 7 abiding, lasting **8** constant, enduring, habitual, periodic **9** confirmed, continual, ingrained, perennial, recurrent, recurring **10** continuous, deep-rooted, deep-seated, inveterate, persistent, persisting **12** intermittent, longstanding

chronicle 3 log **4** epic, list, note, post, saga **5** diary, enter, story **6** annals, docket, record, relate, report **7** account, history, journal, narrate, recount, set down **8** archives **9** narrative **10** chronology

Chronicles of England, Scotland, and Ireland
   author: 16 Raphael Holinshed

chronological 5 dated **6** serial **7** ordered, sequent **10** sequential, succeeding, successive **11** consecutive, progressive, time-ordered **12** chronometric, chronoscopic **13** chronographic

chronology 6 annals, record **7** history **9** chronicle **13** order of events

chronometer 5 clock **8** horologe **9** timepiece

chrysanthemum
   varieties: 3 Max **4** Corn **5** Daisy, Tansy **6** Nippon **7** Garland **8** Florist's, Tricolor **10** Portuguese

chrysoberyl
   variety: 7 cat's-eye **11** alexandrite

chrysolite 4 iron, lava **5** beryl, green, stone **6** yellow **7** mineral, olivine, peridot **8** silicate **9** magnesium **10** aquamarine

chrysoprase
   species: 6 quartz
   color: 5 green

Chrysothemis
   father: 9 Agamemnon
   mother: 12 Clytemnestra
   brother: 7 Orestes
   sister: 7 Electra **9** Iphigenia
   daughter: 5 Rhoeo

Chthonian
   form: 5 deity **6** spirit
   habitat: 10 underworld

Chthonius
   member of: 6 Sparti

epithet of: 4 Zeus
means: 15 of the underworld

Chuang-tzu, Chwang-tse
   author: 9 Chuang-tzu

chubby 3 fat **5** buxom, plump, podgy, pudgy, stout, tubby **6** chunky, flabby, fleshy, portly, rotund, stocky, zaftig **7** paunchy **8** heavyset, roly-poly, thickset **9** corpulent **10** overweight **15** pleasingly plump

chuck 3 pat, pet, tap **4** cast, toss **5** fling, heave, pitch, sling, throw **6** tickle

chuckle 5 cluck, laugh **6** clumsy **7** cackle, chortle, snicker

chum 3 pal **4** bait **5** buddy, crony **6** cohort, friend **7** comrade **8** intimate, playmate, sidekick **9** companion, confidant **10** bosom buddy, playfellow **11** close friend

chummy 5 close, palsy **7** devoted **8** familiar, friendly, intimate **9** congenial **10** buddy-buddy, palsy-walsy **12** affectionate

chump 4 dolt, dupe, fool, goof, goon, head **5** champ, munch **6** sucker **9** blockhead

chunk 3 gob, wad **4** clod, hunk, lump, mass **5** batch, block, piece **6** nugget, square

chunky 5 beefy, dumpy, lumpy, pudgy, squat, stout, thick **6** chubby, portly, stocky, stodgy, stubby **7** squabby **8** heavyset, thickset **11** thick-bodied

church 4 cult, sect **5** faith **6** belief, chapel, mosque, temple **7** service **8** basilica, religion **9** cathedral, devotions, synagogue **10** house of God, Lord's house, persuasion, tabernacle **11** affiliation **12** denomination **13** divine worship **14** house of worship

Church, Frederick Edwin
   born: 10 Hartford CT
   artwork: 14 Andes of Ecuador, Falls of Niagara (Niagara Falls) **18** The Heart of the Andes **19** Morning in the Tropics

Churchill, Frank
   character in: 4 Emma
   author: 6 Austen

Churchill, Sarah
   father: 19 Sir Winston Churchill
   born: 6 London **7** England
   roles: 12 Royal Wedding

Churchill, Winston Spencer
   born: 7 England **14** Blenheim Palace
   father: 8 Randolph
   mother: 12 Jennie Jerome
   wife: 16 Clementine Hosier
   daughter: 5 Sarah
   school: 6 Harrow **9** Sandhurst
   captured by: 5 Boers
   position: 13 prime minister
   author of: 11 Marlborough, My Early Life **14** The World Crisis **17** The Second World War **35** A History of the

English-Speaking Peoples
   won: 10 Nobel Prize

churchly 8 clerical, pastoral, priestly **9** parochial **11** ministerial **14** ecclesiastical

churchman 5 vicar **6** bishop, cleric, curate, deacon, parson, pastor, priest, rector **7** prelate **8** chaplain, minister, preacher **9** clergyman **12** ecclesiastic

church official 5 elder **6** beadle, deacon **9** presbyter

churchyard 8 cemetery **9** graveyard **12** burial ground **13** burying ground

churl 3 cad, oaf **4** boor, lout **7** bounder

churlish 4 rude, sour, tart **5** crude, surly, testy **6** crusty, sullen **7** bearish, bilious, boorish, brusque, crabbed, grouchy, ill-bred, uncivil, uncouth, waspish **8** arrogant, captious, choleric, impolite, impudent, insolent, petulant **9** dastardly, insulting, irascible, irritable, obnoxious, rancorous, splenetic **10** unmannerly **11** ill-mannered, ill-tempered, quarrelsome **12** contemptible, discourteous

churn 4 beat, foam, rage, roil, roll, toss, whip **5** heave, shake, swirl, whisk **6** stir up **7** agitate, disturb, pulsate, shake up, vibrate **8** convulse **9** palpitate

chute 5 rapid, slide, slope **7** incline, passage **9** parachute

chutzpa, chutzpah 4 gall **5** brass, cheek, nerve **8** audacity, boldness, temerity **9** brashness, impudence **10** brazenness, effrontery **11** forwardness, presumption

Chwatt, Aaron
   real name of: 10 Red Buttons

ciao 2 hi **5** hello **6** so long **7** goodbye **11** see you later

Cicero, Marcus Tullius
   lived in: 11 ancient Rome
   noted as: 6 author, lawyer, orator **9** statesman **11** philosopher **12** letter writer
   position: 6 aedile, consul **7** praetor
   author of: 9 De finibus, De oratore **10** De amicitia, De officiis **11** De republica, De senectute, In Catilinam **14** De natura deorum, Pro lege Manilia **23** Tusculanae Disputationes

cicerone 5 guide, pilot **8** conductor **9** explainer

cicisbeo 5 lover

Cid, The
   also: 11 Poema del Cid
   author: 7 unknown **15** Pierre Corneille
   character: 7 Chimene **8** Rodrigue
   Cid also called: 14 el Cid Campeador **18** Rodrigo Diaz de Bivar
   horse: 7 Babieca

ci-devant 6 former **7** retired **10** heretofore

cierge 3 dip, wax **5** light, taper **6** bougie, candle, tallow

cigar 4 toby **5** claro **6** corona, havana, maduro, stogie **7** cheroot **8** panatela, panetela, perfecto **9** cigarillo, panatella
  ingredient: 11 tobacco leaf
  part: 6 binder, filler **7** wrapper
  made in: 4 Cuba **6** Havana
  kept in: 7 humidor

cigarette, cigaret 3 cig, fag **4** biri, rett **5** smoke **6** gasper, grette, reefer **10** coffin nail
  ingredient: 3 tar **7** menthol, tobacco **8** nicotine

Cimabue
  real name: 11 Cenni di Pepi
  born: 5 Italy **8** Florence
  artwork attributed: 18 The S Trinita Madonna **29** Madonna Enthroned with St Francis **45** Madonna and Child Enthroned with Angels and Prophets

Cimarron
  author: 10 Edna Ferber
  director: 13 Wesley Ruggles
  cast: 10 Irene Dunne, Richard Dix **13** Estelle Taylor
  Oscar for: 7 picture **10** screenplay

Cimarron Strip
  character: 8 (US Marshal) Jim Crown **9** Mac Gregor **12** Francis Wilde **17** Dulcey Coopersmith
  cast: 10 Randy Boone **12** Jill Townsend, Percy Herbert **13** Stuart Whitman

Cimino, Michael
  director of: 11 Heaven's Gate **13** The Deer Hunter (Oscar)

Cimmerian
  mentioned by: 5 Homer
  form: 10 Westerners
  live in: 8 darkness

cinch 4 band, snap **5** girth **6** clinch, ensure, girdle, shoo-in **8** lead-pipe **9** pull tight, sure thing **11** piece of cake

Cincinnati
  baseball team: 4 Reds
  football team: 7 Bengals

cincture 4 band, belt, cord, sash **6** girdle

cinder 3 ash **4** slag **5** ashes, dross, ember **6** embers, scoria **8** clinkers, iron slag **10** burned coal, burned wood

Cinderella
  author: 7 unknown
  source: 8 Perrault
  character: 14 Fairy Godmother, Handsome Prince **15** Ugly Stepsisters **16** Wicked Stepmother
  coach: 7 pumpkin
  horses: 9 white mice
  footman: 4 frog
  loses: 12 glass slipper

cinema 5 films **6** flicks, movies **7** theater **14** motion pictures, moving pictures

cinnamon 5 spice
  botanical name: 20 Cinnamomum zeylanicum
  variety: 6 cassia, Ceylon **10** zeylanicum
  color: 4 buff **5** tawny **6** auburn **8** nut-brown **11** golden- brown, yellow-brown **12** reddish-brown **13** chestnut- brown **14** yellowish-brown
  origin: 5 China **7** Vietnam **9** Indonesia **10** East Indies

Cinyras
  king of: 6 Cyprus
  son: 5 Melus
  daughter: 6 Myrrha
  introduced worship of: 9 Aphrodite
  crime: 6 incest
  death by: 7 suicide

cipher 3 nil, zip **4** code, zero **5** aught **6** naught, nobody **7** anagram, nothing, nullity **8** acrostic, goose egg **9** nonentity, obscurity **10** cryptogram **11** cryptograph

Circe
  form: 11 enchantress
  father: 6 Helios
  mother: 5 Perse
  brother: 6 Aeetes
  son: 6 Agrius **7** Latinus **9** Telegonus
  home: 5 Aeaea
  turned men into: 4 pigs **5** swine

circle 3 orb, set **4** belt, curl, gird, girt, halo, hoop, knot, loop, reel, ring, turn **5** arena, bound, cabal, crowd, curve, cycle, field, girth, group, hem in, orbit, pivot, range, reach, realm, round, sweep, swing **6** border, bounds, clique, cordon, corona, course, domain, girdle, region, sphere **7** circlet, circuit, company, compass, coterie, enclose, envelop, hedge in, revolve, ringlet, society, theater **8** dominion, encircle, province, sequence, surround **9** bailiwick, encompass, territory, wind about **10** move around, revolution, ring around **11** curve around, progression **12** circumrotate, circumscribe **13** revolve around **14** circumnavigate

Circle 6 gilgal

circlet 4 band, halo, ring **5** tiara **6** diadem, fillet, wreath **7** chaplet, coronet, ringlet

circuit 3 lap, run **4** area, beat, edge, tour, trek, walk **5** jaunt, limit, round, route **6** border, bounds, course, margin, sphere **7** compass, confine, journey **8** circling, frontier, orbiting, pivoting **9** excursion, extremity, perimeter, revolving, territory **10** revolution **13** circumference **14** distance around

circuitous 7 devious, turning, winding **8** circular, indirect, rambling, tortuous, twisting **10** meandering, roundabout, serpentine **12** labyrinthine **14** circumlocutory

circular 4 bill **5** flier, round **6** curved,
notice, rotary **7** coiling, curling, leaflet, rocking, rolling, rounded, turning, winding **8** bulletin, gyrating, handbill, pivoting, spinning, twirling **9** revolving, spiraling, swiveling, throwaway **10** circuitous, ring-shaped **12** announcement **13** advertisement

circulate 4 flow **5** issue, strew **6** circle, course, spread, travel **7** give out, go forth, journey, publish, radiate, scatter **8** announce, disperse, go around, put about **9** broadcast, get abroad, make known, move about, publicize **10** distribute, make public, move around, pass around, put forward **11** disseminate, pass through, visit around **13** make the rounds

circulation 4 flow **6** motion **7** flowing **8** circling, rotation **9** diffusion, radiation **10** dispersion **11** propagation **12** distribution, promulgation, transmission **13** dissemination

circulatory system
  part: 4 vein **5** heart **6** artery **9** capillary **15** lymphatic vessel
  carries: 6 plasma **9** platelets **13** red blood cells **15** white blood cells

circumcision
  Hebrew: 4 Bris, Brit **5** Berit, Brith **6** Berith
  performed by: 5 Mohel

circumference 3 rim **4** edge **5** girth **6** border, bounds, fringe, girdle, limits, margin **7** circuit, compass, outline **8** boundary **9** extremity, perimeter, periphery **14** distance around

circumlocution 8 rambling, verbiage **9** garrulity, verbosity, wordiness **10** digression, meandering **14** discursiveness, long-windedness, roundaboutness

circumlocutory 5 wordy **7** diffuse, verbose **8** rambling **9** wandering **10** digressive, discursive, maundering, roundabout

circumnavigate 5 skirt **6** bypass, circle **8** encircle, go around **10** circumvent

circumnavigation 8 circling, skirting **9** bypassing **11** going around **12** encirclement **13** circumvention

circumscribe 3 fix **4** curb **5** check, hem in, limit **6** bridle, circle, corset, define, impede **7** confine, enclose, outline **8** encircle, restrain, restrict, surround **9** constrain, delineate, encompass, proscribe

circumscribed 6 narrow **7** limited **10** restricted

circumscription 5 limit **7** outline **9** hemming in, restraint **10** constraint **11** confinement **12** encirclement **14** restrictedness

circumspect 4 sage, wary **5** alert **7** careful, guarded, prudent **8** cautious, discreet, vigilant, watchful **9** judicious, sagacious, wide-awake **10** deliberate, discerning, particular, thoughtful **13** contemplative, perspicacious **14** discriminating

circumspection 4 care, heed **7** caution **8** prudence **10** discretion, precaution, steadiness **11** carefulness, heedfulness, mindfulness **12** deliberation

circumstance 4 fact, item **5** event, point, thing **6** detail, factor, matter, ritual **7** element **8** ceremony, incident, splendor **9** condition, formality, happening, pageantry **10** brilliance, occurrence, particular, phenomenon **11** vicissitude **12** happenstance, magnificence, resplendence **14** state of affairs

circumstances 5 state **9** situation **11** environment **16** living conditions

circumstantial 4 full **6** minute **7** deduced, hearsay, implied, precise **8** accurate, complete, detailed, explicit, inferred, presumed, thorough **9** secondary **10** blow-by- blow, evidential, exhaustive, extraneous, incidental, particular, unabridged **11** conjectural, inferential, provisional **12** nonessential

circumvent 4 miss, shun **5** avoid, dodge, elude, evade, skirt **6** bypass, circle, escape, outwit, thwart **8** go around **9** frustrate **12** keep away from **14** circumnavigate

circumvention 7 dodging, ducking, eluding, evasion **9** avoidance, bypassing **11** frustration **12** sidestepping

circus 4 ring **5** arena **6** big top, circle, uproar **8** carnival, coliseum **9** spectacle **10** exhibition, hippodrome **11** ampitheater **12** intersection
  act: 5 clown, flyer **7** acrobat, juggler, trapeze **8** side show **9** lion tamer, menagerie **10** equestrian **13** flying trapeze
  famous: 6 Astley **12** Cirque d'Hiver **15** Barnum and Bailey **16** Ringling Brothers

Cist
  form: 9 sacred box
  used for: 8 utensils

cistern 3 box, tub, vat **4** tank, well **6** cavity, vessel **8** aqueduct **9** reservoir

citadel 4 fort **7** bastion, rampart **8** fortress **10** stronghold **13** fortification

citation 4 cite **5** award, honor, kudos, medal, quote **7** example, excerpt, extract, passage **8** instance **9** quotation **12** commendation, illustration **14** official praise

cite 4 name, note **5** honor, quote **6** praise **7** advance, commend, mention, present, refer to, specify **8** allude to, document, indicate **9** enumerate, exemplify **12** bring forward **13** give as example

Cithaeronian see **4** Zeus

citified 5 urban **6** urbane **12** cosmopolitan **13** sophisticated

citizen 6 native **7** denizen, subject **8** national, resident **10** inhabitant
  French: 7 citoyen

Citizen Kane
  director: 11 Orson Welles
  script: 11 Orson Welles **17** Herman J Mankiewicz
  cast: 11 Orson Welles **12** Joseph Cotten **13** Everett Sloane **14** Agnes Moorehead
  score: 15 Bernard Herrmann
  sled: 7 Rosebud

citizenry 4 folk **6** people, public **7** society **8** populace **9** community **10** population

citoyen 7 citizen

citrine
  species: 6 quartz
  color: 6 yellow

citron 3 rue **4** lime, rind **5** lemon **6** cedrat, orange, yellow **8** Rutaceae **9** tangerine **10** watermelon **12** citrus medica
  Jewish: 6 ethrog

city 4 burg, town **7** big town **8** denizens, township **9** residents **10** metropolis **11** inhabitants, megalopolis, townspeople **12** municipality **16** incorporated town, metropolitan area

city hall
  French: 12 hotel de ville

City Life
  author: 15 Donald Barthelme

City Lights
  director: 14 Charles Chaplin
  cast: 8 Hank Mann **10** Harry Myers **14** Charlie Chaplin **16** Virginia Cherrill

City of God, The (De Civitate Dei)
  author: 11 St Augustine

City of the Lion see **9** Singapore

city slicker 4 dude **8** urbanite **11** cosmopolite **12** sophisticate

City Without Walls and Other Poems
  author: 7 W H Auden

Ciudad Trujillo
  capital of: 17 Dominican Republic

Civ 17 second Hebrew month

civic 5 local **6** public **8** citizen's, communal **9** community

civil 3 lay **4** city **5** civic, state **6** genial, polite, public **7** affable, amiable, citizen, cordial, secular **8** citizen's, communal, decorous, gracious, mannerly, obliging **9** civilized, community, courteous, municipal **10** individual, neighborly, respectful **11** gentlemanly, nonmilitary **12** conciliatory, well-mannered

Civil Disobedience
  author: 17 Henry David Thoreau

civilian 9 lay person **14** private citizen **17** nonmilitary person **18** nonuniformed person

civility 4 tact **7** manners, respect **8**

courtesy **10** affability, amiability, cordiality, good temper, politeness **11** good manners **12** graciousness, pleasantness **13** agreeableness, courteousness **14** respectfulness

civilization 7 culture, society **10** refinement **11** cultivation, worldliness **13** enlightenment **14** sophistication

civilize 5 edify, teach, train **6** inform, polish, refine **7** culture, develop, educate, elevate **8** humanize, instruct **9** cultivate, enlighten **11** acculturate **12** sophisticate

civil law
  Latin: 9 jus civile

Civil War
  admirals: 6 DuPont, Semmes
  battles: 6 Shiloh **7** Bull Run **8** Antietam **9** Nashville, Vicksburg **10** Cold Harbor, Gettysburg **11** Chattanooga, Chickamauga **14** Fredericksburg
  coin: 10 copperhead
  Confederate commanders: 3 Lee **4** Hill, Hood **5** Bragg, Early, Ewell, Mosby, Smith **6** Stuart, Toombs **7** Buckner, Hampton, Jackson **10** Beauregard **12** Breckinridge
  Union commanders: 5 Banks, Buell, Grant, Logan **6** Butler, Custer, Hooker, Porter **7** Sherman, Hancock

clad 6 garbed **7** arrayed, attired, clothed, dressed **9** outfitted

Claggart
  character in: 9 Billy Budd
  author: 8 Melville

claim 3 ask **4** avow, call, plea, take **5** exact, right, title **6** access, affirm, allege, assert, avowal, charge, demand, pick up **7** call for, collect, command, declare, profess, request **8** exaction, insist on, maintain, proclaim **9** assertion, ownership, seek as due, statement **10** allegation, lay claim to, pretension, profession **11** affirmation, declaration, postulation, requirement **12** proclamation, protestation

claimant 6 suitor **9** applicant, pretender **10** petitioner

clairvoyant 7 psychic **8** divining, oracular **9** prescient, prophetic **10** telepathic **11** foreknowing, telekinetic **12** extrasensory, precognitive, psychometric **13** psychokinetic, second-sighted

clam 4 vise **5** clamp, clasp **6** dollar, marine **7** bivalve, mollusk
  kind: 5 pismo, razor **6** butter, quahog **7** geoduck, steamer **10** little neck **11** cherrystone
  part: 4 foot, palp **5** gills, shell, valve **6** mantle, siphon **7** sinuses **8** ligament
  habitat: 3 mud **4** sand
  relative: 6 mussel, oyster

clamber up 5 climb, mount, scale **10** scramble up, struggle up

clamminess 4 damp **7** wetness **8**

dampness, dankness **10** stickiness, sweatiness

clammy 3 wet **4** damp **5** pasty, slimy **6** sticky, sweaty **10** perspiring **11** cold and damp

clamor 3 cry, din **4** call, howl, yell **5** blast, chaos, noise, shout, storm **6** bedlam, bellow, cry out, hubbub, jangle, outcry, racket, rumpus, tumult, uproar **7** bluster, call out, clangor, thunder **8** brouhaha, shouting **9** commotion, hue and cry **10** hullabaloo, vociferate, wild chorus

clamorous 4 loud **5** noisy **10** boisterous, uproarious

clamp 4 clip, grip, vise **5** brace, clasp **6** clench, clinch, fasten, secure **7** bracket **8** fastener

clan 4 gang, knot, line, ring **5** breed, cabal, crowd, group, guild, house, party, stock **6** circle, league, strain **7** company, dynasty, lineage, society **8** alliance, pedigree **10** fraternity **11** affiliation, association, brotherhood, family group, lineal group **12** tribal family

clandestine 6 covert, hidden, masked, secret, veiled **7** cloaked, furtive, private **8** secluded, sneaking, stealthy **9** concealed, secretive, underhand **10** undercover, unrevealed **11** underground, underhanded, undisclosed **12** confidential **13** surreptitious

clang 3 din **4** bong, gong, peal, toll **5** chime, clank, clash, knell **6** jangle **7** clangor, resound, ringing, tolling **8** clashing **10** resounding, ring loudly

clangor 3 din **5** noise **6** clamor, hubbub, jangle, racket, uproar

clank 5 chink, clang, clash, clink **6** jangle, rattle **7** clangor, clatter **8** clashing

clannish 4 cold **5** aloof **6** narrow **7** distant, insular **8** cliquish, snobbish **9** exclusive, parochial, sectarian **10** provincial, restricted, unfriendly **11** unreceptive

Clan of the Cave Bear, The
   author: 9 Jean M Auel

clap 3 bat, hit, rap, tap **4** bang, bump, cast, cuff, dash, hurl, peal, push, roar, rush, slam, slap, swat, toss **5** burst, clack, crack, drive, fling, force, pitch, shove, smack, smite, thump, whack **6** buffet, plunge, propel, strike, thrust, thwack, wallop **7** applaud, clatter **9** explosion **11** set suddenly

claptrap 3 rot **4** bosh, bull, bunk, sham, **5** bilge, hokum, hooey, stuff, trash, tripe **6** bunkum, drivel, hot air, humbug, tinsel **7** baloney, blarney, fustian, hogwash, spinach, twaddle **8** buncombe, nonsense, quackery, tommyrot **9** gaudiness, poppycock, staginess **10** applesauce, flapdoodle, tawdriness, tomfoolery **11** foolishness **15** pretentiousness **16** stuff and nonsense

claque 10 sycophants **15** cheering section

Clare, Ada
   character in: 10 Bleak House
   author: 7 Dickens

claret 3 red **5** blood **7** carmine, deep red, red wine **8** blood-red, Bordeaux, cardinal **11** purplish red, wine-colored

clarification 10 commentary **11** elucidation, explanation, explication **14** further comment
   French: 15 eclaircissement

clarify 5 clear, purge, solve **6** purify, refine **7** clear up, explain, lay open, resolve **9** elucidate, explicate, make clear, make plain **10** illuminate **11** disentangle, shed light on **12** bring to light **18** make understandable

clarinet 4 wind **8** woodwind **11** transposing **13** locorice stick
   mouthpiece: 4 reed
   ancestor: 9 chalumeau
   musician: 12 Benny Goodman

clarion 5 acute, clear, sharp **6** shrill **7** blaring, ringing **8** distinct, piercing, resonant, sonorous, stirring **10** commanding, compelling, imperative **11** high-pitched

Clarissa Harlowe
   author: 16 Samuel Richardson
   character: 8 Miss Howe **11** John Belford **14** Robert Lovelace **20** Colonel William Morden

clarity 6 purity **8** lucidity, radiance **9** clearness, exactness, plainness, precision **10** brightness, brilliance, directness, effulgence, glassiness, luminosity, simplicity **12** explicitness, translucence, transparency **15** intelligibility **17** comprehensibility

Clark, Mark W
   served in: 3 WWI **4** WWII **9** Korean War
   rank: 22 allied commander in Italy **24** commander of forces in Korea **30** chief of staff of army ground forces **42** commander of Allied occupation forces in Austria
   president of: 7 Citadel

Clark, Walter Van Tilburg
   author of: 16 The Ox-Bow Incident

Clarke, Arthur C
   author of: 10 (2010) Odyssey Two **13** (2001) A Space Odyssey, Childhood's End **18** Rendezvous with Rama

clash 4 bang, boil, feud, fray, tiff **5** argue, clang, clank, crash, fight, set-to **6** battle, combat, fracas, jangle, rattle, tussle **7** clangor, clatter, contend, contest, discord, dispute, grapple, jarring, quarrel, wrangle **8** conflict, crashing, friction, skirmish, squabble, struggle **9** altercate, encounter, lock horns **10** antagonism, difference, disharmony, dissidence, opposition **11** cross

swords **12** disagreement **13** exchange blows

clash of arms 5 fight **6** battle, combat **8** conflict, skirmish, struggle **9** encounter **10** engagement

clash with 9 fight with **12** do battle with **14** contend against **15** cross swords with

clasp 3 hug **4** bolt, clip, grip, hasp, hold, hook, link, lock, snap **5** catch, clamp, grasp, latch, press **6** buckle, clinch, clutch, couple, fasten, secure **7** coupler, embrace, grapple, squeeze **8** fastener **9** fastening

clasp in the arms 3 hug **4** hold **6** enfold **7** embrace

class 3 set **4** form, kind, rank, rate, size, sort, type **5** brand, breed, caste, genre, genus, grade, group, index, label, order, state **6** circle, clique, codify, course, lesson, number, sphere, status **7** arrange, catalog, section, session, species, station, variety **8** category, classify, division, pedigree, position **9** condition, designate **10** categorize, pigeonhole, social rank **11** set of pupils **13** social stratum **14** classification **15** departmentalize, graduating group

classic, classical 4 epic **5** model **6** heroic **7** ageless, paragon **8** absolute, accepted, enduring, masterly **9** archetype, excellent, exemplary, first-rate, prototype **10** archetypal, consummate, definitive, first-class, Greco-Roman, prototypal **11** masterpiece, outstanding, traditional **12** ancient Greek, ancient Roman, standard work **13** authoritative, distinguished **14** distinguishing **17** first-class example

classification 4 kind, rank, sort, type **5** class, genus, group, order **6** family, series **7** section, species **8** category, classing, division, grouping, labeling, ordering, taxonomy **9** arranging, gradation **10** assortment, organizing **11** arrangement, designation, disposition **12** categorizing, codification, organization **14** categorization **15** systematization

classified 5 secret **6** sorted **7** classed **8** assorted **10** restricted **11** categorized **12** confidential

classify 3 tag **4** list, rank, rate, size, sort, type **5** brand, class, grade, group, index, label, order, range **6** assort, codify, number, ticket **7** arrange, catalog **8** organize **9** segregate **10** categorize, pigeonhole **11** distinguish

classy 4 chic, posh, tony **5** nifty, nobby, ritzy, smart, swank, swell **6** dressy, modish, spiffy, swanky **7** elegant, genteel, opulent, refined, stylish **8** cultured, polished, tasteful **9** highclass **10** ultrasmart **11** fashionable, in good taste **12** aristocratic, wellmannered

clatter 4 bang **5** clack, clang, clank, clash, clink, clump, crash **6** clamor, jangle, racket, rattle **7** chatter **8** crashing, rattling

clattering 3 din **6** clamor, hubbub, racket, uproar **7** clangor

Claude
real name: **12** Claude Gellee
also called: **14** Claude Lorraine
born: **6** France **9** Champagne
artwork: **7** The Mill **16** Hagar and the Angel **18** Ascanius and the Stag, The Enchanted Castle **27** The Rest on the Flight into Egypt **31** The Embarkation of the Queen of Sheba

Claudel, Paul
author of: **6** L'Otage **10** The Hostage **13** Partage de Midi **15** The Satin Slipper **20** Tidings Brought to Mary

Claudia Quinta
freed: **12** grounded ship
feat proved: **8** chastity

Claudio
character in: **17** Measure for Measure **19** Much Ado About Nothing
author: **11** Shakespeare

Claudius
character in: **6** Hamlet
author: **11** Shakespeare

Claudius the God
author: **12** Robert Graves
sequel to: **9** I Claudius

clause 4 term **7** article, proviso **8** covenant **9** condition, provision **11** proposition, stipulation **13** specification **14** simple sentence

claustrophobia
fear of: **12** closed spaces **14** confined spaces

Clavell, James
author of: **6** Shogun, Tai-Pan **7** King Rat **9** Whirlwind **10** Noble House

clavicle
bone of: **10** collarbone

claw 3 paw **4** foot, grip, maul, tear **5** seize, slash, talon **6** clutch, pincer, scrape **7** scratch **8** lacerate **10** animal nail

Clay, Cassius
former name of: **11** Muhammad Ali

Clayburgh, Jill
born: **9** New York NY
roles: **9** Semi-Tough **12** Starting Over **16** An Unmarried Woman, North Dallas Forty **21** I'm Dancing as Fast as I Can

Clayhanger Trilogy, The
author: **13** Arnold Bennett

clean 3 mop **4** dust, fine, neat, pure, tidy, trim, wash **5** bathe, clear, fresh, moral, order, scour, scrub, sweep **6** bathed, chaste, decent, neaten, tidy up, vacuum, washed **7** cleaned, cleanse, healthy, launder, orderly, perfect, scoured, shampoo, upright **8** cleansed, decorous, flawless, innocent, sanitary, scrubbed, spotless, unsoiled, virtuous, well-made **9** exemplary, faultless, honorable, laundered, stainless, undefiled, unspotted, unstained, unsullied, untainted, wholesome **10** immaculate, uninfected, unpolluted **11** unblemished **13** unadulterated **14** uncontaminated

cleaner, cleanser 4 soap **5** borax **6** washer **7** ammonia, janitor **8** purifier, scrubber **9** detergent **14** scouring powder

cleaning 7 bathing, washing **8** scouring **9** cleansing, going-over, scrubbing, tidying up **10** laundering

cleanse 3 rid **4** free, wash **5** bathe, clean, clear, erase, flush, scour, scrub **7** absolve, deliver, expunge, launder, release, shampoo **8** sweep out, unburden **9** expurgate

clean-shaven 6 smooth **9** unbearded **11** unwhiskered **12** smooth-shaven

cleansing 7 bathing, healing, purging, washing **8** flushing, scouring **9** expunging, purifying, scrubbing **10** absolution

cleanup 4 gain **6** profit **8** windfall
baseball: **12** fourth batter

clear 3 rid **4** fair, free, keen, make, open **5** alert, clean, empty, gauzy, lucid, plain, sharp, sunny **6** acquit, bright, patent, remove, serene, unstop, wholly **7** absolve, audible, audibly, certain, clearly, evident, express, fly over, glowing, halcyon, hop over, lighten, obvious, plainly, radiant, unblock **8** apparent, brighten, clear-cut, dazzling, definite, distinct, entirely, explicit, gleaming, leap over, luminous, manifest, pass over, pellucid, positive, skip over, unhidden **9** all the way, bound over, brilliant, cloudless, exculpate, exonerate, sparkling, unblocked, unclouded, unimpeded, unmuddled, vindicate, wide-awake **10** articulate, become fair, completely, diaphanous, discerning, distinctly, glistening, pronounced, unconfused, undeniable, unobscured **11** crystalline, inescapable, self-evident, translucent, transparent, unambiguous, unconcealed, undisguised, unequivocal, unqualified **12** articulately, intelligible, recognizable, unencumbered, unmistakable, unobstructed **14** comprehensible **15** distinguishable, straightforward

clearance 4 room, sale **6** margin, permit **7** removal **8** clearing **10** offsetting **11** elimination **13** authorization, certification

clear as day 5 plain **7** obvious **8** apparent, clear-cut, manifest **11** self-evident

clear-cut 4 open **5** exact, lucid, plain **6** patent **7** evident, express, obvious, precise **8** definite, detailed, distinct, explicit, manifest **10** clear as day, unconfused, undeniable **11** appreciable, conspicuous, self-evident, substantial, unambiguous, undisguised, unequivocal, well-defined **12** crystal-clear, unmistakable **14** comprehensible, understandable **15** straightforward

clearheaded 5 acute, alert, awake, aware, sharp **6** astute **8** rational, sensible **9** on the ball, practical, realistic, wide-awake **10** discerning, insightful, on one's toes, on the stick, perceptive **13** perspicacious

clearheadedness 7 insight **8** sagacity **9** alertness, sharpness **10** perception **11** discernment **12** perspicacity

clearing 5 glade

clearly 6 surely **7** plainly **8** markedly, palpably, patently **9** assuredly, certainly, decidedly, evidently, obviously **10** distinctly, manifestly, noticeably, observably, undeniably **11** beyond doubt, indubitably, perceptibly, undoubtedly **12** recognizably, unmistakably **13** unequivocally **14** beyond question, unquestionably

clearly expressed 8 coherent **10** articulate **11** unambiguous **12** intelligible

clearness 7 clarity **10** brightness, brilliance **12** explicitness **15** unmistakability

clear-sighted 4 sage, wise **5** acute, sharp **6** astute, shrewd **8** piercing **9** judicious, sagacious, sensitive **10** discerning, perceptive **11** intelligent, keen-sighted, penetrating **12** sharp-sighted **13** perspicacious

clear up 6 settle **7** clarify, unsnarl **8** untangle **11** disentangle **12** uncomplicate **13** straighten out

Cleary, Beverly
author of: **6** Ramona **7** Fifteen **12** Henry Huggins **13** Jean and Johnny **15** Beezus and Ramona **16** Sister of the Bride

cleat 5 block, chock, spike, wedge **6** batten **7** bollard

cleavage 3 gap **4** rent, rift, slit **5** cleft, crack, notch, split **6** furrow, trench, trough **7** crevice, fissure, opening **8** crevasse

cleave 3 cut, hew **4** chop, fuse, hack, hold, open, part, plow, rend, rive, slit, tear **5** cling, crack, halve, sever, slash, slice, split, stick, unite **6** adhere, be true, bisect, cut off, detach, divide, furrow, sunder, uphold **7** abide by, chop off, disjoin, lay open, stand by **8** be joined, break off, hold fast, separate **9** disengage, dismember

cleaver 3 axe **4** tool **5** knife ridge

cleft 3 gap **4** rent, rift, slit **5** break, crack, notch, split **6** breach, cloven, cranny, divide, forked, furrow, trench, trough **7** crevice, divided, fissure, notched, opening, slotted **8** aperture, bisected, branched, cleavage, crevasse, division **10** separation **11** indentation

clemency 5 mercy **7** charity **8** humanity, kindness, leniency, mildness, softness, sympathy **9** tolerance **10** compassion, indulgence, moderation, temperance **11** benevolence, forbearance, magnanimity **12** mercifulness, pleasantness **13** forgivingness

clement 4 kind, mild, warm **5** balmy **6** benign, gentle, humane **7** lenient **8** merciful, tolerant **9** not severe, not strict **10** benevolent **13** compassionate

clench 3 set **4** grip **5** clasp, tense **6** clinch, clutch **7** stiffen, tighten **8** fasten on, hold fast **11** grasp firmly, strain tight **12** close tightly

Clennam, Arthur
  character in: 12 Little Dorrit
  author: 7 Dickens

Cleopatra
  queen of: 5 Egypt
  father: 7 Ptolemy
  brother/husband: 7 Ptolemy
  lover: 10 Mark Antony **12** Julius Caesar
  son: 9 Caesarion **15** Alexander Helios **19** Ptolemy Philadelphos
  daughter: 15 Cleopatra Selene
  death by: 3 asp **7** suicide

Cleopatra
  director:
    1934 version: 13 Cecil B DeMille
    1963 version: 17 Joseph L Mankiewicz
  cast:
    1934 version: 13 Henry Wilcoxon, Warren William **16** Claudette Colbert
    1963 version: 11 Rex Harrison **13** Richard Burton, Roddy McDowall **15** Elizabeth Taylor

clergy 6 rabbis **7** clerics, pastors, priests **8** ministry, prelates, the cloth **9** churchmen, clergymen, clericals, ministers, pastorate, preachers, rabbinate, the church, the pulpit **10** priesthood **14** the first estate

clergyman 5 padre, rabbi **6** cleric, father, parson, pastor, priest **7** prelate **8** chaplain, minister, preacher, reverend, sky pilot **9** churchman **13** man of the cloth

cleric 6 parson, pastor **8** chaplain, preacher **9** churchman, clergyman **13** man of the cloth

clerical 6 cleric, filing, office, typing **7** clerkly **8** churchly, of clerks, pastoral, priestly **10** accounting, rabbinical **11** bookkeeping, ministerial **13** recordkeeping **14** ecclesiastical

clerical worker 5 clerk **6** typist **9** file clerk **10** bookkeeper, keypuncher **12** office worker **13** data processor

clerk 6 typist **8** salesman **9** file clerk **10** bookkeeper, salesclerk, sales-

woman **11** salesperson **12** office worker

Cleta
  member of: 6 Graces
  worshipped at: 6 Sparta

Cleveland
  baseball team: 7 Indians
  basketball team: 7 Rockers **9** Cavaliers
  football team: 6 Browns

Cleveland, Grover
  name at birth: 22 Stephen Grover Cleveland
  nickname: 5 Grove
  presidential rank: 12 twenty-fourth, twenty-second
  party: 8 Democrat
  state represented: 2 NY
  defeated: 4 (Simon) Wing **6** (Benjamin Franklin) Butler, (James Baird) Weaver, (James Gillespie) Blaine, (John Pierce) St John **7** (John) Bidwell **8** (Belva Ann Bennett) Lockwood, (Benjamin) Harrison
  vice president: 9 (Adlai Ewing) Stevenson, (Thomas Andrews) Hendricks
  cabinet:
    state: 5 (Richard) Olney **6** (Thomas Francis) Bayard **7** (Walter Quinton) Gresham
    treasury: 7 (Daniel) Manning **8** (John Griffin) Carlisle **9** (Charles Stebbins) Fairchild
    war: 6 (David Scott) Lamont **8** (William Crowninshield) Endicott
    attorney general: 5 (Richard) Olney **6** (Judson) Harmon **7** (Augustus Hill) Garland
    interior: 5 (Hoke) Smith, (Lucius Quintus Cincinnatus) Lamar, (William Freeman) Vilas **7** (David Rowland) Francis
  born: 2 NJ **8** Caldwell
  died/buried: 2 NJ **9** Princeton
  education:
    high school: 16 Liberal Institute
  religion: 12 Presbyterian
  interests: 7 fishing **8** shooting **13** gun collecting
  political career:
    mayor of: 7 Buffalo
    governor of: 7 New York
  civilian career: 6 lawyer
  notable events of lifetime/term: 5 Panic (of 1893) **10** gold crisis (of 1895)
    Act: 6 Tariff **14** Dawes Severalty **18** Interstate Commerce
    strike: 7 Pullman
  father: 13 Richard Falley
  mother: 4 Anne (Neal)
  siblings: 7 Ann Neal **9** Mary Allen **11** Susan Sophia, William Neal **12** Richard Cecil **13** Rose Elizabeth **14** Lewis Frederick **20** Margaret Louise Falley
  wife: 7 Frances (Folsom)

  children: 4 Ruth **6** Esther, Marion **13** Francis Grover, Richard Folsom

clever 4 able, cute, deft, keen **5** acute, quick, sharp, smart, witty **6** adroit, artful, astute, bright, crafty, expert, shrewd **8** creative, humorous, original **9** ingenious, inventive **11** imaginative, intelligent, quick-witted, resourceful

cleverly 6 deftly **7** sharply, smartly, wittily **8** adroitly, artfully, craftily, expertly **10** creatively, humorously **11** ingeniously, inventively **13** imaginatively, intelligently

cleverness 3 wit **6** acumen **8** ableness, deftness, keenness **9** expertise, ingenuity, quickness, sharpness, smartness **10** adroitness, artfulness, astuteness, brightness, craftiness **12** intelligence, skillfulness **13** inventiveness **15** imaginativeness, quick-wittedness

clew see **4** clue

Clew
  thread in: 9 Labyrinth
  showed way to: 7 Theseus
  given by: 7 Ariadne

cliche 3 saw **6** old saw **7** bromide **8** banality, old story **9** platitude **10** stereotype **11** trite phrase

cliche-ridden 5 corny, stale, tired, trite, vapid **6** jejune **8** bromidic **9** hackneyed **10** unoriginal **13** platitudinous, unimaginative

click 3 tap **4** clap, snap **5** clack, clink, crack **6** rattle **7** crackle

client 5 buyer **6** patron **7** advisee, shopper **8** customer **9** purchaser **17** person represented

cliff 3 tor **4** crag **5** bluff, ledge **8** palisade **9** precipice **10** promontory

Cliff Dwellers see **6** Pueblo

Clift, Montgomery
  real name: 21 Edward Montgomery Clift
  nickname: 5 Monty
  born: 7 Omaha NE
  roles: 9 The Search **10** The Heiress, The Misfits **14** A Place in the Sun **18** From Here to Eternity, Suddenly Last Summer

climactic 7 crucial **8** critical, dramatic **11** sensational, suspenseful

climate 3 air **4** mood, tone **5** pulse **6** spirit, temper **7** quality, weather **8** ambience, attitude **9** character, condition **10** atmosphere **11** disposition, frame of mind, weather zone **12** usual weather **13** weather region **14** general feeling, weather pattern

climax 4 acme, apex, peak **5** crown **6** crisis, height, summit **8** best part, pinnacle **9** high point **10** denouement **11** culmination **12** highest point, turning point **13** critical point, crowning point, decisive point, supreme moment **18** moment of revelation

climb 4 go up, rise **5** mount, scale **6**

ascend, ascent, come up **8** climbing **9** clamber up **10** scramble up

climb down 6 go down **7** descend **8** back down, come down

clinch 3 cap, fix, win **4** bind, bolt, grip, nail **5** cinch, clamp, clasp, close, crown, grasp, screw **6** assure, clutch, couple, decide, fasten, obtain, secure, settle, verify, wind up **7** confirm, grapple **8** complete, conclude, make fast, make sure **9** culminate, establish, finish off **10** grab hold of, hold firmly **12** seize and hold **13** ensure victory

cling 3 hug **4** fuse, grip, hold **5** clasp, grasp, stick **6** adhere, be true, cleave, clutch **7** stand by **8** hang on to, hold fast, hold on to, maintain **9** stay close **10** be constant, be faithful, grab hold of

clinging 6 sticky **7** holding **8** adherent, adhering, adhesive, clasping, cleaving, grasping, gripping, sticking **9** hanging on, holding on **11** holding fast **12** grabbing hold

clinic 9 infirmary **10** polyclinic **13** medical center **15** outpatients' ward

clink 4 ting **5** clack, clank, click **6** jangle, jingle, rattle, tinkle **11** ring sharply

clinkers 4 duds, slag **5** dross, flops **6** cinder, scoria **8** failures

Clinton, William Jefferson
  original last name: 6 Blythe
  nickname: 4 Bill
  presidential rank: 11 forty-second
  party: 10 Democratic
  state represented: 2 AR **8** Arkansas
  defeated: 4 (George) Bush, (Bob) Dole
  vice president: 4 (Albert) Gore
  cabinet:
    state: 11 (Warren) Christopher
    treasury: 7 (Lloyd) Bentsen
    attorney general: 4 (Janet) Reno
    interior: 7 (Bruce) Babbitt
    labor: 5 (Robert) Reich
    HUD: 8 (Henry) Cisneros
  born: 2 AR **4** Hope
  education: 6 Oxford **7** Yale Law **10** Georgetown
  honor: 13 Rhodes Scholar
  political career:
    governor of: 7 Arkansas
    attorney general of: 7 Arkansas
  notable events of lifetime/term: 4 Waco **5** NAFTA **10** Whitewater **13** Anticrime Bill, Rhodes Scholar **15** Branch Davidians **17** Health Security Act
    Supreme Court appointments: 13 Stephen Breyer **17** Ruth Bader Ginsburg
  father: 13 William Blythe
  mother: 12 Virginia Cassidy Blythe
  stepfather: 12 Roger Clinton
  sibling: 12 Roger Clinton

wife: 13 Hillary Rodham
children: 7 Chelsea

Clio
  muse of: 7 history

clip 3 bob, cut, fix **4** crop, grip, hook, snip, trim **5** clamp, clasp, shear **6** attach, buckle, clinch, couple, cut off, cut out, fasten, paring, secure, staple **7** cutting, shorten **8** clipping, cropping, cut short, fastener, shearing, snipping

clipper 4 boat, ship **6** cutter, shears **8** aircraft, airplane, sailboat, scissors **9** racehorse

clipping 7 cutting, pruning, snippet **8** trimming

clique 3 set **4** clan, gang **5** crowd, group **6** circle **7** coterie, faction

cliquish 4 cold **5** aloof **7** distant **8** clannish, snobbish **9** exclusive **10** unfriendly **11** unreceptive

cloak 4 cape, hide, mask, robe, veil, wrap **5** cover, tunic **6** mantle, screen, shield, shroud **7** conceal, curtain, pelisse, secrete **8** burnoose, disguise **10** camouflage **11** concealment

cloaked 7 covered, muffled, wrapped **9** disguised

cloaking 7 masking, veiling **8** covering **9** obscuring **10** disguising

cloakroom 8 anteroom, coatroom

clobber 3 hit **4** beat, belt, drub, lick, maul, rout, slug, sock, trim, whip **5** clout, pound, punch, smash, smear, whack **6** batter, beat up, strike, subdue, thrash, wallop **7** conquer, shellac, trounce **8** beat up on, lambaste

clock 5 watch **8** horologe **9** timepiece **11** chronometer

Clockwork Orange, A
  author: 14 Anthony Burgess
  director: 14 Stanley Kubrick
  cast: 12 Patrick Magee **13** Adrienne Corri **15** Malcolm McDowell
  protagonist: 4 Alex

clod 3 oaf, wad **4** boor, dolt, dope, glob, hunk, lout, rube **5** chunk, clown, clump, dummy, dunce, moron, yokel **7** bumpkin, fathead **8** imbecile, numskull **9** blockhead, ignoramus, simpleton

clodhopper 3 oaf **4** boot, clod, hick, lout, rube, slob **5** booby, clown, yokel **6** galoot, lubber, lummox, rustic **7** bumpkin, hayseed, peasant, plowboy, redneck **8** clodpole, lunkhead **9** heavy shoe, hillbilly **10** provincial

clog 4 stop **5** block, check, choke, close, dam up **6** stop up **7** barrier, congest **8** blockage, obstacle, obstruct, stoppage **9** restraint **10** impediment **11** obstruction

clogged 6 choked, halted, jammed **7** clotted, impeded **8** choked up, filled up, hampered, hindered, restrained **10** encumbered, obstructed, overloaded

cloister 4 stoa, walk **5** abbey, aisle **6** arcade, closet, coop up, friary, hole up, immure, shut up, wall up **7** conceal, confine, convent, embower, gallery, nunnery, passage, portico, seclude, walkway **8** shut away **9** colonnade, courtyard, monastery, promenade, sequester **10** ambulatory, passageway

cloistered 5 alone, aloof, apart **6** hidden **7** immured, recluse **8** closeted, confined, detached, isolated, secluded, secreted, separate, solitary **9** concealed, insulated, sheltered, withdrawn **11** dissociated, sequestered

clone 4 copy **5** robot **6** double **7** android, replica **9** automaton, duplicate, replicate **10** carbon copy **12** doppelganger **13** identical copy

close 3 end, hot, pen **4** akin, clog, fast, fill, firm, fuse, halt, join, keen, link, near, neat, nigh, plug, shut, stop, trim, warm **5** alert, block, cease, dense, fixed, humid, muggy, pen in, sharp, short, solid, stuff, tight, unite **6** allied, at hand, clog up, coop up, couple, ending, fill in, fill up, finale, finish, hard by, intent, jammed, loving, narrow, nearby, next to, plug up, recess, secure, shut in, shut up, smooth, stingy, stop up, stuffy, windup **7** adjourn, careful, close up, closing, compact, confine, connect, cramped, crowded, devoted, dismiss, enclose, intense, miserly, pinched, seal off, shut off, similar, stuffed, suspend, teeming **8** attached, blockade, break off, conclude, confined, familiar, friendly, grudging, imminent, intimate, leave off, obstruct, populous, shut down, squeezed, stagnant, stifling, stinting, swarming, thorough, vigilant, watchful **9** attentive, congested, impending, niggardly, penurious, scrimping, terminate **10** almost like, completion, compressed, conclusion, nearly even, nip-and-tuck, resembling, restricted, sweltering, ungenerous **11** almost alike, approaching, approximate, close-fisted, discontinue, forthcoming, impermeable, in proximity, inseparable, nearly equal, neighboring, suffocating, termination, tight-fisted, well-matched **12** bring to an end, impenetrable, parsimonious, unventilated **13** bring together, near to the skin, penny-pinching, uncomfortable **14** thick as thieves

closed 6 secret **7** private **9** exclusive

closed-minded 5 rigid **7** adamant, uptight **8** obdurate, stubborn **9** hidebound, obstinate, pig-headed, unbending **10** inflexible, unyielding **12** intransigent **14** uncompromising

Close Encounters of the Third Kind
  director: 15 Steven Spielberg

cast: 8 Teri Garr **13** Melinda Dillon **15** Richard Dreyfuss **16** Francois Truffaut
score: 12 John Williams

closefisted 4 mean **5** cheap, close, mingy, tight **6** stingy **7** miserly **8** grudging **9** niggardly, penurious **10** economical, ungenerous **11** close-handed, tightfisted **12** parsimonious **13** penny-pinching

close-fitting 4 snug **5** tight **9** skintight **11** constricted, form-fitting **12** constricting, tight-fitting **15** like a second skin

close friend 3 pal **4** chum, mate **5** buddy, crony **6** cohort **7** best pal **8** alter ego, intimate **9** companion, confidant **10** bosom buddy **17** intimate confidant

close loudly 4 bang, clap, slam

closely 6 keenly **7** alertly, sharply **8** intently **9** carefully, heedfully, intensely **10** diligently, vigilantly, vigorously, watchfully **11** attentively

close-mouthed 3 shy **4** cool **5** terse **7** bashful, distant **8** reserved, reticent, retiring, taciturn **9** diffident, secretive, withdrawn **11** tight-lipped **15** uncommunicative

closeness 8 meanness, nearness **10** stinginess **11** familiarity, miserliness **15** tightfistedness

close of day 3 eve **4** dusk, even **6** sunset **7** evening, sundown **8** eventide, gloaming, twilight **9** nightfall

closet 2 WC **4** eury, safe **5** ambry, cuddy **6** covert, hidden, locker pantry, secret, toilet **7** armoire, cabinet, private **8** coatroom, cupboard, imprison, secluded **9** cloakroom, storeroom, visionary **11** speculative, theoretical, unpractical, water closet

close tightly 3 set **4** seal, slam **5** latch **6** clench, secure **13** press together

close to 4 near **6** almost, around **9** just about **12** on the point of **13** approximately

closure 3 lid, tap **4** bung, cork, plug, stop **6** cover, ending, faucet, finish, spigot **7** barring, bolting, closing, cloture, locking, sealing, stopper **8** securing, shutting, stoppage **9** cessation **10** conclusion, stoppering **11** termination **14** discontinuance **15** discontinuation

clot 3 gob **4** lump, mass **7** congeal, thicken **8** embolism, solidify, thrombus **9** coagulate, occlusion **11** coagulation

Cloten
character in: 9 Cymbeline
author: 11 Shakespeare

cloth 5 goods **6** fabric **7** textile **8** dry goods, material **9** yard goods **10** piece goods

clothe 3 don **4** case, coat, deck, garb, robe, veil, wrap **5** array, cloak, cloud,

cover, drape, dress **6** attire, bedeck, encase, enwrap, outfit, rig out, screen, shroud **7** bedizen, costume, deck out, envelop, sheathe, swaddle **8** accouter

clothed 4 clad **5** robed **6** draped **7** cloaked, couched, covered, dressed, mantled, wearing **8** equipped, provided **9** expressed, furnished

clothes 4 duds, garb, rags, togs, wear **5** dress **6** attire, finery **7** apparel, costume, raiment, regalia **8** clothing, ensemble, garments, wardrobe **11** habiliments

clotheshorse 3 fop **4** dude **5** dandy, model **12** Beau Brummell, fashion plate, man of fashion, sharp dresser **14** woman of fashion

clothing see **7** clothes

Clotho
member of: 5 Fates
spinner of: 12 thread of life

cloud 3 dim, mar **4** blur, hide, veil **5** blind, cloak, cover, muddy, shade, sully, upset **6** darken, impair, muddle, screen, shadow, shroud **7** conceal, confuse, curtain, distort, disturb, eclipse, obscure, tarnish **8** overcast **9** discredit, make vague **10** overshadow **11** cast doubt on **14** call to question **19** place under suspicion

cloudburst 6 deluge **8** downpour, rainfall **9** rainstorm

clouded 3 dim **5** dusky, murky **7** blurred, obscure, sullied, tainted, unclear **8** confused, darkened, obscured **10** ill-defined, indistinct

cloudless 4 fair **5** clear, sunny **6** bright **7** halcyon **8** sunshiny **9** unclouded **10** unobscured

Clouds
goddess of: 3 Fri **5** Frigg, Frija **6** Frigga

Clouds, The (Nephelai)
author: 12 Aristophanes
character: 8 Just Plea, Socrates **10** Unjust Plea **11** Strepsiades **12** Pheidippides

cloudy 4 dark, gray, hazy **5** murky, vague **6** dreary, gloomy, leaden, veiled **7** clouded, obscure, sunless, unclear **8** confused, nebulous, overcast **9** confusing, undefined **10** indefinite, mysterious **11** overclouded

Clouet, Jean
born: 8 Flanders
artwork attributed: 13 Guillaume Bude **16** Madame de Canaples, Man with Gold Coins **17** The Count of Brissac, The Dauphin Francis **22** Man with a Book by Petrarch

clout 3 box, hit, jab **4** bash, belt, blow, pull, sock **5** crack, knock, punch, smack, thump, whack **6** wallop **9** influence **10** importance

clove
botanical name: 16 Eugenia aroma-

tica **18** Syzygium aromaticum
origin: 5 Pemba **7** Far East **8** Moluccas, Zanzibar **9** Mauritius **10** Madagascar
use: 3 ham **8** pickling, pomander **16** yellow vegetables

cloven 5 cleft, split **7** divided, notched, slotted **8** bisected

clover 9 Trifolium
varieties: 3 bur, elk, hop, low, pin, red **4** bush, holy, Kura, musk, owl's, tick **5** Alyce, Hubam, lucky, sweet, water, white **6** Alsike, cow hop, indoor, Korean, Ladino, yellow **7** Bukhara, crimson, Italian, mammoth, Mexican, Persian, prairie **8** four-leaf, Japanese, large hop, reversed, small hop, stinking **9** Hungarian **10** strawberry, toothed bur, white Dutch, white sweet **11** yellow sweet **12** silky prairie, subterranean, white prairie **13** European water **16** strawberry-headed

clown 3 wag, wit **4** card, fool, jest, joke, mime, zany **5** comic, cut up, joker **6** jester, madcap **7** buffoon **8** comedian, humorist **7** harlequin, kid around **10** comedienne, fool around **11** funny person, merry-andrew

Clown, The
author: 12 Heinrich Boll

clownishness 6 antics **10** buffoonery, tomfoolery **12** monkeyshines **14** playing the fool

Clowns of God, The
author: 11 Morris L West

cloy 3 gag **4** bore, glut, pall, sate, tire **5** choke, weary **6** benumb, overdo **7** exhaust, satiate, surfeit **8** nauseate, saturate

cloying 5 sweet **6** sugary **9** excessive, satiating **10** saccharine

club 3 bat, hit **4** bash, beat, flog, slug **5** billy, flail, group, guild, lay on, lodge, stick, union **6** batter, buffet, cudgel, league, pommel, pummel, strike **7** society **8** alliance, bludgeon, sorority **9** billyclub, clubhouse, truncheon **10** fraternity, shillelagh, sisterhood **11** affiliation, association, brotherhood, country club

clubhouse 4 club, hall **5** lodge **11** locker rooms **12** meeting house

clue 3 cue, key **4** clew, hint, mark, sign **5** guide, scent, trace **7** glimmer, inkling, pointer **8** evidence **9** indicator, inference **10** indication, intimation, suggestion **11** insinuation

clump 4 bulb, bump, knob, knot, lump, mass, plod, thud **5** batch, bunch, clomp, clunk, copse, group, grove, plunk, shock, stamp, stomp, thump, tramp **6** lumber **7** cluster, thicket **9** aggregate **10** assemblage, collection

clumsiness 9 gawkiness **10** ineptitude **11** awkwardness **12** carelessness, ungainliness **13** gracelessness, maladroitness

clumsy 5 bulky, crude, gawky, inept, rough **6** klutzy **7** awkward, unhandy **8** bungling, careless, ungainly, unwieldy **9** graceless, makeshift, maladroit, unskilled **10** blundering, cumbersome, ungraceful **11** heavy-handed **12** ill-contrived, unmanageable **14** butterfingered **21** like a bull in a china shop

cluster 4 band, bevy, heap, herd, knot, mass, pack, pile **5** amass, batch, block, bunch, clump, crowd, flock, group, sheaf, shock, swarm **6** gather, muster, throng **7** collect, company **8** assemble, converge **9** aggregate **10** accumulate, assemblage, collection, congregate **12** accumulation, congregation **13** agglomeration **14** conglomeration

cluster around 6 gather **7** collect **10** congregate **12** herd together **13** flock together

clutch 3 hug **4** grip, hold **5** clasp, grasp **6** clench **7** cling to, embrace, squeeze **8** hang on to

clutter 4 fill, heap, mess, pile **5** chaos, strew **6** jumble, litter, tangle **7** scatter **8** disarray, disorder **9** confusion **10** hodgepodge

cluttered 5 messy **7** chaotic, crowded, jumbled, muddled **8** confused, littered **9** scattered **10** disordered, disorderly

Clytemnestra
father: **9** Tyndareus
mother: **4** Leda
brother: **6** Castor, Pollux
sister: **5** Helen **8** Timandra
cousin: **8** Perilaus
husband: **9** Agamemnon
son: **7** Orestes
daughter: **7** Electra, Erigone **9** Iphigenia **12** Chrysothemis
lover: **9** Aegisthus
killed: **9** Agamemnon
killed by: **7** Orestes

coach 3 bus **5** drill, guide, sedan, stage, teach, train, tutor **6** advise, direct, mentor **7** omnibus, trainer **8** carriage, instruct **9** limousine, preceptor **10** automobile, four-in-hand, motor coach, stagecoach **11** four-wheeler, second class **12** economy class **14** private teacher **16** athletic director

coachman 3 fly **4** jehu, whip **5** pilot **6** driver **10** charioteer

Coactrice 14 poisonous snake

coagulate 3 gel, set **4** clot, jell **6** curdle, harden **7** congeal, jellify, thicken **8** solidify

coagulation 3 gob **4** clot, mass **8** clotting, curdling, thrombus **10** thickening

coal 4 ash, bass, char, coke, coom, culm, dust, fuel, slag, smut, swad **5** ember **6** cannel, cinder **7** lignite, clinker **8** charcoal **10** fossil fuel **11** charred wood

box: **3** hod **7** scuttle
made from: **6** carbon
type: **4** hard, soft **7** lignite **10** anthracite, bituminous
mining method: **4** deep **8** opencast **10** strip auger **11** underground
mine: **5** drift, shaft, slope, strip
size: **3** egg, nut, pea **5** stove

coal-black 3 jet **4** dark, inky **5** black, ebony, raven, sable **9** pitch-dark

coalesce 3 mix **4** ally, form, fuse, join, meld **5** blend, merge, unify, unite **6** cohere **7** combine **9** become one, integrate **10** amalgamate, join forces **11** agglutinate, consolidate **12** band together, come together **14** form an alliance

coalition 5 union **6** fusion, league **7** society **8** alliance **9** syndicate **10** federation **11** affiliation, association, combination, confederacy, partnership **12** amalgamation **13** agglomeration, consolidation **14** conglomeration

Coal Miner's Daughter
director: **12** Michael Apted
cast: **9** Levon Helm **11** Sissy Spacek (Loretta Lynn) (Oscar) **13** Tommy Lee Jones **14** Beverly D'Angelo
Oscar for: **7** actress (Spacek)
screenplay: **10** Tom Rickman

Coaluitecan
tribe: **6** Payaya

coarse 4 lewd, rude, vile **5** crass, crude, dirty, gross, harsh, rough **6** common, nubbly, odious, ribald, shaggy, sordid, vulgar **7** boorish, bristly, brutish, ill-bred, loutish, obscene, prickly, uncouth **8** impolite, improper, indecent, scratchy **9** bristling, inelegant, offensive, repulsive, revolting, sandpaper, unrefined **10** disgusting, indecorous, indelicate, lascivious, licentious, scurrilous, unladylike, unpolished **11** foul-mouthed, ill-mannered **12** lacking taste **13** rough-textured, ungentlemanly

coarse-grained 5 crude, harsh, nubby, rough **6** coarse, grainy, shaggy **7** bristly **8** scratchy **9** unrefined **13** rough- textured

coarseness 9 crudeness, grossness, roughness, vulgarity **10** indelicacy, inelegance **11** boorishness **16** lack of refinement

coast 4 skim, slip, waft **5** drift, float, glide, shore, slide, sweep **6** strand **7** seaside **8** glissade, littoral, seaboard, seacoast, seashore **9** shoreline

coaster 3 mat **4** ship, sled, tray **5** wagon **6** cradle, glider, slider **8** toboggan **9** tray stand **13** decanter stand, roller coaster

coat 3 fur **4** hair, hide, pelt, wrap **5** cover, glaze, layer, paint, smear **6** blazer, enamel, encase, jacket, spread **7** coating, encrust, envelop, lacquer, overlay, plaster, slicker, topcoat **8**

covering, laminate, mackinaw, overcoat, raincoat **9** whitewash **10** mackintosh, sports coat

coating 4 coat, film, skin **5** layer, sheet **6** veneer **7** overlay **8** covering, envelope

coat of arms 4 arms **5** crest **6** creast **8** insignia **9** blaconwry **10** escutcheon **14** heraldic emblem **16** armorial bearings

coat of mail 4 mail **5** armor **9** chain mail **11** suit of armor

Coat of Varnish, A
author: **6** C P Snow

coax 6 cajole **7** wheedle **8** butter up; inveigle, soft-soap, talk into **9** sweet-talk

cobalt 4 blue **5** azure **7** element, sky blue **10** bright blue **12** greenish blue
chemical symbol: **2** Co

Cobb, Lee J
born: **9** New York NY
roles: **10** Willy Loman **12** The Virginian **14** Twelve Angry Men **16** On the Waterfront **16** Death of a Salesman

Cobb, Ty (Tyrus Raymond)
nickname: **12** Georgia Peach
sport: **8** baseball
position: **8** outfield
team: **13** Detroit Tigers

cobbler 3 pie **9** bootmaker, shoemaker **12** shoe repairer **16** deepdish fruit pie

cobra
also: **3** asp **5** mamba **11** hooded snake
native to: **4** Asia **6** Africa
kind: **4** king **6** hooded, Indian **8** Egyptian
enemy: **8** mongoose

Coburn, Charles
born: **10** Savannah GA
roles: **9** Boss Tweed **17** The More the Merrier

Coburn, James
born: **8** Laurel NE
roles: **10** Hudson Hawk **11** In Like Flint, Our Man Flint **14** The Great Escape, The Muppet Movie **17** The Nutty Professor **19** The Magnificent Seven

Coca, Imogene
partner: **9** Sid Caesar
born: **14** Philadelphia PA
roles: **15** Your Show of Shows

cock 3 tip **4** knob **5** raise, valve **6** faucet, handle, perk up **7** rooster, stand up **8** cockerel, male bird, set erect **9** bristle up **11** chanticleer **13** turn to one side **16** raise the hammer of **17** draw back the hammer

cockade 4 knot **5** badge **6** ribbon **7** rosette **8** ornament **10** party badge

Cockade State
nickname of: **8** Maryland

cock-and-bull story 3 fib, lie **4** myth, yarn **5** fable **7** fiction, untruth, whop-

per 9 fairy tale, falsehood, fish story, invention, tall story **11** fabrication **13** prevarication

Cockcroft, John Douglas
  field: 7 physics
  nationality: 7 British
  developed: 24 Cockcroft-Walton generator
  worked with: 6 Walton
  awarded: 10 Nobel Prize

cockeyed 3 mad **4** awry, wild **5** askew, crazy, goofy, inane, nutty, weird **6** absurd, aslant, insane, tilted **7** crooked, foolish, twisted **8** lopsided, sideways **9** irregular, off-center, senseless **10** cockamamie, out of whack, ridiculous, unbalanced **11** nonsensical **12** asymmetrical, preposterous

Cockpit of Europe *see* **7** Belgium

cockscomb 4 comb **5** crest **7** celosia, coxcomb **8** amaranth, caruncle

cocksure 4 pert, smug, vain **5** brash, cocky, pushy **6** cheeky, snooty **8** arrogant, positive **9** assertive, audacious, bumptious, conceited **10** aggressive, swaggering **11** overbearing, self-assured, swell-headed **13** overconfident, self-confident

cocktail 5 drink, fruit, horse **6** shrimp **10** docked tail, semi-formal
  type: 4 grog **6** brandy, gibson, gimlet, mai tai, rob roy, zombie **7** Bellini, gin fizz, martini, negroni, sidecar, stinger **8** daiquiri, highball, hot toddy, pink lady **9** cuba libre, hurricane, gin rickey, manhattan, margarita, mint julep, rusty nail **10** bloody mary, tom collins **11** boilermaker, gin and tonic, grasshopper, screwdriver, sloe gin fizz **12** black russian, cosmopolitan, old-fashioned, tom and jerry, whiskey sour **13** planter's punch **15** brandy alexander
  mixer: 4 soda **5** tonic, water **7** bitters, seltzer **9** ginger ale
  garnish: 4 lime **5** lemon, olive, orange, twist **16** maraschino cherry
  stirrer: 7 muddler

cocktail lounge 3 bar **6** saloon, tavern **7** gin mill, taproom

cocky 5 brash, saucy **6** jaunty **8** arrogant, cocksure, impudent **9** conceited, egotistic **10** swaggering

Coco, James
  born: 9 New York NY
  roles: 11 Sancho Panza **13** Man of La Mancha **21** Last of the Red Hot Lovers

cocoa 5 brown, cacao **9** chocolate **12** hot chocolate

cocoon
  covering for: 5 larva
  stage: 5 pupal
  made of: 4 silk

Cocteau, Jean
  author of: 7 Orpheus **8** Antigone **12** Blood of a Poet **18** The Infernal Machine **19** Les Enfants Terribles, Les Parents Terribles **20** The Beauty and the Beast

Cocytus
  river in: 5 Hades

coddle 3 pat, pet **4** baby **5** humor, spoil **6** caress, cuddle, dote on, fondle, pamper **7** indulge **11** mollycoddle

code 4 laws **5** rules **6** cipher **7** statute **8** precepts **9** ordinance, standards **10** cryptogram, guidelines, principles **11** cryptograph, proprieties, regulations **13** secret writing **14** secret language

codger 5 crank, miser **6** geezer, oddity, old man **9** eccentric, odd person

codicil 5 rider **8** addendum, addition, appendix **9** extension, subscript **10** postscript, supplement **11** added clause

codify 4 rank, rate **5** grade, group, index, order **7** arrange, catalog **8** classify, organize, tabulate **9** methodize **10** categorize, coordinate, regularize **11** systematize

coelenterate 5 coral, hydra, polyp **6** Medusa **7** acaleph, radiate **8** acalephe **9** jellyfish **10** sea anemone
  habitat: 5 ocean **9** salt water

Coelophysis
  type: 8 dinosaur, therapod
  location: 7 Arizona
  period: 8 Triassic

coequal 5 equal **10** coordinate **16** equally important

coequality 6 parity **8** equality, evenness, sameness **10** uniformity **11** equivalency **14** correspondence

coerce 3 cow **4** make **5** bully, drive, force **6** compel, oblige **7** dragoon **8** browbeat, bulldoze, pressure, threaten **9** constrain, strong-arm **10** intimidate

coercer 5 bully **9** oppressor, tormenter, tormentor **10** browbeater **11** intimidator, petty tyrant

coercion 5 force **6** duress **7** threats **8** bullying, pressure **10** compulsion, constraint **11** browbeating **12** intimidation

coercive 8 enforced, forcible **10** compulsory, obligatory **11** threatening

coexist with 12 go hand in hand, go side by side, live together **13** go hand in glove

coffee 6 Coffea **13** Coffea arabica
  varieties: 4 Java, Kona, Wild **5** Irish, Mocha **6** Almond, Common **7** Arabian, Arabica, Robusta, Vanilla **8** Liberian, Liberica, Zanzibar **9** Colombian **11** French Roast, Wild robusta **13** Decaffeinated **20** Jamaican Blue Mountain
  beverage: 5 decaf, latte **6** kahlua **8** espresso **10** cafe au lait, cappuccino
  small cup: 9 demitasse

coffee (black)
  French: 8 cafe noir **10** cafe nature

coffee brandy 6 Kahlua **8** Tia Maria

coffee with milk 5 latte
  French: 10 cafe au lait

coffer 3 box **4** case **5** chest **9** strongbox **10** depository, repository **13** treasure chest

coffers 5 safes **6** vaults **8** treasury **9** cash boxes **11** money supply

coffin 3 box **4** pall **6** casket **10** catafalque **11** sarcophagus

cog 3 cam, lie **4** gear **5** cheat, cozen, tenon, tooth, wedge, wheel **8** small boat **10** projection

cogent 5 sound, valid **6** potent **7** weighty **8** forceful, powerful **9** effective, trenchant **10** compelling, convincing, persuasive, undeniable **11** meritorious, well-founded **12** well-grounded **16** incontrovertible

cogitate 5 study, think, weigh **6** ponder **7** reflect **8** meditate, mull over, ruminate **9** think over **10** deliberate, think about **11** contemplate, reflect upon **18** consider thoroughly

cogito ergo sum 18 I think therefore I am
  said by: 9 Descartes

cognac
  type: 6 brandy **7** liqueur
  origin: 6 France
  brand: 7 Bisquit, Martell **8** Hennessy **10** Remy Martin **11** Courvoisier
  label: 2 VO (very old), VS (very special), XO (extra old) **3** XXO (extra extra old) **4** VSOP (very superior old pale) **8** Napoleon (5 year premium)
  drink: 9 Andalusia
  with Cointreau: 10 Rolls Royce
  with Triple Sec: 7 Chicago **10** Rolls Royce
  with vodka: 7 Cossack

cognate 4 akin, like **5** alike, close **7** kindred, related, similar **8** familial, parallel, relative **9** affiliate **10** derivative **11** consanguine

cognition 7 knowing **9** awareness, knowledge **11** familiarity **13** comprehension, understanding

cognizance 4 heed, note **5** grasp **6** notice, regard **8** scrutiny **9** attention, awareness, cognition, knowledge **10** perception **11** familiarity, observation, recognition, sensibility **12** apprehension **13** comprehension, consciousness, understanding

cognizant 5 aware **6** posted **7** knowing, mindful **8** familiar, informed, versed in **9** conscious **10** acquainted, conversant, instructed **11** enlightened **13** knowledgeable, understanding

cognomen 4 name **6** handle **7** epithet, moniker, surname **11** appellation, designation

cognoscenti 6 judges **7** experts **8** insiders **11** authorities **12** connoisseurs **14** those in the know

cohere 3 fit, set 4 bind, fuse, glue, hold, jibe, join 5 agree, cling, match, stick, tally, unite 6 cement, concur, square 7 combine, conform, congeal 8 coalesce, coincide, dovetail, solidify 9 coagulate, harmonize 10 correspond 11 consolidate, synchronize 12 hold together 13 stick together

coherence 5 logic, unity 7 clarity, concord, harmony 8 cohesion 9 congruity 10 accordance, conformity, consonance 11 consistency, rationality 12 organization

coherent 5 clear, lucid 7 logical, orderly 8 cohesive, rational 9 congruous, connected, in keeping, organized 10 articulate, consistent, harmonious, meaningful, systematic 11 in agreement 12 intelligible 13 corresponding 14 comprehensible, understandable

cohesion 4 bond 5 union, unity 7 bonding 8 adhesion 10 attraction, solidarity

cohesive 3 set 5 solid 6 sticky 7 viscous 8 cemented, coherent, cohering, sticking 9 connected 11 indivisible, inseparable 12 consolidated 13 agglutinative

Cohn, Ferdinand Julius
  field: 6 botany
  nationality: 6 German
  founded: 12 bacteriology

Cohn, Robert
  character in: 15 The Sun Also Rises
  author: 9 Hemingway

cohort 3 pal 4 chum 5 buddy, crony 6 fellow, friend 7 comrade 8 follower, myrmidon 9 associate, companion 10 accomplice

coif 3 cap 4 hood, veil 6 beggin, burlet, hairdo 8 biggonet, coiffure, skull cap 9 head-dress

coiffed 6 capped, styled 7 dressed 8 arranged

coiffeur 7 stylist 11 hairdresser 15 male hairdresser

coiffure 2 DA, GI 3 bob, bun 4 Afro, coif, perm, shag, trim, updo, wave 6 hairdo 7 beehive, blowcut, comb-out, flattop, haircut, pageboy, upsweep 8 cold wave, cornrows, ducktail 9 hairstyle, permanent, pompadour

coil 4 curl, loop, ring, roll, wind 5 braid, twine, twist 6 circle, spiral, writhe 7 entwine 8 encircle

coin 4 mint 5 hatch, money, piece 6 change, create, devise, invent, make up, silver, strike 7 concoct, dream up, think up 8 conceive 9 fabricate, originate

coin/currency
  of Afghanistan: 3 pul 5 abaze, riyal, rupee 6 abbasi, amania 7 afghani
  of Albania: 3 lek 5 franc 6 qintar 7 quintar
  of Algeria: 5 dinar 7 centime
  of Andorra: 5 franc 6 peseta

of Angola: 6 escudo, kwanza, macuta, macute 7 angolar, centavo
of Argentina: 4 peso 7 centavo 9 argentino
of Armenia: 5 ruble
of Australia: 4 dump, tray, zack 5 pound 6 dollar 8 shilling
of Austria: 4 lira 5 crown, ducat, krone 6 florin, gulden, heller, zehner 8 albertin, groschen, kreutzer 9 schilling
of Azerbaijan: 5 manat
of Bahrain: 5 dinar
of Bangladesh: 4 taka 5 paisa
of Belarus: 5 ruble
of Belgium: 5 belga, franc 7 brabant, centime, crocard
of Benin: 5 franc 7 centime
of Bhutan: 5 paisa, rupee 7 chetrum 8 ngultrum
of Bolivia: 4 peso 7 centavo 9 boliviano
of Bosnia-Herzegovina: 5 dinar
of Botswana: 4 pula, rand
of Brazil: 3 joe 4 reis 5 dobra 7 centara, halfjoe, milreis 8 cruzeiro
of Bulgaria: 3 lev 8 stotinki
of Burkina Faso: 5 franc 7 centime
of Burundi: 5 franc 7 centime
of Cambodia: 3 sen 4 quan, riel 6 puttan 7 piaster
of Cameroon: 5 franc 7 centime
of Canada: 6 loonie, toonie
of Canary Islands: 6 peseta
of Cape Verde: 6 escudo 7 centavo
of Central African Republic: 5 franc 7 centime
of Chad: 5 franc 7 centime
of Chile: 4 peso 5 libra 6 condor, escudo
of China: 4 cash, cent, fyng, mace, tael, tiao, yuan 5 sycee 12 jen nin piao pu
of Colombia: 4 peso, real 6 condor, peseta 7 centavo
of Comoros: 5 franc 7 centime
of Congo: 5 franc 7 centime
of Costa Rica: 5 colon 6 colone 7 centimo
of Crete: 7 drachma
of Croatia: 5 dinar
of Cuba: 4 peso 7 centavo 8 cuarenta
of Cyprus 4 para 5 pound
of Czechoslovakia/ Czech Republic: 5 crown, ducat 8 heller, koruna
of Denmark: 3 one, ora, ore 4 fyrk 5 krone 8 frederik, skilling 9 rigsdaler
of Djibouti: 5 franc 7 centime
of Dominican Republic: 3 oro 4 peso 6 franco
of Ecuador: 5 sucre 7 centavo
of Egypt: 4 fils, kees, para 5 asper, dinar, fodda, gersh, girsh, medin, pound, riyal 6 ahmadi, dirham, foddah, guinea, junayh, maidin, medine, medino 7 piaster, piastre, tallard 8 bedidlik, millieme
of El Salvador: 4 peso 5 colon 7 centavo

of England: 3 ora 4 rial 5 achey, crown, groat, noble, pence, penny, pound 6 bawbee, florin, guinea 7 angelet, hapenny 8 farthing, shilling, sixpence, tuppence, tuppenny 13 pound sterling
of Equatorial Guinea: 6 ekuele, peseta 7 centimo
of Estonia: 3 lat 4 sent 5 kroon 7 estmark
of Ethiopia: 4 besa, birr, harf 5 amole, girsh 6 dollar, kharaf, levant, pataca, talari 7 ashrafi, menelik, plaster, tallero 12 maria theresa
of European Community: 3 ecu
of Fiji: 6 dollar
of Finland: 4 mark 5 penni 6 markka 7 markkaa
of France: 5 franc 7 centime 8 napoleon
of Gabon Republic: 5 franc 7 centime
of the Gambia: 5 pound 6 butbut, dalasi
of Georgia: 5 ruble
of Germany: 4 mark 7 Ostmark, pfennig 12 Deutsche mark
of Ghana: 4 cedi, cidi 5 ackey
of Greece: 5 lepta 7 drachma
of Greenland: 3 ore 5 krone
of Guatemala: 4 peso 7 centavo, quetzal
of Guinea: 4 iliy, syli 5 franc 6 cauris
of Guinea-Bissau: 4 peso 6 escudo 7 centavo
of Haiti: 6 gourde 7 centime
of Honduras: 4 peso 7 centavo, lempira
of Hungary: 4 gara 5 balas, krone, pengo 6 filler, forint, gulden, korona, ongara, ungara
of Iceland: 5 aurar, eyrir, krona 6 kronur
of India: 3 lac, pie 4 anna, fels, lakh, pice, tara 5 abidi, crore, paisa, rupee
of Indonesia: 3 sen 6 rupiah
of Iran: 3 pul 4 asar, gran, lari, rial 5 bisti, daric, dinar, larin, shahi, toman 6 stater 7 ashrafi, kasbeke, pahlavi
of Iraq: 4 fils 5 dinar
of Ireland: 3 rap 4 real 5 pence, pound 6 turney 8 shilling
of Israel: 3 mil 5 agora, agura, pound, pruta 6 agorot, shekel
of Italy: 4 lira, lire, tara 5 grano, paoli, paolo, scudo, soldo 6 danaro, denaro, ducato, sequin 7 testone 8 zecchino 9 centesini
of Ivory Coast: 5 franc 7 centime
of Jamaica: 7 quattie
of Japan: 2 bu 3 mon, rin, rio, sen, shu, yen 4 cash, mibu, oban 5 koban, obang, tempo 6 cobang, ichebu, ichibu, itzebu, kogang 7 itzeboo, itziboo
of Jordan: 4 fils 5 dinar
of Kazakhstan: 5 ruble

of Kenya: 4 cent **5** pound **8** shilling
of Kiribati: 4 cent **6** dollar
of Korea: 3 woh, won **4** chun, hwan, kwan
of Kuwait: 4 fils **5** dinar
of Kyrgyzstan: 3 som
of Laos: 2 at **3** att, kip
of Latvia: 3 lat **4** latu **6** rublis, santim **7** kapeika, santima
of Lebanon: 5 livre, pound **7** piastre
of Lesotho: 4 cent, rand **6** maloti
of Liberia: 4 cent **6** dollar
of Libya: 5 dinar
of Liechtenstein: 5 franc **6** rappen **7** franken
of Lithuania: 3 lit **5** litas, marka **6** centas, fennig **7** ostmark, skatiku **8** auksinas, skatikas
of Luxembourg: 5 franc **7** centime
of Macao: 3 avo **6** pataca, pataco
of Macedonia: 5 denar
of Madagascar: 5 franc **7** centime
of Malawi: 6 kwacha **7** tambala
of Malaysia: 3 sen, tra **4** taro, trah **7** ringgit, tampang
of Maldives: 5 laree, rupee **7** rufiyaa
of Mali: 5 franc **7** centime
of Malta: 4 cent **5** grain, grano, pound
of Mauritania: 5 khoum **7** ouguiya
of Mauritius: 4 cent **5** rupee
of Mexico: 4 onza, peso **5** adobe, claco, tlaco **6** azteca, cuarto, dinero **7** centavo, piaster
of Moldova: 5 ruble
of Monaco: 5 franc **7** centime
of Mongolia: 5 mongo, mungo **6** tugrik **7** tughrik
of Montenegro: 4 para **6** florin **7** perpera
of Morocco: 4 flue, okia, rial **5** floos, franc, okieh, ounce **6** dirham, miskal **8** mouzouna
of Mozambique: 6 escudo **7** centavo, metical
of Myanmar: 3 pya **4** kyat
of Namibia: 4 cent, rand
of Nauru: 4 cent **6** dollar
of Nepal: 4 anna, pice **5** mohar, rupee
of the Netherlands: 4 doit, oord, raps **5** crown, daler, rider, ryder **6** florin, gulden, stiver, suskin **7** daalder, ducaton, escalan, escalin, guilder, stooter, stuiver **8** albertin, ducatoon **9** dubbeltje **12** rijksdaalder **13** albertustaler
of New Guinea: 4 kina, toea
of New Zealand: 4 cent **6** dollar
of Nicaragua: 4 peso **7** centavo, cordoba
of Niger: 5 franc **7** centime
of Nigeria: 4 kobo **5** naira
of Norway: 3 ore **5** krone **6** kroner
of Oman: 3 gaj, gaz **4** rial **5** baiza, ghazi **7** mahmudi
of Pakistan: 4 anna, pice **5** paisa, rupee

of Panama: 4 cent **6** balboa **9** centesimo
of Paraguay: 4 peso **7** centimo, guarani
of Peru: 3 sol **5** libra **6** dinero, reseta **7** centavo
of the Philippines: 4 peso **6** conant, peseta **7** centavo
of Poland: 4 abia **5** dalar, ducat, grosz, marka, zloty **6** fening, groszy, gulden, halerz, korona **8** groschen
of Portugal: 3 avo, joe **4** peca, real **5** conto, crown, dobra, indio, justo, rupia **6** escudo, macuta, octave, pataca, testad, tostao, vintem **7** angalar, centavo, crusado, miereis, moidore, testone **8** equipaga, johannes
of Qatar: 5 riyal **6** dirham
of Rumania: 3 ban, lei, leu, lev, ley **4** bani **5** uncia **6** triens
of Russia: 5 altin, bisti, copec, genga, grosh, kopek, ruble, shaur **6** abassi, copeck, grivna, kopeck, piatak, rouble **7** poltina, valiuta **8** auksinas, deneshka, imperial, polushka **9** poltinnik **10** altininink, chervonets
of Rwanda: 5 franc **7** centime
of San Marino: 4 lira, lire **9** centesimi
of Samoa: 4 tala
of Sao Tome and Principe: 5 dobra **6** escudo **7** centavo
of Sardinia: 7 carline
of Saudi Arabia: 5 girsh, gursh, pound, riyal
of Scotland: 3 ecu **4** demy, doit, lion, mark, rial, ryal **5** bodle, broad, groat, plack, rider, turne **6** bawbee, folles **7** unicorn **8** atchison, hardhead **9** halfpenny **11** bonnetpiece
of Senegal: 5 franc **7** centime
of Sicily: 5 litra, oncia, uncia **6** carlin **7** carline, oncetta
of Sierra Leone: 4 cent **5** leone
of Singapore: 4 cent **6** dollar
of Slovakia: 6 koruna
of Slovenia: 5 tolar
of Solomon Islands: 4 cent **6** dollar
of Somalia: 4 besa **6** somalo **8** shilling **9** centesimi
of South Africa: 4 cent, pond, rand **5** pound **6** florin **7** daalder **9** krugerand
of Spain: 3 cob **4** duro, peso, real **5** dobla **6** cuarto, dinero, doblon, escudo, peseta **7** alfonso, centimo, pistole, realdor **8** doubloon
of Sri Lanka: 4 cent **5** rupee
of Sudan: 5 pound **7** piastre
of Suriname: 4 cent **7** guilder
of Swaziland: 4 rand **9** lilangeni
of Sweden: 3 ore **5** krona, krone **7** carolin **8** skilling **9** rigsdaler
of Switzerland: 5 franc, rappe **6** hallar, rappen **7** angster, centime, duplone **8** baetzner, blaffert
of Syria: 4 lira **5** pound **6** talent **7** piaster

of Taiwan: 4 yuan **6** dollar
of Tajikistan: 5 ruble
of Tanzania: 4 cent **8** shilling
of Thailand: 2 at **3** att **4** baht **5** cutty, fuang, tical **6** pynung, salung, satang **11** bullet money
of Tibet: 5 tanga
of Togo: 5 franc **7** centime
of Tonga: 6 paanga, seniti
of Trinidad and Tobago: 4 cent **6** dollar
of Tunisia: 5 dinar **6** dollar **7** millime
of Turkey: 4 lira, para **5** akcha, asper, attun, kurus, pound, rebia **6** akcheh, sequin, zequin **7** aetilik, beshlik, pataque, piaster **8** medjidie, zecchino
of Turkmenistan: 5 ruble
of Tuvalu: 4 cent **6** dollar
of Uganda: 4 cent **8** shilling
of Ukraine: 6 grivna **10** karbovanet
of United Arab Emirates: 3 fil **6** dirham
of Uruguay: 4 peso **9** centesimo, centisimo
of Uzbekistan: 5 ruble
of Vanuatu: 5 franc **6** dollar
of Venezuela: 4 peso, real **5** medio **6** fuerte **7** bolivar, centimo **8** morocota **10** venezolano
of Vietnam: 2 xu **4** dong **7** piaster
of Western Samoa: 4 sene, tala
of Yemen: 4 fils, rial **5** dinar, riyal
of Yugoslavia: 4 para **5** dinar
of Zaire: 5 zaire **6** makuta
of Zambia: 5 ngwee **6** kwacha
of Zimbabwe: 4 cent **6** dollar
coincide 3 fit **4** jibe, meet **5** agree, cross, match, tally **6** accord, concur, square **7** conform **8** converge, dovetail **9** harmonize **10** correspond **11** synchronize **12** be concurrent, come together **19** occur simultaneously
coincidence 4 fate, luck **6** chance **8** accident **11** concurrence, synchronism **12** happenstance **22** simultaneous occurrence
coincident 10 coexistent, concurrent **12** contemporary, simultaneous **15** contemporaneous
coincidental 6 chance **9** unplanned **10** accidental, contiguous, synchronal **11** concomitant, synchronous **12** happenstance, simultaneous
cointreau
type: 7 liqueur
variety: 7 curacao **9** triple sec
origin: 6 France
flavor: 6 orange
drink: 8 Applecar
with bourbon: 10 Temptation
with brandy: 7 Sidecar
with cognac: 10 Rolls Royce
with gin: 7 Florida **9** White Lady **13** Sweet Patootie **14** Flying Dutchman
with rum: 8 Acapulco **10** Casa Blanca **11** Beachcomber **12** Blue Hawaiian
with rye: 10 Temptation

with tequila: 9 Margarita
with whiskey: 16 Canadian Cocktail

Colavito, Rocky (Rocco Domenico)
sport: 8 baseball
team: 16 Cleveland Indians

Colbert, Claudette
real name: 22 Claudette Lily Chauchoin
born: 5 Paris **6** France
roles: 8 Tovarich **9** Cleopatra **14** Palm Beach Story **18** It Happened One Night (Oscar)

cold 3 icy, old **4** cool, dead, flat, hard **5** aloof, brisk, chill, crisp, cruel, faded, faint, gelid, harsh, nippy, polar, sharp, stale, stiff, stony **6** arctic, biting, bitter, chilly, cooled, frigid, frosty, frozen, inured, numbed, remote, severe, snappy, steely, wintry **7** callous, chilled, cutting, distant, frosted, glacial, haughty, nipping, passive, unmoved **8** chilling, coolness, detached, freezing, hardened, piercing, reserved, reticent, stinging, uncaring, unheated, unloving, unwarmed **9** apathetic, heartless, impassive, insensate, unfeeling, unstirred **10** disdainful, forbidding, impervious, insensible, phlegmatic, unfriendly **11** frozen stiff, indifferent, passionless, penetrating, unconcerned, unconscious, unemotional, unexcitable **12** antipathetic, bone-chilling, inaccessible, supercilious, uninterested, unresponsive **13** uninteresting, unsympathetic **14** marrow-chilling, unapproachable **15** teeth-chattering, uncommunicative, undemonstrative **16** chilled to the bone, unimpressionable **18** chilled to the marrow

cold-blooded 4 evil, hard **5** cruel, harsh, stiff, stony **6** brutal, flinty, formal, frigid, inured, savage, steely **7** callous, demonic, inhuman, passive, satanic, unmoved **8** detached, fiendish, hardened, inhumane, pitiless, reserved, ruthless, uncaring **9** barbarous, heartless, impassive, merciless, unfeeling, unpitying, unstirred **10** deliberate, diabolical, disdainful, impervious, implacable, unfriendly, unmerciful, villainous **11** calculating, hardhearted, indifferent, insensitive, passionless, unconcerned, unemotional, unexcitable **12** bloodthirsty, contemptuous, uninterested, unresponsive **13** disinterested, unimpassioned, unimpressible, unsympathetic **16** unimpressionable

cold-hearted 5 cruel **9** heartless, unfeeling **11** hard-hearted **13** unsympathetic

coldness 5 chill **7** iciness **9** aloofness **10** chilliness, frostiness **12** indifference **13** unfeelingness **14** unfriendliness **15** hardheartedness

Cole, Janet
real name of: 9 Kim Hunter

Cole, Thomas
born: 7 England **13** Bolton-le-Moors
artwork: 8 The Ox-Bow **15** The Voyage of Life **17** The Course of Empire

coleoptera
class: 8 hexopoda
phylum: 10 arthropoda
group: 6 beetle, weevil

Coleridge, Samuel Taylor
author of: 9 Kubla Khan **10** Christabel **14** Dejection An Ode, Lyrical Ballads (with Wordsworth) **19** Biographia Literaria **26** The Rime of the Ancient Mariner

Colette (Sidonie)
author of: 4 Gigi, Sido **5** Cheri **8** Claudine **11** La Vagabonde **14** The Evening Star

coliseum 4 bowl **5** arena **6** circus **7** stadium, theater **9** Colosseum **10** hippodrome **12** amphitheater **14** exhibition hall

collaborate 4 join **5** unite **6** assist, team up **7** collude **9** cooperate **10** join forces **12** work together **14** work side by side

collaborationist 6 puppet **7** traitor **8** quisling

collaborator 4 ally **6** puppet **7** traitor **8** co-worker, quisling, teammate **9** associate, colleague, co-partner **11** confederate

collapse 4 coma, fail, fall, flop, fold **5** faint, swoon **6** attack, buckle, cave-in, fizzle **7** break up, crack-up, crumple, failure, give way, seizure **8** be in vain, buckling, downfall, flounder, keel over, take sick **9** become ill, break down **10** be stricken, break apart, run aground **11** fall through **12** disintegrate, falling apart, fall helpless, fall to pieces **13** come to nothing, sudden illness **14** disintegration **17** become unconscious

collapsed 4 limp **7** caved in, compact **8** deflated, fallen in, folded up **13** disintegrated

Collapse of the Third Republic, The
author: 14 William L Shirer

collapsible 7 folding **8** foldable **10** deflatable

collar 3 nab **4** eton, grab **5** catch, fichu, pinch, seize **6** arrest, bertha **7** capture **9** apprehend, neckpiece **12** take prisoner **15** take into custody

collate 5 order **6** bestow, verify **7** compare **8** assemble, organize **9** integrate **11** put together

collateral 4 bond **5** extra **6** pledge, surety **7** warrant **8** parallel, security, warranty **9** accessory, ancillary, auxiliary, guarantee, insurance, secondary **10** additional, incidental, supporting,

supportive **11** endorsement, subordinate **12** contributory **13** supplementary

collation 3 tea **4** meal **5** lunch **6** brunch, repast, sermon **7** address, reading **8** hotchpot, luncheon, treatise **10** comparison **11** description

colleague 4 mate **6** fellow **7** partner **8** confrere, co-worker, teammate **9** associate, co-partner **11** confederate **12** collaborator, fellow worker

collect 3 get **4** calm, meet **5** amass, raise, rally **6** gather, heap up, muster, obtain, pick up, pile up, summon **7** call for, compile, compose, control, convene, marshal, prepare, receive, solicit **8** assemble, gather up, scrape up **9** aggregate, get hold of **10** accumulate, congregate **11** concentrate, get together

collectanea 8 analects, treasury **9** anthology, gleanings **10** collection, miscellany, selections **11** miscellanea

collected 4 calm, cool **5** quiet **6** placid, poised, serene, steady **8** composed, peaceful, tranquil **9** confident, unruffled **10** cool-headed, restrained **11** level-headed, self-assured, undisturbed, unemotional, unflappable, unperturbed **12** even-tempered **13** self-possessed **14** self-controlled

collection 3 mob **4** bevy, body, gift, heap, mass, pack, pile **5** array, bunch, clump, crowd, drove, flock, group, hoard, store, swarm **6** corpus, jumble, muster, throng **7** cluster, clutter, variety **8** amassing, assembly, oblation, treasury **9** anthology, gathering, offertory, receiving **10** assemblage, assortment, hodgepodge, miscellany, soliciting **11** aggregation, compilation **12** accumulating, accumulation

Collection of Ten Thousand Leaves (Manyoshu)
author: 7 unknown

collective 5 joint **6** common, mutual, united **7** unified **8** combined, gathered **9** aggregate, composite **10** cumulative, integrated **11** accumulated, cooperative

collector 6 grouper **7** dustman **8** antiquer, compiler, composer, gatherer, zamindar **9** assembler **10** garbageman **11** anthologist

Collector, The
author: 10 John Fowles

college 7 academy **8** seminary **9** institute **10** university **11** institution

college-preparatory 4 prep **8** academic **11** liberal-arts **12** nontechnical **13** nonvocational

collegiate 8 academic **10** scholastic, university **11** educational

collide 3 hit **4** meet **5** clash, crash, smash **7** crack up, diverge, run into **8** bump into, conflict, disagree **9** knock into **10** meet head on **11** beat against **13** hurtle against, strike against

Collier, Lucille Ann
   real name of: **9** Ann Miller

Collins, Mary Catherine
   real name of: **7** Bo Derek

Collins, Mr
   character in: **17** Pride and Prejudice
   author: **6** Austen

Collins, Wilkie
   author of: **6** No Name **12** The Moonstone **15** The Woman in White

collision 4 bump **5** clash, crash, fight, smash **6** battle, combat, impact **7** smash-up **8** accident, conflict, skirmish, struggle **9** encounter **10** engagement **11** clash of arms

colloquial 5 homey, plain **6** casual, chatty, common, folksy **8** everyday, familiar, homespun, informal, ordinary, workaday **9** idiomatic **10** vernacular **14** conversational **15** unsophisticated

colloquy 4 chat, talk **6** caucus, parley **7** council, palaver, seminar **8** commerce, congress, converse, dialogue **9** communion, discourse **10** conference, discussion, rap session **11** interchange, intercourse **12** conversation **13** confabulation

collude 4 plot **7** connive **8** conspire, intrigue **9** cooperate **11** collaborate

collusion 5 fraud **7** treason **8** intrigue **10** complicity, connivance, conspiracy **13** collaboration **15** secret agreement **17** guilty association

Colman, Ronald
   born: **7** England **8** Richmond
   roles: **9** Beau Geste **10** Arrowsmith **11** A Double Life (Oscar), Lost Horizon **16** A Tale of Two Cities

cologne 5 scent **7** essence, perfume **9** fragrance **11** toilet water

Colomba
   author: **14** Prosper Merimee

Colombia
   other name: **6** Darien **10** New Granada
   capital/largest city: **6** Bogota
   others: **3** Ten **4** Amza, Buga, Cali, Mitu, Muzo, Paez, Sipi, Tado, Tolu, Yari **5** Bello, Chinu, Guapi, Neiva, Pasto, Tulua, Tunja **6** Cucuta, Ibaque, Lorica, Quibdo, Sangil, Tumaco **7** Cartago, Ipiates, Leticia, Palmira, Pereira, Popayan **8** Girardot, Maganque, Medellin, Monteria **9** Cartagena, Manizales **10** Santa Marta **11** Bucaramanga **12** Barranquilla, Buenaventura
   school: **5** Andes, Valle **20** Instituto Caro y Cuervo **21** Industrial de Santander
   measure: **4** vara **7** azumbre, celemin
   monetary unit: **4** peso, real **6** condor, peseta **7** centavo
   weight: **3** bag **4** saco **5** libra **7** quin-tal

island: 4 Baru **5** Naipo **6** Fuerte **7** Gorgona, Malpelo **8** Cusachon **9** San Andres **11** Providencia
lake: 4 Tota
mountain: 5 Abibe, Andes, Baudo, Chita, Cocuy, Huila, Pasto **6** Ayapel, Perija, Purace, Tolima, Tunahi **7** Chamusa, del Ruiz **8** Oriengal **10** Santa Marta **17** Central Cordillera, Eastern Cordillera, Western Cordillera
   highest point: 14 Cristobal Colon
river: 3 Uva **4** Bita, Meta, Muco, Sinu, Tomo, Yari **5** Cauca, Cesar, Isana, Mesai, Nechi, Pauto, Sucio **6** Amazon, Arauca, Ariari, Atrato, Atroto, Caguan, Pattia, Yapura **7** Apapois, Caqueta, Guainia, Inirida, Truando, Vichada **8** Casanare, Guaviara, Putumayo **9** Magdalena
sea: 7 Pacific **9** Caribbean
physical feature:
   cape: 4 Vela **5** Aguja, Marzo, Punta **7** Augusta **8** Gallinas
   falls: 10 Tequendama
   gulf: 5 Uraba **6** Cupica, Darien, Tibuga **8** Tortugas
   inlet: 6 Tumaco
   plains: 6 Ilanos
   point: 6 Cruces, Lacruz, Solano **8** Caribana, Gallinas
people: 4 Boro, Cuna, Duit, Hoka, Macu, Muso, Muzo, Paez, Tama, Tapa **5** Carib, Catio, Choco, Cofan, Cogui, Cubeo, Guane, Haida, Mocoa, Paeze, Pijao, Seona, Yagua **6** Arawak, Betoya, Calima, Colima, Ingano, Mirana, Saliva, Tahami, Ticunu, Tucano, Tunebo, Witoto, Yahuna **7** Achagua, Andaqui, Chibcha, Chimila, Churoya, Guahibo, Guajiro, Panches, Puinave, Puitoto, Quechua, Shuswap, Tairona, Telembi **8** Coconuco, Guarauno, mestizos, Motilone, Puinavis, Quimbaya, Sinsigas **9** Cocanucos, Coconucan, mulattoes, Panaquita **10** Bellacoola
   leader: 7 Bolivar
language: 7 Spanish
religion: 13 Roman Catholic
place:
   museum: 4 Gold **8** Colonial
   palace: 11 Inquisition
feature:
   dance: 7 bambuco **8** merengue
   game: 4 tejo
   guitar: 5 tiple
   poncho: 5 ruana
   shoes: 10 alpargatas
   shoulder bag: 7 carriel
   tree: 8 arboloco
   woven hat: 5 jipas

Colombo
   capital of: **8** Sri Lanka

colon 4 coin **6** farmer, vitals **7** pioneer, planter, settler, viscera **9** hemistich,

intestine **15** plantation owner, punctuation mark

colonize 5 found, plant **6** gather, settle **7** migrate **8** establish **10** infiltrate

colonnade 3 row **4** stoa **5** porch **6** arcade, piazza **7** portico, terrace **8** cloister **9** peristyle

colony 3 set **4** band, body **5** flock, group, swarm **7** mandate **8** dominion, province **9** community, territory **10** dependency, possession, settlement **12** protectorate **14** satellite state

colophon 6 design, device, emblem **7** insigne **8** insignia **11** inscription

color 3 dye, hue **4** bias, burn, cast, glow, mood, tint, tone, warp, wash **5** bloom, blush, chalk, drift, flame, flush, force, paint, sense, shade, slant, stain, taint, tinge, twist **6** affect, aspect, crayon, effect, import, intent, redden, spirit, stress **7** distort, feeling, meaning, pervert, pigment, redness, skin hue **8** dyestuff, rosiness **9** go crimson, influence, intention, prejudice **10** intimation **11** connotation, implication, insinuation **12** become florid, pigmentation, significance **17** natural complexion

Colorado
   abbreviation: **2** CO **4** Colo
   nickname: **10** Centennial
   capital/largest city: **6** Denver
   others: **4** Vail **5** Aspen, Delta, Lamar, Ouray **6** Arvada, Aurora, Denver, Golden, Pueblo, Salida **7** Alamosa, Boulder, Durango, Greeley, Manassa, Manitou **8** Gunnison, Loveland, Trinidad **9** Purgatory, Silverton, Telluride **11** Central City **12** Cripple Creek **13** Grand Junction **15** Colorado Springs
   baseball team: **7** Rockies
   college: **5** Regis **6** Denver **7** Boulder **17** US Air Force Academy
   feature: **11** Four Corners **15** Garden of the Gods **17** Continental Divide
      national monument: **8** Dinosaur **14** Great Sand Dunes
      national park: **5** Estes **9** Mesa Verde **13** Rocky Mountain
   tribe: **3** Ute **7** Arapaho **8** Cheyenne
   people: **11** Jack Dempsey **12** Ralph Edwards **14** Scott Carpenter **18** Douglas Fairbanks Sr
   lake: **6** Frozen
   land rank: **6** eighth
   mountains: **5** Longs, Rocky **7** San Juan **9** Pikes Peak **14** Sangre de Cristo
      highest point: **6** Elbert
   physical feature:
      canyon: **5** Black
      gorge: **5** Royal
      plains: **5** Great
      wind: **7** Chinook
   river: **4** Gila **5** Yampa **6** Platte **7** Dolores **8** Apishapa, Arikaree, Arkansas, Gunnison **9** Rio Grande **10** Purgatoire

state admission: 12 thirty-eighth
state bird: 11 lark bunting
state flower: 22 Rocky Mountain columbine
state motto: 24 Nothing Without Providence
state song: 22 Where the Columbines Grow
state tree: 18 Colorado blue spruce
colored 4 dyed, hued **5** dusky **6** biased, shaded, tinged, tinted **7** blushed, excused, flushed, glossed, labeled, painted, stained **8** affected, labelled, reddened **9** chromatic, distorted, pigmented **10** influenced, prejudiced **12** complexioned **13** characterized **14** misrepresented
colorful 3 gay **4** loud **5** showy, vivid **6** bright, florid, unique **7** dynamic, graphic, unusual, vibrant, zestful **8** animated, forceful, spirited, vigorous **9** brilliant, full-toned, vivacious **10** compelling, variegated **11** distinctive, interesting, many-colored, picturesque **12** multicolored, particolored
coloring 3 dye **4** tint **5** color, shade, stain **10** coloration, complexion
colorless 3 wan **4** ashy, drab, dull, flat, pale **5** ashen, dingy, faded, pasty, vapid, white **6** anemic, boring, dreary, grayed, pallid, sallow, sickly, undyed **7** ghastly, ghostly, insipid, natural, neutral, prosaic **8** blanched, bleached, lifeless, ordinary, whitened **9** bloodless, washed out **10** cadaverous, lackluster, monotonous, spiritless, unanimated, unexciting, uninspired **11** commonplace **13** uninteresting
Color Purple, The
  author: 11 Alice Walker
  director: 15 Steven Spielberg
  cast: 11 Danny Glover **12** Adolph Caesar, Oprah Winfrey **13** Margaret Avery **14** Whoopi Goldberg
colors 4 flag, jack **6** banner, ensign, pennon **7** pennant **8** standard
colossal 4 huge, vast **5** giant, grand, great **6** mighty **7** extreme, immense, mammoth, massive, titanic **8** enormous, gigantic, imposing **9** exceeding, excessive **10** incredible, inordinate, monumental, prodigious, tremendous **11** extravagant, spectacular **12** aweinspiring, overwhelming
Colossus of Rhodes
  statue of: 6 Apollo
colt 4 foal **5** horse **6** novice **8** equuleus, yearling **9** fledgling, youngster
  constellation of: 8 Equuleus
columbium
  chemical symbol: 2 Cb
Columbo
  character: 9 Lt Columbo
  cast: 9 Peter Falk
column 3 row **4** file, line, post **5** pylon, queue, shaft, train **6** parade, pillar, string **7** caravan, phalanx, sup-port, upright **8** pilaster **9** cavalcade, formation **10** procession **11** vertical row **12** vertical list
columnist 6 writer **7** analyst
  famous: 7 Heloise **8** Dear Abby, Herb Caen **9** HL Mencken, Jack Smith **10** Ann Landers **11** Miss Manners **15** Abigail van Buren
coma 6 stupor, torpor **8** collapse **15** unconsciousness
Comanche
  language family: 10 Shoshonean
  location: 5 Texas **6** Kansas, Mexico **8** Oklahoma
  noted as: 8 horsemen
comatose 3 lax **4** dull, idle, lazy **5** inert **6** leaden, torpid **7** drugged, languid, passive **8** inactive, indolent, lifeless, listless, slothful, sluggish **9** apathetic, catatonic, lethargic, stuporous **10** cataleptic, insensible, narcotized, phlegmatic, spiritless **11** indifferent, unconcerned, unconscious **12** unresponsive
comb 4 card, tuft **5** curry, dress, groom, plume, scour, style **6** search **7** arrange, explore, panache, ransack, topknot **8** head tuft, hunt over, untangle **9** cast about, cockscomb, currycomb **11** look through **14** rummage through
combat 5 clash, fight **6** action, attack, battle, oppose, resist **7** contest, go to war, wage war **8** conflict, fighting, skirmish, struggle **9** encounter **10** contention, engagement, war against **11** come to blows, grapple with, make warfare, work against **12** do battle with, march against **13** confrontation **14** military action
Combat
  character: 4 Caje (Caddy Cadron) **5** Kirby **8** (Pvt) Braddock **9** Doc Walton, (Lt) Gil Hanley **12** (Sgt) Chip Saunders
  cast: 9 Jack Hogan, Rick Jason, Vic Morrow **12** Shecky Greene, Steven Rogers **13** Pierre Jalbert
combatant 7 fighter, soldier, warrior **9** man-at-arms **10** serviceman **11** fighting man
combating 8 battling, clashing, fighting, opposing **9** waging war **10** contention, contesting, opposition, struggling **11** doing battle **13** grappling with **17** coming to blows with
combative 6 bantam **8** militant **9** agonistic, bellicose **10** aggressive, pugnacious **11** belligerent, contentious **12** antagonistic
combativeness 9 hostility, pugnacity **10** antagonism **12** belligerence **14** aggressiveness **15** contentiousness
combination 3 mix **5** alloy, blend, union **6** fusion, league, medley, merger, mixing **7** amalgam, joining, mixture, pooling, variety **8** alliance, blending, compound **9** coalition, composite, synthesis **10** assortment, coalescing, federation **11** association, composition, confederacy **12** amalgamation **13** confederation
combine 3 mix **4** fuse, join, pool **5** blend, merge, unify, unite **6** couple, league, mingle **8** compound **9** commingle **10** amalgamate, synthesize **11** consolidate, incorporate
combo 4 band **5** group **11** aggregation, combination
comb out 4 curl **5** dress **7** arrange, unsnarl **8** untangle
combustible 8 burnable **9** flammable, ignitable **10** combustive, incendiary **11** inflammable **13** conflagrative
combustion 6 firing **7** burning, flaming **8** ignition, kindling **12** incineration **13** conflagration
combustive 8 burnable **9** flammable, ignitable **11** combustible, inflammable **13** conflagrative
come 2 be, go **3** bud **4** fall, loom, rise **5** arise, issue, occur, range, reach **6** appear, arrive, be made, drop in, emerge, extend, follow, happen, impend, show up, spread, spring, turn up **7** advance, descend, emanate, stretch **8** approach, draw near, go toward, grow to be **9** be a native, germinate, take place **10** be imminent, move toward **11** be a resident, be in the wind, materialize, originate in, spring forth
come about 5 occur **6** chance, happen **7** turn out **10** come to pass
come afterward 5 ensue **6** derive, follow, result **7** succeed
come apart 6 detach **7** disjoin, unstick **8** separate
come back 5 rally **6** answer, retort, return **7** rebound **8** recovery
Come Back Little Sheba
  director: 10 Daniel Mann
  based on play by: 11 William Inge
  cast: 10 Terry Moore **12** Shirley Booth **13** Burt Lancaster
  Oscar for: 7 actress (Booth)
come clean 4 sing **5** own up **7** confess **14** unbosom oneself **18** make a clean breast of
come close to 7 verge on **8** approach, border on **11** approximate, nearly equal
comedian 3 wag **4** fool, zany **5** clown, comic, cutup, joker **6** jester, madcap **7** buffoon **8** humorist, jokester **9** prankster **10** comedienne, comic actor **14** practical joker
comedown 4 drop **8** lowering **10** anticlimax
come down 4 dive, drop, fall, sink **6** plunge, tumble **7** descend, plummet **8** decrease
come down a peg 5 deign, stoop **6**

unbend **7** descend **10** condescend **12** lower oneself **13** humble oneself

comedy 3 fun, wit **5** farce, humor **6** banter, joking, pranks, satire **7** foolery, jesting **8** drollery, raillery, travesty **9** burlesque, cutting up, horseplay, silliness **10** buffoonery, pleasantry, tomfoolery **13** fooling around

Comedy of Errors, The
    author: 18 William Shakespeare
    character: 6 Aegeon, Dromio **7** Adriana, Aemilia, Luciana, Solinus **10** Antipholus

come face to face with 4 meet **8** confront **9** encounter

come first 7 precede, predate **8** antecede, antedate, go before **10** anticipate

come into being 4 dawn, show **5** arise, begin, occur, set in, start **6** appear, be born, crop up, emerge, sprout **8** commence, spring up **9** germinate, originate **11** come to light

come into port 4 dock **5** berth

come into view 4 show **6** appear, come up, emerge, show up **7** surface **11** come to light **13** become visible

come loose 5 let go **6** detach, loosen **7** slip off **8** break off, separate, unfasten **9** break away **10** come undone, come untied, disconnect **11** come unglued, come unstuck

comely 4 fair, nice **5** bonny **6** pretty, proper, seemly, simple **7** correct, fitting, natural, sightly, winning, winsome **8** becoming, blooming, charming, decorous, engaging, fetching, pleasant, pleasing, suitable, tasteful **9** agreeable, appealing, wholesome **10** attractive, unaffected **11** well-favored

come near 4 loom, near **6** appear **8** approach **9** draw close **10** move toward

come-on 4 bait, hook, lure, trap **5** decoy, snare **6** magnet **9** seduction **10** allurement, attraction, bewitchery, enticement, inducement, seducement, temptation **12** inveiglement

comestibles 5 foods **7** edibles **8** victuals **10** foodstuffs, provisions

come to a decision 6 decide, settle **7** resolve **8** conclude **9** determine

come to an understanding 5 agree **6** settle **11** come to terms **12** agree to marry **16** reach an agreement

come to a standstill 4 halt, quit, stop **5** abate, cease **7** die away **8** quit cold

come to blows 5 fight **7** contest **8** do battle **9** square off **12** start to fight

come together 4 meet **5** flock, group, rally **6** gather **7** collect, convene **8** assemble **10** congregate **11** get together

come to light 4 dawn **5** arise **6** appear, crop up, emerge, evolve, show

up, turn up, unfold **7** develop, surface, turn out

come to nothing 4 fail, flop, fold **6** fizzle **8** be in vain, collapse **9** break down **11** fall through **12** come to naught **17** fail to materialize

come to pass 5 ensue, occur **6** arrive, befall, follow, happen **9** take place

come to terms 5 agree, yield **6** give up, settle **7** succumb **8** contract, cry quits **9** make a deal, negotiate, surrender **10** capitulate, compromise **11** come to grips, meet halfway, sue for peace **13** resign oneself **14** strike a bargain **15** lay down one's arms **16** reach an agreement **17** acknowledge defeat, hoist the white flag **18** split the difference

come unglued 6 detach, loosen **8** separate **9** fall apart **11** come unstuck

come unstuck 4 lift **6** detach, loosen **8** break off, unfasten **9** break away, come apart, come loose, fall apart **11** come unglued

come up 4 rise **5** arise **7** quicken, sharpen **8** heighten, increase **9** intensify **10** accelerate, strengthen **12** be referred to

come upon 4 find, meet **7** learn of, run into **8** discover **9** encounter

comfit 5 candy, sweet **9** sweetmeat **10** confection, sugar candy **13** confectionery

comfort 4 calm, ease, help **5** cheer, peace, quiet **6** luxury, relief, solace, soothe, succor, warmth **7** cheer up, compose, console, hearten **8** coziness, opulence, pleasure, reassure, serenity, snugness **9** bolster up, comforter, composure, encourage, well-being **10** cheering up, relaxation **11** consolation, contentment, reassurance **12** satisfaction **13** encouragement, gratification **14** quiet one's fears **16** source of serenity **17** lighten one's burden **18** bolster one's spirits

Comfort, Alex
    author of: 11 The Joy of Sex **12** More Joy of Sex

comfortable 4 cozy, easy **6** at ease, at home, serene **7** relaxed **8** adequate, pleasant, suitable **9** agreeable, congenial, contented **10** giving ease, gratifying, untroubled **11** pleasurable, undisturbed **12** satisfactory **16** free from distress

comforter 4 balm, puff **5** quilt, scarf **6** afghan, solace **7** anodyne, blanket, comfort, soother **8** coverlet **10** palliative

comic, comical 4 rich **5** droll, funny, merry, silly, witty **6** absurd, jocose, jovial **7** amusing, jocular, risible **8** farcical, humorous, mirthful **9** facetious, laughable, ludicrous, whimsical **10** ridiculous **11** nonsensical **12** nimble-witted

coming 4 next **6** advent, future, in view, to come **7** arrival, nearing **8** approach, arriving, imminent, on the way **9** advancing, emergence, imminence, impending, in the wind, proximity **10** appearance, occurrence, subsequent **11** approaching, forthcoming, prospective **12** on the horizon **13** materializing

Coming Home
    director: 8 Hal Ashby
    cast: 9 Bruce Dern, Jane Fonda, Jon Voight **15** Robert Carradine
    Oscar for: 5 actor (Voight) **7** actress (Fonda) **10** screenplay

Coming into the Country
    author: 10 John McPhee

Coming of Age, The
    author: 16 Simone de Beauvoir

Coming of Age in Samoa
    author: 12 Margaret Mead

Coming Race, The
    author: 18 Edward Bulwer-Lytton

command 3 bid, get **4** boss, call, draw, fiat, grip, head, hold, lead, rule **5** edict, evoke, grasp, guide, order, power **6** adjure, behest, charge, compel, decree, demand, direct, elicit, enjoin, govern, incite, induce, kindle, manage, ordain, prompt, summon **7** call for, conduct, control, deserve, extract, inspire, mastery, provoke, receive, require, summons **8** call upon, instruct, motivate **9** authority, call forth, direction, directive, governing, knowledge, ordinance, supervise, ultimatum **10** administer, be master of, domination, injunction, leadership, management **11** familiarity, instruction, superintend, supervision **12** have charge of **13** comprehension, understanding **14** administration **17** have authority over

commandant 7 captain **9** commander **12** chief officer

commandeer 4 take **5** seize, usurp **8** shanghai **11** appropriate, expropriate

commander 4 boss, head **5** chief, ruler **6** leader **7** manager **8** director **9** conductor

commanding 4 head **5** chief, grand, lofty **6** ruling, senior, strong **7** dynamic, leading, ranking, stately **8** forceful, gripping, imposing, powerful, striking, towering **9** arresting, directing, governing, important, prominent **10** compelling, dominating, impressive **11** controlling, significant **13** authoritative, distinguished, overshadowing

commandment
    Hebrew: 7 mitsvah, mitzvah

comme il faut 6 proper **7** fitting **12** as it should be

commemorate 4 hail, mark **5** extol, honor **6** hallow, revere, salute **7** acclaim, glorify, observe **8** venerate **9** celebrate, solemnize **11** acknowledge, memorialize, pay homage to **12** pay tribute to

commence 5 begin, start **8** get going, initiate **10** get started, inaugurate, originated

commencement 4 dawn **5** birth, onset, start **6** outset **7** genesis, morning **9** beginning, first step, inception **10** graduation, initiation **11** origination **12** inauguration **13** graduation day **20** graduation ceremonies

commend 2 OK **4** back, give, laud **5** extol **6** commit, confer, convey, praise **7** acclaim, approve, consign, endorse, entrust, stand by, support **8** delegate, give over, hand over, pass over, relegate, transfer **13** speak highly of

commendable 6 worthy **7** notable **8** laudable **9** admirable, deserving, estimable, exemplary, honorable **10** creditable **11** meritorious **12** praiseworthy

commendation 5 honor **6** praise **7** support **8** approval **10** acceptance **11** acclamation, approbation

commendatory 8 admiring, praising **9** laudatory, praiseful **10** plauditory **13** complimentary **14** congratulatory

commensurate, commensurable 4 even, meet **5** equal **6** square **7** fitting **8** balanced, in accord, parallel, relative, suitable **10** comparable, compatible, consistent, equivalent **11** appropriate, in agreement **13** corresponding, proportionate **14** on a proper scale

comment 4 note, word **6** remark **7** clarify, discuss, explain, expound **8** expand on **9** assertion, criticism, elucidate, shed light, statement, talk about, touch upon, utterance **10** annotation, expression, reflection **11** elucidation, explanation, explication, observation **13** clarification **15** exemplification

commentary 6 review **8** critique, scholium, treatise **9** criticism **10** exposition **11** explanation, explication **12** dissertation **14** interpretation **16** explanatory essay

commentator 6 critic, writer **7** speaker **8** panelist, reporter, reviewer **9** columnist, explainer **10** newscaster **11** interpreter, news analyst

comment upon 7 clarify, clear up, explain **8** spell out **9** delineate, elucidate, explicate, interpret, make plain **10** illuminate, illustrate **14** throw light upon

commerce 5 trade **6** barter **7** trading, traffic **8** business, exchange, industry **12** mercantilism **16** buying and selling **god of: 6** Hermes **7** Mercury

commercial 2 ad **5** sales, trade **8** business **10** mercantile, sales pitch **12** profit-making **13** advertisement **16** buying-and-selling

commingle 3 mix **4** fuse **5** blend,

merge, unify **7** combine **10** amalgamate

commiserate 7 feel for **8** show pity **10** grieve with, lament with **13** express sorrow **14** sympathize with **15** share one's sorrow **17** have compassion for

commiseration 4 pity **8** sympathy **10** compassion, tenderness **13** fellow feeling

commission 3 act, bid, cut, fee **4** duty, hire, name, rank, role, task **5** board, doing, order, piece, power, proxy, trust **6** agency, assign, charge, direct, employ, engage, office **7** appoint, certify, charter, conduct, council, empower, license, mandate, mission, portion, rake-off, stipend, warrant **8** capacity, contract, delegate, dividend, document, exercise, function, position **9** acting out, allotment, allowance, authority, authorize, committal, committee **10** assignment, commitment, committing, delegation, deputation, entrusting, percentage, performing **11** appointment, carrying out, certificate, performance, transacting **12** officer's rank, perpetration **13** authorization, written orders **14** give the go-ahead **15** representatives **16** piece of the action **17** appointment papers, grant officer's rank

commissioner 5 envoy, trier **7** officer, pristaw **8** delegate, official **9** authority, commissar

commissioning 10 assignment, delegation **11** appointment, designation, entrustment **13** authorization

commit 2 do **3** act, put **4** bind, pull **5** enact, place **6** assign, decide, effect, engage, intern, pursue **7** confine, consign, deliver, deposit, entrust, execute, perform, pull off, resolve **8** carry out, give over, obligate, practice, transact, transfer **9** determine **10** make liable, perpetrate **13** participate in **16** institutionalize

commitment 3 vow **4** bond, word **5** stand **6** pledge **7** promise **8** decision, delivery, transfer, warranty **9** assurance, detention, guarantee, liability, restraint **10** assignment, giving over, internment, obligation, resolution **11** confinement, consignment, dispatching **12** imprisonment **13** determination, incarceration **14** responsibility **18** institutionalizing

commit oneself 3 act **7** resolve **8** dedicate, obligate **9** determine

committed 6 active, liable **8** confined, detained, interned **9** concerned, delivered, entrusted, obligated **10** interested, responsive **11** responsible **17** institutionalized

committee 4 body, jury **5** bench, board, group, junta, table **6** bureau, soviet **7** cabinet, council **9** gathering,

syndicate **10** assemblage **12** organization

commode 6 bureau, toilet **7** cabinet, dresser **9** washstand **14** chest of drawers

commodious 5 ample, large, roomy **8** spacious **9** capacious, uncramped **11** unconfining

commodity 4 ware **5** asset, goods, stock **6** staple **7** chattel, holding, product **8** property **9** advantage, belonging **10** possession **11** convenience, merchandise **14** article of trade **17** article of commerce

common 3 bad, low **4** base, lewd, mean, rude, vile **5** brash, cheap, crass, crude, gross, joint, lowly, minor, plain, stock **6** brazen, brutal, coarse, lesser, normal, old-hat, public, ribald, shared, simple, smutty, tawdry, vulgar **7** average, boorish, callous, general, ignoble, ill-bred, loutish, low-bred, obscene, obscure, popular, prosaic, regular, routine, settled, uncouth, unknown, worn-out **8** communal, everyday, familiar, frequent, homespun, impolite, informal, mediocre, middling, nameless, ordinary, plebeian, shameful, standard, workaday, worn thin **9** bourgeois, customary, deficient, household, low-minded, moth-eaten, obnoxious, offensive, pervasive, shameless, tasteless, unexalted, universal, unnoticed, unrefined, well-known **10** collective, colloquial, despicable, dime-a-dozen, inglorious, threadbare, unblushing, uncultured, unpolished, widespread **11** disgraceful, established, ill-mannered, insensitive, middle-class, oft-repeated, subordinate, traditional, unimportant, widely known, without rank **12** contemptible, conventional, disagreeable **13** garden-variety, insignificant **15** undistinguished

commoners 5 plebs **6** masses **8** plebians

common law Latin: **13** lex non scripta

commonly 5 often **6** widely **7** as a rule, usually **8** normally, of course **9** generally, in general, most often, popularly, regularly, routinely **10** by and large, familiarly, frequently, habitually, informally, ordinarily, repeatedly **11** customarily **13** traditionally **14** by force of habit, conventionally, for the most part **15** in most instances **17** generally speaking

common people 5 demos, plebs **6** masses **8** populace **9** hoi polloi, plebeians **11** bourgeoisie

commonplace 3 old **4** dull **5** adage, banal, stale, trite, usual **6** cliche, old-hat, truism **7** bromide, general, humdrum, regular, routine, worn-out **8** banality, everyday, familiar, ordinary, standard, worn thin **9** customary, hackneyed, moth-eaten, platitude **10** pedestrian, threadbare, un original, widespread **11** oft-repeated, stereotyped, traditional **12** received idea, run-of-the-mill **13** unimaginative, uninteresting

commonplace book 9 anthology, gleanings, scrapbook

Common Sense
  author: **11** Thomas Paine

common-sense 5 sound **8** everyday, sensible **9** mother wit, practical, pragmatic, realistic **10** no-nonsense **11** down-to-earth, levelheaded, serviceable, utilitarian **12** matter-of-fact

commonwealth 5 state **6** nation **8** republic
  Latin: **10** res publica

commotion 3 ado **4** fuss, stir, to-do **5** furor **6** bustle, racket, ruckus, tumult, uproar **7** clatter, turmoil **9** agitation **10** excitement, hullabaloo **11** disturbance **12** perturbation

communal 5 joint **6** common, mutual, public, shared **9** community **10** collective

commune 3 gab, rap, yak **4** chat, chin, farm, talk, town **5** visit **6** babble, confer, gossip, parley, powwow **7** chatter, palaver, prattle **8** converse, schmooze **9** discourse **10** chew the fat, chew the rag **11** communicate, confabulate **14** shoot the breeze

communicable 8 catching **10** contagious, infectious **12** transferable **13** transmissible, transmittable

communicate 3 say **4** give, show, talk, tell **5** state, write **6** advise, convey, impart, notify, pass on, relate, reveal **7** declare, divulge, exhibit, mention, publish, signify **8** announce, converse, disclose, inform of, proclaim, transmit **9** apprise of, bring word, broadcast, make known, publicize **10** correspond

communication 4 news, note, wire **5** cable **6** letter, missal, report **7** liaison, message, missive, notices, rapport, writing **8** bulletin, dispatch, document, speaking, telegram **9** broadcast, cablegram, directive, statement **10** communique **11** declaration, information **12** conversation, intelligence, proclamation, radio message **13** telephone call **14** correspondence

communicative 4 open **5** frank **6** candid, chatty **7** voluble **8** friendly, outgoing, sociable **9** revealing, talkative **10** expressive, forthright, free-spoken, loquacious, revelatory, unreserved **11** informative

communion, Communion 6 accord **7** concord, harmony, rapport, sharing **8** affinity, sympathy **9** agreement **12** the Eucharist **13** communication, contemplation

communique 4 note, wire **5** aviso, cable, flash **6** report, letter, notice **7** epistle, message, missive, release, telegram **8** bulletin, dispatch **9** directive, statement **10** memorandum **12** announcement, intelligence, notification **13** communication

Communist 3 red **6** soviet **7** comrade, marxist **8** Leninist **9** bolshevik, socialist **10** bolshevist **12** totalitarian

Communist Manifesto
  author: **8** Karl Marx **15** Friedrich Engels

community 4 area, folk, town **5** arena, field, group, range, realm, scope **6** locale, people, public, sphere, suburb **7** quarter, society **8** affinity, district, environs, likeness, populace, province, sameness, vicinity **9** agreement, citizenry **10** population, similarity **11** environment, social group **12** commonwealth, neighborhood, surroundings

commute 4 ride, trip **5** alter **6** adjust, change, redeem, soften, switch, travel **7** convert, journey, replace, reverse **8** diminish, exchange, mitigate **9** alleviate, supersede, transform, transmute, transpose **10** substitute **11** transfigure **12** metamorphose, transmogrify

comodo
  music: **9** leisurely

Comoros
  other name: **26** lost pearls of the Indian Ocean
  capital/largest city: **6** Moroni
  others: **6** Bambao **7** Fomboni **8** Dzaoudzi **9** Mutsamudu **11** Mitsamiouli
  monetary unit: **5** franc **7** centime
  island: **6** Moheli **7** Anjouan, Mayotte **12** Grande Comoro
  highest point: **7** Kartala **8** Karthala
  sea: **6** Indian
  physical feature:
    channel: **10** Mozambique
  people: **4** Arab **5** Bantu, Malay **7** African **8** Malagasy
  language: **6** Arabic, French **7** Swahili **8** Malagasy
  religion: **5** Islam **13** Roman Catholic

compact 4 bond, cram, deal, pack, pact, snug, tidy **5** close, dense, press, small, stuff **6** little, treaty **7** bargain, crammed, pressed, squeeze, stuffed **8** alliance, compress, contract, covenant **9** agreement, clustered, concordat **10** compressed **11** arrangement, pack closely **12** concentrated **13** tightly packed, understanding

compactness 7 density **8** snugness **9** smallness **10** littleness **11** compression **13** concentration

companion 3 pal **4** chum, mate **5** buddy, crony **6** escort, friend, helper **7** comrade **9** assistant, associate, attendant

companionable 6 social **7** amiable, cordial **8** friendly, sociable **9** agreeable, congenial, convivial

companionate 4 warm **6** genial **7** cordial **8** amicable, friendly, platonic, suitable **9** accordant, agreeable, consonant, easygoing, nonsexual, spiritual, unfleshly **10** compatible, concordant, harmonious **11** nonphysical, passionless, warm-hearted **12** affectionate **13** companionable

companionship 4 pals **5** chums **7** buddies, company, friends **8** comrades **10** associates, companions, fellowship, friendship **11** camaraderie, comradeship, familiarity, sociability **17** close acquaintance, friendly relations

company 3 mob **4** band, firm, gang **5** bunch, group, guest, party **6** guests, outfit, people, throng **7** callers, concern, friends, society, visitor **8** assembly, comrades, presence, visitors **9** gathering, multitude, syndicate **10** assemblage, companions, fellowship, friendship **11** camaraderie, comradeship, corporation, sociability **12** conglomerate, congregation **13** companionship, establishment **15** business concern

comparable 4 like, up to **5** close, equal **6** akin to **7** similar **8** as good as, parallel **9** a match for, analogous **10** equivalent, on a par with, tantamount **11** approaching, approximate **12** commensurate, in a class with **13** commensurable

comparative 4 near **8** relative **11** approximate

compare 5 equal, liken, match **6** be up to, equate, relate **7** vie with **8** approach, contrast **9** correlate **11** compete with **12** be on a par with **13** hold a candle to **14** be in a class with **20** draw a parallel between

compare notes 6 confer **7** consult **8** talk over **13** exchange views

comparison 7 analogy, kinship **8** contrast, equality, likeness, parallel, relation **10** connection, similarity **11** correlation, resemblance **13** comparability

compartment 3 box, pew **4** brig, cell, crib, hold, hole, nook, room **5** berth, booth, cabin, crypt, niche, stall, vault **6** alcove, bunker, closet **7** chamber, cubicle, section **8** anteroom, roomette **9** cubbyhole **10** pigeonhole **11** antechamber

compass 5 bound, range, reach, scope, sweep **6** domain, extent **8** boundary, province **13** circumference

Compass, Mariner's Compass
  constellation of: **5** Pyxis

Compasses, Pair
  constellation of: **8** Circinus

compassion 4 pity **5** heart **7** empathy, feeling **8** humanity, sympathy **10** ten-

derness **13** commiseration, fellow feeling **17** tender-heartedness
Latin: 12 misericordia

compassionate 4 kind **6** humane **7** pitying **8** merciful **10** benevolent, charitable **11** kindhearted, sympathetic **13** tender-hearted

compatibility 6 accord **7** concord, harmony, rapport **8** affinity **9** agreement, unanimity **12** congeniality **14** like- mindedness

compatible 3 apt, fit **6** seemly **7** fitting **8** in accord, suitable **9** congenial, in harmony, in keeping **10** likeminded **11** appropriate

compel 4 make **5** drive, force **6** oblige **7** require **11** necessitate

compelled 4 must **5** bound, urged **6** driven, forced **7** coerced, obliged, pressed **8** commanded, dragooned, enforced, impelled, obsessed, pressured, required **11** constrained, overpowered

compelling 7 driving, dynamic **8** forceful **10** commanding **12** overwhelming

compel obedience to 5 force **6** coerce **7** enforce **8** carry out, insist on **10** administer

compendium 4 list **5** brief **6** apercu, digest, precis, survey **7** abstract, capsule, catalog, epitome, summary **8** syllabus, synopsis **9** catalogue **11** abridgement, compilation **12** condensation

compensate 3 pay **5** cover, repay **6** make up, offset, redeem, square **7** balance, pay back, redress **9** indemnify, reimburse **10** make amends, recompense, remunerate **14** counterbalance **15** make restitution

compensation 3 fee, pay **4** gain **5** wages **6** income, profit, return, reward, salary **7** payment, redress **8** benefits, earnings, gratuity **9** indemnity, repayment **10** recompense, settlement **11** restitution **12** remuneration, satisfaction **13** consideration, reimbursement

compete 3 vie **5** fight **6** battle, combat, oppose **7** contend, contest **8** be rivals **9** lock horns, match wits

competence 5 skill **7** ability, knowhow, mastery **8** ableness **9** expertise **10** capability, competency, expertness **11** proficiency

competent 3 fit **6** expert, versed **7** skilled, trained **8** skillful **9** efficient, practiced, qualified **10** dependable, proficient **11** experienced, responsible, trustworthy

competition 4 game **5** event, match, rival **7** contest, rivalry, tourney **8** conflict, opponent, struggle **9** contender **10** contention, opposition, tournament

competitive 8 fighting, opposing,

striving **9** combative **10** aggressive, contending

competitor 5 rival **7** fighter **8** opponent **9** adversary, contender **10** contestant, opposition

compilation 4 body **5** group **9** collating, garnering, gathering, mustering **10** assemblage, assembling, assortment, collecting, collection, compendium, marshaling **11** aggregating, aggregation, marshalling **12** accumulating, accumulation

compile 5 amass **6** garner, gather, heap up, muster **7** collate, collect, marshal **8** assemble **10** accumulate

complacent 4 smug **6** at ease **7** content **9** contented **10** self-secure, unbothered, untroubled **13** self-satisfied

complain 3 nag **4** beef, carp, kick, moan, pick **5** cavil, gripe, whine **6** grouch, grouse, squawk **7** grumble **9** bellyache, criticize, find fault **15** state a grievance

complaint 4 beef, kick **5** gripe **6** malady, squawk, tirade **7** ailment, illness, protest **8** debility, disorder, sickness **9** criticism, grievance, infirmity, objection **10** impairment **12** faultfinding **15** dissatisfaction

complaisance 7 pliancy **8** docility **10** affability, amiability, compliance **12** acquiescence

complaisant 4 warm **7** affable, amiable, cordial **8** friendly, gracious, obliging, pleasant, pleasing **9** agreeable, compliant, congenial, easygoing **10** solicitous **11** good-humored, goodnatured

Compleat Angler, The
author: **11** Izaak Walton

complement 3 cap **5** crown, match, total, whole **7** balance, perfect **8** ensemble, entirety, parallel, round out **9** aggregate, companion **10** completion, consummate, full amount, full number, supplement **11** counterpart, rounding-out **12** consummation **14** required number

complementary 7 matched **8** integral, opposite **9** companion **10** additional, compatible, completing **11** correlative **12** interrelated, supplemental **13** correspondent, corresponding

complete 3 cap, end **4** full **5** crown, total, utter, whole **6** entire, finish, intact, settle, wrap up **7** achieve, execute, fulfill, perfect, perform, plenary, settled **8** absolute, achieved, carry out, conclude, executed, round out, thorough, unbroken **9** discharge, make whole, performed, polish off, terminate, undivided **10** accomplish, carried out, complement, conclusive, consummate, unabridged **11** consummated **12** accomplished

completed 4 done **5** ended, whole **6** closed, entire, filled **7** matured,

through **8** achieved, finished, realized **9** concluded, executed, fulfilled, perfected **10** terminated, wrapped up **11** consummated **12** accomplished

completeness 8 fullness, richness **9** wholeness **10** perfection **12** thoroughness

completion 3 end **5** close **6** ending, finish, windup **7** closing **9** finishing **10** concluding, conclusion, expiration **11** fulfillment, terminating, termination **12** consummation

complex 4 maze **5** mixed **6** knotty, system **7** network, tangled **8** compound, involved, manifold, multiple, puzzling **9** aggregate, composite, difficult, enigmatic, fixed idea, intricate, obsession **10** perplexing, variegated **11** bewildering, complicated **12** conglomerate, labyrinthian, labyrinthine, multifarious **13** preoccupation

complexion 3 hue **4** look, tone **5** color, guise, image, slant **6** aspect **7** outlook **8** coloring **9** character **10** appearance, coloration, impression **11** countenance, skin texture **12** pigmentation, skin coloring

complexity 6 puzzle **9** intricacy, obscurity **10** bafflement, involution, perplexity **11** crabbedness, elaboration, involvement **12** complication, entanglement **15** inextricability **17** unintelligibility **19** incomprehensibility

compliance 6 assent **7** pliancy **8** docility, giving in, meekness, yielding **9** deference, obedience, passivity **10** conforming, conformity, submission **12** acquiescence, complaisance **13** nonresistance

compliant 8 flexible, yielding **9** agreeable **10** submissive

complicate 4 knot **5** ravel, snarl **6** muddle, tangle **7** confuse, involve **8** confound, entangle **11** make complex **13** make difficult, make intricate

complicated 7 complex **8** involved **9** elaborate, intricate

complication 4 snag **5** hitch **7** dilemma, problem **8** drawback, handicap, obstacle, quandary **9** hindrance **10** difficulty, impediment, perplexity **11** aggravation, obstruction, predicament **12** disadvantage **14** stumbling block

complicity 8 abetment, intrigue, plotting, schemery, scheming **9** collusion, finagling **10** connivance, conspiracy **11** confederacy, contrivance, implication, involvement **12** entanglement

compliment 5 honor, kudos **6** homage, praise **7** tribute **8** flattery **9** adulation, laudation **11** acclamation **12** commendation **14** congratulation

complimentary 4 free **6** gratis **8** admiring, praising **9** adulatory, extolling, laudatory, panegyric, praiseful **10** flattering, gratuitous, plauditory **12** appreciative, commendatory **13** without charge **14** congratulatory

compliments 4 best, laud **5** exalt, extol, toast **6** homage, praise, salute **7** applaud, commend, regards **8** respects **9** greetings **10** best wishes, good wishes **11** salutations **13** felicitations **15** congratulations

comply 3 bow **4** bend, meet, mind, obey **5** defer, yield **6** accede, adhere, follow, give in, submit **7** abide by, conform, consent, fulfill, observe, satisfy **9** acquiesce, surrender

component 4 item, part **5** piece **6** detail, member, module **7** element, modular, segment **8** material **9** composing, elemental, essential, intrinsic **10** elementary, ingredient, particular **11** constituent, fundamental **13** component part

component part 4 item, part **5** piece **6** detail, member **7** element **10** ingredient, particular **11** constituent, fundamental

comport 3 act **4** bear **5** carry **6** acquit, behave, deport **7** conduct

comportment 7 bearing, conduct **8** attitude, behavior, carriage, demeanor, presence **9** acquittal **10** appearance, deportment

comport oneself 3 act **6** behave **13** acquit oneself **14** conduct oneself

compose 4 calm, form, lull, make **5** frame, quell, quiet, relax, shape, write **6** create, devise, make up, pacify, settle, soothe **7** collect, fashion, placate **8** be part of, belong to, comprise, conceive, modulate **9** formulate **10** constitute

composed 4 calm, cool **5** quiet **6** at ease, placid, poised, sedate, serene, steady **8** peaceful, tranquil **9** collected, quiescent, unexcited, unruffled **10** controlled, cool- headed, restrained, unagitated, untroubled **11** level- headed, undisturbed, unemotional, unflappable, unperturbed **12** even-tempered **13** dispassionate, imperturbable **15** undemonstrative

composer 4 bard, poet **6** author, writer **7** creator **8** musician, producer **10** compositor, typesetter

composite 6 mosaic **7** blended **8** combined, compound **10** compounded

composition 4 form, opus, work **5** essay, etude, piece **6** design, layout, make-up, making **7** forming, framing, product, shaping **8** creating, creation, devising, exercise **9** framework, structure **10** concoction, fashioning, organizing, production **11** arrangement, combination, compilation, formulation, preparation **12** constitution, organization **13** configuration

compos mentis 4 sane **13** mentally sound

composure 4 calm, cool, ease **5** poise

6 aplomb **7** control, dignity **8** calmness, coolness, patience, serenity **9** sang-froid **10** equanimity **11** self-control **13** self-assurance, self-restraint **14** cool-headedness, self-possession, unexcitability, unflappability **15** levelheadedness **16** even-temperedness, imperturbability

compound 3 mix **4** fuse, make **5** add to, alloy, blend, boost, mixed, union, unite **6** devise, fusion, mingle **7** amalgam, amplify, augment, blended, combine, complex, concoct, enlarge, magnify, mixture, prepare **8** combined, heighten, increase **9** composite, fabricate, formulate, reinforce **10** synthesize **11** combination, complicated, composition, incorporate, put together **12** conglomerate **14** conglomeration

comprehend 3 dig, get **5** catch, grasp, savvy **6** absorb, digest, fathom **7** make out **8** conceive, perceive **9** penetrate **10** appreciate, assimilate, understand

comprehensible 5 clear, plain **7** evident **8** apparent **11** unambiguous **12** intelligible

comprehension 5 grasp **7** insight **9** awareness **10** conception, perception **11** realization **12** acquaintance, appreciation, apprehension **13** consciousness, understanding

comprehensive 4 full **5** broad **7** copious, general, overall **8** complete, sweeping, thorough **9** expansive, extensive, universal **10** exhaustive, widespread **11** compendious **12** all-embracing, all-inclusive

compress 4 cram, pack **5** press **6** reduce, shrink **7** abridge, bandage, compact, curtail, plaster, shorten, squeeze **8** condense, dressing **10** abbreviate

compressed 5 dense **6** jammed, packed **7** crowded **8** squashed, squeezed **9** compacted **12** concentrated

compressed form 6 digest **7** summary **8** cake form, synopsis **10** shortening **11** abridgement, contraction, curtailment **12** abbreviation, condensation

compression 9 narrowing, squeezing, stricture, tightness **10** compaction, constraint **12** constriction

compressor 4 pump **7** presser, reducer **8** squeezer **9** compactor, condenser

comprise 4 form **6** make up **7** compose, contain, include **8** be made of **9** consist of **10** constitute **12** be composed of

compromise 4 risk **5** agree, truce **6** settle **7** balance, compact, imperil **8** endanger, undercut **9** agreement, discredit, embarrass, implicate, make a deal, prejudice **10** adjustment, jeopardize, settlement **11** arrangement,

come to terms, happy medium, make suspect, meet halfway **12** conciliation **13** accommodation, rapprochement **14** make vulnerable, strike a bargain **16** mutual concession **18** split the difference **21** come to an understanding German: **9** Ausgleich

compromising 7 risking **8** settling **9** adjusting **10** bargaining **11** give and take, making a deal **12** embarrassing, jeopardizing **13** accommodating, coming to terms **14** meeting halfway

Compsognathus
type: 8 dinosaur, theropod
characteristic: 8 smallest
location: 6 Europe **7** Bavaria
period: 8 Jurassic

Compson, Quentin
character in: 14 Absalom Absalom **18** The Sound and the Fury
author: 8 Faulkner

Compson family
characters in: 18 The Sound and the Fury
member: 5 Benjy, Caddy, Jason **7** Candace, Quentin **8** Benjamin
author: 8 Faulkner

compte rendu 6 record, report, review **7** account **15** account rendered

comptroller 7 auditor **9** treasurer **10** accountant, bookkeeper, controller

compulsion 5 force **6** demand, duress, urging **8** coercion, pressure **9** necessity **10** obligation **11** domineering, requirement

compulsive 6 driven, hooked **7** driving, fanatic **8** addicted, habitual **9** compelled, obsessive **10** compelling **14** unable to resist, uncontrollable

compulsory 7 binding **8** coercive, demanded, enforced, forcible, required **9** mandatory, requisite **10** compulsive, imperative, obligatory **11** unavoidable **12** prescriptive

compunction 5 demur, qualm, shame **6** regret, unease **7** anxiety, concern, remorse, scruple **9** misgiving **10** contrition **16** pang of conscience

computation 5 tally, total **8** figuring **9** numbering, reckoning **10** numeration **11** calculation, enumeration

compute 3 add **5** add up, sum up, tally, total **6** figure, reckon **7** count up, work out **9** ascertain, calculate, figure out

computer 5 adder **9** processor **10** calculator
language: 3 Ada, APL **4** Java, LISP, HTML, LOGO **5** ALGOL, BASIC, COBOL **6** Pascal **7** FORTRAN
term: 2 PC **3** bit, bug, CAD, CAM, CPU, DOS, FAQ, RAM, ROM web, www **4** boot, byte, chip, file, hack, icon, spam, Unix **5** CD-Rom, crash, debug, drive, input, modem, mouse, pixel, queue, virus **6** analog, backup, cursor, glitch, hacker, laptop, mem-

ory, online, output, readme, window **7** digital, network, offline, program **8** database, hardware, lightpen, printout, software, terminal **9** hypertext interface, mainframe **10** binary code, floppy disk **11** application, interactive, spreadsheet **12** minicomputer, World Wide Web **13** microcomputer, word processor **14** microprocessor *see also* **18** *desktop publishing*

comrade 3 pal **4** ally, chum **5** buddy, crony **6** friend **7** partner **8** confrere, co-worker, helpmate, intimate **9** associate, colleague, companion, confidant **10** bosom buddy **11** confederate **12** collaborator **13** boon companion **Russian: 8** tovarich

comradeship 8 alliance **10** fellowship, friendship **11** association, camaraderie **13** companionship

comte 5 count

Comte Ory, Le
also: 8 Count Ory
opera by: 7 Rossini
character: 13 Countess Adele

Comus
author: 10 John Milton
subtitle: 7 A Masque

Comus
origin: 5 Roman
god of: 7 revelry **8** drinking

con 3 gyp **4** anti, bilk, coax, fool, gull, hoax, lure, rook **5** cheat, cozen, felon, trick **6** delude **7** against, beguile, convict, defraud, mislead, swindle **8** hoodwink, jailbird, prisoner, yardbird **9** bamboozle

Conakry
capital of: 6 Guinea

concatenation 4 link **5** union **6** hookup **7** joining, linking, reunion **8** coupling, junction **10** bracketing, confluence, connection **11** conjunction **12** interlinking **15** interconnection **16** interassociation **18** intercommunication

concave 6 hollow, sunken **8** indented **9** depressed **13** curving inward

conceal 4 hide, mask **5** cloak, cover **6** screen, shield **7** cover up, obscure, secrete **8** disguise **10** camouflage, keep secret

concealed 5 blind, doggo **6** covert, hidden, latent, masked, perdue, secret, veiled **7** cloaked, covered, obscure, unknown, wrapped **8** abstruse, shrouded, ulterior **9** disguised, incognito **11** clandestine

concealment 5 cover **6** hiding **7** hideout, masking **8** covering, hideaway **9** screening, secreting, secretion **10** covering up, under cover

concede 3 own **4** cede **5** admit, agree, allow, grant, yield **6** accept, give up, resign, tender **7** abandon, confess, deliver **8** hand over **9** acquiesce, recognize, surrender, vouchsafe **10** relinquish **11** acknowledge, be persuaded

conceit 3 ego **5** pride **6** vanity **7** ego trip, egotism **8** bragging, self-love **9** vainglory **10** self-esteem **12** boastfulness **14** self-importance

conceited 4 smug, vain **7** stuck-up **8** arrogant, boasting, bragging, puffed up **9** bombastic, overproud, strutting **11** egotistical, swellheaded **12** vainglorious **13** self-important

conceivable 8 credible, knowable, possible **9** thinkable **10** believable, imaginable, supposable **11** perceivable

conceive 4 form **5** frame, hatch, start **6** create, ideate, invent **7** concoct, dream up, imagine, produce, think of, think up **8** consider, contrive, envisage, envision, initiate **9** originate **10** comprehend, understand

concentrate 4 mass **5** amass, bunch, focus, hem in **6** center, gather, heap up, reduce **7** close in, cluster, pay heed, thicken **8** assemble, attend to, condense, converge, fasten on **10** accumulate, congregate **11** bring to bear **12** direct toward

concentrated 5 dense **7** crowded, focused, thought **8** centered **10** compressed

concentration 4 mass **5** focus **7** cluster **9** diligence, gathering, reduction **10** absorption, assemblage, collection, intentness, thickening **11** aggregation, boiling down, convergence, deep thought, engrossment **12** accumulation **13** concentrating, consolidation **14** centralization

concept 4 idea, view **5** image **6** belief, notion, theory **7** opinion, surmise, thought **9** postulate **10** conviction, hypothesis, impression **11** supposition

conception 4 idea **5** birth, image, start **6** notion **7** forming, genesis, inkling, picture **8** creating, devising, hatching **9** beginning, formation, imagining, inception, invention, launching **10** conceiving, concocting, initiation, perception **11** envisioning, formulation, originating **12** apprehension **13** fertilization, understanding **16** becoming pregnant

conceptual 8 abstract **9** visionary **11** conjectural, ideological, speculative, theoretical **12** experimental, hypothetical **15** impressionistic

concern 3 job **4** care, duty, firm, heed **5** chore, house, store, touch, worry **6** affair, affect, charge, matter, occupy, regard **7** anxiety, apply to, company, disturb, involve, mission, trouble **8** bear upon, business, distress, interest, relate to **9** attention, pertain to **10** disconcert, enterprise, solicitude **11** appertain to, corporation, disturbance, involvement, undertaking **12** apprehension **13** consideration, establishment **14** thoughtfulness

concerned 5 upset **6** active, caring,

uneasy **7** alarmed, anxious, engaged, fearful, worried **8** involved, troubled **9** attentive, committed, disturbed **10** disquieted, distressed, interested, solicitous **12** apprehensive **13** participating

concerning 2 of, on, re **3** for **4** as to, over, upon **5** about, anent **7** apropos **8** engaging, touching, worrying **9** affecting, involving, mattering, regarding **10** relating to, respecting

concert 5 union, unity **6** accord, settle **7** concord, harmony **8** teamwork **9** agreement, congruity, unanimity **10** accordance, complicity **11** association, cooperation **13** collaboration **14** correspondence **18** musical performance

concerted 5 joint **6** united **7** planned **8** by assent **10** agreed upon **11** cooperative, prearranged **12** premeditated **13** predetermined

concert hall 5 odeum **6** lyceum **7** theater **9** music hall **10** auditorium **12** symphony hall

concession 5 lease **6** assent **8** giving in, yielding **9** admission, franchise, privilege **10** adjustment, compromise, indulgence **12** acquiescence, modification **14** acknowledgment

Conch
form: 7 trumpet
made of: 5 shell
owned by: 7 Tritons

Conchobar
origin: 5 Irish
king of: 6 Ulster
nephew: 10 Cuchulainn

concierge 7 janitor **9** custodian **10** doorkeeper

conciliate 6 pacify **7** appease, placate **9** make peace, reconcile **11** accommodate

conciliation 11 appeasement, peacemaking **12** propitiation **13** accommodation **14** reconciliation

conciliatory 8 friendly **9** appeasing, pacifying, placatory **10** mollifying, reassuring **11** peacemaking, reconciling **13** accommodative

concise 5 brief, pithy, short, terse **7** compact **8** succinct **9** condensed **10** to the point **11** abbreviated

conciseness 7 brevity **9** terseness **11** compactness **12** condensation, succinctness

conclave 6 parley, powwow **7** council, meeting, session **8** assembly **10** conference, convention **11** convocation **13** secret council

conclude 3 end **4** halt, stop **5** close, infer, judge **6** decide, deduce, effect, finish, gather, reason, settle **7** arrange, resolve, surmise **8** break off, carry out, complete **9** determine, terminate **10** accomplish **11** bring to pass, discontinue **12** draw to a close

concluded 5 bound, ended, guess **6** closed, judged **7** decided, deduced, expired, settled, wound up **9** completed **10** culminated, determined, restrained, terminated

conclusion 3 end **5** close **6** finale, finish, result, upshot, windup **7** finding, outcome **8** decision, judgment **9** agreement, deduction, final part, inference, summation **10** completion, denouement, resolution, settlement, working out **11** arrangement, presumption, termination **13** determination

conclusive 5 clear **6** patent **7** certain, obvious **8** absolute, decisive, definite, manifest, palpable **9** clinching **10** compelling, convincing, undeniable **11** categorical, determining, inescapable, irrefutable **12** demonstrable, unanswerable **13** incontestable, unimpeachable **14** unquestionable **16** incontrovertible

concoct 3 mix **4** brew **5** frame, hatch **6** cook up, create, devise, invent, make up **7** think up **8** compound, contrive **9** fabricate, formulate

concoction 4 brew **5** blend **6** jumble, medley **7** mixture **8** compound, creation **9** invention, potpourri **11** contrivance, fabrication **14** conglomeration

concomitant 7 related **9** accessory, attendant, connected, corollary, secondary **10** additional **12** accompanying, contributing, supplemental **13** complementary

concord 5 amity, peace **6** accord **7** harmony **8** goodwill **9** agreement **10** friendship **11** amicability, cooperation **16** cordial relations **19** mutual understanding

concordance 5 index **6** accord **7** concord **9** agreement, consensus, unanimity **17** meeting of the minds

concordant 6 unison **7** calming **8** agreeing, unifying **9** assenting, consonant **10** concurrent, harmonious

concordat 4 pact **8** covenant **9** agreement

Concorde 3 jet, SST **10** supersonic airline **9** Air France **14** British Airways

Concordia
  origin: 5 Roman
  goddess of: 5 peace **7** harmony

concourse 7 conflux, joining, linkage, meeting **8** junction **9** amassment **10** assembling, concursion, confluence **11** aggregation, association, convergence **12** congregation, focalization **13** concentration **14** conglomeration **15** flowing together **16** flocking together

concrete 4 real **5** solid **6** cement **7** express, factual, precise **8** definite, distinct, explicit, material, specific, tangible **10** particular **11** fused stones, substantial **12** alloyed rocks

concupiscence 4 itch, lust **6** desire **7** craving, lechery, longing, passion **8** appetite, hot pants, lewdness, satyrism **9** horniness, lubricity, prurience, randiness **10** wantonness **11** goatishness, libertinism, lustfulness **12** sexual desire **13** lecherousness **14** lasciviousness, libidinousness

concur 5 agree, match, tally **6** square **7** conform **8** coincide, hold with **9** be uniform **10** be in accord, correspond **11** go along with **12** go hand in hand

concur in 7 approve **9** agree with **11** go along with

concurrence, concurrency 6 accord **7** concord, consent, harmony **8** approval **9** agreement, consensus, unanimity **10** acceptance, conformity **11** affirmation, coexistence, coincidence, conjuncture, cooperation, synchronism **12** acquiescence **13** collaboration, mutual consent **14** correspondence **15** working together **17** meeting of the minds **22** simultaneous occurrence

concurrent 5 at one **6** allied **7** aligned **8** agreeing, matching **9** congenial, congruous, consonant **10** coexisting, coincident, coinciding, compatible, harmonious **11** in agreement, sympathetic, synchronous **12** commensurate, contemporary, in accordance, simultaneous **13** correspondent, of the same mind **15** contemporaneous

concurring 8 agreeing **10** consenting **11** affirmative, in agreement, synchronous **12** coincidental, simultaneous **13** corresponding

concussion 3 jar **4** blow, bump **5** clash, shock **6** buffet, impact **7** shaking **8** pounding **9** agitation, collision **11** brain injury

condemn 4 damn, doom **5** decry **6** rebuke **7** censure **8** denounce, sentence **9** criticize, proscribe, reprehend **10** disapprove

condemnation 6 rebuke **7** censure, reproof **8** judgment, reproach, sentence **9** criticism **10** conviction, punishment **11** disapproval **12** denunciation, reprehension **14** disapprobation **20** pronouncement of guilt

condensation 6 digest **9** reduction **10** abridgment **13** shortened form **16** condensed version

condense 3 cut **4** trim **6** digest, reduce **7** abridge, compact, liquefy, shorten, thicken **8** boil down, compress, contract, pare down **10** abbreviate, bluepencil **11** concentrate, consolidate, precipitate

condensed form 6 digest, precis **7** summary **8** synopsis **10** shortening **11** abridgement, compression, contraction, curtailment **12** abbreviation

condescend 5 deign, stoop **6** submit, unbend **7** descend, disdain **9** patronize **10** look down on, talk down to **12**

come down a peg, lower oneself **13** humble oneself

condescending 7 high-hat **8** superior **10** disdainful **11** overbearing, patronizing

condescension 4 airs **7** disdain, hauteur, modesty **8** humility **9** deference, loftiness **10** humbleness **11** haughtiness **12** graciousness **13** selfabasement **14** self-effacement **19** patronizing attitude **20** assumption of equality **21** high-and-mighty attitude

condign 3 due **4** fair, just, meet **5** right **6** earned, proper, worthy **7** fitting, merited **8** deserved, suitable **9** warranted **11** appropriate

condiment 4 herb **5** sauce, spice **8** dressing, flavorer, seasoner **9** seasoning
  kind: 3 bay **4** dill, mace, mint, sage, salt **5** caper, clove, curry, onion, thyme **6** catsup, garlic, ginger, nutmeg, pepper, pickle, relish **7** caraway, chutney, ketchup, mustard, parsley, oregano, paprika, pimento, tabasco, vinegar **8** cardamon, marjoram, turmeric **9** pimpernel **10** bell pepper, mayonnaise

condition 3 fit **4** term **5** adapt, equip, ready, shape, state, train **6** demand, fettle, malady, status, tone up **7** ailment, prepare, problem, proviso **8** accustom, position, standing **9** agreement, complaint, provision, requisite, situation **10** limitation, make used to, put in shape **11** arrangement, contingency, malfunction, reservation, restriction, stipulation **12** prerequisite **13** circumstances, qualification, state of health **14** state of affairs **15** physical fitness

conditional 7 limited **9** dependent, qualified, tentative **10** contingent, restricted **11** provisional, stipulative **16** with reservations

condolence 4 pity **6** solace **7** comfort **8** sympathy **10** compassion **11** consolation **13** commiseration

Condon, Richard
  author of: 11 Winter Kills **18** Death of a Politician **22** The Manchurian Candidate

condonation 11 forgiveness, overlooking **12** disregarding **13** putting up with

condone 6 excuse, forget, ignore, pardon, wink at **7** absolve, forgive, justify, let pass **8** overlook **9** disregard, put up with

conduce 3 aid **4** help, lead, tend **5** bring, favor, guide **6** effect **7** advance, forward, further, promote **10** contribute

conducive 7 helpful **8** salutary **9** favorable, promotive **10** beneficial **11** expeditious **12** contributive, contributory, instrumental **19** calculated to produce **22** helpful in bringing about

conduct 3 act **4** bear, lead, rule, ways **5** carry, chair, deeds, enact, guide, pilot, steer, usher **6** action, attend, behave, convey, convoy, direct, escort, govern, manage, manner **7** carry on, comport, control, execute, marshal, operate, perform **8** behavior, carry out, dispatch, guidance, regulate, transact **9** accompany, direction, discharge, look after, supervise **10** administer, deportment, government, leadership, management **11** comportment, generalship, preside over, superintend, supervision **14** administration

conduct oneself 3 act **6** behave **13** acquit oneself **14** comport oneself

conductor 3 cad **5** guide **6** carman, escort, leader **7** cathode, channel, maestro, manager **8** aqueduct, batonist, cicerone, conveyor, director, operator, stickman, trainman **9** collector, drum major **10** impresario, supervisor **11** choirmaster, transmitter **13** concert master

conduit 4 duct, main, pipe, tube **5** canal, drain, flume, sewer **6** gutter, trough **7** channel, passage **8** aqueduct **11** watercourse

cone 5 bevel, shape, spire **6** bobbin, conoid, funnel **7** pyramid, volcano **8** pyramid

   kind: 3 fir **4** pine **5** larch **7** conifer, retinal **8** ice cream

confabulate 4 chat, talk **6** confer, patter **7** chatter, discuss **8** chitchat, converse, talk idly

confabulation 4 chat, talk **8** chitchat **10** conference, discussion **12** conversation

confection 3 jam **5** candy **6** pastry **7** dessert **8** conserve, delicacy **9** preserves, sweetmeat **10** sugar candy

confectionery 5 candy **6** sweets **7** goodies, pasties **10** sugar candy, sweetmeats

confederacy, Confederacy 3 CSA **4** band, bloc **5** guild, union **6** fusion, league **7** combine, society **8** alliance, the South **9** coalition, syndicate **10** federation **11** association **13** confederation **14** Southern states **18** secessionist states **26** Confederate States of America

   capital: 8 Richmond

   leader: 14 Jefferson Davis

   flag: 12 Stars and Bars

   See also **8** Civil War

confederate 4 ally **5** merge, unite **6** cohort, helper **7** abettor, comrade, partner **8** coalesce, coworker **9** accessory, affiliate, associate, colleague, companion **10** accomplice, cooperator, join forces **11** consolidate, helping

hand **12** band together, collaborator, right hand man **17** fellow conspirator

Confederates

   author: 14 Thomas Keneally

confederation 4 band **5** guild, union **6** fusion, league **7** combine, society **8** alliance **9** coalition, syndicate **10** federation **11** association, confederacy

confer 4 give **5** award **6** accord, parley **7** consult, discuss, palaver **8** converse **9** present to **10** bestow upon **12** compare notes, talk together **15** hold a conference **18** deliberate together

conference 4 talk **6** parley **7** council, meeting, seminar **8** conclave **9** symposium **10** convention, discussion **12** consultation, deliberation

conferment 4 gift **5** award **8** bestowal **12** presentation

confess 3 own **4** avow, sing **5** admit, own up **6** expose, reveal **7** declare, divulge, lay bare **8** blurt out, disclose **9** come clean, make known **11** acknowledge **12** bring to light **14** unbosom oneself **18** make a clean breast of

confessed 6 avowed **8** admitted **9** professed **12** self-declared **14** self-proclaimed

confession 6 avowal, shrift **9** admission **10** disclosure, divulgence, revelation **11** declaration **12** confessional **14** acknowledgment

Confessions of an English Opium Eater

   author: 15 Thomas DeQuincey

Confessions of Nat Turner, The

   author: 13 William Styron

confidant, confidante 5 crony **6** friend **8** intimate **10** bosom buddy **15** trusty companion

confide 6 impart, reveal **7** confess, divulge, lay bare, let in on, let know **8** disclose **9** make known **12** tell secretly **13** tell privately **14** unbosom oneself

confidence 4 grit, guts **5** faith, nerve, pluck, spunk, trust **6** belief, daring, mettle, secret, spirit **7** courage **8** audacity, boldness, credence, intimacy, reliance **9** certainty, certitude **10** conviction **11** intrepidity **12** self-reliance **13** private matter, self-assurance **14** faith in oneself **17** inside information

confidence man 5 cheat **6** con man **8** swindler **9** charlatan, trickster **10** mountebank

confident 4 bold, sure **5** cocky **6** daring, secure **7** assured, certain **8** cocksure, intrepid, positive **9** convinced, dauntless, expectant **10** optimistic **11** self-assured, self-reliant **13** sure of oneself

confidential 5 privy **6** secret **7** private **8** hush-hush **9** top- secret **10** classi-

fied **11** undisclosed **12** off-the-record **16** not to be disclosed

confidentially 7 sub rosa **8** in secret, secretly **9** privately **16** between ourselves **17** behind closed doors

   French: 9 entre nous

confiding 6 trusty **7** reliant **8** trustful, trusting **9** confident **11** trustworthy

configuration 4 form **6** design, makeup **11** arrangement, composition

confine 3 pen, tie **4** bind, cage, hold, jail, keep **5** limit **6** coop up, govern, keep in, lock up, shut in, shut up **7** fence in, impound **8** imprison, regulate, restrain, restrict **9** sequester **11** incarcerate **13** hold in custody

confined 4 pent **5** close, tight **6** jailed, narrow **7** cramped **8** locked up **10** imprisoned, restricted

confinement 7 custody, lying in **9** cooping up, detention, restraint **10** childbirth, constraint, limitation, shutting in **11** parturition, restriction **12** accouchement, imprisonment **13** incarceration **15** circumscription

confines 4 edge **6** border, bounds, limits **7** margins **8** precinct **10** boundaries **13** circumference

confirm 5 prove **6** accept, clinch, ratify, uphold, verify **7** agree to, approve, bear out, certify, sustain **8** make firm, validate **9** authorize, establish **11** acknowledge, corroborate, make binding, make certain **12** authenticate, substantiate

confirmation 5 proof **6** assent **8** approval, sanction **9** agreement **10** acceptance, validation **11** affirmation, endorsement **12** ratification, verification **13** corroboration **14** authentication, substantiation

confirmed 3 set **5** fixed **7** chronic **8** hardened, verified **9** ingrained, validated **10** deep-rooted, deep-seated, inveterate, proven true **11** established **12** corroborated **13** authenticated, dyed-in-the-wool, substantiated

confiscate 4 take **5** seize **7** impound, possess, preempt **8** take over **9** sequester **10** commandeer **11** appropriate, expropriate

confiscation 7 seizure **10** impounding, preemption **13** appropriation, commandeering, expropriation

conflagration 4 fire **5** blaze **7** bonfire, inferno **8** conflict, fighting, wildfire **9** brush fire, firestorm, holocaust **10** forest fire, raging fire, wall of fire **11** sea of flames **12** sheet of flame

conflagrative 8 burnable **9** flammable, ignitable **10** combustive, incendiary **11** combustible, inflammable

conflict 4 fray **5** clash, fight, melee, set-to **6** action, battle, combat, fracas, oppose, strife, tussle **7** collide, discord, dissent, scuffle, warfare **8** disagree, division, friction, skirmish, struggle, variance **9** encounter, hostility **10** antagonism, be contrary, difference, dissension, engagement **12** disagreement **13** confrontation **14** be inharmonious **15** be contradictory **Spanish: 9** mano a mano

conflicting 7 warring **8** clashing, opposing **10** ambivalent **13** contradictory

confluence 5 union **7** conflux, joining, linkage, meeting **8** junction, juncture **9** concourse, gathering **10** assembling, concursion **11** association, convergence **13** concentration **14** coming together **15** flowing together

conform 3 fit **4** obey **5** adapt **6** adjust, follow **8** adhere to, jibe with, submit to **9** agree with, reconcile, tally with **10** be guided by, comply with, fall in with, square with **11** acquiesce in **12** correspond to

conformable 8 amenable **9** agreeable, malleable **10** submissive **12** in compliance

conformance 7 harmony **9** agreement **10** accordance, compliance, conformity **13** compatibility

conformation 4 form **5** build, shape **6** figure **7** anatomy **9** formation, framework, structure **11** arrangement **13** configuration

conformist 12 well-adjusted **13** unadventurous

conformity 6 accord, assent **7** harmony **8** likeness **9** agreement, obedience **10** compliance, observance, similarity, submission, uniformity **11** resemblance **12** acquiescence **14** correspondence **15** conventionality

confound 5 amaze, mix up **6** baffle, puzzle, rattle **7** astound, confuse, fluster, mystify, nonplus, perplex, startle **8** astonish, bewilder, dumfound, surprise, unsettle **10** disconcert **11** flabbergast **16** strike with wonder, throw off the scent

confounded 8 confused **10** bewildered, nonplussed **11** dumbfounded **12** disconcerted

confraternity 4 body **5** guild, union **7** society **8** sodality **9** confrairy **11** association, brotherhood

confrere 3 pal **4** ally, chum **5** buddy **6** friend **7** brother, comrade, partner **9** associate, colleague

confront 3 dare, defy, face, meet **5** brave **8** cope with, face up to **9** challenge, encounter, withstand

confrontation 5 clash, run-in, set-to **6** battle, combat, debate **7** contest, dispute, face-off **8** conflict, showdown, skirmish **9** encounter **10** engagement, opposition **11** controversy **17** face-to-face meeting **Spanish: 9** mano a mano

Confucius
  author of: 10 Book of Odes **11** The Analects
confuse 5 addle, befog, mix up, stump **6** baffle, muddle, puzzle, rattle **7** fluster, mistake, mystify, nonplus, perplex **8** befuddle, bewilder, confound, unsettle **10** discompose, disconcert **11** make unclear **12** make baffling **14** make perplexing **17** throw into disorder

confused 5 fazed **6** addled **7** abashed, baffled, chaotic, jumbled, mixed-up, muddled, tangled **8** rambling **9** befuddled, illogical, perplexed, unsettled **10** bewildered, disjointed, distracted, incoherent, nonplussed **11** dumbfounded **12** disconcerted, disorganized **13** disharmonious, heterogeneous

confusing 7 addling **8** baffling, blinding, blurring, dizzying, jumbling, mixing up, muddling **9** deranging, mistaking **10** befuddling, disorderly, flustering, mystifying, perplexing, stupefying **11** bewildering, confounding **13** disconcerting, unintelligible

confusion 4 mess, riot **5** chaos, snarl **6** bedlam, hubbub, jumble, muddle, tangle, tumult, uproar **7** clutter, ferment, turmoil **8** disarray, disorder, madhouse, shambles, upheaval **9** abashment, commotion **10** bafflement, hodgepodge, hullabaloo, perplexity, puzzlement, untidiness **11** disturbance, pandemonium **12** bewilderment, discomposure, stupefaction **13** mystification **14** disarrangement, disconcertment **15** disorganization **French: 14** bouleversement

confutation 6 denial **7** counter **8** negation, rebuttal **10** refutation **13** contradiction

confute 4 deny **5** rebut **6** impugn, oppose, refute **7** counter, gainsay **10** contradict, controvert **12** be contrary to

congeal 3 set **4** clot, jell **6** curdle, freeze, harden **7** stiffen, thicken **8** solidify **9** coagulate **10** gelatinize

congenial 4 like **6** genial, social **7** affable, cordial, kindred, related, similar **8** agreeing, amenable, gracious, pleasant, pleasing, sociable **9** agreeable, convivial **10** compatible, consistent, harmonious, well-suited **11** sympathetic **13** companionable, corresponding **French: 9** en rapport **German: 9** gemutlich

congeniality 7 harmony, rapport **8** affinity **11** sociability **12** conviviality, friendliness, pleasantness **13** compatibility **14** like-mindedness

congenital 6 inborn, inbred, innate, native **7** natural **8** inherent **9** ingrained, inherited, intrinsic **10** hereditary

congested 6 filled, gorged, jammed, packed **7** crowded **9** saturated **11** overcrowded

congestion 3 jam, mob **4** mass **5** snarl **6** pile-up **8** crowding **10** bottleneck **11** obstruction **12** overcrowding

conglomerate 4 heap, mass, pile **5** amass, blend, stack **7** mixture **8** assemble **9** aggregate **10** accumulate, assemblage **12** accumulation **16** large corporation

conglomeration 6 jumble, medley **7** mixture **8** mishmash **9** aggregate, potpourri **10** assortment, collection, hodgepodge **11** aggregation, combination **13** agglomeration

Congo
  other name: 10 Moyen Congo **11** Middle Congo
  capital/largest city: 11 Brazzaville
  others: 3 Ewo **4** Boko **5** Epena, Kayes, Kelle, Okoyo, Sembe **6** Dongou, Komono, Makoua, Matadi, M'Binda, M'Vouti, Ouesso, Sibiti, Zanaga **7** Cabinda, Dolisie, Etoumbi, Gamboma, Kinkala, Loubomo, Loudima, Madingo, Mossaka, Souanke **8** Djambala, Impfondo, Kibangou, Madingou, Mindouli **9** Mossendjo **11** Fort- Rousset, Pointe-Noire **17** Mayombe Escarpment
  school: 13 Marien Ngoubai
  monetary unit: 5 franc **7** centime
  lake: 5 Mweru, Tumba **6** Albert, Nyanza, Upemba **7** Leopold **11** Stanley Pool
  highest point: 6 Leketi
  river: 3 Dja **4** Uele **5** Alima, Congo, Kasal, Kwilu, Lulua, Ngoko, Niari, Sanga, Swilu, Wamba, Zahir, Zaire **6** Kwango, Kwenge, Loange, Lobaye, Lomami, Ogooue, Ubangi **7** Aruwima, Kouilou, Lualaba, Luapula, N'Gounie **8** Itimbiri, Likouala, Lubilash
  sea: 8 Atlantic
  physical feature:
    plateau: 6 Bateke
  people: 3 Rua **4** Akka, Susa, Teke, Vili **5** Amadi, Bantu, Figot, Kongo, Mantu, Pygmy, Sanga, Warua, Zambi **6** Ababua, Bafyot, Bateke, Mbochi, Nzambi, Wabuma **7** Bacongo, Bakongo, Bangala, Batetla, Manyema **10** Binga Pygmy
    discoverer: 3 Cam
  language: 4 Susu **5** Bantu, Fiote **6** French, Kituba **7** Bangala, Lingala
  religion: 5 Islam **7** animism **10** Protestant **13** Roman Catholic
  place:
    church: 9 Saint Anne
    stadium: 5 Eboue
  feature:
    tree: 5 limba

congratulate 4 hail **6** salute **10** compliment, felicitate, wish one joy **11** rejoice with **18** give one's best wishes

28 wish many happy returns of the day

congratulations 6 salute **8** mazelov **9** blessings, greetings **10** best wishes, good wishes **11** well-wishing **13** felicitations **24** many happy returns of the day

congregate 4 mass **5** amass, flock, swarm **6** gather, throng **7** cluster, collect **8** assemble **12** come together **13** crowd together

congregation 5 crowd, flock, group, horde, laity **6** parish, throng **8** assembly, audience, brethren **9** gathering, multitude **12** parishioners **16** church membership **17** religious assembly

congress, Congress 4 diet **6** caucus **7** council **8** assembly **9** delegates, gathering **10** conference, convention, parliament **11** legislature **14** federal council **15** discussion group, legislative body, national council, representatives **17** chamber of deputies

Congreve, William
   author of: 11 Love for Love **15** The Double-Dealer **16** The Mourning Bride, The Way of the World

congruity 7 harmony **9** agreement, coherence **10** consonance **11** consistency **12** congeniality **13** compatibility **14** correspondence **15** appropriateness

congruous 4 meet **6** seemly **7** apropos **8** becoming, relevant, suitable **9** congenial, consonant, in keeping **10** harmonious **11** appropriate, in agreement **13** corresponding

conifer
   means: 11 cone bearing
   order: 11 coniferales
   class: 10 gymnosperm
   kind: 3 fir, yew **4** pine **5** cedar, larch, pinal **6** ginkgo, pinale, spruce, torrey **7** cypress, hemlock, juniper, redwood, sequoia **8** softwood **9** evergreen

Coningsby
   author: 16 Benjamin Disraeli

conjectural 7 reputed **8** abstract, academic, doubtful, putative, supposed, surmised **11** inferential, speculative, theoretical **12** hypothetical **13** suppositional **14** supposititious

conjecture 4 idea, view **5** fancy, guess, infer, judge, think **6** augury, notion, reckon, theory **7** imagine, opinion, presume, suppose, surmise **8** estimate, forecast, judgment, theorize **9** calculate, deduction, guesswork, inference, speculate, suspicion **10** assumption, guestimate, hypothesis, presuppose **11** guesstimate, hypothesize, speculation, supposition **13** shot in the dark

conjoin 4 join, knit, link **5** touch, unite **7** combine, connect, overlap **8** together **9** associate

conjoined 6 joined, linked, united **7**

knitted, meeting **8** combined, touching **9** connected **10** associated **11** overlapping **14** joined together

conjugal 6 wedded **7** marital, married, nuptial, spousal **9** connubial **11** matrimonial

conjugate 4 join, pair, yoke **5** mated, unite, yoked **6** couple, joined, paired, united **9** connect, coupled, related **10** connected **10** paronymous

conjunction 3 and, but **5** union **7** joining, meeting **11** association, coincidence, combination, concurrence

conjuration 5 charm, spell, trick **11** incantation

conjure 5 allay, charm, raise **6** invoke, summon **7** bewitch, command, enchant **8** call away, call upon **9** call forth **10** cast a spell, make appear **13** make disappear **15** practice sorcery

conjurer 6 wizard **8** magician

conk 3 die, hit **4** bean, blow, fail, head **5** decay, faint, sleep, stall **6** fungus, strike **7** bracket **8** knock out **9** break down **10** straighten

Conn, Katherine
   real name of: 13 Kitty Carlisle

connect 3 tie **4** join **5** hinge, merge, unite **6** attach, couple, relate **7** combine, compare **9** associate, correlate **14** fasten together

connected 4 tied **6** joined, merged, united **7** coupled **8** abutting, adjacent, attached, combined, touching **9** bordering, proximate **10** connecting, contiguous, juxtaposed **12** conterminous **16** fastened together

connected group 5 cycle **6** series **8** sequence **11** progression

Connecticut
   abbreviation: 2 CT **4** Conn
   nickname: 6 Nutmeg **7** Blue Law **9** Freestone **12** Constitution **18** Land of Steady Habits
   capital/largest city: 8 Hartford
   others: 4 Avon **6** Bethel, Canaan, Cos Cob, Darien, Hamden, Mystic, Sharon, Storrs **7** Ansonia, Bristol, Danbury, Enfield, Madison, Meriden, Milford, Niantic, Norwalk, Norwich, Shelton, Tolland, Windsor **8** Guilford, New Haven, Simsbury, Stamford, Westport **9** Greenwich, Naugatuck, New London, Stratford, Waterbury **10** Bridgeport, Manchester, New Britain, Torrington **11** Wallingford
   college: 4 Yale **7** Trinity **8** Hartford, St Joseph, Wesleyan **9** Fairfield **10** Bridgeport, Quinnipiac **11** Connecticut, Sacred Heart **12** U S Coast Guard
   feature: 10 Charter Oak
      museum: 8 PT Barnum
      seaport: 6 Mystic
      theater: 27 American Shakespeare Festival

   tribe: 6 Pequot **7** Mohegan, Niantic **10** Quinnipiac
   people: 8 PT Barnum **9** John Brown **10** Nathan Hale **11** Noah Webster **12** Thomas Hooker **19** Harriet Beecher Stowe
   lake: 10 Candlewood
   land rank: 11 forty-eighth
   mountain: 4 Bear **7** Taconic
      hills: 10 Berkshires
      highest point: 8 Frissell
   physical feature: 15 Long Island Sound
   river: 6 Thames **9** Naugatuck **10** Housatonic **11** Connecticut
   state admission: 5 fifth
   state bird: 5 robin
   state flower: 14 mountain laurel
   state motto: 30 He Who Transplanted Still Sustains
   state song: 12 Yankee Doodle
   state tree: 8 white oak

Connecticut Yankee in King Arthur's Court, A
   author: 9 Mark Twain
   character: 5 Sandy **6** Merlin **8** Alisande, Clarence **11** Morgan le Fay **12** Hello-Central **18** Sir Kay the Seneschal

connection 3 kin, tie **4** bond, link **5** nexus **6** family, friend **7** contact, coupler, kinfolk, kinsman, linkage **8** affinity, alliance, coupling, junction, kinsfolk, relation, relative **9** associate, connector, fastening **10** attachment, kith and kin **11** association, correlation **12** acquaintance, relationship **13** flesh and blood, interrelation

Connelly, Marc
   author of: 16 The Green Pastures
      with Frank Elser: 19 The Farmer Takes a Wife
      with George S Kaufman: 5 Dulcy **11** To the Ladies **17** Beggar on Horseback, Merton of the Movies

Connery, Sean
   real name: 13 Thomas Connery
   born: 8 Scotland **9** Edinburgh
   roles: 6 Marnie **7** The Rock **10** Highlander **14** Robin and Marian **15** The Untouchables **16** The Molly Maguires **20** The Great Train Robbery, The Man Who Would Be King **28** Darby O'Gill and the Little People **29** Indiana Jones and the Last Crusade
      James Bond: 4 Dr No **10** Goldfinger **11** Thunderball **16** You Only Live Twice **18** Diamonds Are Forever, From Russia with Love, Never Say Never Again

connivance 4 plot **5** cabal **6** design, scheme **8** intrigue **9** collusion **10** complicity, conspiracy **11** machination

connive 3 aid **4** abet, plan, plot **5** allow **6** wink at **7** collude **8** conspire **10** be a party to **13** be accessory to, lend oneself **14** shut one's eyes to

17 be in collusion with, cooperate secretly

conniving 4 wily **6** artful, crafty **7** cunning **8** plotting, scheming **9** designing **10** intriguing **11** calculating

connoisseur 5 judge, maven, mavin **6** expert **7** epicure, gourmet **9** authority **11** cognoscente **17** person of good taste

Connolly, Maureen
nickname: **8** Little Mo
sport: **6** tennis

Connor, Dale
creator/artist of: **9** Mary Worth

connotation 5 drift **6** import, spirit **8** coloring **9** evocation, undertone **10** intimation, suggestion **11** implication, insinuation **12** significance

connote 5 imply **6** hint at **7** suggest **8** intimate **9** insinuate **11** bring to mind

connubial 6 wedded **7** marital, married, nuptial **8** conjugal **11** matrimonial

conquer 4 beat, best, drub, lick, rout, rule, trim, whip **5** floor, quell **6** defeat, humble, master, occupy, subdue, thrash **7** possess, win over **8** overcome, surmount, vanquish **9** overpower, rise above, subjugate **11** prevail over, triumph over **14** get the better of

conqueror 6 victor, winner **7** subduer **8** champion **10** subjugator, vanquisher **12** conquistador

conquest 3 fan **4** sway **5** lover **6** adorer, defeat **7** captive, mastery, triumph, victory, winning **8** adherent, follower, whip hand **9** upper hand **10** ascendancy, conquering, domination, overcoming **11** acquisition, subjugation **12** vanquishment **17** captured territory

Conrad, Joseph
real name: **29** Josef Teodor Konrad Korzeniowski
author of: **6** Chance **7** Lord Jim, Typhoon, Victory **8** Nostromo **13** Almayer's Folly **14** The Secret Agent **15** Heart of Darkness **16** Under Western Eyes **21** An Outcast of the Islands **23** The Nigger of the Narcissus

consanguine 4 akin **7** cognate, kindred, related **8** relative

consanguineous 3 kin **4** akin **7** kindred, related **9** connected **21** having a common ancestor

conscience 8 scruples **10** moral sense, principles **15** ethical feelings **20** sense of right and wrong

conscience-stricken 6 guilty **7** ashamed **8** contrite, penitent **9** chastened, regretful, repentant **10** remorseful **13** guilt-stricken

conscientious 5 exact **6** honest **7** careful, dutiful, ethical, upright **10**

fastidious, meticulous, particular, scrupulous **11** painstaking, responsible, trustworthy **12** conscionable **14** high-principled

conscious 5 aware **7** alert to, alive to, awake to, studied **8** noticing, sensible, sentient **9** cognizant, in the know, observing **10** calculated, deliberate, discerning, perceiving **12** apperceptive, premeditated **13** knowledgeable

consciousness 4 mind **6** senses **8** feelings, thoughts **9** awareness **10** cognizance, perception **11** discernment, sensibility

conscript 3 PFC **4** boot, hire, levy **5** draft **6** call up, employ, engage, enlist, enroll, induct, muster, rookie, seaman, select, take on **7** draftee, impress, private, recruit **8** enlistee, inductee, mobilize, register, selectee, shanghai **9** conscribe **11** buck private

consecrate 5 bless **6** hallow **7** glorify **8** sanctify **10** make sacred **11** immortalize **13** declare sacred

consecrated 4 holy **7** blessed **8** hallowed **10** sanctified

consecutive 6 in turn, serial **8** unbroken **10** continuous, sequential, successive **11** progressive **13** uninterrupted **19** following one another

consensus 6 accord **7** concord **9** unanimity **11** concurrence **13** common consent **14** general opinion **15** majority opinion **16** general agreement

consent 5 agree, allow, yield **6** accede, accept, accord, assent, concur, permit, ratify, submit **7** approve, concede, concord, confirm, endorse **8** approval, sanction **9** acquiesce, agreement **10** acceptance, fall in with, permission **11** concurrence, endorsement, willingness **12** acquiescence, confirmation, ratification

Consenting Adults
author: **12** Peter DeVries

consent to 2 OK **4** okay **6** permit **7** approve **8** accede to **10** concur with **11** acquiesce to, go along with **14** give the go-ahead

consequence 3 end **4** note **5** avail, fruit, issue, value, worth **6** import, moment, result, sequel, upshot **7** account, gravity, outcome **9** aftermath, influence, magnitude, outgrowth **10** importance, notability, prominence, usefulness **11** development, distinction, seriousness **12** significance

consequent 7 ensuing **8** eventual **9** following, resulting

consequential 7 crucial, epochal **8** historic **9** important, momentous **10** meaningful **11** significant

consequently 2 so **4** ergo, then **5** and so, hence, later **9** as a result, therefore **11** accordingly **12** subsequently

conservation 4 care **6** upkeep **9** hus-

bandry **10** careful use, protection **11** maintenance, safekeeping **12** preservation

conservative 5 quiet **6** square **7** old-line **8** cautious, moderate, undaring **9** right-wing **10** nonliberal, unchanging **11** reactionary, right-winger, traditional **13** unprogressive **15** middle-of-the-road **16** opponent of change **17** middle-of-the-roader **22** champion of the status quo

conservatoire 11 music school **12** conservatory, music academy

conservatory 7 nursery **8** hothouse **9** arboretum **10** glasshouse, greenhouse **11** music school **12** music academy **13** conservatoire

conserve 4 save **5** guard **7** care for, cut back, husband, use less **8** maintain, not waste, preserve **9** safeguard **12** use sparingly

consider 4 deem, hold, note **5** gauge, honor, judge, opine, study, think, weigh **6** ponder, regard, review **7** believe, examine, pay heed, respect **8** appraise, envision, hold to be, mull over **9** be aware of, reflect on **10** bear in mind, cogitate on, think about **11** contemplate **12** deliberate on **17** make allowances for **18** turn over in one's mind

considerable 4 tidy **5** ample, great, large **6** goodly **7** notable, sizable **8** not small **9** estimable, important **10** impressive, noteworthy, noticeable, of some size, remarkable **11** a good deal of, significant, substantial

considerably 5 amply **7** greatly, largely, notably, sizably **9** estimably **10** abundantly, noticeably, remarkably **13** significantly, substantially

considerate 4 kind **6** kindly **7** mindful **8** obliging **9** attentive, concerned **10** solicitous, thoughtful

consideration 4 heed, tact **5** cause, honor, point, study **6** factor, ground, motive, notice, reason, regard, review **7** concern, respect, thought **8** interest, judgment **9** attention **10** advisement, cogitation, inducement, kindliness, meditation, reflection, solicitude **11** examination **12** deliberation **13** contemplation **14** thoughtfulness **15** considerateness

consider closely 7 pay heed **11** concentrate **12** pay attention **13** put one's mind to **21** give one's full attention

considered 5 mused **6** deemed, heeded, judged, mulled **7** advised, express, honored, noticed, studied, thought, weighed, willful **8** believed, esteemed, looked on, pondered, regarded, supposed **9** reflected, respected, ruminated **10** deliberate, looked upon, thought out **11** deliberated, entertained, intentional **12** contemplated, premeditated, thought about

consign 5 remit 6 assign, commit, convey, remand 7 deliver, entrust 8 delegate, hand over, relegate, transfer 9 commend to 11 deposit with

consignment 8 delivery, shipment, transfer 10 assignment, committing, consigning, delegation, depositing, entrusting, relegation 11 handing over 12 goods for sale, goods shipped 19 goods sent on approval

consist 3 lie 6 reside 7 contain, include 10 be made up of 11 to be found in 13 be comprised of 14 to be composed of

consistency, consistence 4 body 5 unity 6 makeup 7 density, harmony, texture 8 firmness 9 agreement, coherence, congruity, stiffness, structure, thickness, viscosity 10 accordance, conformity, connection, uniformity 11 compactness, composition, persistence 12 construction, faithfulness, steady effort 13 compatibility, steadfastness 14 correspondence 16 uniform standards 19 constant performance, undeviating behavior

consistent 4 meet 6 steady 7 regular, unified 8 agreeing, constant, of a piece, suitable 9 congenial, congruous, consonant 10 compatible, harmonious, persistent, unchanging 11 in agreement, undeviating 13 correspondent 16 conforming to type

consolation 4 help 5 cheer 6 relief, solace, succor 7 comfort, support 8 easement, soothing, sympathy 10 condolence 11 alleviation, assuagement 13 encouragement

Consolation of Philosophy (De Consolatione Philosophiae)
author: 31 Anicius Manlius Severinus Boethius

console 4 calm, ease 5 cheer 6 soothe, succor 7 comfort, support, sustain 10 lament with, sympathize 11 condole with 13 express sorrow 15 commiserate with 18 express sympathy for

consolidate 4 fuse, join 5 merge, unify, unite 6 league 7 combine, fortify 8 coalesce, compress, condense, federate, make firm, make sure, solidify 9 integrate, make solid 10 amalgamate, centralize, strengthen 11 concentrate, incorporate 12 band together 13 bring together

consolidation 5 union 6 fusion, merger 8 alliance 9 coalition 11 unification 12 amalgamation 13 agglomeration 14 conglomeration

consommé 4 soup 5 broth 9 madrilene

consonance 5 amity, unity 6 accord, unison 7 concord, harmony, oneness 9 agreement, coherence, congruity, unanimity 10 accordance, conformity,

congruence, consonancy 11 concordance, consistency, homogeneity 13 compatibility 14 correspondence, likemindedness

consonant 8 in accord 9 agreeable, congruous, in harmony 10 concordant, consistent 11 in agreement

consort 3 mix 4 club, mate, wife 6 mingle, spouse 7 hang out, husband, pair off, partner 8 go around, sidekick 9 accompany, associate, companion, other half, pal around, rub elbows 10 fraternize 11 keep company

conspicuous 5 clear, great, overt, plain 6 famous, patent 7 eminent, evident, glaring, notable, obvious 8 distinct, flagrant, glorious, manifest, renowned, splendid, striking 9 arresting, brilliant, memorable, notorious, prominent, well-known 10 celebrated, easily seen, remarkable 11 illustrious, outstanding, standing out 13 distinguished, easily noticed, highly visible

conspicuousness 9 celebrity, flagrance, notoriety 10 prominence, visibility 11 obviousness 13 noticeability

conspiracy 4 plot 7 treason 8 intrigue, sedition 9 collusion, treachery 10 connivance, secret plan 11 machination 12 criminal plan 14 treasonous plan

conspirator 7 plotter, schemer, traitor 8 conniver 9 intriguer 10 subversive

conspire 5 unite 6 concur, scheme 7 collude, combine, connive 8 intrigue 9 cooperate, machinate 11 plot treason 12 work together

Constable, John
born: 7 England 12 East Bergholt
artwork: 10 The Haywain 12 Cloud Studies 14 Hadleigh Castle 39 Salisbury Cathedral from the Bishop's Grounds

constancy 6 fealty 7 loyalty 8 devotion 9 fixedness, stability 10 allegiance, permanence 12 faithfulness, immutability 13 dependability, invariability, steadfastness 15 trustworthiness 16 unchangeableness

constant 4 even, true 5 fixed, loyal 6 stable, steady, trusty 7 abiding, devoted, endless, eternal, regular, staunch, uniform 8 diligent, enduring, faithful, resolute, stalwart, unbroken, unvaried 9 ceaseless, continual, immutable, incessant, permanent, perpetual, steadfast, sustained, unceasing, unfailing 10 dependable, invariable, persistent, unchanging, unflagging, unswerving, unwavering 11 everlasting, never-ending, trustworthy, unalterable, undeviating, unrelenting 12 interminable, tried-and-true 13 uninterrupted

Constant Nymph, The
director: 14 Edmund Goulding
cast: 11 Alexis Smith 12 Charles

Boyer, Joan Fontaine 14 Brenda Marshall

constellation 4 host 5 group, rally 6 circle, galaxy, nebula, spiral, throng 7 cluster, company, pattern 9 gathering 10 assemblage, collection 12 spiral nebula 13 configuration 14 island universe
name: 3 Ara, Leo 4 Apus, Crux, Grus, Lynx, Lyra, Pavo, Vela 5 Aries, Cetus, Draco, Hydra, Indus, Lepus, Libra, Lupus, Mensa, Musca, Norma, Orion, Pyxis, Virgo 6 Antlia, Aquila, Auriga, Bootes, Caelum, Cancer, Carina, Corvus, Crater, Cygnus, Dorado, Fornax, Gemini, Hydrus, Octans, Pictor, Pisces, Puppis, Scutum, Taurus, Tucana, Volans 7 Cepheus, Columba, Lacerta, Pegasus, Perseus, Phoenix, Sagitta, Serpens, Sextans 8 Aquarius, Circinus, Equuleus, Eridanus, Hercules, Leo Minor, Scorpius, Sculptor 9 Andromeda, Centaurus, Delphinus, Monoceros, Ophiuchus, Reticulum, Ursa Major, Ursa Minor, Vulpecula 10 Canis Major, Canis Minor, Cassiopeia, Chamaeleon, Horologium, Triangulum 11 Capricornus, Sagittarius, Telescopium 12 Microscopium 13 Canes Venatici, Coma Berenices 14 Camelopardalis, Corona Borealis 15 Corona Australis, Piscis Austrinus 18 Triangulum Australe

consternation 5 alarm, panic, shock 6 dismay, fright, horror, terror 11 trepidation 12 apprehension

constituent 4 atom, part 5 piece, voter 6 factor, member 7 elective, element, essence 8 electing, integral, making up 9 component, formative, principal, supporter 10 appointing, ingredient

constitute 4 form, make, name 5 found, set up 6 create, invest, make up 7 appoint, compose, empower, produce 8 compound, delegate 9 authorize, establish, institute 10 commission

constitution 6 figure, health, make-up, mettle 7 charter, stamina, texture 8 physique, strength, vitality 9 basic laws, formation, structure 10 figuration 11 composition 12 construction 13 configuration 16 governing charter 17 physical condition 21 fundamental principles

constitutional 4 turn, walk 5 basic 6 inborn, ramble, stroll, vested 7 natural, organic 8 inherent, internal, physical 9 chartered, intrinsic 10 congenital 11 fundamental

Constitution State
nickname of: 11 Connecticut

constrain 4 curb, urge 5 check, crush, drive, force, quash 6 coerce, compel, oblige, subdue 7 confine, enforce, put down, repress, squelch 8 hold back, pressure, restrain, restrict, suppress **9** fight down, necessity, strong-arm **14** put the screws on

constrained 3 shy **5** timid **6** forced **7** bashful **8** reserved, reticent **9** compelled, diffident **10** restricted **11** embarrassed

constraint 5 force **6** duress **7** reserve **8** coercion, pressure **9** restraint **10** compulsion, diffidence, inhibition, obligation **11** enforcement **13** necessitation

constrict 4 bind **5** choke, cramp, pinch **6** shrink **7** squeeze **8** compress, contract, strangle **11** strangulate

constriction 7 binding, choking **8** cramping, pinching **9** narrowing, shrinking, squeezing, stricture, tightness **10** constraint, strangling **11** compression, contraction

construct 4 form, make **5** build, erect, frame, set up, shape **6** create, design, devise **7** arrange, fashion **8** organize **9** fabricate, formulate

construction 4 form, make **5** build, style **6** format **7** edifice, raising, reading, rearing, version **8** building, creation, erecting **9** rendition, structure **10** fashioning, production **11** composition, elucidation, explanation, explication, fabrication, manufacture **12** conformation, constructing **13** configuration **14** interpretation **15** putting together

constructive 5 handy **6** useful **7** helpful **8** valuable **9** practical **10** beneficial, productive **12** advantageous

construe 4 read, take **7** explain, make out **8** decipher **9** elucidate, figure out, interpret, translate **10** comprehend, understand

Consuelo
author: **10** George Sand

consul 5 envoy **8** emissary, minister **14** foreign officer, representative **15** diplomatic agent

Consul, The
opera by: **7** Menotti
character: **10** Magda Sorel

consult 6 confer, parley, regard **7** refer to **8** consider, talk over **9** inquire of **11** ask advice of, have an eye to **12** compare notes **13** exchange views **15** discuss together, seek counsel from, take into account **16** seek the opinion of **18** deliberate together

consultant 6 expert **7** adviser, advisor, counsel **9** discusser

consultation 7 council, hearing, meeting, palaver **9** interview **10** conference, discussion **12** deliberation

consumable 6 edible **7** eatable **10** comestible

consume 3 eat **4** gulp **5** drain, eat up, spend, use up, waste **6** absorb, devour, expend, guzzle, ravage **7** de-

plete, destroy, drink up, engross, exhaust **8** demolish, lay waste, squander **9** devastate, dissipate, swallow up **10** annihilate

consumed 4 used **5** burnt, drank, drunk, eaten, spent **6** used up, wasted **7** drained, outworn **8** absorbed, burned up, expended, perished **9** destroyed, engrossed, exhausted, swallowed **10** squandered **11** annihilated

consume greedily 5 eat up, snarf **6** devour, inhale **7** stuff in **8** bolt down, gobble up, gulp down, wolf down **12** swallow whole **13** eat ravenously **14** eat voraciously

consumer 4 user **5** buyer, drain **6** client, patron, waster **7** spender **8** customer **9** purchaser **10** dissipater, squanderer

consummate 2 do **5** sheer, total, utter **6** effect, finish **7** achieve, execute, fulfill, perfect, perform, realize, supreme **8** absolute, carry out, complete, finished, thorough **9** faultless **10** accomplish, bring about, undisputed **11** unmitigated **12** accomplished, unquestioned **13** unconditional **17** through-and-through

consummation 3 end **5** close **6** finish **9** execution **10** attainment, completion, conclusion **11** achievement, culmination, fulfillment, realization **14** accomplishment

consumption 2 TB **3** use **7** using up **9** consuming, depletion **10** exhaustion **11** expenditure, utilization **12** exploitation, tuberculosis

Consus
origin: **5** Roman
god of: **11** good counsel, horse racing
protector of: **5** grain
corresponds to: **3** Ops

contact 4 join, meet **5** reach, touch, union **7** connect, meeting **8** abutment, junction, touching **9** adjacency, get hold of **10** connection **11** association **13** communication **14** get in touch with **15** communicate with

contagion 7 disease **8** epidemic, outbreak **9** infection, spreading **13** contamination

contagious 8 catching **9** spreading **10** infectious, spreadable **12** communicable **13** transmittable

contain 4 curb, hold **5** check **6** embody, hold in **7** control, embrace, enclose, include, inhibit, involve, repress **8** hold back, keep back, restrain, suppress **11** accommodate, incorporate **12** keep the lid on **16** keep within bounds

container 3 bag, box, can, jar, vat **4** pail **6** barrel, bottle, bucket, carton, holder, vessel **10** receptacle

containment 7 control **9** restraint, retention

contaminate 4 foul, soil **5** dirty, spoil,

taint **6** befoul, blight, debase, defile, infect, poison **7** corrupt, pollute **8** besmirch **10** adulterate, make impure

contamination 5 filth **7** fouling, soiling **8** dirtying, foulness, impurity, spoiling **9** dirtiness, poisoning, polluting, pollution, putridity **10** defilement **11** uncleanness **12** adulteration

Conte, Richard
real name: **18** Nicholas Peter Conte
born: **12** Jersey City NJ
roles: **8** Barabbas **13** A Bell for Adano **24** The Greatest Story Ever Told

contemplate 4 note, plan, scan **5** weigh **6** expect, gaze at, intend, ponder, regard, survey **7** examine, imagine, inspect, observe, project, stare at, think of **8** aspire to, envision, mull over, ruminate **9** muse about **10** anticipate, cogitate on, have in view, meditate on, think about **11** reflect upon **12** deliberate on **13** consider fully, look at fixedly, look forward to **14** speculate about **15** view attentively

contemplation 5 study **6** gazing, musing, seeing, survey **7** looking, reverie, thought, viewing **8** scanning, thinking **9** pondering **10** cogitation, inspection, meditation, reflection, rumination **11** examination, observation **12** deliberation **13** consideration

contemplative 6 musing **7** pensive **8** studious **9** engrossed **10** cogitative, meditative, reflective, ruminating, thoughtful **11** speculative **13** introspective, lost in thought

contemporaneous 6 coeval **10** coexistent, coincident, concurrent **11** synchronous **12** contemporary, simultaneous

contemporary 3 new **4** late **6** modern, recent, with-it **7** current **8** advanced, brand-new, up-to-date **10** coexistent, coincident, concurrent, newfangled, present-day **11** ultramodern **12** simultaneous **13** of the same time, up-to-the-minute **15** contemporaneous

contempt 4 hate **5** scorn, shame **6** hatred **7** disdain, disgust **8** aversion, derision, disfavor, disgrace, dishonor, distaste, ignominy, loathing, ridicule **9** antipathy, disregard, disrepute, revulsion **10** abhorrence, repugnance **11** detestation, humiliation

contemptible 3 low **4** base, mean, vile **5** cheap **6** abject, paltry, shabby **8** shameful, unworthy, wretched **9** miserable, repugnant, revolting **10** despicable, detestable, disgusting **11** ignominious

contemptuous 6 lordly **7** haughty, pompous **8** arrogant, derisive, insolent, scornful, snobbish **10** disdainful **12** supercilious **13** condescending, disrespectful

contemptuousness 5 scorn 7 disdain 8 contempt, rudeness 9 arrogance, insolence

contend 3 vie, war 4 aver, avow, hold, spar 5 argue, claim, clash, fight 6 allege, assert, battle, combat, debate, insist, jostle, strive, tussle 7 compete, contest, declare, dispute, grapple, quarrel, wrestle 8 be a rival, maintain, propound, skirmish, struggle 10 put forward

content 4 area, core, gist, load, size, text 5 cheer, happy, heart, ideas, peace 6 at ease, at rest, matter, please, serene, thesis, volume 7 appease, comfort, essence, gratify, insides, meaning, pleased, satisfy, suffice, unmoved 8 capacity, make easy, pleasure, serenity 9 contented, gratified, happiness, satisfied, set at ease, substance 10 complacent, untroubled 11 comfortable, contentment, peace of mind, unconcerned 12 satisfaction 13 gratification

contented 5 happy 6 at ease, serene 7 at peace, content, pleased 9 gratified, satisfied 11 comfortable

contentedness 4 ease 5 peace 7 comfort, content 8 pleasure, serenity 9 happiness 11 contentment 12 satisfaction 13 gratification

contention 5 clash, fight 6 battle, combat, strife 7 contest, discord, dispute, rivalry 8 argument, conflict, disunity, fighting, friction, skirmish, struggle, variance 9 assertion, encounter, wrangling 10 dissension, quarreling 11 competition, discordance 12 disagreement 13 confrontation

contentious 5 angry, cross 7 bateful, scrappy 8 captious 9 bellicose 10 pugnacious 11 belligerent, competitive, quarrelsome 12 cantankerous, disputatious 13 argumentative, controversial

contentment 4 ease 5 peace 7 comfort, content 8 pleasure, serenity 9 happiness 12 satisfaction 13 contentedness, gratification

conterminous 8 abutting, adjacent, touching 9 bordering 11 right beside 14 contiguous with

contest 3 war 4 bout, game 5 fight, match 6 battle, combat, debate, oppose, vie for 7 dispute, rivalry, tourney 8 conflict, fight for, object to, struggle 9 battle for, challenge, combat for, encounter 10 compete for, contend for, controvert, engagement, tournament 11 competition, struggle for 12 argue against 14 call in question

contestant 5 rival 6 player 7 entrant, fighter 8 competer, prospect 9 combatant, contender 10 challenger, competitor

context 6 milieu 7 climate, meaning, setting 8 ambience 9 framework, precincts, situation 10 atmosphere, background, conditions, connection 11 environment 12 relationship, surroundings 13 circumstances 16 frame of reference

contiguous 5 close, handy 6 nearby 7 close-by, tangent 8 abutting, adjacent, next-door, touching 9 adjoining, bordering, in contact 10 juxtaposed 11 neighboring 12 conterminous

continence 6 purity 8 chastity, sobriety 10 abstinence, moderation, temperance 11 forbearance 13 self-restraint

continent 4 Asia, pure 6 Africa, chaste, Europe 7 Eurasia 8 celibate, land mass, mainland, virginal 9 abstinent, Australia, temperate 10 abstemious, Antarctica 12 North America, South America

contingency 7 urgency 8 accident 9 emergency, extremity 10 likelihood 11 possibility, predicament 15 unforeseen event

contingent 9 dependent, subject to 11 conditioned 12 controlled by

continual 7 endless, eternal 8 constant, frequent, habitual, unbroken, unending 9 ceaseless, incessant, perennial, perpetual, recurring, unceasing 10 continuous, persistent 11 everlasting, never-ending, oft-repeated, unremitting 12 interminable 13 uninterrupted

continually 3 aye 4 ever 6 always, steady 7 endless, eternal, forever, on and on 8 steadily 9 recurring 10 constantly, frequently, repeatedly

continuance 4 stay, term 6 extent, period 7 lasting 8 duration 9 extension 10 continuing, permanence 11 adjournment, persistence, protraction 12 continuation, perseverance, prolongation

continuation 6 sequel 8 addition, sequence 9 extension 10 continuing, supplement 11 continuance, protraction 12 prolongation

continue 4 go on, last, stay 5 abide 6 drag on, endure, extend, keep on, keep up, remain, resume, stay on 7 carry on, persist, proceed 9 persevere

continued 6 kept on, kept up, lasted, went on 7 endured 8 extended 9 carried on, persisted, proceeded, prolonged 10 persevered, protracted

continuing 6 steady 7 abiding, eternal, ongoing 8 constant, enduring, extended, unbroken, unending 9 ceaseless, incessant, perpetual, prolonged 10 dragged out, persistent, protracted 11 persevering, unremitting 12 interminable 13 uninterrupted

continuity 4 flow 5 chain 9 continuum 10 succession 11 continuance, progression 12 continuation

continuous 6 linked, steady 7 endless, eternal, lasting 8 constant, enduring, unbroken 9 ceaseless, connected, continual, extensive, incessant, perpetual, prolonged, unceasing 10 continuing, persistent, protracted, successive 11 consecutive, everlasting, persevering, progressive, unremitting 12 interminable 13 uninterrupted

continuum 4 flow 5 chain 8 sequence 10 continuity, succession 11 continuance, progression 12 continuation

contort 4 bend, warp 5 twist 6 deform 7 distort 11 be misshapen

contorted 4 bent 7 crooked, twisted 8 deformed 9 distorted

contortion 7 bending 8 twisting 10 distortion 11 crookedness

contour 4 form 5 lines, shape 6 figure 7 outline, profile 10 silhouette 11 physiognomy

contraband 11 bootlegging 13 smuggled goods 14 illegal exports, illegal imports 15 unlicensed goods 17 black-marketeering 18 prohibited articles 19 unlawful trafficking

contract 3 get 4 pact, take 5 agree, incur 6 absorb, assume, narrow, pledge, reduce, shrink, treaty 7 acquire, compact, develop, dwindle, promise, shorten, tighten 8 compress, condense, covenant, engender 9 constrict, enter into, negotiate, undertake 11 arrangement, come to terms 12 draw together, make a bargain 13 become smaller, legal document 15 sign an agreement 16 written agreement

contracted form 6 digest 7 summary 8 synopsis 9 short form 11 abridgement, compression 12 abbreviation, condensation

contraction 8 decrease 9 drawing in, lessening, narrowing, reduction, shrinkage 10 shortening, shriveling, tightening 11 compression 12 abbreviation, condensation, constriction

contradict 4 deny 5 belie, rebut 6 impugn, oppose, refute 7 confute, counter, dispute, gainsay 8 disprove 10 controvert 12 be contrary to, disagree with

contradiction 6 denial 7 counter 8 negation, rebuttal 10 refutation 11 confutation 12 disagreement

contradictory 8 contrary, opposing 10 discrepant, dissenting, refutatory 11 conflicting, disagreeing 12 antithetical, inconsistent 14 countervailing, irreconcilable

contradistinction 8 contrast 10 difference 13 dissimilarity

contraption 6 device, gadget 9 apparatus, invention 11 contrivance

contrariety 9 deviation 10 difference, divergence 13 contradiction

contrary 5 balky 6 ornery 7 adverse,

counter, froward, hostile, opposed, wayward, willful **8** converse, inimical, opposite, stubborn, untoward **9** disparate, obstinate, unfitting **10** at variance, discordant, headstrong, refractory, unsuitable **11** conflicting, disagreeing, intractable, unfavorable **12** antagonistic, antithetical, disagreeable, inauspicious, incompatible, recalcitrant, unpropitious **13** contradictory **15** at cross purposes, unaccommodating

contrast 6 depart, differ **7** deviate, diverge **8** variance **9** disparity **10** comparison, difference, divergence, unlikeness **11** distinction **12** disagree with **13** differentiate, dissimilarity **15** differentiation, set in opposition

contrasting 8 clashing, dividing, opposing **9** comparing, differing **10** discordant, juxtaposed **14** distinguishing **15** differentiating

contravene 4 deny **5** annul, fight, spurn **6** abjure, breach, combat, disown, negate, offend, oppose, reject, resist **7** disobey, exclude, gainsay, infract, nullify, violate **8** abrogate, disclaim, overstep **9** overreach, repudiate **10** act against, contradict, infringe on, transgress **12** encroach upon **15** trespass against

contretemps 4 spat **5** clash, set-to **7** dispute, quarrel **8** argument, squabble **10** difference, falling out **12** disagreement **18** embarrassing mishap

contribute 4 give **5** endow, grant **6** bestow, confer, donate, lead to **7** advance, forward, hand out, present **9** bear a part, influence **11** have a hand in **13** be conducive to **14** help bring about

contribution 4 alms, gift **5** grant **7** charity, subsidy **8** bestowal, donation, offering **9** endowment **11** benefaction **12** dispensation

contributive 8 valuable **9** favorable **10** beneficial

contributory 9 accessory, ancillary, auxiliary **13** supplementary

contrite 6 rueful **7** humbled **8** penitent **9** chastened, regretful, repentant, sorrowful **10** apologetic, remorseful **18** conscience-stricken

contrition 6 regret **7** penance, remorse **9** atonement, penitence **10** repentance **11** compunction **12** self-reproach **18** qualms of conscience

contrivance 4 plan, plot, tool **5** gizmo, trick **6** design, device, doodad, gadget **7** machine, measure **8** artifice, intrigue **9** apparatus, implement, invention, mechanism, stratagem **10** instrument **11** contraption, machination, thingamajig **12** Rube Goldberg

contrive 4 plan, plot **6** create, design, devise, invent, manage, scheme **7**

concoct **8** maneuver **9** improvise **11** devise a plan **17** effect by stratagem

contrived 7 labored, studied **8** mannered **9** unnatural **10** artificial

contriver 7 creator, deviser **8** designer, inventor **9** architect

control 4 curb, rule, sway **5** brake, steer **6** bridle, charge, govern, manage, master, subdue **7** command, contain, mastery, repress **8** dominate, dominion, regulate, restrain, restrict **9** authority, direction, reign over, restraint, supervise **10** domination, management, manipulate, regulation **11** superintend, supervision, suppressant **12** have charge of, jurisdiction

controlled 5 ruled **6** curbed, steady, swayed **7** checked, managed, powered, servile, subdued **8** directed, governed, held back, kept down, reserved, verified **9** commanded, contained, dominated, moderated, regulated, repressed **10** authorized, regimented, restrained, supervised **11** manipulated

controlling 6 ruling **8** dominant **9** governing **10** commanding **11** influencing, predominant **13** predominating

controversial 7 at issue **8** arguable **9** debatable, polemical **10** disputable **12** questionable **13** causing debate **15** widely discussed **16** open to discussion

controversy 6 debate **7** dispute, quarrel, wrangle **8** argument, squabble **10** contention, discussion, dissension **11** altercation **12** disagreement

controvert 4 deny **5** belie, rebut **6** negate, oppose, refute **7** confute, dispute, gainsay, protest **8** confound, disprove, question **9** challenge, disaffirm **10** contradict, contravene, invalidate **12** give the lie to

contumacious 6 unruly **7** froward **8** contrary, factious, insolent, mutinous, perverse **9** fractious, seditious **10** headstrong, rebellious, refractory **11** disobedient, intractable **12** ungovernable, unmanageable **13** disrespectful, insubordinate

contumely 5 abuse, insult, scorn **7** disdain, obloquy **8** contempt, diatribe, reproach, rudeness **9** arrogance, insolence, invective, pomposity **10** opprobrium, scurrility **11** brusqueness, haughtiness **12** billingsgate, vituperation **15** overbearingness

contusion 4 hurt, mark, sore **5** mouse **6** bruise, injury, shiner **7** blemish **8** abrasion, black eye **9** black mark **13** discoloration **16** black-and-blue mark

conundrum 5 poser, rebus **6** enigma, puzzle, riddle **7** arcanum, mystery, paradox, problem, puzzler, stopper, stumper **11** brain-teaser **13** Chinese puzzle

convalesce 4 mend **5** rally **6** revive **7** improve, recover, restore **8** progress **9** get better **10** recuperate

convalescence 7 recruit **8** recovery **11** restoration **12** recuperation **14** return to health

convene 6 gather, muster, summon **7** collect, convoke, round up **8** assemble **12** call together, come together, hold a session **13** bring together

convenience 3 use **4** ease **6** chance **7** benefit, comfort, service, utility **8** facility, pleasure **9** appliance, enjoyment, handiness, work saver **10** usefulness **11** opportunity **12** availability, satisfaction, suitable time **13** accessibility, accommodation

convenient 5 handy **6** at hand, nearby, suited, useful **7** adapted, helpful **8** suitable **9** easy to use **10** beneficial **11** serviceable **12** advantageous **16** easily accessible

convent 7 nunnery **8** cloister **13** society of nuns

convention 4 code **6** caucus, custom **7** meeting, precept **8** assembly, conclave, congress, practice, propriety, protocol, standard **9** formality, gathering **10** conference, social rule **11** convocation

conventional 5 usual **6** common, normal, proper **7** regular, routine **8** accepted, orthodox, standard **9** customary **11** traditional

converge 4 meet **5** focus **8** approach **11** concentrate **12** come together **13** bring together

convergence 6 accord **8** junction **9** congruity **10** confluence **12** meeting place **14** correspondence

conversant 4 up on **5** aware **6** au fait **7** erudite, privy to, skilled, tutored **8** familiar, informed, sensible, sentient **9** au courant, cognizant, practiced **10** acquainted, proficient **12** well-informed **13** knowledgeable

conversation 3 rap **4** chat, talk **7** gabfest, palaver **8** chit- chat, dialogue **9** discourse, tete-a-tete **11** bull session **13** confabulation
Italian: **13** conversazione

Conversation, The
director: **18** Francis Ford Coppola
cast: **10** John Cazale **11** Gene Hackman **13** Allen Garfield

conversational 6 casual, chatty **8** everyday, informal **9** idiomatic **10** colloquial, vernacular

conversazione 12 conversation

converse 3 gab, jaw, rap **4** chat, chin, talk **7** palaver, reverse **9** chitchat, contrary, opposite **10** antithesis, chew the fat, chew the rag **11** confabulate **13** speak together **14** shoot the breeze

conversely 12 contrariwise **14** antithetically, on the other hand

conversion 6 change **10** changeover **12** modification **13** change of heart, metamorphosis, transmutation **14** transformation **15** change in beliefs, transfiguration **16** change of religion

convert 4 turn **6** change, modify, novice **8** neophyte **9** proselyte, transform **11** proselytize

convex 7 bulging, rounded **11** protuberant **13** curved outward

convey 4 bear, cede, deed, give, move, tell, will **5** bring, carry, grant, leave **6** impart, relate, reveal **7** conduct, consign, deliver, divulge **8** bequeath, disclose, dispatch, transfer, transmit **9** confide to, make known, transport **11** communicate

conveyance 3 bus, car, rig, van **4** cart **5** buggy, truck, wagon **7** vehicle **8** carriage, carrying, movement, transfer **9** conveying, transport **12** transmission **14** transportation

convict 3 con **4** doom **5** felon **7** condemn **8** jailbird, prisoner, yardbird **10** find guilty **11** prove guilty **13** declare guilty

conviction 4 view, zeal **5** ardor, creed, dogma, faith, fever, tenet **6** belief, fervor **7** opinion **8** doctrine, judgment, position **9** assurance, certainty, certitude, intensity, principle, viewpoint **10** persuasion **11** earnestness **13** steadfastness

convince 4 sway **6** assure **7** satisfy, win over **8** persuade **9** influence **11** bring around, prevail upon

convincing 5 sound, valid **6** cogent, potent **7** evident **8** assuring, forceful, powerful **9** plausible **10** persuading, persuasive, satisfying

convivial 6 merry **6** genial, jovial **7** affable, festive **8** friendly, sociable **9** agreeable, fun-loving **10** gregarious **13** companionable

convocation 6 caucus, muster, roster **7** council, meeting, roundup **8** assembly, conclave, congress **9** gathering **10** conference, convention **11** ingathering

convoke 4 meet, open **6** gather, muster **8** assemble, converse **11** call to order **12** call together

convolute 4 coil, wave, wavy, wind **5** twirl, twist **6** coiled, rolled, spiral, tangle **7** contort, sinuous, twisted **8** involved, spiraled **9** intricate **11** complicated **12** turn and twist

convolution 4 coil, maze **5** twist **7** coiling, winding **8** twisting **9** labyrinth, sinuosity **10** contortion, undulation **11** sinuousness **12** tortuousness

convoy 5 fleet, usher **6** column, escort **7** conduct **9** accompany, formation, safeguard **10** armed guard, protection

convulse 4 rock, stir **5** laugh, shake, spasm, wring **6** excite **7** agitate, disturb, perturb, trouble **8** double up

convulsion 3 fit **5** spasm **6** tumult **7** seizure **8** outburst, paroxysm **9** agitation, commotion **10** contortion **11** disturbance

convulsive 6 fitful **7** hurtful, rending, shaking **8** exciting, stirring **9** agitating, epileptic, spasmodic, troubling **10** disturbing

Conway, Tim
    real name: 18 Thomas Daniel Conway
    born: 12 Willoughby OH
    roles: 11 McHale's Navy **16** Carol Burnett Show **17** The Steve Allen Show

coo 4 bill **6** babble, gurgle, murmur **20** whisper sweet nothings

Coogan, Jackie
    real name: 16 Jack Leslie Coogan
    wife: 11 Betty Grable
    born: 12 Los Angeles CA
    roles: 6 The Kid **9** Tom Sawyer **11** Oliver Twist, Peck's Bad Boy **15** Huckleberry Finn

cook 3 fix **4** chef, fire, heat, make **5** occur **6** cookie, doctor, happen, seethe **7** concoct, falsify, prepare, process **8** work well **9** improvise
    method: 3 fry **4** bake, boil, brew, sear, stew **5** baste, broil, grill, poach, roast, saute, scald, shirr, steam **6** braise, coddle, simmer **7** parboil, stir-fry **8** barbecue **9** fricassee

Cooke, Alistair
    author of: 14 One Man's America **18** A Generation on Trial **26** Around the World in Fifty Years
    TV host of: 18 Masterpiece Theatre

cooked sufficiently 4 done **5** ready **7** al dente **11** done to a turn

cookie 3 bar, gal, gul **4** cake, cook **5** wafer **6** person **7** biscuit, brownie **10** shortbread
    type: 4 oreo **5** sugar **7** oatmeal **8** macaroon, molasses **9** girl scout, tollhouse **10** gingersnap, lorna doone **12** peanut butter **13** chocolate chip

cooking, fine/gourmet
    French: 12 haute cuisine

cooking term 3 a la, cut, dot, fry **4** bake, beat, boil, chop, coat, cube, dice, dust, flan, fold, lard, roux, sear, snip, stew, toss, whip **5** aspic, au jus, baste, blend, bread, broil, brush, candy, cream, crepe, devil, dough, flake, glace, glaze, grate, grill, knead, plank, puree, roast, saute, scald, score, shirr, steep, stock, swear, torte **6** au lait, blanch, braise, coddle, devein, dredge, fillet, flambe, fondue, render, simmer, skewer, sliver **7** a la mode, compote, crouton, garnish, goulash, liquefy, parboil, precook, preheat, rissole, scallop, stir-fry **8** aperitif, au gratin, barbecue, conserve, consomme, julienne, marinate, pot roast **9** brochette, demitasse,

drippings, forcemeat, fricassee, lyonnaise, macedoine **10** caramelize, cracklings
    boneless strips of meat/ fish: 6 fillet
    clear soup: 8 bouillon, consomme
    cubed toasted bread: 7 crouton
    food cooked and served in foil or paper: 11 en papillote
    fruit preserve with nuts/raisins: 8 conserve
    fruits in syrup: 7 compote
    in the fashion: 7 a la mode
    remove veins: 6 devein
    skewered meat: 5 kebab **9** brochette
    small cup of black coffee: 9 demitasse
    thin strips: 6 sliver **8** julienne
    with cheese: 8 au gratin
    with ice cream: 7 a la mode
    with juice/with its own juices: 5 au jus
    with milk: 6 au lait

cook up 3 mix **4** brew **5** hatch **6** create, devise, invent, make up **7** concoct, think up **8** compound, contrive **9** fabricate, formulate

cool 3 icy **4** calm, cold **5** aloof, chill **6** chilly, frosty, offish, serene **7** distant, not warm **8** composed, lose heat, make cool, reserved **9** collected, impassive, uncordial, unexcited **10** become cool, cool-headed, deliberate, nonchalant, unfriendly, unsociable, untroubled **11** indifferent, standoffish, undisturbed, unemotional, unflappable **12** slightly cold, somewhat cold, unresponsive **13** dispassionate, imperturbable, self-possessed

cooler 3 ade, can, fan, jug **4** coop, icer, jail **5** drink, icier **6** calmer, icebox, lockup, prison **11** refrigerant **12** refrigerator **14** air conditioner

Cool Hand Luke
    director: 15 Stuart Rosenberg
    cast: 8 J D Cannon **10** Jo Van Fleet, Lou Antonio, Paul Newman **12** Anthony Zerbe, Dennis Hopper **13** George Kennedy **14** Strother Martin
    Oscar for: 15 supporting actor (Kennedy)

Coolidge, Calvin
    name at birth: 18 John Calvin Coolidge
    nickname: 9 Silent Cal
    presidential rank: 9 thirtieth
    party: 10 Republican
    state represented: 2 MA
    succeeded: 7 Harding
    defeated: 5 (Frank Thomas) Johns, (Herman P) Faris, (John William) Davis **6** (William Zebulon) Foster **7** (Gilbert O) Nations, (William James) Wallace **10** (Robert Marion) La Follette
    vice president: 4 none (first term) **5** (Charles Gates) Dawes
    cabinet:
        state: 6 (Charles Evans) Hughes **7**

(Frank Billings) Kellogg

treasury: 6 (Andrew William) Mellon

war: 5 (Dwight Filley) Davis, (John Wingate) Weeks

attorney general: 5 (Harlan Fiske) Stone **6** (Charles B) Warren **7** (John Garibaldi) Sargent **9** (Harry Micajah) Daugherty

navy: 5 (Edwin) Denby **6** (Curtis Dwight) Wilbur

postmaster general: 3 (Harry Stewart) New

interior: 4 (Hubert) Work, (Roy Owen) West

agriculture: 4 (Howard Mason) Gore **7** (Henry Cantwell) Wallace, (William Marion) Jardine

commerce: 6 (Herbert Clark) Hoover **7** (William Fairfield) Whiting

labor: 5 (James John) Davis

born: 2 VT **13** Plymouth Notch

died: 2 MA **11** Northampton

buried: 2 VT **8** Plymouth

education:
  College: 7 Amherst
  later studied: 3 law

religion: 17 Congregationalist

vacation spot: 10 Black Hills

author: 32 The Autobiography of Calvin Coolidge

political career: 13 vice president
  state senator/lieutenant governor/governor of: 2 Ma **13** Massachusetts

civilian career: 6 lawyer **17** bank vice president **18** newspaper columnist

notable events of lifetime/term: 22 Pennsylvania coal strike
  Act: 8 Volstead **10** Boulder Dam **11** Immigration **17** Japanese Exclusion
  bribery case: 8 Elks Hill
  conference: 11 Geneva Naval
  flight by: 16 Charles Lindbergh
  Lindbergh's plane: 15 Spirit of St Louis
  Pact: 13 Kellogg-Briand
  trial: 6 Scopes **12** Scopes monkey
  quote: 35 (After all) the chief business of America is business **43** Spend less than you make and make more than you spend

father: 10 John Calvin

mother: 8 Victoria (Josephine Moor)
  stepmother: 8 Caroline (Brown)

sibling: 13 Abigail Gratia

wife: 5 Grace (Anna Goodhue)

children: 4 John **6** Calvin

coolness 5 chill **7** dislike, reserve **8** distance **9** aloofness, composure, sangfroid **10** chilliness, detachment, frostiness **11** impassivity **12** indifference **13** lack of emotion, lack of feeling **14** unfriendliness **15** emotionlessness, standoffishness **16** imperturbability, unresponsiveness

coop 3 mew, pen, sty **4** auto, cage, cote **5** cramp, hutch, roost **6** encase, prison **7** confine **8** imprison **9** enclosure **11** cooperation, cooperative

Cooper, Gary
  real name: 16 Frank James Cooper
  born: 8 Helena MT
  roles: 8 High Noon (Oscar) **9** Beau Geste **12** Sergeant York (Oscar), The Virginian **15** A Farewell to Arms **17** Mr Deeds Goes to Town **19** For Whom the Bell Tolls, The Cowboy and the Lady **20** The Pride of the Yankees **22** North West Mounted Police

Cooper, James Fenimore
  author of: 6 The Spy **8** The Bravo, The Pilot **9** Wyandotte **10** The Prairie **11** The Pioneers, The Red Rover **13** The Deerslayer, The Pathfinder, The Water-Witch **20** Leatherstocking Tales, The Last of the Mohicans
  character: 4 Cora **5** Alice, Magua, Uncas **7** Hawkeye **11** Natty Bumppo **12** Chingachgook

cooperate 4 join **5** unite **7** go along, pitch in, share in **8** take part **9** join hands **10** act jointly, bear part in, join forces **11** collaborate, participate **12** pull together, work together **14** work side by side

cooperation 7 concert, detente **8** teamwork **9** agreement **10** accordance **11** concurrence, cooperating, give and take, joint action **13** collaboration, participation **15** pulling together, working together

coop up 3 pen **4** cage **5** pen in **6** closet, encage, shut in **7** confine, impound **8** restrain, restrict

coordinate 4 mesh **5** equal, match, order **6** relate **7** arrange, coequal **8** organize, parallel **9** correlate, harmonize **11** correlative, systematize **16** equally important

coordination 4 bond **5** skill **6** accord **7** harmony, liaison **10** adaptation, adjustment **12** equalization, organization **15** synchronization

cop 3 bag, nab, rob, win **4** bull, grab, take **5** bobby, catch, filch, pinch, snare, steal, swipe **6** peeler, pilfer, snatch **7** capture **8** flat foot, gendarme, purchase **9** policeman **11** acquisition, policewoman **13** police officer

cope 4 face, spar **6** handle, hurdle, manage, strive, tussle **7** contend, wrestle **8** struggle **11** hold one's own

copious 4 full **5** ample **6** lavish **7** liberal, profuse **8** abundant, generous **9** bountiful, extensive, plenteous, plentiful

copiousness 6 bounty, plenty, wealth **7** surfeit **8** fullness, plethora **9** abundance, ampleness, plenitude, profusion **10** lavishness, oversupply

Copland, Aaron
  born: 10 Brooklyn NY
  composer of: 5 Rodeo **9** Quiet City **10** Statements **11** Billy the Kid **12** Connotations **13** Dance Symphony, El Salon Mexico, The Tender Land **15** Outdoor Overture **17** Appalachian Spring **18** Music for a Great City, Music for the Theater

Copley, John Singleton
  born: 8 Boston MA
  artwork: 11 Samuel Adams **19** The Siege of Gibraltar **21** The Boy with the Squirrel **22** Brook Watson and the Shark, The Death of Major Pierson **26** The Death of the Earl of Chatham

copper
  chemical symbol: 2 Cu

copper-colored 5 henna **6** auburn, russet **11** golden-brown, rust-colored **12** reddish-brown

coppice 4 bosk, wood **5** bluff, copse, firth, grove **6** forest, growth **7** boscage, thicket

Coppola, Francis Ford
  director of: 12 The Godfather (Part I) (Part II, Oscar) **13** Apocalypse Now, The Cotton Club **15** The Conversation

copse 5 brush, clump, grove **6** forest **7** coppice, thicket **8** woodland

copy 3 ape **4** fake, sham, text **5** clone, mimic, story, Xerox **6** follow, mirror, parody, repeat **7** emulate, forgery, imitate, replica **8** likeness **9** duplicate, facsimile, imitation, photostat, reportage, reproduce **10** carbon copy, manuscript **11** counterfeit, make a copy of **12** reproduction **14** representation **15** written material

coquette 4 vamp **5** flirt, tease **12** heart-breaker

coquettish 3 coy **9** kittenish **11** flirtatious

coral 3 red **4** fire, pink, rose **5** horny, polyp, snake **6** orange, sea fan **8** acropora, hydrozoa, staghorn **9** gorgonian **10** sea feather **12** coelenterata

coram populo 8 publicly **15** before the public

corban 8 offering

Corbett, James (John)
  nickname: 12 Gentleman Jim
  sport: 6 boxing
  class: 11 heavyweight

cord 5 braid, twine **8** thin rope **11** heavy string
  abbreviation: 2 cd

Cordelia
  character in: 8 King Lear
  author: 11 Shakespeare

cordial 4 warm **6** genial, hearty **7** affable, amiable, sincere **8** friendly, gracious **9** heartfelt **11** good-natured **12** affectionate, wholehearted

cordiality 6 warmth **8** goodwill **9** affection, geniality, sincerity **10** affability, amiability, heartiness **11** amicability, earnestness **12** friendliness, graciousness, pleasantness **13** agreeableness

cordial relations 5 amity **6** accord **7** concord, harmony **8** goodwill **9** agreement **10** friendship **11** amicability **15** entente cordiale

cordon 4 cord, ring, rope **6** circle **8** encircle

cordon bleu 4 bird **5** finch **7** waxbill **10** red cheeked **11** estrildidae
  school for: 5 chefs **7** cooking
    where: 5 Paris **6** France
  founded by: 13 Marthe Distell
  means: 10 blue ribbon

core 3 nub, nut **4** crux, gist, guts, meat, pith **5** heart **6** center, kernel **7** essence, nucleus **9** substance **10** brass tacks **11** central part, nitty-gritty **13** essential part, innermost part **15** sum and substance

Corelli, Arcangelo
  born: 5 Imola, Italy
  composer of: 7 La Folia (sonata No 12) **14** Concerti Grossi

coriander
  botanical name: 17 Coriandrum sativum
  origin: 13 Mediterranean
  color: 5 brown, white **6** yellow
  flavor: 4 sage **5** cumin **7** caraway **9** lemon peel
  candy: 6 comfit

Corinth, Lovis
  born: 6 Tapiau **7** Prussia
  artwork: 6 Salome **8** Ecce Homo **10** Apocalypse **29** The Walchensee with a Yellow Field

Coriolanus
  author: 18 William Shakespeare
  character: 8 Cominius, Virgilia, Volumnia **12** Junius Brutus, Titus Lartius **14** Tullus Aufidius **15** Menenius Agrippa, Sicinius Velutus **22** Caius Marcius Coriolanus

cork 3 bob, oak **4** bark, bung, plug, seal, stop **5** check, close, float **7** confine, filling stopper, stopple **8** restrain, suppress **10** insulation

corker 3 ace **4** lulu, oner, whiz **7** stopper **8** clencher, striking, top notch **9** excellent, humdinger **10** remarkable **11** astonishing

corkscrew 4 coil, curl **5** twist **6** spiral **7** winding **10** serpentine **12** bottle opener

Corleone family
  characters in: 12 The Godfather
  author: 4 Puzo
  member: 5 Fredo, Sonny **7** Don Vito, Freddie, Michael

corn 4 cure **5** grain **6** callus **7** Zea Mays **8** preserve, schmaltz **9** vegetable
  varieties: 3 Pod **4** Crow, Dent, Rice, Sand **5** Broom, Flint, Kafir, maize, Sugar, Sweet **6** Indian, Turkey **8** Egyptian, Squirrel
  bread/cake: 4 pone **7** hoecake **8** tortilla **9** hushpuppy **10** johnnycake
  beverage: 7 bourbon, whiskey

Corncracker State
  nickname of: 8 Kentucky

Corneille, Pierre
  author of: 5 Cinna, Le Cid, Medea, Medee **6** Horace, The Cid **8** Nicomede **9** Polyeucte

Cornelius, Peter von (van)
  born: 7 Germany **10** Dusseldorf
  artwork: 12 Last Judgment **24** The Wise and Foolish Virgins **30** The Four Horsemen of the Apocalypse

Cornell, Katherine
  nickname: 21 first lady of the theater
  born: 6 Berlin **7** Germany
  roles: 8 Dear Liar **9** Saint Joan **18** Antony and Cleopatra **26** The Barretts of Wimpole Street

corner 3 fix, jam, nab **4** bend, grab, hole, nail, nook, spot, trap **5** angle, seize **6** collar, pickle, plight, scrape **7** dead end, dilemma, impasse **10** blind alley, pigeonhole **11** predicament

cornerstone 4 base **5** basis **9** principle **10** foundation **11** fundamental

cornet 4 cone, horn **7** trumpet **9** cornopean

Cornhuskers, The
  author: 12 Carl Sandburg

Cornhusker State
  nickname of: 8 Nebraska

cornice 4 drip **5** ancon, crown **7** molding, valance **8** astragal

Cornwallis, Charles
  also: 10 second Earl **13** first Marquess
  nationality: 7 British
  served in: 5 India **7** Ireland **18** American Revolution
  battle: 8 Yorktown **10** Brandywine
  captured: 10 Charleston **12** Philadelphia
  surrendered at: 8 Yorktown

Cornwell, David
  real name of: 11 John Le Carre

corny 5 banal, hokey, inane, stale, tired, trite, vapid **6** jejune, square **7** fatuous, insipid **8** bromidic, ordinary, shopworn **9** hackneyed **10** threadbare, unoriginal **11** commonplace, stereotyped **12** cliche-ridden, old-fashioned **13** platitudinous, unimaginative **15** unsophisticated

corona 4 halo, ring **5** cigar **6** circle, nimbus

coronet 5 tiara **6** diadem **7** chaplet, circlet **10** small crown

Corot, Jean-Baptiste-Camille
  born: 5 Paris **6** France
  artwork: 9 Pastorale **11** Ville d'Avray, Woman in Blue **15** Woman with a Pearl **16** The Farnese Garden, Woman in the Studio **21** Memory of Mortefontaine **23** Souvenir de Mortefontaine

corporal 3 NCO **6** bodily **8** physical **9** corporeal

corporation 7 combine, company **9** syndicate **11** association **14** conglomeration

corporeal 6 bodily, mortal **7** worldly **8** material, physical **11** perceptible **12** nonspiritual

corps 4 band, crew, team **5** force, party, squad, troop **6** outfit

corpse 4 body **5** stiff **7** cadaver, remains **8** dead body

corpselike 4 pale **5** ashen **6** pallid **9** bloodless, deathlike **10** cadaverous

corpulent 3 fat **5** dumpy, hefty, obese, plump, pudgy, stout **6** chubby, chunky, fleshy, portly, rotund **7** lumpish, well-fed **8** roly-poly **10** overweight, well-padded

corral 4 herd **5** pen in **6** shut in **7** enclose, fence in, round up

correct 3 fit, fix **4** true **5** alter, amend, chide, emend, exact, right, scold **6** adjust, berate, change, modify, proper, punish, rebuke, remedy, repair, revamp, revise, rework, seemly **7** censure, chasten, factual, fitting, improve, lecture, perfect, precise, rectify, reprove **8** accurate, admonish, becoming, chastise, flawless, regulate, suitable, unerring **9** castigate, dress down, faultless, make right, reprimand **10** acceptable, discipline, take to task **11** appropriate **12** conventional **16** haul over the coals, read the riot act to

correction 6 change **8** revision **10** adjustment, alteration, discipline, emendation, punishment **11** castigation, improvement, reformation **12** chastisement, modification **13** rectification

corrective 7 counter **8** remedial **9** improving **10** palliative, rectifying **11** reformatory, restorative, therapeutic **12** ameliorative, compensatory **13** counteractive **16** counterbalancing

correctness 8 accuracy **9** exactness, precision, propriety, rightness **10** exactitude, seemliness **11** suitability **12** becomingness, flawlessness **13** acceptability

Correggio
  real name: 14 Antonio Allegri
  born: 5 Italy **6** Emilia **9** Correggio
  artwork: 5 Danae **12** Jupiter and Io **14** Leda and the Swan **17** The Rape of Ganymede **21** The Madonna of St Francis **23** Adoration of the Shepherds **28** Mystic Marriages of St Catherine

correlate 7 compare, connect **8** parallel **10** correspond

correlation 8 parallel **10** comparison, connection **14** correspondence

correlative 4 akin **7** related **8** agreeing, parallel **9** analogous **10** comparable, connecting, equivalent **13** corresponding

correspond 3 fit **4** jibe, suit **5** agree, match, tally **6** accord, be like, concur, equate, square **7** conform **8** coincide, dovetail, parallel **9** harmonize **11** communicate, drop a line to, keep in touch

correspondence 4 mail **7** analogy, letters **8** epistles, missives, relation **9** bulletins **10** dispatches, similarity **11** association, communiques, resemblance

corresponding 4 akin **5** alike, equal **7** similar **8** agreeing, matching, tallying **9** according **10** equivalent **11** correlative **12** proportional

corridor 3 way **4** hall, road **5** aisle **6** artery **7** hallway, passage **8** approach **10** passageway

Corridors of Power
    author: **6** C P Snow

corroborate 4 back **5** prove **6** affirm, back up, uphold, verify **7** bear out, certify, confirm, endorse, support, sustain **8** validate **9** vindicate **12** authenticate, substantiate

corroborated 6 backed, proved, proven, upheld **7** factual **8** affirmed, backed up, borne out, verified **9** certified, confirmed, supported, sustained, validated **10** vindicated **11** well-founded **12** well-grounded **13** authenticated, substantiated

corroboration 5 proof **7** support **8** evidence **10** validation **11** affirmation, endorsement, vindication **12** confirmation, verification **13** certification, documentation **14** authentication, substantiation

corroborative 7 proving **9** affirming, backing up, upholding, verifying **10** bearing out, concurring, confirming, supporting, validating **11** affirmative **12** confirmative **14** substantiating

corrode 4 rust **7** oxidize **12** disintegrate

corrosive 4 acid **7** burning, caustic, erosive, mordant **8** abrasive **9** corroding **11** destructive

corrugated 6 fluted, ridged **7** creased, grooved, pleated **8** crinkled, furrowed, puckered, wrinkled **10** crenulated

corrupt 3 low **4** base, evil, mean **5** shady **6** debase, poison, seduce, sinful, wicked **7** crooked, debased, debauch, deprave, immoral, pervert, subvert **8** depraved **9** dishonest, unethical **10** fraudulent, iniquitous **11** contaminate **12** dishonorable, unprincipled, unscrupulous

corruption 4 vice **5** fraud, graft **7** bribery **8** iniquity **9** decadence, depravity, looseness, turpitude **10** debauchery, degeneracy, dishonesty, immorality, perversion, sinfulness, wickedness, wrongdoing **11** malfeasance

corsair 6 pirate, sea dog, Viking **7** brigand, sea wolf **8** marauder, picaroon, sea rover **9** buccaneer, plunderer, privateer, sea looter, sea robber **10** Blackbeard, freebooter **11** Captain Kidd **14** Long John Silver

corset 5 laces **6** girdle **8** corselet **17** foundation garment

Corsica 6 island
    located in: **16** Mediterranean Sea
    capital: **7** Ajaccio
    colony of: **4** Rome
    purchased by: **6** France
    birthplace of: **8** Napoleon
    industry: **7** tourism **10** wine making **12** sheep raising, cheese making

Corsican Brothers, The
    author: **14** Alexandre Dumas (pere)

Cortazar, Julio
    author of: **7** Rayuela **9** A Model Kit, Bestiario, Hopscotch **10** The Winners **12** Book of Manuel, End of the Game **15** All Fires the Fire **18** We Love Glenda So Much

cortege 4 line **5** court, staff, suite, train **6** column, escort, parade, string **7** caravan, company, retinue **9** cavalcade, entourage, following, motorcade **10** attendants, procession **17** funeral procession

corundum
    variety: **4** ruby **8** sapphire, star ruby **12** star sapphire

coruscate 4 beam **5** flash, gleam **7** glimmer, glitter, shimmer, sparkle

Corybant
    attendant of: **6** Cybele

Corythosaurus
    type: **8** dinosaur **10** ornithopod
    period: **10** Cretaceous
    characteristic: **10** duck-billed

Cosby, Bill
    born: **14** Philadelphia PA
    roles: **4** I Spy **8** Ghost Dad **12** The Cosby Show **19** Mother Juggs and Speed, Uptown Saturday Night
    nickname: **3** Cos

Cosby Show, The
    character: **4** Rudy, Theo **6** Denise, Sondra **7** Vanessa **13** Clair Huxtable, (Dr) Cliff (Heathcliff) Huxtable
    cast: **9** Bill Cosby, Lisa Bonet **14** Sabrina LeBeauf **15** Tempestt Bledsoe **18** Malcolm Jamal-Warner **19** Keshia Knight Pulliam, Phylicia Ayers-Rashad

Cosi fan tutte
    also: **11** So Do They All **16** Women Are Like That
    opera by: **6** Mozart
    character: **7** Despina **8** Ferrando **9** Dorabella, Guglielmo **10** Don Alfonso, Fiordiligi

cosmetic 5 blush, liner, paint, rouge **6** makeup, powder **7** mascara, surface **8** artifice, eyeliner, lipstick **9** cold cream, eye shadow **10** foundation, nail polish **11** beautifying **13** eyebrow pencil

cosmic 4 vast **7** immense **8** colossal, enormous, infinite **9** grandiose, universal **10** stupendous, widespread **12** interstellar **14** interplanetary **16** extraterrestrial

cosmopolitan 5 suave **6** urbane **7** worldly **8** traveler **11** broad- minded, worldly-wise **12** globetrotter, sophisticate **13** international, sophisticated

cosmos 5 stars **8** universe **9** macrocosm **10** starry host **13** vault of heaven
    book by: **5** Sagan

Cossack 7 czarist, Russian, trooper **8** horseman **10** cavalry man

cosset 3 pet **6** caress, coddle, fondle, pamper

cost 3 fee, run, tab **4** bill, harm, hurt, loss, pain, take, toll **5** fetch, go for, price, value, worth **6** amount, burden, charge, come to, damage, injure, injury, outlay **7** bring in, expense, penalty, sell for, set back **8** amount to, distress **9** face value, sacrifice, suffering, valuation, weigh down **11** expenditure, market price

Costa-Gavras, Constantine
    director of: **7** Missing

Costard
    character in: **16** Love's Labour's Lost
    author: **11** Shakespeare

Costa Rica
    name means: **9** rich coast
    other name: **19** Land of Eternal Spring
    capital/largest city: **7** San Jose
    others: **5** Canas, Limon, Vesta **6** Boruca, Nicoya **7** Cartago, Golfito, Heredia, Liberia, Negrita **8** Alajuela, Colorado, Guapiles **9** Turrialba **10** Puntarenas
    measure: **4** vara **5** cafiz, cahiz **6** fanega, tercia **7** cajuela, cantaro, manzana **10** caballeria
    monetary unit: **5** colon **7** centimo
    weight: **3** bag **4** caja **5** libra
    island: **4** Cano, Coco
    lake: **6** Arenal
    mountain: **4** Poas **5** Barba, Irazu **6** Blanco **7** Central, Gongora **9** Talamanca, Turrialba **10** Guanacaste
    highest point: **14** Chirripo Grande
    river: **4** Poas **5** Irazu **6** Matina **7** San Juan, Sixaola, Tenoria **8** Tarcoles
    sea: **7** Pacific **9** Caribbean
    physical feature:
        bay: **7** Salinas **8** Coronada
        cape: **5** Velas **6** Blanco **8** Matapalo **10** Santa Elena

crater: 4 Poas
gulf: 5 Dulce **6** Nicoya **8** Papagayo
hot springs spa: 12 Agua Caliente
peninsula: 3 Osa **6** Nicoya
point: 5 Judas **6** Blanca, Burica, Quepos **7** Cahuito, Galonos, Guionos, Llerena
valley: 8 Tarcoles **10** Reventazon
people: 4 Voto **6** Boruca, Bribri, Guaymi **7** Guatuso, mestizo, Spanish
explorer: 8 Columbus, Coronado
language: 7 Spanish
religion: 13 Roman Catholic
place:
shrine: 18 Our Lady of the Angels
theater: 14 Teatro Nacional
feature:
barbecue: 5 asado
dance: 6 torito **9** botijuela, zapateado **11** baile suelto **17** punto guanacasteco
drum: 8 quijonga
gourd: 4 caro
outdoor concerts: 7 retreta
plantation: 5 finca
wind instrument: 8 chirimia
food:
hearts of palm salad: 7 palmito
pudding: 10 tamal asado

Costello, Lou
real name: 21 Louis Francis Cristillo
partner: 9 Bud Abbott
born: 10 Paterson NJ
roles: 11 Who's on First

costly 4 dear **5** steep, stiff **7** harmful **8** damaging, precious **9** expensive **10** disastrous, exorbitant, high-priced **11** deleterious, extravagant **12** catastrophic

Costner, Kevin
born: 2 CA **10** Los Angeles
films: 3 JFK **9** Silverado, Wyatt Earp **10** Bull Durham, The Postman, Waterworld **12** The Bodyguard **13** Field of Dreams, A Perfect World **15** The Untouchables **16** Dances With Wolves **24** Robin Hood: Prince of Thieves

costume 4 garb **5** dress **6** attire, livery, outfit **7** apparel, clothes, raiment, uniform **8** clothing, garments

costuming 8 disguise **10** masquerade

cot 3 bed, hut, pen **4** coop, crib **5** cover, stall **7** cottage

cotelette 3 cut **4** chop **5** slice **6** cutlet

coterie 3 set **4** band, camp, clan, club, crew, gang **5** crowd, group **6** circle, clique **7** faction

cottage 3 cot, hut **5** lodge, shack **6** chalet **8** bungalow

Cotten, Joseph
born: 12 Petersburg VA
roles: 8 Gaslight **11** Citizen Kane, The Third Man **12** Duel in the Sun **14** Shadow of a Doubt **15** Journey into Fear **16** Portrait of Jennie **23** The Magnificent Ambersons

cotton 9 Gossypium
varieties: 3 bog **4** tree, wild **6** kidney, levant, upland **8** lavender **9** sea island **11** Arizona wild
fabric: 4 duck, jean, lawn, pima **5** baize, chino, denim, drill, khaki, lisle, pique, scrim, terry, twill **6** burlap, calico, canvas, chintz, dimity, madras, muslin, nankin, oxford, poplin, sateen **7** batiste, buckram, cambric, flannel, fustian, gingham, holland, jaconet, oilskin, organdy, percale, ticking **8** chambray, cretonne, sheeting **9** crinoline, sailcloth **10** broadcloth, hopsacking, printcloth, seersucker, terrycloth **11** cheesecloth, dotted Swiss

Cotton Club, The
director: 18 Francis Ford Coppola
cast: 9 Diane Lane **11** Richard Gere **12** Gregory Hines

cotton gin
invented by: 7 Whitney

Cotton State
nickname of: 7 Alabama

cottonwood 7 Populus **16** Populus deltoides
varieties: 5 black, Jack's, swamp **7** Fremont **9** Rio Grande **10** Wislizenus **11** Great Plains

Cotyleus
epithet of: 9 Asclepius
means: 13 of the hip joint

couch 3 put **4** sofa, word **5** divan, draft, frame, state, utter, voice **6** daybed, draw up, lounge, phrase, settee **7** express **8** love seat, set forth **9** davenport **12** chesterfield

couch potato
activity: 7 viewing
loves: 10 television

cougar 3 cat **4** lion, puma **7** panther **9** catamount **12** mountain lion

cough 4 hack **6** tussis **9** pertussis

cough up 3 pay **5** eject, expel **7** deliver **8** disgorge, hand over **9** surrender **11** regurgitate

Coulomb, Charles Augustin de
field: 7 physics
nationality: 6 French
invented: 14 torsion balance
discovered: 16 inverse square law

council 5 board, panel, synod **7** cabinet, chamber **8** assembly, colloquy, conclave, congress, ministry **9** committee, gathering, sanhedrin **10** conference, convention **11** convocation **12** congregation **15** representatives

counsel 4 urge, warn **6** advice, advise, charge, lawyer, prompt **7** call for, caution, opinion, suggest **8** admonish, advocate, attorney, guidance, instruct **9** barrister, counselor, recommend, solicitor **10** advisement, suggestion **12** consultation **14** recommendation

counsel house
German: 7 Rathaus

Counsellor-at-Law
director: 12 William Wyler
based on play by: 9 Elmer Rice
cast: 11 Bebe Daniels, Doris Kenyon **12** Isabel Jewell **13** John Barrymore, Melvyn Douglas, Onslow Stevens

counselor, counsellor 5 tutor **6** lawyer, mentor **7** adviser **8** advocate, attorney, minister **9** barrister, solicitor **10** instructor

counselor-at-law 6 lawyer **8** advocate, attorney **9** barrister, solicitor **10** mouthpiece

count 4 deem, hold, lord, rate, tell **5** add up, judge, noble, tally, total **6** impute, look on, matter, number, reckon, regard **7** ascribe, include, tick off **8** consider, estimate, look upon, numerate **9** attribute, enumerate, numbering, reckoning **10** numeration **11** calculation, computation, enumeration
German: 4 Graf
French: 5 comte
Italian: 5 conte
famous: 7 Dracula **8** Almaviva **11** Monte Cristo

countenance 3 aid, air **4** back, face, help, look, mien **5** build, favor **6** aspect, permit, traits, uphold, visage **7** advance, approve, condone, endorse, forward, further, profile, promote, support, work for **8** advocacy, advocate, approval, auspices, champion, contours, features, presence, sanction **9** promotion **10** appearance, assistance, expression, silhouette **11** approbation, physiognomy **12** championship, moral support **13** encouragement

counter 3 bar, man **4** defy, disk **5** piece, stand, table **6** buffet, contra, offset, oppose, resist **7** against, get even, hit back, opposed, pay back, reverse **8** contrary, fountain, opposite **9** fight back, retaliate **11** conflicting **13** contradictory

counteract 4 curb, undo **5** check, fight **6** defeat, hinder, negate, offset, oppose, resist, thwart **7** assuage, nullify, repress **8** overcome, restrain **9** alleviate, frustrate, overpower **10** annihilate, contravene, neutralize

counteraction 8 negation **10** offsetting, opposition **13** contravention, nullification **14** neutralization

counteractive 7 adverse **8** inimical **10** corrective **11** unfavorable **12** antagonistic, neutralizing

counteractor 7 negator **9** nullifier, offsetter **11** neutralizer

counteragent 3 spy **4** mole **8** antidote **9** antitoxin **10** antipoison **11** double agent

counterbalance 5 amend, check **6** cancel, offset, redeem, set off **7** correct, rectify **8** atone for, equalize,

make good, outweigh **9** make up for **10** balance out, neutralize, outbalance, recompense **12** compensation

counterfeit 4 copy, fake, sham **5** bogus, fraud, phony **6** ersatz, forged **7** feigned, forgery **8** spurious **9** facsimile, imitation, simulated **10** artificial, fraudulent, substitute **11** make-believe

Counterfeiters, The
author: **9** Andre Gide

countermand 4 void **5** annul, quash **6** cancel, recall, repeal, revoke **7** abolish, nullify, rescind, retract, reverse **8** abrogate, call back, disenact, override, overrule, set aside, withdraw, write off **12** disestablish

counterpart 4 copy, mate, twin **5** equal, match **6** double, fellow **8** parallel **9** duplicate **11** correlative **12** doppelganger **13** correspondent, spitting image

counterpoise 7 balance **9** stability **11** equilibrium

countersign 4 sign **7** certify, confirm, endorse **8** validate **9** authorize **11** corroborate **12** authenticate

countess
French: **8** comtesse
Italian: **8** contessa

countless 6 myriad, untold **7** endless **8** infinite **9** limitless, unlimited **10** numberless, unnumbered **11** innumerable, measureless **12** immeasurable, incalculable **13** multitudinous

Count of Monte Cristo, The
author: **14** Alexandre Dumas (pere)
character: **6** Albert, Haydee, Morrel **7** Fernand (Comte de Morcerf) **8** Danglars, Mercedes **9** Abbe Faria, Valentine, Villefort **10** Caderousse, Maximilian **12** Edmond Dantes
prison: **10** Chateau d'If

count on 6 expect **7** hope for **10** anticipate

countrified 5 rural **6** rustic **9** backwoods **15** unsophisticated

country 4 area, farm, land **5** realm, rural, state **6** nation, people, public, region, rustic, simple, sticks **7** boonies, farming, kingdom, natives, scenery, terrain **8** citizens, district, homeland, populace **9** backwoods, boondocks, community, landscape, territory **10** fatherland, native land, native soil, population, provincial, rural areas **11** farming area, hinterlands, inhabitants, nationality **12** commonwealth **15** unsophisticated

Country Cousin
author: **16** Louis Auchincloss

Country Girl, The
director: **12** George Seaton
based on play by: **13** Clifford Odets
cast: **10** Bing Crosby, Grace Kelly (Oscar) **11** Anthony Ross **13** William Holden
Oscar for: **7** actress (Kelly)

countryman 4 hick, rube **5** yokel **6** farmer, rustic **7** bumpkin, hayseed, peasant **8** landsman **10** clodhopper, compatriot, provincial

Country of the Pointed Firs, The
author: **15** Sarah Orne Jewett

country place 4 farm **5** manor **6** estate

countryside 6 sticks **7** boonies **9** backwater, backwoods, boondocks, rural area **10** hinterland

count up 3 add **5** tally, total **6** reckon **7** compute **9** calculate

count upon 6 expect **7** foresee **10** anticipate

coup 3 act **4** blow, deed, feat **6** stroke **12** master stroke

coup de grace 9 deathblow **11** mercy stroke **12** decisive blow **15** finishing stroke
literally: **11** blow of mercy

coup de main 14 surprise attack **17** sudden development
literally: **15** blow from the hand

coup d'etat 6 mutiny **8** uprising **9** overthrow, rebellion **10** revolution, subversion

coup de theatre 15 theatrical trick

coup d'oeil 11 quick glance
literally: **14** stroke of the eye

Couperin, Francois (Le Grand)
born: **5** Paris **6** France
composer of: **9** La Sultane, Les Fastes (de la grande et ancienne) **13** Concert Royaux **16** Apotheose de Lulli, Pieces de Clavecin **17** Lecons des Tenebres **20** Les Follies Francoises **31** Le Parnasse on l'Apotheose de Corelli

couple 3 duo, tie **4** bind, join, link, pair, yoke **5** hitch **6** fasten **7** connect, doublet, twosome **10** man and wife **11** man and woman **14** husband and wife

coupler 4 link, lock **5** clasp, hitch **6** buckle **8** fastener **9** fastening

Couples
author: **10** John Updike

coupling 5 clasp, hatch **6** hookup, yoking **7** joining, pairing **8** hitching **9** attaching, fastening **10** attachment, connecting, connection

courage 4 grit, guts, sand **5** nerve, pluck, spunk, valor **6** daring, mettle **7** bravery **8** boldness **9** derring-do, fortitude **11** intrepidity **12** fearlessness **13** dauntlessness **16** stout-heartedness

courageous 4 bold **5** brave, manly **6** dogged, heroic **7** dashing, doughty, gallant, valiant **8** fearless, intrepid, resolute, stalwart, unafraid, valorous **9** dauntless **10** chivalrous **11** indomitable **12** bold-spirited **13** stronghearted

Courbet, Jean Desire Gustave
born: **6** France, Ornans

artwork: **16** The Artist's Studio, The Stonebreakers **17** The Burial at Ornans **19** The Peasants of Flagey **25** Self-Portrait with a Black Dog

courier 4 mule **5** envoy **6** herald, legate, runner **7** Gabriel, mailman, Mercury, postman **8** emissary **9** go-between, harbinger, messenger, postrider **11** herald angel, internuncio

course 3 run, way **4** flow, gush, mode, path, pour, race, road **5** march, orbit, round, route, surge, track **6** action, circle, method, policy, stream **7** channel, circuit, classes, conduct, lessons, passage, subject **8** behavior, lectures, sequence **9** direction, procedure, unfolding **10** curriculum, racecourse, trajectory **11** development, progression

court 3 bar, woo **4** hall, quad, seek, suit, yard **5** bench, manor, plaza, staff, train **6** atrium, castle, homage, induce, invite, palace, pursue, wooing **7** address, attract, chateau, cortege, council, flatter, hearing, meeting, provoke, retinue, session **8** advisers, assembly, audience, blandish, fawn upon, pander to, respects, run after **9** entourage, following **10** attendants, quadrangle **13** solicitations

Courtenay, Tom
born: **4** Hull **7** England
roles: **9** Billy Liar **10** The Dresser **36** The Loneliness of the Long Distance Runner

courteous 4 kind, mild **5** civil **6** polite **7** refined, tactful **8** gracious, mannerly, well-bred **10** diplomatic, respectful, soft-spoken **11** considerate, well-behaved **12** well-mannered

courtesy 5 favor **7** manners, regards, respect **8** civility, kindness, respects **9** deference, gallantry, gentility **10** indulgence, politeness, refinement **11** cultivation **12** graciousness **13** consideration

courtier 4 beau **7** gallant **8** cavalier **9** attendant **18** gentleman-in-waiting

Courtier, The
author: **21** Baldassare Castiglione

Court Jester
director: **11** Melvin Frank **12** Norman Panama
cast: **9** Danny Kaye **11** Glynis Johns **13** Basil Rathbone **14** Angela Lansbury

courtly 5 suave **6** polite **7** elegant, gallant, genteel, refined, stately **8** debonair, decorous, highbred, ladylike, mannerly, polished **9** civilized, courteous, dignified **10** chivalrous **11** blue-blooded, gentlemanly **12** aristocratic **14** silk-stockinged

courtship 4 suit **6** wooing **14** keeping company

Courtship of Eddie's Father, The
character: **4** Tina **10** Tom Corbett **12** Eddie Corbett, Norman Tinker **13**

Mrs Livingston
cast: 9 Bill Bixby **11** Brandon Cruz, James Komack **12** Miyoshi Umeki **15** Kristina Holland

Courtship of Miles Standish, The
author: 24 Henry Wadsworth Longfellow
character: 9 John Alden, Priscilla

courtyard 4 area, quad **6** atrium **9** curtilage, enclosure **10** quadrangle

cousin 7 kinsman **8** relation, relative **9** kinswoman

Cousin Bette
author: 14 Honore de Balzac
character: 6 Crevel **7** Adeline **10** Baron Hulot **11** Mme Marneffe **13** Hortense Hulot, Marechal Hulot **14** Lisbeth Fischer **23** Count Wenceslas Steinbock

Cousin Pons
author: 14 Honore de Balzac

Cousy, Bob
nickname: 12 Mr Basketball
sport: 10 basketball
position: 5 guard
team: 13 Boston Celtics

couturier, couturiere 8 designer **9** midinette **10** dressmaker, seamstress

cove 3 bay **5** inlet **6** lagoon **7** estuary

covenant 3 vow **4** bond, oath, pact **6** pledge, treaty **7** bargain, promise **8** contract **9** agreement **15** solemn agreement
Hebrew: 4 Brit **5** Berit, Brith **6** Berith

Covenant, The
author: 13 James Michener

cover 3 cap, lid, top **4** case, hide, hood, mask, veil, wrap **5** cloak, cross, guard, lay on, put on, quilt **6** asylum, clothe, defend, embody, enwrap, jacket, refuge, report, screen, sheath, shield, shroud, take in, tell of **7** binding, blanket, conceal, contain, defense, embrace, envelop, include, involve, obscure, overlay, protect, put over, secrete, sheathe, shelter, wrapper, write up **8** comprise, deal with, describe, disguise, envelope, pass over, traverse **9** chronicle, comforter, eiderdown, encompass, sanctuary **10** camouflage, comprehend, encasement, protection **11** concealment, hiding place

coverage 7 payment **8** analysis **9** indemnity, reporting **10** protection, publishing **11** description **12** broadcasting **13** reimbursement

covered 4 clad **6** hidden **7** aimed at, cloaked, guarded, insured **8** included, overlaid, screened **9** blanketed, concealed, protected, sheltered, traversed **10** overspread

covering 6 casing, sheath **7** wrapper **8** envelope, wrapping **11** descriptive, explanatory **12** introductory

coverlet 5 quilt, throw **6** afghan,

spread **7** blanket **9** bedspread, comforter

Coverly, Sir Roger de
character in: 12 The Spectator
authors: 6 Steele **7** Addison

covert 6 hidden, secret, veiled **7** sub rosa, unknown **9** concealed, disguised **11** clandestine **13** surreptitious

cover up 4 hide, mask, veil **6** hush up **7** conceal **8** disguise, keep back, suppress, withhold **9** gloss over, whitewash

cover-up 4 mask **5** blind **6** screen **8** disguise **9** whitewash **11** concealment

covet 4 want **5** crave, fancy **6** desire **7** long for

covetous 6 greedy **7** craving, envious, jealous, lustful, selfish **8** desirous, grasping, yearning **9** mercenary, rapacious **10** avaricious

covetousness 4 envy **5** greed **7** avarice **8** jealousy, rapacity **10** greediness **12** graspingness **13** mercenariness

covey 4 bevy **5** flock, group **6** family

cow 4 beef **5** abash, Bossy, bully, deter, Elsie, scare **6** bovine, cattle, dismay **7** terrify **8** browbeat, bulldoze, frighten, threaten **9** terrorize **10** discourage, dishearten, intimidate, make cringe
young: 4 calf **6** heifer

coward 3 cad **5** sissy **6** craven **7** caitiff, chicken, dastard, milksop **8** poltroon **11** Milquetoast, mollycoddle, yellow-belly

Coward, Sir Noel
author of: 8 Hay Fever **9** Cavalcade **10** Sigh No More **12** Blithe Spirit, Private Lives **14** In Which We Serve, Nude with Violin **15** Design for Living

cowardliness 8 timidity **10** yellowness **12** irresolution **13** pusillanimity, spinelessness **18** chicken-heartedness

cowardly 5 shaky, timid **6** afraid, craven, yellow **7** anxious, chicken, fearful, gutless, nervous **8** timorous **9** dastardly, tremulous **10** frightened **11** lily-livered **12** apprehensive, fainthearted, uncourageous **13** pusillanimous, yellow-bellied **14** chickenhearted

Cowardly Lion
character in: 13 The Wizard of Oz
author: 4 Baum
played by: 8 Bert Lahr

cowboy 6 drover, gaucho **7** vaquero **8** buckaroo **10** roughrider **12** broncobuster, cattle-herder

cowed 5 fazed **7** abashed, crushed, subdued **8** dismayed **11** intimidated **12** disconcerted **14** under one's thumb

cower 5 crawl, quail, toady **6** cringe, flinch, grovel, recoil, shrink **7** tremble, truckle **8** bootlick, draw back

cowl 4 cope, hood **5** cloak

Cowley, Malcolm
author of: 12 Exile's Return **16** A Second Flowering **27** And I Worked at the Writer's Trade **28** The Dream of the Golden Mountains

coworker 7 partner **8** teammate **9** associate, colleague **10** accomplice **11** confederate **12** collaborator

Cowper, William
author of: 7 The Task **11** The Cast-Away

Cowperwood, Frank
character in: 8 The Titan **12** The Financier
author: 7 Dreiser

coxcomb 3 fop **4** beau **5** dandy **8** popinjay

coy 3 shy **5** timid **6** demure, modest **7** bashful, prudish **8** blushing, sheepish, skittish, timorous **9** diffident, kittenish, shrinking **10** coquettish, overmodest

Coyote State
nickname of: 11 South Dakota

cozen 3 con, gyp **4** bilk, coax, dupe, gull, rook **5** cheat, trick **6** fleece **7** deceive, defraud, swindle, wheedle **9** bamboozle, victimize

cozener 4 fake **5** cheat, fraud, quack **6** con man **8** deceiver, swindler **9** charlatan, trickster **10** mountebank **13** confidence man

coziness 6 warmth **7** comfort **8** intimacy, snugness **11** contentment

cozy 4 easy, snug **5** comfy, homey **7** restful **8** homelike, relaxing **9** gemutlich, simpatico **11** comfortable **16** snug as a bug in a rug
French: 6 intime

Cozzens, James Gould
author of: 12 Guard of Honor **15** By Love Possessed

CPA 7 auditor **10** accountant, bookkeeper **25** certified public accountant

crab 4 carp **5** crank, gripe, grump **6** grouch, grouse **8** complain, sourball **9** shellfish **10** crustacean, curmudgeon
constellation of: 6 Cancer

Crabbe, Buster
real name: 20 Clarence Linden Crabbe
nickname: 16 King of the Serials
born: 9 Oakland CA
roles: 6 Tarzan **10** Buck Rogers **11** Flash Gordon **15** King of the Jungle

crabbed 4 mean, sour **6** cranky, morose **7** grouchy, peevish, pinched **8** churlish, spiteful **9** irascible, irritable, rancorous

crabby 5 cross, testy **6** cranky, touchy **7** grouchy, peevish **8** petulant, snappish **9** irritable **10** ill-humored, out of sorts **11** ill-tempered **12** cantankerous

crack 3 gag, jab, pop **4** chip, clap, gash, gibe, jest, joke, quip, rent, rift,

slit, snap 5 break, burst, cleft, split, taunt **6** cleave, insult, report **7** crackle, crevice, fissure, give way, rupture, thunder **8** fracture, splinter **9** break down, wisecrack, witticism **10** go to pieces

cracked 3 mad **4** daft, nuts **5** crazy, nutty **6** crazed, insane **8** demented, deranged, unhinged **10** unbalanced **12** mad as a hatter **13** off one's rocker, out of one's head **14** off one's trolley **15** mad as a March hare

cracker 5 snack, wafer **7** biscuit, redneck **10** party favor **11** backsettler **12** backwoodsman

crackerjack 2 A-1 **3** ace **4** a-one, fine **5** super **6** superb, tip-top **8** splendid, terrific **9** excellent, fantastic, first-rate, wonderful **10** first-class

Cracker State
   nickname of: 7 Georgia

crackle 4 snap **5** craze, crink **9** crepitate

crackpot 3 nut, odd **4** fool, kook **5** balmy, crank, flake, freak, kinky, kooky, loony, nutty, wacko **6** freaky, insane, looney, madman, maniac, weirdo **7** dingbat, foolish, lunatic, oddball **9** character, eccentric, screwball **11** impractical

cracksman 4 yegg **7** burglar **10** cat burglar **14** second- story man

crackup 5 crash, smash, split, wreck **6** mishap, pileup **7** breakup, debacle, smashup **8** accident, calamity, collapse, disaster **9** breakdown, collision, splitting **10** exhaustion, shellshock **11** catastrophe, prostration **14** disintegration

cradle 3 hug **4** crib, font, rock **6** cuddle, enfold, origin, source, spring **7** nursery, snuggle **8** bassinet, fountain **10** birthplace, wellspring **12** fountainhead

craft 3 art **4** boat, ruse, ship, wile **5** guile, knack, plane, skill, trade **6** deceit, vessel **7** ability, calling, cunning, know-how, mastery, perfidy, pursuit **8** airplane, artifice, business, commerce, deftness, fineness, industry, intrigue, trickery, vocation **9** adeptness, chicanery, deception, duplicity, expertise, technique **10** adroitness, artfulness, competency, craftiness, employment, expertness, handicraft, occupation **11** proficiency

craftiness 4 ruse, wile **5** guile **7** cunning, slyness **8** artifice, foxiness, scheming, trickery, wiliness **9** chicanery **10** artfulness **11** machination

craftsman 4 hand **5** smith **6** worker, wright **7** artisan **8** mechanic

crafty 3 sly **4** foxy, wily **5** canny, sharp **6** artful, astute, shifty, shrewd, tricky **7** cunning, devious **8** guileful, plotting, scheming **9** deceitful, deceptive, designing, dishonest, underhand,

unethical 10 intriguing, perfidious, suspicious **11** calculating

crag 3 tor **4** rock **5** bluff, cliff **9** precipice

craggy 5 rocky, rough, sheer, steep, stony **6** abrupt, jagged, ragged, rugged, snaggy **7** scraggy **8** bouldery **9** rockbound **10** rock-ribbed **11** precipitous

Crain, Jeanne
   born: 9 Barstow CA
   roles: 5 Pinky **6** Margie **9** State Fair **17** Cheaper by the Dozen **19** A Letter to Three Wives

cram 3 jam **4** fill, pack **5** crowd, force, grind, press, stuff **7** congest, squeeze **8** compress **9** overcrowd, study hard

Cram, Ralph
   architect of: 17 US Military Academy (West Point) **29** Cathedral of Saint John the Divine (NYC)
   style: 13 Gothic Revival

crammed 4 full **6** filled, packed **7** studied, stuffed **9** jam- packed **11** overflowing, well-stocked

cramp 4 pang **5** block, check, crick, limit, spasm **6** hamper, hinder, stitch, stymie, thwart **7** prevent, seizure **8** handicap, obstruct, restrain, restrict **9** frustrate **12** charley horse

cramped 5 close, tight **6** narrow **7** compact, pinched **8** confined **10** compressed, restrained, restricted

Cranach, Lucas (Lukas) (the Elder)
   born: 7 Kronach, Germany
   artwork: 6 Luther **10** Adam and Eve **11** Crucifixion **14** Apollo and Diana **15** Rest on the Flight **18** The Judgment of Paris **22** Duke and Duchess of Saxony

Cranaus
   king of: 6 Athens, Attica
   wife: 6 Pedias
   daughter: 6 Atthis, Cranae
   renamed Athens: 6 Attica

cranberry 9 Vaccinium **19** Vaccinium vitis-idaea **20** Vaccinium macrocarpon
   varieties: 3 bog **4** rock, tree **5** large, small **8** American, European, highbush, mountain **10** Australian

crane 4 bird, boom **5** davit, heron **7** derrick **10** wading bird
   group of: 5 sedge, siege
   constellation of: 4 Grus

Crane, Bob
   born: 11 Waterbury CT
   roles: 12 Colonel Hogan, Hogan's Heroes

Crane, Hart
   author of: 9 The Bridge **14** White Buildings

Crane, Ichabod
   character in: 23 The Legend of Sleepy Hollow
   author: 6 Irving

Crane, Roy

creator/artist of: 9 Buz Sawyer, Wash Tubbs **11** Captain Easy

Crane, Stephen
   author of: 11 The Open Boat **20** The Red Badge of Courage **23** Maggie: A Girl of the Streets **24** The Bride Comes to Yellow Sky

Cranford
   author: 10 Mrs Gaskell

cranium 4 head **5** skull **6** noggin **8** brain box, brainpan **9** brain case

crank 4 turn, whim **5** brace, winch **6** grouch, handle **7** fanatic **8** crotchet **9** eccentric

cranky 5 cross, testy **6** crabby, touchy **7** bearish, grouchy, peevish, waspish **8** captious, petulant **9** crotchety, irascible, splenetic **10** ill-humored, out of sorts **11** ill-tempered **12** cantankerous

cranny 3 gap **4** nook, slit **5** break, chink, cleft, crack, notch, split **7** crevice, fissure **8** cleavage

crash 3 din **4** bang, boom, bump, dash, ruin **5** crack, slump, smash, wreck **6** hurtle, invade, pileup, plunge, racket, slip in, topple, tumble **7** bumping, clangor, clatter, collide, crackup, decline, failure, hitting, intrude, setback, shatter, smashup, sneak in **8** accident, smashing, toppling, tumbling **9** collision, recession **10** bankruptcy, depression, shattering

crass 5 crude, cruel, gross **6** coarse, oafish, vulgar **7** boorish **8** uncaring **9** inelegant, unfeeling, unrefined **10** unpolished **11** hardhearted, insensitive **13** unsympathetic

crassness 9 crudeness, grossness, vulgarity **10** coarseness, inelegance, oafishness **11** boorishness **13** insensitivity

Cratchit, Bob
   character in: 15 A Christmas Carol
   author: 7 Dickens
   son: 7 Tiny Tim

crate 3 box, car **4** auto, case, pack **5** plane **6** jalopy, pallet **8** airplane **9** container

crater 3 pit **4** hole **6** cavity **10** depression

cravat 3 tie **5** ascot, scarf, stock **7** necktie **11** neckerchief

crave 4 need, want **5** covet **6** desire **7** hope for, long for, pine for, require, sigh for, wish for **8** yearn for **9** hunger for, lust after, thirst for **11** hanker after, have a yen for **13** have a fancy for

craven 3 low **4** base **5** timid **6** scared, yellow **7** fearful, lowdown **8** cowardly, timorous **9** dastardly **10** frightened **11** lily-livered **12** mean-spirited **13** pusillanimous **14** chicken-hearted

craving 3 yen **4** need **6** desire, hunger, thirst **7** longing **9** hankering

Crawford, Broderick

real name: 24 William Broderick Crawford
wife: 11 Jan Sterling
born: 14 Philadelphia PA
roles: 6 The Mob **10** The Interns **12** Of Mice and Men **13** Born Yesterday, Highway Patrol **14** All the King's Men (Oscar)

Crawford, Henry
    character in: 13 Mansfield Park
    author: 6 Austen

Crawford, Joan
    real name: 17 Lucille Fay Le Sueur
    husband: 12 Franchot Tone **18** Douglas Fairbanks Jr
    daughter: 6 Cheryl **9** Christina
    born: 12 San Antonio TX
    biography: 13 Mommie Dearest
    roles: 8 The Women **10** Grand Hotel **13** Mildred Pierce (Oscar) **26** What Ever Happened to Baby Jane

crawl 4 drag, inch, poke, worm **5** creep, mosey **6** squirm, wiggle, writhe **7** slither, wriggle

Crawley, Rawdon
    character in: 10 Vanity Fair
    author: 9 Thackeray

crayon 5 chalk, draft **6** pastel, pencil, sketch **7** drawing **8** charcoal

craze 3 fad **4** rage **5** furor, mania **6** dement **7** derange, passion, unhinge **11** infatuation

crazed 3 mad **6** insane **7** cracked, lunatic **8** demented, deranged

crazy 3 mad, odd **4** avid, daft, gaga, keen, nuts, wild **5** nutty, rabid, silly, weird **6** absurd, far-out, insane, stupid, unwise **7** berserk, bizarre, cracked, excited, foolish, frantic, idiotic, strange, touched, unusual, zealous **8** demented, deranged, maniacal, peculiar, uncommon, unhinged **9** fanatical, foolhardy, imprudent, laughable, senseless **10** hysterical, infatuated, outrageous, passionate, ridiculous, unbalanced **11** smitten with **12** enthusiastic, mad as a hatter **13** out of one's head **15** mad as a March hare

creak 4 rasp **5** grate, grind **6** scrape, screak, squeak **7** screech

Creakle
    character in: 16 David Copperfield
    author: 7 Dickens

cream 3 top **4** beat, best, drub **5** elite **6** choice, flower **7** the pick, trounce **8** greatest, off-white **14** creme de la creme

Cream, Arnold Raymond
    real name of: 10 Joe Walcott

cream of the cream
    French: 14 creme de la creme

Cream of the Jest, The
    author: 17 James Branch Cabell

creamy 5 thick, foamy **6** smooth, yellow **8** emulsive

crease 4 fold **5** crimp, pleat, ridge **6** furrow, pucker, ruffle, rumple **7** crimple, crinkle, wrinkle **9** corrugate **11** corrugation

create 4 form, make, mold **5** cause, erect, found, set up **6** design, devise, invent **7** appoint, concoct, develop, fashion **8** conceive, contrive, organize **9** construct, establish, fabricate, formulate, institute, originate

creation 5 world **6** making, nature **8** building, devising, erection, founding **9** all things, formation, handiwork, invention **10** brainchild, conception, concoction, fashioning, production **11** development, fabrication, institution, origination **12** construction **13** establishment

Creation
    author: 9 Gore Vidal

creative 8 fanciful, original **9** ingenious, inventive **11** imaginative, resourceful

creator 5 maker **6** author, father, framer **7** founder **8** begetter, designer, inventor, producer **9** architect, generator, initiator **10** originator

creature 3 man **4** bird, fish **5** beast, human **6** animal, insect, mammal, mortal, person **7** critter, reptile **9** earthling, quadruped **10** individual, vertebrate **12** invertebrate

credence 5 faith, trust **6** belief, credit **8** reliance **9** certainty, certitude **10** confi- dence **11** reliability **13** believability **14** acceptableness, dependableness **15** trustworthiness

credentials 6 permit **7** diploma, license, voucher **9** reference **11** certificate, testimonial **13** authorization

credenza 5 shelf, table **6** buffet **8** bookcase **9** sideboard

credible 6 likely **7** tenable **8** possible, probable, reliable **9** plausible, thinkable **10** believable, dependable, imaginable, reasonable **11** conceivable, trustworthy

credit 3 buy **4** time **5** glory, honor, trust **6** accept, assign, esteem, rely on **7** acclaim, ascribe, believe, fall for, swallow **9** allowance, attribute, recognize **10** prepayment **11** acknowledge, recognition **12** commendation **14** acknowledgment

creditable 6 worthy **8** laudable **9** admirable, estimable, reputable **11** commendable, meritorious, respectable **12** praiseworthy

credo 4 code, rule **5** maxim, motto, tenet **8** doctrine **10** philosophy

credulous 5 naive **8** gullible, trusting **9** believing **12** overtrustful, unsuspecting, unsuspicious **13** unquestioning **15** unsophisticated

Cree
    language family: 9 Algonkian **10** Al-
gonquian
    tribe: 10 Plains Cree **13** Woodlands Cree
    location: 6 Canada **8** Manitoba
    related to: 8 Chippewa

creed 5 dogma **6** belief, canons, gospel **8** doctrine

creek 3 run **4** rill **5** brook **6** branch, spring, stream **7** freshet, rivulet **10** millstream, small river

Creek
    language family: 10 Muskhogean
    location: 7 Alabama, Florida, Georgia **11** Mississippi
    leader: 8 Red Eagle **15** William McIntosh **20** Alexander McGillivray

Creek Mary's Blood
    author: 8 Dee Brown

creep 4 inch, worm **5** crawl, sneak, steal **6** dawdle, squirm, writhe **7** slither, wriggle

creeper 3 ivy **4** bird, iron, vine, worm **5** snake **7** climber, crawler, grapnel, trailer

creepy 4 eery **5** eerie, scary **6** crawly, spooky, uneasy **12** apprehensive

cremate 4 burn, char, fire, sear **5** roast **6** ignite, kindle, scorch **8** enkindle **10** incinerate **11** conflagrate **17** consume with flames

creme de banane
    type: 7 liqueur
    flavor: 6 banana
    color: 6 yellow

creme de cacao
    type: 6 brandy **7** liqueur
    origin: 6 France
    flavor: 9 chocolate
    color: 5 brown, white
    drink: 11 Fifth Avenue
    with rum: 6 Panama
    with tequila: 8 Toreador
    with vodka: 9 Ninotchka **11** Russian Bear **12** Velvet Hammer, White Russian

creme de cassis
    type: 7 liqueur
    origin: 6 France **8** Burgundy
    flavor: 12 black currant
    with gin: 8 Parisian

creme de fraise
    type: 7 liqueur
    flavor: 10 strawberry

creme de framboise
    type: 7 liqueur
    flavor: 9 raspberry

creme de la creme 3 top **4** best **5** cream, elite **6** choice, flower **8** choicest, very best **12** choicest part **15** cream of the cream

creme de menthe
    type: 7 liqueur
    flavor: 4 mint
    color: 5 green, white
    with brandy: 7 Stinger

with cream: 11 Grasshopper
with gin: 6 Caruso, Virgin

creme de noyau
  type: 7 liqueur
  flavor: 6 almond

creme de violette
  type: 7 liqueur
  flavor: 7 violets
  color: 8 lavender

creme Yvette
  type: 7 liqueur
  origin: 12 United States
  flavor: 7 violets
  with gin: 9 Union Jack

Crenna, Richard
  born: 12 Los Angeles CA
  roles: 9 Death Ship **13** Our Miss
  Brooks, The Real McCoys

Creole 6 patois **7** criollo, dialect, Haitian **10** West Indian

Creole State
  nickname of: 9 Louisiana

Creon
  king of: 6 Thebes **7** Corinth
  father: 9 Lycaethus, Menoeceus
  sister: 7 Jocasta
  daughter: 6 Creusa, Glauce
  nephew: 7 Oedipus **8** Eteocles **9** Polynices
  niece: 6 Ismene **8** Antigone
  defeated: 18 Seven against Thebes

crescendo
  music: 22 gradually getting louder
    abbreviation: 5 cresc

crescent 3 arc, bow **4** arch **5** curve **8** half-moon

crescit eundo 15 it grows as it goes
  motto of: 9 New Mexico

Cressida
  also: 8 Criseyde **9** Crisseyde
  based on characters of: 7 Bryseis **8** Chryseis
  setting: 9 Trojan War
  loved: 7 Troilus
  deserted Troilus for: 8 Diomedes

crest 3 tip, top **4** apex, arms, comb, peak, tuft **5** crown, plume **6** emblem, height, summit **7** topknot **8** pinnacle **10** coat of arms, escutcheon

crestfallen 8 dejected, downcast **9** depressed, woebegone **10** despondent, dispirited **11** discouraged, downhearted, low-spirited **12** disappointed, disheartened

Cretaceous period
  dinosaur from: 9 Euhelopus, Iguanodon **10** Allosaurus, Antrodemus **11** Anatosaurus, Ankylsaurus, Deinonychus, Gorgosaurus, Triceratops **12** Lambeosaurus, Ornithomimus **13** Albertosaurus, Corythosaurus, Hypselosaurus, Hypsilophodon, Palaeoscincus, Protoceratops, Struthiomimus, Styracosaurus, Tyrannosaurus **14** Psittacosaurus, Thescelosaurus **15** Parasaurolophus, Procheneosaurus

Cretan bull
  also: 15 Marathonian bull
  form: 4 bull
  son: 8 Minotaur
  captured on: 5 Crete
  captured by: 8 Hercules
  roamed: 8 Marathon
  recaptured by: 7 Theseus

Cretan Mythology
  goddess of fishermen/hunters/ sailors: 11 Britomartis
    corresponds to Greek: 7 Artemis
  goddess of the sea: 8 Dictynna
  maze: 9 labyrinth
  monster: 8 Minotaur

Crete
  other name: 5 Kriti **6** Candia
  capital/largest city: 5 Canea **8** Iraklion
  others: 3 Hag **4** Lato **5** Khora, Sitia, Zakro **6** Anoyia, Candia, Khania, Lisamo, Mallia, Meleme, Retimo **7** Malerni **8** Kastelli, Nikolaos, Sphakion **9** Heraclion, Heraklion, Rethymnon, Tympakion **11** Palaiophora
  government: division of: 6 Greece
  monetary unit: 7 drachma
  mountain: 3 Ida **5** Dikte, Phino **6** Juktas **7** Lasithi, Madaras **8** Leuka Ori, Theodore, Thriphte **9** Psiloriti
  highest point: 3 Ida
  sea: 5 Crete **6** Aegean **13** Mediterranean
  physical feature:
    bay: 4 Suda **5** Kanca **6** Kisamo, Mesara
    cape: 4 Buza **5** Liano **6** Salome, Sidero, Spatha **7** Stavros **8** Lithinon, Sidheros
    gulf: 6 Khania **9** Merabello
  people: 7 Candiot, Cretans, Minoans **9** Caphtorim, Sphakiots **11** Philistines
    artist: 7 El Greco
    author: 11 Kazantzakis
    conqueror: 8 Metellus
    king: 5 Minos
  language: 5 Greek **6** Minoan **7** Linear A, Linear B
  religion: 14 Greek Orthodoxy
  place:
    ruins: 15 Palace at Knossos

Creusa
  also: 6 Glauce
  father: 5 Creon, Priam **8** Cychreus **10** Erechtheus
  mother: 6 Hecuba
  husband: 6 Aeneas **7** Telamon
  son: 3 Ion **8** Ascanius
  bride of: 5 Jason
  killed by: 5 magic, Medea

crevasse 3 gap **4** rift **5** abyss, break, chasm, cleft, gorge, gulch, gully, split **6** breach, divide **7** fissure

crevice 4 rent, rift, slit **5** chasm, cleft, crack, split **6** breach **7** fissure **8** crevasse, fracture

crew 3 men, mob **4** band, body, herd, mass, pack, team **5** corps, force, group, hands, horde, party, squad, troop **6** seamen, throng **7** company, haircut, sailors **8** mariners **9** multitude, seafarers **10** assemblage, complement

crib 3 bed, bin, cot, hut, key **4** pony, trot **5** cheat, shack, stall, steal **6** creche, manger **7** purloin **8** bassinet **10** plagiarism

cribbage
  scorer: 3 peg
  score kept on: 5 board
  points/game: 8 sixty-one
  third hand: 4 crib
  jack: 7 his nobs

Crich, Gerald
  character in: 11 Women in Love
  author: 8 Lawrence

Crichton, Michael
  author of: 5 Congo **6** Sphere **8** Airframe **9** Rising Sun **10** Disclosure **12** Jurassic Park **14** The Terminal Man **15** Eaters of the Dead **18** The Andromeda Strain **20** The Great Train Robbery

cricket
  players/team: 6 eleven
  equipment: 3 bat **4** bail, ball **5** stump **6** wicket
  position: 5 gully, mid on, slops **6** bowler, long on, mid off **7** batsman, fine leg, long off **8** third man **9** mid wicket, square leg **10** cover point, extra cover, silly mid on **11** silly mid off **12** wicket keeper **13** deep mid wicket **16** backward short leg
  lines: 7 creases
  period of play: 4 over **7** innings
  championship game: 9 test match
  England/Australia match: 8 the Ashes

cricket
  variety: 4 bush, cave, fair, sand, tree **5** camel, field, house **6** ground **9** Jerusalem, pygmy mole

Cries and Whispers
  director: 12 Ingmar Bergman
  cast: 10 Liv Ullmann **12** Ingrid Thulin **16** Harriet Andersson

crime 3 sin **4** tort **5** wrong **6** felony **7** misdeed, offense, outrage **8** foul play, iniquity, villainy **10** misconduct, wrongdoing **11** abomination, lawbreaking, malfeasance, misdemeanor **13** transgression

Crime and Punishment
  author: 16 Fyodor Dostoevsky
  character: 5 Sonya **6** Dounia **7** Porfiry **9** Razumihin **11** Raskolnikov

criminal 4 hood **5** crook, felon, wrong **6** guilty, outlaw **7** crooked, culprit, illegal, illicit, lawless **8** culpable, offender, unlawful, wasteful **9** felonious, senseless, wrongdoer **10** abominable, delinquent, indictable, lawbreaker, malefactor, outrageous, villainous **11** blameworthy, disgraceful, lawbreaking **12** transgressor

crimp 4 curl, fold, kink, wave **5** clamp, flute, frill, frizz **7** crinkle, frizzle, wrinkle **8** obstacle

crimple 4 curl **6** pucker **7** crinkle, crumple, wrinkle **9** corrugate

crimson 3 red **4** ruby **5** blush, flush **6** redden **7** carmine, scarlet

cringe 4 duck **5** cower, dodge, quail, toady **6** blench, flinch, grovel, recoil, shrink **7** truckle

cringing 6 abject **7** fawning, ignoble, servile, wincing **8** cowering, toadying **9** flinching, groveling, shrinking, sniveling

crinkle 5 crush **6** rumple, rustle **7** crumple, wrinkle

crinkly 4 wavy **5** curly, kinky **6** crimpy, frizzy **7** cockled, crimped, crimply, puckery, ruffled, rumpled, twisted, wrinkly **8** crimpled, frizzled, puckered, wrinkled **9** shriveled

crinoline 4 hoop **5** skirt **9** hoopskirt, petticoat **10** underskirt

cripple 4 gimp, halt, harm, maim, stop **6** damage, impair **7** disable **8** make lame, paralyze **9** hamstring **10** debilitate, inactivate **12** incapacitate

crisis 6 climax **9** emergency

crisp 5 brisk, fresh, nippy, sharp, terse, witty **6** candid, chilly, crispy, lively, snappy **7** bracing, brittle, crunchy, pointed **8** incisive **9** energetic, sparkling, vivacious **10** potato chip, refreshing **12** invigorating

crisscross 4 awry **5** cross **8** confused, traverse

Crisseyde see **8** Cressida

Cristillo, Louis Francis
    real name of: 11 Lou Costello

criterion 3 law **4** norm, rule **5** gauge, model **7** example, measure **8** standard **9** guidepost, precedent, principle, yardstick **10** touchstone

critic 5 judge, mavin, scold **6** carper, censor, expert, rapper **7** analyst, arbiter, knocker, reviler **8** attacker, reviewer, vilifier, virtuoso **9** authority, backbiter, detractor, evaluator **10** antagonist, criticizer **11** cognoscente, commentator, connoisseur, faultfinder

critical 5 fussy, grave, hairy, picky, risky, vital **6** urgent **7** carping, crucial, finicky, judging, nagging, serious **8** caviling, decisive, perilous, pressing **9** dangerous, harrowing, hazardous, judicious, momentous, sensitive **10** analytical, censorious, derogatory, diagnostic, nitpicking, precarious **11** disparaging **12** disapproving, faultfinding

critical situation 3 jam **4** mess **6** crisis, pickle **7** straits, trouble **8** hot water **9** deep water **10** difficulty **11** predicament

critical stage 5 H-hour **6** climax, crisis **9** emergency

critical success
    French: 13 succes d'estime

criticism 4 fire, flak, slam **5** blame, knock **6** review **7** censure, comment **8** analysis, critique, judgment **9** aspersion, stricture **10** commentary, evaluation **12** faultfinding

criticize 4 carp, fuss, pick **5** cavil, nag at **7** censure, nitpick, reprove **8** denounce, reproach **9** disparage

critique 6 review **8** analysis

Crna Gora see **10** Montenegro

croak 3 caw, die **4** kill, moan, roup **7** grumble, kick off **8** complain, harsh cry **13** kick the bucket

Croatia
    capital/largest city: 5 Zagreb
    others: 4 Knin **5** Split, Zadar **6** Osijek, Rijeka (Fiume) **7** Vukovar, Sibenik **8** Karlovac, Varazdin, Vinkovci **9** Dubrovnik **10** Kostajnica
    head of state: 9 president
    government: 9 democracy
    monetary unit: 5 dinar
    mountain: 10 Julian Alps **11** Styrian Alps
    sea: 8 Adriatic
    people: 5 Serbs **6** Croats **7** Muslims **9** Yugoslavs
    language: 8 Croatian **10** Serbo Croat
    religion: 17 Catholic Christian, Orthodox Christian

Crocetti, Dino Paul
    real name of: 10 Dean Martin

crock 3 jar, pot **4** olla **9** container

crockery 5 china **6** dishes, plates **7** pottery **8** clayware **9** chinaware, tableware **11** ceramic ware, earthenware **14** cups and saucers

Crock of Gold
    author: 13 James Stephens

crocodile 4 croc **6** cayman, gavial, lizard **7** reptile, asurian

crocus
    varieties: 4 fall, wild **5** dutch **6** autumn, scotch **7** Chilean, saffron **8** tropical **9** celandine **12** iris-flowered

Crome Yellow
    author: 12 Aldous Huxley

Crommyonian sow
    also: 5 Phaea
    killed by: 7 Theseus

Cromwell, Oliver
    also: 13 Lord Protector
    served in: 15 English Civil War
    fought against: 8 Charles I **9** Cavaliers
    fought for: 10 Parliament, Roundheads
    regiment: 9 Ironsides
    battle: 6 Naseby, Oxford **7** Preston **11** Marston Moor

crone 3 hag **5** witch **6** beldam **7** beldame, old wife

Cronus
    also: 6 Cronos, Kronos
    form: 5 Titan
    father: 6 Uranus
    mother: 4 Gaea
    sister: 4 Rhea
    wife: 4 Rhea
    son: 4 Zeus **5** Hades **8** Poseidon
    daughter: 4 Hera **6** Hestia **7** Demeter
    corresponds to: 6 Saturn

crony 3 pal **4** ally, chum, mate **5** buddy **6** bunkie, cohort, friend **7** comrade **8** bunkmate, intimate, shipmate, sidekick **9** accessory, associate, companion, old friend **10** accomplice, bosom buddy **11** confederate **12** acquaintance, collaborator **13** coconspirator

Cronyn, Hume
    wife: 12 Jessica Tandy
    born: 6 London **7** Canada, Ontario
    roles: 13 The Fourposter **17** Phantom of the Opera **19** Sunrise at Campobello

crook 3 arc, bow **4** bend, hook, thug, turn **5** angle, cheat, curve, knave, thief, twist **6** bandit, outlaw, robber **7** burglar **8** criminal, swindler **9** curvature, embezzler

crooked 4 awry, bent, wily **5** askew, bowed, shady **6** crafty, curved, hooked, shifty, sneaky, spiral, warped, zigzag **7** corrupt, sinuous, twisted, winding **8** criminal, deformed, tortuous, twisting, unlawful **9** deceitful, deceptive, dishonest, distorted, nefarious, unethical **10** fraudulent, meandering, perfidious, serpentine **11** underhanded **12** dishonorable, unscrupulous

crookedness 10 dishonesty **11** deviousness **13** deceitfulness, double-dealing

Crookes, William
    nationality: 7 British
    invented: 8 thallium **10** radiometer **11** Crookes tube

croon 3 hum **4** sing **6** murmur, warble

crop 3 bob, cut, lop **4** clip, snip, trim **5** prune, shear, yield **6** growth **7** harvest, reaping **8** cut short, gleaning **9** gathering ·**10** production

crop-raising 7 farming, tillage **11** agriculture **12** agribusiness, truck farming **15** market gardening

crop up 5 arise, ensue, occur **6** appear **7** develop, surface **11** come to light

croquet
    equipment: 4 ball, hoop **6** mallet, wicket
    variation: 5 roque
    term: 5 rover
    site: 4 lawn

Crosby, Bing
    real name: 17 Harry Lillis Crosby
    partner: 7 Bob Hope **10** Hedy Lamarr **13** Dorothy Lamour

nickname: 8 Der Bingle

wife: 8 Dixie Lee **12** Kathryn Grant

born: 8 Tacoma WA

roles: 10 Going My Way (Oscar), Holiday Inn **11** High Society **14** The Country Girl, White Christmas **17** The Bells of St Mary's **22** Christmas in Connecticut

    Road to: 3 Rio **4** Bali **7** Morocco **8** Hong Kong, Zanzibar **9** Singapore

cross 3 mad, mix, tau **4** crux, ford, meet, rood **5** angry, blend, erase, gruff, surly, testy, trial **6** burden, cancel, cranky, delete, go over, hybrid, ordeal, shirty, touchy **7** amalgam, annoyed, athwart, grouchy, oblique, peevish, trouble, waspish **8** captious, choleric, churlish, contrary, crucifix, distress, intermix, pass over, petulant, snappish, traverse **9** adversity, crotchety, half-breed, hybridize, intersect, irascible, irritable, querulous, splenetic, strike out, suffering **10** affliction, difficulty, ill-humored, interbreed, misfortune, obliterate, out of sorts, transverse **11** combination, ill-tempered, intractable, tribulation **12** cantankerous, disagreeable, intersecting

crossbar 3 bar **4** spar **5** sprit **6** stripe

crossbreed 3 mix **8** intermix **9** hybridize **10** interbreed

cross-fertilize 9 hybridize

crossing 4 pass **7** mixture, passage **8** blocking, opposing, traverse **9** thwarting **10** traversing **11** hybridizing, intersection **13** hybridization

cross over 4 span **5** cross **6** bridge **8** traverse

crosspiece 3 bar **4** spar **5** sprit

cross-pollinate 9 hybridize

crossroad 12 intersection, turning point

cross swords 5 clash, fight **6** battle, combat, tussle **7** contend, contest **8** skirmish

crossways 7 athwart **12** transversely

crosswise 6 across **7** athwart **8** sideways, traverse **10** transverse

crotchet 3 tat **4** bent, whim **5** habit, quirk, trait **6** foible, hang-up, oddity, vagary, whimsy **7** caprice **8** quiddity **9** mannerism **10** eraticism **11** peculiarity **12** eccentricity, idiosyncrasy, irregularity **14** characteristic

crotchety 3 odd **5** fussy **6** cranky **7** erratic, grouchy **8** contrary, peculiar **9** eccentric

crouch 4 bend, duck **5** cower, squat, stoop **6** cringe, recoil, shrink **9** hunch over **10** hunker down **11** scrooch down, scrunch down

crow 3 daw, jay, kae **4** blow, brag, rook **5** boast, crake, exult, gloat, raven, strut, vaunt **6** cackle, chough, corbie, magpie **7** corvine, jackdaw,

rejoice, swagger, triumph, trumpet **8** jubilate **14** cock-a-doodle-doo

group of: 6 murder

Crow

    constellation of: 6 Corvus

Crow

    language family: 6 Siouan

    tribe: 9 River Crow **12** Mountain Crow

    location: 7 Montana, Wyoming

    related to: 7 Hidatsa

crowbar 3 bar, pry **5** jimmy, lever

crowd 3 jam, mob, set **4** cram, gang, herd, host, mass, push **5** crush, flock, group, horde, press, shove, surge, swarm **6** circle, claque, clique, gather, huddle, legion, throng **7** cluster, coterie, elbow in, squeeze **8** assemble **9** gathering, multitude **10** assemblage, congregate **11** concentrate **12** congregation

Crowd, The

    director: 9 King Vidor

    cast: 9 Bert Roach **11** James Murray **15** Eleanor Boardman

crowded 4 full **6** filled, jammed, mobbed, packed **7** crammed, teeming **8** swarming, thronged **9** congested, jampacked **11** overflowing

crowd out 8 displace **9** overwhelm

crown 3 cap, top **4** acme, apex, head, pate, peak **5** crest, tiara **6** climax, diadem, noggin, noodle, summit, top off, wreath, zenith **7** chaplet, circlet, coronet, fulfill, garland, perfect, royalty **8** complete, monarchy, pinnacle, round out **11** sovereignty

Crowne, Lenina

    character in: 13 Brave New World

    author: 6 Huxley

crowning point 3 cap, tip **4** apex, peak **6** summit, vertex, zenith **8** pinnacle

crown of thorns 4 bane **5** cross **6** burden, ordeal **7** torment **8** vexation **10** affliction **11** tribulation

crow over 5 gloat **9** brag about **10** boast about

crucial 5 grave **6** knotty, urgent **7** serious, weighty **8** critical, decisive, pressing **9** essential, important, momentous **11** determining, significant

Crucible, The

    author: 12 Arthur Miller

crude 3 raw **5** crass, gross, rough **6** coarse, vulgar **7** obscene, sketchy, uncouth **9** imperfect, tasteless, unrefined **10** incomplete, unfinished, unpolished, unprepared **11** uncompleted, undeveloped, unprocessed

crudeness 7 rawness **8** bad taste **9** crassness, grossness, obscenity, vulgarity **10** coarseness, indelicacy **13** tastelessness

cruel 6 brutal, savage **7** inhuman, vicious **8** inhumane, pitiless, ruthless,

sadistic **9** heartless, merciless, unfeeling **10** unmerciful **11** cold-blooded, hardhearted, remorseless **15** uncompassionate

cruelty 6 sadism **8** ferocity, savagery **9** barbarity, brutality **10** bestiality, inhumanity **11** viciousness **12** ruthlessness **13** heartlessness

cruet 3 jar, jug **6** bottle **7** urceole **9** dispenser

cruise 4 sail, scud, skim **5** coast, drift, float, glide, sweep **6** stream, voyage **7** seafare **8** navigate

Cruise, Tom

    original name: 21 Thomas Cruise Maypother

    born: 10 Syracuse NY

    wife: 10 Mimi Rogers **12** Nicole Kidman

    films: 4 Taps **6** Top Gun **7** The Firm, Rain Man **8** Cocktail **10** Far and Away **11** Endless Love, A Few Good Men **12** Jerry Maguire, The Outsiders **13** Days of Thunder, Risky Business **15** The Color of Money **16** All the Right Moves **17** Mission Impossible **21** Born on the Fourth of July, Interview with a Vampire

crumb 3 bit, ort **5** grain, scrap, shred, speck **6** morsel, sliver **8** fragment, particle

crumble 5 crush, decay, grate, grind **6** powder **8** fragment, splinter **9** decompose, pulverize **12** disintegrate

crumbly 7 brittle, friable **9** breakable

Crummles, Vincent

    character in: 16 Nicholas Nickleby

    author: 7 Dickens

crummy 5 awful, lousy **6** rotten **8** terrible

crumple 4 fall **5** crush **6** cave in, crease, pucker, rumple **7** crimple, crinkle, wrinkle **8** collapse **9** corrugate

crunch 4 chew, gnaw **5** chomp, gnash, grind, munch **7** squeeze **8** showdown **9** masticate

Cruncher, Jerry

    character in: 16 A Tale of Two Cities

    author: 7 Dickens

crunchy 3 dry **5** crisp **6** crispy **7** crackly

crusade 5 drive, rally **8** campaign, movement

Crusader 6 knight, zealot **7** pilgrim, Templar **8** champion **11** Hospitaller

Crusades

    time: 10 Middle Ages

    cry: 8 deus vult

    foe: 4 turk **7** infidel, Saladin, saracen

    leader: 7 Tancred

    port: 4 Acre

crush 4 mash **5** break, press, quash, quell, smash **6** enfold, quench, squash, subdue **7** crumble, crumple, embrace, put down, shatter, squeeze, squelch **8** compress, overcome, sup-

press 9 granulate, overpower, over-whelm, pulverize **10** extinguish

crushed 3 sad **5** cowed **6** broken, mashed, woeful **7** abashed, doleful, forlorn, pressed, put down, quashed, quelled, smashed, subdued **8** crumbled, crumpled, dejected, desolate, overcame, overcome, quenched, squashed, squeezed, wretched **9** flattened, miserable, squelched, woebegone **10** compressed, despondent, pulverized, suppressed **11** overpowered, overwhelmed **12** disconsolate, extinguished, inconsolable **13** broken-hearted

crushing 7 mashing **8** decisive, quelling, smashing **10** shattering **11** humiliating, putting down, stamping out, suppression **12** obliterating, overwhelming **13** pulverization

crust 4 coat, gall, hull, rind, scab **5** brass, nerve, shell **6** harden **7** coating **8** chutzpah, covering, pie shell **9** impudence **11** pastry shell

crustacean 4 crab, flea **5** louse, prawn **6** isopod, shrimp **7** lobster **8** barnacle, crawfish, crayfish **9** shellfish, water flea

crusty 4 curt **5** blunt, gruff, rough, short, stern, surly, testy **6** abrupt, crabby, cranky, shirty, snippy, sullen **7** brusque, peevish, waspish **8** choleric, snappish, snippety **9** irascible, splenetic **10** ill-natured **11** ill-tempered **13** short-tempered

crux 3 nub **4** core, gist **5** basis, heart **7** essence **9** essential **10** brass tacks **11** nitty-gritty

cry 3 beg, sob, sue **4** bawl, call, hawk, howl, keen, moan, plea, roar, wail, weep, yell, yelp **5** blare, cheer, groan, mourn, plead, shout, utter, whoop **6** appeal, bellow, blazon, boohoo, clamor, hurrah, huzzah, lament, outcry, prayer, scream, shriek, snivel **7** blubber, call out, exclaim, implore, request, screech, trumpet, whimper **8** entreaty, petition, proclaim **9** advertise, importune **10** adjuration, promulgate **11** exclamation **12** solicitation, supplication

Cry, the Beloved Country
    author: 9 Alan Paton
    locale: 11 South Africa

cry out 4 bark, bawl, call, howl, roar, yell **5** shout **6** bellow, clamor, holler **7** exclaim **8** proclaim **9** ejaculate

cry over 5 mourn **6** bemoan, bewail, lament

crypt 4 tomb **5** vault **8** catacomb **9** mausoleum, sepulcher

cryptic 4 dark **5** vague **6** arcane, hidden, occult, secret **7** obscure, strange **8** esoteric, mystical, puzzling **9** ambiguous **10** cabalistic, mysterious, perplexing **11** enigmatical

cryptogram 4 code **6** cipher

cryptograph 4 code **6** cipher, encode

crystal 3 ice **5** clear, flake, glass, lucid **6** quartz **7** diamond **8** stemware **9** glassware, snowflake, watch part **10** rhinestone **11** transparent

crystallize 3 fix, gel **4** firm, jell **5** candy **6** harden **8** solidify **9** granulate

Csonka, Larry (Lawrence Richard)
    nickname: 9 Lawnmower
    sport: 8 football
    position: 8 fullback
    team: 13 Miami Dolphins, New York Giants

cub 3 boy, pup **4** bear, lion **5** scout, whelp **6** novice **8** reporter **9** youngling, youngster **10** apprentice

Cuba
    other name: 18 pearl of the Antilles
    capital/largest city: 6 Havana **8** Le Habana
    others: 5 Bauta, Colon, Duabi, Guane, Manes **6** Baines, Bayamo, Gibara, Guines, Mayari **7** Antilla, Baracoa, Fomento, Holguin, Holquin, Jiguani, Niquero, Palmira, Sanhuis **8** Artemisa, Camaguey, Cardenas, Guaimaro, Guayabal, Marianao, Matanzas, Nuevitas, Varadero, Yaguajay **9** Cabaiguan, Camajuani, Cienfuego **10** Cienfuegos, Guanabacoa, Guantanamo, Manzanillo, Santa Clara **11** Campechuela, Pinar del Rio, Puerto Padre **12** Ciego de Avila **13** Sagua de Tanamo **14** Sancti Spiritus, Santiago de Cuba **17** Aguada de Pasajeros, Consolacion del Sur
    measure: 4 vara **5** bocoy, cocoy, tarea **6** cordel, fanega **10** caballeria
    monetary unit: 4 peso **7** centavo **8** cuarenta
    weight: 5 libra **6** tercio
    island: 5 Pines, Pinos **6** Sabana **8** Camaguey, Juventud **9** Canarreos **17** Jardines de la Reina
      cay: 4 Coco **5** Largo **6** Romano **7** Guajaba, Rosareo, Sabinal **8** Cantiles **9** San Felipe **10** Santa Maria
    mountain: 6 Copper **7** Cristal, Maestra, Organos **8** Camaguey, Trinidad **9** Las Villas **11** Pinar del rio **12** Guaniguanico **14** Sancti-Spiritus
    highest point: 8 Turquino
    river: 4 Zaza **5** Cauto **8** San Pedro
    sea: 8 Atlantic **9** Caribbean
    physical feature:
      bay: 4 Nipe, Pigs **6** Jiguey **8** Cochinos **10** Buena Vista, Guantznamo
      cape: 4 Cruz **5** Maisi **8** Lucrecia **10** Corrientes, San Antonio
      channel: 8 Nicholas **9** Old Bahama
      falls: 3 Toa **7** Agabama, Caburni
      gulf: 6 Mexico **7** Cazones **8** Anamaria, Batabano **12** Guancanayabo
      inlet: 4 Broa **10** Corrientes
      peninsula: 6 Zapata
      point: 7 Guarico
      swamp: 6 Zapata

    people: 5 Carib, Negro, Taino, white **6** Arawak **7** Ciboney, mestizo **8** Ciboneye
      conqueror: 9 Velazquez
      explorer: 8 Columbus
      leader: 6 Castro **7** Batista **10** Che Guevara
    language: 7 Spanish
    religion: 13 Roman Catholic
      cult: 6 Chango, Yemaya
    places:
      castle: 5 Morro
      cathedral: 8 Santiago
    feature:
      dance: 5 conga, rumba **6** danzon, rhumba **8** guaracha, pachanga
      harvest: 5 zafra
      peasant: 7 guajiro
      tree: 5 jique, jiqui
      witch doctor: 7 nanigos
    food:
      dish: 6 paella
      drink: 4 pina

cubbyhole 4 nook **5** niche **6** cranny **10** pigeonhole **11** compartment

cube of deep-fried pork
    American Spanish: 10 cuchifrito

cubic centimeter
    abbreviation: 4 cu cm

cubic dekameter
    abbreviation: 5 cu dkm

cubic foot
    abbreviation: 4 cu ft

cubic inch
    abbreviation: 4 cu in

cubicle 3 bay **4** cell, nook **5** booth, niche **6** alcove, carrel, recess

cubic meter
    abbreviation: 3 cu m

cubic millimeter
    abbreviation: 4 cu mm

cubic yard
    abbreviation: 4 cu yd

cubit 15 Biblical measure

cuchifrito 19 cube of deep-fried pork

Cuchulainn
    origin: 5 Irish
    hero of: 6 Ulster
    uncle: 9 Conchobar
    guarded house of: 10 Smith Culan
    killed by: 6 Lugaid

cuckoo 3 ani **4** bats, bird, fool, gaga, nuts **5** balmy, batty, crazy, daffy, dotty, goofy, loony, nutty, silly, wacky **6** screwy **7** idiotic **9** screwball **12** crackbrained **13** off one's rocker **14** off one's trolley

cucumber 14 Cucumis sativus
    varieties: 3 bur **4** mock, star, wild **6** bitter, pickle **7** prickly, serpent **9** squirting **13** African horned

cuddle 3 hug, pet **5** clasp **6** caress, curl up, fondle, huddle, nestle, nuzzle **7** cling to, embrace, lie snug, snuggle

Cuddly Dudley
    nickname of: 11 Dudley Moore

cudgel 4 club 5 baton, staff, stick 8 bludgeon 9 billy club, blackjack, truncheon 10 shillelagh 12 quarterstaff

cue 3 key, tip 4 clue, hint, sign 6 signal 7 inkling 10 intimation, suggestion 11 insinuation

cuff 3 box, hit, rap 4 blow 5 clout, smack, thump, whack 6 thwack, wallop

cui bono 10 for what use, of what good 15 for whose benefit

cuisine 4 fare, food, menu 5 table 6 viands 7 cookery, cooking, edibles 8 victuals, vittles 11 comestibles

Cukor, George
  director of: 7 Camille 8 Adam's Rib, Gaslight, The Women 10 My Fair Lady (Oscar) 11 A Double Life, A Star Is Born, Little Women 13 Born Yesterday, Dinner at Eight 14 Romeo and Juliet 16 David Copperfield 18 A Bill of Divorcement 20 The Philadelphia Story

cul-de-sac 6 pocket 7 dead-end, impasse 10 blind alley

cull 4 junk, pick, sift, take 5 dross, glean, scrap, trash, waste 6 choose, divide, garner, gather, jetsam, reject, second, select, winnow 7 castoff, collect, discard, excerpt, extract, leaving 8 abstract, scouring, separate 9 segregate

culminate 3 cap, end, top 5 crown, end up 6 climax, finish, result, top off, wind up 8 complete, conclude 9 terminate 10 consummate

culmination 4 acme, apex, peak 6 apogee, climax, height, zenith 7 epitome 8 pinnacle 10 conclusion 11 fulfillment, realization 12 consummation

Culp, Robert
  born: 10 Berkeley CA
  roles: 4 I Spy 20 Greatest American Hero

culpability 4 onus 5 blame, fault, guilt 9 liability 14 accountability, responsibility

culpable 6 guilty, liable 7 at fault, to blame 8 blamable 10 censurable 11 blameworthy

culprit 5 felon 6 sinner 8 criminal, evildoer, offender 9 miscreant, wrongdoer 10 lawbreaker, malefactor 12 transgressor

cult 4 sect 7 faction, zealots 8 admirers, devotees, devotion 9 disciples, followers 10 admiration

cultivable 6 arable 7 fertile, friable 8 farmable, plowable, tillable

cultivate 3 dig, hoe, sow 4 farm, grow, plow, seek, till, weed 5 court, plant, spade 6 enrich, garden 7 acquire, advance, develop, elevate, enhance, improve

cultivated 3 dug 4 fine, grew, hoed 6 farmed, forked, sought, spaded, tilled,

weeded 7 courted, planted 8 advanced, cultured, elevated, enhanced, enriched, finished, improved, polished 9 developed

cultivation 5 grace 6 polish, sowing 7 farming, manners, tilling 8 agronomy, planting 9 elevation, gardening, gentility, good taste, husbandry 10 refinement 11 agriculture

culture 3 art 5 music 7 the arts 8 learning 9 erudition, knowledge 10 enrichment, literature, refinement 12 civilization 13 enlightenment 15 accomplishments

Culture and Anarchy
  author: 13 Matthew Arnold

cultured 7 elegant, erudite, genteel, learned, refined 8 polished, well-bred, well-read 11 enlightened 12 accomplished, well-educated 13 sophisticated

culture medium 4 agar 8 agar-agar

culvert 5 ditch, drain, sewer 6 trench 7 channel, conduit, fox-hole

cumbersome 5 bulky, hefty 6 clumsy 7 awkward 8 cumbrous, ungainly, unwieldy 9 ponderous 12 unmanageable

cum grano salis 15 not too seriously 16 with a grain of salt

cumin
  botanical name: 14 Cuminum cyminum
  other name: 6 comino, jiraka, kummel
  origin: 5 Egypt
  family: 7 parsley
  symbol of: 5 greed
  guards against straying: 7 pigeons 8 chickens, husbands
  use: 4 fish, meat, rice, soup, stew 5 bread, curry 6 cheese 7 pickles, sausage 8 potatoes 11 chili powder

cum laude 10 with praise

Cummings, E. E. (Edward Estlin)
  author of: 12 in just spring 15 The Enormous Room 17 Tulips and Chimneys 18 Chansons Innocentes

Cummings, Robert
  real name: 29 Clarence Robert Orville Cummings
  born: 8 Joplin MO
  roles: 8 King's Row 14 Dial M for Murder 18 The Bob Cummings Show

cumulate 5 amass 6 gather, heap up, pile up 10 accumulate

cumulative 7 amassed, piled up 8 additive, heaped up 9 aggregate 10 collective 12 accumulative, conglomerate

Cunegonde
  character in: 7 Candide
  author: 8 Voltaire

cunning 3 art, sly 4 foxy, wily 5 canny, craft, guile, knack, skill 6 artful, crafty, deceit, genius, shifty, shrewd, talent, tricky 7 ability, devious, finesse, slyness 8 aptitude, arti-

fice, deftness, foxiness, guileful, subtlety, trickery, wiliness 9 chicanery, deceitful, deception, deceptive, dexterity, duplicity, ingenious, underhand 10 adroitness, artfulness, cleverness, craftiness, expertness, shrewdness 11 deviousness 13 Machiavellian
  god of: 6 Hermes

Cunning Little Vixen, The
  opera by: 7 Janacek

cup 3 cup 5 glass, grail, stein 6 beaker, goblet, vessel 7 chalice, tankard 8 half pint, schooner
  abbreviation: 1 c

Cup
  constellation of: 6 Crater

cupbearer of gods 8 Ganymede

cupboard 6 buffet, bureau, closet 7 armoire, cabinet 9 sideboard, storeroom 10 chiffonier 11 china closet 12 clothespress

Cupid 6 cherub
  also: 4 Amor
  origin: 5 Roman
  god of: 4 love
  mother: 5 Venus
  corresponds to: 4 Eros
  features: 3 bow 5 arrow, wings

cupidity 5 greed 7 avarice, avidity 8 rapacity 10 greediness 11 selfishness 12 covetousness, graspingness 13 concupiscence, insatiability, rapaciousness 14 avariciousness 15 acquisitiveness

cupola 4 dome, roof 5 tower, vault 6 belfry, turret 7 ceiling

cur 3 cad 4 mutt 5 rogue 6 rascal, varlet, wretch 7 mongrel, varmint, villain 9 scoundrel 10 blackguard

curacao
  type: 7 liqueur
  origin: 19 Netherlands Antilles
  flavor: 6 orange
  with gin: 8 Blue Moon, Napoleon 9 Blue Devil 14 Flying Dutchman
  with rum: 6 Mai-Tai 8 Blue Lady 12 Blue Hawaiian
  with vodka: 8 Aqueduct

curate 5 vicar 6 cleric, deacon, parson, pastor, priest, rector 8 minister, preacher 9 churchman, clergyman 12 ecclesiastic

curative 4 balm 7 healing 11 restorative

curator 5 doyen 6 keeper 7 steward 8 director, overseer 9 caretaker, custodian

curb 3 rim 4 edge, rein 5 brink, check, ledge, limit 6 border, bridle, halter, retard, slow up 7 control, harness, inhibit, repress, slacken 8 hold back, moderate, restrain, restrict, slow down, suppress 9 curbstone, hindrance, restraint 10 decelerate, limitation 11 restriction, retardation

curdle 3 rot 4 clot, curd, sour, turn 5 decay, go bad, go off, spoil 7 clabber, congeal, ferment, putrefy, thicken **8** putresce, solidify **9** coagulate **11** deteriorate

cure 3 dry **4** heal, salt **5** smoke **6** remedy **8** antidote, make well, preserve **10** corrective

cure-all 4 balm **6** elixir, remedy **7** panacea **10** catholicon

cured 5 dried **6** healed, mended, smoked **8** made well, remedied **9** preserved, recovered

Curie, Marie Sklodowska and Pierre
  field: 7 physics **9** chemistry
  discovered: 6 radium **8** polonium **13** radioactivity
  awarded: 10 Nobel Prize
  daughter: 5 Marie (Joliot-Curie, Nobelist)

curio 7 bibelot, trinket **9** bric-a-brac, objet d'art

curiosity 5 freak, sight **6** marvel, oddity, prying, rarity, wonder **7** novelty **8** interest, nosiness **10** phenomenon, rare object **11** questioning **15** inquisitiveness

curious 3 odd **4** nosy, rare **5** funny, novel, queer, weird **6** prying, quaint, unique **7** bizarre, strange, unusual **8** peculiar, singular, snooping, uncommon **9** inquiring, searching **11** inquisitive, questioning

curl 4 coil, lock, wave, wind **5** crimp, frizz, swirl, twirl, twist **6** spiral **7** frizzle, ringlet, scallop **8** curlicue **9** corkscrew

curled 3 set **5** kinky, waved, wound **6** coiled, frizzy, permed, spiral **7** crimped, frizzed, twisted **8** crinkled, scrolled **9** curlicued

curlicue 4 coil **5** twist **6** spiral **8** flourish

curly 4 wavy **5** kinky **6** frizzy **7** rippled **8** crinkled **9** ringleted

curmudgeon 4 crab **5** crank, grump **6** grouch **8** grumbler, sourball

currant 5 Ribes
  varieties: 3 red **5** black, fetid, skunk, squaw, stink **6** alpine, cherry, common, garden, Indian, Sierra **7** Buffalo **8** Missouri, mountain, swamp red **9** chaparral, wild black **11** northern red **12** bristly black **13** American black, European black, northern black, white-flowered **15** California black

currency 4 cash, coin **5** bills, money, vogue **6** specie **7** coinage **9** bank notes **10** acceptance, popularity, prevalence **12** predominance, universality

current 3 now **4** flow, flux, mood, tide **5** draft, drift, trend **6** modern, spirit, stream, with-it **7** feeling, in style, in vogue, popular, present **8** existing, tendency, up-to-date **9** prevalent, zeitgeist **10** atmosphere, present-day, prevailing **11** inclination **12** contemporary, undercurrent

current of air 4 wind **5** draft **6** breeze, zephyr

curricle 3 gig **4** cart, trap **6** chaise **8** carriage

curry powder
  origin: 5 India
  ingredient: 5 cumin **6** cloves **8** capsicum, turmeric **9** coriander, fenugreek, red pepper **13** cayenne pepper
  use: 5 kebab, kebob **6** kofta, malai **6** kormas **7** curries **8** meat loaf, vindaloo, zucchini **11** potato salad

curse 3 vex **4** bane, cuss, damn, oath **5** blast, cross, swear, trial **6** burden, ordeal, plague, whammy **7** afflict, condemn, evil eye, scourge, swear at, torment, trouble **8** anathema, denounce, execrate, swearing, vexation **9** annoyance, blasphemy, damnation, evil spell, expletive, obscenity, profanity **10** affliction, execration, misfortune **11** imprecation, malediction, tribulation **12** anathematize, denunciation

cursory 5 brief, hasty, quick, swift **6** casual, random **7** hurried, offhand, passing **8** careless **9** desultory, haphazard **11** inattentive, perfunctory, superficial

curt 4 rude **5** bluff, blunt, gruff, short, terse **6** abrupt, crusty, snappy **7** brusque, summary **8** petulant **10** peremptory

curtail 3 cut **4** clip, trim **6** reduce **7** abridge, shorten **8** condense, contract, cut short, decrease, diminish, pare down **10** abbreviate

curtailed 3 cut **7** checked, concise, cut back, reduced, slashed **8** abridged, cut short **9** shortened **10** retrenched

curtailment 7 cutback, cutting, halting, pruning **8** clipping, decrease, trimming **9** lessening, reduction, restraint **10** limitation, shortening **11** abridgement, contraction **12** abbreviation, condensation

curtain 3 end **4** mask, veil **5** blind, cover, drape, shade, sheet **6** screen, shroud **7** conceal, drapery, hanging **8** portiere

Curtis, Tony
  real name: 15 Bernard Schwartz
  wife: 10 Janet Leigh
  daughter: 9 Jamie Lee
  born: 9 New York NY
  roles: 7 Houdini, Trapeze **12** The Great Race **13** Some Like It Hot **14** The Defiant Ones **16** The Great Imposter **18** The Boston Strangler **22** The Sweet Smell of Success

Curtius
  also: 6 Marcus
  volunteered as: 17 sacrificial victim

Curtiz, Michael
  director of: 10 Casablanca (Oscar), The Sea Hawk **12** Captain Blood **13** Mildred Pierce **14** Life with Father **17** Yankee Doodle Dandy **24** The Adventures of Robin Hood (with William Keighley) **26** The Charge of the Light Brigade **34** The Private Lives of Elizabeth and Essex

curtsy, curtsey 3 bob, bow, dip **5** honor **6** homage **9** obeisance, reverence **11** bend the knee

curvature 3 arc **4** arch, bend **5** crook **6** bowing

curve 3 arc, bow, ess **4** arch, bend, coil, hook, loop, turn, wind **5** crook, twist **6** spiral, swerve

curved 4 bent **5** bowed **6** arched, looped, turned

curved span 3 bow **4** arch, dome **5** vault **6** bridge

Curve of Binding Energy, The
  author: 10 John McPhee

curving 4 bent **5** bowed **6** arched **7** bending, looping, turning, winding **8** twisting

curving inward 6 hollow, sunken **7** concave **8** hollowed **9** depressed

curving outward 5 bowed **6** convex **7** bulging, rounded **8** bellying **11** protuberant

Cuscatlan *see* **10** El Salvador

Cush
  father: 3 Ham
  grandfather: 4 Noah
  brother: 6 Canaan
  son: 6 Nimrod
  Hebrew for: 8 Ethiopia

cushion 3 mat, pad **4** damp **5** quiet **6** dampen, deaden, muffle, pillow, soften, stifle **7** bolster **8** suppress

Cushitic
  language family: 11 Afro-Asiatic **13** Hamito-Semitic
  branch: 6 Somali **8** Gallinya
  spoken in: 7 Somalia **8** Ethiopia, Tanzania

cusp 4 apex, barb, horn, peak **5** angle, point, tooth **6** corner

custard 4 flan, fool **5** creme **6** junket **7** dessert, pudding **8** flummery **10** blanc-mange, zabaglione

Custer, George A
  served in: 8 Civil War **10** Indian Wars
  side: 5 Union
  battle: 13 Little Big Horn
  defeated: 11 Black Kettle
  defeated by: 10 Crazy Horse

custodian 6 duenna, keeper, warden **7** janitor **8** chaperon, guardian, watchman **9** attendant, caretaker, chaperone, concierge **14** superintendent

custody 4 care **5** watch **6** charge **9** detention **10** possession, protection **11** confinement, safekeeping, trusteeship **12** conservation, guardianship, preservation

custom 4 form, mode 5 habit, usage 7 fashion 10 convention

customarily 7 as a rule, usually 8 commonly, normally 9 generally, regularly 10 frequently, habitually, ordinarily 13 traditionally

customary 5 usual 6 common, normal, wonted 7 general, regular, routine, typical 8 everyday, habitual, ordinary 10 accustomed 11 traditional 12 conventional

customer 5 buyer 6 client, patron 7 habitue, shopper 9 purchaser

customs 4 duty, levy, toll 6 excise, tariff 9 import tax 10 assessment

cut 3 mow, saw 4 chop, clip, crop, cube, dice, fall, gash, hack, move, nick, pare, part, rent, rive, slit, snip, snub, trim 5 carve, cross, lance, mince, piece, prune, sever, share, shave, shear, slash, slice, split, wound 6 bisect, course, delete, divide, furrow, hollow, ignore, incise, pierce, reduce, sunder, trench 7 abridge, channel, curtail, decline, dissect, opening, passage, portion, section, segment 8 condense, contract, decrease, diminish, incision, lacerate 9 abatement, intersect, lessening, reduction, shrinkage 10 abbreviate, diminution, excavation, shortening 11 contraction, curtailment, indentation

cut and run 4 bolt, flee, skip 6 escape 7 abscond, get away, make off, run away 8 slip away 9 break free 10 break loose, fly the coop 12 make a getaway

cut apart 7 dissect 9 anatomize

cutback 8 decrease, trimming 9 reduction 11 abridgement, curtailment

cut back 4 trim 5 prune 6 reduce 7 abridge, curtail 8 decrease

cut costs 4 save 5 skimp, stint 6 scrimp 7 husband 8 conserve, downsize 9 economize 15 tighten one's belt

cut down 4 kill, trim 5 limit 6 lessen, reduce 7 abridge, curtail, destroy, disable, remodel, shorten 8 condense, decrease, diminish, restrict 10 abbreviate

cut-down form 6 digest, precis 7 summary 8 synopsis, trimming 10 shortening 11 abridgement, contraction, curtailment 12 abbreviation, condensation

cut down to size 5 abase 6 humble 7 mortify 8 belittle, bring low, disgrace 9 humiliate 13 bring down a peg

cute 5 sweet 6 dainty, pretty 7 darling, lovable 8 adorable, handsome, precious 9 beautiful 10 attractive

cut expenses 4 save 5 skimp, stint 6 scrimp 8 conserve 9 economize 12 pinch pennies 15 tighten one's belt

cut in half 5 halve 6 bisect

cut in two 5 halve, sever 6 bisect

cutlet 3 cut 4 chop 5 slice 9 cotelette, croquette

cut off 4 dock, trim 5 apart, sever 6 detach, remove 7 chop off, divorce, isolate 8 amputate, divorced, isolated, separate 10 disconnect

cut out 2 go 4 blow, exit 5 be off, erase, leave, scram, split 6 beat it, delete, depart, escape, excise, go away, remove, set out 7 abolish 8 designed, get rid of, set forth 9 eliminate 10 do away with, hit the road, make tracks 11 exterminate, take a powder

cut short 4 clip, crop, dock, trim 7 abridge, shorten 8 truncate 10 abbreviate

cutter 4 boat 5 blade, hewer, knife 6 sledge, sleigh, tailor 11 cutting edge

cutthroat 5 cruel 6 outlaw 7 brigand, hoodlum, ruffian 8 ruthless 9 merciless

cutting 3 raw 4 acid, cold 5 harsh, nasty, sharp 6 biting, bitter 7 acerbic, caustic, nipping, pruning, searing 8 clipping, derisive, piercing, scathing, smarting, snubbing, stinging, trimming 9 reduction, sarcastic, stringent 11 abridgement, acrimonious, compression, contraction, curtailment, disparaging, penetrating 12 abbreviation, condensation

cutting edge 5 blade 8 vanguard 9 forefront

cutting off 8 severing 9 severance 10 detachment, separation 13 disconnection, disengagement

cutting remark 3 dig 4 gibe, jeer 5 taunt

Cuttle
   character in: 12 Dombey and Son
   author: 7 Dickens

cut up 4 chop, hack, maim, rend 5 caper, carve, halve, mince, slash, slice, split 6 cleave, deface, deform, divide 7 portion, quarter 8 dissever, mutilate 9 apportion, kid around 10 fool around 11 clown around, play the fool

Cuvier, Georges
   field: 7 geology, zoology
   nationality: 6 French
   founded: 12 paleontology 18 comparative anatomy

Cybele
   also: 9 Dindymene 10 Berecyntia, Magna Mater 11 Great Mother 12 Mater Turrita 17 Great Idaean Mother
   origin: 8 Phrygian 9 Asia Minor
   goddess of: 6 nature
   priest: 5 Galli 10 Corybantes
   corresponds to: 3 Ops 4 Rhea
   epithet: 6 Antaea

Cyclades 3 Dos, Zea 4 Keos, Nios, Sira, Syra 5 Delos, Melos, Naxos,

Paros, Siros, Syros, Tenos, Tinos 6 Andros 7 Amorgos, islands, Kythnos 13 Aegean islands

cycle 3 run 6 series 8 sequence 10 succession 11 progression 14 connected group

cyclone 4 gale, gust, wind 5 storm 7 tornado, twister, typhoon 9 whirlwind, windstorm
   Australian: 10 willy-nilly

Cyclone (Cy)
   nickname of: 15 Denton True Young

Cyclops, Cyclopes
   form: 5 giant
   number of eyes: 3 one
   father: 6 Uranus
   mother: 2 Ge
   blinded by: 8 Odysseus

Cycnus
   father: 4 Ares
   killed in: 4 duel
   killed by: 8 Hercules
   changed into: 4 swan

cylinder 3 can, tin 4 drum, pipe, roll, tube 5 spool 6 barrel, column, pillar, piston, platen, roller 13 piston chamber

cylindrical 5 round 6 tarete 7 tubular 8 columnar

Cymbeline
   author: 18 William Shakespeare
   character: 6 Cloten, Imogen 7 Iachimo, Pisanio 9 Bellarius 17 Leonatus Posthumus

Cymru see 5 Wales

cynic 7 scoffer, skeptic 9 pessimist 10 misogynist 11 faultfinder, misanthrope

cynical 8 derisive, sardonic, scoffing, scornful, sneering 9 misogynic, sarcastic, skeptical 12 misanthropic

cypress 8 Taxodium 9 Cupressus
   varieties: 3 toy 4 bald, berg, pond 5 false, Gowen, Modoc, Piute 6 Bhutan, Hinoki, Lawson, MacNab, Nootka, Sawara, summer, Tecate 7 African, Arizona, Italian, Mexican, Sargent 8 Cuyamaca, golf-ball, Monterey, mourning, Siskiyou, standing 9 Guadalupe, Mendocino, Montezuma, red summer, Santa Cruz 10 Portuguese, tennis-ball 12 Chinese swamp 18 rough-barked Arizona 19 smooth-barked Arizona

Cyprian see 9 Aphrodite

Cyprus
   biblical name: 6 Kittim
   capital/largest city: 7 Nicosia
   city: 6 Paphos 7 Kyrenia, Larnaca 8 Limassol 9 Famagusta
   monetary unit: 4 para 5 pound
   mountain: 7 Kyrenia, Troodos
   highest point: 7 Olympus
   river: 6 Pedias
   sea: 13 Mediterranean
   physical feature:
      bay: 8 Episkopi
      cape: 4 Gata 5 Greco 7 Andreas,

Arnauti **9** Kormakiti
peninsula: 6 Karpas
plain: 8 Mesaoria **9** Messaoria
people: 5 Greek, Turks **9** Cypriotes
ruler: 5 Turks **6** Greeks, Romans **7** British **9** Egyptians, Lusignans, Venetians **10** Byzantines **11** Phoenicians
language: 5 Greek **7** Turkish
religion: 5 Islam **6** Muslim **13** Greek Orthodoxy **16** Eastern Orthodoxy

Cyrano de Bergerac
director: 13 Michael Gordon
author: 13 Edmond Rostand
cast: 10 Jose Ferrer (Cyrano), Mala Powers **13** William Powers
character: 6 Roxane **22** Christian de Neuvillette
setting: 5 Paris
Oscar for: 9 best actor (Ferrer)

Cyrano de Bergerac, Savinien
author of: 25 Voyages to the Moon and the Sun
play based on his life by: 13 Edmond Rostand

cytology
study of: 5 cells

czar, tsar 4 king **5** ruler **6** caesar, despot, tyrant **7** emperor, monarch **8** dictator, overlord **9** potentate, sovereign

czarina 7 empress

czaristic 10 autocratic **11** all-powerful, dictatorial, monarchical

Czechoslovakia/Czech Republic
see also **8** Slovakia
capital/largest city: 5 Praha **6** Prague
others: 2 As **4** Asch, Brno, Cheb, Most **5** Brunn, Nitra, Opava, Plzen, Tabor, **6** Aussig, Bilina, Kladno, Kosice, Pilsen, Presov, Sadowa, Trnava, Vsetin **7** Budweis, Jihlava, Liberec, Olomouc, Ostrava, Teplitz **8** Carlsbad, Jachymov, Karlsbad **9** Pressburg **10** Austerlitz, Bratislava, Koniggratz **11** Reichenberg
university: 7 Charles
division: 7 Bohemia, Moravia, Silesia **8** Ruthenia, Slovakia
measure: 3 Lan **4** Mira **5** Korec, Liket, Stopa **6** Merice, Strych
monetary unit: 5 crown, ducat **6** heller, Koruna
mountain: 3 Erz, Ore **5** Giant, Tatra **6** Sumava **7** Sudeten, Sudetes **8** Krkonose **10** Carpathian
highest point: 7 Gerlach **11** Gerlachovka
river: 2 Uh, **3** Mze, Vag, Vah **4** Dyje, Eger, Elbe, Gran, Hron, Ipel, Iser, Labe, Nisa, Oder, Odra, Ohre, Olse, Waag **5** Becva, Dunaj, March, Nitra, Slana, Tisza **6** Danube, Moldau, Morava, Ondava, Sazava, Torysa, Vltava **7** Laborec, Luznice **8** Berounka

physical feature:
plateau: 8 Bohemian **11** Sudetenland
people: 4 Slav **5** Czech **6** Slovak **8** Bohemian, Moravian
author: 5 Capek, Hasek, Havel **7** Kundera, Seifert
composer: 6 Dvorak **7** Janacek, Martinu, Smetana
director: 11 Milos Forman
philosopher/reformer: 8 Comenius, John Huss
language: 5 Czech **6** German, Magyar, Slovak **7** Russian **9** Hungarian
religion: 6 Uniate **8** Lutheran **9** Orthodoxy **13** Roman Catholic
place:
castle: 8 Hradcany
cathedral: 7 St Vitus **10** St Nicholas
resort/spa: 8 Carlsbad, Piestany **9** Marienbad **10** Luhacovice **11** Karlovy Vary **14** Marianske Lazne
square: 9 Wenceslas
feature:
dance: 5 polka **6** redowa, talian **7** furiant
gymnastics festival: 11 spartakiada
song: 7 Ma Vlast
food:
beer: 6 pilsen
sausage: 5 parky **6** vursty

dab 3 bit, pat, tap **6** stroke **7** smidgen, soupcon

dabble 5 slosh **6** fiddle, putter, splash **7** spatter, toy with **8** sprinkle

dabbler 7 amateur, trifler **10** dilettante **12** experimenter **15** nonprofessional

da capo
  music: 22 repeat from the beginning
  abbreviation: 2 DC

Dacca
  capital of: 10 Bangladesh

d'accord 2 OK **6** agreed **7** granted

Dactyls
  also: 7 Daktyls
  dwellers of: 8 Mount Ida

dad 2 da, pa **3** pop **4** papa, pops, sire **5** daddy, pappy, pater **6** father, parent **11** the old man

Daedalus
  occupation: 9 architect
  father: 6 Metion
  son: 5 Iapyx **6** Icarus
  nephew: 5 Talos **6** Perdix
  killed: 5 Talos
  built: 9 labyrinth
    for: 5 Minos
  made: 5 wings

Daedalus, Stephen *see* **30** Portrait of the Artist as a Young Man

daffodil 9 Narcissus **24** Narcissus pseudonarcissus
  varieties: 3 sea **6** winter **8** Peruvian **9** petticoat **13** hoop-petticoat

daft 3 mad **4** loco **5** balmy, batty, crazy, daffy, dizzy, goofy, loony, nutty, silly, wacky **6** cuckoo, insane, screwy **7** foolish, lunatic, witless

Dagan
  origin: 12 Mesopotamian
  god of: 5 earth **11** agriculture
  corresponds to: 5 Dagon

dagger 4 dirk, snee **5** blade, knife **6** weapon **7** poniard **8** stiletto **11** snickersnee

Dagon
  origin: 10 Philistine, Phoenician
  god of: 5 earth **11** agriculture
  corresponds to: 5 Dagan

Daguerre, Louis J M
  nationality: 6 French
  inventor of: 11 photography **13** daguerreotype

Dagwood 8 sandwich
  see also **7** Blondie

dahlia

varieties: 3 sea **4** tree **6** common, garden **7** bedding **8** bell tree **10** candelabra

Dahomey, Republic of *see* **5** Benin

daily 7 diurnal, per diem **9** circadian, quotidian

Daimler, Gottlieb
  nationality: 6 German
  inventor of: 10 carburetor, motorcycle **14** gasoline engine **18** gasoline automobile **25** compression ignition engine

daimyo 4 lord **10** feudal lord

dainty 4 fine **5** fussy, tasty **6** choice, choosy, lovely, pretty, savory **7** choosey, elegant, refined **8** delicate, pleasing **9** beautiful, delicious, exquisite **10** attractive, fastidious, particular

Daira
  father: 7 Oceanus

dais 5 stage **6** podium **7** rostrum **8** platform

daisy 6 Bellis **23** Chrysanthemum frutescens **25** Chrysanthemum leucanthemum
  varieties: 4 blue, cape, high, lazy **5** crown, giant, globe, oxeye, Paris, veldt, white **6** butter, Easter, Nippon, shas- ta, sleepy, Tahoka **7** African, English, painted, seaside, turfing **8** Dahlberg, mountain, panamint **9** Barberton, Englemann, Swan River, Transvaal **10** Kingfisher, Michaelmas, Portuguese **11** Clanwilliam, Livingstone, Namaqualand **12** Boston yellow, double orange **15** blue-eyed African

Daisy Miller
  author: 10 Henry James
  character: 10 Giovanelli **12** Winterbourne

Dakar
  capital of: 7 Senegal

Dakota (Sioux)
  language family: 6 Siouan
  tribe: 5 Teton **6** Lakota, Nakota, Santee **7** Yankton **8** Sisseton, Wahpeton, Wiciyela **9** Wahpekute, Yanktonai **11** Mdewakanton
  location: 7 Montana **9** Minnesota **11** North Dakota, South Dakota
  leader: 4 Gall **10** Crazy Horse **11** Sitting Bull **13** Jashunca-Uiteo
  noted for: 15 military prowess
  deity: 10 Wakan Tanka

dale 4 dell, dene, glen, vale **6** dingle, hollow, valley

D'Alembert
  author of: 12 Encyclopedia

Dali, Salvador
  born: 5 Spain **7** Figuras
  artwork: 10 Last Supper **17** Atomic Leda and Swan **19** Persistence of Memory **22** Accommodations of Desire **24** Christ of St John of the Cross

Dalibor
  opera by: 7 Smetana
  character: 6 Milada

Dallas
  airport: 23 Dallas-Fort Worth Regional
  basketball team: 4 Mavs **9** Mavericks
  football team: 7 Cowboys
  landmark: 15 Turtle Creek Park **16** Museum of Fine Arts **19** Dallas Theater Center **25** Margo Jones Memorial Theater
  river: 7 Trinity
  stadium: 10 Cotton Bowl
  university: 3 SMU **13** Bishop College **17** Southern Methodist

Dallas
  character: 7 JR Ewing **9** Jack Ewing, Jenna Wade, Jock Ewing, Miss Ellie, Ray Krebbs **10** Bobby Ewing **11** Christopher, Cliff Barnes, Mandy Winger, Mark Graison **12** Digger Barnes **13** Clayton Farlow, John Ross Ewing, Sue Ellen Ewing **16** Donna Culver Krebs **17** Pamela Barnes Ewing **22** Eleanor Southworth Ewing
  cast: 8 John Beck **9** Dack Rambo, Linda Gray **10** Howard Keel **11** Larry Hagman, Steve Kanaly, Susan Howard **12** Ken Kercheval, Patrick Duffy **16** Barbara Bel Geddes, Priscilla Presley **17** Victoria Principal
  ranch: 9 Southfork
  business: 3 oil **8** Ewing Oil

dalliance 6 affair, toying **7** romance **8** fiddling, trifling **10** flirtation, lovemaking

dally 3 toy **4** play **5** flirt **6** dawdle, loiter, trifle

Dalmatia *see* **10** Yugoslavia

Dalmatian (dog) 5 spots **12** firehouse dog **13** black and white

Dalton, John
  field: 7 physics **9** chemistry
  nationality: 7 British
  formulated: 12 atomic theory

first: 18 atomic weights table
described: 14 color blindness

dam 3 bar, cow **4** clog, mare, plug, stop, wall **5** bitch, block, check **6** bridle, hinder, hold in, impede, plug up, stanch, stop up **7** barrier, block up, confine, congest, inhibit, repress, stopper, stuff up **8** blockade, hold back, obstruct, restrain **9** barricade, hindrance **11** obstruction

damage, damages 3 mar **4** cost, harm, hurt, loss **6** impair, injure, injury, ravage **10** impairment, reparation, settlement **11** destruction **12** compensation, despoliation

damaging 7 harmful, hurtful, ruinous **9** injurious **11** destructive, detrimental

Damascus
ancient kingdom: 8 Aramaean
Arabic: 7 Dimashq
capital of: 5 Syria
monastery: 22 Suleiman the Magnificent
mosque: 5 Great **7** Umayyad
mount: 6 Qasyun
museum: 8 National **9** Qasr al-Azm
river: 4 Awaj **6** Barada
rulers: 5 Arabs, Timur **6** Romans **7** Mongols, Saladin **8** Assyrian **9** Caliphate, Seleucids **12** Ottoman Turks **15** Byzantine Empire **17** Alexander the Great
tomb: 7 Saladin

Damastes *see* **10** Procrustes

Dame Pliant
character in: 12 The Alchemist
author: 6 Jonson

Damia
spirit of: 9 fertility

damn 4 doom **5** blast **6** rail at **7** censure, condemn **8** denounce **9** criticize, disparage

damned 4 lost **6** cursed, darned, doomed, fallen **7** doggone, dratted, godless **8** accursed, doggoned **9** condemned, execrated, reprobate **12** unregenerate

Damocles
of: 8 Syracuse
offended: 9 Dionysius
seated under: 14 suspended sword

Damon
friend: 7 Pythias

damp 3 wet **4** curb, dank, dash, dewy, dull, mist **5** check, foggy, humid, misty, moist, muggy, rainy, soggy, spoil **6** clammy, deaden, hamper, hinder, reduce, soaked, sodden **7** depress, drizzly, inhibit, sopping, wettish **8** dankness, diminish, dripping, humidity, moisture, restrain **9** mugginess, restraint **10** clamminess, discourage **14** discouragement

dampen 3 wet **4** mute **7** moisten, wet down

dampen one's spirits 5 daunt, un-

man **6** deject **7** depress **10** discourage, dishearten

damper 4 curb, mute **8** obstacle **9** hindrance, restraint **10** constraint, impediment, wet blanket **14** discouragement

damsel 4 girl, lass **6** maiden **9** young lady

damselfly
varieties: 8 forktail **10** civilbluet **11** black-winged, broad-winged **12** narrow-winged, spread-winged, violet dancer

dam up 4 clog, plug **5** block, choke **6** plug up, stop up **7** congest **8** obstruct

Dan
means: 5 judge
father: 5 Jacob
mother: 6 Bilhah
brother: 3 Gad **4** Levi **5** Asher, Judah **6** Joseph, Reuben, Simeon **7** Zebulun **8** Benjamin, Issachar, Naphtali
sister: 5 Dinah
descendant of: 6 Danite

Dana *see* **4** Danu

Dana, Richard Henry
author of: 21 Two Years Before the Mast

Danae
form: 6 maiden
father: 8 Acrisius
mother: 8 Eurydice
imprisoned by: 8 Acrisius
lover: 4 Zeus
son: 7 Perseus

Danai
members of: 6 Greeks **7** Argives

Danaides
daughters of: 6 Danaus
number of daughters: 5 fifty

Dan August
character: 9 (Sgt) Joe Rivera **14** (Sgt) Charles Wilentz **16** (Chief) George Untermeyer
cast: 9 Ned Romero **10** Norman Fell **12** Burt Reynolds **15** Richard Anderson

Danaus
ruler of: 5 Argos
father: 5 Belus
twin brother: 8 Aegyptus
daughters called: 8 Danaides
number of daughters: 5 fifty

dance 3 hop, jam **4** ball, jump, leap, prom, reel, skip **5** lindy, party, polka, twist **6** bounce, cavort, frolic, gambol, prance, square **7** fox-trot, perform **8** cakewalk **9** jitterbug **10** Charleston **11** Boston waltz **12** choreography, Virginia reel **15** hesitation waltz
Renaissance/17th century: 3 jig **5** galop, gigue **6** branle, pavane, redowa **7** bourree, gavotte, lancers, lavolta, mazurka **8** canaries, chaconne, courante, galliard, rigadoon, rigaudon, tourdion **9** allemande, passepied, polonaise, sarabande **10** danse basse, danse haute

18th century: 6 minuet **9** cotillion **11** contre danse **12** country dance
19th century: 5 waltz **9** quadrille
early 1900's: 7 foxtrot, one-step, two-step **8** bunny hug **10** turkey trot **11** grizzly bear
1920's: 5 tango **6** shimmy, toddle **10** Charleston **11** black bottom
1930's: 4 shag **5** conga, rumba, samba, Suzy-Q **7** pecking **8** big apple, lindy hop, trucking **9** jitterbug
1940's: 5 mambo **8** cha-cha
1950's and 1960's: 4 frug, go-go **5** twist **6** monkey **9** rock-'n'-roll
1970's: 5 disco
1980's: 7 lambada
1990's: 8 macarena
Argentine: 5 tango
Austrian: 13 schuhplattler
Balinese: 6 legong
Brazilian: 5 samba **6** maxixe **7** lambada
Cuban: 5 conga, rumba **6** cha-cha
Czech: 5 polka
Dominican: 8 marengue, merengue
folk: 6 Morris **7** maypole
French: 6 can-can **8** galliard **9** ecossaise
German: 11 schottische
Indian: 6 kathak **8** manipuri **9** kathakali **13** bharata nat yam
Japanese: 6 bugaku **7** dengaku **8** sarugaku
dance/theater: 2 no **3** noh **6** kabuki
Mexican: 3 hat
Polish: 7 mazurka **9** krakoviak, polonaise **11** varsovienne
Scottish: 5 sword
Siamese: 6 wayang wong
Spanish: 4 jota **6** bolero **8** flamenco **9** sevillana **10** seguidilla
modern dancer/choreographer: 4 Juba **8** Ted Shawn **9** Eliot Feld, Gene Kelly, Ray Bolger **10** Alvin Ailey, Mary Wigman, Paul Draper, Twyla Tharp **11** Anna Sokolow, Antony Tudor, Eric Hawkins, Fred Astaire, Irene Castle, Ruth St Denis **12** Bill Robinson, Ginger Rogers, Martha Graham, Vernon Castle **13** Alwin Nikolais, Doris Humphrey, Isadora Duncan **14** Charles Weidman **15** Merce Cunningham
see also **6** ballet

dance of death
French: 12 danse macabre

Dandelion Wine
author: 11 Ray Bradbury

dander 3 ire **5** anger, Irish **6** temper

Dandie Dinmont terrier 24 soft-coated wheaten terrier, Staffordshire bull terrier, West Highland white terrier

dandy 3 fop **4** beau, dude, fine **5** beaut, great, super, swell **6** beauty, superb **7** coxcomb, peacock **8** terrific **9** excellent **12** clotheshorse

danger 4 risk **5** peril **6** hazard, menace, threat **8** jeopardy **12** endangerment

dangerous 5 hairy, risky **6** chancy, unsafe **8** menacing, perilous **9** hazardous **10** precarious **11** threatening, treacherous

danger signal 5 alarm, alert **7** red flag, warning

dangle 3 sag **4** drag, hang, sway **5** droop, swing, trail **6** depend **7** draggle, hang out, suspend **8** hang down, hang over **9** oscillate

Daniel
Babylonian name: **12** Belteshazzar
companion: **7** Meshach **8** Abednego, Shadrach

Daniel Boone
character: **5** Mingo **6** Yadkin **11** Cincinnatus, Israel Boone, Jemima Boone **12** Rebecca Boone
cast: **6** Ed Ames **10** Fess Parker **11** Albert Salmi, Dal McKennon, Darby Hinton **13** Patricia Blair **18** Veronica Cartwright

Danielovitch, Issur
real name of: **11** Kirk Douglas

dank 3 wet **4** cold, damp **5** humid, moist, muggy, soggy **6** chilly, clammy, sodden, sticky

danke 8 thank you

danke schon 16 thank you very much

dankness 4 damp **7** wetness **8** dampness, humidity **9** humidness, moistness, mugginess **10** clamminess

Danner, Blythe
born: **14** Philadelphia PA
roles: **8** Betrayal **15** The Great Santini **16** Man Woman and Child
daughter: **14** Gwyneth Paltrow

Danny Deever
story in: **18** Barrack-Room Ballads
author: **14** Rudyard Kipling

Danny Thomas Show, The
character: **6** Clancy **12** Uncle Tonoose **13** Danny Williams, Linda Williams, Rusty Williams, Terry Williams **16** Mrs Kathy Williams **18** Uncle Charley Halper
cast: **9** Sid Melton **10** Rusty Hamer **11** Hans Conried **12** Marjorie Lord, Penney Parker **13** Sherry Jackson **16** Angela Cartwright

danse macabre 12 dance of death

Dante (Alighieri)
author of: **9** Vita Nuova **15** The Divine Comedy
Divine Comedy Part I: **10** The Inferno
Divine Comedy Part II: **9** Purgatory **10** Purgatorio
Divine Comedy Part III: **8** Paradise, Paradiso
heroine: **8** Beatrice
guide: **6** Virgil

Dantes, Edmond
character in: **21** The Count of Monte Cristo
author: **5** Dumas (pere)

Danton, Ray
born: **9** New York NY
roles: **14** I'll Cry Tomorrow **18** The George Raft Story **27** The Rise and Fall of Legs Diamond

Danu
also: **4** Dana
origin: **5** Irish
mother of: **14** Tuatha De Danann

Danvers, Mrs
character in: **7** Rebecca
author: **9** Du Maurier
played by: **14** Judith Anderson

Daphnaea
epithet of: **7** Artemis
means: **11** of the laurel

Daphne
form: **5** nymph
father: **5** Ladon **6** Peneus
pursued by: **6** Apollo **9** Leucippus
changed into: **7** bay tree

Daphnis
occupation: **7** cowherd **8** shepherd
father: **6** Hermes
originated: **14** pastoral poetry
blinded by: **5** Nomia

Daphnis and Chloe
characters in: **12** Greek romance
author: **6** Longus

Daphnis et Chloe
ballet by: **5** Ravel
choreographer: **12** Michel Fokine

dapper 4 neat, trim **5** natty, smart **6** jaunty, modish, spiffy, sporty, spruce **7** stylish

dapple 3 dab, dot **4** spot **6** mottle

dappled 7 flecked, mottled, spotted **10** variegated

Darcy, Fitzwilliam
character in: **17** Pride and Prejudice
author: **6** Austen

Dardanus
father: **4** Zeus
mother: **7** Electra
twin brother: **6** Iasion
wife: **6** Myrina
son: **12** Erechthonius
ancestor of: **7** Trojans

dare 3 bet **4** defy **5** taunt **7** venture **9** challenge **11** provocation

daredevil 4 bold, rash **5** risky **8** heedless, reckless, stuntman **9** audacious, breakneck, risk-taker **11** adventurous, Evel Knievel **12** death-defying, devil-may-care **13** adventuresome

daredevilry 6 daring **8** rashness **9** derring-do **10** imprudence **12** carelessness, heedlessness, recklessness **13** foolhardiness

Dar es Salaam
former capital of: **8** Tanzania

Darien *see* **8** Colombia

daring 4 bold, game **5** brave **6** plucky

7 bravery, courage, gallant, valiant **8** audacity, boldness, intrepid **9** audacious, dauntless, undaunted **10** courageous **11** adventurous, venturesome **13** audaciousness **15** adventurousness

daring deed 4 feat **7** exploit **11** achievement

dark 3 dim **4** deep, evil, inky **5** angry, black, bleak, dingy, dusky, murky, night, shady **6** dismal, dreary, gloomy, hidden, opaque, secret, somber, sullen, wicked **7** evening, joyless, obscure, ominous, shadowy, sunless **8** eventide, frowning, hopeless, overcast, sinister, twilight **9** concealed, nightfall, nighttime, sorrowful **10** forbidding **11** threatening **12** discouraging **13** disheartening

darken 3 dim, dye **4** tint **5** cloud, color **6** sadden **7** blacken, obscure **8** dispirit

darkened 3 dim **5** dusky, unlit **6** cloudy, gloomy **7** clouded **9** blackened, tenebrous, unlighted **10** blacked out **13** unilluminated

darkening 7 eclipse, shading **8** clouding, lowering **9** obscuring, shadowing **10** blackening **12** clouding over

Dark Frontier, The
author: **10** Eric Ambler

dark-hued 5 black, dusky, ebony, raven **6** somber **7** swarthy

Dark Is Light Enough, The
author: **14** Christopher Fry

Dark Lady, The
author: **16** Louis Auchincloss

Dark Laughter
author: **16** Sherwood Anderson

darkness 4 dusk **5** night, shade **7** dimness, evening **8** eventide, twilight **9** blackness, nightfall, nighttime

Darkness at Noon
author: **14** Arthur Koestler

Darkness Visible
author: **14** William Golding

Dark Victory
director: **14** Edmund Goulding
cast: **10** Bette Davis **11** George Brent **12** Ronald Reagan **14** Humphrey Bogart **19** Geraldine Fitzgerald
remade as: **11** Stolen Hours

darling 4 cute, dear, love **5** loved, sweet **6** adored, lovely **7** beloved, dearest, lovable **8** adorable, charming, precious **9** cherished **10** attractive, enchanting, sweetheart **11** captivating

Darling
director: **15** John Schlesinger
cast: **11** Dirk Bogarde **13** Julie Christie **14** Laurence Harvey
Oscar for: **6** script **7** actress (Christie)

Darling, Wendy
character in: **8** Peter Pan
author: **6** Barrie

darn 4 damn, dang, dash, drat, mend **5** blast, patch, sew up **6** hang it, stitch

7 consarn, doggone, goldang **8** confound **10** confound it

Darnay, Charles
character in: **16** A Tale of Two Cities
author: **7** Dickens

darnel 12 Biblical weed

Darnell, Linda
real name: **20** Monetta Eloyse Darnell
born: **8** Dallas TX
roles: **12** Blood and Sand, Forever Amber **14** The Mark of Zorro **17** Unfaithfully Yours

Darren, James
real name: **13** James Ercolani
born: **14** Philadelphia PA
roles: **6** Gidget **13** The Time Tunnel

dart 3 run **4** bolt, dash, flit, jump, leap, race, rush, tear **5** bound, fling, hurry, spear, spurt **6** hasten, spring, sprint **7** javelin, missile **10** projectile

D'Artagnan
character in: **18** The Three Musketeers
author: **5** Dumas (pere)

Dartle, Rosa
character in: **16** David Copperfield
author: **7** Dickens

Darwin, Charles
author of: **15** The Descent of Man **18** The Origin of Species **20** The Voyage of the Beagle
studied: **16** Galapagos Islands
field: **6** nature **7** biology
nationality: **7** British
theory of: **9** evolution **16** natural selection
ship: **6** Beagle

dash 3 bit, run, zip **4** bolt, dart, drop, elan, foil, hurl, race, ruin, rush, slam, tear, zeal **5** bound, crash, flair, fling, hurry, oomph, pinch, smash, speed, spoil, throw, touch, verve, vigor **6** dampen, energy, hasten, pizazz, spirit, splash, sprint, thrust, thwart **7** a little, panache, shatter, soupcon, spatter **8** splatter, splinter, vivacity **9** animation, frustrate **10** disappoint, discourage

dashing 4 bold **5** brave **6** daring, plucky **7** gallant **8** fearless, spirited, unafraid **9** audacious, impetuous **10** courageous **13** swashbuckling

dash one's hopes 5 daunt, unman **6** deject **7** depress **8** dispirit **10** discourage, dishearten

Dashwood, Elinor and Marianne
characters in: **19** Sense and Sensibility
author: **6** Austen

Da Silva, Howard
real name: **17** Harold Silverblatt
born: **11** Cleveland OH
roles: **8** Oklahoma **12** Sergeant York **14** The Great Gatsby **20** Abe Lincoln in Illinois

Dass, Secundra
character in: **21** The Master of

Ballantrae
author: **9** Stevenson

dastard 3 cad **6** coward, craven **7** bounder, caitiff, chicken **8** poltroon **11** yellow-belly

dastardly 3 low **4** base, mean, vile **6** sneaky **8** cowardly, shameful **9** atrocious **10** despicable

data 4 dope, info **5** facts, input **7** dossier, figures **8** evidence **9** documents **11** information

Datchery, Mr
character in: **22** The Mystery of Edwin Drood
author: **7** Dickens

date 3 age, era **5** court, epoch, stage **6** escort, period **7** partner, take out **9** companion, originate **10** engagement, rendezvous **11** appointment

date 18 Phoenix dactylifera
varieties: **5** cliff **6** Ceylon **7** Chinese **9** Jerusalem **12** Canary Island

dated 5 passe **6** old hat **8** obsolete, outmoded **9** out-of-date **10** antiquated **12** old-fashioned **13** unfashionable

daub 4 blot, coat, soil, spot **5** cover, dirty, paint, smear, stain **6** blotch, smirch, smudge **7** splotch

Daudet, Alphonse
author of: **6** Sappho **15** The Woman of Arles **17** Letters from My Mill **18** Tartarin of Tarascon

Daughter of the Regiment, The
opera by: **9** Donizetti

Daumier, Honore
born: **6** France **10** Marseilles
artwork: **7** Bathers **9** Gargantua **12** Men of Justice **13** Bluestockings **14** The Washerwoman **16** The Good Bourgeois **18** The Legislative Body **19** Professors and Pupils **20** Stories from Antiquity **21** The Third-Class Carriage

daunt 3 cow **4** dash, faze **5** abash, alarm, scare **6** deject, dismay, menace, subdue **7** depress, unnerve **8** affright, browbeat, frighten, threaten **10** discourage, dishearten, intimidate

dauntless 4 bold **5** brave, gutsy **6** daring, heroic **7** gallant, valiant **8** fearless, resolute, unafraid, valorous **10** courageous **12** stouthearted

dauntlessness 4 grit, guts, sand **5** nerve, pluck, spunk, valor **6** daring, mettle **7** bravery, courage, resolve **8** boldness **9** fortitude **10** resolution **12** fearlessness, resoluteness **16** stoutheartedness

Davers, Lady
character in: **6** Pamela
author: **10** Richardson

David 6 statue
by: **12** Michelangelo
site: **8** Florence
size: **6** heroic

David

king of: **6** Israel
father: **5** Jesse
wife: **6** Maacah, Michal **7** Abigail, Ahinoam, Haggith **9** Bathsheba
son: **5** Amnon **7** Absalom, Chileab, Solomon **8** Adonijah
daughter: **5** Tamar
brother: **5** Eliab **7** Shammah **8** Abinadab
sister: **7** Abigail
friend: **5** Abner **8** Jonathan
nephew: **5** Amasa
city of: **9** Bethlehem, Jerusalem
anointed by: **6** Samuel
killed: **7** Goliath
wrote: **6** Psalms
comforter: **7** Abishag
conspirators against: **4** Joab **8** Abiathar, Adonijah
pertaining to: **7** Davidic

David, Jacques-Louis
born: **5** Paris **6** France
artwork: **13** Mme de Verninac **15** The Death of Marat **19** The Oath of the Horatii **23** The Coronation of Napoleon **26** View of the Luxembourg Gardens **31** The Intervention of the Sabine Women

David Copperfield
author: **14** Charles Dickens
character: **3** Ham **6** Barkis, Mr Dick **7** Creakle **8** Traddles **9** Mr Spenlow, Uriah Heep **10** Aunt Betsey, Little Em'ly, Mr Micawber, Rosa Dartle, Steerforth **11** Dora Spenlow, Little Emily, Mr Murdstone, Mr Wickfield, Mrs Gummidge **13** Clara Peggotty **14** Agnes Wickfield, Betsey Trotwood
director: **11** George Cukor
cast: **8** W C Fields **10** Madge Evans **11** Frank Lawton, Roland Young **13** Basil Rathbone, Edna May Oliver **15** Lionel Barrymore **16** Maureen O'Sullivan **18** Freddie Bartholomew

David Harum
author: **19** Edward Noyes Westcott

Davies, Arthur Bowen
born: **7** Utica NY
artwork: **5** Dream **8** Unicorns **9** Crescendo **13** Every Saturday **15** Dancing Children, Sacramental Tree **17** Along the Erie Canal **18** Leda and the Dioscuri

Davies, Marion
real name: **19** Marion Cecilia Douras
lover: **21** William Randolph Hearst
born: **10** Brooklyn NY
roles: **12** Cain and Mable **13** Runaway Romany **15** Tillie the Toiler

Da Vinci, Leonardo
born: **5** Italy, Vinci
artwork: **8** Mona Lisa **10** La Gioconda **13** The Last Supper **15** The Annunciation **19** The Battle of Anghiari **21** The Adoration of the Magi

Davis, Bette

real name: 18 Ruth Elizabeth Davis
husband: 11 Gary Merrill
born: 8 Lowell MA
roles: 7 Jezebel (Oscar) **9** Dangerous (Oscar), The Letter **10** Now Voyager, The Old Maid **11** All About Eve, Dark Victory **14** Of Human Bondage, The Little Foxes **18** The Petrified Forest **22** Hush Hush Sweet Charlotte **26** What Ever Happened to Baby Jane?

Davis, H L
author of: 14 Honey in the Horn

Davis, Ossie
wife: 7 Ruby Dee
born: 9 Cogdell GA
author: 16 Purlie Victorious
roles/films: 7 Jamaica **15** A Raisin in the Sun **18** No Time for Sergeants **19** Cotton Comes to Harlem

Davis, Sammy Jr
wife: 8 May Britt
group: 14 Will Master Trio
born: 9 New York NY
autobiography: 7 Yes I Can
roles: 11 Mr Wonderful **12** Porgy and Bess **20** The Benny Goodman Story

Davis, Stuart
born: 14 Philadelphia PA
artwork: 4 Visa **9** Eggbeater **11** Lucky Strike, Ready to Wear **11** Owh! In Sao Pao **12** The Mellow Pad **14** Colonial Cubism **15** Cigarette Papers

Davy, Humphrey
field: 9 chemistry
nationality: 7 British
isolated: 5 boron **6** barium, sodium **7** calcium **8** chlorine **9** magnesium, potassium, strontium
invented: 8 Davy lamp **10** miner's lamp

dawdle 4 idle, loaf **5** dally, delay **6** loiter **10** dillydally **12** putter around **13** procrastinate

dawdler
French: 7 flaneur

dawdling
French: 8 flanerie

dawn 4 rise **5** begin, birth, occur, start, sunup **6** advent, appear, Aurora, emerge, origin, strike, unfold **7** develop, sunrise **8** commence, daybreak, daylight **9** beginning, emergence, inception, unfolding **12** commencement
god of: 8 Heimdall
goddess of: 3 Eos **6** Aurore, Matuta

dawning 5 sunup **7** morning, sunrise **8** daybreak, daylight

Dawn Patrol, The
director: 14 Edmund Goulding
cast: 10 David Niven, Errol Flynn **11** Donald Crisp **13** Basil Rathbone **14** Melville Cooper **15** Barry Fitzgerald

day 3 age, era **4** date, time **5** epoch **6** period

Day, Clarence (Jr)
author of: 14 God and My Father, Life with Father, Life with Mother

Day, Doris
real name: 18 Doris von Kappelhoff
born: 12 Cincinnati OH
autobiography: 19 Doris Day Her Own Story
roles: 10 Pillow Talk **12** Calamity Jane **13** The Pajama Game **15** Move Over Darling, The Doris Day Show **23** Please Don't Eat the Daisies

daybed 5 couch **6** lounge **12** chaise longue

day book 3 log **5** diary **6** agenda **7** journal **8** calendar, schedule

daybreak 4 dawn, morn **5** sunup **7** sunrise

daydream 4 muse **5** fancy **7** fantasy, imagine, reverie **9** fantasize **10** woolgather **14** castle in the air

Day for Night
director: 16 Francois Truffaut
cast: 15 Jean-Pierre Leaud **16** Francois Truffaut, Jacqueline Bisset, Jean-Pierre Aumont
Oscar for: 11 foreign film

daylight 4 dawn **5** sunup **7** morning, sunrise **8** full view, openness, sunlight, sunshine

Days and Nights
author: 17 Konstantin Simonov

day's end 3 een, eve **4** dusk, even **6** sunset **7** evening, sundown **8** gleaming, twilight **9** nightfall

Days of Heaven
director: 14 Terrence Malick
cast: 9 Linda Manz **10** Sam Shepard **11** Brooke Adams, Richard Gere
Oscar for: 14 cinematography

Days of Wine and Roses
director: 12 Blake Edwards
cast: 9 Lee Remick **10** Jack Lemmon **11** Jack Klugman **15** Charles Bickford
score: 12 Henry Mancini

daze 4 numb, stun **5** amaze, shock **6** benumb, dazzle, excite, muddle, stupor **7** astound, confuse, stagger, startle, stupefy **8** astonish, bewilder, surprise **9** disorient, electrify **11** flabbergast **12** astonishment, bewilderment, blow one's mind **14** discombobulate

dazed 5 woozy **6** groggy **7** confused, dazzled, stunned **9** befuddled, stupefied **10** bewildered, punch-drunk

dazzle 3 awe **4** blur, daze **5** blind **6** excite **7** confuse, overawe **9** electrify, overpower, overwhelm

dazzling 7 radiant **8** blinding **9** sparkling **10** impressive, staggering **11** coruscating **12** breathtaking, electrifying, overwhelming **14** flabbergasting

deacon 6 cleric **9** churchman, clergyman **12** ecclesiastic

deactivate 6 defuse **9** switch off **10** neutralize

Dead, The
author: 10 James Joyce

dead, the dead 4 beat, cold, dull, flat **5** depth, exact, midst, quiet, spent, tired, total, utter, vapid **6** entire, middle, unused **7** defunct, expired, extinct, insipid, precise, useless, utterly, worn-out **8** abruptly, absolute, complete, deceased, entirely, inactive, lifeless, obsolete, perished, stagnant, suddenly, thorough, unerring **9** exhausted, inanimate, inorganic **10** absolutely, completely, lackluster, unemployed, unexciting **11** ineffectual, inoperative **12** unproductive, unprofitable
Latin: 8 ad patres
god of: 6 Osiris **7** Veiovis

dead body 5 stiff **6** corpse **7** cadaver, remains

deaden 4 dope, drug, dull, mute, numb **5** abate, blunt **6** lessen, muffle, soothe, subdue, weaken **7** assuage, smother **8** diminish, mitigate, moderate **9** alleviate **11** anesthetize

deadened 5 muted **6** dulled, numbed **7** muffled, subdued

Dead Father, The
author: 15 Donald Barthelme

Dea Dia
origin: 5 Roman
goddess of: 11 agriculture
corresponds to: 13 Acca Laurentia

deadlock 7 impasse **8** standoff **9** stalemate **10** standstill

deadly 3 wan **4** dull **5** ashen, awful, fatal, fully, undue **6** boring, lethal, mortal, pallid **7** awfully, baneful, destroy, extreme, ghostly, tedious, totally **8** dreadful, entirely, horribly, terrible, terribly, tiresome **9** excessive, malignant, wearisome **10** cadaverous, completely, implacable, inordinate, relentless, thoroughly **11** destructive, unrelenting

deadpan 5 sober **8** detached **9** impassive **10** poker-faced **11** unemotional **13** straight-faced

dead ringer 4 copy, mate, twin **6** double **9** duplicate **11** counterpart **12** doppelganger **13** spitting image

Dead Souls
author: 12 Nikolai Gogol

dead to the world 6 asleep **7** out cold **9** konked out **10** fast asleep, slumbering **11** sound asleep

dead weight 7 ballast **9** inert mass

Dead Zone, The
author: 11 Stephen King

deal 3 act **4** give, hand **5** round, see to, trade, treat **6** behave, handle, market **7** bargain, concern, deliver, dole out, give out, mete out, oversee **8** consider, dispense **9** agreement, apportion **10** administer, distribute **11** arrangement **12** distribution **13** apportionment

dealer 5 agent **6** monger, trader, vendor **8** merchant **10** trafficker **11** distributor

dealing, dealings 5 trade **7** traffic **8** business, practice **9** relations, treatment **12** transactions

dealing out 8 dividing **9** allotting, bestowing **10** conferring, consigning, dispensing **12** apportioning, distributing

Dea Marica see **6** Marica

Dean, Dizzy (Jay Hanna)
 sport: **8** baseball
 position: **7** pitcher
 team: **16** St Louis Cardinals
 part of: **12** Gashouse Gang
 brother: **4** Paul

Dean, James (Jimmy)
 real name: **14** James Byron Dean
 born: **8** Marion IN
 roles: **5** Giant **10** East of Eden **18** Rebel Without a Cause

Deane, Seneca
 character in: **7** Babbitt
 author: **5** Lewis

Dean's December
 author: **10** Saul Bellow

dear 4 love **5** angel, loved **6** costly **7** beloved, darling **8** esteemed, favorite, precious **9** cherished, expensive, respected **10** sweetheart
 French: **5** cheri **6** cherie

Dear Antoine
 author: **11** Jean Anouilh

Dear Brutus
 author: **12** James M Barrie

dearest 7 beloved, darling

dearth 4 lack **7** paucity **8** scarcity, shortage **10** deficiency

death, Death 5 dying **6** demise **7** decease, passing **9** departure **10** expiration, grim reaper
 goddess of: **3** Hel **7** Berchta, Perchta **10** Ereshkigal

Death Be Not Proud
 author: **9** John Donne

death blow
 French: **11** coup de grace

Death Comes for the Archbishop
 author: **11** Willa Cather
 character: **7** Jacinto **9** Kit Carson **16** Bishop Jean Latour **20** Father Joseph Vaillant

death-dealing 5 fatal **6** lethal, mortal **7** killing **11** destructive

death-defying 4 bold, rash **5** risky **6** daring **8** reckless **9** audacious, breakneck, daredevil

Death in the Family, A
 author: **9** James Agee
 filmed as: **13** All the Way Home

Death in Venice
 director: **15** Luchino Visconti

 author: **10** Thomas Mann
 cast: **9** Mark Burns **11** Dirk Bogarde **14** Marisa Berenson

deathless 7 eternal **8** immortal **9** perpetual **11** everlasting

deathlike 3 wan **4** pale **5** ashen **6** pallid **7** ghastly **9** bloodless **10** cadaverous, corpselike

deathly 4 very **7** extreme, intense **8** terrible **9** extremely **12** overwhelming **15** resembling death

Death of a Salesman
 director: **12** Laslo Benedek
 author: **12** Arthur Miller
 character: **4** Biff **5** Happy, Linda **7** Bernard, Charley **8** Uncle Ben **10** Willy Loman
 cast: **13** Frederic March, Kevin McCarthy **14** Mildred Dunnock **15** Cameron Mitchell

Death of Ivan Ilyich, The
 author: **10** Leo Tolstoy

Death of the Gods, The
 author: **17** Dmitri Merejkowski

Death of the Heart
 author: **14** Elizabeth Bowen

Death on the Nile
 author: **14** Agatha Christie

Death Takes a Holiday
 director: **14** Mitchell Leisen
 cast: **11** Guy Standing **13** Evelyn Venable, Frederic March (Death)

Death Valley Days
 host: **12** Robert Taylor, Ronald Reagan **13** Dale Robertson **14** Stanley Andrews

debacle 4 rout, ruin **5** havoc, wreck **8** collapse, disaster, downfall **9** breakdown, cataclysm, overthrow, ruination **10** bankruptcy **11** catastrophe, devastation, dissolution **12** vanquishment **14** disintegration

debar 3 ban **6** reject **7** exclude, keep out **8** preclude, prohibit **9** blackball, blacklist

debark 4 land

debarment 7 removal **8** omission **9** exception, exclusion, exemption, rejection **11** elimination, prohibition **12** nonadmission

debase 5 lower **6** befoul, defile **7** corrupt, degrade **8** disgrace, dishonor **9** desecrate **10** adulterate **11** deteriorate **16** impair the worth of **18** reduce the quality of

debased 4 vile **6** impure **7** corrupt, defiled, lowered **8** degraded, depraved **9** debauched, disgraced, dissolute, perverted **10** degenerate, dissipated **11** adulterated

debasement 9 decadence, depravity **10** corruption, debauchery, degeneracy, immorality, perversion **13** dissoluteness

debatable 4 iffy **6** unsure **7** dubious **8** arguable, doubtful **9** uncertain, unde-

cided **10** disputable **12** questionable **13** problematical

debate 5 argue **6** ponder **7** discuss, dispute, reflect **8** argument, cogitate, consider, hash over **10** cogitation, deliberate, discussion, meditation, reflection, think about **12** deliberation, meditate upon **13** consideration

debauch 4 orgy **5** revel, spree **6** debase **7** carouse, corrupt, deprave, revelry, subvert **8** carousal **9** bacchanal **10** lead astray, saturnalia

debauched 4 lewd **6** wanton **7** corrupt, debased, immoral **8** degraded, depraved, perverse, vitiated **9** abandoned, corrupted, dissolute, lecherous, led astray, pervert- ed, reprobate, shameless **10** degenerate, dissipated, lascivious, libidinous, licentious, profligate **12** disreputable

debauchery 6 excess **11** dissipation **12** immoderation, intemperance **14** self-indulgence

DeBeck, Billy
 creator/artist of: **12** Barney Google **20** Parlor Bedroom and Sink

debilitate 6 weaken **7** wear out **8** enervate **10** devitalize, make feeble **17** deprive of strength

debilitated 5 frail **6** feeble, infirm **7** worn out **8** delicate, weakened **9** enervated **11** devitalized

debilitation 8 handicap, weakness **9** infirmity **10** affliction, disability, impairment, inadequacy **11** disablement

debility 7 fatigue, frailty **8** asthenia, handicap, senility, weakness **9** infirmity, lassitude, weakening **10** affliction, enervation, exhaustion, feebleness, impairment, invalidism, sickliness **11** decrepitude, prostration

debit 4 debt **6** red ink **7** account, payable **9** liability **10** balance due, obligation **11** ledger entry, shortcoming

debonair 5 suave **6** dapper, jaunty, urbane **7** buoyant, elegant, genteel, refined **8** carefree, charming, gracious, well-bred **9** sprightly **11** free and easy **12** lighthearted **13** sophisticated

Deborah 11 Hebrew judge
 companion: **7** Rebekah
 summoned: **5** Barak

debouch 5 drain **6** emerge, let out **7** flow out **9** discharge

debris 4 crap, junk **5** dreck, dregs, dross, ruins, scrap, trash, waste **6** litter, rubble, shards **7** clutter, garbage, rubbish **8** detritus, wreckage **9** fragments

debt 4 bill **5** debit **7** arrears **9** liability **10** obligation **15** deferred payment, that which is owed

debunk 4 bare **5** strip **6** expose, send up, show up, unmask **7** deflate, lampoon, take off, uncloak, uncover

8 ridicule, satirize **9** burlesque, demystify, disparage **13** demythologize

Debussy, Claude Achille
  born: 6 France **15** St Germain-en-Laye
  composer of: 5 La Mer **6** Gigues, Iberia, Images **8** Estampes **9** Nocturnes, Printemps **11** Clair de Lune **13** En Blanc et Noir **15** Children's Corner, L'Enfant prodigue **16** La Demoiselle Elue, Suite Bergamasque **17** Rondes de Printemps, The Blessed Damozel **18** Pelleas et Melisande **24** The Girl with the Flaxen Hair **26** Prelude a l'apres-midi d'un faune **28** Prelude to the Afternoon of a Faun

debut 9 coming out **12** presentation

decadence 5 decay **7** decline **10** corruption, debasement, degeneracy, immorality **12** degeneration **13** deterioration

decadent 7 corrupt, debased, immoral **8** decaying, depraved, perverse **9** debauched, dissolute, perverted **10** degenerate
  French: 11 fin de siecle

Decalogue 15 Ten Commandments

Decameron, The
  author: 17 Giovanni Boccaccio

decamp 7 move off, run away, take off **8** march off, sneak off

decampment 6 escape, flight **7** getaway

decant 4 pour **7** draw off, pour out

decanter 6 bottle, carafe, vessel

decathlon winner 11 Bruce Jenner

Decatur, Stephen
  served in: 11 Algerine War, Barbary Wars **13** Tripolitan War **19** War of Eighteen Twelve
  commander of ship: 12 United States
  defeated ship: 10 Macedonian (British)
  saying: 22 "Our country right or wrong"

decay 3 rot **5** spoil **7** corrode, putrefy, rotting **8** spoiling **9** decompose **12** disintegrate, putrefaction **13** decomposition
  goddess of: 4 Hour **5** Horae

decayed 3 bad **6** putrid, rotted, rotten, ruined **7** corrupt, gone bad, spoiled **10** decomposed **12** deteriorated **13** disintegrated

deceased *see* **4** dead

deceit 5 fraud **8** cheating, trickery **9** duplicity **10** dishonesty, trickiness **11** fraudulence **13** double-dealing **15** underhandedness **17** misrepresentation

deceitful 5 false **6** crafty, sneaky, tricky **7** cunning **9** dishonest, insincere **11** duplicitous, treacherous, underhanded **12** hypocritical **13** double-dealing, untrustworthy

deceive 3 con **4** fool **5** cheat, put on,

trick **6** delude **7** defraud, mislead, swindle

deceiver 4 fake **5** cheat, fraud, quack **6** con man **7** cozener **8** impostor, swindler **9** charlatan, trickster **10** mountebank **13** confidence man

decelerate 5 brake **8** slow down

deceleration 7 braking, slowing

December
  event: 11 Pearl Harbor (7), Winter solstice (21, 22)
  flower: 5 holly **9** narcissus
  French: 8 Decembre
  gem: 4 ruby **6** zircon **9** turquoise
  German: 8 Dezember
  holiday: 8 Hanukkah **9** Boxing Day (26), Christmas (25) **16** Saint Nicholas Day (6)
  Italian: 8 Dicembre
  number of days: 9 thirty-one
  origin of name: 5 decem (Latin meaning ten)
  place in year:
    Gregorian: 7 twelfth
    Roman: 5 tenth
    Julian: 7 twelfth
  Spanish: 9 Diciembre
  Zodiac sign: 9 Capricorn **11** Sagittarius

decency 7 decorum, modesty **9** propriety **14** respectability **15** appropriateness

decent 4 fair, nice **5** ample **6** proper, seemly **7** correct, fitting **8** adequate, gracious, obliging, passable, suitable **9** courteous **10** acceptable, sufficient **11** appropriate **12** satisfactory **13** accommodating

deception 3 con **4** scam **5** fraud, sting, trick **7** cunning, slyness **8** artifice, illusion, trickery **9** duplicity, falseness, hypocrisy, treachery **10** craftiness, dishonesty, sneakiness, trickiness **11** fraudulence, insincerity **13** deceitfulness, double-dealing **15** underhandedness **17** untrustworthiness

deceptive 5 phony **9** dishonest **10** fraudulent, misleading

decibel
  abbreviation: 2 dB

decide 4 rule **5** elect, judge **6** choose, decree, select, settle **7** resolve **9** determine

decided 4 firm **7** certain **8** clear-cut, definite, emphatic, resolute **9** assertive **10** deliberate, determined, unwavering **12** indisputable, strong-willed, unhesitating, unmistakable **14** unquestionable

decidedly 9 certainly **10** absolutely **11** indubitably, undoubtedly **12** indisputably, unmistakably **13** unequivocally **14** unquestioningly

decidedness 7 purpose, resolve **10** resolution **12** resoluteness **13** determination **14** purposefulness

decide on 5 adopt, elect **6** choose, opt for, select, settle **7** appoint, arrange, embrace, espouse, pick out **8** settle on **9** deter- mine, establish, single out

decigram
  abbreviation: 2 dg

deciliter
  abbreviation: 2 dL

decimate 6 reduce **7** destroy **8** massacre **9** slaughter **13** greatly reduce

decimeter
  abbreviation: 2 dm

decipher 4 read **5** solve **6** decode, deduce, render **7** decrypt, dope out, explain, make out, unravel **8** construe, untangle **9** interpret, translate **12** cryptanalyze

decision 6 decree, ruling **7** finding, outcome, purpose, resolve, verdict **8** judgment **10** conclusion, resolution **12** resoluteness **13** determination **14** purposefulness

decisive 4 firm **5** final **8** absolute, definite, positive, resolute **10** conclusive, convincing, definitive, determined, undeniable **12** indisputable

decisive blow 9 deathblow **11** coup de grace

decisiveness 7 purpose, resolve **10** resolution **12** resoluteness **14** purposefulness

decisive point 3 nut **4** core, crux, gist **5** basis, heart **6** kernel **7** essence **9** essential

deck 4 garb, trim **5** adorn, array, dress, prank **6** clothe, doll up, enrich, outfit, tog out **7** apparel, bedizen, festoon, furbish, garnish, gussy up **8** accouter, beautify, ornament, spruce up **9** embellish

Decker, Mary
  sport: 7 running
  married name: 6 Slaney

deck out 5 adorn, array, dress **6** attire, clothe, fit out, outfit, rig out **7** costume

declaim 4 rail **5** orate **6** recite **7** inveigh **9** sermonize **11** pontificate

declaration 6 avowal, notice **8** document **9** assertion, statement, testimony **10** deposition **11** affirmation, attestation, publication **12** announcement, notification, proclamation **14** acknowledgment

declare 4 show **6** affirm, reveal **7** express **8** announce, proclaim **9** pronounce

declare null and void 6 cancel, repeal, revoke **7** abolish, rescind, retract **8** abrogate, set aside **9** repudiate **10** invalidate **11** countermand

declare untrue 4 deny **9** repudiate **10** contradict

decline 3 ebb **4** drop, fail, flag, sink, wane **5** decay, slump, spurn **6** balk at, eschew, lessen, refuse, reject, weaken, worsen **7** dwindle **8** decrease, diminish, downfall **9** downgrade, downswing **11** deteriorate **13** deterioration

Decline and Fall
    author: **11** Evelyn Waugh

Decline and Fall of the Roman Empire, The
    author: **12** Edward Gibbon

declivity 4 drop **5** slant, slope **6** plunge **7** descent

decompose 3 rot **5** decay, spoil **7** putrefy **8** separate **10** go to pieces **12** disintegrate

decomposed 6 putrid, rotted, rotten **7** decayed, spoiled **9** putrefied **13** disintegrated

decontaminate 6 purify **9** disinfect, sterilize

decor 13 ornamentation

decorate 4 trim **5** adorn, array, honor **7** festoon, garnish **8** beautify, ornament **9** embellish

decorated 5 fancy **6** decked, ornate **7** adorned, trimmed **8** bedecked **9** bemedaled, bedizened, garnished **10** ornamented **11** embellished

decoration 4 trim **5** award, badge, medal **6** emblem, ribbon **7** garnish **8** ornament, trimming **9** adornment **13** embellishment, ornamentation **14** beautification

decorous 3 fit **6** decent, polite, proper, seemly **7** correct **8** becoming, mannerly, suitable **9** dignified **10** respectful **11** appropriate

decorum 4 tact **5** taste **7** dignity **8** good form **9** gentility, propriety **10** politeness **14** respectability

decoy 4 bait, lure **5** plant, snare **6** allure, come-on, entice **10** enticement, inducement **11** smoke screen

decrease 4 drop, ease, loss **5** abate, taper **6** lessen, reduce **7** cutback, decline, dwindle, fall-off, slacken, subside **8** diminish **9** abatement, dwindling, lessening, reduction **10** de-escalate, diminution **12** de-escalation

decree 3 law **5** edict, order **6** dictum, ruling **7** command, mandate, statute **8** proclaim **9** authorize **12** proclamation

decrepit 7 rickety **8** battered **10** broken-down **11** dilapidated

decrescendo
    music: **22** gradually getting softer
    abbreviation: **4** decr

decry 7 censure, condemn **8** denounce **9** criticize, deprecate, disparage

Dedalus, Stephen
    character in: **7** Ulysses **30** Portrait of the Artist as a Young Man
    author: **5** Joyce

dedicate 6 commit, devote, launch, pledge **7** address, present **8** inscribe

dedication 8 devotion **10** commitment

11 devotedness **16** prefatory address **20** prefatory inscription

Dedlock, Sir Leicester and Lady
    characters in: **10** Bleak House
    author: **7** Dickens

deduce 5 infer **6** gather, reason **8** conclude **10** comprehend, understand

deduct 4 take **6** remove **8** subtract, take from, withdraw **10** decrease by

deduction 5 guess **6** belief, credit, rebate **7** removal **8** analysis, decrease, discount, judgment, markdown, rollback **9** abatement, allowance, exemption, gathering, inference, lessening, reasoning, reduction **10** assumption, concession, conclusion, diminuition, hypothesis, reflection, taking away, withdrawal **11** calculation, presumption, speculation, subtraction, supposition **13** comprehension, consideration, understanding **14** interpretation

Dee, Ruby
    real name: **14** Ruby Ann Wallace
    husband: **10** Ossie Davis
    born: **11** Cleveland OH
    roles: **15** A Raisin in the Sun **16** Purlie Victorious

Dee, Sandra
    real name: **13** Alexandra Zuck
    husband: **10** Bobby Darin
    born: **9** Bayonne NJ
    roles: **6** Gidget **12** A Summer Place **15** Tammy Tell Me True

deed 3 act **4** feat **5** title **6** action, effort **11** achievement **14** accomplishment

deeds are manly, words are womanish
    Italian: **24** fatti maschii parole femine
    motto of: **8** Maryland

deem 4 hold, view **5** judge, think **6** regard **7** believe **8** consider

de-emphasize 8 play down **9** underplay

deep 3 far, sea **4** dark, late, lost, rich, wise **5** far in, midst, ocean, vivid **6** astute, strong **7** extreme, intense, learned **8** absorbed, immersed, involved, profound, resonant, sonorous **9** engrossed, sagacious **10** discerning **11** intelligent **13** philosophical

Deep, The
    author: **13** Peter Benchley

deeply 6 richly **7** acutely, gravely, greatly, vividly **8** entirely **9** intensely, seriously **10** completely, profoundly, resonantly, sonorously, thoroughly **12** passionately

deeply felt 6 ardent, fervid **7** earnest, fervent, intense, sincere, zealous **9** heartfelt **10** passionate **11** impassioned **12** wholehearted

deepness 10 profundity

deep-rooted 7 abiding, lasting **8** enduring **9** confirmed, ingrained

deep-seated 7 abiding, lasting **8** enduring **9** confirmed, ingrained

deep thought 10 absorption, brown study, intentness **11** engrossment **13** concentration

deep water 3 jam **4** mess **5** ocean **6** pickle **7** trouble **8** distress **10** difficulty **11** dire straits, predicament **12** over one's head

deer
    young: **4** fawn
    female: **3** doe
    male: stag

Deer Hunter, The
    director: **13** Michael Cimino
    cast: **10** John Cazale, John Savage **11** Meryl Streep **12** Robert De Niro **17** Christopher Walken
    Oscar for: **7** picture **8** director **15** supporting actor (Walken)

Deerslayer, The
    author: **19** James Fenimore Cooper
    first of: **20** Leatherstocking Tales
    character: **4** Hist **5** Hetty **6** Judith **10** Hurry Harry **11** Natty Bumppo (Deerslayer) **12** Chingachgook, Thomas Hutter

de-escalate 5 limit **6** lessen, narrow **8** contract, minimize

deface 3 mar **4** mark, scar **5** spoil **6** bruise, damage, impair, injure **9** disfigure

de facto 4 real **6** actual, really **8** actually

defalcate 8 embezzle **14** misappropriate

defamation 5 libel **7** calumny, slander **12** vilification **13** disparagement

defamatory 8 libelous **9** vilifying **10** calumnious, derogatory, slanderous **11** disparaging

defame 5 libel **6** malign, vilify **7** degrade, slander **8** derogate **9** denigrate, discredit, disparage **10** calumniate

Defarge, Madame
    character in: **16** A Tale of Two Cities
    author: **7** Dickens

default 10 nonpayment

defeat 4 foil, loss, rout **5** cream, crush, elude, quell **6** baffle, thwart **7** conquer, setback, shellac, trounce **8** confound, overcome, vanquish **9** frustrate, overpower, overthrow, overwhelm, thwarting **11** frustration **14** disappointment

defeated 4 beat **5** upset **6** beaten, bested, licked, routed **7** outdone, whipped, worsted **8** overcame **9** conquered, overthrew, put to rout **10** frustrated, overthrown **11** overpowered, overwhelmed **12** hors de combat

defect 4 flaw, scar, spot **5** break, crack, fault, stain **6** blotch, foible **7** blemish, default, failing, frailty **8** omission, weakness **10** deficiency **11** shortcoming **12** imperfection **14** incompleteness

defective 6 broken, faulty, flawed

7 lacking, wanting **8** abnormal, impaired **9** deficient, imperfect, subnormal **10** inadequate, out of order **11** inoperative **12** insufficient

Defence of Poetry
author: **18** Percy Bysshe Shelley

defend 5 guard **6** secure, shield, uphold **7** endorse, protect, shelter, stand by, support, sustain **8** advocate, champion, maintain, preserve **9** safeguard

defender 8 advocate, champion, guardian, upholder **9** protector, supporter

Defender of the Faith
Latin: **13** Fidei Defensor
title of: **17** English sovereigns

Defenders, The
character: **10** Joan Miller **14** Helen Donaldson, Kenneth Preston **15** Lawrence Preston
cast: **10** E G Marshall, Robert Reed **11** Joan Hackett, Polly Rowles

defense 4 care **5** guard **7** custody, support **8** advocacy, security **9** barricade, safeguard, upholding **10** protection, stronghold **11** maintenance, safekeeping **12** preservation **13** fortification, justification

defenseless 7 unarmed **8** helpless **10** on one's back, vulnerable, weaponless **11** unprotected, unresisting

defensible 3 fit **5** valid **6** proper **7** tenable **8** sensible, suitable **9** allowable, excusable **10** admissible, condonable, forgivable, pardonable, vindicable **11** justifiable, permissible, supportable, warrantable

defer 4 obey **5** delay, table, yield **6** accede, give in, put off, shelve, submit **7** respect, suspend **8** postpone **10** capitulate

deference 5 honor **6** esteem, regard **7** respect **9** obedience, reverence **12** capitulation **13** consideration

deferential 5 civil **6** polite **7** dutiful **8** obedient, reverent **9** courteous, regardful **10** respectful, submissive **11** acquiescent, considerate, reverential

deferment 4 stay **5** delay **9** extension **12** postponement

deferral 5 pause **6** hiatus, recess **8** abeyance **10** suspension **12** postponement **14** discontinuance

defiance 9 hostility, obstinacy, rebellion **12** disobedience **14** rebelliousness

defiant 4 bold **9** truculent **10** aggressive, rebellious **11** disobedient, provocative

Defiant Ones, The
director: **13** Stanley Kramer
cast: **10** Tony Curtis **11** Lon Chaney Jr **12** Cara Williams **13** Charles McGraw, Sidney Poitier, Theodore Bikel
Oscar for: **10** screenplay

deficiency 4 flaw **6** defect **7** failing, frailty **8** shortage, weakness **10** inadequacy **11** shortcoming **12** imperfection **13** insufficiency

deficient 4 weak **6** flawed **7** lacking, short on **8** inferior **9** defective **10** inadequate **11** substandard **12** insufficient **14** unsatisfactory

deficit 8 shortage **9** shortfall **10** deficiency

de fide 10 of the faith

defile 4 soil **5** dirty, smear, spoil, stain, taint **6** befoul, debase **7** degrade, profane, tarnish **8** besmirch, disgrace, dishonor **9** desecrate

defiled 5 dirty **6** fouled, impure, soiled **7** debased, dirtied, stained, sullied, tainted, unclean **8** befouled, polluted, ravished, smirched, violated **9** blackened, corrupted, tarnished **10** besmirched **12** contaminated

define 5 state **7** clarify, explain, specify **8** describe, spell out **9** delineate, designate

definite 3 set **4** sure **5** exact, fixed **7** certain, precise **8** clear-cut, positive

definitely 5 truly **6** indeed, surely **7** for sure, no doubt **9** assuredly, certainly, decidedly, doubtless, expressly **10** absolutely, decisively, explicitly, positively, undeniably **11** indubitably, inescapably, unavoidably, undoubtedly **12** unmistakably **13** categorically, unequivocally **14** unquestionably **16** incontrovertibly

definiteness 8 sureness **9** certainty, precision **10** exactitude **11** unambiguity

definition 6 limits **7** clarity, purpose **11** description **15** distinctiveness

definitive 5 exact **7** decided, perfect **8** complete, decisive, reliable **10** conclusive, consummate

deflate 6 reduce **7** flatten **8** contract **9** devaluate

deflect 6 divert, swerve

Defoe, Daniel
author of: **6** Roxana **11** Colonel Jack **12** Moll Flanders **14** Robinson Crusoe **23** A Journal of the Plague Year

DeForest, Lee
invented/worked on: **10** audion tube, television **13** sound pictures

deform 3 mar **4** maim **5** twist **6** mangle **7** blemish, contort, distort **9** disfigure

deformation 9 deformity **10** distortion **12** malformation **13** disfigurement

deformed 6 marred, warped **7** defaced, mangled, spoiled, twisted **8** crippled **9** misshapen, monstrous **10** disfigured

defraud 3 con **4** bilk, rook **5** cheat **6** fleece, rip off **7** swindle

defray 3 pay **5** cover **11** foot the bill

deft 3 apt **4** able, sure **5** quick **6** adroit, expert **8** skillful **9** dexterous

deftness 5 knack, skill **7** ability **8** facility **9** adeptness, dexterity, handiness **10** adroitness, competency **11** proficiency **12** skillfulness

defunct 4 dead **7** extinct

defy 5 spurn **6** oppose, resist **7** disdain **8** confront **9** challenge, disregard, withstand

degage 4 easy **8** detached **10** disengaged **13** unconstrained

Degas, (Hilaire Germain) Edgar
born: **5** Paris **6** France
artwork: **14** The Ballet Class, The Morning Bath **15** Ballet Rehearsal **16** The Millinery Shop **17** The Glass of Absinth **23** Woman with Chrysanthemums **30** The Little Fourteen-Year-Old Dancer

degeneracy 9 decadence, depravity **10** debasement, debauchery, immorality, perversion **11** dissolution

degenerate 3 rot **4** base, sink, vile **5** decay **6** revert, wanton, wicked, worsen **7** corrupt, debased, decline, go to pot, immoral, pervert, vicious **8** decadent, degraded, depraved **9** abandoned, backslide, debauched, dissolute, perverted **10** dissipated, go downhill, profligate, retrograde, retrogress **11** deteriorate, hit the skids **12** disintegrate

degeneration 7 decline **9** depravity **10** corruption, debasement, immorality, perversion **11** degradation, dissolution, viciousness **13** deterioration

degradation 8 disgrace **11** humiliation

Degradation of the Democratic Dogma, The
author: **10** Henry Adams

degrade 5 lower, shame **6** debase, demote **7** corrupt **8** disgrace, dishonor

degraded 4 vile **6** wicked **7** corrupt, debased, lowered **8** depraved, shameful, unworthy **9** debauched, perverted, reprobate **10** degenerate **11** undignified **12** unregenerate

degrading 3 low **6** menial **8** shameful **11** humiliating

degree 4 mark, step, unit **5** grade, level, order, phase, point, stage **8** division, interval
abbreviation: **3** deg

De Guiche, Lillian
real name of: **11** Lillian Gish

de gustibus non est disputandum 29 there is no disputing about tastes

De Havilland, Joan de Beauvoir
real name of: **12** Joan Fontaine

De Havilland, Olivia
sister: **12** Joan Fontaine
born: **5** Japan, Tokyo
roles: **7** Melanie **10** The Heiress (Oscar) **11** The Snake Pit **12** Captain Blood, To Each His Own (Oscar) **14** Anthony Adverse, My Cousin Rachel **15** Gone With the Wind, Hold Back

the Dawn **16** Light in the Piazza **22** Hush Hush Sweet Charlotte **24** The Adventures of Robin Hood

dehydrate 3 dry **5** parch **6** dry out

dehydrated 3 dry **7** parched, thirsty **8** dried-out **9** shriveled **10** desiccated

deification 7 worship **8** idolatry **10** exaltation **13** glorification

deify 5 exalt **7** glorify, idolize, worship

Deighton, Len
　author of: 4 SS-GB **14** The Ipcress File **15** Funeral in Berlin **16** Catch a Falling Spy

deign 4 deem **5** stoop **6** see fit **7** consent **8** think fit **10** condescend

Dei gratia 15 by the grace of God

Deiphobus
　father: 5 Priam
　mother: 6 Hecuba
　brother: 6 Hector
　wife: 5 Helen
　killed by: 8 Menelaus

Deirdre
　origin: 5 Irish
　husband: 6 Naoise
　father-in-law: 6 Usnach
　uncle: 9 Conchobar

Deirdre of the Sorrows
　author: 19 John Millington Synge

deity, the Deity 3 god **4** idol **7** goddess, godhead, Jehovah **8** Almighty, divinity, immortal, Olympian

deja vu 11 already seen

dejected 3 low, sad **4** blue, down **7** doleful, unhappy **8** desolate **9** depressed, sorrowful **10** despondent, dispirited, spiritless **11** discouraged, downhearted, low-spirited **12** disconsolate, disheartened

dejection 5 gloom **7** sadness **10** depression, low spirits, melancholy **11** despondency **15** dispiritedness, downheartedness

dejeuner 5 lunch

de jure 7 by right **14** according to law

dekagram
　abbreviation: 3 dkg

dekaliter
　abbreviation: 3 dkL

dekameter, decameter
　abbreviation: 3 dkm

Dekker, Thomas
　author of: 11 Westward Ho! (with John Webster) **20** The Shoemaker's Holiday

de Kooning, Willem
　born: 9 Rotterdam **14** The Netherlands
　artwork: 5 Woman **8** Painting **15** Woman and Bicycle

Delacroix, Eugene
　born: 6 France **18** Charenton-St Maurice
　artwork: 8 Paganini **14** Women of Algiers **15** Massacre at Chios **16** The

Barque of Dante **19** Chopin and George Sand **20** Dante and Virgil in Hell **22** Liberty at the Barricades, The Death of Sardanapalus

Delaroche, Paul
　born: 5 Paris **6** France
　artwork: 24 The Death of Queen Elizabeth, The Death of the Duke of Guise **26** The Execution of Lady Jane Grey **36** Children of Edward Imprisoned in the Tower

Delaunay, Robert
　born: 5 Paris **6** France
　artwork: 5 Disks **6** Cities, Rhythm **7** Runners, Windows **10** Cathedrals **11** City of Paris, Eiffel Tower **14** The Cardiff Team **19** Cosmic Circular Forms **28** Simultaneous Prismatic Windows

Delaware
　abbreviation: 2 DE **3** Del
　nickname: 5 First **7** Blue Hen, Diamond
　capital: 5 Dover
　largest city: 10 Wilmington
　others: 5 Acoma, Lewes **6** Easton, Newark, Smyrna **7** Briston, Elsmere, Milford **8** Claymont **9** New Castle **10** Georgetown
　college: 6 Wesley **10** Brandywine, Wilmington **12** Goldey Beacom
　feature: 10 Winterthur **15** Old Swedes Church **17** E I du Pont de Nemours
　tribe: 4 Leni **5** Lenni **6** Lenape, Munsee
　people: 10 Howard Pyle
　island: 7 Fenwick
　land rank: 10 forty-ninth
　physical feature:
　　bay: 8 Delaware, Rehoboth
　　sea: 8 Atlantic
　river: 8 Delaware **9** Christina, Nanticoke **10** Brandywine
　state admission: 5 first
　state bird: 14 blue hen chicken
　state flower: 12 peach blossom
　state motto: 22 Liberty and Independence
　state song: 11 Our Delaware
　state tree: 13 American holly

Delaware (Lenni-Lenape)
　language family: 9 Algonkian **10** Algonquian
　tribe: 5 Munsi, Unami **6** Munsee **11** Unalachtigo
　location: 7 New York **8** Delaware **9** Manhattan, New Jersey **10** Long Island **12** Pennsylvania, Staten Island
　leader: 7 Tamanen, Tammany
　deity: 11 Kitanitowet

delay 4 slow, stay **5** check, table, tarry **6** dawdle, detain, hamper, hinder, hold up, impede, linger, put off, retard, shelve **7** inhibit, slowing, suspend **8** dawdling, obstruct, postpone, reprieve, stoppage, tarrying **9** deferment, lingering, loitering **10** suspen-

sion **12** postponement, prolongation **13** procrastination

delayed 4 late **6** put off, slowed **7** held up, stalled, tarried **8** arrested, deferred, detained, retarded **9** postponed, slackened **12** dillydallied **14** procrastinated **15** dragged one's feet

Delbruck, Max
　field: 7 biology **17** molecular genetics
　researched: 20 genetic recombination
　awarded: 10 Nobel Prize

delectable 5 tasty, yummy **8** pleasant **9** agreeable, delicious, enjoyable **10** delightful, gratifying **11** pleasurable

delegate 3 rep **4** give, name **5** agent, envoy, proxy **6** assign, charge, deputy **7** entrust **8** give over, transfer **9** authorize, designate **10** commission **14** representative

delegation 11 designation, entrustment **13** authorization, commissioning

delete 3 cut **4** omit **5** erase **6** cancel, remove

deleterious 7 harmful, hurtful, ruinous **9** dangerous, injurious **11** destructive, detrimental

Delia
　festival of: 6 Apollo

deliberate 4 easy, slow, wary **5** weigh **6** confer, debate **7** careful, discuss, examine, express, planned, prudent, willful **8** cautious, cogitate, consider, measured, meditate, mull over **9** leisurely, unhurried **10** calculated, considered, purposeful, thoughtful **11** circumspect, contemplate, intentional, prearranged **12** premeditated

deliberate together 6 confer **7** consult, discuss

deliberation 4 care **6** debate **10** conference, discussion, steadiness **11** calculation, carefulness, forethought **13** premeditation **14** circumspection

Delibes, C P (Clement Philibert) Leo
　born: 6 France **14** St Germain-du-Val
　composer of: 5 Lakme **6** Sylvia **8** Coppelia **10** Le Roi l'a dit

delicacy 4 tact **5** taste **7** frailty **8** accuracy, elegance, fineness, softness, weakness **9** fragility, frailness, lightness, precision **10** perfection, smoothness **11** savoir-faire, sensibility, sensitivity, unsoundness **13** consideration, exquisiteness, sensitiveness **14** discrimination

delicate 4 fine, soft **5** frail, muted **6** ailing, dainty, feeble, flimsy, infirm, minute, savory, sickly, touchy, unwell **7** careful, elegant, fragile, refined, subdued, tactful **8** detailed, luscious, tasteful, ticklish, weakened **9** breakable, delicious, difficult, exquisite, palatable, sensitive, toothsome **10** appetizing, diplomatic, fastidious, perishable, precarious, scrupulous **11** debilitated

Delicate Balance, A
   author: **11** Edward Albee

delicious 5 tasty, yummy **6** joyful, savory **8** charming, luscious, pleasant **9** palatable **10** appetizing, delectable, delightful **11** pleasurable **13** mouthwatering

delight 3 joy **5** amuse, charm, cheer, revel **6** please **7** enchant, gratify, rapture **8** pleasure **9** enjoyment, fascinate, happiness **13** gratification

delighted 6 elated **7** pleased, psyched **8** ecstatic **9** enchanted **10** captivated, enraptured, enthralled **11** on cloud nine

delightful 6 peachy **7** amiable, amusing **8** charming, engaging, pleasing **9** agreeable, congenial, enjoyable **10** enchanting **11** pleasurable **12** entertaining

delight in 4 love **5** adore, eat up, enjoy, fancy, savor **6** dote on, relish **7** cherish **8** treasure **10** appreciate

Delilah
   lover: **6** Samson
   betrayed: **6** Samson

delineate 4 draw **5** draft **6** define, depict, design, lay out, sketch **7** outline, portray **8** describe **9** represent **12** characterize

delineation 9 depiction, portrayal **11** description **12** illustration **14** representation **16** characterization

delineavit 6 he drew (this) **7** she drew (this)

delinquency 7 misdeed **10** misconduct, negligence **11** dereliction, misbehavior **19** neglect of obligation

delinquent 3 due **4** late **6** remiss **7** hoodlum, misdoer, overdue **8** derelict **9** in arrears, miscreant, negligent, wrongdoer **10** neglectful

delirious 6 raving **7** excited, frantic **8** ecstatic, frenzied **10** incoherent **11** carried away **13** hallucinating

delirium 5 fever **6** frenzy, raving **7** madness, ranting **8** insanity **10** brain fever

Deliro
   character in: **22** Every Man Out of His Humour
   author: **6** Jonson

Delisle, Guillaume
   field: **9** geography
   nationality: **6** French
   founder of: **15** modern geography

Delius, Frederick
   born: **7** England **8** Bradford
   composer of: **5** Paris **6** Koanga **7** Eventyr, Irmelin **8** Sea-Drift **9** Brigg Fair **10** Appalachia **11** A Mass of Life, Sur les Cimes **17** Fennimore and Gerda **20** North Country Sketches **22** A Village Romeo and Juliet, Over the Hills and Far Away

deliver 3 aim, say **4** bear, deal, free, give, save **5** bring, carry, throw, utter **6** convey, direct, launch, rescue, strike **7** release, set free **8** give over, hand over, liberate, proclaim, turn over **9** surrender **10** emancipate

deliverance 6 rescue **7** release **9** salvation **10** liberation **12** emancipation

Deliverance
   director: **11** John Boorman
   author: **11** James Dickey
   cast: **8** Ronny Cox **9** Jon Voight, Ned Beatty **12** Burt Reynolds
   song: **13** Dueling Banjos

deliver up 4 cede, give **5** grant, yield **8** fork over, hand over, transfer **9** surrender **10** relinquish

delivery 8 transfer **11** transferral, transmittal **12** transmission

delivery service 3 DHL, UPS **4** USPS **5** FedEx **8** Airborne **11** Express mail

dell 4 dale, dene, glen, vale **5** glade **6** dingle, hollow, valley

Della Robbia, Luca
   born: **5** Italy **8** Florence
   artwork: **8** Cantoria (Singing Gallery) **12** The Ascension **13** Altman Madonna **15** Madonna and Child, The Resurrection

Dello Joio, Norman
   born: **9** New York NY
   composer of: **7** The Ruby **12** Psalm of David **15** New York Profiles, The Trial at Rouen, Triumph of St Joan **20** Proud Music of the Storm, The Lamentation of Saul

Delon, Alain
   born: **6** France, Sceaux
   roles: **10** Purple Noon, The Leopard **13** The Black Tulip **14** Is Paris Burning? **19** Rocco and His Brothers

Delphic
   pertains to: **6** Apollo, Delphi

Delphic oracle
   oracle of: **6** Apollo
   located at: **6** Delphi
   priestess: **6** Pythia

Delphinia
   festival of: **6** Apollo

Del Rio, Dolores
   real name: **21** Lolita Dolores Negrette
   born: **6** Mexico **7** Durango
   roles: **11** The Fugitive **13** Madame duBarry **15** Flying Down to Rio, Journey into Fear, Maria Candelaria

Delta Wedding
   author: **11** Eudora Welty

delude 3 con **4** dupe, fool **5** put on, trick **7** deceive, mislead

deluge 4 bury, glut **5** drown, flood, spate, swamp **6** engulf **7** barrage, torrent **8** inundate, overflow, submerge **10** inundation

DeLuise, Dom
   born: **10** Brooklyn NY
   roles: **5** Fatso **6** The End **11** Silent Movie **14** Blazing Saddles

delusion 8 illusion **9** misbelief **10** aberration **11** derangement **13** hallucination, irrationality, misconception, self-deception

Delusions, Etc. of John Berryman
   author: **12** John Berryman

deluxe 4 fine, posh **5** grand **6** choice, classy **7** elegant **8** splendid **9** luxurious

delve 5 probe **6** search **7** examine, explore **8** look into

demagogue 6 ranter **7** hothead, spouter **8** agitator, fomenter, inflamer **9** firebrand, haranguer **10** incendiary, malcontent, tub-thumper **12** rabble-rouser, troublemaker

demand 4 call, need, want **5** exact, order **7** command, require **11** requirement

demanding 4 hard **5** harsh, rigid **6** strict **8** exacting **9** difficult

demantoid
   species: **6** garnet

demarche 4 gait, plan

demean 5 lower, shame **6** debase, humble **7** degrade **8** disgrace **9** humiliate

demeanor 4 mien **6** manner **7** bearing, conduct **8** behavior, presence **10** appearance, deportment **11** comportment

demented 3 mad **4** nuts **5** crazy **6** crazed, cuckoo, insane **7** lunatic **8** deranged

dementia praecox 13 schizophrenia

dementophobia
   fear of: **8** insanity

demesne 4 land **5** realm **6** domain, estate **8** property

Demeter
   origin: **5** Greek
   goddess of: **5** earth **9** fertility
   protectress of: **8** marriage **11** social order
   father: **6** Cronus
   mother: **4** Rhea
   daughter: **10** Persephone
   corresponds to: **5** Brimo, Ceres **8** Despoena
   epithet: **5** Chloe, Lusia, Mysia **6** Antaea, Erinys, Stiria **7** Chamyne, Thesmia **8** Stiritis **9** Anesidora, Thermasia **11** Carpophorus **13** Thesimophorus

Demetrius
   character in: **21** A Midsummer Night's Dream
   author: **11** Shakespeare

De Mille, Agnes
   choreographer of: **5** Rodeo **15** Fall River Legend

DeMille, Cecil B
   director of: **9** Cleopatra **18** The Ten Commandments **22** The Greatest Show on Earth
   niece: **5** Agnes (choreographer)

Demiphon
form: **4** king
sacrificed: **7** maidens
to prevent: **6** plague
demise 3 end **4** fall, ruin **5** death **7** decease, passing **8** collapse **10** expiration
demobilization 7 release **9** discharge **10** disbanding
demobilize 7 disband, release **9** discharge
Democoon
father: **5** Priam
birth: **12** illegitimate
killed by: **8** Odysseus
democracy 8 equality, fairness
Democracy
author: **10** Henry Adams
Democracy in America
author: **19** Alexis de Tocqueville
Democratic Party
symbol: **6** donkey
president belonging to: **4** Polk **6** Carter, Pierce, Truman, Wilson **7** Clinton, (Lyndon Baines) Johnson, Jackson, Kennedy **8** Buchanan, Van Buren **9** Cleveland, (Franklin D) Roosevelt
Democratic Republican Party
president belonging to: **5** (John Quincy) Adams **6** Monroe **7** Madison **9** Jefferson
demode 8 outmoded **13** unfashionable
demoiselle 4 girl
demolish 4 raze, ruin **5** level, total, wreck **7** destroy **9** devastate
demolition 6 razing **8** leveling, wrecking **11** destruction
demon 3 imp **4** jinn, ogre **5** afrit, devil, fiend, genie, harpy, jinni, lamia, satan, troll **6** afreet, dybbuk, goblin **7** incubus, monster, vampire, warlock **8** go-getter, succubus
demonic, demoniacal 6 hectic **7** frantic, hellish **8** devilish, fiendish, frenzied
demonstrable 7 evident **8** apparent, manifest, palpable **11** supportable
demonstrate 4 show **5** march, prove, teach **6** parade, picket, reveal **7** display, exhibit, explain **8** describe, manifest **9** establish **10** illustrate
demonstration 5 march, rally **6** parade **7** display **9** picketing **10** exhibition, exposition, expression **12** illustration, presentation **13** manifestation
demonstrative 7 gushing **8** effusive **12** affectionate
demonstrativeness 9 gushiness **12** effusiveness, emotionalism
demoralize 8 dispirit **9** undermine **10** disconcert, discourage, dishearten **11** disorganize
de mortuis nil nisi bonum 26 of the dead say nothing but good

demos 5 plebs **6** masses, people **7** commons **8** populace **9** commoners
demote 4 bust **5** abase **7** degrade
Dempsey, Jack (William Harrison)
nickname: **13** Manassa Mauler
sport: **6** boxing
class: **11** heavyweight
demur 5 qualm **6** object **7** protest, scruple **8** disagree **9** misgiving, objection **10** hesitation **11** compunction
demure 3 shy **4** prim **6** modest **7** bashful **8** reserved
demurrer 5 doubt, qualm **7** dissent, protest, scruple **8** objector, question, rebuttal **9** challenge, exception, misgiving, objection, protester, protestor, stricture **11** compunction **12** remonstrance
den 4 lair **5** haunt, study **6** hotbed **7** hangout, library, retreat, shelter **9** sanctuary
denial 7 refusal **9** disavowal, disowning, rejection **10** disclaimer
denigrate 4 soil **5** abuse, smear, sully **6** defame, dump on, malign, revile, vilify **7** asperse, blacken, degrade, run down, slander, traduce **8** backbite, badmouth, belittle, besmirch, tear down **9** call names, discredit, disparage, downgrade **10** calumniate, stigmatize
De Niro, Robert
born: **9** New York NY
roles: **4** Heat **6** Brazil **8** Cape Fear, Sleepers **10** A Bronx Tale, Angel Heart, Awakenings, Goodfellas, Raging Bull (Oscar), Taxi Driver **11** Mean Streets **13** The Deer Hunter **14** New York New York, The Godfather II **15** The King of Comedy, The Untouchables, True Confessions **17** Bang the Drum Slowly
denizen 7 dweller **8** resident **10** inhabitant
Denmark
other name: **17** Kongeriget Danmark
capital/largest city: **9** Kobenhavn **10** Copenhagen
others: **3** Hov **4** Hals, Koge, Nibe, Ribe, Soro **5** Arhus, Kosor, Vejle **6** Aarhus, Abenra, Alborg, Dorsor, Dragor, Nyberg, Odense, Skagen, Struer, Viborg **7** Aalborg, Esbjerg, Horsens, Kolding, Morsens, Randers **8** Ballerup, Elsinore, Gentofte, Glostrup, Hillerod, Naestred, Roskilde, Slagelse **9** Haderslev, Helsingor, Svendborg **10** Fredericia **13** Frederikshavn
school:
university institute of: **18** Theoretical Physics
folk high school: **14** folkehojskoler
continuation school: **11** efterskoler
division: **3** Fyn **7** Jutland, Lolland **9** Schleswig, Sjaelland
measure: **3** ell, fod, mil, pot **4** alen, favn, last, rode **5** album, anker,

kande, linje, paegl, tomme **6** achtel, paegel, skeppe **7** landmil, oltonde, ortonde, skieppe, viertel **8** fjerding **9** ottingkar **10** korntonmde
monetary unit: **3** one, ora, ore **4** fyrk **5** krone **8** frederik, skilling **9** rigsdaler
weight: **2** es **3** lod, ort, vog **4** last, mark, pund, unze **5** carat, kvint, pound, quint, tonde **6** toende **7** centner, lispund, quintin **8** lispound, skippund **9** skibslast, skippound **10** bismerpund
island: **2** Oe **3** Als, Fyn, Mon, Rum, Thy **4** Aaro, Aero, Fano, Fohr, Moen, Mors, Romo **5** Baago, Faero, Faroe, Funen, Laeso, Samso, Sando **6** Amager, Sandoy, Sejero, Sudero **7** Faeroes, Falster, Hesselo, Laaland, Lolland, Seeland, Zealand **8** Bornholm, Eysturoy, Sudhuroy **9** Greenland, Langeland, Sjaelland **10** Vendsyssel
lake: **6** Arreso
hill: **12** Ejer Bavnehoj **14** Himmelbjaerget
highest point: **12** Yding Skovhoj
river: **3** Asa **4** Holm, Omme, Stor **5** Skive, Susaa, Varde **6** Gelsaa, Gudena, Vorgod **7** Gudenaa, Lilleaa, Lonborg
sea: **5** North **6** Baltic **7** Oresund **8** Atlantic, Kattegat **9** Skagerrak
physical feature:
fjord: **3** Ise **4** Isse **5** Lamme
inlet: **3** Ise **5** Fjord, Vejle **6** Nissum, Odense **7** Horsens, Logstor **8** Limfjord, Mariager
peninsula: **7** Jutland
strait: **7** Otesund **8** Kattegat **9** Skagerrak
people: **4** Dane, Jute **5** Angle **6** Cimbri, Eskimo, German, Ostmen, Teuton, Viking **12** Scandinavian
astronomer: **10** Tycho Brahe
author: **11** Isak Dinesen **21** Hans Christian Andersen
founder: **4** Axel **7** Absalon
king: **4** Hans, Knud **6** Canute **8** Frederik **9** Christian **10** Gorm the Old **15** Harold Bluetooth
philosopher: **11** Kierkegaard
physicist: **9** Niels Bohr
queen: **9** Margrethe **12** Thyra Danebod
sculptor: **11** Thorvaldsen
teacher: **4** Kold
language: **4** Odan **6** Danish, German **8** Faeroese **11** Greenlander
religion: **19** Evangelical Lutheran
place:
airport: **7** Kastrup
castle: **7** Egeskov **8** Kronborg **13** Frederiksborg
museum: **6** Rebild **9** Glyptotek **11** Thorvaldsen **15** Rosenborg Castle
park: **10** Langelinie **13** Tivoli Gardens

royal palace: 11 Amalienborg
statue: 13 Little Mermaid
stock exchange: 5 Borse **6** Borsen
feature:
  dance: 6 sextur
  drink: 5 glogg **7** aquavit
  beer: 6 Tuborg **9** Carlsberg
food:
  cheese: 3 Ost **4** Blue, Tybo **5** Esrom, Samso **6** Samsoe **7** Havarti, Mycella
  meat patty: 11 frikadeller
  pudding: 15 rodgrod med flode

Dennis, Patrick
author of: 10 Auntie Mame

Dennis, Sandy
real name: 16 Sandra Dale Dennis
born: 10 Hastings NE
roles: 12 Any Wednesday **15** A Thousand Clowns **18** Up the Down Staircase **25** Who's Afraid of Virginia Woolf?

Dennis the Hangman
character in: 12 Barnaby Rudge
author: 7 Dickens

Dennis the Menace
creator: 11 Hank Ketcham
character: 9 Mrs Elkins **10** John Wilson **12** Eloise Wilson, George Wilson, Joey McDonald, Martha Wilson **13** Alice Mitchell, Henry Mitchell, Tommy Anderson **14** Dennis Mitchell
dog: 4 Ruff
cast: 8 Gil Smith, Jay North **10** Billy Booth, Gale Gordon, Sara Seeger **11** Gloria Henry, Irene Tedrow, Sylvia Field **12** Joseph Kearns **15** Herbert Anderson

denomination 4 name, sect, size **5** class, value **8** category, grouping **10** persuasion **11** designation

denotation 4 mark, name, sign **6** symbol **7** meaning **10** indication

denote 4 mark, mean, name **6** signal **7** signify **8** indicate

denouement 3 end **6** finale, upshot **7** outcome **8** solution **10** conclusion **11** termination

denounce 6 accuse, vilify **7** censure, condemn **9** criticize

denouncement 7 censure **12** condemnation, denunciation

de novo 4 anew **5** again **6** afresh **16** from the beginning

dense 4 dull, dumb, slow **5** close, heavy, thick **6** stupid **7** compact, crowded, intense **8** ignorant **9** dimwitted **10** compressed **11** thickheaded **12** concentrated, impenetrable

Densher, Merton
character in: 17 The Wings of the Dove
author: 5 James

density 4 mass **6** weight **7** opacity **8** dullness, solidity **9** stupidity, thickness **10** obtuseness, opaqueness **11** compactness

dent 3 pit **4** nick **6** hollow **10** depression **11** indentation

denude 4 bare **5** strip **6** divest **7** lay bare **8** unclothe

denuded 4 bare **5** naked **6** barren **8** stripped **9** unclothed, uncovered

denunciation 7 censure **12** condemnation, denouncement **13** attack against

Denver
basketball team: 7 Nuggets
football team: 4 Gold **7** Broncos

deny 6 refuse, refute **7** disavow **8** disallow, disclaim **9** disaffirm **10** contradict

deny oneself 5 avoid, forgo **6** eschew, give up, refuse **7** abstain, forbear **8** renounce **9** sacrifice

deny responsibility 7 disavow

Deo gratias 13 thanks be to God

Deo volente 10 God willing

DePalma, Brian
director of: 6 Carrie **8** Scarface **11** Carlito's Way, Raising Cain **13** Dressed to Kill **15** The Untouchables **17** Mission Impossible **20** Bonfire of the Vanities

depart 2 go **4** exit **5** leave **6** embark **7** deviate, digress, entrain

departed 4 dead, gone, late, left, past, went **6** at rest, bygone **7** gone off **8** gone away **10** passed away **11** gone to glory **12** late-lamented **20** gone the way of all flesh

depart for 8 leave for **9** adjourn to, set off for, set out for **10** head toward, move toward

depart hastily 3 fly **4** flee **5** elope **6** decamp, escape **7** abscond **9** skedaddle

department 4 unit **6** branch, bureau, sector **7** section **8** district, division, province

departure 4 exit **5** going **6** exodus **7** leaving **9** deviation **10** digression, divergence

depend 4 rely, rest **5** count, hinge **6** hang on

dependable 4 sure, true **5** loyal **6** steady, trusty **7** trusted **8** faithful, reliable **9** steadfast, unfailing **11** trustworthy

dependence 5 trust **8** reliance **10** confidence, dependency

dependency 10 dependence

dependent 7 reliant

depict 4 draw, limn **5** carve, chart, draft, paint **6** define, detail, map out, recite, record, relate, sculpt, sketch **7** diagram, narrate, picture, portray, recount **8** describe **9** chronicle, delineate, dramatize, represent, verbalize **10** illustrate **12** characterize

depiction 6 sketch **7** drawing, picture **8** portrait **9** picturing, portrayal **11** de-

lineation **12** illustration **14** representation **16** characterization

deplete 5 drain, use up **6** lessen, reduce **7** consume, exhaust **8** decrease **10** impoverish

depleted 5 empty, spent, waste **6** barren, used up **7** drained, emptied, reduced, worn out **8** bankrupt, consumed, expended, lessened **9** exhausted, infertile **10** unfruitful

deplorable 5 awful **8** wretched **9** miserable **11** blameworthy **13** reprehensible **17** deserving reproach

deplore 5 mourn **6** bemoan, bewail, lament **7** censure, condemn **9** grieve for **12** disapprove of

deport 3 act **4** oust **5** carry, exile, expel **6** banish, behave **7** cast out **10** expatriate **14** conduct oneself

deported person 2 DP **5** exile **8** deportee **10** expatriate **14** banished person

deportment 7 conduct **8** behavior, demeanor **11** comportment

depose 4 oust **6** unseat **8** dethrone **16** remove from office

deposit 3 put **4** pile **5** place **7** put down, set down **8** sediment **10** accumulate **11** down payment, give in trust, installment **12** accumulation **14** partial payment

deposition 7 deposit **9** statement, testimony **11** declaration **12** accumulation

depository 4 bank, safe **5** vault **6** museum **7** library **8** archives **10** storehouse

depot 4 dump **7** station **8** terminal, terminus **10** bus station **15** railroad station **20** military storage place

depraved 4 vile **6** wicked **7** corrupt, debased **8** degraded **9** debauched, perverted **10** degenerate

depravity 8 vileness **9** decadence **10** corruption, debasement, debauchery, degeneracy, immorality, perversion, wickedness **11** degradation, dissolution

deprecate 6 insult **7** condemn, protest **8** belittle, object to, play down **10** depreciate **15** take exception to

deprecated 7 defamed, put down **8** despised **9** belittled, derogated, disdained

deprecation 4 slur **5** abuse **7** protest, put-down **9** aspersion **10** aspersions, belittling, defamation, derogation **11** disapproval **12** condemnation **13** disparagement

deprecatory 8 critical **9** insulting, maligning, vilifying **10** belittling, defamatory, derogatory, slanderous **11** disparaging **12** disapproving

depreciate 5 scorn **7** run down **8** belittle, diminish **9** denigrate, disparage, downgrade, lose value **13** reduce in value, lower the value

depreciation 5 scorn **7** disdain **8** contempt **9** criticism, deflation **10** belittling, disrespect **11** devaluation **13** disparagement

depredation 4 sack **6** rapine, ravage **7** looting, pillage, plunder, robbery, sacking **8** spoiling **9** marauding **10** brigandage, ravishment, spoliation **11** desecration, devastation, freebooting, laying waste

depress 5 lower **6** deject, lessen, reduce, sadden, weaken **7** cut back **8** diminish, dispirit **9** press down **10** dishearten **14** lower in spirits

depressed 3 sad **4** blue **7** unhappy **8** dejected, downcast **10** despondent, dispirited, melancholy **11** low-spirited **12** disconsolate, inconsolable

depressing 3 sad **6** gloomy **8** lowering **9** dejecting, saddening **10** oppressing **11** casting down, dispiriting, melancholic, pushing down **12** discouraging, pressing down, weighing down **14** causing sadness

depression 5 gloom **6** dimple, hollow **7** sadness **9** dejection, recession **10** desolation, melancholy **11** despondency, indentation, melancholia **14** discouragement **15** downheartedness, economic decline

deprive 5 strip **6** divest **8** take from **10** confiscate, dispossess

deprived 8 divested, stripped **11** handicapped **12** dispossessed, impoverished **13** disadvantaged **15** underprivileged

deprive of honor 5 abase, shame, sully **6** defame **7** blacken, tarnish **8** disgrace, dishonor **9** discredit **10** stigmatize

deprive of strength 6 hinder, weaken **7** disable, wear out **8** enervate, enfeeble, handicap **10** debilitate, devitalize

de profundis 13 from the depths

depth 6 timbre **10** deepness **10** profundity **19** downward measurement **24** perpendicular measurement

depths 4 deep **6** bowels **8** interior, recesses

deputation 9 committee **10** commission, delegation **15** representatives

deputize 6 assign **7** appoint **8** delegate **10** commission

deputy 4 aide **5** agent, envoy, proxy **6** second **8** delegate, emissary, minister **9** alternate, assistant, go-between, messenger, middleman, surrogate **10** ambassador, substitute **11** pinch hitter **12** spokesperson **14** representative **15** second-in-command

DeQuincey, Thomas
  author of: 19 The English Mail-Coach **31** On the Knocking at the Gate in

Macbeth **32** Confessions of an English Opium-Eater

derail 3 bar **4** balk, foil **5** block, check, spike **6** hinder, impede, thwart **7** inhibit, prevent **8** obstruct **14** throw off course

deranged 3 mad **5** crazy **6** insane **8** demented **10** irrational, unbalanced

derangement 6 lunacy **7** madness **8** insanity **9** craziness **11** peculiarity **13** irrationality, mental illness **14** mental disorder

Der Bingle
  nickname of: 10 Bing Crosby

Derby 4 race
  site: 5 Epsom **8** Kentucky **14** Churchill Downs

Derek, Bo
  husband: 4 John
  roles: 3 Ten (10) **6** Bolero, Tarzan

derelict 3 bum **4** hobo **5** tramp **6** remiss **7** outcast, vagrant **8** careless, deserted **9** abandoned, negligent **10** delinquent, neglectful

dereliction 7 failure, neglect **9** disregard **10** negligence **11** delinquency **13** noncompliance, nonobservance

De rerum natura
  author: 9 Lucretius

deride 4 mock **5** scoff, scorn **7** sneer at **8** ridicule

de rigueur 11 fashionable **16** strictly required

derision 5 scorn **7** disdain, mockery **8** ridicule, sneering

derivation 5 stock **6** origin, source **7** descent, getting, lineage **8** ancestry, deriving, heritage **9** acquiring, etymology, parentage **10** background, beginnings, extraction **21** historical development

derive 4 gain **5** arise, enjoy, glean **6** obtain **7** descend **8** stem from **9** originate

dermaptera
  class: 8 hexapoda
  phylum: 6 arthropoda
  group: 6 earwig

dermatitis 4 rash **6** eczema **9** psoriasis **12** inflammation

Dern, Bruce
  born: 9 Chicago IL
  roles: 6 Marnie, Tattoo **10** Coming Home, Family Plot **11** Black Sunday **13** The Wild Angels **14** The Great Gatsby **22** The King of Marvin Gardens

dernier 4 last **5** final **8** ultimate

dernier cri 9 latest cry **10** latest word **13** latest fashion

derogate 4 blot **5** taint **6** smirch **8** disgrace **9** disparage

derogation 4 blot **5** odium, stain **7** blemish **8** contempt, disfavor, disgrace, ignominy **9** disesteem, disre-

pute **10** disrespect **11** humiliation **13** disparagement

derogatory 9 injurious **10** belittling **11** disparaging, unfavorable **12** unflattering **15** uncomplimentary

derrick 3 rig **5** crane, hoist, tower **9** framework
  kind: 3 oil **6** sheers **7** gin-pole
  part: 3 gin, leg **4** boom, mast **6** pulley **7** guy line

derring-do 6 daring **8** audacity, boldness **11** daredevilry **12** daredeviltry, recklessness **15** venturesomeness

dervish 5 fakir **6** Muslim **7** ascetic

De Sapientia Veterum
  author: 12 Francis Bacon

Descartes, Rene
  author of: 17 Discourse on Method
  field: 11 mathemathics
  nationality: 6 French
  developed: 18 analytical geometry
  quote: 13 Cogito ergo sum **18** I think therefore I am
  pertaining to: 9 Cartesian

descend 3 dip **4** drop, pass **5** slant, slope, swoop **6** go down, invade **7** incline **8** come down, inherited **11** come in force **12** be handed down, move downward

descendant 5 issue, scion **7** progeny **9** offspring

descend upon 6 assail, attack, charge **7** assault, set upon **12** bear down upon

descent 4 drop, fall, raid **5** slant, slope **6** origin **7** assault, decline, lineage **8** ancestry **9** declivity, incursion **10** coming down **11** sneak attack, sudden visit

describe 4 draw **5** trace **6** depict, detail, recite, relate **7** explain, mark out, narrate, outline, portray, recount, speak of **9** delineate **10** illustrate **12** characterize

description 3 ilk **4** kind, sort, type **5** brand, class, genus **6** manner, nature **7** account, species, variety **9** depiction, narration, portrayal **12** illustration **16** characterization

descry 3 see **4** spot **6** behold, notice **7** discern, observe, pick out **8** discover **12** catch sight of

Desdemona
  character in: 7 Othello
  author: 11 Shakespeare

desecrate 6 defile **7** profane, violate **8** dishonor

desecration 8 dishonor **9** violation **10** defilement **11** profanation

desert 3 dry **4** arid, wild **5** leave, waste **6** barren **7** abandon, forsake **8** desolate, untilled **9** infertile, wasteland **10** arid region **11** run away from, uninhabited **12** uncultivated **16** barren wilderness
  world: 4 Gobi, Thar **6** Gibson, Lib-

yan, Mohave, Nubian, Sahara, Syrian **7** Arabian, Atacama, Kara Kum, Painted, Sonoran **8** Kalahari **9** Patagonia **10** Great Sandy **11** Death Valley
   watering spot: 5 Oasis

deserted 4 AWOL, left **5** empty **6** lonely, vacant **7** cast off, forlorn, reneged **8** defected, desolate, forsaken, marooned **9** abandoned, absconded **12** quit one's post **14** left in the lurch

desertedness 9 emptiness **10** desolation **13** uncrowdedness

Deserted Village, The
   author: 15 Oliver Goldsmith

desertion 8 quitting **9** forsaking **11** abandonment **14** relinquishment

desertlike 3 dry **4** arid, sere **5** sandy **6** barren **7** dried up, parched **9** waterless

deserts 3 due **5** worth **6** reward **7** payment

deserve 4 rate **5** merit **7** warrant **9** earn as due **10** be worthy of, qualify for **12** be entitled to **13** be deserving of

deserving 6 worthy **9** qualified

deserving reproach 8 blamable **10** deplorable, punishable, reprovable **11** blameworthy **12** reproachable **13** reprehensible

De Sica, Vittorio
   director of: 15 The Bicycle Thief **27** The Garden of the Finzi-Continis

desiccate 5 dry up, parch **6** wither **7** shrivel **9** dehydrate

design 3 aim, end **4** draw, form, goal, plan, plot **5** draft, motif, set up **6** devise, intend, scheme, sketch, target **7** destine, diagram, drawing, fashion, outline, pattern, project, purpose **8** conceive, intrigue **9** blueprint, intention, objective **11** arrangement **14** draw up plans for

designate 4 call, name, term **5** elect, label **6** assign, choose, select **7** appoint, signify, specify **8** identify, indicate, nominate, pinpoint

designation 5 label **6** naming **10** delegation **11** appointment **13** specification **14** identification

designer 7 creator, deviser, planner **9** contriver **10** originator

designing 4 wily **6** artful, crafty **7** cunning **8** plotting, scheming **9** conniving

desirable 4 fine **8** in demand, pleasing **9** advisable **10** beneficial **11** worth having **12** advantageous

desire 3 yen **4** need, urge, want, wish **5** crave **6** ask for, hunger, thirst **7** craving, longing, long for, request **8** yearning, yearn for **9** hunger for, thirst for

Desire Under the Elms
   author: 12 Eugene O'Neill

character: **4** Eben **5** Peter **6** Simeon **11** Abbie Putnam **12** Ephraim Cabot

desirous 4 avid, keen **5** eager **7** hopeful, longing, wishful **8** yearning

desist 4 stop **5** cease **6** lay off **7** suspend **8** leave off **11** discontinue, refrain from

Desk Set
   director: 10 Walter Lang
   cast: 8 Gig Young **11** Dina Merrill **12** Joan Blondell, Spencer Tracy **16** Katharine Hepburn

desolate 3 sad **4** bare, ruin **5** bleak, empty **6** barren, grieve, ravage, sadden **7** depress, destroy, forlorn **8** dejected, demolish, deserted, distress, downcast, forsaken, lay waste, wretched **9** abandoned, depressed, devastate, miserable, sorrowful **10** despondent, discourage, dishearten, melancholy **11** downhearted, uninhabited

desolating 6 tragic **7** ruinous **8** dreadful, grievous, terrible **10** calamitous, horrendous **11** devastating **12** catastrophic

desolation 4 ruin **6** misery, sorrow **7** sadness **8** bareness, distress, solitude **9** bleakness, dejection, emptiness, seclusion **10** barrenness, depression, dreariness, loneliness, melancholy, wilderness **11** destruction, devastation, unhappiness **12** solitariness

despair 5 gloom, trial **6** burden, ordeal **9** lose heart **10** depression, have no hope **11** despondency, lose faith in **12** hopelessness **14** discouragement

despair of 5 doubt **8** give up on **10** have no hope

desperado 4 thug **5** rowdy **6** bandit, gunman, outlaw **7** brigand, convict, hoodlum, ruffian **8** criminal, fugitive, hooligan **9** terrorist **10** lawbreaker

desperate 4 dire, rash, wild **5** grave, great **6** daring, urgent **7** extreme, frantic, serious **8** critical, hopeless, reckless, wretched **9** dangerous, incurable **10** beyond hope, despairing, despondent

Desperate Hours, The
   director: 12 William Wyler
   cast: 8 Gig Young **11** Dewey Martin, Martha Scott **13** Arthur Kennedy, Frederic March **14** Humphrey Bogart

Desperately Seeking Susan
   director: 14 Susan Seidelman
   cast: 7 Madonna **15** Rosanna Arquette

desperation 7 despair **12** hopelessness, recklessness

despicable 4 base, mean, vile **10** detestable, outrageous **11** disgraceful **12** contemptible **13** reprehensible

despise 5 abhor, scorn **6** detest, loathe **7** contemn, disdain, dislike **10** look down on

despoil 3 rob **4** loot **6** ravage **7** pillage, plunder

despoiler 6 looter, robber, vandal **7** brigand **8** pillager **9** plunderer

despondency 5 gloom **6** dismay **7** despair, sadness **9** dejection, pessimism **10** depression, desolation, low spirits, melancholy **11** melancholia **12** hopelessness **14** discouragement **15** downheartedness

despondent 3 low **4** blue, down **8** dejected, downcast, hopeless **9** depressed **11** discouraged, downhearted **12** disconsolate, disheartened

despot 4 czar, tsar **6** tyrant **8** autocrat, dictator **9** oppressor

despotic 9 imperious **10** autocratic, tyrannical **11** dictatorial **13** authoritarian

despotism 7 tyranny **9** autocracy **10** absolutism

dessert 3 pie **4** cake, nuts, tart **5** fruit, sweet, treat **6** pastry **7** cobbler **8** ice cream **11** final course

destination 3 aim, end **4** goal, plan **6** object, target **7** purpose **8** ambition **9** objective **11** journey's end

destiny 3 lot **4** fate **5** karma, moira **6** future, kismet **7** fortune **9** necessity
   goddess of: 5 Fates, Morae, Parca **6** Moerae, Moirai, Parcae

destitute 4 poor **5** broke, needy **6** busted **8** indigent **9** penniless **15** poverty-stricken

destitution 4 lack, want **6** penury **7** beggary, poverty **9** indigence, privation **11** extreme want **13** pennilessness **14** impoverishment

destroy 4 ruin **5** waste, wreck **6** ravage **8** demolish **9** devastate

destroy completely 3 end **4** rase, raze **5** total **7** abolish, wipe out **8** lay waste **9** eradicate, extirpate, liquidate **10** annihilate, obliterate **11** exterminate

destroyer 4 bane **6** blight, killer **7** gunboat, warship **10** affliction **11** annihilator

destruct 3 gut **4** raze, ruin **5** wreck **7** despoil, destroy, wipe out **8** decimate, demolish, desolate, pull down, tear down **9** devastate **10** lay in ruins

destruction 4 ruin **5** havoc **8** wreckage, wrecking **10** demolition **11** devastation

destructive 7 harmful, hurtful, ruinous **8** damaging **9** injurious **11** detrimental, devastating **15** not constructive

Destry Rides Again
   director: 14 George Marshall
   based on a story by: 8 Max Brand
   cast: 12 Brian Donlevy, James Stewart **15** Marlene Dietrich **16** Charles Winninger

song: 35 See What the Boys in the Back Room Will Have

desultory 4 idle **6** casual, chance, fitful, random **7** aimless, cursory **9** haphazard **10** without aim **11** unconnected

detach 5 sever **6** loosen **7** unhitch **8** separate, unfasten **9** disengage **10** disconnect **11** disentangle

detached 4 fair **5** aloof **7** distant, neutral, severed **8** reserved, unbiased **9** impartial, objective, separated, uncoupled, unhitched **10** disengaged, fairminded, unfastened **11** indifferent, unconnected **12** disconnected, unprejudiced **13** disinterested, dispassionate **French: 6** degage

detachment 4 unit **5** force **8** coolness, fairness, severing **9** aloofness, isolation, severance **10** cutting off, neutrality, separation **11** objectivity **12** impartiality, indifference **13** disconnection, disengagement, preoccupation **16** special task force

detail 4 fact, iota, item **6** aspect, relate **7** appoint, feature, itemize, recount, respect, specify **9** component, delineate, designate, enumerate **10** detachment, particular **11** special duty **13** assign to a task, particularize **14** special service **20** particular assignment

detailed 6 minute **8** itemized, thorough **10** item by item **12** point by point

detailed list 9 breakdown **11** itemization **14** categorization

detain 4 hold, slow, stop **5** delay **6** arrest, hinder, retard, slow up **7** confine **8** slow down **13** keep in custody

detainment 7 custody, holding **9** detention **11** confinement **12** imprisonment **13** incarceration

detect 3 see **4** espy, note, spot **5** catch **6** notice **7** observe, uncover **8** discover, perceive

detectable 10 noticeable **11** appreciable, discernible, perceivable, perceptible **13** ascertainable

detective 2 PI **3** tec **6** shamus, sleuth **7** gumshoe **10** private eye **12** investigator **19** special investigator

detectives 5 Kojak **7** Columbo, Matlock **8** Sam Spade, Magnum P.I. **9** James Bond, Nancy Drew, Hardy Boys **10** Bertha Cool, Goldfinger, Mike Hammer, Miss Marple, Perry Mason **11** Charlie Chan, Ellery Queen **13** Hercule Poirot, Father Dowling, Philip Marlowe **14** Sherlock Holmes **15** Jessica Fletcher

detention 7 custody, holding **9** keeping in **10** detainment **11** confinement, holding back **12** imprisonment **13** incarceration

deter 4 stop **5** daunt **6** divert, hinder, impede **7** prevent **8** dissuade **10** discourage

deteriorate 3 ebb **4** fade, wane **5** decay, lapse **6** worsen **7** crumble, decline, fall off **10** degenerate **12** disintegrate

deteriorated 6 shabby **7** rickety **8** decaying, worsened **9** crumbling **10** broken-down, tumble-down **11** dilapidated, in disrepair **13** disintegrated

deterioration 5 decay, lapse **6** fading, waning **7** decline **9** crumbling, decadence, worsening **12** degeneration, dilapidation **14** disintegration

determination 4 grit **5** pluck, power, spunk **6** fixing **7** finding, resolve, verdict **8** boldness, decision, judgment, settling, solution, tenacity **9** reasoning, resolving **10** conclusion, resolution **11** determining, persistence **12** perseverance, resoluteness **13** act of deciding, steadfastness **16** stick-to-itiveness

determine 5 learn **6** affect, decide, detect, settle **7** control, find out, resolve **8** conclude, discover, regulate **9** ascertain, establish, figure out, influence **15** come to a decision, give direction to

determined 7 dead set, decided, settled **8** found out, obdurate, resolute, stubborn **9** obstinate, tenacious **10** figured out **11** ascertained, established **15** come to a decision

deterrent 4 curb **5** check **9** hindrance, restraint **14** discouragement

detest 4 hate **5** abhor **6** loathe **7** despise **10** recoil from **16** dislike intensely

detestable 4 vile **6** odious **7** hateful **9** abhorrent, loathsome, obnoxious, offensive, repulsive, revolting **10** disgusting, unpleasant **12** disagreeable

detestation 4 hate **6** hatred **7** disgust, dislike **8** aversion, distaste, loathing **9** antipathy, repulsion, revulsion **10** abhorrence, repugnance

dethrone 4 oust **6** depose, unseat

detonate 4 fire **5** blast, burst, erupt, go off, shoot **6** blow up, ignite, report, set off **7** explode **8** touch off **9** discharge, fulminate

detonation 5 blast, burst **6** report **9** discharge, explosion

detour 5 skirt **6** bypass, byroad, divert **7** digress **9** deviation, diversion **10** digression

detract 5 lower **6** lessen, reduce **8** diminish **12** subtract from, take away from

detraction 4 flaw **11** shortcoming **12** disadvantage

detractor 5 enemy **6** critic **8** opponent **9** adversary, belittler, slanderer **10** antagonist, bad mouther, disparager

detriment 4 harm, loss **6** damage, injury **10** impairment **12** disadvantage

detrimental 7 adverse, harmful **8** damaging **9** injurious **10** pernicious **11** deleterious, destructive, unfavorable **15** disadvantageous

Detroit
baseball team: 6 Tigers
basketball team: 5 Shock **7** Pistons
football team: 5 Lions
hockey team: 8 Redwings

de trop 7 too many, too much **8** in the way **9** not wanted

Deucalion
father: 10 Prometheus
mother: 7 Pronoia
wife: 6 Pyrrha
son: 6 Hellen
founded: 9 human race
after: 6 deluge

deus ex machina 15 god from a machine **18** improbable solution

Deus vobiscum 12 God be with you

Deus vult 8 God wills (it)
cry of: 9 Crusaders

devaluate 6 lessen, reduce **7** deflate, degrade **10** depreciate

devaluation 4 drop **7** decline **12** depreciation

devalue 5 lower, taint **6** debase, defile, infect **7** cheapen, corrupt, degrade, pervert, pollute, revalue **8** mark down **9** devalu- ate, underrate, write down **10** adulterate, degenerate, demonetize, depreciate, remonetize **11** contaminate

devastate 4 ruin **5** level, spoil, waste, wreck **6** ravage **7** despoil, destroy **8** demolish, desolate, lay waste

devastating 7 ruinous **8** damaging **9** injurious **10** calamitous, disastrous **11** cataclysmic, destructive, detrimental **12** catastrophic

devastation 4 ruin **9** ruination **10** demolition **11** destruction

develop 4 grow **5** print, ripen **6** evolve, expand, finish, flower, mature, pick up, unfold **7** acquire, advance, amplify, augment, broaden, build up, convert, enlarge, improve, process, turn out **8** contract, energize **9** cultivate **10** come to have **11** come to light, elaborate on

development 5 event **6** growth, result **7** advance, history **8** progress **9** evolution

deviant 4 warp **5** shift **7** deviate, pervert **8** aberrant, abnormal **9** deflected, divergent

deviate 4 part, vary, veer **5** stray **6** depart, swerve, wander **8** go astray **9** sidetrack, turn aside

deviation 6 change **7** veering **8** rambling, straying **9** wandering **10** aberration, digression, divergence **11** abnormality, fluctuation

device 4 plan, plot, ploy, ruse, wile

5 angle, trick **6** design, gadget, scheme **7** gimmick **8** artifice, strategy **9** apparatus, invention, mechanism, stratagem **11** contraption, contrivance

devil, the Devil 3 guy **5** rogue, Satan, thing **6** Azazel, fellow, wretch **7** hellion, Lucifer, ruffian, serpent, villain **8** creature **9** Archfiend, Beelzebub, scoundrel **11** unfortunate **12** spirit of evil **13** mischief-maker **16** prince of darkness

Devil and Daniel Webster, The
author: **19** Stephen Vincent Benet
director: **15** William Dieterle
character: **5** Devil **7** Webster **9** Mr Scratch
cast: **10** James Craig **11** Anne Shirley **12** Edward Arnold, Walter Huston
score: **15** Bernard Herrmann
Oscar for: **5** score
also titled: **18** All That Money Can Buy

devilish 4 evil **6** wicked **7** demonic, heinous, impious, satanic, vicious **8** demoniac, fiendish **9** nefarious **10** demoniacal, diabolical, villainous

devil-may-care 4 bold, rash, wild **5** risky **6** daring, rakish **8** heedless, reckless **9** audacious, daredevil

devil's advocate
Latin: **16** advocatus diaboli

Devil's Advocate
author: **14** Taylor Caldwell

Devil's Disciple, The
author: **17** George Bernard Shaw

Devine, Andy
real name: **16** Jeremiah Schwartz
born: **11** Flagstaff AZ
roles: **7** Jingles **9** Andy's Gang **14** Wild Bill Hickok

devious 3 sly **4** wily **6** sneaky, tricky **7** crooked **9** deceitful, dishonest **11** treacherous **12** dishonorable **13** double-dealing

devise 4 plot **5** forge, frame **6** design, invent, map out **7** concoct, prepare, think up **8** block out, conceive, contrive **9** construct, formulate

deviser 6 author, framer **7** creator, planner **8** inventor **9** architect, contriver **10** originator

devitalize 4 kill **6** deaden, weaken **8** enervate **10** debilitate

DeVito, Danny
born: **9** Neptune, NJ
wife: **11** Rhea Perlman
roles: **4** Taxi **5** Twins, Hoffa **6** Tin Men **7** Matilda **9** Get Shorty **11** Mars Attacks **13** Batman Returns, War of the Roses **14** Ruthless People **22** Throw Mamma From the Train

devoid 5 empty **6** barren **7** lacking, wanting, without **8** bereft of **9** destitute **11** unblest with

devote 5 apply **6** direct **7** address, utilize **8** dedicate **10** consecrate, give

over to **11** concentrate **15** give oneself up to **22** center one's attentions on

devoted 4 fond, true **5** loyal **6** ardent, loving **7** earnest, staunch, zealous **8** adhering, faithful **9** dedicated, steadfast **10** passionate, unwavering **17** strongly committed

devotedness 8 devotion **10** commitment, dedication **13** attentiveness **17** earnest attachment

devoted to luxury 9 epicurean, sybaritic **10** hedonistic, voluptuous

devotee 3 fan **6** rooter **7** booster, groupie **8** adherent, advocate, champion, disciple, follower **10** aficionado, enthusiast

devotion, devotions 4 love, zeal **5** ardor, piety **6** fealty, regard **7** loyalty **8** fondness, holiness **9** adherence, godliness, reverence **10** allegiance, commitment, concern for, dedication, devoutness, meditation **11** religiosity **12** faithfulness, spirituality **13** attentiveness, prayer service **15** religious fervor **17** earnest attachment **19** religious observance

De Voto, Bernard A
author of: **21** Across the Wide Missouri

devour 7 stuff in **8** bolt down, gobble up, gulp down, knock off, wolf down **9** go through **13** read widely **14** eat voraciously **15** absorb oneself in, consume greedily **16** read compulsively, take in ravenously **17** become engrossed in

devout 5 pious **6** ardent **7** earnest, fervent, intense, serious, zealous **8** orthodox, reverent **9** religious **10** passionate, worshipful

devoutness 5 piety **8** devotion, holiness **9** godliness, reverence **12** spirituality **15** religious fervor

DeVries, Hugo
field: **6** botany
nationality: **5** Dutch
researched: **8** heredity, mutation

DeVries, Peter
author of: **16** Consenting Adults **24** Slouching Toward Kalamazoo

dew 8 moisture **12** condensation **18** droplets of moisture

Dewar, James
field: **7** physics **9** chemistry
nationality: **8** Scottish
liquified: **8** hydrogen
solidified: **8** hydrogen
developed: **7** cordite **10** Dewar flask **12** liquid oxygen

Dewey, George
served in: **18** Spanish-American War
battle: **9** Manila Bay
destroyed: **12** Spanish fleet

Dewhurst, Colleen
husband: **12** George C Scott
born: **6** Canada **8** Montreal

roles: **12** The Nun's Story **18** Desire Under the Elms **22** A Moon for the Misbegotten

De Wilde, Brandon
born: **10** Brooklyn NY
roles: **3** Hud **5** Shane **11** All Fall Down

dewy 4 damp **5** moist **7** bedewed

dexterity 8 deftness, facility **9** handiness **10** adroitness, nimbleness **11** manual skill, proficiency

dexterous 4 able, deft **5** agile, quick **6** active, adroit, gifted, nimble **8** skillful **9** efficient, ingenious **11** resourceful

diabolic, diabolical 4 evil, foul **6** wicked **7** baleful, demonic, heinous, impious, satanic, vicious **8** devilish, fiendish **9** monstrous, nefarious **10** malevolent, villainous

diadem 4 halo **5** crown, tiara **7** circlet, coronet **8** headband

diagnosis 5 study **8** analysis, scrutiny **11** examination **13** investigation, medical report **16** scientific report **22** conclusion from symptoms, specification of illness

diagonal line 4 bias **5** angle, slant

diagram 3 map **4** plan **5** chart **6** sketch **7** drawing, outline **9** breakdown **11** line drawing **12** illustration **14** representation **15** rough projection

dialect 5 argot, idiom, lingo **6** accent, jargon, patois **8** localism **10** vernacular **11** regionalism **13** colloquialism, provincialism **15** language variety

Dial M for Murder
director: **15** Alfred Hitchcock
based on play by: **14** Frederick Knott
cast: **10** Grace Kelly, Ray Milland **14** Robert Cummings

dialogue, dialog 4 talk **5** lines **6** parley, speech **8** conclave **10** conference **12** conversation **14** verbal exchange **15** personal meeting **16** formal discussion

diamond
characteristic: **7** hardest
color: **4** blue, pink **9** blue-white **12** canary yellow
element: **6** carbon
famous: **4** Hope **6** Jonker **8** Cullinan, Idol's Eye, Koh-i-Noor **9** Excelsior **12** Star of Africa, Star of the East **17** Star of Sierra Leone
quality: **3** cut **4** fire **5** color **7** clarity **10** brilliance
source: **5** Congo, India **6** Africa, Borneo, Brazil, Guyana **8** Tanzania **9** Australia, Venezuela **11** South Africa, Soviet Union **12** South America **15** South West Africa
weight: **5** carat, point

Diamond State
nickname of: **8** Delaware

Diana
origin: **5** Roman

goddess of: 4 moon **6** slaves **7** hunting
protectress of: 5 women
corresponds to: 6 Phoebe **7** Artemis
epithet: 10 Nemorensis
  means: 10 of the grove

Diana of the Crossways
author: 14 George Meredith
character: 9 Mr Warwick **11** Diana Merion, Percy Dacier **12** Lady Dunstane **14** Thomas Redworth **15** Lord Dannisburgh

diaphanous 5 filmy, gauzy, lucid, sheer **6** flimsy, limpid **8** gossamer, pellucid **11** translucent, transparent

diary 3 log **7** daybook, journal **9** chronicle **12** daily journal **14** day-to-day record

Diary of Anne Frank, The
author: 9 Anne Frank
director: 13 George Stevens
cast: 6 Ed Wynn **9** Lou Jacobi **10** Diane Baker **13** Millie Perkins, Richard Beymer **14** Shelley Winters (Mrs Van Daan) **17** Joseph Schildkraut (Father Frank)
Oscar for: 17 supporting actress (Winters)

Diasia
festival of: 4 Zeus

diatribe 6 tirade **9** contumely, invective **11** castigation **12** vituperation **13** stream of abuse **14** bitter harangue **18** accusatory language **19** violent denunciation

dice 4 chop, cube **5** bones, cubes, cut up, mince
singular: 3 die

Dick, Mr
character in: 16 David Copperfield
author: 7 Dickens

Dickens, Charles
author of: 9 Hard Times **10** Bleak House **11** Oliver Twist **12** Barnaby Rudge, Dombey and Son, Little Dorrit **14** Pickwick Papers **15** A Christmas Carol, Our Mutual Friend **16** A Tale of Two Cities, David Copperfield, Martin Chuzzlewit, Nicholas Nickleby **17** Great Expectations **19** The Old Curiosity Shop **22** The Mystery of Edwin Drood

dicker 4 deal **6** haggle, higgle, outbid **7** bargain, chaffer, quibble, wrangle **8** beat down, talk down, underbid **9** negotiate **17** drive a hard bargain

Dickey, James
author of: 9 The Zodiac **11** Deliverance **16** Strength of Fields **17** Buckdancer's Choice

Dickinson, Angie
real name: 13 Angeline Brown
husband: 13 Burt Bacharach
born: 6 Kulm ND
roles: 8 Rio Bravo **11** Police Woman **13** Dressed to Kill **19** The Sins of Rachel Cade

Dick Tracy
creator: 12 Chester Gould
character: 8 BO Plenty, Moonmaid **12** Gravel Gertie **13** Sparkle Plenty **16** Jeremiah Truehart
  wife: 12 Tess Truehart
  daughter: 11 Bonny Braids
  assistant: 9 Pat Patton
  protege: 6 Junior
  villain: 5 Itchy **6** B-B Eyes **7** Flattop, Flyface, Measles, Mumbles, The Brow, The Mole **8** The Blank **9** Pruneface, The Midget, The Rodent
equipment: 16 two-way wrist radio

Dick Van Dyke Show, The
character: 9 Alan Brady, Rob Petrie **11** Jerry Helper, Laura Petrie, Sally Rogers **12** Buddy Sorrell, Melvin Cooley, Millie Helper **13** Ritchie Petrie
cast: 9 Rose Marie **10** Carl Reiner, Jerry Paris **13** Larry Matthews, Richard Deacon **14** Mary Tyler Moore, Morey Amsterdam **17** Ann Morgan Guilbert

dictate 4 rule **5** edict, order **6** decree, dictum, direct, enjoin, impose, ordain, ruling, urging **7** bidding, counsel, lay down, mandate **8** set forth **9** determine, ordinance, prescribe, prompting, pronounce, stricture **11** exhortation, inclination, requirement

dictator 4 czar, duce, tsar **6** caesar, despot, fuhrer, kaiser, tyrant **7** emperor **8** autocrat **13** absolute ruler
Argentinian: 5 Peron
German: 6 Hitler
Italian: 9 Mussolini
Russian: 5 Lenin **6** Stalin
Spanish: 6 Franco
Ugandan: 7 Idi Amin

dictatorial 6 lordly **7** haughty, willful **8** absolute, arrogant, despotic **9** arbitrary, imperious, unlimited **10** autocratic, peremptory, tyrannical **11** categorical, domineering, magisterial, overbearing **12** supercilious, unrestricted **13** authoritative **17** inclined to command

diction 7 wording **8** delivery, rhetoric, verbiage **9** elocution **10** intonation, use of idiom, vocabulary **11** enunciation, phraseology, verbal style **12** articulation **13** choice of words, pronunciation **16** turn of expression **17** command of language **18** manner of expression

dictum 3 saw **4** fiat **5** adage, axiom, edict, maxim, order **6** decree, saying, truism **7** dictate, precept, proverb **11** commandment **13** pronouncement **15** dogmatic bidding **22** authoritative statement

Dictys
occupation: 9 fisherman

found: 5 chest
  containing: 5 Danae **7** Perseus

didactic 7 donnish, preachy **8** academic, edifying, pedantic, tutorial **9** doctrinal, homiletic, pedagogic **10** expository, moralizing **11** educational, instructive, lecturelike, overbearing **12** prescriptive **17** inclined to lecture

didactics 8 teaching **9** education, teachings **10** pedagogics **11** instruction

Diderot, Denis
author of: 12 Encyclopedia **13** Rameau's Nephew

Didion, Joan
author of: 8 Salvador **10** White Album **14** Play It as It Lays **19** A Book of Common Prayer **24** Slouching Toward Bethlehem

Dido
queen of: 8 Carthage
father: 5 Mutto
brother: 9 Pygmalion
sister: 4 Anna
husband: 8 Sychaeus
lover: 6 Aeneas
corresponds to: 6 Elissa

Dido and Aeneas
opera by: 7 Purcell
character: 4 Dido (Queen of Carthage) **6** Aeneas

die 3 ebb, rot **4** ache, fade, fail, long, pass, stop, wane **5** croak, yearn **6** depart, expire, go flat, pass on, perish, recede, run out, wither **7** be eager, decline, die away, go stale, run down, subside **8** fade away, melt away, pass away, pass over, wear away **9** be anxious, break down, lose force, lose power, meet death **10** degenerate, want keenly **11** come to an end, suffer death **12** wish ardently **13** come to one's end, desire greatly, go to one's glory, kick the bucket **14** leave this world, pine with desire, become inactive **15** slowly disappear **17** become inoperative
plural: 4 dice

die away 4 fade **5** abate, cease **8** diminish

die down 5 abate **7** subside **8** diminish, slack off

die out 6 vanish **9** cease to be, disappear **13** become extinct

Diesel, Rudolf
field: 11 engineering
invented: 12 Diesel engine

diet 5 board, synod **7** edibles, nurture **8** congress, victuals **9** nutriment, nutrition **10** assemblage, convention, parliament, provisions, sustenance **11** comestibles, convocation, legislature, nourishment, subsistence **12** eating habits, eat sparingly **13** eating regimen, lawmaking body **14** eat judiciously **15** eat abstemiously, eat restrictedly, general assembly

16 limitation of fare, regulate one's food **17** bicameral assembly **18** nutritional regimen, representative body, restrict one's intake

Dietrich, Marlene
real name: 22 Maria Magdalene Dietrich
born: 7 Germany
roles: 8 Lola Lola **11** Blonde Venus **12** The Blue Angel **15** Rancho Notorious **16** Destry Rides Again, The Garden of Allah **17** The Scarlet Empress **24** Witness for the Prosecution

Dietrich von Bern
origin: 8 Germanic
king of: 10 Ostrogoths
Latin name: 9 Theodoric

Diety 3 Bel, God **4** Baal **6** Marduk, Molech, Moloch, Yahweh **7** Chemosh, Jehovah **10** Anammelech **11** Adrammelech

Dieu et mon droit 13 God and my right
motto of: 18 royal arms of England

differ 5 demur **7** dispute, dissent **8** be unlike, contrast, disagree **9** take issue **10** be distinct, depart from, stand apart **11** be disparate, deviate from, diverge from **12** be at variance, be dissimilar, stand opposed

difference 4 spat **5** clash, set-to **7** dispute, quarrel **8** argument, contrast, squabble **9** deviation, disparity, variation **10** divergence, falling out, unlikeness **11** contrariety, contretemps, discrepancy, distinction **12** disagreement **13** contradiction, dissimilarity, dissimilitude **17** contradistinction, lack of resemblance

different 4 rare **6** divers, sundry, unique, unlike **7** bizarre, diverse, foreign, several, strange, unusual, various **8** aberrant, atypical, distinct, manifold, not alike, peculiar, separate, singular, uncommon **9** anomalous, disparate, divergent, other than, unrelated **10** dissimilar, individual, variegated **11** contrasting, distinctive, diversified, not ordinary **12** not identical **13** miscellaneous **14** unconventional

differential 8 contrast **11** distinction

differentiate 6 set off **8** contrast, separate, set apart **11** distinguish, draw the line **12** discriminate **13** make different

differentiation 8 contrast **10** comparison, separation **11** discernment, distinction

differing 6 unlike **7** variant **8** distinct, opposing **9** deviating, disparate, dissident, divergent **10** dissenting, dissimilar **11** contrasting, disagreeing

difficult 4 grim, hard **5** hairy, rough, tough **6** knotty, thorny, trying, unruly, uphill **7** arduous, complex, forward, not easy, onerous, tedious, willful **8** critical, exacting, perverse, stubborn,

ticklish, toilsome **9** demanding, enigmatic, fractious, Herculean, intricate, laborious, obstinate, Sisyphean, strenuous, wearisome **10** burdensome, exhausting, fastidious, formidable, inflexible, perplexing, unyielding **11** bewildering, complicated, hard to solve, intractable, troublesome **12** hard to manage, hard to please, obstreperous, rambunctious, recalcitrant, unmanageable **13** hard to satisfy, problematical, unpredictable **14** hard to deal with **15** unaccommodating

difficulty 3 jam, rub **4** mess, snag **5** trial **6** crisis, muddle, pickle, puzzle **7** barrier, dilemma, problem, straits, trouble **8** hot water, obstacle, quandary, tough job **9** deep water, hindrance, intricacy **10** impediment, perplexity, rough going, uphill work **11** arduousness, obstruction, predicament **12** hard sledding **13** laboriousness **14** stumbling block **15** troublesomeness **17** critical situation

diffidence 7 reserve, shyness **8** meekness, timidity **9** hesitancy, timidness **10** constraint, humbleness, insecurity, reluctance **11** bashfulness **12** introversion, sheepishness, timorousness **14** extreme modesty **15** unassertiveness **19** lack of self-assurance, retiring disposition

diffident 3 shy **6** modest **7** anxious, bashful **8** doubtful, hesitant, reserved, reticent, retiring **11** distrustful, unassertive **12** apprehensive

diffuse 5 wordy **7** verbose **8** rambling **9** desultory, dispersed, scattered, spread out, wandering **10** digressive, discursive, disjointed, long-winded, maundering, meandering, roundabout **14** circumlocutory, extended widely, unconcentrated, vaguely defined **15** not concentrated **18** lacking conciseness

diffuseness 8 rambling **9** prolixity, verbosity, wandering, wordiness **10** dispersion **11** indirection **14** circumlocution, long-windedness

diffusion 6 spread **8** rambling, verbiage **9** dispersal, prolixity, verbosity, wordiness **10** maundering, scattering **11** indirection, profuseness **14** circumlocution, discursiveness, disjointedness, roundaboutness

dig 3 jab **4** gibe, jeer, like, poke, prod, slur **5** aside, drive, gouge, punch, taunt **6** exhume, thrust **7** put-down, salvage, unearth **8** disinter, excavate, pinpoint, retrieve, scoop out **9** extricate, find among, hollow out **10** come up with, excavation, wry comment **11** bring to view **12** verbal thrust **13** cutting remark, search and find

digest 3 dig **5** grasp **6** absorb, fathom, precis, resume **7** realize, summary **8** abstract, dissolve, synopsis **10** abridg-

ment, appreciate, assimilate, comprehend, understand **12** condensation, take in wholly **14** take in mentally

digestive system
component: 5 liver, mouth, teeth **6** tongue **7** stomach **8** appendix, pancreas **9** esophagus, intestine **11** gall bladder **13** salivary gland

dig in 3 eat **4** root **5** begin, embed, imbed, plant **6** anchor **7** pitch in **8** entrench, go to work **10** begin to eat **12** apply oneself

digit 3 one, six, two, toe **4** five, four, nine, unit, zero **5** light, seven, three **6** cipher, figure, finger, number **7** integer, numeral

dignified 5 proud **6** august, proper **7** upright **8** decorous, reserved **9** honorable **10** upstanding **11** circumspect **13** distinguished **14** self-respecting

dignify 5 raise **6** uplift **7** elevate, inflate, promote

dignitary 3 VIP **7** notable **8** luminary **9** personage **12** person of note

dignity 5 honor **7** decorum, majesty, station **9** loftiness, solemnity **10** augustness, importance **11** comportment, stateliness **12** high position, lofty bearing **13** proud demeanor **14** self-possession

digress 5 stray **6** back up, wander **7** deviate **8** divagate **9** turn aside **15** go off on a tangent **17** depart from subject

digression 6 detour **8** straying **9** departure, deviation, diversion, wandering **10** divagation, divergence, side remark **12** obiter dictum

digressive 7 diffuse **9** wandering **10** disjointed, maundering, roundabout **11** off the point **14** circumlocutory

dig up 6 locate **7** find out, root out, uncover, unearth **8** discover **9** ferret out **12** bring to light

dike 4 bank **5** levee, ridge **10** embankment

Dike *see* **4** Dice

dikerion 11 candelabrum, candlestick **12** candleholder

dilapidated 4 shot **6** beat-up, ruined, shabby **7** rickety, run-down, worn-out **8** battered, decaying, decrepit **10** broken-down, ramshackle, tumble-down **11** in disrepair **12** deteriorated, falling apart **15** falling to pieces

dilate 5 swell, widen **6** expand, extend **7** broaden, distend, enlarge, inflate, puff out **9** make wider

dilation 8 swelling, widening **9** expansion **10** broadening, distension, distention

dilatory 4 lazy, slow **5** tardy **6** remiss **8** dawdling, indolent, slothful, sluggish **9** negligent, reluctant **10** phlegmatic **13** lackadaisical **15** inclined to delay, procrastinating

dilemma 4 bind **6** crunch, plight **7** impasse, problem **8** deadlock, quandary **9** stalemate **11** predicament **13** Hobson's choice **15** difficult choice

dilettante 7 amateur, dabbler, trifler **12** experimenter **16** cultured hobbyist

diligence 4 zeal **8** industry **10** commitment, dedication **11** persistence **12** perseverance

diligent 6 active **7** careful, earnest, patient, zealous **8** plodding, sedulous, studious, thorough, untiring **9** assiduous, concerted **10** persistent **11** hardworking, industrious, painstaking, persevering **12** pertinacious **15** well-intentioned

dill 4 anet
  botanical name: 17 Anethum graveolens
  origin: 9 Asia Minor **13** Mediterranean
  family: 7 parsley
  guards against: 7 Evil Eye **10** witchcraft
  use: 6 sauces **7** pickles **10** vegetables

Dillon, Matt
  roles: 3 Tex **10** Rumblefish **12** The Outsiders

dillydally 3 lag **4** idle, loaf **5** dally, delay **6** dawdle, loiter **8** kill time **9** waste time **10** fool around **13** procrastinate

Dilsey
  character in: 18 The Sound and the Fury
  author: 8 Faulkner

dilute 4 thin, weak **6** reduce, temper, watery, weaken **7** diffuse, diluted, thin out **8** decrease, diminish, make weak, mitigate, weakened **9** attenuate, liquidify, water down **10** add water to, adulterate, thinned out **11** adulterated, make thinner, watered down

diluted 4 weak **6** dilute, watery **8** weakened **10** thinned out **11** adulterated, watered down

dilution 8 thinning **9** weakening **12** watering down

dim 3 low **4** hazy, soft, weak **5** dusky, faint, foggy, murky, muted, vague **6** blurry, feeble, gloomy, remote **7** blurred, clouded, muffled, shadowy **8** darkened, nebulous, obscured **9** not bright, tenebrous **10** adumbrated, ill-defined, indefinite, indistinct, intangible **13** unilluminated

DiMaggio, Joe
  nickname: 9 Joltin Joe
  sport: 8 baseball
  position: 8 outfield
  team: 14 New York Yankees
  wife: 13 Marilyn Monroe

dime-a-dozen 6 common **7** humdrum **8** ordinary, workaday **9** plentiful **10** ubiquitous **11** commonplace **12** easy to come by **13** garden-variety **15** undistinguished

dimension, dimensions 4 bulk, mass, size **5** range, scope, width **6** extent, height, length, volume, weight **7** measure **9** amplitude, greatness, magnitude, thickness **10** importance, proportion **11** massiveness **12** measurements **14** physical extent

diminish 3 ebb **4** wane **5** abate, lower **6** lessen, narrow, reduce, shrink **7** decline, dwindle, fall off, shorten, shrivel, subside **8** decrease, peter out **9** be reduced **11** make smaller **13** become smaller

diminuendo
  music: 22 gradually getting softer
  abbreviation: 3 dim

diminution 6 ebbing, waning **7** decline **8** decrease, lowering **9** dwindling, lessening, reduction, shrinkage **10** falling off, shortening, shriveling, subsidence **11** petering out, slacking off

diminutive 3 wee **4** tiny **5** elfin, short, small, teeny **6** little, minute, petite, slight **7** pet name, stunted **8** dwarfish, half-pint, nickname **9** miniature, short form **10** pocket-size, undersized, vest-pocket **11** lilliputian, small-scale, unimportant **13** insignificant **14** inconsiderable

Dimmesdale, Arthur
  character in: 16 The Scarlet Letter
  author: 9 Hawthorne

dimness 4 dusk **5** gloom, shade **8** darkness **14** indistinctness

dimwit 4 fool **5** dummy, dunce, idiot, moron **6** cretin, nitwit **7** dingbat, dullard, dumbell, pinhead **8** dumbbell, dummkopf, imbecile, meathead, numskull **9** birdbrain, blockhead, ding-a-ling, lamebrain, numbskull, simpleton **11** chowderhead, knucklehead

dim-witted 4 dull, dumb **5** dense **6** stupid **7** foolish, idiotic, moronic, witless **8** retarded **9** cretinous, imbecilic

din 4 stir, to-do **5** bruit **6** babble, clamor, hubbub, racket, ruckus, tumult, uproar **7** clangor **9** commotion **10** clattering, hullabaloo

Dinah
  father: 5 Jacob
  mother: 4 Leah
  brother: 3 Dan, Gad **4** Levi **5** Asher, Judah **6** Joseph, Reuben, Simeon **7** Zebulun **8** Benjamin, Issachar, Naphtali
  violated by: 7 Shechem

dine 3 eat, sup **4** feed **5** feast, lunch **6** fall to, supper **7** banquet, partake **9** breakfast, eat dinner **10** break bread, gluttonize, have dinner **11** gourmandize **14** take sustenance

Dine see **6** Navajo

Dinesen, Isak
  real name: 18 Karen Blixen-Finecke
  author of: 9 Last Tales **11** Out of Africa **12** Winter's Tales **16** Seven Gothic Tales

dinghy 5 skiff **7** rowboat **8** sailboat **9** small boat

dingy 4 dull **5** dusty, grimy, murky, tacky **6** dismal, dreary, gloomy, shabby **12** dirty and drab

dining room
  French: 12 salle a manger

dinner 4 food, meal **5** feast **6** repast, supper **7** banquet
  French: 8 dejeuner **10** table d'hote

Dinner at Eight
  director: 11 George Cukor
  author: 10 Edna Ferber **14** George S Kaufman
  cast: 8 Lee Tracy **10** Jean Harlow **11** Billie Burke **12** Wallace Beery **13** John Barrymore, Marie Dressler **15** Lionel Barrymore

dinosaur
  means: 14 fearfully great, terrible lizard
  subclass: 11 Archosauria
  characteristic: 7 diapsid **14** teeth in sockets, two-arched skull **18** three-element pelvis
  group: 11 Saurischian **13** Ornithischian
    flesh-eating biped: 8 therapod
    plant-eating quadruped: 8 sauropod
    plant-eating biped: 10 ornithopod
    armored: 10 ceratopsid
  of Africa: 9 Iguanodon **13** Brachiosaurus **17** Heterodontosaurus
  of Asia: 13 Hypselosaurus, Protoceratops
  of Europe: 9 Iguanodon **12** Plateosaurus **13** Compsognathus, Hypselosaurus, Hypsilophodon
  of North America: 10 Diplodocus, Edmontonia, Nodosaurus **11** Anatosaurus, Anchisaurus, Gorgosaurus, Monoclonius, Saurolophus, Scolosaurus, Stegosaurus, Triceratops **12** Ankylosaurus, Camarasaurus, Camptosaurus, Coelophysics, Lambeosaurus, Paleoscincus **13** Brachiosaurus, Styracosaurus, Tyrannosaurus **14** Thescelosaurus **15** Parasaurolophus, Procheneosaurus
  of South America: 12 Pisanosaurus
  fictional: 4 Puff **6** Barney **12** Jurassic Park

dint 4 push, will **5** drive, force, labor, might, power **6** charge, effort, energy, strain, stress **8** endeavor, exertion, strength, struggle **10** insistence **12** forcefulness **13** determination **14** relentlessness

diocese 3 see **7** eparchy **9** bishopric **14** church district
  jurisdiction of: 6 bishop

Diomedes
  king of: 6 Thrace
  father: 4 Ares **6** Tydeus

mother: 6 Cyrene **7** Deipyle
member of: 7 Epigoni
kept: 9 wild mares
fed mares on: 10 human flesh
death planned by: 8 Hercules

Dione
consort of: 4 Zeus

Dionysia
festival of: 8 Dionysus

Dionysus *see* **7** Bacchus

Dioscuri *see* **15** Castor and Pollux

dip 4 bail, dish, dunk, sink, skim, soak **5** droop, ladle, scoop, slope, spoon **6** dabble, dish up, peruse, shovel **7** decline, descend, dish out, run over **8** drop down, glance at, submerge, turn down **13** study slightly **14** immerse briefly, lift by scooping, try tentatively **15** incline downward

dip into 4 scan, skim **5** ladle **6** browse, peruse **7** deplete **8** look over **13** glance through, make inroads in

Diplodocus
type: 8 dinosaur, sauropod
period: 8 Jurassic
location: 12 North America

diplomacy 4 tact **5** craft, skill **7** finesse **8** delicacy, prudence, subtlety **10** artfulness, discretion **11** maneuvering, savoir-faire **13** statesmanship **14** foreign affairs **16** artful management **18** foreign negotiation **21** international politics

diplomat 5 envoy **6** consul **7** attache **8** emissary, minister **9** statesman **10** ambassador, negotiator **12** interlocutor **13** tactful person
acceptable: 12 persona grata
unacceptable: 15 persona non grata

diplomatic 5 adept, suave **6** artful, urbane **7** attuned, politic, prudent, tactful **8** discreet **9** sensitive, strategic **13** ambassadorial **14** foreign-service **15** state-department

Dipper
nickname of: 15 Wilt Chamberlain

Dipsas
form: 7 serpent

dipsomaniac 3 sot **4** lush, soak, wino **5** drunk, rummy, souse, toper **6** barfly, boozer **7** tippler **8** drunkard **9** alcoholic, inebriate

diptera
class: 8 hexapoda
phylum: 10 arthropoda
group: 7 true fly

Dirae *see* **6** Furies

dire 4 grim **5** awful, grave **6** dismal, urgent, woeful **7** crucial, extreme, fearful, ominous, ruinous **8** critical, dreadful, horrible, terrible **9** appalling, desperate, harrowing, ill-boding, ill-omened **10** calamitous, disastrous, portentous **11** apocalyptic, cataclysmic **12** catastrophic, inauspicious

direct 3 aim **4** head, lead, urge **5**
blunt, clear, focus, frank, guide, order, pilot, usher **6** advise, candid, charge, enjoin, handle, head-on, honest, manage **7** address, command, conduct, control, earmark, forward, level at, oversee, pointed, sincere, train at **8** explicit, indicate, instruct, navigate, personal **9** conduct to, designate, firsthand, intend for, supervise **10** administer, face-to-face, forthright, point-blank, show the way, unmediated **11** plain-spoken, point the way, point toward, preside over, superintend **15** straightforward

direction 3 aim, ENE, ESE, NNE, NNW, SSE, SSW, way, WNW, WSW **4** bent, care, east, path, west **5** drift, north, order, route, south, track, trend **6** charge, course, recipe **7** bearing, command, control, current **8** guidance, headship, tendency **9** alignment **10** guidelines, leadership, management, regulation **11** inclination, instruction, line of march, supervision **12** line of action, prescription, surveillance **13** line of thought **14** administration, point of compass **15** superintendence

directive 5 ukase **8** bulletin **9** statement **10** communique **11** declaration **12** instructions, proclamation **13** communication

directly 4 soon **6** at once, openly **7** exactly, frankly **8** candidly, honestly, in person, promptly, straight **9** forthwith, precisely, presently, right away **10** face-to-face, in a beeline, personally **11** immediately, momentarily **12** in plain terms, not obliquely, unswervingly **13** unambiguously, unequivocally **14** as the crow flies **15** in a straight line **16** as soon as possible **17** on a straight course, straightforwardly

directness 6 candor **9** bluntness, frankness **10** candidness **14** forthrightness **19** straightforwardness

direct opposite 7 reverse **8** converse **10** antithesis

director 4 boss, head **5** chief **6** leader, master **7** curator, foreman, manager **8** chairman, governor, overseer **9** commander, conductor, organizer **10** controller, supervisor **13** administrator **14** superintendent

dirge 6 lament **7** requiem **8** threnody **9** death song **10** burial hymn, death march **11** funeral song **13** mournful sound **19** mournful composition

dirigo 7 I direct
motto of: 5 Maine

dirk 3 sny **4** snee, stab **5** knife, skean **6** dagger, skiver **7** poniard
origin: 8 Scotland

Dirks, Rudolph
creator/artist of: 12 Hans and Fritz **17** Captain and the Kids **19** The Katzenjammer Kids

dirt 3 mud **4** dust, loam, mire, muck, scum, slop, smut, soil, soot **5** dross, earth, filth, grime, humus, offal, rumor, slime, trash **6** gossip, ground, refuse, sludge, smudge **7** garbage, rubbish, scandal, slander **8** impurity, leavings, vileness **9** excrement, indecency, obscenity, profanity, sweepings **10** foul matter, moral filth, scurrility **11** pornography, scuttlebutt, squalidness **12** scabrousness **13** salaciousness **14** defamatory talk **15** filthy substance, unclean language **17** sensational expose

dirt-cheap 6 a steal **7** bargain **11** inexpensive **14** very reasonable **15** bargain-basement

dirty 4 base, foul, hard, lewd, mean, soil, spot, vile **5** grimy, messy, muddy, nasty, smear, stain, sully **6** coarse, filthy, grubby, mess up, muck up, risque, rotten, shabby, slop up, smudge, smudgy, smutty, soiled, sordid, untidy, vulgar **7** begrime, besmear, blacken, corrupt, crooked, devious, illegal, illicit, immoral, lowdown, muddied, obscene, pollute, squalid, sullied, tarnish, unclean **8** befouled, begrimed, indecent, off-color, polluted, prurient, scabrous, unwashed **9** besmeared, deceitful, difficult, dishonest, tarnished, unsterile **10** despicable, fraudulent, licentious, perfidious, unpleasant, villainous **11** distasteful, treacherous **12** contemptible, disagreeable, dishonorable, pornographic, unscrupulous **14** morally unclean

Dirty Dozen, The
director: 13 Robert Aldrich
cast: 8 Jim Brown **9** Lee Marvin **10** Robert Ryan, Trini Lopez **11** Clint Walker **13** George Kennedy **14** Charles Bronson, Ernest Borgnine, John Cassavetes, Richard Jaeckel **16** Donald Sutherland

Dis
also: 8 Dis Pater
means: 5 Hades
god of: 10 underworld
corresponds to: 5 Orcus, Pluto

dis 6 insult **9** disparage

disability 5 minus **6** defect **8** handicap, weakness **9** infirmity, unfitness **10** affliction, impairment, impediment, inadequacy **11** shortcoming **12** debilitation, disadvantage **16** disqualification

disable 6 damage, hinder, impair, weaken **7** cripple **8** handicap **12** incapacitate

disabled
French: 12 hors de combat

disabuse 8 set right **9** relieve of **10** disenchant **11** disillusion, set straight

disaccord 7 discord **10** disharmony **12** disagreement **15** incompatibility

disacknowledge 4 deny **6** disown **7** disavow **8** disallow, disclaim **9** repudiate

disadvantage 4 flaw **6** burden **7** trouble **8** drawback, handicap, hardship, nuisance, weakness **9** detriment, hindrance, in arrears, weak point **10** impediment **12** weak position **13** inconvenience **16** fly in the ointment

disadvantaged 8 deprived, emergent, emerging, troubled **10** struggling **11** handicapped **12** impoverished **14** underdeveloped **15** underprivileged

disadvantageous 7 harmful **9** injurious **11** detrimental, inadvisable, inexpedient, undesirable, unfavorable, unfortunate

disaffect 4 wean **8** alienate, estrange **10** drive apart

disaffected 5 upset **7** hostile **8** agitated, inimical **9** alienated, disturbed, estranged, withdrawn **10** unfriendly **11** belligerent, discomposed, disgruntled, quarrelsome **12** antipathetic, discontented, dissatisfied **14** irreconcilable

disaffection 7 dislike **8** aversion, distaste **9** antipathy **10** alienation, discontent, disloyalty **12** estrangement

disaffirm 4 deny **5** annul **6** disown **7** decline, disavow **8** abnegate, disclaim, forswear, renounce **9** repudiate **15** wash one's hands of

disaffirmation 6 denial **9** annulment, disavowal **10** abnegation, disclaimer **11** repudiation **12** renunciation **13** contradiction

disagree 4 vary **5** clash, upset **6** depart, differ **7** deviate, diverge, make ill **8** be unlike, conflict, distress **9** discomfit **10** disconcert, stand apart **11** be injurious, fail to agree, not coincide **12** be at variance, be discordant, be dissimilar **13** cause problems **14** be unreconciled **15** be at loggerheads, differ in opinion **16** oppose one another, think differently

disagreeable 5 cross, harsh, nasty, surly, testy **7** grating, grouchy, peevish **8** churlish, petulant **9** difficult, irascible, irritable, obnoxious, offensive, repellent, repugnant, repulsive, unamiable, unwelcome **10** disgusting, ill-natured, uninviting, unpleasant **11** acrimonious, bad-tempered, displeasing, distasteful, ill-tempered, uncongenial, unpalatable **13** uncomfortable

disagreeing 6 at odds **7** deviant, varying **8** clashing **9** deviating, differing, disputing **10** quarreling **11** conflicting **13** at loggerheads

disagreement 5 clash, fight **7** discord, dispute, quarrel **8** argument, squabble, variance **9** deviation, disaccord, disparity, diversity **10** difference, divergence, falling-out, unlikeness **11** discrepancy, incongruity **13** dissimilarity, dissimilitude, lack of harmony **15** incompatibility **16** misunderstanding

disallow 4 deny, veto **6** abjure, forbid, refuse, reject **8** prohibit **9** repudiate

disallowance 4 veto **6** denial **7** refusal **9** rejection **11** prohibition, repudiation

disallowed 6 vetoed **7** abjured, refused **8** rejected **9** forbidden **10** repudiated **12** inadmissible, unacceptable

disappear 2 go **3** end **4** exit, fade, flee **5** leave **6** be gone, depart, die out, retire, vanish **8** be no more, fade away, melt away, withdraw **9** evaporate **12** be lost to view, cease to exist, leave no trace **13** cease to appear, cease to be seen **14** become obscured, cease to be known, pass out of sight **15** vanish from sight

disappearance 9 vanishing **11** evanescence **16** passing from sight

disappoint 4 foil **6** hinder, sadden, thwart **7** chagrin, let down, mislead **9** frustrate **10** dishearten **11** disillusion

disappointing 11 frustrating **12** unfulfilling **13** dissatisfying **14** unsatisfactory

disappointment 3 dud **4** bomb, loss **6** defeat, fiasco, fizzle **7** failure, letdown, setback, washout **8** disaster **9** the knocks **11** frustration **13** unfulfillment, unrealization **15** disillusionment, dissatisfaction

disapprobation 7 censure **8** disfavor **9** criticism, disesteem, objection **11** disapproval, displeasure **12** condemnation **15** dissatisfaction

disapprove 4 veto **5** decry **6** refuse, reject **7** censure, condemn, deplore, dislike **8** denounce, disallow, object to, turn down **9** criticize, deprecate, disparage, frown upon **10** think ill of **13** look askance at, regard as wrong **14** discountenance, refuse assent to **15** take exception to **16** find unacceptable, view with disfavor

disapprove of 7 censure, condemn, deplore **8** object to

disarm 4 move, sway **5** charm **6** entice **7** attract, bewitch, enchant, win over **8** convince, persuade **9** captivate, fascinate, influence, prevail on

disarming 7 melting, winning, winsome **8** charming, magnetic **9** appealing, beguiling, ingenuous, seductive **10** bewitching, entrancing **11** captivating **12** ingratiating, irresistible

disarrange 5 mix up, upset **6** jumble, mess up, muddle, ruffle, rumple **7** confuse, scatter **8** disarray, dishevel, disorder, displace, put askew, scramble **11** disorganize **13** put out of order **14** turn topsy-turvy

disarranged 5 messy **6** mussed, sloppy, untidy **7** jumbled, ruffled, rumpled, tousled, unkempt **8** uncombed **9** cluttered **10** disarrayed, disheveled, disordered, disorderly, in disorder **11** in a shambles

disarrangement 4 mess **5** chaos, mix-up, upset **6** jumble, mixing, muddle **7** clutter **8** disarray, disorder, scramble, shambles **9** confusion, messiness, messing up **10** disharmony, disruption, sloppiness, untidiness **12** dishevelment **14** disorderliness **15** disorganization, heaping together

disarray 5 chaos, mix-up, upset **6** jumble **7** clutter **8** disorder, scramble, shambles **9** confusion, messiness **10** disharmony, sloppiness, untidiness **12** dishevelment **14** disarrangement **15** disorganization

disarrayed 5 messy **6** mussed, sloppy, untidy **7** chaotic, jumbled, mixed up **10** disheveled, disordered, disorderly, in disorder **11** disarranged

disarticulate 6 detach **7** unhinge **8** disjoint, disunite, separate **9** disengage, dislocate **10** disconnect **13** put out of joint

disarticulated 5 apart **7** divided **8** unhinged **9** disunited, separated **10** disengaged, disjointed, dislocated, unattached **11** unconnected **12** disconnected **13** helter-skelter

disassemble 7 disband, scatter **8** disperse **9** knock down, take apart

disassociate 7 divorce **8** separate **10** disconnect **12** disaffiliate

disassociation 5 break, split **6** schism **7** divorce **8** division **10** separation

disaster 4 harm **5** wreck **6** blight, fiasco **7** scourge, tragedy, trouble **8** accident, calamity **9** adversity, cataclysm, ruination **10** misfortune **11** catastrophe, great mishap **12** misadventure

disastrous 4 dire **5** fatal **6** tragic **7** adverse, hapless, harmful, ruinous **8** dreadful, grievous, ill-fated, terrible **9** harrowing **10** calamitous, desolating, horrendous, ill-starred **11** destructive, devastating, unfortunate **12** catastrophic, inauspicious

disavow 4 deny **6** abjure, disown, recant, reject **7** gainsay, retract **8** denounce **9** repudiate **10** contradict

disavowal 6 denial **8** demurrer **9** rejection **10** abjuration, disclaimer, refutation **11** repudiation **13** contradiction

disband 7 adjourn, dismiss, scatter **9** disperse, dissolve **11** disassemble

disbelief 5 doubt **7** dubiety **8** distrust, mistrust, unbelief **10** skepticism **11** incredulity **12** doubtfulness **14** lack of credence

disbelieve 5 doubt **6** refuse, reject **7** suspect **8** discount, distrust **9** discredit, unbelieve **10** misbelieve

disbeliever 7 atheist, skeptic **8** apostate

disbursable 7 payable **9** available, spendable **10** expendable

disburse 6 lay out, pay out **7** fork out **8** allocate, shell out **10** distribute

disbursement 6 outlay **7** payment **8** spending **9** paying out **10** dispensing **11** expenditure **12** dispensation, distribution

discard 4 drop, dump, junk, shed **5** scrap **6** remove, shelve **7** abandon, weed out **8** get rid of, jettison, throw out **9** cast aside, dispose of, eliminate, throw away **10** relinquish **11** thrust aside **12** dispense with, have done with **14** throw overboard

discarded 6 dumped, junked **7** cast off, dropped **8** deserted, forsaken, rejected, scrapped **9** abandoned, cast aside, tossed out **10** jettisoned, left behind, thrown away

discern 3 see **4** espy **6** behold, descry, detect, notice **7** make out, observe, pick out **8** perceive **9** ascertain **12** catch sight of

discernible 7 visible **8** apparent **10** detectable, noticeable **11** perceivable, perceptible

discerning 4 sage, wise **5** acute, sharp **6** astute, shrewd **8** piercing **9** judicious, sagacious, sensitive **10** perceptive **11** intelligent, keen-sighted, penetrating **12** clear-sighted, sharp-sighted **13** perspicacious **14** discriminating

discernment 6 acumen, senses **7** insight **8** feelings, sagacity, thoughts **10** cognizance, discretion, perception **11** distinction **13** consciousness, judiciousness **14** discrimination **15** differentiation

discharge 3 axe, can **4** emit, fire, flow, free, gush, ooze, oust, sack, shot **5** blast, burst, eject, expel, exude, issue, let go, shoot **6** bounce, firing, launch, lay off, let fly, propel, report, set off **7** cashier, dismiss, explode, fire off, project, release, seepage, set free, trigger **8** activate, detonate, drainage, emission, get rid of, liberate, throw off, touch off **9** allow to go, exploding, explosion, firing off, fusillade, give forth, pour forth, secretion, send forth, terminate **10** activating, detonating, detonation, triggering **11** send packing, suppuration **13** give the gate to, walking papers **14** demobilization **15** release document **16** remove from office

disciple 3 nut **5** freak, pupil **7** admirer, convert, devotee, pursuer, student **8** adherent, believer, follower, neophyte, partisan **9** proselyte, supporter **10** aficionado **11** afficionado

Disciple, The
author: **11** Paul Bourget

Disciples *see* **8** Apostles

disciplinarian 8 martinet **13** authoritarian **16** stickler for rules, strict taskmaster

disciplinary 8 punitive **9** punishing **10** corrective **13** authoritarian

discipline 5 drill, prime, rigor, train **6** method, punish **7** break in, chasten, regimen **8** chastise, drilling, instruct, practice, training **9** schooling **11** preparation **14** indoctrination **15** prescribed habit, teach by exercise **16** course of exercise

disclaim 4 deny **6** disown **7** decline, disavow **8** abnegate, forswear, renounce **9** disaffirm, repudiate

disclaimer 6 denial **8** demurrer **9** disavowal **10** abnegation **11** repudiation **12** renunciation

disclose 4 bare, leak, show, tell **6** expose, impart, reveal, unveil **7** divulge, lay bare, publish, uncover **9** broadcast, make known **10** make public **11** communicate **12** bring to light **13** allow to be seen, bring into view, cause to appear

disco 4 club **5** agogo, dance **7** cabaret **9** dance club, nightclub

discolor 4 spot **5** stain, tinge **6** bleach, streak **7** tarnish

discoloration 4 blot, mark, spot **5** smear, stain **6** blotch, bruise, smudge **7** blemish **9** contusion

discolored 4 doty **5** dingy, dirty, faded, livid **6** soiled, tinged **7** bruised, stained **9** tarnished

discomfit 5 upset **6** thwart **7** chagrin **8** confound, distress **9** embarrass, frustrate **10** disconcert

discomfited 5 upset **6** uneasy **7** ashamed **8** thwarted **9** chagrined, ill at ease **10** distressed **11** embarrassed **12** disconcerted

discomfiture 7 anxiety **9** agitation, confusion **10** uneasiness **11** disquietude, distraction, nervousness **12** discomposure, perturbation **13** embarrassment

discomfort 3 try **4** ache, hurt, pain **5** trial **6** misery **7** malaise, trouble **8** disquiet, distress, hardship, nuisance, soreness, vexation **9** annoyance, discomfit, embarrass **10** affliction, discompose, irritation, make uneasy **11** disquietude

discompose 5 abash, upset **6** rattle **7** agitate, confuse, disturb, fluster, nonplus, perturb, trouble, unnerve **8** disquiet, distract, distress, unsettle **9** discomfit, embarrass **10** disconcert

discomposed 5 upset **6** jolted, rocked, shaken, uneasy **7** anxious, nervous, worried **8** agitated, confused, troubled **9** disturbed, flustered, perturbed **10** disquieted, distracted **11** discomfited, uncollected

discomposure 6 flurry **7** anxiety **8** disquiet **9** agitation, confusion **10** discomfort, uneasiness **11** awkwardness, disquietude, distraction, nervousness **12** discomfiture, perturbation **13** embarrassment **17** self-consciousness

disconcert 5 abash, annoy, upset **6** raffle, ruffle **7** agitate, confuse, disturb, nonplus, perturb, trouble **8** unsettle **10** discompose

disconcerted 5 fazed, upset **7** annoyed, rattled, ruffled **8** agitated, confused, troubled **9** disturbed, perturbed, thrown off, unsettled **10** distracted, nonplussed

disconcertment 8 rattling **9** abashment, agitation, confusion **11** disturbance **12** discomposure

disconnect 6 detach **8** separate, uncouple **9** disengage

disconnected 5 split **6** cut off **7** jumbled, mixed-up, severed **8** confused, detached, rambling **9** illogical, separated, uncoupled **10** disengaged, disjointed, incoherent, irrational, unattached, unfastened **12** disorganized

disconnection 8 severing **9** severance **10** cutting off, detachment, separation **13** disengagement

disconsolate 3 sad **4** blue, down **6** woeful **7** crushed, doleful, forlorn, unhappy **8** dejected, desolate, downcast, wretched **9** depressed, miserable, sorrowful, woebegone **10** despondent, dispirited, melancholy **11** discouraged, low-spirited, pessimistic **12** heavy-hearted, inconsolable **13** broken-hearted **14** down in the dumps, down in the mouth

discontent 9 displease **10** discomfort, disgruntle **11** displeasure, unhappiness **15** dissatisfaction

discontented 5 bored **7** fretful, unhappy **9** miserable, regretful **10** displeased, malcontent **11** disgruntled **12** dissatisfied

discontinuance 3 end **4** halt, stop **6** ending, recess **7** ceasing, halting **8** abeyance, giving up, quitting, stoppage, stopping, surcease **9** cessation, desisting **10** concluding, leaving off, suspension **11** abandonment, breaking off, termination

discontinue 3 end **4** drop, quit, stop **5** cease **6** desist, give up **7** abandon, abstain, suspend **8** break off, leave off **9** interrupt, terminate **10** put an end to

discontinuous 8 discrete, episodic, sporadic **9** segmented, spasmodic **10** occasional **11** interrupted **12** disconnected, intermittent

discord 6 strife **7** dispute **8** clashing, conflict, disunity, division, friction **9** cacophony, harshness, wrangling **10** contention, disharmony, dissension, dissonance, quarreling **11** being at odds, differences, discordance **12** disagreement, grating noise **13** lack of

concord **15** incompatibility **16** unpleasant sounds
goddess of: 4 Eris **9** Discordia

discordance 6 strife **7** discord, dispute **8** clashing, conflict, disunity, division, friction **9** wrangling **10** contention, disharmony, dissension, quarreling **12** disagreement **15** incompatibility

discordant 6 at odds **9** disparate, dissonant **10** at variance, discrepant **11** conflicting, disagreeing **12** unharmonious

Discordia
origin: 5 Roman
goddess of: 7 discord
corresponds to: 4 Eris

discount 3 cut **5** break **6** rebate **7** cut rate **9** abatement, allowance, deduction, exemption, reduction **10** concession **11** subtraction

discountenance 7 condemn, despise, disdain, dislike **8** object to **9** frown upon **10** disapprove, think ill of **12** look down upon **13** look askance at, regard as wrong **14** hold in contempt **15** take exception to

discourage 4 do in **5** daunt, deter, unman **6** deject, dismay **7** depress, unnerve **8** decimate, dispirit, dissuade, keep back, restrain **9** disparage, prostrate **10** dishearten, disincline, divert from **13** advise against, dash one's hopes **17** dampen one's spirits

discouraged 3 low **7** daunted **8** dejected, downcast, hopeless **9** depressed **10** despondent, dispirited **11** downhearted, pessimistic **12** disconsolate, disheartened

discouragement 4 curb **5** gloom, worry **6** damper, dismay **7** despair **8** obstacle **9** dejection, hindrance, pessimism, restraint **10** constraint, depression, impediment, low spirits, melancholy, moroseness **11** despondency **12** hopelessness, lack of spirit **13** consternation **15** downheartedness

discourse 3 gab **4** chat, talk **5** essay **6** confer, sermon, speech **7** address, discuss, lecture, oration **8** colloquy, converse, dialogue, diatribe, harangue, treatise **10** discussion **11** intercourse **12** conversation, dissertation, talk together **16** formal discussion

Discourse on Method
author: 13 Rene Descartes

discourteous 4 rude **5** fresh, surly **6** cheeky **7** boorish, ill-bred, uncivil, uncouth **8** impolite, impudent, insolent **9** uncourtly, ungallant **10** ill-behaved, ungracious, unladylike, unmannerly **11** ill-mannered, impertinent **13** disrespectful, ungentlemanly

discourtesy 8 rudeness **9** impudence, insolence **10** incivility **11** boorishness **12** impoliteness

discover 3 see **4** find, spot **5** dig up **6** detect, locate, notice **7** discern, find

out, learn of, realize, root out, uncover, unearth **8** come upon, perceive **9** ascertain, determine, ferret out, light upon, recognize **10** chance upon **11** gain sight of, stumble upon **12** bring to light

discredit 4 deny, slur **5** abuse, smear, sully, taint **6** debase, defame, demean, reject, smirch, vilify **7** degrade, dispute, tarnish, vitiate **8** disallow, disgrace, dishonor, disprove, question **9** challenge, disparage, undermine **10** prove false, stigmatize **16** shake one's faith in **17** drag through the mud

discreditable 8 shameful, shocking **9** appalling **10** outrageous, scandalous **11** disgraceful, ignominious **12** dishonorable, disreputable

discreet 6 polite **7** careful, politic, prudent, tactful **8** cautious **9** judicious, sensitive **10** diplomatic, thoughtful **11** circumspect

Discreet Charm of the Bourgeoisie, The
director: 10 Luis Bunuel
cast: 11 Fernando Rey **14** Delphine Seyrig, Stephane Audran
Oscar for: 11 foreign film

discrepancy 3 gap **8** variance **9** disparity **10** difference, divergence **11** discordance, incongruity **12** disagreement **13** dissimilarity, inconsistency

discrepant 6 at odds **8** contrary, opposing **9** disparate **10** at variance, discordant, dissimilar, refutatory **11** conflicting, contrasting, disagreeing **12** antithetical, inconsistent **13** contradictory **14** countervailing, irreconcilable

discrete 7 several, various **8** detached, distinct, separate **9** different **10** unattached **11** disjunctive, independent **12** disconnected, unassociated **13** discontinuous

discretion 4 tact **6** acumen, option **8** judgment, prudence, sagacity, volition **9** good sense **10** preference **11** discernment, inclination **12** good judgment, predilection **13** judiciousness, sound judgment **14** discrimination **15** power of choosing **16** individual choice

discretionary 8 optional **9** voluntary **10** nonbinding **11** nonrequired, unnecessary **12** nonrequisite, unimperative **13** nonobligatory

discriminate 7 disdain **8** separate **11** distinguish **12** disfranchise **13** differentiate

discriminating 5 acute **6** astute, biased, shrewd **7** bigoted, refined **9** judicious, sensitive **10** cultivated, discerning, fastidious **11** intelligent, prejudicial **13** perspicacious **15** differentiating

discrimination 4 bias **5** taste **6** acumen **7** bigotry **8** inequity, judgment, keenness, sagacity **9** prejudice **10** as-

tuteness, discretion, favoritism, refinement, shrewdness **11** discernment, distinction **12** perspicacity **21** differential treatment

discursive 7 diffuse **8** rambling **9** wandering **10** circuitous, digressive, long-winded, meandering, roundabout

discursiveness 8 rambling **10** digression, meandering **14** circumlocution

discuss 6 debate, parley, review **7** dissect, examine, speak of **8** consider, talk over **9** talk about **13** converse about, exchange views **14** discourse about

discussion 3 rap **4** talk **6** debate, parley, powwow, review **7** inquiry **8** analysis, argument, colloquy, dialogue, scrutiny **9** discourse **10** hashing-out **11** disputation **12** deliberation **13** consideration, investigation

disdain 4 snub **5** abhor, scorn, spurn **6** deride, detest, loathe **7** despise, dislike **8** contempt, distaste **9** frown upon **10** abhorrence, brush aside, disrespect **11** intolerance **12** icy aloofness, look down upon **14** deem unbecoming, discountenance

disdained 7 derided, scorned, spurned **8** abhorred, despised **10** deprecated, disparaged **14** held in contempt

disdainful 4 cold **5** aloof **7** haughty, high-hat **8** derisive, scornful, superior **11** overbearing, patronizing **12** contemptuous, supercilious **13** condescending

disease 6 malady **7** ailment, illness **8** sickness **9** ill health, infirmity **10** affliction **15** morbid condition **16** physical disorder

disembark 4 land **7** deplane, detrain, pile out **10** leave a ship **11** get off a ship

disenchant 6 put off **7** turn off **8** alienate, disabuse, turn away **9** undeceive **11** disenthrall **12** open one's eyes **13** break the spell **15** burst one's bubble **16** bring down to earth

disencumber 3 rid **8** unburden **9** disburden, extricate **11** disentangle

disengage 5 sever **6** detach **7** disjoin **8** separate **9** extricate **10** disconnect

disengaged 7 unmoved **8** detached **9** apathetic, disjoined, separated **11** indifferent, uncommitted, unconcerned **12** disconnected, unresponsive
French: 6 degage

disengagement 6 apathy **8** severing **9** severance, unconcern **10** detachment, separation **12** indifference **13** disconnection **16** unresponsiveness

disentangle 4 free **6** detach, loosen, remove **7** unravel **9** extricate

disenthrall 9 undeceive **10** disenchant **11** disillusion **12** open one's eyes

13 break the spell **15** burst one's bubble **16** bring down to earth

disesteem 7 dislike **8** disfavor **9** disrepute **11** disapproval, displeasure **14** disapprobation

disfavor 5 odium **7** dislike, ill turn **8** disgrace, ignominy **9** disesteem, disregard **10** disrespect, disservice, harmful act **11** disapproval, discourtesy, displeasure **14** disapprobation **15** dissatisfaction **16** unacceptableness

disfigure 3 mar **4** maim, scar **5** cut up **6** damage, deface, deform, impair **7** blemish, scarify **8** make ugly, mutilate

disfigurement 4 blot, flaw, mark, scar, spot **6** blotch, defect **7** blemish **12** imperfection

disfranchise, disenfranchise 15 deprive of a right **19** discriminate against

disgorge 4 spew **5** eject, expel, spout, vomit **6** cast up, spew up **7** cough up, throw up **8** dislodge **9** discharge **10** vomit forth **11** regurgitate

disgrace 4 blot **5** abase, shame, stain, taint **6** debase, smirch **7** blemish, degrade, eyesore, scandal, tarnish **8** contempt, derogate, disfavor, dishonor, ill favor, reproach **9** discredit, disparage, disrepute, embarrass, humiliate **13** embarrassment, in the doghouse **14** bring shame upon

disgraceful 3 low **4** base, mean, vile **6** odious **8** infamous, shameful, shocking, unseemly, unworthy **9** appalling, degrading, obnoxious **10** despicable, detestable, inglorious, outrageous, scandalous, unbecoming **11** ignominious, opprobrious **12** dishonorable, disreputable **13** discreditable, reprehensible

disgruntled 5 sulky, testy, vexed **6** grumpy, shirty, sullen **7** grouchy, peevish **8** petulant **9** irritated **10** displeased, malcontent **12** discontented, dissatisfied

disguise 4 garb, hide, mask, pose, sham, veil **5** blind, cloak, cover, feign, getup, guise **6** facade, muffle, screen, shroud, veneer **7** conceal, cover-up, dress up, falsify **8** pretense, simulate **9** costuming, dissemble, gloss over **10** camouflage, false front, masquerade **11** concealment, counterfeit **12** misrepresent **13** false identity **15** false appearance

disguised 6 masked, veiled **7** cloaked **9** dressed up, incognito **10** undercover **11** camouflaged **14** unrecognizable

disgust 5 repel **6** appall, hatred, offend, put off, revolt, sicken **7** dislike **8** aversion, contempt, distaste, loathing, nauseate **9** antipathy, disrelish, repulsion, revulsion **10** abhorrence, repugnance **11** detestation, displeasure **12** disaffection **13** be repulsive to, cause aversion **15** turn one's stomach

disgusting 4 vile **5** hasty **6** horrid, odious **7** hateful **9** abhorrent, appalling, loathsome, offensive, repellent, repugnant, repulsive, revolting, sickening **10** abominable, despicable, nauseating **13** reprehensible

dish 4 dole, fare, food **5** ladle, place, plate, scoop, serve, spoon **6** recipe, saucer, vessel **7** bowlful, dishful, edibles, helping, platter, portion, serving **8** dispense, plateful, transfer, victuals **10** comestible **11** shallow bowl

dishabille 7 undress **8** bathrobe, disarray, disorder, informal, negligee **9** housecoat

disharmonious 7 chaotic **8** clashing, confused **9** dissonant, illogical **10** discordant, incoherent **11** conflicting, contentious **12** incompatible **13** heterogeneous

disharmony 5 chaos **6** strife **7** discord **8** clashing, conflict, disarray, disunity, division, friction **9** cacophony, confusion, disaccord, harshness **10** contention, dissension, dissonance **11** discordance **12** disagreement, grating noise **15** disorganization, incompatibility

dishearten 4 dash, faze **5** abash, crush, daunt **6** deject, dismay, sadden **7** depress **8** dispirit **10** discourage

disheartened 3 low **4** dismal **8** dejected, desolate, downcast **9** depressed **10** despondent, dispirited **11** discouraged **12** disconsolate

disheartening 4 dark **7** adverse **8** hopeless **11** dispiriting **12** discouraging, inauspicious

disheveled 5 messy **6** blowsy, frowzy, mussed, sloppy, untidy **7** ruffled, rumpled, tousled, unkempt **8** uncombed **10** bedraggled, disarrayed, disorderly, in disorder **11** disarranged

dishevelment 5 chaos, mix-up, upset **6** jumble **7** clutter **8** disarray, disorder, scramble, shambles **9** messiness **10** sloppiness, untidiness **14** disarrangement **15** disorganization

dishonest 5 false **7** corrupt, crooked **8** cheating, specious, spurious, two-faced **9** deceitful, deceptive, faithless, insincere, not honest **10** fraudulent, mendacious, misleading, perfidious, untruthful **11** underhanded **12** disingenuous, false-hearted, unprincipled, unscrupulous **13** untrustworthy

dishonesty 8 cheating **9** duplicity, falseness, mendacity **10** corruption **11** crookedness **12** speciousness **14** untruthfulness

dishonor 4 blot **5** abase, odium, shame, stain, sully **6** debase, defame, infamy, insult, slight, stigma **7** affront, blacken, blemish, degrade, offense, scandal, tarnish **8** disfavor, disgrace, ignominy **9** discredit, disparage, disre-

pute, humiliate, ill repute **10** derogation, stigmatize **11** discourtesy, humiliation **12** bring shame on **14** public disgrace

dishonorable 4 base **7** debased, ignoble **8** shameful **10** despicable **12** contemptible, disreputable **13** reprehensible

dishonorableness 4 blot **5** odium, shame, stain **6** stigma **7** blemish **8** disfavor, disgrace, ignominy **9** discredit, disrepute, ill repute **10** derogation **11** humiliation

dishonoring 8 disgrace **10** debasement **11** degradation, humiliation

dish up 3 dip **5** ladle, serve, spoon **7** dish out, serve up

disillusion 6 clue in **8** disabuse **9** undeceive **10** disenchant **11** disenthrall **13** break the spell, open the eyes of **14** burst the bubble **16** bring down to earth

disinclination 8 aversion **9** hesitancy **10** reluctance **13** indisposition, unwillingness

disincline 5 deter **8** dissuade, keep back, restrain **10** discourage, divert from **13** advise against **16** attempt to prevent

disinclined 5 loath **6** averse **8** hesitant **9** reluctant, unwilling **10** indisposed

disinfect 6 purify **7** cleanse **8** sanitize **9** kill germs, sterilize **13** decontaminate **15** destroy bacteria

disinfectant 9 germicide **10** antiseptic, germ killer **11** bactericide

disinherit 6 cut off, disown **15** deprive of rights

disintegrate 7 break up, crumble, shatter **8** splinter **9** fall apart **10** break apart, go to pieces

disintegration 4 ruin **5** decay **7** breakup, erosion **8** biolysis **9** crumbling **10** dispersion, dissolving, separation **11** decomposing **12** falling apart **13** decomposition, deterioration, pulverization

disinter 5 dig up **6** exhume **7** unearth

disinterest 6 apathy **9** disregard, unconcern **12** indifference

disinterested 7 neutral, outside **8** unbiased **9** impartial **10** impersonal, uninvolved **12** free from bias, unprejudiced **13** dispassionate

disinterment 9 digging up **10** exhumation, unearthing

disjecta membra 15 disjointed parts **16** scattered members

disjoin 4 part, undo **5** break, sever **6** detach, divide **8** disunite, separate **9** disengage

disjoint 6 detach **7** unhinge **8** disunite, separate **9** dislocate **10** disconnect **13** disarticulate

disjointed 5 apart, split **7** chaotic, divided, jumbled, mixed-up, tangled

8 confused, detached, rambling **9** illogical, spasmodic **10** incoherent, irrational, unattached **11** unconnected **12** disconnected, disorganized **13** discontinuous, disharmonious, helter-skelter, heterogeneous **14** disarticulated

disjointedness 8 rambling **11** indirection **14** discursiveness **16** disconnectedness

disjointed parts
Latin: **14** disjecta membra

disk, disc 3 cam **4** aten, coin, dial, face, plow, puck **5** plate, wafer, wheel **6** harrow, record, sequin **7** discuss **8** diskette **9** cultivate, videodisc **11** discotheque
type: **4** hard **5** fixed **6** floppy **8** magnetic **10** Winchester

dislike 4 hate **5** abhor, scorn **6** animus, detest, enmity, hatred, loathe, malice, rancor **7** despise, disdain, disgust, not like **8** aversion, distaste, loathing, object to **9** abominate, animosity, antipathy, hostility, repulsion, revulsion **10** abhorrence, antagonism, repugnance **11** abomination, detestation **12** disaffection

disliked 5 hated **7** loathed, unloved **8** abhorred, despised, detested **10** abominated

dislike intensely 4 hate **5** abhor **6** detest, loathe **7** despise **9** abominate **10** recoil from

dislocate 6 uproot **7** unhinge **8** disjoint, disunite, separate **9** disengage **10** disconnect **13** disarticulate, put out of joint

dislodge 4 oust **5** eject, expel **6** dig out, dispel, remove, uproot **7** disturb **8** displace, force out **9** extricate **11** disentangle

disloyal 6 untrue **8** recreant **9** faithless, seditious, undutiful **10** inconstant, perfidious, subversive, traitorous, unfaithful **11** treacherous, treasonable **12** dishonorable

disloyalty 7 falsity, perfidy, treason **8** apostasy, betrayal, sedition **9** falseness, rebellion, recreancy, treachery **10** infidelity, subversion **11** inconstancy **12** insurrection **13** breach of trust, deceitfulness, double-dealing, faithlessness **14** lack of fidelity, perfidiousness, unfaithfulness **15** betrayal of trust, breaking of faith **18** subversive activity

dismal 3 sad **4** drab, grim, poor **5** awful, bleak **6** dreary, gloomy, morbid, rueful, somber, woeful **7** abysmal, doleful, forlorn, joyless, unhappy, very bad, visaged **8** dejected, desolate, dolorous, downcast, dreadful, hopeless, horrible, mournful, terrible **9** cheerless, depressed, long-faced, sorrowful, woebegone **10** abominable, despondent, in the dumps, lugubrious, melancholy **11** pessimistic **12** discon-

solate, disheartened, heavy-hearted **13** unmentionable **14** down-in-the-mouth

dismantle 5 strip **6** denude, divest **9** take apart

dismay 3 cow **5** abash, alarm, daunt, dread, panic, scare **6** appall, fright, horror, put off, terror **7** anxiety, concern, horrify, unnerve **8** affright, distress, frighten **10** disappoint, discourage, dishearten, intimidate **11** disillusion, trepidation **12** apprehension, exasperation, intimidation, perturbation **13** consternation **14** disappointment, discouragement **15** disillusionment

dismayed 7 abashed, daunted **8** appalled **10** confounded, nonplussed **12** disconcerted

dismember 4 limb **6** hack up **8** disjoint **16** tear limb from limb

dismiss 3 can **4** fire, free, oust, sack **5** let go **6** bounce, excuse, reject **7** adjourn, cashier, disband, discard, release **8** disclaim, disperse, dissolve, lay aside, liberate, pink-slip, set aside **9** disregard, eliminate, repudiate, send forth, terminate **10** permit to go **11** send packing **12** allow to leave, put out of a job, put out of mind **14** give the heave-ho **17** remove from service, give walking papers **19** discharge from office

dismissal 6 firing **7** release **9** discharge, dispersal, disregard **10** disclaimer **11** adjournment, repudiation

Disney
theme parks **10** Disneyland, EuroDisney **15** Disneyland Paris, Tokyo Disneyland, Walt Disney World

Disney, Walt
creator/artist of: **5** Goofy, Pluto **10** Donald Duck **11** Mickey Mouse, Minnie Mouse

disobedience 8 defiance **9** rebellion **10** resistance **13** noncompliance, nonconformity **14** rebelliousness

disobedient 6 unruly **7** defiant, forward, haughty, wayward **8** contrary, mutinous, perverse, stubborn **9** fractious, insurgent, obstinate, seditious, undutiful **10** disorderly, rebellious, refractory, unyielding **11** intractable **12** noncompliant, recalcitrant, ungovernable, unmanageable, unsubmissive **13** insubordinate

disobey 4 defy **5** break **6** ignore, resist **7** violate **8** overstep **9** disregard **10** infringe on, transgress **11** go counter to **12** rebel against

disoblige 5 annoy **6** bother **7** trouble **13** inconvenience

disobliging 4 rude **8** churlish **9** unhelpful **13** inconsiderate

disorder 4 mess, riot **5** chaos **6** fracas, jumble, malady, muddle, ruckus, uproar **7** ailment, clutter, disease, illness, turmoil **8** disarray, sickness **9**

commotion, complaint, confusion **10** affliction, disruption, dissension **11** disturbance **13** indisposition, minor uprising **14** disarrangement **15** disorganization

disordered 7 jumbled **8** confused, messed up **9** haphazard **11** disarranged **12** disorganized

disorderliness 4 mess **5** chaos **6** muddle **8** disarray **9** confusion **10** disruption **14** disarrangement **15** disorganization

disorderly 3 bad **4** awry, wild **5** amiss, messy, noisy, rowdy **6** sloppy, unruly, untidy **7** chaotic, jumbled, lawless, riotous, unkempt, wayward **8** careless, confused, improper, pellmell, rowdyish, slipshod, slovenly, unlawful, unsorted **10** boisterous, disheveled, disordered, disruptive, rebellious, straggling, topsy-turvy **11** disarranged **12** disorganized, disreputable, obstreperous, unrestrained, unsystematic **13** helter-skelter, undisciplined **14** rough-and-tumble, unsystematized

disorganization 4 mess **5** chaos, upset **6** jumble, muddle **7** clutter **8** disarray, disorder, shambles **9** confusion, messiness **10** disharmony, disruption, sloppiness, untidiness **12** dishevelment **14** disarrangement, disorderliness

disorganize 5 mix up, upset **6** jumble, mess up, muddle **7** confuse, scatter **8** disarray, disorder, put askew, scramble **10** disarrange **13** put out of order **14** turn topsy-turvy

disorganized 5 messy, upset **7** chaotic, jumbled, mixed-up, muddled **8** confused, rambling **9** haphazard, illogical **10** disordered, disorderly, incoherent, in disarray, irrational **12** unsystematic **16** at sixes and sevens

disoriented 7 mixed-up **8** confused, unstable **10** distracted, out of joint, out of touch **11** not adjusted

disown 4 deny **6** reject **7** cast off, disavow, forsake **8** denounce, disclaim, renounce **9** repudiate **10** disinherit **17** refuse to recognize **19** refuse to acknowledge

disparage 4 mock **6** demean, slight **7** put down, run down **8** belittle, derogate, ridicule **9** denigrate, discredit, underrate **10** depreciate, undervalue **11** detract from

disparagement 5 abuse, libel **7** slander **8** ridicule **9** criticism **10** belittling, defamation, derogation, detraction **11** denigration, putting down **12** vilification **17** defamatory remarks

disparaging 5 snide **10** belittling, derogatory **11** unfavorable **15** uncomplimentary

disparate 6 at odds, unlike **9** different **10** at variance, discordant, discrepant, dissimilar **11** contrasting

disparity 3 gap 8 contrast, imparity, variance 10 difference, divergence, inequality, unlikeness 11 discrepancy, incongruity 12 disagreement, dissemblance 13 contradiction, disproportion, dissimilarity, dissimilitude, inconsistency

dispassion 6 apathy 8 coolness 10 detachment 12 indifference

dispassionate 4 calm, cool, fair 6 serene 7 neutral, unmoved 8 composed, detached, unbiased 9 collected, impartial, unexcited, unruffled 10 impersonal, uninvolved 11 levelheaded, undisturbed, unemotional 12 unprejudiced 13 disinterested, imperturbable

dispatch 4 item, kill, post, slay 5 flash, haste, piece, speed, story 6 finish, letter, murder, report, settle, wind up 7 bump off, execute, forward, message, missive, send off 8 alacrity, bulletin, carry out, celerity, complete, conclude, expedite, massacre, rapidity 9 finish off, quickness, slaughter, swiftness 10 communique, expedition, promptness, put an end to, put to death 11 assassinate, news account 12 send on the way 14 execute quickly, summarily shoot, swift execution 15 make short work of, transmit rapidly 16 carry out speedily, dispose of rapidly 18 telegraphic message 21 official communication

Dis Pater *see* 3 Dis

dispel 4 rout 5 allay, expel, repel 6 banish, remove 7 diffuse, dismiss, resolve, scatter 8 drive off 9 dissipate, drive away, eliminate 10 put an end to 11 disperse 13 make disappear

dispensable 8 nonvital 9 accessory, extrinsic, secondary 10 disposable, expendable, extraneous 11 superfluous, unessential, unimportant, unnecessary 12 nonessential

dispensation 6 decree 8 approval, bestowal, division 9 allotment, diffusion, exemption, meting out 10 allocation, conferment, credential, dealing out, dispensing, permission, reparation 11 consignment, designation 12 apportioning, distribution, remuneration 13 authorization, dissemination

dispense 6 confer 7 dole out, mete out 8 allocate 9 apportion 10 administer, distribute

dispense with 4 drop, dump, junk, shed 5 scrap 6 shelve 7 abandon, discard 9 dispose of

dispensing 9 bestowing, doling out, meting out 10 allocating, conferring 12 distributing

dispersal 7 breakup, parting 9 dismissal 10 breaking up, scattering 12 distributing, distribution

disperse 4 rout 6 dispel 7 diffuse, disband, scatter, send off 8 drive off 9

dissipate 10 distribute 11 disseminate 13 send scurrying 16 spread throughout

dispersed 7 diffuse 9 scattered, spread out 10 dissipated 11 distributed 14 extended widely, unconcentrated

dispersion 9 dispersal 10 disbanding, scattering 11 dissipation 12 distribution

dispirit 5 cloud 6 darken, deject, sadden 7 depress 10 demoralize, dishearten

dispirited 3 sad 4 blue, down, glum 5 moody 6 morose 7 forlorn, unhappy 8 dejected, downcast, listless 9 cheerless, depressed 10 melancholy 11 crestfallen, demoralized, discouraged, downhearted, pessimistic 12 disconsolate, disheartened 14 down in the dumps, down in the mouth, unenthusiastic

dispiriting 4 cold, dark 6 chilly, dismal, gloomy 9 dampening 10 depressing 12 discouraging 13 disheartening

displace 4 bump, move, oust 5 shift 6 unseat 7 replace 8 crowd out, dislodge, force out, supplant 9 dislocate, supersede

displaced person 2 DP 5 exile 6 emigre 7 refugee 8 expellee 10 expatriate

display 4 show 6 reveal 7 exhibit 8 manifest 10 exhibition 11 demonstrate, make visible 12 presentation 13 bring into view, demonstration, manifestation 15 put in plain sight

display case 7 cabinet, vitrine 8 showcase

displease 3 irk 5 annoy, pique 6 offend 7 disturb, incense, provoke 8 irritate

displeasing 8 annoying 9 loathsome, offensive, repellent, repugnant 10 irritating 11 distasteful, distressing 12 disagreeable

displeasure 5 wrath 7 dislike 8 vexation 9 annoyance 10 irritation 11 disapproval, indignation 15 dissatisfaction

disport 3 act 4 play, romp 5 amuse, caper, sport 6 divert, frolic, gambol 7 display, pastime 9 amusement, entertain 10 recreation 13 entertainment

disposal 5 array, order, power 7 command, control, dumping, junking, pattern, ridding 8 grouping, riddance 9 authority, clearance, direction, placement 10 discarding, government, management, regulation, settlement 11 arrangement, destruction, disposition, supervision 12 distribution, organization, throwing away 13 authorization, configuration, juxtaposition 14 administration

dispose 4 rank 5 array, order, place 7 arrange, deal out, incline 8 classify,

get rid of, motivate, organize 9 be willing 10 distribute

dispose of 4 dump 5 scrap 6 unload 7 discard 8 get rid of, throw out 9 cast aside, throw away

disposition 6 nature, spirit 7 control 8 bestowal, grouping, tendency 9 placement 11 arrangement, inclination, temperament 12 distribution, organization 14 predisposition 15 final settlement

dispossess 4 oust 5 evict, expel 8 take away, take back 9 deprive of

disproportionate 7 unequal 9 disparate 10 dissimilar, unbalanced

disprove 6 refute 9 discredit 10 controvert

disputable 7 dubious 8 doubtful 9 debatable, uncertain 12 questionable 14 controvertible

disputant 5 rival 7 opposer 8 opponent 9 adversary 10 antagonist, competitor, contestant

disputation 6 debate, review 8 argument, dialogue 10 discussion

dispute 4 feud 5 argue, clash, doubt 6 debate, impugn 7 quarrel, wrangle 8 argument, question, squabble 9 bickering, challenge 10 contradict 11 altercation, controversy 12 disagreement

disputed 6 argued 8 wrangled 9 debatable, in dispute, quarreled 10 in question, unverified 12 questionable 13 controversial 15 unsubstantiated

disqualification 5 minus 8 handicap 10 disability 11 shortcoming 13 ineligibility

disqualify 7 disable 9 make unfit 17 declare ineligible, deny participation

disquiet, disquietude 3 awe 6 unease 7 anxiety 8 distress 9 agitation 10 uneasiness 11 fretfulness, trepidation 12 apprehension, discomposure, perturbation 13 consternation

disquieted 6 uneasy 7 anxious, worried 9 concerned 10 distressed 12 apprehensive

disquieting 6 vexing 8 annoying 9 troubling, upsetting 10 bothersome, disturbing, irritating, perturbing, unsettling 11 distressing 13 disconcerting

disquisition 8 tractate, treatise 9 discourse, monograph 12 dissertation

disregard 6 ignore 8 overlook 11 pay no heed to 13 lack of respect 14 take no notice of 15 lack of attention 16 willful oversight

disregardful 8 careless, heedless 9 unmindful 11 insensitive, thoughtless 13 inconsiderate

disreputable 5 shady 8 infamous, shameful, shocking 9 notorious 10 scandalous 11 disgraceful 12 dishonorable, unprincipled **14** not respectable, of bad character

disrespect 6 insult **8** contempt, dishonor, rudeness **9** disregard **11** discourtesy, irreverence **12** impoliteness

disrespectful 4 rude **8** impolite **11** impertinent **12** contemptuous, discourteous

disrobe 5 strip **7** undress **16** divest of clothing

disrupt 5 upset **9** interrupt **13** interfere with **17** throw into disorder

disruption 5 upset **8** disorder **9** confusion **11** disturbance **12** interference, interruption **14** disarrangement **15** disorganization

dissatisfaction 4 veto **7** protest **9** rejection **10** discontent **11** disapproval, displeasure, unhappiness

dissatisfied 7 unhappy **10** displeased **12** discontented

dissect 5 study **7** analyze, lay open **8** cut apart, separate **9** anatomize, break down

dissemble 4 hide, mask **5** feign **7** conceal **8** disguise **10** camouflage **11** dissimulate

disseminate 6 spread **7** diffuse, scatter **8** disperse **9** broadcast, circulate

dissemination 9 diffusion, dispersal, spreading **10** scattering **12** broadcasting, distribution

dissension 7 discord, dispute **8** conflict, disunity, division **9** rebellion **10** contention, disharmony, quarreling **11** discordance **12** disagreement **14** rebelliousness

dissent 6 object, oppose **7** discord, protest **8** disagree **10** difference, dissension, opposition **12** disagreement **14** withhold assent **16** withhold approval

dissenter 5 rebel **9** dissident, protester **13** nonconformist

dissenting 9 differing, dissident **11** disagreeing

dissertation 6 memoir, thesis **8** tractate, treatise **9** discourse, monograph **12** disquisition

disservice 4 harm, hurt **5** wrong **6** injury **7** bad turn **9** injustice

dissever 3 saw **4** hack, rend **5** carve, sever, slash, slice, split **6** cleave, divide **8** disunite, separate

dissident 5 rebel **8** agitator, opposing **9** differing, dissenter **10** dissenting **11** disagreeing

dissimilar 6 unlike **8** distinct **9** different, disparate

dissimilarity 8 contrast, variance **9** disparity **10** difference, dissonance, divergence, inequality, unlikeness **11** discrepancy **12** disagreement **13** inconsistency **17** lack of resemblance

dissimilitude 8 variance **9** disparity

10 difference, unlikeness **11** incongruity **12** disagreement **17** lack of resemblance

dissimulate 4 hide, mask **7** conceal **8** disguise **9** dissemble **10** camouflage

dissipate 5 waste **6** dispel **7** carouse, deplete, scatter **8** disperse, misspend, squander **11** fritter away, overindulge **13** be intemperate **14** spend foolishly

dissipated 6 wasted **8** misspent **9** abandoned, debauched, dispelled, dispersed, dissolute, scattered **10** squandered **11** intemperate **12** disreputable **13** frittered away

dissipater 5 waste **7** wastrel **8** prodigal **10** profligate, squanderer **11** spendthrift

dissipation 6 excess **7** wasting **9** dispersal **10** debauchery, dispelling, scattering **11** dissolution, loose living **12** immoderation, intemperance **14** disintegration, frittering away, self-indulgence

dissociate 8 separate **10** disconnect **12** break off with

dissociation 7 breakup **10** separation

dissolute 5 loose **7** corrupt, immoral **9** abandoned, debauched **10** dissipated **12** unrestrained

dissolution 9 annulment **10** separation **11** termination **14** disintegration

dissolve 3 end, run **4** fade, melt, thaw, void **5** annul, sever **6** finish, render, soften, vanish **7** break up, disband, liquefy, thaw out **8** abrogate, conclude, evanesce **9** disappear, dissipate, terminate **10** deliquesce **12** disintegrate **13** dematerialize

dissonance 5 clash **7** discord **9** cacophony, harshness **10** difference, disharmony **11** discordance **12** disagreement **13** dissimilarity

dissonant 5 harsh **7** grating, hostile, jarring, raucous, warring **8** clashing, jangling **10** discordant, discrepant **11** cacophonous, disagreeing, incongruent, incongruous, unmelodious **12** incompatible, inconsistent, inharmonious **13** contradictory **14** irreconcilable

dissuade 9 urge not to **10** discourage **13** advise against, persuade not to

distance 3 gap **4** span **7** reserve, stretch **8** coldness, coolness, interval **9** aloofness, formality, restraint, stiffness **11** reservation **16** intervening space

distant 3 far **4** cold, cool **5** aloof **6** far-off, remote **7** faraway **8** detached, reserved **10** far-removed, restrained, unfriendly **11** standoffish **17** not closely related

Distant Mirror, A
  author: **15** Barbara W Tuchman

distaste 7 disgust, dislike **8** aversion **9** antipathy **10** repugnance **11** displeasure

distasteful 9 loathsome, repugnant **10** disgusting, unpleasant **11** displeasing **12** disagreeable

distastefulness 13 offensiveness **14** unpleasantness **16** disagreeableness

distasteful work 8 drudgery **11** menial labor

distend 5 bloat, bulge, swell **6** billow, expand **7** inflate, puff out **8** swell out

distended 4 full, taut **5** puffy, tumid **7** blown up, bloated, dilated, swelled, swollen **8** enlarged, expanded, extended, inflated, patulant **9** edematous, stretched

distill 7 draw out, extract **8** condense, vaporize **9** draw forth, evaporate

distillate 7 essence, extract **11** concentrate **13** concentration

distilled 9 condensed, extracted, vaporized **10** evaporated

distinct 5 clear, lucid, plain **7** diverse, supreme **8** clear-cut, definite, explicit, separate **9** different **10** dissimilar, individual **11** unmitigated, well-defined **12** not identical, unmistakable **13** extraordinary **14** unquestionable

distinction 6 renown **8** contrast, eminence **9** greatness **10** difference, excellence, importance, notability, prominence, separation **11** discernment, preeminence, superiority **12** differential **14** discrimination **15** differentiation

distinctive 6 unique **7** special **8** atypical, original, singular, uncommon **9** different **10** individual **13** extraordinary **14** characteristic

distinctiveness 7 clarity **9** character **10** definition, uniqueness **11** personality **13** individuality

distingue 13 distinguished

distinguish 6 decide, define **7** discern **8** set apart **9** single out **10** make famous **12** characterize, discriminate **13** differentiate, make prominent, make well known **14** make celebrated **15** make distinctive, note differences

distinguished 5 grand, great **6** famous, superb **7** elegant, eminent, notable, refined **8** renowned, splendid **9** acclaimed, dignified, distingue, prominent **10** celebrated **11** illustrious, magnificent
  French: **9** distingue

distort 6 deform **7** contort **8** misshape **9** disfigure **11** misconstrue **12** misrepresent **15** twist out of shape, twist the meaning

distorted 4 awry **5** askew **6** belied, loaded, warped **7** altered, colored, crooked, twisted **8** cockeyed, deformed, wrenched **9** contorted, falsified, grotesque, irregular, misshapen, misstated, perverted **13** unsymmetrical **14** misrepresented **15** misproportioned

distortion 7 skewing **8** twisting **10** aberration, caricature **11** crookedness, deformation **12** malformation **17** misrepresentation

distract 5 amuse, craze, worry **6** divert, madden **7** agitate, confuse, disturb, perplex, torment, trouble **8** bewilder, disorder **9** entertain

distracted 3 mad **4** wild **6** amused, crazed, insane, raving **7** frantic, pleased, puzzled **8** agitated, confused, deranged, diverted, frenzied, harassed, heedless, occupied **9** disturbed, stirred up **10** bewildered, distraught, irrational **11** entertained, turned aside

distraction 5 fazed, upset **6** frenzy **7** frantic, madness, pastime, rattled, ruffled **8** agitated, confused **9** amusement, diversion, unsettled **10** distraught, distressed, nonplussed, recreation **11** desperation **12** disconcerted **13** entertainment **14** mental distress

distractive 9 confusing **10** disturbing, unsettling **11** distressing, troublesome

distraught 3 mad **7** anxious, frantic **8** agitated, frenzied, seething **10** distracted, distressed **13** beside oneself

distress 4 need, pain, want **5** agony, upset **6** danger, grieve **7** anguish, disturb, torment, torture, trouble **14** acute suffering

distressed 5 upset **7** anxious, fearful, frantic, grieved, unhappy, worried **8** agitated, troubled **9** anguished, concerned, disturbed, tormented **10** distracted, distraught

distressing 5 acute **7** nagging, painful **8** grievous **9** agonizing, upsetting **10** disturbing, tormenting, unpleasant **11** displeasing, troublesome, unfortunate **13** uncomfortable

distribute 5 allot, class **6** divide, parcel **7** arrange, catalog, deliver, dole out, give out, scatter **8** classify, dispense, disperse, separate, tabulate **9** apportion, circulate, methodize, spread out **11** disseminate, systematize

distribution 7 sorting **8** division, grouping **9** allotment, spreading **10** allocation, dispersion, scattering **11** arrangement, circulation, disposition **12** organization **13** apportionment, dissemination

distribution center
French: **8** entrepot

district 4 area, ward **6** parish, region **8** precinct **12** neighborhood

distrust 5 doubt **7** suspect **8** question **9** misgiving, suspicion **11** lack of faith

distrustful 3 shy **4** wary **5** leery **7** dubious, jealous **8** cautious, doubtful, doubting **9** diffident **10** suspicious, untrusting **11** incredulous, mistrustful **12** disbelieving

disturb 5 annoy, upset, worry **6** bother **7** disrupt, perturb, trouble **8** distress, unsettle **9** dislocate, interrupt, intrude on **10** disarrange **11** disorganize

disturbance 5 upset, worry **6** bother, hubbub, ruckus, tumult, uproar **7** rioting, turmoil **8** disorder, distress, outbreak **9** annoyance **11** distraction **12** interruption, perturbation

disturbance of peace 4 riot **6** fracas, ruckus, uproar **7** turmoil **8** disorder **9** commotion **13** breach of order

disturbed 5 upset **6** uneasy **7** annoyed, anxious, nervous, rattled **8** agitated, confused, troubled **9** perturbed **10** disquieted **11** discomfited **12** disconcerted

disunion 7 divorce **8** division **9** secession **10** separation **14** disintegration

disunite 4 part **6** divide **7** divorce **8** separate **9** disengage **10** disconnect **12** disintegrate **13** disarticulate

disunited 6 parted **8** diverged, divorced, unallied **9** came apart, dispersed, separated **10** uncombined **13** disassociated

disunity 6 strife **7** discord **8** clashing, conflict, division, friction **9** wrangling **10** contention, dissension, separation **11** being at odds, discordance **12** disagreement **15** incompatibility

ditat Deus 11 God enriches
motto of: **7** Arizona

ditch 3 pit **4** junk **5** scrap **6** hollow, trench **7** abandon, discard **8** get rid of **10** excavation

dither 4 flap, fuss **5** tizzy, waver, whirl **6** bother, flurry, lather, quiver, shiver, thrill **7** fluster, tremble, twitter **8** hesitate **9** agitation, commotion, confusion, vacillate, vibration **10** excitement

Dithyrambus
epithet of: **8** Dionysus
means: **20** child of the double door

ditty 3 lay **4** song, tune **6** ballad **7** refrain

Dius Fidius
origin: **5** Roman
god of: **5** oaths **11** hospitality **20** international affairs
corresponds to: **6** Sancus **10** Semo Sancus

divagation 8 straying **9** wandering **10** digression, divergence

divan 4 book, hall, poem, room, salon, seat, sofa **5** couch, court **6** canape, daybed, leewan, lounge, settee **7** chamber, council, ottoman, davenport

dive 4 dash, fall, jump, leap **5** lunge **6** plunge **7** gin mill **9** honky-tonk, shabby bar **15** sleazy nightclub

Diver, Dick and Nicole
characters in: **16** Tender Is the Night
author: **10** Fitzgerald

diverge 6 differ, swerve **7** deflect,

deviate **8** be at odds, conflict, disagree, separate, split off

divergence 7 parting **8** conflict, rambling, straying, variance **9** deviation, disparity, wandering **10** difference, separation **11** discrepancy, incongruity **13** dissimilarity, inconsistency

divergent 8 separate **9** different **11** conflicting, disagreeing **12** drawing apart, splitting off

diverse 6 sundry, varied **8** eclectic, far-flung, opposite **9** different, differing, disparate **10** dissimilar **11** conflicting, of many kinds **13** contradictory

diversified 6 divers **7** various **8** manifold **9** different, unrelated **13** miscellaneous

diversify 4 vary **7** diffuse **8** divide up **9** spread out, variegate

diversion 5 hobby **7** pastime **9** amusement, avocation **10** deflection **11** distraction, drawing away **12** turning aside
French: **14** divertissement

diversity 7 variety **8** variance **10** assortment, difference **13** heterogeneity

divert 5 amuse **7** deflect **8** distract **9** entertain, sidetrack, turn aside

diverting 7 amusing **10** deflecting **11** distracting **12** entertaining, sidetracking

divertissement 9 diversion **13** entertainment

divest 3 rid **4** free **5** strip **7** deprive, disrobe, peel off, take off **8** get out of **10** dispossess **14** remove clothing

divest oneself of 6 give up **7** take off **8** get rid of, give over, hand over, put aside, strip off **9** surrender **10** relinquish

divide 4 part, sort **5** share, split **7** arrange, deal out, divvy up **8** allocate, classify, disunite, separate **9** apportion, partition **10** distribute, put in order

divide and rule
Latin: **14** divide et impera
maxim of: **11** Machiavelli

divided 5 apart, split **6** parted **8** meted out **9** disunited, separated **10** unattached **11** apportioned **12** disconnected, portioned out

divide et impera 13 divide and rule
maxim of: **11** Machiavelli

divide in two 5 halve, split **6** bisect **8** cut in two, separate **9** cut in half **10** break in two **11** split in half **18** split down the middle

dividing line 4 edge **5** brink, verge **6** border, margin **8** boundary **9** threshold

divination 5 guess **6** augury **8** prophecy **10** conjecture, foreboding, prediction, prescience **11** premonition, soothsaying **15** prognostication

divine 4 holy **5** guess **6** fathom, sacred

7 predict, surmise, suspect 8 forecast, foretell, heavenly, prophesy 9 admirable, celestial, excellent, marvelous, wonderful

divine being 3 god 5 deity 7 goddess 8 divinity 14 celestial being

Divine Comedy
author: 14 Dante Alighieri
part: 7 Inferno 8 Paradiso 10 Purgatorio
guide: 6 Virgil 8 Beatrice

diviner 4 seer 5 augur 10 soothsayer 14 prognosticator

Divine retribution
goddess of: 7 Nemesis 8 Adrastea

Divine Sarah
nickname of: 14 Sarah Bernhardt

divining rod 4 twig, wand 5 dowse 9 doodlebug

divinity 3 god 5 deity 7 goddess 8 holiness, religion, theology 9 theosophy 12 science of God 14 celestial being

division 4 part, unit, wing 5 split 6 branch 7 discord, divider, section 8 disunion, variance 9 partition 10 department, difference, divergence, separation 11 splitting up 12 disagreement

divorce 4 rift 5 split 6 breach, divide 7 rupture 8 disunite, separate 9 segregate 10 dissociate, separation

divulge 4 tell 6 impart, relate, reveal 8 disclose 9 make known 11 communicate

divulgence 7 telling 8 exposure 9 imparting 10 disclosure, giving away, laying open, revelation 13 communication 15 bringing to light 17 bring out in the open

divulge to 4 tell 6 advise, inform, notify, reveal 7 apprise 8 acquaint, disclose 9 enlighten, make aware 11 familiarize 13 spill the beans 20 let the cat out of the bag

Dix, Otto
born: 7 Germany 11 Unterhausen
artwork: 6 The War 7 The City 12 The Procuress 15 Sylvia von Harden 18 Parents of the Artist 39 Prague Street Dedicated to My Contemporaries

Dixie Dugan
creator: 8 J P McEvoy 13 John H Striebel

dizzy 5 fleet, giddy, quick, rapid, shaky, swift 6 whirly 7 confuse, reeling 8 bewilder, unsteady 9 make giddy 11 lightheaded, vertiginous 12 make unsteady

Djawa see 4 Java

Djebel al-Tarik see 9 Gibraltar

Djibouti
other name: 16 French Somaliland 39 The French Territory of the Afars and the Issas
capital/largest city: 8 Djibouti
others: 5 Obock 6 Dikhil 8 Tadjoura

9 Ali-Sabieh
monetary unit: 5 franc 7 centime
lake: 4 Abbe 5 Assal
mountain: 5 Gouda
highest point: 9 Moussa Ali
sea: 3 Red
physical feature:
    gulf: 4 Aden 8 Tadjoura
    strait: 11 Bab el-Mandeb
people: 4 Afar, Arab 5 Issas 6 French 8 European
language: 4 Afar 6 Arabic, French, Somali
religion: 5 Islam

do 3 act 4 fare 5 clean, cover, get on, serve, visit 6 behave, finish, look at, stop in 7 achieve, arrange, carry on, conduct, execute, fulfill, make out, perform, prepare, proceed, suffice 8 be enough, carry out, complete, conclude, organize 10 accomplish, administer, bring about, put in order 13 travel through 14 be satisfactory, comport oneself, conduct oneself

do a favor 4 help 6 assist, oblige 7 help out 11 accommodate, do a kindness

do away with 3 end 4 junk, kill, void 5 erase, quash 6 banish, cancel, cut out, give up, remove, repeal, revoke, rub out 7 abolish, blot out, nullify, rescind, weed out, wipe out 8 abrogate, stamp out, throw out 9 eliminate, eradicate, terminate 10 annihilate, put an end to 11 exterminate

Dobbin, Captain William
character in: 10 Vanity Fair
author: 9 Thackeray

Dobie Gillis, The Many Loves of
character: 11 Zelda Gilroy 13 Maynard G Krebs 14 Herbert T Gillis, Milton Armitage, Winifred (Winnie) Gillis 15 Thalia Menninger 19 Chatsworth Osborne Jr
cast: 9 Bob Denver 11 Frank Faylen, Sheila James, Tuesday Weld 12 Warren Beatty 13 Dwayne Hickman 14 Florida Friebus, Stephen Franken
Dobie imitated pose of: 7 Thinker

do business 4 deal 5 trade 10 buy and sell

docile 4 tame 7 willing 8 obedient, obliging 9 agreeable, compliant, tractable 10 manageable 11 complaisant

docility 7 pliancy 8 meekness 9 passivity 10 placidness 12 acquiescence, complaisance 13 nonresistance

dock 4 crop, join, pier, quay 5 berth, wharf 6 couple, cut off, deduct, hook up, link up 7 landing 8 cut short 10 waterfront 12 come into port 13 subject to loss 14 fasten together

dock 5 Rumux
varieties: 3 Bur 4 Sour 5 Green 6 Golden 7 Prairie, Spinach, Tanner's, Western 8 Patience 9 Purple-wen 10 Giant water

docket 4 bill, card, list 5 slate 6 agenda, lineup, roster 7 program 8 calendar, schedule 9 timetable 14 things to be done 15 order of business

doctor 2 GP, MD 3 PhD 5 alter, treat 6 change 7 dentist, falsify, surgeon 9 internist, osteopath, physician 10 podiatrist, tamper with 11 pathologist 12 gynecologist, obstetrician, pediatrician, psychiatrist, veterinarian 15 ophthalmologist 17 apply medication to 19 general practitioner, medical practitioner

Doctor Brodie's Report
author: 15 Jorge Luis Borges

Doctor Faustus
author: 10 Thomas Mann 18 Christopher Marlowe

Doctor Grimshaw's Secret
author: 18 Nathaniel Hawthorne

Doctor J
nickname of: 12 Julius Erving

Doctorow, E L
author of: 7 Ragtime 15 The Book of Daniel

Doctor's Dilemma, The
author: 17 George Bernard Shaw

Doctor Zhivago
director: 9 David Lean
author: 14 Boris Pasternak
cast: 10 Omar Sharif (Zhivago), Rod Steiger 12 Alec Guinness, Tom Courtenay 13 Julie Christie (Lara) 14 Rita Tushingham 15 Ralph Richardson 16 Geraldine Chaplin

doctrinaire 5 rigid 6 mulish 8 absolute, dogmatic, stubborn 9 arbitrary, imperious, pigheaded 10 bullheaded, inflexible, pontifical 11 dictatorial, opinionated, overbearing, stiff-necked 12 narrow-minded 13 authoritarian 14 disciplinarian

doctrinal 8 didactic, dogmatic, edifying, tutorial 11 educational, instructive 12 prescriptive

doctrine 5 dogma, tenet 6 belief, gospel 7 precept 8 teaching 9 principle 10 conviction, philosophy

document 6 back up, record, verify 7 certify, support 9 legal form 10 instrument 12 give weight to, substantiate 13 official paper

documentation 5 proof 7 support 8 evidence 12 verification 13 corroboration 14 substantiation

doddering 4 weak 6 feeble, senile 7 shaking 8 decrepit 9 tottering, trembling

dodge 4 duck, wile 5 avoid, elude, evade, hedge, trick 6 device, swerve 7 fend off 8 sidestep 9 jump aside, stratagem, turn aside 10 equivocate 11 machination

dodging 7 ducking, eluding, evading

8 shunning 12 sidestepping 13 circumventing

Dodgson, Charles Lutwidge
real name of: 12 Lewis Carroll

Dodoma
capital of: 8 Tanzania

Dodsworth
director: 12 William Wyler
author: 13 Sinclair Lewis
character: 4 Fran 12 Arnold Israel 14 Edith Cortright, Renee de Penable 15 Samuel Dodsworth 16 Kurt von Obersdorf 17 Major Clyde Lockert
cast: 9 Mary Astor, Paul Lukas 10 David Niven 12 Walter Huston 14 Ruth Chatterton

doer 6 dynamo 7 hustler 8 activist, go-getter 12 active person

doff 4 bare, drop, junk, shed 5 scrap, strip 6 put off, remove 7 abandon, cast off, discard, disrobe, take off, toss off, undress 8 throw off, throw out 9 eliminate, step out of 10 do away with

dog 3 cur, pup 4 heel, mutt 5 beast, puppy 6 canine 7 mongrel, villain 9 scoundrel 10 blackguard
Alaskan: 5 husky 8 malamute, malemute
anatomy: 3 hip, lip, pad, paw, toe 4 arch, back, hock, loin, rump, stop 5 cheek, crest, croup, flews, skull 6 carpus, dewlap, muzzle, stifle, tarsus 7 brisket, cushion, knuckle, occiput, pastern, withers 8 heelknob, shoulder 10 metacarpus, metatarsus
Australian: 5 dingo 8 warragal
barkless: 7 basenji
breed:
  herding group: 5 pulik 6 briard, collie 12 border collie 13 bearded collie 14 German Shepherd 15 Belgian malinois, Belgian sheepdog, Belgian tervuren 16 Shetland sheepdog 18 Cardigan Welsh corgi, Old English sheepdog, Pembroke Welsh corgi 19 Australian cattle dog, Bouviers des Flandres
  hound group: 6 beagle, borzoi, saluki 7 basenji, harrier, whippet 9 dachshund, greyhound 10 bloodhound, otter hound 11 Afghan hound, basset hound, Ibizan hound 12 pharaoh hound 14 Irish wolfhound 15 English foxhound 16 American foxhound 17 Norwegian elkhound, Scottish deerhound 18 Rhodesian ridgeback 20 black and tan coonhound
  nonsporting group: 6 poodle 7 bulldog 8 chow chow, keeshond 9 dalmatian, lhasa apso 10 keeshonden, schipperke 11 Bichon frise 13 Boston terrier, French bulldog 15 Tibetan spaniel, Tibetan terrier
  sporting group: 6 vizsla 7 pointer 8 Brittany 10 weimaraner 11 Irish setter 12 field spaniel, Gordon set-

ter 13 cocker spaniel, English setter, Sussex spaniel 14 Clumber spaniel 15 golden retriever 17 Irish water spaniel, Labrador retriever 19 flat-coated retriever 20 American water spaniel, curly-coated retriever, English cocker spaniel, Welsh springer spaniel 22 Chesapeake Bay retriever, English springer spaniel 23 German wirehaired pointer 24 German shorthaired pointer 25 wirehaired pointing griffon
  terrier group: 10 fox terrier 11 bull terrier, Skye terrier 12 Cairn terrier, Irish terrier, Welsh terrier 13 border terrier 14 Norfolk terrier, Norwich terrier, wire fox terrier 15 Airedale terrier, Lakeland terrier, Scottish terrier, Sealyham terrier 16 Kerry blue terrier, smooth fox terrier 17 Australian terrier, Bedlington terrier, Manchester terrier 18 Jack Russell Terrier, miniature schnauzer 20 Dandie Dinmont terrier 24 soft-coated wheaten terrier, Staffordshire bull terrier, West Highland white terrier 28 American Staffordshire terrier
  toy group: 3 pug 7 Maltese, shih tzu 8 papillon 9 chihuahua, pekingese, toy poodle 10 pomeranian 12 Japanese chin, silky terrier 13 affenpinscher 15 Brussels griffon 16 Italian greyhound, Yorkshire terrier 17 English toy spaniel, Manchester terrier, miniature pinscher 26 Cavalier King Charlea Spaniel
  working group: 5 akita, boxer 7 mastiff, samoyed 8 kuvaszok 9 great Dane, St Bernard 10 komondorok, rottweiler 11 bullmastiff 12 Newfoundland 13 great Pyrenees, Siberian husky 14 giant schnauzer 15 Alaskan malamute 16 doberman pinscher 17 standard schnauzer 18 Bernese mountain dog, Portuguese water dog
Buster Brown's: 4 Tige
Charles, Nick and Nora's: 4 Asta
Chinese: 7 shih tzu
coach: 9 dalmatian
combining form: 3 cyn 4 cani, cyno
constellation: 12 Canis Majoris
Dorothy's: 4 Toto
family: 7 Canidae
FDR's: 4 Fala 5 Falla
female: 3 dam, gip, gyp 4 slut 5 bitch, brach 7 brachet
genus: 5 Canis
group: 4 pack 5 leash 6 kennel
"His Master's Voice": 6 Nipper
Hungarian: 4 puli 6 kuvasz, vizsla
Indian: 5 dhole
Japanese: 5 akita
Little Orphan Annie's: 5 Sandy
male: 3 dog

movie/TV: 4 Asta, Lady 5 Benji, Tramp 6 Lassie 9 Old Yeller, Rin Tin Tin
mythical: 8 Cerberus
Nixon's: 8 Checkers
Punch and Judy's: 4 Toby
Russian: 6 borzoi 7 samoyed
star: 6 Sirius 8 Canicula
Thin Man movies, in: 4 Asta
Welsh: 5 corgi
wild: 5 adjag, dhole, dingo, guara, rabid 6 jackal 7 agouara 8 cimarron
young: 3 pup 5 puppy, whelp

Dogberry
character in: 19 Much Ado About Nothing
author: 11 Shakespeare

Dog Day Afternoon
director: 11 Sidney Lumet
cast: 8 Al Pacino 10 John Cazale 14 Charles Durning

dogged 8 stubborn 9 tenacious 10 determined, persistent 11 unremitting

dogie 4 calf 14 motherless calf

dogies 6 calves, cattle 16 motherless calves

dogma 5 credo, tenet 7 beliefs 8 doctrine 9 teachings 10 philosophy, principles 11 convictions

dogmatic 6 biased 8 stubborn 9 arbitrary, doctrinal, imperious, obstinate 10 prejudiced 11 dictatorial, domineering, opinionated

Dog Star
constellation of:
  Hunting Dogs: 13 Canes Venatici
  Larger Dog: 10 Canis Major
  Smaller Dog: 10 Canis Minor

dogwood 6 Cornus
varieties: 5 Brown, Creek, False, Giant, Silky, Stiff 6 Pagoda, Poison 7 Chinese 8 American, Jamaican, Mountain, Panicled, Redosier, Siberian, Tatarian 9 Blood-twig, Flowering, Tartarian 10 Golden-twig, West Indian 11 Round-leaved 13 White Mountain

Doha, al-Dawha
capital of: 5 Qatar

do in 4 kill 6 murder 7 destroy, exhaust, tire out

Doktor Faust
opera by: 6 Busoni
character: 5 Faust 14 Duchess of Parma 14 Mephistopheles

dolce
music: 7 sweetly

dolce far niente 18 pleasing inactivity 20 it is sweet to do nothing

dolce vita 9 sweet life

Dol Common
character in: 12 The Alchemist
author: 6 Jonson

doldrums 5 blues, dumps, gloom 10 depression, melancholy

dole 4 deal, give 5 share 6 parcel

7 charity, handout, welfare **9** allotment **10** allocation **13** apportionment

doleful 3 sad **6** dismal, dreary, gloomy, woeful **7** joyless, unhappy **9** sorrowful

dolente
music: **9** sorrowful

dole out 4 give, mete **5** allot **6** parcel **7** portion **8** allocate, dispense **9** apportion **10** distribute

doling out 7 dealing **9** allotment, parceling **10** allocation, assignment **12** distribution **13** apportionment

doll 5 dolly, dummy, honey **6** beauty, puppet **7** darling, rag doll **8** baby doll, figurine, golliwog **9** teddy bear **10** marionette, sweetheart **11** pretty child

dollar 3 one **4** bean, bill, buck, coin, note, skin, yuan **5** money, tater, token **6** single **7** ironman, smacker **8** cartwheel, simolean

Dollar A Second
host: **9** Jan Murray

Dollar Bill
nickname of: **11** Bill Bradley

dollop 3 dab **4** blob, dash, lump **11** small amount

Doll's House, A
author: **11** Henrik Ibsen
character: **8** Krogstad **10** Nora Helmer **13** Torvald Helmer

dolly 3 toy **4** cart, doll **9** plaything **15** wheeled platform

dolor 5 grief **6** sorrow **7** anguish, sadness

dolorous 3 sad **6** rueful, woeful **7** doleful, tearful, unhappy **8** dejected, downcast, grievous, mournful, pathetic, pitiable, wretched **9** anguished, cheerless, harrowing, miserable, sorrowful, woebegone **10** calamitous, despondent, lamentable, melancholy **11** distressing **12** disconsolate, heavyhearted **13** grief-stricken

Dolphin
constellation of: **9** Delphinus

Dolphin, The
author: **12** Robert Lowell

dolt 4 clod, fool, jerk **5** idiot, moron **6** nitwit **7** half-wit, jackass **8** bonehead, imbecile, numskull **9** blockhead

doltish 4 dumb, slow **5** thick **6** simple, stupid **7** asinine, foolish, idiotic, moronic, witless **8** ignorant, retarded **9** brainless, imbecilic **10** half-witted, slow-witted **12** dunderheaded, muddleheaded, simple-minded **13** rattlebrained **14** featherbrained

domain 4 area, fief, land **5** field **6** empire, estate, region, sphere **7** kingdom **8** dominion, property, province **9** bailiwick, territory

Dombey and Son
author: **14** Charles Dickens
character: **4** Paul **5** Toots **6** Carker, Cuttle **8** Florence, Mr Dombey **9** Dr

Blimber, Walter Gay **11** Joe Bagstock, Susan Nipper **12** Cousin Feenix, Edith Granger, Solomon Gills

dome
Italian: **5** duomo

Domenichino
real name: **16** Domenico Zampieri
born: **5** Italy **7** Bologna
artwork: **11** Hunt of Diana **16** Monsignor Agucchi **18** The Four Evangelists, The Life of St Cecilia **23** Last Communion of St Jerome **30** Landscape with Tobias and the Angel

domestic 4 cook, maid, tame **6** au pair, butler, native **7** endemic, servant **8** homemade, houseboy **9** attendant, home-grown **10** indigenous, not foreign **11** housebroken, native-grown, not imported **12** domesticated, hearthloving **13** household help

domesticated 4 tame **11** housebroken

domicile 4 home **5** house **8** dwelling **9** residence **14** legal residence

dominance 4 edge **8** hegemony **9** advantage, authority, upper hand **10** precedence **11** preeminence, superiority

dominant 5 chief, major **6** ruling **8** superior **9** principal **10** commanding **11** controlling, outstanding **13** authoritative, most important, most prominent

dominate 4 rule **5** dwarf **6** direct, govern **7** command, control **8** domineer **9** tower over **11** preside over

dominating 6 lordly, ruling **7** topmost **8** dominant **9** directing, governing, principal, prominent **10** commanding **11** controlling, domineering, outstanding **12** advantageous **13** authoritative, most important **15** most outstanding

domination 4 rule **5** power **7** command, control, mastery **9** authority **11** superiority

domineer 7 control **8** dominate, lord over **9** dictate to, tyrannize

domineering 8 arrogant, despotic, dogmatic **9** imperious **10** commanding, oppressive, tyrannical **11** dictatorial, overbearing **13** authoritative

Dominican Republic
capital/largest city: **12** Santo Domingo **14** Ciudad Trujillo
others: **4** Azua, Bani, Moca, Pena, Polo **5** Bonao, Cotui, Nagua, Neiba, Nizao, Sosua **6** Higuey, La Vega, Oviedo **7** Sanchez **8** Barahona, Santiago **11** Puerto Plata **17** San Pedro de Macoris **21** San Francisco de Macoris
measure: **3** ona **5** tarea **6** fanega
monetary unit: **3** oro **4** peso **6** franco
island: **5** Beata, Saona **8** Altovelo, Catalina **10** Hispaniola
lake: **10** Enriquillo
mountain: **4** Tina **5** Gallo, Neiba **7** Baoruco, Central **8** Bahoruco, Oriental **13** Sententrional

highest point: **6** Duarte
river: **4** Yuna **5** Ozama **11** Yaque del Sur **13** Yaque del Norte
sea: **8** Atlantic **9** Caribbean
physical feature:
  bay: **4** Ocoa, Yuma **5** Neiba **6** Rincon, Samana **7** Isabela **8** Calderas, Escocesa
  cape: **5** Beata, Falso **6** Cabron, Engano **7** Caucedo, Isabela, Macoris
  valley: **4** Real **5** Neyba
people: **5** Negro, Taino **6** Indian **7** mulatto, Spanish **9** Caucasian
  discoverer: **8** Columbus
language: **6** French **7** English, Spanish
religion: **13** Roman Catholic
feature:
  dance: **8** merengue
  religious pilgrimage: **8** romerias
food:
  dessert: **8** pinonate
  fish/meat pastry: **10** pastelitos
  stew: **8** sancocho

dominion 4 land, rule **5** realm **6** domain, empire, region **7** command, mastery **9** authority, supremacy, territory **11** sovereignty **12** jurisdiction
Hindu: **3** raj

Dominus 3 God **4** Lord

Dominus vobiscum 16 the Lord be with you

don 4 wear **5** put on **6** pull on **7** dress in, get into

Don
origin: **5** Welsh
form: **7** goddess
son: **7** Gwydion
daughter: **8** Arianrod

dona 4 lady **5** madam

Dona Flor and Her Two Husbands
author: **10** Jorge Amado

Donalbain
father: **6** Duncan
brother: **7** Malcom

Donald Duck
creator: **10** Walt Disney
character:
  girlfriend: **5** Daisy
  nephew: **4** Huey **5** Dewey, Louie
  uncle: **7** Scrooge

Donar
origin: **8** Germanic
god of: **7** thunder

donate 4 give **6** bestow **7** present **8** bequeath **10** contribute **11** make a gift of

Donatello
real name: **15** Donato di Niccolo
born: **5** Italy **9** Florence
artwork: **5** David **6** St Mark **7** Zuccone **8** Jeremiah, St George **11** Gattamelata **12** Mary Magdalen **19** Judith and Holofernes, St John the Evangelist **22** Cavalcanti Annunciation

donation 4 gift **7** present **12** contribution

Don Careless
author: **8** Rex Beach

Don Carlos
author: **14** Johann Schiller
opera by: **5** Verdi
character: **7** Rodrigo **8** Philip II **9** Don Carlos **13** Princess Eboli **15** Grand Inquisitor **17** Elizabeth de Valois

Dondi
creator: **8** Gus Edson **10** Irwin Hasen
dog: **7** Queenie

done 5 ready **8** finished, prepared **9** completed **12** cooked enough **18** cooked sufficiently

done for 4 dead, gone, over, sunk **5** all up, ended, kaput, spent **6** beaten, doomed, ruined **7** all over, damaged, through **8** finished **9** exhausted

done in 4 beat **5** all in, slain, spent, tired, weary **6** bushed, killed, pooped **7** drained, wearied, worn out **8** dog tired, fatigued, murdered, tired out **9** bone weary, dead tired, played out **10** knocked off

Don Giovanni
also: **7** Don Juan **15** The Rake Punished
opera by: **6** Mozart
setting: **7** Seville
character: **7** Masetto, Zerlina **9** Donna Anna, Leporello **10** Don Ottavio **11** Donna Elvira **15** The Commendatore

Donizetti, Gaetano
born: **5** Italy **7** Bergamo
composer of: **10** Anna Bolena, La Favorita **11** Don Pasquale **12** Elixir of Love, Maria Stuarda **13** L'elisir d'amore, Marino Faliero, Torquato Tasso **14** Lucrezia Borgia **15** Roberto Devereux **16** Linda di Chamounix **17** Lucia di Lammermoor **21** Daughter of the Regiment

Don Juan 3 man **4** beau, wolf **5** Romeo, swain, wooer **6** fellow, squire, steady, suitor **7** admirer, courter, gallant, pursuer **8** Casanova, lothario, lover boy, paramour, young man **9** boyfriend, Lochinvar **10** lady-killer **15** gentleman caller

Don Juan
author: **21** George Gordon Lord Byron
character: **6** Haidee **9** Donna Inez **10** Donna Julia

donkey 3 ass **4** fool, mule **5** burro, idiot **7** jackass

Donlevy, Brian
wife: **12** Marjorie Lane
born: **7** Ireland **9** Portadown
roles: **9** Beau Geste **15** The Great McGinty **21** Two Years Before the Mast

Donn, Arabella
character in: **14** Jude the Obscure
author: **5** Hardy

donna 4 lady **5** madam

Donna Reed Show, The
character: **9** Jeff Stone, Mary Stone **10** Donna Stone **11** Dr Alex Stone, Midge Kelsey, Trisha Stone **12** Dr Dave Kelsey
cast: **8** Bob Crane, Carl Betz **9** Ann McCrea, Donna Reed **12** Paul Peterson **13** Patty Peterson **14** Shelley Fabares

Donne, John
author of: **7** Sermons **10** The Ecstasy, The Extasie **11** Holy Sonnets **15** Death Be Not Proud, Songs and Sonnets, The Canonization **20** Paradoxes and Problems **30** A Valediction Forbidding Mourning

donnish 7 preachy **8** academic, didactic, pedantic **9** pedagogic

Donnithorne, Arthur
character in: **8** Adam Bede
author: **5** Eliot

donnybrook 3 row **4** fray **5** brawl, fight, melee, set-to **6** affray, dustup, fracas, ruckus, rumpus **7** ruction, scuffle **8** skirmish **10** free-for-all **19** knock-down-and-drag-out

donor 5 giver **10** benefactor **11** contributor **12** humanitarian **14** philanthropist

do-nothing 5 idler **6** loafer **14** good-for-nothing

do not prosecute
Latin: **13** nolle prosequi

do not repeat
Latin: **12** non repetatur

Don Pasquale
opera by: **9** Donizetti
character: **6** Norina **7** Ernesto **11** Dr Malatesta

Don Quixote de la Mancha
also: **38** El ingenioso hidalgo Don Quijote de la Mancha
author: **17** Miguel de Cervantes (Saavedra)
character: **10** Pedro Perez **11** Sancho Panza **17** Dulcinea del Toboso
horse: **9** Rosinante
musical: **13** Man of La Mancha

doodad 5 gizmo **6** device, gadget **8** ornament **9** doohickey **10** decoration **11** contraption, contrivance, thingamabob, thingamajig **15** whatchamacallit

doohickey 5 gizmo, thing **6** device, dingus, gadget, object, widget **7** dojiggy, whatsis **8** dojigger **9** thingummy **11** thingamabob, thingamajig **14** thingamadoodle **15** whatchamacallit

Dooley, Thomas Anthony
founded: **6** MEDICO **31** Medical International Corporation
worked in: **13** Southeast Asia

doolie 4 USAF **8** freshman

Doolittle, Eliza

character in: 9 Pygmalion **10** My Fair Lady
author: **4** Shaw

doom 3 end, lot **4** fate, ruin **5** death, judge **7** condemn, convict, destiny, portion, verdict **8** judgment **10** Armageddon **11** destruction, Judgment Day **13** consign to ruin, end of the world, pronouncement **15** resurrection day, the Last Judgment **17** mark for demolition

doomed 5 fated **6** damned, ruined **8** ill-fated **9** condemned

doomsday 11 Judgment Day **13** Day of Judgment, end of the world **15** the Last Judgment

do one's best 3 try **6** strive **7** attempt **8** endeavor, go all out **9** take pains **12** make an effort **13** give all one has **15** knock oneself out

Doonesbury
creator: **12** Garry Trudeau
character: **2** B D **5** Honey, Rufus **6** Calvin, Zonker **7** Boopsie **9** Uncle Duke **12** Joanie Caucus **14** Mark Slackmeyer **18** Michael J Doonesbury

door 4 exit **5** entry **6** egress, portal **7** hallway, ingress **8** entrance **11** entranceway

doorway 5 entry **7** ingress, opening **8** entrance

Doorways
god of: **5** Janus

dope 3 pot, tip **4** drip, drug, fool, jerk, junk, nerd, news **5** creep, drugs, dummy, klutz, scoop **6** heroin, sedate, uppers **7** downers, opiates **8** additive **9** narcotics, narcotize, substance **10** antiseptic, astringent, medication **11** anesthetize, preparation **12** disinfectant **17** inside information

dope fiend 4 head, user **5** doper, freak **6** addict, junkie **7** hophead **8** cokehead **10** dope addict, drug abuser, drug addict

do penance 5 atone **7** expiate **10** make amends

dopey 4 dumb **6** leaden, stupid, torpid **7** asinine, idiotic, witless **8** comatose, mindless, sluggish **9** brainless, lethargic **10** dull-witted, slow-witted, slumberous **11** block-headed, thickheaded **12** simple-minded

Doppelganger 6 double **13** ghostly double
literally: **12** double-walker

Doppler, Christian Johann
field: **7** physics
nationality: **8** Austrian
discovered: **13** Doppler Effect

Dorcas
also called: **7** Tabitha
revived by: **5** Peter
hometown: **5** Joppa

Doris
father: **7** Oceanus

mother: 6 Tethys
husband: 6 Nereus
mother of: 7 Nereids

dormancy 7 latency **8** inaction **10** inactivity, quiescence, somnolence **11** hibernation

dormant 4 idle **8** inactive, sleeping **9** quiescent, somnolent **11** hibernating

Dorothy
character in: 13 The Wizard of Oz
author: 4 Baum
dog: 4 Toto

Dorset, Bertha and George
characters in: 15 The House of Mirth
author: 7 Wharton

dorsum 5 chine, spine **8** backbone

dose 2 OD **3** cut, nip **4** dram, pill, shot, slug **5** quota, share, slice **6** amount, needle, ration, tablet **7** capsule, measure, portion, section, segment **8** division, overdose, quantity **9** allotment, allowance, daily dose, injection **10** percentage

Dos Passos, John
author of: 3 U S A **11** The Big Money **13** Three Soldiers **16** Nineteen Nineteen **17** Manhattan Transfer **22** The Forty-Second Parallel

dossier 4 file **5** brief **6** record **9** portfolio **14** detailed report

Dostoevsky, Fyodor Mikhailovich
author of: 8 The Idiot **9** The Double **10** The Gambler **12** The Possessed **18** Crime and Punishment **20** The Brothers Karamazov **23** Notes from the Underground

dot 3 dab **4** mark, spot **5** fleck, point, speck **6** dapple, period **7** stipple **9** small spot

dotage 8 senility **15** second childhood **16** feeblemindedness

dote 8 be senile, fuss over

dote on 5 adore, prize, spoil, value **6** pamper **7** cherish, indulge **8** fuss over, treasure **15** lavish affection

doting 4 fond **6** loving **9** indulgent, pampering **12** affectionate

double 4 dual, twin **5** clone **6** paired **7** replica, two-part **8** two-sided **9** ambiguous, duplicate **10** dead ringer **11** again as much, counterpart, meant for two, twice as much **12** twice as great **13** multiply by two, spitting image **15** increase twofold
German: 12 Doppelganger

Double, The
author: 16 Fyodor Dostoevsky

double-cross 5 rat on **6** betray, do dirt, tell on, turn in **7** abandon, deceive, let down, sell out, two-time **8** denounce, inform on, run out on, snitch on **9** play Judas **10** be disloyal **13** be treacherous, inform against, play false with **14** break faith with **16** blow the whistle on, sell down the river

double-crosser 5 cheat **7** traitor **8** betrayer, deceiver, informer

Double-Dealer, The
author: 15 William Congreve

double-dealing 5 false **6** deceit, sneaky, tricky **7** crooked, devious, perfidy **8** bad faith, betrayal, disloyal **9** deceitful, duplicity, falseness, treachery, two-timing **10** disloyalty, perfidious, sneakiness **11** crookedness, double-cross, duplicitous, treacherous **12** dishonorable **13** breach of faith, faithlessness

double entendre 12 off-color joke, risque remark **18** ambiguous statement

double entente 9 ambiguity

Double Indemnity
director: 11 Billy Wilder
cast: 13 Fred MacMurray **15** Barbara Stanwyck, Edward G Robinson
script: 9 James Cain **15** Raymond Chandler

Double Life, A
director: 11 George Cukor
cast: 10 Signe Hasso **12** Edmond O'Brien, Ronald Colman **14** Shelley Winters
Oscar for: 5 actor (Colman)
script: 10 Ruth Gordon **11** Garson Kanin

double meaning 9 ambiguity
French: 13 double entente **14** double entendre

doublet 4 pair **5** tunic **6** couple, jacket **10** two of a kind

double-talk 4 bunk, jazz **5** hokum **6** bunkum, drivel, gabble, jabber **7** baloney, blather, palaver, prattle, twaddle **8** flimflam, flummery, nonsense **9** gibberish **10** balderdash, hocus-pocus, mumbo jumbo **11** obfuscation **12** gobbledygook

double-walker
German: 12 Doppelganger

Double X
nickname of: 9 Jimmy Foxx

doubt 5 qualm **6** wonder **7** suspect **8** distrust, mistrust, question **9** misgiving, skeptical, suspicion **10** be doubtful, indecision **11** uncertainty **12** apprehension **13** feel uncertain **14** waver in opinion **15** have doubts about **16** lack confidence in, lack of conviction

Doubter *see* **6** Thomas

doubtful 5 vague **7** dubious, obscure, suspect, unclear **9** tentative, uncertain, undecided, unsettled **10** hesitating, irresolute, suspicious **11** unconvinced **12** inconclusive, questionable

doubtfulness 5 doubt **7** dubiety **8** distrust, mistrust, unbelief **9** disbelief, suspicion **10** skepticism **11** incredulity **14** lack of credence

Doubting *see* **6** Thomas

doucement
music: 6 gently

douceur 3 tip **5** bribe **8** gratuity **9** sweetness

dough 4 cash, duff, spud **5** bread, crust, money, paster **6** batter, change, leaven, noodle **8** doughboy **11** infantryman

doughnut 4 cake, tire **5** bagel, torus **6** cymbal, dunker, sinker **7** beignet, cruller, twister

doughty 4 bold **5** brave **6** strong **8** fearless, intrepid, unafraid **9** confident, dauntless **10** courageous, determined **12** stout-hearted

Douglas, Archibald
character in: 7 Marmion
author: 5 Scott

Douglas, Kirk
real name: 17 Issur Danielovitch
son: 7 Michael
born: 11 Amsterdam NY
roles: 8 Champion **9** Spartacus **10** The Vikings **11** Lust for Life **14** Detective Story, Seven Days in May **17** The Glass Menagerie, Young Man with a Horn **18** Letter to Three Wives **22** Mourning Becomes Electra

Douglas, Lloyd C
author of: 7 The Robe **23** The Magnificent Obsession

Douglas, Melvyn
real name: 23 Melvyn Edouard Hesselberg
wife: 12 Helen Gahagan
born: 7 Macon GA
roles: 3 Hud **9** Ninotchka **10** Being There

Douglas, Michael
father: 4 Kirk
roles: 4 Coma **7** The Game **10** Disclosure, Wall Street (Oscar) **11** Star Chamber **13** Basic Instinct **14** Jewel of the Nile **15** Fatal Attraction **16** The China Syndrome, The Perfect Murder **17** Romancing the Stone

dour 4 sour **6** gloomy, morose, solemn, sullen **9** cheerless **10** forbidding, unfriendly

Douras, Marion Cecilia
real name of: 12 Marion Davies

douse 4 soak **5** souse **6** drench **7** immerse **8** saturate, submerge **15** plunge into water

Dove, Noah's
constellation of: 7 Columba

Dover Beach
author: 13 Matthew Arnold

dovetail 4 jibe, join **5** match, tally, unite **8** coincide **9** harmonize **11** fit together **12** interlocking

dowager 5 widow **6** relict **7** elderly

dowdy 4 drab **5** tacky **6** frumpy, shabby, sloppy **8** slovenly **12** unattractive

dowel 3 peg, pin, rod 4 pole 5 stick 7 spindle

down 3 ill 4 blue, deck, drop, fell, gulp, sick 5 drink, floor 6 ailing 7 put away, swallow 8 dejected, downcast, feathers 9 depressed 10 dispirited 12 disheartened

down-and-out 4 sick 5 broke 9 penniless 12 impoverished, on one's uppers 13 incapacitated 15 under the weather

downcast 3 low, sad 4 blue 7 unhappy 8 dejected 9 cheerless, depressed 11 discouraged 12 disconsolate, disheartened

downfall 4 fall, ruin 6 shower 8 collapse, downpour 9 rainstorm, ruination 10 rain shower 11 destruction

downgrade 4 drop 5 lower 6 debase 7 decline, descent, way down 8 belittle, minimize 9 declivity, denigrate, devaluate 10 depreciate

downhearted 3 sad 7 unhappy 8 dejected, downcast 9 depressed, sorrowful 10 dispirited 11 discouraged 12 disheartened

downheartedness 5 gloom 6 dismay 7 despair, sadness 9 dejection, pessimism 10 depression, low spirits, melancholy 11 despondency 12 hopelessness 14 discouragement

down in the dumps 4 blue, glum 6 gloomy 7 in a funk 9 depressed 10 despondent 13 in the doldrums

down in the mouth 3 sad 6 dismal, woeful 7 joyless, unhappy 8 dejected, downcast 9 depressed, sorrowful, woebegone 10 lugubrious 12 disconsolate

downpayment 6 binder 7 advance, deposit 9 money down

downpour 6 shower 9 rainstorm 10 cloudburst, rain shower

downright 4 open 5 blunt, frank, total, utter 6 candid, direct, honest, really 7 in truth, plainly, sincere, utterly 8 absolute, actually, complete 9 out-and-out 10 aboveboard, completely, thoroughly 12 unmistakably 13 thoroughgoing, unequivocally 15 straightforward

Downright
  character in: 19 Every Man in His Humour
  author: 6 Jonson

downstairs 5 below 6 cellar 8 basement 10 first floor 11 ground floor

down the drain 4 gone, lost 9 up in smoke 12 out the window

down-to-earth 5 crass, plain, sober, solid 6 casual, coarse, earthy, simple 7 relaxed 8 informal, sensible 9 practical, pragmatic, realistic 10 hardheaded, hard-boiled, no-nonsense 11 plain-spoken, substantial 12 matter-of-fact, unidealistic 13 unsentimental

downtown 9 inner city, urban area 10 center city, metropolis 16 business district, metropolitan area

downtrodden 9 exploited, oppressed 10 tyrannized 11 subservient 12 harshly ruled

downturn 3 dip, sag 4 drop, fall, skid, slip 5 slide, slump 6 plunge, waning 7 decline, reverse, setback 8 decrease 9 downslide, downswing, downtrend, dwindling, recession 10 depression, diminution 12 degeneration 13 deterioration

Down Under *see* 9 Australia

down with
  French: 4 a bas

downy 4 soft 5 fuzzy, nappy, plumy, quiet 6 fleecy, fluffy 7 cunning, knowing 8 feathery 9 featherbed

do wrong 3 err, sin 8 go astray 9 misbehave 11 transgress

Doyle, Sir Arthur Conan
  see also 14 Holmes, Sherlock
  author of: 13 The Sign of Four 15 A Study in Scarlet, The White Company 25 The Hound of the Baskervilles 26 Adventures of Sherlock Holmes
  character: 10 Irene Adler 12 Dr John Watson 13 Mycroft Holmes 14 Sherlock Holmes 17 Inspector Lestrade, Professor Moriarty

doze 3 nap 6 catnap, siesta, snooze 10 forty winks, light sleep 12 sleep lightly

dozy 4 lazy 6 drowsy, sleepy 7 languid 9 lethargic, somnolent

D P 5 exile 6 emigre 7 outcast, refugee 8 deportee 10 expatriate 14 banished person, deported person 15 displaced person 16 political refugee

drab 4 dull, gray 5 dingy 6 dismal, dreary, gloomy, somber 9 cheerless, dull brown 10 lackluster

drabness 8 dullness 9 dinginess 10 dreariness, gloominess 13 colorlessness

Dracula
  author: 10 Bram Stoker
  character: 8 Dr Seward 10 Mina Murray 12 Count Dracula, Dr Van Hesling, Lucy Westenra 14 Arthur Holmwood, Jonathan Harker

draft 4 drag, gulp, haul, pull, wind 5 drink 6 breeze, induct, sketch 7 diagram, outline, swallow 9 conscript, induction 10 money order 11 postal order, rough sketch 12 conscription, current of air 15 military service 16 drawing from a cask 18 preliminary version 22 call for military service

drafty 6 breezy, chilly

drag 3 lug 4 bore, haul, pull 5 bring, crawl, trail 6 dredge 7 be drawn 9 inch along 10 creep along, move

slowly, spoilsport, wet blanket 11 party-pooper

Dragnet
  character: 8 (Sgt) Ed Jacobs 9 (Sgt) Ben Romero, (Sgt) Joe Friday 10 (Officer) Bill Gannon, (Officer) Frank Smith
  cast: 8 Jack Webb 9 Herb Ellis 11 Harry Morgan 12 Ben Alexander 14 Barney Phillips 16 Barton Yarborough
  setting: 10 Los Angeles

Dragon 14 Leviathan
  constellation of: 5 Draco

drag on 4 last 6 endure, keep on, keep up 7 persist 8 continue 9 persevere

drag one's feet 5 crawl, creep 6 dawdle 9 waste time 10 move slowly 13 procrastinate

dragonfly
  varieties: 5 biddy 6 darner 7 skimmer 8 clubtail, grayback 9 amberwing 12 elisa skimmer

Dragon Seed
  author: 10 Pearl S Buck

Dragon's teeth
  sown by: 6 Cadmus
  location: 6 Thebes
  grew into: 8 warriors

dragoon 5 bully, force 6 coerce, compel 7 trooper 8 browbeat, bulldoze, cavalier, horseman, pressure 9 strongarm 10 cavalryman 12 horse soldier, horse trooper 14 mounted soldier

drag through the mud 5 smear, sully, taint 6 debase, defame, smirch, vilify 7 degrade, tarnish, vitiate 8 disgrace, dishonor 9 discredit, disparage 10 stigmatize

drain 3 sap 4 drag, pipe, tube 5 empty, sewer, use up 6 outlet, strain 7 channel, conduit, debouch, deplete, flow out, pump off 8 empty out 9 depletion, discharge, dissipate 10 impoverish

drainage 4 flow 9 discharge

drained 4 beat 5 all in, empty, spent, tired, weary 6 bushed, done in, pooped, used up 7 emptied, wearied, worn out 8 con- sumed, depleted, dog tired, expended, fatigued, finished, tired out 9 dead tired, enervated, exhausted, played out

Drake, Stan
  creator/artist of: 21 The Heart of Juliet Jones

Drake, Temple
  character in: 9 Sanctuary
  author: 8 Faulkner

dram
  abbreviation: 2 dr

drama 4 play 6 acting 8 the stage 9 direction, vividness 10 excitement, the theater 11 mise-en-scene 15 dramatic quality, intense interest, theatrical

piece
god of: 7 Bacchus

dramatic 8 striking **9** climactic, emotional **10** theatrical **11** sensational, suspenseful **12** melodramatic **13** for the theater

dramatics 6 acting **7** emoting **9** theatrics **10** dramaturgy, stagecraft **11** hamming it up, histrionics, thespianism

dramatis personae 4 cast **6** actors **7** players **10** performers **16** cast of characters, list of performers

dramaturgy 5 drama **7** theater **10** stagecraft **11** dramatic art

Drambuie
type: 7 liqueur
origin: 8 Scotland
flavor: 5 herbs, honey
with scotch: 9 Rusty Nail

drape 4 deck, garb, veil, wrap **5** adorn, array, cloak, cover, dress **6** attire, bedeck, enrobe, enwrap, shroud, swathe, wrap up **7** apparel, bedight, envelop, festoon, sheathe, swaddle **8** enshroud, enswathe

drastic 4 dire, rash **7** bizarre, extreme, radical **8** dreadful **9** dangerous **10** outlandish **11** deleterious

Dravidian
language group: 3 Kui **5** Ghond, Tamil **6** Teluga **8** Kanarese **9** Malayalam
spoken in: 5 India **6** Ceylon **8** Sri Lanka

draw 3 get, tie, tow **4** drag, etch, haul, limn, lure, pick, pull, take **5** charm, draft, drain, evoke, infer, write **6** allure, come-on, deduce, elicit, entice, extend, make up, siphon, sketch **7** attract, distort, draw out, extract, make out, pick out, pull out, pump out, stretch, suck dry, take out, wrinkle **8** contract, deadlock, elongate, protract **9** attenuate, pull along, stalemate **10** attraction, bring forth, enticement, inducement, make appear **14** make a picture of

draw away 2 go **5** leave **6** go back, shrink **7** retreat **8** withdraw

drawback 8 handicap, obstacle **9** detriment, hindrance **10** impediment **12** disadvantage **14** stumbling block

draw back 6 flinch, recoil **7** back off, retreat **8** move away, withdraw

draw close 3 hug **4** come, near **6** arrive, enfold **7** embrace **8** approach, come nigh, gain upon **10** move toward

drawers 5 pants **6** shorts **7** panties **8** bloomers, calzoons, trousers **9** pantalets, underwear **10** underpants

draw forth 5 evoke **6** elicit **7** distill, extract

drawing 5 study **6** sketch **7** lottery,

picture **9** depiction, selection **11** delineation **12** illustration

drawing apart 8 dividing **9** diverging **10** separating **12** splitting off

drawing out 9 expansion, extension **10** elongation, stretching **11** attenuation, lengthening, protraction **12** prolongation

drawing power 4 pull **6** allure, appeal **9** magnetism **10** attraction, enticement **11** fascination

drawing room 5 salon **6** parlor **10** living room **11** sitting room **13** reception room

drawn out 4 long **7** lengthy **8** extended **9** elongated, prolonged **10** lengthened, protracted

draw out 5 educe, evoke **6** elicit, expand, extend, extort **7** distill, enlarge, extract, prolong, spin out, stretch **8** elongate, lengthen, protract **9** attenuate, call forth **10** stretch out

draw the line 5 limit **8** contrast, separate **12** fix a boundary **13** differentiate

draw to a close 3 end **6** finish **8** conclude **11** come to an end

draw together 4 herd, mass, pack **5** bunch, crowd, flock, group **6** gather, huddle **7** cluster, collect, tighten **8** assemble, compress, contract **9** constrict **10** congregate

draw up 3 map **5** draft **6** make up, map out **7** charter, diagram, outline **9** blueprint

draw up plans 5 draft **6** design, sketch **7** outline

dray 4 cart **5** wagon **7** tipcart, tumbrel **8** dumpcart

dread 4 fear **5** awful **6** fright, terror **7** anguish, anxiety, cower at, fearful **8** alarming, cringe at **10** be afraid of, horrifying, shrink from, terrifying **11** fearfulness, frightening, trepidation **12** apprehension **20** anticipate with horror

dreaded object
French: 9 bete noire

dreadful 5 awful **6** tragic **7** fearful **8** alarming, horrible, shocking, terrible **9** frightful **11** distressing

dream 3 joy **4** goal, hope, muse, wish **5** think **6** desire, vision **7** delight, fantasy, hope for, incubus, reverie, think up **8** consider, pleasure, prospect **9** nightmare **11** expectation, have as a goal **13** look forward to, lost in thought

Dream Merchants, The
author: 13 Harold Robbins

Dream of the Golden Mountains, The
author: 13 Malcolm Cowley

Dreams
god of: 6 Icelus, Oniros **7** Oneiros **8** Morpheus **9** Phantasus

Dream Songs, The
author: 12 John Berryman

dream up 5 frame, hatch **6** create, invent **7** concoct **8** conceive, contrive

dreamy 4 airy **5** blank, empty, vague **6** absent, musing, unreal **8** ethereal, fanciful, illusory, soothing **9** fantastic, wonderful **10** delightful **11** preoccupied, unrealistic **13** unsubstantial **14** out of this world

dreariness 9 bleakness **10** desolation, dismalness, gloominess, melancholy **13** cheerlessness

dreary 3 sad **4** drab **5** bleak **6** dismal, gloomy **7** forlorn **8** mournful **9** cheerless **10** depressing, melancholy

dregs 6 rabble **7** deposit, grounds, residue **8** canaille, riffraff, sediment **9** settlings, worst part **11** lower depths

Dreiser, Theodore
author of: 8 The Titan **12** Sister Carrie, The Financier **17** An American Tragedy

drench 3 wet **4** soak **5** douse **8** saturate

dress 4 curl, deck, do up, garb, gown, robe, trim **5** adorn, frock, groom, treat **6** attire **7** apparel, arrange, bandage, cleanse, clothes, comb out, costume, garnish **8** clothing, decorate, ornament **9** disinfect, embellish **12** put on clothes **13** clothe oneself

Dressed to Kill
director: 12 Brian De Palma
cast: 10 Nancy Allen **11** Keith Gordon **12** Michael Caine **14** Angie Dickinson

dressed up 7 adorned, duded up **8** costumed, dolled up, tarted up **9** decorated, disguised, in costume **10** ornamented **11** embellished

dresser 6 bureau **7** cabinet, commode **8** cupboard **10** chiffonier **14** chest of drawers

dressing-down 6 rebuke **7** censure, chiding, reproof **8** reproach, scolding **9** reprimand **10** bawling-out, chewing-out, upbraiding **11** castigation, reprobation **12** remonstrance **13** tongue-lashing

dressing-gown
French: 13 robe-de-chambre

dressmaker 9 couturier, midinette **10** couturiere, seamstress

dress up 5 adorn **6** doll up **7** enhance, improve **8** beautify, ornament, spruce up **9** embellish, embroider, smarten up **10** exaggerate

Dreyfuss, Richard
born: 10 Brooklyn NY
roles: 4 Jaws **6** Tin Men **8** Stakeout **9** The Big Fix, Stand by Me **14** Mr. Holland's Opus, The Goodbye Girl (Oscar) **15** Moon Over Parador **16** American Graffiti **20** Postcards from the Edge **24** Down and Out in Bev-

erly Hills **29** Close Encounters of the Third Kind **31** The Apprenticeship of Duddy Kravitz

dribble 4 drip, kick **6** bounce **7** drizzle, trickle **11** fall in drops, run bit by bit

driblet 4 drip, drop, tear **7** droplet, globule

dried up 4 arid **7** drained, parched **9** prunelike, shriveled **10** dehydrated, desiccated

drift 3 aim **4** flow, gist, heap, mass, pile **5** amass, amble, sense **6** course, gather, object, pile up, ramble, stream, wander **7** current, meander, meaning, purpose, scatter **8** movement **9** direction, intention, objective **10** accumulate **11** implication, peregrinate **12** accumulation, be borne along

drifter 3 bum **4** hobo **5** idler, tramp **6** loafer **8** derelict, vagabond **16** ne'er-do-well

drill 4 bore **5** punch, train **6** pierce **8** exercise, practice, puncture, training, work with **10** boring tool, repetition **11** instruction **17** repeated exercises **type: 4** hand **5** twist **8** electric

drilling 4 rote **6** boring **8** practice, training **9** schooling **10** discipline **11** preparation

drink 3 sip **4** gulp, swig **5** booze, taste, toast **6** absorb, imbibe, ingest, salute, take in **7** alcohol, swallow **8** beverage, libation **9** partake of, the bottle **10** alcoholism **11** drunkenness **15** alcoholic liquor **17** liquid refreshment **type of: 3** cup, fix **4** fizz, flip, mull, puff, sour **5** daisy, julep, punch, shrub, sling, smash **6** cooler, frappe, rickey **7** cob- bler, stinger **8** highball

drinker 3 sot **4** lush, wino **5** dipso, drunk, rummy, souse **6** bibber, boozer, sponge **7** guzzler, imbiber, tippler, waterer **8** drunkard **9** alcoholic, inebriate

drink in 6 absorb, digest, soak up, take in **10** assimilate **14** immerse oneself

Drinking god of: 5 Comus

drinking spree 4 orgy, toot **5** binge, drunk **6** bender **8** beer-bust, carousal **9** bacchanal

drink up 4 gulp **5** quaff **6** absorb, guzzle, soak up **7** consume, swallow

drip 3 ass **4** bore, jerk, nerd **5** creep, dummy, klutz **6** splash **7** dribble, driz- zle, trickle **8** sprinkle

dripping 3 wet **4** damp **5** soggy **6** soaked, sodden **10** soaking wet

drive 4 goad, lead, mean, move, prod, push, ride, rush, spur, urge **5** force, guide, impel, motor, press, steer, surge **6** co- erce, compel, incite, intend, outing **7** advance, conduct, go by car, impulse, operate, suggest **8** ambition, campaign, motivate **9** ex-

cursion, insinuate, trip by car, urge along **10** motivation

drive apart 8 alienate, estrange **9** disaffect

drive away 4 rout, shoo **5** chase, deter, repel **6** rebuff **7** repulse **8** alienate **11** put to flight, send packing

drive home 7 impress **8** hammer at

drivel 5 drool **6** babble, ramble, slaver **7** dribble, slobber **8** babbling, nonsense, rambling **9** gibberish **12** talk nonsense **13** senseless talk, talk foolishly

drive out 4 fire **5** chase, depel, eject, evict, exile, expel, force, roust **6** compel, remove **7** dismiss, repulse **8** discharge, exorcise

driver 6 cowboy, drover **8** herdsman **9** chauffeur

drizzle 3 fog **4** mist, rain **7** dribble **8** sprinkle

drizzly 3 wet **4** damp **5** foggy, misty, rainy

Dr Jekyll and Mr Hyde author: 20 Robert Louis Stevenson **character: 5** Poole **10** Mr Utterson **13** Dr Henry Jekyll **14** Dr Hastie Lanyon

Dr Kildare character: 14 Dr James Kildare **18** Dr Leonard Gillespie **cast: 13** Raymond Massey **18** Richard Chamberlain **hospital: 12** Blair General

Dr No author: 10 Ian Fleming

droll 5 funny **7** offbeat, strange **8** humorous **9** eccentric, laughable, whimsical **12** oddly amusing

drollery 3 wit **5** humor **6** banter, comedy, whimsy **7** jesting

Dromio character in: 17 The Comedy of Errors **author: 11** Shakespeare

drone 3 hum **4** buzz, whir **5** idler **6** loafer **7** vibrate **8** parasite **9** murmuring, vibration **10** lazy person

drool 6 drivel, slaver **7** dribble, slobber **8** salivate **15** water at the mouth

droop 3 dim, sag **4** flag, sink **5** lower **6** weaken, wither **8** diminish, hang down **9** lose vigor **14** hang listlessly **15** incline downward

droopy 4 bent, blue, down, limp **5** baggy, bowed, slack **6** dashed, pining **7** doleful, sagging, subdued **8** cast down, dangling, dejected, downcast **9** depressed **10** despairing, despondent, dispirited, spiritless, world-weary **11** downhearted, hanging down, languishing **14** down in the mouth

drop 3 can, dab **4** bead, dash, deck, dive, drip, fall, fell, fire, omit, sack, sink, tear **5** abyss, floor, leave, lower, pinch, slide, slope, smack, trace **6** give up, lessen, plunge **7** abandon,

decline, descend, descent, dismiss, dribble, driblet, dwindle, forsake, globule, plummet, slacken, smidgen, soupcon, trickle **8** decrease, diminish, leave out, lowering **9** declivity, discharge, knock down, precipice, terminate **10** sprinkling **12** bring to an end **13** fail to include **15** cease to consider, fail to pronounce

drop anchor 4 dock, moor **5** tie up

drop in 4 call, come **5** visit **6** appear, come by, look in, show up, stop by, turn up **7** stop off **9** pay a visit

droplet 4 bead, drop, tear **7** driblet, globule **8** spherule

droplets of moisture 3 dew, fog **4** mist **5** sweat **12** condensation

drop out 4 quit **5** leave **6** resign, retire

dross 4 scum, slag **5** waste **6** cinder, scoria **8** clinkers, impurity

drought, drouth 4 lack, need, want **6** dearth **7** aridity, paucity **8** scarcity, shortage **10** deficiency, dry weather, lack of rain **13** insufficiency

drover 6 cowboy, driver **7** cowpoke **8** herdsman, shepherd **10** cowpuncher

drown 4 soak **5** flood **6** deluge, drench, engulf **7** immerse **8** inundate, overcome, submerge **9** overpower, overwhelm, suffocate, swallow up **10** asphyxiate

drowse 3 nap, nod **4** doze, laze **5** dover, drone, sleep **6** snooze **7** slumber **8** languish **10** sleepiness

drowsy 4 dozy, lazy, slow **5** tired **6** sleepy **7** languid **8** hypnotic, listless, sluggish, soothing **9** lethargic, somnolent, soporific

Dr Strangelove or How I Learned to Stop Worrying and Love the Bomb director: 14 Stanley Kubrick **cast: 9** Peter Bull **10** Keenan Wynn **11** Slim Pickens **12** George C Scott, Peter Sellers **14** James Earl Jones, Sterling Hayden

drub 3 hit **4** beat, cane, flog, whip **5** whale **6** thrash **9** bastinado

drubbing 6 caning **7** beating, licking, tanning **9** trouncing **11** shellacking

drudge 4 grub, hack, plod, toil **5** labor, slave **6** lackey, menial, toiler **7** grubber **8** inferior, struggle **9** underling **11** subordinate

drudgery 4 toil **5** grind **7** travail **8** hack work **11** menial labor **15** distasteful work

Druk-Yul *see* **6** Bhutan

drum 3 din, keg, rap, tap, tub **4** beat, cask, roar, roll **5** expel, force **6** barrel, harp on, rumble, tattoo **7** dismiss, pulsate **8** drive out, hammer at **9** discharge, drive home, reiterate **11** beat a tattoo, din in the ear, reverberate

Drums author: 9 James Boyd

Drums Along the Mohawk
author: 14 Walter D Edmonds
character: 4 Lana 9 Blue Black, John Wolff 11 Joseph Brant, Mark Demooth 12 Mrs McKlennan 13 Gilbert Martin 20 Magdelena Borst Martin

drunk 3 sot 4 bust, lush, soak 5 binge, rummy, souse, tipsy, toper 6 barfly, bender, looped, sodden, soused, stewed, zapped, zonked 7 smashed 8 beer-bust, besotted, carousal 9 alcoholic, plastered 10 inebriated 11 dipsomaniac, intoxicated 13 drinking spree, under the influence

drunkard 3 sot 4 lush, soak, wino 5 rummy, souse, toper 6 barfly 9 alcoholic 11 dipsomaniac

drunkenness 10 alcoholism 11 inebriation 12 intoxication

Drury, Allen
author of: 14 Capable of Honor, Return to Thebes 15 The Promise of Joy 16 Advise and Consent 19 Come Nineveh Come Tyre

Druse 5 Syria 6 Muslim 7 Lebanon

dry 4 arid, blot, dull, wipe 5 droll 6 boring, low-key 7 deadpan, parched, tedious, thirsty 8 rainless 9 dehydrate, desiccate, shrivel up, wearisome 10 dehydrated, monotonous 13 uninteresting

Dryad
form: 5 deity, nymph
location: 5 woods

dry as dust 4 arid, dull, sere 7 parched 8 pedantic, withered 9 shriveled 13 unimaginative

Dryden, John
author of: 10 All for Love 11 Mac Flecknoe 14 Annus Mirabilis 15 Alexander's Feast, Marriage-a-la-Mode 20 Absalom and Achitophel, Essay on Dramatic Poesy, The Hind and the Panther 22 Fables Ancient and Modern

dry goods 5 cloth, goods 6 fabric 8 material 9 yard goods 10 piece goods

dryness 7 aridity, drought 8 aridness 11 dehydration

Dry Salvages
author: 7 T S Eliot

dry up 6 wither 7 shrivel 9 dehydrate, desiccate, evaporate

Dr Zhivago
author: 14 Boris Pasternak
character: 4 Lara
setting: 17 Russian Revolution

dual 6 double 7 twofold, two-part

dub 4 call, name 5 label 6 knight 7 baptize 8 christen, nickname 9 designate

Dubai
part of: 3 UAE

dubiety 5 doubt 8 unbelief 9 disbelief 10 skepticism 11 incredulity 12 doubtfulness 14 lack of credence

Dubin's Lives
author: 14 Bernard Malamud

dubious 5 shady 6 unsure 7 suspect 8 doubtful 9 skeptical, uncertain 10 suspicious, unreliable 11 unconvinced 12 questionable, undependable 13 untrustworthy

Dublin
brewery: 8 Guinness
capital of: 7 Ireland
Irish: 8 Dubh Linn (black pool) 15 Baile Atha Cliath (town of the Hurdle Ford)
landmark: 10 Four Courts 11 Custom House 12 Abbey Theater, Christ Church, Dublin Castle 13 Leinster House 18 Kilmainham 19 St Patrick's Cathedral
mountain: 7 Wicklow
museum: 8 National 10 James Joyce
park: 7 Phoenix
river: 6 Liffey
rulers: 7 English, Vikings
scene of: 12 Easter Rising (1916)
university: 14 Trinity College

Dubliners
author: 10 James Joyce

DuBois, Blanche
character in: 21 A Streetcar Named Desire
author: 8 Williams

Du Bois, W E B
founded: 5 NAACP
author of: 19 The Souls of Black Folk

Dubonnet
type: 8 aperitif
origin: 6 France
ingredient: 7 quinine, red wine
with gin: 3 BVD 8 Napoleon
with rum: 10 Bushranger

duc 4 duke

Duccio di Buoninsegna
born: 5 Italy 6 Sienna
artwork: 6 Maesta 18 The Rucellai Madonna (attributed)

duce, il duce 6 despot, leader, tyrant 8 dictator 9 Mussolini

Duchamp, Marcel
born: 6 France 8 Normandy 10 Blainville
artwork: 5 LHOOQ 9 Given That 11 Etant Donnes 12 Bicycle Wheel 13 The Large Glass (The Bride Stripped Bare by Her Bachelors Even) 24 Nude Descending a Staircase 37 The King and Queen Surrounded by Swift Nudes

Duchess of Malfi, The
author: 11 John Webster
character: 6 Bosola 7 Antonio 8 Giovanna 9 Ferdinand 11 The Cardinal

duck 4 clee, coot, lory, smew, teal, veer 5 avoid, dodge, drake, eider, elude, evade, goose, ruddy, shirk, stoop 6 canard, canvas, crouch, gannet, Peking, scoter, swerve 7 gadwall,

mallard, Muscovy, pintail, pochard 8 baldpate, freckled, redshank, shelduck, shoveler, sidestep, submerge 9 merganser, whistling 10 bufflehead, canvasback 11 wood steamer 13 give the slip to
male: 5 drake
group of: 5 brace

Duck Soup
director: 10 Leo McCarey
cast: 5 Chico, Harpo, Zeppo 7 Groucho (Rufus T Firefly) 12 Louis Calhern, Raquel Torres 14 Margaret Dumont
setting: 9 Freedonia

duct 4 pipe, tube 6 vessel 7 channel, conduit

ductile 6 docile, pliant, supple 7 elastic, plastic, pliable, tensile 8 amenable, bendable, flexible, formable, moldable, shapable, swayable 9 adaptable, compliant, malleable, tractable 10 extensible, manageable, submissive 11 complaisant, manipulable, stretchable, susceptible

dud 3 dog 4 bomb, bust, flop, hash 5 botch, lemon, loser 6 bummer, fiasco, fizzle 7 clinker, debacle, failure, washout 11 lead balloon, miscarriage 14 disappointment

dude 3 fop 4 beau 5 dandy 7 peacock 11 city dweller, city slicker 12 Beau Brummell

Dudevant, Aurore
real name of: 10 George Sand

duds 4 togs 5 flops 6 attire 7 apparel, clothes, fizzles, threads 8 clothing, failures, garments

due 4 owed 5 ample, owing 6 enough, proper, unpaid 7 fitting, merited 8 adequate, becoming, deserved, expected, plenty of, rightful, suitable 9 in arrears, scheduled 10 sufficient 11 appropriate, outstanding

duel
French: 15 affaire d'honneur

Duel, The
author: 15 Alexander Kuprin

duenna 8 guardian 9 attendant, chaperone, custodian, protector

dues 4 fees 7 charges 10 assessment

Duessa
character in: 15 The Faerie Queene
author: 7 Spenser

duet 3 duo, two 4 pair 6 couple 7 twosome

Dufy, Raoul
born: 6 France 7 Le Havre
artwork: 7 The Palm 15 Riders in the Wood 16 Chateau and Horses 18 Deauville Racetrack, Posters at Trouville

dugout 3 den 4 cave 5 canoe 6 cavity, hollow 7 shelter

Duino Elegies
author: 16 Rainer Maria Rilke

Dukas, Paul
born: **5** Paris **6** France
composer of: **6** La Peri **18** Ariane et
Barbe-Bleue **19** Ariadne and Bluebeard **22** The Sorcerer's Apprentice

duke
French: **3** duc

Duke
nickname of: **9** John Wayne

Duke, Patty (Patty Duke Astin)
real name: **13** Anna Marie Duke
husband: **9** John Astin
born: **10** Elmhurst NY
roles: **11** Helen Keller **16** The Miracle
Worker, The Patty Duke Show, Val-
ley of the Dolls

Dukenfield, William Claude
real name of: **8** W C Fields

Duke Snider
nickname of: **11** Edwin Snider

dulcet 7 lyrical, musical, tuneful **8**
pleasing, sonorous **9** melodious **11**
mellifluous

Dulcinea del Toboso
character in: **10** Don Quixote
author: **9** Cervantes

dull 4 slow **5** blunt, dense, muted,
quiet, thick, trite, vapid **6** boring, obtuse, stupid **7** muffled, not keen, prosaic, subdued, vacuous **8** deadened,
inactive, not brisk, not sharp **9** dim-
witted **10** indistinct, lackluster, uneventful **13** unimaginative, uninteresting

Dull
character in: **16** Love's Labour's Lost
author: **11** Shakespeare

dullard 4 dolt **5** dummy, dunce **6** nitwit **7** halfwit **8** dumbbell, imbecile

Dullea, Keir
born: **11** Cleveland OH
roles: **12** David and Lisa **18** Butterflies Are Free **27** Two Thousand
One: A Space Odyssey

dullness 6 idiocy, tedium **8** dumbness,
lethargy, monotony, slowness **9** bluntness, ignorance, stupidity, vapidness
10 boringness, imbecility, obtuseness
11 tediousness **13** dim-wittedness **15**
thick-headedness

dull-witted 5 dazed, fuzzy **7** bemused, muddled, stunned **8** confused
9 stupefied

Dulong, Pierre-Louis
field: **7** physics **9** chemistry
nationality: **6** French
discovered: **19** nitrogen trichloride
studied: **4** heat **13** atomic weights

duly 6 on time **8** properly, suitably **9**
correctly **10** deservedly, punctually,
rightfully **13** appropriately **15** at the
proper time

Dumaine
character in: **16** Love's Labour's Lost
author: **11** Shakespeare

Dumas, Alexandre (fils)

author of: **7** Camille **11** Le Demi-
Monde **17** La Dame aux Camelias **21**
The Lady of the Camellias
Camille inspired: **10** La Traviata
opera by: **5** Verdi

Dumas, Alexandre (pere)
author of: **17** The Queen's Necklace
18 The Three Musketeers **19** The
Man in the Iron Mask **21** The Count
of Monte Cristo **22** The Vicomte de
Bragelonne

Du Maurier, Daphne
author of: **7** Rebecca **10** Jamaica Inn
11 Don't Look Now **14** My Cousin
Rachel **15** Frenchman's Creek **19**
The House on the Strand

Du Maurier, George
author of: **6** Trilby **10** The Martian
13 Peter Ibbetson

dumb 3 mum **4** dull, mute **5** dense,
dopey **6** silent, stupid **7** foolish, aphasic **8** aphasiac **9** dim-witted **13** unintelligent **17** incapable of speech

dumbbell 3 ass, oaf **4** clod, dolt, dope,
fool **5** booby, clown, dummy, dunce,
idiot, moron, ninny **6** dimwit, nitwit **7**
dullard, halfwit **8** dumb-dumb,
dummkopf, imbecile, lunkhead, meathead, numskull **9** birdbrain, blockhead, ignoramus, lamebrain, numbskull, simpleton **10** noodlehead

dumbfound, dumfound 4 stun **5**
amaze **7** startle **8** astonish **11** flabbergast

dumbfounded 5 agape **6** amazed **7**
stunned **9** astounded, stupefied **10** astonished, speechless **11** openmouthed **13** flabbergasted

dumbness 6 idiocy **8** dullness **9** asininity, stupidity, thickness **10** imbecility **11** witlessness **12** wordlessness **14**
speechlessness **15** thickheadedness

dumbstruck 5 agape **6** amazed, gaping **7** riveted **9** awestruck, stupefied
10 speechless **11** electrified, openmouthed **13** flabbergasted

dump 3 hut **4** hole, toss **5** empty,
hovel, shack **6** shanty, unload **8** get
rid of, junkyard **9** dispose of **10** refuse pile **11** rubbish heap

dumpy 5 squat **7** lumpish **13** short
and stout

Dunaway, Faye
real name: **18** Dorothy Faye
Dunaway
born: **8** Bascom FL
roles: **6** Barfly, Milady **7** Network
(Oscar) **8** The Champ **9** Chinatown
13 Mommie Dearest **14** Bonnie and
Clyde **15** Towering Inferno **17** The
Four Musketeers **18** The Three Musketeers

Duncan
character in: **7** Macbeth
author: **11** Shakespeare

Duncan, Sandy
born: **11** Henderson TX

roles: **8** Peter Pan **9** Funny Face **12**
The Boyfriend

dunce 4 fool **5** dummy, idiot, moron **6**
dimwit, nitwit **8** imbecile, numskull **9**
blockhead, numbskull, simpleton

Dunciad, The
author: **13** Alexander Pope

dune 4 bank **5** mound **8** sandbank,
sandpile

dunk 3 dip, sop **4** duck, soak **5** bathe,
douse, drown, slosh, souse, steep **6**
deluge, drench, engulf, plunge **7** baptize, immerse **8** inundate, saturate,
submerge

Dunne, John Gregory
author of: **11** Dutch Shea Jr **18** Quintana and Friends

Dunnock, Mildred
born: **11** Baltimore MD
roles: **8** Baby Doll **12** The Nun's
Story **14** The Corn Is Green **16** Butterfield Eight, Cat on a Hot Tin Roof,
Death of a Salesman

duo 4 pair **5** combo **6** couple **7** twosome **11** combination

duomo 4 dome **9** cathedral

dupe 4 fool, pawn **5** patsy, trick **6**
humbug, sucker **7** cat's paw, deceive,
fall guy, mislead **8** hoodwink **9** bamboozle

duplicate 4 copy **5** clone, match **6** repeat **7** replica **8** parallel **9** facsimile,
imitation, make again, photocopy,
photostat **10** carbon copy **12** reproduction

duplicity 5 fraud, guile **6** deceit **7** cunning **9** deception, falseness **10** dishonesty **13** deceitfulness

Du Pont Labs
founder: **17** E I du Pont de Nemours
inventor of: **5** nylon **6** Teflon **7** Gore-
Tex

Duquesnoy, Francois
born: **8** Brussels, Flanders
nickname: **11** Il Fiammingo
artwork: **8** St Andrew **9** St Susanna

dur
musical term: **5** major **8** major key

durability 7 stamina **8** strength **9** endurance, toughness **10** sturdiness

durable 5 sound, tough **6** strong,
sturdy **7** lasting **8** enduring **11** long-
wearing, substantial

Durand, Asher Brown
born: **18** Jefferson Village NJ
artwork: **14** Kindred Spirits

Durant, Will and Ariel
authors of: **20** The Story of Philosophy **21** Rousseau and Revolution **22**
The Story of Civilization

Durante, Jimmy
real name: **19** James Francis Durante
nickname: **10** Schnozzola **15** Inka
Dinka Doo Man
born: **9** New York NY

roles: 5 Jumbo **21** It's a Mad Mad Mad Mad World

duration 4 term **6** extent, period **11** continuance **12** continuation

Durdles
character in: **22** The Mystery of Edwin Drood
author: **7** Dickens

Durer, Albrecht
born: **7** Germany **9** Nuremberg
artwork: **10** Adam and Eve, Apocalypse, The Triumph **11** Wehlsch Pirg **12** Four Apostles, Large Passion, Melancholia I **13** Castle of Trent **15** Life of the Virgin **18** St Jerome in his Study **19** Virgin with the Siskin **21** Christ Among the Doctors **22** Knight Death and the Devil **24** Crowned Death on a Thin Horse **25** The Feast of the Rose Garlands **28** The Festival of the Rose Garlands

duress 5 force **6** threat **8** coercion, pressure **10** compulsion, constraint

Durgin, Francis Timothy
real name of: **11** Rory Calhoun

during litigation
Latin: **12** pendente lite

Durocher, Leo
nickname: **9** Leo the Lip
sport: **8** baseball
position: **7** manager
team: **11** Chicago Cubs **13** New York Giants **15** Brooklyn Dodgers
saying: **18** Nice guys finish last

Durrenmatt, Friedrich
author of: **5** Traps **8** The Visit **9** The Pledge, The Quarry **13** The Physicists **21** The Judge and His Hangman **27** The Marriage of the Mississippi

Durrie, James and Henry
character in: **21** The Master of Ballantrae
author: **9** Stevenson

dusk 6 sunset **7** sundown **8** twilight **9** nightfall

dusky 3 dim **4** dark **5** murky **6** cloudy, gloomy, veiled **7** swarthy **8** dark-hued

dust 4 dirt, lint **5** brush, motes **8** sprinkle

duster 3 rag **4** coat, robe **5** brush, cloth, whisk **9** housecoat **10** whisk broom

Dutch Guiana see **8** Suriname

Dutch Shea, Jr
author: **16** John Gregory Dunne

dutiful 5 loyal **8** diligent, faithful, obedient **9** compliant **13** conscientious

duty 3 tax **4** levy, onus, task **6** charge, excise, tariff **7** customs **8** business, function, province **10** assignment, obligation **14** responsibility

Duval, Armand
character in: **7** Camille
author: **5** Dumas (fils)

Duvall, Robert
born: **10** San Diego CA
roles: **4** MASH **10** The Apostle **11** Falling Down, Godfather II **12** Lonesome Dove, The Godfather **13** Apocalypse Now, Days of Thunder, Tender Mercies (Oscar) **15** The Great Santini, True Confessions **16** The Handmaid's Tale, The Scarlet Letter **18** To Kill a Mockingbird

Duvall, Shelley
born: **9** Houston TX
roles: **6** Popeye **9** Nashville **10** The Shining, Three Women **15** Brewster McCloud

Dvorak, Antonin
born: **11** Nelahozeves **14** Czechoslovakia
composer of: **5** Dumky **6** Hymnus, Te Deum **8** Carnival (overture) **10** St Ludmilla **11** Stabat Mater **15** American Quartet, From the New World (Symphony in E Minor) **16** The Specter's Bride **17** The Bells of Zlonice

dwarf 3 dim, elf, imp **4** baby, tiny **5** fairy, gnome, pixie, pygmy, small, troll **6** bantam, goblin, petite, sprite **8** diminish **9** miniature **10** diminutive, leprechaun, overshadow

dwarfish 3 wee **4** tiny **5** pygmy, short, small **6** bantam, little, midget **7** compact, squatty **10** diminutive, undersized **13** foreshortened

dweeb 4 fool, geek, nerd, wonk **5** grind

dwell 4 live **5** abide **6** harp on, reside **7** inhabit **10** linger over

dwelling 4 home **5** abode **8** domicile **9** residence **10** habitation

dwelling place 4 home **5** abode, house **7** habitat, lodging **8** domicile **9** residence **10** habitation **14** living quarters

dwell on 6 accent, stress **7** feature, iterate **9** emphasize, press home

dwindle 4 fade, wane **6** lessen, shrink **7** decline **8** decrease, diminish **13** become smaller

dye 4 tint **5** color, shade, stain **8** coloring **10** coloration

dyed-in-the-wool 9 confirmed, ingrained **10** deep-rooted, inveterate **11** established

dyestuff 14 coloring matter

dynamic 5 vital **6** active **7** driving **8** forceful, powerful, vigorous **9** energetic

dynamism 3 pep **4** life **5** verve, vigor **6** energy, spirit **8** vitality, vivacity **9** animation **10** liveliness

dynamite 4 raze, ruin **5** blast, trash, wreck **6** blow up, charge **7** destroy, shatter, wipe out **8** decimate, demolish **9** devastate, dismantle, eradicate, explosive **10** annihilate, extinguish, obliterate **11** exterminate

dynamo 4 doer **7** hustler **8** activist, go-getter **9** generator **12** active person **14** bundle of energy, mover and shaker

Dynasts, The
author: **11** Thomas Hardy
subject: **17** Napoleon Bonaparte

dynasty 4 line **5** crown, reign **6** regime **7** lineage, regency **8** dominion, hegemony, kingship, monarchy, regnancy **9** authority **10** government, suzerainty **11** ruling house **12** jurisdiction **14** administration

Dynasty
character: **9** Dex Dexter, Jeff Colby **12** Alexis (Morel Carrington Colby) Dexter **14** Adam Carrington **15** Blake Carrington **16** Amanda Carrington, Steven Carrington **17** Krystle Carrington **18** Dominique Devereaux, Krystina Carrington **21** Fallon Carrington Colby
cast: **9** John James **10** Linda Evans **11** Joan Collins **12** John Forsythe
setting: **6** Denver **8** Colorado
hotel: **8** La Mirage

dyspeptic 4 mean **6** crabby, grumpy, ornery, shirty, touchy **7** grouchy, waspish **8** choleric **9** crotchety, fractious, irascible, irritable **10** ill-humored, ill-natured **11** bad-tempered, contentious, hot-tempered **12** cantankerous, sour-tempered **13** short-tempered

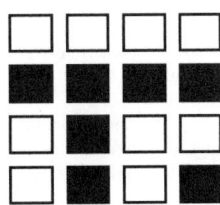

each 3 per **4** a pop **5** every **6** apiece **7** that one, this one **8** everyone, separate **12** respectively

Eagels, Jeanne
  born: 12 Kansas City MO
  roles: 4 Rain **8** Jealousy **9** The Letter **13** Sadie Thompson **14** Man Woman and Sin

eager 3 hot **4** agog, avid, keen **6** ardent, fervid, intent, raring **7** athirst, earnest, excited, fervent, intense, longing, zealous **8** desirous, diligent, resolute, spirited, yearning **9** ambitious, hungering, impatient, thirsting **10** aggressive, passionate **11** hardworking, impassioned, industrious, persevering **12** enterprising, enthusiastic

eagerly 6 avidly, keenly **8** ardently, desiring, fervidly, intently **9** anxiously, earnestly, fervently, zealously **16** enthusiastically

eagerness 4 zeal, zest **5** ardor **6** fervor **7** avidity **9** readiness **10** enthusiasm **11** willingness

eagle
  young: 6 eaglet

Eagle
  constellation of: 6 Aquila

Eakins, Thomas
  born: 14 Philadelphia PA
  artwork: 11 Agnew Clinic **13** Mrs Edith Mahon **14** The Gross Clinic **24** Max Schmitt in a Single Scull

ear
  section: 5 inner, outer **6** middle
  part: 4 drum **5** anvil, canal **6** hammer **7** cochlea, stirrup **8** hair cell **14** eustachian tube

earl 4 lord, peer **5** noble **8** nobleman
  wife: 8 countess

earlier 6 before, in time, sooner **9** before now, in advance **10** beforehand **11** ahead of time **13** before the fact

earliest 5 first **6** oldest, primal **7** ancient, initial, primary, soonest **8** original, primeval **9** beginning, primitive **10** aboriginal, indigenous **11** fundamental

Earl of Baltimore
  nickname of: 10 Earl Weaver

Earl the Pearl
  nickname of: 10 Earl Monroe

early 5 first **6** primal **7** ancient, archaic, betimes, initial, too soon, very old **8** primeval **9** in advance, premature, primitive **10** beforehand, in good time, primordial **11** ahead of time, prehistoric, prematurely

Early Autumn
  author: 14 Louis Bromfield

early man 6 Peking **9** Cro-Magnon, Steinheim **11** Neanderthal **18** Trobriand Islanders **24** Australopithecus robustus **25** Australopithecus africanus

earmark 3 tag **4** band, hold, sign **5** allot, label, stamp, token, trait **6** aspect, assign, dogear **7** feature, put away, quality, reserve **8** allocate, property, set aside **9** attribute, designate **11** peculiarity, singularity **14** characteristic

earn 3 get, net **4** draw, gain, make, rate, reap **5** clear, merit **6** attain, pick up, secure **7** achieve, collect, deserve, realize, receive, warrant **9** bring home **12** be entitled to

earn as due 4 rate **5** merit **7** deserve **10** be worthy of **12** be entitled to **13** be deserving of

earnest 4 firm **5** eager, fixed, grave, sober, staid **6** ardent, fervid, honest, intent, sedate, solemn, stable, steady, urgent **7** devoted, fervent, intense, serious, sincere, zealous **8** constant, diligent, resolute, spirited, vehement **9** ambitious, assiduous, heartfelt, insistent **10** deeply felt, determined, passionate, purposeful, thoughtful **11** hard-working, impassioned, industrious, persevering **12** enthusiastic, wholehearted

earnest request 4 plea **6** appeal **8** entreaty, petition **11** importunity **12** supplication

earnings 3 pay **5** wages **6** income, salary **7** payment, profits **8** proceeds, receipts, takehome **12** compensation

Earnshaw, Catherine
  character in: 16 Wuthering Heights
  author: 6 Bronte

ear-splitting 7 blaring **8** piercing **9** clamorous, deafening **10** thunderous

earth 3 sod **4** clay, dirt, dust, land, loam, soil, turf **5** terra **6** ground **7** topsoil
  god of: 3 Geb, Keb **5** Dagan, Dagon **10** Trophonius
  goddess of: 2 Ge **4** Gaea, Gaia **6** Hecate, Hekate, Tellus

earthen pot
  Spanish: 4 olla

earthenware 5 china **7** pottery **8** clayware, crockery **11** ceramic ware

earthly 6 bodily **7** mundane, secular, ungodly, worldly **8** feasible, material, physical, possible, temporal **9** corporeal, practical **10** imaginable **11** conceivable, terrestrial **12** nonspiritual **13** materialistic

earthquake 5 quake, seism, shock **6** tremor **8** tremblor, upheaval **11** earth tremor

earth tremor 5 quake, seism, shock **6** tremor **8** tremblor, upheaval **10** earthquake

earthy 5 bawdy, crude, dirty, funky, gross, lusty, rough **6** coarse, filthy, ribald, robust, smutty, vulgar **7** obscene, peasant, raunchy **8** indecent **9** primitive, unrefined **10** unblushing, uncultured **12** uncultivated

Earwicker family
  characters in: 13 Finnegans Wake
  author: 5 Joyce

earwig
  variety: 5 black **6** little **10** long horned

ease 4 calm, rest, slip **5** abate, allay, poise, quiet, slide, still **6** aplomb, lessen, luxury, pacify, plenty, relief, repose, solace, soothe **7** assuage, comfort, console, leisure, lighten, mollify, relieve **8** diminish, easement, easiness, facility, maneuver, mitigate, palliate, security, serenity **9** abundance, affluence, alleviate, composure, disburden, readiness **10** confidence, prosperity, relaxation **11** assuagement, naturalness, peace of mind, restfulness **12** tranquillity, unconstraint **13** luxuriousness, move carefully, relaxed manner **14** effortlessness, handle with care, unaffectedness

easel 5 frame, stand **6** tripod

easement 4 ease **6** relief, solace, succor **7** comfort **8** soothing **10** right of way **11** assuagement

easily 5 by far **6** freely, surely **7** clearly, handily, lightly, plainly, readily **8** facilely, smoothly, with ease **9** certainly **10** far and away, undeniably **11** beyond doubt, undoubtedly **12** effortlessly, with facility **13** without a hitch **14** beyond question, without trouble **17** without difficulty **23** beyond the shadow of a doubt

easily embarrassed 3 shy 5 timid 7 bashful 8 blushing, skittish, timorous 9 diffident, shrinking 11 constrained, unconfident

easily noticed 5 clear, plain 6 patent 7 evident, glaring, obvious, visible 8 flagrant, striking 9 arresting, prominent 10 noticeable 11 conspicuous, outstanding

easily ruffled 9 emotional, excitable 11 hot-tempered 13 quick-tempered

easiness 4 ease 10 equanimity, simplicity 11 naturalness 12 indifference 13 impassiveness

East, the 4 Asia 9 the Orient 10 the Far East 11 the Near East 17 Eastern Hemisphere

East Bengal see 10 Bangladesh

East Berlin
former capital of: 11 East Germany

East Coker
author: 7 T S Eliot

Eastern Slavic
language family: 12 Indo-European
group: 11 Balto-Slavic
branch: 6 Slavic
language: 7 Russian 9 Ukrainian 12 White Russian

Easter Parade
director: 14 Charles Walters
based on musical by: 12 Irving Berlin
cast: 9 Ann Miller 11 Fred Astaire, Judy Garland 12 Peter Lawford

East Germany see 11 Germany, East

East Indies see 8 Malaysia 9 Indonesia

Eastman, George
nationality: 8 American
founder of: 14 Eastman Kodak Co
inventor of: 9 Kodak film 11 Kodak camera 20 transparent photo film

East of Eden
author: 13 John Steinbeck
director: 9 Elia Kazan
cast: 8 Burl Ives 9 James Dean 10 Jo Van Fleet 11 Julie Harris 13 Raymond Massey
Oscar for: 17 supporting actress (Van Fleet)
characters: 4 Abra, Adam, Aron 5 Caleb, Trask

East wind
associated with: 5 Eurus 9 Volturnus

Eastwood, Clint
born: 14 San Francisco CA
roles: 7 Firefox, Rawhide 10 Dirty Harry, Hang Em High, Unforgiven 11 Magnum Force, The Dead Pool 12 Coogan's Bluff, Kelly's Heroes, Sudden Impact 13 A Perfect World 14 Play Misty for Me 15 In The Line of Fire, Where Eagles Dare 17 A Fistful of Dollars, Any Which Way You Can, High Plains Drifter 18 Escape from Alcatraz, For a Few Dollars More 21 Two Mules for Sister Sara 23 The Good the Bad and the Ugly 25 The Bridges of Madison County
director of: 10 Unforgiven (Oscar) 12 Sudden Impact 13 Absolute Power, A Perfect World 14 Play Misty For Me 25 The Bridges of Madison County 32 Midnight in the Garden of Good and Evil
mayor of: 6 Carmel

easy 4 calm, mild, open, soft 5 cushy, frank, light, naive 6 benign, calmly, candid, docile, easily, gentle, secure, serene, simple 7 lenient, natural, not hard, relaxed, restful, wealthy 8 affluent, carefree, composed, friendly, gracious, gullible, informal, outgoing, painless, peaceful, pleasant, scarcely, serenely, tranquil, unforced, well-to-do, yielding 9 compliant, indulgent, leisurely, luxurious, tractable, unworried 10 effortless, peacefully, permissive, unaffected, untroubled 11 comfortable, comfortably 12 not difficult, unsuspicious 13 accommodating, unconstrained

easygoing 4 calm 6 casual 7 offhand, patient, relaxed 8 carefree, laidback 9 unruffled, unworried 10 insouciant, nonchalant 11 unconcerned, unexcitable 12 even-tempered, happy-go-lucky, mild-tempered

Easy Rider
director: 12 Dennis Hopper
cast: 10 Karen Black, Peter Fonda 11 Luana Anders 12 Dennis Hopper, Robert Walker 13 Jack Nicholson

easy to use 7 adapted, helpful 9 adaptable 10 convenient 11 serviceable 12 advantageous, user friendly

eat 3 sup 4 bolt, dine, feed, gulp, rust, take 5 feast, lunch 6 devour, gobble, ingest, nibble 7 consume, corrode 8 dispatch, dissolve, wear away, wolf down 9 breakfast, take a meal, waste away 10 break bread, gormandize 14 take sustenance 15 take nourishment

eatable 4 food 6 edible 8 fit to eat 10 comestible, consumable

eat away 4 rust 5 erode 7 corrode, oxidize

eating habits 4 diet 7 regimen

eat into 4 bite 5 erode 6 nibble 7 consume, corrode 8 wear away 9 swallow up

eat one's fill 5 feast, gorge 6 pig out 7 banquet 10 stuff oneself

eat rapidly 4 bolt, gulp, wolf 5 scarf 6 gobble 12 swallow whole

eat up 5 enjoy, savor 6 devour, relish 7 consume, swallow 9 delight in, rejoice in 13 be pleased with, get a kick out of 14 take pleasure in

eat voraciously 6 cram in, devour, gobble 7 stuff in 8 bolt down, gulp down, wolf down 10 gormandize 12 swallow whole

eau, eaux 5 water

eau de vie 6 brandy 11 water of life

eaves 8 overhang

eavesdrop 3 bug, pry, spy, tap 5 snoop 6 attend, harken 7 monitor, wiretap 8 listen in, overhear 9 bend an ear 11 cock one's ear 14 strain one's ears 15 prick up one's ears

ebb 5 abate, go out 6 go down, lessen, recede, shrink, weaken 7 decline, dwindle, retreat, slacken, subside 8 decrease, diminish, fade away, fall away, flow away, flow back, move back, withdraw 9 waste away 10 degenerate 11 deteriorate

ebony 3 jet 4 dark, inky 5 black, raven, sable 8 hardwood 9 coal-black 15 Diospyros Ebenum
varieties: 5 Green, Texas 8 Macassar, Mountain 10 East Indian, Queensland

Ebsen, Buddy
real name: 23 Christian Rudolph Ebsen Jr
born: 12 Belleville IL
roles: 12 Barnaby Jones, Davy Crockett 21 The Beverly Hillbillies

ebullience 3 zip 7 elation 8 buoyancy 9 animation 10 enthusiasm, exuberance, joyousness, liveliness 11 high spirits 12 exhilaration 13 effervescence

ebullient 6 elated, joyful, joyous 9 exuberant 11 exhilarated 12 effervescent, enthusiastic, high-spirited

ecce homo 12 behold the man
said by: 13 Pontius Pilate
spoken of: 6 Christ

eccentric 3 nut, odd 4 kook, rash, sick 5 curio, flake, funny, kooky, nutty, queer, weird 6 freaky, insane, quaint, unique, weirdo 7 bizarre, curious, erratic, oddball, offbeat, strange, unusual, weirdie 8 aberrant, abnormal, crackpot, freakish, peculiar, quixotic, singular, uncommon 9 character, irregular, odd person, off center, parabolic, psychotic, screwball, unnatural, whimsical 10 capricious, elliptical, outlandish, unorthodox 13 extraordinary 14 unconventional

eccentricity 6 oddity, whimsy 7 caprice 9 deviation, queerness 10 aberration 11 abnormality, peculiarity, strangeness 12 idiosyncrasy, irregularity

ecclesiastic, ecclesiastical 5 rabbi, vicar 6 cleric, curate, deacon, parson, pas- tor, priest, rector 7 prelate 8 chaplain, churchly, clerical, minister, pastoral, preacher 9 churchman, clergyman, episcopal, parochial, religious

echelon 4 file, line, rank, rung, tier 5 grade, level 6 office 8 position 9 authority, hierarchy

Echidna 8 anteater
feature: 5 snout

echinoderm 9 sea animal

characteristic: 10 spiny shell
form: 6 radial
kind: 6 cystid **7** crinoid **8** starfish **9** sea urchin **10** basket star **11** sea cucumber

echo 3 ape **4** copy, ring **5** match **6** follow, mirror, parrot, repeat **7** imitate, reflect, resound **8** parallel, simulate **9** duplicate, reproduce, take after **11** reverberate **13** reverberation

Echo
form: 5 nymph
location: 8 mountain
loved: 9 Narcissus
loved by: 3 Pan
changed into: 4 echo

eclair 6 pastry **7** dessert **9** creampuff

eclaircissement 11 explanation **13** clarification, (the) Enlightenment

eclat 4 fame, pomp **5** glory, honor **6** praise, renown, repute **7** acclaim, display, success

eclipse 3 dim **4** hide, loss, mask **5** cloak, cover, excel, outdo **6** darken, exceed **7** blot out, conceal, erasing, masking, obscure, surpass, veiling, wipe out **8** cloaking, clouding, covering, outrival, outshine **9** darkening, shadowing, transcend **10** obliterate, overshadow, tower above **11** blotting out, diminishing, eradicating, obscuration **12** annihilation, obliteration **13** overshadowing

eclogue 4 idyl, poem **5** idyll **7** bucolic **8** dialogue, pastoral

Eclogues
author: 6 Vergil, Virgil

ecole 6 school

economic 6 fiscal **8** material, monetary **9** budgetary, financial, pecuniary **10** productive **12** distributive

economical 5 chary, cheap **6** frugal, modest, saving **7** careful, prudent, sparing, spartan, thrifty **8** economic **9** low-priced, niggardly, penurious, scrimping **10** reasonable **11** close-fisted, tightfisted **12** parsimonious

economic decline 8 downturn **9** recession **10** depression

economics
term: 3 GNP **5** labor **7** capital, Marxism, surplus **8** property **9** commodity, Communism, inflation, Keynesian, recession **10** capitalism, monetarist, supply-side **11** bourgeoisie, central bank, competition, consumption, marketplace, proletariat, stagflation **12** distribution, econometrics, fiscal policy, interest rate, laissez-faire, mercantilism **14** federal deficit, macroeconomics, microeconomics, monetary policy **17** trickledown theory **20** gross national product

economist
American: 6 George, Hansen, Sumner, Veblen **7** Commons **8** Friedman,

Laughlin **9** Greenspan **10** Schumpeter
British: 4 Mill **5** Smith **6** Keynes **7** Malthus, Ricardo **8** Marshall
French: 3 Say **7** Quesnay
German: 4 Marx **7** Schacht
Italian: 6 Pareto
Scottish: 5 Smith

economize 4 save **5** pinch, skimp, stint **6** scrimp **7** husband **8** be frugal, conserve, cut costs **9** be prudent **10** avoid waste **11** cut expenses **12** be economical, use sparingly **14** be parsimonious **15** practice economy, tighten one's belt

economizing 10 conserving **11** cutting down **13** penny-pinching **14** belt-tightening **15** pinching pennies **18** tightening one's belt

economy 6 thrift **8** prudence **9** frugality **10** providence **11** thriftiness **15** financial status, productive power

ecstasy 3 joy **5** bliss **6** frenzy, thrill, trance **7** delight, emotion, madness, rapture **8** delirium, gladness, pleasure **9** cloud nine, happiness, transport **10** enthusiasm, exultation

ecstatic 4 glad, rapt **5** happy **6** elated, joyful, joyous **7** exalted, excited **8** blissful **9** delighted, delirious, ebullient, entranced, overjoyed, rapturous **10** enraptured **11** transported **12** enthusiastic **13** beside oneself

Ecuador
name means: 7 equator
other name: 5 Quito
capital: 5 Quito
largest city: 9 Guayaquil
others: 4 Jama, Loja, Napo, Puyo, Tena **5** Guano, Manta, Pajan, Pinas, Piura, Pojan, Yaupi **6** Ambato, Cuenca, Ibarra, Tulcan, Zaruma **7** Azogues, Cayambe, Guamote, Guapulo, Machala, Pelileo, Pillaro, Salinas **8** Riobamba **10** Esmeraldas, Portoviejo
division: 5 Costa **6** Sierra **7** Oriente
measure: 5 libra **6** cuadra, fanega
monetary unit: 5 sucre **7** centavo
weight: 5 libra
island: 4 Puna, Wolf **5** Colon, Mocha, Pinta **6** Baltra, Chaves, Darwin, Pinzon, Rabida, Wenman **7** Isabela, La Plata, Sante Fe, Tortuga **8** Espanola, Floreana, Genovesa, Marchena, Santiago **9** Culpepper, Galapagos, Santa Cruz **10** Fernandina, Santa Maria **11** San Salvador **12** San Cristobal
mountain: 5 Andes **6** Condor, Sangay **7** Cayambe **8** Antisana, Cotopaxi **9** Cotacachi, Pichincha
highest point: 10 Chimborazo
river: 4 Coca, Mira, Napo **5** Cocoa, Daule, Paute, Pindo, Tigre **6** Blanco, Guayas, Tumbes, Zamora **7** Conambo, Curaray, Jubones, Pastaza, Puyango **8** Aguarico, Bobonaza, Cononaco, Naranjal, Putumayo **9** San

Miguel **10** Esmeraldas, Nangaritza **12** Guaillabamba
sea: 7 Pacific
physical feature:
bay: 5 Manta **7** Isabela **9** Elizabeth **11** Santa Elenas **15** Ancon de Sardinas
cape: 4 Rosa **6** Pasado **8** Marshall, Puntilla **10** San Lorenzo
channel: 7 Jambeli
gulf: 9 Guayaquil, Pichincha
peninsula: 10 Santa Elena
point: 4 Jama **5** Essex **6** Galera **9** Albemarle **10** Christobal
people: 4 Cara, Cixo, Inca **5** Ardan, Aucas, Macoa, Maina, Palta, Quitu, Yumbo **6** Canelo, Jibaro, Jivaro, Puruha **7** Cayapas, Jivaros, mestizo, mulatto **8** Barbacoa, Colorado, Montuvio, Serranos **9** Montubios
artist: 4 Egas **8** Santiago **9** Caspicara **10** Guayasamin
author: 6 Espejo **14** Carrera Andrade
conqueror: 7 Pizarro **10** Benalcazar **11** Huayna-Capac
god: 5 umina
leader: 6 Alfaro, Flores **10** Plaza Lasso, Rocafuerte **12** Garcia Moreno **13** Velasco Ibarra
language: 6 Jibaro **7** Quechua, Spanish
religion: 13 Roman Catholic
feature:
animal: 6 vicuna
dictator: 8 caudillo
estate: 8 hacienda
festival: 5 Yamor
hat: 6 Panama **8** jipijapa, toquilla
tree: 5 balsa
food:
baked guinea pig: 3 cuy
corn tamale: 6 humita
drink: 6 chicha
marinated raw shrimp/fish: 7 ceviche, seviche
potato/cheese patty: 11 llapingacho
potato soup: 5 locro

ecumenical 6 global **7** general **8** catholic **9** communist, planetary, universal, worldwide **10** heavenwide **11** communalist **12** all-embracing, all-including, all-inclusive, all-pervading, collectivist, cosmopolitan **13** communitarian, comprehensive, international

eczema 4 rash **8** eruption **10** dermatitis **12** inflammation

eddy 6 vortex **9** maelstrom, whirlpool **14** countercurrent

Eddy, Nelson
partner: 17 Jeanette MacDonald
born: 12 Providence RI
roles: 9 Rose Marie **15** Naughty Marietta **16** Northwest Outpost

Eden 8 Paradise
see also **4** Adam

Eden, Anthony 10 Earl of Avon **13** prime minister

Eden, Barbara
role: **7** Jeannie
TV: **15** I Dream of Jeannie
costar: **11** Larry Hagman

edentate 5 manis, sloth **7** antbear **8** aardvark, anteater **9** armadillo, toothless

Edgar Huntly
author: **20** Charles Brockden Brown

edge 3 hem, rim **4** bind, inch, line, side, trim **5** bound, brink, creep, limit, sidle, slink, sneak, steal, verge **6** border, fringe, margin **7** contour, outline **9** extremity, periphery, threshold **12** boundary line, dividing line, move sideways

Edgeworth, Maria
author of: **7** Belinda **11** The Absentee **14** Castle Rackrent

edging 3 hem **4** trim **5** limit **6** border, fringe, margin, ruffle **7** binding, curbing, salvage **8** boundary, fringing, trimming

edgy 5 sharp, testy **7** anxious, nervous **8** snappish **9** excitable, impatient, irascible, irritable **10** highstrung

edible 7 eatable **10** comestible, consumable, digestible **12** fit to be eaten, nonpoisonous **13** safe for eating

edict 3 law **4** bull, fiat **5** order, ukase **6** decree, dictum, ruling **7** command, dictate, mandate, statute **9** enactment, manifesto, ordinance, prescript **10** injunction, regulation **12** proclamation, public notice **13** pronouncement **14** pronunciamento

edification 8 guidance, teaching **9** direction, education, elevation, uplifting **11** advancement, information, instruction **13** enlightenment **14** indoctrination

edifice 8 building **9** structure **12** construction

edify 5 teach **6** inform **7** educate, improve **8** instruct **9** enlighten

edifying 8 didactic, tutorial **11** educational, instructive **12** enlightening

Edinburgh
bay: **12** Firth of Forth
capital of: **8** Scotland
Celtic: **11** Dune-eideann (Eidin's Fort)
church: **7** St Giles
landmark: **14** Holyrood Palace **15** Edinburgh Castle
port: **5** Leith
rocks: **10** Castle Rock **11** Arthur's Seat

Edison, Thomas Alva
nickname: **17** Wizard of Menlo Park
home: **11** Menlo Park, NJ
inventor of: **6** (wax cylinder) record **9** light bulb, (quadruplex) telegraph **10** phonograph **11** kinetoscope, stock ticker **14** movie projector **16** incandescent lamp **18** automatic telegraph (transmitter and receiver) **21** flexible celluloid film **22** alkaline storage battery

edit 5 adapt, emend **6** censor, polish, redact, revise **7** abridge, clean up, correct, expunge, rewrite, touch up **8** annotate, condense, copy-edit, rephrase **9** expurgate **10** blue-pencil, bowdlerize

edition 4 book, copy, kind **5** issue **6** number **7** imprint, version **8** printing **9** redaction

editor 2 ed **6** writer **7** newsman, reviser **8** compiler, redactor **10** journalist

Edmonds, Walter D
author of: **8** Rome Haul **19** Drums Along the Mohawk

Edmonton
hockey team: **6** Oilers

Edmontonia
type: **8** dinosaur **10** ornithopod
location: **12** North America

Edmund Campion
author: **11** Evelyn Waugh

Edom
name given: **4** Esau
descendants: **8** Edomites

Edson, Gus
creator/artist of: **5** Dondi **8** The Gumps

Ed Sullivan Show, The
regular cast: **17** June Taylor Dancers **23** Ray Bloch and His Orchestra
noted appearances: **7** Beatles, Bob Hope **9** Topo Gigio (mouse) **10** Walt Disney **11** Senor Wences **12** Elvis Presley **14** Martin and Lewis

educate 5 coach, edify, teach, train, tutor **6** inform, school **7** develop **8** civilize, instruct **9** enlighten

education 5 study **7** culture **8** learning, pedagogy, teaching, training, tutelage **9** didactics, erudition, knowledge, schooling **10** pedagogics **11** cultivation, edification, information, instruction, scholarship **13** enlightenment

Education of Henry Adams, The
author: **10** Henry Adams

educe 5 evoke **6** elicit, extort **7** draw out, extract **8** bring out **9** draw forth **12** bring to light

Edward II
author: **18** Christopher Marlowe

Edwards, Blake
director of: **3** SOB, Ten **14** The Pink Panther, Victor Victoria **18** Days of Wine and Roses **19** Breakfast at Tiffany's
wife: **12** Julie Andrews

Edwards, Vince
real name: **18** Vincent Edward Zoimo
roles: **8** Ben Casey **13** Devil's Brigade **14** The Desperadoes **15** Three Faces of Eve

Edwin Drood, The Mystery of
author: **14** Charles Dickens
character: **7** Durdles, Mr Tatar, Rosa Bud **8** Mr Sapsea **10** John Jasper, Mr Datchery **11** Mr Grewgious **12** Mr Crisparkle **13** Deputy Bazzard **14** Helena Landless, Miss Twinkleton, Mr Honeythunder **15** Neville Landless

eel 6 conger
young: **5** elver

eerie 3 odd **5** queer, weird **6** creepy, spooky, uneasy **7** bizarre, fearful, ghostly, ominous, strange, uncanny **10** mysterious, portentous **11** frightening **12** apprehensive

Eeyore 6 donkey
character in: **13** Winnie-the-Pooh
author: **5** Milne

efface 4 raze **5** erase **6** cancel, delete, excise, rub out **7** blot out, destroy, expunge, wipe out **9** eradicate, extirpate **10** annihilate, obliterate

effect, effects 4 fact, gist, make **5** cause, drift, force, goods, power, tenor, truth **6** action, assets, attain, create, impact, import, intent, result, sequel, things, upshot, weight **7** achieve, essence, execute, meaning, outcome, perform, produce, purport, reality, realize **8** carry out, chattels, efficacy, function, holdings, movables, validity **9** actuality, aftermath, execution, furniture, influence, intention, operation, outgrowth, trappings **10** accomplish, bring about, impression **11** commodities, consequence, development, enforcement, general idea, implication, possessions **12** significance **14** accomplishment

effective 4 real **6** active, actual, cogent, moving, potent, strong, useful **7** capable, current, dynamic, telling **8** a reality, eloquent, forceful, forcible, incisive, powerful, striking **9** activated, competent, effectual, efficient, operative **10** compelling, convincing, impressive, persuasive, productive, successful **11** efficacious, influential, in operation, serviceable

effectiveness 5 power **6** effect, impact **7** potency **8** efficacy, strength **9** influence **10** efficiency, usefulness **14** serviceability

effectual 6 acting, active, useful **7** working **8** adequate **9** effective, efficient, operative **11** efficacious, functioning

effectuate 6 effect **7** achieve, execute, realize **8** carry out, complete **9** discharge **10** accomplish, consummate, perpetrate **12** carry through **13** put into effect

effeminate 7 unmanly **8** sissyish, womanish **9** sissified

effervesce 4 fizz, foam **5** froth **6** bubble, fizzle **7** sparkle

effervescence 3 zip **4** dash, fizz, life **5** froth, vigor **6** fizzle, gaiety, spirit **7** foaming **8** bubbling, buoyancy, vitality, vivacity **9** animation, fizziness **10** bubbliness, bubbling up, ebullience, enthusiasm, liveliness

effervescent 3 gay **5** fizzy, merry **6** bubbly, lively **7** fizzing, foaming **8** animated, bubbling **9** ebullient, exuberant, sparkling, vivacious **13** irrepressible

effete 5 spent **6** barren, wasted **7** sterile, worn-out **8** decadent, depraved **9** enervated, exhausted **10** degenerate, unprolific **12** unproductive

efficacious 9 effective, effectual, efficient

efficacy 6 impact **10** efficiency **13** effectiveness

efficiency 5 skill **6** energy **8** efficacy, facility **9** apartment **10** competence **11** proficiency **13** effectiveness

efficient 3 apt **7** capable **8** skillful **9** competent, effective, effectual **10** productive, proficient, timesaving, unwasteful, work-saving **11** crackerjack, efficacious, workmanlike **12** businesslike

effigy 4 doll **5** dummy, image **6** puppet, statue **8** likeness, straw man **9** mannequin, scarecrow **10** marionette **14** representation

effluence 6 efflux **7** outflow, outpour **8** effluent **9** discharge

effluent 5 waste **6** efflux, sewage **7** outflow **9** effluence

effluvium 4 aura, odor, ooze, reek **5** vapor **6** efflux, flatus **8** outgoing

efflux 7 outflow **8** effluent, emission **9** discharge, effluence

effort 3 try **4** toil, work **5** force, labor, pains, power **6** energy, strain, stress **7** attempt, travail, trouble **8** endeavor, exertion, industry, struggle **11** elbow grease

effortless 4 easy **6** facile, simple, smooth **8** graceful, painless **12** not difficult **13** uncomplicated

effortlessness 4 ease **8** easiness, facility **9** readiness **12** painlessness

effrontery 4 gall **5** brass, cheek, nerve **8** audacity, temerity **9** arrogance, brashness, impudence, insolence **10** brazenness **11** presumption **12** impertinence **13** shamelessness
Yiddish: 7 chutzpa **8** chutzpah

effulgence 6 dazzle **8** radiance, splendor **10** brilliance **12** resplendence

effulgent 6 bright **7** radiant **8** dazzling, splendid **9** brilliant **11** resplendent

effusive 5 gushy **6** lavish **7** copious, gushing, profuse **9** ebullient, expansive, exuberant **10** unreserved **11** extravagant, free-flowing, overflowing **12** unrestrained

eft 4 newt **5** again **6** lizard **9** afterward

egalitarian 10 democratic **11** equalrights **14** constitutional

egalite 8 equality

Egeria
 instructed: 4 Numa **5** nymph **7** advisor

egg 3 ova, roe **4** bomb, goad, mine, oval, ovum, seed, spur **6** embryo, fellow, incite, person **7** albumen **9** instigate, stimulate

Eggar, Samantha
 born: 6 London **7** England
 roles: 12 The Collector, Walking Stick **15** Doctor Doolittle, The Lady in the Car **16** The Molly Maguires

egghead 8 highbrow **13** intellectual

Eggleston, Edward
 author of: 15 The Circuit Rider **19** The Hoosier Schoolboy **22** The Hoosier Schoolmaster

egg on 4 abet, back, goad, spur **6** exhort, incite **8** talk into **9** encourage

egg-shaped 4 oval **5** ovoid **7** oviform **10** elliptical

Egmont
 author: 12 Johann Goethe

egocentric 8 egoistic **11** egomaniacal, egotistical, on an ego trip, self-seeking, self-serving **12** narcissistic, self-absorbed, self-centered, self-involved, self-obsessed **13** self-concerned **14** megalomaniacal, stuck on oneself **18** wrapped up in oneself

egoism 6 vanity **8** self-love **10** narcissism **14** self-absorption, self-importance **16** overweening pride, self-centeredness

egoist 10 narcissist, selfish one **13** selfish person **18** self-centered person

Egoist, The
 author: 14 George Meredith

egoistic 7 selfish **12** narcissistic, self-centered

egotism 6 vanity **7** conceit **8** bragging, smugness **9** arrogance, immodesty, vainglory **10** self-praise **11** braggadocio **12** boastfulness

egotist 6 gascon **7** boaster, peacock **8** blowhard, braggart **9** swaggerer **11** braggadocio

egotistic 4 vain **10** egocentric **12** self-centered **13** self-important

egregious 5 gross **7** extreme, glaring, heinous **8** flagrant, grievous, shocking **9** monstrous, notorious **10** outrageous **11** intolerable **12** insufferable

egress 4 exit, vent **5** issue **6** escape, outlet, way out **7** leakage, outflow, seepage **8** aperture **9** departure, discharge **10** passage out, withdrawal

Egypt
 other name: 3 UAR **5** Kemet **6** Tomeri **11** The Two Lands **12** The Black Land
 capital/largest city: 5 Cairo

 others: 3 Tor **4** Edfu, Gaza, Giza, Idfu, Said, Suez **5** Altur, Aswan, Tanta **6** Boolak, Dumyat, Faiyum, Quseir, Safaga, Sallum **7** Alemein, Memphis, Raschid, Rosetta, Zagazig **8** Damietta, Hurghada, Ismailia, Mansurah **10** Alexandria
 school: 5 Cairo **7** Al-Azhar **8** American
 division: 5 Lower, Nubia, Upper
 measure: 3 apt, dra, hen, rob **4** arab, dira, draa, khet, nief, ocha, roub, theb, wudu **5** abdat, ardab, cubit, farde, fedan, keleh, kerat, kilah, sahme **6** artaba, aurure, baladi, kantar, keddah, robhah, schene **7** choryos, daribah, malouah, roubouh, toumnah **8** kassabah, kharouba **10** diramimari, diribaladi
 monetary unit: 4 fils, kees, para **5** asper, dinar, fodda, gersh, girsh, medin, pound, riyal **6** ahmadi, dirham, foddah, guinea, junayh, maidin, medine, medino **7** piaster, piastre, tallard **8** bedidlik, millieme
 weight: 3 kat, ket, oka, oke **4** dera, heml, khar, okia, rotl **5** artal, artel, deben, kerat, minae, minas, okieh, pound, ratel, uckia **6** hamlah, kantar **7** drachma, quintal
 island: 4 Roda **6** Philae **7** Shadwan **11** Elephantine
 lake: 4 Edku, Idku **5** Qarun **6** Maryut, Moeris, Nasser **7** Manzala **8** Burullus, Mareotis
 mountain: 5 Sinai, Uekia **6** Gharib **13** Shayib al-Banat
 highest point: 8 Katerina **9** Katherina
 river: 4 Bahr, Nile
 Nile branch: 7 Rosetta **8** Damietta
 sea: 3 Red **13** Mediterranean
 physical feature:
  cape: 4 Sudr **5** Banas **8** Rasbanas
  desert: 3 Tih **5** Dakla, Scete, Sinai, Skete **6** Libyan, Nubian, Sahara **7** Arabian
  gulf: 4 Suez **5** Aqaba
  isthmus: 4 Suez
  oasis: 4 Siwa **6** Dakhel, Dakhla, Kharga **7** Farafra, Khargeh **8** Bahariya **9** Bahariyeh **12** Wahel-Khargeh
  peninsula: 5 Sinai **6** Pharos
  plain: 7 Asaseff
  plateau: 3 Tih
 people: 3 Kem **4** Arab, Copt, Misr, Wafd **5** Gippy, Gyppy, Gypsy, Nilot **6** Ababda, Berber, Hyksos, Nubian, Tasian **7** Mizraim, Pharian **8** Badarian, Bisharin, Memphian
  leader: 5 Jawar, Sadat **6** Nasser **7** Mubarak, Saladin **10** King Farouk **11** Ismail Pasha, Mohammed Ali, Tawfiq Pasha
  pharaoh: 5 Khufu, Menes, Zoser **6** Khafre, Ptulol, Ramses **8** Horemheb, Menkaure **9** Akhenaten, Amenemhet, Amenhotep **10** Men-

tuhotep **11** Tutankhamen
queen: 9 Cleopatra, Nefertari, Nefertiti **10** Hatshepsut, Hetepheres
language: 6 Arabic, French **7** English
for liturgy: 6 Coptic
religion: 5 Islam **18** Coptic Christianity
ancient god: 2 Ra **3** Geb, Nut, Shu **4** Aton, Atum, Isis, Ptah, Seth **5** Horus, Thoth **6** Anubis, Hathor, Osiris, Tefnut **8** Nephthys
place:
dam: 4 Sadd, Sudd **5** Aswan **6** Assuan
mosque: 5 Rifai **9** Alabaster **11** Sultan Hasan
palace: 6 Kubbeh
pyramids: 4 Giza **5** Khufu **6** Cheops **7** Saqqara
ruins: 5 Miroe **6** Abydos, Sphinx, Thebes **7** Memphis **8** Berenice **9** Abu Simbel **13** Valley of Kings, Valley of Tombs
temple: 4 Idfu **5** Edoon, Luxor, Thoth **6** Abydos, Karnak, Osiris **7** Dendera
feature:
dynasty: 5 Saite **7** Ayyubid, Fatimid **8** Mameluke **9** Ptolemaic
long robe: 10 gallabiyea
peasant: 6 fellah **8** fellahin **9** fellaheen
sacred bird: 4 benu, ibis **5** bennu
sailboat: 7 felucca
statue: 6 Sphinx **15** Colossi of Memnon
food:
bean: 5 lotus
beer: 6 zythum
bread: 6 herisa
dish: 3 ful
drink: 4 bosa, boza **5** bozah
Egyptian
language family: 11 Afro-Asiatic **13** Hamito-Semitic
later form: 6 Coptic
Egyptian cross 4 ankh
Egyptian Mythology
deities: 6 Ennead
eight gods: 3 Heh **6** Ogdoad
goddess of evil: 7 Sekhmet
goddess of fertility: 2 Io **4** Isis
goddess of law/righteousness: 4 Maat
goddess of love/joy/music/dance: 6 Hathor
goddess of sky: 3 Nut
goddess personifying sky: 6 Hathor
god of bricks: 5 Kulla
god of creation: 4 Ptah
god of dead/Nile: 6 Osiris
god of earth: 3 Geb, Keb
god of ocean: 3 Nun **4** Nunu
god of sun: 2 Ra, Re **5** Horus
corresponds to Greek: 10 Harcorates
god of tombs/embalming: 6 Anubis
god of wisdom/magic/learning:

5 Thoth
corresponds to Greek: 6 Hermes
immortal spirit: 2 Ka
judge of dead: 6 Osiris
king of dead: 6 Osiris
king of gods: 4 Amen, Amon **5** Ammon **6** Amen Ra, Amon Ra
corresponds to Greek: 4 Zeus
corresponds to Roman: 4 Jove **7** Jupiter
personification of femininity: 5 Neith
corresponds to Greek: 6 Athena
ram god: 5 Khnum
vulture: 7 Nekhbet
Ehrlich, Paul
field: 12 bacteriology
nationality: 6 German
studied: 6 toxins **8** immunity **10** antitoxins
discovered: 9 salvarsan
coined term: 12 chemotherapy
awarded: 10 Nobel Prize
Eichmann in Jerusalem
author: 12 Hannah Arendt
eiderdown 4 puff **5** cover, quilt **8** coverlet **9** comforter **10** featherbed
Eight and a Half, 8 1/2
director: 15 Federico Fellini
cast: 10 Anouk Aimee **16** Claudia Cardinale **19** Marcello Mastroianni
Eighteen Seventy-Six, 1876
author: 9 Gore Vidal
Eijkman, Christiaan
nationality: 5 Dutch
discovered: 19 antineuritic vitamin
researched: 8 beriberi
awarded: 10 Nobel Prize
Einstein, Albert
birthplace: 3 Ulm
field: 7 physics
theory of: 10 relativity **14** uranium fission
awarded: 10 Nobel Prize
Eire see **7** Ireland
Eisenhower, Dwight David
nickname: 3 Ike
changed name from: 21 David Dwight Eisenhower
presidential rank: 12 thirty-fourth
party: 10 Republican
state represented: 2 NY
defeated: 4 (Eric) Hass, (Harry Flood) Byrd **5** (Farrell) Dobbs **6** (Darlington) Hoopes, (William Ezra) Jenner **7** (Stuart) Hamblen, (Thomas Coleman) Andrews **8** (Enoch Arden) Holtwick, (Vincent William) Hallinan **9** (Adlai Ewing) Stevenson
vice president: 5 (Richard Milhous) Nixon
cabinet:
state: 6 (Christian Archibald) Herter, (John Foster) Dulles
treasury: 8 (George Magoffin) Humphrey, (Robert Bernard) Anderson

defense: 5 (Thomas Sovereign) Gates (Jr) **6** (Charles Erwin) Wilson **7** (Neil Hesler) McElroy
attorney general: 6 (William Pierce) Rogers **8** (Herbert) Brownell (Jr)
postmaster general: 11 (Arthur Ellsworth) Summerfield
interior: 5 (Douglas) McKay **6** (Frederick Andrew) Seaton
agriculture: 6 (Ezra Taft) Benson
commerce: 5 (Sinclair) Weeks **7** (Frederick Henry) Mueller, (Lewis Lichtenstein) Strauss
labor: 6 (Martin Patrick) Durkin **8** (James Paul) Mitchell
HEW: 5 (Oveta Culp) Hobby **6** (Marion Bayard) Folsom **8** (Arthur Sherwood) Flemming
born: 9 Denison TX
died: 12 Washington DC
buried: 9 Abilene KS
education: 9 West Point **17** US Military Academy
religion: 12 Presbyterian
interest: 4 golf **6** flying **7** fishing, hunting **8** football, painting
vacation spot: 2 CA **11** Palm Springs
author: 11 Waging Peace **15** Crusade in Europe **16** Mandate for Change **27** At Ease: Stories I Tell to Friends
political career: 4 none (prior to presidency)
civilian career:
president of: 18 Columbia University
military service: 7 general **9** World War I **10** World War II **16** Army Chief of Staff
supreme commander of: 6 Allies **15** European Defense (NATO) **18** US occupation forces (Europe)
head of: 18 Joint Chiefs of Staff
notable events of lifetime/term: 4 D-Day, NATO
Acts: 11 Civil Rights
battle of the: 5 Bulge
conference: 7 Big Four **10** NATO Summit **11** Paris Summit
Cuba taken over by: 11 Fidel Castro
invasion: 8 Normandy
trial/execution of: 14 Ethel Rosenberg **15** Julius Rosenberg
USSR shot down: 9 U-Two plane
father: 10 David Jacob
mother: 3 Ida (Elizabeth Stover)
siblings: 3 Roy **4** Earl, Paul **5** Edgar **6** Arthur, Milton
wife: 5 Marie (Geneva Doud)
nickname: 5 Mamie
children: 10 Doud Dwight **15** John Sheldon Doud
ejaculate 4 howl, yell, yelp **5** shout **6** bellow, cry out **7** exclaim **10** vociferate
ejaculation 3 cry **4** howl, yell, yelp **5** shout **6** bellow, outcry, shriek, squeal

7 screech **11** exclamation **12** vociferation

eject 4 emit, oust, spew **5** evict, exile, expel, exude, spout **6** banish, bounce, deport, remove **7** cast out, kick out, spit out, turn out **8** disgorge, drive out, force out, throw out **9** discharge **10** dispossess

ejection 4 gush **5** spurt **6** ouster **7** issuing, removal **8** emission, eruption, eviction **9** dismissal, expelling, expulsion **10** banishment **11** throwing out

Ekdal, Hjalmar
  character in: 11 The Wild Duck
  author: 5 Ibsen

eke 3 add **4** also **7** augment, enlarge, stretch **8** increase, lengthen, likewise, moreover **10** in addition, supplement

elaborate 5 fancy, gaudy, showy **6** expand, flashy, garish, ornate **7** clarify, complex, elegant, labored, specify **8** involved, overdone **9** embellish, intricate **10** add details **11** complicated, painstaking **12** ostentatious **13** particularize

elaborate on 6 expand **7** amplify, develop **9** embellish **10** supplement **11** expatiate on

elaboration 11 added detail, rounding out **12** augmentation **13** amplification, embellishment

Elaine
  character in: 16 Arthurian romance
  called: 8 lily maid
  home: 7 Astolat
  lover: 8 Lancelot
  son: 7 Galahad
  father: 6 Pelles

Elais
  father: 5 Anius
  mother: 7 Dorippe
  changed things into: 3 oil

elan 4 dash, zeal **5** flair, verve, vigor **6** energy, spirit **8** vivacity **9** animation **10** enthusiasm

eland 3 elk **8** antelope **11** taurotragus

elapse 4 go by, pass **5** lapse **6** pass by, roll by, slip by **7** glide by, slide by **8** slip away **9** intervene

elastic 6 pliant, supple **7** pliable, rubbery, springy **8** flexible, tolerant, yielding **9** adaptable, recoiling, resilient **10** rebounding, responsive **11** complaisant, stretchable **12** recuperative **13** accommodating

elate 5 cheer, exalt **6** excite, lift up, please **7** animate, delight, elevate, enliven, gladden, gratify, inspire **10** exhilarate

elated 4 glad **5** happy, proud **6** joyful, joyous **7** exalted, excited, gleeful, pleased **8** animated, blissful, ecstatic, jubilant **9** overjoyed, rejoicing **10** delightful **11** exhilarated **13** in high spirits **18** flushed with success

elation 3 joy **4** glee **5** pride **7** triumph

8 gladness **9** happiness **10** excitement, exultation, jubilation **12** cheerfulness

elbow grease 4 work **5** force, labor **6** effort, energy, muscle **8** exertion, hard work **11** application

elbow in 4 push **5** force, press, shove **6** horn in **7** crowd in

El Cordobes (Manuel Benitez Perez)
  sport: 12 bullfighting

elder 4 head **5** older **6** senior **8** oldtimer **9** firstborn, patriarch, presbyter **14** church official **15** church dignitary
  French: 4 aine

elder, elderberry 8 Sambucus
  varieties: 3 Box **4** Blue **5** Dwarf, Sweet **6** Ground, Poison, Yellow **8** American, European, Stinking **10** Red-berried **11** American red, European red **15** Pacific Coast red

elderly 3 old **4** aged **9** venerable **11** over the hill **13** past one's prime

Eldorado
  nickname of: 10 California

Eleanor and Franklin
  author: 11 Joseph P Lash

Eleazar
  father: 4 Dodo **5** Aaron, Elind, Mahli **6** Parosh **7** Phineas **8** Abinadab
  mother: 8 Elisheba
  brother: 5 Abihu, Nadab **7** Ithamar
  succeeded: 5 Aaron

elect 4 pick **5** adopt **6** choose, opt for, select, take up **7** embrace, espouse, fix upon, pick out **8** decide on, settle on **9** single out

election 4 poll, vote **6** choice, option, voting **7** resolve **8** decision **9** balloting, selection **10** resolution **11** alternative **13** determination

electioneer 3 run **5** stump **8** campaign **11** whistle-stop **12** beat the drums, solicit votes

elective 8 optional **9** selective, voluntary **11** not required **12** open to choice, passed by vote **13** discretionary, not obligatory

Electra
  author: 9 Euripides, Sophocles
  character: 7 Orestes, Pylades **8** Dioscuri **9** Aegisthus **12** Clytemnestra
  father: 9 Agamemnon
  mother: 9 Clytemnestra
  brother: 7 Orestes
  sister: 9 Iphigenia **12** Chrysothemis
  husband: 7 Pylades
  son: 5 Medon **9** Strophius

electric 7 dynamic, rousing **8** exalting, exciting, spirited, stirring **9** inspiring, thrilling **10** full of fire **11** galvanizing, power-driven, stimulating **12** electrifying, soul-stirring

electric battery
  invented by: 5 Volta

electricity measure 3 ohm **4** volt, watt **5** joule **6** ampere **10** horsepower

Electric Kool-Aid Acid Test, The
  author: 8 Tom Wolfe

electrify 4 daze, stir, stun **5** amaze, rouse **6** dazzle, excite, fire up, thrill **7** animate, astound, quicken, startle **8** astonish, surprise **9** fascinate, galvanize, stimulate **18** take one's breath away

electrifying 8 dazzling, shocking, stunning **10** astounding, stupefying **11** astonishing

electromagnet
  invented by: 8 Sturgeon

Electryon
  king of: 7 Mycenae
  father: 7 Perseus
  mother: 9 Andromeda
  brother: 6 Mestor **9** Sthenelus
  wife: 5 Anaxo
  son: 9 Licymnius
  daughter: 7 Alcmene
  grandson: 8 Hercules

eleemosynary 10 altruistic, beneficent, benevolent, charitable **13** philanthropic **15** non-profitmaking

elegance 5 class, grace, taste **6** purity **7** balance **8** delicacy, grandeur, richness, symmetry **10** refinement **12** gracefulness **13** exquisiteness, luxuriousness, sumptuousness

elegant 4 fine, rich **5** grand **6** classy, dapper, lovely, ornate, polite, urbane **7** classic, courtly, genteel, refined, stylish **8** artistic, charming, debonair, delicate, graceful, gracious, handsome, polished, tasteful, well-bred **9** beautiful, dignified, exquisite, luxurious, sumptuous **10** attractive, cultivated **11** fashionable, symmetrical **16** wellproportioned

elegiac 3 sad **8** funereal, mournful **10** melancholy

elegy 7 requiem, sad poem **11** funeral song **14** melancholy poem **16** lament for the dead **17** poem of lamentation, song of lamentation **22** melancholy piece of music

Elegy Written in a Country Churchyard
  author: 10 Thomas Gray

Elektra see **7** Electra

element, elements 3 air **4** fire **5** earth, water **6** basics, member, milieu **7** essence, factors, origins **8** original **9** basic part, basic unit, component, rudiments **10** basic ideas, ingredient, principles, simple body **11** constituent, environment, foundations, native state, subdivision **13** building block, component part, natural medium **14** natural habitat

elemental 5 basal, basic **10** elementary **11** fundamental, rudimentary

elementary 4 easy **5** basal, basic,

crude, first, plain **6** simple **7** primary **8** original **9** elemental, primitive **11** fundamental, rudimentary, undeveloped **13** uncomplicated

elephant
group of: **4** herd
types: **5** Asian **7** African
features: **5** trunk, tusks
famous: **5** Babar, Dumbo
elephant boy: **4** Sabu **6** mahout
extinct: **7** mammoth **8** mastodon
produce: **5** ivory

elephantine 4 huge **7** immense, mammoth, titanic **8** colossal, enormous, gigantic **9** ponderous **10** gargantuan, tremendous **14** Brobdingnagian

Elephant Man, The
director: **10** David Lynch
cast: **8** John Hurt **11** John Gielgud, Wendy Hiller **12** Anne Bancroft **14** Anthony Hopkins

Eleusinian mysteries
in memory of: **10** Persephone
in honor of: **7** Bacchus, Demeter
celebrated at: **6** Athens **7** Eleusis
founded by: **8** Eumolpus
god of: **7** Bacchus

elevate 4 lift **5** boost, cheer, elate, heave, hoist, raise **6** better, excite, lift up, move up, perk up, refine, uplift **7** advance, animate, dignify, enhance, ennoble, improve, inspire, promote, upraise **8** heighten **9** place high **10** exhilarate, raise aloft

elevated 4 high **5** lofty **6** raised **7** exalted **8** improved, uplifted **9** prominent **10** heightened

elevation 4 hill, lift, rise **5** boost **6** ascent, height **8** altitude, mountain **9** acclivity, bettering, high place, promotion **10** prominence, refinement **11** advancement, cultivation, improvement

elevator 4 cage, lift, silo, wing **5** hoist **7** granary **10** dumbwaiter
inventor: **4** Otis

elevator brake
invented by: **4** Otis

elf 4 puck **5** fairy, gnome, pixie, troll **6** goblin, sprite **7** brownie, gremlin **9** hobgoblin **10** leprechaun

elfin 3 fey, wee **4** tiny **7** pixyish **9** fairylike **10** diminutive

Elgar, Sir Edward William
born: **7** England **10** Broadheath
composer of: **8** Falstaff **9** Cockaigne, Froissart **10** Caractacus, The Kingdom **11** The Apostles **14** The Black Knight, The Light of Life **16** Enigma Variations **19** Pomp and Circumstance, The Banner of St George, The Dream of Gerontius **30** Scenes from the Bavarian Highlands

Eli
son: **6** Hophni **7** Phineas
home: **6** Shiloh **10** high priest
teacher of: **6** Samuel

Eli, Eli, Lama sabachthani
means: **31** My God My God why hast thou forsaken me?

Elia see **11** Lamb, Charles

elicit 5 cause, educe, evoke, exact, fetch, wrest **6** derive, extort **7** draw out, extract **9** call forth, draw forth **10** bring forth **12** bring to light

elide 4 omit, slur **5** annul **6** delete **7** neglect **8** slur over, suppress **9** eliminate, strikeout **10** abbreviate

Eliezar
father: **5** Moses
mother: **8** Zipporah
brother: **7** Gershom

eligible 6 proper **7** fitting **8** suitable **9** desirable, qualified **10** acceptable, applicable, authorized, worthwhile **11** appropriate

Elihu
brother: **5** David
friend: **3** Job **6** Bildad, Zophar **7** Eliphaz

Elijah 7 prophet
opposed: **4** Ahab, Baal **7** Jezebel
successor: **6** Elisha

Elimelech
wife: **5** Naomi

eliminate 4 drop, omit, oust **5** eject, erase, exile, expel **6** banish, cut out, delete, except, reject, remove, rub out **7** abolish, cast out, dismiss, exclude, weed out **8** get rid of, leave out, stamp out, throw out **9** eradicate **10** annihilate, do away with **11** exterminate

Eliot, George
real name: **13** Mary Anne Evans
author of: **6** Romola **8** Adam Bede **11** Middlemarch, Silas Marner **17** The Mill on the Floss

Eliot, John
author of: **12** Bay Psalm Book

Eliot, T S
author of: **9** East Coker, Gerontion, Hollow Men **11** Burnt Norton, Dry Salvages **12** Ash Wednesday, Four Quartets, The Waste Land **13** Little Gidding, The Sacred Wood **16** The Family Reunion **20** Murder in the Cathedral **27** Sweeney Among the Nightingales **28** The Love Song of J Alfred Prufrock
inspiration for: **4** Cats

Eliphaz
father: **4** Adah, Esau
friend: **3** Job **5** Elihu **6** Bildad, Zophar

Elisabeth see **9** Elizabeth

Elisha 7 prophet
home: **11** Abelmeholah
succeeded: **6** Elijah

elite 3 top **4** best **5** cream **6** choice, flower **7** bigwigs, society, the pick, wealthy **8** big shots, notables **9** haut monde **10** blue bloods, personages,

select body, upper class **11** aristocracy, celebrities, high society **14** creme-de-la-creme

elixir 6 potion, remedy **7** essence, extract, panacea, spirits **8** tincture **11** concentrate **17** alcoholic solution

Eliza
character in: **14** Uncle Tom's Cabin
author: **5** Stowe

Elizabeth
husband: **9** Zacharias, Zechariah
son: **14** John the Baptist

Elizabeth I
queen of: **7** England
father: **10** Henry Tudor **14** Henry the Eighth
mother: **10** Anne Boleyn
sister: **4** Mary **10** Bloody Mary
brother: **14** Edward the Sixth
advisor: **5** Cecil **8** Burghley **10** Walsingham
suitor: **5** Essex **6** Dudley **9** Leicester
victory over: **13** Spanish Armada

Elizabeth II
father: **14** George the Sixth
mother: **9** Elizabeth
husband: **17** Philip Mountbatten
son: **6** Andrew, Edward **7** Charles
daughter: **4** Anne
daughter-in-law: **5** Diana, Sarah (Fergie)

Elizabeth the Queen
author: **15** Maxwell Anderson

elk
group of: **4** gang

Ellas see **6** Greece

Ellerbee, Linda 6 writer **10** newscaster
book: **11** And So It Goes

Ellice Islands see **6** Tuvalu

Ellington, Duke
real name: **22** Edward Kennedy Ellington
born: **12** Washington DC
composer of: **10** Mood Indigo **14** Creole Love Call, Creole Rhapsody, Hot and Bothered **17** Concerto for Cootie **18** Black and Tan Fantasy

Elliot family
characters in: **10** Persuasion
member: **4** Anne **7** William **9** Elizabeth, Sir Walter
author: **6** Austen

Ellison, Harlan
author of: **7** Paingod **10** Spider Kiss **13** A Boy and His Dog **16** Deathbird Stories **19** Approaching Oblivion **20** Alone Against Tomorrow

Ellison, Ralph
author of: **12** Invisible Man

elm 5 Ulmus
varieties: **3** red **4** bush, cork, rock, vase, wych **5** cedar, Dutch, dwarf, globe, wahoo, water, white **6** Exeter, horned, Jersey, moline, Scotch, willow, winged **7** Belgian, Chinese, Cor-

nish, English, Holland **8** American, fern-leaf, Guernsey, Japanese, Siberian, slippery, tabletop, wheatley **9** September **10** camperdown, Chichester, Huntingdon, smooth-leaf **11** small-leaved **13** European white

Elmer Gantry
   author: 13 Sinclair Lewis
   director: 13 Richard Brooks
   cast: 10 Dean Jagger **11** Jean Simmons **12** Shirley Jones **13** Arthur Kennedy, Burt Lancaster
   Oscar for: 5 actor (Lancaster) **17** supporting actress (Jones)

elocution 6 speech **7** diction, oratory **10** intonation **11** enunciation **12** articulation **13** pronunciation **14** public speaking

Elohim 3 God

Eloisa to Abelard
   author: 13 Alexander Pope

Elon 11 Hebrew judge

elongate 6 extend **7** draw out, prolong **8** lengthen, protract **10** stretch out

elongated 4 long **8** drawn out, extended **9** prolonged **10** attenuated, lengthened, protracted **12** stretched out

eloquence 5 force, grace **7** fluency, oratory **8** rhetoric **9** elocution, speakwell, vividness **10** expression **12** silver tongue
   god of: 4 Ogma **6** Ogmios **7** Mercury

eloquent 5 vivid **6** moving, poetic **8** emphatic, forceful, spirited, stirring, striking **10** articulate, passionate, persuasive **11** impassioned

El Salvador
   other name: 9 Cuscatlan
   capital/largest city: 11 San Salvador
   others: 6 Cutuco, Izalco **7** Corinto, Metapan **8** Acajutla, Libertad, Santa Ana, Usulutan **9** San Miguel, Sonsonate **10** San Vicente, Santa Tecla **11** Union-Cutuco **12** Chalatenango
   school: 15 Jose Simeon Canas **16** Alberto Masferrer
   measure: 4 vara **5** cafiz, cahiz **6** fanega **7** batella, botella, cantara, manzana
   monetary unit: 4 peso **5** colon **7** centavo
   weight: 3 bag **4** caja **5** libra
   lake: 5 Guiha, Guija **8** Ilopango **10** Coatepeque
   mountain: 6 Izalco
   highest point: 8 Santa Ana
   river: 5 Jiboa, Lempa, Lopaz **6** Torola **7** de la Paz **9** Goasoaran **17** Grande de San Miguel
   sea: 7 Pacific
   physical feature:
      bay: 10 Jiquilisco
      coast: 6 Balsam
      gulf: 7 Fonseca
      point: 7 Amapala **8** Remedios
      valley: 7 Hamacas

people: 5 Lenca, Pipil **6** Indian, Mangue **7** mestizo, Spanish **9** Matagalpa
   artist: 8 Salarrue **10** Mejia Vides
   author: 8 Salarrue **14** Antonio Gavidia
   conqueror: 8 Alvarado
   leader: 6 Osorio **8** Jose Arce **13** Matias Delgado **15** Manuel Rodriguez **17** Hernandez Martinez
   philosopher/journalist: 9 Masferrer
language: 7 Spanish
religion: 13 Roman Catholic
place:
   ruins: 7 Tazumal
feature:
   blouse: 9 volcanena
   dance: 7 pasillo **15** los historiantes
   drum: 8 huehuetl
   estate: 5 finca
   musical instrument: 7 caramba
food:
   bread: 10 quesadilla
   cheese pancake: 6 pupusa

Elscheimer, Adam
   born: 7 Germany **15** Frankfurt am Main
   artwork: 17 Tobias and the Angel **21** The Stoning of St Stephen **24** Rest on the Flight into Egypt

else 3 and, too **4** also, more **5** if not, other **7** besides, instead **9** different, otherwise **10** additional, contrarily, in addition

elsewhere 4 away **6** except **7** absence, not here

Elsinore
   castle in: 6 Hamlet **7** Denmark
   author: 11 Shakespeare

Elton, Mr
   character in: 4 Emma
   author: 6 Austen

elucidate 6 detail **7** clarify, clear up, explain, expound **8** describe, spell out **9** delineate, explicate, interpret, make plain **10** illuminate, illustrate **11** comment upon **14** throw light upon

elucidation 7 account **10** commentary **11** description, explanation, explication **13** clarification **14** interpretation **15** exemplification

elude 4 shun **5** avoid, dodge, evade **6** escape, slip by **10** circumvent, fight shy of **11** get away from, keep clear of

eluding 7 dodging, ducking, evading, evasion **8** avoiding **9** avoidance **12** escaping from, sidestepping **13** circumventing **15** getting away from

Elul 16 sixth Hebrew month

elusive 4 foxy, wily **6** crafty, shifty, tricky **7** evasive **8** baffling, puzzling, slippery **11** hard to catch, hard to grasp

elusory 4 wily **6** shifty **7** devious, dodging, elusive, evasive, hedging **8** slippery **9** ambiguous, deceitful,

deceptive, equivocal **10** misleading **12** equivocating

Elvsted, Thea
   character in: 11 Hedda Gabler
   author: 5 Ibsen

elysian 7 sublime **8** blissful, empyreal, empyrean, ethereal, heavenly **9** celestial, unearthly **12** otherworldly, paradisiacal

Elysium
   also: 17 islands of the blest
   afterworld of the: 7 blessed

Elytis, Odysseus
   real name: 19 Odysseus Alepoudelis
   author of: 10 Seemly It Is **20** Heroic and Elegiac Song

emaciated 4 lank, lean, thin **5** gaunt **6** sickly, skinny, wasted **7** haggard, scrawny, wizened **8** skeletal, starving, underfed **10** cadaverous **14** undernourished

emanate 4 flow, rise, stem, well **5** exude, issue **6** spring **7** give off, proceed **8** come from **9** come forth, originate, send forth

emanation 6 coming **7** arising, flowing, issuing **8** effusion **9** effluence, radiation, springing **10** exhalation **11** coming forth

emancipate 4 free **7** manumit, release, set free, unchain **8** liberate, unfetter **9** unshackle **12** set at liberty

emancipation 7 freedom, liberty **10** liberation **11** manumission **12** independence

emasculate 4 geld **5** alter **6** soften, weaken **8** castrate **9** undermine **10** devitalize

Emaux et Camees
   author: 16 Theophile Gautier

Embalming
   god of: 6 Anubis

embankment 4 bank, dike, wall **5** levee

embargo 3 ban **8** shutdown, stoppage **10** impediment, inhibition, injunction, quarantine, standstill **11** prohibition, restriction **12** interdiction, proscription **16** restraint of trade

embark 5 begin, board, start **6** launch, set out **7** enplane, entrain **8** commence, go aboard **9** board ship, enter upon

embark on 5 begin, start **8** approach, commence, initiate, set about **9** enter upon, undertake

embarras de richesses 13 overabundance **21** embarrassment of riches

embarrass 4 faze **5** abash, shame, upset **6** rattle **7** agitate, chagrin, confuse, fluster, mortify, nonplus **8** distress **9** discomfit **10** discompose, disconcert **13** make ill at ease **14** discountenance **17** make self-conscious

embarrassed 7 abashed **8** red-faced

9 chagrined, mortified **10** nonplussed **11** discomfited **13** self-conscious

embarrassing 7 awkward **8** confused, crushing **9** bothering **10** disturbing, mortifying, unpleasant **12** demoralizing, discomfiting **13** discomforting, disconcerting, uncomfortable

embarrassment 4 blot **5** stain **6** smirch **7** blemish, scandal, tarnish **8** disgrace **9** discredit **19** financial difficulty

embattled 8 fighting **9** embroiled, fortified **11** battle-ready, hard-pressed

embed 3 fix, set **4** bond **5** plant **6** fasten **8** ensconce **9** establish

embedded 3 set **5** fixed **6** bonded **7** engaged, planted **8** immersed, inserted **9** ensconced **11** established

embellish 4 gild **5** adorn, color **6** set off **7** dress up, enhance, fancy up, garnish, gussy up **8** beautify, decorate, ornament **9** elaborate, embroider **10** exaggerate

embellished 6 ornate **7** adorned, flowery **8** brocaded **9** decorated **10** beautified, elaborated, ornamented, rhetorical **11** embroidered

embellishment 5 frill **6** accent **7** garnish **8** furbelow, ornament, trimming **9** adornment **10** decoration, embroidery **11** elaboration **14** beautification **15** fuss and feathers

ember 3 ash **4** slag **6** cinder **7** clinker **8** live coal

embezzle 4 bilk, rook **5** cheat, filch **6** fleece **7** defraud, swindle **9** defalcate **14** misappropriate

embezzler 5 cheat, crook, thief **8** swindler

Embezzler, The
　　author: 16 Louis Auchincloss

embitter 4 sour **6** rankle **7** envenom **10** make bitter **11** make cynical **13** make rancorous, make resentful **15** make pessimistic

Embla
　　origin: 12 Scandinavian
　　first: 5 woman
　　made by: 4 gods
　　made from: 4 tree

emblem 4 sign **5** badge **6** design, device, symbol **8** colophon, hallmark, insignia

emblematic 7 typical **8** symbolic **10** indicative **11** distinctive **14** characteristic, representative

embodiment 6 avatar **7** epitome, essence **14** representation **15** exemplification, personification

embody 4 fuse **5** blend, merge **6** typify **7** collect, contain, embrace, express, include, realize **8** manifest, organize **9** exemplify, personify, represent, symbolize **10** assimilate **11** consolidate, incorporate **12** substantiate

embolden 7 fortify, hearten, inspire **8** inspirit **9** encourage

emboldened 6 poised **7** assured, unfazed **9** confident, heartened, unabashed **10** courageous, encouraged, inspirited

embonpoint 9 plumpness, stoutness **15** in good condition

emboss 4 knob, knot, stud **5** adorn, chase **6** indent **7** engrave, exhaust **8** decorate

embossed 4 bold **6** raised **7** adorned, antique, knotted **8** engraved, indented **9** decorated, exhausted

embrace 3 hug **5** adopt, clasp, cover, grasp **6** accept, embody **7** contain, espouse, include, involve **8** comprise **9** encompass **10** comprehend **11** consolidate, incorporate

embroider 5 color **7** dress up **9** elaborate, embellish, fabricate **10** exaggerate **11** romanticize

embroidery 8 tapestry **9** adornment, gros point **10** crewelwork, decoration, needlework, petit point **11** imagination **12** exaggeration **13** ornamentation

embroil 4 trap **6** enmesh **7** ensnare, involve **8** entangle **10** complicate

embroiled 8 enmeshed **9** embattled, entangled **11** hard-pressed

embroilment 3 row **4** fray, tilt **5** brawl, brush, clash, melee **6** fracas, ruckus, rumpus, uproar **7** scuffle **8** conflict, disorder, struggle **9** confusion, imbroglio **10** contention **11** altercation **12** entanglement

embryo 3 bud, egg **4** germ **5** fetus, larva, ovule **6** budding, source **8** immature, rudiment **9** beginning **11** rudimentary, undeveloped

embryonic 5 rough **6** unborn **7** nascent **8** immature, inchoate **9** beginning, imperfect, incipient **10** incomplete, unfinished **11** rudimentary, undeveloped

emend 4 edit **6** change, revise **7** correct, improve, rectify

emendation 8 revision **10** alteration, correction **11** improvement

emerald
　　species: 5 beryl
　　source: 4 Muzo **5** Egypt, India **6** Chivor **8** Colombia, Rhodesia, Zimbabwe **11** South Africa, Soviet Union **13** Ural Mountains
　　color: 5 green

Emerald City
　　setting in: 13 The Wizard of Oz
　　author: 4 Baum

Emerald Isle see **7** Ireland

emerge 3 run **4** dawn, emit, flow, gush, loom, pour, rise **5** arise, issue **6** appear, come up, crop up, escape, stream, turn up **7** develop, surface **9** come forth, discharge **11** come to

light **12** come into view **13** become visible **14** become apparent, become manifest

emergence 4 dawn **7** dawning **10** appearance **11** development **13** coming to light, manifestation **15** materialization

emergency 5 pinch **6** crisis **7** urgency **8** exigency **11** contingency, predicament **16** unforeseen danger

Emergency
　　character: 8 (Dr) Joe Early, (Paramedic) John Gage **9** (Paramedic) Roy DeSoto **11** (Nurse) Dixie McCall **13** (Dr) Kelly Brackett
　　cast: 10 Bobby Troup, Kevin Tighe **11** Julie London **12** Robert Fuller **16** Randolph Mantooth

Emerson, Ralph Waldo
　　nickname: 13 Sage of Concord
　　author of: 4 Fate **6** Brahma, Nature **10** Friendship, The Rhodora **12** Compensation, Self-Reliance **14** The Concord Hymn **18** The American Scholar
　　philosophy: 17 Transcendentalism

emeute 4 riot

emigrant 6 emigre **8** wanderer, wayfarer **10** expatriate

Emigrants, The
　　author: 10 Johan Bojer

emigrate 4 move, quit **5** leave **6** depart, remove **7** migrate

emigration 5 exile **6** exodus **12** expatriation

emigre 2 DP **5** alien, exile **7** evacuee, refugee **8** defector, emigrant, expellee, fugitive **9** immigrant **10** expatriate **15** displaced person **16** political refugee

Emile
　　author: 19 Jean Jacques Rousseau
　　treatise on: 9 education

Emilia
　　character in: 7 Othello
　　husband: 4 Iago
　　author: 11 Shakespeare

eminence 4 fame, hill, note, peak, rise **5** bluff, cliff, glory, knoll, ridge **6** height, repute, summit, upland **7** hillock, hummock **8** mountain, standing **9** celebrity, elevation, greatness, high place, high point **10** excellence, importance, notability, prominence, promontory, reputation **11** distinction, preeminence **12** elevated rank, high position, public esteem **15** conspicuousness

eminence grise 15 unofficial power
　　literally: 12 gray eminence

eminent 3 top **5** grand, great, noted **6** famous, signal, utmost **7** exalted, notable, unusual **8** elevated, esteemed, glorious, imposing, laureate, renowned **9** important, memorable, paramount, prominent, well-known **10** celebrated, noteworthy, preeminent, remarkable **11** high-ranking, illustrious, outstanding **13** distinguished, extraordinary

emir 4 amir, Arab, Turk **5** chief, emeer, ruler **6** leader, prince **9** chieftain, commander, dignitary

emissary 5 agent, envoy **6** deputy, herald, legate **7** courier **8** delegate **9** go-between, messenger **10** ambassador **14** representative

emission 5 fumes, smoke, waste **8** ejection, emitting, impurity, issuance, voidance **9** discharge, emanation, excretion, expulsion, extrusion, pollutant **10** sending out **11** throwing out **12** transmission

emit 4 beam, give, shed, vent **5** expel, issue **7** cast out, excrete, secrete, send out **8** dispatch, throw out, transmit **9** discharge, give forth, pour forth

Emma
author: **10** Jane Austen
character: **7** Mr Elton **9** Miss Bates, Mrs Weston **11** Jane Fairfax **12** Harriet Smith, Robert Martin **13** Emma Woodhouse **14** Frank Churchill **15** George Knightley

Emmanuel 7 Messiah **11** Jesus Christ
means: **9** God with us

emollient 3 oil **4** balm **5** balmy, cream, salve **6** lotion **7** calming, easeful, healing, unguent **8** allaying, lenitive, ointment, relaxing, soothing **9** assuasive, lubricant, relieving **10** palliative **11** alleviative, restorative

emolument 3 fee, pay **4** gain, wage **6** income, profit, salary **7** benefit, stipend **9** advantage **10** honorarium **12** compensation, remuneration

emotion 4 fear, hate, heat, love, zeal **5** anger, ardor, pride **6** fervor, sorrow, warmth **7** concern, despair, passion, sadness **8** jealousy **9** agitation, happiness, sentiment, vehemence **10** excitement **12** satisfaction

emotional 4 warm **5** fiery **6** ardent, moving **7** fervent, zealous **8** stirring, touching **9** excitable, impetuous, thrilling, wrought-up **10** high-strung, hysterical, passionate, responsive, vulnerable **11** impassioned, sentimental, tear-jerking **12** enthusiastic, heartwarming, heart-rending, soul-stirring **13** demonstrative, temperamental **14** hypersensitive

emotionalism 8 hysteria **9** gushiness, hysterics, melodrama, theatrics **11** mawkishness **13** melodramatics, show of emotion **14** sentimentality **17** demonstrativeness

emotionless 6 stolid **7** unmoved **9** apathetic, impassive, unfeeling **11** passionless, unemotional

emperor, empress 4 czar, king, shah **5** queen, ruler **6** caesar, kaiser, mikado, sultan **7** czarina, monarch, sultana **9** sovereign **14** dowager empress

Emperor Jones, The

author: **12** Eugene O'Neill
character: **4** Jeff **8** Smithers **11** Brutus Jones

Emperor's New Clothes, The
author: **21** Hans Christian Andersen

emphasis 6 accent, stress, weight **7** feature **10** focal point **12** accentuation, underscoring

emphasize 6 accent, stress **7** dwell on, feature, iterate, point up **9** press home, punctuate, underline **10** accentuate, underscore

emphatic 4 flat **6** marked, strong **7** certain, decided, express, telling **8** absolute, decisive, definite, distinct, forceful, striking, vigorous **9** assertive, insistent, momentous **10** pronounced, undeniable, unwavering, unyielding **11** categorical, conspicuous, significant, unequivocal, unqualified **12** unmistakable

empire 4 rule **5** realm **6** domain **8** dominion, imperium **11** sovereignty **12** commonwealth

Empire State
nickname of: **7** New York

Empire State of the South
nickname of: **7** Georgia

Empire Strikes Back, The
director: **13** Irvin Kershner
cast: **10** Kenny Baker, Mark Hamill (Luke Skywalker) **11** David Prowse, Peter Mayhew **12** Alec Guinness, Carrie Fisher (Princess Leia), Harrison Ford (Han Solo) **14** Anthony Daniels (C3PO) **16** Billy Dee Williams (Lando Calrissian)
sequel to: **8** Star Wars
sequel: **15** Return of the Jedi

empirical 9 firsthand, practical, pragmatic **12** experiential, experimental

employ 3 use **4** hire **5** apply **6** devote, engage, occupy, retain, take on **7** service, utilize **8** exercise, keep busy, put to use **9** make use of **10** commission, employment **12** retainership

employee 6 member, worker **8** hireling **9** job holder, underling **10** wage earner

employer 4 boss, firm **6** outfit **7** company **8** business **10** proprietor **12** organization **13** establishment

employment 3 job, use **4** line, task, work **5** chore, field, trade, using **6** employ **7** calling, pursuit, service **8** business, exercise, exertion, vocation **9** employing **10** engagement, occupation, profession **11** application, utilization **13** preoccupation

emporium 5 store **6** bazaar, market **9** warehouse **10** large store **12** general store **15** department store

empower 4 vest **5** allow, endow **6** enable, invest, permit **7** license **8** delegate, sanction **9** authorize **10** commission

empress 5 queen, ruler **7** czarina, monarch, sultana, tsarina **9** sovereign

emprise 7 venture **9** adventure **10** enterprise **11** undertaking

emptied 6 used up **7** drained, vacated **8** consumed, depleted, finished **9** evacuated, exhausted

emptiness 4 void **6** vacuum **7** vacancy **8** bareness **10** barrenness, desolation, hollowness

empty 4 bare, dump, flow, idle, void **5** banal, drain, inane **6** futile, hollow, vacant **7** aimless, debouch, insipid, pour out, shallow, trivial, vacuous **8** evacuate **9** discharge, frivolous, worthless **10** unoccupied **11** meaningless, purposeless, unfulfilled, uninhabited **13** insignificant

empty space 3 gap **4** void **5** blank **6** cavity, lacuna, vacuum **7** vacancy

empyrean 7 elysian, sublime **8** blissful, heavenly **9** celestial **12** paradisiacal

emu
also: **4** emeu
form: **4** bird
habitat: **9** Australia
characteristic: **9** nonflying, three toed

emulate 3 ape **4** copy **5** mimic, rival **6** follow **7** imitate

emulative 5 model **9** exemplary

enable 3 aid **5** allow **6** assist, permit **7** benefit, empower, qualify, support **8** make able **10** capacitate, facilitate **15** make possible for

enact 4 pass **6** decree, ratify **7** approve **8** proclaim, sanction **9** authorize, institute, legislate **11** pass into law **12** vote to accept

enactment 3 law **4** bill **5** canon, edict, ukase **6** decree **7** statute **9** ordinance, prescript **11** legislation **12** proclamation, ratification

enamel 4 coat **5** paint **7** coating **10** nail polish **12** glossy finish, tooth coating

enamor 5 charm **6** allure, attach, draw to, excite **7** bewitch, enchant **8** enthrall, entrance **9** captivate, enrapture, fascinate, infatuate **12** take a fancy to

enamored 6 in love **7** amorous **8** lovesick **10** infatuated

en arriere 8 backward

en avant 6 onward **7** forward

en bloc 8 as a whole

encage 3 pen **4** cage **5** pen in **6** coop up, lock up, shut in **7** confine **8** restrain **11** incarcerate

encamp 4 camp **7** bivouac **9** set up camp **10** pitch a tent

encampment 4 camp **5** tents **7** bivouac **8** tent city

encase 4 wrap **5** cover **6** enfold, enwrap **7** enclose, envelop, sheathe

enceinte 8 pregnant

Enceladus
form: **5** giant
hit by: **5** stone
stone flung by: **6** Athena
location: **6** Sicily
buried under: **9** Mount Etna

enchain 7 enslave, shackle **8** enthrall **11** put in chains **13** hold in bondage

enchant 3 hex **5** charm **7** bewitch, delight **8** enthrall, entrance **9** captivate, enrapture, fascinate, hypnotize, mesmerize, transport **14** cast a spell over **16** place under a spell

enchanted 7 charmed, pleased **9** bewitched, delighted, entranced **10** captivated, enraptured, enthralled, spellbound **11** under a spell

enchanting 8 charming, pleasant **9** agreeable, wonderful **10** bewitching, delightful, entrancing **11** captivating, enthralling, fascinating, hypnotizing **12** spellbinding **15** casting a spell on **17** casting a spell over

enchantment 5 spell **6** allure, appeal **9** magnetism **10** attraction **11** captivation, fascination

enchantress 4 vamp **5** siren, witch **7** charmer, vampire **9** sorceress, temptress **10** seductress **11** femme fatale

Enchiridion
author: **11** St Augustine

encircle 4 gird, ring, wall **5** fence, hem in **6** circle, girdle **7** enclose, wreathe **8** surround **9** encompass **12** circumscribe

enclose, inclose 4 ring **6** circle, girdle, insert, wall in **7** close in, fence in, include **8** encircle, surround **9** encompass, send along **12** circumscribe

enclosed area 4 quad **5** court, patio **6** atrium **9** courtyard **10** quadrangle

enclosure 3 sty **4** cage, coop, jail, wall **5** fence, hedge, stall **6** corral, kennel, pigsty **7** paddock, wrapper **8** envelope, stockade **9** cartridge, inclosure **10** receptacle

encomium 5 kudos, paean **6** eulogy **7** plaudit, tribute **8** citation **9** laudation, panegyric **11** acclamation

encompass 4 hold, ring **5** cover, hem in **6** circle, embody, girdle, take in, wall in **7** contain, embrace, enclose, fence in, include, involve, touch on **8** comprise, encircle, surround **11** incorporate **12** circumscribe

encounter 4 bout, face, meet **5** brush, clash, fight **6** affray, battle, combat, endure, fracas, suffer **7** run into, sustain, undergo **8** come upon, confront, meet with, skirmish **9** clash with **10** chance upon, engagement, experience **11** grapple with **12** do battle with, meet and fight, skirmish with **13** confrontation **14** contend against, engage in combat, hostile meeting **18** come face to face with

Encounters with the Archdruid
author: **10** John McPhee

encourage 3 aid **4** help, spur, sway **5** boost, cheer, egg on, favor, impel, rally **6** assist, exhort, foster, induce, prompt **7** advance, forward, further, hearten, inspire, promote **8** embolden, inspirit, reassure **10** give hope to

encouragement 4 lift **5** boost **6** praise **7** backing, support **11** approbation, encouraging, reassurance **12** shot in the arm **13** reinforcement

encroach 6 invade **7** impinge, intrude, overrun, violate **8** infringe, overstep, trespass **9** break into, interfere **10** transgress **11** make inroads

encumber 3 tax **4** lade, load **6** burden, hinder, impede, saddle **8** handicap, load down, obstruct, slow down **9** weigh down **13** inconvenience

encumbrance 4 load, onus **6** burden **9** hindrance **10** impediment **11** obstruction **13** inconvenience

Encyclopedia
author: **9** D'Alembert **12** Denis Diderot

encyclopedic 5 broad **7** erudite **9** scholarly, universal **10** exhaustive **11** wide-ranging **13** comprehensive **15** all-encompassing

end 3 aim **4** edge, goal, halt, kill, ruin, stop **5** cease, close, death, issue, limit, scrap **6** border, demise, design, effect, ending, finale, finish, object, result, run out, upshot, windup **7** destroy, outcome, purpose, remnant **8** boundary, conclude, fragment, leave off, leftover, terminus **9** cessation, eradicate, extremity, finish off, intention, objective, terminate **10** annihilate, completion, conclusion, denouement, expiration, extinction, extinguish, put an end to, settlement **11** consequence, culmination, destruction, exterminate, fulfillment, termination **12** annihilation, consummation, draw to a close **13** extermination **19** bring down the curtain

endanger 4 risk **6** expose, hazard **7** imperil **8** threaten **10** compromise, jeopardize **11** put in danger

endear 8 make dear **10** ingratiate **11** make beloved

endearment 7 pet name **9** sweet talk **10** loving word **12** sweet nothing **13** fond utterance

endeavor 3 aim, job, try **4** seek, work **5** essay, labor **6** aspire, career, effort, strive, work at **7** attempt **8** exertion, interest, striving, struggle, vocation **9** take pains, undertake **10** do one's best, enterprise, occupation **11** undertaking **12** make an effort **13** preoccupation

ended 4 done, over **6** ceased, closed, halted, runout **7** expired, stopped, wound up **8** finished, over with,

resulted 9 completed, concluded, destroyed **10** terminated **11** annihilated **12** discontinued, exterminated

Enderby
author: **14** Anthony Burgess

end from which
Latin: **12** terminus a quo

ending 3 end **5** close **6** finale, finish, windup **9** cessation **10** completion, conclusion, expiration **11** culmination, termination **12** consummation

ending point
Latin: **14** terminus ad quem

Ending Up
author: **12** Kingsley Amis

endless 7 eternal **8** constant, infinite, unbroken, unending **9** boundless, continual, perpetual, unlimited **10** continuous, persistent, without end **11** everlasting, measureless, never-ending **12** interminable **13** uninterrupted

endlessly 7 forever **10** constantly **11** ceaselessly, continually, perpetually **12** continuously
Latin: **11** ad infinitum

endocrine system
component: **5** ovary **6** testes, thymus **7** adrenal, thyroid **9** pituitary **11** parathyroid

endocuticle
consists of: **6** chitin

end of the century
French: **11** fin de siecle

End of the Road, The
author: **9** John Barth

end of the world 8 doomsday **10** Armageddon **11** Judgment Day **13** Day of Judgment **15** the Last Judgment

End of the World News, The
author: **14** Anthony Burgess

endorse, indorse 2 OK **4** back, sign **6** affirm, ratify, second **7** approve, certify, support **8** advocate, champion, sanction, validate, vouch for **9** authorize, recommend **11** countersign, stand behind, subscribe to **14** lend one's name to

endorsement 2 OK **7** support **8** approval **9** signature **10** acceptance **12** commendation, ratification **14** seal of approval **16** official sanction

endow 4 will **5** award, bless, equip, favor, grace, grant, leave **6** accord, bestow, confer, invest, supply **7** furnish, provide **8** bequeath, settle on

endowed 6 graced **7** blessed, favored **8** bestowed, enriched, provided **10** bequeathed

endowment 4 gift **5** award, flair, grant **6** legacy, talent **7** ability, bequest, faculty **8** aptitude, donation **9** attribute **10** capability **11** benefaction, natural gift

end to which
Latin: **14** terminus ad quem

endue 5 dress, endow, equip, indue,

put on 6 bestow, clothe, outfit, supply **7** furnish

endurable 8 bearable **9** tolerable **11** sustainable

endurance 7 stamina **8** strength, tenacity **9** fortitude, hardihood, stability **10** durability, permanence, resolution **11** durableness, persistence **12** immutability, perseverance, staying power **13** tenaciousness **14** changelessness **16** stick-to-itiveness

endure 4 bear, last, live **5** brave, brook, stand **6** live on, remain, suffer **7** persist, prevail, sustain, undergo, weather **8** continue, cope with, tolerate **9** go through, withstand **10** experience **11** bear up under, countenance

enduring 7 abiding, durable, eternal, lasting **8** constant, unending **9** immutable, permanent, steadfast **10** changeless, continuing, unchanging **11** everlasting, long-lasting **12** indissoluble

Endymion
    author: 9 John Keats
    form: 5 youth
    father: 8 Aethlios
    mother: 6 Calyce
    loved by: 4 Moon **6** Selene
    son: 5 Epeus, Paeon **7** Aetolus
    number of daughters: 5 fifty
    granddaughter: 7 Hyrmina

enemy 3 foe **5** rival **7** nemesis **8** armed foe, attacker, opponent **9** adversary, assailant, detractor **10** antagonist, competitor

Enemy of the People, An
    author: 11 Henrik Ibsen

energetic 5 alert, brisk, peppy, zippy **6** active, lively, robust **7** dynamic **8** animated, forceful, restless, spirited, vigorous **9** go-getting **11** hardworking, high-powered, industrious, quick-witted **12** enthusiastic

energize 7 animate, enliven, quicken **8** vitalize **9** galvanize, stimulate **10** invigorate, strengthen

energy 2 go **3** pep, vim, zip **4** elan, zeal, zest **5** drive, force, power, verve, vigor **6** hustle **8** dynamism, vitality, vivacity **9** animation **10** enterprise, liveliness

enervate 3 fag **4** bush, tire **5** weary **6** tucker, weaken **7** deplete, disable, exhaust, fatigue, wash out **8** enfeeble **9** prostrate **10** debilitate, devitalize **13** sap one's energy

enervated 5 spent **6** effete, wasted **7** languid, worn-out **8** fatigued, listless, sluggish, unmanned, unnerved, weakened **9** enfeebled, exhausted, lethargic, washed out **11** debilitated, devitalized, emasculated

enervation 7 fatigue **9** tiredness, weariness **10** exhaustion

en famille 11 in the family

Enfants Terribles, Les
    author: 11 Jean Cocteau

enfant terrible 16 indiscreet person **17** incorrigible child **19** irresponsible person

enfeeble 3 sap **6** impair, weaken **8** enervate **10** debilitate

enfin 7 finally **8** in the end **12** in conclusion

enfold 4 veil, wrap **5** cloak, cover **6** encase, enwrap, shroud **7** blanket, contain, embrace, enclose, envelop, sheathe **8** surround

enforce 5 apply, exact **6** defend, impose **7** execute, support **8** carry out, insist on **9** implement **10** administer

enforcement 5 force **6** duress **7** defense, support **8** coercion, pressure **9** execution **10** compulsion, constraint, imposition, obligation **11** carrying out **13** necessitation, strengthening **14** implementation

engage 4 hire **6** absorb, combat, employ, occupy, pledge, retain, secure, take on **7** betroth, engross, involve, partake, promise, war with **8** affiance, embark on, set about, takepart **9** enter into, fight with, undertake **10** commission **11** busy oneself, participate **12** give battle to **15** take into service

engaged 5 hired, in use **6** active, took on **7** partook, pledged, secured **8** absorbed, employed, involved, occupied, promised, retained, took part **9** affianced, betrothed, engrossed, undertook **10** embarked on **11** entered into, particpated **15** took into service

engagement 3 gig, job **4** bout, date, duty, fray, post **5** banns, berth, brush, fight, troth **6** action, battle, billet, combat **7** contest, meeting, scuffle **8** conflict, position, skirmish **9** betrothal, encounter, situation **10** affiancing, commitment, employment, obligation **11** appointment, arrangement

engage pleasantly 5 amuse, charm **6** divert, please **7** beguile, delight **8** enthrall, interest **9** entertain

engaging 7 likable, lovable, winning, winsome **8** charming, fetching, pleasing **9** agreeable, appealing, disarming **10** attractive, enchanting **11** captivating **12** ingratiating

engender 5 beget, breed, cause **7** produce **8** generate, occasion **10** bring about, give rise to **11** precipitate

engine
    inventor:
        of compression ignition: 7 Daimler
        of electric ignition: 4 Benz
        of gas (compound): 10 Eickemeyer
        of gasoline: 7 Brayton, Daimler
        of piston steam: 4 Watt **8** Newcomen

engineer 5 pilot **6** driver, hogger **7** builder, hoghead, planner **8** maneu-

ver, motorman, operator **10** accomplish

England
    other name: 6 Albion **7** Britain **9** Britannia
    capital/largest city: 6 London
    others: 3 Ely **4** Bath, Deal, Hull, Ryde, Ware, York **5** Blyth, Brent, Derby, Dover, Erith, Flint, Leeds, Ripon, Truro, Wigan **6** Barnet, Bolton, Bootle, Camden, Durham, Ealing, Exeter, Henley, Jarrow, Leyton, Oldham, Oxford, Yeovil **7** Bristol, Bromley, Burnley, Chelsea, Croydon, Enfield, Grimsby, Halifax, Hornsey, Ipswich, Lambeth, Newport, Norwich, Preston, Salford, **8** Bradford, Brighton, Cornwall, Coventry, Dewsbury, Hastings, Plymouth **9** Cambridge, Greenwich, Liverpool, Newcastle, Sheffield **10** Birmingham, Manchester **15** Stratford-on-Avon
    school: 4 Eton **5** Leeds, Rugby **6** Harrow, London, Oxford **9** Cambridge, Sandhurst **23** London School of Economics
    division: 4 Avon, Kent **5** Devon, Essex, **6** Dorset, Durham, Surrey, Sussex **7** Norfolk, Suffolk **8** Cheshire, Cornwall, Somerset **9** Hampshire, Wiltshire, Yorkshire **10** Derbyshire, East Sussex, Humberside, Lancashire, Merseyside, Shropshire, West Sussex **11** Oxfordshire, Tyne and Wear **12** Bedfordshire, Lincolnshire, Warwickshire, West Midlands **13** Hertfordshire, Staffordshire, West Yorkshire **14** Cambridgeshire, Leicestershire, Northumberland, North Yorkshire, South Yorkshire **15** Buckinghamshire, Gloucestershire, Nottinghamshire **16** Northamptonshire **20** Hereford and Worcester
    head of state: 4 king **5** queen **7** monarch
    measure: 3 cut, lea, pin, rod, ton, tun, vat **4** acre, bind, butt, comb, coom, foot, gill, goad, hand, hank, heer, hide, inch, last, line, mile, nail, pace, palm, peck, pint, pipe, pole, pool, rood, rope, sack, seam, span, trug, typp, wist, yard, yoke **5** bodge, chain, coomb, cubit, digit, float, floor, fluid, hutch, jugum, minim, ounce, perch, point, prime, quart, skein, stack, truss **6** barrel, bovate, bushel, cranne, fathom, firkin, gallon, hobbet, hobbit, league, manent, oxgang, pottle, runlet, square, strike, sulung, thread, tierce **7** auchlet, furlong, kenning, quarter, rundlet, seamile, spindle, tertian, virgate **8** carucate, chaldron, hogshead, landyard, puncheon, quadrant, standard
    monetary unit: 3 ora **4** rial **5** ackey, crown, groat, noble, pence, penny, pound, sprat, unite **6** bawbee, florin, guinea, seskin **7** angelet, hapenny **8**

farthing, shilling, sixpence, tuppence
weight: 3 bag, kip, tod, ton **4** keel, last, mast, maun **5** barge, fagot, grain, pound, score, stone, truss **6** bushel, cental, fangot, fother, fotmal, pocket **7** quarter, sarpler
island: 3 Man **4** Holy **5** Farne, Lundy, Wight **6** Coquet, Mersea, Scilly, Thanet, Tresco, Walney **7** Bardsey, Channel, Hayling, Ireland, Sheppey **8** Anglesea, Anglesey, Foulness, Holyhead
lake: 8 Grasmere **9** Ennerdale, Ullswater, Wastwater **10** Buttermere, Windermere **12** Derwentwater **13** Coniston Water
mountain: 5 Black **7** Pennine, Snowdon **8** Cambrian, Cumbrian
  hill: 6 Formby, Lizard, Mendip **7** Brendon, Cemmaes, Trevose
highest point: 11 Scafell Pike
river: 3 Cam, Dee, Don, Esk, Exe, Lea, Nen, Ure, Wye **4** Aire, Avon, Eden, Lune, Nene, Nidd, Ouse, Penk, Tame, Tees, Till, Tyne, Wear, Yare **5** Anker, Colne, Deben, Stour, Swale, Tamar, Tawar, Trent, Tweed **6** Humber, Kennet, Mersey, Rother, Severn, Thames, Wharfe, Witham **7** Derwent, Parrett, Waveney, Welland **8** Torridge **9** Yorkshire **12** Wensum Ribble
sea: 5 Irish, North **6** Celtic **8** Atlantic
physical feature:
  bay: 3 Tor **4** Lyme, Wash **5** Start **6** Mounts **7** Bigbury **8** Bideford, Cardigan, Falmouth, Tremadoc, Weymouth
  chalk cliffs: 5 Dover
  channel: 6 Solent **7** Bristol, English **8** Spithead
  firth: 6 Solway
  forest: 5 Arden **6** Exmoor **8** Dartmoor, Sherwood
  point: 4 Naze **5** Lynas, Morte, Sales **6** Dodman, Lizard, Prawle **8** Hartland, Landsend
  region: 5 Weald **8** Midlands **10** West Riding **11** North Riding **12** Lake District
  valley: 4 Coom, Eden, Tees, Tyne **5** Combe, Coomb **6** Coquet
people: 4 Celt, Pict **5** Jutes, Norse, Saxon **6** Angles, Briton, Norman, Viking
  artist: 6 Romney, Turner **7** Hogarth **8** Reynolds, Rossetti **9** Constable **12** Gainsborough
  author: 3 Kyd **4** Bede, Hume, Pope, Shaw **5** Auden, Bacon, Blake, Burke, Byron, Defoe, Donne, Eliot, Hardy, Joyce, Keats, Scott, Swift, Waugh, Wilde, Woolf **6** Austen, Bronte, Bunyan, Conrad, Dryden, Gibbon, Jonson, Milton, Newton, Ruskin, Sterne, Thomas **7** Boswell, Chaucer, Dickens, Kipling, Marlowe, Shelley, Spenser,

Walpole **8** Browning, Fielding, Lawrence, Sheridan, Smollett, Tennyson, Trollope **9** Churchill, Coleridge, Stevenson, Thackeray **10** Galsworthy, Richardson, Thomas More, Wordsworth **11** Shakespeare
king: 3 Hal **4** Cnut, John, Lear **5** Henry, James **6** Alfred, Arthur, Canute, Edmund, Edward, Egbert, George, Harold **7** Charles, Richard, Stephen, William **9** Cymbeline **18** Richard Coeur de Lion **19** Richard the Lionheart
  leader: 4 Eden, Grey, Lamb, Peel, Pitt **5** Heath, Major **6** Attlee, Wilson **7** Baldwin, Balfour, Canning, Fitzroy, Spencer, Stanley, Walpole **8** Disraeli, Stanhope, Thatcher **9** Cavendish, Churchill, Gladstone, Grenville, MacDonald, Macmillan **10** Palmerston, Wellington **11** Chamberlain, Douglas-Home, Lloyd George
  queen: 3 Mab **4** Anne, Bess, Jane, Mary **7** Eleanor **8** Boadicea, Victoria **9** Catherine, Charlotte, Elizabeth, Guinivere **10** Bloody Mary **11** Jane Seymour
language: 7 English
religion: 6 Jewish **8** Anglican **9** Methodist, Unitarian **13** Roman Catholic **15** Church of England
place:
  bridge: 5 Tower **6** London **11** Westminster
  cathedral: 4 York **6** Exeter **7** St Pauls **8** St Albans **9** Salisbury **10** Canterbury, Winchester **16** Westminster Abbey
  clock: 6 Big Ben
  fortification: 12 Hadrian's Wall
  museum: 4 Tate **7** British **9** Ashmolean **17** Madame Tussauds Wax
  palace: 7 St James, Windsor **10** Buckingham **12** Hampton Court
  racetrack: 5 Ascot
  ruins: 10 Stonehenge
  street: 4 Grub **5** Fleet **12** Threadneedle **16** Piccadilly Circus
  tower: 6 London
feature:
  dance: 6 morris
food:
  bacon: 6 gammon, rasher **7** streaky
  beer: 5 grout, stout
  cookie: 7 biscuit
  dessert: 6 trifle **11** plum pudding
  dish: 12 fish and chips **14** Cornish pasties **15** bubble and squeak **16** Yorkshire pudding
  drink: 3 ale, tea **6** squash
English, Julian
  character in: 20 Appointment in Samarra
  author: 5 O'Hara
English Mail-Coach, The
  author: 15 Thomas DeQuincey

engrave 3 cut **4** etch **5** carve, stamp **6** chisel **7** decorate, stipple
engraving 3 cut, die **5** print, stamp **7** etching, gravure **9** woodblock **11** copperplate, lithography **12** photogravure
engross 4 hold **6** absorb, arrest, engage, occupy, take up **7** immerse, involve **9** preoccupy
engrossed 4 busy, deep **6** intent **7** engaged **8** absorbed, immersed, involved, occupied **11** preoccupied
engrossing 8 engaging, exciting **9** absorbing, arresting, thrilling **10** intriguing **11** captivating, fascinating, interesting
engrossment 9 immersion **10** absorption, intentness **11** involvement **13** concentration, preoccupation
engulf 4 bury **5** swamp **6** deluge **7** envelop, immerse, overrun **8** inundate, submerge **9** swallow up
enhance 4 lift **5** add to, boost, raise **7** augment, elevate, magnify **8** heighten, redouble **9** embellish, intensify **10** complement
enhancement 11 heightening, improvement **15** intensification
Enid
  character in: 12 The Mabinogion **15** Idylls of the King **16** Arthurian romance
  husband: 7 Geraint
  known for: 9 constancy
  author: 8 Tennyson
enigma 6 puzzle, riddle, secret **7** mystery **8** question **9** conundrum **10** perplexity
enigmatic, enigmatical 7 cryptic, elusive **8** baffling, puzzling **9** ambiguous, equivocal, secretive **10** mysterious, perplexing **11** inscrutable, paradoxical **12** unfathomable **14** indecipherable
Eniwetok 5 atoll
  location: 15 Marshall Islands
  known for: 5 A bomb, H bomb (tests)
enjoin 3 ask, ban, bar, beg, bid **4** urge, warn **6** advise, charge, direct, forbid **7** command, counsel, entreat **8** admonish, call upon, instruct, prohibit, restrain, restrict **9** interdict, proscribe
enjoy 3 own **4** have, like **5** eat up, fancy, savor **6** admire, relish **7** possess **9** delight in, rejoice in **10** appreciate **11** think well of **13** be blessed with, be pleased with, get a kick out of **14** take pleasure in **16** have the benefit of
enjoyable 8 pleasant, pleasing **9** agreeable, fun-filled, rewarding **10** delightful, gratifying, satisfying **11** pleasurable
enjoyment 3 fun, joy **4** zest **5** gusto, right **6** relish **7** benefit, delight **8** blessing, exercise, good time, pleasure

9 advantage, amusement, diversion, happiness, privilege **10** possession, recreation **11** prerogative **12** satisfaction **13** entertainment, gratification

enlarge 4 grow **5** add to, swell, widen **6** expand, extend **7** amplify, augment, broaden, develop, expound, inflate, magnify **8** elongate, increase, lengthen, multiply **9** discourse, elaborate, expatiate

enlarged 7 swollen, widened **8** expanded, extended, inflated **9** amplified, broadened, distended, elongated, magnified

enlargement 6 growth **8** addition, increase, swelling, widening **9** expansion, extension, inflation **10** broadening, elongation **11** development, elaboration, expatiation, lengthening **12** augmentation **13** amplification, magnification **14** multiplication

enlighten 5 edify **6** advise, inform, wise up **7** apprise, clarify, educate **8** civilize, instruct **9** make aware **10** illuminate **12** sophisticate

enlightenment 8 learning **9** erudition, knowledge **11** edification, instruction
  French: 15 Eclaircissement
  German: 10 Aufklarung

enlist 4 join **6** engage, enroll, join up, obtain, secure, sign up **7** procure, recruit **8** register **9** volunteer **19** gain the assistance of

enlistment 9 signing up **10** admittance, enrollment, recruiting

enliven 4 fire **5** pep up, renew **6** excite, vivify, wake up **7** animate, cheer up, quicken **8** brighten, vitalize **10** make lively, rejuvenate

enlivened 7 revived **8** animated, vivified **9** refreshed **11** invigorated

en masse 7 in a body **8** as a group, as a whole, in a group, together **11** all together

enmesh 4 trap **5** catch, snare, snarl **6** tangle **7** embroil, ensnare, entwine, involve **8** entangle

enmity 6 animus, hatred, malice, rancor, strife **7** ill will **8** acrimony, bad blood **9** animosity, antipathy, hostility **10** bitterness

Ennead 7 dieties
  origin: 8 Egyptian
  number: 4 nine

ennoble 5 raise **6** refine **7** dignify, elevate

ennui 6 apathy, tedium **7** boredom, languor **9** lassitude, weariness **12** indifference, listlessness
  Latin: 12 taedium vitae

Enoch
  father: 4 Cain **5** Jared
  son: 10 Methuselah
  grandfather: 4 Adam

Enoch Arden
  author: 18 Alfred Lord Tennyson

character: 8 Annie Lee **9** Philip Ray **10** Miriam Lane

enology see **8** oenology

enormity 8 baseness, evilness, hugeness, vastness, vileness, villainy **9** depravity, immensity, largeness, malignity **10** wickedness **11** heinousness, viciousness **12** enormousness **13** atrociousness, monstrousness, offensiveness **14** outrageousness

enormous 4 huge, vast **7** immense, mammoth, massive, titanic **8** colossal, gigantic **10** gargantuan, prodigious, tremendous **11** elephantine **14** Brobdingnagian

enormousness 8 enormity, hugeness, vastness **9** amplitude, immensity, largeness **11** massiveness

Enormous Room, The
  author: 10 e e cummings

Enos
  father: 4 Seth
  grandfather: 4 Adam

enough 5 ample, amply **6** plenty **7** copious **8** abundant, adequate, passably **9** tolerably **10** abundantly, adequately, competence, plentitude, reasonably, sufficient **11** ample supply, full measure, sufficiency **12** sufficiently **14** satisfactorily

enounce 8 set forth **9** enunciate **10** articulate

en passant 8 by the way **9** chess term, in passing

enrage 5 anger **6** madden **7** incense, inflame **9** aggravate, infuriate **11** make furious **13** make one see red **14** throw into a rage **17** make one's blood boil

enraged 3 mad **5** angry, irate **7** angered, furious, violent **8** incensed, inflamed, maddened, provoked **9** irritated **10** aggravated, infuriated **11** exasperated

en rapport 8 in accord **9** congenial **10** in sympathy **11** in agreement

enrapture 5 charm **6** thrill **7** beguile, bewitch, delight, enchant **8** enthrall, entrance, hold rapt **9** captivate, transport

enraptured 4 rapt **8** beatific, blissful, ecstatic **9** delighted, enchanted **10** enthralled **11** transported

enravel 5 snare, snarl, twist **6** enmesh, tangle **7** ensnare, ensnarl, entwine **8** entangle **10** intertwine

enrich 5 adorn, endow **6** refine **7** elevate, enhance, fortify, improve, upgrade **8** make rich **9** embellish **10** ameliorate **11** make wealthy **15** feather one's nest

enroll 4 join **5** admit, enter **6** accept, engage, enlist, join up, sign up, take on **7** recruit **8** register

enrollment 6 roster **9** enrolling, signing up **10** admittance, enlistment, re-

cruiting **12** registration **13** matriculation

en route 8 on the way **9** in transit, on the road

ensconce 4 bury, hide, seat **5** lodge **6** settle **7** conceal, secrete, shelter **9** establish

ensemble 5 getup **6** attire, outfit, troupe **7** company, costume **8** assembly, entirety, grouping, totality **9** aggregate

ensign 4 flag, jack, mark, sign **5** badge **6** banner, colors, emblem, pennon, symbol **7** pennant **8** insignia, standard

enslave 6 addict, subdue **7** capture, control, enchain, shackle **8** dominate, enthrall **9** indenture, subjugate **13** hold in bondage, put in shackles

enslavement 4 yoke **6** chains, thrall **7** bondage, serfdom, slavery **9** captivity, servitude, thralldom, vassalage **11** subjugation

ensnare 4 trap **5** catch **6** enmesh, entrap, tangle **7** enravel **8** entangle

Ensor, James
  born: 6 Ostend **7** Belgium
  artwork: 8 Intrigue **19** Bourgeois Living Room **25** Entry of Christ into Brussels **26** The Tribulations of St Anthony **29** Self-Portrait Surrounded by Masks

enstatite
  source: 5 Burma, Mogok

ensue 6 derive, follow, result **7** succeed **10** come to pass **13** come afterward

ensuing 8 eventual **9** following, resulting **10** consequent, succeeding

en suite 6 in a set **9** in a series **12** in succession

ensure, insure 5 guard **6** assure, clinch, secure **7** protect, warrant **8** be sure of, make safe, make sure **9** guarantee, safeguard **13** make certain of

entail 6 demand **7** call for, include, involve, require **8** occasion **11** incorporate, necessitate

entangle 4 trap **5** catch, mix up, snare, snarl **6** enmesh, foul up, muddle, tangle **7** confuse, embroil, enravel, ensnare, involve **8** encumber **9** embarrass, implicate **10** complicate, compromise, intertwine

entanglement 5 mixup, snarl **6** foul-up, muddle **7** problem **9** confusion, imbroglio **10** difficulty, entrapment **11** embroilment **12** complication

entente 4 pact **6** accord, treaty **7** compact **8** alliance, covenant **9** agreement, consensus, unanimity **10** consortium **12** conciliation **13** rapprochement, understanding **14** likemindedness

entente cordiale 21 friendly understanding

enter 4 go in, join, list, post **6** arrive,

come in, record **8** enlist in, enroll in, inscribe, pass into, set out on, trespass **9** penetrate, sign up for **10** embark upon, take part in

enterprise 4 push, task, zeal **5** drive, vigor **6** daring, effort, energy, spirit **7** attempt, program, project, venture **8** ambition, boldness, campaign, endeavor, industry **9** alertness, eagerness, ingenuity, operation **10** enthusiasm, initiative **11** undertaking, willingness **14** aggressiveness **15** adventurousness

enterprising 4 bold, keen **5** alert, eager **6** active **7** earnest, zealous **8** intrepid **9** ambitious, energetic, inventive, wide-awake **10** aggressive **11** hardworking, industrious, self-reliant, up-and-coming, venturesome **12** enthusiastic

entertain 4 heed **5** admit, amuse, charm **6** absorb, divert, foster, harbor, please, ponder, regale **7** beguile, delight, dwell on, engross, imagine, nurture, support **8** consider, enthrall, interest, muse over, play host **10** cogitate on, give a party, have guests, keep in mind, think about **11** contemplate **13** keep open house

entertainer 4 host **5** actor **6** amuser, artist, dancer, singer **7** hostess **8** magician, musician **9** performer

entertaining 3 fun **7** amusing, hosting **8** charming, pleasing **9** beguiling, diverting, enjoyable **10** delightful, hostessing **11** playing host **12** having guests **14** having people in

entertainment 3 fun **4** play **7** novelty, pastime **8** good time, pleasure **9** amusement, diversion, enjoyment **10** recreation **11** distraction **12** satisfaction
French: 14 divertissement

enter upon 5 begin **6** assume **9** undertake

enthrall, enthral 5 charm, rivet **6** seduce, thrill **7** beguile, bewitch, enchant, enslave **8** entrance, intrigue, transfix **9** captivate, enrapture, fascinate, hypnotize, overpower, spellbind, subjugate, transport **13** keep in bondage **14** put into slavery

enthralled 4 rapt **8** beguiled, enslaved **9** bewitched, enchanted, entranced, in bondage, intrigued **10** captivated, enraptured, fascinated, hypnotized, spellbound, subjugated

enthusiasm 4 love, rage, zeal, zest **5** ardor, craze, hobby, mania **6** fervor, relish **7** elation, passion **8** devotion, interest, keenness **9** diversion, eagerness **10** excitement, exuberance, hobbyhorse **11** distraction, pet activity **12** anticipation

enthusiast 3 bug, fan, nut **4** buff **5** freak **6** addict **7** devotee, fanatic **10** aficionado

enthusiastic 5 eager **6** ardent, fervid **7** fervent, zealous **8** spirited **9** exuberant **10** passionate, unstinting **11** unqualified **12** wholehearted

entice 4 coax, lure **5** tempt **6** allure, incite, induce, seduce **7** attract, beguile, wheedle **8** inveigle, persuade

enticement 4 bait, draw, lure **6** allure **9** seduction, siren song **10** attraction, temptation

entire 4 full **5** gross, total, whole **6** in toto, intact **8** absolute, complete, thorough, unbroken **9** undamaged **10** unimpaired **12** all-inclusive

entirely 5 fully **6** wholly **7** totally, utterly **10** absolutely, altogether, completely, thoroughly **12** unreservedly **13** unqualifiedly
French: 9 tout a fait

entitle 3 dub, tag **4** call, name **5** allow, label, style, title **6** enable, permit **7** qualify **9** authorize, designate **12** make eligible

entity 4 body **5** being, thing **6** matter, object **7** article **8** creature, presence, quantity **9** real thing, structure, substance **10** individual

entomb 4 bury **5** inter **7** confine

entombment 6 burial **9** interment **10** inhumation

Entommeures, Frere Jean des
character in: 22 Gargantua and Pantagruel
author: 8 Rabelais

entourage 5 court, staff, suite, train **6** convoy, escort **7** cortege, retinue **9** followers, following **10** associates, attendants, companions

entrails 4 guts **5** offal **6** bowels **7** innards, insides, viscera **10** intestines

entrance 4 door, gate **5** charm, entry, way in **6** access, entree, portal **7** beguile, bewitch, delight, doorway, gateway, gladden, ingress, opening **8** approach, coming in, enthrall **9** captivate, enrapture, fascinate, hypnotize, mesmerize, spellbind, transport **10** admittance, appearance, passageway **12** introduction

entranced 4 rapt **7** charmed **8** beguiled **9** entralled, rapturous **10** enraptured, fascinated, spellbound **11** carried away, transported

entranceway 5 entry, foyer, way in **7** doorway, ingress **8** entryway **9** front hall, vestibule

entrancing 6 lovely **8** adorable, charming **9** appealing, beautiful, beguiling, disarming **10** bewitching, delightful **11** captivating, fascinating **12** irresistible

entrap 3 bag, nab **4** hook, land, nail **5** catch, snare, tempt **6** allure, collar, drag in, draw in, entice, rope in, seduce, suck in **7** beguile, capture, ensnare **8** inveigle

entreat 3 beg **6** adjure, enjoin, exhort **7** beseech, implore, request **8** appeal to, petition **9** importune, plead with **10** supplicate

entreaty 4 plea **6** appeal, prayer **8** petition **11** importunity **12** supplication

entree 4 pull **5** entry **6** access **7** ingress **8** entrance, main dish **9** admission **10** acceptance, admittance, main course

entremets 8 side dish

entrench, intrench 3 fix, set **4** root **5** dig in, embed, plant **6** anchor **7** implant, ingrain, install, solidly **8** ensconce **12** establish

entrenched leaders 11 ruling class **12** powers that be **13** Establishment **14** power structure

entre nous 9 between us, privately **14** confidentially **15** between you and me **16** between me and thee, between ourselves **18** in strict confidence

entrepot 5 depot **9** warehouse **18** distribution center

entrepreneur 7 manager **8** director **9** organizer **10** impresario **11** coordinator

entrust, intrust 5 trust **6** assign, commit **7** consign **8** delegate, hand over, turn over **9** authorize **10** charge with

entrustment 10 delegation **13** authorization, commissioning

entry 3 way **4** door, gate, item, memo, note **5** foyer, way in **6** access, entree, minute, portal, record **7** account, doorway, gateway, ingress, jotting **8** approach, entrance **9** admission, vestibule **10** admittance, appearance, competitor, contestant, memorandum, passageway **11** entranceway **12** entrance hall, introduction, registration

entwine, intwine 4 fold, lace, wind **5** braid, plait, twine, twist, weave **9** interlace **10** interweave

enumerable 6 finite **7** limited **11** denumerable

enumerate 3 add **4** cite, list **5** add up, count, sum up, tally, total **6** detail, number, relate **7** count up, recount, specify, tick off **8** numerate, spell out, tabulate

enumeration 4 list **5** tally **7** account, listing **8** adding up, addition, citation, tallying, totaling **9** checklist, detailing, numbering, reckoning, summing up **10** counting up, recounting, tabulation, ticking off **11** spelling out

enunciate 5 sound, speak, voice **8** vocalize **10** articulate **15** utter distinctly **16** pronounce clearly

enunciation 6 accent, speech **7** diction **9** utterance **12** articulation **13** pronunciation

envelop 4 hide, veil, wrap **5** cloak, cover **6** encase, enfold, engulf, enwrap, shroud, swathe **7** blanket, conceal, contain, enclose, obscure, sheathe, swaddle **8** encircle, surround **9** encompass

envelope 5 cover **6** jacket **8** covering, wrapping

envenom 4 sour **6** rankle **8** embitter **13** make poisonous

enviable 5 lucky **8** salutary **9** agreeable, covetable, desirable, excellent, fortunate **10** beneficial **12** advantageous

envious 5 green **7** jealous **8** covetous, grudging, spiteful **9** jaundiced, resentful

enviousness 4 envy **8** jealousy **10** resentment **12** covetousness **13** resentfulness **19** the green-eyed monster

environment 5 scene **6** locale, medium, milieu **7** climate, element, habitat, setting **8** ambience **9** situation **10** atmosphere, background **12** surroundings **13** circumstances
French: 11 mise en scene

environs 6 exurbs **7** suburbs **8** vicinity **9** outskirts, precincts **11** outer limits **12** outlying area **15** surrounding area

envisage 5 fancy **7** dream of, dream up, imagine, picture **8** conceive, envision **9** conjure up, visualize **11** contemplate **13** conceptualize **14** have a picture of **16** picture to oneself

envoy 5 agent **6** deputy, legate **7** attache, courier **8** delegate, emissary, minister **9** messenger, middleman **10** ambassador **12** intermediary **14** representative

envy 5 greed, spite **6** resent **8** begrudge, grudging, jealousy **10** resentment **11** be jealous of, enviousness, malevolence **12** covetousness **13** resentfulness **16** be spiteful toward **19** the green-eyed monster

enwrap 6 absorb, engage, enrobe **7** engross, envelop **9** preoccupy

Enyo
origin: 5 Greek
goddess of: 3 war
companion of: 4 Ares
member of: 6 Graeae, Graiae
corresponds to: 7 Bellona

enzyme 7 protein **8** molecule **13** macromolecule
function: 8 catalyst
acts on: 9 substrate
kind: 5 amino, malic **6** lactic, lipase, pepsin, rennin, urease **7** amylase, glucose, trypsin **8** aldehyde, glutamic, glycolic, lipozyme, thrombin, xanthine **9** cellulase **12** ribonuclease

eon 3 age, era **8** eternity, long time **9** many years **15** one billion years

Eos
origin: 5 Greek
goddess of: 4 dawn
father: 8 Hyperion
mother: 5 Theia
brother: 6 Helios
sister: 6 Selene
husband: 8 Astraeus, Tithonus **10** Eosophorus
son: 6 Memnon **8** Phaethon, Zephyrus **10** Eosophorus
horse: 6 Lampos **8** Phaethon
mother of: 5 stars, winds
corresponds to: 6 Aurore **7** Hermera

Epha, Ephah, Epheh 15 Biblical measure

ephemeral 5 brief **7** passing **8** fleeting, flitting, fugitive, temporal **9** fugacious, momentary, temporary, transient **10** evanescent, fly-by-night, inconstant, nondurable, short-lived, transitory, unenduring **11** impermanent **21** here today gone tomorrow

ephemeroptera
class: 8 hexapoda
phylum: 10 arthropoda
group: 6 mayfly

Ephraim
father: 6 Joseph
mother: 7 Asenath
brother: 8 Manasseh
blessed by: 5 Jacob
descendant of: 10 Ephraimite

Ephraimi 16 Greek unical codex

epic 4 saga **5** drama, great, noble **6** fabled, heroic **7** exalted, storied **8** fabulous, imposing, majestic **9** legendary **10** heroic poem, superhuman **14** larger than life

Epicaste see **7** Jocasta

epicure 7 glutton, gourmet **8** gourmand, hedonist, sybarite **9** bon vivant **10** gastronome

epicurean 4 rich **6** lavish **7** gourmet, sensual **8** hedonist, Lucullan, sybarite **9** libertine, luxurious, sybaritic **10** hedonistic, sensualist, voluptuary, voluptuous **11** intemperate **13** self-indulgent

epidemic 4 rife **6** plague **7** rampant, scourge **8** catching, outbreak, pandemic **9** contagion, infection, pervasive, prevalent **10** infectious, pestilence, prevailing, widespread **11** far-reaching

Epigoni
sons of: 18 Seven against Thebes

epigram 4 quip **5** adage, maxim **6** bon mot **8** aphorism, apothegm **9** witticism

epilogue 4 coda **5** rider **7** codicil **8** addendum **9** afterword **10** supplement **12** final section

Epione
husband: 9 Asclepius

episcopal 8 churchly, diocesan, pastoral **12** ecclesiastic(al)

episode 4 part **5** event, scene **6** affair, period **7** chapter, passage, section **8** incident **9** adventure, happening, milestone **10** experience, occurrence **11** installment

Episode of Sparrows, An
author: 11 Rumer Godden

episodic 7 halting **8** rambling **9** segmented, wandering **10** digressive, discursive, meandering **13** discontinuous

epistle 6 letter **7** message, missive **10** encyclical

Epistle to a Godson and Other Poems
author: 7 W H Auden

Epistle to Dr Arbuthnot
author: 13 Alexander Pope

Epithalamion
author: 13 Edmund Spenser

epithet 5 curse **6** insult **8** nickname **9** blasphemy, expletive, obscenity, sobriquet **10** ascription **11** appellation, designation

Epithet
of Aphrodite: 6 Acraea, Scotia **7** Doritis, Erycina, Limenia **8** Melaenis, Nymphaea, Pandemos **9** Migonitis **11** Aphrogeneia, Apostrophia
of Apollo: 6 Loxias **7** Acesius, Agraeus, Agyieus, Carneus, Phyteus, Spodius **8** Grynaeus **9** Parnopius, Smintheus **10** Alexicacus, Archegetes, Boedromius, Delphinius **11** Argyrotoxus, Epibaterius **12** Platanistius
of Ares: 8 Enyalius **14** Gynaecothoenas
of Argus: 8 Panoptes
of Artemis: 6 Orthia **7** Eurippa, Laphria, Limnaea, Pyronia **8** Aeginaea, Agrotera, Calliste, Caryatis, Daphnaea **9** Hemerasia, Lygodesma **10** Polymastus **11** Leucophryne
of Asclepius: 8 Cotyleus
of Athena: 4 Alea **5** Meter, Xenia **6** Ergane, Itonia, Polias **7** Agoraea, Cissaea, Paeonia, Pronaus, Pronoea **8** Anemotis, Poliates, Zosteria **9** Oxyderces, Parthenia, Poliuchus, Promachus **10** Axiopoenus, Chalinitis, Cyparissia **11** Promachorma
of Cybele: 6 Antaea
of Demeter: 5 Chloe, Lusia, Mysia **6** Antaea, Erinys, Stiria **7** Chamyne, Thesmia **8** Stiritis **9** Anesidora, Thermasia **11** Carpophorus **12** Thesmophorus
of Dionysus: 6 Lyaeus **7** Bromius, Cresius **8** Thyoneus, Triambus **9** Pyrigenes **11** Dithyrambus, Mitrephorus
of Hera: 6 Anthea, Bunaea **8** Henioche **9** Prodromia
of Hercules: 7 Charops **8** Buphagus **9** Ipoctonus
of Hermes: 6 Dolius **8** Agoraeus **9** Spelaites **10** Criophorus **11** Argiphontes **12** Argeiphontes, Psychopompus
of Icelus: 8 Phobetor

of Juno: 6 Moneta **7** Curitis, Pronuba, Sospita

of Jupiter: 5 Ultor **7** Elicius, Pluvius

of Mopsus: 9 Ampycides

of Nestor: 7 Nelides

of Odin: 7 Alfader, Alfadir

of Odysseus: 10 Laertiades

of Persephone: 11 Carpophorus

of Pheriphetes: 9 Corynetes

of Poseidon: 11 Ennosigaeus, Hippocurius **12** Prosclystius

of Rhea: 6 Antaea

of Sinis: 12 Pityocamptes

of Vulcan: 8 Mulciber

of Zeus: 5 Areus, Soter **6** Aqueus, Areius, Nemean, Philus **7** Alastor, Apemius, Ctesius, Lycaeus, Polieus, Stenius **8** Agoraeus, Aphesius, Apomyius, Cappotas, Cosmetas, Dodonian, Herceius, Leucaeus, Tropaean **9** Aegiochus, Chthonius, Coccygius, Hecaleius, Lecheates, Mechaneus **10** Cataebates, Catharsius, Coryphaeus, Homagyrius, Laphystius, Meilichius **11** Eleutherius **12** Panhellenius

epitome 4 peak **5** ideal, model **6** height **7** essence, summary **9** summation **10** embodiment **12** typification **14** representation **15** exemplification, sum and substance

e pluribus unum 12 out of many one
motto of: **12** United States

epoch 3 age, era **4** time **6** period **8** interval

epochal 7 weighty **8** historic **9** important, momentous **11** significant **13** consequential

Eppie
character in: **11** Silas Marner
author: **5** Eliot

Eppie
nickname of: **10** Ann Landers

Epstein, Sir Jacob
born: **9** New York NY
artwork: **4** Adam **7** Genesis **8** Ecce Homo, Einstein **9** Rock Drill **10** Visitation **11** Night and Day, Paul Robeson **12** Behold the Man, Joseph Conrad **13** Haile Selassie **14** Consummatum Est **19** Social Consciousness **20** Monument to Oscar Wilde, St Michael and his (the) Devil

equable 4 calm, even **5** sunny **6** placid, serene, stable, steady **7** regular, uniform **8** constant, pleasant, tranquil, unvaried **9** agreeable, easygoing, unruffled **10** consistent, dependable, unchanging **11** goodnatured, predictable, unexcitable, unflappable **12** even-tempered **13** imperturbable

equably
Latin: **9** pari passu

equal 4 even, like, peer **5** match **7** matched, the same, uniform **8** balanced, be even to, equalize, jibe with, of a piece, parallel **9** agree with, identical, tally with **10** accord with, comparable, equate with, equivalent, square with, tantamount **11** balance with, be the same as, correlative, counterpart, symmetrical **12** commensurate, correspond to, proportional **13** be identical to, corresponding, evenly matched, one and the same

equality 6 parity **7** balance, justice **8** evenness, fair play, fairness, sameness **10** similarity, uniformity **11** equivalency **12** impartiality **13** fair treatment **14** correspondence
French: **7** egalite

Equality
author: **13** Edward Bellamy

Equality State
nickname of: **7** Wyoming

equalization 7 balance **9** stability **11** equilibrium **14** counterbalance
German: **9** Ausgleich

equalize 7 balance **9** make equal **11** make uniform **13** compensate for

equal to 3 fit **4** able, up to **5** adept **7** capable **8** adequate, master of **9** competent, qualified

equanimity 4 cool **5** poise **6** aplomb **8** calmness, coolness **9** composure, sangfroid **10** steadiness **11** self-control, tranquility **12** tranquillity **14** presence of mind, self-possession **16** imperturbability

equate 5 liken, match **7** average, balance, compare, even out **8** equalize, equal out **9** think of as **10** consider as **14** be commensurate, be equivalent to **17** be proportionate to

Equatorial
language family: **16** Andean-Equatorial
group: **8** Arawakan **11** Tupi-Guarani

Equatorial Guinea
other name: **13** Spanish Guinea
capital/largest city: **6** Malabo
others: **4** Bata **9** Rio Benito
division: **5** Bioko **7** Rio Muni
monetary unit: **6** ekuele, peseta **7** centimo
island: **5** Bioko **6** Pagalu **7** Corisco **11** Chico Elobey **12** Grande Elobey
mountain: **5** Mitra
highest point: **11** Santa Isabel
river: **5** Mbini
physical feature:
  gulf: **6** Guinea
people: **4** Bubi, Fang **5** Benge, Combe **6** Bujeba **10** Fernandino
  explorer: **2** Po
  leader: **12** Nguema Biyogo
language: **4** Bubi, Fang **7** Spanish **13** pidgin English
religion: **7** animism **10** Protestant **13** Roman Catholic

equilibrium 7 balance **8** symmetry **9** equipoise, stability **14** sense of balance

equip 3 rig **5** stock **6** fit out, outfit, supply **7** appoint, furnish, prepare, provide **8** accoutre **9** caparison, provision

equipage 4 gear **6** outfit **8** carriage **9** equipment **13** accoutrements

equipment 4 gear **5** stuff **6** tackle **8** equipage, material, materiel, supplies **9** apparatus **11** furnishings, outfittings **13** accoutrements, paraphernalia

equipoise 7 balance **9** stability **11** equilibrium

equitable 3 due **4** fair, just **6** proper **8** unbiased **9** impartial **10** evenhanded, reasonable **12** unprejudiced

equity 4 cash **5** value **6** assets, profit **7** justice **8** fairness, justness **9** cash value **10** investment **12** fair dealings, impartiality **14** evenhandedness, fairmindedness, reasonableness

equivalency 6 parity **7** balance **8** equality **10** coequality, uniformity **14** correspondence

equivalent 4 even, peer **5** equal, match **8** of a piece, parallel **9** the same as **10** comparable, tantamount **11** correlative, counterpart, equal amount

equivocal 4 hazy **5** vague **7** dubious **8** doubtful **9** ambiguous, enigmatic, imprecise, qualified, uncertain, undecided **10** ambivalent, indefinite, suspicious **11** nonspecific **12** undetermined **13** indeterminate

equivocate 5 dodge, evade, fudge, hedge, stall **9** pussyfoot **10** mince words **11** be ambiguous, prevaricate **13** avoid the issue **16** straddle the fence **17** beat around the bush

equivocating 6 shifty **7** devious, dodging, elusive, elusory, evasive, hedging **8** stalling **9** ambiguous, deceptive, equivocal **10** misleading **11** dissembling

ERA
abbr. for: **16** earned run average (baseball) **20** equal rights amendment (failed)

era 3 age **4** time **5** epoch **6** period **8** interval

eradicate 5 erase **6** remove **7** abolish, blot out, destroy, expunge, wipe out **8** get rid of **9** eliminate, extirpate, liquidate **10** annihilate, do away with, extinguish, obliterate **11** exterminate

eradication 7 erasure, removal **9** abolition **11** blotting out, destruction, elimination **12** obliteration

erase 6 delete, remove, rub out **7** expunge, scratch **8** wipe away **9** eliminate, eradicate, strike out

Erasistratus
field: **10** physiology
nationality: **5** Greek
described: **5** brain, heart

Erasmus, Desiderius

author of: 14 Encomium Moriae **16** The Praise of Folly

Erato
    muse of: 10 love poetry

Ercolani, James
    real name of: 11 James Darren

erect 5 build, put up, raise, rigid, stiff **6** unbent **7** stand up, upright **8** straight, vertical **9** construct, unstooped **12** place upright

erection 7 raising **8** building **9** putting up **11** fabrication **12** construction

eremite 4 monk **6** essene, hermit **7** ascetic, recluse **9** anchorite, religious

Erewhon
    author: 12 Samuel Butler
    title spelled backwards, modified: 7 nowhere
    character: 5 Higgs **6** Strong **7** Chowbok **8** Arowhena

erg
    metric unit of: 4 work **6** energy

ergo 4 work **6** hence **7** because **9** therefore **11** accordingly

Eriboea
    husband: 6 Aloeus

Ericson 4 Leif
    son of: 10 Eric the Red
    discovered: 7 Vinland
    home: 6 Norway

Erie 4 lake, port **5** canal **9** Iroquoian

Erigone
    father: 7 Icarius **9** Aegisthus
    mother: 12 Clytemnestra
    brother: 6 Aletes
    death by: 7 suicide

Erin *see* **7** Ireland

Erin go bragh 14 Ireland forever

Erinys
    also: 6 Furies
    epithet of: 7 Demeter
    means: 4 fury

Eris
    origin: 5 Greek
    goddess of: 7 discord
    brother: 4 Ares
    threw: 14 apple of discord
    corresponds to: 9 Discordia

Eritrea
    capital/largest city: 6 Asmara
    others: 5 Assab, Keren **6** Ghinda **7** Massawa
    formerly division of: 8 Ethiopia
    river: 5 Mareb
    highest point: 5 Soira
    strait: 11 Bab el Mandeb
    sea: 3 Red
    language: 7 Amharic
    religion: 5 Islam **6** Coptic, Muslim

Erlking
    origin: 8 Germanic **12** Scandinavian
    form: 6 spirit
    personifies: 6 nature
    works: 8 mischief
    poem by: 6 Goethe
    song by: 8 Schubert

ermine 3 fur **4** duty, rank **6** weasel **7** ermalin **8** position

Ernani
    opera by: 5 Verdi
    setting: 6 Aragon
    character: 6 Ernani **11** Donna Elvira

Ernst, Max
    born: 5 Bruhl **7** Germany
    co-founder of: 7 Dadaism **10** Surrealism
    artwork: 7 Moon Man **8** Lady Bird **11** A Little Calm, Femme Oiseau **12** The Whole City **13** The Table Is Set, Totem and Taboo **14** Lunar Asparagus

erode 3 eat **5** spoil, waste **6** ravage **7** corrode, despoil, eat away **8** wear away **12** disintegrate

Eros
    origin: 5 Greek
    god of: 4 love
    mother: 9 Aphrodite
    corresponds to: 4 Amor **5** Cupid

erosion 8 abrasion, ravaging **9** corrosion **10** eating away **11** wearing away, wearing down

erosive 7 burning, caustic **9** corrosive

erotic 3 hot **4** lewd, sexy **5** bawdy, lusty **6** ardent, carnal, impure, ribald, risque **7** amatory, amorous, obscene, raunchy **8** immodest, indecent, unchaste **9** salacious **10** lascivious, passionate, suggestive

err 3 sin **6** mess up, slip up **7** blunder, do wrong **8** go astray **9** be in error, misbehave **10** transgress **12** make a mistake, miscalculate **13** slip from grace

errand 4 duty, task **6** office **7** mission **10** assignment

errant 5 wrong **6** arrant, astray, erring, roving **7** erratic, wayward **8** mistaken, straying **9** incorrect, wandering, wayfaring **11** adventurous

errare humanum est 12 to err is human

erratic 3 odd **5** queer **6** fitful **7** strange, unusual, wayward **8** aberrant, abnormal, peculiar, shifting, unstable, variable **9** eccentric, unnatural **10** capricious, changeable **11** vacillating **12** inconsistent **13** unpredictable

erroneous 5 false, wrong **6** all wet, faulty, untrue **7** off base, unsound **8** mistaken, spurious **9** incorrect, unfounded **10** fallacious, inaccurate **12** full of hot air **13** unsupportable

error 4 flaw **5** boner, botch, fault **6** boo-boo, bungle, howler **7** blooper, fallacy, mistake **9** oversight **10** inaccuracy **13** misconception **14** miscalculation **15** misapprehension **16** misunderstanding **17** misinterpretation

ersatz 4 fake, sham **5** bogus, phony **9** imitation, pretended, synthetic **10** artificial, not genuine **11** counterfeit

Erse 4 Celt, Gael, Scot **5** Irish **6** Celtic, Gaelic **7** Ireland **8** Scottish **10** Highlander

erstwhile 2 ex **4** past **6** bygone, former **7** onetime **8** previous

eruct 4 burp **5** belch

eructation 4 burp **5** belch

erudite 4 wise **7** learned, sapient **8** cultured, literate, well-read **9** scholarly **10** cultivated, thoughtful, well-versed **11** intelligent **12** well-educated, well-informed, well-reasoned

erudition 5 skill **7** culture **8** learning, literacy **9** education, expertise, knowledge, schooling **10** refinement **11** cultivation, learnedness, scholarship **12** book learning **13** enlightenment

Erulus
    king of: 5 Italy
    mother: 7 Feronia
    gift: 10 three lives

erupt 4 emit, gush, vent **5** eruct **6** blow up **7** explode **8** break out, throw off **9** be ejected, discharge, flow forth, pour forth **10** belch forth, burst forth

eruption 4 rash **6** eczema **7** flare-up, gushing, venting **8** ejection, emission, outbreak, outburst **9** blowing up, discharge, explosion, festering **10** dermatitis, outpouring **11** breaking out **12** flowing forth, inflammation, pouring forth **13** belching forth, bursting forth

Erving, Julius
    nickname: 7 Doctor J
    sport: 10 basketball
    position: 7 forward
    team: 11 New York Nets **15** Virginia Squires **25** Philadelphia Seventy-Sixers

Erymanthian boar
    form: 4 boar
    plagued: 7 Arcadia
    captured by: 8 Hercules

erythrophobia
    fear of: 8 blushing

Esau
    also called: 4 Edom
    father: 5 Isaac
    mother: 7 Rebekah
    twin brother: 5 Jacob
    wife: 6 Judith **8** Makalath
    son: 7 Eliphaz
    birthright sold to: 5 Jacob

escadrille 6 armada **8** flotilla, squadron

escalate 4 rise **5** boost, mount, swell **6** ascend, expand, extend, step up **7** advance, amplify, broaden, elevate, enlarge, magnify **8** increase **9** intensify **10** accelerate, aggrandize

Escalus
    character in: 17 Measure for Measure
    author: 11 Shakespeare

escapade 4 lark **5** antic, caper, fling, prank, revel, spree, trick **7** caprice **8** mischief **9** adventure **11** high old time

escape 3 lam 4 bolt, exit, flee, flow, gush, leak, seep, shun, skip 5 avoid, dodge, elude, issue, skirt 6 efflux, egress, emerge, eschew, exodus, flight, stream 7 abscond, emanate, getaway, leakage, make off, outflow, outpour, run away, seepage 8 breakout, emission, outburst, slip away, steal off 9 be emitted, break free, cut and run, discharge, diversion, effluence, pour forth 10 break loose, decampment, fly the coop 11 avoid danger, deliverance, distraction, extrication, safe getaway 12 make a getaway

escargot 5 snail

escarpment 4 bank, crag 5 bluff, cliff, ridge, slope 8 headland, palisade 9 precipice 10 promontory

eschew 4 shun 5 avoid, forgo 6 give up 7 forbear 9 keep shy of 11 abstain from 12 steer clear of

eschewal 7 refusal 8 forgoing, shunning 9 avoidance 10 abnegation, abstention, self-denial 11 forbearance 13 nonindulgence 16 nonparticipation

Escoffier, Auguste
 nationality: 6 French
 profession: 4 chef
 worked in: 4 Ritz 6 London

escort 4 date, take 5 guard, guide, train, usher 6 squire 7 company, conduct, cortege, retinue 8 chaperon 9 companion, conductor, entourage 10 attendants, lead the way

escritoire 4 desk 5 table 9 secretary 10 secretaire 11 writing desk

escutcheon 4 arms 5 crest 6 shield 10 coat of arms 16 armorial bearings
 see also 8 Heraldry

Eskimo (Eskimantsic, Askkimey, Inuit, Yuit)
 tribe: 5 Aleut
 location: 6 Alaska, Arctic, Canada 9 Greenland
 noted for: 7 fishing 9 mechanics

Eskimo-Aleut
 language branch: 5 Aleut, Yupik
 spoken in: 6 Alaska 7 Siberia 15 Aleutian Islands

Esmeralda
 character in: 23 The Hunchback of Notre Dame
 author: 4 Hugo

esoteric 6 arcane, covert, hidden, occult, secret, veiled 7 cloaked, cryptic, obscure, private 8 abstruse, mystical 9 concealed, enigmatic, recondite 10 inviolable, mysterious 11 inscrutable, undisclosed 12 confidential 16 incomprehensible

ESP 7 insight 9 foresight, intuition 10 sixth sense 11 premonition, second sight 12 clairvoyance 22 extrasensory perception

espanol 7 Spanish 13 Spanish person 15 Spanish language

especial *see* 7 special

especially 6 really 7 notably 9 expressly, intensely, primarily, unusually 10 singularly, uncommonly 11 exclusively, principally 12 particularly, specifically 13 exceptionally, outstandingly 15 extraordinarily

espiegle 7 playful, roguish

espieglerie 12 playful trick

esplanade 4 mall, path, walk 5 drive 9 boardwalk 10 quadrangle

espousal 7 backing, support, wedding 8 adoption, advocacy, marriage, taking up 9 betrothal, promotion 10 supporting 12 championship

espouse 3 wed 4 back, tout 5 adopt, boost, marry 6 take up 7 embrace, further, promote, support 8 advocate, champion, side with 10 stand up for

espressivo
 music: 12 expressively
 abbreviation: 4 espr

esprit de corps 10 fellowship, group pride, group unity, high morale, solidarity, team spirit 11 camaraderie

espy 3 see, spy 4 spot, view 6 behold, descry, detect, locate, notice 7 discern

essay 3 try 5 paper, theme, tract 6 effort, take on 7 article, attempt, venture 8 critique, endeavor, treatise 9 editorial, undertake 10 commentary, experiment 11 make a stab at, undertaking 12 dissertation, take a crack at, take a fling at 14 make an effort at 16 short composition

Essay on Criticism, An
 author: 13 Alexander Pope

Essay on Man, An
 author: 13 Alexander Pope

Essays
 author: 12 Francis Bacon

Essays in Criticism
 author: 13 Matthew Arnold

esse 5 being 9 existence

essence 4 core, germ, gist, pith, soul 5 heart, point, scent 6 elixir, nature, spirit 7 cologne, extract, meaning, perfume, spirits 8 tincture 9 fragrance, lifeblood, principle, substance 11 concentrate, toilet water 12 basic quality, quintessence, significance 15 sum and substance

essential, essentials 3 key 4 main 5 basic, vital 6 basics, needed 7 crucial, leading 8 cardinal, inherent 9 basic need, important, ingrained, intrinsic, necessary, necessity, principal, requisite, rudiments, vital part 10 key element, principles 11 fundamental, nitty-gritty 12 fundamentals 13 indispensable

essential ingredient 9 necessity 10 sine qua non 22 indispensable component

establish 3 fix 4 form, open, show 5 begin, found, prove, set up, start 6 create, settle, uphold, verify 7 confirm, implant, install, justify, situate, sustain, warrant 8 initiate, organize, validate 9 institute 10 bring about, inaugurate, make secure 11 corroborate, demonstrate 12 authenticate 16 win acceptance for 18 bring into existence

established 6 common 7 regular 8 accepted, familiar 9 customary 10 recognized

establishment, Establishment 4 firm 5 plant 6 office, outfit, system 7 company, concern, factory 8 building, business, creation, founding 9 formation, setting up 10 foundation 11 corporation, development, instituting, institution, ruling class 12 organization, powers that be 13 bringing about

estaminet 4 cafe 6 bistro

estate 4 rank, will 5 class, grade, manor, money, order, state 6 assets, legacy, status, wealth 7 bequest, fortune, station 8 compound, holdings, property 9 condition, situation 10 belongings, plantation 11 inheritance 12 country place

esteem 4 deem, hold 5 honor, judge, prize, think, value 6 admire, reckon, regard, revere 7 believe, cherish, respect 8 approval, consider, estimate, look up to, treasure, venerate 9 calculate, reverence 10 admiration, set store by, veneration 12 appreciation 13 think highly of 16 favorable opinion, hold in high regard 18 attach importance to

esteemed 5 great, noted 6 prized, valued, worthy 7 admired, eminent, honored, notable, revered 9 admirable, important, respected 10 looked up to, preeminent 11 illustrious 13 distinguished, well thought of 14 highly regarded

Estella
 character in: 17 Great Expectations
 author: 7 Dickens

Estevez, Ramon
 real name of: 11 Martin Sheen

Esther
 author: 10 Henry Adams

Esther
 Persian name of: 8 Hadassah
 father: 7 Abihail
 grandfather: 6 Shimei
 cousin: 8 Mordecai
 husband: 9 Ahasuerus
 displaced: 6 Vashti
 enemy: 5 Haman
 holiday: 5 Purim

Esther Waters
 author: 11 George Moore

esthetic 7 refined 8 artistic 9 sensitive 10 cultivated, fastidious 12 aesthetic 14 discriminating

estimable 4 good 6 prized 7 admired, revered 8 laudable 9 admirable, honorable, important, reputable, respected, treasured **10** worthwhile **11** commendable **12** praiseworthy **14** highly regarded

estimate 4 view **5** assay, guess, judge, opine, think, value **6** assess, belief, fig- ure, reckon **7** believe, opinion, surmise **8** appraise, conclude, consider, evaluate, judgment, thinking **9** appraisal, calculate, reckoning **10** assessment, conjecture, evaluation **11** calculation

estimation 4 view **6** belief, esteem, regard **7** opinion, respect **8** approval, judgment **9** appraisal, reckoning **10** admiration, evaluation **13** consideration

estimator 7 analyst **8** assessor **9** appraiser, evaluator **10** calculator

Estonia
    capital/largest city: 7 Tallinn
    others: 5 Narva, Paide, Parnu, Tartu, Valga **6** Dorpat **7** Petseri **8** Paldiski **11** Kohtla-Jarve
    government: 8 republic
    measure: 3 tun **4** elle, liin, sund, toll, toop **5** verst **6** sagene, versta **7** kulimet **8** tonnland
    monetary unit: 3 lat **4** sent **5** kroon **7** estmark
    weight: 4 lood, nael, puud
    island: 4 Dago, Muhu **5** Kihnu, Oesel, Saare **6** Sarema, Vormsi **7** Hiiumaa **8** Saaremaa
    lake: 5 Pskov **6** Peipus **9** Vortsjarv
    highest point: 8 Munamagi
    river: 3 Ema **5** Narva, Parnu
    sea: 6 Baltic
    physical feature:
        gulf: 4 Riga **5** Parnu **7** Finland
        strait: 4 Irbe
    people: 4 Esth, Finn **5** Aesti **6** Jewish **8** Estonian **9** Ukrainian **11** Belorussian
    language: 5 Tartu **10** Finno-Ugric
    religion: 8 Lutheran

estop 3 bar **4** fill, plug, stop **7** prevent **8** obstruct

esto perpetua 17 may she live forever
    motto of: 5 Idaho

Estragon
    character in: 15 Waiting for Godot
    author: 7 Beckett
    French for: 8 tarragon

estrange 4 part **8** alienate **9** disaffect **10** antagonize, dissociate, drive apart

estranged 5 aloof **6** cut off **7** distant **8** detached, divorced **9** alienated, separated **10** unfriendly

estrangement 8 coolness **10** alienation **12** disaffection

estuary 5 firth, inlet **10** river mouth, tidal basin

eta 10 Greek vowel **22** estimated time of arrival

etagere 7 whatnot **11** open shelves

etc (&c) 4 et al **7** and so on, whatnot

8 et cetera, whatever **9** and others **10** and so forth, and the rest

etch 3 cut, fix **5** carve, stamp **7** corrode, engrave, impress, scratch

Eteocles
    father: 7 Oedipus
    mother: 7 Jocasta **10** Euryganeia
    uncle: 5 Creon
    brother: 9 Polynices
    sister: 6 Ismene **8** Antigone
    son: 8 Laodamas
    slain by: 9 Polynices

eternal 7 abiding, endless **8** constant, immortal, infinite, timeless, unending **9** ceaseless, continual, perpetual **10** persistent, relentless, without end **11** everlasting, never-ending **12** interminable **13** uninterrupted

eternity 4 Zion **6** Heaven **7** forever, nirvana **8** infinity, paradise **11** ages and ages, endlessness, eons and eons, immortality **12** New Jerusalem, the hereafter, the next world **13** the afterworld **14** the world to come, time without end **15** everlasting life

Ethan Frome
    author: 12 Edith Wharton
    character: 5 Zeena **7** Zenobia **12** Mattie Silver

Ethanim 18 seventh Hebrew month

ether 5 ester, ethyl, ozone, vapor **7** diethyl, solvent **10** anesthetic **11** refrigerant

ethereal 4 airy, rare **6** aerial **7** elusive, refined, sublime **8** delicate, rarefied **9** celestial, exquisite, unearthly, unworldly

ethical 4 fair, just **5** moral, right **6** decent, kosher, proper **7** correct, fitting, upright **8** virtuous **9** honorable **10** aboveboard, scrupulous **15** straightforward **17** open and aboveboard

ethical feelings 9 integrity **10** conscience, moral sense **16** incorruptibility

ethics, ethic 8 morality **9** integrity, moral code **10** conscience, principles **11** moral values, sense of duty **14** moral standards, rules of conduct

Ethics of Ambiguity
    author: 16 Simone de Beauvoir

Ethiopia
    Biblical name: 4 Cush
    other name: 9 Abyssinia
    capital/largest city: 10 Addis Ababa
    others: 3 Edd **4** Axum, Bako, Dori, Goba, Gore, Thio **5** Adola, Adowa, Aduwa, Aksum, Assab, Awash, Dimtu, Elfud, Harar, Jidda, Jimma, Kecha, Meroe, Mojjo **6** Antalo, Asmara, Dessye, Dunkur, Gondar, Harrar, Makale, Napata **7** Ankober, Gambela, Gardula, Magdala, Massawa, Nakamti **8** Dire Dawa, Lalibala, Mustahil
    school: 13 Haile Selassie
    division: 5 Tigre **6** Amhara, Ogaden

    former division: 7 Eritrea
    measure: 3 tat **4** cubi, kuba **5** derah, messe **6** cabaho, sinjer, sinzer, tanica **7** entelam, farsakh, farsang, ghebeta
    monetary unit: 4 besa, birr, harf **5** amole, girsh **6** dollar, kharaf, levant, pataca, talari **7** ashrafi, menelik, plaster, tallero **12** maria theresa
    weight: 3 pek **4** kasm, natr, oket, rotl **5** alada, artal, mocha, neter, ratel, wakea **6** wogiet **8** farasula **9** mutagalla
    island: 6 Dahlak
    lake: 3 Abe **4** Tana **5** Abaya, Shola, Tanna, Tsana, Tzana, Zeway **6** Dambea, Dembea **7** Rudolph **8** Stefanie **11** The Blue Nile
    mountain: 4 Amba, Batu, Guge, Guna, Talo **5** Ahmar, Choke **9** Rasdashan
    highest point: 9 Ras Deshen
    river: 3 Omo **4** Baro, Dawa, Gibe, Gila, Juba **5** Abbai, Akoho, Albai, Awash, Fafan, Mareb, Mofer, Rahad, Webbe **6** Tekeze **7** Tacazze, Takkaze **8** Gashgash, Shebante **11** The Blue Nile
    sea: 3 Red
    physical feature:
        desert: 17 Danakil Depression
        falls: 7 Tisisat **8** Blue Nile
        valley: 4 Rift
    people: 4 Afar, Agau, Beja, Doko, Kafa, Kala, Saho, Shoa **5** Afara, Agows, Galas, Galla, Negro, Tigre **6** Abigar, Amhara, Annuak, Gondar, Hamite, Harari, Sidama, Sidamo, Somali, Tigrai, Wolamo **7** Cushite, Danakil, Donakus, Falasha, Somalis **8** Assamite, Blemmyes **10** Abyssinian, Troglodyte
    leader: 7 Menelik **8** Mengistu **13** Haile Selassie
    language: 3 Giz **4** Afar, Agow, Geez, Saho **5** Geeze, Ghese, Smali, Tigre **6** Arabic, Harari **7** Amharic, English, Italian, Russian **8** Gallinya, Irob-Saho, Tigrinya
    religion: 5 Islam **7** Falasha, Judaism **18** Ethiopian Orthodoxy
    place:
        cathedral: 8 St George
        hall: 6 Africa
        palace: 7 Jubilee **9** Menelik II
        park: 4 Lion
    feature:
        flower: 7 brayera
        game: 5 dulla **8** shum-shir
        garment: 4 toga **5** kamis **6** barnos, chamma, netela, shamma
        tree: 4 koho, koso **5** cusso
    food:
        banana: 4 musa **6** ensete
        beer: 5 talla
        bread dish: 6 injera
        cereal: 4 teff

honey liquor: 3 tej
spicy sauce: 3 wat
ethnic 6 native, racial, unique **8** cultural, national, original **10** indigenous
ethnic group
of Afghanistan: 5 Aimak, Aymak, Kafir, Nuris **6** Baloch, Baluch, Chahar, Durani, Hasara, Hazara, Kaffir, Kirgiz, Pathan, Tajiks, Uzbeks **7** Beluchi, Belucki, Ghilzai, Pakhton, Pakhtun, Pashtun, Pukhtun, Pushtun, Sistani, Taimani, Taimuri, Taliban **8** Jamshidi, Siah Push **9** Firuz-kuhi, Safed Push, Safid Push
of Albania: 3 Geg **4** Cham, Gheg, Gueg, Tost **6** Arnaut, Arnout **8** Illyrian, Skipetar
of Algeria: 4 Arab **6** Berber, Kabyle, Shawai, Tuareg **7** Haratin
of Andorra: 7 Catalan
of Angola: 5 Bantu, Kongo, Lundu **6** Chokwe, Herero, Mbundi, Ovambo **7** Bakongo, Kangela, Kikongo **8** Kimbundu, Kwangare **9** Ovinbundu **12** Nyaneka-Humbi
of Antigua and Barbuda: 7 African, British **8** Lebanese **10** Portuguese
of Argentina: 3 Api **4** Lule **5** Vejoz **6** Abipon, Vilela **7** Guarani, Puelche, Ranquel, Taluhet **8** Querandi, Querendy
of Armenia: 5 Armen, Ermyn, Gomer, Hadji
of Australia: 3 Abo **4** Koko, Mara, Wong **5** Anzac, Bieri, Binge, Maori, Myall **6** Aranda, Arunta, Aussie, Binghi, Digger, Kipper, Papuan **7** Arawong, Billjim, Ilpirra **8** Antipode, Barkinji, Euahlayi, Warragal, Warrigal **9** Aborigine **10** Austroloid, Melanesian, Sandgroper **12** Jindyworobak
of Austria: 4 Pole **5** Croat, Czech, Gypsy **6** German **7** Slovene **9** Hungarian
of Azerbaijan: 5 Azeri **11** Azerbaijani
of the Bahamas: 5 black **7** Haitian
of Bahrain: 4 Arab **6** Indian **7** Persian **8** European **9** Pakistani
of Bangladesh: 7 Bengali
of Barbados: 5 Bajan **9** Barbadian
of Belarus: 12 Byelorussian
of Belgium: 4 Remi **6** Nervii **7** Belgian, Fleming, Flemish, Walloon **9** Bellovaci
of Benin: 3 Fon, Pla **4** Adja, Aizo, Mina, Peul **5** Pedah, Peuhl, Somba **6** Bariba, Fulani, Yoruba **8** Pilapila **9** Dahomeyan
of Bhutan: 5 Monpa **6** Bhutia **7** Tibetan **8** Assamese, Nepalese
of Bolivia: 6 Aymara **7** mestizo, Quechua
of Borneo: 4 Iban **5** Bukat, Dajak, Dayak, Dusan, Malay, Punan **6** Illano **7** Bakatan, Chinese, Illanun
of Bosnia-Herzegovina: 4 Serb **5** Croat **8** Yugoslav
of Botswana: 5 Bantu **6** Tswana

7 Bakatla, Bakwena, Bushman **8** Bamalete, Baralong, Batawana, Batlokwa, Botswana **10** Bamangwato **11** Bangwaketse
of Brazil: 2 Ge **4** Anta **5** Acroa, Arara, Araua, Bravo, Carib, Guana, Negro **6** Arawak, Caraja **7** Carayan, Javahai, mulatto, Tariana **8** Botocudo, Chambioa, mameluco **9** Caucasian **10** Portuguese **11** Tupi-Guarani
of Bruneii: 4 Iban **5** Dayak, Malay **7** Chinese, Kadazan
of Bulgaria: 4 Slav, Turk **5** Gypsy, Pomak, Tatar **6** Bulgar, Slavic **7** Chuvash **9** Cheremiss **10** Macedonian
of Burkina Faso: 4 Bobo, Lobi, Samo **5** Bella, Bissa, Dyula, Fulbe, Hausa, Mande, Marka, Mossi, Puchl **6** Fulani, Senufo, Tuareg **7** Grunshi, Voltaic, Yatenga **8** Mandingo **9** Gourounsi **15** Bunsansi Gambaga
of Burundi: 3 Twa **4** Hutu **5** Bantu, Batwa, Pygmy, Tutsi **6** Bahutu, Watusi **7** Barundi
of Cambodia: 4 Cham, Thai **5** Khmer **7** Chinese **10** Vietnamese
of Cameroon: 3 Abo, Edo, Ibo **4** Beti, Bulu, Ekoi, Ijaw, Sara **5** Bantu, Bassa, Kirdi, Pygmy, Tikar **6** Bamoun, Donala, Ewondo, Fulani, Ibibio **7** Bakweri **8** Bamileke
of Canada: 6 Canuck, Eskimo, French, Innuit **7** English
of the Canary Islands: 7 Spanish
of Cape Verde: 6 Creole **7** African, mulatto **8** European **10** Portuguese
of Central African Republic: 4 Baya, Sara **5** Banda, Bwaki, Sango **6** Azande, Yakoma **7** Banziri, Mandjia, Nzakara
of Chad: 4 Arab, Daza, Maba, Sara, Teda, Tubu **5** Barma, Hakka, Kroda, Massa **6** Fulani, Kotoko, Toubou, Wadaii **7** Kamadja, Kanembu **8** Moundang
of Chile: 3 Ona **4** Auca, Inca, Onan **6** Arauca, Chango, Yahgan **7** Mapuche, mestizo, Moluche, Pampean, Patagon, Puegian, Ranquel **8** Alikuluf, Picunche, Tsonecan
of China: 3 Han, Yis **4** Huis, Lolo, Miao, Pu-is **5** Hakka, Hoklo, Seres, Sinic **6** Cataia, Chuang, Johnny, Korean, Manchu, Mongol, Serian, Uighun **7** Sinaean, Tibetan
of Colombia: 4 Boro, Cuna, Duit, Hoka, Macu, Muso, Muzo, Paez, Tama, Tapa **5** Carib, Catio, Choco, Cofan, Cogui, Cubeo, Guane, Haida, Mocoa, Paeze, Pijao, Seona, Yagua **6** Arawak, Betoya, Calima, Colima, Ingano, Mirana, Saliva, Tahami, Ticunu, Tucano, Tunebo, Witoto, Yahuna **7** Achagua, Andaqui, Chibcha, Chimila, Churoya, Guahibo, Guajiro, mestizo, mulatto, Panches,

Puinave, Puitoto, Quechua, Shuswap, Tairona, Telembi **8** Coconuco, Guarauno, Motilone, Puinavis, Quimbaya, Sinsigas **9** Cocanucos, Coconucan, Panaquita **10** Bellacoola
of Comoros: 4 Arab **5** Bantu, Malay **7** African **8** Malagasy
of the Congo: 3 Rua **4** Akka, Susa, Teke, Vili **5** Amadi, Bantu, Figot, Kongo, Mantu, Pygmy, Sanga, Warua, Zambi **6** Ababua, Bafyot, Bateke, Mbochi, Nzambi, Wabuma **7** Bacongo, Bakongo, Bangala, Batetla, Manyema **10** Binga Pygmy
of Costa Rica: 4 Voto **6** Boruca, Bribri, Guaymi **7** Guatuso, mestizo, Spanish
of Crete: 6 Cretan, Minoan **7** Candiot **8** Sphakiot **9** Caphtorim **10** Philistine
of Croatia: 4 Serb **5** Croat **8** Yugoslav
of Cuba: 5 Carib, Negro, Taino **6** Arawak **7** Ciboney, mestizo **8** Ciboneye **9** Caucasian
of Czechoslovakia/Czech Republic: 4 Slav **5** Czech **6** Slovak **8** Bohemian, Moravian
of Denmark: 4 Dane, Jute **5** Angle **6** Cimbri, Eskimo, German, Ostmen, Teuton, Viking **12** Scandinavian
of Djibouti: 4 Afar, Arab **5** Issas **6** French **8** European
of Dominican Republic: 5 Negro, Taino **6** Indian **7** mulatto, Spanish **9** Caucasian
of Ecuador: 4 Cara, Cixo, Inca **5** Ardan, Aucas, Macoa, Maina, Palta, Quitu, Yumbo **6** Canelo, Jibaro, Jivaro, Puruha **7** Cayapas, Jivaros, mestizo, mulatto **8** Barbacoa, Colorado, Montuvio, Serranos **10** Montubious
of Egypt: 3 Kem **4** Arab, Copt, Misr, Wafd **5** Gippy, Gyppy, Gypsy, Nilot **6** Ababda, Berber, Hyksos, Nubian, Tasian **7** Mizraim, Pharian **8** Badarian, Bisharin, Memphian
of El Salvador: 5 Lenca, Pipil **6** Indian, Mangue **7** mestizo, Spanish **9** Matagalpa
of England: 4 Celt, Jute, Pict **5** Norse, Saxon **6** Angles, Briton, Norman, Viking
of Equatorial Guinea: 4 Bubi, Fang **5** Benge, Combe **6** Bujeba **10** Fernandino
of Estonia: 4 Esth, Finn **5** Aesti **6** Jewish **8** Estonian **9** Ukrainian **11** Belorussian
of Ethiopia: 4 Afar, Agau, Beja, Doko, Kafa, Kala, Saho, Shoa **5** Afara, Agows, Galas, Galla, Negro, Tigre **6** Abigar, Amhara, Annuak, Gondar, Hamite, Harari, Sidama, Sidamo, Somali, Tigrai, Wolamo **7** Cushite, Danakil, Donakus, Falasha **8** Assamite, Blemmyes **10** Abyssinian, Troglodyte
of Fiji: 6 Fijian, Indian **7** Chinese

10 Melanesian, Polynesian **11** Micronesian

of Finland: 3 Jew, Vod, Vot, Yak **4** Avar, Finn, Hame, Lapp, Turk, Veps **5** Fioun, Gypsy, Ijore, Inger, Suomi, Vepse, Zyrin **6** Magyar, Ostiak, Ostyak, Tarast, Tavast, Ugrian **7** Lappish, Mordvin, Permiak, Samoyed, Uralian **8** Cheremis, Estonian, Karelian, Livonian, Swekoman **9** Tavastian **11** Karjalaiset, Suomalaiset

of France: 5 Frank

of the Gabon Republic: 4 Fang **6** Adouma, Bakota, Bateke, Echira, Okande, Omyene **7** Eshiras **8** Bandjabi, Bapounou

of The Gambia: 4 Fula, Jola **5** Foula, Wolof **6** Fulani **8** Mandingo, Serahuli **9** Seranuleh

of Georgia: 5 Azeri **7** Russian **8** Armenian, Georgian, Ossetian

of Germany: 3 Hun **4** Slav, Sorb, Wend **5** Saxon

of Ghana: 2 Ga **3** Ewe **4** Akan, Akim, Akra, Aksa **5** Ahafo, Brong, Inkra **7** Akwapim, Ashanti, Dagomba, Maprusi **11** Mole-Dagbani

of Gibraltar: 6 Jewish **7** British, Italian, Maltese, Spanish **10** Portuguese

of Greece: 5 Greek **6** Achean, Dorian, Ionian **7** Aeolian, Hellene

of Greenland: 3 Ita **6** Eskimo **8** European

of Grenada: 5 Negro **6** Indian

of Guatemala: 3 Mam **4** Chol, Itza, Ixil, Maya **5** Xinca **6** Caribe, Quiche **7** ladinos, mestizo, Pocomam **13** Guatemaltecos

of Guinea: 4 Koma, Loma, Nalu, Susu, Toma **5** Kissi, Manon **6** Fulani, Guerzi **7** Landoma, Malinke **8** Kouranke, Landuman **11** Kissi-Sherbo **12** Guerze- Kpelle

of Guinea-Bissau: 6 Fulani **7** Balanta, Balante, mulatto **8** Mandingo, Mandyako

of Guyana: 6 Akawai, Arawak, Creole, Taruma **7** African, Chinese, mulatto **10** Portuguese

of Haiti: 5 Taino **7** African, mulatto

of Honduras: 4 Maya, Paya, Sumo, Ulva **5** Carib, Lenoa, Pipil **6** Tauira **7** Jicaque, mestizo, Miskito **8** Mosquito

of Hong Kong: 5 Hakka, Haklo, Punti, Tanka **7** British, Chinese **8** American, Japanese **9** Cantonese **10** Portuguese

of Hungary: 3 Hun **4** Serb **5** Croat, Gypsy **6** Cigany, Magyar, Slovak, Ugrian

of Iceland: 6 Celtic, Viking **8** Norseman **9** Norwegian

of India: 2 Ao **3** Gor **4** Bhil **5** Aryan **6** Badaga, Pathan **7** Sherani **9** Dravidian **10** Andamanese

of Indonesia: 4 Dyak **5** Batak, Dayak, Malay **6** Battak, Papuan, Toraja **7** Chinese, Igorots **8** Acehnese, Achi-

nese, Balinese, Javanese, Madurese, Sudanese **11** Minang Kabau

of Iran: 3 Lur, Tat **4** Arab, Kurd, Turk **5** Medes **6** Galcha, Gilani, Jewish, Shugni **7** Baluchi, Persian **8** Armenian, Bactrian, Bartangi, Parthian, Scythian **9** Bakhtiari **11** Azerbaijani, Mazandarani

of Iraq: 4 Arab, Kurd **7** Bedouin

of Ireland: 4 Celt, Erse, Gael **5** Irish **6** Celtic **9** Hibernian

of Israel: 3 Jew **4** Arab **5** Druze **10** Circassian

of Italy: 5 Latin **6** Sabine **7** Italian, Lombard **8** Etruscan

of Ivory Coast: 3 Abe, Dan, Kru, Kwa **4** Akan, Bete, Dida, Guro, Koua, Lobi, Wobe **5** Abron, Abure, Attie, Baule, Guere, Mande, Mossi **6** Baoule, Lagoon, Senufo, Senufu **7** Kroumen, Malinke, Voltaic **8** Dan-Gouro **10** Anyi-Baoule **11** Lobi-Kulango **12** Agnis-Ashanti

of Jamaica: 7 African, Chinese **10** East Indian

of Japan: 3 Eta **6** Korean **8** Japanese, Okinawan **10** Buramkumin

of Java: 5 Krama, Kromo **6** Kalang **8** Javanese, Madurese, Sudanese

of Jordan: 4 Arab, Kurd **7** Bedouin, Checher **8** Armenian, Assyrian **10** Circassian **11** Palestinian

of Kazakhstan: 6 Kazakh

of Kenya: 3 Luo **4** Arab, Meru **5** Bantu, Elgey, Galla, Kamba, Kisii, Luhya, Masai, Nandi, Tugen **6** Kikuyu, Ogaden, Somali **7** Baluyha, Hamitic, Hilotic, Kipsigi, Swahili, Turkana **8** Kalenjin, Marakwet

of Kiribati: 8 Banabans **10** Polynesian **11** Micronesian

of Korea: 6 Korean

of Kuwait: 4 Arab **5** Iraqi, Saudi **6** Indian **7** Bedouin **8** Egyptian **9** Pakistani **11** Palestinian

of Kyrgyzstan: 5 Uzbek **6** Kyrgyz **7** Kirghiz

of Laos: 2 Lu **3** Kha, Lao, Man, Meo, Tai, Yao, Yun **4** Miao, Thai **5** Hmong **8** Lao Teung **10** Phoutheung

of Latvia: 3 Kur, Liv **4** Balt, Cour, Lett **7** Latgale, Latvian, Russian, Zemgale

of Lebanon: 4 Arab **9** Canaanite **10** Phoenician **11** Palestinian

of Lesotho: 4 Zulu **5** Bantu, Tembu **6** Basuto **7** Basotho

of Liberia: 2 Gi **3** Gio, Kra, Kru, Kwa, Vai, Vei **4** Gola, Kroo, Krou, Loma, Mano, Toma **5** Bassa, Gibbi, Gissi, Grebo **6** Gbande, Kpelle, Kpuesi, Krooby, Kruman **7** Krooboy, Krooman **8** Mandingo **15** Americo-Liberian

of Libya: 4 Arab, Tebu **6** Berber, Tuareg **7** Gaetuli **8** Getulans, Harratin

of Liechtenstein: 8 Alamanni, Ale-

manni

of Lithuania: 4 Balt, Lett, Pole **5** Zhmud **6** Jewish, Litvak **7** Aistian, Russian, Yatvyag **10** Lithuanian, Samogitian **11** Belorussian

of Luxembourg: 6 French, German **12** Luxembourger

of Macao: 6 Macaon **7** Chinese **10** Portuguese

of Macedonia: 4 Turk **8** Albanian **10** Macedonian

of Madagascar: 4 Arab, Bara, Hova **5** Malay **6** Merina, Tanala **7** African **8** Betsileo, Mahafaly, Malagasy, Sakalava **9** Antaimoro, Antaisaka, Antandroy, Tsimihety **10** Indonesian, Polynesian **13** Betsimisaraka

of Malawi: 3 Yao **4** Sena **5** Bantu, Lomwe, Ngoni **6** Cheiva, Maravi, Ngonde, Nyanja **7** Tumbuka

of Malaysia: 4 Iban **5** Dayak, Malay **6** Indian **7** Chinese, Kadazan **9** Pakistani, Sri Lankan **10** Bangladesh, Indonesian

of Maldives: 4 Arab **6** Indian **9** Sinhalese **10** Singhalese

of Mali: 3 Bwa **4** Fula, Kyan, Moor, Peul **5** Dogon, Dyula, Fulbe, Marka **6** Berber, Dognon, Fulani, Senufo, Tuareg **7** Bembara, Fellata, Malinke, Miniaka, Songhai, Soninke **8** Khasonke, Mandingo, Senoulfo

of Malta: 7 Maltese

of Mauritania: 4 Arab, Fula, Moor **5** Black, Fulbe, Wolof **6** Bafour, Berber, Fulani **7** African, Soninke, Tukulor **8** Sarakole **9** Sarakolle **10** Toucouleur **12** Halphoolaren

of Mauritius: 6 Creole, French, Indian **7** African, Chinese **8** European **13** Indo-Mauritian

of Mexico: 3 Ixe, Mam, Mie, Ser **4** Chol, Cora, Jova, Meco, Mixe, Pame, Pima, Roto, Seri, Teca, Teco, Texo, Xova **5** Aztec, Chizo, Chora, Mayan, Nahua, Opata, Otomi, Zoque **6** Eudeve, Indian, Mixtec, Pueblo, Toltec, Zotzil **7** Chincha, mestizo, Nahuatl, Nayarit, Spanish, Tehueco, Tepanec, Totonac, Zacatec, Zapotec **8** Lagunero, Mazateca, Tezcucan, Totonaco, Tzapotec, Yucateco, Zacateco, Zapoteca **9** Tlascalan **10** Coahuiltec, Cuitlateco, Tarahumara

of Moldova: 7 Gagauzi **8** Moldovan **9** Moldovian

of Monaco: 6 French **7** Italian **10** Monegasque

of Mongolia: 5 Oirat, Tungu **6** Buryat, Darbet, Khoton, Mongol **7** Kazakhs, Khalkha **8** Tuvinian **9** Dariganga

of Montenegro: 4 Serb, Slav **11** Montenegrin

of Morocco: 4 Arab, Moor **6** Berber, French **7** Spanish

of Mozambique: 3 Yao **5** Bantu, Chopi, Lomue, Lomwe, Macua,

Makua, Ngoni, Nguni, Shona **6** Maravi, Thouga **7** Maconde, Makonde **10** Portuguese

of Myanmar: 4 Shan **7** Burmese, Siamese

of Namibia: 4 Nama **5** Bantu **6** Damara, Herero, Ovambo, Tswara **7** Bushman, Colored **8** Okavango **9** Hottentot

of Nauru: 7 Chinese **10** Melanesian, Polynesian **11** Micronesian

of Nepal: 3 Rai **4** Aoul **5** Limbu, Magar, Murmi, Newar, Tharu **6** Gurkha, Gurung, Nepali, Sherpa, Tamang **7** Bhutias, Kiranti **8** Gorkhali, Nepalese

of the Netherlands: 5 Dutch **7** Frisian **9** Hollander **10** Surinamese **12** Netherlander **13** South Moluccan

of New Guinea: 5 Pygmy **6** Papuan **7** Negrito **10** Melanesian

of New Zealand: 3 Ati **5** Arawa, Dutch, Maori **7** British, Ringatu **10** Polynesian

of Nicaragua: 4 Mico, Mixe, Rama, Smoo, Ulva **5** Cukra, Diria, Lenca, Sambo, Toaca **6** Mangue **7** mestizo, Miskito **8** Mosquito **9** Matagalpa

of Niger: 4 Daza, Idjo, Idyo, Idzo, Peul, Teda **5** Hausa, Warri **6** Djerma, Fulani, Kanuri, Songha, Toubou, Tuareg **13** Djerma-Songhai

of Nigeria: 3 Abo, Aro, Djo, Ebo, Edo, Ibo, Ijo, Tiv, Vai **4** Beni, Bini, Eboe, Efik, Egba, Ejam, Ekoi, Idyo, Igbo, Ijaw, Nupe **5** Angas, Benin, Gwari, Hausa **6** Chamba, Fulani, Ibibio, Kanuri, Yoruba **11** Hausa-Fulani

of Norway: 4 Lapp **5** Samme **6** Nordic, Viking

of Oman: 4 Arab

of Pakistan: 5 Sindi, Wazir **6** Afridi, Bengal, Mahsud, Pathan, Puktun, Sindhi **7** Baluchi, Brahuis, Punjabi, Pushtun, Sherani **8** Khattack, Shinwari, Yusefazi **11** Mohammedzai

of Panama: 4 Cuna **5** Choco **6** Guaymi **7** mestizo

of Qatar: 4 Arab **6** Pushtu, Yemeni **7** Baluchi, Iranian **9** Pakistani

of Romania: 6 Dacian **8** Romanian, Rumanian

of Russia: 4 Slav **5** Kulak **6** Jewish, Soviet, Velika **7** Chukchi, Latvian, Russian, Turkmen **8** Armenian, Estonian, Georgian, Siberian, Ukrainian **10** Lithuanian **11** Belorussian

of Rwanda: 3 Twa **4** Hutu **5** Batwa, Pygmy, Tutsi **6** Bahutu, Watusi **7** Batutsi

of Samoa: 6 Samoan **10** Polynesian

of San Marino: 7 Italian **11** San Marinese

of Sao Tome and Principe: 7 African **10** Portuguese **11** Cape Verdean

of Saudi Arabia: 4 Arab **7** Bedouin

of Scotland: 4 Gael, Pict, Scot **5** Norse

of Senegal: 4 Lebu, Peul, Soce

5 Diola, Dyola, Foula, Laobe, Peulh, Serer, Wolof **6** Fulani, Serere **7** Bambara, Malinke, Tukuler, Tukulor **8** Mandingo

of Seychelles: 5 Asian **6** Creole, French, Indian **7** African, Chinese

of Sicily: 5 Elymi, Sican, Sicel **6** Sicani, Siculi

of Sierra Leone: 3 Vai **4** Kono, Loko, Susu **5** Bulom, Kissi, Limba, Mande, Mendi, Temne **6** Creole, Fulani, Syrian **7** Gallina, Koranko, Kuranko, Sherbro, Yalunka **8** Lebanese, Mandingo

of Sikkim: 4 Rong **5** Bhote **6** Bhotia, Bhutia, Indian, Lepcha **7** Tibetan **8** Nepalese **9** Mongoloid

of Singapore: 5 Malay **6** Indian **7** Chinese **9** Malaysian, Pakistani, Sri Lankan

of Slovakia: 5 Czech **6** Slavic, Slovak **9** Hungarian

of Slovenia: 7 Slovene

of the Solomon Islands: 7 Chinese **8** European **10** Melanesian, Polynesian

of Somalia: 3 Sab **4** Asha **5** Galla **6** Hawiya, Isbaak, Somali **7** Danakil, Hamitic, Marehan, Samaale, Shuhali **8** Rahanwin

of South Africa: 4 Boer, Yosa, Zulu **5** Asian, Bantu, Namas, Nguni, Pondo, Sotho, Swazi, Tembu, Venda **6** Damara, Kaffir **7** African, British, Bushmen, English, Swahili **8** Bechuana, Coloured, Khoikhoi, San Xhosa **9** Afrikaner, Hottentot

of Spain: 4 Pict **5** Diego, Gente, Latin **6** Basque, Espana **7** Catalan, Espanol, Iberian **8** Galician, Gallegos, Maragato

of Sri Lanka: 5 Malay, Tamil, Vedda **6** Veddah, Weddah **7** Burgher, Mahinda, Malabar **8** Eurasian **9** Cingalese, Dravidian, Sinhalese **10** Ginghalese **12** Bandaranaike

of the Sudan: 3 Bor, Dor, Fur **4** Arab, Bari, Beri, Bobo, Daza, Egba, Fula, Golo, Nuba, Nuer, Poul, Sere **5** Anuak, Bongo, Dinka, Fulah, Hausa, Joluo, Junje, Mosgu, Mossi, Negro, Tibbu, Volta **6** Acholi, Azande, Gurusi, Hamite, Lotuho, Makari, Nilote, Nubian, Senufo, Surhai, Taureg **7** Balante, Baqqara, Gubayna, Jaaliin, Nilotes, Shilluk, Songhai, Songhay, Songhoi, Sourhai **8** Kababish, Mandingo, Menkiera **9** Sarakille **10** Gurmantshi, Shaiquiyya

of Suriname: 4 Boni, Bush, Trio **5** Djuka, Dutch **6** Creole, Wayana **7** African, Chinese **10** Amerindian, Boschneger, West Indian **11** Asian Indian

of Swaziland: 5 Asian, Bantu, Swazi **10** Eurafrican

of Sweden: 4 Lapp **5** Norse, Swede **6** Viking

of Switzerland: 5 Swiss, **6** Franks

8 Alamanni, Alemanni, Italians **12** Rhaeto-Romans

of Syria: 4 Arab, Kurd, Turk **5** Alawi, Aptal, Druse, Druze **6** Afshar, Aissor, Aushar, Avshar, Awshar **7** Amorite, Ansarie, Bedouin, Nosaris, Saracen, Shemite **8** Ansarieh, Armenian **9** Ansariyah **10** Circassian **12** Khachaturian

of Taiwan: 4 Yami **5** Hakka, Hoklo **7** Chinese, Malayan **9** Fukienese, Taiwanese **10** Indonesian, Polynesian **12** Kwangtungese

of Tajikistan: 5 Tajik, Uzbek **7** Tadzhik

of Tanzania: 2 Ha **4** Arab, Gogo, Goma, Haya, Hehe **5** Asian, Bantu, Masai **6** Arusha, Chagga, Sukuma, Wagogo, Wagoma **7** African, Makonde, Sambara, Sandawe, Shirazi, Swahili, Wabunga, Zongora **8** Nyakyusa, Nyamwezi

of Thailand: 3 Lao, Mon **4** Lawa, Shan, Thai **5** Malay **6** Indian, Khymer **7** Chinese, Siamese **9** Cambodian **10** Vietnamese

of Tibet: 4 Asian, Balti, Bodpa, Drupa **6** Bhotia, Champa, Drokpa, Khamba, Khambu, Mongol, Panaka, Sherpa, Tangut **7** Bhotiya, Bhutani, Gyarung, Taghlik, Tibetan

of Togo: 3 Ana, Ewe, Twi **4** Mina **5** Hausa **6** Akposa, Kabrai **7** Bassari, Cabrais, Kabrais, Ouatchi **8** Konkomba, Kotokoli, Lotokoli

of Tongo: 10 Polynesian

of Trinidad and Tobago: 5 Irish **6** French, Indian, Syrian **7** African, Chinese, English, Spanish **8** European, Lebanese **10** East Indian, Portuguese, Venezuelan **11** Asian Indian **13** Latin American

of Tunisia: 4 Arab **6** Berber, Jewish

of Turkey: 4 Arab, Kurd, Turk **6** Seljuk

of Turkmenistan: 7 Turkmen **10** Turkmenian

of Tuvalu: 6 Samoan **10** Polynesian

of Uganda: 4 Alur, Gisu, Soga, Teso **5** Ateso, Bantu, Chiga, Ganda, Langi, Lango, Nkole, Pygmy **6** Acholi, Ankole, Bagisu, Bakega, Basoga, Batoro **7** Baganda, Banyoro, Bunyoro, Hamitic, Lugbara, Nilotic, Sudanic **9** Nyoro-Toro **10** Banyankole, Karamojong

of Ukraine: 7 Russian **9** Ukrainian

of United Arab Emirates: 4 Arab **6** Indian **7** African, Iranian **9** Pakistani **10** South Asian

of Uruguay: 4 Yaro **5** Swiss **6** Indian **7** Italian, mestizo, Russian, Spanish **8** Charrusa

of Uzbekistan: 5 Uzbek

of Vanuatu: 8 European **10** Melanesian, Polynesian **11** Micronesian

of Venezuela: 4 Bare, Pume **5** Bello, Carib, pardo, zambo **6** Arawak,

Creole, Timote **7** Charoya, Guahibo, Kaliana, mestizo, mulatto, Otomaca, Timotex **8** Caquetio, Guarauno, Matilone **11** Maquiritare

of Vietnam: 3 Hoa, Man, Meo, Tai, Tay **4** Cham, Kinh, Nung, Thai **5** Khmer, Malay, Muong **7** Chinese **8** Annamese, Annamite **9** Cambodian **10** montagnard, Vietnamese

of Wales: 4 Celt, Kelt **5** Cymry, Kymry, Welsh **7** Brython, Silures, Taffies **8** Awabokal, Cambrian **9** Siluridan

of Western Sahara: 4 Arab **6** Berber

of Western Samoa: 6 Samoan **10** Melanesian, Polynesian

of Yemen: 4 Arab **5** Zaidi **6** Shafai, Yemeni **8** Yemenite

of Yugoslavia: 4 Serb, Slav **5** Croat **7** Bosnian, Slovene **8** Albanian, Croatian **9** Hungarian **10** Macedonian **11** Montenegrin **13** Herzegovinian

of Zaire: 4 Kuba, Luba, Yaka **5** Bantu, Bashi, Bemba, Kongo, Lulue, Lunda, Mongo, Pygmy **6** Azande, Baluba, Watusi **7** Bakongo, Nilotes, Tshokwe **8** European, Mangbetu, Sudanese

of Zambia: 4 Lozi **5** Bantu, Bemba, Ngoni, Tonga

of Zimbabwe: 3 Ila **4** Sena **5** Asian, Bantu, Bemba, Sotho, Tongo, white **6** Indian **7** Barotse, Chinese, English, Mashoma, Mashona, Ndebele **8** Coloured, Japanese, Matabele **9** Afrikaner **10** Balakwakwa

etiquette 5 usage **7** decorum, manners **8** behavior, courtesy, good form, protocol **9** amenities, gentility, good taste **10** civilities, politeness **11** conventions, proprieties **15** rules of behavior

etoile 4 star **9** ballerina

Etruscan
native of: (ancient) **7** Etruria
location: 7 Tuscany
king: 7 Tarquin **11** Lars Porsena

Ettarre
character in: 16 Arthurian romance

ET The Extra-Terrestrial
director: 15 Steven Spielberg
cast: 10 Dee Wallace **11** Henry Thomas, Peter Coyote **13** Drew Barrymore **17** Robert MacNaughton

et tu, Brute 13 and thou Brutus
spoken by: 12 Julius Caesar

etymology 7 history **10** derivation

Etzel
origin: 8 Germanic
mentioned in: 14 Nibelungenlied
represents: 6 Attila
wife: 9 Kriemhild

Eucharist 8 viaticum **9** Communion, sacrament **13** Holy Communion

euchre
number of players: 3 two **4** four **5** three
derived from: 8 triomphe

five tricks won: 5 march
jack of trump: 10 right bower
second highest trump: 9 left bower

Euclid
field: 11 mathematics
nationality: 5 Greek
founder of: 8 geometry
author of: 8 Elements

Eugene Onegin
author: 16 Alexander Pushkin
opera by: 11 Tchaikovsky
character: 4 Olga **6** Lensky, Onegin **7** Tatyana **12** Prince Gremin, Tatyana Larin **14** Vladimir Lensky

Eugenie Grandet
author: 14 Honore de Balzac
character: 5 Nanon **7** Charles, Eugenie **11** Mme d'Aubrion

Euhelopus
type: 8 dinosaur, sauropod
period: 10 Cretaceous

Euler, Leonhard
field: 7 physics **11** mathematics
nationality: 5 Swiss
first: 12 calculus book

eulogize 4 hail, laud, tout **5** boost, exalt, extol **7** acclaim, commend, glorify, magnify **9** celebrate **10** compliment, panegyrize **12** pay tribute to, praise highly

eulogy 5 paean **6** homage **7** hosanna, plaudit, tribute **8** citation, encomium **9** laudation, panegyric **10** high praise **11** acclamation

Eumenides
author: 9 Aeschylus
character: 6 Apollo, Athene, Furies **7** Orestes
see **6** Furies

Eunice
son: 7 Timothy

Eunomia
member of: 5 Horae
personifies: 5 order

Eunuch 6 Biztha, Careas, Zethar **7** Abagtha, Harbona, Mehuman **8** castrato

Eunuch, The
author: 7 Terence

euphemism 11 prudishness, refined term **12** delicate term, overdelicacy **13** prudish phrase **14** mild expression, overrefinement

euphoria 7 ecstasy, elation, rapture **9** well-being

Euphrosyne
member of: 6 Graces

Euphues
character in: 20 Euphues and His England **22** Euphues The Anatomy of Wit
author: 4 Lyly

Euripides
author of: 3 Ion **5** Medea **6** Hecuba **7** Electra, Orestes **8** Alcestis, Heracles **10** Andromache, Heraclidae,

Hippolytus, Phoenissae, The Bacchae **13** The Suppliants **14** The Trojan Women **16** Iphigenia in Aulis **17** Iphigenia in Tauris **21** The Children of Heracles

Europa
also: 6 Europe
father: 6 Agenor
mother: 10 Telephassa
brother: 5 Cilix **6** Cadmus **7** Phoenix
son: 5 Minos **8** Sarpedon **12** Rhadamanthus
daughter: 5 Crete
abducted by: 4 Zeus

Europe *see* **6** Europa

Europe
country: 5 Italy, Malta, Spain, Wales **6** France, Greece, Latvia, Monaco, Norway, Poland, Russia, Sweden **7** Albania, Andorra, Armenia, Austria, Belarus, Belgium, Croatia, Denmark, England, Estonia, Georgia, Germany, Hungary, Iceland, Ireland, Romania, Ukraine **8** Bulgaria, Portugal, Scotland, Slovakia, Slovenia **9** Lithuania, Macedonia, San Marino **10** Azerbaijan, Luxembourg, Yugoslavia **11** Byelorussia, Netherlands, Switzerland, Vatican City **13** Czech Republic, Liechtenstein **14** Czechoslovakia **17** Bosnia Herzegovina

city: 4 Bern, Bonn, Oslo, Rome **5** Paris, Sofia, Vaduz **6** Athens, Dublin, Lisbon, London, Madrid, Monaco, Moscow, Prague, Tirana, Vienna, Warsaw **7** Cardiff **8** Belgrade, Brussels, Budapest, Helsinki, Valletta **9** Amsterdam, Bucharest, Edinburgh, Reykjavik, San Marino, Stockholm **10** Bratislava, Copenhagen, Luxembourg **14** Andorra la Vella

river: 3 Don **4** Ebro, Elbe, Oder **5** Loire, Neman, Rhine, Rhone, Seine, Tagus, Volga **6** Danube, Thames **7** Dnieper, Pechora, Vistula **8** Dniester

island: 3 Man **4** Skye **5** Crete, Malta **6** Faeroe, Sicily **7** Corsica, Iceland, Ireland **8** Balearic, Sardinia **12** British Isles

mountain/mountain range: 4 Alps **7** Balkans **8** Caucasus, Pyrenees **9** Apennines **11** Carpathians **12** Sierra Nevada

highest point: 11 Mount Elbrus
lowest point: 10 Caspian Sea
sea: 4 Aral, Azov, Kara **5** Black, North, White **6** Aegean, Baltic **7** Caspian, Marmara **8** Adriatic **13** Mediterranean

people: 3 Hun **4** Gael, Pict, Serb **5** Celts, Croat, Danes, Dutch, Jutes, Kymry, Marur, Poles, Scots, Slavs, Tatar, Welsh **6** Czechs, Franks **7** Basques, Britons, Gypsies, Iberian, Magyars, Slovaks, Slovene **8** Alamanni, Cossacks, Tyrolean, Walloons

language: 5 Czech, Irish **6** Basque, Danish, French, Gaelic, German, Polish, Slovak **7** English, Italian, Romance, Russian, Spanish, Swedish **8** Germanic **9** Bulgarian, Portugese **11** Balto-slavic

religion: **5** Islam **6** Jewish, Muslim **8** Anglican, Lutheran **9** Methodist **10** Protestant **12** Presbyterian **13** Dutch Reformed, Greek Orthodox, Roman Catholic **15** Church of England, Eastern Orthodox

holiday: **11** Bastille Day, National Day **12** Guy Fawkes Day **13** Liberation Day, St Patricks Day **14** Queens Birthday **15** Independence Day **19** Heroes of the Republic

Eurus
origin: **5** Greek
personifies: **8** east wind **13** southeast wind

Euryale
member of: **7** Gorgons

Euryanthe
opera by: **5** Weber
character: **6** Adolar **7** Lysiart **9** Eglantine

Euryclea
nurse of: **10** Telemachus

Eurydamas
member of: **9** Argonauts

Eurydice
also: **7** Agriope
form: **5** dryad
husband: **7** Orpheus
daughter: **8** Themiste
pursued by: **9** Aristaeus

Eurynome
father: **7** Oceanus
mother: **6** Tethys
sister: **6** Thetis
daughters: **6** Graces

Eurysthenes
origin: **7** Spartan
father: **11** Aristodemus
twin brother: **7** Procles
shared: **6** throne
shared throne with: **7** Procles

Eurystheus
king of: **6** Tiryns **7** Mycenae
father: **9** Sthenelus
mother: **7** Nicippe
cousin: **8** Hercules
son: **9** Perimedes
imposed: **6** labors
number of labors: **6** twelve
imposed on: **8** Hercules

Euterpe
member of: **5** Muses
muse of: **5** music **11** lyric poetry

evacuate 4 quit **5** leave **6** desert, remove, vacate **7** abandon, forsake, move out, take out **8** order out **12** withdraw from

evade 4 duck, shun **5** avoid, dodge, elude, hedge, parry **6** escape, eschew **7** fend off **8** sidestep **10** circumvent, equivocate **12** steer clear of

evaluate 4 rate **5** assay, gauge, judge,

value, weigh **6** assess, size up **8** appraise, estimate

evaluation 4 test **8** analysis, judgment **9** appraisal **10** assessment, estimation

evaluator 5 judge **6** critic, tester **7** analyst, arbiter **8** assessor, reviewer **9** appraiser, estimator

evanesce 6 vanish **8** fade away, pass away **9** disappear, dissipate, evaporate

evanescence 9 vanishing **10** fading away **12** ephemerality **13** disappearance **14** transitoriness

evanescent 8 fleeting **9** ephemeral, transient **10** short- lived, transitory

evangel 6 gospel

Evangeline
author: **24** Henry Wadsworth Longfellow
character: **17** Gabriel Lajeunesse **23** Evangeline Bellefontaine

evangelist 4 John, Luke, Mark **7** apostle, Matthew **8** disciple, minister, preacher, reformer **9** apostolic, missioner, soul-saver **10** missionary, revivalist **12** Bible Thumper, propagandist, proselytizer **17** religious crusader

Evan Harrington
author: **14** George Meredith
character: **6** Louisa **10** Jack Raikes **11** Rose Jocelyn **12** Tom Cogglesby **13** Count de Saldar, Juliana Bonner **14** Caroline Strike **15** Andrew Cogglesby, Ferdinand Laxley, Melville Jocelyn **16** Countess de Saldar, Harriet Cogglesby **21** Melchisedek Harrington

Evans, Dame Edith
born: **6** London **7** England
roles: **8** Tom Jones **11** A Doll's House **13** The Whisperers **14** The Chalk Garden **27** The Importance of Being Earnest

Evans, Mary Anne
real name of: **11** George Eliot

Evans, Maurice
born: **6** Dorset **7** England **10** Dorchester
roles: **9** Saint Joan **13** Rosemary's Baby **14** Man and Superman, Romeo and Juliet **15** Heartbreak House, Planet of the Apes **17** The Devil's Disciple **18** Gilbert and Sullivan **19** Androcles and the Lion

evaporate 5 dry up **6** dispel, vanish **7** scatter **8** dissolve, evanesce, fade away, melt away, vaporize **9** dehydrate, desiccate, disappear, dissipate

evasion 7 dodging, ducking, eluding **8** shunning **9** avoidance **12** sidestepping **13** circumventing, shrinking from **15** attempt to escape

evasive 6 shifty **7** devious, dodging, elusive, elusory, hedging **9** ambiguous, deceitful, deceptive, equivocal **10** misleading **11** dissembling **12** equivocating

Eva Trout
author: **14** Elizabeth Bowen

eve 4 dusk **6** female, sunset **7** evening, sunset **8** eventide **9** day before

Eve
husband: **4** Adam
son: **4** Abel, Cain, Seth
home: **4** Eden

Evelina
author: **11** Fanny Burney

even 4 calm, fair, flat, just, true **5** equal, flush, level, plane, plumb **6** placid, smooth, square, steady **7** balance, equable, flatten, regular, the same, uniform **8** balanced, constant, equalize, matching, parallel, straight, unbiased **9** equitable, identical, impartial, make flush, unruffled, unvarying **10** straighten, unwavering **11** make uniform, unexcitable **12** even-tempered, make parallel **13** dispassionate

evening 3 e'en, eve **4** dusk, even **6** sunset **7** day's end, sundown **8** eventide, gloaming, twilight **9** nightfall **10** close of day

evenly matched 5 equal **8** of a piece **9** identical **10** well suited **13** one and the same

evenness 7 balance **8** calmness, equality, fairness, flatness, sameness **9** placidity **10** regularity, smoothness, steadiness, uniformity **11** equivalency

event 4 bout, game **7** contest, episode **8** incident, occasion **9** happening, milestone **10** experience, occurrence, tournament **11** competition

even-tempered 4 calm **6** serene **7** equable, patient **11** good-natured, unflappable **12** mild-tempered, well-adjusted

eventful 7 crucial, epochal, fateful, notable, weighty **8** critical, exciting, historic **9** important, memorable, momentous, thrilling **10** noteworthy **11** significant **13** consequential, unforgettable

eventide 4 dusk **6** sunset **7** evening, sundown **8** gloaming, twilight **9** nightfall

eventual 5 final, later **6** coming, future **7** ensuing **8** imminent, ultimate, upcoming **9** following, impending, resulting **10** consequent, subsequent **11** prospective

eventually 6 one day **7** finally **8** in the end, sometime **10** ultimately **12** in the long run **13** sooner or later **17** in the course of time **20** when all is said and done

even up 3 tie **5** align **8** make even **10** straighten

Eve of St Agnes, The
author: **9** John Keats

ever 5 at all **6** always **7** forever **9** at any time, eternally, in any case **10** at all times, constantly **11** incessantly, perpetually **12** continuously

Everdene, Bathsheba
 character in: **22** Far From the Madding Crowd
 author: **5** Hardy

Everglade State
 nickname of: **7** Florida

evergreen 3 fir, yew **4** pine **5** heath, holly **6** jujube, laurel, myrtle, needle, privet **7** arbutus, casiope, conifer, jasmine, juniper **8** camellia, hawthorn, oleander, rosemary **9** mistletoe, sugarbush **11** conebearing **12** rhododendrum

Evergreen State
 nickname of: **10** Washington

everlasting 7 durable, endless, eternal, lasting, tedious, undying **8** constant, immortal, infinite, timeless, tiresome **9** ceaseless, continual, incessant, perpetual, unceasing, wearisome **10** continuous, ever-living **11** long-lasting, never-ending **12** imperishable, interminable **14** indestructible

evermore 6 always **7** forever **9** eternally **10** for all time **13** everlastingly

ever upward
 Latin: **9** excelsior
 motto of: **7** New York (state)

everybody
 French: **11** tout le monde

everyday 4 dull **5** daily, stock, trite, usual **6** common, square **7** mundane, regular, routine **8** familiar, ordinary, workaday **9** customary, hackneyed, quotidian **11** commonplace, day after day, established, stereotyped **12** conventional, run-of-the-mill **13** unimaginative

Everyman
 author: **7** unknown
 character: **3** God **5** Death, Goods **6** Beauty **7** Kindred **8** Strength **9** Good Deeds, Knowledge, Messenger **10** Fellowship

every man for himself
 French: **12** sauve qui peut

Every Man in His Humour
 author: **9** Ben Jonson
 character: **6** Kitely **7** Bridget **8** Bobadill, Wellbred **9** Brainworm, Downright **13** Edward Knowell **14** Justice Clement

Every Man out of His Humour
 author: **9** Ben Jonson
 character: **6** Deliro **7** Fungoso, Sordido **9** Macilente, Sogliardo **10** Puntarvolo **12** Carlo Buffone **15** Fastidious Brisk

everyone
 French: **11** tout le monde

everywhere 7 all over **10** every place, far and near, far and wide, throughout **11** extensively, in all places, uni-

versally **12** the world over, ubiquitously **14** to the four winds

evict 4 oust **5** eject, expel **6** remove **7** kick out, turn out **8** dislodge, get rid of, throw out **10** dispossess

evidence 4 fact, sign **5** proof, token **7** exhibit, grounds **9** testimony **10** indication **11** affirmation **12** confirmation, illustration **13** corroboration, documentation, material proof **14** authentication, substantiation **15** exemplification

evident 5 clear, plain **6** patent **7** certain, obvious, visible **8** apparent, manifest, tangible **10** noticeable, undeniable **11** conspicuous, perceptible **12** demonstrable, unmistakable **14** unquestionable **24** plain as the nose on your face

evidently 7 clearly, plainly **9** assumedly, certainly, doubtless, obviously **10** apparently, undeniably **11** doubtlessly **12** unmistakably **14** unquestionably **16** to all appearances

evil 3 bad, sin **4** base, vice, vile **5** venal **6** sinful, wicked **7** heinous, immoral, vicious **8** baseness, iniquity, sinister **9** depravity, malicious, malignant, nefarious, turpitude **10** corruption, immorality, iniquitous, malevolent, pernicious, villainous, wickedness, wrongdoing **12** black-hearted, unprincipled, unscrupulous
 goddess of: **7** Sekhmet

evildoer 6 sinner **7** culprit, villain **9** miscreant, wrongdoer **10** malefactor **12** transgressor

evil-minded 4 base **5** nasty **6** wicked **7** ignoble, immoral **8** depraved **10** despicable, iniquitous, villainous **12** dishonorable, unprincipled

evilness 6 malice **7** cruelty **8** villainy **9** barbarity, malignity **10** sinfulness, wickedness

evince 4 show **6** convey, reveal **7** display, exhibit, express **11** communicate, demonstrate **12** give evidence

Evius *see* **7** Bacchus

Evnissyen
 origin: **5** Welsh
 brother: **4** Bran **10** Manawyddan
 sister: **7** Branwen
 caused: **3** war
  between: **5** Irish **7** British
 killed: **6** nephew

evoke 4 stir **5** rouse, waken **6** arouse, awaken, call up, elicit, excite, induce, invite, invoke, summon **7** produce, provoke, suggest **9** call forth, conjure up, stimulate **10** bring forth

evolution 4 rise **6** change, growth **8** fruition, increase **9** expansion, unfolding **10** maturation **11** development, enlargement, progression **13** metamorphosis
 founder of theory: **13** Charles Darwin

forerunner of theory: 12 Charles Lyell **18** Chevalier de Lamarck

evolve 4 grow **5** ripen **6** expand, mature, unfold, unroll **7** develop, enlarge **8** increase

Ewell, Tom
 real name: **14** Yewell Tompkins
 born: **11** Owensboro KY
 roles: **8** Adam's Rib **9** State Fair **14** The Great Gatsby **16** Tender Is the Night, The Seven Year Itch

ewer 3 jug, urn **5** basin **6** vessel **7** pitcher

Ewing, Patrick
 sport: **10** basketball
 team: **13** New York Knicks **15** Georgetown Hoyas

exacerbate 3 irk **5** anger **6** deepen, worsen **7** inflame, magnify, provoke, sharpen **8** heighten, increase, irritate **9** aggravate, intensify **10** exaggerate **12** fan the flames **16** pour oil on the fire **17** add insult to injury **18** add fuel to the flames **19** rub salt into the wound

exact 4 take, true **5** claim, force, mulct, right, wrest **6** compel, demand, extort, strict **7** careful, correct, extract, literal, precise, require, squeeze **8** accurate, clear-cut, exacting, explicit, specific **9** on the head, on the nose **10** methodical, meticulous, scrupulous, systematic **11** painstaking, punctilious, to the letter, unequivocal

exacting 4 hard **5** harsh, rigid, stern, tough **6** severe, strict, trying **7** arduous **8** critical **9** demanding, difficult, hard-nosed, strenuous, unbending, unsparing **10** hard-headed, meticulous, no-nonsense

exactly 4 just **5** fully, quite, truly **6** indeed, just so, wholly **7** quite so **8** entirely, of course, strictly **9** assuredly, certainly, correctly, literally, precisely **10** absolutely, accurately, definitely, explicitly, that's right **12** specifically

exactness 8 accuracy **9** precision **10** exactitude **12** accurateness

exact satisfaction 6 avenge, punish **7** get back, get even, revenge **9** retaliate **14** get one's own back

exaggerate 5 boast **6** overdo **7** amplify, lay it on, magnify, stretch **9** embellish, embroider, enlarge on, overstate **11** hyperbolize

exaggerated 7 extreme, intense **10** inordinate, overstated **14** overemphasized

exalt 4 laud **5** cheer, elate, extol, honor **6** praise, uplift **7** acclaim, applaud, commend, elevate, ennoble, glorify, inspire, magnify, worship **8** venerate **9** celebrate, stimulate **10** exhilarate, make much of **12** pay tribute to

exaltation 4 high **5** bliss, glory, honor **6** praise **7** dignity, ecstasy, elation, rapture, tribute, worship **8** grandeur, nobility, praising **9** happiness, panegyric, transport **10** eulogizing, exultation, veneration **11** celebration, deification **12** exhilaration

exalted 2 up **5** grand, happy, lofty, noble **6** august, elated, lordly **7** excited, notable **8** blissful, ecstatic, elevated, glorious, inspired, uplifted **9** dignified, honorable, rapturous, venerable **10** heightened **11** high-ranking, illustrious, magnificent

exaltedness 5 bliss **6** height **7** ecstasy, elation, heights, rapture **8** highness, nobility **9** elevation, loftiness, transport

examination 4 exam, quiz, test **5** assay, audit, final, orals, probe, study **6** review, survey **7** midterm, perusal **8** analysis, scrutiny **10** inspection **11** looking over **13** investigation **15** physical checkup

examine 4 pump, quiz, scan, test, view **5** audit, grill, probe, query, study **6** peruse, ponder, review, survey **7** explore, inspect, observe **8** consider, look into, look over, question **10** scrutinize **11** inquire into, interrogate, investigate, take stock of

examiner 6 tester **8** inquirer, reviewer, surveyor **12** interrogator, investigator

example 5 ideal, model **6** sample **7** paragon, pattern **8** exemplar, specimen, standard **9** archetype, prototype **11** case in point **12** illustration **14** representation **15** exemplification

exasperate 3 bug, irk, vex **4** rile **5** anger, annoy, chafe, pique **6** bother, enrage, harass, madden, offend, rankle, ruffle **7** incense, provoke, turn off **8** irritate **9** aggravate, infuriate **15** try one's patience

exasperating 7 irksome **8** annoying **9** vexatious **10** irritating **11** infuriating

Excalibur 5 sword
  drawn from: 5 stone
    by: 6 Arthur
  given by: 5 Nimue **7** Viviane **13** Lady of the Lake

ex cathedra 12 from the chair **13** with authority **22** from the seat of authority

excavate 3 dig **4** mine **5** dig up, gouge **6** burrow, cut out, dig out, furrow, groove, quarry, tunnel **7** uncover, unearth **8** scoop out **9** hollow out **11** make a hole in

excavation 3 dig, pit **4** hole, mine, sump **5** ditch, grave, shaft, space **6** cavity, dugout, trench, trough **7** digging, opening

exceed 4 pass **5** excel **6** go over, outrun, overdo **7** outpace, outrank, surpass **8** go beyond, outreach, outrival, outstrip, surmount **9** come first, overshoot, transcend **10** be superior **11** predominate

exceedingly 4 very **6** vastly **7** greatly, notably **9** amazingly, eminently, extremely, supremely, unusually **10** enormously, especially, unwontedly, very highly **11** excessively **12** immeasurably, impressively, inordinately, preeminently, surpassingly **13** astonishingly, outstandingly, superlatively **15** extraordinarily

excel 5 outdo **6** exceed **7** prevail, surpass **8** outrival, outstrip **9** rank first **10** tower above **11** predominate, take the cake **20** walk off with the honors

excellence 5 merit **7** quality **8** eminence **9** greatness **10** perfection **11** distinction, high quality, preeminence, superiority **13** transcendence

excellent 4 aces, A-one, fine, tops **5** great, nifty, prime, super, swell **6** bang-up, choice, grade A, superb **7** capital, classic, notable **8** peerless, sterling, superior, terrific, top-notch **9** admirable, exemplary, first-rate, matchless, superfine, wonderful **10** first-class, preeminent, tremendous **11** exceptional, outstanding, superlative

excelsior 10 ever upward
  motto of: 7 New York (state)
Excelsior State
  nickname of: 7 New York

except 3 ban, bar, but **4** omit, save **6** enjoin, excuse, exempt, reject, remove, saving **7** barring, besides, exclude, shut out **8** count out, disallow, pass over **9** eliminate, excepting, excluding, other than **11** exclusive of

excepted 6 exempt **7** excused **8** excluded **11** not included

exception 6 oddity, rarity **7** anomaly, removal **8** omission **9** debarment, deviation, exclusion, exemption, isolation, rejection, seclusion **10** difference, leaving out, separation **11** elimination, peculiarity, repudiation, segregation, shutting out, special case **12** disallowment, irregularity, renunciation **13** inconsistency

exceptional 3 odd **4** rare **5** great, queer **6** unique **7** special, strange, unusual **8** aberrant, abnormal, atypical, freakish, peculiar, singular, superior, terrific, uncommon, unwonted **9** anomalous, excellent, irregular, marvelous, unheard of, unnatural, wonderful **10** first-class, inimitable, noteworthy, out-of-sight, phenomenal, remarkable **11** outstanding **12** incomparable **13** extraordinary, unprecedented **17** better than average

exception to the rule 7 anomaly **11** abnormality **12** irregularity

excerpt 4 part **5** piece **7** extract, portion, section **8** abstract, fragment **9** quotation, selection **13** quoted passage

excess 4 glut **5** extra, flood, spare **7** residue, surfeit, surplus, too much

8 fullness, overflow, plethora **9** avalanche, excessive, profusion, remainder, repletion **10** inundation, lavishness, oversupply **11** undue amount **13** overabundance **14** superabundance

excessive 5 undue **6** excess **7** extreme, profuse, too much **8** needless **9** senseless **10** immoderate, inordinate **11** exaggerated, extravagant, superfluous, unnecessary **12** overabundant, unreasonable **16** disproportionate

excessively 5 enorm **7** greatly **9** extremely, intensely **11** exceedingly, fanatically **12** boisterously, exorbitantly, inordinately **14** overabundantly

exchange 4 swap **5** trade **6** barter, switch **8** bandying, trade off **9** tit for tat **10** quid pro quo **11** convert into, give-and-take, interchange, reciprocate, reciprocity

exchange blows 3 box **5** clash, fight **6** battle, combat, tussle **7** contend, contest, grapple **8** skirmish **11** cross swords

exchange of viewpoints 6 debate, parley **8** dialogue **10** conference, discussion

exchange premium 4 agio

exchange views 6 confer, debate **7** consult, discuss **8** consider, talk over **12** compare notes

excise 3 tax **4** duty **6** cut off, cut out, impost, remove **7** extract **8** pluck out **9** eradicate, surcharge

excitable 4 edgy **5** jumpy **7** jittery, nervous **8** feverish, frenzied, skittish **9** flappable, hotheaded **10** highstrung, passionate **11** combustible, inflammable

excite 4 fire, move, whet **5** evoke, pique, rouse, waken **6** arouse, awaken, elicit, foment, incite, kindle, spur on, stir up, thrill **7** agitate, animate, inflame, provoke **8** energize **9** electrify, galvanize, instigate, stimulate, titillate **13** get a kick out of

excited 4 daft **5** afire, astir **6** ablaze **7** aroused **8** agitated, ecstatic, frenzied, inflamed, turned on **9** disturbed, stirred up **10** magnetized **11** electrified

excitement 3 ado **4** flap, stir, to-do **5** furor, kicks **6** action, flurry, frenzy, hoopla, thrill, tumult **7** elation, ferment, flutter, turmoil **8** activity, brouhaha, interest **9** adventure, agitation, animation, commotion, fireworks **10** enthusiasm **11** stimulation

exciting 5 spicy **6** moving, risque **7** rousing, zestful **8** dazzling, stirring **9** affecting, impelling, inspiring, thrilling **11** hair-raising, provocative, sensational, stimulating, titillating **12** breathtaking, electrifying **13** spinetingling

exclaim 4 howl, yell **5** shout **6** bellow,

cry out **7** call out **8** proclaim **9** ejaculate **10** vociferate

exclamation 3 cry **4** howl, yell, yelp **5** shout **6** bellow, outcry, shriek, squeal **7** screech **9** expletive **11** ejaculation **12** interjection, vociferation

exclamation of:
  approval: **3** ole, rah **5** bravo
  despair: **4** alas **5** alack **7** woe is me
  dicovery: **3** aha, oho
  disdain: **3** duh, hah, tsk **4** bosh, bunk, pooh
  disgust: **3** bah, ugh **4** damn, darn, drat, pfui, rats **5** shoot **6** humbug, phooey
  joy: **3** yay **4** whee, yeah **6** hooray, hurrah, hurray **7** whoopie
  pain: **4** ouch **5** yipes
  relief: **4** phew, whew
  other: **3** fie, hah, hey, tut, wow **4** oops, scat, shoo, ta-da **5** voila **6** hoopla
  bacchanalian cry: 4 evoe

exclude 3 ban, bar **4** omit, oust **5** eject, evict, expel **6** banish, except, forbid, refuse, reject, remove **7** boycott, keep out, rule out, shut out **8** disallow, leave out, prohibit, set aside, throw out **9** blackball, repudiate **13** shut the door on

excluding 3 but **4** save **6** except, saving **7** banning, barring, besides **9** excepting, other than **10** keeping out

exclusion 6 ouster **7** barring, refusal, removal **8** ejection, eviction **9** debarment, dismissal, expelling, expulsion, rejection, restraint **10** banishment, keeping out, preclusion, prevention **11** prohibition, throwing out **12** nonadmission

exclusive 4 full, posh, sole **5** aloof, total **6** closed, entire, single **7** private **8** absolute, clannish, cliquish, complete, snobbish, unshared **9** undivided, selective **10** restricted **11** restrictive

exclusive of 3 but **4** save **6** except, saving **7** barring, besides **9** excepting, excluding, other than

excommunicate 3 ban **4** oust **5** eject, expel **6** banish, remove **8** unchurch **12** anathematize

excommunication 3 ban **6** ouster **8** anathema **10** banishment **12** proscription

excoriate 4 flay **5** curse **6** berate, revile **7** censure **8** denounce, execrate **9** skin alive

excrescence 4 bump, hump, knob, knot, lump **5** bulge, gnarl **6** nodule **8** swelling **10** protrusion **12** protuberance

excrete 4 void **5** expel **8** evacuate **9** discharge, eliminate

excruciating 5 acute **6** fierce, severe **7** cutting, extreme, intense, racking, violent **9** agonizing, exquisite, torturous **10** lacerating, tormenting, unbearable **11** unendurable **12** insufferable

exculpate 5 clear **6** acquit, excuse, pardon **7** absolve **9** exonerate, let one off, vindicate

excursion 4 hike, ride, tour, trek, trip, walk **5** drive, jaunt, sally, tramp **6** cruise, flight, junket, outing, ramble, sortie, stroll, voyage **10** expedition **12** pleasure trip

excusatory 9 defensive **10** apologetic **11** extenuatory, vindicatory **13** justificatory

excuse 4 free **5** alibi, clear, spare **6** acquit, defend, exempt, let off, pardon, reason **7** absolve, condone, defense, explain, forgive, indulge, justify, release **8** argument, bear with, mitigate, overlook, palliate, pass over **9** disregard, exculpate, exemption, exonerate, extenuate, gloss over, let one off, relieve of, vindicate, whitewash **10** absolution **11** exoneration, vindication **12** apologize for **13** justification **16** make allowance for **17** accept one's apology

execrable 4 vile **5** awful **8** dreadful, terrible **9** atrocious, revolting **10** abominable

execrate 4 hate **5** abhor **6** detest, loathe **7** despise **9** abominate, can't stand, excoriate **10** shrink from **11** can't stomach **12** be revolted by **13** be nauseated by, find repulsive **15** be disgusted with **20** regard with repugnance

execration 4 hate **6** hating **7** disgust **8** loathing **9** despising, repulsion, revulsion **10** repugnance **11** abomination, detestation

execute 2 do **3** act **4** kill, play, slay **5** enact **6** effect, murder, render **7** achieve, enforce, fulfill, perform, realize, sustain **8** carry out, complete, massacre **9** discharge **10** accomplish, administer, consummate, effectuate, perpetrate, put to death **11** assassinate **12** carry through **13** put into effect

execution 5 doing **7** killing, slaying **9** discharge, effecting, rendition **10** completion **11** achievement, carrying out, fulfillment, performance, realization, transaction **14** accomplishment, administration, implementation, interpretation, putting to death

executioner 6 hit man, killer, slayer **7** butcher, hangman **8** assassin, murderer

Executioner's Song, The
  author: **12** Norman Mailer
  subject: **11** Gary Gilmore

executive 3 CEO, CFO **4** suit **7** manager **8** chairman, director, overseer **9** president **10** leadership, managerial, supervisor **11** directorial, supervisory **13** administrator **14** administrative, superintendent

executives 5 suits **7** leaders **8** managers, officers **9** directors **13** governing body **14** administration

executor 4 doer **5** agent **9** performer **13** administrator

exegesis 10 exposition **11** explanation **14** interpretation **18** explication de texte

exemplar 5 ideal, model **7** example, pattern **8** original, specimen, standard **9** archetype, prototype

exemplary 5 ideal, model **6** sample **7** typical **8** laudable, sterling **9** admirable, emulative, estimable, nonpareil **10** noteworthy **11** commendable, meritorious **12** illustrative, praiseworthy **14** characteristic, representative

exemplification 7 epitome, essence, example **8** citation, evidence **10** embodiment **11** case in point **12** illustration **13** documentation **14** representation **15** personification

exemplify 6 depict, embody, typify **8** instance **9** epitomize, personify, represent **10** illustrate **11** demonstrate **12** characterize

exempli gratia 6 such as **10** for example **19** for the sake of example
  abbreviation: 2 eg

exempt 4 free **5** clear, freed, spare **6** except, excuse, immune, pardon, spared **7** absolve, cleared, excused, release, relieve **8** absolved, excepted, relieved **9** not liable, privilege **10** privileged

exemption 6 excuse **7** expense, freedom, release **8** immunity **9** allowance, deduction, exception **10** absolution **12** dispensation

exercise 3 use **4** show **5** apply, drill, exert, teach, train, tutor, wield **6** employ, school, warm-up **7** break in, develop, display, execute, exhibit, perform, prepare, program, utilize, workout **8** accustom, aerobics, carry out, ceremony, movement, practice, training **9** discharge, inculcate, schooling **10** daily dozen, discipline, employment, gymnastics, isometrics **11** application, demonstrate, give lessons, performance, utilization **12** calisthenics **14** do calisthenics

exert 3 use **5** apply, wield **6** employ, expend **7** utilize **8** exercise, put forth, resort to **9** discharge, make use of **11** put in action, set in motion

exertion 4 toil, work **5** labor, pains **6** effort, energy **7** travail, trouble **8** activity, endeavor, industry, strength, struggle **11** application, elbow grease

ex facie 9 on the face **10** apparently **11** from the face

ex facto 8 actually **15** according to fact

exhalation 4 puff **6** breath, wheeze,

whoosh **10** expiration **12** breathing out

exhale 4 huff, pant, puff **6** expire **7** breathe, respire **10** breathe out

exhaust 3 fag, tax **4** bush, poop, tire **5** drain, empty, spend, use up **6** expend, finish, strain, weaken **7** consume, deplete, disable, draw off, draw out, fatigue, wear out **8** enervate, overtire **9** dissipate **10** debilitate, devitalize, run through **13** sap one's energy

exhausted 4 beat, gone **5** all in, spent **6** bushed, done in, pooped, used up **7** drained, emptied, wearied, worn out **8** bankrupt, consumed, depleted, expended, fatigued, finished, tired out **9** dead tired, enervated, played out **11** devitalized **12** impoverished

exhausting 5 tough **6** tiring, uphill **7** arduous **8** toilsome **9** difficult, fatiguing, Herculean, laborious, Sisyphean, wearisome **10** burdensome

exhaustion 7 fatigue, using up **8** draining, spending **9** depletion, tiredness, weariness **10** enervation **11** consumption

exhaustive 6 all-out **7** in-depth **8** complete, profound, sweeping, thorough **9** intensive **12** all-embracing, all-inclusive **13** comprehensive

exhibit 3 air **4** show **6** flaunt, parade, reveal, unveil **7** display **8** brandish **9** put on view **10** exhibition, exposition, make public **11** demonstrate **12** bring to light **13** public showing

exhibition 4 show **5** array **7** display, exhibit, showing **9** unveiling **10** exposition **13** demonstration, public showing

exhibitionist 7 flasher, show-off **15** attention-seeker

exhilarate 4 lift **5** cheer, elate **6** excite, perk up **7** animate, delight, enliven, gladden, hearten, quicken **9** stimulate **10** invigorate

exhilaration 6 gaiety **7** delight, elation **8** gladness, vivacity **9** animation **10** exaltation, excitement, joyousness, liveliness **11** high spirits **16** lightheartedness

exhort 3 bid **4** goad, prod, spur, urge **5** egg on, press **6** advise, enjoin **7** beseech, implore **8** admonish, advocate, appeal to, persuade **9** encourage, plead with, recommend **14** give a pep talk to

exhortation 6 sermon, urging **7** bidding, lecture, pep talk **8** dictates, harangue, prodding **9** prompting

exhumation 9 digging up **12** disinterment **13** disentombment

exhume 5 dig up **8** disinter

exigency 3 fix, jam **5** needs, pinch **6** crisis, pickle, plight, scrape, strait **7** demands **8** hardship, quandary

9 emergency, extremity, urgencies **10** difficulty **11** constraints, contingency, necessities, predicament **12** circumstance, requirements

exigent 5 vital **6** urgent **8** critical, exacting, pressing **9** demanding, difficult, necessary

exile 2 DP **4** oust **5** eject, expel **6** banish, deport, emigre, pariah **7** outcast, refugee **8** drive out, expellee **9** expulsion **10** banishment, expatriate

Exile, The
author: 9 Pearl Buck

exiled person 5 exile **6** emigre **7** outcast **8** expellee **10** expatriate

Exile's Return
author: 13 Malcolm Cowley

exist 4 last, live, stay **5** abide, ensue, occur **6** endure, happen, obtain, remain **7** breathe, prevail, survive

existence 4 life **5** being **7** reality **8** presence, survival **9** actuality, animation, endurance **11** continuance, materiality, subsistence, tangibility

existent 4 real **5** alive **6** actual, extant, living **7** present **8** existing, tangible **9** surviving, to be found **11** in existence

existing 4 real **5** being **6** actual, extant, living **7** ongoing, present **9** existence, surviving, to be found **10** continuing, prevailing **11** established, in existence **12** accomplished

exit 4 blow **5** go out, leave, split **6** cut out, depart, egress, escape, exodus, way out **7** retreat **8** withdraw **9** departure **10** withdrawal **11** take a powder

ex libris 15 out of the books of **16** from the library of

ex nihilo nihil fit 25 out of nothing nothing is made **27** nothing is created from nothing

exocuticle
consists of: 9 sclerotin

exodus 4 exit **5** exile **6** flight, hegira **9** departure, migration **10** emigration, going forth

Exodus
author: 8 Leon Uris
story of founding of: 6 Israel

exonerate 4 free **5** clear **6** acquit **7** absolve, forgive **9** exculpate, vindicate **12** find innocent

exoneration 8 clearing **10** absolution **11** exculpation, vindication

exorbitant 4 dear **5** undue **6** costly **7** extreme **8** enormous **9** egregious, excessive, expensive, out-of-line **10** high-priced, inordinate, oppressive, outrageous, overpriced **11** extravagant **12** extortionate, preposterous, unreasonable

exorcise 5 expel **7** cast out **8** get rid of
Exorcist, The
author: 18 William Peter Blatty
director: 15 William Friedkin

cast: 8 Lee J Cobb **10** Linda Blair **11** Jason Miller, Max von Sydow **12** Ellen Burstyn
Oscar for: 10 screenplay

exoskeleton
of insect: 5 shell **8** body wall
part: 10 epicuticle, exocuticle **11** endocuticle

exoteric 4 open **6** public, simple **7** popular **8** exterior, external, outsider

exotic 5 alien **6** quaint, unique **7** foreign, strange, unusual **8** colorful, peculiar, striking **9** different, not native **10** from abroad, intriguing, outlandish, unfamiliar **11** exceptional **13** not indigenous

expand 4 grow, open **5** swell, widen **6** dilate, evolve, extend, fatten, spread, unfold, unfurl, unroll **7** amplify, augment, develop, distend, enlarge, inflate, magnify, stretch, unravel **8** heighten, increase, multiply **9** outspread, spread out **10** aggrandize

expanded 4 grew **5** grown **7** dilated, swelled, swollen, widened **8** enlarged, extended, unfolded, unfurled, unrolled **9** augmented, broadened, increased, outspread, spread out, stretched **10** heightened **11** aggrandized

expanse 4 area **5** field, range, reach, space, sweep **6** extent **7** breadth, compass, stretch **9** magnitude

expansion 6 growth **8** dilation, increase, swelling, widening **9** enlarging, extension, spreading **10** amplifying, distention, magnifying, stretching **11** development, enlargement, lengthening, multiplying **12** augmentation **13** amplification

expansive 4 free, open, vast, wide **5** broad **6** genial **7** affable, amiable, general, liberal **8** effusive, generous, outgoing **9** bounteous, bountiful, capacious, extensive, exuberant **10** voluminous **11** extroverted, far-reaching, uninhibited, unrepressed, wide-ranging **12** unrestrained **13** comprehensive

expatiate 6 expand **7** amplify, enlarge, expound **9** discourse, elaborate

expatriate 2 DP **5** exile **6** emigre, pariah **7** outcast, refugee **15** displaced person

expatriation 5 exile **9** expulsion **10** banishment

expect 5 guess, trust **6** assume, demand, plan on, reckon **7** believe, count on, foresee, hope for, imagine, look for, presume, require, suppose, surmise **8** envision, reckon on, rely upon **9** calculate **10** anticipate, bargain for, conjecture, reckon upon **11** contemplate **13** look forward to

expectancy 11 expectation **12** anticipation

expectant 4 agog **5** eager, ready **7** anxious, hopeful, waiting **9** expecting

10 looking for, optimistic **12** anticipating, apprehensive

expectation 4 hope **5** trust **6** belief, chance **8** prospect, reliance **9** assurance **10** confidence, expectancy, likelihood **11** presumption **12** anticipation **13** contemplation

expedient 4 help, wise **5** means **6** resort, tactic, useful **7** benefit, helpful, measure, politic, selfish, stopgap **9** advantage, advisable, conniving, desirable, effective, judicious, makeshift, opportune, practical, strategem **10** beneficial, instrument, profitable, worthwhile **11** calculating, self-seeking, self-serving **12** advantageous **14** self-interested

expedite 4 rush **5** hurry **6** hasten **7** advance, forward, further, promote, quicken, speed up **8** dispatch **10** accelerate, facilitate **11** precipitate, push through

expedition 4 trek **6** voyage **7** journey, mission **8** campaign, voyagers **9** explorers, travelers, wayfarers **10** enterprise **11** adventurers, exploration

expeditious 4 fast **5** alert, awake, hasty, quick, rapid, ready, swift **6** prompt, snappy, speedy **7** instant **8** punctual **9** effective, immediate **10** bright-eyed **11** efficacious

expel 4 fire, oust, sack, spew, void **5** eject, evict, exile **6** banish, bounce, remove **7** cashier, cast out, dismiss, drum out, excrete **8** dislodge, drive out, evacuate, force out, throw out **9** discharge, eliminate

expellee 2 DP **5** exile **14** banished person **15** displaced person

expend 3 pay **4** give **5** drain, empty, spend, use up **6** donate, lay out, pay out **7** consume, exhaust, fork out, wear out **8** disburse, dispense, shell out, squander **9** dissipate, go through **10** contribute

expendable 7 payable **9** available, forgoable, spendable **10** consumable, extraneous **11** disbursable, dispensable, replaceable, superfluous **12** nonessential **14** relinquishable

expended 5 spent **6** used up **7** drained, emptied, paid out **8** consumed **9** disbursed, exhausted **10** dissipated

expenditure 3 use **4** cost **5** price **6** charge, outlay, output **7** payment **8** exertion, expenses, spending **9** expending, paying out **10** employment, money spent **11** application, consumption **12** disbursement

expense 4 cost, rate **5** drain, price **6** amount, charge, figure, outlay **9** depletion, quotation

expensive 4 dear **6** costly **9** excessive **10** exorbitant, high-priced, immoderate, overpriced **11** extravagant **12** un-

economical, unreasonable **15** beyond one's means

experience 3 see **4** bear, feel, know, meet, view **5** doing, event, sense **6** affair, behold, endure, suffer **7** episode, observe, sustain, undergo **8** exposure, incident, perceive, practice, training **9** adventure, encounter, go through, happening, seasoning, withstand **10** occurrence **11** familiarity, live through, observation **17** personal knowledge **18** firsthand knowledge

experienced 4 able, wise **6** expert, master **7** capable, knowing, skilled, trained, veteran **8** seasoned **9** competent, efficient, practical, qualified **10** well-versed **11** worldly-wise **12** accomplished **13** sophisticated

experiential 9 empirical, firsthand, practical

experiment 4 test **5** assay, flier, trial **6** feeler, try out **7** analyze, examine, explore, venture **8** analysis, research **11** examination, investigate **12** seek proof for, verification **13** investigation **14** mess around with

experimental 3 new **4** test **5** fresh, rough, trial **7** radical **9** tentative **10** conceptual, first-draft **11** conjectural, speculative **13** developmental, trial-and-error

experimentation 7 testing **8** analysis, research **10** experiment **11** examination, exploration **13** investigation, trial and error

experimenter 6 tester **10** researcher **15** experimentalist

expert 3 ace, apt, pro, wiz **4** able, deft, whiz **5** adept, crack, doyen, maven, mavin, shark **6** adroit, artist, facile, master, wizard **7** artiste, capable, perfect, skilled, trained, veteran **8** masterly, skillful, virtuoso **9** authority, competent, masterful, practiced, qualified **10** first-class, past-master, proficient, specialist **11** connoisseur, crackerjack, experienced **12** accomplished, professional **13** knowledgeable
French: 6 au fait

expertise 5 savvy, skill **7** know-how **10** expertness **12** special skill **14** specialization **15** professionalism

expertness 5 savvy, skill **7** ability, know how **8** training **9** expertise **10** capability, competence, experience **11** proficiency **12** special skill **13** qualification **14** accomplishment, specialization **15** professionalism

expiate 7 appease **8** atone for **13** make amends for **16** pay the penalty for

expiation 6 amends, shrift **7** penance **9** atonement **11** appeasement **16** paying the penalty

expiration 3 end **5** death, dying **6** demise, ending, finish **7** passing, closing

8 decrease, exhaling **10** conclusion **11** termination **12** breathing out

expire 3 die, end **5** cease, lapse **6** finish, perish, run out **7** decease, kick off, succumb **8** conclude, pass away **9** terminate **11** come to an end, discontinue **13** kick the bucket **14** give up the ghost

expired 4 dead, died **6** lapsed, ran out, run out **7** defunct, laspsed **8** deceased, lifeless, perished **10** passed away **11** came to an end, come to an end **14** gave up the ghost

explain 6 fathom **7** clarify, clear up, justify, resolve **8** describe, spell out **9** elucidate, explicate, interpret, make clear, make plain **10** account for, illuminate, illustrate **11** demonstrate, rationalize **14** give a reason for **20** give an explanation for

explainer 6 critic **7** analyst **8** reviewer **10** translator **11** commentator, interpreter

explanation
French: 15 eclaircissement

explicate 7 analyze, clarify, develop, explain **8** annotate **9** elucidate, interpret **10** elucidated, illuminate, illustrate

explication 8 analysis **10** commentary **11** elucidation, explanation **12** illumination **13** clarification **14** interpretation

explication de texte 8 exegesis **11** explanation **14** interpretation **17** literary criticism

explicit 5 blunt, clear, exact, frank, plain **6** candid, direct **7** certain, express, pointed, precise **8** absolute, definite, distinct, specific **9** outspoken **10** unreserved **11** categorical, unequivocal, unqualified **15** straightforward **16** clearly expressed

explicitness 7 clarity **9** clearness, precision **11** unambiguity

explode 5 belie, blast, burst, erupt, go off **6** blow up, expose, refute, set off **7** destroy **8** detonate, disprove **9** discredit, repudiate **10** invalidate, prove false, prove wrong **11** burst loudly **12** utter noisily **14** burst violently, express noisily **18** discharge violently **19** burst out emotionally

exploit 4 feat **5** abuse **6** misuse **7** utilize **8** profit by, put to use **9** adventure, brave deed, heroic act, make use of **10** daring deed **11** achievement **12** capitalize on **14** accomplishment, use to advantage **15** take advantage of **16** make selfish use of **21** take unfair advantage of **22** turn to practical account

exploited 6 abused **7** ill used, misused **11** downtrodden **15** took advantage of **16** taken advantage of

exploration 5 probe **7** inquiry **8** scrutiny **9** discovery **10** expedition, experiment **11** examination **12** scouting trip **13** investigation

explore 3 try **5** plumb, probe, scout **6** survey, try out **7** analyze, examine, feel out, pry into **8** look into, research, traverse **9** delve into, penetrate, range over **10** scrutinize, search into, travel over **11** inquire into, investigate, reconnoiter **14** experiment with

explorer
  American: 4 Byrd, Pike **5** Boone, Clark, Lewis, Peary, Perry
  Australian: 4 Hume **5** Sturt **6** Stuart **8** Mitchell
  British: 4 Bell, Cook, Park **5** Baker, Bligh, Bruce, Cabot, Davis, Drake, Grant, Puget, Scott, Smith, Speke **6** Baffin, Burton, Hudson, Lander **7** Raleigh, Stanley **8** Franklin **9** Frobisher, MacKenzie, Vancouver **11** Livingstone
  Danish: 6 Bering **7** Niebuhr
  Dutch: 6 Tasman **7** Barents, Le Maire **8** Schouten **10** Linschoten
  French: 6 Joliet **7** Cartier, Jolliet, La Salle **9** Champlain, Marquette **12** Bougainville
  Italian: 8 Columbus **9** Marco Polo, Verrazano **15** Amerigo Vespucci
  Moslem: 8 Ibn Battuta
  Norwegian: 8 Amundsen
  Portuguese: 3 Cam, Cao **4** Dias, Diaz **6** Cabral, Da Gama **7** Almeida **8** Covilhao, Magellan **11** Albuquerque **23** Prince Henry the Navigator
  Russian: 10 Middendorf **11** Przhevalsky
  Spanish: 6 Balboa, Cortes, De Soto **7** Pizarro **8** Coronado, Orellana, Valdivia **11** Ponce de Leon
  Swedish: 12 Nordenskjold
  Viking: 10 Eric the Red **11** Leif Ericson

explosion 3 fit **4** clap **5** blast, burst, crack **6** report **7** tantrum **8** eruption, outbreak, outburst, paroxysm **9** blowing up, discharge **10** detonation **11** fulmination

explosive 3 TNT **5** shaky, tense **6** touchy **7** cordite, keyed up **8** critical, dynamite, perilous, strained, ticklish, unstable, volatile **9** dangerous, emotional, gelignite **10** ammunition, precarious **12** pyrotechnics **13** nitroglycerin

exponent 6 backer **8** advocate, champion, defender, promoter **9** expounder, proponent, spokesman, supporter **12** propagandist

export 7 send out **8** dispatch **10** sell abroad **11** foreign sale **12** ship overseas

expose 4 bare, risk, show **5** brand, offer, strip **6** betray, denude, divest, hazard, let out, reveal, submit **7** display, divulge, exhibit, imperil, let slip, subject, uncover, unearth **8** denounce, disclose, endanger **10** jeopardize, reveal to be **12** acquaint with, bring to light **16** leave unprotected

exposé 6 baring **8** exposure **10** divulgence, revelation

exposed 4 open **5** bared **8** divulged, laid open, revealed, unmasked **9** denounced, disclosed, displayed, uncovered, unearthed **11** unprotected, unsheltered

exposition 4 expo, fair, mart, show **6** bazaar, market **7** account, display, exhibit, picture **8** exegesis **9** trade fair, trade show **10** commentary, exhibition, world's fair **11** description, elucidation, explanation, explication **12** illustration, presentation **13** clarification, demonstration **14** interpretation

expostulate 5 argue **6** enjoin, exhort, object, reason **7** caution, counsel, protest **8** forewarn **9** plead with **11** remonstrate **13** cry out against, reason against **14** inveigh against

exposure 4 view **5** vista **6** expose **7** outlook **8** frontage, prospect **9** divulging, unmasking **10** disclosure, divulgence, laying bare, laying open, revelation, subjection, submission, uncovering **11** perspective **12** public notice **15** bringing to light

expound 6 defend, uphold **7** explain **8** describe **9** elucidate, explicate, hold forth, make clear

express 3 say **4** fast, show, word **5** clear, couch, exact, lucid, plain, quick, rapid, speak, state, swift, utter, vivid, voice **6** convey, direct, evince, phrase, relate, reveal **7** certain, declare, divulge, exhibit, nonstop, precise **8** definite, describe, disclose, evidence, explicit, forceful, specific, vocalize **9** high-speed, make known, verbalize **10** articulate, particular **11** categorical, communicate, unequivocal **12** put into words

expression 4 look, mien, term, tone, word **5** idiom, style **6** airing, aspect, phrase, saying **7** emotion, meaning, stating, telling, venting, voicing, wording **8** language, locution, phrasing, relating, speaking, uttering **9** assertion, eloquence **10** appearance, modulation **11** countenance, declaration, enunciation, phraseology **12** articulation, setting forth, turn of phrase **13** communication

expressionless 5 blank, empty **6** vacant **7** deadpan **12** inexpressive

expressive 5 vivid **6** moving **7** telling **8** eloquent, forceful, poignant, powerful, striking **9** effective **10** compelling, indicative, meaningful, thoughtful **11** significant **14** characteristic

expressly 7 clearly, plainly **9** decidedly, pointedly, precisely, specially

10 definitely, distinctly, explicitly **12** particularly, specifically **13** categorically, unequivocally **18** in no uncertain terms

express sorrow 3 cry **4** weep **6** grieve, lament **7** condole, console **10** sympathize **11** commiserate

expropriate 4 take **5** seize **8** take over **10** commandeer, confiscate **11** appropriate

expropriation 7 seizure **10** arrogation, taking over **12** confiscation **13** commandeering

expulsion 5 exile **6** ouster **7** ousting, removal **8** ejection, eviction **9** debarment, discharge, dismissal, exclusion, expelling **10** banishment **11** elimination, prohibition, throwing out **12** proscription

expunge 5 erase **6** delete, efface, rub out **7** blot out, destroy, wipe out **9** eradicate, strike out **10** obliterate

expurgate 3 cut **4** blip, edit **5** bleep, purge **6** censor, cut out, delete, excise, remove **8** bleep out **10** blue-pencil, bowdlerize

exquisite 4 fine **5** dainty **6** choice, lovely, superb **7** elegant, perfect **8** delicate, flawless, peerless, precious, splendid **9** admirable, excellent, faultless, matchless **10** consummate, fastidious, impeccable, meticulous **11** superlative **12** incomparable **14** discriminating

exquisiteness 6 beauty **8** delicacy, elegance, fineness **10** loveliness, perfection **12** flawlessness

extant 6 living **7** present **8** existent, existing **9** surviving, to be found **11** in existence

Extasie, The
  author: 9 John Donne

extemporaneous 5 ad-lib **7** offhand **9** extempore, impromptu **10** improvised, off the cuff, unprepared **11** extemporary, spontaneous, unrehearsed **12** without notes **13** without notice **14** unpremeditated **15** spur-of-the-moment **19** off the top of one's head

extemporary 5 ad-lib **9** extempore, impromptu **10** improvised, off the cuff, unprepared **14** extemporaneous **19** off the top of one's head

extempore 5 ad-lib **7** offhand **9** impromptu **10** improvised, off the cuff, unprepared **11** extemporary, unrehearsed **12** without notes **14** extemporaneous, unpremeditated **15** spur-of-the-moment **19** off the top of one's head

extemporize 5 ad-lib **6** make up **9** improvise **14** speak impromptu **15** speak off the cuff

extend 4 give **5** grant, offer, widen **6** bestow, expand, impart, put out, spread, submit **7** advance, amplify, augment, broaden, draw out, enlarge, hold out, proffer, prolong, stretch **8** continue, elongate, increase, lengthen, protract, reach out **10** make longer, stretch out **12** stretch forth

extended 4 long **7** widened **8** drawn out, enlarged, expanded, thorough, unfolded, unfurled **9** broadened, continued, extensive, prolonged, spread out **10** lengthened, protracted, widespread **12** stretched out **13** comprehensive

extending 8 full form **9** expansion **10** drawing out, elongation, proffering, stretching **11** enlargement, lengthening **12** putting forth

extension 3 arm, ell **4** wing **5** annex, delay **6** branch, length, outlay **7** adjunct **8** addition, appendix, increase **9** appendage, expansion, outgrowth **10** drawing out, proffering **11** enlargement, lengthening **12** continuation, postponement, prolongation

extensive 4 huge, long, vast, wide **5** broad, great, large **7** lengthy **8** enormous, extended, far-flung, thorough **9** capacious, universal **10** protracted, voluminous **12** all-inclusive, considerable **13** comprehensive

extensiveness 4 span **5** range, reach, scope **6** extent, spread **7** breadth, compass, expanse, stretch

extent 4 area, size, time **5** range, reach, scope, sweep **6** amount, degree, length **7** breadth, compass, expanse, stretch **8** duration **9** amplitude, magnitude **10** dimensions

extenuate 6 excuse, temper **7** explain, justify, qualify **8** mitigate, moderate

extenuating 9 lessening, tempering **10** mitigating, moderating, qualifying **11** attenuating, diminishing, explanatory, justifiable

exterior 4 face, skin **5** alien, outer, shell **6** exotic, facade, finish, manner **7** bearing, coating, foreign, outside, outward, surface **8** covering, demeanor, external **9** extrinsic, outer side, outermost **10** extraneous **11** superficial

exterminate 3 zap **4** kill **5** erase, waste **7** abolish, destroy, expunge, root out, wipe out **8** demolish, massacre **9** eliminate, eradicate, slaughter **10** annihilate, extinguish

external 5 alien, outer **7** foreign, outside, outward, surface **8** exterior **9** extrinsic, outermost **10** extraneous **11** superficial

extinct 4 dead, gone, lost **6** put out **7** defunct, died out, gone out **8** quenched, vanished **12** extinguished

extinction 5 death **7** eclipse **9** wiping out **11** destruction, eradication **13** disappearance

extinguish 3 end, zap **4** dash, do in, kill **5** crush, douse, quash **6** cancel,

dispel, put out, quench, stifle **7** abolish, blow out, destroy, smother, wipe out **8** demolish, snuff out **9** eliminate, eradicate, suffocate

extinguished 6 put out **7** gone out **8** quenched **15** no longer burning

extirpate 5 erase **7** abolish, destroy, extract, pull out, root out, wipe out **8** demolish **9** eradicate **10** annihilate, extinguish, obliterate **11** exterminate

extol 4 laud **6** praise **7** acclaim, applaud, commend, glorify **8** eulogize **9** celebrate **10** compliment **16** sing the praises of

extort 5 educe, exact **6** coerce, elicit **7** extract **9** shake down

extortion 5 force, graft **6** payola, ransom **7** threats, tribute **8** coercion **9** blackmail, hush money, shakedown **14** forced payments

extortionate 5 undue **7** extreme **9** excessive, out-of-line **10** exorbitant, inordinate **12** unreasonable

extra 4 more **5** spare **7** adjunct, further, surplus **9** accessory, auxiliary, redundant, unusually **10** additional, attachment, complement, especially, remarkably, uncommonly **11** superfluous, unnecessary **12** additionally, appurtenance, particularly, supplemental **13** exceptionally **15** extraordinarily

extract 3 get **4** cite, cull **5** educe, evoke, exact, gleen, juice, quote, wrest **6** choose, deduce, derive, elicit, obtain, pry out, remove, select **7** copy out, distill, draw out, essence, excerpt, passage, pull out, root out, take out **8** abstract, bring out, citation, pluck out, press out, separate **9** extirpate, extricate, quotation, selection **10** distillate, squeeze out **11** concentrate

extraction 5 stock **7** descent, removal **8** ancestry **10** derivation, drawing out, pulling out

extraneous 5 alien **6** exotic **7** foreign, strange **9** extrinsic, unrelated **10** immaterial, incidental, irrelevant, not germane **11** superfluous **12** adventitious, inadmissible, nonessential, not pertinent **13** inappropriate

extraordinary 3 odd **4** rare **5** queer **6** unique **7** amazing, notable, strange, unusual **8** uncommon **9** fantastic, monstrous, unheard of **10** incredible, phenomenal, remarkable **11** exceptional **12** unbelievable **13** inconceivable

extraterrestrial 2 ET **3** Alf **6** cosmic **10** outer-space **12** interstellar, otherworldly **14** interplanetary

extravagance 5 folly, waste **6** excess **7** caprice **9** absurdity **10** profligacy **11** prodigality, squandering, unrestraint **12** immoderation, improvidence, overspending, recklessness, wastefulness **13** excessiveness **14** capriciousness **16** inordinate outlay, unreasonableness

extravagant 4 wild **6** absurd, costly, unreal **7** foolish **8** fabulous, lavishly, prodigal, spending, wasteful **9** excessive, expensive, fantastic, high-flown, imprudent **10** exorbitant, high-priced, immoderate, inordinate, openhanded, outlandish, outrageous, overpriced, profligate **11** improvident, spendthrift, squandering **12** overspending, preposterous, unreasonable, unrestrained

extravaganza 4 fair **5** opera **6** ballet **7** pageant **8** carnival, operetta **9** spectacle, stage show **10** exposition, vaudeville **11** opera bouffe, spectacular **12** Broadway show, opera comique, son et lumiere, wild west show **14** phantasmagoria **17** sound and light show

extreme 3 end **5** depth **6** excess, height, severe **7** intense, radical, unusual **8** advanced, boundary, farthest, uncommon **9** excessive, extremity, nth degree, outermost, very great **10** avant-garde, immoderate, inordinate, outrageous **11** exaggerated, extravagant, most distant **13** extraordinary

extremely 4 very **5** quite **7** awfully **8** terribly **9** curiously, intensely, unusually **10** abnormally, especially, freakishly, peculiarly, remarkably, singularly, uncommonly **11** exceedingly, excessively, unnaturally **12** immoderately, surprisingly **13** exceptionally **15** extraordinarily

extremely painful 7 racking **9** agonizing, torturous **10** tormenting, unbearable **11** intolerable, unendurable **12** excruciating, insufferable

extremity 3 arm, end, leg, tip, toe **4** edge, foot, hand, limb **5** bound, brink, limit, reach **6** border, finger, margin **7** confine, extreme **8** boundary, terminus **9** outer edge, periphery

extricate 4 free **5** loose **6** get out, rescue **7** deliver, release **8** liberate, untangle **9** disengage **11** disencumber, disentangle **12** wriggle out of

extrication 6 escape **7** loosing, release **10** liberation **11** deliverance **13** disengagement **15** disentanglement

extrinsic 5 alien **7** foreign **9** accessory **10** accidental, extraneous, incidental **11** dispensable **12** nonessential

extrovert 7 show-off **13** exhibitionist **14** life of the party **17** hail-fellow-well-met

extroverted 8 outgoing, sociable **9** expansive **10** gregarious **12** unrestrained

extrude 4 spew **5** eject, expel **7** project, push out **8** force out, protrude, stickout **9** thrust out

exuberance 3 zip **4** elan, life, zeal **5** vigor **6** energy, spirit **8** buoyancy, vitality, vivacity **9** animation, eagerness **10** enthusiasm, excitement, liveliness **13** effervescence, sprightliness

exuberant 4 lush, rich **5** eager

6 lavish, lively **7** copious, excited, profuse, zealous **8** abundant, animated, spirited, vigorous **9** bounteous, energetic, luxuriant, plenteous, plentiful, sprightly **12** enthusiastic **13** superabundant

exudation 3 sap, tar **4** ooze **5** pitch, sweat **7** leakage, seepage **8** bleeding, drainage **9** discharge, excretion

exude 4 drip, emit, ooze **5** sweat **7** secrete **9** discharge

exult 4 crow **5** gloat, glory **7** rejoice **8** be elated **10** be jubilant, jump for joy **11** be delighted **13** be exhilarated **15** be in high spirits

exultant 5 happy **6** elated, joyful **7** crowing **8** boasting, ecstatic, euphoric, gloating, jubilant **9** rapturous, rejoicing **10** triumphant

exultation 3 joy **7** elation, ovation, rapture, triumph **9** rejoicing **10** jubilation

Eyck, Jan van
   born: 8 Flanders, Maaseyck **10** Maastricht
   artwork: 9 Timotheos **15** Ghent Altarpiece **18** Adoration of the Lamb, The Man in a Red Turban, The Virgin in a Church **20** The Arnolfini Marriage **24** Arnolfini Wedding Portrait **29** The Madonna with Chancellor Rolin **30** The Madonna with Canon van der Paele

eye 3 orb **4** scan, view **5** sight, study, taste, watch **6** behold, gaze at, look at, peeper, regard, survey, take in, vision **7** inspect, observe, stare at **8** eyesight, glance at **10** perception, scrutinize **14** discrimination
   part: 4 iris, lens, rods **5** cones, nerve, pupil **6** cornea, muscle, retina **11** blood vessel

eyeful 4 doll **5** beaut, peach, Venus **6** beauty **7** stunner **8** knockout **10** good-looker **13** beautiful girl **14** beautiful woman

eyeglass, eyeglasses 4 lens **5** specs **6** eyecup, lenses **7** goggles, monocle **8** bifocals, cheaters, contacts, pincenez **9** lorgnette **10** spectacles

Eye of the Needle
   author: 10 Ken Follett

eyesight 4 eyes **5** sight **6** vision

eyewitness 5 gaper, gazer **6** gawker, viewer **7** witness **8** attester, attestor, beholder, informer, looker-on, observer, onlooker, passerby **9** bystander, spectator, testifier **10** rubberneck

eyre 4 lake, tour **7** circuit

Ezekiel
   father: 4 Buzi

Ezra
   father: 7 Seraiah

Fabares, Ruby Bernadette Nanette
real name of: **13** Nanette Fabray
aunt of: **14** Shelley Fabares

fable 3 fib, lie **4** hoax, myth, tale, yarn **6** legend **7** fiction, leg-pull, parable, romance, untruth, whopper **8** allegory **9** fairy tale, falsehood, invention, tall story **11** fabrication

fabled 6 unreal **7** storied **8** fabulous, fanciful, mythical **9** imaginary, legendary **10** fictitious **12** mythological

Fables
author: **5** Aesop **16** Jean de La Fontaine
ends with: **5** moral
feature: **4** hare **8** tortoise **10** sour grapes

Fabray, Nanette
real name: **28** Ruby Bernadette Nanette Fabares
partner: **9** Sid Caesar
born: **10** San Diego CA
roles: **7** Baby Nan **12** The Band Wagon **13** Sid Caesar Hour **15** High Button Shoes, Our Gang comedies

fabric 5 cloth, frame, stuff **6** makeup **7** textile, texture **8** dry goods, material **9** framework, structure, substance, yard goods **10** foundation **12** organization, substructure **14** infrastructure, superstructure
cotton: **4** duck **5** denim, drill, scrim, terry **6** burlap, calico, canvas, chintz, dimity, madras, muslin, oxford, poplin **7** batiste, buckram, flannel, gingham, organdy, percale, ticking **8** chambray **9** crinoline, sailcloth **10** broadcloth, printcloth, seersucker **11** cheesecloth, dotted Swiss
linen: **6** canvas, damask **7** butcher, cambric **8** birds-eye **9** huckaback
natural: **4** jute, silk, wool **5** linen **6** cotton **8** asbestos
silk: **3** raw **4** tram **7** organza **8** organzie **9** organzine
synthetic: **5** nylon, orlon, rayon **6** olefin **7** acetate, acrylic **9** polyester
type: **4** felt, lace, lame **5** crepe, gauze, moire, serge, voile **6** damask, faille, jersey, melton, velour, velvet **7** brocade, chiffon, flannel, foulard, gingham, taffeta **8** chenille, corduroy, tapestry **9** gabardine, velveteen
wool: **4** felt **5** crepe, serge, tweed, twill **6** boucle, covert, faille, melton, woolen **7** challis, doeskin, Donegal,

worsted **8** homespun, Shetland **9** Astrakhan, gabardine, sharkskin **10** hopsacking **11** Harris tweed, herringbone
from goats: **8** cashmere
sheep: **5** Iraqi **6** Hirrik, merino, Romney, Somali **7** Lincoln **8** Cotswold, Tatarian **9** Hampshire, Southdown **10** Corriedale, Dorset Down, Dorset Horn, Shropshire, Sikkim Bera **13** Hampshire Down
other wool-bearing animals:
5 camel, llama **6** alpaca, vicuna

fabricate 4 fake, form, make **5** build, erect, feign, forge, frame, hatch, shape **6** design, devise, invent, make up **7** compose, concoct, falsify, fashion, produce, trump up **8** assemble, contrive, simulate **9** construct, embroider, formulate **11** counterfeit, manufacture

fabrication 3 fib, lie **4** myth, yarn **5** fable **6** makeup **7** fiction, forgery, untruth **8** building, creation, erection **9** fairy tale, falsehood, invention **10** assemblage, concoction, fashioning, production **11** composition, manufacture **12** constructing, construction **13** prevarication **16** cock-and-bull story

Fabritius, Carel
real name: **13** Carel Pietersz
born: **14** Midden-Beemster, The Netherlands
artwork: **11** View of Delft **12** The Goldfinch **19** The Raising of Lazarus

fabulous 5 great **6** fabled, superb **7** amazing, storied **8** fanciful, invented, mythical, smashing **9** fantastic, imaginary, legendary, marvelous, wonderful **10** apocryphal, astounding, fictitious, incredible, stupendous **11** astonishing, spectacular **12** mythological, unbelievable **13** extraordinary

facade 4 face, mask **6** veneer **8** frontage, pretense **9** front view **10** false front **13** building front

face 3 air, mug, pan **4** coat, gall, grit, look, pout, puss, sand **5** brass, cheek, cover, front, image, nerve, pluck, spunk **6** aspect, daring, facade, kisser, mettle, repute, visage **7** bravado, dignity, front on, grimace, obverse, overlay, surface **8** boldness, confront, features, forepart, frontage, good name, overlook, prestige **9** encounter, hardihood, impudence, semblance **10** appearance, confidence, effrontery, ex-

pression, give toward, look toward, reputation, turn toward **11** countenance, physiognomy, self-respect

Face
character in: **12** The Alchemist
author: **6** Jonson

facet 3 cut **4** part, side **5** angle, phase, plane **6** aspect **7** surface

facetious 5 comic, droll, funny, witty **6** clever, jocose, joking, jovial **7** amusing, comical, jesting, jocular, playful **8** humorous **12** wisecracking

face-to-face 6 direct **8** one-on-one, personal **9** firsthand

facile 3 apt **4** glib **5** adept, handy, quick, slick **6** adroit, artful, casual, clever, fluent, smooth **7** cursory, shallow **8** careless, skillful **10** effortless, proficient **11** superficial

facilitate 3 aid **4** ease **6** foster, help in, smooth **7** advance, forward, further, lighten, promote, speed up **8** expedite, simplify **10** accelerate, make easier

facility 3 aid **4** bent, ease **5** knack, means, skill **7** aptness, fluency **8** deftness, easiness, resource **9** advantage, appliance, dexterity, readiness **10** adroitness, capability, competence, efficiency, expertness, smoothness **11** convenience, proficiency **14** effortlessness, practicability

facsimile 3 fax **4** copy **5** clone, xerox **7** replica, reprint **8** likeness **9** duplicate, imitation, photostat **10** transcript **12** reproduction

fact 3 act **4** deed **5** event, truth **6** verity **7** reality **8** incident, specific **9** actuality, certainty, happening, thing done **10** occurrence, particular **12** circumstance

faction 3 set **4** bloc, gang, ring, sect, side, unit **5** cabal, clash, group, split **6** breach, circle, clique, schism, strife **7** combine, coterie, discord, rupture, section **8** conflict, division, minority, sedition **9** rebellion **10** contention, disruption, dissension, dissidence, insurgency, quarreling **11** subdivision **12** disagreement **13** splinter group **15** incompatibility

factious 7 warring **8** divisive, fighting, mutinous **9** alienated, bickering, combative, estranged **10** contending, rebellious **11** belligerent, contentious, disaffected, disagreeing, dissentious, quarrelsome **12** disputatious **13** at loggerheads, insubordinate **15** insurrectionary **16** at sixes and sevens

factitious 4 sham **5** phony **9** pretended, synthetic, unnatural **10** artificial **12** manufactured

factor 4 part **5** agent, cause **6** reason **7** element **9** component, influence **11** constituent **12** circumstance **13** consideration

factory 4 mill, shop **5** plant, works **8** workshop **11** manufactory

factotum 4 aide **6** Figaro **8** handyman **9** gal Friday, guy Friday, man Friday **10** girl Friday **12** right-hand man **15** jack-of-all-trades

factual 4 real, true **5** exact, plain **6** actual **7** certain, correct, genuine, literal **8** accurate, concrete, definite, faithful **9** authentic, unadorned **10** scrupulous, verifiable

faculty, faculties 4 bent, gift, wits **5** flair, knack, power, skill **6** genius, reason, talent **7** quality **8** aptitude, capacity, function, penchant, teachers **9** adeptness, endowment **10** capability, professors **12** mental powers, skillfulness **13** teaching staff

fad 4 mode, rage, whim **5** craze, fancy, mania, vogue **6** whimsy **7** fashion **10** dernier cri, latest word **11** latest thing

faddish 2 in **6** trendy **10** innovative **11** fashionable

fade 3 die, dim, ebb **4** blur, dull, fail, flag, pale, wane **5** droop, taper **6** bleach, lessen, recede, whiten, wither **7** crumble, decline, dwindle, fall off, grow dim, shrivel **8** diminish, dissolve, evanesce, languish, make pale, melt away, pass away **9** disappear dissipate, evaporate, lose color

fade away 3 die, ebb **6** recede **7** subside **8** diminish

faded 4 drab, dull, pale **5** dingy **6** grayed **7** died out **8** bleached, dwindled, whitened, withered **9** colorless, shriveled, washed out

Faerie Queene, The
author: **13** Edmund Spenser
character: **3** Una **5** Guyon **6** Duessa **8** Artegall, Gloriana (the Faerie Queen) **9** Archimago, Britomart **12** Prince Arthur **14** Red Cross Knight

Fafnir
origin: **12** Scandinavian
form: **6** dragon
father: **8** Hreidmar
brother: **5** Otter, Regin
killed: **8** Hreidmar
killed by: **6** Sigurd

fag 4 bush, butt, poop, tire, weed **5** weary **6** tucker **7** exhaust **9** cigarette

Fagin
character in: **11** Oliver Twist
author: **7** Dickens

Fahrenheit
abbreviation: **1** F

Fahrenheit 451
author: **11** Ray Bradbury

Fahrenheit, Gabriel Daniel
field: **7** physics
nationality: **6** German
invented: **16** thermometer scale **18** alcohol thermometer, mercury thermometer

fail 3 die, ebb **4** bomb, flag, flop, fold, wane **5** abort, crash, droop, flunk **6** desert, slip up **7** decline, dwindle, forsake, founder, give out, go under, let down, misfire **8** be in vain, collapse, fade away, languish, lay an egg, miscarry **9** disappear, fall short, fizzle out **10** end in smoke, go bankrupt, not succeed, run aground **11** be stillborn, come to grief, deteriorate, fall through, go up in smoke, miss the mark **12** come to naught, turn out badly **13** come to nothing **15** go out of business **16** meet one's Waterloo, meet with disaster

fail at 11 fall short of **12** be defeated in, not succeed at **16** be unsuccessful at

failed
French: **6** manque

failing 4 weak **5** fault, shaky **6** defect, ebbing, foible, waning **7** folding, frailty **8** drooping, flagging, giving up, slipping, weakness **9** deficient, dwindling, giving out, weakening, weak point **10** deficiency, going under **11** shortcoming **12** unsuccessful **13** insufficiency

fail to include 4 drop, omit **5** elide **8** leave out, pass over

failure 3 dud **4** bomb, flop, mess, ruin **5** botch, crash, loser **6** fizzle, mishap, muddle, turkey **7** decline, default, failing, folding, misfire, washout **8** collapse, downfall **9** breakdown, ruination **10** bankruptcy, ne'er-do-well

Fainall, Mrs
character in: **16** The Way of the World
author: **8** Congreve

faint 3 dim, low **4** pale, soft, thin, weak **5** dizzy, faded, frail, giddy, muted, small, swoon, timid **6** dulcet, feeble, little, meager, remote, slight, subtle, torpid **7** fearful, fragile, languid, muffled, obscure, pass out, worn out **8** black out, collapse, cowardly, delicate, drooping, fatigued, timorous **9** exhausted, inaudible, lethargic, whispered **10** indistinct **11** lightheaded, lily-livered, vertiginous **13** inconspicuous **17** lose consciousness

fainthearted 4 weak **5** timid **6** feeble **8** cowardly **10** irresolute **11** halfhearted, indifferent, lily-livered

faintheartedness 9 cowardice **12**

cowardliness, yellow streak **13** pusillanimity, yellow feather **17** pusillanimousness **18** chickenheartedness

fair 4 fine, just, pale, so-so **5** blond, bonny, sunny **6** blonde, bright, comely, creamy, decent, honest, justly, kosher, lovely, medium, pretty, proper, square **7** average, cricket, legally, not dark, upright **8** adequate, candidly, carnival, honestly, mediocre, middling, moderate, ordinary, passable, pleasant, rainless, squarely, sunshiny, unbiased **9** beautiful, cloudless, equitable, ethically, honorable, honorably, impartial, justified, objective, tolerable, unclouded **10** aboveboard, attractive, evenhanded, exhibition, legitimate, pretty good, reasonable, truthfully **11** indifferent, respectable **12** forthrightly, light-colored, lightskinned, on the up-and-up, run-of-themill, satisfactory, unprejudiced **13** disinterested, dispassionate **19** according to the rules

Fair, A A
pseudonym of: **18** Erle Stanley Gardner

Fairbanks, Douglas
real name: **17** Douglas Elton Ulman
wife: **12** Mary Pickford
son: **18** Douglas Fairbanks Jr
born: **8** Denver CO
roles: **9** Robin Hood **11** The Iron Mask **14** The Black Pirate, The Mark of Zorro **16** The Thief of Bagdad **18** The Three Musketeers **23** The Private Life of Don Juan

Fairbanks, Douglas Jr
father: **16** Douglas Fairbanks
wife: **12** Joan Crawford
born: **9** New York NY
roles: **8** Gunga Din **12** Little Caesar **15** Sinbad the Sailor **16** That Lady in Ermine **17** Catherine the Great **18** The Prisoner of Zenda **19** The Corsican Brothers

fair dealing 7 honesty **8** fairness **15** trustworthiness

Fairfax, Gwendolen
character in: **27** The Importance of Being Earnest
author: **5** Wilde

Fairfax, Jane
character in: **4** Emma
author: **6** Austen

Fairfax, Mrs
character in: **8** Jane Eyre
author: **15** Charlotte Bronte

Fair Land, Fair Land
author: **11** A B Guthrie Jr

fairly 5 fully **6** justly, rather, really **7** rightly **8** actually, honestly, passably, properly, somewhat, squarely **9** equitably, honorably, so to speak, tolerably **10** absolutely, completely, moderately, positively, reasonably **11** impartially, objectively **12** evenhand-

edly, legitimately **15** dispassionately **19** in a manner of speaking
Latin: 9 pari passu

fairness 7 balance, honesty, justice **8** equality, fair play **11** objectivity **12** impartiality **14** even-handedness **16** equal opportunity

fair play 7 cricket, justice **8** equality, fairness **12** impartiality **16** equal opportunity

fair-skinned 4 pale **5** blond, light **6** blonde **17** light-complexioned

fairy 3 elf **5** pixie **6** sprite **10** leprechaun

fairy tale 3 fib **4** myth **5** fable **6** legend **7** fantasy, fiction **8** tall tale **9** invention **11** fabrication **16** cock-and-bull story, Mother Goose story
German: 7 Marchen

fait accompli 16 accomplished fact, thing already done

faith 4 sect **5** creed, trust **6** belief, church, fealty **7** loyalty, promise **8** credence, fidelity, reliance, religion, security **9** assurance, certainty, certitude, constancy **10** confidence, conviction, obligation, persuasion

faithful 4 true **5** close, exact, loyal, tried **6** honest, strict, trusty **7** devoted, factual, precise, similar, staunch, upright **8** accurate, constant, lifelike, reliable, resolute, truthful **9** steadfast **10** dependable, scrupulous, true-to-life, unswerving, unwavering, verifiable **11** trustworthy **13** conscientious, incorruptible

faithfulness 6 fealty **7** loyalty **8** devotion, fidelity **9** constancy **10** allegiance **11** reliability **13** steadfastness

faithless 5 false **6** fickle **8** disloyal **10** inconstant, perfidious, unreliable **11** treacherous **13** untrustworthy

faithlessness 5 doubt **7** perfidy **9** disbelief, falseness, treachery **10** disloyalty, fickleness, infidelity, skepticism **11** inconstancy **13** unreliability **14** perfidiousness, unfaithfulness

fake 4 hoax, ruse, sham **5** bogus, dodge, dummy, faker, false, feign, forge, fraud, phony, put-on, quack, trick **6** deceit, forged, humbug, poseur, pseudo **7** falsify, forgery, not real, pretend, trump up **8** artifice, contrive, deceiver, delusion, imposter, invented, simulate, specious, spurious **9** charlatan, concocted, contrived, deception, dissemble, fabricate, imitation, imposture, pretender, simulated **10** artificial, fabricated, fictitious **11** contrivance, counterfeit, dissimulate, fabrication, make-believe

faker 5 fraud, phony **6** humbug **8** imposter **9** charlatan, pretender

fakir 5 Hindu **6** Muslim **7** ascetic, dervish

falcon 4 eyas **5** hobby, saker **6** desert,

lanner, merlin **7** goshawk, kestrel, prairie, shaheen, tiercel **8** caracara, falconet **9** gyrfalcon, peregrine
cover eyes: 4 seel

Falcon and the Snowman, The
author: 13 Robert Lindsey
director: 15 John Schlesinger
cast: 8 Sean Penn (Andrew Daulton Lee, the Snowman) **13** Timothy Hutton (Christopher John Boyce, the Falcon)

Falconer
author: 11 John Cheever

Falconet, Etienne-Maurice
born: 5 Paris **6** France
artwork: 9 The Bather **12** Bathing Nymph **13** Milo of Crotona, Peter the Great **19** Pygmalion and Galatea

falconry 7 hawking
equipment: 4 lure **5** cadge **6** jesses **7** creance

Falk, Lee
creator/artist of: 10 The Phantom **19** Mandrake the Magician

Falk, Peter
born: 9 New York NY
roles: 7 Columbo **9** Murder Inc **12** The Great Race **13** Murder by Death, Wings of Desire **17** The Cheap Detective **19** Pocketful of Miracles **21** It's a Mad Mad Mad Mad World, Robin and the Seven Hoods

fall, falls 3 die, ebb, err, sin **4** drop, plop, ruin, slip, wane **5** droop, lapse, occur, slope, slump, spill **6** autumn, crop up, defeat, happen, perish, plunge, topple, tumble **7** be slain, be taken, capture, cascade, cheapen, come off, crumple, decline, descend, descent, falling, plummet, sinking, succumb **8** cataract, collapse, come down, decrease, diminish, disgrace, downfall, drop down, dropping, go astray, hang down, lowering **9** crash down, overthrow, reduction, surrender, take place, waterfall **10** capitulate, come to pass, corruption, debasement, depreciate, diminution, subsidence, subversion, transgress **11** be destroyed, harvest time **12** capitulation, depreciation, Indian summer **15** loss of innocence

Fall, The
author: 11 Albert Camus

Falla, Manuel de
born: 5 Cadiz, Spain
composer of: 11 El Amor Brujo, La Atlantida, La Vida Breve, Life Is Short **14** Fantasia Betica **15** Love the Magician **19** The Three-Cornered Hat **21** El sombrero de tres picos **25** Nights in the Gardens of Spain

fallacious 5 false, wrong **6** faulty, flawed, untrue **8** delusive, mistaken **9** deceptive, erroneous, illogical, incorrect **10** inaccurate, misleading, untruthful

fallacy 4 flaw **5** catch, error, fault **7** mistake, pitfall **8** delusion, illusion **9** misbelief **10** faultiness **11** false belief, false notion **13** inconsistency, misconception **15** misapprehension

fall apart 5 decay **7** break up, crumble, shatter **8** fragment, splinter **10** go to pieces **11** fragmentize **12** disintegrate

fall away 4 fade, wane **5** abate **7** drop off, slacken, subside **8** mitigate, taper off

fall back 6 recede **7** back off, retreat

fallen 4 dead **5** loose, slain **6** ousted, ruined, sinful **7** debased, deposed, dropped, immoral, spilled, toppled, tumbled **8** sprawled **9** butchered, disgraced, massacred, turned out **10** discharged, overthrown **11** slaughtered

fallen short
French: 6 manque

fall for 7 believe, swallow

fall guy 4 dupe, pawn, tool **5** patsy **7** cat's-paw

fallible 5 frail, human **6** faulty, mortal, unsure **9** imperfect **10** unreliable

fall in drops 4 drip, rain **7** dribble, drizzle **8** sprinkle

falling apart 6 ruined, shabby **7** rickety, run-down **8** decaying, decrepit **9** crumbling **10** broken-down, collapsing, ramshackle, tumbledown **11** dilapidated **13** deteriorating

Falling in Place
author: 10 Ann Beattie

falling into decay 6 ruined, shabby **7** rotting, run-down **8** decrepit **9** crumbling, moldering **10** broken-down, tumbledown **11** dilapidated, in disrepair **13** deteriorating

falling off 3 ebb **4** fall, wane **7** decline **8** decrease **9** dwindling, lessening, reduction **10** diminution **13** deterioration

falling out 4 spat **7** dispute, quarrel **8** argument, squabble **10** difference **12** disagreement

fall in with 6 concur **7** conform **8** accede to **9** acquiesce **11** go along with

fall off 4 drop, wane **6** lessen, plunge, reduce, topple **7** decline, drop off, plummet, slacken, subside **8** decrease, diminish, moderate, peter out

Fall of the House of Usher, The
author: 13 Edgar Allan Poe
character: 8 Narrator **13** Madeline Usher, Roderick Usher

fallow 4 arid, idle **5** inert **6** barren, unused **7** dormant, unsowed, worn out **8** depleted, inactive, untilled **9** exhausted, unplanted **10** unfruitful **12** uncultivated, unproductive

fall short 6 be less, fail at, give up **9** be lacking, lag behind **10** have too few **11** fail to reach, miss the mark **12** be inadequate **14** be insufficient

fall to one's lot 4 fall **5** occur **6** befall, chance, happen **7** turn out **9** come about **10** come to pass

fall upon 5 fly at **6** assail, attack, dive at **7** embrace, lunge at, set upon **8** thrust at, tuck into

false 4 fake, sham **5** bogus, phony, wrong **6** ersatz, faulty, forged, pseudo, tricky, unreal, untrue **7** devious, feigned, inexact, invalid, unsound **8** delusive, disloyal, mistaken, spurious, two-faced **9** deceitful, deceiving, deceptive, dishonest, erroneous, faithless, imitation, incorrect, unfounded **10** apocryphal, artificial, factitious, fallacious, inaccurate, inconstant, misleading, not correct, perfidious, traitorous, unfaithful, untruthful **11** counterfeit, make-believe, treacherous **12** hypocritical **13** double-dealing

false front 4 mask, sham, show **6** facade, screen, veneer **8** pretense

false-hearted 8 two-faced **9** deceitful, deceiving, faithless **10** perfidious **13** double-dealing, untrustworthy

falsehood 3 fib, lie **5** lying, story **6** canard, deceit **7** fiction, figment, perfidy, perjury, untruth, whopper **8** bad faith, white lie **9** deception, duplicity, hypocrisy, invention, mendacity **10** dishonesty, distortion, inaccuracy **11** dissembling, fabrication, insincerity **12** misstatement, two-facedness **13** deceptiveness, dissimulation, double-dealing, falsification **17** misrepresentation

falseness 5 fraud **6** deceit **7** perfidy **9** duplicity, treachery **10** dishonesty **12** spuriousness **13** deceitfulness, double-dealing, faithlessness **14** untruthfulness

falsified 5 false, phony **6** forged, made-up **7** assumed **10** fictitious

falsify 4 fake **5** belie, rebut **6** doctor, misuse, refute **7** confute, distort, pervert **8** disprove **10** tamper with **12** misrepresent

Falstaff
  opera by: 5 Verdi
  character: 4 Anne **6** Fenton, Pistol **7** Dr Caius **8** Bardolph **11** Dame Quickly **12** Mistress Ford, Mistress Page **15** Mistress Quickly, Sir John Falstaff

Falstaff, Sir John
  character in: 12 Henry IV Part I **13** Henry IV Part II **22** The Merry Wives of Windsor
  author: 11 Shakespeare

falter 3 lag **4** halt, reel **5** demur, waver **6** dodder, mumble, shrink, teeter, totter **7** shamble, shuffle, stagger, stammer, stumble, stutter **8** hesitate **9** fluctuate, vacillate **10** dillydally **11** be undecided **12** be irresolute, show weakness **14** blow hot and cold

fame 4 note **5** eclat, glory **6** renown, repute **7** laurels **8** eminence, prestige **9** celebrity, notoriety **10** notability, popularity, prominence, reputation **11** distinction, preeminence **15** illustriousness

famed 5 noted **6** famous **7** notable **8** renowned **9** prominent, well-known **10** celebrated

familiar 3 pal **4** bold, chum, cozy, free, snug **5** buddy, close, crony, known, stock, usual **6** chummy, common, friend **7** forward, general **8** accepted, amicable, at home in, everyday, frequent, friendly, habitual, informal, intimate, ordinary, seasoned, versed in **9** abreast of, brotherly, confidant, customary, fraternal, gemutlich, intrusive, simpatico, skilled in, well-known **10** accessible, accustomed, acquainted, apprised of, conversant, proverbial, unreserved **11** cognizant of, commonplace, impertinent, traditional **12** confidential, conventional, hand and glove, no stranger to, proficient at **13** boon companion, companionable, disrespectful **15** taking liberties

familiarity 4 ease **5** amity, skill **7** know-how, mastery **8** coziness, intimacy **9** closeness, impudence, indecorum, knowledge, unreserve **10** casualness, chumminess, cognizance, disrespect, experience, fellowship, fraternity, friendship **11** association, brotherhood, conversance, forwardness, impropriety, informality, naturalness, presumption, proficiency **12** acquaintance, impertinence, unconstraint, undue liberty, unseemliness **13** brotherliness, comprehension, intrusiveness, understanding, undue intimacy **16** acquaintanceship

familiarize 4 edify, teach, tutor **6** inform, orient (oneself), school, season **7** educate **8** accustom, acquaint, instruct **9** enlighten, habituate, inculcate **11** acclimatize

family 3 kin, set **4** clan, kind, line, race, sept **5** blood, breed, brood, class, group, house, issue, order, stock, tribe **7** dynasty, kinfolk, kinsmen, lineage, progeny **8** ancestry, category, division, kinsfolk **9** forebears, genealogy, offspring, parentage, relations, relatives **10** extraction, kith and kin **11** forefathers **14** classification
  goddess of: 6 Cardea

Family Affair
  character: 4 Jody **5** Buffy, Cissy **8** Mr (Giles) French **9** Bill Davis
  cast: 10 Brian Keith **11** Anissa Jones, Kathy Garver **14** Sebastian Cabot **15** Johnnie Whitaker

family line 4 tree **7** lineage **8** ancestry **9** blood line, genealogy, parentage

Family Moskat, The
  author: 19 Isaac Bashevis Singer

Family Reunion, The
  author: 7 T S Eliot

Family Ties
  character: 4 Nick **5** Ellen **6** Skippy **10** Alex Keaton **11** Elyse Keaton **12** Andrew Keaton, Steven Keaton **13** Mallory Keaton **14** Jennifer Keaton
  cast: 9 Marc Price **11** Michael J Fox, Tina Yothers **12** Michael Gross **14** Justine Bateman **20** Meredith Baxter-Birney

family tree 7 lineage **8** ancestry, pedigree **9** blood line, genealogy

famine 4 lack, want **6** dearth, hunger **7** paucity, poverty **8** scarcity **9** depletion **10** deficiency, exhaustion, famishment, meagerness, scantiness, starvation **11** destitution, half rations, short supply **13** acute shortage, extreme hunger, insufficiency

famished 6 hungry **7** starved

famous 5 noted **7** eminent, notable **8** far-famed, renowned, well-known **9** notorious, prominent **10** celebrated **11** conspicuous, illustrious **13** distinguished

famous person 4 name, star **7** notable **8** luminary, somebody **9** celebrity, personage, superstar **11** personality

fan 3 bug, nut **4** buff **5** fiend, freak **6** addict, rooter, zealot **7** booster, fanatic **8** follower, partisan

fanatic 5 crazy **6** maniac, zealot **7** hothead, radical **8** activist, militant **9** extremist **10** enthusiast **24** member of the lunatic fringe

fanaticism 6 fervor **8** activism, zealotry **9** dogmatism, extremism, monomania, obsession **10** enthusiasm, radicalism **11** extreme zeal, militantism **12** intemperance **13** ruling passion **15** opinionatedness

fancied 5 liked **6** dreamt, took to, unreal **7** assumed, desired, dreamed, thought **8** imagined, supposed **9** conceived, imaginary, preferred

fanciful 3 odd **6** unreal **7** bizarre, curious, flighty, unusual **8** fabulous, humorous, illusory, mythical, quixotic, romantic **9** eccentric, fantastic, imaginary, invective, legendary, visionary, whimsical **10** apocryphal, capricious, chimerical, fictitious **11** imaginative

fanciful talk 7 blarney **9** hyperbole, tall tales **11** fish stories **12** exaggeration

fancy 3 yen **4** fine, idea, like, want **5** crave, dream, enjoy, favor, opine, showy, taste, think **6** assume, custom, deluxe, desire, florid, liking, notion, ornate, relish, rococo, take it, take to, vagary, vision, whimsy **7** baroque, caprice, conceit, dream of, elegant, fantasy, figment, gourmet, imagine, leaning, longing, long for, picture, presume, reverie, special, suppose, surmise, suspect, unusual **8** be fond of, crotchet, daydream, fondness, illusion, not plain, penchant, superior, weakness, yearn for **9** elaborate, epicurean, expensive, hankering, superfine **10** be bent upon, conceive of, conjecture, decorative, high-priced, ornamental, partiality **11** distinctive, exceptional, extravagant, gingerbread, hanker after, have a mind to, imagination, inclination **12** have an eye for, predilection **13** be pleased with, take a liking to

fancy house 4 stew **5** house **6** bagnio **7** brothel **8** bordello, cathouse **10** bawdy house, whorehouse **13** sporting house **14** house of ill fame **16** house of ill repute **19** house of prostitution

fang 4 claw, nail, root, take, tang, tusk **5** prong, seize, tooth **6** obtain **7** capture, procure **8** eyetooth **9** chelicera

fanny 3 bum **4** buns, rump, seat, tush **6** behind, bottom **8** backside, buttocks, derriere **9** fundament

Fanny
    author: **9** Erica Jong

Fanny
    character in: **13** Joseph Andrews
    author: **8** Fielding

fan out 7 scatter **8** disperse **9** spread out

fantasize 5 dream, fancy **7** imagine **8** daydream

fantastic 3 mad, odd **4** huge, wild **5** antic, crazy, great, queer, weird **6** absurd, superb **7** amazing, bizarre, extreme, strange **8** enormous, fabulous, fanciful, freakish, illusory, quixotic, romantic, terrific **9** grotesque, imaginary, marvelous, visionary, wonderful **10** chimerical, far-fetched, incredible, irrational, outlandish, ridiculous, tremendous **11** extravagant, implausible, sensational **12** preposterous, unbelievable

fantasy 4 mind **5** dream, fancy **6** mirage, notion, vision, whimsy **7** caprice, chimera, fiction, figment, phantom, reverie **8** daydream, illusion, phantasm **9** imagining, invention, nightmare, unreality **10** apparition **11** fabrication, imagination, make-believe, supposition **13** hallucination, realm of dreams, visionary idea

Fantasy Island
    character: **6** Tattoo **8** Mr Roarke
    cast: **16** Herve Villechaize, Ricardo Montalban

far 4 afar, much **6** deeply, remote, way-off, yonder **7** distant, greatly **11** beyond range, out-of-the-way **12** considerably, immeasurably, incomparably

Faraday, Michael
    field: **7** physics **9** chemistry

worked in: 11 electricity
developed: 9 generator **12** electrolysis
liquified: 8 chlorine
discovered: 6 carbon **7** benzene **24** electromagnetic induction
named for him: 5 farad

far and near 10 every place, everywhere, far and wide **11** in all places

far and wide 10 every place, everywhere, far and near **11** in all places

Far Away and Long Ago
    author: **8** W H Hudson

farce 4 sham **6** parody **7** mockery **8** drollery, nonsense, pretense, travesty **9** absurdity, burlesque, horseplay, low comedy **10** buffoonery, tomfoolery **11** broad comedy, make-believe **12** harlequinade **14** ridiculousness

farceur 3 wag **5** joker

farcical 5 droll, funny, silly **6** absurd, stupid **7** asinine, comical, foolish **8** humorous **9** laughable, ludicrous, senseless **10** irrational, ridiculous

fare 2 do **3** fee **4** diet, food, menu **5** board, get on, rider, table **6** charge, client, manage **7** make out, perform, regimen, turn out **8** customer, get along, victuals **10** provisions **11** comestibles, ticket price **12** food and drink, passage money **15** paying passenger **20** cost of transportation

farewell 6 so long **7** good-bye, parting **8** Godspeed **9** departing, departure **11** leave-taking, parting wish, valediction **17** parting compliment
    French: **5** adieu **8** au revoir
    German: **14** auf Wiedersehen
    Hawaiian: **5** aloha
    Italian: **4** ciao **5** addio **11** arrivederci
    Japanese: **8** sayonara
    Latin: **4** vale
    Spanish: **5** adios

Farewell to Arms, A
    author: **15** Ernest Hemingway
    character: **13** Frederic Henry **16** Catherine Barkley

far-fetched 7 dubious **8** doubtful, strained, unlikely **10** cockamamie, improbable **11** implausible **12** preposterous, unconvincing

Far From the Madding Crowd
    author: **11** Thomas Hardy
    character: **10** Fanny Robin, Gabriel Oak **12** Sergeant Troy **14** Farmer Boldwood **17** Bathsheba Everdene
    setting: **6** Wessex

farina 4 meal, mush **5** flour **6** cereal, pollen, starch **8** semolina

farm 3 sow **4** plow, reap **5** plant, ranch, tract **6** grange, spread **7** harvest **9** cultivate **10** plantation **11** till the soil **12** country place

farmable 6 arable **7** friable **8** plowable, tillable **10** cultivable

farm animal 2 ox **3** cow, ewe, hen,

hog, pig, ram, sow **4** bull, goat **5** beast, brute, horse, sheep **7** chicken, rooster

farm boundaries
    god of: **8** Silvanus, Sylvanus

farmer 6 grower, raiser, reaper **7** granger, planter, rancher **8** agrarian **9** harvester **10** agronomist, husbandman **12** sharecropper **13** agriculturist, truck gardener **15** tiller of the soil

farming
    god of: **4** Thor

far-off 6 remote **7** distant, far-away **11** unreachable **12** inaccessible **13** unforeseeable

farouche 3 shy **6** fierce, sullen **10** unsociable

far-out 3 mad **4** wild **5** crazy, weird **7** bizarre, strange **10** outlandish **14** fantastic

Far Pavilions, The
    author: **6** M M Kaye

Farragut, David
    served in: **8** Civil War **10** Mexican War **19** War of Eighteen Twelve
    captured: **9** Mobile Bay **10** New Orleans
    saying: **30** Damn the torpedoes full speed ahead

far-reaching 4 wide **5** broad **8** sweeping **9** expansive, extensive, universal, unlimited **11** wide-ranging

Farrell, James T
    author of: **11** Judgment Day **12** Studs Lonigan, Young Lonigan **29** The Young Manhood of Studs Lonigan

far-removed 6 far-off, remote **7** distant, faraway

farrow 6 barren **7** piglets, sterile **9** infertile **10** unpregnant

Farrow, Mia
    real name: **27** Maria de Lourdes Villier Farrow
    father: **10** John Farrow
    mother: **16** Maureen O'Sullivan
    husband: **11** Andre Previn **12** Frank Sinatra
    companion: **10** Woody Allen
    born: **12** Los Angeles CA
    roles: **5** Zelig **11** John and Mary, Peyton Place **12** The Hurricane **13** Rosemary's Baby **14** The Great Gatsby **16** Allison MacKenzie **19** Hannah and Her Sisters **20** The Purple Rose of Cairo

far side 4 back **7** reverse **8** back side

Far Side, The
    creator/artist: **10** Gary Larson

farsighted 4 wise **5** acute **6** shrewd **7** prudent **9** farseeing, hyperopic, judicious, prescient, provident **10** forehanded, foreseeing **11** clairvoyant, levelheaded

farther 6 beyond, deeper, longer **7** further, remoter **9** lengthier **10** more remote **11** more distant, more removed

farthermost 7 extreme **8** farthest, furthest **11** furthermost, most distant

farthest 3 end **4** most **7** extreme, longest **8** furthest, remotest, ultimate **9** uttermost **11** farthermost, furthermost

fascia 4 band, sash **5** board, strip **6** fillet, girdle, ribbon, tissue **7** bandage **8** membrane **9** dashboard

fascinate 5 charm, rivet **6** absorb, allure **7** beguile, bewitch, delight, enchant, engross **8** enravish, enthrall, entrance, transfix **9** captivate, enrapture, overpower, spellbind **14** hold spellbound

fascinating 8 alluring, charming, gripping, riveting **9** absorbing, beguiling **10** bewitching, delightful, enchanting, engrossing, entrancing **11** captivating, enthralling, interesting **12** overpowering, spellbinding

fascination 4 draw, lure **5** charm **6** allure **9** magnetism **10** attraction **11** captivation

fascism 6 Nazism **9** autocracy, oligarchy **10** plutocracy **11** corporatism, police state **13** corporativism **14** corporate state **15** totalitarianism **17** national socialism **21** right-wing dictatorship

fascist 8 dictator **9** Mussolini, rightwing **10** black shirt, brown shirt, repressive, tyrannical **11** dictatorial, doctrinaire **12** storm trooper

fashion 3 air, fad, hew, way **4** form, make, mode, mold, rage **5** carve, craze, forge, frame, habit, shape, style, tenor, trend, usage, vogue **6** create, custom, design, devise, manner **7** compose, pattern, produce **8** attitude, behavior, contrive, demeanor **9** construct, fabricate **10** convention **11** manufacture

fashionable 2 in **3** hip **4** chic **5** smart **6** modish, with-it **7** current, in style, in vogue, popular, stylish, voguish **9** in fashion **10** all the rage, prevailing
French: 9 de rigueur

fashionable world
French: 10 grand monde

fashion designer 4 (Christian) Dior **5** Kenzo, (Jean) Patou, Prada **6** Adolfo, (Georgio) Armani, Lanvin, Poiret, (Coco) Chanel **7** Galanos, (Gianni) Versace, Halston, Missoni, (Pierre) Balmain **8** Givenchy **9** Courreges, Mary Quant, Valentino **10** Balenciaga, Donna Karan, Mainbocher, Perry Ellis **11** Calvin Klein, Emilio Pucci, Ralph Lauren **12** Liz Claiborne, Lucien Lelong, Norman Norell, Pierre Cardin, Schiaparelli **13** Karl Lagerfeld, Rudi Gernreich **14** Pauline Trigere **15** Claire McCardell **16** Gloria Vanderbilt, Yves Saint-Laurent
Empress Eugenie's: 5 (Charles Frederick) Worth
Marie Antoinette's: 10 Rose Bertin

Empress Josephine's: 19 Louis Hippolyte Leroy

fashioned 4 made **5** built **6** formed, framed, molded, shaped, styled **7** adapted, crafted, created, devised, managed, modeled **9** contrived, patterned **11** constructed **12** accommodated

fashion plate 4 dude **5** dandy **12** Beau Brummell, clotheshorse, man of fashion, sharp dresser **14** woman of fashion

fast 4 firm, taut, true, wild **5** ahead, brisk, fleet, fully, hasty, loose, loyal, quick, rapid, rigid, swift, tight **6** famish, firmly, fly- ing, rakish, secure, speedy, stable, starve, steady, wanton, winged **7** abiding, devoted, durable, fasting, fast day, fixedly, hastily, hurried, immoral, lasting, lustful, quickly, rapidly, solidly, soundly, staunch, swiftly, tightly **8** constant, enduring, faithful, fastened, go hungry, immodest, reckless, resolute, securely, speedily, unfading **9** debauched, dissolute, hurriedly, immovable, immovably, in advance, permanent, resistant, steadfast **10** completely, dissipated, firmly tied, lascivious, licentious, profligate, starvation, stationary, unswerving, unwavering **11** accelerated, expeditious, extravagant, intemperate, pleasure-mad, tenaciously **12** hunger strike, ineradicable, lickety-split

Fast, Howard
author of: 9 Spartacus **11** Freedom Road **13** The Immigrants **15** Citizen Tom Paine

fasten 3 bar, fix, pin, tie, wed **4** bind, bolt, clip, fuse, hold, hook, join, lash, link, lock, moor, snap, weld, yoke **5** affix, clamp, clasp, dowel, focus, hitch, close, latch, rivet, screw, stick, truss, unite **6** adhere, anchor, attach, button, cement, couple, direct, pinion, secure, solder, tether **7** connect **8** dovetail **11** put together

fastener 3 peg, pin, tie **4** clip, glue, grip, hook, line, nail, snap, tack **5** catch, clamp, clasp, cleat, latch, screw, strap, truss **6** buckle, button, cement, staple, thread, zipper **7** bracket **8** barrette **9** fastening, safety pin, thumbtack **10** clothespin, connection, hook and eye

fastening 4 snap **5** clasp **8** coupling **9** attaching **11** attachment, connection

fasten together 3 tie **4** dock, join **6** couple, hook up, link up

fastidious 5 fussy, picky **6** choosy, dainty, proper, queasy **7** finicky **8** exacting, precious **9** difficult, squeamish **10** meticulous, particular **11** overprecise, overrefined, persnickety **12** hard to please, overdelicate **13** hypercritical

Fastidious Brisk
character in: 22 Every Man out of His Humour
author: 6 Jonson

fastidiousness 4 care **12** exactingness **14** discrimination **15** persnicketiness

fat 4 full, oily **5** beefy, fatty, flush, heavy, obese, palmy, plump, pudgy, stout, suety **6** chubby, fleshy, grease, greasy, portly, rotund **7** copious, fertile, lumpish, paunchy, replete, stuffed **8** abundant, blubbery, chockful, fruitful, thickset, unctuous **9** animal fat, corpulent, fortunate, lucrative, plenteous, plentiful, rewarding **10** overweight, potbellied, productive **11** wellstocked **12** remunerative

fatal 6 deadly, lethal, mortal **7** ruinous **8** terminal, virulent **10** calamitous, disastrous **11** destructive **12** catastrophic, causing death

fatalism 8 stoicism **11** resignation **12** acquiescence, helplessness **13** powerlessness **14** predestination

fatality 5 death **8** casualty **9** lethality, mortality **10** deadliness, malignancy **11** banefulness

fatal woman see **11** femme fatale

fate 3 lot **4** doom **5** karma, moira **6** effect, future, kismet, upshot **7** chances, destiny, fortune, outcome, portion **8** prospect **10** providence **11** consequence **12** will of heaven **14** predestination

fated 4 sure **5** bound, meant **6** doomed **7** certain **8** destined

fateful 5 fatal **7** crucial, ominous **8** critical, decisive **9** momentous **10** disastrous, portentous **11** significant

Fates
also: 5 Morae **6** Moerae, Moirai, Parcae
named: 6 Clotho **7** Atropos **8** Lachesis
goddesses of: 7 destiny
number of goddesses: 5 three
called: 12 weird sisters
parents: 4 Zeus **5** Night **6** Themis

father 3 dad, pop **4** abbe, cure, papa, sire **5** beget, begin, daddy, found, hatch, maker, padre, pater **6** author, create, design, old man, parson, pastor, priest **7** creator, founder **8** ancestor, begetter, designer, engender, forebear, inventor, preacher **9** architect, confessor, originate, procreate **10** forefather, male parent, originator, progenitor
French: 4 pere

Father 4 Abba

Father, The
author: 16 August Strindberg

Father Knows Best
character: 11 Jim Anderson **13** Betty Anderson (Princess), Kathy Anderson (Kitten) **15** James Anderson Jr (Bud) **16** Margaret Anderson
cast: 9 Billy Gray, Jane Wyatt **11** Ro-

bert Young **12** Lauren Chapin **13** Elinor Donahue

fatherland 6 Heimat, patria, patrie **8** homeland **10** birthplace, motherland, native land, native soil **13** mother country, native country

fatherly 6 benign, kindly, tender **8** parental, paternal **9** indulgent **10** beneficent, benevolent

father of his country
Latin: **12** Pater Patriae

father of stars/wind 8 Astraeus

Father of the Bride
director: **16** Vincente Minnelli
cast: **11** Billie Burke, Joan Bennett, Leo G Carroll **12** Spencer Tracy **15** Elizabeth Taylor
sequel: **21** Father's Little Dividend

father of the family
Latin: **13** paterfamilias

Father of the Rivers see **4** Nile

Fathers and Sons
author: **12** Ivan Turgenev
character: **5** Katya, Pavel **6** Arkady, Vasily **8** Bazaroff, Fenichka **9** Kirsanoff **15** Madame Odintzoff

fathom 5 probe **6** divine, follow **7** hunt out, root out, uncover, unravel **8** discover **9** ferret out, figure out, penetrate **10** comprehend, understand **16** get to the bottom of

fathom
abbreviation: **4** fath

fatigue 3 fag **4** bush, tire **5** drain, weary **6** tedium, tucker, weaken **7** exhaust, languor, wear out **8** enervate, overtire **9** heaviness, lassitude, tiredness, weariness **10** debilitate, drowsiness, enervation, exhaustion **12** debilitation, listlessness **13** overtiredness

fatigued 4 beat **5** all in, jaded, spent, tired, weary **6** bushed, done in, fagged, pooped **7** worn out **8** dogtired, weakened **9** dead tired, enervated, exhausted, overtaxed **10** overworked **11** debilitated, tuckered out

fatiguing 6 tiring **7** arduous, tedious **8** tiresome **9** wearisome **10** exhausting

Fatima
character in: **9** Bluebeard

fatti maschii, parole femine 29 deeds are manly words are womanish
motto of: **8** Maryland

fatty 4 oily **5** lardy, suety **6** greasy **7** buttery **8** blubbery **9** shortened

fatuous 5 inane, silly, vapid **6** obtuse, simple, stupid **7** asinine, foolish, idiotic, moronic, puerile, vacuous, witless **8** besotted, imbecile **9** brainless, senseless **10** ridiculous

faucet 3 tap **4** cock **5** spout, valve **6** nozzle, outlet, spigot **7** bibcock

Faulkland
character in: **9** The Rivals
author: **8** Sheridan

Faulkner, William

author of: **7** The Bear **8** Sartoris **9** Sanctuary, The Hamlet **10** The Reivers **11** As I Lay Dying **13** Light in August **15** Absalom Absalom! **17** Intruder in the Dust **18** The Sound and the Fury
fictional county: **13** Yoknapatawpha

fault 3 bug, sin **4** flaw, slip, snag **5** blame, crime, error, guilt, stain, taint, wrong **6** defect, foible, glitch, impugn **7** blemish, blunder, censure, failing, frailty, misdeed, mistake, offense, reprove **8** drawback, weakness **9** criticize, infirmity, oversight, weak point **10** deficiency, impediment, negligence, peccadillo, wrongdoing **11** culpability, dereliction, misdemeanor, shortcoming **12** imperfection, indiscretion **13** answerability, transgression **14** accountability, responsibility

faultfind 3 nag **4** beef, carp, kick **5** cavil, gripe, knock **6** deride, squawk **7** nitpick **8** complain **9** criticize

faultfinder 3 nag **4** bear, crab **5** crank **6** carper, censor, critic, grouch **7** caviler, grouser **8** quibbler, sorehead **9** derogator, detractor, Mrs Grundy, nitpicker **10** bellyacher, complainer, curmudgeon, fuddy-duddy, fussbudget

faultfinding 4 beef, kick **5** gripe **6** squawk **7** beefing, carping, griping, kicking, nagging **9** complaint, criticism, squawking **10** nitpicking **11** complaining, criticizing

faultless 5 ideal **7** correct, perfect **8** accurate, flawless **9** exemplary **10** immaculate, impeccable **11** unblemished **13** unimpeachable **14** irreproachable, without blemish

faulty 3 bad **4** awry **5** amiss, false, wrong **7** injured, unsound **8** impaired, inferior, mistaken **9** defective, deficient, erroneous, imperfect, incorrect **10** inadequate, out of order, unreliable **14** unsatisfactory

faun
form: **5** deity, satyr **7** goat-man
location: **5** rural

Fauna see **7** Bona Dea

Faunus
origin: **5** Roman
form: **5** deity
location: **5** woods
also called: **5** Inuus **6** Fatuus
king of: **6** Latium
father: **5** Picus
son: **7** Latinus
corresponds to: **3** Pan

Faure, Gabriel Urbain
born: **6** France **7** Pamiers
composer of: **5** Dolly **6** Pavane **7** Ballade, Mirages, Requiem, Shylock **8** Penelope **9** Fantaisie, Promethee **12** Le Jardin Clos **13** La Chanson d'Eve **14** La Bonne Chanson **18** L'Horizon Chimerique, Pelleas et

Melisande **21** Masques et Bergamasques

Faust
author: **12** Johann Goethe
character: **6** Wagner **8** Gretchen **10** Homunculus **11** Helen of Troy **14** Mephistopheles

Faust
opera by: **6** Gounod
character: **6** Siebel **8** Valentin **10** Marguerite **14** Mephistopheles

Faustulus
vocation: **8** herdsman, shepherd
raised: **5** Remus **7** Romulus

faute de mieux 24 for lack of something better

faux pas 4 goof **5** boner, error, gaffe, lapse **6** boo-boo, howler, slip-up **7** blooper, blunder, mistake **9** false step **11** impropriety **12** indiscretion

favela 4 slum **10** shanty town

Favell, Jack
character in: **7** Rebecca
author: **9** Du Maurier

Favonius
origin: **5** Roman
personifies: **8** west wind

favor 3 aid **4** abet, back, gift, help, like **5** be for, fancy, humor **6** assist, esteem, foster, oblige, pamper, prefer, succor, uphold **7** approve, commend, endorse, go in for, indulge, kind act, memento, present, service, support **8** advocacy, approval, courtesy, espousal, good deed, good turn, goodwill, largesse, look like, resemble, sanction, side with, souvenir **9** encourage, patronage, patronize, smile upon, take after, use gently **10** act of grace, use lightly **11** accommodate, approbation, be partial to, benefaction, countenance, good opinion **12** be the image of, championship, commendation, dispensation, kindly regard **13** accommodation, goodwill token

favorable 4 fair, good, kind **6** benign, timely **7** helpful, hopeful **8** amicable, friendly, salutary **9** approving, conducive, opportune, promising **10** auspicious, beneficial, convenient, propitious **11** predisposed, serviceable, sympathetic **12** advantageous, commendatory, well-disposed

favorable opinion 6 esteem, regard **7** respect **8** approval **10** admiration **12** appreciation

favorably disposed 7 willing **8** amenable, inclined, obliging **9** agreeable **11** sympathetic

favorite 3 pet **5** fancy, jewel **6** choice **7** darling, special **9** best-liked, preferred **11** front-runner, most popular **13** fair-haired one **14** apple of one's eye

favoritism 4 bias **10** partiality **12** one-sidedness, partisanship

Fawley, Jude and Drusilla
 characters in: **14** Jude the Obscure
 author: **5** Hardy

fawn 5 toady **6** pander **7** flatter, truckle **8** pay court **9** be servile, seek favor **12** be obsequious, bow and scrape

fawning 7 servile **8** flattery, toadying **9** adulating, adulation, truckling **10** flattering, obsequious **11** sycophantic **12** ingratiating **14** obsequiousness

fax 4 send **8** transmit **9** facsimile

faze 4 fret **5** abash, daunt, upset, worry **6** bother, flurry, rattle **7** disturb, fluster, perturb **8** confound **9** discomfit, embarrass **10** discompose, disconcert

fazed 5 upset **7** abashed, ruffled **8** agitated, bothered, confused **9** chagrined, unsettled **10** confounded, distracted, nonplussed **11** embarrassed **12** disconcerted

FBI, The
 character: **10** Arthur Ward **21** Inspector Lewis Erskine
 cast: **12** Philip Abbott **16** Efrem Zimbalist Jr

fealty 7 loyalty **8** devotion, fidelity **9** adherence, constancy **10** allegiance, attachment **12** faithfulness

fear 3 awe **4** care **5** alarm, bogey, dread, panic, qualm, worry **6** dismay, esteem, fright, horror, phobia, revere, terror, threat, wonder **7** anxiety, bugaboo, bugbear, concern, quaking, specter **8** affright, venerate **9** cowardice, nightmare, reverence, shudder at, tremble at **10** be afraid of, be scared of, feel awe for, foreboding, take fright, veneration **11** trepidation **12** apprehension, perturbation **13** consternation **14** be frightened of

fearful 4 dire **5** awful, dread, eerie, lurid, timid **6** afraid, aghast, horrid, scared, uneasy **7** alarmed, anxious, ghastly, macabre, nervous, ominous, panicky, worried **8** alarming, dreadful, horrible, shocking, sinister, skittish, terrible, timorous **9** appalling, concerned, diffident, frightful, tremulous **10** formidable, frightened, portentous, terrifying **11** distressing, frightening, intimidated **12** apprehensive, fainthearted **13** panic-stricken **14** chicken-hearted

fearfulness fear **5** alarm, dread, panic **6** fright, terror **7** anguish, anxiety **8** timidity **11** trepidation **12** apprehension

fearless 4 bold **5** brave **6** daring, gritty, heroic, plucky **7** doughty, gallant, valiant **8** intrepid, unafraid, valorous **9** audacious, confident, dauntless, unabashed, undaunted **10** courageous, undismayed **11** adventurous, indomitable, lionhearted, unflinching, unshrinking, venturesome, without fear **12** stout-hearted

fearlessness 4 grit **5** pluck, valor **7** bravery, courage **8** boldness **10** confidence **13** dauntlessness

Fear of Flying
 author: **9** Erica Jong

feasible 6 doable, viable **7** fitting, politic **8** possible, suitable, workable **9** advisable, desirable **10** achievable, attainable, reasonable **11** appropriate, conceivable, practicable

feast 4 dine, fete **5** festa, gorge **6** bounty **7** banquet, holiday, jubilee, surplus **8** feast day, festival **9** bacchanal, saint's day **10** gluttonize, gormandize, have a feast, rich supply **11** celebration, eat one's fill, elegant meal, wine and dine

feat 3 act **4** deed, task **6** action, stroke **7** exploit, triumph **8** maneuver **9** adventure **10** attainment, enterprise **11** achievement, performance, tour de force **14** accomplishment

feather 4 down, kind, sort **5** adorn, eider, pinna, plume, quill **7** bristle, plumage, variety **9** character, turn an oar

featherbrained 4 dumb **5** silly **6** simple, stupid **7** foolish, witless **9** brainless **12** muddleheaded, simple-minded **13** rattle-brained **14** scatterbrained

feather in one's cap 5 honor **6** credit **11** distinction

feather one's nest 6 enrich **15** fill one's pockets

feature, features 3 see **4** mark, star **5** fancy, trait **6** aspect, play up, visage **7** display, earmark, imagine, picture, present, quality **8** envision, hallmark, headline, main item, property **9** attribute, character, highlight, specialty, spotlight **10** conceive of, lineaments **14** characteristic

February
 event: **4** Lent **5** Purim **8** Leap year **9** Mardi Gras **12** Ash Wednesday, Groundhog Day (2)
 flower: **6** violet **8** primrose
 French: **7** Fevrier
 gem: **8** amethyst
 German: **7** Februar
 holiday: **9** Candlemas (2) **13** President's Day Valentine's Day (14) **14** Chinese New Year **16** Lincoln's Birthday (12) **19** Washington's Birthday (22)
 Italian: **8** Febbraio
 Latin: **6** Februa
 number of days: **10** twenty-nine (every 4 years) **11** twenty-eight
 origin of name: **7** Februus
  Roman god of: **12** purification
 place in year:
  Gregorian: **6** second
  Roman: **7** twelfth
 Spanish: **7** Febrero
 Zodiac signs: **6** Pisces **8** Aquarius

Fechner, Gustav Theodore

 nationality: **6** German
 founder of: **22** experimental psychology

fecit 6 he made (it) **7** she made (it)

feckless 3 lax **5** slack **6** remiss **8** careless, heedless **9** negligent, worthless **10** neglectful **11** thoughtless **13** irresponsible

Fecundity
 goddess of: **5** Freia, Freya

Fed
 Federal Reserve System: **6** the Fed
 FBI agent: **4** G-man **6** feebie, fibbie
 Treasury agent: **4** T-man
 head: **14** Alan Greenspan

Federalist Party
 president belonging to: **5** Adams **10** Washington

federate 5 unite **7** combine **12** join together

federation 5 union **6** league **7** combine **8** alliance **9** coalition, syndicate **10** sisterhood **11** association, brotherhood, confederacy **12** amalgamation **13** confederation

fee 4 fare, hire, toll, wage **5** price **6** charge, salary, tariff **7** payment, stipend **9** emolument **10** commission, honorarium **12** compensation, remuneration **13** consideration

feeble 4 flat, lame, poor, puny, tame, thin, weak **5** faint, frail, vapid **6** ailing, flabby, flimsy, infirm, meager, paltry, senile, sick- ly, slight **7** fragile, insipid **8** decrepit, delicate, disabled, impotent, weakened **9** colorless, declining, doddering, enervated, enfeebled, forceless, not strong, powerless **10** inadequate, spiritless, wishy-washy **11** debilitated, ineffective, ineffectual

feeble-minded 4 dull, dumb **6** senile, stupid **7** moronic **8** backward, childish, retarded **9** imbecilic, senseless, subnormal **10** half-witted, weakminded **12** mentally slow

feeble-mindedness 6 dotage, idiocy **8** dullness, senility, slowness **9** denseness, stupidity **11** retardation

feed 3 eat **4** fare, fuel, mash **5** cater, feast, graze **6** devour, fodder, forage, foster, viands **7** augment, bolster, consume, gratify, nourish, nurture, pasture, satisfy, support, sustain **8** maintain, take food, victuals **9** encourage, foodstuff, provender **10** minister to, provisions, strengthen **11** comestibles, nourishment, wine and dine

feeder 6 branch **7** channel **9** tributary

feel 3 paw, see **4** know **5** grope, press, probe, reach, sense, think, touch **6** fin- ger, fumble, handle, makeup, notice **7** believe, discern, feeling, observe, palpate, texture **8** perceive **9** be aware of, be moved by, character, sensation **10** comprehend, experience, manipulate, suffer from, understand

11 be convinced, be stirred by, be touched by, composition

feel aversion toward 4 hate **5** abhor **6** detest **7** despise **9** abominate, can't abide, can't stand **11** can't stomach **12** be revolted by **13** find repugnant, find repulsive **14** view with horror

feeler 7 antenna **8** proposal, tentacle **10** experiment **12** trial balloon

feel indebted 10 appreciate, be beholden, be grateful **13** feel obligated

feeling 4 aura, pity, view, zeal **5** ardor, gusto, sense, verve **6** fervor, spirit, thrill, warmth **7** concern, emotion, opinion, passion **8** attitude, instinct, reaction, response, sympathy **9** affection, awareness, intuition, sensation, sentiment, vehemence **10** atmosphere, compassion, enthusiasm, impression **11** earnestness, inclination, point of view, sensibility, sensitivity

feeling life is wearisome
   Latin: **12** taedium vitae

feelings 3 ego **5** pride **8** emotions, passions **10** self- esteem **13** sensibilities, sensitivities **16** susceptibilities

feel pain 4 ache, hurt **5** smart **6** suffer **7** agonize **9** be in agony **11** be tormented **12** be in distress

Feenix, Cousin
   character in: **12** Dombey and Son
   author: **7** Dickens

feet 4 dogs, pads, paws **5** hoofs **6** hooves **8** gunboats, tootsies

feign 4 fake, sham **5** forge, put on **6** affect, assume, cook up, invent, make up **7** concoct, pretend **8** simulate **9** fabricate **11** counterfeit, make a show of, make believe

feigned 4 fake, sham **5** bogus, phony **6** ersatz **8** spurious **9** imitation, insincere, pretended, simulated **10** artificial **11** counterfeit, make-believe

feint 4 hoax, mask, move, pass, ploy, ruse, wile **5** blind, bluff, dodge, trick **6** gambit **7** pretext **8** artifice, maneuver, pretense **9** stratagem **10** subterfuge **13** feigned attack

Feldman, Marty
   born: **6** London **7** England
   roles: **11** Silent Movie **17** Young Frankenstein **24** The Last Remake of Beau Geste

feldspar
   varieties: **8** sunstone **9** amazonite, moonstone

felicitate 4 hail **6** salute **10** wish one joy **11** rejoice with **12** congratulate **18** give one's best wishes **28** wish many happy returns of the day

felicitations 3 joy **6** cheers **9** blessings, greetings **10** best wishes, good wishes **11** compliments, salutations **12** pat on the back **15** congratulations **24** many happy returns of the day

felicitous 3 apt **5** happy **6** joyful, joy-

ous **7** fitting, germane, well-put **8** inspired, pleasing, relevant, suitable, well-said **9** effective, fortunate, pertinent **10** propitious, well-chosen **11** appropriate

felicity 5 bliss, charm, grace, knack, skill **6** heaven, nicety **7** aptness, delight, ecstasy, fitness **8** paradise **9** beatitude, happiness **12** blissfulness **13** effectiveness **15** appropriateness

Felix the Cat
   creator: **11** Pat Sullivan

fell 4 raze **5** level **7** cut down, destroy, hew down **8** demolish **9** knock down, prostrate

Feller, Bob (Robert)
   nickname: **11** Rapid Robert
   sport: **8** baseball
   position: **7** pitcher
   team: **16** Cleveland Indians

Fellini, Federico
   director of: **8** Amarcord, Casanova, La Strada **11** La Dolce Vita **15** Nights of Cabiria **18** Juliet of the Spirits

fellow 3 boy, guy, mac, man, pal **4** chap, chum, dude, gent, mate, peer **5** equal **6** friend **7** comrade, consort **8** coworker **9** associate, colleague, companion **10** compatriot

fellow conspirator 4 ally **6** cohort **7** abettor **8** henchman **9** accessory **11** confederate **12** collaborator

fellow creature 5 human **6** mortal, person **10** individual

fellow feeling 6 regard **7** empathy, kinship **8** affinity, fondness **10** attraction, partiality

fellowship 5 amity **7** society **8** intimacy **10** affability, cordiality, fraternity, friendship **11** amicability, association, brotherhood, comradeship, familiarity, sociability **12** friendliness **13** companionship

felon 5 crook, cruel, thief **6** fierce, outlaw, wicked **7** convict, illegal, villain, whitlow **8** criminal, gangster, jailbird, murderer **10** law-breaker, malefactor **11** public enemy **12** inflammation

felony 5 arson, crime **6** murder **7** assault, misdeed, offense, robbery **8** burglary **9** blackmail **10** kidnapping, wrongdoing **12** capital offense

female 3 cow, dam, hen, sow **4** girl, mare **5** bitch, tabby, woman **6** heifer **7** distaff, womanly **8** feminine, ladylike **9** womanlike

feminine 4 soft **5** woman **6** dainty, female, gentle **7** distaff, girlish, womanly **8** delicate, ladylike **10** femalelike, like a woman **14** of the female sex

femininity 8 softness **10** femaleness, gentleness **11** girlishness, womanliness **12** feminineness **13** female quality

femme 4 wife **5** woman

femme de chambre 9 lady's maid **11** chambermaid

femme fatale 4 vamp **5** siren **7** charmer **10** fatal woman, seductress **11** enchantress

femur
   bone of: **5** thigh **8** upper leg

fen 3 bog **4** moor, sump **5** marsh, swale, swamp **6** bottom, morass, slough **7** lowland, wetland **8** quagmire

fence 3 pen **4** coop, duel, gird, rail **5** hedge, hem in **6** corral, secure, wall in **7** barrier, confine, palings **8** encircle, palisade, stockade, surround **9** barricade, encompass **11** cross swords

fencing
   equipment: **4** epee, foil, mask **5** saber, sword **8** plastron
   part of weapon: **5** blade, forte, guard **6** foible, handle, medium, pommel
   term: **3** hit **5** prime, sixte, touch **6** octave, quarte, quinte, tierce **7** en garde, on guard, seconde, septime
   deceptive move: **5** feint
   movement: **4** beat **5** lunge, parry **6** double, fleche, thrust **7** advance, cutover, recover, retreat, riposte **9** disengage **11** froissement

fend 2 do **5** avert, avoid, parry, repel, shift **6** manage **7** keep off, make out, provide, repulse, support, survive, ward off **8** push away

fender 3 pad **4** curb **5** guard **6** buffer, bumper, shield, sluice **7** cushion, railing **9** fireguard, protector **10** cowcatcher, fire screen, protection, wheel guard

fend off 5 avert, dodge, evade, parry, repel **6** escape **7** ward off **8** sidestep, stave off

fennel
   botanical name: **17** Foeniculum vulgare
   family: **7** parsley
   varieties: **3** dog **4** wild **5** giant **8** Florence **9** common dog **11** common giant
   mythical aid to: **9** fortifier **11** aphrodisiac, slenderizer **12** rejuvenation, stops hiccups **16** restores eyesight
   use: **4** duck, fish **5** bread, rolls **7** chicken **8** apple pie **16** seafood casserole

Fenrir
   also: **6** Fenris
   origin: **12** Scandinavian
   form: **4** wolf **7** monster
   father: **4** Loki
   mother: **9** Angerboda, Angrbodha, Angurboda
   sister: **3** Hel
   brother: **11** Iormungandr, Jormungandr **14** Midgard Serpent
   ate: **4** Odin **5** Othin
   killed by: **5** Vidar

Fenris *see* **6** Fenrir

Fenton
  character in: **22** The Merry Wives of Windsor
  author: **11** Shakespeare

feral 4 wild **6** brutal, deadly, ferine, fierce, savage **7** bestial, untamed, vicious **9** ferocious **12** uncultivated **14** undomesticated

Ferber, Edna
  author of: **5** Giant, So Big **8** Cimarron, Show Boat **9** Ice Palace, Stage Door (with George S Kaufman) **13** Dinner at Eight (with George S Kaufman), Saratoga Trunk **14** The Royal Family (with George S Kaufman)

Ferdinand
  king of: **5** Spain
  wife: **8** Isabella
  patron of: **8** Columbus

Ferdinand
  character in: **10** The Tempest
  author: **11** Shakespeare

Ferdinand
  character in: **16** Love's Labour's Lost
  author: **11** Shakespeare

Ferdinand the Bull
  author: **9** Munro Leaf
  disliked: **12** bullfighting

Ferd'nand
  creator: **3** Mik **13** Dahl Mikkelsen

Feria
  origin: **5** Roman
  form: **7** holiday

Fermat, Pierre de
  field: **11** mathematics
  nationality: **6** French
  discovered: **16** analytic geometry

ferment 4 foam, mold, sour, turn **5** froth, yeast **6** enzyme, fester, leaven, seethe, tumult, unrest, uproar **7** agitate, inflame, smolder, turmoil **8** bubble up, disquiet **9** agitation, commotion, leavening **10** disruption, effervesce, turbulence **11** be turbulent, fomentation

fermented 6 soured, worked **7** seethed **8** agitated

Fermi, Enrico
  field: **7** physics
  nationality: **7** Italian
  developed: **10** atomic bomb **20** uranium fission theory
  awarded: **10** Nobel Prize

fern
  varieties: **3** air, cup, lip, man, oak, saw **4** ball, blue, claw, deer, dish, felt, fire, gold, hand, iron, king, lace, lady, male, moss, nest, pine, sago, tara, tree, wall, wart, wood **5** beard, beech, chain, cloak, fancy, glade, glory, grape, grass, hedge, holly, marsh, plume, royal, strap, swamp, sweet, sword, table, water, whisk **6** adder's, bamboo, basket, Boston, button, carrot, coffee, cotton, cuplet, dagger, ladder, meadow, mother, ribbon, shield, silver, tongue, turnip, winter **7** bladder, boulder, brittle, bulblet, crested, emerald, feather, Fee's lip, fragile, Goldie's, hacksaw, Halberd, hammock, leather, New York, ostrich, parsley, peacock, rainbow, walking **8** bear-foot, bear's-paw, cinnamon, climbing, elk's-horn, fishtail, floating, florist's, fragrant, hairy lip, Hartford, licorice, mosquito, Nebraska, Savannah, snuffbox, soft tree, staghorn **9** asparagus, bird's-nest, black tree, blond tree, Christmas, common cup, deer's-foot, downy wood, flowering, glossy cup, hare's foot, long beech, sensitive, vegetable, Venus hair, viscid lip, wavy cloak, woolly lip **10** Alabama lip, Boott's wood, broad beech, deer-tongue, Duff's sword, erect sword, five-finger, hay-scented, lady ground, maidenhair, scented oak, shoestring, silver tree, silver-back, silver-lace, silver-leaf, slender lip, strawberry, upside-down, woolly tree **11** Braun's holly, coastal wood, Coville's lip, crested felt, crested wood, dwarf Boston, elephant-ear, Fendler's lip, hart's-tongue, interrupted, Jamaica gold, leatherleaf, leatherwood, narrow beech, netted chain, Northern oak, Parry's cloak, Pursh's holly, rabbit's-foot, rattlesnake, Sierra water, walking leaf **12** Adder's-tongue, American wall, berry bladder, Clinton's wood, Dudley's holly, Eaton's shield, English hedge, Hawaiian tree, Java staghorn, limestone oak, mountain wood, Northern lady, resurrection, Southern lady, squirrel-foot, toothed sword, Western holly, Western sword **13** California lip, Cleveland's lip, Dudley's shield, European chain, fan maidenhair, Fendler's cloak, Florida ribbon, leathery grape, Malay climbing, mountain holly, Northern holly, prickly shield, Prince-of-Wales, spinulose wood, Tasmanian tree, triangle water, Virginia chain, wild bird's nest **14** Anderson's holly, Australian tree, bulblet bladder, California gold, common staghorn, dissected grape, dwarf asparagus, hen-and-chickens, imbricate sword, silver-king tree, West Indian tree **15** American parsley, California cloak, California holly, Delta maidenhair, East Indian holly, European parsley, mountain bladder, mountain parsley **16** black-stemmed tree, daisy-leaved grape, Farley maidenhair, Tassel maidenhair, Tracy's maidenhair **17** Bermuda maidenhair, brittle maidenhair, climbing bird's nest, walking maidenhair **18** Aleutian maidenhair, American maidenhair, Barbados maidenhair, Northern maidenhair, Trailing maidenhair, Triangular staghorn **20** Australian maidenhair, California maidenhair

fernet-branca
  type: **8** aperitif
  origin: **5** Italy
  flavor: **4** herb

Fern Hill
  author: **11** Dylan Thomas

ferocious 6 brutal, deadly, fierce, savage **7** bestial, brutish, enraged, violent **8** fiendish, maddened, ravening, ruthless **9** atrocious, barbarous, merciless, murderous, predatory, rapacious **10** relentless **11** cold-blooded **12** bloodthirsty

ferocity 7 cruelty **8** savagery **9** barbarity, brutality, harshness **10** fierceness, inhumanity, savageness **11** brutishness, viciousness **12** ruthlessness

Ferrer, Jose
  real name: **33** Jose Vincente Ferrer de Otero y Cintron
  wife: **8** Uta Hagen **15** Rosemary Clooney
  son: **6** Miguel
  born: **8** Santurce **10** Puerto Rico
  roles: **7** I Accuse **9** Joan of Arc **11** Moulin Rouge, Ship of Fools **14** The Caine Mutiny **16** Cyrano de Bergerac (Oscar), Lawrence of Arabia **24** The Greatest Story Ever Told

ferret out 5 dig up **6** detect **7** find out, root out, uncover, unearth **8** discover **9** ascertain

fertile 4 rich **5** loamy **6** fecund **8** creative, fruitful, original, prolific **9** fructuous, ingenious, inventive, luxuriant, plenteous **10** fecundated, fertilized, fructified, generative, productive, vegetative **11** imaginative, resourceful **12** reproductive

Fertility
  god of: **7** Bacchus, Mutinus **8** Lupercus, Picumnus
  goddess of: **4** Isis **5** Fauna **6** Athena, Athene, Brigit, Libera, Pallas, Saitis, Tellus **7** Astarte, Berchta, Bona Dea, Demeter, Perchta **11** Tritogeneia **12** Pallas Athena **16** Alalcomean Athena

fertilize 6 enrich, manure **8** fructify **9** fecundate, pollinate **10** impregnate, inseminate

fertilizer 4 dung, muck **5** guano, niter **6** manure, potash **7** compost **8** bonemeal, dressing **10** enrichener **14** superphosphate

fervent 4 keen **5** eager, fiery **6** ardent, devout, fervid, fierce, hearty, heated **7** burning, earnest, intense, zealous **8** spirited, vehement **9** heartfelt **10** passionate **11** impassioned, warmhearted **12** enthusiastic, wholehearted

fervid 5 eager **6** ardent, raging **7** burning, earnest, fanatic, fervent, intense, zealous **8** spirited **10** passionate **11** impassioned **12** all-consuming

fervor 4 fire, zeal, zest **5** ardor, gusto,

piety, verve **6** warmth **7** passion **9** animation, eagerness, intensity, vehemence **10** devoutness, enthusiasm, heartiness **11** earnestness, seriousness **14** purposefulness

Feste
clown in: **12** Twelfth Night
author: **11** Shakespeare

Fester *see* **12** Addams Family

fester 3 rot, vex **4** fret, gall, grow, rile **5** chafe, pique **6** nettle, plague, rankle **7** blister, form pus, inflame, putrefy, smolder, torment **8** irritate, ulcerate **9** intensify, suppurate

festering 6 putrid **7** rotting **8** infected, inflamed, rankling **10** putrefying **11** suppurating

festina lente 15 make haste slowly

festival 4 fete, gala **5** feast **6** fiesta **7** gala day, holiday, jubilee **8** carnival, jamboree **11** celebration, festivities

Festival of
Adonis: **6** Adonia
Apollo: **5** Delia **8** Didymaea **9** Delphinia **12** Daphnephoria
Athena: **6** Lenaea **8** Diipolia **9** Pyanepsia **11** Oschophoria
Attica: **13** Rural Dionysia **14** Lesser Dionysia
Bacchus: **11** Bacchanalia
Boeotians: **7** Daedala **13** Little Doedala
Demeter: **5** Haloa
Dionysus: **5** Haloa **8** Dionysia
flowers: **11** Anthesteria
Greeks: **6** Heraea **9** Pyanepsia **11** Scirophoria, Skirophoria **13** Thesmorphoria
Persephone: **5** Haloa
Roman: **8** Floralia, Matralia **9** Lemuralia, Liberalia **10** Larentalia, Lupercalia, Matronalia, Parentalia, Saturnalia
spring: **11** Anthesteria
wine: **11** Anthesteria
Zeus: **6** Diasia **8** Didymaea

festive 3 gay **4** gala **5** jolly, merry **6** festal, joyous **7** larkish, playful **8** sportive **9** convivial **10** frolicsome **11** celebratory **12** lighthearted

festivity 3 joy **4** fete, gala **5** feast, mirth **6** fiesta, gaiety, levity **7** fanfare, jollity, jubilee, revelry **8** festival, jamboree **9** merriment, rejoicing **11** celebration, merrymaking

festoon 3 lei **4** swag **5** chain, curve **6** wreath **7** garland, hanging **8** decorate

fetch 3 get **4** cost **5** bring, go for, yield **6** afford, obtain **7** procure, realize, sell for **8** amount to, retrieve

fetching 6 divine, lovely **8** adorable, becoming, charming, engaging, pleasing **9** appealing **10** attractive, delightful **11** captivating

fete 4 gala **5** feast, party, treat **6** regale **7** banquet, holiday **8** carnival, festival **9** bal masque **11** celebration, garden

party, wine and dine **13** fete champetre

fete champetre 11 garden party **15** outdoor festival

fetid 4 foul, gamy, rank **5** fusty, moldy, musty, nasty **6** putrid, rancid, rotten **7** noisome, stenchy, tainted **8** mephitic, stifling, stinking **9** stenchful **10** malodorous **11** ill-smelling, suffocating

fetish 4 idol, joss **5** charm, craze, image, mania, totem **6** amulet, scarab **7** passion **8** idee fixe, talisman **9** obsession **10** golden calf, phylactery **11** magic object **12** superstition **13** preoccupation

fetter 4 bind, bond, cage, curb, yoke **5** chain, tie up **6** duress, hamper, hinder, hobble, impede, shut in, tether **7** confine, durance, manacle, pin down, shackle, tie down, trammel, truss up **8** bracelet, encumber, handcuff, hold back, restrain **9** hindrance, restraint **13** put into bilbos **15** bind hand and foot

feud 3 row **4** fuss, spat, tiff **5** argue, brawl, clash, set-to **6** affray, bicker, breach, enmity, fracas, schism, strife **7** discord, dispute, faction, ill will, quarrel, rupture, wrangle **8** argument, bad blood, be at odds, clashing, conflict, disagree, squabble, vendetta **9** animosity, bickering, hostility **10** falling out **11** altercation, controversy **12** disagreement, hard feelings
famous: **6** McCoys **9** Hatfields

Feud, The
author: **12** Thomas Berger

feudal lord
Japanese: **6** daimyo

Feuerbach, Anselm
born: **6** Speyer **7** Germany
artwork: **9** Iphigenia **15** Judgment of Paris, Plato's Symposium **18** The Fall of the Titans

fever 4 fire, heat **5** ardor, craze, flush, furor **6** desire, frenzy, warmth **7** ferment, illness, pyrexia **8** delirium, sickness **9** agitation **10** enthusiasm, excitement **11** temperature **12** restlessness

feverish 3 hot **5** fiery **6** ardent, red-hot **7** burning, excited, fanatic, febrile, fervent, fevered, flushed, parched, pyretic, zealous **8** frenzied, inflamed, restless **9** impatient, overeager, wrought-up **10** high-strung, passionate **11** impassioned

few 4 rare, some, thin **5** scant **6** meager, paltry, scanty, scarce, skimpy, sparse, unique **7** handful, limited, not many, several, unusual **8** exiguous, piddling, sporadic, uncommon **9** hardly any **10** infrequent, occasional **11** scarcely any, small number **13** infinitesimal, insignificant **14** inconsiderable

Fezziwig
character in: **15** A Christmas Carol
author: **7** Dickens

fiance, fiancee 6 future **7** engaged, pledge **8** intended, promised **9** affianced, betrothed, bride-to-be, groom-to-be **10** bride-elect, groom-elect

fiasco 4 bomb, flop **5** botch **6** fizzle **7** debacle, washout **8** disaster **10** non-success

fiat 3 act, law **4** rule **5** edict, order, ukase **6** decree, dictum, ruling **7** command, mandate **11** commandment

fiat lux 15 let there be light

fib 3 lie **5** hedge **7** fiction, untruth **8** white lie **9** half-truth, invention **10** equivocate **11** fabrication, harmless lie, prevaricate **13** falsification, prevarication, tell a white lie **15** stretch the truth **17** misrepresentation

fiber 4 hemp, jute, silk **5** fibre, linen, nylon, rayon, shred, sinew, sisal **6** cotton, dacron, manila, nature, strand, thread **7** quality, texture **8** filament **9** character, polyester, structure

fibrolite
source: **5** Burma, Mogok

fibula
bone of: **8** lower leg

fickle 5 giddy **6** fitful **7** erratic, flighty **8** shifting, unstable, unsteady, variable, volatile, wavering **9** frivolous, mercurial, spasmodic, whimsical **10** capricious, changeable, inconstant, irresolute, unreliable **11** fluctuating, light-headed, vacillating **12** inconsistent **13** feather-headed, unpredictable, untrustworthy **14** feather-brained

fiction 3 fib, lie **4** play, tale, yarn **5** fable, novel **7** fantasy, forgery, novella, romance, whopper **8** tall tale **9** falsehood, invention, narrative **10** concoction, short novel, short story **11** fabrication, imagination, made-up story **12** storytelling **13** prevarication **16** cock-and-bull story

fictional 6 made-up **8** invented, literary, mythical **9** storybook **10** fictitious **11** theoretical **12** hypothetical

fictitious 4 fake, sham **5** bogus, false, phony **6** forged, made-up, unreal, untrue **7** assumed, feigned **8** fanciful, invented, mythical, spurious **9** imaginary, legendary, simulated, trumped-up, unfounded **10** apocryphal, artificial, fabricated, fraudulent, not genuine **11** counterfeit **14** supposititious

fiddle 3 bow, saw, toy **4** fool **5** cheat, dally, fraud **6** dawdle, monkey, potter, putter, tamper, trifle, violin **7** falsify, finagle, fritter, swindle **9** deception **10** fool around, mess around **12** monkey around

Fidei Defensor 18 Defender of the Faith
title of: **17** English sovereigns

Fidelio
  opera by: **9** Beethoven
  character: **5** Rocco **7** Leonora (Fidelio), Pizarro **8** Fernando **9** Florestan

fidelity 5 honor **6** fealty **7** honesty, loyalty, probity **8** accuracy, devotion **9** adherence, closeness, constancy, exactness, good faith, integrity, precision, sincerity **10** allegiance, exactitude **11** earnestness, reliability, staunchness **12** faithfulness, truthfulness **14** correspondency **15** trueheartedness, trustworthiness

Fides
  origin: **5** Roman
  personifies: **9** good faith

fidget 4 fret, fuss, jerk, stew, toss **5** chafe, worry **6** jiggle, squirm, twitch, wiggle, writhe **7** twiddle, wriggle

fidgety 5 antsy, fussy, jerky, jumpy **6** uneasy **7** jittery, nervous, restive, squirmy, twitchy, unquiet **8** restless **9** impatient, irritable, tremulous **12** apprehensive

fief 4 land **6** domain, estate **9** territory

field 3 lea **4** area, grab, lawn, line, mead, turf, yard **5** arena, catch, court, front, glove, green, heath, lists, orbit, range, reach, realm, scope, sward, sweep **6** circle, common, course, domain, extent, meadow, pick up, region, sphere **7** acreage, calling, diamond, expanse, pasture, run down, stretch **8** clearing, province, retrieve, spectrum **9** bailiwick, grassland, territory **10** department, occupation, profession **12** battleground

Field, Sally
  born: **10** Pasadena CA
  roles: **5** Sybil **6** Gidget **8** Norma Rae (Oscar) **9** Punchline, Surrender **12** The Flying Nun **14** Murphy's Romance **15** Absence of Malice **16** Places in the Heart (Oscar) **18** Smokey and the Bandit

Fielding, Cecil
  character in: **15** A Passage to India
  author: **7** Forster

Fielding, Henry
  author of: **6** Amelia **7** Shamela **8** Tom Jones, Tom Thumb **12** Jonathan Wild **13** Joseph Andrews

Field of Blood 8 Aceldama

Fields, W C
  real name: **23** William Claude Dukenfield
  born: **14** Philadelphia PA
  roles: **5** Poppy **8** Micawber **11** The Bank Dick **16** David Copperfield **17** My Little Chickadee **27** Never Give a Sucker an Even Break

Fields of Mourning
  location: **10** underworld
  inhabited by: **14** shades of lovers
    lovers who died by: **7** suicide

Fields of Visions, The
  author: **12** Wright Morris

fiend 5 beast, brute, demon, devil, Satan **6** dybbuk **7** incubus, monster, villain **8** succubus **9** barbarian, hellhound, scoundrel **10** evil spirit **12** wicked person **14** devil incarnate **16** prince of darkness

fiendish 4 evil, foul **5** cruel **6** wicked **7** demonic, heinous, impious, satanic, vicious **8** barbaric, demoniac, devilish **9** monstrous, nefarious **10** demoniacal, diabolical, villainous

fierce 4 fell, wild **5** cruel, feral, fiery **6** bru-tal, fervid, raging, savage, strong **7** enraged, extreme, fearful, fervent, furious, intense, leonine, untamed, violent **8** horrible, menacing, powerful, ravening, ravenous, terrible, tigerish, uncurbed, vehement **9** barbarous, bellicose, ferocious, impetuous, merciless, truculent, unbridled, voracious **10** immoderate, inordinate, passionate **11** threatening **12** bloodthirsty, overpowering, overwhelming, unrestrained
  French: **8** farouche

fierceness 4 zeal **7** passion **8** ferocity, wildness **9** pugnacity, vehemence **10** savageness

fiery 5 afire, angry, irate **6** ablaze, alight, ardent, fervid, fierce, red-hot, torrid **7** blazing, burning, febrile, fervent, fevered, flaming, glaring, glowing, peppery, pyretic, violent, zealous **8** choleric, feverish, flashing, headlong, inflamed, spirited, vehement, wrathful **9** excitable, hotheaded, impetuous, impulsive, irascible, irritable **10** full of fire, high-strung, mettlesome, passionate, sweltering **11** hot-tempered, impassioned, precipitate **12** enthusiastic

fiesta 4 fete, gala **5** feast, party **6** picnic **7** funfair **8** carnival, feast day, festival, jamboree **9** saint's day **10** block party, observance, street fair **11** celebration **13** com-memoration **15** festive occasion

fig 5 Ficus
  varieties: **3** keg, sea **4** bush, cape, Java, Zulu **5** cedar, clown, Congo, rusty **6** common, Devil's, exotic, golden, Indian, Kaffir, Mysore, sacred **7** Barbary, cluster, oak-leaf, spotted, weeping **8** climbing, creeping, Dracaena, mulberry, sycamore **9** Hottentot, mistletoe, strangler **10** East Indian, fiddle-leaf, glossy-leaf, little-leaf, Moreton Bay, Philippine **11** Port Jackson **16** West Indian laurel

Figaro
  character in: **18** The Barber of Seville **19** The Marriage of Figaro
  author: **12** Beaumarchais

fight 3 box, row, war **4** bout, duel, feud, fray, grit, spar, spat, tiff, tilt, wage **5** ar-gue, brawl, brush, clash, event, joust, match, melee, pluck, round, scrap, set-to **6** battle, bicker, combat, engage, fracas, mettle, oppose, resist, spirit, strife, tussle **7** carry on, conduct, contend, contest, discord, dispute, go to war, quarrel, repulse, scuffle, tourney, wage war, wrangle **8** confront, dogfight, gameness, skirmish, squabble, struggle **9** bickering, encounter, pugnacity, scrimmage, toughness, wrangling **10** contention, difference, dissension, prizefight, strive with, tournament **11** altercation, armed action, battle royal, bellicosity, clash of arms, controversy **12** belligerency, do battle with, rise up in arms, struggle with **13** armed conflict, combativeness, confrontation, exchange blows, pitched battle

fight back 7 counter, get even, hit back, pay back **9** retaliate **10** strike back **13** counterattack

fighter 5 boxer **7** soldier, sparrer, warrior **8** pugilist, scrapper **9** combatant **10** militarist **11** belligerent

fighting 3 war **4** fray **5** brawl, melee **6** action, battle, bicker, combat, rumpus, tumult, tussle **7** contest, dispute, quarrel, warfare **8** battling, brawling, conflict, skirmish, squabble **9** bickering, disputing **10** engagement, quarreling, squabbling **11** clash of arms, controversy, hostilities

Fighting Marine
  nickname of: **10** Gene Tunney

fighting men 4 army **6** legion, troops **7** legions, militia **8** military, soldiers, soldiery **13** military force **15** military machine

fighting spirit 9 animosity, hostility, pugnacity **10** antagonism **11** bellicosity **12** belligerence **14** aggressiveness

fight shy of 5 avoid, dodge, elude, evade, skirt **6** escape **8** sidestep

figment 5 fable, fancy, story **6** canard **7** fantasy, fiction, product **8** creation **9** falsehood, invention **10** concoction **11** fabrication

figuration 4 form **7** outline **9** formation, structure **12** constitution

figurative 6 florid, ironic, ornate **7** flowery **8** humorous, symbolic **9** satirical **10** not literal **11** allegorical **12** hyperbolical, metaphorical

figure, figures 3 cut, man, sum **4** body, cast, cost, foot, form, mark, plan, rate, sign, sums **5** add up, adorn, build, count, digit, force, frame, guess, judge, mo-tif, price, shape, think, total, tot up, value, woman **6** amount, appear, assess, cipher, design, device, emblem, factor, leader, number, person, reckon, schema, symbol **7** anatomy, believe, compute, contour, count up, diagram, drawing, imagine, notable, numeral, outline, pattern, presume, suppose **8** appraise, be placed, eminence, estimate, ornament, physique, presence **9** calculate, character, diversify, embellish, have a part, personage, play a part, quotation, variegate **10** arithmetic, conjecture, shine forth, silhouette **11** be mentioned, be prominent **12** calculations, computations, illustration

figurehead 4 tool **5** dummy, front, token **6** cipher, puppet **8** ornament **9** nonentity

figure out 6 reckon **7** compute, find out, work out **8** discover **9** ascertain, calculate, determine

figure roughly 5 guess **6** reckon **8** estimate **11** approximate, make a stab at

figure up 3 add **5** add up, total, tot up **6** reckon **7** compute, count up **9** calculate

figurine 7 bibelot **8** ornament **9** statuette

Fiji
  capital/largest city: 4 Suva
  others: 3 Mba **4** Mbua **5** Navua **6** Labasa **7** Lautoka, Nausori, Vaileka, Vunisea **8** Korolevu, Savusavu **9** Singatoka
  school: 12 South Pacific
  head of state: 14 British monarch **15** governor general
  monetary unit: 6 dollar
  island: 4 Ngau **6** Ovalau, Rotuma, Yasawa **7** Kandavu, Taveuni **8** Viti Levu **9** Vanua Levu
  highest point: 8 Victoria **9** Tomaniivi
  river: 4 Rewa **8** Ndreketi
  sea: 4 Koro **7** Pacific
  people: 6 Fijian, Indian **7** Chinese **10** Melanesian, Polynesian **11** Micronesian
  language: 5 Hindi **6** Fijian **7** English
  religion: 5 Hindu, Islam **9** Methodist **13** Roman Catholic
  feature:
    cluster houses: 5 mbure

filament 4 hair, line, wire **5** fiber, fibre **6** cilium, ribbon, strand, string, thread

filbert 7 Corylus
  varieties: 3 red **4** cork, Momi, plum **5** azure, China, giant, Greek, joint, Nikko, noble, white **6** alpine, balsam, Fraser, Korean, needle, Scotch, silver, summer **7** cascade, Douglas, lowland, Spanish **8** Algerian, Japanese, Sakhalin, Southern **9** Himalayan, Shasta Red **10** dwarf Nikko, Santa Lucia **11** bristle-cone **13** Pacific silver **14** Southern balsam

filch 3 cop, rob **4** copy, crib, hook, lift **5** boost, heist, steal, swipe **6** pilfer, pirate **7** purloin **8** arrogate **10** plagiarize **11** appropriate, expropriate

file 3 row **4** data, line, list, rank, tier **5** ap-ply, chain, index, put in, queue,

store **6** drawer, folder, record, stacks, string **7** catalog, dossier, put away, records, request **8** archives, classify, petition **9** catalogue, chronicle
  type: 4 mill, nail, rasp, wood **5** round **9** half-round **13** three-cornered

filial 7 dutiful, sonlike **10** daughterly, respectful

fill 3 act **4** cram, glut, lade, load, meet, pack, puff, sate **5** crowd, gorge, lay by, lay in, serve, stock, store **6** answer, as-sign, blow up, charge, dilate, do duty, expand, infuse, make up, occupy, outfit, supply, take up **7** distend, execute, furnish, inflate, pervade, preside, provide, satiate, satisfy, suffuse, surfeit **8** carry out, function, permeate, saturate **9** discharge, provision, replenish **10** full amount, impregnate, overspread

filled in 7 stood in **9** completed, **11** substituted

filled out 6 marked **7** matured **9** completed

fillet 4 band **5** slice, strip **6** ribbon **7** bandeau, circlet

fillip 3 tap **4** flip, snap, toss **5** flick, tonic **6** buffet **8** stimulus

Fillmore, Millard
  presidential rank: 10 thirteenth
  party: 4 Whig
  state represented: 2 NY
  defeated: 5 no one
    succeeded upon death of: 6 Taylor
  vice president: 4 none
  cabinet:
    State: 7 (Daniel) Webster, (Edward) Everett
    Treasury: 6 (Thomas) Corwin
    War: 6 (Charles Magill) Conrad
    Attorney General: 10 (John Jordan) Crittenden
    Navy: 6 (William Alexander) Graham **7** (John Pendleton) Kennedy
    Postmaster General: 4 (Nathan Kelsey) Hall **7** (Samuel Dickinson) Hubbard
    Interior: 6 (Alexander Hugh Holmes) Stuart
  born: 7 Locke NY
  died/buried: 9 Buffalo NY
  education:
    college: 4 none
    studied: 3 law
  religion: 9 Unitarian
  interests: 5 civic
    first chancellor of University of: 7 Buffalo
    founder: 22 Buffalo General Hospital **24** Buffalo Historical Society
  author: 21 Millard Fillmore Papers
  political career: 13 state assembly, Vice President **24** US House of Representatives
  civilian career: 6 lawyer (New York Supreme Court) **7** teacher **10** wool

carder **12** cloth dresser
  notable events of lifetime/term: 25 Compromise of Eighteen-Fifty
    act: 13 Fugitive Slave
  father: 9 Nathaniel
  mother: 6 Phoebe (Millard)
  siblings: 5 Cyrus, Julia **11** Phoebe Maria **12** Almon Hopkins, Calvin Turner **13** Charles DeWitt **14** Darius Ingraham, Olive Armstrong
  wife: 7 Abigail (Powers) **8** Caroline (Carmichael McIntosh)
  children: 11 Mary Abigail **13** Millard Powers

fill with air 5 bloat **6** billow, blow up, expand **7** balloon, distend, inflate, puff out **8** swell out

fill with dread 5 alarm, panic **6** dismay **7** perturb, terrify, unnerve **8** disquiet, frighten

fill with gloom 6 darken, sadden **8** dispirit

fill with wonder 3 awe **5** amaze **7** astound **8** astonish **9** fascinate

film, films 4 cine, coat, haze, mist, skin, veil **5** cloud, flick, movie, sheet, shoot **6** cinema, flicks, movies, screen **7** coating **8** membrane

filmy 3 dim **4** fine, hazy, thin **5** gauzy, misty, sheer, wispy **8** cobwebby, finespun, gossamer **10** diaphanous, seethrough

fils 3 son

filter 4 leak, ooze, seep **5** drain, exude, sieve **6** effuse, purify, refine, screen, strain **7** clarify, cleanse, dribble, trickle, well out **8** filtrate, strainer

filth 3 mud **4** dirt, dung, mire, muck, porn, slop, smut **5** offal, slime, slush, trash **6** manure, ordure, refuse, sewage, sludge **7** carrion, excreta, garbage, squalor **8** impurity, lewdness, ribaldry, vileness **9** excrement, grossness, indecency, nastiness, obscenity, pollution **10** corruption, defilement, immorality, indelicacy, putridness **11** pornography, squalidness **13** contamination **14** suggestiveness

filthy 4 foul, vile **5** black, dirty, grimy, gross, messy, nasty **6** grubby, impure, odious, soiled **7** defiled, dirtied, obscene, smirchy, squalid, unclean **8** befouled, slovenly, unwashed **9** repulsive **10** besmirched, disgusting **12** contaminated

finagle 3 con, gyp **4** plot, rook **5** cheat, mulct, trick **6** chisel, fleece, scheme, wangle **7** defraud, swindle **8** engineer, intrigue, maneuver

final 4 last, rear **6** ending, latest **7** closing, extreme **8** complete, decisive, finished, hindmost, rearmost, terminal, thorough, ultimate **10** concluding, conclusive, definitive, exhaustive, hindermost **11** irrevocable, terminating **12** unappealable, unchangeable

13 determinative
French: 7 dernier

finale 3 end **5** close, finis **6** finish, windup **7** curtain **8** epilogue, last part, swan song **10** conclusion **11** culmination, termination

final limit
Latin: 14 terminus ad quem

finally 6 lastly **10** eventually, inexorably, ultimately **11** inescapably **12** conclusively, definitively, in conclusion **16** incontrovertibly
French: 5 enfin
Latin: 10 ad extremum

final section 4 coda **5** rider **6** ending **7** last act **8** addendum, epilogue **9** afterword **10** conclusion

final settlement 8 solution **11** disposition

finance 6 pay for **7** banking **8** accounts **9** economics **10** underwrite

financial backer 5 angel **6** patron **7** sponsor **9** supporter **10** benefactor

financial support 7 backing, subsidy **10** assistance **12** contribution

financier 5 angel **6** backer, banker, broker **7** rich man **10** capitalist **11** millionaire, underwriter

Financier, The
author: 15 Theodore Dreiser
character: 12 Aileen Butler, Edward Butler **15** Henry Cowperwood **16** Frank A Cowperwood **23** Lillian Semple Cowperwood

Finch, Peter
real name: 15 Peter Ingle-Finch
born: 6 London **7** England
roles: 7 Network (Oscar) **11** Lost Horizon **12** The Nun's Story **15** The Pumpkin Eater **18** Sunday Bloody Sunday

Finchley, Sondra
character in: 17 An American Tragedy
author: 7 Dreiser

find 3 get, see, win **4** earn, espy, gain, meet, rule, spot **5** award, catch, dig up, judge, learn **6** attain, come by, decide, decree, detect, expose, locate, regain **7** achieve, acquire, adjudge, bargain, bonanza, discern, get back, godsend, good buy, hit upon, procure, recover, uncover, unearth **8** bump into, come upon, discover, disinter, lucky hit, meet with, retrieve, windfall **9** ascertain, determine, discov-ery, encounter, pronounce, repossess **10** adjudicate **11** acquisition

fin de siecle 8 decadent **15** end of the century

find fault 3 nag **4** beef, carp **5** blame, cavil, gribe **6** grouse, squawk **7** nitpick **8** complain **9** bellyache, criticize, disparage **10** disapprove

find guilty 5 blame **6** indict **7** condemn, convict **8** sentence **9** implicate

finding 6 decree, ruling **7** verdict **8** decision

find innocent 5 clear **6** acquit **9** exonerate

find out 5 learn **6** detect, locate **7** uncover, unearth **8** discover **9** ascertain, determine, establish

find repulsive 4 hate **5** abhor **6** detest, loathe **7** despise **8** execrate, recoil at **9** abominate

fine 4 airy, chic, fair, keen, neat, nice, rare, thin **5** bonny, clear, dandy, gauzy, mulct, nifty, sharp, sheer, silky, small, smart, sunny, swell **6** assess, bonnie, bright, charge, choice, comely, dainty, flimsy, ground, lovely, minute, modish, pretty, silken, slight, spiffy, subtle, superb **7** damages, elegant, forfeit, fragile, penalty, perfect, powdery, precise, refined, slender, stylish, tenuous **8** cobwebby, delicate, ethereal, flawless, gossamer, handsome, penalize, pleasant, polished, powdered, rainless, skillful, splendid, superior, tasteful **9** admirable, beautiful, brilliant, cloudless, excellent, exquisite **10** assessment, attractive, consummate, diaphanous, fastidious, pulverized, swimmingly **11** excellently, exceptional, lightweight, magnificent, transparent, well-favored **12** accomplished **13** hairsplitting, unsubstantial
music: 3 end

fine clothes 8 glad rags **10** Sunday best **16** best bib and tucker

fine-looking 4 fair **5** bonny **6** bonnie, comely, lovely, pretty, seemly **8** gorgeous, handsome **9** beauteous, beautiful, exquisite, ravishing **10** attractive **11** resplendent **15** pulchritudinous

fineness 6 beauty **8** delicacy, elegance, thinness **10** perfection, smoothness **12** flawlessness **13** exquisiteness

fine points 3 art **7** finesse, nuances **8** niceties **10** subtleties **11** refinements **12** distinctions

finer 6 better **8** superior

finery 6 frills, tinsel **7** baubles, gaudery, gewgaws **8** frippery, spangles, trinkets **9** trappings, trimmings **13** paraphernalia

finesse 4 ruse, tact, wile **5** craft, dodge, guile, savvy **7** cunning **8** artifice, delicacy, intrigue, trickery **9** deception, stratagem **10** artfulness, discretion, subterfuge
French: 11 savoir-faire

fine workmanship 8 delicacy **9** precision **13** craftsmanship

finger 4 paw **5** feel, poke, ring **5** digit, index, punch, thumb, touch **6** caress, feeler, handle, middle, pinkie, pollex **7** pointer, squeeze, toy with, twiddle **8** identify, play with **10** manipulate

finicky 5 fussy, picky **6** choosy **8** niggling **10** fastidious, meticulous, nit-

picking, overprecise, particular, pernickety **11** persnickety **14** discriminating, overparticular

finish 3 end **4** coat, face, gild, goal, kill, last, seal, stop **5** cease, close, glaze, use up **6** clinch, defeat, devour, ending, finale, settle, veneer, wind up **7** achieve, coating, consume, curtain, destroy, fulfill, get done, lacquer, realize, surface, varnish **8** carry out, complete, conclude, dispatch, epilogue, exterior, get rid of, knock off, make good **9** discharge, eradicate, objective, polishing, terminate **10** accomplish, completion, conclusion, consummate, denouement **11** discontinue, exterminate, termination

finished 4 full **5** ended, final, ideal, whole **6** entire, urbane **7** classic, elegant, perfect, refined, shapely, skilled, trained, well-set **8** complete, flawless, polished, well-bred **9** beautiful, completed, concluded, exquisite, faultless **10** consummate, cultivated, impeccable **11** consummated **12** accomplished

finishing stroke 9 death blow
French: 11 coup de grace

finish off 4 kill, slay **7** destroy, execute, wipe out **8** complete, dispatch **9** eradicate, polish off **10** annihilate **11** exterminate

finite 7 bounded, limited **8** confined, temporal **9** countable **10** measurable, restricted, short-lived, terminable **13** circumscribed

Finland
other name: 5 Suomi **15** Suomen Tasavalta
capital/largest city: 8 Helsinki **11** Helsingfors
others: 3 Aba, Abo, Kem **4** Kemi, Ouli, Oulu, Ouou, Pori, Vasa **5** Enare, Espoo, Kotka, Lahti, Rauma, Turku, Vaasa **6** Imatra, Kuopio **7** Joensuu, Kajaani, Kokkola, Mikkeli, Tampere, Tapiola **9** Jyvaskyla, Mariehamn, Rovaniemi **12** Lappeenranta
measure: 5 kannu, verst **6** fathom, kannor **8** otlinger, skalpund, tunnland
monetary unit: 4 mark **5** penni **6** markka
island: 5 Aland, Karlo **6** Aaland **7** Hailuto **9** Vallgrund **10** Ahvenanmaa
lake: 3 Juo, Muo **4** Kemi, Kiui, Nasi, Oulu, Puru, Pyha, Simo **5** Enara, Enare, Hauki, Inari, Kalla, Lappa, Lesti, Puula, Saima **6** Ladoya, Lentua, Saimaa, Sounne, Syvari **7** Koitere, Nilakka, Pielien **9** Kallavesi, Pielavesi
mountain: 7 Laltiva **10** Saari Selka
highest point: 6 Haltia **11** Haldetsokka
river: 4 Kala, Kemi, Kymi, Oulu, Pats, Simo, Teno **5** Ivalo, Lotta, Ounas, Siika, Torne **6** Iijoki, Lapuan, Muonio, Pasvik, Tornoi, Vuoski **7** Kitinen **8** Kokemaki

sea: 6 Baltic **8** Atlantic
physical feature:
    gulf: 7 Bothnia, Finland
    isthmus: 7 Karelia
    peninsula: 13 Fennoscandian
people: 3 Jew, Vod, Vot, Yak **4** Avar, Finn, Hame, Lapp, Turk, Veps **5** Fioun, Gypsy, Ijore, Inger, Suomi, Vepse **6** Magyar, Ostiak, Ostyak, Tarast, Tavast, Ugrian, Zyrian **7** Lappish, Mordvin, Permiak, Samoyed, Uralian **8** Cheremis, Estonian, Karelian, Livonian, Swekoman **9** Tavastian **11** Karjalaiset, Suomalaiset
    athlete: 10 Paavo Nurmi
    composer: 8 Sibelius
    designer: 9 Marimekko
language: 4 Avar, Lapp **5** Karel, Ugric, Vogul **6** Magyar, Ostyak, Tarast **7** Finnish, Olonets, Samoyed, Swedish **8** Estonian **10** Olonetsian
religion: 19 Evangelical Lutheran
place:
    canal: 6 Saimaa
    castle: 10 Saint Olaf's **11** Olavinlinna
    fortress: 8 Sveaborg **11** Suomenlinna
    memorial: 8 Sibelius
    pine ridge: 10 Punkaharju
feature:
    game: 9 pesapallo
food:
    dish: 11 Karelian pie
    fruit: 16 yellow cloudberry
    liqueur: 9 Mesimarja
Finn
    also: 5 Fionn **13** Fionn MacCumal
    origin: 5 Irish
    king of: 4 gods **14** Tuatha De Danann
    son: 6 Ossian
    father: 5 Cumal **6** Comhal
Finnegans Wake
    author: 10 James Joyce
    family: 9 Earwicker
Finney, Albert
    wife: 10 Anouk Aimee
    born: 7 England, Salford
    roles: 5 Annie **7** Scrooge **8** Tom Jones **10** The Dresser **12** Shoot the Moon **13** Two for the Road **17** Under the Volcano **29** Saturday Night and Sunday Morning
Finnish Mythology *see* **21** Scandinavian Mythology
Finno-Ugric
    language family: 6 Uralic
    Finnic group: 4 Lapp **6** Votyak, Zyryan **7** Finnish, Mordvin, Permian **8** Estonian **9** Cheremiss
    Ugric group: 5 Vogul **6** Ostyak **7** Ob-Ugric **9** Hungarian
Fionn, Fionn MacCumal *see* **4** Finn
fiord, fjord 5 firth, inlet **7** estuary
    location: 6 Norway
fir 4 pine **5** cedar, larch **6** alpine, bal-

sam, linden, spruce **7** conifer, cypress, douglas **9** evergreen
Firbolg
    origin: 5 Greek, Irish
    defeated by: 9 Fomorians
    ousted by: 4 gods **14** Tuatha De Danann
fire 3 can, vim **4** bake, boot, burn, cook, dash, dump, elan, hurl, oust, sack, stir **5** ardor, blaze, eject, flame, flare, flash, force, gusto, let go, light, power, punch, rouse, salvo, shell, shoot, spark, verve, vigor **6** arouse, bounce, depose, excite, fervor, foment, genius, ignite, incite, kindle, luster, spirit, stir up, vivify, volley **7** animate, bombard, bonfire, cashier, dismiss, inferno, inflame, inspire, project, quicken, sniping, trigger **8** enfilade, fervency, inspirit, radiance, splendor, vivacity **9** broadside, cannonade, discharge, eagerness, fusillade, galvanize, holocaust, instigate, intensity, stimulate, vehemence **10** brilliance, effulgence, enthusiasm **11** bombardment, earnestness, inspiration **13** conflagration, sharpshooting **15** imaginativeness
    god of: 4 Loki **5** Ishum **6** Vulcan **10** Hephaestus, Hephaistos
    goddess of: 6 Brigit
Fire and Ice
    author: 11 Robert Frost
firearm 3 gun, rod **5** piece, rifle **6** pistol **7** shotgun **8** revolver **10** machine gun **12** shooting iron **13** submachine gun **20** Saturday-night special
firefight 5 clash **6** battle, combat **8** skirmish
firefly 8 glowworm, lampyrid **9** candlefly **12** lightning bug
Fire Next Time, The
    author: 12 James Baldwin
fire off 5 eject, shoot **6** launch **8** detonate **9** discharge
Fireside Theatre
    host: 9 Jane Wyman **11** Frank Wisbar, Gene Raymond
Firestarter
    author: 11 Stephen King
fire up 4 fuel, rile **5** anger, light, rouse **6** arouse, excite, ignite, incite, kindle **7** animate, enthuse, inspire **8** activate, energize, irritate, vitalize **9** galvanize, stimulate
firm 4 bent, fast, grim, hard, taut **5** close, dense, fixed, house, rigid, rocky, solid, stiff, stony, tight, tough **6** dogged, flinty, intent, moored, rooted, secure, stable, steady, steely **7** compact, company, dead set, decided, earnest, serious, settled, staunch **8** anchored, business, constant, definite, fearless, obdurate, resolute, resolved, unshaken **9** confirmed, hard-nosed, immovable, obstinate, steadfast, tenacious, unbending **10** adamantine,

compressed, determined, inexorable, inflexible, invincible, persistent, unwavering, unyielding **11** corporation, established, partnership, unalterable, unfaltering, unflinching **12** conglomerate, indissoluble, organization **13** establishment
firmament 3 air, sky **5** ether, space, vault **6** canopy, welkin **7** heavens, the blue, the void **10** outer space
firmness 8 tenacity **9** obstinacy **10** resolution **11** persistence, staunchness **12** resoluteness **13** determination, inflexibility, steadfastness
first 4 head, main **5** basic, prime, start, vital **6** before,eldest, maiden, outset, primal, rather, sooner **7** highest, leading, premier, primary, ranking, supreme **8** earliest, foremost, original, primeval, superior **9** beginning, essential, inception, initially, paramount, primitive, principal **10** aboriginal, elementary, preeminent, preferably, primordial **11** fundamental, rudimentary **12** commencement, introduction, introductory
first among equals
    Latin: 16 primus inter pares
first appearance 4 dawn **5** debut **9** beginning **12** introduction
firstborn 5 elder, older **6** eldest, oldest
Firstborn, The
    author: 14 Christopher Fry
First Circle
    author: 23 Aleksandr Solzhenitsyn Jr
first god *see* **8** god, first
firsthand 6 direct **8** personal **9** empirical **10** unmediated **12** experimental
First Lady of the Theater
    nickname of: 10 Helen Hayes **16** Katherine Cornell
first-line 4 main **5** chief **7** primary **8** foremost
first moving thing
    Latin: 12 primum mobile
first-rate 3 ace **4** A-one, best, fine, tops **5** crack, elite, great, prime **6** choice, finest, select **7** top-hole **8** splendid, superior, top-notch, very good **9** admirable, estimable, excellent, exclusive, nonpareil, top drawer, topflight, wonderful **10** noteworthy, stupendous **11** commendable, outstanding **12** above-average, incomparable **13** distinguished
First State
    nickname of: 8 Delaware
first step 5 start **9** beginning **12** commencement
firth 5 fjord, inlet **7** estuary
fiscal 8 economic, monetary **9** budgetary, financial, pecuniary
fish 3 net **4** cast, hook, hunt **5** angle, grope, seine, trawl, troll **6** ferret, search **7** rummage
fish

class: 7 Agnatha 12 Osteichthyes 14 Chondrichthyes

fin: 4 anal, tail 6 caudal, dorsal, median, paired, pelvic 7 adipose, ventral 8 pectoral

kind: 3 cod, eel, gar, ray 4 bass, carp, hake, opah, pike, tuna 5 brill, perch, shark, skate, sword, trout 6 bichir, blenny, marlin, minnow, mullet, salmon, tarpon 7 anchovy, catfish, dogfish, dolphin, hagfish, herring, lamprey, piranha, sunfish 8 bluefish, cavefish, crayfish, flounder, goldfish, lungfish, mackerel, menhaden, moray eel, pilchard, sea horse, squirrel, sturgeon 9 killifish, pygmy goby, swordfish 10 coelacanth, flying fish, paddlefish, rabbit fish, rocksucker, whale shark 11 anemonefish, electric eel, electric ray, lanternfish, longnose gar 13 butterflyfish 14 largemouth bass

part: 3 fin 4 gill 5 scale 6 cirrhi 10 gas bladder 11 swim bladder 12 rete mirabile

shellfish:
   crustacean: 4 crab 6 shrimp 7 lobster 8 blue crab, king crab, snow crab 9 langouste 11 langoustine 13 Dungeness crab, horseshoe crab
   mollusk: 4 clam 6 mussel, oyster, quahog 8 surf clam 9 horse clam, razor clam 11 geoduck clam

young: 3 fry 10 fingerling

Fisher, Bud
creator/artist of: 11 Mutt and Jeff

Fisher, Carrie
father: 11 Eddie Fisher
mother: 13 Debbie Reynolds
role: 12 Princess Leia
films: 7 Shampoo 8 Star Wars 12 This Is My Life 16 The Blues Brothers 17 When Harry Met Sally 18 The Return of the Jedi 19 The Empire Strikes Back, Hannah and Her Sisters
author: 20 Postcards from the Edge

Fisher, Ham
creator/artist of: 10 Joe Palooka

Fisher, Vardis
author of: 10 The Mothers 13 Children of God 17 The Testament of Man

fisherman 5 eeler 6 angler, caster, jacker, netter, seiner 7 trawler, troller 8 piscator 9 flycaster, Waltonian 17 the compleat angler

Fishermen
goddess of: 11 Britomartis

Fishes
constellation of: 6 Pisces

fish story 3 fib, lie 7 fiction, whopper 9 falsehood, tall story 16 cock-and-bull story

fishy 3 odd 4 dull 5 blank, queer, shady, weird 6 vacant 7 dubious, strange, suspect 8 doubtful, peculiar, slippery 9 dishonest 10 farfetched, glassy-eyed, improbable, suspicious, unreliable 11 exaggerated, extravagant 12 questionable, unscrupulous 14 expressionless

fission 7 atomize 8 breaking, cleavage, scission 9 severance, splitting 10 breaking up, sunderance 12 disseverance, reproduction

fissure 3 gap 4 rift, slit 5 chink, cleft, crack, gully, split 6 breach, cranny, groove, hiatus 8 aperture, cleavage

fit 4 able, good, hale, meet, ripe, suit, well, whim 5 adapt, agree, alter, burst, equal, equip, hardy, match, ready, right, shape, sound, spasm, spell, train 6 access, accord, adjust, become, concur, enable, in trim, mature, primed, proper, robust, seemly, strong, timely, worthy 7 adapted, apropos, capable, caprice, conform, correct, empower, fashion, healthy, prepare, qualify, rectify, seizure, toned up, trained 8 apposite, becoming, coincide, crotchet, decorous, eligible, graduate, grand mal, outbreak, outburst, paroxysm, petit mal, prepared, relevant, suitable 9 calibrate, competent, consonant, deserving, efficient, explosion, harmonize, initiated, opportune, pertinent, qualified 10 acceptable, applicable, capacitate, convenient, convulsion, correspond, seasonable 11 appropriate, capacitated

fitful 4 weak 6 broken, random, uneven 7 erratic 8 listless, off-and-on, periodic, sporadic, unsteady, variable 9 irregular, spasmodic 10 capricious, changeable, convulsive 11 fluctuating 12 disconnected, intermittent

fitness
Hebrew: 7 kashrut 8 kashruth

fit out 4 robe 5 array, dress, equip 6 attire, clothe, supply 7 appoint, deck out, prepare

fitting 3 apt 4 meet 6 proper, seemly 8 decorous, suitable 9 congruous 11 appropriate
French: 11 comme il faut

fit to be eaten 6 edible 9 palatable 10 comestible, consumable, digestible

fit together 4 join 5 hinge, unite 6 hook up 7 connect 8 dovetail 9 interlock 10 articulate

Fitzgerald, Barry
real name: 20 William Joseph Shields
born: 6 Dublin 7 Ireland
roles: 10 Going My Way 11 The Quiet Man 19 How Green Was My Valley

FitzGerald, Edward
author of: 24 The Rubaiyat of Omar Khayyam (translation)

Fitzgerald, F Scott
wife: 10 Zelda Sayre
author of: 10 The Crack-Up 13 The Last Tycoon 14 The Great Gatsby 16 Tender Is the Night 18 This Side of Paradise 24 The Beautiful and the Damned
coined term: 7 Jazz Age

Fitzgerald, George Francis
field: 7 physics
nationality: 5 Irish
theory of: 24 electromagnetic radiation

Fitzgerald, Geraldine
born: 6 Dublin 7 Ireland
roles: 11 Dark Victory 12 Ah Wilderness, Rachel Rachel 15 Watch on the Rhine 16 Wuthering Heights 24 Long Day's Journey into Night

Fitzsimmons, Bob (Robert Prometheus)
sport: 6 boxing

Fitzsimmons, Maureen
real name of: 12 Maureen O'Hara

Five, The
group of: 16 Russian composers
member: 3 Cui 7 Borodin 9 Balakirev 10 Mussorgsky 14 Rimsky-Korsakov

Five Easy Pieces
director: 11 Bob Rafelson
cast: 10 Karen Black 11 Fannie Flagg 12 Susan Anspach 13 Jack Nicholson 14 Billy Breen Bush, Sally Struthers

Five Men and Pompey
author: 19 Stephen Vincent Benet

five-o'clock shadow 5 beard 7 stubble 8 bristles, whiskers

fix 3 jam, put, set 4 bind, make, mend, mess, moor, spot 5 place, rivet 6 adjust, anchor, attach, decide, fasten, harden, impose, muddle, pickle, plight, repair, scrape, secure, settle 7 congeal, connect, correct, dilemma, impasse, implant, patch up, prepare, rebuild 8 assemble, hot water, make fast, make firm, quandary, regulate, renovate, set right, solidify 9 establish, prescribe, retaliate, stabilize 10 difficulty 11 consolidate, involvement, predicament 12 entanglement

fixation 5 quirk 6 fetish 7 complex 8 crotchet, delusion 9 monomania, obsession 13 preoccupation

fixed 3 set 4 fast, firm 5 rigid, still 6 intent, rooted, stable, steady 8 constant, fastened, resolute, unpliant 9 immovable, unbending 10 determined, inflexible, motionless, persistent, stationary, unwavering

fixed idea 4 bias 5 slant 9 obsession 13 preconception
French: 8 idee fixe

fixedness 8 firmness 9 constancy, stability 10 immobility 12 immutability 16 unchangeableness

fixed regard 7 staring 9 diligence 10 absorption, intentness 11 engrossment 13 concentration

Fixer, The
author: 14 Bernard Malamud

fixing 6 repair 7 mending, mooring, placing, putting, setting 8 deciding, imposing, righting, riveting, settling, trimming 9 adjusting, anchoring, attaching, fastening, hardening, preparing, repairing 10 adjustment, assembling, congealing, connecting, correcting, implanting, rectifying, regulating, regulation 11 determining, prescribing, solidifying, stabilizing 12 establishing 13 consolidating

fixture 6 addict 7 devotee, habitue, regular 8 equipage 9 apparatus, appendage, appliance, equipment 10 attachment 11 appointment 12 appurtenance 13 paraphernalia

fix up 4 plan 6 design, devise 7 arrange, prepare 8 renovate, schedule

fix upon 4 pick 6 choose, opt for, select 7 call out, extract, pick out

fizz 4 foam 5 froth 7 bubbles 11 carbonation 13 effervescence

fizziness 9 foaminess 10 bubbliness, frothiness 13 effervescence

fizzing 6 bubbly 7 foaming 8 bubbling 9 sparkling 12 effervescent, effervescing

fizzle 3 dog, dud 4 bomb, fail, flop, hiss, mess 5 abort, botch 6 bubble, fiasco, gurgle, muddle, turkey 7 failure, founder, misfire, sputter, washout 8 collapse, disaster, miscarry

fizzy 6 bubbly 8 bubbling 9 sparkling 12 effervescent

flabbergast 4 stun 5 amaze, shock 6 puzzle 7 astound, stagger, stupefy 8 astonish, bewilder, bowl over, confound, overcome 9 dumbfound

flabbergasted 5 agape 6 amazed, gaping 9 awestruck, stupefied 10 astonished, dumbstruck, spellbound 11 dumbfounded 12 hornswoggled 13 thunderstruck

flabby 4 lame, limp, soft, weak 5 baggy, slack 6 doughy, effete, feeble, flimsy, floppy, spongy 7 flaccid 8 impotent, listless, yielding 9 enervated, inelastic 10 out of shape, spiritless 11 adulterated, emasculated

flag 3 ebb, sag 4 fade, fail, pall, sink, tire, wane, warn, wave, wilt 5 abate, faint, slump 6 banner, colors, dodder, emblem, ensign, signal, totter 7 decline, give way, pennant, subside, succumb 8 grow weak, languish, Old Glory, standard, streamer 9 grow weary, Union Jack 12 Stars and Bars 15 Stars and Stripes

flagellant 7 ascetic 8 penitent 13 self-mortifier

flagon 3 gun, jug, mug 4 ewer 5 flask, stein 6 bottle, carafe, vessel 7 canteen 8 schooner

flagrant 5 gross, sheer 6 arrant, bra-

zen, crying 7 blatant, glaring, heinous, obvious 8 immodest 9 audacious, barefaced, flaunting, monstrous, notorious, shameless 10 outrageous, scandalous 11 conspicuous

Flaherty, Margaret (Pegeen)
character in: 24 Playboy of the Western World
author: 5 Synge

flail 4 beat, lash, whip 5 swing 6 thresh 7 scourge

flair 4 bent, dash, feel, gift 5 knack, style, taste, touch, verve 6 genius, talent 7 faculty, feeling, panache 8 aptitude, capacity 9 ingenuity 11 discernment

flake 3 bit 4 chip, peel 5 fleck, layer, patch, scale, sheet, strip 7 chip off, crumble, peel off, shaving 8 scale off

flaky 4 bats, gaga, nuts 5 balmy, batty, crisp, daffy, dotty, goofy, loony, nutty, scaly, short, wacky 6 scabby, screwy, scurfy 8 scabious, squamous 9 eccentric 10 flocculent

flamboyant 4 wild 5 gaudy, jazzy, showy 6 flashy, florid, garish, ornate, rococo 7 baroque, dashing 8 colorful, exciting 10 theatrical 11 sensational 12 ostentatious

flame 4 beau, fire, glow 5 ardor, blaze, blush, flare, flash, flush, glare, gleam, light, lover, spark, swain 6 fervor, ignite, kin-dle, redden, warmth 7 passion 8 fervency 9 affection, boyfriend, intensity 10 enthusiasm, excitement, girlfriend, sweetheart 13 conflagration

flaming 5 afire, fiery 6 ablaze, alight, ardent, bright, fervid, stormy 7 blazing, burning, fervent, glaring, glowing, igneous, intense, shining, violent 8 flagrant, vehement 9 brilliant, egregious 10 passionate, smoldering 11 conspicuous, inflammable

flammable 7 igneous 10 combustive, incendiary 11 combustible, inflammable

flan 3 pie 4 gust, puff, tart 6 expand, pastry 7 custard, dessert 12 creme caramel

flanerie 8 dawdling, idleness

flaneur 5 idler 6 loafer 7 dawdler

flank 3 hip 4 edge, line, loin, side, wing 5 cover, skirt 6 border, fringe, haunch, screen, shield

Flannagan, John Bernard
born: 7 Fargo ND
artwork: 6 New One, Not Yet 9 Beginning 11 Dragon Motif 15 Triumph of the Egg 16 Jonah and the Whale

flap 3 bat, fly, tab 4 bang, beat, flop 5 apron, shake, skirt 6 lappet 7 agitate, banging, flutter, vibrate 9 oscillate

flare 4 burn, glow 5 blaze, erupt, flame, flash, glare, gleam, taper, torch, widen 6 blow up, dilate, expand, ignite, signal, spread 7 bell out,

broaden, distend, explode, stretch 8 boil over, break out 9 coruscate 10 incandesce

flash 4 glow, wink 5 blaze, blink, burst, flame, flare, glare, gleam, jiffy, shake, shine, spark, touch, trice 6 minute, moment, second, streak 7 flicker, glimmer, glisten, glitter, instant, sparkle 8 instance, outburst, radiance 9 coruscate 10 occurrence 11 coruscation, fulmination, scintillate 13 incandescence

Flash Gordon
creator: 8 Dan Berry 11 Alex Raymond 12 Austin Briggs
character: 11 Emperor Ming 12 Princess Aura
companion: 4 Dale
portrayed by: 12 Buster Crabbe

flashy 4 loud 5 gaudy, jazzy, showy, smart 6 garish, sporty, tawdry, tinsel, vulgar 7 raffish 8 dazzling 9 bedizened 10 flamboyant, tricked out 11 pretentious 12 ostentatious

flask 6 bottle 7 canteen 9 container

flat, flats 3 low 4 dead, dull 5 clear, equal, flush, level, marsh, plain, plane, prone, shoal, shoes, stale, total, vapid 6 direct, planar, smooth, supine 7 blowout, exact-ly, insipid, laid low, leveled, levelly, loafers, prairie, regular, shallow 8 absolute, complete, definite, lowlands, positive, puncture, thorough, unbroken 9 apartment, downright, precisely, prostrate, reclining, recumbent, tasteless 10 flavorless, horizontal, peremptory 11 unequivocal, unpalatable, unqualified 12 deflated tire, horizontally, unmistakable

flatfish 3 ray 4 sole 5 brill, fluke 6 turbot 7 halibut, sand dab, sunfish, teleost 8 flounder

Flathead *see* 5 Salis 7 Chinook

flatness 8 dullness 9 levelness, staleness 10 insipidity 13 tastelessness 14 flavorlessness

flatten 4 deck, even, fell 5 crush, floor, level, plane 6 defeat, ground, smooth 7 deflate 8 compress, overcome 9 overwhelm, prostrate

flatter 4 fool, laud 5 court, extol, honor, toady 6 become, cajole, delude 7 adulate, beguile, deceive, mislead, wheedle 8 blandish, bootlick, butter up, eulogize, soft-soap 9 brown-nose, sweet-talk, truckle to 10 compliment, overpraise, panegyrize

flatterer 5 toady 6 fawner, yes man 8 eulogist, truckler, wheedler 9 sycophant 10 bootlicker 11 lickspittle 13 apple-polisher

flattering 7 lauding 8 praising 9 extolling, favorable, laudatory 10 gratifying 13 complimentary

flattering attention 5 court 7 fawning

flattery 6 eulogy 7 blarney, fawning, snow job 8 cajolery, encomium, jollying, soft soap, toadying, toadyism 9 adulation, panegyric, servility, truckling, wheedling 10 sycophancy 12 blandishment 14 obsequiousness

Flaubert, Gustave
author of: 8 Salammbo 12 Madame Bovary 21 A Sentimental Education 24 The Temptation of St Anthony

flaunt 3 air 4 brag, wave 5 boast, sport, strut, vaunt 6 blazon, dangle, parade 7 exhibit, show off 8 brandish, flourish 9 advertise, broadcast

flavor 4 aura, lace, soul, tang, tone 5 gusto, imbue, savor, spice, style, tenor 6 aspect, infuse, lacing, relish, season, spirit 7 essence, instill 8 ambience, piquancy 9 attribute, seasoning

flavorful 4 rich 5 nutty, sapid, spicy, tangy, tasty, zesty 6 savory 7 peppery, piquant 8 aromatic 9 palatable, toothsome 10 appetizing

flavoring 4 herb, salt 5 spice 6 pepper 7 essence, extract, vanilla 8 additive, seasoner 9 chocolate, condiment, seasoning

flavorless 4 dull, flat, thin, weak 5 bland, stale, vapid 6 watery 7 insipid 9 tasteless

flaw 3 mar 4 blot, harm, spot, vice 5 error, fault, speck, stain 6 blotch, deface, defect, foible, impair, injure, injury, smudge, weaken 7 blemish, failing, fallacy, frailty, mistake 8 weak spot, weakness 9 deformity, disfigure 10 compromise, defacement 11 shortcoming 12 imperfection 13 disfigurement

flawed 6 faulty 8 impaired 9 defective, imperfect

flawless 5 sound 7 perfect 9 errorless, faultless 10 immaculate, impeccable

flawlessness 8 accuracy 10 perfection 11 correctness 14 immaculateness

flay 4 bark, pare, peel, skin 5 scalp, scold, strip 6 assail, fleece, punish, rebuke 7 plunder, upbraid 9 castigate, excoriate 11 decorticate

flea
varieties: 3 bat, dog, rat 5 mouse 6 rodent 9 carnivore 10 sticktight

fleck 3 dot, jot 4 drop, mark, mole, spot 5 flake, speck 6 bespot, dapple, mottle, streak, tittle 7 blemish, freckle, spatter, speckle, stipple 8 particle, small bit 9 bespeckle 10 besprinkle

Fledermaus, Die
also: 6 The Bat
operetta by: 7 (Johann) Strauss
character: 5 Adele, Falke, Frank 6 Alfred 9 Rosalinda 14 Prince Orlofsky 18 Baron von Eisenstein

fledgling 4 tyro 6 novice 8 beginner,

freshman 9 greenhorn 10 apprentice, tenderfoot

flee 4 shun, skip 5 avoid, dodge, elude, evade, split 6 decamp, desert, vanish 7 abscond, fly away, make off 8 speed off 9 cut and run, disappear 10 fly the coop

fleece 3 gyp 4 bilk, dupe, gull, rook, wool 5 cheat, cozen, trick 7 deceive, defraud, swindle 9 bamboozle, victimize

fleet 3 run 4 band, fade, fast, flow, navy, skim, spry, swim, unit 5 agile, array, brief, creek, drift, float, hasty, inlet, light, quick, rapid, shift, ships, short, swift 6 abound, active, armada, nimble, number, speedy, sudden, vanish 7 caravan, cursory, hurried 8 flotilla, squadron 9 disappear, momentary, transient 10 evanescent, transitory 11 expeditious 13 instantaneous

fleeting 5 brief, quick 7 passing 8 flitting, fugitive, temporal 9 ephemeral, fugacious, momentary, temporary, transient 10 evanescent, perishable, transitory 11 impermanent, precarious, unenduring

Fleming, Alexander
field: 12 bacteriology
nationality: 7 British
discovered: 10 penicillin
awarded: 10 Nobel Prize

Fleming, Henry
character in: 20 The Red Badge of Courage
author: 5 Crane

Fleming, Ian
author of: 4 Dr No 9 Moonraker 10 Goldfinger 11 Thunderball 12 Casino Royale 13 Live and Let Die 15 For Your Eyes Only 16 The Spy Who Loved Me, You Only Live Twice 18 From Russia with Love 20 Chitty Chitty Bang Bang
character: 1 M, Q 6 Oddjob 7 Blofeld, SPECTRE (organization) 9 James Bond 14 Miss Moneypenny 15 Auric Goldfinger

Fleming, Victor
director of: 13 The Wizard of Oz 14 Treasure Island 15 Gone With the Wind (Oscar) 18 Captains Courageous

flesh 3 fat, man 4 body, meat, pulp 5 brawn, power, vigor 6 embody, fatten, people 7 fatness, fill out, mankind, realize 8 humanity, physique, strength 9 carnality, substance 10 sensuality 11 materiality 13 individualize, particularize

flesh and blood 3 kin 4 real 5 a body, child 6 family 7 kindred 8 children 9 corporeal, offspring, relations, relatives 10 kith and kin 11 substantial

flesh-eating 9 predatory 10 predaceous 11 carnivorous

fleshy 3 fat 5 beefy, obese, plump, stout, tubby 6 chubby, portly, rotund, stocky 7 paunchy 8 roly-poly, thickset 9 corpulent, succulent 10 overweight, potbellied

Fletcher, Louise
born: 12 Birmingham AL
roles: 17 The Cheap Detective 25 One Flew Over the Cuckoo's Nest (Oscar)

Fletcher, Susanna Yolande
real name of: 12 Susannah York

flex 4 bend 5 curve

flexible 4 mild, soft 5 lithe 6 docile, genial, gentle, limber, pliant, supple 7 amiable, ductile, elastic, plastic, pliable, springy 8 bendable, yielding 9 adaptable, compliant, malleable, resilient, tractable 10 changeable, extensible, manageable, responsive, submissive 11 complaisant

Flibbertigibbet
character in: 10 Kenilworth
author: 5 Scott

flick 4 film 5 brush, graze, movie, sweep, whisk

Flicka
nickname of: 17 Frederica Von Stade

Flicka 5 horse
in: 14 My Friend Flicka

flicker 4 flit, glow, sway 5 blaze, flame, flare, flash, gleam, glint, shake, spark, throb, trace, waver 6 quaver, quiver, waggle 7 flutter, glimmer, glisten, glitter, modicum, pulsate, shimmer, sparkle, tremble, vestige, vibrate, wriggle 8 undulate 9 coruscate, fluctuate, oscillate, scintilla, vacillate

Flickertail State
nickname of: 11 North Dakota

flicks 5 films 6 cinema, grazes, movies, sweeps, whisks 7 brushes

flier 4 bill 5 pilot 6 notice 7 aviator, leaflet, venture 8 brochure, bulletin, circular, handbill 10 experiment 12 announcement 13 advertisement

flight 4 rout, rush, wing 5 flock 6 escape, exodus, flying, hegira 7 fleeing, retreat, soaring, winging 8 squadron 10 withdrawal 11 aeronautics

flighty 5 dizzy, giddy 6 fickle 8 quixotic, reckless, unstable, volatile 9 frivolous, mercurial, whimsical 10 capricious, changeable, inconstant, indecisive, irresolute 11 harebrained, impractical, light-headed, thoughtless 13 irresponsible 14 scatterbrained

flimsy 5 poor, thin, weak 5 cheap, filmy, frail, gauzy, petty, sheer 6 feeble, shab-by, shoddy, sleazy, slight, trashy 7 foolish, fragile, ill-made, shallow, trivial 8 cobwebby, delicate, gossamer, trifling 9 frivolous, worthless 10 diaphanous, inadequate, jerry-built, ramshackle **11** dilapidated, superficial **13** unsubstantial

flinch 3 fly, shy **4** jerk **5** cower, quail, quake, start, wince **6** blench, cringe, falter, quaver, quiver, recoil, shiver, shrink **7** contort, grimace, retreat, shudder

fling 2 go **3** try **4** ball, bash, cast, dash, emit, hurl, lark, toss **5** eject, expel, heave, pitch, sling, spree, trial **6** let fly, propel **7** attempt **8** bit of fun **11** precipitate

Flintstones, The
  character: 7 Pebbles **8** Bamm Bamm **11** Betty Rubble **12** Barney Rubble **14** Fred Flintstone **15** Dino the Dinosaur, Wilma Flintstone
  voice: 8 Alan Reed, Mel Blanc **10** Don Messick **12** Bea Benaderet, Gerry Johnson **13** Jean Vander Pyl
  city: 7 Bedrock
  creator: 12 Hanna-Barbera

Flintwinch
  character in: 12 Little Dorrit
  author: 7 Dickens

flinty 4 cold, hard **5** cruel, harsh, stern, stony **6** inured, steely **7** callous **8** hardened **10** unyielding **11** hardhearted, insensitive

flip 3 tap **4** bold, pert, spin, toss, turn **5** brash, flick, fresh, throw, thumb **6** cheeky, fillip **8** impudent, insolent, turn over **9** unabashed

flippant 4 glib, pert, rude **5** brash, lippy, saucy **6** cheeky, nimble **7** voluble **8** impudent, insolent, trifling **9** bumptious, frivolous, talkative **11** impertinent **12** presumptuous **13** disrespectful

Flipper
  character: 8 Bud Ricks **10** Sandy Ricks **11** Porter Ricks
  cast: 10 Brian Kelly, Luke Halpin **11** Tommy Norden
  Flipper played by: 4 Suzy

flirt 3 toy **4** play, vamp **5** dally, tease **6** trifle **8** coquette **12** heartbreaker

flit 4 dart, scud, skim, wing **5** speed **6** hasten, scurry **7** flicker, flutter

Flitch of Bacon, The
  author: 16 William Ainsworth

Flite, Miss
  character in: 10 Bleak House
  author: 7 Dickens

flivver 3 car **4** auto, heap **5** motor **6** jalopy, wheels **7** machine, vehicle **8** motorcar **9** tin lizzie **10** automobile

float 3 bob **4** waft **5** drift, hover, slide **6** bear up, buoy up, hold up, launch **8** levitate

floating 4 free **5** awash, loose **6** adrift, afloat, errant **7** buoyant, wafting **8** drifting **9** fluctuant, wandering **10** unattached

flock 2 go **3** mob, run **4** band, bevy, gang, herd, mass, pack, rush **5** bunch,

crowd, crush, drove, group, surge, troop **6** clique, gather, huddle, muster, stream, throng **7** cluster, company, coterie **8** converge **9** gathering, multitude **10** assemblage, collection, congregate **11** aggregation **12** congregation
  of fish: 6 school
  of game birds: 5 covey
  of geese: 6 gaggle
  of insects: 5 swarm
  of lions: 5 pride
  of seals or whales: 3 pod
  of young birds: 5 brood

flocks
  god of: 3 Pan

flock together 6 gather, mingle **7** convene **8** assemble **9** associate **10** congregate

flog 4 beat, cane, club, cuff, drub, hide, lash, maul, whip **5** birch, flail, smite, strap **6** cudgel, paddle, strike, switch, thrash **7** scourge **8** lambaste **9** horsewhip **10** flagellate

flood 4 flow, glut, gush, tide **6** deluge, drench, shower, stream **7** cascade, current, torrent **8** downpour, flow over, inundate, overflow, saturate, submerge, wash over **9** overwhelm **10** cloudburst, inundation, outpouring, oversupply
  period before: 12 antediluvian

Flood
  author: 16 Robert Penn Warren

flooded 6 flowed, surged **7** deluged, glutted, overran, swamped **8** drenched, engulfed **9** inundated, outpoured, washed out **10** downpoured, overflowed

floor 2 KO **4** base, deck, fell, kayo, tier **5** level, stage, story **6** bottom, ground **7** minimum, parquet **8** base rate, flooring, pavement **9** prostrate

flop 4 bomb, bust, drop, fail, fold, plop **5** close **6** fiasco, fizzle, topple, tumble, turkey **7** failure, go under, shutter, washout **8** disaster, lay an egg **14** disappointment

Flora
  origin: 5 Roman
  goddess of: 7 flowers

floral 6 bloomy **7** verdant **8** blossomy **9** botanical **10** herbaceous

Floralia
  origin: 5 Roman
  form: 8 festival

Florence
  artist: 6 Giotto **7** Cimabue **8** Ghiberti **9** Donatello **10** Michelozzi **11** della Robbia **12** Brunelleschi, Michelangelo
  capital of: 7 Tuscany **15** Firenze province
  cathedral/church: 10 San Lorenzo, San Miniato, Santa Croce **18** Santa Maria del Fiore
  Italian: 7 Firenze

  landmark: 5 David, Pieta **6** Uffizi **8** Bargello **11** Pitti Palace **12** Ponte Vecchio **13** Boboli Gardens **14** Loggia dei Lanzi, Palazzo Vecchio **19** Piazza della Signoria **22** Baptistry of San Giovanni, Ospedale degli Innocenti
  mountain: 9 Apennines
  religious reformer: 10 Savonarola
  river: 4 Arno
  ruler: 5 Goths **6** Medici, Romans **8** Lombards **9** Etruscans **15** Byzantine Empire
  tomb of: 7 Galileo, Rossini **11** Machiavelli **12** Michelangelo **15** Lorenzo de Medici

florescence 5 bloom **9** flowerage **10** blossoming

florid 4 rosy **5** gaudy, ruddy, showy **6** blowsy, hectic, ornate, rococo **7** baroque, flowery, flushed, reddish **8** inflamed, red-faced, rubicund, sanguine **9** elaborate **10** flamboyant, ornamented **12** ostentatious **13** grandiloquent

Florida
  abbreviation: 2 FL **3** Fla
  nickname: 6 Flower **8** Sunshine **10** Peninsular
  capital: 11 Tallahassee
  largest city: 12 Jacksonville
  others: 4 Tice **5** Cocoa, Miami, Ocala, Tampa **7** Hialeah, Orlando, Palatka, Sebring **8** Sarasota **9** Bradenton, Palm Beach, Pensacola **10** Clearwater **11** Brooksville, Coral Gables, Gainesville, St Augustine **12** Daytona Beach, Ft Lauderdale, St Petersburg
  baseball team: 7 Marlins
  college: 4 Nova **5** Barry, Miami, Tampa **6** Eckerd **7** Rollins, Stetson
  explorer: 11 Ponce de Leon
  feature:
    amusement park: 5 Epcot **10** Marineland **11** Disney World
    canal: 5 Miami **7** Tamiami
    museum: 8 Ringling
    national park: 10 Everglades
  tribe: 3 Ais **5** Ocale, Utina **6** Calusa, Chatot, Potano **7** Timucua **8** Seminole
  people: 5 conch **7** cracker, Osceola
  island: 7 Bahamas, Sanibel **8** Biscayne
    key: 4 Long, Vaca, West **5** Largo **7** Big Pine **8** Biscayne **9** Sugarloaf
    lake: 4 Dora **6** Apopka, Harney, Jessup, Newnan **7** Ledwith **8** Arbuckle **9** Kissimmee **10** Okeechobee
  land rank: 12 twenty-second
  physical feature:
    bay: 8 Biscayne **9** Apalachee **10** Waccasassa
    cape: 5 Sable **7** Kennedy **9** Canaveral
    gulf: 6 Mexico
    sea: 8 Atlantic
    springs: 6 Silver **7** Rainbow

swamp: 10 Everglades, Okefenokee
river: 6 Banana, Indian **7** Aucilla, Manatee, Scambia, St Johns, Suwanee **9** Ochlawaha **12** Apalachicola
state admission: 13 twenty-seventh
state bird: 11 mockingbird
state fish: 16 Atlantic sailfish
state mammal: 7 dolphin
state flower: 13 orange blossom
state motto: 12 In God We Trust
state song: 11 Swanee River **14** Old Folks at Home
state tree: 13 sabal palmetto **15** cabbage palmetto

florilegium 7 garland **8** chapbook, treasury **9** anthology

Florizel
character in: 14 The Winter's Tale
author: 11 Shakespeare

floruit 12 he flourished **13** she flourished

flotilla 5 fleet **6** armada

Flotow, Friedrich von
born: 7 Germany **11** Mecklenburg
composer of: 6 Martha **11** Die Matrosen **19** Alessandro Stradella

flotsam 4 junk **6** debris, refuse **7** garbage **8** castoffs

flounce 3 hem **4** edge, leap, skip, trim, trip **5** bound, caper, frill, stamp, stomp, storm, strut **6** bounce, edging, fringe, gambol, prance, ruffle, sashay, spring **7** valance **8** furbelow, ornament, skirting, trimming

flounder 4 fish, flop, halt, limp **5** lurch, waver **6** falter, hobble, muddle, totter, tumble, wallow, welter **7** blunder, shamble, stagger, stumble **8** flatfish, hesitate, struggle

Flounder, The
author: 11 Gunter Grass

flourish 4 curl, dash, grow, pomp, rant, show, turn **5** bloom, bluff, get on, shake, strut, sweep, swing, swish, twirl, twist, wield **6** flaunt, flower, hot air, parade, splash, thrive, waving **7** blossom, bravado, burgeon, cadenza, fanfare, fustian, glitter, prosper, shaking, succeed, swagger **8** boasting, brandish, curlicue, fare well, get ahead, swinging, vaunting, wielding **9** agitation, grace note, thrashing **10** decoration **11** braggadocio, brandishing, fanfaronade, ostentation **12** appoggiatura **13** embellishment, magniloquence, swashbuckling **14** grandiloquence

flourishing 8 swinging, swishing, thriving, wielding **9** flaunting **10** prospering, successful **11** brandishing

flout 3 rag **4** defy, mock, twit **5** chaff, scorn, spurn, taunt **6** gibe at, insult

flow 3 jet, run **4** flux, gush, pass, pour, rush, seep, tide **5** drain, drift, float, flood, glide, issue, spout, spurt, surge, sweep, swirl, train **6** abound, course, deluge, efflux, effuse, filter, plenty,

rapids, stream **7** cascade, current, debouch, torrent, well out **8** effusion, millrace, plethora, sequence **9** abundance, discharge, effluence, emanation **10** outpouring, succession **11** debouchment, progression

flower 3 bud **4** best, blow, open, pick, posy **5** bloom, cream, elite, ripen **6** mature **7** blossom, bouquet, burgeon, develop, nosegay, prosper **8** flourish **11** aristocracy

flower arranging, art of
Japanese: 7 ikebana

Flower Fables
author: 15 Louisa May Alcott

flowering 4 peak **5** bloom **6** height, heyday **8** blooming, maturing **10** blossoming, developing, prospering **11** flourishing

Flowering Judas
author: 19 Katherine Anne Porter

flowers
goddess of: 5 Flora

Flowers of Evil
author: 17 Charles Baudelaire
French title: 14 Les Fleurs du Mal

Flower State
nickname of: 7 Florida

flowery 5 fancy **6** floral, florid, ornate **8** blooming **10** blossoming, burgeoning, euphuistic, figurative, florescent, ornamental, rhetorical **11** embellished **12** efflorescent, magniloquent **13** grandiloquent

Flowery Kingdom *see* **5** China

flowing 4 flux **5** fluid **6** ebbing, fluent, smooth **7** current, copious, gliding, running **8** abundant **9** liquefied, plentiful **10** continuity, pouring out, proceeding

fluctuate 4 sway, vary, veer **5** shift, swing, waver **6** dawdle, falter, wobble **8** hesitate, undulate **9** alternate, oscillate, vacillate **10** dillydally

fluctuation 5 shift **6** change **7** veering **8** shifting, swinging **9** deviation, variation **11** alternation, oscillation, vacillation

flue 3 net **4** barb, down, pipe, tube, vent **5** fluff, fluke, shaft **6** funnel **7** channel, chimney, passage **9** smokejack

fluent 4 glib **5** vocal **6** facile **7** voluble **8** effusive, eloquent **9** garrulous, talkative **10** articulate, effortless

fluff 3 err, nap **4** down, flub, fuzz, lint, miss, puff, slip, soft **5** botch, floss, froth, primp **6** forget **7** blunder **8** feathers

fluffy 5 downy, fuzzy, nappy, wooly **6** fleecy, woolly **8** feathery

fluid 6 liquid, watery **7** unfixed **8** flexible, floating, shifting, solution, unstable **9** adaptable, liquefied, unsettled **10** adjustable, changeable, indefinite

fluid ounce
abbreviation: 4 fl oz

fluke 3 hap **5** freak **6** chance **7** miracle **8** accident, windfall **9** mischance **11** vicissitude **12** stroke of luck

flummery 7 dessert, pudding **9** gibberish **10** doubletalk, mumbo jumbo **11** obfuscation

flunky 6 lackey, menial, minion **7** servant **9** attendant, underling

fluorine
chemical symbol: 1 F

flurry 3 ado **4** fuss, gust, heat, puff, stir **5** alarm, fever, flush, haste, panic **6** breeze, bustle, pother, rattle, shower, squall, tumult **7** agitate, confuse, disturb, fidgets, fluster, flutter, perturb **8** confound, disquiet **9** agitation, commotion, confusion **10** discompose, disconcert, turbulence **11** disturbance, hurry-scurry, trepidation **12** discomposure, perturbation, restlessness

flush 4 even, glow, swab, tint, wash **5** bloom, blush, color, elate, flood, level, rinse, scour, scrub, shock, spray **6** access, dampen, deluge, douche, drench, excite, puff up, quiver, redden, sponge, thrill, tremor **7** animate, flutter, glowing, impulse, moisten, redness, wash out **8** rosiness, rosy glow, squarely, strength **9** freshness, make proud, ruddiness **10** exultation, jubilation

flushed 3 hot, red **4** rosy, ruby **5** aglow, **6** florid, torrid **7** crimson, excited, scarlet **8** blushing, feverish **10** prosperous

flushed with success 5 proud **6** elated

fluster 4 daze **5** shake, upset **6** dither, flurry, hubbub, muddle, ruffle **7** agitate, confuse, disturb, flutter, perplex, per-turb, startle, turmoil **8** befuddle, bewilder **9** agitation, commotion, confusion, discomfit **10** discompose, disconcert **12** bewilderment, discomfiture, discomposure **14** discombobulate

flute 4 fife, fold, pipe, roll, tube, wind **5** crimp **6** furrow, groove **7** piccolo, whistle **8** recorder **9** wine glass **14** champagne glass

flutter 3 bob **4** flap, flit, soar, stir, wave, wing **5** hurry, shake, throb **6** flurry, quiver, ripple, thrill, tremor, wobble **7** beating, flitter, fluster, pulsate, tremble, twitter **8** flapping, tingling **9** agitation, commotion, confusion, palpitate, sensation, vibration **12** perturbation

fluvial 7 aquatic

fluviatile 7 aquatic

flux 4 flow, tide **5** flood **6** course, motion, stream, unrest **7** current **8** mutation, shifting **10** alteration, transition **11** fluctuation **12** modification **14** transformation

fly 4 flap, flee, sail, skip, soar, wave, wing **5** coast, float, glide, hover, hurry, split, swoop **6** hasten, hustle **7** flutter, run away, take off, vibrate **8** take wing, undulate

fly
varieties: **3** bat, bot **4** blow, deer, dung, gnat, horn, moth, rust, sand **5** beach, black, crane, dance, drone, flesh, fruit, horse, house, march, marsh, midge, mydas, punky **6** bee fly, cactus, maggot, pomace, robber, stable, tsetse, warble, window **7** chalcid, seaweed, skipper, soldier, tachima **8** lousefly, mosquito, stiletto **9** leaf miner **10** flat-footed, fungus gnat, humpbacked **11** thickheaded **14** black scavenger

fly apart 5 burst **6** blow up **7** explode, shatter **8** detonate, fragment

fly at 6 assail, attack

fly-by-night 5 shady **6** shifty **7** crooked **8** unstable, untrusty **9** dishonest **10** unreliable **12** disreputable, undependable **13** irresponsible, untrustworthy

Flying Dutchman, The
opera by: **6** Wagner
character: **4** Erik **5** Senta **6** Daland **11** The Dutchman

Flying Fish
constellation of: **6** Volans

Flying Nun, The
character: **9** Sister Ana **11** Sister Sixto **13** Carlos Ramirez **14** Mother Superior **15** Sister Bertrille **16** Sister Jacqueline
cast: **10** Sally Field **12** Alejandro Rey, Linda Dangcil, Marge Redmond **14** Shelly Morrison **17** Madeleine Sherwood

fly in the ointment 5 hitch **7** problem, trouble **8** drawback, nuisance **9** hindrance **10** impediment **12** disadvantage

Flynn, Errol
real name: **17** Leslie Thomas Flynn
born: **6** Hobart **8** Tasmania **9** Australia
roles: **10** The Sea Hawk **12** Captain Blood **14** Too Much Too Soon **15** The Sun Also Rises **24** The Adventures of Robin Hood **26** The Charge of the Light Brigade

fly off the handle 6 see red

fly the coop 4 bolt, flee **6** escape, run off **7** abscond, get away, make off, run away, skip out, take off

foal 4 cade, colt **5** filly, young **9** fledgling

foam 4 fizz, head, scum, suds **5** froth, spume **6** lather **7** sparkle **8** bubbling **13** effervescence

foaming 5 sudsy **6** bubbly, frothy **7** lathery **8** bubbling, frothing

foamy 5 fizzy **6** frothy **7** lathery **8** bubbling **9** sparkling **12** effervescent

fob 5 chain, medal, strap **6** ribbon **8** ornament **9** medallion

focal 3 key **4** main **5** chief **7** central, pivotal **8** foremost **9** principal

Foch, Ferdinand
served in: **3** WWI
nationality: **6** French
rank: **7** marshal **16** commander-in-chief
battle: **5** Marne, Somme

Foch, Nina
real name: **20** Nina Consuelo Maud Fock
born: **6** Leyden **11** Netherlands
roles: **9** Spartacus **14** Executive Suite, Song to Remember **17** An American in Paris, My Name Is Julia Ross **18** The Ten Commandments

Fock, Nina Consuelo Maud
real name of: **8** Nina Foch

focus 3 aim, fix, hub **4** core **5** haunt, heart **6** adjust, center, direct, middle, resort **7** nucleus, retreat **8** converge **9** limelight, spotlight **10** rendezvous **11** concentrate **12** headquarters

focusing 6 aiming **9** adjusting, centering, directing **10** adjustment, converging **11** pinpointing **13** concentrating

fodder 4 feed, food **6** forage, silage **7** rations **9** provender

foe 5 enemy, rival **8** attacker, opponent **9** adversary, assailant, combatant, contender, disputant **10** antagonist, competitor

fog 3 dim **4** daze, haze, smog, soup **5** brume, cloud **6** darken, muddle, stupor, trance **7** confuse, obscure, pea soup, perplex **8** bewilder **9** murkiness **10** cloudiness **12** bewilderment

Fogg, Phileas
character in: **26** Around the World in Eighty Days
author: **10** Jules Verne
valet: **12** Passepartout

foggy 3 dim **4** dark, hazy **5** dusky, filmy, fuzzy, misty, murky, musty, soupy, vague **6** cloudy, smoggy, spacey **7** brumous, clouded, obscure, shadowy, unclear **8** confused, nebulous, overcast, vaporous **9** beclouded **10** indistinct

foible 4 kink **5** quirk **6** defect, whimsy **7** failing, frailty **8** crotchet, weak side, weakness **9** infirmity **10** deficiency **11** shortcoming **12** imperfection

Foible
character in: **16** The Way of the World
author: **8** Congreve

foil 3 nip **4** balk, film, leaf **5** check, flake, match, sheet, wafer **6** hinder, lamina, set off, thwart **7** enhance, prevent **8** backdrop, contrast **9** frustrate

10 antithesis, complement, supplement **11** correlative, counterpart

foist 6 impose, unload **7** palm off, pass off

fold 3 hug, lap, pen, sty **4** bend, curl, sect, tuck, wrap, yard **5** clasp, close, crimp, flock, group, layer, pleat **6** corral, crease, dog-ear, double, encase, enfold, fur-row, gather, parish, pucker, ruffle, rumple, wrap up **7** crinkle, crumple, embosom, embrace, entwine, envelop, flounce, overlap, wrinkle **8** barnyard, compound, doubling, stockade **9** community, corrugate, enclosure **12** congregation

folder 7 booklet, leaflet **8** brochure, circular, pamphlet **9** portfolio

foliage 6 leaves **7** leafage, verdure

folklore 5 myths **6** fables **7** legends **10** traditions

folks 3 kin **6** family, people **7** kinsmen, parents **8** everyone **9** relatives **10** kith and kin

folksy 6 casual, chatty **8** familiar, friendly, homespun, informal, sociable **10** neighborly **14** conversational **15** unsophisticated

folk tale
German: **7** Marchen

Follett, Ken
author of: **14** Eye of the Needle **15** On Wings of Eagles, The Key to Rebecca **22** The Man from St Petersburg

follow 3 dog **4** copy, heed, hunt, mind, note, obey, tail **5** aim at, chase, grasp, hound, stalk, trace, track, trail, watch **6** attend, notice, pursue, regard, shadow, take up **7** cherish, emulate, imitate, observe, replace, succeed **8** practice, supplant **9** accompany, cultivate, prosecute **10** comprehend, understand

follower 3 fan **4** tail **5** pupil, toady **6** chaser, hunter, shadow, stooge **7** admirer, apostle, convert, devotee, protege, pursuer, servant, stalker **8** adherent, advocate, disciple, hanger-on, henchman, parasite, partisan, retainer, servitor **9** accessory, attendant, dependent, proselyte, satellite, supporter, sycophant

following 4 next **5** below, suite, train **6** public **7** ensuing, retinue **8** audience **9** adherents, clientele, entourage, partisans, patronage **10** attendance, consequent, sequential, subsequent, succeeding, successive **11** consecutive

Follow the Fleet
director: **12** Mark Sandrich
cast: **11** Fred Astaire **12** Ginger Rogers **13** Randolph Scott **21** Harriet Hilliard Nelson
song: **11** We Saw the Sea **13** Let Yourself Go **24** Let's Face the Music and Dance

follow-up **7** ensuing **8** sequence **9** aftermath **10** subsequent

folly **6** idiocy, levity **7** inanity, mistake **8** nonsense, trifling **9** absurdity, asininity, frivolity, giddiness, silliness **10** imbecility, imprudence, tomfoolery **11** doltishness, fatuousness, foolishness **12** indiscretion **13** brainlessness, irrationality, senselessness

foment **4** goad, spur, urge **5** rouse **6** arouse, excite, foster, incite, kindle, stir up **7** agitate, inflame, promote, provoke, quicken **8** irritate **9** aggravate, galvanize, instigate, stimulate **10** exacerbate

fond **5** naive **6** ardent, doting, loving, tender **7** amorous, devoted **8** desirous, enamored, harbored, held dear **9** cherished, indulgent, preserved, sustained **10** infatuated, passionate **11** impassioned, sentimental **12** affectionate **16** overaffectionate

Fonda, Henry
  wife: **16** Margaret Sullavan
  son: **5** Peter
  daughter: **4** Jane
  born: **13** Grand Island NE
  roles: **7** Jezebel, Warlock **8** Fail Safe **10** Fort Apache, In Harm's Way, The Best Man, The Lady Eve **12** On Golden Pond (Oscar) **13** Mister Roberts, Ox-Bow Incident, The Longest Day **14** Twelve Angry Men, Young Mr Lincoln **16** Advise and Consent, Battle of the Bulge, How the West Was Won, The Grapes of Wrath **18** The Boston Strangler **19** My Darling Clementine, The Immortal Sergeant **21** Sometimes a Great Notion

Fonda, Jane
  father: **5** Henry
  brother: **5** Peter
  husband: **9** Ted Turner, Tom Hayden **10** Roger Vadim
  born: **9** New York NY
  roles: **5** Julia, Klute (Oscar) **10** Barbarella, Coming Home (Oscar) **11** A Doll's House **12** Any Wednesday, On Golden Pond **13** China Syndrome **17** Barefoot in the Park **23** They Shoot Horses Don't They?

Fonda, Peter
  father: **5** Henry
  sister: **4** Jane
  born: **9** New York NY
  roles: **7** The Trip **9** Easy Rider **13** The Wild Angels

fondle **3** hug, neck, pet **4** neck **5** spoon **6** caress, cuddle, nestle, nuzzle, smooch, stroke **7** embrace, make out **8** canoodle **10** bill and coo

fondness **4** bent, care, love **5** ardor, fancy **6** desire, liking **7** passion **8** devotion, penchant, weakness **9** affection **10** attachment, partiality, preference, propensity, tenderness **11**

amorousness, inclination **12** predilection **14** susceptibility

fond utterance **9** sweet talk **10** endearment **12** sweet nothing

Fons
  origin: **5** Roman
  god of: **7** springs

fons et origo **15** source and origin

Fontaine, Joan
  real name: **25** Joan de Beauvoir de Havilland
  sister: **17** Olivia de Havilland
  husband: **11** Brian Aherne
  born: **5** Japan, Tokyo
  roles: **3** Ivy **7** Ivanhoe, Rebecca **8** Casanova, Gunga Din, Jane Eyre, The Women **9** Suspicion (Oscar) **12** The Devil's Own **15** Frenchman's Creek, September Affair **16** Tender Is the Night, The Constant Nymph

Fontanne, Lynn
  husband: **10** Alfred Lunt
  born: **6** London **7** England
  roles: **8** The Visit **9** Quadrille, The Pirate **10** The Sea Gull **13** O Mistress Mine **15** Design for Living **18** The Great Sebastians **19** The Taming of the Shrew

food **4** chow, feed, grub **5** board **6** fodder, forage, silage, viands **7** edibles, nurture, pasture, rations **8** eatables, victuals **9** nutrition, pasturage, provender **10** provisions, sustenance **11** comestibles, nourishment, subsistence

food, miraculous **5** manna

fool **3** ass, con, oaf **4** bilk, clod, dolt, dupe, gull, hoax, jest, joke **5** cheat, chump, clown, cozen, cut up, dummy, dunce, feign, goose, idiot, klutz, moron, nin-ny, tease, trick **6** diddle, fleece, frolic, hum-bug, jester, nitwit, rip off, stooge **7** beguile, buffoon, deceive, defraud, half-wit, Pierrot, pretend **8** bonehead, dummkopf, flimflam, hoodwink, imbecile, lunkhead, meathead, numskull **9** bamboozle, blockhead, harlequin, ignoramus, numbskull, simpleton **10** dunderhead, nincompoop, scaramouch **11** Punchinello

fool around **3** toy **4** idle **5** clown, dally **6** dawdle, loiter, trifle

foolhardy **4** rash **5** brash, hasty **6** madcap **8** careless, heedless, reckless **9** daredevil, hotheaded, impetuous, imprudent, impulsive **10** headstrong, incautious **11** harebrained, thoughtless

foolish **5** inane, silly **6** absurd, stupid, unwise **7** asinine, fatuous, idiotic, moronic, witless **9** brainless, imbecilic, imprudent, ludicrous, senseless **10** boneheaded, incautious, indiscreet, ridiculous **12** preposterous **13** irresponsible, unintelligent

foolishness **5** folly **6** idiocy, lunacy **8** unwisdom **9** absurdity, asininity, pu-

erility, silliness, stupidity **10** imbecility, imprudence **11** fatuousness, witlessness **12** childishness, extravagance, indiscretion **13** brainlessness, senselessness **14** ridiculousness **15** injudiciousness **16** irresponsibility, preposterousness

Fool of Quality, The
  author: **11** Henry Brooke

foot **3** dog, pad, paw **4** base, hoof **6** bottom, tootsy **7** trotter **8** infantry **10** foundation
  abbreviation: **2** ft

football
  term: **3** end **4** bomb, down, draw, flat, punt, sack **5** blitz, guard, zebra **6** center, fumble, option, pocket, safety, tackle **7** audible, bootleg, flanker, holding, kickoff, lateral, offside, platoon, reverse, rollout, shotgun **8** clipping, gridiron, halfback, turnover **9** crackback, field goal, nose guard, scrimmage, touchback **10** conversion, cornerback, linebacker, nose tackle **11** quarterback **12** encroachment

Hall of Fame:
  1963: **4** Bell (Bert), Carr (Joe), Hein (Mel), Mara (Tim) **5** Baugh (Sammy), Clark (Dutch), Halas (George), Henry (Pete) **6** Hutson (Don), Nevers (Ernie), Thorpe (Jim) **7** Hubbard (Cal), Lambeau (Curly), McNally (John Blood) **8** Nagurski (Bronko), Marshall (George P)
  1964: **5** Lyman (Link) **6** Healey (Ed), Hinkle (Clarke), Rooney (Art) **7** Trafton (George) **9** Conzelman (Jimmy), Michalske (Mike)
  1965: **6** Graham (Otto), Grange (Red) **7** Luckman (Sid) **8** Driscoll (Paddy), Fortmann (Daniel J), Van Buren (Steve) **10** Chamberlin (Guy), Waterfield (Bob)
  1966: **3** Ray (Hugh "Shorty") **5** Guyon (Joe), Owens (Steve) **6** Dudley (Bill), Herber (Arnie), McAfee (George), Turner (Clyde "Bulldog") **8** Kiesling (Walt)
  1967: **5** Brown (Paul E), Layne (Bobby) **6** Reeves (Dan), Strong (Ken) **7** Bidwill (Charles W), Tunnell (Emlen) **8** Bednarik (Chuck), Stydahar (Joe)
  1968: **6** Hirsch (Elroy), Motley (Marion), Trippi (Charley) **7** Battles (Cliff), Donovan (Art), Millner (Wayne) **13** Wojciechowicz (Alex)
  1969: **5** Neale (Earle "Greasy"), Perry (Joe) **7** Edwards (Albert Glen "Turk") **8** Stautner (Ernie) **9** Nomellini (Leo)
  1970: **5** Fears (Tom), Pihos (Pete) **9** McElhenny (Hugh) **12** Christiansen (Jack)
  1971: **5** Brown (Jim) **6** Hewitt (Bill), Kinard (Frank "Bruiser"), Tittle (Y A) **8** Lombardi (Vince) **10** Robustelli

(Andy) **11** Van Brocklin (Norm)
1972: 4 Hunt (Lamar) **6** Matson (Ollie), Parker (Ace) **9** Marchetti (Gino)
1973: 5 Berry (Raymond) **6** Parker (Jim) **7** Schmidt (Joe)
1974: 4 Lane (Dick "Night Train") **5** Groza (Lou "The Toe") **6** George (Bill) **7** Canadeo (Tony)
1975: 5 Brown (Roosevelt), Moore (Lenny) **6** Connor (George) **7** Lavelli (Dante)
1976: 4 Ford (Len) **6** Taylor (Jim) **8** Flaherty (Ray)
1977: 5 Gregg (Forrest), Starr (Bart) **6** Sayers (Gale), Willis (Bill) **7** Gifford (Frank)
1978: 6 Ewbank (Weeb), Wilson (Larry) **7** Alworth (Lance), Leemans (Tuffy) **8** Nitschke (Ray)
1979: 3 Mix (Ron) **4** Lary (Yale) **6** Butkus (Dick), Unitas (Johnny)
1980: 4 Otto (Jim) **5** Jones (David "Deacon"), Lilly (Bob) **8** Adderley (Herb)
1981: 5 Davis (Willie), Ringo (Jim) **6** Badgro (Morris "Red"), Blanda (George)
1982: 4 Huff (Sam) **5** Musso (George), Olsen (Merlin) **6** Atkins (Doug)
1983: 4 Bell (Bobby) **6** Gilman (Sid) **8** Mitchell (Bobby), Warfield (Paul) **9** Jurgensen (Sonny)
1984: 5 Brown (Willie) **6** Taylor (Charley) **9** McCormack (Mike) **11** Weinmeister (Arnie)
1985: 6 Gatski (Frank), Namath (Joe) **7** Rozelle (Pete), Simpson (OJ) **8** Staubach (Roger)
1986: 6 Lanier (Willie), Walker (Doak) **7** Hornung (Paul), Houston (Ken) **9** Tarkenton (Fran)
1987: 6 Csonka (Larry), Dawson (Len), Greene (Joe), Langer (Jim), Upshaw (Gene) **7** Johnson (John Henry), Maynard (Don)
1988: 3 Ham (Jack) **4** Page (Alan) **5** Ditka (Mike) **11** Biletnikoff (Fred)
1989: 4 Wood (Willie) **5** Shell (Art) **6** Blount (Mel) **8** Bradshaw (Terry)
1990: 6 Griese (Bob), Harris (Franco), Landry (Tom) **7** Lambert (Jack), St Clair (Bob) **8** Buchanan (Buck) **9** Hendricks (Ted)
1991: 5 Jones (Stan) **6** Hannah (John) **7** Schramm (Tex) **8** Campbell (Earl), Stenerud (Jan)
1992: 5 Davis (Al) **6** Barney (Lem), Mackey (John) **7** Riggins (John)
1993: 4 Noll (Chuck) **5** Fouts (Dan), Walsh (Bill) **6** Little (Larry), Payton (Walter)
1994: 5 Grant (Bud), Kelly (Leroy), Smith (Jackie), White (Randy) **7** Dorsett (Tony), Johnson (Jimmy)
other player/coach: 8 Don Shula, Kyle Rote **9** Amos Stagg, Dan Marino, Earl Blaik, Jerry Rice, Lou Little, **10** Bear Bryant, Bruce Smith, Bubba Smith, Joe Montana, Joe Paterno, Ken Stabler, Larry Brown, Troy Aikman, Walter Camp, Warren Moon **11** Ahmad Rashad, Craig Morton, Deion Sanders, Earl Morrall, Floyd Little, Jim Plunkett, Knute Rockne, Reggie White **12** Bud Wilkinson, Joe Thiesmann, Ozzie Newsome, Roman Gabriel, William Perry **13** Ara Parseghian, Eric Dickerson, **14** Lawrence Taylor, Lydell Mitchell

football bowl games 3 Sun **4** Rose **5** Aloha, Gator, Peach, Sugar, Super **6** Citrus, Copper, Cotton, Fiesta, Orange **7** Holiday, Liberty **10** Bluebonnet, California **12** Independence

football leagues
National Football League (NFL): 11 New York Jets **12** Buffalo Bills, Chicago Bears, Detroit Lions **13** Dallas Cowboys, Denver Broncos, Miami Dolphins, New York Giants **14** Atlanta Falcons, Los Angeles Rams **15** Baltimore Ravens, Cleveland Browns, Green Bay Packers, Seattle Seahawks, Tennessee Oilers (formerly Houston) **16** Kansas City Chiefs, Minnesota Vikings, New Orleans Saints, Phoenix Cardinals (formerly St Louis), San Diego Chargers **17** Cincinnati Bengals, Indianapolis Colts (formerly Baltimore), Los Angeles Raiders (formerly Oakland) **18** New England Patriots, Philadelphia Eagles, Pittsburgh Steelers, Tampa Bay Buccaneers, Washington Redskins **23** San Francisco Forty-Niners
United States Football League (USFL): 10 Denver Gold **12** Chicago Blitz **14** Baltimore Stars, Boston Breakers **15** Houston Gamblers, Oakland Invaders, Oklahoma Outlaws, Tampa Bay Bandits **16** Arizona Wranglers, Memphis Showboats, Michigan Panthers, Orlando Renegades, Portland Breakers **17** Jacksonville Bulls, Los Angeles Express, New Jersey Generals, Philadelphia Stars **18** Washington Federals **19** Birmingham Stallions **21** San Antonio Gunslingers

football team (NFC)
Atlanta: 7 Falcons
    stadium: 11 Georgia Dome
Chicago: 5 Bears
    stadium: 12 Soldier Field
Dallas: 7 Cowboys
    stadium: 5 Texas
Detroit: 5 Lions
    stadium: 17 Pontiac Silverdome
Green Bay: 7 Packers
    stadium: 9 Milwaukee **12** Lambeau Field
Los Angeles: 4 Rams
    stadium: 7 Anaheim
Minnesota: 7 Vikings
    stadium: 9 Metrodome

New Orleans: 6 Saints
    stadium: 18 Louisiana Superdome
New York: 6 Giants
    stadium: 6 Giants
Philadelphia: 6 Eagles
    stadium: 8 Veterans
Phoenix: 9 Cardinals
    stadium: 8 Sun Devil
    formerly in: 7 St Louis
San Francisco: 11 Forty-Niners
    stadium: 15 Candlestick Park
Tampa Bay: 10 Buccaneers
    stadium: 5 Tampa
Washington: 8 Redskins
    stadium: 14 Robert F Kennedy
football team (AFC)
Buffalo: 5 Bills
    stadium: 4 Rich
Cincinnati: 7 Bengals
    stadium: 10 Riverfront
Cleveland: 6 Browns
    stadium: 9 Cleveland
Denver: 7 Broncos
    stadium: 8 Mile High
Houston: 6 Oilers
    stadium: 9 Astrodome
Indianapolis: 5 Colts
    stadium: 11 Hoosier Dome
    formerly in: 9 Baltimore
Kansas City: 6 Chiefs
    stadium: 9 Arrowhead
Los Angeles: 7 Raiders
    stadium: 16 Memorial Coliseum
    formerly in: 7 Oakland
Miami: 8 Dolphins
    stadium: 9 Joe Robbie
New England: 8 Patriots
    stadium: 7 Foxboro
New York: 4 Jets
    stadium: 6 Giants
Pittsburgh: 8 Steelers
    stadium: 11 Three Rivers
San Diego: 8 Chargers
    stadium: 8 San Diego
Seattle: 8 Seahawks
    stadium: 8 Kingdome
footfall 3 pad **4** pace, step **5** tread **8** footstep
foothold 4 grip, hold **7** support **8** purchase
footloose 4 free **8** carefree **9** fancy-free **10** unattached **11** uncommitted **12** unencumbered
footnote 5 gloss **9** reference **10** annotation **11** explanation **12** afterthought
footnote abbreviations 2 ca, ms, nd, qv **3** mss **4** et al, ibid **5** et seq, infra, op cit, pseud, supra **6** loc cit
footpad 5 thief **6** bandit, mugger, outlaw, robber **10** highwayman
footpath 4 lane, ramp **5** jetty, trail **8** sidewalk
foot soldiers 8 infantry **10** fusilliers, musketeers
footstool 6 buffet **7** hassock, ottoman **8** footrest

footwear
French: 9 chaussure

fop 4 beau, dude 5 dandy, swell 7 coxcomb 8 popinjay 9 prettyboy 11 Beau Brummel

foppish 4 vain 5 gaudy, showy 6 ornate 7 finical 8 affected, dandyish 9 dandified 12 ostentatious 13 overelaborate

forage 4 feed, food, hunt, raid, seek 6 fodder, ravage, search, silage 7 despoil, explore, pasture, plunder, rummage 8 scavenge, scrounge 9 pasturage, provender 10 provisions

foray 4 raid 5 sally 6 attack, inroad, invade, ravage, thrust 7 pillage, plunder, venture 8 invasion 9 incursion 10 expedition 11 depredation

forbear 4 quit, stop 5 cease, forgo 6 desist, endure, eschew, forego, give up, suffer 7 abstain, refrain 8 abnegate, renounce, tolerate

forbearance 4 pity 5 mercy 6 pardon 8 clemency, eschewal, leniency, meekness, mildness, patience 9 endurance, tolerance 10 abstention, abstinence, continence, indulgence, moderation, submission, temperance 11 longanimity, resignation 12 mercifulness

forbearing 6 denial 7 lenient, refusal 8 eschewal, tolerant 9 indulgent 10 abnegation, abstention, abstinence, permissive, refraining 13 nonindulgence 16 nonparticipation

forbid 3 ban, bar 4 veto 5 taboo 6 enjoin, hinder, impede, oppose, refuse, reject 7 exclude, gainsay, inhibit, obviate, prevent 8 disallow, obstruct, preclude, prohibit, restrain 9 interdict, proscribe

forbiddance 3 ban 4 no-no 5 taboo 7 barring, embargo 9 exclusion, interdict 11 prohibition 12 interdiction, proscription

forbidden 4 no-no, tabu 5 taboo 6 banned 8 debarred 10 prohibited, proscribed
German: 8 verboten

forbidden fruit
type: 6 brandy 7 liqueur
origin: 7 America
flavor: 5 honey 6 orange 10 grapefruit

forbidding 4 dour, grim, ugly 6 odious 7 hideous, ominous 8 horrible, sinister 9 abhorrent, offensive, repellent, repulsive 10 unfriendly, unpleasant 11 prohibitive, prohibitory, threatening 12 disagree-able, inhospitable 14 unapproachable

force 3 pry, vim 4 army, body, coax, crew, drag, gang, make, pull, push, team, unit, urge 5 break, clout, corps, drive, group, impel, might, power, press, squad, value, vigor, wrest 6 coerce, compel, duress, effect, elicit, energy, enjoin, extort, impact, import, impose, induce, oblige, propel, stress, thrust, weight, wrench 7 cogency, intrude, meaning, obtrude, potency, require, squeeze, stamina 8 charisma, coercion, division, efficacy, emphasis, momentum, persuade, pressure, squadron, strength, validity, violence, vitality 9 animation, battalion, constrain, magnetism, overpower, puissance 10 attraction, compulsion, constraint, detachment 11 necessitate, weightiness 12 significance 13 effectiveness
Latin: 3 vis

forced 5 slave 7 binding, coerced, labored, obliged 8 affected, enslaved, grudging, mannered, required, strained 9 compelled, impressed, insincere, mandatory, unwilling 10 artificial, compulsory, obligatory 11 constrained, involuntary

forceful 5 pithy, valid, vivid 6 cogent, potent, robust, strong, virile 7 dynamic, intense 8 emphatic, powerful, puissant, vigorous 9 effective, energetic 10 impressive

forceless 4 weak 8 impotent

force measurement 4 dyne 6 newton 7 poundal

Force of Circumstance
author: 16 Simone de Beauvoir

Force of Destiny, The
also: 17 La Forza del Destino
opera by: 5 Verdi
character: 7 Leonora 8 Don Carlo 9 Don Alvaro

forcible 8 coercive 10 compulsory

ford 3 car 4 span, wade 5 cross, shoal 6 bridge, stream 7 passage 8 crossing, tin lizzy

Ford, Gerald Rudolph
born: 17 Leslie Lynch King Jr
adopted by/named after: 10 step father
nickname: 5 Jerry 7 Mr Clean
presidential rank: 12 thirty-eighth
party: 10 Republican
state represented: 2 MI
defeated: 5 no one
elected to neither: 10 presidency 14 vice presidency
vice president: 11 (Nelson A) Rockefeller
cabinet:
  state: 9 (Henry A) Kissinger
  treasury: 5 (William E) Simon
  defense: 8 (Donald H) Rumsfeld 11 (James) Schlesinger
  attorney general: 4 (Edward H) Levi 5 (William B) Saxbe
  interior: 6 (Rogers Clark Ballard) Morton, (Thomas S) Kleppe 8 (Stanley K) Hathaway
  agriculture: 4 (Earl Lauer) Butz 6 (John A) Knebel
  commerce: 4 (Frederick B) Dent 6

(Rogers Clark Ballard) Morton 10 (Elliot L) Richardson
  labor: 5 (W J) Usery (Jr) 6 (John T) Dunlop 7 (Peter J) Brennan
  HEW: 7 (F David) Mathews 10 (Caspar W) Weinberger
  HUD: 4 (James T) Lynn 5 (Carla Anderson) Hills
  transportation: 7 (William T) Coleman (Jr) 8 (Claude S) Brinegar
born: 7 Omaha NE
education:
  University: 8 Michigan
  Law School: 4 Yale
religion: 12 Episcopalian
interests: 4 golf 6 boxing, skiing 8 football, swimming
vacation spot: 2 CO 4 Vail
author: 21 Portrait of the Assassin (with John R Stiles) 27 A Time To Heal: An Autobiography
political career: 13 vice president 19 House minority leader 24 US House of Representatives
civilian career: 6 lawyer
  assistant football coach at: 4 Yale
military service: 6 US Navy 10 lieutenant, World War II
notable events of lifetime/term: 9 recession 12 Bicentennial
  assassination attempts on: 4 Ford
  clemency for: 12 draft dodgers, draft evaders
  kidnapping/trial/conviction of: 11 Patty Hearst
  scandal: 8 Lockheed 10 Hays Affair
  talks: 4 SALT
quotes: 19 I am a Ford not a Lincoln 41 Indebted to no man{hp}---{hp}the president of all the people 50 Our long national nightmare is over Our constitution works
father:
  natural: 15 Leslie Lynch King
  adoptive: 17 Gerald Rudolph Ford
mother: 7 Dorothy (Gardner King Ford)
siblings:
  half-brothers: 12 James Francis 13 Thomas Gardner 14 Richard Addison
wife: 9 Elizabeth (Bloomer Warren)
  nickname: 5 Betty
children: 4 John 5 Susan 6 Steven 7 Michael

Ford, Glenn
real name: 11 Gwyllyn Ford
wife: 13 Eleanor Powell
born: 6 Canada, Quebec
roles: 4 Rage 5 Gilda, Jubal 6 Santee 8 Cimarron 11 The Rounders 14 Is Paris Burning? 17 Interrupted Melody 18 Don't Go Near the Water 19 The Blackboard Jungle 23 Teahouse of the August Moon

Ford, Harrison
born: 9 Chicago IL
roles: 7 Frantic, Witness 8 Star Wars

11 Blade Runner **15** Return of the Jedi **16** American Graffiti **19** Raiders of the Lost Ark **20** The Empire Strikes Back **30** Indiana Jones and the Temple of Doom

Ford, John
author of: **13** Perkin Warbeck **17** 'Tis Pity She's a Whore **19** The Lover's Melancholy

Ford, John
director of: **10** Stagecoach **11** The Informer (Oscar), The Quiet Man (Oscar) **12** The Hurricane, The Searchers **13** Grapes of Wrath (Oscar), Mister Roberts (with Mervyn LeRoy), The Lost Patrol **17** The Long Voyage Home **19** How Green Was My Valley (Oscar), My Darling Clementine **27** The Man Who Shot Liberty Valence

Ford, Thelma Booth
real name of: **12** Shirley Booth

Ford and Mistress Ford
characters in: **22** The Merry Wives of Windsor
author: **11** Shakespeare

Ford automobiles 3 LTD **5** Edsel, Pinto, T-Bird **6** Model T, Taurus **7** Mustang **11** Thunderbird

fore 5 front **7** frontal **8** anterior, headmost

forearm 4 ulna **5** prime, ready **7** prepare

forebear 8 ancestor, begetter **10** antecedent, procreator, progenitor

foreboding 4 omen **5** dread **6** augury, boding **7** portent **9** intuition, misgiving **10** prescience, prognostic **11** premonition **12** apprehension, presentiment

forecast 5 augur **6** augury, divine, expect **7** outlook, portend, predict, presage, project **8** envisage, envision, prophesy **9** calculate, prevision, prognosis **10** anticipate, conjecture, prediction, prescience, projection **11** extrapolate **12** anticipation, precognition, presentiment **13** prognosticate **15** prognostication

forefather 6 author **8** ancestor, begetter **9** patriarch, precursor **10** antecedent, originator, procreator, progenitor **12** primogenitor

forefront 4 fame, head, lead **8** vanguard **9** celebrity

foreign 5 alien **6** exotic, remote **7** distant, strange, unknown, unusual **8** imported **9** barbarous, extrinsic, irregular, unrelated **10** extraneous, heathenish, introduced, irrelevant, outlandish, unfamiliar **11** incongruous, inconsonant, unconnected **12** antipathetic, inadmissible, inapplicable, incompatible, inconsistent **13** inappropriate **16** uncharacteristic

Foreign Correspondent
director: **15** Alfred Hitchcock
cast: **10** Joel McCrea, Laraine Day **13** George Sanders **14** Robert Benchley **15** Albert Basserman, Herbert Marshall

foreigner 5 alien, pagan **6** emigre **8** newcomer, outsider, stranger **9** barbarian, immigrant, nonnative, outlander
German: **9** Auslander

foreign officer 6 consul **8** diplomat, minister **10** ambassador **14** representative **15** charge d'affaires

foreknowledge 9 intuition, prevision **10** prescience **11** premonition **12** anticipation, apprehension, clairvoyance, precogni-tion, presentiment

foreman 4 boss **7** manager **8** chairman, overseer **9** president, spokesman **10** supervisor **11** coordinator **14** superintendent

foremost 4 head, main **5** chief, vital **7** capital, leading, supreme **8** cardinal **9** essential, paramount, principal **10** preeminent

forerunner 4 omen, sign **5** token **6** augury, herald **7** portent, presage **8** ancestor **9** harbinger, precursor, prototype **10** progenitor, prognostic **11** predecessor, premonition

foresee 5 augur **6** divine, expect **7** predict, presage **8** envision, prophesy **10** anticipate **13** prognosticate

foreshadow 5 augur **7** presage, promise **9** prefigure

foresight 6 wisdom **8** planning, prudence, sagacity **9** prevision **10** discretion, precaution, prescience, providence, shrewdness **12** anticipation, clairvoyance, perspicacity, precognition, preparedness **13** premeditation **14** farsightedness

forest 4 bush, wood **5** copse, grove, stand, woods **6** jungle **7** thicket **8** wildwood, woodland **10** timberland, wilderness

forestall 5 avert, avoid, block, deter **6** thwart **7** head off, obviate, prevent, ward off **8** preclude **10** anticipate, circumvent, counteract

Forester, C S (Cecil Scott)
author of: **6** The Gun **14** A Ship of the Line **15** Payment Deferred, The African Queen **24** Captain Horatio Hornblower

forests
god of: **3** Pan **7** Silenus, Virbius
pertaining to: **6** silvan, sylvan
nymph: **5** dryad

foretell 5 augur **6** divine **7** portend, predict, presage **8** prophesy, soothsay **9** apprehend **13** prognosticate

forethought 4 heed **7** caution **8** prudence, sagacity, wariness **10** discretion, precaution, providence, shrewdness **11** carefulness **12** anticipation, deliberation **13** consideration, premed-itation **14** circumspection, farsightedness

forever 6 always **9** eternally, undyingly **10** constantly **11** ceaselessly, continually, incessantly, perpetually, unceasingly **12** interminably **13** everlastingly, unremittingly
Latin: **11** in perpetuum

forewarn 4 bode **5** alert **6** advise, notify, signal, tip off **7** caution, portend, presage, prewarn **8** cry havoc

foreword 7 preface, prelude **8** preamble, prologue **12** introduction

Forewords and Afterwords
author: **7** W H Auden

for example
Latin: **2** eg **13** exempli gratia

forfeit 4 fine, miss **5** waive, waste, yield **6** waiver **7** damages, default, let slip, penalty **8** squander **9** surrender **10** assessment

Forfeit
author: **11** Dick Francis

forge 4 copy, form, make **5** clone, shape **6** devise, hearth, smithy **7** falsify, fashion, furnace, imitate, produce, turn out **8** contrive, simulate **9** fabricate, ironworks **11** counterfeit, manufacture

forgery 4 copy, fake, hoax, sham **5** clone, fraud **7** cloning **9** deception, imitation **11** counterfeit, fraudulence **13** falsification **14** counterfeiting **17** misrepresentation

forget 6 slight **7** neglect **8** overlook, pass over **9** disregard

forgetful 6 remiss **7** out of it **8** amnesiac, careless, heedless, mindless **9** negligent, oblivious, unmindful **10** neglectful **11** inattentive

forget-me-not 8 Myosotis
varieties: **5** white **6** alpine, garden **7** Chinese **8** creeping

forgive 5 clear **6** acquit, excuse, pardon **7** absolve, condone, release, set free **8** overlook, reprieve **9** discharge, exculpate, exonerate

forgiveness 6 pardon **7** amnesty **9** remission **10** absolution

forgiving 6 benign, kindly **8** excusing **9** benignant, pardoning **11** kindhearted

forgo 4 skip **5** waive, yield **6** eschew, give up **8** abnegate, renounce **9** sacrifice, surrender **10** relinquish

fork 4 bend, stab **5** angle, elbow, split **6** branch, crotch, divide, impale, pierce, ramify, skewer **7** diverge, trident **8** division **9** bifurcate, pitchfork **10** divergence, separation **11** bifurcation **12** intersection

forked 5 cleft, tined **6** horned, zigzag **7** angular, divided, pronged **8** branched **9** ambiguous, deceitful, equivocal **10** bifurcated

For Kicks
  author: **11** Dick Francis
fork out 5 spend **6** expend **8** disburse, dispense
for lack of something better
  French: **12** faute de mieux
forlorn 4 lone **6** abject, bereft, dismal, dreary, lonely **7** unhappy **8** bereaved, dejected, deserted, desolate, forsaken, helpless, hopeless, lonesome, pathetic, pitiable, solitary, wretched **9** abandoned, depressed, desperate, destitute, forgotten, miserable, woebegone **10** despairing, despondent, dispirited, friendless **11** comfortless **12** disconsolate, inconsolable **13** brokenhearted
form 3 cut, hew, way **4** body, cast, kind, make, mode, mold, plan, rite, rule, sort, trim, type **5** being, brand, build, carve, class, forge, found, frame, genre, genus, guise, habit, image, model, order, phase, set up, shape, stamp, style, usage **6** aspect, chisel, create, custom, design, devise, fettle, figure, manner, matrix, person, ritual, sculpt, system **7** acquire, anatomy, compose, conduct, contour, decorum, develop, fashion, fitness, harmony, liturgy, manners, outline, pattern, produce, species, variety **8** ceremony, comprise, contract, likeness, physique, practice, presence, rough-hew, symmetry **9** character, construct, establish, etiquette, fabricate, framework, propriety, sculpture, semblance, structure **10** appearance, constitute, deportment, figuration, proceeding, proportion, regularity **11** arrangement, description, incarnation, manufacture, orderliness, shapeliness **12** denomination **13** configuration, manifestation **15** conventionality
formal 4 cool, prim **5** aloof, fancy, fixed, grand, legal, rigid, smart, stiff **6** dressy, lawful, proper, solemn, strict **7** distant, outward, pompous, prudish, regular, settled, stilted, stylish **8** decorous, definite, expli-cit, external, official, positive, reserved, starched **9** customary **10** ceremonial, inflexible, prescribed **11** ceremonious, highfalutin, perfunctory, punctilious, ritualistic, standoffish, straitlaced **12** conventional **13** authoritative **14** uncompromising
formal discussion 6 debate, parley **8** dialogue **10** conference
formality 4 rite **6** custom, motion, ritual **7** decorum, reserve **8** ceremony, coolness **9** etiquette, propriety, punctilio **10** ceremonial, convention **15** conventionality
Forman, Milos
  director of: **7** Amadeus (Oscar), Ragtime **25** One Flew Over the Cuckoo's Nest (Oscar)
formation 3 set **6** makeup **7** genesis **8** building, creation **9** structure **10** generation, production **11** arrangement, composition, development, fabrication, manufacture **12** organization **13** configuration, constellation, establishment
formative 7 plastic, shaping **9** sensitive **10** accessible **11** susceptible **13** determinative **14** impressionable
former 2 ex **4** gone, past **5** olden, prior **6** bygone, gone by, lapsed, of yore, whilom **7** ancient, earlier, elapsed, old-time, quondam **8** anterior, previous **9** aforesaid, erstwhile, preceding **10** antecedent, first-named **14** aforementioned
  French: **8** ci-devant
formerly 4 once **5** of old **6** ere now, lately, of yore, whilom **7** long ago **8** hitherto **9** anciently **10** originally, previously
former student 6 alumna **7** alumnus, dropout **8** graduate
formidable 6 taxing **7** awesome, fearful, mammoth, onerous **8** alarming, dread-ful, imposing, menacing, terrific **9** dangerous, demanding, difficult **10** forbidding, impressive, portentous, terrifying **11** threatening **12** overpowering, overwhelming
formless 5 vague **9** amorphous, shapeless
Formosa see **6** Taiwan
formula 4 cant, plan, rule **5** chant **6** cliche, recipe, saying, slogan **7** precept **9** blueprint, guideline, platitude, principle, rigmarole **10** pleasantry **11** incantation **12** prescription
formulate 5 draft, frame, state **6** define, devise, invent **7** compose, itemize, specify **11** systematize **13** particularize
Fornax
  origin: **5** Roman
  goddess of: **6** baking
fornication 8 adultery
for one's country
  Latin: **9** pro patria
Forrest, Nathan Bedford
  served in: **8** Civil War
  side: **11** Confederate
  known for: **12** cavalry raids
forsake 4 deny, drop, flee, quit **5** leave, spurn, waive, yield **6** abjure, depart, desert, give up, reject, resign, vacate **7** abandon, cast off, disavow, discard, lay down **8** abdicate, disclaim, go back on, jettison, part with, renounce **9** repudiate, surrender **10** relinquish
forsaken 4 bare **5** empty **8** deserted, desolate, rejected **9** abandoned, discarded, neglected **11** uninhabited
Forsete see **7** Forseti
Forseti
  also: **7** Forsete
  origin: **12** Scandinavian
  god of: **7** justice
  father: **5** Baldr **6** Balder, Baldur
  mother: **5** Nanna
  dwelling place: **7** Glitnir
Forster, E M (Edward Morgan)
  author of: **7** Maurice **10** Howards End **14** A Room with a View **15** A Passage to India **17** The Longest Journey **22** Where Angels Fear to Tread
  member of: **15** Bloomsbury Group
forswear 4 deny **5** spurn **6** abjure, disown, eschew, give up, recant, reject, revoke **7** disavow, gainsay, retract **8** abdicate, disclaim, renounce, take back **9** disaffirm, repudiate **10** contravene
Forsyte Saga, The
  author: **14** John Galsworthy
  trilogy including: **5** To Let **10** In Chancery **16** The Man of Property
  character: **3** Jon **4** June **5** Fleur **6** Dartie **7** Annette **8** Winifred **9** Old Jolyon **11** Young Jolyon **12** Irene Forsyte **13** Soames Forsyte **14** Philip Bosinney
Forsythe, John
  real name: **17** John Lincoln Freund
  born: **12** Penn's Grove NJ
  roles: **5** Topaz **7** Dynasty, Madame X **11** In Cold Blood **14** Bachelor Father, Charlie's Angels **15** Blake Carrington **16** And Justice for All **19** The Trouble with Harry **23** Teahouse of the August Moon
fort 4 base, camp **6** castle **7** bastion, bulwark, citadel, station **8** fastness, garrison **10** stronghold
forte 4 bent **5** knack, skill **6** talent **8** strength **9** specialty **11** proficiency
  music: **4** loud
  abbreviation: **1** f
forth 5 ahead **6** onward **7** outward
forthcoming 5 handy, on tap **6** at hand **7** helpful **8** imminent **9** available, impending **10** accessible, obtainable, openhanded **11** approaching, cooperative, prospective
for the greater glory of God
  Latin: **19** ad majorem Dei gloriam
for the public good
  Latin: **14** pro bono publico
for the time being
  Latin: **10** pro tempore
For the Time Being
  author: **7** W H Auden
for this purpose only
  Latin: **5** ad hoc
forthright 4 open **5** blunt, frank **6** candid, direct, openly **7** bluntly, frankly, up-front **8** candidly, directly, straight **9** outspoken **10** truthfully **11** outspokenly, plain-spoken **15** straightforward **17** straightforwardly
forthrightness 6 candor **7** honesty **8**

openness **9** frankness, sincerity **19** straightforwardness

forthwith 4 ASAP, stat **6** at once, pronto **7** quickly **8** directly, in a jiffy, promptly, right off **9** instantly **11** immediately **12** straightaway

fortification 5 tower **7** bastion, bulwark, citadel, rampart **8** fortress, garrison **9** earthwork **10** breastwork, stronghold

fortify 4 lace **5** boost, brace, cheer **6** buoy up, enrich, harden, secure, shield, urge on **7** build up, bulwark, hearten, protect, shore up, stiffen, support, sustain **8** buttress, embolden, garrison, reassure **9** encourage, reinforce, stimulate **10** invigorate, strengthen

fortissimo
music: **8** very loud
abbreviation: **2** ff

fortitude 4 dash, grit, guts, sand **5** nerve, pluck, spunk, valor **6** daring, mettle, spirit **7** bravery, courage, heroism, prowess **8** backbone, boldness, firmness, tenacity **9** endurance, hardihood **10** resolution **11** intrepidity **12** fearlessness, resoluteness **13** dauntlessness, determination

Fortitude
author: **11** Hugh Walpole

Fort-Lamy
former name of: **8** N'Djamena
capital of: **4** Chad

fortress 7 bastion, bulwark, citadel, rampart **8** buttress **9** acropolis **10** stronghold

Fortress, The
author: **11** Hugh Walpole

fortuitous 5 happy, lucky, stray **6** casual, chance, random **9** haphazard, hitor-miss **10** accidental, incidental, undesigned, unexpected, unintended, unpurposed **11** inadvertent **12** adventitious **13** serendipitous, unintentional **14** unpremeditated

fortuity 6 chance **8** accident **12** happenstance

Fortuna
origin: **5** Roman
goddess of: **7** fortune
corresponds to: **5** Tyche

fortunate 4 fair, rich, rosy **5** happy, lucky, palmy **6** benign, bright, timely **7** blessed, booming, favored, halcyon, well-off **8** well-to-do **9** favorable, opportune, promising **10** auspicious, convenient, felicitous, profitable, propitious, prosperous, successful **11** encouraging, flourishing **12** advantageous, providential

Fortunate Isles see **13** Canary Islands

Fortunato
character in: **20** The Cask of Amontillado
author: **3** Poe

fortune, fortunes 3 lot **4** doom, fate, luck, mint, pile, star **5** karma, means **6** chance, es-tate, income, kismet, riches, wealth **7** bonanza, capital, destiny, godsend, portion, revenue **8** accident, fatality, gold mine, good luck, lady luck, opulence, property, treasure, windfall **9** affluence, haphazard, substance **10** prosperity, providence **11** dame fortune **12** circumstance **13** circumstances
goddess of: **5** Tyche **7** Fortuna

Fortunes of Nigel, The
author: **14** Sir Walter Scott

fortuneteller 4 seer **5** augur, Gypsy, sibyl **6** medium, oracle **7** palmist, prophet **8** magician **10** soothsayer **11** chiromancer, clairvoyant **12** crystal gazer

for two
French: **5** a deux

Forty Days of Musa Dagh, The
author: **11** Franz Werfel

42nd Parallel, The
author: **13** John Dos Passos

Forty-Second Street
director: **10** Lloyd Bacon
cast: **9** Guy Kibbee, Una Merkel **10** Dick Powell, Ruby Keeler **11** Bebe Daniels, George Brent **12** Ginger Rogers, Warner Baxter
choreographer: **13** Busby Berkeley
song: **15** Young and Healthy **17** Forty-second Street **19** Shuffle Off to Buffalo **28** You're Getting to Be a Habit with Me

Forty Thieves, The
story in: **13** Arabian Nights
character: **7** Ali Baba
code word: **10** Open Sesame

forty winks 3 nap **4** doze **6** catnap, snooze

forum 6 medium, outlet **7** rostrum, seminar **8** platform **9** symposium **10** colloquium

forward, forwards 3 out **4** back, bold **5** ahead, brash, fresh, relay, sassy **6** assist, brazen, cheeky, hasten, onward, pass on, send on, spread **7** advance, frontal, further, go-ahead, promote, quicken, re-route **8** anterior, champion, immodest, impudent, insolent, up-to-date **9** advancing, barefaced, intrusive, offensive, presuming, readdress, shameless **10** accelerate, unmannerly **11** impertinent, progressive **12** enterprising, presumptuous **13** overconfident
French: **7** en avant

forwardness 4 gall **5** brass, cheek **8** audacity, boldness **10** brazenness, effrontery **11** presumption **13** bumptiousness, obtrusiveness

for what use
Latin: **7** cui bono

For Whom the Bell Tolls
author: **15** Ernest Hemingway

director: **7** Sam Wood
character: **5** Maria, Pablo, Pilar **6** Andres, Rafael **7** Anselmo, El Sordo **8** Augustin, Fernando **12** Robert Jordan
cast: **10** Gary Cooper **12** Akim Tamiroff **13** Ingrid Bergman, Joseph Calleia, Katina Paxinou **15** Arturo de Cordova
score: **11** Victor Young
Oscar for: **17** supporting actress (Paxinou)

for whose benefit
Latin: **7** cui bono

For Your Eyes Only
author: **10** Ian Fleming

Forza del Destino, La see **17** Force of Destiny, The

Fosse, Bob
director of: **5** Lenny **7** Cabaret (Oscar) **11** All That Jazz

fossil 4 fogy, rock **5** fogey, oldie, relic, stone **7** imprint, antique **9** remainder **13** petrification

foster 3 aid **4** back, feed, rear, tend **5** favor, nurse, raise **6** foment, harbor, mother, rear up, take in **7** advance, bring up, care for, cherish, forward, further, nourish, nurture, promote, protect, support, sustain **8** advocate, befriend, hold dear, sanction, side with, treasure **9** encourage, patronize, stimulate **11** accommodate, countenance

Foster, Alicia Christian
real name of: **11** Jodie Foster

Foster, Harold
creator/artist of: **6** Tarzan **13** Prince Valiant

Foster, Jodie
real name: **21** Alicia Christian Foster
born: **7** Bronx NY
roles: **7** Contact **8** Maverick **9** Tom Sawyer **10** Taxi Driver, The Accused (Oscar) **11** Bugsy Malone **13** Little Man Tate **20** The Silence of the Lambs (Oscar)

Foster, Stephen Collins
born: **15** Lawrenceville PA
composer of: **11** Swanee River **13** Camptown Races **16** Beautiful Dreamer **17** My Old Kentucky Home, The Old Folks at Home **27** Jeanie with the Light Brown Hair

Foucault, Jean Bernard Leon
field: **7** physics
nationality: **6** French
proved: **19** Earth spins on its axis
measured: **15** velocity of light
named for him: **8** pendulum **16** Foucault currents

Foucault's Pendulum
author: **10** Umberto Eco

foul 3 wet **4** base, clog, evil, lewd, soil, vile **5** dirty, foggy, grimy, gross, gusty, misty, muddy, murky, nasty, rainy, sully, taint **6** choked, cloudy, coarse, defile, filthy, grubby, odious, putrid, risque, scurvy, smelly, smutty, soiled, sordid, stormy, tangle, turbid, vulgar, wicked **7** abusive, begrime, drizzly, ensnare, hateful, heinous, impeded, obscene, pollute, profane, smeared, squalid, squally, stained, sullied, tangled, unclean **8** begrimed, besmirch, blustery, ensnared, entangle, immodest, indecent, infamous, stinking, unseemly **9** atrocious, besmeared, entangled, insulting, loathsome, monstrous, nefarious, notorious, obnoxious, repulsive, revolting **10** abominable, bedraggled, detestable, disgusting, encumbered, flagitious, indelicate, malodorous, putrescent, scurrilous, villainous **11** blasphemous, disgraceful **12** contemptible

foul-mouthed 4 lewd, rude, vile **5** dirty, gross **6** coarse, filthy, vulgar **7** abusive, obscene, profane **9** offensive **10** indelicate

foul play 5 crime **6** murder **8** violence **9** treachery

foul-smelling 4 rank **5** acrid, fetid, musty **6** putrid, smelly **7** noisome, reeking **8** stinking **10** malodorous

foul up 3 mar **4** goof, muff, ruin **5** botch, mix up, spoil **6** bungle, mess up, muddle **7** blunder, butcher, confuse, louse up, screw up **9** mismanage

found 4 base, rear, rest **5** build, erect, raise, set up, start **6** create, ground, locate, settle **7** develop, sustain **8** colonize, organize **9** construct, establish, institute, originate

foundation 3 bed **4** base, foot, fund, rock, root **5** basis, cause **6** bottom, cellar, ground, motive, origin, reason, source **7** charity, premise, purpose, support **8** basement, creation, pedestal **9** endowment, rationale **10** assumption, groundwork, settlement **11** benefaction, institution **12** commencement, installation, philanthropy, substructure, underpinning **13** establishment, justification **14** infrastructure, understructure

foundational 3 key **4** base, core **5** basic, prime **7** primary **9** essential **10** elementary

foundation garment 6 corset, girdle **8** corselet

founder 4 fall, limp, reel, sink, trip **5** abort, drown, lurch, swamp **6** author, father, go down, go lame, hobble, perish, plunge, sprawl, topple, tumble **7** break up, builder, capsize, creator, go under, planner, stagger, stumble, succumb **8** collapse, miscarry **9** architect, organizer, shipwreck **10** originator, strategist **12** disintegrate

foundered 4 sank **6** failed **7** beached, swamped **8** capsized, went down **9** collapsed

founding 5 birth **8** creation, settling **9** beginning **11** institution, origination **12** introduction, organization **13** establishment

found on 6 base on **7** model on **8** stem from **10** derive from **11** establish on

fountain 3 jet **4** flow, gush, well **5** birth, cause, spout **6** cradle, feeder, origin, reason, source, spring **7** genesis **8** purveyor, supplier **9** beginning, reservoir, upswelling **10** derivation, wellspring

fountainhead 4 font **6** origin, source, spring **9** beginning **10** wellspring

Fountainhead, The
    author: 7 Ayn Rand
    character: 11 Howard Roark
    profession: 9 architect

fourgon 3 van **7** tumbril

Four Horsemen of the Apocalypse, The
    author: 19 Vicente Blasco Ibanez
    based on: 10 Revelation

400 Blows, The
    director: 16 Francois Truffaut
    cast: 10 Albert Remy **13** Claire Maurier **14** Patrick Auffray **15** Jean-Pierre Leaud

Four Quartets
    author: 7 T S Eliot

Four-Season Recreation State
    nickname of: 7 Vermont

fourth class mail 10 parcel post

fourth dimension 4 time

fourth estate 5 press **10** journalism

fowl 3 hen **4** cock, duck, game **5** banty, capon, chick, goose, quail **6** bantam, grouse, pigeon, turkey **7** chicken, cornish, leghorn, poultry **8** duckling

Fowles, John
    author of: 8 Mantissa, The Magus **10** The Aristos **12** Daniel Martin, The Collector **13** The Ebony Tower **25** The French Lieutenant's Woman

fox 9 scavenger
    young: 3 kit, pup
    group of: 5 leash, skulk

Fox (Mesquakie, Red Earth People)
    language family: 9 Algonkian **10** Algonquian
    location: 4 Iowa **9** Wisconsin
    allied with: 4 Sauk **8** Kickapoo

Fox, Fontaine
    creator/artist of: 16 Toonerville Folks **18** Toonerville Trolley

foxglove 9 digitalis
    varieties: 5 false, rusty **6** common, yellow **7** Grecian, Mexican **10** downy false **12** willow-leaved

foxiness 5 guile **7** cunning, slyness **8** artifice, trickery, wiliness **10** craftiness, shrewdness

fox-trot 5 dance **13** ballroom dance

Foxx, Jimmy (James Emory)
    nickname: 7 Double X
    sport: 8 baseball
    team: 12 Boston Red Sox **21** Philadelphia Athletics

Foxx, Redd
    real name: 16 John Elroy Sanford
    born: 9 St Louis MO
    roles: 13 Sanford and Son **19** Cotton Comes to Harlem

foxy 3 sly **4** wily **5** canny, sharp, slick **6** artful, astute, clever, crafty, shifty, shrewd, sneaky, tricky **7** cunning, devious, oblique **8** guileful, scheming, stealthy **9** conniving, deceitful, deceptive, designing, insidious, underhand **10** intriguing

foyer 4 hall **5** lobby **6** loggia **8** anteroom **9** vestibule **11** antechamber

fracas 3 row **4** fray, to-do **5** brawl, broil, clash, fight, melee, scrap **6** battle, ruckus, rumpus, strife, uproar **7** scuffle **9** imbroglio **10** donnybrook, free-for-all **11** altercation, embroilment

fraction 3 bit, few **4** chip **5** crumb, piece, ratio, scrap **6** morsel, trifle **7** cutting, portion, section, segment, shaving **8** fragment, particle, quotient **10** proportion **11** subdivision

fractious 5 cross, huffy **6** shirty, touchy, unruly **7** fretful, grouchy, peevish, pettish, waspish, wayward, willful **8** contrary, perverse, petulant, shrewish, snappish **9** irascible, irritable, querulous **10** rebellious, refractory **11** quarrelsome **12** disputatious, recalcitrant, unmanageable

fracture 4 rend, rift **5** break, crack, fault, sever, split **6** breach, cleave **7** disrupt, rupture, shatter **8** cleavage, division **9** severance **10** separation

Fra Diavolo, ou L'Hotellerie de Terracine
    also: 31 Brother Devil or The Inn at Terracina
    comic opera by: 5 Auber
    character: 7 Lorenzo, Zerlina **11** Lady Allcash, Lord Allcash **17** Marquis di San Marco

fragile 4 soft, weak **5** crisp, frail **6** dainty, feeble, flimsy, infirm, sleazy, slight, tender **7** brittle, crumbly, friable, rickety, shivery **8** decrepit, delicate **9** breakable, ephemeral, frangible, splintery **10** evanescent, tumbledown **11** dilapidated **13** unsubstantial

fragility 7 frailty **8** delicacy, weakness **9** frailness **10** feebleness **11** brittleness **12** frangibility

fragment 3 bit **4** chip, snip **5** crumb, cut up, piece, scrap, shard, shred, trace **6** chop up, divide, morsel **7** break up, crumble, portion, remnant, section, segment, shatter, vestige **8** disunite, fraction, separate, splinter, survival **12** disintegrate

fragmentary 6 broken, choppy **7** scrappy **8** detached **9** piecemeal, scattered, segmented **10** disjointed, fractional, incomplete, unfinished **12** disconnected

Fragonard, Jean-Honore
  born: 6 France, Grasse
  artwork: 8 The Swing **10** Stolen Kiss, The Bathers, The Warrior **12** Le Billet Doux **14** Progress of Love **16** La Chemise Enlevee **18** Storming the Citadel **40** Coresus Sacrificing Himself to Save Callirhoe

fragrance 4 aura, balm **5** aroma, scent **7** bouquet, incense, perfume **9** redolence, sweetness

fragrant 5 balmy, spicy **7** odorous **8** aromatic, perfumed, redolent **11** odoriferous

Fragrant Harbor *see* **8** Hong Kong

frail 4 puny, weak **6** feeble, flimsy, infirm, sleazy, slight, weakly **7** brittle, crumbly, fragile, rickety, shivery **8** decrepit, delicate, fallible **9** breakable, frangible, splintery **10** perishable, vulnerable **11** dilapidated **13** unsubstantial

frailness 8 delicacy, weakness **9** fragility **11** unsoundness

frailty 3 sin **4** flaw, vice **5** fault **6** defect, foible **7** blemish, failing **11** fallibility **12** imperfection **14** susceptibility

Fra Lippo Lippi
  author: 14 Robert Browning

frame 3 rim, set **4** body, case, cast, form, make, mold, mood, plan **5** build, draft, hatch, humor, set up, shape, state **6** border, casing, design, devise, edging, figure, indite, invent, map out, nature, scheme, sketch, system, temper **7** anatomy, backing, chassis, concoct, contour, housing, outline, setting **8** attitude, conceive, contrive, mounting, organize, physique, skeleton **9** formulate, structure **11** disposition, scaffolding, systematize, temperament **12** constitution, construction

frame of mind 4 mood **7** climate **8** attitude **10** atmosphere **11** disposition

framer 6 author, shaper **7** creator, planner **10** formulator

framework 5 shell, truss **7** carcass **8** skeleton, template **9** structure **10** foundation **11** scaffolding **14** infrastructure

Framley Parsonage
  author: 15 Anthony Trollope

France
  other name: 4 Gaul
  anthem: 14 La Marseillaise
  capital/largest city: 5 Paris
  others: 4 Nice, St.-Lo **5** Brest, Lille, Lyons, Rouen, Vichy **6** Amiens, Calais, Cannes, Carnac, Cognac, Dieppe, Grasse, Nantes, Prades, Rheims **7** Antibes, Avignon, Bayonne, Dunkirk, Le Havre, Les Baux **8** Bordeaux, Boulogne, Chartres, Grenoble, Poitiers, Toulouse **9** Cherbourg, Roquefort **10** La Rochelle, Marseilles, Saint-Denis, Strasbourg **12** Saint-Nazaire **13** Aix-en- Provence, Fontainebleau
  school: 8 Grenoble, Saint Cyr, Sorbonne **10** Montpelier
  division: 5 Anjou, Bearn, Berry, Maine, Savoy **6** Alsace, Artois, Marche, Poitou **7** Gascony, Guienne, Picardy **8** Auvergne, Bordeaux, Brittany, Burgundy, Dauphine, Flanders, Lorraine, Lyonnais, Normandy, Provence, Touraine **9** Aquitaine, Champagne, Languedoc **11** Ile de France **12** Bourbonnaise, Franche-Comte
  measure: 3 pot, sac **4** aune, mine, muid, pied, velt **5** arpen, carat, ligne, minot, pinte, point, pouce, velte **6** arpent, hemine, league, quarte, setier
  monetary unit: 5 franc **7** centime
  weight: 3 sol **4** gros, kilo, once **5** carat, livre, pound, tonne **6** gramme **7** tonneau **8** esterlin **9** esterling
  island: 2 Re **3** Yeu **4** Cite **5** Groix, Hyere **6** Comoro, Oleron, Tahiti, Ushant **7** Corsica, Leeward, Reunion **8** Windward **10** Guadeloupe, Martinique **12** New Caledonia
  lake: 6 Annecy, Cazaux, Geneva
  mountain: 4 Jura **5** Pelat **6** Vosges **8** Ardennes, Pyrenees **10** French Alps **11** Pic Montcalm
  highest point: 5 Blanc **9** Mont Blanc
  river: 3 Lys **4** Oise, Yser **5** Aisne, Eiser, Isere, Loire, Meuse, Rhine, Rhone, Saone, Seine **7** Garonne, Gironde
  sea: 5 North **8** Atlantic **13** Mediterranean
  physical feature:
    bay: 6 Biscay **7** Arachon
    beach: 4 Utah **5** Omaha
    cape: 5 Hague, Talma
    channel: 7 English **8** La Manche
    gulf: 4 Lion
  people: 6 Franks
    artist: 5 Corot, David, Degas, Manet, Monet **6** Braque, Ingres, Millet, Renoir, Seurat **7** Cezanne, Daumier, Gauguin, Matisse, Utrillo **8** Pissarro **9** Delacroix, Fragonard, Gericault
    author: 4 Gide, Hugo, Zola **5** Camus, Dumas **6** France, Proust, Racine, Sartre, Villon **7** Moliere **8** Rabelais, Rousseau, Voltaire **9** Corneille, Descartes, Giraudoux, Montaigne **10** Baudelaire
    composer: 5 Bizet, Ravel, Satie **6** Franck, Gounod **7** Berlioz, Debussy, Poulenc
    king: 5 Henri, Louis **6** Clovis, Philip **7** Charles **9** Hugh Capet **11** Charlemagne **13** Louis Philippe **14** Henry of Navarre
    leader: 6 Danton, Petain **7** Colbert, Mazarin **8** de Gaulle, D'Estaing, Pompidou **9** Joan of Arc, Richelieu **10** Mitterrand **11** Robespierre **17** Napoleon Bonaparte
    queen: 7 Eugenie **9** Josephine **13** Marie de Medici **15** Marie Antoinette
  language: 6 French
  expressions: 6 deja vu **7** apropos, detente, en masse, faux pas, vis-a-vis **8** de riguer **9** bete noire, c'est la vie, coup d'etat **10** bon appetit **11** coup de grace, joie de vivre, raison d'etre, savoir faire, tour de force **12** carte blanche, cause celebre, je ne sais quoi, nouveau riche, fait accompli **14** creme de la creme, noblesse oblige
  religion: 5 Islam **7** Judaism **8** Huguenot **10** Protestant **13** Roman Catholic
  place:
    cathedral: 6 Rheims **8** Chartres **9** Madeleine, Notre Dame **10** Sacre-Coeur **14** Sainte-Chapelle **15** Mont-Saint-Michel
    chapel: 8 Ronchamp
    gardens: 9 Tuileries
    hall of mirrors: 16 Galerie des Glaces
    museum: 6 Louvre
    palace: 6 Elysee **10** Luxembourg, Versailles **12** Grand Trianon, Petit Trianon, **13** Fontainebleau
    prison: 8 Bastille
    racetrack: 7 Le Mans **7** Auteuil **10** Longchamps
    resort: 3 Pau **5** Vichy **6** Cannes, Menton **7** Antibes, Mentone, Riviera **8** Biarritz, Chamonix, Grenoble **9** Cote d'Azur **10** Aix-les-Bains
    section of Paris: 8 Left Bank **9** Right Bank **10** Montmartre, Rive Droite, Rive Gauche **12** Latin Quarter
    street: 13 Champs-Elysees **17** Place de la Concorde
    woods: 14 Bois de Boulogne **15** Bois de Vincennes
  possession: 12 French Guiana
    island: 6 Futuna, Hoorne, Wallis **7** Reunion **8** Miquelon **10** Guadeloupe, Martinique **11** Saint Pierre **12** New Caledonia **15** French Polynesia
  feature:
    airport: 4 Orly **9** Le Bourget **15** Charles de Gaulle
    bicycle race: 12 Tour de France
    dance: 5 gavot **6** branle, canary, cancan **7** boutade, gavotte
    fortification: 11 Maginot Line
    holiday: 11 Bastille Day
    monument: 13 Arc de Triomphe **14** Tomb of Napoleon
    national theater: 16 Comedie Francaise
    sightseeing boat: 12 bateau mou-

che
tower: 6 Eiffel
food:
  cheese: 4 bleu, Brie **6** bonbel **7** boursin **8** Muenster **9** camembert, marcillat, port-salut, Roquefort **11** coulommiers
  dessert: 6 mousse
  dish: 4 pate **5** crepe **6** canape, quiche **7** souffle **8** escargot, piperade, pot au feu **9** cassoulet, tournedos **14** pate de foie gras
  drink: 6 cognac **8** bordeaux, burgundy **9** champagne
  french fries: 12 pommes frites
  pastry: 7 brioche **8** napoleon **9** croissant
  soup: 8 a l'oignon **13** bouillabaisse
  steak: 7 bifteck
France, Anatole
  real name: 30 Jacques Anatole Francois Thibault
  author of: 5 Thais **12** Golden Verses **13** My Friend's Book, Penguin Island **17** The Gods Are Athirst **20** The Revolt of the Angels **25** Le Crime de Sylvestre Bonnard **27** At the Sign of the Reine Pedauque
franchise 5 grant, right **6** ballot **7** charter, freedom, license **8** immunity, suffrage **9** privilege **10** permission **11** prerogative **13** authorization
Franciosa, Anthony
  real name: 14 Anthony Papales
  born: 9 New York NY
  wife: 14 Shelley Winters
  roles: 12 The Naked Maja **13** A Hatful of Rain, Long Hot Summer, Name of the Game, Wild Is the Wind **15** Assault on a Queen
Francis, Dick
  author of: 4 Bolt, Risk **5** Nerve, Proof **6** Banker, Reflex **7** Break In, Enquiry, Forfeit, Rat Race **8** Dead Cert, For Kicks, Slayride, Trial Run, Twice Shy, Whip Hand **9** Bonecrack, The Danger, Knockdown **10** Blood Sport, High Stakes, In the Frame **11** Smokescreen **12** Flying Finish
Franck, Cesar
  born: 5 Liege **7** Belgium
  composer of: 4 Ruth **5** Hulda **6** Psyche **7** Rebecca **8** Ghiselle **9** Les Djinns **10** Les Eolides, Redemption **13** La Tour de Babel, Les Beatitudes, The Beatitudes **16** Le Chasseur Maudit **17** The Accursed Hunter
Franco, Francisco
  dictator of: 5 Spain
  title: 10 el caudillo
  party: 7 falange, fascist
  followers: 11 fifth column
frank 4 bold, free, open **5** clear, plain, round **6** candid, direct, honest, patent **7** artless, evident, genuine, natural, sincere, up-front **8** apparent, distinct, explicit, manifest **9** downright, ingen-

uous, outspoken **10** aboveboard, forthright, unreserved **11** plain-spoken, transparent, unambiguous, undisguised, unequivocal **12** unmistakable **15** straightforward
Frank, Anne
  author of: 19 The Diary of Anne Frank
Frankenstein
  author: 17 Mary Godwin Shelley
  character: 7 Clerval, Justine, William **9** Elizabeth **10** The Monster **12** Robert Walton **18** Victor Frankenstein
Franklin, Benjamin
  author of: 20 Poor Richard's Almanack
  inventor of: 12 lightning rod **13** bifocal lenses, Franklin stove
frankness 6 candor **7** honesty **8** openness **9** bluntness, sincerity **10** directness **11** artlessness **13** guilelessness **14** forthrightness **19** straightforwardness
frantic 3 mad **4** wild **5** crazy, rabid **6** hectic, insane, raging, raving **7** berserk, excited, furious, nervous, violent **8** agitated, deranged, frenetic, frenzied **9** delirious **10** distracted, distraught, infuriated **11** impassioned, overwrought **12** ungovernable
Frasier
  network: 3 NBC
  cast: 5 Eddie (dog) **10** Peri Gilpin (Roz), Jane Leeves (Daphne) **11** John Mahoney (Martin) **13** Kelsey Grammer (Frasier) **15** David Hyde Pierce (Niles)
  characters: 5 Eddie **8** Roz Doyle **10** Niles Crane, Daphne Moon **11** Martin Crane **12** Frasier Crane
  spinoff of: 6 Cheers
fraternal 6 hearty, loving, social **7** devoted, kindred, related **8** amicable, friendly **9** brotherly **11** warmhearted **12** affectionate **14** consanguineous
fraternity 4 clan, club **5** Greek, union **6** circle, clique, league **7** company, coterie, kinship, society **8** alliance **9** coalition **10** federation **11** association, brotherhood, confederacy, propinquity **13** brotherliness, consanguinity, interrelation
Fraternity
  author: 14 John Galsworthy
fraternize 3 mix **5** unite **6** concur, hobnob, mingle **7** combine, consort **8** coalesce **9** associate, cooperate, harmonize, pal around, socialize **10** sympathize **11** confederate
Fratres Arvales *see* **5** Arval
frau 4 lady, wife **12** married woman
fraud 4 fake, hoax, hype, ruse, sham **5** cheat, craft, guile, knave, quack, rogue, trick **6** deceit, humbug, rascal **7** swindle **8** artifice, cheating, cozenage, impostor, swindler, trickery **9** charlatan, chicanery, con artist, decep-

tion, duplicity, impos-ture, pretender, stratagem, swindling, treachery **10** dishonesty, mountebank, subterfuge **11** counterfeit, four-flusher, machination **13** dissimulation
fraudulence 6 deceit **8** trickery **9** deception **13** deceitfulness, deceptiveness **17** misrepresentation
fraudulent 4 sham, wily **5** bogus, false **6** crafty, tricky **7** crooked, cunning, knavish **8** cheating, guileful, spurious **9** deceitful, deceptive, dishonest **11** counterfeit, treacherous, underhanded **12** dishonorable, unprincipled
fraught 4 full **5** heavy, laden **6** filled, loaded **7** charged, replete, teeming **8** attended, pregnant **9** abounding
fraulein 4 miss **9** young lady **14** unmarried woman
fray 3 rub **4** fret, fuss, riot, spat, tiff **5** brawl, chafe, fight, melee, ravel, set-to **6** bat-tle, combat, fracas, rumble, rumpus, strain, tatter, tumult, tussle **7** contest, dispute, frazzle, quarrel, scuffle, warfare, wear out, wrangle **8** conflict, skirmish, squabble **9** bickering, commotion **10** contention, dissension, engagement **11** altercation, controversy **12** disagreement
Frazer, Sir James G
  author of: 14 The Golden Bough
freak 3 fad, odd **4** kink, turn, whim **5** craze, fancy, humor, queer, quirk, sport, twist **6** marvel, oddity, vagary, whimsy, wonder **7** anomaly, bizarre, caprice, erratic, monster, strange, unusual **8** crotchet, mutation, peculiar **9** curiosity, deviation **10** aberration **11** abnormality, monstrosity **12** irregularity
freakish 3 odd **5** queer, weird **7** bizarre, strange, unusual **8** peculiar, singular, uncommon **9** eccentric, fantastic **10** outlandish **13** extraordinary
Frederick
  character in: 11 As You Like It
  author: 11 Shakespeare
Frederick I
  nickname: 10 Barbarossa
  position: 16 Holy Roman Emperor
  dynasty: 12 Hohenstaufen
  wife: 7 Beatrix
  battle: 7 Legnano
Frederick the Great
  nickname: 8 Old Fritz
  position: 13 King of Prussia
  invaded: 7 Silesia
  war: 13 Seven Years' War **18** Austrian Succession
free 3 big, lax **4** able, bold, easy, idle, idly, open, save **5** clear, extra, let go, loose, rid of, spare **6** daring, devoid, exempt, giving, gratis, lavish, parole, ransom, redeem, unbond, uncage, wanton **7** allowed, assured, forward, liberal, loosely, manumit, release, un-

chain, unleash **8** at no cost, careless, costless, devoid of, familiar, fearless, generous, handsome, immune to, informal, let loose, liberate, prodigal, released, unfasten **9** abandoned, audacious, available, boundless, bounteous, bountiful, confident, delivered, discharge, disengage, dissolute, expansive, extricate, footloose, lacking in, leisurely, liberated, permitted, unblocked, unbridled, unchained, unclogged, unimpeded, unmuzzled, unshackle **10** autonomous, bighearted, carelessly, chargeless, emancipate, gratuitous, licentious, manumitted, munificent, openhanded, unattached, unconfined, unfettered, unhampered, unoccupied, unreserved, unshackled **11** emancipated, enfranchise, independent, uncluttered, uncommitted, uninhibited, unrepressed **12** enfranchised, overfamiliar, uncontrolled, unencumbered, unobstructed, unrestrained **13** complimentary, unceremonious, unconstrained

free-and-easy 6 breezy, casual, jaunty **7** buoyant, relaxed **8** debonair, informal **12** lighthearted, presumptuous, unrestrained **13** unconstrained

freed 6 exempt, loosed, spared **7** cleared, excused **8** absolved, let loose, released, relieved **11** emancipated

freedom 4 play **5** range, scope, sweep, swing **6** candor, margin **7** abandon, license, release **8** autonomy, boldness, latitude, openness, rudeness **9** bluntness, frankness, impudence, indecorum **10** directness, disrespect, liberation **11** abandonment, forwardness, impropriety, normality, manumission, naturalness, sovereignty, unrestraint **12** emancipation, impertinence, unconstraint **13** downrightness **14** unreservedness **15** enfranchisement

Freedom of the Poet, The
    author: 12 John Berryman

free-flowing 7 copious, gushing, profuse **8** effusive

free-for-all 3 row **4** fray **5** brawl, fight, melee, scrap **6** affray, fracas, ruckus, tussle **7** rhubarb, ruction, wrangle **9** brannigan **10** donnybrook

free from bias 7 neutral **9** impartial, unbigoted **12** unprejudiced **13** disinterested

free from moisture 3 dry **4** arid, sere **5** parch **6** dry out **7** parched **8** dried out, rainless **9** dehydrate **10** dehydrated, desertlike, desiccated

free hand 12 carte blanche, open sanc-tion **13** full authority

free rein 12 carte blanche, open sanction **13** full authority

free-spoken 6 chatty **7** voluble **9** talkative **10** loquacious, unreserved **13** communicative

Free State
    nickname of: 8 Maryland

Freestone State
    nickname of: 11 Connecticut

Free to Choose
    author: 14 Milton Friedman (with Rose Friedman)

Freetown
    capital of: 11 Sierra Leone

freeze 3 nip **4** bite, cool, halt, stop **5** chill, frost, sting **6** arrest, benumb, harden, pierce **7** ceiling, congeal, terrify **8** glaci-ate, solidify **11** anesthetize, refrigerate, restriction

freezing 3 icy **6** arctic, frigid **7** glacial

Frege, Gottlieb
    field: 11 mathematics
    nationality: 6 German
    founded: 13 symbolic logic

Freia *see* **5** Freya

freight 4 haul, lade, load, ship **5** cargo, carry, goods **6** burden, charge, convey, lading **7** baggage, cartage, luggage, portage **8** transmit, truckage **9** transport **10** conveyance **13** transshipment

Freischutz, Der
    also: 11 The Marksman
    opera by: 5 Weber
    character: 3 Max **6** Agathe, Caspar, Samiel

Freki
    origin: 12 Scandinavian
    form: 4 wolf
    owner: 4 Odin **5** Othin
    received: 4 food
    exception: 4 meat
    fellow wolf: 4 Geri

French, Daniel Chester
    born: 8 Exeter NH
    artwork: 7 (seated) Lincoln (at Lincoln Memorial) **21** The Minute Man of Concord

French-American
    French: 9 Franglais

French civil code 12 Code Napoleon

French Connection, The
    director: 15 William Friedkin
    cast: 11 Fernando Rey, Gene Hackman (Popeye Doyle), Roy Scheider
    Oscar for: 5 actor (Hackman) **7** editing, picture **8** director **10** screenplay
    sequel: 21 The French Connection II

French-English
    French: 9 Franglais

French Guinea *see* **6** Guinea

French Indonesia *see* **7** Vietnam

French is spoken here
    French: 18 ici on parle francais

French Lieutenant's Woman, The
    director: 10 Karel Reisz
    author: 10 John Fowles
    cast: 9 Leo McKern **11** Hilton McRae, Jeremy Irons, Meryl Streep
    script: 12 Harold Pinter

French national anthem 12 Marseillaise

French national theater 16 Comedie Francaise

French parliament
    formal sessions: 12 lit de justice

French Somaliland *see* **8** Djibouti

French Sudan, Soudan *see* **4** Mali

French Togoland *see* **4** Togo

frenzied 3 mad **4** wild **7** excited, frantic, furious **8** agitated, ecstatic **9** delirious

frenzy 3 fit **4** fury **5** craze, furor, mania, state **6** access **7** mad rush, madness, seizure, turmoil **8** delirium, hysteria, outburst **9** obsession, transport **11** distraction

Frenzy
    director: 15 Alfred Hitchcock
    cast: 8 Jon Finch **10** Anna Massey **11** Barry Foster **16** Barbara Leigh-Hunt

frequency 9 iteration **10** recurrence, regularity, repetition **11** persistence, reiteration

frequent 5 daily, haunt, usual **6** common, wonted **7** regular **8** constant, everyday, familiar, habitual, numerous, ordinary, resort to **9** continual, customary, incessant, perpetual, recurrent **10** accustomed **11** reiterative

frequently 5 often **7** usually **8** ofttimes **9** generally **10** constantly, habitually, ordinarily, repeatedly **11** continually, customarily, incessantly, perpetually, recurrently

frere 4 monk **5** friar **7** brother

Frescobaldi, Girolamo
    born: 5 Italy **7** Ferrara
    composer of: 13 Fiori Musicali **14** Musical Flowers

fresh 3 fit, hot, new **4** bold, cool, fair, keen, late, pert, pure, rare, rosy, rude **5** alert, brisk, chill, clear, green, nervy, novel, ready, ruddy, sassy, saucy, stiff, sweet **6** active, biting, brassy, brazen, bright, cheeky, lively, modern, recent, rested, snotty, unique, unused, unworn **7** bracing, cutting, forward, glowing, just out, nipping, strange, uncured, undried, unfaded, untried, unusual **8** assuming, blooming, brand-new, creative, flippant, gleaming, impudent, insolent, original, stinging, unabated, undimmed, unsalted, unsmoked, unwilted, up-to-date **9** energetic, inventive, obtrusive, refreshed, sparkling, undecayed, unpickled, unspoiled, unwearied, wholesome **10** meddlesome, new-fangled, refreshing, unfamiliar, unimpaired, unwithered **11** flourishing, invigorated, modernistic, smartalecky, untarnished **12** presumptuous, unaccustomed

freshen 4 wash **5** brace, calve, clean, groom, renew **6** air out, breeze, desalt, revive **7** cool off, sweeten **8** renovate, spruce up **9** deodorize

freshet 5 crest, flood **11** overflowing

Freshman, The
director: **9** Sam Taylor **12** Fred Newmeyer
cast: **11** Harold Lloyd **13** Jobyna Ralston **14** Brooks Benedict

Fresnel, Augustin Jean
field: **7** physics
nationality: **6** French
worked in: **6** optics

fret 3 eat, rub, vex **4** fray, fume, gall, gnaw, mope, pine, pout, stew, sulk **5** brood, chafe, erode, sulks, worry **6** abrade, lament, ruffle, tatter **7** agonize, corrode, fidgets **8** disquiet, distress, irritate, vexation, wear away **9** annoyance, excoriate **10** irritation **11** displeasure, peevishness **12** discomposure

fretful 5 cross, huffy, sulky, tense **6** cranky, shirty, touchy **7** grouchy, nervous, peevish, pettish, waspish **8** contrary, petulant, snappish **9** crotchety, irritable, querulous **11** complaining **12** cantankerous

fretfulness 5 worry **6** unease **7** anxiety **10** crankiness **11** peevishness **12** irritability

Freud, Sigmund
lived in: **6** Vienna
collaborator: **6** Breuer
disciple: **4** Jung **5** Adler
daughter: **4** Anna
method: **15** free association **19** dream interpretation
coined: **2** id **8** superego **14** psychoanalysis
author of: **13** Totem and Taboo **22** Interpretation of Dreams **37** Group Psychology and the Analysis of the Ego, Jokes and Their Relation to the Unconscious

Freund, John Lincoln
real name of: **12** John Forsythe

Frey
also: **5** Freyr
origin: **12** Scandinavian
god of: **5** peace **8** marriage **10** prosperity
race: **5** Vanir
father: **5** Niord, Njord
home: **7** Alfheim

Freya
also: **5** Freia
origin: **8** Teutonic
goddess of: **4** love **6** beauty **9** fecundity
race: **5** Vanir
leader of: **9** Valkyries
father: **5** Niord, Njord

Fri *see* **5** Frigg

friable 7 crumbly **9** breakable, frangible

friar
French: **5** frere

Friar Lawrence
character in: **14** Romeo and Juliet
author: **11** Shakespeare

Friar Tuck
character in: **9** Robin Hood

friary 5 abbey **6** priory **8** cloister **9** hermitage, monastery

friction 6 strife **7** chafing, discord, grating, quarrel, rubbing **8** abrasion, bad blood, conflict, fretting **9** animosity, attrition, hostility **10** antagonism, contention, dissension, dissidence, opposition, resentment, resistance **12** disagreement **13** counteraction

Friday
character in: **14** Robinson Crusoe
author: **5** Defoe

Friday
from: **5** Freya, Frigg
heavenly body: **5** Venus
French: **8** vendredi
Italian: **7** venerdi
Spanish: **7** viernes
German: **7** freitag

Friedan, Betty
author of: **19** The Feminine Mystique
co-founder of: **3** NOW **28** National Organization for Women

Friedkin, William
director of: **11** The Exorcist **19** The French Connection (Oscar)

Friedman, Milton
author of: **12** Free to Choose (with Rose Friedman) **20** Capitalism and Freedom

Friedrich, Caspar David
born: **7** Germany **10** Greifswald
artwork: **22** The Cross on the Mountains **26** Man and Woman Gazing at the Moon, The Ruined Monastery of Eldena, Two Men Contemplating the Moon

friend 3 pal **4** ally, beau, chum, date, mate **5** amigo, buddy, crony, lover **6** backer, cohort, escort, fellow, intime, minion, patron **7** brother, comrade, consort, partner **8** adherent, advocate, confrere, co-worker, defender, favorite, follower, henchman, intimate, mistress, myrmidon, paramour, partisan, playmate, retainer, sidekick, soul mate **9** associate, bedfellow, colleague, companion, confidant, copartner, supporter **10** benefactor, encourager, playfellow, well-wisher **12** acquaintance
French: **3** ami **4** amie **9** bonne amie
Spanish: **5** amiga, amigo

friendliness 5 amity **8** bonhomie, good will **9** geniality **10** affability, amiability, cordiality, fraternity **11** amicability, camaraderie, sociability **14** neighborliness **16** companionability

friendly 4 kind **6** allied, ardent, benign, chummy, clubby, genial, kindly, loving, social **7** affable, amiable, cordial, devoted, helpful **8** amicable, fa-

miliar, generous, gracious, intimate, salutary **9** brotherly, convivial, favorable, fortunate, fraternal, opportune **10** accessible, auspicious, beneficial, hospitable, neighborly, not hostile, propitious **11** kindhearted, sympathetic, warmhearted **12** advantageous, affectionate **13** companionable

Friendly, Fred W
president of: **7** CBS News
collaborator: **13** Edward R. Murrow
show: **8** See It Now

Friendly Fire
author: **8** C D B Bryan

Friendly Islands *see* **5** Tongo

friendly understanding
French: **15** entente cordiale

friend of the court
Latin: **12** amicus curiae

Friends
network: **3** NBC
cast: **10** Lisa Kudrow **11** Matt LeBlanc **12** Courteney Cox, Matthew Perry **14** David Schwimmer **15** Jennifer Aniston
characters: **10** Ross Geller **11** Rachel Green **12** Chandler Bing, Phoebe Buffay, Monica Geller **13** Joey Tribiani

friendship 5 amity **6** accord, comity **7** concord, harmony **8** close tie, goodwill, intimacy, sympathy **10** consonance, cordiality, fellowship, fraternity **11** brotherhood, comradeship, familiarity **12** amicableness **13** companionship, understanding **14** neighborliness **16** acquaintanceship

Frigg
also: **3** Fri **5** Frija **6** Frigga
origin: **8** Teutonic
goddess of: **3** sky **6** clouds **8** marriage
husband: **4** Odin **5** Othin
race: **4** Asar **5** Aesir

Frigga *see* **5** Frigg

fright 4 fear, funk **5** alarm, dread, panic, scare **6** dismay, horror, terror, tremor **7** anxiety, concern, flutter, quaking **8** cold feet **9** misgiving, quivering, the creeps **10** the jitters, the willies **11** disquietude, palpitation, trepidation **12** apprehension, intimidation, perturbation **13** consternation

frighten 5 alarm, daunt, scare, shock **6** affray, excite **7** agitate, horrify, petrify, startle, terrify **8** disquiet **9** terrorize **10** intimidate

frightened 6 afraid, scared **7** alarmed, panicky **9** horrified, petrified, terrified **10** terrorized

frightening 5 awful, dread **7** fearful **8** alarming, dreadful **10** horrifying, terrifying **11** hair-raising

frightful 5 awful, lurid, nasty **6** grisly, horrid **7** baleful, extreme, fearful, ghastly, hideous, macabre, ogreish **8** alarming, dreadful, fearsome, freakish, gruesome, horrible, horrific, shocking, sinister, terrible, terrific **9** appalling, loathsome, monstrous, offensive, repellent, repulsive, revolting **10** abominable, detestable, disgusting, horrendous **12** insufferable

frigid 3 icy, raw **4** cold, cool, prim **5** aloof, bleak, gelid, stiff **6** biting, bitter, chilly, formal, frosty **7** austere, cutting, distant, glacial, nipping **8** freezing, piercing **10** forbidding **11** straitlaced **12** unresponsive

frigidity 7 iciness **8** coldness **9** aloofness **10** frostiness **16** unresponsiveness

Frija *see* **5** Frigg

frill 3 air **5** extra **6** edging, fringe, ruffle **7** flounce **8** falderal, frippery, furbelow, ornament **9** gathering, mannerism **10** decoration **11** affectation, superfluity **13** embellishment

fringe 3 hem, rim **4** edge, mane **5** limit, skirt **6** border, edging, margin, tassel **7** enclose, outline, selvage **8** decorate, frontier, skirting, surround, trimming **9** embellish, periphery

frisk 3 hop **4** jump, lark, leap, romp, skip, trip **5** bound, caper, cut up, dance, sport **6** bounce, cavort, frolic, gambol, prance, search, spring **7** disport, examine, inspect, ransack **8** look over

frisky 4 spry **5** agile, peppy **6** active, lively, nimble **7** jocular, playful, waggish **8** animated, mirthful, prankish, spirited, sportive **9** vivacious **10** frolicsome, rollicking

fritter 4 blow **5** use up, waste **7** deplete, pancake **8** fool away, idle away, squander **9** dissipate

fritter away 4 blow **5** waste **6** misuse **8** misspend, squander **9** dissipate

fritter away time 4 idle **6** dawdle **10** dillydally

Fritzi Ritz
  aunt to: **5** Nancy
  creator: **15** Ernie Bushmiller **16** Larry Whittington
  character: **4** Phil **5** Nancy, Rollo **6** Sluggo

frivolity 3 fun **4** jest, play **5** folly, sport **6** levity, whimsy **7** abandon **8** airiness, dallying, frippery **9** emptiness, flippancy, giddiness, lightness **10** fickleness, triviality, wantonness **11** flightiness **15** thoughtlessness

frivolous 4 airy, vain **5** barmy, dizzy, emp- ty, inane, light, minor, petty, silly **6** flimsy, frothy, paltry, slight, stupid **7** fatuous, flighty, foolish, trivial, witless **8** careless, flippant, heedless, niggling, piddling, trifling **9** brainless, imprudent, pointless, senseless, unserious, worthless **10** insouciant **11** extravagant, harebrained, impractical, improvident, nonsensical,

superficial, unimportant **13** insignificant, rattlebrained **14** shallowbrained

frizzle 4 curl **5** crimp

frock 4 coat, gown, robe, suit **5** cloak, dress, smock **6** blouse **7** cassock, soutane **8** chasuble, surplice, vestment **9** clericals **10** canonicals

frog 3 pad, pod **4** knot, wood **5** frosh, hitch, track **6** holder, peeper, toggle **7** crawler, croaker, cushion, leopard, tadpole **8** bullfrog, fastener, pickerel, pollywog **9** amphibian, plow frame **12** flower holder

Frogs, The
  author: **12** Aristophanes
  character: **5** Pluto **6** Charon **7** Bacchus **8** Dionysus, Hercules, Xanthias **9** Aeschylus, Euripides

Froissart, Jean
  author of: **8** Meliador **10** Chronicles

frolic 3 fun **4** lark, play, romp, skip **5** act up, antic, caper, frisk, mirth, prank, sport, spree **6** cavort, gaiety, gambol **7** disport, jollity, make hay **8** escapade **9** amusement, festivity, joviality, merriment **10** buffoonery, pleasantry, recreation, skylarking, tomfoolery **11** merrymaking **13** entertainment

frolicsome 5 antic, jolly, merry **6** cheery, jaunty, lively **7** playful **8** cheerful, mirthful, prankish **9** sprightly **12** lighthearted

Frollo, Claude
  character in: **23** The Hunchback of Notre Dame
  author: **4** Hugo

from 2 de, ex, of **3** for, fro **5** off of, out of **7** against **8** starting **9** beginning

from abroad 5 alien **6** exotic **7** foreign **8** imported

fromage 6 cheese

from behind
  Latin: **6** a tergo

From Here to Eternity
  director: **13** Fred Zinnemann
  author: **10** James Jones
  cast: **9** Donna Reed **11** Deborah Kerr **12** Frank Sinatra, George Reeves **13** Burt Lancaster **14** Ernest Borgnine **15** Montgomery Clift
  setting: **11** Pearl Harbor
  Oscar for: **7** picture **8** director **12** screenwriter **15** supporting actor (Sinatra) **17** supporting actress (Reed)

from inside
  Latin: **7** ab intra

from outside
  Latin: **7** ab extra

From Russia With Love
  author: **10** Ian Fleming

from scratch 4 anew **14** from ground zero **16** from the beginning **20** from fresh ingredients

from side to side 4 over, sway **5**

cross **7** athwart, swaying, zigzag **12** back and forth

from the beginning
  Latin: **5** ab ovo **6** de novo **8** ab initio

from the chair
  Latin: **10** ex cathedra

from the depths
  Latin: **11** de profundis

from the face
  Latin: **7** ex facie

from the fact
  Latin: **7** de facto

from the founding of the city
  Latin: **13** ab urbe condita

from the library of
  Latin: **8** ex libris

from the seat of authority
  Latin: **10** ex cathedra

front 3 air, top **4** face, fore, head, lead, mask, mien **5** first **6** facade, give on, regard **7** bearing, initial, look out **8** anterior, carriage, demeanor, presence, pretense, trenches, vanguard **9** beginning, semblance

Front, The
  director: **10** Martin Ritt
  cast: **10** Lloyd Gough, Woody Allen, Zero Mostel **13** Joshua Shelley, Michael Murphy **16** Herschel Bernardi

frontage 7 outlook **8** exposure, prospect

frontier 4 edge **5** march, verge **6** border, limits **7** extreme, marches **8** boundary, confines, outposts **9** backlands, backwoods, outskirts, perimeter **10** hinterland **11** territories

front matter 8 foreword **9** title page **12** introduction **15** table of contents **20** introductory material

Front Page, The
  author: **8** Ben Hecht **16** Charles MacArthur
  director: **11** Billy Wilder **14** Lewis Milestone
  actor: **9** Mae Clarke, Mary Brian, Pat O'Brien **10** Jack Lemmon, David Wayne **12** George E Stone, Carol Burnett **13** Adolphe Menjou, Allen Garfield, Susan Sarandon, Walter Catlett, Walter Matthau **14** Charles Durning **15** Andrew Pendleton, Vincent Gardenia **19** Edward Everett Horton
  character: **4** Earl **5** Burns, Grant, Hildy, Peggy **6** Walter **7** Hartman, Johnson **8** Williams

frost 4 rime **5** chill **7** iciness **8** coolness, distance **9** aloofness, cold spell, frigidity **10** chilliness, glaciality **13** inhospitality **14** unfriendliness

Frost, Robert
  author of: **7** Birches **10** Fire and Ice, Home Burial **11** Mending Wall **13** Brown's Descent **15** The Road Not Taken **17** After Apple-Picking **21** The

Death of the Hired Man **30** Stopping by Woods on a Snowy Evening

frostiness 3 nip **4** bite **5** chill **7** iciness **8** coldness, coolness **9** crispness, frigidity, hoariness, sharpness **10** chilliness, wintriness

frosting 3 mat **4** trim **5** glass, icing **7** cooling, topping **8** chilling, divinity, freezing, trimming **13** embellishment, ornamentation

frosty 3 icy **4** cold, cool **5** bleak, chill, hoary **6** frigid, wintry **8** freezing

froth 4 bosh, fizz, foam, fume, head, scum, suds, surf **5** spume, trash, yeast **6** lather, trivia **7** bubbles, rubbish **8** flummery, frippery, nonsense, trumpery, whitecap **9** frivolity **10** balderdash, triviality **12** fiddle-faddle

frothy 5 fizzy, foamy, light **6** bubbly **7** trivial **9** frivolous **15** inconsequential

froward 5 balky **6** unruly **7** wayward, willful **8** contrary, perverse, stubborn **9** difficult, fractious, obstinate **10** headstrong, refractory **11** disagreeing, intractable **12** recalcitrant **13** contradictory **15** unaccommodating

frown 4 fret, mope, muse, pout, sulk **5** glare, scowl **6** glower, ponder **14** discountenance

frowning 4 dark **5** angry **6** gloomy, somber, sullen **8** scowling **9** glowering

frown upon 7 condemn, dislike **8** object to **14** discountenance

frowsy, frowzy 5 fusty, musty, stale **6** sloppy, untidy **7** tousled, unkempt **8** slovenly

frozen 3 icy **4** cold, iced, numb **5** chill, gelid, polar **6** arctic, chilly, cooled, wintry **7** chilled, clogged, glacial, stymied **8** benumbed, hibernal, icebound **10** obstructed, stalemated **11** frostbitten, immobilized **12** refrigerated

fructify 5 bloom **6** sprout, thrive **7** blossom, prosper, succeed **8** flourish

frugal 4 slim **5** scant, tight **6** skimpy, stingy **7** ascetic, sparing, thrifty **9** niggardly, penny-wise **10** abstemious, economical, unwasteful **12** parsimonious

frugality 6 thrift **7** economy **8** prudence, stinting **9** parsimony **10** scantiness, stinginess **11** thriftiness **12** cheeseparing **13** niggardliness, pennypinching **16** parsimoniousness

fruit 4 crop **5** award, issue, yield, young **6** effect, profit, result, return, reward, upshot **7** benefit, harvest, outcome, produce, product, progeny, revenue **8** earnings **9** advantage, emolument, offspring, outgrowth **10** production **11** consequence **12** remuneration

fruitful 6 fecund **7** fertile **8** blooming, prolific, yielding **9** effective **10** productive, profitable, successful **11** efficacious **12** advantageous, fructiferous

fruition 8 maturity, ripeness **10** attainment **11** achievement, fulfillment, realization **12** consummation, satisfaction **13** actualization, gratification **15** materialization

fruitless 4 arid, vain **5** empty, inept **6** barren, futile, hollow **7** sterile, useless **8** abortive, bootless, nugatory **9** infertile, pointless, worthless **10** profitless, unavailing, unprolific **11** incompetent, ineffective, ineffectual, inoperative, purposeless, unrewarding **12** unproductive, unprofitable, unsuccessful **13** inefficacious

fruit trees
  goddess of: 6 Pomona

frumpy 4 drab **5** dowdy **8** slovenly **10** slatternly **12** unattractive

frustrate 3 bar **4** balk, foil **5** block, check, upset **6** baffle, cancel, defeat, hinder, impede, thwart **7** counter, cripple, fluster, inhibit, nullify, prevent **8** dispirit, obstruct, prohibit, suppress **9** forestall, hamstring, undermine **10** circumvent, disappoint, disconcert, discourage, dishearten

frustration 6 defeat **7** balking, chagrin, failure, foiling, letdown **8** futility **9** hindrance, thwarting **10** bafflement, inhibition, nonsuccess **11** obstruction **12** discomfiture, interference **13** contravention, counteraction **14** disappointment, nonfulfillment **15** dissatisfaction

fry 4 cook **5** brown, grill, saute **7** frizzle **9** fricassee

fry 4 fish **5** child, young **8** children, small fry

Fry, Christopher
  author of: 9 Yard of Sun **12** The Firstborn **13** Venus Observed **20** The Dark Is Light Enough **21** The Lady's Not for Burning

frying pan 3 wok **6** frypan **7** browner, griddle, skillet

fuchsia
  varieties: 4 cape, tree **5** hardy **10** California **11** honeysuckle

fuddled 5 bosky, dopey, drunk, tipsy **6** boozed, groggy **7** maudlin, muddled, sozzled, tippled **8** confused **9** stupefied **10** inebriated **11** intoxicated

fudge 3 lie **4** bosh, fake **5** candy, cheat, evade, hedge, hunch, patch, welch **7** falsify, penuche **8** divinity

fuel 3 fan, gas, oil **4** coal, feed, fire, wood **5** light, means, stoke **6** charge, fill up, fodder, ignite, incite, kindle **7** impetus, inflame, sustain **8** activate, energize, gasoline, material, recharge, stimulus **9** petroleum, stimulate **10** ammunition, motivation, sustenance **11** inspiration, wherewithal

fugitive 4 hobo **5** brief, exile, hasty, nomad, rover, short, tramp **6** errant, fading, flying, loafer, outlaw **7** cursory, elusive, erratic, escaped, escapee, fleeing, hurried, passing, refugee, runaway, summary, vagrant **8** apostate, deserter, escaping, fleeting, flitting, renegade, shifting, unstable, vagabond, volatile, wanderer **9** ephemeral, fugacious, itinerant, momentary, straggler, temporary, transient, uncertain **10** evanescent, expatriate, short-lived, transitory **11** impermanent

Fugitive, The
  character: 9 Donna Taft **11** Fred Johnson (one-armed man) **12** (Lt) Philip Gerard **13** (Dr) Richard Kimble
  cast: 10 Barry Morse, Bill Raisch **12** David Janssen **15** Jacqueline Scott

fuhrer, Fuhrer, der fuhrer 4 Nazi **6** Hitler, leader, tyrant **8** dictator **11** Adolf Hitler

fulfill 2 do **4** heed, keep, meet, obey, suit **6** answer, effect, follow, redeem **7** achieve, execute, observe, perfect, perform, realize, satisfy **9** discharge, establish, implement **10** accomplish, consummate, effectuate

fulfillment, fulfilment 7 delight **8** crowning, pinnacle, pleasure **9** execution, happiness **10** attainment, completion **11** achievement, contentment, culmination, realization **12** effectuation, satisfaction **13** contentedness, establishment, gratification **14** accomplishment, implementation

Fulks, Sarah Jane
  real name of: 9 Jane Wyman

full 3 big **4** rich, very, wide **5** ample, broad, flush, laden, large, plump, quite, round, sated, total, whole **6** entire, gorged, in-tact, loaded, mature, packed, rotund **7** brimful, crammed, exactly, fraught, glutted, heaping, maximum, perfect, plenary, replete, shapely, stuffed, teeming **8** brimming, bursting, complete, resonant, swarming, thorough **9** abounding, capacious, perfectly, precisely, saturated, surfeited **10** unabridged, voluminous

full amount 3 all, sum **5** total, whole **8** entirety, totality **9** aggregate **10** complement

full-bodied 3 fat **4** rich **5** ample, lofty **6** hearty, mature, robust **9** flavorful **10** meaningful

Fuller, R Buckminster
  architect of: 10 US Pavilion (Expo '67 Montreal) **13** Dymaxion House
  form: 12 geodesic dome

full-fledged 5 adept **6** expert, mature **7** skilled, trained **8** complete, masterly, schooled **9** qualified, topflight **10** proficient **11** experienced **13** authoritative

full form 9 extension **10** elongation **11**

enlargement **12** augmentation **13** amplification

full-grown 4 ripe **5** adult, manly, of age, matured, womanly **9** developed

full measure 6 enough, plenty **9** abundance, plenitude **10** competence **11** sufficiency

Full Moon
author: **11** P G Wodehouse

fullness 7 satiety **8** richness **9** amplitude, roundness, satiation **12** completeness **14** voluminousness

full of fire 7 rousing **8** electric, exciting, spirited **9** thrilling **11** galvanizing, stimulating **12** electrifying, soulstirring

full of life 5 vital **8** animated, spirited, vigorous **9** ebullient, energetic, exuberant, vivacious

full of pep 5 vital **6** lively **8** animated

full of vim and vigor 5 peppy **6** lively **11** invigorated

full view 7 the open **8** daylight, openness

fully 5 amply, quite **6** richly, wholly **7** totally, utterly **8** entirely **9** copiously, perfectly **10** abundantly, altogether, completely, positively, throughout **11** plentifully **12** sufficiently **13** substantially

fully realized 7 perfect **8** achieved, complete, executed, finished **9** completed, perfected, performed **11** consummated **12** accomplished

fulminate 4 boil, rage, rant **7** explode **8** denounce

fulminate against 5 roast **6** berate **7** scourge **8** call down, chastise **9** castigate

fulmination 7 violent **8** bursting, eruption **9** discharge, explosion

fulsome 3 fat **4** foul **5** suave **6** lavish, odious **7** cloying, lustful, noisome, obscene **8** overdone, unctuous **9** excessive, obnoxious, offensive, repulsive, tasteless **10** disgusting, obsequious

Fulton, Robert
nationality: **8** American
inventor of: **9** steamboat (Clermont), submarine **12** Fulton's folly **13** marine torpedo

fumble 3 err, mar **4** blow, muff **5** grope, spoil **6** bobble, boggle, bollix, bungle, goof up, mess up, muddle **7** butcher, louse up, screw up **9** mishandle

fume 3 gas **4** boil, burn, emit, foam, haze, puff, rage, rant, rave, reek, waft **5** exude, scent, smell, smoke, stink, vapor **6** bil-low, exhale, miasma, seethe, stench **7** carry on, explode, flame up, flare up, smolder **10** exhalation

fun 3 gas **4** ball, game, jest, lark, play, romp, trip **5** antic, blast, cheer, mirth, prank, sport, spree **6** frolic, gaiety, joking **7** jollity, revelry, whoopee **8** escapade, good time, pleasure **9** amusement, diversion, enjoyment, horseplay, joviality, merriment **10** buffoonery, recreation, relaxation, skylarking, tomfoolery **11** distraction, playfulness, waggishness **13** entertainment

Funafuti
capital of: **6** Tuvalu

function 3 act, job **4** duty, fete, gala, help, role, task, work **5** feast, field, niche, party, place, power, range, scope, serve **6** affair, behave, do duty, office, soiree, sphere **7** banquet, benefit, concern, faculty, operate, perform, purpose **8** activity, business, capacity, ceremony, occasion, province **9** festivity, objective, operation, reception **13** entertainment

functional 6 useful **7** working **8** operable **9** operative, practical **11** serviceable, utilitarian

functionary 8 employee, official **10** bureaucrat **13** administrator

functioning 5 in use **6** active, at work, usable **7** working **9** effectual, operating, operative

fund 3 pot **4** bank, foot, lode, mine, pool, vein, well **5** endow, float, fount, hoard, kitty, stock, store **6** pay for, spring, supply **7** finance, nest egg, reserve, savings, support **8** treasure **9** endowment, patronize, reservoir **10** foundation, investment, repository, storehouse, underwrite **12** accumulation

fundament 3 can **4** buns, rump, seat **5** fanny **6** behind, bottom **8** backside, buttocks, haunches **9** posterior **12** hindquarters

fundamental 3 key **4** ABC's, base, main **5** axiom, basic, basis, chief, first, major, vital **7** central, crucial, element, primary **8** cardinal, integral **9** component, essential, necessary, principal, principle, requisite **10** elementary, foundation, groundwork, underlying **11** cornerstone **13** indispensable

funds 4 cash, jack, pelf **5** bread, dough, lucre, means, money, moola **6** assets, income, wampum, wealth **7** capital, scratch **8** finances, property **9** resources **11** wherewithal

funeral 4 wake **5** rites **6** burial **7** requiem **9** cremation, interment, obsequies **10** entombment, inhumation

funeral song 5 dirge, elegy **6** lament **7** requiem **8** threnody **11** lamentation

funereal 3 sad **4** grim **5** weepy **6** dismal, dreary, gloomy, solemn, somber, woeful **7** doleful **8** desolate, dirgeful, grieving, mournful **9** cheerless, woebegone **10** depressing, lachrymose, lugubrious **13** brokenhearted

fun-filled 5 happy **6** joyful, joyous **8** pleasant, pleasing **9** enjoyable **10** delightful **11** pleasurable

Fungoso
character in: **22** Every Man Out of His Humour
author: **6** Jonson

fungus, fungi 4 mold, myco, rust, smut **5** ergot, yeast **6** mildew **7** truffle **8** mushroom **9** toadstool **11** thallophyte

fun-loving 5 jolly, merry **6** genial, jovial **7** affable **8** sociable **9** convivial **10** gregarious

funnel 4 cone, duct, flue, pipe, pour **5** focus, shaft **6** direct, filter, siphon **7** channel, chimney, conduit **9** stovepipe **10** smokestack, ventilator **11** concentrate

funny 3 odd **5** antic, comic, droll, merry, queer, weird, witty **6** absurd, jocose **7** amusing, bizarre, comical, curious, jesting, jocular, offbeat, strange, unusual, waggish **8** farcical, humorous, mirthful, peculiar, sporting, uncommon **9** diverting, facetious, hilarious, laughable, ludicrous **10** outlandish, ridiculous

Funny Girl
director: **12** William Wyler
cast: **8** Lee Allen **10** Kay Medford, Omar Sharif **11** Anne Francis **13** Walter Pidgeon **15** Barbra Streisand (Fanny Brice)
score: **9** Jule Styne **10** Bob Merrill
sequel: **9** Funny Lady
song: **6** People **18** Don't Rain on My Parade

funnyman 3 wag, wit **4** card, fool, mime, zany **5** clown, comic, joker **6** jester, madcap **7** buffoon **8** comedian, humorist, jokester **9** harlequin

fuoco, con
music: **8** with fire

fur 3 fox **4** down, hair, lamb, mink, pelt, seal **5** coney, lapin, otter, sable **6** beaver, fleece, jaguar, kit fox, nutria, rabbit, red fox **7** blue fox, cheetah, leopard, muskrat, opossum, raccoon **8** black fox, cross fox, squirrel, white fox **9** silver fox **10** animal skin, chinchilla **11** karakul lamb, Persian lamb **13** broadtail lamb **14** mouton-dyed lamb

furbelow 5 frill **6** fringe **7** falbala, flounce **8** trimming

furbish 4 buff **5** renew, shine **6** polish **7** burnish **8** renovate

Furiae see **6** Furies

Furies
5 Dirae **6** Erinys, Furiae, Semnai **7** Allecto, Erinyes, Megaera **9** Eumenides, Tisiphone
form: **7** spirits
sex: **6** female
mother: **4** Gaea
father: **6** Uranus
born of the blood of: **6** Uranus

Greek name: 6 Erinys **7** Erinyes **9** Eumenides
Roman name: 5 Dirae **6** Furiae

furious 3 mad **4** wild **5** angry, fiery, irate, rabid **6** enrage, fierce, fuming, raging, savage, stormy **7** intense, rampant, violent **8** frenetic, frenzied, heedless, maddened, provoked, reckless, up in arms, vehement, wrathful **9** fanatical, irascible, turbulent **10** infuriated, passionate, tumultuous, unbalanced **11** tempestuous **12** ungovernable, unrestrained

furl 4 coil, curl, fold, roll, wrap **5** truss **6** curl up, fold up, furdle, roll up, spiral

furlong
abbreviation: 3 fur

furnace 4 kiln, oven **5** forge, stove **6** boiler, heater **11** incinerator

Furnace
constellation of: 6 Fornax

furnish 3 arm, rig **4** gird, give, vest **5** array, dress, endow, equip, favor, fit up, grant, stock **6** fit out, outfit, purvey, render, supply **7** appoint, indulge, prepare, provide **8** accoutre, bestow on, decorate **9** provision **11** accommodate

furnishings 5 decor **9** equipment **11** accessories **12** haberdashery

furnish room for 5 lodge, put up **6** billet **7** shelter **11** accommodate

furniture 7 effects **8** chattels, movables, property **11** possessions **12** appointments

furor 3 fad **4** flap, rage, to-do, word **5** craze, mania, noise, thing, vogue **6** fervor, frenzy, hoopla, lunacy, raving, uproar **7** fashion, madness, passion **8** brouhaha, insanity, reaction **9** agitation, commotion, obsession, transport **10** dernier cri, enthusiasm, excitement, fanaticism

furrow 3 cut, dig, rut **4** knit, line, plow, rift, seam **5** cleft, crack, ditch, ridge, track **6** crease, groove, pucker, trench, trough **7** channel, crevice, fissure, wrinkle **10** depression **11** corrugation

furry 4 soft **5** downy, hairy, scary **6** cuddly, fleecy, pelted, shaggy **8** fearsome, horrible **11** hair-raising

further 3 aid, new, too, yet **4** also, back, help, more **5** again, extra, favor, fresh, other, spare, speed **6** abroad, assist, back up, beyond, foster, hasten, oblige, to boot, yonder **7** advance, afar off, besides, farther, forward, promote, quicken, stand by, work for **8** champion, expedite, likewise, moreover **9** accessory, ancillary, auxiliary, encourage, propagate **10** accelerate, additional, strengthen **11** accommodate **12** additionally, contributory, supplemental **13** supplementary

furtherance 3 aid **4** help, lift **5** favor **6** succor **7** advance, defense, support **8** advocacy, interest **9** patronage, promotion **10** assistance **11** advancement, cooperation, countenance **12** championship

furthering 3 aid **6** aiding, growth **8** abetting, advocacy, espousal **9** assisting, fostering, promoting, promotion **10** assistance, supporting **11** advancement, encouraging, propagating, propagation **12** accelerating, acceleration, encouragement **13** strengthening

furthermore 3 too **4** also **6** as well, to boot **7** besides **8** likewise, moreover **10** in addition **12** additionally

furthermost 7 extreme **8** farthest **11** farthermost

furtive 3 sly **4** wily **5** shady **6** covert, crafty, hidden, masked, secret, shifty, sneaky, unseen, veiled **7** cloaked, elusive, evasive, private **8** secluded, shrouded, skulking, sneaking, stealthy **9** collusive, secre-tive, underhand **10** mysterious, undercover, unrevealed **11** clandestine **12** confidential **13** surreptitious **14** conspiratorial

fury 3 fit, hag, ire, pet **4** gall, huff, rage, snit **5** force, might, shrew, vixen, wrath **6** attack, choler, frenzy, spleen, virago **7** assault, bluster, dudgeon, hellcat, tantrum **8** acerbity, acrimony, ferocity, outburst, severity, she-devil, spitfire, violence **9** intensity, termagant, vehemence, virulence **10** excitement, fierceness, turbulence **11** impetuosity

fuse 4 join, link, meld, melt, weld, wick **5** blend, merge, smelt, torch **6** league, mingle, solder **7** combine **8** coalesce, federate, ignition, solidify **9** associate, detonator **10** amalgamate, assimilate **11** confederate, consolidate, incorporate, intermingler

fusillade 4 hail, rain **5** salvo, spray **6** volley **7** barrage, battery **8** drumfire, enfilade **9** broadside, cannonade **11** bombardment

fusion 5 blend, union **6** league **7** combine, melding, melting, merging **8** alliance, blending, compound, smelting **9** coalition, synthesis **10** commixture, dissolving, federation **11** association, coalescence, combination, commingling, confederacy, unification **12** amalgamation, intermix-ture, liquefaction **13** agglomeration, confederation

fuss 3 ado, nag **4** carp, fool, fret, fume, pomp, spat, stew, stir, tiff, to-do **5** annoy, cavil, labor, set-to, worry **6** bother, bustle, excite, fidget, flurry, hubbub, hustle, niggle, pester, pother, potter, putter, rattle, scurry, tinker **7** agitate, confuse, dispute, fluster, flutter, nitpick, quarrel, quibble, perturb, trouble, turmoil **8** ceremony **9** agitation, commotion, confusion **10** discconcert, hurly-burly, turbulence **11** disturbance, superfluity **12** perturbation **15** ceremoniousness
Yiddish: 7 tzimmes

fuss over 6 dote on

fussy 4 busy **6** ornate **7** finical, finicky, nervous **8** bustling, critical, exacting **9** assiduous, cluttered, crotchety, demanding, squeamish **10** compulsive, fastidious, meticulous, nitpicking, old-maidish, particular, scrupulous **11** painstaking, persnickety

fusty 5 moldy, musty, stale **6** foisty, rancid, stuffy **8** obsolete **9** out of date **10** malodorous **12** old fashioned

Futabatei, Shimei
author of: 16 The Drifting (Floating) Cloud

futile 4 idle, vain **5** empty, petty **7** trivial, useless **8** abortive, bootless, nugatory, trifling **9** frivolous, fruitless, valueless, worthless **10** profitless, unavailing **11** ineffective, ineffectual, unimportant **12** unprofitable, unsuccessful **13** insignificant

future 4 hope **5** after, later **6** coming, lat-ter, morrow, offing, to come **7** by-and-by, ensuing, outlook **8** eventual, prospect, tomorrow, ultimate **9** following, hereafter, impending, projected **10** in prospect, subsequent, succeeding **11** anticipated, expectation, opportunity, prospective **12** anticipation
Spanish: 6 manana

Future Shock
author: 12 Alvin Toffler

fuzz 4 down, lint **5** fluff **6** police

fuzzy 3 dim **4** hazy **5** downy, foggy, linty, misty, murky, vague, wooly **6** fluffy, frizzy, woolly **7** blurred, obscure, shadowy, unclear **8** confused **9** pubescent **10** indefinite, indistinct

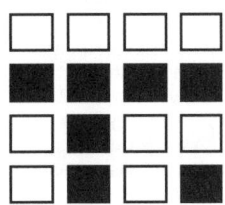

gab 3 jaw, rap, yak **4** blab, chat **5** prate **6** babble, gibber, gossip, jabber, patter **7** baloney, blarney, blather, chatter, prattle **8** chitchat, idle talk, talk idly **10** balderdash **12** conversation

gabble 3 rap **4** blab **5** prate **6** babble, drivel, gossip, jabber **7** blather, chatter, prattle, twaddle **8** babbling, chitchat, idle talk **9** gibbering, jabbering **10** blathering, chattering **14** chitterchatter

gabfest 3 rap **4** chat, talk **7** palaver **8** chitchat **10** discussion **12** conversation **13** confabulation

gable 4 edge, peak, roof, wall **6** detail, dormer, pinion **7** aileron **8** pediment, triangle

Gable, Clark
real name: 17 William Clark Gable
wife: 13 Carole Lombard
nickname: 7 The King
born: 7 Cadiz OH
roles: 7 Red Dust **8** Saratoga **10** The Misfits **11** Rhett Butler **15** Gone With the Wind **18** It Happened One Night (Oscar)

Gabo, Naum
real name: 17 Naum Neemia Pevsner
born: 6 Russia **7** Brainsk
founder: 14 Constructivism
artwork: 6 Column **11** Spiral Theme **16** Sculptural Models **19** Kinetic Construction **24** Variations of Spheric Theme

Gabon Republic
capital/largest city: 10 Libreville
others: 4 Oyem **5** Bongo, Kango **6** Mitzic, Moanda, Mouila, Omvane **7** Makokou, Mounana **9** Lambarene **10** Port-Gentil **11** Franceville
monetary unit: 5 franc **7** centime
lake: 7 Anengue, Azinguo
mountain: 5 Mpele **7** Chaillu, Cristal, Mikongo **8** Balaquri, Birougou
highest point: 8 Iboundji
river: 4 Como **6** Abanga, Ivindo, Ogooue **7** Ngounie
sea: 8 Atlantic
physical feature:
  cape: 5 Lopez
people: 4 Fang **6** Adouma, Bakota, Bateke, Echira, Okande, Omyene **7** Eshiras **8** Bandjabi, Bapounou
  leader: 3 Mba **5** Bongo
  philanthropist: 16 Albert

Schweitzer
language: 6 French
religion: 5 Islam **7** animism **10** Protestant **13** Roman Catholic
feature:
  tree: 6 okoume
food: 6 manioc **9** Dika bread

Gabor, Eva
mother: 5 Jolie
sister: 5 Magda **6** Zsa Zsa
born: 7 Hungary **8** Budapest
roles: 4 Gigi **10** Green Acres **12** My Man Godfrey **13** A Royal Scandal, Forced Landing **15** Youngblood Hawke **18** The Truth About Women **20** The Last Time I Saw Paris

Gabor, Zsa Zsa
real name: 9 Sari Gabor
mother: 5 Jolie
sister: 3 Eva **5** Magda
husband: 10 Nick Hilton **13** George Sanders
born: 7 Hungary **8** Budapest
roles: 4 Lili **11** Moulin Rouge **14** Lovely To Look At **20** The Story of Three Loves

Gaborone, Gaberones
capital of: 8 Botswana

Gabriel 9 archangel
means: 8 man of God **11** God is strong
spoke to: 4 Mary **9** Zacharias, Zechariah

Gad
father: 5 Jacob
mother: 6 Zilpah
brother: 3 Dan **4** Levi **5** Asher, Judah **6** Joseph, Reuben, Simeon **7** Zebulun **8** Benjamin, Issachar, Naphtali
sister: 5 Dinah
descendant of: 6 Gadite

gadget 4 tool **6** device, doodad, jigger **7** gimmick, novelty **9** accessory, doohickey **10** attachment **11** contraption, contrivance, thingamabob, thingamajig

Gaea
also: 2 Ge **4** Gaia
origin: 5 Greek
goddess of: 5 earth
husband: 6 Uranus
children: 6 Pontus, Titans, Uranus **7** Cyclops, Erinyes **9** mountains **13** Hecatonchires
son: 6 Nereus **7** Iapetus, Oceanus
daughter: 4 Rhea **5** Theia **6** Phoebe,

Tethys, Themis **9** Mnemosyne
corresponds to: 6 Tellus

Gaelic
language family: 12 Indo-European
branch: 4 Erse **6** Celtic
subgroup: 4 Manx **5** Irish **8** Scottish

gaffe 4 goof **5** boner **6** boo-boo **7** blunder **11** impropriety **12** indiscretion
French: 7 faux pas **9** gaucherie

gag 4 hoax, hush, jest, joke, stop **5** block, choke, heave, retch **6** muffle, muzzle, stifle **7** cloture, foolery, silence, smother **8** stoppage, suppress **9** horseplay, restraint **13** facetiousness

Gaia see **4** Gaea

gaiety, gayety 3 fun **4** show **5** mirth **6** frolic, tinsel **7** elation, glitter, jollity, spirits **8** airiness, frippery, trumpery, vivacity **9** amusement, animation, brummagem, gaudiness, merriment, showiness **10** brightness, brilliance, garishness, jauntiness, joyousness, liveliness **11** celebration, merrymaking **12** cheerfulness, colorfulness, exhilaration, sportiveness **13** effervescence, sprightliness

gain, gains 3 add, bag, get, hit, net, win **4** jump, leap, plus, reap **5** bloom, bonus, fetch, glean, put on, reach, wages, yield **6** attain, come to, gather, income, obtain, pick up, profit, return, salary, secure, thrive **7** achieve, acquire, blossom, capture, collect, improve, procure, produce, prosper, recover, revenue **8** addition, arrive at, black ink, dividend, earnings, flourish, increase, overtake, proceeds, winnings **9** accretion, advantage, increment **10** attainment **11** improvement **12** accumulation, compensation, remuneration

Gaines, Ernest J
author of: 33 The Autobiography of Miss Jane Pittman

gainful 4 rich **6** paying **9** lucrative **10** productive, profitable **12** remunerative

gainfully 8 usefully **10** profitably **11** lucratively **12** productively **14** remuneratively

gain recognition 9 establish

gainsay 4 deny **6** abjure, oppose, refute **7** disavow, dispute **9** repudiate **10** contradict, controvert

Gainsborough, Thomas
born: 7 England, Sudbury

artwork: 10 The Blue Boy **14** The Morning Walk **15** Mr and Mrs Andrews, The Hon Mrs Graham **16** Viscount Ligonier **26** Peasant Girl Gathering Sticks

gait 4 pace, step, walk **5** tread **6** stride **7** bearing **8** carriage **10** deportment **French: 8** demarche

gaiter 4 boot, shoe, spat, vamp **5** chaps, strad **6** gaskin, hugger, puttee **7** legging **8** cuttikin, overshoe

gala 3 gay **5** grand, party **7** benefit, festive, opulent **8** festival, majestic, splendid **9** festivity, glamorous, sumptuous **10** ceremonial, fancy-dress, glittering **11** celebration, celebratory, magnificent, spectacular, star-studded **French: 4** fete

Galahad
character in: 16 Arthurian romance
father: 8 Lancelot
mother: 6 Elaine
quest: 9 Holy Grail
symbol of: 6 purity **8** nobility

Galatea
form: 6 maiden, statue **8** sea nymph
father: 6 Nereus
mother: 5 Doris
courted by: 10 Polyphemus
lover: 4 Acis
killed: 4 Acis
statue carved by: 9 Pygmalion
brought to life by: 9 Aphrodite
son: 6 Paphos

gale 3 fit **4** blow, gust, stir **6** flurry, squall, tumult, uproar **7** cyclone, tempest **8** eruption, outbreak, outburst **9** agitation, commotion, windstorm

Galileo Galilei
nationality: 7 Italian
birthplace: 4 Pisa
inventor of: 6 sector **11** thermometer
studied: 6 motion **8** pendulum
discovered: 18 Jupiter's satellites
constructed: 9 telescope
formulated: 18 law of falling bodies
author of: 8 Dialogue **10** Discourses **18** The Starry Messenger
condemned for: 6 heresy

gall 3 bug, irk, vex **4** bile, flay, fret, miff, rile **5** anger, annoy, brass, chafe, cheek, gripe, nerve, score, sting, venom **6** abrade, bruise, enrage, harass, injure, nettle, offend, rancor, ruffle, spleen **7** affront, incense, provoke, rub sore **8** acrimony, audacity, boldness, irritate, rudeness, temerity **9** animosity, assurance, displease, excoriate, impudence, insolence, malignity, sauciness, virulence **10** bitterness, brazenness, effrontery, exacerbate, exasperate **11** presumption

gallant 3 fop **4** bold, dude, game, stud **5** blood, brave, dandy, gutsy, noble, suave, swell **6** daring, heroic, kindly, plucky, polite, urbane **7** courtly, dashing, valiant **8** cavalier, fearless, gay

blade, intrepid, mannerly, obliging, resolute, stalwart, valorous, well-bred **9** attentive, courteous, dauntless **10** chivalrous, courageous, thoughtful **11** considerate, gentlemanly, lionhearted **12** stouthearted

gallantries 10 attentions **11** compliments **12** pleasantries

gallantry 4 grit, sand **5** nerve, pluck, valor **6** daring, mettle, spirit **7** bravery, courage, dashing, heroism, prowess, suavity **8** chivalry, courtesy, urbanity **9** derring-do, fortitude, gentility **10** politeness **11** courtliness, intrepidity **12** fearlessness, resoluteness **13** attentiveness, dauntlessness, determination **14** courageousness

gallery 4 stoa **5** salon **6** arcade, loggia, piazza **7** balcony, passage, portico **8** cloister, corridor **9** bleachers, colonnade, mezzanine, triforium **10** ambulatory, grandstand, passageway

Gallia Belgica *see* **7** Belgium

galliano
type: 7 liqueur
origin: 5 Italy
flavor: 5 herbs, spice
color: 6 yellow
with creme de cacao: 14 Golden Cadillac
with rum: 9 Bossa Nova
with vodka: 16 Harvey Wallbanger

gallinule 3 hen **4** coot, fowl, rail, sora **7** moorhen **8** dabchick, hyacinth, rallidae, ricebird, swamphen

Gallipoli
director: 9 Peter Weir
cast: 7 Mark Lee **8** Bill Kerr **9** Mel Gibson **11** Robert Grubb

gallivant, galavant 3 gad **4** kite, roam, rove **5** jaunt, range, stray **6** ramble, travel, wander **7** gallant, meander, traipse, **8** gad about **9** philander

gallon
abbreviation: 3 gal

gallop 3 fly, hie, jog, run **4** bolt, dart, dash, flit, race, rush, scud, skim, trot, whiz **5** bound, hurry, scoot, shoot, speed, whisk **6** hasten, scurry, spring, sprint **7** mad dash, scamper, scuttle, tear off **8** fast clip, fast gait **9** skedaddle

Galloping Ghost
nickname of: 9 Red Grange

gallows 4 rope **5** noose **6** gibbet, halter **8** scaffold

galore 7 aplenty, to spare

galosh, galoche 4 boot, clog, shoe **6** arctic, patten, rubber **8** overshoe

Galsworthy, John
author of: 5 To Let **6** Strife **7** Justice **9** Loyalties **10** In Chancery **11** The Skin Game **13** A Modern Comedy **14** The Forsyte Saga **15** End of the

Chapter **16** The Man of Property **22** Indian Summer of a Forsyte

Galt, John
character in: 13 Atlas Shrugged
author: 7 Ayn Rand

galvanize 4 fire, move, stir, wake **5** rally, rouse, treat **6** arouse, awaken, charge, excite, foment, spur on, thrill **7** inspire, provoke, quicken **8** activate, energize, vitalize **9** electrify, stimulate

galvanizing 7 rousing **8** electric, exciting, spirited **9** inspiring, thrilling **11** stimulating **12** electrifying, soul-stirring

Galveston Giant
nickname of: 11 Jack Johnson

Gamaliel
father: 6 Simeon **8** Pedahzur
grandfather: 6 Hillel
taught: 4 Paul

Gambia
capital/largest city: 6 Banjul **8** Bathurst
others: 5 Bakau, Basse, Mansa **7** Bintang, Brikama, Kuntaur **10** Georgetown
monetary unit: 5 butut, pound **6** dalasi
island: 7 Ft James, St Mary's **8** Elephant
river: 3 Bao **6** Gambia **7** Bintang, Nianija **9** Sandougou
sea: 8 Atlantic
people: 4 Fula, Jola **5** Foula, Wolof **6** Fulani **7** Mandingo, Serahuli **9** Seranuleh
language: 4 Fula **5** Wolof **6** Fulani **7** English, Malinke **8** Mandingo
religion: 5 Islam **10** Protestant **13** Roman Catholic

gambit 4 ploy, ruse **5** feint, trick **6** scheme **8** artifice, maneuver **9** stratagem

gamble 3 bet **4** back, risk **5** flyer, wager **6** chance, hazard, toss-up **7** trust in, venture **9** speculate **11** speculation, uncertainty

gambler 5 dicer, shark, sharp, sport **6** banker, bettor, bookie, dealer, player **7** hustler **8** gamester, hazarder **10** speculator

Gambler, The
author: 16 Fyodor Dostoevsky
character: 6 Astley, Polina **10** The General **11** Mlle Blanche **15** Marquis de Grieux **16** Alexey Ivanovitch **22** Antonida Tarasyevitchev

gambol 3 hop **4** leap **5** bound, caper, frisk, sport, vault **6** bounce, cavort, frolic, prance, spring **7** disport, rollick

game 3 bad, fun **4** golf, halt, lame, lark, play, polo, pool, prey, romp **5** antic, brave, cocky, darts, gimpy, jacks, match, rugby, sport, spree **6** boccie, boxing, daring, frolic, gaiety, gambol, heroic, plucky, quarry, soccer, spunky, squash, tennis **7** archery, bowling, contest, crooked, croquet, curling, fencing, frisbee, gallant, hawking, hunting, hurling, jai alai, limping, pastime, tourney, valiant, willing **8** baseball, crippled, deformed, disabled, fearless, football, handball, hobbling, intrepid, lacrosse, ping pong, resolute, skittles, spirited, valorous, wild fowl **9** amusement, badminton, billiards, dauntless, diversion, festivity, merriment, wrestling **10** basketball, courageous, determined, horseshoes, ice-skating, lawn tennis, recreation, tournament, volleyball **11** competition, distraction, merrymaking, racquetball, table tennis, unflinching **12** shuffleboard **13** entertainment, incapacitated, roller-skating

board game: 4 Clue, Life, ludo **5** chess **7** Othello **8** checkers, cribbage, dominoes, draughts, fanorona, Monopoly, Scrabble **10** backgammon **14** Trivial Pursuit

   Chinese: 6 Ma-jong, wei-ch'i **7** mahjong **8** Mah-jongg
   Egyptian: 5 Senat
   Indian: 7 pachisi **8** parchesi, shatranj **9** ashtapada, parcheesi **10** shaturanga
   Japanese: 2 Go **3** I-go **5** Sho-gi
   Korean: 5 Nyout, Pa-tok
   Swedish: 6 tablut

card game: 3 loo, war **4** brag, fish, skat, vint **5** ombre, poker, rummy, tarot, whist **6** boston, bridge, casino, chemmy, ecarte, euchre, go fish, hearts, memory, piquet, pocher **7** bezique, canasta, cooncan, old maid, plafond, primero **8** baccarat, conquian, cribbage, gin rummy, napoleon, patience, pinochle, slapjack **9** blackjack, pelmanism, solitaire, spoil five, twenty-one **11** chemin de fer, crazy eights **13** concentration **14** contract bridge **16** beggar-my-neighbor, trente et quarante

gamete 3 egg **4** ovum **5** sperm **6** oocyte, zygote **8** germ cell, oosphere **12** spermatozoan, spermatozoon

Gamow, George
   field: 7 physics **9** cosmology
   proponent of: 13 big bang theory
   deciphered: 11 genetic code
   proposed: 13 quantum theory
   established: 17 Gamow-Teller theory

Gamp, Sarah
   character in: 16 Martin Chuzzlewit
   author: 7 Dickens

gamut 3 ken **5** reach, scope, sweep **6** extent **7** compass, purview

Gandhi
   director: 19 Richard Attenborough
   cast: 11 Ben Kingsley **13** Candice Bergen
   Oscar for: 5 actor (Kingsley) **7** picture

gang 3 mob **4** band, body, crew, pack, pals, ring, team **5** chums, crowd,

flock, group, party, relay, shift, squad, troop **6** clique, outfit **7** buddies, company, coterie, cronies, friends, phalanx **8** comrades **9** coworkers, neighbors **10** associates, classmates, companions, contingent, detachment **11** schoolmates

gangster 4 goon, hood, thug **5** crook, felon, tough **6** bandit, gunman **7** hoodlum, mafioso, mobster, ruffian **8** criminal, hooligan **9** racketeer

Gant, Eugene
   character in: 17 Look Homeward Angel, Of Time and the River
   author: 5 Wolfe

Ganymede
   also: 9 Catamitus
   cupbearer of: 4 gods

gap 3 cut **4** gash, hole, rent, rift, slit, slot, void **5** abyss, break, chasm, chink, cleft, crack, gulch, gully, notch, pause **6** breach, canyon, cavity, divide, hiatus, lacuna, ravine, recess, vacuum, valley **7** crevice, fissure, interim, opening **8** aperture, crevasse, fracture, interval, puncture **9** disparity, interlude **10** difference, divergence **12** intermission, interruption

gape 4 gasp, gawk, gaze, ogle, part, peer, yawn **5** split, stare **6** cleave, expand **7** fly open **8** wide open, separate **10** rubberneck

gaping 6 astare **7** gawking, staring, yawning **13** rubbernecking

garb 3 rig **4** gear, gown, robe, suit, togs **5** dress, getup, habit **6** attire, finery, livery, outfit **7** apparel, clothes, costume, raiment, uniform, vesture **8** clothing, garments, vestment, wardrobe **9** trappings **11** habiliments

garbage 4 dirt, junk **5** offal, swill, trash, waste **6** debris, litter, refuse **7** carrion, rubbish **9** sweepings

garbage in, garbage out 4 GIGO
   term in: 9 computers

garble 5 mix up **6** jumble **7** confuse, distort **8** fragment

Garbo, Greta
   real name: 21 Greta Louisa Gustaffson
   born: 6 Sweden **9** Stockholm
   roles: 4 Love **7** Camille **8** Conquest, Mata Hari **9** Ninotchka **10** Grand Hotel **12** Anna Christie, Anna Karenina **13** Queen Cristina, Two-Faced Woman **14** The Painted Veil **16** Flesh and the Devil

Garcia Lorca, Federico
   author of: 5 Yerma **12** Blood Wedding, Gypsy Ballads **19** House of Bernarda Alba

Garcia Marquez, Gabriel
   author of: 9 Leaf Storm **23** The Autumn of the Patriarch **25** One Hundred Years of Solitude

garcon 3 boy **6** waiter **7** servant

garden 4 Eden, lawn, plot, yard **7** Arcadia **8** paradise **10** Gethsemane
   type: 4 herb, rock, rose **5** truck **6** flower, formal **7** kitchen **9** botanical, vegetable

gardenia
   varieties: 5 crape **9** butterfly

Garden of the Finzi Continis, The
   director: 14 Vittorio De Sica
   author: 14 Giorgio Bassani
   cast: 10 Fabio Testi **11** Romolo Valli **12** Helmut Berger **14** Dominique Sanda **15** Lino Capolicchio
   Oscar: 11 foreign film

Garden of the West
   nickname of: 6 Kansas

garden party
   French: 13 fete champetre

gardens
   god of: 9 Vertumnus
   goddess of: 5 Venus

Garden State
   nickname of: 9 New Jersey

garden variety 5 plain **6** common, simple **7** regular **8** everyday, familiar, ordinary **11** commonplace

Gardner, Ava
   husband: 9 Artie Shaw **12** Frank Sinatra, Mickey Rooney
   born: 12 Smithfield NC
   roles: 7 Mogambo **8** Show Boat **9** Mayerling, Naked Maja **10** On the Beach **15** The Sun Also Rises **18** Snows of Kilimanjaro **19** The Barefoot Contessa, The Night of the Iguana

Gardner, Erle Stanley
   character: 9 Paul Drake **10** Perry Mason **11** Della Street **14** Hamilton Burger
   also wrote as: 6 A A Fair

Gardner, John
   author of: 7 Grendel **12** October Light **14** Nickel Mountain, The Art of Living, The King's Indian **17** Michelsson's Ghosts **20** The Sunlight Dialogues, The Wreckage of Agathon

Gareth
   character in: 16 Arthurian romance

Garfield, James Abram
   presidential rank: 9 twentieth
   party: 10 Republican
   state represented: 2 OH
   defeated: 3 (Neal) Dow **6** (James Baird) Weaver, (John Wolcott) Phelps **7** (Winfield Scott) Hancock
   vice president: 6 (Chester Alan) Arthur
   cabinet:
      state: 6 (James Gillespie) Blaine
      treasury: 6 (William) Windom
      war: 7 (Robert Todd) Lincoln
      attorney general: 8 (Isaac Wayne) MacVeagh
      navy: 4 (William Henry) Hunt
      postmaster general: 5 (Thomas Lemuel) James

interior: 8 (Samuel Jordan) Kirkwood
born: 2 OH **6** Orange **8** log cabin
died: 9 Elberon NJ
died by: 13 assassination
buried: 11 Cleveland OH
education:
  seminary: 6 Geauga
  college: 5 Hiram (Eclectic Institute) **8** Williams
  studied: 3 law
religion: 17 Disciples of Christ
political career: 8 US Senate (declined seat) **11** state Senate **24** US House of Representatives
civilian career: 6 lawyer **7** teacher **11** lay preacher
military service: 6 US Army **8** Civil War **12** major general
notable events of lifetime/term:
  exposure of: 15 Star Route frauds
father: 7 Abraham
mother: 8 Eliza (Ballou)
siblings: 4 Mary **5** James **6** Thomas **9** Mehitabel
wife: 8 Lucretia (Rudolph)
  nickname: 5 Crete
children: 4 Mary **5** Abram, Eliza **6** Edward **12** James Rudolph **13** Harry Augustus, Irvin McDowell

Garfield, John
real name: 15 Julius Garfinkle
born: 9 New York NY
roles: 6 Juarez **10** Humoresque **11** Body and Soul **26** The Postman Always Rings Twice

Gargamelle
character in: 22 Gargantua and Pantagruel
author: 8 Rabelais

Gargantua and Pantagruel
author: 16 Francois Rabelais
character: 7 Panurge **10** Gargamelle, Grangosier, Picrochole **23** Frere Jean des Entommeures

gargantuan 4 huge, vast **5** great **7** hulking, immense, mammoth, massive, titanic **8** colossal, enormous, gigantic, lubberly, towering **9** herculean, monstrous, overgrown **10** prodigious, stupendous, tremendous **11** elephantine **13** amplitudinous

Gargery, Joe
character in: 17 Great Expectations
author: 7 Dickens

garish 4 loud **5** cheap, gaudy, showy **6** brassy, bright, flashy, tawdry, tinsel, vulgar **7** blatant, glaring **9** flaunting, obtrusive **11** pretentious **12** ostentatious **13** overelaborate

garland 3 bay, lei **4** halo **5** crown **6** corona, diadem, fillet, laurel, wreath **7** chaplet, circlet, coronet, festoon **8** chapbook, headband, treasury **9** anthology **10** collection **11** florilegium

Garland, Hamlin

author of: 18 Main-Travelled Roads **20** Rose of Dutcher's Coolly

Garland, Judy
real name: 11 Frances Gumm
husband: 7 Sid Luft **16** Vincente Minnelli
daughter: 9 Lorna Luft **12** Liza Minnelli
costar: 12 Mickey Rooney
born: 13 Grand Rapids MN
roles: 7 Dorothy **11** A Star Is Born, Babes in Arms **12** Easter Parade **13** The Wizard of Oz **14** The Harvey Girls **15** A Child Is Waiting, Meet Me in St Louis

garlic
botanical name: 13 Allium sativum
origin: 4 Asia **13** Mediterranean
charm against: 7 poverty, witches **13** whooping cough
use: 4 fish, fowl, meat **5** salad **10** vegetables **13** Italian dishes, salad dressing
varieties: 4 crow, hog's, wild **5** bear's, false, field, giant, grace, mouse, stag's, sweet **6** levant **7** serpent, society, Spanish, striped **8** daffodil, oriental **11** great-headed, round-headed **16** fragrant-flowered

Garm
origin: 12 Scandinavian
form: 8 watchdog
watches over: 3 Hel
location: 8 Niflheim

garment, garments 4 garb, gear, togs **5** dress, habit **6** attire, outfit **7** apparel, clothes, costume, raiment **8** clothing, vestment **10** habiliment

garner 4 reap **5** amass, hoard **6** gather, heap up **7** acquire, collect **8** assemble **10** accumulate

Garner, James
real name: 15 James Baumgarner
born: 8 Norman OK
roles: 8 Maverick, Sayonara **11** Jim Rockford **12** Bret Maverick, Hour of the Gun **13** Darby's Rangers, Rockford Files **14** Murphy's Romance, Victor Victoria **23** Support Your Local Sheriff **25** The Americanization of Emily

garnet
varieties: 6 syrope **9** almandite, demantoid, hessonite, rhodolite **12** grossularite
month: 7 January

garnish 4 deck, gild, trim **5** adorn, array **6** bedeck, doll up, set off **7** festoon, furbish, smarten **8** beautify, decorate, emblazon, ornament, spruce up, trimming **9** adornment, embellish, embroider **10** decoration **13** embellishment

garret 4 loft **5** attic

garrison 4 fort **5** guard **6** patrol, secure **7** battery, bivouac, brigade, platoon, station **8** division, regiment,

squadron **10** detachment, escadrille **13** fortification

garrulity 8 verbiage **9** loquacity, prosiness, verbosity, wordiness **13** talkativeness

garrulous 5 gabby, windy, wordy **6** chatty **7** gossipy, prating, verbose, voluble **8** babbling, chattery, effusive **9** prattling, talkative **10** loquacious

Garry Moore Show, The
cast: 9 Allen Funt, Denise Lor, John Byner, Ken Carson **11** Chuck McCann, Marion Lorne **12** Carol Burnett, Durward Kirby, Jackie Vernon, Pete Barbutti **13** Dorothy Loudon

Garson, Greer
born: 7 Ireland **10** County Down
roles: 10 Mrs Miniver (Oscar) **11** Madame Curie **12** Her Twelve Men **13** Mrs Parkington, Random Harvest **14** Goodbye Mr Chips **16** That Forsyte Woman **17** Pride and Prejudice **19** Sunrise at Campobello

gas 4 fuel, fume **5** vapor **6** petrol **7** essence

gascon 7 boaster, bragger, egotist **8** blowhard, braggart **9** swaggerer **11** braggadocio

gasconade 4 brag, crow **5** boast **7** bravado **8** boasting **11** braggadocio

gash 4 hack, rend, rent, slit, tear **5** carve, cleft, crack, lance, slash, slice, split, wound **6** cleave, incise, pierce **7** dissect, fissure, quarter **8** incision, lacerate

Gaskell, Elizabeth
author of: 4 Ruth **8** Cranford **10** Mary Barton **13** North and South **24** The Life of Charlotte Bronte

Gaslight
director: 11 George Cukor
cast: 10 Terry Moore **12** Charles Boyer **13** Dame May Whitty, Ingrid Bergman **14** Angela Lansbury **15** Halliwell Hobbes

Gasoline Alley
creator: 9 Bill Perry, Frank King **10** Dick Moores
character: 3 Eve **4** Adam, Hope **6** Clovia, Gideon, Nubbin **7** Chipper, Gabriel **10** Walt Wallet
wife: 14 Phyllis Blossom
children: 4 Judy **5** Corky **7** Skeezix
daughter-in-law: 9 Nina Clock
dog: 5 Punky

gasp 4 gulp, pant, puff **5** blurt **6** suck in, wheeze **10** vociferate

gastronome 7 epicure, gourmet **9** bon vivant

gastronomy 9 epicurism

gastropod, gasteropod 4 slug **5** cowry, snail, whelk **6** cowrie, limpet, nerite **7** abalone, mollusk **8** univalve

gate 3 tap **5** crowd, house, valve **6** por- tal, sluice, spigot **7** doorway

8 audience, hatchway **9** turnstile **10** attendance

gateau 4 cake **7** dessert

gatekeeper 5 guard **6** porter **7** St. Peter **8** watchman

Gates, Horatio
served in: 16 Revolutionary War **18** French and Indian War
battle: 6 Camden **8** Saratoga
defeated: 8 Burgoyne
defeated by: 10 Cornwallis

gateway 4 adit **5** entry **6** access, portal **7** doorway, opening **8** entrance, entryway **10** passageway

Gath 14 Philistine city

gather 4 fold, mass **5** amass, group, infer, learn, pleat, shirr, stack **6** assume, deduce, heap up, muster, pile up, pucker, ruffle **7** cluster, collect, convene, marshal, observe **8** assemble, conclude **9** stockpile **10** accumulate, congregate, understand **11** concentrate

gathering 3 mob **4** gang, pack **5** bunch, crowd, crush, drove, flock, horde, party, press **6** throng **7** company, meeting, roundup, turnout **8** assembly, conclave **9** concourse, multitude **10** assemblage, collection, conference, convention **11** aggregation, convergence, convocation **12** accumulation, congregation **13** concentration

gather together 4 herd **5** amass, hoard, rally **6** muster **7** collate, collect, compile, marshal, round up, sweep up **8** assemble, shepherd **9** aggregate, stockpile **10** accumulate, congregate

Gatling, Richard Jordan
nationality: 8 American
inventor of: 10 machine gun **16** steam-powered plow

gatophobia
fear of: 4 cats

gauche 5 inept **6** clumsy, oafish **7** awkward, boorish, ill-bred, uncouth **8** bungling, plebeian, tactless **9** inelegant, maladroit, tasteless, unrefined **10** blundering, uncultured, ungraceful, unmannerly, unpolished **11** proletarian **13** ungentlemanly

gaucherie 5 gaffe **7** blunder, faux pas **11** impropriety **12** indiscretion

Gaudeamus igitur 22 Let us therefore be joyful

gaudy 4 loud, sham **5** cheap, showy, vivid **6** flashy, flimsy, garish, tawdry, tinsel, vulgar **7** glaring, intense **8** colorful, dazzling, lustrous, striking **9** brilliant, sparkling, tasteless, worthless **10** bespangled, glittering **11** pretentious **12** ostentatious

gauge, gage 4 rate, size **5** guess, judge, meter **6** assess **7** adjudge, measure **8** appraise, estimate, evalu-

ate, standard **9** ascertain, calculate, criterion, yardstick **11** measurement
type: 4 ring **5** bevel

Gauguin, Paul Eugene Henri
born: 5 Paris **6** France
artwork: 9 Nevermore **12** The Tahitians **13** The White Horse **15** The Yellow Christ **18** Horsemen on the Beach **23** The Vision after the Sermon (Jacob Wrestling with the Angel) **25** Be in Love and You Will Be Happy **26** The Spirit of the Dead Watching **36** Where Do We Come From? Who Are We? Where Do We Go?
book: 6 Noa Noa

Gaul *see* **6** France

gaunt 4 bony, grim, lank, lean, slim, thin **5** bleak, lanky, spare **6** barren, meager, skinny, wasted **7** haggard, pinched, scraggy, scrawny, slender, spindly, starved **8** deserted, desolate, forsaken, raw-boned, skeletal, withered **9** emaciated, shriveled **10** cadaverous, forbidding **14** spindle-shanked

Gauss, Carl Friedrich
field: 7 physics **9** astronomy **11** mathematics
nationality: 6 German
worked in: 9 magnetism **11** electricity **12** number theory
named for him: 9 Gauss's Law

Gautier, Marguerite
character in: 7 Camille
author: 5 Dumas (fils)

Gautier, Theophile
author of: 6 La Peri **7** Giselle **8** Albertus **11** Young France **13** Emaux et Camees **16** Enamels and Cameos **20** Mademoiselle de Maupin, The Romance of the Mummy
doctrine: 14 Art for art's sake

gauzy 5 filmy, sheer **6** flimsy, sleazy **10** diaphanous **11** translucent, transparent

gave up 4 quit **5** ceded **7** dropped, forsook, yielded **8** forswore, resigned **9** abandoned, abdicated, forfeited, renounced **11** surrendered **12** discontinued, relinquished

Gawain
character in: 16 Arthurian romance
opponent: 11 Green Knight

gawk 4 gape, gaze, peer **10** rubberneck

gawky 6 clumsy, klutzy **7** awkward, lumpish **8** bungling, fumbling, lubberly, ungainly, unwieldy **9** all thumbs, graceless, ham-fisted, hamhanded, maladroit **10** blundering, ungraceful

gay 3 fun **4** airy, glad **5** happy, jolly, merry, showy, sunny, vivid **6** blithe, bright, cheery, elated, frisky, genial, jaunty, jocose, jovial, joyful, joyous, lively, social **7** buoyant, chipper, coltish, dashing, festive, gleeful, glowing, intense, jocular, playful, smiling, wag-

gish **8** animated, cheerful, colorful, exultant, gladsome, humorous, jubilant, lustrous, skittish, spirited, splendid, sportive, volatile **9** brilliant, convivial, frivolous, hilarious, rejoicing, sparkling, sprightly, sumptuous, vivacious **10** flamboyant, frolicsome, glittering, homosexual, insouciant, theatrical, variegated **12** effervescent, lighthearted, multicolored

Gay, John
author of dialogue/lyrics for: 15 The Beggar's Opera

Gay, Walter
character in: 12 Dombey and Son
author: 7 Dickens

gay blade 3 fop **4** beau **5** blade, dandy **7** playboy **8** cavalier **9** ladies' man **12** boulevardier, man-about-town

Gay Divorcee, The
director: 12 Mark Sandrich
cast: 10 Alice Brady, Erik Rhodes **11** Betty Grable, Fred Astaire **12** Ginger Rogers **19** Edward Everett Horton
song: 11 Continental, Night and Day

Gay-Lussac, Joseph
field: 7 physics **9** chemistry
nationality: 6 French
discovered: 24 law of combining gas volumes
invented: 10 hydrometer

Gaynor, Mitzi
real name: 20 Franceska Mitzi Gerber
husband: 8 Jack Bean
born: 9 Chicago IL
roles: 8 Les Girls **10** Golden Girl **12** Anything Goes, South Pacific **14** The Joker Is Wild **32** There's No Business Like Show Business

gaze 3 eye **4** gape, ogle, peek, peer, scan **5** glare, lower, stare, study, watch **6** behold, glance, glower, peruse, regard, survey **7** examine, inspect, observe, witness **8** look long, pore over, scrutiny **10** rubberneck, scrutinize **11** contemplate

gaze at 4 view **5** watch **6** behold, look at **7** stare at **8** look upon **11** contemplate

gazpacho 4 soup
ingredients: 6 onions **7** peppers **8** tomatoes **9** cucumbers

Gazza Ladra, La
also: 17 The Thieving Magpie
opera by: 7 Rossini

Ge *see* **4** Gaea

gear 3 cam, rig **4** duds, garb, togs **5** dress, tools **6** attire, outfit, tackle, things **7** apparel, clothes, rigging **8** clothing, cogwheel, flywheel, garments, material, property **9** apparatus, equipment, trappings **10** belongings, implements **11** accessories, instruments **12** contrivances **13** accouterments, paraphernalia

Geb
also: 3 Keb

origin: 8 Egyptian
god of: 5 earth
daughter: 4 Isis
son: 6 Osiris
sister: 3 Nut

Geer, Will
born: 11 Frankfort IN
roles: 7 Grandpa **10** The Waltons **11** In Cold Blood

Gehenna 4 hell

Gehrig, Lou (Henry Louis)
nickname: 9 Iron Horse
sport: 8 baseball
position: 9 first base
team: 14 New York Yankees

Geist 4 mind **6** spirit

gelatin 4 agar, glue **5** aspic, gelee, jelly **6** glutin, pectin **7** protein, sericin

gelatinize 3 set **4** jell **7** congeal, stiffen, thicken **9** coagulate

gelatinous 7 colloid, viscous **8** muculent **9** jelly-like

geld 5 alter **8** castrate **10** emasculate

gelid 3 icy **6** frigid, frozen **8** freezing

gem 4 dear, doll, rock **5** beaut, bijou, jewel, peach, prize **6** marvel, wonder **8** treasure
type: 4 jade, opal, ruby, sard **5** agate, amber, beryl, coral, pearl, topaz **6** garnet, pyrope, quartz, spinel, zircon **7** apatite, cat's-eye, citrine, diamond, emerald, jadeite, kunzite, olivine, peridot **8** amethyst, corundum, feldspar, hematite, lazurite, nephrite, sapphire, steatite, sunstone **9** almandite, amazonite, carnelian, demantoid, enstatite, fibrolite, malachite, moonstone, morganite, rhodolite, scapolite, spodumene, tiger's-eye, turquoise **10** aquamarine, bloodstone, chalcedony, hessionite, rose quartz, tourmaline **11** alexandrite, chrysoberyl, chrysocolla, chrysoprase, lapis lazuli, rock crystal, topaz quartz **12** grossularite

Gemini
symbol: 5 twins
planet: 7 Mercury
rules: 14 communications
born: 3 May **4** June
twins: 6 Castor, Pollux

Gemini Contenders, The
author: 12 Robert Ludlum

Gem State
nickname of: 5 Idaho

gemutlich 4 easy **9** agreeable, congenial, simpatico **11** comfortable

gendarme 9 policeman

gender 3 sex **4** kind, male, sort, type **5** class **6** female, neuter **8** feminine **9** masculine

genealogy 4 line **5** birth, house, stock **7** lineage **8** ancestry, pedigree **9** parentage **10** derivation, extraction

Gene Autry Show, The
cast: 10 Pat Buttram

horse: 8 Champion
theme song: 20 Back in the Saddle Again

general 5 basic, broad, usual, vague **6** common, normal, public, wonted **7** blanket, current, generic, inexact, natural, overall, popular, regular, typical **8** everyday, frequent, habitual, ordinary, pandemic, sweeping **9** customary, extensive, imprecise, panoramic, prevalent, universal, worldwide **10** accustomed, collective, ecumenical, prevailing, widespread **11** unspecified **12** conventional, nonexclusive, nontechnical **13** comprehensive, miscellaneous

General Electric Theater
host: 12 Ronald Reagan

general idea 4 gist **5** drift, tenor **6** effect, import **7** purport **10** impression **11** implication

generality 6 cliche, truism **9** platitude **12** universality **14** collectiveness **17** miscellaneousness **18** indiscriminateness

generalization 3 law **5** axion **7** bromide **9** inference, statement

generalize 5 infer, judge **8** conclude

generally 5 often **6** always, mainly, mostly **7** as a rule, chiefly, largely, usually **9** currently, typically **10** frequently, habitually, ordinarily, repeatedly **11** extensively, principally, universally

general/military leader
American:
Revolutionary War: 3 (Light Horse Harry) Lee **5** Allen, Barry, Gates, Jones, Wayne **6** Arnold, Greene, Marion, Morgan **10** Washington
War of 1812: 4 Hull **5** Perry, Scott **7** Decatur
Mexican War: 5 Scott **6** Kearny
Civil War: 3 Lee **5** Early, Grant, Meade **6** Thomas, (JEB) Stuart **7** Forrest, Pickett, Sherman, (Stonewall) Jackson **8** Farragut, Sheridan **9** McClellan **10** Beauregard, Longstreet
Indian Wars: 6 Custer **7** Houston **10** Crazy Horse
WWI: 4 Sims **8** Mitchell, Pershing
WWII: 4 King **5** Clark **6** Arnold, Halsey, Nimitz, Patton **7** Bradley, Merrill **8** Marshall, Stilwell **9** Chennault, Doolittle, MacArthur **10** Eisenhower, Wainwright
Korean War: 5 Clark **9** MacArthur
Vietnam War: 6 Abrams **12** Westmoreland
Gulf War: 6 Powell **11** Schwarzkopf
British: 4 Byng, Haig, Howe, Slim **5** Wolfe **6** French, Gordon, Harris, Nelson, Wavell **7** Allenby, Clinton, Dowding, Wingate **8** Braddock, Burgoyne, Cromwell, Jellicoe, Lawrence

9 Alexander, Kitchener **10** Cornwallis, Montgomery, Wellington **11** Marlborough, Mountbatten
Carthagenian: 8 Hannibal **13** Hamilcar Barca
French: 3 Ney **4** Foch **5** Murat **6** Giraud, Joffre, Petain, Roland **7** Nivelle **8** De Gaulle, Montcalm, Napoleon **9** Lafayette **10** Bernadotte
German: 5 Kluck **6** Moltke, Paulus, Rommel, Scheer **7** Blucher, Goering, Tirpitz **8** Bismarck, Goebbels, Guderian **9** Rundstedt **10** Falkenhayn, Hindenburg, Kesselring, Ludendorff, Schlieffen **17** Frederick the Great
Israeli: 5 Dayan
Japanese: 10 Tojo Hideki **15** Yamamoto Isoroku
Macedonian: 7 Ptolemy **8** Philip II **9** Alexander (the Great)
Norman: 7 William (the Conqueror)
Roman: 5 Sulla **6** Brutus, Pompey, Seneca, Trajan **7** Crassus, Hadrian, Lepidus **8** Gracchus, Octavian (Caesar Augustus), Tiberius **9** Vespasian **10** Flamininus, Mark Antony **11** Gaius Marius **12** Julius Caesar **15** Cassius Longinus, Scipio Africanus **18** Tarquinius Superbus
Russian: 6 Zhukov **7** Kutuzov, Voronov **8** Brusilov, Kerensky, Kornilov, Samsonov **9** Bagration **10** Timoshenko, Vasilevsky

generate 4 bear, coin, form, make, sire **5** beget, breed, cause, frame, spawn, yield **6** create, evolve, father, induce, invent **7** develop, fashion, produce **8** contrive, engender, fructify, occasion **9** construct, fabricate, fecundate, fertilize, institute, originate, procreate, propagate, reproduce **10** effectuate, impregnate **11** proliferate

generation 3 kin **4** clan, line, race **5** breed, house, issue, stock, tribe **6** family, growth, strain **7** genesis, lineage, progeny **8** breeding, creation **9** begetting, causation, evolution, formation, offspring **10** production **11** development, engendering, origination, procreation, propagation **12** impregnation, reproduction **13** fertilization, proliferation

generic 6 common **7** general **8** sweeping **9** universal **10** collective **11** generalized, unspecified **12** nonexclusive **13** comprehensive **14** nonrestrictive

generosity 6 bounty **7** charity **8** altruism, courtesy, kindness, largesse **9** abundance, nobleness **10** liberality **11** benevolence, hospitality, magnanimity

generous 5 ample, large, lofty, noble **6** humane, lavish **7** copious, liberal **8** abundant, effusive, obliging, princely, prodigal **9** bounteous, bountiful, honorable, plenteous, plentiful, plethoric, unselfish, unstinted **10** altruistic, beneficent, benevolent, bighearted, charitable, freehanded, free-giving, high-minded, hospitable, munificent, open-handed, ungrudging, unstinting **11** considerate, extravagant, magnanimous, overflowing **12** humanitarian, largehearted, unrestricted **13** accommodating, philanthropic

genesis 4 rise, root **5** birth **6** origin **8** creation **9** begetting, beginning, inception **10** generation **11** engendering **12** commencement

geneticist
American: 5 Temin **6** Morgan, Muller

genetics
science of: 8 heredity
researcher: 6 Mendel

Genghis Khan
also: 11 Jenghiz Khan
name means: 14 universal ruler
position: 13 Mongol emperor
defeated: 6 Russia **10** Chin empire
occupied: 6 Peking

genial 3 gay **4** glad, kind, warm **5** civil, happy, jolly, merry, sunny **6** bright, cheery, hearty, jaunty, jocund, jovial, joyful, joyous, kindly, lively, social **7** affable, amiable, chipper, cordial, festive **8** cheerful, friendly, gracious, mirthful, pleasant, sociable **9** agreeable, congenial, convivial, courteous, expansive, sparkling, vivacious **10** neighborly **12** lighthearted **13** companionable

geniality 10 affability, cordiality **11** sociability **12** conviviality, friendliness **13** expansiveness

genius 3 ace, wit **4** bent, gift, mind, whiz **5** brain, flair, knack **6** expert, master, wisdom **7** faculty, insight, prodigy **8** aptitude, judgment, penchant, sagacity, wizardry **9** ingenuity, intuition, invention **10** mastermind, perception, proclivity, propensity **11** imagination, percipience **12** intelligence, predilection **13** understanding

Genius, The
author: 15 Theodore Dreiser

genius loci 16 guardian of a place

genre 4 kind, sort, type **5** breed, class, genus, group, order, style **6** school **7** fashion, species, variety **8** category, division **11** description **14** classification

genteel 4 tony **5** civil, elite, ritzy, swank, swell **6** modish, poised, polite, urbane **7** courtly, elegant, high-hat, refined, stylish **8** cultured, decorous, ladylike, mannerly, polished, well-bred **9** courteous, high-class, high-toned, patrician **10** cultivated, well-spoken **11** fashionable, gentlemanly, highfalutin, over-refined, pretentious **12** aristocratic, silk-stocking, thoroughbred

gentian 8 Gentiana
varieties: 5 blind, green, horse **6** alpine, bottle, closed, Sierra, yellow

7 crested, fringed, prairie, spurred **8** Catesby's, soapwort, stemless **9** Mendocino **10** pine barren

gentil 4 kind **5** noble **6** gentle

gentile
Yiddish: 3 goy
man: 7 shegetz
woman: 6 shiksa

gentility 6 polish **7** decorum, suavity **8** breeding, chivalry, civility, courtesy, urbanity **9** gallantry, propriety, punctilio **10** refinement **11** cultivation, savoir-faire **12** mannerliness

gentle 3 low **4** calm, easy, kind, meek, mild, soft, tame **5** balmy, bland, light, quiet **6** benign, broken, docile, kindly, placid, serene, slight, smooth, tender **7** lenient, pacific, subdued **8** harmless, merciful, moderate, peaceful, tolerant, tranquil **9** indulgent, temperate, tractable **10** manageable, thoughtful, untroubled **11** considerate, sympathetic **12** domesticated **13** compassionate, tenderhearted
French: 6 gentil

gentleman 3 don, guy, man, one **4** chap, gent **5** swell **6** fellow, person, squire **7** esquire, hidalgo **8** cavalier **9** caballero, chevalier, patrician **10** aristocrat, individual

Gentleman Jim
nickname of: 12 James Corbett

gentlemanly 6 polite **7** courtly, gallant, refined **8** cultured, decorous, mannerly, polished, well-bred **9** courteous, dignified **10** cultivated

Gentleman's Agreement
director: 9 Elia Kazan
based on novel by: 12 Laura Z Hobson
cast: 10 Anne Revere **11** Celeste Holm, Gregory Peck **12** John Garfield **14** Dorothy McGuire
Oscar for: 7 picture **17** supporting actress (Holm)

Gentlemen Prefer Blondes
author: 9 Anita Loos

gentleness 8 calmness, docility, mildness, serenity, tameness **10** compassion, tenderness **12** mercifulness, peacefulness, tractability

gentle wind 4 waft **6** breath, breeze, zephyr

gently 6 easily, kindly, meekly, mildly, softly, tamely **7** amiably, lightly **8** benignly, placidly, smoothly, tenderly **9** gradually **10** delicately, moderately, pleasantly, soothingly **15** compassionately, sympathetically

gentry 5 elite **7** society **8** nobility **10** blue bloods, gentlefolk **11** aristocracy, aristocrats

genuflect 4 bend **6** kowtow

genuine 4 open, pure, real, true **5** frank, naive, plain, solid **6** actual, candid, hon- est, proven, simple **7** art-

less, earnest, natural, sincere **8** bona fide, sterling, true-blue **9** authentic, guileless, heartfelt, ingenuous, simon-pure, unalloyed, veritable **10** legitimate, unaffected **13** unadulterated **15** straightforward, unsophisticated

genuineness 7 honesty **9** frankness, sincerity **10** candidness, simplicity **11** artlessness **13** guilelessness **14** unaffectedness **19** straightforwardness

genus 4 kind, sort, type **5** class, group **7** variety **8** category, division **14** classification

geologist
British: 4 Hall
German: 6 Werner
Scottish: 6 Hutton

geoponics 7 tillage **8** agronomy **9** husbandry **10** agronomics **11** agriculture, cultivation

George Burns and Gracie Allen Show, The
character: 9 Mr Beasley (Mailman) **11** Harry Morton **13** Blanche Morton
theme song: 8 Love Nest

Georgetown
capital of: 6 Guyana

Georgia (former Soviet Union)
capital/largest city: 7 Tbilisi
others: 6 Batumi **7** Kutaisi, Rustavi, Sukhumi
division: 7 Ossetia **8** Abkhazia, Adzharia
head of state: 9 president
government: 8 republic
monetary unit: 5 ruble
mountain: 8 Caucasus
river: 4 Kura **5** Rioni
sea: 5 Black
people: 5 Azeri **7** Russian **8** Armenian, Georgian, Ossetian **9** Abkhazian
language: 8 Georgian
religion 14 Georgian Church **15** Russian Orthodox

Georgia (US)
abbreviation: 2 GA
nickname: 5 Peach **7** Cracker **21** Empire State of the South
capital/largest city: 7 Atlanta
others: 4 Rome **5** Jesup, Macon **6** Albany, Athens, Dalton, Plains, Sparta **7** Augusta, Conyers, Cordele, Decatur, Griffen, Vidalia **8** Columbus, LaGrange, Marietta, Moultrie, Savannah, Valdosta, Waycross **9** Brunswick **11** College Park, Gainesville, Thomasville **13** Andersonville
college: 4 Tift **5** Clark, Emory, Paine **6** Mercer **7** Atlanta, Spelman **8** Wesleyan **9** Morehouse **10** Agnes Scott **11** Georgia Tech
explorer: 15 James Oglethorpe
feature: 16 Little White House
amusement park: 19 Six Flags Over Georgia
national cemetery: 13 Anderson-

ville
national monument: 8 Ocmulgee **11** Fort Pulaski **13** Fort Frederica
tribe: 5 Creek, Guale, Yuchi **6** Chiaha, Oconee, Uchean **7** Yamasee **8** Hitchiti
people: 6 Ty Cobb **7** cracker **10** Bobby Jones **11** Juliette Low **15** Erskine Caldwell **16** Margaret Mitchell **18** Joel Chandler Harris
island: 3 Sea **6** Jekyll, Sapelo **7** Ossabaw **10** Cumberland
lake: 6 Lanier, Martin **7** Harding, Nottely **8** Bankhead, Hartwell, Sinclair
land rank: 11 twenty-first
mountain: 5 Stone **7** Lookout **8** Kennesaw **9** Blue Ridge **11** Alleghenies **13** High Point Peak
   highest point: 17 Brasstown Bald Peak
physical feature:
   sea: 8 Atlantic
   springs: 4 Warm
   swamp: 10 Okefenokee
president: 11 Jimmy Carter
river: 3 Pea **5** Flint **6** Etowah, Oconee, Pigeon **7** Conecuh, Satilla, St Mary's, Tugaloo **8** Altamaha, Ocmulgee, Ogeechee, Savannah, Suwannee **9** Chattooga **13** Chattahoochie
state admission: 6 fourth
state bird: 13 brown thrasher
state fish: 14 largemouth bass
state flower: 12 Cherokee rose
state motto: 6 Wisdom **20** Justice and Moderation
state song: 7 Georgia
state tree: 7 live oak
Georgia Peach
   nickname of: 6 Ty Cobb
Georgics, The
   author: 6 Vergil, Virgil
Geraint
   character in: 16 Arthurian romance
   wife: 4 Enid
geranium 11 Pelargonium
   varieties: 3 ivy **4** fish, lime, mint, pine, rock, rose, show, wild **5** apple, fancy, house, lemon, regal, zonal **6** almond, alpine, cactus, jungle, nutmeg, orange **7** apricot, bedding, coconut, feather, hanging, knotted, polecat **8** crowfoot, fern-leaf, horsehoe **9** beefsteak, oak-leaved **10** California, gooseberry, peppermint, strawberry, sweetheart, village-oak **11** grape-leaved, herb-scented, maple-leaved, rose-scented **12** silverleaved, southernwood, sweet-scented **13** black-flowered, pansy-flowered, pheasant's-foot **14** Lady Washington, little-leaf rose **15** mint-scented rose **16** Martha Washington **17** English finger-bowl
Gerber, Franceska Mitzi
   real name of: 11 Mitzi Gaynor
Gerd, Gerda

origin: 12 Scandinavian
husband: 4 Frey **5** Freyr
Gere, Richard
   roles: 5 Yanks **10** Breathless, Cotton Club **11** Pretty Woman **12** Days of Heaven **14** American Gigolo **19** Looking for Mr Goodbar **22** An Officer and a Gentleman
   former wife: 13 Cindy Crawford
   cause 5 Tibet
germ 3 bud, bug, egg **4** ovum, root, seed **5** ovule, spark, spore, virus **6** embryo, origin, source, sprout **7** microbe, nucleus, seed bud **8** bacillus, offshoot, rudiment **9** bacterium, beginning **12** fountainhead **13** microorganism
German 3 Hun **4** balt, Goth **5** boche, heine, jerry, kraut, Saxon **6** Teuton **7** tedesco **8** Prussian, Teutonic **9** deutscher
   article: 3 das, dem, den, der, des, die, ein **4** eine, eins
   empire: 5 reich
   pronoun: 3 ich, mir, sie, uns
   man: 4 herr
   storm and stress: 13 sturm und drang
   thank you: 5 danke **10** danke schon
   toast: 6 prosit **10** gesundheit
   woman: 4 frau **8** fraulein
German-Dutch
   language family: 12 Indo-European
   branch: 8 Germanic
   group: 15 Western Germanic
   language: 9 Low German **10** High German
germane 3 apt, fit **6** native, proper **7** apropos, fitting, related **8** material, relative, relevant, suitable **9** connected, intrinsic, pertinent **10** applicable **11** appropriate **12** appertaining
germaneness 9 relevance **10** pertinence **13** applicability **15** appropriateness
Germanic
   language family: 12 Indo-European
   group: 6 Gothic **15** Western Germanic
Germanic Mythology
   chief of gods: 5 Wotan
     corresponds to Scandinavian: 4 Odin
   dwarf: 15 Rumpelstiltskin
   dwarves: 8 Niblungs **9** Nibelungs
   emperor: 15 Dietrich von Bern
   epic: 14 Nibelungenlied
   goddess of clouds/sky/marriage: 3 Fri **5** Frigg, Frija **6** Frigga
   goddess of death/fertility: 7 Berchta, Perchta
   goddess of love/ beauty/fecundity: 5 Freya
   goddess of moon/ witch: 5 Holle
   god of thunder: 5 Donar
   god of winter sports: 4 Ullr **5** Uller
   hero: 6 Sigurd **9** Siegfried

   heroine: 6 Gudrun, Kudrun **7** Guthrun **8** Brunhild **9** Kriemhild
   king: 7 Siggeir
   king of dwarves: 8 Alberich
   knight of the holy grail: 9 Lohengrin
   magic cloak: 9 Tarnkappe
   maidens: 9 Valkyries
   nature spirit: 7 Eriking
   nymph: 7 Lorelei, Lurelei
   water spirit: 3 Nix
German is spoken here
   German: 25 hier wird Deutsch gesprochen
German literary movement (18th cent) 13 sturm und drang
Germany (see also *Germany, East* and *Germany, West*)
   capital: 6 Berlin
   government leader: 10 chancellor, Helmut Kohl
   monetary unit: 12 Deutsche mark
   people: 3 Hun **4** Slav, Sorb, Wend **5** Saxon
     artist: 4 Marc **5** Durer **7** Barlach, Cranach, Gropius, Holbein **9** Grunewald **14** Mies van der Rohe
     author: 4 Mann, Marx **5** Grass **6** Brecht, Elsner, Goethe **7** Johnson, Lessing **8** Hochhuth
     composer: 4 Bach **5** Weill **6** Brahms, Handel, Wagner **7** Strauss **8** Schumann **9** Beethoven, Hindemith **11** Mendelssohn
     conductor: 5 Henze **6** Walter **9** Klemperer **11** Furtwangler, Stockhausen
     historical leader: 6 Hitler, Kaiser **8** Bismarck **10** Barbarossa
     Prussian noble: 6 Junker
     religious leader: 6 Luther
   language: 6 German **10** High German **11** Hochdeutsch
   religion: 8 Lutheran **10** Protestant **13** Roman Catholic **17** Evangelical Church
   food:
     bread: 12 pumpernickel
     dish: 9 lebkuchen
     dumpling: 6 knodel
     frankfurter: 15 wiener wurstchen
     fruit bread: 7 stollen
     ham: 11 Westphalian
     potato salad: 14 kartoffelsalat
     pot roast: 11 sauerbraten
     sausage: 5 wurst **9** blutwurst, bratwurst **10** brockwurst, knackwurst, leberwurst
     sole: 8 seezunge
Germany, East (former) (see also *Germany*)
   capital/largest city: 10 East Berlin
   others: 4 Jena **5** Halle, Waren **6** Erfurt, Weimar **7** Cottbus, Dresden, Leipzig, Meissen, Potsdam, Rostock, Schwedt, Wannsee, Zwickau **9** Frankfurt, Magdeburg **10** Angermunde, Warnemunde, Wittenberg **11** Neustrelitz **13** Karl-Marx-Stadt

(Chemnitz)
school: 8 Humboldt
division: 6 Saxony **9** Thuringia **11** Brandenburg, Mecklenburg **12** Saxony-Anhalt
government: 11 Volkskammer (Peoples' Chamber)
monetary unit: 4 mark **7** Ostmark, pfennig
lake: 6 Muritz
mountain: 3 Ore **4** Harz **10** Erzgebirge
highest point: 11 Fichtelberg
river: 4 Elbe, Oder **5** Havel, Saale, Spree **6** Neisse, Warnow
sea: 6 Baltic
physical feature:
　forest: 10 Thuringian
　place: 10 Berlin Wall **17** Checkpoint Charlie
　castle: 9 Sans Souci
　church: 8 St Thomas **12** Thomaskirche
　city center: 13 Karl Marx Platz **14** Alexanderplatz, Neubrandenberg
　comic opera: 12 Komische Oper
　gate: 11 Brandenburg
　museum: 7 Zwinger **8** Pergamon **10** Goethe Haus
　opera house: 18 Deutsche Staatsoper
feature:
　china: 7 Dresden
　fair: 7 Leipzig
　theater company: 16 Berliner Ensemble
Germany, West (former) (see also *Germany*)
capital: 4 Bonn
largest city: 10 West Berlin
others: 4 Kiel **5** Essen, Mainz, Trier **6** Aachen, Bochum, Bremen, Kassel, Lubeck, Minden, Munden, Munich **7** Cologne, Hamburg, Hanover, Krefeld, Munster **8** Augsburg, Biberach, Dortmund, Duisberg, Duisburg, Freiburg, Mannheim, Solingen **9** Darmstadt, Karlsruhe, Nuremberg, Oldenburg, Stuttgart, Wiesbaden, Wuppertal **10** Dusseldorf, Heidelberg, Steingamen **11** Saarbrucken **12** Oberammergau **13** Gelsenkirchen **15** Frankfurt am Main **16** Mulheim an der Ruhr
school: 4 Bonn **7** Hamburg **10** Heidelberg **16** Ludwig- Maximilian
division: 4 Saar **5** Baden, Hesse **6** Bremen **7** Bavaria **9** Rhineland **10** Palatinate, Westphalia **11** Lower Saxony, Wurttemberg **17** Schleswig-Holstein
head of government: 10 chancellor
monetary unit: 4 mark **7** pfennig **12** Deutsche mark
island: 11 East Frisian **12** North Frisian
lake: 9 Constance **11** Inner Alster, Outer Alster
mountain: 4 Harz **8** Feldberg

11 Black Forest **12** Bavarian Alps
highest point: 9 Zugspitze
river: 3 Ems **4** Elbe, Main, Nahe, Ruhr, Saar, Wese **5** Donau, Rhine, Weser **6** Danube, Neckar **7** Moselle, Pegnitz
sea: 5 North **6** Baltic
physical feature:
　canal: 4 Kiel **10** Mittelland
　forest: 5 Black **7** Bohemia **9** Teu Toburg
　place: 17 Checkpoint Charlie
　botanical garden: 18 Pflantzen und Blumen
　boulevard: 14 Kurfurstendamm
　church: 12 Frauenkirche (Cathedral of Our Lady) **13** Kaiser Wilhelm **16** Gadachtniskirche
　city center: 12 Marienplatz
　fortress: 9 Marksburg
　fountain: 14 Schoner Brunnen
　garden: 10 Englischer
　hall: 9 Beethoven
　museum: 8 Residenz **9** Durer Haus **12** Schatzkammer **14** Alte Pinakothek
　opera house: 18 Deutsches Opern Haus
　park/zoo: 18 Hagenbecks Tierpark
　residential district: 11 Hansa Vierte **12** Hanse Viertel
　resort (on Baltic): 10 Travemunde
　theater: 9 Cuvillies
feature:
　beer cellar: 11 bierkellern
　beer garden: 10 biergarten
　beer hall: 10 bierhallen
　beer room: 10 bierstuben
　cars: 3 BMW **4** Opel **7** Porsche **10** Volkswagen **12** Mercedes-Benz
　children: 6 kinder
　city hall: 5 Romer **7** Rathaus
　festival: 11 Oktoberfest
　folk songs: 11 volkslieder
　kitchen: 5 kuche
　old city: 8 Altstadt
　pre-Lent carnival: 8 Fasching
　secondary school: 9 gymnasium
　states: 6 lander
　wine street: 11 Weinstrasse
germicide 11 bactericide **12** disinfectant
Germinal
　author: 9 Emile Zola
germinate 3 bud **4** blow, open **5** bloom, shoot **6** flower, push up, sprout **7** blos- som, burgeon, develop **8** generate, spring up, vegetate
germination 9 sprouting **11** propagation
Gershom
　father: 5 Moses
　mother: 8 Zipporah
　brother: 12 Eliezar
Gershwin, George
　born: 10 Brooklyn NY
　partner/lyricist: 11 Ira Gershwin
　composer of: 9 Funny Face **11** Of

Thee I Sing **12** Porgy and Bess **13** Cuban Overture **14** Rhapsody in Blue **15** Strike Up the Band **17** An American in Paris
Gertrude
　character in: 6 Hamlet
　author: 11 Shakespeare
　husband: 8 Claudius
　widow of: 6 Hamlet
Gervin, George
　nickname: 6 Iceman
　sport: 10 basketball
　team: 15 San Antonio Spurs
Gesta Romanorum
　author: 7 unknown
gestation 9 evolution, pregnancy **10** epigenesis, generation, incubation, maturation **11** development, propagation
gesticulate 3 nod **4** wink **5** nudge, shrug **6** beckon, motion, signal **8** indicate **9** pantomime
gesture 3 nod **4** sign, wave, wink **5** nudge, shrug, touch **6** beckon, motion, signal **8** courtesy, dumb show, flourish, high sign **9** formality, pantomime **13** demonstration
get 3 bag, fix, net, wax, win **4** beat, coax, earn, gain, grab, grip, grow, have, hear, move, reap, sway, take, turn **5** annoy, catch, fetch, glean, grasp, learn, reach, seize, sense, upset **6** arrive, attain, baffle, become, collar, come by, come to, enlist, entrap, fathom, follow, induce, obtain, pick up, pocket, prompt, puzzle, secure, snatch, suborn, take in, turn to **7** achieve, acquire, capture, confuse, contact, dispose, ensnare, go after, incline, inherit, mystify, perplex, prepare, procure, realize, receive, wheedle, win over **8** bewilder, confound, contract, irritate, perceive, persuade **9** influence, transport **10** comprehend, disconcert, predispose, understand
get a kick out of 4 like **5** eat up, enjoy, fancy, savor **6** relish **10** appreciate
getaway 6 escape, exodus, flight **10** decampment
get done 2 do **6** finish **8** complete **10** accomplish
get even 6 avenge **7** counter, hit back, pay back, revenge **9** retaliate
Gethsemane 6 garden
get into 3 don **5** enter, put on
get in touch with 5 reach **7** contact
get lost 4 scat, shoo **5** be off, leave, scram **6** beat it, begone, depart, go away **7** vamoose
get one's dander up 4 gall, rile **5** anger **6** enrage, madden, nettle, ruffle **7** incense, inflame, outrage **9** infuriate
get out of bed 4 rise **5** arise **12** rise and shine
get rid of 4 drop, dump, junk, shed **5**

get rid of 4 drop, dump, junk, shed **5** ditch, scrap **6** banish, cut out, delete, remove, unload **7** abolish, discard, weed out **8** jettison, stamp out, throw out **9** eliminate, eradicate **10** annihilate **11** exterminate

Get Smart
character: 5 Hymie (CONTROL robot) **7** Agent 99, Carlson, Starker **8** Larrabee, The Chief (Thaddeus) **12** Maxwell Smart (Agent 86) **15** Conrad Siegfried
cast: 8 Don Adams **9** King Moody **10** Stacy Keach **11** Dave Ketchum, Dick Gautier, Edward Platt **12** Bernie Kopell **13** Barbara Feldon **14** Robert Karvelas
Max worked for: 7 CONTROL
foe: 4 KAOS

get the better of 4 foil, rout **5** crush, quell **6** baffle, defeat, thwart **7** conquer **8** confound, overcome **9** frustrate, overthrow

get the upper hand of 5 quell **6** master **7** conquer **8** dominate, overcome, surmount

get the worst of 4 fail, fall, lose

Getting Even
author: 10 Woody Allen

get to 5 reach **8** approach

get-together 2 do **3** bee **4** meet **5** agree, party, visit **6** affair, gather, hobnob **7** meeting **8** assemble, assembly **9** gathering

getup 3 rig **6** attire, outfit **7** costume **8** disguise, ensemble

get up 4 find, rise **5** arise, rouse, stand **8** assemble

get used to 5 adapt, inure **6** adjust **8** accustom **9** acclimate, habituate

gewgaws 7 baubles, doodads, trifles **8** trinkets **9** bric-a-brac, gimcracks, kickshaws, ornaments **11** knickknacks

Ghana
other name: 9 Gold Coast
capital/largest city: 5 Accra, Akkra
others: 3 Oda **4** Axim, Fian, Keta, Tala, Tema **5** Bawku, Enchi, Lawra, Legon, Sampa, Yapei **6** Dunkwa, Karaga, Kpandu, Kumasi, Nsawam, Obuasi, Swedru, Tamale, Tarkwa, Wasipe **7** Antubia, Damongo, Mampong, Prestea, Sekondi, Sunyani, Winneba **8** Akosombo, Kintampo, Takoradi **9** Cape Coast **15** Sekondi-Takoradi
school: 6 Kumasi **9** Cape Coast
monetary unit: 4 cedi **5** ackey
lake: 5 Volta **8** Bosumtwi
mountain: 12 Akwapim Hills
highest point: 8 Afadjato
river: 3 Oti, Pra **4** Daka, Tano **5** Afram, Volta **7** Ankobra, Kulpawn **10** Black Volta, White Volta
sea: 8 Atlantic
physical feature:
  gulf: 6 Guinea

people: 2 Ga **3** Ewe **4** Akan, Akim, Akra, Aksa **5** Ahafo, Brong, Inkra **7** Akwapim, Ashanti, Dagomba **8** Mamprusi **11** Mole-Dagbani
language: 2 Ga **3** Ewe, Gur, Kwa, Twi **5** Fanti, Hausa **7** Dagomba, English
religion: 5 Islam **7** animism **13** Roman Catholic
feature:
  castle: 14 Christiansborg
  dam: 8 Akosombo
  national dress: 5 kente

ghastly 3 wan **4** grim, ugly **5** ashen, pasty, weird **6** dismal, glassy, grisly, horrid, odious, pallid **7** fearful, ghostly, haggard, hideous, uncanny **8** blanched, dreadful, gruesome, horrible, shocking, spectral, terrible **9** appalling, colorless, deathlike, frightful, ghostlike, loathsome, repellent, repulsive, revolting **10** cadaverous, corpselike, forbidding, horrendous, lackluster, terrifying

Ghiberti, Lorenzo
born: 5 Italy **8** Florence
artwork: 9 St Matthew, St Stephen **15** Gates of Paradise (baptistry doors) **16** St John the Baptist **19** The Sacrifice of Isaac

ghost 4 hint **5** demon, shade, spook, trace **6** goblin, shadow, sprite, wraith **7** banshee, chimera, phantom, specter **8** phantasm **9** hobgoblin, phantasma, semblance **10** apparition, suggestion **12** Doppelganger **13** manifestation **15** materialization

Ghost and Mrs Muir, The
character: 11 Candice Muir, Martha Grant **12** Jonathan Muir **13** Claymore Gregg **14** Mrs Carolyn Muir **18** Captain Daniel Gregg
TV cast: 8 Reta Shaw **9** Hope Lange **13** Edward Mulhare **14** Harlen Carraher, Kellie Flanagan **19** Charles Nelson Reilly
setting: 11 Gull Cottage
director: 17 Joseph L Mankiewicz
movie cast: 8 Edna Best **11** Gene Tierney, Rex Harrison **13** George Sanders

Ghostbusters
director: 11 Ivan Reitman
screenplay: 10 Dan Aykroyd **11** Harold Ramis
cast: 10 Bill Murray, Dan Aykroyd **11** Harold Ramis **15** Sigourney Weaver

ghostly 4 pale **5** eerie, weird **6** spooky, unreal **7** ghastly, phantom, shadowy, uncanny **8** illusive, spectral **9** unearthly **10** phantasmal, wraithlike **11** phantomlike **12** supernatural

ghostly double
German: 12 Doppelganger

Ghosts
author: 11 Henrik Ibsen
character: 7 Manders **12** Oswald

Alving **14** Jacob Engstrand, Mrs Helen Alving **15** Regina Engstrand

ghoulish 5 eerie, scary, weird **7** demonic, hellish, macabre, ogreish, satanic **8** diabolic, fiendish, gruesome, infernal, sinister **9** monstrous **10** horrifying, zombielike **11** hair-raising, necrophilic

Giacometti, Alberto
born: 11 Switzerland **12** Stampa-Tessin
artwork: 3 Dog **7** The Cage **8** Caroline **10** City Square **11** Head of Diego, Man Pointing **14** Reclining Woman **17** The Palace at Four Am **19** Hands Holding the Void

Gianni Schicchi
opera by: 7 Puccini
character: 11 Buoso Donati

giant 3 big **4** huge **5** titan **7** Goliath, spanker, thumper, whopper **8** behemoth, colossus, strapper **9** Gargantua **14** Brobdingnagian

Giant
director: 13 George Stevens
author: 10 Edna Ferber
cast: 9 James Dean **10** Chill Wills, Rock Hudson **11** Jane Withers **12** Carroll Baker **15** Elizabeth Taylor
setting: 5 Texas
Oscar for: 8 director

Giant see **8** Gigantes

giant people 6 Anakim

Giants in the Earth
author: 9 O E Rolvaag
character: 3 Ole **5** Beret **8** Per Hanea **9** Anna Marie **12** Hans Kristian **15** Peder Victorious

gibber 3 gab **4** blab **5** prate **6** babble, gabble, jabber **7** blabber, blather, chatter, prattle **8** chitchat

gibberish 4 blab, bosh **6** babble, drivel, gabble **7** blather, twaddle **8** nonsense **10** balderdash, double-talk, flapdoodle, hocus-pocus, mumbo-jumbo **12** gobbledegook

Gibbon, Edward
author of: 33 The (History of the) Decline and Fall of the Roman Empire

gibbous 6 convex, curved, humped **7** bulging, rounded, swollen **8** swelling **10** humpbacked, protuberant

Gibbs family
characters in: 7 Our Town
member: 6 George **7** Rebecca
author: 6 Wilder

gibe, jibe 3 rag **4** jeer, mock, quip, razz, twit **5** chaff, flout, knock, toast, scoff, sneer, taunt **6** deride, needle, rail at **7** mockery, poke fun, sarcasm **8** brickbat, derision, ridicule, taunting **9** criticism, wisecrack

Gibraltar
other name: 11 rock of Tarik **13** Djebel al-Tarik **15** rock of Gibraltar

largest city: 9 Gibraltar
government: 18 British crown colony
head of government: 15 governor
general
mountain: 6 Misery
sea: 13 Mediterranean
physical feature:
bay: 5 Ceuta, Rosia, Sandy **6** Ca-
tlan **9** Algeciras
cliffs: 17 Pillars of Hercules
people: 6 Jewish **7** British, Maltese,
Spanish **8** Italians **10** Portuguese
language: 7 English, Spanish
feature: 12 King's Bastion
gardens: 7 Alameda **11** Barbary
apes

Gibson, Mel
roles: 6 Mad Max **9** Gallipoli, The
Bounty **10** Braveheart **12** Lethal
Weapon **14** The Road Warrior **26**
The Year of Living Dangerously

Giddens, Regina
character in: 14 The Little Foxes
author: 7 Hellman

giddy 5 dizzy, faint, silly **6** fickle, fitful
7 awesome, erratic, flighty, muddled,
reeling **8** careless, dizzying, fainting,
fanciful, reckless, swimming, unsteady, volatile, whirling **9** befuddled,
frivolous, impulsive, mercurial, whimsical **10** capricious, changeable, inconstant **11** hare-brained, harum-scarum,
lightheaded, thoughtless, vacillating,
vertiginous **12** inconsistent, overpowering **13** irresponsible, rattlebrained

Gide, Andre
author of: 13 The Immoralist **15**
Strait Is the Gate **17** The Counterfeit-
ers **18** Lafcadio's Adventure (The
Vatican Swindle) **19** The Pastoral
Symphony

Gideon 11 Hebrew judge
father: 5 Joash, Ophra
son: 9 Abimelech
also called: 9 Jerubbaal

Gidget
character: 5 Larue **10** Anne Cooper,
John Cooper **16** Francine (Gidget)
Lawrence **21** Professor Russ Lawrence
cast: 9 Don Porter **10** Peter Deuel,
Sally Field **11** Betty Conner **13** Lynette Winter
film role: 9 Sandra Dee

Gielgud, Sir John
born: 6 London **7** England
roles: 6 Arthur, Becket, Hamlet **7**
Macbeth **9** Saint Joan **26** The Barretts of Wimpole Street **27** The Importance of Being Earnest

gift 3 aid, dot, fee, sop, tip **4** alms,
bent, boon, dole, help, turn **5** award,
bonus, bribe, craft, dower, dowry, favor, flair, forte, graft, grant, knack,
power, prize, skill **6** genius, legacy,
talent, virtue **7** aptness, bequest,
faculty, handout, largess, premium,

present, quality, tribute **8** aptitude, capacity, donation, facility, gratuity, offering, property **9** attribute, endowment, expertise, ingenuity **10**
adroitness, capability, competency **11**
benefaction, proficiency **12** contribution **13** consideration, qualification

gifted 4 able, deft **5** adept, crack,
handy, quick, slick **6** adroit, bright,
clever, expert, facile, master, wizard **7**
capable, skilled **8** finished, masterly,
polished, superior, talented **9** brilliant,
ingenious, inventive, practiced, qualified **10** proficient **11** crackerjack, experienced, resourceful **12** accomplished

Gift From the Sea, The
author: 19 Anne Morrow Lindbergh

gig 3 job **4** trap **5** stint **6** chaise **7** dog-
cart **8** carriage, curricle **10** engage-
ment

Gigantes
single member: 5 giant
father: 6 Uranus
mother: 4 Gaea
heads of: 3 men
bodies of: 8 serpents
attacked: 4 gods

gigantic 4 huge, vast **5** bulky, jumbo
6 mighty **7** hulking, immense, lumpish, mammoth, massive, titanic **8** colossal, enormous, lubberly, towering,
unwieldy **9** herculean, monstrous,
ponderous, strapping **10** gargantuan,
prodigious, stupendous, tremendous,
voluminous **11** elephantine

giggle 6 cackle, hee-hee, simper, tee-
hee, titter **7** chuckle, snicker, snigger,
twitter

Gigi
director: 16 Vincente Minnelli
based on story by: 7 Colette
cast: 8 Eva Gabor **11** Leslie Caron **12**
Louis Jourdan **15** Hermione Gingold,
Jacques Bergerac **16** Maurice Chevalier
score: 14 Lerner and Loewe
Oscar for: 7 picture **8** director
song: 4 Gigi **15** I Remember It Well
25 Thank Heaven for Little Girls **29**
The Night They Invented Champagne

Gilbert, Cass
architect of: 14 US Customs House
(NYC) **17** Woolworth Building (NYC)
20 Supreme Court Building (Washington DC) **21** Minnesota State Capitol (St Paul) **22** George Washington
Bridge

Gilbert, John
real name: 11 John Pringle
wife: 9 Ina Claire **11** Leatrice Joy **13**
Virginia Bruce
born: 7 Logan UT
roles: 4 Love **12** The Big Parade **13**
The Merry Widow **15** A Woman of
Affairs **16** Flesh and the Devil

Gilbert, William

field: 7 physics
nationality: 7 British
father of: 11 electricity
named for him: 27 CGS unit of
magnetomotive force

**Gilbert, W S, and Sullivan, Arthur
Seymour**
composers of: 7 Ivanhoe **8** Iolanthe,
Patience **9** Ruddigore, The Mikado
11 H M S Pinafore, Princess Ida, The
Sorcerer, Trial by Jury **12** The Grand
Duke **13** The Gondoliers, Utopia
Limited **19** The Yeoman of the
Guard **20** The Pirates of Penzance
24 Thespis or The Gods Grown Old
produced by: 10 D'Oyly Carte
devotees: 9 Savoyards

Gilbert Islands *see* **8** Kiribati

Gil Blas (of Santillane)
author: 11 Alain LeSage
character: 6 Scipio **11** Don Alphonso

Gilbreth, Frank B, Jr
author of: 17 Cheaper by the Dozen
(with Ernestine Gilbreth Carey)

gild 4 bend **5** slant, twist **7** cover up,
stretch, touch up **10** exaggerate

Gilded Age, The
authors: 9 Mark Twain **19** Charles
Dudley Warner

gilded youth
French: 13 jeunesse doree

Gileadite password 10 Shibboleth

Giles Goat-Boy
author: 9 John Barth

Gilgal 5 wheel **6** circle

Gilgamesh
origin: 8 Sumerian
king of: 4 Uruk **5** Erech
servant: 6 Enkidu
event: 5 flood

gill
abbreviation: 2 gi

Gilligan's Island
character: 7 Skipper (Jonas Grumby)
8 Gilligan **9** Mrs Howell (Lovey),
Professor (Roy Hinkley) **11** Ginger
Grant **14** Mary Ann Summers **17**
Thurston Howell III
cast: 9 Bob Denver, Dawn Wells, Jim
Backus **10** Alan Hale Jr, Tina Louise
14 Natalie Schafer, Russell Johnson
ship: 6 Minnow

Gills, Solomon
character in: 12 Dombey and Son
author: 7 Dickens

gimcrack 5 bijou, curio **6** bauble, gewgaw, trifle **7** trinket, whatnot **8** kick-
shaw, ornament **9** bagatelle, plaything
10 knickknack **11** contrivance, thingamabob, thingamajig

gimmick 4 plan, ploy, ruse, wile **5** angle, dodge, stunt **6** design, device,
gadget, scheme **7** wrinkle **9** stratagem
10 subterfuge **11** contrivance

gin
origin: 11 Netherlands

ingredient: 4 sloe **6** grains **12** juniper berry

type: 6 Geneva **8** Plymouth **9** London dry

drink: 5 Allen **6** Gibson, gimlet **7** Belmont, Bennett, gin Fizz, swizzle **8** Pink Lady **9** Gin Rickey **10** Tom Collins **11** Alabama Fizz, gin and tonic **12** Grand Passion **14** Casino Cocktail

with anisette: 8 Snowball **11** Bachio Punch

with apricot brandy: 14 Boston Cocktail

with brandy: 15 Bermuda Highball

with Chartreuse: 5 Bijou **9** Green Lady

with cherry brandy: 14 Singapore Sling

with Cointreau: 7 Florida **9** White Lady **13** Sweet Patootie **14** Flying Dutchman

with creme de cacao: 9 Alexander

with creme de cassis: 8 Parisian

with creme de menthe: 6 Caruso, Virgin

with creme Yvette: 9 Union Jack

with Curacao: 8 Blue Moon, Napoleon **9** Blue Devil **14** Flying Dutchman

with Dubonnet: 3 BVD **8** Napoleon

with Grand Marnier: 7 Red Lion

with grapefruit juice: 8 Salty Dog

with kirsch, kirschwasser: 7 Florida **10** Lady Finger

with onions: 6 Gibson

with orange juice: 5 Abbey **13** Orange Blossom

with Pernod: 7 Dubarry

with rum: 3 BVD

with scotch: 12 Barbary Coast

with sherry: 11 Renaissance

with strawberries: 10 Bloodhound

with Swedish Punch: 5 Biffy

with vermouth: 5 Bijou, Bronx, Tango **6** Caruso **7** Bermuda, Cabaret, Martini **10** Bloodhound

with vodka: 15 Russian Cocktail

ginger 3 pep, tan **5** brown, spice **6** energy

varieties: 3 red **4** wild **5** crape, crepe, shell, torch, white **6** canton, common, Kahili, orchid, spiral, yellow **9** butterfly **10** small shell, variegated

botanical name: 8 Zingiber **12** Z officinales

Sanskrit: 9 singabera

origin: 4 Asia **5** China, India **7** Jamaica

use: 6 tongue **7** vinegar **9** beef stock **11** baked dishes, gingerbread **12** chicken stock

gingerly 6 warily **7** charily, timidly **8** daintily **9** carefully, finically, guardedly, heedfully, mincingly, prudently **10** cautiously, delicately, discreetly, hesitantly, vigilantly, watchfully **11** squeamishly **12** fastidiously, suspiciously **13** circumspectly

gingham 5 cloth **6** cotton, fabric, striped **8** chambray **9** checkered

gin mill 3 bar **4** dive **6** saloon, tavern **9** honky-tonk, roadhouse

Ginnungagap
origin: **12** Scandinavian
void filled with: **4** mist
between: **9** Nifelheim **10** Muspelheim

Ginsberg, Allen
author of: **4** Howl **7** Kaddish **10** Planet News **11** Mind Breaths **16** The Fall of America **20** Reality and Sandwiches

Giordano, Umberto
born: **5** Italy **6** Foggia
composer of: **6** Fedora **8** Mala Vita **13** Andrea Chenier **14** Madame Sans-Gene

Giorgione da Castelfranco
born: **5** Italy **12** Castelfranco
artwork: **10** The Tempest **13** Ordeal of Moses, Sleeping Venus **17** Judgment of Solomon **19** The Concert Champetre (disputed) **20** The Three Philosophers **23** Adoration of the Shepherds

Giotto di Bondone
born: **5** Italy **8** (near) Florence
artwork attributed: **17** Ognissanti Madonna **31** Presentation of Christ in the Temple **32** St Francis Surrounded by his Brothers

Giovanelli
character in: **11** Daisy Miller
author: **5** James

Giovanni's Room
author: **12** James Baldwin

giraffe
constellation of: **14** Camelopardalis
kin: **5** okapi
other name: **10** camelopard

girandole 11 candelabrum, candlestick **12** candleholder

Girardon, Francois
born: **6** France, Troyes
artwork: **13** Bathing Nymphs **14** Galley of Apollo, Virgin of Troyes **16** Rape of Persephone **17** (tomb for) Cardinal Richelieu **23** Apollo Tended by the Nymphs

Giraudoux, Jean
author of: **5** Bella **6** Judith, Ondine, Racine **7** Electra **12** Amphitryon 38 **15** Tiger at the Gates **18** Madwoman of Chaillot **20** My Friend from Limousin

gird 3 pen, tie **4** belt, girt, loop, ring **5** brace, hem in, hitch, steel, strap, truss **6** circle, fasten, girdle, harden, secure, wall in **7** besiege, confine, enclose, fortify, hedge in, prepare, stiffen, sustain, tighten **8** blockade, buttress, encircle, lay siege, surround **9** encompass **10** strengthen **12** circumscribe

girder 4 beam **5** brace, truss **6** binder, rafter **7** support, tie-beam

girdle 3 hem **4** band, belt, ring, sash **5** girth, hedge, stays **6** bodice, circle, corset **7** baldric, circlet, contour **8** boundary, cincture, corselet **9** surcingle, waistband **10** cummerbund **12** waist cincher **17** foundation garment

girl 4 bird, cook, help, lass, maid, minx, miss **5** angel, chick, nymph, wench **6** damsel, kitten, lassie, maiden, pigeon, virgin **7** baggage, colleen, darling, fiancee, ingenue, nymphet **8** daughter, domestic, handmaid, lady love, mistress, scullion **9** affianced, betrothed, inamorata, lady's maid, soubrette **10** sweetheart **11** maidservant
French: **10** demoiselle, jeune fille

girl Friday 4 aide **6** helper **9** assistant, secretary **10** amanuensis **12** office worker **23** administrative assistant

girlfriend 6 steady **7** beloved, sweetie **8** best girl **10** one and only, sweetheart

Girl in a Swing
author: **12** Richard Adams

girlish 8 girl-like, maidenly, youthful **10** maidenlike

Girl of the Golden West, The
opera by: **7** Puccini
setting: **8** Gold Rush **10** California
character: **6** Minnie **7** Johnson, Sheriff

Girl Scouts
founded by: **11** Juliette Low
abbr: **5** GSUSA
rank: **7** brownie **10** tenderfoot

girt 4 belt, bind, gird, ring **5** bound, girth **6** belted, circle, girdle, ringed **7** circled, girdled **9** encircled

girth 5 cinch **9** perimeter **10** saddle band **13** circumference

Giselle
ballet by: **4** (Adolphe Charles) Adam

Gish, Lillian
real name: **12** Lillian Gishi **15** Lillian de Guiche
born: **13** Springfield OH
roles: **8** La Boheme **10** Enoch Arden **11** Annie Laurie, Intolerance, Way Down East **12** Duel in the Sun **13** Scarlet Letter **14** Broken Blossoms **16** Portrait of Jennie **17** Orphans of the Storm, The Birth of a Nation

Gissing, George
author of: **5** Demos **13** New Grub Street **14** The Nether World

gist 3 nut **4** core, crux, meat, pith **5** drift, force, heart, sense, tenor, theme **6** burden, center, effect, import, kernel, marrow, spirit **7** essence, purport **8** main idea **9** main point, substance **11** implication **12** significance

give 3 buy, pay, tip **4** bend, ease, emit, hire, lend, show, sink **5** admit, allot, allow, apply, award, bribe, deign, endow, grant, issue, leave, offer, relax, utter, voice, yield **6** accord, addict, afford, assign, attach, bestow, bounce, commit, confer, convey, devote, donate, enable, enrich, hand to, impart, loosen, notify, open on, permit, recede, relent, render, shrink, supply, tender, unbend, vest in **7** concede, consign, deliver, entrust, fork out, furnish, hand out, let know, present, proffer, provide, requite, retreat, slacken **8** announce, bequeath, collapse, dispense, exchange, fork over, hand over, lead on to, make over, move back, put forth, shell out **9** apportion, break down, dispose of, equip with, favor with, look out on, present to, pronounce, subscribe, surrender, vouchsafe **10** articulate, become soft, compensate, contribute, deliquesce, distribute, recompense, remunerate, resilience, supply with **11** communicate, flexibility, provide with, springiness

give aid to 4 help **6** assist, succor **7** help out **8** befriend **9** look after **10** minister to

give a leg up 3 aid **4** help, lift **5** boost, hoist, raise **6** assist **7** elevate

give and take 8 exchange **10** compromise **11** interchange, reciprocity

give a pep talk to 4 goad, prod, spur **5** press **6** exhort **9** encourage

give a reason for 7 clarify, clear up, explain, justify **9** elucidate **10** account for

give as security 4 pawn **6** pledge **7** deposit, pay down, put down

give away 6 bestow, betray, donate, reveal **7** hand out

give birth 4 bear **5** hatch **6** create, invent **7** deliver, develop **9** originate **10** bring forth

give confidence to 7 inspire **8** embolden, inspirit **9** encourage

give courage 5 brace **6** buck up **7** hearten **8** inspirit, motivate

give energy to 7 animate, enliven **8** activate, energize, vitalize **9** stimulate **10** invigorate

give enjoyment 5 amuse, charm **6** divert, please **7** beguile, delight **8** enthrall **9** entertain

give forth 4 emit, gush **5** exude, issue **7** send out **8** throw off, transmit **9** discharge

give full attention 7 pay heed **8** fasten on **11** concentrate

give in 5 defer, yield **6** accede, cave in, submit **7** succumb **9** surrender **10** capitulate **12** knuckle under

give in to 7 yield to **9** indulge in, partake of **16** abandon oneself to

give leave 3 let **5** allow **6** permit **8** sanction **9** authorize **14** give permission

give moral support to 3 aid **4** abet,

back, help **6** assist, uphold **7** support, sustain **8** sanction **9** encourage

given 3 apt **4** wont **5** prone **6** likely, wonted **7** awarded, donated, granted, offered **8** accorded, bestowed **9** committed, conferred, entrusted, presented **10** accustomed, handed over, in the habit **11** contributed **13** furnished with, made a donation, presented with **17** made a contribution

give new life to 3 fan **4** fire **6** awaken, revive **8** revivify **10** rejuvenate **11** reincarnate

give oneself to 8 dedicate **10** buckle down, consecrate

give one's word 3 vow **5** swear **6** assure, pledge **7** certify, promise, warrant **9** guarantee

give one walking papers 3 axe, can **4** fire, oust, sack **5** let go **6** bounce, lay off **7** cashier, dismiss, release **8** get rid of **9** discharge, terminate **11** give the gate, send packing

give out 4 quit, tell, tire **6** assign, inform, reveal, run out **7** divulge, dole out, mete out **8** allocate, announce, disclose, dispense, proclaim **9** apportion, broadcast, parcel out **10** distribute, make public, portion out **11** disseminate

give over 4 cede **5** yield **9** surrender **10** relinquish

give permission 3 let **5** allow **6** accede, permit **7** approve **8** sanction **9** acquiesce, authorize, give leave

give rise to 4 sire **5** breed, cause **6** lead to **7** produce **8** engender, generate, occasion **9** call forth **10** bring about

give support to 3 aid **4** abet **5** serve **6** defend, prop up, second **7** bolster, comfort, sustain **8** buttress, champion **10** contribute, minister to, provide for, stick up for

give the go-ahead 4 okay **5** order **6** direct **7** appoint, charter, empower **8** contract **9** authorize **10** commission

give the lie to 5 belie **8** disprove **9** repudiate **10** contradict, controvert

give the raspberry 3 boo, pan **4** razz **6** deride, hoot at **8** ridicule **11** give the bird **17** give the Bronx cheer

give the right to 5 allow **6** permit **7** entitle, qualify **9** authorize

give the slip 4 duck **5** avoid, dodge, elude, evade

give up 4 cede, drop, lose, quit, skip **5** forgo, let go, waive, yield **6** eschew, resign **7** abandon, forfeit, forsake **8** abdicate, forswear, renounce **9** sacrifice, surrender **10** relinquish **11** discontinue

give up the ghost 3 die **6** expire, pass on, perish **7** decease **8** pass away **15** breathe one's last

give vent 4 free **5** let go **7** release **8** let loose, liberate **12** give free rein

give way 4 fall **6** buckle, cave in **7** crumple **8** collapse **10** break apart

giving birth 7 bearing **8** creating, creation, delivery, hatching **9** inventing, invention **10** childbirth, delivering **11** originating, origination, parturition

giving up 7 refusal **8** dropping, quitting, yielding **9** resigning **10** abandoning, abdicating, abdication, abstinence, continence, forbearing, forfeiting, forfeiture, self-denial **11** abandonment, forswearing, resignation **12** renunciation, surrendering **14** relinquishment

gizmo 4 tool **6** device, doodad, gadget **7** whatsis **9** apparatus, implement, invention, mechanism **10** instrument **11** contraption, contrivance, thingamabob, thingamajig

glacial 3 icy, raw **4** cold **5** chill, gelid, polar **6** arctic, biting, bitter, frigid, frosty, frozen, wintry **8** hostile **9** freezing, inimical, piercing **9** congealed **10** disdainful, unfriendly **12** antagonistic, bone-chilling, contemptuous

Glackens, William James
  born: 14 Philadelphia PA
  artwork: 9 Promenade **11** Chez Mouquin **15** Nude with an Apple **16** Washington Square (A Holiday in the Park) **17** Luxembourg Gardens

glad 5 happy **6** elated, joyful, joyous **7** elating, gleeful, pleased, tickled **8** blissful, cheerful, cheering, pleasing, rejoiced **9** contented, delighted, joygiving **10** delightful, entrancing, gratifying **11** exhilarated, tickled pink **12** exhilarating

gladden 5 cheer, elate **6** please **7** animate, cheer up, delight, enliven, gratify, hearten, rejoice **8** inspirit, pleasure **9** make happy **10** exhilarate

gladdened 5 happy **6** joyful, joyous **8** cheerful

glade 4 dell, glen, lawn, vale, wood **5** grove, marsh, vista **6** canada, hollow, valley **7** opening **8** clearing

gladness 3 joy **4** glee **5** bliss, cheer, mirth **7** delight, gaiety, jollity **8** pleasure **9** happiness **10** joyfulness **11** contentment **12** cheerfulness

glad rags 5 array **6** attire, finery **10** Sunday best

Gladsheim
  origin: 12 Scandinavian
  palace of: 4 Odin **5** Othin
  location: 8 Valhalla

gladsome 3 gay **5** happy, merry **6** cheery, joyful, joyous **8** cheerful **12** lighthearted

glamor, glamour 5 charm, magic **6** allure **7** glitter, romance **8** illusion **9** adventure, challenge, magnetism **10**

excitement **11** enchantment, fascination **14** attractiveness

glamorous, glamourous 8 alluring, charming, dazzling, exciting, magnetic **10** attractive, bewitching, enchanting **11** captivating, charismatic, fascinating

glance 4 kiss, peek, peep, scan, skim, slip **5** brush, graze, shave, touch **6** bounce, careen, squint **7** glimpse, rebound **8** ricochet **9** brief look, quick look, quick view
French: **6** apercu

glance through 4 scan, skim **6** browse, peruse **7** dip into **8** look over **9** check over

gland
part of: **15** endocrine system
type: **4** duct **8** ductless
kind: **3** oil **5** sweat **7** adrenal, thyroid **8** pancreas **9** pituitary **11** parathyroid
ductless gland secretes: **8** hormones

glare 4 glow **5** blaze, flame, flare, flash, gleam, glint, gloss, lower, scowl, sheen **6** dazzle, glower **7** flicker, glimmer, glisten, glitter, radiate, shimmer, sparkle, twinkle **8** radiance **9** angry look, black look, dirty look **10** brightness, harsh light, luminosity **12** resplendence

glaring 4 rank **5** gross, harsh, vivid **6** arrant, bright, strong **7** blatant, flaring, intense, obvious **8** blinding, dazzling, flagrant, piercing **9** audacious, brilliant, egregious **10** glittering, outrageous, shimmering **11** conspicuous, penetrating, resplendent, unconcealed, undisguised **12** unmistakable

Glasgow, Ellen
author of: **10** Vein of Iron **12** Barren Ground **13** In this Our Life, Sheltered Life **18** They Stooped to Folly **20** The Romantic Comedians

glass 6 beaker, goblet **7** chalice, tumbler **10** tumblerful
type of: **4** fizz, sour **5** flute, tulip **6** jigger, sherry **7** balloon, collins, cordial, red wine, snifter **8** cocktail, highball **9** champagne, white wine **10** hollow-stem, pousse cafe **12** old-fashioned

glasshouse 7 nursery **8** hothouse **10** greenhouse **12** conservatory

glassiness 7 clarity **8** dullness, flatness **9** shininess **10** brilliance, luminosity **12** lifelessness, transparency

Glass Key, The
author: **15** Dashiell Hammett
character: **9** Shad O'Rory **10** Janet Henry, Opal Madvig, Paul Madvig **11** Ned Beaumont **12** Senator Henry **13** Bernie Despain

Glass Menagerie, The
director: **12** Irving Rapper
author: **17** Tennessee Williams
character: **5** Laura **6** Amanda **12** Tom Wingfield
cast: **9** Jane Wyman **11** Kirk Douglas **13** Arthur Kennedy **16** Gertrude Lawrence

glassware 5 agata **6** aurene **7** crystal, favrile, steuben, vitrics **8** amerina, stemware
worker: **7** glazier

glassy 4 dull **5** clear, shiny **6** glazed, smooth **8** lifeless **10** glittering **11** transparent

Glauber, Johann Rudolf
field: **9** chemistry
nationality: **6** German
prepared: **12** tartar emetic **13** sodium sulfate (Glauber's salt) **16** hydrochloric acid

Glaucus
god of: **3** sea
father: **5** Minos
ally of: **7** Trojans
loved by: **5** Circe **6** Scylla **10** Amphitrite

glaze 4 blur **5** gloss **6** enamel, finish **7** grow dim, varnish **8** film over **9** glass over

glazed 4 iced **5** filmy **6** coated, glassy, shined, smooth **7** glossed, sugared **8** enameled, lustrous, polished **9** burnished, varnished

Glazunoff, Alex K (Glazunov, Alexander Konstantinovich)
born: **6** Russia **12** St Petersburg
composer of: **10** Chopiniana, The Seasons **11** Stenka Razin **13** Hymn to Pushkin **15** Memorial Cantata

gleam 3 bit, jot, ray **4** beam, drop, glow, hint, iota **5** blink, flare, flash, glare, glint, gloss, grain, sheen, shine, spark, speck, trace **6** luster, streak **7** flicker, glimmer, glimpse, glisten, glitter, inkling, shimmer, sparkle, tiny bit, twinkle **8** least bit, radiance **9** coruscate **10** brightness, brilliance, effulgence **11** coruscation, scintillate

gleaming 5 clear, shiny **6** bright, flashy, glossy **7** shining, radiant **8** dazzling, glinting, luminous, lustrous, polished, splendid **9** brilliant, burnished, sparkling **10** glistening

glean 4 cull **5** amass **6** gather, pick up **7** harvest **10** accumulate **13** piece together **14** scrape together

gleanings 8 analects, extracts **10** miscellany, selections **11** collectanea, miscellanea **15** commonplace book

Gleason, Jackie
real name: **18** Herbert John Gleason
nickname: **15** Mr Saturday Night
born: **10** Brooklyn NY
roles: **5** Gigot **6** The Toy **10** The Hustler **11** Life of Riley, The Poor Soul **12** Ralph Kramden **15** Joe the Bartender, The Honeymooners **17** Don't Drink the Water, Jackie Gleason Show, The Time of Your Life **22**

Requiem for a Heavyweight **24** Reggie Van Gleason the Third

glebe 3 sod **4** clod, land, plot, soil **5** earth, field **6** termon **8** kirktown **10** church land

glee 3 joy **5** mirth, verve **6** gaiety **7** delight, ecstasy, jollity, rapture **8** gladness, hilarity, laughter **9** joviality, merriment **10** exultation, jocularity, joyfulness, joyousness, liveliness **11** playfulness **12** cheerfulness, exhilaration, sportiveness **13** jollification, sprightliness

glee club 6 chorus **12** singing group **13** choral society

gleeful 3 gay **4** glad **5** happy, jolly, merry **6** elated, jocund, jovial, joyful, joyous, lively **7** festive **8** blissful, cheerful, exultant, mirthful **9** delighted **11** exhilarated **12** lighthearted

Gleipnir
origin: **12** Scandinavian
chain that bound: **6** Fenrir, Fenris

glen 4 dale, dell, vale **6** bottom, hollow

Glencaire Cycle
author: **12** Eugene O'Neill

glib 4 oily **5** gabby, quick, ready, suave **6** facile, fluent, smooth **7** devious, voluble **8** flippant, slippery, unctuous **9** insincere, talkative

glide 3 run **4** flow, roll, sail, skim, slip, soar **5** coast, drift, float, issue, skate, slide, steal **6** elapse, stream **7** proceed **8** glissade

glider 5 swing **7** aviator **9** sailplane **10** hydroplane

glimmer 3 bit, ray **4** beam, drop, glow, hint **5** blink, flare, flash, glare, gleam, grain, shine, speck, trace **7** flicker, glimpse, glisten, glitter, shimmer, sparkle, twinkle **9** coruscate, scintilla **10** flickering, intimation **11** scintillate

glimpse 3 see, spy **4** espy, peek, peep, spot **6** glance, peek at, peep at, squint **9** brief look, quick look, quick view **12** catch sight of, fleeting look
French: **6** apercu

Glinka, Mikhail Ivanovich
born: **6** Russia **8** Smolensk
composer of: **12** Ivan Sussanin, Karaminskaya **13** Jota Aragonesa **18** Russlan and Ludmilla

glint 4 gaze, look, peep **5** flash, gleam, sheen, shine, stare **6** glance **7** appear, glimmer, glimpse, glisten, glitter, shim- mer, sparkle, twinkle **9** coruscate **11** scintillate

glissade 5 coast, glide, slide

glissando
music: **7** sliding

glisten 4 glow **5** flash, gleam, glint, shine **7** flicker, glimmer, glister, glitter, radiate, shimmer, sparkle, twinkle **9** coruscate **11** scintillate

glitter 4 fire, glow, pomp, show **5**

flare, flash, gleam, glint, sheen, shine **6** luster, thrill, tinsel **7** beaming, display, glamour, glimmer, glisten, radiate, sparkle, twinkle **8** grandeur, radiance, splendor **9** pageantry, showiness **10** brilliance, excitement, refulgence **11** electricity

glittering 6 bright **7** radiant, shining **8** luminous, lustrous **9** brilliant, sparkling **11** coruscating

gloaming 4 dusk **7** evening **8** twilight

gloat 4 bask, brag **5** exult, strut, vaunt **7** revel in, swagger, triumph **8** crow over **9** glory over

global 5 world **6** all-out **7** general **9** planetary, unbounded, universal, unlimited, worldwide **10** widespread **13** comprehensive, international **16** intercontinental

globe 3 orb **4** ball **5** Earth, world **6** planet, sphere **7** globule **8** spheroid, spherule **9** biosphere

globule 4 ball, bead, bleb, blob, drop **5** globe **6** bubble, pellet, sphere **7** blister, droplet **8** particle, spheroid

glogg
   type: **5** punch
   origin: **6** Sweden

gloom 3 woe **4** dark, dusk, murk **5** blues, dolor, grief, shade **6** misery, sorrow **7** despair, dimness, sadness, shadows **8** darkness, distress, doldrums **9** blackness, dejection, dinginess, duskiness, murkiness, obscurity **10** cloudiness, depression, gloominess, low spirits, melancholy, mopishness, moroseness, oppression **11** despondency, forlornness, unhappiness **12** hopelessness **13** cheerlessness **16** disconsolateness, heavy-heartedness

gloomy 3 dim, sad **4** dark, dour, down, dull, glum, grim, mopy, sour **5** dusky, moody, mopey, murky, shady **6** cloudy, dismal, dreary, morbid, morose, shaded, somber **7** doleful, forlorn, shadowy, sunless, unhappy **8** dejected, desolate, downcast, frowning, funereal, overcast **9** cheerless, depressed, heartsick, miserable, sorrowful, woebegone **10** chapfallen, despondent, dispirited, ill-humored, melancholy **11** comfortless, crestfallen, discouraged, downhearted, low-spirited, pessimistic **12** disconsolate, disheartened, heavy-hearted **13** in the doldrums **14** down in the dumps, down in the mouth

Gloria in Excelsis Deo 22 Glory in the highest to God

Gloriana
   character in: **15** The Faerie Queene
   author: **7** Spenser

Gloriana
   opera by: **7** Britten
   character: **10** Elizabeth I **11** Earl of Essex

glorification 7 worship **8** devotion **9**

adoration, adulation **10** exaltation, veneration **13** magnification

glorify 4 laud **5** adore, deify, exalt, extol, honor **6** praise, revere **7** beatify, dignify, elevate, ennoble, idolize, worship **8** canonize, enshrine, sanctify, venerate **9** celebrate, glamorize **10** consecrate **11** apotheosize, immortalize, romanticize

glorious 4 fine **5** grand, great, noble, noted **6** august, divine, famous, superb **7** eminent, glowing, honored, notable, radiant, shining, stately, sublime, supreme **8** dazzling, gorgeous, imposing, lustrous, majestic, renowned, splendid **9** beautiful, brilliant, dignified, excellent, marvelous, sparkling, wonderful **10** celebrated, delightful, impressive, preeminent **11** illustrious, magnificent, resplendent **12** praiseworthy **13** distinguished

glory 4 fame, mark, name **5** boast, honor, revel, vaunt **6** esteem, homage, praise, renown, repute **7** dignity, majesty, worship **8** blessing, eminence, grandeur, nobility, prestige, splendor **9** adoration, celebrity, gratitude, solemnity, sublimity **10** admiration, excellence, notability, veneration **11** benediction, distinction, preeminence, stateliness **12** magnificence, resplendence, thanksgiving **14** impressiveness **15** illustriousness

Glory in the highest to God
   Latin: **19** Gloria in Excelsis Deo

gloss 4 glow, mask, veil **5** cloak, color, glaze, gleam, japan, sheen, shine **6** enamel, excuse, luster, polish, veneer **7** cover up, lacquer, shimmer, varnish **8** annotate, disguise, mitigate, radiance **9** whitewash **10** annotation, brightness, brilliance, commentary, smooth over **11** explain away, explanation, rationalize **12** luminousness, treat lightly **14** interpretation

gloss over 4 hide, mask, veil **7** conceal, cover up **9** dissemble, whitewash **12** misrepresent

glossy 5 photo, shiny, showy, silky, sleek, slick **6** bright, satiny, smooth **7** picture, shining **8** gleaming, lustrous, magazine, polished **9** burnished

glove 3 kid **4** cuff, mitt **5** catch, thumb **6** gusset, mitten, muffle **7** chevron **8** gauntlet

glow 4 fill, heat **5** ardor, bloom, blush, color, flush, gleam, gusto, shine **6** fervor, thrill, tingle, warmth **7** flicker, glimmer, glisten, glitter, radiate, shimmer, smolder, twinkle **8** radiance **9** eagerness, intensity, radiation, reddening, vividness **10** brightness, enthusiasm **11** earnestness

glower 4 pout, sulk **5** frown, glare, lower, scowl, stare

glowing 3 hot, red **4** rave **5** ruddy, vivid **6** ardent, bright, florid, raving **7**

fervent, flaming, flushed **8** ecstatic, exciting **9** rhapsodic, thrilling **10** passionate **11** luminescent, sensational, stimulating **12** enthusiastic

Glubbdubdrib
   fictional land in: **16** Gulliver's Travels
   author: **5** Swift

Gluck, Christoph Willibald (von)
   born: **7** Bavaria **8** Neumarkt
   composer of: **5** Orfeo **6** Armide **7** Alceste **13** Paride ed Elena **14** Echo et Narcisse **17** Iphigenie en Aulide **18** Iphigenie en Tauride

glue 3 fix, gum **5** affix, epoxy, paste, putty, stick **6** adhere, cement, fasten, mortar **7** plaster, stickum **8** adherent, adhesive, concrete, fixative, mucilage **11** agglutinate

gluey 5 gooey, gummy, mucid, ropey, slimy, tacky, thick, **6** sticky, viscid **7** stringy, viscous **8** adhesive **12** mucilaginous

glum 6 gloomy, morose **8** dejected **9** cheerless **10** melancholy **14** down in the mouth

glut 4 bolt, clog, cram, drug, fill, gulp, jade, load, sate **5** choke, flood, gorge, stuff **6** burden, deluge, devour, excess, gobble **7** congest, overeat, satiate, surfeit, surplus **8** gobble up, obstruct, overdose, overfeed, overload, plethora, saturate **10** gormandize, oversupply, saturation **11** obstruction, superfluity **13** overabundance, supersaturate **14** superabundance **15** supersaturation

glutinous 5 gluey, bummy, mucid, ropey, slimy, tacky, thick **6** sticky, viscid **7** viscous **8** adhesive **10** gelatinous **12** musilaginous

glutton 3 hog, pig **6** gorger **7** stuffer **8** gourmand **9** chowhound, overeater **10** belly-slave **11** gormandizer, trencherman

gluttonous 6 greedy **7** hoggish, piggish, swinish **8** edacious, grasping, ravening, ravenous **9** excessive, voracious **10** insatiable, omnivorous **11** intemperate

gluttony 8 rapacity, voracity **10** overeating **11** gourmandism, hoggishness, piggishness **12** gormandizing, intemperance, ravenousness **13** voraciousness

gnarled 6 knotty, rugged, snaggy **7** crooked, knotted, nodular, twisted **8** leathery, wrinkled **9** contorted, distorted **11** full of knots **13** weatherbeaten

gnash 4 gnaw **5** chomp

gnat 7 no-see-um
   group of: **5** cloud, horde

gnaw 4 bite, chew, fret, gall **5** chafe, chomp, eat at, grate, graze, munch, worry **6** browse, crunch, harrow, nibble, rankle **7** torment, trouble **8**

distress, nibble at, ruminate **9** eat away at, masticate

gnome 3 elf **4** pixy **5** dwarf, troll **6** goblin, sprite **10** leprechaun

gnostic 4 sage, wise **6** clever, shrewd **7** knowing **8** mandaean, simonian **10** insightful

gnothi seauton 11 know thyself

gnu 7 brindle **8** antelope **10** wildebeest
type: 5 C gnou **9** C taurinus **12** Connochaetes

go 3 act, end, fit, fly, pep, run, try, vim **4** blow, dash, elan, fare, flee, flow, jibe, lead, life, pass, quit, stir, turn, wend, work **5** agree, begin, be off, blend, drive, force, get on, lapse, leave, reach, scram, slide, split, steam, tally, trial, verve, vigor, whirl **6** beat it, be used, belong, chance, decamp, depart, effort, elapse, energy, expire, extend, mettle, pass by, repair, result, retire, spirit **7** advance, attempt, be given, be known, comport, fall out, glide by, move out, operate, perform, proceed, slip off, take off, turn out, vamoose, work out **8** ambition, endeavor, function, move away, progress, slip away, sneak off, spread to, start for, steal off, vitality, vivacity, withdraw **9** animation, harmonize, terminate, transpire **10** enterprise, experiment, initiative

goad 4 move, prod, push, spur, urge, whet **5** drive, egg on, impel, press, prick, set on **6** arouse, exhort, fillip, incite, motive, propel, stir up **8** pressure, stimulus **9** constrain, incentive, stimulant, stimulate **10** cattle prod, inducement, motivation **11** instigation

goal 3 aim, end **4** home, mark, wire **5** point, score, tally **6** design, intent, object, target **7** end line, purpose **8** ambition, goal line, terminus **9** intention, objective **10** finish line

go along with 5 usher **6** assent, convoy, escort **8** accede to, shepherd **9** accompany, agree with, chaperone, consent to **10** comply with

go ashore 4 land **6** debark **9** disembark

go astray 3 err, sin **6** wander **7** deviate, do wrong **9** misbehave **10** transgress **13** fall from grace

goat 3 kid **4** buck, butt **5** billy, nanny **6** victim **7** fall guy **9** scapegoat **11** whipping boy **13** laughingstock
breed: 6 Angora, Chamal, Nubian, Saanen **7** Granada **8** La Mancha **10** Toggenburg **11** Anglo-Nubian **12** French Alpine **13** British Alpine
combining form: 4 aego **5** capri
family: 7 Bovidae
female: 3 doe **5** capra, nanny **7** doeling
genus: 5 Capra
goat-boy: 5 Giles
goat-milk cheese: 7 chevret

goat-man: 5 satyr
god: 3 Pan **5** satyr **7** Aegipan
group of: 4 herd **5** tribe
hair: 5 kasha, tibet
hair of Angora goat: 6 mohair
male: 4 buck **5** billy
meat: 7 cabrito
star: 7 capella
young: 3 kid

Goat, Horned Goat
constellation of: 11 Capricornus

goat god 3 Pan **5** satyr

go away 3 ebb **4** fade, scat, wane **5** abate, leave, scram **6** depart, lessen, retire **8** withdraw **9** disappear

gob 3 dab, tar **4** clot, glob, lump, mass **6** sailor **7** Jack Tar

go back 6 return **7** retreat

gobble 3 caw **4** bolt, gulp, wolf **5** raven, stuff **6** cackle, devour, gabble, gaggle **8** bolt down, cram down, gulp down

gobbledygook 4 bosh, bunk, cant, tosh **6** jargon **7** rubbish, twaddle **8** buncombe, nonsense, tommyrot **9** gibberish, moonshine **10** balderdash, double-talk, hocus-pocus, mumbo jumbo **11** foolishness **12** fiddle-faddle

gobble up 6 devour **8** bolt down, gulp down, wolf down

go before 7 precede, predate **8** antecede, antedate **9** come first, go ahead of **10** anticipate

go-between 5 agent, envoy, fixer, proxy **6** deputy, second **7** arbiter **8** delegate, emissary, mediator **9** messenger, middleman, moderator **10** arbitrator, interceder, negotiator **12** intermediary **13** intermediator **14** representative

goblet 3 cup **5** glass **6** vessel **7** chalice

goblin 4 ogre **5** bogey, demon, troll **7** gremlin **8** bogeyman

Gobseck
author: 14 Honore de Balzac

go by 4 pass **6** elapse, pass by, roll by, rush by, slip by **7** glide by, slide by **8** slip away

go by car 4 ride **5** drive, motor

go-cart 4 cart **5** buggy **6** barrow **8** carriage, handcart, pushcart, stroller **11** wheelbarrow

go crimson 4 burn, glow **5** blush, color, flame, flush **6** redden

God, god 4 Lord **5** Allah, deity **6** Elohim, Jahveh, Yahweh **7** Holy One, Jehovah, Skaddai **8** divinity, the Deity **9** Our Father **10** the Creator, the Godhead **11** divine being, God Almighty, the Almighty **13** the Omnipotent, the Omniscient **14** the All-Merciful, the Man Upstairs **15** the Supreme Being
Hebrew: 6 Adonai
Latin: 7 Dominus

god, first

origin: 12 Scandinavian
known as: 7 Forsete, Forseti

God and Man at Yale
author: 17 William F Buckley Jr

God and my right
French: 14 Dieu et mon droit
motto of: 18 royal arms of England

God be with us
German: 10 Gott mit uns

God be with you
Latin: 12 Deus vobiscum

Godbole, Professor
character in: 15 A Passage to India
author: 7 Forster

Goddard, Jean-Luc
director of: 10 Breathless

Goddard, Paulette
real name: 10 Marion Levy
husband: 14 Charlie Chaplin **15** Burgess Meredith **18** Erich Maria Remarque
born: 11 Great Neck NY
roles: 11 Modern Times, Unconquered **15** So Proudly We Hail **16** Standing Room Only, The Great Dictator **19** Diary of a Chambermaid

Goddard, Robert Hutchings
nationality: 8 American
inventor of: 12 rocket engine **22** liquid propellant rocket

Godden, Rumer
author of: 8 The River **14** Black Narcissus, Kitchen Madonna **16** The Peacock Spring **18** In This House of Brede, The Greengage Summer **19** An Episode of Sparrows **23** The Battle of Villa Fiorita

God enriches
Latin: 9 ditat Deus
motto of: 7 Arizona

Godfather, The
author: 9 Mario Puzo
family: 8 Corleone
director: 18 Francis Ford Coppola
cast: 8 Al Pacino (Michael) **9** James Caan (Sonny) **10** John Cazale (Fredo), John Marley, Talia Shire **11** Diane Keaton **12** Marlon Brando (Don Vito Corleone), Richard Conte, Robert Duvall **14** Sterling Hayden **17** Richard Castellano
Oscar for: 5 actor (Brando) **7** picture **10** screenplay
sequel: 18 The Godfather Part II

Godfather, The, Part II
director: 18 Francis Ford Coppola
cast: 8 Al Pacino **10** John Cazale, Talia Shire **11** Diane Keaton **12** Lee Strasberg, Robert DeNiro, Robert Duvall
Oscar for: 7 picture **10** screenplay **15** supporting actor (DeNiro)
sequel to: 12 The Godfather

godforsaken 5 bleak **6** lonely, remote **8** deserted, desolate, wretched **9** abandoned, neglected

god from a machine
  Latin: **13** deux ex machina
God is with us
  German: **10** Gott mit uns
godless 4 evil **6** wicked **7** heathen, impious, profane, ungodly **8** agnostic, depraved **9** atheistic **10** unhallowed **11** blasphemous, irreligious, unrepentant, unrighteous **12** sacrilegious, unsanctified
godlessness 7 atheism **8** apostasy, unbelief **9** disbelief **10** irreligion
godlike 4 holy **5** godly, pious **6** deific, divine, sacred **8** immortal, olympian
godliness 5 piety **8** devotion, holiness **9** reverence **10** devoutness **12** spirituality
godly 4 good, holy **5** moral, pious **6** devout, divine, sacred **7** devoted, saintly **8** faithful, hallowed, reverent **9** believing, God-loving, pietistic, religious, righteous, spiritual **10** God-fearing, sanctified **11** consecrated, pure in heart, reverential
go down 3 ebb **4** drop, fade, wane **5** abate, lower, slide **6** lessen, plunge, reduce, weaken **7** descend, plummet, slacken, subside **8** decrease, diminish, moderate
God Save the Queen
  author: **17** William F Buckley Jr
God's Grace
  author: **14** Bernard Malamud
God's Little Acre
  author: **15** Erskine Caldwell
Godthaab
  capital of: **9** Greenland
God willing
  Latin: **10** Deo volente
God wills it
  Latin: **8** Deus vult
  cry of: **9** Crusaders
Goes, Hugo van der
  born: **5** Ghent **8** Flanders
  artwork: **7** The Fall **14** The Lamentation **19** The Death of the Virgin **21** The Adoration of the Magi **22** The Adoration of the Child **26** The Adoration of the Shepherds
Goethe, Johann
  author of: **5** Faust **6** Egmont **24** The Sorrows of Young Werther **29** Wilhelm Meister's Apprenticeship
go-getter 4 doer **7** hustler **8** achiever, live wire
go-getting 7 driving, dynamic **8** forceful, hustling **9** ambitious, assertive, energetic **10** aggressive **11** hard-driving, hard-working, industrious
Gogol, Nikolai
  author of: **7** The Nose **9** Dead Souls **10** Taras Bulba **11** The Overcoat **19** The Inspector-General
go hand in hand 5 match, tally **6** concur, square **7** coexist **9** accompany

go hungry 4 fast **6** famish, starve **7** abstain
Going My Way
  director: **10** Leo McCarey
  cast: **10** Bing Crosby (Father O'Malley) **12** Gene Lockhart **15** Barry Fitzgerald
  Oscar for: **4** song **5** actor (Crosby) **7** picture **8** director **15** supporting actor (Fitzgerald)
  song: **15** Swinging on a Star
gold 3 bar **4** gilt **5** aurum, ingot **6** beauty, nugget, purity, yellow **7** bullion **8** goodness, goodwill, humanity, kindness **11** beneficence
  chemical symbol: **2** Au
gold and silver
  Spanish: **9** oro y plata
  motto of: **7** Montana
Gold Bug, The
  author: **13** Edgar Allan Poe
Gold Coast see **5** Ghana **11** Sierra Leone
golden 4 best, gilt, rosy **5** blest, blond, great, happy, palmy **6** bright, gilded, joyous, timely **7** aureate, halcyon, richest, shining **8** beatific, glorious, happiest, splendid **9** favorable, opportune, priceless, promising **10** auspicious, delightful, propitious, seasonable **11** exceptional, flourishing, resplendent **12** advantageous, bright-yellow **13** extraordinary
Golden Age
  first age of: **3** man
  world ruled by: **6** Cronus, Saturn
Golden Ass, The
  author: **14** Lucius Apuleius
  character: **4** Milo **5** Fotis **6** Lucius **8** Charites, Pamphile **9** Lepolemus **10** Thrasillus
Goldenberg, Emmanuel
  real name of: **15** Edward G Robinson
Golden Bough, The
  branch of: **9** mistletoe
  sacred to: **10** Proserpina
  used by: **6** Aeneas
  at shrine of: **5** Diana **7** Virbius
  author: **15** Sir James G Frazer
Golden Bowl, The
  author: **10** Henry James
  character: **8** Mr Verver **12** Maggie Verver, Mrs Assingham **13** Prince Amerigo **14** Charlotte Stant
Golden Boy
  nickname of: **11** Paul Hornung
golden brown 3 tan **5** tawny, toast **6** sienna **7** tobacco **8** chestnut
Golden Cockerel, The
  also: **8** Le Coq d'Or **15** Zolotoy Petushok
  opera by: **14** Rimsky-Korsakov
  character: **9** King Dodon **14** Queen of Shemaka
golden egg-layer

form: 5 goose
  made of: **4** gold
Golden Fleece
  made of: **4** gold
  kept at: **7** Colchis
  kept by: **10** King Aeetes
  stolen by: **5** Jason **9** Argonauts
  accomplice: **5** Medea
Golden Legend
  author: **13** William Caxton
goldenrod 8 Solidago
  varieties: **5** sweet, white **6** Wreath **7** seaside **8** blue- stem, European **10** California
Golden State
  nickname of: **10** California
golden youth
  French: **13** jeunesse doree
goldfinch
  group of: **5** charm
Goldfinger
  director: **11** Guy Hamilton
  author: **10** Ian Fleming
  cast: **9** Gert Frobe (Auric Goldfinger) **10** Bernard Lee (M) **11** Lois Maxwell (Miss Moneypenny) **12** Harold Sakata (Oddjob), Shirley Eaton **13** Honor Blackman (Pussy Galore), Sean Connery (James Bond, 007)
Golding, William
  author of: **8** Free Fall **13** A Moving Target **14** Lord of the Flies, Rites of Passage **15** Darkness Visible
gold mine 7 bonanza **10** mother lode
Gold Rush, The
  director: **14** Charlie Chaplin
  cast: **9** Mack Swain, Tom Murray **11** Georgia Hale **14** Charlie Chaplin (Little Tramp)
  setting: **5** Yukon
Goldsmith, Oliver
  author of: **18** She Stoops to Conquer, The Deserted Village **19** The Vicar of Wakefield
goldwasser
  form: **7** liquor
  origin: **6** France **7** Germany
  flavor: **4** herb **5** spice **7** caraway
  flecked with: **8** gold leaf
golf
  average number strokes to reach a hole: **3** par
  ball in another's path: **6** stymie
  championship: **6** US Open **9** Grand Slam **11** British Open **17** Masters' Tournament
  club: **4** iron, wood **6** driver, putter **7** brassie **8** long iron **9** sand wedge, short iron **10** middle iron **13** pitching wedge
  club carrier: **6** caddie
  course also called: **5** links
  golf ball formerly called: **6** guttie **8** feathery
  hole scored in one stroke: **3** ace **9** hole-in-one
  one stroke less than par: **6** birdie

one stroke more than par: 5 bogey
part of the course: 3 cup, tee **4** hole **5** apron, green, rough **6** bunker, hazard **7** fairway **8** sand trap
position: 3 lie
stance: 4 open **6** closed, square **7** address
two strokes less than par: 5 eagle
type of competition: 5 match, skins **6** stroke
uprooted turf: 5 divot
warning cry: 4 fore

golfer 8 Ben Hogan, Ernie Els, Lee Elder, Sam Snead **9** Carol Mann, Hale Irwin, Patty Berg, Tom Watson **10** Betsy Rawls, Bobby Jones, Deane Beman, Gary Player, Hubie Green, Jim Demaret, Judy Rankin, Lee Trevino, Nancy Lopez, Tiger Woods **11** Ben Crenshaw, Billy Casper, Byron Nelson, Calvin Peete, Donna Caponi, Gene Sarazen, Julius Boros, Tom Weiskopf, Walter Hagen **12** Arnold Palmer, Jack Nicklaus, Joanne Carner, Johnny Miller, Mickey Wright, Sandra Haynie **14** Cary Middlecoff, Kathy Whitworth **16** Roberto DeVicenzo **19** Susie Maxwell Berning **20** Severiano Ballesteros **21** Babe Didrikson Zaharias

Golgotha 7 Calvary
  means: 10 skull place

Goliath 5 giant
  home: 4 Gath **9** Philistia
  slain by: 5 David
  weapon: 9 slingshot

golliwogg 3 toy **4** doll **9** plaything

Gomer Pyle USMC
  character: 5 Bunny **7** Frankie **9** Corp Boyle **11** Duke Slayter, (Sgt) Vince Carter
  cast: 9 Jim Nabors, Roy Stuart **10** Ted Bessell **11** Frank Sutton **12** Ronnie Schell **13** Barbara Stuart

Gomorrah
  destroyed with: 5 Sodom **6** Zeboim **10** Admah

Gondoliers, The
  operetta by: 18 Gilbert and Sullivan
  character: 4 Luiz **5** Tessa **7** Casilda **8** Gianetta **13** Marco Palmieri **15** Duke of Plaza-Toro **16** Giuseppe Palmieri

gone 3 ago, out **4** away, dead, left, lost, past **6** absent, ruined, used up **7** defunct, died out, extinct, missing **8** departed, finished, hopeless, vanished **11** disappeared

Goneril
  character in: 8 King Lear
  author: 11 Shakespeare

Gone With the Wind
  author: 16 Margaret Mitchell
  character: 5 Mammy **6** Big Sam, Prissy **7** Dr Meade **10** Ellen (Robillard) O'Hara **11** Gerald O'Hara, Honey Wilkes, India Wilkes **12** Ashley Wilkes, Aunt Pittypat, Belle Watling **13** Scarlett O'Hara, Tarleton twins **15** Mrs Merriweather **21** Melanie Hamilton Wilkes
  Scarlett's husband: 11 Rhett Butler **12** Frank Kennedy **15** Charles Hamilton
  Scarlett's children: 4 Emma, Wade **6** Bonnie
  Scarlett's sister: 7 Carreen, Suellen
  director: 13 Victor Fleming
  cast: 9 Ona Munson **10** Clark Gable (Rhett Butler) **11** Evelyn Keyes, Vivien Leigh (Scarlett O'Hara) **12** Leslie Howard (Ashley Wilkes) **13** Ann Rutherford **14** Hattie McDaniel (Mammy), Thomas Mitchell (Gerald O'Hara) **16** Butterfly McQueen (Prissy) **17** Olivia de Havilland (Melanie Hamilton Wilkes)
  score: 10 Max Steiner
  Oscar for: 7 actress (Leigh), picture **8** director **12** screenwriter **17** supporting actress (McDaniel)
  producer: 14 David O Selznick

good 3 ace, fit, new **4** best, boon, fine, full, gain, kind, pure, real **5** ample, crack, favor, great, large, merit, moral, pious, prize, right, solid, sound, sunny, valid, value, worth **6** adroit, choice, devout, entire, genial, honest, humane, kindly, lively, newest, profit, proper, seemly, select, tiptop, useful, virtue, wealth, worthy **7** adapted, benefit, capable, capital, dutiful, fitting, genuine, godsend, healthy, orderly, service, sizable, skilled, success, upright, welfare **8** adequate, becoming, blessing, bonafide, cheerful, complete, decorous, gracious, innocent, interest, kindness, obedient, obliging, pleasant, precious, reliable, salutary, skillful, smartest, sociable, splendid, suitable, thorough, topnotch, valuable, virtuous, windfall **9** admirable, advantage, agreeable, authentic, convivial, deserving, efficient, enjoyable, enjoyment, excellent, exemplary, expensive, favorable, firstrate, happiness, healthful, honorable, priceless, qualified, religious, righteous, unsullied, untainted, wholesome, wonderful **10** altruistic, beneficent, beneficial, benevolent, excellence, first-class, legitimate, proficient, prosperity, sufficient, worthwhile **11** appropriate, commendable, considerate, improvement, kindhearted, substantial, sympathetic, well-behaved **12** advantageous, considerable, praiseworthy, satisfactory **13** companionable, conscientious, righteousness
  French: 3 bon **4** bien
  Spanish: 5 bueno
  German: 3 gut

Good as Gold
  author: 12 Joseph Heller

Good Book 5 Bible

good breeding 5 grace **6** polish **7** manners **9** gentility **10** refinement **11** cultivation

good buy 4 deal **5** steal **7** bargain

goodby, goodbye 3 bye **6** bye-bye, bye now, so long **7** parting, send-off **8** farewell, Godspeed **9** departure **10** separation **11** be seeing you, leave-taking, see you later **12** God be with you **15** till we meet again
  French: 5 adieu **8** au revoir
  German: 14 auf Wiedersehen
  Hawaiian: 5 aloha
  Italian: 4 ciao **5** addio **11** arrivederci
  Japanese: 8 sayonara
  Latin: 4 vale
  Spanish: 5 adios **12** hasta la vista

Goodbye, Mr Chips
  director: 7 Sam Wood
  author: 11 James Hilton
  cast: 11 Greer Garson, Paul Henreid (von Henreid), Robert Donat
  Oscar for: 5 actor (Donat)
  character: 7 Mr Chips **10** Mrs Wickett **12** Kathy Bridges
  school: 10 Brookfield

Goodbye Girl, The
  director: 11 Herbert Ross
  based on play by: 9 Neil Simon
  cast: 11 Marsha Mason **13** Quinn Cummings **15** Richard Dreyfuss
  Oscar for: 5 actor (Dreyfuss)

Good Companions, The
  author: 11 J B Priestley

good counsel
  god of: 6 Consus

good day
  French: 7 bonjour
  German: 8 guten tag
  Spanish: 10 buenos dias
  Italian: 10 buon giorno

good deal 3 buy **5** steal **7** bargain

good deed 8 kindness **11** benefaction **12** philanthropy
  Hebrew: 7 mitsvah, mitzvah

Good Earth, The
  author: 10 Pearl S Buck
  character: 4 O-Lan **6** Nung En **7** Nung Wen, The Fool **8** Wang Lung **11** Pear Blossom **12** Lotus Blossom
  director: 14 Sidney Franklin
  cast: 8 Keye Luke, Paul Muni **10** Tilly Losch **11** Jessie Ralph, Luise Rainer **14** Walter Connolly **15** Charley Grapewin
  Oscar for: 7 actress (Rainer)

good feelings 3 era **8** good will **11** benevolence **12** friendliness

good form 9 etiquette, good taste **10** politeness **11** good manners

good-for-nothing 5 idler **6** loafer **7** useless **9** no-account, shiftless, worthless

good fortune 4 luck **7** bonanza **8** fortuity, lady luck, windfall **9** blessings **10** lucky break

good friend
French: 6 bon ami 9 bonne amie

good health 5 vigor 7 fitness 8 vitality 10 robustness

Goodhue, Bertram Grosvenor
architect of: 13 St Bartholomew (NYC) 14 St Thomas Church (NYC) 25 Chapel at US Military Academy (West Point), National Academy of Sciences (Washington DC) 28 Nebraska State Capitol Building (Lincoln)
style: 13 Gothic Revival 15 Spanish Colonial

good humor 10 affability, amiability, cheeriness, kindliness, mellowness 12 cheerfulness, complaisance, pleasantness 15 kindheartedness

good-humored 4 mild, warm 6 cheery, genial, gentle, kindly, mellow 7 affable, amiable 8 cheerful, pleasant 9 congenial, easygoing 11 complaisant

good-looker 3 fox 4 doll, hunk 5 beaut, Venus 6 Adonis, beauty, eyeful 7 stunner 8 knockout 11 handsome Dan

good-looking 4 fair, foxy, sexy 5 bonny 6 comely, lovely, pretty 8 alluring, clean-cut, gorgeous, handsome, stunning 9 beauteous, beautiful, exquisite, ravishing 10 attractive, bewitching, enchanting 11 captivating, eye-catching, well-favored 15 pulchritudinous

good looks 6 beauty 10 comeliness, loveliness 11 pulchritude 12 handsomeness 14 attractiveness

good luck
Yiddish: 8 mazel tov

goodly 4 tidy 5 ample, large 7 sizable 11 substantial 12 considerable

good manners 8 courtesy 9 amenities, etiquette, gentility 10 politeness, refinement

good name 4 face 5 image 10 reputation 11 self-respect

good nature 6 warmth 9 geniality, good humor 10 affability, amiability, cordiality, likability 12 complaisance, pleasantness 13 agreeableness

good-natured 4 warm 5 sunny 6 genial, kindly 7 affable, amiable 8 cheerful, friendly, obliging, pleasant 9 agreeable, congenial, easygoing 11 complaisant, good-humored, warmhearted 13 accommodating

goodness 3 boy, gee, hey, say, wow 5 favor, honor, mercy, merit, piety, value, worth, wowee 6 profit, purity, virtue 7 benefit, decorum, gee whiz, heavens, honesty, probity, service 8 boy-oh-boy, devotion, gracious, kindness, morality 9 advantage, innocence, integrity, land alive, landsakes, nutrition, propriety, rectitude 10 generosity, kindliness, sakes alive, usefulness 11 benevolence, nourishment

12 virtuousness 13 righteousness, wholesomeness 14 heavens to Betsy

good night
French: 7 bon soir 9 bonne nuit
German: 9 gute nacht
Spanish: 12 buenas noches
Italian: 10 buona notte

good opinion 6 esteem, regard 7 respect 8 approval 10 admiration

good person 4 dear, love 5 angel 7 darling 10 sweetheart

goods 4 gear 5 cloth, stock, wares 6 fabric, things 7 effects, fabrics 8 chattels, material, movables, property, textiles 9 inventory, trappings 11 commodities, furnishings, merchandise, possessions 13 appurtenances, paraphernalia

good sense 6 brains, wisdom 8 judgment 12 intelligence

good taste 10 refinement 11 cultivation, discernment 14 discrimination

good-tempered 5 sunny 7 amiable, smiling 8 cheerful 12 sweet-natured

good time 3 fun 9 amusement, diversion, enjoyment 13 entertainment

good times 4 boom 8 fat years

good turn 5 favor 7 service 8 good deed

goodwill 5 amity 8 kindness 9 benignity 10 cordiality, kindliness 11 amicability, benevolence 12 friendliness 15 kindheartedness

good wishes 4 best 5 favor 6 regard 7 consent, regards 8 approval, blessing, respects, sanction 11 compliments

Goodwood, Caspar
character in: 18 The Portrait of a Lady
author: 5 James

good word 6 praise 10 compliment 11 approbation 12 commendation 14 congratulation

Goodyear, Charles
nationality: 8 American
developed: 16 vulcanized rubber

goof 3 err 4 boob, flub, fool, mess 5 botch, error, gum up 6 bollix, booboo, bungle, fumble, slip up 7 blunder, mistake 9 oversight

Goolagong Cawley, Evonne
sport: 6 tennis
heritage: 19 Australian Aborigine

go on all fours 5 crawl, creep

goose
young: 7 gosling
group of: 5 flock, skein 6 gaggle

goose egg 3 nil, zip 4 zero 5 aught 6 cipher, naught 7 nothing 11 horse collar

go over 5 audit, check 6 review 7 examine, inspect 10 scrutinize 11 investigate

Gopher State
nickname of: 9 Minnesota

Gorbachev, Mikhail Sergeyevich
party: 9 Communist
country: 4 USSR 6 Russia 31 Union of Soviet Socialist Republics
born: 9 Stavropol 10 Privolnoye 16 Krasnogvardeisky
education: 21 Moscow State University
political career: 9 Politburo 16 General Secretary 20 Agriculture Secretary 23 Stavropol Communist Party 35 Deputy Supreme Soviet Central Committee
policy: 8 glasnost 11 perestroika
distinguishing characteristic: 19 strawberry birthmark (head)
wife: 15 Raisa Maksimovna
  occupation: 7 teacher
daughter: 5 Irisa
  occupation: 6 doctor 9 physician
grandchild: 6 Oksana

Gorcey, Leo
born: 9 New York NY
roles: 4 Spit 10 Bowery Boys 11 Dead End Kids

Gordimer, Nadine
author of: 11 July's People 12 The Lying Days 13 A Guest of Honor 15 Burger's Daughter 16 A Soldier's Embrace 21 The Late Bourgeois World
award: 10 Nobel Prize

Gordon, Ruth
real name: 15 Ruth Gordon Jones
husband: 11 Garson Kanin
born: 11 Wollaston MA
roles: 11 Where's Poppa? 13 Rosemary's Baby 14 Harold and Maude 17 Inside Daisy Clover 20 Abe Lincoln in Illinois

gore 5 blood 7 carnage 8 butchery 9 bloodshed, slaughter

Gore, Albert
born: 10 Washington (DC)
wife: 6 Tipper 13 Mary Elizabeth
children: 5 Sarah 6 Albert 7 Karenna, Kristin
education: 7 Harvard 10 Vanderbilt
profession: 10 journalist
author of: 17 Earth in the Balance
political career: 6 Senate 13 vice president 22 House of Representatives

Gorgas, William Crawford
field: 8 medicine
position: 18 army surgeon general
conquered: 7 malaria 11 yellow fever
location: 11 Panama Canal

gorge 3 gap, ire 4 bolt, cram, craw, dale, dell, fill, glen, glut, gulp, pass, sate, vale 5 abyss, anger, blood, chasm, cleft, gulch, gully, mouth, stuff, wrath 6 canyon, defile, devour, gobble, gullet, hatred, hollow, muzzle, nausea, ravine, throat 7 disgust, indulge, overeat, satiate **8** crevasse **9** animosity, esophagus, repulsion, revulsion **10** gluttonize, gormandize, repugnance **11** overindulge

gorgeous 4 fine, rich **5** grand **6** bright, costly, lovely **7** elegant, opulent, shining **8** dazzling, glorious, imposing, splendid, stunning **9** beautiful, brilliant, exquisite, luxurious, ravishing, sumptuous **10** attractive, glittering, impressive **11** good-looking, magnificent, resplendent, splendorous **13** splendiferous

Gorgons
 form: **7** maidens **8** monsters
 names: **6** Medusa, Stheno **7** Euryale, Sthenno
 father: **7** Phorcys
 mother: **4** Ceto
 protectress: **6** Graeae, Graiae
 hair of: **6** snakes
 hands of: **5** brass
 turned viewers to: **5** stone

Gorgosaurus
 type: **8** dinosaur, theropod
 location: **7** Alberta **12** North America
 period: **10** Cretaceous

gorilla
 group of: **4** band
 studied by: **10** Dian Fossey

Gorky, Arshile
 real name: **21** Vosdanig Manoog Adokian
 born: **7** Armenia **11** Khorkomvari
 artwork: **5** Agony **15** Diary of a Seducer **17** Making the Calendar **21** The Artist and his Mother, Water of the Flowery Hill **22** The Liver is the Cock's Comb

Gorky, Maxim (Maksim)
 real name: **25** Alekseimaksimovich Peshkov
 author of: **7** V I Lenin **11** My Childhood **14** The Lower Depths **18** The Small Town Okurov **20** City of the Yellow Devil, Twenty-six Men and a Girl **27** The Life of Matthew Kozhemyakin

gormandize 5 feast, raven **6** devour
gory 5 scary **6** bloody, creepy **9** murderous **10** horrifying, sanguinary, terrifying **11** bloodsoaked, ensanguined, frightening **12** bloodstained, bloodthirsty **13** bloodcurdling

gospel, Gospel 5 credo, creed **8** doctrine **11** the good news, the last word **12** the final word **13** the whole truth, ultimate truth
 the first four books of the New Testament: **4** Luke, John, Mark **7** Matthew

Gospel writers 4 John, Luke, Mark **7** Matthew **9** synoptist
gospodin (Russian) 2 Mr **6** Mister
gossamer 5 filmy, gauzy, sheer **8** cobwebby **10** diaphanous **13** insubstantial

gossip 4 news **6** babble, report, tattle **7** comment, hearsay, prattle, scandal, twaddle **8** idle talk **10** backbiting **12** tittle-tattle **13** newsmongering

gossiper 3 pry **4** blab **5** prate, snoop, yenta **6** gabble, magpie, meddle, tattle **7** babbler, meddler, prattle, snooper, tattler **8** busybody **9** chatterer **10** chatterbox, newsmonger, talebearer, tattletale **11** rumormonger **12** blabbermouth, gossipmonger **13** scandalmonger

Go Tell It on the Mountain
 author: **12** James Baldwin

Gothic
 language family: **12** Indo-European
go through 4 bear **6** endure, suffer **7** sustain, undergo **9** encounter, withstand **10** experience
go to 3 see **5** visit **6** attend **8** appear at, frequent
go to bed 6 retire, turn in **7** lie down, sack out **8** flake out **9** hit the hay **10** call it a day, hit the sack **11** catch some z's
go to pieces 5 break, crack **7** break up, crack up, crumble, give way, shatter **8** splinter **9** break down, fall apart **11** lose control **12** disintegrate
go to work on 6 attack, tackle **8** set about **9** undertake
go to wrack and ruin 5 decay **7** crumble **9** fall apart **12** disintegrate
Gotterdammerung 17 Twilight of the Gods
 see: **8** Ragnarok
Gott mit uns 11 God be with us, God is with us
gouge 5 carve, drill, scoop **6** chisel, extort **10** overcharge
gouge out 5 drill **6** hollow **8** carve out, scoop out **9** chisel out, hollow out **10** whittle out
Gould, Chester
 creator/artist of: **9** Dick Tracy
Gould, Elliott
 real name: **16** Elliott Goldstein
 wife: **15** Barbra Streisand
 born: **10** Brooklyn NY
 roles: **4** MASH **13** Little Murders **14** The Long Goodbye **15** California Split, Getting Straight **19** Bob & Carol & Ted & Alice
Goulding, Edmund
 director of: **10** Grand Hotel **11** Dark Victory **13** The Dawn Patrol
go under 4 fail, fall, sink **9** go belly up **10** go bankrupt
Gounod, Charles Francois
 born: **5** Paris **6** France
 composer of: **5** Faust **6** Gallia, Sappho, Te Deum **8** Cinq-Mars, Mireille **9** La Colombe, Polyeucte **10** Mors et Vita **11** Marie Stuart, Stabat Mater **13** La Reine de Saba **14** Romeo and Juliet **16** La Nonne Sanglante, Phile-

mon et Baucis **17** La Tribute de Zamora **18** Le Medecin Malgre Lui
gourd 4 pepo **9** Cucurbita
 varieties: **3** ash, ivy, rag, wax **4** club **5** snake, white **6** bitter, bottle, dipper, sponge, teasel, viper's **7** fig-leaf, Malabar, serpent, trumpet **8** calabash, hedgehog, Missouri **9** dishcloth **10** goareberry, gooseberry, knobkerrie, silver-seed **11** sugar- trough **12** Hercules'-club **14** scarlet-fruited
gourmand 7 glutton **8** big eater **9** bon vivant, chowhound **11** gormandizer, trencherman
gourmet 7 epicure **9** bon vivant **10** gastronome **11** connoisseur, gastronomer **12** gastronomist
gourmet cooking
 French: **12** haute cuisine
gout 5 style, taste **10** preference
govern 3 run **4** boss, curb, form, head, lead, rule, sway, tame **5** check, guide, pilot, steer **6** bridle, direct, manage **7** command, control, incline, inhibit, oversee **8** dominate, restrain **9** influence, supervise **10** administer, discipline, hold in hand **11** hold in check, superintend **13** be at the helm of **14** pull the strings **16** keep under control **17** exercise authority **18** be in the driver's seat
governed 3 led **5** ruled **6** guided **7** steered, subject **8** directed **9** dependent **10** controlled, supervised **12** administered **13** superintended
governing 6 ruling **7** curbing, guiding, heading, leading, swaying **8** bridling, checking, managing, piloting, reigning, steering **9** directing, inclining **10** inhibiting, management, overseeing **11** controlling, influencing, restraining, supervision **13** administering **14** administrating, administration, superintending
governing body 10 government, management, parliament **12** powers that be **14** administration **16** board of directors, board of governors **18** executive committee
government 3 law **4** rule **5** state **6** regime **7** command, control **8** dominion, guidance **9** authority, direction **10** domination, management, regulation **11** supervision **13** governing body, statesmanship **14** administration
 absence of: **7** anarchy
 absolute: **7** czarism, tsarism, tyranny **9** autocracy, despotism
 by the best: **11** aristocracy
 by church: **9** theocracy
 by elders: **12** gerontocracy
 by technologists: **11** technocracy
 by few: **9** oligarchy
 by mob: **10** ochlocracy
 by people: **9** democracy
 by rich: **10** plutocracy
 by three: **8** triarchy **11** triumvirate

by two: 7 biarchy 10 duumvirate
by women: 8 gynarchy 10 matriarchy

governor
Turkish: 3 bey
Barbary States: 3 dey

Gowan
character in: 12 Little Dorrit
author: 7 Dickens

go with 6 convey, convoy, escort 7 conduct 9 accompany

gown 4 robe 5 dress, frock 10 nightdress

goy 6 non-Jew 7 Gentile

Goya (y Lucientes, Francisco Jose de)
born: 5 Spain 13 Fuente de todos
artwork: 8 Proverbs 10 Disparates 11 Tauromaquia 12 Los Caprichos, The Naked Maja 15 Majas on a Balcony 17 The Disasters of War 21 Charles IV and his Family

grab 3 bag, nab 4 grip, hold, pass 5 catch, clasp, grasp, lunge, pluck, seize 6 clutch, collar, snatch 7 capture

grace 4 deck, love, tact, trim 5 adorn, charm, endow, exalt, favor, honor, mercy, merit, piety, skill, taste 6 beauty, bedeck, enrich, pardon, polish, set off, virtue 7 charity, culture, decorum, dignify, dress up, elevate, enhance, garnish, glorify, manners, smarten, suavity 8 beautify, clemency, decorate, elegance, felicity, fluidity, God's love, holiness, lenience, ornament, reprieve, sanctity, spruce up, urbanity 9 embellish, endowment, etiquette, exemption, extra time, God's favor, good looks, propriety 10 aggrandize, comeliness, devoutness, excellence, indulgence, refinement 11 cultivation, forgiveness, lissomeness, pulchritude, saintliness, willowiness 12 dispensation, gracefulness, mannerliness, mercifulness 14 accomplishment, divine goodness
French: 11 savoir faire

graceful 5 lithe 6 comely, limber, lovely 7 elegant, lissome, shapely, sinuous, willowy 8 delicate 9 beautiful, lithesome, sylphlike 10 attractive 11 light-footed

gracefulness 8 delicacy, fluidity 10 suppleness 11 lissomeness

graceless 5 gawky, inept 6 clumsy 7 awkward 10 ungraceful 11 heavy-handed

Graces
also: 7 Gratiae 9 Charities
goddesses of: 6 beauty
father: 4 Zeus
mother: 8 Eurynome
names: 4 Auxo 5 Cleta 6 Aglaia, Thalia 7 Phaenna 8 Hegemone 10 Euphrosyne

gracious 2 my 3 boy, gee, wow 4 kind 5 civil, mercy, oh boy 6 benign, humane, kindly, polite, tender, ye gods 7 affable, amiable, clement, cordial, courtly, gee whiz, lenient, my stars 8 friendly, goodness, merciful, obliging, pleasant 9 benignant, courteous, landsakes 10 benevolent, charitable, chivalrous, hospitable 11 good heavens, good natured, kindhearted 13 compassionate 14 heavens to Betsy

gradation 4 step 5 stage 6 degree 7 shading 8 grouping, ordering 9 arranging 11 arrangement 12 organization 14 classification

grade 4 bank, even, hill, mark, ramp, rank, rate, sort, step 5 brand, caste, class, level, order, pitch, place, slope, stage, value 6 degree, estate, rating, smooth, sphere, status 7 flatten, incline, quality, station 8 classify, gradient, position, standing 9 acclivity, condition, declivity, intensity

grade-A 2 A-1 4 aces, a-one, fine, tops 5 grade, great, prime, super 6 choice, superb, tip-top 7 capital 8 peerless, sterling, superior, top-notch 9 excellent, first-rate, matchless, superfine 10 first-class, preeminent, tremendous 11 outstanding, superlative

Gradgrind, Thomas and Louisa
characters in: 9 Hard Times
author: 7 Dickens

gradient 4 ramp, tilt 5 pitch, slant, slope 6 ascent 7 incline, leaning 9 steepness 11 inclination

gradual 4 slow 6 gentle, steady 7 regular 8 measured 9 graduated, piecemeal 10 continuous, deliberate, drop-by-drop, inch-by-inch, step-by-step, successive 11 incremental, progressive 13 imperceptible, slow-but-steady 14 little-by-little

graduate 5 grade 6 alumna 7 alumnus, mark off 9 calibrate 10 measure out 14 grant a degree to, receive a degree

Graduate, The
director: 11 Mike Nichols
cast: 12 Anne Bancroft (Mrs Robinson) 13 Dustin Hoffman, Katharine Ross 14 Murray Hamilton, William Daniels
score: 17 Simon and Garfunkel
Oscar for: 8 director

Graeae
also: 6 Graiae
goddesses of: 3 sea
number: 5 three
names: 4 Enyo 5 Deino 9 Pemphredo
father: 7 Phorcys
mother: 4 Ceto
sisters: 7 Gorgons
protectresses of: 7 Gorgons
personified: 6 old age
three shared: 6 one eye 8 one tooth
eye stolen by: 7 Perseus
corresponds to: 4 Enyo

Graeme, Alison
character in: 21 The Master of Ballantrae
author: 9 Stevenson

Graf 5 count

graffito, graffiti 4 name 6 slogan 7 drawing, scratch 8 scribble 10 defacement

graft 3 bud 4 join, last, slip, swag 5 booty, infix, inset, plant, scion 6 bribes, payola, splice, spoils, sprout 7 bribery, implant, ingraft, payoffs, plunder, rake-off 8 kickback 9 hush money 10 corruption, transplant 12 implantation 13 inserted shoot

Graham, Bruce
architect of: 17 John Hancock Center (Chicago)

Grahame, Kenneth
author of: 19 The Wind in the Willows

Graiae see 6 Graeae

grain 3 bit, dot, jot, rye 4 atom, corn, dash, iota, mite, oats, seed, whit 5 crumb, grist, maize, ovule, pinch, spark, speck, touch, trace, wheat 6 barley, cereal, kernel, millet, morsel, pellet, tittle, trifle 7 granule, modicum 8 fragment, molecule, particle 9 scintilla
abbreviation: 2 gr
god of: 7 Robigus
goddess of: 6 Ribigo

Grain Coast see 11 Sierra Leone

Grainger, Percy Aldridge
born: 9 Australia, Melbourne
composer of: 14 Country Gardens 17 Handel in the Strand 19 Rosenkavalier Ramble

gram
abbreviation of: 1 g

Gram
origin: 12 Scandinavian
mentioned in: 8 Volsunga
form: 5 sword
owned by: 7 Sigmund
used by: 6 Sigurd
killed: 6 Fafnir

grand 2 A-1 3 big 4 fine, full, good, head, huge, keen, main 5 chief, fancy, great, large, lofty, noble, regal, royal, showy, super, swell 6 august, choice, groovy, kingly, lordly, superb 7 dashing, elegant, exalted, haughty, mammoth, opulent, pompous, queenly, stately, sublime, supreme 8 arrogant, complete, elevated, fabulous, glorious, imperial, imposing, majestic, palatial, princely, real cool, real gone, smashing, splendid, striking, terrific 9 admirable, dignified, excellent, first-rate, grandiose, luxurious, marvelous, principal, sumptuous, wonderful 10 impressive, monumental, out-of-sight 11 highfalutin, magnificent, pretentious, sensational 12 ostentatious 13 comprehensive, distinguished

Grand Canyon State
nickname of: **7** Arizona
grande dame 9 great lady
grandee 5 noble **8** nobleman **9** blue blood **10** aristocrat
Grandees
author: **17** Stephen Birmingham
grandeur 4 fame, pomp **5** glory, state **6** luster **7** dignity, majesty **8** eminence, nobility, splendor **9** celebrity, loftiness, solemnity, sublimity **10** augustness, excellence, importance **11** distinction, stateliness **12** magnificence, resplendence **14** impressiveness
Grand Hotel
author: **9** Vicki Baum
character: **9** Miss Flamm **12** Baron Gaigern **14** Dr Otternschlag, Otto Kringelein **27** Herr Generaldirektor Preysing **32** Elisaveta Alexandrovna Grusinskaya
director: **14** Edmund Goulding
cast: **10** Greta Garbo **12** Joan Crawford, Wallace Beery **13** John Barrymore **15** Lionel Barrymore
setting: **6** Berlin
Grand Illusion
director: **10** Jean Renoir
cast: **5** Dalio **7** Carette **9** Dita Parlo, Jean Gabin **13** Pierre Fresnay **16** Erich von Stroheim
grandiloquent 5 lofty **6** florid, turgid **7** flowery, pompous, stilted, swollen **8** inflated **9** bombastic, grandiose, high-flown **10** rhetorical **11** highfalutin, pretentious **12** high-sounding, magniloquent
grandiose 5 grand **7** pompous, splashy **8** affected **9** high-flown **10** flamboyant, theatrical **11** extravagant, highfalutin, pretentious
Grand Marnier
type: **6** brandy, cognac **7** liqueur
origin: **6** France
flavor: **6** orange
with gin: **7** Red Lion
grand monde 10 great world **11** best society **16** fashionable world
grand prix 10 grand prize
grand prize
French: **9** grand prix
Grange, Red (Harold)
nickname: **14** Galloping Ghost
sport: **8** football
team: **11** U of Illinois **12** Chicago Bears
Granger, Edith
character in: **12** Dombey and Son
author: **7** Dickens
Grangosier
character in: **22** Gargantua and Pantagruel
author: **8** Rabelais
Granite State
nickname of: **12** New Hampshire

grant 4 boon, cede, gift, give **5** admit, allot, allow, award, endow, favor, yield **6** accord, assign, bestow, confer, donate, permit **7** agree to, bequest, concede, consent, deal out, largess, present, subsidy, tribute **8** accede to, allocate, bestowal, dispense, donation, gratuity, offering **9** allotment, allowance, apportion, consent to, endowment, vouchsafe **10** assignment, concession, indulgence **11** benefaction **12** contribution, presentation **13** appropriation
Grant, Cary
real name: **23** Archibald Alexander Leach
wife: **10** Dyan Cannon **13** Barbara Hutton
born: **7** England **8** Bristol
roles: **6** Topper **9** Dream Wife, Houseboat **10** Indiscreet **11** Blonde Venus **12** To Catch a Thief **14** Bringing Up Baby, Monkey Business, The Bishop's Wife **15** She Done Him Wrong **16** North by Northwest **17** Arsenic and Old Lace, I Was a Male War Bride **18** Operation Petticoat **20** The Philadelphia Story **21** None But the Lonely Heart
Grant, Lee
real name: **21** Lyova Haskell Rosenthal
born: **9** New York NY
roles: **7** Shampoo **10** Plaza Suite **11** Peyton Place, The Landlord **14** Detective Story **19** In the Heat of the Night **20** Divorce American Style
Grant, Ulysses Simpson
real name: **17** Hiram Ulysses Grant
nickname: **3** Sam **4** Lyss **27** Unconditional Surrender Grant
presidential rank: **10** eighteenth
party: **10** Republican
state represented: **2** IL
defeated: **5** (David) Davis, (James) Black **6** (Charles) O'Conor **7** (Horace) Greeley, (Horatio) Seymour **9** (William Slocomb) Groesbeck
vice president: **5** (Thomas W) Ferry (acting) **6** (Henry) Wilson (died in office 1875), (Schuyler) Colfax
cabinet:
  state: **4** (Hamilton) Fish **9** (Elihu Benjamin) Washburne
  treasury: **7** (Alexander Turney) Stewart, (Benjamin Helm) Bristow, (Lot Myrick) Morrill **8** (George Sewall) Boutwell **10** (William Adams) Richardson
  war: **4** (Alphonso) Taft **7** (James Donald) Cameron, (John Aaron) Rawlins, (William Worth) Belknap
  attorney general: **4** (Alphonso) Taft, (Ebenezer Rockwood) Hoar **7** (Amos Tappan) Akerman **8** (George Henry) Williams **10** (Edwards) Pierrepont
  navy: **5** (Adolph Edward) Borie **7**

(George Maxwell) Robeson
  postmaster general: **5** (James Noble) Tyner **6** (Marshall) Jewell **8** (James William) Marshall, (John Angel James) Creswell
  interior: **3** (Jacob Dolson) Cox **6** (Columbus) Delano **8** (Zachariah) Chandler
born: **15** Point Pleasant OH
died: **15** Mount McGregor NY
buried: **9** New York NY
education: **9** West Point **17** US Military Academy
religion: **9** Methodist
author: **24** Personal Memoirs of US Grant **30** Around the World with General Grant
political career:
  secretary of: **3** War (interim appointment)
civilian career: **6** farmer
military service: **6** US Army **8** Civil War **10** Mexican War **18** Illinois Volunteers **20** Commander of Union Army
notable events of lifetime/career: **5** Panic (of 1873) **11** Black Friday (gold panic) **16** Custer's Last Stand
  Act: **10** Salary Grab
  conspiracy: **11** Whiskey Ring
  scandal: **14** Credit Mobilier
quote: **60** "No terms except unconditional and immediate surrender can be accepted"
father: **9** Jesse Root
mother: **6** Hannah (Simpson)
siblings: **5** Clare **10** Orvil Lynch **11** Mary Frances **13** Samuel Simpson, Virginia Paine
wife: **5** Julia (Boggs Dent)
children: **5** Ellen **9** Jesse Root **13** Frederick Dent **14** Ulysses Simpson
granted
French: **7** d'accord
grantee 8 receiver **9** recipient **11** beneficiary
grant immunity to 4 free **5** clear, spare **6** except, excuse, exempt **7** absolve, release, relieve **9** privilege
grantor 5 giver **8** bestower **10** benefactor
granulate 5 crush **6** powder **9** pulverize **11** crystallize
granulated 6 ground **7** crushed **8** powdered **10** pulverized **12** crystallized
granule 5 grain **7** crystal **8** particle
grape 5 Vitis **13** Vitis vinifera
varieties: **3** cat, red, sea **4** amur, blue, bush, cape, rock, sand, tail **5** bear's, bunch, frost, Javan, sugar, veldt **6** canyon, Damson, Miller, Oregon, pigeon, possum, summer, winter **7** African, Bullace, catbird, chicken, Concord, Spanish **8** European, mountain **9** evergreen, panhandle, river-bank **10** silver-leaf **11**

southern fox **13** sweet mountain

wine: 5 Gamay **6** Cayuga, Duriff, Merlot, Muscat, Shiraz **7** Barbera, Catawba **8** Baco Noir, Dolcetto, Labrusca, Nebbiolo, Verduzzo **9** Aglianico, Fume Blanc, Huxelrebe, Pinot Noir, Primitivo, Trebbiano, Zinfandel **10** Chardonnay, Sangiovese **11** Chenin Blanc, Petite Sirah, Pinot Bianco, Seyval Blanc **13** Cabernet Franc, Montepulciano **14** Sauvignon Blanc **15** Gewurtztraminer **17** Cabernet Sauvignon **20** Johannisberg Riesling

Grapes of Wrath, The
author: 13 John Steinbeck
character: 4 Noah **6** Connie, Ma Joad, Pa Joad **7** Jim Casy, Tom Joad **12** Rose of Sharon
director: 8 John Ford
cast: 10 Henry Fonda **11** Jane Darwell **12** Dorris Bowden **13** John Carradine **15** Charley Grapewin
Oscar for: 17 supporting actress (Darwell)

graphic 4 seen **5** clear, drawn, lucid, vivid **6** visual **7** painted, printed, visible, written **8** distinct, explicit, forcible, lifelike, pictured, striking **9** pictorial, realistic, trenchant **10** expressive **11** descriptive, picturesque **12** illustrative

grappa
type: 6 brandy **7** liqueur
origin: 5 Italy
made from: 9 grape pulp

grapple 4 face, grip, hold, meet **5** catch, clasp, fight, grasp, seize **6** breast, clutch, combat, engage, fasten, tackle, take on **7** contend, grapnel, wrestle **8** confront, deal with, do battle, make fast, struggle **9** encounter, large hook, lay hold of **11** hold tightly

grasp 3 get, ken **4** grab, grip, hold, sway, take **5** catch, clasp, infer, power, range, reach, savvy, scope, seize, sense, skill, sweep **6** clinch, clutch, deduce, fathom, follow, master, snatch, take in, talent **7** catch at, compass, control, embrace, grapple, mastery, seizing, seizure **8** clutches, gripping, perceive **9** handclasp, knowledge, seize upon **10** comprehend, perception, understand **13** comprehension, understanding

grasping 5 venal **6** greedy **7** hoggish, miserly, selfish, wolfish **8** covetous **9** mercenary, predatory, rapacious **10** avaricious **11** acquisitive

graspingness 5 greed **7** avarice **8** rapacity, venality **10** greediness **12** covetousness

grass
varieties: 3 cup, cut, dog, eel, elk, mat, nut, oat, oil, pin, rib, rye, Uva **4** barn, bear, bent, blue, chee, cord, crab, deer, fish, hair, lace, love, Lyme, moor, Nard, palm, Para, rice, rush, silk, star, tape, worm, yard **5** arrow, Bahia, beach, beard, Brome, Carib, China, cloud, curly, Ditch, fever, goose, lemon, Means, Melic, Mondo, natal, quack, sedge, shave, shore, Smilo, spike, squaw, Sudan, sword, Vasey, wheat, white, witch, zebra **6** Aleppo, alkali, basket, Bengal, Buffel, Canary, carpet, Dallis, Dudder, finger, gallow, Guinea, Indian, Korean, Manila, Napier, orange, orchid, Pampas, Rescue, Rhodes, ribbon, ripple, scurvy, signal, starry, switch, Tobosa, velvet, vernal, viper's, Zoysia **7** Bermuda, Brahman, Bristle, Buffalo, Esparto, Harding, Johnson, Kleberg, Pangola, poverty, pudding, quaking, Ravenna, sea lyme, serpent, tall oat, Wallaby, Widgeon **8** Angleton, blue-eyed, blue love, Boer love, elephant, fountain, hairy cup, lazy- man's, molasses, Ree wheat, sand love, scorpion, tuber oat **9** blue conch, centipede, common rye, hairy crab, hare's-tail, Hungarian, Malojilla, Mascarene, Oregon rye, rancheria, tall wheat, water star, yellow nut **10** Amur silver, beavertail, big quaking, blue finger, citronella, English rye, false wheat, golden-eyed, Indian rice, Italian rye, Korean lawn, Kuma bamboo, purple-eyed, rabbit-foot, rabbit-tail, reed canary, tufted hair, Washington, western rye, yellow-eyed **11** annual beard, branched cup, desert wheat, domestic rye, dwarf meadow, feather love, giant finger, green needle, Lehmann love, Nepal silver, Pentz finger, prairie cord, ringed beard, St Augustine, sweet vernal, Texas needle, Texas winter, weeping love **12** Common carpet, crested wheat, crinkled hair, European dune, Indian basket, Japanese lawn, Japanese love, Korean velvet, perennial rye, slender wheat, squirreltail, western wheat **13** American beach, Australian rye, billion-dollar, European beach, Himalaya fairy, Japanese sedge, little quaking, Paraguay Bahia, plains bristle, Siberian wheat **14** African Bermuda, bluebunch wheat, Japanese carpet, Pensacola Bahia, perennial veldt, pubescent wheat, Saint Augustine, stiff-hair wheat **15** European feather, Wilmington Bahia **16** creeping windmill, Pacey's English rye **17** Australian rye, intermediate wheat, Mediterranean salt, Transvaal dog-tooth **18** Australian windmill, California blue-eyed, Mexican everlasting **19** Fairway crested wheat **20** standard crested wheat

Grass, Gunter
author of: 6 Floods **8** Dog Years **10** The Tin Drum **11** Cat and Mouse, The Flounder **16** Local Anaesthetic **18** The Meeting at Telgte **20** From the Diary of a Snail **33** Headbirths or The Germans Are Dying Out

grasshopper
variety: 5 pygmy **6** meadow, monkey **7** katydid **10** band winged, cone headed, long-horned, slant-faced **11** bush katydid, leaf-rolling, short-horned **12** shield-backed, spur-throated

grassland 3 lea **4** farm, vale, veld **5** field, pampa, plain, range, veldt **6** meadow **7** pasture, prairie, savanna **8** farmland, flatland, savannah **10** plantation

grate 3 irk, jar, rub, vex **4** bars, burr, buzz, gall, rasp **5** annoy, chafe, clack, grill, grind, mince, shred **6** abrade, gnaw at, hearth, jangle, rankle, scrape, scream, screen **7** firebed, firebox, grating, lattice, scratch, screech **8** irritate **9** fireplace, pulverize **10** exasperate, firebasket **11** latticework

grateful 7 obliged **8** beholden, indebted, thankful **9** gratified, obligated **12** appreciative

gratefulness 6 thanks **9** gratitude **12** appreciation, thankfulness

Gratiae *see* **6** Graces

Gratiano
character in: 19 The Merchant of Venice
author: 11 Shakespeare

gratification 3 joy **4** glee, kick **5** bliss **6** relish, solace, thrill **7** comfort, delight, ecstasy, elation, rapture **8** gladness, humoring, pleasing, pleasure, soothing **9** enjoyment, happiness, transport **10** indulgence, jubilation, satisfying **11** contentment, enchantment **12** exhilaration, satisfaction

gratified 5 happy **7** content, pleased **9** satisfied **11** comfortable

gratify 4 suit **5** amuse, favor, humor **6** coddle, divert, pamper, please, regale, soothe, thrill, tickle **7** appease, delight, enchant, flatter, gladden, indulge, refresh, satisfy **8** enthrall, entrance, interest, recreate **9** enrapture, entertain, transport **10** compliment, exhilarate

gratifying 8 humoring, pleasant, pleasing, soothing **9** agreeable, enjoyable, indulging, pampering, rewarding **10** delightful, satisfying **11** pleasurable

grating 4 bars, fret, grid **5** grate, harsh, raspy **6** creaky, grille, shrill **7** jarring, lattice, rasping, raucous, squeaky, tracery, trellis **8** abrasive, annoying, filigree, fretwork, gridiron, jangling, piercing, scraping, strident **9** offensive, vexatious **10** discordant, gate of bard, irritating, unpleasant **11** cacophonous, displeasing, high-pitched **12** disagreeable, exacerbating, exasperating

grating noise 7 discord, rasping **8** grinding **9** cacophony, harshness **10** disharmony, dissonance

gratis 4 free **10** gratuitous, on the house **13** complimentary, without charge

gratitude 6 thanks **10** obligation **11** recognition **12** appreciation, beholdenness, gratefulness, thankfulness, thanksgiving **14** acknowledgment

gratuitous 4 free **6** gratis, wanton **7** donated, willing **8** baseless, unproven **9** unfounded, voluntary **10** free of cost, groundless, irrelevant, unasked for, unprovoked **11** conjectural, impertinent, presumptive, spontaneous, uncalled for, unjustified, unwarranted **13** complimentary, unrecompensed

gratuity 3 tip **4** gift **8** donation
French: **7** douceur **9** pourboire

Graustark
author: **20** George Barr McCutcheon

grave 4 dour, sage, tomb **5** acute, crypt, mound, quiet, sober, staid, vault, vital **6** gloomy, sedate, solemn, somber, urgent **7** crucial, earnest, ossuary, serious, subdued, weighty **8** catacomb, cenotaph, critical, frowning, pressing **9** dignified, important, long-faced, mausoleum, momentous, sepulcher **10** thoughtful **11** burial ground, grim visaged, significant **13** consequential, philosophical **16** last resting place, place of interment
music: **6** solemn **7** serious

Graves, Robert
author of: **9** I Claudius, King Jesus **14** Claudius the God **15** The White Goddess **16** Goodbye to All That

graveyard 7 charnel, ossuary **8** boneyard, boot hill, cemetery **10** churchyard, necropolis **12** memorial park, potter's field **13** burying ground

gravitate 4 fall, head, move, sink, tend **6** settle **7** be drawn, descend, incline **8** converge, zero in on **9** be prone to **10** lean toward

gravity 4 pull **6** danger, import, moment **7** concern, dignity, urgency **8** calmness, enormity, grimness, serenity, sobriety **9** emergency, magnitude, solemnity, staidness **10** attraction, gloominess, importance, sedateness, solemnness, somberness **11** consequence, earnestness, gravitation, seriousness **12** significance, tranquillity **13** consideration, crucial nature **14** critical nature, pull of the earth, thoughtfulness **16** mutual attraction

gray, grey 3 dun **4** ashy, dark, drab, pale **5** ashen, foggy, hoary, misty, murky, slate **6** cloudy, dismal, gloomy, silver, somber **7** clouded, grayish, grizzly, neutral, silvery, sunless **8** overcast **9** cheerless, pearl-gray **10** depressing, gray-haired, grayheaded **11** dove-colored, hoary-headed **12** mouse-colored, silver-haired **13** salt and pepper

Gray, Harold
creator/artist of: **17** Little Orphan Annie

Gray, Thomas
author of: **32** Elegy Written in a Country Churchyard

grayness 4 murk **6** pallor **8** drabness **9** bleakness **10** somberness

Grayson, Kathryn
real name: **19** Zelma Kathryn Hedrick
born: **14** Winston-Salem NC
roles: **8** Show Boat **10** Kiss Me Kate **13** Anchors Aweigh, The Desert Song **15** The Vagabond King

graze 3 rub **4** crop, rasp, skim, skin **5** brush, grind, swipe **6** abrade, browse, bruise, glance, scrape **7** pasture, scratch **8** abrasion, eat grass **16** turn out to pasture

grease 3 fat, oil **4** balm, lard **5** salve **6** anoint, tallow **7** unguent **8** ointment **9** drippings, lubricant, lubricate

grease the palm 3 tip **5** bribe **6** buy off, pay off

greasy 3 fat **4** oily, waxy **5** fatty, lardy, slick **7** buttery **8** slippery, slithery **10** lardaceous, oleaginous

great 3 apt, big **4** able, a-one, cool, fine, good, high, huge, kind, many, phat, vast, well **5** chief, crack, grand, grave, gross, heavy, large, noble, noted, super, swell **6** adroit, choice, expert, famous, groovy, humane, loving, strong, superb **7** awesome, crucial, decided, eminent, extreme, grandly, immense, leading, mammoth, notable, serious, titanic, weighty **8** abundant, colossal, critical, enormous, esteemed, fabulous, generous, gigantic, glorious, gracious, manifold, renowned, skillful, smashing, splendid, superbly, superior, terrific, very well **9** boundless, countless, cyclopean, excellent, fantastic, first-rate, important, marvelous, momentous, monstrous, prominent, unlimited, wonderful **10** altruistic, celebrated, gargantuan, high-minded, inordinate, out-of-sight, prodigious, proficient, pronounced, remarkable, splendidly, stupendous, tremendous, voluminous **11** crackerjack, excellently, extravagant, illustrious, magnanimous, magnificent, outstanding, sensational, significant, superlative, wonderfully **12** considerable **13** consequential, distinguished, inexhaustible, magnificently, multitudinous **14** out of this world

Great Ajax
origin: **5** Greek
hero of: **9** Trojan War

greater 4 more **5** finer **6** better, bigger, larger **8** superior

Great Escape, The
director: **11** John Sturges
cast: **11** James Coburn, James Garner **12** Steve McQueen **13** David McCallum **14** Charles Bronson **15** Donald Pleasance **19** Richard Attenborough
setting: **7** Germany, POW camp

greatest 4 best, most **5** ultra **6** picked, select, utmost **7** extreme, highest, maximal, maximum, noblest, supreme **8** champion **9** first-rate **11** superlative, unsurpassed

Greatest Show on Earth, The
director: **13** Cecil B DeMille
cast: **11** Betty Hutton, Cornel Wilde **12** James Stewart **13** Dorothy Lamour, Gloria Grahame **14** Charlton Heston
Oscar for: **7** picture

Great Expectations
author: **14** Charles Dickens
character: **3** Pip **7** Estella **9** Compeyson, Mr Jaggers **10** Joe Gargery **12** Abel Magwitch, Miss Havisham **13** Herbert Pocket
director: **9** David Lean
cast: **9** John Mills **11** Martita Hunt **12** Alec Guinness, Bernard Mills **13** Valerie Hobson **16** Francis L Sullivan

Great Gatsby, The
author: **16** F Scott Fitzgerald
character: **9** Jay Gatsby **11** Tom Buchanan **12** Myrtle Wilson, Nick Carraway **13** Daisy Buchanan

Great God Brown, The
author: **12** Eugene O'Neill

great lady
French: **10** grande dame

Great Lake 4 Erie **5** Huron **7** Ontario **8** Michigan, Superior

Great Land
nickname of: **6** Alaska

greatly 6 vastly **7** largely, notably **8** markedly, mightily, very much **9** immensely **10** abundantly, enormously, infinitely, powerfully, remarkably **12** considerably, immeasurably, tremendously

great mishap 5 wreck **6** blight, fiasco **7** tragedy **8** calamity, disaster **9** cataclysm, ruination **11** catastrophe

greatness 8 eminence, nobility **9** loftiness **10** excellence, importance, notability, prominence **11** preeminence, superiority **12** magnificence **15** illustriousness

Great Profile
nickname of: **13** John Barrymore

Great Railway Bazaar, The
author: **11** Paul Theroux

great world
French: **10** grand monde

Great Ziegfeld, The
director: **14** Robert Z Leonard
cast: **9** Myrna Loy **10** Fanny Brice **11** Frank Morgan, Luise Rainer (Anna Held) **13** Virginia Bruce, William

Powell
Oscar for: 7 actress (Rainer), picture
grebe 4 bird, fowl, loon **5** diver **6** dipper **7** henbill **8** dabchick **9** hell-diver **10** water witch
Grecco, Al
character in: 20 Appointment in Samarra
author: 5 O'Hara
Greco, El Greco
real name: 23 Domenikos Theotokopoulos
born: 5 Crete **6** Candia
artwork: 7 Espolio (Disrobing of Christ), Laocoon **12** View of Toledo **19** Cleaning of the Temple **20** Healing of the Blind Man **21** Burial of the Count Orgaz **27** Christ Stripped of his Garments **28** San Ildefonso at his Writing Desk **29** Cardinal Fernando Nino de Guevara **42** Christ Driving the Money-Changers from the Temple
Greece
other name: 5 Ellas **16** Hellenic Republic
capital/largest city: 6 Athens
others: 4 Enor **5** Canea, Corfu, Pylos, Volos **6** Delphi, Patras, Sparta **7** Chalcis, Corinth, Olympia, Piraeus **8** Salonika, Thessaly **9** Epidaurus, Gallipoli **10** Herakleion **11** Hermoupolis
school: 5 Crete **6** Athens, Patras, Thrace **8** Ioannina, Salonika
division: 6 Attica, Epirus, Thrace **7** Boeotia **8** Thessaly **9** Macedonia
measure: 3 pik **4** bema, piki, pous **5** baril, chous, cubit, diote, doron, maris, pekhe, podos, pygon, xylon **6** acaena, bacile, barile, cotula, dichas, gramme, hemina, koilon, lichas, milion, orgyia, palame, pechys, schene, xestes **7** amphora, bacvhel, chenica, choenix, cyathos, diaulos, metreta, stadium, stremma **8** condylos, daktylos, dekapode, dolichos, medimnos, medimnus, metretes, palaiste, plethron, plethrum, stathmos **9** hemiekton, oxybaphon
monetary unit: 5 lepta **7** drachma
weight: 3 mna, oke **4** mina, obol **5** livre, pound **6** diobol, kantar, obolos, obolus, talent **7** chalcon, drachma **8** diobolon
island: 3 Ios **5** Chios, Corfu, Crete, Delos, Melos, Naxos, Paros, Samos, Syros, Tenos, Thera, Zante **6** Andros, Euboea, Ionian, Ithaca, Lemnos, Lesbos, Patmos, Rhodes, Skyros, Thasos **7** Mykonos **8** Cyclades, Mytilene, Skiathos, Skopelos **9** Alonnisos **10** Cephalonia, Dodecanese, Samothrace **16** Northern Sporades
lake: 5 Karla, Volve **6** Copais, Kopais, Prespa, Voweis **8** Ioannina, Koroneia, Vistonis **9** Trichonis, Vegoritis
mountain: 3 Ida **4** Idhi, Oeta, Oite,

Ossa **5** Athos **6** Ithome, Peleon, Pelion, Pindus **7** Grammos, Helicon, Rhodope **8** Hymettos, Smolikas, Taygetos, Taygetus **9** Parnassus **10** Hagion Oros, Lycabettus, Pentelicus
highest point: 7 Olympus
river: 4 Arta **6** Peneus, Struma, Vardar **7** Hellada, Maritsa **8** Achelous, Aliakmon
sea: 5 Crete **6** Aegean, Ionian **7** Mirtoon **13** Mediterranean
physical feature:
gulf: 7 Corinth, Saronic
peninsula: 6 Balkan **10** Chalcidice **12** Peloponnesus
plain: 7 Boeotia **8** Thessaly
plateau: 7 Arcadia
valley: 5 Nemea
people: 5 Greek **6** Achean, Dorian, Ionian **7** Aeolian, Hellene
artist: 7 El Greco
author: 5 Homer **6** Hesiod, Pindar **8** Menander **9** Aeschylus, Euripides, Sophocles **11** Kazantzakis **12** Aristophanes
god: 4 Ares, Hera, Leto, Zeus **5** Cupid **6** Apollo, Cronus, Hermes, Hestia **7** Artemis, Demeter **8** Dionysus, Poseidon **9** Aphrodite **10** Hephaestus, Persephone **12** Pallas Athena **13** Phoebus Apollo
historian: 9 Herodotus **10** Thucydides
king: 11 Constantine
lawmaker: 5 Draco, Solon **8** Lycurgus, Pericles
leader: 10 Papandreou
mathematician: 6 Euclid **10** Archimedes, Pythagoras
mythological: 5 Atlas, Helen, Jason, Medea, Paris **6** Hector, Medusa **7** Ariadne, Chimera, Pandora, Pegasus, Perseus, Theseus **8** Achilles, Heracles, Minotaur, Odysseus **9** Agamemnon, Andromeda, Iphigenia, King Minos **10** Prometheus **11** Bellerophon
orator: 11 Demosthenes
philosopher: 5 Plato **8** Socrates **9** Aristotle
physician: 11 Hippocrates
sculptor: 5 Myron **7** Phidias **10** Praxiteles
tycoon: 7 Onassis
language: 5 Greek
religion: 14 Greek Orthodoxy
place:
ruins: 5 Delos, Pella, Pylos, Samos **6** Delphi, Sparta, Thebes, Tiryns **7** Corinth, Eleusis, Elevsis, Knossos, Mycenae, Olympia **9** Acropolis, Epidaurus, Parthenon **13** Palace of Minos
feature:
coffeeshop: 7 kaphene
marketplace: 5 agora
port 7 Piraeus
presidential guard: 7 Evzones

village square: 7 plateia
food:
dish: 4 gyro **7** baklava, mousaka **8** moussaka, souvlaki, dolmades **10** shish kabob
liquor: 4 ouzo
wine: 7 retsina
greed 7 avarice, avidity, craving **8** cupidity, rapacity **11** itching palm, money-hunger, piggishness, selfishness **12** covetousness **13** rapaciousness **14** avariciousness
greediness 7 avarice **8** gluttony, rapacity, voracity **12** covetousness, graspingness **15** acquisitiveness
greedy 4 avid **5** eager **6** ardent, hungry **7** anxious, burning, craving, fervent, hoggish, piggish, selfish, swinish, wolfish **8** covetous, famished, grasping, ravenous **9** devouring, impatient, mercenary, predatory, rapacious, thirsting, voracious **10** avaricious, gluttonous, insatiable **11** acquisitive, money-hungry **12** gormandizing
Greek
language family: 12 Indo-European
ancient branch: 5 Attic, Doric, Ionic **6** Aeolic
Greek alphabet 5 alpha **4** beta **5** gamma **5** delta **7** epsilon **4** zeta **3** eta **5** theta **4** iota **5** kappa **6** lambda **2** mu **2** nu **2** xi **7** omicron **2** pi **3** rho **5** sigma **3** tau **7** upsilon **3** phi **3** chi **3** psi **5** omega
Greek Anthology, The
author: 8 Cephalas, Meleager
Greek measure 4 mina **5** cubit **6** obolos, talent **7** drachma, stadion
Greek Mythology
afterworld of the blessed: 7 Elysium
amber islands: 10 Electrides
architect of labyrinth: 8 Daedalus
blood-sucking monster: 5 Lamia
cupbearer to the gods: 8 Ganymede **9** Catamitus
dragon: 8 basilisk
drink of the gods: 6 nectar
eagle/lion monster: 7 griffin, griffon, gryphon
enchantress: 5 Circe
female warrior: 6 Amazon
fire-breathing monster: 7 Chimera
first man: 12 Alalcomeneus
food/drink/perfume of the gods: 8 ambrosia
the Furies: 5 Dirae **6** Erinys, Furiae, Semnai **7** Erinyes **9** Eumenides
names: 7 Allecto, Megaera **9** Tisiphone
goat god: 7 Aegipan
goddess of beauty: 6 Graces **7** Gratiae **9** Charities
names: 4 Auxo **5** Cleta **6** Aglaia, Thalia **7** Phaenna **8** Hegemone **10** Euphrosyne
goddess of childbirth: 8 Ilithyia **10** Eileithyia

corresponds to Roman: **6** Lucina
goddess of the dawn: **3** Eos
corresponds to Roman: **6** Aurora
goddesses of destiny: **5** Fates, Morae
6 Moerae, Moirai
names: **5** Moira **6** Clotho **8** Lachesis
corresponds to Roman: **6** Parcae
goddess of discord: **4** Eris
corresponds to Roman: **9** Discordia
goddess of divine punishment/
recklessness: **3** Ate
goddess of divine retribution: **8** Adrastea
goddess of the earth: **2** Ge **4** Gaea, Gaia
corresponds to Roman: **6** Tellus
goddess of earth/fertility: **7** Demeter
corresponds to Roman: **5** Ceres
goddess of earth/Hades: **5** Brimo **6** Hecate, Hekate
goddess of fortune: **5** Tyche
corresponds to Roman: **7** Fortuna
goddess of healing: **4** Iaso
goddess of health: **6** Hygeia
corresponds to Roman: **5** Salus
goddess of the hearth: **6** Hestia
corresponds to Roman: **5** Vesta
goddess of justice: **4** Dice, Dike **6** Astrea **7** Astraea
goddesses of literature/the arts: **5** Muses **7** the Nine **8** Pierides **10** Castalides
names: **4** Clio **5** Aoede, Erato, Mneme **6** Melete, Thalia, Urania **7** Euterpe **8** Calliope **9** Melpomene **10** Polyhymnia **11** Terpsichore
corresponds to Roman: **7** Camenae
muse of astronomy: **6** Urania
muse of dancing/choral song: **11** Terpsichore
muse of history: **4** Clio
muse of idyllic poetry/comedy: **6** Thalia
muse of love poetry: **5** Erato
muse of meditation: **6** Melete
muse of memory: **5** Mneme
muse of music/lyric poetry: **7** Euterpe
muse of poetry/epic: **8** Calliope
muse of sacred music/dance: **10** Polyhymnia
muse of song: **5** Aoede
muse of tragedy: **9** Melpomene
goddess of love/beauty: **6** Urania **7** Cyprian, Paphian **8** Cytherea **9** Aphrodite **10** Anadyomene
corresponds to Roman: **5** Venus
goddess of memory: **9** Mnemosyne
goddess of the night: **3** Nyx
goddess of peace: **5** Irene
corresponds to Roman: **3** Pax
goddess of the rainbow: **4** Iris
goddess of sailors: **5** Brizo
goddess of the sea: **10** Amphitrite
goddesses of the sea: **6** Graeae,

Graiae
names: **4** Enyo **5** Deino **9** Pemphredo
goddesses of seasons/growth/
decay/social order: **4** Hour **5** Horae
names: **4** Dice, Dike **5** Carpo, Irene **6** Thallo **7** Eunomia
goddess of spring flowers: **6** Thallo
goddess of summer fruit: **5** Carpo
goddess of victory: **4** Nike
corresponds to Roman: **6** Athena **8** Victoria
goddess of war: **4** Enyo
corresponds to Roman: **7** Bellona
goddess of wisdom/fertility/arts/
warfare: **6** Athena, Athene, Pallas, Saitis **11** Tritogeneia **12** Pallas Athena **18** Alalcomenean Athena
corresponds to Roman: **7** Minerva
goddess of youth/spring: **4** Hebe
god of beekeeping/winemaking/
husbandry: **9** Aristaeus
god of censure/ridicule: **5** Momos, Momus
god of dreams: **6** Icelus, Oniros **7** Oneiros **8** Morpheus
god of earth: **10** Trophonius
god of Eleusinian mysteries: **7** Bacchus
god of erotic desire: **7** Himeros
god of fire/metalworking/
handicrafts: **10** Hephaestus, Hephaistos
corresponds to Roman: **6** Vulcan
god of the heavens: **4** Zeus
corresponds to Roman: **4** Jove **7** Jupiter
corresponds to Egyptian: **4** Amen, Amon **5** Ammon **6** Amen Ra, Amon Ra
god of light/healing/music/poetry/
prophecy/beauty: **6** Apollo
god of love: **4** Eros
corresponds to Roman: **4** Amor **5** Cupid
god of male power/procreation: **7** Priapus
corresponds to Roman: **7** Mutinus
god of marriage: **5** Hymen **9** Hymenaeus
corresponds to Roman: **8** Talassio
god of medicine/healing: **9** Asclepius
corresponds to Roman: **11** Aesculapius
god of oaths: **6** Horcus
god of recovery from illness: **11** Telesphorus
god of sea/caused earthquakes: **8** Poseidon
corresponds to Roman: **7** Neptune
god of shepherds/flocks/pastures/
forests: **3** Pan **7** Sinoeis
god of sleep: **6** Hypnos, Hypnus
corresponds to Roman: **6** Somnus
god of the sun: **6** Helios **8** Hyperion
corresponds to Roman: **3** Sol
god of the underworld: **6** Infiri

god of war: **4** Ares **8** Theritas
corresponds to Roman: **4** Mars
god of wine/fertility/drama: **5** Evius **7** Bacchus **8** Dionysus
Gorgon monster: **6** Medusa
hundred-headed monster: **5** Ladon **8** Typhoeus
islands of the blessed: **10** Hesperides
man/horse monster: **7** centaur
messenger of gods/god of roads/
commerce/invention/cunning/
thieves: **6** Hermes
corresponds to Roman: **7** Mercury
monster that asked riddles: **6** Sphinx
monsters that turn people to stone: **7** Gorgons
moon goddess/huntress/virgin: **6** Phoebe, Selene **7** Artemis
corresponds to Roman: **5** Diana
corresponds to Cretan: **11** Britomartis
nine-headed water serpent: **5** Hydra
nymph: **7** Calypso
one-eyed giant: **7** Cyclops
oracle of Apollo: **13** Delphic oracle
personification of death: **4** Mors **8** Thanatos
personification of punishment/
revenge: **5** Poena, Poine
personification of soul: **6** Psyche
physician to gods of Olympia: **5** Paeon
prophetess: **9** Alexandra, Cassandra
queen of heaven: **4** Hera, Here
corresponds to Roman: **4** Juno
race of gods: **6** Titans
names: **4** Rhea, Thia **5** Coeus, Crius **6** Cronus, Phoebe, Tethys, Themis **7** Iapetus, Oceanus **8** Hyperion **9** Mnemosyne
river god: **6** Asopus, Peneus, Simois **7** Inachus, Pelegon **8** Achelous
river in Hades: **4** Styx **5** Lethe **7** Acheron, Cocytus
ferryman: **6** Charon
river of forgetfulness: **5** Lethe
ruler of the winds: **6** Aeolus
satyr/god of the forest: **7** Silenus
sea god: **6** Nereus, Triton **7** Glaucus, Phorcys, Proteus
sea monster: **6** Scylla
seer: **6** Mopsus **8** Tiresias
serpent: **6** dipsas
serpent of darkness: **5** Apepi **7** Apophis
seven against Thebes: **6** Tydeus **8** Adrastus, Capaneus **9** Polynices **10** Amphiaraus, Hippomedon **13** Parthenopaeus
seven sisters: **8** Pleiades
names: **4** Maia **6** Merope **7** Alcyone, Celaeno, Electra, Sterope, Taygete
sorceress: **5** Medea
spirits of disease/evil/old age/death: **5** Keres
three-headed dog that guards un-

derworld: **8** Cerberus
twins: **8** Dioscuri **15** Castor and Pollux
two-headed serpent: **11** Amphisbaena
underworld: **5** Hades,
   corresponds to Roman: **3** Dis **5** Orcus, Pluto **8** Dis Pater
underworld darkness: **6** Erebus
underworld spirit: **9** Chthonian
virgin huntress: **8** Atalanta, Atalante
whirlpool: **9** Charybdis
winged horse: **5** Arion **7** Pegasus
woman/beast monster: **6** Python **8** Delphyne
woman/bird monster: **5** Harpy
woman/serpent monster: **7** Echidna
wood nymph: **5** dryad
Greek uncial codex 4 Syri **6** Regius **8** Ephraemi **9** Laudianus, Vaticanus **10** Sinaiticus **11** Basiliensis **12** Alexandrinus, Sangallensis **13** Koridethianus
green 3 raw **4** jade, lawn, lime, turf **5** crude, heath, olive, rough, sward, young **6** callow, campus, common, tender, unripe **7** awkward, emerald, verdant, verdure **8** greenish, gullible, ignorant, immature, inexpert, not cured, not dried, pea-green, sea-green, unsmoked, untanned, unversed **9** blue-green, credulous, grassplot, lime-green, unfledged, unskilled, untrained **10** aquamarine, chartreuse, golf course, grass-green, greensward, kelly-green, olive green, uninformed, unmellowed, unpolished, unseasoned **11** cobalt green, forest green, undeveloped, yellow-green **12** easily fooled, green-colored, not fully aged, putting green, village green **13** inexperienced, undisciplined **14** underdeveloped **15** unsophisticated
Green Acres
  character: **7** Mr Haney **8** Eb Dawson **10** Fred Ziffel, Sam Drucker **11** Doris Ziffel, Hank Kimball, Lisa Douglas **20** Oliver Wendell Douglas
  cast: **8** Eva Gabor, Fran Ryan **9** Alvy Moore, Frank Cady, Tom Lester **10** Pat Buttram **11** Eddie Albert **13** Barbara Pepper, Hank Patterson
  pig: **6** Arnold
  town: **11** Hooterville
green at the gills 6 queasy, sickly **7** bilious **8** nauseous **9** nauseated, sickening
greenback 4 bill **8** banknote **12** treasury note **15** legal-tender note **17** silver certificate
Green Bay
  football team: **7** Packers
Green Bay Tree, The
  author: **14** Louis Bromfield
Greene, Graham
  author of: **11** The Third Man **12** Brighton Rock, Ways of Escape **14** The Human Factor **16** Monsignor

Quixote **17** The End of the Affair, The Ministry of Fear, Travels with My Aunt **19** The Heart of the Matter, The Power and the Glory
Greene, Joe
  nickname: **7** Mean Joe
  sport: **8** football
  position: **7** lineman
  team: **18** Pittsburgh Steelers
Greene, Lorne
  born: **6** Canada, Ottawa **7** Ontario
  roles: **5** Adama **7** Bonanza **11** Peyton Place **12** Autumn Leaves, The Buccaneer **13** Ben Cartwright **16** The Silver Chalice **19** Battlestar Galactica
Greene, Nathanael
  served in: **16** Revolutionary War
  rank: **16** brigadier general **20** quartermaster general
  battle: **7** Cowpens, Trenton **12** Eutaw Springs, Hobkirk's Hill **18** Guilford Court House
green-eyed monster 4 envy **8** jealousy **12** covetousness
Green for Danger
  director: **13** Sidney Gilliat
  cast: **7** Leo Genn **9** Sally Gray **11** Alastair Sim **12** Rosamund John, Trevor Howard
greenhorn 4 rube, tyro **6** novice, rookie **7** learner **8** beginner, neophyte, newcomer **9** fledgling **10** apprentice, tenderfoot **14** babe in the woods
Green Hornet, The
  character: **4** Kato **9** Britt Reid (The Green Hornet)
  cast: **8** Bruce Lee **11** Van Williams
  car: **11** Black Beauty
  creator: **11** Bert Whitman
  sidekick: **4** Kato
Green House, The
  author: **16** Mario Vargas Llosa
Greening of America, The
  author: **12** Charles Reich
greenish 6 sickly **7** bilious
Greenland
  alternate name: **14** Kalaalit Nunaat
  capital/largest city: **3** Nuk **8** Godthaab, The Point
  others: **4** Etah, Nord **5** Thule **6** Ivigut, Umanak **7** Godhavn, Ivigtut **10** Nanortalik **11** Julianehaab **12** Angmagssalik, Sukkertoppen **14** Christianshaab
  government: **20** home rule under Denmark
  monetary unit: **3** ore **5** krone
  island: **5** Disko
  mountain: **5** Forel, Payer **7** Khardyu **8** Peterman **15** Petermannsbjerg
  highest point: **9** Gunnbjorn **16** Gunnbjornsfjaeld
  sea: **6** Arctic **9** Greenland
  physical feature: **9** Inland Ice
    bay: **5** Disko **6** Baffin **8** Melville
    cape: **4** Jaal **6** Grivel, Walker **8** Bismarck, Brewster, Farewell, Lowen-

orn **11** Morris Jesup
    glacier: **10** Jacobshavn
    strait: **5** Davis **7** Denmark
  people: **3** Ita **6** Eskimo **8** European
    explorer: **10** Eric the Red
  language: **6** Danish, Eskimo **11** Greenlandic
  religion: **19** Evangelical Lutheran
  feature:
    airbase: **4** Etah **5** Thule
    animal: **7** caribou
Green Mansions
  author: **8** W H Hudson
  character: **4** Rima **5** Nuflo **6** Mr Abel
Greenmantle
  author: **10** John Buchan
Green Mountain State
  nickname of: **7** Vermont
Greenough, Horatio
  born: **8** Boston MA
  artwork: **16** George Washington **18** The Chanting Cherubs
Green Pastures, The
  author: **12** Marc Connelly
Greenstreet, Sydney
  born: **7** England **8** Sandwich
  roles: **9** The Fat Man **10** Casablanca **16** The Maltese Falcon **19** Passage to Marseilles
green with envy 7 envious, jealous **8** covetous
greet 4 hail, meet **5** admit **6** accept, accost, salute **7** receive, speak to, welcome **9** smile upon, recognize **10** bid welcome
greeting 6 salute **7** welcome **8** saluting **9** reception, welcoming **10** salutation **12** introduction, presentation
greetings 4 best **5** hello **7** regards **8** respects **10** best wishes, good wishes, salutation **11** compliments, remembrance, well-wishing **13** felicitations
  Latin: **5** salve
gregarious 6 genial, lively, social **7** affable **8** friendly, outgoing, sociable **9** convivial, talkative, vivacious **11** extroverted **13** companionable
gremlin 3 imp **5** demon, gnome **6** goblin
Grenada
  other name: **11** Isle of Spice
  capital/largest city: **9** St Georges
  others: **8** Sauteurs
  head of state: **14** British monarch **15** governor general
  island: **8** Windward **9** Carriacou **10** Grenadines
  lake: **10** Grand Etang
  highest point: **11** St Catherine
  sea: **9** Caribbean
  physical feature:
    bay: **9** St Georges'
  people: **5** Black, Negro **6** Indian
    discoverer: **8** Columbus
  language: **7** English
  religion: **8** Anglican **10** Protestant **13** Roman Catholic

food:
    spice: 4 mace **6** nutmeg
grenade 7 missile **9** pineapple
Grendel
    character in: 7 Beowulf
    author: 11 John Gardner
Grewgious, Mr
    character in: 22 The Mystery of Edwin Drood
    author: 7 Dickens
Grey, Joel
    real name: 8 Joel Katz
    born: 13 Cleveland Ohio
    roles: 7 Cabaret, George M **13** Come September **23** The Seven Percent Solution
Grey, Zane
    author of: 18 Valley of Wild Horses **20** The Spirit of the Border **21** Riders of the Purple Sage, The Last of the Plainsmen
greyhound
    group of: 5 leash
Greystoke, Lord
    real identity of: 6 Tarzan
griddle cake 6 blintz, waffle **7** crumpet, hot cake, pancake **8** corncake, flapjack, flapjack **10** battercake **11** flannel cake **13** buckwheat cake
    French: 5 crepe **12** crepe suzette
    German: 11 pfannkuchen
    Hungarian: 10 palacsinta
    Indian: 8 chapatty
Gride, Arthur
    character in: 16 Nicholas Nickleby
    author: 7 Dickens
grief 3 woe **4** care **5** agony, worry **6** burden, misery, ordeal, sorrow **7** anguish, anxiety, concern, despair, remorse, sadness, trouble **8** distress, grieving, hardship, nuisance, vexation **9** grievance, heartache, suffering **10** affliction, desolation, discomfort, heartbreak **11** despondency, tribulation **12** wretchedness **13** inconvenience
griefstricken 7 joyless, unhappy **8** saddened, wretched **9** sorrowful **13** brokenhearted
Grieg, Edvard Hagerup
    born: 6 Bergen, Norway
    composer of: 5 I Host **8** Bergljot, In Autumn, Peer Gynt **11** Lyric Pieces **12** Landjaenning **14** Fra Holbergs Tid, Lyriske Stykker **15** Sigurd Jorsalfar **16** From Holberg's Time **17** Recognition of Land **18** Foran Sydens Kloster **22** At a Southern Convent Gate
grievance 4 beef, hurt **5** wrong **6** injury **7** outrage **8** hardship, iniquity **9** complaint, injustice **10** affliction, bone to pick, disservice
grieve 3 cry, rue, sob **4** moan, pain, wail, weep **5** be sad, mourn **6** bemoan, deject, harass, lament, sadden, sorrow **7** afflict, agonize, depress, op-

press, torture **8** disquiet, distress **10** discomfort **11** be anguished
grieve over 5 mourn **6** bemoan, bewail, lament **7** cry over **8** moan over, weep over
grievous 3 sad **5** acute, grave, harsh, heavy **6** severe, tragic, woeful **7** crucial, glaring, harmful, heinous, painful, serious, very bad **8** critical, shameful, shocking **9** agonizing, appalling, atrocious, monstrous, nefarious, sorrowful **10** burdensome, calamitous, deplorable, iniquitous, lamentable, outrageous, unbearable **11** destructive, distressing, intolerable, significant **12** insufferable **13** heartbreaking
griffin
    also: 7 griffon, gryphon
    form: 7 monster
    head of: 5 eagle
    wings of: 5 eagle
    body of: 4 lion
    guards of: 4 gold
    location: 7 Scythia
Griffith, Andy
    real name: 20 Andrew Samuel Griffith
    born: 8 Mt Airy NC
    roles: 7 Matlock **13** Will Stockdale **15** A Face in the Crowd, Angel in My Pocket **18** No Time for Sergeants **19** The Andy Griffith Show
Griffith, D W
    director of: 11 Intolerance **14** Broken Blossoms **17** Orphans of the Storm, The Birth of a Nation
Griffith, Hugh
    born: 5 Wales **8** Anglesey **10** Marian Glas
    roles: 6 Ben-Hur **8** Lucky Jim, Tom Jones
griffon see **7** griffin
grill 3 fry **4** cook, grid, pump, quiz, sear **5** broil, query **7** broiler, grating, griddle **8** gridiron, question **9** crossbars **11** interrogate **12** cross-examine
grim 4 foul, hard, ugly **5** cruel, harsh, lurid, stern, sulky **6** brutal, fierce, gloomy, grisly, grumpy, horrid, morose, odious, severe, somber, sullen **7** austere, ghastly, hideous, inhuman, macabre, squalid, vicious **8** dreadful, fiendish, gruesome, horrible, resolute, scowling, shocking, sinister **9** appalling, ferocious, frightful, heartless, loathsome, merciless, obstinate, repellent, repugnant, repulsive, revolting **10** determined, forbidding, implacable, inexorable, relentless, unyielding
grimace 4 face **5** scowl, smirk, sneer **6** glower **7** wry face
    French: 4 moue
grime 4 dirt, dust, smut, soil, soot **5** filth **6** smudge
Grimhild
    origin: 12 Scandinavian

    mentioned in: 8 Volsunga
    form: 9 sorceress
    husband: 5 Giuki, Gjuki
    daughter: 6 Gudrun, Kudrun **7** Guthrun
    son: 6 Gunnar
    tricked Sigurd to marry: 6 Gudrun, Kudrun **7** Guthrun
Grimm Brothers (Jakob and Wilhelm)
    editors of: 15 Hansel and Gretel **16** Grimm's Fairy Tales
grim reaper 5 death **12** angel of death
grim-visaged 8 frowning, scowling **9** long-faced **10** stern-faced
grin 4 beam **5** smile, smirk **6** rictus, simper **11** crack a smile
grind 4 file, grit, mill, rasp, whet **5** chore, crush, gnash, grate **6** abrade, drudge, polish, powder, scrape **7** crammer, hard job, plodder, sharpen, slavery **8** bookworm, drudgery **9** granulate, pulverize, triturate
Gringoire
    character in: 23 The Hunchback of Notre Dame
    author: 4 Hugo
grip 3 bag **4** grab, hilt, hold **5** clasp, grasp, rivet, seize **6** clench, clutch, handle, retain, snatch, valise **7** attract, control, impress, mastery, satchel **8** clutches, hold fast, suitcase **9** gladstone, handclasp, handshake, retention, spellbind **10** domination, perception
gripe, gripes 4 beef, carp, fret, kick, pain, pang, rail **5** cavil, colic, spasm, whine **6** cramps, grouch, grouse, kvetch, mutter, squawk, twinge, twitch **7** grumble, protest, whining **8** complain, distress, grousing, bellyache, complaint, find fault, grievance, grumbling **10** affliction
Grisham, John
    author of: 7 The Firm **9** The Client **10** The Chamber, The Partner **11** A Time to Kill **12** The Rainmaker **14** The Runaway Jury **15** The Pelican Brief, The Street Lawyer
    movie: 7 The Firm
        actors: 9 Tom Cruise **11** Gene Hackman
    movie: 9 The Client
        actors: 13 Tommy Lee Jones, Susan Sarandon **17** Jeanne Tripplehorn
    movie: 15 The Pelican Brief
        actors: 12 Julia Roberts **16** Denzel Washington
grisly 4 foul, gory, grim **5** lurid **6** horrid, odious **7** ghastly, hideous, macabre **8** dreadful, gruesome, horrible, shocking, sinister **9** abhorrent, appalling, frightful, loathsome, repellent, repugnant, repulsive, revolting **10** abominable, forbidding, horrendous
grit 3 rub **4** dirt, dust, guts, muck,

rasp, sand, soot **5** filth, gnash, grate, nerve, pluck, spunk **6** crunch, mettle, scrape **7** courage, stamina **8** backbone, tenacity **9** fortitude **10** doggedness, resolution **12** perseverance **13** determination, grind together

Grizzly Bear State 10 California

groan 4 howl, moan, roar, wail **5** bleat, crack, creak, whine **6** bellow, bemoan, lament, murmur, squeak **7** grumble, screech, whimper **8** complain

grocery store
Spanish: 6 bodega

groggy 5 dazed, dizzy, dopey, shaky, woozy **6** addled, punchy **7** muddled, reeling, stunned **8** confused, sluggish, unsteady **9** befuddled, lethargic, perplexed, stupefied **10** bewildered, punch-drunk, staggering

groom 4 comb, wash **5** boots, brush, curry, dress, drill, preen, prime, primp, train, valet **6** flunky, lackey, spouse **7** clean up, consort, develop, educate, footman, freshen, hostler, husband, prepare, refresh, rub down, servant **8** exercise, initiate, make neat, make tidy, practice, spruce up **9** currycomb, make ready, stableboy **10** bridegroom, manservant **12** indoctrinate **13** livery servant

groove 3 cut, rut, use **4** rule **5** flute, habit, score, usage **6** custom, furrow, gutter, hollow, trench **7** channel, cutting, scoring **8** practice **9** procedure **10** beaten path, convention **11** corrugation **12** fixed routine, second nature

grope 3 paw **5** probe **6** finger, fumble **7** fish for, venture **9** feel about **11** feel one's way, move blindly, try one's luck **13** search blindly

Gropius, Walter
architect of: 5 Fagus (factory) **7** Bauhaus (Dessau) **13** Pan Am Building (NYC) **31** Harvard University Graduate Center

gross 3 bag, big, fat **4** bulk, earn, huge, lewd, mass, rank, reap, vast **5** bulky, crude, great, heavy, large, obese, plain, sheer, total, utter, whole **6** carnal, coarse, earthy, entire, pick up, ribald, smutty, sordid, take in, vulgar **7** glaring, heinous, immense, lump sum, massive, obscene, obvious, titanic, uncouth **8** colossal, complete, enormous, flagrant, gigantic, improper, indecent, manifest, unseemly, unwieldy **9** aggregate, downright, egregious, lecherous, monstrous, offensive, unrefined **10** gargantuan, indelicate, lascivious, licentious, outrageous, overweight, prodigious, stupendous **11** unequivocal, unmitigated, unqualified

grossness 7 obesity **8** hugeness, lewdness, ribaldry **9** crudeness, heaviness, indecency, obscenity, roughness, vul-

garity **10** coarseness, indelicacy, inelegance **14** lasciviousness

grossularite
species: 6 garnet

grotesque 3 odd **4** wild **5** antic, weird **6** absurd, exotic, far-out, rococo, way-out **7** baroque, bizarre, strange **8** deformed, fanciful, peculiar **9** contorted, distorted, eccentric, fantastic, misshapen, odd-shaped, unnatural **10** outlandish **11** extravagant, incongruous **12** preposterous

grotto 4 cave **6** burrow, cavern, hollow, recess, tunnel **8** catacomb

grouch 3 cry **4** beef, carp, crab, fret, kick, mope, pout, rail, sulk **5** cavil, crank, gripe, growl, moper, whine **6** grouse, mutter, pouter **7** grumble, killjoy, protest **8** complain, grumbler **9** bellyache, find fault **10** complainer, curmudgeon, spoilsport, wet blanket

grouchy 5 cross, testy **6** crabby, cranky, grumpy, touchy **8** snappish **10** ill-humored, out of sorts **11** ill-tempered **12** cantankerous **13** short-tempered

ground, grounds 3 set, sod **4** area, base, call, dirt, farm, land, loam, soil, turf, yard **5** acres, basis, beach, cause, dregs, drill, earth, field, found, lawns, realm, teach, train **6** campus, domain, estate, excuse, inform, motive, object, reason, region, secure, settle, sphere, strand **7** account, confirm, deposit, dry land, educate, founder, gardens, habitat, prepare, purpose, support, terrain **8** district, exercise, firm land, initiate, instruct, occasion, organize, practice, premises, property, province, sediment, the earth **9** arguments, bailiwick, establish, fix firmly, institute, principle, rationale, settlings, territory **10** discipline, inducement, real estate, terra firma **11** pros and cons **12** indoctrinate **14** considerations

grounded 5 based **6** kept in, taught **7** aground, beached, bounded, drilled, founded, secured, trained **8** informed, prepared, stranded **9** foundered, initiated **10** kept at home, instructed, restricted **11** disciplined, established **12** washed ashore **13** indoctrinated

grounding 8 training **9** education **10** background, experience **11** preparation **14** indoctrination **15** familiarization

groundless 4 idle **5** empty, false **6** faulty, flimsy, unreal, untrue **8** baseless, needless, unproved **9** erroneous, illogical, imaginary, unfounded **10** chimerical, fallacious, gratuitous **11** uncalled for, unjustified, unsupported, unwarranted **13** unjustifiable, without reason

groundwork 4 base, root **5** basis **6** cradle, ground, origin, source, spring **7** bedrock, footing, grounds, taproot **8**

keystone, learning, planning, practice, training **9** spadework **10** foundation **11** cornerstone, fundamental, preparation **12** fundamentals, underpinning **14** apprenticeship, indoctrination

group 3 set **4** band, clan, file, gang, herd, pack, sift, size, sort **5** align, bunch, class, crowd, flock, grade, hoard, index, party, place, range, swarm, tribe, troop **6** as- sign, branch, circle, clique, family, hobnob, league, line up, mingle, throng **7** arrange, catalog, cluster, combine, company, consort, coterie, faction, marshal, section, species, variety **8** classify, division, graduate, organize, register **9** associate, gathering **10** assemblage, collection, coordinate, detachment, fraternity, fraternize **11** aggregation, alphabetize, association, brotherhood, subdivision **12** congregation **14** classification, representation

Group, The
author: 12 Mary McCarthy

grouping 7 sorting **8** arraying, ordering **10** assemblage, assortment **11** arrangement, disposition **12** distribution, organization

group of performers 6 troupe **7** company **8** ensemble

Group Portrait of a Lady
author: 12 Heinrich Böll

grouse 4 beef, crab, fret, fume, fuss, kick **5** gripe **6** grouch, mutter, squawk, take on **7** carry on, grumble **8** complain, gamebird **9** bellyache

grove 4 bosk **5** brake, copse **6** forest, pinery, timber **7** coppice, orchard, thicket, wood lot **8** wildwood, woodland **9** shrubbery **10** plantation

grovel 4 fawn **5** cower, crawl, stoop, toady **6** cringe, kowtow, snivel **7** flatter, truckle **12** bow and scrape **13** demean oneself, humble oneself **14** lick the boots of

groveling 6 abject **7** fawning, servile **8** cowering, crawling, cringing, toadying **9** kowtowing, truckling **11** bootlicking **17** bowing and scraping

grow 3 bud, sow, wax **4** boom, farm, rise, till **5** bloom, breed, plant, raise, ripen, surge, swell, widen **6** become, expand, extend, flower, garden, mature, spread, sprout, thrive **7** advance, amplify, blossom, develop, enlarge, fill out, get to be, improve, magnify, produce, prosper, shoot up, stretch, succeed **8** come to be, flourish, fructify, increase, mushroom, progress, spring up, vegetate **9** cultivate, germinate, propagate, skyrocket **10** aggrandize

Growing Up in New Guinea
author: 12 Margaret Mead

growl 4 fret, snap **5** croak, grind, gripe, groan, grunt, snarl, whine **6**

grouse, murmur, mutter, rumble **7** grumble **8** complain, talk back

grown-up 3 big, man **4** lady, ripe **5** adult, of age, woman **6** mature, senior **7** worldly **9** full-blown, full-grown, gentleman **11** full-fledged **13** sophisticated

growth 4 crop, hump, lump, rise **5** gnarl, prime, surge, swell, tumor **6** sowing, spread **7** advance, harvest, produce, success **8** increase, maturity, planting, progress **9** expansion, extension, flowering, increment **10** burgeoning, matureness, production, prospering **11** advancement, cultivation, development, enlargement, excrescence, flourishing, improvement, propagation **12** augmentation, mass of tissue **13** amplification
   goddess of: 4 Hour **5** Horae

Groza, Lou
   nickname: 6 The Toe
   sport: 8 football
   team: 15 Cleveland Browns

grub 3 bum, dig **4** food, toil, worm **5** cadge, dig up, larva, mooch, slave **6** drudge, sponge **7** rummage

grubber 5 slave **6** drudge, toiler **7** laborer

grubby 4 foul **5** dirty, grimy, messy, muddy, nasty, seedy, tacky **6** beat-up, filthy, frowzy, frumpy, shabby, shoddy, sloppy, smudgy, soiled, sordid **7** squalid, unclean, unkempt **8** begrimed, slovenly, unwashed **9** besmeared **10** bedraggled

grudge 4 envy **5** pique, spite **6** animus, hatred, malice, rancor, resent **7** dislike, ill will **8** aversion, begrudge **9** animosity **10** resentment **11** malevolence **12** hard feelings

grudging 7 envious **8** hesitant, spiteful **9** reluctant, resentful, unwilling **10** ungenerous **13** penny-pinching

grueling 4 hard **6** brutal, tiring **7** racking **9** fatiguing, punishing, torturous **10** exhausting

gruesome 4 gory, grim **5** awful **6** grisly, horrid **7** fearful, ghastly, hideous, macabre **8** horrible, shocking, terrible **9** frightful, loathsome, repellent, repulsive, revolting **10** forbidding, horrendous, horrifying **13** bloodcurdling, spine-chilling

gruff 4 curt, rude, sour, tart **5** bluff, blunt, harsh, husky, raspy, rough, sharp, short, stern, sulky, surly **6** abrupt, croaky, crusty, grumpy, hoarse, ragged, sullen **7** bearish, brusque, caustic, crabbed, cracked, grouchy, peevish, throaty, uncivil, waspish **8** churlish, guttural, impolite, snarling, strident **9** bristling, insulting **10** illhumored, ill-natured, ungracious **11** ill-tempered **12** discourteous

grumble 4 fret **5** chafe, gripe, growl **6**

grouch, grouse, mutter **8** complain **9** find-fault

grump 4 crab **5** crank **6** grouch **8** grumbler, sourball **10** curmudgeon

grumpy 4 sour **5** moody, sulky, surly, testy **6** crabby, cranky, crusty, sullen **7** grouchy, peevish, pettish **8** churlish **9** irritable, splenetic **10** ill-humored, out of humor, out of sorts **11** disgruntled, ill-disposed, ill-tempered **12** cantankerous

grunt 3 cry **4** bark, call, gasp, howl **5** burro, croak, groan, snort, utter **6** bellow, grouch, mumble, murmur, mutter, shriek **7** howling, whisper **8** complain **9** ululation **11** foot soldier, infantryman

Grunwald, Matthais (Grunewald, Mathis)
   real name: 23 Mathis Gothardt Neithardt
   born: 7 Germany **8** Wurzburg
   artwork: 14 The Crucifixion **15** The Resurrection **20** Altarpiece at Isenheim

Grushenka
   character in: 20 The Brothers Karamazov
   author: 11 Dostoyevsky

Gryce, Percy
   character in: 15 The House of Mirth
   author: 7 Wharton

gryphon see **7** griffin

Guam
   capital: 5 Agana
   largest city: 8 Tamuning
   others: 4 Agat, Apra, Toto, Yigo **5** Magua **6** Dededo, Merizo **8** Inarajan, Mangilao, Mongmong, Sinajana, Talofofo, Tamuning **9** Barrigada, Finegayan, Santa Rita
   member of: 7 Mariana (islands)
   mountain: 5 Tenjo
   highest point: 6 Lamlam
   sea: 7 Pacific **10** Philippine
   people: 7 Spanish **8** American, Chamorro, Filipino **11** Micronesian
     explorer: 8 Magellan
     ruler: 5 Japan, Spain **12** United States
   language: 7 English **8** Chamorro
   religion: 16 Roman Catholicism
   feature: 7 typhoon **10** coral reef
   Air Force base: 8 Andersen
   product: 5 copra **6** banana, papaya

guarantee, guaranty 4 avow, bail, bond, pawn, word **5** swear **6** affirm, allege, assure, attest, avowal, insure, pledge, surety **7** deposit, endorse, promise, sponsor, testify, voucher, warrant **8** contract, covenant, security, vouch for, warranty **9** agreement, answer for, assurance, insurance, testimony **10** collateral, underwrite **11** affirmation, endorsement, word of honor **12** give one's word

guard 4 mind, save, tend **5** watch **6** at-

tend, convoy, defend, escort, patrol, picket, screen, secure, sentry, shield, warder **7** conduct, defense, protect, shelter **8** defender, garrison, guardian, keep safe, preserve, security, sentinel, watchdog, watchman **9** bodyguard, concierge, custodian, guardsman, protector, safeguard, watch over **10** doorkeeper, gatekeeper, protection **12** preservation **13** keep watch over

guard against 6 beware **10** look out for **11** take warning, watch out for

guarded 4 wary **5** cagey, chary, leery **7** careful, heedful, mindful, prudent **8** cautious, discreet, hesitant **9** in custody, protected, tentative **10** restrained, suspicious, under guard **11** circumspect, on one's guard

guardian 5 guard **6** convoy, escort, keeper, patrol, patron, picket, sentry, warden, warder **7** curator, trustee **8** advocate, champion, defender, sentinel, shepherd, wardsman, watchdog **9** attendant, bodyguard, caretaker, conductor, custodian, preserver, protector, safeguard, vigilante **10** benefactor **11** conservator **13** friend at court, guardian angel **14** legal custodian

guardian of a place
   Latin: 10 genius loci

guardianship 4 care **6** charge **7** custody, keeping **10** protection **11** safekeeping, supervision, trusteeship

Guatemala
   capital/largest city: 13 Guatemala City
   others: 4 Ocos **5** Coban, Vieja **6** Chahal, Chisec, Cuilco, Flores, Iztapa, Jalapa, Salama, Solola, Tacana, Tecpan, Yaloch, Zacapa **7** Antigua, Cuilapa, Jutiapa, San Jose **8** Progreso **9** Escuintla, Tiquisate **10** Livingston **11** Totonicapan **13** Puerto Barrios, Quezaltenango **14** San Pedro Carcha **16** Chichicastenango
   school: 9 San Carlos
   measure: 4 vara **6** cuarta, tercia **7** cajuela, manzana **10** caballeria
   monetary unit: 4 peso **7** centavo, quetzal
   weight: 4 caja **5** libra
   lake: 5 Dulce, Guija, Peten **6** Izabal **7** Atitlan **9** Amatitlan, Peten Itza
   mountain: 4 Agua, Mico **5** Fuego, Madre **6** Pacaya, Tacana **7** Atitlan, Toliman **8** La Candon, Las Minas **10** Acatenango, Santa Maria **12** Cuchumatanes
   highest point: 8 Tajumuko **9** Tajamulco
   river: 4 Azul **5** Bravo, Dulce, Lapaz **6** Belize, Chixoy, Negino, Pasion, Samala **7** Chiapas, Motagua, Sarstun, Sastoon **8** Polochic, Rio Dulce, Sarstoon **10** Usumacinta
   sea: 7 Pacific **8** Atlantic **9** Caribbean
   physical feature:
     bay: 8 Amatique

gulf: 8 Honduras
people: 3 Mam **4** Chol, Itza, Ixil, Maya **5** Xinca **6** Caribe, Quiche **7** ladinos, mestizo, Pocomam **13** Guatemaltecos
language: 6 Quiche **7** Spanish
religion: 13 Roman Catholic
place:
    church: 10 Santo Tomas
    ruins: 5 Mayan, Tikal **8** Uaxactun
feature:
    bird: 7 quetzal
    clarinet: 8 chirimta
    dance: 5 elson **8** guarimba
    flute: 3 xul
    military dictator: 8 Caudillo
food:
    dish: 6 pepian **10** enchiladas **13** gallo en chicha
    fruit: 4 anay
guava 7 Psidium **16** Psidium guineense
    varieties: 5 apple **6** common, purple, yellow **7** Cattley, Chilean **9** pineapple **10** Costa Rican, strawberry **13** yellow cattley **16** purple strawberry, yellow strawberry

Gudrun
also: 6 Kudrun **7** Guthrun
origin: 12 Scandinavian
mentioned in: 8 Volsunga
father: 5 Giuki, Gjuki **6** Hertel
mother: 8 Grimhild
brother: 6 Gunnar
husband: 4 Atli **6** Herwig, Sigurd
killed: 4 Atli
corresponds to: 9 Kriemhild

guess 4 deem, view **5** fancy, judge, opine, think **6** assume, belief, deduce, divine, gather, reckon, regard, theory **7** believe, daresay, feeling, imagine, opinion, predict, suppose, surmise, suspect, venture **8** conclude, estimate, theorize **9** postulate, speculate, suspicion **10** assumption, conjecture, divination, hypothesis, prediction **11** hypothesize, make a stab at, postulation, presumption, speculation, supposition
guesswork 7 surmise **10** conjecture, hypothesis **11** supposition **13** shot in the dark
guest 5 diner **6** caller, client, friend, inmate, lodger, patron, roomer **7** boarder, company, habitue, invitee, patient, visitor **8** customer **9** sojourner **10** frequenter **14** paying customer

Guest, Edgar A
author of: 12 A Heap of Livin'
Guest, Judith
author of: 14 Ordinary People
Guevara 3 Che **7** Ernesto
born: 9 Argentina
active in: 15 Cuban Revolution
friend: 5 Castro
role in: 5 Evita
killed in: 7 Bolivia
guffaw 4 howl **6** scream **10** belly laugh, horse laugh

guidance 3 tip **4** clue, help, hint, lead **6** advice, escort **7** conduct, counsel, pointer **8** auspices **9** direction **10** leadership, management, protection, suggestion **11** information, instruction, supervision **12** intelligence **13** enlightenment
guide 4 lead, rule **5** model, pilot, steer, usher **6** beacon, convoy, direct, escort, govern, handle, leader, manage, marker, master, mentor **7** adviser, command, conduct, control, example, marshal, monitor, oversee, pattern, steerer, teacher **8** chaperon, cicerone, director, engineer, helmsman, landmark, lodestar, maneuver, polestar, regulate, shepherd, signpost **9** accompany, attendant, conductor, counselor **10** manipulate
guidebook 5 bible **6** manual **8** Baedeker, handbook **13** reference book
Guidry, Ron (Ronald Ames)
nickname: 18 Louisiana Lightning
sport: 8 baseball
position: 7 pitcher
team: 14 New York Yankees
guild 5 hansa, hanse, order, union **6** league **7** company, society **8** alliance **9** coalition **10** craft union, federation, fraternity, labor union, sisterhood, trade union **11** association, brotherhood, confederacy, corporation
Guildenstern
character in: 6 Hamlet
author: 11 Shakespeare
guile 5 craft, fraud **6** deceit, tricks **7** cunning, slyness **8** artifice, strategy, trickery, wiliness **9** chicanery, deception, duplicity, treachery **10** artfulness, craftiness, dishonesty, hankypanky, stratagems, trickiness **11** fraudulence **13** sharp practice
guileless 4 open **5** frank, naive **6** candid, honest, simple **7** artless, natural, sincere **8** harmless, innocent, truthful **9** ingenuous, innocuous **10** aboveboard, unaffected **11** undesigning, unoffending **15** straightforward, unselfconscious, unsophisticated
guilelessness 6 candor **9** innocence, sincerity **10** candidness, directness **11** artlessness **13** ingenuousness
guilt 3 sin **4** blot, vice **5** shame, wrong **6** infamy, stigma **7** misdeed **8** disgrace, dishonor, misdoing, trespass **9** black mark, turpitude **10** guiltiness, misconduct, sinfulness, wrongdoing **11** criminality, culpability, degradation, delinquency, dereliction, humiliation, misbehavior, self-disgust **13** transgression
guiltless 4 good, pure **5** clean **6** chaste **7** angelic, sinless **8** innocent, unfallen, virtuous **9** blameless, childlike, faultless **10** immaculate, inculpable, unblamable **11** uncorrupted
French: 12 sans reproche

guilt-stricken 7 ashamed **18** conscience-stricken
guilty 5 sorry, wrong **6** erring, sinful **7** ashamed, corrupt, hangdog, immoral **8** blamable, contrite, criminal, culpable, penitent, sheepish **9** offensive, regretful, repentant **11** blameworthy **18** conscience-stricken

Guinea
other name: 12 French Guinea **13** Rivieres du Sud
capital/largest city: 7 Conakry
others: 4 Boke, Fria, Labe **5** Beyla **6** Dabola, Kankan, Kindia **7** Dubreka, Siguiri **8** Kerouane **9** Kouroussa, Nzerekore
measure: 7 jacktan
monetary unit: 4 iliy, syli **5** franc **6** cauris
weight: 4 akey, piso, uzan **5** benda, seron **6** quinto **8** aguirage
island: 3 Los **5** Tombo **7** Tristao
mountain: 4 Loma **6** Tamgue **11** Fouta Djalon
highest point: 5 Nimba
river: 4 Milo **5** Kogon, Niger **6** Bafing, Faleme, Gambia **7** Kolente, Senegal **8** Konkoure, Tinkisso **13** Great Scarcies
sea: 8 Atlantic
physical feature:
    cape: 5 Verga
people: 4 Koma, Loma, Nalu, Susu, Toma **5** Kissi, Manon **6** Fulani, Guerzi **7** Landoma, Malinke **8** Kouranke, Landuman **11** Kissi-Sherbo **12** Guerze-Kpelle
language: 5 Fulbe, Mande **6** Arabic, French, Fulani **7** English
religion: 5 Islam **7** animism
feature:
    plant: 11 globeflower
    tree: 4 akee **5** dalli

Guinea-Bissau
other name: 16 Portuguese Guinea
capital/largest city: 6 Bissau
others: 4 Buba **5** Catio, Farim **6** Bafata, Bolama, Cacheu, Cacine, Dandum, Mansoa **7** Bissora, Bubaque, San Joav **9** Fulacunda **10** Nova Lamego **11** Madina do Boe, Madine do Boe, Sao Domingos
monetary unit: 4 peso **6** escudo **8** centavos
island: 4 Roxa **6** Orango **7** Bijagos, Formosa
river: 4 Geba **6** Cacheu, Mansoa **7** Corubal
sea: 8 Atlantic
people: 6 Fulani **7** Balanta, Balante, mulatto **8** Mandingo, Mandyako
language: 5 Fulah **7** Balante, Crioulo **8** Mandingo **10** Portuguese **21** Cape Verde-Guinea Creole
religion: 5 Islam **7** animism **12** Christianity

Guinevere
character in: 16 Arthurian romance

husband: 6 Arthur
lover: 8 Lancelot

Guinness, Sir Alec
  born: 6 London **7** England
  roles: 8 Star Wars **11** Oliver Twist **13** Doctor Zhivago **14** Our Man in Havana, The Ladykillers **15** A Passage to India, Ben Obi Wan Kenobi, Lavender Hill Mob **16** Lawrence of Arabia **17** Great Expectations **21** Kind Hearts and Coronets **22** Tinker Tailor Soldier Spy **23** The Bridge on the River Kwai (Oscar)

guise 4 garb, mode **5** dress, habit **6** attire **7** apparel, clothes, costume, fashion **8** clothing, disguise, pretense **10** masquerade

Gulag Archipelago, The
  author: 23 Aleksandr Solzhenitsyn Jr

gulch 3 gap **4** rift **5** abyss, chasm, cleft, crack, gorge, gully, split **6** arroyo, breach, divide, ravine **8** crevasse

gulf 4 cove, rent, rift **5** abyss, chasm, cleft, firth, fjord, gully, inlet, split **6** canyon, lagoon **7** estuary, opening **8** crevasse **10** separation

gull 3 gyp **4** dupe, rook **5** cozen, trick **7** deceive, defraud, sea gull, sea bird, swindle **9** bamboozle, victimize

gullet 3 maw **4** craw, crop **5** belly, gorge, tummy **6** dewlap, throat **7** abdomen, channel, stomach, weasand **9** beer belly, esophagus

gullible 5 green, naive **6** simple **8** innocent, trustful, trusting **9** credulous **11** easily duped **12** easily fooled, overtrusting, unsuspicious **13** easily cheated, inexperienced **14** easily deceived **15** unsophisticated

Gulliver's Travels
  author: 13 Jonathan Swift
  character: 14 Lemuel Gulliver
  visited: 6 Laputa, Yahoos **8** Blefuscu, Lilliput, Luggnagg **9** Balnibari **10** Houyhnhnms **11** Brobdingnag **12** Glubbdubdrib

gully 3 gap **5** ditch, gorge, gulch **6** defile, furrow, gutter, ravine, trench **7** channel **11** small canyon, small valley, watercourse **13** drainage ditch

gulp 4 bolt, swig, wolf **5** quaff, swill **6** devour, guzzle **7** swallow, toss off **8** mouthful

gulp down 4 bolt **6** devour, gobble **7** swallow **8** gobble up, wolf down

gum 3 wax **5** latex, resin **6** chicle **8** mucilage **10** Eucalyptus
  varieties: 3 cup, red **4** blue, cape, gray, rose, snow, sour **5** apple, black, cider, coral, giant, gully, Karri, Manna, sug- ar, swamp, sweet **6** cotton, Deane's, desert, gimlet, salmon, snappy, Tupelo **7** Barbary, cabbage, Fuchsia, maiden's, Morocco, scarlet, spotted **8** Formosan, Lehmann's, mountain, scribbly, spinning **9** forest red, Murray red, steedman's **10** Australian, candle-bark, red-spotted, Sydney blue, Timor white, tumble-down, urn-fruited **11** Blakely's red, blue weeping, salmon white, small-leaved, strickland's **12** lemon-scented, red-flowering, silver-dollar **13** American sweet, Oriental sweet, Tasmanian blue, Tasmanian snow **14** yellow-flowered **15** Omeo round-leaved, round-leaved snow **16** rough-barked manna, scarlet-flowering **17** heart-leaved silver **20** silver-leaved mountain

gummed 5 glued, gummy, stuck **6** sticky **8** adhering, adhesive

Gummidge, Mrs
  character in: 16 David Copperfield
  author: 7 Dickens

gummy 5 gluey, gooey, gunky **6** gloppy, sticky, viscid **7** rubbery, viscous **8** adhesive **10** gelatinous **12** mucilaginous

gumption 3 zip **4** dash, push **5** drive, spunk, verve **6** energy, hustle, pizazz, spirit **7** courage **10** enterprise, get-up-and-go, initiative **12** forcefulness **14** aggressiveness **15** resourcefulness

gumshoe 3 tec **4** dick **6** shamus **9** detective **10** private eye **12** investigator

gun 3 aim, gat, rod, try **4** Colt, hunt, iron **5** piece, rifle, shoot **6** cannon, Magnum, mortar, musket, pistol **7** attempt, carbine, firearm, Gatling, go after, Long Tom, shotgun **8** howitzer, ordnance, revolver **9** automatic, Big Bertha, derringer, equalizer, flintlock, forty-five, twenty-two, Remington **10** fieldpiece, machine gun, six-shooter, three-fifty, Walther PPK, Winchester **11** blunderbuss, thirty-eight, trusty-rusty **12** fowling piece, muzzle loader, shooting iron **13** Kentucky rifle **14** artillery piece, Smith and Wesson
  invented by:
    breechloader: 8 Thornton
    magazine: 9 Hotchkiss
    silencer: 5 Maxim

Gunga Din
  story in: 18 Barrack-Room Ballads
  author: 14 Rudyard Kipling
  director: 12 George Stevens
  cast: 8 Sam Jaffe **9** Cary Grant **12** Joan Fontaine **14** Victor McLaglen **18** Douglas Fairbanks Jr
  setting: 5 India
  remade as: 13 Soldiers Three **14** Sergeants Three

gunman 6 bandit, outlaw, robber, sniper **7** hoodlum **9** assailant, desperado, holdup man

Gunn, Ben
  character in: 14 Treasure Island
  author: 9 Stevenson

Gunnar
  origin: 12 Scandinavian
  father: 5 Giuki, Gjuki

mother: 8 Grimhild
sister: 6 Gudrun, Kudrun **7** Guthrun
wife: 8 Brynhild
Brynhild won by: 6 Sigurd

Gunsmoke
  character: 3 Sam (the bartender) **8** Doc (Dr Galen) Adams **10** Quint Asper **11** Newly O'Brien **12** Chester Goode, Festus Haggen, Kitty Russell (Miss Kitty) **18** Marshall Matt Dillon **24** Clayton Thaddeus (Thad) Greenwood
  cast: 9 Ken Curtis **10** Buck Taylor, Roger Ewing **11** Amanda Blake, James Arness **12** Burt Reynolds, Dennis Weaver, Glenn Strange, Milburn Stone
  setting: 9 Dodge City
  saloon: 10 Longbranch

Guns of August, The
  author: 15 Barbara W Tuchman

Guns of Navarone, The
  director: 12 J Lee Thompson
  based on novel by: 15 Alistair MacLean
  cast: 10 David Niven **11** Gregory Peck, James Darren **12** Anthony Quinn, Stanley Baker **13** Anthony Quayle

Gunther
  origin: 8 Germanic
  mentioned in: 14 Nibelungenlied
  king of: 8 Burgundy
  wife: 8 Brunhild
  sister: 9 Kriemhild
  killed by: 9 Kriemhild

Guppy
  character in: 10 Bleak House
  author: 7 Dickens

gurgle 5 plash **6** babble, bubble, burble, murmur, ripple **7** sputter **8** bubbling, gurgling

guru 5 guide **6** leader, master **7** teacher **9** preceptor **10** instructor

gush 3 gab, gas, jet, run **4** blab, bull, rush, well **5** issue, prate, spout, spurt **6** bab- ble, burble, drivel, hot air, splash, squirt, stream **7** baloney, blabber, blather, chatter, pour out, prattle, rubbish, torrent, twaddle **8** nonsense, outburst, rattle on **10** outpouring **11** mawkishness **12** emotionalism **14** sentimentalism, talk effusively **16** run off at the mouth

gushiness 12 effusiveness, emotionalism **17** demonstrativeness

gushing 6 lavish **7** pouring, profuse **8** effusive, spurting **10** flattering **11** free-flowing **12** demonstative, unrestrained **16** overenthusiastic

gushy 8 effusive **12** unrestrained **13** demonstrative **16** overenthusiastic

gussy up 5 adorn **7** dress up, enhance **8** beautify, decorate, ornament **9** embellish

gust 3 fit **4** blow, puff, wind **5** blast, burst, draft **6** breeze, flurry, squall, zephyr 8 outbreak, outburst, paroxysm 9 explosion

Guster
character in: 10 Bleak House
author: 7 Dickens

gusto 3 joy 4 zeal, zest 5 savor 6 fervor, relish 7 delight 8 appetite, pleasure 10 enthusiasm 12 appreciation, exhilaration, satisfaction

gusto, con
music: 9 with style, with taste

gusty 5 blowy, windy 6 breezy 7 squally 8 blustery

gut 4 raze 5 belly, clean, level, tummy 6 bowels, paunch, ravage 7 abdomen, consume, midriff, stomach, viscera 8 entrails, lay waste 9 bay window, beer belly, spare tire 10 disembowel, eviscerate, intestines, midsection 11 breadbasket

guten abend 11 good evening

Gutenberg
nationality: 6 German
inventor of: 11 movable type
printer of: 14 Gutenberg Bible

guten morgen 11 good morning

guten tag 7 good day

Guthrie, A B Jr
author of: 6 Arfive 9 The Big Sky 10 The Way West 13 The Last Valley 16 Fair Land Fair Land, The Blue Hen's Chick, The Thousand Hills

Guthrun see 6 Gudrun

Gutman, Casper
character in: 16 The Maltese Falcon
author: 7 Hammett

guts 4 dash, grit 5 nerve, pluck, spunk 6 bowels, daring, mettle, spirit, vitals 7 bravado, bravery, courage, gizzard, innards, insides, viscera 8 audacity, backbone, boldness 9 fortitude 10 intestines 11 intrepidity

gutsy 4 game 5 brave 6 heroic, plucky 7 doughty, valiant 8 fearless, intrepid, stalwart, unafraid, valorous 9 dauntless, undaunted 10 courageous 11 lionhearted, unflinching 12 stouthearted

guttural 3 low 4 deep 5 gruff, harsh, husky, raspy, thick 6 hoarse 7 throaty 8 croaking 12 inarticulate

guy 3 boy, joe, kid, man 4 body, chap, dude, gent, rope 5 bloke, human, joker 6 fellow, hombre, person 8 blighter, up-holder 9 supporter 10 individual

Guyana
name means: 12 land of waters
other name: 13 British Guiana
capital/largest city: 10 Georgetown
others: 7 Charity 8 Hyde Park, Rosignol 9 Jonestown, Mackenzie
island: 6 Leguan 8 Wakenaam
mountain: 5 Amuku, Ariwa, Kamoa 6 Akarai, Kanuku 7 Caburai 9 Pacaraima
highest point: 7 Roraima
river: 5 Waini 6 Barama 7 Amakura, Baruima, Berbice 8 Demerara, Mazaruni, Rupununi 9 Essequibo 10 Burro-Burro
ocean: 8 Atlantic
physical feature:
falls: 5 Great, Tiger 7 Kamaria 8 Kaieteur 9 Serikoeng 10 Surwakwima 15 Fredrik Willem IV
people: 6 Akawai, Arawak, Creole, Taruma 7 African, Chinese, mulatto 10 Portuguese
language: 5 Hindi 7 English
religion: 5 Hindu, Islam 8 Anglican 13 Roman Catholic

Guy Fawkes
author: 16 William Ainsworth

Guy Mannering
author: 14 Sir Walter Scott

Guyon
character in: 15 The Faerie Queene
author: 7 Spenser

Guys and Dolls
director: 17 Joseph L Mankiewicz
based on story by: 11 Damon Runyon
cast: 10 Stubby Kaye 11 Jean Simmons 12 Frank Sinatra, Marlon Brando, Vivian Blaine
setting: 11 New York City
score: 12 Frank Loesser
song: 11 Luck Be a Lady 12 Guys and Dolls 26 Sit Down You're Rocking the Boat

guzzle 4 bolt, swig 5 quaff, swill 6 devour, imbibe, tipple 7 toss off 8 gulp down

guzzler 5 drunk 6 boozer 7 imbiber, tippler 8 devourer, drunkard 9 alcoholic

Gwawl
origin: 5 Welsh
mentioned in: 10 Mabinogion
rival of: 5 Pwyll
sought hand of: 8 Rhiannon

Gwydion
origin: 5 Welsh
son: 14 Llew Llaw Gyffes
sister: 9 Arianrhod
lover: 9 Arianrhod

Gwyn
origin: 7 British
god of: 7 rebirth 9 afterlife

Gyas
companion of: 6 Aeneas

Gyes see 5 Gyges

Gygaea, Gyge
form: 5 nymph
location: 4 lake

Gyges
also: 4 Gyes
member of: 13 Hecatonchires

gymnasium 5 arena 6 circus 7 stadium 10 hippodrome

gymnast 10 Olga Korbut 13 Mary Lou Retton, Nadia Comaneci

gymnastics 9 exercises 10 acrobatics 11 contortions 16 physical training

Gynaecothoenas
epithet of: 4 Ares
means: 17 feasted by the women

gynophobia
fear of: 5 women

gyp 3 con 4 bilk, burn, fake, hoax, rook, scam, soak 5 cheat, cozen, fraud, phony, trick 6 diddle, fleece, humbug, ripoff 7 con game, defraud, swindle 8 flimflam, hoodwink 9 bamboozle, deception

gypsy
Italian: 7 zingara, zingaro

gyrate 5 swirl, twirl, wheel, whirl 6 circle, rotate, spiral 7 revolve 9 pirouette 10 spin around

habeas corpus 11 have the body **23** produce the person in court
legal writ guards against: 19 illegal imprisonment

habiliments 4 garb, wear **5** dress **6** attire, outfit **7** clothes, costume, raiment, regalia **8** clothing, wardrobe **9** vestments

habit 3 rut, way **4** garb, gear, robe, rule, wont **5** dress, trait, usage **6** attire, custom, groove, livery, manner, outfit **7** apparel, clothes, costume, garment, leaning, raiment, routine, uniform, vesture **8** clothing, fondness, habitude, nun's wear, practice **9** mannerism, trappings **10** beaten path, convention, observance, partiality, proclivity, propensity **11** habiliments, inclination, peculiarity **12** predilection, second nature **13** accoutrements, fixed practice **14** matter of course, predisposition **15** behavior pattern

habitat 3 pad **4** digs, home, spot, zone **5** abode, haunt, place, range, realm, roost **6** domain, locale, milieu, region **7** housing, lodging, setting, terrain **8** domicile, dwelling, home base, lodgment, precinct, quarters **9** territory **10** habitation **11** environment, natural home **12** place of abode **13** dwelling place **14** stamping ground **15** natural locality **17** native environment

habitation 3 pad **4** digs, home **5** abode, haunt, house, roost **6** colony **7** habitat, housing, lodging, shelter, tenancy **8** domicile, dwelling, lodgment, quarters **9** community, occupancy, residence **10** occupation, settlement **12** place of abode **13** dwelling place, temporary stay **16** place of residence

Habit of Being, The
author: 15 Flannery O'Connor

habitual 5 fixed, usual **6** common, normal, wonted **7** chronic, natural, regular, routine, typical **8** addicted, constant, expected, familiar, frequent, periodic, repeated **9** confirmed, continual, customary, incessant, ingrained, perpetual, recurrent **10** accustomed, deep- rooted, deep-seated, inveterate, methodical, systematic **11** established, traditional **12** conventional, second nature **14** by force of habit

habitual practice 4 wont **5** habit **6** custom

habituate 5 adapt, drill, imbue, inure, train **6** harden, school, season **7** break in, instill **8** accustom, initiate **9** inculcate **10** discipline, make used to **12** indoctrinate

habitue 7 regular **10** frequenter **13** regular patron **15** frequent visitor **16** constant customer

hacek 13 inverted caret **15** diacritical mark

hack 3 cab, cut, hew, nag **4** bark, chip, chop, gash, plug, rasp, slit, taxi **5** coach, cut up, notch, slash, slice, whack **6** cleave, mangle **7** hackney, taxicab **8** lacerate, mutilate **9** cart horse, dray horse, scribbler, workhorse **10** cough drily, cut roughly, draft horse, hired horse, shaft horse **11** common horse, penny-a-liner **12** hackney coach, worn- out horse **13** carriage horse **16** grubstreet writer **18** horse-drawn carriage

hackle 3 peg **4** card, comb, hack, hook, ruff **5** curry, plume, quill **6** heckle, mangle **7** bristle, feather, plumage

Hackman, Gene
born: 15 San Bernardino CA
roles: 8 Superman **11** Popeye Doyle **14** Bonnie and Clyde **15** The Conversation **19** The French Connection (Oscar) **20** The Poseidon Adventure

hackneyed 4 dull, worn **5** banal, inane, stale, stock, trite, vapid **6** common, jejune **7** cliched, humdrum, insipid, routine, worn-out **8** bromidic, ordinary, shopworn, well-worn **9** moth-eaten **10** pedestrian, threadbare, uninspired **11** commonplace, stereotyped **12** conventional **13** platitudinous, unimaginative

Hadassah 6 Esther

Hades 4 hell
also: 3 Dis **5** Pluto **10** lower world, Underworld
corresponds to: 5 Orcus
god of: 5 Orcus, Pluto
goddess of: 6 Hecate, Hekate

Haenigsen, Harry
creator/artist of: 5 Penny **7** Our Bill

hafnium
chemical symbol: 2 Hf

hag 3 bat, nag **4** drab, fury **5** biddy, crone, frump, harpy, shrew, vixen, witch **6** beldam, gorgon, ogress, vi-

rago **7** hellcat **8** battle-ax, harridan **9** termagant

Hagar
servant of: 5 Sarah
husband: 7 Abraham
son: 7 Ishmael

Hagar the Horrible
creator: 9 Dik Browne

Hagen
origin: 8 Germanic
mentioned in: 14 Nibelungenlied
killed by: 9 Kriemhild
killed: 9 Siegfried

Haggadah 7 parable **8** anecdote
source: 6 Talmud
read at: 5 seder **8** Passover

haggard 4 beat, wild, worn **5** gaunt, spent, tired, upset, weary **6** bushed, fagged, pooped, raging, wasted **7** ranting **8** careworn, drooping, fatigued, flagging, frenzied, harassed, harrowed, overcome, toilworn, wild-eyed **9** exhausted, woebegone **10** hollow-eyed **11** debilitated, overwearied, overwrought, tuckered out, wild-looking **12** tired-looking

Haggard, H Rider
author of: 3 She **17** King Solomon's Mines
noted phrase: 18 She who must be obeyed

haggle 6 barter, bicker, dicker, higgle **7** bargain, dispute, quarrel, quibble, wrangle **8** beat down, squabble

Hagiographa
Hebrew: 7 Ketubim

hagiographer 19 writer of saints' lives

Hagman, Larry
mother: 10 Mary Martin
born: 13 Weatherford TX
roles: 6 Dallas **7** J R Ewing **15** I Dream of Jeannie

Hahn, Otto
field: 9 chemistry
nationality: 6 German
discovered: 13 protoactinium **14** nuclear isomers
awarded: 10 Nobel Prize

Haida
language family: 6 Masset, Na-Dene **10** Skidegatta
tribe: 7 Kaigani
location: 6 Alaska **15** British Columbia **21** Queen Charlotte Islands

related to: 7 Tlingit 9 Tsimshian
associated with: 9 totem pole 13 wood sculpture

hail 3 ave 4 call 5 cheer, exalt, extol, greet, hello, honor, shout 6 accost, call to, esteem, salute 7 acclaim, address, applaud, commend, glorify, receive, shout at, usher in, welcome 8 cry out to, eulogize, greeting 9 accosting 10 calling out, compliment, panegyrize, salutation 11 make welcome
German: 4 heil
Latin: 3 ave 5 salve

Hailey, Arthur
author of: 5 Hotel 6 Wheels 7 Airport 12 In High Places 14 Final Diagnosis 16 The Moneychangers

hail-fellow-well-met 8 familiar, friendly, intimate, outgoing, sociable 9 extrovert 10 gregarious

Hail Mary
Latin: 8 Ave Maria 12 rosary prayer

Hail the Conquering Hero
director: 14 Preston Sturges
cast: 10 Ella Raines 12 Eddie Bracken 14 Raymond Walburn 15 William Demarest 16 Franklin Pangborn

hail to victory
German: 8 sieg heil

Hair
writers: 9 James Rado 11 Gerome Ragni
composer: 13 Galt MacDermot
character: 3 Hud 4 Woof 6 Berger, Claude, Crissy, Dionne, Jeanie, Sheila
songs: 4 3500 8 Aquarius 9 Ain't Got No 12 Colored Spade 17 Manchester England

hair 3 fur, mop 4 coat, down, iota, mane, pelt, wool 5 bangs, curls, locks 6 fleece 7 tresses 8 ringlets 12 narrow margin
loss: 8 alopecia, baldness

haircut, hairdo 3 bob, bun, cut 4 Afro, clip, crop, fade, perm, shag, trim, updo 5 bangs, braid, butch, swirl 6 boogie, mohawk 7 beehive, buzzcut, chignon, cornrow, crewcut, flattop, fuzz cut, natural, pachuco, page boy, pigtail, shingle, tonsure, upsweep 8 bouffant, brushcut, coiffure, ducktail, ponytail, razorcut 9 barbering, hairstyle, permanent, pompadour 10 feathercut, french knot

haircutter 6 barber 11 hairdresser, hair stylist

hairdresser 8 coiffeur 9 coiffeuse 10 beautician, haircutter 11 beauty salon 12 beauty parlor
French: 8 coiffeur

hair-raising 5 eerie 7 bristle 8 exciting 9 thrilling 10 terrifying 11 astonishing 12 breathtaking, electrifying 13 horripilation, spine-tingling

hairsplitting 4 fine 6 minute, subtle 7 carping 8 caviling, delicate, hairline,

niggling 9 minuscule, quibbling 10 nitpicking, unapparent 12 faultfinding, overcritical 13 imperceptible, inappreciable, infinitesimal 15 inconsequential

hairy 5 bushy, furry, wooly 6 fleecy, pilose, shaggy, woolly 7 hirsute

Hairy Ape, The
author: 12 Eugene O'Neill

Haiti
name means: 15 mountainous land
other name: 12 Santo Domingo
capital/largest city: 12 Port-au-Prince
others: 5 Aquin, Furcy, Limbe 6 Hinche, Jacmel, St Marc 7 Jeremie, Leogane, Saltrou 8 Gonaives, Kenscoff, Les Cayes 10 Cap-Haitien
monetary unit: 6 gourde 8 centimes
island: 5 Vache 6 Gonave, Tortue 7 Navassa, Tortuga 8 Caymites 10 Hispaniola 14 Grande Cayemite 15 Greater Antilles
lake: 8 Saumatre
mountain: 4 Nord 5 Cahos 6 Macaya, Noires 7 Lahotte 8 Troudeau
highest point: 7 La Selle, Laselle
river: 9 Guayamoul 10 Artibonite
sea: 8 Atlantic 9 Caribbean
physical feature:
   gulf: 6 Gonave
   passage: 8 Windward
people: 5 Taino 7 African, mulatto
   discoverer: 8 Columbus
   liberator: 19 Toussaint Louverture
   ruler: 7 Papa Doc 8 Duvalier
language: 6 Creole, French, patois
religion: 6 voodoo 13 Roman Catholic
feature:
   dance: 5 mambo
   festival: 9 Mardi Gras
   fortress: 10 La Ferriere 24 Citadelle du Roi Christophe
   security force: 8 bogeymen 15 Tontons Macoutes
food:
   sweet potato: 6 batata

Hakenkreuz 11 hooked cross 12 Nazi swastika

HAL
character in: 14 Two Thousand One (2001)
author: 6 Clarke

Halas, George
nickname: 8 Papa Bear
sport: 8 football
position: 5 coach
team: 12 Chicago Bears

halcyon 4 calm, fair 5 happy, quiet, sunny 6 blithe, golden, hushed, joyous, placid, serene 7 pacific 8 carefree, cheerful, peaceful, tranquil 9 cloudless, contented, reposeful, unclouded, unruffled 10 unagitated, untroubled

hale 3 fit 4 well 5 hardy, sound 6 hearty, robust, rugged, sturdy 7

healthy, in shape 8 vigorous 9 energetic, in the pink, strapping 10 ablebodied, robustious 12 in fine fettle

Hale, Edward Everett
author of: 21 The Man Without a Country
hero: 11 Phillip Nolan

Hale, George Ellery
field: 9 astronomy
initiated: 20 Mt Palomar Observatory
invented: 17 spectroheliograph

Hale, Nathan, 7 patriot
hanged as a: 3 spy

Hale-Bopp 5 comet

Haley, Alex
author of: 5 Roots 26 The Autobiography of Malcolm X

Haley, Jack
born: 8 Boston MA
roles: 6 Tin Man 13 The Wizard of Oz

half 4 part, some 6 all but, barely, fairly, feebly, halved, in part, meager, partly, rather, scanty, skimpy, slight, weakly 7 divided, faintly, limited, partial, portion, section 8 fraction, middling, moderate, passable, passably, slightly 9 deficient, imperfect, partially, tolerable, tolerably 10 fractional, inadequate, incomplete, moderately, relatively 12 fifty percent, inadequately, insufficient, pretty nearly 13 after a fashion, comparatively 14 insufficiently

half-asleep 6 drowsy, groggy, unwary 7 out-of-it, unaware 8 sluggish 9 not-with-it, oblivious

half-hearted 4 cold, cool, tame 5 blase, faint 7 languid, passive 8 listless, lukewarm 9 apathetic, lethargic 10 ambivalent, irresolute, lackluster, phlegmatic, spiritless, unaspiring 11 indifferent, perfunctory 13 lackadaisical 14 unenthusiastic

half homer 15 Biblical measure

half-moon 3 arc, bow 4 arch 5 curve 8 crescent

Half Moon 4 ship
of: 11 Henry Hudson

halfway 6 almost, in part, medial, medium, middle, midway, nearly, partly, rather 7 midmost 8 somewhat 9 partially, to a degree 10 middlemost, moderately 11 equidistant, in the middle 12 intermediate, pretty nearly, to some extent 13 in some measure 18 between two extremes

half-wit 4 dolt, dope, fool 5 dummy, dunce, idiot, moron, ninny 6 dimwit, nitwit 7 dullard 8 dumb-dumb, imbecile, numskull 9 blockhead, numbskull, simpleton 10 nincompoop 15 mental defective, mental deficient

half-witted 4 dumb 5 silly 6 stupid 7 asinine, foolish, idiotic, moronic 9 dimwitted, imbecilic, senseless

11 lamebrained **12** feeble-minded, simple-minded

hall 5 entry, foyer, lobby **6** arcade **7** chamber, gallery, hallway, passage **8** anteroom, club room, corridor, entrance **9** vestibule **10** auditorium, dining hall, passageway **11** antechamber, banquet hall, concert hall, waiting room **12** amphitheater, assembly room, meeting place **13** reception room

Hall, Diane
real name of: **11** Diane Keaton

Hall, James
field: **7** geology **9** chemistry
nationality: **7** British
founded: **12** geochemistry **19** experimental geology

Hall, James Norman
author of: **17** Mutiny on the Bounty
co-author: **15** Charles Nordhoff

Hallel 6 praise **16** liturgical prayer

Haller, Albrecht von
field: **7** biology
nationality: **5** Swiss
founded: **15** modern neurology

Haller, Harry
character in: **11** Steppenwolf
author: **5** Hesse

Halley, Edmund
field: **9** astronomy
nationality: **7** British
discovered: **12** Halley's Comet

hallmark 4 sign **5** badge, stamp **6** device, emblem, symbol **14** characteristic

halloo 3 cry **4** call, hail, yell **5** shout **6** cry out, holler

hallow 5 bless **7** respect **8** dedicate, sanctify, venerate **10** consecrate

hallowed 4 holy **6** sacred **7** blessed, honored **9** beatified, dedicated **10** sacrosanct, sanctified **11** consecrated

Halloween
date: **7** October (31)
also called: **13** All Hallows Eve
symbol: **7** pumpkin **12** jack-o-lantern
saying: **12** trick or treat

hallucination 5 dream **6** mirage, vision **7** chimera, fantasy, figment **8** delusion, illusion **9** nightmare **10** aberration, apparition **14** phantasmagoria

hallway 4 hall **5** entry, foyer **7** passage **8** corridor, entryway **10** passageway

halo 4 aurora, corona, luster, nimbus **7** aureole, dignity, majesty **8** grandeur, holiness, radiance, sanctity, splendor **9** solemnity, sublimity **11** ring of light **12** chromosphere, luminousness, magnificence, resplendence **13** spiritual aura **15** illustriousness

Hals, Franz
born: **7** Antwerp, Holland
artwork: **9** Gypsy Girl **10** Hille Bobbe (The Witch of Haarlem) **13** The Jolly Toper **14** Jacobus Zaffius **15** The Merry Company **19** The Laughing Cavalier **22** Portrait of a Standing Man **24** The Regents of the Almshouse **26** Yonker Ramp and his Sweetheart **28** The Regentesses of the Almshouse **33** The Banquet of the St George Civic Guard

Halsey, William F
served in: **3** WWI **4** WWII
rank: **12** fleet admiral
battle: **9** Leyte Gulf **11** Philippines **14** Solomon Islands

halt 3 end **4** balk, curb, foil, quit, rest, rout, stay, stem, stop, wait, whoa **5** abate, block, brake, break, cease, check, close, crush, delay, pause, quash, quell, stall, tarry **6** bridle, cut off, defeat, draw up, hamper, hinder, impede, linger, pull up, recess, rein in, scotch, subdue, thwart, wind up **7** heave to, inhibit, prevent, put down, repress, respite, squelch, suspend, time out **8** break off, breather, choke off, don't move, hang fire, interval, knock off, leave off, overturn, prohibit, restrain, restrict, shut down, suppress, vanquish **9** cessation, frustrate, interlude, interrupt, overthrow, terminate **10** call it a day, extinguish, shut up shop, standstill, suspension **11** come to a halt, come to a stop, discontinue, hold in check, termination **12** intermission, interruption, throttle down **13** spike one's guns **14** breathing spell, discontinuance

halting 6 ending **7** curbing **8** episodic, hesitant, stopping **9** faltering, stumbling **10** calling off, discursive, suspending **11** restraining, terminating **13** discontinuous **14** calling a halt to, putting a stop to

halting place
Spanish: **6** posada

halutz 7 pioneer **26** person who emigrates to Israel

halve 6 bisect **9** cut in half **10** split in two **13** divide equally

ham, 6 emoter **9** overactor **20** amateur radio operator

Ham
character in: **16** David Copperfield
author: **7** Dickens

Ham
father: **4** Noah
brother: **4** Shem **7** Japheth
son: **3** Put **4** Cush **6** Canaan **7** Mizraim
descendant of: **6** Hamite

Hamadryad
form: **5** dryad
spirit of: **4** tree

Haman
served: **9** Ahasuerus also see **6** Esther

Hamill, Mark
born: **9** Oakland CA
roles: **8** Star Wars **13** Luke Skywalker **15** Return of the Jedi **20** The Empire Strikes Back

Hamilton
capital of: **7** Bermuda

Hamilton, Alexander
1st Secretary:, **8** Treasury
slain by: **9** Aaron Burr
in: **4** duel

Hamilton, Charles
character in: **15** Gone With the Wind
author: **8** Mitchell

Hamilton, Iain
composer of: **6** Aurora **7** Alastor **8** Sinfonia **9** Pharsalia **11** The Bermudas **18** Threnos In Time of War **20** The Royal Hunt of the Sun **21** The Catiline Conspiracy

Hamilton, Margaret
real name: **23** Margaret Hamilton Meserve
born: **11** Cleveland OH
roles: **4** Cora **13** The Wizard of Oz **23** The Wicked Witch of the West

Hamito-Semitic
language also known as: **11** Afro-Asiatic
branch: **6** Berber, Chadic **7** Semitic **8** Cushitic, Egyptian

hamlet 4 burg **7** village **8** hick town, tank town **10** crossroads **11** whistle stop **12** one-horse town, small village **13** jerkwater town

Hamlet
author: **18** William Shakespeare
character: **7** Horatio, Laertes, Ophelia **8** Claudius, Gertrude, Polonius, The Ghost **11** Rosencrantz **12** Guildenstern
soliloquy: **13** To be or not to be
skull: **6** Yorick
castle: **8** Elsinore
setting: **7** Denmark
director: **15** Laurence Olivier
cast: **11** Basil Sydney, Felix Aylmer, Jean Simmons **12** Eileen Herlie **15** Laurence Olivier
Oscar for: **5** actor (Olivier) **7** picture

Hamlet, The
author: **15** William Faulkner
character: **4** Eula, Jody **6** Labove **8** Ab Snopes **9** V K Ratliff **10** Flem Snopes, Mink Snopes, Will Varner **11** Isaac Snopes **12** Henry Armstid

Hamlin, Vincent T
creator/artist of: **8** Alley Oop

Hammarskjold, Dag 7 Swedish **13** United Nations **16** secretary-general

hammer 3 hit, tap **4** bang, form, make, nail **5** drive, forge, knock, pound, punch, shape, whack **6** pummel, rammer, strike **7** beat out, fashion
type: **4** claw, jack, tack **5** gavel, steam **6** mallet, sledge **8** ballpeen **10** pile driver **12** upholsterers

Hammer, Mike

detective created by: 14 Mickey Spillane

hammered 5 drunk **6** banged, beaten, shaped **7** knocked, pounded, whipped, wrought **8** battered, repeated **10** terrorized

Hammett, Dashiell
author of: 10 Red Harvest, The Thin Man **11** The Glass Key **12** The Dain Curse **16** The Maltese Falcon
character: 4 Asta (dog) **8** Sam Spade **11** Miles Archer, Nick Charles, Nora Charles **13** Continental Op

hamper 3 gag **4** balk, curb, stem **5** block, check, stall **6** fetter, hinder, hog-tie, hold up, impede, muzzle, retard, thwart **7** inhibit, prevent, shackle **8** encumber, handicap, obstruct, restrain, restrict **9** frustrate **13** interfere with

Hampton, Hope
nickname: 22 The Duchess of Park Avenue
born: 14 Philadelphia PA
roles: 8 Star Dust **13** Lawful Larceny, The Road to Reno **16** The Price of a Party

hamstring 6 impair, muscle, tendon **7** cripple, disable **8** handicap **10** debilitate

Hamsun, Knut
author of: 3 Pan **6** August, Hunger **8** Victoria **9** Mysteries, Vagabonds **16** Children of the Age **18** The Growth of the Soil

Hananiah *see* **8** Shadrach

hand, hands 3 aid, man, paw **4** care, fist, give, help, hold, lift, mitt, palm, pass **5** guide, power, reach **6** assist, charge, convey, helper, menial, script, worker **7** command, control, custody, deliver, keeping, laborer, ovation, present, support, workman **8** auspices, dominion, employee, guidance, handyman, hired man, longhand, meat-hook **9** assistant, associate, authority, hired hand **10** assistance, domination, management, minister to, penmanship, possession, turn over to, workingman **11** calligraphy, furnish with, handwriting, supervision **12** jurisdiction **13** member of a crew **15** burst of applause, manual extremity, round of applause

handbag 3 bag **4** grip **5** purse **6** clutch, valise **7** satchel **8** moneybag, reticule **10** pocketbook, portmanteau

handbill 5 flier, tract **6** notice **7** leaflet **8** bulletin, circular **12** announcement **13** advertisement

handbook 5 bible **6** manual **8** baedeker **9** guidebook, vade mecum **13** reference book

handcart 4 cart **6** barrow **8** pushcart **10** handbarrow **11** wheelbarrow

handcuffs 5 cuffs, irons **6** chains **7** fetters **8** manacles, shackles **9** bracelets

hand down 4 will **5** leave **6** hand on, pass on **8** bequeath

Handel, George Frederick (Georg Friedrich)
born: 5 Halle **7** Germany
lived in: 7 England
composer of: 4 Nero, Saul **5** Serse, Silla, Siroe, Teseo **6** Admeto, Alcina, Almira, Esther, Flavio, Jeptha, Joseph, Ottone, Samson, Semele, Xerxes **7** Amadigi, Athalia, Deborah, Lotario, Messiah, Rinaldo, Rodrigo, Solomon, Tolomeo **8** Atalanta, Berenice, Hercules, Scipione, Theodora **9** Agrippina, Radamisto, Rodelinda, Tamerlano **10** Alessandro, Belshazzar, Floridante, Water Music **12** Giulio Cesare, Il Pastor Fido, Muzio Scevola **13** Israel in Egypt, Riccardo Primo **14** Acis and Galatea, Fireworks Music **15** Alexander's Feast, Judas Maccabaeus **16** Hornpipe Concerto **19** Julius Caesar in Egypt, Ode for St Cecilia's Day **22** The Royal Fireworks Music **23** Hallelujah Organ Concerto, The Harmonious Blacksmith **24** The Triumph of Time and Truth

handful 7 minimum, modicum **10** scattering, smattering, sprinkling, thimbleful, tiny amount **11** scant amount, small number **13** small quantity

handgun 3 rod **5** piece, rifle **6** pistol, weapon **7** firearm, shotgun **8** revolver **9** automatic, twenty-two **12** shooting iron **20** Saturday night special

handicap 4 curb **5** limit **6** burden, defect, hamper, hinder, impede, retard, thwart **7** barrier, inhibit, repress, shackle **8** deafness, drawback, encumber, hold back, lameness, obstacle, restrain, restrict, suppress **9** blindness, detriment **10** difficulty, impediment, inhibition, limitation **11** encumbrance, restriction, shortcoming **12** disadvantage **13** inconvenience **14** stumbling block

handicapped 7 limited **8** burdened, disabled, held back, hindered, impaired, retarded **10** encumbered, restrained, restricted **13** disadvantaged

handicrafts
god of: 10 Hephaestus, Hephaistos
handicraftsman 7 artisan **10** handworker **12** handicrafter

handiness 7 utility **8** deftness **9** dexterity **10** adroitness, usefulness **11** convenience **12** availability **13** accessibility

hand in glove 5 as one **10** side by side **13** close together

handle 3 paw, ply, run, tag, use **4** feel, grip, hilt, hold, knob, name, poke, pull, sell, work **5** carry, grasp, guide, knead, pilot, pinch, shaft, shank, steer, swing, touch, treat **6** caress, CB name, deal in, employ, finger, fondle, manage, market, pick up, stroke **7** care for, command, conduct, control, massage, moniker, operate, paw over, trade in, utilize **8** cognomen, deal with, maneuver **9** traffic in **10** manipulate, take care of **11** appellation, merchandise **12** offer for sale **13** bring into play

handout 4 alms, dole **7** freebie **19** something for nothing

hand out 4 deal, give **5** grant **6** bestow, confer, donate **7** dole out, mete out, present **8** dispense **9** apportion **10** contribute, distribute

hand over 4 cede **5** grant, yield **6** give up, tender **7** abandon, release **8** transfer **9** deliver up, surrender **10** relinquish

handsome 4 fair **5** ample, bonny, noble **6** benign, comely, lovely, pretty **7** elegant, liberal, sightly, sizable, stately **8** abundant, generous, gracious, imposing, merciful, princely, splendid, stunning, tasteful **9** beauteous, beautiful, bountiful, exquisite, unselfish **10** attractive, benevolent, big-hearted, impressive, sufficient, well-formed **11** fine-looking, good-looking, magnanimous **12** considerable, easy to look at, humanitarian **13** compassionate, easy on the eyes **16** well-proportioned

hand to hand
Spanish: 9 mano a mano

handy 4 deft, near, nigh **5** adept, on tap **6** adroit, at hand, clever, expert, on call, on hand, useful, wieldy **7** capable, helpful, skilled **8** skillful **9** available, competent, dexterous, easy to use, efficient, practical **10** accessible, convenient, manageable, obtainable, proficient **11** at one's elbow, close at hand, in readiness, ready to hand, serviceable **12** accomplished **14** nimble-fingered **15** within easy reach **16** easily accessible **17** at one's beck and call

hang 3 bow, sag **4** drop, gist, rest **5** affix, hinge, knack, lie in, lower, lynch, point, trail **6** append, attach, dangle, depend **7** incline, meaning, suspend, thought **8** lean over, let droop, repose in, string up, turn upon **9** be pendant, be pendent **11** be dependent, be subject to, bend forward, swing freely **12** be contingent, bend downward **13** revolve around **15** die on the gallows, fasten from above **16** execute by hanging, send to the gallows

hangdog 6 abject **7** ashamed **8** defeated, degraded, hopeless, resigned, wretched **9** miserable **10** browbeaten, chapfallen, humiliated, shamefaced **11** crestfallen, embarrassed, intimidated **13** guilty-looking

hang down 3 sag 5 droop

hanger-on 7 admirer, groupie 8 follower 9 sycophant

hanging object
Japanese: 8 kakemono

hang loosely 3 bag, sag 5 droop

hangout 3 den 5 haunt

hang out 3 mix 4 live 5 dwell 6 hobnob, loiter, mingle, reside 7 consort 9 associate, be friends, pal around, run around 10 fraternize, hang around 11 keep company

hanker after 4 want 5 covet, crave, fancy 6 desire 7 long for, pine for 8 aspire to, yearn for 9 lust after 11 have a yen for, have an eye on, hunger after, thirst after

hankering 3 yen 4 itch, urge 6 aching, desire, hunger, pining, thirst 7 craving, longing 8 yearning

Hanna-Barbera
creators of: 6 Top Cat 7 Jetsons 8 Yogi Bear 11 Tom and Jerry 15 Quickdraw McGraw 16 Huckleberry Hound 14 The Flintstones

Hannah
husband: 7 Elkanah
son: 6 Samuel

Hanoi
capital of: 7 Vietnam 12 North Vietnam
river: 3 Red 4 Yuan 7 Song Koi
delta: 6 Tonkin
airport: 6 Gia Lam

Hans Brinker
author: 5 (Mary Elizabeth Mapes) Dodge
character: 4 Raff 5 Gleck, Hilda 6 Gretel 7 Boekman, Mevrouw
feature: 12 silver skates

Hansel and Gretel
author: 13 Grimm Brothers (Jakob and Wilhelm)
opera by: 11 Humperdinck
character: 5 Witch
feature 4 oven 16 gingerbread house

Hans Kristian
character in: 16 Giants of the Earth
author: 7 Rolvaag

Hanson, Howard
born: 7 Wahoo NE
composer of: 5 Sacra (symphony No 5) 6 Nordic (symphony No 1) 7 Requiem (symphony No 4) 8 Romantic (symphony No 2) 10 Merry-Mount

haphazard 6 casual, chance, fitful, random 7 aimless, chaotic 8 careless, on-and-off, slapdash, sporadic 9 arbitrary, hit-or-miss 10 accidental, disordered, disorderly, fortuitous, undesigned, undirected, unthinking 11 purposeless, unorganized 12 disorganized, unmethodical, unsystematic 14 indiscriminate, unpremeditated 15 catch-as-catch-can

hapless 6 cursed, jinxed, no-good, rotten, woeful 7 forlorn, unhappy, unlucky 8 accursed, hopeless, ill- fated, luckless, wretched 9 miserable 10 ill-starred 11 star-crossed, unfortunate

happen 5 arise, ensue, occur 6 appear, befall, betide, crop up, result 7 turn out 8 become of, spring up 9 be borne by, be the case, come about, eventuate, take place, transpire 10 be one's fate, come to pass 11 be endured by 12 be suffered by 13 be one's fortune, fall to one's lot, present itself

happening 4 case 5 event 6 advent, affair, matter 7 episode 8 accident, incident, occasion 9 adventure, incidence 10 experience, occurrence, proceeding 11 vicissitude 12 circumstance, happenstance 20 just one of those things

happenstance 4 luck 6 chance 8 accident, fortuity

happiness 3 joy 4 glee 5 bliss, cheer, mirth 6 gaiety 7 comfort, content, delight, ecstasy, elation, jollity, rapture 8 blessing, felicity, gladness, pleasure 9 beatitude, enjoyment, merriment, rejoicing, transport 10 cheeriness, exuberance, exultation, jubilation 11 blessedness, contentment, high spirits 12 cheerfulness, satisfaction 13 gratification 16 lightheartedness, sense of well-being

happy 3 fit, gay 4 glad, meet 5 lucky 6 elated, joyful, joyous, timely 7 content, fitting, gleeful, pleased, tickled 8 blissful, cheerful, cheering, ecstatic, exultant, jubilant, pleasant, pleasing 9 agreeable, contented, delighted, exuberant, favorable, fortunate, gratified, opportune, overjoyed, rapturous, rhapsodic 10 auspicious, convenient, delightful, felicitous, gratifying, propitious, seasonable 11 exhilarated, tickled pink, transported 12 advantageous 13 in high spirits 15 in seventh heaven

Happy Days
character: 6 Arnold, Fonzie 10 Ralph Malph 11 Potsie Weber 12 Chachi Arcola 14 Pinky Tuscadero 15 Chuck Cunningham 16 Alfred Delvecchio, Arthur Fonzarelli, Howard Cunningham, Joanie Cunningham, Leather Tuscadero, Marion Cunningham, Richie Cunningham
cast: 8 Roz Kelly 9 Donny Most, Erin Moran, Pat Morita, Ron Howard, Scott Baio, Tom Bosley 10 Al Molinaro, Marion Ross, Suzi Quatro 12 Henry Winkler 13 Anson Williams, Gavan O'Herlihy 15 Randolph Roberts

happy-go-lucky 6 blithe 7 buoyant, flighty, relaxed 8 carefree, careless, feckless, heedless, skittish 9 easygoing, unworried 10 insouciant, noncha-

lant, optimistic, untroubled 11 free-and-easy, unconcerned 12 devil- may-care, light-hearted 13 irresponsible 14 scatterbrained 23 without a worry in the world

harangue 6 speech, tirade 7 lecture, oration 8 diatribe, scolding 9 contumely, sermonize 12 denunciation, vituperation

Harare
capital of: 8 Zimbabwe

harass 3 cow, irk, vex 4 bait, ride 5 annoy, beset, bully, harry, hound, tease, worry 6 attack, badger, bother, heckle, hector, pester, plague 7 assault, bedevil, besiege, disturb, torment 8 browbeat, distress, irritate 9 persecute 10 discommode, exasperate, intimidate 14 raid frequently

harbinger 4 clue, omen 5 token 6 herald, symbol 7 portent 8 signaler 9 announcer, first sign, precursor 10 forerunner, indication, proclaimer

Harbonna 6 eunuch

harbor 3 bay 4 cove, dock, feel, goal, hide, hold, keep, pier, port, quay 5 basin, haven, house, inlet, lodge, wharf 6 asylum, billet, foster, lagoon, refuge, retain, shield, take in 7 care for, cling to, conceal, nurture, protect, quarter, retreat, shelter 8 hideaway, keep safe, maintain, muse over, terminus 9 brood over, sanctuary 11 concealment, destination, hiding place 12 give refuge to 13 bear in the mind, terminal point 18 protected anchorage

Harcorates see 5 Horus

hard 3 sad 4 cold, firm, mean, ugly 5 cruel, eager, harsh, heavy, rigid, rough, solid, stern, stiff, stony, tight, tough 6 bitter, brutal, fierce, firmly, keenly, knotty, severe, steely, strict, strong, sullen, thorny, unkind 7 angrily, arduous, callous, closely, complex, cryptic, eagerly, earnest, harmful, heavily, hostile, hurtful, inhuman, intense, onerous, sharply, solidly, tightly, to heart, vicious, violent, willing, zealous 8 animated, baffling, critical, diligent, exacting, fiercely, forceful, forcibly, hardened, intently, involved, pitiless, powerful, puzzling, rocklike, ruthless, severely, spirited, spiteful, steadily, strongly, stubborn, untiring, venomous, vigorous 9 arduously, assiduous, bellicose, confusing, difficult, earnestly, energetic, furiously, Herculean, insulting, intensely, intricate, laborious, malicious, merciless, painfully, rancorous, seriously, strenuous, stringent, unbending, unpliable, unsparing, violently, wearisome 10 burdensome, diligently, forcefully, formidable, impervious, implacable, inexorable, inflexible, lamentable, melancholy, oppressive, perplexing, persistent, powerfully, relentless, resolutely, rigorously, tormenting, unbearable, unflagging, unfriendly, unpleasant, untiringly, unyielding, vigorously, vindictive **11** acrimonious, agonizingly, assiduously, belligerent, bewildering, complicated, distressing, emotionally, hardhearted, industrious, insensitive, intolerable, laboriously, persevering, troublesome, unceasingly, unmalleable, unrelenting, unremitting, unsparingly **12** antagonistic, cantankerous, determinedly, disagreeable, enterprising, impenetrable, persistently, relentlessly, thick-skinned, unfathomable, unflaggingly **13** conscientious, disheartening, distressfully, energetically, indefatigable, industriously, with much anger **14** uncompromising, with much sorrow **15** conscientiously **16** with all one's might **18** with strong feelings

hard-and-fast 3 set **6** strict **7** binding **8** exacting, rigorous **9** mandatory, unbending **10** compelling, compulsory, inflexible, obligatory, undeniable, unyielding **11** irrevocable, unalterable, unremitting **12** indisputable **13** incontestable **14** uncompromising

Hardcastle family
  characters in: 18 She Stoops to Conquer
  author: 9 Goldsmith

hard drinker 3 sot **4** lush, soak, wino **5** drunk, rummy, souse, toper **6** barfly, boozer **7** guzzler, imbiber, tippler **8** drunkard **9** alcoholic **11** dipsomaniac **14** problem drinker **16** two-fisted drinker

harden 3 dry, gel, set **4** cake, fire, firm **5** adapt, adjust, blunt, enure, inure, steel **6** anneal, freeze, season, temper **7** calcify, callous, congeal, fortify, petrify, stiffen, thicken, toughen **8** accustom, solidify **9** fossilize, make tough, reinforce **10** discipline, invigorate, strengthen **11** crystallize, turn to stone **12** restrengthen **13** make unfeeling

hard feelings 5 anger **6** grudge, hatred, rancor **7** ill will **8** acrimony **9** animosity, hostility **10** antagonism, bitterness **12** spitefulness

hardheaded 4 cool **5** balky **6** astute, mulish, poised, shrewd **7** willful **8** contrary, sensible, stubborn **9** immovable, objective, obstinate, pigheaded, practical, pragmatic, realistic, unbending, unfeeling **10** coolheaded, impersonal, inflexible, refractory, self-willed, unyielding **11** down-to-earth, intractable, tough-minded, unemotional, unflappable **14** self-controlled

hardhearted 4 cold, hard, mean **5** cruel, stony **6** brutal, Hannah **7** callous, inhuman **8** pitiless, ruthless, uncaring **9** heartless, merciless, unfeeling, unpitying, unsparing **11**

coldblooded, indifferent, insensitive, remorseless, unforgiving **12** cruel-hearted, thick-skinned **13** unsympathetic

hardihood 4 grit **5** pluck, spunk **6** mettle **7** courage **8** strength **9** endurance, fortitude **10** resolution **12** resoluteness

Harding, Warren Gamaliel
  presidential rank: 11 twenty-ninth
  party: 10 Republican
  state represented: 2 OH
  defeated: 3 (James Middleton) Cox, (William Wesley) Cox **4** (Eugene Victor) Debs **7** (Aaron Sherman) Watkins **8** (Robert Charles) Macauley **11** (Parley Parker) Christensen
  vice president: 8 (Calvin) Coolidge
  cabinet:
    state: 6 (Charles Evans) Hughes
    treasury: 6 (Andrew William) Mellon
    war: 5 (John Wingate) Weeks
    attorney general: 9 (Harry Micajah) Daugherty
    navy: 5 (Edwin) Denby
    postmaster general: 3 (Harry Stewart) New **4** (Hubert) Work, (William Harrison) Hays
    interior: 4 (Albert Bacon) Fall, (Hubert) Work
    agriculture: 7 (Henry Cantwell) Wallace
    commerce: 6 (Herbert Clark) Hoover
    labor: 5 (James John) Davis
  born: 9 Corsica OH (now Blooming Grove)
  died: 2 CA (while in office) **12** San Francisco
  buried: 8 Marion OH
  education:
    College: 11 Ohio Central
  religion: 7 Baptist
  interests: 5 poker
    played musical instrument: 6 cornet **7** helicon
  political career: 8 US Senate **15** Ohio State Senate
    lieutenant governor of: 4 Ohio
  civilian career: 9 publisher **13** schoolteacher **15** newspaper editor **17** insurance salesman
  notable events of lifetime/term:
    Act: 21 Fordney-McCumber Tariff
    peace treaty with: 7 Austria, Germany, Hungary
    scandal: 10 Teapot Dome (oil)
    Treaty: 9 Five-Power, Nine-Power **16** Four-Power Pacific
  father: 11 George Tryon
  mother: 6 Phoebe (Elizabeth Dickerson)
    stepmother: 4 Mary (Alice Severns) **6** Eudora (Kelley Luvisi)
  siblings: 11 George Tryon **12** Mary Clarissa **14** Charity Malvina, Phoebe Caroline **15** Abigail Victoria **16**

Charles Alexander, Eleanor Priscilla
  wife: 8 Florence (Kling DeWolfe)
  children:
    illegitimate daughter: 21 Elizabeth Ann Christian (by mistress Nan Britton)

hardly 4 just, only **6** barely, rarely **7** faintly, in no way **8** not often, not quite, scarcely **9** almost not, by no means **10** in no manner, uncommonly **12** certainly not, infrequently **13** not by any means **15** not by a great deal

hardnosed 4 hard **5** harsh, rigid, stern, tough **6** severe, shrewd, strict **8** critical, hard-line, exacting, stubborn **9** demanding, unbending, unsparing **10** hardheaded, inflexible, nononsense, unyielding **11** calculating, intractable **12** unsentimental **14** uncompromising

Hardouin-Mansart, Jules
  architect of: 8 Orangery (Versailles) **12** Chateau du Val (St Germain-en-Laye), Grand Trianon (Versailles), Place Vendome (Paris) **15** Chateau de Clagny (Versailles) **16** Galerie des Glaces (Hall of Mirrors at Versailles), Les Invalides (Church of the Dome, Paris)

hard-pressed 7 harried, put-upon **9** embattled **10** overworked

hardship 3 woe **4** load **5** agony, grief **6** burden, misery, ordeal, sorrow **7** problem, travail, trouble **8** handicap **9** adversity, privation, suffering **10** affliction, difficulty, misfortune **11** cross to bear, encumbrance, tribulation, unhappiness **12** wretchedness

hard sledding 8 tough job **10** difficulty, tough going, uphill work **11** arduousness **13** laboriousness

hard times 4 bust **5** slump **8** bad times **9** recession **10** depression

Hard Times
  author: 11 Studs Terkel

Hard Times
  author: 14 Charles Dickens
  character: 9 Sissy Jupe **10** Mrs Sparsit **11** Mr Bounderby **12** Tom Gradgrind **14** James Harthouse **15** Louisa Gradgrind, Thomas Gradgrind **16** Stephen Blackpool

hard to catch 3 sly **4** foxy, wily **6** crafty, shifty, tricky **7** elusive, evasive **8** slippery

hard to grasp 6 arcane **7** complex, elusive **8** abstruse, baffling, puzzling, slippery **9** difficult, enigmatic **10** perplexing **16** incomprehensible

hard to manage 6 unruly **7** froward, willful **8** perverse, stubborn **9** difficult, fractious, obstinate **10** inflexible, refractory, unyielding **11** intractable **12** obstreperous, unmanageable

hard to please 5 fussy, picky **7** exigent, finicky **8** critical **10** fastidious, meticulous, particular

Hardwick, Elizabeth
  author of: **11** Simple Truth **12** A View of My Own **15** Sleepless Nights **20** Seduction and Betrayal
Hardwicke, Sir Cedric
  born: **3** Lye **7** England
  roles: **14** On Borrowed Time **21** Livingstone and Stanley **36** A Connecticut Yankee in King Arthur's Court
hardwood 4 wood **8** leadwood
  kind: **3** ash, elm, oak **4** teak **5** beech, birch, maple **6** cherry, linden, walnut **7** hickory **8** mahogany, rosewood, sycamore
hardworking 8 diligent, sedulous **9** assiduous **11** industrious, persevering **12** enterprising **13** conscientious
hardy 3 fit **4** hale **5** tough **6** hearty, mighty, robust, rugged, strong, sturdy **7** healthy **8** stalwart, vigorous **9** strapping **10** able-bodied **12** in fine fettle **13** physically fit **15** in good condition
Hardy, Oliver
  partner: **10** Stan Laurel
  born: **8** Harlem GA
  roles: **8** Pardon Us **9** Saps at Sea **10** Way Out West
Hardy, Thomas
  author of: **10** The Dynasts **14** Jude the Obscure **20** The Return of the Native **21** Tess of the D'Urbervilles **22** Far from the Madding Crowd, The Mayor of Casterbridge
  mythical county: **6** Wessex
  represents: **11** Dorsetshire
hare
  constellation of: **5** Lepus
  group of: **4** down, husk
harebrained 5 silly, wacko, wacky **7** asinine, flighty, foolish **8** skittish **9** dimwitted, senseless **10** half-witted **11** empty-headed **12** simple-minded **13** rattlebrained **14** featherbrained, scatterbrained
Haredale, Reuben
  character in: **12** Barnaby Rudge
  author: **7** Dickens
harem 5 serai, wives **6** purdah, serail, senana, zenana **8** love nest, seraglio **10** concubines
  room: **3** oda
  guard **6** eunuch
Hargreaves, James
  nationality: **7** English
  inventor of: **13** spinning jenny
Harker, Jonathan
  character in: **7** Dracula
  author: **6** Stoker
harlot 3 pro **4** bawd, doxy, jade, pros, slut, tart **5** whore **6** chippy, wanton **7** jezebel, trollop **8** call girl, mistress, strumpet **9** courtesan, kept woman **10** prostitute **11** fallen woman **12** painted woman, scarlet woman, streetwalker
Harlow, Jean
  real name: **16** Harlean Carpenter
  nickname: **15** Blonde Bombshell
  born: **12** Kansas City MO
  roles: **7** Red Dust **8** Riffraff, Saratoga **9** Bombshell, China Seas **11** Hell's Angels, Libeled Lady **13** Dinner at Eight
harm 3 ill, mar, sin **4** evil, hurt, maim, pain, ruin, vice **5** abuse, agony, havoc, spoil, wound, wrong **6** damage, debase, deface, ill-use, impair, injure, injury, malice, misuse, trauma **7** blemish, cripple, degrade, scourge **8** aggrieve, calamity, hardship, iniquity, maltreat, mischief, villainy **9** adversity, detriment, disfigure, suffering, undermine **10** defacement, immorality, impairment, misfortune, sinfulness, wickedness **11** destruction, devastation, malevolence **12** do violence to **13** deterioration, maliciousness
harmful 3 bad **7** adverse, baneful, hurtful, ruinous **8** damaging **9** dangerous, injurious, unhealthy **10** pernicious **11** deleterious, destructive, detrimental, unhealthful, unwholesome **17** counterproductive
harmless 4 mild, safe **6** benign, gentle **7** sinless **8** innocent, nontoxic **9** blameless, guiltless, incorrupt, innocuous, peaceable **10** not hurtful **11** inoffensive **12** not dangerous **15** unobjectionable
harmlessness 6 safety **9** innocence **10** gentleness **11** nontoxicity **12** nonvirulence **13** innocuousness **15** inoffensiveness
Harmon, Young John
  character in: **15** Our Mutual Friend
  author: **7** Dickens
Harmonia
  father: **4** Ares
  mother: **9** Aphrodite
  husband: **6** Cadmus
  daughter: **3** Ino
harmonious 5 sweet **6** dulcet **7** amiable, cordial, unified **8** amicable, friendly, in accord, matching **9** agreeable, congenial, in harmony, melodious **10** compatible, consistent, euphonious, likeminded **11** coordinated, harmonizing, in agreement, mellifluous, sympathetic **12** synchronized **13** sweet-sounding **17** agreeably combined
harmonium 9 reed organ
harmonize 3 fit **4** jibe, mesh **5** agree, blend, chime, tally **6** accord, adjust, attune **7** conform **8** be in tune **9** reconcile **10** complement, correspond, go together **13** sing in harmony
harmony 5 amity, order, peace, unity **6** accord **7** balance, concord **8** matching, symmetry, sympathy **9** agreement, unanimity **10** conformity, fellowship, friendship, proportion **11** amicability, cooperation, correlation, parallelism **12** congeniality, coordination, mutual regard **13** compatibility, mutual fitness **14** like-mindedness **15** organic totality **17** good understanding **19** harmonious relations, pleasing consistency **21** concurrence in opinions
Harmony
  goddess of: **9** Concordia
harness 4 curb, rein, tugs, yoke **5** lines, reins, rig up **6** bridle, collar, employ, halter, muzzle, straps, tackle, traces **7** exploit, hitch up, utilize **8** restrain **9** caparison, trappings **12** put in harness, render useful **13** control and use, turn to account **14** make productive **22** direct to a useful purpose
Harper, Joe
  character in: **9** Tom Sawyer
  author: **5** Twain
harp on 7 dwell on **9** reiterate **18** repeat persistently
Harpy
  form: **7** monster
  head of: **5** woman
  body of: **4** bird
  father: **7** Thaumas
  mother: **7** Electra
  names: **5** Aello **7** Celaeno, Ocypete, Podarge
harridan 3 hag **5** crone, shrew, witch **6** virago **8** battle-ax, old crone **12** mean old woman
harried 5 upset **7** worried **8** harassed, troubled **10** distraught
Harris, Joel Chandler
  author of: **10** Uncle Remus (His Songs and Sayings)
  character: **7** Brer Fox, tar baby **8** Brer Bear **10** Brer Rabbit
Harris, Julie
  real name: **14** Julia Ann Harris
  born: **18** Grosse Pointe Park MI
  roles: **6** Harper **10** East of Eden, I Am a Camera **11** The Haunting **14** A Shot in the Dark, The Hiding Place **19** The Last of Mrs Lincoln **21** The Member of the Wedding **22** Requiem for a Heavyweight **27** And Miss Reardon Drinks a Little
Harris, Richard
  born: **7** Ireland **8** Limerick
  roles: **7** Camelot **8** Cromwell **15** A Man Called Horse **16** The Molly Maguires, This Sporting Life **17** Mutiny on the Bounty, The Guns of Navarone **20** The Cassandra Crossing **26** The Return of a Man Called Horse
Harris, Roy
  composer of: **16** Folksong Symphony **17** American Portraits **27** When Johnny Comes Marching Home (overture)
Harrison, Benjamin
  nickname: **3** Ben **9** Little Ben
  presidential rank: **11** twenty-third
  party: **10** Republican
  state represented: **2** IN

defeated: 4 (Clinton Bowen) Fisk **6** (James Langdon) Curtis **7** (Robert Hall) Cowdrey **8** (Albert) Redstone, (Alson Jenness) Streeter, (Belva Ann Bennett) Lockwood **9** (Grover) Cleveland
vice president: 6 (Levi Parsons) Morton
cabinet:
  state: 6 (James Gillespie) Blaine, (John Watson) Foster
  treasury: 6 (Charles) Foster, (William) Windom
  war: 6 (Stephen Benton) Elkins **7** (Redfield) Proctor
  attorney general: 6 (William Henry Harrison) Miller
  navy: 5 (Benjamin Franklin) Tracy
  postmaster general: 9 (John) Wanamaker
  interior: 5 (John Willock) Noble
  agriculture: 4 (Jeremiah McLain) Rusk
born: 11 North Bend OH
died/buried: 14 Indianapolis IN
education:
  prep school: 14 Farmer's College
  University: 21 Miami University of Ohio
  later studied: 3 law
religion: 12 Presbyterian
interests: 7 fishing, hunting **8** swimming
author: 17 This Country of Ours **20** Views of An Ex- President
political career: 8 US Senate
  city attorney: 12 Indianapolis
  reporter of: 19 Indiana supreme court
  secretary of: 31 Republican state central committee
civilian career: 6 lawyer **12** law professor
military service: 8 Civil War **16** brigadier general
notable events of lifetime/term:
  Act: 16 Dependent Pension, Sherman Anti-Trust **21** Sherman Silver Purchase
  Tariff: 8 McKinley
father: 9 John Scott
mother: 9 Elizabeth (Ramsey Irwin)
siblings: 8 Mary Jane **9** John Irwin, John Scott **10** Anna Symmes, James Irwin **12** James Findlay **13** Carter Bassett **14** Archibald Irwin
  half sisters: 9 Elizabeth **13** Sarah Lucretia
wife: 4 Mary (Scott Lord Dimmick) **8** Caroline (Lavinia Scott)
children: 9 Elizabeth, Mary Scott **15** Russell Benjamin

Harrison, Lou
born: 10 Portland OR
composer of: 8 Rapunzel, Solstice **13** Changing World **15** Four Strict Songs, Johnny Appleseed **17** The Perilous Chapel **19** Almanac of the Seasons **22** At the Tomb of Charles Ives

Harrison, Peter
architect of: 11 Brick Market (Newport RI), King's Chapel (Boston) **14** Redwood Library (Newport RI), Touro Synagogue (Newport RI)

Harrison, Rex
real name: 21 Reginald Carey Harrison
nickname: 8 Sexy Rexy
wife: 10 Kay Kendall **11** Lilli Palmer **13** Rachel Roberts
born: 6 Huyton **7** England
roles: 9 Cleopatra **10** My Fair Lady (Oscar) **12** Blithe Spirit, Henry Higgins **14** Doctor Dolittle **16** The Foxes of Harrow **17** Unfaithfully Yours **18** The Ghost and Mrs Muir **20** Anna and the King of Siam

Harrison, Wallace K
architect of: 13 Lincoln Center (NYC) **14** Socony Building (NYC) **17** Rockefeller Center (NYC) **22** Metropolitan Opera House (NYC) **25** United Nations Headquarters (NYC) **34** Nelson A Rockefeller Empire State Plaza (Albany NY), ALCOA Building (Pittsburgh, with Max Abramovitz)

Harrison, William Henry
nickname: 6 Old Tip **22** The Washington of the West
presidential rank: 5 ninth
party: 4 Whig
state represented: 2 OH
defeated: 6 (James G) Birney **8** (Martin) Van Buren
vice president: 5 (John) Tyler
cabinet:
  state: 7 (Daniel) Webster
  treasury: 5 (Thomas) Ewing
  war: 4 (John) Bell
  attorney general: 10 (John Jordan) Crittenden
  navy: 6 (George Edmund) Badger
  postmaster general: 7 (Francis) Granger
born: 2 VA **17** Charles City County **18** Berkeley plantation
died: 12 Washington DC
buried: 11 North Bend OH
education: 16 privately tutored (at home)
  College: 13 Hampden-Sydney (did not graduate)
  later studied: 8 medicine
religion: 12 Episcopalian
political career: 8 US Senate **11** state Senate **24** US House of Representatives
  governor of: 16 Indiana Territory
  minister: 8 Columbia
civilian career: 6 farmer **7** soldier
military service: 6 US Army **12** major general **19** War of Eighteen Twelve
  battle: 6 (the) Thames **8** Lake Erie **10** Tippecanoe
notable events of lifetime/term: 24 Land Act of Eighteen Hundred
  campaign slogan: 21 Tippecanoe and Tyler too
  treaty of: 10 Greenville
father: 8 Benjamin
mother: 9 Elizabeth (Bassett)
siblings: 3 Ann **4** Lucy **5** Sarah **8** Benjamin **9** Elizabeth **13** Carter Bassett
wife: 4 Anna (Tuthill Symmes)
children: 8 Benjamin **9** John Scott **10** Mary Symmes **11** Anna Tuthill **12** James Findlay, William Henry **13** Carter Bassett, Lucy Singleton **16** Elizabeth Bassett, John Cleves Symmes

Harrow 10 prep school
rival: 4 Eton

harrowing 7 fearful, painful **8** alarming, chilling **9** traumatic, upsetting **10** disturbing, terrifying, tormenting **11** distressing, frightening **13** bloodcurdling

harry 3 irk, vex **4** bait, gall, raid, ride, sack **5** annoy, beset, bully, haunt, hound, tease, worry **6** badger, bother, harass, heckle, hector, pester, plague **7** disturb, pillage, plunder, torment, trouble **8** distract, distress, irritate **9** terrorize **10** exasperate, intimidate **16** attack repeatedly

harsh 4 hard, mean **5** cruel, raspy, rough, sharp, stern **6** bitter, brutal, hoarse, severe, shrill, unkind **7** abusive, caustic, glaring, grating, jarring, rasping, raucous, squawky **8** piercing, pitiless, ruthless, scratchy, strident, ungentle **9** Draconian, heartless, merciless, too bright, unmusical, unsparing **10** discordant, overbright, unpleasant, vindictive **11** cacophonous, hardhearted **12** uncharitable, unharmonious

harshness 5 rigor **7** cruelty, discord **9** brutality, cacophony, raspiness, roughness, sternness, stridency **10** dissonance, shrillness, unkindness **12** ungentleness **13** heartlessness **14** unpleasantness **15** hardheartedness

Hart, Johnny
creator/artist of: 2 B C **13** The Wizard of Id

Hart, Moss
author of: 15 Once in a Lifetime **20** You Can't Take It with You (with George S Kaufman) **21** The Man Who Came to Dinner (with George S Kaufman)

Harte, Bret
author of: 20 The Luck of Roaring Camp **22** The Outcasts of Poker Flat

Hartford
hockey team: 7 Whalers

Harthouse, James
character in: 9 Hard Times
author: 7 Dickens

Hartley, Vivian Mary
real name of: **11** Vivien Leigh

harum-scarum 5 giddy **6** wildly **7** erratic, flighty, foolish **8** careless, confused **9** aimlessly, haphazard, impetuous, impulsive, unplanned, unsettled **10** bewildered, recklessly, unreliable **11** haphazardly, harebrained, impulsively **12** absent-minded, capriciously, disorganized, inconsistent, undependable **13** rattlebrained **14** featherbrained, scatterbrained

Harun ar-Rashid 6 caliph **7** Baghdad **13** Arabian Nights

harvest 3 cut, mow **4** crop, gain, pick, reap **5** amass, fruit, pluck, yield **6** gather, haying, mowing, output, result, return, reward **7** benefit, collect, cutting, picking, produce, product, reaping **8** fruition, gleaning, proceeds **9** aftermath, amassment, gathering, outgrowth **10** accumulate, collection, harvesting **12** accumulation **13** season's growth

harvest time 4 fall **6** autumn **8** maturity **12** Indian summer

Harvey
director: **11** Henry Koster
based on play by: **9** Mary Chase
cast: **6** rabbit **8** Peggy Dow **12** James Stewart (Elwood P Dowd) **13** Cecil Kellaway, Josephine Hull
Oscar for: **17** supporting actress (Hull)

Harvey, Laurence
real name: **19** Larushka Misch Skikne
wife: **16** Margaret Leighton
born: **9** Lithuania, Yomishkis
roles: **7** Darling **12** Life at the Top, Room at the Top **14** Of Human Bondage, Summer and Smoke **16** Butterfield Eight **17** Walk on the Wild Side

Harvey, William
field: **7** anatomy
nationality: **7** British
discovered: **18** circulation of blood

Hasen, Irwin
creator/artist of: **5** Dondi **9** Goldbergs **11** Wonder Woman **12** Green Lantern

hash out 6 review **7** discuss **8** consider, talk over

hasp 4 lock **5** catch, clasp, latch **7** closure **8** fastener

Hassam, (Frederick) Childe
born: **12** Dorchester MA
artwork: **13** Southwest Wind **14** Summer Sunlight, Washington Arch **15** Against the Light **23** Boston Commons at Twilight

hassle 3 bug, row, vex **5** annoy, fight, harry, hound, scrap, set-to **6** badger, battle, bother, harass, tussle **7** contest, dispute, quarrel **8** argument, conflict, squabble, struggle **9** persecute

hassock 4 boss, pess, seat, tuft, weed **5** bunch, chair, group, trush **6** buffet, plants, tuffet **7** ottoman, tussock **9** footstool, vegetable

hasta la vista 6 good-by, so long **7** goodbye **12** until I see you **16** until we meet again

hasta manana 13 until tomorrow **14** see you tomorrow

haste 4 rush **5** hurry, speed **8** celerity, dispatch, rapidity, rashness **9** fleetness, quickness, swiftness **10** expedition, speediness, undue speed **11** hurriedness **12** recklessness **13** careless hurry, impetuousness, impulsiveness, precipitation

hasten 3 fly, run **4** bolt, dart, dash, flit, jump, race, rush **5** egg on, hurry, impel, speed, whisk **6** hustle, incite, scurry, sprint, urge on **7** advance, drive on, hurry on, hurry up, promote, quicken, scamper, scuttle, speed up **8** expedite, make time **10** accelerate, lose no time **11** go full blast, precipitate, push forward **12** step on the gas **13** go on the double **14** step right along **15** go like lightning, make short work of, work against time **20** go hell-bent for leather

hastily 4 fast **5** apace **6** pronto, rashly **7** quickly **8** promptly, speedily **9** hurriedly, like a shot, posthaste, summarily **10** carelessly, heedlessly, recklessly, too quickly **11** impetuously, impulsively, on the double **12** lickety-split, straightaway **13** precipitately, thoughtlessly **18** hell-bent for leather **20** like greased lightning, on the spur of the moment

Hastings, Thomas *see* **17** Carrere, John Merven

hasty 4 fast, rash **5** brief, fleet, quick, rapid, swift **6** abrupt, prompt, rushed, speedy **7** cursory, hurried, passing **8** fleeting, headlong, heedless, reckless **9** impetuous, impulsive, momentary **10** breathless **11** precipitate, superficial, unduly quick **12** quick as a wink **19** without deliberation

hat
French: **7** chapeau

hatch 4 plan, plot **5** frame **6** cook up, create, design, devise, evolve, invent, make up **7** concoct, dream up, fashion, produce, think up **8** conceive, contrive **9** construct, fabricate, formulate, improvise, originate **10** bring forth **11** give birth to, manufacture

hatchlings 5 brood, young **6** chicks **9** offspring

hate 5 abhor, dread, venom **6** animus, detest, enmity, hatred, loathe, malice, rancor **7** be sorry, despise, dislike, wince at **8** acrimony, aversion, be sick of, distaste, execrate, loathing **9** abominate, animosity, antipathy, be tired of, disliking, hostility, not care to **10** abhorrence, be averse to, feel sick at, recoil from, repugnance, resentment, shrink from **11** abomination, be hostile to, be reluctant, be unwilling, detestation, malevolence, wish to avoid **12** be repelled by **14** have no taste for, hold in contempt, revengefulness, vindictiveness **16** bear malice toward, have no stomach for **17** feel disinclined to, not have the heart to **19** regard as distasteful

hateful 4 evil, foul, mean, ugly, vile **5** nasty **6** odious, sinful, wicked **7** heinous **8** infamous, scornful **9** abhorrent, atrocious, loathsome, monstrous, obnoxious, offensive, repellent, repugnant, revolting, sickening **10** abominable, deplorable, despicable, detestable, disdainful, disgusting, forbidding, full of hate, irritating, unbearable, unpleasant, villainous **11** distasteful, intolerable, unendurable **12** contemptible, contemptuous, insufferable **13** objectionable

Hathaway, Anne
husband: **11** Shakespeare

Hathor
origin: **8** Egyptian
goddess of: **3** joy **4** love
symbol: **4** ears, head **5** horns
patron of: **5** dance, music
personifies: **3** sky

Hat on the Bed, The
author: **9** John O'Hara

hatred 4 hate **5** venom **6** animus, enmity, malice, rancor **7** disgust, dislike, ill will **8** acrimony, aversion, bad blood, distaste, loathing **9** animosity, antipathy, hostility, revulsion **10** abhorrence, antagonism, bitterness, repugnance, resentment **11** abomination, detestation, malevolence **14** revengefulness, vindictiveness

haughtiness 4 airs **5** pride **7** conceit, hauteur **8** snobbery **9** arrogance **10** snootiness **13** condescension **14** disdainfulness, high-handedness **16** superciliousness

haughty 5 aloof **6** lordly, snooty, uppish, uppity **7** high- hat, stuck-up **8** arrogant, scornful, snobbish **9** conceited, officious **10** disdainful, high-handed, hoity-toity **11** highfalutin, overbearing, overly proud, patronizing, swell-headed **12** contemptuous **13** condescending, high and mighty

haul 3 bag, lug, tow, tug **4** cart, drag, draw, gain, jerk, move, pull, swag, take, tote, yank **5** booty, bring, carry, catch, fetch, heave, truck, yield **6** convey, profit, remove, spoils, wrench **7** capture, takings **9** transport

haunches 4 buns, rear, rump, seat **5** nates **7** rear end **8** buttocks **9** fundament, posterior **12** hindquarters

haunt 3 vex **5** beset, worry **6** live in, obsess, plague, prey on **7** disturb, terrify, torment, trouble, weigh on **8** distress, frequent, frighten **9** hang out at, preoccupy, terrorize **10** hang around, hover about, loiter near, visit often **11** beat a path to **12** linger around

haunts 3 den **4** cave, hole, lair, nest **6** burrow **7** hangout **8** hideaway **9** waterhole **10** rendezvous **12** meeting place **14** gathering place **15** stamping grounds

Hauptmann, Gerhart
  author of: **10** Before Dawn, The Weavers

haute couture 11 high fashion

haute cuisine 11 fine cooking **14** gourmet cooking

hauteur 5 swank **7** conceit, disdain **8** snobbery **9** arrogance, loftiness **10** snootiness **11** haughtiness **12** affectedness, snobbishness **13** condescension **14** disdainfulness, highhandedness **16** superciliousness **19** patronizing attitude

haut monde 5 elite **10** blue bloods, upper class, upper crust **11** aristocracy, high society **14** creme de la creme

Havana
  capital of: **4** Cuba
  gulf: **6** Mexico
  landmark: **15** Cabaret Parisien **16** Castillo del Morro **17** Castillode la Punta, Jose Marti Monument **18** Castillo de la Atares, Castillo de la Fuerza, Garcia Lorca Theater **19** Maximo Gomez Monument **21** Latinamericano Stadium **22** Academy of Science of Cuba
  river: **10** (Rio) Almendares
  Spanish: **8** La Habana

Havasupai, Supai
  location: **7** Arizona **11** Grand Canyon
  related to: **7** Yavapai **8** Hualapai

have 3 buy, eat, get, own, use **4** bear, fool, gain, gull, hold, host, keep, make, must **5** beget, carry, cheat, drink, enjoy, force, grasp, ought, smoke, trick **6** accept, affirm, compel, harbor, obtain, outwit, permit, retain, suffer **7** achieve, acquire, defraud, exhibit, possess, realize, receive, swindle **8** comprise, maintain, manifest, outsmart, perceive, tolerate **9** encompass, encounter, partake of, recognize, victimize **10** comprehend, experience, understand

have a go at 3 try **6** hazard, tackle **7** attempt **8** give a try **9** undertake **10** give a whirl **12** take a crack at, take a whack at

have a good opinion of 5 favor **6** admire, revere **7** approve, respect **9** believe in **10** appreciate

have a hand in 7 advance, forward **9** influence **10** take part in **12** contribute to **13** be conducive to, participate in **14** help bring about

have an eye on 4 want **5** covet,

crave, fancy **6** desire **7** long for, pine for **8** aspire to, yearn for **9** lust after **11** have a yen for

have a yen for 4 want **5** covet, crave **6** desire **7** long for, wish for **8** yearn for **9** lust after **11** hanker after **13** have a fancy for

have bearing on 5 apply, refer **6** relate **7** concern, pertain **9** appertain, touch upon **13** be pertinent to, have respect to

have done with 4 drop, junk, shed **7** abandon, discard **9** dispose of **10** relinquish **12** dispense with

have faith in 5 trust **6** rely on **9** believe in **16** have confidence in

have guests 8 play host **9** entertain **10** give a party **13** keep open house **16** offer hospitality

Have Gun Will Travel
  character: **6** Hey Boy **7** Hey Girl, Paladin
  cast: **6** Lisa Lu **7** Kam Tong **12** Richard Boone
  setting: **12** San Francisco **13** Hotel Carleton

have in mind 4 mean, want, wish **6** desire, intend **10** think about

haven 4 port **5** cover **6** asylum, harbor, refuge **7** hideout, retreat, shelter **8** hideaway **9** sanctuary

have no hope 6 give up **7** despair **11** be desperate

have plenty 6 abound, be rich **8** flourish, overflow **10** be numerous, have enough **11** be plentiful **14** be well supplied **18** have more than enough

have the body
  Latin: **12** habeas corpus
  legal writ guards against: **19** illegal imprisonment

have too few 4 lack, want **7** be scant **9** fall short **13** be deficient in, have a dearth of **14** have a paucity of **15** be in short supply, have a scarcity of, not have enough of

having life 5 alive, vital **6** living, viable **7** animate

having the means 3 fit **4** able **6** fitted **7** capable, equal to **8** adequate **9** qualified **12** being solvent **20** having the wherewithal

Havisham, Miss
  character in: **17** Great Expectations
  author: **7** Dickens

havoc 4 ruin **5** chaos **8** calamity, disaster, disorder, upheaval **9** cataclysm, ruination **11** catastrophe, destruction, devastation **12** wrack and ruin **16** widespread damage

Havoc, June, **7** actress
  sister: **12** Gypsy Rose Lee
  dramatized as: **5** Gypsy
  billed as: **8** Baby June

Hawaii

abbreviation: 2 HI
nickname: 5 Aloha **15** Sandwich Islands **20** Paradise of the Pacific
capital/largest city: 8 Honolulu
others: 3 Ewa **4** Aiea, Hana, Hilo, Laie, Paia **5** Kapaa, Kapaa, Lihue, Maili **6** Kailua, Kekaha **7** Kahului, Kaneohe, Lanikae, Wahiawa, Waianae, Wailuku
college: 9 Chaminade, Hawaii Loa **12** Brigham Young **13** Hawaii Pacific
dance: 4 hula
explorer: 4 Cook **7** Gaetano
feature:
  district: **7** Lahaina
  national park: **9** Haleakala **15** Hawaii Volcanoes
festivity: 4 luau
food: 3 poi **4** taro
foreigner: 5 haole
gift: 3 lei
greeting: 5 aloha
goddess: 4 Pele
king: 10 Kamehameha
medicine man: 6 Kahuna
musical instrument: 3 uke **7** ukulele, ukelele
native woman: 6 wahine
people: 5 Don Ho **9** Hiram Fong **10** Polynesian **11** Sanford Dole, Bette Midler **12** Daniel Inouye, Father Damien
porch: 5 lanai
queen: 12 Liliuokalani
island name: 4 Kure **9** Kahoolawe
  big isle: **6** Hawaii
  friendly isle: **7** Molokai
  garden isle: **5** Kauai
  gathering place: **4** Oahu
  house of the sun: **9** Haleakala
  mystery isle: **6** Niihau
  pineapple isle: **5** Lanai
  valley isle: **4** Maui
lake: 5 Waiau
land rank: 12 forty-seventh
mountain: 3 Kea, Loa **5** Kaala **6** Kohala, Kohala, Koolau **7** Kamakou, Waianae **8** Maunaloa **9** Lanaihale
  highest point: **8** Maunakea
physical feature:
  bay: **5** Pohue **6** Halawa, Kiholo, Mamala **7** Kamohio, Kaneohe, Waiagua **8** Kawaihae, Maunalua
  beach: **7** Waikiki
  canyon: **6** Waimea
  channel: **3** Aua **5** Kaiwi **6** Kalohi **7** Pailolo
  crater: **7** Kilauea **9** Punchbowl
  desert: **3** Kau
  harbor: **5** Pearl
  promontory: **11** Diamond Head
  valley: **3** Iao **5** Manoa
  volcano: **7** Kilauea **8** Maunakea, Maunaloa **9** Haleakala
state admission: 8 Fiftieth
state bird: 4 nene **13** Hawaiian goose
state flower: 5 lehua **11** red hibiscus **15** scarlet hibiscus

state motto: 44 The Life of the Land is Perpetuated in Righteousness

state song: 11 Hawaii Ponoi **12** Our Own Hawaii

state tree: 5 kukui **9** candlenut

Hawaii
author: 13 James Michener

Hawaiian swimmer 14 Duke Kahanamoku

Hawaii Five-O
character: 4 Kono **5** Wo Fat **8** Ben Kokua **11** Chin Ho Kelly **13** Danny Williams **14** Steve McGarrett
cast: 4 Zulu **7** Kam Fong **8** Jack Lord **11** Khigh Dhiegh **12** Al Harrington **14** James MacArthur

hawk 4 bird, sell, vend **6** falcon, peddle **8** militant **9** accipiter, warmonger
young: 4 eyas
group of: 4 cast

Hawk, Sir Mulberry
character in: 16 Nicholas Nickleby
author: 7 Dickens

Hawkes, John
author of: 10 Second Skin **11** The Cannibal, The Lime Twig **12** The Beetle Leg **15** The Blood Oranges

Hawkeye 11 Natty Bumppo
author: 6 Cooper

Hawkeye Pierce 4 Mash **8** Alan Alda

Hawkeye State
nickname of: 4 Iowa

Hawkins, Jim
character in: 14 Treasure Island
author: 9 Stevenson

Hawkline Monster, The
author: 16 Richard Brautigan

Hawks, Howard
director of: 8 Red River, Rio Bravo, Scarface **11** The Big Sleep **12** Sergeant York **13** His Girl Friday **14** Bringing Up Baby **16** To Have and Have Not, Twentieth Century

Hawn, Goldie
husband: 12 Gus Trinkonis
born: 12 Washington DC
roles: 7 Laugh-In, Shampoo **8** Foul Play **12** Cactus Flower **15** Private Benjamin **18** Butterflies Are Free

hawser 4 line, rope **5** cable **7** mooring

hawthorn 9 Crataegus
varieties: 5 water, yeddo **6** Indian **7** English

Hawthorne, Nathaniel
author of: 13 The Marble Faun **14** Twice-told Tales **16** The Scarlet Letter **20** Mosses from an Old Manse **24** The House of the Seven Gables

Haydee
character in: 21 The Count of Monte Cristo
author: 5 Dumas (pere)

Haydn, Franz Joseph
born: 6 Rohrau **7** Austria
called: 9 Papa Haydn
composer of: 7 The Bird, The Joke

10 Gypsy Rondo, The Seasons **11** The Creation **12** Emperor's Hymn, Wild Band Mass **13** The Apothecary **14** Lord Nelson Mass, Theresienmesse **15** Mass in Time of War **16** Il Mondo della Luna, Mariazellermesse **17** The World of the Moon **38** The Seven Last Words of Our Savior on the Cross
quartet: 3 Sun **4** Bird, Frog, Lark, Tost **5** Dream, Razor, Witch **6** Fifths, Maiden **7** Emperor, Erdoedy, Russian, Sunrise, The Bell, The Hunt **8** Farmyard, Horseman, The Jokes **9** The Donkey **14** The House on Fire, The Row in Vienna
symphony: 4 Fire **5** Paris **6** Le Midi, Le Soir, Loudon, Merkur, Oxford, The Hen **7** Evening, Le Matin, Mercury, Morning, Salomon, The Bear, The Hunt **8** Abschied, Alleluia, Drum Roll, Farewell, Military, Mourning, Surprise, The Clock, The Queen, The Storm **9** Children's, Christmas **10** La Passione, La Tempesta, The Miracle, The Passion **11** The Imperial **12** Der Philosoph, Maria Theresa, The Afternoon **13** Auf dem Anstand **14** The Philosopher **15** The Schoolmaster, Trauersymphonie, With the Horn Call **17** At the Hunting Place **18** Mit dem Hornersignal

Hayes, Elvin
nickname: 4 Big E
sport: 10 basketball
team: 8 San Diego **14** Houston Rockets

Hayes, Helen
real name: 15 Helen Hayes Brown
nickname: 29 First Lady of the American Theater
son: 14 James MacArthur
roles: 7 Airport **9** Anastasia **22** The Sin of Madelon Claudet (Oscar)

Hayes, Rutherford B (Birchard)
nickname: 8 Rud Hayes
presidential rank: 10 nineteenth
party: 10 Republican
state represented: 2 OH
defeated: 5 (Green Clay) Smith **6** (James B) Walker, (Peter) Cooper, (Samuel Jones) Tilden
vice president: 7 (William Almon) Wheeler
cabinet:
state: 6 (William Maxwell) Evarts
treasury: 7 (John) Sherman
war: 6 (Alexander) Ramsey **7** (George Washington) McCrary
attorney general: 6 (Charles) Devens
navy: 4 (Nathan) Goff (Jr) **8** (Richard Wigginton) Thompson
postmaster general: 3 (David McKendree) Key **7** (Horace) Maynard
interior: 6 (Carl) Schurz

born: 10 Delaware OH
died/buried: 9 Fremont OH
education:
preparatory school: 4 Webb
College: 6 Kenyon
Law School: 7 Harvard
religion: 9 Methodist
political career: 24 US House of Representatives
city solicitor of: 10 Cincinnati
governor of: 4 Ohio
civilian career: 6 farmer, lawyer
military service: 6 US Army **8** Civil War **12** Ohio infantry **18** brevet major general
notable events of lifetime/term: 10 Depression (of 1873) **15** railroad strikes (of 1877) **18** civil service reform **24** specie payments resumption **Act: 26** Bland-Allison Silver Purchase
father: 10 Rutherford
mother: 6 Sophia (Birchard)
siblings: 7 Lorenzo **11** Sarah Sophia **13** Fanny Arabella
wife: 4 Lucy (Ware Webb)
children: 5 Fanny **9** James Webb (renamed Webb Cook) **11** George Crook **12** Manning Force, Scott Russell **14** Joseph Thompson, Sardis Birchard (renamed Birchard Austin) **15** Rutherford Platt

hayseed 4 hick, rube **5** yokel **6** rustic **7** bumpkin, peasant **10** clodhopper

Hayward, Susan
real name: 14 Edythe Marrener
husband: 10 Jess Barker
born: 10 Brooklyn NY
roles: 11 I Want to Live (Oscar) **14** I'll Cry Tomorrow, My Foolish Heart **18** With a Song in My Heart **23** Smash Up The Story of a Woman

Hayworth, Rita
real name: 22 Margarita Carmen Cansino
husband: 7 Aly Khan **10** Dick Haymes **11** Orson Welles
born: 10 Brooklyn NY
roles: 5 Gilda **9** Cover Girl **14** Separate Tables **17** Miss Sadie Thompson, You'll Never Get Rich

hazan 18 cantor of a synagogue

hazard 3 bet **4** dare, luck, risk **5** fluke, guess, offer, peril, stake, wager **6** chance, danger, expose, gamble, menace, mishap, submit, threat **7** advance, daresay, imperil, pitfall, presume, proffer, suppose, venture **8** accident, chance it, endanger, jeopardy, theorize, threaten, throw out **9** mischance, speculate, tempt fate, volunteer **10** conjecture, jeopardize, misfortune **11** coincidence, hypothesize, imperilment, take a chance, trust to luck **12** endangerment, happenstance, stroke of luck

Hazard of New Fortunes, A
author: 18 William Dean Howells

hazardous 4 iffy **5** risky, shaky **6** chancy, unsafe, unsure **7** dubious, unsound **8** doubtful, insecure, perilous, unstable **9** dangerous, uncertain **10** precarious, unreliable **11** speculative, threatening **13** untrustworthy

haze 3 fog **4** daze, film, mist, pall, veil **5** cloak, cloud, smoke, vapor **6** mantle, muddle, screen **9** fogginess **12** befuddlement, bewilderment **16** state of confusion

hazel 3 nut **4** tree **5** brown, shrub, tawny **8** brownish **14** yellowish-brown

varieties: **4** tree **5** Chile, witch **6** winter **7** Chinese, Turkish **8** American, European, Japanese **11** spike winter **12** Chinese witch **13** Japanese witch **15** buttercup winter

Hazel

character: **12** George Baxter, Harold Baxter **13** Dorothy Baxter
cast: **9** Don DeFore **12** Shirley Booth, Whitney Blake **13** Bobby Buntrock
creator: **6** Ted Key

hazelnut 7 Corylus

varieties: **6** beaked **7** Chinese, Turkish **8** American, European, Japanese

Hazlitt, William

author of: **6** essays **17** The Spirit of the Age **32** The Characters of Shakespeare's Plays

hazy 3 dim **5** dusky, faint, filmy, foggy, misty, murky, smoky, vague **6** bleary, blurry, cloudy, smoggy, veiled **7** bleared, general, muddled, obscure, unclear **8** confused, nebulous, overcast **9** ambiguous, uncertain **10** ill-defined, indefinite

head 2 go, IQ **3** aim, CEO, end, hie, tip, top **4** acme, apex, bent, boss, czar, duce, font, fore, gift, jefe, king, lead, main, mind, peak, rise, rule, tsar, turn, well **5** begin, brain, chief, crest, crown, drive, first, front, guide, pilot, prime, queen, ruler, start, steer **6** climax, crisis, direct, genius, govern, honcho, launch, leader, manage, origin, ruling, source, spring, summit, talent, vertex, zenith **7** ability, admiral, captain, command, conduct, control, foreman, general, go first, highest, leading, make for, manager, marshal, monarch, precede, premier, primary, proceed, ranking, supreme, topmost **8** aptitude, be head of, big wheel, capacity, chairman, dictator, director, dominant, foremost, fountain, fruition, headmost, initiate, judgment, managing, pinnacle, start off, superior, suzerain, upper end **9** acuteness, beginning, commander, commodore, extremity, forefront, front rank, governing, intellect, introduce, mentality, paramount, potentate, president, principal, sovereign, supervise, uppermost **10** administer, be master of,

birthplace, cleverness, commandant, commanding, conclusion, first place, gray matter, inaugurate, lead the way, move toward, perception, preeminent, supervisor, wellspring **11** be at the helm, controlling, culmination, discernment, forward part, highest rank, officiate at, preside over, superintend, take the lead, termination **12** apprehension, field marshal, fountainhead, guiding light, place of honor, take charge of, take the reins, turning point, utmost extent **13** administrator, go at the head of, most prominent, prime minister, understanding **14** chief executive, highest ranking, superintendent **15** be in the vanguard, make a beeline for, quickness of mind **16** commander-in-chief, direct one's course, inevitable result **17** commanding general, have authority over **18** be in the driver's seat, chairman of the board, go in the direction of **21** chief executive officer

head

contains: **4** eyes **5** brain, mouth, skull **9** braincase **10** optic nerve **12** ocular muscle **13** cranial cavity, lacrimal organ, orbital cavity **14** buccaval cavity

headache 5 trial **6** strain, stress **7** problem, trouble **8** migraine, nuisance **10** affliction, difficulty **13** inconvenience, pain in the neck

headdress 3 cap, hat **6** bonnet **7** chapeau **12** headcovering

headgear 3 cap, fez, hat, tam **4** cowl, hood, kepi, topi, veil **5** beret, busby, crown, derby, miter, mitre, opera, shako, shawl, snood, straw, terai, tiari, topee, toque **6** beanie, boater, bonnet, bowler, cloche, fedora, helmet, mobcap, panama, sailor, trilby, turban **7** bicorne, biretta, chapeau, hardhat, homberg, pillbox, porkpie, stetson, **8** babushka, kerchief, mantilla, nightcap, skullcap, snap-brim, sombrero, tarboosh, tricorne, yarmulke **9** stovepipe, sunbonnet, tengallon **10** pith helmet **11** deerstalker, dolly varden

headland 4 bank, crag **5** bluff, cliff **8** palisade **9** precipice **10** promontory

headlong 6 abrupt **8** abruptly, heedless, pell-mell, reckless **9** headfirst, impetuous **10** heedlessly, recklessly **11** impetuously, precipitate, precipitous **13** head over heels, precipitously

headman 5 chief **6** leader **7** foreman **8** alderman, princeps **9** commander **10** councilman, supervisor **14** public official, superintendent

head-on 6 direct **7** frontal **10** face-to-face

headshrinker 6 shrink **7** analyst **12** psychiatrist **13** psychoanalyst

headstrong 4 rash **6** dogged, mulish,

unruly **7** defiant, froward, willful **8** contrary, obdurate, reckless, stubborn **9** hotheaded, imprudent, impulsive, obstinate, pigheaded **10** bullheaded, incautious, refractory **11** intractable **12** incorrigible, recalcitrant, ungovernable, unmanageable **14** uncontrollable **22** bent on having one's own way

heady 4 hard **6** potent, strong **8** alluring, exciting, inviting, stirring, tempting **9** seductive, thrilling **10** high-octane **11** high-voltage, tantalizing **12** exhilarating, intoxicating

heal 4 cure, knit, mend **5** right, salve, treat **6** heal up, remedy, settle, soothe **7** compose, get well, improve, recover, rectify, relieve **8** heal over, make well **9** alleviate, make whole, reconcile **10** conciliate, convalesce, recuperate **11** set to rights **14** make harmonious, return to health **20** restore good relations

healed 4 knit **5** cured **6** mended **7** got well **8** relieved

healing 6 curing **7** mending **8** knitting, soothing **9** emollient, improving, restoring **10** making well **11** restorative **13** strengthening

god of: **6** Apollo **7** Phoebus, Pythius **9** Asclepius, Musagetes **11** Aesculapius

goddess of: **4** Iaso

health 5 vigor **7** fitness, stamina **8** strength, vitality **9** hardihood, hardiness, well-being **10** robustness **16** general condition **17** physical condition

goddess of: **6** Hygeia

healthful 7 healthy **8** hygienic, salutary **9** wholesome **10** beneficial, nourishing, nutritious, salubrious **12** healthgiving, invigorating

healthiness 6 health **9** good shape, soundness **10** good health, robustness **12** salutariness **13** good condition, healthfulness, wholesomeness **14** salubriousness

healthy 3 fit **4** hale **5** hardy, sound **6** hearty, robust, strong, sturdy **8** vigorous **9** in the pink **10** able-bodied **12** in fine fettle **18** sound of mind and limb

heap 3 gob, lot **4** fill, gobs, hunk, load, lots, lump, mass, mess, pack, pile, slew **5** amass, award, batch, bunch, flood, group, mound, ocean, slews, stack, store, world **6** accord, assign, bundle, deluge, engulf, gather, jumble, load up, oceans, oodles, pile up, plenty, worlds **7** barrels, cluster, collect, mete out, present **8** good deal, inundate, pour upon **9** abundance, gathering, great deal, multitude, profusion **10** assemblage, collection, shower upon **11** aggregation, concentrate **12** accumulation **13** agglomeration

heap up 5 amass **6** pile up **7** stack up **10** accumulate

hear 4 heed **5** admit, favor, grant, judge, learn **6** attend, be told, gather, look on **7** approve, concede, examine, find out, receive, witness **8** accede to, appear at, discover, hear tell, hold with, listen to **9** acquiesce, ascertain, hearken to **10** understand **11** acknowledge

hear!
French: **4** oyez
cry used by: **10** court crier
precedes: **5** trial **12** proclamation

hearing 5 probe, sound **6** review **7** council, earshot, inquiry **8** audience **9** interview **10** conference **11** examination, questioning **12** consultation **13** interrogation, investigation

hearken to 4 heed, mark, mind **6** attend **8** listen to **11** take to heart **14** pay attention to

Hearns, Thomas
nickname: **6** Hitman
sport: **6** boxing
class: **12** middleweight, welterweight

hearsay 4 talk **5** rumor **6** gossip, report **8** idle talk **9** grapevine **11** scuttlebutt

heart 3 hub, nub **4** base, core, crux, guts, love, meat, mood, pith, root, soul **5** humor, pluck, spunk, valor **6** center, daring, desire, kernel, middle, nature, source, spirit **7** bravery, charity, courage, emotion, essence, nucleus, stomach **8** audacity, backbone, boldness, clemency, feelings, firmness, fondness, gameness, interior, main part, sympathy **9** affection, fortitude, gallantry, inner part, rudiments, sentiment, tolerance **10** brass tacks, compassion, enthusiasm, essentials, foundation, gentleness, indulgence, manfulness, principles, resolution, tenderness, true nature **11** busiest part, central part, disposition, forgiveness, nitty-gritty, temperament **12** fearlessness, fundamentals, quintessence, resoluteness **13** audaciousness
part: **5** aorta, valve **6** atrium **7** chamber **9** ventricle
pumps: **5** blood

heartache 3 woe **4** pain **5** grief **6** misery, sorrow **7** anguish, sadness, torment, trouble **8** distress **9** suffering **11** tribulation, unhappiness

heartbreaker 4 vamp **5** flirt, tease **8** coquette

Heartbreak House
author: **17** George Bernard Shaw

hearten 4 abet **5** cheer **6** assure, solace **7** animate, cheer up, comfort, console, enliven, gladden **8** brighten, embolden, energize, inspirit, reassure **9** encourage **10** invigorate

heartening 7 hopeful **9** favorable **10** auspicious, reassuring **11** encouraging

heartfelt 4 deep, full **5** total **6** ardent, devout, entire, honest **7** earnest, fervent, genuine, intense, sincere **8** complete, profound, thorough **10** keenly felt **12** all-inclusive, wholehearted

hearth 4 home **5** abode, house **8** fireside **9** fireplace, household **10** family life **12** family circle **13** chimney corner
goddess of: **4** Caca **5** Salus, Vesta **6** Hestia

Heart Is a Lonely Hunter, The
author: **15** Carson McCullers
character: **8** Mr Singer **9** Mick Kelly **10** Dr Copeland, Jake Blount **11** Biff Brannon

heartless 4 cold, mean **5** cruel **6** brutal, savage, unkind **7** callous, inhuman, unmoved **8** pitiless, ruthless, uncaring **9** unfeeling, unpitying, unstirred **10** unmerciful **11** coldhearted, cold-blooded, hardhearted, insensitive **12** cruelhearted, unresponsive **13** unsympathetic

Heart of Darkness
author: **12** Joseph Conrad
character: **5** Kurtz **7** Marlowe

Heart of Dixie
nickname of: **7** Alabama

Heart of Juliet Jones, The
creator: **9** Stan Drake
character: **3** Eve

Heart of Midlothian, The
author: **14** Sir Walter Scott

Heart of the Matter, The
author: **12** Graham Greene
character: **5** Yusef **6** Wilson **7** Mrs Rolt **9** Mrs Scobie **11** Major Scobie

heart-stopper 5 belle **6** beauty **7** charmer, stunner **8** knockout **10** good-looker **13** beautiful girl **14** beautiful woman

hearty 4 hale, warm, well **5** ample, hardy, sound **6** lively, robust, strong **7** cordial, genuine, healthy, profuse, sincere, zestful **8** complete, effusive, generous, thorough, vigorous **9** heartfelt, unbounded **10** unreserved **12** enthusiastic, unrestrained, wholehearted **13** physically fit

hearty appetite
French: **10** bon appetit

Heaslop, Ronald
character in: **15** A Passage to India
author: **7** Forster

heat 3 fry **4** bake, boil, cook, sear, stew, warm, zeal **5** ardor, broil, roast, steam **6** braise, climax, fervor, height, simmer, stress, thrill, warmth, warm up **7** hotness, make hot, passion, rapture, swelter **8** fervency, hot spell, warmness **9** eagerness, intensity, transport **10** enthusiasm, excitement **12** bring to a boil

heated 3 hot **5** angry, fiery, irate **6** bitter, fierce, raging, stormy **7** excited, fervent, furious, intense, violent **8** frenzied, inflamed, vehement **9** emotional **10** infuriated, passionate **11** impassioned, tempestuous

heated discussion 7 dispute **8** argument **10** war of words **11** controversy **12** disagreement

heath 5 Erica
varieties: **4** Tree **5** Berry, Besom, Irish, Otago, Spike **6** Dorset, Scotch, Spring **7** Cornish, Fringed, Spanish, Twisted **9** Cranberry **11** Cross-leaved

Heathcliff
character in: **16** Wuthering Heights
loved: Cathy
author: **6** Bronte

heathen 3 goy **4** boor **5** pagan **6** savage **7** atheist, gentile, infidel **8** agnostic, idolator **9** barbarian, ignoramus **10** polytheist, troglodyte, unbeliever **11** non-believer **17** uncivilized native

heather 7 Calluna
varieties: **3** Bog, Red **4** Bell, Snow **5** Beach, False, White **6** French, Golden, Scotch **8** Corsican, Mountain **9** Christmas **11** White winter **13** Mediterranean **18** Everblooming French

heat up 3 fan, zap **4** goad, nuke, warm, whet **6** arouse **7** enhance, sharpen **8** increase **9** aggravate, intensify **10** strengthen

heave 3 peg, pry, sob **4** arch, blow, cast, emit, fire, hurl, lift, moan, pant, puff, puke, toss **5** boost, bulge, chuck, eject, fling, groan, hoist, lever, pitch, raise, retch, sling, surge, swell, throw, vomit **6** dilate, drag up, draw up, exhale, expand, haul up, launch, let fly, propel, pull up, tilt up, yank up **7** elevate **8** thrust up **9** discharge, palpitate **11** regurgitate

heaven, Heaven, the Heavens 3 wow **4** Zion **5** bliss, glory, mercy, space **6** my oh my, utopia **7** delight, ecstasy, Elysium, my stars, nirvana, Olympus, rapture **8** boy oh boy, goodness, land sake, paradise, Valhalla **9** afterlife, dreamland, next world, Shangri-la **10** afterworld, Beulah Land, life beyond, outer space, perfection, sheer bliss **11** enchantment, the Holy City, world beyond, world to come **12** eternal bliss, good gracious, New Jerusalem, the City of God, the firmament **13** Abraham's bosom, Elysian fields, seventh heaven **14** heavens to Betsy, our eternal home **15** life everlasting, our Father's house, the heavenly city **16** goodness gracious, Isle of the Blessed, supreme happiness, the abode of saints, the Celestial City, the vault of heaven **17** complete happiness, the wild blue yonder **18** Island of the Blessed, the celestial sphere, the heavenly kingdom, the kingdom of Heaven **19** the celestial expanse **21** the happy hunting ground god of: **2** An **3** Anu **4** Jove, Zeus **7** Jupiter

Heaven Can Wait (1943)
director: **13** Ernst Lubitsch
cast: **9** Don Ameche **11** Gene Tierney **12** Marjorie Main **13** Charles Coburn

Heaven Can Wait (1978)
director: **9** Buck Henry **12** Warren Beatty
cast: **10** Dyan Cannon, Jack Warden **12** Warren Beatty **13** Julie Christie
remake of: **17** Here Comes Mr Jordan

heavenly 6 divine **7** angelic, blessed, saintly, sublime **8** beatific, blissful

Heavens and Earth
author: **19** Stephen Vincent Benet

Heaven's My Destination
author: **14** Thornton Wilder

heavy 3 big, fat, sad **4** deep, dull, full, hard, lazy, slow **5** broad, bulky, dense, grave, gross, harsh, hefty, large, obese, plump, rough, stout, thick **6** clumsy, coarse, deadly, dreary, fierce, gloomy, leaden, pained, portly, raging, rugged, savage, solemn, strong, sturdy, torpid, woeful **7** awesome, complex, copious, doleful, forlorn, furious, intense, joyless, languid, lumpish, massive, notable, onerous, profuse, roaring, ruinous, serious, tearful, tedious, violent, weighty **8** abundant, agonized, burdened, crushing, cumbrous, damaging, dejected, desolate, downcast, forceful, grieving, grievous, imposing, lifeless, listless, mournful, pedantic, profound, seething, sluggish, stricken, tiresome, unwieldy **9** apathetic, cheerless, corpulent, depressed, difficult, excessive, extensive, harrowing, important, injurious, laborious, lethargic, lumbering, miserable, momentous, ponderous, rampaging, sorrow- ful, turbulent, wearisome **10** burden- some, calamitous, cumbersome, dis- tressed, full of care, immoderate, impressive, inordinate, melancholy, monotonous, noteworthy, oppressive, overweight, pernicious, phlegmatic, unbearable, unstinting **11** crestfallen, deleterious, destructive, detrimental, distressing, extravagant, intemperate, intolerable, significant, tempestuous, unendurable, unrelenting, unremitting **12** considerable, disconsolate, hard to endure, overwhelming, unrestrained **13** consequential, grief- stricken, of great import **16** laden with sorrows **18** of great consequence

heavy-handed 5 harsh **6** clumsy **7** awkward **8** bungling **9** graceless, maladroit **10** blundering, oppressive, ungraceful

heavyhearted 3 sad **4** glum **6** dismal, gloomy, morose **7** doleful, forlorn, joyless, unhappy **8** dejected, downcast **9** cheerless, depressed, sorrowful **10**

despondent, melancholy **11** downhearted **14** down in the dumps, down in the mouth

Hebe
goddess of: **5** youth **6** spring
father: **4** Zeus
mother: **4** Hera
brother: **4** Ares
husband: **8** Hercules
handmaiden to: **4** gods
corresponds to: **8** Juventas

Hebrew alphabet
or: **5** aleph
b/v: **4** beth
g: **5** gimel
d: **6** daleth
h: **2** he **5** cheth
v/w: **3** vav
z: **5** zayin
y/j/i: **3** yod
k/kh: **4** kaph
l: **5** lamed
m: **3** men
n: **3** nun
`: **4** ayin
p/f: **2** pe
k: **4** koph
r: **4** resh
sh/s: **4** shin
s: **3** sin **4** sadi **6** samekh
t: **3** tav **4** teth

Hebrew Judge 4 Ehud, Elon, Jair, Tola **5** Abdon, Ibzan **6** Gideon, Samson, Samuel **7** Deborah, Othniel, Shamgar **8** Jephthah

Hebrew months
first: **4** Ahib, Nisn **6** Ehanim, Tishri
second: **3** Bul, Civ **4** Iyar **7** Heshvan
third: **5** Sivan **6** Kislev
fourth: **5** Tebet **6** Tammuz, Tebeth
fifth: **2** Ab **7** Shelbat
sixth: **4** Adar, Elul **6** Veadar
seventh: **4** Abib **5** Nisan **6** Tishri **7** Ethanim
eighth: **3** Zif **4** Iyer **11** Marcheshvan
ninth: **5** Sivan **7** Chislev
tenth: **6** Tabeth, Tammuz
eleventh: **2** Ab **6** Shebat
twelfth: **4** Adar, Elul

he carved it
Latin: **8** sculpsit

Hecate
also: **6** Hekate
goddess of: **5** earth, Hades
associated with: **6** hounds **7** sorcery **10** crossroads
corresponds to: **5** Brimo

heckle 3 boo **4** bait, hiss, hoot, mock, razz, ride, twit **5** annoy, bully, chivy, harry, hound, taunt **6** badger, harass, harrow, hector, jeer at, molest, needle **7** provoke **9** shout down

Heckle and Jeckle 7 magpies **8** cartoons

hectare
abbreviation of: **2** ha

hectic 3 mad **4** wild **6** stormy **7** cha-

otic, frantic, furious **8** feverish, frenetic, frenzied, headlong **9** breakneck, turbulent **10** tumultuous

hectoliter
abbreviation of: **2** hl

hectometer
abbreviation of: **2** hm

hector 4 bait, ride **5** bully, harry, hound, tease, worry **6** badger, harass, needle, plague **7** torment, swagger **8** browbeat

Hector
father: **5** Priam
mother: **6** Hecuba
brother: **5** Paris
sister: **9** Cassandra
wife: **10** Andromache
son: **8** Astyanax
hero of: **9** Trojan War
killed by: **8** Achilles

Hecuba
also: **5** Maera **6** Hecabe
father: **5** Atlas
husband: **5** Priam **8** Tegeates
son: **5** Paris **6** Hector **7** Helenus, Polites, Troilus **9** Deiphobus, Polydorus
daughter: **6** Creusa **7** Laodice **8** Polyxena **9** Cassandra
changed into: **3** dog **5** bitch
hound of: **7** Icarius

Hecuba
author: **9** Euripides
character: **8** Odysseus, Polyxena **9** Agamemnon, Polydorus **10** Polymestor

Hedda Gabler
author: **11** Henrik Ibsen
character: **10** Judge Brack **11** Hedda Tesman, Thea Elvsted **12** George Tesman **13** Eilert Lovberg **17** Miss Juliana Tesman

heder 12 Jewish school

hedge 3 hem **4** duck, edge, ring, wall **5** bound, dodge, evade, fence, guard, hem in, limit **6** border, margin, shut in, waffle **7** barrier, enclose, mark off, outline **8** encircle, hedgerow, surround **9** be evasive, delineate, demarcate, insurance, pussyfoot, temporize **10** equivocate, protection **11** delineation, row of bushes **12** compensation **13** circumference, fence of shrubs **14** beg the question, counterbalance **17** beat around the bush

he died
Latin: **5** obiit

he does not pursue
Latin: **14** non prosequitur

hedonist 8 Sybarite **9** debauchee, libertine **10** dissipater, profligate, sensualist, voluptuary **14** pleasure seeker

hedonistic 7 sensual **9** epicurean, libertine, sybaritic **10** voluptuous **11** intemperate **13** self-indulgent **15** pleasure-seeking

he drew this
Latin: **10** delineavit

heed 4 care, mind, obey 5 bow to, pains, study 6 concur, follow, hold to, notice, regard 7 defer to, observe, perusal, respect, yield to 8 accede to, consider, listen to, prudence, scrutiny, submit to 9 attention, be ruled by, give ear to 10 bear in mind comply with, precaution, take note of 11 carefulness, examination, heedfulness, mindfulness, observation, take to heart 12 take notice of 13 attentiveness 14 fastidiousness, meticulousness, pay attention to, scrupulousness 17 conscientiousness

heedful 4 wary 5 alert, aware, cagey, chary 7 alive to, careful, mindful, prudent 8 cautious, discreet, vigilant, watchful 9 attentive, concerned, conscious

heedless 3 lax 4 rash 5 slack 6 remiss, unwary 7 foolish, unaware, witless 8 careless, mindless, reckless, uncaring 9 foolhardy, frivolous, impetuous, imprudent, negligent, oblivious, unheeding, unmindful 10 incautious, neglectful, unthinking, unwatchful 11 harebrained, improvident, inattentive, thoughtless, unconcerned, unobservant, unobserving 12 happy-go-lucky 14 scatterbrained

heedlessly 5 blind 6 rashly 8 headlong 9 foolishly, witlessly 10 carelessly, mindlessly, recklessly 11 frivolously, impetuously, impulsively, negligently, unmindfully 12 neglectfully, unthinkingly 13 inattentively, thoughtlessly, unconcernedly 15 inconsiderately, uncooperatively

heedlessness 8 rashness 9 unconcern 10 negligence 11 inattention, unawareness 12 carelessness, indiscretion, mindlessness, recklessness 13 unmindfulness 15 thoughtlessness 16 irresponsibility

heel 3 cad, cur, end, rat 4 list, rind, tilt 5 churl, crust, louse 6 rotter 7 bounder, caitiff, dastard

he engraved it
　　Latin: 8 sculpsit

Heep, Uriah
　　character in: 16 David Copperfield
　　author: 7 Dickens

he flourished
　　Latin: 7 floruit

hefty 3 big 5 beefy, bulky, burly, heavy, husky, large, stout 6 brawny, hearty, mighty, robust, rugged, strong, sturdy 7 hulking, massive, sizable, weighty, well-fed 8 muscular, powerful, stalwart, thickset 9 corpulent, strapping 11 substantial

hegemony 7 control 9 authority, dominance, influence, supremacy

Heggen, Thomas
　　author of: 9 Mr Roberts

hegira 6 exodus, flight 7 journey

he himself said it
　　Latin: 9 ipse dixit

Heidi 4 girl
　　location: 9 Swiss Alps
　　author 12 Johanna Spyri
　　friend: 5 Peter

Heifetz, Jascha
　　born: 6 Russia
　　instrument: 6 violin

height 4 acme, apex, hill, peak, rise 5 bluff, cliff, crest, knoll, limit, mound, tower 6 apogee, heyday, summit, zenith 7 hilltop, maximum, plateau 8 altitude, eminence, highland, highness, mountain, palisade, pinnacle, tallness, ultimate 9 elevation, extremity, flowering, high point, loftiness, supremacy 10 perfection, promontory 11 culmination 12 consummation, upward extent, utmost degree, vantage point

heighten 5 raise 7 elevate 8 increase 9 aggravate, intensify

heil 4 hail

Heimberger, Eddie Albert
　　real name of: 11 Eddie Albert

Heine, Heinrich
　　author of: 9 Atta Troll 11 Book of Songs 19 Germany A Winter's Tale

Heinlein, Robert
　　author of: 10 Double Star 16 Starship Troopers 20 The Green Hills of Earth 22 Stranger in a Strange Land 23 The Moon Is a Harsh Mistress

heinous 4 evil, foul, vile 5 gross, nasty 6 grisly, horrid, odious, sinful, wicked 7 beastly, ghastly, hideous, inhuman, vicious 8 infamous, shocking, terrible 9 abhorrent, atrocious, loathsome, monstrous, nefarious, offensive, repugnant, repulsive, revolting, sickening 10 abominable, deplorable, despicable, detestable, disgusting, iniquitous, outrageous, scandalous, villainous 11 disgraceful, distasteful 12 contemptible 13 objectionable, reprehensible

heinousness 4 evil 7 outrage 8 atrocity, baseness, enormity, foulness, savagery, vileness, villainy 9 barbarity, depravity, malignity 10 inhumanity 13 loathsomeness, monstrousness 14 outrageousness

heir, heiress 7 legatee 9 inheritor 10 inheritrix 11 beneficiary, inheritress 12 heir apparent 15 heir presumptive

Heiress, The
　　director: 12 William Wyler
　　based on novel by: 10 Henry James
　　　film title: 16 Washington Square
　　cast: 13 Miriam Hopkins 15 Montgomery Clift, Ralph Richardson 17 Olivia de Havilland
　　score: 12 Aaron Copland
　　Oscar for: 7 actress (de Havilland)

Hekate see 6 Hecate

Hel
　　origin: 12 Scandinavian

　　goddess of: 5 death
　　rules: 8 Niflheim 10 underworld
　　father: 4 Loki
　　mother: 9 Angerboda, Angrbodha, Angurboda
　　brother: 6 Fenrir, Fenris 11 Iormungandr, Jormungandr 14 Midgard Serpent
　　color of body: 4 blue 5 flesh
　　home of: 4 dead

Helen
　　father: 4 Zeus
　　mother: 4 Leda
　　brother: 6 Castor, Pollux
　　sister: 8 Timandra 12 Clytemnestra
　　husband: 8 Menelaus
　　abducted by: 5 Paris
　　carried off to: 4 Troy
　　abduction caused: 9 Trojan War
　　quote: 33 the face that launched a thousand ships

Helena
　　character in: 20 All's Well That Ends Well 21 A Midsummer Night's Dream
　　author: 11 Shakespeare

helicopter
　　invented by: 8 Sikorsky
　　also: 8 autogyro 9 eggbeater

Helios
　　origin: 5 Greek
　　god of: 3 sun
　　father: 8 Hyperion
　　mother: 4 Thia
　　children: 5 Circe 6 Aeetes 8 Phaethon
　　corresponds to: 3 Sol

heliotrope 12 Heliotropium
　　varieties: 6 garden, winter, yellow 7 seaside

helium
　　chemical symbol: 2 He

hell, Hell 5 agony, grief, Hades 6 misery, the pit 7 Abaddon, anguish, despair, Gehenna, inferno, remorse, torment 8 Appolyons, hell fire, the abyss 9 martyrdom, perdition, suffering 10 lake of fire 12 hopelessness, wretchedness 13 bottomless pit, Satan's kingdom, the lower world, the underworld 14 place of the lost, the Devil's house, the nether world, the shades below 15 everlasting fire, home of lost souls, infernal regions 16 abode of the damned

Hellen
　　king of: 8 Thessaly
　　father: 9 Deucalion
　　mother: 6 Pyrrha
　　wife: 6 Orseis
　　son: 5 Dorus 6 Aeolus, Xuthus
　　ancestor of: 8 Hellenes

Hellenic Republic see 6 Greece

Heller, Joseph
　　author of: 7 Catch-22 10 Good as Gold 17 Something Happened

hellion 5 devil, rogue, scamp 9 scoundrel 13 mischief-maker

hellish 4 foul, vile **5** awful **6** brutal **7** hateful **8** accursed, damnable, dreadful, horrible, infernal **9** atrocious, revolting **10** abominable, disgusting

Hellman, Lillian
author of: 5 Maybe **10** Pentimento **13** Scoundrel Time **14** The Little Foxes, Toys in the Attic **15** Watch on the Rhine **16** The Children's Hour **17** An Unfinished Woman **22** Another Part of the Forest

hello
French: 7 bonjour
German: 8 guten tag
Spanish: 10 buenos dias
Hebrew 6 shalom
Italian: 4 ciao **10** buon giorno
Latin: 3 ave

Hello-Central
character in: 36 A Connecticut Yankee in King Arthur's Court
author: 5 Twain

help 3 aid **4** back, balm, calm, care, crew, cure, ease, gift, lift, save **5** allay, emend, force, guide, hands, salve, serve, staff **6** advice, advise, assist, give to, menial, relief, remedy, rescue, soothe, succor, uphold **7** advance, backing, console, correct, endorse, further, helpers, improve, nurture, promote, rectify, relieve, servant, service, stand by, support, welfare, workers, workmen **8** advocate, befriend, champion, domestic, factotum, farmhand, guidance, laborers, maintain, mitigate, retainer, retrieve, side with **9** alleviate, chip in for, employees, encourage, extricate, lend a hand, make whole, promotion, put at ease, underling, workhands, work force **10** ameliorate, apprentice, assistance, assistants, bring round, corrective, friendship, go to bat for, hired hands, kind regard, minister to, preventive, protection, stick up for **11** advancement, benevolence, cooperation, endorsement, furtherance, good offices, helping hand, make healthy, restorative **12** bring through, contribute to, contribution, hired helpers, intercede for **13** collaboration, cooperate with, encouragement, take the part of

helper 3 aid **4** aide **5** angel **6** backer, deputy, patron, second **7** adjunct, partner, servant **8** adjutant, advocate, champion, confrere, co-worker, employee, retainer **9** assistant, associate, auxiliary, colleague, man Friday, right hand, supporter **10** accomplice, aide-de-camp, apprentice, benefactor, girl Friday **11** confederate, helping hand, subordinate **12** collaborator, right-hand man **13** good samaritan **14** fairy godmother

helpful 4 fine, good, kind, nice **6** usable, useful **8** obliging, splendid, valuable **9** excellent, favorable, practical **10** beneficial, profitable, supportive **11** considerate, cooperative, serviceable **12** advantageous, constructive **13** accommodating

helping hand 3 aid **4** aide, hand **5** boost **6** assist, hand up, helper, succor **7** abettor, support **9** assistant **10** assistance

helplessness 8 weakness **9** impotence, inability, infirmity **10** dependence, feebleness, ineptitude **12** incapability, incompetence, inefficiency **13** powerlessness, vulnerability

Helsinki
capital of: 7 Finland

hem 3 box, rim **4** bind, brim, edge, welt **5** bound, brink, skirt, verge **6** border, edging, fringe, impede, margin, turn up **7** confine, enclose, stammer, stutter, turning **8** compress, encircle, restrain, surround

he made it
Latin: 5 fecit

hem in 4 best **5** fence **7** besiege, confine, enclose **8** encircle, surround

Hemingway, Ernest
author of: 9 In Our Time **14** A Moveable Feast **15** A Farewell to Arms, The Sun Also Rises **16** To Have and Have Not **18** Islands in the Stream, The Old Man and the Sea **19** For Whom the Bell Tolls **21** The Snows of Kilimanjaro **34** The Short Happy Life of Francis Macomber

hemlock 5 Tsuga **15** Conium maculatum
varieties: 5 Dwarf, Water **6** Canada, Ground, Poison **7** Siebold, Spotted, Western **8** Carolina, Japanese, Mountain

hemp 14 Cannabis sativa
varieties: 3 Bog **5** Cuban, Sisal **6** Deccan, Indian, Manila **7** African **8** Deckaner **9** Bowstring, Mauritius **10** New Zealand **13** Colorado River **15** Ceylon bowstring, Indian bowstring **16** African bowstring

hen
young: 6 pullet **7** lobster

Henchard, Michael
character in: 22 The Mayor of Casterbridge
author: 5 Hardy

henchman 4 goon, thug **6** flunky, lackey, minion, stooge, yes-man **7** gorilla **8** hanger-on, hireling, retainer **9** attendant, bodyguard **10** hatchet man, lieutenant **12** right-hand man, strongarm man

Henderson, Marge
creator/artist of: 10 Little Lulu

henna 3 dye **5** rinse **6** auburn, russet **8** cinnamon **11** rust-colored **12** reddish-brown **13** copper-colored

henpecked 4 meek **5** timid **6** docile **8** obedient **10** browbeaten, submissive, wife-ridden **11** unassertive

Henry, Frederic
character in: 15 A Farewell to Arms
author: 9 Hemingway

Henry Esmond
author: 16 William Thackeray
character: 5 Frank **7** Beatrix **9** Lord Mohun **10** Father Holt **11** James Stuart **12** Rachel Esmond **13** Francis Esmond

Henry IV
author: 18 William Shakespeare
character: 7 Hotspur **11** Prince Henry, Thomas Percy **14** Edmund Mortimer, Sir Walter Blunt **15** John of Lancaster, Mistress Quickly, Sir John Falstaff **18** Earl of Westmoreland, King Henry the Fourth

Henry V
author: 18 William Shakespeare
character: 7 Dauphin, Montjoy **15** Charles the Sixth (King of France) **17** Princess Katharine
director: 15 Laurence Olivier
cast: 11 Leslie Banks **12** Robert Newton **13** Renee Asherson **15** Laurence Olivier

Henry VI
author: 18 William Shakespeare
character: 6 Edward (Prince of Wales) **7** Charles (Dauphin of France), Eleanor, Louis XI (King of France) **8** Lady Bona, Lady Grey **9** Joan of Arc **10** Lord Talbot **11** Bolingbroke **12** John Beaufort, Lord Clifford, Lord Hastings **13** Henry Beaufort, Joan La Pucelle **15** Margaret of Anjou, Margery Jourdain **16** Bastard of Orleans, Cardinal Beaufort
duke: 4 York (Richard Plantagenet) **7** Bedford, Suffolk **8** Somerset **10** Gloucester
earl: 7 Suffolk, Warwick **9** Salisbury
Richard Plantagenet's son: 6 Edmund, Edward, George **7** Richard

Henry VIII
author: 18 William Shakespeare
character: 7 Cranmer **8** Gardiner **10** Anne Boleyn **12** Thomas Wolsey **14** Queen Katharine, Thomas Cromwell **16** Cardinal Campeius
duke: 7 Norfolk, Suffolk **10** Buckingham

Henze, Hans Werner
born: 7 Germany **10** Westphalia
composer of: 6 Ariosi, Ondine **8** King Stag **10** El Cimarron **11** Konig Hirsch **12** The Bassarids, The Young Lord **14** Being Beauteous **15** The Runaway Slave **17** Boulevard Solitude **18** Der Prinz von Homburg, The Raft of the Medusa **19** Elegy for Young Lovers **48** The Long and Weary Journey to the Flat of Natasha Ungeheur

Heorot
great hall in: 7 Beowulf

he painted it
  Latin: **6** pinxit
Hepburn, Audrey
  real name: **19** Audrey Hepburn-Ruston
  husband: **9** Mel Ferrer
  born: **7** Belgium **8** Brussels
  roles: **6** Ondine **7** Charade, Sabrina **9** Bloodline, Funny Face **10** My Fair Lady **11** War and Peace **12** Roman Holiday (Oscar), The Nun's Story **13** Green Mansions, Wait Until Dark **18** Love in the Afternoon **19** Breakfast at Tiffany's
Hepburn, Katharine
  co-star: **12** Spencer Tracy
  born: **10** Hartford CT
  roles: **7** Desk Set, Holiday **8** Adam's Rib **10** Alice Adams, Pat and Mike, Summertime **12** Morning Glory (Oscar), On Golden Pond (Oscar), The Rainmaker **14** Woman of the Year **15** The African Queen, The Lion in Winter (Oscar) **18** Suddenly Last Summer **20** The Philadelphia Story **23** Guess Who's Coming to Dinner (Oscar) **24** Long Day's Journey into Night
Hephaestus
  also: **10** Hephaistos
  father: **4** Zeus
  mother: **4** Hera
  god of: **4** fire **11** handicrafts **12** metalworking
  vocation: **5** smith
  wife: **9** Aphrodite
  corresponds to: **6** Vulcan
Hephzibah
  husband: **8** Hezekiah
  son: **8** Manasseh
Hepzibah see **9** Hephzibah
Hera
  also: **4** Here
  origin: **5** Greek
  queen of: **6** Heaven
  father: **6** Cronos, Cronus, Kronos
  mother: **4** Rhea
  brother: **4** Zeus
  husband: **4** Zeus
  son: **4** Ares
  daughter: **9** Eilithyia **10** Hephaestus
  birthplace: **5** Samos
  festival: **7** Daedala
  counterfeit: **7** Nephele
  corresponds to: **4** Juno
  epithet: **6** Anthea, Bunaea **8** Henioche **9** Prodromia
Heracles see **8** Hercules
Heracles, Children of
  author: **9** Euripides
  character: **6** Hyllus, Iolaus **7** Alcmene, Macaria **8** Demophon **10** Eurystheus
Heracles, Madness of
  author: **9** Euripides
  character: **4** Hera **5** Lycus **6** Megara **7** Theseus **8** Heracles **10** Amphitryon

Herakles see **8** Hercules
herald 4 clue, omen, sign **5** crier, envoy, token, usher **6** augury, inform, report, reveal, symbol **7** courier, divulge, portent, presage, publish, usher in, warning **8** announce, forecast, foregoer, foretell, proclaim **9** advertise, harbinger, indicator, make known, messenger, precursor, prefigure, publicize **10** forerunner, indication, proclaimer **11** bruit abroad, communicate, give voice to, predecessor **13** give tidings of
heraldic emblem 4 arms **5** crest **8** blazonry, insignia **10** coat of arms
heraldry
  also called: **4** arms **10** coat of arms
  band: **3** bar **4** bend, fess, orle
  black: **5** sable
  blue: **5** azure
  border: **4** orle
  bottom: **4** base
  center: **5** fesse
  coat of arms of cities/countries/colleges: **14** impersonal arms
  coat of arms on shield/crest/helmet/motto: **19** armorial achievement
  colors: **8** tincture
  concerns family's: **8** heritage **9** genealogy
  described as: **9** blazoning
  divided diagonally: **7** per bend
  divided vertically and horizontally: **9** quartered
  expert: **8** armorist
  for holding shield: **10** supporters
  fur: **4** vair **6** ermine
  gold/yellow: **2** or
  green: **4** vert
  helmet top: **5** crest
  horizontal band: **4** fess
  illegitimacy mark: **5** baton **6** baston **11** bar sinister **12** bend sinister
  intrafamily distinctions: **12** differencing
    daughter: **7** lozenge
    eldest son: **5** label
    younger son: **7** cadency
  left part: **8** sinister
  main figure: **6** charge **8** ordinary **14** heraldic device
  metal: **2** or **6** argent
  motto in: **6** scroll
  orange: **5** tenne
  placed on lord's: **6** banner, shield **8** garments **14** horse trappings
  portrayed as: **6** emblem, symbol
  position: **7** courant, dormant, passant, rampant, salient **8** couchant, trippant
  purple: **7** purpure
  red: **5** gules
  red-purple: **8** sanguine
  right part: **6** dexter
  shield: **10** escutcheon
  sunshade: **8** mantling
    held by: **6** wreath
    made of: **4** silk

  surface/background: **5** field
  top: **5** chief
  two or more colors: **16** lines of partition
  vertical band: **4** pale
  wavy: **4** ente, onde, unde
  when worn by followers: **5** badge **6** livery
  white/silver: **6** argent
herb 4 drug **5** plant, spice **6** annual, physic **7** herbage, perfume **8** aromatic, biennial, medicine **9** flavoring, perennial, seasoning, succulent
  kind: **3** bay, rue **4** corn, dill, hemp, mint, rose, sage **5** anise, basil, curry, chili, grass, onion, peony, thyme, wheat **6** catnip, celery, chives, clover, fennel, garlic, pepper, sesame **7** boneset, caraway, ginseng, lavender, mustard, oregano, parsley **8** camomile, licorice, rosemary, tarragon **9** buttercup, marijuana, spearmint **10** peppermint **11** wintergreen
Herbert, George
  author of: **9** The Temple
Herbert, Victor
  born: **6** Dublin **7** Ireland
  composer of: **14** Babes in Toyland, Hero and Leander **15** Naughty Marietta
herbivorous 10 vegetarian **11** plant-eating **14** noncarnivorous
Herceius
  epithet of: **4** Zeus
  means: **14** of the courtyard
herculean, Herculean 4 hard **5** burly, hefty, tough **6** brawny, mighty, robust, rugged, strong, sturdy **7** arduous, onerous **8** muscular, powerful, toilsome, wearying **9** difficult, fatiguing, laborious, strapping, strenuous **10** burdensome, exhausting, formidable, prodigious **12** backbreaking
Hercules
  also: **7** Alcides **8** Heracles, Herakles **9** Carnopian
  father: **4** Zeus
  mother: **7** Alcmene
  cousin: **10** Eurystheus
  wife: **4** Hebe **6** Megara **8** Deianira
  son: **5** Lamus **6** Hyllus **8** Telephus **11** Therimachus
  daughter: **7** Macaria
  teacher: **6** Chiron
  gift: **8** strength
  performed: **6** labors
  number of labors: **6** twelve
  epithet: **7** Charops **8** Buphagus **9** Ipoctonus
  corresponds to: **6** Sancus **10** Semo Sancus
Hercyna
  form: **5** nymph
  location: **8** fountain
  playmate: **10** Persephone
herd 3 lot, mob **4** army, band, body, gang, goad, host, lead, mass, pack,

spur **5** array, bunch, crowd, drive, drove, flock, force, group, guide, horde, party, press, rally, swarm, tribe, troop **6** gather, huddle, legion, muster, number, throng **7** cluster, collect, company, convene, round up **8** assemble, assembly, conclave **9** gathering, multitude **10** assemblage, collection **11** convocation **12** congregation

Herds
    god of: 8 Silvanus, Sylvanus
    herdsman 6 cowboy, driver, drover **7** cowpoke **8** shepherd

Herdsman
    constellation of: 6 Bootes

herd together 5 flock, group **6** gather **7** cluster, collect **10** congregate **12** band together

hereafter 5 limbo **6** heaven **8** paradise **9** afterlife, from now on, next world, Purgatory **10** afterworld, future life, henceforth, life beyond, ultimately **11** in the future, world to come **12** at a later date, at a later time, henceforward, subsequently **14** life after death **15** heavenly kingdom

here and there 6 around **11** at intervals **18** in this place and that
    Latin: 6 passim

Here Comes Mr Jordan
    director: 13 Alexander Hall
    cast: 11 Claude Rains, Evelyn Keyes, Rita Johnson **16** Robert Montgomery
    remade as: 13 Heaven Can Wait

hereditary 6 inborn, inbred **7** genetic **9** ancestral, heritable, inherited **10** congenital, handed-down **11** established, inheritable, traditional

here lies
    Latin: 8 hic jacet

heresy 7 dissent, fallacy **8** apostasy **10** dissension, heterodoxy, iconoclasm, irreligion **11** unorthodoxy **13** nonconformity **15** unsound doctrine

heretic 7 skeptic **8** apostate, recreant, recusant, renegade **9** dissenter **10** backslider **11** freethinker, misbeliever **12** deviationist **13** nonconformist

heretical 7 radical **9** dissident **10** unorthodox **12** iconoclastic **13** nonconforming, nonconformist **14** unconventional

heretofore
    French: 8 ci-devant

Hereward the Wake
    author: 15 Charles Kingsley

Hergesheimer, Joseph
    author of: 8 Java Head **19** The Three Black Pennys

heritage 6 estate, legacy **7** portion **9** patrimony, tradition **10** birthright **11** inheritance **16** family possession

Hermaphroditus
    father: 6 Hermes
    mother: 9 Aphrodite

    loved by: 8 Salmacis
    joined with: 8 Salmacis
    became: 8 bisexual

Hermes
    origin: 5 Greek
    occupation: 6 herald
    messenger of: 4 gods
    father: 4 Zeus
    mother: 4 Maia
    son: 3 Pan **6** Prylis **7** Abderus, Daphnis **14** Hermaphroditus
    birthplace: 7 Arcadia
    god of: 4 luck **5** roads, sleep **6** dreams, wealth **7** cunning, thieves **8** commerce **9** fertility, invention, merchants
    invented: 4 lyre
    sandals had: 5 wings
    epithet: 6 Dolius **8** Agoraeus **9** Spelaites **10** Criophorus **11** Argiphontes **12** Argeiphontes, Psychopompus
    corresponds to: 5 Thoth **7** Mercury

hermetic 6 mystic, occult **7** obscure **8** abstruse, airtight, esoteric, mystical **9** recondite

Hermia
    character in: 21 A Midsummer Night's Dream
    author: 11 Shakespeare

hermine, L'
    author: 11 Jean Anouilh

Hermione
    character in: 14 The Winter's Tale
    author: 11 Shakespeare

Hermione
    father: 8 Menelaus
    mother: 5 Helen
    husband: 7 Orestes
    son: 9 Tisamenus

hermit 7 eremite, recluse **8** cenobite, monastic, solitary **9** anchorite **11** desert saint **14** solitudinarian **16** religious recluse

hermitage 5 abbey **6** friary, priory **7** convent, retreat **8** cloister **9** monastery

hero, heroine 4 idol, star **7** gallant **8** brave man, champion, great man, male lead, male star, noble man **9** daredevil, daring man, main actor **10** adventurer, leading man **11** protagonist, valorous man **12** man of courage, man of the hour **13** chivalrous man, popular figure **15** fearless fighter, idealized person, intrepid warrior, legendary person

Hero
    character in: 19 Much Ado About Nothing
    author: 11 Shakespeare

Hero
    vocation: 9 priestess
    priestess of: 9 Aphrodite
    lover: 7 Leander
    death by: 7 suicide **8** drowning

Herod Antipas
    father: 13 Herod the great

    mother: 8 Malthace
    grandfather: 9 Antipater
    wife: 8 Herodias
    half brother: 6 Philip
    beheaded: 14 John the Baptist

Herodias
    husband: 6 Philip **12** Herod Antipas
    daughter: 6 Salome

Herodotus
    called: 15 Father of History
    wrote history of: 11 Persian Wars

Herod Philip
    daughter: 6 Salome

heroic 4 bold, epic **5** brave, grand, noble **6** daring **7** classic, exalted, gallant, Homeric, valiant **8** elevated, fearless, highbrow, inflated, intrepid, mythical, resolute, valorous **9** bombastic, dauntless, dignified, grandiose, high-flown, legendary, undaunted **10** chivalrous, courageous **11** exaggerated, extravagant, lionhearted, pretentious, unflinching **12** mythological, ostentatious, stouthearted

heroic act 4 feat **7** exploit **9** brave deed

heroism 5 valor **6** daring **7** bravery, courage, prowess **8** boldness, chivalry, nobility **9** fortitude, gallantry **11** intrepidity **12** fearlessness **13** dauntlessness **14** courageousness **15** lionheartedness

Herophilus
    field: 7 anatomy
    nationality: 5 Greek
    experimented with: 15 post-mortem exams

Heros
    author: 8 Menander

herpetophobia
    fear of: 8 reptiles

Herrenvolk 10 master race

Herrick, Robert
    author of: 10 Hesperides **20** Corinna's Going A Maying **26** Gather ye rosebuds while ye may

Herriman, George
    creator/artist of: 8 Krazy Kat

Herschel, William
    field: 9 astronomy
    nationality: 7 British
    discovered: 6 Uranus

Hersey, John
    author of: 7 The Wall **9** Hiroshima **13** A Bell for Adano, The Conspiracy **22** My Petition for More Space

Hertz, Heinrich
    field: 7 physics
    nationality: 6 German
    discovered: 13 electric waves **18** wireless telegraphy
    named for him: 13 hertzian waves
    unit of: 9 frequency

Herzog
    author: 10 Saul Bellow

he sculptured it
 Latin: **8** sculpsit
Hesiod
 author of: **8** Theogony **12** Works and Days
hesitancy 10 indecision, reluctance, unsureness **11** uncertainty, vacillation **12** irresolution
hesitant 5 loath **6** unsure **7** halting **8** doubtful, wavering **9** diffident, faltering, reluctant, tentative, uncertain, undecided **10** hesitating, indecisive, irresolute **11** half- hearted, hanging back, vacillating **15** shilly-shallying **17** lacking confidence, sitting on the fence
hesitate 4 balk, halt **5** delay, pause, shy at, waver **6** falter **7** scruple, stick at **8** be unsure, hang back **9** stickle at, vacillate **10** dillydally, shrink from, think twice **11** be reluctant, be uncertain, be undecided, be unwilling, stop briefly **12** be irresolute, shilly-shally **16** straddle the fence
hesitating 8 doubtful, hesitant **10** indecisive, irresolute, on the fence
he speaks
 Latin: **8** loquitur
Hesperia
 also: **5** Italy **16** Iberian Peninsula
Hesperides
 author: **13** Robert Herrick
Hesperides
 form: **6** nymphs
 guarded: **12** golden apples
 guarded with: **5** Ladon **6** dragon
 names: **5** Aegle **6** Hestia **7** Erythea, Hespera **8** Arethusa **9** Hespereia, Hesperusa
 islands of the: **7** blessed
 form of: **6** heaven
Hess, Victor Francis
 field: **7** physics
 discovered: **10** cosmic rays
 awarded: **10** Nobel Prize
Hesse, Hermann
 author of: **6** Demian **9** Rosshalde **10** Siddhartha **11** Steppenwolf **12** Magister Ludi **14** Peter Camenzind **15** Beneath the Wheel **16** Death and the Lover, Journey to the East, The Glass Bead Game
Hesselberg, Melvyn Edouard
 real name of: **13** Melvyn Douglas
Hessian
 native of: **5** Hesse **7** Germany
 soldier: **9** mercenary
 aided: **7** British
 in: **16** Revolutionary War
Hestia
 origin: **5** Greek
 goddess of the: **6** hearth
 father: **6** Cronos, Cronus, Kronos
 mother: **4** Rhea
 corresponds to: **5** Vesta
Heston, Charlton

real name: **13** Charles Carter
 born: **10** Evanston IL
 roles: **5** El Cid, Moses **6** Ben-Hur (Oscar) **15** Planet of the Apes **18** The Ten Commandments **21** The Agony and the Ecstasy **22** The Greatest Show on Earth
heterogeneous 5 mixed **6** motley, unlike, varied **7** diverse, jumbled **8** assorted **9** composite, disparate, divergent, unrelated **10** dissimilar, variegated **11** diversified **13** miscellaneous
hew 2 ax **3** cut, lop **4** chop, form, hack, mold **5** carve, model, prune, sever, shape **6** chisel, cut out, devise **7** cut down, fashion, whittle **8** chop down **9** sculpture
He Who Gets Slapped
 author: **14** Leonid Andreyev
he wrote it
 Latin: **8** scripsit
hex 4 harm, jinx, sign **5** curse, spell, witch **6** hoodoo, voodoo, whammy **7** bewitch, enchant, evil eye, ill wind, possess **8** sorcerer **9** sorceress **11** malediction
Hexateuch 27 first six books of Old Testament
 see also **7** Books of **12** Old Testament
heyday 4 acme **5** bloom, crest, flush, prime, vigor **6** zenith **9** flowering, salad days
Heyerdahl, Thor
 author of: **7** Kon-Tiki **16** The Ra Expeditions
Hi and Lois
 creator: **9** Dik Browne **10** Mort Walker
 character:
  brother: **12** Beetle Bailey
  children: **3** Dot **4** Chip **5** Ditto **6** Trixie
  dog: **4** Dawg
  friend: **7** Thirsty
hiatus 3 gap **4** void **5** blank, break, lapse, space **6** lacuna, vacuum **7** interim **8** interval **10** disruption **12** interruption
Hiawatha, The Song of
 author: **24** Henry Wadsworth Longfellow
 character: **5** Nahma **7** Kwasind, Nokomis, Wenonah **8** Mondamin **9** Chibiabos, Minnehaha **11** Mudjekeewis **12** Pau-Puk-Keewis, Pearl-Feather
hibernate 5 sleep **6** retire **8** withdraw **13** become dormant
hibernating 6 asleep **7** dormant **8** inactive, sleeping **9** quiescent
Hibernia *see* **7** Ireland
hibiscus
 varieties: **7** Chinese **8** Hawaiian, Japanese
hic jacet 8 here lies
hick 4 boor, rube **5** yokel **6** rustic **7** hayseed

Hickock, James B 5 scout **7** marshal
 called: **8** Wild Bill
hickory 5 Carya
 varieties: **4** Pale, Sand **5** Broom, Swamp, Water **6** Pignut **7** Chinese **8** Mountain, Shagbark **9** Mockernut, Shellbark **10** White-heart **12** Small-fruited
Hicks, Edward
 born: **11** Attleboro PA
 artwork: **19** The Peaceable Kingdom
hidden away 6 buried, cached **7** stashed **8** closeted, pocketed, secluded, secreted **9** concealed **10** out of sight **11** stashed away **12** inaccessible, undiscovered
hidden meaning 6 enigma, puzzle, riddle, secret **7** mystery
hidden motive
 French: **13** arriere pensee
hide 4 mask, pelt, skin, veil **5** cache, cloak, cloud, cover **6** lie low, screen, shroud **7** conceal, curtain, leather, obscure, repress, seclude, secrete **8** disguise, suppress
hideaway 7 hideout, retreat **11** hiding place, secret place
hideous 4 grim, ugly, vile **5** awful **6** horrid, odious **7** ghastly, macabre **8** dreadful, gruesome, horrible, shocking **9** abhorrent, appalling, frightful, grotesque, loathsome, monstrous, repellent, repugnant, repulsive, revolting, sickening **10** abominable, detestable, disgusting, horrendous
hiding place 5 cache **8** hideaway **9** hidey hole **10** repository **11** secret place
Hieronimo
 character in: **17** The Spanish Tragedy
 author: **3** Kyd
hier wird Deutsch gesprochen 18 German is spoken here
Higgins, Henry
 character in: **9** Pygmalion **10** My Fair Lady
 author: **4** Shaw
Higgs
 character in: **7** Erewhon
 author: **6** Butler
high 3 gay, top **4** main, tall **5** aloft, chief, far up, grand, great, jolly, lofty, merry, noble, prime, sharp, undue, way up **6** alpine, august, elated, jovial, joyful, joyous, shrill **7** capital, eminent, exalted, excited, extreme, gleeful, leading, notable, playful, primary, serious, soaring, soprano **8** cheerful, elevated, exultant, foremost, imposing, jubilant, mirthful, peerless, piercing, strident, superior, towering, uncurbed **9** ascendant, excellent, excessive, exuberant, important, overjoyed, principal, prominent, unbridled, uppermost **10** exorbitant, immoderate, inordinate, preeminent **11** cloud-capped, exaggerated, exhilarated, ex-

travagant, high-pitched, illustrious, intemperate, predominant, significant, sky- scraping **12** earsplitting, high-reaching, lighthearted, unreasonable, unrestrained **13** consequential, distinguished

high-and-mighty 5 lofty **6** lordly **7** haughty **8** arrogant **9** imperious **11** overbearing

highborn 5 noble **8** highbred, well-born **9** patrician **10** of high rank, upper-class **12** aristocratic, of high degree, silk-stocking **13** of gentle blood

highbred 5 noble, regal **6** lordly **7** refined **8** highborn, wellborn **9** patrician **11** aristocracy, blue-blooded

highbrow 4 snob **5** brain **7** bookish, Brahmin, egghead, elitist, erudite, scholar, thinker **8** cultured, mandarin, snobbish **9** scholarly **10** cultivated, double-dome, mastermind **12** intellectual **13** knowledgeable

highest good
    Latin: 11 summum bonum

highest point
    Latin: 11 ne plus ultra

high fashion
    French: 12 haute couture

high-flown 4 wild **5** lofty, proud **6** absurd, florid, lordly, turgid, unreal **7** flowery, orotund, pompous **8** elevated, fabulous, inflated **9** bombastic, excessive, fantastic, grandiose **10** flamboyant, immoderate, inordinate, outrageous **11** exaggerated, extravagant, highfalutin, pretentious, sententious **12** magniloquent, preposterous, presumptuous, unreasonable, unrestrained **13** grandiloquent, self-important

High German
    language family: 12 Indo-European
    branch: 8 Germanic
    group: 15 Western Germanic
    subgroup: 11 German-Dutch
    division: 6 German **7** Yiddish

high-hat 5 aloof **6** formal, la-di-da, snooty **7** haughty **8** snobbish **12** supercilious

highjinks, hijinks 6 antics, capers, pranks, stunts **11** shenanigans **12** monkeyshines

highland, Highlands 4 rise **7** heights, plateau, uplands **8** headland **9** tableland **10** promontory **11** hill country **17** mountainous region
    refers especially to: 8 Scotland
    dance: 5 fling

highlight 4 peak **6** accent, climax, stress **7** feature, point up **9** emphasize, high point, underline **10** accentuate, focal point, make bright

highly qualified 3 fit **4** able **7** trained **8** eligible, prepared, skillful **9** practiced **10** proficient **11** experienced **12** accomplished

highly regarded 6 prized **7** admired, revered **8** esteemed **9** respected, treasured **13** well thought of

highly valued 4 dear **5** loved **6** adored **7** beloved, revered **8** esteemed, precious **9** cherished, treasured

highly visible 7 glaring, obvious **8** distinct **9** prominent **11** conspicuous, outstanding

high-minded 4 fair, just **5** lofty, moral, noble **6** honest, worthy **7** ethical, sincere, upright **8** truthful, virtuous **9** exemplary, honorable, reputable, righteous, uncorrupt **10** chivalrous, idealistic, principled, scrupulous **13** conscientious, square-dealing

High Noon
    director: 13 Fred Zinnemann
    cast: 10 Gary Cooper (Will Kane), Grace Kelly **12** Lloyd Bridges **14** Thomas Mitchell
    score: 14 Dimitri Tiomkin
    Oscar for: 5 actor (Cooper)

high old time 4 ball, lark **5** fling, revel, spree **8** escapade

high-pitched 5 acute, sharp **6** shrill **7** clarion, squeaky **8** piercing

high place 3 tor **4** hill, peak, rise **5** aerie, bluff, cliff, knoll, ridge **6** height, summit, upland **7** hillock, hummock, plateau **8** eminence, mountain **9** elevation **10** prominence, promontory

high point, highest point 3 cap, top **4** acme, apex, peak **5** crest, crown **6** apogee, climax, height, heyday, summit, tiptop, vertex, zenith **8** eminence, pinnacle **9** flowering **10** prominence **11** culmination

high position 4 note **8** eminence, high rank, standing **9** supremacy **10** ascendancy, importance, notability, prominence **11** distinction, preeminence

high-powered 7 driving, dynamic **8** forceful **9** ambitious, assertive, energetic, go-getting **10** aggressive **11** hard- driving

high praise 5 kudos, paean **6** eulogy **7** hosanna, plaudit **8** encomium **9** laudation, panegyric **11** acclamation

high-priced 4 dear, high **6** costly, pricey **9** expensive **10** exorbitant, overpriced **11** extravagant

high-principled 5 moral, noble **6** chaste, honest, worthy **7** ethical, upright **9** honorable, reputable **10** idealistic **11** responsible, trustworthy **13** conscientious

high quality 5 merit **7** quality **9** greatness **10** excellence, perfection **11** distinction, superiority

high-ranking 3 top **5** grand, great, lofty, regal, royal **6** august **7** eminent, exalted, supreme **8** elevated, es-

teemed, imposing **9** important, paramount, venerable **10** preeminent **11** illustrious **13** distinguished

High Sierra
    director: 10 Raoul Walsh
    cast: 9 Ida Lupino **10** Alan Curtis, Joan Leslie **13** Arthur Kennedy **14** Humphrey Bogart (Mad Dog Earle)
    remade as: 17 Colorado Territory **19** I Died a Thousand Times

high society 5 elite **6** jet set **9** haut monde, top drawer **11** aristocracy **14** creme de la creme
    French: 9 haut monde

High Society
    director: 14 Charles Walters
    cast: 10 Bing Crosby, Grace Kelly **11** Celeste Holm **12** Frank Sinatra, Louis Calhern **14** Louis Armstrong
    score: 10 Cole Porter
    remake of: 20 The Philadelphia Story
    song: 8 True Love **10** Did You Evah? **16** You're Sensational

high-speed 4 fast **5** quick, rapid, swift **6** speedy **7** express

high-spirited 5 vital **6** lively **8** animated **9** exuberant, vivacious **12** effervescent, enthusiastic

high spirits 5 vigor **6** gaiety **7** delight, elation **8** gladness, vitality, vivacity **9** animation **10** enthusiasm, exaltation, excitement, joyousness, liveliness **12** exhilaration **16** lightheartedness

high-strung 4 edgy **5** jumpy, moody, tense **6** uneasy **7** jittery, nervous, uptight **8** neurotic, restless, skittish **9** emotional, excitable, impatient, wrought-up **10** hysterical **13** oversensitive, temperamental **14** easily agitated, hypersensitive

High Tor
    author: 15 Maxwell Anderson

highway 7 freeway, parkway, thruway **8** hard road, highroad, main road, speedway, turnpike **9** paved road **10** expressway, interstate, main artery **12** four-lane road, thoroughfare
    British: 9 coach road, royal road **12** King's highway **13** Queen's highway

highwayman 5 crook, thief **6** bandit, outlaw, robber **7** brigand, footpad

hike 4 rise, roam, rove, trek, walk **5** leg it, march, raise, tramp **6** draw up, hoof it, jerk up, pull up, ramble, trudge, wander **7** hitch up, raise up **8** addition, increase **9** expansion **10** escalation **12** augmentation **13** journey on foot **14** go by shank's mare

hilarious 3 gay **5** jolly, merry, noisy **6** jocund, jovial, joyful, joyous, lively **7** comical, gleeful, riotous **8** jubilant, mirthful **9** exuberant, laughable, very funny **10** boisterous, hysterical, rollicking, uproarious, vociferous **11** exhilarated **12** high-spirited **13** highly amusing **14** laugh- provoking

hilarity 3 fun, gig, joy **4** glee, riot **5**

laugh, mirth, noisy **6** comedy, gaiety, giggle, levity **7** chortle, chuckle, jollity **8** hysteria, laughter **9** amusement, funniness, joviality, jubilance, merriment **10** exuberance **12** exhilaration, humorousness **14** uproariousness

Hilbert, David
field: **8** geometry **11** mathematics
nationality: **6** German
formulated: **12** modern axioms

Hilda Lessways
author: **13** Arnold Bennett

hill 4 bank, dune, heap, pile, ramp, rise **5** bluff, butte, cliff, climb, grade, knoll, mound, mount, slope **6** height **7** hillock, hilltop, hummock, incline, upgrade **8** eminence, foothill, highland, hillside **9** acclivity, declivity, downgrade, elevation **10** prominence, promontory

Hill, Arthur
born: **6** Canada **7** Melfort **12** Saskatchewan
roles: **13** All the Way Home **15** The Ugly American **17** Look Homeward Angel **25** Who's Afraid of Virginia Woolf?

Hill, George Roy
director of: **8** The Sting (Oscar) **23** The World According to Garp **29** Butch Cassidy and the Sundance Kid

Hillary, Edmund
born: **10** New Zealand
climbed: **9** Mt. Everest
explored: **9** South Pole

Hiller, Arthur
director of: **25** The Americanization of Emily

hillock 4 hill, rise **5** knoll, mound **7** hummock **8** eminence

Hill Street Blues
character: **5** LaRue, Renko **9** Bobby Hill, Jablonski, Joe Coffey, Lucy Bates **10** Fay Furillo, Mick Belker, Washington **11** (Lt) Norman Buntz **12** Howard Hunter, (Captain) Frank Furillo **13** Henry Goldblum **14** Joyce Davenport
cast: **8** Joe Spano **10** Bruce Weitz, Ed Marinaro, Kiel Martin **11** Betty Thomas, Charles Haid, Dennis Franz **12** Robert Prosky **13** James B Sikking, Michael Warren, Veronica Hamel **14** Taurean Blacque **15** Daniel J Travanti

Hilton, James
author of: **11** Lost Horizon **14** Good-Bye Mr Chips

Himalayas 9 mountains
countries **5** India, Nepal, Tibet, **6** Bhutan **8** Pakistan
peak: **7** Everest **9** Annapurna
native: **6** sherpa
Climber: **7** Hillary **13** Tenzing Norkay
legendary creature: **4** yeti **17** Abominable Snowman

Hind see **5** India

Hind and the Panther, The
author: **10** John Dryden

Hindemith, Paul
born: **5** Hanau **7** Germany
composer of: **8** The Demon **9** Cardillac **10** Heriodiade **12** Ludus Tonalis, Neues vom Tage, News of the Day **13** Sancta Susanna **14** Cupid and Psyche, Mathis Der Maler **15** In Praise of Music **17** Murder Hope of Women **18** Die Harmonie der Welt, Nobilissima Visione **19** The Four Temperaments **23** Morder Hoffnung der Frauen

hinder 3 bar **4** curb, foil, stay, stop **5** block, check, delay, deter, spike, stall **6** arrest, detain, fetter, hamper, hobble, hog-tie, hold up, impede, retard, stifle, stymie, thwart **7** inhibit **8** encumber, handicap, hold back, obstruct, restrain, slow down **9** frustrate, hamstring **13** interfere with

Hindi
language family: **12** Indo-European
branch: **11** Indo-Iranian
group: **5** Indic
official language of: **5** India

hindmost 4 last, rear **7** tail end **12** farthest back

hindpart 4 tail **6** far end **7** rear end **8** backside, buttocks, haunches **9** afterpart, posterior

hindquarters 4 rear, rump **7** rear end, tail end **8** back legs, backside, buttocks, haunches **9** posterior

hindrance 3 bar **4** clog, curb, snag **5** catch **6** fetter **7** barrier, shackle **8** blockade, blockage, handicap, obstacle **9** barricade, restraint, retardant **10** constraint, difficulty, impediment, limitation **11** encumbrance, obstruction, restriction **12** interference **14** stumbling block

hinge 4 hang, rest, turn **5** pivot, swing **6** depend **7** be due to **9** arise from **10** result from **11** be subject to, emanate from **13** revolve around

hint 3 bit, jot, tip **4** clue, idea, iota **5** grain, imply, pinch, tinge, touch, trace, whiff **6** little, notion, tip off **7** inkling, pointer, signify, soupcon, suggest, whisper **8** allusion, indicate, innuendo, intimate **9** insinuate, suspicion **10** impression, indication, intimation, smattering, suggestion **11** implication, indirection, insinuation **12** flea in the ear, slight amount **13** word to the wise

hinted 7 implied, oblique **8** implicit, indirect **9** suggested

hinterland 6 sticks **7** boonies, country **8** interior, midlands **9** backwater, backwoods, boondocks, rural area **11** countryside

Hippalectryon
form: **7** monster

Hippocampus
form: **7** monster
body of: **5** horse
tail of: **4** fish

Hippocrene
form: **6** spring
location: **12** Mount Helicon

hippodrome 5 arena **6** circus **7** stadium **8** coliseum

Hippogriff
form: **7** monster
combined: **5** horse **7** griffin

Hippolyte
also: **7** Antiope **9** Hippolyta
queen of: **7** Amazons
husband: **7** Theseus
son: **10** Hippolytus
Hercules stole her: **6** girdle

Hippolytus
author: **9** Euripides
character: **7** Artemis, Phaedra, Theseus **9** Aphrodite

Hippolytus
father: **7** Theseus
mother: **9** Hippolyta
stepmother: **7** Phaedra
loved by: **7** Phaedra
killed by: **8** Poseidon

hire 3 fee, get, let, pay **4** cost, gain, rent **5** lease, wages **6** charge, employ, engage, income, obtain, profit, retain, reward, salary, secure, take on **7** appoint, charter, payment, procure, stipend **8** earnings, receipts **9** emolument **10** recompense **12** compensation, remuneration

hireling 4 goon, thug **6** flunky, lackey, menial, minion, stooge **7** gorilla **8** henchman, retainer **9** strong-arm **10** hatchet man

Hiroshima
author: **10** John Hersey

hirsute 5 bushy, downy, hairy, nappy, wooly **6** shaggy, woolly **7** bearded, bristly, prickly, unshorn **8** bristled, unshaven **9** whiskered **11** bewhiskered

His Girl Friday
director: **11** Howard Hawks
cast: **9** Cary Grant **12** Gene Lockhart, Ralph Bellamy **15** Rosalind Russell
remake of: **12** The Front Page

Hispania see **5** Spain

hiss 3 boo **4** mock, razz **6** deride, heckle, hoot at, jeer at, revile **7** catcall, scoff at, sneer at **9** shout down **10** Bronx cheer **16** give the raspberry

histology
study of: **6** tissue

historian
American: **4** Webb **5** Adams **6** Brooks, De Voto, Durant, Fisher, Miller, Nevins, Sparks, Turner **7** Morison, Parkman, Taussig, Tuch-

man **8** Bancroft, Channing, Prescott, Robinson **10** Hofstadter
British: 4 Bede (the Venerable) **6** Gibbon, Turner **7** Toynbee **8** Macaulay **9** Trevelyan
Chinese: 10 Ssu-ma Ch'ien, Ssu-Ma Kuang
French: 5 Bayle, Blanc, Bloch, Taine **7** Braudel **8** Mabillon, Michelet, Voltaire **11** Tocqueville
German: 5 Ranke **7** Mommsen **8** Spengler **10** Burckhardt, Treitschke
Greek: 8 Polybius **9** Herodotus **10** Thucydides
Islamic: 8 al Tabari **10** Ibn Khaldun
Italian: 4 Polo, Vico **5** Croce **11** Machiavelli **12** Guicciardini
Latin: 4 Livy **7** Sallust, Tacitus
Scottish: 7 Carlyle

historic 5 famed **7** notable **8** renowned **9** memorable, well-known **10** celebrated **11** outstanding

historical 4 past, real, true **6** actual, bygone, former **7** ancient, factual **8** attested, recorded **9** authentic **10** chronicled, documented

historical period 3 age, era **4** date, time **5** epoch, stage

history 4 epic, saga, tale **5** story **6** annals, change, growth, record, resume, review **7** account, the past **8** old times **9** chronicle, days of old, narration, narrative, portrayal, tradition, yesterday **10** bygone days, days of yore, olden times, the old days, yesteryear **11** bygone times, development, former times, local events, major events, world events **12** actual events **13** an unusual past, human progress **14** military action, national events, recapitulation **15** political change

History of Colonel Jacque, The
   author: 11 Daniel Defoe
History of Henry VII
   author: 12 Francis Bacon
History of Mr Polly, The
   author: 7 H G Wells
   character: 6 Miriam **8** Uncle Jim **13** The Plump Woman
History of the English-Speaking Peoples, A
   author: 17 Winston S Churchill
His Toy, His Dream, His Rest
   author: 12 John Berryman

histrionics 4 fuss **6** acting, tirade **7** bluster, bombast **8** outburst **9** dramatics, hamminess, staginess, theatrics **10** dramaturgy, playacting **11** performance, rodomontade **13** melodramatics, temper tantrum, theatricality **16** ranting and raving

hit 3 bat, jab, lob, rap, tap **4** bang, bash, beat, belt, blow, boon, bump, butt, clip, club, coup, cuff, damn, drub, find, flog, hurt, move, pelt, poke, slam, slap, slug, sock, stir, swat **5** abash, baste, clout, crack, crush, flail, knock, paste, pound, punch, reach, rouse, smack, smash, smite, thump, touch, upset, whack **6** affect, arouse, assail, attack, attain, batter, cudgel, effect, impact, incite, pommel, revile, strike, thrash, thwack, wallop, winner **7** achieve, assault, censure, clobber, condemn, execute, godsend, impress, inflame, provoke, quicken, realize, shatter, success, triumph, trounce, victory **8** arrive at, bang into, blessing, bring off, denounce, lambaste, overcome, reproach **9** criticize, deal a blow, devastate, lash out at, overwhelm, sensation, smash into **11** collide with, connect with, deal a stroke, strike out at **12** go straight to **13** make a bull's-eye, send to the mark **14** popular success, strike together **16** mount an offensive

hit back 7 counter, get even, pay back **9** fight back, retaliate **10** strike back

hitch 3 tie, tug **4** curb, draw, halt, haul, hike, jerk, knot, loop, pull, snag, stop, yank, yoke **5** catch, check, clamp, delay, raise, tying **6** attach, couple, fasten, mishap, secure, tether **7** bracket, connect, harness, joining, mistake, problem, trouble **8** coupling, handicap, make fast, obstacle **9** attaching, fastening, hindrance, mischance, restraint **10** connection, difficulty, impediment, limitation **11** restriction **12** complication, interruption, loop together, put in harness **14** stumbling block

Hitchcock, Alfred
   director of: 6 Frenzy, Marnie, Psycho **7** Rebecca, Vertigo **8** Lifeboat, The Birds **9** Notorious, Suspicion **10** Family Plot, Rear Window, Spellbound **13** To Catch a Thief **14** Dial M for Murder, Shadow of a Doubt **15** The Lady Vanishes **16** North by Northwest **17** Strangers on a Train **18** The Thirty-Nine Steps **19** The Trouble with Harry **20** Foreign Correspondent

hither 2 on **4** here, near **5** close **6** closer, nearby, nearer, onward **7** close by, forward **8** over here **11** to this place **12** to the speaker

hitherto 6 ere now, hereto **7** thus far, till now, up to now **8** until now **10** before this, heretofore

Hitler, Adolf
   author of: 9 Mein Kampf

hit man 6 killer, slayer **8** assassin, hired gun, murderer **11** executioner **12** exterminator

Hitman
   nickname of: 12 Thomas Hearns

hit-or-miss 3 lax **6** casual, fitful **7** aimless, cursory **8** slapdash **9** haphazard **10** incomplete **11** purposeless, superficial, unorganized **12** unsystematic **15** catch-as-catch-can

hive 3 hub **5** heart **6** center, colony **7** cluster **9** busy place **11** swarm of bees

H M S Pinafore
   subtitle: 23 The Lass That Loved a Sailor
   operetta by: 18 Gilbert and Sullivan
   character: 11 Dick Deadeye **14** Ralph Rackstraw **15** Captain Corcoran, Little Buttercup, Sir Joseph Porter **17** Josephine Corcoran

Hoagland, Edward
   author of: 15 African Calliope **17** The Tugman's Passage

hoar 3 old **4** aged, rime **5** frost, moldy, mushy, passe, stale, white **6** old hat **7** ancient, antique, elderly, grayish **8** grizzled **9** out of date

hoard 4 fund, heap, mass, pile **5** amass, buy up, cache, lay up, store **6** save up, supply **7** acquire, collect, lay away, reserve **8** quantity **9** amassment, gathering, stockpile, store away **10** accumulate, collection **12** accumulation

hoarse 5 gruff, harsh, husky, raspy, rough **6** croaky **7** cracked, rasping, raucous, throaty **8** gravelly, guttural, scratchy

hoary 3 old **4** aged, gray, hoar **5** dated, passe, white **6** grayed, old hat **7** ancient, antique, grizzly **8** grizzled, whitened **9** out-of-date **11** gray with age **12** white with age

hoax 3 gyp **4** bilk, dupe, fake, fool, gull, yarn **5** bluff, cheat, cozen, fraud, prank, spoof, trick **6** canard, delude, humbug, take in **7** deceive, defraud, fiction, mislead, swindle **8** hoodwink **9** bamboozle, chicanery, deception, fish story, victimize **10** hocus-pocus

Hoban, James
   architect of: 13 The White House, Great Hotel (Washington, DC)
Hobbes, Thomas
   author of: 9 Leviathan
Hobbit, The
   prelude to: 14 Lord of the Rings
   author: 10 J R R Tolkien
   character: 5 Bilbo **7** Baggins
   wizard:: 7 Gandalf

hobble 4 bind, gimp, halt, limp **5** block, check, cramp **6** fetter, hamper, hinder, hog-tie, impede, lumber, stymie, thwart, toddle **7** inhibit, manacle, shackle, shamble, shuffle, stagger, stumble **8** encumber, handicap, hold back, lame gait, obstruct, restrain, restrict **9** constrain, frustrate, hamstring **10** uneven gait, walk lamely **13** interfere with

hobby 7 pastime, pursuit **8** sideline **9** amusement, avocation, diversion **10** relaxation **13** entertainment **14** divertissement

hobbyhorse 5 hobby 7 pastime 8 interest, toy horse 9 diversion 10 enthusiasm 11 distraction 12 rocking horse

hobgoblin 3 imp 4 ogre 5 bogey 6 goblin 7 bugaboo, bugbear 9 betenoire

hobnob 3 mix 4 club 6 mingle 7 consort, hang out 9 associate, rub elbows 10 fraternize

hobo 3 beg, bum 5 stiff, tramp 6 beggar, cadger, loafer 7 drifter, migrant, moocher, vagrant 8 derelict, vagabond, wanderer 9 scrounger 11 beachcomber

hoc est 6 this is

Ho Chi Minh City
formerly: 6 Saigon
river: 6 Saigon
delta: 6 Mekong
former capital of: 9 Indochina 11 Cochin China 12 South Vietnam

hockey
athlete: 8 Bobby Orr, Brad Park 9 Bobby Hull, Ken Dryden, Mike Bossy 10 Doug Harvey, Eddie Shore, Ed Giacomin, Gordie Howe, Guy Lafleur, Ray Bourque, Rod Gilbert, Stan Mikita 11 Bobby Clarke, Brian Leetch, Denis Potvin, Eric Lindros, Jean Ratelle, Mark Messier 12 Emile Francis, Jean Beliveau, Marcel Dionne, Mario Lemieux, Phil Esposito, Wayne Gretzky 13 Bernard Parent, Jacques Plante, Larry Robinson, Pat La Fontaine 14 Alex Delvecchio, Maurice Richard 15 Bernie Geoffrion 18 Yvan Serge Courneyer

hockey team
Anaheim: 11 Mighty Ducks
Atlanta: 9 Thrashers
Boston: 6 Bruins
Buffalo: 6 Sabres
Calgary: 6 Flames
Carolina: 10 Hurricanes
Chicago: 10 Black Hawks
Columbus: 11 Blue Jackets
Dallas: 5 Stars
Detroit: 8 Red Wings
Edmonton: 6 Oilers
Florida: 8 Panthers
Hartford: 7 Whalers
Los Angeles: 5 Kings
Montreal: 9 Canadiens
New Jersey: 6 Devils
New York: 7 Rangers 9 Islanders
Ottawa: 8 Senators
Philadelphia: 6 Flyers
Phoenix: 7 Coyotes
Pittsburgh: 8 Penguins
Quebec: 9 Nordiques
St Louis: 5 Blues
San Jose: 6 Sharks
Tampa Bay: 9 Lightning
Toronto: 10 Maple Leafs
Vancouver: 7 Canucks
Washington: 8 Capitals
Winnipeg: 4 Jets

hocus-pocus 4 bosh, bull, hoax, sham 5 chant, charm, cheat, magic, spell 6 bunkum, deceit, fakery, humbug 7 con game, hogwash, rubbish, swindle 8 delusion, flimflam, tommyrot, trickery 9 deception, moonshine, poppycock 10 dishonesty, flapdoodle, hanky-panky, magic spell, magic words, mumbo jumbo, subterfuge 11 bewitchment, incantation, legerdemain, magic tricks 12 fiddle-faddle, magic formula 13 sleight of hand

Hoder
also: 5 Hodur
origin: 12 Scandinavian
brother: 5 Baldr 6 Balder, Baldur
father: 4 Odin 5 Othin
killed: 5 Baldr 6 Balder, Baldur

hodgepodge, hotchpotch 3 mix 4 hash, mess, olio 6 jumble, medley, muddle 7 melange, mixture 8 mishmash 9 composite, confusion, patchwork, potpourri 10 miscellany

Hoff, Jacobus Hendricus van't
field: 9 chemistry
nationality: 5 Dutch
researched: 7 gas laws 10 carbon atom 14 thermodynamics
awarded: 10 Nobel Prize

Hoffman, Dustin
born: 12 Los Angeles CA
roles: 5 Lenny 6 Ishtar 7 Tootsie 8 Papillon 10 Ratso Rizzo 11 The Graduate 12 Little Big Man 14 Kramer vs Kramer (Oscar), Midnight Cowboy 19 All the President's Men

Hofmann, Hans
born: 7 Germany 11 Weissenberg
artwork: 6 Spring 7 The Gate 13 Effervescence 14 Fantasia in Blue, Magenta and Blue 16 Sanctum Sanctorum

Hofstadter, Richard
author of: 14 The Age of Reform

hog 3 pig, sow 4 arch, boar, trim 5 broom, sheep, swine 6 gorger, porker 7 baconer, glutton, take all 9 razorback 10 locomotive

Hogan, Paul
country: 9 Australia
roles: 10 Mick Dundee 15 Crocodile Dundee

Hogan's Heroes
character: 7 (Peter) Newkirk 8 Lt Carter 10 Sgt (Hans) Schultz 11 Louis LeBeau 14 Col Robert Hogan 15 Col Wilhelm Klink
cast: 8 Bob Crane 10 John Banner, Larry Hovis 11 Robert Clary 13 Richard Dawson 15 Werner Klemperer

Hogarth, William
born: 6 London 7 England
artwork: 12 Captain Coram 14 A Rake's Progress 15 Marriage a la Mode, The Beggar's Opera 16 A Harlot's Progress 19 Garrick as Richard III

hogshead 3 keg, tun, vat 4 butt, cask, drum 6 barrel

hogwash 3 rot 4 bull, bunk 5 hokum, hooey, stuff 6 bunkum, drivel, hot air, humbug 7 baloney, blather, spinach, twaddle 8 claptrap, nonsense, tommyrot 9 poppycock 10 applesauce 11 foolishness 13 horsefeathers 16 stuff and nonsense

hoi polloi 6 rabble, the mob 7 the herd 8 canaille, populace, riffraff, the crowd, the plebs 9 the masses, the proles, the vulgar 10 commonalty 12 the multitude 14 the lower orders, the proletariat, the rank and file 15 the common people, the lower classes, the working class

hoist 4 lift 5 heave, raise, run up 6 bear up, pull up, take up, uplift 7 elevate, raise up, upraise 9 bear aloft

Hokusai, Katsushika
born: 3 Edo 5 Japan, Tokyo
artwork: 5 Crabs, Manga 10 Waterfalls 11 Chushingura 25 Thirty-six Views of Mount Fuji

Holabird, William
partner: 11 Martin Roche
architect of: 12 Gage Building 13 Cable Building, Crerar Library (City Hall, Chicago) 14 Tacoma Building 15 McClurg Building 17 Marquette Building

Holbein, Hans (the Elder)
born: 7 Germany 8 Augsburg
son: 11 Hans Holbein (the Younger)
artwork: 11 St Sebastian 14 Fountain of Life 18 Kaisheim Altarpiece 31 Presentation of Christ in the Temple

Holbein, Hans (the Younger)
born: 7 Germany 8 Augsburg
father: 11 Hans Holbein (the Elder)
artwork: 7 Erasmus 9 Henry VIII 11 Jane Seymour 12 Dance of Death 13 The Dead Christ

hold 4 bear, bind, bond, curb, deem, grip, halt, have, hilt, keep, knob, lock, prop, rule, stay, sway, take, urge 5 block, brace, carry, check, clasp, cling, count, defer, grasp, guard, limit, offer, power, shaft, shore, stall, stand, stick, strap, think, unite, watch 6 adhere, affirm, assert, assume, cleave, clinch, clutch, deduct, detain, direct, enfold, handle, hinder, hold up, join in, manage, occupy, reckon, regard, retain, submit, take in, tender, thwart, uphold 7 advance, believe, carry on, command, conduct, confine, contain, control, declare, embrace, enclose, enforce, execute, hold off, include, inhibit, mastery, possess, present, presume, prevent, profess, propose, protect, repress, reserve, support, suppose, surmise, suspend, toehold, venture 8 advocate, conceive, conclude, consider, engage in, foothold, handhold, hold back, hold down, leverage, maintain, obligate, postpone, purchase, put forth, restrain, restrict, set aside, suppress, withhold **9** advantage, anchorage, authority, be in force, dominance, forestall, frustrate, influence, keep valid, ownership, stay fixed, stick fast **10** ascendancy, attachment, desist from, domination, possession, put forward, understand **11** accommodate, preside over

hold a candle to 5 equal, match **6** be up to **7** compare **8** approach **10** be as good as **11** come close to, compete with **12** be comparable **14** bear comparison

hold against 6 resent **8** begrudge

hold back 3 lag **4** curb, deny, keep, slow **5** check, dally, limit, stall **6** arrest, bridle, falter, refuse **7** contain, inhibit, keep out, reserve, retrain **8** hesitate, keep back, maintain, restrain, withhold **9** constrain

hold close 3 hug **5** clasp **6** cuddle, harbor **7** cherish, embrace, snuggle

Holden, William
  real name: 23 William Franklin Beedle Jr
  nickname: 4 Bill
  born: 9 O'Fallon IL
  roles: 6 Picnic **7** Network, Sabrina **9** Golden Boy **13** Born Yesterday **14** The Country Girl **15** Stalag Seventeen (Oscar), Sunset Boulevard **23** The Bridge on the River Kwai

hold fast 4 fuse, hold **5** cling, stick **6** adhere

hold firmly 4 grip **5** clasp, grasp **6** clench, clinch, clutch **10** grab hold of

hold forth 5 orate **7** expound **9** discourse, expatiate, speechify

hold in abeyance 5 table **6** recess, shelve **7** suspend **8** lay aside, postpone

hold in bondage 7 control, enchain, enslave, entrall **8** dominate **9** subjugate **12** make a slave of

holdings 6 assets **8** property **10** securities **11** commodities

hold in high regard 5 honor, prize, value **6** admire, esteem, revere **7** cherish, respect **8** look up to, treasure, venerate **10** rate highly, set store by **13** think highly of **18** attach importance to

hold one's own 4 cope **6** manage **7** contend **11** be a match for **20** maintain one's position **22** keep one's head above water

hold rapt 5 charm **7** beguile, bewitch, enchant **8** enthrall, entrance **9** captivate, enrapture, fascinate, spellbind, transport

hold to 4 bind **8** obligate

hold together 4 bind, fuse, glue, hold, join **5** cling, stick, unite **6** ce-

ment, cohere **7** combine **11** consolidate

holdup 3 rob **4** bear, halt, stay, stop **5** delay, heist, steal, theft **6** hijack, retain, uphold **7** robbery, stickup, support, sustain **8** stoppage **9** hindrance **12** interruption

hold up 4 prop, slow **5** block, brace, check, delay **6** bear up, detain, endure, hinder, impede, manage **7** bolster, present, stand up, support, sustain **8** keep back, obstruct **13** rob at gunpoint

hold up under 4 bear **6** endure, manage **8** tolerate

hold warmly 3 hug **5** clasp **6** cuddle **7** embrace, snuggle

hole 3 den, gap, pit **4** brig, cage, cave, flaw, keep, lair, rent, slit, slot **5** break, crack, fault, shaft **6** breach, burrow, cavern, cavity, crater, defect, dugout, lockup, pocket, prison, tunnel **7** dungeon, fallacy, opening, orifice, slammer **8** aperture, dark cell, puncture **9** concavity, open space **10** depression, excavation **11** discrepancy, hollow place, indentation, perforation **13** inconsistency

Holgrave, Mr
  character in: 24 The House of the Seven Gables
  author: 9 Hawthorne

holiday 3 gay **4** fete, gala **5** feria **6** cheery, fiesta, joyful, joyous, junket, outing **7** festive, holy day, jubilee **8** cheerful, feast day, festival, vacation **11** celebrating, celebration, merrymaking
  American: 6 Easter **8** Arbor Day, Labor Day **9** Christmas (Dec 25), Halloween (Oct 31) **10** Father's Day, Good Friday, Mother's Day **11** Columbus Day, Election Day, Memorial Day, New Year's Day (Jan 1), Veterans' Day (Nov 11) **12** Children's Day, Thanksgiving **15** Independence Day (July 4), St Valentine's Day (Feb 14) **23** National Grandparents' Day
    birthday: 8 Lincoln's **11** Robert E Lee's (Jan 19), Washington's **17** Martin Luther King's (Jan 15)
    Hawaiian: 13 Kamehameha Day (June 11)
  British: 8 Hogmanay (Dec 31) **9** Boxing Day (Dec 26) **11** Harvest Home **12** Guy Fawkes Day (Nov 5), Twelfth Night (Jan 5) **14** Queen's Birthday (June) **15** Commonwealth Day (May 24), Mothering Sunday **19** Feast of Saint Swithin (July 15)
  Canadian: 11 Victoria Day **14** Queen's Birthday, Remembrance Day
  Chinese: 7 New Year **15** Lantern Festival **17** Confucius' Birthday (Sept 28) **18** Dragon Boat Festival
  French: 11 Bastille Day (May 14)
  German: 11 Oktoberfest

  Greek: 7 Genesia **11** Feast of Pots
  Indian: 4 Holi **6** Basant, Diwali (New Year) **17** Hindu fire festival **22** Mahatma Gandhi's Birthday (Oct 2)
  Irish: 16 Saint Patrick's Day (March 17)
  Italian: 13 Liberation Day (April 25)
  Japanese: 11 Hina-Matsuri **12** Children's Day (May 5), Feast of Dolls (March 3) **15** Constitution Day (May 3) **17** Girls' Doll Festival
  Jewish: 5 Purim **6** Sukkot **7** Shavuot, Sukkoth **8** Hanukkah, Passover **9** Yom Kippur **12** Rosh Hashanah **20** Hamishah Assar B'Shevat, The New Year of the Trees **21** Feast of the Tabernacles
  Korean: 6 Ch'usok
  Latin American: 12 Day of the Race
  Moslem: 7 Mouloud **8** Id-al-Adha, Id-al-Fitr **12** Maulid-an-Nabi **14** month of Ramadan
  religious: 6 Advent **7** Lady Day (Mar 25) **8** Epiphany, Shabuoth **9** Candlemas, Mardi Gras, Martinmas (Nov 11), Pentecost **10** Whitsunday **11** All Souls' Day (Nov 2) **12** Ascension Day, Ash Wednesday, Feast of Weeks **13** Shrove Tuesday, Trinity Sunday **15** Annunciation Day (Mar 25) **16** Feast of All Saints **20** Feast of Corpus Christi **23** Day of Our Lady of Guadalupe (Dec 12) **27** Purification of the Virgin Mary **30** Feast of the Immaculate Conception (Dec 8)
  Roman: 7 Feralia **10** Saturnalia
  Scottish: 8 Hogmanay **12** Candlemas Day **19** Festival of the Virgin
  South American: 21 Simon Bolivar's Birthday (July 24)
  Sri Lankan: 5 Wesak
  Soviet Union: 6 May Day (May 1) **14** Lenin's Birthday (April 22) **39** Day of the Great October Socialist Revolution (Nov 7)
  Swedish: 13 Santa Lucia Day (Dec 13)
  Thai: 11 Visakha Puja
  Vietnamese: 3 Tet

holiness 8 sanctity **9** godliness **10** sacredness **11** blessedness, saintliness

Holland *see* **11** Netherlands

holler 4 bark, roar, yell **5** gripe, shout **6** bellow, cry out, grouse **8** complain **9** hue and cry

Holliday, Judy
  real name: 11 Judith Tuvim
  born: 9 New York NY
  roles: 8 Adam's Rib **13** Born Yesterday (Oscar) **15** Bells Are Ringing

Hollinshed, Raphael
  author of: 37 Chronicles of England Scotland and Ireland

hollow 3 dip, low, rut **4** cave, dale, deep, dell, dent, dull, hole, sink, vain, vale, void **5** ditch, empty, false, muted **6** cavern, cavity, crater, dig out, dimple, furrow, futile, groove, pocket, sunken, vacant, vacuum, valley **7** channel, concave, useless **8** crevasse, empty out, excavate, gouge out, indented, not solid, nugatory, rumbling, scoop out, specious, unfilled **9** cavernous, concavity, deceptive, depressed, fruitless, pointless, valueless, worthless **10** depression, profitless, sepulchral, unavailing, unresonant **11** indentation, meaningless, nonresonant **12** unprofitable **13** curving inward, disappointing, reverberating **14** expressionless, unsatisfactory **15** inconsequential

Holloway, Stanley
born: 6 London **7** England
roles: 10 My Fair Lady **15** Alfred Doolittle **18** The Lavender Hill Mob

Hollow Men
author: 7 T S Eliot

hollowness 4 void **6** vacuum **7** vacancy **9** emptiness

hollow out 4 bore **5** drill **6** dig out **8** carve out, gouge out, scoop out **9** chisel out **13** tunnel through

holly 4 Ilex
varieties: 3 box, sea **4** dune **5** Cuban, Dutch, dwarf, false, Furin, Kashi, swamp, Tsuru **6** desert, horned, Oregon, Sarvis, Soyogo, summer **7** African, Chinese, English, Georgia, Madeira **8** American, European, hedgehog, Japanese, Kurogane, mountain **9** box- leaved, Highclere, miniature, moonlight, porcupine, Singapore **10** Costa Rican, luster-leaf, West Indian **11** large-leaved, Puerto Rican, screw-leaved **12** Canary Island, gold hedgehog, myrtle-leaved, smooth-leaved **14** silver hedgehog

hollyhock 6 mallow **7** Antwerp, figleaf **8** biennial **9** ficifolia, Malvaceae **10** alcea rosea

Hollywood's Mermaid
nickname of: 14 Esther Williams

Hollywood Squares
host: 9 Jon Bauman **12** John Davidson **13** Peter Marshall
regular: 8 Wally Cox **10** Joan Rivers **13** Cliff Arquette (Charley Weaver), Shadoe Stevens

Holmes, Oliver Wendell
author of: 12 Old Ironsides **30** The Autocrat of the Breakfast Table

Holmes, Sherlock
address: 11 (221B) Baker Street
appears in: 13 The Sign of Four **14** The Naval Treaty **15** A Study in Scarlet, The Speckled Band **16** Scandal in Bohemia, The Blue Carbuncle, The Copper Beeches **18** The Red-Headed League, The Solitary Cyclist **22** Hound of the Baskervilles
assistants: 21 Baker Street Irregulars
author: 16 (Sir) Arthur Conan Doyle
brother: 7 Mycroft
femme fatale 10 Irene Adler

foe: 17 Professor Moriarty
hat: 11 deerstalker
hobby: 6 violin
housekeeper/landlady: 9 Mrs Hudson
keeps tobacco in: 7 slipper **14** Turkish slipper
police: 17 Inspector Lestrade
sidekick: 12 Dr John Watson

Holmwood, Arthur
character in: 7 Dracula
author: 6 Stoker

holocaust 4 ruin **5** havoc **6** ravage **7** bonfire, carnage, inferno, killing **8** butchery, genocide, massacre **10** deadly fire, mass murder **11** devastation **12** annihilation **13** conflagration

Holofernes
character in: 16 Love's Labour's Lost
author: 11 Shakespeare

Holofernes
general of: 14 Nebuchadnezzar
killed by: 6 Judith

Holst, Gustav Theodore
born: 7 England **10** Cheltenham
composer of: 7 Savitri **10** Egdon Heath, Ode to Death, The Planets **11** Hammersmith **12** St Paul's Suite **13** Fugal Concerto **14** The Hymn of Jesus, The Perfect Fool **16** Somerset Rhapsody **17** The Cloud Messenger **19** Hymns from the Rig-Veda

holy 4 pure **5** godly, moral, pious **6** adored, devout, divine, sacred, solemn **7** angelic, blessed, from God, revered, saintly, sinless **8** faithful, hallowed, heavenly, reverent, virtuous **9** from above, guileless, religious, righteous, spiritual, undefiled, unspotted, unstained, unworldly, venerated, worshiped **10** heaven-sent, immaculate, inviolable, sacrosanct, sanctified, worshipped **11** consecrated, pure in heart, uncorrupted
Latin: 7 sanctus

Holy Ark
Hebrew: 10 Aron Kodesh

holy of holies
Latin: 16 sanctum sanctorum

Holy one *see* **5** Jesus

Holy Spirit, Holy Ghost 9 Paraclete **13** presence of God **23** third person of the Trinity
Latin: 15 Spiritus Sanctus
Greek: 12 Hagion Pneuma

holy war
Arabic: 5 jehad, jihad

Holy Willie's Prayer
author: 11 Robert Burns

Homadus
form: 7 centaur
killed by: 8 Hercules

homage 5 honor **6** esteem, praise, regard **7** respect, tribute, worship **8** devotion **9** adoration, adulation, deference, obeisance, reverence **10** exaltation, veneration **13** glorification

Homagyrius
epithet of: 4 Zeus
means: 9 assembler

hombre 3 man

home 5 abode, haunt, haven, house **6** asylum, cradle, refuge **7** habitat, hangout **8** domicile, dwelling, hospital **9** orphanage, poorhouse, residence **10** habitation, native land, sanatorium **11** institution **12** fountainhead **13** dwelling place, home sweet home **14** stamping ground **16** place of residence **18** natural environment **25** place where one hangs one's hat

Home Burial
author: 11 Robert Frost

homegrown 5 local **6** native **8** domestic **10** indigenous

Home Is the Sailor
author: 10 Jorge Amado

homelike 4 cozy **5** comfy, homey **6** simple **8** cheerful, domestic, familiar, informal, inviting **11** comfortable

homely 4 cozy, drab, snug **5** comfy, homey, plain **6** modest, rustic, simple **7** artless, natural **8** everyday, familiar, homelike, homespun, ordinary, uncomely **9** graceless **10** ill-favored, provincial, unaffected, unassuming, ungraceful, unhandsome **11** comfortable **12** plain-looking, unattractive **13** unpretentious

Homer
author of: 5 Iliad **7** Odyssey

Homer, Winslow
born: 8 Boston MA
painter of: 9 seascapes
artwork: 9 High Cliff **10** Breezing Up, Eight Bells **11** Marine Coast, Northeaster, The Life Line **13** The Fog Warning, The Gulf Stream **21** Inside the Bar Tynemouth, Prisoners from the Front

home rule 8 autonomy **11** sovereignty **12** independence **14** self-government

homespun 5 plain **6** folksy, homely, modest, native, simple **7** artless, natural **8** down-home, homemade **9** handwoven **10** hand-loomed, unaffected **11** hand-crafted, hand-wrought **13** unpretentious

homey 4 cozy **6** casual, folksy **8** down-home, homelike, homespun, informal **15** unsophisticated

homicide 6 killer, murder, slayer **7** slaying **8** foul play, murderer, regicide, vaticide **9** bloodshed, man killer, manslayer, matricide, parricide, patricide, uxoricide **10** fratricide **11** infanticide **12** manslaughter

homiletic 7 preachy **8** didactic **10** moralizing

homily 6 sermon **7** lecture **10** preachment **11** exhortation

homogeneous 4 akin, pure **7** kindred, similar, uniform, unmixed **8** all alike, constant, of a piece **9** identical, unvarying **10** consistent **13** of the same kind, unadulterated

homology 7 analogy **8** likeness, relation **10** similarity **12** relationship **14** correspondence

Honduras
name means: 6 depths
capital/largest city: 11 Tegucigalpa
others: 4 Tela, Yoro **5** Copan, Danli, Lapaz **6** Roatan **7** Gracias, La Ceiba **8** Trujillo, Yuscaran **9** Choluteca, Juticalpa **10** El Progreso **11** Comayaguela **12** Puerto Cortes, San Pedro Sula
measure: 4 vara **5** milla **6** mecate **7** cajuela
monetary unit: 4 peso **7** centavo, lempira
island: 3 Bay **5** Bahia, Utila **6** Roatan **7** Bonacca, Guanaja
lake: 5 Criba, Yojoa **6** Brewer
mountain: 4 Pija **6** Agalta **7** Celaque **9** Esperanza
highest point: 8 Las Minas
river: 4 Coco, Sico, Ulua **5** Aguan, Lempa, Negro, Tinto, Wanks **6** Patuca, Sulaco **7** Olancho, Paulaya, Segovia **8** Guiavope, Santiago **9** Choluteca **10** Chameleton
sea: 7 Pacific **8** Atlantic **9** Caribbean
physical feature:
  coast: 5 North **8** Mosquito **10** Costa Norte
  gulf: 7 Fonseca **8** Honduras
  port: 7 Laceiba **8** Trujillo
people: 4 Maya, Paya, Sumo, Ulva **5** Carib, Lenca, Pipil **6** Tauira **9** Jicaque, mestizo, Miskito **8** Mosquito
  discoverer: 8 Columbus
  farmer: 9 campesino
language: 7 English, Spanish
religion: 13 Roman Catholic
place:
  ruins: 5 Copan **8** Tenampua
feature:
  bird: 9 zenzontle
  dance: 5 sique **7** mascaro
  estate: 10 latifundia
  farm: 6 milpas **10** minifundia
  musical instrument: 7 caramba, marimba
  tree: 8 cockspur
food:
  beans: 8 frijoles
  beef dish: 6 tapado
  corn: 5 maize
  stuffed corn cake: 10 naca tamale
  tripe stew: 8 mondongo
hone 4 long, moan, pine, tool, whet **5** stroke, strope, whine, yearn **6** hanker, grumble, mutter, sharpen **9** whetstone

Honegger, Arthur
born: 5 Havre **6** France
nationality: 5 Swiss
member of: 6 Les Six, The Six
composer of: 5 Rugby **6** Judith **7** L'Aiglon **8** Antigone **9** The Eaglet

10 Le Roi David **13** Pastorale d'ete **18** Jeanne d'Arc au Bucher, Liturgical Symphony **19** Pacific Two-Thirty-One

honest 4 fair, just, open, real, true **5** blunt, frank, legal, plain, solid, valid **6** candid, decent, lawful, proper, square **7** artless, ethical, genuine, sincere, upright **8** bona fide, clear-cut, faithful, innocent, reliable, straight, true-blue, truthful, virtuous **9** authentic, blameless, guileless, honorable, ingenuous, reputable, righteous **10** aboveboard, dependable, forthright, law-abiding, legitimate, on the level, principled, reasonable, scrupulous, unaffected, unreserved **11** plainspoken, trustworthy, undisguised **12** on the up-and-up, tried and true **13** conscientious, fair and square **15** straightforward, unsophisticated **16** as good as one's word, straight-shooting **17** open and aboveboard
honest man: 10 Abe Lincoln
Searcher: 8 Diogenes

honesty 4 word **5** honor **7** probity **8** fairness, good name, morality, scruples, veracity **9** innocence, integrity, rectitude, sincerity **10** principles **11** just dealing, uprightness **12** faithfulness, reputability, truthfulness **13** guiltlessness, square dealing **15** trustworthiness **16** incorruptibility, straight shooting

honeybee
classification: 6 social
live in: 4 hive **6** colony
headed by: 5 queen
male: 5 drone
laborer: 6 worker
food-gatherer: 7 forager
gather: 6 nectar, pollen
produce: 5 honey
queen's food: 10 royal jelly
pertaining to: 5 apian
keeper: 8 apiarist

honeyed 4 kind **5** sweet **6** sugary **7** cloying, fawning **10** flattering, saccharine **12** ingratiating **13** complimentary

honeyed words 4 line **7** blarney **8** cajolery, flattery, soft soap **9** sweet talk

Honey in the Horn
author: 7 H L Davis

Honeymooners, The
character: 8 Ed Norton **12** Alice Kramden, Ralph Kramden, Trixie Norton
cast: 8 Jane Kean **9** Art Carney **12** Sheila MacRae **13** Audrey Meadows, Jackie Gleason, Joyce Randolph
Ralph's job: 9 bus driver
Ed's job: 5 sewer
lodge: 8 Raccoons
Saying: 16 You're the greatest **38** One of these days Alice, pow, right in the kisser

honeysuckle 8 Lonicera **19** Aquilegia canadensis, Justicia californica **24** Rhododendron prinophyllum
varieties: 3 fly **4** bush, cape **5** coral, giant, grape, hairy, swamp **6** desert, French, purple, yellow **7** Arizona, Jamaica, trumpet **8** Himalaya, Japanese, swamp fly, Tatarian **9** chaparral, Tartarian **10** yellow cape **11** European fly **12** giant Burmese, long-flowered, South African **13** Hall's Japanese

Honeythunder, Mr
character in: 22 The Mystery of Edwin Drood
author: 7 Dickens

Hong Kong
name means: 13 incense harbor **14** fragrant harbor
capital: 8 Victoria
largest city:
  section: 7 Kowloon **8** Hong Kong, Victoria
  others: 4 Tai O **5** Tai Po **8** Aberdeen, Pingshan, Yuenlong **9** Shataukok **10** Sheungshui
division: 7 Kowloon **8** Hong Kong **14** New Territories
government: 18 British crown colony
head of state: 14 British monarch **15** governor general
island: 5 Lamma **6** Lan Tao, Lantau, Middle, Poi Toi **8** Hong Kong **9** Ap Lei Chau **11** Stonecutter
mountain: 6 Castle **8** Victoria
highest point: 9 Tai Mo Shan
river: 5 Pearl **6** Canton **8** Sham Chun
sea: 10 South China
physical feature:
  bay: 4 Mirs **6** Quarry **7** Kowloon, Repulse **9** Deep Water
  harbor: 4 Tolo **8** Aberdeen, Hong Kong, Victoria
  peak: 8 Victoria
  peninsula: 7 Kowloon
people: 5 Hakka, Haklo, Punti, Tanka **7** British, Chinese **8** American, Japanese **9** Cantonese **10** Portuguese
language: 7 Chinese, English **9** Cantonese
religion: 5 Hindu, Islam **6** Taoism **8** Buddhism **12** Christianity
feature:
  airport: 6 Kai Tak
  clothing: 6 samfoo **9** cheongsam
  houseboat: 6 sampan
  rock: 5 Amahs **6** Sha Tin
  temple: 18 Ten Thousand Buddhas

Honiara
capital of: 14 Solomon Islands

honi soit qui mal y pense 31 shamed be the one who thinks evil of it
motto of: 16 Order of the Garter

honk 4 toot **5** blare, blast **7** trumpet

honky-tonk 4 dive **7** gin mill **9** roadhouse, nightclub

honor 3 pay 4 cash, fame, laud, note, take 5 adore, exalt, extol, favor, glory, grant, leave, power, right, truth, value 6 accept, admire, credit, esteem, homage, praise, redeem, regard, renown, repute, revere, virtue 7 acclaim, commend, decency, dignify, glorify, honesty, liberty, probity, respect, tribute, worship 8 eminence, fairness, good name, goodness, justness, look up to, make good, pleasure, prestige, sanction, venerate, veracity 9 adoration, celebrity, constancy, deference, greatness, integrity, principle, privilege, rectitude, reverence, sincerity 10 admiration, compliment, exaltation, good report, importance, notability, permission, prominence, veneration 11 acknowledge, approbation, distinction, pay homage to, recognition, think much of, uprightness 12 commendation, faithfulness, high standing, pay tribute to, truthfulness 13 authorization, bow down before, glorification, have regard for, honorableness, make payment on 14 high-mindedness, scrupulousness 15 illustriousness, trustworthiness 17 a feather in one's cap, conscientiousness

honorable 4 good 5 noble, title 6 decent, honest, lordly, square 7 upright 9 elevated, reputable, respected 10 creditable 11 distinctive, illustrious, respectable, trustworthy 12 considerable 13 distinguished

hood 4 cowl, lout, punk 5 bully, rowdy, scarf, tough 6 vandal 7 hoodlum, ruffian 8 hooligan 9 barbarian, roughneck 10 delinquent 12 headcovering, neighborhood

Hood, Raymond
   architect of: 11 RCA Building (Rockefeller Center) 17 Daily News Building (NYC) 18 McGraw-Hill Building (NYC) 22 Chicago Tribune Building 24 American Radiator Building
   style: 13 International

hoodlum 4 hood, punk, thug 5 crook, rowdy, tough 6 gunman 7 bruiser, gorilla, mobster, ruffian 8 criminal, gangster, hooligan, plug-ugly 9 desperado, strong arm 10 delinquent

hoodwink 3 gyp 4 dupe, fool, gull, hoax, rook 5 cheat, cozen, trick 7 deceive, defraud, mislead, swindle 8 inveigle 9 bamboozle, victimize

hook 3 arc, bag, bow, nab, net 4 arch, bend, bill, curl, gaff, grab, loop, take, trap, wind 5 angle, catch, crook, curve, elbow, fluke, hitch, latch, seize, snare 6 buckle, collar, fasten, peavey, secure 7 capture, crampon, ensnare, grapnel, grapple, pothook 8 crescent, make fast 9 horseshoe

Hooke, Robert
   field: 7 physics 9 astronomy
   nationality: 7 British

discovered: 9 Orion star 15 Jupiter rotation 20 moon's center of gravity 21 earth's center of gravity
invented: 10 microscope
named for him: 15 law of elasticity

hooked 8 addicted 9 compelled, obsessive 10 compulsive, habituated 14 uncontrollable

hooked cross
   German: 10 Hakenkreuz

hook up 4 ally, dock, join 5 hinge 6 couple, link up 7 connect 8 assemble 10 articulate 11 fit together 14 fasten together

hooligan 4 hood, lout, punk 5 bully, rowdy, tough 6 vandal 7 hoodlum, ruffian 9 barbarian, roughneck 10 delinquent

hoopla 4 hype 8 ballyhoo 9 promotion, publicity 10 hullabaloo, propaganda 11 advertising 15 public relations

Hoosier Schoolmaster, The
   author: 15 Edward Eggleston
Hoosier State
   nickname of: 7 Indiana

hoot 3 boo, din 4 bawl, blow, hiss, honk, howl, jeer, moan, mock, razz, roar, wail, yelp, yowl 5 shout, sneer, taunt, whoop 6 bellow, chorus, cry out, deride, outcry, racket, scream, shriek, shrill, tumult, uproar 7 catcall, cry down, scoff at, screech, sing out, sneer at, snicker, ululate, wailing, whistle 8 proclaim, shouting 9 caterwaul, commotion, raspberry, screaming, snicker at 10 Bronx cheer, screeching

Hoover, Herbert Clark
   nickname: 13 Great Engineer 14 Great Secretary 17 Great Humanitarian 18 Great Public Servant
   presidential rank: 11 thirty-first
   party: 10 Republican
   state represented: 2 CA
   defeated: 5 (Alfred Emanuel) Smith 6 (George William) Norris, (Norman) Thomas, (William Frederick) Varney, (William Zebulon) Foster 8 (Verne L) Reynolds
   vice president: 6 (Charles) Curtis
   cabinet:
      state: 7 (Henry Lewis) Stimson
      treasury: 5 (Ogden Livingston) Mills 6 (Andrew William) Mellon
      war: 4 (James William) Good 6 (Patrick Jay) Hurley
      attorney general: 8 (William DeWitt) Mitchell
      navy: 5 (Charles Francis) Adams
      postmaster general: 5 (Walter Folger) Brown
      interior: 6 (Ray Lyman) Wilbur
      agriculture: 4 (Arthur Mastick) Hyde
      commerce: 6 (Robert Patterson) Lamont, (Roy Dikeman) Chapin

      labor: 4 (William Nuckles) Doak 5 (James John) Davis
   born: 12 West Branch IA
   died: 13 New York City NY
   buried: 12 West Branch IA
   education:
      University: 8 Stanford
   religion: 5 Quaker 16 Society of Friends
   interests: 7 fishing
   vacation spot: 10 Camp Hoover 11 Rapidan Camp 22 Shenandoah National Park
   author: 7 Memoirs 11 On Growing Up 14 An American Epic 16 Years of Adventure 18 Principles of Mining, The Great Depression 20 America's First Crusade 21 American Individualism, The Challenge to Liberty 24 The Ordeal of Woodrow Wilson 25 The Problems of Lasting Peace 26 The Cabinet and the Presidency 28 Addresses Upon the American Road 51 The State Papers and Other Public Writings of Herbert Hoover
   political career: 19 US Food Administrator
      head of: 23 American Relief Committee 28 Commission for Relief in Belgium
      director: 38 General Relief and Reconstruction of Europe
      member/chairman: 22 Supreme Economic Council
      secretary of: 8 Commerce
      chairman of: 17 Hoover Commissions
   civilian career: 6 author 14 mining engineer 18 consulting engineer
   notable events of lifetime/term: 15 Great Depression
      conference: 11 London Naval
      crash of: 11 stock market
      independence for: 11 Philippines
      Tariff: 11 Hawley-Smoot
   named for him: 11 Hoover apron, Hoover plate (clean plate), Hooverville (shantytown)
   father: 10 Jesse Clark
   mother: 6 Huldah (Randall Minthorn)
   siblings: 3 May 13 Theodore Jesse
   wife: 3 Lou (Henry)
   children: 10 Allan Henry 12 Herbert Clark
   first lady:
      vice president of: 10 Girl Scouts

hop 3 bob 4 ball, jump, leap, prom, romp, skip, step, trip 5 bound, caper, dance, frisk, mixer, vault 6 bounce, gambol, prance, soiree, spring 7 Humulus
   varieties: 4 Wild 5 False 6 Common 8 European, Japanese

hope 3 yen 4 help, wish 5 crave, dream, faith, fancy, trust 6 aspire, belief, chance, desire, expect, hunger, rescue, yen for 7 believe, count on, craving, dream of, longing, long for 8 ambition, daydream, feel sure, optimism, prospect, reckon on, reliance, yearn for, yearning **9** assurance, hankering, have faith, hunger for, salvation, take heart **10** anticipate, aspiration, assumption, be bent upon, confidence, conviction, expectancy **11** be confident, contemplate, expectation, have an eye to, possibility, presumption, reassurance, saving grace **12** anticipation, be optimistic, heart's desire **13** encouragement, have a fancy for, look forward to **14** have a hankering **17** great expectations **18** have one's heart set on **19** look on the bright side

Hope, Anthony
　real name: 21 Sir Anthony Hope Hawkins
　author of: 15 Rupert of Hentzau **18** The Prisoner of Zenda

Hope, Bob
　real name: 16 Leslie Townes Hope
　co-star: 10 Bing Crosby **13** Dorothy Lamour
　born: 6 Eltham **7** England
　roles:
　　Road to: **3** Rio **4** Bali **6** Utopia **7** Morocco **8** Hong Kong, Zanzibar **9** Singapore
　performed for: 3 USO

hopeful 7 assured, in hopes **8** cheering, sanguine, trusting **9** confident, expectant, favorable, fortunate, promising **10** auspicious, heartening, of good omen, optimistic, propitious, reassuring **11** encouraging **12** anticipative

hopeless 3 sad **4** lost, vain **6** abject, futile **7** forlorn, useless **8** dejected, downcast **9** depressed, incurable, pointless **10** beyond help, despairing, despondent, impossible, melancholy, past remedy **11** downhearted, heartbroken, irreparable, irrevocable, pessimistic, sick at heart **12** beyond recall, disconsolate, heavyhearted, irredeemable, irreversible **13** grief-stricken, irretrievable **14** down in the mouth, sorrow-stricken

hopelessness 7 despair **8** futility **9** pessimism **11** uselessness

Hopi (Hopitu, Moki)
　language family: 10 Shoshonean
　location: 7 Arizona
　adapted culture of: 6 Pueblo
　ceremony: 10 snake dance

Hopkins, Anthony
　born: 5 Wales **10** Port Talbot
　roles: 10 Audrey Rose **11** A Doll's House **12** Young Winston **14** The Elephant Man **15** The Lion in Winter

Hopper, Edward
　born: 7 Nyack NY
　artwork: 10 Nighthawks **18** Early Sunday Morning, House by the Railroad **19** Second Story Sunlight **20** Sunlight in a Cafeteria **21** Lighthouse at Two Lights

Horae
　also: 5 Hours
　goddesses of: 5 decay **6** growth **7** seasons **11** social order
　names: 4 Dice, Dike **5** Irene **7** Eunomia

Horatio
　character in: 6 Hamlet
　author: 11 Shakespeare

Horatio
　character in: 17 The Spanish Tragedy
　author: 3 Kyd

Horatius
　origin: 5 Roman
　defended: 6 bridge
　　over: 5 Tiber
　　against: 9 Etruscans

horde 3 mob **4** band, gang, host, pack **5** bunch, crowd, crush, drove, party, swarm, tribe, troop **6** legion, throng **7** company **8** assembly **9** gathering, multitude **10** assemblage **12** congregation

Horgan, Paul
　author of: 10 Whitewater **13** Lamy of Santa Fe **18** The Thin Mountain Air

horizon 4 area **5** field, range, realm, scope, vista, world **6** bounds, domain, sphere **7** compass, expanse, outlook, purview, stretch **8** frontier, prospect **11** perspective

horizontal 4 even, flat **5** flush, level, plane, plumb, prone **6** supine **8** parallel (to something) **9** lying down, prostrate, reclining, recumbent **14** flat on one's back

horizontal support 3 tie **4** beam **5** brace, joist **6** girder, header, lintel **8** crossbar

hormone 4 ACTH **5** auxin **6** cortin **7** estrone, insulin, steroid **8** endocrin, estrogen, galactin, lactogen, secretin **9** adrenalin, cortisone **12** progesterone, testosterone

horn 4 tusk **5** cornu, point, spike **6** antler **11** excrescence
　brass instrument: 4 oboe, tuba **5** bugle **6** cornet **7** bassoon, trumpet **8** alto horn, baritone, clarinet, trombone **9** euphonium, saxophone **10** French horn, mellophone, sousaphone **11** English horn

Horn of Africa *see* **7** Somalia

Hornung, Paul
　nickname: 9 Golden Boy
　sport: 8 football
　position: 6 runner **11** placekicker
　team: 15 Green Bay Packers

horny 4 hard **5** tough **7** callous, lustful **8** callused, hardened **12** thick-skinned **14** pachydermatous

horologe 5 clock **9** timepiece **11** chronometer

horoscope *see* **9** astrology

horrendous 4 gory **5** awful **6** horrid **7** ghastly, hideous **8** dreadful, horrible, shocking, terrible **9** appalling, frightful, repellent, repulsive, revolting **10** horrifying

horrible 3 bad **4** foul, rank, vile **5** awful, nasty **6** grisly, horrid, odious **7** ghastly, hideous **8** dreadful, gruesome, shocking, terrible, unsavory **9** abhorrent, appalling, atrocious, frightful, harrowing, loathsome, monstrous, obnoxious, repellent, repulsive, revolting, sickening **10** abominable, despicable, detestable, disgusting, forbidding, nauseating, unbearable, unpleasant **11** disquieting, distasteful, unspeakable **12** disagreeable, insufferable

horrid 3 bad **4** foul, grim, ugly **5** awful, nasty, rough **6** bratty, horror, shaggy, wicked **7** fearful, hideous **8** dreadful, gruesome, horrible, shocking, terrible **9** bristling, frightful, offensive, revolting, vexatious **10** abominable, detestable, unpleasant **11** troublesome **12** disagreeable

horrific 4 dire **5** awful **7** fearful, ghastly **8** dreadful, horrible, shocking, terrible **9** appalling

horrified 6 aghast **8** appalled **9** petrified, terrified **10** frightened **13** thunderstruck **14** terror-stricken

horrify 5 daunt, repel, shock **6** appall, dismay, revolt, sicken **7** disgust, petrify, terrify **8** affright, disquiet, frighten, nauseate **10** disconcert, dishearten **11** make one sick **15** make one turn pale **18** make one's flesh creep **22** make one's hair stand on end

horrifying 5 awful, dread **8** alarming, dreadful **10** terrifying **11** frightening, hair-raising

horror 3 woe **4** fear **5** alarm, crime, dread, panic **6** dismay, hatred, misery, terror **7** anguish, cruelty, disgust, dislike, outrage, torment **8** atrocity, aversion, distaste, distress, hardship, loathing **9** antipathy, awfulness, privation, repulsion, revulsion, suffering **10** abhorrence, affliction, discomfort, inhumanity, repugnance **11** abomination, detestation, hideousness, trepidation **12** apprehension, terribleness, wretchedness

horror-struck 6 aghast **7** fearful **8** appalled **9** horrified, terrified **10** frightened **13** scared to death

hors de combat 8 disabled **13** out of the fight

hors d'oeuvre 3 dip **6** canape, relish, tidbit **9** antipasto, appetizer **10** finger food

horse 4 colt, foal, hack, jade, mare, plug, pony, sire, stud **5** bronc, filly, mount, pacer, pinto, steed **6** bronco, dobbin, equine, nellie **7** cavalry,

charger, cow pony, gelding, hackney, hussars, lancers, mustang, palfrey, trotter **8** cossacks, dragoons, galloper, stallion, troopers, yearling **9** broodmare, racehorse **10** cavalrymen, draft horse **12** horse cavalry, horse marines, quarter horse, thoroughbred **13** horse soldiers, mounted troops **15** mounted troopers, mounted warriors
Achilles': **7** Xanthus
Alexander the Great's: **10** Bucephalus
anatomy: **4** hock, hoof, loin, mane, tail **5** croup, flank, shank **6** cannon, gaskin, haunch, stifle **7** coronet, crupper, fetlock, gambrel, nostril, pastern, withers **11** throatlatch
Australian: **5** myall **8** warragal, warrigal, yarraman
breed: **6** Morgan, Nubian, Tarpan **7** Arabian, Belgian, mustang **8** Galloway, Shetland **9** Appaloosa, Percheron **10** Clydesdale, Lippizaner **12** Narragansett, Standardbred, Thoroughbred **15** Tennessee-Walker
Bellerophon's: **7** Pegasus
Caligula's: **9** Incitatus (made a senator)
castrated: **7** gelding
color: **3** bay, dun **4** gray, pied, roan, zain **5** morel, pinto **6** calico, dapple, sorrel **7** piebald **8** chestnut, palomino, schimmel (gray)
combining form: **4** eque, equi **5** hippo
Dick Turpin's: **9** Black Bess
Don Quixote's: **9** Rosinante
family: **7** Equidae **9** Miohippus, Orohippus
female: **3** dam **4** mare **5** filly
French: **6** cheval
gear: **3** bit **4** rein, tack **6** saddle **7** blinder, harness, snaffle **9** surcingle **11** saddlecloth
Gen Custer's: **8** Comanche
Gen Grant's: **10** Cincinnati
Gen Robert E Lee's: **9** Traveller
Gen Sherman's: **6** Rienzi
genus: **5** equus
Gulliver's Travels: **9** Houyhnhnm
kind: **3** cob **4** race **6** bronco, hunter, jumper **7** charger, mustang, palfrey, quarter, trotter **8** destrier
legendary: **6** Trojan
Lone Ranger's: **6** Silver
male: **4** colt **8** stallion
measure: **4** hand
Mohammed's: **7** Alborak
movie/story: **6** Flicka **8** Champion **11** Black Beauty **14** National Velvet **16** The Black Stallion
Napoleon's: **7** Marengo
Odin's: **8** Sleipnir
Orlando's: **11** Vegliantino
pace: **4** lope, trot **5** amble **6** canter, gallop
pair of: **4** span, team **6** tandem
race: **5** derby, plate **6** exacta **7** pick

six **8** claiming, handicap **9** allowance **11** daily double, sweepstakes **12** steeplechase, weight-for-age
  Triple Crown: **7** Belmont **9** Preakness **13** Kentucky Derby
riding show: **8** gymkhana
riding sport: **4** polo
Rinaldo's: **6** Bayard
Roy Rogers': **7** Trigger
Siegfried's: **5** Grani
small: **4** pony
Stonewall Jackson's: **12** Little Sorrel
Tom Mix's: **4** Tony
Tonto's: **5** Scout
television: **4** Mr. Ed
three: **6** random, troika **7** unicorn
Wellington's (at Waterloo): **10** Copenhagen
wild: **5** fuzzy **6** bramby, kumrah, outlaw, tarpan **7** jughead **8** bangtail, fuzztail, warragal, warrigal
Will Rogers': **8** Soapsuds **10** Bootlegger
winged: **7** Pegasus
young: **4** colt, foal **5** filly **8** yearling

horseback riding
athlete: **11** Frank Chapot **17** William Steinkraus
horse collar 3 zip **4** zero **5** aught, zilch **6** cipher, naught **8** goose egg
Horse Knows the Way, The
author: **9** John O'Hara
horseman 5 groom, rider **6** hussar, jockey, lancer, ostler **7** cossack, dragoon, hostler, trainer, trooper **9** postilion, stableboy, stableman **10** cavalryman, equestrian, roughrider **11** horse marine, horse breeder, horse soldier, stable keeper **14** cavalry soldier, horseback rider, mounted trooper
horseplay 6 pranks **7** foolery **9** cutting up **10** buffoonery, tomfoolery **13** fooling around, horsing around
horse racing
jockey: **8** Del Insko **11** Bill Hartack, Eddie Arcaro **12** Angel Cordero, Bill Haughton, Laffit Pincay, Steve Cauthen **13** Johnny Longden, Stanley Dancer **15** Willie Shoemaker
god of: **6** Consus
Horseshoe Robinson
author: **12** John P Kennedy
horse soldier 6 hussar, lancer **7** dragoon, trooper **8** cavalier, horseman **10** cavalryman
horse trooper 6 hussar, lancer **7** dragoon, Mountie **8** cavalier, horseman **10** cavalryman **12** horse soldier **14** mounted soldier **16** mounted policeman
Horton, Edward Everett
sidekick of: **11** Fred Astaire
born: **10** Brooklyn NY
roles: **15** Cinderella Jones, Her Primitive Man **18** Springtime for Henry
Horus

origin: **8** Egyptian
god of: **3** sun
Greek name: **10** Harcorates
symbol: **6** falcon
mother: **4** Isis
father: **6** Osiris
enemy: **3** Set **4** Seth
hosannas 4 yeas **5** kudos **6** bravos, cheers, paeans **7** acclaim, hurrahs, huzzahs, yippees **8** applause **10** hallelujas **11** halleluiahs
hose, hosiery 5 socks **6** nylons, tights **7** anklets, argyles, hosiery **9** kneehighs, pantyhose, stockings **10** bobbysocks
Hosea
father: **5** Beeri
hospitable 4 open, warm **6** genial **7** cordial **8** amenable, amicable, friendly, gracious, sociable, tolerant **9** agreeable, convivial, receptive, welcoming **10** accessible, gregarious, neighborly, openhanded, openminded, responsive **12** approachable
hospital 4 home **6** asylum, clinic **7** sick bay **8** pavilion, rest home **9** infirmary **10** polyclinic, sanatorium **11** nursing home **12** medical center
French: **9** hotel Dieu
hospital, private
French: **13** maison de sante
hospitality 5 cheer **6** warmth **7** welcome **8** openness **9** geniality **10** cordiality, heartiness, kindliness **11** amicability, sociability **12** congeniality, conviviality, friendliness **13** Gemutlichkeit **14** hospitableness, neighborliness **15** warmheartedness
god of: **6** Sancus **10** Dius Fidius, Semo Sancus
host, hostess 3 lot, mob **4** army, band, body, crew, gang, mess **5** array, crowd, drove, emcee, group, horde, party, swarm, troop **6** legion, throng **7** company, maitre d', meeting **8** conclave, congress, hosteler, hotelier, landlord, welcomer **9** gathering, innkeeper, multitude **10** confluence, convention, headwaiter, party giver, proprietor **11** convocation, hotel keeper **12** congregation, head waitress, hotel manager, proprietress, receptionist **17** restaurant manager **18** master of ceremonies **20** mistress of ceremonies
hostage 6 pledge **7** captive **8** prisoner
Hostage, The
author: **12** Brendan Behan
hostel 3 inn **4** hall **5** hotel, lodge **7** hospice, lodging, shelter **8** hospital, hostelry
hostile 3 icy **4** cold, mean, ugly **5** angry, at war, enemy, testy **6** at odds, at outs, bitter, chilly, cranky, malign, touchy, unkind **7** opposed, vicious, warring **8** battling, clashing, contrary, fighting, opposing, snappish, spiteful, venomous **9** bellicose, bristling, dissi-

dent, malicious, malignant, truculent **10** contending, ill-natured, malevolent, on bad terms, unfriendly **11** belligerent, contentious, disagreeing, ill-disposed, quarrelsome **12** antagonistic, cantankerous, disagreeable, disputatious, incompatible **13** argumentative, at loggerheads, unsympathetic

hostile act 4 raid **6** strike, threat **7** assault, offense **8** act of war, invasion **9** hostility, incursion **10** aggression

hostile nation 3 foe **5** enemy **7** invader

hostility 3 war **4** duel, feud, fray, hate **5** anger, clash, fight, venom **6** battle, combat, enmity, fracas, hatred, malice, rancor, spleen **7** contest, dispute, ill will, scuffle, warfare, warring **8** act of war, argument, battling, conflict, fighting **9** animosity, antipathy, bickering **10** antagonism, bitterness, contention, dissidence, opposition, state of war **11** altercation, malevolence, viciousness **12** belligerence, contrariness, disagreement **14** unfriendliness, vindictiveness

hot 3 new, top **4** good, late, live, near, warm **5** fiery, fresh, nippy, sharp **6** ardent, baking, biting, fervid, fierce, heated, hectic, latest, molten, raging, recent, red-hot, stormy, sultry, torrid **7** boiling, burning, earnest, excited, furious, intense, melting, peppery, piquant, popular, pungent, searing, violent **8** agitated, animated, broiling, feverish, frenzied, roasting, scalding, sizzling, steaming, vehement, very warm **9** emotional, excellent, scorching, simmering, very close, wrought-up **10** attractive, blistering, passionate, smoldering, successful, sweltering **11** electrified, fast-selling, most popular, radioactive, sought after, tempestuous **12** incandescent **14** fast and furious, highly seasoned, in close pursuit

hot air 7 bombast **8** rhetoric **9** hyperbole **12** exaggeration **13** overstatement

hotel de ville 9 a city hall
  literally: **16** mansion of the city

hotel Dieu 9 a hospital **12** mansion of God

Hotel New Hampshire, The
  author: **10** John Irving

hothouse 6 tender **7** fragile, nursery **8** delicate **10** glasshouse, greenhouse **12** conservatory **13** over-protected

hot temper 4 fire **5** anger **6** pepper **8** acrimony **9** short fuse

hot-tempered 7 peppery **9** emotional, excitable **13** easily ruffled, quick-tempered

hot water 3 jam **4** mess **6** pickle **7** trouble **10** difficulty **11** predicament

Houghston, Walter
  real name of: **12** Walter Huston

hound 3 dog, fan, nag, nut, pup **4** bait, buff, hunt, mutt, tail **5** annoy, chase, doggy, freak, harry, lover, pooch, puppy, stalk, track, trail, whelp, worry **6** addict, badger, canine, follow, harass, hector, keep at, needle, pester, pursue **7** bedevil, poochie **9** keep after **10** aficionado, hunting dog **11** afficionado
  dog breed: **6** beagle, borzoi, saluki **7** basenji, harrier, whippet **9** dachshund, greyhound **10** bloodhound, otter hound **11** Afghan hound, basset hound, Ibizan hound **12** pharaoh hound **14** Irish wolfhound **15** English foxhound **16** American foxhound **17** Norwegian elkhound, Scottish deerhound **18** Rhodesian ridgeback **20** black and tan coonhound
  group of: **3** cry **4** mute, pack

Hound of the Baskervilles, The
  author: **19** Sir Arthur Conan Doyle
  character: **8** Dr Watson **11** Sherlock Holmes **19** Sir Henry Baskerville

hour 3 day **4** span, time **5** space **6** period **8** interval
  abbreviation: **2** hr

Hour *see* **5** Horae

house, House 4 clan, firm, hall, home, keep, line, shop **5** abode, board, lodge, put up, store **6** billet, church, family, garage, harbor, strain, temple **7** Commons, company, concern, contain, council, descent, dynasty, lineage, quarter, shelter, theater **8** ancestry, assembly, audience, building, business, congress, domicile, dwelling **9** ancestors, household, residence **10** auditorium, family tree, habitation, hippodrome, opera house, spectators **11** accommodate, concert hall, corporation, legislature, noble family, partnership, royal family **12** business firm, lower chamber, meeting place, organization **13** dwelling place, establishment
  god of: **8** Silvanus, Sylvanus

housebreaker 5 thief **6** robber **7** burglar **8** pilferer **9** purloiner **10** cat burglar **14** second-story man

housebreaking 5 theft **7** break-in, robbery **8** burglary, stealing **12** burglarizing **19** breaking and entering

House Divided, A
  author: **9** Pearl Buck

House for Mr Biswas, A
  author: **9** V S Naipaul

household 4 home **5** house **6** family, hearth, menage **8** of a house **9** for a house **10** for a family, for home use **12** family circle
  goddess of: **6** Brigit

household gods 5 lares, Roman **7** penates

household help 4 cook, maid **7** foot-

man, steward **8** domestic, gardener, handyman, houseboy **9** charwoman, chauffeur, domestics, majordomo, nursemaid **11** housekeeper

household of three
  French: **12** menage a trois

House of Atreus, The
  author: **9** Aeschylus
  character: **7** Electra, Orestes **9** Aegisthus, Agamemnon, Cassandra **12** Clytemnestra

house of health
  French: **13** maison de sante

House of Mirth, The
  author: **12** Edith Wharton
  character: **8** Lily Bart, Mr Selden **9** Gus Trenor **10** Judy Trenor, Mr Rosedale, Percy Gryce **12** Bertha Dorset, George Dorset

House of the Seven Gables, The
  author: **18** Nathaniel Hawthorne
  character: **10** Mr Holgrave **14** Phoebe Pyncheon **16** Clifford Pyncheon **20** Judge Jaffrey Pyncheon, Miss Hepzibah Pyncheon

house of worship 6 chapel, church, mosque, temple **8** basilica **9** cathedral, synagogue **10** house of God, Lord's house, tabernacle

housewife 4 wife **8** hausfrau **9** homemaker **11** housekeeper

housing 4 case, home **5** abode, house **6** casing, jacket, sheath, shield **7** lodging, shelter **8** covering, domicile, dwelling, envelope, lodgment, quarters **9** enclosure, residence **10** habitation **14** accommodations

Housman, A E
  author of: **14** A Shropshire Lad

Houston
  baseball team: **6** Astros
  basketball team: **6** Comets **7** Rockets
  canal: **11** Houston Ship
  channel: **12** Buffalo Bayou
  football team: **6** Oilers **8** Gamblers
  landmark: **4** NASA **12** Alley Theater **14** Jesse Jones Hall **22** Manned Spacecraft Center **29** San Jacinto Battlefield Monument
  battleship: **5** Texas
  named after: **10** Sam Houston
  planned by: **7** A C Allen, J K Allen
  stadium: **9** Astrodome
  street: **15** Old Spanish Trail
  university: **4** Rice **12** Texas Medical **13** Texas Southern

Houston, Sam
  position: **9** US Senator
  governor of: **5** Texas **9** Tennessee
  president of: **15** Republic of Texas
  served in: **9** Creek Wars **15** Texas Revolution
  battle: **10** San Jacinto
  defeated: **9** Santa Anna

Houyhnhnms
  race of horses in: **16** Gulliver's

Travels
author: 5 Swift

hovel 3 hut **4** dump, hole **5** cabin, shack **6** shanty

hover 4 flit, hang **5** float, haunt, pause, poise, waver **6** attend, falter, seesaw **7** flitter, flutter **9** fluctuate, hang about, vacillate

Hovhaness, Alan
born: 12 Somerville MA
composer of: 10 Magnificat

how
Latin: 7 quo modo

Howard, Catherine
husband: 9 Henry VIII
number: 5 fifth
fate: 8 beheaded

Howard, Ron
born: 2 OK **6** Duncan
roles: 4 Opie **9** Happy Days **16** American Graffiti, Richie Cunningham **19** The Andy Griffith Show
director of: 6 Cocoon, Gung Ho, Splash, Willow

Howard, Sidney
author of: 13 The Silver Cord **22** They Knew What They Wanted

Howard, Trevor
born: 7 England **12** Cliftonville
roles: 6 The Key **13** Ryan's Daughter, Sons and Lovers **14** Brief Encounter **23** The Invincible Mr Disraeli

Howards End
author: 9 E M Forster
character: 9 Jacky Bast **10** Paul Wilcox, Ruth Wilcox **11** Henry Wilcox, Leonard Bast **13** Charles Wilcox, Helen Schlegel **16** Margaret Schlegel, Theobald Schlegel

how are you
German: 8 wie geht's **9** wie geht es

Howe, Elias
nationality: 8 American
invented: 13 sewing machine

Howells, William Dean
author of: 12 Indian Summer **15** A Modern Instance **20** A Hazard of New Fortunes, The Rise of Silas Lapham

How Green Was My Valley
author: 16 Richard Llewellyn
director: 8 John Ford
character: 6 Marged **7** Bronwen **10** Beth Morgan **11** Iestyn Evans **12** Gwilym Morgan
Morgan children: 4 Davy, Huur, Ivor, Owen **5** Ianto **6** Gwilym **8** Angharad
cast: 7 Anna Lee **9** John Loder **11** Donald Crisp **12** Maureen O'Hara **13** Roddy McDowall, Walter Pidgeon
Oscar for: 7 picture **8** director **15** supporting actor (Crisp)

howl 3 bay, cry **4** bark, hoot, roar, wail, yell, yelp, yowl **5** groan, shout, whine **6** bellow, clamor, cry out, outcry, scream, shriek, uproar **7** ululate

howler 4 goof **5** error **6** boo-boo **7** blooper, blunder, mistake

How To Win Friends and Influence People
author: 12 Dale Carnegie

hoyden 3 imp **4** brat, chit **6** tomboy

Hoyle, Edmund 9 authority, (card games)

Hoyle, Fred
field: 9 astronomy
nationality: 7 British
developed: 17 steady-state theory

Hoyt, Rosemary
character in: 16 Tender Is the Night
author: 10 Fitzgerald

Hsitsang *see* **5** Tibet

Hualapai
language family: 5 Yuman
location: 7 Arizona
related to: 7 Yavapai **9** Havasupai

hub 3 nub **4** axis, core **5** focus, heart, pivot **6** center, middle **10** focal point

Hubble, Edwin Powell
field: 9 astronomy
studied: 15 galactic nebulae
named for him: 14 Hubble constant, space telescope

hubbub 3 din **4** fuss, stir, to-do **5** noise **6** babble, bedlam, bustle, clamor, pother, racket, ruckus, tumult, uproar **7** ferment, turmoil **8** disorder **9** agitation, commotion, confusion, hue and cry **10** hullabaloo, hurly-burly **11** disturbance, pandemonium **12** perturbation

Hubert
creator: 11 Dick Wingert

huckleberry 9 Vaccinium **11** Gaylussacia
varieties: 2 He **3** Box, Red **4** Blue, Shot **5** Black, Dwarf, Hairy, Squaw, Sugar **6** Garden **8** Thin-leaf **9** Evergreen **10** California, Little-leaf

Huckleberry Finn (The Adventures of)
author: 9 Mark Twain
character: 3 Jim **9** Tom Sawyer **12** Widow Douglas **13** Judge Thatcher

huckster 5 adman **6** badger, hawker, kidder, seller, vendor **7** haggler, peddler

Hud
director: 10 Martin Ritt
cast: 10 John Ashley, Paul Newman **12** Patricia Neal **13** Melvyn Douglas **14** Brandon de Wilde
Oscar for: 7 actress (Neal) **15** supporting actor (Douglas)

huddle 4 heap, herd, mass, mess **5** bunch, crowd, group **6** cuddle, curl up, jumble, medley, muddle, nestle, throng **7** cluster, collect, meeting, snuggle **8** converge, disarray, disorder **9** confusion, gathering **10** conference, discussion, hodge-podge **12** think session

Hudibras
author: 12 Samuel Butler
character: 6 Ralpho **8** Crowders **9** Sidrophel

Hudson, Rock
real name: 12 Roy Scherer Jr
co-star: 8 Doris Day
born: 10 Winnetka IL
roles: 5 Giant **10** Pillow Talk **15** A Farewell to Arms, McMillan and Wife **20** Magnificent Obsession

Hudson, W H
author of: 13 Green Mansions, The Purple Land **17** Far Away and Long Ago
bird-girl: 4 Rima

hue 4 cast, tint, tone **5** color, shade, tinge **8** tincture **10** coloration

hue and cry 4 call, howl, roar, yell, yowl **5** alarm, alert, shout, storm **6** bellow, clamor, hubbub, outcry, shriek, uproar **7** thunder **10** cry of alarm, hullabaloo

huff 3 pet **4** fury, rage, snit **7** bad mood, dudgeon, outrage **8** ill humor, vexation **9** annoyance, petulance **10** fit of anger, fit of pique, resentment

huffy 4 curt, hurt **5** angry, cross, irate, moody, sulky, surly, testy **6** cranky, grumpy, moping, morose, shirty, sullen, touchy **7** in a snit, peevish, waspish, wounded **8** churlish, offended, petulant, snappish **9** glowering, in a lather, in a pucker, irritable, querulous, rancorous, resentful, sensitive **10** ill-humored, out of sorts **11** disgruntled, quarrelsome, thin-skinned **12** discontented **14** easily offended, hard to live with, hypersensitive

hug 4 hold **5** clasp **6** clutch, cuddle, nestle **7** cling to, embrace, snuggle, squeeze **9** hold close, hover near **11** keep close to **13** cling together, follow closely **15** parallel closely, press to the bosom

huge 4 vast **5** giant, great, jumbo **6** mighty **7** immense, mammoth, massive, titanic **8** colossal, enormous, gigantic, imposing **9** cyclopean, extensive, herculean, leviathan, monstrous **10** gargantuan, monumental, prodigious, staggering, stupendous **11** elephantine, extravagant, spectacular **12** overwhelming **14** Brobdingnagian

hugeness 4 bulk **8** enormity, vastness **9** great size, immensity, largeness, magnitude **11** massiveness

Huggins, Charles Brenton
field: 10 physiology
researched: 6 cancer **12** chemotherapy
awarded: 10 Nobel Prize

Hughes, Langston
author of: 9 The Big Sea **12** One-Way Ticket **13** The Weary Blues **19** Shakespeare in Harlem **20** The Panther and the Lash

Hughes, Richard
author of: **18** A High Wind in Jamaica

Hughes, Thomas
author of: **19** Tom Brown's Schooldays

Hugh the Drover
opera by: **15** Vaughan Williams
character: **4** Mary **12** The Constable **14** John the Butcher

Hugin
origin: **12** Scandinavian
form: **5** raven
owned by: **4** Odin **5** Othin
personifies: **7** thought
duty: **10** newsbearer
other raven: **5** Munin

Hugo, Victor
author of: **7** Ruy Blas **13** Les Miserables **16** Notre Dame de Paris **23** The Hunchback of Notre Dame
character: **6** Javert **9** Esmeralda, Quasimodo **11** Jean Valjean

hulk 4 ship **5** giant, wreck **8** behemoth

hulking 3 big **5** bulky, heavy, husky **7** massive **8** powerful, unwieldy **9** oversized, ponderous **10** cumbersome

hull 3 pod **4** case, husk, peel, rind, skin **5** shell, shuck **7** coating **8** carapace **9** epidermis, tegmentum **10** integument

Hull, Isaac
served in: **19** War of Eighteen-Twelve
sunk ship: **9** Guerriere (British)
commander of ship: **12** Constitution

hullabaloo 3 din **4** stir **5** babel **6** bedlam, clamor, hubbub, ruckus, tumult, uproar **9** confusion **11** pandemonium
Yiddish: **7** tzimmes

hum 4 buzz, purr, whir **5** croon, drone, thrum **6** be busy, bustle, intone, murmur, thrive **7** buzzing, droning, purring, vibrate **8** be active, whirring **9** vibration **10** faint sound **13** be in full swing

human 3 man **5** of man, of men **6** gentle, humane, kindly, mortal, person **7** hominid, like man, manlike **8** merciful, personal **10** anthropoid, individual **11** Homo sapiens, sympathetic

Human Comedy, The
author: **14** Honore de Balzac, William Saroyan

Human Condition, The
author: **12** Hannah Arendt

humane 4 kind **5** human **6** kindly, tender **7** pitying **8** merciful **9** unselfish **10** benevolent, bighearted, charitable, goodwilled **11** magnanimous, sympathetic, warmhearted **12** humanitarian **13** compassionate, philanthropic

Human Factor, The
author: **12** Graham Greene

humanitarian 4 kind **6** humane **8**
generous **10** altruistic, benevolent, charitable **11** kind-hearted **12** largehearted **13** compassionate, philanthropic **14** philanthropist

humanity 3 man **4** love **5** mercy **6** people **7** charity, mankind, mortals **8** goodwill, kindness, sympathy **9** humankind, humanness, mortality **10** compassion, gentleness, humaneness, kindliness, tenderness **11** benevolence, Homo sapiens, human beings, human nature, magnanimity **12** the human race **13** brotherly love, fellow feeling **15** warmheartedness **16** fraternal feeling

humanum est errare 12 to err is human

Humbert Humbert
character in: **6** Lolita
author: **7** Nabokov

humble 3 low **4** meek, poor **5** abase, abash, crush, lower, lowly, plain, shame **6** common, debase, demean, demure, gentle, modest, shabby, simple, subdue **7** chasten, conquer, degrade, mortify, obscure, put down **8** bring low, derogate, disgrace, dishonor, inferior, ordinary, plebeian, pull down, wretched **9** bring down, embarrass, humiliate, make lowly, miserable **10** inglorious, low-ranking, make humble, obsequious, put to shame, respectful, unassuming **11** deferential, subservient, unimportant, unpresuming **12** self-effacing, take down a peg **13** insignificant, unpretentious **14** unostentatious **15** inconsequential, undistinguished

humbled 5 cowed **7** abashed, debased, subdued **9** conquered, disgraced **10** brought low, humiliated

Humboldt, Alexander von
nationality: **6** German
originator of: **7** ecology **10** geophysics

Humboldt's Gift
author: **10** Saul Bellow

humbug 3 fib, gyp, lie **4** bull, bunk, dupe, fake, fool, gull, hoax, liar, lies, sham **5** cheat, cozen, dodge, faker, fraud, hokum, lying, quack, spoof, trick **6** bunkum, con man, deceit, fibber, phooey, take in **7** beguile, blather, cheater, deceive, falsify, fiction, forgery, mislead, rubbish, sharper, swindle **8** artifice, claptrap, flimflam, flummery, hoodwink, impostor, nonsense, perjurer, pretense, swindler, trickery **9** bamboozle, charlatan, deception, fabricate, falsehood, hypocrisy, hypocrite, imposture, mendacity, poppycock, trickster **10** balderdash, hocus-pocus, mountebank, pretension **11** counterfeit, make-believe **12** equivocation, misrepresent **13** confidence man, double-dealing, falsification **15** pretentiousness

humdinger 4 lulu, oner **5** dandy, doozy **6** beauty, hummer, marvel **8** Jim dandy, superior **10** ripsnorter **12** lollapalooza **13** extraordinary

humdrum 4 blah, dull, dumb, flat **5** banal, trite **6** boring, common, dreary **7** insipid, mundane, routine, tedious, trivial **8** everyday, lifeless, mediocre, ordinary, tiresome, wearying **9** hackneyed, unvarying, wearisome **10** monotonous, pedestrian, uneventful, unexciting, uninspired **11** commonplace, indifferent, uninspiring **12** conventional, run-of-the-mill **13** unexceptional, uninteresting

humerus
bone of: **8** upper arm

humid 4 damp, dank **5** moist, muggy, soppy **6** clammy, steamy, sticky, sultry

humidity 4 smog **8** dampness, moisture **9** mugginess **10** stickiness

humiliate 5 abash, crush, shame **6** debase, humble, subdue **7** chagrin, chasten, degrade, mortify, put down **8** belittle, bring low, disgrace, dishonor **9** discomfit, embarrass **11** make ashamed **13** bring down a peg

humiliated 7 abashed, crushed, debased, humbled **8** degraded **9** chagrined, disgraced, mortified

humiliation 5 shame **7** chagrin **8** disgrace, dishonor **9** abasement **10** debasement **11** degradation **12** discomfiture **13** embarrassment, mortification

humility 7 modesty, shyness **8** meekness, timidity **9** lowliness **10** demureness, diffidence, humbleness **11** bashfulness **13** self-abasement **17** unpretentiousness

hummock 4 hill, rise **5** knoll, mound **7** hillock, tussock

Humologumena 17 New Testament books

humor 3 wit **4** baby, gags, mood, puns **5** farce, jests, jokes, spoil **6** cajole, comedy, joking, pamper, parody, satire, soothe, suffer, temper, whimsy **7** appease, flatter, foolery, fooling, indulge, jesting, mollify, placate, spirits, waggery **8** drollery, give in to, jocosity, low humor, nonsense, raillery, ridicule, tolerate, travesty, wordplay **9** burlesque, funniness, low comedy, put up with, slapstick, wittiness **10** buffoonery, caricature, comicality, comply with, high comedy, jocoseness, jocularity, tomfoolery, wisecracks, witticisms **11** broad comedy, disposition, foolishness, frame of mind, go along with **12** monkeyshines **13** ludicrousness **14** ridiculousness

humorist 3 wag, wit **4** card **5** comic **8** comedian

humorous 5 comic, droll, funny, witty **6** jocose **7** amusing, comical, jocular, waggish **8** farcical, mirthful, sportive

9 facetious, laughable, ludicrous, satirical, whimsical 10 ridiculous 11 nonsensical, rib-tickling 13 sidesplitting

hump 4 arch, bend, bump, knob, lift, lump, rise 5 bulge, hunch, knurl, mound, put up, tense 8 swelling 9 convexity 10 projection, prominence 11 excrescence

Humperdinck, Engelbert
born: 4 Bonn 7 Germany
composer of: 10 The Miracle 15 Hansel and Gretel

Humphry Clinker
author: 19 Tobias George Smollet
character: 10 Mr Dennison 12 Jerry Melford, Lydia Melford 14 George Dennison, Matthew Bramble 15 Winifred Jenkins 18 Miss Tabitha Bramble 26 Lieutenant Obadiah Lismahago

Humpty Dumpty
character in: 12 nursery rhyme 22 Through the Looking Glass
author: 7 Carroll

hunch 4 arch, bend, clue, hump, idea 5 tense 7 feeling, glimmer, inkling 8 good idea 9 intuition, suspicion 10 foreboding 11 premonition 12 presentiment

Hunchback of Notre Dame, The
author: 10 Victor Hugo
character: 9 Esmeralda, Gringoire, Quasimodo 12 Claude Frollo 20 Phoebus de Chateaupers

hunched 4 bent 7 crooked, slumped, stooped 9 contorted

hundredweight
abbreviation: 3 cwt

Hungary
capital/largest city: 8 Budapest
others: 4 Gyor, Pecs 5 Harta 6 Mohacs, Sopron, Szeged 7 Komarom, Miskolc, Szentes 8 Dubrecen, Kaposuar, Szegedin 9 Kecskemet 10 Albertirsa 11 Nagykanizsa, Szombathely
measure: 3 ako 4 hold, yoke 5 itcze, marok, metze 7 huvelyk
monetary unit: 4 gara 5 balas, krone, pengo 6 filler, forint, gulden, korona, ongara, ungara
weight: 7 vamfont 8 vammazsa
island: 8 Margaret
lake: 5 Ferto 7 Balaton, Velence 9 Blatensee 10 Neusiedler, Plattensee
mountain: 4 Alps, Bukk 5 Matra, Tatra 6 Bakony, Mecsek, Vertes 7 Cserhat, Gerecse 8 Borzsony, Zempleni 9 Korishegy 10 Carpathian
highest point: 5 Kekes
river: 3 Mur, Sio 4 Duna, Raab, Raba, Sajo, Zala 5 Bodva, Drava, Drave, Ipoly, Kapos, Koros, Maros, Tarna, Tisza 6 Danube, Henrad, Poprad, Szamos, Theiss, Zagyva 7 Vistula 8 Berretyo
physical feature:
    canal: 3 Sio 6 Sarviz

forest: 6 Bakony
plain: 6 Puszta
port: 5 Fiume
people: 3 Hun 4 Serb 5 Croat, Gypsy 6 Cigany, Magyar, Slovak, Ugrian
    composer: 5 Lehar, Liszt 6 Bartok, Kodaly
    national hero: 5 Arpad
    playwright: 6 Molnar
language: 6 German, Magyar, Slovak 8 Croatian 9 Hungarian 10 Finno-Ugric
religion: 8 Lutheran 9 Calvinism 13 Roman Catholic 16 Eastern Orthodoxy
place:
    church: 32 Gothic Coronation Church of Matthias
    ruins: 8 Aquincum
    square: 6 Heroes
    tomb: 14 Turbe of Gul Baba 16 Father of the Roses
feature:
    dance: 3 kos 7 czardas 10 varsoviana
    dog: 4 puli
    musical instrument: 8 taragata 9 czimbalom
food:
    dish: 6 gulyas 7 goulash 15 chicken paprikas
    pastry: 4 rete 5 torte
    wine: 5 Tokay 10 Bulls Blood

hunger 3 yen 4 itch, love, lust, want, wish 5 crave, greed 6 desire, famine, hanker, liking, relish, thirst 7 burn for, craving, itch for, long for, pant for 8 appetite, fondness, voracity, yearn for, yearning 9 hankering, lust after 10 greediness, starvation 11 have a yen for, thirst after 12 malnutrition, ravenousness

hungry 5 eager 6 greedy 7 starved 8 ravenous, starving 9 voracious

hunk 3 gob, wad 4 clod, glob, lump, mass 5 block, chunk, piece 6 gobbet 7 portion 8 quantity

hunt 4 seek 5 chase, probe, shoot, stalk, trace, track, trail 6 course, follow, pursue 7 explore, go after, look for 8 coursing, drive out 9 ferret out, search for, try to find 11 go in quest of, inquire into 14 riding to hounds 20 leave no stone unturned

Hunt, Richard Morris
architect of: 8 Biltmore (Asheville NC) 11 Marble House (Newport RI), The Breakers (Newport RI) 12 Lenox Library (NYC) 14 Studio Building (NYC) 19 National Observatory (Washington DC) 22 William Vanderbilt House (NYC) 23 Metropolitan Museum of Art (NYC)

hunter
constellation of: 5 Orion
French: 8 chasseur

Hunter, Jim

nickname: 7 Catfish
sport: 8 baseball
position: 7 pitcher
team: 14 New York Yankees 16 Oakland Athletics

Hunter, Kim
real name: 8 Jane Cole
born: 9 Detroit MI
roles: 16 Stairway to Heaven, The Seventh Victim 21 A Streetcar Named Desire

Hunting
god of: 7 Verbius
goddess of: 5 Diana 7 Artemis

Hunting Dogs
constellation of: 13 Canes Venatici

hurdle 4 jump, leap, snag, wall 5 bound, clear, fence, hedge, vault 6 hazard 7 barrier 8 obstacle, surmount 9 hindrance, roadblock 10 difficulty, impediment, spring over 11 obstruction 12 interference 14 stumbling block

hurl 4 cast, toss 5 chuck, fling, heave, pitch, sling, throw 6 launch, let fly, propel 7 fire off, project 9 discharge

hurly-burly 4 stir 5 furor 6 action, bustle, hubbub, hustle, uproar 8 activity 9 commotion 10 hullabaloo

hurrah, hurray 4 fine, good 5 bravo, cheer, great, huzza 6 huzzah, salute 7 acclaim, hosanna 9 excellent, halleluia, wonderful 10 exaltation, hallelujah

hurricane 7 cyclone, monsoon, tempest, typhoon 9 windstorm

Hurricane, The
director: 8 John Ford
cast: 7 Jon Hall 9 Mary Astor 12 C Aubrey Smith 13 Dorothy Lamour, Raymond Massey
setting: 9 Manikoora

hurried 4 fast 5 hasty 6 hectic, rushed, speedy 7 cursory, frantic 8 careless, feverish, frenetic, headlong, slapdash, slipshod 9 breakneck, haphazard, impulsive 11 precipitate, superficial

hurry 3 ado, zip 4 bolt, dart, dash, fuss, goad, prod, rush, stew, whiz 5 egg on, haste, speed 6 flurry, hasten, hustle, push on, scurry, tumult, urge on 7 drive on, flutter, press on, scuttle, speed up, turmoil 8 make time, move fast, pressure, scramble, step on it 9 commotion, go quickly, make haste, step along 10 accelerate, get a move on, get hopping, lose no time, make tracks 11 come quickly, get cracking, go like a shot, go like sixty 12 step on the gas 13 go like the wind 14 cover the ground 15 hustle and bustle

hurt 3 cut, mar 4 ache, balk, burn, foil, harm, lame, maim, mark, maul, pain, pang, scar 5 agony, block, check, grief, limit, lower, pique, smart, spike, sting, stung 6 aching, bruise, damage, deface, dismay, grieve, hamper, hinder, impair, impede, injure, lessen, mangle, marked, miffed, misery, morose, narrow, offend, oppose, pained, piqued, reduce, retard, thwart, weaken **7** agonize, bruised, chagrin, cripple, crushed, damaged, disable, exclude, inhibit, injured, mangled, painful, scarred, scratch, torment, torture, trouble, wounded **8** aggrieve, crippled, decrease, dejected, diminish, disabled, dismayed, distress, encumber, hold back, minimize, mutilate, obstruct, offended, preclude, restrain, smarting, soreness, wretched **9** aggrieved, annoyance, chagrined, dejection, disfigure, forestall, frustrate, heartsick, indignant, miserable, mortified, mutilated, resentful, scratched, suffering **10** discomfort, distressed, heartbreak, melancholy, resentment **11** aggravation, crestfallen, heartbroken **12** disheartened, wretchedness **13** embarrassment, mortification

Hurt, John
  born: 7 England **22** Chesterfield Derbyshire
  roles: 5 Alien **8** Partners **9** I Claudius (TV; Caligula) **14** The Elephant Man **15** Midnight Express
Hurt, William
  roles: 8 Body Heat **9** Gorky Park **10** Eyewitness **11** The Big Chill **13** Broadcast News **20** Kiss of the Spider Woman, Children of a Lesser God
hurtful 5 cruel **6** deadly **7** abusive, baleful, harmful **8** crushing, improper, stinging, wounding **9** injurious
hurtle 3 fly, hie, run, zip **4** bolt, dart, dash, race, rush, tear, whiz **5** bound, lunge, scoot, shoot, speed, spurt, whisk **6** charge, gallop, plunge, scurry **7** scamper, scuttle **11** go like a shot **13** go like the wind **14** go lickety-split
husband 3 man **4** keep, mate, save **5** amass, groom, hoard, hubby, store **6** old man, retain, save up, spouse **7** consort **8** conserve, maintain, preserve, set aside **10** accumulate, bridegroom, married man
husbandry 7 farming **9** geoponics **11** agriculture, crop- raising **12** conservation
  god of: 9 Aristaeus
hush 4 calm **5** quell, quiet, shush, still **6** shut up, soothe **7** be quiet, be still, keep mum, mollify, silence **8** be silent, pipe down, quietude **9** quiet down, quietness, stillness **10** knock it off **11** tranquility **12** peacefulness, tranquillity
hushed 4 calm **5** quiet, still **6** calmed, gentle, lulled, silent **7** allayed, quieted, soothed, stifled **8** pacified, silenced, tranquil **12** tranquilized **13** tranquillized

hush money 5 bribe **6** payoff, payola **7** tribute **9** blackmail, extortion
huskiness 5 brawn **9** beefiness **10** hoarseness, robustness, ruggedness, sturdiness **11** muscularity
husky 3 big **5** beefy, burly, gruff, harsh, hefty, plump, rough, solid, stout, thick **6** brawny, coarse, hoarse, robust, stocky, strong, sturdy **7** cracked, grating, rasping, raucous, throaty **8** athletic, croaking, guttural, muscular, powerful, thickset **9** strapping **10** overweight **12** strong as an ox **15** broad-shouldered
husky, **8** Siberian
  work: 7 sled dog
hussar 8 cavalier, horseman **10** cavalryman **12** horse soldier, horse trooper **14** mounted soldier
hussy 4 bawd, jade, minx, slut, tart **5** wench, whore **6** harlot, wanton **7** baggage, trollop **8** strumpet **9** brash girl, lewd woman, saucy miss **10** adulteress, loose woman, prostitute **11** brazen woman, fallen woman **12** scarlet woman **17** woman of easy virtue
hustle 3 ado, fly **4** bolt, dart, dash, fuss, prod, push, rush, stir, toss **5** elbow, hurry, nudge, scoot, shove, throw **6** bounce, bustle, flurry, hasten, hubbub, jostle, scurry, tumult **7** flutter, scuttle, speed up, turmoil **8** make time, scramble, shoulder, step on it **9** commotion, make haste, step along **10** lose no time **11** hurry-scurry, move quickly **12** be aggressive
hustler 4 doer **6** con man, dynamo, hooker **8** go-getter, live-wire, swindler **10** prostitute **12** streetwalker
Hustler, The
  director: 12 Robert Rossen
  cast: 10 Paul Newman **11** Piper Laurie **12** George C Scott **13** Jackie Gleason (Minnesota Fats)
Huston, John
  director of: 8 Key Largo **10** The Misfits **11** Moulin Rouge **12** Prizzi's Honor **13** Asphalt Jungle **15** The African Queen **16** The Maltese Falcon **19** The Night of the Iguana **27** The Treasure of the Sierra Madre (Oscar)
  father: 12 Walter Huston
  wife: 11 Evelyn Keyes
  born: 8 Nevada MO
  daughter: 8 Anjelica
  roles: 9 Chinatown **11** Winter Kills
Huston, Walter
  real name: 15 Walter Houghston
  son: 10 John Huston
  born: 6 Canada **7** Toronto
  roles: 9 Dodsworth **18** All That Money Can Buy **27** The Treasure of the Sierra Madre
hut 4 shed **5** cabin, hutch, shack **6** lean-to, shanty **7** cottage, shelter

hutch 3 pen, sty **4** cage, coop, cote, crib, shed **5** stall **9** enclosure
Hutchinson, A S M
  author of: 13 If Winter Comes
Hutton, Betty
  real name: 18 Betty June Thornburg
  born: 13 Battle Creek MI
  roles: 15 Annie Get Your Gun **19** Greatest Show on Earth
Hutton, James
  field: 7 geology
  nationality: 8 Scottish
  founder of: 7 geology
Hutton, Timothy
  father: 9 Jim Hutton
  roles: 4 Taps **6** Daniel **14** Ordinary People **22** The Falcon and the Snowman
Huxley, Aldous
  author of: 11 Crome Yellow **13** Brave New World **17** Point Counter Point
  brother: 6 Julian
Huxley, Julian
  field: 7 biology
  nationality: 7 British
  promoted theory of: 9 evolution
Huygens, Christiaan
  nationality: 5 Dutch
  invented: 13 pendulum clock
  discovered: 12 Saturn's rings
  formulated: 17 wave theory of light
hyacinth 10 Hyacinthus **20** Hyacinthus orientalis
  varieties: 4 musk, pine, star, wild, wood **5** Dutch, grape, Roman, water **6** common, garden, meadow, nutmeg, starry, summer, Tassel **7** feather, peacock **11** common grape
Hyacinthus
  father: 7 Amyclas
  daughter: 7 Orthaea
  loved by: 6 Apollo **8** Zephyrus
  killed by: 5 quoit **6** discus
  from his blood sprang: 6 flower
    petals marked: 4 AI-AI
    means: 4 alas
Hyades
  also: 5 Hyads **10** Palilicium
  form: 6 nymphs
  father: 5 Atlas **7** Oceanus
  mother: 6 Tethys **7** Pleione
  sisters: 8 Pleiades
  nurtured: 8 Dionysus
  placed among: 5 stars
hybrid 5 cross **7** amalgam, mixture **9** composite, half- breed **10** crossbreed
hybridize 5 cross **14** cross-fertilize, cross-pollinate
Hydra
  form: 12 water serpent
  number of heads: 4 nine
  killed by: 8 Hercules
hydrangea
  varieties: 4 Wild **6** French, Peegee **8** Climbing

hydrogen
chemical symbol: **1** H
hydrophobia 6 rabies
fear of: **5** water
Hygeia
father: **9** Asclepius
goddess of: **6** health
corresponds to: **5** Salus
hygienic 4 pure **5** clean **7** aseptic, healthy, sterile **8** germ- free, harmless, salutary, sanitary **9** healthful, wholesome **10** salubrious, unpolluted **11** disease-free, disinfected, uninjurious **12** prophylactic **14** uncontaminated
Hylaeus
form: **7** centaur
born on: **5** cloud
Hymen
also: **9** Hymenaeus
god of: **8** marriage
holds: **5** torch
corresponds to: **8** Talassio
hymenoptera
class: **8** hexapoda
phylum: **10** arthropoda
group: **3** ant, bee **4** wasp **6** chacid, sawfly **12** ichneumon fly
hymn 5 paean, psalm **6** anthem **12** song of praise **14** devotional song **17** song in praise of God
Hymn to Proserpine
author: **24** Algernon Charles Swinburne
Hypatia
author: **15** Charles Kingsley
hyper 7 keyed-up **10** high-strung, overactive
hyperbole 8 metaphor **11** enlargement **12** exaggeration **13** magnification, overstatement **14** figure of speech
hyperbolize 6 overdo **7** amplify, magnify, stretch **9** embroider, overstate **10** exaggerate
hyperborean 6 arctic **8** freezing, northern **13** septentrional

Hyperborean
inhabitant of: **8** Paradise
Hyperion
also: **6** Helios
form: **5** Titan
father: **6** Uranus
mother: **4** Gaea
sister: **5** Theia
son: **6** Helios
daughter: **3** Eos **6** Selene
corresponds to: **6** Apollo
Hyperion
author: **9** John Keats **24** Henry Wadsworth Longfellow
hypersensitive 6 touchy **9** emotional **13** temperamental
Hypnos
also: **6** Hypnus
god of: **5** sleep
father: **6** Erebus
mother: **3** Nyx
brother: **8** Thanatos
corresponds to: **6** Somnus
hypnotic 9 soporific **11** mesmerizing **12** spellbinding
hypnotize 7 control **9** mesmerize, spellbind
hypocrisy 6 deceit, fakery **7** falsity **9** duplicity, mendacity, phoniness **10** dishonesty **11** dissembling, insincerity **12** two-facedness
hypocrite 5 phony **8** deceiver **9** pretender **10** dissembler
Hypocrite 15 whited sepulcher
hypocritical 5 false, phony **7** feigned **8** feigning, two- faced **9** deceitful, deceptive, dishonest, insincere, truthless **11** counterfeit
hyporchema
form: **9** choral ode
origin: **5** Greek
honored: **6** Apollo **8** Dionysus
hypothalamus
regulates: **15** body temperature
located in: **5** brain

hypothesis 6 theory, thesis **7** premise, theorem **8** proposal **9** assertion, postulate **10** assumption, conclusion, conjecture **11** explanation, guesstimate, presumption, proposition, speculation, supposition
hypothesize 5 infer **6** assume **7** imagine, presume, suppose **8** theorize **9** postulate, speculate **10** conjecture
hypothetical 7 assumed, dubious **8** possible, supposed **9** imaginary, uncertain **10** contingent, postulated **11** conditional, conjectural, presumptive, speculative, theoretical **12** questionable **13** suppositional
Hypselosaurus
type: **8** dinosaur, sauropod
location: **6** France **8** Mongolia
period: **10** Cretaceous
Hypsilophodon
type: **8** dinosaur **10** ornithopod
location: **7** England
period: **10** Cretaceous
Hyrie
transformed into: **4** swan
hyssop 8 Hyssopus **18** Hyssopus officialis
varieties: **5** anise, giant, water **9** blue giant **10** nettle-leaf **11** fennel giant, purple giant, yellow giant **12** Mexican giant **13** fragrant giant, wrinkled giant
Hyssop 13 Biblical plant
hysteria 3 fit **5** panic **6** frenzy **8** delirium
hysterical 5 crazy, droll **6** absurd, crazed, raving **7** amusing, comical **8** farcical, frenzied, worked-up **9** laughable, ludicrous, wrought-up **10** distracted, distraught, ridiculous, uproarious **11** carried away, overwrought, wildly funny **13** beside oneself, out of one's wits **14** uncontrollable
hysterics 3 fit **12** emotionalism

I, Claudius
  author: 12 Robert Graves
  story of: 36 Tiberius Claudius Drusus Nero Germanicus (Emperor of Rome) (on Masterpiece Theater) **actors: 8** John Hurt **11** Derek Jacobi, Sheila White **12** Brian Blessed, Sian Phillips **14** Patrick Stewart, Margaret Tyzack

I, the Jury
  author: 14 Mickey Spillane
  hero: 10 Mike Hammer

I Am a Fugitive from a Chain Gang
  director: 11 Mervyn LeRoy
  cast: 8 Paul Muni **11** Helen Vinson **13** Glenda Farrell, Preston Foster

I am unwilling to contend
  Latin: 14 nolo contendere

Ibanez, Vicente Blasco
  author: 30 The Four Horsemen of the Apocalypse

Iberian Peninsula
  also: 8 Hesperia
  comprising: 5 Spain **8** Portugal

Ibsen, Henrik
  author of: 6 Ghosts **8** Peer Gynt **11** A Doll's House, Hedda Gabler, Rosmersholm, The Wild Duck **16** The Master Builder **18** An Enemy of the People, John Gabriel Borkman

I came, I saw, I conquered
  Latin: 12 veni vidi vici
  author: 12 Julius Caesar

Icarus
  father: 8 Daedalus
  built: 5 wings
  flew too near: 3 sun
  death by: 8 drowning

ICC 28 Interstate Commerce Commission

ice 3 gem **4** berg, floe, gems, rime **5** chill, frost, glace **6** freeze, icicle, jewels **7** crystal, dessert, glacier, jewelry, sherbet **8** diamonds **11** refrigerant, refrigerate

ice-cold 3 icy **4** cold **5** gelid, polar **6** arctic, bitter, frigid, frosty, wintry **7** chilled, frosted, glacial, subzero **8** chilling, freezing, Siberian, unheated, unwarmed **9** stone-cold, supercold **11** hyperborean, supercooled **12** bone-chilling

ice cream 7 dessert, sherbet **4** soda **5** glace **6** frappe, sundae **7** dessert, parfait, sherbet, spumoni, tortoni

Iceland
  other name: 15 Lydveldid Island
  capital/largest city: 9 Reykjavik
  others: 3 Hof **6** Geysir **7** Akranes, Husavik **8** Akureyri, Keflavik, Kopasker **9** Kopavogur **10** Hveragerdi, Isafjordur **12** Siglufjordur **13** Hafnarfjordur, Neskaupstadur, Seydisfjordur
  government:
    general assembly: 7 Althing
  measure: 3 set **4** alin **5** almud **6** almenn, ferfet, pattur **7** fathmur, fermila, oltunna
  monetary unit: 5 aurar, eyrir, krona
  weight: 4 pund **5** pound, tunna **6** smjors
  island: 7 Heimaey, Surtsey, Westman
  lake: 6 Myvatn **10** Thorisvatn **14** Thingvallavatn
  mountain: 5 Jokul **10** Orafajokul
    volcano: 4 Laki **5** Askja, Hekla, Katla **7** Surtsey
  highest point: 17 Hvannadalshnjukur
  river: 5 Hvita **7** Fnjoska, Thjorsa **15** Jokulsa a Fjollum
  sea: 9 Greenland **13** North Atlantic
  physical feature:
    fjord: 4 Eyja
    geyser: 5 gryla **6** geysir **11** Great Gusher
    glacier: 6 Jokull **11** Orafajokull, Vatnajokull
    plain: 15 Skeidharasandur
    waterfall: 8 Godafoss, Gullfoss **9** Dettifoss
  people: 6 Celtic, Viking **8** Norseman **9** Norwegian
    first settler: 8 Arnarson
    hero: 4 Bele, Eric, Leif **10** Sigurdsson
  language: 5 Norse **9** Icelandic
  religion: 19 Evangelical Lutheran
  place:
    national shrine: 11 Thingvellir
  feature:
    airport: 9 Kopavogur
    bird: 4 gull **6** falcon **9** gyrfalcon
    literary genre: 4 saga
    wrestling: 5 glima
  food:
    dish: 4 skyr, svio **7** bloomor **8** harofisk

Iceman
  nickname of: 12 George Gervin

Iceman Cometh, The
  author: 12 Eugene O'Neill
  role: 6 Hickey

Ice Palace
  author: 10 Edna Ferber

ice skating
  athlete: 9 Janet Lynn, John Curry **10** Carol Heiss, Dick Button, Eric Heiden, Sonja Henie **11** Sheila Young **12** Peggy Fleming, Tara Lipinski **13** Dorothy Hamill, Scott Hamilton **14** Linda Fratianne

ich dien 6 I serve
  motto of: 13 Prince of Wales

I Ching 30 ancient Chinese book of divination

ichor
  form: 5 fluid
  in veins of: 4 gods

Ichthyocentaur
  form: 8 creature
  location: 3 sea
  head/torso: 5 human
  legs: 5 horse
  tail: 4 fish

iciness 4 cold **5** chill **9** frigidity **10** chilliness, frostiness, wintriness **12** slipperiness

ici on parle francais 18 French is spoken here **19** here one speaks French

icky 5 gluey, gooey, gross, gucky, gummy, mushy, nasty, tacky, weepy **6** sticky, syrupy, viscid **7** maudlin, viscous **8** bathetic **9** glutinous, offensive, repulsive, revolting **10** disgusting **12** mucilaginous

icon, ikon 4 idol **5** image **6** effigy, figure, statue **7** picture **8** likeness **11** sacred image

iconoclast 5 rebel **7** radical, upstart **9** dissenter **13** nonconformist, revolutionary

icy 3 raw **4** cold, cool **5** aloof, gelid **6** arctic, chilly, frigid, frosty, frozen, glazed, sleety, wintry **7** distant, glacial, haughty, hostile **8** chilling, freezing, slippery **9** impassive **10** forbidding, unfriendly **11** coldhearted, unemotional

Ida
  form: 5 nymph
  watched over: 4 Zeus
  mount: 5 Crete **7** Phrygia

Idaea
  form: 5 nymph
  domain: 8 Mount Ida

husband: 7 Phineus **9** Scamander
son: 6 Teucer

Idaho
abbreviation: 2 ID **3** Ida
nickname: 3 Gem
capital/largest city: 5 Boise
others: 4 Buhl **5** Malad, Nampa **6**
Moscow **7** Orofino, Rexburg **8** Caldwell, Lewiston **9** Pocatello, Twin
Falls **10** Idaho Falls **11** Coeur
d'Alene
college: 17 Northwest Nazarene
explorer: 13 Lewis and Clark
feature: 9 Sun Valley **17** Continental
Divide
  dam: 5 Oxbow **8** Brownlee
  national monument: 16 Craters of
  the Moon
tribe: 5 Banak, Shake **6** Cayuse, Paiute, Spokan **7** Bannock, Kutenai,
Spokane **8** Kalispel, Nez Perce, Sahaptin, Shoshone, Shoshoni **9** Shos-
honee **11** Coeur d'Alene
people: 9 Ezra Pound, Sacagawea **11**
Chief Joseph **17** William Edgar Borah
lake: 4 Bear **5** Grey's **6** Priest **11**
Coeur d'Alene, Pend Oreille **22**
American Falls Reservoir
land rank: 10 thirteenth
mountain: 4 Ryan **5** Rocky **6** Rhodes,
Taylor, Tetons **7** Cabinet **8** Ban-
nocks, Big Baldy, Bluenose, Saw-
tooth **9** Wasatches **10** Clearwater **11**
Beaverheads, Bitterroots **13** Selkirk
Ranges
  highest point: 5 Borah
physical feature:
  falls: 5 Moyie **8** Shoshone **9** Upper
  Mesa
  springs: 4 Soda **6** Hooper **7** Lava-
  hot
river: 4 Bear **5** Boise, Snake, St Joe **6**
Locksa, Salmon **7** Payette, Spokane
8 Kootenai **11** Coeur d'Alene, Pend
Oreille
state admission: 10 forty-third
state bird: 16 mountain bluebird
state flower: 7 syringa
state motto: 13 It Is Perpetual **16** Let
It Be Perpetual
state song: 15 Here We Have Idaho
state tree: 16 western white pine

Idas
father: 8 Aphareus
mother: 5 Arene
brother: 7 Lynceus
wife: 8 Marpessa
daughter: 9 Cleopatra

idea 4 clue, hint, view **6** belief, notion
7 concept, feeling, inkling, insight,
opinion, outlook, thought **8** approach,
proposal, solution **9** sentiment **10**
conception, conclusion, conviction,
impression, indication, intimation,
suggestion **12** apperception, appreciation **13** approximation, mental pic-

ture, understanding **14** interpretation,
recommendation

ideal 3 aim **4** hero, idol **5** dream,
model **7** epitome, optimal, pattern,
perfect **8** exemplar, last word, paradigm, standard, ultimate **9** archetype,
criterion, excellent, exemplary, faultless, matchless, objective **10** impeccable **11** inspiration

idealism 8 optimism **9** meliorism **10**
utopianism **11** romanticism

idealist 7 dreamer, utopian **8** romantic
9 Pollyanna, stargazer, visionary **11**
romanticist **13** perfectionist

idealized 6 dreamy **7** utopian, wishful
8 fanciful, illusory, romantic **10** optimistic **11** pie-in-the-sky, unrealistic **13**
insubstantial

idea man 7 advisor **8** inventor **9** innovator **10** consultant **12** entrepreneur

idee fixe 9 fixed idea
  music: 14 recurring motif

idem 24 the same as previously given
28 the same as previously mentioned

identical 4 twin **7** uniform **8** selfsame, very same **9** duplicate **15** interchangeable **17** indistinguishable

identification 2 ID **5** badge, label **6**
dogtag **7** license **8** passport **9** detection **10** connection, revelation **11** affiliation, association, credentials, pinpointing, recognition **12** confirmation,
verification **13** ascertainment

identify 4 know **5** place **6** finger, verify **7** combine, pick out, specify **9** associate, designate, determine, recognize, single out **11** distinguish

identifying device 4 logo, mark, sign
5 badge **6** emblem, ensign, symbol **8**
insignia, logotype

identity 4 name, self **6** accord **7** harmony, oneness, rapport **9** unanimity
11 delineation, duplication, personality **13** individuality **15** differentiation,
distinctiveness

ideology 5 dogma, ethos **6** ideals, theory **7** program **8** doctrine **9** rationale
10 principles

Ides of March, The
author: 14 Thornton Wilder

id est 6 that is
  abbreviation: 2 ie

idiocy 5 folly **6** lunacy **7** fatuity, inanity, madness, suicide **8** insanity **9** absurdity, asininity, cretinism, mongol-
ism, stupidity **11** foolishness **13**
foolhardiness, senselessness

idiom 5 argot, lingo, slang **6** brogue,
jargon, patois, phrase, speech **7** dialect **8** language, localism, parlance **10**
vernacular **13** colloquialism

idiomatic 6 common **8** informal, ordinary **10** vernacular **14** conversational

idiosyncrasy 3 tic **5** quirk **6** oddity **7**
anomaly **9** mannerism **11** distinction,
peculiarity **12** eccentricity

idiot 3 ass **4** boob, dolt, dope, fool,
jerk **5** cluck, dummy, dunce, moron,
ninny **6** cretin, dimwit, nitwit **7** half-
wit **8** dumbbell, numskull **9** blockhead, numbskull, simpleton **10** nincompoop

Idiot, The
author: 16 Fyodor Dostoevsky
character: 7 Myshkin **11** Mme
Epanchin **14** Aglaya Epanchin, Par-
fen Rogozhin **16** Natasya Filipovna
19 Ganya Ardalionovitch **22** Prince
Lef Nicolaievitch

idiotic 5 crazy, dopey, nutty **6** absurd,
addled, stupid **7** asinine, doltish, foolish, moronic **9** foolhardy, imbecilic,
senseless **10** half-witted, irrational, ridiculous **12** feebleminded **13** rattlebrained

I direct
Latin: 6 dirigo
motto of: 5 Maine

idle 4 laze, lazy, loaf, vain **5** empty, inert, petty, vapid, waste, while **6**
drowsy, fallow, futile, otiose, putter,
torpid, unused **7** aimless, fritter, jobless, languid, trivial, useless, wait out
8 baseless, bootless, fool away, inactive, indolent, listless, slothful, sluggish, trifling **9** at leisure, enervated,
fruitless, lethargic, out of work, pointless, somnolent, valueless, worthless
10 not working, unemployed, unoccupied **11** unimportant **12** unproductive
15 unsubstantiated

idleness 5 sloth **7** inertia **8** laziness,
lethargy **9** indolence **10** inactivity **11**
joblessness, languidness **12** sluggishness, unemployment
French: 8 flanerie

idler 3 bum **6** loafer **7** drifter, vagrant
10 ne'er-do-well
French: 7 flaneur

idol 4 hero, icon **5** relic **6** effigy, statue
7 darling **8** artifact **9** superstar **10**
simulacrum, golden calf **11** graven
image, inspiration

idolatry 5 mania **7** madness, passion,
worship **8** devotion **9** adoration, obsession **10** veneration **11** idolization,
infatuation **12** image worship **13** preoccupation

idolization 7 worship **9** adulation, reverence **10** exaltation, veneration

idolize 5 adore, deify, honor, prize **6**
admire, revere **7** worship **8** treasure,
venerate **9** reverence **11** apotheosize

Idomeneo, re di Creta
also: 20 Idomeneus King of Crete
opera by: 6 Mozart
character: 4 Ilia **7** Electra **8** Ida-
mante, Poseidon

Idomeneus
king of: 5 Crete
father: 9 Deucalion

I don't know what
French: 12 je ne sais quoi

I Dream of Jeannie
  character: 7 Jeannie 9 Dr Bellows 10 (Captain) Tony Nelson 11 Gen Peterson, (Captain) Roger Healey 13 Amanda Bellows
  cast: 9 Bill Daily 11 Barbara Eden, Hayden Rorke, Larry Hagman 13 Barton MacLane, Emmaline Henry
  Tony's job: 9 astronaut

idyllic 6 rustic, sylvan 7 bucolic 8 arcadian, pastoral, peaceful, romantic 9 unspoiled

Idylls of the King, The
  author: 18 Alfred Lord Tennyson
  based on story of: 10 King Arthur

if 2 an 6 though 7 whether 8 although, provided 9 condition, supposing 10 even though 11 stipulation, supposition

iffy 4 moot 5 risky 6 chancy, unsure 7 dubious, erratic 8 arguable, doubtful 9 debatable, uncertain, undecided, unsettled, whimsical 10 capricious, disputable, unresolved 11 conjectural, speculative 12 questionable 13 problematical, unpredictable

If Winter Comes
  author: 13 A S M Hutchinson

if you please
  French: 12 s'il vous plait

ignitable 8 burnable 9 flammable 10 combustive, incendiary 11 combustible, inflammable 13 conflagrative

ignite 4 burn, fire 5 blaze, flame, light 6 blow up, kindle 7 explode, inflame 8 take fire, touch off 9 catch fire, set fire to, set on fire 11 catch on fire

ignoble 3 low 4 base, foul, mean, vile 6 craven 7 debased, heinous 8 cowardly, degraded, depraved, indecent, infamous, inferior, shameful, unworthy 9 dastardly, nefarious 10 degenerate, despicable 11 disgraceful 12 contemptible, dishonorable 13 discreditable, pusillanimous 14 unconscionable

ignominious 3 low 5 sorry 6 abject 8 grievous, shameful, wretched 9 degrading 10 despicable, inglorious, unbearable 11 disgraceful, humiliating 12 dishonorable, disreputable 13 discreditable

ignominy 5 shame 6 infamy 8 contempt, disgrace, dishonor 11 degradation, humiliation

ignoramus 4 fool 5 dunce 6 nitwit 7 low-brow 8 numskull 9 numbskull, simpleton 10 illiterate 11 know-nothing

ignorance 9 confusion 10 illiteracy 11 unawareness 12 backwardness 13 obliviousness, unfamiliarity 15 unenlightenment

ignorant 4 dumb 5 naive 6 stupid 7 asinine, blind to, fatuous, shallow, unaware 8 innocent, untaught 9 in the dark, unknowing, unlearned, un-trained, untutored, unworldly 10 illiterate, uneducated, uninformed, unlettered, unschooled 11 insensitive, uncognizant 12 unperceptive 13 irresponsible, unenlightened, unintelligent 15 unknowledgeable

ignore 4 omit, skip, snub 5 scorn 6 eschew, slight 7 neglect 8 overlook, pass over 9 disregard

Igraine
  character in: 16 Arthurian romance
  son: 6 Arthur
  by: 14 Uther Pendragon

Iguanodon
  type: 8 dinosaur 10 ornithopod
  means: 11 iguana tooth
  found by: 13 Gideon Mantell
  location: 6 Africa, Europe, Sussex 7 Belgium, England
  period: 10 Cretaceous
  characteristic: 10 duck-billed

ikebana
  Japanese: 21 art of arranging flowers

Ile de France *see* 9 Mauritius

Ilha Formosa *see* 6 Taiwan

Iliad, The
  author: 5 Homer
  character: 5 Paris, Priam 6 Hector 8 Achilles, Menelaus 9 Agamemnon, Patroclus 11 Helen of Troy
  subject: 9 Trojan War

Iliniwek *see* 8 Illinois

Ilion
  Greek name for: 11 ancient Troy

Ilium
  Latin name for: 11 ancient Troy

ill, ills 3 woe 4 evil, foul, harm, sick, vile 5 abuse, cross, no way, surly, trial 6 ailing, damage, hardly, injury, laid up, malady, malice, nowise, plague, poorly, sickly, sorrow, unkind, unwell, wicked 7 ailment, cruelty, disease, failing, harmful, invalid, not well, ominous, outrage, peevish, trouble, unlucky, unsound 8 diseased, mischief, scarcely, sinister, vengeful 9 afflicted, complaint, infirmity, malicious, unhealthy 10 affliction, disturbing, foreboding, indisposed, misfortune, wickedness 11 abomination, acrimonious, malefaction, threatening, unfavorable 12 inauspicious, unpropitious 15 under the weather

ill-advised 4 dumb, rash 5 hasty, silly 6 myopic, stupid, unwise 7 foolish 9 foolhardy, ill-judged, impolitic, imprudent, misguided, senseless 10 indiscreet, unthinking 11 injudicious 12 shortsighted 13 ill-considered, irresponsible

ill-at-ease 3 shy 4 edgy 6 on edge, uneasy 7 abashed, fidgety, nervous 8 bothered, troubled 9 disturbed, nonplused, perturbed 10 disquieted, nonplussed 11 discomfited, discomposed, embarrassed 12 disconcerted 13 self-conscious, uncomfortable 15 discountenanced

ill-boding 4 dire 7 ominous 9 ill-omened 11 apocalyptic 12 inauspicious

ill-bred 4 rude 5 crude 7 boorish, uncivil, uncouth 8 churlish, impolite 10 unmannerly 11 ill-mannered 12 discourteous

ill-defined 3 dim 4 hazy 5 faint, murky 6 blurry 7 blurred, clouded, shadowy 8 nebulous, obscured 10 indistinct

illegal 5 wrong 6 banned 7 illicit 8 criminal, not legal, outlawed, unlawful 9 felonious, forbidden 10 actionable, prohibited, proscribed 12 illegitimate, unauthorized, unsanctioned 13 against the law

illegible 7 unclear 8 obscured 9 scribbled 10 unreadable 14 indecipherable, undecipherable, unintelligible

illegitimate 7 bastard, illegal, illicit, lawless, natural 8 baseborn, improper, unlawful 10 prohibited 11 misbegotten, unwarranted 12 unauthorized, unsanctioned

ill-fated 6 doomed, jinxed 7 hapless, unlucky 8 blighted, luckless 9 ill-omened 10 ill-starred

ill-favored 4 ugly 5 plain 6 homely 8 unlovely 9 repulsive, unsightly 12 disagreeable, unattractive

ill-fortune 6 mishap 7 bad luck 8 calamity, disaster, hardship 9 adversity 10 misfortune 11 catastrophe

ill health 6 malady 7 ailment, disease, illness 8 sickness 9 infirmity

ill-humored 5 sulky, testy 6 crabby, grumpy, sullen 7 grouchy 10 in a bad mood, unfriendly, unsociable

illiberal 5 petty, small 6 biased, narrow 7 bigoted 10 hidebound 11 brassbound, intolerant, prejudiced, ungenerous 11 opinionated, small-minded 12 narrow-minded, short-sighted

illicit 7 illegal, lawless 8 criminal, improper, not legal, unlawful 9 felonious 10 prohibited 11 black-market, clandestine 12 illegitimate, not permitted, unauthorized 13 against the law, impermissible 15 under-the-counter

Illinois
  abbreviation: 2 IL 3 Ill
  nickname: 4 Tall 6 Sucker 7 Prairie 13 Land of Lincoln
  capital: 11 Springfield
  largest city: 7 Chicago
  others: 4 Pana 5 Alton, Cairo, Elgin, Flora, Olney, Pekin 6 Albion, Berwyn, Canton, Herrin, Joliet, Peoria, Skokie 7 Batavia, Decatur, Genesco, Mendota, Nokomis 8 Evanston, Rockford, Waukegan 9 Centralia 10 Barrington 11 Bloomington
  college: 4 Knox 5 Barat 6 Aurora, DePaul, Eureka, Loyola, Olivet,

Quincy, Shimer **7** Bradley, Chicago, Wheaton **8** Millikin **9** Augustana **12** Northwestern **16** Illinois Wesleyan **23** Illinois Institute of Tech
explorer: 6 Joliet **7** Jolliet **9** Marquette
feature: 10 stockyards
  airport: 5 O'Hare
  museum: 18 Science and Industry
  seaway: 10 St Lawrence
  trail: 7 Lincoln
tribe: 3 Fox **4** Sauk **9** Kaskaskia
people: 9 Black Hawk, Jack Benny **10** Jane Addams, Walt Disney **12** Carl Sandburg **15** Ernest Hemingway **18** Engineer Casey Jones **20** William Jennings Bryan
lake: 3 Fox **5** Grass **7** Calumet **8** Michigan, Pistakee
land rank: 12 twenty-fourth
mountain: 6 Ozarks
  highest point: 12 Charles Mound
physical feature:
  hills: 7 Shawnee
president: 14 Abraham Lincoln
river: 4 Ohio, Rock **5** Spoon **6** Wabash **7** Chicago, Elkhorn **8** Big Muddy, Illinois, Mackinaw, Sangamon **9** Kaskaskia **10** Des Plaines **11** Mississippi
state admission: 11 twenty-first
state bird: 8 cardinal
state flower: 6 violet
state motto: 29 State Sovereignty, National Union
state song: 8 Illinois
state tree: 7 burl oak **8** white oak

Illinois (Iliniwek)
language family: 9 Algonkian **10** Algonquian
tribe: 6 Peoria **7** Cahokia, Tamaroa **9** Kaskaskia, Moingwena **10** Michigamea
location: 4 Iowa, Ohio **7** Indiana **8** Illinois, Michigan, Missouri **9** Wisconsin
built: 12 Cahokia Mound
murdered: 7 Pontiac
related to: 5 Miami **6** Ojibwa **7** Ojibway

illiterate 7 witless **8** childish, ignorant, unversed **9** unlearned, untutored **10** amateurish, incoherent, uneducated, uninformed, unlettered, unreliable, unschooled **11** not educated, uninitiated, unscholarly **12** uninstructed **13** unenlightened, ungrammatical **15** unknowledgeable

ill-made 6 shoddy **7** awkward **8** deformed, inferior **9** makeshift, malformed **10** jerry-built, jury-rigged **15** misproportioned

ill-mannered 4 rude **5** crude **6** coarse **7** boorish, ill-bred, loutish, uncivil **8** impolite **9** offensive, ungallant **10** ill-behaved, ungracious **12** discourteous **13** disrespectful

ill-natured 4 sour **5** cross, nasty, surly **6** bitter, cranky, malign **7** caustic, grouchy, peevish **8** captious, churlish, spiteful, venomous **9** crotchety, irascible, irritable, malignant, rancorous, splenetic **10** ill-humored, unfriendly **11** acrimonious, contentious, quarrelsome **12** antagonistic, cantankerous

illness 6 malady **7** ailment, disease **8** disorder, sickness **9** complaint, ill health, infirmity **10** affliction, disability, poor health **11** malfunction **13** indisposition

illogical 4 wild **5** crazy, dopey, nutty, silly, wacky **6** absurd, far-out, screwy **7** asinine, offbeat, unsound **9** erroneous, senseless **10** fallacious, irrational, off-the-wall, ridiculous **11** incongruent, incongruous, nonsensical, unreasoning **12** inconsistent, preposterous, unreasonable **13** contradictory

ill-omened 4 dire **7** adverse, ominous **9** ill-boding **11** apocalyptic, unfavorable **12** inauspicious, unpropitious

ill-smelling 4 foul, high, olid, rank **5** fetid, fusty **6** putrid, rancid, smelly, stinky, strong **7** reeking **8** stinking **10** malodorous

ill-starred 4 dire **5** fatal **6** tragic **7** adverse **8** ill-fated **10** calamitous, disastrous **11** unfortunate **12** catastrophic, inauspicious

ill-suited 5 inapt **8** mismated, unsuited **9** misjoined, unfitting **10** ill-adapted, ill-matched, malapropos, mismatched, unbecoming, unsuitable **11** incongruous, unbefitting, uncongenial **12** incompatible, inconsistent **13** inappropriate

ill-tempered 4 mean, rude, sour **5** angry, cross, harsh, nasty, testy **6** bitter, cranky, shirty **7** acerbic, furious, grouchy, peevish, waspish **8** choleric, churlish, petulant **9** crotchety, irascible, irritable **10** bad-natured, ill-humored, ill-natured, in a bad mood, unpleasant **11** acrimonious **12** cantankerous

ill-treatment 4 harm **5** abuse **6** ill-use, injury, misuse **7** cruelty **13** mortification

illuminate 5 edify, light **7** clarify, enhance, explain, light up **8** brighten, illumine, instruct, spell out **9** elucidate, enlighten, exemplify, irradiate, make clear **12** throw light on **13** cast light upon

illuminated 3 lit **5** lit up **6** bright **7** lighted **9** clarified, decorated, illumined **10** brightened, elucidated, irradiated

illumination 6 lights, wisdom **7** insight **8** lighting **9** education, knowledge **10** illumining, lighting up, perception, revelation **11** edification, information, instruction, irradiation **13** comprehension, enlightenment

Illuminations, Les
author: 13 Arthur Rimbaud
illumined 3 lit **7** lighted **8** luminous **11** illuminated

ill-use 4 harm, hurt **5** abuse **6** injure, misuse **7** assault, cruelty, harming **8** maltreat, mistreat **10** bodily harm **12** maltreatment, mistreatment

illusion 5 error, fancy **6** mirage, vagary, vision **7** caprice, chimera, fallacy **8** delusion, phantasm **9** deception, false idea, misbelief, semblance, unreality **10** apparition, false image, hocus-pocus, humbuggery, impression **11** false belief, fata morgana **13** hallucination, misconception, misimpression **15** misapprehension

illusive 5 false **6** unreal **7** phantom, seeming **8** apparent, chimeric, fanciful, fantastic, illusory **9** deceptive **10** ostensible **11** illusionary

illusory 4 sham **5** false **6** unreal **7** seeming **8** apparent, delusive, fanciful, illusive, spurious **9** deceptive, erroneous, imaginary **10** fallacious, misleading, ostensible **11** counterfeit, unrealistic **13** hallucinatory

illustrate 4 show **6** define **7** clarify, explain, picture, point up, portray **8** decorate, ornament **9** bring home, delineate, elucidate, emphasize, make clear, represent **10** illuminate **11** demonstrate **12** pictorialize, throw light on **16** make intelligible

illustration 5 image, plate **6** figure **7** drawing, example, picture **8** instance, specimen **9** portrayal **10** photograph **14** representation **15** exemplification

illustrious 5 famed, great, noted **6** famous **7** eminent, honored, notable **8** glorious, lustrous, peerless, renowned, splendid **9** acclaimed, brilliant, exemplary, matchless, prominent **10** celebrated **11** magnificent **13** distinguished

illustriousness 8 grandeur **9** greatness **11** distinction **12** magnificence

ill will 4 gall **5** anger, spite **6** animus, enmity, hatred, malice, rancor, spleen **7** dislike **8** acrimony, aversion, bad blood, loathing **9** animosity, antipathy, hostility **10** abhorrence, antagonism, bitterness, contention **11** malevolence **12** hard feelings, spitefulness

ill wind 7 bad luck **8** bad break, hard luck **9** adversity, mischance **10** misfortune

Illyrius
father: 6 Cadmus
Ilmarinen
origin: 7 Finnish
form: 10 blacksmith
hero in: 8 Kalevala
forged: 5 Sampo
Sampo's owner: 5 Louhi
I Love Lucy
character: 9 Fred Mertz **10** Ethel

Mertz **11** Little Ricky, Lucy Ricardo **12** Ricky Ricardo
cast: 9 Desi Arnaz **11** Lucille Ball, Vivian Vance **14** William Frawley
Ricky's club: 7 Babaloo **9** Tropicana

Il Penseroso
  author: 10 John Milton
  companion piece: 8 L'Allegro

image 4 copy, icon, idea, idol **6** double, effigy, fetish, figure, memory, simile, statue, symbol, visage **7** concept, picture, replica **8** likeness, metaphor, portrait **9** depiction, duplicate, facsimile, mirroring, semblance **10** photograph, reflection, simulacrum **11** countenance, delineation, incarnation **12** recollection, reproduction **13** mental picture **14** figure of speech, representation

imaginable 8 feasible **9** thinkable **11** conceivable

imaginary 4 sham **5** fancy, phony **6** made-up, unreal **7** fancied, fiction, figment **8** delusion, fabulous, fanciful, illusion, illusory, invented, mythical, romantic **9** fantastic, figmental, legendary **10** factitious, fictitious **11** counterfeit, make-believe

imagination 5 fancy **7** cunning, thought **9** ingenuity, invention **10** astuteness, creativity, enterprise **12** creativeness **13** inventiveness **14** thoughtfulness **15** creative thought, resourcefulness

imaginative 6 clever **7** unusual **8** creative, inspired, original **9** ingenious, inventive **10** innovative **11** resourceful **12** enterprising **16** off the beaten path, out of the ordinary

imagine 5 fancy, guess, infer, judge **6** assume, gather **7** believe, dream up, picture, presume, pretend, project, suppose, surmise, suspect **8** conceive, envisage, envision **9** fantasize, visualize **10** conjecture

imbecile 3 ass **4** dolt, dope, fool, jerk **5** dummy, dunce, idiot, moron, ninny **6** nitwit **7** dingbat **8** dumbbell **9** blockhead, simpleton **10** nincompoop

imbecilic 4 dumb **5** inane, silly **6** absurd, stupid **7** asinine, foolish **8** careless, mindless **11** thoughtless

imbecility 6 idiocy **8** dullness, dumbness **9** asininity, stupidity, thickness **16** simplemindedness

imbibe 4 swig, tope **5** drink, quaff **6** guzzle, ingest, tipple **7** consume, partake, swallow **8** chugalug, toss down, wash down

imbiber 3 sot **4** wino **5** drunk, toper **7** drinker, tippler **8** consumer, drunkard, ingester

imbroglio 3 row **4** fray **5** brawl, broil, clash, fight, melee, scrap **6** fracas, ruckus, rumpus, uproar **7** scuffle **8** argument **9** confusion **11** altercation,

embroilment **12** entanglement **13** embarrassment

imbue 4 fill, fire, tint **5** bathe, color, endow, steep, tinge **6** arouse, infuse **7** animate, impress, ingrain, inspire, instill, pervade, suffuse **8** permeate, tincture **9** inculcate

Imhotep
  father: 4 Ptah
  mother: 7 Sekhmet
  position: 6 scribe, vizier, writer **9** architect, physician
  architect of pyramid: 8 Sakkarah

imitate 3 ape **4** copy, mime **5** mimic **6** mirror, parody, parrot **7** emulate, pass for **8** look like, simulate **9** duplicate, represent **10** caricature **11** counterfeit, impersonate

imitation 4 fake, mock, sham **5** aping, phony **6** ersatz, parody **7** man-made, mimicry, takeoff **8** travesty **9** burlesque, facsimile, semblance, simulated, synthetic **10** adaptation, artificial, caricature, impression, similarity, simulation **11** counterfeit, duplication, make-believe **12** reproduction **13** impersonation **14** representation

Imitation of Christ, The
  author: 13 Thomas a Kempis

immaculate 4 pure **5** clean, ideal **6** chaste, intact, virgin **7** perfect, saintly, sinless **8** flawless, innocent, spotless, unsoiled, virginal, virtuous **9** faultless, guiltless, shipshape, stainless, unstained, unsullied **11** spic and span, untarnished **13** above reproach, unimpeachable **14** irreproachable **15** unexceptionable

immanent 6 inborn, inbred, innate **7** natural **8** inherent **9** ingrained, intrinsic **10** congenital, deep-rooted, deep-seated, indigenous, indwelling **11** instinctive, instinctual

Immanuel 7 Messiah **11** Jesus Christ
  means: 9 God with us

immaterial 7 ghostly, shadowy, trivial **8** bodiless, ethereal, mystical, noumenal, spectral, trifling, unbodied **9** spiritual, unearthly **10** evanescent, extraneous, impalpable, intangible, irrelevant, of no moment **11** disembodied, incorporeal, not relevant, unimportant **12** extramundane, extrasensory **13** insignificant, insubstantial, unsubstantial **14** of no importance **15** inconsequential, of little account

immature 5 green, young **6** callow, unripe **7** babyish, kiddish, puerile **8** childish, juvenile, unformed, youthful **9** embryonic, half-grown, infantile, not mature, pubescent **10** unfinished, unmellowed **11** out of season, rudimentary, undeveloped **16** wet behind the ears

immeasurable 7 endless, immense **8** infinite **9** boundless, limitless, unbounded, unlimited **10** fathomless **11**

illimitable, inestimable, measureless, never-ending **12** incalculable, interminable, unfathomable **13** inexhaustible

immediate 4 near, next, nigh **5** close, hasty, local, swift **6** abrupt, nearby, prompt, recent, speedy, sudden **7** express, instant, nearest **8** adjacent, punctual **9** proximate, undelayed **10** contiguous **13** instantaneous

immediately 3 now **4** ASAP, stat **9** instantly, right away **10** this minute **12** without delay
  French: 11 tout de suite

immemorial 5 olden **7** ageless, ancient **8** dateless, hallowed, timeless **9** ancestral, legendary, venerable **11** time-honored **12** long-standing, mythological **15** long-established

immense 4 huge, vast **5** great **7** mammoth, massive **8** colossal, enormous, gigantic **9** extensive, monstrous **10** prodigious, stupendous, tremendous **11** measureless **14** Brobdingnagian

immensity 8 enormity, hugeness, vastness **9** largeness **12** enormousness

immerse 3 dip **4** duck, dunk, sink, soak **5** bathe, douse, lower, steep **6** absorb, drench, engage, occupy, plunge **7** engross **8** submerge

immerse briefly 3 dip **4** dunk

immersion 7 bathing, dunking **8** drowning **10** absorption, submersion **11** engrossment, involvement, submergence **13** concentration, preoccupation

immigrant 5 alien **7** migrant, settler **8** colonist, newcomer **9** foreigner, nonnative

immigrate 6 move to, settle **7** migrate **8** colonize

imminent 4 near **7** looming **8** menacing, perilous **9** immediate, impending **10** near at hand **11** approaching, close at hand, threatening

immobile 4 fast **5** fixed, quiet, rigid, stiff, still **6** at rest, laid up, rooted, secure, stable, static **7** riveted **9** immovable, not moving, quiescent, steadfast **10** motionless, stationary, stock-still **11** unbudgeable **13** incapacitated

immobilize 3 fix, set **4** stud **6** disarm, freeze, splint **7** disable **8** paralyze, transfix **12** incapacitate

immoderate 5 undue **7** extreme **8** whopping **9** excessive, unbridled **10** exorbitant, gargantuan, inordinate, prodigious **11** extravagant, intemperate, uncalled-for **12** unreasonable, unrestrained **14** unconscionable

immoderation 6 excess **10** debauchery **11** dissipation, prodigality, unrestraint **12** extravagance, intemperance, recklessness **13** excessiveness **14** prodigiousness

immodest 4 lewd, vain **5** gross, loose **6** brazen, coarse, risque, wanton **7**

pompous 8 boastful, braggart, indecent, inflated, unchaste **9** bombastic, conceited, shameless **10** indecorous, indelicate, peacockish, suggestive **11** exaggerated, pretentious **12** self-centered

immoral 4 evil, lewd **5** dirty, wrong **6** sinful, wicked **7** corrupt, heinous, obscene, raunchy, vicious **8** depraved, indecent, infamous, prurient **9** debauched, dissolute, nefarious, salacious, unethical **10** dissipated, iniquitous, licentious, profligate **12** pornographic, unprincipled

Immoralist, The
author: 9 Andre Gide

immorality 3 sin **4** evil **9** decadence, depravity, indecency, obscenity, prurience **10** corruption, debasement, degeneracy, sinfulness **13** salaciousness

immortal 3 god **6** divine **7** abiding, eternal, undying **8** enduring **9** deathless **11** everlasting **12** imperishable

Immortals 6 giants, greats, titans **7** the gods **8** demigods **13** all-time greats
Greek/Roman: 8 pantheon

immovable 3 icy, set **4** cold, fast **5** fixed **6** dogged, secure, steely, stolid **7** adamant, settled **8** detached, fastened, immobile, obdurate, resolute, stubborn **9** heartless, impassive, unfeeling **10** inexorable, inflexible, stationary, unbendable **11** coldhearted, unbudgeable **12** unchangeable **13** unimpressible, unsympathetic **16** unimpressionable

immune 4 free, safe **5** clear **6** exempt **9** protected, resistant **12** invulnerable **13** unsusceptible

immunity 7 freedom **9** exemption **10** resistance **16** unsusceptibility

immure 3 hem, pen **4** cage, coop, jail, wall **6** entomb, intern, wall in, wall up **7** confine, enclose, seclude **8** cloister, imprison **11** incarcerate

immutability 9 endurance, stability **14** changelessness

immutable 4 firm **5** fixed, solid **6** stable **7** lasting **8** constant, enduring **9** permanent, unaltered, unvarying **10** changeless, inflexible, unchanging **11** unalterable **12** unchangeable, unmodifiable **14** intransmutable **16** incontrovertible

Imogen
character in: 9 Cymbeline
author: 11 Shakespeare

imp 3 elf **4** brat **5** demon, devil, gnome, pixie, scamp **6** goblin, hoyden, rascal, sprite, urchin **7** upstart **9** hobgoblin **10** evil spirit, leprechaun

impact 4 jolt **5** brunt, crash, force, shock, smash **6** burden, effect, thrust **7** contact **9** collision, influence **10** concussion **11** implication **12** repercussion

impair 3 mar **4** harm, hurt **6** damage, hinder, injure, lessen, reduce, weaken, worsen **7** cripple, subvert, vitiate **8** decrease, enervate, enfeeble, undercut **10** debilitate **11** detract from

impaired 6 broken, faulty, flawed **7** damaged **9** defective, deficient, imperfect

impairment 4 flaw, harm **5** fault **6** damage, defect, injury, malady **7** ailment, illness **8** debility, disorder, handicap, sickness, weakness **9** detriment, hindrance, infirmity **10** disability, impediment, inadequacy **12** debilitation

impale 3 fix, pin **4** gore, stab, tack **5** affix, stick **8** transfix **10** run through

impart 4 give, lend, tell **5** grant, offer, share **6** accord, afford, pass on, relate, render, report, reveal **7** confide, consign, deliver, divulge, mention **8** bestow on, confer on, disclose, dispense **9** make known **10** contribute **11** communicate

impartial 4 fair, just **7** neutral **8** detached, unbiased **9** equitable, objective **10** evenhanded, fair-minded, open-minded **11** nonpartisan **12** unprejudiced **13** disinterested, dispassionate

impartiality 7 justice **8** equality, fair play, fairness **10** detachment, neutrality **11** objectivity

impasse 4 snag **7** dead end, dilemma **8** cul-de-sac, deadlock, quandary, standoff **9** stalemate **10** blind alley, bottleneck, standstill **11** predicament

impassioned 5 eager, fiery **6** ardent, heated **7** earnest, excited, fervent, intense, rousing, zealous **8** animated, forceful, inspired, stirring

impassive 4 calm, cool **5** aloof, stony **6** sedate, stolid **7** stoical, unmoved **8** reserved **9** apathetic, untouched **10** impervious, insensible, phlegmatic **11** emotionless, indifferent, inscrutable, unemotional, unperturbed **13** dispassionate, imperturbable, unimpressible **16** unimpressionable

impassiveness 8 coldness **9** aloofness, stolidity **12** indifference **15** emotionlessness

impassivity 6 apathy **8** coolness, stoicism **9** aloofness, stolidity **10** dispassion **15** emotionlessness **16** imperturbability

impatient 4 edgy **5** fussy, hasty, itchy, rabid, tense, testy **6** ardent, touchy **7** annoyed, anxious, brusque, hurried, nervous, peevish, restive **8** agitated, feverish, restless **9** excitable, irascible, irritable, irritated **10** high-strung, intolerant, passionate **12** enthusiastic

impeach 4 slur **6** accuse, assail, attack, charge, impugn, indict **7** arraign, slander **8** badmouth, belittle, question **9** challenge, discredit, disparage, incul-

pate **11** incriminate **16** call into question

impeccable 7 perfect **8** flawless **9** blameless, excellent, faultless **10** immaculate **11** unblemished **12** irreprovable, unassailable **13** unimpeachable **14** irreproachable **15** unexceptionable

impecunious 4 poor **5** broke, needy **6** hard-up **7** pinched **8** bankrupt, indigent **9** destitute, insolvent, penniless **10** down-and-out, straitened **12** impoverished **15** poverty-stricken

impede 5 block, check, delay, deter, stall **6** arrest, halter, hamper, hinder, retard, stymie, thwart **7** disrupt, inhibit **8** hold back, obstruct, slow down **9** frustrate, interrupt, sidetrack **13** interfere with

impediment 4 flaw **5** block, delay **6** defect **7** barrier **8** blockage, drawback, handicap, obstacle **9** deformity, hindrance **10** detraction **11** obstruction **12** interference **14** stumbling block

impedimenta 4 gear **7** baggage **9** equipment **13** accoutrements, paraphernalia

impel 4 goad, prod, push, spur, urge **5** drive, force **6** compel, incite, induce, prompt **7** require **8** motivate **9** constrain, stimulate **11** necessitate

impend 4 brew, hang, loom **5** hover, lower **6** menace **8** approach, draw near, overhang, threaten

impending 4 near **6** coming **7** brewing, looming **8** imminent, menacing, oncoming **9** immediate **11** approaching, forthcoming, threatening

impenetrable 5 dense, solid, thick **6** sealed **7** elusive, obscure **8** puzzling **9** insoluble **10** impassable, impervious, insensible, intangible, inviolable, mysterious, unpalpable **11** inscrutable, unenterable **12** inaccessible, inexplicable, invulnerable, unfathomable **16** incomprehensible

impenitent 4 lost **6** inured **7** callous, defiant **8** hardened, obdurate **9** unashamed **10** uncontrite **11** remorseless, unrepentant, unrepenting **12** incorrigible, unapologetic **13** irreclaimable

imperative 6 urgent **7** crucial, needful **8** critical, pressing **9** essential, mandatory, necessary, requisite **10** compulsory, obligatory **11** unavoidable

imperceptible 5 minor, scant, small **6** hidden, minute, slight, subtle **7** minimal **8** academic **10** indistinct **12** undetectable, unnoticeable **13** infinitesimal, insignificant, unappreciable, unperceivable **14** inconsiderable

imperceptive 5 blind **9** unfeeling **11** insensitive, unobservant **12** inpercipient, unperceptive **13** unsympathetic

imperfect 6 faulty, flawed **8** deformed, fallible, impaired **9** blemished, defective

imperfection 4 flaw 5 fault 6 defect 7 blemish 8 weakness 9 deformity 10 faultiness, impairment, inadequacy 11 fallibility, shortcoming 13 insufficiency 14 incompleteness

imperial 5 bossy 6 feudal, lordly 8 despotic 9 arbitrary, imperious 10 autocratic, high-handed, peremptory, repressive, tyrannical 11 dictatorial, domineering, magisterial, overbearing 13 authoritarian

Imperial Presidency, The
   author: 20 Arthur M Schlesinger Jr

imperil 4 risk 6 chance, expose, gamble, hazard 8 endanger 10 compromise, jeopardize 13 put in jeopardy

imperious 5 bossy, lofty 6 lordly 7 haughty 8 arrogant, despotic, imperial 10 autocratic, commanding, peremptory, tyrannical 11 dictatorial, domineering, overbearing 13 high-and-mighty

imperiousness 9 arrogance, loftiness 11 haughtiness

imperishable 6 stable 7 durable, lasting 14 indestructible

imperium 4 rule 5 realm 6 domain, empire 8 dominion 11 sovereignty

impermanent 7 passing 8 fleeting, fugitive, not fixed, unstable 9 ephemeral, temporary, transient 10 evanescent, transitory, unenduring

impermeable 5 dense, solid, tight 6 opaque 9 nonporous 10 impervious, waterproof

impersonal 4 dead 6 remote 7 general, inhuman, neutral 8 detached, lifeless, soulless 9 impartial, impassive, inanimate, inorganic, objective 10 spiritless 11 perfunctory 13 disinterested, dispassionate

impersonate 3 ape 4 copy, mime 5 mimic 6 pose as 7 imitate, portray 9 personify, represent 11 pretend to be 12 masquerade as

impertinence 4 sass 5 cheek, sauce 7 affront 8 audacity, boldness, rudeness 9 freshness, impudence, insolence, sauciness 10 cheekiness, disrespect, effrontery, incivility 11 irrelevance 17 disrespectfulness, inappropriateness

impertinent 4 rude 5 fresh, surly 6 brassy, brazen, smarty 7 uncivil 8 arrogant, impudent, insolent 9 extrinsic, insulting, unrelated 10 extraneous, immaterial, irrelevant, not germane, peremptory, unmannerly 11 unimportant 12 discourteous, presumptuous 13 disrespectful, inappropriate 14 beside the point

imperturbability 5 poise 6 aplomb 8 calmness, coolness 9 composure, sangfroid 10 equanimity, steadiness 11 self-control, tranquility 12 tranquillity 14 presence of mind, self-possession

imperturbable 4 calm, cool 6 sedate, serene 8 composed 9 collected, impassive, unanxious, unfazable, unruffled 10 impervious 11 levelheaded, undisturbed, unexcitable, unflappable, unflustered 13 dispassionate, unsusceptible

impervious 6 closed 8 immune to 11 impermeable 12 impenetrable, inaccessible, invulnerable 14 unapproachable

impetuosity 8 rashness 11 spontaneity, unrestraint 12 recklessness 13 impulsiveness 14 capriciousness

impetuous 4 rash 5 hasty 6 abrupt, stormy 7 rampant, violent 8 forcible, headlong, vehement 9 impulsive 10 capricious, inexorable, relentless, unexpected 11 precipitate 14 unpremeditated

impetus 4 prod, push, spur 5 boost, drive, force, start 6 motive 7 impulse 8 momentum, stimulus 9 impulsion, incentive 10 motivation, propulsion 11 moving force, stimulation

impiety 9 blasphemy, sacrilege 10 disrespect, irreligion 11 irreverence, ungodliness

impinge 7 intrude, obtrude, violate 8 encroach, infringe, trespass 10 transgress

impious 7 godless, immoral, profane, ungodly 8 apostate, renegade 9 perverted 10 iniquitous, irreverent 11 blasphemous, irreligious 12 iconoclastic, sacrilegious 13 disrespectful

impiousness 7 impiety 9 blasphemy, sacrilege 10 disrespect 11 irreverence, ungodliness

impish 5 elfin 7 implike, puckish, roguish 8 prankish, rascally, sportive 11 mischievous

implacable 10 inexorable, inflexible, relentless, unamenable 11 intractable, unrelenting 12 unappeasable, unpacifiable 14 irreconcilable, uncompromising

implant 3 fix, set, sow 4 root 5 embed, graft, imbed, inlay, teach 6 infuse, insert 7 impress, instill 8 entrench 9 establish, inculcate 10 impregnate

implausible 8 doubtful, unlikely 9 illogical, senseless 10 far-fetched, improbable, incredible, outrageous, ridiculous 12 preposterous, unbelievable, unreasonable 13 inconceivable

implement 4 tool 5 begin, enact, piece, start 6 device 7 achieve, article, fulfill, realize, utensil 8 activate, carry out 9 apparatus, appliance, equipment, materials 10 accomplish, bring about, instrument 11 set in motion 13 put into effect

implicate 7 connect, embroil, ensnare, involve 8 entangle 9 associate, inculpate 11 incriminate

implication 6 effect 7 outcome 8 innuendo, overtone 9 inference 10 connection, intimation, suggestion 11 association, connotation, consequence, insinuation, involvement 12 entanglement, ramification, significance

implicit 5 total 6 hinted, innate 7 certain, implied, staunch 8 absolute, complete, inferred, inherent, profound, resolute 9 deducible, steadfast, suggested 10 understood, unreserved, unshakable 13 unquestioning

implied 5 tacit 7 oblique 8 indirect 9 implicitly, indicated

implode 11 burst inward 17 compress violently

implore 3 beg 4 urge 6 obtest 7 beseech, entreat 9 importune, plead with 10 supplicate

imply 4 hint, mean 6 denote 7 bespeak, betoken, connote, presume, signify, suggest 8 evidence, indicate, intimate 9 insinuate 10 presuppose

impolite 4 rude 7 ill-bred, uncivil 9 impolitic, unfitting, ungenteel, unrefined 10 undecorous, unmannerly 12 discourteous 13 disrespectful, inconsiderate

impoliteness 8 rudeness 10 bad manners, incivility 11 boorishness, discourtesy

import 6 burden, moment, thrust 7 meaning 9 overtones 10 importance 11 connotation, implication 12 ramification, significance

importance 4 rank 5 value, worth 6 esteem, import, moment, repute, weight 7 stature 8 eminence, position 9 influence, relevance 11 consequence, seriousness, weightiness 12 significance 13 essentialness, momentousness

Importance of Being Earnest, The
   author: 10 Oscar Wilde
   character: 12 Cecily Cardew, Jack Worthing, Letitia Prism 16 Gwendolen Fairfax 17 Algernon Moncrieff (Algy) 20 Lady Augusta Bracknell 21 Reverend Canon Chasuble

important 5 great, major 7 leading, notable, seminal, serious, weighty 8 creative, esteemed, foremost, original 9 momentous, prominent 10 imperative, meaningful, preeminent, remarkable 11 distinctive, influential, significant 13 consequential

imported 5 alien 6 exotic 7 foreign 9 not native

importunate 7 begging 8 pleading 9 imploring 10 entreating, persistent 11 troublesome 12 supplicating

importune 3 beg, sue 4 pray 5 plead 6 adjure, exhort 7 beseech, entreat, implore 8 appeal to, petition 10 supplicate

importunity 4 plea 6 appeal 7 request 8 entreaty, petition 12 supplication

impose 3 set 4 levy 5 apply, enact, foist, force, lay on 6 peddle, slap on 7 command, dictate, inflict, palm off, place on 9 establish, institute, introduce, prescribe 10 thrust upon

impose upon 5 annoy 6 bother, ill-use 8 ill-treat, maltreat, mistreat 15 take advantage of

imposing 5 grand, lofty 7 massive, stately 8 majestic, striking, towering 10 commanding, impressive, monumental 11 outstanding 12 awe-inspiring

imposition 5 abuse 6 burden, ill use 8 foisting 10 obligation 15 taking advantage

impossible 8 stubborn 9 insoluble 10 unbearable, unsolvable, unyielding 11 intolerable, intractable, not possible 12 insufferable, intransigent, unachievable, unanswerable, unattainable, unimaginable, unmanageable 13 inconceivable 16 out of the question

impost 3 fee, tax 4 duty, fine, toll 6 charge, excise, tariff 10 assessment

impostor 4 sham 5 cheat, duper, fraud, phony, quack 6 con man 7 bluffer, shammer 8 deceiver 9 charlatan, defrauder, pretender, trickster 10 dissembler, mountebank 11 counterfeit, flimflam man, masquerader, pettifogger 12 impersonator

imposture 4 fake, hoax, play, ruse, sham 5 cheat, fraud, trick 6 deceit, humbug 7 forgery, swindle 8 artifice, delusion, pretense, quackery 9 deception, falsehood, imitation 10 pretension 11 charlatanry, counterfeit, fraudulence 12 charlatanism 13 impersonation, mountebankery

impotence 8 weakness 9 paralysis 10 disability, incapacity, inefficacy 12 helplessness 13 powerlessness 14 ineffectuality 15 ineffectiveness

impotent 4 weak 5 frail 6 feeble 7 hapless 8 disabled, feckless, helpless 9 paralyzed, powerless 11 ineffective

impound 3 pen 4 cage 5 pen in, seize 6 coop up, encage, lock up, shut in 7 confine 13 hold in custody

impoverish 4 bust, ruin 5 break, drain 6 beggar, pauper, reduce 7 deplete, exhaust 8 bankrupt, make poor 9 pauperize 18 send to the poorhouse

impoverished 4 poor 6 abject, barren, bereft, effete, used up 7 drained, sterile, wanting, worn out 8 depleted, indigent, wiped out 9 destitute, exhausted 10 down-and-out, pauperized 11 impecunious 12 unproductive, without means

impractical 6 sloppy, unwise 8 careless, quixotic, romantic 10 loose-ended, starry-eyed 11 unrealistic 12 disorganized 13 helter-skelter, unintelligent

imprecation 5 curse 8 anathema 11 malediction

impregnable 6 mighty, potent, strong, sturdy 8 powerful 10 invincible 12 invulnerable, unassailable, unattackable 13 unconquerable

impregnate 3 wet 4 soak 5 steep 6 dampen, drench, imbrue, infuse 7 moisten, suffuse 8 fructify, inundate, permeate, saturate 9 fecundate, fertilize 10 inseminate

impresario 7 manager, sponsor 8 director 9 conductor, organizer 12 entrepreneur

impress 4 grab, move, stir, sway 5 reach, touch 6 affect, excite, sink in, strike 8 bedazzle 9 electrify, influence, overpower, overwhelm

impression 4 idea, mark, mold, view 5 hunch, stamp, trace, track 6 belief, effect, impact, notion 7 contour, feeling, impress, imprint, opinion, outline, surmise 9 influence, reception, sensation 10 conviction 11 indentation 13 understanding

impressionable 8 gullible, passible, sentient 9 affective, receptive 10 vulnerable 11 suggestible

impressive 5 grand 6 august, moving 8 exciting, imposing, majestic, striking 9 memorable, thrilling 11 magnificent, outstanding 12 awe-inspiring, overpowering, soul-stirring 13 unforgettable

imprimis 15 in the first place

imprint 3 fix 4 etch, mark, sign 5 infix, press, stamp, title 6 indent 7 engrave, impress 8 inscribe 9 engraving 10 depression, impression 11 indentation

imprison 3 pen 4 jail 6 coop up, engage, entomb, immure, lock up 7 confine, fence in, impound, shackle 8 restrain 11 hold captive, incarcerate

improbable 8 doubtful, unlikely 9 illogical 11 implausible 12 unreasonable 13 unforeseeable

improbable solution in a play's plot
Latin: 13 deus ex machina

impromptu 6 sudden 7 offhand 9 impulsive, makeshift, on the spot 10 improvised, off the cuff, unexpected, unprepared 11 spontaneous, unrehearsed 14 extemporaneous, unpremeditated, without warning 15 spur-of-the-moment 16 extemporaneously, on a moment's notice 19 off the top of one's head

improper 4 lewd 5 inapt, unfit 8 indecent, off-color, unseemly 9 ill-suited, irregular 10 indecorous, malapropos, out of place, suggestive, unbecoming,

unsuitable 12 inharmonious 13 inappropriate, unconformable
French: 5 outre

impropriety 5 gaffe 7 blunder, faux pas 9 gaucherie, indecorum, vulgarity 10 bad manners 11 boorishness 12 impoliteness, indiscretion

improve 4 help 5 rally 6 better, enrich, repair 7 correct, develop, enhance 9 cultivate 10 ameliorate, recuperate

improvement 4 gain 6 reform, repair 7 advance, upswing 8 additive, progress 9 amendment 10 betterment, emendation, refinement 11 advancement, enhancement, reclamation 12 amelioration 14 reconstruction

improvidence 10 imprudence 11 prodigality 12 extravagance, wastefulness 13 shiftlessness 16 shortsightedness

improvident 6 lavish 8 prodigal, reckless, wasteful 9 imprudent, negligent, unthrifty 10 thriftless 11 extravagant, spendthrift 12 shortsighted 14 unparsimonious

improvise 5 ad-lib 6 make up, wing it 11 extemporize

improvised 5 ad-lib 7 devised, offhand 8 invented 9 concocted, contrived, dreamed-up, extempore, hatched-up, impromptu, makeshift 10 off-the-cuff, originated, unprepared 11 extemporary, spontaneous, unrehearsed 12 extemporized 14 extemporaneous, unpremeditated 15 improvisational, spur-of-the- moment

imprudent 4 rash 5 crazy, dopey 6 unwise 7 foolish 8 heedless, mindless, untoward 9 foolhardy 10 ill-advised, incautious, indiscreet, unthinking 11 inadvisable, injudicious, thoughtless 13 ill-considered

impudence
Yiddish: 7 chutzpa 8 chutzpah

impudent 4 bold, rude 5 brash, fresh, nervy, saucy 6 brazen, cheeky 7 forward, upstart 8 impolite, insolent 9 bumptious, shameless 11 impertinent, smart-alecky, wiseacreish 12 discourteous 13 disrespectful

impugn 4 deny 5 knock, libel 6 assail, attack, berate, negate, oppose 7 asperse, slander 8 denounce, question 9 challenge, criticize 10 contradict 14 call in question, cast aspersions 16 call into question

impugnment 7 slander 10 aspersions

impulse 4 bent, goad, push, spur, urge, whim 5 drive, fancy, force 6 desire, motive, notion, thrust, whimsy 7 caprice, impetus, whimsey 8 instinct, momentum, movement, stimulus, stirring 9 incentive 10 incitement, motivation 11 inclination, inspiration, instigation

impulsive 4 rash 7 driving, offhand 8

forceful, forcible, notional **9** impelling, impetuous, impromptu, unplanned, whimsical **10** capricious, incautious, propellant, propelling **11** involuntary, spontaneous **12** devil-may-care **13** unpredictable **14** extemporaneous, unpremeditated **15** spur-of-themoment

impulsiveness 8 rashness **11** impetuosity, spontaneity, unrestraint **12** recklessness, whimsicality **14** capriciousness

impunity 8 immunity **9** clearance, exemption, privilege **10** absolution **11** prerogative **12** dispensation

impure 4 foul, lewd **5** dirty **6** coarse, filthy, smutty **7** debased, defiled, immoral, lustful, noisome, noxious, obscene, sullied, tainted, unclean **8** degraded, devalued, immodest, improper, indecent, polluted, prurient, unchaste, vitiated **9** lecherous, salacious, unrefined **10** indecorous, indelicate, libidinous, licentious **11** adulterated, depreciated, unwholesome **12** contaminated

impurity 5 alloy, dross, filth, taint **8** foulness **9** dirtiness, pollutant, pollution **10** adulterant, corruption, defilement **11** contaminant, taintedness, uncleanness **12** adulteration **13** contamination, foreign matter **15** unwholesomeness

imputation 6 charge **10** accusation, allegation, ascription **11** attribution

impute 5 refer **6** assign, charge, credit, relate **7** ascribe **9** attribute

inability 10 inaptitude, incapacity, ineptitude **12** helplessness, incapability, incompetence **13** maladroitness, powerlessness

in absence
　Latin: **10** in absentia

in absentia 9 in absence

inaccessible 9 not at hand **11** unreachable **12** unattainable, unobtainable **14** unapproachable

in accord 9 agreeable, approving, in harmony, of one mind **10** concurring, consenting **11** in agreement
　French: **9** en rapport

inaccuracy 4 goof, slip **5** error, fault, wrong **6** boo-boo **7** blunder, erratum, fallacy, mistake **9** unclarity **10** faultiness **11** imprecision, inexactness **13** incorrectness, unreliability **14** fallaciousness

inaccurate 3 off **5** false, wrong **6** faulty **7** inexact **8** mistaken **9** erroneous, imprecise, incorrect, off target **10** fallacious, unreliable **11** not on target, off the track **13** wide of the mark

inaction 8 abeyance, deferral, dormancy, dullness, idleness **9** cessation, indolence **10** inactivity, quiescence, somnolence, suspension **11** complacency

inactive 4 dull, idle, lazy **5** inert, quiet, still **6** low-key, otiose, static, torpid, unused **7** dormant, languid **8** indolent, slothful, sluggish **9** donothing, easygoing, leisurely, sedentary, somnolent **10** on the shelf **11** inoperative **12** out of service

inactivity 4 rest **5** quiet **6** disuse **7** inertia **8** dormancy, idleness, inaction **9** stillness **10** quiescence

in actuality
　Latin: **6** in esse

in addition 3 and, too **4** also, more, plus, then **5** above, added, again, extra **6** as well, beyond **7** besides, further **8** moreover **10** additional **12** additionally, supplemental

inadequacy 4 lack **7** failing **10** deficiency, impairment **11** shortcoming **13** insufficiency

inadequate 5 inept, short, unfit **6** meager, scanty, too raw **7** lacking, not up to, wanting **8** below par, unfitted **9** deficient, imperfect, incapable **11** incompetent, unqualified **12** insufficient

inadmissible 10 disallowed, extraneous **11** intolerable **12** not permitted, unacceptable **14** nonpermissible

in advance 6 before, in time, sooner **7** earlier **9** before now **10** beforehand **11** ahead of time **13** before the fact

inadvertent 7 unmeant **10** accidental, fortuitous, unintended, unthinking **11** involuntary **13** unintentional **14** unpremeditated

inadvisable 5 risky **6** chancy, unwise **9** impolitic, imprudent **10** ill-advised **11** inexpedient, injudicious, inopportune

in aeternum 7 forever

in agreement
　French: **9** en rapport

inalienable 6 sacred **8** absolute, defended, inherent **9** protected **10** inviolable, sacrosanct **12** unassailable **13** unforfeitable, unimpeachable

in all
　Latin: **6** in toto

in all places 10 every place, everywhere, far and near, far and wide

in a low voice
　Latin: **9** sotto voce

inamorata 4 lady, love **5** lover **7** beloved, darling **8** ladylove, mistress, paramour, truelove **10** sweetheart

inane 4 dumb **5** dopey, empty, silly, vapid **6** absurd, jejune, stupid **7** asinine, fatuous, foolish, idiotic, insipid, shallow, vacuous **9** pointless, senseless **10** ridiculous, unthinking **11** meaningless, nonsensical **13** unintelligent

inanimate 4 cold, dead, dull **5** inert **6** asleep, stolid **8** lifeless, soulless **9** inorganic, insensate, nonliving, sense-

less, unfeeling **10** insensible, insentient **11** unconscious

inanity 6 drivel **7** hogwash, vacuity **8** nonsense, vapidity **9** absurdity, asininity, silliness **11** foolishness **13** pointlessness, senselessness **14** ridiculousness

Inanna
　origin: 8 Sumerian
　goddess of: 3 war **4** love
　sister: 10 Ereshkigal
　realm: 6 heaven
　corresponds to: 6 Ishtar **7** Astarte, Mylitta **9** Ashtoreth

in any case 6 anyhow, anyway **9** at any rate **10** in any event

inapplicable 5 unfit **6** not apt **8** unsuited **10** inapposite, irrelevant, not germane, unsuitable **12** incompatible, not pertinent **13** inappropriate

inappropriate 5 inapt **8** ill-timed, improper, unsuited **9** unfitting **10** indecorous, in bad taste, out of place, unbecoming, unsuitable **11** incongruous **12** incompatible, infelicitous
　French: **10** mal a propos

inapt 8 improper, unseemly, unsuited **9** ill-suited, incorrect, unfitting **11** incongruous **13** inappropriate

inaptness 9 inability, ineptness **10** clumsiness, inaptitude, ineptitude **12** incompetence **13** maladroitness **14** unskillfulness

in arrears 4 late **7** overdue **10** delinquent

inarticulate 4 dumb, mute **7** babbled, blurred, garbled, mumbled **8** confused, wordless **9** paralyzed **10** incoherent, indistinct, speechless, tongue-tied **12** inexpressive **14** unintelligible **15** uncommunicative

inartistic 9 graceless, inelegant, tasteless **10** ungraceful **11** unaesthetic **12** unattractive

in a series
　French: **7** en suite

in a set
　French: **7** en suite

in attendance 4 here **7** present, serving **9** appearing, caring for, on the spot, waiting on **12** accompanying, looking after, taking care of

inattention 6 apathy **10** negligence **12** carelessness **14** lack of interest **16** absentmindedness, unresponsiveness

inattentive 7 unaware **8** careless, heedless **9** forgetful, negligent, unmindful **10** distracted **11** daydreaming, thoughtless, unobservant **12** absentminded

inaugurate 5 set up, start **6** induct, launch **7** instate, kick off, usher in **8** initiate **9** institute, undertake **10** embark upon **11** set in action

inauguration 5 start **9** beginning, induction **10** dedication **11** origination **12** commencement

inaugurator 6 author, father **7** creator, founder, starter **9** initiator, organizer **10** originator, prime mover

inauspicious 7 unlucky **9** ill-chosen, ill-omened **10** badly timed, disastrous **11** unfavorable, unfortunate, unpromising **12** infelicitous, unpropitious

in a vacuum
    Latin: **7** in vacuo

in bad faith
    Latin: **8** mala fide

in being
    Latin: **6** in esse

inborn 5 basic **6** inbred, innate, native **7** natural **8** inherent **9** inherited, intrinsic, intuitive **10** congenital **11** fundamental, instinctive **14** constitutional

inbred 6 inborn, innate, primal **7** natural **8** inherent **9** ingrained, inherited, intrinsic, intuitive **10** congenital, deep-rooted, deep-seated, hereditary, indwelling **11** instinctive, instinctual **12** deeply rooted **14** constitutional

Inca
    language family: **7** Quechua
    location: **4** Peru **5** Chili **7** Bolivia, Ecuador **9** Argentina **12** South America
    leader: **7** Huascar **8** Topa Inca **9** Atahualpa, Pachacuti **10** Manco Capac **11** Huayna Capac
    conquered by: **7** Pizarro
    ruins: **11** Machu Picchu, Sacsahuaman, Tambo Machay

incalculable 7 dubious **8** infinite **9** countless, uncertain **11** inestimable, innumerable, measureless, uncountable **12** immeasurable, incomputable **13** unforeseeable, unpredictable

incandesce 4 burn, glow **5** flare, flash

incandescent 7 dynamic, glowing, radiant **8** electric, galvanic, magnetic, white-hot **9** brilliant **11** high-powered **12** electrifying **13** scintillating

incantation 3 hex **4** jinx **5** chant, charm, magic, spell **6** voodoo **7** sorcery **8** wizardry **10** black magic, hocus-pocus, invocation, mumbo-jumbo, necromancy, witchcraft **11** abracadabra, conjuration

incapable 5 inept, unfit **6** unable **8** helpless, impotent, inferior **9** powerless, unskilled, untrained **10** inadequate **11** incompetent, ineffective, inefficient, unqualified

incapacitate 4 maim, undo **5** lay up **7** cripple, disable **8** enfeeble, handicap, paralyze, sideline **9** make unfit **10** disqualify **13** make powerless **14** put out of action **15** render incapable

incapacitated 6 laid up **8** crippled, disabled, disarmed, helpless, stricken **9** hamstrung, paralyzed, sidelined **10** on the shelf, prostrated **11** immobi-lized, out of action **12** hors de combat **14** flat on one's back

incapacity 7 illness **8** sickness **9** crippling **10** deficiency, disability **12** incapability

incarcerate 3 pen **4** jail **6** commit, coop up, immure, intern, lock up **7** confine, impound **8** imprison, restrain

incarceration 9 detention **10** commitment, internment **11** confinement, durance vile **12** imprisonment **18** institutionalizing

incarnate 8 embodied, manifest **9** personify **10** actualized, in the flesh **11** objectified, personified

Incarnations
    author: **16** Robert Penn Warren

incautious 4 rash **5** brash **6** unwary **8** careless, heedless, reckless **9** hotheaded, impetuous, imprudent, impulsive, overhasty **10** headstrong, indiscreet, unthinking **11** injudicious, thoughtless

incendiary 8 agitator, arsonist **12** inflammatory

incense 3 ire **5** anger **6** burn up, enrage, madden **7** inflame, provoke **9** infuriate, make angry **13** make indignant
    spice: **6** stacte

incensed 3 mad **5** angry, irate **6** fuming, raging **7** enraged, furious **8** burned up, inflamed, outraged, provoked **9** affronted, indignant **10** infuriated

incentive 4 lure, spur **6** come-on, motive **8** stimulus **10** enticement, inducement, motivation **11** inspiration **13** encouragement

inception 5 birth, debut, onset, start **6** origin, outset **7** arrival **9** beginning **12** commencement, inauguration

incessant 8 constant, unbroken, unending **9** ceaseless, continual, perpetual, unceasing **10** continuous, persistent **11** everlasting, unrelenting, unremitting **12** interminable **13** uninterrupted

inch
    abbreviation: **2** in

In Chancery
    author: **14** John Galsworthy
    part of trilogy: **11** Forsyte Saga

inchoate 7 budding, nascent **8** formless, unformed, unshaped **9** amorphous, beginning, embryonic, incipient, shapeless **10** commencing, disjointed, uncohesive **11** unorganized **12** disconnected

incidence 4 rate **5** range, scope **6** extent **8** occasion **9** frequency, happening **10** commonness, occurrence, phenomenon **11** routineness

incident 5 clash, event, scene **6** affair **7** episode, related **8** occasion **9** hap-pening **10** incidental, occurrence **11** contretemps, disturbance

incidental 5 minor **9** accessory, secondary **10** extraneous, unexpected **11** subordinate, unlooked-for

incidentally 7 apropos, by the by **8** by the way **9** in passing **14** speaking of that **15** parenthetically **21** while we're on the subject

incidentals 6 extras **8** minutiae **10** minor items **11** accessories, odds and ends **13** appurtenances

incinerate 4 burn **7** consume, cremate **9** carbonize **13** reduce to ashes

incineration 6 firing **7** burning, flaming **8** ignition, kindling **9** cremation **10** combustion **13** carbonization

incinerator 4 oven **6** burner **7** furnace

incipient 7 budding, nascent **8** inchoate **9** beginning, embryonic, fledgling, promising **10** developing, half-formed **11** rudimentary

in circulation 4 rife **6** abroad, around **7** at large **9** all around **11** going around **12** spread around **14** around and about **15** making the rounds

incise 4 etch **5** carve **7** cut into, engrave

incision 3 cut **4** scar, gash, nick, slit **5** cleft, notch, score, slash, slice, wound **6** furrow

incisive 4 curt, keen **5** acute, brisk, crisp, sharp **6** biting, shrewd **7** cutting, express, mordant, precise, probing, summary **8** analytic, piercing **9** trenchant, well-aimed **10** perceptive **11** intelligent, penetrating

incite 4 goad, prod, stir **5** drive, egg on, impel, rouse **6** arouse, excite, fire up, foment, induce, prompt, stir up, urge on **7** actuate, agitate, inflame, provoke **8** activate **9** instigate, stimulate

incitement 6 urging **7** arousal, driving, goading **8** egging on, exciting, firing up, stirring **9** agitating, fomenting, inflaming, prompting, provoking **10** activation, stirring up **11** provocation, stimulation

incivility 8 rudeness **9** barbarism, impudence, indecorum, surliness, vulgarity **10** bad manners, coarseness, disrespect **11** boorishness, discourtesy, misbehavior, uncouthness **12** impoliteness, tactlessness **14** unpleasantness

inclement 3 raw **4** foul **5** harsh, nasty, rough **6** bitter, severe, stormy **7** violent **11** tempestuous

inclination 3 bow, dip, nod **4** bend, bent, hill, rake, rise **5** grade, pitch, slant, slope **6** liking **7** bending, leaning, sloping **8** fondness, lowering, penchant, tendency **9** acclivity, inclining, proneness **10** preference, proclivity, propensity **11** disposition **12** predilection **14** predisposition

incline 3 bow **4** bend, cant, hill, lean, like, rake, seem, tend, tilt, wont **5** be apt, enjoy, pitch, slant, slope **6** prefer **7** decline **8** be likely, gradient **9** acclivity **10** lean toward **11** bend forward, have a mind to

inclined 3 apt **5** prove **6** liable, likely **7** given to **10** disposed to **11** predisposed

incline downward 3 dip, sag **4** sink **5** droop, slant, slope

inclined to delay 4 slow **5** tardy **6** remiss **8** dawdling, dilatory, sluggish **9** reluctant **12** foot-dragging **13** dillydallying **15** procrastinating

include 5 cover **6** enfold, entail, take in **7** contain, embrace, involve, subsume **8** comprise **9** encompass **10** comprehend **11** incorporate

inclusive 7 general, overall **8** sweeping, taking in **9** embracing, including **10** comprising, encircling **11** surrounding **12** encyclopedic **13** comprehending, comprehensive, incorporating **15** all-encompassing

incognito 7 unknown, unnamed **8** nameless **9** concealed, disguised, protected **10** in disguise, uncredited, undercover, unrevealed **11** undisclosed **12** unidentified **14** unacknowledged, unrecognizable

incognizant 6 obtuse **7** unaware **8** ignorant, unseeing **9** unknowing **13** unconscious of **15** uncomprehending

incoherent 7 muddled, unclear **8** confused, rambling **9** illogical **10** disjointed, irrational **11** bewildering, nonsensical **12** inconsistent **14** unintelligible

In Cold Blood
   author: 12 Truman Capote
   director: 13 Richard Brooks
   cast: 11 Paul Stewart, Robert Blake, Scott Wilson **12** John Forsythe

income 5 means, wages **6** salary **7** revenue **8** earnings **9** emolument **10** livelihood

income, annual
   French: 5 rente

incomparable 8 peerless **9** matchless, unequaled, unrivaled **10** inimitable **11** ne plus ultra, superlative **12** transcendent **13** beyond compare **14** unapproachable

incompatibility 6 strife **7** discord **8** friction, variance **9** disaccord, wrangling **10** antagonism **11** being at odds, discordance **13** lack of harmony

incompatible 6 at odds **7** jarring **8** clashing, contrary, unsuited **10** at variance, discordant, mismatched **11** disagreeing, incongruous, uncongenial **12** antagonistic, inconsistent, inharmonious **13** contradictory, inappropriate

incompetency 9 inability, unfitness **10** ineptitude **11** lack of skill **12** inefficiency **15** ineffectiveness

incompetent 5 inept, unfit **8** inexpert **9** incapable, unskilled, untrained **11** ineffective, ineffectual, inefficient, unqualified **14** lacking ability

incomplete 6 broken **7** partial, wanting **9** defective, deficient **10** unfinished **11** fragmentary

incompleteness 8 omission **10** deficiency **11** shortcoming **15** unfinished state

incomprehensible 7 obscure **8** abstruse, baffling **9** confusing **10** befuddling **11** bewildering, inscrutable, ungraspable **12** impenetrable, unfathomable **14** unintelligible **19** beyond comprehension, beyond understanding

incomprehension 10 bafflement, puzzlement **12** bewilderment **19** failure to understand

inconceivable 7 strange **8** unlikely **10** improbable, incredible **11** unthinkable **12** beyond belief, unbelievable, unimaginable **14** highly unlikely

in conclusion
   French: 5 enfin

inconclusive 4 open **9** unsettled **10** indecisive, indefinite, unresolved, up in the air **11** not definite **12** unconvincing, undetermined **13** indeterminate

incongruity 8 variance **9** disparity **10** aberration, disharmony, divergence **11** abnormality, discrepancy **13** dissimilarity, inconsistency, unsuitability **17** inappropriateness

incongruous 5 odd **6** far-out **8** contrary **10** at variance, discrepant, out of place, outlandish, unsuitable **11** conflicting, disagreeing **12** incompatible, inconsistent, out of keeping **13** contradictory, inappropriate **14** irreconcilable

inconsequential 5 petty **6** slight **7** trivial **8** nugatory, picayune, piddling, trifling **9** valueless **10** negligible, of no moment **11** meaningless, unimportant **13** insignificant **15** of no consequence

inconsiderable 5 light, minor, petty, small **6** little, modest, paltry, slight **7** minimal, trivial **8** picayune, trifling **9** no big deal **10** negligible **11** unimportant **13** insignificant, no great shakes **15** inconsequential

inconsiderate 4 rash, rude **6** remiss, unkind **7** uncivil **8** careless, impolite, tactless, uncaring **9** negligent **10** ungracious, unthinking **11** insensitive, thoughtless **12** disregardful, uncharitable

inconsistency 8 variance **9** disparity **10** difference, divergence **11** discrep-

ancy, incongruity **12** disagreement **13** dissimilarity

inconsistent 6 fickle **7** erratic, wayward **8** contrary, notional, unstable, variable **9** changeful, dissonant **10** changeable, discrepant, inconstant, irresolute **11** inaccordant, incongruous, inconsonant, vacillating **12** incompatible, inharmonious **13** contradictory, unpredictable **14** irreconcilable

inconsolable 7 crushed **8** dejected, desolate, wretched **9** miserable **10** despondent **12** disconsolate **13** brokenhearted

inconsonant 10 discordant **12** out of keeping, unharmonious

inconspicuous 3 dim **5** faint, muted **6** modest **9** unnoticed **10** unapparent, unassuming **11** unobtrusive **12** not egregious, unnoticeable **14** unostentatious

inconstancy 10 fickleness, infidelity **11** instability **14** capriciousness, changeableness, unfaithfulness

inconstant 6 fickle, untrue **7** erratic **8** cavalier, disloyal, unstable **9** mercurial **10** capricious, changeable, unfaithful **11** interrupted, uncommitted, undedicated, unsteadfast

incontinence 8 rashness **12** recklessness **13** lack of control **16** irresponsibility

incontinent 8 unchaste **12** unrestrained

incontrovertibility 8 sureness **9** certainty **12** absoluteness, definiteness **13** undeniability **14** irrefutability, conclusiveness **15** indisputability **16** incontestability **17** unquestionability

incontrovertible 9 apodictic **10** unarguable, undeniable **11** established, irrefutable **12** indisputable **14** beyond question, unquestionable

inconvenience 6 bother, put out **7** trouble **8** hardship, headache, nuisance **9** annoyance, disoblige, put one out **10** discomfort **13** be a nuisance to, pain in the neck

inconvenient 7 awkward, unhandy **8** annoying, tiresome, untimely **10** bothersome, burdensome **11** distressing, inopportune, troublesome

Incoronazione di Poppea, L'
   also: 22 The Coronation of Poppaea
   opera by: 10 Monteverdi
   character: 4 Nero **6** Ottone **7** Ottavia

incorporate 4 fuse **6** embody, work in **7** include **10** amalgamate, assimilate **11** consolidate

incorporated 6 united **8** embodied, included **11** amalgamated, assimilated **12** consolidated

incorporeal 6 occult, unreal **7** ghostly, phantom **8** bodiless **9** spiritual, unearthly, unfleshly, unworldly **10** immaterial, intangible **11** disembodied **12** supernatural **13** insubstantial

incorrect 5 false, wrong **6** untrue **7** inexact **8** mistaken **9** erroneous **10** fallacious, inaccurate

incorrectness 5 error **9** wrongness **10** inaccuracy **12** carelessness, slovenliness

incorrigible 6 unruly **8** hardened, hard-core, hopeless **10** beyond help, delinquent **11** intractable **12** beyond saving, past changing, unmanageable **14** uncontrollable

incorrigible child
French: **14** enfant terrible

incorruptible 4 pure **6** honest **7** upright **8** reliable **9** faultless, righteous **10** unbribable **11** trustworthy **14** irreproachable

increase 3 wax **4** grow **5** add to, swell **6** enrich, expand **7** advance, augment, burgeon, enhance, enlarge **8** multiply **12** become larger

increasing 7 growing **9** enlarging, expansion, extending, extension **10** drawing out **11** enlargement **12** augmentation

incredible 6 absurd **7** amazing, awesome **10** astounding, farfetched, remarkable **11** astonishing **12** preposterous, unbelievable, unimaginable **13** extraordinary, inconceivable

Incredible Hulk, The
character: **9** Jack McGee **11** David Banner
cast: **9** Bill Bixby **10** Jack Colvin **11** Lou Ferrigno

incredulous 7 dubious **8** doubtful **9** skeptical **10** suspicious **11** distrustful **12** disbelieving

increment 4 gain, rise **5** raise **6** growth, profit **7** benefit **8** addition, increase **9** accretion **10** supplement **11** enlargement **12** accumulation, appreciation, augmentation **13** proliferation

incriminate 5 blame **6** accuse, charge, indict

incrimination 5 blame **7** charges **10** accusation, indictment

incubate 3 set, sit **4** plot **5** breed, brood, clock, cover, hatch **6** scheme **7** develop, gestate, sit upon **8** generate

incubus 5 demon **8** bad dream **9** nightmare

inculcate 5 drill, imbue, infix, teach, train **6** impart, infuse **7** implant, impress, instill **8** instruct **9** brainwash, condition, enlighten **12** indoctrinate

inculpable 5 clear **8** innocent **9** blameless, guiltless, not guilty **10** not at fault, unblamable **14** not responsible

incur 6 arouse, assume, incite, stir up **7** acquire, bring on, involve, provoke **8** bring out, contract, fall into

incurable 8 cureless, hopeless **9** ceaseless **10** beyond cure, inveterate, relentless, unflagging **12** incorrigible, irremediable **13** dyed-in-the-wool, uncorrectable

incursion 4 push, raid **5** foray **6** attack, inroad, sortie **7** assault **8** invasion **11** advance into, impingement **12** encroachment, infiltration

indebted 5 bound **7** bounden **8** beholden, grateful, thankful **9** obligated **10** chargeable **11** accountable **15** under obligation

indebtedness 4 debt **5** debit **7** arrears **9** liability **10** balance due, obligation **11** liabilities

indecency 10 immorality **12** unseemliness **13** offensiveness, salaciousness **14** indecorousness

indecent 4 blue, lewd, rude **5** bawdy, dirty **6** filthy, smutty, vulgar **7** ignoble, ill-bred, immoral, obscene, uncivil **8** immodest, improper, prurient, unseemly **9** offensive, salacious **10** in bad taste, indecorous, indiscreet, licentious, unbecoming **11** unwholesome **12** pornographic

Indecent Obsession, An
author: **17** Colleen McCullough

indecipherable 7 cryptic **9** enigmatic, illegible **10** unreadable **11** inscrutable

indecision 5 doubt **6** acrisy **7** dilemma, swither **8** wavering **10** hesitation **11** fluctuation, vacillating, vacillation, uncertainty **12** irresolution

indecisive 4 weak **7** dubious, unclear **8** doubtful, hesitant, wavering **9** confusing, debatable, mercurial, uncertain, unsettled **10** disputable, hesitating, irresolute, wishy-washy **11** halfhearted, vacillating **12** inconclusive **13** indeterminate **17** blowing hot and cold

indecorous 5 gross **6** sinful, wicked **7** ill-bred **8** immodest, improper, low-class, unseemly **9** unfitting **10** unbecoming, unsuitable **11** blameworthy **13** inappropriate, reprehensible

indecorum 8 bad taste **9** immodesty, indecency, vulgarity **11** impropriety **12** impoliteness, unseemliness

indeed 5 truly **6** in fact, really **7** for sure, in truth **8** actually, to be sure **9** certainly, in reality, veritably **10** positively, to be honest, undeniably **11** joking apart **13** in point of fact, with certainty **14** to tell the truth **15** as a matter of fact, without question **16** strictly speaking

indefatigable 6 dogged **7** staunch **8** diligent, sedulous, tireless, untiring **9** energetic **10** persistent, unflagging, unwearying **11** persevering, unfaltering **13** inexhaustible

indefensible 8 improper, vincible **9** pregnable, untenable **10** vulnerable **11** defenseless, inexcusable, unpro-

tected, unspeakable **12** open to attack, unpardonable **13** unjustifiable

indefinite 3 dim **5** vague **6** unsure **7** inexact, obscure, unknown **8** doubtful **9** ambiguous, amorphous, limitless, tentative, uncertain, unsettled **10** ill-defined, indecisive, indistinct, inexplicit **11** illimitable, measureless, unspecified **12** undetermined **13** indeterminate

indefiniteness 6 vagary **9** ambiguity, vagueness **10** indecision **11** uncertainty **12** equivocation

indelible 4 fast **5** fixed, vivid **7** lasting **8** deep-dyed **9** ingrained, memorable, permanent **10** unerasable **11** unremovable **12** ineradicable **13** unforgettable

indelicate 4 lewd, rude **5** broad, crude, gross **6** clumsy, coarse, risque, vulgar **7** awkward, obscene **8** immodest, improper, indecent, off-color, unseemly **9** offensive, unrefined **10** indecorous, indiscreet, suggestive, unbecoming

in demand 7 popular **9** desirable **11** sought after

indemnification 7 payment **10** recompense, reparation **12** compensation

indemnify 3 pay **5** atone, cover, repay **6** insure, secure **7** pay back, protect, rectify, requite, satisfy **8** make good **9** make right, make up for, reimburse **10** compensate, make amends, recompense, remunerate **15** make restitution

indemnity 7 redress **8** coverage, security **9** insurance, repayment **10** protection **11** restitution **12** compensation **15** indemnification

indent 5 notch, set in **6** recess **7** set back

indentation 3 bay, cut, pit **4** dent, nick **5** gouge, inset, niche, notch, score **6** cavity, furrow, pocket, recess **8** incision **9** concavity **10** depression

indented 6 hollow, sunken, zigzag **7** concave, notched **9** depressed

indenture 4 bind **8** contract **10** apprentice

indentured 5 bound **10** contracted **11** apprenticed

independence 7 freedom, liberty **8** autonomy **10** liberation **11** sovereignty **12** emancipation, self-reliance **14** self-government **17** self-determination

independent 4 free **7** solvent, well-off **8** affluent, separate, unallied, well-to-do **9** apart from, exclusive, on one's own, sovereign, uncoerced, well-fixed **10** autonomous, well-heeled **11** self-reliant, unconnected **12** unassociated, uncontrolled **13** self-directing, self-governing, unconstrained **15** individualistic, self-determining

indescribable 9 ineffable 11 beyond words, indefinable, unutterable 12 overwhelming 13 inexpressible 17 beyond description 20 beggaring description

indestructible 8 enduring 9 permanent 11 everlasting, infrangible, unbreakable 12 imperishable

indeterminate 5 vague 7 obscure, unclear 8 not clear 9 ambiguous, uncertain, undefined 10 indefinite, perplexing, unresolved 11 problematic, unspecified 12 undetermined, unstipulated

index 4 clue, mark, sign 5 proof, token 7 catalog, symptom 8 evidence, glossary, register 9 catalogue, indicator 10 indication 13 manifestation 16 alphabetical list

Index Librorum Prohibitorum 22 index of prohibited books

index of prohibited books
    Latin: 25 Index Librorum Prohibitorum

India
    other name: 4 Hind 6 Bharat 12 Bharat Varsha
    capital: 8 New Delhi
    largest city: 8 Calcutta
    others: 4 Agra, Gaya, Pune 5 Dacca, Poona, Surat 6 Bombay, Jaipur, Kanpur, Lahore, Madras, Madura, Mysore, Nagpur 7 Banaras 8 Kolhapur, Mandalay, Mirzapur, Shahpura, Srinagar 9 Ahmedabad, Bangalore, Hyderabad 10 Darjeeling
    division: 3 Goa 5 Assam, Bihar, Jammu 6 Kerala, Orissa, Punjab, Sikkim 7 Gujarat, Haryana, Kashmir, Manipur, Tripura 8 Nagaland 9 Karnataka, Meghalaya, Rajasthan, Tamil Nadu 10 West Bengal 11 Daman and Diu, Maharashtra, Pondicherry 12 Uttar Pradesh 13 Andhra Pradesh, Madhya Pradesh 15 Himachal Pradesh
    measure: 3 ady, gaz, gez, jow, lan 4 byee, coss, depa, doph, hath, koss, kunk, raik, rati, seit, taun, tola 5 bigha, covid, crosa, denda, depoh, drona, erosa, garce, hasta, krosa, parah, ratti, salay, yojan 6 adhaka, amunam, covido, cudava, dumbha, geerah, moolum, mushti, ouroub, palgat, parran, prasha, ropani, tipree, unglee, yojana 7 dhanush, gavyuti, khahoon, niranga, prastha 8 okthabah
    monetary unit: 3 lac, pie 4 lakh, pice 5 abidi, rupee
    weight: 3 mod, pai, vis 4 drum, hoen, kona, pala, pank, pice, ruay, tael, tali, tola, wang, yava 5 adpad, candy, hubba, maund, tical 6 karsha 8 mangelin
    island: 6 Agatti, Chilka 7 Andaman, Minicoy, Nicobar 8 Amindivi 9 Laccadive 11 Lakshadweep
    lake: 5 Jheel, Lonar, Wular 6 Chilka, Colair, Dhebar, Kolair 7 Kolleru, Pulicat, Pushkar, Sambahr
    mountain: 8 Aravalli 9 Broad Peak, Distaghil, Himalayas, Karakoram, Nanda Devi, Rakaposhi 10 Gasherbrum, Masherbrum 11 Nanga Parbat 12 Eastern Ghats, Kanchenjunga, Western Ghats
        hills: 4 Chin, Naga 5 Khasi 6 Lushai 7 Nilgiri
    highest point: 12 Godwin Austen
    river: 3 Son 4 Beas, Kosi, Tapi 5 Gogra, Indus, Jumna, Tapti 6 Gandak, Ganges, Jhelum, Kaveri, Kistna, Sutlej, Yamuna 7 Cauveri, Cauvery, Chambal, Damodar, Hooghly, Krishna, Narbada, Narmada 8 Godavari, Mahanadi 10 Bhagirathi 11 Brahmaputra
    sea: 6 Indian 7 Arabian
    physical feature:
        bay: 6 Bengal
        cape: 7 Comorin
        desert: 4 Thar 9 Rajasthan
        forest: 3 Gir
        gulf: 5 Kutch 6 Cambay, Mannar
        pass: 9 Karakoram
        plain: 12 Indo-Gangetic
        plateau: 6 Deccan 7 Shillon 11 Chota Nagpur
        rains: 7 monsoon
        strait: 4 Palk
        swamp: 9 Sundarban 11 Rann of Kutch
        valley: 13 Vale of Kashmir
    people: 2 Ao 3 Gor 4 Bhil 5 Aryan 6 Badaga, Pathan 7 Sherani 9 Dravidian 10 Andamanese
        caste: 3 Jat 5 Sudra 6 Rajput, Shudra 7 Brahman, Brahmin, Harijan, Maratha, Vaishya 9 Kshatriya 11 Untouchable
        dynasty: 5 Gupta, Mogul 6 Maurya, Rajput 8 Marathas 14 Delhi Sultanate
        god: 4 Kali, Rama, Siva 5 Durga, Laxmi, Shiva 6 Brahma, Kumara, Vishnu 7 Ganesha, Hanuman, Krishna, Lakshmi 9 Kartikeya 10 Subramanya
        ruler: 5 Akbar, Asoka, Babur, Timur 7 Humayun 8 Hyder Ali, Jahangir 9 Aurangzeb, Shah Jahan 11 Rajiv Gandhi, Tippu Sultan 12 Indira Gandhi 13 Queen Victoria 15 Jawaharlal Nehru, Mohandas K (Mahatma) Gandhi 18 Chandragupta Maurya
    language: 4 Urdu 5 Hindi, Oriya, Tamil 6 Sindhi, Telugu 7 Bengali, English, Kannada, Malayam, Marathi, Punjabi 8 Assamese, Gujarati, Kashmiri, Sanskrit 9 Malayalam
    religion: 4 Sikh 5 Hindu, Islam, Parsi 7 Jainist, Judaism 8 Buddhism 11 Zoroastrian 12 Christianity
    place:
    cathedral: 10 Saint Thome
    fortress: 3 Red 11 Saint George
    mausoleum: 8 Taj Mahal
    minaret: 9 Qutb Minar
    mosque: 10 Jama Masjid
    park: 6 Maidan
    president's residence: 17 Rashtrapati Bhavan
    railway station: 8 Victoria
    shrine: 7 Raj Ghat
    street: 7 Raj Path 11 Chowringhee, Marine Drive 12 Chandni Chauk 14 Connaught Place
    temple: 5 Birla 6 Ellora, Golden 7 Kailasa 10 Ajanta Cave
    feature:
        dance: 6 nautch 7 cantico
        religious text: 7 Rig Veda
        shrine: 5 stupa
    food:
        beer: 5 apong
        bread: 7 chapati
        liquor: 4 soma, sura 5 shrab
        tea: 5 assam

Indian
    constellation: 5 Indus

Indiana
    abbreviation: 2 IN 3 Ind
    nickname: 7 Hoosier
    capital/largest city: 12 Indianapolis
    others: 4 Gary, Peru 6 Brazil, Goshen, Hobart, Jasper, Kokomo, Marion, Muncie, Wabash 7 Elkhart, Ft Wayne, Hammond, LaPorte, Whiting 8 Columbus, Richmond 9 Lafayette, Mishawaka, South Bend, Vincennes 10 Evansville, Huntington, Logansport, Terre Haute 11 Bloomington, East Chicago 12 Connorsville, Michigan City
    college: 4 Ball 6 Bethel, Butler, DePauw, Goshen, Marion, Purdue, Wabash 9 Notre Dame 10 Evansville, Valparaiso
    explorer: 7 La Salle
    feature: 10 New Harmony 12 Indian mounds
        national memorial: 14 Lincoln boyhood
    tribe: 3 Wea 5 Miami 7 Shawnee
    people: 7 Hoosier 10 Cole Porter, Eugene Debs, Gus Grissom, Red Skelton 12 Wilbur Wright 15 Booth Tarkington, Theodore Dreiser 18 James Whitcomb Riley
    lake: 5 Clear, James 6 Monroe 7 Manitou, Wawasee 8 Michigan 9 Mansfield 11 Maxinkuckee
    land rank: 12 thirty-eighth
    mountain: 13 Greensfort Top
    physical feature:
        cave: 9 Wyandotte
    river: 4 Ohio 5 White 6 Maumee, Wabash 8 Kankakee 10 Tippecanoe, Whitewater
    state admission: 10 nineteenth
    state bird: 8 cardinal
    state flower: 5 peony 6 zinnia

state motto: 19 Crossroads of America

state song: 28 On the Banks of the Wabash Far Away

state tree: 5 tulip **11** tulip poplar

Indiana

basketball team: 6 Pacers

Indiana

author: 10 George Sand

character: 4 Noun **7** Delmare **13** Rodolphe Brown **15** Raymon de Ramiere

Indianapolis

football team: 5 Colts

Indic

language family: 12 Indo-European

branch: 11 Indo-Iranian

subgroup: 5 Hindi, Oriya **6** Nepali, Sindhi **7** Bengali, Marathi, Pakrits, Panjabi **8** Assamese, Gujarati, Kashmiri **9** Sinhalese

indicate 4 mean, show, tell **5** imply **6** denote, evince, record, reveal **7** bespeak, point to, signify, specify, suggest **8** point out, register, stand for **9** be a sign of, designate, establish, make known, represent, symbolize

indication 4 clue, hint, mark, omen, sign **5** token **6** augury, boding, signal **7** gesture, mention, portent, presage, showing, symptom, telling, warning **8** evidence, pointing **9** foretoken **10** foreboding, indicating, intimation, signifying, suggestion **11** designation, premonition **13** demonstration, manifestation

indicative 8 symbolic **10** denotative, emblematic, evidential, expressive, indicatory, suggestive **11** connotative, designative, significant, symptomatic **13** symptomatical **14** characteristic, representative

indicator 4 clue **5** guide **7** pointer **10** indication

indict 4 cite **6** accuse, charge, have up, impute, pull up **7** arraign, bring up, impeach **9** criminate, inculpate, prosecute **11** incriminate **13** prefer charges

indifference 6 apathy **7** disdain, neglect **8** coldness, no import **9** aloofness, unconcern **10** negligence, paltriness, triviality **11** disinterest, impassivity, inattention, insouciance, nonchalance **12** carelessness, unimportance **13** impassiveness, insensibility, insensitivity **14** insignificance, lack of interest

indifferent 4 cool, fair, rote, so-so **5** aloof **6** medium, modest **7** average, unmoved **8** detached, mediocre, middling, moderate, ordinary, passable **9** apathetic, impassive, not caring, unmindful **10** impervious, insensible, insouciant, nonchalant, second-rate, uninspired **11** commonplace, perfunctory, unconcerned **12** uninterested **13** insusceptible **15** undistin-

guished **17** betwixt and between, neither good nor bad

indigence 4 need, want **6** penury **7** beggary, poverty **9** pauperism, privation **11** destitution, dire straits **13** pennilessness

indigenous 6 native **7** endemic **8** domestic, homebred **9** home-grown **10** aboriginal **13** autochthonous, originating in

indigent 4 poor **5** needy **6** hard-up, in need, in want **7** pinched **8** badly off **9** destitute, moneyless, penniless **12** impoverished **15** poverty-stricken

indiges

title in: 4 Rome

suggests: 11 deification

for service to: 7 country

indigestible 4 rich **13** unassimilable

indignant 3 mad **4** sore **5** angry, huffy, irate, riled **6** fuming, miffed, peeved, piqued, put off, put out **8** incensed, offended, provoked, steaming, worked up, wrathful **9** resentful, wrought up **10** displeased, infuriated **15** on one's high horse

indignation 3 ire **4** fury, huff, rage **5** pique, wrath **6** animus, choler, dismay, uproar **7** umbrage **8** vexation **9** annoyance **10** irritation, resentment **11** displeasure

indignity 4 slur **5** abuse **6** insult, slight **7** affront, offense, outrage **8** dishonor, rudeness **9** injustice **11** discourtesy, humiliation **12** mistreatment **13** slap in the face

indigo 3 dye **4** blue **8** dark blue, deep blue, navy blue **10** Indigofera

varieties: 4 wild **5** false **7** bastard **8** wild blue **9** blue false **10** plains wild, white false **12** prairie false **13** fragrant false

indirect 5 vague **6** remote, zigzag **7** crooked, devious, distant, evasive, hedging, oblique, winding **8** rambling, tortuous **9** ancillary, secondary **10** circuitous, derivative, digressive, discursive, incidental, meandering, roundabout, unintended **13** unintentional

indirection 8 rambling **10** digression, meandering, zigzagging **14** circuitousness, circumlocution, roundaboutness

indiscernible 6 hidden **9** invisible **10** indistinct **12** undetectable, unnoticeable **13** imperceptible

indiscreet 6 unwise **7** foolish **8** careless, tactless, unseemly **9** foolhardy, ill-judged, impolitic, imprudent, tasteless, untactful **10** incautious **11** improvident, injudicious, thoughtless, unbefitting, uncalled-for **12** undiplomatic **13** inconsiderate, uncircumspect

indiscretion 8 rashness **10** imprudence **12** carelessness, heedlessness, recklessness, tactlessness **13** foolhardiness, insensitivity **15** thoughtlessness **16** irresponsibility

indiscriminate 6 motley, random **7** aimless, chaotic, jumbled, mongrel **8** confused, slapdash, unchoosy **9** haphazard, hit-or-miss **10** hodgepodge **11** promiscuous, unselective **12** disorganized, unsystematic **16** higgledy-piggledy, undistinguishing

in disorder 5 messy **6** blowsy, frowsy, mussed, sloppy, untidy **7** ruffled, rumpled, tousled, unkempt **8** uncombed **10** disarrayed, disheveled, disordered, disorderly **11** disarranged

indispensable 5 basic, vital **6** needed **7** crucial, needful **8** required **9** essential, mandatory, necessary, requisite **10** compulsory, imperative, obligatory **11** fundamental

indispensable condition

Latin: 10 sine qua non

indispensable element 9 basic need, essential, necessity, requisite **10** sine qua non **11** requirement

indisposed 3 ill **5** loath **6** ailing, averse, laid up, sickly, unwell **7** opposed **8** hesitant, taken ill **9** bedridden, reluctant, unwilling **10** not oneself **11** disinclined **15** under the weather

indisposition 5 upset **6** malady **7** ailment, illness **8** sickness **9** complaint, ill health

indisputable 4 sure **7** assured, certain, decided, evident, obvious **8** absolute, apparent, clear-cut, definite, positive **10** conclusive, unarguable, undeniable **11** indubitable, irrefutable **12** unassailable, unmistakable **13** incontestable **14** unquestionable **16** incontrovertible **20** beyond a shadow of doubt

indissoluble 5 fixed **7** abiding, lasting **8** constant, enduring **9** immutable, indelible, permanent, perpetual **11** everlasting **12** imperishable, ineradicable

indistinct 3 dim **4** weak **5** faint, muddy, murky, vague **6** cloudy, hidden **7** blurred, clouded, muffled, obscure, shadowy, unclear **8** confused, nebulous, puzzling **9** ambiguous, enigmatic, illegible, inaudible, uncertain **10** ill-defined, incoherent, indefinite, mysterious, out of focus **11** not distinct **13** indeterminate **14** indecipherable, unintelligible **16** incomprehensible

indistinguishable 7 obscure, unclear **9** invisible **10** indistinct, unapparent **12** unnoticeable, unobservable **13** a carbon copy of, identical with, imperceptible, inconspicuous, indiscernible

individual 6 person, unique **7** one's own, private, special, unusual **8** distinct, especial, original, personal, separate, singular, somebody, specific, uncommon **9** different, exclusive **10** particular **11** distinctive, independent

12 personalized **14** characteristic, unconventional

individuality 6 cachet **10** uniqueness **11** distinction, singularity, specialness **13** particularity **15** distinctiveness

individually 4 each **5** apart **6** apiece, singly **8** a la carte, uniquely **10** one at a time, peculiarly, personally, separately **12** respectively **13** distinctively **18** characteristically

Indochina 9 peninsula
　includes: 4 Laos **6** Malaya **7** Myanmar, Vietnam **8** Cambodia, Thailand

indoctrinate 5 brief, drill, teach, train, tutor **6** infuse, school **7** educate, implant, instill **8** initiate **9** brainwash, inculcate **12** propagandize

indoctrination 5 drill **8** drilling, teaching, training **9** education, schooling **10** initiation, instilling **11** inculcation, instruction

Indo-European
　language branch: 5 Greek **6** Celtic, Italic **7** Romance **8** Albanian, Armenian, Germanic **9** Anatolian, Tocharian **11** Balto-Slavic, Indo-Iranian

Indo-Iranian
　language family: 12 Indo-European
　ancient: 7 Avestan **8** Sanskrit **10** Old Persian
　modern Iranian: 5 Indic, Tajik **6** Pashto **7** Baluchi, Kurdish, Persian
　modern Indic: 4 Pali **5** Hindi, Oriya **6** Nepali, Sindhi **7** Bengali, Marathi, Panjabi **8** Assamese, Gujarati, Kashmiri **9** Sinhalese

indolence 5 sloth **7** inertia, languor, laxness **8** idleness, laziness **10** inactivity

indolent 4 lazy **5** inert, slack **7** lumpish **8** dawdling, dilatory, inactive, listless, slothful, sluggish **9** do-nothing, easygoing, lethargic, shiftless **13** lackadaisical

indomitable 6 dogged **7** doughty, staunch, valiant **8** cast-iron, fearless, intrepid, resolute, stalwart, stubborn **9** dauntless, steadfast, undaunted **10** courageous, formidable, invincible, unwavering, unyielding **11** insuperable, persevering, unflinching, unshrinking **12** invulnerable, unassailable **13** indefatigable, irrepressible, unconquerable

Indonesia
　other name: 9 Nusantara **12** Tanah Airkita **21** Netherlands East Indies
　capital/largest city: 7 Jakarta **8** Djakarta
　others: 5 Bogor, Medan **6** Malang, Manado **7** Bandung **8** Macassar, Semarang, Surabaya **9** Hollandia, Palembang, Surakarta **10** Jogjakarta, Yogyakarta **11** Banjarmasin
　measure: 5 depah, depoh
　monetary unit: 3 sen **6** rupiah
　weight: 5 catty, ounce, thail **6** soekoe

　island: 3 Aru **4** Bali, Buru, Java **5** Ambon, Ceram, Seram, Spice, Sumba, Timor **6** Bangka, Borneo, Flores, Lombok, Madura, Tidore **7** Belawan, Celebes, Morotai, Sumatra, Sumbawa, Ternate **8** Belitung, Moluccas, Sulawesi **9** Halmahera, New Guinea **10** Kalimantan **11** Lesser Sunda **12** Greater Sunda
　lake: 4 Toba **5** Ranau **6** Towuti
　river: 4 Hari, Musi, Solo **5** Rokan **6** Asahan, Barito, Kampar **7** Brantas, Kaptuas **9** Indrogiri, Mamberamo, Martapura
　sea: 4 Java, Savu **5** Banda, Ceram, Timor **6** Flores, Indian **7** Arafura, Celebes, Molucca, Pacific **10** Philippine, South China
　physical feature:
　　strait: 5 Sunda **7** Makasar, Malacca **8** Makassar
　　volcano: 6 Slamet **8** Krakatoa
　people: 5 Batak, Dayak, Dyaks, Malay **6** Papuan, Toraja **7** Battaks, Chinese, Igorots **8** Acehnese, Achinese, Balinese, Javanese, Madurese, Sudanese **11** Minang Kabau
　　leader: 7 Suharto, Sukarno
　language: 5 Tetum **6** Bahasa, Igorot **7** English, Gyarung, Malayan **8** Balinese, Chamorro, Javanese, Madurese, Sudanese **10** Indonesian, Polynesian
　religion: 5 Hindu, Islam **7** animism **8** Buddhism **12** Christianity, Confucianism
　place:
　　palace: 6 Kraton
　　pyramid: 5 Stupa **9** Borobudur
　　shrine: 6 Dagoba, Kraton
　feature:
　　cap: 5 pitji
　　cloth: 5 batik
　　jacket: 6 kebaja
　　lizard: 12 Komodo dragon
　　scarf: 9 selendang
　　shadow play: 6 wajang, wayang
　　skirt: 4 kain **6** sarong
　　tree: 4 supa
　food:
　　ceremonial dinner: 9 selamatan

indoors 6 at home, inside, shut in, shut up, within **10** in the house **11** sequestered

Indo-Pacific
　language subgroup: 4 Kate **5** Kiwai **7** Andaman, Merauke **8** Highland, Tasmania **9** Ekari-Moni, Hollandia, Timor-Alor **10** New Britain **12** Astrolabe Bay, Bougainville **14** Vogelkop-Kamoro **16** Eastern New Guinea, Northern Salomons **17** Northern Halmahera

indorse *see* **7** endorse

In Dubious Battle
　author: 13 John Steinbeck

indubitable 4 sure **7** certain **9** undoubted **10** conclusive **11** irrefutable,

unequivocal **12** indisputable, unmistakable **14** unquestionable **16** incontrovertible

indubitably 6 surely **7** for sure **8** of course **9** certainly, doubtless **10** for certain **11** undoubtedly **12** without doubt **14** unquestionably, with no question

induce 3 get **4** coax, spur, sway **5** cause, impel **6** arouse, effect, incite, lead to, prompt **7** actuate, bring on, dispose, incline, inspire, produce, provoke, win over **8** activate, motivate, occasion, persuade **9** encourage, influence, instigate, prevail on **10** bring about, bring round, give rise to **11** prevail upon, set in motion

inducement 4 bait, goad, spur **5** cause **6** ground, motive, reason **8** stimulus **9** incentive **10** allurement, attraction, enticement, incitement, persuasion, temptation **11** inspiration, instigation, provocation

induct 5 crown, draft, frock **6** enlist, invest, lead in, ordain, sign up **7** bring in, install, instate, usher in **8** enthrone, initiate, register **9** conscript, establish, introduce **10** consecrate, inaugurate

in due course 4 then **6** thence **10** eventually **11** accordingly **15** at the proper time **19** in the fullness of time

indulge 4 baby **5** favor, humor, serve, spoil, treat **6** coddle, cosset, oblige **7** appease, cater to, gratify, yield to **8** pander to **9** give way to **11** accommodate, go along with, mollycoddle

indulgence 6 excess, luxury **8** kindness, lenience, patience **9** allowance, benignity, tolerance **10** compassion, debauchery, profligacy, sufferance **11** dissipation, forbearance, forgiveness **12** extravagance, graciousness, immoderation, intemperance **13** understanding **14** permissiveness

indulgent 4 kind **6** benign, tender **7** clement, lenient, patient, sparing **8** humoring, obliging, tolerant, yielding **9** easygoing, forgiving, pampering **10** forbearing, permissive **11** complaisant, forebearing **12** conciliatory **13** understanding

Indus
　constellation near: 4 Grus, Pavo
　river in: 4 Asia **5** India, Tibet **8** Pakistan
　into: 10 Arabian Sea

industrious 4 busy **6** active **7** zealous **8** diligent, occupied, sedulous, tireless **9** assiduous, energetic **10** productive, purposeful, unflagging **11** hardworking, painstaking, persevering, unremitting **12** businesslike, enterprising **13** indefatigable

industry 2 go **4** toil, zeal **5** field, labor, trade **6** bustle, energy, hustle **8** activity, business, commerce, hard work **9** assiduity, diligence **10** enterprise **11** application, manufacture **12** perseverance, sedulousness **13** assiduousness **15** industriousness **16** indefatigability

inebriate 3 sot **4** lush, soak, wino **5** drunk, rummy, souse, toper **6** barfly, boozer **7** tippler **8** drunkard **9** alcoholic **11** dipsomaniac

inebriated 4 high **5** drunk, oiled, tight, tipsy **6** bombed, loaded, potted, stoned, tanked, zonked **7** drunken, smashed, sozzled, wrecked **8** besotted **9** befuddled, plastered **10** in one's cups **11** intoxicated **12** drunk as a lord **17** under the influence **20** three sheets to the wind

ineffable 5 ideal **6** divine, sacred **9** spiritual **10** indefinite, untellable **11** indefinable, unspeakable, unutterable **12** transcendent **13** indescribable, inexpressible **14** incommunicable, transcendental

in effect 6 active **8** a reality **9** activated, effective, operative **11** in operation

ineffective 4 vain, weak **6** futile **7** useless **8** impotent **9** fruitless, incapable, powerless, worthless **10** inadequate **11** inefficient, inoperative, not much good, of little use **12** unproductive

ineffectual 4 lame, vain, weak **5** inept **6** feeble, futile **7** hapless, useless **8** impotent **10** inadequate, not up to par, profitless, unavailing **11** incompetent, ineffective, inefficient **12** unproductive, unprofitable, unsuccessful **13** inefficacious **14** unsatisfactory

inefficient 5 inept, slack **6** futile **8** slipshod **9** pointless, unskilled **10** inadequate **11** incompetent, indifferent, ineffective, ineffectual **12** not efficient, unproductive **13** inefficacious **14** good-for-nothing

inelegance 9 crudeness, grossness, roughness, vulgarity **10** coarseness **13** tastelessness

inelegant 4 ugly **6** coarse, common **8** inferior **9** tasteless, unrefined **10** ungraceful

ineligible 5 unfit **10** unentitled, unsuitable **11** not eligible, unqualified **12** disqualified, unacceptable

ineluctable 4 sure **5** fated **7** certain **10** ineludible, inevasible, inevitable, inexorable, sure as fate, unevadable **11** inescapable, irrevocable, unavoidable, unstoppable **13** unpreventable

inept 5 empty, inane, silly, unapt **6** clumsy **7** asinine, awkward, fatuous, foolish **8** bungling **9** maladroit, pointless, senseless, unfitting, unskilled, untrained **10** out of place, unsuitable **11** incompetent, ineffective, ineffectual, inefficient, nonsensical, unqualified **13** inappropriate, inefficacious

ineptitude 9 inability **10** clumsiness, inadequacy **11** awkwardness **12** incompetence **14** ineffectuality **15** ineffectiveness

inequality 8 imparity, inequity **9** disparity, diversity, prejudice **10** difference, divergence, favoritism, unfairness, unlikeness **11** inconstancy, unequalness **12** irregularity, variableness **13** disproportion, dissimilarity, dissimilitude

inequity 4 bias **9** injustice, prejudice **10** favoritism, inequality, unfairness **14** discrimination

ineradicable 7 lasting **9** indelible, permanent **10** inerasable **12** ineffaceable **14** indestructible

inert 4 dull, numb **5** slack, still **6** leaden, static, supine, torpid **7** languid, passive **8** immobile, inactive, listless, sluggish **9** impassive, inanimate, quiescent **10** motionless, phlegmatic, stationary

inertia 6 apathy, stupor, torpor **7** languor **8** dullness, inaction, laziness, lethargy **9** indolence, inertness, lassitude, passivity, torpidity, weariness **10** inactivity, supineness **11** passiveness **12** listlessness, sluggishness

inertness 6 apathy **8** lethargy **9** passivity **10** quiescence **12** sluggishness **14** motionlessness

inescapable 4 sure **7** certain, evident **8** manifest, positive **10** inevitable **11** ineluctable, predestined, unavoidable

in esse 7 in being **11** in actuality **16** actually existing

inestimable 7 sumless **8** precious **9** priceless **10** invaluable **11** beyond price, measureless **12** immeasurable, incalculable, unmeasurable

inevitable 4 sure **5** fated **7** certain **8** destined **10** ineludible **11** ineluctable, inescapable, predestined, unavoidable **13** predetermined, unpreventable

inexact 3 off **6** faulty, sloppy **8** careless, slovenly **9** defective, imperfect, imprecise **10** inaccurate, unspecific **11** approximate

in exactly the same words
Latin: **19** verbatim et literatim

inexcusable 10 unbearable **11** intolerable, unallowable **12** indefensible, unforgivable, unpardonable **13** unjustifiable

inexhaustible 7 endless **8** infinite, tireless, unending **9** boundless **13** indefatigable **15** measurelessness

in existence 5 alive **6** extant, living **8** existent, existing **9** surviving, to be found

inexorable 4 firm **5** cruel, stiff **6** dogged **7** adamant **8** obdurate, pitiless, ruthless **9** immovable, merciless, unbending **10** adamantive, determined, inflexible, relentless, unyield-

ing **11** inescapable, intractable **12** irresistible **14** uncompromising

inexpedient 6 futile, unwise **7** useless **11** detrimental, impractical, inadvisable, injudicious, undesirable **13** not worthwhile **15** disadvantageous

inexpensive 5 cheap **8** moderate **9** low-priced **10** economical, reasonable **13** nominal-priced, popular-priced

inexpensive table wine
French: **12** vin ordinaire

inexperienced 5 fresh, green, naive **6** callow **7** untried **8** inexpert, unversed **9** unfledged, unskilled, untrained, untutored **10** unfamiliar, unschooled, unseasoned **11** uninitiated, unpracticed **12** unaccustomed, unacquainted, unconversant **15** unsophisticated

inexpert 5 inept **6** clumsy, gauche **7** awkward **8** bungling **9** incapable, maladroit **10** amateurish, unpolished, unskillful **11** incompetent, ineffective, inefficient, unqualified **14** unaccomplished

inexplicable 8 abstruse, baffling, puzzling **9** insoluble **10** insolvable, mysterious, mystifying, perplexing **11** enigmatical, inscrutable **12** unfathomable **13** unaccountable, unexplainable **14** undecipherable **16** incomprehensible

inexpressive 5 blank, empty **6** vacant **14** expressionless

in extenso 12 at full length

in extremis 9 near death **11** in extremity **15** on the outer edges **19** at the uttermost limit

in extremity
Latin: **10** in extremis

in fact
Latin: **7** de facto

infallible 4 sure **7** assured, certain, perfect **8** flawless, inerrant, positive, reliable, surefire, unerring **9** apodictic, faultless, foolproof, unfailing **10** dependable, impeccable **11** irrefutable **13** unimpeachable **16** incontrovertible

infamous 3 low **4** base, evil, foul, vile **6** odious, sinful, sordid, wicked **7** corrupt, heinous, ignoble, immoral, knavish **8** damnable, recreant, shameful **9** abhorrent, monstrous, nefarious, notorious **10** abominable, detestable, iniquitous, of evil fame, outrageous, perfidious, profligate, scandalous, scurrilous, villainous **11** disgraceful, of ill repute, opprobrious, treacherous **12** dishonorable, disreputable

infamy 4 evil **5** odium, shame **7** scandal **8** contempt, disgrace, dishonor, ignominy, villainy **9** discredit, disesteem, disrepute, notoriety **10** corruption, opprobrium, wickedness **11** abomination **13** despicability, notoriousness

infancy 6 cradle, nonage **8** babyhood,

minority **9** beginning, childhood, inception **10** immaturity

infant 3 kid **4** babe, baby **5** child **7** neonate, newborn, preemie, toddler **8** nursling, suckling

infantile 7 babyish **8** childish, juvenile **9** childlike, infantine **10** infantlike, sophomoric

infantryman 6 Zouave **7** dogface, dragoon **8** chasseur, doughboy, sorefoot **11** foot soldier

infatuated 7 charmed, smitten **8** beguiled, enamored, inflamed, obsessed **9** bewitched, enchanted, entranced **10** captivated, enraptured, enthralled, spellbound **11** carried away, intoxicated **12** having a crush

infatuation 4 rave **5** craze, crush, folly, mania **6** desire **7** passion **9** obsession, puppy love **10** enthusiasm **11** fascination, foolishness **12** passing fancy

infect 4 ruin **5** spoil, taint, touch **6** blight, damage, poison **7** afflict, corrupt **9** indispose, influence **11** contaminate

infected 6 impure, morbid, septic **7** corrupt, tainted **8** cankered, diseased, poisoned **12** contaminated

infection 6 blight **7** disease **9** contagion, virulence **11** suppuration

infectious 8 catching, epidemic, virulent **9** catchable, infective, spreading **10** compelling, contagious, inoculable **11** captivating **12** communicable, irresistible

infecund 6 barren, farrow **7** sterile **9** infertile **12** unproductive

infer 4 deem **5** glean, guess, judge, opine **6** deduce, gather, reason, reckon **7** presume, suppose, surmise **8** conclude **9** speculate **10** conjecture

inference 4 clue **10** intimation, suggestion **11** insinuation

inferior 4 poor **6** junior **8** low-grade, mediocre **9** secondary **10** low-quality, second-rate, subsidiary **11** indifferent, subordinate, subservient, substandard **12** not up to snuff

infernal 4 vile **5** awful, black, lower **6** cursed, Hadean, nether **7** heinous, hellish, Stygian, vicious **8** accursed, damnable, devilish, fiendish, horrible, terrible **9** atrocious, execrable, malicious, monstrous, nefarious, Plutonian **10** abominable, demoniacal, diabolical, flagitious, horrendous, iniquitous
also: 9 Tartarean
refers to: 10 underworld

inferno 4 hell, oven **5** abyss, Hades **6** hotbox, the pit, Tophet **7** furnace, roaster, sizzler **8** hellfire, hellhole, scorcher **9** perdition **10** lower world, underworld **11** netherworld **12** fiery furnace **13** nether regions **15** infernal

regions **16** fire and brimstone, the bottomless pit

Inferno
part I of: 12 Divine Comedy
author: 14 Dante Alighieri

infertile 4 arid, bare **6** barren, effete, fallow **7** drained, sterile **8** depleted, desolate, impotent, infecund **9** exhausted, fruitless **10** unfruitful, unprolific **12** unproductive **13** nonproductive

infest 4 team **5** beset, crawl, creep, swarm **6** abound, infect, plague, ravage **7** overrun, torment **9** crawl with, swarm with

infestation 6 plague, ravage **9** lousiness, pervasion **11** overrunning **12** overswarming

in few words
Latin: 12 paucis verbis

infidel 5 pagan **6** savage **7** atheist, heathen, heretic, skeptic **8** agnostic, apostate, idolater **9** barbarian **10** unbeliever **11** nonbeliever

infidelity 6 breach **7** falsity, perfidy **8** adultery, betrayal **9** disregard, violation **10** disloyalty, infraction **12** nonadherence **13** nonobservance, transgression **14** unfaithfulness

infiltrate 4 leak, seep **5** imbue, steep **6** absorb, seep in **7** pervade **8** colonize, permeate **9** insinuate, penetrate

infinite 4 vast **5** great **7** endless, immense **8** enormous **9** boundless, limitless, unbounded, unlimited **10** tremendous, without end **11** illimitable, measureless **12** immeasurable, incalculable, interminable **13** inexhaustible **15** uncircumscribed

infinitesimal 3 wee **4** puny, tiny **6** minute **10** diminutive, negligible **11** microscopic **13** imperceptible, inappreciable, insignificant, undiscernible **14** extremely small, inconsiderable

infinity 7 forever **8** eternity **10** infinitude, perpetuity **11** endlessness, eternal time **12** sempiternity **13** boundlessness, limitlessness **14** illimitability **15** everlastingness, immeasurability, incalculability, measurelessness **16** inexhaustibility **19** incomprehensibility

Infiri
gods of: 10 underworld

infirm 3 ill **4** weak, worn **5** anile, frail, shaky **6** ailing, feeble, poorly, sickly **7** failing, fragile, unsound **8** decrepit, disabled, helpless, unstable, weakened **9** doddering, emaciated, enervated, enfeebled, powerless **11** debilitated **12** strengthless

infirmary 6 clinic **7** sick bay **8** hospital

infirmity 4 flaw **5** fault **6** defect, malady **7** ailment, failing, frailty, illness **8** debility, disorder, handicap, sickness **9** fragility, frailness **10** deficiency, dis-

ability, infirmness **11** instability **12** debilitation, imperfection, unstableness **13** indisposition, vulnerability

in flagrante delicto 8 in the act **9** red-handed

inflame 4 fire, rile **5** craze, rouse **6** arouse, enrage, excite, heat up, ignite, incite, kindle, madden, stir up, work up **7** agitate, incense, provoke **8** enkindle **9** electrify, stimulate **10** intoxicate

inflamed 3 mad **5** angry, irate, riled **6** crazed, fuming, roused **7** aroused, enraged, excited, fired up, furious, incited **8** agitated, incensed, provoked, reddened **9** steamed up, stirred up **10** infuriated **11** intensified

inflame with love 6 enamor **9** enrapture, impassion, infatuate

inflammable 5 fiery **8** choleric, volatile **9** excitable, flammable, ignitable, impetuous, overhasty, sensitive **10** high-strung, incendiary **11** combustible, precipitate **12** inflammatory

inflammation 4 acne, fire, gout, sore **6** canker, firing **7** arousal, chafing **8** bursitis, ignition, kindling, soreness, sore spot, swelling **9** agitation **10** incitement, irritation **13** conflagration, rabblerousing
suffix: 4 itis

inflammatory 5 fiery, rabid **8** arousing, enraging, inciting, mutinous, volcanic **9** demagogic, explosive, insurgent **10** incendiary, rebellious **11** combustible, fulminating, inflammable, intemperate, provocative **13** rabble-rousing, revolutionary

inflate 5 bloat, swell **6** blow up, dilate, expand, fill up, pump up **7** distend, improve, puff out **10** appreciate **11** rise in value

inflated 5 blown, gassy, tumid, wordy **6** blew up, turgid **7** bloated, blown up, dilated, flowery, pompous, swollen, verbose **8** boastful, enlarged, expanded **9** bombastic, distended, overblown, swelled up **10** rhetorical, swelled out **11** exaggerated, pretentious

inflection 4 tone **5** tenor **6** accent **10** modulation **11** enunciation, tone of voice **12** articulation **13** pronunciation

inflexible 4 firm, hard, taut **5** fixed, rigid, solid, stiff **6** dogged, mulish **7** adamant **8** obdurate, resolute, stubborn **9** hidebound, immovable, immutable, ironbound, obstinate, pigheaded, stringent, tenacious, unbending, unplastic **10** adamantine, determined, headstrong, impervious, implacable, inexorable, unwavering, unyielding **11** hard and fast, intractable, not flexible, unmalleable **12** unchangeable **14** uncompromising

inflict 4 dump **5** lay on, wreak **6** impose, unload **7** put upon **9** visit upon

10 administer, perpetrate **11** bring to bear

inflorescence 5 bloom **6** flower **7** blossom, cluster **8** blooming **9** flowering **10** blossoming

type: 4 cyme **5** spike, umbel **6** corymb, raceme, spadix **7** panicle **9** capitulum **14** verticillaster

influence 4 hold, move, pull, stir, sway **5** clout, guide, impel, power **6** arouse, effect, incite, induce, prompt, weight **7** act upon, actuate, control, dispose, incline, inspire, mastery, potency, provoke **8** dominion, leverage, persuade, pressure, prestige **9** advantage, authority **10** ascendancy, domination, predispose

influential 6 moving, potent, strong **7** leading, weighty **8** forceful, powerful, puissant **9** effective, effectual, important, inspiring, momentous **10** activating **11** efficacious, significant **12** instrumental **13** consequential

influx 5 entry **6** inflow **7** arrival, indraft, ingress **9** flowing in, incursion, inpouring **10** converging, inundation **12** infiltration

in force 6 extant **7** en masse **8** in

inform 3 rat on **4** fink, tell **5** edify **6** advise, clue in, notify, snitch, squeal, tattle, tell on, tip off **7** apprise, let know **8** acquaint, denounce, forewarn, report to **9** declare to, enlighten **11** communicate, familiarize, serve notice **14** blow the whistle

inform against 5 rat on **6** betray, fink on, tell on **7** sell out **8** denounce, squeal on **11** double-cross **16** blow the whistle on

informal 4 easy **6** casual, simple **7** natural, offhand **8** familiar **9** easygoing, not formal **10** unofficial **11** spontaneous **12** come-as-you-are **13** unceremonious, unconstrained **14** unconventional

informal preliminary conference
French: **10** pourparler

informant 6 source **7** adviser, tipster **8** appriser, informer, notifier, reporter **9** announcer, spokesman **10** respondent **11** enlightener, horse's mouth, spokeswoman

information 4 data, news **5** facts, notes **6** notice, papers, report **7** account, tidings **8** briefing, bulletin, evidence, material **9** documents, knowledge, materials **10** communique **11** fact-finding **12** announcement, intelligence, notification **13** enlightenment

informed 4 told, up on, wise **5** aware, posted, talked, taught, warned **7** abreast, advised, knowing, learned, tattled **8** apprised, betrayed, educated, notified, reported, snitched, up to date **9** au courant, permeated **10** acquainted, instructed **11** enlightened, intelligent **13** knowledgeable

informer 3 rat **4** fink **5** Judas **6** canary **7** blabber, stoolie, tattler, traitor **8** betrayer, mouchard, snitcher, squealer **11** stool pigeon

Informer, The
author: **13** Liam O'Flaherty
director: **8** John Ford
cast: **10** Una O'Connor **11** Wallace Ford **12** Heather Angel **13** Margot Grahame, Preston Foster **14** Victor McLaglen
score: **10** Max Steiner
remade as: **7** Up Tight

infraction 6 breach **8** trespass **9** violation **10** peccadillo **11** lawbreaking **12** disobedience, encroachment, infringement, unobservance **13** nonobservance, transgression

infrastructure 4 base, root **5** basis **6** bottom, fabric, ground **7** bedrock, footing, support **9** framework, substrate **10** foundation, groundwork, substratum **12** substructure, underpinning **14** understructure

infrequent 3 few **4** rare **6** fitful, seldom, unique **7** unusual **8** sporadic, uncommon **9** spasmodic **10** occasional **16** few and far between

infringe 5 break **6** butt in, invade **7** disobey, impinge, infract, intrude, violate **8** encroach, overstep, trespass **10** contravene, transgress

in front 5 ahead, first **6** before **7** forward

in full possession of one's faculties
Latin: **12** compos mentis

infuriate 3 vex **4** gall, rile **5** anger, chafe **6** enrage, madden, offend **7** incense, inflame, outrage, provoke **8** irritate **9** aggravate, burn one up, make angry **10** exasperate **15** raise one's dander

infuriating 7 irksome **8** annoying, enraging **9** maddening, provoking **10** irritating **11** aggravating **12** exasperating, inflammatory

infuse 5 imbue **7** fortify, implant, inspire, instill **8** impart to, pour into **9** inculcate, insinuate, introject

in futuro 9 in the future

Inge, William
author of: **6** Picnic **7** Bus Stop **19** Come Back Little Sheba **26** The Dark at the Top of the Stairs

in general 7 as a rule, usually **10** by and large, on the whole

ingenious 4 deft **6** adroit, artful, clever, crafty, shrewd **7** cunning **8** masterly, original, skillful, stunning **9** brilliant, dexterous, inventive, masterful **11** resourceful

ingenuity 5 flair, skill **7** cunning, know-how, mastery **8** aptitude, deftness, facility **9** adeptness, dexterity, expertise, sharpness **10** adroitness, as-

tuteness, brilliance, cleverness, shrewdness **11** imagination **12** good thinking, skillfulness **13** ingeniousness, inventiveness **15** imaginativeness, quick-wittedness, resourcefulness

ingenuous 4 open **5** frank, naive **6** direct, honest **7** artless, genuine, natural, up front **8** trusting **9** guileless **10** unaffected **11** openhearted **13** simplehearted **15** straightforward, unsophisticated **16** straight-shooting

ingenuousness 7 naivete **8** openness **9** frankness **11** artlessness

ingest 3 eat **4** gulp, take **5** drink **6** absorb, devour, imbibe, take in **7** consume, swallow **8** gulp down

inglorious 3 low **4** base, evil, mean, vile **6** odious **7** corrupt, heinous, ignoble **8** depraved, flagrant, infamous, shameful, shocking **9** atrocious, degrading, nefarious **10** despicable, detestable, outrageous, scandalous **11** disgraceful, ignominious, opprobrious **12** contemptible, dishonorable

in good condition
French: **10** embonpoint

in good health 2 OK **4** fine, hale, well **6** hearty, robust, tiptop **7** healthy **8** all right, blooming, vigorous **9** full of pep, in the pink **17** full of vim and vigor

in good time 5 early **7** betimes **11** ahead of time

ingot 3 bar **5** block

ingrained 4 deep, firm **5** fixed **6** inborn, inbred, innate, rooted **8** inherent, thorough **9** confirmed, implanted, indelible, intrinsic **10** deep-rooted, deep-seated, inveterate **14** constitutional

Ingram, Blanche
character in: **8** Jane Eyre
author: **6** Bronte

ingratiating 4 oily **5** sweet **6** genial, smarmy **7** affable, amiable, cordial, fulsome, gushing, likable, lovable, winning, winsome **8** charming, engaging, friendly, gracious, magnetic, pleasing, unctuous **9** appealing, congenial **10** attractive, enchanting, obsequious, oleaginous, personable, persuasive **11** captivating, good-humored, self-serving **12** presumptuous

ingratiation 7 blarney **8** flattery **9** sweet talk **12** inveiglement **13** blandishments

ingratitude 14 ungratefulness **18** lack of appreciation

ingredient 4 part **6** aspect, factor **7** element, feature **9** component, essential, principle **11** constituent, contributor **12** integral part

Ingres, Jean-Auguste-Dominique
born: **6** France **9** Montauban
artwork: **9** Odalisque, The Source **13**

Mme Moitessier **14** The Turkish Bath **15** Valpincon Bather **16** Roger and Angelica **17** The Vow of Louis XIII **21** Comtesse d'Haussonville **25** The Ambassadors of Agamemnon **26** The Vow of Louis the Thirteenth

ingress 5 entry, way in **6** access **8** entrance

inhabit 5 lodge **6** live in, occupy, people, settle, tenant **7** dwell in **8** populate, reside in

inhabitant 6 inmate, lessee, lodger, native, renter, tenant **7** boarder, citizen, denizen, dweller, settler **8** occupant, occupier, resident, villager **9** inhabiter

inhalation 4 gasp **5** sniff **6** breath **11** breathing in

inhale 5 sniff, snuff **6** suck in **7** inspire, respire **9** breathe in, inbreathe

inherent 6 inborn, inbred, innate, native **7** natural **9** essential, ingrained, intrinsic **10** deep-rooted, hereditary, inveterate **11** inalienable, inseparable **14** constitutional

inherit 3 get **6** be left, come by **7** acquire **8** come into **9** come in for **10** fall heir to

inheritance 6 devise, estate, legacy **7** bequest **8** bestowal, heritage **9** endowment, patrimony **10** bequeathal, birthright

inherited 8 came into, heirloom, unearned **10** handed down

inheritor 4 heir **7** legatee **11** beneficiary

Inherit the Wind
  director: 13 Stanley Kramer
  based on play by: 10 Robert E Lee **14** Jerome Lawrence
  cast: 8 Dick York **9** Gene Kelly **10** Elliot Reid **11** Harry Morgan **12** Spencer Tracy (Clarence Darrow) **13** Frederic March (William Jennings Bryan) **16** Florence Eldridge

inhibit 3 bar, gag **4** curb, stop **5** block, check **6** arrest, enjoin, forbid, hinder, impede, muzzle **7** control, harness, prevent, repress, smother **8** hold back, obstruct, prohibit, restrain, restrict, suppress **9** constrain **11** hold in leash

inhibited 4 cold **6** barred, curbed, frigid **7** bridled, checked, guarded **8** hindered, reserved **9** repressed **10** controlled, obstructed, restrained **11** constrained, discouraged, held in check **12** unresponsive **14** under restraint

inhibition, inhibitions 5 check **7** reserve **8** blockage **9** misgiving, restraint, stricture **10** constraint, impediment **11** guardedness, mental block, obstruction, restriction **12** constriction **17** self-consciousness

in high spirits 2 up **3** gay **5** happy,

merry **6** elated, jaunty, joyful, joyous **7** buoyant **8** carefree, ecstatic, exultant, jubilant **9** overjoyed **11** exhilarated, on cloud nine **13** up in the clouds **15** on top of the world

in hoc signo vinces 26 in this sign shalt thou conquer
  motto of: 19 Constantine the Great
  from vision of: 5 cross

inhospitable 4 cold, cool, rude **5** aloof **6** unkind **7** distant, hostile **8** impolite **10** unfriendly, ungracious, unobliging, unsociable **11** standoffish, uncongenial, unreceptive, unwelcoming **12** discourteous, unneighborly **13** inconsiderate **14** unapproachable **15** unaccommodating

inhuman 5 cruel **6** brutal, savage **7** brutish, satanic, vicious **8** barbaric, demoniac, fiendish, pitiless, ruthless, venomous **9** barbarous, heartless, malignant, merciless, monstrous, unfeeling **10** diabolical, malevolent **11** cold-hearted, cold-blooded, hardhearted

inhumane 6 brutal, savage **7** inhuman **8** fiendish, pitiless, ruthless **9** barbarous, heartless, merciless, unfeeling, unpitying **10** unmerciful **11** cold-blooded, hardhearted **12** bloodthirsty **13** unsympathetic

inhumanity 6 sadism **7** cruelty **8** atrocity, savagery **9** barbarism, barbarity, brutality **11** brutishness, heinousness, malevolence, viciousness **12** fiendishness, ruthlessness **13** heartlessness, mercilessness **15** cold-bloodedness **16** bloodthirstiness

inhumation 6 burial **9** interment **10** entombment

inimical 5 toxic **6** at odds **7** harmful, hateful, hostile, hurtful, ruinous **8** venomous, virulent **9** dangerous, ill-willed, injurious, on the outs, poisonous, rancorous **10** unfriendly **11** acrimonious, deleterious, destructive, detrimental, ill-disposed **12** antagonistic, antipathetic, disputatious **13** at loggerheads, at sword's point

inimitable 4 rare **6** unique **7** supreme **8** peerless **9** matchless, nonpareil, unequaled, unmatched, unrivaled **10** consummate, preeminent, unexcelled **11** superlative, unsurpassed **12** incomparable, unparalleled **13** beyond compare

iniquitous 4 base, evil, vile **6** sinful, wicked **7** corrupt, debased, immoral, vicious **8** depraved, infamous **9** nefarious **10** evil-minded **12** blackhearted **13** reprehensible

iniquity 3 sin **4** evil, vice **5** wrong **6** infamy **7** knavery, outrage, roguery **8** inequity, villainy **9** depravity, evildoing, flagrancy, turpitude **10** corruption, dishonesty, immorality, miscreancy, profligacy, sinfulness, unfairness, unjustness, wickedness,

wrongdoing **11** abomination **13** transgression **14** gross injustice **15** unrighteousness

in isolation
  Latin: 7 in vacuo

initial 5 first **6** maiden, primal **7** opening, primary **8** germinal, original, starting **9** beginning, inaugural, incipient **10** commencing, initiatory **12** introductory

initiate 4 haze, open **5** begin, found, set up, start **6** induct, invest, launch, take in **7** bring in, install, kick off, receive, usher in **8** be opened, commence, get going, set afoot, set going **9** enter upon, establish, institute, introduce, originate **10** inaugurate, lead the way **11** break ground, get under way, take the lead **12** acquaint with **13** blaze the trail **15** familiarize with **16** lay the first stone, lay the foundation **19** start the ball rolling

initiation 5 onset, start **6** outset **7** genesis, opening **8** entrance, guidance, outbreak, starting **9** beginning, inception, induction **10** admittance, initiating, ushering in **11** inculcation **12** commencement, inauguration, introduction **14** indoctrination **15** formal admission

initiative 4 lead **8** dynamism **9** first move, first step **10** creativity, enterprise, get-up-and-go, leadership **11** originality **12** forcefulness **14** aggressiveness

in its original place
  Latin: 6 in situ

inject 3 put **4** pump **5** force, imbue, infix **6** infuse, insert **7** instill, throw in **8** intromit **9** interject, introduce **11** interpolate

injection 4 hypo, shot **7** booster, vaccine **9** antitoxin, insertion **10** hypodermic **11** inoculation, vaccination **12** shot in the arm

injudicious 4 dumb, wild **5** crazy **6** stupid, unwise **7** foolish, unsound **8** heedless, reckless **9** audacious, foolhardy, hotheaded, imprudent, senseless **10** self-willed, unsuitable **11** inadvisable

injunction 4 writ **5** edict, order **7** command **10** admonition, court order

Injun Joe
  character in: 9 Tom Sawyer
  author: 9 Mark Twain

injure 3 mar **4** harm, hurt, lame, maim **5** abuse, spoil, stain, sting, sully, wound, wrong **6** bruise, damage, debase, deface, deform, impair, malign, mangle, misuse, offend, scathe **7** afflict, affront, blemish, violate, vitiate **8** do harm to, ill-treat, lacerate, maltreat, mutilate **9** disfigure

injured 4 hurt, lame **6** abused, harmed, maimed, marred, piqued **7** bruised, damaged, defaced, grieved, scathed, wounded, wronged **8** crippled, deformed, impaired, insulted, offended **9** afflicted, affronted, aggrieved **10** disfigured

injurious 7 abusive, adverse, harmful, hurtful, noxious, ruinous **8** damaging, inimical **9** corrosive **10** calamitous, disastrous, pernicious **11** deleterious, destructive, detrimental

injury 3 cut **4** blow, gash, harm, hurt, stab **5** abuse, wound **6** bruise, damage, lesion **7** affront, outrage, scratch **9** aspersion, contusion, indignity, injustice **10** affliction, defamation, detraction, disservice, impairment, laceration, mutilation **12** vilification

injustice 3 sin **4** bias, evil **5** wrong **6** injury **7** bigotry, offense, tyranny **8** foul play, inequity, iniquity **9** prejudice, unjust act **10** disservice, favoritism, inequality, infraction, partiality, unfairness, unjustness, wrongdoing **11** malpractice, persecution **12** encroachment, infringement, partisanship **13** transgression

in keeping 6 normal **7** natural **8** becoming **9** congruous, consonant **10** consistent **11** appropriate, in agreement **12** in compliance, in conformity

inkling 3 cue, tip **4** clue, hint, idea **6** notion **7** glimmer, whisper **8** innuendo **9** suspicion, vague idea **10** conception, glimmering, indication, intimation, suggestion **11** insinuation, supposition

inky 3 jet **4** dark **5** black, raven, sable **7** stygian **9** coal-black

inlet 3 bay **4** cove, gulf **5** bight, fiord, firth, fjord **6** harbor, strait **7** estuary, narrows **8** waterway

in line 4 even **6** in a row **7** aligned, in order **8** queued up, straight **12** under control

in loco 7 in place **16** in the proper place

in loco parentis 16 replacing a parent **19** in the place of a parent

inmate 3 con **5** felon **6** lodger, tenant **7** convict, denizen **8** prisoner, resident **10** inhabitant

in medias res 19 in the middle of things **21** in the middle of the story

in memoriam 10 in memory of **13** as a memorial to, to the memory of

In Memoriam A H H
    author: 18 Alfred Lord Tennyson

in memory of
    Latin: 10 in memoriam

In Memory of W B Yeats
    author: 7 W H Auden

inmost 5 inner **6** inside **7** central **8** interior **9** innermost

in motion 5 afoot, astir **6** active, moving **7** on the go, working **8** under way **9** on the move, operating, operative **10** responsive

In My Father's Court
    author: 19 Isaac Bashevis Singer

inn 5 hotel, lodge, motel, serai **6** hostel, imaret, tavern **7** hospice, pension **8** hostelry **9** roadhouse **11** caravansary, public house
    French: 7 auberge
    Spanish: 6 posada

innards 4 guts **6** bowels, vitals **7** gizzard, insides, viscera **10** intestines **14** liver and lights

innate 6 inborn, inbred, native **7** natural **8** inherent **9** essential, ingrained, inherited, intrinsic, intuitive **10** congenital, hereditary, indigenous **11** instinctive **14** constitutional

inner 6 hidden, inside, inward, mental, middle **7** central, private, psychic **8** esoteric, interior, internal, personal **9** concealed, emotional, spiritual, unobvious **10** more secret **12** more intimate **13** psychological

inner circle 4 core **5** bosom, cadre, heart **6** center **7** nucleus

inner city 8 core city, downtown **9** urban area **10** city limits, metropolis **11** central city **12** metropolitan area

Inner Mongolia
    other name: 9 Neimenggu, Neimengku
    capital: 6 Hohhot **7** Huhehot
    desert: 4 Gobi
    tent: 4 yurt

innermost 6 inmost, secret **7** deepest **10** deep-rooted, deep-seated **11** most private **12** most intimate, most personal

innermost part 4 core, crux, pith, soul **6** center, kernel **7** essence, nucleus

Inness, George
    born: 10 Newburgh NY
    artwork: 7 The Monk **14** Home of the Heron, Peace and Plenty **16** Delaware Water Gap **17** The Delaware Valley **19** The Lackawanna Valley

Innisfail *see* **7** Ireland

innkeeper 4 host, oste **6** tapper, venter **7** padrone **8** boniface, hosteler, hotelier, landlord, publican **10** proprietor **12** maitre d'hotel, restaurateur

innocence 6 purity **7** naivete **8** chastity **9** freshness **10** clean hands, simplicity **11** artlessness, sinlessness **12** incorruption, spotlessness **13** blamelessness, guilelessness, guiltlessness, impeccability, inculpability, ingenuousness, stainlessness **14** immaculateness

innocent 3 tot **4** baby, naif, open, pure, tyro **5** clean, naive **6** chaste, honest, novice, simple **7** artless, ingenue, sinless, upright **8** harmless, pristine, spotless, virginal, virtuous **9** blameless, childlike, faultless, greenhorn, guileless, guiltless, ingenuous, innocuous, little one, stainless, uncor-

rupt, undefiled, unstained, unsullied, unworldly, well-meant **10** artless one, immaculate, impeccable, inculpable, tenderfoot, young child **11** inoffensive, unblemished, uncorrupted, unmalicious, unoffending **12** unsuspicious **13** meaning no harm, unimpeachable **14** above suspicion, irreproachable **15** unsophisticated
    Latin: 12 integer vitae

Innocents, The
    director: 11 Jack Clayton
    based on story by: 10 Henry James (The Turn of the Screw)
    cast: 11 Deborah Kerr, Megs Jenkins **13** Peter Wyngarde **15** Michael Redgrave
    script: 12 Truman Capote **16** William Archibald

Innocents Abroad, The
    author: 9 Mark Twain (Samuel Clemens)

innocuous 4 dull, mild **5** banal, empty, trite, vapid **6** barren **7** insipid **8** harmless, innocent, painless **9** pointless **11** commonplace, inoffensive, meaningless

innocuousness 6 safety **9** blandness, innocence **12** harmlessness **15** inoffensiveness

in no uncertain terms 7 clearly, plainly **9** expressly **10** definitely, distinctly **13** categorically, unequivocally

innovation 5 shift **7** novelty **8** updating **10** alteration, dernier cri, new measure, remodeling, renovation **11** institution, latest thing **12** commencement, inauguration, introduction, streamlining **13** modernization

innovator 7 deviser, planner **9** contriver **10** instigator, originator **11** inaugurator

Inns of Court 8 Gray's Inn **11** Inner Temple, Lincoln's Inn **12** Middle Temple **14** legal societies
    in: 6 London
    member: 9 barrister

innuendo 4 hint **7** whisper **8** overtone **9** inference **10** imputation, intimation **11** implication, insinuation

innumerable 6 myriad **8** numerous **9** countless **10** numberless, unnumbered **12** incalculable **13** multitudinous

Ino
    also: 9 Leucothea
    goddess of: 3 sea
    father: 6 Cadmus
    mother: 8 Harmonia
    sister: 5 Hgave **6** Semele **7** Autonoe
    husband: 7 Athamas
    son: 8 Learchus **10** Melicertes
    stepson: 7 Phrixus
    stepdaughter: 5 Helle
    saved: 7 Odysseus
    cared for infant: 8 Dionysus
    changed into: 10 sea goddess

inoculate 5 imbue, shoot **6** infuse, inject, insert **7** implant, instill **8** immunize **9** inculcate, vaccinate

inoculation 4 shot **6** needle **7** booster **9** injection **10** hypodermic **11** vaccination **12** immunization

inoffensive 4 mild, safe **5** bland **7** neutral **8** harmless, innocent **9** endurable, innocuous, tolerable **10** sufferable **11** unoffending **15** unobjectionable

inoffensiveness 6 safety **9** innocence **10** neutrality **12** harmlessness **13** innocuousness

in one's debt 7 obliged **8** beholden, indebted **9** obligated **15** under obligation

in one's own person
Latin: **16** in propria persona

in one's own place
Latin: **7** suo loco

in one's own right
Latin: **7** suo jure

in one's rightful place
Latin: **7** suo loco

inoperable 6 broken **10** broken down, unworkable **11** ineffective

in operation 5 in use **7** in force, working **8** in effect **9** operating, operative

inoperative 4 dead, down **8** inactive **10** not working, out of order

inopportune 7 awkward **8** ill-timed, untimely **10** badly timed, ill-advised, unsuitable **11** troublesome, undesirable, unfavorable, unfortunate **12** inauspicious, incommodious, inconvenient, unpropitious, unseasonable **13** inappropriate **15** disadvantageous

in order 2 OK **4** neat, tidy **6** proper **7** correct, perfect **8** all right

inordinate 5 undue **6** lavish, wanton **7** extreme, profuse, surplus **8** needless, overmuch, shocking **9** excessive **10** deplorable, exorbitant, immoderate, irrational, outrageous, scandalous **11** disgraceful, extravagant, intemperate, overflowing, superfluous, uncalled-for, unnecessary **12** unreasonable, unrestrained **13** superabundant **14** super-saturated, unconscionable **16** disproportionate

inordinately 6 overly, unduly **9** extremely **11** excessively **12** immoderately, outrageously, prodigiously **13** extravagantly, intemperately, superfluously, unnecessarily

inorganic 4 dead **7** mineral **8** lifeless **9** inanimate, nonliving **10** artificial

in passing
French: **9** en passant

in perpetuum 7 forever

in petto 11 in the breast **12** not disclosed

in pieces 6 broken **7** asunder, smashed **8** in shreds, sundered **9** torn apart **13** in smithereens

in place
Latin: **6** in loco, in situ

in plain sight 7 exposed, obvious **10** in full view, noticeable **12** out in the open **17** in front of one's nose

in posse 11 potentially **13** in possibility

in possibility
Latin: **7** in posse

In Praise of Darkness
author: **15** Jorge Luis Borges

in propria persona 15 in one's own person

inquest 5 probe **7** autopsy, delving, hearing, inquiry, probing **8** necropsy **10** postmortem **11** inquisition **13** investigation

inquire 3 ask **5** probe, query, study **6** search **7** examine, explore, inspect **8** check out, look into, look over, question **9** track down **10** look deeper, scrutinize **11** investigate

inquirer 5 asker, snoop **6** seeker **7** auditor, querier, quizzer, student **8** pollster, searcher **9** catechist **10** inquisitor, questioner **12** interlocutor, interrogator, investigator

inquiry, enquiry 4 hunt, quiz **5** probe, query, quest, study **6** search, survey **7** inquest **8** analysis, question, research, scrutiny **9** interview **10** inspection **11** examination, exploration, inquisition, questioning **13** interrogation, investigation

inquisitive 4 nosy **6** prying, snoopy **8** meddling, snooping **9** inquiring, intrusive, searching **10** meddlesome, too curious **11** interfering, overcurious, questioning

in re 13 in the matter of

in reality
Latin: **7** de facto

in rem 15 against the thing
of a legal proceeding: **18** against the property

in rerum natura 19 in the nature of things

in retreat 10 backing off, retreating **11** withdrawing, backing away

in reverse 8 backward **9** backing up **22** in the opposite direction

insalubrious 7 harmful, noisome, noxious **8** inimical, virulent **9** injurious, unhealthy **10** pernicious **11** deleterious, detrimental, unhealthful, unwholesome

insane 3 mad **4** bats, daft, dumb, loco, nuts, wild, zany **5** balmy, batty, crazy, loony, manic, nutty, potty **6** absurd, crazed, raving **7** berserk, bizarre, bonkers, cracked, foolish, idiotic, lunatic, tetched, touched, unsound **8** demented, frenzied, maniacal, unhinged **9** eccentric, imbecilic, imprudent, insensate, paranoiac, psychotic, senseless **10** ridiculous, un-

balanced **11** injudicious **12** mad as a hatter, off one's chump, round the bend, unreasonable **13** off one's rocker, out of one's head, out of one's mind, out of one's wits, schizophrenic **15** bats in the belfry, mad as a March hare, stark staring mad **17** nutty as a fruitcake

insanity 5 folly, mania **6** idiocy, lunacy, raving **7** madness **8** dementia, paranoia **9** aberrance, absurdity, craziness, monomania, psychosis, stupidity **10** aberration **11** derangement, foolishness, unsoundness **12** loss of reason **13** hallucination, mental illness, schizophrenia, senselessness

insatiable 8 ravenous **9** insatiate, limitless, voracious **10** bottomless, gluttonous, implacable, omnivorous **12** unappeasable, unquenchable

inscribe 3 pen **4** etch, mark, seal, sign **5** blaze, brand, carve, write **6** chisel, incise, letter, scrawl **7** engrave, impress, imprint **8** scribble **9** autograph

inscription 5 motto, title **6** legend, rubric **7** address, caption, epigram, epitaph, heading, titulus, writing **8** colophon, epigraph, graffiti **9** engraving, lettering **10** dedication

inscrutable 6 arcane, hidden, masked, veiled **7** deadpan, elusive **8** baffling, puzzling **9** concealed, enigmatic **10** mysterious, mystifying, perplexing, poker-faced, unknowable, unreadable, unrevealed **12** inexplicable, unfathomable, unsearchable **14** indecipherable, unintelligible **16** incomprehensible

In Search of Identity
author: **12** Anwar el-Sadat

insect 3 ant, bee, bug, fly **4** flea, gnat, moth, pest, wasp **5** aphid, imago **6** bedbug, beetle, cicada, earwig, hornet, mantis, mayfly, vermin **7** chigger, cricket, firefly, katydid, ladybug, termite **8** horsefly, housefly, lacewing, mosquito **9** arthropod, butterfly, cockroach, dragonfly **10** silverfish **11** grasshopper
study of: 10 entomology
young: 4 grub, pupa **5** larva, nymph **6** larvae, maggot **9** chrysalis **11** caterpillar
anatomy: 4 palp **5** cerci, notum **6** cercus, feeler, labium, labrum, ocelli, thorax **7** antenna, maxilla, ocellus **8** antennae, mandible, maxillae **9** proboscis, spiracles **10** ovipositor **11** exoskeleton

insectivore 4 mole **5** shrew **6** desman, tenrec **7** moon rat **8** alamiqui, anteater, hedgehog **9** solenodon

insecure 4 weak **5** frail, risky, shaky **6** infirm, unsafe, unsure, wobbly **7** dubious, exposed, not firm, not sure, rickety, unsound **8** critical, doubtful, in danger, perilous, unstable, unsteady **9** dangerous, diffident, hazardous, in a bad way, tottering, unassured, uncertain, under fire **10** endangered, precarious, ramshackle, unreliable, unshielded, vulnerable **11** defenseless, dilapidated, unprotected, unsheltered

insecurities 4 risk **5** peril **6** danger, hazard **7** pitfall **8** jeopardy **11** contingency

insecurity 5 doubt **9** self-doubt, shakiness **10** diffidence, unsafeness **11** dubiousness, incertitude, instability, uncertainty **12** doubtfulness, endangerment, insecureness, unsteadiness **13** vulnerability **14** precariousness **15** defenselessness, lack of assurance **16** apprehensiveness

insensate 4 cold **5** cruel **6** brutal **8** inhumane **9** heartless, unfeeling **11** unconscious

insensibility 4 coma **5** swoon **6** apathy, torpor, trance **8** blackout, dullness, lethargy, numbness, obduracy, oblivion, stoicism **9** analgesia, catalepsy **10** anesthesia, obtuseness **12** incognizance, indifference, mindlessness **13** insensitivity, unfeelingness **15** unconsciousness

insensible 4 cold **9** insensate, senseless **11** unconscious

insensitive 4 cold, dead, numb **5** blase **7** callous **8** hardened **9** apathetic, impassive, insensate, unaware of, unfeeling **10** impervious, insensible **11** indifferent, unconcerned **12** thick-skinned **15** uncompassionate

insensitiveness 8 rudeness **10** coarseness, indelicacy **12** tactlessness **13** insensibility, insensitivity **17** inconsiderateness

inseparable 8 attached **11** indivisible, unseverable **12** indissoluble

insert 3 add **5** embed, enter, imbed, infix, inlay, inset, pop in, put in, set in **6** infuse, inject, push in, tuck in **7** drive in, implant, intrude, place in, press in, slide in, stick in, stuff in, wedge in **8** thrust in **9** interject, interlard, interpose, introduce **10** put between **11** interpolate, intersperse

insertion 2 ad **5** entry, graft, inlay, inset **7** implant **11** insinuation, parenthesis **12** interjection **13** advertisement

inset 4 gore **5** embed, godet, imbed, inlay, panel **6** insert **9** insertion

in seventh heaven 6 elated, joyful, joyous **8** ecstatic, euphoric **9** exuberant, rapturous **11** on cloud nine **13** up in the clouds

inside 2 in **5** inner **6** inmost, inward, secret **7** private **8** cliquish, esoteric, interior, internal, intimate **9** inner part, inner side, innermost **12** confidential

inside information 3 tip **10** inside dope

inside out 9 backwards **10** in disorder, topsy turvy **11** wrong side to

insides 4 guts **6** bowels, vitals **7** gizzard, innards, viscera **10** intestines

insidious 3 sly **4** foxy, wily **5** shady **6** artful, covert, crafty, sneaky, subtle, tricky **7** crooked, cunning, devious, furtive **8** guileful, slippery, sneaking, stealthy **9** concealed, deceitful, designing, disguised, secretive, underhand **10** contriving, perfidious, pernicious, undercover, undetected **11** clandestine, deleterious, treacherous, underhanded **12** disingenuous, falsehearted **13** Machiavellian, surreptitious

insight 6 acumen **9** intuition **10** perception **11** discernment, penetration **12** apprehension, perceptivity, perspicacity **13** comprehension, intuitiveness **14** perceptiveness
French: 6 apercu

insignia 3 bar **4** mark, sign, star **5** badge, medal, patch **6** emblem, stripe, symbol **7** chevron, epaulet, oak leaf **10** decoration **13** badge of office

insignificance 8 puniness **9** pettiness, smallness **10** meagerness, triviality **11** irrelevance **12** unimportance

insignificant 4 puny **5** petty, small **6** flimsy, meager, minute, paltry **7** trivial **8** niggling, not vital, nugatory, picayune, piddling, trifling **9** minuscule, worthless **10** immaterial, irrelevant, negligible, of no moment, second-rate **11** indifferent, meaningless, unimportant **12** nonessential **13** small potatoes **14** inconsiderable **15** inconsequential, of little account, of no consequence **18** not worth mentioning

insincere 5 false, lying **6** untrue **7** devious, evasive **8** guileful, two-faced, uncandid **9** deceitful, dishonest, equivocal **10** fraudulent, perfidious, untruthful **11** dissembling **12** disingenuous, hypocritical, mealymouthed **13** dissimulating, double-dealing

insincerity 4 sham **6** deceit **8** pretense, uncandor **9** deception, falseness, hypocrisy, mendacity **11** affectation, shallowness, unfrankness **12** uncandidness **13** artificiality **16** disingenuousness

insinuate 5 imply **6** inject, insert **7** asperse, let fall, suggest, wheedle, whisper **8** intimate **10** ingratiate **11** worm one's way

insinuation 4 hint **8** allusion, infusion, innuendo **9** aspersion, insertion, intrusion **10** allegation, imputation, intimation, suggestion **11** implication, penetration **12** ingratiation, interjection

insipid 4 arid, blah, drab, dull, flat, lean **5** banal, bland, empty, inane, stale, trite, vapid **6** barren, boring, jejune, stupid **7** prosaic **8** lifeless, zestless **9** pointless, savorless, tasteless,

wearisome **10** monotonous, namby-pamby, wishy-washy **11** commonplace **12** unappetizing **13** characterless, uninteresting

insist 4 aver, hold, urge, warn **5** claim, vouch **6** assert, demand, exhort, repeat, stress **7** caution, command, contend, persist, protest, require **8** admonish, maintain **9** reiterate **10** asseverate **13** lay down the law **14** take a firm stand **15** stand one's ground

insistence 6 demand, urging **7** urgency **8** exigency, pressure **9** clamoring **11** persistence **12** perseverance **14** imperativeness

insistent 4 firm **7** adamant **8** emphatic, repeated, stubborn **9** assertive, demanding **10** determined, unyielding **11** unrelenting

in situ 7 in place **18** in its original place

insolence 4 gall **7** disdain, hauteur **8** audacity **9** arrogance, impudence **10** brazenness, disrespect, effrontery, incivility, lordliness **11** haughtiness, presumption **12** disobedience, impertinence, impoliteness **13** bumptiousness, imperiousness **14** unmannerliness **16** superciliousness

insolent 4 rude **5** fresh, nervy **6** brazen, cheeky **7** defiant, galling, haughty **8** arrogant, impolite, impudent **9** audacious, bumptious, insulting **10** disdainful, outrageous, unmannerly **11** impertinent, overbearing **12** contemptuous, discourteous, presumptuous, supercilious **13** disrespectful

insoluble 12 inexplicable, unanswerable **13** undissolvable, unexplainable **14** undecipherable **16** incomprehensible

insolvent 5 broke **6** ruined **8** bankrupt, wiped out **9** destitute, moneyless, penniless **10** down-and-out, out of money **11** impecunious **12** impoverished, overextended

insomnia 11 nuit blanche, pervigilium, wakefulness **12** insomnolence **13** sleeplessness

insouciant 4 airy **5** perky **6** breezy, casual, jaunty **7** buoyant, offhand **8** carefree, debonair, flippant **9** easygoing, mercurial, unruffled, sans souci, whimsical **10** capricious, nonchalant, untroubled **11** free and easy, indifferent, unconcerned **12** devil-may-care, happy-go-lucky, lighthearted

inspect 3 eye **4** scan **5** probe, study **6** peer at, peruse, review, survey **7** examine, explore, observe **8** pore over **10** scrutinize **11** contemplate, investigate, reconnoiter

inspection 4 scan **5** audit, check, probe, study **6** review, survey **7** perusal **8** checking, scrutiny **9** appraisal, oversight **11** examination

inspector 7 analyst, auditor **8** analyzer, examiner, overseer, reviewer **9** appraiser, detective **11** scrutinizer **12** investigator
    famous: 3 Fix, Fox **4** Japp **5** Queen **6** Alleyn, Bucket, Gerard, Gideon, Javert **7** Maigret **8** Clouseau, Lestrade **9** Dalgliesh

Inspector-General, The
    author: 12 Nikolai Gogol
    character: 4 Anna, Osip **5** Maria **26** Ivan Alexandrovich Hlestakov **35** Anton Antonovich Skvoznik-Dmukhanovsky

inspiration 4 idea, spur **5** fancy, flash **6** motive **7** impulse **8** afflatus, stimulus **9** incentive, influence, prompting **10** compulsion, incitement, motivation, revelation **13** encouragement

inspire 4 fire, stir **5** cause, exalt, impel, rouse **6** arouse, excite, induce, prompt, vivify **7** animate, enliven, hearten, produce, promote, provoke, quicken **8** embolden, engender, enkindle, illumine, inspirit, motivate, occasion **9** encourage, galvanize, influence, stimulate **10** give rise to, illuminate

inspired 3 apt **5** fired, moved **6** elated **7** elegant, exalted, excited, incited, touched, well-put **8** creative, original, prompted **9** impressed, ingenious, inventive, motivated **10** encouraged, felicitous, influenced, stimulated, well-chosen **11** exhilarated, imaginative **13** well-expressed

inspiring 5 grand **6** moving **7** awesome **8** eloquent, stirring **9** affecting, brilliant **10** impressive **11** encouraging, magnificent, stimulating

inspirit 5 boost, cheer, rouse **6** buoy up, uplift **7** animate, comfort, enliven, hearten, inspire **9** encourage, give a lift

in spite of himself
    French: 9 malgre lui

instability 8 wavering, weakness **9** hesitancy **10** fitfulness, hesitation, indecision, insecurity **11** flightiness, fluctuation, inconstancy, vacillation **12** irresolution, unstableness, unsteadiness **13** changeability, inconsistency, mercurialness, vulnerability **14** capriciousness, changeableness

install, instal 3 lay **4** seat **5** crown, embed, imbed, lodge, plant **6** induct, invest, locate, move in, ordain **7** arrange, emplace, instate, receive, situate, station, usher in **8** coronate, initiate, position **9** establish **10** inaugurate, set in place

installation 5 plant **6** agency **8** facility **9** formation, induction **10** foundation, initiation, ordination **11** appointment, institution, investiture **12** inauguration, military base, organization **13** establishment

installment 4 part, unit **5** issue **6** laying **7** chapter, payment, section, segment **8** division, fragment, locating

instance 4 case, time **6** sample **7** example **8** occasion, specimen **9** precedent, prototype **10** antecedent **11** case in point **12** circumstance, illustration

instant 5 flash, jiffy, quick, trice **6** abrupt, minute, moment, prompt, second, sudden **8** premixed **9** immediate, on the spot, precooked, twinkling **10** ready-to-use **11** split second **12** unhesitating

instantaneous 5 rapid, swift **6** abrupt, direct, prompt, speedy, sudden **9** immediate **13** quick as a flash

instantaneously 6 at once **7** quickly, rapidly **8** in a flash, in no time, instanter, right now **9** on the spot, right away **11** immediately **21** in the twinkling of an eye

instantly 6 at once **7** quickly **8** directly, in a flash, promptly, right now **9** instanter, on the spot **10** here and now **11** immediately **12** quick as a wink, without delay **15** instantaneously **17** without hesitation

instar
    insect period between: 5 molts **7** molting

in statu quo 17 in the state in which (something is or was)

Instauratio Magna
    author: 12 Francis Bacon

instead 6 in lieu, rather **10** in its place

instigate 4 goad, spur, urge **5** begin, rouse, start **6** foment, incite, kindle, prompt, stir up **7** provoke **8** initiate **9** stimulate **10** bring about **11** set in motion

instigator 6 shaper **7** inciter **9** architect, innovator **10** prime mover, ringleader

instill, instil 4 pour **5** mix in, teach **6** impart, induce **7** implant, inspire **8** engender **9** inculcate

instinct 4 gift **5** knack **6** genius, nature **7** faculty **8** aptitude, capacity, tendency **9** intuition, mother wit **10** proclivity

instinctive 6 inborn, inbred, innate, native **7** natural **8** inherent, inspired **9** automatic, impulsive, intuitive, unlearned **10** deep-seated, unacquired **11** instinctual, involuntary, spontaneous

institute 4 pass **5** begin, enact, found, set up, start **6** ordain, school **7** academy, college, society **8** commence, get going, initiate, organize **9** establish, introduce, originate, prescribe, undertake **10** constitute, foundation, inaugurate **11** association, get under way **13** put into effect **14** bring into being

institution 4 rite **5** habit, usage **6** custom, prison, ritual, school **7** academy,

college, company, fixture **8** bughouse, madhouse, nuthouse, seminary **9** institute **10** convention, crazy house, foundation, university **11** association **12** organization **13** establishment

institutionalize 6 commit, detain **7** confine, put away **8** imprison **11** incarcerate

in strict confidence 7 sub rosa **9** between us, entre nous, privately **14** confidentially **15** between you and me **16** between me and thee, between ourselves

instruct 3 bid **5** brief, coach, drill, guide, order, teach, train, tutor **6** advise, direct, inform, notify, school **7** apprise, command, educate **8** acquaint **9** catechize, enlighten **12** indoctrinate

instruction 8 coaching, guidance, pedagogy, teaching, training, tutelage, tutoring **9** education **11** instructing **14** indoctrination

instructions 4 rule **5** maxim, moral, motto **6** advice, homily, lesson **7** precept **9** direction, guideline **11** explanation, information **12** prescription **13** specification **14** recommendation

instructive 8 didactic, edifying **11** educational **12** enlightening

instructor 3 don **4** guru **5** coach, guide, tutor **6** mentor **7** counsel, maestro, teacher, trainer **8** educator, lecturer **9** governess, pedagogue, preceptor, professor **10** schoolmarm **12** schoolmaster **13** schoolteacher **14** schoolmistress

instrument 4 deed, tool **5** agent, grant, means, paper **6** agency, device, gadget, medium **7** charter, machine, utensil, vehicle **8** contract **9** apparatus, appliance, equipment, expedient, implement, mechanism **11** contrivance

Instrument, The
    author: 9 John O'Hara

instrumental 5 vital **6** active, useful **7** crucial, helpful **8** a means to, decisive, valuable **9** assisting, conducive, effective, effectual, essential **10** functional **12** contributory

instrumentality 5 force, means **6** agency, charge **9** influence, mediation **12** intervention

insubordinate 6 unruly **7** defiant **8** insolent, mutinous **9** fractious **10** disorderly, rebellious, refractory **11** disobedient, intractable, uncompliant **12** recalcitrant, ungovernable, unsubmissive

insubordination 6 mutiny, revolt **7** anarchy **8** sedition **9** rebellion **10** dissension, insurgence, unruliness **12** disobedience, insurrection **13** noncompliance **14** refractoriness

insubstantial 4 airy, weak **5** frail, shaky, small **6** flimsy, modest, paltry, slight, unreal **7** fragile, trivial, unsound **8** baseless, bodiless, delicate, ethereal, gossamer, piddling, trifling, unstable **9** imaginary, visionary **10** groundless, immaterial, impalpable, intangible **12** apparitional **14** inconsiderable

in succession
French: **7** en suite

insufferable 7 hateful **8** dreadful **10** abominable, detestable, disgusting, outrageous, unbearable **11** intolerable, unendurable, unspeakable **13** insupportable

insufficiency 4 lack, need, want **6** dearth **7** drought, paucity **8** scarcity, shortage **10** deficiency, inadequacy, meagerness, scantiness **11** undersupply

insufficient 6 scanty, skimpy, sparse **7** lacking, wanting **8** impotent **9** deficient, not enough **10** inadequate **11** incompetent **14** unsatisfactory

insular 5 petty **6** biased, narrow **7** bigoted, limited **8** isolated **9** illiberal, insulated, parochial **10** intolerant, prejudiced, provincial **12** narrow-minded

insulate 5 cover **6** cut off, detach, enisle, shield **7** cushion, isolate, protect, seclude **8** separate **9** segregate, sequester **10** disconnect

insult 3 cut **4** slap **5** abuse, cheek, scorn **6** deride, offend, slight **7** affront, offense, outrage **8** be rude to, belittle, rudeness **9** disparage, impudence, indignity **11** discourtesy, lese majesty

insulting 4 rude **5** nasty **7** abusive, uncivil, vicious **8** impolite, insolent **9** invidious, offensive **10** defamatory, derogatory **11** disparaging **12** discourteous **13** disrespectful

insuperable 8 crushing **9** defeating **10** impassable, impossible, invincible, unbeatable, unyielding **12** inexpugnable, overpowering, overwhelming **13** overmastering, unconquerable **14** insurmountable

insurance 6 policy **8** coverage, security, warranty **9** assurance, guarantee, indemnity

insure 6 secure **10** underwrite

insurgent 5 rebel **7** lawless **8** mutineer, mutinous, partisan, renegade, resister, revolter **9** breakaway, dissident, guerrilla **10** disorderly, rebellious **11** disobedient **13** insubordinate, revolutionary, revolutionist **15** insurrectionist

insurmountable 8 hopeless, too great **10** unbeatable **11** beyond reach, insuperable **13** unconquerable

insurrection 4 riot **6** mutiny, revolt, rising **8** outbreak, uprising **9** rebellion **10** insurgence, revolution

intact 4 safe **5** sound, whole **6** unhurt **7** perfect **8** complete, integral, unbro-

ken, unharmed **9** undamaged, uninjured, untouched **10** in one piece, unimpaired **11** in good shape **15** without a scratch

intangible 5 vague **7** elusive, shadowy **8** abstract, ethereal, fleeting, fugitive **9** transient **10** accidental, evanescent, immaterial, impalpable **11** abstraction, untouchable **12** imponderable **13** imperceptible, insubstantial

integer 5 digit, whole **6** entity, figure, number **7** numeral **11** whole number

integer vitae 8 innocent **15** blameless in life

integral 4 full **5** basic, total, whole **6** entire, intact **7** perfect, rounded **8** complete, finished, inherent **9** component, essential, fulfilled, necessary, requisite **10** fulfilling **11** constituent, well-rounded **13** indispensable

integrate 3 mix **4** fuse **5** blend, merge, unify, unite **6** mingle **7** combine **8** intermix **10** amalgamate **11** desegregate **13** bring together

integrated 6 entire, joined, linked, united **7** blended, merged, unified, unitary **8** combined **9** composite, undivided **10** harmonized, reconciled **11** coordinated, synthesized **12** desegregated, unsegregated

integration 5 union **6** fusion, mixing **8** blending **9** combining, synthesis **11** combination **12** assimilation **13** desegregation

integrity 5 unity **6** purity, virtue **7** decency, honesty, probity **8** cohesion, morality, strength **9** character, coherence, principle, rectitude, wholeness **11** reliability, self-respect, uprightness **12** completeness

integument 4 coat, hide, husk, rind, skin **5** shell, **7** coating, cuticle, epiderm, exoderm **8** covering, envelope, membrane

integumentary system
component: **4** hair, skin **5** nails

intellect 3 wit **4** mind **5** brain, sense **6** brains, wisdom **7** thinker **9** cognition, mentality **10** perception **11** mental power, rationality **12** intellectual, intelligence **13** consciousness, understanding

intellectual 4 sage **5** brain **6** brainy, mental, pundit, savant **7** bookish, egghead, scholar, thinker **8** abstract, academic, cerebral, highbrow, longhair, mandarin, rational, studious **9** intellect, of the mind, reasoning, scholarly **10** thoughtful **11** intelligent
French: **9** bel-esprit

intelligence 4 dope, news **6** acumen, advice, brains, notice, report, wisdom **7** tidings **8** sagacity **9** intellect, knowledge **10** advisement, shrewdness **11** information **12** notification, perspicacity **13** comprehension, understanding

intelligent 4 keen, sage, wise **5** alert,

canny, quick, sharp, smart **6** astute, brainy, bright, clever, shrewd **7** knowing, prudent **8** informed, sensible, thinking **9** brilliant, sagacious **10** perceptive, thoughtful **11** clearheaded, quick-witted, sharp-witted **12** well-informed **13** perspicacious

intelligentsia 5 mensa **7** academe **8** thinkers **10** ivory tower **13** intellectuals

intelligible 5 clear, lucid **7** evident, obvious **8** apparent, clear-cut, coherent, definite, distinct **11** unambiguous, well-defined **12** unmistakable **14** comprehensible, understandable

intemperance 10 alcoholism, insobriety **11** dissipation, drunkenness, inebriation **12** immoderation, recklessness **13** excessiveness **16** irresponsibility

intemperate 5 harsh **6** brutal, rugged, severe **7** extreme, violent **8** bibulous, uncurbed **9** dissolute, excessive, inclement **10** dissipated, gluttonous, immoderate, inordinate **11** extravagant, inabstinent, incontinent **12** unrestrained **13** overindulgent

intend 3 aim **4** mean, plan, wish **6** aspire, design, expect **7** project, propose, resolve **9** calculate, determine **10** have in mind **11** contemplate

intended 5 meant **6** fiance, future **7** engaged, fiancee, implied, willful **8** proposed, purposed **9** affianced, betrothed, bride-to-be, groom-to-be, voluntary **10** calculated, deliberate **11** intentional

intense 4 deep, keen **5** acute, sharp **6** ardent, potent, strong **7** burning, earnest, extreme, fervent, violent **8** emphatic, forceful, forcible, powerful, vehement **10** passionate **12** concentrated, considerable

intensely 4 very **5** hotly **6** deeply, keenly **7** acutely, eagerly, vividly **8** ardently, heatedly, terribly **9** extremely, fervently, seriously, violently, zealously **10** forcefully, powerfully, profoundly, vehemently, vigorously **11** excessively, exquisitely, strenuously **12** considerably, passionately **13** energetically

intensify 5 boost **6** deepen, worsen **7** magnify, quicken, sharpen **8** escalate, heighten, increase, redouble **9** aggravate, reinforce **10** accelerate, strengthen

intensifying 9 worsening **10** increasing, magnifying, redoubling, sharpening **11** aggravating, heightening, reinforcing **12** exacerbating **13** strengthening

intensity 4 zeal **5** ardor, depth, force, power, vigor **6** energy, fervor **7** emotion, passion, potency **8** severity, strength **9** magnitude, vehemence **11** earnestness **12** forcefulness

intensive 6 all-out **7** growing, radical **8** complete, sweeping, thorough **10** exhaustive, increasing **11** comprehensive **12** concentrated **13** thoroughgoing

intent 3 aim, end, set **4** bent, gist, plan **5** drift, fixed **6** burden, design, import, steady **7** earnest, intense, meaning, purport, purpose **8** absorbed, piercing, resolved **9** engrossed, insistent, intention, steadfast, substance, tenacious, unbending **10** determined, unwavering **11** preoccupied **12** concentrated, significance, undistracted **13** determination, premeditation

intention 3 aim, end **4** goal, plan **6** design, intent, object, target **7** purpose, resolve **9** objective **10** resolution **13** determination

intentional 6 willed **7** planned **8** designed, intended **9** voluntary **10** calculated, deliberate, purposeful **12** contemplated, premeditated **13** done on purpose

intently 6 deeply, raptly **9** fervently, zealously **10** absorbedly **11** attentively **12** passionately **18** without distraction **22** with undivided attention

intentness 10 absorption **11** engrossment **13** concentration

inter 4 bury **5** inurn **6** entomb, inhume **7** inearth, lay away **9** lay to rest **11** ensepulcher

interact 4 join, mesh **5** coact, unite **6** engage **7** combine, conjoin **8** dovetail **9** cooperate, interlace, intermesh, interplay, interwork **10** coordinate, interreact

inter alia 16 among other things

inter alios 17 among other persons

interbreed 3 mix **5** cross **8** intermix **10** crossbreed

intercede 5 plead **6** step in **7** mediate, speak up **9** arbitrate, interpose, intervene, offer help **12** offer support **14** put in a good word **16** lend a helping hand

intercept 3 nab **4** grab, stay, stop, take **5** catch, seize **6** ambush, arrest, cut off, detain **7** deflect, reroute

intercessor 5 agent **6** bishop, broker **8** advocate, mediator **9** go-between, middleman **12** intermediary, spokesperson

interchange 5 shift **6** switch **7** trading **8** exchange, junction, swapping, transfer **9** alternate, crossover **10** substitute **11** give and take, reciprocity

interchangeable 8 parallel, tradable **9** analogous **10** equivalent, switchable, synonymous **12** exchangeable, transposable **13** corresponding

interconnected 8 adjacent **10** contiguous, juxtaposed **12** conterminous, labyrinthine

intercourse 4 talk **5** trade **6** coitus, parley **7** pairing, traffic **8** colloquy, commerce, congress, coupling, dealings, exchange **9** communion, discourse, relations **10** connection, copulation **12** conversation **14** communications, correspondence

interdict 3 ban, bar **5** taboo **6** enjoin, forbid **7** barring, censure **8** prohibit, restrain, restrict **9** proscribe **11** forbiddance, prohibition **12** proscription

interdiction 3 ban **7** barring **11** forbiddance, prohibition **12** proscription

interest, interests 4 gain, good, part, weal **5** bonus, hobby, share, stake, touch, yield **6** absorb, affect, behalf, divert, engage, notice, profit, regard **7** attract, benefit, concern, holding, involve, pastime, portion, pursuit, service **8** dividend **9** advantage, attention, avocation, curiosity, preoccupy, suspicion **10** absorption, investment **11** engrossment **13** preoccupation

interested 6 active **7** engaged **8** diverted **9** committed, concerned **10** fascinated, responsive

interesting 7 curious **8** engaging, magnetic, pleasing, riveting, striking **9** absorbing, appealing, arresting **10** attractive, suspicious **11** fascinating, stimulating **12** entertaining

interfere 3 jar, mix **6** butt in, horn in, meddle, rush in, step in **7** counter, intrude **8** conflict **9** frustrate, intercede, interpose, intervene **11** get in the way **14** be a hindrance to, be an obstacle to, be inconsistent, stick in one's oar

interference 3 bar **6** static **8** clashing, conflict, friction, invasion, meddling **9** collision, hindrance, intrusion **12** interception, interruption, intervention

interfere with 6 hinder, impede, thwart **7** disrupt **9** interrupt

interim 7 stopgap **8** interval, meantime, temporal **9** interlude, temporary, tentative **10** pro tempore **11** provisional

interior 4 bush **5** inner **6** inmost, inside, inward **8** internal **9** backwoods, heartland, innermost, upcountry **10** hinterland

Interiors
director: **10** Woody Allen
cast: **10** E G Marshall **11** Diane Keaton **12** Marybeth Hurt **13** Geraldine Page **15** Kristin Griffith **16** Maureen Stapleton
screenplay: **10** Woody Allen

interject 5 put in **6** inject, insert, slip in **7** force in, sneak in, throw in **9** interpose, introduce **11** interpolate

interjection 2 ah, er, lo, oh, ow, um **3** aha, cry, fie, hey, huh, ugh, wow **4** ahem, alas, darn, dear, drat, egad, gosh, heck, jeez, oops, ouch, phew, rats **5** aside, golly, zowie **6** eureka, hooray, hurrah, hurray **7** gee-whiz, jeepers **9** insertion **11** ejaculation, exclamation **13** interpolation, interposition

interlace 3 mix **4** knit, link **5** braid, plait, twine, twist, weave **7** wreathe **9** alternate **10** intertwine, interweave **11** intersperse

interlaced 5 woven **6** linked, twined **7** braided, knitted, plaited, twisted **8** entwined, latticed, wreathed **9** interknit **10** interwoven **11** intertwined **12** interspersed

interlocutor 8 minstrel **9** converser, dialogist **12** interrogator **14** man in the middle

interlope 6 invade, meddle **7** intrude, obtrude **8** encroach, infringe, trespass **9** interfere

interloper 7 invader, meddler **8** intruder, outsider **10** interferer, trespasser **11** gatecrasher **15** persona non grata

interlude 5 break, event, letup, pause **6** recess **7** episode, respite **8** incident, interval **12** intermission **14** breathing spell

intermediary 6 midway, umpire **7** referee **8** bridging, mediator **9** go-between, in-between, mediating, middleman **10** arbitrator **11** adjudicator, arbitrating

intermediate 3 mid **4** fair, mean, so-so **6** median, medium, middle, midway **7** average, halfway, mediate, midmost **8** mediocre, middling, moderate **11** intervening

interment 6 burial **7** funeral **10** entombment, inhumation

Intermezzo
director: **13** Gregory Ratoff
cast: **8** Edna Best **12** Leslie Howard **13** Cecil Kellaway, Ingrid Bergman

interminable 6 prolix **7** endless **8** infinite, unending **9** boundless, ceaseless, incessant, limitless, perpetual, unlimited **10** continuous, long-winded **11** illimitable **12** long-drawn-out

intermingle 3 mix **4** fuse **5** blend, merge, mix up, unite **6** commix **7** combine **8** emulsify, intermix **9** commingle, interfuse, interlace **10** amalgamate, homogenize, interblend **12** conglomerate

intermission 3 gap **4** halt, rest, stop **5** break, pause **6** hiatus, recess **7** interim **8** interval, stoppage **9** interlude **10** suspension

intermittent 6 fitful **8** on and off, periodic, sporadic **9** irregular, recurrent, spasmodic **10** occasional **13** discontinuous **15** on-again-off-again

intermix 3 mix **5** blend, cross, mix in **6** mingle **10** crossbreed, interbreed **11** intermingle, intersperse

intern 6 commit, detain **7** confine, impound **8** imprison, restrain

internal 5 inner, state **6** inmost **8** domestic, interior **9** executive, political, sovereign **12** governmental **14** administrative

international 9 worldwide **12** cosmopolitan

international affairs
  god of: 6 Sancus **10** Dius Fidius, Semo Sancus

Internet
  terms: 3 AOL, FAQ, FTP, net, URL, web, WWW **4** chat, host, link, post **5** cyber, flame, Lycos, Yahoo, e-mail, TCP/IP **6** dial-up, Gopher, online, server, Usenet, Excite **7** browser, Web site **8** firewall, Username **9** hypertext, newsgroup, webmaster, AltaVista **11** interactive **12** search engine, World Wide Web
  based on: 7 ARPAnet

internment 9 detention **10** commitment, impounding **11** confinement **12** imprisonment

inter nos 16 between ourselves

interpolate 3 add **5** put in **6** inject, insert, work in **7** implant, intrude, stick in, throw in, wedge in **8** sandwich **9** insinuate, interject, interlard, interline, intervene, introduce **11** intercalate, intersperse

interpose 6 butt in, impose, inject, insert, meddle, step in **7** intrude, mediate, obtrude **9** arbitrate, insinuate, intercede, interfere, interject, interrupt, intervene, negotiate **11** come between, interpolate

interpret 3 see **4** read, take **6** accept, define, render, reword **7** clarify, explain, make out, restate, unravel **8** construe, decipher **9** elucidate, explicate, figure out, make clear, puzzle out, translate **10** account for, paraphrase, understand

interpretation 7 reading, version **8** analysis **9** rendition **10** commentary **11** explanation **12** construction

interpreter 7 analyst **9** explainer **10** translator **11** commentator

interrelated 9 companion, connected **10** compatible, correlated **13** complementary, correspondent, corresponding

interrelation 10 connection **11** association, correlation **12** relationship

interrogate 3 ask **4** test **5** grill, probe, query **7** examine **8** question **9** catechize **11** investigate **12** cross-examine **18** give the third degree

interrogation 4 quiz **5** probe, query **7** inquiry **8** grilling, querying, question, quizzing **9** catechism, inquiring **11** examination, inquisition, questioning

interrupt 4 stop **5** sever **7** cut in on, disjoin, disturb **8** break off **9** break in on, intersect, punctuate **10** disconnect **11** discontinue **13** interfere with

interrupted 6 broken, cut off, halted

7 checked, stalled, stopped **8** arrested, broke off, deferred **9** broken off, disturbed, suspended **11** broke in upon, intercepted **12** discontinued

interruption 3 gap **4** halt, rift, stop **5** break, pause **6** hiatus, lacuna **9** hindrance, interlude **11** obstruction **12** interference, intermission **13** disconnection, discontinuity

inter se 15 among themselves **17** between themselves

intersect 4 meet **5** cross **6** bisect, divide **7** overlap **8** crosscut, transect, traverse **9** cut across **10** crisscross

intersection 6 corner **8** crossing, junction **10** crossroads **11** interchange

intersperse 3 dot, mix **5** strew **6** mingle, pepper **7** bestrew, scatter, wedge in **8** disperse, intermix, sprinkle **9** broadcast, interfuse, interject, interlard, interpose **11** intercalate, interpolate

interstice 4 slit, slot **5** crack, space **7** opening, orifice **8** aperture, interval

intertwine 4 lace **5** braid, plait, twine, twist, weave **7** entwine **8** entangle **9** interlace

interval 3 gap **4** gulf, rest, rift **5** break, cleft, pause, space, spell **6** breach, hiatus, recess, season **7** interim, opening **9** interlude **10** interspace, separation **12** intermission, interruption

intervene 4 pass **6** befall, butt in, step in **7** break in, intrude, mediate **9** arbitrate, intercede, interfere, interpose, interrupt, take place **10** come to pass **11** come between

intervention 9 butting in, intrusion, mediation **10** breaking in, stepping in **11** arbitration **12** intercession, interference **13** interposition **14** intermediation

interview 4 chat, talk **6** parley **7** meeting **8** audience **10** conference, evaluation, round table **11** questioning **12** consultation, conversation

interweave 3 mix **4** fuse, join, knit, lace, link **5** blend, braid, plait, twine, twist **6** splice **7** wreathe **9** interlace, interknit **10** intertwine **11** intersperse

intestinal 5 inner **7** enteric **8** internal, visceral

intestines 4 guts **6** bowels **7** insides, viscera **8** entrails

in the air 2 up **5** above, aloft **7** skyward **8** all about, in the sky, overhead **10** everywhere **11** in the clouds

in the doghouse 9 in bad odor **10** in disfavor, in disgrace, in ill favor **11** in disrepute

in the end 6 one day **7** finally **8** sometime **10** eventually, ultimately **13** sooner or later **17** in the course of time
  French: 5 enfin

in the family
  French: 9 en famille

in the first place
  Latin: 8 imprimis

in the future
  Latin: 8 in futuro
  Spanish: 6 manana

In the Heat of the Night
  director: 13 Norman Jewison
  cast: 8 Lee Grant **10** Rod Steiger **11** Warren Oates **13** Sidney Poitier (Virgil Tibbs)
  score: 11 Quincy Jones
  Oscar for: 5 actor (Steiger) **7** picture **10** screenplay

in the know 9 cognizant **11** on the inside **13** fully informed, knowledgeable **23** having inside information

in the manner of
  French: 3 a la

in the matter of
  Latin: 4 in re

in the meantime
  Latin: 9 ad interim

in the middle of things
  Latin: 11 in medias res

in the midst of 5 among **7** amongst **12** surrounded by **13** in the middle of

in the nature of things
  Latin: 13 in rerum natura

in the neighborhood of 6 almost, around, nearly **7** close to **9** generally, just about **10** more or less, not far from **13** approximately **15** in the vicinity of

in the place cited
  Latin: 6 loc cit **10** loco citato

in the place of a parent
  Latin: 14 in loco parentis

in the same manner that
  Latin: 7 quo modo

in the same place
  Latin: 4 ibid **6** ibidem

in the state in which
  Latin: 10 in statu quo

in the style of
  French: 7 a la mode

in the very act of committing the crime
  Latin: 18 in flagrante delicto

in the vicinity of 4 near **6** almost, around, nearly **7** close to **9** just about **10** more or less, not far from **13** approximately **19** in the neighborhood of

in the way
  French: 6 de trop

in the whole
  Latin: 6 in toto

in the work cited
  Latin: 5 op cit **11** opere citato

in the year of the reign
  Latin: 9 anno regni

in the year of the world
  Latin: 9 anno mundi

In This House of Brede
  author: **11** Rumer Godden

in this sign shalt thou conquer
  Latin: **16** in hoc signo vinces
  motto of: **19** Constantine the Great
  from vision of: **5** cross

intimacy 5 amity **6** caring, warmth **8** dearness, fondness **9** affection, closeness **10** chumminess, endearment, fraternity, lovemaking, tenderness **11** brotherhood, camaraderie, familiarity **12** friendliness

intimate 3 pal **4** chum, dear, deep, hint **5** bosom, buddy, close, crony, imply, rumor **6** allude, direct **7** guarded, private, special, suggest **8** detailed, familiar, indicate, personal, profound, thorough **9** cherished, confidant, first-hand, innermost, insinuate **12** confidential
  French: **6** intime

intimately 7 closely **8** secretly, very well **9** privately **10** familiarly, personally **11** essentially **13** intrinsically **14** confidentially

intimation 4 clue, hint, sign **5** rumor **7** inkling, portent **8** allusion, innuendo **10** indication, suggestion **11** insinuation **13** veiled comment

Intimations of Immortality
  author: **17** William Wordsworth

intime 4 cozy **8** intimate

in time 6 before, sooner **7** earlier **9** before now, in advance **10** beforehand, eventually **11** ahead of time **13** before the fact, sooner or later

intimidate 3 cow **5** alarm, bully, daunt, scare **6** coerce, menace, subdue **7** buffalo, terrify **8** browbeat, frighten **9** terrorize

intimidated 5 cowed, fazed **6** scared **7** crushed, daunted, subdued **10** browbeaten, frightened, terrorized

intimidation 7 tyranny **8** bullying, coercion **9** despotism **11** browbeating, terrorizing, tyrannizing **12** scare tactics

intimidator 5 bully **6** despot **7** coercer **9** oppressor, tormenter, tormentor **10** browbeater

into 2 in, to **5** among **6** inside, toward, within **7** against

intolerable 7 hateful, racking **9** abhorrent, agonizing, excessive, loathsome, torturous **10** abominable, outrageous, unbearable **11** unendurable **12** excruciating, insufferable, unreasonable **13** insupportable

intolerance 4 bias **6** racism **7** bigotry **8** weak spot **9** no stomach, prejudice **10** chauvinism, xenophobia **12** low tolerance **16** hypersensitivity, narrow-mindedness

Intolerance
  director: **10** D W Griffith
  cast: **8** Mae Marsh **11** Lillian Gish

12 Robert Harron **17** Constance Talmadge

intolerant 7 bigoted, hostile, jealous **9** fanatical, parochial, resentful, sectarian **10** prejudiced, xenophobic **11** mistrustful **12** chauvinistic, closed-minded, narrow-minded

intonation 4 tone **5** pitch **6** accent **8** chanting **10** modulation, inflection

intone 3 hum, say **4** song **5** chant, croon, drawl, mouth, speak, utter, voice **6** murmur, recite **8** intonate, modulate, singsong, vocalize **9** enunciate, pronounce **10** articulate

in toto 5 in all, uncut **6** entire, wholly **7** totally **8** as a whole, entirely, outright **10** completely, in the whole, unabridged **11** all together, uncondensed

intoxicant 3 gin, rum **4** beer, grog, wine **5** booze, drink **6** liquor, tipple, whisky **7** alcohol, spirits, whiskey **8** cocktail, highball **9** inebriant

intoxicated 4 high, rapt **5** drunk, oiled, tight, tipsy **6** bombed, elated, loaded, stewed, stinko, stoned, zonked **7** drunken, exalted, smashed, wrecked **9** delighted, enchanted, entranced, plastered **10** enthralled, inebriated, infatuated, in one's cups **11** exhilarated, transported

intoxicating 4 hard **5** heady **6** potent **7** elating **9** alcoholic, spiritous **11** inebriating **12** exhilarating

intoxication 3 joy **5** bliss **7** elation, rapture **8** euphoria **9** poisoning, tipsiness **10** excitement, insobriety **11** drunkenness, inebriation **12** befuddlement, stupefaction

intractable 6 mulish, ornery, unruly **7** froward, willful **8** obdurate, perverse, stubborn **9** fractious, obstinate **10** headstrong, inflexible, refractory **11** unmalleable **12** contumacious, incorrigible, ungovernable, unmanageable **14** hard to cope with, uncontrollable

intransigent 7 diehard **8** obdurate, stubborn **9** steadfast, unmovable **10** inflexible, iron-willed, unyielding **11** intractable, unbudgeable **14** uncompromising

intrepid 4 bold **5** brave **6** daring, heroic **7** doughty, valiant **8** fearless, resolute, valorous **9** audacious, dauntless **10** courageous, undismayed **11** adventurous

intrepidity 4 guts **5** spunk, valor **6** mettle **7** bravery, courage **8** backbone **9** fortitude, sangfroid **12** fearlessness **13** dauntlessness

intricacy 10 complexity **11** involvement **12** complication, entanglement **15** complicatedness

intricate 6 knotty, tricky **7** complex, devious, tangled **8** involved **9** entangled **11** complicated

intrigue 3 spy **4** fire, plot **5** amour **6**

absorb, arrest, scheme **7** attract, collude, knavery, romance **8** conspire, enthrall, scheming **9** fascinate, machinate, titillate **10** conspiracy, love affair **11** machination **13** double-dealing **15** interest greatly, tickle one's fancy

intriguer 7 cheater, plotter, schemer **8** conniver, finagler **9** trickster **10** machinator, wirepuller **11** conspirator, Machiavelli, manipulator

intriguing 8 engaging, exciting **9** absorbing, beguiling **11** captivating, enthralling, fascinating, interesting

intrinsic 5 basic, per se **6** inborn, inbred, innate, native **7** natural **8** inherent **9** essential, ingrained **10** indigenous, underlying **11** fundamental

introduce 3 add **4** show, urge **5** begin, offer, put in, start **6** create, expose, import, inform, infuse, insert **7** advance, bring in, kick off, lead off, present, propose, sponsor, throw in **8** acquaint, initiate, lead into **9** establish, institute, interject, interpose, make known, originate, recommend **10** put forward **11** familiarize, interpolate

introduction 6 change **7** novelty, opening, preface, prelude **8** foreword, preamble, prologue **9** insertion, precursor **10** bringing in, conducting, innovation, ushering in **11** instituting, institution

introductory 7 initial **9** beginning, prefatory **10** initiatory, precursory **11** acquainting, preliminary **13** get-acquainted

introspection 8 brooding **10** meditation, reflection, rumination **12** deliberation, self-analysis, self-scrutiny **13** contemplation, soul-searching **15** self-examination, self-observation, self-questioning

introspective 7 pensive **10** reflective **13** contemplative, lost in thought

introversion 7 reserve **8** brooding **10** constraint, diffidence, withdrawal **13** introspection

introvert 5 loner **7** brooder, thinker **13** contemplative, private person

introverted 3 shy **5** stiff **8** reserved **9** inhibited, repressed, withdrawn **10** antisocial, restrained **13** inner-directed, introspective

intrude 4 push **6** butt in, impose, meddle, thrust **7** obtrude **8** encroach, trespass **9** interfere, interlope, interpose, intervene

intruder 10 encroacher, interferer, interloper, intervener, trespasser **11** gate-crasher

Intruder in the Dust
  author: **15** William Faulkner

intrusive 4 nosy **5** pushy **6** prying, snoopy **8** in the way, invasive **9** hindering, obtrusive, officious, unwelcome **10** meddlesome **11** impertinent, interfering, interruptive

intuition 5 flash, hunch **7** insight, surmise **8** instinct **9** guesswork, telepathy **10** sixth sense **11** second sight **12** clairvoyance, precognition

intuitive 6 inborn, inbred, innate, native **7** natural, psychic **10** telepathic **11** clairvoyant, instinctive, intuitional, nonrational **12** extrasensory

Inuit *see* **6** Eskimo

inundate 4 glut **5** drown, flood, swamp **6** deluge, drench, engulf **8** load down, overcome, overflow, saturate, submerge **9** overwhelm **10** overburden, overspread

inundation 4 glut **5** flood **6** deluge **9** avalanche

in unison 5 as one **8** in chorus **9** all at once **11** all together

inure 5 adapt, steel, train **6** adjust, custom, harden, season, temper **7** toughen **8** accustom **9** acclimate, get used to, habituate **10** discipline, naturalize, strengthen **11** acclimatize, desensitize, familiarize **12** become used to **15** learn to live with **16** become hardened to

in use 8 employed **9** operating **11** functioning, operational

in vacuo 9 in a vacuum **11** in isolation

invade 5 flood, limit **6** assail, attack, engulf, infect, infest **7** assault, overrun, violate **8** permeate, restrict, strike at, trespass **9** intrude on, march into, penetrate

invader 6 raider **8** attacker, intruder, marauder **9** aggressor, assailant **10** trespasser

invalid 4 null, sick, void, weak **5** false **6** ailing, infirm, sickly, unwell **7** amputee, cripple, unsound, useless **8** disabled, not valid, nugatory, weakened **9** enfeebled, forceless, illogical, paralytic, powerless, worthless **10** dead letter, fallacious, paraplegic **11** debilitated, ineffective, inoperative, unsupported **12** unconvincing **13** incapacitated, unsupportable **14** good-fornothing, valetudinarian

invalidate 5 annul **6** cancel, refute, repeal, weaken **7** nullify, vitiate **8** abrogate, make void, undercut **9** discredit, undermine **11** countermand

invalidation 7 voiding **9** annulment **10** abrogation **12** cancellation **13** nullification

invaluable 4 rare **6** choice **9** priceless **11** beyond price, inestimable

invariable 7 uniform **8** constant **9** immutable, unfailing, unvarying **10** changeless, consistent, unchanging, unwavering **11** unalterable, undeviating **12** unchangeable

invariably 4 ever **6** always **7** forever **9** every time, uniformly **10** all the time,

constantly **11** perpetually, universally **15** in every instance **16** without exception

invasion 4 raid **5** foray **6** attack, breach, inroad, sortie **7** assault **8** trespass **9** incursion, intrusion, onslaught **10** aggression, juggernaut, usurpation **11** penetration **12** encroachment, infiltration, infringement, overstepping

Invasion of the Body Snatchers
  director:
    1956 version: 9 Don Siegel
    1978 version: 13 Philip Kaufman
  cast:
    1956 version: 10 Dana Wynter, Larry Gates **11** King Donovan **13** Kevin McCarthy
    1978 version: 11 Brooke Adams **12** Jeff Goldblum, Leonard Nimoy **16** Donald Sutherland

invective 4 rant **5** venom **6** insult **7** censure, railing, sarcasm **8** diatribe **9** contumely **10** execration, harsh words, revilement **11** verbal abuse **12** billingsgate, denunciation, vilification, vituperation

inveigh 4 rail, slam **5** abuse, knock, scold **6** rebuke, revile **7** censure, put down, run down, upbraid **8** belittle, denounce, harangue, reproach **9** castigate, criticize, dress down **10** vituperate

inveigh against 5 abuse **6** defame, rail at, revile **7** protest **8** denounce **9** castigate

inveigle 4 coax, lure **5** tempt, trick **6** allure, cajole, entice, rope in, seduce, suck in **7** beguile, ensnare, flatter, mislead, wheedle **8** persuade, softsoap **9** bamboozle, sweet-talk

inveiglement 7 coaxing **8** cajolery, flattery **9** wheedling **10** enticement, persuasion **13** blandishments

invent 4 coin **6** cook up, create, devise, make up **7** concoct, develop, fashion, think up, trump up **8** conceive, contrive **9** conjure up, fabricate, formulate, originate **10** come up with **11** put together

invented 6 fabled, made up **8** fabulous, fanciful, mythical **9** fantastic, imaginary, legendary **10** apocryphal, fictitious

Inventing America
  author: **10** Garry Wills

invention 3 lie **4** fake, sham **6** design, device, gadget **7** fiction, forgery, machine **8** creation, trumpery **9** apparatus, discovery, fertility, implement, ingenuity, inventing **10** concoction, creativity, production **11** contraption, contrivance, development, fabrication, imagination, originality, origination **13** dissimulation, inventiveness, prevarication **15** resourcefulness

invention
  god of: **6** Hermes

inventive 6 bright, clever **9** ingenious **11** resourceful

inventiveness 9 ingenuity **10** cleverness, creativity **11** imagination, originality **15** imaginativeness

inventor 5 maker **6** author **7** creator, deviser **8** engineer, producer, tinkerer **9** architect, generator, innovator **10** discoverer, originator
  of air brake: **12** Westinghouse
  of automobile: **7** Daimler
  of barometer: **10** Torricelli
  of camera: **7** Eastman
  of cotton gin: **7** Whitney
  of cylinder lock: **4** Yale
  of dynamite: **5** Nobel
  of elevator: **4** Otis
  of gyrocompass: **6** Sperry
  of helicopter: **8** Sikorsky
  of linotype: **12** Mergenthaler
  of machine gun: **7** Gatling
  of movable type: **9** Gutenberg
  of phonograph, incandescent lamp, mimeograph, dictating machine, fluoroscope: **6** Edison
  of photography: **6** Niepce, Talbot **8** Daguerre
  of Polaroid: **4** Land
  of quick-freezing: **8** Birdseye
  of reaper: **9** McCormick
  of radio: **7** Marconi
  of revolver: **4** Colt
  of rocket engine: **7** Goddard
  of sewing machine: **4** Howe
  of sleeping car: **7** Pullman
  of steamboat: **6** Fulton
  of steam engine: **4** Watt
  of steam locomotive: **10** Stephenson
  of telegraph: **5** Morse
  of telephone: **4** Bell
  of wireless telegraph: **7** Marconi
  of vulcanized rubber: **8** Goodyear

inventory 4 roll **5** goods, index, stock **6** roster, supply **7** catalog **8** register, schedule **9** stock list **10** accounting **11** merchandise, stock-taking

inverse 8 backward, contrary, converse, indirect, inverted, opposite, reversed **11** back to front, bottom-to-top, right-to-left

inversion 7 turning **8** reversal **9** ectropion, turnabout **10** transposal **12** resupination **13** transposition

inverted 7 inverse **8** bottom up **10** upside-down

invest 4 fill, garb, give **5** adorn, allot, array, color, cover, dress, endow, imbue **6** clothe, devote, enable, enrich, infuse, supply **7** appoint, license **8** set aside **9** apportion

investigate 4 sift **5** probe, query, study **6** survey **7** analyze, dissect, explore, inspect **8** ask about, look into, pore over, question, research **9** anatomize, delve into **10** scrutinize

investigation 5 probe, study **6** review, search, survey **7** anatomy, inquiry **8** analysis, research, scrutiny **10** dissection, inspection **11** fact-finding

investigator 6 shamus **7** analyst, gumshoe **8** examiner, inquirer, observer **9** detective **10** private eye, researcher

investment 4 ante, risk **5** share, stake **7** venture **8** offering

inveterate 6 inured **7** adamant, chronic, diehard **8** constant, habitual, hardened **9** confirmed, incurable, ingrained, recurrent, steadfast **10** continuous, deep-rooted, deep-seated **11** established **12** long-standing, unregenerate **15** unreconstructed

invidious 7 vicious **8** spiteful **9** insulting, malicious, offensive, rancorous, resentful, slighting **10** malevolent

invigorate 4 stir **5** brace, cheer, liven, pep up, renew, rouse, zip up **6** jazz up, vivify **7** animate, enliven, fortify, refresh, restore **8** energize, vitalize **9** stimulate **10** exhilarate, rejuvenate, strengthen

invigorated 6 braced **7** revived **8** animated, restored, vivified **9** energized, full of pep, quickened, refreshed **10** stimulated **11** rejuvenated **12** strengthened **17** full of vim and vigor

invigorating 7 bracing **9** animating, healthful **10** energizing, enlivening, quickening, refreshing, vitalizing **11** restorative, stimulating **12** rejuvenating **13** strengthening

invincible 10 unbeatable **11** impregnable, indomitable, insuperable **12** invulnerable, undefeatable **13** irrepressible, unconquerable **14** insurmountable

in vino veritas 18 in wine there is truth

inviolable 4 holy, pure **6** chaste, divine, sacred, secret **7** blessed **8** hallowed **9** dedicated, inviolate, undefiled **10** sacrosanct **11** consecrated, impregnable, trustworthy **12** impenetrable, invulnerable, unassailable **13** incorruptible

inviolate 4 pure **6** intact, sacred, secret **8** hallowed **9** unaltered, unchanged, undefiled, unstained **10** inviolable, sacrosanct

invisible 6 covert, hidden, unseen, veiled **7** obscure **9** concealed, unseeable **10** unapparent **13** imperceptible, undiscernible

Invisible Man
  author: **12** Ralph Ellison

Invisible Man, The
  author: **7** H G Wells
  character: **4** Hall **6** Dr Kemp, Marvel **7** Griffin **11** Colonel Ayde

invitation 3 bid **4** call, lure **5** offer **7** bidding, summons **8** open door **9** challenge **10** allurement, enticement, inducement, temptation **12** solicitation

invite 3 bid **4** call, lure, urge **5** tempt

6 entice, induce **7** attract, solicit, welcome **9** encourage

inviting 4 warm **8** alluring, charming, engaging, enticing, magnetic, tempting **9** appealing, welcoming **10** attractive, intriguing

invocation 4 plea **6** appeal, orison, prayer **8** petition **9** summoning **12** supplication

in vogue 2 in **6** modish **7** a la mode, current, in style, stylish **9** in fashion **11** fashionable **12** le dernier cri

invoke 3 beg, use **5** apply **6** ask for, employ **7** beseech, conjure, entreat, implore, pray for **8** call upon, petition, resort to **9** appeal for, call forth, implement, importune, introduce **10** supplicate

involuntary 6 forced, reflex **7** coerced **8** unchosen, unwilled **9** automatic, reluctant, unwilling **10** compulsory **11** inadvertent, instinctive, spontaneous, unconscious **13** unintentional **15** against one's will

involve 5 imply, mix up **6** commit, engage, entail, wrap up **7** contain, embroil, include **8** comprise, depend on, entangle **9** implicate, preoccupy

involved 7 complex, engaged, mixed up, wound up **8** absorbed, immersed **9** committed, elaborate, embroiled, engrossed, entangled, intricate, wrapped up **10** implicated **11** complicated, preoccupied

involve deeply 5 mix up **6** absorb, commit, wrap up **7** embroil, engross, immerse **8** entangle **9** implicate, preoccupy

invulnerable 10 formidable, invincible, unbeatable **11** impregnable, indomitable, insuperable **12** imperishable, inexpugnable, unassailable, undefeatable **13** unconquerable, undestroyable

inward, inwards 5 inner **6** mental, toward **7** going in, ingoing, private **8** incoming, interior, inwardly, personal **9** spiritual, the inside **10** interiorly

in what way
  Latin: **7** quo modo

in which case 4 then, when **6** thence **9** whereupon **11** accordingly **12** at which point

In Which We Serve
  director: **9** David Lean **10** Noel Coward
  script: **10** Noel Coward
  cast: **9** John Mills **10** Noel Coward **12** Bernard Miles, Celia Johnson

in wine there is truth
  Latin: **13** in vino veritas

Io
  father: **7** Inachus
  husband: **9** Telegonus
  loved by: **4** Zeus
  son: **7** Epaphus

  changed into: **6** heifer
  color of heifer: **5** white
  guarded by: **5** Argus
  pursecuted by: **6** gadfly
    sent by: **4** Hera
  corresponds to: **4** Isis

iodine
  chemical symbol: **1** I

Iolanthe
  author: **9** W S Gilbert

Iole
  father: **7** Eurytus
  loved by: **8** Heracles
  captive of: **8** Heracles, Hercules

Ion
  author: **9** Euripides
  character: **6** Apollo, Athene, Crensa, Xuthus

ion 15 charged particle
  part of: **8** molecule
  charge: **8** negative, positive
  loses or gains: **8** electron
  called: **5** anion **6** cation **12** dissociation

Ionesco, Eugene
  born: **7** Romania, Slatina
  author of: **9** The Lesson, The Chairs **10** Rhinoceros **14** The Bald Soprano

iota 3 bit, jot **4** atom, spot, whit **5** shred, spark, speck **7** smidgin **8** particle **9** scintilla **11** faint degree, small amount **15** tiniest quantity

IOU 4 chit, debt, note **6** marker **10** obligation **12** promise to pay **14** promissory note

Iowa
  abbreviation: **2** IA
  nickname: **7** Hawkeye
  capital/largest city: **9** Des Moines
  others: **4** Ames **5** Amana, Mason, Perry **6** Algona, Keokuk, Le Mars, Marion, Newton **7** Anamosa, Clinton, Dubuque, Ft Dodge, Ottumwa **8** Waterloo **9** Davenport, Ft Madison, Marquette, Mason City, Sioux City **10** Burlington, Cedar Falls, West Branch **11** Cedar Rapids **12** Marshalltown **13** Council Bluffs
  college: **3** Coe **5** Corot, Drake, Loras **7** Cornell, Parsons **8** Grinnell, Wartburg **12** Iowa Wesleyan
  explorer: **6** Joliet, Jolliet **9** Marquette **13** Lewis and Clark
  feature: **13** Amana Colonies **17** first apple orchard
    church: **11** Little Brown
    national historical site: **13** Herbert Hoover
    national monument: **12** Effigy Mounds
    state fair: **4** Iowa
  tribe: **3** Fox **4** Sauc **5** Ioway, Omaha **9** Muscoutin, Winnebago
  people: **7** Hawkeye **9** Grant Wood **10** John L Lewis **11** Billy Sunday **15** Buffalo Bill Cody, Charles Ringling
  lake: **5** Clear, Storm **6** Spirit **7** Rath-

bun **11** East Okoboji, West Okoboji
land rank: 11 twenty-fifth
president: 13 Herbert Hoover
river: 4 Iowa **5** Cedar, Floyd, Skunk **8** Big Sioux, Missouri **9** Des Moines **11** Mississippi, Nishnabotna **12** Wap-sipinicon
state admission: 11 twenty-ninth
state bird: 16 eastern goldfinch
state flower: 8 wild rose
state motto: 45 Our Liberties We Prize and Our Rights We Will Maintain
state song: 13 The Song of Iowa
state tree: 3 oak

Iowa, Ioway
  language family: 6 Siouan
  location: 4 Iowa
  related to: 3 Oto **8** Missouri

Iphigenia
  father: 9 Agamemnon
  mother: 12 Clytemnestra
  brother: 7 Orestes
  sister: 7 Electra **12** Chrysothemis
  saved by: 7 Artemis

Iphigenia in Aulis
  author: 9 Euripides
  character: 8 Achilles, Menelaus **9** Agamemnon **12** Clytemnestra

Iphigenia in Tauris
  author: 9 Euripides
  character: 5 Thoas **6** Athena **7** Orestes, Pylades

Iphigenie en Aulide
  also: 16 Iphigenia in Aulis
  opera by: 5 Gluck
  character: 7 Artemis, Calchas **8** Achilles **9** Agamemnon **12** Clytemnestra

Iphigenie en Tauride
  also: 17 Iphigenia in Tauris
  opera by: 5 Gluck
  character: 5 Diana, Thoas (King of Scythia) **7** Orestes, Pylades **9** the Furies

ipse dixit 15 he himself said it **21** assertion without proof

ipsissima verba 8 verbatim **12** the very words

ipso facto 15 by the fact itself **24** by the very nature of the deed

ipso jure 14 by the law itself **16** by operation of law

IRA 19 Irish Republican Army **27** Individual Retirement Account

Iraklion
  capital of: 5 Crete

Iran
  name means: 15 land of the Aryans
  earlier name: 5 Media **6** Persia
  capital/largest city: 6 Tehran **7** Teheran
  others: 3 Qum **4** Shah **5** Ahwaz, Urmia **6** Abadan, Bandar, Kashan, Meshed, Shiraz, Tabriz **7** Birjand, Hamadan, Isfahan, Mashhad, Zahidan **11** Bandar Abbas
  supreme head of state: 5 faghi **17** religious guardian

measure: 3 gaz, zar, zer **4** cane **5** gareh, kafiz, makuk, qasab **6** charac, chebel, ghalva **7** capicha, chenica, farsakh, mansion, mishara **8** parasang, piamaneh, stathmos

monetary unit: 3 pul **4** asar, gran, rial **5** bisti, daric, dinar, larin, shahi, toman **6** stater **7** ashrafi, pahlavi

weight: 3 ser **4** dung, rotl, seer **5** abbas, artel, pinar, ratel **6** batman, dirhem, karwar, miscal, nimman **7** abbassi **8** tcheirek

lake: 5 Niris, Tasht, Tuzlu, Urmia **6** Sahweh, Sistan **7** Maharlu **8** Nemekser, Urumiyeh

mountain: 6 Elburz, Zagros

highest point: 8 Demavend

river: 4 Aras **5** Araks, Atrak, Atrek, Karun, Safid, Sefid **6** Gargan

sea: 7 Arabian, Caspian

physical feature:
  desert: 9 Dasht-i-Lut **11** Dasht-i-Kavir
  gulf: 4 Oman **7** Persian
  strait: 6 Hormuz

people: 3 Lur, Tat **4** Arab, Kurd, Turk **5** Medes **6** Galcha, Gilani, Jewish, Shugni **7** Baluchi, Persian **8** Armenian, Bactrian, Bartangi, Parthian, Scythian **9** Bakhtiari **11** Azerbaijani, Mazandarani
  mister: 4 agha
  dynasty: 5 Qajar **7** Arsacid, Pahlavi, Safavid **8** Parthian, Seleucid **9** Sassanian **10** Achaemenid
  statesman, mathematician, poet: 11 Omar Khayyam
  ruler: 5 Abbas, Cyrus **6** Darius, Xerxes **10** Rafsanjani **23** Shah Mohammed Reza (Riza) Pahlavi **25** Ayatollah Ruhollah Khomeini

language: 4 Luri, Zend **5** Farsi, Turki **6** Arabic **7** Baluchi, Kurdish, Persian **8** Armenian **11** Azerbaijani

religion: 5 Baha'i, Islam **7** Judaism **9** Shia Islam **11** Zoroastrian **12** Christianity

place:
  dam: 5 Karaj
  mosque: 4 Shad **5** Royal **12** Masjidi-i-Shah **18** Madreseh Chahar Bagh
  ruins: 4 Susa **10** Persepolis
  feature: 13 Peacock Throne
  head cloth: 6 chador **7** chawdar
  parliament: 6 majlis
  underground water channel: 5 qanat
  food: 5 kabob
  soured milk: 4 mast
  stuffed vegetables/leaves: 5 dolma **6** dolmeh

Iraq
  capital/largest city: 7 Baghdad
  others: 2 Ur **3** Kut **4** Al Faw, Amara, Ashur, Basra, Erbil, Mosul, Najaf, Qurna **6** Hillah, Kirkuk, Tikrit **7** Karbala, Mandali, Samarra, Umm Qasr **8** Al Zubair

division:
  ancient: 5 Akkad, Sumer **7** Assyria **9** Babylonia **11** Mesopotamia
  monetary unit: 4 fils **5** dinar
  lake: 6 al-Milh **7** Sanniya **8** al-Hammar
  mountain: 6 Qalate, Zagros **7** Qaarade **9** Kurdistan
  highest point: 7 Halgurd
  river: 6 Diyala, Hawran, Tigris **8** Great Zab **9** al-Ubayyid, Euphrates, Little Zab **11** Shatt-al-Arab
  physical feature:
    desert: 6 Syrian **8** al-Hajava
    gulf: 7 Persian
  people: 4 Arab, Kurd **7** Bedouin
  leader: 6 Faisal, Sargon **7** Abbasid, Hussein, Ottoman **9** Hammurabi **13** Harun al-Rashid, Saddam Hussein **14** Nebuchadnezzar **16** Abbasid Caliphate
  language: 5 Farsi **6** Arabic **7** Kurdish, Persian, Turkish
  religion: 5 Islam **12** Christianity
  place:
    ancient: 14 Hanging Gardens
    arch: 9 Ctesiphon
    mosque: 5 Great **9** Kadhimain
    ruins: 2 Ur **7** Babylon, Nineveh, Samarra
    Sumerian temple tower: 8 Ziggurat
  feature:
    marketplace: 4 souk
    war: 4 Gulf **11** Desert Storm **12** Desert Shield

irascibility 8 acerbity **9** bad temper, crossness, testiness **10** crabbiness, crankiness **11** peevishness, waspishness **12** irritability **16** cantankerousness

irascible 5 cross, testy **6** cranky, grumpy, ornery, touchy **7** grouchy, peevish, waspish **8** choleric **9** irritable, splenetic **10** ill-humored **11** badtempered, hot-tempered, intractable **12** cantankerous

irate 3 mad **5** angry, livid, rabid, riled, vexed **6** galled **7** angered, annoyed, enraged, furious **8** burned up **9** indignant, irritated **10** infuriated

ire 4 fury, rage **5** anger, wrath **6** choler **7** outrage, umbrage **8** vexation **10** resentment **11** indignation

Ireland
  other name: 4 Eire, Erin **5** Ierne **8** Hibernia **9** Innisfail **11** Emerald Isle
  capital/largest city: 6 Dublin
  others: 4 Cobh, Cork, Erne, Suir, Tara **5** Adare, Ennis, Sligo **6** Bangor, Galway, Lurgan, Mallow, Tralee, Ulster **7** Athlone, Belfast, Donegal, Dundalk, Kildare, Wexford **8** Drogheda, Kilkenny, Limerick **9** Craigavon, Tipperary, Waterford **10** Queenstown **11** Londonderry

school: 7 Trinity
division: 4 Cork, Down, Mayo **5** Clare, Kerry, Meath **6** Antrim, Armagh, Galway, Tyrone, Ulster **7** Donegal, Kildare, Wexford, Wicklow **8** Kilkenny, Limerick **9** Fermanagh, Killarney, Tipperary, Waterford **11** Londonderry
  ancient: 6 Ulster **7** Munster **8** Connacht, Leinster
head of government: 9 taoiseach (prime minister)
measure: 4 mile **6** bandle **8** crannock
monetary unit: 3 rap **4** real **5** pence, pound **6** turney **8** shilling
island: 3 Man **4** Aran, Bear, Holy, Tory **5** Clare, Clear, Magee **6** Achill, Saltee, Whiddy **7** Blasket, Gorumna, Rathlin **8** Aranmore, Inisheer **9** Inishmore **10** Inishbofin
lake: 3 Doo, Key, Ree, Tay **4** Conn, Derg, Erne, Mask **5** Allen, Barra, Capra, Gowna, Leane, Lough, Neagh **6** Boderg, Cooter, Corrib, Ennell **7** Dromore, Gougane, Oughter, Sheelin **9** Killarney
mountain: 5 Galty **6** Croagh, Mourne **7** Errigal, Muckish, Patrick, Wicklow **8** Comeragh **10** Benna Beola, Twelve Bens, Twelve Pins **13** Knockmealdown **19** Macgillycuddy's Reeks
highest point: 13 Carrantuohill
river: 3 Lee, May **4** Bann, Deel, Erne, Nore, Suir **5** Boyne, Clare, Feale, Flesk, Foyle, Laune **6** Bandon, Barrow, Corrib, Liffey, Slaney **7** Kenmare, Munster, Shannon **10** Blackwater
sea: 5 Irish **8** Atlantic
physical feature:
  bay: 4 Clew **5** Sligo **6** Bantry, Dingle, Galway, Tralee **7** Donegal, Dundalk
  cape: 5 Clear
  channel: 5 North **9** St George's
  cliffs: 5 Moher
  point: 6 Cahore **8** Carnsore
people: 4 Celt, Erse, Gael **6** Celtic **9** Hibernian
  author: 4 Shaw **5** Behan, Burke, Joyce, Swift, Synge, Wilde, Yeats **6** O'Casey, Steele **7** Beckett, O'Connor **8** O'Faolain, Sheridan, Stephens **9** Goldsmith, O'Flaherty **13** St John Gogarty
  leader: 4 Tone **6** Devlin, Valera **7** Grattan, Parnell, Redmond **8** O'Connell **9** Brian Boru **12** Saint Patrick
  legend: 9 Cuchulain **11** Finn MacCool
language: 4 Erse **5** Irish **6** Gaelic **7** English
religion: 8 Anglican **13** Roman Catholic
feature:
  airport: 7 Shannon
  castle: 4 Tara **7** Blarney

crystal: 9 Waterford
dance: 3 jig **4** reel
game: 7 hurling
lottery: 16 Irish Sweepstakes
manuscript: 11 Book of Kells
museum: 10 James Joyce
political movement: 8 Sinn Fein
race: 10 Irish Derby
relic: 13 Ardagh Chalice
revolutionary society: 6 Fenian
stone: 7 Blarney
street: 8 O'Connell
theater: 5 Abbey
food:
  beer: 5 stout
Ireland forever
  Gaelic: 11 Erin go bragh
I Remember Mama
  director: 13 George Stevens
  based on play by: 13 John Van Druten
  cast: 10 Ellen Corby, Irene Dunne, Philip Dorn **12** Oscar Homolka **16** Barbara Bel Geddes
  setting: 12 San Francisco
Irene
  member of: 5 Horae, Hours
  personifies: 5 peace
  corresponds to: 3 Pax
iridescence 7 glitter **11** opalescence, pearliness **12** nacreousness, play of colors
iridescent 5 shiny **7** glowing **8** colorful, nacreous **9** prismatic **10** changeable, opalescent **11** rainbowlike
iris
  varieties: 3 fan, red **4** roof, wall, wild **5** Dutch, dwarf, house **6** copper, German, orchid, Sierra, Spuria, violet, yellow **7** African, bearded, crested, English, Evansia, Lamance, peacock, Persian, Prairie, Spanish, walking **8** Japanese, mourning, Siberian, stinking **9** beachhead, beardless, butterfly, Palestine **10** snake's-head
Iris
  goddess of: 7 rainbow
  messenger of: 4 gods
  father: 7 Thaumas
  mother: 7 Electra
  sisters: 7 Harpies
  husband: 8 Zephyrus
Irish 4 Erse **4** Celtic, dander, Gaelic, temper
  accent: 6 brogue
  death spirit: 7 banshee
  flower: 8 shamrock
  girl: 7 colleen
  king: 9 Brian Boru
  legislature: 4 Dail
  saint: 7 Patrick
  society: 8 Sinn Fein
  theater: 5 Abbey
Irish gods 14 Tuatha De Danann
Irishman 4 Celt, Gael, Kelt, Mick **5**

Paddy **7** Irisher **9** Hibernian, orangeman **10** bogtrotter
Irish Mythology
  cats: 8 Kilkenny
  fairies: 4 Side
  god of love/beauty/youth: 7 Angus Og
  god of poetry/eloquence: 4 Ogma
  god of sea: 8 Manannan
  gods: 14 Tuatha De Danann
  hero: 10 Cuchulainn
  invaders/ancestors: 9 Milesians
  king: 4 Bres **5** Ronan **9** Conchobar **10** Matholwych
  king of gods: 4 Finn **5** Fionn
  pirate/demon: 8 Fomorian
  sea goddess: 3 Ler, Lir
  spirit: 4 Puca **5** Pooka
    corresponds to British: 4 Puck
irk 3 bug, vex **4** gall **5** annoy **6** bother, pester, ruffle **7** provoke **8** irritate
irksome 5 pesky **6** plaguy, vexing **7** plaguey, tedious **8** annoying, tiresome, wearying **9** difficult, provoking, vexatious, wearisome **10** bothersome, irritating, nettlesome **11** troublesome
iron
  chemical symbol: 2 Fe
Iron Age
  period of: 4 time
  followed age of: 6 Bronze
ironclad 5 fixed **6** strict **9** immutable, permanent **10** inexorable, inflexible, rigoristic, unchanging **11** irrevocable, unalterable **12** irreversible, unchangeable, unmodifiable
Iron Horse
  nickname of: 9 Lou Gehrig
ironic, ironical 3 odd **5** funny, weird **6** biting **7** abusive, caustic, curious, cutting, mocking, strange **8** derisive, sardonic, sneering, stinging **9** facetious, insincere, pretended, sarcastic **10** surprising, unexpected **11** implausible, incongruous **12** inconsistent **13** contradictory
irons 5 bonds **6** chains **7** fetters, presses, smooths **8** manacles, shackles **9** golf clubs, handcuffs **10** restraints
Ironside
  character: 7 (Det Sgt) Ed Brown **10** Mark Sanger **11** Fran Belding **12** Eve Whitfield **14** Robert Ironside
  cast: 11 Don Galloway, Don Mitchell, Raymond Burr **13** Elizabeth Baur **15** Barbara Anderson
irony 7 mockery, sarcasm **9** absurdity **11** incongruity, indirection **12** contrariness **13** facetiousness **14** implausibility
Iroquoian
  tribe: 6 Cayuga, Mohawk, Oneida, Seneca **8** Cherokee, Iroquois, Onandaga **9** Tuscarora **12** Kanienghaga
Iroquois
  language family: 9 Iroquoian
  tribe: 6 Cayuga, Mohawk, Oneida,

Seneca **8** Onondaga **9** Tuscarora
location: 6 Canada **7** New York **11** Connecticut **13** Massachusetts
leader: 11 Cornplanter, Joseph Brant
formed: 10 Six Nations **19** League of the Iroquois
supernatural force: 6 Orenda
prophet: 10 Ganiodaiyo

irrational 6 absurd **7** foolish, unsound **8** baseless **9** illogical, unfounded **10** ill-advised, unthinking **11** nonsensical, unreasoning **12** unreasonable

irreclaimable 4 lost **6** wicked **7** corrupt, debased **9** abandoned, reprobate **12** disreputable, irredeemable, irreformable **16** beyond redemption

irreconcilable 7 opposed **12** incompatible, inconsistent, intransigent, unadjustable, unappeasable, unbridgeable

irreformable 6 wicked **7** corrupt **9** abandoned, reprobate, shameless **11** unrepentant **12** disreputable **13** irreclaimable

irrefutable 10 undeniable **12** indisputable, not refutable **13** proof positive **14** unquestionable **16** incontrovertible

irrefutably 6 surely **10** definitely, positively, undeniably **12** conclusively, indisputably **13** incontestably **14** unquestionably **16** incontrovertibly

irregular 3 odd **5** bumpy, queer, rough **6** broken, uneven **7** crooked, unusual **8** aberrant, abnormal, improper, peculiar, singular **9** anomalous, desultory, eccentric, haphazard, not smooth, out of line, unaligned, unfitting **10** indecorous, unexpected, unsuitable **12** asymmetrical, unmethodical, unsystematic **13** inappropriate, nonconforming **14** unconventional **16** uncharacteristic

irregularity 7 anomaly **9** asymmetry, deviation **10** aberration, divergence, unevenness **11** abnormality, peculiarity **12** constipation, eccentricity

irrelevant 5 inapt **7** foreign, off base **9** unfitting, unrelated **10** extraneous, immaterial, malapropos, not apropos, not germane **11** impertinent, unconnected **12** nonpertinent **14** beside the point

irreligion 7 atheism **8** apostasy, unbelief **9** disbelief **11** godlessness

irreligious 6 unholy **7** godless, impious, profane, ungodly **8** agnostic **9** atheistic **10** irreverent **11** unbelieving **12** not religious, sacrilegious

irremediable 8 hopeless **9** incurable **11** irreparable **12** beyond remedy

irreparable 9 unfixable **10** remediless **12** irremediable, irreversible **13** beyond redress, uncompensable, uncorrectable

irreplaceable 6 unique **9** essential **13** indispensable

irrepressible 7 vibrant **8** bubbling, galvanic, undamped **9** ebullient **10** boisterous, full of life **11** tempestuous **12** unquenchable **13** unsquelchable **14** uncontrollable, unrestrainable

irreproachable 8 flawless **9** blameless, faultless, stainless, unspotted **10** impeccable, inculpable **11** unblemished **12** above reproof, without fault **13** unimpeachable

irresistible 8 alluring, enticing **9** beckoning, seductive **10** enchanting, superhuman **11** tantalizing **12** overpowering, overwhelming

irresolute 4 weak **6** fickle, unsure **8** doubtful, hesitant, unsteady, wavering **9** faltering, uncertain, undecided, unsettled **10** changeable, hesitating, indecisive, unresolved **11** vacillating

irresolution 5 doubt **9** hesitancy **10** hesitation, indecision

irresponsibility 8 rashness **10** immaturity, imprudence **11** foolishness **12** carelessness, heedlessness, indifference, indiscretion, recklessness **13** unreliability **15** thoughtlessness, undependability **17** untrustworthiness

irresponsible 4 rash **7** foolish **8** careless, immature, reckless **9** imprudent, overhasty **10** capricious, incautious, unreliable **11** harebrained, indifferent, injudicious, thoughtless **12** undependable **13** ill-considered, untrustworthy **14** not responsible, scatterbrained

irresponsible person
French: 14 enfant terrible

irreverence 7 impiety **9** blasphemy, sacrilege **10** irreligion

irreverent 5 saucy **6** brazen **7** impious, profane **8** critical, impudent, sneering **9** debunking, shameless, skeptical, slighting **11** blasphemous, disparaging, irreligious **12** nosethumbing **13** disrespectful

irrevocable 5 final **10** conclusive **11** unalterable **12** irreversible, unchangeable

irritability 6 spleen **8** acerbity, edginess **9** crossness, huffiness, petulance, testiness **10** crabbiness, crankiness, impatience **11** fretfulness, peevishness, short temper, waspishness **12** irascibility

irritable 5 testy **6** grumpy, touchy **7** fretful, grouchy, peevish, pettish, waspish **8** snappish **9** impatient, irascible **10** ill-humored **11** easily vexed, ill-tempered

irritate 3 irk, vex **5** anger, annoy, chafe, peeve **6** nettle, worsen **7** inflame, provoke **8** make sore **9** aggravate, make angry **10** exasperate

irritated 3 mad, raw **4** sore **5** cross, irked, irate, testy, vexed **6** chafed, crabby, galled, miffed, peeved, piqued, put out **7** annoyed, burning, nettled, peevish **8** burned up, choleric, incensed, inflamed, provoked **9**

impatient, irascible **10** aggravated **11** exasperated

irritating 5 acrid, harsh, rough **7** caustic, chafing, galling, irksome, rasping **8** abrasive, annoying **9** provoking, vexatious **10** bothersome **11** infuriating, troublesome **12** exasperating

irritation 6 bother **7** chafing **8** distress, vexation **9** annoyance **10** discomfort **11** irksomeness

irruption 4 raid **5** break, foray **6** inroad **7** upsurge **8** bursting, invasion **9** incursion, intrusion

Irving, John
author of: 16 A Widow for One Year **18** The Cider-House Rules **19** A Prayer for Owen Meany **20** The Hotel New Hampshire **23** The World According to Garp

Irving, Washington
author of: 10 Salmagundi **12** Rip Van Winkle **13** The Sketch Book **23** The Legend of Sleepy Hollow

Isaac
father: 7 Abraham
mother: 5 Sarah
brother: 7 Ishmael
wife: 7 Rebekah
son: 4 Esau **5** Jacob
birthplace: 5 Gerar
burial place: 9 Machpelah
blessed: 5 Jacob
sacrificed at: 6 Moriah

Isaac of York
character in: 7 Ivanhoe
author: 5 Scott

Isabella
character in: 17 Measure for Measure
author: 11 Shakespeare

Isaiah
means: 12 Jehovah saves
father: 4 Amoz
son: 11 Shearzashub **18** Maharshalalhashbaz

Iscariot *see* **5** Judas

Isenstein
origin: 12 Scandinavian
home of: 8 Brunhild
location: 8 Isenland

I serve
German: 7 ich dien
motto of: 13 Prince of Wales

Iseult, Isolde, Isolt
character in: 16 Arthurian romance
lover: 7 Tristan **8** Tristram
betrothed to: 8 King Mark

I shall rise again
Latin: 8 resurgam

Isherwood, Christopher
author of: 10 I Am a Camera **13** Berlin Stories **17** Down There on a Visit
character: 11 Sally Bowles

Ishmael
narrator in: 8 Moby Dick
author: 8 Melville

Ishmael

father: 7 Abraham
mother: 5 Hagar
means: 11 God will hear
brother: 5 Isaac
son: 5 Kedar **7** Kedemah
descendant of: 10 Ishmaelite

Ishtar
also: 7 Mylitta
origin: 8 Assyrian **10** Babylonian
goddess of: 3 war **4** love
queen of: 6 heaven
corresponds to: 6 Inanna **7** Astarte **9** Ashtoreth

Isis
origin: 8 Egyptian
goddess of: 9 fertility
hieroglyphic symbol: 6 throne
husband: 6 Osiris
brother: 6 Osiris
son: 5 Horus
father: 3 Geb, Keb
mother: 3 Nut
horns of: 3 cow
headdress: 9 solar disk
corresponds to: 2 Io

Islam
adherent: 4 Sufi **5** Shiah **6** Moslem, Muslim, Shiite, Wahabi **7** Sunnite **8** Islamite **9** Mussulman **10** Mohammedan
crusade: 5 Jahad, Jihad
deity: 5 Allah
flight from Mecca: 6 hegira
founder/prophet: 8 Mohammed, Muhammad
holy city: 5 Mecca **6** Medina
other names: 9 Moslemism **13** Mohammedanism
pilgrimage to Mecca: 4 hadj
priest: 4 imam
scripture: 5 Koran

Islamabad
capital of: 8 Pakistan

Islamic 6 Moslem, Muslim **10** Mohammedan

island 4 isle **5** atoll, haven, islet, oasis **6** refuge **7** enclave, retreat, shelter **9** sanctuary

Islands of the Blessed *see* **10** Hesperides

isle, islet 3 ait, cay, key **4** holm **5** atoll, islet **6** island

Isle of Cloves *see* **8** Tanzania

Isle of Spice *see* **7** Grenada

Isleta (Tuei)
language family: 6 Pueblo, Tanoan
location: 9 New Mexico, Rio Grande

isn't that so?
French: 9 n'est-ce pas?
German: 9 nicht wahr?

isolate 6 banish, detach, enisle **7** seclude **8** insulate, separate, set apart **9** segregate, sequester **10** disconnect, place apart, quarantine

isolated 4 lone, solo **5** alone, apart **6** cut off, lonely, remote, unique **7** insular, removed **8** detached, secluded, set

apart, solitary **9** separated, unrelated **10** segregated **11** out-of-the-way, quarantined, sequestered

isolation 7 privacy **8** solitude **9** aloneness, apartness, hermitism, seclusion **10** desolation, detachment, insularity, insulation, quarantine, separation **11** confinement, segregation **12** separateness

isoptera
class: 8 hexapoda
phylum: 10 arthropoda
group: 7 termite **8** white ant

Ispahan
also: 7 Isfahan **8** Aspadana
location: 4 Iran
capital of: 6 Persia
river: 8 Zayandeh

I Spy
character: 13 Kelly Robinson **14** Alexander Scott
cast: 9 Bill Cosby **10** Robert Culp
Kelly's cover: 9 tennis bum

Israel
former name: 5 Jacob
means: 12 soldier of God
wrestled with: 5 angel

Israel
other name: 4 Zion **6** Canaan, Yishuv **9** Palestine **12** Promised Land
capital: 9 Jerusalem
largest city: 12 Tel Aviv-Jaffa
others: 4 Acre, Elat, Gaza **5** Eilat, Elath, Haifa, Holon, Jaffa, Jenin **6** Ashdod, Bat Yam, Dimona, Hebron, Nablus **7** Netanya, Rehovot, Tel Aviv **8** Nazareth, Ramallah, Ramat Gan **9** Beersheba, Bene Beraq, Bethlehem
school: 6 Hebrew **14** Technion-Israel **26** Weizmann Institute of Science
division: 5 Judea, Negev, Sinai **7** Galilee **8** West Bank **9** Gaza Strip **12** Golan Heights
government:
  legislature: 7 Knesset
  political parties: 5 Labor, Likud, Mapam
measure: 3 cab, car, hin, kab, kor **4** bath, ezba, omer, reed **5** cubit, donum, dunam, ephah, ganeh, homer, kaneh
monetary unit: 3 mil **5** agora, agura, pound, pruta **6** agorot, shekel
lake: 5 Huleh **7** Dead Sea **8** Kinneret, Tiberias **12** Sea of Galilee
mountain: 4 Nafh, Sagi **5** Harif, Ramon, Tabor **6** Atzmon, Carmel, Hatira
highest point: 5 Meron **6** Meiron
river: 4 Qarn **5** Faria, Malik, Sareq **6** Hadera, Jordan, Kishon, Qishon, Sarida, Yarkon, Yarmuk **7** Lakhish
sea: 3 Red **4** Dead **7** Galilee **13** Mediterranean
airline: 4 El Al
physical feature:
  bay: 5 Haifa

desert: 5 Negev, Sinai
gulf: 5 Aqaba
plain: 5 Judea **6** Sharon **7** Zebulun **9** Esdraelon
people: 3 Jew **4** Arab **5** Druze **10** Circassian
  ancient: 6 Hebrew
  immigrant: 4 olim
  Jew born in Israel: 5 sabra
  leader: 4 Eban, Meir **5** Begin, Dayan, Herzl, Peres, Rabin **6** Ben-Zvi, Eshkol **7** Sharett **8** Weizmann **9** Ben- Gurion
language: 6 Arabic, French, Hebrew **7** English, Yiddish
religion: 5 Baha'i, Islam **7** Judaism **12** Christianity
place:
  church: 13 Holy Sepulcher
  gates to Old Jerusalem: 3 New **4** Dung, Zion **5** Jaffa **6** Herod's **8** Damascus **10** St Stephen's
  mosque: 13 Dome of the Rock
  mount: 4 Zion **6** Olives, Scopus
  shrine: 3 Bab **4** Book **11** Wailing Wall, Western Wall **18** Garden of Gethsemane
  tomb: 9 Sanhedrin **10** King David's
  way of sorrows: 11 Via Dolorosa
feature: 14 Dead Sea Scrolls
  collective village: 7 kibbutz **9** kibbutzim
  cooperative village: 6 moshav **8** moshavim
  dance: 4 hora
  movement: 7 Zionism
  Palestinian uprising: 8 intifada
  peace agreement: 16 Camp David Accords
  tree: 5 judas
  wave of immigration: 5 aliya **6** aliyot
food:
  dish: 4 pita **6** hummus **7** falafel

Israel, tribes of 3 Dan, Gad **4** Levi **5** Asher, Judah **6** Joseph, Reuben, Simeon **7** Zebulun **8** Benjamin, Issachar, Naphtali

Israel-born
Hebrew: 5 sabra

Israelite 3 Jew **6** Hebrew, Jewish, Semite **7** Judaist **8** Hebraist
descended from: 5 Jacob
king: 4 Ahab, Elah, Jehu, Omri, Saul **5** David, Hosea, Nadab, Zimri

Issachar
father: 5 Jacob
mother: 4 Leah
brother: 3 Dan, Gad **4** Levi **5** Asher, Judah **6** Joseph, Reuben, Simeon **7** Zebulun **8** Benjamin, Naphtali
sister: 5 Dinah
descendant: 11 Issacharite

Is Sex Necessary?
author: 7 E B White **12** James Thurber

issuance 8 emission **9** allotment, discharge, emanation **12** dispensation, distribution

issue 4 gush, rise, stem **5** allot, arise, ensue, erupt, go out, heirs, spout, yield **6** emerge, follow, number, result, spring **7** dispute, emanate, flow out, give out, outcome, outflow, pass out, problem, proceed, product, progeny **8** children, dispense, drainage, eruption, granting, heritors, issuance, question **9** circulate, discharge, effluence, grow out of, offspring, posterity, pour forth **10** distribute, outpouring **11** consequence, descendants, publication **12** dispensation, distributing

Istanbul
  area: 7 Beyoglu **8** Stamboul
  capital of: 6 Turkey
  formerly: 9 Byzantium **14** Constantinople
  landmark: 10 Hippodrome **11** Hagia Sophia **12** Galata Bridge **14** Bosporus Bridge **26** Palais de la Culture d'Istanbul
  mosque: 3 New **8** Mihrimah **9** Yeni Camii **11** Suleymaniye
  museum: 13 Topkapi Palace **14** Archaeological **20** Turkish and Islamic Art
  rulers: 4 Rome **6** Athens, Darius, Rhodes, Sparta **8** Persians, Suleiman **9** Macedonia **11** Latin Empire **12** Ottoman Turks **15** Byzantine Empire, Turkish Republic **19** Constantine the Great
  sea: 5 Black **7** Marmara **8** Bosporus **10** Golden Horn
isthmus 4 neck, spit **5** point, strip **6** narrow, strait, tongue **7** narrows
  name: 4 Suez **6** Panama **7** Corinth
I sustain the wings
  Latin: 12 sustineo alas
  motto of: 10 US Air Force
Italic
  language family: 12 Indo-European
  branch: 5 Latin, Oscan **7** Umbrian
italics 11 slanted type
Italy
  also: 8 Hesperia
  capital/largest city: 4 Roma, Rome
  others: 4 Pisa **5** Genoa, Milan, Padua, Turin, Udine **6** Amalfi, Ancona, Assisi, Naples, Rimini, Savona, Venice, Verona **7** Bologna, Bolzano, Brescia, Catania, Messina, Palermo, Ravenna, Taranto, Trieste **8** Florence
  division: 6 Apulia, Latium, Marche, Molise, Umbria, Veneto **7** Abruzzi, Liguria, Tuscany **8** Calabria, Campania, Lombardy, Piedmont **10** Basilicata **12** Valle d'Agosta **13** Emilia-Romagna **17** Trentino-Alto Adige **19** Friuli-Venezia Giulia
    independent enclave: 9 San Marino **11** Vatican City
  measure: 3 pie **4** orna **5** palma, palmo, punto, salma, stero **6** barile,

miglie, moggio, rubbio, tomolo **7** braccio, secchio **8** giornata, quadrato
monetary unit: 4 lira, lire, tara **5** grano, paolo, soldo **6** danaro, denaro, ducato **7** testone **8** zecchino **9** centesini
weight: 5 carat, libra, oncia, pound **6** denaro, libbra
island: 4 Elba **5** Capri, Egadi, Eolie **6** Ischia, Istria, Linosa, Lipari, Sicily, Ustica **7** Aeolian, Trieste, Vulcano **8** Lampione, Sardinia **9** Borromean, Lampedusa, Stromboli **10** Isola Bella **11** Pantelleria
lake: 4 Como, Iseo, Nemi **5** Garda **6** Albano, Lesina, Lugano, Varano **7** Bolsena, Perugia **8** Maggiore **9** Bracciano, Trasimeno
mountain: 4 Alps, Etna, Visa **5** Amaro, Blanc, Corno, Somma **6** Cimone, Ortles **9** Apennines, Dolomites, Maritimes **11** Gennargentu **12** Gran Paradiso **16** Abruzzi Apennines
  Alps: 6 Apuane, Carnic, Julian, Otztal **7** Bernina **8** Ligurian **9** Lepontine
  volcano: 4 Etna **7** Vulcano **8** Vesuvius **9** Stromboli
highest point: 4 Rosa
river: 2 Po **4** Adda, Agri, Arno, Liri, Nera, Reno, Sele, Taro **5** Adige, Crati, Mannu, Oglio, Parma, Piave, Salso, Stura, Tiber, Tirso **6** Aniene, Belice, Isonzo, Mincio, Ofanto, Panaro, Rapido, Sangro, Simeto, Tanaro, Tevere, Ticino **7** Biferno, Bradano, Chienti, Metauro, Montone, Ombrone, Pescara, Rubicon, Secchia, Trebbia **8** Volturno
sea: 6 Ionian **8** Adriatic, Ligurian **10** Tyrrhenian **13** Mediterranean
physical feature:
  bay: 6 Naples
  channel: 5 Malta
  grotto: 4 Blue
  gulf: 5 Gaeta, Genoa **6** Venice **7** Salerno, Taranto **11** Manfredonia
  hills of Rome: 7 Caelian, Viminal **8** Aventine, Palatine, Quirinal **9** Esquiline **10** Capitoline
  lagoon: 6 Venice
  pass: 5 Resia **6** Maloja **7** Bernina, Brenner, Simplon **9** Mont Cenis **13** Saint Gotthard **17** Great Saint Bernard
  resort: 14 Italian Riviera
  strait: 6 Sicily **7** Messina, Otranto **9** Bonifacio
people: 7 Italian
  ancient: 5 Latin, Remus **6** Sabine **7** Lombard, plebian, Romulus **8** Etruscan **9** patrician
  architect: 5 Nervi, Ponti, Salvi **6** Vasari **7** Alberti, Guarini, Juvarra, Vignola **8** Ammanati, Bramante, Palladio **9** Borromini, De Sanctis **12** Brunelleschi, Michelangelo
  artist: 5 Balla, Carra **6** Batoni,

Gaulli, Guardi, Titian **7** Bellini, Chirico, Cimabue, Cortona, Da Vinci, Raphael, Tiepolo, Uccello **8** Carracci, Mantegna, Masaccio, Severini **9** Benvenuti, Canoletto, Giorgione **10** Botticelli, Caravaggio, Modigliani, Tintoretto **11** Buoninsegna, Fra Angelico **12** Michelangelo **13** Giotto Bondone **14** della Francesca
composer: 5 Verdi **7** Bellini, Cavalli, Corelli, Puccini, Rossini, Vivaldi **8** Mascagni, Piccinni **9** Donizetti, Scarlatti **10** Monteverdi, Palestrina **11** Leoncavallo
emperor: 4 Nero, Otho **5** Galba, Nerva, Titus **6** Trajan **7** Hadrian **8** Caligula, Claudius, Commodus, Domitian, Octavian, Tiberius **9** Caracalla, Vespasian, Vitellius **10** Diocletian **11** Constantine **13** Antoninus Dius **14** Caesar Augustus, Marcus Aurelius
film director: 6 de Sica **7** Fellini **8** Visconti **9** Antonioni **10** Bertolucci, Rossellini, Wertmuller, Zeffirelli
god: 4 Juno, Mars **5** Ceres, Diana, Janus, Lares, Venus **6** Apollo, Vulcan **7** Bacchus, Jupiter, Minerva, Neptune, Penates **8** Quirinus
Italian author: 3 Eco **4** Levi **5** Bembo, Bruno, Pulci, Tasso **6** Artino, Vasari **7** Ariosto, Bassani, Deledda, Moravia **8** Bandello, Petrarch **9** Boccaccio, D'Annunzio, Sannazaro **10** Cavalcanti, Guinicelli, Metastasio, Pirandello, Straparola **11** Castiglione, Machiavelli **12** Guicciardini, Michelangelo **14** Dante Alighieri
Latin author: 4 Cato, Livy, Ovid **5** Pliny, Varro **6** Cicero, Gallus, Horace, Seneca, Vergil, Virgil **7** Donatus, Juvenal, Martial, Plautus, Sallust, Tacitus, Terence **8** Boethius, Catullus, Lucilius, St Jerome **9** St Ambrose, Suetonius **11** St Augustine
ruler: 4 Moro **6** Cavour, Enrico **7** Mazzini **9** Mussolini **10** Berlinguer **14** Victor Emmanuel **15** Alcide de Gasperi
ruler/military leader: 5 Sulla **6** Brutus, Pompey, Seneca **7** Crassus, Lepidus **8** Gracchus **10** Mark Antony **12** Gaius Marious, Julius Caesar **15** Cassius Longinus, Scipio Africanus **18** Tarquinius Superbus
old ruling family: 4 Este **6** Borgia, Medici, Sforza **8** Visconti
sculptor: 6 Canova, Marini, Pisano **7** Bernini, Bologna, Cellini **8** Antelami, Boccioni, Ghiberti **9** Donatello, Sansovino **10** Giacometti, Pollaiuolo, Verrocchio **11** Della Robbia **12** Michelangelo

wife: 7 Poppaea **9** Agrippina, Messalina **13** Livia Drusilla

language: 5 Ladin, Latin **6** French, German, Italian, Slovene **8** Friulian **9** Sardinian

expressions: 4 ciao **5** bella **10** primadonna

religion: 13 Roman Catholic

place:

   arch: 11 Constantine

   baths: 9 Caracalla

   bridge: 5 Sighs **12** Ponte Vecchio

   cathedral/church: 5 Siena **7** St Mark's, Vatican **8** San Marco, St Peter's **13** Sistine Chapel

   fountain: 5 Trevi

   museum: 5 Duomo **6** Uffizi **8** Bargello, National **10** Capitoline **11** Pitti Palace, Villa Giulia **16** Gallerio Borghese

   opera house: 7 La Scala

   palace: 5 Doges

   road: 9 Appian Way

   ruins: 5 Forum **7** Capitol, Pompeii **8** Pantheon **9** Catacombs, Colosseum **11** Herculaneum **13** Circus Maximus

   steps: 7 Spanish

   tower: 18 Leaning Tower of Pisa

feature:

   unification movement: 12 Risorgimento

food:

   cheese: 6 romano **7** fontina, ricotta **8** parmesan

   dish: 5 pizza **6** scampi **7** gnocchi, lasagna, lasagne, polenta, ravioli, risotto **9** antipasti, antipasto **17** chicken cacciatora, cacciatore

   ice cream: 6 gelato **7** spumoni

   meat: 6 salami **9** pepperoni **10** mortadella, prosciutto

   soup: 8 caciucco **10** minestrone

   wine: 7 Chianti

itch 3 yen **4** ache, long, pine **5** crave, crawl, creep, yearn **6** desire, hanker, hunger, thirst, tickle **7** craving, prickle **8** appetite, have a yen, pruritis, tingling, yearning **9** hankering

it does not follow

   Latin: 11 non sequitur

item 4 unit **5** entry, piece, point, story, thing **6** detail, matter, notice, report **7** account, article, feature, subject **8** dispatch, notation **9** paragraph **10** particular **11** news article

itemization 4 list **7** listing **11** enumeration

itemize 6 detail **7** specify **8** spell out **9** enumerate

items of business 4 list **6** agenda, docket **7** program **8** schedule

iterate 6 repeat **7** restate **9** reiterate

It Girl

   nickname of: 8 Clara Bow

it grows as it goes

   Latin: 12 crescit eundo

   motto of: 9 New Mexico

Ithaca

   ancient home of: 8 Odysseus, Penelope

   modern home of: 7 Cornell (University)

It Happened One Night

   director: 10 Frank Capra

   cast: 8 Alan Hale, Ward Bond **10** Clark Gable **11** Roscoe Karns **14** Walter Connolly **16** Claudette Colbert

   Oscar for: 5 actor (Gable) **7** actress (Colbert), picture **8** director

   remade as: 16 Eve Knew Her Apples **20** You Can't Run Away from It

I think therefore I am

   Latin: 13 cogito ergo sum

   said by: 9 Descartes

itinerant 5 nomad, rover **6** roamer, roving **7** migrant, nomadic, roaming, vagrant **8** vagabond, wanderer, wayfarer **9** footloose, transient, traveling, wandering, wayfaring **11** peripatetic

itinerary 3 log **5** diary, route **6** course **7** account, circuit, day book, journal **8** schedule **9** timetable **10** travel plan

it is not clear; it is not evident

   Latin: 9 non liquet

it is not lawful; it is not permitted

   Latin: 8 non licet

it is sweet to do nothing

   Italian: 14 dolce far niente

It's a Gift

   director: 13 Norman Z McLeod

   cast: 8 W C Fields **9** Baby LeRoy, Tommy Bupp **10** T Roy Barnes **13** Charles Sellon, Morgan Wallace **14** Kathleen Howard

   remake of: 17 It's the Old Army Game

It's a Wonderful Life

   director: 10 Frank Capra

   cast: 9 Donna Reed **11** Beulah Bondi **12** Henry Travers, James Stewart **13** Gloria Grahame **15** Lionel Barrymore

   remade as: 22 It Happened One Christmas

itsy-bitsy 3 wee **4** tiny **5** dwarf, pygmy, small, teeny **6** bantam, little, minute, petite **9** miniature, miniscule **10** diminutive, teeny-weeny **11** microscopic, pocket-sized

It Takes a Thief

   character: 8 Noah Bain **12** Alister Mundy, Wallie Powers **14** Alexander Mundy

   cast: 11 Edward Binns, Fred Astaire **12** Robert Wagner **13** Malachi Throne

Itza

   language family: 6 Toltec

   location: 6 Mexico **7** Chichen, Yucatan **14** Central America

Iulus *see* **8** Ascanius

Ivan 4 czar, tsar **8** the Great **11** the Terrible **18** grand duke of Muscovy

   English equivalent: 4 John

   personifies: 6 Russia

Ivanhoe

   author: 14 Sir Walter Scott

   character: 7 Rebecca **8** Guilbert **9** Robin Hood **10** Lady Rowena **11** Isaac of York **12** King Richard I **14** Cedric the Saxon, Sir Brian de Bois **16** Wilfred of Ivanhoe **19** King Richard the First

Ivanhoe, Burle Icle

   real name of: 8 Burl Ives

I've Got a Secret

   host: 10 Bill Cullen, Garry Moore, Steve Allen

Ives, Burl

   real name: 16 Burle Icle Ivanhoe

   nickname: 17 Wayfaring Stranger

   born: 6 Hunt IL

   roles: 8 Big Daddy **10** East of Eden **13** The Big Country **14** Our Man in Havana **16** Cat on a Hot Tin Roof **18** Desire Under the Elms

Ives, Charles

   born: 9 Danbury CT

   composer of: 11 Putnam's Camp **13** Concord Sonata **19** Washington's Birthday **20** Central Park in the Dark **21** The Unanswered Question **23** Three Places in New England

ivory 4 tusk **6** dentin

   source: 6 walrus **8** elephant

   used for: 4 dice **9** piano keys **13** billiard balls

   color: 5 cream **8** off-white

Ivory Coast

   capital/largest city: 7 Abidjan

    new capital: 12 Yamoussoukro

   others: 3 Man **4** Divo **5** Daloa, Tabou **6** Adzobe, Bonoua, Bouake, Danane, Gagnoa **7** Korhogo, Odienne, Seguela **8** Dimbokro **9** Agboville, Bondoukou, Sassandra **10** Abengourou **11** Grand Bassam **14** Ferkessedougou

   monetary unit: 5 franc **7** centime

   highest point: 5 Nimba

   river: 3 Bia **5** Comoe, Komoe **7** Bandama, Cavally **9** Sassandra

   ocean: 8 Atlantic

   physical feature:

    cape: 6 Palmas

    gulf: 6 Guinea

    lagoon: 3 Aby **5** Ebrie

    wind: 9 harmattan

   people: 3 Abe, Dan, Kru, Kwa **4** Akan, Bete, Dida, Guro, Koua, Lobi, Wobe **5** Abron, Abure, Attie, Baule, Guere, Mande, Mossi **6** Baoule, Lagoon, Senufo, Senufu **7** Dan Guro, Kroumen, Malinke, Voltaic **10** Anyi-Baoule **11** Lobi-Kulango **12** Agnis-Ashanti

   language: 4 Akan **6** Dioula, French

   religion: 5 Islam **7** animism **13** Roman Catholic

place:
  canal: 5 Vridi
  dam: 7 Bandama
  game reserve: 9 Sassandra
  feature: 7 kola nut

Ivory Coast *see* **11** Sierra Leone

ivory-towered 6 remote **8** academic, romantic **11** conjectural, impractical, theoretical, unrealistic **12** hypothetical

ivy 6 Cissus, Hedera **15** Kalmia latifolia
  varieties: 3 fan, red **4** baby, tree **5** grape, Irish, Nepal, water **6** aralia, Baltic, Boston, canary, devil's, German, ground, marine, parlor, poison, spider, switch **7** colchis, English, Italian, Madeira, Mexican, parsley, Persian, Swedish **8** Algerian, American, coliseum, fragrant, Japanese, red-flame **9** bird's-foot, ghost-tree, heart-leaf **10** five-leaved, Kenilworth, variegated **12** Hagenburger's **13** Solomon Island **14** miniature grape **15** Gloire-de-Marengo

Ivy League colleges 4 Yale **5** Brown **7** Cornell, Harvard **8** Columbia **9** Dartmouth, Princeton **12** Pennsylvania (Penn)

I Want to Live!
  director: 10 Robert Wise
  cast: 12 Simon Oakland, Susan Hayward (Barbara Graham) **13** Theodore Bikel **15** Virginia Vincent
  score: 12 Johnny Mandel
  Oscar for: 7 actress (Hayward)

I will defend
  Latin: 6 tuebor

IWW 8 Wobblies **10** labor union **27** Industrial Workers of the World
  leader: 4 Debs **6** DeLeon **7** Haywood

members: 6 miners **9** lumbermen **16** migratory workers

Ixion
  king of: 8 Lapithae
  wife: 3 Dia
  son: 9 Pirithous
  children: 8 centaurs
  loved: 4 Hera
  punished by: 4 Zeus
  bound to: 5 wheel

Iyar 17 second Hebrew month

Iynx
  father: 3 Pan
  mother: 4 Echo

Izmir
  formerly: 6 Smyrna
  location: 6 Turkey **9** Aegean Sea **11** Gulf of Izmir
  settle by: 7 Ionians **8** Aeolians
  ruled by: 13 Ottoman Empire

izzard 3 zed, zee

ja 3 yes

jab 3 cut, dig, hit, rap, tap **4** belt, blow, bump, clip, goad, lick, pelt, plug, poke, poke, prod, sock, stab, swat **5** elbow, nudge, paste, swing **6** strike, stroke

jabber 3 gab, gas **4** blab **5** clack, prate **6** babble, cackle, drivel, gibber, gossip, hot air, patter, ramble, rattle, raving **7** blabber, blather, chatter, gushing, maunder, palaver, prating, prattle, ranting, twaddle, twattle **8** chitchat, idle talk, nonsense, talk idly **9** gibberish **10** maundering **14** chitter-chatter

jack 4 flag **5** knave, money **6** ensign, sailor

jackass 3 ass **4** fool, mule **5** burro, dummy, idiot **6** donkey

Jack Benny Show, The
  cast: 8 Mel Blanc **9** Dennis Day, Don Wilson **11** Frank Nelson **13** Artie Auerbach, Eddie (Rochester) Anderson **14** Mary Livingston
  Jack's car: 7 Maxwell
  Jack played: 6 violin

jacket 4 case, coat **5** cover **6** blazer, casing, folder, sheath **7** wrapper **8** envelope, mackinaw, wrapping **9** container, enclosure, short coat, sport coat **10** dinner coat **11** windbreaker

Jackson, Andrew
  nickname: 10 Old Hickory
  presidential rank: 7 seventh
  party: 10 Democratic
  state represented: 2 TN **9** Tennessee
  defeated: 4 (Henry) Clay **5** (John Quincy) Adams
  vice president: 7 (John Caldwell) Calhoun **8** (Martin) Van Buren
  cabinet:
    state: 6 (Louis) McLane **7** (John) Forsyth **8** (Martin) Van Buren **10** (Edward) Livingston
    treasury: 5 (William John) Duane **6** (Louis) McLane, (Samuel Dulucenna) Ingham **8** (Levi) Woodbury
    war: 4 (Lewis) Cass **5** (John Henry) Eaton
    attorney general: 5 (Roger Brooke) Taney **6** (Benjamin Franklin) Butler **7** (John McPherson) Berrien
    navy: 6 (John) Branch **8** (Levi) Woodbury **9** (Mahlon) Dickerson
    postmaster general: 5 (William Taylor) Barry **7** (Amos) Kendall

  born: 8 Waxhaw SC
  died/buried: 11 Nashville TN
  education:
    college: 4 none
    studied: 3 law
    admitted to: 3 bar
  religion: 12 Presbyterian
  political career: 8 US Senate **24** US House of Representatives
    judge: 22 Tennessee Superior Court
  civilian career: 6 lawyer
  military service: 12 major general **16** brigadier general
    defeated: 6 Creeks **9** Cherokees
    captured: 9 Pensacola
    military governor of: 7 Florida
  notable events of lifetime/term:
    battle: 5 Alamo **10** New Orleans
    fought: 5 duels
    scandal/wife suspected of: 6 bigamy
    war: 8 Creek War **13** Revolutionary **16** First Seminole War **19** War of Eighteen Twelve
  father: 6 Andrew
  mother: 9 Elizabeth (Hutchinson)
  siblings: 4 Hugh **6** Robert
  wife: 6 Rachel (Donelson Robards)
  children:
    adopted: 11 wife's nephew **15** Andrew Jackson Jr

Jackson, Anne
  husband: 10 Eli Wallach
  born: 10 Millvale PA
  roles: 3 Luv **10** The Typists

Jackson, Charles
  author of: 14 The Lost Weekend

Jackson 5 4 Tito **6** Jackie, Marlon **7** Michael **8** Jermaine
  songs: 3 ABC **10** I'll Be There **12** I Want You Back **14** The Love You Save

Jackson, Glenda
  born: 7 England **10** Birkenhead
  roles: 10 Elizabeth R **11** Women in Love (Oscar) **13** A Touch of Class (Oscar) **14** The Music Lovers **16** Mary Queen of Scots **18** Sunday Bloody Sunday
  politics: 11 Labour Party **18** Member of Parliament

Jackson, Jesse Louis
  title: 8 Reverend
  party: 10 Democratic
  born: 12 Greenville SC
  education: 20 University of Illinois

26 Chicago Theological Seminary **49** North Carolina Agricultural and Technical State College
  religion: 7 Baptist
  political career: 17 Democratic primary
  civilian career: 4 SCLC **9** PUSH Excel **13** Operation PUSH **20** Operation Breadbasket **24** National Rainbow Coalition **37** Southern Christian Leadership Conference

Jackson, Michael
  born: 2 IN **4** Gary
  father: 6 Joseph
  mother: 9 Katherine
  siblings: 4 Tito **5** Janet, Randy **6** Jackie, La Toya, Marlon **7** Maureen **8** Jermaine
  wife: 16 Lisa Marie Presley
  trademark: 5 glove
  recordings: 3 Bad **7** Triumph, Victory **8** Thriller **9** Dangerous **10** Off the Wall
  film: 6 The Wiz
  group: 8 Jacksons **11** Jackson Five

Jackson, Reggie
  nickname: 13 Mister October
  sport: 8 baseball
  position: 8 outfield
  known for: 7 hitting
  team: 9 Oakland A's **14** New York Yankees **16** California Angels

Jackson, Shirley
  author of: 10 The Lottery **28** We Have Always Lived in the Castle

Jackson, Stonewall (Thomas)
  served in: 8 Civil War **10** Mexican War
  side: 11 Confederate
  battle: 7 Bull Run **8** Antietam, Richmond **9** Seven Days **14** Fredericksburg **16** Chancellorsville, Shenandoah Valley

Jacksonville
  football team: 5 Bulls **7** Jaguars

Jacob
  father: 5 Isaac
  mother: 7 Rebekah
  brother: 4 Esau
  wives: 4 Leah **6** Rachel
  concubines: 5 Bilah **6** Zilpah
  son: 3 Dan, Gad **4** Levi **5** Asher, Judah **6** Joseph, Reuben, Simeon **7** Zebulun **8** Benjamin, Issachar, Naphtali
  daughter: 5 Dinah

dream of: 6 ladder
wrestled with: 5 angel
name changed to: 6 Israel
burial place: 9 Machpelah

Jacob, Francois
field: 7 biology
nationality: 6 French
discovered: 3 RNA
awarded: 10 Nobel Prize

jacuzzi 4 bath **9** whirlpool

jade
species: 7 jadeite **8** nephrite
source: 5 Burma, China **6** Mexico **7** Mogaung **10** New Zealand **12** United States

jaded 5 blase, bored, sated, spent, stale, tired, weary **6** cloyed, dulled, fagged **7** glutted, satiate, spoiled, wearied, worn-out **8** dog-tired, fatigued, overused, satiated, shopworn, tired out **9** exhausted, played out, surfeited **11** overwearied **12** overindulged

jadeite
variety: 4 jade

jagged 5 jaggy, rough, spiny **6** barbed, broken, craggy, nicked, ridged, rugged, snaggy, spiked, thorny, uneven, zigzag **7** angular, bristly, cragged, notched, pointed, spinous, studded **8** indented, serrated **9** irregular, knifelike **10** crenulated, saw-toothed **12** sharp-toothed

Jagger, Mick
born: 12 Dartford, Kent (UK)
musician for: 13 Rolling Stones
songs: 8 Star, Star, Lady Jane **9** Start Me Up **10** Brown Sugar, The Citadel, She's So Cold, Wild Horses **11** Ruby Tuesday **12** Paint It Black **13** Get Off My Cloud, Honky Tonk Woman **15** Jumpin' Jack Flash
body feature: 4 lips
wife: 6 Bianca
companion: 9 Jerri Hall

Jaggers, Mr
character in: 17 Great Expectations
author: 7 Dickens

jaguar 3 cat **5** tiger **6** feline **7** panther **8** uturuncu

jail 3 bag, can, jug, nab, pen **4** book, brig, bust, cell, keep, stir **5** clink, pinch, pound, run in, seize **6** arrest, collar, cooler, lockup, prison, take in **7** arraign, bring in, capture, confine, dungeon, slammer **8** bastille, big house, hoosegow, imprison, stockade **9** apprehend, black hole, calaboose, guardroom, workhouse **10** guardhouse **11** incarcerate, reformatory **12** halfway house, penitentiary, reform school, station house **13** hold in custody, police station **14** detention house **16** penal institution **17** house of correction

jailbird 3 con **5** felon, lifer **7** convict **8** prisoner

jailer 5 guard, screw **6** gaoler, keeper, warden **7** turnkey **9** custodian

Jair 11 Hebrew judge

Jakarta, Djakarta
capital of: 9 Indonesia

Jake's Thing
author: 12 Kingsley Amis

jalopy 3 car **4** auto, heap **5** motor **6** wheels **7** flivver, machine, vehicle **8** motorcar **9** tin lizzie **10** automobile

jam 3 fix, mob, ram, sea **4** army, cram, herd, host, mess, pack, push, stop **5** block, cease, crowd, crush, drove, flock, horde, pinch, press, shove, stall, stick, stuff, swarm, tie-up, wedge **6** arrest, edge in, pickle, plight, scrape, strait, throng, thrust, work in, worm in **7** congest, dilemma, foist in, force in, squeeze, suspend, trouble **8** hot water, obstruct, quandary, sandwich **9** interrupt, multitude, overcrowd **11** malfunction, predicament **13** agglomeration

Jamaica
name means: 18 land of wood and water
capital/largest city: 8 Kingston
others: 6 May Pen **8** Ocho Rios **9** Morant Bay, Port Maria, Port Royal **10** Mandeville, Montego Bay **11** Port Antonio, Spanish Town **12** Saint Ann's Bay, Savanna-la-Mar
head of state: 14 British monarch **15** governor general
monetary unit: 7 quattie
island: 4 Navy **15** Greater Antilles
mountain: 8 Sir John's
highest point: 4 Blue
river: 5 Black, Cobre, Great, Minho, White **9** Rio Grande
sea: 8 Atlantic **9** Caribbean
physical feature: 13 Portland Bight
area: 14 Cockpit Country
bay: 4 Buff, Hope, Long **6** Morant **9** Discovery **10** Black River, Bluefield's, Old Harbour
point: 6 Galina **8** Portland **9** North East, North West, South East **11** North Negril, South Negril
people: 7 African, Chinese **10** East Indian
ancient: 6 Arawak **7** Ciboney
discoverer: 8 Columbus
leader: 5 Seaga **6** Garvey, Manley **10** Bustamente
language: 6 Creole **7** English
religion: 7 Baptist **8** Anglican **9** Methodist **11** Church of God, Rastafarian **13** Roman Catholic
place:
beach: 11 Doctor's Cave
botanical garden: 4 Hope
racetrack: 12 Caymanas Park
feature:
evil spirits: 7 duppies
guerrilla fighters: 7 Maroons
tree: 4 poui **5** cedar, ceiba, mahoe, saman **6** cassia, guango **7** logwood

8 mahogany **9** casuarina, poinciana **10** silkcotton **11** lignum vitae
witch doctor: 8 obeah man
food:
coffee: 12 Blue Mountain
drink: 3 rum **4** jake **8** tia maria
fruit: 5 guava, mango **6** pawpaw
spicy soup: 9 pepper pot

jamboree 2 do **4** bash, gala **5** party, revel, spree **6** fiesta, frolic **7** blowout, jubilee, shindig **8** carnival, carousal, festival **9** festivity **11** celebration
French: 4 fete **13** fete champetre

James 7 apostle
also called: 12 James the Less
father: 7 Zebedee **8** Alphaeus
brother: 4 John, Levi **5** Judas
disciple of: 5 Jesus
killed by: 12 Herod Agrippa
with John called: 13 sons of thunder

James, Henry
author of: 11 Daisy Miller, The American **13** The Bostonians, The Golden Bowl **14** Roderick Hudson, The Ambassadors **15** The Aspern Papers **16** Washington Square **17** The Turn of the Screw, The Wings of the Dove **18** The Portrait of a Lady **19** Princess Casamassima

James, P D
author of: 12 Cover Her Face **13** Innocent Blood **15** Unnatural Causes **17** Devices and Desires **21** Shroud for a Nightingale **22** Death of an Expert Witness
character: 13 Adam Dalgliesh

James the Less see **5** James

jammed 4 full **5** stuck **6** filled, loaded, massed, packed, rammed, wedged **7** blocked, crammed, crowded, crushed, pressed, stuffed **8** overfull, squeezed **10** obstructed, sandwiched **11** overcrowded

Janacek, Leos
born: 8 Hukvaldy **14** Czechoslovakia
composer of: 5 Mladi, Youth **6** Jenufa **9** In the Mist **10** Taras Bulba **13** Katya Kabanova **14** Glagolitic Mass **17** On an Overgrown Path **18** The Makropoulos Case **21** From the House of the Dead, The Cunning Little Vixen **24** The Diary of One Who Vanished, The Excursions of Mr Broucek

Jane
character in: 6 Tarzan
author: 9 Burroughs

Jane Eyre
author: 15 Charlotte Bronte
character: 5 Mason **7** Mrs Reed **10** Grace Poole, Mary Rivers, Mrs Fairfax **11** Adele Varens, Bertha Mason, Diana Rivers **12** Bessie Leaven, St John Rivers **13** Blanche Ingram **15** Edward Rochester
school: 6 Lowood
house: 10 Thornfield

director: 15 Robert Stevenson
cast: 11 Orson Welles **12** Joan Fontaine **14** Margaret O'Brien

jangle 3 din, jar **4** ring **5** annoy, chime, clang, clank, clash, crash, upset **6** jingle, racket, rattle **7** clangor, clatter, grate on **8** irritate **9** cacophony **11** reverberate **13** reverberation **14** tintinnabulate

janitor 5 super **6** porter **8** handyman **9** caretaker, custodian, janitress **11** cleaning man **12** cleaning lady **13** cleaning woman **14** maintenance man, superintendent

Janssen, David
real name: 16 David Harold Meyer
born: 9 Naponee NE
roles: 6 Harry O **11** The Fugitive **14** Richard Diamond **15** Dr Richard Kimble

January
event: 15 Inauguration Day (every 4 years)
flower: 8 snowdrop **9** carnation
French: 7 Janvier
gem: 6 garnet
German: 6 Januar
holiday: 8 Epiphany (6) **11** New Year's Day (1) **12** Twelfth Night (5)
Italian: 7 Gennaio
number of days: 9 thirty-one
origin of name: 5 Janus
   Roman god of: 5 doors **8** doorways **10** beginnings
place in year:
   Gregorian: 5 first
   Julian/Roman: 8 eleventh
Spanish: 5 Enero
Zodiac sign: 8 Aquarius **9** Capricorn

Janus
origin: 5 Roman
god of: 8 doorways **9** rising sun **10** beginnings, setting sun

Japan
other name: 5 Nihon **6** Nippon
name means: 18 Land of the Rising Sun
capital/largest city: 3 Edo **5** Tokyo
others: 4 Kobe, Naha **5** Kyoto, Osaka **6** Nagoya, Sendai **7** Fukuoka, Niigata, Sapporo **8** Kanazawa, Kawasaki, Nagasaki, Yokohama **9** Hiroshima, Kagoshima **10** Kitakyushu
school: 4 Chuo, Keio **5** Hosei, Kyoto, Nihon, Tokyo **6** Sophia, Waseda **7** Fukuoka **8** Doshisha
head of state: 7 emperor
measure: 2 go **3** boo, cho, djo, fun, inc, ken, kin, kon, rin, shi, sho, sun, tan **4** hiro, isse, kati, koku, niyo, shoo **5** carat, catty, issho, ittan, momme, picul, shaku **6** kwamme **8** hiyak-kin **9** hiyak-hiro **11** komma-ichida, kujira-shaku
monetary unit: 2 bu **3** mon, rin, rio, sen, shu, yen **4** cash, mibu, oban **5** koban, obang, tempo **6** cobang, ichebu, ichibu, itzebu, kobang **7** itze-boo, itziboo

weight: 2 mo **3** fun, kon, rin **4** kati, kwan **5** carat, catty, momme **8** hiyakkin

island: 3 Iki, Izu, Oki, Tsu **4** Oita, Sado, Yaku **5** Amami, Awaji, Bonin, Hondo, Kuril, Rebun, Sikok **6** Honshu, Kiushu, Kyushu, Loochu, Marcus, Riukiu, Tanega, Tyukyu **7** Cipango, Hachijo, Iwo Jima, Okinawa, Rishiri, Shikoko, Shikoku, Volcano **8** Hokkaido, Miyajima, Okigunto, Okushiri, Tsushima, Yakujima
lake: 4 Biwa, Suwa, Toya **6** Towada **8** Kutchawa, Shikotsu
mountain: 3 Uso, Zao **5** Asahi, Asama, Hondo, Yesso **6** Asosan, Enasan, Hiuchi, Kiusiu, Yariga **7** Hakusan, Kujusan, Tokachi **8** Fujiyama **9** Japan Alps
highest point: 4 Fuji **7** Fujisan
river: 4 Tone, Yalu **8** Ishikari, Tonegawa **11** Shinano- gawa
sea: 3 Suo **5** Japan **6** Inland **7** Amakusa, Okhotsk, Pacific **8** Tsushima
physical feature:
   bay: 3 Ise **4** Miku, Tosa, Yedo **5** Amort, Mutsu, Osaka, Otaru, Tokyo **6** Ariake, Atsumi, Sendai, Suruga, Toyama, Wakasa **7** Uchiura
   cape: 3 Iro, Oki, Oma, Toi **4** Daio, Esan, Jizo, Mela, Mino, Noma, Nomo, Sada, Sawa, Shio, Soya, Suzu **5** Erimo, Kyoga, Rurui **6** Todoga **7** Shiriya **8** Ashizuri, Shakotan **12** Muroto Nojima
   channel: 3 Kii **5** Bungo
   current: 5 Japan **7** Okhotsk **8** Kuro Shio
   divine wind: 8 kamikaze
   gulf: 6 Sagami
   plain: 4 Nobi **5** Kanto
   strait: 4 Soya **5** Korea, Osumi **6** Nemuro, Tanega, Tokara **7** Tsugaru **8** Tsushima **9** La Perouse
people: 3 Eta **6** Korean **8** Japanese, Okinawan **10** Buramkumin
   ancient: 4 Ainu **5** Jomon, Yayoi
   artist: 4 Okyo **5** Buson, Jocho, Korin, Taiga, Unkei **6** Buncho, Eitoku, Kenzan, Koetsu, Reisai, Sesshu, Sesson, Shubun **7** Baiitsu, Choshun, Foujita, Gyokudo, Hokusai, Josetsu, Sanraku, Sharaku, Sotatsu, Utamaro **8** Harunobu, Kiyonaga, Motonobu **9** Hiroshige, Mitsunobu
   author: 5 Basho **7** Abe Kobo **8** Mori Ogai **11** Ueda Akinari **12** Ihara Saikaku, Mishima Yukio, Sakyo Komatsu **13** Natsume Soseki, Zeami Motokiyo **14** Shimazaki Toson, Tsubouchi Shoyo **15** Motoori Norinaga, Murasaki Shikibu **16** Fujiwara Nokisaki, Kawabata Yasunari **17** Tanizaki Junichiro **19** Chikamatsu Monzaemon

dynasty: 5 Meiji, Taira **6** Yamato **8** Fujiwara, Minamoto
leader: 4 Hojo **5** Kammu, Meiji **6** Go-Toba, Ieyasu **7** Akihito, Go-Daigo **8** Hirohito, Nobunaga, Yoritomo **9** Hideyoshi, Yoshimasa **10** Tojo Hideki, Yoshimitsu **11** Hara Takashi, Ito Hirobumi **12** Tanaka Kakuei **13** Konoe Fumimaro, Shotoku Taishi **14** Yoshida Shigeru **15** Ashikaga Takauji **18** Matsukata Mayayoshi
legendary ruler: 5 Jimmu, Jingo **7** Izanagi
shogunate: 8 Ashikaga, Kamakura, Tokugawa
language: 8 Japanese
alphabet/characters: 4 kana **5** kanji **8** hiragana, katakana
dialect: 5 Kanto
religion: 6 Tendai **7** Shingon **8** Buddhism **9** Shintoism **12** Confucianism
place:
   castle: 4 Nijo
   hall: 5 Hoodo **7** Phoenix **12** Golden Buddha
   mausoleum: 4 Ojin **7** Nintoku
   palace: 7 Akasaka, Katsura
   shrine: 5 Heian **11** Itsukushima **16** Grand Shrine of Ise
   temple: 6 Kotoku **7** Byodoin, Horyuji, Ryoanji, Senso-ji, Todaiji **8** Enkakuji, Kenchoji, Kofukuji **9** Kinkakuji **13** Asakusa Kannon
feature:
   abacus: 7 soroban
   bed: 5 futon
   clothing: 6 kimono
   festival: 13 Cherry Blossom
   firm: 4 Sony **5** Honda **6** Mitsui, Nissan, Toyota, Yasuda **7** Iwasaki **8** Sumitomo **10** Mitsubishi
   flower arranging: 7 ikebana
   painting style: 4 kano, tosa **5** nanga, nisee, onnae, rarae, rimpa, shijo **6** chinso, otokoe, sesshu, ukiyoe **7** konpeki, nihonga, yamatoe
   paper folding art: 7 origami
   poem: 4 waka **5** haiku, tanka
   puppet theater: 7 bunraku
   rush floor covering: 6 tatami
   sport: 4 judo **6** karate **13** sumo wrestling
   statue: 8 Daibutsu **11** Great Buddha
   tea ceremony: 7 chanoyu
   theater: 2 no **3** noh **6** kabuki
   the way of the warrior/code of honor: 7 bushido
   tree: 6 bonsai
   wood block print: 6 ukiyoe
food:
   beverage: 4 sake **8** green tea
   dish: 5 sushi **7** sashimi, tempura **8** sukiyaki, teriyaki, yakitori
   noodle: 4 soba
Japanese

independent language of: 5 Japan **13** Ryukyu Islands

jape 4 gibe, joke **5** antic, caper, prank **7** mockery

Japheth
father: 4 Noah
brother: 3 Ham **4** Shem

Jaques
character in: 11 As You Like It
author: 11 Shakespeare

jar 3 din, jug, pot, urn **4** bong, bray, buzz, daze, faze, jolt, rock, stir, stun **5** blare, blast, brawl, clang, clank, crash, crock, flask, floor, quake, shake, shock, throw, upset **6** beaker, bottle, impact, jangle, jiggle, joggle, racket, rattle, vessel **7** agitate, astound, clangor, clatter, confuse, disturb, fluster, perturb, shake up, startle, stupefy, trouble, upheave, vibrate **8** befuddle, bewilder, bleating, canister, clashing, convulse, decanter, demijohn, disquiet, distract, unsettle **9** agitation, cacophony, container **10** concussion, discompose, disconcert, receptacle **11** discordance
Spanish: 4 olla

jargon 4 bosh, bull, bunk, cant **5** argot, fudge, hooey, idiom, lingo, prate, usage **6** babble, brogue, drivel, patois, pidgin, piffle **7** baloney, blabber, blather, dialect, fustian, hogwash, prattle, rubbish, twaddle **8** folderol, malarkey, nonsense, parlance, tommyrot, verbiage **9** gibberish, moonshine, poppycock, rigmarole **10** balderdash, flapdoodle, hocus-pocus, rigamarole, vernacular, vocabulary **11** abracadabra, jabberwocky, phraseology, shibboleths **12** gobbledygook, lingua franca **14** grandiloquence

Jarley, Mrs
character in: 19 The Old Curiosity Shop
author: 7 Dickens

Jarndyce, John
character in: 10 Bleak House
author: 7 Dickens

jarring 4 rude **5** harsh, rough **6** jangly **7** grating, jolting, rasping, shaking **8** clashing, grinding, jangling, rattling, strident **9** dissonant, wrenching **10** discordant **12** nerve- racking **13** nerve-wracking

Jarry, Alfred
author of: 7 King Ubu **11** Ubu in Chains **13** Ubu the Cuckold

jasmine 8 Jasminum
varieties: 4 blue, cape, rock, star **5** crape, night, royal **6** orange, yellow **7** Arabian, Chilean, Italian, Spanish **8** Carolina, cinnamon, Japanese, Paraguay, pinwheel, primrose, windmill **9** angel-wing **10** Catalonian, Madagascar **11** Confederate

Jason
leader of: 9 Argonauts

father: 5 Aeson
mother: 8 Alcimede, Polymede
half-brother: 6 Pelias
son: 5 Thoas **6** Euneus, Pheres **7** Medeius **8** Mermerus, Tisander **9** Alcimenes, Thessalus
daughter: 7 Eriopis
teacher: 6 Chiron **7** centaur, Cheiron
retrieved: 12 Golden Fleece
ship: 4 Argo
loved by: 5 Medea
loved: 6 Glauce

Jasper, John
character in: 22 The Mystery of Edwin Drood
author: 7 Dickens

jaundiced 5 blase, bored **6** bitter **7** cynical, envious, hostile, jealous **8** covetous, doubting, satiated **9** green-eyed, resentful, skeptical **10** embittered, suspicious **11** mistrustful

jaunt 4 spin, tour, trip **6** airing, flight, junket, outing, ramble, stroll **9** adventure, excursion, promenade, short trip **10** expedition

jaunty 4 airy, neat, trim **5** natty, perky **6** blithe, bouncy, breezy, dapper, lively, sporty, spruce **7** buoyant **8** carefree, debonair **9** sprightly, vivacious **12** lighthearted, high-stepping, high-spirited

Java
other name: 5 Djawa
capital/largest city: 7 Jakarta **8** Djakarta
others: 5 Bogor, Dessa **6** Kediri, Malang **7** Bandung, Batavia **8** Semarang, Surabaja, Surabaya **9** Surakarta **11** Djokjakarta **13** Pelabuhanratu
government: 17 island of Indonesia
measure: 3 kan **4** paal, rand **5** palen
weight: 4 amat, pond, tali **5** pound **6** soekel
island: 4 Bali **5** Sunda **6** Lombok, Madura
mountain: 4 Amat, Gede **5** Lawoe, Murjo, Prahu **6** Raoeng, Slamet **8** Soembing
highest point: 6 Semuru **7** Semeroe
river: 4 Solo **7** Brantas
sea: 4 Java **6** Indian **7** Pacific
physical feature:
plateau: 4 Ijen
strait: 5 Sunda
people: 5 Krama, Kromo **6** Kalang **8** Javanese, Madurese **9** Sundanese
dynasty: 7 Mataram **9** Majapahit, Srivijaya
language: 4 Kavi, Kawi **5** Malay **6** Sassak **8** Balinese, Madurese, Sudanese **16** Bahasa Indonesian
religion: 5 Hindu, Islam **7** animism **8** Buddhism
place:
temple: 6 Chandi, Thandi **9** Borobudur, Prambanan
feature:
cloth: 3 kat **5** batik, kapok

dance: 7 seri mpi
dancer: 6 bedoyo
fishing boat: 4 prau
ornamental dagger: 4 kris
puppet play: 6 wajang, wayang
food:
fruit: 6 durian, lomboy, nangca **7** gondang

javelin 4 dart **5** lance, shaft, spear **10** projectile

jaw 3 gab, rap **4** chat, chin, talk **7** jawbone, palaver **8** chitchat, converse, mandible **10** chew the fat, chew the rag **11** confabulate

Jaws
author: 13 Peter Benchley
director: 15 Steven Spielberg
cast: 10 Robert Shaw **11** Roy Scheider **12** Lorraine Gary **15** Richard Dreyfuss
score: 12 John Williams
Oscar for: 5 score

Jayhawker State
nickname of: 6 Kansas

jazz musician 8 Art Tatum **9** Bud Powell **10** Miles Davis **11** Lester Young **12** Benny Goodman, John Coltrane **13** Charles Mingus, Charlie Parker, Duke Ellington, Thelonius Monk **14** Dizzy Gillespie, Louis Armstrong, Ornette Coleman, Wynton Marsalis

jealous 4 wary **7** anxious, envious, mindful **8** covetous, grudging, watchful **9** concerned, green-eyed, regardful, resentful **10** possessive, protective, suspicious **11** mistrustful, mistrusting **12** apprehensive

jealousy 4 envy **8** distrust, jaundice, mistrust **9** suspicion **10** resentment **12** covetousness **14** possessiveness **16** green-eyed monster
color: 5 green

Jebus
city captured by: 5 David
renamed: 9 Jerusalem
inhabitant: 8 Jebusite

jeer 3 boo, bug, dig, rap **4** barb, hiss, hoot, mock, razz, slam, slur **5** abuse, flout, hound, knock, scoff, scorn, sneer, taunt, whoop **6** deride, harass, heckle, hector, insult, revile **7** catcall, laugh at, mockery, obloquy **8** derision, ridicule, scoffing **9** aspersion, contumely, poke fun at, whistle at

Jeffers, Robinson
author of: 5 Medea, Tamar **6** Cawdor **8** Solstice **9** Dear Judas **12** Roan Stallion **14** Thurso's Landing **18** The Women at Point Sur **21** The Tower Beyond Tragedy

Jefferson, Thomas
nickname: 16 Sage of Monticello
presidential rank: 5 third
party: 20 Democratic-Republican
state represented: 2 VA
defeated: 5 (John) Adams **8** (Charles

Cotesworth) Pinckney
vice president: 4 (Aaron) Burr **7** (George) Clinton
cabinet:
  state: 7 (James) Madison
  treasury: 6 (Samuel) Dexter **8** (Albert) Gallatin
  war: 8 (Henry) Dearborn
  attorney general: 6 (Caesar Augustus) Rodney **7** (Levi) Lincoln **12** (John) Breckenridge
  navy: 5 (Robert) Smith
born: 2 VA **14** Shadwell estate **15** Goochland (Albemarle) County
died/buried: 10 Monticello
education: 14 William and Mary
interests: 6 violin **7** writing **11** agriculture **12** architecture
favorite foods: 10 French food **11** French wines
vacation: 12 Poplar Forest
author: 25 Declaration of Independence, Notes on the State of Virginia **39** A Summary View of the Rights of British America
political career: 8 governor **16** House of Burgesses **19** Virginia legislature **25** Declaration of Independence, Second Continental Congress
  secretary of: 5 state
  minister to: 6 France
civilian career: 6 farmer, lawyer
notable events of lifetime/term:
  expedition: 13 Lewis and Clark
  prohibition of: 19 importation of slaves
  purchase: 9 Louisiana
father: 5 Peter
mother: 4 Jane (Randolph)
siblings: 4 Jane, Lucy, Mary **6** Martha **8** Randolph **9** Anna Scott, Elizabeth **10** Peter Field
wife: 6 Martha (Wayles Skelton)
children: 4 Mary **6** Martha
Jeffersons, The
  character: 8 Florence **9** Tom Willis **11** Helen Willis **12** Harry Bentley **15** George Jefferson, Lionel Jefferson, Louise Jefferson, Ralph the Doorman **20** Jenny Willis Jefferson
  cast: 9 Mike Evans **10** Damon Evans, Marla Gibbs, Roxie Roker **11** Ned Wertimer **12** Paul Benedict **13** Franklin Cover, Isabel Sanford **14** Sherman Hemsley **15** Berlinda Tolbert
  George's business: 11 dry cleaning
  spinoff from: 14 All in the Family
Jeffreys, Harold
  field: 7 physics **9** astronomy
  nationality: 7 British
  explained: 7 weather
  studied: 10 Earth's core **11** solar system
Jeffries, James Jackson
  nickname: 14 The Boilermaker
  sport: 6 boxing
  class: 11 heavyweight

jehad, jihad 6 strife **7** holy war **8** struggle
Jehioada
  father: 7 Paseach
  son: 7 Benaiah
  means: 12 Jehovah knows
Jehoshaphat
  father: 3 Asa **6** Ahitub, Nimshi, Parnah
  mother: 8 Jehorani
  means: 13 Jehovah judges
Jehovah 3 god **4** YHWH **5** diety
Jehu
  father: 6 Hanani **11** Jehoshaphat **14** reckless driver
jejune 4 dull **5** banal, inane, stale, trite, vapid **7** humdrum, insipid, puerile **8** ordinary **9** hackneyed **10** pedestrian, unexciting, unoriginal, wishy-washy **11** commonplace **12** conventional **13** uninteresting
jell 3 gel, jam, set **4** clot, firm **5** jelly **7** congeal, thicken **9** coagulate **10** gelatinize
Jellyby, Mrs
  character in: 10 Bleak House
  author: 7 Dickens
jellyfish 5 hydra, polyp, softy **6** coward, medusa, nettle **7** sunfish **8** weakling **10** ctenophore, pantywaist **11** milquetoast, mollycoddle **12** coelenterate, invertebrate, siphonophore **18** Portuguese man-of-war
je ne sais quoi 13 I don't know what **18** indefinable quality
Jenner, Bruce
  sport: 13 track and field
  known for: 9 decathlon
  won: 8 Olympics
Jenner, Edward
  nationality: 7 British
  discovered: 11 vaccination **19** smallpox inoculation
Jenney, William Le Baron
  architect of: 21 Home Insurance Building (Chicago)
jeopardize 4 risk **6** expose, hazard **7** imperil **8** endanger **10** compromise **11** put into danger
jeopardy 4 risk **5** peril **6** danger, hazard **8** exposure, unsafety **9** liability **10** insecurity **11** imperilment **12** endangerment **13** vulnerability **14** precariousness
Jephthah 11 Hebrew judge
  father: 6 Gilead
Jeremiah
  father: 7 Hilkiah **10** Habazaniah
  daughter: 7 Mamutal
  grandson: 7 Jehohaz
  friend, scribe: 6 Baruch
jerk 3 ass, tic, tug **4** dope, dupe, fool, pull, snap, yank **5** dummy, dunce, idiot, klutz, pluck, shake, spasm, start, twist **6** quiver, reflex, thrust, twitch,

wrench **7** tremble **8** convulse **9** trembling
jerky 4 beef, meat **5** jolty, jumpy **6** choppy, elboic, jouncy **7** biltong, charqui, fidgety, twitchy **9** dried beef, spasmodic, twitching
Jeroboam
  father: 5 Joash, Nebat
  successor: 9 Zachariah
Jerry
  (British): 6 German
jerry-built 4 weak **5** frail, run-up, shaky, tacky **6** faulty, flimsy, shoddy, sleazy **7** rickety, unsound **8** gimcrack, slipshod, thrown-up, unstable **9** cheap-jack, defective **10** ramshackle **13** unsubstantial **14** thrown-together
jersey 3 cow **5** maillot, shirt **6** tricot **7** sweater **8** camisole, guernsey, pullover **10** undershirt
Jersey Joe
  nickname of: 10 Joe Walcott
Jerusalem
  author: 12 William Blake
Jerusalem
  former name: 5 Jebus
  pool of: 6 Siloam **8** Bethesda
Jerusalem
  Arabic: 14 Bayt al-Muqaddas
  capital of: 6 Israel
  Hebrew: 12 Yerushalayim
  hills: 7 Judaean
  landmark: 6 al-Aqsa **11** Wailing Wall, Western Wall **12** Israel Museum **13** Dome of the Rock **14** Dead Sea Scrolls **15** Shrine of the Book **17** Rockefeller Museum **24** Church of the Holy Sepulcher
  mount: 6 Olives, Scopus
  river: 6 Kidron
  ruler: 5 Arabs, David, Herod **6** Persia, Romans **7** British, Saladin, Seljuks, Solomon **8** Ayyubids, Fatimids, Ptolemy I **9** Crusaders, Maccabees, Mamelukes **10** Canaanites **12** Antiochus III **13** Pontius Pilate **15** Byzantine Empire **17** Alexander the Great, Antiochus the Third
  street: 11 Via Dolorosa
Jerusalem Delivered
  author: 13 Torquato Tasso
Jervis, Mrs
  character in: 6 Pamela
  author: 10 Richardson
jessamine 8 Jasminum
  varieties: 3 day **5** night, poet's **6** orange, yellow **12** willow-leaved **13** night-blooming **14** Carolina yellow
Jesse
  father: 4 Obed
  grandfather: 4 Boaz
  grandmother: 4 Ruth
  great-grandfather: 5 Rahab
  son: 5 David, Eliab **7** Shammah **8** Abinadab
jest 3 gag, pun **4** fool, game, gibe, jape, joke, josh, quip **5** act up, crack,

laugh, prank, tease, trick **6** banter, bon mot **9** wisecrack, witticism **10** crack jokes, pleasantry **11** horse around

jester 3 wag, wit **4** card, fool, mime, zany **5** clown, comic, joker, mimer, mimic **6** madcap, mummer **7** buffoon **8** comedian, funnyman, humorist, quipster **9** harlequin **10** motley fool **11** merry-andrew, pantomimist, punchinello

jesting 6 joking **7** teasing **8** sportive **9** bantering, unserious **12** wisecracking

Jesus
also called: 7 Holy One, Messiah **8** Nazarene, Son of God **9** the Christ **12** Man of Sorrows **13** Prince of Peace **14** Savior Anointed
mother: 4 Mary
stepfather: 6 Joseph
birthplace: 9 Bethlehem
lived in: 8 Nazareth
death place: 9 Jerusalem
buried by: 17 Joseph of Arimathea
disciples: 4 John, Jude **5** James, Peter, Simon **6** Andrew, Philip, Thomas **7** Matthew **12** James the Less **13** Judas Iscariot **20** Bartholomew Nathanael
secret follower: 9 Nicodemus
famous discourse: 16 Sermon on the Mount

jet 4 gush **5** flush, issue, shoot, spout, spray, spurt, surge, swash **6** effuse, nozzle, rush up, squirt, stream **7** sparger, sprayer, Spritze, syringe **8** atomizer, fountain, shoot out, Spritzer **9** discharge, sprinkler

Jethro
daughter: 8 Zipporah
son-in-law: 5 Moses

Jetsons, The
character: 5 Astro **10** Jane Jetson, Judy Jetson **11** Elroy Jetson **12** George Jetson **13** Cosmo G Spacely
voices: 8 Mel Blanc **10** Daws Butler, Don Messick, Janet Waldo **13** George O'Hanlon **14** Penny Singleton

jettison 4 dump **5** eject, scrap **6** unload **7** cast off, discard **8** throw out **9** discharge, eliminate, pitch over, throw over **13** toss overboard

jetty 4 dike, dock, mole, pier, quay, slip **5** black, ebony, groin, levee, raven, sable, wharf **6** bridge **7** sea wall **8** buttress **10** breakwater

jeu de mots 3 pun **11** play on words

jeu d'esprit 9 witticism **17** witty literary work
literally: 12 play of spirit

jeune fille 4 girl **9** young girl **13** unmarried girl

jeunesse doree 11 gilded youth, golden youth

Jew 6 Essene, Hebrew, Judean, Semite **7** Edomite, Judaist, Moabite **8** Hebraist, Sephardi **9** Israelite

jewel 3 ace, gem, pip **4** bead, dear, find, ring, whiz **5** honey, pearl, prize, stone, tiara **6** bangle, bauble, brooch, locket, winner **7** earring, pendant, trinket **8** bracelet, knockout, necklace, ornament, pure gold, treasure **9** humdinger, lavaliere **10** topnotcher **11** crackerjack, masterpiece

jewelry 4 gems, gold **6** silver **7** bangles, gewgaws, regalia **8** trinkets **10** adornments **14** precious stones

Jewett, Sarah Orne
author of: 26 The Country of the Pointed Firs

Jewish 6 Hebrew, Judaic **7** Hebraic, Semitic
bread: 5 matzo **6** matzoh **7** challah
candelabrum: 7 menorah
ceremonial robe: 5 kitel
color: 5 white
coming of age: 10 bar mitzvah, bat mitzvah
dietary laws: 7 kashrut **8** kashruth
fit to eat: 6 kosher
not fit to eat: 4 tref
group: 8 Hadassah **9** B'nai B'rith
holy day/festival: 5 Purim, seder **6** Sukkot **7** Shavuot **8** Chanukah, Hanukkah, Passover **9** Yom Kippur **12** Rosh Hashanah
law/scripture: 5 Torah **6** Gemara, Talmud, Tanach **7** Mishnah
liturgical prayer: 6 Yigdal **8** Kol Nidre
recited on eve of: 9 Yom Kippur
marriage canopy: 6 chupah
months:
1st: 6 Tishri
2nd: 7 Heshvan
3rd: 6 Kislev
4th: 5 Tevet
5th: 6 Shevat
6th: 4 Adar
7th: 5 Nisan
8th: 4 Iyar
9th: 5 Sivan
10th: 6 Tammuz
11th: 2 Av
12th: 4 Elul
prayerbook: 6 mahzor, siddur **7** machzor
quarter: 6 ghetto, mellah
school: 5 heder **6** cheder
skullcap: 5 kipah **8** yarmulka
service to commemorate the dead: 6 Yizkor
synagogue: 4 shul **5** schul
toast: 8 mazel tov

Jewkes, Mrs
character in: 6 Pamela
author: 10 Richardson

Jew of Malta, The
author: 18 Christopher Marlowe
character: 7 Abigail, Barabas **8** Ithamore **15** Governor of Malta

Jezebel
director: 12 William Wyler
cast: 10 Bette Davis, Fay Bainter,

Henry Fonda **11** Donald Crisp, George Brent **15** Margaret Lindsay
Oscar for: 7 actress (Davis) **17** supporting actress (Bainter)

Jezebel
father: 7 Ethbaal
husband: 8 King Ahab
daughter: 8 Athaliah
opposed: 6 Elijah
killed: 6 Naboth
father-in-law: 4 Omri

jib 3 arm, shy **4** balk, boom, sail, tack **5** demur, gigue, stick **6** recoil **7** scruple

jibe 2 go **3** fit **4** mesh, tack **5** agree, fit in, match, shift, tally **6** accord, concur, square **7** conform **8** coincide, dovetail **9** harmonize **10** correspond, go together **11** fit together

jiffy 3 sec **4** jiff **5** flash, shake, trice **6** minute, moment, second **7** half a mo, instant **9** twinkling **10** nanosecond **11** microsecond, millisecond, split second

jigger 4 dram, shot **5** glass **6** device, doodad, gadget, object **7** bicycle, gimmick, measure **9** doohickey, shot glass **10** boneshaker **11** contraption, thingumabob

jiggle 4 jerk **5** shake **6** bounce, fidget, joggle, jostle, twitch, wiggle **7** agitate, wriggle

jihad *see* **5** jehad

jilt 5 leave **6** betray, desert **7** forsake, let down **12** break off with **17** break an engagement

Jim
character in: 15 (The Adventures of) Huckleberry Finn
author: 5 Twain

jimmy 3 bar, pry **5** force, lever **7** crowbar

jingle 4 ring **5** clang, clank, clink, ditty **6** jangle, tinkle **7** clatter, ringing **8** doggerel, facetiae, limerick **10** catchy poem, catchy song **12** product theme **13** reverberation **14** commercial tune **16** tintinnabulation

Jingle, Alfred
character in: 14 Pickwick Papers
author: 7 Dickens

jingoism 10 chauvinism, flag-waving, patriotism **11** nationalism **14** overpatriotism, spread-eagleism **15** superpatriotism **16** ultranationalism

jinn 3 imp **5** afrit, demon, genie, jinni **6** afreet, spirit **8** jinniyeh

jinx 3 hex **5** curse **6** plague, whammy **7** bugaboo, bugbear, evil eye, ill wind, nemesis **9** evil spell
French: 9 bete noire

jitney 3 bus, cab

jitterbug 5 dance, lindy **8** lindy hop **12** boogie-woogie

jitters 6 shakes **7** anxiety, fidgets, jimjams, shivers, willies **9** jumpiness, quivering, shakiness, tenseness, the

creeps, whim-whams **10** uneasiness
11 butterflies, fidgetiness, nervousness
12 skittishness **13** heebie- jeebies **16**
screaming-meemies

jittery 5 jumpy **6** uneasy **7** anxious,
nervous

Jivaro, Shuara, Jibaro
tribe: 6 Achual, Antipa **8** Aguaruna,
Huambiza
location: 4 Peru **7** Ecuador **12** South
America
noted for: 7 tsantsa (shrunken
heads)

Joab
mother: 7 Zeruiah
brother: 6 Asahel **7** Abishai
commanded: 10 David's army
killed: 5 Abner, Amasa **7** Absalom
killed by: 7 Benaiah
conspired to overthrow: 5 David

Joad family
characters in: 16 The Grapes of
Wrath
members: 2 Ma, Pa **3** Tom **4** Noah **6**
Connie **12** Rose of Sharon
author: 9 Steinbeck

job 3 lot **4** care, duty, part, role, spot,
task, work **5** chore, craft, field, place,
quota, share, stint, trade, trust **6** affair, career, charge, errand, living, metier, office, output **7** calling, concern,
mission, opening, portion, product,
pursuit **8** activity, business, capacity,
contract, exercise, function, position,
province, vocation **9** allotment, piece-
work, situation **10** assignment, commission, engagement, enterprise, livelihood, occupation, profession **11**
achievement, appointment, performance, undertaking **14** accomplishment, responsibility

Job 8 sufferer
father: 8 Issachar
friend: 5 Elihu **6** Bildad, Zophar **7** Eliphaz

job holder 6 worker **8** employee, hireling

job seeker 7 hopeful **8** aspirant **9** applicant, candidate

Jocasta
also: 8 Epicaste
queen of: 6 Thebes
father: 9 Menoeceus
brother: 5 Creon
husband: 5 Laius **7** Oedipus
son: 7 Oedipus **8** Eteocles **9** Polynices
daughter: 6 Ismene **8** Antigone
death by: 7 hanging, suicide

Jochebed
father: 4 Levi
husband: 5 Amram
nephew: 5 Amram
son: 5 Aaron, Moses

jockey 5 Baeza, Krone **6** Arcaro, Pincay **7** Cauthen, Cordero, Cruguet, Hartack **8** McCarron, McHargue, Turcotte
9 Shoemaker, Velasquez

jocose 3 fun **4** arch **5** comic, droll,
funny, jolly, merry, witty **6** joking, jovial **7** amusing, comical, jesting, jocular, playful, roguish, teasing, waggish
8 humorous, mirthful, prankish, sportive **9** facetious

jocular 3 gay **5** droll, funny, jolly,
merry, witty **6** jocose, jocund, joking,
jovial **7** amusing, jesting, playful, roguish, rompish, waggish **8** humorous,
mirthful, prankish, sportive **9** facetious **10** frolicsome **12** entertaining,
lighthearted

jocund 5 jolly, merry **6** breezy, cheery,
elated, jovial, lively **8** cheerful, debonair, pleasant **9** easygoing **10** untroubled **12** happy-go-lucky, lighthearted

Joel
means: 12 Jehovah is God
father: 4 Nebo **6** Samuel **7** Azariah,
Pedaiah, Pethuel
brother: 6 Nathan

Joe Palooka
creator: 9 Ham Fisher **11** Tony Di-
Preta
character:
children: 3 Joe **5** Buddy **7** Joannie
friend: 9 Little Max **10** Jerry Leemy
manager: 11 Knobby Walsh
valet: 6 Smokey
wife: 8 Anne Howe
profession: 5 boxer

jog 3 bob, jar, tug **4** jerk, pull, rock,
stir, trot, yank **5** nudge, shake, twist
6 bounce, jiggle, jostle, jounce,
prompt, twitch, wrench **7** actuate, animate **8** activate, energize **9** stimulate

jogger 4 memo **6** layboy, runner **7**
trotter **8** reminder **10** memorandum

Johannesburg
airport: 8 Jan Smuts
area: 4 Rand **9** Transvaal
capital of: 11 South Africa
landmark: 13 Carlton Centre **14** Afri-
cana Museum **16** Union Observatory
17 Zoological Gardens **20** Melrose
Bird Sanctuary
township: 6 Soweto **7** Lenasia **10**
Nancefield
university: 13 Rand Afrikaans, Witwatersrand

John
father: 7 Zebedee
brother: 5 James
son: 5 Peter
called, with brother: 9 Boanerges **13**
sons of thunder
pertaining to John or his writings: 9
Johannine

John Barleycorn
personification of: 6 liquor **7** whiskey

John Brown's Body
author: 19 Stephen Vincent Benet

John Bull
personification of: 7 England **10**
Englishman

John Gabriel Borkman
author: 11 Henrik Ibsen

John Mark *see* **4** Mark

Johnny Belinda
director: 13 Jean Negulesco
cast: 8 Lew Ayres **9** Jane Wyman **15**
Charles Bickford
Oscar for: 7 actress (Wyman)

Johnny Cash Show, The
cast: 9 Jim Varney **10** Howard Mann
11 Carl Perkins, Steve Martin **14**
June Carter Cash, Tennessee Three
15 Statler Brothers **32** Mother May-
belle and the Carter Family

Johnny-come-lately 8 newcomer **9**
latecomer **10** new arrival **11** late arrival

Johnny U
nickname of: 12 Johnny Unitas

Johns, Glynis
born: 8 Pretoria **11** South Africa
roles: 11 Mary Poppins **13** The Sundowners **17** A Little Night Music **26**
Around the World in Eighty Days

Johns, Jasper
born: 9 Augusta GA
artwork: 4 Flag **6** Studio, Target **8**
Watchman **10** Fool's House **12** Device Circle **13** Painted Bronze (Beer
Cans) **14** The Barber's Tree **19** Target with Four Faces **22** Target with
Plaster Casts

Johnson, Andrew
presidential rank: 11 seventeenth
party: 8 Democrat
state represented: 2 TN
defeated: 5 no one
succeeded upon death of: 7 Lincoln
vice president: 4 none
cabinet:
state: 6 (William Henry) Seward
treasury: 9 (Hugh) McCulloch
war: 7 (Edwin McMasters) Stanton
9 (John McAllister) Schofield
attorney general: 5 (James) Speed
6 (William Maxwell) Evarts **8**
(Henry) Stanbery
navy: 6 (Gideon) Welles
postmaster general: 7 (Alexander
Williams) Randall **8** (William) Dennison
interior: 5 (John Palmer) Usher **6**
(James) Harlan **8** (Orville Hickman) Browning
born: 9 Raleigh NC
died: 16 Carter's Station TN
buried: 13 Greeneville TN
education: 9 no college **12** self-
educated
political career: 8 US Senate **13** vice
president **22** House of Representatives
only president to be: 9 impeached
(1868)
found: 9 not guilty
mayor of: 11 Greeneville (TN)

governor of: 9 Tennessee
civilian career: 6 tailor
military service: 8 Civil War **12** US Volunteers **16** brigadier general
　military governor of: 9 Tennessee
notable events of lifetime/term: 14 Reconstruction
　Purchase: 6 Alaska
father: 5 Jacob
mother: 4 Mary (McDonough)
　stepfather: 15 Turner Dougherty
sibling: 7 William
wife: 5 Eliza (McCardle)
children: 4 Mary **6** Andrew, Martha, Robert **7** Charles

Johnson, Don
born: 10 Flatt Creek (MO)
roles: 7 Melanie **8** Dead-Bang, Paradise **9** Miami Vice, Cease Fire **11** Guilty as Sin **16** In Pursuit of Honor, The Long Hot Summer
wife: 15 Melanie Griffith

Johnson, Earvin
nickname: 5 Magic
sport: 10 basketball
position: 5 guard
team: 16 Los Angeles Lakers

Johnson, Jack (John Arthur)
nickname: 11 Little Artha **14** Galveston Giant
sport: 6 boxing
class: 11 heavyweight

Johnson, Lyndon Baines
nickname: 3 LBJ **15** Landslide Lyndon
presidential rank: 11 thirty-sixth
party: 10 Democratic
state represented: 2 TX
succeeded upon death of: 7 Kennedy
defeated: 4 (Earle Harold) Munn, (Eric) Hass **6** (John) Kasper **7** (Clifton) DeBerry **9** (Barry Morris) Goldwater
vice president: 4 none (first term) **8** (Hubert Horatio) Humphrey
cabinet:
　state: 4 (David Dean) Rusk
　treasury: 4 (Joseph William) Barr **6** (Clarence Douglas) Dillon, (Henry Hamill) Fowler
　defense: 8 (Clark McAdams) Clifford, (Robert Strange) McNamara
　attorney general: 5 (William Ramsey) Clark **7** (Robert Francis) Kennedy **10** (Nicholas deBelleville) Katzenbach
　postmaster general: 6 (Lawrence Francis) O'Brien, (William Marvin) Watson **9** (John Austin) Gronouski
　interior: 5 (Stewart Lee) Udall
　agriculture: 7 (Orville Lothrop) Freeman
　commerce: 5 (Cyrus Rowlett) Smith **6** (John Thomas) Connor, (Luther Hartwell) Hodges **10** (Alexander Buel) Trowbridge
　labor: 5 (William Willard) Wirtz

HEW: 5 (Wilbur Joseph) Cohen **7** (John William) Gardner **10** (Anthony Joseph) Celebrezze
HUD: 4 (Robert Colwell) Wood **6** (Robert Clifton) Weaver
transportation: 4 (Alan Stevenson) Boyd
born: 11 (near) Stonewall TX
died/buried: 13 (near) Johnson City TX
education:
　teachers' college: 19 Southwest Texas State
　law school: 10 Georgetown
religion: 17 Disciples of Christ
vacation spot: 8 LBJ Ranch
author: 15 The Vantage Point
political career: 8 US Senate **13** vice president **24** US House of Representatives
civilian career: 7 teacher
military service: 6 US Navy **10** World War II **11** World War Two
notable events of lifetime/term: 9 race riots **12** Great Society
　act: 11 Civil Rights **12** Voting Rights **19** Economic Opportunity
　assassination of: 14 Robert F Kennedy **18** Martin Luther King Jr
　capture of: 6 Pueblo
　Pueblo captured by: 10 North Korea
　treaty: 23 Nuclear Non-Proliferation
　war: 7 Vietnam **11** Arab-Israeli
father: 7 Sam Ealy
mother: 7 Rebekah (Baines)
siblings: 10 Sam Houston **12** Lucia Huffman **13** Josefa Hermine, Rebekah Luruth
wife: 7 Claudia (Alta Taylor)
　nickname: 8 Lady Bird
children: 9 Lynda Bird **10** Luci Baines
First Lady:
　responsible for: 24 Highway Beautification Act
　author: 16 A White House Diary

Johnson, Philip Cortelyou
architect of: 10 Glass House (New Canaan CT), Wiley House (New Canaan CT) **12** Hodgson House (New Canaan CT) **13** Pennzoil Place (Houston TX) **14** Bolssonas House (New Canaan CT) **16** Amon Carter Museum (Ft Worth TX) **17** Sheldon Art Gallery (Lincoln NE) **18** A T and T Headquarters (NYC), Kline Science Center (Yale) **19** New York State Theater (Lincoln Center)

Johnson, Samuel
author of: 8 Rasselas, The Idler **18** The Lives of the Poets **22** The Vanity of Human Wishes **30** Dictionary of the English Language

Johnson, Walter
nickname: 8 Big Train
sport: 8 baseball

position: 7 pitcher
team: 18 Washington Senators

John the Baptist
father: 9 Zechariah
mother: 9 Elizabeth
descendant of: 5 Aaron
precurser of: 5 Jesus **10** the Messiah

joie de vivre 11 joy of living **19** delight in being alive

join 3 hug, mix **4** abut, ally, band, bind, fuse, glue, link, meet, pool **5** affix, brush, chain, enter, graze, marry, merge, paste, reach, skirt, stick, touch, unify, unite **6** adjoin, attach, bridge, cement, cohere, couple, fasten, scrape, solder, splice **7** combine, connect, verge on **8** border on, enlist in, enroll in, federate, hold fast **9** associate, cooperate, syndicate **10** amalgamate, fraternize **11** confederate, consolidate **12** conglomerate

joined 3 met, wed **4** tied **5** bound, fused, glued, mated, yoked **6** allied, bonded, linked, merged, paired, seamed, united, welded **7** coupled, married, related, spliced **8** attached, cemented, combined, enlisted, fastened **9** bracketed, connected **10** associated, hand-in- hand, integrated **11** hand-in-glove

join forces 4 ally **5** merge, unite **6** league, team up **7** combine **8** coalesce **9** affiliate, cooperate **11** consolidate **12** band together

joint 4 hock, knee, knot, link **5** elbow, hinge, nexus **6** allied, common, mutual, shared, united **7** knuckle, unified **8** combined, communal, coupling, junction, juncture **9** associate, community, conjoined, corporate, unanimous **10** associated, collective, connection, hand-in- hand, like-minded **11** coalitional, conjunctive, cooperative **12** articulation, consolidated **13** collaborative
　kind:
　　ball and socket: 3 hip **8** shoulder
　　fused: 5 skull **11** base of spine
　　hinged: 4 knee **5** elbow
　　unfused: 3 hip, jaw **4** knee **5** elbow **8** shoulder

joint action 7 concert **8** teamwork **11** cooperating, cooperation, give-and-take **13** collaboration, participation

joint effort 7 concert **8** teamwork **11** cooperation **13** collaboration

jointly 8 arm in arm, in common, in unison, mutually, together, unitedly **10** conjointly, hand-in-hand, side by side **12** collectively **13** in association, in conjunction

join together 3 wed **4** fuse, weld **5** marry, unify, unite **6** solder **9** integrate **10** amalgamate **11** consolidate, incorporate

join up 6 enlist, enroll, sign up **9** volunteer

joist 4 beam **5** brace **6** timber **7** support

joke 3 gag, pun, wit **4** butt, dupe, fool, gibe, goof, gull, jape, jest, josh, lark, mock, quip **5** antic, caper, cinch, clown, farce, prank, put-on, roast, tease, trick **6** banter, bon mot, deride, frolic, gambol, gibe at, jeer at, parody, satire, take in, target, trifle, whimsy **7** buffoon, bumpkin, chortle, lampoon, laugh at, nothing, scoff at, smile at, snicker **8** anecdote, badinage, poohpooh, pushover, repartee, ridicule, town fool, travesty **9** burlesque, diversion, horseplay, simpleton, wisecrack, witticism **10** pleasantry **11** horse around, monkeyshine **13** facetiousness, laughingstock

joker 3 wag, wit **4** snag, trap, zany **5** catch, clown, hitch, mimic, rider, snare, trick **6** jester, madcap **7** codicil, pitfall, punster **8** addendum, comedian, funnyman, humorist **10** subterfuge, supplement **11** wisecracker
French: 7 farceur

jokester 3 wag **5** comic, cutup, joker **8** comedian **9** prankster

Joliba *see* **5** Niger

Joliot-Curie, Frederic
field: 9 chemistry
nationality: 6 French
discovered: 23 artificial radioisotopes
awarded: 10 Nobel Prize
wife: 16 Irene Joliot-Curie

Joliot-Curie, Irene
field: 7 physics
nationality: 6 French
discovered: 23 artificial radioisotopes
awarded: 10 Nobel Prize
husband: 14 Frederic Joliot
father: 11 Pierre Curie
mother: 11 Marie Curie

jollity 3 fun **4** glee, play, romp **5** cheer, mirth, revel, sport **6** frolic, gaiety **7** revelry, whoopee **8** hilarity **9** amusement, festivity, jocundity, joviality, merriment, pleasure **10** jocularity **12** merrymaking **12** conviviality

jolly 3 gay **5** droll, funny, happy, merry **6** jocund, jovial **7** gleeful, jocular, playful **8** cheerful, mirthful, sportive **9** fun-loving **10** delightful, rollicking **12** high-spirited

Jolly Roger 11 pirate's flag **18** skull and crossbones

jolt 3 bob, jar, jog **4** bump, jerk, jump, stun **5** lurch, quake, shake, shock, start, throw, upset **6** bobble, bounce, jiggle, joggle, jostle, jounce, quiver, trauma, twitch **7** disturb, perturb, setback, shake up, shaking, startle **8** convulse, reversal **9** agitation, take aback **11** thunderbolt

Joltin' Joe
nickname of: 11 Joe DiMaggio

Jonah
father: 7 Amittai

swallowed by: 9 large fish
preached in: 7 Nineveh
hometown: 10 Gathhepher

Jonathan
means: 11 Jehovah gave
father: 4 Jada, Saul **6** Joiada, Kereah **8** Abiathar
friend: 5 David
son: 9 Meribbaal **12** Mephibosheth

Jonathan Livingston Seagull
author: 11 Richard Bach

Jonathan Wild
author: 13 Henry Fielding

Jones, Carolyn
born: 10 Amarillo TX
roles: 8 Morticia **15** The Addams Family

Jones, Inigo
architect of: 11 Queen's House (Greenwich) **14** Banqueting Hall (Whitehall Palace, London)
restoration: 16 St Paul's Cathedral

Jones, James
author of: 7 Whistle **14** The Thin Red Line **15** Some Came Running **18** From Here to Eternity

Jones, James Earl
born: 11 Arkabutla MS
roles: 6 The Man **7** Othello **8** Star Wars **15** The Emperor Jones **17** The Great White Hope
voice of: 10 Darth Vader

Jones, John Paul
served in: 11 Russian navy **16** Revolutionary War **21** British merchant marine
commander of ship: 6 Ranger **10** Providence **15** Bonhomme Richard
defeated ship: 7 Serapis
saying: 23 "I have not yet begun to fight"

Jones, Shirley
husband: 11 Jack Cassidy, Marty Ingels
born: 10 Smithton PA
roles: 8 Carousel, Oklahoma **11** Elmer Gantry, The Music Man **18** The Partridge Family

Jones, Tom
born: 5 Wales **10** Pontypridd
songs: 7 Delilah **9** She's a Lady **11** Thunderball **13** Love Me Tonight **15** Letter to Lucille **16** What's New Pussycat **21** Green Green Grass of Home

Jong, Erica
author of: 5 Fanny **12** Fear of Flying **18** At the Edge of the Body **20** How to Save Your Own Life

jonquil 4 bulb, lily **8** daffodil **9** narcissus

Jonson, Ben
author of: 6 The Fox **7** Sejanus, Volpone **11** A Tale of a Tub **12** The Alchemist **15** Bartholomew Fair **18** Every Man in His Humo(u)r **21**

Every Man out of His Humo(u)r **23** Epicene or the Silent Woman

Jordan
other name: 24 Hashemite Kingdom of Jordan
capital/largest city: 5 Amman
ancient name: 12 Philadelphia
others: 4 Krak, Ma'an, Salt **5** Agaba, Ariha, Irbid, Jenin, Karak, Kerak, Sarga, Zarga, Zerke **6** Bethel, Hebron, Jarash, Jerash, Madaba, Nablus, Ramtha **7** Al-Agaba, Bethany, El-Kerak, El Zerga, Jericho, Kirmoab, Nabulus, Samaria **8** Al-Khalil, Ram Allah **9** Bethlehem, Jerusalem
school: 7 yarmouk
division: 8 East Bank, West Bank **11** Transjordan
ancient state: 4 Edom, Moab **5** Ammon, Judah **6** Gilead
head of state: 11 King Hussein
wife: 4 Noor (nee Lisa Walaby)
monetary unit: 4 fils **5** dinar
mountain: 3 Hor **4** Nebo **5** Bukka, Dabab **6** Ataiba, Gilead, Mubrak
highest point: 9 Jabal Ramm, Jebel Ramm
river: 6 Jordan, Yarmuk **11** Nahr-az-Zarga
sea: 3 Red **4** Dead **7** Galilee **13** Mediterranean
physical feature:
desert: 6 Syria
gulf: 5 Aqaba
plateau: 11 Transjordan
valley: 4 Ghor **9** Great Rift
wind: 7 Khamsin
people: 4 Arab, Kurd **7** Bedouin, Checher **8** Armenian, Assyrian **10** Circassian **11** Palestinian
ancient: 8 Armonite **9** Nabataean
ruler: 5 Talal **6** Faisal, Greeks, Romans **7** Hussein **8** Abdullah, Selucidas **9** Crusaders **10** Ibn Hussein, Nabataeans **12** Ottoman Turks **18** Abdullah Ibn Hussein
tribe: 5 Qaysi **6** Yamani
language: 6 Arabic
religion: 5 Islam **13** Greek Orthodox
place:
canal: 8 East Gher
ruins: 5 Ajlun, Petra **6** Jarash **7** Al Karak
feature:
headdress: 8 kaffiyeh
village headman: 7 mukhtar
village square: 5 sahah
food:
dessert: 7 baklava
pastry: 7 katayif

Jordan, Robert
character in: 19 For Whom the Bell Tolls
author: 9 Hemingway

Jormungandr
also: 10 Jormungand **11** Iormungandr **14** Midgard Serpent
origin: 12 Scandinavian

form: 7 serpent
father: 4 Loki
mother: 9 Angerboda, Angrbodha, Angurboda
brother: 6 Fenrir, Fenris
sister: 3 Hel
wrapped around: 5 world
killed by: 4 Thor
death place: 6 Vigrid
killed: 4 Thor

Jo's Boys
author: 15 Louisa May Alcott
sequel to: 11 Little Women

Joseph
father: 4 Bani 5 Aseph, Jacob 10 Mattathias
mother: 6 Rachel
brother: 3 Dan, Gad 4 Levi 5 Asher, Judah 6 Reuben, Simeon 7 Zebulun 8 Benjamin, Issachar, Naphtali
wife: 4 Mary 7 Asenath
stepson: 5 Jesus
also called: 20 Barsabbas of Arimathea 21 Barsabbas of Arimathaea
buried: 5 Jesus
slave of: 8 Potiphar

Joseph Andrews
author: 13 Henry Fielding
character: 5 Fanny 9 Lady Booby 11 Mrs Slipslop, Parson Adams, Peter Pounce 13 Pamela Andrews

josh 3 guy, kid, rag, rib 4 dish, haze, jape, jest, jive, joke, quiz, razz, ride, twit 5 chaff, jolly, put on, roast, tease 6 banter, needle 8 ridicule

Joshua
means: 18 Jehovah is salvation
father: 3 Nun
succeeded: 5 Moses
captured: 7 Jericho, Lachish
hid spies: 5 Rahab

jostle 3 jab 4 bump, butt, poke, prod, push 5 crowd, elbow, shove 7 collide 8 shoulder 10 hit against, run against 12 knock against

jot 3 bit, dot 4 iota, list, mite, note, snip, whit 5 enter, speck, trace 6 record, trifle 7 modicum, one iota, put down, set down, smidgen, snippet 8 flyspeck, particle, register, scribble, take down 9 scintilla

Jo the crossing sweeper
character in: 10 Bleak House
author: 7 Dickens

jotting 4 memo, note 6 doodle 8 scribble 10 memorandum, scribbling

Jotun
origin: 12 Scandinavian
form: 5 giant
conflicts with: 4 gods
enemy: 4 Asar 5 Aesir

Joule, James Prescott
field: 7 physics
nationality: 7 British
established law of: 20 conservation of energy
named for him: 10 unit of work

jounce 3 bob 6 bounce 7 rebound 8 ricochet

Jourdain, Monsieur
character in: 21 The Bourgeois Gentleman 22 Le Bourgeois Gentilhomme
author: 7 Moliere

Jourdan, Louis
real name: 11 Louis Gendre
born: 6 France 9 Marseille
roles: 4 Gigi 6 Can Can 9 Octopussy 15 The Paradine Case 23 Three Coins in the Fountain 24 Letter from an Unknown Woman

journal 3 log 5 album, daily, diary, paper, sheet 6 annual, ledger, memoir, record, weekly 7 almanac, daybook, gazette, history, logbook, monthly, tabloid 8 calendar, magazine, notebook, register, yearbook 9 chronicle, newspaper, quarterly, scrapbook 10 chronology, confession, memorandum, memory book, periodical, record book 11 account book, daily record, publication 13 autobiography

journalism 15 the fourth estate

journalist 6 author, editor, writer 7 byliner, diarist, newsman 8 reporter 9 columnist, newswoman 12 newspaperman 13 correspondent 14 newspaperwoman

Journal of the Plague Year, A
author: 11 Daniel Defoe

journey 3 fly, way 4 roam, rove, sail, tour, trek, trip, wend 5 jaunt, quest, route, tramp 6 course, cruise, flight, junket, outing, ramble, roving, travel, voyage, wander 7 circuit, meander, odyssey, passage, transit 8 divagate, navigate, sightsee, vagabond 9 excursion, itinerary, take a trip, wandering 10 divagation, expedition, pilgrimage 11 peregrinate 13 peregrination

Journey Into Fear
author: 10 Eric Ambler

journey's end 4 goal 9 objective 11 destination

joust 4 tilt 5 combat, jostle 7 contend, contest, tourney 8 run a tilt 10 contention, tournament

Jove see 7 Jupiter

jovial 3 gay 5 jolly, merry, sunny 6 blithe, cheery, hearty, jocose, jocund 7 buoyant, gleeful, jocular, playful, zestful 8 cheerful, humorous, laughing, mirthful, sportive 9 convivial, fun-loving, hilarious 10 delightful, frolicsome, rollicking

joviality 3 fun 4 glee 5 cheer, gaity, mirth 7 delight, jollity, revelry 8 buoyancy 9 jocundity, merriment 10 joyfulness, liveliness 11 high spirits

jowl 3 jaw 5 cheek, chops 6 muzzle 8 mandible

joy 3 gem 4 glee 5 jewel, pride, prize 6 gaiety 7 delight, ecstasy, elation, rap-

ture 8 gladness, pleasure, treasure 9 enjoyment, happiness 10 excitement, exultation, jubilation 11 contentment, delectation 12 cheerfulness, exhilaration, satisfaction
goddess of: 6 Hathor

Joyce, James
author of: 7 Ulysses 9 Dubliners 13 Finnegans Wake 31 A Portrait of the Artist as a Young Man

joyful 4 glad, rosy 5 happy 6 bright, elated 7 blessed, pleased 8 cheerful, ecstatic, exultant, gladsome, jubilant, pleasing 9 delighted, full of joy, overjoyed 10 delightful, enraptured, gratifying, heartening 11 pleasurable, transported 12 heartwarming

joyless 3 sad 4 glum, grim 5 black 6 dismal, gloomy, morbid, woeful 7 doleful, forlorn, unhappy 8 dejected, desolate, dolorous, downcast, mournful 9 cheerless, depressed, sorrowful, woebegone 10 despondent, in the dumps, lugubrious, melancholy 11 downhearted, pessimistic 12 disconsolate, heavyhearted 14 down in the mouth

joy of living
French: 11 joie de vivre

Joy of Sex, The
author: 11 Alex Comfort

joyous 3 gay 4 glad 5 happy, merry 7 festive, gleeful 8 cheerful, gladsome, mirthful 9 rapturous, wonderful 10 delightful, gratifying, heartening 11 pleasurable 12 heartwarming, lighthearted

joyousness 4 glee 8 gladness 9 happiness, merriment 10 blitheness, exuberance 11 high spirits 16 lightheartedness

jubilant 3 gay 4 glad 5 happy, jolly, merry 6 blithe, cheery, elated, enrapt, joyful, joyous 7 buoyant, charmed, gleeful, pleased, radiant, smiling 8 cheerful, ecstatic, exultant, gladsome, laughing, mirthful 9 delighted, delirious, exuberant, gladdened, gratified, overjoyed, rapturous, rejoicing, rhapsodic 10 blithesome, captivated, enraptured 11 exhilarated, intoxicated, tickled pink 12 happy as a lark, lighthearted 13 in high spirits

jubilation 5 bliss 9 rejoicing 11 celebration 12 exhilaration

jubilee 2 do 4 bash, fete, gala 5 blast, party 6 frolic, revels 7 blowout, holiday, revelry, shindig 8 festival, wingding 9 festivity 10 jubilation, observance 11 anniversary, celebration, merrymaking 12 conviviality 13 commemoration

Judah
father: 5 Jacob
mother: 4 Leah
brother: 3 Dan, Gad 4 Levi 5 Asher, Judah 6 Joseph, Reuben, Simeon 8

Benjamin, Issachar, Naphtali
sister: 5 Dinah
wife: 5 Shuah
son: 2 Er **4** Onan **5** Perez, Zerah **6** Baruch, Shelah
daughter-in-law: 5 Tamar
last king of: 8 Zedekiah
descendant of: 8 Judahite

Judah, tribes of *see* **14** Israel, tribes of

Judas
brother: 5 James
also called: 8 Thaddeus
disciple of: 5 Jesus

Judas Iscariot 8 betrayer
disciple of: 5 Jesus
betrayed: 5 Jesus
replaced by: 8 Matthias

Jude 7 apostle
brother: 5 James

Jude the Obscure
author: 11 Thomas Hardy
character: 10 Jude Fawley **12** Arabella Donn, Sue Bridehead **14** Drusilla Fawley **16** Little Father Time **17** Richard Phillotson

judge 3 try **4** deem, find, hear, rank, rate **5** fancy, gauge, guess, infer, juror, value, weigh **6** assess, assume, censor, critic, decide, deduce, expert, reckon, regard, review, rule on, settle, size up, umpire **7** adjudge, analyze, arbiter, believe, conduct, discern, imagine, justice, referee, resolve, suppose, surmise **8** appraise, assessor, conclude, consider, estimate, official, reviewer **9** appraiser, arbitrate, ascertain, authority, determine, evaluator, moderator **10** adjudicate, arbitrator, conjecture, magistrate **11** adjudicator, connoisseur, distinguish **12** pass sentence

judgment, judgement 4 view **5** sense, taste **6** acumen, belief, decree, ruling **7** finding, opinion, verdict **8** decision, estimate, sentence **9** appraisal, deduction, valuation **10** assessment, conclusion, conviction, discretion, perception, persuasion, shrewdness **11** arbitration, discernment, percipience **14** discrimination, perceptiveness

Judgment at Nuremberg
director: 13 Stanley Kramer
cast: 11 Judy Garland **12** Spencer Tracy **13** Burt Lancaster **14** Richard Widmark, William Shatner **15** Marlene Dietrich, Montgomery Clift **16** Maximilian Schell (Oscar)

Judgment Day 8 doomsday **13** end of the world **14** day of reckoning **15** the Last Judgment

Judgment Day
author: 13 James T Farrell

Judgment of Paris *see* **5** Paris

judicial 5 legal **8** imposing, juristic, majestic, official **9** magistral **11** magisterial **13** distinguished

judiciary 5 bench, court **11** court system

judicious 4 just, sage, wise **5** acute, sober, sound **6** astute, shrewd **7** knowing, politic, prudent, tactful **8** sensible **9** sagacious **10** diplomatic, discerning, percipient, reasonable, reflective, thoughtful **11** levelheaded **13** perspicacious **14** discriminating

judiciousness 4 tact **6** acumen, wisdom **8** prudence, sagacity **9** good sense **10** discretion **11** discernment, percipience **12** perspicacity **14** discrimination

Judique, Mrs Tanis
character in: 7 Babbitt
author: 5 Lewis

Judith
husband: 4 Esau
killed: 10 Holofernes

Judith Paris
author: 11 Hugh Walpole

jug 3 jar, urn **4** ewer **5** crock, stein **6** bottle, carafe, flagon, vessel **7** pitcher, tankard **8** decanter, demijohn **9** container

juggle 4 redo **5** alter **6** modify **7** falsify **8** disguise, fool with **9** keep aloft **10** manipulate, meddle with, reorganize, tamper with, tinker with **12** misrepresent

juggler 5 cheat **6** jester **8** conjuror, deceiver, jongleur, magician, shuffler **15** prestidigitator

Juice
nickname of: 9 O J Simpson

juicy 3 wet **4** lush, racy **5** fluid, lurid, moist, pulpy, runny, sappy, spicy, vivid **6** fluent, liquid, risque, watery **7** flowing, graphic **8** colorful, dripping, exciting, luscious **9** succulent, thrilling **10** intriguing **11** captivating, fascinating, picturesque, provocative, sensational, tantalizing

Jules and Jim
director: 16 Francois Truffaut
cast: 10 Henri Serre **11** Marie Dubois, Oskar Werner **12** Jeanne Moreau

Julia
character in: 20 Two Gentlemen of Verona
author: 11 Shakespeare

Julia
character: 10 Corey Baker, Eddie Edson, Julia Baker **11** Hannah Yarby **14** Earl J Waggedorn, Marie Waggedorn **15** Dr Morton Chegley
cast: 10 Lloyd Nolan, Marc Copage **11** Betty Beaird, Michael Link **12** Eddie Quillan, Lurene Tuttle, Paul Winfield **14** Diahann Carroll

Julia
director: 13 Fred Zinnemann
based on story by: 14 Lillian Hellman (Pentimento)
cast: 9 Jane Fonda (Lillian Hellman) **11** Hal Holbrook **12** Jason Robards (Dashiell Hammett) **15** Vanessa Redgrave (Julia) **16** Maximilian Schell
Oscar for: 12 screenwriter **15** supporting actor (Robards) **17** supporting actress (Redgrave)

Julius Caesar
author: 18 William Shakespeare
character: 6 Brutus (Marcus Brutus), Portia **7** Cassius (Gaius Cassius) **9** Calpurnia **10** Mark Antony (Marcus Antonius)
director: 17 Joseph L Mankiewicz
cast: 10 James Mason **11** Deborah Kerr, Greer Garson, John Gielgud **12** Edmond O'Brien, Louis Calhern, Marlon Brando

July
flower: 8 larkspur **9** water lily
French: 7 Juillet
holiday: 11 Bastille Day (14), Dominion Day (1) **15** Independence Day (4) **16** Saint Swithin's Day (15)
gem: 4 ruby
German: 4 Juli
Italian: 6 Luglio
number of days: 9 thirty-one
origin of name: 12 Julius Caesar
place in year:
Gregorian: 7 seventh
Roman: 5 fifth
Spanish: 5 Julio
Zodiac sign: 3 Leo **6** Cancer

jumble 3 mix **4** heap, mess, olio, stew **5** bunch, chaos, mix up, pitch, snarl **6** ball up, medley, muddle, pile up, tangle, tumble **7** clutter, farrago, melange, mixture, scatter **8** disarray, mishmash **9** aggregate, confusion, patchwork, potpourri **10** hodgepodge, miscellany, salmagundi **11** gallimaufry **12** accumulation **14** conglomeration

jumbled 5 messy **7** chaotic, mixed up, snarled, tangled **8** confused **9** cluttered, illogical **10** disjointed, incoherent **11** disarranged **12** disconnected, disorganized

jumbo 4 huge, vast **5** giant **6** mighty **7** immense, mammoth, titanic **8** colossal, enormous, gigantic, towering **9** cyclopean, monstrous, oversized **10** monumental, stupendous **11** elephantine, mountainous

jump 3 hop **4** buck, leap, pass, skip **5** boost, bound, pitch, start, surge, vault, wince **6** ambush, attack, blench, bounce, flinch, gambol, go over, hurdle, prance, recoil, spring, switch, upturn, zoom up **7** advance, barrier, digress, maunder, overrun, upsurge **8** fall upon, obstacle **9** barricade, increment, skyrocket **10** impediment **11** obstruction **12** augmentation

jumper 4 frog, sled, toad **5** dress, horse, shirt, smock **6** blouse, hopper, jacket, leaper **7** overall **8** coverall, kangaroo

jump for joy 5 exult **7** rejoice

jumpy 5 nervy, shaky **6** goosey, uneasy **7** alarmed, anxious, fidgety, fretful, jittery, nervous, panicky, twitchy, uptight **8** aflutter, agitated, fluttery, skittish **9** trembling, twitching **10** frightened **12** apprehensive

junction 6 linkup **7** conflux, joining **10** confluence, crossroads **11** concurrence, convergence, interchange **12** intersection

juncture 4 pass, seam **5** joint **6** crisis, linkup, moment **7** closure, joining, meeting **8** interval, occasion **10** confluence, connection **11** convergence, point in time **12** intersection **13** critical point

June
  characteristic: 8 weddings
  event: 12 Midsummer Day (24), Midsummer Eve (23) **14** summer solstice (21)
  flower: 4 rose
  French: 4 Juin
  gem: 5 pearl **9** moonstone **11** alexandrite
  German: 4 Juni
  holiday: 7 Flag Day (14) **10** Father's Day (third Sunday) **13** Kamehameha Day (11) **22** Jefferson Davis' birthday (3)
  Italian: 6 Giugno
  number of days: 6 thirty
  origin of name: 4 Juno (Roman goddess) **6** Junius (Roman clan) **8** juniores (youths)
  place in year:
    Gregorian: 5 sixth
    Roman: 6 fourth
  saying: 24 What is so rare as a day in June
  Spanish: 5 Junio
  Zodiac sign: 6 Cancer, Gemini

jungle 4 bush, wild **5** woods **10** rain forest, wilderness **11** undergrowth **12** swampy forest, virgin forest

Jungle, The
  author: 13 Upton Sinclair
  character: 3 Ona **5** Jonas **6** Marija **8** Elzbieta **12** Jurgis Rudkus **13** Antanas Rudkus
  criticism of: 19 meat-packing industry

Jungle Books, The
  author: 14 Rudyard Kipling
  character: 3 Kaa **5** Akela, Baloo, Hathi **6** Buldeo, Messua, Mowgli **8** Bagheera **9** Shere Khan **11** Gray Brother

Jungle Jim
  creator: 11 Alex Raymond
  character: 4 Joan, Kolu

junior 5 later, lower, minor, newer **6** lesser **7** younger **8** inferior **9** secondary **11** subordinate

juniper 9 Juniperus

varieties: 4 ashe, plum **5** Greek, Irish, shore **6** common, ground, needle, Polish, Sierra, Syrian **7** African, incense, prickly, Sargent **8** creeping, drooping, mountain, red-berry, Waukegan **9** alligator, blue-spire, Himalayan, prostrate **10** California **11** cherrystone **12** Canary Island, sweetfruited **13** Rocky Mountain

junk 4 dump **5** scrap, trash, waste **6** debris, litter, refuse **7** clutter, discard, garbage, rubbish, rummage **8** castoffs, oddments, throw out **9** dispose of, throw away **11** odds and ends

junket 4 tour, trip **7** journey **9** excursion

Juno
  origin: 5 Roman
  queen of: 6 heaven
  father: 6 Saturn
  brother: 7 Jupiter
  husband: 7 Jupiter
  son: 4 Mars
  protectress of: 5 women **8** marriage
  epithet: 6 Lucina, Moneta **7** Curitis, Pronuba, Sospita
  festival: 10 Matronalia
  corresponds to: 4 Hera, Here

Juno and the Paycock
  author: 10 Sean O'Casey

junta 5 cabal **7** council **9** committee **18** military government

Jupe, Sissy
  character in: 9 Hard Times
  author: 7 Dickens

Jupiter
  also: 4 Jove
  god of: 5 light **7** heavens, weather **9** lightning **11** thunderbolt
  epithet: 5 Ultor **7** Elicius, Pluvius
  corresponds to: 4 Zeus

Jupiter
  position: 5 fifth
  satellite: 2 Io **6** Europa **8** Amalthea, Callisto, Ganymede
  characteristic: 7 red spot

Jura 11 Swiss canton **13** mountain range

Jurassic period
  dinosaur from: 10 Diplodocus **11** Apatosaurus, Stegosaurus **12** Brontosaurus, Camarasaurus, Camptosaurus, Ceratosaurus, Megalosaurus **13** Brachiosaurus, Compsognathus, Ornitholestes

Jurgen
  author: 17 James Branch Cabell

Jurgens, Curt
  also: 11 Curd Jurgens
  born: 6 Munich **7** Germany
  roles: 12 The Blue Angel **16** The Spy Who Loved Me

jurisdiction 3 say **4** area, beat, rule, sway, zone **5** field, range, reach, scope **6** bounds, domain, sphere **7** circuit, command, compass, control, quarter **8** district, dominion, hegem-

ony, latitude, precinct, province **9** authority, bailiwick **10** legal right **11** prerogative

jurist 5 judge **6** lawyer **7** counsel, justice **8** advocate, attorney **9** barrister, counselor, solicitor **10** magistrate **12** legal adviser **13** attorney-at-law

jury 5 panel, peers **6** assize, twelve **9** committee, makeshift, veniremen

jury-rigged 9 improvised, makeshift, temporary

jus 3 law **5** right

jus civile 8 civil law

jus gentium 12 law of nations

jus naturale 11 law of nature

jus sanguinis 12 right of blood (law) citizenship of child is same as: **7** parents

jus soli 11 right of land, right of soil (law) citizenship of child based on place of: **5** birth

just 3 but, due **4** fair, firm, good, only, sane **5** fully, moral, quite, solid, sound **6** at most, barely, decent, hardly, honest, lately, merely, proper, simply, strong, worthy **7** condign, ethical, exactly, fitting, logical, merited, only now, upright **8** adequate, balanced, deserved, entirely, narrowly, recently, scarcely, sensible, suitable, unbiased **9** befitting, blameless, equitable, honorable, impartial, justified, objective, perfectly, precisely, reputable, righteous, unbigoted, uncorrupt **10** aboveboard, absolutely, acceptable, completely, evenhanded, fair-minded, high-minded, no more than, nothing but, not long ago, principled, reasonable, scrupulous, upstanding **11** appropriate, justifiable, trustworthy, well-founded **12** conscionable, open to reason, unprejudiced, well-grounded **13** conscientious, disinterested, dispassionate

just about 6 almost, around, barely, nearly **7** close to **10** not far from **12** on the point of **13** approximately

Just Above My Head
  author: 12 James Baldwin

just a moment ago
  French: 11 tout a l'heure

justice 5 honor, right, truth **6** amends, equity, the law, virtue **7** honesty, payment, penalty, probity, redress **8** fair play, fairness, goodness, legality **9** atonement, integrity, rightness **10** correction, lawfulness, legitimacy, reparation **11** just desserts, proper cause, uprightness **12** chastisement, compensation, equitability, remuneration, satisfaction **13** due punishment, equitableness, justification, righteousness **17** constitutionality
  god of: 7 Forsete, Forseti
  goddess of: 4 Dice, Dike **6** Astrea **7** Astraea

Justice
   author: 14 John Galsworthy
Justice Clement
   character in: 19 Every Man in His
      Humour
   author: 6 Jonson
justice to all
   Latin: 15 justitia omnibus
   motto of: 18 District of Columbia
justifiable 9 excusable **10** defensible
   11 explanatory, extenuating, support
   able
justification 5 alibi **6** excuse **7** apology, defense, pretext, support **8** sanction **10** accounting, adjustment, validation **11** explanation, vindication **12**
   confirmation **13** rectification **14** reconciliation

justification for existence
   French: 11 raison d'etre
justify 6 back up, defend, excuse, uphold **7** bear out, confirm, explain,
   support, sustain, warrant **8** sanction,
   validate **9** vindicate **10** account for,
   prove right
justitia omnibus 12 justice to all
   motto of: 18 District of Columbia
just now
   French: 11 tout a l'heure
just the same 6 anyhow, anyway **12**
   nevertheless
just the thing 7 apropos **8** suitable
   11 appropriate **12** exactly right
Justus *see* **5** Titus
jut 5 bulge **6** beetle, extend **7** poke out,
   project **8** overhang, protrude, shoot

out, stand out, stick out **13** thrust
forward
jute 19 Corchorus capsularis
   varieties: 5 Bimli, China, Tossa,
      white **7** bastard **10** Bimlipatum
juvenile 5 child, minor, young, youth
   6 boyish, callow, infant, junior **7** girlish **8** childish, immature, teenager,
   youthful **9** childlike, pubescent, stripling, youngster **10** adolescent, sophomoric **15** unsophisticated
juxtaposed 6 next to **8** adjacent,
   touching **9** proximate **10** contiguous,
   side by side **12** conterminous
juxtaposition 5 touch **7** balance, contact **8** contrast, nearness **9** adjacency,
   proximity **10** apposition, contiguity

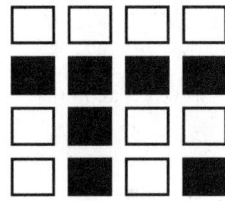

K
character in: **9** The Castle
author: **5** Kafka

Ka
origin: **8** Egyptian
form: **6** spirit
trait: **11** immortality

kabob 5 cabab, cobob, kabab, kebab, kebob **7** shaslik **8** shashlik **9** shashlick

Kabul
capital of: **11** Afghanistan

Kafka, Franz
author of: **7** Amerika **8** The Trial **9** The Castle **16** The Metamorphosis

kahlua
type: **6** brandy
origin: **6** Mexico
flavor: **6** coffee
with rum: **10** Black Maria
with tequila: **9** Brave Bull
with vodka: **12** Black Russian

Kahn, Albert
architect of: **15** River Rouge Plant **17** Highland Park Plant **20** Athletic Club Building (Detroit) **21** General Motors Building (Detroit)

Kahn, Louis Isadore
architect of: **16** Kimbell Art Museum (Ft Worth TX) **23** Yale Center for British Art **24** Yale University Art Gallery **28** Phillips Exeter Academy Library (NH) **31** Richards Medical Research Building (U of PA) **33** Salk Institute for Biological Studies (La Jolla CA)

Kahn, Madeline
born: **8** Boston MA
roles: **5** Cosby **9** Paper Moon **10** What's Up Doc? **14** Blazing Saddles **17** Young Frankenstein

kaiser 5 ruler **7** emperor, Wilhelm **8** autocrat

kakemono 6 scroll **13** hanging object

kale 16 Brassica oleracea (Acephala Group)
varieties: **3** sea **4** Ruvo, tall, tree **6** Indian, Scotch **7** cabbage, Chinese, Italian, kitchen **8** Siberian **9** flowering, Tronchuda **10** decorative, ornamental, Portuguese **13** dwarf Siberian **16** ornamental-leaved

kaleidoscopic 6 mobile, motley **7** protean **8** shifting, unstable, variable **9** checkered **10** changeable, variegated **11** fluctuating, many colored, rainbowlike, vacillating **12** ever-changing

Kaleva 8 folk hero
origin: **7** Finnish **8** Estonian

Kali
also: **3** Uma **5** Durga **7** Parvati
husband: **4** Siva **5** Shiva
festival: **6** dewali
goddess of: **5** death **7** disease

Kalimantan see **6** Borneo

Kalki
author: **9** Gore Vidal

Kampala
capital of: **6** Uganda

Kampuchea see **8** Cambodia

Kandinsky, Wassily (Vasily)
born: **6** Moscow, Russia
artwork: **7** Striped **8** Twilight **10** Black Lines **11** Impressions **12** Blue Mountain (no 84), Compositions, Violet Orange **13** Black Relation **14** Improvisations **15** Capricious Forms **17** Bavarian Mountains, The Street in Murnau **23** Painting with White Border

Kanga
character in: **13** Winnie the Pooh
author: **5** Milne
child: **3** Roo

kangaroo
young: **4** joey
group of: **3** mob **5** troop

Kaniengehaga see **6** Mohawk

Kansas
abbreviation: **2** KS **4** Kans
nickname: **5** Wheat **9** Jayhawker, Sunflower **15** Garden of the West
capital: **6** Topeka
largest city: **7** Wichita
others: **4** Hays, Iola **5** Colby, Dodge **6** Salina **7** Abilene, Chanute, Emporia, Liberal **8** Atchison, Lawrence **9** Great Bend **10** Belleville, Hutchinson, Kansas City **11** Coffeeville, Leavenworth **12** Junction City
college: **5** Baker, Tabor **7** Bethany **8** Sterling, Washburn
explorer: **8** Coronado
feature: **16** Eisenhower Center
  fort: **5** Riley, Scott
  Indian training school: **16** Haskell Institute
  penitentiary: **11** Leavenworth
  reservoir: **11** Tuttle Creek
tribe: **3** Kaw **4** Pani **5** Kansa, Kiowa, Osage **6** Pawnee **7** Arapaho, Wichita **8** Cheyenne, Comanche, Kickapoo
people: **7** Jayhawk **11** Damon Runyon **13** Amelia Earhart, Karl Menninger **14** Walter Chrysler **15** Edgar Lee Masters
lake: **6** Cheney, Kerwin, Neosho **7** Milford
land rank: **10** fourteenth
mountain:
  highest point: **9** Sunflower
physical feature:
  plains: **5** Great, Osage
president: **17** Dwight D Eisenhower
river: **3** Kaw **6** Kansas **8** Arkansas, Cimarron, Missouri **9** Smoky Hill **10** Republican
state admission: **12** thirty-fourth
state bird: **17** western meadowlark
state flower: **9** sunflower
state motto: **29** To the Stars Through Difficulties
state song: **14** Home on the Range
state tree: **10** cottonwood

Kansas City
baseball team: **6** Royals
football team: **6** Chiefs
landmark: **12** Union Station **22** Nelson-Atkins Art Gallery
river: **6** Kansas **8** Missouri

Kant, Immanuel
author of: **20** Critique of Pure Reason

Kantor, MacKinlay
author of: **13** Andersonville

Karloff, Boris
real name: **17** William Henry Pratt
born: **7** Dulwich, England
roles: **12** Frankenstein

karma 3 act **4** aura, deed, duty, fate, rite **5** force, power **6** action, kismet, spirit **7** destiny **9** vibration

Kasdan, Lawrence
director of: **11** The Big Chill

Kashmiri
language family: **12** Indo-European
branch: **11** Indo-Iranian
group: **5** Indic
spoken in: **5** (northern) India

kashruth, kashrut 7 fitness **17** Jewish dietary laws

Katharina
character in: **19** The Taming of the Shrew
author: **11** Shakespeare

Katmandu, Kathmandu
capital of: **5** Nepal

Katzenjammer Kids
also: 17 Captain and the Kids
creator: 12 Rudolph Dirks
character: 4 Hans **5** Fritz, Momma **10** der Captain **12** der Inspector

Kaufman, George S
author of:
with Edna Ferber: 9 Stage Door **13** Dinner at Eight **14** The Royal Family
with Moss Hart: 15 Once in a Lifetime **20** You Can't Take It with You **21** The Man Who Came to Dinner

Kay (Sir Kay)
character in: 16 Arthurian romance
foster brother: 6 Arthur

Kaye, Danny
real name: 19 David Daniel Kaminski
born: 10 Brooklyn NY
wife: 10 Sylvia Fine
roles: 14 The Court Jester **19** The Inspector General **21** Hans Christian Andersen **26** The Secret Life of Walter Mitty

Kaye, M M
author of: 9 Trade Wind **12** Death in Kenya **15** Death in Zanzibar, Shadow of the Moon, The Far Pavilions

Kazakhstan
capital/largest city: 7 Alma-Ata
others: 9 Karaganda **13** Petropavlovsk, Semipalatinsk
head of state: 9 president
government: 8 republic
monetary unit: 5 ruble
sea: 4 Aral **7** Caspian
physical feature: 7 steppes **12** Lake Balkhash
people: 6 Kazakh
language: 6 Kazakh

Kazan, Elia
director of: 10 East of Eden, Viva Zapata **15** On the Waterfront (Oscar) **18** Splendor in the Grass **19** Gentleman's Agreement (Oscar) **20** A Tree Grows in Brooklyn **21** A Streetcar Named Desire

Kazantzakis, Nikos
author of: 13 Zorba the Greek **14** Freedom or Death, The Greek Passion **25** The Last Temptation of Christ

kazoo 5 bazoo, zarah **6** hewgag **11** eunuch flute
French: 8 mirliton

Keach, Stacy
real name: 18 Walter Stacy Keach Jr
born: 10 Savannah GA
brother: 5 James
roles: 3 Doc **6** Luther **10** Mike Hammer **24** Twinkle Twinkle Killer Kane

Kearny, Stephen Watts
served in: 10 California, Mexican War
commander of: 13 Army of the West

occupied: 9 New Mexico
battle: 10 San Gabriel, San Pasqual

Keaton, Buster
real name: 19 Joseph Francis Keaton
born: 7 Piqua KS
roles: 6 Go West **7** College **10** The General **12** The Cameraman

Keaton, Diane
real name: 9 Diane Hall
born: 12 Los Angeles CA
roles: 4 Reds **7** Sleeper **8** Baby Boom **9** Annie Hall (Oscar) **12** Shoot the Moon, The Godfather **13** The Good Mother **14** Play It Again Sam **19** Looking for Mr Goodbar **20** The Little Drummer Girl

Keats, John
author of: 5 Lamia **8** Endymion, Hyperion, Isabella **11** Ode to Autumn, Ode to Psyche **14** Ode on Indolence **15** Ode on Melancholy, The Eve of St Agnes **16** Ode on a Grecian Urn **17** Ode to a Nightingale **20** La Belle Dame Sans Merci **31** On First Looking into Chapman's Homer

Kedemah
also called: 5 Kedar
father: 7 Ishmael
mother: 5 Hagar
descendant of: 8 Kedarite

Keel (of Argo)
constellation of: 6 Carina

Keel, Howard
real name: 17 Harry Clifford Leek
costar: 14 Kathryn Grayson
born: 11 Gillespie IL
roles: 6 Dallas, Kismet **8** Show Boat **10** Kiss Me Kate **13** Clayton Farlow **15** Annie Get Your Gun **27** Seven Brides for Seven Brothers

Keeler, Ruby
husband: 8 Al Jolson
costar: 10 Dick Powell
born: 6 Canada **7** Halifax
roles: 15 Footlight Parade **17** Forty-Second Street **32** Gold Diggers of Nineteen Thirty Three

keel over 5 faint, swoon, upset **7** capsize, tip over **8** collapse, fall down, fall flat, flip over, overturn, turn over **10** turn turtle

keen 4 avid, fine **5** acute, alert, eager, sharp **6** ardent, astute, clever, fervid, fierce, shrewd **7** earnest, excited, fervent, intense, zealous **8** incisive **9** impatient, paper thin, razorlike **10** discerning **11** finely honed, impassioned, penetrating, quick-witted **12** enthusiastic **13** perspicacious **14** discriminating

Keene, Carolyn
created: 18 Nancy Drew mysteries
father 17 Edward Stratemeyer

keen-eyed 5 alert **9** vigilant, watchful **9** attentive, eagle-eyed, observant, sharp-eyed, wide-awake

keen-minded 5 acute, sharp, smart **6**

astute, clever, shrewd **10** perceptive **11** penetrating

keenness 4 zeal, zest **5** ardor **6** acumen, fervor **7** passion **9** acuteness, eagerness, sharpness **10** astuteness, cleverness, enthusiasm, excitement, shrewdness **11** discernment **12** anticipation, intelligence, perspicacity

keen-sighted 4 sage, wise **5** acute, sharp **6** astute, shrewd **8** piercing **9** eagle-eyed, judicious, sagacious, sharp-eyed **10** discerning **11** intelligent, penetrating **12** clear-sighted, sharp-sighted **13** perspicacious

keep 3 bar **4** clog, fort, have, heap, hold, mind, pile, stay **5** abide, block, carry, cramp, delay, deter, guard, honor, lay in, place, stack, stall, stand, stick, stock, store, tie up, tower **6** arrest, castle, detain, donjon, endure, hamper, hinder, hobble, hold up, impede, living, pay for, remain, retain, retard **7** care for, carry on, citadel, deposit, furnish, inhibit, observe, possess, prevent, shackle, support, sustain **8** conserve, continue, encumber, fortress, hang on to, hold back, maintain, obstruct, preserve, restrain **9** celebrate, constrain, hamstring, persevere, persist in, ritualize, safeguard, solemnize, watch over **10** accumulate, daily bread, livelihood, provide for, stronghold, sustenance **11** commemorate, maintenance, memorialize, subsistence **12** room and board **13** fortification

keep an eye on 5 watch **7** oversee **9** chaperone, look after, watch over

keep apart 7 isolate **8** separate **9** segregate

keep at bay 7 beat off, fend off, ward off **8** stave off

keep back 5 check, delay **6** detain, hold up, retain **8** withhold

keep busy 3 use **6** employ, engage, occupy **7** utilize

keep clear of 4 shun **5** avoid, dodge, elude, evade, skirt **6** escape

keep company 4 date **5** court **7** consort, hang out **8** go around, go steady **9** accompany, associate **10** fraternize, go together

keeper 5 guard, nurse **6** duenna, escort, jailer, sentry, warden **7** curator **8** chaperon, guardian, retainer, sentinel, wet nurse **9** attendant, bodyguard, caretaker, chaperone, custodian, governess, nursemaid, protecter, protector **11** conservator, nurserymaid **13** guardian angel

keep in mind 8 consider, remember **10** think about

keep mum 13 button one's lip

keep off 7 fend off, stay off, ward off **8** stave off

keep one's counsel 12 remain silent 13 button one's lip

keep open 8 hold open 16 leave unscheduled

keep out 6 reject 8 prohibit 9 blackball, blacklist

keep out of sight 4 hide 5 cover 6 lay low, lie low 7 conceal, cover up, secrete 10 camouflage

keep private 4 hide 7 conceal, reserve 8 withhold

keepsake 5 relic, token 6 emblem, memory, symbol 7 memento 8 memorial, reminder, souvenir 11 remembrance 18 token of remembrance

keep secret 4 hide 6 hush up 7 conceal, cover up 8 suppress, withhold

keep silent 10 remain dumb 15 not breathe a word

keep steady 5 poise 7 balance 9 stabilize

keep to 5 cling, stick 6 adhere, be true, cleave, hold to 7 be loyal, stand by 8 maintain

keg 3 tub, tun, vat 4 butt, cask, drum, tank 6 barrel 7 rundlet 8 hogshead, puncheon 9 container, kilderkin

Keller, Helen
born: 4 deaf 5 blind
teacher: 12 Anne Sullivan
play and film: 16 The Miracle Worker
author: 13 William Gibson
actors: 9 Patty Duke 12 Anne Bancroft
both won: 6 Oscars

Kellerman, Sally
born: 11 Long Beach CA
roles: 4 MASH 15 Hot Lips Houlihan

Kelly, Gene
real name: 17 Eugene Curran Kelly
born: 12 Pittsburgh PA
roles: 7 Pal Joey 9 Brigadoon, On the Town 13 Anchors Aweigh 15 Singin' in the Rain 17 An American in Paris 18 The Three Musketeers

Kelly, Grace
husband: 21 Prince Rainier Grimaldi
nickname: 11 Ice Princess
born: 14 Philadelphia PA
princess of: 6 Monaco
roles: 7 Mogambo 8 High Noon 10 Rear Window 11 High Society 13 To Catch a Thief 14 Dial M for Murder, The Country Girl (Oscar)

Kelly, Walt
creator/artist of: 4 Pogo

kelp 3 ash 4 agar, alga, leag 5 varec, varic, wrack 7 seaweed
source of: 4 soda 6 iodine 9 potassium

Kelpie
origin: 8 Scottish
form: 5 horse 6 spirit
habitat: 4 lake 5 river

causes: 8 drowning
warns of: 8 drowning

Kelvin
abbreviation: 1 K

Kelvin, William Thomson
field: 7 physics 11 mathematics
nationality: 7 British
worked on: 4 heat 11 electricity
invented: 12 electrometer, galvanometer 13 tide predictor
named for him: 22 Kelvin temperature scale

Kempis, Thomas a
author of: 20 The Imitation of Christ

Keneally, Thomas
author of: 12 Confederates 14 Schindler's List

Kenilworth
author: 14 Sir Walter Scott
character: 6 Alasco, Dudley (Earl of Leicester) 10 Amy Robsart 12 Wayland Smith 13 Richard Varney 14 Queen Elizabeth 15 Flibbertigibbet 16 Edmund Tressilian

Kennedy, Arthur
real name: 17 John Arthur Kennedy
born: 11 Worcester MA
roles: 6 Becket 9 All My Sons 11 Peyton Place 12 Blind Victory 16 Death of a Salesman

Kennedy, Frank
character in: 15 Gone With the Wind
author: 8 Mitchell

Kennedy, John Fitzgerald
nickname: 3 JFK 4 Jack
presidential rank: 11 thirty-fifth
party: 10 Democratic
state represented: 2 MA
defeated: 5 (Richard Milhous) Nixon
vice president: 7 (Lyndon Baines) Johnson
cabinet:
  state: 4 (David Dean) Rusk
  treasury: 6 (Clarence Douglas) Dillon
  defense: 8 (Robert Strange) McNamara
  attorney general: 7 (Robert Francis) Kennedy
  postmaster general: 3 (James Edward) Day 9 (John Austin) Gronouski
  interior: 5 (Stewart Lee) Udall
  agriculture: 7 (Orville Lothrop) Freeman
  commerce: 6 (Luther Hartwell) Hodges
  labor: 5 (William Willard) Wirtz 8 (Arthur J) Goldberg
  HEW: 8 (Abraham Alexander) Ribicoff 10 (Anthony Joseph) Celebrezze
born: 11 Brookline MA
died: 8 Dallas TX
  died by: 13 assassination
  assassinated by: 6 (Lee Harvey) Oswald

buried: 25 Arlington National Cemetery
education:
  prep school: 6 Choate
  University: 7 Harvard 9 Princeton 23 London School of Economics
religion: 13 Roman Catholic
interests: 7 sailing 8 football 13 touch football
vacation spot: 9 Cape Cod MA 13 Hyannis Port MA
author: 15 Strategy of Peace, Why England Slept 17 Profiles in Courage (Pulitzer Prize)
political career: 9 US Senator 24 US House of Representatives
civilian career: 17 newspaper reporter
military service: 6 US Navy 10 lieutenant 11 World War Two
  commander of: 6 PT boat
notable events of lifetime/term: 9 Bay of Pigs 10 Berlin Wall, Peace Corps 18 Cuban missile crisis
  march: 11 Civil Rights
  treaty: 14 Nuclear Test-Ban
quote: 17 Ich bin ein Berliner (I am a Berliner) 35 We stand today on the edge of a New Frontier 61 Ask not what your country can do for you ask what you can do for your country
father: 13 Joseph Patrick
mother: 4 Rose (Fitzgerald)
siblings: 4 Jean 6 Eunice, Joseph 8 Kathleen, Patricia, Rosemary 11 Edward Moore 13 Robert Francis
wife: 10 Jacqueline (Lee Bouvier)
  nickname: 6 Jackie
  second marriage to: 7 Onassis
children: 14 John Fitzgerald (John-John, JFK Jr.), Patrick Bouvier (died in infancy) 15 Caroline Bouvier

Kennicott, Dr Will and Carol
characters in: 10 Main Street
author: 5 Lewis

Kentucky
abbreviation: 2 KY
nickname: 9 Bluegrass 11 Corncracker
capital: 9 Frankfort
largest city: 10 Louisville
others: 5 Berea 6 Corbin, Hazard 7 Ashland, Glasgow, Newport, Paducah, Shively 8 Danville 9 Covington, Henderson, Lexington, Owensboro 12 Bowling Green, Hopkinsville, Madisonville
college: 5 Berea 6 Centre 7 Ashbury, Brescia 8 Ursuline 12 Transylvania
explorer: 11 Daniel Boone
feature: 7 Obelisk
  birthplace: 14 Abraham Lincoln
  fort: 4 Knox
  national park: 11 Mammoth Cave
  race: 13 Kentucky Derby
  racetrack: 14 Churchill Downs
  trail: 10 Wilderness
tribe: 7 Shawnee 8 Cherokee,

Iroquois
people: 11 corncracker, John M Harlan **13** Louis Brandeis **16** Frederick M Vinson, Robert Penn Warren
lake: 8 Kentucky **10** Cumberland
land rank: 13 thirty-seventh
mountain: 4 Pine **10** Cumberland
  highest point: 5 Black **8** Big Black
physical feature:
  basin: 9 Bluegrass
  cave: 7 Mammoth
  gap: 10 Cumberland
  plain: 7 Coastal
  plateau: 10 Cumberland
president: 14 Abraham Lincoln
  Confederate president: 14 Jefferson Davis
river: 3 Dix **4** Ohio, Salt **5** Green **6** Barren **7** Licking **8** Big Sandy, Kentucky **9** Tennessee **10** Cumberland **11** Mississippi
state admission: 9 fifteenth
state bird: 8 cardinal
state flower: 9 goldenrod
state motto: 26 United We Stand Divided We Fall
state song: 17 My Old Kentucky Home
state tree: 10 coffee tree **11** tulip poplar **12** yellow poplar
Kenya
capital/largest city: 7 Nairobi
others: 5 Nyeri, Thika, Wajir **6** Kisumu, Kitale, Lodwar, Moyale, Nakuru, Webuye **7** Eldoret, Kericho, Malindi, Mandera, Mombasa, Nanyuki **9** Lokitaung
measure: 4 wari
monetary unit: 4 cent **5** pound **8** shilling
island: 5 Manda, Patta
lake: 6 Magadi, Nakuru, Natron, Rudolf **7** Turkana **8** Naivasha, Victoria
mountain: 5 Elgon, Kulai, Nyira, Nyiru **6** Matian **7** Logonot **8** Aberdare
highest point: 5 Kenya **6** Kinyaa **9** Kirinyaga
river: 3 Lak **4** Athi, Dawa, Kuja, Tana **5** Nzoia **6** Galana **8** Turkwell
sea: 6 Indian
physical feature:
  bay: 7 Formosa
  desert: 6 Chalbi
  escarpment: 3 Mau
  gulf: 9 Kavirondo
  highlands: 5 Kenya, Kisii, Luyla **7** Kericho
  plain: 4 Kano
  plateau: 5 Nandi, Yatta **6** Elgeyo
  valley: 9 Great Rift
people: 3 Luo **4** Arab, Meru **5** Bantu, Elgey, Galla, Kamba, Kisii, Luhya, Masai, Nandi, Tugen **6** Kikuyu, Ogaden, Somali **7** Baluhya, Hamitic, Hilotic, Kipsigi, Swahili, Turkana **8** Kalenjin, Marakwet
  god: 4 Ngai
  leader: 5 Mboya **12** Jomo Kenyatta

13 Daniel Arap Moi
language: 3 Luo **5** Bantu, Luhya, Masai **6** Kikuyu **7** English, Swahili **8** Guyerati **10** Hindustani
religion: 5 Islam **7** animism **8** Anglican **13** Roman Catholic
place:
  archeological excavation: 11 Gamble's Cave
  mosque: 5 Khoja
  museum: 9 Fort Jesus
  national park/wildlife preserve: 4 Meru **5** Nyeri, Tsavo **6** Arusha **7** Manyara, Nairobi, Samburu **8** Aberdare, Amboseli **10** Lake Nakuru, Mount Kenya, Rift Valley
  ruins: 4 Gedi
feature:
  garment: 5 kanga **7** kitenge
  round house: 6 shamba
  secret organization: 6 Mau Mau
  tree: 6 ayieke, baobab
food:
  fish: 7 tilapia
  wine: 5 tembo
Kepler, Johannes
nationality: 6 German
invented: 14 convex eyepiece **21** astronomical telescope
formulated:
  three laws of planetary motion (Kepler's Laws): 10 law of areas **11** harmonic law **24** elliptical orbit of planets
author of: 14 Astronomia nova, Harmonice mundi **16** Rudolphine Tables **23** Mysterium cosmographicum **30** Epitome astronomiae Copernicanae
kerchief 5 cloth, scarf **7** muffler **8** babushka, bandanna, kaffiyah, neckwear **9** headpiece, neckcloth **11** neckerchief **12** handkerchief
Keres
origin: 5 Greek
spirits of: 4 evil **5** death **6** old age **7** disease
Keres-Siouan
language branch: 5 Keres **7** Caddoan **9** Iroquoian **11** Siouan-Yuchi
kernel 3 nub, nut, pip, pit **4** core, germ, gist, pith, seed **5** grain, stone **6** center, marrow **7** nucleus **12** quintessence
Kerouac, Jack
author of: 6 Big Sur **9** On the Road **13** The Dharma Bums **16** Lonesome Traveler
Kerr, Deborah
real name: 22 Deborah Jane Kerr-Trimmer
born: 8 Scotland **11** Helensburgh
roles: 11 Edward My Son, The King and I **12** The Hucksters **13** The Sundowners **14** Separate Tables, The Chalk Garden **18** From Here to Eternity **19** The Night of the Iguana **20** Heaven Knows Mr Allison

Kesey, Ken
author of: 21 Sometimes a Great Notion **25** One Flew Over the Cuckoo's Nest
Ketcham, Hank
creator/artist of: 15 Dennis the Menace
kettle 3 pan, pot, tub, vat **6** boiler, teapot, tureen **8** cauldron, crucible, saucepan
Ketubim 8 writings **11** Hagiographa
Keturah
husband: 7 Abraham
kewpie 4 doll
originator: 9 Rose O'Neil **13** carnival prize
key 3 cue, fit **4** clue, gear, mode, suit **5** adapt, light, point, scale **6** adjust, answer, direct, opener **7** address, finding, meaning, pointer **8** indicant, solution, tonality **9** indicator **10** exposition, indication, resolution **11** elucidation, explanation, explication, translation **14** interpretation
Key, Ted
creator/artist of: 5 Hazel
keyboard instrument 5 organ, piano **6** spinet **8** psaltery, virginal **9** harmonium **10** clavichord, pianoforte **11** harpsichord
keyed up 5 tense **7** excited, nervous **8** volatile **9** emotional, explosive
key element 9 essential, vital part **18** primary constituent **20** indispensable element
Key Largo
director: 10 John Huston
based on story by: 15 Maxwell Anderson
cast: 12 Claire Trevor, Lauren Bacall **14** Humphrey Bogart **15** Edward G Robinson, Lionel Barrymore
Oscar for: 17 supporting actress (Trevor)
Keynes, John Maynard
author of: 44 The General Theory of Employment Interest and Money
keynote 3 nub **4** core, gist, pith **5** heart, theme **6** marrow **7** essence, nucleus, pattern **8** main idea, quiddity **9** substance **11** nitty-gritty, salient idea **12** central point
keystone 4 base, crux, root **5** basis **8** gravamen, linchpin **9** principle **10** foundation, mainspring
Keystone State
nickname of: 12 Pennsylvania
Key to Rebecca, The
author: 10 Ken Follett
KGB 4 USSR **14** security police **18** intelligence agency
Khachaturian, Aram Ilich
born: 6 Tiflis **7** (Soviet) Georgia
composer of: 6 Gayane **9** Spartacus **12** Song of Stalin

khaki 5 cloth **6** fabric **7** uniform **9** olive-drab **14** yellowish- brown

khan, kahn 3 inn **4** lord **5** chief, ruler **6** prince **7** emperor **9** chieftain, sovereign **11** caravansary
famous: **3** Aga, Ali **4** Yuan **6** Kublai **7** Genghis **8** Ghenghis

Khartoum
capital of: **5** Sudan

Khayyam, Omar
born: **6** Persia
famous as: **4** poet **9** statesman **13** mathematician
name means: **9** tentmaker
author of: **11** The Rubaiyat

Khoisan
language spoken by: **3** San **7** Bushmen **9** Khoikhoin **10** Hottentots
includes: **5** Hatsa **7** Sandawe
distinguishing sound: **5** click

Khomeini, Ruholla
title: **9** ayatollah
ruled: **4** Iran

Khruschev, Nikita
premier of: **4** USSR
followed: **8** Bulganin
preceded: **7** Kosygin

Khyber Pass
between: **8** Pakistan and **11** Afghanistan
range: **9** Hindu Kush

kibbutz 10 collective **11** Israeli Farm

kibitzer 3 pry **5** prier, snoop **6** butt-in **7** advisor, meddler, snooper, watcher **8** busybody, onlooker **9** buttinsky

kick 3 fun, hit, out, pep, vim **4** beef, boot, dash, fret, fume, fuss, life, punt, snap, tang, zest **5** eject, force, gripe, growl, power, punch, verve, vigor **6** flavor, grouch, grouse, object, recoil, remove, return, strike, stroke, thrill **7** boot out, cast out, grumble, fly back, protest, rebound, sparkle, turn out **8** backlash, complain, jump back, piquancy, pleasure, pungency, reaction, throw out, vitality **9** amusement, animation, complaint, enjoyment, find fault, grievance, intensity, make a fuss, objection **10** excitement, spring back **11** give the gate, remonstrate, send packing, show the door **12** protestation **13** gratification, remonstration

Kickapoo
language family: **9** Algonkian **10** Algonquian
location: **5** Texas **6** Kansas, Mexico **9** Chihuahua, Wisconsin
related to: **3** Fox, Sac **4** Sauk

kickback 3 cut **5** bribe, graft, share **6** boodle, payoff, payola **9** hush money **10** commission, percentage, protection, recompense **12** compensation, remuneration **15** protection money

kick downstairs 4 bust **6** demote **7** degrade

kickoff 5 start **7** opening **9** beginning, inception, launching **12** inauguration

kick out 4 oust **5** eject, evict, expel **8** throw out **9** discharge

kicks 3 fun **7** thrills **8** pleasure **10** excitement **11** stimulation

kick upstairs 5 boost **7** advance, elevate, promote

kid 3 rag, rib, tot **4** baby, fool, gull, jest, joke, josh, mock, ride, tyke **5** bluff, child, cozen, harry, put on, tease, trick, youth **6** delude, infant, moppet, plague, shaver, squirt **7** beguile, deceive, laugh at, mislead **8** goat hide, goatskin, hoodwink, juvenile, ridicule, teenager, yearling **9** bamboozle, billy goat, little one, make fun of, nanny goat, offspring, young goat, youngster **10** adolescent **11** goat leather, young person **12** little shaver

Kid, The
nickname of: **11** Ted Williams **13** William Bonney (Billy)

kid around 5 clown, cut up **10** fool around, play around **11** clown around

Kidd, William 13 pirate captain
born: **8** Scotland
end: **6** hanged

Kidder, Margot
born: **6** Canada **11** Yellow Knife
roles: **7** Sisters **8** Lois Lane, Superman **14** Some Kind of Hero **19** The Amityville Horror

Kiddush 6 prayer **8** blessing **14** sanctification

kidnap 5 seize, steal **6** abduct, hijack, snatch **7** bear off, capture, impress, skyjack **8** bear away, carry off, shanghai **10** run off with **11** make off with **13** hold for ransom

Kidnapped
author: **20** Robert Louis Stevenson
character: **9** Alan Breck **10** Rankeillor **12** David Balfour **15** Ebenezer Balfour

Kigali
capital of: **6** Rwanda

Kiley, Richard
born: **9** Chicago IL
roles: **7** Redhead **13** Man of La Mancha **16** Advise and Consent

Kilimanjaro, Mount
in **6** Africa **8** Tanzania
feature: **15** highest in Africa
see also **9** Hemingway

Kilkenny Cats
origin: **5** Irish
form: **4** cats
number: **3** two
left after fight: **5** tails

kill 4 beat, do in, halt, hang, ruin, slay, stay **5** break, check, drown, erase, lynch, quell, shoot, waste **6** behead, defeat, murder, poison, rub out, stifle **7** bump off, butcher, cut down, destroy, execute, garrote, silence,

smother, squelch, wipe out **8** blow away, dispatch, get rid of, knock off, massacre, strangle, string up **9** dismember, finish off, shoot down, slaughter, suffocate **10** asphyxiate, decapitate, disembowel, extinguish, guillotine, put a stop to, put an end to, put to death **11** assassinate, burn to death, electrocute, exterminate **13** mortally wound

killer 6 hit man, slayer **7** butcher **8** assassin, murderer **11** executioner **12** exterminator

Killers, The
director: **13** Robert Siodmak
based on story by: **15** Ernest Hemingway
cast: **10** Ava Gardner **12** Edmond O'Brien **13** Burt Lancaster

killer whale 4 orca **7** grampus **11** Orcinus orca

killing 4 coup **5** fatal **6** big hit, deadly, lethal, mortal, murder **7** bonanza, cleanup, deathly, hanging, slaying, success, suicide **8** butchery, fatality, homicide, lynching, massacre, regicide, shooting, smash hit, stabbing, windfall **9** bloodshed, execution, garroting, martyrdom, matricide, murderous, patricide, poisoning, slaughter, uxoricide **10** cleaning up, decimation, fratricide, immolation, impalement, sororicide, strangling **11** crucifixion, devastating, elimination, infanticide **12** annihilation, death-dealing, decapitation, excruciating, guillotining, manslaughter, master stroke, stroke of luck, violent death **13** electrocution, extermination, strangulation **17** capital punishment

Killing Fields
director: **11** Roland Joffe
based on article by: **15** Sydney Schanberg (The Death and Life of Dith Pran)
cast: **10** Haing S Ngor **12** Sam Waterston
setting: **8** Cambodia
Oscar for: **15** supporting actor (Ngor)

Killing Time
author: **12** Thomas Berger

killjoy 6 grouch **8** grumbler, sourball, sourpuss **9** Cassandra, gloomy Gus, worrywart **10** complainer, malcontent, spoilsport, wet blanket **11** crapehanger, party-pooper

kill time 4 idle **6** dawdle **9** waste time **10** fool around

Kilmer, Joyce
author of: **5** Trees

kiln 3 ost **4** bake, burn, fire, oast, oven **5** drier, glaze, stove, tiler **7** furnace **8** calciner, limekiln **9** oasthouse

kiloliter
abbreviation: **2** kL

kilometer
abbreviation: **2** km

Kim
  author: 14 Rudyard Kipling
  character: 9 Mahbub Ali **11** Tibetan Lama **12** Kimball O'Hara **16** Colonel Creighton **22** Hurree Chunder Mookerjee

kimono 4 gown, robe
  traditional costume of: 5 Japan
  sash: 3 obi
  ornament: 7 netsuke

kin 4 akin, clan, kith, race **5** folks, tribe **6** family, people **7** kinfolk, kinsmen, related **8** clansmen, kinfolks **9** next of kin, relations, relatives, tribesmen **10** kith and kin **11** connections, consanguine, distaff side, spindle side **13** flesh and blood **14** kissing cousins

kind 3 ilk **4** cast, make, mold, sort, type **5** brand, breed, caste, civil, class, genre, genus, style **6** benign, gentle, kidney, kindly, nature, polite, strain, tender **7** amiable, cordial, variety **8** amicable, friendly, generous, gracious, merciful, obliging **9** courteous **10** bighearted, charitable, neighborly, thoughtful **11** considerate, description, designation, good-hearted, good-humored, good-natured, softhearted, sympathetic, warmhearted, well-meaning **12** affectionate, well-disposed **13** accommodating, compassionate, tenderhearted, understanding **French: 6** gentil

kindhearted 4 good, warm **6** benign, gentle, humane, kindly, loving **7** helpful **8** amicable, generous, gracious, merciful **10** altruistic, charitable, thoughtful **11** considerate, good-hearted, good-natured, softhearted, sympathetic, warmhearted, well-meaning **12** affectionate, humanitarian **13** accommodating, compassionate, philanthropic, tenderhearted, understanding

kindheartedness 5 mercy **8** altruism, goodness, goodwill, humanity, sympathy **10** compassion, humaneness, tenderness **11** benefaction, benevolence, magnanimity **12** graciousness, philanthropy **13** consideration, understanding, unselfishness **14** charitableness **15** humanitarianism

kindle 4 fire, goad, prod, stir, urge, whet **5** awake, light, rouse, waken **6** arouse, excite, foment, ignite, incite, induce, stir up **7** agitate, animate, inflame, inspire, provoke, quicken, sharpen **8** enkindle **9** call forth, intensify, set fire to, set on fire, stimulate **10** invigorate

kindling 4 fuel **5** brush, paper, twigs **6** firing, tinder **7** burning, flaming **8** firewood, igniting, ignition, lighting, shavings **9** brushwood **10** combustion, enkindling

kindly 4 good, warm **6** benign, gentle, gently, humane, tender, warmly **7**

amiable, amiably, civilly, cordial, devoted, patient **8** amicable, amicably, benignly, friendly, generous, gracious, humanely, merciful, tenderly **9** cordially, courteous **10** benevolent, bighearted, charitable, charitably, generously, graciously, mercifully, neighborly **11** considerate, good-humored, good-natured, magnanimous, softhearted, sympathetic, warmhearted, well-meaning **12** affectionate, benevolently, bigheartedly, humanitarian **13** compassionate, considerately, good-humoredly, good-naturedly, magnanimously, philanthropic, softheartedly, tenderhearted, understanding, warmheartedly, well-meaningly **14** affectionately, well-manneredly **15** compassionately, sympathetically, tenderheartedly, understandingly **17** philanthropically

kindness 3 aid **4** gift, help **5** favor, grace, mercy **6** bounty **7** charity **8** good deed, good turn, goodness, goodwill, humanity, patience, sympathy **9** tolerance **10** act of grace, assistance, compassion, generosity, humaneness, kind office, toleration **11** benefaction, beneficence, benevolence, magnanimity **12** act of charity, graciousness, philanthropy **13** consideration, understanding, unselfishness **14** charitableness **15** humanitarianism

Kind of Anger, A
  author: 10 Eric Ambler

kindred 4 akin, like **5** alike **6** allied, united **7** related, similar **8** agreeing, familial, matching **9** accordant, analogous, congenial, simpatico **10** harmonious, resembling **11** consanguine, sympathetic **13** corresponding

kine 4 cows, oxen **6** cattle **9** livestock

kinfolk 3 kin **6** family **7** kinsmen **8** clansmen **9** relations, relatives **10** kith and kin

king 3 HRH **5** liege, ruler **7** monarch **8** suzerain **9** potentate, protector, sovereign **10** His Majesty **11** crowned head, royal person, the anointed **18** defender of the faith
  Latin: 3 rex

king/emperor/dynasty
  of Afghanistan: 8 Barakzai
  of Albania: 3 Zog **9** Ahmet Zogu
  of Algeria: 3 bey, dey **6** disawa **8** Jugurtha **9** bevlerbay, Masinissa
  of Austria: 7 Charles, Francis **9** Ferdinand, Habsburgs **10** Franz Josef
  of Bahrain: 9 al-Khalifa
  of Belgium: 7 Leopold **8** Baudouin
  of China: 3 Han, Sui **4** Chou, Ch'in, Ming, Sung, T'ang **5** Ch'ing, Shang **6** Manchu
  of Crete: 5 Minos
  of Denmark 4 Hans, Knud **6** Canute **8** Frederik **9** Christian **10** Gorm the Old **15** Harold Bluetooth

  of Egypt: 5 Khufu, Menes, Zoser **6** Farouk, Khafre, Ptulol, Ramses **7** Saladin **8** Horemheb, Menkaure **9** Akhenaten, Amenemhet, Amenhotep **10** Mentuhotep **11** Tutankhamen
  of England: 3 Hal **4** Cnut, John, Lear **5** Henry, James **6** Alfred, Arthur, Canute, Edmund, Edward, Egbert, George, Harold **7** Charles, Richard, Stephen, William **9** Cymbeline **18** Richard Coeur de Lion **19** Richard the Lionheart **21** Richard the Lionhearted
  of France: 5 Henri, Louis **6** Clovis, Philip **7** Charles **8** Napoleon **9** Hugh Capet **11** Charlemagne **21** Richard the Lionhearted **13** Louis Philippe **14** Henry of Navarre
  of Germany: 6 Kaiser **7** Wilhelm **9** Frederick **10** Barbarossa
  of Greece: 5 Creon **6** Atreus **7** Theseus **8** Menelaus **10** Agammemnon **11** Constantine
  of India: 5 Akbar, Asoka, Babur, Gupta, Mogul, Timur **6** Maurya, Rajput **7** Humayun **8** Hyder Ali, Jahangir, Marathas **9** Aurangzeb, Shah Jahan **11** Tippu Sultan **14** Delhi Sultanate **18** Chandragupta Maurya
  of Iran: 5 Abbas, Cyrus, Qajar **6** Darius, Xerxes **7** Arsacid, Pahlavi, Safavid **8** Parthian, Seleucid **9** Sassanian **10** Achaemenid **15** Shah Reza Pahlavi
  of Iraq: 6 Faisal, Sargon **7** Hussein **9** Hammurabi **13** Harun al-Rashid **14** Nebuchadnezzar
  of Ireland: 9 Brian Boru
  of Italy/Rome: 4 Nero, Otho **5** Galba, Nerva, Titus **6** Trajan **8** Hadrian **8** Caligula, Claudius, Commodus, Domitian, Octavian, Tiberius **9** Caracalla, Vespasian, Vitellius **10** Diocletian **11** Constantine **13** Antoninus Dius **14** Caesar Augustus, Marcus Aurelius, Victor Emmanuel
  of Japan: 5 Jimmu, Jingo, Meiji, Taira **6** Yamato **7** Akihito, Izanagi **8** Ashikaga, Fujiwara, Hirohito, Kamakura, Minamoto, Tokugawa
  of Java: 7 Mataram **9** Majapahit, Srivijaya
  of Jordan: 5 Talal **6** Faisal **7** Hussein **8** Abdullah, Selucidas **10** Ibn Hussein, Nabataeans
  of Korea: 2 Yi **4** Choe **5** Ki-tse, Koryo **6** Chi-tsi, Chi-tzu, Tangun
  of Kuwait: 5 Ahmad, Sabah, Salem **7** Mubarak **12** Jaber al-Ahmed, Sabah al-Salim **15** Abdullah al-Salim
  of Liechtenstein: 7 Florian **13** Francis Joseph **16** von Liechtenstein
  of Luxembourg: 8 Sigefroi, Wencelas **12** Jean l'Aveugle **21** House of Nassau-Weilburg
  of Madagascar: 6 Merina
  of Malawi: 6 Maravi
  of Maldives: 4 Didi

of Mexico: 10 Maximilian

of Monaco: 5 Louis **6** Albert, Honore **7** Antoine, Charles, Rainier **9** Florestan

of Mongolia: 8 Jahangir, Jehangir **10** Kublai Khan, Tsendenbal **11** Genghis Khan

of Morocco: 7 Alawite, Almohad **9** Almoravid

of Nepal: 8 Mahendra **9** Tribhuwan **10** Birenda Bir **12** Bikram Sha Dev **17** Prithwi Narayan Sha

of the Netherlands: 7 William

of Nigeria: 3 Ife, Nok, Oyo **5** Benin **6** Fulani **10** Kanem- Borno

of Norway: 4 Olaf, Olav **5** Olave, Oscar **6** Haakon, Harold, Magnus, Sverre

of Peru: 7 Huascar **9** Atahualpa **10** Manco Capac

of Poland: 5 Piast **7** Casimir, Jagello **8** Augustus

of Portugal: 6 Manuel, Philip, Sancho **7** Alfonso **9** Ferdinand, Sebastian **23** Prince Henry the Navigator

of Qatar: 18 Ahmad bin Ali al-Thani **22** Khalifa bin Hamad al-Thani

of Rumania: 5 Carol **7** Michael

of Russia: 4 Ivan, Paul **5** Peter **6** Alexis **8** Nicholas **9** Alexander **12** Boris Godunov

of Sardinia: 12 Charles Felix **13** Charles Albert **14** Victor Emmanuel

of Saudi Arabia: 4 Fahd, Saud **6** Faisal, Khalid **7** Ibn Saud **9** Abdul Aziz

of Scotland: 5 David, James **6** Duncan **7** Kenneth, Macbeth, Malcolm, Stuarts, William **9** Alexander **14** Robert the Bruce **19** Bonnie Prince Charlie

of Sicily: 4 Eryx **5** Bomba, Henry, Peter, Roger **7** Charles, Cocalus, Leontes **9** Ferdinand, Frederick

of Spain: 6 Pelayo, Philip, Ramiro, Sancho, Witiza **7** Alfonso, Almohad, Charles, Umayyad **8** al-Mansur, Reccared, Roderick **9** Almoravid, Ferdinand, Leovigild **10** Juan Carlos **11** Abd al-Rahman, Reccosvinth

of Swaziland: 3 Kbe **5** Nyama **6** Mswati, Sozisa **7** Sobhuza

of Sweden: 4 Vosa, Wasa **5** Oscar **6** Gustav **8** Gustavus **10** Carl Gustav **12** Gustav Adolph **13** Charles Gustav **22** Jean Baptiste Bernadotte

of Syria: 5 Rezin **6** Faisal, Hazael **8** Benhadad **9** Antiochus

of Thailand: 4 Rama **7** Chakkri, Mongkut **10** Chao Phraya **12** Prahjadhipok **13** Chulalongkorn **17** Bhumibol Adulyadej

of Tongo: 11 George Tupou **14** Taufaahau Tupou

of Tunisia: 6 Hafsid **7** Fatimid **8** Aghlabid, Almohade **10** Husseinite

of Turkey: 8 Mausolus

of Uganda: 6 Mutesa, Mwanga **8** Kabarega

of Upper Volta: 4 Naba **5** Mogho

of Zimbabwe: 9 Lobengula, Mzilikaze

King, Frank
creator/artist of: **13** Gasoline Alley

King, Martin Luther
born: **7** Atlanta, Georgia
died: **7** Memphis **9** Tennessee
wife: **12** Coretta Scott
career: **8** minister (Southern Baptist), activist
notable moments: **17** "I Have A Dream" speech **26** march from Selma to Montgomery

King, Stephen
author of: **2** It **4** Cujo **6** Carrie, Misery **9** Christine, Salem's Lot, The Stand **10** Night Shift, The Shining **11** Firestarter, Pet Sematary, The Dead Zone **12** Skeleton Crew, The Dark Tower **16** Different Seasons, The Tommyknockers

King and I, The
director: **10** Walter Lang
cast: **10** Rita Moreno, Yul Brynner **11** Deborah Kerr **12** Martin Benson
score: **21** Rodgers and Hammerstein
from the book: **20** Anna and the King of Siam
song: **12** Shall We Dance? **16** Getting to Know You, Hello Young Lovers **18** Something Wonderful

King Arthur
opera by: **7** Purcell
character: **6** Merlin, Osmond, Oswald **8** Emmeline, Philadel **14** Duke of Cornwall

kingdom 4 land **5** duchy, field, realm, state **6** domain, empire, nation, sphere **7** country, dukedom **8** dominion, monarchy **9** territory **12** principality

King John
author: **18** William Shakespeare
character: **6** Elinor **9** Constance **11** Prince Henry **13** Hubert de Burgh **15** Blanch of Castile, Lewis the Dauphin **16** Arthur of Bretagne Cardinal Pandulph, William Longsword, William Mareshall **19** Philip Faulconbridge, Robert Faulconbridge

King Kong
director: **13** Merian C Cooper **17** Ernest B Schoedsack
cast: **7** Fay Wray **10** Bruce Cabot **11** James Flavin **12** Noble Johnson **15** Robert Armstrong
setting (final scene): **19** Empire State Building
score: **10** Max Steiner

King Lear
author: **18** William Shakespeare
character: **5** Edgar, Regan **6** Edmund **7** Goneril **8** Cordelia **10** Earl of Kent **12** Duke of Albany, King of France **14** Duke of Cornwall **16** Earl of Gloucester

kingly 5 grand, noble, regal, royal **6**

august, lordly, mighty **7** queenly, stately **8** absolute, despotic, glorious, kinglike, imperial, majestic, princely, splendid **9** imperious, monarchal, patrician, sovereign **10** autocratic, commanding, tyrannical **11** magnificent **12** awe- inspiring

Kingman, Dave
nickname: **4** Kong
sport: **8** baseball
position: **8** outfield **9** first base
team: **11** Chicago Cubs, New York Mets **14** New York Yankees, San Diego Padres **16** California Angels **18** San Francisco Giants

king of gods 4 Amen, Amon, Finn, Zeus **5** Ammon, Enlil, Fionn, Wotan **6** Marduk **7** Jupiter **8** Merodach **12** Baal Merodach **13** Fionn MacCumal

King of Hearts
character in: **28** Alice's Adventures in Wonderland
author: **7** Carroll

King of Righteousness 11 Melchizedek

Kingsley, Ben
roles: **6** Gandhi (Oscar) **8** Betrayal **14** Schindler's List

Kingsley, Charles
author of: **7** Hypatia **10** Alton Locke **11** Westward Ho! **14** The Water Babies **15** Hereward the Wake

King Solomon's Mines
author: **13** H Rider Haggard
character: **5** Twala **6** Gagool, Umbopa **14** Sir Henry Curtis **15** Allan Quatermain, Captain John Good

King's Row
author: **14** Henry Bellamann
director: **7** Sam Wood
cast: **10** Betty Field **11** Ann Sheridan, Claude Rains **12** Ronald Reagan **13** Charles Coburn **14** Judith Anderson, Robert Cummings
score: **21** Erich Wolfgard Korngold
character: **11** Drake McHugh, Elise Sandor **13** Randy Monaghan **14** Cassandra Tower, Parris Mitchell

Kingston
capital of: **7** Jamaica

kink 4 coil, flaw, knot, pang **5** cramp, crick, crimp, frizz, gnarl, hitch, quirk, snarl, spasm, twist **6** defect, foible, glitch, oddity, tangle, twinge, vagary **7** crinkle, frizzle **8** crotchet **9** queerness, stiffness, weirdness **10** difficulty **11** peculiarity, singularity **12** charley horse, complication, eccentricity, freakishness, idiosyncrasy, imperfection

kinky 3 odd **4** sick, wiry **5** kooky, queer **6** frizzy, matted, quirky, twisty **7** bizarre, deviant, frizzly, knotted, strange, tangled, twisted, unusual **8** aberrant, abnormal, crinkled, freakish, frizzled, peculiar, perverse **9** eccentric, unnatural **10** unorthodox **13** idiosyncratic

Kinshasa
capital of: **5** Zaire

kinsman 3 sib, son **4** aunt, heir **5** child, uncle **6** cousin, father, mother, parent, sister **7** brother **8** daughter, landsman, relation, relative **9** offspring **10** countryman **11** grandfather, grandmother **13** blood relation, blood relative

Kiowa
language family: **6** Tanoan
location: **6** Plains **7** Montana **8** Colorado, Oklahoma
allied with: **7** Arapaho **8** Comanche **11** Kiowa Apache
deity: **5** Taime

Kiowa Apache
language family: **12** Shapwailutan
location: **6** Plains

Kipling, Rudyard
author of: **3** Kim **8** Gunga Din, Mandalay **11** Danny Deaver **12** The Seven Seas **13** Just So Stories, The Jungle Book **18** Barrack-Room Ballads, Captains Courageous

Kipps
author: **7** H G Wells

Kirchhoff, Gustav Robert
field: **7** physics
nationality: **6** German
discovered: **6** cesium **8** rubidium
developed: **12** spectroscope
named for him: **19** electric circuit laws

Kirchner, Ernst Ludwig
born: **7** Germany **13** Aschaffenburg
artwork: **11** Street Scene **12** Street Berlin **13** Moonlit Winter **21** Self-portrait with Model

Kirghiz see **10** Kyrgyzstan

Kiribati
other name: **14** Gilbert Islands
capital/largest city: **6** Tarawa
others: **5** Betio **7** Bairiki, Bonriki **9** Bikenibeu
school: **12** South Pacific
monetary unit: **4** cent **6** dollar
island: **5** Flint, Ocean **6** Banaba, Canton, Malden, Tarawa **7** Abemama, Fanning, Gilbert, Marakei, Nonouti, Phoenix, Vostock **8** Caroline, Starbuck **9** Christmas, Enderbury, Tabiteuea **10** Butaritari, Equatorial, Washington **12** Northern Line, Southern Line
sea: **7** Pacific
people: **8** Banabans **10** Polynesian **11** Micronesian
language: **6** Samoan **7** English **10** Gilbertese
religion: **5** Baha'i **8** Anglican **9** Methodist **11** Church of God **13** Roman Catholic **19** Seventh Day Adventist

kirsch, kirschwasser
type: **6** brandy **7** liqueur
origin: **6** France **7** Germany **11** Switzerland
flavor: **6** cherry
with gin: **7** Florida **10** Lady Finger
with vodka: **12** Volga Boatman

kismet 3 end, lot **4** doom, fate **5** karma, moira **7** destiny, fortune, portion **8** God's will **10** Providence **11** will of Allah **12** circumstance **13** inevitability **14** predestination

kiss 4 buss, neck **6** smooch, salute **8** osculate

Kiss for Cinderella, A
author: **12** James M Barrie

Kissinger, Henry
born: **6** Fuerth **7** Germany
career: **9** statesman **11** businessman **16** Secretary of State
won: **10** Nobel Prize

kit 3 rig **4** gear **5** tools **6** outfit, tackle, things **7** devices **8** supplies, utensils **9** equipment, trappings **10** implements, provisions **11** furnishings, impediments, instruments, necessaries **13** accoutrements, paraphernalia

Kitasato, Shibasaburo
field: **12** bacteriology
nationality: **8** Japanese
isolated: **7** anthrax, tetanus **9** dysentery **13** bubonic plague
developed: **19** diphtheria antitoxin

kitchen 6 bakery, cocina, galley **7** cuisine **8** cookroom, scullery **9** bakehouse, cookhouse

Kitchener, Horatio Herbert
also: **18** first Earl Kitchener
nationality: **7** British
served in: **7** Boer War **15** South African War
battle: **8** Khartoum, Omdurman
governor of: **8** the Sudan
commander in chief of: **5** India **12** Egyptian army
consul general of: **5** Egypt

kitel 20 Jewish ceremonial robe
color: **5** white

Kitely
character in: **19** Every Man in His Humour
author: **6** Jonson

kittenish 3 coy **7** playful **10** coquettish

Klamath
language family: **8** Penutian
location: **6** Oregon **10** California
related to: **5** Modoc **6** Cayuse, Molala

Klee, Paul
born: **11** Switzerland **14** Munchenbuchsee
artwork: **9** Locksmith **11** Ad Parnassum **18** Barbarian Sacrifice, Demon above the Ships **20** The Twittering Machine **22** Revolution of the Viaduct **23** Dance-Play of the Red Skirts **24** Dance Monster to my Soft Song **35** The Vocal Fabric of the Singer Rosa Silber

Kleist, Heinrich von
author of: **11** Penthesilea **14** The Marquise of O **16** The Broken Pitcher **18** The Prince of Homburg

Kline, Kevin
roles: **4** Dave **8** In and Out **11** The Big Chill **13** Sophie's Choice **16** A Fish Called Wanda **17** Pirates of Penzance

Klugman, Jack
born: **14** Philadelphia PA
roles: **6** Quincy **12** Oscar Madison, The Odd Couple

klutz 5 dummy **9** blockhead **11** satchelfoot **13** fumblefingers

klutzy 4 dumb **6** clumsy, stupid **7** awkward **9** graceless

knack 4 bent, gift, turn **5** flair, forte, skill **6** genius, talent **7** ability, faculty, finesse **8** aptitude, capacity, facility **9** dexterity, expertise, ingenuity, quickness, readiness **10** adroitness, capability, cleverness, competence, efficiency, propensity **11** inclination, proficiency **13** dexterousness

knave 3 cad, cur, dog, rat **4** jack (cards) **5** phony, rogue, scamp **6** con man, rascal, rotter, varlet, wretch **7** bounder, culprit **8** scalawag, swindler **9** charlatan, con artist, reprobate, scoundrel **10** blackguard **11** rapscallion **14** good for nothing

knee breeches 8 breeches, jodhpurs, knickers **9** plus fours **14** knickerbockers

kneel 3 bow **6** curtsy, kowtow, salaam **7** bow down **9** genuflect **13** make obeisance **16** prostrate oneself

knell 4 peal, ring, toll **5** chime, sound **6** stroke **7** pealing, ringing, tolling

Knickerbocker Holiday
author: **15** Maxwell Anderson

knickknack, nicknack 3 toy **6** bauble, gewgaw, trifle **7** bibelot, trinket **8** frippery, gimcrack **9** bagatelle, bric-a-brac, plaything **11** thingamajig

knife 3 cut **4** dirk, shiv, stab **5** blade, slash, wound **6** cutter, pierce **7** cut down, cutlery **8** cut apart, lacerate, mutilate
type: **3** pen **4** jack **5** bowie, bread, putty, table **6** dagger, paring, pocket **7** butcher, carving, hunting, machete, palette, pruning, scalpel **8** skinning, stiletto, surgical **11** switchblade

knight 4 hero **7** fighter, gallant, paladin, soldier, Templar, warrior **8** cavalier, champion, defender, guardian, horseman, Lancelot **9** gentleman, man-at-arms, protecter, protector **10** equestrian, vindicator

Knight
character in: **18** The Canterbury Tales
author: **7** Chaucer

Knightley, George

character in: **4** Emma
author: **6** Austen

Knights, The
author: **12** Aristophanes
character: **5** Demus **6** Nicias **11** Demosthenes **20** Cleon the Paphlagonian

knit 3 tat **4** ally, bind, draw, join, knot, link **5** braid, plait, twist, unify, unite, weave **6** attach, crease, fasten, furrow, stitch **7** connect, crochet, wrinkle **10** intertwine, interweave **12** draw together

knob 3 nub **4** bulb, bump, grip, hold, hump, knot, knur, lump, node, snag **5** bulge, gnarl, knurl, latch, lever, swell **6** handle, nubbin **8** handhold, swelling, tubercle **9** convexity **10** projection, prominence, protrusion **12** protuberance, protuberancy

knock 3 bat, hit, pat, rap, tap **4** bang, beat, belt, blow, bomb, bump, clip, cuff, dash, kick, lick, push, slam, slap, sock, swat, thud **5** abuse, cavil, clout, crack, crash, decry, pound, punch, smack, smash, smite, thump, whack **6** batter, carp at, defeat, hammer, jostle, murder, peck at, pummel, strike, stroke, thwack, wallop **7** censure, condemn, failure, setback **8** belittle, lambaste **9** criticism, criticize, deprecate, disparage, reprehend **12** condemnation, faultfinding, reprehension

knock down 4 deck, down, drop, fell **5** floor **7** flatten **8** bowl over, discount **9** take apart **11** disassemble

knock off balance 6 rattle **7** shake up **8** unsettle **9** take aback **11** disorganize

knockout 2 KO **4** doll **5** beaut, Venus **6** beauty, eyeful **7** stunner

knock out of shape 4 maul **5** crush **6** batter, beat up, mangle

knoll 4 hill, rise **5** mound

knot 3 bun **4** bump, frog, heap, hump, loop, lump, mass, pack, pile, star, tuft **5** braid, bunch, clump, group, hitch, knurl, plait, twist **6** bundle, circle **7** cat's-paw, chignon, cluster, epaulet, rosette **8** ornament **9** gathering **10** assemblage, collection, intertwist **13** interlacement
type: **3** bow, top **4** flat, slip **5** slide **6** double, single, square **7** running **8** hangman's, overhand, shoulder, surgeon's **9** half-hitch **11** figure-eight, midshipman's

Knots Landing
character: **9** Abby Ewing, Gary Ewing **10** Greg Sumner **11** Valene Ewing **12** Mac Mackenzie **14** Karen Mackenzie, Paige Forrester
cast: **10** Donna Mills, Joan Van Ark **11** Julie Harris, Kevin Dobson, Michelle Lee **13** William Devane **14** Douglas Sheehan, Ted Shackelford **17** Nicolette Sheridan

knotty 4 hard **5** bumpy, rough, tough **6** coarse, flawed, knobby, knurly, rugged, snaggy, thorny, tricky, uneven **7** complex, gnarled, knurled, nodular **8** baffling, involved, puzzling, ticklish, unsmooth **9** blemished, difficult, intricate **10** perplexing **11** complicated, troublesome **12** rough-grained **13** coarse-grained, problematical

know 3 see **6** be sure, be wise, notice **7** be smart, discern, make out, realize **8** identify, perceive **9** apprehend, be assured, be aware of, be certain, be close to, get wise to, recognize **10** be informed, be positive, understand **11** be confident, be sagacious, be thick with, distinguish, feel certain, have down pat, have no doubt **12** discriminate, have down cold, have the ear of **13** be cognizant of, be intelligent, have knowledge, rub elbows with **14** be familiar with

knowable 9 thinkable **11** conceivable, discernible, perceivable **14** understandable

Knowell, Edward
character in: **19** Every Man in His Humour
author: **6** Jonson

know for sure 9 be certain **10** be positive

know-how 3 art **4** bent, gift **5** craft, flair, knack, savvy, skill **6** talent **7** ability, mastery **8** aptitude, capacity, deftness **9** adeptness, expertise, knowledge, technique **10** adroitness, capability, competence, experience, expertness **12** proficiency **12** skillfulness **15** professionalism
French: **11** savoir-faire

knowing 4 deep, wise **5** aware, canny, sharp, smart, sound **6** astute, brainy, bright, clever, shrewd **7** erudite, fraught, learned, sapient **8** academic, educated, eloquent, highbrow, literary, profound, schooled, sensible **9** conscious, judicious, revealing, sagacious **10** discerning, expressive, meaningful, perceptive, percipient, scholastic, widely read **11** enlightened, intelligent, significant **12** intellectual, well-informed **13** comprehending, knowledgeable, perspicacious, philosophical, sophisticated, understanding

knowing how to live
French: **11** savoir-vivre

knowing just what to do
French: **11** savoir-faire

know-it-all 5 brash **13** overconfident

knowledge 3 ken, tip **4** data, hint, lore, news **5** sense **6** memory, notice, report, wisdom **7** inkling, mention, tidings **8** learning **9** awareness, education, erudition, schooling, statement **10** cognizance, intimation, perception **11** cultivation, declaration, familiarity, information, realization, recognition, revelation, scholarship **12** announcement, book learning, intelligence, notification **13** communication, comprehension, consciousness, enlightenment, pronouncement
god of: **4** Odin **5** Othin

knowledgeable 3 hip **4** up on **8** at home in, versed in **12** familiar with, well-informed **14** acquainted with, conversant with
French: **9** au courant

knowledge of the world
French: **11** savoir-vivre

known 5 noted, plain **6** common, famous, patent **7** evident, obvious, popular **8** apparent, definite, distinct, familiar, manifest, palpable **9** notorious, prominent **10** celebrated, recognized **11** self-evident

know thyself
Greek: **13** gnothi seauton

knuckle under 5 yield **6** give in, submit **7** bow down **9** surrender **10** capitulate

knurled 5 bumpy, lumpy **6** gnarly, knobby, knotty, knurly, nubbly, ridged **7** bulging, gnarled, knotted, nodular

koala
family: **9** marsupial
habitat: **9** Australia
food: **10** eucalyptus
resembles: **9** small bear
kin of: **6** wombat

Koch, Robert
field: **12** bacteriology
nationality: **6** German
isolated: **2** TB **12** tuberculosis
awarded: **10** Nobel Prize

Kodaly, Zoltan
born: **7** Hungary **9** Kecskemet
composer of: **9** Hary Janos **11** Czinka Panna, Missa Brevis, Szekely Fono **14** Budavari Te Deum **15** Dances of Galanta **17** Dances of Marosszek, Peacock Variations, Psalmus Hungaricus **28** The Spinning Room of the Szekelys

Koestler, Arthur
author of: **14** Darkness at Noon **15** The Sleepwalkers

Kohinoor, Koh-i-noor 7 diamond **6** (106) carats
from: **5** India
part of: **18** British Crown Jewels

kohoutek 5 comet
named for: **15** Czech astronomer

Kojak
character: **5** (Det) Rizzo **7** (Det) Stavros **9** (Lt) Theo Kojak **10** (Det) Saperstein **11** Frank McNeil **12** (Lt) Bobby Crocker
cast: **9** Dan Frazer **10** Vince Conti **11** Kevin Dobson, Mark Russell **12** Telly Savalas **13** George Savalas (Demosthenes)

trademark: 8 lollipop
phrase: 14 Who loves ya baby?

Kollwitz, Kathe
real name: 12 Kathe Schmidt
born: 10 Konigsberg **11** East Prussia
artwork: 3 War **5** Death, Pieta **11** Proletariat **13** Weavers' Revolt (Weaver's Rebellion) **14** Mother and Child, The Peasants' War **18** Death Seizing a Woman

Kol Nidre 4 vows **8** promises **22** Jewish liturgical prayer
recited on eve of: 9 Yom Kippur

Kong
nickname of: 11 Dave Kingman

Kon-Tiki
author: 13 Thor Heyerdahl
name of: 4 raft

kook 3 nut **5** crazy, flake, loony, wacko **6** cuckoo, weirdo **7** dingbat **8** crackpot **9** ding-a-ling, eccentric, fruitcake, harebrain, screwball **10** crackbrain

Koran 5 Islam, Quran **9** Word of God **10** Sacred book
revelations to: 8 Mohammed
division: 4 sura
dictated by: 7 Gabriel **9** archangel

Korea
other name: 6 Chosen **17** land of morning calm
capital:
  North Korea: 9 Pyongyang
  South Korea: 5 Seoul
largest city: 5 Seoul
others: 5 Masan, Mokpo, Pusan, Sinpo, Suwon, Taegu, Wonju **6** Chonju, Inchon, Kangso, Kunsan, Taejon, Wonsan **7** Hanyang, Hungnam, Kaesong, Kangson, Kwangju **8** Chongjin, Chunchon, Kimchaek
school: 5 Busan **6** Yonsei **7** Hanyang **8** Kim Chaek, Kyung Hee **9** Kim Il Sung
division:
  ancient: 5 Silla **6** Chosen **7** Koguryo, Paekche
monetary unit: 3 woh, won **4** chun, hwan, kwan
weight: 3 won
island: 4 Chin, Koje **5** Cheju, Sinmi **6** Anmyon, Huksan, Namhae **7** Tokchok **8** Quelpart **10** Paengnyong
mountain: 4 Wang **5** Chiri, Halla **6** Kwanmo, Sobaek **7** Diamond, Kyebang, Nangnim, Taebaek **8** Changpai, Hamgyong, Myohyang **9** Paektusan **10** Kumgang-san
highest point: 6 Paektu **9** Paektu-san
river: 3 Han, Kin, Kum, Kun, Nam **4** Lobk, Yalu **5** Amnok, Imjin, Tumen **6** Namhan, Pukhan, Somjin, Soyang, Yesong **7** Naktong, Taedong **8** Changjin, Youngsan **9** Chongchon
sea: 5 Japan **6** Yellow **9** East China
physical feature:
  bay: 5 Korea **6** Yongil **7** Kanghwa,

Kyonggi **9** Tongjoson
cape: 4 Musu
point: 7 Changgi **8** Changsan
strait: 5 Korea
valley: 7 Naktong
people: 6 Korean
artist: 8 Chong Son **10** Kimtlong-do
dynasty: 2 Yi **4** Choe **5** Koryo
leader: 6 Sejong **8** Yi Sung-gy **9** Kim Il Sung **11** Chun Doo Hwan, Syngman Rhee **12** Park Chung Hee
legendary leader: 5 Ki-tse **6** Chitse, Chi-tzu, Tangun
poet: 10 Hwang Chini
Unification Church Leader 12 Sun Myung Moon
language: 6 Korean
alphabet: 6 hangul
religion: 6 Taoism **7** animism **8** Buddhism **9** Chondogyo **12** Christianity, Confucianism
place:
  palace: 8 Kyongbok
  temple: 7 Haein-sa **17** Hall of Eternal Life
  tomb: 14 Dancing Figures
feature:
  clothing: 5 chima
  game: 3 yut **5** akoan **6** ho-hpai **7** kol-ye-si **9** ryong-hpai, sang-ryouk **10** ke-pouk-hpai, sin-syo-tyen **12** tjak-ma- tchi-ki **15** kko-ri-pouk-tchi-ki
  martial art: 9 tae-kwon-do
  musical instrument: 6 chaing **7** kayagum, komungo
  porcelain: 7 Celadon
  porch: 4 maru
  pottery: 8 pun-chong
food:
  bean curd: 4 tubu
  hot pickle: 6 kimchi
  meat-filled dumpling: 5 mandu
  noodle: 5 kuksu

Korman, Harvey
born: 9 Chicago IL
roles: 11 High Anxiety **13** Danny Kaye Show **14** Blazing Saddles **16** Carol Burnett Show

Kornberg, Arthur
field: 12 biochemistry
sythesized: 3 DNA, RNA **15** ribonucleic acid **20** deoxyribonucleic acid
awarded: 10 Nobel Prize

kosher 5 right **6** proper **7** ethical **8** fit to eat **10** aboveboard **12** on the up and up

Kosinski, Jerzy
author of: 5 Steps **7** Cockpit **9** Blind Date **10** Being There **11** Passion Play **12** The Devil Tree **14** The Painted Bird

Kowalski, Stanley
character in: 21 A Streetcar Named Desire
wife: 6 Stella
sister-in-law: 7 Blanche
author: 8 Williams

kowtow 4 bend, fawn **5** cower, stoop, toady **6** bow low, cringe, curtsy, grovel, salaam **7** truckle **8** bootlick, butter up, softsoap **9** genuflect **11** apple-polish **12** bow and scrape **16** prostrate oneself
kowtowing 7 fawning, servile **8** toadying **9** groveling **10** obsequious

Kraken
origin: 9 Norwegian
form: 7 monster
habitat: 3 sea
caused: 10 whirlpools

Kramer, Stanley
director of: 10 On the Beach **11** Ship of Fools **14** Inherit the Wind, The Defiant Ones **19** Judgment at Nuremberg

Kramer vs Kramer
director: 12 Robert Benton
based on novel by: 11 Avery Corman
cast: 10 Howard Duff **11** Justin Henry, Meryl Streep **13** Dustin Hoffman, Jane Alexander
Oscar for: 5 actor (Hoffman) **7** picture **8** director **10** screenplay **17** supporting actress (Streep)

Krantz, Judith
author of: 8 Scruples **13** Princess Daisy **16** I'll Take Manhattan, Mistral's Daughter

Krazy Kat
creator: 14 George Herriman
character:
  cop: 12 Offissa B Pupp
  mouse: 6 Ignatz
prop: 5 brick
place: 4 jail **14** Coconino County **24** Kelly's Exclusive Brick Yard

Krebs, Hans Adolf
field: 9 chemistry
nationality: 6 German
discovered: 15 citric acid cycle
awarded: 10 Nobel Prize

Kreisler, Fritz
born: 6 Vienna **7** Austria
composer of: 7 Allegro **10** Praeludium **15** Caprice Viennois **16** Tambourin Chinois

Kreutzer, Rodolphe
born: 6 France **10** Versailles
composer of: 16 Etudes ou Caprices

Kreutzer Sonata, The
author: 10 Leo Tolstoy
character: 13 Mme Pozdnishef, Trukhashevsky **16** Vasyla Pozdnishef

Krieg 3 war

Kriemhild
origin: 8 Germanic
mentioned in: 14 Nibelungenlied
brother: 7 Gunther
husband: 9 Siegfried
slew: 5 Hagan **7** Gunther
avenged: 6 murder **9** Siegfried
corresponds to: 6 Gudrun, Kudrun **7** Guthrun

Kristin Lavransdatter
author: **12** Sigrid Undset

Kronos *see* **6** Cronus

Krook
character in: **10** Bleak House
author: **7** Dickens

Kropp, Albert
character in: **25** All Quiet on the Western Front
author: **8** Remarque

krypton
chemical symbol: **2** Kr

Kuala Lumpur
capital of: **8** Malaysia

Kubla Khan
author: **15** Samuel Coleridge
city: **6** Xanadu
river: **4** Alph

Kubrick, Stanley
director of: **6** Lolita **9** Spartacus **11** Barry Lyndon **12** Paths of Glory **13** Dr Strangelove (or How I Learned to Stop Worrying and Love the Bomb) **16** A Clockwork Orange **30** Two Thousand and One A Space Odyssey

kudos 4 fame **5** award, glory, honor, prize **6** esteem, praise, renown, repute **7** acclaim, plaudit **8** citation, prestige **9** celebrity, laudation **10** admiration, decoration **12** commendation **14** celebratedness

Kudrun *see* **6** Gudrun

Kukla, Fran & Ollie
hostess: **11** Fran Allison
puppet: **5** Kukla, Ollie (Oliver J Dragon) **8** Mercedes **9** Cecil Bill **10** Col Crackie **11** Beulah Witch **12** Olivia Dragon **13** Delores Dragon **14** Fletcher Rabbit **18** Mme Ophelia Oglepuss

kummel
origin: **7** Germany
flavor: **7** caraway

kumquat 10 Fortunella
varieties: **4** oval **5** round **6** Marumi, Nagami **16** Australian desert

Kung Fu
character: **8** Master Po **9** Master Kan **14** Kwai Chang Caine
cast: **8** Keye Luke **9** Philip Ahn **11** Radames Pera **14** David Carradine
Caine raised in: **13** Shaolin Temple

kunzite
species: **9** spodumene

Kupka, Frank (Frantisek)
born: **6** Opocno **7** Bohemia **14** Czechoslovakia
artwork: **12** Black Accents, The Cathedral **16** Etude pour la Fugue **17** Fugue in Red and Blue **23** Fugue in Two Colors Amorpha **25** Philosophical Architecture

Kuprin, Aleksandr
author of: **7** The Duel **10** Yama the Pit

Kurosawa, Akira
director of: **3** Ran **8** Rashomon **12** Seven Samurai

Kurtz
character in: **15** Heart of Darkness
author: **6** Conrad

Kuwait
name means: **9** small fort
capital/largest city: **10** Kuwait City
others: **6** Ahmadi **7** Hawalli **8** Abdullah, al-Jahrah, Fahaheel, Shuwaykh **9** al-Shuayba **12** Mena al- Ahmadi, Mina Abd Allah, Mina al-Ahmadi
head of state: **4** emir
monetary unit: **4** fils **5** dinar
island: **5** Warba **7** Bubiyan, Failaka
physical feature:
bay: **6** Kuwait **12** Khor Abdullah
duststorm: **4** kaus
gulf: **7** Persian
oasis: **6** Jahrah
people: **4** Arab **5** Iraqi, Saudi **6** Indian **7** Bedouin **8** Egyptian **9** Pakistani **11** Palestinian
ruling family: **5** Sabah
sheikh (Sabah family): **5** Ahmad, Salem **7** Mubarak **12** Jaber al-Ahmed, Sabah al-Salim **15** Abdullah al-Salim
religion: **5** Islam
war: **4** Gulf **11** Desert Storm, Persian Gulf **12** Desert Shield
enemy: **4** Iraq **13** Saddam Hussein

Kwa
language family: **16** Niger-Kordofanian
group: **10** Niger-Congo
includes: **3** Ewe, Ibo, Twi **4** Bini, Nupe, Togo **6** Yoruba **7** Dahomey

Kwakiutl
language family: **8** Wakashan
location: **6** Canada **15** British Columbia, Vancouver Island **20** Queen Charlotte Island
related to: **6** Nootka **10** Bellabella
noted for: **10** totem poles **15** Cannibal Society, wooden sculpture
called: **14** potlatch people

Kwanza, Kwanzaa 15 harvest festival
celebrated by: **16** African-Americans

Kyd, Thomas
author of: **17** The Spanish Tragedy

Kyrgyzstan
formerly: **10** Kirghiz SSR
capital/largest city: **6** Frunze **7** Bishkek
head of state: **9** president
government: **8** republic
monetary unit: **3** som
mountain: **8** Tian Shan
people: **5** Uzbek **6** Kyrgyz **7** Kirghiz, Russian
language: **6** Turkic **7** Kirghiz, Russian
religion: **6** Muslim **10** Sunni Islam

Kyrie eleison 13 Lord have mercy

Laban
   father: 7 Bethuel
   grandfather: 5 Nahor
   daughter: 4 Leah **6** Rachel
   sister: 7 Rebekah
   son-in-law: 5 Jacob

label 3 tag **4** mark, name, note, seal,
sign, slip **5** brand, stamp, tally, title **6**
define, docket, ticket **7** earmark, mark
off, sticker **8** classify, describe **9** designate **10** denominate, put a mark on
11 appellation, designation, inscription **12** characterize **13** specification
14 classification, identification **16**
characterization

labor, labour 4 plod, toil, work **5**
slave, sweat **6** drudge, effort, suffer **7**
agonize, travail, workers, workmen **8**
drudgery, exertion, laborers, manpower, plodding, plug away, struggle
9 employees, grind away, work force
10 birth pangs, childbirth, menial
work, smart under **11** birth throes,
manual labor, parturition **12** accouchement, be affected by, be burdened by, be troubled by **13** be the
victim of **14** employ one's time, work
like a slave

labored 5 heavy, stiff **6** clumsy,
forced, wooden **7** awkward, cramped,
halting, studied **8** drawnout, overdone, strained **9** contrived, difficult,
laborious, maladroit, ponderous, unnatural **13** self-conscious, unsponta-
neous

laborer 4 esne, hand, peon, serf **6** coolie, drudge, menial, toiler, worker **7**
plodder, workman **8** handyman, hired
man, hireling, workhand **9** hired hand
10 roustabout, wage earner, workingman **11** proletarian **12** manual worker
16 blue- collar worker

laborious 4 hard **6** brutal, severe, uphill **7** arduous, irksome, labored, onerous, wearing **8** rigorous, tiresome,
toilsome, wearying **9** demanding, difficult, effortful, fa- tiguing, herculean,
strenuous, wearisome **10** burdensome,
oppressive, struggling **11** troublesome

laboriously 4 hard **9** arduously **14**
with difficulty **15** with great effort

laboriousness 5 trial **8** tough job **10**
difficulty, rough going, uphill work **11**
arduousness **12** hard sledding **15**
troublesomeness

labor omnia vincit 15 work conquers
all
   motto of: 8 Oklahoma

Labors of Hercules *see* **8** Hercules

labyrinth 3 web **4** knot, maze **5** snarl
6 jungle, morass, riddle, tangle **7**
complex, network **9** intricacy, mare's
nest **10** complexity, perplexity, wilderness **11** convolution

Labyrinth
   form: 4 maze
   location: 5 Crete
   built by: 8 Daedalus
   for: 9 King Minos
   challenged by: 7 Theseus
   he was aided by: 7 Ariadne
   with: 6 thread
   housed: 8 Minotaur

Lacaille, Nicholas Louis de
   field: 9 astronomy
   nationality: 6 French
   mapped: 14 constellations

lace 3 tie **4** beat, bind, cane, dope,
lash, whip **5** braid, cinch, close, flail,
spank, spike, strap, tie up, truss **6**
dope up, fasten, flavor, infuse, punish, secure, switch, tether, thrash **7**
fortify, spice up, suffuse, tighten **8**
chastise, make fast, make taut **10**
strengthen **11** add liquor to **12** add
spirits to, draw together, give a beating

Lacedaemon
   founder of: 6 Sparta
   father: 4 Zeus
   mother: 8 Taygete
   wife: 6 Sparta
   son: 7 Amyclas
   daughter: 8 Eurydice
   descendants: 5 Helen **6** Castor, Pollux **8** Dioscuri **9** Hippocoon, Tyn-
   darius **12** Clytemnestra

lacerate 3 cut, rip **4** gash, hurt, pain,
scar, stab, tear **5** lance, sever, slash,
slice, wound **6** deface **7** agonize,
scratch, torment, torture **8** distress,
give pain, puncture **10** excruciate **11**
inflict pain

lacerating 5 acute **6** fierce, severe **7**
cutting, extreme, intense, violent **12**
excruciating

laceration 3 cut, rip **4** tear **5** wound
10 mutilation

Lachaise, Gaston
   born: 5 Paris **6** France
   artwork: 12 Standing Nude **13** Standing Woman **14** Floating Figure

Lachesis
   form: 4 Fate
   holds: 12 thread of life
   determines: 6 length **7** destiny

lachrymose 3 sad **5** teary, weepy **6**
crying **7** maudlin, tearful, weeping **8**
mournful **10** melancholy

lack 4 miss, need, want **6** dearth **7** absence **8** omission, scarcity, shortage **9**
be missing, be short of, depletion,
neediness, privation, scantness **10** deficiency, exhaustion **11** deprivation,
fall short of **12** be inadequate **13** be
caught short, be deficient in **14** be
found wanting, be insufficient

lackadaisical 4 idle **7** languid, loafing
8 lifeless, listless, mindless **9** apathetic, lethargic, unexcited **10** inani-
mated, phlegmatic, spiritless, unaspiring, uninspired **11** indifferent,
languishing, unambitious, unconcerned, unexcitable, unmotivated **12**
uninterested **13** dillydallying

lackey 4 page **5** slave, toady, usher,
valet **6** butler, flunky, helper, menial,
minion, squire, waiter **7** servant,
steward **8** employee, follower, hanger-on, hireling, inferior, retainer **9** assistant, attendant, cupbearer, mercenary, underling

lacking 7 needing, wanting **9** deficient
10 inadequate **12** falling short, insufficient
   French: 6 manque

lackluster 4 blah, dead, drab, dull **5**
bland, muted **6** boring, dreary,
leaden, pallid, somber **7** humdrum,
nothing, prosaic, subdued **8** lifeless,
mediocre, ordinary **9** colorless **10** lusterless **11** commonplace **12** run-of-
the-mill **13** uninteresting

lack of conviction 5 doubt **8** question **9** misgiving **10** hesitation, indecision **11** uncertainty
   trait of: 14 Doubting Thomas

lack of faith 5 doubt **7** atheism **8** distrust, mistrust **9** disbelief, suspicion

lack of feeling 6 apathy **8** coldness,
numbness **11** impassivity **15** emotionlessness, hardheartedness, passionless-
ness

lack of interest 5 ennui **6** apathy **7**
boredom **9** unconcern **12** indifference

lack of respect 8 contempt, rudeness

9 disregard **10** disrespect **11** discourtesy, irreverence **12** impoliteness

lack of skill 9 inability **10** clumsiness, ineptitude **11** awkwardness **12** incompetency

Laclos, Pierre Choderlos de
author of: **22** Les Liaisons Dangereuses

Lacombe, Lucien
director: **10** Louis Malle
cast: **12** Pierre Blaise **13** Aurore Clement **16** Holger Lowenadler

laconic 4 curt **5** blunt, brief, pithy, short, terse **7** compact, concise, pointed, spartan, summary **8** succinct **9** condensed **10** to the point **12** concentrated **14** sparing of words

lacquer 4 coat **5** glaze **7** coating, shellac, varnish

lacrimoso
music: **7** tearful

lacrosse
Indian name: **9** bagataway
circle around goal: **6** crease
played with: **6** crosse **14** pouched racquet
players/team: **3** ten
position: **6** goalie **9** attackman **10** defenseman, midfielder
term: **6** riding **8** clearing

lacuna 3 gap, pit **4** gulf, hole, void **5** blank, break, crack, ditch, pause, space **6** breach, cavity, hiatus **7** caesura, fissure, interim, opening, vacancy **8** interval, omission **10** interstice, suspension **12** interruption **13** discontinuity

lacustrine 7 aquatic **8** riparian **11** lake-growing **12** lake-dwelling

lacy 4 fine **5** filmy, gauzy, meshy, netty, sheer, webby **6** barred, frilly, netted, porous, webbed **7** gridded, netlike **8** cobwebby, delicate, filigree, gossamer, lacelike, retiform **9** filigreed **10** diaphanous, reticulate **11** latticelike, transparent

lad 3 boy, kid **5** sprig, youth **6** shaver, sprout **8** juvenile, young man **9** schoolboy, stripling, young chap, youngster **11** young fellow

Ladd, Alan
son: **5** David **6** Alan Jr
co-star: **12** Veronica Lake
born: **12** Hot Springs AR
roles: **5** Shane **13** The Blue Dahlia **14** The Great Gatsby, This Gun for Hire

ladies' man 4 beau, stud **5** spark **6** escort, gigolo **7** playboy **8** cavalier, gay blade

Ladino
also: **7** Judezmo **12** Judeo-Spanish
spoken by: **9** Sephardim
based on: **10** Old Spanish
script: **6** Hebrew **7** mestizo

Ladoga, Lake

largest in: **6** Europe
located in: **6** Russia

La Dolce Vita
director: **15** Federico Fellini
cast: **9** Lex Barker, Nadia Gray **10** Anouk Aimee **11** Anita Ekberg **19** Marcello Mastroianni

ladrone 5 thief **6** bandit, outlaw

lady 4 wife **5** woman **6** female, matron, spouse **7** duchess, peeress **8** baroness, countess **10** aristocrat, noblewoman **11** gentlewoman, marchioness, viscountess, woman of rank **13** well-bred woman
German: **4** frau
Italian: **5** donna
Spanish/Portuguese: **4** dona

Lady Chatterley's Lover
author: **10** D H Lawrence
character: **7** Mellors **19** Constance Chatterley

Lady Eve, The
director: **14** Preston Sturges
cast: **10** Henry Fonda **13** Charles Coburn **14** Eugene Pallette **15** Barbara Stanwyck, William Demarest

Lady for a Day
director: **10** Frank Capra
based on story by: **11** Damon Runyon
cast: **9** Guy Kibbee, May Robson **13** Warren William
remade as: **19** Pocketful of Miracles

Lady from Dubuque, The
author: **11** Edward Albee

Lady from the Sea, The
author: **11** Henrik Ibsen

Lady in Chair
constellation of: **10** Cassiopeia

ladylike 5 civil **6** modest, polite, proper **7** courtly, elegant, genteel, refined **8** cultured, decorous, mannerly, polished, well-bred **9** courteous, dignified **10** cultivated **11** respectable **12** well mannered **13** well brought up

Lady of the Camellias, The *see* **7** Camille

Lady of the Lake, The
author: **14** Sir Walter Scott
character: **9** Allan Bane **11** Roderick Dhu **12** Ellen Douglas **13** Malcolm Graeme **14** James Fitz-James, James of Douglas

Lady Oracle
author: **14** Margaret Atwood

lady's maid
French: **14** femme de chambre

Lady's Not for Burning, The
author: **14** Christopher Fry

lady's-slipper, lady-slipper
varieties: **4** pink **5** showy **6** orchid **8** mountain, ram's-head **9** two-leaved **10** small white **11** large yellow, small yellow

Lady Vanishes, The
director: **15** Alfred Hitchcock

cast: **9** Paul Lukas **13** Dame May Whitty **15** Michael Redgrave **16** Margaret Lockwood

Lady Windermere's Fan
author: **10** Oscar Wilde
character: **10** Mrs Erlynne **14** Lord Darlington, Lord Windermere **18** Lord Augustus Lorton

Laertes
son: **8** Odysseus

Laertes
character in: **6** Hamlet
sister: **7** Ophelia
father: **8** Polonius
author: **11** Shakespeare

La Farge, John
born: **9** New York NY
artwork: **14** Maua Our Boatman **17** The Muse of Painting **18** Red and White Peonies

La Fayette, Comtesse de
author of: **19** La Princesse de Cleves

Lafayette, Marquis de
also: **38** Marie Joseph Paul Yves Roch Gilbert du Motier
nationality: **6** French
served in: **14** July Revolution **16** French Revolution **18** American Revolution
battle: **8** Yorktown **10** Brandywine

Lafcadio's Adventures (The Vatican Swindle)
author: **9** Andre Gide

La Fontaine, Jean de
author of: **6** Fables

lag 4 drag, halt, inch, limp, snag **5** dally, delay, hitch, tarry, trail **6** be idle, be late, be slow, dawdle, falter, hold up, linger, loiter, trudge **7** be tardy, setback, slacken, stagger **8** be behind, hang back, slowdown **9** be overdue, inch along **10** drag behind, slackening **11** slowing down **12** bide one's time, take one's time **13** falling behind, procrastinate

laggard 4 mope, poke, slow, slug **5** idler, snail, tardy **6** loafer, remiss **7** dallier, dawdler, lounger **8** lingerer, loiterer, potterer, putterer, slowfoot, slowpoke, sluggard, sluggish **9** donothing, straggler **12** dilly-dallier **13** stick-in-the-mud

lagniappe, lagnappe 3 tip **4** gift, perk **5** bonus, favor, prize **7** largess, memento, present **8** gratuity, largesse **9** pourboire

Lagos
former capital of: **7** Nigeria

Lahr, Bert
real name: **14** Irving Lahrheim
born: **9** New York NY
roles: **12** Cowardly Lion **13** The Wizard of Oz

laic 3 lay **5** civil **6** laical **7** amateur, popular, profane, secular, worldly **8** temporal **11** nonclerical, nonpastoral

12 secularistic **13** inexperienced **15** nonprofessional **17** nonecclesiastical

lair 3 den, lie, mew **4** hole, nest **5** cover, haunt **6** burrow, cavern, covert **7** hideout, retreat **8** hideaway **9** sanctuary **12** resting place

laissez-faire, laisser-faire 8 hands off **9** let them be, unconcern **12** indifference **14** let-alone policy, live and let live **15** noninterference, nonintervention

laissez-passer 4 pass **6** permit **11** allow to pass

Laius
  king of: 6 Thebes
  father: 8 Labdacus
  great-grandfather: 6 Cadmus
  wife: 7 Jocasta
  son: 7 Oedipus
  killed by: 7 Oedipus

Lajeunesse, Gabriel
  character in: 10 Evangeline
  author: 10 Longfellow

lake
  of Afghanistan: 7 Helmand **13** Hamud-i-Helmand
  of Albania: 4 Ulze **5** Matia, Ohrid **6** Prespa **7** Ochrida, Scutari, Shkoder **8** Ohridsko
  of Algeria: 5 Hodna **6** Sabkha **7** Cherqui, Fedjadj, Meirhir **10** Azzel Matti, Meherrhane
  of Andorra: 11 Engolasters
  of Argentina: 6 Viedma **7** Cardiel, Fagnano, Musters **11** Buenos Aires, Mar Chiquita, Nahuel Huapi
  of Armenia: 3 Van **5** Sevan, Urmia **8** Urumiyah
  of Australia: 4 Eyre **5** Carey, Cowan, Frome, Moore, Wells **6** Austin, Barlee, Bulloo, Dundas, Harris, Mackay **7** Amadeus, Blanche, Everard, Torrens **8** Carnegie, Gairdner **9** MacDonald **10** Yammayamma **14** Disappointment
  of Austria: 6 Almsee **7** Fertoto, Mondsee **8** Bodensee, Traunsee **9** Constance **10** Neusiedler
  of Benin: 5 Aheme **6** Nokoue
  of Bolivia: 5 Poopo **7** Allagas, Coipasa, Rogagua **8** Titicaca **10** Desaguader
  of Botswana: 3 Dow, Xau **5** Ngami
  of Brazil: 4 Aima, Feia **5** Mirim **13** Logo dos Platos
  of Burundi: 7 Rugwero **8** Tshohoha **10** Tanganyika
  of Cambodia/Kampuchea: 8 Tonle Sap
  of Cameroon: 4 Chad
  of Canada: 4 Cree, Erie, Gras, Seul **5** Garry, Huron, Rainy **6** Louise, St John **7** Abitibi, Dubawnt, Nipigon, Ontario, Testlin **8** Kootenay, Manitoba, Okanagan, Reindeer, Superior, Winnipeg **9** Athabaska, Great Bear, Nipissing **10** Great Slave, Mistassini **12** Winnipegosis

  of Central African Republic: 4 Assa
  of Chad: 4 Chad
  of Chile: 5 Ranco **6** Yelcho **7** Puyehue, Rupanco **8** Cochrane **10** General Paz, Llanquihue **11** Buenos Aires
  of China: 3 Tai **4** Chao, Na-mu **5** Kaoyu, Oling, Telli **6** Bamtso, Bornor, Ebinor, Erhhai, Khanka, Lopnor, Namtso, Poyang **7** Chaling, Hungtse, Karanor, Kokonor **8** Hulunnor, Montcalm, Taroktso, Tellinor, Tienchih, Tsinghai, Tungting
  of Colombia: 4 Tota
  of the Congo: 5 Mweru, Tumba **6** Albert, Nyanza, Upemba **7** Leopold **11** Stanley Pool
  of Costa Rica: 6 Arenal
  of Denmark 6 Arreso
  of Djibouti: 4 Abbe **5** Assal
  of Dominican Republic: 10 Enriquillo
  of Egypt: 4 Edku, Idku **5** Qarun **6** Maryut, Moeris, Nasser **7** Manzala **8** Burullus, Mareotis
  of El Salvador: 5 Guiha, Guija **8** Ilopango **10** Coatepeque
  of England: 8 Grasmere **9** Ennerdale, Ullswater, Wastwater **10** Buttermere, Windermere **12** Derwentwater **13** Coniston Water
  of Estonia: 5 Pskov **6** Peipus **9** Vortsjarv
  of Ethiopia: 3 Abe **4** Tana **5** Abaya, Shola, Tanna, Tsana, Tzana, Zeway **6** Dambea, Dembea, Rudolf **8** Blue Nile, Stefanie
  of Finland: 3 Juo, Muo **4** Kemi, Kiui, Nasi, Oulu, Puru, Pyha, Simo **5** Enara, Enare, Hauki, Inari, Kalla, Lappa, Lesti, Puula, Saima **6** Ladoya, Lentua, Saimaa, Sounne, Syvari **7** Koitere, Nilakka **8** Pielinen **9** Kallavesi, Pielavesi
  of France: 6 Annecy, Cazaux, Geneva
  of Gabon Republic: 7 Anengue, Azinguo
  of Germany, East: 6 Muritz
  of Germany, West: 9 Constance **11** Inner Alster, Outer Alster
  of Ghana: 5 Volta **8** Bosumtwi
  of Greece: 5 Karla, Volve **6** Copais, Kopais, Prespa, Voweis **8** Ioannina, Koroneia, Vistonis **9** Trichonis, Vegoritis
  of Grenada: 10 Grand Etang
  of Guatemala: 5 Dulce, Guija, Peten **6** Izabal **7** Atitlan **9** Amatitlan, Peten Itza
  of Haiti: 8 Saumatre
  of Honduras: 5 Criba, Yojoa **6** Brewer
  of Hungary: 5 Ferto **7** Balaton, Velence **9** Blatensee **10** Neusiedler, Plattensee
  of Iceland: 6 Myvatn **10** Thorisvatn **14** Thingvallavatn
  of India: 5 Jheel, Lonar, Wular **6** Chilka, Colair, Dhebar, Kolair **7** Kol-

  leru, Pulicat, Pushkar, Sambahr
  of Indonesia: 4 Toba **5** Ranau **6** Towuti
  of Iran: 5 Niris, Tasht, Tuzlu, Urmia **6** Sahweh, Sistan **7** Maharlu **8** Nemekser, Urumiyeh
  of Iraq: 6 al-Milh **7** Sanniya **8** al-Hammar
  of Ireland: 3 Doo, Key, Ree, Tay **4** Conn, Derg, Erne, Mask **5** Allen, Barra, Carra, Gowna, Leane, Lough, Neagh **6** Boderg, Cooter, Corrib, Ennell **7** Dromore, Gougane, Oughter, Sheelin **9** Killarney
  of Israel: 5 Huleh **7** Dead Sea **8** Kinneret, Tiberias **12** Sea of Galilee
  of Italy: 4 Como, Iseo, Nemi **5** Garda **6** Albano, Lesina, Lugano, Varano **7** Bolsena, Perugia **8** Maggiore **9** Bracciano, Trasimeno
  of Japan: 4 Biwa, Suwa, Toya **6** Towada **8** Kutchawa, Shikotsu
  of Kazakhstan: 8 Balkhash
  of Kenya: 6 Magadi, Nakuru, Natron, Rudolf **7** Turkana **8** Naivasha, Victoria
  of Lebanon: 5 Quran **6** Qirawn
  of Lithuania: 5 Dysna
  of Luxembourg: 8 Haut Sure
  of Macedonia: 5 Ohrid **6** Prespa **7** Ochrida
  of Madagascar: 5 Itasy **7** Alaotra, Kinkony
  of Malawi: 5 Nyasa **6** Chilwa, Malawi
  of Mali: 2 Do **4** Debo **5** Garou **7** Korarou **9** Faguibine
  of Mexico: 7 Chapala, Texcoco **9** Patzcuaro
  of Mongolia: 3 Uvs **5** Har Us **6** Bor Nor **7** Ghirgis, Ubsa Nor **8** Airik Nor, Durga Nor, Hobsogol, Khara Usu **9** Khubsugul, Khukhu-Nur **10** Khirgis Nor
  of Montenegro: 7 Scutari, Shkoder
  of Mozambique: 5 Nyasa **6** Chuali, Nyassa **8** Nhavarre
  of Myanmar: 4 Inle
  of Nauru: 11 Buada Lagoon
  of the Netherlands: 7 Haarlem **10** Ijsselmeer **11** Grevelingen, Hazinguliet
  of New Zealand: 3 Ada **4** Gunn, Ohau **5** Hawea, Taupo **6** Pukaki, Pupuke, Te Anau, Tekapo, Wanaka **7** Brunner, Diamond, Kanieri, Okareka, Rotorua **8** Okataina, Paradise, Rotoaira, Wakatipi **9** Manapouri
  of Nicaragua: 7 Managua **9** Nicaragua
  of Niger: 4 Chad
  of Nigeria: 4 Chad
  of the Nile: 4 Tana **5** Kyoga, Tsana **6** Albert, Edward, Nasser **8** Victoria
  of Norway: 4 Alte **5** Ister, Mjosa, Snasa **6** Femund **7** Rostavn, Tunnsjo
  of Panama: 5 Gatun
  of Paraguay: 4 Vera, Ypoa **8** Ypa-

carai
of Peru: 8 Titicaca
of Poland: 5 Goplo, Mamry **8** Niegocin, Sniardwy **13** Stettin Lagoon
of Puerto Rico: 5 Loiza **6** Carite **8** Dos Bocas **9** Caonillas, Guatajaca
of Romania: 5 Sinoe **6** Snagov
of Russia: 3 Seg **4** Azov, Kola, Neva **5** Byelo, Chany, Elton, Erara, Ilmen, Lacha, Onega, Vozhe **6** Baikal, Ladoga **10** Caspian Sea
of Rwanda: 4 Kivu **5** Ihema **6** Bufera, Bulera, Mohasi **7** Rugwero, Ruhnodo **8** Mugesera, Tshohoha
of Sardinia: 6 Omodeo
of Scotland: 3 Awe, Dee, Lin, Tay **4** Earn, Fyne, Gair, Gare, Linn, Ness, Oich, Ryan, Sloy **5** Duich, Leven, Lochy, Lough, Morar, Maree, Nevis **6** Laggan, Linnhe, Lomond **7** Katrine, Rannoch, St Marys
of Senegal: 6 Guiers
of Sicily: 7 Pergusa **8** Camarina
of Slovenia: 4 Bled
of Spain: 4 Lago **9** Albrifera
of the Sudan: 2 No **4** Chad, Toad **6** Nasser
of Sweden: 4 Ster **5** Asnen, Malar, Silja, Vaner **6** Vanern, Vatter, Wennen **7** Hielmar, Malaren, Vattern **8** Dalalven **9** Hjalmaren
of Switzerland: 3 Uri, Zug **4** Biel, Thon, Thun **5** Ageri, Leman, Morat **6** Bienne, Brienz, Geneva, Lugano, Sarnen, Wallen, Zurich **7** Hallwil, Lucerne, Lungern **8** Maggiore, Vierwald **9** Bielersee, Constance, Neuchatel, Sarnersee, Thunersee
of Syria: 5 Merom **7** Djeboid **8** Tiberias
of Tanzania: 5 Eyasi, Nyasa, Rukwa **6** Malawi, Natron, Nyassa **7** Manyara **8** Victoria **10** Tanganyika
of Thailand: 9 Nong Lahan
of Tibet: 3 Aru, Bam, Bum, Nam **4** Mema, Tosu **5** Jagok, Tabia **6** Dagtse, Garhur, Kashun, Nam Iso, Seling, Tangra, Yamdok **7** Kyaring, Terinam, Tsaring, Zilling **8** Jiggitai **9** Tengrinor **11** Manasarowar
of Tunisia: 6 Achkel, Djerid **7** Bizerte
of Turkey: 3 Tuz, Van **7** Egridir **8** Beysehir
of Uganda: 5 Kioga, Kyoga **6** Albert, Edward, George **8** Victoria
of the United States: 4 Erie, Mead **5** Huron, Tahoe **6** Cayuga, Finger, George, Itasca, Oneida, Seneca **7** Iliamma, Ontario **8** Michigan, Superior **9** Champlain, Great Salt, Salton Sea, Teshekpuk, Winnebago **10** Okeechobee **11** Yellowstone **13** Pontchartrain, Wallenpaupack, Winnipesaukee **14** Lake of the Woods
of Uruguay: 5 Merin, Mirim **18** Embalse del Rio Negro
of Venezuela: 9 Maracaibo, Tacarigua

of Wales: 4 Bala **6** Vyrnwy
of Yugoslavia: 4 Bled **5** Ohrid **6** Prespa **7** Ochrida, Scutari
of Zaire: 4 Kivu **5** Mweru, Tumba **6** Albert, Edward, Upemba **9** Mai-Ndombe **10** Tanganyika
of Zambia: 5 Mweru **6** Kariba **9** Bangweulu **10** Tanganyika
of Zimbabwe: 4 Kyle **6** Kariba

Lake, Veronica
real name: 29 Constance Frances Marie Ockelman
co-star: 8 Alan Ladd
born: 10 Brooklyn NY
roles: 13 The Blue Dahlia **14** I Married a Witch, This Gun for Hire **16** Sullivan's Travels

Lake Isle of Innisfree, The
author: 7 W B Yeats

L'Allegro
author: 10 John Milton
companion piece: 11 Il Penseroso

Lalo, (Victor Antoine) Edouard
born: 5 Lille **6** France
composer of: 7 Namouna **8** Le Roi d'Ys **11** The King of Ys **15** Spanish Symphony **18** Symphonie Espagnole

lama 4 monk **6** priest
in: 7 Lamaism
high priest: 9 Dalai Lama
locale: 5 Tibet

Lamar, Ruby
character in: 9 Sanctuary
author: 8 Faulkner

Lamarck, Jean B
field: 7 biology
forerunner of theory of: 9 evolution
author of: 21 Philosophie Zoologique

La Mare, Walter de
author of: 16 Memoirs of a Midget

Lamarr, Hedy
real name: 21 Hedwig Eva Maria Kiesler
born: 6 Vienna **7** Austria
roles: 7 Ecstasy **16** Samson and Delilah

Lamas, Fernando
wife: 10 Arlene Dahl **14** Esther Williams
son: 7 Lorenzo
born: 9 Argentina **11** Buenos Aires
roles: 13 The Merry Widow **16** Dangerous When Wet **23** The Girl Who Had Everything

Lamb, Charles
author of: 12 Essays of Elia **13** Dream Children **20** Tales From Shakespeare **25** A Dissertation upon Roast Pig **31** Specimens of English Dramatic Poets
pseudonym: 4 Elia
sister: 4 Mary

lambaste 4 beat, drub, lick, pelt, whip **5** scold, smear **6** berate, defeat, pummel, rebuke, subdue, thrash, wallop **7** bawl out, censure, chew out, clobber, cuss out, shellac, trounce **8** bludgeon,

denounce, vanquish **9** castigate, dress down, light into, overwhelm, reprimand

lambent 6 bright **7** radiant, shining **8** luminous, lustrous **10** flickering, shimmering

Lambert, Constant
born: 6 London **7** England
composer of: 9 Horoscope, Rio Grande **14** Romeo and Juliet **17** Music for Orchestra **27** Summer's Last Will and Testament

lame 4 game, halt, weak **5** sorry **6** clumsy, feeble, flimsy, infirm, maimed; uncool **7** failing, halting, hobbled, limping, unsound, wanting **8** crippled, deformed, disabled **9** deficient, faltering **10** inadequate **11** ineffectual **12** insufficient, unconvincing, unpersuasive **14** unsatisfactory

lamebrain 3 ass, sap **4** fool **5** booby, dunce, idiot, moron, ninny **6** dimwit, nitwit **7** fathead, half-wit **8** bonehead, dumb-dumb, imbecile, lunkhead, numskull **9** blockhead, numbskull **10** dunderhead, nincompoop **11** chowderhead

lamebrained 4 dumb **6** stupid **7** asinine, foolish, idiotic, moronic **8** crackpot **9** dimwitted, imbecilic **10** halfwitted **12** feeble-minded, simpleminded

Lamech
father: 9 Methusael **10** Methuselah
wives: 6 Adah **6** Zillah
son: 5 Jabal, Jubal **9** Tubalcain
daughter: 6 Naamah

lament 3 cry, sob **4** moan, wail, weep **5** dirge, mourn **6** bewail, outcry, plaint, regret **7** deplore, keening, requiem, whimper **8** mourning **9** death song **11** condole with, lamentation **12** funeral music **13** complain about **14** express pity for, show concern for, sympathize with **15** commiserate with

lamentable 4 dire **6** woeful **7** piteous **8** dreadful, grievous, pathetic, pitiable, shameful, terrible, wretched **9** miserable **10** deplorable **11** distressing, regret- table, unfortunate **13** disheartening, heart- breaking

Lamia
author: 9 John Keats

Lamia
form: 7 monster
characteristic: 12 blood-sucking

La Motta, Jake (Jacob)
nickname: 9 Bronx Bull
sport: 6 boxing
class: 12 middleweight
movie biography: 10 Raging Bull

Lamour, Dorothy
real name: 23 Mary Leta Dorothy Kau- meyer
trademark: 6 sarong
co-star: 7 Bob Hope **10** Bing Crosby
born: 12 New Orleans LA

roles:
    Road to: 3 Rio **4** Bali **6** Utopia **7** Morocco **8** Hong Kong, Zanzibar **9** Singapore

L'Amour, Louis
    author of: 5 Hondo, Lando **7** Sackett, Shalako **8** Conagher **10** Key-Lock Man, Rivers West **14** The Californios, The Daybreakers **15** Westward the Tide **16** How the West Was Won, Over on the Dry Side **21** The Man from Broken Hills, To the Far Blue Mountains

lamp 4 bulb **5** light, torch **6** beacon **7** blinker, lantern **9** headlight, spotlight **10** chandelier, floodlight, Kleig light, night light **11** searchlight **12** ceiling light, reading light **14** ceiling fixture
    invented by:
        arc: 6 Staite
        incandescent: 6 Edison
        incandescent frosted: 6 Pipkin
        incandescent gas: 8 Langmuir
        Kleig: 7 Kleigel
        mercury vapor: 6 Hewitt
        miner's safety: 4 Davy
        neon: 6 Claude

Lampedusa, Giuseppe di
    author of: 10 The Leopard

lampoon 5 farce, put-on, spoof, squib **6** parody, satire, send up **7** mockery, takeoff **8** diatribe, ridicule, satirize, travesty **9** broadside, burlesque **10** caricature, pasquinade **11** make light of

Lamus
    father: 8 Hercules
    mother: 7 Omphale
    attacked: 5 ships

Lamy of Santa Fe
    author: 10 Paul Horgan

lanai 4 deck **5** porch **7** terrace, veranda

Lancaster 17 English royal house
    faction in: 13 War of the Roses
    founder: 11 John of Gaunt
    symbol: 7 red rose

Lancaster, Burt
    real name: 22 Burton Stephen Lancaster
    born: 9 New York NY
    roles: 5 Moses **9** All My Sons, Local Hero **11** Elmer Gantry (Oscar) **12** Atlantic City, The Rainmaker **13** The Rose Tattoo **14** Seven Days in May **16** Sorry Wrong Number **17** Birdman of Alcatraz **18** From Here to Eternity **19** Come Back Little Sheba, Sweet Smell of Success

lance 4 gaff, pike **5** shaft, spear **7** assegai, halberd, harpoon, javelin

Lancelot, Launcelot
    character in: 16 Arthurian romance
    also called: 13 Lancelot du Lac
    father: 3 Ban
    son: 7 Galahad
    lover: 6 Elaine **9** Guinevere
    home: 10 Joyous Gard

lancer 8 cavalier, horseman **10** cavalryman **12** horse soldier, horse trooper **14** mounted soldier

Lanchester, Elsa
    real name: 17 Elizabeth Sullivan
    husband: 15 Charles Laughton
    born: 7 England **8** Lewisham
    roles: 15 Come to the Stable **22** The Bride of Frankenstein **24** Witness for the Prosecution **25** The Private Life of Henry VIII **31** The Private Life of Henry the Eighth

land 3 get, lea, nab, net **4** area, dirt, dock, gain, grab, lawn, loam, moor, park, soil, take, ward, zone **5** acres, catch, earth, grass, green, humus, light, put in, realm, seize, shire, snare, state, tie up, tract **6** alight, anchor, canton, clinch, colony, county, debark, domain, empire, fields, ground, meadow, nation, parish, realty, region, secure **7** acreage, capture, country, descend, dry land, grounds, kingdom, pasture, section, set down, subsoil, terrain, win over **8** come down, district, dominion, farmland, homeland, location, mainland, make land, make port, precinct, property, province, republic, vicinity **9** cornfield, disembark, grassland, lay anchor, lay hold of, lead one to, reach land, territory **10** bring one to, carry one to, come to land, drop anchor, fatherland, motherland, native land, native soil, real estate, settle down, settlement, terra firma, wheat field **11** countryside, put into port **12** commonwealth, put into shore, real property, village green **13** the old country

Landau, Lev Davidovitch
    field: 7 physics
    nationality: 7 Russian
    discovered: 12 liquid helium **14** ferromagnetism
    awarded: 10 Nobel Prize

landed property 5 manor **6** estate **8** compound **12** countryplace

land force 4 army **6** legion, troops **7** legions **8** infantry, soldiers, soldiery **9** artillery

Landless, Neville and Helena
    characters in: 22 The Mystery of Edwin Drood
    author: 7 Dickens

landlord 5 owner **6** holder, squire **8** landlady **9** landowner, possessor **10** freeholder, landholder, proprietor **13** property owner **14** lord of the manor

landmark 8 keystone, monument, signpost **9** benchmark, guidepost, highlight, high point, milestone, watershed **11** cornerstone **12** turning point **16** historic building

Landmarks
    god of: 8 Terminus

Land of Enchantment
    nickname of: 9 New Mexico

Land of Lincoln
    nickname of: 8 Illinois

Land of Opportunity
    nickname of: 8 Arkansas

Land of Sky-blue Waters
    nickname of: 9 Minnesota

Land of Steady Habits
    nickname of: 11 Connecticut

Land of Ten Thousand Lakes
    nickname of: 9 Minnesota

Land of the Dakotas
    nickname of: 11 North Dakota

Land of the Midnight Sun
    nickname of: 6 Alaska

Landon, Michael
    real name: 20 Eugene Maurice Orowitz
    born: 13 Forest Hills NY
    roles: 7 Bonanza **15** Highway to Heaven **19** Little Joe Cartwright **20** I Was a Teenage Werewolf **23** Little House on the Prairie

landscape 4 view **5** scene, sight, vista **6** aspect **7** scenery **8** panorama, prospect **9** spectacle **10** rural scene, scenic view **14** natural scenery

landscape architect 7 Le Notre, Olmsted

landsman 10 countryman **13** fellow citizen

Landsteiner, Karl
    field: 8 medicine **9** pathology
    distinguished: 10 blood types
    identified: 8 RH factor
    awarded: 10 Nobel Prize

lane 3 way **4** pass, path, road **5** alley, byway, drive, route, track, trail **6** access, avenue, bypath, course **7** passage, roadway **8** alleyway, approach, footpath **10** passageway

Lang, Walter
    director of: 7 Desk Set **11** The King and I

Lange, Jessica
    born: 9 Cloquet MN
    roles: 7 Country, Frances, Tootsie **8** Cape Fear, King Kong **11** All That Jazz **16** Crimes of the Heart **26** The Postman Always Rings Twice

Langella, Frank
    born: 9 Bayonne NJ
    roles: 9 Dracula **23** The Diary of a Mad Housewife

Langland, William
    author of: 12 Piers Plowman

Langmuir, Irving
    field: 9 chemistry
    invented: 15 atomic blowtorch **17** gas-tungsten lights
    awarded: 10 Nobel Prize

language 4 cant, jive **5** argot, idiom, lingo, prose, slang, words **6** jargon, patois, speech, tongue **7** cursing, cussing, dialect, diction, wording **8** parlance, rhetoric, swearing, verbiage **9** discourse, elocution, profanity **10** expression, use of words, vernacular, vocabulary **11** imprecation, phraseology, profane talk **12** mother tongue, native tongue **13** colloquialism **14** public speaking, self-expression **16** manner of speaking, mode of expression **17** oral communication, reading and writing, verbal intercourse

of Afghanistan: 4 Dari **5** Farsi **6** Afghan, Pashto, Pushtu **7** Balochi, Baluchi, Persian

of Albania: 3 Geg **4** Cham, Gheg, Hish, Tosk **5** Greek **8** Albanian

of Algeria: 6 Arabic, Berber, French, Zenata **7** Senhaja

of Andorra: 6 French **7** Catalan, Spanish

of Angola: 5 Bantu **8** Kimbundu, Oumbundu **9** Ovimbundu **10** Portuguese

of Antigua and Barbuda: 7 English

of Argentina: 7 Spanish

of Armenia: 7 Russian **8** Armenian

of Australia: 6 Yabber **7** English **9** aborigine (dialects)

of Austria: 5 Czech **6** German, Magyar **8** Croatian **9** Slovenian

of Azerbaijan: 6 Turkic

of the Bahamas: 6 Creole **7** English

of Bahrain: 4 Urdu **5** Farsi **6** Arabic **7** English, Persian

of Bangladesh: 6 Bihari **7** Bengali, English

of Barbados: 7 English

of Belgium: 5 Dutch **6** French, German **7** Flemish

of Benin: 3 Fon **5** Dendi **6** Bariba, French, Fulani, Yoruba

of Bermuda: 7 English

of Bhutan: 5 Hindi, Lhoke **7** Tibetan **8** Dzongkha, Nepalese

of Bolivia: 6 Aymara **7** Quechua, Spanish

of Borneo: 5 Malay **7** Chinese, English

of Bosnia-Herzegovina: 13 Serbo Croatian

of Botswana: 5 Bantu, Click **6** Tswana **7** English, Khoisan **8** Setswana

of Brazil: 10 Portuguese

of Brunei: 4 Iban **5** Malay **7** Chinese, English

of Bulgaria: 9 Bulgarian

of Burkina Faso: 4 Bobo, Lobi, More, Samo **5** Dyula, Mande, Mossi **6** French

of Burundi: 6 French **7** Kirundi, Swahili

of Cambodia/Kampuchea: 5 Khmer **6** French

of Cameroon: 4 Bulu **5** Bantu, Bassa, Hausa **6** Douala, Ewondo, French, Fulani **7** English **8** Bamileke, Fulfulde

of Canada: 6 Eskimo, French **7** English

of Canary Islands: 7 Spanish

of Cape Verde: 7 Crioulo **10** Portuguese **13** Verdean Creole

of Central African Republic: 5 Sango, Zande **6** French

of Chad: 4 Sara **5** Turku **6** Arabic, French

of Chile: 7 Spanish

of China: 7 Chinese **8** Mandarin, Shanghai **9** Cantonese

of Colombia: 7 Spanish

of Comoros: 6 Arabic, French **7** Swahili **8** Malagasy

of Congo: 4 Susu **5** Bantu, Fiote **6** French, Kituba **7** Bangala, Lingala

of Costa Rica: 7 Spanish

of Crete: 5 Greek **6** Minoan **7** Linear A, Linear B

of Croatia: 8 Croatian **10** Serbo Croat

of Cuba: 7 Spanish

of Cyprus: 5 Greek **7** Turkish **8** Armenian

of Czechoslovakia/Czech Republic: 5 Czech **6** German, Magyar, Slovak **7** Russian **9** Hungarian

of Denmark: 4 Odan **6** Danish **8** Faeroese **11** Greenlander

of Djibouti: 4 Afar **6** Arabic, French, Somali

of Dominican Republic: 6 French **7** English, Spanish

of Ecuador: 6 Jibaro **7** Quechua, Spanish

of Egypt: 6 Arabic, Coptic, French **7** English

of El Salvador: 7 Spanish

of England: 7 English

of Equatorial Guinea: 4 Bubi, Fang **6** pidgin **7** Spanish

of Eritrea: 7 Amharic

of Estonia: 5 Tartu **10** Finno-Ugric

of Ethiopia: 3 Giz **4** Afar, Agow, Geez, Saho **5** Geeze, Ghese, Smali, Tigre **6** Arabic, Harari **7** Amharic, English, Italian, Russian **8** Gallinya, Irob-Saho, Tigrinya

of Fiji: 5 Hindi **6** Fijian **7** English

of Finland: 4 Avar, Lapp **5** Karen, Ugric, Vogul **6** Magyar, Ostyak, Tarast **7** Finnish, Olonets, Samoyed, Swedish **8** Estonian **10** Olenetsian

of France: 6 French

of Gabon Republic: 6 French

of The Gambia: 4 Fula **5** Wolof **6** Fulani **7** English, Malinke **8** Mandingo

of Georgia: 8 Georgian

of Germany: 6 German **10** High German **11** Hochdeutsch

of Ghana: 2 Ga **3** Ewe, Gur, Kwa, Twi **5** Fanti, Hausa **7** Dagomba, English

of Gibraltar: 7 English, Spanish

of Greece: 5 Greek

of Greenland: 6 Danish, Eskimo **11** Greenlandic

of Grenada: 7 English

of Guatemala: 6 Quiche **7** Spanish

of Guinea: 5 Fulbe, Mande **6** Arabic, French, Fulani **7** English

of Guinea-Bissau: 5 Fulah **7** Balante, Crioulo **8** Mandingo **10** Portuguese **21** Cape Verde--Guinea Creole

of Guyana: 5 Hindi **7** English

of Haiti: 6 Creole, French, patois

of Honduras: 7 English, Spanish

of Hong Kong: 7 Chinese, English **9** Cantonese

of Hungary: 6 German, Magyar, Slovak **8** Croatian **9** Hungarian **10** Finno-Ugric

of Iceland: 5 Norse **9** Icelandic

of India: 4 Urdu **5** Hindi, Oriya, Tamil **6** Sindhi, Telugu **7** Bengali, English, Kannada, Malayam, Marathi, Punjabi **8** Assamese, Gujarati, Kashmiri, Sanskrit **9** Malayalam

of Indonesia: 5 Tetum **6** Bahasa, Igorot **7** English, Gyarung, Malayan **8** Balinese, Chamorro, Javanese, Madurese, Sudanese **10** Indonesian, Polynesian

of Iran: 4 Luri, Zend **5** Farsi, Turki **6** Arabic **7** Baluchi, Kurdish, Persian **8** Armenian **11** Azerbaijani

of Iraq: 5 Farsi **6** Arabic **7** Kurdish, Persian, Turkish

of Ireland: 4 Erse **5** Irish **6** Gaelic **7** English

of Israel: 6 Arabic, French, Hebrew **7** English

of Italy: 5 Ladin, Latin **6** French, German **7** Italian, Slovene **8** Friulian **9** Sardinian

of Ivory Coast: 4 Akan **6** Dioula, French

of Jamaica: 6 Creole **7** English

of Japan: 5 Kanto **8** Japanese

of Java: 4 Kavi, Kawi **5** Malay **6** Sassak **8** Balinese, Madurese, Sudanese **16** Bahasa Indonesian

of Jordan: 6 Arabic

of Kazakhstan: 6 Kazakh

of Kenya: 3 Luo **5** Bantu, Luhya, Masai **6** Kikuyu **7** English, Swahili **8** Buyerati **10** Hindustani

of Kiribati: 6 Samoan **7** English **10** Gilbertese

of Korea: 6 Korean

of Kuwait: 6 Arabic

of Kyrgyzstan: 6 Turkic **7** Kirghiz

of Laos: 3 Lao, Man, Meo **6** French **7** English

of Latvia: 7 Lettish

of Lebanon: 6 Arabic, French, Syriac **7** English, Turkish **8** Armenian

of Lesotho: 5 Sotho **7** English, Sesotho

of Liberia: 3 Kru, Kwa **5** Mande **7** English

of Libya: 6 Arabic, Berber **7** English, Italian

of Liechtenstein: 6 German **10** Alemannish

of Lithuania: 5 Zmudz **6** Baltic **10** Lithuanian

of Luxembourg: 6 French, German **7** English **13** Letzeburgesch

of Macao: 7 Chinese, English **9** Cantonese **10** Portuguese

of Macedonia: 10 Macedonian

of Madagascar/Malagasy Republic: 6 French **8** Malagasy, Malgache

of Malawi: 3 Yao **4** Cewa **5** Bantu, Ngoni, Tonga **6** Nyanja **7** English, Tumbuka **8** Chichewa **10** Chitumbuka

of Malaysia: 4 Bugi, Dyak **5** Malay, Tamil **6** Battok, Rejang **7** Chinese, English, Lampong, Niasese **8** Achinese, Javanese, Makassar **14** Bahasa Malaysia

of Maldives: 6 Arabic, Divehi

of Mali: 5 Dogon, Dyula, Feulh, Mande, Marka **6** Berber, French, Fulani **7** Bambara, Malinke, Senoufo, Songhai

of Malta: 7 English, Italian, Maltese

of Mauritania: 4 Fula **5** Wolof **6** Arabic, French **7** Phoolor, Tukulor **8** Fulfulde, Mandingo **9** Sarakolle **10** Hassaniyya

of Mauritius: 4 Urdu **5** Hindi, Tamil **6** Creole, French **7** English

of Mexico: 5 Mayan, Otomi **6** Mixtec **7** Mazahua, Mazatec, Nahuatl, Spanish, Totonac, Zapotec **8** Tarascan

of Moldova: 8 Romanian **9** Moldovian

of Monaco: 6 French **7** English, Italian **10** Monegasque

of Mongolia: 6 Kazakh **16** Khalkha Mongolian

of Montenegro: 13 Serbo-Croatian

of Morocco: 6 Arabic, Berber, French **7** Spanish

of Mozambique: 3 Yao **5** Makua **6** Nyanji, Thonga **7** Swahili **10** Portuguese

of Myanmar: 3 Lai **4** Chin, Kuki, Pegu, Shan **5** Karen **6** Kachin **7** Burmese

of Namibia: 5 Bantu **6** German **7** English, Khoisan **9** Afrikaans

of Nauru: 7 English, Nauruan

of Nepal: 6 Nepali, Newari **7** English

of the Netherlands: 5 Dutch **7** English, Frisian

of New Guinea: 4 Motu **7** English **16** Melanesian Pidgin

of New Zealand: 5 Maori **7** English

of Nicaragua: 7 English, Spanish

of Niger: 5 Hausa, Mande **6** Djerma, French, Fulani, Tuareg **8** Mandingo, Tamashek

of Nigeria: 3 Ibo **4** Efik, Igbo **5** Hausa **6** Yoruba **7** English

of Norway: 4 Lapp **5** Norse **6** Bokmal **7** Nynorsk, Riksmal **8** Landsmal, Samnorsk **9** Landsmaal, Norwegian

of Oman: 4 Urdu **5** Hindi **6** Arabic **7** Baluchi

of Pakistan: 4 Urdu **6** Pushtu, Sindhi **7** Baluchi, Bengali, English, Punjabi

of Panama: 7 English, Spanish

of Paraguay: 6 German **7** Guarani, Spanish

of Peru: 6 Aymara **7** English, Quechua, Spanish

of the Philippines: 4 Moro **5** Bicol, Bikol **6** Ibanag **7** Cebuano, English, Ilocano, Spanish, Tagalog, Visayan **8** Filipino **9** Pampangan, Philipino **10** Samar-Leyte **13** Bamboo-English **14** Panay-Hiligayon

of Poland: 6 Kaszub, Polish **10** Pomeranian

of Polynesia: 4 Niue, Uvea **5** Maori **6** Samoan, Tongan **7** Austral, Tagalog, Tokelau **8** Hawaiian, Tahitian **9** Marquesan, Tuamatuan **10** Mangarevan

of Portugal: 10 Portuguese

of Qatar: 6 Arabic

of Romania: 6 French, Magyar **7** Russian **8** Romanian, Rumanian **9** Hungarian

of Russia: 5 Evenk **6** Buriat, Kalmyk **7** Finnish, Russian **8** Ossetian

of Rwanda: 6 French **7** Swahili **11** Kinyarwanda

of Samoa: 6 Samoan **7** English

of San Marino: 7 Italian

of Sao Tome and Principe: 10 Portuguese

of Sardinia: 7 Italian

of Saudi Arabia: 6 Arabic

of Scotland: 4 Erse **6** Celtic, Gaelic, Keltic, Lallan **7** English, Lalland

of Senegal: 5 Wolof **6** French

of the Seychelles: 6 Creole, French **7** English

of Sierra Leone: 4 Krio **5** Limba, Mende, Mendi, Temne **6** Creole **7** English

of Singapore: 5 Malay, Tamil **7** Chinese, English **8** Mandarin

of Slovakia: 6 Slovik Slovak

of Slovenia: 7 Slovene

of the Solomon Islands: 7 English **13** Pidgin English **16** Melanesian Pidgin

of Somalia: 6 Arabic, Somali **7** English, Italian

of South Africa: 4 Taal, Zulu **5** Bantu, Hindi, Nguni, Sotho, Swazi, Tamil, Venda, Xhosa **6** Telegu, Thonga **7** English, Khoisan, Ndebele, Sesotho **8** Bujarati, Fanakalo **9** Afrikaans **13** Kitchen-Kaffir

of Spain: 6 Basque **7** Catalan, Spanish **8** Balearic, Galician **9** Castilian, Valencian

of Sri Lanka: 4 Pali **5** Tamil **7** English **9** Sinhalese

of Sudan: 2 Ga **3** Efe, Ewe, Ibo, Kru, Vak, Vei **4** Efik, Mole, Tshi **6** Arabic, Nubian, Yoruba **7** English **8** Mandango, Mandingo **9** Ta Bedawie

of Suriname: 5 Carib, Dutch, Hindi **6** Arawak **7** English **8** Javanese, Taki-Taki **10** Hindustani **11** Sranan Tongo **12** Sranang Tongo

of Swaziland: 5 Ngumi **7** English, Siswati **9** Afrikaans **10** Portuguese

of Sweden: 4 Lapp **7** Swedish

of Switzerland: 5 Ladin **6** French, German **7** Italian **8** Romansch **14** Switzerdeutsch

of Syria: 6 Arabic, French, Syriac **7** Aramaic, English, Kurdish, Turkish **8** Armenian

of Taiwan: 4 Amon, Amoy **5** Hakka, Kuo Yu **6** Minnan **9** Taiwanese **15** Mandarin Chinese

of Tajikistan: 5 Tajik **7** Tadzhik

of Tanzania: 5 Bantu **6** Arabic **7** English, Khoisan, Nilotic, Swahili **8** Cushitic, Gujarati

of Thailand: 3 Lao, Tai **4** Ahom, Shan, Thai **5** Kadai **7** Bangkok, English **9** Krung Thep **12** Chinese Malay

of Tibet: 5 Balti **6** Ladkhi **7** Bhutani, Bodskad **8** Sanskrit **9** Bhutanese

of Togo: 3 Ana, Ewe, Twi **4** Mina **5** Hausa **6** French, Kabrai, Kabrie **7** Bassari, Dagomba, Quatchi **8** Kotokoli, Lotocoli

of Tonga: 6 Tongan **7** English

of Trinidad and Tobago: 6 French **7** Chinese, English, Spanish **10** Portuguese **12** French Patois

of Tunisia: 6 Arabic, Berber, French

of Turkey: 6 Arabic **7** Kurdish, Turkish

of Turkmenistan: 6 Turkic **10** West Turkic

of Tuvalu: 6 Samoan **7** English **8** Tuvaluan **10** Polynesian

of Uganda: 5 Ateso, Ganda **7** English, Luganda, Swahili

of Ukraine: 9 Ukrainian

of United Arab Emirates: 5 Farsi **6** Arabic **7** English, Persian

of Uruguay: 7 Italian, Spanish

of Uzbekistan: 5 Uzbek

of Vanuatu: 6 French **7** Bislama, English **16** Melanesian Pidgin

of Venezuela: 4 Pume **7** Spanish

of Vietnam: 3 Yue **4** Cham **5** Khmer, Rhade **6** French **7** Chinese, English **9** Cantonese **10** Vietnamese

of Wales: 5 Welsh **6** Celtic, Cymric, Keltic, Kymric **7** Cymraeg, English

of Western Sahara: 16 Hassaniyya Arabic

of Western Samoa: 6 Samoan **7** English

of Yemen: 6 Arabic

of Yugoslavia: 7 Bosnian, Slovene **8** Albanian, Croatian **9** Hungarian, Slovenian **10** Macedonian **11** Montenegrin **13** Herzegovinian, Serbo-Croatian

of Zaire: 5 Bantu **6** French **7** Chiluba, Kikongo, Lingala, Swahili **8** Sudanese, Tshiluba

of Zambia: 4 Lozi **5** Bemba, Lunda, Tonga **6** Luvale, Nyanja **7** English **9** Afrikaans

of Zimbabwe: 3 Ila **5** Bantu, Shona **7** English, Ndebele

language, artificial

of James Cooke Brown: 6 Loglan

of Hans Freudenthal: 6 Lincos **13** Lingua Cosmica
of Alexander Gode: 11 Interlingua
of C K Ogden: 12 Basic English
of J M Schleyer: 7 Volapuk
of Jean Francois Sudre: 8 Solresol
of L L Zamehof: 9 Esperanto

language, extinct 6 Dacian, Hattic, Lycian, Lydian, Palaic **7** Cornish, Elamite, Hittite, Hurrian **8** Etruscan, Illyrian, Phrygian, Sumerian, Thracian, Urartian **9** Dalmatian **15** Cuneiform Luwian **18** Hieroglyphic Luwian

languid 4 dull, slow, weak **5** faint, heavy, inert, shaky, spent, weary **6** feeble, infirm, leaden, sickly, supine, torpid **7** rickety, unsound, worn-out **8** drooping, fatigued, inactive, lifeless, listless, sluggish, unstable **9** apathetic, declining, doddering, enervated, exhausted, inanimate, lethargic, trembling, unhealthy **10** indisposed, spiritless **11** debilitated **12** on the decline **13** lackadaisical

languidness 6 apathy, torpor **7** inertia **8** lethargy **12** listlessness, sluggishness **13** indisposition

languish 3 ebb **4** fade, fail, flag, wane, wilt **5** covet, droop, faint **6** desire, hunger, sicken, thirst, wither **7** dwindle, long for, pine for, sigh for **8** diminish, give away, take sick, yearn for **9** become ill, break down, hanker for, hunger for, thirst for, waste away **10** go downhill **11** deteriorate, have a yen for, hunger after **12** be desirous of **13** go into decline

Languish, Lydia
  character in: 9 The Rivals
  author: 8 Sheridan

languor 5 ennui **6** torpor **7** inertia **8** dullness, hebetude, lethargy **9** indolence, lassitude, torpidity, weariness **10** dispassion, dreaminess **11** languidness, leisureness **12** lifelessness, listlessness, sluggishness

lank 4 bony, lean, limp, thin **5** gaunt, spare **6** skinny, slight **7** angular, scrawny **8** straight

lanky 4 bony, lean **5** gaunt, gawky, rangy, spare, weedy **6** skinny **7** angular, scrawny **8** gangling, rawboned **11** tall and thin

La Nouvelle Heloise
  author: 10 J J Rousseau

Lansbury, Angela
  born: 6 London **7** England
  roles: 4 Mame **8** Gaslight **10** JB Fletcher **11** Sweeney Todd **14** Murder She Wrote **15** Jessica Fletcher **22** The Manchurian Candidate

Laocoon
  vocation: 6 priest
  father: 5 Priam
  mother: 6 Hecuba
  sons: 3 two (unnamed)
  warned: 7 Trojans
  warned of: 11 Trojan horse
  killed by: 11 sea serpents

Laomedon
  king of: 4 Troy
  father: 4 Ilus
  wife: 6 Strymo
  son: 5 Priam **6** Lampus **7** Clytius **8** Hicetaon, Tithonus
  daughter: 7 Hesione **8** Themiste

Laos
  other name: 7 Lan Xang **23** land of a million elephants
  capital/largest city: 9 Viengchan, Vientiane
  others: 4 Nape **5** Pakse, Xieng **6** Paklay **7** Thakhek **11** Savannakhet, Xiang Khoang **12** Luang Prabang **14** Louangphrabang
  school: 12 Sisavangvong
  measure: 3 bak
  monetary unit: 2 at **3** att, kip
  mountain: 3 Lai, Loi, San **4** Copi, Khat **5** Atwat **6** Khoung, Tiubia **15** Annam Cordillera
  highest point: 3 Bia **7** Phou Bia
  river: 3 Noi **4** Done **5** Khong **6** Mekong, Sebang
  physical feature:
    plain: 4 Jars
    plateau: 8 Bolovens
  people: 2 Lu **3** Kha, Lao, Man, Meo, Tai, Yao, Yun **4** Miao, Thai **5** Hmong **8** Lao Teung **10** Phoutheung
    leader: 7 Fa Ngoun **13** Souphanouvong **14** Souligna Vongsa, Souvanna Phouma
  language: 3 Lao, Man, Meo **6** French **7** English
  religion: 7 animism **8** Buddhism **17** Theravada Buddhism
  feature:
    Buddhist priest: 5 bonze
    Communist guerrilla group: 9 Pathet Lao
    musical instrument: 5 khene
    temple: 3 wat
    trail: 9 Ho Chi Minh

Laothoe
  concubine of: 5 Priam
  son: 6 Lycaon **9** Polydorus

Lao-tzu, Lao-tze, Lao-Tse, Lao-tsze
  author of: 10 Tao Te Ching
  founder of: 6 Taoism

lap 3 sip **4** lick, wash **5** awash, drink, plash, slosh **6** babble, bubble, gurgle, lick up, murmur, ripple, splash, tongue

La Paz
  administrative capital of: 7 Bolivia

Laphria
  epithet of: 7 Artemis

Laphystius
  epithet of: 4 Zeus

lapidary 11 stonecutter
  expert in: 4 gems

lapis lazuli 9 azure-blue **17** semiprecious stone
  species: 8 lazurite
  source: 10 Badakhshan **11** Afghanistan

Laplace, Pierre S
  field: 7 physics **9** astronomy
  nationality: 6 French
  hypothesis of: 18 nebular solar system

Lapland
  region of: 6 Norway, Sweden **7** Finland
  peninsula: 4 Kola
  native: 4 Lapp
  herders of: 8 reindeer

lapse 3 gap, sag **4** drop, fall, flaw, go by, loss, sink, slip, stop, wane **5** boner, break, cease, droop, error, fault, pause, slump **6** breach, elapse, expire, hiatus, laxity, pass by, period, recede, recess, run out, slip by, wither, worsen **7** blunder, decline, descent, failing, failure, faux pas, interim, passage, relapse, respite, subside **8** collapse, downfall, elapsing, interval, omission, slip away **9** backslide, disregard, interlude, oversight, slump down, terminate **10** degenerate, falling off, forfeiture, infraction, negligence, peccadillo, regression **11** backsliding, delinquency, dereliction, deteriorate, shortcoming **12** degeneration, intermission, interruption, lose validity **13** deterioration, process of time, slight mistake **14** become obsolete, fall into disuse

lapsus linguae 16 a slip of the tongue

Laputa 12 Flying Island
  inhabitants: 11 visionaries
  in: Gulliver's Travels

lar *see* **5** lares

Lara
  character in: 9 Dr Zhivago
  author: 9 Pasternak

larboard 8 left side
  same as: 4 port

larceny 5 fraud, theft **7** bilking, forgery, looting, robbery, sacking **8** burglary, cheating, fleecing, stealing **9** extortion, pilferage, pilfering, swindling **10** absconding, peculation, plagiarism, purloining **11** defalcation, depredation **12** embezzlement, grand larceny, petit larceny, petty larceny, safecracking **13** appropriation, housebreaking **16** misappropriation

larder 5 cuddy **6** pantry, spence **7** buttery **8** food room **9** stillroom, storeroom **10** supply room **11** storage room

Lardner, Ring
  author of: 11 The Love Nest, You Know Me Al **12** Treat Em Rough **16** Gullible's Travels

Larentalia
  origin: 5 Roman
  event: 8 festival

lares

form: 7 spirits
watched over: 5 house **6** hearth **9** community **10** crossroads
single member: 3 lar
companions: 7 penates
correspond to: 8 Dioscuri

large 3 big, fat **4** high, huge, vast, wide **5** ample, broad, grand, great, heavy, hulky, obese, plump, roomy **6** goodly, mighty, portly, rotund **7** copious, immense, liber- al, massive, sizable **8** colossal, enormous, gigantic, imposing, man-sized, outsized, spacious, sweeping, towering **9** boundless, capacious, expansive, extensive, giantlike, kingsized, limitless, monstrous, overgrown, ponderous, strapping, unlimited, unstinted **10** exorbitant, gargantuan, stupendous **11** extravagant, far- reaching, magnificent, substantial **12** considerable **13** comprehensive **14** Brobdingnagian

large-hearted 8 generous **10** altruistic, benevolent, charitable **12** humanitarian **13** philanthropic

largely 6 mainly, mostly, widely **7** chiefly, greatly **9** generally, primarily **10** on the whole **11** extensively, principally **12** considerably **13** predominantly, substantially **14** for the most part, to a great extent

large-scale 3 big **4** epic, huge, vast, wide **5** broad, great **6** all-out, heroic, mighty **8** colossal, far-flung, gigantic **9** extensive, monstrous **10** gargantuan, stupendous, tremendous **11** far-reaching, wide-ranging **15** allencompassing

largess, largesse 3 aid **4** boon, gift, help **5** favor, mercy **6** bounty, reward **7** charity, payment **8** bestowal, donation, gratuity, kindness, offering **9** benignity **10** assistance, generosity **11** benefaction, benevolence **12** philanthropy, remuneration

large store 8 emporium **11** supermarket **15** department store

largo
music: 4 slow **14** dignified tempo

lark 3 gag **4** game, jape, romp, whim **5** antic, caper, fling, prank, spree, trick **6** frolic, gambol **7** caprice **8** escapade **11** high old time **12** sportiveness
group of: 10 exaltation

larkspur 9 Consolida **10** Delphinium
varieties: 4 Tall **5** Dwarf **6** Rocket

La Rochefoucauld, Francois
author of: 6 Maxims **7** Maximes

larva
insect stage after: 3 egg
insect stage before: 4 pupa
legless: 6 maggot

lascivious 4 foul, lewd **5** bawdy, dirty, gross, lurid **6** coarse, filthy, impure, rib- ald, sordid, vulgar, wanton **7** immoral, lustful, obscene, ruttish, squalid **8** depraved, immodest, improper, indecent, prurient **9** lecherous, salacious, shameless **10** indelicate, licentious, unblushing **11** dirty-minded, unwholesome

lash 3 fix, hit, tie **4** beat, bind, blow, flog, moor, rope, whip **5** brace, curse, flail, hitch, knock, leash, pound, scold, smack, strap, thong, tie up, truss **6** attach, be- rate, buffet, fasten, hammer, pinion, revile, secure, strike, stroke, tether, thrash, whip up **7** lecture, scourge, upbraid **8** lambaste, make fast **9** castigate, horsewhip **10** take to task, tongue-lash **11** rail against **13** cat-o'- nine-tails

Lash, Joseph P
author of: 18 Eleanor and Franklin

lashed together 4 tied **5** bound **6** tied up **7** secured, trussed **8** fastened

lash out at 5 fly at **6** assail, attack, strike **8** fall upon

Las Palmas
capital of: 13 Canary Islands

lass 4 girl, maid, miss **5** wench **6** damsel, female, lassie, lovely, maiden, pretty, virgin **7** colleen **10** schoolgirl, young woman

Lasser, Louise
father: 8 S J Lasser
husband: 10 Woody Allen
born: 9 New York NY
roles: 22 Mary Hartman Mary Hartman

lassie 4 girl, lass, maid **6** maiden **7** colleen **10** young woman

Lassie
character: 5 Timmy **9** Doc Weaver **10** Jeff Miller, Paul Martin, Ruth Martin **11** Corey Stuart, Ellen Miller **12** Gramps Miller **17** Sylvester (Porky) Brockway
cast: 10 Jan Clayton, Jon Provost, Jon Shepodd, Robert Bray **11** Arthur Space, Tommy Rettig **12** Donald Keeler, June Lockhart **14** Cloris Leachman, George Chandler **15** George Cleveland
type of dog: 6 collie

lassitude 5 ennui **6** apathy, torpor **7** boredom, fatigue, inertia, languor, malaise **8** debility, doldrums, dullness, lethargy, weakness **9** faintness, indolence, tiredness, torpidity, weariness **10** droopiness, drowsiness, enervation, exhaustion, feebleness, supineness **11** languidness, prostration **12** indifference, lack of energy, listlessness, sluggishness

lasso 4 lash, rope **5** catch, noose, reata, riata, thong **6** lariat

last 3 end **4** go on, keep, live, stay, wear **5** abide, after, exist, final, stand **6** behind, ending, endure, extend, finale, finish, hold on, hold up, remain, utmost **7** carry on, closing, extreme, finally, hold out, outlive, outwear, persist, stand up, subsist, survive, tail-
ing **8** at the end, continue, doomsday, farthest, final one, furthest, hindmost, hold good, in back of, maintain, rearmost, terminal, terminus, trailing, ultimate **9** in the rear, persevere **10** Armageddon, concluding, conclusion, conclusive, eventually, terminally, ultimately **11** crack of doom, crucial time **12** in conclusion, tagging along **13** Day of Judgment
French: 7 dernier

Last Analysis, The
author: 10 Saul Bellow

Last Days of Pompeii, The
author: 18 Edward Bulwer-Lytton
character: 4 Ione **5** Nydia **7** Arbaces, Glaucus **9** Apaecides

Last Frontier
nickname of: 6 Alaska

lasting 4 firm **5** fixed, solid **7** abiding, chronic, durable, eternal **8** constant, enduring, immortal, lifelong, long-term **9** incessant, lingering, long-lived, permanent, perpetual, steadfast, unceasing **10** continuing, deep-rooted, deep-seated, persistent, protracted **11** established, never-ending **12** indissoluble **14** indestructible, of long duration **17** firmly established

Last Lion, The
author: 17 William Manchester

lastly 6 at last **7** finally, to sum up **8** after all, in the end **10** on the whole **12** in conclusion **19** all things considered **33** taking everything into consideration

Last of the Barons, The
author: 18 Edward Bulwer-Lytton

Last of the Mohicans, The
author: 19 James Fenimore Cooper
character: 5 Magua, Uncas **9** Cora Munro **10** Alice Munro **11** Natty Bumppo **12** Chingachgook **18** Major Duncan Heyward

last part 3 end **6** ending, finale, finish **8** third act **10** denouement **12** final chapter

Last Picture Show, The
director: 16 Peter Bogdanovich
based on story by: 13 Larry McMurtry
cast: 10 Ben Johnson **11** Jeff Bridges **12** Ellen Burstyn **13** Eileen Brennan **14** Cloris Leachman, Cybill Shepherd, Timothy Bottoms
Oscar for: 15 supporting actor (Johnson) **17** supporting actress (Leachman)

Last Puritan, The
author: 15 George Santayana

La Strada
director: 15 Federico Fellini
cast: 11 Aldo Silvana **12** Anthony Quinn **15** Giulietta Masina, Richard Basehart

score: 8 Nino Rota
Oscar for: 11 foreign film

last resort
French: 8 pis aller

Last Tango in Paris
director: 18 Bernardo Bertolucci
cast: 12 Marlon Brando 14 Maria Schneider

Last Things
author: 6 C P Snow

Last Valley, The
author: 11 A B Guthrie Jr

Last Waltz, The
director: 14 Martin Scorsese
cast: 7 The Band 8 Bob Dylan 9 Neil Young 10 The Staples 11 Eric Clapton, Muddy Waters, Neil Diamond, Van Morrison 12 Joni Mitchell 13 Emmylou Harris

last word
French: 10 dernier cri

latch 3 bar 4 bolt, clip, hasp, hook, lock, loop, shut, snap 5 catch, clamp, close 6 buckle, button, clinch, fasten, secure 8 make fast 9 fastening

late 3 new 4 dead, gone, slow 5 fresh, tardy 6 held up, put off, recent 7 delayed, newborn, overdue, tardily 8 departed, detained, dilatory, passed on 9 after time, postponed 10 behindhand, behind time, dilatorily, unpunctual 16 recently deceased

late arrival 7 laggard 8 lateness, newcomer 9 immigrant, latecomer, tardiness 16 Johnny-come-lately

Late George Apley, The
author: 10 J P Marquand

lately 6 of late 7 just now 8 latterly, recently, right now 9 currently, presently, yesterday 10 not long ago 13 a short time ago

Late Mattia Pascal, The
author: 15 Luigi Pirandello

latency 8 abeyance, deferral, dormancy, inaction 10 quiescence, suspension

Late Night with David Letterman
feature: 11 Ask Mr Melman 15 Stupid Pet Tricks 18 Brush with Greatness, Stupid People Tricks
bandleader: 10 Paul Shafer
city: 7 New York

latent 6 covert, hidden 7 abeyant, dormant, lurking, passive 8 inactive, sleeping 9 concealed, potential, quiescent, suspended, unaroused, unexposed 10 in abeyance, intangible, unapparent, unrealized 11 not manifest, undeveloped, unexpressed 13 inconspicuous

later 4 next 5 since 6 behind, in time, mature 7 ensuing, tardily 8 in a while, in sequel 9 afterward, following, presently, thereupon 10 consequent, more re- cent, most recent, subsequent, succeeding, successive,

thereafter 11 after a while, consecutive 12 subsequently, successively, toward the end

lateral 4 side 5 sided 7 flanked, oblique, sloping 8 edgeways, edgewise, flank- ing, sidelong, sideward, sideways, sidewise, skirting, slanting

latest fashion
French: 10 dernier cri

lather 4 foam, head, scum, soap, suds 5 froth, spume, sweat 6 soap up 8 make foam, soapsuds 9 make froth 11 shaving foam

Latin
language family: 12 Indo-European
branch: 6 Italic
group: 7 Romance
subgroup: 6 French 7 Catalan, Italian, Romansh, Spanish 8 Romanian 9 Provencal 10 Portuguese 13 Rhaeto- Romanic

Latino, Latina 8 Hispanic 13 Latin American

Latinus
king of: 6 Latium
father: 6 Faunus
mother: 6 Marica
wife: 5 Amata
daughter: 7 Lavinia

latitude 5 range, scope, sweep 6 leeway, margin 7 license 8 free play 9 amplitude, elbowroom, full swing 10 indulgence, liberality 11 opportunity, unrestraint 12 independence 15 freedom of action, freedom of choice 16 unrestrictedness

Latona see 4 Leto

La Tour, Georges de
born: 3 Vic 6 France 8 Lorraine
artwork: 7 Peasant 10 The New Born 12 Peasant's Wife, The Card Cheat 15 St Peter Penitent 16 The Fortune Teller 18 The Denial of St Peter 23 The Education of the Virgin 31 St Sebastian Tended by the Holy Women

Latrobe, Benjamin Henry
architect of: 9 US Capitol 15 Sedgeley Mansion (PA) 18 Baltimore Cathedral 22 Philadelphia Waterworks
style: 12 Greek Revival, Neoclassical 13 Gothic Revival

latter 3 end 4 last 5 final, later 6 ending, latest, modern 7 ensuing 8 terminal 10 most recent, subsequent, succeeding, successive 13 last-mentioned 15 second-mentioned

lattice 4 fret, grid 5 frame, grate 6 grille, screen 7 framing, grating, network, trellis, webwork 8 fretwork, openwork 9 framework, reticulum 11 trelliswork 12 reticulation

Latvia
former name: 30 Latvian Soviet Socialist Republic
capital/largest city: 4 Riga
others: 5 Cesis, Libau 6 Dvinsk, Li-

bava, Tukums 7 Jelgava, Jurmala, Liepaja, Rezekne 8 Dunaberg, Dunaburg, Valmiera 9 Ventspils 10 Daugavpils
government: 8 republic
measure: 3 let 4 stof 5 stoff, verst 6 arshin, kulmet 7 verchoc, verchok 8 krouchka, pourvete 9 deciatine, lofstelle, pourvette 10 tonnseteel
monetary unit: 3 lat 4 latu 6 rublis, santim 7 kapeika, santima
weight: 9 liespfund
lake: 7 Aluksne
river: 4 Ogre 5 Gauja, Venta 6 Salaca 7 Daugava, Lielupe 12 Western Dvina
sea: 6 Baltic
physical feature:
  cape: 8 Domesnes
  gulf: 4 Riga
  strait: 4 Irbe
people: 3 Kur, Liv 4 Balt, Cour, Lett 7 Latgale, Latvian, Russian, Zemgale
  former ruler: 15 Teutonic Knights
language: 7 Lettish
religion: 8 Lutheran 13 Roman Catholic

laud 5 extol, honor 6 praise 7 acclaim, commend, glorify

laudable 5 model, noble 8 sterling 9 admirable, estimable, excellent, exemplary 10 creditable 11 commendable, meritorious 12 praiseworthy 13 unimpeachable 17 deserving of esteem 18 worthy of admiration

laudation 6 praise 7 acclaim 8 applause, approval 11 approbation 12 commendation

laudatory 8 admiring, honoring, praising 9 adulatory, approving, extolling, favorable 10 eulogistic, eulogizing, flattering, glorifying 11 acclamatory, approbatory, celebratory, encomiastic, panegyrical 12 commendatory 13 complimentary

laugh 4 glee, ha-ha, ho-ho, howl, roar 5 mirth 6 cackle, giggle, guffaw, titter 7 break up, chortle, chuckle, snicker, snigger 10 bellylaugh, horselaugh 12 express mirth 14 roll in the aisle, split one's sides

laughable 5 comic, dopey, droll, funny, inane, merry, silly, witty 6 absurd, stupid 7 amusing, asinine, comical, foolish, risible 8 farcical, tickling 9 diverting, grotesque, hilarious, ludicrous 10 outlandish, outrageous, ridiculous 11 rib-tickling 12 preposterous 13 sidesplitting

Laugh-In, Rowan & Martin's
regular: 8 Dan Rowan 9 Gary Owens, Judy Carne, Ruth Buzzi 10 Dick Martin, Goldie Hawn, Larry Hovis, Lily Tomlin 11 Arte Johnson, Henry Gibson 12 Jo Anne Worley 13 Eileen Brennan
saying: 10 Sock it to me 15 Here

come de judge, You bet your bippy **24** Beautiful downtown Burbank **31** Look that up in your Funk and Wagnalls

laughingstock 3 ass **4** butt, dupe, fool, joke **8** fair game **11** figure of fun

laugh off 6 deride **7** dismiss, put down **8** belittle, ridicule **9** disparage

laughter 3 joy **4** glee **5** mirth **6** gaiety **7** jollity, revelry **8** hilarity **9** joviality, merriment **11** merrymaking **12** conviviality, exhilaration

Laughton, Charles
wife: 14 Elsa Lanchester
born: 7 England **11** Scarborough
roles: 9 Rembrandt **10** Jamaica Inn **13** Les Miserables **15** Ruggles of Red Gap, The Paradine Case **16** Advise and Consent **17** Mutiny on the Bounty **23** Barretts of Wimpole Street, The Hunchback of Notre Dame **24** Witness for the Prosecution **25** The Private Life of Henry VIII (Oscar)

launch 4 fire, hurl **5** begin, eject, float, found, impel, shoot, start, throw **6** let fly, propel, unveil **7** fire off, project, send off **8** catapult, initiate, premiere, put to sea **9** cast forth, discharge, establish, institute, introduce, set afloat **10** embark upon, inaugurate, set forth on **11** set in mo- tion, venture upon **13** thrust forward **15** set into the water

launder 4 soak, wash **5** clean, rinse, scour, scrub **7** cleanse, wash out **11** wash and iron

Launfal
knight of: 10 round table

Laura
director: 13 Otto Preminger
cast: 11 Clifton Webb, Dana Andrews, Gene Tierney **12** Vincent Price **14** Judith Anderson

laurel 6 Kalmia, Laurus **13** Laurus nobilis **14** Ficus benjamina **15** Cordia alliodora
varieties: 3 bog, pig **4** pale **5** black, dwarf, great, sheep **6** Alpine, cherry, ground, Indian, purple, Sierra, spurge, tropic **7** Chinese, English, red-twig, weeping, western **8** American, drooping, Himalaya, Japanese, mountain, Portugal **9** Tasmanian **10** Australian, California, variegated **11** Alexandrian

Laurel, Stan
real name: 22 Arthur Stanley Jefferson
partner: 11 Oliver Hardy
born: 7 England **9** Ulverston
roles: 8 Pardon Us **9** Saps at Sea **10** Way Out West

laurels 4 fame **5** award, glory, honor, kudos, prize **6** credit, praise, renown, reward **7** acclaim, tribute **8** accolade, applause, citation **9** celebrity **10** deco-

ration, popularity **11** acclamation, distinction, recognition **12** commendation **15** illustriousness

Laurie
also: 16 Theodore Laurence
character in: 11 Little Women
author: 6 Alcott

laus Deo 11 praise to God **13** praise be to God

lavation 7 bathing, washing **8** ablution, cleaning **9** cleansing

lavender 4 herb, mint **5** aspic, behen, lilac, spick, spike **6** purple **7** inkroot **8** amethyst, stichado **9** lavendula
represents: 6 purity
uses: 6 sachet **7** perfume **8** medicine **9** cosmetics

laver 11 footed basin

Laverne and Shirley
character: 12 Frank De Fazio **13** Carmine Ragusa, Lenny Kolowski, Mrs Edna Babish, Shirley Feeney **14** Laverne De Fazio **15** Andrew (Squiggy) Squiggman
cast: 10 Eddie Mekka, Phil Foster **12** Betty Garrett, David L Lander **13** Cindy Williams, Michael McKean, Penny Marshall
girls worked in: 12 Shotz Brewery
theme song: 23 Making Our Dreams Come True
spinoff from: 9 Happy Days

Lavinia
father: 7 Latinus
mother: 5 Amata
husband: 6 Aeneas

lavish 4 free, lush, wild **5** plush, waste **6** shower **7** copious, opulent, pour out, profuse **8** abundant, effusive, generous, prodigal, squander **9** bounteous, bountiful, dissipate, excessive, exuberant, impetuous, luxuriant, plenteous, plentiful, sumptuous, unsparing **10** immoderate, munificent, profligate, unstinting **11** extravagant, fritter away, intemperate, overindulge, overliberal, spend freely **12** give overmuch, greathearted, overwhelming, unrestrained, without limit

lavishness 6 bounty **8** lushness, opulence **9** profusion **10** luxuriance **11** munificence, prodigality **12** extravagance, immoderation **13** bountifulness, plenteousness, sumptuousness

Lavoisier, Antoine
field: 9 chemistry
nationality: 6 French
founder: 15 modern chemistry
named: 6 oxygen **8** hydrogen

law 3 act **4** bill, code, fuzz, rule, writ **5** axiom, bylaw, canon, dogma, edict, model, truth **6** decree, police **7** justice, mandate, precept, statute, theorem **8** absolute, legality, standard **9** criterion, enactment, gendarmes, legal form, ordinance, postulate, principle **10** civil peace, convention, due proc-

ess, invariable, regulation **11** commandment, formulation, fundamental, orderliness, working rule **13** jurisprudence, standing order **14** generalization, rules of conduct **15** legal profession
Latin: 3 jus
goddess of: 4 Maat

law-abiding 6 honest **7** upright **9** honorable **10** aboveboard, principled

lawbreaker 3 con **4** hood, thug **5** crook, felon **6** outlaw **7** convict, culprit **8** criminal, jailbird, offender, scofflaw **9** miscreant, wrongdoer **10** delinquent, malefactor, recidivist **11** perpetrator **12** transgressor

lawful 3 due **5** legal, licit **6** proper, titled **7** allowed, granted **8** rightful **9** legalized, statutory, warranted **10** authorized, legitimate, prescribed **11** legitimized, permissible **15** legally entitled **16** legally permitted

lawless 6 unruly, wanton **7** chaotic, defiant, illegal, riotous, wayward **8** anarchic, mutinous, unlawful, wide open **9** insurgent, out of hand, unbridled **10** disorderly, licentious, rebellious, refractory, ungoverned **11** disobedient, lawbreaking, terroristic **12** disorganized, freewheeling, illegitimate, noncompliant, unrestrained **13** insubordinate, transgressive **14** uncontrollable

lawlessness 5 chaos **7** anarchy **8** disorder

lawn 4 park, turf, yard **5** glade, grass, sward **7** grounds, terrace **10** grassy plot, green field, greensward, meadowland **12** grassy ground

law of a place
Latin: 7 lex loci

Law of Moses 5 Torah **10** Pentateuch **15** Ten Commandments

law of nations
Latin: 10 jus gentium

law of nature
Latin: 11 jus naturale

Lawrence, Carol
real name: 16 Carol Maria Laraia
husband: 12 Robert Goulet
born: 13 Melrose Park IL
roles: 5 Maria **13** West Side Story

Lawrence, D H
author of: 10 The Rainbow **11** Women in Love **13** Sons and Lovers **20** Lady Chatterley's Lover

Lawrence, Ernest Orlando
field: 7 physics
invented: 9 cyclotron
awarded: 10 Nobel Prize

Lawrence, Gertrude
real name: 29 Alexandra Dagmar Lawrence Klasen
born: 6 London **7** England
roles: 9 Pygmalion **11** The King and I **17** The Glass Menagerie

Lawrence, T E
  also: **16** Lawrence of Arabia
  served in: **3** WWI **10** Arab Revolt
  advisor to: **6** Faisal **12** Husayn Ibn Ali
  fought against: **5** Turks **8** Ottomans
  author of: **20** Seven Pillars of Wisdom

Lawrence of Arabia
  director: **9** David Lean
  cast: **10** Jose Ferrer, Omar Sharif **11** Claude Rains, Jack Hawkins, Peter O'Toole (T E Lawrence) **12** Alec Guin- ness, Anthony Quinn **13** Anthony Quayle
  Oscar for: **7** picture **8** director **14** cinematography

Lawrence Welk Show, The
  champagne lady: **8** Alice Lon **11** Norma Zimmer
  cast: **7** Aladdin **11** Larry Hooper, Myron Floren **12** Bobby Burgess **13** Barbara Boylan, Lennon Sisters
  Welk played: **9** accordion

lawyer 6 jurist, legist **7** counsel, shyster **8** advocate, attorney **9** barrister, counselor, solicitor **10** mouthpiece, prosecutor **11** pettifogger **12** legal advisor **14** special pleader **15** ambulance chaser

lax 4 hazy, limp, weak **5** agape, loose, slack, vague **6** casual, flabby, floppy, remiss **7** cryptic, flaccid, inexact, lenient, not firm, relaxed **8** careless, derelict, droop- ing, heedless, nebulous, slipshod, uncaring, yielding **9** confusing, imprecise, negligent, oblivious, undutiful, unheeding, unmindful **10** ill-defined, incoherent, neglectful, permissive **11** hanging open, indifferent, thoughtless, unconcerned **12** loosemuscled, unstructured **13** irresponsible **15** unconscientious

laxness 7 neglect **9** looseness, slackness **10** negligence **11** imprecision **12** carelessness, indifference

Laxness, Halldor Kiljan
  author of: **12** Iceland's Bell **14** The Atom Station **17** Independent People **25** The Great Weaver from Kashmir
  won: **10** Nobel Prize

lay 3 air, bet, put, set **4** bear, fell, fine, form, give, laic, lend, levy, make, plan, poem, raze, rest, seat, song, tune **5** align, allot, apply, ditty, exact, floor, hatch, level, offer, place, stage, wager **6** assess, assign, ballad, charge, demand, depict, devise, gamble, ground, hazard, impose, impute, laical, layout, locate, melody, repose, strain **7** amateur, arrange, concoct, contour, deposit, dispose, forward, present, produce, profane, proffer, refrain, secular, set down, situate, station **8** allocate, assemble, beat down, give odds, inexpert, organize, oviposit, position **9** attribute, elucidate, enunci-

ate, formulate, knock down, knock over, prostrate, roundelay, situation **10** cause to lie, topography **11** arrangement, disposition, nonclerical, orientation, put together **12** conformation **13** configuration, inexperienced, nonspecialist **14** partly informed, unprofessional **15** nonprofessional **17** nonecclesiastical

lay at the door of 6 assign **7** ascribe **8** charge to **9** attribute

lay bare 4 bare, show **6** expose, reveal, unmask, unveil, unwrap **7** divulge, exhibit, publish, uncover **8** disclose **9** broadcast, make known **10** make public **11** communicate

lay down arms 5 yield **6** give up **7** succumb **8** cry quits **9** surrender **10** capitulate **11** come to terms, sue for peace **13** declare a truce **17** acknowledge defeat

layer 3 bed, lap, ply **4** coat, fold, leaf, seam, slab, tier, zone **5** level, plate, scale, sheet, stage, story **6** lamina **7** stratum **9** thickness

layman 4 laic **6** sister **7** amateur, brother **8** outsider **9** churchman **10** catechumen **11** churchwoman, communicant, parishioner **15** nonprofessional **16** member of the flock

layoff 4 fire **6** firing, idling, ouster, the axe **7** dismiss, release, sacking, the boot, the gate, the sack **8** pink slip, shutdown **9** closedown, discharge, dismissal, hard times, the bounce **10** cashiering, depression, the heave-ho **11** furloughing, termination **12** unemployment **13** disemployment, walking papers **20** discharge temporarily

lay off 7 dismiss, forfeit, release, set free **8** get rid of, liberate **9** discharge, terminate **11** give the gate, send packing

Lay of the Last Minstrel, The
  author: **14** Sir Walter Scott
  character: **8** Margaret, The Dwarf **13** Lady Buccleuch, Lord Cranstoun **17** Master of Buccleuch **19** Ghost of Michael Scott **21** Sir William of Deloraine

lay on 6 bestow, confer, supply **7** present, provide

lay open 4 open **6** expose, open up **7** clarify **9** make plain **18** make understandable

layout 4 form, plan **5** chart, draft, dummy, model, motif, spend **6** design, expend, pay out, sketch, spread **7** diagram, drawing, fork out, outline, pattern **8** disburse, delineate, placement, spread out, structure **11** arrangement, composition

lay waste 4 ruin **5** level, wreck **6** ravage **7** despoil, destroy, wipe out **8** demolish, desolate **9** devastate, eradicate **10** annihilate, obliterate

Lazarus 6 beggar
  means: **8** God helps
  sister: **4** Mary **6** Martha
  hometown: **7** Bethany
  resurrected by: **5** Jesus

Lazarus
  author: **14** Leonid Andreyev

Lazarus, Mell
  creator/artist: **5** Momma **9** Miss Peach

lazurite
  variety: **11** lapis lazuli

lazy 3 lax **4** idle, slow **5** inert, slack **6** drowsy, sleepy, torpid **7** laggard, languid **8** inactive, indolent, listless, slothful, sluggish **9** apathetic, easygoing, lethargic, shiftless **10** languorous, slow-moving **13** unindustrious **15** unwilling to work

lazy person 5 drone, idler **6** loafer **14** good-for-nothing

l'chaim, l'chayim 5 toast **6** Hebrew, to life

Leachman, Cloris
  born: **11** Des Moines IA
  roles: **7** Phyllis **11** High Anxiety **12** Kiss Me Deadly **17** Young Frankenstein **18** Mary Tyler Moore Show, The Last Picture Show

lead 2 go **3** aim, top **4** clue, draw, edge, have, head, hero, hint, live, lure, pass **5** charm, excel, guide, model, outdo, pilot, steer, tempt **6** allure, convey, direct, en- tice, extend, induce, manage, margin, pursue, seduce **7** advance, attract, bring on, command, conduct, control, example, go first, incline, issue in, marshal, pioneer, precede, proceed, produce, stretch, surpass, undergo **8** domineer, go before, guidance, moderate, outstrip, persuade, priority, result in, shepherd, star part **9** advantage, come first, direction, go through, headliner, influence, plurality, rank first **10** branch into, experience, first place, indication, precedence, precedency, set the pace, show the way, tend toward **11** antecedence, be in advance, leading role, preside over, protagonist

lead
  chemical symbol: **2** Pb
  mineral: **10** fiedlerite
  ore: **6** galena, pyrite

lead astray 4 dupe, lure **6** delude **7** beguile, deceive, ensnare, mislead **19** lead up the garden path

leaden 4 dark, dull, glum, gray **5** inert, murky **6** dreary, gloomy, numbed, somber, torpid **7** grayish, languid **8** burdened, careworn, darkened, deadened, listless, sluggish, unwieldy **9** depressed, inanimate **10** cumbersome, hard to move

leader 4 boss, guru, head **5** chief, guide, mogul **6** bigwig, honcho, master, mentor, tycoon **7** captain, foreman, kingpin, magnate, manager, pioneer, prophet **8** director, superior **9** chieftain, commander, conductor, godfather, pacemaker, patriarch **10** forerunner, pacesetter, pathfinder, supervisor **11** frontrunner, torchbearer, trailblazer

leadership 4 helm, lead, sway **5** reins, wheel **7** command, primacy **8** charisma, guidance, headship, hegemony **9** captaincy, supremacy **10** domination, mastership **11** managership, preeminence, stewardship **12** directorship, governorship, guardianship, self-reliance **13** ability to lead, self-assurance **14** administration **15** managerial skill, superintendency **17** authoritativeness

leading 3 top **4** head, main **5** basic, chief, first, great, prime **6** ruling **7** advance, guiding, initial, leadoff, notable, primary, ranking, stellar, supreme, topmost **8** advanced, dominant, foremost **9** directing, essential, governing, nonpareil, paramount, principal, prominent, sovereign, unrivaled **10** motivating, preeminent, underlying **11** controlling, outstanding, pacesetting **12** unchallenged, unparalleled **13** most important **14** quintessential **15** most influential, most significant

lead on 4 goad **5** egg on **6** entice **7** mislead, support **9** encourage **19** lead up the garden path

lead the way 4 lead, show, take **5** guide **6** escort **7** conduct

leaf 4 flip, foil, page, skim **5** blade, bract, folio, frond, green, inset, petal, sheet, thumb **6** browse, glance, insert, needle **7** foliole, lamella, leaflet **9** cotyledon, extension, turn green **10** lamination **12** sheet of metal
  edge: 5 erose **7** crenate, dentate
  angle: 4 axil
  aperture: 5 stoma
  kind: 5 calyx, petal, sepal **7** corolla

leaflet 2 ad **4** bill **5** flier, flyer, tract **6** folder, notice **7** booklet, handout **8** brochure, bulletin, circular, handbill, pamphlet **9** broadside, throwaway **10** broadsheet **12** announcement **13** advertisement

league 4 ally, band **5** cabal, group, guild, merge, union **6** cartel **7** combine, compact, company, network, society **8** alliance **9** coalition **10** conspiracy, federation, frater- nity, join forces **11** association, confederacy, confederate, consolidate, cooperative, partnership **13** collaboration, confederation, confraternity

Leah
  means: 7 wild cow
  father: 5 Laban
  husband: 5 Jacob
  sister: 6 Rachel
  slave: 6 Zilpah
  son: 4 Levi **5** Judah **6** Reuben, Simeon **7** Zebulun **8** Issachar
  daughter: 5 Dinah
  burial place: 9 Machpelah

leak 3 ebb, rip **4** blab, gash, hole, ooze, rent, rift, seep, vent **5** break, chink, cleft, crack, drain, exude, fault, spill **6** breach, efflux, escape, filter, let out, reveal, take in **7** confide, crevice, divulge, dribble, fissure, let slip, opening, outflow, rupture, seepage **8** aperture, disclose, draining, give away, puncture **9** discharge, percolate **10** interstice, make public **11** be permeable, perforation **12** admit leakage **16** let enter or escape

leakage 5 issue **7** outflow, seepage **9** discharge

Leakey, Louis S Bazett
  field: 12 anthropology
  discovered: 8 early man
  worked at: 8 Tanzania **12** Olduvai Gorge
  wife: 4 Mary
  son: 7 Richard

lean 3 aim, bow, tip **4** bend, cant, lank, list, poor, rely, rest, slim, tend, thin, tilt **5** gaunt, lanky, lurch, scant, slant, slope, small, spare, weedy **6** barren, depend, meager, modest, nonfat, prefer, scanty, skinny, sparse, svelte **7** angular, count on, incline, recline, scraggy, scrawny, slender, spindly, trust in, willowy **8** exiguous, rawboned, resort to, skeletal **9** emaciated **10** inadequate, set store by **11** be partial to, have faith in, prop oneself **12** insufficient, seek solace in **14** rest one's weight, support oneself

Lean, David
  director of: 10 Summertime **11** Oliver Twist **13** Doctor Zhivago, Ryan's Daughter **15** A Passage to India **16** Lawrence of Arabia (Oscar) **17** Great Expectations **23** The Bridge on the River Kwai (Oscar)

Leander
  loved: 4 Hero
  swam nightly: 10 Hellespont
  death by: 8 drowning

leaning 4 bent, turn **5** slant **7** relying **8** affinity, tendency **9** proneness **10** dependence, partiality, preference, proclivity, propensity **11** inclination **14** predisposition

leap 3 hop **4** jete, jump, romp, rush, skip **5** bound, caper, frisk, vault **6** bounce, cavort, frolic, gambol, hasten, hurtle, prance, spring **7** hop over **8** jump over **9** bound over, saltation **10** hurtle over, jump across, spring over

Lear, Norman
  TV producer of: 5 Maude **13** The Jeffersons **14** All in the Family

Learchus
  father: 7 Athamas
  mother: 3 Ino
  killed by: 7 Athamas

learn 3 con **4** hear **6** detect, master, pick up **7** find out, uncover, unearth **8** discover, memorize **9** ascertain, determine, ferret out **10** become able **12** find out about

learned 4 deep, wise **7** erudite **8** cultured, educated, informed, lettered, literate, profound, schooled, well-read **9** scholarly **10** cultivated **12** accomplished, intellectual, well-educated **13** knowledgeable

Learned, Michael
  roles: 5 Nurse **10** The Waltons

learner 4 tyro **5** pupil, tutee **6** novice, rookie **7** draftee, recruit, scholar, student, trainee **8** beginner, disciple, enlistee, follower, freshman, neophyte **9** fledgling, greenhorn, novitiate, proselyte, schoolboy **10** apprentice, schoolgirl, tenderfoot **11** schoolchild

learning 4 lore **5** study **6** wisdom **7** culture **8** teaching **9** education, erudition, knowledge, schooling **11** cultivation, edification, information, instruction, scholarship **13** comprehension, enlightenment, understanding

Learning
  god of: 5 Thoth

Leary, Timothy
  phrase: 19 Tune in, turn on, drop out

leash 4 curb, lead, line, rein, ruin **5** strap, thong **6** bridle, choker, fasten, hold in, stifle, string, tether **7** contain, control, harness **8** restrain, suppress

leatherneck 6 gyrene, marine

Leather-Stocking Tales
  author: 19 James Fenimore Cooper
  includes: 10 The Prairie **11** The Pioneers **13** The Deerslayer, The Pathfinder **20** The Last of the Mohicans
  hero of: 7 Hawkeye **10** Pathfinder, The Trapper **11** Natty Bumppo **13** The Deerslayer **15** Leather-stocking **16** Le Longue Carabine

leave 2 go **3** fly **4** cede, exit, flee, jilt, keep, quit, will **5** allot, be off, cause, endow, forgo, going, split, waive, yield **6** assign, bug out, commit, decamp, depart, desert, eschew, forego, give up, legate, move on, recess, resign, retain, set out **7** abandon, abscond, bequest, consent, consign, deposit, entrust, forsake, holiday, let stay, liberty, parting, produce, push off, release, respite, retreat, sustain, take off, time off **8** approval, bequeath, farewell, furlough, generate, give over, maintain, result in, sanction, shove off, vacation **9** allowance, apportion, departure, hotfoot it, let remain, surrender, tolerance **10** concession, depart from, embark from, go away from, indulgence, permission, relinquish, retire from, sabbatical, sufferance, withdrawal **11** bid farewell, endorsement **13** absent oneself, understanding

leave a ship 4 land **6** debark **8** go ashore **9** disembark **11** abandon ship

leave behind 4 jilt **6** desert, vacate **7** abandon, discard, forsake **8** evacuate **9** cast aside **10** relinquish **11** outdistance

leave cold 4 bore **12** leave unmoved **15** leave unaffected

Leave It To Beaver
character: **11** June Cleaver, Ward Cleaver **12** Eddie Haskell, Wally Cleaver **13** Beaver (Theodore) Cleaver
cast: **7** Tony Dow **9** Ken Osmond **12** Hugh Beaumont, Jerry Mathers **18** Barbara Billingsley

leave off 3 end **4** halt, quit, stop **5** cease **6** desist, finish **7** suspend **8** conclude **11** discontinue, refrain from

leave out 4 drop, omit **6** except, reject **7** exclude

Leaves of Grass
author: **11** Walt Whitman

leave suddenly 3 fly **4** flee **6** cut out, decamp, run off **7** abscond, make off, run away, rush off, take off **11** take a powder **15** be off and running

leave-taking 4 exit **5** adieu **7** goodbye, leaving, parting, send-off **8** au revoir, farewell **9** departure **10** withdrawal

leave undone 4 quit **6** give up **7** abandon, forsake, neglect **8** give up on

Lebanon
ancient name: **9** Phoenicia
capital/largest city: **6** Beirut **8** Beyrouth
others: **3** Sur **4** Arca, Tyre **5** Ehden, Halba, Hamat, Sahle, Saida, Sayda, Sidon, Sofar, Zahla, Zahle **6** Byblos, Ghazir, Juniye, Tibnin **7** Baalbek, Batroun, Bsherri, Rachaya, Tripoli, Zgharta **8** Djezzine, El Hermel, Hasbaiya, Merjuyun **9** Broummana, Marjayoun **10** Beited Dine, Heliopolis
ancient city: **8** Carthage
school: **4** Arab **8** American, Lebanese **11** Saint Joseph
division:
ancient: **4** Tyre **5** Arwad, Sidon **6** Byblos, Jubayl
monetary unit: **5** livre, pound **7** piastre
lake: **5** Quran **6** Qirawn
mountain: **4** Mzar **5** Aruba **6** Hermon **7** Lebanon, Sannine **8** Kadischa, Kenisseh **9** Kennisseh **10** al- Mukammal **11** Anti-Lebanon
highest point: **7** es Sauda **13** Qurnat al-Sawda
river: **3** Dog, Joz **5** Barid, Kebir, Lycos **6** Auwali, Barada, Damour, Litani **7** Hasbani, Leontes, Orontes **8** Kasemieh

sea: **13** Mediterranean
physical feature:
cape: **10** Pigeon Rock **11** Ras esh Shiqa **12** Qadisha Gorge
plain: **4** Bika **5** Bekaa
valley: **5** Beqaa **6** al-Biqa **9** Great Rift
wind: **7** khamsin
people: **4** Arab **11** Palestinian
ancient: **9** Canaanite **10** Phoenician
leader: **6** Bashir, Sarkis **7** Chamoun **8** Franjieh **9** al-Din Maan **11** Amin Gemayel **13** Bashir Gemayel
poet: **11** Kahlil Gibran
rulers: **5** Arabs **6** French, Greeks, Romans **8** Hittites, Ottomans, Persians **9** Assyrians, Crusaders, Egyptians, Mamelukes **11** Babylonians
language: **6** Arabic, French, Syriac **7** English, Turkish **8** Armenian
religion: **5** Druse, Druze, Islam **8** Maronite, Melchite **10** Protestant **11** Monophysite **12** Christianity **13** Greek Catholic **14** Greek Orthodoxy **17** Armenian Orthodoxy
place:
dam: **5** Qarun
ruins: **7** Baalbek **15** Temple of Bacchus, Temple of Jupiter
feature:
Christian group: **10** Phalangist
dance: **6** dabkeh, dabkey
tree: **5** cedar
food:
dish: **6** kibbeh **8** tabouleh
drink: **4** arak **6** arrack

Le Bel, Joseph Achille
field: **9** chemistry
nationality: **6** French
founded: **15** stereochemistry

Le Bourgeois Gentilhomme
author: **7** Moliere
character: **7** Cleonte, Dorante **9** M Jourdain **16** Monsieur Jourdain

Le Carre, John
real name: **13** David Cornwell
author of: **11** A Perfect Spy **13** Smiley's People **18** The Looking Glass War **19** A Small Town in Germany **20** The Little Drummer Girl **21** The Honorable Schoolboy **22** Tinker Tailor Soldier Spy **26** The Spy Who Came in from the Cold

lechayim, lehayim 6 to life

lecherous 4 lewd **5** randy **6** carnal **7** goatish, lustful, ruttish **8** prurient **9** sala- cious, satyrlike **10** lascivious, libidinous, licentious, lubricious

lechery 4 lust **8** lewdness **9** carnality, prurience **10** satyriasis **11** lustfulness, nym- phomania **13** salaciousness **14** lasciv- iousness

Le Cid
author: **9** Corneille
composer: **21** Leconte Dehisle, Charles **13** Jules Massenet

Leconte de Lisle, Charles
author of: **14** Poemes Antiques, Poemes Barbares

Le Corbusier
real name: **23** Charles Edouard Jeanneret
architect of: **10** La Tourette (monastery) **15** Notre Dame du Haut (Ronchamp France) **16** Unite d'Habitation (Marseilles)
planned city of: **10** Chandi garh (capital of the Punjab)
style: **6** Purism **12** New Brutalism

lecture 4 talk **5** chide, scold, speak **6** homily, preach, rail at, rebuke, sermon, speech **7** address, censure, chiding, expound, oration, reading, re proof, reprove, upbraid, warning **8** admonish, call down, harangue, moralize, reproach **9** discourse, hold forth, reprimand, sermonize, talking-to **10** preachment, take to task **12** chastisement, disquisition, remonstrance

lecture hall 9 classroom **10** auditorium **12** amphitheater, assembly hall

lecturelike 7 donnish, preachy **8** academic, didactic, pedantic **9** homiletic **10** moralizing

LED 18 light emitting diode **19** alphanumeric display

Leda
father: **8** Thestius
husband: **9** Tyndareus
lover: **4** swan, Zeus
son: **6** Castor, Pollux **8** Dioscuri **10** Polydeuces
daughter: **5** Helen **6** Phoebe **8** Philonoe, Timandra **12** Clytemnestra

Leda and the Swan
author: **7** W B Yeats

ledge 4 sill, step **5** ridge, shelf **6** mantel, offset **8** foothold, shoulder **10** projection **11** mantelpiece, mantelshelf, outcropping

Lee, Bruce
born: **12** San Francisco
son: **7** Brandon
roles: **7** Marlowe **11** Fists of Fury, Game of Death **14** The Green Hornet, Enter the Dragon **17** Return of the Dragon, Chinese Connection **24** Bruce Lee: Curse of the Dragon

Lee, Christopher
born: **6** London
roles: **5** Jocks **6** Albino, Serial **7** The Girl **8** Caravans **9** Shaka Zulu, The Keeper, The Gorgon **10** Dark Places **11** Eye for an Eye, Horror Hotel, Moulin Rouge, Killer Force **12** Count Dracula, The Wicker Man, The Oblong Box, Scream of Fear **13** The Death Train **14** Treasure Island **15** Journey of Horror **16** Castle of Fu Manchu, The Creeping Flesh, A Tale of Two Cities **17** The Four Musketeers **23** Return from Witch Mountain

25 The Hound of the Baskervilles **30** The Private Life of Sherlock Holmes

Lee, Gypsy Rose
  born: 7 Seattle
  author of: 5 Gypsy 8 Doll Face 15 Lady of Burlesque
  roles: 11 The Stripper, My Lucky Star 13 Screaming Mimi

Lee, Harper
  author of: 18 To Kill a Mockingbird

Lee, Johnny
  born: 8 Alta Loma (TX)
  roles: 11 Urban Cowboy 12 School Spirit

Lee, Henry
  nickname: 15 Light Horse Harry
  served in: 16 Revolutionary War
  member of: 10 US Congress 19 Continental Congress
  governor of: 8 Virginia
  suppressed: 16 Whiskey Rebellion
  son: 7 Robert E

Lee, Peggy
  born: 9 Jamestown (ND)
  roles: 7 Mr. Music 13 The Jazz Singer 15 Pete Kelly's Blues 18 Ladies Sing the Blues

Lee, Robert E
  father: 5 Henry 15 Light Horse Harry
  born: 11 Stratford VA 18 Westmoreland County
  wife: 21 Mary Ann Randolph Custis
  served in: 8 Civil War 10 Mexican War
  commander of: 22 Army of Northern Virginia
  suppressed raid: 9 John Brown 12 Harper's Ferry
  battle: 7 Bull Run 8 Antie tam 10 Gettysburg 14 Fredericksburg 16 Chancellorsville, Seven Days' Battles
  surrendered at: 20 Appomattox Court House
  president of: 17 Washington College

Lee, Spike
  original name: 17 Sheldon Jackson Lee
  born: 2 GA 7 Atlanta
  wife: 17 Tonya Linette Lewis
  films: 8 Malcolm X 10 School Daze 11 Jungle Fever 15 Do the Right Thing, She's Gotta Have It
  company: 18 Forty Acres and A Mule
  ads for: 4 Nike

Lee, Stan 10 cartoonist
  of: 9 Spider-Man

leek 18 Allium ampeloprasum
  emblem of: 5 Wales
  varieties: 4 lily, rose, sand, wild 5 lady's 6 meadow

leer 4 ogle 5 fleer, smirk 6 goggle

leery 4 wary 5 cagey, chary 6 unsure 7 guarded 8 cautious, doubtful, hesitant 9 skeptical, undecided 10 suspicious 11 circumspect, distrustful, mistrustful

Leeuwenhoek, Anton van

field: 10 microscopy
father of: 12 microbiology
discovered: 13 red blood cells

leeway 4 play 5 scope, slack 6 margin 7 cushion, headway, reserve 8 headroom, latitude 9 allowance, clearance, elbow room, extra time, tolerance 11 flexibility 13 room for choice 14 margin for error 15 maneuverability

left behind 7 vacated 8 deserted, forsaken, forsook 9 abandoned, discarded, evacuated 12 relinquished

leftover 6 excess, legacy, unused 7 overage, residue, surplus, uneaten 8 leavings, oddments, residual, survivor 9 carry-over, remainder, remaining

left-wing 7 leftist, liberal, radical 9 socialist 11 progressive

left-winger 7 leftist, liberal, radical 9 socialist 11 progressive

Lefty
  nickname of: 5 Gomez 12 Steve Carlton

leg 3 gam, lap, pin 4 limb, part, post, prop 5 brace, femur, shank, stage, stump, tibia 6 column, fibula, member, pillar 7 portion, section, segment, stretch, support, upright

legacy 4 gift 6 devise, estate 7 bequest, vestige 8 heirloom, heritage, leftover, survivor 9 carry-over, throwback, tradition 10 birthright, hand-me-down 11 inheritance

legal 4 fair 5 licit, of law, valid 6 kosher, lawful 7 cricket 8 forensic, judicial, juristic, rightful 9 courtroom, juridical 10 legiti- mate, sanctioned 11 permissible

legal advisor 6 lawyer 7 counsel 8 advocate, attorney 9 barrister, counselor, so licitor 13 attorney-at-law 14 counselor-at-law

legal form 4 writ 8 document 10 instrument

legality 8 validity 9 licitness 10 lawfulness, legitimacy 17 constitutionality

legalization 8 sanction 9 enactment 10 permission, validation 13 authorization 14 legitimization

legalize 5 enact 6 permit 8 sanction, validate 9 authorize 10 legitimize

legal residence 4 home 8 domicile, dwelling

legal tender 4 cash 5 money 8 currency

legate 5 agent, envoy 6 deputy 8 emissary 14 representative

legatee 4 heir 7 heiress 9 inheritor 11 beneficiary

legation 7 embassy, mission 8 ministry 9 consulate 10 delegation 11 chancellery

legend 3 key 4 edda, lore, myth, saga, tale 5 fable, motto, story, title 7 caption, fiction, proverb 8 folklore 11 inscription

legendary 5 famed 6 fabled, famous, mythic 7 storied 8 fabulous, fanciful, mythical 9 imaginary 10 apocryphal, celebrated, fictitious, proverbial

Legend of Good Women, The
  author: 15 Geoffrey Chaucer
  character: 4 Dido 5 Medea 6 Thisbe 7 Alceste, Ariadne, Lucrece, Phyllis 9 Cleopatra, Hypsipyle, Philomela 12 Hypermnestra

Legend of Sleepy Hollow, The
  author: 16 Washington Irving
  character: 12 Brom Van Brunt (Brom Bones), Ichabod Crane 16 headless horseman, Katrina Van Tassel

Leger, Fernand
  born: 6 France 8 Argentan
  artwork: 8 Bargeman 10 Adam and Eve, The Wedding, Three Women 11 The Builders, The Cyclists, The Mechanic, The Stairway 14 The Great Parade 15 Le Grand Dejeuner 16 Contrasting Forms, Nudes in the Forest 21 Butterflies and Flowers

legerdemain 7 cunning 8 deftness, jugglery, juggling, trickery 9 deception 10 adroitness, artfulness 11 maneuvering 13 sleight of hand 16 prestidigitation

legible 4 neat 5 clear, plain 7 visible 8 clear-cut, distinct, readable 12 decipherable 14 comprehensible, understandable

legion 3 mob, sea 4 army, host, mass 5 corps, drove, horde, spate, swarm 6 myriad, throng, troops 7 brigade 8 division 9 multitude

leg irons 5 bonds, irons 6 chains 7 fetters 8 shackles

legislation 3 act 4 bill 6 ruling 7 measure, statute 9 amendment, enactment, law making, ordinance

legislator 7 senator 8 alder man, delegate, lawgiver, lawmaker 10 councilman 11 assemblyman, congressman 13 congresswoman 14 representative 15 parliamentarian

legislature 4 diet 5 house 6 senate 7 chamber, council 8 assembly, congress 10 parliament

legitimacy 8 legality, validity 10 lawfulness 11 correctness, genuineness 12 authenticity, rightfulness 15 appropriateness

legitimate 4 fair, just, true 5 legal, licit, sound, valid 6 lawful, proper 7 correct, genuine, logical, tenable 8 rightful 9 authentic, justified, plausible 10 believable, reasonable 11 appropriate, well-founded

leg-pull 4 hoax 9 deception 13 practical joke

Legree, Simon 13 cruel overseer
  character in: 14 Uncle Tom's Cabin
  author: 5 Stowe

LeGuin, Ursula K

author of: 13 Lathe of Heaven **14** Rocannon's World **15** The Dispossessed **16** Always Coming Home **21** The Left Hand of Darkness

Lehar, Franz (Ferencz)
born: 7 Komarno (then Hungary, now Czechoslovakia)
composer of: 9 Gipsy Love **13** The Merry Widow **20** The Count of Luxembourg

Lehmbruck, Wilhelm
born: 7 Germany **9** Meiderich
artwork: 11 Rising Youth **12** Man Flung Down, Praying Woman, Seating Youth **13** Kneeling Woman, Standing Woman, Standing Youth

Leigh, Janet
husband: 10 Tony Curtis
daughter: 14 Jamie Lee Curtis
born: 8 Merced CA
roles: 6 Psycho, The Fog **10** The Vikings **11** Little Women, Touch of Evil

Leigh, Vivien
real name: 17 Vivian Mary Hartley
husband: 15 Laurence Olivier
born: 5 India **10** Darjeeling
roles: 11 Ship of Fools **12** Anna Karenina **13** Blanche du Bois, Scarlett O'Hara **14** Waterloo Bridge **15** Gone With the Wind (Oscar) **17** That Hamilton Woman **21** A Streetcar Named Desire (Oscar), Roman Spring of Mrs Stone

Leighton, Margaret
husband: 12 Max Reinhardt **14** Laurence Harvey, Michael Wilding
born: 7 England **10** Barnt Green **14** Worcestershire
roles: 12 The Go-Between **13** The Winslow Boy **14** Separate Tables **19** The Night of the Iguana

leisure 4 ease, rest **6** recess, repose **7** holiday, respite, time off **8** free time, vacation **9** diversion, idle hours, spare time **10** recreation, relaxation

leisurely 4 idle, slow **6** casual, slowly **7** languid, relaxed, restful **9** unhurried **10** slow-moving **11** lingeringly, unhurriedly **12** without haste **13** lackadaisical

Lemmon, Jack
real name: 18 Jack Uhler Lemmon III
wife: 11 Felicia Farr
born: 8 Boston MA
roles: 7 Missing **10** April Fools **12** Grumpy Old Men, Save the Tiger (Oscar), The Apartment, The Great Race, The Odd Couple **13** China Syndrome, Mister Roberts, Some Like It Hot **18** Days of Wine and Roses, Under the Yum-Yum Tree **19** How to Murder Your Wife

lemon 11 Citrus limon
varieties: 4 wild **5** dwarf, giant, Meyer, water **6** garden, wonder **9** wild water **12** Chinese dwarf

14 American wonder
slang for: 3 dud **9** defective

lemures
form: 6 ghosts
characteristic: 10 maleficent **11** troublesome

lend 4 give, loan **6** impart, in vest, supply **7** advance, furnish **10** contribute

lend a hand 3 aid **6** assist **7** help out

lend assistance 3 aid **4** abet, help **6** succor **7** relieve **16** give a helping hand

lend one's name to 7 endorse, support **9** recommend

length 3 run **4** span, term, time **5** piece, range, reach **6** extent, period **7** com- pass, measure, portion, section, segment, stretch **8** distance, duration, end to end **9** longitude, magnitude **11** elapsed time, measurement

lengthen 3 pad **5** add to **6** expand, extend, let out, pad out **7** augment, drag out, draw out, fill out, prolong, spin out, stretch **8** elongate, flesh out, increase, protract **9** attenuate, string out

lengthening 8 full form **9** extending, extension **10** elongation, stretching **11** extenuation, protraction **12** prolongation

lengthy 5 windy, wordy **6** padded, prolix **7** endless **8** drawn out, extended, over- long, rambling **9** elongated, extensive, garrulous, longdrawn, prolonged **10** digressive, discursive, long- winded, protracted **12** interminable

leniency 5 mercy **7** charity **8** clemency **9** tolerance **10** compassion **11** forbearance, magnanimity **12** mercifulness **13** forgivingness

lenient 4 kind, mild, soft **6** gentle **7** clement, liberal, patient, sparing **8** merciful, moderate, tolerant **9** easygoing, forgiving, indulgent **10** benevolent, charitable, forbearing, permissive **11** kindhearted, soft-hearted, sympathetic **13** compassionate, tenderhearted

Lenin, Vladimir Illyich
surname: 7 Ulyanov
also called: 7 Nikolai
founder of: 10 Bolshevism
leader of: 17 Russian Revolution
premier of: 4 USSR

Lenni-Lenape see **8** Delaware

Lennon, John
born: 9 Liverpool (UK)
songs: 5 Woman **6** Mother **9** Stand By Me **10** Jealous Guy
see also **7** Beatles

Lenny
director: 8 Bob Fosse
cast: 8 Jan Miner **11** Stanley Beck **13**

Dustin Hoffman (Lenny Bruce) **14** Valerie Perrine (Honey Harlowe)

Leno, Jay
host of: 14 The Tonight Show
author of: 9 Headlines (Books I-IV) **17** Leading with My Chin

Le Notre, Andre
landscape architect of: 6 Clagny **9** Tuileries **10** Ver sailles **12** Saint Germain **13** Fontainebleau **22** Chateau de Vaux-le-Vicomte

lens
invented by:
   achromatic: 7 Dollond
   bifocal: 8 Franklin
   fused bifocal: 6 Borsch

Lenya, Lotte
real name: 16 Karoline Blamauer
husband: 9 Kurt Weill
born: 7 Austria, Hitzing
roles: 5 Jenny **18** From Russia with Love, The Seven Deadly Sins, The Three-penny Opera

Leo
symbol: 4 lion
planet: 3 Sun
rules: 7 romance **10** creativity
born: 4 July **6** August

Leonard, Elmore
author of: 4 Swag **5** Glitz, Stick **6** Hombre **7** La Brava **9** Cat Chaser, Gold Coast, Gunsights, The Hunted **10** Mr Majestyk **12** The Big Bounce **14** Fifty-Two Pick-Up, Valdez Is Coming **16** Double Dutch Treat, The Bounty Hunters **18** Forty Lashes Less One

Leonato
character in: 19 Much Ado About Nothing
author: 11 Shakespeare

Leoncavallo, Ruggiero
born: 5 Italy **6** Naples
composer of: 8 Serafita **10** I Pagliacci

Leontes
character in: 14 The Winter's Tale
author: 11 Shakespeare

Leonteus
leader of: 6 Greeks
leader at: 4 Troy
suitor of: 5 Helen

leopard 3 cat **7** panther **10** spotted cat
group of: 4 leap

Leo the Lip
nickname of: 11 Leo Durocher

lepidoptera
class: 8 hexapoda
phylum: 10 arthropoda
group: 4 moth **9** butterfly

leprechaun 3 elf, imp **5** dwarf, gnome **6** sprite **12** little person

Ler
also: 3 Lir
origin: 5 Irish
personifies: 3 sea

son: 8 Manannan
corresponds to: 4 Llyr
Lerner, Alan J.
born: 7 New York
author of: 4 Gigi **7** Camelot **9** Brigadoon **10** My Fair Lady **17** An American in Paris
composer of: 7 Tribute **15** The Little Prince
producer of: 14 Paint Your Wagon
Lesage, Le Sage, Alain
author of: 7 Gil Blas **8** Turcaret
Lesbos
island in: 6 Aegean
home of: 6 Sappho
Lescaze, William
architect of: 18 Borg-Warner Building (Chicago) **38** Philadelphia Savings Fund Society Building
Lescot, Pierre
architect of: 10 Cour Carree **20** Fontaine des Innocents
rebuilding of: 6 Louvre
lese-majeste, lese majesty 5 crime **7** treason
against: 12 king's dignity
Lesotho
other name: 10 Basutoland
capital/largest city: 6 Maseru
others: 4 Roma **5** Joels **6** Leribe, Morija **7** Quthing, Sekakes **8** Mafeteng, Matsieng **9** Marakabei, Qachas Nek, Semonkong **10** Butha Buthe, Mokhotlong, Thaba Bosiu **11** Mohales Hoek **12** Sehlabathebe, Teyateyaneng
head of state: 4 king
monetary unit: 4 cent, rand
mountain: 6 Maloti, Maluti **7** Central **8** Injasuti, Machache **10** Ben Macdhui **11** Drakensberg, Thaba Putsoa
highest point: 16 Thabana Ntlenyana
river: 5 Senqu **6** Orange, Tugela **7** Caledon **9** Makhaleng
physical feature:
gorge: 5 Oxbow
people: 4 Zulu **5** Bantu, Tembu **6** Basuto **7** Basotho
leader: 7 Moshesh **9** Mosheshwe **10** Moshoeshoe **14** Leabua Jonathan
language: 5 Sotho **7** English, Sesotho
religion: 7 animism **13** Roman Catholic **18** Lesotho Evangelical
feature:
blanket: 4 kobo
house: 8 rondavel
water project: 11 Malibamatso
less 5 fewer **6** barely, little **7** smaller **8** meagerly, slighter **10** not as great **11** more limited
lessen 3 ebb **4** ease, sink, thin, wane **5** abate, lower **6** dilute, reduce, shrink **7** abridge, decline, dwindle, lighten, slacken, subside **8** contract, decrease, diminish, mitigate, wind down **9** alleviate **10** depreciate

lessening 6 waning **8** decrease, dilution **9** abatement, deduction, dwindling, reduction, shrinkage **10** diminution, lightening, mitigation, shortening, slackening **11** abridgement, alleviation, contraction, diminishing, slacking off **12** abbreviation, condensation, depreciation
Lesseps, Ferdinand 8 engineer **9** Suez Canal
lesser 4 less **5** minor **7** humbler, smaller **8** inferior, slighter **9** secondary **11** sec- ondarily
Lessing, Doris
author of: 8 Shikasta **16** The Four-Gated City **17** The Golden Notebook **20** The Sirian Experiments **21** The Children of Violence **37** Marriages Between Zones Three Four and Five **42** The Making of the Representative for Planet Eight
lesson 5 class, drill, guide, model, moral, study **6** caveat, notice, rebuke **7** cau- tion, example, message, reading, segment, warning **8** exemplar, exercise, homework **9** deterrent **10** admonition, advisement, assignment, punishment, recitation, Scriptures **11** instruction **12** remonstrance
Lestrade, Inspector
character in: 14 (The Adventures of) Sherlock Holmes
author: 10 Conan Doyle
let 4 make, rent **5** admit, allow, cause, grant, lease, leave **6** enable, permit, sublet, suffer **7** approve, charter, concede, empower, endorse, hire out, license, warrant **8** sanction, sublease, tolerate **9** authorize
let
term in: 6 tennis
serve touches: 3 net
let down 4 drop **5** lower **6** betray **8** push down **10** disappoint **11** disillusion
letdown 3 rue **4** balk, blow **6** fizzle, regret **7** chagrin, set back **8** comedown **9** anticlimax, bafflement, bitter pill, dashed hope, discontent **11** frustration **12** blighted hope, discomfiture **13** mortification **14** disappointment, disenchantment, disgruntlement **15** disillusionment, dissatisfaction
let fall 4 drop **5** let go **7** release
let fly 4 cast, hurl **5** eject, fling, heave, sling, throw **6** launch, propel
let go 3 axe, can **4** fire, free, lose, oust, sack **6** bounce, give up
lethal 5 fatal, toxic **6** deadly, mortal **7** baneful, killing **8** venomous, virulent **9** dan gerous, malignant, poisonous **11** destructive **13** mortally toxic
lethargic 4 dull, idle, lazy **5** inert **6** drowsy, sleepy, torpid **7** languid, passive **8** comatose, indolent, listless, slothful, sluggish **9** apathetic, enervated, somnolent, soporific **10** dispir-

ited, lackluster, unspirited **11** debilitated, indifferent
lethargy 5 sloth **6** apathy, stupor, torpor **7** inertia, languor **8** dullness, laziness **9** indolence, lassitude, torpidity **10** drowsiness, inactivity **12** indifference, listlessness, slothfulness, sluggishness
Lethe
form: 5 river
location: 5 Hades
caused: 13 forgetfulness
let in 5 admit **7** receive **12** allow to enter
let loose 4 free **5** let go **6** let fly **7** release, set free, unleash **8** give vent, liberate **12** give free rein
Leto
also: 6 Latona
father: 5 Coeus
mother: 6 Phoebe
son: 6 Apollo
consort: 4 Zeus
daughter: 5 Diana **7** Artemis
let off 5 let go **6** acquit, excuse, exempt **7** release, set free **8** liberate **9** discharge
let slip 6 betray, expose, reveal **7** divulge, uncover **8** blurt out, disclose, give away
Let's Make a Deal
host: 9 Monty Hall
announcer: 10 Jay Stewart
letter 4 note **7** epistle, message, missive **8** dispatch, document **9** substance **10** billet-doux
Letter, The
director: 12 William Wyler
based on story by: 15 Somerset Maugham
cast: 10 Bette Davis **14** Frieda Inescort **15** Gale Sondergaard, Herbert Marshall, James Stephenson
setting: 6 Malaya
Letterman, David
Host of: 26 Late Show with David Letterman
letter ordering imprisonment
French: 14 lettre de cachet
carried seal of: 4 king **9** sovereign
letters 8 learning **9** erudition **10** literature **13** belles lettres
Letters from the Underground
author: 16 Fyodor Dostoevsky
Letter to Three Wives, A
director: 17 Joseph L Mankiewicz
cast: 10 Ann Sothern **11** Jeanne Crain, Jeffrey Lynn, Kirk Douglas, Paul Douglas **12** Linda Darnell, Thelma Ritter
Oscar for: 6 script **8** director
let the buyer beware
Latin: 12 caveat emptor
let the people rule
Latin: 13 regnat populus
motto of: 8 Arkansas

let there be light
 Latin: **7** fiat lux

lettre de cachet 26 letter ordering imprisonment **28** letter under the sovereign's seal

lettuce 7 Lactuca
 varieties: **3** cos **5** chalk, frog's, lamb's, water **6** Boston, garden, miner's **7** iceberg, prickly, romaine **8** escarole **9** asparagus **11** common lamb's

letup 4 lull **5** pause **6** relief **7** respite **8** decrease, interval, slowdown, stopping, surcease, vacation **9** abatement, cessation, interlude, lessening, remission **10** slackening **11** retardation

Let Us Now Praise Famous Men
 author: **9** James Agee

Let us therefore be joyful
 Latin: **15** Gaudeamus igitur

Le Vau, Louis
 architect of: **6** Louvre **10** Versailles **12** Hotel Lambert **22** Chateau de Vaux-le-Vicomte **24** College des Quatres Nations

levee 3 dam **4** bank, dike, pier, quay, wall **5** ditch, jetty, ridge, wharf **6** durbar **9** reception **10** embankment

level 3 aim, bed **4** even, flat, rank, raze, tied, vein, zone **5** align, floor, flush, grade, layer, plane, point, stage, story, wreck **6** direct, height, lay low, reduce, smooth, topple **7** aligned, even out, flatten, landing, on a line, station, stratum, uniform **8** equalize, make even, position, tear down, together **9** devastate, elevation, knock down **10** consistent, horizontal, on a par with, unwrinkled **11** achievement, neck and neck **12** on an even keel

level-headed 4 sage **5** sound **6** poised, stable, steady **7** prudent **8** balanced, cautious, composed, sensible **9** collected, judicious, practical, unruffled **10** cool-headed, dependable, thoughtful **11** circumspect **12** eventempered **13** dispassionate **14** self-controlled

levelheadedness 6 aplomb **9** good sense, soundness, stability **10** equanimity **11** common sense **13** judiciousness

Levene, Sam
 real name: **12** Samuel Levine
 born: **6** Russia
 roles: **12** Guys and Dolls **13** Nathan Detroit **15** The Sunshine Boys

lever 3 bar, pry **5** jimmy, raise **7** crowbar

Lever, Charles
 author of: **14** Charles O'Malley

Leverrier, Urbain Jean Joseph
 field: **9** astronomy
 nationality: **6** French
 co-discovered: **7** Neptune
 worked with: **14** John Couch Adams

Levi
 father: **5** Jacob **6** Melchi, Symeon
 mother: **4** Leah
 son: **6** Kohath, Merari **7** Gershom
 brother: **3** Dan, Gad **5** Asher, Judah **6** Joseph, Reuben, Simeon **7** Zebulun **8** Benjamin, Issachar, Naphtali
 sister: **5** Dinah
 violated: **5** Dinah
 also called: **7** Matthew
 descendant of: **6** Levite

Leviathan 6 dragon **10** sea monster
 means: **13** spirally bound
 represents: **14** terrible powers

Leviathan
 author: **12** Thomas Hobbes

Levin, Ira
 author of: **6** Sliver **13** Rosemary's Baby **16** The Stepford Wives

Levin, Konstantin
 character in: **12** Anna Karenina
 author: **7** Tolstoy

Levi-Strauss, Claude
 method: **13** structuralism
 author of: **13** Mythologiques, The Savage Mind **16** Tristes Tropiques **22** Structural Anthropology **29** Elementary Structures of Kinship

Levitch, Joseph
 real name of: **10** Jerry Lewis

levity 3 fun **5** mirth **6** joking, whimsy **8** hilarity, trifling **9** flippancy, frivolity, lightness, silliness **10** jocularity, pleasantry, triviality **11** flightiness, foolishness **16** lightheartedness

levy 3 fee, tax **4** duty, make, toll, wage **5** draft, exact, start **6** assess, call up, charge, demand, enlist, excise, impose, muster, pursue, tariff **7** carry on, collect **9** calling up, conscript, prosecute **10** assess ment, imposition **12** conscription

Levy, Marion
 real name of: **15** Paulette Goddard

Lew Archer, Private Detective
 author: **13** Ross MacDonald

lewd 5 bawdy **6** ribald, risque, vulgar, wanton **7** goatish, immoral, lustful, obscene **8** indecent, prurient **9** lecherous, libertine, salacious **10** lascivious, libidinous, licentious, lubricious **11** Rabelaisian **12** pornographic

Lewis, C S
 author of: **10** Perelandra **13** Prince Caspian, The Last Battle **14** Surprised by Joy, The Silver Chair, Til We Have Faces **17** The Horse and His Boy **18** The Magician's Nephew **19** The Screwtape Letters **20** Out of the Silent Planet **21** The Chronicles of Narnia **25** The Voyage of the Dawn Treader **29** The Lion the Witch and the Wardrobe

Lewis, Jerry
 real name: **13** Joseph Levitch
 partner: **10** Dean Martin
 born: **8** Newark NJ

 roles: **8** The Caddy **10** The Bellboy, The Sad Sack **11** Cinderfella **12** The Geisha Boy **16** Artists and Models **17** The Nutty Professor **20** The Disorderly Orderly

Lewis, Sinclair
 author of: **7** Babbitt **9** Dodsworth **10** Arrowsmith, Main Street **11** Elmer Gantry **14** Cass Timberlane

lexicon 5 gloss, index **8** code book, glossary, synonymy, wordbook, wordlist **9** thesaurus, wordstock **10** dictionary, vocabulary **11** concordance, onomasticon

lex loci 11 law of a place

lex non scripta 9 common law **12** unwritten law

lex scripta 10 statute law, written law

Leyden, Lucas (Lukas) van
 born: **6** Leiden, Leyden **14** The Netherlands
 artwork: **12** Last Judgment **14** The Card Players, The Game of Chess **26** Mohammed and the Murdered Monk

Lhasa
 capital of: **5** Tibet

liability 4 debt, drag, duty, onus **5** debit, minus **6** arrear, burden **8** drawback, handicap, obstacle **9** hindrance **10** impediment, obligation **11** encumbrance, shortcoming **12** disadvantage, indebtedness **13** inconvenience **14** responsibility, stumbling block

liable 3 apt **4** open **5** prone **6** likely **7** exposed, ripe for, subject **8** disposed, inclined **9** obligated, sensitive **10** answerable, chargeable, vulnerable **11** accountable, responsible, susceptible

liaison 4 bond, link **5** amour, union **7** contact **8** alliance, intrigue, mediator **9** ad- venture, dalliance, go-between **10** connection, flirtation, love affair **11** association, cooperation, interchange **12** coordination, entanglement **13** communication

liar 6 fibber **8** perjurer **9** falsifier **10** fabricator **11** story teller **12** prevaricator

libation 4 wine **5** drink, water **6** liquid **8** ambrosia, beverage, offering, potation **9** sacrifice

libel 4 slur **5** smear **6** defame, malign, revile, vilify **7** asperse, blacken, calumny, obloquy, slander **8** derogate **9** aspersion, discredit, disparage **10** calumniate, defamation **12** vilification

Libeled Lady
 director: **10** Jack Conway
 cast: **8** Myrna Loy **10** Jean Harlow **12** Spencer Tracy **13** William Powell **14** Walter Connolly
 remade as: **9** Easy to Wed

Libera
 origin: **7** Italian
 goddess of: **4** wine **9** fertility, vineyards

husband: 5 Liber
corresponds to: 10 Persephone
liberal 5 ample, broad **6** casual, lavish **7** leftist, lenient **8** abundant, advanced, flexible, generous, handsome, left-wing, prodigal, reformer, tolerant, unbiased **9** bounteous, bountiful, impartial, not strict, plenteous, reformist, unbigoted, unspar- ing **10** fair-minded, forbearing, left-winger, munificent, not literal, openhanded, open-minded, unrigorous, unstinting **11** broad-minded, enlightened, extravagant, libertarian, magnanimous, progressive **12** freethinking, humanitarian, open to reason, unprejudiced **14** latitudinarian

liberal arts
7 trivium: 5 logic **7** grammar **8** rhetoric
10 quadrivium: 5 music **8** geometry **9** astronomy **10** arithmetic

liberality 10 generosity **11** benevolence, munificence **12** philanthropy **13** bountifulness **14** openhandedness

liberate 5 let go **6** let out, redeem, rescue, spring **7** absolve, deliver, manumit, release, set free **8** let loose **9** discharge, disengage, extricate, unshackle **10** emancipate **11** disencumber

liberated 5 freed, let go **7** rescued, set free **8** let loose, released **10** discharged, extricated **11** emancipated

liberation 6 escape, rescue **7** freedom, freeing, release **8** delivery **9** letting go, releasing **11** manumission **12** emancipation

Liberia
capital/largest city: 8 Monrovia
others: 4 Sino **5** Gribo, Rebbo **6** Bopora, Gbanga, Harper, Kakata **7** Bgarnga, Kolahun, Nanakru, Tappita, Vonjama **8** Buchanan, Garraway, Marshall, Nanakaru, Sass Town **9** Grand Cess, River Cess, Roysville **10** Careysburg, Green ville, Sanoquelli **11** Robertsport **12** Sanniquellie
school: 7 Liberia **10** Cuttington **15** Our Lady of Fatima **16** Booker Washington
religious school/secret society: 4 poro **5** sande
measure: 4 kuba
monetary unit: 4 cent **6** dollar
mountain: 3 Uni **4** Bong, Putu **5** Niete, Nimba **9** Bomi Hills
highest point: 6 Wutivi
river: 4 Cess, Lofa, Mano **5** Duobe, Lotta, Manna, Morro, Sinoe **6** Cestos, Douobe **7** Cavalla, Cavally **8** San Pedro **9** Saint John, Saint Paul, Sehnk-wehn
sea: 8 Atlantic
physical feature:
wind: 9 harmattan
people: 2 Gi **3** Gio, Kra, Kru, Kwa, Vai, Vei **4** Gola, Kroo, Krou, Loma,

Mano, Toma **5** Bassa, Gibbi, Gissi, Grebo **6** Gbande, Kpelle, Kpuesi, Krooby, Kruman **7** Krooboy, Krooman **8** Mandingo **15** Americo-Liberian
leader: 3 Doe **6** Tubman **7** Roberts, Tolbert
language: 3 Kru, Kwa **5** Mande **7** English
religion: 5 Islam **7** animism **10** Protestant **12** Christianity
feature:
clothing: 5 lappa
rubber plantation: 9 Firestone

Libertas
origin: 5 Roman
personifies: 7 liberty

liberte egalite fraternite 25 liberty equality fraternity
motto of: 16 French Revolution

liberties 6 misuse **7** license **9** violation **10** distortion **11** familiarity, impropriety **13** falsification

libertine 4 goat, lewd, rake, roue **5** loose, satyr **6** lecher, wanton **7** immoral, lustful, seducer **8** unchaste **9** debauchee, dissolute, lecherous, reprobate, womanizer **10** immoralist, lascivious, libidinous, licentious, profligate, sensualist, voluptuary

liberty 5 leave, right **7** freedom, license **8** autonomy, delivery, free time, furlough, sanction, vacation **9** privilege **10** liberation, permission, shore leave **11** citizenship, manumission **12** carte blanche, dispensation, emancipation, independence **15** enfranchisement **17** self- determination

liberty equality fraternity
French: 24 liberte egalite fraternite
motto of: 16 French Revolution

Libra
symbol: 6 scales **7** balance
planet: 5 Venus
rules: 8 marriage
born: 7 October **9** September

Libreville
capital of: 13 Gabon Republic

Libya
capital/largest city: 7 Tripoli
summer capital: 8 Benghazi
others: 4 Homs, Marj, Surt **5** Beida, Darna, Derna, Khums, Kufra, Sebha, Sidri, Zawia **6** Garian, Murzuq, Tobruk **7** Es Sidar, Gharyan, Misrata **8** Ajdabiya, Misurata, Rashanuf **12** Marsa el Brega
school: 7 Alfateh **9** Garyounis
division: 6 Fezzan **9** Cyrenaica **12** Tripolitania
measure: 3 dra, pik, saa **4** kele **5** bozze, donum, jabia, teman, uckia **6** barile, gorraf, misura **7** mattaro, termino **8** kharouba
weight: 4 kele **6** gorraf **8** kharouba
monetary unit: 5 dinar
mountain: 5 Green **13** Jabal al Akh-

dar, Tibesti Massif
highest point: 9 Bette Peak
sea: 13 Mediterranean
physical feature:
desert: 6 Libyan, Sahara **9** Calanscio
gulf: 5 Bomba, Sidra, Sirte
oasis: 4 Ghat **5** Kufra, Sebha **7** Tazerbo **8** Al-Kufrah, Ghudamis
plain: 6 al Marj, Gefara **7** Jaffara
plateau: 12 Gebel Nefuisa, Jabal Nafusah
wind: 6 ghibli
people: 4 Arab, Tebu **6** Berber, Tuareg **7** Gaetuli **8** Getu lans, Harratin
leader: 6 Battus **7** Jalloud, Qadhafi **8** Aegyptus **9** al- Qaddafi, Karamanli **13** Idris al-Senusi
religious leader: 8 al-Senusi
ruler: 4 Rome **5** Italy **6** Greece **9** Phoenicia **12** Ottoman Turks
language: 6 Arabic, Berber **7** English, Italian
alphabet: 8 tifinagh
religion: 5 Islam
feature: 14 Tropic of Cancer
clothing: 5 lanaf **9** barracano
festival: 3 Mez **7** Fantasi
Islamic law: 6 sharia
leader: 6 sheikh
ruins: 11 Leptis Magna
food:
dish: 5 bazin **8** couscous
red pepper: 6 filfil

license 3 let **4** pass, visa **5** allow, grant, leave, right **6** enable, laxity, permit **7** anarchy, approve, certify, charter, empower, endorse, freedom, liberty, warrant **8** accredit, audacity, disorder, latitude, passport, sanction, temerity **9** admission, allowance, authorize, franchise, looseness, privilege, slackness **10** brazenness, commission, debauchery, unruliness **11** certificate, free passage, lawlessness, libertinism, presumption, safe- conduct **12** carte blanche, dispensation, recklessness

licentious 4 lewd **5** dirty, loose **6** amoral, sleazy, wanton **7** brutish, goatish, immoral, lawless, lustful, raunchy, ruttish **8** depraved, prodigal **9** abandoned, debauched, dissolute, excessive, lecherous, libertine, salacious **10** dissipated, lascivious, libidinous, lubricious, profligate, ungoverned **11** promiscuous **12** unprincipled, unrestrained, unscrupulous **13** irresponsible, unconstrained

licentiousness 7 abandon **8** lewdness **10** immorality, wantonness

licit 5 legal, legit, valid **6** kosher, lawful **9** allowable, statutory **10** acceptable, admissible, authorized, legitimate, sanctioned **11** permissible **12** authorizable, sanctionable **14** constitutional

lick 3 bit, dab, hit, jot, lap **4** beat, blow, drub, fire, hint, iota, rout, slap, snip, sock, suck, whip **5** crack, punch, sally, shred, spank, speck, taste, touch, trace **6** defeat, ignite, kindle, master, sample, stroke, subdue, thrash, tongue, wallop **7** clobber, conquer, modicum, smidgen, trounce **8** outmatch, overcome, particle, vanquish **9** overpower, overthrow, scintilla, subjugate **10** smattering **12** denunciation

lid 3 cap, top **4** cork, curb, plug **5** cover, limit **7** ceiling, maximum, stopper, stopple **9** operculum, restraint

lie 3 fib **4** loll, rest, stay **5** abide, exist, range, story **6** belong, deceit, extend, inhere, lounge, obtain, remain, repose, sprawl **7** falsify, fiction, perjury, recline, romance, untruth **8** misstate, tall tale **9** deception, embellish, embroider, fabricate, falsehood, invention **10** equivocate **11** fabrication, prevaricate **12** equivocation **13** falsification, prevarication **17** misrepresentation

Liechtenstein
capital/largest city: 5 Vaduz
others: 4 Haag **6** Balzer, Eschen, Iradug, Schaan **7** Balzers, Bendern, Nendeln, Planken, Triesen **12** Schellenberg
division:
  ancient province: 6 Rhaeti **7** Rhaetia
government:
  legislature: 7 Landtag
monetary unit: 6 rappen **7** franken
mountain: 4 Alps **8** Naafkopf, Rhatikon **12** Three Sisters
highest point: 15 Vorder-Grauspitz
river: 5 Rhine
physical feature:
  valley: 6 Lavena, Samina
people: 8 Alemanni
  leader: 7 Florian **15** Francis Joseph II **16** von Liechtenstein
language: 6 German **10** Alemannish
religion: 13 Roman Catholic
place:
  castle: 9 Gutemburg, Gutenberg
feature:
  legendary dwarf: 10 wildmannli
  wine: 7 Vaduzer

lie down 6 retire **7** go to bed, recline **8** take a nap **11** take a snooze **15** catch forty winks

life 4 path, soul, zest **5** being, human, plant, story, verve, vigor **6** animal, career, course, energy, memoir, person, spirit **8** creature, duration, life span, lifetime, lifework, organism, survival, vitality, vivacity **9** animation, biography, existence, life story, longevity **11** subsistence **13** autobiography
French: 3 vie

Life Before Man
author: 14 Margaret Atwood

Lifeboat
director: 15 Alfred Hitchcock
cast: 10 John Hodiak **12** Mary Anderson **13** William Bendix **16** Tallulah Bankhead

life-giving 5 vital **9** vivifying **12** invigorating

life jacket 7 Mae West

lifeless 4 dead, dull, flat, late **5** inert, stiff, vapid **6** boring, hollow, static, torpid, wooden **7** defunct **8** deceased, departed, inactive, lifeless, sluggish **9** colorless, inanimate **10** lackluster, spiritless

lifelessness 5 death **7** inertia **8** dullness, limpness, vapidity **9** blandness **10** flaccidity, inactivity **13** colorlessness

Life Magazine
founder: 9 Henry Luce

Life of Dante
author: 17 Giovanni Boccaccio

Life of Emile Zola
director: 15 William Dieterle
cast: 8 Paul Muni **11** Donald Crisp **12** Gloria Holden **15** Gale Sondergaard **17** Joseph Schildkraut (Dreyfus)
Oscar for: 7 picture

Life of Man, The
author: 14 Leonid Andreyev

Life of Riley, The
character: 4 Babs **6** Dangle, Junior **8** Peg Riley **9** Jim Gillis **10** Cunningham, Digby (Digger) O'Dell **11** Waldo Binney **13** Chester A Riley **14** Honeybee Gillis
cast: 9 John Brown, Lanny Rees, Sid Tomack **10** Tom D'Andrea **12** Emory Parnell, Wesley Morgan **13** Gloria Winters, Jackie Gleason, Lugene Sanders, Robert Sweeney, William Bendix **14** Gloria Blondell, Rosemary DeCamp **16** Douglas Dumbrille, Marjorie Reynolds, Sterling Holloway

Life of Samuel Johnson, The
author: 12 James Boswell

life of the party 7 show-off **9** extrovert **13** exhibitionist **17** hail-fellow-well-met

Life on the Mississippi
author: 9 Mark Twain

life span 4 life **8** lifetime **14** life expectancy

Life Studies
author: 12 Robert Lowell

Life With Father
author: 13 Clarence Day Jr
director: 13 Michael Curtiz
cast: 9 ZaSu Pitts **10** Irene Dunne **11** Edmund Gwenn **13** William Powell **15** Elizabeth Taylor
setting: 11 New York City

lifework 6 career **7** calling **8** vocation **10** livelihood, occupation, profession

lift 4 high, palm, pick, rear, rise, soar, take **5** boost, climb, exalt, filch, heave, hoist, pinch, raise, steal, swipe **6** ascend, ascent, banish, cancel, pilfer, pirate, pock- et, remove, revoke, snatch, thieve, uplift, vanish **7** elation, elevate, purloin, raise up, raising, rescind, scatter, upraise **8** disperse **9** disappear, dissipate, float away **10** ascendance, move upward, plagiarize, put an end to **11** appropriate, countermand, inspiration, make off with, reassurance **12** give a boost to, shot in the arm **13** encouragement, enheartenment

ligament
holds: 5 bones

Ligeia
author: 13 Edgar Allan Poe
character: 19 Lady Rowena Trevanion

light 3 gay **4** airy, beam, easy, fair, fall, find, fire, glow, lamp, land, pale, puny, side, soft, stop **5** aglow, angle, blaze, blond, faint, flame, funny, glare, guide, happy, jolly, match, model, perch, petty, put on, roost, shine, slant, small, spare, spark, sunny, torch **6** alight, aspect, beacon, blithe, bright, candle, chance, frugal, gentle, get off, ignite, jaunty, kindle, luster, meager, paltry, scanty, settle, simple, slight, turn on **7** amusing, buoyant, chipper, clarify, come off, descend, get down, gleeful, insight, lantern, lighten, lighter, lucifer, not dark, not rich, paragon, radiant, radiate, sparkle, sunbeam, trivial **8** approach, attitude, bleached, blondish, brighten, carefree, cheerful, come upon, discover, dismount, ethereal, exemplar, gossamer, graceful, illumine, jubilant, luminous, meet with, moderate, moonbeam, not heavy, paradigm, radiance, sportive, step down, switch on, trifling, untaxing **9** brilliant, catch fire, direction, encounter, frivolous, irradiate, light-hued, set fire to, sprightly, stumble on, sylphlike, viewpoint **10** abstemious, brightness, brilliance, burdenless, come across, come to rest, effortless, effulgence, floodlight, happen upon, illuminate, light-toned, luminosity, manageable, restricted, set burning, weightless **11** conflagrate, elucidation, illuminated, information, make radiant, superficial, undemanding, underweight **15** inconsequential
god of: 6 Apollo **7** Mithras, Phoebus, Pythius **8** Heimdall **9** Musagetes
Latin: 3 lux
measurement: 7 candela **11** candlepower

light-colored 4 pale **5** beige, blond **6** blonde, flaxen, pastel **7** neutral, whitish **9** yellowish

light-complexioned 4 fair, pale **12** white-skinned

lighten 4 buoy, ease, lift **5** abate, allay, blaze, elate, flare, flash, gleam, shine **6** buoy up, lessen, reduce, revive, temper, unload, uplift **7** assuage, enliven, gladden, inspire, light up, relieve **8** brighten, mitigate, moderate, unburden **9** alleviate, coruscate, disburden, irradiate **10** illuminate, make bright **11** become light, disencumber, make lighter, scintillate

light-filled 5 sunny **6** bright **7** well-lit **11** illuminated

lighthearted 3 gay **4** airy, glad **5** jolly, merry, sunny **6** blithe, cheery, joyful, joyous, lively **7** buoyant, cheered, chipper **8** carefree, cheerful, sanguine **9** sprightly **10** insouciant, untroubled **11** free and easy **12** effervescent

lightheartedness 3 joy **4** glee **5** mirth **8** gladness **9** happiness, merriment **10** blitheness, exuberance, joyfulness, joyous ness **11** high spirits

Light in August
  author: **15** William Faulkner
  character: **8** Doc Hines, Joe Brown **9** Lena Grove, McEachern **10** Byron Bunch **12** Joanna Burden, Joe Christmas

lightless 4 dark **5** black, murky **7** stygian **9** unlighted **13** unilluminated

lightly 6 airily, easily, gently, nimbly, softly, thinly, weakly **7** blandly, faintly, quickly, readily, swiftly, timidly **8** blithely, fac- ilely, gingerly, meagerly, slightly, sparsely **9** buoyantly, sparingly **10** carelessly, flippantly, hesitantly, moderately **11** frivolously, slightingly **13** indifferently, thoughtlessly, unconcernedly, without effort **14** without concern

lightness 8 airiness, radiance **10** brightness, fluffiness, luminosity **12** illumination, luminousness

lightning rod
  invented by: **8** Franklin

light of day 8 daylight, sunlight, sunshine

light sleep 3 nap **4** doze **6** catnap, snooze **10** forty winks

light wind 4 waft **6** breeze, zephyr **10** gentle wind **11** breath of air

Lightwood, Mortimer
  character in: **15** Our Mutual Friend
  author: **7** Dickens

lignum vitae 10 wood of life
  tree species: **8** Guaiacum

likable, likeable 4 nice **6** genial **7** amiable, lovable, winsome **8** charming, engaging, loveable, pleasant, pleasing **9** agreeable, appealing, simpatico **10** attractive **11** complaisant, sympathetic

like 4 akin, care, dote, same, wish **5** enjoy, equal, fancy, favor, savor **6** admire, allied, choose, esteem, relish **7** approve, cognate, endorse, matched, related, similar, support, uniform **8** be fond of, parallel, selfsame, think fit **9** analogous, congru- ent, have a mind, identical **10** comparable, equivalent,

homologous, resembling **11** be partial to, much the same **12** feel in clined, have a crush on, take a shine to **13** cor- responding, find agreeable **14** take plea- sure in

Like a Bulwark
  author: **13** Marianne Moore

likelihood 8 prospect **10** good chance **11** possibility, probability **12** potentiality

likely 3 apt, fit **4** able **6** liable, proper **8** credible, destined, inclined, probable, probably, rational, reliable, suitable **9** befitting, plausible, promising, qualified **10** believable, presumably, reasonable **11** appropriate, verisimilar **16** in all probability

like-mindedness 6 accord **7** concord, harmony, rapport **8** affinity **9** agreement **12** congeniality **13** compatibility

likeness 5 image, model, study **6** effigy **7** analogy, picture, replica **8** affinity, portrait **9** agreement, depiction, facsimile, portrayal, rendition, semblance **10** similarity, similitude **11** delineation, resemblance **14** correspondence, representation

likes 9 favorites **10** prejudices **11** preferences **12** inclinations, partialities

likewise 3 and, eke, too **4** also **5** ditto **6** as well **7** be sides, equally, the same **8** moreover **9** similarity **10** in addition

liking 4 bent **5** fancy, taste **7** leaning **8** affinity, appetite, fondness, penchant, soft spot, weakness **9** affection **10** partiality, preference, proclivity, propensity **11** inclination **12** predilection

Li'l Abner
  creator: **6** Al Capp
  character: **5** Pappy **7** Salomey (pig), Wolf Gal **10** Joe Btfsplk, Mammy Yokum, Marryin' Sam **11** Adam Lazonga, Hairless Joe **12** Lena the Hyena, Tobacco Rhoda **13** Joanie Phoanie **14** Daisy Mae Scragg, Evil-Eye Flee gle, Stupefyin' Jones **15** Fearless Fosdick, Henry Cabbage Cod, Lonesome Polecat, Moonbeam McSwine **16** General Bullmoose, Sir Cecil Cesspool **17** Sen Jack S Phogbound **18** J Roaringham Fatback **21** Appassionata von Climax
  brewery: **23** Big Barnsmell's Skonk Works
  event: **15** Sadie Hawkins Day
  juice: **16** Kickapoo Joy Juice
  kingdom: **14** Lower Slobbovia
  mountain: **11** Onnecessary
  animal: **6** Schmoo
  people: **7** kygmies
  place: **8** Dogpatch
  railroad: **11** West Po'k Chop
  ruler: **14** King Nogoodnick

lilac 7 Syringa
  varieties: **4** late, vine, wild **6** common, Indian, summer **7** Chinese, cut-

leaf, Persian **9** Himalayan, Hungarian **12** Japanese tree **16** Catalina mountain

Lili
  director: **14** Charles Walters
  cast: **9** Mel Ferrer **11** Leslie Caron, Zsa Zsa Gabor **16** Jean-Pierre Aumont

Lilies of the Field
  director: **11** Ralph Nelson
  cast: **8** Lisa Mann **10** Lilia Skala **13** Sidney Poitier
  Oscar for: **5** actor (Poitier)

Liliom
  author: **12** Ferenc Molnar
  source for: **8** Carousel

lillet
  type: **8** aperitif
  origin: **6** France
  flavor: **6** orange
  color: **3** red **5** white

Lilliput
  fictional land in: **16** Gulliver's Travels
  inhabitants: **10** tiny people
  author: **5** Swift

lilliputian 3 wee **4** tiny **5** dwarf, short, small, teeny, weeny **6** little, midget, minute, petite **9** miniature **10** diminutive, teeny-weeny **11** pocket-sized

Lilongwe
  capital of: **6** Malawi

lily 6 Lilium
  varieties: **3** Alp, cow, day, pig **4** Arum, bell, boat, corn, fawn, fire, flax, herb, palm, pine, pond, rain, roan, rock, sand, Sego, star, toad, wood **5** adobe, Aztec, blood, bugle, calla, coast, cobra, crane, Cuban, fairy, globe, glory, Gray's, Ifafa, lemon, magic, natal, queen, regal, royal, showy, snake, spear, swamp, sword, tiger, torch, trout, water, wheel **6** Alpine, Amazon, Canada, Crinum, desert, Easter, eureka, ginger, hidden, Kaffir, Marhan, meadow, one-day, orange, Oregon, shasta, Sierra, spider, sunset, tartar, turban, voodoo, yellow, Zephyr **7** African, Bermuda, chamise, checker, garland, leopard, madonna, Nankeen, panther, redwood, thimble, toad-cup, triplet, trumpet, western **8** Atamasco, Barbados, bluebead, Carolina, climbing, Columbia, flamingo, gloriosa, Guernsey, Humboldt, Jacobean, Japanese, long's red, Mariposa, Martagon, Michigan, mountain, paradise, Peruvian, plan tain, Siberian, Solomon's, St Bruno's, St James's, turk's cap **9** alligator, avalanche, butterfly, caucasian, celestial, chaparral, checkered, Eucharist, Kamchatka, naked-lady, orange-cup, pineapple, pinewoods, pot-of-gold, red ginger, red spider, St Joseph's **10** belladonna, blackberry, blue funnel,

fairy water, giant water, globe spear, gold-banded, Josephine's, orange-bell, pink Easter, pygmy water, royal water, small tiger, St Bernard's, Washington, white water, wild yellow, yellow-bell, yellow pond **11** African corn, Amazon water, blue African, candlestick, dwarf ginger, golden-rayed, milk-and-wine, Palmer spear, Scarborough, southern red, yellow water **12** African blood, Chinese white, golden spider, prickly water, resurrection, speckled wood, white trumpet **13** Bermuda Easter, cape blue water, Chinese sacred, Egyptian water, fragrant water, India red water, lavender globe, magnolia water, minor Turk's-cap, per fumed fairy, pink porcelain, scarlet ginger, showy Japanese, tuberous water, wild orange-red **14** Chinese-lantern, lesser Turk's cap, little Turk's-cap, Santa Cruz water, yellow Turk's-cap **15** Australian water, backhouse hybrid, golden hurricane, scarlet Turk's-cap **16** American Turk's cap, Bellingham hybrid, Cape Cod pink water, fragrant plantain, Japanese Turk's-cap, western orange-cup **17** midsummer plantain **18** European white water, seer sucker plantain **20** narrow-leaved plantain

lily-livered 6 afraid, craven, scared, yellow **7** chicken, fearful, gutless **8** cowardly **9** dastardly **12** fainthearted **13** pusillanimous, yellow-bellied **14** chicken-hearted, chicken-livered **22** showing the white feather

lily-white 4 good, pure **6** biased, decent, proper, racist **7** bigoted, upright **8** all-white, innocent, virtuous **9** blameless, exclusive, exemplary, faultless, guiltless, honorable, righteous **10** impeccable, inculpable, prejudiced, segregated, upstanding **11** uncorrupted **12** unintegrated **13** unimpeachable **14** discriminatory, irreproachable

Lima
capital of: 4 Peru
foothills of: 5 Andes
founder: 7 Pizarro
nickname: 11 city of kings
ocean: 7 Pacific
port: 6 Callao
river: 5 Rimac
square: 12 Plaza de Armas

limb 3 arm, gam, leg, pin **4** part, spur, twig, wing **5** bough, shoot, sprig **6** branch, member **9** appendage, extension, outgrowth **10** projection, prosthesis

limber 5 agile, lithe, relax **6** loosen, pliant, supple **7** bending, elastic, lissome, pliable **8** flexible **9** lithesome, malleable

lime 18 Citrus aurantifolia
varieties: 3 key **4** wild **7** Mexican,

Persian, Rangpur, Spanish **8** Mandarin **10** West Indian **14** Australian wild **15** Australian round **16** Australian desert, Australian finger

Limenia
epithet of: 9 Aphrodite
means: 11 of the harbor

Limerick
county in: 7 Ireland
gave name to: 12 nonsense poem
rhyme scheme: 5 aabba
popularized by: 10 Edward Lear

limit 3 end **4** curb **8** boundary, end point, restrain, ultimate **13** breaking point

limitation 4 curb **5** quota **8** boundary, decrease **9** lessening, reduction, restraint **10** shortening **11** abridgement, restriction, shortcoming **13** qualification, specification

limited 5 fixed **6** finite, narrow **7** bounded, cramped, defined, minimal, special **8** confined **9** delimited, specified **10** controlled, restrained, restricted **13** circumscribed

limitless 7 endless, eternal, unbound **8** infinite, unending **9** boundless, unlimited **11** measureless **12** immeasurable

limits 3 rim, top **4** curb, edge **5** bound, check, quota **6** border, define, fringe, margin, narrow **7** ceiling, confine, delimit, inhibit, maximum, qualify **8** confines, frontier, restrain, restrict **9** perimeter, periphery, prescribe, restraint **10** boundaries **11** limitations **12** restrictions

limn 4 draw **6** sketch **7** picture **9** delineate

Limnaea
epithet of: 7 Artemis
means: 9 of the lake

limp 3 lax **4** gimp, halt, soft, weak **5** crawl, loose, skulk, slack **6** droopy, falter, flabby, floppy, hobble **7** flaccid **8** drooping, lameness, yielding **9** dead tired, enervated, exhausted

limpid 4 pure **5** clear, lucid **8** clear-cut, pellucid, vitreous **11** crystalline, perspicuous, translucent, transparent, unambiguous **15** straightforward

Lincoln, Abraham
nickname: 9 Honest Abe **20** Illinois Rail Splitter
presidential rank: 9 sixteenth
party: 4 Whig **10** Republican
state represented: 2 IL
defeated: 4 (John) Bell **7** (John Charles) Fremont, (Stephen Arnold) Douglas **9** (George Brinton) McClellan **12** (John Cabell) Breckinridge
vice president: 6 (Hannibal) Hamlin **7** (Andrew) Johnson
cabinet:
  state: 6 (William Henry) Seward
  treasury: 5 (Salmon Portland) Chase **9** (Hugh) McCulloch, (William Pitt) Fessenden

  war: 7 (Edwin McMasters) Stanton, (Simon) Cameron
  attorney general: 5 (Edward) Bates, (James) Speed
  navy: 6 (Gideon) Welles
  postmaster general: 5 (Montgomery) Blair **8** (William) Dennison
  interior: 5 (Caleb Blood) Smith, (John Palmer) Usher
born: 2 KY **8** log cabin **11** Larue County **17** Sinking Spring farm
died: 12 Washington DC, Fords Theater
  died by: 13 assassination
  assassinated by: 15 John Wilkes Booth
buried: 13 Springfield IL
education:
  educated by: 4 self
  studied: 3 law
interests: 7 theater
  received patent for: 25 adjustable buoyant chambers (for lifting boats)
political career: 16 state legislature **24** US House of Representatives
civilian career: 6 lawyer **8** surveyor **10** postmaster
military service:
  War: 9 Black Hawk
  US Army: 7 private
  captain of company of: 10 volunteers
notable events of lifetime/term: 8 Civil War **24** Emanci pation Proclamation
  Act: 9 Homestead, Income Tax, Judiciary **12** Conscription
  debates: 14 Lincoln-Douglas
  speech: 17 Gettysburg Address
father: 6 Thomas
mother: 5 Nancy (Hanks)
  stepmother: 5 Sarah (Bush Johnston)
siblings: 5 Sarah **6** Thomas
  stepbrother: 4 John
  stepsister: 7 Matilda **9** Elizabeth
wife: 4 Mary (Ann Todd)
children: 6 Thomas **10** Robert Todd **11** Edward Baker **14** William Wallace

Lind, James
field: 8 medicine
nationality: 8 Scottish
eliminated: 6 scurvy

Lindbergh, Anne Morrow
author of: 14 Gift from the Sea **15** Bring Me a Unicorn **16** North to the Orient **19** War Within and Without

linden 5 Tilia
varieties: 6 Indoor **7** Crimean **8** American, Japanese **9** Mongolian **10** Manchurian **11** Large-leaved **13** Pendent silver **19** Small-leaved European

lindy 5 dance **8** lindy hop **9** jitterbug
nickname for: 16 Charles Lindbergh

line, lines 4 card, cord, dash, draw,

file, idea, mark, note, part, race, rank, rope, rule, tier, word **5** align, array, breed, cable, craft, front, house, model, queue, range, score, slash, stock, trade **6** belief, border, column, crease, family, furrow, letter, method, metier, policy, report, scheme, series, stance, strain, strand, streak, stripe, system, thread **7** calling, circuit, conduit, contour, cordage, example, lineage, marshal, outline, pattern, purpose, pursuit, queue up, routine, towline, wrinkle **8** ancestry, business, dialogue, doctrine, fishline, ideology, inscribe, position, postcard, trenches, vanguard, vocation **9** conductor, crow's foot, direction, frontline, genealogy, intention, principle **10** barricades, convention, firing line, livelihood, long stroke, occupation, procession, profession, underscore **11** demarcation

lineage 4 line **5** blood, stock **7** descent **8** ancestry, heredity, pedigree **9** genealogy, parentage **10** derivation, extraction

linen
   fabric: 6 canvas, damask **7** butcher, cambric **8** birds-eye **9** huckaback
   plant: 4 flax
   finest from: 7 Belgium, Ireland
   processing term: 6 shives, sliver **7** carding, hackled, retting **8** beetling, breaking, rippling, spinning **9** scutching

line of march 4 path **5** route, track **11** parade route

line of reasoning 4 case **7** premise **8** argument **10** hypothesis

line up 4 book **5** align **6** engage, even up **7** arrange, procure, program, queue up **8** schedule **9** form a line, put in a row **10** arrange for

line-up 5 slate **6** roster **8** schedule

linger 3 lag **4** idle, last, stay, wait **5** dally, delay, tarry, trail **6** dawdle, hang on, loiter, remain **7** persist, survive **9** die slowly **10** dillydally, hang around

lingering 4 slow **7** abiding, chronic, delayed, lagging, lasting, staying, waiting **8** dawdling, delaying, dragging, drawn out, dwelling, enduring, hovering, tarrying **9** loitering, remaining **10** protracted, sauntering **15** procrastinating

lingo 4 cant, talk **5** argot, idiom, slang **6** jargon, patois, tongue **7** dialect **8** language, parlance **10** vernacular

linguist 8 polyglot **10** grammarian, translator **11** etymologist, interpreter, philologist, phonetician, phonologist, semanticist **12** morphologist **13** lexicographer

liniment 4 balm **5** salve **7** unguent **8** ointment **9** emollient

link 3 tie **4** bind, bond, fuse, loop, ring **5** group, joint, tie in, unite **6** couple, relate, splice **7** bracket, combine, conjoin, connect, involve, liaison **8** junction, relation **9** associate, implicate **10** connection, connective **11** association **12** interconnect, relationship

linkage 3 tie **4** bond **6** hookup **10** connection **11** affiliation, association, correlation

link up 4 dock, join **6** couple, hook up **7** connect **9** affiliate **14** fasten together

Linnaeus, Carolus
   field: 6 botany
   nationality: 7 Swedish
   developed: 8 taxonomy **18** nomenclature system

linotype
   invented by: 12 Mergenthaler

Linton, Edgar
   character in: 16 Wuthering Heights
   author: 6 Bronte

Linus
   vocation: 4 poet **8** musician
   father: 6 Apollo
   mother: 8 Psamathe
   inventor of: 6 melody, rhythm
   identified with: 5 crops **9** withering **10** harvesting
   student: 8 Hercules
   killed by: 8 Hercules

lion 3 cat **6** cougar **7** wildcat **9** celebrity **12** man of the hour **15** king of the jungle
   group of: 5 pride
   constellation of: 3 Leo

lionhearted 4 bold **5** brave **6** heroic **7** valiant **8** fearless, intrepid, stalwart, unafraid, valorous **9** audacious, dauntless **10** courageous **11** indomitable **12** stouthearted
   see **8** Richard I

Lion in Winter, The
   director: 13 Anthony Harvey
   cast: 10 Jane Merrow **11** Peter O'Toole (Henry II) **13** Timothy Dalton **14** Anthony Hopkins **16** Katharine Hepburn (Eleanor of Aquitaine)
   Oscar for: 7 actress (Hepburn)

lionize 5 exalt **6** admire, praise, revere **7** acclaim, adulate, ennoble, flatter, glorify **8** enshrine, eulogize **9** celebrate, glamorize **10** aggrandize **11** immortalize

lion's share 4 bulk, most **8** majority **9** major part **11** greater part **13** preponderance

lip 3 lap, rim **4** brim, edge, kiss, lick, wash **5** apron, mouth, spout, utter **6** labial, labium, margin **8** backtalk, labellum **9** insincere **10** embouchure, mouthpiece **11** superficial

Lipchitz, Jacques
   real name: 17 Chaim Yakob Lipchiz
   born: 9 Lithuania **11** Druskieniki **12** Druskininkai
   artwork: 4 Head **6** Bather, Figure **7** Harpist **9** Sacrifice **10** Prometheus **11** Benediction, Joie de Vivre **12** Peace on Earth **14** Man with a Guitar **15** Acrobats on a Ball, Man with Mandolin, Song of the Vowels **17** Notre Dame de Liesse, Sailor with a Guitar **19** Pierrot with Clarinet, Return of the Prodigal **24** Virgin of the Inverted Heart

Lipizzaner 11 stocky horse
   bred in: 7 Austria
   color: 5 white
   used in: 8 dressage **18** jumping exhibitions

Lipmann, Fritz Albert
   field: 12 biochemistry
   discovered: 9 Coenzyme A
   awarded: 10 Nobel Prize

Lippi, Filippino
   born: 5 Italy, Prato
   father: 15 Fra Filippo Lippi
   artwork: 20 The Vision of St Bernard **24** The Life of St Thomas Aquinas **26** The Lives of Sts Philip and John

Lippi, Fra Filippo
   born: 5 Italy **8** Florence
   son: 9 Filippino
   artwork: 15 Madonna and Child, The Feast of Herod **19** The Tarquinia Madonna **21** Coronation of the Virgin **25** The Madonna Adoring Her Child

liqueur 5 booze, drink, hooch **7** alcohol, potable, spirits **8** beverage, potation **9** aqua vitae, drinkable, inebriant, moonshine **10** intoxicant
   almond: 8 amaretto
   anise: 8 absinthe
   apple: 8 calvados
   apricot: 10 abricotine
   caraway: 6 kummel **7** aquavit
   chocolate: 12 creme de cacao
   citrus: 10 goldwasser, liquor d'or
   coffee: 6 Kahlua
   grape: 6 Metaxa
   herb: 6 pernod **7** raspail **10** vielle cure **11** fiori alpini
   honey: 8 Drambuie
   medicinal: 11 Benedictine
   mint: 13 creme de menthe
   orange: 6 strega **7** curacao **9** cointreau **12** Grand Marnier
   raspberry: 9 framboise

liquid 5 drink, fluid **6** melted, molten, thawed **7** potable **8** beverage, solution

liquidate 3 hit, pay **4** kill **5** clear, erase, waste **6** cancel, murder, pay off, rub out, settle, wind up **7** abolish, break up, destroy, wipe out **8** close out, conclude, demolish **9** discharge, dispose of, eradicate, put to rest, terminate **10** account for, do away with **11** assassinate

liquor 3 gin, rum, rye **5** booze, broth, hooch, juice, sauce, vodka **6** brandy, liquid, redeye, rotgut, Scotch **7** bourbon, extract, spirits, whiskey **9** drippings, moonshine **10** inebriants

11 intoxicants

measure: 4 pint, pony, shot **5** fifth, quart **6** jigger, magnum

symbol: 14 John Barleycorn

Lir *see* **3** Ler

Lisbon
capital of: 8 Portugal
landmark:
  castle: 11 Saint George
  monastery: 9 Jeronimos
  square: 10 Black Horse
  tower: 5 Belem
Moorish name: 7 Lixbuna
ocean: 8 Atlantic
Portuguese: 6 Lisboa
river: 5 Tagus
Roman name: 14 Felicitas Julia
rulers: 5 Moors **6** French, Romans **7** British, Germans, Spanish **11** Phoenicians

lissome 5 agile, lithe, quick **6** limber, lively, nimble, pliant, supple **7** slender **8** flexible, graceful **9** lithesome, sprightly **11** light-footed

list 3 tip **4** bend, heel, lean, roll, tilt **5** index, slant, slate, slope, table **6** careen, muster, record, roster **7** catalog, in cline, leaning **8** register, schedule, tabulate **9** catalogue, inventory

listen 4 hark, hear, heed, list **6** attend **7** give ear, hearken **8** give heed, listen in, overhear **9** be all ears, bend an ear, eavesdrop **10** take notice **12** pay attention

listener 3 ear **6** hearer **7** auditor **10** overhearer **12** eavesdropper

Lister, Joseph
field: 7 surgeon **8** medicine
nationality: 7 British
pioneer of: 17 antiseptic surgery

listless 4 down, dull, lazy **6** dreamy, drowsy, leaden, mopish, torpid **7** languid **8** in active, indolent, lifeless, sluggish **9** apathetic, enervated, lethargic, soporific **10** phlegmatic, spiritless **11** indifferent, unconcerned **12** uninterested **13** lackadaisical

Liston, Charles
nickname: 5 Sonny
sport: 6 boxing
class: 11 heavyweight

Liszt, Franz (Ferencz)
born: 7 Hungary, Raiding
teacher: 6 Czerny
daughter: 6 Cosima
son-in-law: 6 Wagner
composer of: 5 Dante (symphony), Faust (symphony) **8** Christus **9** Psalm XIII **10** Nuages gris **13** Psalm Thirteen **17** Years of Pilgrimage **18** Annees de Pelerinage **19** Hungarian Rhapsodies **22** The Legend of St Elizabeth

litany 4 list **7** account, catalog, recital **9** catalogue, narration, rendition **10** recitation, repetition **11** description, enumeration

literacy 7 culture **8** learning **9** erudition **11** edification, eruditeness, learnedness, scholarship **12** intelligence **13** enlightenment

literal 4 real, true **5** exact **6** actual, direct, honest, strict **7** correct, factual, precise, prosaic **8** accurate, faithful, reliable, truthful, verbatim **9** authentic **10** adlitteram, dependable, meticulous, scrupulous, un-disputed **11** trustworthy, undeviating, word-for-word **12** matter-of-fact **13** authoritative, conscientious, unimaginative, unimpeachable

literary 6 poetic **7** bookish, of books **8** artistic, lettered, literate **12** intellectual

literate 7 learned **8** cultured, educated, lettered, literary, schooled, well-read **12** well-informed **13** knowledgeable

literati 9 highbrows **12** connoisseurs **13** intellectuals **14** intelligentsia

literature 4 lore **5** books, works **6** papers, theses **7** letters **8** classics, writings **9** treatises **11** scholarship **12** publications **13** belles lettres, dissertations

lithe 5 agile **6** limber, nimble, pliant, supple **7** lissome, pliable **8** bendable, flexible, graceful

Lithgow, John
roles: 9 Footloose **17** Terms of Endearment **19** Third Rock From the Sun **21** Harry and the Hendersons **23** The World According to Garp **29** The Adventures of Buckaroo Banzai

lithium
chemical symbol: 2 Li

Lithuania
other/former name: 5 Litva **7** Lietuva **33** Lithuanian Soviet Socialist Republic
capital/largest city: 5 Vilna **6** Kaunas **7** Vilnius
others: 4 Balt, Lett **5** Aesti, Kouno, Memel **6** Kovnac **7** Jel gava, Palanga, Telsiai **8** Ignalina, Kapsukas, Klaipeda, Siauliai **9** Panevezys **10** Elektrenai
government: 8 republic
monetary: 3 lit **5** marka **6** centas **7** ostmark, skatiku **8** auksinas
lake: 5 Dysna
mountain: 15 Samogitian Hills
highest point: 9 Juozapine
river: 5 Neman, Neris, Rusne **6** Dubysa, Nieman, Viliya **7** Nemunas, Nevezis, Nevezys **8** Pregolya
sea: 6 Baltic
physical feature:
  lagoon: 8 Courland, Kuronian
people: 4 Balt, Lett **5** Zhmud **6** Jewish, Litvak, Polish **7** Aistian, Russian, Yatvyag **10** Lithuanian, Samogitian **11** Belorussian
language: 5 Zmudz **6** Baltic **10** Lithuanian

religion: 8 Lutheran **13** Roman Catholic

litigation 4 suit **7** contest, dispute, lawsuit **10** contention, day in court **11** controversy, disputation, legal action, prosecution

litter 3 bed **4** heap, junk, lair, mess, nest, pile **5** issue, strew, trash, young **6** de- bris, jumble, pallet, refuse **7** bedding, clutter, kittens, progeny, puppies, rubbish, scatter **8** leavings **9** offspring, stretcher

little 3 bit, dot, jot, wee **4** dash, drop, hint, iota, mean, mild, tiny, whit **5** brief, crumb, elfin, faint, fleet, hasty, never, petty, pinch, pygmy, quick, scant, short, small, speck, trace **6** bantam, hardly, meager, minute, narrow, paltry, petite, rarely, seldom, skimpy, slight, trifle **7** minimum, modicum, not much, passing, stunted, trivial **8** dwarfish, fragment, inferior, mediocre, not at all, not often, particle, piddling, pittance, scarcely, slightly, some what, trifling, unworthy **9** by no means, deficient, hardly any, itsy- bitsy, itty-bitty, miniature, momentary, pint-sized, third- rate, worthless **10** diminutive, inflexible, negligible, short-lived, suggestion, undersized **11** commonplace, Lilliputian, microscopic, of no account, opinionated, pocket-sized, scarcely any, small amount, unimportant **12** insufficient, run-of-the-mill, short-sighted **13** infinitesimal, insignificant, next to nothing

Little America
on: 10 Antarctica **12** Ross Ice Shelf
bases established by: 11 Admiral Byrd

Little Annie Rooney
creator: 14 Darrell McClure

Little Artha
nickname of: 11 Jack Johnson

Little Bighorn 5 river **7** Wyoming
battle site of: 5 Sioux **6** Custer, Dakota **8** Cheyenne
called: 16 Custer's last stand
see also **13** Custer, George A.

Little Big Man
author: 12 Thomas Berger
director: 10 Arthur Penn
cast: 11 Faye Dunaway **12** Martin Balsam **13** Dustin Hoffman (Jack Crabb) **14** Chief Dan George **15** Richard Mulligan

little by little
French: 7 peu a peu
Spanish: 9 poco a poco

Little Caesar
director: 11 Mervyn LeRoy
cast: 13 Glenda Farrell **15** Edward G Robinson (Rico) (Caesar Enrico Bandello) **18** Douglas Fairbanks Jr

Little Corporal 8 Napoleon

Little Dipper 11 star cluster
  in: **9** Ursa Minor **10** Little Bear
Little Dorrit
  author: **14** Charles Dickens
  character: **3** Amy (Little Dorrit), Tip
  4 Rugg **5** Casby, Fanny, Flora,
  Gowan **6** Affery, Merdle, Pancks, Rigaud (Blandois) **7** Meagles **8** Mr F's
  Aunt **9** Mrs Merdle **10** Flintwinch **13**
  Arthur Clennam, William Dorrit **16**
  Monsieur Blandois, Young John
  Chivery
Little Drummer Girl, The
  author: **11** John Le Carre
Little Emily, Little Em'ly
  character in: **16** David Copperfield
  author: **7** Dickens
Little Fox
  constellation of: **9** Vulpecula
Little Foxes, The
  author: **14** Lillian Hellman
  character: **13** Regina Giddens
  director: **12** William Wyler
  cast: **10** Bette Davis (Regina) **12** Teresa Wright **14** Richard Carlson **15**
  Herbert Marshall
  prequel: **22** Another Part of the Forest
Little Gidding
  author: **7** T S Eliot
Little House on the Prairie
  author: **18** Laura Ingalls Wilder
  character: **6** Albert **7** Dr Baker **8** Rev
  Alden **9** Mr Edwards **10** Andy Garvey, Lars Hanson, Nels Oleson **11**
  Adam Kendall, Alice Garvey, Mary
  Ingalls **12** Grace Ingalls, Laura In-
  galls, Nellie Oleson, Willie Oleson **13**
  Carrie Ingalls, Harriet Oleson **14**
  Charles Ingalls, Eva Beadle Simms,
  Jonathan Garvey **15** Caroline Ingalls
  cast: **10** Dabbs Greer, Kevin Hagen
  11 Karl Swenson, Merlin Olsen,
  Richard Bull **12** Hersha Parady, Ka-
  ren Grassle, Victor French **13** Alison
  Arngrim, Linwood Boomer, Michael
  Landon **14** Melissa Gilbert **15**
  Jonathon Gilbert, Sidney Greenbush,
  Wendy Turnbeaugh **16** Brenda Turn-
  beaugh, Charlotte Gilbert, Lindsay
  Greenbush **17** Katherine McGregor,
  Matthew Laborteaux, Patrick Laborteaux **18** Melissa Sue Anderson
  setting: **6** Winoka **9** Minnesota, Plum
  Creek **11** Walnut Grove
Little John
  character in: **9** Robin Hood
Little King, The
  creator: **10** Otto Soglow
  technique: **9** pantomine
little-known 6 unsung **7** obscure, unnoted **10** unrenowned
Little Learning, A
  author: **11** Evelyn Waugh
Little Lord Fauntleroy
  author: **15** Frances H Burnett

Little Lulu
  creator: **14** Marge Henderson
Little Match Girl, The
  author: **21** Hans Christian Andersen
Little Men
  author: **15** Louisa May Alcott
Little Mermaid, The
  author: **21** Hans Christian Andersen
Little Minister, The
  author: **12** James M Barrie
Little Mo
  nickname of: **15** Maureen Connolly
Little Nemo in Slumberland
  creator: **11** Winsor McCay
  character: **6** Dr Pill **8** cannibal, princess
    clown: **4** Flip
    dog: **6** Blutch
little one 3 tot **4** babe, baby, tyke **5**
  child **6** infant, wee one **7** toddler
Little Orphan Annie
  creator: **10** Harold Gray
  character:
    foster father: **13** Daddy Warbucks
    dog: **5** Sandy
  saying: **13** Leapin' Lizards
little people 5 elves **6** dwarfs **7** fairies, midgets **11** leprechauns
Little Prince, The
  author: **21** Antoine de Saint-Exupery
Little Rhody
  nickname of: **11** Rhode Island
Little Rock *see* **8** Arkansas
Little Tramp
  nickname of: **14** Charlie Chaplin
Little Women
  author: **15** Louisa May Alcott
  character: **6** Laurie (Theodore Laurence), Marmee **10** John Brooke **14**
  Professor Bhaer
    March sisters: **2** Jo **3** Amy, Meg **4**
    Beth
  director:
    1933 version: 11 George Cukor
    1949 version: 11 Mervyn LeRoy
  cast (1933): **9** Paul Lukas **10** Frances
  Dee, Jean Parker **11** Joan Bennett **16**
  Katharine Hepburn (Jo)
  cast (1949): **9** Mary Astor **10** Janet
  Leigh **11** June Allyson **12** Peter Lawford **14** Margaret O'Brien **15** Elizabeth Taylor
liturgical 6 ritual **10** ceremonial **11**
  ceremonious, sacramental
liturgy 4 mass, rite **6** ritual **7** service,
  worship **8** ceremony, services **9** communion, sacrament
lituus
  form: **5** staff
  shape: **7** crooked
Lityerses
  father: **9** King Midas
  held: **15** reaping contests
  killed: **6** losers
livable, liveable 4 cozy, snug **5**
  comfy, homey **8** bearable, passable,

pleasant, suitable **9** agreeable, endurable, enjoyable, habitable, tolerable **10**
acceptable, convenient, gratifying, satisfying, worthwhile **11** comfortable
live 2 be **3** hot **4** bunk, feed, stay **5**
  abide, afire, aglow, alive, dwell, exist,
  fiery, lodge, quick, stand, vital **6**
  ablaze, active, aflame, alight, at hand,
  billet, bodily, endure, hold on, living,
  obtain, occupy, red-hot, remain, reside, settle, thrive **7** animate, at issue,
  be alive, blazing, breathe, burning,
  current, flaming, fleshly, going on, ignited, persist, prevail, subsist, survive
  8 existent, flourish, get ahead, get
  along, have life, increase, multiply,
  physical, pressing, take root, up- to-
  date, white-hot **9** breathing, corporeal
  10 draw breath
live and keep well
  Latin: **11** vive valeque
Live and Let Die
  author: **10** Ian Fleming
live dissolutely 7 carouse, debauch **9**
  dissipate **11** overindulge
livelihood 3 job **5** trade **6** career, living, metier **7** calling, support, venture
  8 business, position, vocation **9** situation **10** enterprise, line of work, occupation, profession, sustenance **11**
  maintenance, subsistence, undertaking
liveliness 3 pep, zip **4** brio, elan **5**
  vigor **7** agility **8** alacrity, vitality, vivacity **9** animation, briskness, eagerness **10** ebullience, nimbleness **13**
  sprightliness
lively 5 alert, brisk, eager, peppy,
  perky, vivid **6** active, ardent, bouncy
  7 buoyant, excited, fervent, intense **8**
  animated, spirited, vigorous **9** energetic, excitable, sprightly, vivacious
  12 enthusiastic
liven 4 buoy **5** cheer, elate, pep up **6**
  perk up, vivify **7** animate, delight, enliven, fortify, gladden, hearten, punch
  up, quicken **8** brighten, embolden, energize, inspirit **10** exhilarate, invigorate, strengthen
liver
  stores: **8** glycogen
  color: **3** red **5** brown
  produces: **4** bile **10** blood cells
Livermore Larruper
  nickname of: **7** Max Baer
livery 4 garb, suit **5** dress **6** attire **7**
  costume, raiment, regalia, uniform **8**
  clothing **9** vestments
Lives of a Bengal Lancer
  director: **13** Henry Hathaway
  cast: **10** Gary Cooper **12** Franchot
  Tone **14** Sir Guy Standing **15** Richard Cromwell
Lives of the Poets, The
  author: **13** Samuel Johnson
live through 4 know **7** survive, undergo **9** go through **10** experience

livid 3 mad **4** pale **5** angry, irate, riled, vexed **6** fuming, galled, purple, raging **7** bruised, enraged, furious **8** contused, incensed, inflamed, outraged, provoked, wrathful **9** indignant, steamed up, ticked off **10** discolored, infuriated **11** exasperated **12** black-and-blue

living 3 job **4** life, live, work **5** alive, being, quick, trade **6** active, bodily, career, extant, income **7** animate, calling, fleshly, going on, organic, venture **8** business, embodied, enduring, existent, existing, material, up-to-date, vocation **9** animation, breathing, corporeal, existence, incarnate, life-style, operative, permanent, remaining, surviving, way of life **10** employment, enterprise, having life, in the flesh, line of work, livelihood, occupation, persisting, prevailing, profession, subsisting, sustenance **11** maintenance, subsistence **13** drawing breath

living being 8 creature, organism

living conditions 10 atmosphere **11** environment **13** circumstances

living picture
    French: 13 tableau vivant

living quarters 4 home **5** abode, house **6** billet **7** housing, lodging, shelter **8** domicile, dwelling, quarters **9** apartment, residence **10** habitation **13** dwelling place

Livy
    also: 11 Titus Livius
    author of: 13 Ab urbe condita **26** From the Foundation of the City

lizard 3 dab, eft, uma **4** adda, gila, newt, seps, tegu, uran **5** agama, anole, anoli, gecko, idler, shrink **6** aguana, dragon, iguana, komodo, moloch **7** lounger, monitor, reptile, saurian **8** dinosaur, lacerata, scorpion **9** alligator, blind worm, chameleon, crocodile, galliwasp **10** chuckwalla, glass snake, horned toad, salamander **11** gila monster **12** Komodo dragon
    characteristic: 6 scales **7** molting **9** oviparous **11** cold-blooded **12** regeneration
    constellation of: 7 Lacerta

llama 6 alpaca, kechua, mammal, vicuna **7** guanaco **8** ungulate **13** Peruvian sheep

llano 11 grassy plain
    in: 12 South America

Llewellyn, Richard
    author of: 19 How Green Was My Valley

Llew Llaw Gyffes
    origin: 5 Welsh
    father: 7 Gwydion
    mother: 9 Arianrhod
    wife: 10 Blodenwedd
    curses bestowed by: 9 Arianrhod

Lloyd
    origin: 5 Welsh

form: 8 magician
cast spells upon: 7 Pryderi

Lloyd, Harold
    born: 10 Burchard NE
    roles: 9 Feet First **10** Safety Last **11** The Freshman **13** The Kid Brother

Lloyd Webber, Andrew
    born: 6 London
    Composer of: 4 Cats **5** Evita **6** Jeeves **12** Song and Dance **13** Aspects of Love **15** Tell Me on a Sunday **16** Starlight Express **20** Jesus Christ Superstar, The Phantom of the Opera **39** Joseph and the Amazing Technicolor Dreamcoat

Llud
    also: 4 Ludd, Nudd
    origin: 5 Welsh
    king of: 7 Britain
    rid kingdom of: 6 plague
    famous for: 10 generosity

Llyr
    origin: 5 Welsh
    son: 10 Manawyddan
    corresponds to: 3 Ler, Lir

load 3 try, vex **4** care, fill, haul, heap, lade, pack, pile **5** cargo, crush, stack, stuff, worry **6** burden, hamper, hinder, lad- ing, misery, strain, weight **7** afflict, carload, freight, oppress, trouble **8** capacity, contents, encumber, handicap, pressure, shipload, shipment **9** overwhelm, plane load, truckload, wagonload, weigh down **10** affliction, deadweight, depression, misfortune, oppression **11** encumbrance

loads 4 lots, much **5** heaps, piles, scads **6** oodles, plenty **14** more than enough

loaf 4 idle, loll **5** dally **6** be lazy **7** goof off **8** kill time, malinger **9** do nothing, gold brick, laze about, waste time **10** take it easy **12** lounge around

loafer 3 bum **4** shoe **5** idler **6** no-good **7** laggard, shirker, sponger, wastrel **8** deadbeat, loiterer, sluggard **9** goldbrick, lazybones **10** lazy person, malingerer, ne'er-do- well **11** couch potato **12** lounge lizard **15** drugstore cowboy
    French: 7 flaneur

loan 4 lend **5** allow **6** credit **7** advance, lending **8** mortgage **9** advancing

loath 4 loth **6** averse **7** against, counter, hostile, opposed **8** inimical **9** reluctant, resisting, unwilling **10** indisposed, set against **11** disinclined

loathe 4 hate **5** abhor, scorn **6** detest, eschew **7** deplore, despise, disdain, dislike **9** abominate **10** blench from, flinch from, recoil from, shrink from **11** keep clear of, shy away from **12** draw back from **14** be unable to bear, find disgusting, view with horror **16** have no stomach for

loathing 4 hate **5** odium **6** hatred **7**

disgust, dislike **8** aversion, distaste **9** antipathy, repulsion, revulsion **10** abhorrence, repugnance **11** abomination, detestation

loathsome 4 foul, mean, rank, vile **5** nasty **6** odious **7** hateful **9** abhorrent, invidious, obnoxious, offensive, repugnant, re- pulsive, revolting, sickening **10** abominable, despicable, detestable, disgusting, nauseating, unbearable **11** distasteful

lobby 5 foyer **8** anteroom, politick **9** vestibule **11** antechamber, pull strings, waiting room **12** entrance hall

lobscouse 4 meat **8** hardtack **10** vegetables **11** sailor's stew

local 6 narrow, native, nearby **7** insular, limited **8** citywide, confined, regional **9** adjoining, homegrown, parochial, sectional **10** provincial **11** territorial **12** neighborhood **13** circumscribed

locale 4 area, site, spot, zone **6** region **7** quarter, section, setting **8** locality, location, precinct, province, vicinity **12** neighborhood

locality 4 area, site, spot, zone **5** place **6** locale, region **7** quarter, section **8** district, location, precinct, province, vicinity **9** territory **12** neighborhood

locate 3 fix, put **4** find, live, post, seat, stay **5** dwell, place **6** detect, move to, reside, settle **7** deposit, discern, hit upon, set down, situate, station, uncover, unearth **8** come upon, meet with, pinpoint **9** establish, ferret out, light upon, search out, stumble on, track down **10** settle down **12** put down roots

location 4 site, spot **5** place **6** locale **8** district, position **9** situation **11** whereabouts **12** neighborhood

Lochinvar
    character in: 7 Marmion
    bride: 5 Ellen
    author: 5 Scott

Loch Ness
    in: 8 Scotland
    home of: 6 Nessie **7** monster

lock 3 bar, dam, pen **4** bang, bolt, cage, coil, curl, grab, grip, hank, hold, hook, jail, join, link, tuft **5** catch, clamp, clasp, grasp, latch, seize, skein, tress, unite **6** clinch, coop up, fasten, lock up, secure, shut in **7** confine, embrace, entwine, grapple, impound, padlock, ringlet **8** dock gate, imprison **9** canal gate, fastening, floodgate, interlink **10** intertwine, sluice gate **11** incarcerate

lock, cylinder
    invented by: 4 Yale

Lockhart, Gene
    daughter: 11 June Lockhart
    granddaughter: 11 Ann Lockhart
    born: 6 Canada, London **7** Ontario
    roles: 12 Madame Bovary **16** Death

of a Salesman **19** The Inspector General **20** Abe Lincoln in Illinois

lock horns 4 feud, tiff **5** argue, brawl, clash, fight **7** dispute, quarrel, wrangle **8** squabble **9** altercate

Lockit 4 Lucy
  character in: 12 Beggar's Opera
  author: 3 Gay

lockup 3 jug, pen **4** jail, stir **5** clink, pokey **6** cooler, prison **7** slammer **8** big house, hoosegow **11** reformatory **12** penitentiary

lock up 3 pen **4** cage, jail **6** coop up, secure **7** confine, impound **8** imprison, restrain, restrict **11** incarcerate

Lockyer, Joseph Norman
  field: 9 astronomy
  nationality: 7 British
  discovered: 6 helium

loco citato 15 in the place cited
  abbreviation: 6 loc cit

locomotive
  invented by:
    electric: 4 Vail
    experimental: 6 Fenton, Hedley **10** Stephenson, Trevithick
    first US: 6 Cooper
    practical: 10 Stephenson

locust 7 Robinia
  varieties: 4 moss **5** black, honey, mossy, swamp, sweet, water **6** clammy, yellow **7** African, bristly **8** ship-mast **10** West Indian **13** Allegheny moss, South American

locution 4 term **5** idiom, trope, usage **6** phrase, saying **7** wording **8** idiolect, phrasing **9** set phrase, utterance, verbalism **10** expression **11** phraseology, regionalism **12** turn of phrase **14** figure of speech

lode 3 bed **4** seam **7** deposit

lodge 3 bed, hut **4** camp, file, room, stay **5** cabin, catch, hotel, house, motel, put up **6** billet, harbor, resort, submit **7** cottage, quarter, shelter, sojourn **8** register

lodging 4 room **8** quarters **13** accommodation

Loewe, Frederick
  born: 6 Vienna
  Composer of: 4 Gigi **7** Camelot **8** Galateya **9** Brigadoon **10** My Fair Lady **14** Paint Your Wagon **15** The Little Prince

loft 3 lob **5** attic, pop up **6** belfry, garret **7** balcony, gallery, hit high, mansard **8** top floor **9** attic room, throw high **10** clerestory

loftiness 5 pride **9** arrogance **11** haughtiness **13** imperiousness **16** superciliousness

Lofting, Hugh
  author of: 10 Dr Dolittle

lofty 4 cold, high, tall **5** aloof, grand, great, noble, proud **6** lordly, mighty, remote, snooty **7** distant, eminent, exalted, haughty, leading, soaring, stately, stuck-up, sublime **8** arrogant, eleva- ted, glorious, imposing, insolent, majestic, puffed-up, scornful, snobbish, superior, towering **9** conceited, dignified, imperi- ous, important **10** disdainful, hoity-toity, preeminent **11** high ranking, illustrious, patronizing **12** high-reaching **13** condescending, distinguished, high-and-mighty, self-important

lofty bearing 7 dignity, majesty **10** augustness **11** stateliness

log 5 block, diary, stump **6** docket, lumber, record, timber **7** account, daybook, journal, logbook **8** calendar, schedule

Logan, Mount
  in: 5 Yukon **12** St. Elias range
  highest mt. in: 6 Canada

loges 5 boxes **7** balcony **9** mezzanine

loggia 5 lanai, porch **6** arcade, piazza **7** balcony, gallery

logic 5 sense **6** reason **7** cogency **8** analysis, argument **9** coherence, deduction, good sense, induction **10** dialectics

logical 5 clear, sound, valid **6** cogent, likely **7** germane **8** coherent, rational, relevant, sensible **9** deducible, pertinent, plausible **10** analytical, consistent, most likely, reasonable **11** enlightened, intelligent **13** well-organized

logos 4 word **5** ratio **6** saying, speech **7** thought **9** discourse, reckoning **10** proportion

logy 4 dull **5** inert, tired, weary **6** drowsy, groggy, sleepy, torpid **8** comatose, life- less, listless, sluggish **9** enervated, inanimate, lethargic **10** phlegmatic **12** hebetudinous

Lohengrin
  opera by: 6 Wagner
  character: 4 Elsa **6** Ortrud **9** Gottfried (Duke of Brabant) **25** Count Frederick of Telramund

Lohengrin
  origin: 8 Germanic
  knight of: 9 Holy Grail
  father: 8 Parsifal, Parzival

loiter 4 idle, laze, loaf, loll, lurk **5** dally, skulk, slink, tarry **6** dawdle **10** dillydally, hang around **11** hover around **12** shilly-shally

Loki
  origin: 12 Scandinavian
  mentioned in: 9 Lokasenna
  god of: 4 fire
  son: 6 Fenrir, Fenris
  daughter: 3 Hel
  fathered: 10 Jormungand **11** lormungandr, Jormungandr **14** Midgard Serpent
  mother of his children: 9 Angerboda, Angrbodha, Angurboda
  caused death of: 5 Baldr **6** Balder, Baldur
  form: 5 giant
  extorted treasure from: 7 Andvari
  function: 4 evil **6** strife **7** discord **8** mischief

Lolita
  author: 15 Vladimir Nabokov
  character: 6 Lolita **14** Humbert Humbert
  director: 14 Stanley Kubrick
  based on novel by: 15 Vladimir Nabokov
  cast: 7 Sue Lyon (Lolita) **10** James Mason (Humbert Humbert) **12** Peter Sellers **14** Shelley Winters

loll 3 sag **4** drag, drop, flap, flop, idle, lean, loaf **5** droop, relax, slump **6** dangle, dawdle, lounge, repose, slouch, sprawl **7** goof off, recline **8** flop over, languish

Lollobrigida, Gina
  born: 5 Italy **7** Subiaco
  roles: 7 Trapeze **14** Anne of Brooklyn, The Wayward Wife **15** Solomon and Sheba **20** Buona Sera Mrs Campbell **27** The World's Most Beautiful Woman

Loman, Willy
  character in: 16 Death of a Salesman
  author: 6 Miller
  epitome of: 8 salesman

Lombard, Carole
  real name: 15 Jane Alice Peters
  husband: 10 Clark Gable
  born: 11 Fort Wayne IN
  roles: 12 My Man Godfrey **13** Nothing Sacred, To Be Or Not To Be **16** Twentieth Century

Lome
  capital of: 4 Togo

London
  airport: 7 Gatwick **8** Heathrow, Stansted
  architect: 4 Wren
  area: 4 Soho **6** Camden **7** Brixton, Chelsea, Holborn, Pimlico **8** Vauxhall **9** Bayswater, Belgravia, Islington, Southwark **10** Bloomsbury, Kensington, Paddington, Shoreditch **11** Notting Hill, St John's Wood **13** Knightsbridge
  capital of: 7 England **12** Great Britain **13** United Kingdom
  landmark: 6 Big Ben **8** Hyde Park **9** Whitehall, Wimbledon **11** Regent's Park, Saint James's, Tate Gallery, Tower Bridge **12** Covent Garden, London Bridge **13** British Museum, Tower of London **14** British Library, Speaker's Corner **15** National Gallery, Trafalgar Square **16** Buckingham Palace, Piccadilly Circus, Westminster Abbey **17** Kensington Gardens, Royal Festival Hall, Westminster Palace **18** Houses of Parliament **19** Saint Paul's Cathedral **23** Victoria and Albert Museum

police: 7 bobbies
  established by: 13 Sir Robert Peel
prime minister's residence: 16 Ten Downing Street
river: 6 Thames
Roman name: 9 Londinium
subway: 11 Underground

London, Jack
  author of: 9 White Fang **10** The Sea Wolf **16** The Call of the Wild

lone 4 only, sole **5** alone **6** single, unique **8** isolated, singular, solitary, unpaired **9** unabetted **10** individual, unattended, unescorted **13** companionless, unaccompanied

loneliness 9 isolation, seclusion **12** lonesomeness, solitariness **14** friendlessness

Loneliness of the Long Distance Runner, The
  author: 12 Alan Sillitoe
  director: 14 Tony Richardson
  cast: 11 Avis Bunnage, Peter Madden **12** Tom Courtenay **15** Michael Redgrave

lonely 6 remote **7** forlorn **8** deserted, desolate, forsaken, hermitic, isolated, lonesome, secluded, solitary, unsocial **9** by oneself, reclusive, withdrawn **10** friendless, unattended **11** uninhabited, unpopulated **12** unfrequented **13** companionless, unaccompanied

Lone Ranger, The
  character: 5 Tonto
  cast: 8 John Hart **12** Clayton Moore **14** Jay Silverheels
  horse: 5 Scout **6** Silver
  saying: 8 kemo sabe
  Lone Ranger used: 13 silver bullets
  theme: 19 William Tell Overture

lonesome 5 alone, aloof **6** lonely **7** forlorn, insular **8** desolate, detached, forsaken **9** alienated, withdrawn **10** friendless, unfriended **13** companionless

Lone Star State
  nickname of: 5 Texas

long 4 hope, lust, pine, sigh, want, wish **5** covet, crave, yearn **6** aspire, hanker, hunger, thirst **7** lengthy, spun out **8** drawn-out, extended, have a yen, in length, unending **9** elongated, extensive, prolonged **10** be bent on, protracted **11** far-reaching, have a desire **12** from end to end, interminable, outstretched

Long, Crawford Williamson
  field: 8 medicine
  first used: 5 ether

Longaville
  character in: 16 Love's Labour's Lost
  author: 11 Shakespeare

Long Day's Journey into Night
  author: 12 Eugene O'Neill
  director: 11 Sidney Lumet
  cast: 13 Dean Stockwell **14** Jason Ro-

bards Jr **15** Ralph Richardson **16** Katharine Hepburn

Longest Day, The
  director: 10 Ken Annakin **12** Andrew Marton, Bernard Wicki
  cast: 9 John Wayne, Mel Ferrer **10** Henry Fonda, Red Buttons, Robert Ryan, Rod Steiger **12** Peter Lawford
  setting: 4 D-Day **8** Normandy (Allied invasion)

long-faced 4 glum **6** dismal, gloomy **7** doleful, unhappy **8** dejected, mournful **10** lugubrious **14** down in the mouth

Longfellow, Henry Wadsworth
  author of: 8 Hyperion, (The Song of) Hiawatha **10** Evangeline **15** Paul Revere's Ride **18** Tales of a Wayside Inn **21** The Wreck of the Hesperus **27** The Courtship of Miles Standish

longing 3 yen **4** wish **6** ardent, pining, thirst **7** craving, wishful **8** desirous, yearning **9** hankering, hungering **10** aspiration **11** languishing

long-lasting 7 chronic, lengthy, tedious **8** enduring, extended **9** prolonged **10** continuing, protracted

long live
  French: 4 vive

long past 3 old **5** olden **6** gone by, of yore **7** ancient, long ago **8** long gone

long-standing 4 long **5** hardy, hoary **6** rooted **7** abiding, ancient, chronic, durable, lasting **8** enduring, habitual, hallowed, unfading **9** confirmed, continual, long-lived, perennial, perpetual, venerable **10** continuous, deep-rooted, deep-seated, inveterate, persistent, persisting **11** long-lasting, time-honored **15** long-established

Longstreet, James
  served in: 8 Civil War
  side: 11 Confederate
  battle: 7 Bull Run **10** Gettysburg **11** Chickamauga **14** Fredericksburg **18** Wilderness Campaign
  after war joined: 11 Republicans
  US minister to: 6 Turkey

Long Voyage Home, The
  director: 8 John Ford
  based on play by: 12 Eugene O'Neill
  cast: 9 Ian Hunter, John Wayne **13** Wilfrid Lawson **14** Thomas Mitchell **15** Barry Fitzgerald

long-wearing 5 tough **6** strong, sturdy **7** durable, lasting **8** enduring **11** substantial

long-winded 5 wordy **6** prolix **7** lengthy, tedious, verbose **8** rambling **9** garrulous **10** digressive, discursive

long-windedness 8 rambling **9** garrulity, prolixity, verbosity, wordiness **14** discursiveness

look 3 air, see **4** cast, face, gape, gaze, mien, ogle, peek, peep, scan, seem, show, view **5** front, glare, guise, sight, stare, study, watch **6** appear, behold, glance, regard, survey **7** bear-

ing, examine, exhibit, glimpse **8** demeanor, manifest, once-over, presence, scrutiny **10** appearance, be directed, cut a figure, expression, scrutinize **11** contemplate, countenance, observation

look after 4 help **6** assist, defend **7** help out, protect **10** minister to **11** watch out for **17** take under one's wing

look askance at 7 condemn **8** object to **9** frown upon **10** disapprove **14** discountenance **15** take exception to **16** find unacceptable, view with disfavor

look at 3 see **4** view **6** behold, notice, regard **7** examine, inspect, witness **10** scrutinize

Look Back in Anger
  director: 14 Tony Richardson
  based on play by: 11 John Osborne
  cast: 7 Mary Ure **10** Edith Evans **11** Claire Bloom **13** Richard Burton **15** Donald Pleasance

look down on 7 despise, disdain **9** frown upon, patronize **10** condescend **13** put on airs with **14** hold in contempt

looker-on 6 viewer **7** watcher, witness **8** beholder, observer, onlooker **9** bystander, spectator

look for 4 seek **5** await **6** expect, pursue **7** hunt for **9** search for **10** anticipate

look for the woman
  French: 15 cherchez la femme

look forward to 5 await **6** expect **7** long for, wait for **9** pin hope on **10** anticipate **17** count the days until

Look Homeward, Angel
  author: 11 Thomas Wolfe
  character: 7 Ben Gant **9** Eliza Gant **10** Eugene Gant, Laura James, Oliver Gant **15** Margaret Leonard

look in the eye 4 defy, face **5** brave **8** confront **9** challenge

look into 5 probe **7** examine, explore **10** scrutinize **11** inquire into, investigate

lookout 4 heed **5** guard, scout, vigil **6** patrol, sentry **7** spotter **8** observer, sentinel, watchdog, watchman **9** alertness, attention, awareness, readiness, vigilance **10** precaution **11** guardedness, mindfulness, watchkeeper **12** surveillance, watchfulness

look out 4 mind **6** beware **8** take care, watch out **9** be careful, be on guard **11** take warning **12** be on the alert

look over 4 scan, skim **5** judge **6** assess, peruse, survey **7** dip into **8** appraise, evaluate **13** browse through, glance through

look through 4 scan, skim **6** browse, peruse **7** dip into **8** look over **9** check over **13** glance through

look toward 7 count on **10** anticipate **13** look forward to

look upon 3 see **4** view **6** be hold, gaze at, look at **7** observe, stare at

look upon as 4 deem, hold **5** count, judge, think **6** regard, view as **7** account, believe **8** consider, take to be

look up to 5 honor **6** admire, esteem, revere **7** respect **8** venerate

loom 4 hulk, rise, soar **5** tower **6** appear, ascend, emerge **8** stand out **9** take shape

loom, power
    invented by: 10 Cartwright

loop 3 eye **4** bend, coil, curl, furl, ring, roll, turn **5** braid, curve, noose, plait, twirl, twist, whorl **6** circle, eyelet, spiral **7** opening, ringlet **8** aperture, encircle, loophole **10** wind around **11** convolution, curve around

Loos, Anita
    author of: 22 Gentlemen Prefer Blondes

loose 4 fast, free, lewd, undo, wild **5** freed, let go, slack, untie, vague **6** freely, loosen, unbind, undone, untied, wanton **7** immoral, inexact, loosely, release, set free, slacken, unbound, uncaged, unchain, unleash, unloose, unyoked **8** careless, heedless, liberate, not tight, rakehell, unbridle, unchaste, unfasten, unjoined, untether **9** abandoned, debauched, dissolute, imprecise, liberated, libertine, unbridled, unchained, unleashed, unmanacle, un shackle **10** dissipated, inaccurate, licentious, not binding, profligate, unattached, unexacting, unfastened, unfettered, unhandcuff, untethered **11** not fastened, unconnected **12** unimprisoned **13** unconstrained

loose-fitting 4 limp **5** baggy, loose, slack **6** draped, droopy **7** sagging **9** overlarge, oversized

loosely connected 5 jerky **6** fitful **8** episodic, rambling **9** spasmodic, wandering **10** digressive, discursive, meandering

loosen 3 lax **4** ease, free, undo **5** break, relax, untie **6** limber, unbend, unbind **7** release, relieve, slacken, unchain, unscrew **8** liberate, unbuckle, unfasten, work free **10** emancipate

looseness 8 fastness, lewdness, wildness **9** slackness, vagueness **10** debauch- ery, immorality, inaccuracy, profligacy, wantonness **11** dissipation, dissolution, imprecision **12** carelessness, heedlessness, inexactitude **14** licentiousness

loot 3 rob **4** haul, raid, sack, swag, take **5** booty, prize, strip **6** boodle, fleece, pilfer, ravage, spoils **7** pillage, plunder, ransack **11** stolen goods

looter 5 thief **6** robber, vandal **7** brigand **8** pillager **9** despoiler, plunderer

lop 3 cut **4** chip, chop, crop, dock, flop, sned, snip, trim **5** droop, prune, sever **6** cut off, deduct, detach, remove, slouch **7** cut back **8** amputate, truncate

Lopez, Nancy
    sport: 4 golf
    husband: 9 Ray Knight
        plays: 8 baseball

lopsided 4 awry **5** askew **6** aslant, tipped, uneven **7** crooked, leaning, listing, slanted, tilting, unequal **8** cockeyed, inclined, slanting **9** irregular **10** asymmetric, off- balance, unbalanced **15** disproportional **16** disproportionate

loquacious 5 gabby, talky, windy, wordy **6** blabby, chatty, prolix **7** prating, verbose, voluble **8** babbling, chattery **9** garrulous, prattling, talkative **10** chattering, long-winded

loquitur 8 he speaks **9** she speaks

lord 4 king **5** chief, crown, ruler **6** leader, master **7** monarch **8** overlord, seign- ior, superior **9** commander, landowner, sovereign **10** landholder, proprietor
    Japanese: 6 daimyo
    Turkish: 3 beg, bey

Lord
    Latin: 7 Dominus

Lord be with you, the
    Latin: 15 Dominus vobiscum

Lord have mercy
    Greek: 12 Kyrie eleison

Lord Jim
    author: 12 Joseph Conrad
    character: 5 Stein **6** Marlow **9** Dain Waris **14** Gentleman Brown

lordliness 7 disdain **8** contempt **9** arrogance, insolence, loftiness **11** haughtiness **13** imperiousness **16** superciliousness

lordly 4 cold **5** aloof, bossy, grand, lofty, noble, proud, regal **6** august, remote, snooty **7** distant, elegant, eminent, exalted, haughty, stately, stuck-up **8** arrogant, despotic, imposing, majestic, princely, puffed-up, scornful, snobbish **9** conceited, dignified, imperious, sumptuous **10** disdainful, hoity-toity, tyrannical **11** dictatorial, domineering, magisterial, magnificent, patronizing **13** condescending, high-and-mighty, self- important

Lord of the Flies
    author: 14 William Golding

Lord of the Rings, The
    author: 10 J R R Tolkien
    creatures: 3 elf, ent, orc **5** dwarf **6** hobbit

Lord Weary's Castle
    author: 12 Robert Lowell

lore 7 beliefs, legends **10** traditions

Lorelei

also: 7 Lurelei
origin: 8 Germanic
form: 5 nymph
dwelling place: 5 cliff, Rhine
lured: 7 boatmen
caused shipwrecks by: 7 singing

Lorelei Lee
    role in: 22 Gentlemen Prefer Blondes
    played by: 6 Monroe **8** Channing
    song: 27 Diamonds Are a Girl's Best Friend

Loren, Sophia
    real name: 14 Sofia Scicolone
    husband: 10 Carlo Ponti
    born: 4 Rome **5** Italy
    roles: 5 El Cid **8** Two Women (Oscar) **9** Arabesque, Houseboat **13** Man of La Mancha **14** The Black Orchid **18** Desire Under the Elms **20** Marriage Italian Style **21** A Countess from Hong Kong, The Pride and the Passion

Lorentz, Hendrik Anton
    field: 7 physics
    nationality: 5 Dutch
    discovered: 17 special relativity
    named for him: 21 Lorentz transformation **34** Lorentz- Fitzgerald Length Contraction
    awarded: 10 Nobel Prize

Loring, Eugene
    choreographer of: 11 Billy the Kid

Lorna Doone
    author: 11 R D Blackmore
    character: 8 John Ridd **9** Tom Faggus **11** Carver Doone **13** Sir Ensor Doone **14** Jeremy Stickles **15** Reuben Huckaback

Lorre, Peter
    real name: 16 Laszlo Lowenstein
    born: 7 Hungary **9** Rosenberg
    roles: 1 M **6** Mr. Moto **7** Mad Love **9** Joel Cairo **10** Casablanca, The Verdict **12** The Big Circus **14** Three Strangers **16** The Maltese Falcon **18** Crime and Punishment, The Mask of Dimitrios

Lorry, Jarvis
    character in: 16 A Tale of Two Cities
    author: 7 Dickens

Los Angeles
    airport: 3 LAX **7** Burbank **23** Los Angeles International
    area: 5 Watts **6** Bel Air, Downey, Venice **7** Anaheim, Compton, Norwalk **8** Mar Vista, Pasadena, Torrance, Westwood **9** Brentwood, Hollywood, Inglewood, Long Beach **10** Culver City **11** Century City, Garden Grove, Palos Verdes, Santa Monica **12** Beverly Hills, Marina del Rey **16** Pacific Palisades
        San Fernando Valley: 6 Encino **7** Tarzana, Van Nuys, Ventura **10** Northridge **11** Sherman Oaks
    baseball team: 7 Dodgers
    basketball team: 6 Lakers, Sparks

8 Clippers
football team: 4 Rams **7** Express, Raiders
hockey team: 5 Kings
landmark: 5 Forum **10** Disneyland **11** Civic Center, Getty Museum, Watts Towers **12** Griffith Park **13** Farmers' Market, Hollywood Bowl, Hollywood Park, La Brea Tar Pits, Magic Mountain **15** Knott's Berry Farm **16** Bonaventure Hotel **17** Norton Simon Museum **22** Grauman's Chinese Theater **23** Griffith Park Observatory
mountains: 10 San Gabriel **11** Santa Monica
nickname: 15 City of the Angels
street: 4 Vine **10** Rodeo Drive **12** Olvera Street **15** Mulholland Drive **16** Van Nuys Boulevard **17** Wilshire Boulevard **18** Hollywood Boulevard **20** Santa Monica Boulevard
university: 3 USC **4** UCLA **7** Caltech **10** Pepperdine **17** Occidental College **31** California Institute of Technology

lose 4 fail, miss **6** forget, ignore, mislay **7** confuse, forfeit **8** misplace **9** fail to win, stray from **10** be the loser, fail to heed **11** be thrown off **12** be defeated in, be deprived of, suffer loss of, take a licking

lose control 5 break, crack **7** crack up **9** fall apart **10** go to pieces **15** go off the deep end

lose faith 6 give up **7** despair **9** lose heart **10** have no hope **18** become disenchanted

lose force 3 die **7** run down **9** lose power

lose heart 6 give up **7** de spair **17** become discouraged

lose one's cool 12 fly into a rage **13** become enraged, throw a tantrum **14** lose one's temper **15** fly off the handle

loser 4 flop **7** failure **8** defeated **9** conquered **10** vanquished

lose track of 4 lose **9** let escape **11** lose sight of

lose vigor 4 flag **5** droop **6** sicken, weaken, wither **7** decline

Losing Battles
   author: 11 Eudora Welty

loss 4 ruin **5** wreck **6** defeat, losing **7** licking, removal, undoing **8** overturn, riddance, wrecking **9** abolition, mislaying, privation **10** amount lost, demolition, extinction, forfeiture, misplacing, number lost **11** bereavement, deprivation, destruction, dissolution, eradication, expenditure, extirpation

loss of life 5 death **8** fatality **9** mortality

lost 5 stray **6** absent, astray, killed, ruined, wasted **7** lacking, mislaid, missing, misused, strayed, wrecked **8** absorbed, murdered, perished, vanished, wiped out **9** abolished, destroyed, engrossed, misplaced, off- course **10** demolished, eradicated, extirpated, gone astray, misapplied, squandered **11** annihilated, misdirected, obliterated, preoccupied **12** exterminated

Lost Honor of Katharina Blum, The
   author: 12 Heinrich Boll

Lost Horizon
   author: 11 James Hilton
   character: 10 Hugh Conway, Rutherford **12** Henry Barnard, Miss Brinklow **14** Father Perrault **20** Captain Mallison Chang
   director: 10 Frank Capra
   cast: 5 Margo **8** H B Warner, Sam Jaffe **9** Jane Wyatt **10** John Howard **12** Isa- bel Jewell, Ronald Colman **14** Thomas Mitchell **19** Edward Everett Horton
   setting: 5 Tibet

Lost Illusions
   author: 14 Honore de Balzac

Lost in America
   director: 12 Albert Brooks
   cast: 12 Albert Brooks, Julie Hagerty

Lost in Space
   character: 5 Robot **7** Don West **12** Judy Robinson, Will Robinson **13** Pen- ny Robinson **14** Dr Zachary Smith **15** Maureen Robinson **16** Prof John Rob- inson
   cast: 9 Billy Mumy **11** Guy Williams, Mark Goddard **12** June Lockhart, Marta Kristen **14** Jonathan Harris **16** Angela Cartwright
   ship: 9 Jupiter II

Lost in the Funhouse
   author: 9 John Barth

Lost in the Stars
   author: 15 Maxwell Anderson

lost in thought 7 pensive **8** absorbed **9** engrossed, wrapped up **13** contemplative, in a brown study, introspective

Lost Lady, A
   author: 11 Willa Cather

Lost Ones, The
   author: 13 Samuel Beckett

Lost Patrol, The
   director: 8 John Ford
   cast: 8 Alan Hale **11** Wallace Ford **12** Boris Karloff **14** Victor McLaglen
   score: 10 Max Steiner

Lost Weekend, The
   author: 14 Charles Jackson
   director: 11 Billy Wilder
   cast: 9 Jane Wyman, Mary Young **10** Frank Falen, Ray Milland **11** Philip Terry **12** Doris Dowling **13** Howard da Silva
   Oscar for: 5 actor (Milland) **7** picture **8** director **10** screenplay

lot 4 fate, lots, many, much, plot **5** field, patch, quota, share, straw, tract **6** oceans, oodles, ration **7** counter, measure **8** beaucoup, property **9** allotment, allowance, great deal

Lot
   grandfather: 5 Terah
   father: 5 Haran
   uncle: 7 Abraham
   son: 5 Ammon
   hometown: 5 Sodom
   rescued by: 6 angels
   fled to: 4 Zoar

lothario 3 rip **4** rake, roue, wolf **5** lover, Romeo, sheik **6** lecher **7** Don Juan, seducer, swinger **8** Casanova, lover- boy **9** debauchee, debaucher, libertine, womanizer **10** lady-killer, profligate, sensualist **11** philanderer, skirt-chaser

Lothario
   character in: 15 The Fair Penitent
   author: 4 Rowe

Loti, Pierre
   author of: 18 An Iceland Fisherman
   pseudonym of: 5 Viaud

lotion 4 balm, wash **5** salve **6** liquid **7** unction, unguent **8** cosmetic, liniment, ointment, solution **9** demulcent, emollient, freshener, skin cream **10** after-shave, astringent **11** conditioner, embrocation, moisturizer

Lotis
   form: 5 nymph
   changed into: 4 tree **5** lotus

lotophagi
   means: 11 lotus-eaters

lots 4 much **5** heaps, loads, plots, scads **10** quantities

lotus 7 Nelumbo **13** Nymphaea lotus
   varieties: 4 blue **5** water, white **6** sacred **8** American, Egyptian **10** East Indian

lotus-eaters 9 lotophagi
   appear in: 7 Odyssey

loud 5 gaudy, noisy, showy, vivid **6** bright, flashy, garish **7** blatant, booming, intense, splashy **8** colorful, sonorous **9** clam- orous, deafening **10** resounding, stentorian, thundering, vociferous **11** ear-piercing, loud-mouthed **12** earsplitting, ostentatious

loud sound 4 bang, boom, clap, honk, howl, peal, roar, slam, toot **5** blare, blast, burst, crash **6** bellow, report, scream, shriek **7** clatter, thunder **9** explosion **10** detonation

Lou Grant
   character: 6 Animal **8** Joe Rossi **10** Art Donovan **11** Charlie Hume **12** Billie Newman **15** Margaret Pynchon
   cast: 10 Jack Bannon, Mason Adams **11** Edward Asner, Linda Kelsey **12** Robert Walden **13** Nancy Marchand **14** Darryl Anderson
   paper: 17 Los Angeles Tribune
   spinoff of: 18 Mary Tyler Moore Show

Louis, Joe
   real name: 14 Joe Louis Barrow

nickname: 11 Brown Bomber
sport: 6 boxing
class: 11 heavyweight
Louis, Morris
 born: 11 Baltimore MD
 artwork: 4 Veil **5** Signa **7** Stripes **8** Unfurled **15** Mountains and Sea
Louise
 opera by: 11 Charpentier
 character: 6 Julian
Louisiana
 abbreviation: 2 LA
 nickname: 5 Bayou, Sugar **6** Creole **7** Pelican
 capital: 10 Baton Rouge
 largest city: 10 New Orleans
 others: 5 Houma **6** Bunkie, Gretna, Kenner, Minden, Monroe, Ruston **7** Bastrop **8** Bogalusa **9** Lafayette, Opelousas **10** Alexandria, Shreveport **11** Lake Charles
 college: 3 LSU **6** Loyola, Tulane **7** Dillard, Newcomb **9** Grambling
 explorer: 7 La Salle **9** Iberville **13** Pierre Lemoyne
 feature:
  area: 5 bayou **13** French Quarter
  festival: 9 Mardi Gras
  music: 4 jazz
  stadium: 9 Sugar Bowl
  street: 7 Bourbon
 tribe: 4 Adai, Ioni, Rees, Waco **5** Caddo, Haini, Washa **6** Eyeish, Pawnee **7** Andarko, Arikara, Atakapa **8** Ovachita **9** Bayogoula, Nachitoch
 people: 5 Cajun **6** Creole **7** Acadian, pelican **8** Huey Long **14** Lillian Hellman, Louis Armstrong
 island: 5 Avery
 lake: 3 Iat **4** Iatt **5** Caddo, Clear, Cross, Larto, White **6** Borgne, Saline **8** Darbonne, Maurepas **9** Bistineau, Calcasieu, Catahoula **10** False River **13** Pontchartrain
 land rank: 11 thirty-first
 mountain:
  highest point: 8 Driskill
 physical feature: 15 Head of the Passes **17** coastal marshlands
  delta: 11 Mississippi
  gulf: 6 Mexico
  salt domes: 11 Five Islands
 river: 3 Red **5** Amite, Bayou, Pearl **6** Tensas **8** Ouachita **11** Mississippi
 state admission: 10 eighteenth
 state bird: 19 eastern brown pelican
 state flower: 8 magnolia
 state motto: 5 Union **7** Justice **10** Confidence
 state song: 15 Give Me Louisiana **16** You Are My Sunshine
 state tree: 11 bald cypress
Louisiana Lightning
 nickname of: 9 Ron Guidry
lounge 4 flop, idle, laze, loaf, loll, rest, sofa **5** couch, dally, divan, lobby, relax, sleep, slump **6** dawdle, daybed, repose, slouch, sprawl **7** recline,

slumber **8** kill time, languish **9** davenport, do nothing, lie around, vestibule **10** dillydally, stretch out, take it easy **12** chaise longue
lourd
 music: 5 heavy
Lourenco Marques
 capital of: 10 Mozambique
louse 3 cad, rat **4** heel **5** churl, knave **6** rascal, rotter, vermin **8** parasite **9** scoundrel
louse up 3 mar **4** goof, muff, ruin **5** botch, spoil **6** bungle, foul up, mess up **7** butcher, do badly, screw up **9** mismanage **11** make a mess of
lousy 3 bad **4** mean **5** awful, nasty **6** crummy, rotten, shabby, unkind **7** hateful, vicious **8** dreadful, inferior, infested, terrible **9** unethical, worthless **10** pediculous, second-rate, unpleasant **12** contemptible
lout 3 ape, oaf **4** boor, clod **5** booby, churl, clown, dummy, dunce, klutz, yokel **6** lummox, rustic **7** bumpkin, dullard
loutish 4 rude **5** crude **6** coarse, gauche, oafish, vulgar **7** boorish, uncouth **9** unrefined **10** unpolished **11** peasantlike
lovable, loveable 4 cute **5** sweet **6** cuddly, lovely, taking **7** darling, winning, winsome **8** adorable, charming, engaging, fetching **9** endearing **10** enchanting **11** captivating
Lovberg, Eilert
 character in: 11 Hedda Gabler
 author: 5 Ibsen
love 3 man **4** beau, bent, dear, girl, mind, turn **5** adore, amity, amour, angel, ardor, enjoy, fancy, flame, honey, lover, savor, taste, woman **6** admire, bask in, choice, esteem, fellow, relish **7** beloved, charity, cherish, concord, darling, dearest, emotion, leaning, passion, rapture, revel in, sweetie **8** affinity, be fond of, devotion, fondness, goodwill, hold dear, loved one, mistress, paramour, penchant, precious, sympathy, treasure, truelove, weakness **9** adoration, affection, boyfriend, delight in, inamorata, rejoice in, sentiment **10** admiration, appreciate, attachment, cordiality, friendship, girlfriend, partiality, proclivity, solicitude, sweetheart, sweetie pie, tenderness **11** amorousness, benevolence, brotherhood, inclination, infatuation **12** be enamored of, congeniality, predilection
 god of: 4 Amor, Eros **5** Cupid **7** Angus Og
 goddess of: 5 Freia, Freya, Venus **6** Hathor, Inanna, Ishtar **7** Astarte, Mylitta **9** Aphrodite
Love, the Magician
 also: 11 El Amor Brujo
 ballet by: 5 Falla

love affair 5 amour **7** liaison, romance **14** affaire de coeur
Love Boat, The
 character: 3 Ace **10** (Cruise Director) Julie McCoy **11** (Dr) Adam Bricker, (Purser Burl) Gopher Smith **14** (Captain) Merrill Stubing **15** (Bartender) Isaac Washington
 cast: 8 Ted Lange **10** Fred Grandy **11** Lauren Tewes **12** Bernie Kopell, Gavin MacLeod
 ship: 15 Pacific Princess
love child 7 bastard **12** natural child **17** illegitimate child
love conquers all
 Latin: 15 omnia vincit amor
loved one 4 love, wife **5** lover **6** fiance, spouse **7** be loved, dearest, fiancee, husband **9** boyfriend **10** girlfriend, sweetheart **12** family member
Love for Three Oranges, The
 opera by: 9 Prokofiev
Love in the Afternoon
 director: 11 Billy Wilder
 cast: 10 Gary Cooper **13** Audrey Hepburn **16** Maurice Chevalier
 setting: 5 Paris
Lovelace, Richard
 author of: 18 To Althea from Prison **23** To Lucasta Going to the Wars
loveliness 6 beauty **9** good looks **11** pulchritude **14** attractiveness
lovely 4 cute, fine, good **5** sweet **6** comely **7** elegant, lovable, winning, winsome **8** adorable, alluring, charming, engaging, fetching, handsome, pleasant, pleasing **9** agreeable, beautiful, endearing, enjoy-able, exquisite **10** attractive, delightful, en-chanting **11** captivating, fascinating **12** irresistible
Love Machine, The
 author: 16 Jacqueline Susann
Love Me Tonight
 director: 15 Rouben Mamoulian
 cast: 8 Myrna Loy **14** Charlie Ruggles **16** Maurice Chevalier **17** Jeanette MacDonald
 score: 14 Rodgers and Hart
 song: 4 Mimi **5** Lover **14** Isn't It Romantic
love of country
 Latin: 11 amor patriae
Love of One's Neighbor
 author: 14 Leonid Andreyev
lover 3 fan, man, nut **4** beau, buff, dear, girl, love **5** flame, freak, honey, Romeo, swain, woman, wooer **6** fellow, suitor **7** admirer, beloved, darling, devotee, Don Juan, fanatic, sweetie **8** Casanova, follower, Lothario, loved one, lover boy, mistress, paramour, truelove **9** boyfriend, inamorata **10** aficionado, enthusiast, girlfriend, sweetheart **11** afficionado
 French: 6 bon ami **9** bonne amie
 Italian: 8 cicisbeo

Lovers and Other Strangers
director: **8** Cy Howard
cast: **8** Gig Young **9** Anne Meara, Bea Arthur **11** Anne Jackson **13** Bonnie Bedelia, Harry Guardino **14** Cloris Leachman, Michael Brandon **17** Richard Castellano

love seat 4 sofa **5** couch **6** settee **13** courting chair

lovesick 7 amorous **8** yearning **10** moonstruck

Love's Labour's Lost
author: **18** William Shakespeare
character: **4** Dull **5** Maria **7** Berowne, Costard, Dumaine **8** Rosaline **9** Ferdinand, Katherine **10** Holofernes, Jaquenetta, Longaville **16** Princess of France **18** Don Adriano de Armado

Love Song of J Alfred Prufrock, The
author: **7** T S Eliot

Love Story
author: **10** Erich Segal

Love-wit
character in: **12** The Alchemist
author: **6** Jonson

loving 4 fond, kind, warm **6** ardent, caring, doting, erotic, tender **7** amatory, amorous, devoted **8** enamored, friendly **10** benevolent, passionate, solicitous **11** sympathetic, warm hearted **12** affectionate

loving word 9 sweet talk **10** endearment **12** sweet nothing

low 4 base, blue, deep, down, evil, glum, mean, soft, vile **5** awful, cruel, dirty, dumpy, faint, gross, lower, lowly, muted, prone, quiet, short, small, squat **6** brutal, coarse, common, cruddy, crummy, fee- ble, gentle, gloomy, humble, hushed, little, paltry, scurvy, softly, sordid, stubby, stumpy, sunken, vulgar, wicked **7** coastal, concave, corrupt, doleful, heinous, muffled, obscene, quietly, snubbed, squalid, subdued, unhappy **8** cowardly, degraded, dejected, depraved, downcast, inferior, low-lying, low-slung, mediocre, murmured, sawed-off, soothing, terrible, trifling, undersea, unworthy **9** dastardly, depressed, lethargic, nefarious, prostrate, repugnant, repulsive, submarine, submerged, truncated, unethical, whispered **10** abominable, despicable, despondent, dispirited, melancholy, outrageous, scandalous **11** ignominious, scoundrelly, underground, unimportant **12** contemptible, disheartened, dishonorable **14** down in the mouth

Low, Juliette
founder of: **10** Girl Scouts

lowbred 4 non-u **6** coarse, common, vulgar **7** lowbrow, peasant **10** lower-class, uncultured

low-down 4 base, mean **5** dirty **10**

despicable **12** contemptible **13** reprehensible

Lowell, James Russell
author of: **12** The Cathedral **15** The Biglow Papers **16** A Fable for Critics **21** The Vision of Sir Launfal

Lowell, Robert
author of: **8** Day by Day **9** Skunk Hour **10** The Dolphin **11** Life Studies **15** For the Union Dead **16** Lord Weary's Castle

lower 3 cut, dim **4** damp, drop, duck, mute, pare, sink, sulk **5** frown, glare, pared, prune, scowl **6** deduct, glower, lop off, muffle, reduce, soften, subdue **7** curtail, depress, immerse, let down, put down, reduced, repress, shorten **8** decrease, diminish, grow dark, lessened, make less, pare down, pull down, submerge, take down, tone down **9** curtailed, decreased, make lower, pared down **10** abbreviate, diminished

lower-case letter 9 minuscule **11** small letter

lower-class 4 poor **6** common **7** lowbred, lowbrow, peasant **9** unrefined **10** blue-collar **12** working-class

lower classes 6 proles, rabble **8** canaille, riffraff **9** hoi polloi, peasantry **11** proletariat **13** the common herd, working people **16** the great unwashed

lower depths 4 pits, scum **5** dregs **6** rabble **8** canaille, riffraff **14** scum of the earth

Lower Depths, The
also called: **11** At the Bottom **14** A Night's Lodging
author: **10** Maxim Gorky

lower in rank 4 bust **6** demote **7** degrade

lower in spirits 6 deject, sadden **7** depress **8** dispirit **10** dishearten

low-key 4 soft **5** loose, muted **6** gentle, subtle **7** muffled, relaxed, subdued **8** laid-back, softened, soft-sell **9** modulated, toned-down **10** low-pitched, restrained **11** low- pressure, understated, unobtrusive **14** unostentatious

lowliness 8 baseness **9** obscurity **10** humbleness

lowly 3 low **6** humble, modest, simple, softly **7** ignoble, low born, lowbred, obscure **8** baseborn, plebeian **10** unassuming **11** proletarian **13** unpretentious

low-minded 4 lewd, vile **5** crude, gross **6** coarse, smutty, vulgar **7** obscene, uncouth **9** obnoxious, offensive **11** disgraceful **12** contemptible

low point, lowest point 4 base, foot, zero **5** depth, nadir, worst **6** bottom **7** perigee **10** rock bottom

low-priced 5 cheap, token **6** budget,

modest **7** bargain, cut-rate, low-cost, nominal, reduced **8** closeout, moderate **9** dirt-cheap **10** discounted, economical, marked-down, reasonable **11** inexpensive **15** bargain-basement

low-ranking 5 minor, petty **11** subordinate, unimportant

low-spirited 3 low, sad **4** blue, down, glum **6** gloomy, morose, woeful **7** doleful, forlorn, unhappy **8** dejected, desolate, downcast **9** depressed, heart sore, sorrowful, woebegone **10** despondent, dispirited, melancholy **11** crestfallen, discouraged, downhearted **12** disconsolate, disheartened **14** down-in-the-mouth

low spirits 4 funk **5** gloom **6** dismay, sorrow **7** despair **8** dejected **9** pessimism **10** depression, desolation, melancholy, moroseness **11** despondency **12** hopelessness **14** discouragement **15** downheartedness

Loy, Myrna
real name: **13** Myrna Williams
co-star: **13** William Powell
born: **13** Raidersburg MT
roles: **10** The Thin Man **11** Nora Charles **17** Cheaper by the Dozen **22** The Best Years of Our Lives

loyal 4 firm, true **6** trusty **7** devoted, dutiful, staunch **8** constant, faithful, reliable, resolute, true-blue **9** steadfast **10** dependable, scrupulous, unswerving, unwavering **11** trustworthy **12** tried and true

loyalist 4 tory **12** conservative

Loyalties
author: **14** John Galsworthy

loyalty 6 fealty **8** devotion, fidelity, firmness **9** adherence, constancy **10** allegiance **11** reliability, staunchness **12** faithfulness **13** dependability, steadfastness **15** trustworthiness

lozenge 4 drop, pill **6** tablet, troche **8** pastille **9** cough drop

Luanda
capital of: **6** Angola

Lubitsch, Ernst
director of: **9** Ninotchka **13** Heaven Can Wait, To Be or Not To Be

Lucas, Charlotte
character in: **17** Pride and Prejudice
author: **6** Austen

Lucas, George
director of: **8** Star Wars **16** American Graffiti

Lucentio
character in: **19** The Taming of the Shrew
author: **11** Shakespeare

Lucerne
German: **6** Luzern
river: **5** Reuss
landmark: **9** Hofkirche **11** Am Rhyn House **15** Mariahilf Church

Lucia di Lammermoor

opera by: 9 Donizetti
based on novel by: 14 Sir Walter Scott
   called: 20 The Bride of Lammermoor

Luciana
  character in: 17 The Comedy of Errors
  author: 11 Shakespeare

Luciani, Albino 13 Pope John Paul I **20** Pope John Paul the First

lucid 5 clear **6** bright, direct, normal **7** certain, precise, radiant, shining **8** accurate, apposite, dazzling, luminous, lustrous, pellucid, positive, rational, specific **9** brilliant, sparkling **10** articulate, perceptive, responsive, to the point **11** clearheaded, crystalline, illuminated, resplendent, transparent **12** crystal clear, intelligible **13** clear thinking, scintillating, well-organized **14** comprehensible, understandable **15** straightforward

Lucifer
  means: 5 Satan **11** fallen angel, light bearer **13** friction match

Lucina
  origin: 5 Roman
  goddess of: 10 childbirth
  corresponds to: 4 Juno **8** Ilithyia **10** Eileithyia

Lucio
  character in: 17 Measure for Measure
  author: 11 Shakespeare

luck 3 lot **4** fate **5** karma **6** chance, kismet **7** destiny, fortune, success, triumph, victory **8** accident, fortuity, good luck, Lady Luck **11** good fortune, piece of luck **12** happenstance
  god of: 12 Bonus Eventus

lucky 4 good **5** happy **6** in luck, timely **7** blessed, favored **9** favorable, fortunate, opportune, promising **10** auspicious, beneficial, felicitous, of good omen, propitious **12** providential

Lucky Jim
  author: 12 Kingsley Amis

lucky piece 4 tiki **5** charm **6** amulet, grigri **8** shamrock, talisman **10** lucky charm **11** rabbit's foot

lucrative 7 gainful **8** fruitful **10** beneficial, high-income, high-paying, profitable **11** moneymaking **12** remunerative

Lucretia
  husband: 26 Lucius Tarquinius Collatinus
  raped by: 16 Sextus Tarquinius
  death by: 7 suicide

Lucretius
  author of: 13 De rerum natura **19** On the nature of things

Lucullan 4 rich **6** lavish **7** gourmet **9** epicurean, luxurious

Lucy Show, The
  also: 9 Here's Lucy
  character: 9 Kim Carter **10** Lucy Carter **11** Craig Carter **12** Harry Conners, Vivian Bagley **13** Mary Jane Lewis, Sherman Bagley **14** Lucy Carmichael **15** Chris Carmichael, Harrison Cheever, Jerry Carmichael, Theodore J Mooney **18** Harrison Otis Carter
  cast: 9 Ralph Hart **10** Candy Moore, Dick Martin, Gale Gordon, Lucie Arnaz, Roy Roberts **11** Desi Arnaz Jr, Lucille Ball, Vivian Vance **12** Jimmy Garrett **13** Mary Jane Croft

ludicrous 4 wild **5** comic, crazy, funny **6** absurd, far-out **7** amusing, comical **8** farcical **9** laughable **10** outlandish, ridiculous **11** nonsensical **12** preposterous

Ludlum, Robert
  author of: 15 The Matlock Paper **17** The Bourne Identity, The Parsifal Mosaic, The Road to Gandolfo **18** The Osterman Weekend **19** The Gemini Contenders **20** The Rhinemann Exchange **23** The Chancellor Manuscript, The Scarlatti Inheritance

Luftwaffe 9 air weapon **18** German Nazi air force

lug 3 tow, tug **4** bear, drag, draw, haul, pull, tote **5** carry, heave **9** transport

luggage 4 bags, gear **6** trunks **7** baggage, effects, valises **9** suitcases **13** accouterments

Luggnagg
  fictional land in: 16 Gulliver's Travels
  author: 5 Swift

Lugnasad
  origin: 5 Irish
  feast date: 11 August first

Lugosi, Bela
  real name: 10 Bela Blasko
  born: 5 Lugos **7** Hungary
  roles: 7 Dracula **21** Murders in the Rue Morgue

lugubrious 4 dour, glum **6** gloomy, morose, rueful, somber, woeful **7** doleful, elegiac **8** dolorous, downcast, funereal, mournful **9** miserable, sorrowful, woebegone **10** depressing, melancholy

Luke
  birthplace: 7 Antioch
  companion: 4 Paul
  occupation: 9 physician
  wrote: 6 Gospel

lukewarm 4 cool, mild, warm **5** aloof, tepid **8** detached, uncaring **9** apathetic, temp- erate **11** halfhearted, indifferent, per- functory, unconcerned **12** uninterested **13** lackadaisical **14** unenthusiastic **15** body-temperature, room- temperature

lull 3 gap **4** calm, ease, halt, hush **5** break, pause, quell, quiet, still **6** hiatus, la- cuna, pacify, recess, soothe, subdue **7** assuage, caesura, compose, mollify, respite **8** breather, calmness **9** interlude **12** brief silence, interruption

Lully, Jean-Baptiste
  born: 5 Italy **8** Florence
  composer of: 4 Atys, Isis **6** Persee, Psyche, Roland, Thesee **7** Alceste, Phaeton **10** Le Sicilien, Proserpine **11** Bellerophon **13** Acis et Galatee, Amadis de Gaule, L'Amour medecin **14** Acis and Galatea, Armide et Renaud, Le mariage force **16** Cadmus et Hermione **17** Achille et Polyxene, Cadmus and Hermione **19** Achilles and Polyxene **20** Les Amants magnifiques **22** Le Bourgeois Gentilhomme, Monsieur de Pourceaugnac

lulu 3 pip **4** oner **5** dandy, doozy **8** Jim Dandy **9** allowance, humdinger, wonderful **10** remarkable

lumber 3 log **4** plod, wood **5** barge, clump, stamp **6** boards, planks, trudge, waddle **7** shamble, shuffle **8** flounder **9** fell trees

Lumber State
  nickname of: 5 Maine

Lumet, Sidney
  director of: 7 Network, Serpico **13** The Pawnbroker **14** Twelve Angry Men **15** Dog Day Afternoon **24** Long Day's Journey Into Night

luminary 3 VIP **5** light, wheel **6** bigwig **7** big shot, notable **8** somebody **9** celebrity, dignitary, personage **10** luminosity **11** illuminator

luminescent 5 aglow **7** glowing **8** gleaming, luminous **9** twinkling **10** flickering, glimmering, glistening, shimmering **11** fluorescent **14** phosphorescent

luminosity 4 glow **5** gleam, sheen, shine **6** luster **8** radiance **10** brightness, brilliance

luminous 6 bright **7** glowing, radiant, shining **8** lustrous **9** brilliant **10** irradiated **11** illuminated, luminescent **15** reflecting light

lump 3 gob, mix **4** bump, cake, clod, fuse, heap, hunk, knob, knot, mass, node, pile, pool **5** amass, batch, blend, bunch, chunk, clump, group, knurl, merge, tumor, unite **6** gather, growth, nodule **7** collect, combine, compile **8** assemble, swelling **9** aggregate **10** protrusion, tumescence **11** excrescence **12** protuberance

lumpish 4 dull, slow **5** bulky, dumpy, heavy, lumpy **6** clumsy **7** awkward **8** clod dish, ungainly, unwieldy **9** corpulent **10** cumbersome, overweight

Lumpkin, Tony
  character in: 18 She Stoops to Conquer
  author: 9 Goldsmith

lump together 4 fuse, pool **7** combine **10** amalgamate **11** consolidate, incorporate

Luna

personifies: 4 moon
Greek: 6 Selene

lunacy 5 folly, mania **6** idiocy **7** madness **8** dementia, insanity **9** absurdity, asininity, craziness, silliness, stupidity **10** imbecility, imprudence, insaneness **11** foolishness **13** foolhardiness, senselessness

lunatic 3 mad, nut **4** daft, loco **5** batty, crazy, loony, nutty, potty **6** cuckoo, in- sane, madman, maniac, screwy **7** bonkers, cracked, touched **8** crackers, demented, demo niac, deranged, maniacal, unhinged **9** psychotic, senseless **10** irrational, psychopath, reasonless, unbalanced **11** crazy person, mentally ill, not all there **12** crackbrained, insane person, psychopathic, round the bend **13** off one's rocker, of unsound mind, out of one's mind

lunch
French: 8 dejeuner

luncheonette 4 cafe **5** diner **7** beanery **8** snack bar **9** hash house, lunchroom **10** coffee shop **11** eating house **12** lunch counter, sandwich shop

lunchroom 4 cafe **5** diner, grill **8** snack bar **9** cafeteria **12** luncheonette

lunge 3 cut, jab **4** dash, dive, pass, rush, stab **5** hit at, lurch, swing, swipe **6** attack, charge, plunge, pounce, thrust **7** set upon **8** fall upon, strike at **9** make a pass

lunkhead 3 ass **4** dope, fool **5** booby, dunce, idiot, moron, ninny **6** dimwit, nitwit **7** fat head, halfwit **8** bonehead, dumb-dumb, imbecile, numskull **9** blockhead, lamebrain, numbskull **10** dunderhead, nincompoop **11** chowderhead

Lunt, Alfred
wife: 12 Lynn Fontanne
born: 11 Milwaukee WI
roles: 12 The Guardsman **13** The Ragged Edge

Lupercalia
origin: 5 Roman
event: 8 festival
honoring: 6 Faunus **8** Lupercus
to procure: 9 fertility

Lupercus
origin: 5 Roman
god of: 9 fertility
corresponds to: 3 Pan **6** Faunus

Lupino, Ida 7 actress **8** director
husband: 10 Howard Duff **12** Collier Young, Louis Hayward
born: 6 London **7** England
roles: 8 Devotion **10** The Hard Way **12** Junior Bonner, Women's Prison **13** Escape Me Never **15** Strange Intruder **17** On Dangerous Ground **18** The Light That Failed, While the City Sleeps

lurch 4 cant, keel, list, reel, roll, sway, tilt, toss **5** lunge, pitch, slant **6** ca-

reen, plunge, swerve, teeter, totter **7** incline, stagger, stumble

Lurch 6 butler
on: 15 The Addams Family

lure 4 bait, coax, trap **5** bribe, decoy, snare, tempt **6** allure, cajole, come-on, entice, induce, seduce **7** attract, beguile **8** cajolery, persuade **9** fascinate, tantalize **10** allurement, attraction, enticement, inducement, temptation **11** drawing card **12** blandishment

Lurelei *see* **7** Lorelei

lurid 4 gory, grim **5** eerie, fiery, vivid **6** bloody **7** carmine, flaming, ghastly, glaring, glowing, graphic, scarlet, shining **8** dramatic, rubicund, sanguine, shocking **9** appalling, bright-red **11** sensational **12** melodramatic **13** bloodcurdling

lurk 4 hide **5** prowl, skulk, slink, sneak **9** lie in wait

Lusaka
capital of: 6 Zambia

luscious 5 tasty **6** savory **7** scented **8** aromatic, fragrant, perfumed **9** delicious, flavorful, succulent, toothsome **10** appetizing, delectable **13** mouthwatering

lush 4 posh, rich **5** dense, fancy, grand **6** ornate **7** elegant, profuse **8** abundant, pro lific, splendid **9** elaborate, luxuriant, lux- urious, sumptuous **11** flourishing, magnificent

lust 5 covet, crave **6** be lewd **7** craving, lechery, passion **8** lewdness **9** carnality, hunger for, sexuality **10** satyriasis **14** lasciviousness, libidinousness

lust after 4 want **5** covet, crave **6** desire **11** have a yen for, have an eye on, hunger after, thirst after

luster 4 fame, glow **5** gleam, glory, gloss, honor, merit, sheen, shine **6** dazzle, burnish, glimmer, glitter, sparkle **8** prestige, radiance **9** radiation **10** brightness, brilliance, luminosity, notability, refulgence **11** distinction **12** luminousness, resplendence **15** illustriousness

lusterless 3 dim, wan **4** dead, drab, dull, flat **5** faded, matte, muted **7** prosaic **9** colorless, tarnished

Lust for Life
author: 11 Irving Stone
director: 16 Vincente Minnelli
based on story by: 11 Irving Stone
cast: 11 James Donald, Kirk Douglas (Vincent Van Gogh), Pamela Brown **12** Anthony Quinn (Gaugin)
Oscar for: 15 supporting actor (Quinn)

lustful 4 lewd **6** carnal **8** prurient **9** lecherous, salacious **10** lascivious, libidinous

lustrous 6 bright, glossy **7** glowing, radiant, shining **8** dazzling, gleaming,

luminous, polished **9** burnished, effulgent **10** glistening **11** coruscating, illuminated **12** incandescent

lusty 4 hale **5** husky, sound **6** brawny, hearty, robust, rugged, sturdy, virile **7** healthy **8** vigorous **9** exuberant, strapping **10** full of life **11** uninhibited **12** unrestrained, wholehearted **13** irrepressible

Lutetia
Latin: 5 Paris

Luther, Martin
born: 7 Germany **8** Eisleben
author: 16 Ninety-Five Theses **27** On the Freedom of a Christian Man **46** Address to the German Nobility of the German Nation **51** A Prelude Concerning the Babylonian Captivity of the Church
excommunicated by: 8 Pope Leo X **15** Pope Leo the Tenth
summoned before: 11 Diet of Worms
founded: 11 Lutheranism, Reformation **13** Protestantism

lux 5 light

Luxembourg
other name: 9 Luxemburg **13** Lucilinburhuc
name means: 10 little fort
capital/largest city: 10 Luxembourg
others: 4 Hamm **5** Roodt, Wiltz **6** Mersch, Remich **7** Kopstal, Lintgen, Petange, Redange, Vianden **8** Capellen, Clervaux, Diekirch, Frisange **9** Dudelange **10** Echternach, Ettelbruck, Hesperange, Larochette **11** Differdange, Wormeldange **12** Grevenmacher, Troisvierges, Wasserbillig **14** Esch-sur-Alzette
division: 6 Esleck **7** Bon Pays, Gutland, Oesling
measure: 5 fuder
monetary unit: 5 franc **7** centime
lake: 8 Haut Sure
mountain: 8 Ardennes
highest point: 8 Huldange **9** Burgplatz **11** Wemperhardt
river: 3 Our **4** Sure, Syre **5** Alert, Clerf, Eisch, Mosel, Sauer, Wiltz **6** Chiers **7** Alzette, Moselle **8** Petrusse **11** Ernz Blanche
physical feature:
   plateau: 4 Bock **8** Ardennes, Lorraine
   valley: 7 Moselle
people: 6 French, German **12** Luxembourger
   ruler: 8 Sigefroi, Wencelas **12** Jean l'Aveugle **21** House of Nassau-Weilburg
   saint: 10 Willibrord
language: 6 French, German **7** English **13** Letzeburgesch
religion: 13 Roman Catholic
food:
   pastry: 20 les pensees brouillees

luxuriant 4 lush, rank **5** dense, fancy, grand **6** florid, ornate **7** elegant, flowery, profuse, teeming **8** abundant, splendid **9** elaborate, exuberant, luxurious, overgrown, sumptuous **10** flamboyant **11** extravagant, flourishing, magnificent

luxuriate 4 bask **6** relish **7** delight **8** wallow in **9** indulge in

luxurious 4 rich **5** grand **6** costly, effete **7** elegant, wealthy **8** decadent, pampered **9** enjoyable, expensive, indulgent, sumptuous **10** gratifying **11** comfortable, pleasurable

luxuriousness 4 ease **6** luxury **7** comfort **8** richness **10** costliness **13** sumptuousness

luxury 5 bliss **6** heaven, riches, wealth **7** delight **8** paradise, pleasure **9** enjoyment **10** high living, indulgence **12** extravagance, nonessential, nonnecessity, satisfaction **13** gratification

LXX *see* **15** Septuagint

Lycaon
 king of: 7 Arcadia
 father: 8 Pelasgus
 son: 8 Maenalus, Tegeates
 tested: 4 Zeus
 turned into: 4 wolf

Lycidas
 author: 10 John Milton
 elegy for: 10 Edward King

Lycus
 king of: 6 Thebes **7** Cilicia

father: 7 Pandion **9** Chthonius
mother: 5 Pylia
brother: 7 Nycteus
wife: 5 Dirce
niece: 7 Antiope
son: 5 Lycus
succeeded: 8 Sarpedon
killed by: 6 Zethus **7** Amphion **12** Antiope's sons

Lydia
 kingdom in: 9 Asia Minor
 king: 7 Croesus
 queen: 7 Omphale
 capital: 6 Sardis
 conquered by: 8 Persians

lying down 5 in bed, prone **6** supine **7** napping, resting **8** snoozing **9** reclining, recumbent **10** taking a nap **13** taking a snooze

Lyle, Albert Walter
 nickname: 6 Sparky
 sport: 8 baseball
 position: 7 pitcher
 team: 12 Boston Red Sox **14** New York Yankees
 author of: 11 The Bronx Zoo

Lyly, John
 author of: 20 Euphues and His England **22** Euphues the Anatomy of Wit

lynch 4 hang **6** gibbet **8** string up

Lynde, Paul

born: 13 Mount Vernon OH
roles: 12 Bye Bye Birdie **16** Hollywood Squares **17** Beach Blanket Bingo **18** Under the Yum-Yum Tree

lynx 3 cat **6** bobcat **7** wildcat

Lyonnesse
 place: 12 near Cornwall **16** Arthurian romance
 birthplace of: 8 Tristram
 fate: 11 sunk into sea

Lyre
 constellation of: 4 Harp, Lyra
 star: 4 Vega

lyric, lyrical 6 poetic **7** lilting, melodic, musical, singing, tuneful **8** songlike **9** melodious **10** euphonious **11** mellifluent, mellifluous **13** sweetsounding

Lyrical Ballads
 author: 17 William Wordsworth **21** Samuel Taylor Coleridge

lyrics 4 poem **5** words

Lysander
 character in: 21 A Midsummer Night's Dream
 author: 11 Shakespeare

Lysistrata
 author: 12 Aristophanes
 character: 7 Lampito **8** Cinesias, Cleonice, Myrrhine **10** Magistrate **14** Old Men of Athens (Chorus)

M
   director: 9 Fritz Lang
   cast: 10 Peter Lorre **11** Inge Landgut
   12 Ellen Widmann **15** Gustav Grundgens
   setting: 6 Berlin
Mabinogian
   origin: 5 Welsh
   tales of: 7 romance
macabre 4 grim **5** eerie, weird **6** grisly, horrid **7** ghastly, ghostly **8** dreadful, gruesome, horrible, horrific **9** frightful, ghostlike, unearthly **11** frightening
Macao
   other name: 5 Ao-men, Macau
   territory of: 8 Portugal
   monetary unit: 3 avo **6** pataca, pataco
   island: 5 Taipa **7** Coloane
   highest point: 5 Hag-Sa
   river: 5 Pearl **6** Canton
   sea: 10 South China
   people: 7 Chinese, Macaoan **10** Portuguese
   language: 7 Chinese, English **9** Cantonese **10** Portuguese
   religion: 6 Taoism **8** Buddhism **13** Roman Catholic
   place:
      street: 11 Praia Grande
   feature:
      houseboat: 6 sampan
Macareus
   father: 6 Aeolus
   mother: 7 Encrete
   sister: 6 Canace
MacArthur, Douglas
   served in: 3 WWI **4** WWII **9** Korean War, World War I **10** World War II **11** World War One, World War Two
   commander of: 15 Rainbow (42nd) Division **19** United Nations forces **24** US Army forces in the Pacific
   rank: 15 five-star general **16** army chief of staff
   battle: 5 Luzon, Pusan **6** Inchon **9** New Guinea **11** Leyte Island, Philippines **14** Bismark Islands, Solomon Islands **15** Bataan Peninsula **16** Admiralty Islands, Corregidor Island
   accepted surrender of: 5 Japan
      surrender occurred aboard: 8 Missouri
   chairman of: 13 Remington Rand
   author of: 13 Reminiscences

   smoked: 11 corncob pipe
   saying: 12 "I shall return"
Macbeth
   author: 18 William Shakespeare
   character: 6 Banquo, Duncan (King of Scotland) **7** MacDuff, Malcolm **11** Lady Macbeth **12** Three Witches
   title: 5 thane
   domain: 6 Glamis
   director: 13 Roman Polanski
   cast: 8 Jon Finch **10** Martin Shaw **13** Nicholas Selby **14** Francesca Annis
Maccabees
   title of: 5 Judas
   patriarch: 10 Mattathias
   means: 8 hammerer
   holiday: 8 Hanukkah
MacDonald, John D
   author of: 11 Condominium
   character: 11 Travis McGee
MacDonald, Ross
   real name: 13 Kenneth Millar
   author of: 8 The Chill **10** Black Money **13** The Blue Hammer **14** The Goodbye Look
   character: 9 Lew Archer
MacDowell, Edward Alexander
   born: 9 New York NY
   composer of: 9 Sea Pieces **11** To a Wild Rose **13** Fireside Tales **15** Poems after Heine **16** Hamlet and Ophelia, New England Idylls, Woodland Sketches **17** Idylls after Goethe
MacDuff
   character in: 7 Macbeth
   author: 11 Shakespeare
mace
   origin: 9 Indonesia
   from same tree as: 6 nutmeg
   tree: 17 Myristica fragrans
   use: 4 fish **7** seafood **9** cherry pie, pound cake **16** chicken fricassee
Macedonia
   capital/largest city: 6 Skopje
   head of state: 9 president
   government: 8 republic
   monetary unit: 5 denar
   river: 6 Struma, Vardar
   people: 4 Turk **9** Albanian **10** Macedonian
   language: 10 Macedonian
   religion: 27 Macedonian Orthodox Christian
macerate 4 fade, mash, pulp, soak **5** souse, steep **6** shrink, soften, squash, wither **7** decline, liquefy, shrivel

   8 dissolve, emaciate, fluidize, permeate, saturate **9** liquidize, waste away **10** lose weight
MacGraw, Ali
   real name: 12 Alice MacGraw
   husband: 8 Bob Evans **12** Steve McQueen
   born: 12 Pound Ridge NY
   roles: 7 Dynasty **9** Love Story **10** The Getaway **13** The Winds of War **15** Goodbye Columbus
Macheath, Captain
   character in: 12 Beggar's Opera
   author: 3 Gay
   see Threepenny Opera
ma chere 6 my dear
Machiavelli, Niccolo
   author of: 9 The Prince **11** The Art of War **16** Discourses on Livy
   home: 8 Florence
   The "Prince": 12 Cesare Borgia
Machiavellian 6 amoral, crafty **7** cunning, devious **8** scheming **9** deceitful, designing **10** perfidious **11** self-serving, treacherous, underhanded **12** falsehearted, unscrupulous
machination 4 plot, rule, ruse **5** dodge **6** design, device, scheme **8** artifice, intrigue, maneuver **9** stratagem **10** conspiracy **11** contrivance
machine 3 set **4** army, body, camp, club, gang, pool, ring **5** corps, crowd, force, group, setup, trust, union **6** device, system **7** combine, coterie, faction, society **9** apparatus, appliance, machinery, mechanism, structure **11** association **12** organization **13** establishment
machine gun
   invented by: 7 Gatling
   improved by: 5 Maxim **9** Hotchkiss
machinery 4 gear **5** setup, tools **6** agency, makeup, system, tackle, wheels **9** apparatus, mechanism, resources, structure **12** contrivances, organization
macho 5 he-man, manly **6** strong, virile
Machpelah
   location: 6 Hebron
   burial place of: 4 Leah **5** Isaac, Jacob, Sarah **7** Abraham, Rebekah
Machu Picchu 5 ruins
   of: 5 Incas
   in: 4 Peru

Macilente
  character in: 22 Every Man out of His Humour
  author: 6 Jonson

MacInnes, Helen
  author of: 13 North from Rome 14 Above Suspicion 16 Decision at Delphi 17 The Venetian Affair 21 The Salzburg Connection

macintosh, mackintosh 7 slicker 8 raincoat 10 waterproof

Mack, Connie
  real name: 30 Cornelius Alexander McGillicuddy
  sport: 8 baseball
  position: 7 manager
  team: 21 Philadelphia Athletics

MacKellar
  character in: 21 The Master of Ballantrae
  author: 9 Stevenson

mackerel
  young: 5 spike 6 tinker 7 blinker

mackinaw 4 coat 6 jacket 8 overcoat

Mack the Knife see 15 Three Penny Opera

MacLaine, Shirley
  real name: 19 Shirley MacLean Beaty
  brother: 12 Warren Beatty
  born: 10 Richmond VA
  roles: 6 Can Can 10 Being There 11 Irma La Douce 12 Sweet Charity, The Apartment 15 Some Came Running, The Turning Point, Two for the Seesaw 16 The Children's Hour 17 Terms of Endearment (Oscar) 19 The Trouble with Harry 20 The Bliss of Mrs Blossom

MacMurray, Fred
  wife: 9 June Haver
  born: 10 Kankakee IL
  roles: 11 My Three Sons 12 The Apartment 14 Above Suspicion, The Caine Mutiny 15 Double Indemnity 20 The Miracle of the Bells

macrocosm 6 cosmos, nature 7 heavens 8 creation, universe 9 firmament

mad 4 avid, daft, loco, nuts, wild 5 angry, balmy, crazy, irate, nutty 6 ardent, crazed, cuckoo, fuming, insane, miffed, screwy, ticked 7 cracked, enraged, excited, fanatic, furious, in a huff, lunatic, riled up, teed off, touched 8 crackers, demented, deranged, frenzied, incensed, maniacal, provoked, unhinged, up in arms, worked up, wrathful 9 devoted to, non compos, seeing red, ticked off, wrought up 10 distracted, distraught, infatuated, infuriated, in love with, irrational, unbalanced 11 boiling over, exasperated, impassioned, not all there 12 enthusiastic, round the bend 13 beside oneself, in high dudgeon, not quite right, off one's rocker, out of one's mind

Madagascar
  other name: 16 Malagasy Republic
  capital/largest city: 10 Tananarive 12 Antananarivo
  others: 6 Tulear 7 Majanga, Nossibe, Toliary 8 Manakara, Tamatave 9 Faradofay, Mananjory, Toamasina 10 Antsirabe 11 Antsiranana, Diego-Suarez, Fort Dauphin
  measure: 7 gantang
  monetary unit: 5 franc 7 centime
  island: 6 Barren, Radama 7 Nossi-Be 11 Sainte-Marie 12 Chesterfield
  lake: 5 Itasy 7 Alaotra, Kinkony
  mountain: 4 Boby 9 Ankaratra 12 High Plateaus, Tsiafajavona 17 Tsaratanana Massif
  highest point: 11 Maromokotro
  river: 5 Ikopa, Mania, Sofia 7 Mangoky, Mangoro, Onilahy 8 Ivoloina, Manambao, Mananara 9 Betsiboka, Manambolo 10 Manarandra 11 Tsiribihina
  ocean: 6 Indian
  physical feature:
    bay: 6 Radama 8 Antongil 9 Mahajamba 10 Sahamalaza
    cape: 5 Amber 10 Saint-Andre 11 Sainte-Marie 14 Saint-Sebestien
    channel: 10 Mozambique
    lagoon: 9 pangalane
    plateau: 9 Ankaizina
  people: 4 Arab, Bara, Hova 5 Malay 6 Merina, Tanala 7 African 8 Betsileo, Mahafaly, Malagasy, Sakalava 9 Antaimoro, Antaisaka, Antandroy, Tsimi-hety 10 Indonesian, Polynesian 13 Betsimisaraka
    dynasty: 6 Merina
    leader: 9 Ratsiraka, Tsiranana 11 Ranamantsoa
  language: 6 French 8 Malagasy, Malgache
  religion: 5 Islam 7 animism 10 Protestant 13 Roman Catholic
  place:
    market: 4 Zoma
    royal estate: 4 Rova
  feature:
    animal: 4 zebu 5 lemur 6 foussa
    musical instrument: 11 jego vaotavo
    proverb: 8 hainteny
    shawl: 5 lamba
  food:
    vegetable: 7 brettes

madam, madame 3 Mrs 4 dame, lady 6 matron 7 dowager 8 mistress
  German: 4 Frau
  Spanish: 6 senora
  Italian: 5 donna 7 signora
  Spanish/Portuguese: 4 dona

Madame Bovary
  author: 15 Gustave Flaubert
  character: 10 Emma Bovary, Leon Dupuis 13 Charles Bovary 17 Rodolphe Boulanger

Madame Butterfly

  also: 15 Madama Butterfly
  opera by: 7 Puccini
  character: 5 Bonze 6 Suzuki 9 Cho-Cho-San, Cio-Cio-San, Sharpless 14 Prince Yamadori 19 Lieutenant Pinkerton
  aria: 7 Un beldi

mad as a hatter 3 mad 4 daft, nuts 5 crazy, nutty 6 insane 7 cracked, touched 8 demented, deranged, unhinged 10 unbalanced 13 off one's rocker, out of one's head 14 off one's trolley 15 mad as a March hare 17 nutty as a fruitcake

mad as a March hare 3 mad 4 daft, nuts 5 crazy, nutty 6 insane 7 cracked, touched 8 demented, deranged, unhinged 10 unbalanced 12 mad as a hatter 13 out of one's head 14 off one's trolley 17 nutty as a fruitcake

madcap 4 rash, wild, zany 5 brash, clown, giddy, joker 6 unruly 7 erratic, flighty, foolish 8 reckless 9 hotheaded, impetuous, impulsive, senseless 10 incautious 11 impractical, thoughtless 12 unconsidered 13 inconsiderate, undisciplined

madden 3 vex 4 gall 5 anger, craze, pique, upset 6 enrage, frenzy 7 derange, incense, inflame, outrage, provoke, torment, unhinge 9 aggravate, infuriate, unbalance 10 exasperate

made 5 built 6 formed 7 created 8 composed, produced 9 assembled, developed 10 fabricated 11 constructed 12 manufactured

madeira
  type: 4 wine 6 brandy 7 liqueur 8 aperitif
  origin: 7 Madeira

Madeira Islands
  capital: 7 Funchal
  city: 5 Monte
  island: 6 Grande 7 Dezerte, Madeira 8 Desertas 9 Selvagens 10 Porto Santo
  ocean: 8 Atlantic
  owned by: 8 Portugal
  stone aqueduct: 7 levadas
  wine: 4 Bual 5 Tinta, Tinto 6 Canary, Gomera 7 Malmsey, Marsala, Sercial 8 Verdelho

made-up 5 false 7 assumed, created 8 fanciful, invented 9 fictional, imaginary, pretended, thought-up 10 fictitious 11 make-believe, theoretical 12 hypothetical

Mad Hatter
  character in: 28 Alice's Adventures in Wonderland
  author: 7 Carroll

madhouse 6 asylum, bedlam, uproar 7 turmoil 8 loony bin, nuthouse

Madison, James
  nickname: 23 Father of the Constitution

presidential rank: **6** fourth
party: **20** Democratic-Republican
state represented: **2** VA
defeated: **7** (DeWitt) Clinton **8**
(Charles Cotesworth) Pinckney
vice president: **5** (Elbridge) Gerry **7**
(George) Clinton
cabinet:
  state: **5** (Robert) Smith **6** (James)
  Monroe
  treasury: **6** (Alexander James) Dallas **8** (Abraham Alfonse Albert)
  Gallatin, (George Washington)
  Campbell, (William Harris) Crawford
  war: **6** (James) Monroe, (William)
  Eustis **8** (William Harris) Crawford
  9 (John) Armstrong
  attorney general: **4** (Richard) Rush
  6 (Caesar Augustus) Rodney **7**
  (William) Pinkney
  navy: **5** (William) Jones **8** (Paul)
  Hamilton **13** (Benjamin Williams)
  Crowninshield
born: **12** Port Conway VA **16** King
George County
died/buried: **2** VA **12** Orange County
16 Montpelier estate
education:
  tutored at home by: **15** Rev
  Thomas Martin
  school: **15** Donald Robertson
  college of: **9** New Jersey (now
  Princeton University)
religion: **12** Episcopalian
interests: **3** law **11** agriculture **14**
natural history
author: **16** Federalist Papers (with
Hamilton and Jay) **24** Memorial and
Remonstrances **29** Journal of the
Federal Convention
political career: **24** US House of Representatives **25** Second Continental
Congress
  secretary of: **5** state
  signed: **12** Constitution
civilian career: **6** farmer **7** planter
military service:
  colonel of: **19** Orange County militia
notable events of lifetime/term: **19**
War of Eighteen Twelve
  battle of: **10** New Orleans
  treaty of: **5** Ghent
  Washington DC burned by: **7** British
father: **5** James
mother: **7** Eleanor (Rose Conway)
siblings: **5** Sarah **6** Reuben **7** Ambrose, Catlett, Francis, William **9**
Elizabeth **11** Nelly Conway **13** Frances Taylor
wife: **8** Dorothea (Payne Todd)
  nickname: **6** Dolley
first lady:
  saved: **11** state papers **25** George
  Washington's portrait
madman **3** nut **5** loony **6** maniac

7 lunatic **8** demoniac **9** psychotic **10**
psychopath
Mad Max
director: **12** George Miller
cast: **9** Mel Gibson
sequel: **14** The Road Warrior **17** Beyond Thunderdome (with Tina
Turner)
madness **6** lunacy, oddity **8** delusion,
dementia, illusion, insanity **9** craziness **11** derangement
Madonna
nickname: **15** The Material Girl
husband: **8** Sean Penn
recordings: **7** Madonna **8** True Blue
11 Like A Prayer, Like A Virgin
films: **9** Dick Tracy **11** Truth or Dare
12 Who's That Girl **14** Body of Evidence **16** Shanghai Surprise **17** A
League of Their Own **23** Desperately
Seeking Susan
tour: **6** Girlie **13** Blond Ambition
books: **3** Sex
Madrid
area: **9** Salamanca **19** Ciudad Univer-
sitaria
capital of: **5** Spain
landmark: **14** National Palace **18** Bi-
blioteca Nacional
  bull ring: **22** Plaza de Toros Monumental
  museum: **5** Prado
mountain: **18** Sierra de Guadaramma
river: **10** Manzanares
square: **10** Plaza Mayor **11** Plaza del
Sol **13** Plaza de Espana
street: **13** Paseo del Prado
Madwoman of Chaillot
author: **13** Jean Giraudoux
maelstrom **4** eddy **5** shoot, swirl **6**
bedlam, rapids, tumult, uproar, vortex
7 riptide, torrent **8** disorder, madhouse, undertow, upheaval **9** confusion, whirlpool **10** white water **11**
pandemonium
location: **6** Norway
maenad, menad **5** lenae **7** bacchae,
bassara **8** clodones, thyiades **9** bacchante **10** mimallones
companion of: **7** Bacchus **8** Dionysus
Maeterlinck, Maurice
author of: **8** The Blind **11** The Blue
Bird, The Intruder **19** Pelleas and
Melisande
ma foi **6** my word, really **7** my faith
magazine **6** weekly **7** arsenal, journal,
monthly **9** quarterly **10** periodical,
powder room **13** military depot,
munitions room
Magdalene see **4** Mary
magenta **6** maroon **7** carmine, crimson, fuchsia **9** vermilion **12** purplish
rose **13** reddish purple
Maggie: A Girl of the Streets
author: **12** Stephen Crane
maggot **4** grub, worm **5** larva **8** meal-
worm

Magi
also called: **7** wise men **11** astrolo-
gers
followed: **15** Star of Bethlehem
visited: **5** Jesus
gifts: **4** gold **5** myrrh **12** frankincense
singular: **5** magus
magic **4** lure **5** charm, spell **6** hoodoo,
voodoo **7** sorcery **8** charisma, jugglery, witchery, wizardry **9** occultism,
voodooism **10** allurement, black
magic, demonology, divination, hocus-
pocus, witchcraft **11** captivation, conjuration, enchantment, fascination,
legerdemain, the black art **12** en-
trancement **13** sleight of hand **16**
prestidigitation
god of: **5** Thoth
Magic
nickname of: **13** Earvin Johnson
Magic Flute, The
also: **14** Die Zauberflote
opera: **6** Mozart
character: **6** Pamina, Tamino **8** Papa-
gena, Papageno, Sarastro **10**
Monostatos **12** Queen of Night
magician **5** magus **6** shaman, wizard
7 juggler, warlock **8** conjurer, sorcerer
9 alchemist **11** illusionist, medicine
man, necromancer, witch doctor **12**
escape artist **15** prestidigitator
Magic Mountain, The
author: **10** Thomas Mann
character: **6** Naphta **7** Clavdia **11**
Hans Castorp, Settembrini **15** Joa-
chim Ziemssen
magisterial **9** imperious **10** autocratic,
peremptory **11** dictatorial, domineering, overbearing **13** condescending
**Magister Ludi: The Glass Bead
Game**
author: **12** Hermann Hesse
magistrate **2** JP **5** judge **7** prefect **17**
justice of the peace
Magna Carta **7** charter
forced by: **6** barons
upon: **8** King John
at: **9** Runnymede
guaranteeing: **14** civil liberties
magna cum laude **15** with great
praise
Magna Graecia **27** ancient Greek colonies in Italy
Magna Mater **3** Ops **4** Rhea **6** Cybele
Magnani, Anna
nickname: **10** Nannerella
roles: **8** Open City **13** The Rose Tattoo (Oscar) **15** The Fugitive Kind **21**
Secret of Santa Vittoria
magnanimous **7** liberal **8** generous,
princely **9** forgiving, unselfish **10** altruistic, beneficent, charitable **12**
largehearted **13** philanthropic
magnate **3** VIP **5** giant, mogul, nabob
6 big gun, bigwig, leader, tycoon **7**
big shot, notable **8** big wheel, great

man **9** celebrity **13** empire builder, industrialist

magnesium
chemical symbol: **2** Mg

magnetic 8 alluring, charming, inviting **9** of a magnet, seductive **10** attractive, enchanting, entrancing, persuasive **11** captivating, charismatic, fascinating **12** irresistible

magnetism 4 lure **5** charm **6** allure **8** charisma **9** mesmerism, seduction **10** allurement, attraction, enticement **11** captivation, enchantment, fascination

magnification 5 honor **7** worship **9** adoration, blowing up, expansion, inflation, reverence **11** acclamation, enlargement, idolization **12** exaggeration **13** amplification, glorification, overstatement

magnificence 4 pomp **5** glory, state **6** luxury **7** glitter, majesty, royalty **8** grandeur, richness, splendor **10** brilliance **13** sumptuousness

magnificent 4 fine **5** grand, noble **6** august, superb **7** elegant, exalted, stately, sublime **8** glorious, imposing, majestic, splendid **9** brilliant, exquisite, wonderful **10** commanding, impressive **11** resplendent **12** transcendent **13** extraordinary

Magnificent Ambersons, The
director: **11** Orson Welles
based on novel by: **15** Booth Tarkington
cast: **7** Tim Holt **10** Anne Baxter **12** Joseph Cotten **14** Agnes Moorehead **15** Dolores Costello

Magnificent Obsession, The
author: **13** Lloyd C Douglas

Magnificent Seven, The
director: **11** John Sturges
cast: **10** Brad Dexter, Eli Wallach, Yul Brynner **11** James Coburn **12** Robert Vaughn, Steve McQueen **13** Horst Buchholz **14** Charles Bronson
setting: **6** Mexico
score: **14** Elmer Bernstein
remake of: **12** Seven Samurai
sequel: **16** Return of the Seven **20** Magnificent Seven Ride

magnify 4 laud **5** adore, boost, exalt, extol **6** blow up, double, expand, praise, puff up, revere **7** acclaim, amplify, enlarge, glorify, greaten, inflate, stretch, worship **8** heighten, maximize, overrate **9** embroider, overstate, reverence **10** exaggerate

magniloquence 7 bombast, fustian **8** euphuism, tumidity **9** pomposity, turgidity **10** orotundity **11** fanfaronade, grandiosity **14** grandiloquence **15** pretentiousness

magniloquent 5 tumid, windy, wordy **6** turgid **7** pompous, verbose **8** inflated **9** bombastic **13** grandiloquent

magnitude 4 bulk, fame, mass, size **6** extent, renown, repute, volume **7** big-ness, expanse, measure **8** eminence, enormity, hugeness, vastness

magnolia
varieties: **4** ashe, star **6** saucer **7** Chinese **8** southern, umbrella **11** great-leaved

Magnum, P. I.
character: **2** TC **4** Rick **7** Higgins **12** Thomas Magnum
cast: **10** Tom Selleck **12** Roger E Mosley **13** John Hillerman
setting: **6** Hawaii

Magog
father: **7** Japheth

Magritte, Rene Francois Ghislain
born: **7** Belgium **8** Lessines
artwork: **14** La Belle Captive, The False Mirror, The Key of Dreams **15** Memory of a Voyage **18** L'Empire des Lumieres (The Empire of Light), The Menaced Assassin

Magua
character in: **20** The Last of the Mohicans
author: **6** Cooper

Magus see **4** Magi

Magwitch, Abel
character in: **17** Great Expectations
author: **7** Dickens

Magyar 9 Hungarian

Mahican see **7** Mohican

mah-jongg 4 game
origin: **7** Chinese
play piece: **4** tile
suit: **3** bam, dot **5** crack, winds
dragon: **3** red **5** white
term: **4** kong, pung **6** flower

Mahler, Gustav
born: **7** Austria, Bohemia
composer of: **12** Resurrection (symphony No 2) **15** Das Klagenlied **16** Songs of a Wayfarer **17** Das Lied von der Erde, Kindertotenlieder, The Song of the Earth **19** Des Knaben Wunderhorn **28** Lieder eines fahrenden Gesellen

mahogany 4 tree, wood **5** brown **8** hardwood **9** Swietenia **12** reddish-brown
varieties: **3** red **5** swamp, white **7** African, big-leaf, Florida, Senegal, Spanish **8** Honduras, mountain **9** Nyasaland, Venezulan **10** West Indian

Mahon, Christopher
character in: **27** The Playboy of the Western World
author: **5** Synge

mahzor, machzor 16 Jewish prayer book

Maia
member of: **8** Pleiades
place in group: **6** eldest
father: **5** Atlas
mother: **7** Pleione
son: **6** Hermes

maid 6 tweeny **7** servant **8** domestic **9** hired girl, housemaid, lady's maid, nursemaid **10** parlor maid **11** maidservant **12** upstairs maid **13** female servant
French: **6** au pair

maiden, maidenly 4 girl, lass, maid, miss **5** chick, first **6** chaste, damsel, lassie, virgin **7** colleen, girlish, ingenue, initial, untried **8** original, virginal, youthful **9** inaugural, soubrette, unmarried **10** demoiselle, initiatory **12** introductory

Maid Marian
beloved of: **9** Robin Hood

maidservant 4 amah, ayah, char, lass, maid **5** bonne **6** au pair, tweeny **7** abigail **8** charlady, domestic **9** hired girl, lady's maid, tirewoman **10** handmaiden, parlormaid

Maidu
language family: **8** Penutian
location: **10** California
noted for: **8** basketry

mail 4 arms, post **5** armor **6** get out **7** airmail, harness, letters, panoply **8** dispatch, packages **9** postcards **10** send by mail, send by post, suit of mail **11** surface mail **12** mail delivery, put in the mail **13** postal service **14** defensive armor, drop in a mailbox **17** post-office service

Mailer, Norman
author of: **15** An American Dream **16** Armies of the Night **18** The Naked and the Dead **19** The Executioner's Song

Maillol, Aristide
born: **6** France **13** Banyuls-sur-mer
artwork: **5** Night, Torso **7** Le Desir (Desire) **11** Ile de France **12** Young Cyclist **14** Action in Chains, The Three Nymphs **16** The Mediterranean (Seated Woman) **17** Monument to Cezanne, Monument to Debussy **18** Venus with a Necklace

maim 3 cut, rip **4** gash, lame, maul, rend, tear **5** slash, wound **6** deface, hobble, injure, mangle, savage **7** cripple, disable **8** lacerate, mutilate **9** disfigure, dismember, hamstring **12** incapacitate

main 4 head **5** chief, prime, vital **6** urgent **7** capital, central, crucial, leading, primary, special, supreme **8** critical, foremost, pressing **9** essential, important, necessary, paramount, principal, requisite **10** particular, preeminent **11** outstanding, predominant **13** consequential, indispensable

Main, Marjorie
real name: **13** Mary Tomlinson
partner: **12** Wallace Beery **13** Percy Kilbride
born: **7** Acton IN
roles: **7** Dead End **8** Ma Kettle

Maine

abbreviation: 2 ME
nickname: 6 Lumber **8** Pine Tree **10** Wonderland
capital: 7 Augusta
largest city: 8 Portland
others: 4 Bath, Saco **5** Hiram, Orono **6** Auburn, Bangor **7** Kittery **8** Boothbay, Lewiston, Ogunquit **9** Bar Harbor, Biddeford, Brunswick, Skowhegan **10** Waterville **11** Millinocket, Presque Isle
college: 5 Bates, Colby **7** Bowdoin
explorer: 6 Cabots **8** Norsemen
feature: 8 lobsters **19** West Quoddy Headlight
  beach: 10 Old Orchard
  national park: 6 Acadia
  waterway: 18 Allagash Wilderness
tribe: 6 Abnaki **7** Wewenoc
people: 10 downeaster **11** Dorothea Dix **19** Edna St Vincent Millay **24** Henry Wadsworth Longfellow
island: 4 Orrs **8** Mt Desert **10** Campobello
lake: 5 Sebec, Wyman **6** Sebago **8** Rangeley, Schoodic **9** Flagstaff, Moosehead **10** Chesuncook
land rank: 11 thirty-ninth
mountain: 5 Kineo, White **7** Bigelow **8** Cadillac
  highest point: 8 Katahdin
physical feature:
  bay: 5 Casco **9** Penobscot **12** Merrymeeting **13** Passamaquoddy
  sand dunes: 13 Desert of Maine
river: 4 Saco **6** St John **7** St Croix **8** Allagash, Kennebec **9** Aroostook, Kennebago, Penobscot **12** Androscoggin
state admission: 11 twenty-third
state bird: 9 chickadee
state fish: 16 land-locked salmon
state flower: 7 thistle **8** pine cone **22** white pine cone and tassel
state motto: 7 I Direct
state song: 16 State of Maine Song
state tree: 16 eastern white pine
mainly 6 mostly **7** chiefly **8** above all **9** in the main, most of all, primarily **10** on the whole **11** principally **12** predominantly **14** for the most part, in great measure **16** first and foremost
main point 3 nut **4** core, crux, gist, meat **5** basis, heart, theme **6** kernel **7** essence **10** brass tacks **11** nitty-gritty **15** sum and substance
mainspring 5 agent, cause **6** motive **9** incentive **10** motivation
mainstay 4 prop **6** anchor, pillar **7** bulwark **8** backbone, buttress **16** pillar of strength
Main Street
  author: 13 Sinclair Lewis
  character: 14 Carol Kennicott **15** Dr Will Kennicott
maintain 4 aver, avow, hold, keep **5** claim, state, swear **6** affirm, allege, assert, defend, insist, keep up, uphold **7** care for, contend, declare, finance, profess, stand by, support, sustain **8** conserve, continue, preserve **9** keep alive, keep going **10** provide for, take care of
maintenance 4 keep **6** living, repair, upkeep **7** keeping, support **10** livelihood, protection, sustenance **11** safekeeping, subsistence, sustainment **12** conservation, preservation, safeguarding
maison de sante 10 sanitarium **13** house of health
maize 4 corn, milo **5** grain **6** cereal, silage, yellow **7** zea mays **10** Indian corn
majestic, majestical 5 grand, lofty, noble, regal, royal **6** august, famous, superb **7** elegant, eminent, stately, sublime **8** esteemed, glorious, imperial, imposing, princely, renowned, splendid **10** impressive **11** illustrious, magnificent **13** distinguished
majesty 4 pomp **5** glory **6** luster **7** dignity **8** elegance, eminence, grandeur, mobility, splendor **9** elevation, loftiness, solemnity, sublimity **10** augustness **11** distinction, stateliness **12** gloriousness, magnificence **14** impressiveness
major 4 main **5** chief, prime, vital **6** larger, urgent **7** capital, crucial, greater, leading, primary, ranking, serious, supreme **8** critical, foremost, pressing **9** essential, important, necessary, paramount, principal, requisite **10** preeminent **11** outstanding, predominant, significant **13** consequential, indispensable
Major Barbara
  director: 13 Gabriel Pascal
  based on play by: 17 George Bernard Shaw
  cast: 11 Deborah Kerr, Rex Harrison, Wendy Hiller **12** Robert Morley, Robert Newton **14** Sybil Thorndike
majority 4 bulk, mass **8** best part, legal age, maturity **9** adulthood, seniority, womanhood **10** lion's share **13** preponderance
major key (in music)
  German: 3 dur
Major prophets *see* **8** prophets
majuscule 7 capital **11** large letter **13** capital letter **15** upper-case letter
make 3 fix **4** form, kind, mark, meet, pass **5** beget, brand, build, catch, cause, enact, erect, force, frame, impel, press, reach, shape, speak, utter **6** attain, compel, create, devise, draw up, effect, foment, makeup, oblige, render **7** appoint, compose, deliver, dragoon, fashion, produce, require **8** arrive at, assemble, engender **9** cause to be, constrain, construct, establish, fabricate, formation, legislate, pronounce, structure **10** bring about,

fashioning **11** composition, manufacture
make a bet 3 bet **4** risk **5** stake, wager **6** chance, gamble, hazard, plunge **7** venture
make a clean breast of 7 confess, lay bare, own up to **8** blurt out **14** come clean about
make a dash 3 fly, run **4** flee **6** escape **7** get away **8** make a run **10** make a break, take flight **12** make a getaway
make a deal 5 agree **6** settle **10** compromise **11** come to terms, meet halfway **14** strike a bargain
make advances 8 approach, come on to, sound out **11** proposition **13** make overtures, put the moves on
make a fuss over 6 dote on **7** protest **8** crow over
make again 4 copy **6** remake, repeat **9** duplicate **11** reconstruct
make a getaway 4 bolt, flee, skip **6** escape **7** get away, make off, run away **8** make a run, slip away **9** break free, cut and run, make a dash **10** break loose, fly the coop, take flight
make a gift of 4 give **6** donate **7** present **8** bequeath **10** contribute
make allowance for 6 excuse, pardon **7** forgive, indulge **8** bear with, pass over
make amends 5 atone **6** make up, square **7** expiate **9** do penance **10** compensate
make a mess of 3 mar **4** goof, muff, ruin **5** botch, spoil **6** bungle, foul up, mess up **7** butcher, do badly, louse up, screw up **9** mismanage
make a mistake 3 err **4** goof **6** mess up, slip up **12** miscalculate
make an effort 3 try **5** essay **6** strive, work at **7** attempt **8** endeavor
make appear 5 evoke **6** elicit **7** produce **9** conjure up **10** bring forth
make a racket 3 cry **4** howl, yell **5** shout **6** bellow, clamor, holler, scream **7** bluster **8** make a din **10** vociferate **12** raise a rumpus
make a stab at 3 try **5** essay, guess **6** reckon, take on **7** attempt, surmise, venture **8** estimate, give a try **9** undertake **10** conjecture **11** approximate **12** take a crack at, take a fling at
make a stand 9 stand fast **13** refuse to yield **17** fight to the last man
make a statement 6 remark **7** clarify, comment, discuss, explain, expound **9** elucidate, talk about
make aware 4 tell **5** edify **6** advise, inform, notify, reveal **7** apprise **8** acquaint, disclose **9** divulge to, enlighten, introduce **11** familiarize **16** bring to (one's) attention
make away with 3 eat **4** kill, take

5 spend, steal **6** kidnap, murder **7** abolish, consume, destroy **8** carry off, embezzle, get rid of **9** dissipate

make-believe 4 fake, sham **5** false, phony **6** made-up, make-up, unreal **7** assumed, charade, fantasy, feigned, fiction **8** creation, imagined, invented, pretense, spurious **9** fantastic, imaginary, invention, pretended, simulated **10** artificial, fictitious **11** counterfeit, fabrication **13** falsification

make certain of 6 assure, clinch, ensure **8** be sure of **10** make sure of

make damp 5 bedew **6** dampen **7** moisten **8** sprinkle

make dark 3 dim **6** darken **7** blacken, obscure

make different 4 vary **5** alter, amend **6** change, modify, mutate **7** convert, remodel **9** transform, transmute **12** metamorphose

make distinctive 8 set apart **9** single out **11** distinguish **12** characterize **13** differentiate

make easy 4 ease **6** smooth **7** explain, lighten **8** simplify **10** clear a path, facilitate

make eligible 5 allow **6** permit **7** entitle, qualify **9** authorize

make evident 4 show **5** prove **6** reveal **7** exhibit **8** manifest **9** establish, make clear, make plain **11** demonstrate

make fast 3 fix **4** moor **5** affix, tie up **6** attach, fasten, secure **7** connect

make feeble 6 weaken **7** wear out **8** enervate **10** debilitate, devitalize

make furious 5 anger **6** enrage, madden **7** incense, inflame **9** infuriate

make giddy 5 dizzy **12** make unsteady **15** make lightheaded

make good 5 repay **6** arrive, make it **7** fulfill, succeed **11** reach the top **15** make restitution

make happy 5 amuse, cheer, elate **6** please **7** delight, gratify **9** entertain

make haste slowly
Latin: **12** festina lente

make hostile 5 repel **6** offend **7** provoke **8** alienate **10** antagonize

make ill 5 repel **6** infect, revolt, sicken **7** afflict, disgust, repulse **8** disagree, distress, make sick, nauseate **9** discomfit **14** turn the stomach

make ill at ease 5 upset **6** rattle **7** fluster **8** distress **9** discomfit, embarrass **10** disconcert

make impure 4 foul, soil **5** dirty, spoil, taint **6** befoul, blight, defile, infect, poison **7** corrupt, pollute **10** adulterate **11** contaminate

make inroads 6 invade **7** impinge, intrude **8** encroach, infringe, trespass **9** penetrate

make known 4 tell **6** advise, impart,
inform, notify, report, reveal, unveil **7** apprise, divulge, lay bare, publish, uncover **8** disclose **9** broadcast **10** give notice, make public **11** communicate

make less forceful 6 soften, weaken **9** undermine **10** devitalize, emasculate

make light of 8 belittle, minimize, pooh-pooh, sneeze at **9** deprecate, disparage, underrate **10** depreciate, undervalue **13** underestimate

make merry 5 revel **7** carouse, roister **9** celebrate, have a ball **15** paint the town red

make much of 5 honor **6** praise **7** acclaim, applaud, commend, flatter **8** fuss over

make nervous 5 annoy, upset **7** agitate, disturb, perturb, trouble, unnerve **10** disconcert

make off with 4 lift **5** boost, steal, swipe **6** abduct, kidnap, snatch **7** bear off **8** carry off **10** run off with **11** get away with

make one's blood boil 5 anger **6** enrage, madden **7** incense, inflame **9** infuriate

make one's eyes pop 4 stun **5** amaze, shock **6** dazzle **7** stagger, startle **8** astonish **9** electrify **11** flabbergast

make out 3 see **4** espy **6** behold, descry, detect, fill in, notice **7** discern, observe, pick out **8** get along, perceive, write out **12** catch sight of

make plain 7 clarify, clear up, explain, lay open **9** elucidate, explicate, make clear **10** illuminate **11** disentangle, shed light on **12** bring to light

make possible for 5 allow **6** enable, permit **7** empower, qualify **10** capacitate

make public 3 air **4** tell, vent **5** print, utter, voice **6** expose, inform, reveal, spread **7** declare, display, divulge, exhibit, express, give out, publish **8** announce, disclose, proclaim, televise **9** broadcast, circulate, publicize

maker, Maker 3 god **4** poet **5** smith **6** author, forger **7** builder, creator, founder **8** declarer, inventor, producer **9** architect, generator **10** originator **12** manufacturer

make ready 5 prime **7** arrange, forearm, prepare

make reparation for 5 atone, repay **6** pay for **10** compensate, recompense, remunerate

make restitution 5 repay **7** pay back **9** reimburse **10** compensate, recompense

make right 3 fix **5** amend, emend **6** remedy, repair **7** correct, improve, rectify

make self-conscious 5 abash **6** rattle **7** chagrin, fluster **9** discomfit, embarrass **10** disconcert

makeshift 6 make-do **7** standby, stopgap **8** slapdash **9** alternate, expedient, temporary, tentative **10** substitute **11** provisional

make sick 6 revolt **7** disgust **8** nauseate

make smaller 6 lessen, reduce, shrink, take in **8** decrease, diminish

make sure 5 cinch **6** assure, clinch, decide, ensure, secure, settle **9** ascertain **11** double-check

make thinner 4 thin **6** dilute **9** water down **10** adulterate

make tracks 2 go **4** scat, shoo **5** be off, leave, scram **6** beat it, cut out, depart, go away **8** withdraw **10** hit the road

make uncomfortable 3 try **7** agitate, perturb **8** disquiet, distress **9** discomfit, embarrass **10** discompose

make uneasy 6 rattle **7** disturb, perturb, trouble, unnerve **8** disquiet, distress **9** discomfit, embarrass **10** discomfort, discompose, disconcert

make uniform 4 even **5** equal **6** smooth **7** balance **8** equalize **10** straighten

makeup 5 frame **9** character, cosmetics, framework, structure **11** composition, personality **12** constitution, organization

make up 4 form **5** cover **6** invent **7** arrange, concoct **8** assemble **9** improvise, reconcile **10** compensate, constitute **11** put together

make up for 5 atone **7** expiate **8** make good **10** make amends **13** compensate for

make up one's mind 6 decide **7** resolve **9** determine

make use of 3 use **5** apply **6** employ, engage, occupy **7** exploit, utilize **8** keep busy, put to use **13** turn to account

make weary 4 do in, poop, tire **7** exhaust, wear out **8** enervate

makeweight 6 weight **7** ballast

make well 4 cure, heal

make wider 5 widen **6** dilate, expand **7** broaden, stretch **9** spread out

make worse 7 worsen **8** heighten, increase **9** aggravate, intensify **10** exacerbate

making excuses 8 alibiing **9** defending **10** justifying **11** apologizing

Making of the President, The (series)
author: **14** Theodore H White

making the rounds 5 about **6** abroad **11** circulating, going around **13** going the route

Malachi
means: **11** my messenger
identified with: **4** Ezra **8** Mordecai, Nehemiah **10** Zerubbabel

maladroit 5 inept **6** clumsy, gauche **7** awkward, unhandy **8** bumbling, bungling, tactless **9** impolitic, unskilled **10** blundering, left-handed, ungraceful

maladroitness 9 gaucherie, inability **10** clumsiness, ineptitude **11** awkwardness, unhandiness **12** incompetence

malady 7 ailment, disease, illness **8** disorder, sickness **9** affection, complaint, infirmity **10** affliction, disability

mala fide 10 in bad faith, not genuine

malaise 4 pang **5** throb **6** twinge **7** anxiety **8** disquiet **9** lassitude **10** uneasiness, discomfort **11** nervousness

Malamud, Bernard
    author of: 8 The Fixer **9** God's Grace **10** The Natural, The Tenants **11** Dubin's Lives **12** The Assistant

Malaprop, Mrs
    character in: 9 The Rivals
    author: 8 Sheridan

Malawi
    other name: 9 Nyasaland
    capital: 8 Lilongwe
    largest city: 8 Blantyre
    others: 4 Bana **5** Dedza, Limbe, Mzuzu, Zomba **6** Kasese, Mzimba, Salima **7** Chipoka, Chiromo, Deep Bay, Karonga, Katumbi **8** Chikwawa, Chilumbe, Kota Kota, Nkata Bay **9** Monkey Bay **10** Port Herald **12** Fort Johnston, Livingstonia
    monetary unit: 6 kwacha **7** tambala
    lake: 5 Nyasa **6** Chilwa, Malawi
    mountain: 11 Livingstone
    highest point: 6 Mlanje **7** Mulanje
    river: 3 Bua **5** Shire **7** Dwangwa **11** South Rukuru
    physical feature:
        highlands: 5 Shire
        plateau: 5 Nyika
        valley: 5 Shire **9** Great Rift
    people: 3 Yao **4** Sena **5** Bantu, Lomwe, Ngoni **6** Cheiva, Maravi, Ngonde, Nyanja **7** Tumbuka
        dynasty: 6 Maravi
        explorer: 16 David Livingstone
        leader: 5 Banda
    language: 3 Yao **4** Cewa **5** Bantu, Ngoni, Tonga **6** Nyanja **7** English, Tumbuka **8** Chichewa **10** Chitumbuka
    religion: 5 Islam **7** animism **10** Protestant **12** Presbyterian **13** Roman Catholic
    feature:
        village: 5 mudzi

Malaysia
    capital/largest city: 11 Kuala Lumpur
    others: 4 Ipoh, Sibu **5** Anson, Davao, Telok **6** Iloilo, Johore, Kupang, Manado, Penang, Pinang **7** Bintulu, Kuantan, Kuching, Melalap **8** Port Weld, Sandakan **10** Georgetown, Kota Baharu **11** Johor Baharu, Port Dickson **12** Kota Kinabulu **14** Port Swettenham
    division: 5 Sabah **6** Malaya **7** Malacca, Sarawak
    head of state:
        supreme head of state: 18 yang di-pertuan agong
    measure: 3 pau, tun **4** para, pipe, tael, wang **5** parah **6** chupak, parrah **7** gantang
    monetary unit: 3 sen, tra **4** taro, trah **7** ringgit, tampang
    weight: 4 chee, mace, tael, wang **7** tampang
    island: 6 Banggi, Borneo, Labuan, Penang, Pinang, Tioman **7** Pangkor, Sebatik **8** Langkawi **10** Perhentian **11** Balambangan
    mountain: 4 Bulu, Hose, Iban, Iran, Main, Mulu, Niut, Raja **5** Murjo, Niapa, Ophir **6** Blumut, Kapuas, Leuser, Slamet **7** Binaija, Brassey, Crocker **8** Rindjani **11** Gunong Korbu, Gunong Tahan
    highest point: 8 Kinabalu
    river: 5 Klang, Kutai, Perak **6** Barito, Pahang, Rajang, Rejang **7** Sarawak **12** Kinabatangan
    sea: 4 Sulu **7** Celebes **10** South China
    physical feature:
        bay: 5 Labuk
        cape: 5 Sirik
        highlands: 7 Cameron
        passage: 6 Sibutu
        peninsula: 5 Malay
        point: 13 Tanjong Gelang
        strait: 6 Johore **7** Balabac, Malacca
    people: 4 Iban **5** Dayak, Malay **6** Indian **7** Chinese, Kadazan **9** Pakistani, Sri Lankan **10** Bangladesh, Indonesian
    language: 4 Bugi, Dyak **5** Malay, Tamil **6** Battok, Rejang **7** Chinese, English, Lampong, Niasese **8** Achinese, Javanese, Makassar **14** Bahasa Malaysia
        alphabet: 5 tagal
    religion: 5 Hindu, Islam **6** Taoism **7** animism **8** Buddhism **12** Christianity, Confucianism
    place:
        mosque: 8 National
    feature:
        cap: 7 songkok
        cloth: 4 tapa **5** batik
        clothing: 4 baju, malo, sari **5** badju, pareu **6** cabaya, kebaya, sam-foo, sarong **9** cheongsam
        dance: 4 haka, hula **5** joget
        game: 9 sepakraga
        hamlet: 7 kampong
        parish: 5 mukim
        rice paddy: 4 padi
        scarf: 9 selendang
        self-defense: 5 silat
        shadow play: 6 menora
        spirit: 5 hantu
    food:
        drink: 4 kava
        fruit: 6 durian **8** rambutan **10** mangosteen

Malcolm
    character in: 7 Macbeth
    author: 11 Shakespeare

Malcolm X
    original name: 13 Malcolm Little
    born: 7 Omaha NE
    religion: 5 Islam **11** Black Muslim **13** Nation of Islam
    assassinated in: 6 Harlem **11** New York City
    book about: 26 The Autobiography of Malcolm X
        author: 9 Alex Haley
    film about: 8 Malcolm X
        director: 8 Spike Lee

malcontent 4 glum, sour **5** rebel **6** grouch, grumpy, morose, sullen, uneasy **7** grouchy, growler, repiner, restive **8** dejected, downcast, grumbler, restless **9** insurgent, irritable **10** complainer, despondent **11** faultfinder **12** discontented, dissatisfied, faultfinding, hard to please

mal de mer 11 seasickness

Malden, Karl
    real name: 16 Mladen Sekulovich
    born: 6 Gary IL
    roles: 6 Patton **8** Baby Doll **15** On the Waterfront **21** A Streetcar Named Desire **24** The Streets of San Francisco

Maldives
    capital/largest city: 4 Male
    government:
        legislature: 6 Majlis
    monetary unit: 5 laree, rupee
    island: 3 Ari, Gan **4** Addu, Male **5** Rasdu **6** Felidu, Hulele, Mulaku **7** Malcolm, Minicoy, Nilandu **8** Maldives, Suvadiva **9** Fadiffolu, Wilingili **10** Haddummati, Kolumadulu **11** Tiladummati **13** Ihavandiffulu, Miladummadulu **16** North Malosmadulu, South Malosmadulu
    sea: 6 Indian **7** Arabian **9** Laccadive
    physical feature:
        channel: 4 Wadu **7** Kardiva **8** Veimandu **10** Equatorial **11** Eight Degree **17** One and a Half Degree
    people: 4 Arab **6** Indian **9** Sinhalese **10** Singhalese
        ruling family/sultans: 4 Didi
    language: 6 Arabic, Divehi
    religion: 5 Islam
    feature:
        coconut fiber: 4 coir
        dried coconut: 5 copra

male 3 boy, man, ram, tom **4** bull **5** manly, youth **6** tomcat **7** manlike, rooster **8** stallion **9** billy goat, masculine

Male
    capital of: 8 Maldives

male bird 4 cock 5 drake 6 gander 7 rooster

maledict 4 damn 5 curse 8 denounce 9 proscribe 12 anathematize

malediction 5 curse 8 anathema, diatribe 9 damnation, evil spell 10 execration 11 fulmination, imprecation 12 denunciation, proscription

malefactor 5 felon, knave, rogue 6 sinner 7 culprit 8 criminal, evil-doer, offender 9 miscreant, scoundrel, wrongdoer 10 malfeasant

male hairdresser
French: 8 coiffeur

malentendu 7 mistake 16 misunderstanding

male power
god of: 7 Priapus

Malevich, Kasimir Severinovich
born: 4 Kiev 6 Russia
artwork: 11 Black Square 15 The Knife Grinder 18 Eight Red Rectangles 19 Woman with Water Pails 34 Suprematist Composition White on White

malevolence 4 evil, hate 5 spite 6 enmity, grudge, hatred, malice, rancor, spleen 7 despite, ill will 9 hostility, malignity 10 antagonism, malignance, malignancy 12 spitefulness 13 maliciousness

malevolent 5 surly 6 malign, sullen 7 baleful, vicious 8 sinister, spiteful, venomous 9 invidious, malicious, malignant, rancorous, resentful 10 ill-natured, pernicious, revengeful 11 acrimonious, ill-disposed 14 ill-intentioned

malfeasance 5 crime 8 misdeeds 10 misconduct, wrongdoing

malformation 9 deformity 10 aberration, distortion 11 abnormality, monstrosity, peculiarity 12 grotesquerie, irregularity 13 disfigurement

malformed 7 twisted 8 deformed 9 contorted, distorted, grotesque, irregular, misshapen

malfunction 6 glitch, malady 7 problem 9 complaint

malgre lui 16 in spite of himself

Mali
other name: 11 French Sudan 12 French Soudan 16 Sudanese Republic
capital/largest city: 6 Bamako
others: 3 Gao 5 Kayes, Mopti, Segou 6 Djenne 7 Sikasso 8 Taoudeni, Timbuktu 10 Tombouctou
division: 5 Sahel 7 Azaouad
monetary unit: 5 franc 7 centime
lake: 2 Do 4 Debo 5 Garou 7 Korarou 9 Faguibine
mountain: 4 Mina 6 Iforas 7 Manding
highest point: 12 Hombori Tondo
river: 4 Bani 5 Bagoe, Bakoy, Diaka,

Niger 6 Bafing, Bakoye, Baoule, Faleme 7 Azaouak, Senegal
physical feature:
desert: 6 Sahara 8 Chech Erg 10 Sekkane Erg 13 Haricha Hamada
plateau: 14 Adrar des Iforas
valley: 5 Niger 7 Tilemsi
people: 3 Bwa 4 Fula, Kyan, Moor, Peul 5 Dogon, Dyula, Fulbe, Marka 6 Berber, Dognon, Fulani, Senufo, Tuareg 7 Bambara, Fellata, Malinke, Miniaka, Songhai, Soninke 8 Khasonke, Mandingo, Senoulfo
leader: 4 Umar 5 Keita 6 Traore 9 Mansa Musa
language: 5 Dogon, Dyula, Feulh, Mande, Marka 6 Berber, French, Fulani 7 Bambara, Malinke, Senoufo, Songhai
religion: 5 Islam 7 animism
place:
ruins: 8 Terhazza
feature:
empire: 4 Mali 5 Ghana 7 Bambara, Songhai

malice 4 hate 5 spite, venom 6 enmity, grudge, hatred, rancor 7 ill will 8 acrimony 9 animosity, malignity 10 antagonism, bitterness, evil intent, resentment 11 malevolence 12 spitefulness

malice aforethought
legal term: 51 planning to commit a crime without just cause or provocation

malicious 7 baleful, harmful, hateful, vicious 8 spiteful 9 invidious, malignant, rancorous, resentful 10 malevolent, revengeful, vindictive 11 acrimonious, ill-disposed

malign 3 bad 4 evil 5 abuse, black 6 defame, revile, vilify 7 baneful, harmful, hateful, noxious, ominous, put down, run down, slander 8 backbite, bad mouth, belittle, derogate, menacing, sinister 9 denigrate, deprecate, disparage, injurious, malicious, malignant 10 malevolent, pernicious, speak ill of 11 deleterious, detrimental, threatening 14 inveigh against

malignancy 5 spite, tumor 6 cancer, malice, rancor 7 ill will, sarcoma 8 acrimony, neoplasm, toxicity 9 carcinoma, hostility, virulence 10 bitterness 11 malevolence, viciousness 12 hard feelings, spitefulness, vengefulness 13 poisonousness

malignant 4 evil 5 fatal, toxic 6 bitter, deadly 7 hateful, hostile, vicious 8 fiendish, spiteful, venomous, virulent 9 invidious, malicious, poisonous, rancorous, resentful 10 diabolical, evil-minded, malevolent, pernicious, revengeful, vindictive 11 acrimonious, ill-disposed

malignant spirit 3 imp 5 demon, devil 7 gremlin

malignity 4 evil 5 spite, venom 6 animus, rancor, spleen 7 ill will 8 acrimony 9 animosity 12 hard feelings, spitefulness, venomousness

malinger 4 loaf 5 dodge, evade, shirk, slack 7 goof off 9 goldbrick

mall 4 yard 5 court, plaza 6 arcade, circus, piazza, square 8 cloister 9 colonnade, esplanade, promenade 10 quadrangle 12 parade ground

Mallarme, Stephane
author of: 8 Herodias 18 L'Apres Midi d'un faune 19 The Afternoon of a Faun

Malle, Louis
director of: 10 Pretty Baby 12 Atlantic City 13 Lacombe Lucien 16 Murmur of the Heart
wife: 13 Candice Bergen

malleable 6 docile, pliant 7 ductile, plastic, pliable 8 flexible, moldable, workable 9 adaptable, compliant, teachable, tractable 10 governable, manageable 12 easily shaped 13 easily wrought 14 impressionable

mallet
type: 6 rubber, wooden 12 plastic-faced

malnutrition 10 emaciation, starvation 16 undernourishment

malodorous 4 rank 5 acrid, fetid, musty 6 putrid, smelly 7 noisome, reeking 8 stinking 12 foul-smelling

Malone, Dorothy
real name: 20 Dorothy Eloise Maloney
husband: 15 Jacques Bergerac
born: 9 Chicago IL
roles: 11 Peyton Place 14 Too Much Too Soon 16 Written on the Wind

Malory, Sir Thomas
author of: 14 Le Morte d'Arthur

Malpighi, Marcello
field: 10 physiology
nationality: 7 Italian
founded: 18 microscopic anatomy

malpractice 10 negligence

Malraux, Andre
author of: 8 Man's Fate 11 Anti-Memoirs, Days of Wrath, The Royal Way 13 The Conquerors 18 The Voices of Silence

Malta
capital: 8 Valletta
largest city: 6 Sliema
others: 5 Marfa, Mdina, Mgarr, Mosta, Nadut, Paola, Rabat 6 Zejtun 7 Senglea, Zeibrun 8 Cospicua, Floriana, Mellieha, Victoria 10 Birkirkara, Birzebbuga, Vittoriosa
measure: 4 rotl 5 artal, canna, parto, ratel, salma 6 kantar 7 caffiso
monetary unit: 4 cent 5 grain, grano, pound
island: 4 Gozo 5 Malta 6 Comino, Filfla 7 Filfola 9 Cominotto 10 Comminotto

highest point: 12 Dingli Cliffs
sea: 13 Mediterranean
physical feature:
    bay: 7 St Paul's **8** Mellieha **10** Mar-saxlokk
    channel: 11 North Comino, South Comino
    harbor: 5 Grand **10** Marsamxett
people: 7 Maltese
    leader: 7 Mintoff **9** Buttigieo **18** Parisot de La Valette
    ruler: 5 Arabs **6** Romans **7** British **8** Napoleon **10** Byzantines **11** Hospitalers, Phoenicians **13** Carthaginians **15** Holy Roman Empire, Knights of St John
language: 7 English, Italian, Maltese
religion: 13 Roman Catholic
feature:
    gondola boat: 7 dghaisa

Maltese Falcon, The
    author: 15 Dashiell Hammett
    director: 10 John Huston
    cast: 9 Mary Astor (Brigid O'Shaughnessy) **10** Peter Lorre (Joel Cairo) **12** Elisha Cook Jr (Wilmer), Gladys George **14** Humphrey Bogart (Sam Spade) **17** Sydney Greenstreet (the Fat Man)
    character: 6 Wilmer **8** Sam Spade **9** Joel Cairo **11** Miles Archer **12** Casper Gutman, Floyd Thursby **18** Brigid O'Shaughnessy
    remade as: 13 Satan Met a Lady

malt liquor 3 ale **4** beer, bock, brew **5** stout **6** porter

maltreat 4 harm, hurt **5** abuse **6** ill-use, injure **8** mistreat

maltreatment 5 abuse **6** ill-use, injury **7** assault, cruelty **10** bodily harm, oppression **11** manhandling, molestation, persecution **12** mistreatment

Malvolio
    character in: 12 Twelfth Night
    author: 11 Shakespeare

Mama
    character: 4 Nels **6** Dagmar, Katrin, TR Ryan **9** Aunt Jenny **10** (Papa) Lars Hansen **11** (Mama) Marta Hansen
    cast: 8 Iris Mann **9** Peggy Wood, Ruth Gates **11** Judson Laire, Robin Morgan **12** Rosemary Rice **13** Dick Van Patten, Kevin Coughlin
    dog: 6 Willie
    based on book: 16 Mama's Bank Account
    author: 13 Kathryn Forbes
    setting: 12 San Francisco
    theme: 12 Holverg Suite **13** The Last Spring

mamma, mama 2 ma **3** mam, mom, mum **4** wife **5** madre, mammy, mater, mommy, mummy, mumsy, woman **6** mother, parent

mammal

bat (chiroptera): 4 tomb **5** fruit, naked, smoky **7** mastiff, vampire **9** fisherman, horseshoe, leaf-nosed, sac-winged, slit-faced, thumbless **10** disk-winged, free-tailed, moustached **11** funnel-eared, hollow-faced, mouse-tailed **12** false vampire, sheath-tailed, sucker-footed, yellow-winged **14** vespertilionid **21** New Zealand short-tailed
carnivore: 3 cat, dog, fox **4** bear, lion, lynx, mink, puma, wolf **5** civet, dingo, fossa, hyena, otter, panda, skunk, tayra, tiger **6** badger, bobcat, coyote, ferret, grison, hyaena, jackal, jaguar, marten, olingo, weasel **7** polecat, raccoon **8** aardwolf, kinkajou, mongoose, suricate **9** wolverine **10** cacomistle, coatimundi
cetacea: 4 gray **5** pilot, right, whale **6** beluga, killer **7** dolphin, rorqual **8** humpback, narwhale, porpoise **10** sperm whale **11** beaked whale **16** bottle-nosed whale
edentata: 5 sloth **8** anteater **9** armadillo, tree sloth
egg-laying: 7 echidna **13** spiny anteater **18** duck-billed platypus
even-toed ungulate: 2 ox **3** elk, hog, pig **4** deer, goat, oxen **5** bison, camel, llama, moose, okapi, sheep **6** alpaca, cattle, duiker, vicuna **7** buffalo, caribou, gazelle, giraffe, guanaco, muntjak, peccary **8** antelope **9** mouse deer **10** chevrotain **12** hippopotamus
hyracoidea: 5 hyrax
insect-eating: 4 mole **5** shrew **6** desman, tenrec **7** gymnure, moon rat **8** hedgehog **9** shrew-mole, solenodon **10** golden mole, otter shrew, water shrew **13** elephant shrew
lagomorpha: 4 hare, pika **6** rabbit
marsupials/pouched: 5 koala **6** cuscus, numbat, possum, wombat **7** opossum, wallaby **8** kangaroo **9** bandicoot, phalanger **14** Tasmanian devil
odd-toed ungulate: 3 ass **5** horse, kiang, tapir, zebra **6** onager, quagga **10** rhinoceros
pinnipedia: 4 seal **6** walrus **7** sea lion
primate: 5 lemur, loris, potto **6** avahis, aye-aye, baboon, galago, gibbon, indris, monkey, people **7** gorilla, tamarin, tarsier **8** marmoset, simpoona **9** orangutan, tree shrew **10** chimpanzee
proboscidea: 8 elephant
rodent: 4 cavy, vole **5** coypu, gundi, hutia, mouse **6** agouti, beaver, coruro, gerbil, gopher, jerboa, nutria **7** blesmol, cane rat, hamster, lemming, mole-rat, rock rat **8** capybara, chipmunk, dormouse, sewellel, spiny rat, squirrel, tucu-tuco, viscacha **9** chozchori, false paca, pacaranas,

porcupine, woodchuck **10** chinchilla, prairie dog, springhare **11** kangaroo rat, pocket mouse, viscacha rat **13** kangaroo mouse **16** Speke's pectinator
sirenia: 6 dugong, sea cow **7** manatee
tubulidentata: 8 aardvark

mammon, Mammon 4 gain, gold **5** money **6** profit, riches, wealth **9** affluence **11** possessions **13** material goods, the god of money

Mammon, Sir Epicure
    character in: 12 The Alchemist
    author: 6 Jonson

mammoth 4 huge **5** great **6** mighty **7** immense, massive **8** colossal, enormous, gigantic, whopping **9** cyclopean, herculean, monstrous, ponderous, very large **10** gargantuan, monumental, prodigious, stupendous, tremendous **11** elephantine, mountainous

Mammy
    character in: 15 Gone With the Wind
    author: 8 Mitchell

Mamoulian, Rouben
    director of: 13 Love Me Tonight, Silk Stockings **14** Queen Christina, The Mark of Zorro

man 3 boy, guy, one **4** chap, gent, hand, male, soul **5** equip, hubby, human, staff **6** anyone, attend, butler, fellow, fit out, helper, outfit, people, person, spouse, waiter, worker **7** footman, husband, laborer, mankind, someone, subject, workman **8** employee, garrison, handyman, henchman, humanity, liegeman, somebody **9** assistant, gentleman, hired hand, humankind **11** Homo sapiens
    Spanish: 6 hombre

Man, first 4 Adam **12** Alalcomeneus
    Nordic: 3 Ask

Man, Isle of
    capital: 7 Douglas
    location: 8 Irish Sea
    native: 4 Manx **7** Manxman
    Manx cat lacks: 4 tail

Man, Woman and Child
    author: 10 Erich Segal

man about town 5 blade **7** playboy **8** cavalier, gay blade **12** boulevardier

manacle, manacles 3 ply, run, use **4** cope, fare, head, rule, work **5** bonds, get on, guide, irons, order, pilot, shift, steer, wield **6** chains, direct, fetter, govern, handle, make go **7** command, conduct, control, operate, oversee, shackle, succeed, survive, work out **8** cope with, deal with, dominate, get along, handcuff, maneuver, shackles **9** bracelets, handcuffs, look after, supervise, watch over **10** accomplish, administer, bring about, manipulate, put in irons, take care of **11** be at the helm, hand-fetters, preside over, put in chains, superintend **12** have charge of, hold the reins

manage 4 care, rule **6** bosses, charge, wheels **7** bigwigs, command, conduct, control, dealing, running, tactics **8** big shots, guidance, handling, ordering, planning, strategy, top brass **9** direction, directors, operation **10** conducting, executives, overseeing, regulation **11** generalship, negotiation, supervision, supervisors, transaction **12** manipulation, organization **14** administration, administrators **15** superintendence

manageable 4 easy **6** docile, pliant, wieldy **8** amenable, flexible **9** compliant, tractable **10** governable, submissive **12** controllable

management 4 boss, head **5** agent, chief **7** foreman, planner **8** overseer **9** budgeteer, majordomo, organizer, tactician **10** impresario, negotiator, supervisor **11** manipulator **13** administrator **14** superintendent

manager 4 boss, head **5** agent, chief **7** foreman, planner **8** overseer **9** budgeteer, majordomo, organizer, tactician **10** impresario, negotiator, supervisor **11** manipulator **13** administrator **14** superintendent

managerial 9 executive **10** management **11** supervisory **14** administrative, organizational

Managua
capital of: 9 Nicaragua

Manala *see* **7** Tuonela

Manama
capital of: 7 Bahrain

manana 6 future **8** tomorrow **11** in the future

Man and Superman
author: 17 George Bernard Shaw

Manassa Mauler
nickname of: 11 Jack Dempsey

Manasseh
father: 6 Joseph
mother: 7 Asenath
great uncle: 4 Esau
grandfather: 5 Jacob
descendant of: 9 Manassite

man-at-arms 7 fighter, soldier, warrior **9** combatant **10** cavalryman

Manchester, William
author of: 11 The Last Lion **14** American Caesar **15** Goodbye Darkness

Manchuria
also: 7 Manchow
city: 5 Aigun, Hulan, Kirin, Peian, Penki **6** Anshan, Antung, Dairen, Fu-Shun, Hailar, Harbin, Hokang, Mukden, Penchi, Yenchi **7** Hulutao, Ikuliho, Ssuping, Tantung **8** Chinchao, Paicheng, Shenyang **9** Changchun, Chiamussu, Manchouli, Miuchwang **10** Port Arthur

11 Chichihaerh, Mutanchiang
peninsula: 8 Liaotung
province: 5 Jehol, Jilin, Kirin **8** Liaoning **12** Heilongjiang, Heilungkiang
river: 4 Amur, Liao, Yalu **5** Argun, Mutan, Nonni, Tumen **6** Ussuri **7** Sungari
tribe: 5 Tungu **6** Manchu, Mongol

Mandalay
found in: 18 Barrack-Room Ballads
author: 14 Rudyard Kipling

mandamus
legal term: 48 writ from a superior court commanding that a thing be done
literally: 9 we command

Mandan
language family: 6 Siouan
location: 11 North Dakota
ceremony: 5 Okipa

Mandarins, The
author: 16 Simone de Beauvoir

mandate 5 edict, order **6** behest, charge, decree **7** bidding, command, dictate **8** approval, sanction **9** authority, direction, directive **10** commission, dependency **11** instruction, requisition **12** protectorate **13** authorization

mandatory 7 binding, exigent, needful **8** required **9** called for, essential, necessary, requisite **10** compulsory, imperative, obligatory, peremptory

Mandelbaum Gate, The
author: 11 Muriel Spark

Manderley
house in: 7 Rebecca
author: 9 Du Maurier

mandible 3 jaw **4** beak, bill, jowl **7** maxilla **8** lower jaw
part: 4 mala **5** angle, molar, ramus **6** corpus

Mandrake the Magician
creator: 7 Lee Falk **9** Phil Davis
character: 5 Narda **6** Lothar

Manes
spirits or souls of: 4 dead

Manet, Edouard
born: 5 Paris **6** France
artwork: 7 Olympia **8** The Fifer **9** Emile Zola **10** Argenteuil **12** The Guitarist **19** Le Dejeuner sur l'Herbe (Luncheon on the Grass) **25** The Bar at the Folies- Bergeres **31** Execution of the Emperor Maximilian

Manette, Dr and Lucie
characters in: 16 A Tale of Two Cities
author: 7 Dickens

maneuver 4 move, plot, ploy **5** dodge, guide, pilot, steer, trick **6** deploy, device, gambit, scheme, tactic **7** finagle **8** arti- fice, contrive, intrigue **9** stratagem **10** manipulate **11** contrivance, machination, pull strings

Man for All Seasons, A

director: 13 Fred Zinnemann
based on play by: 10 Robert Bolt
cast: 9 Leo McKern **10** Robert Shaw **11** Orson Welles, Wendy Hiller **12** Paul Scofield (Sir Thomas More), Susannah York **14** Nigel Davenport **15** Vanessa Redgrave
Oscar for: 5 actor (Scofield) **7** picture **8** director

man Friday 4 aide **8** adjutant, employee **9** assistant **10** aide de camp **12** right-hand man
source: 14 Robinson Crusoe

Man from St Petersburg, The
author: 10 Ken Follett

Man from UNCLE, The
character: 9 Mr Waverly **12** Napoleon Solo **13** Illya Kuryakin
cast: 11 Leo G Carroll **12** Robert Vaughn **13** David McCallum
foe: 6 THRUSH

manful 5 brave **8** resolute **10** courageous

manganese
chemical symbol: 2 Mn

mangle 3 cut **4** harm, hurt, lame, maim, maul, ruin, tear **5** crush, press, slash **6** damage, impair, injure **7** flatten **8** lacerate, mutilate **9** disfigure

manhandle 4 maul **5** abuse **6** batter **7** rough up **8** maltreat, mistreat **9** pull about, push about **10** knock about, slap around

Manhattan
director: 10 Woody Allen
cast: 9 Anne Byrne **10** Woody Allen **11** Diane Keaton, Meryl Streep **13** Michael Murphy **15** Mariel Hemingway

Manhattan Transfer
author: 13 John Dos Passos

manhood 5 prime **8** legal age, machismo, majority, maleness, maturity, virility **9** adulthood, manliness, mature age **10** manfulness **11** masculinity

mania 4 rage **5** craze **6** frenzy, lunacy, raving **7** craving, madness, passion **8** delirium, delusion, dementia, fixation, hysteria, insanity **9** monomania, obsession **10** aberration, compulsion, enthusiasm, fanaticism **11** fascination, infatuation

maniac 3 ass, nut **4** fool **5** loony **6** cuckoo, madman, nitwit **7** half-wit, lunatic **9** psychotic, screwball, simpleton **10** crackbrain, psychopath

manic 2 up **4** high **7** excited, frantic, hyped up **8** agitated, frenzied, worked up **9** wrought up **10** freaked out, switched on **11** hyperactive

manifest 4 bare, open, show **5** clear, frank, plain **6** candid, evince, expose, patent, reveal, unveil **7** display, divulge, evident, exhibit, express, obvious, uncover, visible **8** apparent, disclose, evidence, indicate, palpable

9 make known **10** noticeable **11** demonstrate, make visible, self-evident, transparent, unconcealed, undisguised

manifestation 4 show **7** display, example, symptom **8** evidence, instance **10** exhibition, expression, indication, revelation **12** illustration, presentation, proclamation, public notice **13** demonstration

manifesto 4 bull **5** edict, ukase **6** notice **9** broadside, statement **10** communique, encyclical **11** declaration **12** announcement, annunciation, notification, proclamation, public notice **13** position paper, pronouncement **14** pronunciamento

manifold 4 many **6** myriad, varied **7** complex, diverse **8** multiple, numerous **9** many-sided, multiform **10** variegated **11** diversified, innumerable **12** multifarious **13** multitudinous

Manila
capital of: 11 Philippines
former name: 8 Maynilad
island: 5 Luzon
landmark: 9 Rizal Park **16** San Agustin Church
river: 5 Pasig
section: 10 Quezon City
university: 10 Santo Tomas

Man in the Gray Flannel Suit, The
author: 11 Sloan Wilson

manipulate 3 pat, ply, use **4** feel, work **5** drive, pinch, wield **6** employ, finger, handle, manage, stroke **7** control, deceive, defraud, massage, operate, squeeze

Manitoba
bay: 6 Hudson
capital: 8 Winnipeg
city: 6 Carman, The Pas **7** Brandon, Caribou, Dauphin, Selkirk **8** Flin Flon, Lynn Lake, Wabowden, Winnipeg **9** Churchill, Killarney, Sherridon, Swan River **10** St Boniface **11** Norway House, York Factory **16** Portage La Prairie
flower: 11 windflower **13** prairie crocus
Indian tribe: 4 Cree **6** Eskimo, Ojibwa **8** Chippewa **10** Assiniboin
lake: 4 God's, Swan **5** Cedar, Moose **6** Island **7** Dauphin, Red Deer **8** Manitoba, Reindeer, St Martin, Waterhen, Winnipeg **9** Granville
mountain: 4 Hart **5** Baldy
name means: 16 lake of the prairies **18** Great Spirit's strait **19** Great Spirit's narrows
nickname: 15 Prairie Province **16** Keystone Province
province of: 6 Canada
river: 3 Red **4** Seal, Swan **5** Hayes **6** Nelson, Roseau, Souris **7** Pembina **8** Winnipeg **9** Churchill **11** Assiniboine **12** Saskatchewan
university: 7 Brandon **10** St Boniface

Mankiewicz, Joseph L
director of: 6 Sleuth **9** Cleopatra **11** All About Eve (Oscar) **12** Guys and Dolls, Julius Caesar **18** The Ghost and Mrs Muir **19** A Letter to Three Wives (Oscar)

mankind 3 man **6** people **7** mortals, persons, society **8** humanity **9** humankind **11** Homo sapiens

manlike 5 macho, manly **6** virile **8** hominoid **9** masculine

manly 4 bold, male **5** brave, hardy, husky, noble **6** brawny, daring, heroic, manful, plucky, robust, strong, sturdy, virile **7** gallant, staunch, valiant **8** athletic, fearless, malelike, muscular, powerful, resolute, stalwart, vigorous **9** masculine, strapping **11** chivalrous, courageous **11** gentlemanly, indomitable, self-reliant **12** stouthearted
Spanish: 5 macho

man-made 4 mock, sham **6** formed **7** crafted, created **8** produced **9** fashioned, ready-made, simulated, synthetic **10** artificial, fabricated, factitious, originated **11** constructed, handcrafted **12** manufactured

Mann, Delbert
director of: 5 Marty (Oscar) **14** Separate Tables

Mann, Thomas
author of: 12 Buddenbrooks **13** Death in Venice, Doctor Faustus **16** The Magic Mountain

manna 4 boon **5** award **6** reward **7** bonanza **16** divine sustenance

mannequin 4 form **5** dummy, model **6** figure

manner 3 air, way **4** form, kind, make, mode, mold, race, rank, sort, type **5** brand, breed, caste, genre, grade, guise, habit, stamp, style **6** aspect, custom, method, strain **7** bearing, conduct, fashion, species, variety **8** behavior, carriage, category, demeanor, practice, presence **9** character **10** appearance, deportment **14** classification

mannered 6 formal **7** stilted, studied **8** affected **9** contrived, unnatural **10** artificial **11** ceremonious

mannerism 4 airs, pose **5** habit **8** pretense **10** pretension **11** affectation, singularity **12** eccentricity, idiosyncrasy

mannerly 5 civil **6** polite **7** courtly, gallant, genteel, refined **8** well-bred **9** courteous **10** chivalrous **11** gentlemanly, well-behaved

manner of living
Latin: 12 modus vivendi

manner of looking at the world
German: 14 Weltanschauung

manner of speaking 7 diction **9** elocution **10** intonation **13** pronunciation

manners 6 polish **7** decorum **8** behavior, breeding, courtesy **9** amenities, deference, etiquette, gallantry, gentility, politesse, propriety **10** deportment, politeness, refinement **11** courtliness

Mannix
character: 9 Joe Mannix, Peggy Fair **10** (Lt) Adam Tobias **13** Lou Wickersham
cast: 10 Gail Fisher, Robert Reed **11** Mike Connors **16** Joseph Campanella

Mannon family
members: 4 Ezra, Orin **7** Lavinia **9** Christine
characters in: 22 Mourning Becomes Electra
author: 6 O'Neill

Manoah
son: 6 Samson

mano a mano 5 alone **8** conflict **13** confrontation, in a small group
literally: 10 hand to hand

Man of a Thousand Faces
nickname of: 9 Lon Chaney

Man of Nazareth
author: 14 Anthony Burgess

Man of Property, The
author: 14 John Galsworthy

Man of Sorrows see **5** Jesus

Manolin
character in: 18 The Old Man and the Sea
author: 9 Hemingway

Manon Lescaut
author: 11 Abbe Prevost

Manor, The
author: 19 Isaac Bashevis Singer

manor house 6 estate, manoir **7** chateau, mansion **11** stately home

manpower 4 help **5** brawn, labor **9** work force, employees

manque 6 failed, missed **7** lacking **11** fallen short, unfulfilled

Mansart, Francois
architect of: 14 Chateau de Berny **18** Hotel de la Vrilliere **33** Church of Sainte Marie de la Visitation
feature: 11 mansard roof

manservant 5 groom, valet **6** butler **7** footman **8** factotum **9** chauffeur

Man's Fate
author: 12 Andre Malraux

Mansfield, Jayne
real name: 14 Vera Jane Palmer
husband: 14 Mickey Hargitay
born: 10 Bryn Mawr PA
roles: 15 Hell on Frisco Bay **26** Will Success Spoil Rock Hunter

Mansfield, Katherine
author of: 5 Bliss **12** The Dove's Nest **14** The Garden Party

Mansfield Park
author: 10 Jane Austen
character: 5 Yates **8** Mrs Grant **9** Mrs Norris, Rushworth **10** Fanny Price

11 Lady Bertram **12** Mary Crawford **13** Henry Crawford **16** Sir Thomas Bertram

> **Bertram children: 3** Tom **5** Julia, Maria **6** Edmund

mansion 5 manor, villa **6** castle, estate, palace **7** chateau **10** manor house

manslaughter 6 murder **7** killing **8** homicide

manta 3 ray **4** cape **5** cloak, shawl **9** devilfish

Mantegna, Andrea
> **born: 5** Italy **14** Isola di Carturo
> **artwork: 9** Parnassus **16** Camera degli Sposi (Bridal Chamber) **18** The Triumph of Caesar, The Triumph of Virtue **20** Madonna della Vittoria

Man That Corrupted Hadleyburg, The
> **author: 9** Mark Twain

Mantius
> **father: 8** Melampus
> **son: 6** Clitus

mantle 4 cape, film, mask, pall, veil **5** cloak, cloud, cover, scarf, tunic **6** canopy, screen, shroud **7** blanket, curtain, wrapper **8** covering, envelope, mantilla

Mantle, Mickey (Charles)
> **sport: 8** baseball
> **position: 8** outfield
> **team: 14** New York Yankees

manual 6 primer **8** handbook, physical, textbook, workbook **9** guidebook **10** done by hand **12** hand-operated, nonautomatic **15** instruction book

manual skill 8 deftness **9** dexterity, handiness **10** adroitness **12** coordination

manufacture 4 form, make, mold **5** build, frame **6** cook up, create, devise, invent, make up **7** concoct, fashion, produce, think up, trump up **8** assemble **9** construct, fabricate **11** mass-produce, put together

manufacturing 8 devising **9** inventing, producing **10** industrial **11** fabricating, nonagrarian

manumission 7 freeing **10** liberation **11** setting free **12** emancipation

manumit 4 free **7** set free **8** liberate **10** emancipate

manure 4 dung **5** feces **6** ordure **7** compost, excreta **8** dressing **10** fertilizer

manuscript 6 script **10** typescript **14** shooting script **15** written document

Manvah
> **son: 6** Samson

Man Who Came to Dinner, The
> **director: 15** William Keighley
> **based on play by: 8** Moss Hart **14** George S Kaufman
> **cast: 10** Bette Davis **11** Ann Sheridan,

Billie Burke **12** Monty Woolley **13** Richard Travis

Man Who Fell to Earth, The
> **director: 12** Nicholas Roeg
> **cast: 7** Rip Torn **9** Buck Henry **10** Candy Clark, David Bowie

Man Who Shot Liberty Valence, The
> **director: 8** John Ford
> **cast: 9** John Wayne, Lee Marvin, Vera Miles **12** Edmund O'Brien, James Stewart

Man Who Was Thursday, The
> **author: 12** G K Chesterton

Man Without a Country, The
> **author: 17** Edward Everett Hale
> **character: 11** Philip Nolan

Manx 3 cat **8** Goidelic
> **spoken in: 10** Isle of Man
> **manx cat lacks: 4** tail

many 4 a lot, lots **5** a heap, heaps, piles **6** divers, dozens, myriad, scores, sundry **7** numbers, several, various **8** numerous **9** countless **10** a profusion, numberless **11** an abundance, innumerable **13** multitudinous

manzanita 14 Arctostaphylos
> **varieties: 4** dune, Ione, Otay **5** hairy, hoary, Morro, Parry, Pecho **6** island, Sonoma, woolly **7** Mexican, Pajarro, pine-mat **8** big-berry, Del Norte, Eastwood, Mariposa, Monterey, shagbark, Stanford **9** Fort Bragg, greenleaf, heart-leaf, little Sur, white-leaf **10** serpentine, silver-leaf **11** brittleleaf, pink-bracted

Maori
> **native of: 10** New Zealand

Mao Tse-Tung
> **also: 8** Mao Zedong
> **born: 5** China
> **leader of: 10** communists
> **title: 8** Chairman
> **led: 9** Long March
> **book: 16** The Little Red Book

map 4 plan, plot **5** chart, graph, ready **6** design, devise, lay out **7** arrange, diagram, prepare, project **8** contrive, organize **9** elevation **10** make a map of, projection **14** representation **18** topographical chart

maple 4 Acer
> **varieties: 3** red **4** Amur, hard, rock, soft, vine **5** black, chalk, field, hedge, Nikko, river, sugar, swamp, white **6** Balkan, canyon, Norway, Oregon, parlor, sierra, silver, Triden **7** big-leaf, Florida, Persian, scarlet, striped **8** big-tooth, Drummond, full-moon, Hawthorn, Hornbeam, Japanese, mountain, Shantung, Sycamore, Tatarian **9** ash-leaved, eagle-claw, flowering, paperbark, Schwedler, Tartarian **11** Montpellier **12** Pennsylvania **13** Rocky Mountain, Southern sugar **18** Rocky Mountain sugar

map out 3 map **5** chart, draft **6** devise, lay out **7** diagram, outline **8** block out **9** delineate, formulate

Maputo
> **capital of: 10** Mozambique

mar 4 hurt, maim, mark, nick, ruin, scar **5** botch, spoil, stain, taint **6** blight, damage, deface, defile, impair **7** blemish, destroy, scratch **8** diminish, mutilate **9** disfigure

Marabar Caves
> **setting in: 15** A Passage to India
> **author: 7** Forster

Maranatha
> **means: 9** O Lord come

maraschino
> **type: 7** liqueur
> **origin: 5** Italy
> **flavor: 6** cherry
> **color: 3** red **5** white

Marathi
> **language family: 12** Indo-European
> **branch: 11** Indo-Iranian
> **group: 5** Indic
> **spoken in: 5** (northern) India

Marathonian bull *see* **10** Cretan bull

marauder 6 looter, pirate, ranger **7** corsair, ravager, spoiler **9** pillager **buccaneer, despoiler, guerrilla, plunderer, privateer **10** depradator, freebooter

marble 3 jet **4** vein **5** agate **6** basalt, blotch, mottle, streak **7** calcite **8** dolomite **9** limestone **10** serpentine, travertine **12** anthraconite
> **quarry: 7** Carrara

Marble Faun, The
> **author: 18** Nathaniel Hawthorne
> **character: 5** Hilda **6** Kenyon, Miriam **9** Donatello

marbles
> **type: 3** mib, taw **4** aggy, duck, immy, migg **5** agate, monny, scrap **6** commie, glassy, hoodle, marine **7** cat's eye, rainbow, shooter **9** carnelian **16** peppermint stripe
> **term: 3** hit **4** shot **6** edgers, ringer **7** bowling, for fair, histing, lagging, lag line, lofting **8** circling, for keeps, hunching **9** pitch line **10** roundsters **11** knuckle down **13** knuckling down

Marc, Franz
> **born: 6** Munich **7** Germany
> **artwork: 10** Blue Horses **12** Yellow Horses **13** Fighting Forms

Marceline
> **character in: 19** The Marriage of Figaro
> **author: 12** Beaumarchais

march 2 go **4** hike, rise, step, trek, walk **5** tramp **6** file by, growth, parade **7** advance, proceed **8** progress **9** group walk **10** go directly, procession, walk in step **11** advancement, development, progression **12** martial music

March

event: 9 Mardi Gras **11** Ides of March (15) **12** Ash Wednesday **13** vernal equinox (21)
flower: 7 jonquil **8** daffodil
French: 4 Mars
gem: 10 aquamarine, bloodstone
German: 4 Marz
holiday: 12 St Joseph's Day (19) **13** St Patrick's Day (17)
Italian: 5 Marzo
number of days: 9 thirty-one
origin of name: 4 Mars
  Roman god of: 3 war
place in year:
  Gregorian: 5 third
  Roman: 5 first
saying: 20 Beware the Ides of March **40** March comes in like a lion and goes out like a lamb
Spanish: 6 Marcha
Zodiac sign: 5 Aries **6** Pisces

March, Fredric
real name: 29 Ernest Frederick McIntyre Bickel
born: 8 Racine WI
roles: 11 A Star Is Born **12** Anna Karenina, The Buccaneer **13** Les Miserables **14** Anthony Adverse, Inherit the Wind, Mary of Scotland, Seven Days in May **16** Death of a Salesman **17** Alexander the Great, Dr Jekyll and Mr Hyde (Oscar), The Desperate Hours **18** Death Takes a Holiday **19** The Affairs of Cellini **22** The Best Years of Our Lives (Oscar) **23** Barretts of Wimpole Street

Marchen 8 folk tale **9** fairy tale

March family
members: 2 Jo **3** Amy, Meg **4** Beth **6** Marmee
characters in: 11 Little Women
author: 6 Alcott

March Hare
character in: 28 Alice's Adventures in Wonderland
author: 7 Carroll

Marchmain family
characters in: 19 Brideshead Revisited
author: 5 Waugh

Marciano, Rocky
real name: 23 Rocco Francis Marchegiano
nickname: 19 Brockton Blockbuster
sport: 6 boxing
class: 11 heavyweight

Marconi, Guglielmo
nationality: 7 Italian
nickname: 16 father of wireless
invented/discovered: 5 radio **12** radio signals **16** magnetic detector **30** wireless high frequency telegraph
shared (1919): 20 Nobel Prize for physics

Marcus Welby MD
character: 11 (Dr) Steven Kiley **13** Consuelo Lopez

cast: 11 James Brolin, Robert Young **12** Elena Verdugo

Mardi (and a Voyage Thither)
author: 14 Herman Melville
character: 4 Alma, Jarl, Mohi, Taji **5** Media, Samoa, Yoomy **6** Yillah **7** Annatoo **10** Babbalanja, Braidbeard **11** Queen Hautia

Mardi Gras 7 holiday **8** carnival, festival, jamboree **10** fat Tuesday **13** Shrove Tuesday
king: 3 rex
social club: 5 krewe

Marduk
also: 8 Merodach **12** Baal Merodach
origin: 10 Babylonian
chief of: 4 gods

mare 3 sea **9** brood-mare **11** female horse

mare nostrum 6 our sea
ancient Roman name for: 13 Mediterranean

margin 3 hem, rim **4** edge, side **5** bound, skirt, verge **6** border, fringe, leeway **7** confine **8** boundary **9** allowance, extra room, safeguard

marginal 9 on the edge **11** in the margin **12** barely usable

mariage de convenance 21 marriage of convenience

marigold 7 Tagetes
varieties: 3 big, bur, fig, pot **4** cape, corn, wild **5** Aztec, fetid, field, marsh, water **6** desert, French, signet **7** African **12** sweet-scented

marijuana, marihuana 3 boo, kif, pot, tea **4** hash, hemp, herb, weed **5** bhang, blunt, dagga, ganja, grass, joint **6** buddha, moocah, reefer **7** chronic, hashish **8** cannabis, locoweed, mary jane

Marin, John Cheri (3rd)
born: 12 Rutherford NJ
artwork: 8 Sea Piece **12** Maine Islands **13** Tunk Mountains **16** Beach Flint Island **19** Movement Fifth Avenue **21** Seaside Interpretation **26** Camden Mountain across the Bay

marine 3 sea **5** naval **6** gyrene **7** aquatic, oceanic, of ships, pelagic **8** maritime, nautical, of the sea, seagoing **9** salt-water, seafaring **10** ocean-going **11** leatherneck **13** oceanographic

mariner 3 gob, tar **4** salt **5** pilot **6** sailor, sea dog, seaman **7** boatman **8** deck hand, helmsman, seafarer **9** navigator, yachtsman **10** bluejacket **12** seafaring man **16** able-bodied seaman

Marion, Francis
nickname: 8 Swamp Fox
served in: 16 Revolutionary War
type of warfare: 9 guerrilla
area fought in: 13 South Carolina
battle: 12 Eutaw Springs

marionette 6 puppet **10** fantoccino

famous: 4 Judy **5** Punch **9** Pinocchio
dummy: 13 Mortimer Snerd **15** Charlie McCarthy
maker: 4 Sarg

marital 6 wedded, wifely **7** married, nuptial, spousal **8** conjugal **9** connubial, husbandly **10** of marriage **11** matrimonial

maritime 5 naval **6** marine **7** aquatic, coastal, oceanic, of ships **8** nautical, of the sea, seagoing **9** seafaring

marjoram
botanical name: 8 Majorana, O vulgare, Origanum **16** M hortensis moench
origin: 4 Asia **13** Mediterranean
family: 4 mint
symbol of: 5 honor **9** happiness
charm against: 10 witchcraft
used as: 12 air sweetener
use: 4 eggs, fish, meat **5** salad **8** stuffing **9** vegetable

Marjorie Morningstar
author: 10 Herman Wouk

mark 3 cut, mar, pit **4** dent, goal, harm, heed, line, mind, nick, note, pock, rate, scar, show, sign, spot **5** badge, brand, grade, label, notch, point, proof, score, stain, stamp, token, track **6** attend, bruise, deface, denote, emblem, evince, injure, intent, rating, regard, reveal, streak, symbol, target, typify **7** betoken, blemish, correct, imprint, measure, scratch, signify, suggest, symptom, write in, write on **8** bull's-eye, colophon, disclose, evidence, hallmark, indicate, manifest, point out, standard, stand for **9** be a sign of, criterion, designate, disfigure, objective, symbolize, yardstick **10** impression, indication, touchstone **11** distinguish **12** characterize **13** differentiate

Mark
also: 8 John Mark
mother: 4 Mary
cousin: 8 Barnabas
wrote: 11 Gospel

Mark (King Mark)
character in: 16 Arthurian romance

Mark Antony
also: 14 Marcus Antonius
character in: 12 Julius Caesar
author: 11 Shakespeare

mark down 4 note **5** enter, lower **6** record, reduce **7** put down **9** write down

marked 5 clear, great, noted, plain **6** dotted, scored, severe, showed, spotty, tabbed, tagged, traced **7** branded, labeled, pointed, specked, spotted, stained, tracked **8** destined, speckled, striking, targeted **9** indicated, prominent **10** emphasized, identified, made note of, noticeable, remarkable, singled out **11** conspicuous, distinctive, outstanding **12** considerable **13** distinguished

marker 3 IOU, peg, run, tab **4** chip, flag, sign **5** score **6** etcher, scorer, tablet, ticket **7** counter **8** bookmark, memorial, monument, recorder

market 4 hawk, sell, vend **5** stand **6** bourse, peddle, retail **7** grocery **9** dispose of **10** curb market, meat market **11** butcher shop, grocer's shop, marketplace

marketplace 4 mart **5** agora, arena, plaza **6** bazaar, market, square **8** exchange

Mark of Zorro, The
director: 15 Rouben Mamoulian
cast: 11 Tyrone Power **12** Linda Darnell **13** Basil Rathbone **15** Gale Sondergaard
score: 12 Alfred Newman

mark out 8 describe **9** delineate

marksman 8 dead shot, good shot, sure shot **9** crack shot **12** sharpshooter

marksmanship 3 aim **5** skill **8** accuracy **13** sharpshooting

Marley's Ghost
character in: 15 A Christmas Carol
author: 7 Dickens

Marlow
character in: 7 Lord Jim
author: 6 Conrad

Marlowe
character in: 15 Heart of Darkness
author: 6 Conrad

Marlowe, Christopher
author of: 8 Edward II **13** Doctor Faustus, The Jew of Malta **14** Hero and Leander **15** Edward the Second **19** Tamburlaine the Great

Marmee
character in: 11 Little Women
author: 6 Alcott

Marmion
author: 14 Sir Walter Scott
character: 11 Lord Marmion **13** Ralph de Wilton **14** Clare Fitz-Clare **16** Archibald Douglas **19** Constance de Beverley

Marnie
director: 15 Alfred Hitchcock
cast: 10 Diane Baker **11** Sean Connery, Tippi Hedren

maroon 4 plum, wine **6** desert, strand **7** abandon, forsake, magenta **8** cast away, jettison **9** put ashore **10** cast ashore, terra cotta **11** brownish-red, leave behind **15** leave high and dry

Marple, Miss Jane
detective created by: 14 Agatha Christie

Marquand, J P
author of: 13 Wickford Point **18** The Late George Apley
character: 6 Mr Moto

marquee 4 tent **6** awning, canopy **8** marquise

marred 6 ruined **7** damaged, injured, spoiled **8** impaired **9** blemished, destroyed **10** disfigured

marriage 7 wedding, wedlock **8** nuptials **9** matrimony
god of: 4 Frey **5** Freyr, Hymen **9** Hymenaeus
goddess of: 3 Fri **5** Frigg, Frija **6** Frigga, Tellus

marriage broker
Yiddish: 8 shadchan **9** schatchen

marriage of convenience
French: 19 mariage de convenance

Marriage of Figaro, The
also: 15 Le Nozze di Figaro
opera: 6 Mozart
character: 7 Susanna **8** Countess **9** Cherubino, Dr Bartolo **10** Marcellina **13** Count Almaviva

Marriage of Figaro, The
author: 12 Beaumarchais
character: 6 Figaro **7** Suzanne **8** Cherubin **9** Marceline **10** Dr Bartholo **13** Count Almaviva **16** Countess Almaviva

Marriages Between Zones Three, Four and Five
author: 12 Doris Lessing

married 3 wed **5** mated **6** joined, united, wedded **7** hitched, marital **8** combined, espoused **9** connubial **11** matrimonial, tied the knot

married woman
German: 4 frau

marry 3 wed **7** espouse, make one **10** get spliced, tie the knot **13** join in wedlock **14** join in marriage, lead to the altar, take in marriage

Marryat, Frederick
author of: 11 Peter Simple **16** Mr Midshipman Easy

Mars
also: 6 Mamers, Mavors
origin: 5 Roman
god of: 3 war
mother: 4 Juno
wife: 5 Nerio
epithet: 5 Ultor **8** Gradivus
corresponds to: 4 Ares

Mars
position: 6 fourth
nickname: 9 Red Planet
satellite: 6 Deimos, Phobos

Marseillaise 20 French national anthem

marsh 3 bog, fen **5** swamp **6** morass, slough **7** bottoms, wetland **8** quagmire **9** everglade, marshland, quicksand

Marsh, Dame Ngaio
author of: 9 Dead Water **12** Final Curtain **13** Death at the Bar **14** Enter a Murderer **19** Singing in the Shrouds

character: 10 Troy Alleyn **14** Roderick Alleyn

Marsh, Reginald
born: 5 Paris **6** France
artwork: 9 The Bowery **10** Pip and Flip **14** Why Not Use the El? **16** Tattoo and Haircut **17** Twenty-Cent Haircut

marshal 5 align, array, chief, group, order **6** deploy, draw up, gather, leader, line up, muster **7** arrange, collect, manager, sheriff **8** assemble, director, marechal, mobilize, organize **9** fire chief **10** law officer, supervisor **11** police chief **12** chief officer, field marshal **13** generalissimo

Marshall, George C
served in: 3 WWI **4** WWII **9** Korean War, World War I **10** World War II **11** World War One, World War Two
rank: 12 chief of staff **16** general of the army
author of: 12 Marshall Plan
secretary of: 5 state **7** defense
winner of: 15 Nobel Peace Prize (1953)

Marshall, Penny
husband: 9 Rob Reiner
born: 7 Bronx NY
roles: 5 Myrna **12** The Odd Couple **14** Laverne DeFazio **17** Laverne and Shirley
director: 3 Big

marshy 3 wet **4** miry **5** boggy, fenny, muddy **6** swampy **7** paludal, paludic **11** waterlogged

marsupial 5 koala **6** numbat, possum, wombat **7** cuscuse, opossum, wallaby **8** kangaroo **9** bandicoot, phalanger **14** Tasmanian devil

mart 4 show **6** market **8** exchange **9** trade fair, trade show **10** exposition

Martha
sister: 4 Mary
brother: 7 Lazarus
home: 7 Bethany

martial 7 hostile, Spartan, warlike **8** militant, military **9** bellicose, combative, soldierly **10** pugnacious **11** belligerent, contentious

Martian Chronicles, The
author: 11 Ray Bradbury

Martin, Dean
real name: 16 Dino Paul Crocetti
partner: 10 Jerry Lewis
born: 14 Steubenville OH
roles: 8 Matt Helm, Rio Bravo, The Caddy **9** The Stooge **10** Living It Up **12** Four for Texas, Sailor Beware **14** Toys in the Attic **15** Some Came Running **16** Artists and Models

Martin, Mary
son: 11 Larry Hagman
born: 13 Weatherford TX
roles: 6 I Do I Do **8** Peter Pan **12** Sound of Music, South Pacific

Martin, Steve

born: 6 Waco TX
roles: 7 The Jerk **17** Pennies From Heaven, Saturday Night Live **19** The Man with Two Brains **20** Dead Men Don't Wear Plaid **26** Planes Trains and Automobiles

Martin Chuzzlewit
author: 14 Charles Dickens
character: 5 Mercy **7** Charity **8** Tom Pinch **9** Pecksniff, Ruth Pinch, Sarah Gamp **10** Mark Tapley, Mary Graham **15** Jonas Chuzzlewit **17** Anthony Chuzzlewit

martinet 6 despot, tyrant **8** dictator **10** hard master, taskmaster **11** drillmaster, Simon Legree **12** little Caesar **13** authoritarian, drill-sergeant

Marty
director: 11 Delbert Mann
cast: 10 Betsy Blair **11** Joe De Santis **14** Ernest Borgnine **15** Esther Minciotti
Oscar for: 5 actor (Borgnine) **7** picture
script: 14 Paddy Chayefsky

martyr 5 saint **8** sufferer

martyrdom 5 agony **6** ordeal **7** anguish, torment, torture **9** bitter cup, suffering **10** affliction **11** cup of sorrow **13** crown of thorns

marvel 4 gape **6** be awed, rarity, wonder **7** miracle **8** be amazed **9** spectacle **10** phenomenon

Marvell, Andrew
author of: 9 The Garden **16** To His Coy Mistress

marvelous, marvellous 4 A-one, fine **5** grand, great, super **6** divine, lovely, superb **7** amazing **8** colossal, fabulous, heavenly, smashing, splendid **9** fantastic, first-rate, wonderful **10** phenomenal, remarkable, stupendous **11** astonishing, magnificent, outstanding, sensational **13** extraordinary

marvelous to relate
Latin: 13 mirabile dictu

Marwood, Mrs
character in: 16 The Way of the World
author: 8 Congreve

Marx, Bernard
character in: 13 Brave New World
author: 6 Huxley

Marx, Karl
author of: 10 Das Kapital **18** Communist Manifesto (with Friedrich Engels)

Marx Brothers 5 Chico (Leonard), Gummo (Milton), Harpo (Adolph, Arthur) Zeppo (Herbert) **7** Groucho (Julius)
costar: 14 Margaret Dumont
born: 9 New York NY
roles: 8 Coconuts, Duck Soup **11** The Big Store **13** Horse Feathers **14** A Day at the Races, Animal Crackers, Monkey Business **16** A Night at the Opera
Groucho's TV show: 14 You Bet Your Life

Mary 6 Virgin **7** Madonna **8** Holy Mary **9** Magdalene, of Cleopas **10** Virgin Mary **11** Mother of God, Regina Coeli **13** Queen of Heaven **15** Mother of Sorrows **17** Mother of the Church
mother: 4 Anna, Anne
husband: 6 Joseph **7** Alpheus, Cleopas
son: 4 Jude, Mark **5** Jesus, Moses, Simon **12** James the Less
sister: 6 Martha
brother: 7 Lazarus **8** Barnabas
cousin: 9 Elizabeth
home: 8 Nazareth
visitor: 7 Gabriel
flower: 4 lily **8** marigold

Mary
author: 10 Sholem Asch

Maryland
abbreviation: 2 MD
nickname: 4 Free **7** Cockade **12** Old Line State
capital: 9 Annapolis
largest city: 9 Baltimore
others: 5 Essex **6** Easton, Laurel, Towson **8** Aberdeen, Bethesda, Pocomoke **9** Frederick, Ocean City, Rockville **10** Cumberland, Hagerstown, Pikesville **11** Catonsville, College Park
college: 4 Hood **7** Goucher, St John's **10** Washington **11** Towson State **12** Johns Hopkins **21** Annapolis Naval Academy
feature:
  fort: 7 McHenry
  national battlesite: 8 Antietam
  presidential retreat: 9 Camp David
  race: 9 Preakness **12** Steeplechase
  racetrack: 5 Bowie **6** Butler, Laurel **7** Pimlico
tribe: 5 Conoy **9** Nanticoke
people: 6 Wesort **8** Terrapin **10** Spiro Agnew **11** crawthumper **14** Sargent Shriver **15** Francis Scott Key
  explorer: 7 Calvert
lake: 8 Patapsco **9** Deep Creek, Loch Raven, Pretty Boy **10** Rocky Gorge **11** Triadelphia
land rank: 11 forty second
mountain: 4 Dans **8** Piedmont **9** Blue Ridge **11** Appalachian
  highest point: 8 Backbone
physical feature:
  bay: 10 Chesapeake
  sea: 8 Atlantic
  swamp: 7 Pocoson
  valley: 5 Great **10** Hagerstown
river: 3 Elk **7** Chester, Potomac **8** Choptank, Patapsco, Patuxent, Pocomoke **11** Susquehanna
state admission: 7 seventh
state bird: 15 Baltimore oriole
state fish: 11 striped bass
state flower: 14 black-eyed Susan
state motto: 22 Manly Deeds Womanly Words **43** Thou Hast Crowned Us With the Shield of Thy Good Will
state song: 18 Maryland My Maryland
state tree: 8 white oak

Mary Poppins
director: 15 Robert Stevenson
based on story by: 9 P L Travers
cast: 6 Ed Wynn **11** Dick Van Dyke (Bert), Glynis Johns **12** Julie Andrews **14** David Tomlinson **16** Hermione Baddeley
score: 13 Robert Sherman **14** Richard Sherman
Oscar for: 4 song **5** score **7** actress (Andrews) **13** visual effects
song: 14 Chim-chim-cheree

Mary Queen of Scots
director: 14 Charles Jarrott
cast: 12 Trevor Howard **13** Glenda Jackson (Elizabeth I), Timothy Dalton **14** Nigel Davenport **15** Patrick McGoohan, Vanessa Redgrave (Mary of Scotland)

Mary Tyler Moore Show, The
character: 8 Lou Grant **9** Ted Baxter **12** Gordon (Gordy) Howard, Mary Richards, Sue Ann Nivens **13** Bess Lindstrom **14** Marie Slaughter **15** Murray Slaughter **16** Phyllis Lindstrom, Rhoda Morgenstern **23** Georgette Franklin Baxter
cast: 8 John Amos **9** Ted Knight **10** Betty White **11** Edward Asner **12** Gavin MacLeod, Georgia Engel **13** Joyce Bulifant, Lisa Gerritsen, Valerie Harper **14** Cloris Leachman
setting: 11 Minneapolis

Mary Worth
creator: 8 Carey Orr **9** Dale Allen **10** Dale Connor **13** Allen Saunders
character: 4 Bill, Slim

Masaccio
real name: 26 Tommaso di Ser Giovanni di Mone
born: 5 Italy **27** Castel San Giovanni di Valdarno
artwork: 14 The Holy Trinity **15** The Tribute Money **24** The Expulsion from Paradise

Mascagni, Pietro
born: 5 Italy **7** Leghorn
composer of: 4 Iris **6** Nerone **7** Isabeau **10** Le Maschere **11** L'Amico Fritz **14** Il Piccolo Marat **19** Cavalleria Rusticana

masculine 4 bold, male **5** brave, hardy, husky, macho, manly **6** brawny, daring, manful, plucky, robust, strong, sturdy, virile **7** staunch, valiant **8** athletic, fearless, forceful, intrepid, muscular, powerful, resolute, vigorous **9** strapping **10** courageous **11** indomitable, self-reliant **12** stouthearted

Masefield, John

author of: 7 Cargoes **8** Sea Fever **16** Salt Water Ballads

Maseru
capital of: 7 Lesotho

mash 4 mush **5** crush, paste, puree, smash **6** squash **8** mishmash **9** pulverize

M*A*S*H (TV Series)
character: 10 (Capt) BJ Hunnicut, (Lt Col) Henry Blake, (Maj) Frank Burns **12** (Corp) Radar O'Reilly **13** Father (John) Mulcahy, (Capt Benjamin Franklin) Hawkeye Pierce, (Col) Sherman Potter **14** (Corp) Maxwell Klinger **15** (Maj Margaret) Hot Lips Houlihan **19** (Capt) Trapper John McIntyre **24** (Maj) Charles Emerson Winchester
cast: 8 Alan Alda **9** Jamie Farr **11** Harry Morgan, Loretta Swit, Mike Farrell, Wayne Rogers **12** Gary Burghoff **13** Larry Linville **15** McLean Stevenson **16** David Ogden Stiers **18** William Christopher
war: 6 Korean
MASH stands for: 26 Mobile Army Surgical Hospital
tent: 5 Swamp
theme: 17 Suicide Is Painless

M*A*S*H (Film)
director: 12 Robert Altman
cast: 10 Jo Ann Pflug **11** Elliot Gould (Trapper John McIntyre), Tom Skerritt (B J Hunnicut) **12** Gary Burghoff (Radar O'Reilly), Robert Duvall (Frank Burns) **14** Sally Kellerman (Margaret Hot Lips Houlihan) **16** Donald Sutherland (Hawkeye Pierce)

masjid 6 mosque

mask 4 hide, veil **5** blind, cloak, cover **6** domino, screen, shroud **7** conceal, cover-up, curtain, obscure **8** disguise **9** face guard, false face **10** camouflage, keep secret

Mask
director: 16 Peter Bogdanovich
cast: 4 Cher **10** Eric Stoltz (Rocky Dennis), Sam Elliott

masked 9 concealed, covered up, disguised **10** in disguise, masquerade

Masked Ball, A
also: 17 Un Ballo in Maschera
opera by: 5 Verdi
character:
    first version: 9 Count Horn **10** King Gustav **12** Count Ribbing
    second version: 3 Sam, Tom **13** Count Riccardo

masking 6 hiding **7** veiling **8** covering **9** eclipsing, obscuring **10** concealing, covering up

Mason, Bertha
character in: 8 Jane Eyre
author: 6 Bronte

Mason, James
wife: 6 Pamela
born: 7 England **12** Huddersfield

roles: 6 Lolita **7** Lord Jim **9** Bloodline **10** Georgy Girl **13** Heaven Can Wait **14** Humbert Humbert, Murder by Decree, The Seventh Veil **15** Prisoner of Zenda **16** North by Northwest **17** The Boys from Brazil

Mason, Marsha
husband: 9 Neil Simon
born: 9 St Louis MO
roles: 10 Chapter Two **11** Blume in Love **14** The Goodbye Girl **15** Max Dugan Returns **17** Cinderella Liberty

Masque of the Red Death, The
author: 13 Edgar Allan Poe

masquerade 4 mask, ruse, veil **5** cloak, cover, guise, trick **6** masque, pose as, scene, shroud **7** cover-up, pretext **8** artifice, pretense **9** bal masque **10** camouflage, masked ball, subterfuge **11** impersonate **12** harlequinade

Masquerade Party
host: 9 Bert Parks **10** Bud Collier **11** Peter Donald **12** Eddie Bracken, Robert Q Lewis **14** Douglas Edwards

mass, Mass 3 jam, lot, mob **4** body, bulk, cake, clot, heap, host, hunk, knot, lump, pack, pile **5** amass, batch, block, bunch, chunk, clump, corps, crowd, crush, group, horde, press, stack, troop **6** bundle, gather, matter, throng, weight **7** collect, pyramid **8** assemble, best part, main body, majority, material **9** aggregate, Eucharist, gathering, plurality **10** accumulate, assemblage, assortment, collection, concretion, congregate, cumulation, lion's share **11** aggregation, consolidate, greater part **12** accumulation, congregation **13** Holy Communion, holy sacrament, preponderance **14** conglomeration

Massachusetts
abbreviation: 2 MA **4** Mass
nickname: 3 Bay **7** Puritan **9** Baked Bean, Old Colony
capital/largest city: 6 Boston
others: 4 Ayer, Lynn, Otis **5** Athol, Barre, Lenox, Salem **6** Agawam, Dedham, Groton, Nahant, Natick, Revere, Saugus, Woburn **7** Belmont, Beverly, Ipswich, Medford, Peabody, Taunton, Waltham **8** Brockton, Chicopee, Cohasset, Plymouth, Scituate, Yarmouth **9** Arlington, Attleboro, Braintree, Brookline, Cambridge, Lexbridge, Lexington, Worcester **10** Gloucester, New Bedford, Pittsfield **11** Springfield **12** Provincetown, Williamstown
college: 3 MIT **5** Clark, Curry, Smith, Tufts **6** Babson **7** Amherst, Harvard, Simmons, Wheaton **8** Brandeis, Williams **9** Hampshire, Holy Cross, Merrimack, Radcliffe, Wellesley **11** Springfield **12** Mount Holyoke, Northeastern **13** Boston College

feature: 10 Walden Pond **12** Plymouth Rock
    national seashore: 7 Cape Cod
    village: 13 Old Sturbridge
tribe: 6 Nauset **8** Pocomtuc **10** Wampanoags
people: 8 Pilgrims **9** Amy Lowell, Elias Howe **10** Cyrus Field, Eli Whitney **11** Clara Barton, John Hancock, Samuel Adams, Samuel Morse **12** Henry Thoreau, Robert Lowell, Winslow Homer **13** James Whistler, Joseph Kennedy, Robert Kennedy **14** Emily Dickinson **15** Henry Cabot Lodge **16** Benjamin Franklin, Edward "Ted" Kennedy **17** Ralph Waldo Emerson **18** Bartholomew Gosnold, James Russell Lowell, Nathanial Hawthorne **19** Oliver Wendell Holmes, William Cullen Bryant **21** John Greenleaf Whittier
    explorer: 8 Norsemen
island: 5 Duke's **9** Nantucket **13** Chappaquidick **15** Martha's Vineyard
lake: 5 Onota **7** Quabbin, Rohunta, Webster **8** Long Pond **11** Watuppa Pond **16** Assawompsett Pond **17** Chaubunagungamaug
land rank: 10 forty-fifth
mountain: 3 Tom **6** Brodie, Potter **7** Alander, Everett, Taconic **10** Berkshires
    highest point: 8 Greylock
physical feature:
    bay: 8 Buzzard's
    cape: 3 Ann, Cod
    sea: 8 Atlantic
president: 9 John Adams **14** Calvin Coolidge **15** John Quincy Adams **21** John Fitzgerald Kennedy
river: 6 Nashua **7** Charles, Concord, Quaboag, Taunton **8** Chicopee **9** Deerfield, Merrimack **10** Blackstone, Housatonic **11** Connecticut
state admission: 5 sixth
state bird: 9 chickadee
state flower: 9 mayflower **15** trailing arbutus
state motto: 37 With the Sword She Seeks Peace Under Liberty **45** By the Sword We Seek Peace But Peace Only Under Liberty
state song: 22 All Hail to Massachusetts
state tree: 11 American elm

massacre 7 butcher, carnage **8** butchery, decimate **9** bloodbath, slaughter **10** mass murder **12** bloodletting

massage 3 rub **4** flex **5** chafe, knead **6** finger, handle, stroke **7** rubbing, rub down, stretch **8** kneading, stroking **10** manipulate **12** manipulation

Massasoit *see* **10** Wampanoags

Massenet, Jules Emile Frederic
born: 6 France **9** St Etienne
composer of: 5 Le Cid, Manon, Thais **7** Werther **9** Herodiade **11** David Rizzio **12** Don Quichotte **13** Le Roi

de Lahore **21** Le Jongleur de Notre-Dame

masses 6 plebes, proles, rabble, the mob **7** the many **8** the crowd **9** hoi polloi, plebeians **11** the populace, the riffraff **12** the multitude **13** the common herd **14** the proletariat, the rank and file **15** the common people, the lower classes, the working class **16** the great unwashed

massive 4 huge, vast **5** ample, bulky, great, heavy, hefty, massy, solid **7** hulking, immense, mammoth, titanic, weighty **8** colossal, enormous, gigantic, imposing, towering, whopping **9** cyclopean, extensive, monstrous, ponderous **10** gargantuan, impressive, monumental, stupendous **11** elephantine, substantial

massiveness 4 bulk, size **6** volume, weight **7** bigness **8** enormity, hugeness, vastness **9** amplitude, bulkiness, greatness, immensity, largeness, magnitude

mast 4 main, nuts, pole, post, spar **5** spirit, staff, stick, stuff **6** acorns, pillar **9** beechnuts, chestnuts
type: 4 fore, main **6** jigger, mizzen
support: 4 bibb

master 3 ace **4** able, A-one, best, boss, curb, deft, head, lord, main, tame, whiz **5** check, chief, crack, grasp, owner, prime, ruler **6** bridle, choice, expert, genius, gifted, govern, leader, manage, subdue, wizard **7** conquer, control, excel at, head man, manager, primary, skilled, skipper, supreme **8** director, dominate, finished, governor, masterly, overcome, overlord, overseer, regulate, suppress, talented, virtuoso **9** authority, conqueror, craftsman, first-rate, paramount, practiced, principal **10** controller, proficient, supervisor **12** get the hang of, ship's captain

Master Builder, The
author: 11 Henrik Ibsen
character: 5 Hilda **7** Solness

master craftsman 7 artisan **12** masterworker **13** skilled worker

masterful 4 able, deft **5** bossy **6** expert, superb **7** dynamic, skilled **8** finished, forceful, masterly, resolute, skillful, virtuoso **9** excellent **10** commanding **11** domineering, self-reliant **12** accomplished, strong-willed **13** authoritarian, self-confident

masterfulness 6 genius **10** capability, competence, excellence **11** proficiency

Master Melvin
nickname of: 6 Mel Ott

mastermind 4 plan, sage **6** direct, expert, genius, master, pundit, wizard **7** old hand, planner **8** conceive, director, engineer, organize, virtuoso **9** authority, initiator, organizer **10** specialist **11** moving force

Master of Ballantrae, The
author: 20 Robert Louis Stevenson
character: 4 Chew **5** Teach **9** MacKellar **11** Henry Durrie, James Durrie **12** Alison Graeme, Francis Burke, Secundra Dass

master of ceremonies 4 host **5** emcee **11** toastmaster

master of the family
Latin: 13 paterfamilias

masterpiece 5 jewel, prize **7** classic, paragon **8** monument, treasure **9** nonpareil **10** brainchild **11** chef d'oeuvre, ne plus ultra, prizewinner

Masterpiece Theater
host: 13 Alistair Cooke

master race
German: 10 Herrenvolk

Masters, Edgar Lee
author of: 19 Spoon River Anthology

Mastersingers of Nuremberg, The
also: 27 Die Meistersinger von Nurnberg
opera by: 6 Wagner
character: 9 Eva Pogner, Hans Sachs **10** Beckmesser **18** Walther von Stolzing

mastery 4 rule, sway **5** grasp **7** ability, command, control **8** deftness, whip hand **9** dominance, supremacy, upper hand **10** adroitness, attainment, domination, leadership **11** achievement, acquirement, proficiency, superiority **14** accomplishment

masticate 4 chew, gnaw **5** chomp, munch **6** nibble

Mastroianni, Marcello
born: 5 Italy **11** Fontana Liri
roles: 13 Eight and a Half **7** La Notte **11** La Dolce Vita, The Stranger, White Nights **19** Divorce Italian Style

mat 3 dim, pad, rug **4** dead, dull, flat **5** doily, muted **6** carpet, matrix, tangle **7** bedding, bolster, coaster, cushion, support **8** entangle **10** lackluster, lusterless
Japanese: 6 tatami

Mata Hari
real name: 21 Gertrud Margarete Zelle
worked as: 3 spy **6** dancer
worked for: 7 Germans
executed by: 6 French

match 3 fit **4** game, join, mate, meet, pair, peer, suit, twin, yoke **5** adapt, agree, equal, event, unite **6** couple, double, oppose **7** be alike, be equal, combine, connect, contend, contest, vie with **8** parallel **9** companion, duplicate, harmonize **10** correspond, equivalent, tournament **11** competition, counterpart

matched 5 equal **8** of a piece **9** identical **11** coordinated

matching 4 twin **5** equal **6** paired

10 equivalent **11** harmonizing **13** corresponding

matchless 4 rare **7** supreme **8** crowning, foremost, peerless, sterling, superior **9** exemplary, first rate, priceless, paramount, unequaled, unmatched, unrivaled **10** invaluable, preeminent, unbeatable, unexcelled **11** inestimable, superlative, unsurpassed **12** incomparable, unparalleled

matchmaker
Yiddish: 8 shadchan **9** schatchen

mate 3 pal **4** chum, twin, wife **5** buddy, crony, hubby, match **6** couple, friend, spouse **7** cohabit, comrade, consort, husband, pair off, partner **8** copulate, coworker, sidekick **9** associate, colleague, companion, duplicate **10** better half, equivalent **11** confederate, counterpart **12** fellow worker, ship's officer

materfamilias 15 mother of a family

material 5 stuff **6** matter **8** elements **9** substance **12** constituents

materialism 5 greed **12** covetousness **15** acquisitiveness

materialistic 6 greedy **8** covetous, grasping **11** acquisitive, unspiritual

materiality 9 existence **11** tangibility

materialization 5 ghost, shade **6** coming, wraith **7** phantom, specter **9** emergence **10** apparition, appearance **13** manifestation

materialize 4 loom, rise, show **5** bob up, issue, pop up **6** appear, crop up, emerge, turn up **9** come forth **10** burst forth **11** come to light, spring forth **12** come into view

materially 7 vitally **8** palpably, tangibly **9** in the main, seriously **10** monetarily **11** corporeally, essentially, financially, in substance **12** considerably, emphatically **13** significantly, substantially **14** for the most part

material possessions 6 assets, estate, wealth **7** fortune **8** property **10** belongings **12** worldly goods

material proof 8 evidence **13** documentation

materials 4 data **5** cloth, facts, notes, tools **6** stocks, stores, timber **7** fabrics, figures **8** concrete, dry goods, supplies, textiles **9** citations, equipment, machinery, yard goods **10** essentials, piece goods, quotations, references **11** impressions **12** observations **15** bricks and mortar

materiel 4 gear **6** stores **8** supplies **9** equipment, materials **10** provisions **16** military supplies

Mater Matuta see **6** Matuta

maternal 4 fond **6** doting **8** motherly **9** of a mother, shielding **10** motherlike, protective, sheltering

maternity 5 labor **8** delivery

9 pregnancy **10** childbirth, motherhood **11** parturition **12** accouchement, childbearing

mathematical, mathematic 5 exact, rigid **6** strict **7** precise **8** accurate, rigorous, unerring **10** meticulous, scientific, scrupulous **11** punctilious, well-defined **13** computational

mathematician
American: 5 Aiken **6** Wiener
British: 6 Newton **7** Babbage
French: 6 Fermat **9** D'Alembert, Descartes
German: 5 Frege, Gauss **6** Bessel **7** Hilbert
Greek: 6 Euclid, Thales **11** Anaximander
Norwegian: 4 Abel
Swiss: 5 Euler **9** Bernoulli

Mathewson, Christy
nickname: 5 Matty **6** Big Six
sport: 8 baseball
position: 7 pitcher
team: 13 New York Giants

Matholwych
king of: 7 Ireland
wife: 7 Branwen

matinee 9 early show **16** early performance **20** afternoon performance

Mating Season, The
author: 11 P G Wodehouse

Matisse, Henri Emile Benoit
born: 6 France **16** Chateau Cambresis (Le Cateau)
artwork: 5 Dance, Music **8** The Slave **10** Odalisques **11** Joie de Vivre **12** Harmony in Red, La Serpentine **13** Head with Tiara, The Open Window **15** Bathers by a River, Memory of Oceanie, Woman with the Hat **16** Heads of Jeannette **19** Torso with Arms Raised **20** Goldfish and Sculpture

matriarch 7 dowager **10** female head, grande dame **11** female ruler **12** female leader **13** materfamilias

matriculate 4 join **5** enter **6** enlist, enroll, sign up **7** check in **8** register

matriculation 9 signing up **10** enrollment **12** registration

matrimonial 6 bridal, wedded, wifely **7** marital, married, nuptial, spousal **8** conjugal, hymeneal **9** affianced, connubial, husbandly **11** epithalamic

matrimony 7 wedlock **8** marriage **11** holy wedlock

matrix 3 die **4** cast, form, mold **5** frame, punch, stamp

matron 4 dame **5** madam **7** dowager **8** forelady, mistress, overseer **9** forewoman **10** directress **11** housekeeper **12** married woman **14** superintendent

matter 3 fix **4** gist, snag, text **5** count, drift, event, sense, stuff, theme, thing, topic **6** affair, crisis, import, moment, object, scrape, strait, thesis **7** content, dilemma, episode, essence, purport, signify, subject, trouble **8** argument, business, elements, exigency, material, obstacle, quandary **9** adventure, emergency, happening, situation, substance **10** difference, difficulty, experience, impediment, importance, occurrence, perplexity, proceeding **11** carry weight, consequence, predicament, transaction **12** circumstance, significance

matter-of-course 5 usual **6** common **7** routine **8** everyday, ordinary, standard **9** customary **11** commonplace, established

matter-of-fact 4 real **5** blunt, frank **6** candid, direct **7** factual, literal, mundane, natural, prosaic **8** ordinary, sensible **9** outspoken, practical, pragmatic, realistic **10** hardheaded, nononsense, unaffected, uninspired, unromantic **11** commonplace, common-sense, down-to- earth, straight-out **13** unimaginative, unsentimental **15** straightforward

matter-of-factness 10 detachment **11** impassivity **12** practicality **13** impassiveness **17** unimaginativeness

Matter of Time, A
author: 12 Jessamyn West

Matthau, Walter
real name: 13 Walter Matthew **23** Walter Matuschanskavasky
born: 9 New York NY
roles: 5 Kotch **8** A New Leaf **10** Plaza Suite **11** Pete n Tillie **12** Bad News Bears, Ensign Pulver, Grumpy Old Men,Oscar Madison, The Front Page, The Odd Couple **15** California Suite, The Sunshine Boys **16** The Fortune Cookie **22** A Guide for the Married Man

Matthew 7 apostle
father: 7 Alpheus
also called: 4 Levi
wrote: 6 Gospel

Matthiessen, Peter
author of: 10 Sand Rivers **14** The Snow Leopard

maturation 6 growth **8** fruition, ripening **9** growing up

mature 4 ripe **5** adult, bloom, grown, manly, of age, ready, ripen **6** flower, grow up, mellow, nubile, virile **7** blossom, develop, grown-up, matured, womanly **8** finished, maturate, seasoned **9** come of age, completed, fullblown, full-grown, perfected, practiced **10** middle- aged **11** become adult, experienced, full-fledged, in one's prime **12** marriageable

Mature, Victor
born: 12 Louisville KY
roles: 7 The Robe **11** After the Fox, Kiss of Death **12** Cry of the City, One Million BC **16** Samson and Delilah **19** Androcles and the Lion

matured 3 big **4** aged, ripe **5** adult, grown **6** formed **7** ripened **8** flowered, mellowed, seasoned **9** blossomed, developed, full-blown, full-grown **11** full-fledged

maturity 7 manhood **8** legal age, majority, practice, ripeness **9** adulthood, composure, full bloom, readiness, seasoning, womanhood **10** completion, experience, full growth, maturation, matureness, perfection **11** culmination, fulfillment **12** age of consent

Matuta
origin: 5 Roman
goddess of: 3 sea **4** dawn **7** harbors **10** childbirth
called: 11 Mater Matuta

Maud
author: 18 Alfred Lord Tennyson

Maude
character: 5 Carol **7** Phillip **10** Henry Evans **12** Florida Evans, Maude Findlay, Mrs Naugatuck **13** Walter Findlay **14** Dr Arthur Harmon **20** Vivian Cavender Harmon
cast: 8 Bill Macy, John Amos **10** Conrad Bain **11** Esther Rolle **13** Brian Morrison, Rue McClanahan **14** Beatrice Arthur, Kraig Metzinger **15** Adrienne Barbeau **16** Hermione Baddeley
spinoff from: 14 All in the Family
spinoff: 9 Good Times

maudlin 5 gushy, mushy, teary **6** slushy **7** gushing, mawkish, tearful **8** bathetic **9** emotional **10** lachrymose **11** sentimental **13** overemotional

maudlinism 6 bathos **11** mawkishness **14** sentimentalism, sentimentality

Maugham, W Somerset
author of: 9 The Circle **10** Our Betters **11** Cakes and Ale **12** Miss Thompson **13** The Razor's Edge **14** Of Human Bondage **15** The Constant Wife **18** The Moon and Sixpence **21** Lady Frederick Ashenden

maul 4 beat **5** batter, beat up, bruise, mangle, pummel, thrash **7** rough up **9** manhandle **10** knock about

Mauldin, Bill
creator/artist of: 7 Up Front **12** Willie and Joe

Mau Mau 13 secret society
of: 6 Kikuyu
in: 5 Kenya

maunder 4 loaf **5** drift, run on, stray **6** babble, dawdle, gabble, gibber, ramble, wander **7** blather, meander, prattle, saunter **8** flounder, ramble on, straggle **9** go on and on, hem and haw **10** dillydally

maundering 7 diffuse **8** rambling **9** wandering **10** digressive, disjointed, roundabout **14** drift, run on, stray **6** babble, dawdle, gabble, gibber, ramble, wander **7** blather, meander, prattle, saunter **8** flounder, ramble on, straggle **9** go on and on, hem and haw **10** dillydally

Maupassant, Guy de
author of: 6 Belami **9** Ball of Fat, Mont-Oriol **11** A Woman's Life, The Necklace **12** Ball of Tallow **16** Mademoiselle Fifi

Mauriac, Francois
author of: 8 Genitrix **10** The Egoists **12** Viper's Tangle **15** A Kiss to the Leper, The Desert of Love **20** A Woman of the Pharisees

Mauritania
capital/largest city: 10 Nouakchott
others: 4 Atar **5** Kaedi, Rosso **6** Fderik **7** Akjoujt **10** Nouadhibou
division: 5 Sahel **7** Chemama
monetary unit: 5 khoum **7** ouguiya
highest point: 11 Kediat Idjil
river: 7 Senegal
sea: 8 Atlantic
physical feature:
desert: 6 Sahara
valley: 7 Chemama **12** Senegal River
people: 4 Arab, Fula, Moor **5** Black, Fulbe, Wolof **6** Bafour, Berber, Fulani **7** African, Soninke, Tukulor **8** Sarakole **9** Sarakolle **10** Toucouleur **12** Halphoolaren
leader: 4 Luly **5** Salek **6** Daddah **8** Haidalla
ruler: 6 France **9** Almoravid **14** Kingdom of Ghana
language: 4 Fula **5** Wolof **6** Arabic, French **7** Phoolor, Tukulor **8** Fulfulde, Mandingo **9** Sarakolle, Hassaniya
religion: 5 Islam
place:
mosque: 5 Grand
feature:
beehive hut: 4 ruga
priest-teacher: 8 marabout
waterskin: 6 guerba
food:
dish: 7 meshuri
tea: 5 attay

Mauritius
other name: 11 Ile de France
capital/largest city: 9 Port Louis
others: 6 Reduit **8** Curepipe **9** Mahebourg **13** Quartre Bornes **19** Grande Riviere Sud-Est
head of state: 14 British monarch **15** governor general
monetary unit: 4 cent **5** rupee
island: 3 Est **4** Flat **5** Ambre, Cerf's, Morne, Round **7** Agalega, Serpent **9** Mauritius, Rodrigues, Rodriguez, St Brandon **12** Gunner's Quoin **15** Cargados Carajos
highest point: 27 Piton de la Petite Riviere Noire
sea: 6 Indian
people: 6 Creole, French, Indian **7** African, Chinese **8** European

13 Indo-Mauritian
leader: 8 Jugnauth **9** Ramgoolam
ruler: 5 Dutch **6** French **7** English
language: 4 Urdu **5** Hindi, Tamil **6** Creole, French

mausoleum 10 family tomb **11** stately tomb **18** sepulchral monument

mauve 4 plum, puce **5** lilac **6** violet **8** lavender **11** light purple **12** bluish purple

maverick 5 loner **8** yearling **9** dissenter, dissident, eccentric **11** independent **13** individualist, noncomformist

Maverick
character: 12 Bart Maverick, Bret Maverick **13** Brent Maverick **16** Samantha Crawford **24** Cousin Beauregard Maverick
cast: 9 Jack Kelly **10** Roger Moore **11** James Garner **13** Diane Brewster, Robert Colbert

maw 4 craw, crop, jaws **5** mouth **6** gullet, muzzle, throat

mawkish 5 gushy, mushy, teary **7** maudlin, tearful **9** emotional, nostalgic, schmaltzy **10** lachrymose **11** sentimental **15** oversentimental

mawkishness 4 mush **5** slush **6** bathos **9** mushiness, soppiness **10** maudlinism, slushiness **14** sentimentalism, sentimentality

maxim 3 saw **4** rule **5** adage, axiom, motto **6** old saw, saying, truism **7** proverb **8** aphorism, apothegm **9** platitude

Maximes
author: 23 Francois La Rochefoucauld

Maxims of the Law
author: 12 Francis Bacon

maximum 3 top **4** most **6** utmost **7** highest, largest, maximal, optimum, supreme **8** foremost, greatest **9** paramount **11** unsurpassed

Maxwell, Elsa 6 author **7** hostess **9** socialite **10** party-giver **23** "The hostess with the mostes'"

May
characteristic: 7 Maypole **13** queen of the May
flower: 8 hawthorn **15** lily of the valley
French: 3 Mai
gem: 7 emerald
German: 3 Mai
holiday: 6 May Day (1) **10** Mother's Day (2nd Sunday) **11** Memorial Day (last Monday) **14** Armed Forces Day (3rd Saturday)
Italian: 7 Maggio
number of days: 9 thirty-one
origin of name: 4 Maia
Roman goddess of: 6 spring
place in year:
Gregorian: 5 fifth
Roman: 5 third
saying: 27 April showers bring May

flowers
Spanish: 4 Mayo
Zodiac sign: 6 Gemini, Taurus

May, Elaine
real name: 12 Elaine Berlin
partner: 11 Mike Nichols
born: 14 Philadelphia PA
roles: 8 A New Leaf **15** California Suite
director of: 16 The Heartbreak Kid
writer/director of: 8 A New Leaf

Maya
city: 4 Coba **5** Tulum, Uxmal **6** Akumal, Cuello, Izamal **8** Calakmul, Palenque **11** Chichen Itza
conqueror: 8 Alvarado
day: 5 uayeb
language family: 5 Mayan **10** Maya-Quiche
location: 5 Tikal **6** Belize, Mexico **7** Chiapas, Mayapan, Tabasco, Yucatan **8** Honduras **9** Guatemala **11** Chichen Itza **14** Central America
month: 5 uinal **6** uninal
noted for: 9 astronomy **12** architecture **19** hieroglyphic writing
rain god: 4 Chac **5** Chaac **7** Chac Mol **8** Chac Mool
ruins: 9 Yaxchilan **20** Temple of Inscriptions
underworld: 7 Xibalba
year: 4 haab

maybe 6 mayhap **7** perhaps **8** feasibly, possibly **9** perchance **10** God willing, imaginably **11** conceivably **12** peradventure

Maybe
author: 14 Lillian Hellman

Mayberry RFD
character: 5 Alice **7** Aunt Bee **8** Sam Jones **9** Mike Jones **10** Goober Pyle **11** Emmett Clark **13** Howard Sprague, Millie Swanson
cast: 8 Ken Berry **10** Jack Dodson **11** Buddy Foster, Paul Hartman **13** Alice Ghostley, Arlene Golonka, Frances Bavier, George Lindsey

mayfly
varieties: 5 small **6** stream **9** burrowing

mayhem 4 maim **6** felony **7** battery, cripple **8** mutilate, violence **9** crippling, dismember **10** mutilation **13** disfigurement

may he rest in peace
Latin: 16 requiescat in pace

may it do good
Latin: 6 prosit

Maylie, Mrs and Rose
characters in: 11 Oliver Twist
author: 7 Dickens

Mayo, Virginia
real name: 13 Virginia Jones
husband: 12 Michael O'Shea
born: 9 St Louis MO
roles: 17 The West Point Story

22 The Best Years of Our Lives **26** The Secret Life of Walter Mitty

Mayor of Casterbridge, The
author: **11** Thomas Hardy
character: **13** Donald Farfrae, Richard Newson **14** Lucetta Le Sueur **15** Michael Henchard **19** Elizabeth Jane Newson, Susan Henchard-Newson

Mays, Willie
nickname: **9** Say Hey Kid
sport: **8** baseball
position: **11** center field
team: **11** New York Mets **13** New York Giants **18** San Francisco Giants

may she live forever
Latin: **12** esto perpetua
motto of: **5** Idaho

may she rest in peace
Latin: **16** requiescat in pace

maze 5 snarl **6** jungle, tangle **7** complex, meander, network **9** labyrinth **11** convolution

mazel tov 8 good luck

Mbabane
capital of: **9** Swaziland

McBeal, Ally see **10** Ally McBeal

McCambridge, Mercedes
real name: **32** Carlotta Mercedes Agnes McCambridge
born: **8** Joliet IL
roles: **5** Giant **8** Cimarron **11** Touch of Evil **14** All the King's Men **15** A Farewell to Arms **18** Suddenly Last Summer

McCarey, Leo
director of: **8** Duck Soup **10** Going My Way (Oscar) **13** The Awful Truth (Oscar) **15** Ruggles of Red Gap **17** The Bells of St Mary's

McCarthy, Mary
author of: **8** The Group
sister of: **5** Kevin

McCay, Winsor
creator/artist of: **23** Little Nemo in Slumberland

McClellan, George B
nickname: **25** Little Mac the Young Napoleon
served in: **8** Civil War **10** Mexican War
side: **5** Union
commander of: **16** Army of the Potomac
battle: **8** Antietam **18** Peninsular campaign
governor of: **9** New Jersey

McCloud
character: **10** Sam McCloud **13** Chris Coughlin, (Sgt) Joe Broadhurst **14** Peter B Clifford
cast: **8** JD Cannon **11** Terry Carter **12** Dennis Weaver, Diana Muldaur

McClure, Darrell
creator/artist of: **17** Little Annie Rooney

McCrea, Joel

wife: **10** Frances Dee
born: **12** Los Angeles CA
roles: **11** Buffalo Bill **14** Palm Beach Story **16** Sullivan's Travels, The Great Man's Lady **17** Reaching for the Sun, The More the Merrier **20** Foreign Correspondent

McCreary, Fainy (Mac)
character in: **3** USA
author: **9** Dos Passos

McCullers, Carson
author of: **17** The Mortgaged Heart **18** Member of the Wedding **21** The Ballad of the Sad Cafe **23** Reflections in a Golden Eye, The Heart Is a Lonely Hunter

McCullough, Colleen
author of: **13** The Thornbirds **19** An Indecent Obsession

McCutcheon, George Barr
author of: **9** Graustark

McEvoy, JP
creator/artist of: **10** Dixie Dugan

McFee, William
author of: **15** Casuals of the Sea

McGinley, Phyllis
author of: **12** Three Decades **15** A Pocketful of Wry **24** The Horse Who Lived Upstairs

McHale's Navy
character: **7** Christy **9** Willy Moss **11** Fuji Kobiaji, Happy Haines **12** Harrison (Tinker) Bell, Lester Gruber **13** Virgil Farrell, (Ensign) Charles Parker, (Lt Cdr) Quinton McHale **14** (Lt) Elroy Carpenter **18** (Capt) Wallace B Binghamton
cast: **8** Joe Flynn **9** Tim Conway **10** Billy Sands, Gary Vinson, John Wright, Yoshio Yoda **11** Bob Hastings, Edson Stroll **12** Gavin MacLeod **14** Carl Ballantine, Ernest Borgnine

McKenna, Siobhan
born: **7** Belfast, Ireland
roles: **11** King of Kings **13** Doctor Zhivago **14** Of Human Bondage **24** Playboy of the Western World

McKim, Charles M
architect of: **27** Lutheran Church of the Redeemer (Houston)

McKim, Mead, and White
partners: **13** Stanford White **18** Charles Follen McKim **21** William Rutherford Mead
architects of: **11** Century Club **14** University Club, Washington Arch **17** Vanderbilt Mansion **18** Columbia University (NYC) **19** Boston Public Library, Pennsylvania Station (NYC), (first) Madison Square Garden (NYC) **21** New York Herald Building, Pierpont Morgan Library (NYC) **31** Madison Square Presbyterian Church
style: **7** Shingle **18** Italian Renaissance

McKinley, William

nickname: **13** Major McKinley
presidential rank: **11** twenty-fifth
party: **10** Republican
state represented: **2** OH
defeated: **4** (Eugene Victor) Debs **5** (Seth Hockett) Ellis, (William Jennings) Bryan **6** (John McCauley) Palmer, (Wharton) Barker **7** (Charles Eugene) Bentley, (John Granville) Woolley, (Jonah Fitz Randolph) Leonard **8** (Charles Horatio) Matchett, (Joseph Francis) Malloney, (Joshua) Levering
vice president: **6** (Garret Augustus) Hobart **9** (Theodore) Roosevelt
cabinet:
state: **3** (John Milton) Hay, (William Rufus) Day **7** (John) Sherman
treasury: **4** (Lyman Judson) Gage
war: **4** (Elihu) Root **5** (Russell Alexander) Alger
attorney general: **4** (Philander Chase) Knox **6** (John William) Griggs **7** (Joseph) McKenna
navy: **4** (John Davis) Long
postmaster general: **4** (James Albert) Gary **5** (Charles Emory) Smith
interior: **5** (Cornelius Newton) Bliss **9** (Ethan Allen) Hitchcock
agriculture: **4** (James) Wilson
born: **7** Niles OH
died: **9** Buffalo NY
died by: **13** assassination
buried: **8** Canton OH
education:
college: **10** Allegheny
law school: **6** Albany
religion: **9** Methodist
author: **37** The Tariff in the Days of Henry Clay and Since
political career: **24** US House of Representatives
governor of: **4** Ohio
civilian career: **6** lawyer
military service: **7** captain **8** Civil War **11** brevet major
notable events of lifetime/term:
Act: **13** Dingley Tariff
Peace Conference: **5** Hague
Treaty of: **5** Paris
war with: **5** Spain
father: **7** William
mother: **5** Nancy (Campbell Allison)
siblings: **4** Anna, Mary **5** Abner, Helen, James **10** Abbie Celia **12** David Allison **14** Sarah Elizabeth
wife: **3** Ida (Saxton)
children: **3** Ida **9** Katherine

McManus, George
creator/artist of: **12** The Newlyweds **16** Bringing Up Father

McMillan, Edwin Mattison
field: **7** physics **9** chemistry
developed: **16** synchrocyclotron
awarded: **10** Nobel Prize

McMillan and Wife
character: **7** Mildred **13** Sally McMil-

lan **14** (Sgt) Charles Enright **15** (Commissioner) Stewart McMillan
cast: 10 John Schuck, Rock Hudson **11** Nancy Walker **15** Susan Saint James

McMurtry, Larry
author of: **10** Texasville **12** Lonesome Dove **14** Horseman Pass By **18** The Last Picture Show

McPhee, John
author of: **16** In Suspect Terrain **20** Coming into the Country **23** The Curve of Binding Energy **26** Encounters with the Archdruid

McQueen, Steve
real name: **21** Terrence Steven McQueen
wife: **10** Ali MacGraw
born: **8** Slater MO **14** Indianapolis IN
roles: **7** Bullitt, The Blob **8** Papillon **14** The Great Escape, The Sand Pebbles **16** The Cincinnati Kid **17** Thomas Crown Affair, Wanted Dead or Alive **19** The Magnificent Seven

McTeague
author: **11** Frank Norris

mea culpa 7 my fault **14** through my fault

Mead, Margaret
author of: **14** My Earlier Years **16** Blackberry Winter **18** Coming of Age in Samoa **20** Growing Up in New Guinea **42** Sex and Temperament in Three Primitive Societies
husband: **14** Gregory Bateson

Meade, Dr and Mrs
characters in: **15** Gone With the Wind
author: **8** Mitchell

Meade, George Gordon
served in: **8** Civil War **10** Mexican War
side: **5** Union
battle: **7** Bull Run **8** Antietam **10** Gettysburg **13** South Mountain **14** Fredericksburg **16** Chancellorsville **18** Peninsular campaign
commander of: **16** Army of the Potomac

meadow 3 lea **4** mead, park **5** field, green **6** forage **7** herbage, pasture, savanna **9** grassland, pasturage

meager 4 bare, lean, slim, thin **5** scant, short, spare, token **6** little, paltry, scanty, scarce, skimpy, slight, sparse **7** scrimpy, slender, stinted, wanting **9** deficient **10** inadequate **12** insufficient **13** insubstantial

meagerness 8 sparsity **9** smallness **10** inadequacy, measliness, scantiness, skimpiness, sparseness **13** insufficiency **14** insignificance

Meagles
character in: **12** Little Dorrit
author: **7** Dickens

meal 4 bran, chow, diet, eats, fare, food, grub, menu **5** feast, flour, grits **6** farina, groats, repast, spread **7** banquet, cooking, cuisine, oatmeal **8** cornmeal, victuals **10** bill of fare **11** nourishment, refreshment

mealymouthed 6 unsure **7** devious **8** hesitant **9** deceptive, insincere

mean 3 low, par, say **4** base, evil, norm, plan, poor, rude, rule, vile, want, wish **5** aim at, cheap, close, cruel, imply, nasty, petty, small, tight, venal **6** denote, flimsy, greedy, hint at, intend, malign, medium, menial, normal, paltry, sleazy, sordid, stingy, tell off, trashy, unfair **7** average, balance, betoken, dream of, drive at, express, hoggish, inhuman, miserly, point to, propose, purpose, regular, resolve, selfish, signify, squalid, suggest, think of, trivial, vicious **8** aspire to, gimcrack, grasping, indicate, inferior, inhumane, intimate, low-grade, picayune, piddling, pitiless, rubbishy, say truly, shameful, standard, stand for, trifling, uncaring, wretched **9** illiberal, low-paying, malicious, mercenary, merciless, miserable, niggardly, penurious, symbolize, unfeeling **10** avaricious, compromise, despicable, have in mind, have in view, jerrybuilt, low-ranking, malevolent, pinchpenny, second-rate, ungenerous, villainous **11** closefisted, commonplace, disgraceful, happy medium, hardhearted, self-seeking, small-minded, tightfisted, unimportant **12** contemptible, disagreeable, dishonorable **13** insignificant, unsympathetic **15** inconsequential

meander 4 loop, rove, wind **5** snake, stray, twist **6** circle, ramble, spiral, wander, zigzag **8** undulate **9** convolute, corkscrew

meandering 7 devious, sinuous, turning, winding **8** indirect, rambling, tortuous, twisting **9** wandering **10** circuitous, roundabout, serpentine

meaning 3 aim, end **4** gist, goal, hint, meat, pith, plan, view **5** drift, force, point, sense, value, worth **6** burden, design, intent, object, scheme, thrust, upshot **7** content, essence, pointer, purport, purpose **9** intention, substance **10** denotation, indication, intimation, suggestion **11** implication **12** significance **15** sum and substance

meaningful 4 deep **5** meaty, pithy **6** useful **7** pointed, serious **8** eloquent, explicit, pregnant **9** designing, important **10** expressive, gratifying, portentous, purposeful, suggestive, worthwhile **11** significant, substantial **13** consequential

meaningless 5 trite **6** absurd, paltry, stupid **7** aimless, fatuous, foolish, idiotic, shallow, trivial, useless **8** baffling, piddling, puzzling **9** enigmatic, facetious, frivolous, illegible, sense-

less, valueless, worthless **10** incoherent, mystifying, perplexing **11** bewildering, inscrutable, nonsensical, purposeless, unessential, unimportant **12** impenetrable, inexplicable, inexpressive, preposterous **13** insignificant, unsubstantial **14** undecipherable

Mean Joe
nickname of: **9** Joe Greene

means 3 way **4** jack, mode **5** bread, dough, funds, money **6** avenue, course, income, method, resort, riches, wealth **7** capital, dollars, measure, process, revenue **8** property **9** affluence, long green, resources, substance **11** alternative, wherewithal

mean-spirited 3 low **4** base, poor, vile **5** cheap, nasty, petty, small, snide, sorry, tight, venal **6** abject, measly, paltry, scurvy, shabby, sordid, stingy **7** ignoble, miserly, selfish, vicious **8** tightwad, wretched **9** miserable, penurious **10** ungenerous **12** parsimonious

Mean Streets
director: **14** Martin Scorsese
cast: **11** Amy Robinson, David Proval **12** Harvey Keitel, Robert DeNiro

meantime 7 interim **8** interval **9** meanwhile

meanwhile 8 meantime **12** concurrently, in the interim **13** at the same time **14** simultaneously

measurable 10 assessable, computable, mensurable, reckonable **11** appraisable **12** determinable

measure 3 act, law **4** bill, plan, rule, size, step, time **5** bound, clock, gauge, judge, limit, means, plumb, quota, range, scale, scope, share, sound, value **6** amount, assess, course, degree, design, extent, method, resort, scheme, survey **7** portion, project **8** appraise, evaluate, proposal, quantity **9** allotment, allowance, enactment, procedure, restraint, yardstick **10** limitation, moderation, proceeding, temperance

measure, unit of
of Afghanistan: **3** paw, sir **5** jerib, karoh **6** khurds **7** kharwar
of Algeria: **3** pik **5** rebis, tarri **6** termin
of Argentina: **4** sino **5** legua **6** cuadra, lastre **7** manzana
of Australia: **4** arna, naut, saum
of Austria: **4** fass, fuss, joch, mass, muth, yoke **5** halbe, linie, meile, metze, pfiff, punkt **6** achtel, becher, leipoa, seidel **7** klafter, viertel **8** dreiling **12** futtermassel
of Belgium: **3** vat **4** aune, pied **5** carat **6** perche **8** boisseau
of Bolivia: **6** league **7** celemin
of Borneo: **7** gantang
of Brazil: **2** pe **4** moio, sack, vara **5** braca, legoa, milha, tonel **6** canada,

cuarto, quarto, tarefa **7** garrafa **8** al-queire

of Bulgaria: 3 oka, oke **5** krine, lekhe, likhe

of Canada: 3 ton **5** minot, perch, point **6** arpent **7** chainon

of the Canary Islands: 8 fanegada

of Chile: 4 vara **5** legua, linea **6** cuadra **7** fanega

of China: 3 cho, fan, fen, pau, tou, tun, yan, yin **4** chek, chih, fang, kish, papa, quei, shih, teke, tsan, tsun **5** catty, chang, ching, sheng, shing **6** chupak, gungli, kungho, kungmu, tching **7** kungfen, kungyin **8** kungchih, kungshih **9** kungching

of Colombia: 4 vara **7** azumbre, celemin

of Costa Rica: 4 vara **5** cafiz, cahiz **6** fanega, tercia **7** cajuela, cantaro, manzana **10** caballeria

of Cuba: 4 vara **5** bocoy, cocoy, tarea **6** cordel, fanega **10** caballeria

of former Czechoslovakia: 3 lan **4** mira **5** korec, liket, stopa **6** merice, strych

of Denmark: 3 ell, fod, mil, pot **4** alen **5** album, anker, kande, linje, paegl **7** landmil, oltonde, ortonde, skieppe, viertel **8** fjerding **9** ottingkar **10** korntonde

of the Dominican Republic: 3 ona **5** tarea **6** fanega

of Ecuador: 5 libra **6** cuadra, fanega

of Egypt: 3 apt, dra, hen, rob **4** arab, dira, draa, khet, nief, ocha, roub, theb, wudu **5** abdat, ardab, cubit, farde, fedan, keleh, kerat, kilah, sahme **6** artaba, aurure, baladi, kantar, keddah, robhah, schene **7** choryos, daribah, malouah, roubouh, toumnah **8** kassabah, kharouba **10** diramimari, diribaladi

of El Salvador: 4 vara **5** cafiz, cahiz **6** fanega **7** batella, botella, cantara, manzana

of England: 3 cut, ell, lea, pin, rod, ton, tun, vat **4** acre, bind, butt, comb, coom, cran, foot, gill, goad, hand, hank, heer, hide, inch, last, line, mile, nail, pace, palm, peck, pint, pipe, pole, pool, rood, rope, sack, seam, span, trug, typp, wist, yard, yoke **5** bodge, chain, cubit, digit, float, floor, fluid, hutch, jugum, minim, ounce, perch, point, prime, quart, skein, stack, truss **6** barrel, bovate, bushel, cranne, fathom, firkin, gallon, hobbet, hobbit, league, manent, oxgang, pottle, runlet, square, strike, sulung, thread, tierce **7** auchlet, furlong, kenning, quarter, rundlet, seamile, spindle, tertian, virgate **8** carucate, chaldron, hogshead, landyard, puncheon, quadrant, standard

of Estonia: 3 tun **4** elle, liin, sund, toll, toop **5** verst **6** sagene, versta

7 kulimet **8** tonnland

of Ethiopia: 3 tat **4** cubi, kuba **5** derah, messe **6** cabaho, sinjer, sinzer, tanica **7** entelam, farsakh, farsang, ghebeta

of Finland: 5 kannu, verst **6** fathom, kannor **8** ottinger, skalpund, tunnland

of France: 3 pot, sac **4** aune, mine, pied, velt **5** arpen, carat, ligne, minot, pinte, point, pouce, velte **6** arpent, hemine, league, quarte, setier

of Greece: 3 pik **4** bema, piki, pous **5** baril, chous, cubit, diote, doron, maris, pekhe, podos, pygon, xylon **6** acaena, bacile, barile, cotula, dichas, gramme, hemina, koilon, lichas, milion, orgyia, palame, pechys, schene, xestes **7** bacvhel, chenica, choenix, cyathos, diaulos, metreta, stadium, stremma **8** condylos, daktylos, dekapode, dolichos, medimnos, medimnys, metretes, palaiste, plethron, plethrum, stathmos **9** hemiekton, oxybaphon

of Guatemala: 4 vara **6** cuarta, tercia **7** cajuela, manzana **10** caballeria

of Guinea: 7 jacktan

of Honduras: 4 vara **5** milla **6** mecate **7** cajuela

of Hungary: 3 ako **4** hold, yoke **5** itcze, marok, metze **7** huvelyk

of Iceland: 3 set **4** alin **5** almud **6** almenn, ferfet, pottur **7** fathmur, fermila, oltunna

of India: 3 ady, gaz, gez, jow, lan **4** byee, coss, depa, doph, hath, koss, kunk, raik, rati, seit, taun, tola **5** bigha, covid, crosa, danda, depoh, drona, erosa, garce, hasta, krosa, parah, ratti, salay, yojan **6** adhaka, amunam, covido, cudava, cumbha, geerah, moolum, mushti, ouroub, palgat, parran, prasha, ropani, tipree, unglee, yojana **7** dhanush, gavyuti, khahoon, niranga, prastha **8** okthabah

of Indonesia: 5 depah, depoh

of Iran: 3 gaz, zar, zer **4** cane **5** gareh, kafiz, makuk, qasab **6** charac, chebel, ghalva **7** capicha, chenica, farsakh, mansion, mishara **8** parasang, piamaneh, stathmos

of Ireland: 4 mile **6** bandle **8** crannock

of Israel: 3 cab, car, hin, kab, kor **4** bath, ezba, omer, reed **5** cubit, donum, dunam, ephah, ganeh, homer, kaneh

of Italy: 3 pie **4** orna **5** palma, palmo, punto, salma, stero **6** barile, miglie, moggio, rubbio, tomolo **7** braccio, secchio **8** giornata, quadrato

of Japan: 2 go **3** boo, cho, djo, fun, inc, ken, kin, kon, rin, shi, sho, sun, tan **4** hiro, isse, kati, koku, niyo, shoo **5** carat, catty, issho, ittan, momme, picul, shaku **6** kwamme

8 hiyak-kin **9** hiyak-hiro **11** komma-ichida, kujira-shaku

of Java: 3 kan **4** paal, rand **5** palen

of Kenya: 4 wari

of Laos: 3 bak

of Latvia: 3 let **4** stof **5** stoff, verst **6** arshin, kulmet **7** verchoc, verchok **8** krouchka, pourvete **9** deciatine, lofstelle, pourvette **10** tonnseteel

of Liberia: 4 kuba

of Libya: 3 dra, pik, saa **4** kele **5** bozze, donum, jabia, teman, uckia **6** barile, gorrah, misura **7** mattaro, termino **8** kharouba

of Luxembourg: 5 fuder

of Madagascar: 7 gantang

of Malaysia: 3 pau, tun **4** para, pipe, tael, wang **5** parah **6** chupak, parrah **7** gantang

of Malta: 4 rotl **5** artal, canna, parto, ratel, salma **6** kantar **7** caffiso

of Mexico: 3 bag, pie **4** alma, onza, vara **5** almud, baril, carga, jarra, labor, legua, libra, linea, marco, sitio **6** adarme, almude, arroba, carega, fanega, ochaua, terceo **7** pulgada, quintal **9** cuarteron, cuartillo **10** caballeria

of Morocco: 4 kala, muhd, rotl, saah, sahh, ueba **5** artal, cadee, gerbe, ratel **6** covado, dirhem, fanega, izenbi, kintar, tangin, tomini **8** quintral

of Myanmar: 2 ly **3** dha, gon, mau, sao, tao, tat **4** byee, phan, seit, taun, that **5** shita, thuoc **6** lamany, palgat **7** chaivai **8** okthabah

of the Netherlands: 2 el **3** aam, ahm, ell, kan, vat **4** duim, mijl, rood, rope **5** anker, roede, wisse **6** bunder, legger, maatje, mutsje, streep **7** schepel **8** mimgelen, steekkan

of Nicaragua: 4 vara **5** cahiz **6** suerte **7** cajuela, manzana **10** cabelleria

of Norway: 3 fot, mal **4** alen **5** kande **6** fathom **7** skieppe **9** korntonde

of Panama: 5 celemin

of Paraguay: 3 pie **4** lino, lira, lire, vara **5** legua **6** cuadra, fanega

of Peru: 4 topo **5** galon **7** celemin **8** fanegada

of the Philippines: 4 loan **5** braza, catty, cavan, chupa, fardo, ganta, picul, punto **6** apatan, balita, lachsa, quinon **7** quilate **8** chinanta

of Poland: 3 cal **4** mila, pret **5** morga, sazen, vloka, wloka **6** cwierc, cwierk, kwarta, lokiec **7** garniec **9** kwarterka

of Portugal: 2 pe **4** bota, moio, vara **5** almud, fanga, geira, linha, milha **6** almude, covado **7** alquier, ferrado, selamin **8** alqueire

of Puerto Rico: 6 cuerda **10** cabelleria

of Rumania: 7 faltche

of Russia: 3 fut, lof **4** duim, fass, loof, pood, quar, stof **5** duime, foute, korec, korek, ligne, osmin, pajak, st-off, stoof, vedro, verst **6** charka, liniya, osmina, paletz, sagene, stekar, tchast, tsarki, versta, verste **7** archine, arsheen, botchka, chkalik, garnetz, verchoc, verchok **8** boutylka, chetvert, krouchka, kroushka **9** chetverik **10** dessiatine **11** polugarnetz

of Scotland: 3 cop **4** boll, cran, fall, mile, peck, pint, rood, rope, span **5** crane, lippy **6** audlet, davach, firlot, lippie, noggin **7** chalder, choppin **8** mutchkin, stimpart, stimpert **9** particate, shaftment, shathmont

of Sicily: 5 salma **7** caffiso

of Sierra Leone: 4 load **6** kettle

of Somalia: 3 top **4** caba **5** chela, darat, tabla **6** cubito **8** parsalah

of South Africa: 4 vara

of Spain: 3 pie **4** codo, dedo, paso, vara **5** braza, cahiz, carga, legua, medio, palmo, sesma **6** cordel, cuarta, fanega, racion, yugada **7** azumbre, celemin, estadel, pulgada **8** fanegada

of Sri Lanka: 4 para, seer **5** parah **6** amunam, parrah

of Sudan: 2 ud

of Suriname: 7 ketting

of Sweden: 3 aln, fot, ref, tum **4** alar, amar, famn, kapp, last, stop **5** carat, foder, kanna, linje, nymil, spann **6** fathom, jumfru **7** oxhuvud, tunland **8** fjarding, koltunna, tunnland

of Switzerland: 3 imi, pot **4** aune, fuss, muid, pied, zoll **5** lieue, linie, maass, pouce, staab, toise **6** perche, strich **7** klafter, viertel **9** quarteron **10** holzlafter **11** holzklafter

of Syria: 5 makuk **6** garava

of Thailand: 2 wa **3** can, ken, niv, rai, sat, sok, wah **4** cohi, keup, niou, tang **5** kwien, leeng, sesti, vouah **6** kabiet, kanahn **7** chaimeu **8** changawn **9** anukabiet

of Tunisia: 3 saa **4** saah **5** cafiz **6** mettar **8** milerole

of Turkey: 3 dra, oka, pik **4** draa, khat, kile, zira **5** berri, kileh, zirai **6** arshin, chinik, fortin, halebi **7** nocktat

of Uruguay: 4 vara **6** cuadra, suerte

of Venezuela: 5 galon, milla **6** fanega **7** estadel

of Vietnam: 4 gang, phan, thon

of Wales: 5 cover **7** cantred, crannoc, listred

of Yugoslavia: 3 oka, rif **4** akov, ralo **5** donum, khvat, lanaz, plaze, stopa **6** motyka, ralico **9** danoranja

measured 5 equal, exact **6** steady **7** precise, regular, studied, uniform **8** verified **10** calculated, deliberate **11** cold-blooded, intentional, well-planned **12** premeditated **13** predetermined

Measure for Measure
   author: 18 William Shakespeare
   character: 5 Lucio **6** Angelo, Juliet **7** Claudio, Escalus, Mariana **8** Isabella **9** Vincentio

measureless 7 endless **8** infinite **9** boundless, unlimited **12** immeasurable

measurement 4 area, mass, size **5** depth, width **6** extent, height, length, volume, weight **7** breadth, content, gauging **8** capacity, plumbing, sounding **9** amplitude, appraisal, dimension, magnitude, measuring, reckoning, surveying **10** assessment, estimation, evaluation **11** mensuration

   Biblical: 4 omer **5** cubit, ephah **6** shekel

   champagne: 6 magnum **8** jeroboam, rehoboam **9** balthazar **10** methuselah, salmanazar **14** Nebuchadnezzar

   cloth: 4 bolt

   cotton: 4 bale

   electricity: 3 ohm **4** volt, watt **5** joule **6** ampere **10** horsepower

   energy: 3 BTU **5** joule **7** calorie **11** kilocalorie **18** British thermal unit

   firewood: 4 cord

   force: 4 dyne **6** newton **7** poundal

   gold/jewelry: 5 carat, karat, point

   Greek: 4 mina **5** cubit **6** obolos, talent **7** drachma, stadion

   gun: 5 gauge **7** caliber

   light: 7 candela **11** candlepower

   liquor/spirits: 4 pint, pony, shot **5** fifth, quart **6** jigger, magnum

   metric system: 5 liter, meter **9** deciliter, decimeter, dekaliter, dekameter, kiloliter, kilometer, nanometer **10** centiliter, centimeter, cubic meter, hectoliter, hectometer, milliliter, millimeter **11** square meter **14** cubic dekameter **15** cubic centimeter, cubic millimeter, square decimeter, square dekameter, square kilometer **16** square centimeter, square hectometer, square millimeter

   metric weight: 3 ton **4** gram **5** tonne **7** quintal **8** dekagram, kilogram **9** centigram, hectogram, microgram, milligram

   paper: 4 ream **5** quire

   pressure: 6 pascal **10** atmosphere

   Roman: 2 as **5** cubit, libra **6** pondus **7** stadium

   sound: 7 decibel

   temperature: 6 degree, Kelvin **7** Celsius **10** Fahrenheit

   time: 3 day **4** hour, week, year **5** month, score **6** decade, minute, second **7** century **10** millennium, nanosecond **11** microsecond, millisecond

   typography: 2 em, en **4** pica **5** point

   unit: 3 cup, rod **4** acre, dram, foot, gill, inch, link, mile, peck, pint, yard **5** chain, minim, ounce, quart **6** barrel, bushel, circle, degree, fathom, gallon **7** furlong, hectare **8** angstrom, hogshead, teaspoon **9** cubic foot, cubic inch, cubic yard, square rod

10 fluid ounce, right angle, square foot, square inch, square mile, square yard, tablespoon **25** international nautical mile

   weight: 3 ton **4** dram **5** grain, ounce, pound **7** scruple **8** short ton **9** ounce troy, pound troy **11** pennyweight **13** hundredweight

measure out 6 ration **7** dole out, mete out **9** apportion

meat 3 nut **4** core, fare, food, gist, grub **5** heart, point **6** kernel **7** edibles, essence, nucleus **8** victuals **9** provender, substance **10** provisions, sustenance **11** comestibles, nourishment

mechanic 6 joiner **7** artisan **9** automatic, craftsman, machinist **11** uninspired **12** grease monkey

mechanical 4 cold **7** routine **9** automatic, unfeeling **10** impersonal, self-acting, unthinking **11** instinctive, involuntary, machinelike, perfunctory, unconscious **13** machine-driven

mechanism 4 tool **5** motor, works **7** machine, utensil **9** apparatus, appliance, implement, machinery **10** instrument **11** contrivance

medal 5 award, honor, prize **6** laurel, reward, ribbon, trophy **8** citation **9** medallion **10** decoration

Medawar, Peter Brian
   field: 7 biology
   nationality: 7 British
   discovered: 23 acquired immune tolerance
   awarded: 10 Nobel Prize

meddle 5 mix in **6** butt in, horn in, kibitz **7** intrude, pry into **9** interfere, interlope, intervene **10** tamper with

meddler 3 pry **5** snoop **7** Paul Pry **8** busybody **10** interferer, Nosy Parker

meddlesome 4 nosy **5** pushy **6** prying, snoopy **7** pushing **8** meddling, snooping **9** intrusive, obtrusive, officious **11** impertinent, interfering **12** presumptuous

Medea
   author: 9 Euripides
   character: 5 Creon, Jason **6** Aegeus, Glauce

Medea
   form: 9 sorceress
   father: 6 Aeetes
   mother: 5 Idyia
   aunt: 5 Circe
   brother: 8 Apsyrtus
   sister: 9 Chalciope
   lover: 5 Jason
   son: 6 Medeus, Pheres **8** Mermerus, Tisander **9** Alcimenes, Thessalus
   killed: 7 her sons
   escaped to: 6 Athens

Medeus
   father: 6 Aegeus
   mother: 5 Medea

Media 14 ancient kingdom
   present day: 4 Iran

capital: 8 Ecbatana
King: 6 Darius, Xerxes **9** Ahasueras
inhabitant: 4 Mede **5** Aryan **7** Persian **8** Parthian

media 5 press, radio **9** magazines **10** billboards, journalism, newspapers, television **11** journalists
singular: 6 medium

medial 4 mean **6** median **7** average

median 3 mid, par **4** mean, norm **5** mesne **6** center, medial, medium, middle **7** average, central, halfway **8** middling, midpoint, moderate **12** intermediate

mediate 6 pacify, step in, umpire **7** referee **8** moderate **9** arbitrate, intercede, interpose, intervene, negotiate, reconcile **10** conciliate, propitiate

mediation 6 parley **10** adjustment, com- promise, discussion **11** arbitration, give- and-take, negotiation, peacemaking **12** conciliation, intercession, intervention, pacification **14** reconciliation

mediator 6 umpire **7** referee **9** go-between, moderator **10** arbitrator, negotiator, peacemaker, reconciler **12** intermediary

medical 7 healing **8** curative, remedial, salutary, sanative **9** medicinal **10** medicative **11** restorative, therapeutic

medical abbreviation
  a c: 11 before meals
  ad lib: 8 as needed **9** as desired
  agit: 5 shake
  aq: 5 water
  b i d: 9 twice a day
  cap: 4 take **7** capsule
  coch: 8 spoonful
  dil: 6 dilute **8** dissolve
  fldxt: 12 fluid extract
  ft: 4 make
  ft mist: 12 make a mixture
  ft pulv: 11 make a powder
  gr: 5 grain
  gt: 4 drop
  gtt: 5 drops
  h s: 9 at bedtime
  in d: 5 daily
  lot: 6 lotion
  mod praesc: 21 in the manner prescribed
  O: 4 pint
  O D: 8 right eye
  O S: 7 left eye
  O U: 9 in each eye
  ol: 3 oil
  p c: 9 after food **10** after meals
  p o: 7 by mouth
  p r n: 25 as circumstances may require
  pil: 3 pill
  pulv: 6 powder
  q i d: 14 four times daily
  rep: 6 repeat
  s o s: 11 if necessary
  ss: 7 one half

  tab: 6 tablet
  t i d: 15 three times daily
  ut dict: 10 as directed

Medical Center
  character: 9 (Dr) Joe Gannon **11** Nurse Wilcox, (Dr) Paul Lochner **13** Nurse Chambers **14** Nurse Courtland, (Dr) Jeanne Bartlett
  cast: 9 James Daly **11** Chad Everett, Chris Hutson **12** Audrey Totter, Jayne Meadows **14** Corinne Camacho

medical practitioner 6 doctor, medico **9** physician

medication 4 balm **5** tonic **6** elixir, remedy **7** nostrum, panacea **8** medicine **10** medicament, palliative **11** restorative

Medici, Giovanni de' 8 Pope Leo X **15** Pope Leo the Tenth

Medici, Giulio 14 Pope Clement VII **21** Pope Clement the Seventh

medicine 4 balm, drug, pill **5** salve, tonic **6** remedy **7** nostrum **10** healing art, medication **11** restorative **12** therapeutics **13** materia medica
  god of: 9 Asclepius **11** Aesculapius

medieval 8 Dark Ages **10** antiquated, Middle Ages **12** old-fashioned **14** pre-Renaissance

mediocre 4 so-so **5** petty **6** common, meager, medium, normal, paltry, slight **7** average **8** inferior, ordinary, passable, trifling **9** tolerable **10** negligible, pedestrian, second-rate **11** commonplace, indifferent, unimportant **12** run-of-the-mill **13** inappreciable, insignificant **14** fair- to-middling, inconsiderable **15** inconsequential, undistinguished

mediocrity 8 poorness **9** pettiness **10** low-quality, meagerness, paltriness, triviality **11** inferiority **12** indifference, ordinariness, unimportance **14** insignificance **15** commonplaceness

meditate 4 muse, plan **5** aim at, study, think **6** devise, ponder **7** concoct, dream of, propose, reflect **8** cogitate, consider, contrive, mull over, ruminate **9** dwell upon **10** deliberate **11** contemplate

meditation 4 yoga **5** study **6** musing, poring **7** mulling, reverie, thought **8** brooding **9** discourse, pondering **10** cogitation, reflection, rumination **12** deliberation **13** consideration, contemplation

Mediterranean
  called by ancient Romans: 11 mare nostrum
  coast: 7 Riviera
  gulf: 5 Lions, Sidra, Tunis **7** Antalya, Catania, Taranto **8** Hammamet **9** Iskenderon
  island: 4 Elba **5** Capri, Corfu, Crete, Ibiza, Malta **6** Cyprus, Euboea, Lesbos, Rhodes, Sicily **7** Corsica, Majorca, Minorca **8** Balearic, Sardinia

  resort: 4 Nice **5** Capri **6** Cannes **7** Riviera **9** Cote d'Azur **10** Costa Brava
  river into: 2 Po **4** Ebro, Nile **5** Rhone
  sea: 5 Black **6** Aegean, Ionian **8** Adriatic, Ligurian **10** Tyrrhenian
  strait: 8 Bosporus **9** Bosphorus, Gibraltar **11** Dardanelles
  wind: 7 mistral, sirocco

medium 3 way **4** form, mean, mode, tool **5** means, organ **6** agency, avenue, common, milieu, normal **7** average, balance, channel, diviner, psychic, setting, vehicle **8** middling, moderate, ordinary **9** go-between, middle way, mid-course **10** atmosphere, compromise, golden mean, instrument, moderation **11** clairvoyant, environment, happy medium **12** crystal-gazer, intermediary, intermediate, middle ground, spiritualist, surroundings **13** fortuneteller **15** instrumentality

The Medium
  composer: 7 Menotti **5** opera

medley 4 hash, mess, olio **6** jumble, mosaic **7** farrago, melange, mixture **8** mishmash, pastiche **9** patchwork, potpourri **10** assortment, hodgepodge, miscellany **11** gallimaufry

Medon
  mentioned in: 5 Iliad **7** Odyssey
  father: 6 Oileus
  mother: 5 Rhene
  position: 6 herald
  friend of: 8 Penelope
  killed by: 6 Aeneas

medulla
  part of: 5 brain
  controls: 6 glands **7** muscles

Medusa
  form: 6 Gorgon
  father: 7 Phorcys
  mother: 4 Ceto
  sisters: 6 Graiae
  loved by: 8 Poseidon
  children: 7 Pegasus **8** Chrysaor
  sight of her caused people to turn to: 5 stone
  killed by: 7 Perseus

meek 4 mild **6** docile, gentle, humble, modest **8** lamblike, retiring, tolerant, yielding **9** compliant, spineless, tractable, weak-kneed **10** spiritless, submissive, unas- suming **11** acquiescent, complaisant, deferential, unassertive, unresisting **13** long-suffering, tenderhearted, unpretentious

meekness 7 pliancy, shyness **8** docility, humility **9** passivity **10** diffidence, humbleness **11** bashfulness **13** nonresistance **14** self-effacement

meet 3 apt, fit **4** abut, face, good, heed, obey **5** cross, equal, greet, match, rally, right **6** adjoin, answer, border, follow, gather, muster, proper, seemly **7** abide by, collect, convene, execute, fitting, fulfill, observe, perform, respect, run into, satisfy, welcome **8** assemble, becoming, bump into, confront, converge, decorous, opposite, relevant, suitable **9** agreeable, allowable, befitting, congruous, discharge, encounter, intersect, permitted, pertinent **10** admissable, comply with, congregate, felicitous **11** acknowledge, appropriate, permissible **12** come together

meet eye to eye 4 face **8** confront, face up to **11** meet vis- a-vis

meet halfway 6 settle **9** make a deal **10** compromise **11** come to terms **14** strike a bargain **18** split the difference

meet head on 4 face **5** crash **6** oppose **7** collide, crack up **8** confront, face up to **9** challenge, encounter

meeting 4 date **5** group, tryst **6** caucus **7** council **8** assembly, conclave, congress **9** encounter, gathering **10** conference, convention, engagement, rendezvous **11** assignation, convocation, get-together **12** introduction, presentation **13** confrontation

Meeting at Telgte
 author: **11** Gunter Grass

meeting of the minds 7 concert, concord, harmony **9** agreement **11** concordance **13** understanding

meeting place 5 mecca **10** focal point, rendezvous

Meet Me in St Louis
 director: **16** Vincente Minnelli
 cast: **8** Leon Ames, Tom Drake **9** Mary Astor **11** Judy Garland **12** June Lockhart, Marjorie Main **13** Lucille Bremer **14** Margaret O'Brien
 song: **11** Trolley Song **14** The Boy Next Door **33** Have Yourself a Merry Little Christmas

Meet the Press
 moderator: **9** Ned Brooks **10** Bill Monroe **11** Edwin Newman **14** Lawrence Spivak, Martha Rountree

meet with 4 meet **6** endure **7** undergo **8** come upon **9** encounter **10** come across, experience

Mefitis
 also: **8** Mephitis
 prevented: **5** winds
 kind of winds: **7** harmful

Megaera
 member of: **6** Furies

Megamede
 husband: **12** King Thespius
 number of daughters: **5** fifty

Megara
 father: **5** Creon
 husband: **8** Hercules
 son: **11** Therimachus

Mehuman 6 eunuch

Mein Kampf
 author: **11** Adolf Hitler
 means: **7** my fight **8** my battle

Meitner, Lise
 field: **7** physics
 nationality: **8** Austrian
 collaborator: **8** Otto Hahn
 contributed to: **21** atomic bomb development
 discovered: **12** protactinium **16** fission of uranium

Melaenis
 epithet of: **9** Aphrodite
 means: **5** black

melancholia 7 despair **10** depression, desolation, melancholy **11** despondency

melancholy 4 blue, glum **5** blues, dumps, gloom, moody **6** dismal, dreary, gloomy, mopish, morose, somber **7** despair, doleful, forlorn, joyless, unhappy **8** dejected, desolate, doldrums, dolorous, downcast, funereal, mournful **9** cheerless, dejection, depressed, heartsick, moodiness, plaintive **10** calamitous, depressing, depression, despondent, dispirited, gloominess, low spirits **11** despondency, discouraged, downhearted, forlornness, languishing, melancholia, sick at heart, unfortunate **12** disconsolate, heavyhearted **14** down in the dumps, down in the mouth **16** disconsolateness
 French: **6** triste **9** tristesse

melange 3 mix **4** olio **6** jumble, medley **7** mixture **8** compound, mishmash, pastiche **9** pasticcio, patchwork, potpourri **10** assemblage, assortment, hodgepodge, miscellany **11** gallimaufry

Melanippe
 form: **4** foal
 foal born to: **6** Euippe
 transformed into: **4** Arne, girl
 father: **4** Ares
 queen of: **7** Amazons

Melanosaurus
 type: **8** dinosaur
 period: **8** Triassic

Melba, Nellie
 title: **4** dame
 born: **9** Australia
 voice: **7** soprano
 named for her: **10** Melba toast, Peach melba

Melbourne
 bay: **7** Hobson's **11** Port Phillip
 landmark: **20** Flemington Racecourse
 river: **5** Yarra **6** Plenty **9** Mary Creek, Patterson **11** Maribyrnong **12** Diamond Creek **13** Kororoit Creek **14** Dandenong Creek, Gardiner's Creek **16** Moonee Ponds Creek
 state: **8** Victoria
 university: **6** Monash **7** La Trobe

Melchizedek
 means: **19** king of righteousness
 hometown: **5** Salem
 contemporary: **7** Abraham

meld 3 mix **4** fuse, join **5** blend, merge, unite **6** jumble, mingle **7** combine **8** coalesce, intermix, scramble **9** commingle **10** amalgamate, intertwine, interweave **11** consolidate, incorporate, intermingle

Meleager
 father: **4** Ares **6** Oeneus
 mother: **7** Althaea
 uncle: **9** Plexippus
 slew: **14** Calydonian boar
 loved: **8** Atalanta
 killed: **15** mother's brothers
 sisters: **11** Meleagrides

melee 3 row **4** fray, riot **5** brawl, scrap, set-to **6** fracas, rumpus, tussle **7** scuffle **8** disorder, dogfight **9** commotion, fistfight **10** free-for-all **11** altercation, pandemonium

Meliad
 form: **5** nymph
 nymph of: **6** flocks **10** fruit trees

mellifluous 4 soft **5** sweet **6** dulcet, mellow, smooth **7** musical **8** resonant **9** full-toned, melodious **10** euphonious, harmonious, sweet-toned **13** sweet-sounding

Mellors
 character in: **20** Lady Chatterley's Lover
 author: **8** Lawrence

mellow 4 rich, ripe, soft **5** drunk, sweet **6** mature, season, soften **7** matured, relaxed **8** luscious, tolerant **9** delicious **10** full-bodied **11** sympathetic **12** full-flavored **13** compassionate, understanding

mellowness 8 full body, fullness, maturity, richness, ripeness, softness **9** tolerance **10** compassion, smoothness **12** lusciousness, pleasantness

melodic 5 lyric **7** tuneful

melodious 4 rich, soft **5** clear, lyric, sweet **6** dulcet, mellow, smooth **7** melodic, musical, ringing, tuneful **8** resonant **9** full-toned **10** euphonious, sweet-toned **11** mellifluent, mellifluous

melodrama 9 theatrics **12** emotionalism **13** theatricality

melodramatic 5 corny, hammy, hokey, stagy **7** maudlin, mawkish **8** cornball, frenzied **10** flamboyant, histrionic **11** exaggerated, overwrought, sensational, sentimental, spectacular **13** overemotional

melody 3 air **4** aria, song, tune **5** ditty, theme **6** ballad, strain, timbre **7** concord, euphony **10** musicality **11** tunefulness **12** mellifluence **13** melodiousness **14** harmoniousness **15** mellifluousness

melon
 varieties: **4** pear **5** mango, snake, stink **6** casaba, citron, Dudaim, netted, nutmeg, orange, winter **7** Persian, serpent **8** honeydew

10 cantaloupe, preserving, watermelon **11** pomegranate **16** Oriental pickling, Queen Anne's pocket **17** Chinese preserving

Melpomene
   member of: 5 Muses
   personifies: 7 tragedy

melt 4 fade, fuse, pass, thaw **5** blend, merge, shade, touch **6** affect, disarm, dispel, soften, vanish **7** appease, dwindle, liquefy, mollify, scatter **8** dissolve **9** disappear, dissipate, evaporate, waste away **10** arouse pity, conciliate, propitiate

melt away 5 dry up **8** vaporize **9** evaporate

Melville, Herman
   author of: 4 Omoo **5** Mardi, Typee **7** Redburn **8** Moby Dick **9** Billy Budd **12** Benito Cereno **16** The Confidence Man **20** Bartleby the Scrivener

Melville, Julia
   character in: 9 The Rivals
   author: 8 Sheridan

Melvin and Howard
   director: 13 Jonathan Demme
   cast: 9 Paul LeMat **12** Jason Robards **15** Mary Steenburgen
   Oscar for: 6 script **17** supporting actress (Steenburgen)

member 3 arm, leg, toe **4** foot, hand, limb, part, tail, wing **5** bough, digit, organ, piece, shoot **6** branch, finger, pinion **7** element, portion, section, segment **8** fragment **9** appendage, component, extremity **10** ingredient **11** constituent

member
   of the bar: 4 beak **7** counsel **8** advocate, attorney **9** barrister, counselor **10** mouthpiece **12** legal advisor **13** attorney-at-law
   of a crew: 4 hand, mate **6** ensign, ganger, gunner, purser, yeoman **7** bowsman, oarsman, steward, swabbie **8** cabin boy, coxswain, deckhand, helmsman **9** first mate, navigator
   of faculty: 3 don, PhD **4** prof **5** tutor **6** doctor, master **7** teacher **8** lecturer **9** professor **10** instructor
   of family: 3 son **4** aunt **5** niece, uncle **6** cousin, father, mother, nephew, sister **7** brother **8** daughter, grandson **11** grandfather, grandmother **13** granddaughter
   of legislature: 4 whip **6** deputy **7** senator, speaker **8** delegate, lawmaker **10** legislator, politician **11** congressman **12** congresswoman **14** representative
   of religious order: 3 nun **4** dame, monk **5** Clare, friar, priest **6** father, hermit, Jesuit, sister **7** Alexian, ascetic, brother, Cluniac, Templar **8** Capuchin, cenobite, minister, Trappist **9** Carmelite, Dominican

10 Carthusian, Cistercian, Franciscan **11** Augustinian, Benedictine **14** mother superior

Member of the Wedding, The
   author: 15 Carson McCullers
   character: 6 Jarvis **11** Janice Evans **13** Frankie Addams, John Henry West **16** Honey Camden Brown **18** Berenice Sadie Brown

membership 4 club **6** league, roster **7** company, society **9** community, personnel **10** connection, fellowship, fraternity **11** affiliation, association, brotherhood

membrane 3 web **4** film, skin **6** lining, sheath **7** coating **8** envelope, pellicle **9** thin sheet **10** integument

memento 5 favor, relic, token **6** record, trophy **8** keepsake, memorial, reminder, souvenir **11** memorabilia, remembrance **12** remembrancer **13** commemoration

memento mori 23 remember that thou must die **31** object serving as a reminder of death

Memnon
   origin: 8 Oriental **9** Ethiopian
   father: 8 Tithonus
   mother: 3 Eos **4** Dawn
   brother: 8 Emathion
   companions: 10 Memnonides
   fought with: 7 Trojans
   killed by: 8 Achilles
   made immortal by: 4 Zeus
   commemorated with: 11 giant statue
   at: 6 Thebes

Memnonides see **6** Memnon

memo
   French: 11 aide memoire

memoir 4 life **5** diary **7** journal **9** biography, life story **10** adventures **11** confessions, experiences, reflections **13** autobiography, recollections, reminiscences

Memoirs of a Dutiful Daughter
   author: 16 Simone de Beauvoir

memorabilia 6 papers **7** records **8** archives **9** documents

memorable 6 famous **7** eminent, notable, salient **8** historic, stirring, striking **9** important, momentous, prominent, red-letter **10** celebrated, impressive, noteworthy, remarkable **11** illustrious, outstanding, significant **13** distinguished, extraordinary, unforgettable

memorandum 4 memo, note **5** brief **6** agenda, minute, record **7** jotting **8** reminder **11** brief report, list of items

memorial 6 homage **7** tribute **8** monument **10** monumental **11** testimonial **13** commemorative

memorialization 11 celebration **13** commemoration

memorialize 4 mark **5** honor

9 celebrate **11** commemorate, pay homage to **12** pay tribute to

memory 4 fame, mark, name, note **5** glory, honor, token **6** esteem, recall, regard, renown, repute **7** memento, respect **8** eminence, keepsake, memorial, prestige, reminder, souvenir **10** estimation, reputa- tion **11** distinction, remembering, remembrance, testimonial **12** recollection, remembrancer, reminiscence **13** commemoration
   goddess of: 9 Mnemosyne

Memphis
   football team: 9 Showboats

menace 3 cow **4** risk **5** bully, daunt, peril **6** danger, hazard, threat **7** imperil, pitfall, portend, presage, terrify **8** browbeat, endanger, forebode, jeopardy, threaten **9** terrorize **10** intimidate, jeopardize **11** be a hazard to, imperilment **12** endangerment

menacing 7 hostile **9** dangerous **11** belligerent, threatening, treacherous **12** antagonistic

menage a trois 9 threesome **16** household of three

Menander
   author of: 5 Heros **13** Perikeiromene **14** The Arbitration, The Misanthrope **16** The Rape of the Lock

Men at Arms
   author: 11 Evelyn Waugh

Mencken, H L
   author of: 10 Prejudices **19** The American Language
   editor of: 10 The Mercury **11** The Smart Set
   coined word: 9 booboisie, eclysiast

mend 3 fix **4** cure, darn, heal, knit **5** amend, emend, patch **6** better, reform, remedy, repair, revise **7** correct, improve, rectify, restore, retouch, touch up **8** overhaul, renovate **9** meliorate **10** ameliorate **11** recondition

mendacious 5 false, lying **8** spurious **9** deceptive **10** misleading, untruthful

mendacity 5 fraud, lying **6** deceit **7** falsity, perfidy **9** chicanery, deception, duplicity, falsehood, hypocrisy **10** dishonesty **11** insincerity **12** doubledealing, falsification, prevarication **14** untruthfulness **17** misrepresentation

Mendel, Gregor Johann
   field: 6 botany
   nationality: 8 Austrian
   discovered: 14 laws of heredity
   founded: 8 genetics

Mendeleyev (Mendeleev), Dimitri Ivanovich
   field: 9 chemistry
   nationality: 7 Russian
   devised: 11 periodic law **13** periodic table

Mendelssohn, (Jakob Ludwig) Felix
   born: 7 Germany, Hamburg
   composer of: 6 Elijah, St Paul

7 Athalie, Italian (symphony No 4), Lorelei, Ruy Blas **8** Antigone, Scottish (symphony No 3) **11** Reformation (symphony No 5), The Hebrides **12** Hymn of Praise (symphony No 2) **17** Songs without Words **21** A Midsummer Night's Dream

mendicant 6 beggar **10** alms-seeker, panhandler

Mending Wall
   author: 11 Robert Frost

Menelaus
   king of: 6 Sparta
   father: 6 Atreus
   mother: 6 Aerope
   brother: 9 Agamemnon
   wife: 5 Helen
   son: 11 Megapenthes, Nicostratus
   daughter: 8 Hermione

mene mene tekel upharsin 20
   handwriting on the wall **30** numbered numbered weighed divided
   foretells destruction of: 10 Belshazzar
   from Biblical book of: 6 Daniel

menhaden 4 pogy **5** pogie **6** bunker **7** alewife, bugfish, ellfish, fatback, herring, oldwife, sardine **8** bonyfish, hardhead, ladyfish **10** mossbunker

menial 3 low **4** mean **5** drone, lowly, slave, toady **6** abject, drudge, flunky, helper, humble, lackey **7** fawning, ignoble, servant, servile, slavish **8** cringing, employee **9** degrading, groveling, sycophant, truckling, underling **10** apprentice, obsequious **11** bootlicking, subordinate, subservient, sycophantic

menial labor 4 toil **5** grind **8** drudgery

Menjou, Adolphe
   born: 12 Pittsburgh PA
   roles: 9 Golden Boy, Pollyanna **11** A Star Is Born **12** The Front Page **13** A Woman of Paris **15** A Farewell to Arms, State of the Union **16** Little Miss Marker **18** A Bill of Divorcement

Mennonite 4 sect
   oppose: 15 military service
   favor: 10 plain dress
   kin to: 5 Amish

meno
   music: 4 less

Menominee, Menomini, Menomonie
   language family: 9 Algonkian **10** Algonquian
   location: 4 Ohio **7** Indiana **8** Illinois, Michigan **9** Wisconsin

menorah 11 candelabrum, candlestick **12** candleholder
   number of candles: 5 seven

Menotti, Gian-Carlo
   born: 5 Italy **10** Cadigliano
   composer of: 9 The Consul, The Medium **12** The Island God, The Tele-

phone **19** Amelia Goes to the Ball **24** Amahl and the Night Visitors

mens sana in corpore sano 22 a sound mind in a sound body

mental 5 crazy, nutty **6** insane, psycho **7** cracked, lunatic, psychic **8** abstract, cerebral, neurotic, rational **9** disturbed, in the mind, of the mind, psychotic **10** disordered, subjective, unbalanced **11** intelligent, mentally ill **12** intellectual, metaphysical **13** psychological

mental application 9 diligence **10** absorption, intentness **11** deep thought, engrossment, fixed regard **13** concentration **14** close attention

mental disorder 5 quirk **6** lunacy, oddity **7** madness **8** delusion, insanity, neurosis **9** craziness, psychosis **10** aberration **11** abnormality, derangement, mental lapse, peculiarity, strangeness **12** eccentricity, idiosyncrasy **13** schizophrenia **15** manic depression

mental hospital 6 asylum **8** madhouse **11** institution

mental institution 6 asylum **8** madhouse **9** funny farm **12** insane asylum

mentality 4 mind **6** acumen, brains, wisdom **8** judgment, sagacity **9** intellect **10** gray matter, perception **11** discernment **12** intelligence, perspicacity

mental lapse 5 quirk **6** lunacy, oddity **7** madness **8** rambling, straying **9** wandering **10** aberration **11** derangement, peculiarity **12** eccentricity **13** forgetfulness

mentally incapable
   Latin: 15 non compos mentis

mentally sound
   Latin: 12 compos mentis

mention 3 say **4** cite, hint, name, tell **5** imply, state **6** hint at, notice, remark, report, tell of **7** comment, divulge, inkling, narrate, observe, recount, refer to, specify **8** allude to, allusion, disclose, intimate **9** insinuate, make known, reference, statement, touch upon, utterance **10** advisement, indication, suggestion **11** designation, insinuation, observation **12** acquaintance, announcement, notification **13** communication, enlightenment, specification

mentor 4 guru **5** guide, tutor **6** master **7** adviser, monitor, proctor, teacher **9** counselor, preceptor, professor **10** instructor

Mentor
   advisor of: 8 Odysseus
   educated: 10 Telemachus

Mephibosheth
   father: 8 Jonathan
   also called: 9 Meribbaal
   grandfather: 4 Saul
   son: 5 Micha

Mephistopheles
   character in: 5 Faust
   author: 6 Goethe

Mephitis *see* **7** Mefitis

mer 3 sea

Merab
   father: 4 Saul
   sister: 6 Michal
   brother-in-law: 5 David

mercantile 5 trade **8** business **10** commercial **16** buying-and-selling

mercantilism 5 trade **8** business, commerce, exchange **13** commercialism

Mercedes
   character in: 21 The Count of Monte Cristo
   author: 5 Dumas (pere)

mercenary 5 venal **6** for pay, greedy **7** for gain, selfish **8** covetous, grasping, hireling, monetary **10** avaricious **11** acquisitive, paid soldier **12** hired soldier

merchandise 4 sell **5** goods, stock, trade, wares **6** deal in, market **7** effects, staples **8** huckster **9** advertise, publicize, traffic in **10** belongings, buy and sell, distribute **11** commodities **12** stock in trade

merchant 6 broker, dealer, hawker, jobber, monger, trader, vendor **7** peddler **8** chandler, retailer, salesman **9** purchaser, tradesman **10** saleswoman, shopkeeper, wholesaler **11** storekeeper, tradeswoman

Merchant of Venice, The
   author: 18 William Shakespeare
   character: 6 Portia **7** Antonio, Jessica, Lorenzo, Nerissa, Shylock **8** Bassanio, Gratiano

merci 8 thank you

merci beaucoup 16 thank you very much

merciful 4 kind **6** benign, humane, tender **7** clement, feeling, lenient, pitying, sparing **8** gracious **9** forgiving **10** beneficent **11** kindhearted, softhearted, sympathetic **13** compassionate, understanding

merciless 4 fell **5** cruel, harsh **6** fierce, severe **7** callous, inhuman **8** inhumane, pitiless, ruthless **9** ferocious, heartless, unpitying, unsparing **10** relentless, unmerciful **11** cold-blooded, hardhearted, remorseless, unrelenting

Mercouri, Melina
   husband: 11 Jules Dassin
   born: 6 Athens, Greece
   roles: 7 Topkapi **10** Gaily Gaily **13** Never on Sunday **15** Once Is Not Enough

mercurial 6 fickle, lively, mobile **7** erratic, flighty, kinetic, protean **8** electric, spirited, unstable, variable, volatile **9** impetuous, impulsive **10** capricious, changeable, inconstant

11 fluctuating **13** irrepressible, unpredictable

mercury
chemical symbol: **2** Hg

Mercury
origin: **5** Roman
messenger of: **4** gods
god of: **7** science, thieves **8** commerce **9** eloquence
corresponds to: **6** Hermes, Ogmios

Mercutio
character in: **14** Romeo and Juliet
author: **11** Shakespeare

mercy 4 pity **5** grace **6** lenity **7** charity **8** blessing, clemency, humanity, kindness, lenience, leniency, sympathy **9** good thing, tolerance **10** compassion, humaneness, lucky break **11** benevolence, forbearance, forgiveness, piece of luck **13** commiseration, fellow feeling **15** softheartedness **17** tenderheartedness
Latin: **12** misericordia

Mercy seat see **16** Ark of the Covenant

Merdle
character in: **12** Little Dorrit
author: **7** Dickens

mere 4 bald, bare, sole **5** plain, scant, sheer, utter **6** common, paltry **7** mundane **8** nugatory, ordinary, trifling **10** negligible, uneventful **11** commonplace, unmitigated **13** insignificant, unappreciable **14** inconsiderable

mere 6 mother

Meredith, Burgess
wife: **15** Paulette Goddard
born: **11** Cleveland OH
roles: **5** Magic, Rocky **6** Batman (the Penguin) **7** Madame X **8** Foul Play **12** Hurry Sundown, Of Mice and Men **15** Magnificent Doll, Such Good Friends **16** Advise and Consent

Meredith, George
author of: **9** The Egoist **10** Modern Love **14** Evan Harrington **16** Beauchamp's Career **19** Diana of the Crossways **25** The Ordeal of Richard Feverel

merely 3 but **4** just, only **5** quite **6** barely, in part, purely, simply, solely **7** utterly **8** scarcely, wholly **10** absolutely

meretricious 4 mock, sham **5** bogus, false, phony **6** pseudo, shoddy, tawdry **8** delusive, specious, spurious **9** deceptive **10** fraudulent, misleading **11** counterfeit

merge 4 fuse, join, weld **5** blend, unify, unite **6** link up **7** combine **8** coalesce, converge, intermix **9** associate, become one, integrate, interfuse, interlock **10** amalgamate, synthesize **11** confederate, consolidate **12** band together, interconnect

mergence 3 mix **5** blend **7** merging,

mixture **8** mingling **10** concoction **11** combination

Mergenthaler, Ottmar
nationality: **8** American
invented: **8** linotype

merger 5 union **7** wedding **8** marriage **9** coalition **12** amalgamation **13** confederation, consolidation

meridian 3 tip, top **4** acme, apex, brow, peak **5** crest, crown, point, ridge **6** apogee, climax, summit, vertex, zenith **7** heights **8** pinnacle **11** culmination

Merimee, Prosper
author of: **6** Carmen **7** Colomba

merit 4 earn, rate **5** value, worth **6** credit, desert, invite, prompt, talent, virtue **7** ability, benefit, deserve, quality, stature, warrant **8** efficacy **9** advantage **10** be worthy of, excellence, worthiness **11** distinction **12** be entitled to, have a right to **13** justification

merited 3 due **5** rated **6** earned **8** deserved, rightful

meritorious 4 fine **6** worthy **8** laudable **9** admirable, estimable, excellent, exemplary **10** creditable, noteworthy **11** commendable, exceptional **12** praiseworthy

Mermaid Tycoon
nickname of: **14** Esther Williams

Merman, Ethel
real name: **20** Ethel Agnes Zimmermann
husband: **14** Ernest Borgnine
born: **9** Astoria NY
autobiography: **6** Merman
roles: **11** Call Me Madam **12** Anything Goes, Panama Hattie **15** Annie Get Your Gun **16** Stage Door Canteen **21** Alexander's Ragtime Band

Mermerus
father: **5** Jason
mother: **5** Medea

Merope
member of: **8** Pleiades
father: **5** Atlas **8** Oenopion
husband: **7** Polybus **8** Sisyphus **11** Cresphontes, Polyphontes
son: **7** Aepytus
raped by: **5** Orion
raised: **7** Oedipus

merrily 5 gaily **6** gladly **7** briskly, happily, lightly, lustick, quickly **8** blithely, jocundly, jovially, joyfully, joyously **9** festively, gleefully **10** cheerfully, laughingly, mirthfully **11** hilariously, vivaciously **14** lightheartedly

Merrimac see **9** Pennacook

merriment 3 fun **4** glee **5** cheer, mirth **6** frolic, gaiety, hoopla, levity **7** good fun, jollity, revelry, whoopee **8** hilarity, laughter **9** amusement, festivity, good humor, jocundity, joviality **10** jocularity, jubilation, liveliness, skylarking **11** celebration, gleefulness,

good spirits, merrymaking **12** conviviality, exhilaration, sportiveness **16** lightheartedness

Merriweather, Mrs
character in: **15** Gone With the Wind
author: **8** Mitchell

merry 3 gay **5** happy, jolly **6** blithe, cheery, jocund, jovial, joyous, lively **7** festive, gleeful, jocular **8** animated, carefree, cheerful, gladsome, laughing, mirthful, partying, reveling, sportive **9** convivial, fun-loving, sprightly, vivacious **10** frolicsome, rollicking, skylarking **12** high-spirited, lighthearted

merrymaking 5 sport **6** frolic, gaiety, hoopla, revels **7** jollity, revelry, whoopee **8** carousal **9** festivity, funmaking, high jinks, merriment, rejoicing, whoop-de-do **10** saturnalia **11** bacchanalia, celebration, festivities **12** conviviality

Merry Wives of Windsor, The
author: **18** William Shakespeare
character: **4** Ford, Page **5** Caius **6** Doctor, Fenton **7** Slender **8** Anne Page **12** Mistress Ford, Mistress Page **15** Mistress Quickly, Sir John Falstaff

mesa 4 hill, peak **5** bench, butte, table **7** plateau, terrace **9** cartouche, tableland

Mescalero
language family: **6** Apache
location: **6** Mexico **9** New Mexico
related to: **5** Lipan **10** Chiricahua

mesh 3 fib, net, web **4** grid, jibe **5** agree, sieve, tally **6** engage, enmesh, grille, plexus, screen **7** connect, engaged, netting, network, webbing, webwork **8** dovetail, interact, lacework, meshwork, openwork **9** grillwork, interlock, inter-mesh **10** coordinate, correspond, interweave, wickerwork **11** fit together, latticework **12** reticulation

Meshach
former name: **7** Mishael
companion: **6** Daniel
friend: **8** Abednego, Shadrach

Mesmer, Franz (Friedrich) Anton
nationality: **6** German
developed: **8** hypnosis

mesmerize 5 charm **7** bewitch **8** enthrall, entrance **9** fascinate, hypnotize, magnetize, spellbind, transport

Mesopotamian mythology
god of agriculture/earth: **5** Dagan
corresponds to Phoenician: **5** Dagon

Mesquakie see **3** Fox

mess 3 fix **4** hash, stew **5** mix-up, pinch **6** crisis, jumble, litter, muddle, pickle, plight, scrape, strait **7** clutter, dilemma, trouble **8** disarray, disorder, hot water, mess hall, mishmash, quandary **9** cafeteria, confusion, imbroglio, refectory, situation **10** commissary, difficulty, dining hall, dining room, hodgepodge **11** predicament **14** conglomeration

message 4 news, note, word **5** moral, point, theme **6** letter, notice, report **7** meaning, missive, purport, tidings **8** bulletin, dispatch **9** statement **10** communique, memorandum **12** intelligence **13** communication

mess around with 4 test **6** try out **8** fool with, play with **10** tinker with **14** experiment with

messenger 5 envoy **6** bearer, runner **7** carrier, courier **8** delegate, emissary **9** deliverer, go-between **11** delivery boy, delivery man **12** intermediary

messenger of gods 4 Iris **6** Hermes **7** Mercury

Messiaen, Olivier Eugene Prosper Charles
    born: 6 France **7** Avignon
    composer of: 11 Exotic Birds, Turangalila **13** Chronochromie **20** Le Nativite du Seigneur **22** Quartet for the End of Time **27** Vingt Regards sur l'Enfant Jesus **33** Et exspecto resurrectionem mortuorum **41** Transfiguration de Notre Seigneur Jesus Christ

Messiah
    means: 11 anointed one
    see also **10** Jesus

Messick, Dale
    creator/artist of: 19 Brenda Starr Reporter

messiness 5 chaos, mix-up, upset **6** jumble **7** clutter **8** disarray, disorder, scramble, shambles **9** confusion **10** disharmony, sloppiness, untidiness **12** dishevelment **14** disarrangement **15** disorganization

mess up 3 mar **4** goof, muff, ruin **5** botch, spoil **6** bungle, foul up, jumble **7** blunder, butcher, disturb, do badly, louse up, screw up **9** mismanage **10** disarrange **11** disorganize, make a mess of, make an error **12** make a mistake

messy 4 ugly **6** blowsy, frowsy, grubby, sloppy, tricky, untidy **7** awkward, chaotic, jumbled, tangled, unkempt **8** confused, littered **9** cluttered, difficult **10** bedraggled, disheveled, disordered, slatternly, topsy-turvy, unenviable, unpleasant **11** disarranged **12** embarrassing, inextricable **13** uncomfortable

mesto
    music: 8 mournful

metal
    alloy: 5 brass, monel **6** bronze, nickel, niello, pewter, solder
    bar: 3 gad **4** risp **5** ingot
    bolt: 5 rivet
    box: 8 canister
    casting: 3 peg
    classification: 5 light, noble **6** alkali, common **7** coinage **8** platinum, precious **9** rare earth **10** low-melting,

refractory, transition **11** high-melting **14** semiconductors
    clippings: 7 scissel
    coarse: 5 matte
    corrosion: 4 rust
    crude: 3 ore **4** slug
    cymbals: 3 tal
    deposit: 4 lode, vein
    design: 7 chasing
    disk or plate: 4 shim **5** medal, paten **6** platen, sequin
    eyelet: 7 grommet
    filings: 5 lemel
    god of: 6 Vulcan **10** Hephaestus
    heaviest: 6 osmium
    kind: 3 tin **4** gold, iron, lead, zinc **6** barium, cerium, cesium, copper, erbium, nickel, osmium, radium, silver, sodium **7** arsenic, bismuth, calcium, holmium, iridium, lithium, rhodium, silicon, terbium, thulium **8** actinium, aluminum, antimony, europium, lutetium, platinum, rubidium, samarium, selenium, titanium, tungsten **9** beryllium, magnesium, palladium, potassium, ruthenium, strontium **10** molybdenum, phosphorus
    layer: 7 plating
    leaf: 4 foil
    lightest: 7 lithium
    liquid: 7 mercury
    mass: 3 pid **5** ingot **7** bullion
    piece: 4 jack, slug
    refuse: 4 slag **5** dross
    shaper: 5 swage
    suit: 4 mail **5** armor **6** armour
    thread: 4 lame, wire
    trademark: 5 monel
    ware: 4 tole **6** Revere
    worker: 5 smith **6** forger, welder **7** armorer, riveter **8** armourer **9** goldsmith, ironsmith **10** blacksmith **11** coppersmith, silversmith **12** metallurgist

Metalious, Grace
    author of: 11 Peyton Place
metalworking
    god of: 6 Vulcan **10** Hephaestus, Hephaistos

metamorphose 6 change, mutate **7** convert **9** transform **11** transfigure

Metamorphoses
    author: 4 Ovid

metamorphosis 8 mutation **10** alteration, conversion **11** permutation **12** change of form, modification **13** radical change, transmutation **14** transformation **15** series of changes, startling change, transfiguration **18** transmogrification

Metamorphosis, The
    author: 10 Franz Kafka
metaphor 5 image, trope **6** simile **7** analogy **8** metonymy, parallel **11** equivalence **14** figure of speech, representation

metaphysical 5 basic, lofty, vague

6 far-out **7** eternal **8** abstract, abstruse, esoteric, mystical, ultimate **9** essential, high-flown, recondite, universal **10** impalpable, intangible, jesuitical, oversubtle **11** existential, fundamental, ontological, speculative **12** cosmological, intellectual, unanswerable **13** philosophical **15** epistemological

Metaphysics
    author: 9 Aristotle
metaxa
    type: 6 brandy **7** liqueur
    origin: 6 Greece

mete, mete out 5 allot **6** assign, divide **7** deal out, dole out **8** allocate, disburse, dispense **9** apportion, parcel out **10** administer, distribute, measure out

meteoric 4 fast **5** fiery, rapid, swift **6** speedy, sudden **7** blazing, flaming, instant **8** flashing, unabated **10** inexorable **11** ineluctable, unstoppable

meter
    abbreviation: 1 m
method 3 way **4** form, mode, plan, tack **5** means, order, style, usage **6** course, design, manner, scheme, system **7** fashion, formula, process, program, purpose, routine **8** approach, efficacy **9** procedure, technique, viability **13** modus operandi

methodical, methodic 4 neat, tidy **5** exact **7** careful, logical, orderly, precise, regular, uniform **10** analytical, deliberate, meticulous, systematic **12** businesslike **13** well-regulated

methodization 5 order **11** arrangement **12** organization **14** categorization, classification **15** systematization

methodize 5 order **7** arrange **8** classify, organize **11** systematize

Methuselah
    father: 5 Enoch
    son: 6 Lamech
    years lived: 23 nine hundred and sixty-nine
    known as: 9 oldest man

meticulous 4 nice **5** exact, fussy **7** finical, finicky, precise **8** exacting, sedulous **10** fastidious, particular, scrupulous **11** painstaking, punctilious **13** conscientious, perfectionist

meticulousness 4 care **5** pains **12** sedulousness, thoroughness **14** fastidiousness, scrupulousness **17** conscientiousness

metier 3 job **4** area, line, work **5** craft, field, forte, trade **7** calling, pursuit **8** activity, business, lifework, province, vocation **9** specialty **10** employment, livelihood, occupation, profession

meting out 8 alloting **9** bestowing, doling out **10** allocating, conferring, consigning, dealing out, dispensing **11** designating **12** apportioning, distributing, measuring out

Metis
 member of: **6** Titans
 father: **7** Oceanus
 mother: **6** Tethys
 consort of: **4** Zeus
 daughter: **6** Athena

Metropolis
 director: **9** Fritz Lang
 cast: **10** Alfred Abel **12** Brigitte Helm

metropolitan area 4 city **8** core city, downtown, environs **9** inner city, precincts, urban area **10** city limits, metropolis **11** central city **16** business district

mettle 3 vim **4** grit, guts **5** nerve, pluck, spunk, valor, vigor **6** spirit **7** bravery, courage, heroism **8** audacity, backbone, boldness, gameness, temerity **9** derring-do, fortitude, gallantry, manliness **10** enthusiasm, resolution **11** intrepidity **12** fearlessness **13** determination

mettlesome 4 bold, edgy **5** brave, fiery **6** ardent, plucky, spunky **7** gingery, peppery **8** restless, skittish, spirited **9** excitable, impatient **10** courageous, high-strung **12** high-spirited

Mexica *see* **5** Aztec

Mexico
 other name: **8** New Spain
 capital/largest city: **10** Mexico City
 others: **4** Leon **5** La Paz, Taxco **6** Cancun, Celaya, Merida, Oaxaca, Puebla, Toluca **7** Durango, Guaymas, Tampico, Tijuana, Torreon **8** Acapulco, Culiacan, Ensenada, Irapuato, Mazatlan, Mexicali, Saltillo, Veracruz **9** Chihuahua, Matamoros, Monterrey, Queretaro, Salamanca, Zacatecas **10** Hermosillo **11** Guadalajara, Nuevo Laredo **12** Ciudad Juarez, Villahermosa **13** Coatzacoalcos, Piedras Negras, San Luis Potosi **14** Puerto Vallarta **15** Netzahualcoyotl
  ancient city: **4** Tula **7** Texcoco **8** Tlacopan **10** Monte Alban **11** Teotihuacan **12** Tenochtitlan **13** Tula de Allende
 division: **6** Colima, Oaxaca, Puebla, Sonora **7** Chiapas, Durango, Hidalgo, Jalisco, Sinaloa, Tabasco, Yucatan **8** Campeche, Coahuila, Tlaxcala, Veracruz **9** Chihuahua, Michoacan, Nuevo Leon, Zacatecas **13** San Luis Potosi **14** Baja California
 measure: **3** bag, pie **4** alma, onza, vara **5** almud, baril, carga, jarra, labor, legua, libra, linea, marco, sitio **6** adarme, almude, arroba, carega, fanega, ochaua, terceo **7** pulgada, quintal **9** cuarteron, cuartillo **10** caballeria
 monetary unit: **4** onza, peso **5** adobe, claco, tlaco **6** azteca, cuarto, dinero **7** centavo, piaster
 weight: **3** bag **4** onza **5** libra, marco **6** arroba, tercio **7** quintal
 island: **6** Carmen, Cedros **7** San Jose,

Tiburon **8** Cerralvo **10** Tres Marias **13** Espiritu Santo **14** Santa Magdelena, Santa Margarita **15** Angel de la Guarda
 lake: **7** Chapala, Texcoco **9** Patzcuaro
 mountain: **6** Colima, Tacana, Toluca **9** Paricutin **11** Ixtacihuatl, Sierra Madre **12** Popocatepetl **14** Sierra Zacateca **16** Chiapas Highlands **24** Transverse Volcanic Sierra
 highest point: **7** Orizaba **12** Citlaltepetl
 river: **4** Mayo **5** Yaqui **6** Balsas, Fuerte, Grande, Panuco **8** Colorado, Grijalva **10** Papaloapan, Usumacinta **13** Bravo del Norte, Coatzacoalcos, Lerma-Santiago
 sea: **7** Pacific **8** Atlantic **9** Caribbean
 physical feature:
  bay: **8** Campeche **9** Olas Atlas
  cape: **10** Corrientes
  desert: **6** Sonora
  gulf: **6** Mexico **8** Campeche **10** California **11** Tehuantepec
  isthmus: **11** Tehuantepec
  peninsula: **7** Yucatan **14** Baja California
  plain: **7** Tabasco
  plateau: **7** Mexican
  valley: **7** Chiapas
 people: **6** Indian **7** Mestizo, Spanish
  architect: **7** O'Gorman
  artist: **6** Orozco, Rivera, Tamayo **9** Siqueiros
  composer: **6** Chavez
  emperor: **6** Maximilian
  explorer: **6** Cortes, Cortez **7** Cordoba **8** Alvarado, Grijalva
  god: **6** Tlaloc **12** Quetzalcoatl **14** Huitzilopochtli
  leader: **3** Gil **4** Diaz **5** Lopez, Rubio, Villa **6** Calles, Huerta, Juarez, Madero, Valdes, Zapata **7** Obregon **8** Carranza, Iturbide, Portillo, Santa Ana **9** Diaz Ordaz, Montezuma, Rodriguez **13** Madrid Hurtado **16** Salinas de Gortari
  revolutionary/priest: **13** Morelos y Pavon **16** Hidalgo y Costilla
  soldier/explorer: **12** conquistador
  viceroy: **7** Mendoza
  writer: **3** Paz **5** Nervo, Reyes, Yanez **6** Azuela, Guzman, Najera **7** Fuentes
 language: **5** Mayan, Otomi **6** Mixtec **7** Mazahua, Mazatec, Nahuatl, Spanish, Totonac, Zapotec **8** Tarascan
 religion: **13** Roman Catholic
 place:
  cathedral: **10** Assumption
  center of Mexico City: **6** Zocalo **21** Plaza de la Constitucion
  floating gardens: **10** Xochimilco
  museum: **28** Shrine of the Virgin of Guadalupe
  park: **7** Alameda **11** Chapultepec
  ruins: **5** Mitla, Uxmal **8** Palenque **10** Monte Alban **11** Chichen Itza,

Teotihuacan **20** Temple of Quetzalcoatl
  street: **13** Avenida Juarez **16** Paseo de la Reforma
  temple/pyramid: **7** Cholula **8** Castillo
 feature:
  agreement: **5** NAFTA
  Christmas tradition: **6** pinata
  coffee plantation: **5** finca
  empire: **4** Maya **5** Aztec, Olmec **6** Mixtec, Toltec **7** Zapotec
  large estate: **8** hacienda
  musician: **8** mariachi
  small farm/commune: **6** ejidos
  sport: **7** jai alai **12** bullfighting
  tree: **9** sapodilla **11** chicozapote
 food:
  corn cake: **8** tortilla
  dish: **4** mole, taco **5** huevo, pollo **6** tamale **7** burrito, chorizo, taquito, tostada **8** empanada **9** enchilada, guacamole, sopadilla **10** chili verde, quesadilla **11** chimichanga **12** chili relleno
  drink: **6** pulque **7** tequila

Mexico City
 Aztec name: **12** Tenochtitlan
 capital of: **6** Mexico
 landmark: **13** Mercado Merced **15** Chapultepec Park **19** Basilica of Guadalupe
  bull ring: **11** Plaza Mexico
  floating gardens: **10** Xochimilco
  pyramids: **11** Teotihuacan
 square: **6** Zocalo **22** Plaza de las Tres Culturas
 street: **16** Paseo de la Reforma

Meyerbeer, Giacomo
 real name: **17** Jacob Liebmann Beer
 born: **6** Berlin **7** Germany
 composer of: **7** Dinorah **10** Le Prophete, The African, The Prophet **12** Les Huguenots, The Huguenots, The North Star **14** Robert le Diable, Robert the Devil

mezza voce
 music: **9** half voice **10** half volume

mezzo
 music: **4** half

Miami
 bay: **8** Biscayne
 county: **4** Dade
 developer: **7** Flagler
 football team: **8** Dolphins
 museum: **4** Lowe **12** Villa Viscaya
 ocean: **8** Atlantic
 people: **5** Cuban **8** Hispanic
 section: **7** Hialeah **10** Bal Harbour **11** Coral Gables
 stadium: **10** Orange Bowl
 tropical garden: **9** Fairchild
 university: **5** Barry **8** St Thomas
 zoo: **11** Crandon Park

Miami (Twightwee)
 language family: **9** Algonkian **10** Algonquian
 tribe: **3** Wea **5** Miami **10** Piankashaw

location: 4 Ohio **7** Indiana **8** Illinois, Michigan **9** Wisconsin
leader: 12 Little Turtle
allied with: 6 Peoria

Miami Vice
character: 4 Gina **5** Trudy **8** (Capt) Castillo **13** Riccardo Tubbs, Sonny Crockett
cast: 10 Don Johnson **11** Olivia Brown **15** Saundra Santiago **16** Edward James Olmos **20** Phillip Michael Thomas

Micah Clarke
author: 19 Sir Arthur Conan Doyle

Micawber, Mr
character in: 16 David Copperfield
author: 7 Dickens

Michael
author: 17 William Wordsworth

Michael
means: 12 Who is like God
father: 8 Izrahiah **11** Jehoshaphat
son: 4 Omri **8** Zabadiah
also: 9 archangel

Michel
father: 4 Saul
husband: 5 David, Palti
sister: 5 Merab

Michelangelo Buonarotti (Simoni)
architect of: 11 Campidoglio (Capitoline Hill) **12** Medici Chapel (Florence) **13** Farnese Palace **21** Palazzo Medici-Riccardi (Florence) **22** Palazzo dei Conservatori (Capitoline Hill) **24** Convent of San Marco Library
born: 5 Italy **7** Caprese
patron: 12 Pope Julius II **14** Lorenzo d'Medici **19** Pope Julius the Second **21** Lorenzo the Magnificent
artwork: 5 David, Moses, Pieta **6** Brutus, Slaves **7** Bacchus **9** The Victor **10** Holy Family **12** Madonna Pitti **15** The Last Judgment **18** Conversion of St Paul **20** Madonna Seated on a Step, Sistine Chapel Ceiling **21** The Flight of the Lapites, The Martyrdom of St Peter

Michelozzo
architect of: 21 Palazzo Medici-Riccardi (Florence) **24** Convent of San Marco Library

Michelson, Albert A
field: 7 physics
established: 12 speed of light **15** velocity of Earth
awarded: 10 Nobel Prize

Michener, James A
author of: 5 Space **6** Alaska, Hawaii, Iberia, Legacy, Poland **8** Caravans, Sayonara **9** The Source **10** Centennial, Chesapeake **11** The Covenant, The Drifters **16** The Fires of Spring **18** The Bridges at Toko-ri **22** Tales of the South Pacific

Michigan
abbreviation: 2 MI **4** Mich

nickname: 4 Lake **9** Wolverine **10** Automobile **15** Water Wonderland **16** Winter Wonderland
capital: 7 Lansing
largest city: 7 Detroit
others: 4 Caro, Troy **5** Flint, Niles, Wayne **6** Adrien, Alpena, Bad Axe, Monroe, Owosso, Warren, Wassar **7** Bay City, Holland, Jackson, Livonia, Midland, Pontiac, Saginaw, Trenton, Wyoming **8** Ann Arbor, Cadillac, Dearborn, Escanaba, Ironwood, Manistee, Muskegon, Petoskey, Royal Oak **9** Cheboygan, Hillsdale, Kalamazoo, Marquette, Port Huron, Roseville, Wyandotte **10** Birmingham, River Rouge **11** Battle Creek, Grand Rapids **12** Benton Harbor, Traverse City **13** Sault Ste Marie, St Clair Shores
college: 4 Alma, Hope **5** Wayne **6** Adrian, Albion, Calvin, Olivet, Owosso **7** Detroit, Oakland **9** Hillsdale, Kalamazoo, Marygrove
feature:
    bridge: 8 Mackinac
    canal: 3 Soo **12** Sault St Marie
    festival: 12 Holland Tulip
    national park: 10 Isle Royale
    village: 10 Greenfield
tribe: 6 Ojibwa, Ottawa **8** Chippewa **10** Potawatomi
people: 9 Henry Ford, wolverine **11** Bruce Catton, Edgar A Guest, Julie Harris, Ralph Bunche, Ring Lardner **16** Charles Lindburgh
    explorer: 6 Joliet **7** La Salle, Nicolet **9** Marquette **12** Etienne Brule, Sault St Marie
island: 8 Mackinaw
lake: 4 Burt, Erie **5** Clear, Huron, Round, Torch **6** Austin, Devils, Moline **7** Bawbees, St Clair **8** Houghton, Michigan, Superior
land rank: 11 twenty-third
mountain: 6 Copper **7** Gogebic **9** Menominee, Porcupine
    highest point: 12 Mount Curwood
physical feature:
    bay: 7 Saginaw, Thunder **8** Keweenaw, Sturgeon
    straits: 8 Mackinac
president: 10 Gerald Ford
river: 4 Cass **5** Grand, Huron **6** Raisin **7** Detroit, Saginaw, St Clair, St Mary's **8** Escanaba, Muskegon **9** Menominee
state admission: 11 twenty-sixth
state bird: 5 robin
state fish: 5 trout
state flower: 12 apple blossom
state motto: 11 I Will Defend **39** If You Seek a Pleasant Peninsula Look About You
state song: 18 Michigan My Michigan
state tree: 16 eastern white pine

Mickey Mouse
creator: 10 Walt Disney

character: 5 Morty **6** Ferdie **11** Minnie Mouse
    cow: 10 Clarabelle

Micklewhite, Maurice Joseph
real name of: 12 Michael Caine

Micmac
language family: 9 Algonkian **10** Algonquian
location: 6 Canada **10** Nova Scotia **12** Newfoundland, New Brunswick **14** Gaspe Peninsula **16** Cape Breton Island **18** Prince Edward Island

microbe 4 germ **5** virus **6** gamete, zygote **8** bacillus, parasite **9** bacterium **10** spirochete **13** microorganism, streptococcus **14** staphylococcus

microbiologist
American: 7 Waksman **9** Baltimore
Dutch: 11 (van) Leeuwenhoek

Micronesia
part of: 7 Oceania
island: 3 Nui **4** Guam, Rota, Truk, Wake **5** Makin, Nauru, Wotho **6** Bikini, Ellice, Majuro, Ponape **7** Gilbert, Mariana **8** Caroline, Kiribati, Marshall

microorganism 3 bug **4** germ **5** virus **7** microbe **8** bacillus, pathogen **9** bacterium

microphobia
fear of: 12 small objects

microscope
invented by:
    compound: 7 Janssen
    electronic: 5 Knoll, Ruska
    field ion: 7 Mueller
single lens model improved by: 11 (van) Leeuwenhoek
first observed: 8 protozoa **13** red blood cells **19** single-celled animals

microscopic, microscopical 4 tiny **5** teeny **6** atomic, minute **9** invisible **10** diminutive, very little **13** imperceptible, infinitesimal

microscopy
founder: 11 Robert Hooke **13** Jan Swammerdam **16** Marcello Malpighi **19** Anton van Leeuwenhoek

Midas
king of: 7 Phrygia
father: 7 Gordius
gift: 11 golden touch
gift from: 7 Silenus
ears changed to those of: 3 ass
changed by: 6 Apollo

midday 4 noon **7** noonday **8** meridian, noontide, noontime

middle 3 act, gut, hub, mid **4** core, main **5** belly, heart, midst, waist **6** center, course, medial, median, midway, throes **7** central, halfway, midmost, midriff, nucleus, process, stomach **8** midpoint **9** heartland **10** midsection **12** intermediate

Middle Ages
French: 8 moyen age

middle-class 4 mass **8** ordinary **9** bourgeois **10** mainstream, middlebrow

middle Europe
  German: **12** Mitteleuropa

middle ground 4 mean **7** balance **8** midpoint **11** equilibrium **12** common ground

Middle Kingdom *see* **5** China

middleman 5 agent **6** broker, dealer, jobber **7** liaison **8** mediator **9** go-between **10** wholesaler **11** distributor, intercessor **12** entrepreneur, intermediary

Middlemarch
  author: **11** George Eliot
  character: **5** Celia **12** Will Ladislaw **13** Rosamond Viney **14** Dorothea Brooke, Edward Casaubon, Tertius Lydgate **15** Sir James Chettam

middlemost 4 mean **5** inner **6** inmost, median **7** central, midmost **8** interior

middle-of-the-road 8 moderate **10** mainstream

middle-of-the-roader 8 moderate **12** mainstreamer

middle way
  Latin: **8** via media

middling 4 fair, so-so **6** medium **7** average, fairish, minimal **8** mediocre, moderate, ordinary, passable **9** tolerable **10** pretty good, second-rate **11** indifferent **12** run-of-the-mill, unremarkable

Midgard
  also: **10** Mithgarthr
  origin: **12** Scandinavian
  means: **10** abode of man
  located between: **8** Niflheim **10** Muspelheim
  connected to Asgard by: **7** bifrost **13** rainbow bridge
  formed from brow of: **4** Ymir

midget 4 doll, runt **5** dwarf, pygmy **6** peewee, puppet, shrimp, squirt **7** manikin **8** half-pint, munchkin, small fry, Tom Thumb **9** pipsqueak **10** fingerling, homunculus **11** hop-o'-my-thumb, lilliputian

Midi 5 skirt **16** the south of France

midlands 8 interior **10** hinterland **13** central region

midmost 5 inner **6** inmost, middle **7** central, pivotal **8** interior **10** middlemost

Midnight Cowboy
  director: **15** John Schlesinger
  cast: **9** Jon Voight **11** John McGiver, Sylvia Miles **13** Brenda Vaccaro, Dustin Hoffman (Ratso Rizzo)
  Oscar for: **7** picture

Midnight Express
  director: **10** Alan Parker
  cast: **8** John Hurt **9** Bo Hopkins, Brad Davis (Billy Hayes) **10** Randy Quaid **12** Irene Miracle
  setting: **13** Turkish prison

score: 14 Giorgio Moroder
  Oscar for: **5** score **6** script

midori
  type: **7** liqueur
  origin: **5** Japan
  flavor: **5** melon

midpoint 4 core, mean **5** focus **6** center, middle **15** point of no return

midriff 3 gut **4** guts **5** belly, tummy **6** paunch **7** abdomen, stomach **9** diaphragm **10** midsection **11** breadbasket

midst 3 eye, hub **4** core **5** bosom, heart, thick **6** center, depths, middle **7** nucleus **8** interior

Midsummer Night's Dream, A
  author: **18** William Shakespeare
  character: **4** Puck (Robin Goodfellow) **6** Bottom, Helena, Hermia, Oberon **7** Theseus, Titania **8** Lysander **9** Demetrius, Hippolyta

midterm 4 exam, test **6** review **11** examination

midwife
  French: **11** accoucheuse

mien 3 air **4** look **5** guise, style **6** aspect, manner, visage **7** bearing, feature **8** attitude, behavior, carriage, demeanor, presence **9** semblance **10** appearance, deportment, expression **11** countenance

Mies van der Rohe, Ludwig
  architect of: **14** German Pavilion (1929 International Exposition, Barcelona), Lake Shore Drive (apartment towers, Chicago), Tugendhat House (Brno Czechoslovakia) **15** National Gallery (West Berlin), Seagram Building (NYC)
  style: **13** International
  principle: **10** less is more

miff 3 irk, vex **4** rile **5** anger, annoy, chafe, pique **6** nettle, offend, rankle **7** affront, provoke **8** irritate **9** put one off **10** exasperate **11** make one sore **14** rub the wrong way **15** raise one's dander

Mifune, Toshiro
  born: **5** China **8** Tsingtao
  roles: **6** Midway, Shogun **8** Rashomon **12** Seven Samurai **13** Throne of Blood

Miggs, Miss
  character in: **12** Barnaby Rudge
  author: **7** Dickens

might 3 may **5** brawn, clout, force, power, vigor **6** energy, muscle **7** potency, prowess **8** strength **9** influence, lustihood, puissance, toughness **10** capability, competence, durability, robustness, sturdiness **11** capableness **12** forcefulness

mighty 4 able, bold, huge, vast, very **5** brave, hardy, husky, lusty, stout, truly **6** brawny, manful, potent, really, robust, strong, sturdy **7** immense, massive, titanic, valiant **8** colossal, enormous, forceful, gigantic, imposing,

majestic, powerful, puissant, stalwart, towering, valorous, vigorous **9** monstrous, strapping **10** courageous, gargantuan, invincible, monolithic, monumental, prodigious, stupendous **11** elephantine, exceedingly, indomitable, of great size **12** overpowering, particularly **13** exceptionally **14** Brobdingnagian

migrate 4 move, trek **6** travel **7** journey **8** emigrate, relocate, resettle **9** immigrate

migration 4 trek **6** exodus, flight, moving **7** passage **8** diaspora, movement

mikado 5 ruler **7** emperor, monarch **9** sovereign **10** locomotive **15** Japanese emperor

Mikado, The
  subtitle: **15** The Town of Titipu
  operetta by: **18** Gilbert and Sullivan
  character: **4** Ko-Ko **6** Mikado, Peep-Bo, Yum-Yum **7** Katisha, Pooh-Bah **8** Nanki-Poo, Pish-Tush **9** Pitti-Sing

Mikkelsen, Dahl
  also: **3** Mik
  creator/artist of: **8** Ferd'nand

mikrophobia
  fear of: **5** germs

mikvah 16 public ritual bath
  used by: **12** Orthodox Jews

mild 4 calm, easy, soft, warm **5** balmy, bland **6** docile, gentle, placid, serene, smooth **7** pacific, summery **8** delicate, moderate, not sharp, pleasant, soothing, tranquil **9** easygoing, emollient, not severe, not strong, temperate **10** forbearing, not extreme, springlike **11** complaisant, uninjurious **12** good-tempered

mildew 4 mold **6** blight, fungus

mildewed 5 fusty, moldy **10** discolored

mildness 8 calmness, delicacy, serenity, softness **9** placidity **10** gentleness, good temper

Mildred Pierce
  director: **13** Michael Curtiz
  based on novel by: **10** James M Cain
  cast: **8** Ann Blyth, Eve Arden **10** Jack Carson **12** Bruce Bennett, Joan Crawford, Zachary Scott
  Oscar for: **7** actress (Crawford)

mild-tempered 7 equable, patient **9** easygoing **11** good-natured, unflappable

mile
  abbreviation: **2** mi

Miles, Sarah
  brother: **11** Christopher
  husband: **10** Robert Bolt
  born: **7** England **11** Ingatestone
  roles: **6** Blow-Up **10** The Servant **11** The Hireling **13** Ryan's Daughter **16** Lady Caroline Lamb

miles gloriosus 15 boastful soldier

Miles Gloriosus
author: **7** Plautus

Milesian
origin: **5** Irish
invaders from: **5** Spain
invaded: **7** Ireland
defeated: **14** Tuatha De Danann
ancestors of: **5** Irish

milestone 7 jubilee **8** milepost, signpost **10** road marker **11** anniversary **12** red-letter day, turning point

Milestone, Lewis
director of: **12** Of Mice and Men, The Front Page **13** A Walk in the Sun **17** Mutiny on the Bounty **25** All Quiet on the Western Front (Oscar)

Milestones
author: **13** Arnold Bennett

milieu 5 scene **7** culture, element, setting **8** ambience, backdrop **10** background **11** environment, mise-en-scene **12** surroundings

militant 7 defiant, extreme, martial, warlike, warring **8** fighting, military **9** assertive, bellicose, combatant, combative **10** aggressive, pugnacious **11** belligerent, contentious **12** disputatious, paramilitary, warmongering **14** uncompromising

military 4 army **5** armed, crisp **6** strict, troops **7** martial, militia, Spartan, warlike **8** generals, soldiers **9** combative, defensive, regulated, soldierly, warmaking **10** regimented **11** armed forces, belligerent, soldierlike

military force 4 army, navy **6** legion, troops **7** legions, militia **8** military, regiment, soldiers, soldiery **9** battalion **11** fighting men **13** fighting force

military machine 4 army **6** legion, troops **11** armed forces **13** fighting force

military rank abbreviation
admiral: **3** adm
brigadier general: **2** bg **7** brig gen
captain: **3** cpt **4** capt
chief petty officer: **3** CPO
colonel: **3** col
commander: **5** comdr
corporal: **3** cpl
ensign: **3** ens
general: **3** gen
lieutenant: **2** lt **5** lieut
lieutenant colonel: **3** ltc **5** lt col
lieutenant general: **5** lt gen **8** lieut gen
major: **3** maj
master sergeant: **4** msgt
non-commissioned officer: **3** nco
private: **3** pvt
private first class: **3** pfc
sergeant: **3** sgt
sergeant first class: **3** sfc
sergeant major: **4** smaj **6** sgt maj
specialist: **4** spec
staff sergeant: **4** ssgt

military storehouse 6 armory **7** arsenal **8** magazine **9** arms depot **13** ordnance depot **14** ammunition dump

military stores 7 arsenal, weapons **8** ordnance **9** munitions **10** ammunition

military unit 4 army, crew, unit **5** corps, force, squad **6** legion, outfit **7** brigade, company **8** regiment, squadron **9** battalion, task force **10** contingent, detachment

milksop 4 baby, wimp **5** mouse, pansy, sissy, softy **6** coward **7** crybaby, nebbish **8** mama's boy, poltroon, weakling **9** fraidy-cat **10** namby-pamby, pantywaist, scaredy-cat, weak sister **11** milquetoast, mollycoddle

mill 4 roam, teem **5** crush, grind, shape, swarm, works **6** finish, groove **7** factory, meander **8** converge **9** granulate, pulverize

Mill, John Stuart
author of: **9** On Liberty **14** Utilitarianism **20** The Subjection of Women **28** Principles of Political Economy

Millais, Sir John Everett
born: **7** England **12** Southampton
artwork: **7** Bubbles **9** Blind Girl **12** Autumn Leaves, Chill October **13** My First Sermon **18** Lorenzo and Isabella **25** Christ in the Carpenter's Shop **36** Young Men of Benjamin Seizing Their Brides

Millament, Mrs
character in: **16** The Way of the World
author: **8** Congreve

Milland, Ray
real name: **21** Reginald Truscott-Jones
born: **5** Neath, Wales
roles: **9** Beau Geste **11** Blonde Crazy **14** Dial M for Murder, The Lost Weekend (Oscar) **22** Bulldog Drummond Escapes

Millay, Edna St Vincent
author of: **11** Second April **13** The Harp Weaver **19** Make Bright the Arrows **20** A Few Figs from Thistles

millennium 13 thousand years **9** age of gold **21** one-thousandth anniversary

Miller
character in: **18** The Canterbury Tales
author: **7** Chaucer

Miller, Ann
real name: **17** Lucille Ann Collier
autobiography: **15** Miller's High Life
born: **9** Chireno TX
roles: **9** On the Town, Stage Door **10** Hit the Deck, Kiss Me Kate **11** Sugar Babies **16** The Kissing Bandit

Miller, Arthur
wife: **13** Marilyn Monroe
author of: **8** The Price **11** The Crucible **12** After the Fall **16** Death of a Salesman **18** A View from the Bridge

Miller, Henry
author of: **5** Nexus, Sexus **6** Plexus **14** Tropic of Cancer **17** Tropic of Capricorn **18** The Rosy Crucifixion **21** The Colossus of Maroussi

Milles, Carl
real name: **23** Wilhelm Carl Emil Anderson
born: **5** Lagga **6** Sweden
artwork: **5** Diana, Jonah **6** Europa **12** Man and Nature, Playing Bears **13** Peace Monument **15** Orpheus Fountain **18** Meeting of the Waters, Saltsjobaden Church (bronze doors)

millet 16 Panicum miliaceum
varieties: **3** hog **5** pearl, Sanwa **6** finger, Indian **7** African, foxtail, Italian **8** barnyard, browntop, Japanese **16** Japanese barnyard

Millet, Jean-Francois
born: **6** France, Gruchy
artwork: **5** Sower **7** Angelus **11** The Gleaners, The Winnower **14** Potato Planters, The Man with a Hoe **23** Oedipus Taken from the Tree

Millett, Kate
author of: **6** Flying **14** Sexual Politics

milligram
abbreviation: **2** mg

milliliter
abbreviation: **2** mL

millimeter
abbreviation: **2** mm

Millionaire, The
character: **14** Michael Anthony
cast: **12** Marvin Miller

Mill on the Floss, The
author: **11** George Eliot
character: **8** Bob Jakin, Mrs Glegg **9** Lucy Deane, Mrs Pullet **11** Philip Wakem, Tom Tulliver **12** Stephen Guest **14** Maggie Tulliver

Mills, Hayley
real name: **15** Rose Vivian Mills
father: **4** John
sister: **6** Juliet
husband: **11** Ray Boulting
born: **6** London **7** England
roles: **8** Tiger Bay **9** Pollyanna **11** Summer Magic **13** The Parent Trap **14** The Chalk Garden **15** The Moon-Spinners **19** In Search of Castaways **20** The Trouble with Angels

Mills, John
daughter: **6** Hayley, Juliet
born: **7** England **10** Felixstowe
roles: **12** Tunes of Glory **13** Ryan's Daughter **14** The Chalk Garden **17** Great Expectations **19** Swiss Family Robinson

Mills, Robert
architect of: **10** Post Office (Washington DC) **12** Patent Office (Washington DC) **14** Circular Church (Charleston) **15** Unitarian Church (Philadelphia) **16** Treasury Building (Washington DC) **18** Washington

Monument **25** Sansom Street Baptist Church (Philadelphia) **29** Egyptian Revival Monument Church (Richmond VA)
style: 12 Greek Revival

millstream 3 run **4** race **5** brook, canal, creek, river **6** branch

Milne, A A
author of: 13 Winnie-the-Pooh **20** The House at Pooh Corner
character: 3 Roo **4** Pooh **5** Kanga **6** Eeyore, Piglet, Tigger **16** Christopher Robin

Milo, Milos
island of: 6 Greece **8** Cyclades **9** Aegean Sea
found: 5 Venus **6** statue
missing: 4 arms

Milosz, Czeslaw
author of: 11 Native Realm, The Usurpers **13** Bells in Winter **14** Seizure of Power, The Captive Mind

milquetoast 4 wimp **7** milksop, nebbish **11** mollycoddle

Milton
author: 12 William Blake

Milton, George
character in: 12 Of Mice and Men
author: 9 Steinbeck

Milton, John
author of: 7 Lycidas **8** L'Allegro **11** Il Penseroso **12** Areopagitica, Paradise Lost **15** Samson Agonistes **16** Paradise Regained **29** On the Morning of Christ's Nativity

Milton Berle Show, The
host: 11 Milton Berle
regulars: 10 Fatso Marco **11** Arnold Stang, Jack Collins, Milton Frome, Ruth Gilbert **12** Irving Benson **13** Bobby Sherwood
announcer: 8 Sid Stone **11** Jimmy Nelson **13** Jack Lescoulie
orchestra: 8 Alan Roth, Billy May **11** Victor Young
theme: 7 Near You
Milton Berle's nickname: 12 Mr Television
sponsor: 5 Buick **6** Texaco

Milwaukee
baseball team: 7 Brewers
basketball team: 5 Bucks
Indian name: 16 Mahn-a-waukee Seepe
lake: 8 Michigan
river: 9 Milwaukee, Menomonee, **12** Kinnickinnic
university: 9 Marquette

mimic 3 ape **4** aper, copy, echo, mime **6** mirror, parrot **7** copycat, copyist, feigner, imitate, take off **8** imitator, simulate **9** reproduce **10** burlesquer **11** counterfeit, impersonate **13** impressionist

Mimir
origin: 12 Scandinavian
god of: 3 sea

decapitated by: 5 Vanir
head sent to: 4 Odin **5** Othin
oracle for: 4 Asar **5** Aesir

mimosa 14 Acacia dealbata **18** Albizia Julibrissin
varieties: 5 Texas **6** golden **7** prairie **8** Egyptian
cocktail contains: 9 champagne **10** orange juice

mince 4 dice, pose **5** grate, shred **6** refine, soften **7** posture, qualify **8** chop fine, hold back, mitigate, moderate, palliate **9** gloss over, put on airs, whitewash **12** attitudinize **14** affect delicacy, affect primness **15** give oneself airs **16** affect daintiness, soften one's speech **18** cut into small pieces **19** be mealymouthed about **20** cut into tiny particles

mince words 5 dodge, hedge, stall **10** equivocate **11** be ambiguous **13** avoid the issue **17** beat around the bush

mind 4 hate, heed, note, obey, tend, will, wits **5** abhor, bow to, brain, focus, sense, watch **6** brains, choice, detest, eschew, follow, intent, liking, memory, notice, notion, reason, recall, regard, resent, sanity **7** dislike, marbles, observe, opinion, outlook, thought **8** adhere to, attend to, be wary of, judgment, object to, reaction, response, submit to, take care, thinking **9** attention, awareness, be careful, cognition, faculties, intellect, intention, look after, sentiment **10** be cautious, comply with, conception, conclusion, gray matter, impression, perception, propensity, recoil from, reflection, shrink from, take care of **11** acquiesce, be wary about, inclination, percipience, point of view, rationality, remembrance **12** apprehension, disapprove of, intelligence, recollection, reminiscence, take charge of, take notice of **13** be conscious of, comprehension, concentration, consciousness, consideration, contemplation, look askance at, preoccupation, ratiocination, retrospection, understanding **14** pay attention to
German: 5 Geist

mindful 4 wary **5** aware **7** alert to, alive to, careful, heedful **8** cautious, sensible, watchful **9** cognizant, conscious, observant, regardful **10** absorbed in, open-eyed to, thoughtful **11** attentive to, engrossed in, taken up with **12** occupied with **15** preoccupied with

mindfulness 9 alertness, awareness **10** perception **12** acquaintance **13** attentiveness, consciousness, understanding

mindless 6 insane, obtuse, stupid **7** asinine, doltish, idiotic, unaware, witless **8** careless, heedless **9** apathetic, cretinous, imbecilic, oblivious, unat-

tuned, unheeding **10** neglectful, regardless, sophomoric, unthinking **11** inattentive, indifferent, nonsensical, thoughtless, unobservant, unreasoning **12** disregardful, simple-minded **13** inconsiderate, unintelligent **14** indiscriminate

mine 3 pit **4** fund **5** cache, hoard, shaft, stock, store **6** dig for, quarry, supply, tunnel, wealth **7** extract, reserve **8** dig under, excavate, treasure **9** abundance, booby-trap **10** excavation **12** accumulation

Mineo, Sal
real name: 14 Salvatore Mineo
born: 7 Bronx NY
roles: 5 Giant, Tonka **6** Exodus **18** Rebel Without a Cause, Who Killed Teddy Bear?

mineral 3 jet, ore **4** coal, gold, iron, mica, opal, spar, talc **5** beryl, topaz **6** augite, barite, blende, cerine, copper, galena, garnet, iolite, pinite, rutile, sandix, silver, sphene, spinel, sulfur **7** amesite, apatite, azurite, biotite, bornite, calcite, citrine, coesite, crystal, cuprite, cyanite, element, gahnite, helvite, jadeite, kernite, kunzite, niobite, olivine, prasine, zeolite, zircon **8** asbestos, borocite, chlorite, cinnabar, corundum, dolomite, epsomite, fayalite, feldspar, fluorite, graphite, hematite, lazulite, siderite, sodalite, stibnite, triplite, wellsite **9** aragonite, argentite, carnelian, celestite, cerussite, danburite, fosterite, kaolinite, lawsonite, magnetite, malachite, muscovite, petroleum, phenakite, scapolite, tridymite, turquoise, wulfenite **10** calaverite, chalcedony, orthoclase, pyrrhotite, sphalerite, tourmaline, wolfachite **11** alexandrite, chrysoberyl, melanterite **12** brazilianite, chalcopyrite, fincalconite, fluorapatite **13** rhodochrosite

Minerva
origin: 5 Roman
goddess of: 3 war **4** arts **6** wisdom **11** handicrafts
corresponds to: 6 Athena

mingle 3 mix **4** fuse, join **5** blend, merge, unite **6** hobnob **7** combine, consort **8** coalesce, intermix **9** associate, circulate, commingle, interfuse, interlard, socialize **10** amalgamate, fraternize, intertwine, interweave **11** intermingle, intersperse **12** rub shoulders

miniature 3 wee **4** tiny **5** elfin, pygmy **6** bantam, little, petite **9** minuscule **10** diminutive, pocket-size, small-scale **11** lilliputian, microcosmic, microscopic

minim
abbreviation: 3 min

minimal 5 token **7** minimum, nominal **13** least possible, unappreciable

minimize 5 dwarf **6** reduce, shrink

8 belittle, mitigate **9** underrate **10** depreciate, undervalue

minimum 4 base **5** basic, least **7** modicum **8** smallest

minister 4 abbe, tend **5** padre, rabbi, serve, vicar **6** answer, cleric, father, oblige, parson, pastor, priest **7** care for, cater to **8** attend to, chaplain, pander to, preacher, reverend **9** clergyman, secretary **10** evangelist, revivalist, take care of **11** accommodate **12** ecclesiastic **13** cabinet member

ministerial 6 cleric **8** churchly, clerical, pastoral, priestly **14** ecclesiastical

ministration 3 aid **4** care **6** charge **7** comfort **9** attention **10** protection **11** supervision

Ministry of Fear, The
    author: 12 Graham Greene

Minnehaha
    character in: 8 Hiawatha
    author: 10 Longfellow

Minnelli, Liza
    father: 8 Vincente
    mother: 11 Judy Garland
    born: 12 Los Angeles CA
    roles: 6 Arthur **7** Cabaret (Oscar) **14** New York New York **16** The Sterile Cuckoo **17** Flora the Red Menace

Minnelli, Vincente
    director of: 4 Gigi (Oscar) **9** Brigadoon **11** Lust for Life **15** Bells Are Ringing, Meet Me in St Louis **16** Father of the Bride **17** An American in Paris

Minnesota
    abbreviation: 2 MN **4** Minn
    nickname: 6 Gopher **9** North Star **19** Land of Sky-blue Waters **22** Land of Ten Thousand Lakes
    capital: 6 St Paul
    largest city: 11 Minneapolis
    others: 3 Ada, Ely **4** Mora **5** Edina **6** Austin, Duluth, Newulm, Winona **7** Babbitt, Bemidji, Fosston, Hibbing, Mankato, Red Wing, St Cloud **8** Brainerd, Moorhead **9** Albertlea, Blue Earth, Richfield, Rochester, Roseville **10** Minnetonka, Robinsdale **11** Bloomington, St Louis Park **14** Brooklyn Center **18** International Falls
    college: 6 Bethel, St Olaf, Winona **7** Bemidji, Hamline **8** Adolphus, Augsburg, Carleton, St Thomas **10** Macalester
    feature:
        monument: 10 Paul Bunyan
        national monument: 9 Pipestone **12** Grand Portage
        national park: 9 Voyageurs'
        Norse artifact: 19 Kensington Rune Stone
    tribe: 5 Sioux **6** Dakota, Ojibwa, Santee **8** Chippewa **9** Menominee
    people: 11 Judy Garland **12** Mayo brothers **13** Harold Stassen, Lauris Norstad, Sinclair Lewis **16** F Scott Fitzgerald
    explorer: 8 Hennepin, Norsemen, Radisson **9** Greysolon **12** Groseilliers **19** Sieur Duluth of du Lhut
    lakes: 3 Red **5** Leech, Rainy **6** Itasca **7** Bemidji **8** Superior **9** Mille Lacs **10** Minnewaska **14** Lake of the Woods, Winnibigoshish
    land rank: 7 twelfth
    mountain: 6 Cuyuna, Mesabi **7** Misquah **9** Vermilion
        highest point: 5 Eagle
    physical feature: 6 Big Bog **14** Northwest Angle
        falls: 9 Minnehaha
    river: 3 Red **5** Rainy **6** Pigeon **7** St Croix, St Louis **9** Des Moines, Minnesota **10** St Lawrence **11** Mississippi
    state admission: 12 thirty-second
    state bird: 10 common loon
    state fish: 7 walleye
    state flower: 14 moccasin flower **24** pink and white lady's slipper
    state motto: 17 The Star of the North
    state song: 13 Hail Minnesota
    state tree: 9 Norway red pine
    baseball team: 5 Twins
    football team: 7 Vikings
    hockey team: 10 North Stars

Minni *see* **7** Armenia

minor 5 child, light, petty, small, youth **6** infant, lesser, paltry, slight **7** trivial **8** nugatory, picayune, piddling, teenager, trifling **9** secondary, youngster **10** adolescent **11** subordinate, unimportant **13** insignificant **14** inconsiderable **15** inconsequential

minority 4 less **5** youth **6** lesser, nonage **7** boyhood, infancy **8** girlhood **9** childhood, juniority **10** immaturity **11** adolescence

minor-league 4 punk **5** dinky, seedy, tacky **6** cheesy, common, lesser, shabby **8** inferior, small-fry **9** secondary, small-time **10** bush-league, second-rate **13** insignificant

Minos
    king of: 5 Crete
    father: 4 Zeus
    mother: 6 Europa
    brother: 8 Sarpedon **12** Rhadamanthys
    wife: 8 Pasiphae
    daughter: 7 Ariadne, Phaedra
    ordered: 9 Labryinth
    became: 5 judge
        in: 5 Hades

Minotaur
    form: 7 monster
    combined: 3 man **4** bull
    father: 10 Cretan bull
    mother: 8 Pasiphae
    home: 9 Labyrinth
    ate flesh of: 6 humans
    killed by: 7 Theseus

minstrel 4 bard, poet **6** dancer, end man, lyrist, player, singer **8** comedian, songster **9** blackface, poetaster, serenader, versifier **11** troubadour **12** interlocutor, vaudevillian **15** song-and-dance man

mint
    varieties: 3 dog, red **4** wood **5** apple, field, lemon, stone, water **6** coyote, dotted, orange, Scotch **7** Meehan's **8** bergamot, Corsican, creeping, Japanese, mountain **9** pineapple
    flavor: 7 menthol **9** spearmint **10** peppermint
    liqueur: 13 creme de menthe
    botanical name: 6 Mentha **8** Labiatae, M spicata **9** M piperita
    origin: 13 Mediterranean
    related herb: 7 oregano **8** marjoram, rosemary
    symbol of: 11 hospitality
    mythical nymph: 6 Mintha
        beloved of: 5 Pluto
        Mintha trod underfoot by: 10 Persephone
    cure for: 7 hiccups
    antidote for: 16 sea serpent stings
    use: 4 lamb **5** salad **6** fruits

Minthe
    form: 5 nymph
    changed into: 9 mint plant
    changed by: 10 Persephone

minuscule 3 wee **4** tiny **5** small **6** minute **10** teeny-weeny **11** small letter **13** infinitesimal **15** lower-case letter

minute 3 wee **4** fine, puny, tiny, wink **5** close, exact, flash, jiffy, petty, scant, shake, teeny, trice **6** breath, little, moment, petite, second, slight, strict **7** careful, instant, minikin, precise **8** detailed, itemized, trifling **9** miniature, twinkling **10** a short time, diminutive, exhaustive, meticulous, negligible, scrupulous **11** lilliputian, microscopic **12** sixty seconds **13** conscientious, imperceptible, inappreciable, infinitesimal, insignificant **14** extremely small, inconsiderable
    abbreviation: 3 min

minute portion 3 bit, sip **4** bite **5** crumb, grain, scrap, shred, speck **6** morsel, sliver **7** swallow **8** fragment, mouthful, particle

minutiae 6 trivia **7** trifles **8** niceties **10** bagatelles, pedantries, subtleties **11** odds and ends, particulars **12** minor details, trivialities **15** particularities

minx 4 jade, slut **5** hussy, huzzy, wench **7** baggage **10** prostitute

Minyades
    daughters of: 6 Minyas

Miolnir
    hammer of: 4 Thor

mir 5 peace, world **21** Russian village commune

mirabile dictu 12 strange to say **17** marvelous to relate

miracle 4 omen, sign **6** marvel, wonder **7** mystery, portent, prodigy **9** divine act, sensation, spectacle **10** phenomenon **11** masterpiece

Miracle of Morgan's Creek, The
director: **14** Preston Sturges
cast: **9** Diana Lynn **11** Betty Hutton **12** Brian Donlevy, Eddie Bracken **15** William Demarest

Miracle on 34th Street
director: **12** George Seaton
based on story by: **15** Valentine Davies
cast: **9** John Payne **11** Edmund Gwenn (Kris Kringle), Natalie Wood **12** Gene Lockhart, Maureen O'Hara, Thelma Ritter
Oscar for: **12** screenwriter **15** supporting actor (Gwenn)

Miracle Worker, The
director: **10** Arthur Penn
cast: **9** Patty Duke (Helen Keller) **10** Victor Jory **11** Inga Swenson **12** Anne Bancroft (Anne Sullivan)
Oscar for: **7** actress (Bancroft) **17** supporting actress (Duke)

miraculous 6 divine **7** amazing, magical **9** marvelous, visionary, wonderful **10** incredible, mysterious, phenomenal, prodigious, remarkable **11** astonishing, astounding, exceptional, spectacular, supernormal **13** extraordinary, preternatural, wonderworking **14** thaumaturgical

miraculous food 5 manna

Miraculous writing
also: **4** mene **5** perez, tekel **8** upharsin
means: **7** divided, weighed **8** numbered
interpreted by: **6** Daniel

mirage 5 fancy **7** fantasy **8** delusion, illusion, phantasm **9** unreality **12** will-o'-the-wisp **13** hallucinations, misconception **14** castle in the air **15** optical illusion

Miranda
character in: **10** The Tempest
author: **11** Shakespeare

Miranda, Carmen
real name: **26** Maria do Carmo Miranda da Cunha
nickname: **18** Brazilian Bombshell
born: **8** Portugal **16** Marco de Canavezes
roles: **10** Copacabana **14** That Night in Rio **15** Weekend in Havana **16** Down Argentine Way **22** Springtime in the Rockies

mire 3 bog, fen, mud **4** cake, muck, ooze, soil **5** marsh, muddy, slime, slush, smear **6** enmesh, sludge **7** begrime, bog down, ensnare, spatter **8** besmirch, entangle, quagmire

Miriam
father: **5** Amram

mother: **8** Jochebed
brother: **5** Aaron, Moses

Miro, Joan
born: **5** Spain **8** Montroig **9** Barcelona
artwork: **9** Help Spain, The Reaper **13** Dutch Interior **14** Constellations **16** Catalan Landscape **19** Dog Barking at the Moon **20** Still Life with Old Shoe **26** Woman and Bird in the Moonlight

mirror 4 copy, show **5** glass, image, model **7** epitome, example, paragon, reflect **8** exemplar, manifest, paradigm, standard **10** reflection **11** cheval glass **12** looking glass

mirth 4 glee **6** gaiety, levity **7** jollity **8** drollery, hilarity, laughter **9** amusement, festivity, happiness, jocundity, joviality, merriment **10** jocularity **11** good spirits, merrymaking, playfulness **12** cheerfulness

mirthful 3 gay **4** glad **5** happy, jolly, merry **6** blithe, jocose, jovial, joyful, joyous **7** gleeful, jocular, risible

mirthless 3 sad **4** dour, glum **6** gloomy, morose **7** joyless, unhappy **8** dejected **9** cheerless, sorrowful **10** in the dumps, melancholy **14** down in the mouth

miry 3 wet **4** oozy **5** boggy, mucky, muddy, slimy, slushy, soggy **6** claggy, swampy **7** sloughy

misadventure 3 ill **4** slip **6** mishap **7** debacle, failure, reverse, setback **8** bad break, calamity, casualty, disaster **9** adversity, mischance **10** infelicity, misfortune **11** catastrophe, contretemps

misanthrope 5 cynic **7** skeptic **9** pessimist **10** misogynist

Misanthrope, Le
author: **7** Moliere
character: **7** Alceste, Arsinoe, Eliante **8** Celimene, Philinte

misanthropic 4 cold **5** surly **6** morose **7** cynical, distant **10** antisocial, unfriendly, unsociable **11** distrustful **12** discourteous, inhospitable, unneighborly, unpersonable, unresponsive **14** unapproachable **15** unaccommodating

misapply 5 abuse **6** misuse **9** misemploy **13** use improperly

misapprehension 5 mixup **7** mistake **11** misjudgment **13** misconception **14** miscalculation **15** false impression, misconstruction **16** misunderstanding **17** misinterpretation

misappropriate 4 bilk **5** abuse, cheat, mulct, steal **6** misuse **7** defraud, purloin, swindle **8** embezzle, misapply, peculate **9** defalcate, misemploy

misappropriation 6 misuse, taking **11** defalcation **12** embezzlement

misbehave 5 act up **7** disobey, do wrong **10** transgress **15** get into mischief

misbehavior 5 lapse **7** misdeed, offense **8** acting up, trespass **9** impudence **10** bad conduct, bad manners, disrespect, misconduct **11** delinquency, dereliction, impropriety, misdemeanor **12** indiscretion **13** transgression **16** obstreperousness, unmanageableness

miscalculate 3 err **8** misjudge **10** guess wrong **11** misestimate

miscalculation 5 error **10** inaccuracy **13** misestimation

miscarriage 4 slip **5** botch **6** fizzle **7** default, failing, failure, misfire, undoing, washout **8** casualty, collapse

miscarry 4 fail **5** abort, botch **6** fizzle, go awry **9** terminate **12** come to naught

miscellanea 8 analects **9** anthology, gleanings, scrapbook **10** collection, miscellany, selections **11** collectanea

miscellaneous 5 mixed **6** divers, motley, sundry, varied **7** diverse, mingled, various **8** assorted, manifold **9** different **11** diversified **13** heterogeneous

miscellaneous collection
Latin/pseudo Latin: **14** omniumgatherum

miscellany 5 blend **6** jumble, medley **7** melange, mixture, variety **8** analects, extracts, mishmash, pastiche **9** anthology, gleanings, potpourri **10** assortment, collection, hodgepodge, salmagundi, selections **11** collectanea, compilation, gallimaufry, miscellanea **14** conglomeration, omnium-gatherum

mischance 6 ill lot, mishap **7** bad luck, ill luck, ill wind **8** accident **9** adversity **10** infelicity, misfortune **12** misadventure

mischief 4 evil **5** wrong **6** injury, malice **7** devilry, knavery, roguery **8** deviltry, foul play, plotting, scheming, villainy **9** depravity, devilment, rascality **10** orneriness, wrongdoing **11** naughtiness, playfulness, roguishness, shenanigans, willfulness **12** prankishness, sportiveness **14** capriciousness

mischief-maker 3 imp **5** demon, devil, scamp **7** gremlin, hellion **9** scoundrel **10** hell-raiser

mischievous 3 sly **5** elfin **6** elfish, impish, malign, vexing, wicked **7** harmful, naughty, noxious, playful, roguish, teasing, vicious, waggish **8** annoying, devilish, prankish, spiteful, sportive **9** injurious, malicious, malignant, uninvited **10** frolicsome, gratuitous, pernicious **11** deleterious, destructive, detrimental, uncalled for **12** exacerbating

misconceive 3 err **4** lose, miss **8** misjudge **12** misinterpret **13** misunderstand

misconception 5 error **8** delusion **11** misjudgment **13** erroneous idea **14** mis- information **15** misapprehension, mis- construction **16** misunderstanding **17** misinterpretation, misrepresentation

misconduct 7 misdeed, misstep **10** mis- prision, peccadillo, wrongdoing **11** delinquency, dereliction, impropriety, malefaction, malfeasance, misbehavior, misdemeanor **13** transgression

misconstrue 7 distort, mistake **8** misjudge **9** misreckon, misrender **12** misapprehend, miscalculate, misinterpret, mistranslate **13** misunderstand

miscreant 3 bum **4** heel **5** knave, scamp **6** bad egg, rascal, sinner, wretch **7** villain **8** evildoer, lost soul, scalawag **9** reprobate, scoundrel **10** blackguard, black sheep, malefactor

misdeed 3 sin **4** slip **5** crime, lapse, wrong **6** felony **7** faux pas, offense, outrage **8** atrocity, trespass **9** violation **10** misconduct, peccadillo **11** malfeasance, misbehavior, misdemeanor **12** indiscretion, infringement **13** transgression

misdemeanor 3 sin **5** crime, fault **7** offense, misdeed **8** disorder **10** peccadillo **11** misbehavior **13** transgression

misdoer 5 crook **8** criminal **9** miscreant, wrongdoer **10** delinquent

mise en scene 6 milieu **7** setting **8** ambience **10** atmosphere, background **11** environment **12** stage setting, surroundings

miser 5 piker **7** hoarder, niggard, Scrooge, skimper **8** tightwad **9** skinflint **10** cheapskate, pinchpenny **12** pennypincher, stingy person

Miser, The
also: **6** L'Avare
author: **7** Moliere
character: **5** Elise **6** Valere **7** Anselme, Cleante, Mariane **8** Harpagon

miserable 3 sad **4** mean **5** inept, needy, sorry **6** abject, scurvy, shabby, sordid, woeful **7** abysmal, crushed, doleful, forlorn, grieved, hapless, unhappy **8** beggarly, degraded, dejected, desolate, dolorous, feckless, inferior, mournful, pathetic, pitiable, rubbishy, very poor, wretched **9** appalling, atrocious, cheerless, depressed, desperate, heartsick, sorrowful, woebegone **10** chapfallen, deplorable, despicable, despondent, heavy- laden, lamentable, second-rate, unbearable **11** crestfallen, heartbroken, unfortunate **12** contemptible, disconsolate, impoverished **13** brokenhearted **14** down in the mouth

Miserables, Les
author: **10** Victor Hugo
character: **6** Javert **7** Cosette, Fantine **10** Thenardier **11** Jean Valjean **15** Father Madeleine, Marius Pontmercy **17** Eponine Thenardier

misericordia 5 mercy **10** compassion

miserliness 6 penury **9** frugality, par-

simony **10** stinginess **13** niggardliness, penny-pinching **15** tight-fistedness

miserly 4 mean, near **5** cheap, tight **6** frugal, greedy, meager, stingy **7** selfish **8** grasping, grudging, pinching **9** illiberal, niggardly, penurious, scrimping **10** avaricious, ungenerous **11** closefisted, closehanded, tight-fisted **12** parsimonious **13** penny-pinching

misery 3 woe **4** blow **5** agony, curse, grief, trial **6** ordeal, regret, sorrow **7** anguish, bad deal, bad news, chagrin, despair, sadness, torment, trouble **8** bad scene, calamity, disaster, distress, exaction, hardship **9** dejection, heartache, privation, suffering **10** affliction, bitter pill, depression, desolation, melancholy, misfortune **11** catastrophe, despondency, tribulation **12** wretchedness

Misfits, The
director: **10** John Huston
based on story by: **12** Arthur Miller
cast: **10** Clark Gable, Eli Wallach **12** Thelma Ritter **13** Marilyn Monroe **15** Montgomery Clift

misfortune 4 blow, loss **6** misery, mishap **7** bad luck, reverse, setback, tragedy, trouble **8** calamity, casualty, disaster, downfall, hard luck, hardship **9** adversity, hard times, ruination **10** affliction, ill fortune **11** catastrophe, tribulation **12** misadventure

misgiving, misgivings 4 fear **5** alarm, doubt, dread, qualm, worry **7** anxiety, dubiety **8** disquiet, mistrust **9** suspicion **10** foreboding, skepticism **11** dubiousness, uncertainty **12** apprehension, doubtfulness, presentiment, reservations **14** second thoughts

misguided 5 at sea **6** adrift, faulty, misled, unwise **7** in error **8** mistaken **9** erroneous, imprudent, led astray, off course **10** ill-advised, indiscreet, misadvised **11** injudicious, misdirected, misinformed

mishap 4 slip, snag **5** botch **6** fiasco, slipup **7** reverse, setback **8** casualty, disaster **9** mischance **10** difficulty, misfortune **11** miscarriage **12** misadventure

mishmash 3 mix **4** hash, stew **5** salad **6** jumble, medley, muddle **7** melange **8** mixed bag, pastiche, scramble **9** patchwork **10** assemblage, crazy quilt, hodgepodge, miscellany, salmagundi **14** conglomeration, omnium-gatherum

misinform 7 deceive, mislead **8** misguide **9** misdirect **10** lead astray **12** misrepresent

misinterpret 11 misconstrue **12** misapprehend **13** misunderstand

misinterpretation 13 misconception **16** misunderstanding **17** misrepresentation

misjudge 3 err **7** mistake **10** exaggerate, understate **11** misconceive, mis-

construe **12** misapprehend, miscalculate, misinterpret, overestimate **13** misunderstand, underestimate

mislay 4 lose, miss **8** displace, misplace

mislead 4 dupe, fool, gull **6** betray, delude, entice, seduce, take in **7** beguile, deceive **8** hoodwink, inveigle, misguide **9** bamboozle, misdirect, misinform, play false, victimize **10** lead astray **11** double-cross, string along

misleading 6 luring **8** deluding **9** deceiving **10** misguiding **11** hoodwinking

mismanage 3 mar **4** flub, muff, ruin **5** botch, spoil **6** bollix, bungle, foul up, mess up **7** louse up, screw up **9** mishandle **11** make a hash of, make a mess of

misnomer 8 misusage, solecism **9** barbarism, misnaming **11** malapropism

misogynic 7 cynical **11** woman-hating **12** misanthropic

misogynist 5 cynic **10** woman-hater **11** misanthrope

misplace 4 lose **5** abuse **6** mislay **11** lose track of

misreckon 8 misjudge **10** guess wrong, miscompute **11** misestimate **12** miscalculate

misrepresent 7 falsify, mislead **8** disguise

misrepresentation 7 mockery **8** altering, travesty, twisting **9** burlesque, doctoring **10** caricature, distortion, falsifying **12** adulteration, exaggeration, misstatement **13** falsification

miss 4 blow, girl, lack, lady, lass, lose, loss, maid, muff, skip, slip, want **5** avert, avoid, error, forgo, let go, woman **6** bypass, damsel, escape, forego, lassie, maiden, miscue, pass by **7** blunder, colleen, default, failure, fly wide, let pass, let slip, long for, mistake, neglect, old maid, overrun, pine for **8** leave out, omission, overlook, pass over, senorita, slip up on, spinster, yearn for **9** disregard, fall short, false step, gloss over, go without, overshoot, oversight, surrender, young lady **10** demoiselle, schoolgirl **12** be absent from **13** feel the loss of, mademoiselle

missal 10 prayer book

missed
French: **6** manque

misshapen 7 twisted **8** deformed **9** contorted, distorted

missile 4 ball, dart **5** arrow, lance, shaft, shell, spear, stone **6** bullet, rocket **7** harpoon, javelin **10** projectile

missing 4 AWOL, gone, lost **6** absent **7** lacking, left out, not here **8** avoiding, skipping **10** longing for, not present **11** overlooking, yearning for **12** disregarding

Missing
director: **22** Constantine Costa-Gavras
cast: **8** John Shea **10** Jack Lemmon
11 Sissy Spacek **13** Melanie Mayron

Missing Persons and Other Essays
author: **12** Heinrich Boll

mission 3 end, job **4** task **5** quest **6** charge **7** calling, mandate, pursuit **8** legation, ministry **9** objective **10** assignment, commission, delegation, enterprise **11** raison d'etre, undertaking

Mission
tribe: **7** Chumash, Juaneno, Luiseno **8** Diegueno **9** Costanoan **10** Gabrielino **11** Fernandario
location: **10** California

Mission: Impossible
character: **5** Casey, Paris **10** Rollin Hand **11** Dana Lambert, James Phelps **12** Daniel Briggs **13** Barney Collier **14** Cinnamon Carter, Willie Armitage
cast: **10** Greg Morris, Peter Lupus, Steven Hill **11** Barbara Bain, Peter Graves **12** Leonard Nimoy, Martin Landau **14** Lynda Day George **15** Lesley Ann Warren

Mississippi
abbreviation: **2** MS **4** Miss
nickname: **5** Bayou **6** Mudcat **8** Magnolia
capital/largest city: **7** Jackson
others: **6** Biloxi, Helena, Laurel, Tupelo, Winona **7** Belzoni, Corinth, Grenada, Natchez **8** Bogalusa, Columbus, Gulfport, Meridian **9** Kosciusko, Vicksburg **10** Clarksdale, Pascagoula **11** Hattiesburg **13** Pass Christian
college: **4** Rust **6** Alcorn **7** Jackson **8** Belhaven, Millsaps, Tougaloo **11** Mississippi **12** Blue Mountain, William Carey
feature: **12** Natchez Trace
  national military park: **9** Vicksburg
  national seashore: **11** Gulf Islands
tribe: **3** Sac **5** Tious **6** Biloxi, Mandan, Tunica **7** Choctaw, Natchez, Tonikan **8** Chicksaw
people: **11** Eudora Welty **15** William Faulkner **17** Tennessee Williams
explorer: **6** DeSoto, Joliet **9** Iberville, Marquette
island: **3** Cat **4** Horn, Ship **9** Petit Bois
lake: **4** Enid **6** Sardis **7** Barnett, Grenada **8** Pickwick **9** Arkabutla, Okatibbee
land rank: **12** thirty-second
highest point: **7** Woodall
physical feature:
  delta: **10** Yazoo Basin
  hills: **8** Fall Line **9** Tennessee **11** Loess Bluffs
  prairie: **5** Black **7** Jackson
  sound: **11** Mississippi
river: **4** Leaf **5** Pearl, Yazoo **8** Big Black **9** Tombigbee, Yalobusha

10 Homochitto, Pascagoula **11** Mississippi **12** Tallahatchie
state admission: **9** twentieth
state bird: **11** mockingbird
state flower: **8** magnolia
state motto: **14** By Valor and Arms
state song: **13** Go Mississippi
state tree: **8** magnolia

missive 4 note **6** billet, letter **7** epistle, message **13** communication **14** correspondence

Miss Julie
author: **16** August Strindberg

Miss Lonelyhearts
author: **13** Nathanael West

Missouri
abbreviation: **2** MO
nickname: **5** Ozark **6** Show-Me **7** Bullion **15** Mother of the West
capital: **13** Jefferson City
largest city: **7** St Louis
others: **5** Eldon, Hayti, Lamar, Macon, Rolla **6** Butler, Joplin, Mexico **7** Bethany, Bolivar, Cameron, Clayton, Lebanon, Moberly, Sedalia **8** Berkeley, Columbia, Hannibal, Kirkwood, Sikeston, St Joseph **10** Bonne Terre, Kansas City **11** Springfield, Warrensburg **12** Independence **13** Cape Girardeau, Webster Groves
college: **5** Avila, Drury **6** Tarkio **7** Lincoln, St Louis, Webster **8** Stephens **10** Washington **11** Westminster
feature:
  dam: **5** Osage
tribe: **3** Fox, Sac **4** Sauk **5** Osage **7** Shawnee **8** Cherokee, Missouri
people: **7** TS Eliot **9** Mark Twain **10** Jesse James **11** Omar Bradley **12** Helen Traubel, Sara Teasdale **13** John J Pershing, Marianne Moore, Samuel Clemens **15** Reinhold Niebuhr **22** George Washington Carver
  explorer: **6** Joliet **7** La Salle **9** Marquette
lake: **7** Norfolk **9** Tablerock, Taneycomo **10** Bull Shoals **14** Kaysinger Bluff **15** Lake of the Ozarks
land rank: **10** nineteenth
mountain: **6** Ozarks **10** St Francois
  highest point: **8** Taumsauk
physical feature: **8** Bootheel **9** Big Spring
  plains: **4** Till **5** Osage
  plateau: **5** Ozark
president: **12** Harry S Truman
river: **4** Salt **5** Grand, Osage, White **6** Platte **7** Current, Meramec **8** Big Muddy, Chariton, Missouri **9** Des Moines, Gasconade, St Francis **11** Mississippi
state admission: **12** twenty-fourth
state bird: **8** bluebird
state flower: **8** hawthorn
state motto: **41** The Welfare of the People Shall Be the Supreme Law

state song: **13** Missouri Waltz
state tree: **7** dogwood

Miss Peach
creator: **11** Mell Lazarus
character: **3** Ira **6** Arthur, Lester, Marcia **8** Francine
place: **9** Kamp Kelly **11** Kelly School

misspend 5 waste **8** squander **9** dissipate, throw away **11** fritter away

misspent 6 wasted **8** depraved **9** debauched, dissolute, idled away **10** misapplied, profitless, squandered, thrown away

misstate 5 alter **6** bollix, garble **7** confuse, distort, falsify, pervert **8** misquote **9** misreport **12** misrepresent

misstatement 3 fib, lie **4** tale **5** error **7** falsity, untruth **9** falsehood **13** prevarication **17** misrepresentation

misstep 3 sin **4** goof, slip, vice **5** boner, error, fault, gaffe, lapse **6** booboo, defect, foul-up **7** blooper, faux pas, offense, screw-up **11** delinquency, dereliction, shortcoming **12** indiscretion **13** transgression

miss the mark 4 fail **9** fall short **11** come up short

miss the point 7 mistake **11** fail to catch, misconceive **12** misapprehend **13** misunderstand

mist 3 fog **4** haze, murk, smog **5** steam, vapor **7** drizzle

mistake 4 slip **5** boner, error, gaffe, mix-up **6** slipup **7** blooper, blunder, confuse, faux pas, misstep **8** confound, misjudge **9** misreckon, oversight **11** misconstrue, misidentify **12** misapprehend, miscalculate, misinterpret **13** misunderstand **14** miscalculation
French: **10** malentendu

mistaken 5 at sea, false, wrong **6** faulty, untrue **7** at fault, in error, unsound **8** deceived **9** erroneous, illogical, incorrect, off course, unfounded **10** fallacious, groundless, inaccurate, ungrounded **11** unjustified

Mister 3 aga, dom, don, pan, reb, sir **4** agha, babu, herr **5** sahib, senor **6** senhor, signor **7** mynheer **8** monsieur

Mister Roberts
author: **12** Thomas Heggen
director: **8** John Ford **11** Mervyn LeRoy
cast: **8** Ward Bond **10** Henry Fonda, Jack Lemmon (Ensign Pulver) **11** Betsy Palmer, James Cagney **13** William Powell
Oscar for: **15** supporting actor (Lemmon)

Mister Saturday Night
nickname of: **13** Jackie Gleason

mistreat 4 harm **5** abuse, bully, hound, wrong **6** harass, ill-use, injure, misuse, molest **7** assault, oppress, outrage, pervert, torment, violate

8 ill-treat, maltreat **9** brutalize, manhandle, mishandle, persecute

mistreatment 5 abuse **6** ill-use, injury **7** assault, cruelty, harming **10** bodily harm, oppression **11** manhandling, molestation, persecution **12** maltreatment

mistress 3 Mrs **4** doxy, lady, Miss **5** lover, Madam **6** matron **8** ladylove, paramour **9** concubine, headwoman, housewife, inamorata, kept woman **10** chatelaine, girlfriend, sweetheart

mistrust 5 doubt, qualm **7** anxiety, dubiety, suspect **8** distrust, question, wariness **9** challenge, chariness, leeriness, misgiving, suspicion **10** disbelieve, skepticism

misty 4 dewy, hazy **5** filmy, foggy, murky **6** cloudy, opaque, steamy **8** nebulous, overcast, vaporous **10** indistinct

misunderstand 7 confuse, misread, mistake **8** misjudge **9** misreckon **11** misconceive, misconstrue **12** misapprehend, miscalculate, misinterpret, miss the point

misunderstanding 4 rift, spat **5** set-to **7** discord, dispute, quarrel, wrangle **8** conflict, squabble **10** difference, dissension, misreading **11** altercation, contretemps, misjudgment **12** disagreement **13** misconception **15** false impression, misapprehension **16** miscomprehension **17** misinterpretation
French: **10** malentendu

misuse 4 harm, hurt **5** abuse, waste, wrong **6** debase, injure **7** corrupt, exploit, outrage, pervert, profane **8** illtreat, maltreat, misapply, mistreat, wrong use **9** misemploy **10** corruption, perversion, prostitute **11** desecration, profanation, squandering **12** ill treatment, maltreatment, mistreatment, prostitution **13** misemployment **14** misapplication **15** take advantage of

Mitchell, Billy (William Lendrum)
advocate of: **8** air power
court-martialed for: **15** insubordination
served in: **3** WWI
rank: **16** brigadier general
commander of: **15** US army air forces

Mitchell, Margaret
author of: **15** Gone With the Wind

Mitchell, Silas Weir
author of: **9** Hugh Wynne (Free Quaker) **11** Roland Blake

Mitchell, Thomas
born: **11** Elizabeth NJ
roles: **7** Our Town **8** Doc Boone **9** The Outlaw **10** Stagecoach **11** Gerald O'Hara, Lost Horizon **15** Gone With the Wind **19** Only Angels Have Wings

Mitchum, Robert
born: **12** Bridgeport CT
roles: **6** Midway **10** Winds of War **11** Thunder Road **13** Ryan's Daughter, The Longest Day, The Sundowners **15** The Story of G I Joe **16** Farewell My Lovely **20** Heaven Knows Mr Allison

mite 3 bit, jot **4** atom, iota, whit **5** scrap, speck **6** spider **7** smidgen **8** arachnid, particle

Mitford, Jessica
author of: **21** The American Way of Death **22** Kind and Usual Punishment

Mitford, Nancy
author of: **14** Noblesse Oblige **16** The Pursuit of Love **18** Love in a Cold Climate
coined term: **1** U **4** non-U

Mithgarthr see **7** Midgard

Mithras
origin: **7** Persian
god of: **5** light, truth
corresponds to: **3** Sol

mitigate 4 ease **5** allay, blunt **6** lessen, reduce, soften, soothe, temper, weaken **7** assuage, lighten, mollify, placate, relieve **8** diminish, moderate, palliate **9** alleviate, extenuate **10** ameliorate

mitigating 6 easing **8** allaying, blunting, reducing **9** assuaging, lessening, relieving, softening, tempering **10** lightening, moderating, palliating, palliative **11** diminishing, extenuating **12** ameliorating

Mitteleuropa 12 middle Europe

mitzvah, mitsvah 8 good deed **11** commandment

mix 3 add **4** beat, club, fold, fuse, join, stir, whip **5** admix, alloy, blend, merge, put in, unite **6** commix, fusion, hobnob, mingle **7** combine, consort, include, mixture **8** assembly, coalesce, compound, intermix, mingling **9** associate, commingle, interfuse, interlard, introduce, socialize **10** amalgamate, fraternize, intertwine, interweave **11** incorporate, intermingle, intersperse, put together

mixed 4 coed **5** fused **6** hybrid, motley **7** alloyed, blended, inmixed, mingled, mongrel, not pure **8** combined **9** composite, uncertain **10** ambivalent, indecisive, interwoven, variegated **11** adulterated, diversified, half and half, put together **12** conglomerate, inconclusive **13** heterogeneous, male-and-female, miscellaneous

mixed-up 6 addled **7** chaotic, jumbled, muddled, tangled **8** confused, rambling **9** befuddled, illogical, nonplused, perplexed **10** bewildered, disjointed, incoherent, irrational, nonplussed **12** disconnected, disorganized **13** disharmonious, heterogeneous

Mixtec
tribe: **7** Zapotec

mixture 3 mix **4** hash, stew **5** alloy, blend, union **6** fusion, jumble, medley **7** amalgam, melange **8** compound, mishmash, pastiche **9** admixture, composite, potpourri **10** commixture, hodgepodge, salmagundi **11** association, combination **12** adulteration, amalgamation, intermixture

mixup 4 mess, riot **5** fight, melee, snafu **6** fracas, muddle, tangle **7** mistake **8** disorder **9** confusion, imbroglio **11** misjudgment **14** miscalculation **16** miscomprehension, misunderstanding

mix up 5 addle **6** mess up, muddle **7** confuse, nonplus, perplex **8** befuddle, bewilder **10** disarrange

Mneme
member of: **5** Muses
personifies: **6** memory

Mnemosyne
origin: **5** Greek
member of: **6** Titans
goddess of: **6** memory
father: **6** Uranus
mother: **4** Gaea
daughters: **5** Muses

Moab
son of: **3** Lot
land near: **7** Dead Sea
home of: **4** Ruth **5** Naomi

Moabite god 7 Chemosh

moan 3 sob **4** keen, wail **5** groan **6** bemoan, bewail, lament, plaint **7** grumble **11** lamentation

moan over 5 mourn **6** bemoan, bewail, lament **7** cry over **8** weep over **10** grieve over

moat 4 foss **5** ditch, fosse, graff **6** gutter, rundel, trench

mob 4 gang, herd **5** crowd, crush, horde, Mafia, swarm **6** masses, rabble, throng **7** flock to **8** assembly, populace, surround **9** gathering, hoi polloi, multitude, plebeians, syndicate **10** converge on **11** proletariat, rank and file **14** organized crime

mobile 6 active, motile **7** kinetic, movable, nomadic **8** portable, rootless **9** footloose, traveling, wandering **10** ambulatory, locomotive

mobilize 6 call up, muster, summon **7** marshal **8** activate, organize **10** call to arms **11** put in motion

mobster 4 hood **6** hitman **7** hoodlum, Mafioso **8** gangster **10** gang member

Moby Dick
author: **14** Herman Melville
character: **4** Ahab **5** Stubb **7** Ishmael **8** Fedallah, Queequeg, Starbuck

mock 3 ape **4** copy **5** belie, mimic, scorn, spurn, taunt **6** deride, insult, jeer at, parody, revile, show up **7** imitate, laugh at, let down, profane, scoff at, sneer at **8** ridicule **9** burlesque, frustrate, make fun of, poke fun at **10** caricature, disappoint, make game of **11** make sport of

mockery 4 joke, sham **5** farce, scorn **7** jeering, mimicry, sarcasm **8** derision, raillery, ridicule, scoffing, travesty **9** burlesque, contumely **10** disrespect, ridiculing **13** laughingstock

Mock Turtle
  character in: 28 Alice's Adventures in Wonderland
  author: 7 Carroll

mode 3 cut, fad, way **4** form, rage, rule **5** craze, means, style, taste, trend, vogue **6** course, custom, manner, method, system **7** fashion, process **8** approach, practice **9** condition, procedure, technique **10** appearance

model 4 cast, copy, form, mold, show, type **5** build, dummy, ideal, shape, sport, style **6** design, mirror, mock-up **7** display, example, fashion, outline, paragon, pattern, perfect, replica, subject, variety, version **8** exemplar, paradigm, peerless, standard **9** archetype, criterion, exemplary, facsimile, mannequin, prototype, simulated **10** simulacrum **14** representation, representative

model on 6 base on **7** found on **10** derive from

mode of operating
  Latin: 2 mo **13** modus operandi

moderate 4 calm, cool, curb, fair, hush, mild, tame **5** abate, chair, sober **6** direct, gentle, lessen, manage, medium, modest, soften, subdue, temper **7** average, careful, conduct, control, oversee **8** diminish, measured, mediocre, middling, ordinary, passable, rational, regulate, restrain, tone down **9** judicious, peaceable, temperate, unruffled **10** not violent, reasonable **11** inexpensive, preside over **12** mainstreamer, medium-priced

moderation 7 abating, economy **8** allaying **9** abatement, frugality, lessening, remission, restraint **10** continence, diminution, mitigation, palliation, relaxation, temperance **11** alleviation, forbearance, self-control **12** moderateness **13** temperateness **14** abstemiousness **19** avoidance of extremes

moderator 8 chairman, mediator **10** chairwoman, negotiator

modern 3 new **6** modish, recent **7** current, in vogue **8** up-to-date **10** present-day **11** fashionable, streamlined **12** contemporary **15** contemporaneous **16** twentieth-century

Modern Comedy, A
  author: 14 John Galsworthy

modernistic 3 neo **6** modern **7** moderne **10** new-fangled **12** contemporary

modernity 5 vogue **7** fashion, new

look, novelty, the rage **8** last word **14** newfangledness **15** contemporaneity **16** new fashionedness

modernize 4 redo **5** renew **6** do over, revamp, update **7** restore **8** redesign, renovate **9** refurbish **10** regenerate, rejuvenate, streamline **11** recondition **13** bring up to date **16** move with the times

modern times 5 today **8** nowadays **10** the present **13** the here and now

Modern Times
  director: 14 Charles Chaplin
  cast: 12 Henry Bergman **14** Charlie Chaplin, Chester Conklin **15** Paulette Goddard **19** Stanley "Tiny" Sandford

modest 3 coy, shy **4** meek, prim **5** plain, quiet, timid **6** demure, humble, proper, simple **7** bashful, limited, nominal, prudish, unshowy **8** blushing, discreet, moderate, reserved, timorous **9** diffident, shrinking **10** unassuming **11** circumspect, constrained, inexpensive, puritanical, straitlaced, unassertive, unobtrusive **12** mediumpriced, not excessive, self-effacing, unpretending **13** unpretentious **14** unostentatious

modesty 7 coyness, prudery, reserve, shyness **8** humility, plainness, timidity **9** propriety, restraint, reticence **10** constraint, demureness, diffidence, humbleness, simplicity **11** bashfulness, naturalness **12** timorousness **14** reasonableness, self-effacement **15** inexpensiveness

modicum 3 bit, dab, jot **4** atom, dash, drop, inch, iota, mite, whit **5** crumb, grain, pinch, scrap, speck, tinge, touch **6** morsel, sliver, snatch, trifle **7** handful, minimum, smidgen **8** fraction, fragment, particle **9** little bit **10** sprinkling **11** small amount **13** small quantity

modification 6 change **8** revision **9** variation **10** adjustment, alteration, conversion, emendation, regulation **14** transformation **15** differentiation

modify 4 redo, vary **5** adapt, alter, limit, lower, remit **6** adjust, change, narrow, reduce, remold, revise, rework, soften, temper **7** control, convert, qualify, remodel, reshape **8** moderate, modulate, restrain, restrict, tone down **9** condition, refashion, transform, transmute **10** reorganize **12** transmogrify

Modigliani, Amedeo
  born: 5 Italy **7** Leghorn, Livorno
  artwork: 10 Seated Nude **13** Reclining Nude, Yellow Sweater **15** Jeanne Hebuterne

modish 2 in **3** now **4** chic **5** natty, nifty, sharp, smart, today **6** dapper, snazzy, spiffy, trendy, with it **7** a la mode, current, faddish, in style, in

vogue, stylish, voguish **9** high-style **11** fashionable **13** up-to-the-minute

Modoc
  language family: 12 Shapwailutan
  division: 10 Lutuamnian
  location: 6 Oregon **10** California
  leader: 14 Chief Kintpuash (Captain Jack)
  related to: 7 Klamath

Modred
  character in: 16 Arthurian romance

Mod Squad, The
  character: 9 Linc Hayes, (Capt) Adam Greer **11** Julie Barnes, Pete Cochran
  cast: 11 Michael Cole, Peggy Lipton, Tige Andrews **19** Clarence Williams III

modulate 4 pass **5** lower **6** accord, attune, change, reduce, soften, temper **8** moderate, progress, regulate, tone down, turn down **9** harmonize

modulation 4 tone **5** pitch **6** accent **9** reduction **10** expression, regulation, transition

modus operandi 15 mode of operating
  abbreviation: 2 mo

modus vivendi 14 manner of living

Mogadishu, Mogadiscio
  capital of: 7 Somalia

mogul 3 VIP **4** czar, lord **5** baron, power, wheel **6** bigwig, tycoon **7** big shot, magnate, notable **8** big wheel **9** personage, potentate

Mohammed
  also: 7 Mahomet, Prophet **8** Muhammad
  born: 5 Mecca
  clan: 6 Hashim
  daughter: 6 Fatima
  deity: 5 Allah
  died: 6 Medina
  father: 8 Abdallah, Abdullah
  father-in-law: 7 Abu Bakr, Abubekr
  flight: 4 hadj **6** hegira, hejira
  follower: 6 Moslem, Muslim, Wahbi **10** Mohammedan
  grandfather: 13 Abd al-Muttalib
  horse: 5 Buraq **7** Alborrak
  mother: 5 Amina
  religion: 5 Islam
  shrine: 5 Kaaba
  son: 7 Ibrahim
    adopted: 3 Ali
  successor: 4 imam **5** calif **6** caliph **7** Abu Bakr
  tribe: 7 Koreish, Quraysh
  uncle: 5 Abbas **8** Abu Talib
  wife: 5 Aisha **6** Ayesha, Safiya **7** Khadija **8** Khadidja, Kadijah

Mohammedan 4 Sufi **6** Moslem, Muslim, Shiite **7** Islamic, Moorish, Sunnite **10** Mahometan, Muhammadan, Muhammedan

Mohave, Mojave
  language family: 5 Yuman
  location: 7 Arizona **10** California

Mohawk (Kaniengehaga)
  language family: **9** Iroquoian
  location: **6** Canada, Quebec **7** New
    York **11** Lake Ontario
  leader: **8** Hiawatha **11** Joseph Brant
  member of: **19** League of the Iro-
    quois

Mohegan, Mohican, Mahican
  language family: **9** Algonkian **10** Al-
    gonquian
  location: **7** New York **9** Wisconsin **11**
    Connecticut **12** Hudson Valley
  leader: **5** Occom, Uncas **12** Chingach-
    gook
  allied with: **6** Pequot
  with Delaware: **11** Loup Indians,
    Wolf Indians
  subject of novel: **20** The Last of the
    Mohicans
    author: **19** James Fenimore Cooper

Moira
  personifies: **4** fate

moist 3 wet **4** damp, dank, dewy **5**
    humid, misty, muggy, rainy **6**
    clammy, drippy, watery **7** aqueous,
    drizzly, tearful, wettish, wet-eyed **8**
    dripping, vaporous **10** lachrymose

moisten 3 dew, wet **4** damp, hose,
    mist, soak **5** spray, water **6** dampen,
    douche, splash, sponge **8** humidify, ir-
    rigate, saturate, vaporize **10** moistur-
    ize

moisture 3 dew, wet **4** damp, mist **5**
    sweat, vapor **7** drizzle, exudate, wet-
    ness **8** dampness, dankness, humidity
    9 moistness, mugginess **10** wateriness
    11 evaporation **12** perspiration

Mojave see **6** Mohave

Moki see **4** Hopi

mold 3 cut, die, ilk **4** cast, form, kind,
    line, make, rust, sort, turn, type **5**
    brand, frame, knead, model, shape,
    stamp, train **6** blight, create, figure,
    fungus, kidney, lichen, matrix, mil-
    dew, render, sculpt, shaper **7** contour,
    convert, develop, fashion, outline, pat-
    tern, quality, remodel **9** character,
    construct, formation, structure, trans-
    form

molding 4 cyma, dado, gula, ogee **5**
    ovolo

Moldova
  other name: **8** Moldavia
  capital/largest city: **8** Chisinau, Kishi-
    nev
  head of state: **9** president
  government: **8** republic
  monetary unit: **5** ruble
  river: **8** Dniester
  people: **7** Gagauzi **8** Moldovan **9**
    Moldavian
  language: **8** Romanian **9** Moldavian
  religion: **15** Russian Orthodox

moldy 5 fusty, hoary, musty, stale **7**
    spoiled **8** mildewed

molest 3 irk, vex **4** fret, harm, hurt **5**
    abuse, annoy, beset, harry, worry

6 attack, bother, harass, hector, in-
    jure, pester, plague **7** assault, disturb,
    torment, trouble **8** maltreat

Moliere (Jean-Baptiste Poquelin)
  author of: **6** Scapin **8** Tartuffe, The
    Miser **10** Amphitryon **13** Le Misan-
    thrope **17** The School for Wives **19**
    The Imaginary Invalid **20** The School
    for Husbands **22** Le Bourgeois Gen-
    tilhomme

Moll Flanders
  author: **11** Daniel Defoe
  character: **5** Robin **6** Jemmy E **10** Sea
    Captain

mollification 8 soothing **9** placation
    11 appeasement, assuagement **12** con-
    ciliation

mollify 4 calm, curb, dull, ease, lull **5**
    abate, allay, blunt, check, quell, quiet,
    still **6** lessen, pacify, reduce, soften,
    soothe, temper **7** appease, assuage,
    lighten, placate **8** decrease, mitigate,
    moderate, palliate, tone down

mollusk 4 clam, slug **5** conch, cowry,
    murex, snail, squid, whelk **6** chiton,
    cockle, cowrie, limpet, mussel, oyster,
    teredo, triton **7** abalone, bivalve, geo-
    duck, octopus, scallop **8** argonaut,
    nautilus, shipworm **9** shellfish **10** cut-
    tlefish, nudibranch, peri- winkle

mollycoddle 3 pet **4** baby, wimp **5**
    sissy, spoil **6** cosset, coward, pamper
    7 cater to, crybaby, indulge, milksop
    8 give in to, mama's boy, weakling **9**
    cream puff **11** milquetoast, overin-
    dulge

Molnar, Ferenc
  author of: **6** Liliom **7** The Swan **12**
    The Guardsman

Moloch 3 god **5** diety
  also: **6** Molech
  worshiped by: **9** Ammonites

molt 4 cast, shed, slip **6** change,
    slough **7** castoff, discard, ecdysis **8**
    exuviate

molten 6 melted, red-hot **7** fusible, ig-
    neous, smelted **8** magmatic **9** lique-
    fied

molto
  music: **4** very

Moly
  form: **4** herb
  given to: **8** Odysseus
  given by: **6** Hermes
  to counteract spells of: **5** Circe

Momaday, N Scott
  author of: **18** The House Made of
    Dawn **21** The Way to Rainy Moun-
    tain

moment 5 flash, jiffy, trice, value,
    worth **6** import, minute, second,
    weight **7** concern, gravity, instant **8**
    interest, juncture **9** twinkling **10** im-
    portance **11** consequence, weightiness
    12 significance

momentary 5 brief, hasty, quick,

short **6** sudden **7** instant, passing **8**
    flashing, fleeting, fugitive, imminent **9**
    ephemeral, immediate, temporary,
    transient **10** short-lived, transitory **13**
    instantaneous

momentous 5 grave **7** crucial, fateful,
    salient, serious, weighty **8** critical, de-
    cisive, eventful **9** essential, important,
    ponderous **11** far-reaching, influential,
    significant, substantial **12** earthshak-
    ing **13** consequential

momentous occurrence 5 event **8**
    occasion **9** milestone **12** red-letter
    day, turning point

momentum 2 go **4** dash, push **5**
    drive, force, speed, vigor **6** energy,
    moment, thrust **7** headway, impetus,
    impulse **8** velocity **10** propulsion

Mommsen, Theodor
  author of: **16** The History of Rome

Momus
  also: **5** Momos
  god of: **7** censure **8** ridicule

Monaco
  capital: **11** Monaco-Ville
  largest city: **10** Monte Carlo
  others: **9** Fontville
  division: **9** Fontville **10** Monte Carlo
    11 La Condamine, Monaco-Ville
  head of government: **15** minister of
    state
  head of state: **6** prince
  monetary unit: **5** franc **7** centime
  river: **7** Vesubie
  sea: **13** Mediterranean
  physical feature: **9** Cote d'Azur
  people: **6** French **7** Italian **10** Mone-
    gasque
    oceanographer: **15** Jacques Cous-
      teau
    prince: **5** Louis **6** Albert, Honore **7**
      Antoine, Charles, Rainier **9** Flore-
      stan
    princess: **10** Grace Kelly
    ruler: **4** Rome **5** Genoa **6** Greece **8**
      Grimaldi, Saracens **9** Phoenicia
  language: **6** French **7** English, Italian
    10 Monegasque
  religion: **13** Roman Catholic
  place:
    beach: **8** Larvotto
    casino: **10** Monte Carlo
    gardens: **6** Exotic
    museum: **12** Oceanography
    park: **18** Princess Antoinette
  feature:
    auto race: **15** Monaco Grand Prix

Monaco-Ville
  capital of: **6** Monaco

Mona Lisa
  also called: **10** La Gioconda
  artist: **15** Leonardo da Vinci
  noted for: **5** smile
  museum: **6** Louvre

monarch 3 HRH **4** czar, doge, emir,
    khan, king, rani, shah, tsar **5** rajah,
    ruler, queen **6** caesar, kaiser, prince

7 czarina, emperor, empress, majesty, pharaoh **8** kaiserin, princess **9** chieftain, potentate

monarchical 9 czaristic **10** autocratic **11** dictatorial

monastery 5 abbey **6** friary, priory **7** convent, nunnery, retreat **8** cloister

monastic 7 ascetic, monkish, recluse **8** celibate, hermitic, secluded, solitary **9** cloistral, reclusive, unworldly **10** cloistered, hermitlike **11** sequestered **13** contemplative

mon cher 6 my dear

Moncrieff, Algernon (Algy)
  character in: **27** The Importance of Being Earnest
  author: **5** Wilde

Mond, Mustapha
  character in: **13** Brave New World
  author: **6** Huxley

Monday
  French: **5** lundi
  German: **6** montag
  heavenly body: **4** moon
  Italian: **6** lunedi
  means: **12** day of the moon
  Spanish: **5** lunes

Mondrian, Piet
  real name: **23** Pieter Cornelis Mondriaan
  born: **10** Amersfoort **14** The Netherlands
  artwork: **5** Trees **10** The Red Tree **12** Ocean and Pier **17** Evening Landscapes **18** Landscape with a Mill **20** Broadway Boogie-Woogie **29** Composition in Red Yellow and Blue

Monet, Claude Oscar
  born: **5** Paris **6** France
  artwork: **7** Poplars **9** Haystacks, The Thames **11** Water Lilies **14** Rouen Cathedral **16** Women in the Garden **17** Impression Sunrise **18** Mornings on the Seine **21** The Bridge at Argenteuil

monetary 6 fiscal **9** budgetary, financial, pecuniary, sumptuary

money 4 cash, coin **5** bread, bucks, dough, funds **6** assets, riches, specie, wealth **7** capital, coinage, payment, revenue, scratch **8** currency, hard cash, proceeds **9** affluence, long green **10** collateral, greenbacks **11** wherewithal

money-carrier
  French: **12** porte-monnaie

moneyed, monied 4 rich **5** flush, swell **6** flashy, loaded **7** elegant, opulent, solvent, wealthy **8** affluent **10** prosperous

money-grubbing 5 venal **6** greedy **8** covetous, grasping **9** mercenary **10** avaricious

money lender 6 banker, lender, usurer **7** lombard, shylock **9** loanshark **10** pawnbroker

money saved 7 nest egg, savings **10** investment

money spent 6 outlay **7** payment **8** expenses **11** expenditure

Mongolia
  other name: **13** Outer Mongolia
  capital/largest city: **9** Ulan Bator
  others: **5** Kobdo **6** Darhan **10** Choibalsan, Sukhe Bator, Tsetserlik, Uliassutai
    ancient capital: **9** Karakoram
  government:
    legislature: **17** People's Great Hural **18** People's Great Khural
  monetary unit: **5** mongo, mungo **6** tugrik **7** tughrik
  weight: **3** lan
  lake: **3** Uvs **5** Har Us **6** Bor Nor **7** Ghirgis, Ubsa Nor **8** Airik Nor, Durga Nor, Hobsogol, Khara Usu **9** Khubsugul, Khukhu-Nur **10** Khirgis Nor
  mountain: **4** Cast, Orog **5** Altai **6** Kentei, Sevrej **7** Ich Ovoo, Khangai, Khentei **8** Tannu-Ola **9** Edrengijn **10** Cagaan Bogd **11** Munky Sardyk **14** Hangayn-Hentiyn, Monch Chajrchan
  highest point: **10** Tabun Bogdo
  river: **3** Tes **4** Egin, Onon, Tuul, Uldz **5** Kobdo, Tesin **6** Orkhon **7** Kerulen, Selenga, Selenge **8** Dzabkhan, Dzavchan
  physical feature:
    desert: **4** Gobi **5** Ordos, Shamo
    plateau: **8** Mongolia
    region: **10** Great Lakes
  people: **5** Oirat, Tungu **6** Buryat, Darbet, Khoton, Mongol **7** Kazakhs, Khalkha **8** Tuvinian **9** Dariganga
    leader: **8** Jahangir, Jehangir **10** Kublai Khan, Tsendenbal **11** Genghis Khan
    ruler: **4** Huns **5** Ching **6** Manchu **7** Kirghiz, Uighurs **8** Hsiung-nu
    spiritual/secular ruler: **12** Living Buddha **21** Jebtsun Damba Khutu Khtu
  language: **6** Kazakh **16** Khalkha Mongolian
  religion: **7** Lamaism **9** Shamanism **15** Tibetan Buddhism
  place:
    monastery: **6** Gandun
  feature:
    felt tent: **4** yurt
    nomadic herder: **4** arat
  food:
    fermented mare's milk: **5** airag

Mongolian
  language family: **6** Altaic
  group: **6** Buryat **7** Khalkha

Mongoose, The
  nickname of: **11** Archie Moore

mongrel 3 cur **4** mutt **5** mixed **6** hybrid **7** bastard **8** offshoot **9** anomalous, crossbred **10** crossbreed

moniker 3 tag **4** name **5** label, title **6** eponym, handle **7** epithet, surname **8** cognomen, nickname, taxonomy

9 sobriquet **11** appellation, designation **12** denomination

monitor 2 TV **4** tend **5** guide, teach **6** censor, direct, pickup, police, screen, sensor **7** oversee, proctor, scanner **8** overseer, watchdog **9** supervise **14** disciplinarian

Monkees, The
  cast/musician: **9** Davy Jones, Peter Tork **10** David Jones **11** Micky Dolenz, Mike Nesmith

monkey 3 ape, ass, toy **4** butt, dupe, fool, jerk **5** clown, jimmy **6** baboon, fiddle, meddle, simian, tamper, tinker, trifle **7** buffoon, primate **13** laughingstock
  group of: **5** troop
  god: **7** Hanuman
  kind: **3** owl **4** saki, titi **5** aotus, lemur, titis **6** baboon, guenon, howler, langur, rhesus, spider **7** colobus, Goeldi's, guereza, macaque, tamarin, tarsier, uakaris **8** capuchin, mandrill, marmoset, squirrel, talapoin **11** douroucouli

monkey business 6 capers **9** highjinks **11** shenanigans

monkeyshines 6 antics, capers, pranks **7** hijinks **10** buffoonery, tomfoolery **11** foolishness

Monks (Edward Leeford)
  character in: **11** Oliver Twist
  author: **7** Dickens

monocle 4 quiz **5** glass **7** lorgnon **8** eyeglass

Monoclonius
  type: **8** dinosaur **10** ceratopsid
  location: **12** North America
  characteristic: **6** horned

Monod, Jacques
  field: **7** biology
  nationality: **6** French
  researched: **3** RNA **8** genetics
  awarded: **10** Nobel Prize

monograph 8 tractate, treatise **9** discourse **12** disquisition, dissertation

monolith 5 stone **6** column, menhir, pillar, statue **7** obelisk **8** memorial, monument

monologue, monolog 6 screed, sermon, speech **7** address, lecture, oration **9** discourse, soliloquy **11** expatiation **12** disquisition

monopolize 3 own **6** absorb, corner, manage, take up **7** consume, control, preempt **8** arrogate, dominate, regulate, take over **9** cartelize **11** appropriate

monopoly 4 bloc **5** trust **6** cartel, corner **7** combine, control **8** dominion **9** copyright, ownership, syndicate **10** consortium, domination **11** sovereignty **12** jurisdiction **14** proprietorship

Monopoly 9 board game
  invented by: **6** Darrow

places: 2 go, RR **4** jail **6** chance **9** Boardwalk, Park Place

piece: 5 hotel, house

monotonous 3 dry **4** dull, flat **5** banal **6** boring, dreary, jejune, stodgy, torpid **7** droning, humdrum, insipid, mundane, prosaic, routine, tedious **8** plodding, singsong, tiresome, toneless, unvaried **9** colorless, soporific, wearisome **10** pedestrian **11** repetitious, somniferous **13** uninteresting

monotony 3 rut **5** ennui **6** tedium **7** boredom, humdrum **8** dullness, flatness, prosaism, sameness **9** iteration **10** dreariness, redundancy, uniformity **11** reiteration, tediousness **13** wearisomeness **14** predictability

Monroe, Earl

  nickname: 12 Earl the Pearl

  sport: 10 basketball

  position: 5 guard

  team: 16 Baltimore Bullets **21** New York Knickerbockers

Monroe, James

  presidential rank: 5 fifth

  party: 20 Democratic-Republican

  state represented: 2 VA

  defeated: 4 (Rufus) King **5** (John Quincy) Adams

  vice president: 8 (Daniel D) Tompkins

  cabinet:

    state: 5 (John Quincy) Adams

    treasury: 8 (William Harris) Crawford

    war: 7 (John Caldwell) Calhoun

    attorney general: 4 (Richard) Rush, (William) Wirt

    navy: 8 (Samuel Lewis) Southard, (Smith) Thompson **13** (Benjamin Williams) Crowninshield

  born: 2 VA **18** Westmoreland County

  died: 13 New York City NY

  buried: 10 Richmond VA

  education: 14 William and Mary (did not graduate)

  religion: 12 Episcopalian

  author: 67 A View of the Conduct of the Executive in the Foreign Affairs of the United States

  political career: 8 US Senate

    governor of: 8 Virginia

    minister: 5 Spain **6** France **12** Great Britain

    secretary of: 3 war **5** state

  civilian career: 6 lawyer

  military service: 5 major **7** captain **10** lieutenant **16** Revolutionary War **17** lieutenant colonel

    wounded in Battle of: 7 Trenton

  notable events of lifetime/term: 5 Panic (of 1819) **14** Monroe Doctrine

    Agreement: 9 Rush-Bagot

    Compromise: 8 Missouri

    war: 8 Seminole

  father: 6 Spence

  mother: 9 Elizabeth (Jones)

  siblings: 6 Andrew, Spence

9 Elizabeth **11** Joseph Jones

  wife: 9 Elizabeth (Kortright)

    nickname: 5 Eliza

  children: 11 Maria Hester **14** Eliza Kortright

Monroe, Marilyn

  real name: 23 Norma Jean Mortenson Baker

  husband: 11 Joe DiMaggio **12** Arthur Miller

  born: 12 Los Angeles CA

  roles: 7 Bus Stop, Niagara **10** The Misfits **13** Some Like It Hot **16** The Seven-Year Itch **22** Gentlemen Prefer Blondes, How To Marry a Millionaire **23** The Prince and the Showgirl

Monrovia

  capital of: 7 Liberia

monseigneur 6 my lord

monsieur 2 Mr **3** sir **6** mister, my lord

Monsieur Beaucaire

  author: 15 Booth Tarkington

Monsignor Quixote

  author: 12 Graham Greene

monster 4 Fury, gila, ogre, yeti **5** argus, beast, brute, demon, devil, fiend, freak, ghoul, giant, golem, harpy, hydra, lamia, satyr, titan **6** dragon, gorgon, marvel, oddity, savage, threat, wonder, wretch, zombie **7** anomaly, caitiff, centaur, chimera, deviant, grendel, incubus, mammoth, mermaid, vampire, variant, villain **8** bogeyman, colossus, gargoyle, Loch Ness, succubus, werewolf **9** barbarian, curiosity, cutthroat, scoundrel **10** blackguard, phenomenon **11** abnormality, miscreation **12** Frankenstein, lusus naturae

monstrous 4 bald, evil, huge **5** cruel, giant **6** grisly, mighty, odious **7** ghastly, harried, heinous, hideous, hulking, immense, mammoth, obscene, obvious, satanic, titanic, vicious **8** colossal, enormous, fiendish, flagrant, gigantic, gruesome, horrible, outright, shocking **9** atrocious, egregious, nefarious, revolting **10** diabolical, gargantuan, outrageous, prodigious, scandalous, stupendous, tremendous, villainous **14** Brobdingnagian

monstrousness 8 baseness, enormity, evilness, vileness, villainy **9** barbarity, depravity, malignity **10** inhumanity, wickedness **11** heinousness, viciousness **13** atrociousness, offensiveness **14** outrageousness

Montague family

  characters in: 14 Romeo and Juliet

  author: 11 Shakespeare

  member: 5 Romeo

Montaigne, Michel de

  author of: 6 Essais, Essays

Montalban, Ricardo

  born: 6 Mexico **10** Mexico City

  roles: 4 Khan **8** Mr Roarke **9** The

Colbys **13** Fantasy Island **24** Star Trek II The Wrath of Khan

Montalvo, Garcia de

  author of: 12 Amadis of Gaul

Montana

  abbreviation: 2 MT **4** Mont

  nickname: 6 Big Sky **7** Bonanza, Stubtoe **8** Mountain, Treasure

  capital: 6 Helena

  largest city: 8 Billings

  others: 4 Kipp **5** Butte, Havre, Malta **6** Hardin **7** Bozeman, Chinook, Choteau, Forsyth, Glasgow, Roundup **8** Anaconda, Missoula **9** Kalispell **10** Great Falls

  college: 7 Carroll **10** Great Falls **13** Rocky Mountain

  feature: 17 Continental Divide

    cemetery: 6 Custer

    national park: 7 Glacier **11** Yellowstone

  tribe: 4 Cree, Crow, Hohe **5** Sioux **6** Atsima, Atsina, Salish **7** Arapaho, Bannock, Kutenai, Siksika **8** Cheyenne, Chippewa, Flatfoot, Flathead, Shoshone **9** Blackfeet **11** Assiniboine

  people: 8 Myrna Loy **9** Will James **10** Gary Cooper **14** Charles Russell **15** Jeannette Rankin

    explorer: 13 Lewis and Clark **16** Pierre Jean de Smet

  lake: 5 Tiber **6** Hebgen **8** Flathead, Fort Peck, Medicine **10** Yellowtail **11** Canyon Ferry, Hungry Horse

  land rank: 6 fourth

  mountain: 4 Ajax **5** Baldy, Cowan, Crazy, Lewis **6** Sphinx, Torrey **7** Bighorn, Big Belt, Hilgard, Purcell, Rockies, Trapper **8** Absaroka, Gallatin, Pentagon, Snowshoe

    highest point: 11 Granite Peak

  physical feature: 10 Great Falls

  river: 3 Sun **4** Milk **5** Clark, Teton **6** Marias, Powder, Tongue, Willow **7** Madison, Shields **8** Columbia, Kootenai, Missouri **9** Blackfoot **10** Bitterroot **11** Musselshell, Yellowstone

  state admission: 10 forty-first

  state bird: 17 western meadowlark

  state fish: 26 black-spotted cutthroat trout

  state flower: 10 bitterroot

  state motto: 13 Gold and Silver

  state song: 7 Montana

  state tree: 13 Ponderosa pine

Montana, Bob

  creator/artist of: 6 Archie

Montand, Yves

  real name: 7 Ivo Livi

  wife: 14 Simone Signoret

  born: 5 Italy **14** Monsummano Alto

  roles: 1 Z **12** Let's Make Love **14** Is Paris Burning?

montani semper liberi 28 mountaineers are always free men

  motto of: 12 West Virginia

Montcalm, Louis Joseph

  also: 17 Marquis de Montcalm

nationality: 6 French
served in: 18 French and Indian War
battle: 6 Oswego, Quebec (siege) **8** Carillon **11** Ticonderoga **16** Fort William Henry
killed in battle at: 6 Quebec **15** Plains of Abraham

mont-de-piete 10 pawnbroker
literally: 10 bank of pity

Montenegro
name means: 13 black mountain
other name: 4 Zeta **8** Crna Gora
capital: 7 Cetinje **8** Titograd **9** Podgorica
cities: 3 Bar **5** Kotor, Tivat **6** Niksic, Ulcinj **8** Antivari, Dulcigno, Ivangrad, Pljevlja **10** Hercegnovi **11** Sveti Stefan
division:
    Roman province: 7 Illyria
governed by: 10 Yugoslavia
monetary unit: 4 para **6** florin **7** perpera
lake: 7 Scutari, Shkoder
mountain: 8 Durmitor **11** Dinaric Alps
river: 3 Lim **4** Piva, Tara, Zeta **6** Moraca **7** Ceotina
sea: 8 Adriatic
physical feature:
    gulf: 5 Kotor
people: 4 Serb, Slav **11** Montenegrin
former ruler (Orthodox bishop): 7 vladike **8** vladlika
language: 13 Serbo-Croatian
religion: 16 Serbian Orthodoxy

Monteverdi, Claudio
born: 5 Italy **7** Cremona
composer of: 5 Adone, Orfeo **7** Arianna **14** La Favola d'Orfeo **17** The Fable of Orpheus **21** The Coronation of Poppea **22** L'incoronazione di Poppea **24** Il Ritorno d'Ulisse in patria **34** Il Combattimento di Tancredi e Clorinda

Montevideo
capital of: 7 Uruguay

Montezuma
emperor of: 6 Aztecs
in: 6 Mexico
conquered by: 6 Cortez

Montgomery, Bernard Law
also: 27 (first) Viscount Montgomery of Alamein
author of: 7 Memoirs **17** A History of Warfare
battle: 9 El Alamein
chief: 19 British general staff
commander of: 17 British Eighth Army **32** British occupation forces in Germany
commando raid: 6 Dieppe
deputy supreme commander: 4 NATO
Eighth Army called: 10 Desert Rats
evacuation of: 7 Dunkirk
fought against: 6 Rommel **11** Africa Corps, Afrika Korps

invasion: 6 Sicily **8** Normandy
member: 12 House of Lords
nationality: 7 British
nickname: 5 Monty
served in: 3 WWI **4** WWII

Montgomery, Robert
real name: 17 Henry Montgomery Jr
daughter: 9 Elizabeth
born: 8 Beacon NY
roles: 11 The Big House **13** Night Must Fall **17** Here Comes Mr Jordan

month
1st day: 7 calends
13th or 15th: 4 ides
9th before ides: 5 nones
half: 9 fortnight
next: 7 proximo
preceding: 3 ult(imo)
present: 4 inst(ant)

Month in the Country, A
author: 12 Ivan Turgenev

Mont-Oriol
author: 15 Guy de Maupassant

Montreal
airport: 6 Dorval **8** St Hubert **12** Cartierville
baseball team: 5 Expos
founder: 11 Maisonneuve
hill: 10 Mount Royal
hockey team: 9 Canadiens
island: 5 Jesus **6** Bizard, Perrot **8** Montreal **9** des Soeurs **14** de Boucherville
lake: 7 St Louis
landmark: 12 Place des Arts **13** Molson Stadium **16** Chateau de Ramezay **17** Church of Notre Dame, St Sulpice Seminary **21** Man and His World Exhibit
original name: 10 Ville-Marie
province: 6 Quebec
river: 6 Ottawa **10** St Lawrence **11** des Prairies **14** des Milles Isles
subway: 5 Metro
university: 6 McGill

Montresor
character in: 20 The Cask of Amontillado
author: 3 Poe

Mont Saint Michel and Chartres
author: 10 Henry Adams

Monty
nickname of: 15 Montgomery Clift **17** (General) Bernard Montgomery

monument 4 slab **5** token **6** shrine **7** memento, obelisk, witness **8** cenotaph, memorial, monolith, reminder **9** testament, tombstone **10** gravestone **11** remembrance, testimonial **13** commemoration

monumental 4 huge **5** fatal, heavy **7** awesome, classic, epochal, immense, lasting, massive **8** colossal, decisive, enduring, gigantic, historic, immortal, statuary **9** cyclopean, egregious, memorable **10** horrendous, monolithic,

shattering, stupendous **11** inestimable **12** catastrophic **13** unprecedented

mooch 3 beg, bum **5** cadge **6** hustle, sponge **7** solicit **8** freeload

mood 5 blues, dumps, humor **6** spirit, temper **7** feeling **8** doldrums, vexation **9** condition **10** depression, gloominess, melancholy **11** disposition, melancholia, temperament **14** predisposition **16** hypersensitivity

moody 4 mean **5** sulky, surly, testy **6** crabby, dismal, fickle, gloomy, mopish, morbid, morose, sullen **7** erratic, flighty, peevish, unhappy **8** brooding, dejected, notional, variable, volatile **9** impetuous, impulsive, irascible, irritable, mercurial, saturnine, whimsical **10** capricious, changeable, despondent, inconstant, lugubrious, melancholy **11** pessimistic **12** inconsistent **13** temperamental, unpredictable

Mookerjee, Hurree Chunder
character in: 3 Kim
author: 7 Kipling

moon 4 gape, lamp, luna, roam **5** dream, month, stare **6** dawdle, wander **8** daydream **9** satellite
god of: 3 Sin **5** Nanna **6** Meztli
goddess of: 4 Luna **5** Diana, Holle, Tanit **6** Hecate, Hekate, Phoebe, Selena, Selene, Tanith **7** Artemis, Astarte, Cynthia
full: 9 plenilune
new: 5 prime
waning: 7 waiand

Moon and Sixpence, The
author: 16 W Somerset Maugham

moonless 4 dark **5** black, murky **7** stygian **9** lightless, unlighted **13** unilluminated

Moonlighting
character: 11 Maddie Hayes **12** Agnes Dipesto, David Addison
cast: 11 Bruce Willis **13** Allyce Beasley **14** Cybill Shepherd
detective agency: 8 Blue Moon

Moon Mullins
creator: 12 Frank Willard
character: 4 Kayo **5** Mamie **9** Mushmouth **11** Uncle Willie **15** Lady Plushbottom, Lord Plushbottom **16** Moonshine Mullins

Moon of the Caribbees, The
author: 12 Eugene O'Neill

moonshine 5 hokum **6** bunkum, humbug **7** bootleg **8** clockade, homebrew, malarky, nonsense **10** balderdash, bathtub gin **11** mountain dew

moonstone
species: 8 feldspar
source: 5 Burma, Mogok

Moonstone, The
author: 13 Wilkie Collins
character: 7 Dr Candy **12** Lady Verinder, Sergeant Cuff **13** Franklin Blake **14** John Herncastle, Rachel

Verinder **15** Rosanna Spearman **16** Godfrey Ablewhite

moor 3 fen **4** dock, down, fell, lash, wold **5** affix, berth, chain, heath, marsh, tie up **6** anchor, attach, fasten, secure, steppe, tether, tundra, upland **7** savanna, tie down **8** make fast **9** wasteland

Moore, Archie
nickname: **11** The Mongoose
real name: **18** Archibald Lee Wright
sport: **6** boxing
class: **16** light-heavyweight

Moore, Clement C
author of: **23** A Visit from Saint Nicholas

Moore, Dick
creator/artist of: **13** Gasoline Alley

Moore, Dudley
nickname: **12** Cuddly Dudley
wife: **11** Suzy Kendall, Tuesday Weld
born: **5** Essex **7** England **8** Dagenham
roles: **3** Ten **6** Arthur **8** Lovesick, Six Weeks **9** Bedazzled **13** Micki and Maude **16** Arthur on the Rocks **17** Like Father Like Son
plays: **5** piano

Moore, George
author of: **12** Esther Waters **15** Hail and Farewell

Moore, Henry
born: **7** England **10** Castleford
artwork: **4** Mask **8** Two Forms **9** North Wind **10** Bird Basket **11** Family Group, Head of a Girl **12** Locking Piece **13** Nuclear Energy **15** Reclining Figure **20** Four-Piece Composition

Moore, Marianne
author of: **12** Like a Bulwark, Nevertheless, O To Be a Dragon, Tell Me Tell Me

Moore, Mary Tyler
husband: **11** Grant Tinker
born: **10** Brooklyn NY
roles: **4** Mary **12** Mary Richards **14** Ordinary People **18** The Dick Van Dyke Show **21** The Mary Tyler Moore Show

Moore, Mrs
character in: **15** A Passage to India
author: **7** Forster

Moore, Roger
born: **6** London **7** England
roles: **8** The Saint **12** Simon Templar
as James Bond: **9** Moonraker, Octopussy **13** Live and Let Die **16** The Spy Who Loved Me **22** The Man with the Golden Gun

Moorehead, Agnes
born: **7** Clinton MA
roles: **6** Endora **9** Bewitched **11** Citizen Kane **13** Johnny Belinda **15** Dear Dead Delilah **20** Magnificent Obsession **23** The Magnificent Ambersons

mooring 4 hook, line, rope **5** cable, chain **6** anchor, hawser

moot 4 open **7** eristic **8** arguable, disputed **9** debatable, undecided, unsettled **10** disputable, unresolved **11** conjectural **12** questionable **13** controversial, problematical **14** controvertible

mope 4 fret, pine, pout, sulk **5** brood, worry **6** grieve, grouse, lament, repine **7** grumble **8** languish

Mopsus
occupation: **4** seer
mother: **5** Manto
grandfather: **8** Tiresias
member of: **9** Argonauts
founded: **6** oracle
location: **6** Mallus **7** Cilicia
cofounder: **11** Amphilochus
epithet: **9** Ampycides

moral 3 tag **4** fair, just, pure **5** adage, maxim, motto, noble, right **6** honest, lesson, proper, saying **7** epigram, ethical, message, proverb, saintly **8** aphorism, didactic, personal, virtuous **9** estimable, homiletic, honorable, preaching **10** aboveboard, high-minded, principled **11** meritorious, sermonizing, tendentious **12** conscionable

moral code 5 ethos **6** ethics **9** integrity, standards **10** principles

morale 4 mood **6** spirit, temper **10** confidence, resolution **11** disposition
French: **13** esprit de corps

morality 5 honor **6** ethics, habits, tastes, virtue **7** modesty, probity **8** fairness, goodness **9** integrity, rectitude **10** chasteness **11** uprightness **13** righteousness

moralize 6 preach **7** lecture

moralizing 7 preachy **8** didactic **9** homiletic

morally corrupt 6 effete **8** decadent, depraved **10** degenerate

moral sense 9 integrity **10** conscience

morass 3 bog, fen **4** mire **5** marsh, swamp **6** slough **8** quagmire, wetlands **9** quicksand

morbid 3 sad **4** dour, glum, grim **5** moody **6** gloomy, morose, somber **8** brooding **9** depressed, saturnine **10** despondent, lugubrious **11** melancholic, pessimistic, unwholesome

morbid condition 6 malady **7** ailment, disease, illness **8** sickness **9** infirmity

Morcerf, Comte de (Fernand)
character in: **21** The Count of Monte Cristo
author: **5** Dumas (pere)

mordant 6 biting, bitter **7** acerbic, caustic, cutting, waspish **8** incisive, piercing, scathing, scornful, stinging, venomous, virulent **9** acidulous, malicious, sarcastic, trenchant **11** acrimonious

Mordecai
cousin: **6** Esther
served: **15** Ahasuerus Xerxes
enemy: **5** Haman

more 5 added, extra, other, spare **6** longer **7** further, reserve **10** additional **12** additionally, supplemental **13** supplementary

More, Thomas
author of: **6** Utopia

Moreau, Frederic
character in: **21** A Sentimental Education
author: **8** Flaubert

Moreau, Gustave
born: **5** Paris **6** France
artwork: **7** Orpheus **13** Dance of Salome (Salome Dancing), The Apparition **16** Hesiod and the Muse **18** The Poet and the Siren **19** Oedipus and the Sphinx **27** Diomedes Devoured by His Horses

Morehouse, J Ward
character in: **3** USA
author: **9** Dos Passos

Morel, Paul
character in: **13** Sons and Lovers
author: **8** Lawrence

Moreno, Rita
real name: **20** Rosita Dolores Alverio
born: **7** Humacao **10** Puerto Rico
roles: **13** Pagan Love Song, The Deerslayer, West Side Story **15** Singin' in the Rain

more or less 5 about **6** around **8** somewhat **9** generally, just about **13** approximately

moreover 3 too **4** also **7** besides, further **11** furthermore **12** more than that

mores 4 code **5** ethos, forms, rules **6** usages **7** customs, rituals **9** etiquette, practices, standards **10** traditions **11** conventions, observances, proprieties

more than enough 5 ample **6** excess, plenty **7** copious, profuse **8** plethora **9** abundance, amplitude, bountiful, excessive, profusion **10** oversupply

Morgan, Daniel
served in: **16** Revolutionary War
commander of: **8** riflemen **13** sharpshooters
battle: **7** Cowpens **8** Saratoga **12** Bemis Heights, Freeman's Farm
helped suppress: **16** Whiskey Rebellion

Morgan, Thomas Hunt
founder of: **8** genetics
awarded: **10** Nobel Prize

Morgan family
characters in: **19** How Green Was My Valley
members: **4** Beth, Davy, Huur, Ivor,

Owen **5** Ianto **6** Gwilym **8** Angharad
author: **9** Llewellyn

morganite
color: **4** pink **5** peach

Morgan le Fay
character in: **16** Arthurian romance

Moriarty, Professor
villain in: **14** (The Adventures of)
Sherlock Holmes
author: **10** Conan Doyle

moribund 5 dying **6** doomed, waning
10 stagnating

Morier, James
author of: **18** Hajji Baba of Ispahan

morituri te salutamus 28 we who
are about to die salute thee
said by: **15** Roman gladiators
said to: **13** Roman emperors

Mork & Mindy
character: **4** Mork **6** Eugene **10** Cora
Hudson **13** Mindy McConnel **17**
Frederick McConnel
cast: **9** Pam Dawber **11** Conrad Janis
13 Elizabeth Kerr, Robin Williams **14**
Jeffrey Jacquet
Mork's planet: **3** Ork
phrase: **8** nanu nanu
spinoff from: **9** Happy Days

Morland, Catherine
character in: **15** Northanger Abbey
author: **6** Austen

Morley, Robert
born: **6** Semley **7** England
roles: **5** Melba **10** Oscar Wilde **11**
Beau Brummel, Edward My Son **12**
Major Barbara **15** Marie Antoinette,
The African Queen **21** The Man Who
Came to Dinner

Mormon State
nickname of: **4** Utah

morning 4 dawn **5** early, sunup **7**
sunrise **8** daybreak, daylight, forenoon
9 matutinal

morning-glory 7 Ipomoea **10**
Calystegia **11** Convolvulus
varieties: **3** red **4** wild **5** beach,
dwarf **6** Ceylon, common, silver,
woolly, yellow **9** Brazilian **16** Imperial Japanese

Morocco
other name: **7** Barbary **8** Maroquin **9**
Al Maghrib **13** Maghrib el Aksa **19**
Mauretania Tingitana
capital: **5** Rabat **6** Rabbat
largest city: **10** Casablanca
others: **3** Fes, Fez, Sla **4** Ifni, Safi,
Sale, Sali, Taza **5** Ceuta, Oujda,
Porte, Saffi **6** Agadir, Meknes, Se-
mara, Tetuan **7** Elarish, Kenitra, Lar-
ache, Mazagan, Mililla, Mogador,
Tangier, Tetouan **8** Kouribga,
Tinerhir **9** Marrakech, Marrakesh **10**
Youssoufia **11** Port-Lyautey
division:
disputed territory: **13** Western Sahara
head of state: **4** king

measure: **4** kala, muhd, rotl, saah,
sahh, ueba **5** artal, cadee, gerbe, ratel **6** covado, dirhem, fanega, izenbi,
kintar, tangin, tomini **8** quintral
monetary unit: **4** flue, okia, rial **5**
floos, franc, okieh, ounce **6** dirham,
miskal **8** mouzouna
weight: **4** rotl **5** artel, ratel **6** dirhem,
kintar **7** quintal
island: **7** Madeira
mountain: **3** Rif **4** Bani **5** Abyla, Atlas, Sarro **8** Tidiguin **9** Anti-Atlas,
High Atlas, Jebel-Musa **11** Middle
Atlas
highest point: **12** Jebel Toubkal **13**
Djebel Toubkal
river: **3** Dra, Ziz **4** Sous **5** Sebou **6**
Gheris **7** Tensift **8** Moulouya **9** Oum
er Rbia
sea: **8** Atlantic **13** Mediterranean
physical feature:
cape: **3** Nun, Sim **4** Juby, Noun,
Rhir **6** Cantin
desert: **6** Sahara
oasis: **8** Tafilelt
plain: **5** Rharb
strait: **9** Gibraltar
valley: **7** Ouergha
wind: **5** leste **7** charqui
people: **4** Arab, Moor **6** Berber,
French **7** Spanish
dynasty: **7** Alawite, Almohad **9** Almoravid
leader: **5** Idris **7** Lyautey **8** Hassan
II **9** Abd el-Krim
philosopher: **8** Averroes
language: **6** Arabic, Berber, French **7**
Spanish
religion: **5** Islam
place:
ruins: **9** Volubilis
feature:
clothing: **4** haik **7** jellaba
hat: **3** fez
Islamic holy war: **5** jehad, jihad
shanty town: **10** bidonville
food:
dish: **8** couscous

moron 3 ass, nut, oaf, sap **4** boob,
dolt, dope, fool **5** dummy, dunce, idiot, loony, ninny **6** dimwit, nitwit **7**
half-wit, jackass **8** bonehead, dumbbell, dumbhead, imbecile, numskull **9**
blockhead, numbskull, simpleton **10**
muttonhead, nincompoop

Moroni
capital of: **7** Comoros

Moros
mother: **3** Nyx
personifies: **4** fate

morose 3 low, sad **4** blue, dour, glum,
sour **5** cross, moody, sulky, surly,
testy **6** cranky, gloomy, grumpy, mopish, solemn, sullen **7** waspish **8** churlish, downcast, mournful **9** depressed,
irascible, saturnine **10** despondent,
melancholy **11** crestfallen

moroseness 5 gloom **8** glumness

9 pessimism, sulkiness, surliness **10**
sullenness

Morpheus
god of: **6** dreams
father: **6** Hypnos

morphology
study of: **9** structure

Morris, Dinah
character in: **8** Adam Bede
author: **5** Eliot

Morris, Willie
author of: **5** Yazoo **10** Good Old Boy
15 North Toward Home

Morris, Wright
author of: **8** Will's Boy **10** Plain's
Song **13** Field of Vision, My Uncle
Dudley

Morrison, Toni
real name: **19** Chloe Anthony Wofford
author of: **4** Sula, Jazz **7** Beloved,
Tar Baby **12** The Bluest Eye **13** Song
of Solomon
honor: **10** Nobel Prize **13** Pulitzer
Prize

Morrow, Vic
born: **7** Bronx NY
roles: **6** Combat **8** Cimarron **14** God's
Little Acre **15** The Twilight Zone **18**
Portrait of a Mobster **19** The Blackboard Jungle
daughter: **18** Jennifer Jason Leigh

Morse, Samuel F B
nationality: **8** American
invented: **9** Morse code **17** electric
telegraph **24** electromagnetic telegraph

morsel 3 bit, nip, sip **4** bite, drop, iota,
whit **5** crumb, grain, piece, scrap,
snack, speck, taste, touch, trace **6** dollop, nibble, sliver, tidbit **7** modicum,
segment, swallow **8** fraction, fragment, mouthful, particle **9** scintilla

mortal 4 deep, type **5** fatal, grave, human **6** deadly, lethal, living, person,
severe **7** earthly, extreme, intense,
mundane **8** creature, enormous, fleeting, temporal **9** character, corporeal,
ephemeral **10** individual, transitory **12**
unimaginable

mortality 7 carnage **8** fatality **9** bloodshed, ephemeral, slaughter **10** transience **11** evanescence **12** impermanence **13** extermination **14**
transitoriness

mortar 6 cannon, cement, vessel **7**
plaster **8** adhesive

Morte d'Arthur, Le
author: **12** Thomas Malory

Mortgaged Heart, The
author: **15** Carson McCullers

mortification 3 rot **5** decay, shame **7**
chagrin, penance **8** ignominy **11** humiliation **12** putrefaction **13** embarrassment

mortified 6 rotted **7** abashed,

mortify ashamed, debased **8** dismayed, festered, tortured **9** chagrined, putrefied **11** discomfited, embarrassed

mortify 3 rot **4** deny, fast **5** abash, decay, shame **6** appall, fester **7** chagrin, horrify, putrefy **9** discomfit, embarrass **10** discipline, disconcert

Mosaic law 10 Pentateuch **15** Ten Commandments

Moscow
airport: 12 Sheremetyevo
canal: 11 Moscow-Volga
capital of: 4 USSR **6** Russia **11** Soviet Union
hills: 5 Lenin
landmark: 7 Kremlin **9** Gorky Park, Red Square **12** Lenin Library **13** Izmailovo Park, Sokolniki Park **14** Bolshoi Theater **16** Moscow Art Theater **21** Luzhniki Sports Complex
museum: 6 Armory **7** Pushkin **10** Historical **16** Tretyakov Gallery **28** Central Museum of the Soviet Army
river: 5 Setun, Volga, Yauza **6** Moscow
Russian: 6 Moskva

Moses
father: 5 Amram
mother: 8 Jochebed
sister: 6 Miriam
brother: 5 Aaron
wife: 8 Zipporah
son: 7 Eliezar, Gershom
father-in-law: 6 Jethro
received: 15 Ten Commandments
patriarch of: 10 Israelites
saw: 11 burning bush
successor: 6 Joshua
pertaining to: 6 Mosaic

Moses, Grandma
real name: 17 Anna Mary Robertson, Mary Anne Robertson
born: 11 Greenwich NY
artwork: 23 Out for the Christmas Trees

mosey 4 poke **5** amble **6** stroll **7** saunter, shuffle

Moslem 4 Moor **5** Islam, Sunni **6** Muslim, Shiite **7** Islamic **10** Mohammadan, Muhammadan

mosque 6 temple
Arabic: 6 masjid, musjid

Mosquito Coast, The
author: 11 Paul Theroux
director: 9 Peter Weir
cast: 11 Helen Mirren **12** Harrison Ford, River Phoenix

Mosquito State
nickname of: 9 New Jersey

moss
varieties: 4 ball, club, gold, rose **5** broom, bunch, coral, ditch, fairy, Irish, spike, water **6** Scotch, spring **7** cushion, haircap, peacock, Spanish **8** floating, fountain, Japanese, mat spike **9** dwarf club, flowering **10** little club, pincushion **11** basket spike, meadow spike, shining club **12** treelet spike **13** Douglas's spike

Mossbauer, Rudolph Ludwig
field: 7 physics
nationality: 6 German
discovered: 15 Mossbauer effect **28** recoil-free gamma ray absorption
awarded: 10 Nobel Prize

Mosses from an Old Manse
author: 18 Nathaniel Hawthorne

most 4 best, very **6** degree **7** maximum **9** extremely

most distant point 5 limit, reach **8** boundary **9** extremity **11** ultima Thule

Mostel, Zero
real name: 16 Samuel Joel Mostel
born: 10 Brooklyn NY
roles: 8 The Front **10** Rhinoceros **11** The Enforcer **12** The Producers **15** Du Barry Was a Lady **16** Fiddler on the Roof **17** Panic in the Streets

most important 3 key, top **4** head, main **5** chief **7** central, highest, leading **8** cardinal, dominant, foremost, greatest **9** paramount, principal, uppermost **10** preeminent **11** outstanding, predominant

mostly 6 mainly **7** as a rule, chiefly, greatly, largely **8** above all **9** generally, primarily, specially **10** especially **11** principally **12** particularly **13** predominantly

most prominent 7 leading **8** dominant **10** preeminent **11** outstanding

most successful 6 banner, record **7** winning **10** triumphant **11** outstanding

mote 3 dot **4** iota **5** speck **8** particle **9** scintilla

moth
varieties: 4 hawk, luna, tent **5** ghost, gypsy, plume, royal, swift, yucca **6** hornet, lappet, miller, urania **7** clothes, emperor, flannel, hook tip, leopard, tussock **8** army worm, forester, imperial, polka dot **9** carpenter, clearwing **10** forest tent **11** pseudosphex **12** African peach **13** American tiger, giant Hercules **14** tropical sphinx **15** Chinese silkworm, glover's silkworm **20** striped morning sphinx

moth-eaten 5 holey **6** old-hat **7** wornout **8** outmoded **10** antiquated, threadbare **11** dilapidated

mother 3 mom, mum **4** bear, mama, mind, mums, rear, tend **5** beget, breed, mammy, mater, momma, mommy, mummy, nurse, raise **6** origin, source **7** care for, indulge, nurture, old lady, produce, protect **8** conceive, stimulus **10** wellspring **11** inspiration
French: 4 mere **5** maman
Spanish: 5 madre
Italian: 5 mamma
of wind: 3 Eos

of stars: 3 Eos
of gods: 5 Nammu

mother country 8 homeland **10** fatherland, native land, native soil, old country **13** native country

Mother Goose in Prose
author: 14 Lyman Frank Baum

motherly 4 kind **6** gentle, loving, tender **7** devoted **8** maternal, parental **9** indulgent **10** protective, sheltering

mother of a family
Latin: 13 materfamilias

Mother of the West
nickname of: 8 Missouri

mother's helper
French: 6 au pair

motif 4 form, idea **5** shape, style, theme, topic **6** design, figure, thread **7** pattern, refrain, subject **9** treatment

motion 3 cue, nod **4** flow, flux, move, sign, stir **5** drift **6** action, beckon, signal, stream **7** gesture, kinesis, passage, request **8** mobility, movement, progress **10** indication, suggestion **11** gesticulate, proposition **13** gesticulation **14** recommendation

motionless 4 calm, dead, idle **5** fixed, inert, still **6** at rest, frozen, stable, static **8** immobile, inactive, lifeless, tranquil, unmoving **9** immovable, quiescent **10** stationary, transfixed **11** immobilized **12** unresponsive

motion picture 3 pic **4** cine, film, show **5** flick, movie **6** cinema, talkie **8** flickers **10** photodrama **11** picture show **13** moving picture

motivate 4 goad, move, stir **5** egg on, impel **6** arouse, induce, prompt, stir up, turn on **7** actuate, provoke **8** activate, persuade **9** influence, stimulate

motivation 5 cause **6** reason **7** impetus, impulse **9** causation, impulsion **11** provocation

motive 3 aim, end **4** goal, spur **5** cause **6** design, object, reason **7** grounds, purpose **8** occasion, stimulus, thinking **9** incentive, intention, prompting, rationale **10** enticement, incitement, inducement **11** inspiration, instigation, provocation

motley 4 pied **5** mixed, tabby **6** hybrid, sundry, unlike, varied **7** dappled, piebald, watered **8** assorted, brindled, speckled **9** checkered, composite, different, disparate, divergent, harlequin, patchwork **10** dissimilar, iridescent, polychrome, variegated **11** diversified, incongruous, varicolored **12** multicolored **13** heterogeneous, kaleidoscopic, miscellaneous

motor 3 car **4** auto, ride, tour **5** drive, pilot, wheel **6** engine, turbine **7** machine **8** efferent **10** automobile

motorcar 4 auto, heap **6** jalopy, wheels **7** flivver, machine, vehicle **9** tin lizzie **10** automobile

motor vehicle 3 bus, cab, car, van **4** auto, heap, jeep, limo, taxi **5** motor, sedan, truck, wagon **6** jalopy, jitney, pickup, wheels **7** flivver, hardtop, machine, omnibus, town car, vehicle **9** limousine, tin lizzie **10** automobile **11** convertible

mottled 4 pied **5** tabby **7** blotchy, flecked, piebald, specked **8** brindled, speckled, stippled **10** iridescent, multicolor, variegated **11** varicolored **12** parti-colored **13** kaleidoscopic, polychromatic

motto 3 saw **4** rule **5** adage, axiom, maxim **6** byword, dictum, saying, slogan, truism **7** epigram, precept, proverb **8** aphorism **9** catchword, principle, watchword

moue 4 pout **7** grimace

Moulin Rouge
  director: 10 John Huston
  cast: 10 Jose Ferrer (Toulouse-Lautrec) **11** Suzanne Flon, Zsa Zsa Gabor **12** Eric Pohlmann
  setting: 5 Paris **10** Montmartre

mound 4 bump, dune, heap, hill, pile, rick **5** knoll, mogul, ridge, stack **7** bulwark, hillock, hummock, rampart **9** earthwork **10** embankment **12** entrenchment

Mound Builders
  location: 15 Ohio River Valley **22** Mississippi River Valley
  known for: 13 earthen mounds

mount 3 fit, fix, rig, set, wax **4** go up, grow, pony, rise, soar **5** affix, camel, climb, equip, frame, horse, scale, steed, surge, swell **6** ascend, fit out, outfit, set off **7** augment, charger, climb up, get over, get upon, install, set into **8** elephant, increase, multiply, straddle **9** intensify

mountain 3 alp **4** peak **5** bluff, butte, range, ridge **6** height, massif **7** volcano **8** eminence, highland **9** elevation
  of Afghanistan: 3 Koh **5** Safeo **6** Chagai, Pamirs **7** Nowshak **8** Koh-i-Baba, Safed Koh, Sulaiman **9** Himalayas, Hindu Kush, Istoro Nal **11** Khwaja Amran, Paropamisus
  of Albania: 5 Shala **6** Pindus **8** Koritnjk **10** Mount Korab **12** Albanian Alps
  of Algeria: 5 Aissa, Atlas, Aures, Dahra, Tahat **6** Chelia **7** Ahaggar, Kabylia, Mouydir **8** Djurjura **9** Djurdjura, Tell Atlas **12** Saharan Atlas
  of Andorra: 6 d'Etats **8** l'Estanyo **8** Pyrenees **10** Cataperdis **11** Como Pedrosa
  of Angola: 4 Moco **5** Chela **6** Loviti **16** Humpata Highlands
  of Antigua and Barbuda: 9 Boggy Peak
  of Argentina: 4 Toro **5** Andes, Chato, Laudo, Potro **6** Conico, Pissis, Rin-

con **8** Famatina, Murallon, Olivares, Tronador, Zapaleri **9** Aconcagua, Tupungato **10** Cordillera **13** Ojos del Salado **15** Cerro Mercedario, Sierra de Cordoba
  of Armenia: 6 Ararat, Taurus **8** Karabekh **7** Aladagh **12** Mount Aragats
  of Australia: 3 Ise **4** Blue, Olga, Ossa, Zeil **5** Bruce, Snowy **6** Cradle, Doreen, Garnet, Gawler, Magnet, Morgan **7** Bongong, Gregory **8** Augustus, Brockman, Cuthbert, Herbert, Jusgrave, Mulligan, Surprise **9** Murchison, Kosciusko, Woodroffe **14** Australian Alps **15** New England Range **18** Great Dividing Range
  of Austria: 4 Alps **6** Tirols, Tyrols, Stubai **8** Eisenerz, Rhatikon **9** Dolomites, Kitzbuhel **10** Hohe Tauern **13** Grossglockner **14** Silvretta Group
  of Azerbaijan: 8 Caucasus
  of Bangladesh: 10 Keokradong **15** Chittagong Hills
  of Barbados: 6 Chalky **7** Hillaby
  of Belgium: 8 Ardennes **16** Signal de Botrange
  of Benin: 7 Atakora
  of Bhutan: 5 Black **9** Himalayas **10** Chomo Lhari, Kula Kangri
  of Bolivia: 4 Jara **5** Andes, Cusco, Cuzco **6** Sajama, Sorata, Sunsas **7** Illampu **8** Ancohuma, Illimani, Mururata, Sansimon, Santiago, Zapaleri **12** Eastern Range, Western Range **18** Cordillera Oriental **20** Cordillera Occidental
  of Borneo: 4 Iran, Raja **5** Saran **6** Kapuas, Muller, Nijaan, Tebang **8** Kinabalu, Kinibalu, Schwaner
  of Bosnia-Herzegovina: 11 Dinaric Alps
  of Brazil: 3 Mar **5** Geral, Organ, Piaui **6** Acarai, Gurupi, Parima, Urucum **7** Amambai, Carajas, Gradaus, Neblina, Oragaos, Roraima **8** Bandeira, Itatiaia, Roncador, Tombador **9** Pacaraima, Sugar Loaf **10** Tumuc-Humac
  of Brunei: 6 Teraja **9** Ulu Tutong **10** Pagon Priok
  of Bulgaria: 3 Kom **5** Botev, Pirin, Sapka **6** Balkan, Musala, Sredna **7** Vikhren **8** Musallah **11** Rila-Rhodope
  of Burkina Faso: 4 Tema **8** Nakourou **10** Tenakourou, Tenekourou
  of Burundi: 8 Nyarwana **9** Nyamisana
  of Cambodia: 3 Pan **7** Dangrek, Dong Rek **8** Cardamom, Elephant **10** Phnom Aoral, Phnom Aural
  of Cameroon: 5 Mbabo **7** Bambuto, Kapsiki, Mandara **8** Batandji, Cameroon **9** Atlantika
  of Canada: 5 Coast, Logan, Royal **6** Robson, Skeena **7** Cariboo, Cascade, Purcell, Rockies, Selkirk, Stelias, St Elias **8** Columbia, Hazelton, Monashee **9** Mackenzie, Notre

Dame, Tremblant **10** Laurentian, Richardson, Shickshock **14** Jacques Cartier
  of Canary Islands: 5 Teide, Teyde **6** La Cruz **8** El Cumbre, Tenerife
  of Cape Verde: 4 Cano, Fogo **10** Pico de Cano
  of Central African Republic: 5 Karre, Tinga **6** Mongos **9** Dar Challa **11** Kayagangiri
  of Chad: 7 Tibesti, Touside **9** Emi Koussi
  of Chile: 4 Maca, Toro **5** Chato, Maipo, Maipu, Paine, Potro, Pular, Torre, Yogan **6** Apiwan, Burney, Conico, Jervis, Poquis, Rincon **7** Chaltel, Copiapo, Fitzroy, Palpana, Velluda **8** Cochrane, Tronador, Yanteles **9** Tupungato **13** Ojos del Salado
  of Colombia: 5 Abibe, Andes, Baudo, Chita, Cocuy, Huila, Pasto **6** Ayapel, Perija, Purace, Tolima, Tunahi **7** Chamusa, del Ruiz **8** Oriengal **10** Santa Marta **14** Cristobal Colon **17** Central Cordillera, Eastern Cordillera, Western Cordillera
  of Costa Rica: 4 Poas **5** Barba, Irazu **6** Blanco **7** Central, Gongora **9** Talamanca, Turrialba **10** Guanacaste **14** Chirripo Grande
  of Crete: 3 Ida **5** Dikte, Phino **6** Juktas **7** Lasithi, Madaras **8** Leuka Ori, Theodore, Thriphte **9** Psiloriti
  of Croatia: 10 Julian Alps **11** Styrian Alps
  of Cuba: 6 Copper **7** Cristal, Maestra, Organos **8** Camaguey, Trinidad, Turquino **9** Las Villas, Pinar del rio **12** Guaniguanico **14** Sancti-Spiritus
  of Czechoslovakia: 3 Ore **5** Grant, Tatra **6** Sumava **7** Gerlach, Sudeten **8** Krkonose **9** High Tatra **10** Carpathian **11** Gerlachovka
  of Denmark: 12 Ejer Bavnehoj, Yding Skovhoj **14** Himmelbjaerget
  of Djibouti: 5 Gouda **9** Moussa Ali
  of Dominican Republic: 4 Tina **5** Gallo, Neiba **6** Duarte **7** Baoruco, Central **8** Bahoruco, Oriental **13** Septentrional
  of Ecuador: 5 Andes **6** Condor, Sangay **7** Cayambe **8** Antisana, Cotopaxi **9** Cotacachi, Pichincha **10** Chimborazo
  of Egypt: 5 Sinai, Uekia **6** Gharib **8** Katerina **9** Katherina **13** Shayib al-Banat
  of El Salvador: 6 Izalco **8** Santa Ana
  of England: 5 Black **7** Pennine, Snowdon **8** Cambrian, Cumbrian **11** Scafell Pike
  of Equatorial Guinea: 5 Mitra **11** Santa Isabel
  of Ethiopia: 4 Amba, Batu, Guge, Guna, Talo **5** Ahmar, Choke **9** Rasdashan, Ras Deshen
  of Finland: 6 Haltia **7** Laltiva

10 Saari Selka 11 Haldetsokka

of France: 4 Alps, Jura **5** Blanc, Pelat **6** Vosges **8** Ardennes, Pyrenees **9** Mont Blanc **10** French Alps **11** Pic Montcalm

of Gabon Republic: 5 Mpele **7** Chaillu, Cristal, Mikongo **8** Balaquri, Birougou, Iboundji

of Georgia: 8 Caucasus

of Germany: 3 Ore **4** Harz **8** Feldberg **9** Zugspitze **10** Erzgebirge **11** Black Forest, Fichtelberg **12** Bavarian Alps

of Ghana: 8 Afadjato **12** Akwapim Hills

of Gibraltar: 6 Misery

of Greece: 3 Ida **4** Idhi, Oeta, Oite, Ossa **5** Athos **6** Ithome, Peleon, Pelion, Pindus **7** Grammos, Helicon, Olympus, Rhodope **8** Hymettos, Smolikas, Targetos, Taygetus **9** Parnassus **10** Hagion Oros, Lycabettus, Pentelicus

of Greenland: 5 Forel, Payer **7** Khardyu **8** Peterman **9** Gunnbjorn **15** Petermannsbjerg **16** Gunnbjornsfjaeld

of Guatemala: 4 Agua, Mico **5** Fuego, Madre **6** Pacaya, Tacana **7** Atitlan, Toliman **8** La Candon, Las Minas, Tajumuko **9** Tajamulco **10** Acatenango, Santa Maria **12** Cuchumatanes

of Guinea: 4 Loma **5** Nimba **6** Tamgue **11** Fouta Djalon

of Guyana: 5 Amuku, Ariwa, Kamoa **6** Akarai, Kanuku **7** Caburai **9** Pacaraima

of Haiti: 4 Nord **5** Cahos **6** Macaya, Noires **7** Lahotte, Laselle **8** Troudeau

of Honduras: 4 Pija **6** Agalta **7** Celaque **8** Las Minas **9** Esperanza **25** Central American Cordillera

of Hong Kong: 6 Castle **8** Victoria **9** Tai Mo Shan

of Hungary: 4 Alps, Bukk **5** Kekes, Matra, Tatra, Vetes **6** Bakony, Mecsek **7** Cserhat, Gerecse **8** Borzsony, Zempleni **9** Korishegy **10** Carpathian

of Iceland: 4 Laki **5** Askja, Hekla, Jokul, Katla **7** Surtsey **10** Orafajokul **16** Hvannadalshnukur

of India: 8 Aravalli **9** Broad Peak, Distaghil, Himalayas, Karakoram, Nanda Devi, Rakaposhi **10** Gasherbrum, Masherbrum **11** Nanga Parbat **12** Eastern Ghats, Godwin Austen, Kanchenjunga, Western Ghats

of Iran: 6 Elburz, Zagros **8** Demavend

of Iraq: 6 Qalate, Zagros **7** Halgurd, Qaarade **9** Kurdistan

of Ireland: 5 Galty **6** Croagh, Mourne **7** Errigal, Muckish, Patrick, Wicklow **8** Comeragh **10** Benna Beola, Twelve Bens, Twelve Pins **13** Carrantuohill, Knockmealdown **19** Macgillycuddy's Reeks

of Israel: 4 Nafh, Sagi **5** Harif, Meron, Ramon, Tabor **6** Atzmon, Carmel, Hatira, Meiron

of Italy: 4 Alps, Etna, Rosa, Viso **5** Amaro, Blanc, Corno, Somma **6** Cimone, Ortles **7** Vulcano **8** Vesuvius **9** Apennines, Dolomites, Maritimes, Stromboli **10** Apuane Alps, Carnic Alps, Julian Alps, Otztal Alps **11** Bernina Alps, Gennargentu **12** Gran Paradiso, Ligurian Alps **13** Lepontine Alps **16** Abruzzi Apennines

of Jamaica: 4 Blue **8** Sir Johns

of Japan: 3 Uso, Zao **4** Fuji **5** Asahi, Asama, Hondo, Yesso **6** Asosan, Enasan, Hiuchi, Kiusiu, Yariga **7** Fujisan, Hakusan, Kujusan, Tokachi **8** Fujiyama **9** Japan Alps

of Java: 4 Amat, Gede **5** Lawoe, Murjo, Prahu **6** Raoeng, Semuru, Slamet **7** Semeroe **8** Soembing

of Jordan: 9 Jabal Ramm, Jebel Ramm

of Kenya: 5 Elgon, Kenya, Kulai, Nyira, Nyiru **6** Kinyaa, Matian **7** Logonot **8** Aberdare **9** Kirinyaga

of Korea: 4 Wang **5** Chiri, Halla **6** Kwanmo, Paektu, Sobaek **7** Diamond, Kyebang, Nangnim, Taebaek **8** Chang-pai, Hamgyong, Myohyang **9** Paektu-san **10** Kumgang-san

of Kyrgyzstan: 8 Tian Shan

of Laos: 3 Bia, Lai, Loi, San **4** Copi, Khat **5** Atwat **6** Khoung, Tiubia **7** Phou Bia **15** Annam Cordillera

of Lebanon: 4 Mzar **5** Aruba **6** Hermon **7** es Sauda, Lebanon, Sannine **8** Kadischa, Kenisseh **9** Kennisseh **10** al-Mukammal **11** Anti-Lebanon **13** Qurnat al-Sawda

of Lesotho: 6 Maloti, Maluti **7** Central **8** Injasuti, Machache **10** Ben Macdhui **11** Drakensberg, Thaba Putsoa **16** Thabana Ntlenyana

of Liberia: 3 Uni **4** Bong, Putu **5** Niete, Nimba **6** Wutivi **9** Bomi Hills

of Libya: 5 Green **9** Bette Peak **13** Jabal al Akhdar, Tibesti Massif

of Liechtenstein: 4 Alps **8** Naafkopf, Rhatikon **12** Three Sisters **15** Vorder-Grauspitz

of Lithuania: 9 Juozapine **15** Samogitian Hills

of Luxembourg: 8 Ardennes, Huldange **9** Burgplatz **11** Wemperhardt

of Madagascar: 4 Boby **9** Ankaratra **11** Maromokotro **12** High Plateaus, Tsiafajavona **17** Tsaratanana Massif

of Malawi: 6 Mlanje **7** Mulanje **11** Livingstone

of Malaysia: 4 Bulu, Hose, Iban, Iran, Main, Mulu, Niut, Raja **5** Murjo, Niapa, Ophir **6** Blumut, Kapuas, Leuser, Slamet **7** Binaija, Brassey, Crocker **8** Kinabalu, Rindjani **11** Gunong Korbu, Gunong Tahan

of Mali: 4 Mina **6** Iforas **7** Manding **12** Hombori Tondo

of Mexico: 6 Colima, Tacana, Toluca **7** Orizaba **9** Paricutin **11** Ixtacihuatl, Sierra Madre **12** Citlaltepetl, Popocatepetl **14** Sierra Zacateca **16** Chiapas Highlands **24** Transverse Volcanic Sierra

of Mongolia: 4 Cast, Orog **5** Altai **6** Kentei, Sevrej **7** Ich Ovoo, Khangai, Khentei **8** Tannu-Ola **9** Edrengijn **10** Cagaan Bogd, Tabun Bogdo **11** Munky Sardyk **14** Hangayn-Hentiyn, Monch Chajrchan

of Montenegro: 8 Durmitor **11** Dinaric Alps

of Morocco: 3 Rif **4** Bani **5** Abyla, Atlas, Sarro **8** Tidiguin **9** Anti-Atlas, High Atlas, Jebel-Musa **11** Middle Atlas **12** Jebel Toubkal **13** Djebel Toubkal

of Mozambique: 5 Binga **7** Lebombo

of Myanmar: 4 Chin, Naga, Pegu, Popa **5** Dawna **6** Arakan, Kachin, Lushai, Patkai **7** Karenni **8** Nattaung, Peguyoma, Saramati, Victoria **10** Tenasserim **11** Hkakabo Razi, Manipur Hill **12** Tanen Taunggi

of Namibia: 9 Brandberg **14** Khomas Highland, Koakoveld Hills

of Nepal: 6 Cho Oyu, Churia, Makalu **7** Everest, Lhotse I, Manaslu, Siwalik **8** Lhotse II **9** Annapurna, Himalayas **10** Dhaulagiri, Gosainthan, Himalchuli **11** Ganesh Himal **12** Kanchenjunga **14** Mahabharat Lekh

of New Guinea: 4 Snow **6** Orange **7** Bismark, Wilhelm **8** Victoria **9** Carstensz **10** Puncak Jaya **11** Owen Stanley **12** Albert Edward

of New Zealand: 4 Cook, Eden, Flat, Owen **5** Allen, Chope, Lyall, Mitre, Ohope, Otari, Young **6** Egmont, Stokes, Tasman **7** Aorangi, Cameron, Coronet, Ernslaw, Huiarau, Pihanga, Ruahine, Ruapehu, Tauhera, Tutamee, Tyndall **8** Aspiring, Richmond, Tauranga **9** Messenger, Murchison, Ngauruhoe, Raukumara, Tongariro **11** Remarkables **12** Southern Alps

of Nicaragua: 4 Leon **5** Negro, Viejo **6** Madera, Telica **7** Managua, Mogoton, Saslaya **9** Momotombo

of Niger: 7 Bagzane, Greboun **9** Air Massif

of Norway: 5 Sogne **6** Kjolen **7** Numedal **8** Blodfjel, Snohetta, Telemark, Ustetind **9** Harteigen, Jotunheim, Langfjell, Ramnanosi **10** Dovrefjell, Galdhoepig, Glitretind, Vibmesnosi **11** Myrdalfjell **12** Galdhopiggen **13** Glittertinden **14** Aardangerjokul, Hallingskarvet, Skagastolstind

of Oman: 4 Qara **5** Green, Hafit, Harim, Nakhl, Tayin **6** al-Sham **8** el-Akhdar **11** Jabal Akhdar **13** Green Mountain

of Pakistan: 3 Pab, Pub **4** Salt **6** Makran **7** Kirthar **8** Himalaya, Safed Koh, Sulaiman **9** Hindu Kush,

Karakoram, Tirich Mir **11** Makran Coast **12** Godwin Austin **13** Central Makran **14** Takht-i-Sulaiman

of Panama: 4 Baru, Maje **5** Chico, Gandi **6** Darien **7** Columan, San Blas, Veragua **8** Chiriqui, Santiago, Tabasara **10** Costa Rican **14** Serrania de Sapo **15** Aspave Highlands **17** Cordillera Central

of Peru: 5 Andes **7** El Misti, Huamina **8** Coropuna **9** Huascaran

of Philippines: 3 Apo, Iba **4** Mayo, Taal **5** Albay, Askja, Hibok, Mayon, Pulog **6** Pagsan **7** Banahao, Canlaon

of Poland: 4 Rysy **5** Tatra **6** Beskid **7** Pieniny, Sudeten **9** Beshchady, High Tatra, Holy Cross **10** Carpathian

of Portugal: 4 Acor, Lapa **5** Gerez, Marao, Mousa **6** Bornes, Peneda **7** Larouco **8** Caramulo **9** Caldeirao, Monchique **11** Pico da Serra **14** Serra da Estrela

of Puerto Rico: 4 Toro **5** Cayey, Punta **6** Yunque **8** Guilarte, Luquilla **10** Torrecilla **17** Cordillera Central

of Romania: 5 Banat, Bihor, Negoi **6** Codrul, Rodnei **7** Apuseni, Balkans, Caliman, Fagaras **8** Pietrosu **9** Moldavian **10** Carpathian, Moldoveanu **17** Transylvanian Alps

of Russia: 5 Altai, Lenin, Sayan, Urals **6** Anadyr, Elbrus, Koryak, Pamirs, Pobedy **7** Belukha, Crimean, Khibiny, Stanovi, Zhiguli **8** Caucasus, Dzhughur, Stanavoi, Tien Shan **9** Kopet Dagh, Narodnaya, Pamir-Alai, Yablonovy **11** Sikhote-Alin, Verkhoyansk

of Rwanda: 7 Mitumba, Virunga **8** Muhavura **9** Karisimbi

of Samoa: 4 Fito, Vaea **5** Alava **6** Savaii **7** Matafao **8** Silisili **9** Rainmaker

of San Marino: 6 Titano **9** Apennines

of Sardinia: 4 Rasu **5** Ferry, Linas **7** Gallura, Limbara **8** Marghine, Serpeddi, Vittoria **11** Gennargentu

of Saudi Arabia: 5 Razih **6** Tuwayq **10** Jebal Sawda

of Scotland: 5 Attow, Ochil **6** Sidlaw **7** Cheviot **8** Ben Nevis, Grampian **9** Ben Lomond, Highlands, Trossachs

of Senegal: 6 Gounou **12** Fouta Djallon

of Sicily: 4 Erei, Etna, Moro, Sori **5** Aetna, Atlas, Erici, Hybla, Iblei, Ibrei **7** Nebrodi, Vulcano **9** Apennines, Le Madonie, Stromboli **10** Peloritani

of Sierra Leone: 4 Loma **9** Bintimani **10** Tingi Hills

of Sikkim: 7 Dongkya, Donkhya **9** Himalayas, Singalili **10** Darjeeling **12** Kanchenjunga

of Singapore: 6 Mandai **7** Panjang **10** Bukit Timah

of Slovakia: 7 Sudetes **8** Low Tatra **9** High Tatra, Slovak Ore **10** Carpathian, Nizke Tatry **11** Visoke Tatry **15** White Carpathian

of the Solomon Islands: 5 Balbi **11** Popomanasiu

of Somalia: 5 Guban **7** Surud Ad **11** Migiurtinia, Ogo Highland

of South Africa: 3 Aux, Kop **5** Table **7** Kathkin **8** Injasuti **9** Stormberg **10** Devil's Peak, Sneeuwberg **11** Drakensberg **12** Giant's Castle **13** Witwatersrand **14** Mont-aux-Sources **15** Great Escarpment

of Spain: 4 Gata **5** Aneto, Rouch, Teide **6** Cuenca, Estats, Europa, Gredos, Magina, Morena, Nethou, Nevada, Teleno, Toledo **7** Alcaraz, Banuelo, Catalan, Cerredo, Demanda, Iberian, La Sagra, Moncayo, Perdido **8** Almanzor, Asturias, Galician, Maladeta, Monegros, Montseny, Mulhacen, Penalara, Pyrenees **10** Albarracin, Cantabrian, Guadarrama, Torrecilla

of Sri Lanka: 5 Pedro **7** Sri Pada **9** Adams Peak **14** Pidurutalagala

of Sudan: 4 Nuba **6** Red Sea **7** Imatong, Kinyeti **9** Dongotona **10** Jabal Marra, Jebel Marra **18** Ethiopian Highlands

of Surinam: 4 Emma **6** Kayser, Oranje **10** Julianatop, Tumuc-Humac, Wilhelmina **13** Eilert's Il Haan, Van Ach Van Wyck **15** Guiana Highlands

of Swaziland: 7 Emlembe **8** Highveld **11** Drakensberg

of Sweden: 4 Sarv **5** Ammar, Kebne **6** Helags, Kjolen, Ovniks, Sarjek **7** Kjollen **10** Kebnekaise

of Switzerland: 3 Dom **4** Alps, Jura, Rigi, Rosa, Todi **5** Adula, Blanc, Cenis, Eiger, Genis, Karpf, Righi **6** Linard, Pizela, Sentis **7** Bernina, Beverin, Grimsel, Pilatus, Rotondo **8** Balmhorn, Jungfrau **9** Weisshorn **10** Diablerets, Matterhorn, St Gotthard, Wetterhorn **11** Burgenstock **12** Dufourspitze **13** Rheinwaldhorn **14** Finsteraarhorn

of Syria: 6 Carmel, Hermon **7** Alawite, Libanus **10** Nusairiyya **11** Anti-Lebanon

of Taiwan: 5 Tatun **6** Tzukao, Yu Shan **7** Taitung **8** Morrison **10** Sinkao Shan **11** Hsin-Kao Shan **15** Chungyang Shanmo

of Tajikistan: 13 Communism Peak

of Tanzania: 4 Kibo, Mero **8** Usambara **11** Kilimanjaro

of Thailand: 5 Dawna, Khieo **6** Phanom **8** Dang Raek, Inthanon, Kao Prawa, Maelamun **9** Khao Luang **11** Bilauktaung, Doi Inthanon

of Tibet: 5 Kamet, Sajum **6** Kailas, Kunlun **7** Bandala, Everest **9** Himalayas, Karakoram

of Togo: 4 Togo **7** Atakora, Baumann, Koronga

of Tunisia: 5 Atlas **6** Chambi, Mrhila **7** Tebessa **8** High Tell, Zaghouan

12 Northern Tell **18** Dorsale Tunnisienne

of Turkey: 2 Ak **3** Ala **4** Alai, Dagh, Kara **5** Hasan, Hinis, Honaz, Murat, Murit **6** Ala Dag, Ararat, Bingol, Bolgar, Pontic, Suphan, Taurus **7** Aladagh, Erciyas **8** Karacali **10** Kackar Dagi

of Uganda: 4 Oboa **5** Elgon **7** Virunga **9** Mufumbiro, Ruwenzori **10** Margherita **18** Mountains of the Moon

of Ukraine: 7 Crimean **10** Carpathian

of United States: 4 Hood **5** Coast, Green, Kenai, Ozark, Rocky, White **6** Alaska, Brooks, DeLong, Elbert, Helena, Mesabi, Pocono, Shasta **7** Cascade, Chugach, Foraker, Harvard, Kilauea, Massive, Olympic, Olympus, Rainier, St Elias, Whitney **8** Catskill, Davidson, Endicott, Katahdin, Mauna Loa, McKinley, Mitchell, Ouachita, St Helens, Wrangell **9** Allegheny, Blue Ridge, Kuskokwim, North Peak, Pike's Peak **10** Black Hills, Blanca Peak, Grand Teton, Washington, Williamson **11** Appalachian, Santa Monica **12** Sierra Nevada **14** Berkshire Hills

of Uruguay: 6 Animas **10** Grand Hills **14** Cuchilla Grande **15** Mirador Nacional

of Vanuatu: 6 Lopevi **11** Tabwemasana

of Venezuela: 3 Pao **4** Pava, Yair **5** Andes, Duida, Icutu **6** Concha, Cuneva, Merida, Parima, Sierra, Yumari **7** Bolivar, Imutaca, Masaiti, Roraima **8** Gurupira **9** Pacaraima **10** Auyan-Tepui **11** Turimiquire **18** Cordillera del Norte

of Vietnam: 6 Badinh, Badink **7** Nindhoa, Ninhhoa **8** Fansipan, Knontran, Ngoklinh, Ngoklink, Tchepone, Tclepore **18** Annamese Cordillera

of Wales: 6 Berwyn **7** Snowdon **8** Cambrian **9** Prescelly **13** Brecon Beacons

of Western Samoa: 4 Fito, Vaea **13** Mauga Silisili

of Yemen: 6 Shuayb, Thamir **7** Djehaff

of Yugoslavia: 5 Karst **6** Balkan **7** Rhodope, Triglav **8** Crna Gora, Durmitor **9** Sar-Pindus **10** Carnic Alps, Julian Alps, Karawanken **11** Dinaric Alps **13** Slovenian Alps **20** Northern Albanian Alps

of Zaire: 7 Crystal, Mitumba, Virunga **9** Ruwenzori **10** Margherita, Nyaragongo **18** Mountains of the Moon

of Zambia: 8 Muchinga **12** Mafinga Hills

of Zimbabwe: 5 Vumba **6** Manica **7** Inyanga **9** Inyangani **11** Chimanimani, Matopo Hills

Mountain
constellation of: **5** Mensa

mountaineers are always free men
Latin: **19** montani semper liberi
motto of: **12** West Virginia

Mountain State
nickname of: **7** Montana **12** West Virginia

Mountbatten, Louis
also: **27** first Earl Mountbatten of Burma
nationality: **7** British
position: **12** first sea lord
supreme allied commander of: **13** Southeast Asia
chief of: **25** British combined operations
viceroy of: **5** India
served in: **3** WWI **4** WWII
directed invasion of: **10** Madagascar
recaptured: **5** Burma

mountebank 5 cheat, fraud, phony, quack **6** con man, humbug **7** hustler, sharper **8** huckster, operator, swindler **9** charlatan, con artist **11** quacksalver

mounted soldier 6 hussar, lancer **7** dragoon **8** cavalier, horseman **10** cavalryman

mourn 3 cry, rue, sob **4** keen, pine, wail, weep **6** bemoan, bewail, grieve, lament, regret, sorrow **7** deplore, despair **8** languish, weep over

mournful 3 sad **5** black, sorry, weepy **6** dismal, rueful, somber, triste, woeful **7** doleful, joyless, unhappy **8** dejected, dirgeful, dolorous, funereal, grievous, saddened **9** depressed, plaintive, sorrowful **10** depressing, dispirited, lamentable, lugubrious, melancholy **11** distressing, melancholic **12** heavy hearted

mourning 3 woe **5** black, crape, dolor, grief, weeds **6** sorrow **7** anguish, despair **8** grieving **9** lamenting, sorrowing **11** bereavement, lamentation

Mourning Becomes Electra
author: **12** Eugene O'Neill
character: **4** Seth **10** Hazel Niles, Peter Niles **16** Captain Adam Brant
Mannon family: **4** Ezra, Orin **7** Lavinia **9** Christine

mourning period
Hebrew: **6** shibah, shivah

mouser 3 cat **4** puss **5** kitty, pussy **6** feline **7** pussycat

Mousetrap, The
author: **14** Agatha Christie

mousseline 6 muslin

mousy 3 shy **4** drab, dull **5** timid, wimpy **7** bashful, fearful **8** timorous **9** colorless, unnoticed, withdrawn **11** unobtrusive **13** inconspicuous

mouth 3 bay, say **4** bell, jaws, lips **5** inlet, speak, voice **6** outlet, portal

7 declare, estuary, opening **8** aperture, propound **9** pronounce

mouthful 3 dab **4** bite **5** taste **6** morsel, nibble

mouthpiece 4 reed **6** lawyer **7** counsel **8** advocate, attorney **9** counselor

mouth-watering 8 inviting, tempting **9** appealing **10** appetizing **11** tantalizing

movable, moveable 4 free **5** loose **6** mobile, motile, moving **8** portable **10** changeable

movables 4 gear **5** goods **7** baggage, effects, luggage **9** equipment **10** belongings **11** impedimenta, possessions **13** accoutrements, paraphernalia

move 2 go **3** act, ask, get **4** bear, deed, fire, lead, pass, ploy, step, stir, sway, turn, urge **5** begin, budge, carry, cause, drive, impel, plead, rouse, shift, touch **6** action, affect, arouse, attack, convey, excite, exhort, incite, induce, motion, prompt, strike, stroke, switch **7** advance, budging, gesture, go ahead, impress, inspire, measure, operate, proceed, propose, provoke, request, suggest **8** function, interest, locomote, maneuver, motivate, persuade, relocate, start off, stirring, transfer, transmit **9** impassion, influence, recommend, stimulate, transport, transpose **10** transplant **11** opportunity

move downward 3 dip **4** dive, drop, fall, sink **6** plunge, tumble **7** decline, descend, plummet **8** decrease

movement 4 part **5** drive, steps, works **6** action, effort, motion **7** crusade, measure, program, section **8** activity, division, gestures, maneuver, progress, stirring **9** agitation, execution, mechanism, operation **10** locomotion **11** undertaking

move out 5 leave **6** depart, vacate **8** evacuate

move quickly 3 fly, run **4** bolt, dash, race, rush, tear **5** hurry **6** hasten, sprint

move sideways 4 edge **5** sidle **8** sidestep

move slyly 4 edge, lurk **5** sidle, skulk, slink, sneak, steal

move up 5 boost, climb, heave, hoist, raise, scale **6** ascend, uplift **7** advance, elevate, promote, upraise

move upward 4 rise, soar **5** climb, mount **6** ascend **7** take off

movie 4 film, show **5** flick **6** cinema **7** feature, picture, showing **9** screening
invented by:
machine: **7** Jenkins
panoramic: **6** Waller
projector: **6** Edison
talking: **14** Warner Brothers

moving 5 motor **6** mobile, motile

8 exciting, poignant, spurring, stirring, touching **9** affecting, inspiring **10** impressive, locomotive, motivating **11** interacting, stimulating

moving about 5 astir **6** active **7** on the go

Moving Target, A
author: **14** William Golding

Mowgli
character in: **14** The Jungle Books
author: **7** Kipling

moxie 4 grit, guts, sand **5** nerve, pluck, spunk **6** mettle, spirit **7** courage, stamina **8** audacity, backbone **9** hardihood, toughness **10** pluckiness **13** dauntlessness

moyen age 10 Middle Ages

Mozambique
capital/largest city: **6** Maputo **15** Lourenco Marques
others: **4** Tete **5** Beira, Pemba, Zumbo **6** Chemba, Nacala, Pafuri, Sofala **7** Nampula **8** Mutarara **9** Inhambane, Quelimane **11** Porto Amelia
school: **15** Eduardo Mondlane
monetary unit: **6** escudo **7** centavo, metical
island: **6** Inhaca **7** Angoche **8** Bazanuto **9** Benguerua
lake: **5** Nyasa **6** Chuali, Nyassa **8** Nhavarre
mountain: **7** Lebombo
highlands: **6** Namuli **9** Gorongosa
highest point: **5** Binga
river: **4** Buzi, Save **5** Lurio, Msalu **6** Rovuma, Ruvuma **7** Ligonha, Limpopo, Lugenda, Messaio, Zambezi **8** Changane
ocean: **6** Indian
physical feature:
cape: **7** Delgado
channel: **10** Mozambique
people: **3** Yao **5** Bantu, Chopi, Lomue, Lomwe, Macua, Makua, Ngoni, Nguni, Shona **6** Maravi, Thouga **7** Maconde, Makonde **10** Portuguese
explorer: **11** Vasco de Gama
leader: **8** Chissano **9** Dos Santos **12** Samora Machel **15** Eduardo Mondlane
language: **3** Yao **5** Makua **6** Nyanji, Thonga **7** Swahili **10** Portuguese
religion: **5** Islam **7** animism **13** Roman Catholic
place:
game reserve: **8** Marromeu **9** Gorongosa, Gorongoza **18** Maputo Elephant Park
reservoir: **11** Cabora Bassa
feature:
bride price: **6** lobolo

Mozart, Wolfgang Amadeus
born: **7** Austria **8** Salzburg
cataloguer: **6** Kochel
composer of: **4** Linz (symphony No 36) **5** Paris (symphony No 31)

6 Prague (symphony No 38) **7** Don Juan, Haffner (symphony No 35), Jupiter (symphony No 41), Requiem, Turkish (concerto) **8** Idomeneo **9** Credo Mass, Mitridate **10** Lucio Silla **11** Don Giovanni, Hunt Quartet, Il Re Pastore, Sparrow Mass **12** A Musical Joke, Cosi Fan Tutte (So Do They All or Women Are Like That), Haydn Quartet, Spatzenmesse **13** The Magic Flute, Trumpet Sonata, Turkish Sonata **14** Coronation Mass, Stadler Quintet, Die Zauberflote **15** Haffner Serenade, La Finta Semplice, Prussian Quartet **16** Dissonant Quartet, La Clemenza di Tito, Posthorn Serenade, Serenata Notturna **17** A Little Night Music **18** Jeunehomme Concerto, La Finta Giardiniera, The Clemency of Titus **19** Bastien und Bastienne, The Marriage of Figaro **20** Eine Kleine Nachtmusik, The Pretender Gardener **21** Der Schauspieldirektor, Ein Musikalischer Spass **22** The Pretending Simpleton **25** Die Entfuhrung aus dem Serail **27** The Abduction from the Seraglio

Mr, Mister
    Russian: 8 gospodin
    French: 8 monsieur
    Yiddish: 3 Reb

Mr B
    character in: 6 Pamela
    author: 10 Richardson

Mr Basketball
    nickname of: 8 Bob Cousy

Mr Britling Sees It Through
    author: 7 H G Wells

Mr Cub
    nickname of: 10 Ernie Banks

Mr Deeds Goes to Town
    director: 10 Frank Capra
    cast: 10 Gary Cooper (Longfellow Deeds), Jean Arthur **14** George Bancroft

Mr Ed
    character: 9 Carol Post **10** Kay Addison, Wilbur Post **12** Roger Addison **14** Gordon Kirkwood, Winnie Kirkwood
    cast: 8 Leon Ames **9** Alan Young **11** Connie Hines, Edna Skinner **12** Larry Keating **18** Florence MacMichael
    Mr Ed was: 12 talking horse

Mr Flood's Party
    author: 22 Edwin Arlington Robinson

Mr Midnight
    nickname of: 10 Steve Allen

Mr Peepers
    character: 9 Mrs Gurney **11** Marge Weskit, Mr Remington **12** Harvey Weskit **14** Nancy Remington **15** Robinson Peepers **20** Superintendent Bascom
    cast: 8 Wally Cox **9** Gage Clark **11** Ernest Truex, Marion Lorne, Tony Randall **14** Patricia Benoit **16** Georgiann Johnson
    Mr Peepers taught: 7 science
    school: 13 Jefferson High

Mr Sammler's Planet
    author: 10 Saul Bellow

Mrs Dalloway
    author: 13 Virginia Woolf
    character: 10 Miss Kilman, Peter Walsh, Sally Seton **15** Richard Dalloway **16** Clarissa Dalloway **17** Elizabeth Dalloway

Mrs Miniver
    director: 12 William Wyler
    cast: 11 Greer Garson **12** Teresa Wright **13** Dame May Whitty, Walter Pidgeon
    Oscar for: 7 actress (Garson), picture **8** director **17** supporting actress (Wright)

Mr Smith Goes to Washington
    director: 10 Frank Capra
    cast: 9 Guy Kibbee **10** Jean Arthur **11** Claude Rains **12** Edward Arnold, James Stewart **14** Thomas Mitchell

Mrs Parkington
    author: 14 Louis Bromfield

Mrs Stevens Hears the Mermaids Singing
    author: 9 May Sarton

Mrs Warren's Profession
    author: 17 George Bernard Shaw

Mr Television
    nickname of: 11 Milton Berle

much 3 far **4** a lot, lots **5** about, ample, heaps, loads, often **6** almost, indeed, nearly, overly, rather, scores **7** copious, greatly **8** abundant, good deal, plenty of, quantity, somewhat, striking **9** decidedly, important, plenteous, plentiful, regularly **10** frequently, impressive, noteworthy, oftentimes, satisfying, sufficient, worthwhile **11** appreciable, exceedingly, excessively, sufficiency **12** considerable **13** approximately, consequential

Much Ado About Nothing
    author: 18 William Shakespeare
    character: 4 Hero **7** Claudio, Don John, Leonato **8** Beatrice, Benedick, Dogberry, Don Pedro

much in little
    Latin: 13 multum in parvo

much loved 4 dear **7** beloved, darling, dearest **8** precious **9** cherished, treasured

mucilage 3 gum **4** glue **5** paste **6** cement **8** adhesive

mucilaginous 5 gluey, gummy, gunky **6** gloppy, sticky **8** adhesive

muck 3 mud **4** dirt, dung, gunk, mire, ooze, slop **5** filth, slime **6** sewage, sludge **7** compost, garbage

muck up 4 soil **5** dirty, muddy **7** pollute

mud 4 dirt, muck, soil, wire

Mudcat State
    nickname of: 11 Mississippi

muddied 5 dirty, grimy **6** grubby, soiled **7** stained **8** begrimed, confused

muddle 3 fog **4** blow, daze, haze, mess, muff, ruin **5** botch, chaos, mix up, spoil, throw **6** boggle, bungle, fumble, goof up, jumble, mess up, pother, rattle **7** blunder, clutter, confuse, nonplus, stupefy **8** bewilder, confound, disarray, disorder **13** disconcertion **14** disarrangement

muddlebrained 5 inept **7** witless **8** confused **11** lamebrained

muddled 5 fuzzy **7** bemused **8** confused **10** bewildered

muddy 4 dull **5** dirty, grimy, vague **6** filthy, grubby **7** obscure **8** begrimed, confused

muff 5 botch, spoil **6** bungle **10** handwarmer

muffle 3 gag **4** dull, hush, mask, mute, veil, wrap **5** cloak, cover, quell, quiet, still **6** dampen, deaden, shroud, soften, stifle, swathe **7** conceal, enclose, envelop, silence, swaddle

muffled 3 low **4** dull, soft **5** faint, muted **6** dulled, feeble, hushed, veiled **7** cloaked, covered, quelled, quieted, stilled, subdued, swathed, wrapped **8** deadened, shrouded, silenced, softened, swaddled **9** concealed, enveloped, inaudible **10** indistinct, suppressed

mug 3 cup **4** face, puss, toby **5** stein, stoup **6** beaker, flagon, goblet, kisser, visage **7** chalice, tankard, toby jug, tumbler **11** countenance

mugger 8 assailer, attacker **9** assailant, assaulter

mugginess 4 damp **8** dampness, dankness, humidity **9** humidness **10** sultriness **14** oppressiveness

muggy 5 close, humid **6** clammy, steamy, sticky, stuffy, sultry, sweaty **8** steaming, vaporous **10** oppressive, sweltering

mulberry 5 Morus
    varieties: 3 red **4** Aino **5** black, paper, white **6** French, Indian **7** Russian **8** American, silkworm

mulct 4 bilk **6** extort **7** defraud, swindle

mule 3 ass **5** burro **6** donkey **7** jackass
    group of: 4 span

mulish 6 balky **7** ornery **8** perverse, stubborn **9** fractious, obstinate **10** refractory **11** intractable **12** recalcitrant

mull, mull over 5 study, weigh **6** ponder **8** consider, meditate, pore over, ruminate **10** deliberate

Muller
    character in: 25 All Quiet on the Western Front
    author: 8 Remarque

Muller, Hermann Joseph

field: 8 genetics
researched: 5 X-rays **8** mutation
awarded: 10 Nobel Prize

Muller, Paul
field: 9 chemistry
nationality: 5 Swiss
established: 16 DDT as insecticide
awarded: 10 Nobel Prize

Mulligan, Buck
character in: 7 Ulysses
author: 5 Joyce

multicolored 10 variegated

multifarious 4 many **5** mixed **6** divers, motley, sundry, varied **7** diverse, protean, several, various **8** manifold, numerous **9** different, multiplex **10** variegated **11** diversified **13** heterogeneous, miscellaneous

multiple 4 many **7** various **8** manifold

multiply 5 add to, beget, breed, raise **6** extend, spread **7** augment, enhance, enlarge, magnify **8** generate, heighten, increase **9** intensify, procreate, propagate, reproduce **11** proliferate

multitude 3 mob **4** army, herd, host, mass, pack, slew **5** array, crowd, crush, drove, flock, flood, horde, troop **6** legion, myriad, scores, throng **7** conflux

multum in parvo 12 much in little **23** a great deal in a small space

mum 4 mute **5** quiet, still, tacit **6** silent **8** taciturn, wordless **9** secretive **12** closemouthed **15** uncommunicative

mumble 5 growl, grunt, mouth **6** murmur, mutter, rumble **7** stammer **9** hem and haw

mumbo jumbo 3 rot **4** blah, bosh, cant, tosh **5** bilge, hokum, hooey, tripe **6** hot air, humbug **7** baloney **8** flummery **9** gibberish, sophistry **10** double talk, hocus pocus **11** doublespeak, jabberwocky, obfuscation **12** fiddle-faddle, gobbledygook, obscurantism

Mummy, The
director: 10 Karl Freund
cast: 10 Zita Johann **12** Boris Karloff, David Manners **16** Bramwell Fletcher

munch 4 chew, gnaw **5** champ, chomp, crush, grind **9** masticate

Munch, Edvard
born: 5 Loten **6** Norway **10** Hedemarken
artwork: 6 The Cry **7** Puberty, The Kiss **9** The Scream **11** Dance of Life **12** Frieze of Life **21** Death in the Sick Chamber

Munchausen, Baron 4 liar **7** solider **10** adventurer **11** exaggerator

Munchkins
characters in: 13 The Wizard of Oz
author: 5 Baum

mundane 4 petty **7** earthly, humdrum, prosaic, routine, worldly **8** day-to-day, everyday, ordinary **9** practical **10** pe-

destrian **11** commonplace, down-to-earth, terrestrial

Muni, Paul
real name: 16 Muni Weisenfreund
born: 7 Austria, Lemberg (now Lvov Ukraine)
roles: 6 Juarez **8** Scarface **10** The Valiant **12** The Good Earth **14** Clarence Darrow, Inherit the Wind **15** The Last Angry Man **18** The Life of Emile Zola **22** The Story of Louis Pasteur (Oscar) **26** I Am a Fugitive from a Chain Gang

municipal 4 city **5** civic **6** public **9** community **14** administrative

municipality 4 city, town **6** parish **7** village **8** township **9** bailiwick

munificence 6 bounty **7** charity **8** largesse **9** patronage **10** generosity, liberality **11** benefaction, beneficence, benevolence **12** philanthropy **13** bounteousness, bountifulness **14** charitableness **15** humanitarianism

munificent 4 free **6** kindly, lavish **7** liberal, profuse **8** generous, princely **9** bounteous, bountiful **10** altruistic, beneficent, benevolent, charitable, freehanded, open-handed **11** extravagant, magnanimous **12** eleemosynary, humanitarian **13** philanthropic

Munin
origin: 12 Scandinavian
form: 5 raven
owned by: 4 Odin **5** Othin
personifies: 6 memory
duty: 10 newsbearer
other raven: 5 Hugin

Munsters, The
character: 11 Lily Munster **12** Eddie (Edward Wolfgang) Munster **13** Herman Munster **14** Grandpa Munster, Marilyn Munster
cast: 7 Al Lewis **9** Pat Priest **10** Fred Gwynne **11** Beverly Owen **12** Butch Patrick **13** Yvonne DeCarlo

Muppet Show, The
character: 4 Rolf **5** Gonzo **6** Animal, Beaker **7** Scooter **9** Miss Piggy **10** Fozzie Bear **13** Kermit the Frog (Kermie)

Murasaki, Lady
author of: 14 The Tale of Genji

murder 4 kill, slay **5** abuse, waste **6** mangle, misuse **7** butcher, corrupt, cut down, killing **8** homicide, knock off **9** agonizing, slaughter **10** bastardize, formidable, impossible, oppressive, unbearable **11** assassinate, intolerable **12** manslaughter **13** assassination, very difficult **14** commit homicide, use incorrectly

Murder, She Wrote
character: 15 Jessica (JB) Fletcher
cast: 14 Angela Lansbury
setting: 9 Cabot Cove

murderer 4 Cain **6** killer, slayer

7 butcher **8** assassin, Barabbas, homicide **9** cutthroat

Murder in the Cathedral
author: 7 T S Eliot

Murder of Roger Ackroyd, The
author: 14 Agatha Christie

Murder on the Orient Express
author: 14 Agatha Christie
detective: 13 Hercule Poirot

murderous 4 gory **5** cruel, rough **6** bloody, brutal, deadly, savage, trying **7** killing **9** dangerous, difficult, ferocious **11** devastating **12** bloodthirsty, disagreeable

Murdoch, Iris
author of: 7 The Bell **11** Under the Net **12** A Severed Head, The Sea the Sea **14** The Black Prince **15** Nuns and Soldiers **17** The Good Apprentice, The Nice and the Good **20** The Philosopher's Pupil **24** The Book and The Brotherhood **30** The Sacred and Profane Love Machine

Murdstone, Mr
character in: 16 David Copperfield
author: 7 Dickens

Murillo, Bartolome (Bartolomeo) Esteban
born: 5 Spain **7** Seville
artwork: 13 Angels' Kitchen **14** Death of St Clare **15** The Two Trinities **17** Vision of St Anthony **23** The Immaculate Conception **24** Dream of the Roman Patrician

murk 3 fog **4** haze, mist **5** gloom **6** miasma **7** pea soup **8** darkness

murky 3 dim **4** dark, gray, hazy **5** dusky, foggy, misty **6** cloudy, dismal, dreary, gloomy, somber **7** obscure, sunless **8** lowering, overcast, vaporous **9** cheerless

murmur 3 hum **4** buzz, purl, purr, sigh **5** drone, sough, swish **6** lament, mumble, mutter, rumble, rustle **7** grumble, lapping, whimper, whisper **8** low sound, susurrus **9** complaint, undertone

murophobia
fear of: 4 mice

Murphy, Eddie
roles: 3 Raw **13** Trading Places **14** The Golden Child **15** Coming to America, Forty-Eight Hours **16** Beverly Hills Cop **17** Saturday Night Live, The Nutty Professor **19** Beverly Hills Cop Two

Murray, Bill
roles: 7 Stripes **9** Meatballs **10** Caddyshack **12** Ghostbusters, Groundhog Day **13** The Razor's Edge **17** Saturday Night Live **27** Not Ready for Prime Time Players

Murray, Don
wife: 9 Hope Lange
born: 11 Hollywood CA
roles: 7 Bus Stop **13** A Hatful of Rain

16 The Bachelor Party, The Hoodlum Priest

Murray, Jeanne
  real name of: **13** Jean Stapleton

Murray, Mina
  character in: **7** Dracula
  author: **6** Stoker

Musaeus
  occupation: **4** poet, seer

Musagetes *see* **6** Apollo

Muscat, Masqat
  capital of: **4** Oman

muscle 4 grit, thew **5** bicep, brawn, force, might, power, sinew, vigor **6** energy, flexor, tendon **7** potency, prowess, stamina **8** virility **9** puissance **10** sturdiness **16** muscular strength
  kind: **4** limb **5** axial **6** smooth **7** dynamic, flexors, special, striped **8** postural, striated **9** abductors, extensors, voluntary **11** involuntary
  fuel: **4** food
  action: **4** pull
  specific: **6** rectus **7** deltoid, oblique **8** omohyoid **9** abdominal, abdominis, sartorius **10** pectoralis **11** intercostal, sternohyoid **13** biceps brachii, rectus femoris **14** vastus medialis **15** brachioradialis, vastus lateralis **16** serratus anterior, tensor fascia lata **17** quadriceps femoris **18** transverse thoracic **19** sternocleidomastoid **20** transversus abdominis
  supplementary structure: **6** sheath **10** deep fascia, retinacula **14** synovial bursae, synovial sheath

muscular 3 fit **5** burly, husky, tough **6** brawny, sinewy, strong **8** athletic, powerful **9** strapping

muscular contraction 3 tic **5** cramp, crick, spasm **6** stitch **12** charley horse

musculoskeletal system
  component: **4** bone **6** muscle, tendon **8** ligament

muse 4 mull **6** ponder, review **7** reflect **8** cogitate, consider, meditate, ruminate **9** speculate **10** deliberate **11** contemplate

Musee des Beaux Arts
  author: **7** W H Auden

Muses
  also: **7** the Nine **8** Pierides **10** Castalides
  form: **9** goddesses
  names: **4** Clio (history) **5** Erato (love poetry) **6** Thalia (comedy), Urania (astronomy) **7** Euterpe (music, lyric poetry) **8** Calliope (epic poetry) **9** Melpomene (tragedy) **10** Polyhymnia (sacred poetry) **11** Terpsichore (dance)
  father: **4** Zeus
  mother: **9** Mnemosyne
  corresponds to: **7** Camenae

Musgrave, Thea
  born: **8** Scotland **9** Edinburgh

composer of: **11** The Decision **16** The Five Ages of Man **17** Beauty and the Beast, The Voice of Ariadne

mush 5 slush **6** drivel **8** porridge **14** sentimentalism, sentimentality

mushiness 5 slush **6** bathos **10** sponginess **11** mawkishness **14** sentimentalism, sentimentality

mushroom 4 grow **5** burst, fungi **6** blow up, expand, fungus, spread, sprout **7** burgeon, explode, shoot up **8** flourish, increase, spring up **9** toadstool **11** proliferate
  part: **3** cap **4** veil **5** gills, stalk, tubes, volva **6** button, hyphae, spores **7** annulus, basidia **10** rhizomorph
  non-poisonous: **5** field, honey, morel, table **6** oyster **7** inky cap, parasol **8** puffball, shiitake **9** fairy-ring, morchella, shaggy cap, stinkhorn **10** champignon **11** chanterelle **12** edible bolete, slippery jack **16** old man of the woods
  poisonous: **7** amanita **8** death cap, sickener **9** fly agaric **12** jack-o-lantern **13** devil's boletus **15** destroying angel
  study of: **8** mycology

mushy 4 soft **5** foggy, misty, pappy, pulpy, vague **6** cloudy, quaggy, spongy **7** maudlin, mawkish, squashy, squishy **8** effusive, romantic, squelchy **10** lovey-dovey **11** sentimental, tearjerking **12** affectionate

Musial, Stan
  nickname: **10** Stan the Man
  sport: **8** baseball
  team: **16** St Louis Cardinals

music 4 song, tune **5** score **6** melody **7** euphony, harmony **8** lyricism **10** minstrelsy **11** tunefulness **13** melodiousness
  god of: **5** Brage, Bragi **6** Apollo **7** Phoebus, Pythius **9** Musagetes

musical 5 lyric, sweet **6** dulcet **7** lilting, lyrical, melodic, tuneful **9** melodious **10** euphonious, harmonious **11** mellifluent

musical instrument 3 lur, sax, saz **4** bass, bell, drum, fife, gong, harp, horn, lute, lyre, oboe, outi, pipe, tuba, viol **5** argul, banjo, bugle, cello, cobza, flute, kazoo, organ, piano, guena, rabob, sansa, shawm, sheng, sitar, viola **6** bagana, chimes, cornet, cymbal, fiddle, guitar, spinet, treble, violin, zither **7** bagpipe, bassoon, cittern, clavier, kithara, marimba, panpipe, pibcorn, piccolo, samisen, strings, tambura, theorbo, timpani, trumpet, ukulele **8** autoharp, bass drum, calliope, clarinet, dulcimer, Jew's harp, mandolin, psaltery, recorder, talharpa, triangle, trombone, virginal **9** accordion, balalaika, castanets, harmonica, harmonium, krummhorn, rommelpot, saxophone, snare

drum, xylophone **10** bongo drums, clavichord, concertina, flugelhorn, French horn, kettledrum, sousaphone, tambourine, vibraphone **11** English horn, harpsichord **12** jouhikantele
  classification: **4** horn, reed, wind **5** brass **6** string **8** keyboard, woodwind **10** electronic, percussion

musical terms
  agitated: **7** agitato
  all players/singers together: **5** tutti
  becoming quicker: **11** accelerando
  continue without a break: **5** segue
  disconnected/each note separate: **8** staccato
  end: **4** fine
  expressively: **10** espressivo
    abbreviation: **4** espr
  fast: **6** veloce **7** allegro
  gentle: **5** soave
  gently: **9** doucement
  getting slower: **10** allargando
  getting weaker and slower: **7** calando
  gradually getting louder: **9** crescendo
    abbreviation: **5** cresc
  gradually getting softer: **10** diminuendo **11** decrescendo
    abbreviation: **3** dim **4** decr
  gradually slowing: **11** rallentando
    abbreviation: **4** rall
  half: **5** mezzo
  half voice/half volume: **9** mezza voce
  heavy: **5** lourd
  in an undertone/in a low voice: **9** sotto voce
  leisurely: **6** comodo
  less: **4** meno
  light: **8** leggiero
  little: **4** poco
  lively: **3** vif
  loud: **5** forte
    abbreviation: **1** f
  moderately slow and even: **7** andante
  more: **3** piu
  mournful: **5** mesto
  not too much: **9** non troppo
  plucked instead of bowed: **9** pizzicato
    abbreviation: **4** pizz
  quick/vivacious: **6** vivace
  repeat from beginning: **6** da capo
    abbreviation: **2** D C
  shaking and quavering/rapid alternation of notes: **5** trill
  silent: **4** tace
  singing/songlike/flowing: **9** cantabile
  sliding: **9** glissando
  slow: **5** lento **6** adagio
  slow dignified tempo: **5** largo
  slow down: **5** cedez
  smooth/connected: **6** legato
  soft: **5** piano
    abbreviation: **1** p
  solemn/serious: **5** grave

sorrowful: 7 dolente
strict time: 10 tempo gusto
sudden accent: 9 sforzando
  abbreviation: 2 sf
sweetly: 5 dolce
tearful: 9 lacrimoso
tenderly: 10 affettuoso
trembling vibrating effect/rapid reiteration of a single pitch: 7 tremolo
very: 5 molto
very loud: 10 fortissimo
  abbreviation: 2 ff
very soft: 10 pianissimo
  abbreviation: 2 pp
with fire: 8 con fuoco
with spirit/vigor: 7 con brio
with style/taste: 8 con gusto
with the mute: 10 con sordino
musician 4 bard **5** piper **6** artist, player, singer, violer **7** bandman, cellist, drummer, pianist, twanger **8** minstrel, organist, virtuoso **9** performer, trumpeter, violinist **11** saxophonist
Music Man, The
  director: 13 Morton Da Costa
  cast: 12 Buddy Hackett, Shirley Jones (Marian the librarian) **13** Robert Preston (Professor Harold Hill) **15** Hermione Gingold
  setting: 9 River City
  score: 15 Meredith Willson
  song: 15 Till There Was You **19** Seventy-six Trombones
music school 12 conservatory
  French: 13 conservatoire
musing 6 absent, dreamy **7** mulling **8** absorbed, pondering **10** meditating, meditative, reflecting, reflective
musjid 6 mosque
Muskogean, Muskhogean
  tribe: 4 Cree **7** Alabama, Alibamu, Choctaw, Natchez **8** Seminole **9** Chickasaw
Muslim *see* **6** Moslem
muslin
  French: 10 mousseline
muss 4 mess **6** foul up, jumble, ruffle, rumple, tangle, tousle **7** crumple, disturb **8** dishevel, disorder **9** bedraggle **10** disarrange
mussed 5 messy **6** frowzy, untidy **7** ruffled, rumpled, tousled, unkempt **8** uncombed **10** disarrayed, disheveled, disordered, disorderly **11** disarranged
Mussorgsky (Moussorgsky), Modest Petrovich
  born: 5 Pskov **6** Russia
  member of: 7 The Five
  composer of: 7 Sunless **10** The Nursery **12** Boris Godunov **13** Khovanshchina **19** Night on Bald Mountain **21** Songs and Dances of Death **22** Pictures at an Exhibition
mustard
  botanical name: 5 B alba **6** B hirta, B nigra **7** B juncea **8** Brassica

also called: 7 sinapis
  origin: 4 Asia **5** China
  use: 6 hotdog, sauces **7** egg roll **9** hamburger **13** salad dressing
muster 4 call **5** amass, raise, rally **6** gather, line up, summon **7** collect, company, convene, convoke, marshal, meeting, round up, turnout **8** assemble, assembly, mobilize **9** convocate, gathering **10** assemblage, confluence, congregate, inspection **11** aggregation **12** accumulation **13** agglomeration
musty 3 old **4** damp, dank, worn **5** banal, dirty, dusty, moldy, stale, tired, trite **6** frousy, frouzy, frowsy, frowzy, old hat, stuffy **7** worn-out **8** familiar, mildewed **9** hackneyed **10** antiquated, threadbare **11** commonplace
mutable 6 fickle **7** pliable **8** flexible, variable **9** adaptable, alterable, mercurial, versatile **10** adjustable, changeable, inconstant, modifiable, permutable **11** convertible, metamorphic **13** transformable
mutate 4 turn **5** alter **6** change **7** convert **9** transform
mutation 6 change **7** anomaly **9** deviation, variation **10** alteration **12** modification **13** metamorphosis **14** transformation **15** transfiguration **18** transmogrification
mutatis mutandis 30 necessary changes having been made
mute 3 mum **4** dumb **5** quiet, tacit **6** silent **8** aphasiac, nonvocal, reserved, reticent **9** unsounded, unuttered, voiceless **10** speechless **12** inarticulate, noncommittal, unpronounced **13** unarticulated **15** uncommunicative
muted 3 dim, low **4** dull, soft, weak **5** quiet **6** dulled, feeble **7** muffled **8** deadened, softened **10** indistinct, lackluster
mutilate 4 lame, maim **6** cut off, deform, excise, mangle **7** butcher, cripple **8** amputate, lacerate, truncate **9** disfigure, dismember
mutineer 5 rebel **9** dissident, insurgent **10** malcontent **15** insurrectionist
mutinous 6 unruly **10** dissenting, rebellious **13** revolutionary
Mutinus
  origin: 5 Roman **7** Italian
  god of: 9 fertility
  fertility in: 8 marriage
  corresponds to: 7 Priapus
mutiny 4 coup **5** rebel **6** revolt, rise up **8** takeover, upheaval, uprising **9** overthrow, rebellion **10** insurgency **12** insurrection
Mutiny on the Bounty
  author: 15 Charles Nordhoff, James Norman Hall
  character: 6 Tehani **9** Roger Byam **12** William Bligh (Captain Bligh) **13** George Stewart **17** Fletcher Christian
  director: 10 Frank Lloyd

  cast: 10 Clark Gable (Fletcher Christian) **12** Eddie Quillan, Franchot Tone **13** Herbert Mundin **15** Charles Laughton (Captain Bligh)
  Oscar for: 7 picture
mutt 3 cur, dog, pup **5** puppy **7** mongrel
Mutt and Jeff
  creator: 7 Al Smith **9** Bud Fisher
  character: 5 A Mutt **6** Cicero **7** Mrs Mutt
mutter 4 carp **5** gripe, growl, grunt **6** grouch, grouse, kvetch, mumble, murmur, rumble **7** grumble, whisper **8** complain
mutual 5 joint **6** common, shared **7** related **8** communal, returned **10** coincident, reciprocal **11** correlative, interactive
mutual understanding 6 accord **9** agreement
muzzle 3 gag **4** bind, curb **5** check, quiet, still **6** bridle, rein in, stifle **7** harness, silence **8** strangle, suppress, throttle
Myanmar
  former name: 5 Burma
  other name: 16 Land of the Pagodas
  capital: 6 Yangon **7** Rangoon
    ancient capital: 3 Ava **4** Pegu **8** Mandalay
  largest city: 7 Rangoon
  others: 2 Ye **3** Ava **4** Pegu **5** Akyab, Bhamo, Katha, Minbu, Namtu, Papun, Prome, Tavoy **6** Hsenwi, Hsipaw, Lashio, Maymyo, Monywa, Shwebo **7** Bassein, Henzada, Pakokku, Toungoo **8** Moulmein, Myingyan
  measure: 2 ly **3** dha, gon, mau, sao, tao, tat **4** byee, phan, seit, taun, that **5** shita, thuoc **6** lamany, palgat **7** chaivai **8** okthabah
  monetary unit: 3 pya **4** kyat
  weight: 2 ta **3** can, pai, vis **4** binh, kyat, ruay, viss **5** behar, candy, ticul **6** abucco **7** peiktha
  lake: 4 Inle
  mountain: 4 Chin, Naga, Pegu, Popa **5** Davna **6** Arakan, Kachin, Lushai, Patkai **7** Karenni **8** Nattaung, Peguyoma, Saramati, Victoria **10** Tenasserim **11** Manipur Hill **12** Tanen Taunggi
  highest point: 11 Hkakabo Razi
  river: 3 Hka **6** Salwin, Sutang **7** Irawadi, Kaladan, Myitnge, Salween, Schweli, Sittang **8** Chindwin, Indawgyi **9** Irrawaddy
  sea: 7 Andaman
  physical feature:
    bay: 4 Siam **6** Bengal, Hunter **7** Heanzay **8** Thailand
    gulf: 8 Martaban
    plateau: 4 Shan
    port: 5 Akyab **7** Bassein, Henzada **8** Moulmein
  people: 2 Ao, Vu, Wa **3** Kaw, Lai,

Lao, Mon, Pyu, Tai, Was **4** Akha, Chin, Juki, Kadu, Laos, Lolo, Miao, Naga, Sema, Shan, Thai, Tsin **5** Karen, Lhota **6** Birman, Burman, Kachin, Peguan, Rengma **7** Akhlame, Burmese, Kakhyen, Palauna, Palaung, Siamese **8** Mon-Khmer **9** Arakanese **12** Tibeto-Berman

language: 3 Lai **4** Chin, Kuki, Pegu, Shan **5** Karen **6** Kachin **7** Burmese, English

religion: 5 Hindu, Islam **8** Buddhism **12** Christianity

place:
  mines: 6 Mawchi **7** Bawdwin
  pagoda: 9 Shwe Dagon
  road: 4 Ledo **5** Burma **9** Stillwell

feature:
  ball game: 7 chin-lon
  festival: 5 Water **6** Lights **10** Thadin-gyut
  silk head band: 10 gaungbaung
  skirt: 6 longyi
  traveling theatrical group: 4 Pwes

My Antonia
  author: 11 Willa Cather
  character: 9 Jim Burden **15** Antonia Shimerda

My Darling Clementine
  director: 8 John Ford
  cast: 7 Tim Holt **8** Ward Bond **10** Henry Fonda (Wyatt Earp) **12** Linda Darnell, Victor Mature (Doc Holliday) **13** Walter Brennan

my dear
  French: 7 ma chere, mon cher

My Fair Lady
  director: 11 George Cukor
  based on play by: 17 George Bernard Shaw (Pygmalion)
  cast: 11 Rex Harrison (Professor Henry Higgins) **13** Audrey Hepburn (Eliza Doolittle) **15** Stanley Holloway **16** Wilfrid Hyde-White
  score: 14 Lerner and Loewe
  Oscar for: 7 picture
  song: 14 The Rain in Spain **24** I Could Have Danced All Night

my faith
  French: 5 ma foi

my fault
  Latin: 8 mea culpa

My Favorite Martian
  character: 8 Tim O'Hara **11** Uncle Martin **15** Mrs Lorelei Brown
  cast: 9 Bill Bixby **10** Ray Walston **13** Pamela Britton

Myles
  king of: 7 Laconia
  invented: 9 grain mill

My Little Margie

character: 7 Charlie **9** Mrs Odetts **11** Mr Honeywell **13** Freddie Wilson **14** Margie Albright, Vernon Albright **15** Roberta Townsend

cast: 9 Don Hayden, Gale Storm **10** Willie Best **12** Clarence Kolb **13** Hillary Brooke **14** Charles Farrell **15** Gertrude Hoffman

my lord
  French: 8 monsieur **11** monseigneur
  Italian: 9 monsignor **10** monsignore

My Man Godfrey
  director: 13 Gregory La Cava
  cast: 10 Alice Brady, Mischa Auer **11** Gail Patrick **13** Carole Lombard, William Powell

myriad 6 untold **7** endless **8** infinite, manifold **9** boundless, countless, limitless, uncounted **11** innumerable, measureless **12** immeasurable, incalculable **13** multitudinous

Myrina
  husband: 8 Dardanus

myrmidon 6 cohort **8** follower, henchman

Myrmidons
  people of: 6 Aegina **8** Thessaly
  created by: 4 Zeus
  created from: 4 ants
  characteristic: 7 warlike
  leader: 6 Peleus **8** Achilles

Myrrha
  also: 6 Smyrna
  father: 11 King Cinyras
  loved: 7 Cinyras
  crime: 6 incest
  son: 6 Adonis
  changed into: 6 myrtle **9** myrrh tree

Myrtilus
  charioteer of: 8 Oenomaus

myrtle 6 Myrtus **10** Vinca minor **14** Myrtus communis **18** Cyrilla racemiflora **23** Umbellularia californica
  varieties: 3 bog, gum, sea, wax **4** cape, Jew's, sand **5** crape, crepe, downy, dwarf, Greek, honey, scent **6** German, Oregon, Polish, willow **7** box sand, classic, running, Swedish **10** Western tea **11** candleberry, Queen's crape, sandverbena **13** Allegheny sand, bracelet honey, California wax **16** Australian willow

Mysia
  epithet of: 7 Demeter

mysophobia
  fear of: 4 dirt

Mysteries of Paris, The
  author: 9 Eugene Sue

Mysteries of Udolpho, The
  author: 15 Mrs Ann Radcliffe

mysterious 4 dark **6** cloudy, covert, hidden, secret **7** cryptic, obscure, strange, unknown **8** baffling, puzzling **9** enigmatic, secretive **10** perplexing, sphinxlike, undercover **11** clandestine, inscrutable **12** impenetrable, inexplicable, supernatural, unfathomable **13** surreptitious **14** undecipherable

Mysterious Stranger, The
  author: 9 Mark Twain

mystery 6 enigma, occult, puzzle, riddle, secret **7** problem, secrecy **9** conundrum, obscurity, symbolism, vagueness **11** ambivalence, elusiveness **12** ineffability, quizzicality **13** ineffableness, mystification

Mystery of Edwin Drood, The see **10** Edwin Drood

mystical, mystic 5 inner **6** hidden, occult **7** cryptic, obscure **8** abstruse, esoteric, ethereal, symbolic **9** enigmatic, secretive **10** cabalistic, symbolical, unknowable **11** inscrutable, nonrational **12** metaphysical, otherworldly **14** transcendental

mystification 9 confusion **10** bafflement, perplexity, puzzlement **12** bewilderment

mystify 4 fool **5** elude **6** baffle, puzzle **7** confuse, deceive, mislead, perplex **8** bewilder, confound **9** bamboozle

myth 3 fib, lie **4** tale, yarn **5** error, fable, story **6** canard, legend **7** fantasy, fiction, hearsay, parable **8** allegory, delusion, illusion, tall tale **9** fairy tale, falsehood **10** shibboleth **13** prevarication

mythical, mythic 6 fabled, unreal **8** illusory **9** imaginary, legendary, pretended **10** conjured-up, fabricated, fantasized, fictitious **13** unsubstantial

mythological, mythologic 6 unreal **8** fabulous, illusory, imagined **9** fantastic, imaginary, legendary, unfactual **10** fictitious

My Three Sons
  character: 11 Chip Douglas, Mike Douglas **12** Steve Douglas **13** Robbie Douglas **18** Katie Miller Douglas, Uncle Charley O'Casey **20** Ernie Thompson Douglas, Michael Francis (Bub) O'Casey
  cast: 8 Don Grady, Tina Cole **12** Tim Considine **13** Fred MacMurray **14** William Frawley **15** Barry Livingston, William Demarest **17** Stanley Livingston
  dog: 5 Tramp

my word
  French: 5 ma foi

nab 4 bust, grab, nail, snag **5** catch, pinch, seize, snare **6** arrest, collar, detain, haul in, pick up, pull in, snatch **7** capture **9** apprehend

nabob 3 VIP **4** lord **5** mogul, nawab **6** deputy, tycoon **7** magnate **8** governor **9** plutocrat **10** capitalist **11** billionaire, millionaire

Nabokov, Vladimir
   author of: 3 Ada **4** Mary, Pnin **6** Lolita **8** Pale Fire

nadir 4 base, zero **5** floor **6** apogee, bottom **7** nothing **8** low point **10** rock bottom **11** lowest point

Nadja
   author: 11 Andre Breton

nag 4 fury, goad, harp **5** annoy, devil, harpy, scold, shrew, vixen **6** badger, bicker, harass, hassle, heckle, hector, nettle, peck at, pester, pick at, pick on, plague, rail at, tartar, virago **7** bedevil, upbraid **8** battle-ax, irritate **9** importune, termagant, Xanthippe

Nahua *see* Aztec

Nahuatl *see* Uto-Aztecan

Naiad
   form: 5 nymph
   location: 5 water

nail 3 fix, pin **4** brad, claw, spad **5** talon **6** fasten, hammer, secure
   part: 3 bed **4** root

Naipaul, V S
   author of: 10 Guerrillas **15** A Bend in the River **17** A House for Mr Biswas **19** The Return of Eva Peron, The Suffrage of Elvira

Nairobi
   capital of: 5 Kenya

naive 4 open **5** green, plain **6** candid, simple, unwary, unwise **7** artless, foolish, natural, unjaded **8** gullible, immature, innocent **9** childlike, credulous, guileless, ingenuous, unspoiled, unworldly **10** unaffected, unassuming **11** susceptible **12** unsuspecting, unsuspicious **15** unsophisticated

naivete, naiveté 6 candor **7** modesty **8** openness **9** credulity, frankness, greenness, innocence, sincerity **10** callowness, simplicity **11** artlessness, foolishness, naturalness **12** childishness, inexperience **13** ingenuousness **14** unaffectedness **16** simplemindedness

naked 4 bald, bare, nude, pure

5 bared, frank, plain, sheer **6** patent, simple, unclad **7** blatant, exposed **8** disrobed, laid bare, manifest, palpable, undraped, wide- open **9** in the buff, unclothed, uncovered, undressed **11** perceptible, unappareled, unqualified, unvarnished **15** in the altogether

Naked and the Dead, The
   author: 12 Norman Mailer

Naked City
   character: 5 Libby **9** (Det) Adam Flint **10** (Det Lt) Dan Muldoon, (Lt) Mike Parker **11** (Det) Jim Halloran, (Sgt) Frank Arcaro **13** Janet Halloran
   cast: 9 Paul Burke **11** Nancy Malone **12** John McIntire **13** Harry Bellaver, Horace McMahon, Suzanne Storrs **15** James Franciscus
   setting: 11 New York City
   theme: 19 Somewhere in the Night

Namath, Joe (Joseph William)
   nickname: 11 Broadway Joe
   sport: 8 football
   position: 11 quarterback
   team: 11 New York Jets

namby-pamby 3 coy **4** dull, prim, weak **5** banal, inane, vapid **6** prissy **7** insipid, mincing, sapless **9** colorless, innocuous, simpering **10** indecisive, wishy-washy **13** characterless

name 3 dub, tag **4** call, term **5** label, title **6** choose, ordain, select **7** appoint, baptize, epithet, specify **8** christen, cognomen, delegate, deputize, nominate, taxonomy **9** authorize, designate, signature, sobriquet **10** commission **11** appellation, designation **12** denomination, nomenclature

nameless 5 minor **7** obscure, unknown, unnamed **8** untitled **9** anonymous, unheard-of, unhonored **12** undesignated

namely
   Latin: 3 viz **9** videlicet

Name of the Game
   character: 8 Andy Hill **9** Joe Sample, Ross Craig **10** Dan Farrell, Jeff Dillon **11** Glenn Howard **12** Peggy Maxwell
   cast: 9 Ben Murphy, Gene Barry **10** Mark Miller **11** Cliff Potter, Robert Stack **13** Tony Franciosa **15** Susan Saint James
   business: 8 magazine **10** publishing

Name of the Rose, The
   author: 10 Umberto Eco

Name That Tune

host: 9 Red Benson **10** Bill Cullen **12** George de Witt
   orchestra: 11 Harry Salter

Namibia
   other name: 15 South West Africa
   capital/largest city: 8 Windhoek
   others: 6 Tsumeb **8** Luderitz **9** Walvis Bay **10** Oranjemund, Swakopmund **12** Keetmanshoop
   monetary unit: 4 cent, rand
   mountain: 14 Khomas Highland, Koakoveld Hills
   highest point: 9 Brandberg
   river: 4 Fish **6** Cunene, Orange **7** Zambezi **8** Okavango
   sea: 8 Atlantic
   physical feature:
      bay: 6 Walvis
      desert: 5 Namib **8** Kalahari
      region: 12 Caprivi Strip
   people: 4 Nama **5** Bantu **6** Damara, Herero, Ovambo, Tswara **7** Bushman, colored **8** Okavango **9** Hottentot
   language: 5 Bantu **6** German **7** English, Khoisan **9** Afrikaans
   religion: 7 animism **8** Lutheran
   feature:
      homeland: 9 bantustan

Nammu
   origin: 8 Sumerian
   mother of: 4 gods
   personifies: 3 sea

Namtar
   origin: 8 Akkadian, Sumerian
   form: 5 demon
   personifies: 5 death

Nana
   author: 9 Emile Zola

Nana (Nurse) (dog)
   character in: 8 Peter Pan
   author: 6 Barrie

Nancy
   character in: 11 Oliver Twist
   author: 7 Dickens

Nancy
   creator: 15 Ernie Bushmiller
   character: 5 Rollo **6** Sluggo **10** Aunt Fritzi

Nanna
   origin: 12 Scandinavian
   husband: 5 Baldr **6** Balder, Baldur
   habitat: 4 moon

Nannerella
   nickname of: 11 Anna Magnani

nanometer
  abbreviation: **2** nm
Naoise
  origin: **5** Irish
  wife: **7** Deirdre
  uncle: **9** Conchobar
  killed by: **9** Conchobar
  father: **6** Usnach, Usnech
Naomi
  husband: **9** Elimelech
  daughter-in-law: **4** Ruth
  son: **6** Mahlon **7** Chilion
nap 3 nod **4** doze, rest **6** cat nap,
  drowse, siesta, snooze **7** doze off,
  drop off, goof off, shut-eye, slumber **8**
  drift off **10** forty winks
napery 5 doily **6** linens, napkin **10** ta-
  blecloth
Naphtali
  father: **5** Jacob
  mother: **6** Bilkah
  brother: **3** Dan, Gad **4** Levi **5** Asher,
    Judah **6** Joseph, Reuben, Simeon **7**
    Zebulun **8** Benjamin, Issachar
  sister: **5** Dinah
  descendant of: **10** Naphtalite
Napoleon Bonaparte
  also: **9** Napoleon I **18** Emperor of the
    French
  battle: **3** Ulm **5** Eylau **6** Lutzen, Mos-
    cow, Toulon (siege), Wagram **7** Bau-
    tzen, Dresden, Leipzig, Marengo,
    Mondovi **8** Borodino, Waterloo **9**
    Friedland **10** Austerlitz **13** Aspern-
    Essling, Jena-Auerstadt, Peninsular
    War **22** War of the Fifth Coalition
  born: **7** Corsica
  exile to: **4** Elba **11** Saint Helena
  fought against: **7** Kutuzov **10** von
    Blucher, Wellington **14** Barclay de
    Tolly
  French fleet destroyed at: **9** Trafal-
    gar
    destroyed by: **6** Nelson
  laws: **14** Napoleonic Code
  marshal/general under: **3** Ney **5** Mu-
    rat **7** Massena **10** Bernadotte
  position: **7** emperor **11** first consul
    13 consul for life
  tomb: **5** Paris **9** Invalides
  wife: **9** Josephine **20** Marie-Louise of
    Austria
Napoleon of Notting Hill, The
  author: **12** G K Chesterton
narcissism 6 egoism, vanity **7** conceit
  8 self-love **11** egocentrism **16** selfcen-
  teredness
narcissist 6 egoist **7** egotist **11** egocen-
  trist **12** self- absorbed, self-admiring
narcissistic 4 smug, vain **6** vanity **7**
  conceit, selfish **8** egotistic, puffed-up
  9 conceited **10** egocentric, egoistical
  11 egomaniacal, egotistical
narcissus
  varieties: **5** poet's **6** poetaz **7** leedsii,
    trumpet **10** paper-white, polyanthus
    16 primrose peerless

Narcissus
  father: **8** Cephisus
  mother: **8** Leiriope
  loved: **7** himself
  loved by: **4** Echo
  punished by: **9** Aphrodite
  changed into: **6** flower
narcotic 4 drug, morphine **5** opium **6**
  herion, opiate **8** medicine, sedative **9**
  soporific **10** medicament, medication,
  painkiller **12** tranquilizer **14** pharma-
  ceutical
Narragansett
  language family: **9** Algonkian **10** Al-
    gonquian
  location: **11** Connecticut, Rhode Is-
    land
  related to: **7** Niantic
  involved in: **9** Pequot War **14** King
    Philip's War **15** Great Swamp Fight
narrate 6 detail, recite, relate, render,
  repeat, retell **7** portray, recount **8** describe, set forth **9** chronicle **10** tell a
  story **15** give an account of
narration 7 recital, telling **8** relating,
  speaking **9** voice-over **10** recitation,
  recounting **11** chronicling, description
  12 storytelling
narrative 4 tale **5** story **6** report **7** account, recital **8** dialogue, episodic **9**
  anecdotal, chronicle, statement **10** historical **12** storytelling
**Narrative of Arthur Gordon Pym,
The**
  author: **13** Edgar Allan Poe
narrow 3 set **4** fine, slim **5** close,
  scant, small, tight **6** biased, scanty **7**
  bigoted, cramped, pinched, shallow,
  slender, tapered **8** confined, dogmatic,
  isolated, squeezed **9** hidebound, illiberal, parochial **10** attenuated, compressed, intolerant, provincial, restricted **11** constricted, incapacious,
  opinionated, reactionary **12** conservative
narrowing 5 taper **8** tapering **9**
  squeezing **11** compressing **12** constricting
narrow-minded 5 petty **7** bigoted,
  prudish **8** one-sided **9** hidebound, parochial, unworldly **10** provincial **11**
  opinionated, reactionary, straitlaced
  12 conservative **15** unsophisticated
narrow-mindedness 4 bias **7** bigotry
  9 prejudice **10** unfairness **11** intolerance
narrows 4 neck, pass **5** canal **6** ravine,
  strait **7** channel, isthmus, passage
Nasca see **5** Nazca
Nascimento, Edson Arantes do
  real name of: **4** Pele
Nash, Ogden
  author of: **6** Versus **9** Hard Lines **20**
    The Private Dining Room **21** I'm a
    Stranger Here Myself
Nashville

director: 12 Robert Altman
cast: 10 Karen Black, Lily Tomlin **11**
  Henry Gibson **12** Ronee Blakley **13**
  Barbara Harris, Michael Murphy **14**
  Keith Carradine **16** Geraldine Chaplin
Oscar for: 4 song
song: 6 I'm Easy
Nassau
  capital of: **7** Bahamas
Nasser, Gamal Abdel
  president of: **5** Egypt **18** United Arab
    Republic
nasty 4 foul, mean, vile **5** awful **6** odious **7** beastly, hateful, vicious **8** horrible **9** repellent, revolting **10** abominable, disgusting, nauseating, unpleasant
  11 distasteful **12** disagreeable
Natchez
  language family: **10** Muskhogean
  tribe: **6** Avoyel, Taensa
  location: **11** Mississippi **13** South Car-
    olina
  allied with: **7** Choctaw
  practiced: **14** head flattening
nates 4 buns, rear, rump, seat **7** rear
  end **8** buttocks, haunches **9** fundament, posterior **12** hindquarters
Nathan
  father: **5** Attai
  served: **5** David **7** Solomon
Nathanael, Nathaniel see **5** Jesus **8**
  Apostles **11** Bartholomew
nation 4 host, race **5** realm, state, tribe
  6 empire, people **7** country, kingdom
  8 republic **9** community **11** sovereignty **12** commonwealth
national park
  Alaska: **13** Mount McKinley
  Arizona: **11** Grand Canyon **15** Petri-
    fied Forest
  Arkansas: **10** Hot Springs
  California: **7** Redwood, Sequoia **8** Yo-
    semite **11** Kings Canyon **14** Channel
    Islands, Lassen Volcanic
  Canada: **4** Yoho **5** Banff, Fundy **6**
    Jasper, Kluane **8** Kootenay **9** Auyuit-
    tuq **13** Waterton Lakes
  Colorado: **5** Estes **9** Mesa Verde **13**
    Rocky Mountain
  Florida: **10** Everglades
  Hawaii: **9** Haleakala **15** Hawaii Volca-
    noes
  Kentucky: **11** Mammoth Cave
  Maine: **6** Acadia
  Michigan: **10** Isle Royale
  Minnesota: **9** Voyageurs
  Montana: **7** Glacier **11** Yellowstone
  New Mexico: **15** Carlsbad Caverns
  North Carolina: **19** Great Smoky
    Mountains (with Tennessee)
  North Dakota: **17** Theodore Roose-
    velt
  Oklahoma: **6** Platte
  Oregon: **10** Crater Lake
  South Dakota: **8** Badlands, Wind
    Cave
  Tennessee: **6** Shiloh **13** Cumberland

Gap **19** Great Smoky Mountains (with North Carolina)
Texas: 7 Big Bend **18** Guadalupe Mountains
Utah: 4 Zion **6** Arches **11** Bryce Canyon, Canyonlands, Capital Reef
Virginia: 10 Shenandoah **26** Colonial National Historical
Washington: 7 Olympic **12** Mount Rainier **13** North Cascades
Wyoming: 10 Grand Teton **11** Yellowstone

National Velvet
director: 13 Clarence Brown
cast: 10 Anne Revere **11** Donald Crisp **12** Mickey Rooney **14** Angela Lansbury **15** Elizabeth Taylor
horse: 6 The Pie
Oscar for: 17 supporting actress (Revere)
sequel: 19 International Velvet

native 4 home **5** basic, local, natal **6** inborn, inbred, innate, savage **7** citizen, endemic, natural **8** domestic, inherent, national, paternal **9** aborigine, elemental, homegrown, ingrained, inherited, intrinsic, primitive **10** congenital, countryman, hereditary, indigenous **11** instinctive **12** countrywoman **13** autochthonous

Native Americans
Registered tribes and/or nations, by state:
AL: 11 Poarch Creek
AK: 5 Aleut, Haida **6** Eskimo **7** Tlingit **10** Athabascan, Tsimpshian
AZ: 4 Hopi, Pima **6** Navajo, Apache, Papago **7** Yavapai
CA: 5 Hoopa, Yurok, Karok **6** Paiute **8** Cherokee
CO: 3 Ute
CT: 18 Mashantucket Pequot
FL: 8 Seminole, Cherokee **10** Miccosukee
ID: 7 Bannock **8** Shoshone, Nez Perce
IA: 9 Sac and Fox
KS: 4 Iowa **8** Kickapoo **10** Potawatomi
LA: 9 Coushatta **10** Chitimacha **12** Tunica-Biloxi
ME: 8 Maliseet **9** Penobscot **13** Passamaquoddy
MA: 9 Wampanoag
MI: 6 Ottawa **8** Cherokee, Chippewa **10** Potawatomi
MN: 5 Sioux **8** Chippewa
MS: 7 Choctaw
MO: 4 Crow **5** Sioux **8** Cheyenne **9** Blackfoot **11** Assiniboine
NE: 5 Omaha **9** Winnebago **11** Santee Sioux
NV: 6 Paiute, Washoe **8** Shoshone
NM: 6 Apache, Navajo, Pueblo
NY: 6 Mohawk, Seneca, Oneida **8** Onondaga
NC: 6 Lumbee **8** Cherokee
ND: 5 Sioux **6** Mandan **7** Arikara,

Hidatsa **8** Chippewa
OK: 5 Creek, Kiowa, Osage **7** Choctaw **8** Cherokee, Cheyenne, Comanche, Arapahoe, Chicasaw
OR: 5 Wasco **6** Siletz, Paiute **11** Warm Springs
RI: 12 Narragansett
SC: 7 Catawba
SD: 5 Sioux
TX: 4 Tiwa **8** Kickapoo **16** Alabama-Coushatta
UT: 3 Ute **6** Navajo **7** Goshute **14** Southern Paiute
WA: 5 Lummi **6** Yakama **8** Quinault
WI 6 Oneida **8** Chippewa **9** Winnebago
WY: 8 Shoshone, Arapahoe
see also Individual Entries

native country 7 country **8** homeland **10** fatherland **13** mother country

native-grown 5 local **8** domestic **9** homegrown **10** indigenous

native land 8 homeland **10** birthplace, fatherland, native soil **13** mother country, native country

native of Israel
Hebrew: 5 sabra

native soil 8 homeland **10** fatherland, native land **13** mother country, native country

Native Son
author: 13 Richard Wright

NATO
members: 5 Italy, Spain **6** Canada, France, Greece, Norway, Turkey **7** Belgium, Denmark, Germany, Iceland **8** Portugal **10** Luxembourg **11** Netherlands **12** United States **13** United Kingdom
proposed: 6 Poland **7** Hungary **13** Czech Republic

natty 4 chic, neat, posh, tidy, trim **5** smart **6** dapper, jaunty, snappy, spruce **7** dashing, modish, stylish **11** fashionable

Natty Bumppo
also: 7 Hawkeye **10** Pathfinder, The Trapper **13** The Deerslayer **15** Leatherstocking **16** Le Longue Carabine
character in: 23 The Leatherstocking Tales
friend: 5 Uncas **12** Chingachgook
author: 6 Cooper

natural 5 plain **6** inborn, native, normal **7** earthly, genuine, regular **8** God-given, inherent **9** essential, intuitive, unstudied **10** unaffected, unmannered **11** instinctive, spontaneous, terrestrial **13** unpretentious **14** characteristic **15** straightforward
in craps: 5 seven **6** eleven

Natural, The
director: 13 Barry Levinson
based on story by: 14 Bernard Malamud
character: 7 Roy Hobbs

cast: 10 Glenn Close **12** Robert Duvall **13** Robert Redford

natural child 7 bastard **9** love child **17** illegitimate child

natural gift 5 flair **6** talent **7** ability, faculty **8** aptitude **9** attribute, endowment

natural habitat 5 range **6** domain, milieu **7** element **9** territory **11** environment

naturalize 5 adapt, adopt **6** adjust **8** accustom **9** acclimate **11** domesticate, familiarize

naturalness 4 ease **9** sincerity **10** simplicity **11** artlessness, genuineness **12** unconstraint **14** unaffectedness

nature 4 bent, kind, mood, sort, type **5** birth, earth, globe, humor, stamp, style, trait **6** cosmos, spirit **7** essence, feature, variety **8** category, creation, instinct, property, universe **9** character **11** disposition, peculiarity **12** constitution **13** particularity **14** characteristic
goddess of: 6 Cybele **9** Dindymene **10** Berecyntia

Nature
author: 17 Ralph Waldo Emerson

naught 3 nil **4** zero **5** nihil, zilch **6** cipher **7** nothing, useless **9** worthless

naughty 3 bad **4** blue **5** bawdy, dirty **6** ribald, risque, vulgar **7** wayward, willful **8** devilish, off-color, perverse **9** fractious, obstinate **11** disobedient, misbehaving, mischievous **12** pornographic, recalcitrant, unmanageable **13** disrespectful

Nauru
other name: 14 Pleasant Island
capital: 13 Yaren District
cities: 3 Boe, Ewa **4** Aiwo, Ijuw **5** Baiti, Buada, Nibok, Uaboe, Yaren **6** Anabar, Anetan, Meneng **7** Anibare **10** Denigomodu
monetary unit: 4 cent **6** dollar
lake: 11 Buada Lagoon
sea: 7 Pacific
physical feature:
  bay: 7 Anibare
  lagoon: 5 Buada
  point: 4 Anna **6** Meneng
people: 7 Chinese **10** Melanesian, Polynesian **11** Micronesian
  explorer: 9 John Fearn
language: 7 English, Nauruan
religion: 10 Protestant **13** Roman Catholic
feature: 9 phosphate

nausea 7 disgust, heaving **8** contempt, loathing, retching, sickness, vomiting **9** repulsion, revulsion **10** queasiness **11** airsickness, biliousness, car sickness, seasickness **12** upset stomach **14** motion sickness, travel sickness

Nausea, Nausee
author: 14 Jean-Paul Sartre

nauseate 5 repel, upset **6** offend,

revolt, sicken **7** disgust, repulse **8** make sick **15** turn one's stomach

nauseated 3 ill **4** sick **5** upset **6** queasy **8** repelled, revolted **9** disgusted

nauseating 9 offensive, repellent, repulsive, revolting, sickening **10** disgusting

nauseous 4 sick **5** upset **6** queasy **9** abhorrent, nauseated, offensive, repellent, repulsive, revolting, sickening, upsetting **10** disgusting, nauseating **12** unappetizing

Nausicaa
 father: 8 Alcinous
 position: 8 princess
 aided: 8 Odysseus

Nausithous
 father: 8 Poseidon
 mother: 8 Periboea
 occupation: 8 helmsman
 employer: 7 Theseus
 became: 4 king
 realm: 8 Phaeacia

nautical 5 naval **6** marine **7** aquatic, boating, oceanic **8** maritime, of the sea, seagoing, yachting

nautical mile
 abbreviation: 3 nmi

Nautilus
 submarine in: 32 Twenty Thousand Leagues Under the Sea
 skipper: 11 Captain Nemo
 author: 5 Verne

Navajo, Navaho (Dine)
 language family: 10 Athapascan, Athapaskan
 location: 4 Utah **7** Arizona **9** New Mexico
 noted for: 7 weaving **14** silversmithing
 dwelling: 5 hogan

navigate 3 fly **4** ride, sail, ship **5** cross, steer **6** cruise, voyage **8** maneuver, sail over **11** plot a course **12** chart a course

navigation 7 boating, sailing **8** cruising, piloting, voyaging **9** traveling **10** seamanship
 god of: 5 Niord, Njord

Navigators Islands see **12** Western Samoa

navy 5 fleet **6** armada, convoy **8** flotilla, warships

navy-blue 6 indigo **8** dark blue, deep blue

nay 4 also, deny, vote **5** never **6** denial, refuse **7** against, but also, refusal **8** negative

Nazarene see **5** Jesus

Nazarene, The
 author: 10 Sholem Asch

Nazca, Nasca
 location: 4 Peru **12** South America
 noted for: 8 ceramics, textiles **10** Nazca lines (sketches on plain)

Nazi 7 facost
 air force: 9 Luftwaffe
 swastika: 10 Hakenkreuz
 collaborator: 8 quisling
 elite guard: 13 schutzstaffel
 leader: 4 Hess **6** Hitler **7** Himmler **8** Goebbels
 police: 7 gestapo
 trials: Nuremberg

N'Djamena
 capital of: 4 Chad

Neal, Patricia
 husband: 9 Roald Dahl
 born: 9 Packard KY
 roles: 3 Hud (Oscar) **15** A Face in the Crowd, The Fountainhead **18** The Subject Was Roses

near 4 nigh **5** about, close **6** all but, almost **7** close by, close to, looming **8** approach, come up to, imminent, next door **9** alongside, close with, impending **10** hereabouts **11** approaching, practically, proximately, threatening **13** approximately

nearby 5 close, handy **6** at hand **7** close by **8** next door **9** adjoining **10** accessible, hereabouts

near death
 Latin: 10 in extremis

near home 5 close **7** close by **10** hereabouts

nearly 4 nigh **5** about **6** all but, almost **7** close to, roughly **11** practically **13** approximately

nearly equal 5 close **7** similar **10** nip-and-tuck **11** approaching

nearly even 5 close **10** head to head, nip-and-tuck **11** neck and neck

nearness 8 intimacy, vicinity **9** adjacency, closeness, handiness, immediacy, proximity **10** contiguity **11** propinquity **12** availability, neighborhood **13** accessibility, approximation

nearsighted 6 myopic
 opposite: 9 hyperopic **10** presbyopic

neat 4 tidy **5** clean, great **6** groovy **7** concise, correct, orderly **8** accurate, exciting, original, straight, striking, succinct **9** competent, dexterous, efficient, ingenious, organized, purposive, shipshape **10** controlled, immaculate, methodical, systematic **11** imaginative, intelligent, uncluttered

neatness 5 order **8** tidiness **11** orderliness **12** organization

Nebraska
 abbreviation: 2 NE **4** Nebr
 nickname: 4 Beef **8** Antelope **10** Blackwater, Cornhusker **12** Tree-planter's
 capital: 7 Lincoln
 largest city: 5 Omaha
 others: 5 Cozad **6** Gering **7** Kearney **8** Beatrice, Hastings **9** Broken Bow **11** Grand Island, North Platte, Scottsbluff
 college: 4 Dana **5** Doane **8** Duchesne,

Hastings **9** Creighton **15** Midland Lutheran
 feature: 8 Boys' Town
  national monument: 11 Scott's Bluff **15** Agate Fossil Beds
 tribe: 3 Oto **4** Otoe **5** Kiowa, Omaha, Ponca, Sioux **6** Pawnee
 people: 10 Henry Fonda **11** Fred Astaire, Roscoe Pound
 lake: 7 Merritt, Sherman, Swanson **10** McConaughy **13** Lewis and Clark
 land rank: 9 fifteenth
 physical feature: 8 Badlands
  hills: 4 Sand **5** Drift, Loess
  plains: 5 Great
 river: 4 Loup **5** Logan **6** Dismal, Nemaha, Platte **7** Big Blue, Elkhorn **8** Missouri, Niobrara **10** Little Blue, Republican **12** Harlan County
 state admission: 13 thirty-seventh
 state bird: 17 western meadowlark
 state flower: 9 goldenrod
 state motto: 20 Equality Before the Law
 state song: 17 Beautiful Nebraska
 state tree: 3 elm **10** cottonwood

nebris
 skin of: 4 fawn

Nebrophonus see **5** Thoon

Nebuchadnezzar
 father: 12 Nabopolassar
 son: 10 Bel shazzar **12** Evilmerodach
 same as: 7 Nabucco **14** Nebuchadrezzar
 king of: 7 Babylon
 conquered: 9 Jerusalem
 destroyed: 6 temple
 deported: 4 Jews
 into: 7 slavery
 general: 11 Holophernes

nebula 4 Crab, Ring, Veil **5** Great **6** Lagoon **7** Rosette **9** Horsehead

nebulous 3 dim **4** dark, hazy **5** murky, vague **6** cloudy **7** obscure, unclear **8** confused **9** ambiguous, uncertain **10** impalpable, indefinite, indistinct, intangible **13** indeterminate

necessarily 8 perforce **9** naturally **10** inevitably, inexorably **11** accordingly **12** compulsorily **13** automatically, axiomatically, unqualifiedly **16** incontrovertibly

necessary 6 needed, urgent, wanted **7** crucial, desired, exigent, fitting, needful **8** required **9** called for, essential, requisite **10** compulsory, imperative, obligatory **13** indispensable

necessary changes having been made
 Latin: 15 mutatis mutandis

necessitate 5 cause, force, impel **6** compel, demand, oblige **7** call for, enforce, require **9** constrain, prescribe

necessitation 5 cause, force **6** demand, duress **8** coercion, pressure **10** compulsion, constraint, obligation **11** enforcement, requirement

necessity, necessities 4 must, need **6** demand, needed **7** urgency **8** exigency, pressure **9** essential, requisite **10** sine qua non **11** requirement **13** indispensable
Latin: 10 sine qua non

neck 3 pet **4** kiss, nape, pass **6** caress, cervix, cuddle, fondle, smooth, strait **7** channel, isthmus, make out **9** narrowing

neckerchief 5 scarf **8** bandanna, kerchief

necklace 3 tie **5** beads, chain, noose **6** choker, collar, locket, pearls, string **7** jewelry, pendant **8** ornament **9** lavaliere

necktie 3 bow **4** band **5** ascot, black, scarf **6** cravat, string **7** Windsor **10** four in hand **11** half Windsor **12** hangman's rope

necromancer 5 hexer, magus, witch **6** wizard **7** charmer, warlock **8** conjurer, exorcist, magician, sorcerer **9** enchanter, occultist, voodooist **10** soothsayer **13** black magician, thaumaturgist

necromancy 5 magic, spell **7** sorcery **8** black art **10** witchcraft **11** enchantment, foretelling

necrophobia
fear of: **5** death **10** dead bodies

necropolis 8 cemetery **9** graveyard **12** burial ground **13** burying ground

nectar
drink of: **4** gods
gives: **4** life

nee 4 born **11** maiden-named

need 4 lack, want, wish **5** crave, exact **6** demand, penury **7** call for, longing, poverty, require, straits **8** distress, exigency, yearn for **9** essential, extremity, indigence, necessity, requisite **10** bankruptcy, insolvency **11** desideratum, destitution, necessitate, requirement **13** impecuniosity, pennilessness

needed 5 vital **7** crucial **9** essential, necessary, requisite **13** indispensable

needful 7 wishful **8** required **9** essential, necessary, requisite **10** imperative **13** indispensable

needle 3 vex **4** josh, leaf, ride, twit **5** annoy, chaff, harry, taunt, tease **6** badger, harass, hector **7** torment **9** indicator
prefix: **3** acu

needle-shaped 5 sharp **6** peaked, spiked **7** pointed **8** piercing **10** bodkin-like

needless 7 useless **9** excessive, pointless, redundant **10** gratuitous, pleonastic, unavailing **11** dispensable, purposeless, superfluous, uncalled-for, unessential, unnecessary **12** overabundant

needlework 6 sewing **7** basting, brocade, darning, tacking, tatting **8** appli-

que, knitting, quilting **9** stitching **10** embroidery **11** cross stitch, needle point

needy 4 poor **5** broke **6** hard-up, in want **8** indigent, strapped **9** destitute, money less, penniless **10** down-and-out **12** impoverished **15** poverty-stricken

ne'er-do-well 3 bum **5** idler, loser **6** loafer, no-good **7** goof-off, sad sack, wastrel **8** layabout **9** do-nothing, no-account **10** black sheep **14** good-for-nothing

nefarious 3 bad, low **4** base, evil, foul, vile **6** odious, wicked **7** beastly, ghastly, heinous, hellish, ungodly, vicious **8** depraved, devilish, infamous, infernal, shameful **9** atrocious, execrable **10** abominable, despicable, detestable, iniquitous, scandalous, villainous **11** disgraceful, opprobrious, unspeakable **12** dishonorable **13** unmentionable

Nefertem
origin: **8** Egyptian
personifies: **5** lotus
true identity: **4** Ptah

Nefertiti
queen: **5** Egypt
husband: **8** Ikhnaton **9** Amenhotep
nephew: **11** Tutankhamen

negate 4 deny, veto, void **5** quash, quell, rebut **6** defeat, disown, refute, repeal, revoke, squash **7** blot out, destroy, disavow, gainsay, nullify, retract, reverse, squelch, wipe out **8** abrogate, disallow, disclaim, set aside, vanquish **9** overthrow, overwhelm, repudiate **10** contradict, invalidate

negating 7 denying, voiding **8** refuting, revoking **9** reversing **10** cancelling, nullifying **11** disallowing **12** invalidating, setting aside **13** contradicting

negation 6 denial **7** counter **8** reversal **9** rejection **10** abrogation, disclaimer, refutation **11** confutation, repudiation **12** invalidation **13** contradiction, nullification

negative 4 blue, dark **5** bleak **6** at odds, gloomy **7** dubious, opposed **8** contrary, doubtful, downbeat, inimical, opposing, refusing **9** declining, demurring, dissident, jaundiced, objecting, rejecting, reluctant, skeptical, unwilling **10** dissenting, fatalistic **11** disagreeing, pessimistic **12** antagonistic, disapproving **13** uncooperative **14** unenthusiastic

neglect 4 fail, omit **5** let go, shirk **6** forget, ignore, laxity, pass by, pass up, slight **7** abandon, default, laxness, let pass, let ride, let slip **8** be remiss, idleness, let slide, omission, overlook, pass over, shake off **9** disregard, oversight, passivity, slackness **10** inaccuracy, negligence, remissness **11** dere-

liction, inattention, inexactness **12** carelessness, fecklessness, indifference, slovenliness **13** noncompliance, unfulfillment **14** nonpreparation **16** underachievement

neglected 7 dropped, ignored, omitted, shirked, unkempt **8** forsaken, untended **9** abandoned, cast aside, forgotten **10** overlooked, uncared for **11** disregarded

neglectful 4 lazy **5** slack **6** remiss, untrue **8** careless, derelict, heedless **9** forgetful, negligent, oblivious, unheeding, unmindful **10** inconstant, thriftless, unfaithful, unthinking, unwatchful **11** improvident, inattentive, indifferent, respectless, thoughtless, unobservant **12** devil-may-care, disregardant, disregardful, happy-go-lucky **15** procrastinating

negligee, neglige 4 robe **6** kimono **7** wrapper **8** bathrobe, peignoir **9** housecoat **12** dressing gown

negligence 6 laxity **7** neglect **11** disregarded **12** carelessness

negligent 3 lax **5** slack **6** remiss, untidy **8** careless, heedless, slovenly **9** forgetful, unheeding, unmindful **10** neglectful, unthinking, unwatchful **11** inattentive, indifferent, thoughtless, unobservant **13** inconsiderate

negligible 5 minor, petty, small **6** minute, paltry, slight **7** trivial **8** piddling, trifling **11** unimportant **13** insignificant **15** inconsequential

negotiate 4 cash, make, pass **6** barter, cash in, convey, dicker, haggle, handle, manage, redeem, settle **7** arrange, consign, deliver, discuss, get over **8** contract, cope with, deal with, hand over, make over, pass over, sign over, transact, transfer, transmit, turn over **10** bargain for **11** come to terms, meet halfway

negotiation 4 deal **6** treaty **8** argument, haggling **9** dickering **10** bargaining **11** arbitration, arrangement **12** compromising

negotiator 7 arbiter **8** mediator **9** go-between **10** arbitrator **12** intermediary

Nehemiah
father: **5** Azbuk **14** Hachaliah

neigh 5 hinny **6** nicker, whinny

neighbor 4 abut, meet **5** touch **6** adjoin, be near, border, friend **7** conjoin **8** borderer, border on **9** associate **12** acquaintance

neighborhood 4 area, part, side, ward **5** place, range **6** locale, parish, region, sphere **7** quarter, section **8** confines, district, environs, precinct, purlieus, vicinity **9** community

neighboring 4 near, next **5** close **6** at hand, nearby **7** close by **8** abutting, adjacent **9** adjoining, bordering **10** contiguous **11** surrounding **12** circumjacent

neighborly 4 kind **5** civil **6** chummy, kindly, polite **7** affable, amiable, cordial, helpful **8** amicable, friendly, gracious, obliging **9** courteous **10** hospitable **11** considerate, warmhearted **12** well-disposed

Neighbors
author: **12** Thomas Berger

Neith
origin: **8** Egyptian
personifies: **10** femininity
son: **2** Ra
corresponds to: **6** Athena

Nekhbet
origin: **8** Egyptian
form: **7** vulture
guardian of: **5** Egypt **10** Upper Egypt

Nelson, Harriet Hilliard
real name: **14** Peggy Lou Snyder
husband: **5** Ozzie
son: **4** Rick **5** David
born: **11** Des Moines IA
roles: **30** The Adventures of Ozzie and Harriet

Nelson, Horatio
also: **14** Viscount Nelson
nationality: **7** British
battle: **9** Trafalgar **11** Bay of Abukir **15** Battle of the Nile **16** Cape Saint Vincent **18** Battle of Copenhagen
defeated: **5** Danes **6** French **7** Spanish
flagship: **7** Victory
killed at: **9** Trafalgar
lover: **16** Emma Lady Hamilton

Nelson, Ozzie
real name: **18** Oswald George Nelson
wife: **15** Harriet Hilliard
son: **4** Rick **5** David
born: **12** Jersey City NJ
roles: **30** The Adventures of Ozzie and Harriet

Nemean
epithet of: **4** Zeus **5** games
precursor of: **8** Olympics

Nemean lion
strangled by: **8** Hercules

nemesis 4 ruin **5** match, **6** rival **7** avenger, goddess, justice, revenge, undoing **8** downfall, punisher, Waterloo **9** overthrow, vengeance **10** punishment **11** destruction, retaliation, retribution **16** instrument of fate

nemine contradicente 11 unanimously **18** no one contradicting

nemine dissentiente 11 unanimously **15** no one dissenting

Nemo
character in: **10** Bleak House
author: **7** Dickens

Nemo, Captain
character in: **32** Twenty Thousand Leagues Under the Sea
author: **5** Verne
submarine: **8** Nautilus

nene 13 Hawaiian goose

neologism, neology 7 coinage **9** nonce word

neon
chemical symbol: **2** Ne

neonate 4 baby **6** infant **7** newborn

neophyte 4 tyro **5** pupil **6** novice, rookie **7** amateur, convert, entrant, learner, recruit, student, trainee **8** beginner, disciple, newcomer **9** greenhorn, novitiate, proselyte **10** apprentice, tenderfoot **11** probationer

neoplasm 5 tumor **6** cancer, growth **7** sarcoma **9** carcinoma **10** malignancy **14** carcinosarcoma

Nepal
other name: **9** Shangri-La
capital/largest city: **8** Katmandu **9** Kathmandu
others: **5** Patan, Patna **6** Gurkha **7** Birganj **8** Bhadgaon, Lalitpur **9** Bhaktapur **10** Biratnagar
university: **9** Tribhuvan
division: **5** Terai **13** High Himalayas
monetary unit: **4** anna, pice **5** mohar, paisa, rupee
mountain: **6** Cho Oyu, Churia, Lhotse, Makalu **7** Manaslu, Siwalik **9** Annapurna, Himalayas **10** Dhaulagiri, Gosainthan, Himalchuli **11** Ganesh Himal **12** Kanchenjunga **14** Mahabharat hekh
highest point: **9** Mt Everest
river: **4** Kali, Kosi, Mugu, Seti **5** Babai, Bheri, Rapti, Sarda, Tamur **6** Gandak **7** Karnali **8** Narayani
physical feature:
  plain: **5** Terai
  valley: **5** Nepal **8** Katmandu
people: **3** Rai **4** Aoul **5** Bhote, Limbu, Magar, Murmi, Newar, Tharu **6** Bhutia, Gurkha, Gurung, Nepali, Sherpa, Tamang **7** Kiranti, Tibetan **8** Gorkhali, Nepalese
  birthplace of: **6** Buddha **13** Gautama Buddha **17** Siddhartha Gautama
  king: **8** Mahendra **9** Tribhuwan **18** Prithwi Narayan Shah **23** Birenda Bir Bikram Shah Dev
  ruler: **4** Rana **5** Malla **6** Rajput
language: **6** Nepali, Newari
religion: **8** Buddhism, Hinduism
place:
  dam: **6** Gandak
  shrine: **9** Swayambhu **10** Gorakhnath
feature:
  animal: **3** dzo, yak **7** dzopkyo
  arch: **6** Juddha
  god/goddess: **5** Indra **6** Kumari
  legend: **4** Yeti **17** abominable snowman
  soldiers: **6** Gurkha

Nepali
language family: **12** Indo-European
branch: **11** Indo-Iranian
group: **5** Indic
spoken in: **5** Nepal

nepenthe 4 drug **5** drink, opium **6** heroin, opiate **7** hashish **8** narcotic

nephrite
variety: **4** jade

ne plus ultra 4 acme **6** finest **8** ultimate **12** highest point

nepotism 10 favoritism
patron of: **9** relatives

Neptune
origin: **5** Roman
god of: **3** sea
corresponds to: **8** Poseidon

Neptune
position: **6** eighth
satellite: **6** Nereid, Triton
color: **4** blue
studied by: **7** Voyager (2)

Nereid
form: **5** nymph
location: **3** sea
father: **6** Nereus

Nereus
god of: **3** sea
father: **6** Pontus
mother: **4** Gaea
father of: **7** Nereids
number of Nereids: **5** fifty
son: **7** Nerites

Nerissa
character in: **19** The Merchant of Venice
author: **11** Shakespeare

neritic 7 aquatic, coastal **8** offshore

Nero
name: **18** Nero Claudius Caesar
emperor of: **4** Rome
mother: **9** Agrippina
father: **19** Domitius Ahenobarbus
stepfather: **8** Claudius
tutor: **6** Seneca
son: **11** Britannicus
wife: **7** Octavia **13** Poppaea Sabina
successor: **5** Galba

nerve 4 dash, gall, grit, guts, sass **5** brass, cheek, crust, pluck, spunk, valor **6** mettle, spirit **7** bravery, courage **8** backbone, boldness, coolness, gameness, strength, tenacity **9** arrogance, assurance, derring-do, endurance, flippancy, fortitude, gallantry, hardihood, hardiness, impudence, insolence, sauciness **10** assumption, brazenness, confidence, effrontery, steadiness **11** intrepidity, presumption **12** fearlessness, impertinence, resoluteness **13** determination **16** stoutheartedness

nerveless 4 calm, dead, weak **5** brave, frail, inert **6** feeble, flabby **7** flaccid **8** cowardly **9** powerless **10** courageous **12** fainthearted

nervous 4 wild **5** jumpy, shaky, tense **6** touchy, uneasy **7** alarmed, anxious, excited, fearful, fidgety, jittery, peevish, ruffled **8** feverish, neurotic, skittish, startled, timorous, unstrung **9** delirious, disturbed, excitable, impatient, irritable, sensitive, trembling, tremulous, unsettled **10** high-strung, hysterical **12** apprehensive

nervousness 6 tremor **7** anxiety, flutter, shaking, tension **8** hysteria, timidity **9** agitation, quivering, the creeps, the shakes, trembling, twitching **10** the fidgets, touchiness **11** disturbance, fidgetiness, stage fright **12** apprehension, excitability, irascibility, irritability, perturbation, timorousness **16** hypersensitivity

nervous system
   component: 3 CNS **4** ears, eyes **5** brain, taste, touch **7** ganglia **8** nerve end **10** nerve fiber, spinal cord

nervy 4 bold, firm, rude **5** brash, gutty, gutsy, sassy **6** brassy, brazen, cheeky, gritty, plucky, strong **7** assured, nervous **10** courageous, determined **12** stouthearted

Nesbitt, Cathleen
   born: 7 England **8** Cheshire
   roles: 10 My Fair Lady **18** Upstairs Downstairs **23** Three Coins in the Fountain

Nessus
   form: 7 centaur
   shot by: 8 Hercules
   caused death of: 8 Hercules

n'est-ce pas? 10 isn't that so?

nestle 3 lie, pet **4** live, snug, stay **5** clasp, dwell, lodge **6** bundle, caress, coddle, cosset, cuddle, enfold, fondle, huddle, nuzzle, occupy, remain, settle **7** embrace, inhabit, lie snug, snuggle **8** lie close **10** settle down

Nestor
   origin: 5 Greek
   attributes: 6 oldest, wisest
   father: 6 Neleus
   son: 10 Thasymedes **11** Pisistratus
   epithet: 7 Nelides

net 3 web **4** earn, gain, grab, grid, grip, mesh, snag, take, trap **5** catch, clasp, grate, seize, snare **6** clutch, enmesh, gather, grille, obtain, pick up, screen, snap up, take in **7** acquire, bring in, capture, collect, ensnare, grating, lattice **8** entangle, gather in, gridiron, Internet, meshwork **9** apprehend, grillwork, lay hold of, screening **10** accumulate **11** latticework
   constellation of: 9 Reticulum

nether 5 basal, below, lower, under **6** bottom, lowest **8** downward, inferior **9** subjacent **10** bottommost

Netherlands
   other name: 7 Holland **12** Low Countries
   capital/largest city: 9 Amsterdam
   others: 3 Urk **5** Delft, Lisse **6** Almelo, Arnhem, Leiden, Velsen **7** Haarlem, Helmond, Hengelo, Limburg, Tilburg, Tilburg, Utrecht **8** Aalsmeer, Enschede, Ijmuiden, Nijmegen, The Hague **9** Apeldoorn, Dordrecht, Eind-

hoven, Groningen, Rotterdam **12** Scheveningen
   division: 6 Twente **7** Drenthe, Limburg, Utrecht, Zeeland **9** Friesland, Groningen **10** Gelderland, Overijssel **12** North Brabant, North Holland, South Holland **19** Netherlands Antilles
   government:
      legislature: 4 Raad **11** Eerste Kamer, Tweede Kamer
   head of state: 5 queen
   measure: 2 el **3** aam, ahm, ell, kan, vat **4** duim, mijl, rood, rope **5** anker, roede, wisse **6** bunder, legger, maatje, mutsje, streep **7** schepel **8** mimgelen, steekkan
   monetary unit: 4 doit, oord, raps **5** crown, daler, rider, ryder **6** florin, gulden, stiver, suskin **7** daalder, ducaton, escalan, escalin, guilder, stooter, stuiver **8** albertin, ducatoon **9** dubbeltje **12** rijksdaalder **13** albertustaler
   weight: 3 ons **4** last, pond **5** bahar **6** korrel **7** wichtje
   island: 5 Texel **7** Ameland, Frisian **8** Antilles, Vlieland
   lake: 7 Haarlem **10** Ijsselmeer **11** Grevelingen, Havingvliet
   highest point: 11 Vaalserberg
   river: 3 Eem, Lek **4** Leck, Maas, Waal, Ysel **5** Donge, Hunse, Meuse, Rhine, Schie, Yssel **6** Dintel, Dommel, Ijssel, Kromme **7** Scheldt
   sea: 5 North
   physical feature:
      canal: 6 Oranje **7** Juliana, Merwede **8** Drentsch, North Sea **10** Wilhelmina **11** New Waterway
      former bay: 9 Zuider Zee
      port: 9 Europoort
   people: 5 Dutch **7** Frisian **9** Hollander **10** Surinamese **12** Netherlander **13** South Moluccan
      artist: 4 Eyck, Hals **5** Appel, Bosch **7** Van Gogh, Vermeer **8** Mondrian, Ruisdael **9** Rembrandt
      author: 6 Vondel **7** Erasmus, Grotius, Spinoza **8** Vestdijk **9** Anne Frank
      explorer: 6 Tasman
      king: 7 William
      queen: 7 Beatrix, Juliana **10** Wilhelmina
      ruler: 5 Spain **13** House of Orange **15** Holy Roman Empire
      scientist: 7 Huygens **11** Leeuwenhoek
   language: 5 Dutch **7** English, Frisian
   religion: 13 Dutch Reformed, Protestantism **16** Roman Catholicism
   place:
      airport: 8 Schiphol
      bird sanctuary: 9 Waddenzee
      miniature town: 9 Madurodam
      museum: 9 Frans Hals, Stedelijk **11** Mauritshuis, Rijksmuseum

14 Vincent Van Gogh **19** Boymans-van Beuninging
   seat of government: 7 Den Haag **8** The Hague **11** 'sGravenhage
   tower: 14 Schreierstoren
   feature:
      cheese market: 9 kaasmarkt
      earth mounds: 6 terpen
      flower: 5 tulip
      flower parade: 12 Bloemencorso
      pottery: 5 Delft
      reclaimed land: 6 polder
      wooden shoes: 7 klompen
   food:
      cheese: 4 Edam **5** Gouda **6** Leyden **7** cottage
      dish: 10 nasi goreng, rijsttafel
      drink: 3 gin **8** anisette, schnapps
      pea soup: 10 erwtensoep

Netherlands East Indies see **9** Indonesia

netherworld 4 hell **5** Hades **10** underworld **14** infernal region

nettle 3 vex **4** bait, gall, miff, rile **5** annoy, beset, chafe, harry, pique, sting **6** bother, harass, ruffle **7** perturb, prickle, provoke **8** irritate **9** displease **10** exasperate

nettle 6 Urtica
   varieties: 4 dead, dumb, hemp, rock **5** false, flame, hedge, horse, Roman **6** spurge **7** painted **8** stinging **9** white dead **11** spotted dead **12** western horse

network 3 web **4** grid, mesh, trap **5** grate, group, snare **6** grille, scheme, system **7** complex, netting, station

Network
   director: 11 Sidney Lumet
   based on story by: 14 Paddy Chayefsky
   cast: 9 Ned Beatty **10** Peter Finch, Wesley Addy **11** Faye Dunaway **12** Robert Duvall **13** William Holden **16** Beatrice Straight
   Oscar for: 5 actor (Finch) **7** actress (Dunaway) **17** supporting actress (Straight)

networks see **18** Television Networks

neuroptera
   class: 8 hexapoda
   phylum: 10 arthropoda
   group: 7 ant lion, fishfly **8** alderfly, lacewing, snakefly

neurotic 4 sick **7** anxious, intense, nervous **8** abnormal, unstable **9** disturbed, obsessive, unhealthy **10** distraught, immoderate **11** overwrought

neuter 5 fixed **6** barren, fallow, gelded, spayed **7** asexual, sexless, sterile **8** impotent **9** infertile

Neutra, Richard J
   architect of: 15 Mathematics Park (Princeton) **16** Lovell Heath House (Los Angeles CA) **17** von Sternberg House (Northridge CA) **22** Orange County Courthouse (Santa Ana CA)

neutral 4 mean **5** aloof **6** medium, middle, normal, remote **7** average **8** pacifist, peaceful, unbiased **9** impartial, in-between, peaceable, withdrawn **10** achromatic, indefinite, of two minds, unaffected, uninvolved **11** half-and-half, indifferent, nonpartisan, unconcerned **12** fence sitting, intermediate, noncombatant **13** disinterested, dispassionate **14** nonbelligerent, noninterfering **16** nonparticipating **18** noninterventionist

neutralize 4 halt, stop **5** annul, block, check **6** cancel, defeat, impede, negate, offset, stymie **7** balance, disable, nullify, prevent **8** overcome, suppress **9** frustrate, overpower **10** counteract **12** counterpoise, incapacitate **14** counterbalance

neutralizer 7 blocker **9** nullifier **12** counteractor, counteragent **15** counterbalancer

Neuvillette, Christian de
character in: **16** Cyrano de Bergerac
author: **7** Rostand

Nevada
abbreviation: **2** NV **3** Nev
nickname: **6** Silver **9** Sagebrush
capital: **10** Carson City
largest city: **8** Las Vegas
others: **3** Ely, Nye **4** Elko, Reno **6** Fallon, Nellis, Sparks, Storey, Washoe **7** Boulder, Gerlach **9** Hawthorne, Henderson **11** Weed Heights **12** Virginia City
explorer: **7** Fremont **13** Jedediah Smith
feature: **12** Comstock Lode
  dam: **5** Davis **6** Hoover
  hot springs: **4** Tule **9** Punch Bowl, Steam Boat
  national monument: **11** Death Valley
tribe: **5** Modoc, Washo **6** Digger, Mohave, Paiute **7** Klamath **8** Achomawi, Atsugewi, Shoshone
lake: **4** Mead, Ruby **5** Tahoe, Weber **6** Mohave, Walker **7** Pyramid **8** Lahontan, Rye Patch **9** Wild Horse
land rank: **7** seventh
mountain: **4** East, Pine, Ruby **5** White **7** Rockies, Toiyabe, Wasatch **13** Sierra Nevadas
  highest point: **12** Boundary Peak
physical feature: **7** geysers **10** hot springs
  basin: **5** Great
  cave: **6** Gypsum
  desert: **7** Sonoran
  plateau: **8** Columbia
river: **5** Reese **6** Carson, Walker **7** Truckee **8** Colorado, Humboldt
state admission: **11** thirty-sixth
state bird: **7** sagehen **16** mountain bluebird
state flower: **9** sagebrush
state motto: **16** All for Our Country
state song: **15** Home Means Nevada

state tree: **9** pinon pine **15** single-leaf pinon

never 4 ne'er **7** not ever **8** at no time, not at all

never-ending 6 steady **7** abiding, eternal, lasting, nonstop **8** constant, enduring, immortal, infinite, repeated, unbroken **9** ceaseless, continual, incessant, perennial, perpetual, recurring, unceasing **10** continuous, persistent, relentless **11** everlasting, unremitting **12** interminable, undiminished **13** uninterrupted

never-failing 4 firm, sure **6** proven, trusty **7** abiding **8** enduring, reliable **9** steadfast **10** dependable **11** trustworthy, undeviating, unfaltering **12** unhesitating, tried-and-true

nevermore 6 no more **10** never again

Never on Sunday
director: **11** Jules Dassin
cast: **11** Jules Dassin, Titos Vandis **14** Georges Foundas, Melina Mercouri
setting: **6** Greece

nevertheless 3 but, yet **6** anyhow, anyway, even so, though **7** however **8** after all, although **10** contrarily, in any event, regardless **12** contrariwise **15** notwithstanding

Neville, Constance
character in: **18** She Stoops to Conquer
author: **9** Goldsmith

new 4 late **5** fixed, fresh, green, novel **6** modern, reborn, recent, remote, unused **7** altered, changed, current, just out, rebuilt, resumed, untried **8** original, reopened, repaired, restored, up-to-date **9** recreated, refreshed, remodeled, renovated, uncharted, unessayed, untouched **10** revivified, unexplored, unfamiliar, ungathered, unseasoned, unventured **11** regenerated, uncollected, unexercised **12** unaccustomed **13** reconstructed, reinvigorated

New Atlantis
author: **12** Francis Bacon

New Brunswick
abbreviation: **2** NB
bay: **5** Fundy, Maces **7** Shepody **9** Chignecto, Miramichi **13** Passamaquoddy
channel: **5** Minas **10** Grand Manan
city: **7** Moncton **8** Bathurst **9** Riverview **10** Edmundston, Saint John **11** Fredericton
island: **4** Deer **6** Miscou **7** Machias **10** Campobello, Grand Manan
known as: **16** Atlantic province, maritime province
lake: **5** Grand **8** Oromocto **12** Magagudavic **14** Chiputneticook
people: **5** Irish **6** French **7** Acadian, English **8** American, Scottish **9** Algonkian **10** Anglo Saxon
religion: **6** Canaan **7** Baptist **8** Angli-

can **10** Protestant **12** Presbyterian, United Church **13** Roman Catholic
river: **5** Cains, Green **6** Renous, Salmon **7** Tobique **8** Kedgwick, Nashwak, Oromocto **9** Miramichi, Patapedia, Saint John **10** Nepisiguit, Richibucto, Saint Croix **11** Petitcodiac, Restigouche, Upsalguitch **12** Kennebecasis

New Centurions, The
author: **14** Joseph Wambaugh

newcomer 4 tyro **5** alien **6** novice **7** entrant **8** intruder, neophyte, outsider, stranger **9** foreigner, immigrant, outlander **10** interloper, trespasser

New Deal Agency 3 AAA, CCC, CWA, FCA, FHA, FSA, NRA, NYA, PWA, REA, SEC, SSB, TVA, WPA **4** FCIC, FDIC, FERA, HOLC, NLRD, USHA

New Delhi
capital of: **5** India
designed by: **7** Lutyens
earlier city: **5** Dilli **8** Dhillika, Din Panah, Kilookai **9** Firozabad **11** Tughlukabad **12** Indraprastha **13** Shah Jahanabad
invader: **5** Timur **6** Abdali **7** British, Rohilas **8** Marathas **9** Nadir Shah
landmark: **7** Red Fort **9** India Gate, Qutb Minar **10** Iron Pillar, Jama Masjid **12** Humayun's Tomb **14** Connaught Place **15** Rajghat Memorial **17** Rashtrapati Bhavan (Presidential Palace) **23** Jantar Mantar Observatory **30** Gandhi National Museum and Library
river: **6** Yamuna
street: **7** Raj Path (Kingsway)
university: **15** Jawaharlal Nehru

New England
capital: **6** Boston **7** Augusta, Concord **8** Hartford **10** Montpelier, Providence
city: **4** Lynn **5** Barre **6** Bangor, Lowell, Nashua **7** Hyannis, Rutland, Warwick **8** Brockton, Cranston, Lawrence, Lewiston, New Haven, Portland, Stamford **9** Cambridge, Fall River, New London, Pawtucket, Waterbury, Worcester **10** Bridgeport, Burlington, Manchester, Pittsfield, Portsmouth, Woonsocket **11** Brattleboro, Springfield
football team: **8** Patriots
Indians: **6** Abnaki, Pequot **7** Mahican, Mohegan, Niantic, Nipmuck, Wangunk **8** Algonkin, Iroquois **9** Algonquin, Pennacook **10** Quinnipiac **12** Narragansett
lake: **6** Sebago, Tiogue **7** Sunapee **9** Champlain, Moosehead **10** Candlewood **11** Pemaduncook **13** Winnipesaukee
mountain: **5** Green, White **8** Greylock, Katahdin **9** Berkshire, Mansfield **10** Washington **11** Appalachian
river: **5** Otter **6** Thames **7** Charles **8** Kennebec, Pawtucket, Winooski

9 Merrimack, Missiquoi, Naugatuck, Pawcatuck, Penobscot, Saint John **10** Housatonic, Providence, Quinnipiac **11** Connecticut **12** Androscoggin
state: 5 Maine **7** Vermont **11** Connecticut, Rhode Island **12** New Hampshire **13** Massachusetts

newfangled 5 novel **6** modern, modish **7** stylish

new-fashioned 6 modern, modish **7** stylish **8** up-to-date

Newfoundland
abbreviation: 4 Nfld
capital: 10 Saint Johns
city: 19 Happy Valley Goose Bay
lake: 7 Jeddore, Melville **8** Meelpaeg **10** Michikamau
mountain: 9 Long Range
river: 5 Eagle **6** Fraser, Gander **8** Exploits, Naskaupi **9** Churchill
section: 8 Labrador

New Granada *see* **8** Colombia

New Guinea
other name: 14 Papua New Guinea
capital/largest city: 11 Port Moresby
others: 3 Lae, Wau **4** Daru **5** Soron, Wewak **6** Aitape, Kikori, Medang, Rabaul **7** Gorolka, Kitbadi
division:
  eastern half of island: 9 Indonesia, Irian Jaya
  western half of island: 14 Papua New Guinea
government: 22 constitutional monarchy
head of state: 14 British monarch **15** governor-general
monetary unit: 4 kina, toea
island: 3 Aru **4** Aroe, Buka **5** Arroe, Ceram, Japen, Jobie, Manus **6** Cretin, Mussau, Ninigo, Waigeu **7** Sainson, Solomon **8** Bismarck, Kiriwina, Schouten, Woodlark **9** Admiralty, Trobriant **10** Louisiande, New Britain, New Ireland **12** Bougainville **14** D'Entrecasteaux
mountain: 4 Snow **6** Orange **8** Bismarck, Victoria **9** Carstensz **11** Owen Stanley **12** Albert Edward
highest point:
  Irian Jaya: 9 Carstensz **10** Puncak Jaya
  Papua New Guinea: 7 Wilhelm
river: 3 Fly **4** Hamu, Hany, Ramu **5** Degul, Sepik **6** Kikori, Purari **7** Amberno, Markham
sea: 5 Ceram, Coral, Sepik **6** Indian **7** Arafura, Pacific, Solomon **8** Bismarck
physical feature:
  bay: 3 Oro **5** Milne **8** Geelvink
  gulf: 4 Huon **5** Papua
  strait: 6 Torres, Vitiaz
people: 5 Pygmy **6** Papuan **7** Negrito **10** Melanesian
  explorer: 15 Jorge de Menesses
  ruler: 7 Germany **9** Australia **12** Great Britain
language: 4 Motu **7** English **16** Melanesian Pidjin
religion: 7 animism **10** Protestant **13** Roman Catholic
feature:
  bird: 7 mudlark **9** cassowary
food:
  dried coconut meat: 5 copra

New Hampshire
abbreviation: 2 NH
nickname: 7 Granite
capital: 7 Concord
largest city: 10 Manchester
others: 5 Dover, Keene **6** Berlin, Durham, Exeter, Nashua **7** Hanover, Laconia **8** Sandwich **9** Claremont, Rochester **10** Portsmouth **12** Bretton Woods
college: 5 Keene **6** Rivier **9** Dartmouth, St Anselms **10** New England
feature: 14 Great Stone Face
  notch: 7 Kinsman, Pinkham **8** Crawford **9** Franconia
tribe: 6 Abnaki **9** Pennacook
people: 11 Robert Frost **12** Daniel French **13** Daniel Webster, Horace Greeley, Mary Baker Eddy
  explorer: 9 Champlain **16** Captain John Smith
island: 4 Star **5** White **6** Shoals **7** Lunging
lake: 5 Squam **7** Ossipee, Sunapee, Umbagog **8** Newfound **10** Winnisquam **13** Winnipesaukee
land rank: 11 forty-fourth
mountain: 5 Flume, White **6** Moriah, Paugus **7** Waumbek **8** Chocorua, Sandwich **9** Franconia, Monadnock **11** Profile Peak **12** Presidential
  highest point: 10 Washington
physical feature:
  bay: 5 Great
president: 14 Franklin Pierce
river: 4 Saco **6** Israel **7** Bellamy **8** Souhegan **9** Merrimack **10** Piscataqua **11** Connecticut, Salmon Falls **12** Androscoggin
state admission: 5 ninth
state bird: 11 purple finch
state flower: 11 purple lilac
state motto: 13 Live Free Or Die
state song: 15 Old New Hampshire **26** New Hampshire My New Hampshire
state tree: 10 paper birch, white birch

Newhart
character: 4 Dick **6** Joanna **7** Michael **9** Stephanie
cast: 9 Mary Frann **10** Bob Newhart, Julia Duffy **12** Peter Scolari

Newhart, Bob
born: 9 Chicago IL
roles: 3 Bob **7** Newhart **10** Cold Turkey **12** George and Leo **17** The Bob Newhart Show
films: 7 catch-22 **8** In and out

New Hebrides *see* **7** Vanuatu

New Jersey
abbreviation: 2 NJ
nickname: 6 Garden **8** Mosquito
capital: 7 Trenton
largest city: 6 Newark
others: 4 Lodi **5** Ewing, Ft Lee **6** Camden, Dumont, Haddon, Kearny, Linden, Nutley, Orange, Rahway, Totowa **7** Bayonne, Cape May, Clifton, Hoboken, Hohokus, Keyport, Madison, Matawan, Netcong, Oradell, Paramus, Passaic, Raritan, Teaneck, Tenafly, Wyckoff **8** Carteret, Cranford, Freehold, Garfield, Hillside, Metuchen, Paterson, Secaucus, Watchung **9** Bridgeton, Elizabeth, Engle wood, Hawthorne, Irvington, Maplewood, Montclair, Ocean City, Princeton **10** Asbury Park, Belleville, Ft Monmouth, Hackensack, Jersey City, Livingston, Long Branch, Morristown, Perth Amboy **11** Bergenfield **12** Atlantic City, Collingswood, New Brunswick
colleges: 4 Drew **6** Upsala **7** Rutgers **8** Caldwell, Monmouth, St Peter's **9** Princeton, Seton Hall **10** Bloomfield **18** Fairleigh-Dickinson
feature: 9 Boardwalk **16** Delaware Water Gap
tribe: 8 Delaware **11** Lenni-Lanape
people: 9 Aaron Burr **11** Joyce Kilmer, Paul Robeson **12** Stephen Crane, Thomas Edison **13** James Lawrence **19** James Fenimore Cooper **21** William Carlos Williams
  explorer: 6 Hudson **9** Verrazano
lake: 6 Mohawk **9** Greenwood, Hopatcong
land rank: 10 forty-sixth
mountain: 8 Piedmont **10** Kittatinny **13** First Watchung **14** Second Watchung
  highest point: 9 High Point
physical feature: 9 Palisades, Sandy Hook
  bay: 8 Delaware
  cape: 3 May
  ocean: 8 Atlantic
president: 15 Grover Cleveland
river: 4 Toms **6** Dennis, Haynes, Hudson, Mantua, Ramapo **7** Mullica, Passaic, Raritan **8** Cohansey, Delaware, Tuckahoe **10** Hackensack
state admission: 5 third
state bird: 16 eastern goldfinch
state flower: 6 violet
state motto: 20 Liberty and Prosperity
state tree: 6 red oak
basketball team: 4 Nets
football team: 8 Generals
hockey team: 6 Devils

Newley, Anthony
wife: 11 Joan Collins
born: 6 London **7** England
roles: 11 Oliver Twist **25** Stop the World I Want to Get Off

41 The Roar of the Greasepaint The Smell of the Crowd

newly 4 anew **6** afresh, lately, of late **7** freshly, just now **8** recently

newly rich person
French: **12** nouveau riche

Newlywed Game, The
host: **10** Bob Eubanks
executive producer: **11** Chuck Barris

Newlyweds, The
creator: **13** George McManus
character: **12** Baby Snookums

Newman, Barnett
born: **9** New York NY
artwork: **7** Abraham, The Wild **8** Onement I **18** Stations of the Cross **19** Vir Heroicus Sublimis

Newman, Christopher
character in: **11** The American
author: **5** James

Newman, John Henry (Cardinal)
author of: **18** Apologia pro Vita Sua

Newman, Paul
wife: **14** Joanne Woodward
born: **11** Cleveland OH
company: **10** Newman's own
roles: **3** Hud **6** Harper, Picnic **8** The Sting, Twilight **10** The Hustler, The Verdict **11** Nobody's Fool **12** Cool Hand Luke **15** Absence of Malice, The Color of Money **16** Cat on a Hot Tin Roof, The Left-Handed Gun, The Long Hot Summer, The Silver Chalice **17** The Hudsucker Proxy **29** Butch Cassidy and the Sundance Kid

New Mexico
abbreviation: **2** NM **4** N Mex
nickname: **8** Sunshine **17** Land of Enchantment
capital: **7** Santa Fe
largest city: **11** Albuquerque
others: **3** Jal **4** Taos **5** Aztec, Belen, Hobbs, Raton **6** Clovis, Deming, Gallup, Grants **7** Artesia, Bananea, Roswell, Socorro, Torreon **8** Carlsbad **9** Las Cruces, Los Alamos **10** Alamogordo **13** Piedras Negras
college: **7** Sante Fe **11** Albuquerque
feature: **7** Four Corners
  dam: **5** Butte **8** Elephant
  labs: **6** Sandia **17** Los Alamos National
  national monument: **10** Aztec Ruins, White Sands **11** Chaco Canyon **17** Gila Cliff Dwelling
  national park: **15** Carlsbad Caverns
  observatory: **14** Sacramento Peak
tribe: **3** Sia **4** Hano, Piro, Tano, Taos, Tewa, Tiwa, Zuni **5** Acoma, Jemez, Kares, Manso, Pecos, Tiqua, Tonoa **6** Apache, Isleta, Laguna, Navaho, Navajo, Pueblo **7** Anasazi, Picuris **8** Santa Ana **9** Mescalero **12** Santo Domingo
people: **9** Kit Carson, Peter Hurd **11** Bill Mauldin
  explorer: **5** Onate **6** de Niza, de

Vaca **8** Coronado
lake: **6** El Vado, Navajo, Sumner **7** Conchas **8** McMillan **10** Alamogordo **13** Elephant Butte
land rank: **5** fifth
mountain: **5** Jemez **6** Sandia **7** Manzano, Mimbres, Rockies, Truchas **8** Mogollon **9** Guadalupe, San Andres **10** Nacimiento, Sacramento **11** Mount Taylor **15** Sangre de Christo
  highest point: **11** Wheeler Peak
physical feature:
  basin: **8** Tularosa
  desert: **15** Jornada de Muerto
  plains: **5** Great
river: **3** Ute **4** Gila **5** Pecos **7** San Jose, San Juan **8** Canadian **9** Rio Grande
state admission: **12** forty-seventh
state bird: **10** roadrunner
state fish: **14** cutthroat trout
state flower: **5** yucca
state motto: **15** It Grows as It Goes
state song: **14** O Fair New Mexico **16** Asi es Nuevo Mexico
state tree: **5** pinon **8** tarantah **15** velvet ash pinyon

New Orleans
basketball team: Jazz
event: **9** Mardi Gras, Sugar Bowl **25** International Jazz Festival
football team: **6** Saints
landmark: **7** Cabildo **9** Old Square, Superdome **10** Vieux Carre **12** Pirate's Alley **13** French Quarter
noted for: **4** jazz
people: **5** Cajun **6** Creole **7** Acadian
river: **11** Mississippi
street: **5** Royal **7** Bourbon
university: **6** Loyola, Tulane

news 4 dirt, dope, talk, word **5** flash, libel, piece, rumor, story **6** babble, expose, gossip, report **7** account, article, chatter, hearsay, lowdown, mention, message, release, scandal, slander, tidings **8** bulletin, dispatch, exposure **10** communique, disclosure, divulgence, revelation **11** information **12** announcement, intelligence

news account 4 item **5** story **6** report **7** release **8** bulletin, dispatch **10** communique

newsmonger 6 gossip **8** busybody, reporter

News of the Day
also: **12** Neues vom Tage
opera by: **9** Hindemith
character: **5** Laura **7** Eduoard

Newsome, Chadwick
character in: **14** The Ambassadors
author: **5** James

New Spain see **6** Mexico

newspaper 3 rag **5** daily, paper, sheet **6** herald, weekly **7** courant, gazette, journal, tabloid, tribune **10** periodical **11** publication

New Testament

books of: 4 Acts, John, Jude, Luke, Mark **5** James, Peter, Titus **6** Romans **7** Hebrews, Matthew, Timothy **8** Philemon **9** Ephesians, Galatians **10** Colossians, Revelation **11** Corinthians, Philippians **13** Thessalonians
books: **12** Humologumena

Newton, Isaac
field: **11** mathematics
nationality: **7** English
discovered laws of: **6** motion **7** gravity **8** calculus
discovered: **13** color spectrum **15** binomial theorem **16** method of fluxions
invented: **21** infinitesimal calculus

New York
abbreviation: **2** NY
nickname: **6** Empire **9** Excelsior
capital: **6** Albany
largest city: **7** New York
others: **3** Rye **4** Rome, Troy **5** Ilion, Islip, Nyack, Olean, Owego, Utica **6** Attica, Auburn, Cohoes, Elmira, Goshen, Ithaca, Oneida, Oswego, Tappan **7** Ardsley, Babylon, Batavia, Buffalo, Congers, Endwell, Geneseo, Hewlett, Mahopac, Merrick, Messena, Mineola, Montauk, Oneonta, Pennyan, Suffern, Syosset, Wantagh, Yaphank, Yonkers **8** Bethpage, Catskill, Endicott, Herkimer, Kingston, Ossining, Pottsdam, Saratoga, Tuckahoe **9** Rochester, Scarsdale **10** Binghamton, Bronxville, Mamaroneck **11** Cooperstown, New Rochelle, Schenectady, White Plains **12** Poughkeepsie
college: **4** Bard, CUNY, Iona, Pace, SUNY **5** Finch, Keuka **6** Hobart, Hunter, Vassar **7** Adelphi, Barnard, Colgate, Cornell, Fordham, St John's **8** Columbia, Skidmore, Syracuse **9** Juilliard, Rochester, West Point **13** Sarah Lawrence **30** Rensselaer Polytechnic Institute
feature:
  prison: **6** Attica **8** SingSing
  tribe: **4** Erie **6** Cayuga, Mohawk, Oneida, Seneca **7** Mohican, Montauk **8** Iroquois, Onondaga **9** Manhattan,
  people: **7** John Jay **8** Walloons **9** Jonas Salk **10** Henry James **11** Rockefeller, Walt Whitman **12** Eugene O'Neill **13** DeWitt Clinton, John Burroughs **14** Herman Melville **15** Peter Stuyvesant **16** Eleanor Roosevelt, Washington Irving **17** Fiorello La Guardia
    explorer: **6** Hudson **9** Champlain, Verrazano **16** Dutch West India Co
  island: **4** Fire, Long **5** Ellis **6** Staten **7** Bedloe's, Fisher's, Liberty, Shelter, Welfare **8** Thousand **9** Governors, Manhattan
  lake: **4** Erie **6** Cayuga, Finger, George, Oneida, Otisco, Otsego, Owasco, Placid, Seneca **7** Conesus, Ontario,

Saranac, Schroon **8** Saratoga **9** Champlain
land rank: 9 thirtieth
mountain: 4 Bear **5** Slide **7** Taconic **9** Catskills **11** Adirondacks
  highest point: 5 Marcy
physical feature:
  bay: 7 Jamaica, Peconic **8** Moriches
  canal: 4 Erie **7** Gowanus
  falls: 7 Niagara
  valley: 6 Mohawk
president: 14 Martin Van Buren **14** Teddy Roosevelt **15** Millard Fillmore **17** Theodore Roosevelt **23** Franklin Delano Roosevelt
river: 4 East **5** Black, Tioga **6** Harlem, Hoosic, Hudson, Mohawk, Oswego **7** Ausable, Genesee, Niagara **10** St Lawrence **11** Susquehanna
state bird: 8 bluebird
state fish: 10 brook trout
state flower: 4 rose
state motto: 9 Excelsior (Ever upward, Still higher)
state tree: 10 sugar maple

New York City
nickname: 6 Gotham **8** Big Apple
airport: 3 JFK **6** Newark **9** La Guardia **12** John F Kennedy
area: 4 Soho **6** Harlem **7** Chelsea, Midtown, Tribeca **8** Broadway **9** Chinatown, Manhattan **10** Stuyvesant **11** Bensonhurst, Brownsville, Little Italy **12** Hell's kitchen **13** Spanish Harlem **16** Greenwich Village **17** Bedford-Stuyvesant
baseball team: 4 Mets **7** Yankees
basketball team: 6 Knicks **7** Liberty **14** Knickerbockers
borough: 5 Bronx **6** Queens **8** Brooklyn, Richmond **9** Manhattan **12** Staten Island
early governor: 10 Stuyvesant
feature:
  building: 11 Empire State
  hall of fame: 8 baseball
  park: 7 Central
  square: 5 Times, Union **6** Herald
  statue: 7 Liberty
  street/avenue: 4 Park, Wall **5** Fifth **7** Madison **8** Broadway
  tomb: 6 Grant's
football team: 4 Jets **6** Giants
former name: 12 New Amsterdam
hockey team: 7 Rangers **9** Islanders
island: 4 City, Long **5** Ellis, Ward's **6** Riker's, Staten **7** Liberty **8** Randall's **9** Governor's, Manhattan, Roosevelt
landmark: 5 Macy's **8** Aqueduct, Bronx Zoo **9** Unisphere **10** Jones Beach **11** Battery Park, Central Park, Coney Island, Penn Station, Shea Stadium, Times Square **12** Carnegie Hall **13** Gracie Mansion, Lincoln Center, Port Authority, Rockaway Beach, Trinity Church, United Nations, Yankee Stadium **14** Waldorf-Astoria **15** NY Public Library, NY

Stock Exchange, Seagram Building, Statue of Liberty **16** Chrysler Building, World Trade Center **17** Arthur Ashe Stadium, Hayden Planetarium, Rockefeller Center, Woolworth Building **18** Astoria Film Studios, Radio City Music Hall **19** Empire State Building, Grand Central Station, Madison Square Garden, St Patrick's Cathedral **22** Metropolitan Opera House **29** Cathedral of Saint John the Divine
mayor: 4 Koch **6** Walker **9** La Guardia
museum: 6 Jewish **7** Whitney **9** Cloisters **10** Guggenheim **12** Cooper-Hewitt, Metropolitan **15** Frick Collection **17** Museum of Modern Art (MoMA) **30** American Museum of Natural History
river: 4 East **6** Harlem, Hudson
street: 6 Bowery **8** Broadway **9** Lexington **10** Park Avenue, Wall Street **11** Central Park, Fifth Avenue, Sutton Place **13** Madison Avenue **17** Forty-Second Street
university: 3 NYU **6** Queens **7** Barnard, Fordham, Yeshiva **8** Brooklyn, Columbia **13** Hunter College **22** Juilliard School of Music **23** City University of New York

New Zealand
native's nickname: 4 Kiwi
other name: 8 Aotearoa **12** Nieuw Zeeland **23** Land of the Long White Cloud
capital: 10 Wellington
largest city: 8 Auckland
others: 5 Leuin, Oreti, Otaki, Taupo **6** Clutha, Foxton, Oamaru, Picton, Timaru **7** Dunedin, Manu Kau, Raetihi, Rotorua **8** Hamilton, Kawakawa, Touranga **9** Lyttelton **10** Queenstown **12** Christchurch, Invercargill, Port Chalmers **13** Port Nicholson **14** Napier-Hastings **15** Palmerston North
school: 5 Otago **6** Massey **7** Waikato **8** Auckland, Victoria **10** Canterbury
division: 11 North Island, South Island
head of state: 14 British monarch **15** governor general
monetary unit: 4 cent **6** dollar
island: 4 Cook, Niue, Otea **5** North, South **6** Bounty, Chatam, Snares **7** Stewart, Tokelau **8** Auckland, Campbell, Kermadec, Puketutu **9** Antipodes **10** Resolution, Three Kings **12** Great Barrier
lake: 3 Ada **4** Gunn, Ohau **5** Hawea, Taupo **6** Pukaki, Pupuke, Te Anau, Tekapo, Wanaka **7** Brunner, Diamond, Kanieri, Okareka, Rotorua **8** Okataina, Paradise, Rotoaira, Wakatipu **9** Manapouri
mountain: 4 Eden, Flat, Owen **5** Allen, Chope, Lyall, Mitre, Ohope, Otari, Young **6** Egmont, Stokes, Tas-

man **7** Cameron, Coronet, Ernslaw, Huiarau, Pihanga, Ruahine, Ruapehu, Tauhera, Tutamoe, Tyndall **8** Aspiring, Richmond, Tauranga **9** Messenger, Murchison, Ngauruhoe, Raukumara, Tongariro **11** Remarkables **12** Southern Alps
highest point: 4 Cook **7** Aorangi
river: 4 Avon **5** Mokau, Waipa **6** Clutha, Rakaia, Tamaki, Waihou, Wairau, Wairoa **7** Waikato, Waitaki **8** Clarence, Manawatu, Wanganui **10** Rangitikei
sea: 6 Tasman **12** South Pacific
physical feature:
  bay: 4 Ohua **5** Evans, Hawke, Lyall **6** Awarua, Cloudy, Golden, Plenty, Tasman **7** Fitzroy, Pegasus, Poverty **8** Halfmoon, Rangaunu
  bight: 7 Karamea **10** Canterbury **13** North Taranaki, South Taranaki
  cape: 4 East, West **5** North **6** Egmont **8** Farewell, Foulwind, Palliser **9** Southwest
  channel: 8 Colville
  falls: 10 Sutherland
  glacier: 3 Fox **6** Tasman **11** Franz Joseph
  gulf: 7 Hauraki
  harbor: 7 Kaipara, Manukau **9** Waitemata
  peninsula: 5 Mahia, Otago
  plains: 10 Canterbury
  sound: 8 Doubtful
  strait: 4 Cook **7** Foveaux
people: 3 Ati **5** Arawa, Dutch, Maori **7** British, Ringatu **10** Polynesian
  author: 5 Frame **9** Mansfield **10** Ngaio Marsh **12** Ashton-Warner
  explorer: 4 Cook **6** Tasman
  mountain climber: 7 Hillary
language: 5 Maori **7** English
religion: 8 Anglican **9** Methodist **10** Protestant **12** Presbyterian **13** Roman Catholic
place:
  national park: 9 Fiordland, Fjordland, Tongariro
feature:
  animal: 7 tuatara
  bird: 3 kea, tui **4** kiwi, weka **6** takahe **7** apteryx **8** bellbird
  tree: 4 rimu, tawa **5** kauri, matai **6** totara
food:
  fish: 4 mako
  fruit: 4 kiwi **9** tamarillo **17** Chinese gooseberry
next-door 8 adjacent **9** adjoining **10** connecting, contiguous, juxtaposed, side-by-side, **12** conterminous
next to 6 beside **8** abutting, adjacent **9** adjoining, bordering **10** contiguous, juxtaposed **12** conterminous
next world, the 6 Heaven **8** eternity, paradise **12** the hereafter **14** the world to come
Nez Perce (Numipu)

language family: 10 Shahaptian
location: 5 Idaho **6** Oregon **10** Washington
leader: 11 Chief Joseph

Niamey
capital of: 5 Niger

nib 3 end, tip, top **4** apex, peak **5** point **6** height, tiptop, vertex **7** extreme **8** pinnacle **9** extremity

nibble 3 nip **4** bite, chew, gnaw, peck **5** crumb, munch, speck, taste **6** crunch, morsel, peck at, tidbit **8** fragment, particle

Nibelung, ring of
origin: 8 Germanic
mentioned in: 14 Nibelungenlied
stolen by: 8 Alberich

Nibelungenlied
origin: 8 Germanic
form: 4 epic
date written: 17 thirteenth century
related to: 8 Volsunga
author: 7 unknown
character: 5 Etzel (Attila), Hagen **6** Gernot **7** Gunther **8** Brunhild, Dankwart, Giselher **9** Kriemhild, Siegfried
inspired: 6 Wagner

Nibelungs, Niblungs
origin: 8 Germanic, Teutonic
followers of: 9 Siegfried
race: 6 dwarfs
possessed: 8 treasure
captured by: 9 Siegfried
family of: 7 Gunther

Nicaragua
capital/largest city: 7 Managua
others: 4 Leon, Rama **6** Masaya **7** Corinto, Granada **8** Jinotega **9** Matagalpa **10** Bluefields, Chinandega
division: 13 Mosquito Coast
measure: 4 vara **5** cahiz **6** suerte **7** cajuela, manzana **10** cabelleria
monetary unit: 4 peso **7** centavo, cordoba
weight: 3 bag **4** caha, caja **8** tonelada
island: 7 Ometepe
lake: 7 Managua **9** Nicaragua
mountain: 4 Leon **5** Negro, Viejo **6** Madera, Telica **7** Managua, Saslaya **9** Momotombo
highest point: 7 Mogoton
river: 4 Coco, Tuma **5** Wanks **6** Grande, Poteca **7** San Juan **8** Tipitapa **9** Escondido
sea: 7 Pacific **9** Caribbean
physical feature:
  gulf: 7 Fonseca
people: 4 Mico, Mixe, Rama, Smoo, Ulva **5** Cukra, Diria, Lenca, Sambo, Toaca **6** Mangue **7** mestizo, Miskito **8** Mosquito **9** Matagalpa
  author: 5 Dario
  explorer: 6 Davila **7** Cordoba **8** Columbus
  group: 6 Contra **10** Sandinista
  leader: 6 Somoza, Walker, Zelaya

7 Nicardo **8** Chamorro
language: 7 English, Spanish
religion: 13 Roman Catholic
place:
  cathedral: 12 Metropolitan
feature:
  dance: 5 sones **10** zapateados, zarabandas
food:
  beans: 8 frijoles
  dish: 10 naca tamale
  drink: 5 tiste **9** pinolillo
  fruit: 6 zapote

nice 4 deft, fine, good, kind **5** dandy, exact, fussy, great, swell **6** divine, genial, lovely, proper, seemly, strict, subtle **7** amiable, amusing, careful, cordial, correct, finicky, genteel, likable, precise, refined, winning **8** accurate, charming, cheerful, delicate, friendly, gracious, jim-dandy, ladylike, pleasant, pleasing, rigorous, skillful, unerring, virtuous, well-bred **9** agreeable, congenial, excellent, fantastic, marvelous, sensitive, wonderful **10** attractive, delightful, enchanting, entrancing, fastidious, methodical, meticulous, scrupulous **11** interesting, painstaking, pleasurable, punctilious, respectable, sympathetic, warmhearted **13** compassionate, understanding, well brought up **17** overconscientious

Nice and the Good, The
author: 11 Iris Murdoch

nicely 6 neatly **7** exactly, fussily, happily **9** carefully, precisely **10** accurately, critically, pleasantly, unerringly **11** faultlessly, fortunately, opportunely **12** attractively, fastidiously

nicety 4 care, tact **5** flair, grace **6** acumen, polish **7** culture, finesse, insight **8** accuracy, delicacy, elegance, subtlety **9** attention, exactness, precision **10** refinement **11** cultivation, penetration, preciseness, sensitivity **12** perspicacity, subtle detail, tastefulness **13** elaborateness, particularity **14** discrimination, fastidiousness, meticulousness

niche 4 cove, nook, slot **5** berth, trade **6** alcove, cavity, corner, cranny, dugout, hollow, metier, recess **7** calling **8** position, vocation **9** cubby hole **10** depression, pigeon hole **11** proper place **13** hole in the wall

Nicholas Nickleby
author: 14 Charles Dickens
character: 5 Smike **11** Arthur Gride, Newman Noggs **12** Kate Nickleby, Madeline Bray **13** Lord Verisopht, Ralph Nickleby **14** Frank Cheeryble **15** Sir Mulberry Hawk, Vincent Crummles, Wackford Squeers **17** Cheeryble Brothers

Nichols, Mike
Wife: 11 Diane Sawyer

director of: 7 Catch-22 **11** The Birdcage, The Graduate (Oscar) **15** Carnal Knowledge **25** Who's Afraid of Virginia Woolf?

Nicholson, Ben
born: 6 Denham **7** England
artwork: 9 Fireworks **11** White Relief **12** Tuscan Relief **13** Painted Relief **14** At the Chat Botte

Nicholson, Jack
born: 9 Neptune NJ
roles: 4 Wolf **5** Hoffa **6** Batman **8** Ironweed **9** Chinatown, Easy Rider **10** The Shining **11** A Few Good Men, Mars Attacks, The Two Jakes **12** Prizzi's Honor, The Passenger **13** The Last Detail **14** As Good As It Gets (Oscar), Five Easy Pieces **15** Carnal Knowledge **17** Terms of Endearment **20** The Witches of Eastwick **22** The King of Marvin Gardens **25** One Flew Over the Cuckoo's Nest (Oscar) **26** The Postman Always Rings Twice

nicht wahr? 10 isn't that so?

nick 3 cut, jag, mar **4** chip, dent, gash, mark, scar **5** cleft, gouge, notch, score, wound **6** damage, deface, indent, injure, injury **7** marking, scarify, scoring, scratch **8** incision, lacerate **10** depression **11** indentation

nickel
chemical symbol: 2 Ni

Nickel Mountain
author: 11 John Gardner

nickname 6 handle **7** agnomen, epithet, moniker, pet name **8** baby name, cognomen **9** pseudonym, sobriquet **10** diminutive **11** appellation, designation

Nicomachean Ethics
author: 9 Aristotle

Nidhogg
origin: 12 Scandinavian
form: 7 serpent
domain: 8 Niflheim
gnaws on lowest root of: 9 Iggdrasil, Yggdrasil

niello 5 alloy
of: 6 sulfur
with: 4 lead **6** copper, silver
used as: 5 inlay

Nielsen, Carl August
born: 6 Odense **7** Denmark
composer of: 9 Maskarade **12** Saul and David **16** Inextinguishable (symphony No 4)

Nietzsche, Friedrich
author of: 14 The Will to Power **17** Beyond Good and Evil, The Birth of Tragedy **20** Thus Spake Zarathustra

Niflheim
origin: 12 Scandinavian
ruler of: 3 Hel
purpose: 10 punish dead
climate: 3 fog **4** cold **8** darkness

nifty 4 chic, fine, neat, posh **5** natty, smart **6** clever, dapper **7** dashing, stylish **8** splendid **10** attractive **11** fashionable

Niger
 other name: 6 Joliba, Kworra, Ramtil
 capital/largest city: 6 Niamey
 others: 5 Goure **6** Agadex, Agadez, Maradi, Tahoua, Zinder
 division:
  region: 3 Air **5** Arlit, Sahel
 monetary unit: 5 franc **7** centime
 lake: 4 Chad
 mountain: 7 Bagzane **9** Air Massif
 highest point: 7 Greboun
 river: 5 Niger **6** Dillia
 physical feature:
  desert: 6 Sahara
  oasis: 6 Kaouar
  plateau: 5 Djado **6** Tegama **7** Tchigai **8** Mengueni **11** Adar Doutchi, Djerma Ganda
  people: 4 Daza, Idjo, Idyo, Idzo, Peul, Teda **5** Hausa, Warri **6** Djerma, Fulani, Kanuri, Songha, Toubou, Tuareg **13** Djerma-Songhai
   conqueror: 13 Usman Dan Fodio
   leader: 5 Diori **6** Saibou **7** Ousmane **8** Kountche
  language: 5 Hausa, Mande **6** Djerma, French, Fulani, Tuareg **8** Mandingo, Tamashek
  religion: 5 Islam **7** animism **12** Christianity
  place:
   ruins: 6 Agadez
  feature:
   cavalry: 5 Dosso
   empire: 4 Mali **6** Fulani **7** Songhai **10** Kanem-Borno
   tree: 6 acacia, baobab

Nigeria
 capital: 5 Abuja
 largest city: 5 Lagos
 new capital: 5 Abuja
 others: 3 Aba, Ado, Ede, Isa, Iwo, Jos, Oyo **4** Bida, Bidi, Buea, Kano, Offa, Yola **5** Benin, Bonny, Enugu, Warri, Zaria **6** Burutu, Ibadan, Ilesha, Ilorin, Kachia, Kaduna, Kadune, Kokoto, Mushin, Takoba **7** Calabar, Onitsha, Oshogbo **8** Abeokuta **9** Maiduguri, Ogbomosho **12** Port Harcourt
 division: 3 Air, Isa, Oyo **4** Kano, Nupe, Ondo **5** Asben, Benin, Bornu, Ijebu, Ogoja, Warri **6** Biafra, Degema, Owerri, Sokoto **7** Adamawa
 monetary unit: 4 kobo **5** naira
 lake: 4 Chad
 highest point: 7 Dimlang
 river: 3 Oli **4** Gana, Yobe **5** Benin, Benue, Cross, Niger **6** Kaduna, Sokoto **7** Calabar, Gongola **8** Komadugu **9** Sambreiro
 sea: 8 Atlantic
 physical feature:
  bight: 5 Benin, Bonny **6** Biafra
  delta: 5 Niger
  gulf: 6 Guinea
  plains: 5 Bornu **9** Hausaland

plateau: 3 Jos, Udi **6** Bauchi
 port: 5 Lagos **7** Calabar **8** Harcourt
 people: 3 Abo, Aro, Djo, Ebo, Edo, Ibo, Ijo, Tiv, Vai **4** Beni, Bini, Eboe, Efik, Egba, Ejam, Ekoi, Idyo, Igbo, Ijaw, Nupe **5** Angas, Benin, Gwari, Hausa **6** Chamba, Fulani, Ibibio, Kanuri, Yoruba **11** Hausa-Fulani
  author: 6 Achebe
  British colonial ruler: 6 Goldie, Lugard
  kingdom: 3 Ife, Nok, Oyo **5** Benin **6** Fulani **10** Kanem-Borno
  leader: 5 Gowon **6** Balewa, Ojukwu, Schick **7** Awolowo, Azikine, Azikiwe, Shagari **8** Obasanjo **9** Babangida **13** Usman dan Fodio
 language: 3 Ibo **4** Efik, Igbo **5** Hausa **6** Yoruba **7** English
 religion: 5 Islam **7** animism **12** Christianity
 place:
  dam: 6 Kainji
  mosque/walled city: 4 Kano
 feature:
  dress: 4 riga **7** agbados
  tree: 5 abura, afara **6** obeche **10** terminalia
  war: 7 Biafran

niggard 4 mean **5** cheap, miser, tight **6** stingy **7** miserly **8** scrimper **9** skinflint **10** ungenerous **12** parsimonious

niggardliness 6 penury **8** meanness **9** closeness, parsimony **10** stinginess **11** miserliness **13** penny-pinching **15** tight-fistedness

niggardly 4 mean, poor **5** cheap, close, sorry, tight **6** flimsy, frugal, meager, measly, paltry, saving, scanty, shabby, stingy, tawdry **7** miserly, scrubby, sparing, thrifty **8** beggarly, grubbing, grudging, stinting, wretched **9** illiberal, mercenary, miserable, penurious **10** hardfisted, second-rate, ungenerous **11** closefisted **12** contemptible, insufficient, parsimonious

niggling 5 fussy, minor, petty, small **7** finicky **8** caviling, nugatory, picayune, piddling, trifling **9** quibbling **10** negligible, nit-picking **12** pettifogging **13** insignificant **15** inconsequential

nigh 4 near **5** close, handy **6** almost, at hand, nearly **7** close by **8** adjacent **9** bordering **11** neighboring, practically

night 4 dark, dusk **7** bedtime, evening, sundown **8** darkness, eventide **9** murkiness, obscurity **13** tenebrousness
 goddess of: 3 Nox

nightclub
 French: 5 boite **11** boite de nuit

nightfall 4 dark, dusk **6** sunset **7** evening, sundown **8** darkness, eventide, gloaming, moonrise, twilight
 French: 10 crepuscule

Night Gallery
 host: 10 Rod Serling

Nightingale, Florence
 birthplace: 7 England
 worked in: 10 Crimean War
 founded: 13 modern nursing
 nickname: 18 The Lady with the Lamp
 first woman to receive: 12 Order of Merit

nightingale
 group of: 5 watch

Nightline
 host: 9 Ted Koppel

nightly 4 dark **7** evening, obscure **9** nocturnal **11** nocturnally

nightmare 7 incubus **8** bad dream, succubus **13** hallucination

Night of the Iguana, The
 director: 10 John Huston
 based on play by: 17 Tennessee Williams
 cast: 7 Sue Lyon **8** Skip Ward **10** Ava Gardner **11** Deborah Kerr **13** Richard Burton
 setting: 6 Mexico

nightshade 16 Solanum dulcamara
 varieties: 4 ball **5** black **6** common, deadly, sticky **7** Malabar **8** stinking **9** melon-leaf, poisonous, soda-apple **10** enchanter's

Nights of Cabiria
 director: 15 Federico Fellini
 cast: 13 Amedeo Nazzari **14** Francois Perier **15** Giulietta Masina
 remade as: 12 Sweet Charity

nightstick 3 rod **4** mace, wand **5** baton, staff **6** cudgel **7** scepter **8** bludgeon **9** billy club, truncheon **10** shillelagh

nighttime 4 late **5** night **9** late-night, nighttide, nocturnal

Night to Remember, A
 director: 8 Roy Baker
 based on story by: 10 Walter Lord
 cast: 9 Jill Dixon **11** Kenneth More **13** David McCallum **16** Laurence Naismith
 setting: 7 Titanic

nihil 7 nothing

nihilism 5 chaos **6** anomie **7** license **9** amorality, anarchism, emptiness, terrorism **10** alienation, iconoclasm, radicalism, skepticism **11** agnosticism, lawlessness, nothingness **12** nonexistence **16** irresponsibility

nihilist 5 rebel **9** anarchist, terrorist **13** revolutionary

Nihon *see* **5** Japan

Nike
 origin: 5 Greek
 goddess of: 7 victory
 father: 11 Titan Pallas
 mother: 4 Styx
 brother: 5 Zelos
 corresponds to: 6 Athena **8** Victoria

nil 4 none, null, zero **6** cipher, naught **7** nothing, nullity **11** nonexistent

Nile
  boat: 5 baris **6** cangia, nuggar, sandal **7** felucca, gaiassa **8** dahabeah
  cities: 3 Qus **4** Abri, Argo, Idfu, Isna, Juba, Qina **5** Aswan, Asyut, Cairo, Kokka, Kusti, Luxor, Meroe, Minya, Rejaf, Saite, Tanis, Tanta **6** Atbara, Faiyum **7** Malakel, Mansura, Rosetta **8** Khartoum, Omdurman, Rusayris **9** Was Madani **10** Alexandria
  dam: 6 Sannar **9** Aswan High, White Nile
  desert bordering: 6 Libyan, Nubian **7** Arabian
  falls: 5 Ripon **8** Kabalega **9** Murchison
  feature: 6 Sphinx
    pyramid: 4 Giza
    temple: 8 Ramses II **9** Abu Simbel **11** Deir el-Bahri, Medinet Habu
  flows into: 13 Mediterranean
  flows through: 5 Egypt, Kenya, Sudan, Zaire **6** Rwanda, Uganda **7** Burundi **8** Ethiopia, Tanzania
  island: 4 Roda **6** Philae
  lake: 4 Tana **5** Kyoga, Tsana **6** Albert, Edward, Nasser **8** Victoria
  other name: 4 Hapi **20** The Father of the Rivers
  people: 3 Jur, Luo, Lwo, Nuo, Suk **4** Bari, Beja, Golo, Luoh, Madi **5** Nilot **7** Shilluk
  plain: 6 Gezira
  plant: 4 sudd **5** lotus
  starting point: 5 Tsana **8** Victoria
  swamp: 4 Sudd
  tributary: 4 Arab **5** Rahad, Sobat **6** Atbara, Ghazai, Kagera **7** Rosetta **8** Blue Nile, Damietta **9** Bahr Jebel, White Nile

Niles, Hazel and Peter
  characters in: 22 Mourning Becomes Electra
  author: 6 O'Neill

nil nisi bonum 21 nothing unless it is good

nil sine numine 27 nothing without the divine will
  motto of: 8 Colorado

nimble 4 deft, spry **5** agile, fleet, light, quick, rapid, ready, swift **6** active, expert, lively, prompt, speedy, supple **8** animated, skillful, spirited **9** dexterous, mercurial, sprightly **10** proficient

nimbleness 7 agility **8** alacrity, spryness **9** dexterity, quickness **10** limberness, suppleness

nimble-witted 5 droll, witty **6** clever **11** resourceful

nimbus 4 aura, disk, halo **5** cloud, vapor **7** aureole **8** radiance

Nimitz, Chester
  served in: 3 WWI **4** WWII
  commander of: 12 Pacific fleet
  rank: 12 fleet (five-star) admiral

22 chief of naval operations
  battle: 6 Midway **9** Leyte Gulf **13** Philippine Sea

Nimoy, Leonard
  born: 8 Boston MA
  films: 7 Mr Spock **8** Star Trek **14** Funny About Love **16** Three men and a Baby **17** Mission: Impossible **21** Star Trek: The Voyage Home **22** Star Trek: The Wrath of Khan **24** Star Trek: The Final Frontier **25** Star Trek: The Search for Spock

Nimrod
  father: 4 Cush
  grandfather: 3 Ham
  great grandfather: 4 Noah
  founded: 5 Accad, Calah, Resen **7** Nineveh **8** Rehoboth
  famed as: 6 hunter

nincompoop 4 boob, dolt, dope, fool, jerk **5** dummy, dunce, idiot, klutz, moron, ninny **6** dimwit, lummox, nitwit **7** half-wit, jackass **8** bonehead, dummkopf, imbecile, lunkhead, numskull **9** blockhead, dumb bunny, harebrain, numbskull, simpleton **10** dunderhead, dunderpate, muddlehead, noodlehead **11** knucklehead, rattlebrain **12** featherbrain, scatterbrain

Nine, the *see* **5** Muses

Nineteen Eighty-Four
  author: 12 George Orwell
  character: 4 Syme **5** Julia **6** O'Brien **11** Charrington **12** Winston Smith

1919
  author: 13 John Dos Passos

Ninety-Five Theses
  author: 12 Martin Luther

Nineveh
  founder: 6 Nimrod

Nine worthies
  mentioned in: 16 medieval romances
  three each of: 4 Jews **6** Pagans **10** Christians
  names: 5 David **6** Arthur, Hector, Joshua **11** Charlemagne **12** Julius Caesar **15** Judas Maccabaeus **17** Alexander the Great **18** Godefroy de Bouillon

ninny 3 ass, sap **4** fool, simp **5** booby, dunce, idiot, moron **6** dimwit, nitwit **7** fathead, half-wit **8** bonehead, dumb-dumb, imbecile, lunkhead, numskull **9** blockhead, dumb bunny, lamebrain, numbskull **10** dunderhead, nincompoop **11** chowderhead

Ninotchka
  director: 13 Ernst Lubitsch
  cast: 9 Ina Claire **10** Bela Lugosi, Greta Garbo **13** Melvyn Douglas
  setting: 5 Paris
  remade as: 13 Silk Stockings

Ninurta
  also: 5 Ninib
  origin: 8 Sumerian **10** Babylonian
  type of god: 4 hero
  personifies: 4 wind **9** south wind

  father: 5 Enlil
  avenger of: 5 Enlil

Ninus
  wife: 9 Semiramis
  founder of: 7 Nineveh

Niobe
  father: 8 Tantalus
  mother: 5 Dione
  brother: 6 Pelops
  husband: 7 Amphion
  children: 9 seven sons **14** seven daughters
  children called: 6 Niobid
  taunted: 4 Leto
  children killed by: 6 Apollo **7** Artemis
  changed into: 5 stone
  changed by: 4 Zeus

Niord
  also: 5 Njord
  origin: 12 Scandinavian
  god of: 4 wind **10** navigation, prosperity
  king of: 5 Vanir
  son: 4 Frey **5** Freyr
  daughter: 5 Freia, Freya

nip 3 cut, lop **4** bite, clip, crop, dock, grab, grip, ruin, snag, snap, snip **5** blast, check, chill, clamp, clasp, crack, crush, frost, grasp, pinch, quash, seize, sever, shear, snare, tweak **6** benumb, clutch, cut off, freeze, pierce, snatch, sunder, thwart **7** curtail, destroy, shorten, squeeze **8** compress, cut short, demolish **9** frustrate **10** abbreviate

nip-and-tuck 5 close

nip in the bud 7 prevent **8** preclude **9** forestall, frustrate

Nipper, Susan
  character in: 12 Dombey and Son
  author: 7 Dickens

Nippon *see* **5** Japan

nippy 3 raw **5** brisk, chill, crisp, sharp **6** biting, chilly **7** cutting

nit-pick 4 carp, pick **5** cavil **9** criticize

nitrate 4 salt **5** ester **6** sodium **9** potassium **10** fertilizer

nitrogen
  chemical symbol: 1 N

nitty-gritty 4 core, crux, gist, meat, pith **5** heart **7** essence **9** substance

nitwit 3 ass **4** clod, dolt, fool **5** booby, dummy, dunce, idiot, klutz, moron, ninny **7** fathead, pinhead **8** bonehead, dumb-dumb, imbecile, lunkhead, meathead, numskull, peabrain **9** birdbrain, blockhead, lamebrain, numbskull **10** dunderhead, nincompoop, noodlehead **11** chowderhead

Niven, David
  real name: 21 James David Graham Niven
  autobiography: 16 The Moon's a Balloon **21** Bring on the Empty Horses
  born: 8 Scotland **10** Kirriemuir

roles: 11 Phileas Fogg **12** Casino Royale, My Man Godfrey **14** The Pink Panther, Separate Tables (Oscar) **16** Stairway to Heaven, Wuthering Heights **18** The Prisoner of Zenda **26** Around the World in Eighty Days

Nix, nixie
origin: 8 Germanic
form: 6 spirit
habitat: 5 water

Nixon, Richard Milhous
presidential rank: 13 thirty-seventh
party: 10 Republican
state represented: 2 CA
defeated: 7 (George Corley) Wallace **8** (Hubert Horatio) Humphrey
vice president: 4 (Gerald Rudolph) Ford **5** (Spiro Theodore) Agnew
cabinet:
  state: 6 (William Pierce) Rogers **9** (Henry A) Kissinger
  treasury: 5 (William E) Simon **6** (George P) Shultz **7** (David Matthew) Kennedy **8** (John Bowden) Connally
  defense: 5 (Melvin Robert) Laird **10** (Elliot L) Richardson **11** (James R) Schlesinger
  attorney general: 5 (William B) Saxbe **8** (John Newton) Mitchell **10** (Elliot L) Richardson **11** (Richard G) Kleindienst
  postmaster general: 6 (Winton Malcolm) Blount
  interior: 6 (Rogers Clark Ballard) Morton, (Walter Joseph) Hinkel
  agriculture: 4 (Earl Lauer) Butz **6** (Clifford Morris) Hardin
  commerce: 4 (Frederick B) Dent **5** (Maurice Hubert) Stans
  labor: 6 (George Pratt) Shultz **7** (James Day) Hodgson, (Peter J) Brennan
  HEW: 5 (Robert Hutchinson) Finch **10** (Caspar W) Weinberger, (Elliot Lee) Richardson
  HUD: 4 (James T) Lynn **6** (George Wilcken) Romney
  transportation: 5 (John Anthony) Volpe **8** (Claude S) Brinegar
born: 2 CA **10** Yorba Linda
died: 7 New York **11** New York City
education:
  college: 8 Whittier
  law school: 14 Duke University
religion: 6 Quaker **16** Society of Friends
interests: 8 football
vacation spot: 11 Key Biscayne (FL), San Clemente (CA)
dog: 8 Checkers **11** King Timahoe
author: 9 Six Crises **10** The Real War **11** Beyond Peace **27** RN: The Memoirs of Richard Nixon
political career: 8 US Senate **13** Vice President **24** US House of Representatives
civilian career: 6 lawyer

military service: 6 US Navy **10** lieutenant, World War II
notable events of lifetime/term:
  Calley court martialed for: 13 Mylai Massacre
  court martial of: 6 Calley
  creation of: 10 Bangladesh
  crisis: 3 oil **6** energy
  embargo on: 3 oil
  first men on: 4 moon
  incident: 11 Wounded Knee
  pardon of Nixon by: 4 Ford
  publication of: 14 Pentagon Papers
  resignation of: 5 Agnew, Nixon
  scandal: 9 Watergate
  student deaths at: 9 Kent State
  treaty: 10 Seabed Arms **32** Non-proliferation of Nuclear Weapons
  trip to: 5 China
  war: 7 Vietnam **10** Middle East **12** East Pakistan
quotes: 31 A respectable Republican cloth coat **35** You won't have Nixon to kick around any more
father: 14 Francis Anthony
mother: 6 Hannah (Milhous)
siblings: 11 Arthur Burdg **12** Harold Samuel **13** Edward Calvert, Francis Donald
wife: 8 (Thelma Catherine) Patricia (Ryan)
  nickname: 3 Pat
children: 5 Julie **8** Patricia
  Julie married: 15 David Eisenhower
  Patricia married: 9 Edward Cox
  Patricia's nickname: 6 Tricia

Njord *see* **5** Niord

no 3 nay, nix, not **4** none, veto
French: 3 non
German: 4 nein
Spanish: 2 no
Italian: 2 no
Russian: 4 nyet

Noah
father: 6 Lamech
grandfather: 10 Methuselah
son: 3 Ham **4** Shem **7** Japheth
grandson: 3 Put **4** Cush **6** Canaan **7** Misraim
great grandson: 6 Nimrod
built: 3 ark
collected: 5 pairs **7** animals
survived: 5 flood
pertaining to: 8 Noachian

Noah's Ark
made of: 10 gopherwood
landfall: 6 Ararat

nob 4 peer, toff **5** swell **9** patrician **10** aristocrat

Nobel, Alfred
nationality: 7 Swedish
invented: 8 dynamite
originated: 10 Nobel Prize

Nobel Prizes
Literature:
  1901: 20 Rene F A Sully-Prudhomme
  1902: 14 Theodor Mommsen
  1903: 20 Bjornstjerne Bjornson
  1904: 13 Jose Echegaray **15** Frederic Mistral
  1905: 17 Henryk Sienkiewicz
  1906: 14 Giosue Carducci
  1907: 14 Rudyard Kipling
  1908: 13 Rudolf C Eucken
  1909: 13 Selma Lagerlof
  1910: 12 Paul von Heyse
  1911: 18 Maurice Maeterlinck
  1912: 16 Gerhart Hauptmann
  1913: 21 Sir Rabindranath Tagore
  1915: 13 Romain Rolland
  1916: 19 Verner von Heidenstam
  1917: 11 K A Gjellerup **17** Henrik Pontoppidan
  1919: 15 Carl F G Spitteler
  1920: 10 Knut Hamsun
  1921: 13 Anatole France
  1922: 25 Jacinto Benavente y Martinez
  1923: 18 William Butler Yeats
  1924: 17 Wladyslaw S Reymont
  1925: 17 George Bernard Shaw
  1926: 13 Grazia Deledda
  1927: 13 Henri Bergson
  1928: 12 Sigrid Undset
  1929: 10 Thomas Mann
  1930: 13 Sinclair Lewis
  1931: 14 Erik A Karlfeldt
  1932: 10 John Galsworthy
  1933: 10 Ivan A Bunin
  1934: 15 Luigi Pirandello
  1936: 12 Eugene O'Neill
  1937: 17 Roger Martin du Gard
  1938: 10 Pearl S Buck
  1939: 15 Frans E Sillanpaa
  1944: 15 Johannes V Jensen
  1945: 15 Gabriela Mistral
  1946: 12 Hermann Hesse
  1947: 9 Andre Gide
  1948: 7 T S Eliot
  1949: 15 William Faulkner
  1950: 15 Bertrand Russell (Earl Russell)
  1951: 14 Par F Lagerkvist
  1952: 15 Francois Mauriac
  1953: 21 Sir Winston L S Churchill
  1954: 15 Ernest Hemingway
  1955: 15 Halldor K Laxness
  1956: 16 Juan Ramon Jimenez
  1957: 11 Albert Camus
  1958: 15 Boris L Pasternak
  1959: 18 Salvatore Quasimodo
  1960: 14 Saint-John Perse
  1961: 9 Ivo Andric
  1962: 13 John Steinbeck
  1963: 13 George Seferis
  1964: 14 Jean Paul Sartre
  1965: 17 Mikhail A Sholokhov
  1966: 10 Nelly Sachs **17** Samuel Joseph (Shmuel Y) Agnon
  1967: 19 Miguel Angel Asturias
  1968: 16 Yasunari Kawabata
  1969: 13 Samuel Beckett
  1970: 22 Aleksandr I Solzhenitsyn

1971: 11 Pablo Neruda
1972: 12 Heinrich Boll
1973: 12 Patrick White
1974: 9 Eyvind Johnson **14** Harry Martinson
1975: 14 Eugenio Montale
1976: 10 Saul Bellow
1977: 17 Vicente Aleixandre
1978: 19 Isaac Bashevis Singer
1979: 14 Odysseus Elytis
1980: 13 Czeslaw Milosz
1981: 12 Elias Canetti
1982: 20 Gabriel Garcia Marquez
1983: 14 William Golding
1984: 15 Jaroslav Seifert
1985: 11 Claude Simon
1986: 11 Wole Soyinka
1987: 13 Joseph Brodsky
1988: 13 Naguib Mahfouz
1989: 10 Camilo Cela
1990: 10 Octavio Paz
1991: 12 Nadine Gordimer
1992: 12 Derek Walcott
1993: 12 Toni Morrison
1994: 11 Kenzaburo Oe
1995: 12 Seamus Heaney
1996: 17 Wislawa Szymborska
1997: 7 Dario Fo

Physiology/Medicine:
1901: 15 Emil A von Behring
1902: 13 Sir Ronald Ross
1903: 12 Niels R Finsen
1904: 9 Ivan P Pavlov
1905: 10 Robert Koch
1906: 12 Camillo Golgi **19** Santiago Ramon y Cajal
1907: 16 Charles L A Laveran
1908: 11 Paul Ehrlich **15** Elie Metchnikoff
1909: 11 Emil T Kocher
1910: 14 Albrecht Kossel
1911: 16 Allvar Gullstrand
1912: 12 Alexis Carrel
1913: 14 Charles R Richet
1914: 12 Robert Barany
1919: 11 Jules Bordet
1920: 12 Shack A S Krogh
1922: 12 Otto Meyerhof **14** Archibald V Hill
1923: 13 John J R Macleod **20** Sir Frederick G Banting
1924: 15 Willem Einthoven
1926: 15 Johannes Fibiger
1927: 19 Julius Wagner-Jauregg
1928: 16 Charles J H Nicolle
1929: 13 Christiaan Eijkman **20** Sir Frederick G Hopkins
1930: 15 Karl Landsteiner
1931: 12 Otto H Warburg
1932: 12 Edgar D Adrian **21** Sir Charles Sherrington
1933: 13 Thomas H Morgan
1934: 12 George R Minot **14** George H Whipple, William P Murphy
1935: 11 Hans Spemann
1936: 9 Otto Loewi **13** Sir Henry H Dale

1937: 31 Albert Szent-Gyorgyi von Nagyrapolt
1938: 16 Corneille Heymans
1939: 13 Gerhard Domagk
1943: 9 Henrik Dam **12** Edward A Doisy
1944: 14 Herbert S Gasser, Joseph Erlanger
1945: 14 Ernst B Chain **16** Sir Howard W Florey **19** Sir Alexander Fleming
1946: 14 Hermann J Muller
1947: 9 Carl F Cori **10** Gerty T Cori **16** Bernardo A Houssay
1948: 11 Paul H Muller
1949: 11 Walter R Hess **21** Antonio C de A F Egas Moniz
1950: 12 Philip S Hench **14** Edward C Kendall **16** Tadeus Reichstein
1951: 10 Max Theiler
1952: 14 Selman A Waksman
1953: 13 Fritz A Lipmann, Sir Hans A Krebs
1954: 11 John F Enders **13** Thomas H Weller **17** Frederick C Robbins
1955: 14 Axel H T Theorell
1956: 13 Andre Cournand **15** Werner Forssmann **20** Dickenson W Richards Jr
1957: 11 Daniel Bovet
1958: 12 Edward L Tatum **13** George W Beadle **15** Joshua Lederberg
1959: 11 Severo Ochoa **14** Arthur Kornberg
1960: 13 Peter B Medawar **15** Sir Frank M Burnet
1961: 14 Georg von Bekesy
1962: 12 James D Watson **14** Francis H C Crick **16** Maurice H F Wilkins
1963: 16 Alan Lloyd Hodgkin **18** Sir John Carew Eccles **20** Andrew Fielding Huxley
1964: 11 Feodor Lynen **12** Konrad E Bloch
1965: 10 Andre Lwoff **12** Jacques Monod **13** Francois Jacob
1966: 17 Francis Peyton Rous **21** Charles Brenton Huggins
1967: 10 George Wald **12** Ragnar Granit **20** Haldan Keffer Hartline
1968: 13 Robert W Holley **14** H Gobind Khorana **18** Marshall W Nirenberg
1969: 11 Max Delbruck **14** Alfred D Hershey, Salvador E Luria
1970: 11 Ulf von Euler **13** Julius Axelrod **14** Sir Bernard Katz
1971: 17 Earl W Sutherland Jr
1972: 13 Rodney R Porter **14** Gerald M Edelman
1973: 12 Konrad Lorenz **13** Karl von Frisch **17** Nikolaas Tinbergen
1974: 12 Albert Claude **15** Christian de Duve **16** George Emil-Palade
1975: 12 Howard M Temin **14** Da-

vid Baltimore, Renato Dulbecco
1976: 15 Baruch S Blumberg **22** Daniel Carleton Gajdusek
1977: 13 Andrew Schally, Rosalyn S Yalow **14** Roger Guillemin
1978: 11 Werner Arber **13** Daniel Nathans, Hamilton Smith
1979: 13 Allan M Cormack **17** Godfrey Hounsfield
1980: 11 Jean Dausset **12** George D Snell **15** Baruj Benacerraf
1981: 11 David H Hubel **12** Roger W Sperry **14** Torsten N Wiesel
1982: 9 John R Vane **15** Bengt Samuelsson **17** Sune Karl Bergstrom
1983: 17 Barbara McClintock
1984: 11 Niels K Jerne **13** Cesar Milstein **16** Georges J F Koehler
1985: 13 Michael S Brown **16** Joseph L Goldstein
1986: 12 Stanley Cohen **18** Rita Levi-Montalcini
1987: 14 Susumu Tonegawa
1988: 10 James Black **14** Gertrube B Elion **16** George H Hitchings
1989: 12 Harold Varmas **14** J Michael Bishop
1990: 12 Joseph Murray **14** E Donnall Thomas
1991: 10 Edwin Neher **11** Bert Sakmann
1992: 10 Edwin Krebs **12** Edmond Fisher
1993: 12 Phillip Sharp **14** Richard Roberts
1994: 12 Alfred Gilman **13** Martin Rodbell
1995: 12 Edward B Lewis **14** Eric F Wieschaus
1996: 13 Peter C Doherty **16** Rolf M Ziwkernagel
1997: 16 Stanley B. Prusiner

Chemistry:
1901: 16 Jacobus H van't Hoff
1902: 11 Emil Fischer
1903: 16 Svante A Arrhenius
1904: 16 Sir William Ramsay
1905: 17 J F W Adolf von Baeyer
1906: 12 Henri Moissan
1907: 13 Eduard Buchner
1908: 19 Sir Ernest Rutherford
1909: 14 Wilhelm Ostwald
1910: 11 Otto Wallach
1911: 11 Marie S Curie
1912: 12 Paul Sabatier **14** Victor Grignard
1913: 12 Alfred Werner
1914: 17 Theodore W Richards
1915: 18 Richard Willstatter
1918: 10 Fritz Haber
1920: 13 Walther Nernst
1921: 14 Frederick Soddy
1922: 13 Francis W Aston
1923: 10 Fritz Pregl
1925: 16 Richard Zsigmondy
1926: 15 Theodor Svedberg
1927: 15 Heinrich Wieland

1928: 12 Adolf Windaus
1929: 15 Sir Arthur Harden **19** Hans von Euler-Chelpin
1930: 11 Hans Fischer
1931: 9 Carl Bosch **16** Friedrich Bergius
1932: 14 Irving Langmuir
1934: 11 Harold C Urey
1935: 16 Irene Joliot-Curie **19** Frederic Joliot-Curie
1936: 12 Peter J W Debye
1937: 10 Paul Karrer **17** Sir Walter N Haworth
1938: 11 Richard Kuhn
1939: 14 Adolf Butenandt, Leopold Ruzicka
1943: 14 Georg von Hevesy
1944: 8 Otto Hahn
1945: 16 Artturi I Virtanen
1946: 12 James B Sumner **13** John H Northrop **15** Wendell M Stanley
1947: 17 Sir Robert Robinson
1948: 12 Arne Tiselius
1949: 15 William F Giauque
1950: 9 Kurt Alder, Otto Diels
1951: 13 Glenn T Seaborg **14** Edwin M McMillan
1952: 14 Archer J P Martin, Richard L M Synge
1953: 17 Hermann Staudinger
1954: 13 Linus C Pauling
1955: 17 Vincent du Vigneaud
1956: 15 Nikolai N Semenov **20** Sir Cyril N Hinshelwood
1957: 17 Sir Alexander R Todd (Baron Todd)
1958: 15 Frederick Sanger
1959: 17 Jaroslav Heyrovsky
1960: 13 Willard F Libby
1961: 12 Melvin Calvin
1962: 10 Max F Perutz **12** John C Kendrew
1963: 11 Giulio Natta, Karl Ziegler
1964: 26 Dorothy Mary Crowfoot Hodgkin
1965: 19 Robert Burns Woodward
1966: 15 Robert S Mulliken
1967: 12 Manfred Eigen **15** Sir George Porter **27** Ronald George Wreyford Norrish
1968: 11 Lars Onsager
1969: 9 Odd Hassel **13** Derek H R Barton
1970: 18 Luis Federico Leloir
1971: 15 Gerhard Herzberg
1972: 13 Stanford Moore **18** Christian B Anfinsen, William Howard Stein
1973: 16 Ernst Otto Fischer **17** Geoffrey Wilkinson
1974: 10 Paul J Flory
1975: 14 John W Cornforth, Vladimir Prelog
1976: 16 William N Lipscomb
1977: 13 Ilya Prigogine
1978: 13 Peter Mitchell
1979: 11 Georg Wittig **13** Herbert C Brown

1980: 8 Paul Berg **13** Walter Gilbert **15** Frederick Sanger
1981: 12 Kenichi Fukui **13** Roald Hoffmann
1982: 9 Aaron Klug
1983: 10 Henry Taube
1984: 21 Robert Bruce Merrifield
1985: 11 Jerome Karle **16** Herbert A Hauptman
1986: 8 Yuan T Lee **12** John C Polanyi **16** Dudley Herschbach
1987: 11 Donald J Cram **16** Charles J Pederson
1988: 11 Robert Huber **13** Hartmut Michel **17** Johann Deisenhofer
1989: 10 Thomas Cich **12** Sidney Altman
1990: 10 Elias Corey
1991: 12 Richard Ernst
1992: 13 Rudolph Marcus
1993: 10 Kary Mullis **12** Michael Smith
1994: 10 George Olah
1995: 11 Paul Crutzen, Mario Molina **16** F Sherwood Rowland
1996: 11 Robert F Curl **15** Richard E Smalley, Sir Harold W Kroto
1997: 9 Jens C Skou **10** Paul D Boyer **11** John E Walker

Physics:
1901: 16 Wilhelm K Roentgen
1902: 16 Pieter Zeeman **15** Hendrik A Lorentz
1903: 11 Marie S Curie, Pierre Curie **15** A Henri Becquerel
1904: 11 John W Strutt (Lord Rayleigh)
1905: 13 Philipp Lenard
1906: 16 Sir Joseph Thomson
1907: 16 Albert A Michelson
1908: 15 Gabriel Lippmann
1909: 10 Karl F Braun **16** Guglielmo Marconi
1910: 22 Johannes D van der Waals
1911: 11 Wilhelm Wien
1912: 10 Nils G Dalen
1913: 20 Heike Kamerlingh Onnes
1914: 10 Max von Laue
1915: 16 Sir William H Bragg, Sir William L Bragg
1917: 14 Charles B Barkla
1918: 9 Max Planck
1919: 13 Johannes Stark
1920: 17 Charles E Guillaume
1921: 14 Albert Einstein
1922: 10 Nils H D Bohr
1923: 15 Robert A Millikan
1924: 14 Karl M G Siegbahn
1925: 11 Gustav Hertz, James Franck
1926: 11 Jean B Perrin
1927: 14 Arthur H Compton **15** Charles T R Wilson
1928: 18 Sir Owen W Richardson
1929: 15 Louis V de Broglie
1930: 23 Sir Chandrasekhara V Raman

1932: 16 Werner Heisenberg
1933: 11 Paul A M Dirac **16** Erwin Schrodinger
1935: 16 Sir James Chadwick
1936: 11 Victor F Hess **13** Carl D Anderson
1937: 16 Clinton J Davisson **17** Sir George P Thomson
1938: 11 Enrico Fermi
1939: 15 Ernest O Lawrence
1943: 9 Otto Stern
1944: 11 Isidor I Rabi
1945: 13 Wolfgang Pauli
1946: 14 Percy W Bridgman
1947: 11 Sir Edward V Appleton
1948: 17 Patrick M S Blackett
1949: 12 Hideki Yukawa
1950: 12 Cecil F Powell
1951: 14 Ernest T S Walton **17** Sir John D Cockcroft
1952: 14 Felix Bloch **14** Edward M Purcell
1953: 12 Frits Zernike
1954: 7 Max Born **12** Walther Bothe
1955: 13 Polykarp Kusch, Willis E Lamb Jr
1956: 11 John Bardeen **15** Walter H Brattain **16** William B Shockley
1957: 11 Tsung Dao Lee **12** Chen Ning Yang
1958: 9 Igor Y Tamm **10** Ilya M Frank **15** Pavel A Cherenkov
1959: 11 Emilio Segre **15** Owen Chamberlain
1960: 13 Donald A Glaser
1961: 16 Robert Hofstadter, Rudolf L Mossbauer
1962: 10 Lev D Landau
1963: 11 J Hans Jensen **16** Eugene Paul Wigner **18** Maria Goeppert Mayer
1964: 17 Charles Hard Townes **25** Nikolai Gennadiyevich Basov **30** Aleksandr Mikhailovich Prokhorov
1965: 18 Shinichiro Tomonaga **22** Julian Seymour Schwinger, Richard Phillips Feynman
1966: 13 Alfred Kastler
1967: 17 Hans Albrecht Bethe
1968: 12 Luis W Alvarez
1969: 14 Murray Gell-Mann
1970: 12 Hannes Alfven **15** Louis Eugene Neel
1971: 11 Dennis Gabor
1972: 11 John Bardeen, Leon N Cooper **20** John Robert Schreiffer
1973: 8 Leo Esaki **11** Ivar Giaever **15** Brian D Josephson
1974: 12 Antony Hewish **13** Sir Martin Ryle
1975: 8 Aage Bohr **13** Ben R Mottelson **15** L James Rainwater
1976: 12 Samuel C C Ting **13** Burton Richter
1977: 13 John H Van Vleck, Sir Nevill Mott **15** Philip W Anderson
1978: 12 Arno A Penzias, Peter

Kapitza (Pyotr Kapitsa) **13** Robert W Wilson
1979: 10 Abdus Salam **14** Sheldon Glashow, Steven Weinberg
1980: 9 Val L Fitch **12** James W Cronin
1981: 12 Kai M Siegbahn **14** Arthur Schawlow **19** Nicolaas Bloembergen
1982: 14 Kenneth G Wilson
1983: 14 William A Fowler **25** Subrahmanyan Chandrasekhar
1984: 11 Carlo Rubbia **15** Simon van der Meer
1985: 16 Klaus von Klitzing
1986: 10 Ernst Ruska, Gerd Binner **14** Heinrich Rohrer
1987: 12 K Alex Mueller **13** J Georg Bednorz
1988: 13 Leon M Lederman **14** Melvin Schwartz **15** Jack Steinberger
1989: 11 Hans Dehmelt **12** Norman Ramsey, Wolfgang Paul
1990: 12 Henry Kendall **13** Richard Taylor **14** Jerome Friedman
1991: 12 Pierre Gennes
1992: 13 George Charpak
1993: 12 Joseph Taylor, Russell Hulse
1994: 13 Clifford Shull **17** Bertram Brockhouse
1995: 11 Martin l Perl **15** Frederick Reines
1996: 9 David M Lee **16** Douglas D Osheroff **17** Robert C Richardson
1997: 9 Steven Chu **16** William D Phillips **20** Claude Cohen-Tannoudji
Peace:
1901: 13 Frederic Passy **15** Jean Henri Dunant
1902: 12 Elie Ducommun **18** Charles Albert Gobat
1903: 17 Sir William R Cremer
1904: 27 Institute of International Law
1905: 24 Baroness Bertha von Suttner
1906: 17 Theodore Roosevelt
1907: 12 Louis Renault **14** Ernesto T Moneta
1908: 12 Fredrik Bajer **14** Klas P Arnoldson
1909: 16 Auguste Beernaert **35** Paul H Balluat d'Estournelles de Constant
1910: 24 International Peace Bureau
1911: 12 Alfred H Fried **13** Tobias M C Asser
1912: 9 Elihu Root
1913: 15 Henri La Fontaine
1917: 30 International Red Cross Committee
1919: 13 Woodrow Wilson
1920: 13 Leon Bourgeois
1921: 15 Christian L Lange **19** Karl Hjalmar Branting

1922: 14 Fridtjof Nansen
1925: 13 Charles G Dawes **26** Sir Joseph Austen Chamberlain
1926: 14 Aristide Briand **16** Gustav Stresemann
1927: 12 Ludwig Quidde **17** Ferdinand E Buisson
1929: 14 Frank B Kellogg
1930: 15 (Lars Olof Jonathan) Nathan Soderblom
1931: 10 Jane Addams **20** Nicholas Murray Butler
1933: 15 Sir Norman Angell
1934: 15 Arthur Henderson
1935: 16 Carl von Ossietzky
1936: 19 Carlos Saavedra Lamas
1937: 13 E A Robert Cecil (Viscount Cecil)
1938: 36 Nansen International Office for Refugees
1944: 30 International Red Cross Committee
1945: 11 Cordell Hull
1946: 9 John R Mott **11** Emily G Balch
1947: 21 Friends Service Council **31** American Friends Service Committee
1949: 11 John Boyd Orr (Baron Orr)
1950: 12 Ralph J Bunche
1951: 11 Leon Jouhaux
1952: 16 Albert Schweitzer
1953: 15 George C Marshall
1954: 51 Office of the United Nations High Commissioner for Refugees
1957: 14 Lester B Pearson
1958: 28 Rev Dominique Georges Henri Pire
1959: 16 Philip J Noel-Baker
1960: 14 Albert J Luthuli
1961: 15 Dag Hammarskjold
1962: 13 Linus C Pauling
1963: 25 League of Red Cross Societies **30** International Red Cross Committee
1964: 18 Martin Luther King Jr
1965: 26 United Nations Children's Fund (UNICEF)
1968: 10 Rene Cassin
1969: 30 International Labor Organization (ILO)
1970: 14 Norman E Borlaug
1971: 11 Willy Brandt
1973: 8 Le Duc Tho **15** Henry A Kissinger
1974: 10 Eisaku Sato **12** Sean MacBride
1975: 15 Andrei D Sakharov
1976: 13 Betty Williams **15** Mairead Corrigan
1977: 20 Amnesty International
1978: 10 Anwar Sadat **13** Menachem Begin
1979: 12 Mother Teresa
1980: 19 Adolfo Perez Esquivel
1981: 51 Office of the United Na-

tions High Commissioner for Refugees
1982: 10 Alva Myrdal **19** Alfonso Garcia Robles
1983: 10 Lech Walesa
1984: 17 Bishop Desmond Tutu
1985: 51 International Physicians for the Prevention of Nuclear War
1986: 10 Elie Wiesel
1987: 17 Oscar Arias Sanchez
1988: 31 United Nations peacekeeping troops
1989: 9 Dalai Lama
1990: 16 Mikhail Gorbachev
1991: 13 Aung San Suu Kyi
1992: 15 Rigoberta Menchu
1993: 9 F W de Klerk **13** Nelson Mandela
1994: 11 Yasir Arafat, Shimon Peres **12** Yitzhak Rabin
1995: 13 Joseph Rotblat
1996: 14 Jose Ramos Horta **23** Carlos Filepe, Ximenes Belo
1997: 12 Jody Williams
Economics:
1969: 12 Jan Tinbergen, Ragnar Frisch
1970: 14 Paul A Samuelson
1971: 13 Simon S Kuznets
1972: 13 Kenneth J Arrow, Sir John R Hicks
1973: 15 Wassily Leontief
1974: 12 Gunnar Myrdal **18** Friedrich A von Hayek
1975: 17 Tjalling C Koopmans **18** Leonid V Kantorovich
1976: 14 Milton Friedman
1977: 11 Bertil Ohlin, James E Meade
1978: 13 Herbert A Simon
1979: 14 Sir Arthur Lewis **15** Theodore Schultz
1980: 14 Lawrence R Klein
1981: 10 James Tobin
1982: 14 George J Stigler
1983: 12 Gerard Debreu
1984: 15 Sir Richard Stone
1985: 16 Franco Modigliani
1986: 19 James McGill Buchanan
1987: 12 Robert M Solow
1988: 13 Maurice Allais
1989: 14 Trygve Haavelmo
1990: 12 Merton Miller **13** William Sharpe **14** Harry Markowitz
1991: 11 Ronald Coase
1992: 10 Gary Becker
1993: 11 Robert Fogel **12** Douglas North
1994: 8 John Nash **12** John Harsanyi **14** Reinhard Selten
1995: 14 Robert E Lucas Jr.
1996: 14 James A Mirrlees **15** William S Vickrey
1997: 13 Myron S Scholes, Robert C Merton

nobility 5 elite, lords **7** dignity, majesty, peerage, primacy, royalty **8** breeding, eminence, grandeur, high rank, prestige, splendor **9** gentility, grandness, greatness, loftiness, sublimity, supremacy **10** blue bloods, mightiness, patricians, patriciate, upper crust **11** aristocracy, distinction, exaltedness, preeminence, stateliness, superiority **12** magnificence

nobility obliges
　French: **14** noblesse oblige

noble 3 don **4** high, just, lord, peer **5** famed, grand, great, lofty, moral, regal, royal **6** famous, gentle, honest, knight, lordly, squire, superb, worthy **7** awesome, courtly, eminent, ethical, exalted, grandee, stately, sublime, supreme, upright **8** baronial, cavalier, elevated, glorious, handsome, highborn, imperial, imposing, lordlike, majestic, princely, renowned, selfless, splendid, superior, virtuous **9** chevalier, dignified, estimable, excellent, exemplary, gentleman, honorable, patrician, personage, reputable **10** aristocrat, impressive, preeminent **11** magnanimous, magnificent, meritorious, pureblooded, trustworthy **12** aristocratic, thoroughbred **13** distinguished, incorruptible
　French: **6** gentil

Noble House
　author: **12** James Clavell

nobleman 4 lord, peer **7** grandee **9** patrician **10** aristocrat

noblesse oblige 15 nobility obliges

noblewoman 4 dame, lady, rani **5** begum, queen **6** milady **7** czarina, duchess, empress, peeress, sultana **8** baroness, contessa, countess, maharani, princess **11** marchioness

Nobody Knows My Name
　author: **12** James Baldwin

nock 5 notch
　in: **5** arrow

nocturnal 4 dark **5** night **7** nightly, obscure **8** darkling **9** nighttime

nod 3 bob **4** doze, hail, show, sign **5** agree, greet, lapse, let up **6** assent, beckon, concur, drowse, motion, reveal, salute, signal **7** consent, drop off, fall off, gesture, signify **9** recognize

node 3 bud **4** bump, burl, hump, knob, knot, lump **5** bulge, joint **6** button **8** swelling **10** prominence, tumescence **11** excrescence **12** protuberance

nodule 3 sac, wen **4** bump, cyst, knob, knot, lump, stud **5** bulge **6** growth **8** swelling **9** outgrowth **10** projection, prominence, protrusion, tumescence **11** excrescence **12** protuberance

noel, Noel 4 yule **5** carol **8** yuletide **9** Christmas **13** Christmastide

No Exit
　author: **14** Jean-Paul Sartre

noggin 3 cup, mug **4** bean, head, pate **5** gourd **6** noodle

Noggs, Newman
　character in: **16** Nicholas Nickleby
　author: **7** Dickens

Noguchi, Hideyo
　field: **12** bacteriology
　nationality: **8** Japanese
　isolated: **8** syphilis

noise 3 ado, din **4** bang, blab, boom, echo, pass, roar, stir, wail **5** babel, blare, blast, bruit, rumor, sound, voice **6** bedlam, clamor, hubbub, racket, repeat, report, rumble, tumult, uproar **7** barrage, bluster, clatter, thunder **8** brawling, gabbling, rumbling, shouting **9** cacophony, cannonade, circulate, commotion, discharge **10** dissonance, hullabaloo **11** pandemonium **12** caterwauling, vociferation **13** reverberation

noiseless 5 quiet, still, tacit **6** hushed, silent **9** soundless, voiceless

noisemaker 4 bell, horn **5** siren **6** rattle **7** clacker, clapper, snapper, whistle

noisome 4 foul, rank **5** acrid, fetid, toxic **6** putrid, rotten, smelly **7** baneful, harmful, hurtful, noxious, reeking **8** mephitic, stinking **9** injurious, offensive, poisonous, unhealthy **10** malodorous, nauseating, pernicious **11** deleterious, detrimental **12** evil-smelling

noisy 4 loud **5** alive **6** lively, raging, shrill, stormy **7** blaring, blatant, furious, grating, jarring, rackety **8** animated, piercing, strident **9** clamorous, deafening, dissonant, turbulent **10** boisterous, clangorous, discordant, rampageous, resounding, thundering, thunderous, tumultuous, uproarious **11** cacophonous, tempestuous **12** earsplitting

Nolan, Lloyd
　born: **14** San Francisco CA
　roles: **22** Lieutenant Colonel Queeg **26** The Caine Mutiny Court Martial

Nolde, Emil
　real name: **10** Emil Hansen
　born: **5** Nolde **7** Germany
　artwork: **7** Prophet **10** Papua Youth **11** Tropical Sun **12** The Magicians, The Pentecost **13** The Last Supper, Three Russians **14** Doubting Thomas **20** Life of Maria Aegyptica **22** Christ Among the Children, Christ and the Adulteress

nolens volens 10 willy-nilly **19** whether willing or not

noli me tangere 10 touch me not

nolle prosequi 14 do not prosecute **19** be unwilling to pursue

nolo contendere 21 I am unwilling to contend

no longer able to fight
　French: **12** hors de combat

no longer in existence 4 dead, gone, lost **7** defunct, died out, extinct **8** vanished

Nolte, Nick
　born: **7** Omaha NE
　roles: **5** U-Turn, Weeds **7** The Deep, Cape Fear **10** Cannery Row **11** Lorenzo's Oil, Mother Night **12** I Love Trouble **13** Prince of Tides **14** Rich Man Poor Man **15** Forty-Eight Hours **16** North Dallas Forty

nomad 4 arab, hobo, okie **5** gypsy, mover, rover, stray, tramp **6** roamer **7** migrant, rambler, refugee, runaway, strayer, tuareg, vagrant **8** bohemian, emigrant, migrator, renegade, traveler, vagabond, wanderer **9** immigrant, itinerant, straggler

nomadic 6 roving **7** migrant, roaming, vagrant **8** drifting, vagabond **9** footloose, itinerant, migratory, strolling, traveling, wandering

nom de guerre 5 alias **7** war name **9** pseudonym **11** assumed name

nom de plume 5 alias **7** pen name **9** false name, pseudonym **11** assumed name, writing name

nomenclature 5 lingo, terms **6** jargon, naming **8** glossary, language, taxonomy **10** nomination, vocabulary

nominal 3 low **5** cheap, small **6** puppet **7** minimum, titular, trivial **8** baseless, moderate, official, so-called, trifling **9** pretended, professed, purported, suggested **10** groundless, ostensible, reasonable

nominate 3 tag **4** call, name, pick, term **5** elect, label, style **6** choose, invest, select **7** elevate, install, propose, suggest **9** authorize, recommend

nomination 8 election **9** accession, selection **10** suggestion

nominee 7 hopeful **8** aspirant, eligible **9** applicant, candidate **10** competitor, contestant

nonadjustable 5 fixed, rigid **9** immovable **10** inflexible

nonalcoholic 4 soft **15** nonintoxicating

nonattendance 3 cut **7** absence, truancy **11** absenteeism

nonbeliever 5 cynic, pagan **7** atheist, doubter, heathen, infidel, skeptic **8** agnostic, apostate **10** backslider, empiricist, questioner, unbeliever **11** disbeliever, freethinker **14** doubting Thomas

nonbinding 8 optional **9** voluntary **12** unimperative **13** discretionary

nonce 6 pro tem **7** present **9** time being

nonchalance 9 composure, unconcern **13** offhandedness
　French: **11** insouciance

nonchalant 3 lax **4** cool, idle, lazy **5** blase, slack **6** casual **7** languid, offhand, unmoved **8** careless, heedless, indolent, listless **9** apathetic, collected, easygoing, lethargic, unexcited, unheeding, unmindful, unruffled, unstirred, withdrawn **10** insensible, insouciant, phlegmatic, unaffected

noncombatant 7 neutral **8** civilian

noncommittal 3 mum **4** cool, mute, safe, wary **5** vague **7** careful, evasive, guarded, neutral, politic, prudent **8** cautious, discreet, reserved **9** ambiguous, equivocal, tentative **10** indecisive, indefinite, unspeaking **11** circumspect, temporizing

noncompliance 6 breach **7** failure, neglect **9** disregard **10** resistance **11** dereliction

noncompliant 6 unruly **7** defiant, froward, naughty, wayward **8** contrary, mutinous, perverse, stubborn **9** differing, dissident, fractious, objecting, obstinate, resistant, resistive, undutiful **10** disorderly, dissenting, rebellious, refractory, unorthodox, unyielding

non compos mentis 14 not of sound mind **17** mentally incapable

nonconfirming 7 denying **8** negating, refuting **9** rejecting **10** disavowing **11** disclaiming, repudiating

nonconformist 3 nut **4** beat, card **5** freak, hippy, loner, rebel **6** oddity, weirdo **7** heretic, oddball, radical **8** bohemian, crackpot, deserter, maverick, original, reformer, renegade, vagabond **9** character, dissenter, dissident, eccentric, exception, insurgent, protester, screwball **10** dissenting, iconoclast, rebellious, schismatic **13** individualist, revolutionary

nonconformity 5 quirk **6** oddity **7** anomaly **9** deviation, rebellion **10** aberration, divergence, resistance

noncongenial 6 unlike **8** opposite **9** different, disparate, ill-suited, unrelated **10** dissimilar **11** disagreeing **12** disagreeable, incompatible **13** unsympathetic

nondescript 5 usual, vague **8** ordinary **9** amorphous, colorless **11** stereotyped **12** unimpressive **13** characterless, undistinctive, unexceptional **15** undistinguished

nonentity 4 zero **6** cipher, nobody **7** nothing, no-count, nullity **8** small-fry, unperson **10** mediocrity

nonessential 5 frill **6** luxury, trivia **7** trivial **9** extrinsic, secondary, trimmings **10** accidental, extraneous, incidental, irrelevant, peripheral, subsidiary

nonexclusive 4 open **6** public, shared **7** divided **12** unrestricted

nonexistence 4 lack, void **7** absence **8** oblivion **11** nothingness

nonexistent 4 gone **5** short **6** absent **7** lacking, missing, wanting **11** unavailable **12** insufficient

nonindulgence 7 refusal **8** eschewal, forgoing **9** avoidance, eschewing

10 abstaining, abstention, refraining **11** forbearance **16** nonparticipation

nonirritating 4 calm **5** bland **6** benign **7** calming **8** soothing, tranquil **9** temperate

non licet 13 it is not lawful **16** it is not permitted

non liquet 12 it is not clear **14** it is not evident

nonmaterialistic 9 spiritual **10** idealistic **12** intellectual

nonmember 5 guest **7** outcast, visitor **8** outsider

nonnatural 7 manmade **9** synthetic **10** artificial, fabricated, factitious **12** manufactured

nonobservance 6 breach **7** failure, neglect **9** disregard **11** dereliction **13** noncompliance

non obstante 15 notwithstanding

no-nonsense 4 grim, hard **5** grave, harsh, rigid, sober, stern **6** ardent, intent, severe, solemn, strict **7** earnest, serious **8** critical, diligent, exacting, resolute **9** committed, dedicated, demanding, hardnosed, practical, pragmatic, unbending, unsparing **10** determined, hardheaded, purposeful, sobersided **12** businesslike

nonpareil 5 elite, ideal, model, super **6** symbol, unique **7** epitome, paragon, pattern, supreme **8** exemplar **9** unequaled, unmatched, unrivaled **10** apotheosis **11** exceptional, unsurpassed **13** extraordinary **14** representative

French: **11** ne plus ultra **14** creme de la creme

nonparticipation 7 refusal **8** eschewal, forgoing **9** avoidance, eschewing **10** abstaining, abstention, refraining, sitting out **11** forbearance

nonpartisan 4 fair, just **8** unbiased, unswayed **9** equitable, impartial, objective, unbigoted **10** impersonal, uninvolved **12** freethinking, unaffiliated, unimplicated, uninfluenced, unprejudiced **13** disinterested

nonpermissible 9 forbidden **10** disallowed **11** intolerable **12** inadmissible, unacceptable

nonplus 4 balk, faze, foil, halt, stop **5** abash, stump, upset **6** baffle, bother, dismay, muddle, puzzle, stymie **7** astound, confuse, disturb, mystify, perplex **8** astonish, bewilder, confound, deadlock **9** dumbfound, embarrass **10** disconcert **11** flabbergast **14** discountenance

nonplussed, nonplused 5 at sea, fazed **7** at a loss, baffled, floored, mixed-up, muddled, puzzled, stumped **8** confused **9** befuddled, mystified, unsettled **10** bewildered, confounded **12** disconcerted

nonpoisonous 4 safe **8** nontoxic **11** nonvenomous, nonvirulent

non possumus 8 we cannot

nonpresence 3 cut **7** absence, truancy **11** absenteeism

nonprofessional 3 lay **4** laic **7** dabbler

French: **7** amateur **10** dilettante

non prosequitur 15 he does not pursue

non repetatur 11 do not repeat

nonresident 7 tourist, visitor **9** transient **11** out-of-towner

nonresistance 6 assent **7** pliancy **8** docility, giving in, meekness, yielding **9** deference, obedience, passivity **10** compliance, conforming, conformity, pliability, submission **12** acquiescence, complaisance

nonresistant 4 meek **6** docile, pliant **7** passive, pliable **8** deferent, obedient, yielding **9** compliant **10** conforming, submissive **11** acquiescent, complaisant, deferential

nonscholarly 8 untaught **9** unlearned **10** uneducated, unlettered, unpedantic, unschooled

nonsectarian 10 ecumenical **11** interchurch **16** undenominational **17** nondenominational **19** interdenominational

nonsense 3 rot **4** bosh, bunk **5** folly, trash **6** antics, babble, drivel, joking, piffle **7** baloney, blather, bombast, chatter, fooling, garbage, hogwash, inanity, prattle, rubbish, trifles, twaddle **8** claptrap, flummery **9** absurdity, frivolity, gibberish, high jinks, horseplay, moonshine, silliness, stupidity **10** balderdash, flapdoodle, tomfoolery, triviality **11** foolishness, shenanigans **12** childishness, extravagance **13** facetiousness, ludicrousness, senselessness **14** ridiculousness **15** meaninglessness

nonsensical 4 wild **5** crazy, funny, inane, silly **6** absurd, stupid **7** asinine, comical, foolish **8** farcical **9** facetious, laughable, ludicrous **10** irrational, ridiculous

non sequitur 15 it does not follow

nonspecialized 11 generalized

nonspecific 4 hazy **5** vague **7** general, inexact **9** imprecise, uncertain **10** indefinite, undetailed **11** approximate, generalized

nonspiritual 7 earthly, profane, secular, worldly **8** material, temporal **13** materialistic

nonstop 7 endless, express **8** constant, unbroken **9** incessant **10** continuous, unrelieved **11** unremitting **12** interminable

nonstudious 9 unlearned **10** uneducated, unlettered, unpedantic, unschooled

nontaxable 9 sheltered **10** deductible

nontechnical 6 simple **8** academic **13** uncomplicated

nontypical 7 unusual **8** abnormal, uncommon **9** anomalous, irregular **16** unrepresentative

non-U *see* **12** Mitford, Nancy

nonuniform 5 mixed **6** unlike **7** altered, changed, erratic, unalike **8** changing, variable **9** deviating, different, irregular, multiform **10** dissimilar **11** fluctuating, nonstandard **12** inconsistent

nonvital 9 accessory, extrinsic **10** disposable, expendable, incidental **11** dispensable, superfluous, unessential, unimportant, unnecessary

nonvocational 8 academic

nonvolitional 6 reflex **8** unwilled **9** automatic **11** instinctive, involuntary, spontaneous **12** uncontrolled

noodle 4 bean, head, pate **5** gourd, pasta **6** noggin **8** practice **9** improvise

nook 3 den **4** cove, lair **5** haven, niche **6** alcove, cavity, corner, cranny, dugout, recess, refuge **7** retreat, shelter **8** hideaway **9** cubbyhole **10** depression **11** hiding place

noon 6 midday, zenith **8** high noon, meridian

no one contradicting
 Latin: 19 nemine contradicente

no one dissenting
 Latin: 18 nemine dissentiente

noose 3 tie **4** bond, hang, loop **5** catch, hitch, lasso, snare **6** choker, entrap, halter, lariat, tether

Nootka
 language family: 8 Wakashan
 tribe: 5 Makah **6** Hoiath, Ozette **7** Ahosath, Nitinat **8** Machlath, Otsosath, Tokwaath **9** Ihatisath, Mowachaht, Nochalath, Qayokwath, Tsishaath, Yoloilath **10** Hishkwiath, Hochoqtlis, Manohisath, Tlaokwiath **11** Chiqtlisath, Hopachasath, Qiltsamaath
 location: 10 Washington **15** Vancouver Island
 leader: 8 Maquinna **10** Wikaninish
 related to: 5 Makah
 noted for: 7 whaling

Nordhoff, Charles
 author of: 17 Mutiny on the Bounty (with James Norman Hall)

Nordic Mythology *see* **21** Scandinavian Mythology

Norge *see* **6** Norway

noria 10 water wheel

norm 3 par **4** rule, type **5** gauge, model **7** average, measure, pattern **8** standard **9** barometer, criterion, yardstick **12** measuring rod

normal 3 fit, par **4** sane **5** sound, usual **6** steady **7** average, healthy, natural, regular, typical, uniform **8** constant, expected, mediocre, mid-dling, ordinary, rational, reliable, standard **9** incessant, steadfast, unceasing **10** conforming, consistent, continuous, dependable, reasonable, unchanging **11** conformable, rightminded, unremitting **12** conventional **13** uninterrupted **14** representative

Normandy, Normandie
 beach: 4 Gold, Juno, Utah **5** Omaha, Sword
 borders: 7 Picardy **8** Brittany **14** English Channel
 church/shrine: 12 Saint Etienne **15** Mont Saint Michel
 city: 4 Caen, St. Lo **5** Rouen **7** Le Havre **9** Cherbourg
 event: 4 D Day **17** Operation Overlord
 region of: 6 France
 river: 5 Seine

Norma Rae
 director: 10 Martin Ritt
 cast: 9 Pat Hingle **10** Ron Liebman, Sally Field **11** Beau Bridges
 Oscar for: 4 song **7** actress (Field)
 song: 16 It Goes Like It Goes

Norn
 origin: 12 Scandinavian
 form: 6 virgin **7** goddess
 personifies: 4 fate
 original Norn: 5 Urdar
 the three: 3 Urd **5** Skuld **8** Verdandi
 known as: 12 weird sisters

Norris, Frank
 author of: 6 The Pit **8** McTeague **10** The Octopus

Norse Mythology
 abode of man: 7 Midgard **10** Mithgarthr
 afterworld: 6 Manala **7** Tuonela
 began race of giants: 4 Ymir
 blacksmith/hero: 9 Ilmarinen
 boar: 10 Saehrimnir
 bridge of gods: 7 Bifrost
 dragon: 6 Fafnir
 dwarf: 5 Skuld **7** Andvari
 earth is made from: 4 Ymir
 elf: 4 Norn **8** Verdandi
 epic: 8 Kaleva
 final battle: 15 Gotterdammerung **17** Twilight of the Gods
 first god: 4 Buri **7** Forsete, Forseti
 first man: 3 Ask
 first woman: 5 Embla
 folk hero: 8 Kalevala
 giant: 4 Loki **5** Jotun, Thrym **6** Thiazi, Thjazi **7** Skrymir
 giantess: 3 Urd **5** Thokk **9** Angerboda, Angrbodha, Angurboda
 giant's realm: 9 Jotunheim
 goat: 7 Heidrun
 goddesses: 7 Asynjur
 goddess of death: 3 Hel
 goddess of forbidden marriages: 4 Lofn
 goddess of marriage: 4 Frey **5** Freyr
 goddess of peace: 4 Frey **5** Freyr
 goddess of prosperity: 4 Frey
 5 Freyr
 goddess of spring: 4 Idun **5** Iduna, Ithun **6** Ithunn
 goddess of the sea: 3 Ran
 god of beauty/radiance: 5 Baldr **6** Balder, Baldur
 god of dawn: 8 Heimdall
 god of farming: 4 Thor
 god of fire: 4 Loki
 god of knowledge: 4 Odin **5** Othin
  corresponds to Germanic: 5 Wotan
 god of justice: 7 Forseti
 god of light: 8 Heimdall
 god of music: 5 Bragi
 god of navigation: 5 Niord, Njord
 god of poetry: 4 Odin **5** Bragi, Othin
  corresponds to Germanic: 5 Wotan
 god of prosperity: 5 Niord, Njord
 god of rain: 4 Thor
 god of sea: 5 Aegir, Mimir
 god of thunder: 4 Thor
 god of underworld: 8 Niflheim
 god of victory: 3 Tyr
 god of war: 4 Odin **5** Othin
  corresponds to Germanic: 5 Wotan
 god of wind: 5 Niord, Njord
 god of wisdom: 4 Odin **5** Othin
  corresponds to Germanic: 5 Wotan
 hero: 11 Vainamoinen **12** Lemminkainen
 home of dead: 3 Hel
 king: 5 Gjuki
 magician: 11 Joukahainen
 magic necklace: 11 Brisingamen
 misty void: 11 Ginnungagap
 mountain: 11 Hindarfjall
 nature spirit: 7 Eriking
 oak tree: 9 Barnstock, Branstock
 Odin's court/hall: 8 Valhalla
 Odin's father: 3 Bor
 Odin's horse: 8 Sleipnir
 Odin's magic ring: 8 Draupnir
 Odin's palace: 9 Gladsheim
 Odin's raven: 5 Hugin, Munin
 Odin's spear: 6 Gungni
 Odin's throne: 10 Hlidskjalf
 Odin's wolf: 4 Geri **5** Freki
 race of gods: 5 Vanir
 saga: 8 Vulsunga
 sea monster: 6 Kraken
 serpent: 7 Nidhogg **11** Jormungandr
 Sigmund's sword: 4 Gram
 slave: 8 Kullervo
 sorceress: 5 Louhi **8** Grimhild
 Thor's hammer: 7 Miolnir
 Thor's servant: 7 Thialfi
 tree with three roots: 9 Iggdrasil, Yggdrasil
 Valkyrie: 8 Brynhild **9** Brunhilde, Sigrdrifa **11** Brunnehilde
 virgin goddess: 3 Urd **4** Norn **5** Skuld, Urdar **8** Verdandi
 warrior: 8 Baresark **9** Berserker

watchdog: 4 Garm
wolf monster: 6 Fenrir, Fenris
north 5 polar, upper **6** arctic
North America
　nation: 4 Cuba **5** Haiti **6** Belize, Canada, Mexico, Panama **7** Bahamas, Jamaica **8** Barbados, Honduras **9** Costa Rica, Guatemala, Nicaragua **10** El Salvador, Puerto Rico, Saint Lucia **12** Saint Vincent, United States **17** Dominican Republic, Trinidad and Tobago **28** Saint Vincent and the Grenadines
　desert: 6 Mojave **7** Painted, Sonoran **11** Death Valley
　island: 4 Long **6** Baffin, Cayman, Kodiak **7** Antigua, Bermuda, Iceland **8** Aleutian, Catalina, Thousand **9** Antilles, Greenland, Nantucket, Vancouver **10** Cape Breton **12** Newfoundland, Prince Edward **14** Queen Charlotte
　ocean/sea/bay: 6 Arctic, Baffin, Bering, Hudson, Mexico **7** Chukchi, Lincoln, Pacific **8** Amundsen, Atlantic, Beaufort, Labrador **9** Caribbean, Greenland **10** California, Chesapeake, St Lawrence
　river: 3 Red **4** Ohio **5** Peace, Snake, Yukon **6** Hudson **8** Arkansas, Colorado, Columbia, Missouri **9** Churchill, Mackenzie, Rio Grande **10** St Lawrence **11** Mississippi **12** Saskatchewan
　lake: 4 Erie **5** Huron **7** Ontario **8** Michigan, Superior, Winnipeg **9** Great Bear, Nicaragua **10** Great Lakes, Great Slave
　mountain range: 5 Ozark, Rocky **6** Alaska **7** Cascade **9** Blue Ridge **10** Laurentian **11** Appalachian, Sierra Madre **12** Sierra Nevada
　highest point: 13 Mount McKinley
　lowest point: 11 Death Valley
　city: 4 Nome **5** Miami **6** Boston, Dallas, Denver, Havana, Ottawa, Quebec **7** Atlanta, Calgary, Chicago, Detroit, Houston, Memphis, New York, Phoenix, Seattle, Toronto **8** Montreal, Portland, San Diego **9** Anchorage, Milwaukee, Reykjavik, Vancouver **10** Kansas City, Los Angeles, Mexico City, New Orleans, Washington **11** Philadelphia, San Antonio, San Francisco
　mineral: 3 oil, tin **4** coal, gold, lead, salt, zinc **6** cobalt, copper, nickel, quartz, silver **7** iron ore, mercury, sulphur, uranium **8** aluminum, antimony, asbestos, chromium, platinum, titanium, tungsten **9** magnesium, manganese, petroleum **10** molybdenum, natural gas
Northanger Abbey
　author: 10 Jane Austen
　character: 8 Mrs Allen **10** John Thorpe **12** James Morland **14** Isabella Thorpe **16** Catherine Morland

Tilney family: 5 Henry **7** Captain, Eleanor, General
North by Northwest
　director: 15 Alfred Hitchcock
　cast: 9 Cary Grant **10** James Mason **11** Leo G Carroll **12** Martin Landau **13** Eva Marie Saint **17** Jessie Royce Landis
　setting (climax): 13 Mount Rushmore
　score: 15 Bernard Herrmann
North Carolina
　abbreviation: 2 NC **4** N Car
　nickname: 7 Tar Heel **8** Old North **10** Turpentine
　capital: 7 Raleigh
　largest city: 9 Charlotte
　others: 4 Bath **6** Durham, Lenoir, Shelby, Wilson **7** Edenton, Hickory, Kinston, New Bern, Roxboro, Tarboro **8** Gastonia **9** Albemarle, Asheville, Goldsboro, Henderson, Kitty Hawk, Lumberton **10** Chapel Hill, Greensboro, Greenville, Kannapolis, Wilmington **11** Statesville, Thomasville, Williamston **12** Fayetteville, Jacksonville, Winston-Salem
　college: 4 Duke, Elon **7** Catawba **8** Davidson **10** Wake Forest
　feature:
　　battle site: 18 Guilford Courthouse
　　national park: 19 Great Smoky Mountains (with Tennessee)
　　national seashore: 11 Cape Lookout **12** Cape Hatteras
　tribe: 3 Eno **5** Coree **6** Cheraw **7** Buffalo, Moratok, Pamlico **8** Chowanoc, Hatteras **9** Tuscarora
　people: 6 O Henry (William Sidney Porter) **7** tarheel **11** Billy Graham, Thomas Wolfe **13** Dolley (Dolly) Madison, Edward R Murrow **14** Richard Gatling
　　explorer: 6 de Soto **8** de Ayllon **9** Verrazano
　island: 7 Roanoke
　lake: 6 Norman, Phelps **7** Fontana **8** Waccamaw **12** Mattamuskeet
　land rank: 12 twenty-eighth
　mountain: 5 Black, Unaka **6** Harris **9** Blue Ridge **10** Great Smoky **13** Clingman's Dome
　　highest point: 8 Mitchell
　physical feature: 10 Outer Banks **11** French Broad **15** Little Tennessee
　　cape: 4 Fear **7** Lookout **8** Hatteras
　　plateau: 8 Piedmont
　　sea: 8 Atlantic
　　sound: 4 Core **5** Bogue **7** Croatan, Pamlico
　　swamp: 6 Dismal
　president: 9 James Polk **13** Andrew Johnson
　river: 3 Haw, Tar **4** Fear **5** Neuse **6** Chowan, Lumber, Peedee, Yadkin **7** Roanoke, Wateree
　state admission: 7 twelfth
　state bird: 8 cardinal
　state fish: 11 channel bass

　state flower: 7 dogwood **9** goldenrod
　state motto: 20 To Be Rather Than To Seem
　state song: 16 The Old North State
　state tree: 4 pine
　state dance: 4 shag
North Dakota
　abbreviation: 2 ND **4** N Dak
　nickname: 5 Sioux **11** Flickertail **16** Land of the Dakotas
　capital: 8 Bismarck
　largest city: 5 Fargo
　others: 5 Minot **9** Bottineau, Jamestown, Williston **10** Grand Forks
　college: 4 Mary **9** Jamestown
　feature:
　　dam: 4 Oahe **8** Garrison
　　garden: 18 International Peace
　　national park: 17 Theodore Roosevelt
　tribe: 5 Sioux **6** Mandan **7** Arikara, Hidatsa **8** Chippewa
　people: 12 Eric Sevareid
　　explorer: 6 Carver **8** Thompson, Varennes **13** Lewis and Clark
　lake: 5 Stump **6** Devils **9** Sakakawea
　land rank: 11 seventeenth
　mountain: 6 Turtle **8** Killdeer **10** Black Butte
　　highest point: 10 White Butte
　physical feature:
　　basin: 9 Williston
　　plain: 8 The Slope
　　valley: 8 Red River
　river: 3 Red **4** Park, Rush **5** Cedar, Goose, Heart, James, Knife, Mouse **6** Souris **7** Deslacs, Pembina **8** Missouri, Cheyenne, Wild Rice **9** Otter Tail **10** Cannonball **11** Yellowstone **12** Boise de Sioux **14** Little Missouri **18** Red River of the North
　state admission: 8 fortieth **11** thirty-ninth (with South Dakota)
　state bird: 17 western meadowlark
　state fish: 12 northern pike
　state flower: 15 wild prairie rose
　state motto: 45 Liberty and Union Now and Forever One and Inseparable
　state song: 15 North Dakota Hymn
　state tree: 11 American elm
North Dallas Forty
　director: 11 Ted Kotcheff
　based on story by: 9 Peter Gent
　cast: 8 Mac Davis **9** Nick Nolte **11** Dayle Haddon **14** Charles Durning
Northern Crown
　constellation of: 14 Corona Borealis
Northern Rhodesia *see* **6** Zambia
North Korea *see* **5** Korea
North Star State
　nickname of: 9 Minnesota
North Vietnam *see* **7** Vietnam
Northwest Passage
　director: 9 King Vidor
　author: 14 Kenneth Roberts
　cast: 10 Ruth Hussey **11** Robert

Young **12** Spencer Tracy **13** Walter Brennan

Northwest Territories
abbreviation: 3 NWT
borders: 7 Alberta **8** Manitoba **9** Baffin Bay, Hudson Bay **11** Arctic Ocean, Beaufort Sea, Labrador Sea **12** Saskatchewan **15** British Columbia
city: 6 Inuvik **8** Hay River **9** Fort Smith **11** Yellowknife **12** Frobisher Bay
country: 6 Canada
Inuit land: 7 Nunavut
island: 5 Banks, Devon **6** Baffin **7** Melville **8** Bathurst, Somerset, Victoria **9** Ellesmere **11** King William **13** Prince of Wales, Prince Patrick **14** Queen Elizabeth
mineral: 3 oil **4** gold, lead, zinc **6** silver **8** tungsten **9** petroleum
mountain: 21 Mount Sir James MacBrien
native: 5 Inuit **6** Eskimo
territory: 8 Franklin, Keewatin **9** Mackenzie

North wind
associated with: 6 Boreas

Norway
other name: 5 Norge **20** Land of the Midnight Sun
capital: 4 Oslo **11** Christiania
largest city: 4 Oslo
others: 3 Gol, Nes **4** Bodo, Moss, Odda, Rena, Voss **5** Bjort, Floro, Hamar, Molde, Skien, Skjak, Vadso **6** Bergen, Horton, Larvik, Narvik, Tromso **7** Alesund, Arendal, Drammen, Harstad, Sandnes **8** Aalesund, Kirkenes **9** Stavanger, Trondheim **10** Hammerfest **12** Kristiansand
division: 3 Amt **4** Oslo **5** Fylke, Troms **6** Bergen, Opland, Tromso **7** Finmark, Hedmark, Ostfold **8** Letemark, Nordland, Rogaland, Vestfold **9** Ostlandet
  former: 11 Kalmar Union
  province called: 6 fylker
government:
  legislature: 8 Storting
head of state: 4 king
measure: 3 fot, mal **4** alen **5** kande **6** fathom **7** skieppe **9** korntonde
monetary unit: 3 ore **5** krone
weight: 3 lod **4** mark, pund **10** bismerpund
island: 4 Vega **5** Bomlo, Donna, Froya, Hitra, Hopen, Senja, Smola, Soroy **6** Alsten, Averoy, Bouvet, Hinnoy, Karmoy, Kvaloy, Solund, Vannoy **7** Gurskoy, Lofoten, Mageroy, Seiland **8** Jan Mayen, Svalbard
lake: 4 Alte **5** Ister, Mjosa, Snasa **6** Femund **7** Rostavn, Tunnsjo
mountain: 5 Sogne **6** Kjolen **7** Numedal **8** Blodfjel, Snohetta, Telemark, Ustetind **9** Harteigen, Jotunheim, Langfjell, Ramnanosi

10 Dovrefjell, Galdhoepig, Glitretind, Vibmesnosi **11** Myrdalfjell **14** Aardangerjokul, Hallingskarvet, Skagastolstind
highest point: 12 Galdhopiggen **13** Glittertinden
river: 3 Ena **4** Alta, Klar, Otra, Rana, Tana, Teno **5** Bardu, Begna, Glama, Lagen, Orkla, Otter, Rauma, Reisa **6** Glomma, Lougen, Namsen, Pasvik
sea: 5 North **6** Arctic **7** Barents **8** Atlantic **9** Norwegian, Skagerrak
physical feature:
  cape: 4 Naze **7** Nordkyn **8** Nordkapp **9** Lindesnes
  fjord: 4 Oslo **5** Sogne
  glacier: 12 Jostedalsbre
  inlet: 2 Is **3** Kob, Ran **4** Alst, Ands, Bokn, Nord, Ofot, Salt, Sunn, Tyri, Vest **5** fiord, fjord, Folda, Lakse, Sogne **6** Bjorna, Hadsel **7** Hortens **9** Trondheim
  plateau: 5 Doure, Dovre, Fjeld **9** Hardanger
people: 4 Lapp **5** Samme **6** Nordic, Viking
  artist: 5 Munch
  author: 5 Ibsen **6** Hamsun, Undset **7** Holberg **8** Bjornson **9** Wergeland
  composer: 5 Grieg **7** Sinding **8** Svendsen
  explorer: 4 Eric, Leif, Mohn, Sars **6** Nansen **8** Amundsen
  explorer/statesman: 6 Nansen **8** Amundsen **9** Heyerdahl
  king: 4 Olaf, Olav **5** Olave, Oscar **6** Haakon, Harold, Magnus, Sverre
  mathematics: 4 Abel
  Nazi collaborator: 8 Quisling
  Norse god/goddess: 3 Sif, Tyr **4** Frey, Idun, Loki, Odin, Thor **5** Bragi, Freya, Hoder, Woden **6** Balder, Eostre, Frigga, Hermod
  sculptor: 8 Vigeland
language: 4 Lapp **5** Norse **6** Bokmal **7** Nynorsk, Riksmal **8** Landsmal, Samnorsk **9** Landsmaal, Norwegian
religion: 19 Evangelical Lutheran **22** National Church of Norway
place:
  castle: 8 Akershus
  cathedral: 7 Nidaras
  museum: 7 Kon Tiki **10** Viking Ship **15** Polar Expedition
  park: 7 Frogner
former colony: 7 Vinland
feature:
  dance: 6 gangar **7** halling **8** springar **9** spingleik
  literature form: 4 edda, saga
food:
  bread: 8 flat brod
  cheese: 3 Ost **7** gjetost **9** gammelost, Jarlsberg
  drink: 7 aquavit

Norwegian Mythology see **21** Scandinavian Mythology

nose

sense of: 5 smell
part: 7 nostril **14** olfactory patch
nosegay 4 posy **7** bouquet **10** tussymussy
nosiness 6 prying **9** curiosity **15** inquisitiveness
nostalgia 6 pining, regret **7** longing **11** remembrance **12** homesickness **13** regretfulness
Nostradamus
  name: 7 Michael **17** Michelde Notredame
  occupation: 7 prophet **9** physician **10** astrologer **13** metaphysicist
  wrote: 9 Centuries
Nostromo
  author: 12 Joseph Conrad
nostrum 4 balm, cure, dose, drug **5** draft **6** elixir, physic, potion, remedy **7** cure-all, formula, panacea **8** medicine **9** treatment **10** medicament **12** prescription
nosy, nosey 6 prying, snoopy **7** all ears, curious **8** snooping **9** intrusive **11** inquisitive, overcurious **13** eavesdropping
nota bene 8 note well **10** take notice
notability 4 fame **6** import, moment, renown **8** eminence **9** celebrity **10** importance, prominence **11** consequence, distinction, preeminence **12** significance
notable 3 VIP **4** name **5** famed, wheel **6** biggie, bigwig, famous, marked **7** eminent, salient **8** luminary, renowned, striking **9** celebrity, dignitary, personage, prominent, reputable **10** celebrated, pronounced, remarkable **11** conspicuous, outstanding, personality **13** distinguished
notably 7 visibly **8** markedly **10** distinctly, strikingly **11** prominently **12** unmistakably **13** conspicuously, outstandingly
not alike 8 distinct **9** different, differing, disparate, divergent **10** dissimilar **11** contrasting
notation 5 entry **10** memorandum
not bright 3 dim **4** dark, dull **5** dense, dusky, murky **6** cloudy, stupid **7** clouded **8** obscured **13** unilluminated
notch 3 cut **4** dent, mark, nick, nock **5** grade, level, score **6** degree **7** scoring, scratch **11** indentation
not disclosed
  Italian: 7 in petto
note 4 bill, fame, line, mark **5** bread, draft, enter, green, money, write **6** regard, renown **7** epistle, jot down, lettuce, message, missive, put down, scratch, set down, voucher **8** currency, dispatch, eminence, mark down, perceive **9** bank draft, celebrity, greenback **10** communique, importance, memorandum, prominence,

reputation 11 certificate, consequence, distinction

notebook 3 log **5** diary **6** record **7** journal **9** looseleaf
French: 6 cahier

noted 6 famous **7** eminent **8** renowned **9** prominent, reputable **10** celebrated, remarkable **11** illustrious, outstanding **13** distinguished

Notes from the Underground
author: 16 Fyodor Dostoevsky

note well
Latin: 8 nota bene

noteworthy 7 unusual **8** singular **9** important **10** remarkable **11** outstanding, significant, substantial **12** considerable **13** distinguished, exceptionable

not far from 4 near **6** all but, almost, nearly **7** close to **8** not quite **13** approximately

not genuine 4 fake, sham **5** bogus, false, phony **6** ersatz, unreal **7** feigned **8** spurious **9** imitation, insincere, pretended, synthetic **10** artificial, fraudulent **11** counterfeit **12** hypocritical
Latin: 8 mala fide

not germane 9 extrinsic, unrelated **10** extraneous, immaterial, irrelevant **11** incongruous, inconsonant, unconnected **12** incompatible, nonessential **13** inappropriate

not guilty 5 clear **8** innocent **9** blameless **10** inculpable, unblamable

nothing 3 air, nix, zip **4** none, zero **5** stuff, trash, zilch **6** bauble, bubble, cipher, gewgaw, naught, trifle, trivia **7** duck egg, nullity, rubbish, trinket **8** goose egg **9** bagatelle, obscurity **14** insignificance **16** inconsequentials
Latin: 5 nihil

nothing is created from nothing
Latin: 16 ex nihilo nihil fit

nothingness 4 void **5** death **8** oblivion **9** emptiness **10** triviality **12** nonexistence **14** insignificance

Nothing Sacred
director: 14 William Wellman
cast: 13 Carole Lombard, Frederic March **14** Walter Connolly
score: 11 Oscar Levant
remade as: 10 Living It Up
script: 8 Ben Hecht

nothing unless it is good
Latin: 12 nil nisi bonum

nothing without the divine will
Latin: 13 nil sine numine
motto of: 8 Colorado

notice 3 eye, see **4** dope, heed, info, mark **5** goods **6** poster, rating, regard, review, take in **7** leaflet, mention, observe, warning **8** brochure, circular, critique, handbill, pamphlet **9** appraisal, attention, knowledge, statement **10** advisement, cognizance, disclosure **11** declaration, information

12 announcement, intelligence **13** advertisement, communication, specification

noticeable 5 clear, plain **7** evident, obvious **8** definite, distinct, manifest, palpable, striking **10** observable **11** appreciable, conspicuous, perceivable, perceptible **12** unmistakable

notification 4 news, word **6** advice, report **7** message, release **8** bulletin, dispatch **9** statement **10** communique **11** information **12** announcement, intelligence **13** communication

notify 4 tell, warn **6** advise, inform **7** apprise, let know **8** acquaint, send word **9** enlighten

not indigenous 5 alien **6** exotic **7** foreign **8** imported **9** nonnative **10** extraneous **11** naturalized

notion 4 idea, view, whim **5** fancy, humor, quirk **6** belief, vagary, whimsy **7** caprice, conceit, concept, opinion **8** crotchet **9** suspicion **10** conception, intimation **12** eccentricity

not native 5 alien **6** exotic **7** foreign **8** imported **10** extraneous **11** naturalized

not of sound mind
Latin: 15 non compos mentis

not ordinary 4 rare **6** exotic, unique **7** bizarre, foreign, strange, unusual **8** peculiar, singular, uncommon **9** anomalous, different, fantastic **11** distinctive, outstanding **14** unconventional

notoriety 4 blot **5** shame, stain **6** infamy, stigma **7** scandal **8** disgrace, dishonor, ignominy **9** discredit, disrepute **11** degradation

notorious 6 arrant **7** blatant, glaring **8** infamous, renowned **9** egregious **10** celebrated, outrageous **11** outstanding

Notorious
director: 15 Alfred Hitchcock
cast: 9 Cary Grant **11** Claude Rains **12** Louis Calhern **13** Ingrid Bergman

not pertinent 9 unrelated **10** extraneous, immaterial, irrelevant **11** incongruous, unconnected **13** inappropriate

not quite 6 all but, almost, nearly

Notre Dame 9 cathedral
style: 6 Gothic
location: 5 Paris
setting for: 20 Hunchback of Notre Dame
feature: 7 statues **9** gargoyles

not required 8 elective, optional **9** voluntary

not too seriously
Latin: 13 cum grano salis

Notus
origin: 5 Greek
personifies: 9 south wind

not wanted
French: 6 de trop

notwithstanding
Latin: 11 non obstante

not working 4 dead **8** inactive **10** unemployed **11** inoperative **12** unresponsive

Nouakchott
capital of: 10 Mauritania

Noumea
capital of: 12 New Caledonia

nourish 4 feed **5** nurse **6** suckle **7** nurture, sustain

nourishing 4 rich **6** hearty **7** healthy **9** fostering, nurturing, wholesome **10** nutritious, sustaining **11** maintaining **12** invigorating **13** strengthening

nourishment 4 chow, eats, food, grub, meat **5** bread **6** viands **8** victuals **9** nutriment, nutrition **10** sustenance **11** comestibles

nouveau riche 9 newly rich (person)

Novak, Kim
real name: 19 Marilyn Pauline Novak
born: 9 Chicago IL
roles: 6 Picnic **7** Pal Joey, Vertigo **14** Of Human Bondage **17** Bell Book and Candle **20** The Jeanne Eagels Story **22** The Man with the Golden Arm **31** Amorous Adventures of Moll Flanders

Nova Scotia
borders: 10 Bay of Fundy **12** New Brunswick **13** Atlantic Ocean **16** Gulf of St Lawrence **20** Northumberland Strait
city: 5 Truro **6** Sydney **7** Amherst, Halifax **8** Glace Bay, Yarmouth **9** Dartmouth **10** New Glasgow
country: 6 Canada
island: 10 Cape Breton
means: 11 New Scotland
mineral: 3 oil **4** lead, salt, sand, zinc **6** barite, gravel, gypsum, silver **9** celestite, petroleum **10** natural gas
mountain: 5 North **8** Cobequid
part of: 6 Acadia **12** Appalachians **17** Maritime Provinces **18** Atlantic Provinces
river: 4 Avon **5** Clyde **6** LaHave, Medway, Mersey **7** St Mary's **12** Shubenacadie

novel 3 new **6** unique **7** unusual **8** original, singular, uncommon **9** different **10** innovative, unorthodox **14** unconventional
French: 5 roman

novelty 5 token **6** bauble, change, gewgaw **7** memento, newness, trinket **8** gimcrack, souvenir, surprise **9** bagatelle, variation **10** innovation, knickknack, uniqueness **11** originality

November
event: 11 Election Day
flower: 13 chrysanthemum
French: 8 Novembre
gem: 5 topaz
German: 8 November
holiday: 11 All Souls' Day (2),

Veterans Day (11) **12** All Saints' Day (1), Guy Fawkes Day (5), Thanksgiving (4th Thursday)
Italian: 8 Novembre
number of days: 6 thirty
origin of name: 5 novem (Latin meaning nine)
place in year:
    Gregorian: 8 eleventh
    Roman: 5 ninth
Spanish: 9 Noviembre
Zodiac sign: 7 Scorpio **11** Sagittarius

novice 4 tyro **5** pupil **7** amateur, learner, student **8** beginner, disciple, newcomer **9** greenhorn **10** apprentice, tenderfoot

Novum Organum
    author: 12 Francis Bacon

novus ordo seclorum 24 a new order of the ages is born
    author: 6 Vergil, Virgil
      work: 8 Eclogues
    motto of: 11 US Great Seal

Now, Voyager
    director: 12 Irving Rapper
    cast: 10 Bette Davis **11** Claude Rains, Janis Wilson, Paul Henreid **12** Gladys Cooper
    score: 10 Max Steiner

now and then 8 on-and-off, periodic, sometime, sporadic **9** irregular, sometimes, temporary **10** infrequent, occasional **11** irregularly **12** infrequently, occasionally, periodically, sporadically

Nox, Nyx
    goddess of: 5 night

noxious 4 foul **6** deadly, lethal, putrid **7** baneful, beastly, harmful, hurtful, noisome **8** damaging, virulent **9** injurious, loathsome, poisonous, revolting **10** abominable, disgusting, pernicious, putrescent **11** deleterious **12** foul-smelling

nth degree 5 limit **6** utmost **7** extreme

nuance 5 shade, touch **6** nicety **7** finesse **8** delicacy, fineness, keenness, subtlety **9** sharpness, variation **10** modulation, refinement **11** discernment

nub 4 core, crux, gist, hump, knob, knot, lump, node **5** bulge, heart **6** kernel **7** essence **8** swelling **10** projection, prominence, tumescence **11** nitty-gritty **12** protuberance

nubbin 3 ear **4** corn, lump, stub **5** bulge, fruit, piece, stump **10** diminutive

Nubbles, Kit
    character in: 19 The Old Curiosity Shop
    author: 7 Dickens

nubbly 5 lumpy, rough **6** coarse, knobby, pebbly

nucleus 3 nub **4** core, pith, seed **5** heart **6** center, kernel

nude 3 raw **4** bare **5** bared, naked **6** unclad **7** exposed **8** in the raw, stripped **9** unadorned, unarrayed, unclothed, uncovered, undressed
French: 9 au naturel

nudge 3 jab, jog, nod **4** bump, jolt, poke, prod, push **5** elbow, press, punch, shove, touch **6** jostle, motion, signal **8** indicate

nugatory 4 idle **5** empty **6** hollow, otiose, paltry **7** trivial, useless **8** piddling, trifling **9** meritless, valueless, worthless **10** profitless **11** ineffectual **12** functionless **15** inconsequential

nugget 4 hunk, lump **5** chunk, piece

nuisance 4 bore, fret, hurt, pain, pest **5** curse, thorn, worry **6** blight, bother, burden, plague **7** scourge, torment, trouble **8** handicap, vexation **9** annoyance, grievance **10** affliction, irritation, misfortune, pestilence **11** aggravation, botheration **13** inconvenience

Nuk
    capital of: 9 Greenland

Nukualofa
    capital of: 5 Tonga

null 2 NG **4** void **6** no good **7** invalid **9** valueless, worthless **10** immaterial **11** inoperative, nonexistent, unimportant **13** insignificant

nullification 6 repeal **7** voiding **8** recision **9** abolition, annulment **10** abrogation, rescinding **11** abolishment **12** cancellation, invalidation

nullify 4 veto, void **5** annul **6** cancel, repeal, revoke **7** abolish, rescind, retract **8** abrogate, make void, override, set aside **10** invalidate

nullity 6 cipher, naught **7** nothing **9** nonentity

numb 4 dead **6** frozen **8** deadened **9** insensate, unfeeling **10** insensible, narcotized **12** anesthetized

number 3 mob, sum, tot **4** army, bevy, book, herd, host, mass, part **5** array, bunch, count, crowd, digit, group, issue, swarm, tally, total **6** amount, cipher, figure, reckon, scores, symbol **7** chapter, company, compute, edition, foliate, integer, numeral, passage, section **8** division, estimate, magazine, numerate, paginate, quantity **9** abundance, aggregate, calculate, character, enumerate, multitude, paragraph, quarterly **10** assemblage, quantities **13** preponderance

numbered numbered weighed divided
    Aramaic: 21 mene mene tekel upharsin
    called: 16 writing on the wall
    foretells destruction of: 10 Belshazzar
    Biblical book of: 6 Daniel

numberless 6 myriad **7** copious, umpteen **8** unending, zillions **9** countless, plenteous, unbounded, uncounted

11 illimitable, uncountable **12** immeasurable **13** multitudinous

numbness 8 deadness **11** insentience

numeral 5 digit **6** cipher, figure, letter, number, symbol **7** integer **9** character

numerate 3 add **5** count, tally, total **6** number, reckon **7** compute, tick off **9** calculate

numerophobia
    fear of: 7 numbers

numerous 4 many **6** myriad **7** copious, profuse **8** abundant **9** plentiful **13** multitudinous

Numidia see **7** Algeria

Numipu see **8** Nez Perce

Numitor
    king of: 9 Alba Longa
    father: 5 Proca
    brother: 7 Amulius
    daughter: 10 Rhea Silvia
    grandson: 5 Remus **7** Romulus

numskull, numbskull 3 sap **4** dolt, dope, fool, jerk **5** dummy, dunce, idiot, klutz, ninny **6** dimwit, nitwit **7** dullard, half-wit **8** bonehead, dummkopf, imbecile, lunkhead, silly ass **9** blockhead, simpleton **10** dunderhead, muttonhead, nincompoop, noodlehead **11** chowderhead, knucklehead **12** scatterbrain

Nun see **4** Nunu

nuncio 5 envoy **6** legate **8** diplomat, minister **9** messenger **10** ambassador **11** papallegate **14** representative

nunnery 5 abbey, order **6** priory **7** cenacle, convent **8** cloister **9** hermitage, monastery **10** sisterhood

Nun's Story, The
    director: 12 Fred Zinneman
    based on story by: 12 Kathryn Hulme
    cast: 10 Dean Jagger, Edith Evans, Peter Finch **13** Audrey Hepburn, Peggy Ashcroft **15** Colleen Dewhurst

Nunu
    also: 3 Nun
    origin: 8 Egyptian
    god of: 5 ocean
    personifies: 5 chaos

nuptial 7 marital **8** conjugal, hymeneal **9** connubial **11** matrimonial

nuptials 7 wedding **8** marriage **9** espousals, hymeneals **12** matrimonials

Nurmi, Paavo
    nickname: 13 The Flying Finn
    sport: 5 track
    won: 8 Olympics

nurse 4 feed **5** nanny, treat **6** attend, doctor, foster, harbor, remedy, sister, succor, suckle **7** care for, nourish, nurture, promote **8** attend to, guardian **9** attendant, cultivate, encourage, governess
    Hindi/Indian: 4 ayah
    Orient: 4 amah

famous: 11 Edith Cavell, Sister Kenny **19** Florence Nightingale

nursery 6 hotbed **9** incubator, preschool **10** greenhouse, schoolroom **12** conservatory, kindergarten

nursery rhyme character 3 Tom **4** Jack, Jill, Mary **5** Peter, Polly **6** Bo-Peep **8** King Cole **9** Jack Sprat **10** Jack Horner, Miss Muffet **11** Mother Goose **12** Humpty Dumpty **13** Little Boy Blue, Mother Hubbard

nurture 4 feed, mess, rear, tend **5** breed, raise, teach, train, tutor **6** foster, school **7** bring up, develop, educate, nourish, prepare, sustain, victual **8** instruct, maintain **9** cultivate, provision **10** discipline, strengthen

Nusantara *see* **9** Indonesia

nut 3 fan, pit **4** buff, seed **5** freak, idiot, loony, stone **6** madman, maniac, zealot **7** devotee, fanatic, lunatic, oddball **8** crackpot **9** eccentric, screwball **10** aficionado, enthusiast, psychopath **11** afficionado

Nut
origin: 8 Egyptian
goddess of: 3 sky

nut-brown 5 tawny **6** auburn, brunet **8** brunette, cinnamon

Nutcracker, The
also: 13 Shchelkunchik
ballet by: 11 Tchaikovsky
based on fairy tale by: 11 ETA

Hoffmann
contains: 17 Waltz of the Flowers **24** Dance of the Sugarplum Fairy
characters: 4 mice **5** Clara, Fritz **6** prince **10** nutcracker **11** toy soldiers **12** Drosselmeyer **14** Sugarplum Fairy

nutmeg
botanical name: 17 Myristica fragrans
from same plant as: 4 mace
origin: 9 Indonesia
use: 5 punch **6** eggnog **8** desserts **10** vegetables **11** baked dishes

Nutmeg State
nickname of: 11 Connecticut

nutriment 4 chow, eats, fare, feed, food, meat, mess **5** board **6** fodder, forage **7** aliment, edibles **8** eatables, victuals **9** foodstuff, groceries, provender **10** provisions, sustenance **11** nourishment, subsistence

nutrition 4 chow, feed, food, grub **6** fodder, forage, silage **7** edibles, rations **8** eatables **9** groceries, pasturage, provender **10** foodstuffs, provisions, sustenance **11** nourishment, subsistence

nutritious 9 wholesome **10** nourishing, sustaining

nuts 3 mad **4** bats, daft **5** balmy, crazy, dotty, loony, potty, wacko, wacky **6** insane **7** bananas, bonkers, cracked, touched **8** demented, deranged, unhinged **10** unbalanced

nutty 3 mad **4** daft **5** balmy, crazy, dippy, dotty, goofy, inane, loony, silly, wacko, wacky **6** cuckoo, insane, screwy, weirdo **7** bonkers, cracked, foolish, lunatic, meshuga, touched **8** bughouse, demented **9** senseless **10** addlepated, squirrelly **11** harebrained **12** crackbrained

nuzzle 3 pat, pet **4** buss, kiss **5** smack **6** caress, coddle, cosset, cuddle, fondle, nestle **7** embrace, snuggle

Nyasaland *see* **6** Malawi

nyctophobia
fear of: 8 darkness **14** the dark of night

nyet
Russian: 2 no

nymph 5 belle, dryad, houri, naiad, nixie, oread, sylph **6** beauty, daphne, kelpie, maenad, nereid, ondine, sprite, undine **7** charmer, galatea **8** Eurydice **9** hamadryad

Nymphaea
epithet of: 9 Aphrodite
means: 6 bridal

Nyx, Nox
form: 7 goddess
personifies: 5 night
originated from: 5 Chaos
children: 3 Ker **4** Eris **5** Fates, Geras, Momus, Moros, Oizys **6** Aether, Hemera, Hypnos, Somnus **7** Nemesis, Oneiroi **8** Thanatos

oaf 3 sap **4** boob, boor, clod, dolt, dope, fool, jerk, lout **5** booby, dummy, dunce, idiot, klutz, moron, ninny **6** lummox, nitwit **7** dullard, half-wit **8** bonehead, imbecile, numskull **9** blockhead, ignoramus, numbskull, simpleton **10** dunderhead, nincompoop

oafish 4 rude **5** crude **6** coarse, gauche, vulgar **7** boorish, doltish, loutish, uncouth **9** unrefined **10** unpolished

oak 7 Quercus

varieties: 3 bur, cow, pin, red, she **4** bear, blue, cork, deer, Holm, jack, live, maul, post, silk **5** black, Emory, holly, scrub, ubame, water, white **6** basket, Belote, canyon, Ceylon, Daimyo, gambel, gander, Havard, Indian, island, Kermes, Konara, laurel, Oregon, poison, possum, Turkey, Turner, valley, willow, yellow **7** Ballota, Bartram, Belloot, Catesby, Durmast, English, Georgia, Italian, Kellogg, leather, Lebanon, overcup, scarlet, shingle, Spanish, tanbark, truffle, western **8** Arkansas, bluejack, chestnut, McDonald, mossy-cup, shinnery, Texas red **9** blackjack, Engelmann, flowering, Jerusalem, Mongolian, pubescent, swamp post **10** Chinquapin, Darlington, ring-cupped, Spanish red, swamp white **11** huckleberry, Japanese red, northern pin, northern red, Shumard's red **12** interior live, laurel-leaved, rock chestnut, southern live, yellow-barked **13** dwarf chestnut, oriental white, swamp chestnut **14** Austrian turkey, California live, yellow chestnut **15** California black, California field, California scrub, California white **16** high- ground willow **17** Japanese evergreen **18** Rocky Mountain scrub
venerated by: 6 Druids

Oak, Gabriel
character in: 22 Far From the Madding Crowd
author: 5 Hardy

Oakie, Jack
real name: 19 Lewis Delaney Offield
born: 9 Sedalia (Sadalia) MO
roles: 16 The Great Dictator **17** Alice in Wonderland

Oakland

baseball team: 2 A's **9** Athletics
football team: 8 Invaders

oar 3 row **4** pole **5** blade, rower, scull **6** paddle, propel **9** propeller
blade: 4 palm, peel
fulcrum: 5 thole **7** oarlock, rowlock
part: 4 loom **5** shaft **6** collar

oarsman 5 pilot, rower **6** bowman **7** mariner, sculler **8** helmsman **9** gondolier, propeller

oasis 5 haven **6** asylum, harbor, refuge **7** retreat, sanctum, shelter **9** green spot, sanctuary, water hole **11** fertile area **13** watering place

oast 4 kiln, oven

oat, oats 5 Avena **11** Avena sativa
varieties: 3 sea **4** wild **6** potato **8** animated **9** Tartarian **11** slender wild

Oates, Joyce Carol
author of: 4 Them **9** Childwold **10** Bellefleur, Wonderland **11** Unholy Loves, Wheel of Love **15** Son of the Morning **18** A Bloodsmoor Romance **19** Do With Me What You Will

oath 3 vow **5** curse **6** avowal, pledge **8** cuss word, swearing **9** affidavit, blasphemy, expletive, obscenity, profanity **10** adjuration, deposition **11** affirmation, attestation, declaration, imprecation, malediction

oaths
god of: 6 Horcus, Sancus **10** Dius Fidius, Semo Sancus

oatmeal 6 cereal **7** pottage **8** drammock, porridge

Obadiah 4 Obad **7** prophet **12** minor prophet
father: 4 Azel **6** Jehiel **8** Izrahiah, Shemaiah
son: 8 Ishmaiah
predicted fall of: 4 Edom

Obata, Gyo
architect of: 20 Dallas--Ft Worth Airport **25** National Air and Space Museum (Smithsonian Institution)

obdurate 5 cruel, harsh **6** mulish **7** adamant, callous, unmoved, willful **8** hardened, pitiless, stubborn, uncaring **9** immovable, merciless, obstinate, pigheaded, unfeeling, unpitying, unsparing, untouched **10** bullheaded, headstrong, inflexible, unmerciful, unyielding **11** cold-blooded, hardhearted, intractable **12** ungovernable, unman-

ageable **13** unsympathetic **14** uncontrollable **15** uncompassionate

obeah 5 charm, magic **6** fetish, voodoo **7** sorcery **10** witchcraft
practiced in: 6 Guiana **10** West Indies

obedience 8 docility, yielding **9** deference, ductility, obeisance **10** accordance, allegiance, compliance, subjection, submission **11** conformance, dutifulness, willingness **12** acquiescence, subservience, tractability **14** conformability, submissiveness

obedient 5 loyal **6** docile **7** devoted, dutiful **8** amenable, faithful, obeisant, yielding **9** compliant, tractable **10** governable, law-abiding, respectful, submissive **11** acquiescent, deferential, subservient

obeisance 3 bow **5** honor **6** curtsy, esteem, fealty, homage, regard **7** loyalty, respect **8** courtesy, fidelity, humility, kneeling **9** deference, obedience, reverence **10** allegiance, humbleness, subjection, submission, veneration **11** prostration **12** genuflection **13** self-abasement

obelisk 5 pylon, shaft, tower **6** column, dagger, needle, pillar **8** memorial, monolith, monument

Oberon
character in: 21 A Midsummer Night's Dream
author: 11 Shakespeare
consort: 7 Titania

Oberon
opera by: 5 Weber
character: 5 Reiza
setting: 18 court of Charlemagne **21** court of Haroun al Rashid

Oberon, Merle
real name: 26 Estelle Merle O'Brien Thompson
husband: 14 Alexander Korda
born: 8 Tasmania
roles: 5 Hotel **7** Desiree **15** A Song to Remember **16** Wuthering Heights **19** The Scarlet Pimpernel **25** The Private Life of Henry VIII **30** The Private Life of Henry the Eighth

obese 3 fat **5** gross, heavy, plump, porky, pudgy, stout, tubby **6** chubby, fleshy, portly, rotund **7** paunchy **9** corpulent **10** overweight, potbellied

obesity 3 fat **7** fatness, liposis **8** adiposis, enormity **9** heaviness, plumpness, stoutness **10** corpulence, overweight

obey 4 heed, mind 5 bow to, serve 6 assent, concur 7 abide by, observe, respect, yield to 8 accede to, submit to 9 acquiesce, conform to, succumb to 10 comply with, toe the line 12 follow orders

obfuscate 4 blur 5 befog 6 garble, mess up, muddle 7 becloud, confuse, distort, fluster, obscure, stupefy 8 confound, scramble 10 complicate

obfuscation 8 flummery 9 confusion 10 doubletalk, mumbo jumbo

obi 4 sash 5 obeah 6 girdle

obiit 6 he died 7 she died

obiter dictum 9 diversion 10 digression, divagation, side remark

object 3 aim, end, use 4 body, butt, dupe, form, gist, goal, pith, prey 5 abhor, basis, cause, knock, point, sense, thing 6 balk at, carp at, design, device, dingus, gadget, intent, loathe, motive, oppose, quarry, reason, target, victim 7 article, cavil at, condemn, dislike, essence, frown on, meaning, mission, protest, purpose, subject 8 be averse, cynosure, denounce 9 abominate, criticize, doohickey, incentive, intention, objective, principle, recipient, substance 10 inducement, phenomenon 11 contrivance, explanation, thingamabob, thingamajig 12 be at odds with, disapprove of, significance 13 find fault with, take exception 18 remonstrate against

objection 4 beef, kick 5 cavil 7 protest 8 demurral, rebuttal 9 challenge, complaint, criticism, exception 10 dissension, opposition 11 disapproval, reservation 12 disagreement 13 contradiction 14 disapprobation, opposing reason 15 counter argument

objectionable 4 foul, vile 5 nasty 6 odious 8 unseemly 9 abhorrent, loathsome, obnoxious, offensive, revolting 10 abominable, despicable, disgusting, unbearable, unpleasant 11 displeasing, distasteful, intolerable, unendurable 12 disagreeable, unacceptable 13 inappropriate

objective 3 aim, end 4 fair, goal, just, mark, real 6 actual, design, intent, target 7 mission, purpose 8 detached, unbiased, unswayed 9 impartial, intention, uncolored 10 impersonal, open-minded 11 destination 12 uninfluenced, unprejudiced 13 disinterested, dispassionate

objectivity 8 fairness 10 detachment, neutrality 12 impartiality

object to 7 condemn, dislike 9 frown upon 12 disapprove of 14 discountenance 15 take exception to 16 find unacceptable

objet d'art 5 bijou, curio 7 bibelot, trinket 9 art object

oblation 4 gift 8 offering 9 offertory 10 collection

obligated 5 bound 6 forced, liable 7 pledged 8 beholden, indebted 9 committed 11 constrained

obligation 4 bond, care, debt, duty, oath, onus, word 6 charge, pledge 7 compact, promise 8 contract, guaranty, warranty 9 agreement, guarantee, liability 10 a favor owed, commitment, constraint 12 indebtedness 13 answerability, understanding 14 accountability, responsibility

obligatory 7 binding 8 coercive, enforced, required 9 mandatory, necessary, requisite 10 compulsory, imperative, peremptory 11 unavoidable

oblige 3 aid 4 bind, help, make 5 favor, force, impel, serve 6 assist, coerce, compel 7 require, support 8 obligate 9 constrain 11 accommodate, do a favor for, necessitate 13 do a service for, to be duty bound

obliged 5 bound 7 favored, pleased 8 assisted, beholden, indebted, required, thankful 9 compelled 12 accommodated

obliging 4 kind 6 polite 7 amiable, helpful 8 cheerful, friendly, gracious 9 agreeable, courteous 10 solicitous 11 complaisant, considerate, cooperative, good-natured, sympathetic 12 well-disposed 13 accommodating

oblique 3 sly 4 awry 5 askew 6 aslant, covert, hinted, masked, tilted, veiled 7 cloaked, devious, furtive, implied, slanted, sloping 8 allusive, diagonal, inclined, indirect, slanting, sneaking 9 suggested, underhand

obliterate 4 raze 5 erase, level 6 cancel, delete, efface, remove, rub out 7 abolish, blot out, destroy, expunge, wipe out 9 eradicate, write over 10 annihilate, strike over

obliteration 8 deletion 9 abolition, expunging, wiping out 11 blotting out, destruction, eradication 12 annihilation

oblivion 5 limbo 7 the void 9 blankness, disregard, obscurity, unconcern 11 blotting out, nothingness 12 nonexistence 13 forgetfulness, insensibility, obliviousness 14 insignificance 15 unconsciousness

oblivious 8 careless 9 forgetful, unaware of, unmindful 10 heedless of, insensible 11 inattentive, unconcerned, unobservant 12 disregardful, undiscerning 13 unconscious of

Oblonsky, Prince Stepan
character in: 12 Anna Karenina
author: 7 Tolstoy

obloquy 5 abuse, odium, shame 6 infamy, rebuke 7 calumny, censure, railing 8 contempt, disfavor, disgrace, ignominy, reviling 9 discredit, invective 10 defamation, opprobrium, scurrility 11 degradation, humiliation, verbal abuse 12 billingsgate,

condemnation, denunciation, dressing-down, vilification

obnoxious 4 foul, vile 5 nasty 6 odious 7 hateful 8 unseemly 9 abhorrent, loathsome, offensive, repellent, repugnant, revolting 10 abominable, despicable, detestable, disgusting, nauseating, unbearable, unpleasant 11 displeasing, intolerable, unendurable 12 disagreeable, insufferable 13 inappropriate, objectionable

oboe family
instruments: 5 shawm 6 curtal, pommer, racket 7 bassoon, bombard, curtall, hautboy 8 crumhorn, schalmey, tenoroon 10 Cor Anglais, oboe d'Amore 11 English horn, heckelphone, sarusophone 12 oboe da caccia, sarrusophone 13 contra bassoon, double bassoon

O'Brian, Hugh
real name: 11 Hugh J Krampe
born: 11 Rochester NY
roles: 9 Wyatt Earp 27 The Life and Legend of Wyatt Earp

O'Brien, Edna
author of: 5 Night 11 A Pagan Place 13 The Lonely Girl 14 The Country Girl 20 August Is a Wicked Month 24 Girls in Their Married Bliss

O'Brien, Margaret
real name: 18 Angela Maxine O'Brien
born: 12 Los Angeles CA
roles: 8 Jane Eyre 11 Little Women 15 Meet Me in St Louis 24 Our Vines Have Tender Grapes

O'Brien, Pat
real name: 26 William Joseph Patrick O'Brien
born: 11 Milwaukee WI
roles: 12 Hildy Johnson, The Front Page 13 Some Like It Hot, The Last Hurrah 20 Angels with Dirty Faces 22 Knute Rockne All American
autobiography: 12 Wind on My Back

obscene 4 blue, foul, lewd 5 bawdy, dirty 6 filthy, smutty, vulgar, x-rated 8 indecent, prurient 9 salacious 10 lascivious, lubricious 12 pornographic, scatological 16 morally offensive

obscenity 8 cuss word, lewdness 9 dirtiness, indecency, profanity, prurience, swear word, taboo word, vulgarity 10 filthiness, smuttiness 11 pornography 13 salaciousness 14 four-letter word, lasciviousness

obscuration 7 eclipse, masking, veiling 8 cloaking, clouding, covering 9 darkening, shadowing 10 concealing 11 concealment

obscure 3 dim, fog 4 blur, dark, hide, mask, veil 5 bedim, befog, block, cloak, cloud, cover, dingy, dusky, faint, murky, vague 6 cloudy, darken, hidden, muddle, screen, shadow, shroud, somber, unsung 7 becloud, conceal, confuse, cryptic, curtain, eclipse, shadowy, unclear, unknown, unnoted **8** befuddle, confused, disguise, nameless, puzzling **9** confusing, enigmatic, forgotten, lightless, obfuscate, uncertain, unheard of, unlighted **10** indefinite, indistinct, overshadow, perplexing, unrenowned **11** indefinable, inscrutable, little known, out-of-the-way, unimportant **12** unfathomable **13** inconspicuous, insignificant, unilluminated **15** inconsequential

obscurity 3 fog **4** mist **5** cloud, shade **6** shadow **7** dimness, mystery, opacity, privacy **8** darkness **9** ambiguity, seclusion, vagueness **10** cloudiness

obsequies 5 rites **6** burial **7** funeral **15** memorial service

obsequious 6 menial **7** fawning, servile, slavish **8** cowering, cringing, toadying **9** kowtowing, truckling **11** bootlicking, deferential, subservient, sycophantic **12** ingratiating, mealy-mouthed **14** apple-polishing

observance 4 rite **6** custom, regard, ritual **7** heeding, keeping, obeying **8** ceremony, practice **9** adherence, attending, attention, following, formality, solemnity **10** ceremonial, compliance **11** celebration, observation **13** commemoration **15** memorialization

observant 5 alert, awake, aware **7** careful, heedful, mindful **8** vigilant, watchful **9** attentive, conscious, regardful, wide-awake **10** perceptive **12** on the lookout

observation 4 heed, idea, view **5** probe **6** eyeing, notice, remark, search, seeing, survey, theory **7** comment, finding, opinion, viewing **8** interest, judgment, scrutiny, spotting, watching **9** assertion, attention, beholding, detection, diagnosis, discovery, glimpsing, observing, statement **10** cognizance, commentary, inspection, reflection **11** description, examination, heedfulness **12** surveillance, watchfulness **13** pronouncement **20** firsthand information

observatory 5 tower **7** lookout **9** satellite **11** planetarium
name: 4 Hale, Lick **6** Yerkes **7** Palomar, Whipple **8** Kitt Peak, Mt Wilson **11** Las Campanas, Mount Wilson **12** Big Bear Solar **14** Royal Greenwich

observe 3 eye, say, see **4** espy, heed, keep, mark, note, obey, ogle, spot, view **5** honor, opine, state, watch **6** assert, behold, detect, follow, notice, peer at, regard, remark, size up, survey **7** abide by, comment, declare, defer to, execute, fulfill, glimpse, inspect, make out, mention, perform, reflect, respect, stare at **8** adhere to, announce, carry out, discover, perceive, sanctify, theorize **9** celebrate, recognize, solemnize **10** be guided by,

comply with, consecrate **11** acknowledge, acquiesce to, commemorate, take stock of **12** catch sight of **14** pay attention to

observer 6 viewer **7** watcher **8** onlooker **12** investigator

obsessed 5 beset **7** haunted **8** hung up on, maniacal **9** dominated, possessed **10** controlled **15** having a fixation

obsession 5 craze, mania, quirk **6** phobia **8** fixation **9** fixed idea, monomania **11** infatuation **13** preoccupation **16** overwhelming fear **18** neurotic conviction

obsolescent 8 dying out **9** declining **11** on the way out **12** disappearing **16** becoming obsolete **17** becoming out-of-date

obsolete 3 out **5** dated, passe **6** bygone **7** antique, archaic, extinct **8** outdated, out of use, outmoded **9** out-of-date **10** antiquated **12** old-fashioned, out of fashion

obstacle 3 bar **4** curb, snag **5** block, catch, check **6** hurdle **7** barrier, problem **8** blockade, stoppage **9** barricade, hindrance, roadblock **10** difficulty, impediment, limitation **11** obstruction, restriction **12** interference **14** stumbling block

obstetrician
French: 10 accoucheur

obstinacy 8 rigidity **10** mulishness, resistance **11** willfulness **12** stubbornness **13** inflexibility, intransigence, pigheadedness

obstinate 6 dogged, mulish **7** staunch, willful **8** obdurate, resolute, stubborn **9** pigheaded, steadfast, tenacious, unbending **10** headstrong, inflexible, refractory, self-willed, unyielding **11** intractable **12** recalcitrant, ungovernable, unmanageable **14** uncontrollable **20** unreasonably stubborn

obstreperous 4 loud **5** noisy **6** unruly **8** perverse **9** clamorous, rampaging **10** boisterous, disorderly, refractory, roistering, uproarious, vociferous **11** disobedient **12** uncontrolled, ungovernable, unmanageable, unrestrained **14** uncontrollable

obstruct 3 bar **4** curb, halt, hide, mask, stop **5** block, check, cloak, close, cover, dam up, debar, delay, limit, stall **6** arrest, hinder, hobble, impede, plug up, retard, shroud, stifle, thwart **7** eclipse, inhibit, shut off **8** blockade, choke off, close off, restrict, suppress, throttle **9** barricade, frustrate **18** bring to a standstill

obstruction 3 bar **4** curb, snag, stop **5** block, check, hitch **6** hurdle **7** barrier **8** blockade, obstacle, stoppage **9** barricade, hindrance **10** bottleneck, impediment **11** encumbrance

obtain 3 get **4** earn, gain, hold, take

5 exist, glean, stand **6** attain, come by, gather, pick up, secure **7** achieve, acquire, prevail, procure, receive **9** get hold of **14** get one's hands on **16** gain possession of

obtainment 11 achievement, acquirement, acquisition, procurement

obtrude 5 eject, expel, force **6** butt in, impose, meddle, thrust **7** presume, project **9** interfere

obtrusive 4 nosy **5** brash **6** prying, snoopy **7** bulging, forward, salient **8** familiar, meddling **9** intruding, intrusive, prominent **10** aggressive, jutting out, meddlesome, projecting, protruding **11** conspicuous, impertinent, interfering, outstanding, protuberant, sticking out, trespassing **12** interrupting, presumptuous

obtuse 4 dull, slow **5** blunt, dense, thick **6** simple, stupid **7** blunted **8** ignorant, not sharp **9** unpointed **10** insensible, not pointed, slow-witted **11** insensitive, unsharpened **12** imperceptive, thick-skinned **15** uncomprehending

obtuseness 8 dullness **9** denseness, ignorance, stupidity **13** insensitivity **14** slow-wittedness **15** thickheadedness **16** lack of perception, simplemindedness **19** lack of comprehension

obverse 4 face **5** front **10** complement **11** counterpart
of coin: 4 head

obviate 5 avert, avoid, parry **6** divert, remove **7** fend off, prevent, ward off **8** preclude, stave off **9** forestall, sidetrack, turn aside **10** circumvent, do away with **11** nip in the bud

obvious 5 clear, plain **6** patent **7** evident, glaring, visible **8** apparent, distinct, man- ifest, palpable, striking, unhidden, unmasked, unveiled **10** undeniable **11** conspicuous, discernible, perceptible, self-evident, unconcealed, undisguised **12** in plain sight, unmistakable **24** plain as the nose on your face

ocarina 11 sweet potato **14** wind instrument

O'Casey, Sean
author of: 10 Purple Dust **12** The Green Crow **17** Juno and the Paycock **18** The Shadow of a Gunman **20** The Plough and the Stars

occasion 4 base, time **5** basis, cause, event **6** advent, affair, chance, elicit, ground, lead to, motive, prompt, reason **7** episode, inspire, opening, provoke, venture **8** incident, instance **9** adventure, happening, rationale, situation **10** bring about, experience, motivation, occurrence **11** celebration, explanation, opportunity, provocation **12** circumstance, special event, suitable time **13** justification,

opportune time
14 convenient time, important event, particular time

occasional 4 rare **6** fitful, random **8** sporadic, uncommon **9** irregular, recurring, scattered, spasmodic, uncertain **10** incidental, infrequent, now and then, unreliable **12** intermittent

occasionally 6 rarely, seldom **7** at times **8** fitfully **9** sometimes **10** now and then **11** irregularly **12** infrequently, once in a while, periodically, sporadically **14** from time to time, intermittently **15** every now and then, once in a blue moon

occidental 7 Western **8** American, European **9** Hesperian, Westerner

occlude 4 clog, plug **5** block, choke, close **6** shut up, stop up **7** congest, shut off, stopper **8** choke off, obstruct **9** barricade, constrict **11** strangulate

occult 4 dark **5** magic **6** arcane, hidden, mystic, secret, veiled **7** obscure, private **8** esoteric, mystical, shrouded **9** concealed **10** cabalistic, mysterious, unrevealed **11** undisclosed **12** supernatural

occupancy 3 use **6** tenure **7** tenancy **8** lodgment **9** enjoyment, habitancy **10** engagement, habitation, occupation, possession **11** inhabitancy

occupant 5 owner **6** lessee, lodger, native, renter, roomer, tenant **7** dweller, settler **8** colonist, occupier, resident **9** addressee **10** inhabitant **11** householder

occupation 3 job **4** line, work **5** craft, forte, trade **6** career, living, metier, sphere **7** calling, control, pursuit, seizure **8** activity, business, capacity, conquest, lifework, vocation **9** specialty **10** employment, line of work, livelihood, possession, profession, subjection **11** foreign rule, subjugation **14** specialization **15** military control **18** military occupation

occupied 5 in use **6** amused, took up, used up **7** dwelt in, engaged, lived in, overran, overrun, taken up **8** absorbed, tenanted **9** concerned, conquered, inhabited, resided in **12** had control of, held in thrall **13** was situated in **16** took possession of

occupy 3 use **4** be in, be on, busy, fill, hold **5** amuse, sit in **6** absorb, employ, engage, fill up, room in, take up **7** concern, conquer, dwell in, engross, enslave, inhabit, lodge in, overrun, pervade, possess **8** permeate, reside in, saturate **9** entertain, subjugate **10** monopolize **11** have control **12** be situated in, hold in thrall **14** be the tenants of **16** take possession of

occur 3 hit **4** rise **5** arise, ensue **6** appear, befall, crop up, emerge, happen, result, strike, turn up **7** be found, come off, develop **8** spring up **9** come

about, eventuate, take place, transpire **10** come to pass **11** materialize **13** cross one's mind, enter one's mind

occurrence 5 event **6** affair **7** episode, venture **8** business, incident, instance, occasion **9** adventure, emergence, happening, situation, unfolding **10** appearance, experience, proceeding **11** development, transaction **12** circumstance **13** manifestation **15** materialization

ocean 3 sea **4** deep, main, pond **5** flood, water **7** big pond, high sea **9** briny deep
  god of: 3 Nun **4** Nanu **7** Neptune, Oceanus **8** Poseidon

Oceania, Oceanica 9 Melanesia, Polynesia **10** Micronesia **11** Australia
  ocean: 12 South Pacific
  island: 4 Cook, Guam, Fiji, Maui, Niue, Wake **5** Aunuu, Bonin, Kauai, Lanai, Tonga **6** Bikini, Futuna, Hawaii, Marcus, Midway, Rurutu, Tahiti, Tubuai, Tuvalu, Wallis **7** Gambier, Gilbert, Iwo Jima, Leeward, Mariana, Molokai, Phoenix, Solomon, Tokelau, Tuamotu, Tutuila, Vanuatu, Volcano **8** Aitu taki, Bismarck, Bora-Bora, Johnston, Kiribati, Marshall, Pitcairn, Windward **9** Australia, Christmas, Marquesas, Trobriand **10** New Zealand **12** New Caledonia, Western Samoa **14** Papua New Guinea **15** French Polynesia

oceanic 6 marine **7** aquatic, pelagic **8** seagoing **9** thalassic

Oceanid
  form: 5 nymph
  location: 3 sea
  father: 7 Oceanus
  mother: 6 Tethys

Oceanus
  member of: 6 Titans
  father: 6 Uranus
  mother: 4 Gaea
  consort of: 6 Tethys
  father of: 8 Oceanids **9** river gods
  son: 7 Proteus
  daughter: 5 Doris, Persa **7** Philyra
  form: 6 stream

ocelot 3 cat **7** wildcat

ochlophobia
  fear of: 6 crowds

Ochoa, Severo
  born: 5 Spain
  profession: 10 biochemist

Ockelman, Constance Frances Marie
  real name of: 12 Veronica Lake

O'Connor, Carroll
  born: 7 Bronx NY
  roles: 12 Archie Bunker, Archie's Place **14** All in the Family
  restaurant: 12 The Ginger Man

O'Connor, Donald
  born: 9 Chicago IL
  roles: 9 Beau Geste **15** Singin' in the

Rain **18** Tom Sawyer Detective **21** Francis the Talking Mule

O'Connor, Flannery
  author of: 9 Wise Blood **15** The Habit of Being **17** Mystery and Manners **20** A Good Man Is Hard to Find, The Violent Bear It Away

Octavia
  brother: 8 Augustus
  husband: 4 Nero **10** Mark Antony
  grandson: 8 Caligula

October
  flower: 6 cosmos **9** calendula
  French: 7 Octobre
  gem: 4 opal **10** tourmaline
  German: 7 Oktober
  holiday: 9 Halloween (31) **11** Columbus Day (12) **16** United Nations Day (24)
  Italian: 7 Ottobre
  number of days: 9 thirty-one
  origin of name: 4 octo (Latin meaning eight)
  place in year:
    Gregorian: 5 tenth
    Roman: 6 eighth
  Spanish: 7 Octubre
  Zodiac sign: 5 Libra **7** Scorpio

October Light
  author: 11 John Gardner

Octopus, The
  author: 11 Frank Norris

odd 4 rare **5** extra, funny, queer, spare, weird **6** casual, far-out, quaint, single, sundry, unique **7** bizarre, curious, not even, strange, surplus, unusual, various **8** freakish, left over, peculiar, periodic, singular, sporadic, uncommon **9** irregular, remaining, spasmodic, unmatched **10** occasional, outlandish **13** miscellaneous **15** being one of a pair **16** out of the ordinary **17** not divisible by two

oddball 3 nut **4** kook **5** freak **6** weirdo **8** crackpot, original **9** character, eccentric, screwball **10** one-of-a-kind

Odd Couple, The
  character: 3 Roy **5** Myrna, Roger, Speed **6** Miriam, Murray, Vinnie **10** Felix Unger **11** Gloria Unger **12** Cecily Pigeon, Oscar Madison **14** Blanche Madison **15** Gwendolyn Pigeon, (Dr) Nancy Cunningham
  cast: 10 Al Molinaro, Archie Hahn **11** Brett Somers, Carol Shelly, Jack Klugman, Larry Gelman, Monica Evans, Tony Randall **12** Garry Walberg, Janice Hansen, Ryan McDonald **13** Elinor Donahue, Joan Hotchkiss, Penny Marshall
  setting: 11 New York City
  Felix's job: 12 photographer
  Oscar's job: 12 sportswriter
  based on play by: 9 Neil Simon

Odd Couple, The
  director: 8 Gene Saks
  based on play by: 9 Neil Simon

cast: 10 Jack Lemmon (Felix Unger) **11** Herb Edelman, John Fiedler **13** Walter Matthau (Oscar Madison)

oddity 5 freak, sight **6** marvel, rarity, wonder **9** curiosity, queerness **10** phenomenon, uniqueness **11** abnormality, bizarreness, peculiarity, singularity, strangeness, unusualness **12** eccentricity, freakishness **13** individuality, unnaturalness **14** outlandishness
Latin: 8 rara avis

oddly amusing 5 droll, kooky **9** laughable, whimsical **10** ridiculous

odd person 3 nut **4** kook **5** flake, freak **6** looney, weirdo **7** oddball **8** crackpot **9** character, eccentric, screwball

odds and ends 4 olio **6** scraps **8** remnants **9** leftovers **10** hodgepodge, miscellany **11** this and that **13** bits and pieces **18** miscellaneous items

ode 4 epic, hymn, poem **5** lyric, paean, psalm, verse **6** ballad **8** canticle
type: 8 Horatian, Pindaric

Ode on a Grecian Urn
author: 9 John Keats

Ode on Indolence
author: 9 John Keats

Ode on Melancholy
author: 9 John Keats

Ode to a Nightingale
author: 9 John Keats

Ode to Autumn
author: 9 John Keats

Ode to Duty
author: 17 William Wordsworth

Ode to Psyche
author: 9 John Keats

Ode to the West Wind
author: 18 Percy Bysshe Shelley

Odets, Clifford
author of: 9 Golden Boy **12** Awake and Sing **14** The Country Girl **15** Waiting for Lefty **17** The Flowering Peach

Odin
also: 5 Othin
brother: 2 Ve **4** Vili
children: 4 Hodr, Thor **5** Baldr **6** Balder, Baldur
counterpart: 5 Woden, Wotan
court: 8 Valhalla
father: 3 Bor
god of: 3 war **6** poetry, wisdom **9** knowledge
grandson: 7 Volsung
home: 9 Gladsheim
horse: 8 Sleipnir
magic ring: 8 Draupnir
Norse myth: 10 chief deity
origin: 12 Scandinavian
raven: 5 Hugin, Munin
remaining eye: 3 sun
ruler of: 5 Aexir
spear: 7 Gungnir
throne: 10 Hlidskjalf

wife: 3 Fri **5** Frigg, Frija **6** Frigga
wolf: 4 Geri **5** Freki

odious 4 evil, foul, vile **5** hated, nasty **6** rotten **7** hateful, heinous, hideous **8** infamous **9** invidious, loathsome, monstrous, obnoxious, offensive, repugnant, repulsive, revolting, sickening **10** abominable, despicable, detestable, disgusting, nauseating, unbearable **11** intolerable, unendurable **12** contemptible **13** objectionable

odium 5 shame **6** hatred, infamy **7** disgust **8** contempt, disfavor, disgrace, dishonor, ignominy **9** antipathy, discredit, disesteem, disrepute **10** abhorrence, disrespect, opprobrium, repugnance **11** detestation, disapproval **14** disapprobation

odonata
class: 8 hexapoda
phylum: 10 arthropoda
group: 9 damselfly, dragonfly

odor 4 aura **5** aroma, scent, smell, stink **6** flavor, stench **7** bouquet, essence, perfume **9** effluvium, fragrance **10** atmosphere

odoriferous 4 rank **5** acrid, fetid **6** putrid, smelly **7** noisome, odorous, pungent, reeking, scented **8** aromatic, fragrant, perfumed, stinking **10** malodorous

odorous 4 rank **5** acrid, fetid **6** smelly **7** noisome, pungent, reeking, scented **8** aromatic, fragrant, perfumed, stinking

Odysseus
also: 7 Ulysses
king of: 6 Ithaca
father: 7 Laertes
mother: 8 Anticlea
hero of: 5 Iliad **7** Odyssey
wife: 8 Penelope **9** Callidice
son: 9 Telegonus **10** Polypoetes, Telemachus **11** Polyporthis
seduced by: 5 Circe
killed by: 9 Telegonus
epithet: 10 Laertiades

Odyssey
author: 5 Homer
character: 4 Zeus **5** Arete, Circe, Helen **6** Athene, Nestor, Scylla, Sirens **7** Calypso, Cyclops **8** Alcinous, Menelaus, Nausicaa, Odysseus, Penelope, Poseidon, Tiresias **9** Charybdis **10** Telemachus **11** Lotus-eaters

Oedipus
king of: 6 Thebes
father: 5 Laius
mother: 7 Jocasta
foster father: 7 Polybus
foster mother: 6 Merope **8** Periboea
wife: 7 Jocasta
son: 8 Eteocles **9** Polynices
daughter: 7 Ismene **8** Antigone
killed: 5 Laius
defeated: 6 Sphinx

Oedipus at Colonus

author: 9 Sophocles
character: 5 Creon **6** Elders, Ismene **7** Theseus **8** Antigone **9** Polynices

Oedipus Rex (Oedipus Tyrannus)
author: 9 Sophocles
character: 5 Creon, Laius **7** Jocasta **8** Tiresias

oeil-de-boeuf 16 small round window
literally: 8 bull's eye

Oeneus
king of: 7 Calydon
wife: 7 Althaea
son: 8 Meleager

oenology
science of: 5 wines **10** winemaking

Oenone
form: 5 nymph
father: 6 Cebren
husband: 5 Paris

Oersted, Hans Christian
field: 7 physics
nationality: 6 Danish
founded: 16 electromagnetism
isolated: 16 metallic aluminum
named for him: 11 oersted unit

oeuvre 4 work **5** works **13** artist's output

O'Faolain, Sean
author of: 15 The Heat of the Sun **17** A Nest of Simple Folk **22** Midsummer Night's Madness

of a piece 5 alike, equal **7** matched, the same **8** all in one **9** analogous, identical **10** equivalent, homogenous, synonymous **13** evenly matched, one and the same

of bad character 5 shady **8** unsavory **11** of ill repute **12** disreputable, unprincipled

off 2 by **3** bad, far, ill, odd **4** afar, away, down, from, kill, poor, stop **5** amiss, apart, aside, crazy, wrong **6** absent, begone, lessen, remote **7** distant, further, in error, stopped, tainted **8** abnormal, canceled, inferior, mistaken **9** imperfect

offal 4 junk, slag **5** dregs, trash, waste **6** debris, refuse **7** carcass, carrion, garbage, grounds, remains, residue, rubbish **8** leavings

off base 5 amiss, wrong **8** improper, mistaken **10** out of order, unsuitable **13** inappropriate

offbeat 3 odd **7** strange **8** peculiar **9** different, eccentric **14** unconventional

off-center 6 askew **7** strange **9** eccentric **10** imbalanced, nonaligned, unbalanced **12** unreasonable **14** unconventional

off-color 4 blue, lewd, racy, sexy **5** bawdy, dirty, salty, spicy **6** earthy, risque, smutty, wicked **7** naughty, obscene, raunchy **8** improper, indecent, scabrous **9** offensive **10** indelicate, indiscreet, suggestive

off duty 8 inactive 9 at leisure 10 unoccupied 13 on one's own time

Offenbach, Jacques
　born: 7 Cologne, Germany
　composer of: 13 La Belle Helene 15 Tales of Hoffmann, La Vie Parisienne 22 Orpheus in the Underworld

offend 3 err, sin, vex 4 fret, gall, miff, rile 5 anger, annoy, chafe, lapse, pique, wound 6 insult, madden, nettle, rankle 7 affront, disgust, incense, inflame 8 irritate 9 aggravate, displease, misbehave 10 antagonize, disgruntle, exasperate, transgress 13 fall from grace

offender 5 crook, felon 6 sinner 7 culprit 8 criminal, violator 9 wrongdoer 10 malefactor, trespasser

offense 3 sin 4 gibe, harm, slap, slip, snub, twit 5 abuse, crime, lapse, taunt 6 attack, charge, felony, insult 7 affront, assault, misdeed, outrage, umbrage 8 atrocity, enormity, evil deed, rudeness 9 impudence, indignity, insolence, offensive, violation 10 aggression, disrespect, infraction, peccadillo, wickedness 11 delinquency, humiliation, malfeasance, misdemeanor, shortcoming 13 embarrassment, transgression 15 breach of conduct

offensive 4 foul, rank, rude, ugly 5 nasty, onset 6 attack, horrid 7 abusive, assault, hideous, offense, uncivil 8 charging, impudent, insolent, storming 9 abhorrent, assailing, attacking, insulting, loathsome, obnoxious, onslaught, repugnant, repulsive, revolting, sickening, ungallant 10 abominable, aggression, aggressive, assaulting, bombarding, detestable, disgusting, nauseating, unmannerly, unpleasant 11 belligerent, distasteful, intolerable 12 disagreeable, embarrassing, insufferable 13 disrespectful, objectionable

offensiveness 8 rudeness 9 impudence, insolence, nastiness 10 disrespect, horridness, incivility 13 repulsiveness 14 unpleasantness 15 distastefulness

offer 3 bid 5 put up 6 bestow, extend, render, submit, tender 7 advance, hold out, present, proffer, propose, suggest 8 bestow on, offering, overture, proposal, propound, put forth 9 be willing, volunteer 10 invitation, put forward, submission, suggestion 11 make a motion, proposition 12 bring forward 14 put on the market 19 place at one's disposal

offer hospitality 4 host 7 welcome 8 play host 9 entertain 10 give a party, have guests 13 keep open house

offering 3 bid 4 alms, gift 5 goods, wares 6 course 7 charity, present, tribute 8 anathema, bestowal, donation, oblation 9 sacrifice 11 benefi-

cence 12 contribution
　to God: 6 corban 7 deodate
　to household deities: 4 bali

offertory 4 gift 8 oblation, offering 10 collection

offhand, offhanded 5 ad-lib, hasty 6 casual, chance, random 7 relaxed 8 careless, cavalier, heedless 9 facetious, haphazard, impromptu, unplanned, unstudied 10 improvised, nonchalant, off-the-cuff, unprepared 11 spontaneous, thoughtless, unconcerned, unrehearsed 12 off-the-record 14 extemporaneous, unpremeditated

office 3 job 4 post, role 8 capacity, function, position 10 commission, occupation 11 appointment

officer 3 cop 4 head 7 manager 8 director, gendarme, governor 9 constable, detective, executive, patrolman, policeman, president, secretary, treasurer 10 bureaucrat 12 commissioner 13 administrator, vice-president

officers 8 managers 10 executives, management 14 administration

Officers and Gentlemen
　author: 11 Evelyn Waugh

offices 4 duty, help, task 5 favor, trust 6 charge 7 service 8 function, province 10 assistance

office seeker 7 hopeful, nominee 8 aspirant 9 candidate

office worker 5 clerk, steno 6 typist 9 file clerk, secretary 10 bookkeeper, keypuncher 13 data processor 14 clerical worker

official 5 agent 6 formal, vested 7 manager, officer 8 approved, chairman, director, licensed 9 authentic, certified, dignitary, executive, warranted 10 accredited, authorized, sanctioned, supervisor 11 functionary 13 administrator, authoritative 14 administrative 18 administrative head

official communication 5 edict, order, ukase 6 report 7 release 8 bulletin 10 communique 12 proclamation

officialdom 10 government 11 authorities, bureaucracy 14 administration

official paper 4 writ 5 order 8 document 10 instrument

officiate 3 run 4 head, lead 5 chair, emcee 6 direct, handle, manage 7 oversee, preside 8 moderate, regulate 9 supervise 10 administer 11 superintend 12 be in charge of

officious 6 prying 7 pompous 8 meddling 9 intrusive, kibitzing, obtrusive 10 high-handed, meddlesome 11 domineering, interfering, overbearing, patronizing 13 high and mighty, self-assertive, self-important 16 poking one's nose in

Offield, Lewis Delaney
　real name of: 9 Jack Oakie

offset 6 redeem 7 balance, nullify 8

equalize, knock out 9 cancel out, make up for 10 counteract, neutralize 11 countervail 13 compensate for, counterweight 14 counterbalance

offshoot 4 limb 5 scion, shoot 6 branch 7 adjunct 9 aftermath, by-product, outgrowth 10 descendant

offspring 3 fry 4 heir, seed 5 brood, child, issue, scion, spawn, young 6 family, litter 7 progeny 8 children, increase 9 posterity 10 descendant, succession 11 descendants

off the mark 5 amiss 6 afield, astray 9 off target 16 off the right track

off-the-record 5 privy 6 secret 7 private 11 undisclosed 12 confidential 16 not to be disclosed 17 not for publication

off the top of one's head 5 ad-lib 7 offhand 9 extempore, impromptu 10 improvised, unprepared 11 extemporary, unrehearsed 14 extemporaneous, unpremeditated

of good quality 4 good 6 worthy 8 superior 9 excellent 10 creditable

of high rank 5 noble, regal, royal 6 lordly, titled 7 courtly 11 blue-blooded 12 aristocratic

Of Human Bondage
　author: 16 W Somerset Maugham
　director: 12 John Cromwell
　character: 5 Weeks 7 Hayward 11 Louisa Carey, Philip Carey 12 Sally Athelny, William Carey 13 Mildred Rogers, Miss Wilkinson, Thorpe Athelny
　cast: 10 Bette Davis, Frances Dee, Kay Johnson 12 Leslie Howard

of its own kind
　Latin: 10 sui generis

Of Mice and Men
　author: 13 John Steinbeck
　director: 14 Lewis Milestone
　character: 4 Slim 5 Candy 6 Crooks, Curley 11 Lennie Small 12 George Milton
　cast: 10 Betty Field 11 Lon Chaney Jr (Lenny) 15 Burgess Meredith, Charles Bickford
　score: 12 Aaron Copland

of one's own right
　Latin: 8 sui juris

of poor quality 5 junky 6 flimsy, shoddy, sleazy, trashy 8 inferior 11 substandard

of secondary importance 8 nonvital 9 accessory, extrinsic 10 incidental 11 dispensable, unnecessary 12 nonessential

often 3 oft 4 much 7 usually 8 commonly, ofttimes 9 generally, regularly 10 constantly, frequently, habitually, oftentimes, repeatedly 11 continually, customarily, over and over, recurrently 12 periodically, time and again

of the dead say nothing but good
Latin: **21** de mortuis nil nisi bonum

of the faith
Latin: **6** de fide

of their own kind
Latin: **10** sui generis

of the old school 5 passe **8** outdated, outmoded **9** out-of-date **12** conservative, old-fashioned **18** establishmentarian

Of Time and the River
author: **11** Thomas Wolfe
character: **10** Eugene Gant

oft-repeated 5 trite **7** popular **8** constant, familiar, frequent, habitual, well-worn **9** continual, recurring, well-known **10** persistent **11** widely known

of what good
Latin: **7** cui bono

Ogdoad
also: **3** Heh
origin: **8** Egyptian
number of gods: **5** eight

ogle 3 eye **6** gape at, gawk at, goggle, leer at **7** stare at **8** goggle at **10** give the eye, scrutinize **15** give the once-over, stare at greedily **16** cast sheep's eyes at, gaze at with desire

Ogma
origin: **5** Irish
god of: **6** poetry **9** eloquence
inventor of: **12** Ogham letters

Ogmios
origin: **6** Gaelic
god of: **9** eloquence
corresponds to: **7** Mercury

ogre, ogress 5 brute, demon, fiend, ghoul, harpy **6** despot, tyrant **7** bugbear, monster **8** bogeyman, dictator, martinet **11** slave driver

Ogygia
island of: **7** Calypso

Ogygus
king of: **7** Boeotia
father: **8** Poseidon

O'Hara, John
author of: **7** Pal Joey **11** A Rage to Live **13** The Instrument **14** From the Terrace, The Hat on the Bed **16** Butterfield Eight **17** Ten North Frederick **19** The Horse Knows the Way **20** Appointment in Samarra

O'Hara, Maureen
real name: **18** Maureen Fitzsimmons
nickname: **18** Queen of Technicolor
born: **7** Ireland **8** Milltown
roles: **10** Lady Godiva **11** The Quiet Man **13** North to Alaska, The Parent Trap **16** The Foxes of Harrow **19** How Green Was My Valley **20** Hunchback of Notre Dame **27** Miracle on Thirty-fourth Street

O'Hara, Scarlett
character in: **15** Gone With the Wind

family: **6** Gerald **7** Carreen, Suellen
author: **8** Mitchell

O Henry
real name: **19** William Sidney Porter
author of: **11** The Last Leaf **16** Cabbages and Kings, The Gift of the Magi **18** The Cop and the Anthem **19** The Ransom of Red Chief

Ohio
abbreviation: **2** OH
nickname: **7** Buckeye
capital: **8** Columbus
largest city: **9** Cleveland
others: **3** Ada **4** Kent, Lima **5** Akron, Berea, Cadiz, Niles, Parma, Piqua, Xenia **6** Athens, Canton, Dayton, Elyria, Lorain, Marion, Newark, Tiffin, Toledo, Warren **7** Ashland, Findlay, Fremont, Norwood, Wooster **8** Alliance, Bluffton, Fostoria, Lakewood, Marietta, Sandusky **9** Ashtabula, Kettering, Lancaster, Massillon, Struthers, Vermilion, Willowick **10** Cincinnati, Huntington, Portsmouth, Rocky River, Willoughby, Youngstown, Zanesville **11** Painesville, Springfield **12** Steubenville
college: **4** Kent **5** Akron, Hiram, Miami **6** Dayton, Kenyon, Xavier **7** Antioch, Oberlin, Wooster **8** Defiance, Dennison, Marietta, Ursuline **10** Wittenberg **11** Case Western **12** Bowling Green, Ohio Wesleyan
feature:
 hall of fame: **11** Pro Football
 race: **12** Soap Box Derby
tribe: **4** Erie **7** Wyandot **13** Mound Builders
people: **7** buckeye, Cy Young **8** Zane Grey **10** Clark Gable, T Hart Crane **11** Annie Oakley, Lillian Gish **12** James Thurber, Lowell Thomas, Norman Thomas **13** Neil Armstrong, Orville Wright, Thomas A Edison **14** Barney Old field, Clarence Darrow **15** William T Sherman **16** Sherwood Anderson **18** Norman Vincent Peale
explorer: **7** La Salle
lake: **4** Erie **5** Grand **6** Berlin, Dillon, Hoover, Indian **8** Delaware **13** Mosquito Creek
land rank: **35** thirty-fifth
mountain:
 highest point: **12** Campbell Hill
physical feature:
 caverns: **4** Ohio, Zane **6** Seneca
 spring: **8** Blue Hole
president: **13** Ulysses S Grant **14** James A Garfield, Warren G Harding **15** William McKinley **16** Rutherford B Hayes **17** William Howard Taft **20** William Henry Harrison
river: **5** Grand, Miami **6** Maumee, Scioto, Wabash **7** Hocking **8** Cuyahoga, Sandusky **9** Muskingum, Tennessee **10** Cumberland **11** Monongahela
state admission: **11** seventeenth
state bird: **8** cardinal

state flower: **16** scarlet carnation
state motto: **27** With God All Things Are Possible
state song: **13** Beautiful Ohio
state tree: **7** buckeye

Ohm, Georg Simon
field: **7** physics
nationality: **6** German
discovered: **20** electrical resistance
named for him: **7** ohm unit

oil 4 balm, lard **5** cream, salve **6** anoint, grease, pomade **7** unguent **8** liniment, ointment **9** lubricant, lubricate, melted fat, petroleum **12** melted grease
type: **4** corn, fuel, hair **5** crude, motor, olive, whale **6** canola **7** cooking, mineral **9** safflower, vegetable

oily 5 fatty, lardy, slick **6** greasy, smarmy **7** buttery, fawning, servile **8** slippery, slithery, toadying, unctuous **9** groveling, sebaceous **10** lubricious, oleaginous **11** bootlicking, subservient **12** ingratiating

ointment 4 balm **5** salve **6** lotion, pomade **7** pomatum, unguent **8** liniment **9** emollient, spikenard

Ojibwa, Ojibway see **8** Chippawa

OK 4 fine, good **7** approve, endorse **8** all right, approval **9** authorize **11** endorsement **13** authorization
French: **7** d'accord

O'Keeffe, Georgia
born: **12** Sun Prairie WI
artwork: **7** Stables **9** Black Iris **14** Patio with Cloud **15** Lake George Barns **22** Light Coming on the Plains **26** Black Flower and Blue Larkspur
husband: **15** Alfred Stieglitz

Oklahoma
abbreviation: **2** OK **4** Okla
nickname: **6** Boomer, Sooner
capital/largest city: **12** Oklahoma City
others: **3** Ada **4** Alva, Enid, Hugo **5** Altus, Miami, Ponca, Tulsa **6** Duncan, El Reno, Guymon, Idabel, Lawton **7** Ardmore, Guthrie, Sapulpa, Shawnee **8** Anadarko, Fort Sill, Muskogee **9** Blackwell, Claremore, McAlester **10** Stillwater **12** Bartlesville
college: **5** Tulsa **6** Norman **7** Cameron **8** Langston, Phillips **10** Stillwater **11** Oral Roberts **12** Oklahoma City **15** Bethany Nazarene **17** American Christian
feature:
 hall of fame: **14** American Indian
 national park: **6** Platte
tribe: **3** Kaw, Oto **4** Iowa, Loup, Otoe, Waco **5** Caddo, Kansa, Osage, Ponca **6** Apache, Ottawa, Pawnee, Quapaw **7** Shawnee, Wichita **8** Arapahoe, Tawakoni
 Five Civilized Tribes: 5 Creek **7** Choctaw **8** Cherokee, Seminole **9** Chickasaw

people: 4 Okie **6** Sooner **9** Jim Thorpe **10** Will Rogers **12** Mickey Mantle **14** Maria Tallchief
  explorer: 8 Coronado
lake: 5 Atoka, Grand, Hulah **6** Texoma, Wister **7** Eufaula, Heyburn, Oologah **8** Keystone **9** Pensacola, Tenkiller **10** Fort Gibson **11** Thunderbird **12** Markham Ferry **17** Lake O' The Cherokees
land rank: 10 eighteenth
mountain: 6 Ozarks **8** Ouachita
  highest point: 9 Black Mesa
physical feature: 9 Panhandle
  plains: 5 Great
river: 3 Red **5** Grand **6** Little, Neosho **7** Washita **8** Arkan sas, Canadian, Cimarron **9** Verdigris **15** Muddy Boggy Creek
state admission: 10 forty-sixth
state bird: 23 scissor-tailed flycatcher
state fish: 9 white bass
state flower: 9 mistletoe
state motto: 22 Labor Conquers All Things
state song: 8 Oklahoma
state tree: 6 redbud

Oklahoma!
director: 13 Fred Zinnemann
cast: 10 Rod Steiger **11** Eddie Albert **12** Gordon MacRae, Shirley Jones **13** Gloria Grahame, James Whitmore **18** Charlotte Greenwood
score: 21 Rodgers and Hammerstein
choreographer: 12 Agnes de Mille
song: 23 People Will Say We're in Love **24** Surrey with the Fringe on Top

Olbers, Heinrich Wilhelm Matthaus
field: 9 astronomy
nationality: 6 German
discovered: 5 Vesta **6** comets, Pellas **9** asteroids

old 4 aged, used **5** hoary, of age **6** beat-up, bygone, of yore **7** ancient, antique, archaic, elderly, outworn, rundown, vintage, wornout **8** battered, decrepit, familiar, grizzled, much-used, obsolete, outdated, timeworn **9** crumbling, hackneyed, out-of-date, venerable, weathered **10** antiquated, broken-down, gray-headed, ramshackle, tumbledown **11** dilapidated, from the past, gray with age, obsolescent, time-honored, traditional **12** deteriorated, old-fashioned, white with age **13** weather-beaten **14** of long standing **15** long established

Old Aches and Pains
nickname of: 11 Luke Appling
old age 6 dotage **7** ripe age **8** maturity, senility **11** advanced age **15** second childhood

Old and the Young, The
author: 15 Luigi Pirandello

Old Bay State
nickname of: 13 Massachusetts
Old Bulgarian
also: 15 Old Church Slavic
language family: 12 Indo-European
group: 11 Balto-Slavic
status: 7 archaic
used in: 14 Orthodox church
Old Chinook
nickname of: 10 Washington
Old Colony State
nickname of: 13 Massachusetts
Old Curiosity Shop, The
author: 14 Charles Dickens
character: 5 Quilp **9** Fred Trent, Mrs Jarley **10** Kit Nubbles, Sally Brass **11** Grandfather **12** Sampson Brass **13** Dick Swiveller **15** Little Nell Trent **18** The Single Gentleman
Old Dominion
nickname of: 8 Virginia
olden 4 past **6** bygone, former, of yore **7** ancient, long-ago **8** departed
Oldest Man 10 Methuselah
old-fashioned 5 corny, dated, passe **7** antique, archaic **8** obsolete, outdated, outmoded **9** out-of-date **10** antiquated, out of style **11** obsolescent, traditional **12** long-standing, out of fashion **13** unfashionable **14** behind the times
Old-Fashioned Girl, An
author: 15 Louisa May Alcott
Old Franklin State
nickname of: 9 Tennessee
old hand 3 pro **6** expert, master **8** virtuoso **9** authority **12** professional
old hat 5 passe, stale **6** demode **7** archaic, outworn **8** obsolete, outdated, outmoded **9** out-of-date **10** antiquated, superseded **11** obsolescent **12** old-fashioned **13** unfashionable **14** behind the times
old-line 11 established, traditional **12** conservative
Old Line State
nickname of: 8 Maryland
Old Love
author: 19 Isaac Bashevis Singer
Old Maid, The
author: 12 Edith Wharton
Old Man and the Sea, The
author: 15 Ernest Hemingway
character: 7 Manolin **8** Santiago
Old Mortality
author: 14 Sir Walter Scott
character: 5 Edith **11** Henry Morton **12** Basil Olifant, Lord Evandale **19** John Balfour of Burley **21** Lady Margaret Bellenden **27** Colonel Grahame of Claverhouse
Old Mortality
author: 19 Katherine Anne Porter
Old North
nickname of: 13 North Carolina

Old Patagonian Express, The
author: 11 Paul Theroux
old saw 5 adage, maxim **6** cliche, saying, truism **7** bromide, proverb **9** old saying **10** expression **11** old chestnut
oldster 5 elder **6** codger, old man **7** ancient **8** old woman **13** senior citizen
Old Testament
first five books: 10 Pentateuch
first six books: 9 Hexateuch
first seven books: 10 Heptateuch
books of: 3 Job **4** Amos, Ezra, Joel, Ruth **5** Hosea, Jonah, Kings, Micah, Na- hum, Songs, Tobit **6** Baruch, Daniel, Esther, Exodus, Haggai, Isaiah, Joshua, Judges, Judith, Psalms, Samuel, Sirach, Wisdom **7** Ezekiel, Genesis, Malachi, Numbers, Obadiah **8** Habakkuk, Jeremiah, Macabees, Nehemiah, Proverbs **9** Leviticus, Zechariah, Zephaniah **10** Chronicles **11** Deuteronomy **12** Ecclesiastes **13** Song of Solomon **14** Ecclesiasticus
Oldtown Folks
author: 19 Harriet Beecher Stowe
Old Wives' Tale, The
author: 13 Arnold Bennett
old-world 6 formal **7** courtly, gallant, old-line **8** European, orthodox **10** ceremonial, chivalrous, prescribed **11** ceremonious, continental, established, traditional **12** conservative, conventional, old-fashioned
Ole
character in: 16 Giants of the Earth
author: 7 Rolvaag
Olenska, Ellen
character in: 17 The Age of Innocence
author: 7 Wharton
oleoresin 3 gum **5** anime, apiol, elemi **6** balsam **7** solvent **10** turpentine
olio 4 stew **6** jumble, medley **7** melange, mixture **8** mishmash **9** potpourri **10** assortment, collection, hodgepodge, hotchpotch, miscellany
olive 12 Olea europaea
varieties: 3 tea **4** wild **5** black, false, holly, sweet **6** common, desert, spurge **7** Russian **8** American, fragrant **11** Californian
olive-drab 5 khaki **13** greenish-brown
Oliver
character in: 11 As You Like It
author: 11 Shakespeare
Oliver!
director: 9 Carol Reed
based on story by: 14 Charles Dickens (Oliver Twist)
cast: 8 Jack Wild, Ron Moody (Fagin) **10** Mark Lester (Oliver), Oliver Reed **11** Shani Wallis
Oscar for: 7 picture **8** director
remake of: 11 Oliver Twist
song: 16 Consider Yourself, Food Glo-

rious Food **17** As Long As He Needs Me

Oliver Twist
  author: 14 Charles Dickens
  character: 5 Fagin, Monks (Edward Leeford), Nancy **6** Bumble **9** Bill Sikes, Mrs Maylie **10** Mr Brownlow, Rose Maylie
  director: 9 David Lean
  cast: 8 Kay Walsh **12** Alec Guinness (Fagin), Robert Newton **13** Anthony Newley (Artful Dodger) **16** Francis L Sullivan, John Howard Davies
  remade as: 7 Oliver!

Olivia
  character in: 12 Twelfth Night
  author: 11 Shakespeare

Olivier, Sir Laurence
  born: 7 Dorking, England
  wife: 11 Vivien Leigh **13** Joan Plowright
  roles: 6 Becket, Hamlet (Oscar), Henry V, Sleuth **7** Rebecca **11** Marathon Man **16** Wuthering Heights **17** Pride and Prejudice, The Boys from Brazil, The Devil's Disciple **19** Shoes of the Fisherman **23** The Prince and the Showgirl

olivine
  variety: 7 peridot

olla 3 jar, pot **10** earthen pot

Olmsted, Frederick Law
  landscape architect of: 11 Central Park (NYC, with Calvert Vaux) **12** Prospect Park (Brooklyn NY) **13** Fairmount Park (Philadelphia) **14** Biltmore Estate (Asheville NC), Mount Royal Park (Montreal)

Olsen, Merlin (Jay)
  sport: 8 football
  team: 14 Los Angeles Rams
  TV roles: 12 Father Murphy **15** Highway to Heaven **23** Little House on the Prairie

O Lucky Man
  director: 15 Lindsay Anderson
  cast: 9 Alan Price **13** Rachel Roberts **15** Malcolm McDowell, Ralph Richardson
  score: 9 Alan Price

Olwen
  origin: 5 Welsh
  form: 8 princess
  father: 16 Yspadaden Penkawr

Olympic Games
  site:
    1896: 6 Athens
    1900: 5 Paris
    1904: 7 St Louis
    1906: 6 Athens
    1908: 6 London
    1912: 9 Stockholm
    1920: 7 Antwerp
    1924: 6 Paris **8** Chamonix
    1928: 8 St Moritz **9** Amsterdam
    1932: 10 Lake Placid, Los Angeles
    1936: 6 Berlin **21** Garmisch-Partenkirchen
    1948: 6 London **8** St Moritz
    1952: 4 Oslo **8** Helsinki
    1956: 9 Melbourne **15** Cortina d'Ampezzo
    1960: 5 Tokyo **11** Squaw Valley
    1968: 8 Grenoble **10** Mexico City
    1972: 6 Munich **7** Sapporo
    1976: 8 Montreal **9** Innsbruck
    1980: 6 Moscow **10** Lake Placid
    1984: 8 Sarajevo **10** Los Angeles
    1988: 5 Seoul **7** Calgary
    1992: 9 Barcelona **11** Albertville
    1994: 11 Lillehammer
    1996: 7 Atlanta
    1998: 6 Nagano
    2000: 6 Sydney

Omaha
  language family: 6 Siouan **7** Dhegiha
  location: 4 Iowa **8** Nebraska, Oklahoma

Oman
  other name: 13 Muscat and Oman
  capital: 6 Masqat, Muscat
  largest city: 5 Matra **6** Matrah
  others: 3 Sur **4** Fida **5** Dubai, Nazwa, Nigwa, Sohar, Wazit **6** Khasab, Marbat, Murbat, Suwaih, Tinouf **7** Khabura, Salalah **8** Ashkhara
  government: 9 Sultanate
  head of state/government: 6 sultan
  monetary unit: 3 gaj, gaz **4** rial **5** baiza, ghazi **7** mahmudi
  island: 6 Masera, Masira **7** Masirah **10** Kuria Muria
  mountain: 4 Qara **5** Hafit, Harim, Nakhl, Tayin **8** el-Akhdar **11** Jabal Akhdar **13** Green Mountain
  highest point: 6 al-Sham
  sea: 6 Indian **7** Arabian
  physical feature:
    cape: 7 Madraka **9** Ras Al Hadd **13** Ras Dharbat 'Ali
    gulf: 4 Oman
    peninsula: 7 Arabian **8** Musandam
    plain: 6 Dhofar **7** Batinah
    strait: 6 Hormuz
  people: 4 Arab
    ruler: 12 Qabus Bin Said **13** Said Bin Taimur
  language: 4 Urdu **5** Hindi **6** Arabic **7** Baluchi
  religion: 5 Islam
  war: 4 Gulf **11** Desert Storm

omega 3 end **4** last **5** final **6** ending **8** terminus
  opposite: 5 alpha

omen 4 sign **5** token **6** augury, herald **7** auspice, portent, presage, warning **9** foretaste, harbinger, precursor **10** foreboding, indication

ominous 7 unlucky **8** menacing, minatory, monitory, sinister **9** dismaying, ill-omened **10** foreboding, ill-starred, portentous

omission 3 gap **4** hole **7** neglect **9** exception, exclusion, oversight **10** leaving out, negligence **11** delinquency, elimination **12** noninclusion **13** neglected item **16** something omitted

omit 3 cut **4** drop, fail, jump, miss, shun, skip **5** avoid, elide **6** bypass, delete, except, forget, ignore, slight **7** excerpt, exclude, let slip, neglect **8** leave out, overlook, pass over, preclude, set aside **11** forget about

omnia vincit amor 15 love conquers all

Omnibus
  host: 13 Alistair Cooke

omnipotent 6 mighty **7** supreme **8** almighty, powerful, puissant **11** all-powerful

omniscient 7 all-wise, supreme **8** infinite **9** all-seeing **10** all-knowing, preeminent

omnium gatherum 23 miscellaneous collection

omnivorous 7 hoggish **8** edacious, ravenous **9** crapulous, rapacious, voracious **10** gluttonous, polyphagic, predacious **12** pantophagous

Omoo
  author: 14 Herman Melville
  character: 10 Captain Bob **15** Doctor Long Ghost

Omphale
  queen of: 5 Lydia
  father: 8 Iardanus
  husband: 6 Tmolus
  son: 5 Lamus
  served by: 8 Hercules

Omri
  father: 6 Becher **7** Michael
  son: 4 Ahab
  daughter-in-law: 7 Jezebel

on 2 at **4** atop, near, over, upon **5** about, above, ahead, along, anent **7** against, forward, planned **8** abutting, adjacent, attached, intended, touching **9** occurring **10** concerning, juxtaposed

on-and-off 6 spotty **8** episodic **9** irregular, spasmodic, temporary **10** now-and-then, occasional

On Beginning and Perishing
  author: 9 Aristotle

once 7 ages ago, long ago, one time **8** formerly, hitherto, years ago **9** at one time **10** heretofore, previously **11** a single time, for the nonce, in times past, some time ago **12** in the old days, some time back **13** once upon a time, on one occasion

once-in-a-lifetime 6 unique **7** special **8** singular **11** one-time-only

once more 4 anew **5** again **9** once again, over again **11** one more time

on cloud nine 6 elated, joyful, joyous **8** ecstatic, euphoric **9** exuberant, rapturous **15** in seventh heaven

oncoming 5 close **7** looming, nearing **8** imminent **9** advancing, impending, onrushing **11** approaching, bearing down

on course 8 on target **15** on the right track

Ondine
   author: **13** Jean Giraudoux

one 2 an **3** you **4** a man, lone, only, sole **5** a body, a soul, whole **6** a thing, entire, single, unique **7** a person, someone **8** complete, singular, solitary, somebody **10** individual, unrepeated

One, Two, Three
   director: **11** Billy Wilder
   cast: **11** James Cagney **12** Pamela Tiffin **13** Arlene Francis, Horst Buchholz
   setting: **10** West Berlin
   score: **11** Andre Previn

O'Neal, Ryan
   real name: **16** Patrick Ryan O'Neal
   born: **12** Los Angeles CA
   daughter: **10** Tatum O'Neal
   roles: **9** Love Story, Paper Moon **10** What's Up Doc **11** Barry Lyndon, Peyton Place **16** Rodney Harrington

O'Neal, Tatum
   born: **12** Los Angeles CA
   father: **9** Ryan O'Neal
   roles: **9** Paper Moon **12** Bad News Bears **14** Little Darlings **19** International Velvet
   husband: **11** John McEnroe

one and the same 5 equal **7** matched **9** identical

one by one 6 singly **10** one at a time, separately, single file **12** individually

One Day at a Time
   character: **9** Ann Romano **11** Julie Cooper **13** Barbara Cooper **15** Dwayne Schneider
   cast: **14** Bonnie Franklin **15** Pat Harrington Jr **17** Mackenzie Phillips, Valerie Bertinelli

One Day in the Life of Ivan Denisovich
   author: **23** Aleksandr Solzhenitsyn Jr

One Flew Over the Cuckoo's Nest
   director: **11** Milos Forman
   based on story by: **8** Ken Kesey
   cast: **13** Jack Nicholson **14** Louise Fletcher, Michael Beryman **15** William Redfield
   Oscar for: **7** actor (Nicholson) **7** actress (Fletcher), picture **8** director **10** screenplay

One Hour with You
   director: **11** George Cukor **13** Ernst Lubitsch
   cast: **14** Genevieve Tobin **16** Maurice Chevalier **17** Jeanette MacDonald
   remake of: **17** The Marriage Circle
   song: **14** What Would You Do

one-hundred percent 5 sheer, total, utter, whole **7** supreme **8** absolute, complete **10** consummate **17** through-and-through

O'Neill, Eugene
   author of: **8** The Straw **11** The Hairy Ape **12** Ah Wilderness, Anna Christie **13** Marco Millions **14** Glencairn Cycle **15** The Emperor Jones, The Iceman Cometh **16** Beyond the Horizon, Strange Interlude, The Great God Brown **18** Desire Under the Elms **20** The Moon of the Caribees **22** A Moon for the Misbegotten, All God's Chillun Got Wings, Mourning Becomes Electra **24** Long Day's Journey into Night
   daughter: **4** Oona
   son-in-law: **7** Chaplin

Oneiros
   also: **6** Oniros
   origin: **5** Greek
   god of: **6** dreams

oneness 5 union, unity **7** concord, harmony **8** entirety, identity, sameness, totality **9** agreement, aloneness, integrity, wholeness **10** uniformity, uniqueness **11** singularity **12** completeness **13** individuality

one-of-a-kind 4 rare **6** unique **7** strange, unusual **8** original **9** eccentric

oneology
   science of: **5** wines **10** winemaking

onerous 5 heavy **6** taxing **7** arduous, painful, weighty **8** crushing, grievous **9** demanding, wearisome **10** burdensome, exhausting, oppressive **11** distressing **12** hard to endure

one thing in return for another
   Latin: **10** quid pro quo

one-time 3 old **4** past **5** early, prior **6** former, recent **7** earlier, quondam **8** previous **9** erstwhile
   French: **8** ci-devant

one voice 4 solo **6** unison **7** concert

one who has a fixed income
   French: **7** rentier

On First Looking Into Chapman's Homer
   author: **9** John Keats

on foot
   French: **5** a pied

ongoing 7 endless, lasting **8** enduring, unbroken, unending **10** continuing, proceeding **11** never-ending, unremitting **13** uninterrupted

On Golden Pond
   director: **10** Mark Rydell
   based on play by: **14** Ernest Thompson
   cast: **9** Jane Fonda **10** Doug McKeon, Henry Fonda (Norman Thayer Jr) **16** Katharine Hepburn
   setting: **5** Maine
   Oscar for: **5** actor (Fonda) **7** actress (Hepburn)

on guard 4 wary **5** alert **7** careful, heedful **8** cautious, vigilant, watchful

on hand 5 handy, on tap **6** at hand **9** available **10** accessible, convenient **14** at one's disposal

on horseback
   French: **7** a cheval

onion 6 Allium **10** Allium cepa
   varieties: **3** red, sea, top **4** leek, tree, wild **5** green, gypsy, pearl, swamp, Welsh, white **6** German, potato, yellow **7** Bermuda, Danvers, nodding, prairie, shallot, Spanish **8** climbing, Egyptian, false sea, scallion, Valencia **9** Catawissa, ever-ready, flowering, two-bladed **10** multiplier, red-skinned **16** Japanese bunching
   origin: **9** Asia Minor
   called by Robert Louis Stevenson: **14** rose among roots

Onion Field, The
   author: **14** Joseph Wambaugh

Oniros *see* **7** Oneiros

On Liberty
   author: **14** John Stuart Mill

onlooker 5 gazer, ogler **6** viewer **7** watcher, witness **8** beholder, kibitzer, observer **9** bystander, spectator **10** eyewitness, rubberneck

only 4 just, lone, sole **5** alone **6** barely, merely, purely, simply, single, singly, solely, unique **7** at least **8** by itself, singular, solitary **9** by oneself, exclusive, unmatched **10** individual, no more than, nothing but, one and only, unrepeated **11** exclusively **12** individually, unparalleled

on one's uppers 5 broke **9** destitute **10** down and out

On Plants
   author: **9** Aristotle

On Revolution
   author: **12** Hannah Arendt

onrush 4 flow, flux, gush, tide, wave **5** flood, onset, storm, surge **6** attack, charge, deluge, spring, stream **7** assault, cascade, current, torrent **9** avalanche

onset 4 push, raid **5** birth, sally, start **6** attack, charge, onrush, outset, thrust **7** assault, genesis, infancy, offense **8** founding, invasion, outbreak, storming **9** beginning, inception, incursion, offensive, onslaught **10** incipience, initiation **12** commencement, inauguration

onslaught 4 coup, push, raid **5** blitz, foray, onset, sally **6** attack, charge, putsch, thrust **7** assault, offense **8** invasion **9** incursion, offensive **10** aggression, blitzkrieg

on tap 5 handy **6** at hand, on hand **9** available **10** accessible, convenient

Ontario
   bay: **6** Hudson
   canal: **5** Trent **6** Rideau
   capital: **7** Toronto
   city: **3** Emo **4** Galt **6** London, Ottawa **7** Windsor **8** Hamilton, Kingston **9** Kitchener
   explored by: **5** French **6** British
   industry: **6** mining **11** agriculture **13**

manufacturing
lake: 6 Simcoe
province of: 6 Canada
river: 6 Ottawa, Thames 7 Niagara 10 St Lawrence
settled by: 9 Loyalists
university: 4 York 5 Brock, Trent 8 McMaster

on the alert 4 wary 7 careful, mindful, on guard 8 cautious, watchful 9 wide awake 12 on the lookout

On the Beach
author: 10 Nevil Shute
director: 13 Stanley Kramer
cast: 10 Ava Gardner 11 Fred Astaire, Gregory Peck 13 Donna Anderson 14 Anthony Perkins

on the contrary
French: 11 au contraire

on the dot 7 exactly 8 promptly 9 on the nose, precisely 10 punctually

on the face
Latin: 7 ex facie

on the go 4 busy 6 active, mobile 8 in motion 9 energetic, on the move 13 indefatigable

On the Heavens
author: 9 Aristotle

On the Morning of Christ's Nativity
author: 10 John Milton

on the move 5 astir 6 active, mobile 7 on the go 8 in motion

on the nose 5 exact 7 exactly, precise 8 accurate, on target 9 precisely 10 accurately, on the money

on the outer edges
Latin: 10 in extremis

on the right track 8 on course, on target

On the Soul
author: 9 Aristotle

On the Town
director: 9 Gene Kelly 12 Stanley Donen
cast: 9 Ann Miller, Gene Kelly, Vera-Ellen 12 Betty Garrett, Frank Sinatra
setting: 11 New York City
score: 11 Adolph Green, Betty Comden 16 Leonard Bernstein
song: 14 New York New York

On the Waterfront
director: 9 Elia Kazan
cast: 8 Lee J Cobb 10 Karl Malden, Pat Henning, Rod Steiger 12 Leif Erickson, Marlon Brando 13 Eva Marie Saint
Oscar for: 5 actor (Brando) 7 picture 8 director 10 screenplay 17 supporting actress (Saint)

on the whole 9 in general 10 by and large 27 considering the circumstances

onto 4 atop, upon 5 aware, privy 6 aboard

onus 4 duty, load 5 cross 6 burden, strain, weight 9 liability 10 obligation 11 encumbrance 13 burden of proof 14 responsibility

onus probandi 13 burden of proof

onward, onwards 5 ahead, along 7 forward, ongoing 9 advancing, frontward 11 moving ahead, progressive
French: 7 en avant, en route

On Wings of Eagles
author: 10 Ken Follett

oodles 4 gobs, lots, many 5 heaps, loads, scads 6 plenty

ooze 4 drip, leak, mire, muck, seep, silt 5 bleed, drain, exude, slime, sweat 6 filter, sludge 7 dribble, leakage, seepage, soft mud, trickle 8 alluvium 9 discharge, exudation, percolate, secretion, transpire

oozing 5 leaky, weepy 6 sweaty 7 exuding, seepage, seeping 8 bleeding, sweating

opal
color: 3 red 5 black, white 6 orange 11 transparent
source: 6 Mexico 9 Australia 14 Lightning Ridge
variety: 8 fire opal

opalescent 5 milky 6 pearly 8 irisated, luminous 10 iridescent

opaque 4 dark, dull, hazy 5 muddy, murky 7 clouded, muddied, obscure, unclear 8 abstruse 9 difficult 12 impenetrable, unfathomable 14 nontranslucent, nontransparent, unintelligible 16 incomprehensible

opaqueness 7 opacity 8 dullness 9 denseness, muddiness, murkiness, obscurity 10 cloudiness 11 unclearness 15 impenetrability 17 unintelligibility 19 incomprehensibility

open 4 ajar, fair, just, wide 5 agape, begin, clear, crack, found, frank, plain, unbar 6 candid, create, direct, expand, gaping, honest, launch, unfold, unlock, unseal, unshut 7 artless, exposed, lay open, natural, not shut, sincere, unblock, unclose, yawning 8 commence, extended, outgoing, unbiased, unclosed, unfasten, unfenced, unfolded, unlocked, unsealed 9 available, coverless, establish, expansive, impartial, institute, not closed, objective, originate, receptive, unbigoted, unbounded, uncovered, uncrowded, undertake, welcoming 10 accessible, forthright, impersonal, inaugurate, responsive, unenclosed, unfastened 11 extroverted, uncluttered, uninhabited 12 permit access, unobstructed, unprejudiced 13 disinterested, doing business 15 straightforward

open-air 7 outdoor, outside 10 unconfined
Italian: 8 al fresco

open and aboveboard 6 candid, honest 7 ethical 10 forthright 12 on the up and up 15 straightforward

Open Boat, The
author: 12 Stephen Crane

Open City
director: 17 Roberto Rossellini
cast: 11 Aldo Fabrizi, Anna Magnani 16 Marcello Pagliero
setting: 4 Rome

open-eyed 5 alert, awake, aware 7 heedful, mindful 8 vigilant, watchful, wide-eyed 9 attentive, wide-awake

open-handed 6 lavish 7 liberal 8 generous, prodigal 9 bounteous, bountiful 10 altruistic, beneficent, benevolent, ungrudging, unstinting 11 magnanimous

openhandedness 10 generosity, liberality 11 benevolence, generousity, munificence 12 extravagance

openhearted 7 artless, sincere 8 trusting 9 ingenuous

opening 3 gap, job 4 gash, hole, rent, rift, slit, slot, spot, tear, vent 5 break, chink, cleft, crack, place, space, start 6 breach, chance 7 fissure, kickoff, preface, prelude, send-off, vacancy 8 aperture, occasion, overture, position 9 be ginning, first part, launching, situation 10 initiation 11 opportunity, possibility 12 commencement, inauguration, installation, introduction

openly 6 freely 7 frankly 8 directly, honestly, publicly 9 obviously

open-minded 4 fair 7 liberal 8 amenable, flexible, tolerant, unbiased 9 adaptable, impartial, objective, receptive 10 responsive, undogmatic 11 broad-minded 12 unprejudiced 13 disinterested, nonjudgmental

openmouthed 4 agog, awed 5 agape 6 aghast, amazed 8 wide-eyed 9 awestruck, bewitched, marveling, staggered, stupefied, surprised 10 astonished, confounded 10 dumbstruck, enthralled, spellbound 11 dumbfounded 12 wonderstruck 13 flabbergasted, thunderstruck

openness 6 candor 7 honesty 8 daylight 9 frankness, sincerity 11 artlessness 13 guilelessness 14 forthrightness 19 straightforwardness

open sanction 8 free hand, free rein 13 full authority
French: 12 catre blanche

open the eyes of 8 disabuse 11 set straight

open to choice 8 elective, optional 9 voluntary

openwork 3 net 4 lace 6 eyelet 7 lattice, Madeira, tracery 8 filigree

opera 5 score 7 musical 8 libretto 11 composition
by Bellini: 5 Norma
by Bizet: 6 Carmen
by Delibes: 5 Lakme
by Donizetti: 10 La Favorita 11 Don

Pasquale **12** Maria Stuarda **13** L'Elisir d'Amore **17** Lucia di Lammermoor **19** La Figlia di Regimente
by Gounod: 5 Faust
by Leoncavallo: 10 I Pagliacci
by Mozart: 8 Idomeneo **10** Magic Flute **11** Don Giovanni **12** Cosi fan tutte **13** Marriage of Figaro
by Offenbach: 15 Tales of Hoffmann
by Ponchielli: 10 La Gioconda
by Puccini: 5 Tosca **8** La Boheme **12** Manon Lescaut **15** Madame Butterfly
by Rossini: 8 Tancredi **11** William Tell **15** The Barber of Seville
by Smetana: 13 The Bartered Bride
by Strauss: 6 Salome **7** Elektra **15** Ariadne auf Naxos **16** Der Rosenkavalier
by Tchaikovsky: 12 Eugene Onegin
by Verdi: 4 Aida **6** Otello **8** Falstaff **9** Rigoletto **10** La Traviata **11** Il Trovatore
by Wagner: 8 Parsifal **9** Lohengrin **10** Tannhauser **16** Tristan and Isolde **17** The Flying Dutchman **21** The Ring of the Nibelungs
comic: 5 buffa **7** comique
glass: 9 lorgnette
hat: 5 crush, gibus
house: 3 Met **6** Sydney **7** La Scala **12** Covent Garden, Metropolitan
singer: 4 bass, diva **5** basso, buffa, buffo, tenor **7** soprano **8** baritone **9** contralto **10** coloratura, prima donna **12** mezzo soprano
singular: 4 opus
solo: 4 aria
text: 8 libretto

operate 2 go **3** run **4** go in, work **6** behave, manage, open up **7** oversee, perform **8** function **11** superintend **14** perform surgery **18** perform an operation

operating 6 active **7** working **8** in motion **9** operative **10** responsive

operation 5 force **6** action, agency, effect **7** conduct, pursuit, running, surgery, working **8** activity, exertion **9** influence, procedure **10** management, overseeing **11** exploratory, performance, supervision **15** instrumentality, superintendence

operative 3 spy **4** dick **5** agent, in use **6** acting, active, shamus, worker **7** in force, working **8** in effect, in motion, workable **9** activated, detective, effective, effectual, operating **10** functional, private eye, responsive **11** efficacious, secret agent

operator 4 doer, user **5** agent, pilot **6** driver, worker **7** manager **9** performer

opere citato 14 in the work cited
abbreviation: 5 op cit

Ophelia
character in: 6 Hamlet
author: 11 Shakespeare

ophidiophobia
fear of: 6 snakes

Ophion
form: 7 serpent
created from: 9 north wind
created by: 8 Eurynome

Ophir
father: 6 Joktan
source of: 4 gold

opiate 4 dope **6** downer **7** anodyne **8** hypnotic, narcotic, nepenthe, sedative **9** analgesic, calmative, soporific, stupefier **10** depressant, painkiller, palliative **12** somnifacient, stupefacient, tranquilizer

opine 3 say **4** deem **5** allow, guess, offer, state, think **6** assume, reckon **7** believe, imagine, presume, suggest, surmise **8** conclude, consider, estimate **9** speculate, volunteer **10** conjecture, have a hunch

opinion 4 idea, view **6** belief, notion, theory **7** surmise **8** estimate, judgment, thinking **9** sentiment, suspicion **10** assessment, assumption, conception, conclusion, conjecture, conviction, estimation, evaluation, impression, persuasion **11** speculation

opinionated 8 dogmatic, obdurate, stubborn **9** obstinate, pigheaded, unbending **10** bullheaded, headstrong, inflexible, unyielding **12** closedminded **14** uncompromising

O Pioneers!
author: 11 Willa Cather

Opis
companion of: 7 Artemis

Opobalsammum 12 Biblical tree

Oppenheimer, Julius Robert
field: 7 physics
directed development of: 10 atomic bomb
  location: 9 Los Alamos, New Mexico
chaired: 3 AEC **22** Atomic Energy Commission

Opper, Frederick
creator/artist of: 13 Happy Hooligan **17** Alphonse and Gaston, And Her Name Was Maud

opponent 3 foe **5** enemy, rival **8** resister **9** adversary, assailant, contender, disputant **10** antagonist, challenger, competitor, opposition

opportune 3 apt **5** happy, lucky **6** proper, timely **7** fitting **8** suitable **9** expedient, favorable, fortunate, well-timed **10** auspicious, convenient, felicitous, profitable, propitious, seasonable **11** appropriate **12** advantageous

opportunity 4 time, turn **5** means **6** chance, moment **7** opening **8** occasion **9** situation **10** good chance **11** contingency

oppose 4 buck, defy **5** fight **6** battle, combat, resist, thwart **7** contest **8** ob-

struct **9** withstand **12** be set against, speak against

opposed 3 con **4** anti **6** averse, pitted **7** adverse, against, counter, hostile **8** contrary, disputed, objected, resisted **9** contested, countered **10** confronted, contrasted, reciprocal **12** contradicted

opposer 5 rival **8** opponent **9** adversary **10** antagonist, competitor

opposite 5 other **6** facing **7** adverse, counter, reverse **8** contrary, converse, opposing **9** differing **11** conflicting **12** antagonistic, antithetical **13** contradictory, counteractive

opposite number 5 equal **8** parallel **10** equivalent **11** correlative, counterpart

opposition 3 foe **5** enemy, rival **6** enmity **8** aversion, defiance, opponent **9** adversary, contender, hostility, other side, rejection **10** antagonism, antagonist, competitor, negativism, resistance **11** contrariety, disapproval **12** disagreement

oppress 3 tax, try, vex **4** pain **5** abuse, worry **6** burden, deject, grieve, sadden, sorrow **7** depress, trouble **8** cast down, dispirit, maltreat **9** despotize, persecute, tyrannize, weigh down **10** discourage, dishearten

oppressed 7 crushed **9** exploited **10** tyrannized **11** downtrodden, subservient

oppressive 5 cruel, harsh **6** brutal, severe, trying, vexing **7** onerous, painful, wearing **8** despotic, grievous, pressing **9** worrisome **10** burdensome, depressing, repressive, tyrannical, unbearable **11** distressing, hardhearted, troublesome **12** discouraging **13** uncomfortable

oppressor 6 despot, tyrant **8** autocrat, dictator

opprobrious 4 base **6** wicked **7** abusive, corrupt, damning **8** infamous, reviling, shameful, shocking **9** malicious, maligning, nefarious, vilifying, vitriolic **10** censorious, deplorable, despicable, malevolent, outrageous, scandalous, scurrilous, unbecoming **11** acrimonious, disgraceful, fulminating **12** condemnatory, denunciatory, dishonorable, disreputable, faultfinding **13** hypercritical, objectionable, reprehensible

opprobrium 5 shame **6** infamy **8** disgrace, dishonor **9** disrepute **12** denunciation

Ops
origin: 5 Roman
goddess of: 6 plenty
husband: 6 Saturn
son: 7 Jupiter
called: 10 Magna Mater
corresponds to: 4 Rhea **6** Cybele **9** Dindymene **10** Berecyntia

opt for 4 pick, take **5** adopt **6** choose,

select, take up **7** embrace, espouse, fix upon, pick out **8** decide on, settle on

optimism 10 confidence **11** hopefulness **12** cheerfulness, sanguineness **13** bright outlook, encouragement

optimistic 6 bright **7** hopeful, roseate **8** buoyed up, cheerful, sanguine **9** confident, favorable, heartened, promising **10** auspicious, encouraged, heartening, propitious **11** encouraging, rose-colored **12** enthusiastic

Optimist's Daughter, The
 author: 11 Eudora Welty

optimum 4 acme, A-one, best, peak **5** crest, ideal, prime **6** choice, height, select, zenith **7** capital, perfect, supreme **8** flawless **9** faultless, first-rate **10** perfection, unexcelled **11** superlative **12** quintessence

option 4 will **5** voice **6** choice, liking **8** decision, election, free will, pleasure **9** franchise, privilege, selection **10** discretion, partiality, preference **11** alternative **12** predilection

optional 4 open **8** elective, unforced **9** allowable, open- ended, voluntary **10** volitional **11** not required **12** discretional **13** discretionary, nonobligatory

opulence 6 bounty, plenty, riches, wealth **7** fortune **8** elegance, luxuries, richness **9** abundance, affluence, amplitude, profusion **10** cornucopia, lavishness, plentitude, prosperity **11** copiousness, great wealth **13** sumptuousness

opus 4 work **5** piece **6** effort **7** attempt, product **8** creation **9** handiwork, invention **10** brainchild, production **11** composition

oracle, Oracle 4 sage, seer **5** augur, sibyl **6** wizard **7** adviser, diviner, prophet **9** predictor, Scripture **10** forecaster, soothsayer **11** clairvoyant

oral 5 vocal **6** spoken, verbal, voiced **7** uttered **8** ingested **9** swallowed **10** of the mouth, verbalized **11** articulated, using speech
 Latin: 8 viva voce

orange
 varieties: 4 king, mock, sour, wild **5** blood, hardy, natal, navel, Osage, sweet **6** bitter, common, Panama, Temple **7** Florida, Mexican, Satsuma, Seville, Spanish **8** Bergamot, Mandarin, Otaheite, Valencia **9** Tachibana, vegetable **10** Chinese box, trifoliate **13** African cherry, Mediterranean **15** Jamaica mandarin **17** houseblooming mock
 liqueur: 7 Curacao

orangutan, orang-outang 3 ape **4** mias **5** satyr **6** primate **10** anthropoid
 characteristic: 8 arboreal **11** herbivorous
 native land: 6 Borneo **7** Sumatra
 species: 13 Pongo pygmaeus

ora pro nobis 9 pray for us

orate 6 recite, speak **7** declaim **11** make a speech

oration 4 talk **5** spiel **6** eulogy, sermon, speech **7** address, lecture, recital **9** discourse, monologue, panegyric **10** peroration **11** declamation **12** disquisition, formal speech

orator 6 talker **7** speaker **8** lecturer, preacher **9** declaimer **10** sermonizer **11** rhetorician, speechmaker, spellbinder **12** elocutionist **13** public speaker

oratory 6 speech **7** bombast **8** delivery, rhetoric **9** elocution, eloquence, preaching **11** declamation **12** speechifying, speechmaking **14** grandiloquence

orb 4 ball, moon **5** globe **6** sphere **7** globule **8** spheroid

orbit 3 way **4** path **5** cycle, route, track **6** circle, course **7** channel, circuit, pathway **10** trajectory **13** revolve around **14** circumnavigate

orchards
 god of: 9 Vertumnus

orchestra 3 pit **4** band **6** stalls **7** parquet **8** ensemble, parterre **12** Philharmonic

orchestrate 5 adapt, score **7** arrange, compose

orchestration 5 score **10** adaptation **11** arrangement **12** organization

orchid
 varieties: 3 bat, bee, fen, fly, nun, nut **4** baby, blue, dove, moth, nun's, rein, swan **5** black, chain, cigar, cobra, coral, giant, jewel, pansy, Salep, showy, snowy, spice, tiger, water, widow **6** bamboo, bottle, cradle, dollar, Easter, helmet, mirror, monkey, pigeon, ragged, sawfly, shower, spider, stream, virgin **7** Alaskan, cowhorn, fringed, hooker's, jumping, peacock, rainbow, rosebud, scarlet, soldier **8** bee-swarm, Cooktown, cranefly, fried-egg, gold-lace, greenfly, hyacinth, nun's-hood, poorman's, Savannah, scorpion, white nun, windmill, woodland **9** bluntleaf, butterfly, chocolate, Christmas, clam-shell, green rein, green swan, white rein **10** buttonhole, fiveleaved, golden swan, hay-scented, late spider, leafy white, Sierra rein, slender bog **11** cockle-shell, crested rein, dancing-doll, dancing-lady, early spider, golden chain, greenwinged, one-leaf rein, pink slipper, purple-spire, rattlesnake, roundleaved **12** green fringed, pink scorpion, purple-hooded, Southern rein, tall white bog, white fringed **13** crested yellow, golden fringed, green woodland, Northern green, ragged fringed, yellow fringed **14** crested fringed, large butterfly, little club-

spur, white butterfly **15** lesser butterfly, lily-of-the-valley **16** downy rattlesnake, Florida butterfly, Northern small bog, purple fringeless, small round-leaved, white-flowered bog **18** large purple fringed, leafy Northern green, small purple fringed, Southern small white **19** lesser purple fringed **20** greater purple fringed

Orcus
 god of: 10 underworld
 punishes: 7 perjury
 corresponds to: 3 Dis **5** Hades, Pluto **8** Dis Pater

ordain 4 name, rule, will **5** elect, enact, frock **6** decree, invest **7** adjudge, appoint, command, dictate **8** delegate, deputize, instruct **9** determine, legislate, prescribe, pronounce **10** commission, consecrate

ordeal 4 care, pain **5** agony, grief, trial, worry **6** burden, misery, sorrow, strain, stress **7** anguish, concern, torment, tragedy, trouble **8** calamity, distress, pressure, vexation **9** heartache, nightmare, suffering **10** affliction, oppression **11** tribulation, unhappiness **12** wretchedness **16** trying experience

order 3 bid, law **4** body, book, calm, club, fiat, form, kind, rank, rule, sort, type **5** breed, caste, class, grade, group, guild, house, lodge, quiet, ukase **6** adjure, ask for, charge, decree, degree, demand, dictum, direct, engage, enjoin, family, status, stripe, system **7** agree to, bidding, caliber, call for, command, company, control, dictate, harmony, pattern, quality, request, reserve, silence, society, species, station **8** alliance, category, division, grouping, instruct, neatness, position, purchase, sorority, standing, tidiness **9** framework, structure, ultimatum **10** discipline, federation, fraternity, imperative, sisterhood, tabulation **11** arrangement, association, brotherhood, commandment, confederacy, designation, instruction, tranquility **12** codification, organization, peacefulness, tranquillity **13** pronouncement **14** categorization, classification

ordered 4 bade, neat, trim **7** regular, uniform **8** arranged **9** shipshape **10** systematic

orderliness 8 neatness, tidiness **10** discipline **12** organization

orderly 4 neat, tidy **5** civil, quiet **6** proper, spruce **8** peaceful **9** organized, peaceable, shipshape, tractable **10** classified, controlled, methodical, restrained, system atic **11** disciplined, uncluttered, well-behaved

ordinance 3 act, law **4** bull, fiat, rule, writ **5** canon, edict, order **6** decree, dictum, ruling **7** command, mandate, statute **9** enactment **10** regulation **11** commandment

ordinarily 7 as a rule, usually **8** commonly, normally **9** generally, regularly, routinely **10** habitually **11** customarily **12** on the average **14** conventionally

ordinary 4 dull, so-so **5** usual **6** common, normal **7** average, humdrum, routine, trivial, typical **8** everyday, familiar, habitual, mediocre, standard **9** customary **10** pedestrian, uninspired **11** commonplace, indifferent, stereotyped, traditional, unimportant **12** conventional, run-of-the-mill, unimpressive **13** insignificant, unexceptional, unimaginative, uninteresting **15** inconsequential, undistinguished

Ordinary People
  director: 13 Robert Redford
  author: 11 Judith Guest
  cast: 10 Judd Hirsch **13** Timothy Hutton **14** Mary Tyler Moore **16** Donald Sutherland
  Oscar for: 7 picture **8** director **12** screenwriter **15** supporting actor (Hutton)

ordinary wine
  French: 12 vin ordinaire

ordnance 4 arms **6** cannon **9** armaments, artillery, munitions

ordnance depot 6 armory **7** arsenal **18** military storehouse

ore 3 tin **4** gold, iron, lead, paco, rock, zinc **5** metal **6** bronze, copper, galena, sulfur **7** halvans, mineral **8** aluminum, cinnabar, hematite **9** melachite
  byproduct: 6 gangue
  deposit: 3 bed **4** lode, mine, vein **7** bonanza
  layer: 4 seam **5** stope
  trough: 6 strake
  worthless: 4 slag **5** dross, matte

Oread
  form: 5 nymph
  location: 8 mountain
  companion of: 7 Artemis

oregano
  name means: 16 joy of the mountain
  botanical name: 8 O vulgare, Origanum
  also: 6 organy, origan **8** marjoram **9** pizza herb **11** Mexican sage, winter sweet
  origin: 13 Mediterranean
  family: 4 mint
  cure for: 11 indigestion **14** loss of appetite
  first aid for: 12 spider stings **14** scorpion stings
  use: 5 pizza **6** broths **8** stuffing **12** tomato dishes **13** Italian dishes

Oregon
  abbreviation: 2 OR **4** Oreg
  nickname: 6 Beaver, Sunset **7** Webfoot **13** Sawdust Empire

capital: 5 Salem
largest city: 8 Portland
others: 5 Nyssa **6** Albany, Eugene **7** Ashland, Astoria, Medford **8** Portland, Roseburg **9** Corvallis, Pendleton **10** Grant's Pass, Willamette **12** Klamath Falls
college: 4 Reed **7** Pacific **8** Linfield, Portland **10** Willamette **13** Lewis and Clark
feature:
  fort: 5 Boise **6** Casper **7** Kearney, Laramie
  national park: 10 Crater Lake
tribe: 4 Coos **5** Alsea, Kusan, Modoc, Wasco, Yanan, Yunca **6** Cayuse, Chetco, Chinoo, Kuitsh, Molala, Siletz, Tenino, Umpqua **7** Bannock, Clatsop, Klamath, Sastean, Shastan, Takelma, Walpapi, Yaquina **8** Clackama, Klikitat, Nez Perce, Sahaptin, Umatilla **9** Kalapuyan, Tillamook **10** Kalapooian, Wallawalla
people: 10 Wayne Morse **12** Linus Pauling **15** Phyllis McGinley
  explorer: 13 Lewis and Clark
lake: 5 Abert, Waldo **6** Harney, McNary **7** John Day, Klamath, Malheur
  deepest in US: 6 Crater
land rank: 5 tenth
mountain: 5 Mazama, Tacoma, Walker, Wilson **7** Elkhorn, Grizzly, Jackass, Rainier, Tidbits, Wallowa **8** Cascades **9** Blue Coast, Marys Peak **10** Strawberry
  highest point: 4 Hood
physical feature:
  bay: 4 Coos
  caves: 11 Marble Halls
  wind: 7 Chinook
river: 5 Rogue, Snake **6** Imnaha, Owyhee, Powder, Umpqua **7** Blitzen, John Day, Klamath, Silvie's **8** Columbia **9** Deschutes **10** Willamette
state admission: 11 thirty-third
state bird: 17 western meadowlark
state fish: 13 Chinook salmon
state flower: 7 mahonia **11** Oregon grape
state motto: 8 The Union
state song: 14 Oregon My Oregon
state tree: 10 Douglas fir

Oregon Trail, The
  author: 14 Francis Parkman

Oresteia
  author: 9 Aeschylus
  trilogy includes: 9 Agamemnon, Eumenides **10** Choephoroe

Orestes
  author: 9 Euripides
  character: 5 Helen **6** Apollo, Furies **7** Electra, Pylades **8** Menelaus

Orestes
  father: 9 Agamemnon
  mother: 12 Clytemnestra
  sister: 7 Electra **9** Iphigenia
  wife: 8 Hermione

son: 9 Tisamenus
killed: 9 Aegisthus **12** Clytemnestra
pursued by: 6 Furies

Orfeo, L'
  also: 17 The Story of Orpheus
  opera by: 10 Monteverdi

Orfeo ed Euridice
  also: 18 Orpheus and Eurydice
  opera by: 5 Gluck
  character: 4 Amor, Zeus **6** Furies

Orff, Carl
  born: 6 Munich **7** Germany
  composer of: 7 Der Mond, The Moon **8** Antigone, Die Kluge **9** Schulwerk **10** Prometheus **13** Carmina Burana, The Clever Girl **14** Catulli Carmina **16** Oedipus der Tyrann, Oedipus the Tyrant

organ 6 agency **7** journal, vehicle **9** harmonium **10** hurdy-gurdy, instrument **11** publication

organic 5 alive, quick **6** living **7** animate, natural, ordered, planned, unified **8** designed, physical **9** patterned **10** anatomical, harmonious, methodical, systematic **12** nonsynthetic **13** physiological **14** constitutional

organism 4 cell **5** plant, whole **6** animal, entity, sys tem **7** complex, network, society **8** creature **9** bacterium **10** federation **11** association, corporation, institution, living thing **13** microorganism

organization 4 club, firm, sect **5** corps, group, order, party, union **6** design, league, making, outfit **7** company, forming, harmony, pattern, society **8** alliance, assembly, business, grouping, ordering **9** arranging, formation **10** federation, fellowship, fraternity **11** arrangement, association, composition, corporation, formulation, structuring **12** constitution, coordination **13** establishment, incorporation

organizational 10 managerial **13** developmental **14** administrative

organize 4 file, form, tidy **5** found, group, index, order, set up **6** codify, create, neaten, tidy up **7** arrange, catalog, develop **8** classify, tabulate **9** establish, formulate, originate **10** categorize, coordinate **11** make orderly, systematize

organized 4 neat, tidy **7** logical, orderly **8** coherent **10** methodical, systematic

orgiastic 4 wild **6** wanton **7** drunken, riotous **9** abandoned, debauched, Dionysian, dissolute, libertine **10** dissipated, licentious **12** bacchanalian, unrestrained **13** overindulgent, undisciplined

orgy 7 debauch, wassail **8** carousal **9** bacchanal **10** saturnalia **11** bacchanalia

orient, the Orient 3 fix, set **4** Asia, find **6** locate, relate, square **7** situate

8 accustom **9** acclimate, reconcile **10** the Far East **11** Eastern Asia, familiarize

oriental 4 Arab, fine, Thai, Turk **5** Asian **6** bright, Indian, Korean **7** Asiatic, Chinese, Eastern, Iranian, shining **8** Japanese, lustrous, precious, superior **10** Vietnamese
animal: 4 zebu **5** rasse
building: 6 pagoda
dish: 5 pilau, pilaw **6** pilaff
drum: 6 tomtom
food fish: 3 tai
garment: 3 aba **6** sarong
inn: 4 Khan **5** serai **6** imaret **11** caravansary
laborer: 6 coolie
market: 3 suk, sug **4** souk **6** bazaar
nurse: 4 amah, ayah
prince: 4 amir, haja
sail: 6 lateen
sash: 3 obi
shrub: 3 tea **5** henna **8** oleander
wagon: 5 araba
weight: 2 mo **4** rotl, tael **5** catty, liang **6** cantar

orientation 8 location **9** alignment, direction, situation **10** adjustment **11** acclimation **15** acclimatization, familiarization

orifice 3 gap, pit **4** hole, slit, slot, vent **5** cleft, inlet, mouth **6** cavity, cranny, hollow, lacuna, pocket, socket **7** crevice, fissure, opening, passage **8** alveolus, aperture, entrance

origami
Japanese art of: 12 paper folding

origin 4 base, line, race, rise, root **5** agent, basis, birth, breed, cause, house, stock **6** author, family, father, ground, growth, mother, reason, source, spring, strain **7** creator, descent, genesis, lineage, taproot **8** ancestry, nativity, producer **9** beginning, emergence, evolution, generator, inception, parentage, principle **10** derivation, extraction, foundation **12** commencement, fountainhead

Origin, The
author: 11 Irving Stone

original 3 new **4** bold **5** basic, basis, first, fresh, novel **6** daring, primal, unique **7** example, initial, pattern, primary, seminal, strange, unusual **8** atypical, creative, ear- liest, germinal, primeval, singular, uncommon **9** different, essential, first copy, formative, inaugural, ingenious, inventive, prototype **10** aboriginal, newfangled, primordial, underlying, unfamiliar, unorthodox **11** fundamental, imaginative **12** introductory **13** extraordinary **14** unconventional

Original Amateur Hour, The
host: 7 Ted Mack

originality 6 daring **7** newness, novelty **8** boldness **9** freshness, ingenuity

10 cleverness, creativity, uniqueness **11** imagination, singularity, unorthodoxy **13** individuality, inventiveness **17** unconventionality

originally 7 at first, by birth **8** uniquely **9** initially, unusually **10** creatively **11** differently, inventively **13** imaginatively

originate 4 come, flow, rise, stem **5** arise, begin, draft, found, issue, start **6** create, crop up, derive, design, devise, emerge, evolve, father, invent, sprout **7** develop, emanate, proceed **8** commence, conceive, envision, initiate, organize, spring up **9** establish, fabricate, formulate, germinate **10** inaugurate

origination 5 birth **7** genesis **9** inception, invention **10** conception, initiation **11** germination **12** commencement **13** establishment

Origin of Species, The
author: 13 Charles Darwin

Origins of Totalitarianism, The
author: 12 Hannah Arendt

Orion
form: 5 giant
vocation: 6 hunter
pursued: 8 Pleiades
killed by: 7 Artemis
became: 13 constellation

Oriya
language family: 12 Indo-European
branch: 11 Indo-Iranian
group: 5 Indic
spoken in: 5 (northern) India

Orkney Islands
county seat: 8 Kirkwall
country: 8 Scotland
firth: 8 Pentland
island: 3 Hay **6** Rousay, Sanday **7** Westray **8** Stronsay **14** South Ronaldsay
largest city: 6 Pomona

Orlando
author: 13 Virginia Woolf
character: 5 Sasha **14** Nicholas Greene **28** Archduchess Harriet of Roumania, Marmaduke Bonthrop Shelmerdine

Orlando
character in: 11 As You Like It
author: 11 Shakespeare

Orlando Furioso
author: 7 Ariosto
character: 6 Rogero **7** Rinaldo **8** Agramant, Angelica, Rodomont **9** Bradamant **11** Charlemagne

Ormazd 10 Ahura Mazda **12** supreme deity
religion: 14 Zoroastrianism

ormolu 5 alloy, brass, paste **6** bronze **7** gilding **8** ornament
imitation of: 4 gold
used to decorate: 5 clock **9** furniture

ornament 4 deck, gild, trim **5** adorn **6** bedeck, enrich, finery, frills **7** festoon,

furbish, garnish **8** beautify, decorate, furbelow, trick out, trimming **9** accessory, adornment, embellish **10** decoration, enrich ment **11** elaboration **13** embellishment **14** beautification

ornamental 4 gilt **5** fancy **6** chichi, rococo **10** decorative
ball: 4 bead **6** pompom
button: 4 stud
grass: 4 neti
loop: 5 picot
metal: 5 niello

ornamentation 7 garnish **8** trimming **9** adornment **10** decoration **13** embellishment

ornate 5 fancy, showy **6** flashy, florid, lavish, rococo **7** adorned, baroque, flowery **9** decorated, elaborate, sumptuous **10** flamboyant **11** embellished, pretentious **12** ostentatious

ornery 4 curt, mean **5** surly, testy **6** crabby, grumpy, shirty **7** grouchy, peevish, waspish **8** snappish **9** dyspeptic, irascible, irritable **10** ill-natured **11** ill-tempered, quarrelsome **12** cantankerous

ornithophobia
fear of: 5 birds

ornithopod
type of: 8 dinosaur
member: 9 Iguanodon **10** Edmontonia, Nodosaurus **11** Anatosaurus, Polacanthus, Saurolophus, Scolosaurus, Stegosaurus **12** Ankylosaurus, Camptosaurus, Lambeosaurus, Pisanosaurus **13** Acanthopholis, Corythosaurus, Hypsilophodon, Palaeoscincus **14** Thescelosaurus **15** Parasaurolophus, Procheneosaurus **17** Heterodontosaurus

orotund 4 full, rich **5** clear **6** strong **7** pompous, ringing, vibrant **8** resonant, sonorous **9** bombastic **10** resounding, rhetorical, stentorian
Latin: 10 ore rotundo

oro y plata 13 gold and silver
motto of: 7 Montana

Orozco, Jose Clemente
born: 6 Mexico **7** Jalisco (Zapotlan) **12** Ciudad Guzman
artwork: 5 Grief **9** Catharsis **11** Omniscience **12** House of Tears **16** National Allegory, Social Revolution **18** Hidalgo and Castillo

Orphans of the Storm
director: 10 D W Griffith
cast: 11 Dorothy Gish, Lillian Gish **17** Joseph Schildkraut

Orpheus
vocation: 4 poet **8** musician
mother: 8 Calliope
wife: 8 Eurydice
member of: 9 Argonauts
went into: 5 Hades
killed by: 7 Maenads

Orpheus in the Underworld

also: 15 Orphee aux Enfers
operetta by: 9 Offenbach

Orsino
character in: 12 Twelfth Night
author: 11 Shakespeare

ort 3 bit **5** crumb, dregs, scrap **6** morsel, refuse, trifle **7** remnant **8** leavings, leftover

orthodox 5 fixed, pious, usual **6** devout, narrow **7** limited, regular, routine **8** accepted, approved, official, ordinary, standard **9** customary, religious **11** commonplace, conformable, established, traditional **12** conventional **13** authoritative, circumscribed

orthoptera
class: 8 hexapoda
phylum: 10 arthropoda
group: 4 leaf **5** stick **6** locust, mantid **7** cricket **9** cockroach **11** grasshopper

Orwell, George
real name: 15 Eric Arthur Blair
author of: 4 1984 **10** Animal Farm **18** Nineteen Eighty- Four **29** Politics and the English Language

oryx 5 beisa **6** pickax **7** gazelle, gemsbok **8** antelope, leucoryx

Osage (Wazhazhe)
language family: 6 Siouan
location: 6 Kansas **8** Arkansas, Missouri, Oklahoma

Oscan
language family: 12 Indo-European
branch: 6 Italic

Oschophoria
origin: 8 Athenian
event: 8 festival
honoring: 7 vintage **8** Dionysus

oscillate 4 vary **5** pulse, swing, waver **6** change, seesaw **7** librate, pulsate, vibrate **8** hesitate **9** alternate, come and go, fluctuate, hem and haw, vacillate **10** ebb and flow, equivocate **12** shilly-shally **16** move back and forth

O'Shaughnessy, Brigid
character in: 16 The Maltese Falcon
author: 7 Hammett

osier 3 rod **4** wand **5** salix, withe **6** willow **7** dogwood, wilgers **9** twig-withy
species: 14 Salix viminalis
use: 6 wicker **8** basketry

Osiris
origin: 8 Egyptian
god of: 4 dead, Nile
judge of: 4 dead
king of: 4 dead
wife: 4 Isis
sister: 4 Isis
son: 5 Horus
brother: 3 Set **4** Seth **5** Horus
killed by: 3 Set **4** Seth

Oskar Matzerath
character in: 7 Tin Drum
author: 5 Grass

Oslo
capital of: 6 Norway
former name: 11 Christiania
landmark: 8 Storting (Parliament) **11** Royal Palace
mountain: 12 Holmenkollen
park: 7 Frogner
peninsula: 8 Akershus
street: 14 Karl Johansgate

Osmond, Gilbert
character in: 18 The Portrait of a Lady
author: 5 James

Ossian
character in: 12 Gaelic poetry

ossify 6 harden **7** stiffen **9** fossilize

ossuary 8 boneyard **10** depository, receptacle

ostensible 6 avowed **7** alleged, assumed, feigned, implied, nominal, outward, seeming, surface, titular, visible **8** apparent, declared, illusory, manifest, specious **9** pretended, professed **10** presumable **11** perceivable

ostentation 4 airs, dash, fuss, pomp, ritz, show **5** glitz, gloss, swank **6** splash **7** display, glitter **8** flourish, pretense **9** pageantry, pomposity, showiness, spectacle
French: 7 etalage

ostentatious 4 loud **5** gaudy, showy **6** flashy, florid, garish **7** pompous **8** affected, immodest, overdone **9** grandiose, obtrusive **10** flamboyant, showing off **11** conspicuous, exaggerated, pretentious **15** flaunting wealth

Osterreich see **7** Austria

ostracize 3 cut **4** oust, shun, snub **5** avoid, expel **6** banish, disown, reject **7** exclude, shutout **9** blackball, blacklist

Ostwald, Wilhelm
field: 9 chemistry
nationality: 6 German
founded: 17 physical chemistry

O'Sullivan, Maureen
born: 5 Boyle **7** Ireland **15** County Roscommon
daughter: 9 Mia Farrow
roles: 6 Jane (Tarzan movies) **16** David Copperfield **17** Pride and Prejudice **19** Hannah and Her Sisters

Otello
also: 7 Othello
opera by: 5 Verdi **7** Rossini

O tempora! O mores! 14 O times! O customs!
said by: 6 Cicero

Othello
director: 11 Stuart Burge
author: 18 William Shakespeare
character: 4 Iago **6** Cassio, Emilia **9** Desdemona
cast: 11 Frank Finlay, Joyce Redman, Maggie Smith **15** Laurence Olivier

other 4 more **5** added, extra, spare **6** unlike **7** further, reverse **8** contrary, opposite **9** alternate, auxiliary, different, remaining **10** additional, contrasted, dissimilar **11** contrasting **13** contradictory, supplementary **14** differentiated

Other Gods
author: 9 Pearl Buck

Other Side of Midnight, The
author: 13 Sidney Sheldon

other than 3 but **4** save **6** except, saving **7** barring, besides **9** excepting, excluding

otherwise 5 if not **6** or else **9** inversely **10** contrarily **11** differently **12** contrariwise

otherworldly 7 sublime **8** heavenly **9** celestial **14** transcendental

O times! O customs!
Latin: 14 O tempora! O mores!

Otionia
father: 10 Erechtheus
sister: 10 Protogonia
death by: 9 sacrifice
  for victory of: 9 Athenians
  over: 11 Eleusinians

otiose 4 idle, lazy **6** futile **7** laggard, resting, useless, worn-out **8** abortive, impotent, inactive, indolent, listless, slothful, sluggish **9** fruitless, lethargic, powerless, somnolent **10** unavailing **11** incompetent, ineffective, inoperative, unrewarding **12** unproductive

Otomi
tribe: 7 Capotec

O'Toole, Peter
born: 7 Ireland **9** Connemara
roles: 6 Becket **7** Creator, Lord Jim **13** Man of La Mancha **14** Goodbye Mr Chips, My Favorite Year, The Last Emperor **15** The Lion in Winter **16** Lawrence of Arabia, What's New Pussycat **18** How to Steal a Millon

O'Trigger, Sir Lucius
character in: 9 The Rivals
author: 8 Sheridan

Ott, Mel
nickname: 9 Boy Wonder **12** Master Melvin
sport: 8 baseball
position: 8 outfield
team: 13 New York Giants

Ottawa
capital of: 6 Canada
early name: 6 Bytown
falls: 6 Rideau **9** Chaudiere
landmark: 18 National Arts Centre **19** Dominion Observatory, Parliament Buildings
river: 6 Ottawa, Rideau **8** Gatineau
university: 8 Carleton

Ottawa
language family: 9 Algonkian **10** Algonquian
location: 4 Ohio **6** Canada, Kansas **7** Ontario **12** Lake Michigan
leader: 7 Pontiac

Otter
origin: **12** Scandinavian
mentioned in: **8** Volsunga
form: **5** otter
father: **8** Hreidmar
killed by: **4** Loki

ottoman, Ottoman 4 seat, Turk **5** couch, divan, stool **7** sultane, Turkish **9** footstool
color: **3** red **9** vermilion
governor: **3** bey, dey **5** pasha
ruler: **5** Osman **8** Suleiman
standard: **4** ale

Ouagadougou
capital of: **10** Upper Volta **11** Burkina Faso

oui 3 yes

ounce
abbreviation of: **2** oz

ounce troy
abbreviation of: **3** oz t

Our Bill
creator: **14** Harry Haenigsen
character: **6** Walter

Our Crowd
author: **17** Stephen Birmingham

Our Miss Brooks
character: **8** Mrs Davis **12** Connie Brooks, Walter Denton **13** Osgood Conklin, Philip Boynton **14** Harriet Conklin
cast: **8** Eve Arden **10** Dick Crenna, Gale Gordon, Jane Morgan **14** Gloria McMillan, Robert Rockwell
Miss Brooks taught: **7** English
school: **11** Madison High

Our Mutual Friend
author: **14** Charles Dickens
character: **4** Wegg **5** Venus **6** Boffin **11** Bella Wilfer **17** Mortimer Lightwood, Young John Harmon (Handford, Rokesmith)

our sea
Latin: **11** mare nostrum
ancient Roman name for: **13** Mediterranean

Our Town
author: **14** Thornton Wilder
character: **12** Simon Stimson
Gibbs family: **2** Dr **3** Mrs **6** George **7** Rebecca
Webb family: **2** Mr **3** Mrs **5** Emily, Wally
director: **7** Sam Wood
cast: **10** Fay Bainter **11** Martha Scott **13** William Holden

oust 4 fire, sack **5** eject, evict, expel **6** banish, bounce, put out, remove, unseat **7** boot out, cashier, cast out, dismiss, kick out **8** throw out **9** discharge, give the ax **11** give the gate, send packing

ouster 6 firing **7** removal, sacking **8** bouncing, ejection, eviction **9** discharge, dismissal, expelling, expulsion, overthrow **10** banishment, cash-

iering **11** dislodgment, drumming out, throwing out **13** dispossession

out 2 ex **4** away **5** aloud, eject, forth, not in, passe **6** absent, begone, excuse, public **7** outside **8** exterior, external, revealed **9** in society, in the open, published **10** extinguish

out-and-out 4 pure, sure **5** sheer, total, utter **6** arrant **7** perfect **8** absolute, complete, hardened, outright, positive, thorough **9** confirmed, downright, unlimited **10** inveterate **11** straight out, unequivocal, unmitigated, unqualified **12** unregenerate, unrestricted **13** dyed-in-the-wool, thoroughgoing, unadulterated, unconditional **14** unquestionable

outbrazen 4 dare, defy, face **8** confront **9** challenge, stand up to

outbreak 5 burst **7** display **8** epidemic, eruption, invasion, outburst **9** explosion **10** outpouring **13** demonstration

outbuilding 4 barn, shed **5** privy **6** garage, stable **7** latrine **8** outhouse, woodshed

outburst 5 blast, burst **7** display, thunder **8** eruption, outbreak **9** explosion **10** outpouring **11** fulmination **13** demonstration

outcast 5 exile, rover **6** ousted, outlaw, pariah, roamer **7** refugee, runaway **8** banished, castaway, deportee, derelict, expelled, fugitive, rejected, vagabond **9** discarded **10** expatriate

Outcast of the Islands, The
author: **12** Joseph Conrad

Outcault, R F
creator/artist of: **11** Buster Brown **12** The Yellow Kid

outcome 3 end **5** fruit, issue **6** effect, payoff, result, upshot **9** aftermath, outgrowth **11** aftereffect, consequence

outcry 3 cry **4** howl, roar, yell, yelp, yowl **5** noise, shout, whoop **6** bellow, clamor, hubbub, scream, shriek, uproar **7** clangor, protest, screech **9** commotion, complaint, crying out, hue and cry, objection **10** cry of alarm, hullabaloo **12** caterwauling, remonstrance

outdated 5 passe **7** antique **8** outmoded **9** out-of-date **10** antiquated **12** old-fashioned

outdo 3 top **4** beat, best **5** excel, worst **6** better, defeat, exceed, outfox, outwit **7** eclipse, outplay, outrank, surpass **8** outclass, outshine, outstrip **9** overcome **9** transcend

outdoor festival
French: **13** fete champetre

outdoor market 5 agora **6** bazaar **10** flea market **11** marketplace

outer 6 distal, remote **7** extreme, farther, outside, outward, without **8** ex-

terior, external, outlying **9** outermost **10** farther out, peripheral

outer edge 3 lip, rim, tip **5** bound **6** margin **8** boundary **9** extremity

Outer Mongolia
also: **24** Mongolian People's Republic
border: **5** China **6** Russia **11** Soviet Union
capital: **4** Urga **5** Kulun **9** Ulan Bator
currency: **5** mongo **6** tugrik
desert: **4** Gobi **5** Shamo
language: **7** Khalka
mountain range: **5** Altai, Altay **7** Khangai

outermost 5 outer **6** utmost **7** extreme, outside, outward, surface **8** exterior, external **11** farthest out, most distant, superficial

outfit 3 fit, rig **4** gear **5** array, dress, equip, getup, habit, rig up **6** clothe, supply **7** appoint, costume, furnish **8** accouter, ensemble, wardrobe **9** equipment, provision, trappings **13** accoutrements, paraphernalia

outflow 5 issue **7** leakage, seepage **8** drainage **9** discharge

outgo 4 beat, cost, exit, pass **5** excel, issue, outdo **6** efflux, egress, outlay, outlet **7** outflow, surpass **8** outstrip **9** departure **11** expenditure

outgoing 4 warm **6** genial, social **7** amiable, cordial, exiting, leaving **8** friendly, going out, outbound, sociable **9** convivial, departing **10** gregarious **11** extroverted, sympathetic, warmhearted

outgoing person 9 extrovert **17** hail-fellow-well-met

outgrowth 3 end **4** knob, knot, node **5** bulge, fruit, issue, shoot **6** result, sequel, sprout, upshot **7** product **8** offshoot **9** aftermath **10** conclusion, projection **11** aftereffect, consequence, culmination, excrescence, outcropping **12** protuberance

outing 4 hike, ride, spin, tour, trip, walk **5** drive, jaunt, tramp **6** airing, junket, ramble **7** holiday **9** excursion **10** expedition

outlander 5 alien, exile **6** emigre **7** invader, settler **8** intruder, newcomer, stranger, wanderer **9** Auslander, barbarian, foreigner, immigrant **10** tramontane **12** ultramontane

outlandish 3 odd **5** kooky, queer, weird **6** far-out **7** bizarre, curious, strange, unusual **8** freakish, peculiar **9** eccentric, fantastic, grotesque, unheard-of **10** incredible, outrageous, ridiculous **12** preposterous, unbelievable, unimaginable, unparalleled **13** inconceivable **14** unconventional

outlast 6 endure, hold on, keep on, remain, stay on **7** carry on, hold out, outstay, outwear, perdure, persist, prevail, survive **8** continue

outlaw 3 ban, bar **4** deny, stop **5** felon

6 bandit, forbid, pariah **7** exclude, outcast **8** criminal, disallow, fugitive, prohibit, suppress **9** desperado, interdict, miscreant, proscribe **10** highwayman

outlay 3 fee **4** cost **5** outgo, price **6** charge **7** expense, payment **8** spending **11** amount spent, expenditure **12** disbursement

outlet 3 way **4** door, duct, exit, gate, path, vent **5** means **6** avenue, egress, escape, portal **7** channel, conduit, gateway, opening, passage

outline 4 plot **5** brief, trace **6** digest, limits, resume, review **7** contour, diagram, profile, summary, tracing **8** abstract, synopsis **9** blueprint, delineate, lineation, perimeter, periphery, sketch out **10** abridgment, silhouette **11** delineation **12** condensation
French: 6 apercu

outlook 4 view **5** scene, sight, vista **6** aspect, chance **7** picture, promise **8** attitude, forecast, panorama, prospect **9** spectacle, viewpoint **10** assumption **11** expectation, frame of mind, perspective, point of view, presumption, probability **12** anticipation

outlying 5 outer, rural **6** far-off, remote **7** distant, exurban **8** exterior, suburban **10** peripheral

outmoded 5 corny, dated, passe, tired **6** demode, old hat **7** antique, archaic, vintage **8** obsolete, old-timey, outdated **9** out-of-date **10** antiquated **12** old-fashioned, out-of-fashion **14** behind the times
French: 6 demode

Out of Africa
director: 13 Sydney Pollack
cast: 11 Meryl Streep (Baroness Karen Blixen, Isak Dinesen) **13** Robert Redford (Denys Finch Hatton) **19** Klaus Maria Brandauer (Baron Bror von Blixen)

out of bed 2 up **5** astir **9** up and at 'em **10** on one's feet, up and about **12** rise and shine

out-of-date 5 dated, passe **8** outmoded **10** antiquated **12** old-fashioned
French: 6 demode

out of doors 3 out **5** forth **6** abroad **7** outside **8** alfresco **12** in the open air

out-of-fashion 5 passe **8** obsolete, outmoded **9** out-of-date **12** old-fashioned
French: 6 demode

out of hand 4 wild **5** rowdy **6** unruly **10** disorderly **12** obstreperous, out of control, unmanageable, unrestrained **14** uncontrollable

out of keeping 8 atypical, peculiar, unseemly **9** anomalous, irregular **11** incongruous **12** inconsistent **13** inappropriate

out of kilter 4 awry **5** askew **6** uneven **7** crooked, oblique

out of line 6 unruly **9** excessive **10** exorbitant **12** presumptuous, unreasonable

out of many one
Latin: 13 e pluribus unum
motto of: 12 United States

out of one's head 3 mad **4** daft, nuts **5** crazy, nutty **6** insane **7** cracked, touched **8** demented, deranged, unhinged **10** unbalanced **12** mad as a hatter, off his rocker **15** mad as a March hare **17** nutty as a fruitcake

out of operation 4 dead, down **8** inactive **10** not working, out of order **11** inoperative

out of order 5 amiss **6** faulty **10** not working **11** inoperative, uncalled-for **13** inappropriate

out of place 3 odd **8** unseemly **10** unsuitable **11** incongruous, inconsonant **13** inappropriate

out of shape 4 bent **5** unfit **6** flabby, warped **7** crooked **8** deformed **9** distorted, untrained

out of sorts 5 cross, huffy, testy **6** crabby, cranky, touchy **7** bearish, grouchy, peevish **8** petulant, snappish **9** crotchety, irritable **10** ill-humored **11** ill-tempered **12** cantankerous **13** short-tempered

out of the books of
Latin: 8 ex libris

out of the fight
French: 12 hors de combat

out of the ordinary 4 rare **6** unique **7** notable, unusual **8** singular, uncommon **10** phenomenal, remarkable **11** exceptional **13** extraordinary

Out of the Past
director: 15 Jacques Tourneur
based on novel by: 13 Geoffrey Homes (Daniel Mainwaring) (Build My Gallows High)
cast: 9 Jane Greer **11** Kirk Douglas, Richard Webb **13** Rhonda Fleming, Robert Mitchum

out of touch 7 mixed-up **8** unstable **11** disoriented **12** out of contact **13** incommunicado

out-of-towner 7 tourist, visitor **9** sojourner, transient **11** nonresident

outpace 4 pass **5** outdo **6** exceed, outrun **8** outstrip

outpouring 6 deluge **7** barrage, gushing, outflow **8** effusion

output 4 crop, gain, take **5** yield **6** profit **7** harvest, produce, product, reaping, turnout **8** gleaning, proceeds **9** gathering **10** production **11** achievement **12** productivity **14** accomplishment

outrage 4 evil, gall, rile **5** anger, shock, wrong **6** arouse, enrage, insult, madden, offend, ruffle **7** affront, incense, provoke, steam up **8** atrocity, disquiet, enormity, iniquity **9** barbarity, indignity, infuriate **10** discompose, disrespect, exasperate, gross crime, scandalize **11** desecration, monstrosity, profanation **13** barbarousness, get one's back up, make one see red, slap in the face, transgression **17** make one's blood boil

outraged 3 mad **5** angry, irate, riled **6** fuming, raging **7** enraged, furious **8** incensed, inflamed, offended **9** affronted, indignant **10** displeased, infuriated

outrageous 4 base, foul, rank, rude, vile **5** gross **6** brutal, odious, wicked **7** abusive, extreme, galling, heinous, immense, inhuman **8** enormous, flagrant, inhumane, insolent, scornful, shocking **9** atrocious, barbarous, excessive, insulting, maddening, monstrous, nefarious, offensive, shameless **10** despicable, exorbitant, horrifying, immoderate, iniquitous, scandalous **11** disgraceful, infuriating, unspeakable, unwarranted **12** contemptible, contemptuous, exasperating, preposterous, unreasonable **13** disrespectful, reprehensible **14** unconscionable

outrageousness 8 enormity **9** immensity **10** wickedness **13** atrociousness, monstrousness, offensiveness **16** preposterousness

outre 8 improper

outreach 6 exceed **7** surpass

outright 4 full **5** sheer, total, utter **6** at once, entire, openly **7** utterly, visibly **8** absolute, complete, entirely, patently, promptly, thorough **9** downright, forthwith, instantly, on the spot, out-and-out **10** absolutely, altogether, completely, manifestly, thoroughly, unreserved **11** immediately, unmitigated, unqualified **12** demonstrably, undiminished **13** thoroughgoing, unconditional

outrival 3 dim **5** excel, outdo **6** exceed **7** eclipse, surpass **8** outshine **9** transcend **10** overshadow, tower above

outrush 4 gust **8** overflow

outset 4 dawn **5** birth, start **7** dawning **9** beginning, departure, threshold **12** commencement

outshine 3 dim **5** excel, outdo **6** exceed **7** eclipse, surpass **9** transcend **10** overshadow

outside 4 case, face, skin **5** alien, faint, outer **6** facade, remote, sheath, slight **7** coating, distant, foreign, obscure, outdoor, outward, strange, surface **8** covering, exterior, external, outdoors **9** nonnative, outer side, outermost **10** extraneous, out-of-doors, unfamiliar

outsider 5 alien **7** outcast **8** onlooker, stranger **9** bystander, foreigner, nonmember **14** nonparticipant

outskirts 3 rim 4 edge 6 limits, verges 7 borders, fringes, margins, suburbs 8 environs 9 periphery, precincts 10 perimeters 11 extremities

outspoken 5 blunt, frank 6 candid, direct, honest 7 artless 9 guileless, ingenuous, unsparing 10 forthright, unreserved 11 opinionated, plainspoken 13 undissembling 15 straightforward, undissimulating

outspread 5 broad 6 opened, spread 7 laid out 8 expanded, extended, unfolded, unfurled, unrolled 9 spread out, stretched 12 outstretched

outstanding 3 due 5 famed, great, owing 6 famous, unpaid 7 eminent, notable, payable 8 foremost, renowned, striking 9 best known, exemplary, in arrears, marvelous, memorable, prominent, unsettled 10 celebrated, noteworthy, phenomenal, remarkable 11 exceptional, magnificent, uncollected 13 distinguished, extraordinary, unforgettable

outstrip 4 pass 6 exceed, outrun 7 outpace, surpass 11 leave behind

outward 5 outer 7 evident, outside, surface, visible 8 apparent, exterior, external, manifest 10 observable, ostensible 11 perceivable, perceptible, superficial

outward appearance 4 mien 6 aspect, facade, manner 7 bearing 8 demeanor, exterior

Outward Bound
  author: 10 Sutton Vane

outwardly 7 clearly, visibly 9 evidently, seemingly 10 apparently, manifestly, ostensibly 13 on the face of it 16 to all appearances

outwards 3 out 4 away

outweigh 6 exceed 7 eclipse, surpass 8 override 9 rise above 10 overshadow 11 predominate, prevail over 13 be heavier than, weigh more than

outwit 4 dupe, foil, fool, trap 5 trick 6 baffle, outfox, take in, thwart 7 ensnare 8 outsmart 9 get around 10 circumvent 11 outmaneuver

outworn 5 dated, passe 6 bygone 7 defunct, disused, extinct 8 obsolete, rejected 9 abandoned, discarded, forgotten, out-of-date 10 antiquated, superseded 12 old-fashioned 13 unfashionable

ouzo
  type: 7 liqueur
  origin: 6 Greece
  flavor: 5 anise
  substitute for: 8 absinthe

oval 5 ovate, ovoid 6 curved, ovular 7 obovate, oviform, rounded 9 egg-shaped 10 elliptical 11 ellipsoidal

ovation 6 cheers, homage, hurrah, hurray, huzzah 7 acclaim, fanfare, tribute 8 applause, cheering 9 adulation 11 acclamation

oven 3 umu 4 kiln, oast 5 baker, range, stove 6 hearth 7 broiler, chamber, kitchen, roaster
  clay: 7 tandoor
  fork: 7 fruggan, fruggin
  mop: 6 scovel

over 3 too 4 also, anew, done, else, gone, past 5 above, again, ended, extra, often 6 afresh, bygone, lapsed, no more, to boot 7 at an end, elapsed, expired, settled, surplus 8 finished, in excess, once more, too great 9 completed, concluded, excessive, remaining 10 additional, all through, in addition, passed away, repeatedly, terminated 11 a second time, superfluous

overabundance 4 glut 6 excess 7 surfeit, surplus 8 plethora 9 abundance, profusion 10 oversupply 11 superfluity 14 superabundance 15 supersaturation 21 embarrassment of riches
  French: 19 embarras de richesses

over again 4 anew 5 again 7 all over 8 once more 9 once again

overall 5 total 6 entire 7 general 8 complete, long-term, sweeping 9 extensive, long-range, panoramic 10 exhaustive, widespread 12 all-embracing, all-inclusive 13 comprehensive, thoroughgoing

over-and-above 5 added, extra 7 added on, besides 10 additional, in addition 13 supplementary

overawe 6 dazzle 9 overpower, overwhelm 10 intimidate

overbalance 5 upset 6 topple 8 outweigh

overbearing 5 cocky 6 lordly, snooty 7 haughty, high-hat, pompous, stuck-up 8 arrogant, despotic, egoistic 9 conceited, imperious, know-it-all 10 autocratic, disdainful, egoistical, high-handed, tyrannical 11 dictatorial, domineering, egotistical 13 high-and-mighty, self-assertive, self-important

overburden 3 tax 4 load, task, tire 5 whelm 7 exhaust, wear out 8 encumber, overwork, surcharge 9 overwhelm

overcast 4 dark, dull, gray, hazy 5 foggy, misty, murky 6 cloudy, dreary, gloomy, leaden 7 sunless 8 lowering 11 overclouded, threatening

overcharge 3 gyp, pad 4 rook, skin, soak 5 bleed, cheat, gouge, stick, sting, usury 6 extort, fleece 7 exploit 10 exaggerate

overcoat 3 mac 5 parka 6 duster, poncho, raglan, tabard, ulster 7 oilskin, paletot, topcoat 8 burberry, mackinaw 9 greatcoat, inverness, pea jacket 10 mackintosh, trenchcoat 12 chesterfield, Prince Albert

Overcoat, The
  author: 12 Nikolai Gogol
  character: 9 Petrovich 26 A Certain Important Personage 28 Akakii Akakiievich Bashmachkin

overcome 4 beat, best, lick 5 crush, quell 6 defeat, master, subdue 7 conquer, put down, survive, win over 8 suppress, surmount, vanquish 9 overpower, overthrow, overwhelm, transcend 11 prevail over, triumph over 14 get the better of

overconfident 5 brash 6 cheeky 8 arrogant, cocksure, egoistic, immodest, impudent 9 conceited 10 egoistical 11 egotistical, self-assured 12 presumptuous

overcrowd 3 jam 4 cram, fill, pack 5 stuff 7 congest

overcrowded 6 filled, jammed, packed 7 crammed, stuffed 9 congested, jampacked

overdecorated 5 gaudy, showy 6 flashy, garish 9 unsightly 12 ostentatious

overdelicacy 11 genteelness, prudishness 12 priggishness 14 overrefinement

overdo 4 gild 6 expand 7 amplify, ham it up, magnify, overact 8 overplay 9 embroider, overstate 10 do to excess, exaggerate 11 carry too far, hyperbolize 12 lay it on thick 13 stretch a point

overdue 4 late, slow 5 tardy 7 belated, delayed, past due 8 dilatory 10 behindhand, behind time, unpunctual 11 long delayed

overdue debt 7 arrears 10 balance due 18 balance outstanding

overflow 4 glut 5 flood 6 excess 7 run over, surplus 8 flow over, inundate, plethora, slop over 9 overspill, profusion 10 overspread, oversupply 11 copiousness, superfluity 13 overabundance 14 superabundance

overflowing 4 full 5 flush 7 replete, swamped 8 abundant, flooding 9 abounding, inundated 11 running over

overgarment 4 cape, coat, robe 5 cloak, habit, parka, shawl, smock 6 blazer, blouse, duster, jacket, kimono, mantle, poncho 7 sweater, topcoat, wrapper 8 cardigan, raincoat 9 gaberdine, housecoat

overgrown 4 rank 5 giant 7 blown-up 8 colossal, enlarged, forested, gigantic 9 luxuriant, oversized

overhang 3 jut 4 eave 5 bulge, drape, eaves, jetty 6 beetle, impend, sadden, shelve 7 project, suspend 8 protrude, threaten 9 projection

overhaul 4 beat, pass 5 catch 6 revamp 7 rebuild, remodel, restore, service 8 overtake, renovate 11 catch up with, recondition, reconstruct

overhead 3 nut 4 atop, roof 5 above, aloft, on top, upper 6 upward 7 ceiling, topmost, up above 8 superior 9 overlying, uppermost 11 overhanging

overindulge 4 baby 5 spoil, stuff 6 overdo, pamper, pig out 7 carouse, overeat 9 dissipate 11 mollycoddle

overjoyed 6 elated, joyous 8 ecstatic, euphoric, exultant, jubilant, thrilled 9 delighted, enchanted, exuberant, gratified 10 enraptured, enthralled 11 carried away, tickled pink, transported 12 happy as a lark

overlay 4 coat 5 cover, layer 6 carpet, veneer 7 blanket, coating 8 covering 11 superimpose

overload 3 tax 4 glut 5 flood, whelm 6 deluge, excess 7 burnout, surfeit 8 encumber 9 innundate, surcharge

overlook 4 miss, omit, skip 6 excuse, forget, give on, ignore, pass up, slight, survey, wink at 7 blink at, command, forgive, let ride, neglect 8 leave out, look over, pass over, shrug off 9 disregard, look out on 10 tower above 11 forget about, have a view of, leave undone

overlord 4 czar, tsar 7 emperor, monarch 8 autocrat 12 supreme ruler 13 absolute ruler

overly 3 too 4 very 6 highly, unduly 7 acutely, too much 8 overmuch, severely, to a fault, unfairly 9 extremely, intensely 10 needlessly 11 exceedingly, excessively 12 exorbitantly, immoderately, inordinately, unreasonably 13 disproportionately

overly trusting 5 naive 8 gullible 9 credulous 12 unsuspicious

overmodest 3 coy 4 prim 7 prudish 8 priggish 11 puritanical

overmuch 3 too 6 excess 7 surplus 8 plethora 9 profusion

overpass 4 span 6 bridge 9 crossover

overpower 4 beat, best, move, sway 5 crush, quell, worst 6 defeat, master, subdue 7 conquer 8 overcome, vanquish 9 influence, overwhelm

overpowering 6 mighty, strong 8 crushing 10 astounding 12 overwhelming

overpraise 4 line 7 blarney, fawning 8 flattery 11 fulsomeness

overpriced 6 costly 7 too high 9 expensive 10 exorbitant

overproud 4 vain 8 arrogant, egoistic 9 conceited 10 egoistical 11 egotistical, swell-headed 13 self-important

overrate 4 overprize, overvalue 10 overesteem, overpraise 12 overestimate 13 make too much of

overrefined 7 genteel, prudish 8 priggish 12 overdelicate

override 5 crush, quash 7 reverse 8 set aside 10 commission 11 countermand

overrule 4 deny, veto 5 annul, eject, repel, waive 6 cancel, refuse, reject, revoke 7 dismiss, nullify, outvote 8 disallow, outweigh, override, overturn, preclude, set aside, throw out 9 repudiate 10 invalidate 11 countermand

overrun 4 loot, raid, sack 5 choke 6 deluge, engulf, infest, invade 7 despoil, pillage, plunder, surplus 8 inundate, overgrow, pour in on, rove over 9 overwhelm, surge over, swarm over

overseas, oversea 5 alien 6 abroad, exotic 7 foreign 8 external 11 ultramarine 12 transoceanic 14 in foreign lands

oversee 3 run 4 boss, rule 5 guide, pilot, see to, steer, watch 6 direct, govern, handle, manage 7 carry on, command 8 attend to, overlook, regulate 9 supervise 10 administer 11 keep an eye on, preside over, superintend 12 have charge of

overseeing 7 bossing, guiding, running 8 guidance, handling, managing 10 leadership, management 11 attending to, supervising, supervision 13 administering 14 administrating, administration, superintending 15 superintendence

overseer 4 boss, head 5 chief 7 captain, foreman, manager 8 director, governor 10 supervisor, taskmaster 11 slave driver 13 administrator 14 superintendent

overshadow 3 fog 4 hide, mask, veil 5 cover, dwarf, shade 6 darken, screen, shroud 7 conceal, eclipse, obscure 8 outshine 9 tower over

overshadowing 7 eclipse, masking, shading, veiling 8 cloaking 9 darkening, eclipsing, obscuring 10 concealing, surpassing 11 concealment, obscuration 12 towering over

overshoe 3 gum 4 boot 6 arctic, gaiter, galosh, patten, rubber 7 galoshe

overshoot 4 pass 6 exceed, go over 8 go beyond

oversight 6 laxity, slight 7 blunder, mistake, neglect 8 omission 9 disregard 10 negligence 11 inattention 12 carelessness, heedlessness, inadvertence 13 careless error 14 neglectfulness 15 thoughtlessness

oversized 4 huge, vast 7 immense, mammoth 8 colossal, enormous, gigantic 10 monumental 14 Brobdingnagian

overspending 12 extravagance, throwing away

overspread 3 fog 4 coat, fill, pave 5 bathe, cloud, cover, paint, plate, smear 6 clothe, infest 7 blanket, diffuse, overlay, overrun, pervade, suffuse 8 disperse 9 whitewash

overstate 6 overdo, play up 7 enlarge,

inflate, lay it on, magnify, stretch, touch up 8 increase, overdraw, oversell 9 embellish, embroider, enlarge on, overpaint 10 exaggerate, overstress 15 spread it on thick

overstep 6 exceed 7 violate 10 transgress

oversupply 4 glut 6 excess 7 surfeit, surplus, too much 8 plethora 11 undue amount 13 overabundance 14 superabundance

overt 4 open 5 plain 6 public 7 evident, obvious, visible 8 apparent, manifest, palpable, revealed 10 easily seen, noticeable, observable, ostensible 11 perceivable, perceptible, unconcealed, undisguised

overtake 4 go by, pass 5 catch, reach 6 befall, gain on 7 run down 8 approach, overhaul 11 catch up with

overtax 4 tire 5 abuse, hoist 6 burden, exceed, strain, stress 7 exhaust 8 overload, overwork 9 misemploy 10 overburden

over the hill 3 old 4 aged 5 aging 7 elderly 11 past the peak 13 past one's prime

overthrow 4 undo 5 crush 6 defeat, mutiny, topple 7 abolish, undoing 8 downfall, overcome, overturn, toppling 9 abolition, bring down, overpower, rebellion 10 do away with, revolution

overtire 3 fag 4 bush, do in, poop 5 drain 7 exhaust, fatigue, wear out 8 enervate

overtone 3 hue 4 hint 5 drift 8 coloring, innuendo 10 intimation, suggestion 11 connotation, implication, insinuation

overtrustful 8 gullible 9 credulous 12 unsuspecting, unsuspicious 13 unquestioning

overture 3 bid 6 motion, signal, tender 7 advance, gesture, preface, prelude 8 approach, foreword, offering, preamble, prologue, proposal 9 beginning 10 invitation, suggestion 11 opening move, proposition 12 introduction

overturn 4 beat, oust 5 crush, upend, upset 6 defeat, depose, thrash, topple 7 capsize, conquer, turn out 8 overcome, push over, vanquish 9 knock down, knock over, overpower, overthrow, overwhelm 14 turn topsyturvy, turn upside down

overturning
French: 14 bouleversement

overweening 5 bossy, cocky, pushy 6 brassy 7 haughty, pompous 8 arrogant, egoistic 9 bigheaded, imperious 10 disdainful, egotistical, high-handed, immoderate 11 domineering, egotistical, overbearing, patronizing 12 presumptuous 13 high-and-mighty, overconfident, self-important

overweight 3 fat 5 dumpy, fatty, gross, hefty, obese, piggy, plump, pudgy, stout, tubby 6 chubby, chunky, fleshy, portly, rotund 7 fattish, well-fed 8 roly-poly 9 corpulent 10 potbellied, well-padded 11 beer-bellied, overstuffed 15 well-upholstered

overwhelm 4 beat, bury 5 crush, quash, quell, swamp 6 defeat, engulf 7 conquer, overrun, stagger 8 bowl over, confound, inundate, overcome, vanquish 9 devastate, overpower, overthrow, subjugate

overwhelming 8 crushing 10 staggering 11 astonishing, devastating 12 overpowering

overwork 3 tax 4 task, tire, toil 5 labor 6 burden, strain 7 exhaust, overtax, wear out 9 misemploy 10 overburden

overwrought 4 wild 5 riled 6 touchy, uneasy 7 excited, nervous, ruffled 8 agitated, frenzied, inflamed, wild-eyed, worked up 9 perturbed, wrought up 10 distracted, high-strung 11 carried away, overexcited

Ovid
author of: 6 Amores 7 Tristia 8 Heroides 11 Ars Amatoria 12 The Art of Love 13 Metamorphoses

ovule 3 egg, nit 4 germ, ovum 6 embryo 7 seedlet

ovum 3 egg 4 cell, germ, seed 5 spore 6 gamete 8 oosphere

owe 8 be in debt 11 be obligated 12 be beholden to, be indebted to

owed 3 due 5 owing 6 unpaid 9 in arrears 11 outstanding

Owen Marshall, Counselor at Law
character: 11 Jess Brandon 12 Frieda Krause 15 Melissa Marshall

cast: 9 Lee Majors 10 Arthur Hill 11 Joan Darling 17 Christine Matchett

owing 3 due 4 owed 6 unpaid 9 in arrears 11 outstanding

own 4 avow, have, hold, keep, tell 5 admit, allow, grant, yield 6 assent, concur, retain 7 concede, possess, private 8 disclose, maintain, personal 9 acquiesce, confess to, consent to, recognize 10 individual, particular 11 acknowledge

owner 6 holder, master 7 partner 8 landlady, landlord, mistress 9 co-partner, landowner, possessor 10 landholder, proprietor 11 house-holder, titleholder 12 proprietress

own up to 5 admit 6 accept 7 confess 8 blurt out 9 recognize 11 acknowledge 14 come clean about

ox 3 oaf 4 bull, clod, musk, urus, zebu 5 aiver, beast, bison, gayal, steer 6 auroch, bantin, bovine 7 banteng, buffalo 10 clodhopper
Cambodian: 7 Kouprey, Kouproh
Celebesian: 3 goa, noa 4 anoa
extinct: 4 urus 7 aurochs
family: 7 bovidae
genus: 3 bos
horned: 4 reem
hornless: 4 moil
Indian: 4 gaur
Paul Bunyan's: 4 Babe
    color: 4 blue
stall: 4 crib
team: 4 yoke
Tibetan: 3 yak
wild: 3 ure 4 anoa
young: 4 stot 5 stirk

Ox-Bow Incident, The
author: 21 Walter Van Tilburg Clark
character: 5 Canby, Croft 6 Davies, Gerald, Martin, Tetley 9 Gil Carter
director: 14 William Wellman
cast: 10 Henry Fonda 11 Dana An-

drews 12 Anthony Quinn 13 William Blythe 14 Mary Beth Hughes

oxen
group of: 4 yoke

oxide 8 compound
afterburn: 4 calx
calcium: 4 calx, lime
cobalt: 6 zaffer, zaffre
element: 6 oxygen
iron: 4 rust 8 hematite, limonite 9 colcothar, magnetite
make by heat: 7 calcine
sodium: 4 soda
zinc: 6 cadmia

oxidize 4 burn, char, rust 7 corrode

Oxyderces
epithet of: 6 Athena
means: 10 bright-eyed

oxygen
chemical symbol: 1 O

Oxylus
origin: 8 Aetolian
punishment: 5 exile
chosen leader of: 10 Heraclidae
led invasion of: 12 Peloponnesus

oyez 4 hear 6 attend
cry used by: 10 court crier
preceded: 12 proclamation

Oz *see Wizard of Oz*

Ozark Jubilee
host: 8 Red Foley 10 Webb Pierce
theme: 12 Sugarfoot Rag

Ozark State
nickname of: 8 Missouri

Ozick, Cynthia
author of: 10 Levitation 17 The Cannibal Galaxy 21 The Messiah of Stockholm

Ozzie and Harriet, The Adventures of
cast: 11 David Nelson, Ozzie Nelson, Ricky (Eric) Nelson 13 Harriet Nelson

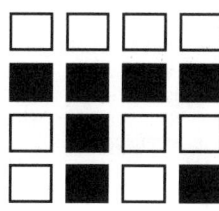

pa 3 dad, paw, pop **4** papa **5** daddy, pater **6** father
mate: 2 ma

pace 4 clip, flow, gait, rate, step, walk **5** amble, speed, tread **6** motion, stride, stroll **7** saunter **8** momentum, slow gait, velocity

Pacelli, Eugenio Maria Giuseppe Giovanni 11 Pope Pius XII

pachyderm 5 hippo, rhino **8** elephant, ungulate **10** rhinoceros **12** hippopotamus
characteristic: 4 tusk **5** ivory, trunk **12** thick-skinned
prehistoric: 7 mammoth **8** mastodon

pachydermatous 4 hard **5** horny, tough **7** callous **8** callused, hardened, leathery **12** thick-skinned **13** elephant-hided

pacific 4 calm **5** quiet, still **6** gentle, placid, serene, smooth **7** halcyon, restful **8** dovelike, peaceful, tranquil **9** pacifying, peaceable, reposeful, unruffled **10** harmonious, untroubled **11** inoffensive, undisturbed **12** conciliatory

pacification 8 soothing **11** appeasement, peacemaking **12** conciliation, nonagression **14** reconciliation

Pacific island 3 Aru, Yap **4** Bali, Fiji, Guam, Maui, Oahu, Rapa, Truk, Wake **5** Mauru, Papua, Samoa **6** Hawaii, Kodiak, Midway, Ryukyu, Tahiti, Taiwan **7** Okinawa **8** Borabora, Eniwetok, Pitcairn, Tasmania **9** New Guinea **12** Bougainville

pacify 4 calm **5** allay, quiet **6** soothe **7** appease, assuage, compose, mollify, placate **9** reconcile **10** conciliate, propitiate

Pacino, Al
real name: 13 Alberto Pacino
born: 9 New York NY
roles: 7 Serpico **8** Scarface **12** Author Author, Donnie Brasco, The Godfather **13** Scent of a Woman (Oscar) **15** Dog Day Afternoon **16** And Justice for All **17** Glengary Glen Ross **22** Does a Tiger wear a Necktie (Tony)

pack 3 box, jam, kit, lot, mob, set, tie **4** bevy, bind, cram, fill, heap, herd, load, mass **5** batch, bunch, clump, covey, crowd, drove, flock, group, horde, stuff, swarm, truss **6** bundle, gaggle, gather, packet, parcel, passel, throng **7** cluster, package **8** assemble **9** container, multitude **10** assortment, collection, miscellany **12** accumulation

package 3 box, kit **4** case, pack, wrap **6** bundle, carton, encase, packet, parcel, wrap up **9** container, wrappings

pack closely 4 cram, pack **5** press, stuff **7** compact **8** compress

packed 4 full **6** filled, jammed, loaded, massed, rammed, wedged **7** crammed, crowded, crushed, pressed, stuffed **8** overfull, squeezed **10** sandwiched **11** overcrowded

packet 3 bag, box **4** bale, pack, roll **5** pouch, sheaf **6** bundle, parcel, quiver **7** package

pact 4 bond **6** treaty **7** compact **8** alliance, contract, covenant **9** agreement, concordat **10** convention **11** concordance **13** understanding

pad 3 mat **4** fill **5** stuff **6** blow up, fatten, tablet **7** bolster, cushion, inflate, protect, puff out **8** mattress, notebook **9** upholster **10** cushioning, stretch out

padding 6 filler, lining **7** filling, packing, surfeit, surplus, wadding **8** stuffing, verbiage, wrapping **9** prolixity, verbosity, wordiness **10** redundancy **11** verboseness **12** extravagance **14** superabundance

Paderewski, Ignace (Ignacy Jan)
born: 6 Poland **9** Kurilowka
composer of: 5 Manru **9** Minuet in G

pad out 5 add to **6** expand, extend **7** amplify, augment, enlarge, stretch **8** elongate, increase, lengthen

padre 6 cleric, father, priest **8** chaplain **9** clergyman

paean 6 anthem, eulogy **7** hosanna **9** laudation, panegyric **10** hallelujah **11** acclamation **12** hymn of praise
form: 4 hymn, song
characteristic: 6 joyful **12** thanksgiving

Paeon
form: 3 god
position: 9 physician
served gods of: 7 Olympia
corresponds to: 6 Apollo

Paezan
language family: 13 Macro-Chibchan
group: 4 Paez **5** Choco **6** Warrau **8** Colorado

pagan 7 atheist, heathen, infidel **8** idolator **9** barbarian **10** heathenish, idolatrous, polytheist, unbeliever **11** nonbeliever **12** polytheistic

Paganini, Niccolo
born: 5 Genoa, Italy
played: 6 violin
composer of: 19 The Carnival of Venice

page 3 boy, lad **4** beep, call, girl, leaf **5** folio, groom, sheet, youth **6** knight, number, summon **7** callboy, contact **8** announce **9** attendant, messenger **10** apprentice, manservant
blank: 7 flyleaf
left-hand: 5 verso
right-hand: 5 recto

Page, Geraldine
born: 12 Kirksville MO
husband: 7 Rip Torn
roles: 5 Hondo **9** Interiors **11** Pete-n-Tillie **14** Summer and Smoke **16** A Trip to Bountiful (Oscar), Sweet Bird of Youth

Page and Mistress Page
characters in: 22 The Merry Wives of Windsor
author: 11 Shakespeare

pageant 4 pomp, rite, show **6** parade, ritual **7** display **8** ceremony **9** spectacle **10** exhibition, procession **12** extravaganza

pageantry 4 pomp, rite, show **5** drama, flair **6** ritual, splash **7** display, glitter, pageant **8** ceremony, grandeur, splendor **9** showiness, spectacle, theatrics **10** flashiness **11** ostentation **12** extravagance, magnificence

Paget, James
field: 7 surgery **8** medicine
nationality: 7 British
founder of: 9 pathology

Pagliacci, I
also: 9 The Clowns
opera by: 11 Leoncavallo
character: 5 Canio, Nedda, Tonio **6** Silvio

Pagnol, Marcel
author of: 5 Cesar, Fanny **6** Marius, Topaze

Pago Pago
capital of: 13 American Samoa

Pahlavi *see* Iran

Paige, Leroy
nickname: 7 Satchel
sport: 8 baseball
position: 7 pitcher

pain 3 vex, woe **4** ache, gall, hell, hurt, pang, rile **5** agony, annoy, chafe, grief, pinch, pique, smart, sting, throb, worry **6** aching, grieve, harass, misery, ordeal, sadden, sorrow, stitch, twinge **7** agonize, anguish, disturb, hurting, malaise, sadness, torment, torture, trouble **8** distress, smarting, soreness **9** displease, heartache, suffering **10** affliction, discomfort, exasperate, heartbreak **11** unhappiness **12** wretchedness

Paine, Thomas
  author of: 9 The Crisis **11** Common Sense **14** The Rights of Man

painful 3 sad **4** dire **5** sharp **6** aching, dismal, dreary, trying **7** arduous, hurtful, racking **8** grievous, grueling, pathetic, piercing, smarting, stinging, very sore **9** agonizing, difficult, sorrowful, throbbing, torturous **10** afflictive, disturbing, lamentable, unpleasant **11** disquieting, distasteful, distressful, distressing **12** disagreeable, excruciating

pain in the neck 4 bane **6** bother **7** torment **8** headache, nuisance **9** annoyance **10** affliction

painstaking 5 fussy **7** careful, earnest, finicky, precise **8** diligent, exacting, thorough **9** assiduous, energetic, strenuous **10** meticulous, scrupulous **11** industrious, persevering, punctilious **13** conscientious, thoroughgoing

paint 4 coat, daub, draw, limn, swab, tint **5** adorn, brush, color, cover, horse, rouge, shade, stain **6** depict, enamel, makeup, opaque, sketch **7** pigment, portray, stipple, touch up **8** cosmetic, decorate, describe, variegate **9** delineate, represent

Painted Bird, The
  author: 13 Jerzy Kosinski

painter 6 artist, drawer **8** sketcher **9** old master **10** delineator **11** illustrator, landscapist, miniaturist **13** watercolorist

Painter, Painter's Easel
  constellation of: 6 Pictor

painting 3 art, oil **5** draft, mural, piece **6** canvas, design, tablet **7** cartoon, daubing, drawing, graphic, picture, tableau **8** panorama, portrait, seascape **9** depiction, landscape, still life **10** cerography, watercolor **11** perspective **12** illustration
  colloidal: 7 tempera
  method: 9 encaustic
  on plaster: 5 secco **6** fresco
  one-color: 8 monotint **10** monochrome
  opaque: 7 gouache
  religious: 5 Pieta
  style: 5 genre
  tool: 5 brush, easel, knife **6** canvas, roller, sponge **7** palette **8** spraygun

pair 3 duo **4** dyad, mate, span, team,

yoke **5** brace, match, unite **6** couple **7** combine, doublet, match up, pair off, twosome

pair off 10 go two by two **11** form couples

Paiute
  language family: 10 Shoshonean
  tribe: 12 Mono-Paviosto, Snake Indians **13** Digger Indians **14** Northern Paiute, Southern Paiute
  location: 4 Utah **5** Idaho **6** Nevada, Oregon **7** Arizona **10** California

Pakistan
  name means: 13 Land of the Holy, Land of the Pure
  capital: 9 Islamabad
  largest city: 7 Karachi
  others: 3 Dir, Sui **4** Mari, Sidi **5** Dacca, Qasim, Ralat **6** Chalna, Khulna, Lahore, Multan, Quetta **7** Larkana, Sialkot **8** Jamalpur, Lyallpur, Peshawar, Sargodha **9** Hyderabad **10** Gujranwala, Rawalpindi
  school: 9 U of Punjab **10** U of Karachi **12** U of Hyderabad **16** Allama Iqbal Open U **22** Pakistan U of Agriculture **39** Pakistan Institute of International Affairs
  division: 3 Dir **4** Sind, Swat **5** Hunza, Kalat **6** Bengal, Kharan, Punjab **7** Chitral **8** Khairpur, Peshawar **10** Bahawalpur, Waziristan **11** Baluchistan
    empire: 5 Gupta, Mogul **6** Kushan, Maurya **7** British, Magadha
    seceded state: 10 Bangladesh
  monetary unit: 4 anna, pice **5** paisa, rupee
  weight: 4 seer, tola **5** maund
  mountain: 3 Pab, Pub **4** Salt **6** Makran **7** Kirthar **8** Himalaya, Safed Koh, Sulaiman **9** Hindu Kush, Karakoram **11** Makran Coast **13** Central Makran **14** Takht-i-Sulaiman
  highest point: 9 Tirich Mir **12** Godwin Austin
  river: 3 Nal **4** Bado, Beas, Ravi, Swat, Zhob **5** Dasht, Indus, Kabul **6** Chenab, Ganges, Jamuna, Jhelum, Kundar, Porali, Sutlej **7** Jamunna
  sea: 7 Arabian
  physical feature:
    bay: 8 Soymiani
    canal: 4 Nara **5** Rohri
    cape: 5 Fasta, Jaddi **6** Jiwani
    delta: 6 Ganges **11** Char-Manpura
    desert: 4 Sind, Thal, Thar
    mountain pass: 5 Bolan **6** Khyber
    plateau: 11 Baluchistan
    valley: 5 Kohat
  people: 5 Sindi, Wazir **6** Afridi, Bengal, Mahsud, Pathan, Sindhi **7** Baluchi, Brahuis, Puktuns, Punjabi, Sherani **8** Khattack, Pushtuns, Shinwari, Yusefazi **11** Mohammedzai
    leader: 6 Jinnah **7** Aly Khan **8** Ayub Khan, Zia Ul-Haq **9** Ali Bhutto, Yahya Khan **13** Benazir Bhutto, Mujibur Rahman **15** Mah-

mud of Ghaznbi
    poet: 5 Igbal, Iqbal
  language: 4 Urdu **6** Pushtu, Sindhi **7** Baluchi, Bengali, English, Punjabi
  religion: 5 Hindu, Islam **8** Buddhism **12** Christianity
  place:
    dam: 6 Mangla **7** Tarbela
    gardens: 8 Shalamar
    mosque: 8 Badshahi
    tomb: 15 Emperor Jahangir
  feature:
    clothing: 5 kurta, pugri, qamis **6** jinnah **7** dupatta, shalwar **8** sherwani **9** churidars
  food:
    bread: 8 chappati
    dish: 5 kebab, pilaf **6** qormas, salans, sautes **10** vermicelli
    yogurt: 4 dahi

Pakula, Alan
  director of: 13 Sophie's Choice **19** All the President's Men

pal 4 chum, mate, pard **5** buddy, crony **6** cohort, friend **7** comrade, partner **8** alter ego, intimate, sidekick **9** associate, colleague, companion, confidant **10** accomplice, bosom buddy **13** boon companion

palace 5 villa **6** castle **7** chateau, mansion **8** hacienda
  French: 6 palais
  Italian: 7 palazzo

palais 6 palace **17** municipal building **18** government building

Palamedes
  lieutenant of: 9 Agamemnon

pal around 7 consort, hang out **9** associate, be friends, run around **10** fraternize

palatable 5 tasty **6** savory **8** pleasant **9** agreeable, toothsome **10** appetizing

palatial 4 posh, rich **5** grand, noble, plush, regal, ritzy, showy **6** swanky **7** elegant, opulent, stately **8** imposing, splendid **9** grandiose, luxurious, sumptuous **10** monumental **11** magnificent

palaver 3 gab **4** chat, talk **5** prate **6** confer, gossip, parley **7** consult, discuss, prattle **8** chitchat, idle talk **10** chew the fat, chew the rag, conference, discussion

palazzo 6 palace

pale 3 pen, wan **4** fold, post **5** ashen, close, light, pasty, stake, white **6** anemic, blanch, paling, pallid, picket, sallow, whiten **7** closure, confine, deathly, ghastly, upright, whitish **8** bleached, palisade **9** bloodless, colorless, deathlike, enclosure, ghostlike **10** ash-colored, cadaverous, light-toned

Pale Horse, Pale Rider
  author: 19 Katherine Anne Porter

paleness 6 pallor **7** wanness **8** dullness **9** whiteness **13** colorlessness

paleontology

study of: 18 correlation of parts
founder: 13 Georges Cuvier

Palermo
capital of: 6 Sicily

Palestine *see* **6** Israel

Palestrina, Giovanni Pierluigi da
born: 5 Italy **10** Palestrina
composer of: 11 Stabat Mater **18** Missa Papae Marcelli

Paley, Grace
author of: 26 The Little Disturbances of Man **30** Enormous Changes at the Last Minute

Palici
origin: 5 Roman
form: 4 gods **5** twins
gods of: 14 sulphur springs

paling 4 pale, rail **5** fence, stake **6** picket

Palinurus
steersman of: 6 Aeneas

palisade 5 close, fence **7** bulwark, rampart **8** stockade **9** enclosure

palisades 4 crag **5** ledge **6** bluffs, cliffs **10** escarpment, promontory

pall 4 cloy, haze, sate **5** gloom, weary **6** shadow, sicken **7** dimness, satiate **8** darkness **10** become dull, be tiresome, depression, desolation, melancholy, moroseness, oppression

Palladio, Andrea
real name: 26 Andrea di Pietro della Gondola
architect of: 12 Villa Rotunda (Vicenza Italy) **14** Teatro Olimpico (Vicenza) **19** Church of Il Redentore (Venice) **26** Church of San Giorgio Maggiore (Venice)
style: 9 Palladian

Pallas *see* **6** Athena

Pallas Athena *see* **6** Athena

pallet 3 bed, cot **4** bunk, tick **5** berth **8** mattress, platform

palliate 4 calm, curb, ease, hush, lull, tame **5** abate, allay, check, quiet, sooth, still **6** lessen, modify, reduce, soften, subdue, temper **7** assuage, comfort, cushion, lighten, relieve **8** decrease, diminish, minimize, mitigate, moderate **9** alleviate **10** ameliorate

palliative 4 balm **6** solace **7** anodyne, comfort **10** comforting

pallid 3 wan **4** ashy, blah, dull, pale **5** ashen, bland, pasty, vapid, waxen **6** boring, chalky, peaked, sallow **7** ghostly, humdrum, insipid, tedious **8** blanched, lifeless **9** bloodless, colorless **10** monotonous **13** anemic looking, unimaginative, uninteresting

pallor 7 wanness **8** paleness **9** pastiness, whiteness **10** ashen color, pallidness **11** ghostliness **13** bloodlessness, colorlessness

palm
varieties: 3 Fan, Ita, Key, Nut, Oil, Wax **4** Cane, Date, Doom, Doub, Doum, Fern, Hair, Hemp, King, Lady, Nipa, Nypa, Rock, Sago, Step, Tala, Wine **5** Areca, Areng, As sai, Betel, Black, Bread, Broom, Curly, Grass, Honey, Inaga, Ivory, Jelly, Latan, Manac, Nikau, Peach, Queen, Royal, Snake, Spine, Sugar, Syrup, Toddy, Yatay, Zombi **6** Bamboo, Barbel, Barrel, Bottle, Cherry, Cohune, Coyoli, Gebang, Gomuti, Gru-gru, Hesper, Kentia, Licuri, Manila, Mazari, Needle, Nibung, Parlor, Pignut, Raffia, Rattan, Ruffle, Sagisi, Sentry, Silver, Thatch, Thread, Yellow **7** Arikury, Cabbage, Calappa, Coconut, Coquito, Feather, Fiji fan, Funeral, Jaggery, Leopard, Mexican, Moriche, Overtop, Palmyra, Prickly, Spindle, Talipot, Weddell **8** Betel nut, Carnauba, Cucurite, Dwarf fan, Fishtail, Good luck, Ivory-nut, Mangrove, Pandanus, Peaberry, Princess, Roebelin, Umbrella, Wild date, Windmill **9** Alexander, Alexandra, Butterfly, Christmas, Desert fan, Gippsland, Guadalupe, Hurricane, India date, Macarthur, Ouricouri, Panama-hat, Petticoat, Piccabeen, Porcupine, Pygmy date, Silver saw, Solitaire, Spiny-club, Traveler's **10** African oil, Black-fiber, Canary date, Chinese fan, Cuban belly, Cuban royal, Everglades, Franceschi, Saw cabbage, Sealing-wax, Thatch-leaf, Washington **11** American oil, Chilean wine, European fan, Gingerbread, Mexican blue, Morass royal, Senegal date, Slender lady, Woolly butia **12** Caribe royal, Egyptian doum, Florida royal, Miniature fan, Walking-stick **13** Australian fan, Australian ivy, Australian nut, Belmore sentry, Feather-duster, Florida silver, Florida thatch, Forster sentry, Golden feather, Miniature date, San Jose hesper **14** Common princess, East Indian wine, Puerto Rican hat, Tufted fish tail, Yellow princess **15** Burmese fishtail, Chinese fountain, Chinese windmill, Yellow butterfly **16** Hispaniolan royal, Northern bangalow, Puerto Rican royal **17** Australian cabbage, Clustered fishtail, Mexican Washington, Piccabeen bangalow **18** South American royal

Palm Beach Story, The
director: 14 Preston Sturges
cast: 9 Mary Astor **10** Joel McCrea, Rudy Vallee **15** William Demarest **16** Claudette Colbert

Palmer, Arnold
sport: 4 golf
noted for: 10 Arnie's Army

Palmer, Lilli
real name: 17 Lillie Marie (Maria Lilli) Peiser
born: 5 Posen **7** Germany
husband: 11 Rex Harrison **14** Carlos Thompson
roles: 11 Body and Soul
autobiography: 22 Change Lobsters and Dance

Palmetto State
nickname of: 13 South Carolina

Palm Sunday
author: 12 Kurt Vonnegut

palmy 4 rosy **5** balmy, sunny **6** golden **7** booming, halcyon **8** blooming, pleasant, thriving **9** agreeable, bounteous, congenial **10** prosperous, successful **11** flourishing, pleasurable

Palmyra
Biblical name: 6 Tadmor

palpable 5 clear, plain **7** evident, obvious, tactile, visible **8** apparent, definite, distinct, feelable, manifest, tangible **9** touchable **10** noticeable **11** discernible, perceivable, perceptible **12** recognizable, unmistakable

palpitate 4 beat **5** pound, shake, throb **6** quaver, quiver, shiver **7** flutter, tremble, vibrate **9** go pit-a-pat

palsied 7 quaking, shaking, spastic **9** trembling

palsy-walsy 5 close, palsy, thick **6** chummy **8** friendly, intimate **10** buddy-buddy **14** thick as thieves

paltriness 10 triviality **12** unimportance **14** insignificance **18** inconsequentiality

paltry 4 poor, puny **5** petty, sorry **6** measly, shabby **7** scrubby, trivial **8** inferior, picayune, piddling, trifling, wretched **11** unimportant **13** insignificant, of little value **14** inconsiderable **15** inconsequential

Pamela
author: 16 Samuel Richardson
character: 3 Mr B **9** Mrs Jervis, Mrs Jewkes **10** Lady Davers **13** Pamela Andrews

pamper 5 humor, spoil **6** coddle, cosset **7** cater to, indulge **8** give in to **11** mollycoddle

pampered 7 coddled, humored **8** indulged **9** catered to, cossetted

pamphlet 5 tract **6** folder **7** booklet, leaflet **8** brochure, bulletin, circular **9** monograph, throwaway

pan 3 boo, map, mug, pot **4** face, hiss **6** kisser **8** ridicule, saucepot **9** criticize

Pan
also: 7 Sinoeis
origin: 5 Greek
form combined: 3 man **4** goat
god of: 6 flocks **7** forests **8** pastures **9** shepherds
father: 4 Zeus **6** Hermes
loved: 4 Echo **5** Pitys **6** Syrinx
invented: 5 pipes **6** syrinx
corresponds to: 6 Faunus

panacea 6 elixir **7** cure-all, nostrum **13** universal cure

panache 4 dash, elan, tuft 5 flair, plume, style, verve 11 flamboyance

Panama
  capital/largest city: 10 Panama City
  others: 4 Daid 5 Ancon, Colon 6 Azuero, Balboa, Gamboa 8 Dos Bocas, Penonome, Santiago 9 Cristobal 10 Portobello
  division: 5 Cocle, Colon 6 Darien, Panama 7 Herrera 8 Chiriqui, Veraguas 9 Los Santos 12 Bocas del Toro
  measure: 7 celemin
  monetary unit: 4 cent 6 balboa 10 centesimos
  island: 5 Coiba, Pearl 6 Cebaco, Multas, Taboga 7 San Blas 10 Isla Del Rey 12 Bocas del Toro, Juan Gallegos 13 Barro Colorado
  lake: 5 Gatun
  mountain: 4 Baru, Maje 5 Chico, Gandi 6 Darien 7 Columan, San Blas, Veragua 8 Santiago, Tabasara 10 Costa Rican 14 Serrania de Sapo 15 Aspave Highlands 17 Cordillera Central
  highest point: 8 Chiriqui
  river: 5 Chepo, Sambu, Tuira 6 Bayano, Panugo 7 Chagres
  sea: 7 Pacific 9 Caribbean
  physical feature:
    bay: 5 Limon 6 Panama
    dam: 5 Gatun
    gulf: 6 Darien, Panama, Parita 7 Montijo, San Blas 8 Chiriqui 9 Mosquitos, San Miguel
    isthmus: 6 Darien, Panama 7 San Blas
    lagoon: 8 Chiriqui
    peninsula: 6 Azuero 8 Valjente
  people: 4 Cuna 5 Choco 6 Guaymi 7 mestizo
    canal builder: 7 Lesseps
    explorer: 6 Balboa 8 Bastidas, Columbus
    leader: 4 Royo 5 Arias 7 Noriega 8 Guerrero, Torrijos 9 Espriella 12 Simon Bolivar
    poet: 4 Miro 5 Korsi, Sinan
  language: 7 English, Spanish
  religion: 13 Roman Catholic
  place:
    church: 7 San Jose 15 Virgen del Carmen
    plaza: 13 Independencia
    ruins: 9 Old Panama
  feature:
    clothing: 7 montuno, pollera
    dance: 4 caja 7 pujador 9 tamborito
    tree: 4 yaya 5 maria, quira 6 alfaje, cativo
    US operation: 9 Just Cause
  food:
    meat: 6 tazajo
    soup: 8 sancocho

Panama City
  capital of: 6 Panama

pancake 4 blin 5 blini, crepe, kisra, latke, lefse 6 blintz, makeup 7 fritter, hotcake 8 flapjack, slapjack 11 griddlecake 12 silverdollar
  day: 13 Shrove Tuesday

Pancks
  character in: 12 Little Dorrit
  author: 7 Dickens

pancreas
  produces: 7 insulin

Pandareus
  father: 6 Lycaon, Merops
  daughter: 5 Aedon 6 Merope 9 Cleothera
  wounded: 8 Menelaus
  stole: 9 golden dog
  turned to: 5 stone
  killed by: 8 Diomedes

Pandarus
  character in: 18 Troilus and Cressida, Troilus and Criseyde
  author: 7 Chaucer 11 Shakespeare

Pandarus
  son: 7 Alcanor
  companion of: 6 Aeneas

pandemic 4 rife 7 rampant 8 epidemic 10 prevailing, widespread 21 dangerously contagious

pandemonium 3 din 5 chaos 6 bedlam, clamor, hubbub, racket, rumpus, tumult, uproar 7 turmoil 8 disorder 9 commotion 10 hullabaloo 11 disturbance

Pandemos
  epithet of: 9 Aphrodite

pander, panderer 4 mack, pimp 5 cadet 7 hustler 8 procurer 9 maquereau, souteneur 12 fleshpeddler

Pandion the Younger
  king of: 6 Athens
  later reigned in: 6 Megara

Pandora
  form: 10 first woman
  created by: 10 Hephaestus
  presented to: 10 Epimetheus
  daughter: 6 Pyrrha
  given by gods: 3 box
    box contained: 4 hope 5 evils

Pandrosos
  position: 9 priestess
  first priestess of: 6 Athena
  father: 7 Cecrops
  mother: 8 Agraulos

panegyric 6 eulogy, homage, praise 7 tribute 8 citation, encomium, good word 9 extolment, laudation 10 compliment 11 testimonial 12 commendation

panegyrize 4 laud 5 extol 6 praise 8 eulogize

panel 4 jury, pane 5 board, group, piece 6 insert 7 divider 8 bulkhead 9 committee, partition 10 round table 11 compartment, expert group, select group 13 advisory group

pang 4 ache, pain 5 agony, pinch, smart, stick, sting, throb 6 stitch, twinge 7 anguish 8 distress 9 suffering 10 discomfort

Pangloss
  character in: 7 Candide
  author: 8 Voltaire
  characteristic: 8 optimism

pang of conscience 5 demur, qualm 6 unease 7 remorse, scruple 9 misgiving 10 uneasiness 11 compunction

panhandle 3 beg, bum 5 cadge, mooch 6 hustle 7 solicit 9 importune

Panhandle State
  nickname of: 12 West Virginia

Panhellenius
  epithet of: 4 Zeus
  means: 14 god of all Greeks

panic 5 alarm, dread, go ape, scare 6 fright, horror, terror 7 anxiety 8 affright, hysteria 9 cold sweat, confusion, fall apart 10 go to pieces 11 nervousness, trepidation 12 apprehension, perturbation 13 consternation

panicky 6 scared 7 alarmed, anxious 9 terrified 10 frightened 13 panic-stricken, scared to death 14 terror-stricken

panic-stricken 6 afraid, scared 7 alarmed, anxious, fearful, panicky 9 terrified 13 scared to death 14 terror-stricken

Panjabi
  language family: 12 Indo-European
  branch: 11 Indo-Iranian
  group: 5 Indic
  spoken in: 5 (northern) India

Pankrits
  language family: 12 Indo-European
  branch: 11 Indo-Iranian
  form of: 5 Indic
  followed use of: 8 Sanskrit

pannier 3 bag 4 hoop 6 basket, dossel, pantry 7 corbeil, drapery 9 framework, overskirt
  literally: 11 breadbasket

Panoptes
  epithet of: 5 Argus
  means: 7 all eyes

panorama 5 scene, vista 6 survey 7 diorama, picture, scenery, tableau 8 long view, overview, prospect 10 scenic view 11 perspective 12 bird's-eye view

panoramic 3 ide 7 overall 8 bird's-eye, extended, sweeping 9 extensive 10 far-ranging 11 far-reaching 12 all-embracing, all-inclusive 15 all-encompassing

pansy 5 Viola
  varieties: 4 Wild 5 Field 6 Garden, Orchid 8 Japanese 9 Miniature 11 Monkey-faced 12 European wild

pant 4 blow, gasp, huff, puff 6 wheeze

pant after 4 seek 5 covet, crave 6 desire, pursue 7 hope for, long for, lust for, wish for **8** yearn for **9** hanker for, hunger for, lust after **11** thirst after, have a yen for **14** set one's heart on

Pantagruel *see* **22** Gargantua and Pantagruel

panther 3 cat **6** cougar **7** leopard

Pantomime Quiz
 host: 10 Mike Stokey **15** Pat Harrington Jr

pantry 5 ambry, store **6** closet, galley, larder **7** butlery, buttery, pannier, spicery **8** cupboard, scullery

pants 5 jeans **6** denims, shorts, slacks **7** drawers, panties **8** breeches, britches, knickers, trousers **9** bluejeans, dungarees **10** underpants **11** undershorts **12** underdrawers

pantywaist 4 wimp **5** sissy, softy **7** crybaby, milksop **8** mama's boy, weakling **10** namby-pamby, sissypants, weak sister **11** Milquetoast, mollycoddle **13** sissy-britches

Panurge
 character in: 22 Gargantua and Pantagruel
 author: 8 Rabelais

Panza, Sancho
 character in: 10 Don Quixote
 author: 9 Cervantes

pap 3 rot **4** bosh, junk, mash, mush, pulp, tosh **5** gruel, paste **6** cereal, drivel, Pablum, trivia **7** rubbish, twaddle **8** soft food **10** balderdash, flapdoodle, triviality

papa 2 pa **3** dad, doc, paw, pop **5** daddy, poppy **6** father, priest **9** Hemingway
 mate: 4 mama

Papa Bear
 nickname of: 11 George Halas

Papago
 language family: 5 Piman **10** Uto-Aztecan
 location: 6 Mexico **7** Arizona
 related to: 4 Pima

papal 9 apostolic, of the pope **10** pontifical

paper 4 bond, deed, news, opus, pulp, work **5** daily, draft, essay, stock, theme **6** record, report, tissue, weekly **7** article, gazette, journal, monthly, tabloid, writing **8** document, gift wrap **9** cardboard, chronicle, newspaper, newsprint, onionskin **10** instrument, manuscript, paperboard, periodical, stationery, typescript **11** certificate, com position, publication

Paper Chase, The
 character: 10 James T Hart, Willis Bell **13** Asheley Brooks **14** Elizabeth Logan, Jonathan Brooks **15** Franklin Ford III **19** Thomas Craig Anderson **29** Professor Charles W Kingsfield Jr
 cast: 10 James Keane **11** Robert Ginty **12** Deka Beaudine, John Houseman **13** James Stephens, Jonathan Segal

14 Francine Tacker, Tom Fitzsimmons
 subject: 9 law school
 Kingsfield's specialty: 11 contract law

paper measure 4 ream **5** quire

Paper Moon
 director: 16 Peter Bogdanovich
 cast: 9 Ryan O'Neal **10** Tatum O'Neal **12** Madeline Kahn (Trixie Delight) **13** John Hillerman
 Oscar for: 17 supporting actress (O'Neal)

Papua New Guinea
 formerly: 16 British New Guinea
 capital: 11 Port Moresby
 town: 3 Thu, Lae **4** Ioma **6** Kikori, Madang
 province of: 9 Indonesia
 province: 9 West Irian
 monetary unit: 4 kina
 island: 6 Misima **10** New Britain
 archipelago: 8 Bismarck
 lake: 6 Murray
 river: 3 Fly **4** Ramu
 sea: 5 Coral **7** Solomon
 strait: 6 Torres
 people: 4 Hula, Kate **5** Kiwai, Kwoma **6** Banaro **7** Arapesh **10** Melanesian
 language: 7 English

papyrus 4 pith, reed **5** paper, sedge **6** scroll **7** bulrush **8** document **10** manuscript
 accordion pleated: 6 orihon
 genus: 7 Cyperus
 origin: 5 Egypt **9** Nile delta **10** Nile valley
 use: 3 mat **4** rope, shoe, sail **5** paper

par 5 level, usual **6** normal, parity **7** average, balance, the norm **8** equality, evenness, identity, sameness, standard **9** stability **11** equilibrium, equivalency **12** equal footing **13** identicalness

parable 4 myth, tale **5** fable, story **6** homily, legend **8** allegory, apologue, folk tale **9** folk story **12** morality tale

Paracelsus
 author: 14 Robert Browning

parade 4 line, pomp, show **5** array, march, strut, train, vaunt **6** column, defile, flaunt, review, string **7** caravan, cortege, display, show off **8** vaunting **9** cavalcade, flaunting, march past, motorcade, pageantry, put on airs, spectacle **10** exposition, grandstand, procession **11** progression **13** demonstration

paradigm 5 ideal, model **6** matrix, sample **7** example, paragon, pattern **8** exemplar, original, standard **9** archetype, criterion, prototype, yardstick

paradise 3 joy **4** Eden **5** bliss **6** heaven, utopia **7** delight, ecstasy, nirvana, rapture **8** pleasure **9** enjoyment, happiness, Shangri-la, transport **11** happy valley **12** Garden of Eden, sat-

isfaction **13** gratification, seventh heaven **15** Land of Cockaigne

Paradise
 also: 9 Paradisio
 part three of: 12 Divine Comedy
 author: 14 Dante Alighieri

Paradise Lost
 author: 10 John Milton
 character: 3 Eve, God **4** Adam **5** Satan **6** Christ **7** Lucifer

Paradise of the Pacific
 nickname of: 6 Hawaii

Paradise Regained
 author: 10 John Milton

paradisiacal 7 elysian, sublime **8** blissful, empyreal, empyrean, ethereal, heavenly **9** celestial, unearthly **12** otherworldly

paradox 5 poser **6** enigma, oddity, puzzle, riddle **7** anomaly **11** incongruity **13** inconsistency

paradoxical 9 ambiguous, enigmatic, equivocal **13** contradictory

paragon 4 norm **5** ideal, model **6** symbol **7** example, pattern **8** exemplar, paradigm, standard **9** archetype, criterion, prototype, yardstick **10** apotheosis

Paraguay
 capital/largest city: 8 Asuncion
 others: 3 Ita **4** Rica, Yuty **5** Belen, Luque, Pilar, Villa **7** Caacupe **8** Trinidad **9** Paraguari **10** Concepcion, Villarrica **11** Encarnacion **26** Puerto Presidente Stroessner
 division: 6 Guaira, Itapua, Olimpo **7** Caazapa **8** Boqueron **10** Concepcion
 measure: 3 pie **4** lino, lira, lire, vara **5** legua **6** cuadra, fanega
 monetary unit: 4 peso **7** guarani, centimo
 weight: 7 quintal
 island:
  floating island: 8 camalote
 lake: 4 Vera, Ypoa **8** Ypacarai
 river: 3 Apa **5** Guazu, Negro, Plata, Verde, Ypane **6** Acaray, Parana **7** Aguaray, Confuso **8** Paraguay **9** Aquidaban, Pilcomayo, Tebicuary, Tibiquare **10** Monte Lindo **14** Riacho Gonzales **15** Riacho Mosquitos
 physical feature:
  falls: 6 Guaira
  plains: 5 Chaco
  plateau: 6 Parana
 people: 6 Abipon, Moskoi **7** Guarani, mestizo **8** Guayaqui
  artist: 7 Bestard
  author: 3 Pla **4** Baez **6** Alcala, Bastos, Correa, O'Leary **7** Cervera **8** Casaccia
  composer: 8 Asuncion
  leader: 5 Lopez **7** Francia **10** Stroessner **16** Antequera y Castro
  sculptor: 8 Guggiari
 language: 6 German **7** Guarani, Spanish

religion: 9 Mennonite **13** Roman Catholic

place:
church: 10 Villarrica **11** Incarnation
dam: 6 Itaipu
memorial: 16 Pantheon of Heroes
museum: 5 Godoi
palace: 10 Government

feature:
animal: 4 puma **5** tapir **6** iguana, jaguar **7** peccary
bird: 6 toucan
clothing: 5 fajas, typoi **6** poncho **7** rebozos **9** bombachas **10** alpargatas
communes: 11 reducciones
dance: 7 Sante Fe **15** Paraguayan polka
fish: 7 piranha
lace: 7 nanduti
music: 8 quarania
townspeople: 9 comuneros
tree: 5 ceiba **7** lapacho **9** quebracho

food:
bread: 5 chipa, mbeyu
dish: 12 sopa paraguay
tea: 9 yerba mate
vegetable: 8 mandioca

parallel 4 akin, like, same, twin **5** alike, equal, match **6** follow **7** abreast, analogy, be alike, similar **8** analogue, likeness, relation **9** alongside, analogous, corollary, duplicate **10** collateral, comparable, comparison, concurrent, connection, equivalent, similarity **11** coextensive, coincidence, comparative, compare with, correlation, correlative, counterpart, equidistant, resemblance **12** correspond to **13** corresponding **14** correspondence

parallelism 8 affinity, likeness, sameness **9** agreement **10** comparison, similarity, similitude **11** resemblance **14** correspondence

parallelogram 5 rhomb **6** square **7** diamond, rhombus **8** rhomboid **9** rectangle **11** plane figure **12** quadrilateral

paralyze 4 stun **6** benumb, deaden, disarm, freeze, weaken **7** cripple, destroy, disable, petrify, stupefy, wipe out **8** demolish, enfeeble **10** debilitate, immobilize, neutralize **12** incapacitate

Paramaribo
capital of: 8 Suriname

paramount 4 main **5** chief **6** utmost **7** capital, highest, leading, premier, supreme **8** cardinal, dominant, foremost, greatest, peerless, superior **9** essential, principal, unmatched **10** preeminent **11** outstanding, predominant **12** incomparable, preponderant, transcendent

paramour 3 man **4** doxy **5** lover, Romeo **6** gigolo **7** Don Juan **8** Casanova, fancy man, lothario, loverboy, mistress **9** boyfriend, concubine, courte-

san, inamorata, inamorato, kept woman **10** girlfriend, lady friend, sugar daddy

paranoid 4 wary **7** deluded **9** paranoiac **11** distrustful **14** oversuspicious

parapet 7 bulwark, rampart **8** abutment, palisade **9** barricade, earthwork **10** battlement, breastwork

paraphernalia 3 rig **4** gear **5** stuff **6** outfit, tackle, things **7** effects, harness, regalia **8** fittings, material, supplies, utensils **9** apparatus, equipment, trappings **10** belongings, implements, properties, provisions **11** accessories, furnishings **13** accoutrements

paraphrase 5 recap **6** rehash, reword **7** restate **8** rephrase **12** recapitulate

parasite 5 leech **6** beggar, cadger, loafer **7** moocher, shirker, slacker, sponger **8** deadbeat **9** goldbrick, scrounger **10** freeloader **11** bloodsucker
inside host: 12 endoparasite
outside host: 12 ectoparasite

parasol 5 shade **6** shadow **7** roundel **8** sunshade, umbrella
mushroom: 7 lepiota

par avion 5 by air

parboil 4 boil **5** scald **6** blanch **7** precook

Parca
origin: 5 Roman
member of: 6 Parcae
goddess of: 7 destiny **10** childbirth

Parcae see **5** Fates

parcel 3 lot **4** bale, pack, part, plot **5** allot, piece, tract **6** bundle, divide, packet **7** carve up, deal out, dole out, package, portion, section, segment, split up **8** allocate, dispense, disperse, division, fraction, fragment, property **9** allotment, allowance, apportion, partition **10** distribute **11** piece of land

parceling out 9 allotment, doling out, meting out **10** allocation, assignment, dealing out **12** distribution **13** apportionment

parcel out 5 allot **7** dole out, give out, mete out **8** allocate, dispense, divide up **9** apportion **10** distribute, portion out

parch 4 bake, burn, char, sear **5** dry up, singe **6** dry out, scorch, sun-dry, wither **7** blister, shrivel **9** dehydrate, dessicate, evaporate

parched 3 dry **4** arid **6** barren **8** withered **9** shriveled **10** dehydrated, desiccated

parchment 6 scroll, vellum **7** papyrus **8** goatskin **9** sheepskin

pardon 5 grace, mercy **6** excuse, wink at **7** absolve, amnesty, blink at, forbear, forgive, indulge, release, set free **8** overlook, reprieve, shrug off **9** discharge, disregard, exculpate, exoner-

ate, remission, vindicate **10** absolution, indulgence **11** deliverance, exculpation, forbearance, forgiveness **12** grant amnesty **16** forgive and forget

Pardoner
character in: 18 The Canterbury Tales
author: 7 Chaucer

pare 3 cut, lop **4** clip, crop, dock, hull, husk, peel, skin, trim **5** lower, prune, shave, shear, shell, shuck, slash, strip **6** lessen, reduce, shrink **7** curtail, cut back **8** decrease, diminish **11** decorticate

pare down 3 cut **4** trim **5** shave **6** reduce **7** abridge, curtail, cut down, shorten **8** condense, cut short, diminish **10** abbreviate

parent 3 dam **4** sire **5** model **6** father, mother **7** creator **8** ancestor, begetter, exemplar, original, producer **9** precursor, prototype **10** antecedent, forerunner, originator, procreator, progenitor **11** predecessor

parentage 5 birth, roots, stock **6** family, origin, strain **7** descent, lineage **8** ancestry, forbears, heredity, pedigree **9** ancestors, genealogy **10** background, derivation, extraction, family tree **11** antecedents

Parentalia
origin: 5 Roman
event: 8 festival

parenthetical 5 aside **6** braced, casual **8** inserted **9** bracketed **10** extraneous, immaterial, incidental, interposed, irrelevant **11** impertinent, intervening, superfluous

par excellence 8 superior **10** preeminent

parfait d'amour
type: 7 liqueur
flavor: 7 violets
color: 6 purple

Paria
form: 5 nymph
loved by: 5 Minos
children: 7 Chryses **9** Eurymedon, Nephalion, Philolaus

pariah 5 exile, rover, stray **6** outlaw, roamer **7** outcast **8** vagabond, wanderer **10** expatriate **11** undesirable, untouchable

paring 4 chip, snip **5** scrap, shred, slice **6** sliver **7** cutting, peeling, shaving **8** fragment

pari passu 6 fairly **7** equably **10** side by side **13** equal progress **17** without partiality

Paris
airport: 4 Orly **9** Le Bourget **15** Charles de Gaulle
area: 5 Passy **6** Clichy, Marais, Ternes, Wagram **7** Auteuil **8** Chaillot, Gobelins, Left Bank, St Honore **9** Les Halles, Right Bank, St Germain **10** Montmartre, Rive Droite, Rive

Gauche, Val de Grace **11** Ile de la Cite **12** Hotel de Ville, Latin Quarter, Montparnasse
capital of: 6 France
city planner: 9 Haussmann
island: 10 Ile St Louis **11** Ile de la Cite
landmark: 8 Pantheon **9** Notre Dame **10** Paris Opera, Sacre Coeur **11** Eiffel Tower, La Madeleine, Palais Royal **12** Elysee Palace, Hotel de Ville, Place Vendome **13** Arc de Triomphe, Palais Bourbon **14** Bois de Boulogne, Place de l'Etoile, Pompidou Center, Sainte Chapelle, Tomb of Napoleon **15** Bois de Vincennes **16** Luxembourg Palace **17** Hotel des Invalides, Place de la Bastille, Place de la Concorde **18** Jardin des Tuileries **20** Place Charles de Gaulle
nickname: 11 city of light
river: 5 Seine
street: 9 Haussmann, Invalides **10** Grand Armee **11** Saint Michel **12** Montparnasse, Saint Germain **13** Champs Elysees **15** Charles de Gaulle
subway: 5 Metro
university: 8 Sorbonne

Paris
character in: 14 Romeo and Juliet
author: 11 Shakespeare

Paris
position: 6 prince
father: 5 Priam
mother: 6 Hecuba
brother: 6 Hector **9** Polydorus
sister: 9 Cassandra
wife: 6 Oenone
abducted: 5 Helen
judgment of: 14 apple of discord
awarded apple to: 9 Aphrodite
killed by: 11 Philoctetes

parish 4 fold **5** flock, shire **6** canton, county **7** diocese, section **8** brethren, district, precinct, province **9** community, pastorate **10** department **11** archdiocese **12** congregation, neighborhood

parity 7 balance **8** equality, sameness **10** coequality, uniformity **11** equivalence, equivalency **14** correspondence

park 4 lawn **5** field, green, grove, woods **6** common, meadow, square **7** grounds, reserve **8** parkland, preserve, woodland **9** grassland, sanctuary **10** public park, quadrangle

Parker, Dorothy
author of: 6 Resume **9** Big Blonde **10** Enough Rope **13** Death and Taxes **18** After Such Pleasures **19** Laments for the Living

parkway 6 avenue **7** thruway **9** boulevard **12** thoroughfare

parlance 4 talk **5** idiom, lingo **6** speech **16** manner of speaking

Parlement of Fowles, The
author: 15 Geoffrey Chaucer

parley 4 talk **6** confab, powwow, summit **7** council, meeting, palaver **8** conclave **9** discourse, mediation, peace talk **10** conference, discussion **11** arbitration, negotiation **12** conversation

parliament 4 diet **5** court, house, junta **6** fan-tan, senate, sevens **7** cabinet, council **8** assembly, congress **9** high court **11** legislature **12** three estates
Communist: 6 Soviet **9** politburo, presidium
estate: 12 House of Lords **14** House of Commons
Germanic: 9 Bundesrat, Bundestag, Bolksraad **11** Volkshammer
Greek: 5 Boule
Icelandic: 7 Althing
Israeli: 7 Knesset **8** Knesseth
Scandinavian: 7 Lagting, Riksdag **8** Lagthing, Storting **9** Odelsting, Storthing
Spanish: 6 Cortes

parlor 5 salon **6** saloon **8** best room **9** front room **10** living room **11** drawing room, sitting room

Parnopius
epithet of: 6 Apollo
means: 9 locust god

parochial 5 local, petty, small **6** church, little, narrow, parish **7** insular, limited **8** regional **9** hidebound, illiberal, religious, sectional, small-town **10** provincial, restricted **11** countrified **12** narrow-minded

parodos
from Greek drama: 9 choral ode

parody 5 mimic **6** satire **7** lampoon, takeoff **8** satirize, travesty **9** burlesque, take off on **10** caricature

Parolles
character in: 20 All's Well That Ends Well
author: 11 Shakespeare

paroxysm 3 fit **5** spasm, spell **7** seizure **10** convulsion

parrot 3 ape **4** bird, echo, lory **5** macaw, mimer, mimic **6** chorus, monkey **7** copycat, imitate **8** cockatoo, imitator, parakeet **9** reiterate

parry 4 duck, shun **5** avert, avoid, dodge, elude, repel **7** beat off, fend off, repulse, ward off **8** sidestep, stave off **10** circumvent, fight shy of

Parsifal
opera by: 6 Wagner
character: 6 Kundry **8** Amfortas, Klingsor **9** Gurnemanz

Parsifal Mosaic, The
author: 12 Robert Ludlum

parsimonious 5 close, tight **6** frugal, saving, stingy **7** miserly, sparing, thrifty **9** niggardly, penurious **10** economical, ungenerous **11** closefisted,

tightfisted **13** money-grubbing, penny-pinching

parsimony 6 thrift **7** economy **8** meanness **10** stinginess **13** niggardliness **15** tightfistedness

parsley 19 Petroselinum crispum
varieties: 5 Horse **7** Chinese, Italian **12** Turnip-rooted
related herb: 4 dill **5** cumin **6** fennel
garland worn by: 8 Hercules
gives speed to: 6 horses
use in: 11 fines herbes **12** bouquet garni

parson 5 clerk, padre **6** cleric, divine, father, pastor, priest, rector **7** dominie **8** minister, preacher, reverend, shepherd, sky pilot **9** clergyman
French: 4 abbe, cure

parsonage 5 glebe, manse **7** deanery, rectory, Vatican **8** vicarage **9** pastorate

part 2 go **3** bit, job **4** care, chip, duty, hunk, item, open, rend, role, slit, task, tear, unit **5** break, chore, crumb, guise, leave, piece, place, scrap, sever, shard, share, sherd, shred, slice, split **6** branch, charge, cleave, depart, detach, detail, divide, go away, member, morsel, region, sector, set out, sliver, sunder **7** concern, cutting, disjoin, element, portion, push off, section, segment, snippet **8** breakoff, business, capacity, disguise, disunite, division, fraction, fragment, function, separate, set forth, start out **9** character, component, disengage, go one's way **10** assignment, break apart, department, disconnect, get up and go, ingredient, mosey along, say good-bye **11** be on one's way, call it quits, constituent, subdivision

partake 5 enjoy, savor, share **6** join in, sample **7** share in **8** engage in **11** participate

part from 5 leave **9** break with **12** separate from

Parthenia
epithet of: 6 Athena
means: 6 virgin

Parthenopaeus
father: 10 Hippomenes
mother: 8 Atalanta
member of: 18 Seven against Thebes

partial 6 biased, unfair, unjust **7** limited, slanted **8** one-sided, partisan **9** factional **10** fractional, incomplete, interested, prejudiced, subjective, unbalanced, unfinished **11** fragmentary, inequitable, predisposed, uncompleted **12** inconclusive, prepossessed

partiality 4 bent, bias, love, tilt **5** fancy, slant, taste **6** choice, liking **7** leaning **8** affinity, fondness, penchant, tendency, weakness **9** prejudice **10** attraction, favoritism, preference, proclivity, propensity **11** inclination **12**

one-sidedness, partisanship, predilection **14** predisposition

partially 6 in part, partly **7** partway **8** somewhat **9** piecemeal **12** fractionally, incompletely

participant 4 ally **5** party **6** cohort, fellow, helper, member, player, sharer, worker **7** partner **8** confrere, partaker **9** accessory, associate, colleague, performer **10** accomplice **11** contributor, shareholder **12** collaborator, participator

participate 5 share **6** join in **7** partake, perform **8** engage in, take part **9** play a part

particle 3 bit, jot **4** atom, iota, mite, snip, whit **5** crumb, grain, scrap, shred, speck, trace **6** morsel, tittle, trifle **7** granule, modicum, smidgen, snippet **9** scintilla

parti-colored 4 pied **5** plaid **6** motley **7** checked, dappled, mottled **8** colorful **9** checkered **10** variegated **11** many-colored **12** multicolored

particular 4 sole **5** exact, fixed, fussy, picky **6** single, strict **7** express, finicky, special **8** concrete, critical, definite, detailed, distinct, especial, exacting, explicit, itemized, personal, separate, specific **9** demanding **10** fastidious, individual, meticulous, scrupulous **11** painstaking, persnickety, punctilious, well-defined **12** hard to please

particularize 6 detail **7** itemize, specify **9** enumerate

particularly 6 mainly **7** notably **8** markedly **9** eminently, expressly, specially, supremely, unusually **10** definitely, distinctly, especially, explicitly, strikingly **11** principally, prominently **13** exceptionally **15** extraordinarily

particulars 5 facts, items **6** events **7** details **9** specifics **13** circumstances

parti pris 15 position decided **20** preconceived attitude

partisan 3 fan **4** ally **6** backer, biased, rooter, zealot **7** booster, devotee, partial, slanted **8** adherent, advocate, champion, follower, one-sided, upholder **9** guerrilla, insurgent, irregular, jayhawker, supporter **10** bushwacker, enthusiast, prejudiced, subjective, unbalanced **11** sympathizer

partition 4 wall **5** allot, fence, panel **6** assign, divide, screen **7** barrier, deal out, divider, mete out, parting, split up **8** allocate, bulkhead, dispense, disperse, dividing, division, separate **9** allotment, apportion, parcel out, separator, severance, splitting, subdivide **10** allocation, assignment, distribute, separation **11** demarcation, segregation **12** distribution, dividing wall **13** apportionment

partly 6 in part **7** part way **8** somewhat **9** not wholly, partially, to a degree **10** relatively **12** fractionally, incompletely **13** after a fashion, comparatively

partly open 4 ajar **5** agape **6** gaping **7** cracked **8** half- open, unclosed **9** squinting **10** half-closed

partner 3 aid, pal **4** ally, chum, mate, wife **5** aider, buddy **6** fellow, friend, helper, sharer, spouse **7** comrade, co-owner, husband **8** confrere, helpmate, partaker, sidekick, teammate **9** accessory, assistant, associate, colleague, companion, co-partner **10** accomplice, better half, joint owner **11** confederate, participant **12** collaborator

Parton, Dolly
  roles: 10 Nine to Five, Rhinestone **30** The Best Little Whorehouse in Texas

partridge
  group of: 5 covey

Partridge
  character in: 8 Tom Jones
  author: 8 Fielding

Partridge Family, The
  character: 13 Reuben Kinkaid **14** Danny Partridge, Keith Partridge, Tracy Partridge **15** Connie Partridge, Laurie Partridge **20** Christopher Partridge
  cast: 8 Susan Dey **11** David Madden **12** Brian Forster, David Cassidy, Shirley Jones **13** Danny Bonaduce, Suzanne Crough **14** Jeremy Gelbwaks
  song: 14 I Think I Love You

parturition 5 birth **8** delivery **10** childbirth **11** giving birth **12** childbearing

party 2 do **4** band, bash, body, crew, fete, gang, team, unit, wing **5** corps, force, group, squad **6** affair, at-home, league, soiree **7** accused, blow out, company, coterie, faction **8** alliance, claimant, conclave, litigant, wingding **9** appellant, coalition, defendant, festivity, gathering, plaintiff, reception **10** contestant, federation, petitioner, respondent **11** celebration, confederacy, get-together, participant, paticipator, perpetrator

party-pooper 4 drag **10** spoilsport, wet blanket

parvenu 4 snob **6** nobody **7** upstart **8** arrivist, mushroom **9** arriviste **12** nouveau riche

Pascal, Blaise
  nationality: 6 French
  invented: 7 syringe **13** adding machine **14** hydraulic press
  author of: 7 Pensees **19** Lettres provinciales **20** Essay pour les coniques

Pascin, Julius
  real name: 6 Pincas
  born: 5 Vidin **8** Bulgaria
  artwork: 6 Femmes **12** Les Deux Amies **17** Ginette et Mireille

Pasiphae
  father: 6 Helios
  mother: 7 Perseis
  husband: 5 Minos
  daughter: 7 Ariadne, Phaedra **9** Acacallis
  became enamored of: 10 Cretan bull
  mother of: 8 Minotaur

Pasithea
  member of: 6 Graces

pass 2 go **3** cap, die, end, gap, hit, top, use, way **4** best, busy, fill, flow, give, go by, go on, hand, kick, lane, meet, toss **5** canal, exact, excel, gorge, gulch, leave, outdo, route, spend, throw, trail **6** accept, affirm, avenue, be over, canyon, convey, course, decree, depart, devote, elapse, employ, engage, exceed, expend, expire, finish, go away, go past, occupy, ordain, permit, pickle, plight, ratify, ravine, slip by, strait, take up, vanish **7** achieve, advance, approve, channel, confirm, consume, deliver, die away, eclipse, freebie, glide by, go ahead, let have, narrows, pathway, present, proceed, qualify, satisfy, slide by, surpass **8** blow over, dissolve, exigency, fade away, furlough, go beyond, go onward, hand over, juncture, legalize, melt away, outshine, outstrip, passaway, peter out, progress, quandary, sanction, transfer, transmit, turn over **9** authorize, disappear, evaporate, extremity, hand along, legislate, situation, terminate **10** accomplish, difficulty, free ticket, get through, move onward, over shadow, passageway **11** predicament, proposition **12** complication, run its course, solicitation, stand the test **13** authorization **15** amorous overture
  French: 13 laissez passer

passable 4 fair, open, so-so **5** clear **6** not bad **8** adequate, fordable, mediocre, middling **9** allowable, crossable, navigable, tolerable **10** acceptable, admissible, pretty good **11** presentable, respectable, traversable **12** unobstructed

passage 3 way **4** hall, pass, path, road, tour, trek, trip **5** aisle, canal, piece, route, verse **6** access, clause, column, course, junket, tunnel, voyage **7** channel, chapter, hallway, journey, passing, portion, section, transit **8** approach, approval, corridor, movement, sanction, sentence **9** enact ment, excursion, paragraph, selection, ship's fare **10** acceptance, expedition, ordainment **11** affirmation, endorsement, legislation, progression **12** confirmation, legalization, ratification **13** authorization

passage out 4 exit **6** egress, outlet

Passages
  author: 10 Gail Sheehy

Passage to India, A

author: 9 E M Forster
character: 6 Dr Aziz 8 Mrs Moore 12 Adela Quested 13 Cecil Fielding, Ronald Heaslop 16 Professor Godbole
setting: 11 Chandrapore 12 Marabar Caves
director: 9 David Lean
cast: 9 Judy Davis 12 Alec Guinness 13 Peggy Ashcroft 15 Victor Bannerjee
Oscar for: 17 supporting actress (Ashcroft)

passageway 4 exit, hall, lane, path, walk 5 aisle 6 access, arcade, tunnel 7 doorway, gangway, gateway, hallway, passage 8 corridor, entrance, entryway, sidewalk 12 companionway

pass away 3 die 6 depart, expire, pass on, perish 7 decease 8 pass over 13 go to one's glory 14 give up the ghost

pass by 4 go by, pass 5 lapse 6 elapse, roll by, slip by 7 glide by, slide by 8 slip away

passe 4 past 5 faded, hoary, stale 6 demode, lapsed, quaint 7 ancient, antique, archaic, disused, outworn, retired 8 obsolete, outdated, outmoded 9 out-of-date 10 antiquated 11 prehistoric 12 antediluvian, old-fashioned, out of fashion 13 superannuated

passenger 4 fare 5 rider 8 commuter, stowaway, traveler, wayfarer

Passepartout
character in: 26 Around the World in Eighty Days
author: 5 Verne

pas seul
ballet: 9 solo dance
literally: 8 solo step

passim 12 here and there, repeated item

passing 5 brief, death, dying 6 demise, fickle 7 decease, passage 8 adequate, fleeting 9 enactment, ephemeral, momentary, temporary, transient 10 evanescent, expiration, not failing, short-lived, transitory 11 impermanent, legislating

passing the bounds of propriety
French: 5 outre

passion 4 fire, idol, love, lust, rage, urge 5 ardor, craze, fancy, flame, gusto, heart, mania 6 desire, fervor, hunger, thirst, warmth 7 beloved, craving, ecstasy, emotion, feeling, rapture 8 loved one 9 carnality, eagerness, inamorata, intensity, obsession, sentiment, transport, vehemence 10 carnal love, enthusiasm 11 amorousness, earnestness, infatuation

passionate 3 hot 4 sexy 5 fiery 6 ardent, carnal, erotic, fervid, fierce, heated, loving, raging 7 amorous, earnest, excited, feeling, fervent, furious, intense, lustful 8 desirous, ecstatic, inflamed, sensuous, vehement 9 emo-

tional, heartfelt, wrought-up 11 tempestuous 12 enthusiastic, intoxicating

passionfruit
type: 7 liqueur
origin: 6 Hawaii
flavor: 5 peach

passionless 4 calm, cold 6 placid, serene 7 passive 8 tranquil 9 apathetic, unfeeling 10 spiritless 11 emotionless, indifferent, unemotional

Passion Play
author: 13 Jerzy Kosinski

passive 5 inert 6 docile 7 dormant, patient, pliable 8 enduring, inactive, lifeless, listless, resigned, yielding 9 apathetic, compliant, impassive, quiescent, tractable 10 spiritless, submissive 11 acquiescent, unassertive, unresisting 12 nonresistant

passiveness 6 apathy 7 inertia 8 docility 10 quiescence 11 resignation 12 acquiescence, lifelessness 14 submissiveness 16 unresponsiveness

passivity 6 apathy 7 inertia 8 docility, meekness 11 resignation 12 complaisance, lifelessness 13 nonresistance 14 submissiveness

pass muster 2 do 5 serve 6 answer 8 be enough 10 be adequate 12 be sufficient 14 be satisfactory

pass on 3 die 6 depart, expire 7 decease 8 pass away 13 go to one's glory 14 give up the ghost, leave this world 15 breathe one's last

pass over 6 ignore, slight 7 neglect 8 overlook 10 brush aside

pass up 4 miss 6 ignore, refuse

password 3 key 4 word 6 by word, slogan 7 keyword, tessera 9 catchword, watchword 10 open sesame, secret word, shibboleth 11 countersign, passe-parole

Password
host: 11 Allen Ludden

past 2 by 4 gone 5 ended, prior 6 beyond, bygone, former, gone by 7 ancient, earlier, elapsed, expired, history, long ago, through 8 departed, finished, previous 9 antiquity, days of old 10 days gone by, days of yore, historical, olden times, passed away, yesteryear 11 dead and gone, former times, times gone by 12 ancient times

pasta 4 orzo, ziti 6 elbows, shells 7 gnocchi, lasagna, pastina, ravioli, rotelli 8 ditalini, linguini, macaroni, rigatoni, tortelli 9 canelloni, cavatelli, fettucine, manicotti, spaghetti 10 tortellini, vermicelli
ingredient: 3 egg 5 flour

pasta sauce 4 ragu 5 pesto, salsa 6 tomato 7 alfredo 8 mushroom, pomodoro 9 bolognese, carbonara

past due 4 late 5 tardy 7 belated, overdue 9 in arrears 10 behindhand

paste 3 gum, hit 4 glue, seal, sock 5

affix, punch, stick 6 attach, cement 7 stickum 8 adhesive, mucilage

pastel 3 dim 4 pale, soft 5 chalk, faded, faint, light, muted 6 crayon 9 washed-out 13 coloring stick 14 coloring pencil

Pasternak, Boris
author of: 9 Dr Zhivago

Pasteur, Louis
field: 9 chemistry
nationality: 6 French
originated: 14 anti-rabies shot, pasteurization
founded: 12 microbiology
disproved: 21 spontaneous generation

pastime 3 fun 4 game, play 5 hobby, sport 9 amusement, avocation, diversion 10 relaxation 11 distraction 13 entertainment 14 divertissement

pastis
type: 7 liqueur
flavor: 8 licorice
substitute for: 8 absinthe

past one's prime 3 old 4 aged 5 aging 7 elderly 9 venerable 11 over the hill 12 in one's dotage

pastor 4 cure, dean 5 padre, vicar 6 cleric, father, parson, priest, rector 8 chaplain, minister, preacher 9 clergyman

pastoral 5 rural 6 rustic 7 bucolic, idyllic 8 arcadian, clerical, priestly 9 episcopal 10 sacerdotal 11 ministerial 14 ecclesiastical

Pastoral Symphony, The
author: 9 Andre Gide

pastorate 6 clergy 8 ministry, the cloth 10 priesthood

pastures
god of: 3 Pan 6 Dumuzi

pasty 3 wan 4 ashy, gray, pale 5 ashen, gluey, gooey, gummy, white 6 anemic, chalky, doughy, pallid, peaked, sallow, sticky 7 deathly, starchy 9 bloodless, colorless, ghostlike, glutinous, like paste 12 mucilaginous

pat 3 apt, dab, hit, pet, rap, tap 4 cake, daub, easy, glib, slap 5 exact, ideal, ready, slick, thump 6 caress, facile, fondle, simple, smooth, stroke, thwack 7 apropos, fitting, perfect, precise, reliant 8 flippant, suitable 9 contrived, pertinent, rehearsed

patch 3 fix, lot 4 area, darn, mend, plot, spot, zone 5 field, sew up, tract 6 garden, repair, stitch 7 expanse, stretch 8 clearing, insignia 9 reinforce 13 reinforcement

patchwork 4 hash, mess 6 jumble, medley, muddle, tangle 7 grab bag, melange, mixture 8 mishmash, mixed bag, pastiche, scramble 9 confusion, potpourri 10 hodgepodge, miscellany, salmagundi 11 gallimaufry 14 conglomeration, omnium-gatherum

pate 3 pie **4** brow, head **5** brain, crown, paste, pastry, patty, skull **6** noddle, noggin, noodle **9** meat paste

patella
bone of: **7** kneecap

patent 4 bald, bold, open, rank **5** clear, gross, overt, plain **6** permit **7** decided, evident, express, glaring, license, obvious **8** apparent, distinct, flagrant, manifest, palpable, registry, striking **9** copyright, downright, prominent **10** pronounced, unreserved **11** conspicuous, copyrighted, indubitable, self-evident, trademarked, transparent, unconcealed, undisguised **12** unmistakable **15** nonprescription

paterfamilias 6 father **17** father of the family, master of the family **20** master of the household

paternal 4 kind **6** tender **8** fatherly, parental, vigilant, watchful **9** concerned, indulgent **10** benevolent, fatherlike, interested, solicitous **11** patriarchal

Pater Patriae 18 father of his country

path 3 way **4** lane, plan, road, walk **5** byway, means, orbit, route, track, trail **6** access, by path, course **7** pathway, process, walkway **8** approach, footpath

pathetic 3 sad **6** moving, rueful, woeful **7** doleful, piteous, pitiful **8** dolorous, grievous, pitiable, poignant, touching, wretched **9** affecting, miserable, plaintive, sorrowful **10** deplorable, lamentable, to be pitied **11** distressing

Pathfinder, The
author: **19** James Fenimore Cooper
character: **9** Arrowhead, Dew-of-June **10** Charles Cap **11** Mabel Dunham, Natty Bumppo **12** Chingachgook **13** Jasper Western **14** Sergeant Dunham **18** Lieutenant Davy Muir

Pathfinders, The
author: **10** Gail Sheehy

pathogen 3 bug **4** germ **5** virus **7** microbe **8** bacillus **9** bacterium **13** microorganism

pathophobia
fear of: **7** disease

pathos 3 woe **5** agony **6** misery **7** anguish, feeling, sadness **8** distress **9** heartache, poignancy, sentiment **10** desolation **12** pitiableness **13** plaintiveness

Paths of Glory
director: **14** Stanley Kubrick
cast: **11** Kirk Douglas, Ralph Meeker **13** Adolphe Menjou

pathway 4 lane, path, road **5** alley, route, track **6** course **7** passage, walkway **8** footpath **10** passageway

patience 5 poise **7** stamina **8** industry, tenacity **9** composure, diligence, fortitude, restraint, tolerance **10** equanimity, resolution, sufferance **11** application, forbearance, longanimity, persistence, self-control **12** perseverance, tirelessness

Patience 8 operetta
by: **7** Gilbert, Sullivan

patient 4 case **6** dogged, serene **8** composed, diligent, enduring, resolute, tireless **9** dauntless, tenacious, undaunted **10** determined, forbearing, persistent, sick person, unflagging, unswerving, unwavering **11** industrious, persevering, unfaltering, unperturbed **13** indefatigable, long-suffering, uncomplaining

patio 4 deck **5** lanai, porch **6** piazza **7** terrace, veranda

patois 5 argot, idiom, lingo **6** jargon **7** dialect **10** vernacular

Paton, Alan
author of: **19** Too Late the Phalarope **20** Cry the Beloved Country **24** Ah but Your Land Is Beautiful

pat on the back 6 praise **7** plaudit **10** compliment **12** commendation

patriarch 5 elder, ruler **6** father, leader, old man **8** male head **9** chieftain **13** paterfamilias

patrician 4 lord, peer **5** noble **6** lordly **7** genteel, stately **8** highborn, imposing, noble man, princely, well-bred **9** blueblood, dignified, gentle man **10** aristocrat, upper- class **12** aristocratic, silk-stocking

patrimony 3 lot **5** dower, share **6** devise, estate, legacy **7** portion **8** bestowal, heritage, jointure **9** endowment **10** bequeathal, birthright **11** inheritance **12** hereditament

patriotism
Latin: **11** amor patriae

Patroclus
father: **9** Menoetius
mother: **8** Periapis
friend: **8** Achilles
killed by: **6** Hector

patrol 5 guard, scout, watch **6** ranger, sentry, warden **7** protect **8** sentinel **9** safe guard, walk a beat, watch man, watch over **10** stand watch

patron 5 angel, buyer **6** backer, client, friend, helper **7** habitue, shopper, sponsor, visitor **8** advocate, attender, champion, customer, defender, financer, promoter, upholder **9** protector, spectator, supporter **10** benefactor, encourager, frequenter, well-wisher **11** sympathizer **12** benefactress **14** philanthropist

patronage 3 aid **4** help **5** favor, plums, trade **6** buying, custom, spoils **7** backing, charity, clients, dealing, support **8** advocacy, auspices, business, commerce **9** clientele, customers, fosterage **10** assistance, friendship, pork barrel, protection, purchasing **11** benefaction, sponsorship **12** philanthropy **13** encouragement

patronize 5 humor **6** shop at **7** buy from **8** deal with, frequent **9** trade with **10** condescend

patsy 4 dupe, pawn, tool **7** cat's-paw, fall guy

patter 3 pad, pat, rap, tap **4** beat, drum **5** pound, thrum **6** tattoo **7** rat-a-tat, spatter, tapping **8** drumming, sprinkle

pattern 4 copy, form, mold, plan **5** draft, guide, ideal, mimic, model, motif, shape **6** design, follow, sample **7** emulate, example, fashion, imitate, paragon **8** exemplar, original, paradigm, parallel, simulate, specimen, standard **9** archetype, criterion, duplicate, prototype **10** apotheosis, stereotype **12** illustration

Patton
director: **17** Franklin Schaffner
cast: **10** Karl Malden (Omar Bradley) **12** George C Scott (George Patton), Stephen Young **13** Michael Strong
Oscar for: **5** actor (Scott), story **7** picture **8** director **10** screenplay (Francis Ford Coppola and Edmund H North)

Patton, George S
nickname: **15** Old Blood and Guts
served in: **3** WWI **4** WWII **11** World War One, World War Two
commander of: **9** Third Army
invasion of: **8** Normandy **11** North Africa
capture of: **6** Sicily
battle: **5** Bulge
wore: **21** ivory-handled revolvers
memoirs: **12** War As I Knew It

Patty Duke Show, The
character: **7** Richard **8** Ross Lane **9** Cathy Lane, Patty Lane **10** Martin Lane **14** Natalie Masters
cast: **9** Jean Byron, Patty Duke **10** Paul O'Keefe **14** Eddie Applegate **16** William Schallert

paucis verbis 10 by few words, in few words **12** with few words

paucity 4 lack **6** dearth **7** fewness, poverty **8** exiguity, poorness, puniness, scarcity, shortage, sparsity, thinness **10** deficiency, meagerness, scantiness, scarceness **13** insufficiency

Paul
former name: **4** Saul
birthplace: **6** Tarsus
teacher: **8** Gamaliel
companion: **5** Silas **7** Timothy **8** Barnabas, John Mark **9** Trophimus
cities visited: **4** Rome **5** Derbe, Perga, Troas **6** Lystra, Paphos **7** Antioch, Corinth, Ephesus, Iconium, Miletus, Salamis **8** Caesarea, Damascus, Neapolis, Philippi **9** Macedonia **12** Thessalonica
conversion place: **14** road to Damas-

cus
wrote: 8 epistles

Paul Bunyan
 author: 12 James Stevens
 character: 9 Shanty Boy **10** Hels Helson **11** King Bourbon **12** Sourdough Sam **13** Babe the Blue Ox **14** Hot Biscuit Slim **16** Johnny Inkslinger

Pauli, Wolfgang
 field: 7 physics
 researched: 13 quantum theory
 established: 14 Pauli principle **18** exclusion principle
 awarded: 10 Nobel Prize

Paulina
 character in: 14 The Winter's Tale
 author: 11 Shakespeare

Pauling, Linus Carl
 field: 12 biochemistry
 worked on: 8 proteins **18** molecular structure
 advocated: 8 Vitamin C
 awarded: 10 Nobel Prize
  awarded for: 5 peace **9** chemistry

paunch 3 gut, pot **5** belly, tummy **7** abdomen, stomach **8** potbelly **9** bay window, beer belly, spare tire **10** midsection **11** breadbasket, corporation

pauper 6 beggar **7** almsman **8** bankrupt, indigent **9** insolvent, mendicant **10** poor person, starveling **11** charity case **12** down-and-outer

pause 3 gap **4** halt, rest, stop, wait **5** break, cease, delay, let up **6** hiatus **7** interim, time out **8** break off, hesitate, interval **9** cessation, interlude **10** deliberate, suspension **12** intermission, interruption

pave 3 tar **4** face **6** cement **7** asphalt, surface **8** black top **9** resurface **10** macadamize

pavement 4 slab **5** brick **6** cement, hearth, street, tarmac **7** asphalt, cobbles, macadam **8** concrete, driveway, flagging, sidewalk **9** flagstone

pavilion 4 tent, ward, wing **5** arbor, kiosk **6** gazebo **7** pergola **9** bandshell **11** summerhouse

Pavlov, Ivan Petrovich
 nationality: 7 Russian
 researched: 9 digestion
 studied: 20 behavior conditioning **21** Pavlovian conditioning
 awarded: 10 Nobel Prize

paw 2 pa **3** dad, pop, toe **4** feel, foot, grab, hand, maul, mitt, papa **5** daddy, flail, touch **6** caress, clutch, father, handle, scrape, strike **7** rough up **8** forefoot **9** mishandle
 mate: 3 maw

pawn 4 bond, dupe, hock, tool **5** agent, patsy **6** flunky, lackey, pledge, puppet **7** cat's-paw **8** borrow on, creature, guaranty, henchman, hireling, security **9** assurance, guarantee, underling **10** instrument **12** raise money on **14** give as security

pawnbroker
 French: 11 mont-de-piete

Pawnbroker, The
 director: 11 Sidney Lumet
 cast: 10 Rod Steiger (Sol Nazerman) **11** Brock Peters **12** Jaime Sanchez **19** Geraldine Fitzgerald
 setting: 6 Harlem

Pawnee (Chahiksichhiks)
 language family: 7 Caddoan
 location: 5 Texas **8** Nebraska, Oklahoma **9** New Mexico
 related to: 7 Arikara
 god: 6 Tirawa

Pawtuxet
 location: 13 Massachusetts
 leader: 7 Squanto

Pax
 origin: 5 Roman
 goddess of: 5 peace
 corresponds to: 5 Irene

pax vobiscum 14 peace be with you

pay 3 fee **4** foot, give, meet **5** grant, honor, remit, repay, serve, wages, yield **6** ante up, chip in, extend, income, profit, render, return, salary, settle **7** benefit, bring in, cough up, payment, present, proffer, stipend **8** be useful, earnings, paycheck, shell out **9** bear fruit, liquidate, reimburse **10** come across, compensate, make good on, recompense **12** compensation **13** reimbursement

payable 3 due **4** owed **5** owing **6** mature, unpaid **8** to be paid **9** in arrears, spendable **10** demandable, expendable, receivable **11** outstanding

pay attention 4 heed, note **6** attend, notice **7** observe

Payaya
 language family: 12 Coahuiltecan
 location: 5 Texas

pay back 5 repay **7** counter, get even **9** reimburse, retaliate **10** recompense, remunerate **15** make restitution

pay for 6 redeem **7** expiate **8** atone for **9** answer for, suffer for **10** compensate, recompense, remunerate **13** make amends for **17** make reparation for

pay heed 6 notice **8** consider **11** concentrate **12** pay attention **13** put one's mind to

pay homage 5 defer, honor **7** acclaim **10** pay tribute

paying back 9 repayment **11** getting even **12** making good on **13** reimbursement

paymaster 6 bursar, purser **7** cashier **10** cashkeeper

payment 3 fee, pay **4** debt **6** outlay, paying, salary **7** premium **8** defrayal, spending **9** allowance, discharge **10** recompense, remittance, settlement **11** expenditure, installment, liquidation **12** compensation, contribution, disbursement, remuneration **13** reimbursement

pay no heed to 4 defy **6** ignore, slight **7** disobey, neglect, violate **8** overlook, pass over **9** disregard **10** brush aside, infringe on **14** shut one's eyes to **16** pay no attention to **17** transgress against

payoff 3 end **4** soap **5** bribe, graft **6** climax, crunch, finale, finish, grease, payola, result, upshot, windup **7** outcome **8** clincher **9** hush money **10** bottom line, conclusion, denouement, protection, resolution **11** culmination

pay off 5 bribe **6** buy off, suborn **13** grease the palm

payola 5 bribe, graft **6** grease, payoff

pay out 5 spend **6** expend, lay out **7** fork out **8** allocate, disburse, dispense, shell out **10** distribute

pay suit 3 woo **5** court **8** pay court

Payton, Walter
 nickname: 9 Sweetness
 sport: 8 football
 position: 11 running back
 team: 12 Chicago Bears

pay tribute to 4 laud, tout **5** boost, toast **6** praise, salute **7** applaud, commend **8** eulogize **10** compliment **16** sing the praises of

pea 5 Pisum **12** Pisum sativum
 varieties: 4 Flat, Love, Snow, Wild **5** Beach, Caley, Chick, Congo, Coral, Field, Glory, Green, Heart, Heath, Hoary, No-eye, Rough, Sugar, Sweet **6** Angola, Canada, Desert, Garden, Marble, Pigeon, Rosary, Scurfy, Winged, Winter **7** Catjang, Darling, English, Rabbit's, Seaside **8** Earthnut, Egyptian, Princess, Shamrock **9** Asparagus, Black-eyed, Butterfly, Chaparral, Jerusalem, Partridge, Perennial **10** Australian, Singletary, Wild winter **11** Everlasting, Sturt desert, Two-flowered, Winter sweet **12** Edible-podded **14** Austrian winter **15** Australian flame

peace 4 calm, ease **5** amity, truce **6** accord, repose **7** concord, content, entente, harmony **8** serenity **9** agreement, armistice, composure, placidity **12** pacification, tranquillity **14** reconciliation
 god of: 4 Frey **5** Freyr
 goddess of: 3 Pax **9** Concordia
 Hebrew: 6 shalom
 Russian: 3 mir

peace be with you
 Latin: 11 pax vobiscum

peaceful 4 calm **5** quiet, still **6** placid, serene, silent **7** pacific, restful **8** amicable, friendly, tranquil **9** agreeable, peaceable, peacetime **10** harmonious, nonviolent, nonwarring, pacifistic, untroubled **11** undisturbed

peacefulness 4 calm **7** concord, harmony **8** calmness, serenity **9** placidity **11** tranquility

peacemaker 8 diplomat, mediator, placater **9** go-between **10** ambassador, arbitrator, negotiator **11** adjudicator, conciliator, pacificator, peacekeeper, peacemonger **12** intermediary

peacemaking 9 pacifying, placating, placatory **11** reconciling **12** conciliating, conciliatory, pacification

peace offering 6 amends **11** appeasement **12** conciliation

peace of mind 8 security, serenity **11** tranquility **16** freedom from worry

peace to you
   Hebrew: 14 shalom aleichem

peach 13 Prunus persica
   varieties: 4 Muir, Peak, Sims, Vine, Wild **5** Gaume, Hiley, Pavie **6** Carmen, Crosby, Desert, Foster, J H Hale, Lovell, Orejon, Paloro, Peen-to, Salwey **7** Dixigem, Dixired, Elberta, Persian, Quadong **8** Champion, Crawford, Isabella, Redhaven, Russelet **9** Alexander, Freestone, Halehaven, Rochester, Southland **10** Clingstone, Goldeneast, Heath Cling, Summer Snow **12** Chinese Cling, Iron Mountain, Mountain Rose, Oldmixon Free **13** Golden Jubilee, Old mixon Cling, Phillips Cling **14** Belle of Georgia
   peach-like: 7 apricot **9** nectarine

Peach State
   nickname of: 7 Georgia

Peachum, Polly
   character in: 12 Beggar's Opera
   author: 3 Gay

peachy 4 fine, keen **5** dandy, super, swell **9** excellent, marvelous, wonderful

peacock
   group of: 6 muster

Peacock
   constellation of: 4 Pavo

Peacock, Thomas Love
   author of: 12 Headlong Hall **14** Crotchet Castle, Nightmare Abbey

Peacock Spring, The
   author: 11 Rumer Godden

peak 3 tip, top **4** acme, apex **5** crest, crown, flood, prime **6** apogee, climax, summit, zenith **8** pinnacle **9** culminate **11** culmination

peaked 3 ill, wan **4** lean, pale, thin, weak **5** ashen, drawn, gaunt, spare, spiked, spiny, white **6** ailing, infirm, pallid, pointy, sallow, sickly, skinny, spiked **7** haggard, pinched, pointed, scrawny, tapered, wizened **9** emaciated, shriveled **11** debilitated

peal 3 din **4** boom, clap, ring, roar, roll, toll **5** blare, blast, clang, crack, crash, knell **6** rumble **7** clangor, resound, ringing **10** resounding **11** re-

verberate **13** reverberation **14** tintinnabulate **16** tintinnabulation

Peale, Charles Willson
   born: 17 Queen Anne County MD
   son: 9 Raphaelle, Rembrandt **12** Titian Ramsay
   artwork: 26 The Exhumation of the Mastodon
      portrait: 8 Franklin **9** Jefferson, John Adams **10** Washington

Peale, Raphaelle
   born: 13 Bucks County PA
   father: 14 Charles Willson
   brother: 9 Rembrandt **12** Titian Ramsay
   artwork: 12 After the Bath

Peale, Rembrandt
   born: 13 Bucks County PA
   father: 14 Charles Willson
   brother: 9 Raphaelle **12** Titian Ramsay
   artwork: 15 The Court of Death
      portrait: 9 Jefferson **10** Washington

peal of bells 7 clangor, ringing **16** tintinnabulation

peanut 3 pod, tot **4** puny, seed **5** petty, small **6** goober, legume, measly, paltry **8** earthpea **9** little one
   species: 15 Arachis hypogaea

Peanuts
   creator: 14 Charles Schultz
   character: 4 Lucy **5** Linus, Sally, Marcy **6** Pig Pen, Snoopy **9** Schroeder, Woodstock **11** Lucy Van Pelt **12** Linus Van Pelt, Charlie Brown **15** Peppermint Patty **19** Little Red Haired Girl
   Halloween figure: 12 Great Pumpkin
   Snoopy's plane: 12 Sopwith Camel
   Snoopy's foe: 8 Red Baron
   saying: 9 Good grief

pear 5 Pyrus **13** Pyrus communis
   varieties: 4 Bosc, Sand **5** Anjou, Asian, Blind, Melon, Smith **6** Balsam, Burrel, Butter, Comice, Common, Garber, Garlic, Orient, Seckel, Warden **7** Chinese, Kieffer, Prickly, Vinegar **8** Bartlett, Japanese, Oriental **9** Alligator, Evergreen, Muscadine **10** Beurre Bosc, Brandywine, Chaumontel **11** Birch-leaved, Bon Chretien, Paper-spined, Winter Nelis **12** Beurre d'Anjou, Easter Beurre, Sacred garlic, Willow-leaved **13** Flemish Beauty, Waite Bergamot **15** Doyenne du Comice **18** Duchesse d'Angouleme

pearl
   grows in: 6 oyster
   genus: 8 Pinctada
   source: 6 Red Sea **9** Caribbean **11** Persian Gulf **12** South Pacific **16** Gulf of California
   composed of: 5 nacre **9** aragonite **10** conchiolin **13** mother-of-pearl
   quality: 6 luster **11** iridescence
   color: 4 blue, rose **5** black, brown,

cream, green, white **6** yellow
   shape: 5 round **7** baroque
   type: 8 cultured, Oriental (saltwater) **9** simulated **10** freshwater

Pearl-Fishers, The
   also: 19 Les Pecheurs de Perles
   opera by: 5 Bizet
   setting: 6 Ceylon

Pearl of the Antilles *see* **4** Cuba

Pearly Gates 7 heaven
   mentioned in: 10 Revelation

peasant 4 boor, esne, peon, serf **5** churl, knave, yokel **6** farmer, rustic, worker **7** laborer, lowlife, villein **10** countryman, dirt farmer
   Arabic: 6 fellah
   Indian: 4 ryot **5** kisan **6** raiyat
   Irish: 4 kern
   Russian: 5 kulak **6** muzhik
   Scottish: 6 cotter

peasantlike 5 crude, rough **6** coarse, oafish, rustic, vulgar **7** boorish, loutish, uncouth **9** unrefined **10** unpolished

peccadillo 4 slip **5** lapse **6** boo-boo **7** blunder, faux pas, misdeed, misstep **8** petty sin, trespass **9** false move, wrong step **10** misconduct, wrongdoing **11** misdemeanor **13** transgression

peck 3 pat, rap, tap **4** buss, gobs, lots, mess **5** a slew, batch, bunch, heaps, scads, smack, snack, stack, thump **6** nibble, oodles, pick at, strike, stroke, worlds **8** light jab **9** abundance, light kiss **11** eight quarts
   abbreviation of: 2 pk

Peck, Gregory
   real name: 17 Eldred Gregory Peck
   born: 9 La Jolla CA
   roles: 8 Moby Dick **10** On the Beach, Spellbound **11** The Yearling **12** Duel in the Sun, Roman Holiday **15** The Paradine Case **16** Twelve O'Clock High **17** The Boys from Brazil, The Guns of Navarone **18** To Kill a Mockingbird (Oscar) **19** Gentleman's Agreement, The Keys of the Kingdom **21** The Snows of Kilimanjaro **26** The Man in the Gray Flannel Suit
   autobiography: 12 An Actor's Life

Peckinpah, Sam
   director of: 9 Straw Dogs **12** The Wild Bunch

Pecksniff
   character in: 16 Martin Chuzzlewit
   author: 7 Dickens

peculiar 3 odd **5** queer, weird **6** farout, quaint, unique **7** bizarre, curious, erratic, private, special, strange, typical, unusual **8** abnormal, distinct, freakish, personal, singular, specific **9** eccentric, exclusive, whimsical **10** capricious, individual, outlandish, particular **11** distinctive **13** idiosyncratic **14** characteristic, distinguishing, representative, unconventional

peculiarity 4 mark **5** badge, stamp,

trait 6 oddity 7 feature, quality 8 odd trait 9 attribute, queerness, weirdness 10 erraticism, uniqueness 11 abnormality, bizarreness, distinction, singularity, strangeness 12 eccentricity, freakishness, idiosyncrasy 13 particularity, unnaturalness 14 characteristic 21 distinguishing quality

pecuniary 6 fiscal 8 economic, monetary 9 budgetary, financial

pedagogic 7 bookish, donnish 8 academic, didactic, pedantic, tutorial 9 scholarly 11 educational 12 professorial 13 instructional

pedagogue, pedagog 5 tutor 7 teacher 8 academic, educator 9 professor 10 instructor, schoolmarm 12 educationist, schoolmaster 13 schoolteacher 14 schoolmistress

pedant 6 purist 8 bookworm 9 dogmatist 13 methodologist

pedantic 5 fussy 7 bookish, finicky, pompous, stilted 8 academic, didactic, dogmatic 10 nitpicking, scholastic 11 doctrinaire, punctilious 13 hairsplitting 14 overparticular

peddle 4 hawk, sell, vend 6 retail 7 deal out 8 dispense

Peder Victorious
    character in: 16 Giants of the Earth
    author: 7 Rolvaag

pedestal 4 base, foot 6 bottom, plinth 10 foundation

pedestrian 6 walker 7 mundane, prosaic, tedious, trekker 8 mediocre, ordinary, stroller 9 itinerant 10 ambulatory, for walking, unexciting 11 commonplace, peripatetic, unimportant 12 foot-traveler, run-of-the-mill 13 insignificant, perambulating, perambulatory, unimaginative 15 inconsequential

pedigree 4 line 6 family, strain 7 descent, lineage 8 ancestry 9 bloodline, parentage 10 derivation, extraction, family tree 13 line of descent

peek 3 pry 4 peep, peer 5 watch 6 glance 7 glimpse

peel 4 bark, hull, husk, pare, rind, skin, tear, zest 5 flake, scale, shuck, spade, strip 6 remove 7 undress 11 decorticate

peel off 6 remove 7 veer off 8 strip off

peep 4 peek, peer, skim, word 5 cheep, chirp, tweet 6 emerge, glance, murmur, mutter, squeak 7 chirrup, glimpse, peeping, peer out, twitter, whimper, whisper 9 come forth, quick look

peeper 3 eye 4 frog 6 voyeur 10 peeping Tom

peer 4 gape, gaze, look, lord, peek, peep 5 equal, noble, stare 6 appear, emerge, squint 7 compeer 8 noble-

man 9 blue blood, gentleman, patrician 10 aristocrat

peerage 8 nobility 10 blue bloods, patricians 11 aristocracy

Peer Gynt
    author: 11 Henrik Ibsen
    character: 3 Ase 6 Anitra 7 Solveig 12 The Great Boyg 16 The Button Moulder
    suite composer: 5 Grieg

peerless 7 supreme 8 flawless 9 faultless, matchless, unequaled, unmatched, unrivaled 10 consummate, inimitable, preeminent, surpassing, unexcelled 11 superlative, unsurpassed 12 incomparable, transcendent

peeve 3 bug, eat, irk, vex 4 fret, gall, rile 5 annoy, chafe, eat at, frost, gripe 6 gnaw at, nettle 7 dislike, perturb, provoke 8 irritate, vexation 9 aggravate, annoyance, complaint, grievance 10 exasperate, irritation 11 aggravation, provocation 12 exasperation, give one a pain 13 pain in the neck 14 thorn in the side

peevish 4 mean 5 cross, huffy, sulky, surly, testy 6 crabby, cranky, grumpy 7 grouchy, pettish 8 churlish, petulant, snappish 9 fractious, irritable, querulous, splenetic 10 ill-humored, ill-natured 11 bad-tempered, ill-tempered, quarrelsome 12 cantankerous

peewee 4 tiny 5 dwarf, small, teeny 6 little, midget, minute 9 itsy-bitsy, itty-bitty, minuscule 10 diminutive, teeny-weeny 11 Lilliputian

Pee Wee
    nickname of: 11 Harold Reese

peg 3 pin 4 nail 5 cleat, dowel, spike, thole 6 skewer, toggle 8 fastener, tholepin

Pegasus
    form: 5 horse
    characteristic: 6 winged
    mother: 6 Medusa
    ridden by: 11 Bellerophon

Peggotty, Clara
    character in: 16 David Copperfield
    author: 7 Dickens

Pei, I M (Ieoh Ming)
    architect of: 12 East Building (National Gallery of Art), L'Enfant Plaza (Washington DC) 14 East-West Center (U of Hawaii), Mile High Center (Denver) 15 Place Ville Marie (Montreal) 16 John Hancock Tower (Boston) 18 Everson Museum of Art (Syracuse NY) 22 Kips Bay Plaza Apartments (NYC) 36 National Center for Atmospheric Research (Boulder CO)

peignoir 4 gown 6 kimono 8 negligee 9 nightgown 12 dressing gown

pejorative 7 mocking 8 debasing, negative, scornful 9 degrading, demeaning, slighting 10 belittling, derogatory,

detracting, disdainful, ridiculing, unpleasant 11 deprecatory, disparaging, downgrading 12 contemptuous, depreciatory, disapproving 15 uncomplimentary

Peking
    also: 7 Beijing
    means: 15 northern capital
    capital of: 5 China
    landmark: 9 Bell Tower, Drum Tower, Ming Tombs 10 Pei-hai Park 12 Palace Museum 13 Forbidden City 14 Hall of Classics, Temple of Heaven 15 Marco Polo Bridge 17 Temple of Confucius 18 Old Legation Quarter 19 Temple of Agriculture 20 Great Hall of the People, Hall of Supreme Harmony 21 Mausoleum of Mao Tse-tung 22 Palace of Heavenly Purity 26 Monument to the People's Heroes 32 Revolutionary and Historical Museum
    mountain: 7 Taihang
    river: 3 Hai 7 Ch'ao-pai 8 Yungting
    square: 9 T'ien-an Men
    university: 8 Tsinghua
    walled city: 5 Inner, Outer, Tatar 7 Chinese

pelagic 6 marine 7 aquatic, oceanic 9 thalassic 11 sea-dwelling

Pele
    real name: 24 Edson Arantes do Nascimento
    sport: 6 soccer
    team: 13 New York Cosmos
    nationality: 9 Brazilian

Peleus
    king of: 6 Phthia 9 Myrmidons
    father: 6 Aeacus
    mother: 6 Endeis
    brother: 7 Telamon
    half-brother: 6 Phocus
    wife: 6 Thetis 8 Antigone
    son: 8 Achilles
    daughter: 8 Polydora

pelf 4 gain 5 booty, lucre, money 6 mammon, riches, spoils

Pelican State
    nickname of: 9 Louisiana

pelisse 4 cape, coat 5 cloak 6 mantle

Pelleas (King Pelleas)
    character in: 16 Arthurian romance
    daughter: 6 Elaine

Pelleas and Melisande
    also: 18 Pelleas et Melisande
    opera by: 7 Debussy
    character: 6 Golaud, Yniold
    author: 18 Maurice Maeterlinck

pellet 3 pea 4 ball, bead, drop, pill 5 pearl, stone 6 marble, pebble, sphere 7 globule

pell-mell 6 rashly 7 hastily 8 slapdash 9 hurriedly, post haste 10 at half cock, carelessly, heedlessly, recklessly 11 hurry-scurry, impetuously, imprudently 12 incautiously 13 helter-skelter, precipitately, thoughtlessly

pellucid 5 clear, lucid **10** articulate **11** crystalline, translucent, transparent **12** intelligible **14** understandable

Pelops
father: **8** Tantalus
sister: **5** Niobe
son: **6** Atreus, Sciron **7** Letreus **8** Pittheus, Thyestes **9** Alcathous **10** Chrysippus
daughter: **7** Nicippe **8** Lysidice **9** Astydamia
resurrected by: **6** Hermes

pelt 3 fur, hit, rap **4** belt, coat, hide, skin, sock **5** pound, punch, whack **6** batter, buffet, fleece, pepper, pummel, strike, thrash, thwack **7** clobber

pen 3 sty **4** cage, coop, crib, fold **5** draft, hutch, pound, quill, stall, write **6** corral, pencil, scrawl **7** compose, paddock **8** compound, scribble, stockade **9** ballpoint, enclosure

penal 7 of jails **8** punitive **9** punishing **10** corrective, penalizing **11** castigatory, retributive **12** disciplinary

penalty 4 fine **7** forfeit **8** handicap **9** suffering **10** assessment, forfeiture, infliction, punishment **11** retribution **12** disadvantage

penance 9 atonement, expiation, hair shirt, penitence **10** contrition, repentance **12** propitiation **13** mortification

penates
protectors of: **4** home
companions: **5** lares

penchant 4 bent, bias, gift, turn **5** fancy, flair, knack, taste **6** liking, relish **7** leaning **8** affinity, fondness, tendency **9** prejudice, proneness, readiness **10** attraction, partiality, preference, proclivity, propensity **11** disposition, inclination **12** predilection **14** predisposition

pendant 3 fob **5** charm **6** locket **15** hanging ornament

Pendennis
author: **25** William Make peace Thackeray
character: **9** Laura Bell **10** Henry Foker **12** Blanche Amory **13** Emily Costigan **14** Helen Pendennis, Major Pendennis **15** Arthur Pendennis

pendent, pendant 7 hanging, jutting, pensile **8** dangling, swinging **9** extending, pendulous, suspended **10** projecting, protruding **11** overhanging, protuberant

pendente lite 16 during litigation **19** with a lawsuit pending

pending 8 imminent **9** undecided, unsettled **10** in suspense, unfinished, unresolved, up in the air **11** in the offing **12** undetermined

pendulous 7 hanging, pendent, pensile, sagging **8** dangling, drooping, swinging **9** suspended

pendulum
invented by: **7** Galileo

Penelope
father: **7** Icarius
mother: **8** Periboea
husband: **8** Odysseus **9** Telegonus
son: **6** Ifalus **10** Telemachus **11** Polyporthis
fended off: **7** suitors

penetrate 3 get **4** bore **5** catch, enter, prick **6** decode, fathom, invade, pierce, seep in **7** cut into, discern, pervade, unravel **8** decipher, perceive, permeate, puncture, saturate, traverse **9** figure out, perforate **10** comprehend, cut through, impregnate, infiltrate, see through, understand **11** pass through

penetrating 4 keen **5** acrid, alert, alive, aware, harsh, heady, sharp, smart **6** astute, biting, clever, shrewd, strong **7** caustic, pungent, reeking **8** piercing, redolent, stinging **9** pervading, pervasive, trenchant **10** discerning, perceptive, percipient, permeating, saturating, thoughtful **11** intelligent, sharp-witted **13** perspicacious

penetration 5 foray, grasp **6** access, boring **7** insight, passage **8** infusion, invasion, keenness, piercing **9** intrusion, quickness, sharpness **10** astuteness, cleverness, perception, puncturing, shrewdness **11** discernment, perforation **12** intelligence, perspicacity

penguin 8 great auk

Penguin Island
author: **13** Anatole France

peninsula 4 cape **5** point **8** headland **10** promontory

Peninsula State
nickname of: **7** Florida

penitence 6 regret, sorrow **7** penance, remorse **9** atonement, attrition, expiation **10** contrition, repentance **11** compunction, humiliation

penitent 5 sorry **6** rueful **7** atoning, devotee, pilgrim **8** contrite **9** regretful, repentant **10** remorseful

penitentiary 3 can, pen **4** jail, stir **5** joint **6** prison **7** slammer **8** big house

Penn, Arthur
director of: **12** Little Big Man **14** Bonnie and Clyde **16** The Miracle Worker

Penn, Sean
wife: **7** Madonna **11** Robin Wright
roles: **5** U-Turn **7** Bad Boys, The Game **11** Carlito's Way **12** She's So Lovely **14** Dead Man Walking **15** Shanghai Express **22** The Falcon and the Snowman **24** Fast Times at Ridgemont High

Pennacook (Merrimac)
language family: **9** Algonkian **10** Algonquian

location: **5** Maine **6** Quebec **7** New York, Vermont **10** New England **12** New Hampshire **13** Massachusetts
leader: **11** Wannalancet **12** Passaconaway
related to: **6** Abnaki

pen name
French: **10** nom de plume

pennant 4 flag, jack **6** banner, burgee, colors, ensign, pennon **7** bunting **8** ensignia, standard, streamer **9** banderole, oriflamme

penniless 4 poor **5** broke, needy **6** busted, ruined **8** bankrupt, indigent, strapped, wiped out **9** destitute, flat broke, insolvent, moneyless **10** down-and-out, pauperized **12** impoverished **15** poverty-stricken

pennon 4 flag, jack **6** banner, colors, ensign **7** pennant **8** standard, streamer

Pennsylvania
abbreviation: **2** PA **5** Penna
nickname: **8** Keystone
capital: **10** Harrisburg
largest city: **12** Philadelphia
others: **4** Erie, Etna, Plum, York **5** Avoca, Baden **6** Beaver, Bethel, Butler, Easton, Emmaus, Radnor, Ridley, Sharon **7** Altoona, Baldwin, Bristol, Chester, Ephrata, Hanover, Hershey, Lebanon, Reading **8** Abington, Braddock, Bradford, Bryn Mawr, Carlisle, Clairton, Harrison, Hazelton, Monessen, Scranton, Shamokin **9** Aliquippa, Allentown, Bethlehem, Charleroi, Haverford, Jeannette, Johnstown, Lancaster, Meadville, Mill Creek, Newcastle, Swissvale, Uniontown, Whitehall **10** Carbondale, Gettysburg, McKeesport, Norristown, Pittsburgh **11** Springfield, Wilkes Barre **12** State College, Williamsport
college: **3** PSU **4** Penn, Pitt **5** Gratz, Thiel **6** Drexel, Lehigh, Temple **7** Juniata, LaSalle, Ursinus **8** Alliance, Bryn Mawr, Bucknell, Duquesne, Lycoming **9** Dickinson, Lafayette, Penn State, St Josephs, Villanova **10** Pittsburgh, Swarthmore **12** Carnegie Tech **17** Pennsylvania State
feature:
  battle site: **10** Gettysburg
  bell: **7** Liberty
  hall: **12** Independence
  historical site: **11** Valley Forge
tribe: **6** Seneca **7** Shawnee **8** Delaware **11** Lenni- Lanape **13** Susquehannock
people: **5** Amish, Dutch **10** Stan Musial **11** Andrew Wyeth, Ethel Waters, Mary Cassatt, Stuart Davis **12** Andrew Mellon, Anthony Wayne, Margaret Mead, Martha Graham, Samuel Barber, Thomas Eakins **13** Clifford Odets, Gertrude Stein **14** George S Kaufman **15** Maxwell Anderson **19**

Stephen Vincent Benet
explorer: 5 Brule **6** Hudson **11** Hendrickson
lake: 4 Erie **7** Harveys **8** Conneaut **10** Pymatuning **13** Wallenpaupack
land rank: 11 thirty-third
mountain: 5 South **6** Pocono **11** Alleghenies
   highest point: 5 Davis
physical feature:
   peninsula: 11 Presque Isle
   valley: 5 Great
president: 13 James Buchanan
river: 4 Ohio **6** Lehigh **7** Clarion, Genesee, Juniata, Licking, Towanda **8** Caldwell, Delaware, Schrader **9** Allegheny **10** Schuylkill **11** Monongahela, Susquehanna
state admission: 6 second
state bird: 12 ruffed grouse
state fish: 10 brook trout
state flower: 14 mountain laurel
state motto: 28 Virtue Liberty and Independence
state tree: 7 hemlock

penny 3 sum **4** cent **5** cheap, pence **6** copper, stiver **7** trivial

penny-pinching 5 close, tight **6** stingy **7** miserly **8** grudging **9** niggardly, penurious **10** ungenerous **11** tight-fisted **12** parsimonious

Penny Serenade
director: 13 George Stevens
cast: 9 Cary Grant **10** Irene Dunne **11** Beulah Bondi **13** Edgar Buchanan

pennyweight
abbreviation of: 3 dwt

Penobscot
language family: 9 Algonkian **10** Algonquian
location: 5 Maine **13** Old Town Island
members of: 17 Abnaki Confederacy

Penrod
author: 15 Booth Tarkington
sequel: 12 Penrod and Sam **13** Penrod Jashber
character: 6 Herman, Verman **9** Sarah Crim **11** Rupe Collins **13** Marjorie Jones **15** Penrod Schofield
dog: 4 Duke

pensee 7 thought **10** reflection

Pensees
author: 12 Blaise Pascal

pension 5 grant **6** income, retire **7** annuity, stipend, subsidy **9** allowance **13** boardinghouse **14** retirement fund

pensive 3 sad **5** grave **6** dreamy, musing, solemn, somber **7** serious, wistful **8** dreaming **10** meditative, melancholy, reflective **11** day dreaming **13** contemplative, introspective **15** sadly thoughtful

Pentateuch 10 Law of Moses **28** first five books of Old Testament
see also **7** books of **12** Old Testament

Penthesilea

queen of: 7 Amazons
father: 4 Ares
mother: 6 Otrere
sister: 9 Hippolyta
killed by: 8 Achilles

Pentheus
king of: 6 Thebes
father: 6 Echion
mother: 5 Agave
grandfather: 6 Cadmus

pent-up 7 boxed-up, checked, stifled **8** hedged-in, held back, penned-in, penned-up, reined in, stored-up **9** bottled-up, repressed **10** restrained, suppressed

penurious 5 close **6** frugal, stingy **7** miserly, sparing **8** stinting **9** niggardly **12** parsimonious **13** penny-pinching

penury 4 need, want **7** poverty **9** indigence, privation **10** bankruptcy, insolvency **11** destitution **14** impoverishment

peon 4 pawn, serf **5** slave **6** drudge, menial, worker **7** footman, laborer, orderly, peasant, servant

peony 7 Paeonia
varieties: 4 Tree **7** Chinese, Tibetan **8** Majorcan **11** Chinese tree **12** Common garden

people 3 kin **5** folks **6** family, humans, the mob **7** kinfolk, mankind, mortals, the herd **8** citizens, humanity, populace, the crowd **9** ancestors, citizenry, commoners, human kind, relatives, the masses, the public, the rabble **10** population **11** Homo sapiens, human beings, individuals, inhabitants, John Q Public, men and women, the millions

People Are Funny
host: 13 Art Linkletter

pep 3 vim, zip **4** dash, life, snap **5** gusto, verve, vigor **6** energy, ginger, spirit **8** vitality, vivacity **9** animation **10** enthusiasm, get-up-and-go, liveliness

Pepe Le Moko
director: 14 Julien Duvivier
cast: 9 Jean Gabin **13** Gabriel Gabrio, Mireille Balin
remade as: 6 Casbah **7** Algiers

peperomia
varieties: 3 Ivy **6** Prayer, Vining **7** Ivy-leaf, Leather, Red-edge **8** Coinleaf, Platinum **9** Flowering **10** Silveredge, Silver-leaf, Watermelon **11** Green-ripple **13** Emerald-ripple, Little fantasy

Pepin
called: 8 the Short
king of: 6 Franks
son: 11 Charlemagne

Pepita
character in: 21 The Bridge of San Luis Rey
author: 6 Wilder

Peppard, George

born: 9 Detroit MI
wife: 15 Elizabeth Ashley
roles: 6 Tobruk **7** Banacek **8** The A-Team **16** The Carpetbaggers **19** Breakfast at Tiffany's

pepper 3 dot **6** shower, strafe **7** bombard **8** sprinkle **9** condiment, vegetable

pepper, peppercorn
botanical name: 5 Piper **7** Pnigrum **8** Capsicum **10** Piperaceae **11** C frutescens
color: 3 red **5** black, green, white
origin: 5 India **6** Brazil, Ceylon **7** Malabar, Sarawak, Sumatra **8** Alleppey, Pandjang, Sri Lanka **11** Tellicherry
varieties: 3 Red **4** Baby, Bell, Bird, Cone, Long, Wild **5** Betle, Black, Chili, Cubeb, Green, Japan, Sweet, White **6** Cherry **7** Cayenne, Celebes, Cluster, Tabasco **8** Capsicum **9** Mild water **10** Australian, Red cluster **12** Mountain long, Tabasco-sauce
French: 6 poivre
German: 7 pfeffer
Italian: 4 pepe
Latin: 5 piper
Persian: 5 biber **6** pilpil
Spanish: 8 pimienta
Swedish: 6 peppar
Sanskrit: 7 pippali

peppermint 6 Mentha
varieties: 4 Gray **5** Black, River, White **6** Silver, Sydney **9** Blackbutt **10** Robert- son's **11** Broad-leaved **15** Mount Wellington **17** Narrow-leaved black **19** Nichol's willow-leaved

peppermint schnapps
type: 7 liqueur
flavor: 4 mint

peppery 3 hot **5** fiery, sharp, spicy **7** burning, piquant, pungent **14** highly seasoned

peppy 4 spry **5** brisk, perky **6** active, bouncy, frisky, lively, snappy **7** dynamic **8** animated, spirited, vigorous **9** energetic, full of pep, sparkling, sprightly, vivacious **12** enthusiastic

pep up 4 fire **6** excite, vivify, wake up **7** animate, enliven, quicken **8** vitalize

Pepys, Samuel
author of: 10 Pepys' Diary

Pepys' Diary
author: 11 Samuel Pepys

Pequot
language family: 9 Algonkian **10** Algonquian
location: 11 Connecticut, Rhode Island

perambulate 4 pace, tour, walk **5** amble, mosey **6** ramble, stroll **7** meander, saunter **9** promenade

perceivable 7 visible **8** apparent, distinct **10** detectable, noticeable, observable **11** discernible, perceptible **13** ascertainable

perceive 3 get, see 4 feel, hear, know, note 5 grasp, savvy, sense, smell, taste 6 deduce, detect, gather, notice 7 discern, make out, observe, realize 8 conclude, discover 9 apprehend, be aware of, recognize 10 comprehend, understand 11 distinguish

perceptible 5 clear, plain 7 evident, notable, obvious, visible 8 apparent, distinct, manifest, palpable, tangible, unhidden 9 prominent 10 detectable, noticeable, observable 11 conspicuous, discernible, perceivable, unconcealed, well-defined 13 discoverable, unmistakable 13 ascertainable

perception 5 grasp, sense 7 faculty 8 judgment 9 awareness, detection 10 cognizance, conception 11 discernment, recognition 12 apprehension 13 comprehension, consciousness, understanding 14 discrimination

perceptive 4 keen 5 acute, aware, quick, sharp 6 astute, shrewd 8 sensible 9 sensitive 10 discerning, insightful, responsive 11 intelligent, penetrating, quick-witted 13 understanding

perch 3 sit 4 land, rest, seat 5 eyrie, light, roost 6 alight, settle

Percival, Perceval
character in: 16 Arthurian romance
also see Parsifal

percolate 4 boil, brew 6 bubble, seethe

percussion instrument 4 gong 5 anvil, bells, tabor 6 chimes, rattle 7 celesta, cymbals, marimba, taboret, timpani 8 bass drum, side drum, triangle 9 castanets, dulcitone, snare drum, tenor drum, typophone, xylophone 10 kettledrum, tambourine 12 Glockenspiel, tubular bells

Percy, Walker
author of: 8 Lancelot 12 The Moviegoer 14 Love in the Ruins 15 The Second Coming 16 The Last Gentleman

Perdita
character in: 14 The Winter's Tale
author: 11 Shakespeare

perdition 4 Hell, ruin 8 hellfire 9 damnation, ruination 11 destruction 12 condemnation

Perdix
also: 9 Polycaste
brother: 8 Daedalus
son: 5 Talus
changed into: 9 partridge

pere 6 father, senior

Pere Goriot
author: 14 Honore de Balzac
character: 15 Monsieur Vautrin 17 Eugene de Rastignac, Madame de Beauseant 18 Victorine Taillefer 26 Countess Anastasie de Restaud, Baroness Delphine de Nucingen

peregrination 4 trip 5 jaunt, sally 6 hiking, junket, roving, travel 7 journey, roaming 8 rambling, trekking 9 excursion, wandering 10 expedition

Peregrine Pickle
author: 14 Tobias Smollett

Pereira, William
architect of: 13 Cape Canaveral 20 Transamerica Building (San Francisco)

Perelman, S J
author of: 10 Eastward Ha 15 One Touch of Venus (with Ogden Nash and Kurt Weill) 16 The Road to Miltown 18 Strictly from Hunger 24 Under the Spreading Atrophy

peremptory 5 final 6 biased, lordly 8 absolute, decisive, dogmatic 9 assertive, imperious 10 aggressive, high-handed, imperative, obligatory, undeniable 11 dictatorial, domineering, irrevocable, opinionated, persistent, unavoidable, unequivocal 12 closed-minded, irreversible 13 authoritative 14 unquestionable 16 incontrovertible

perennial 5 fixed 7 durable, lasting, undying 8 constant, enduring, timeless 9 ceaseless, continual, immutable, incessant, long-lived, permanent, perpetual, unceasing, unfailing 10 changeless, continuous, persistent, unchanging 11 everlasting, long-lasting, unremitting 12 imperishable 14 indestructible

Perez, Manuel Benitez
nickname: 10 El Cordobes

perfect 4 pure, true 5 exact, ideal, whole 6 effect, entire, evolve, strict 7 achieve, develop, fulfill, precise, realize, sublime, supreme 8 absolute, accurate, complete, faithful, finished, flawless, peerless, thorough, unbroken, unerring 9 blameless, faultless, matchless, undamaged, unequaled, unrivaled, untainted 10 accomplish, consummate, immaculate, impeccable, scrupulous, unimpaired 11 superlative, unblemished, unmitigated, unqualified

perfection 6 purity 9 achieving, evolution, exactness, precision, sublimity 10 completion, excellence, ideal state 11 development, fulfillment, perfectness, realization, superiority 12 accurateness, consummation, flawlessness 13 faultlessness, impeccability 14 accomplishment

perfectly 5 fully, quite 6 purely, wholly 7 totally, utterly 8 entirely, superbly 9 downright, supremely 10 absolutely, altogether, completely, flawlessly, impeccably, infinitely, positively, thoroughly 11 faultlessly, wonderfully 12 consummately, preeminently, to perfection, without fault 13 without defect 14 to the nth degree, without blemish

perfidious 5 false, lying 6 shifty, sneaky 7 corrupt 8 cheating, disloyal, two-faced 9 deceitful, dishonest, faithless 10 traitorous, treasonous, unfaithful, untruthful 11 treacherous, treasonable 12 dishonorable, undependable, unscrupulous 13 double-dealing, untrustworthy

perfidy 6 deceit 7 treason 8 bad faith, betrayal 9 falseness, recreancy, treachery, two-timing 10 disloyalty, infidelity 11 double-cross, inconstancy 13 breach of faith, deceitfulness, double-dealing, faithlessness 14 unfaithfulness

perforate 4 bore, gash, hole, slit, stab 5 drill, prick, punch, slash, split, stick 6 pierce 8 puncture 9 lancinate, penetrate

perform 2 do 3 act 4 meet, play 5 enact 6 attain, depict, effect, finish, render, troupe 7 achieve, execute, fulfill, portray, present, pull off, realize 8 carry out, knock off 9 discharge, dispose of, polish off, represent 10 accomplish, bring about, consummate, perpetrate, take part in

performance 4 play, show 5 doing, opera 6 ballet 7 concert, conduct, recital 8 ceremony, dispatch, exercise 9 acquittal, discharge, execution, rendering, spectacle 10 attainment, completion, exhibition, performing, production 11 achievement, fulfillment, realization, transaction 12 consummation, effectuation, perpetration, presentation 13 entertainment 14 accomplishment

perfume 4 odor 5 aroma, scent, smell 7 bouquet, cologne, essence, extract, sweeten 9 aromatize, fragrance

perfumed 7 odorous, scented 8 aromatic, fragrant 11 odoriferous 12 sweet-scented 13 sweet-smelling

perfunctory 3 lax 5 hasty 6 casual 7 cursory, offhand, routine 8 careless, listless, lukewarm 9 apathetic, negligent 10 mechanical, spiritless, unthinking 11 halfhearted, inattentive, indifferent, passionless, superficial, unconcerned 13 disinterested

pergola 5 arbor, bower 6 ramada 7 balcony, trellis

Per Hanea
character in: 16 Giants of the Earth
author: 7 Rolvaag

perhaps 5 maybe 6 mayhap 8 peut-etre, possibly 9 perchance 10 God willing, imaginably 11 conceivably 12 peradventure

Periboea
father: 9 Alcathous, Hipponous
husband: 6 Oeneus 7 Polybus
son: 6 Tydeus 7 Olenias, Pelegon 14 Telamonian Ajax
foster son: 7 Oedipus

Perichole, La
character in: 21 The Bridge of San

Luis Rey
author: **6** Wilder

Pericles, Prince of Tyre
author: **18** William Shakespeare
character: **5** Cleon **6** Marina, Thaisa
7 Dionyza **9** Antiochus **10** Lysima-
chus

Periclymenus
father: **6** Neleus **8** Poseidon
grandfather: **8** Poseidon
gift: **13** shape-changing
killed by: **8** Hercules

periderm 4 bark **8** covering **9** sheathing

peridot
species: **7** olivine
source: **5** Burma, Mogok **8** Zebirget
color: **11** yellow-green

perigee 5 depth, nadir **8** low point

**Perikeiromene (The Rape of the
Ringlets)**
author: **8** Menander

peril 4 risk **6** danger, hazard, menace,
threat **7** pitfall **8** jeopardy, unsafety
10 insecurity **11** uncertainty **13** cause
for alarm, vulnerability

perilous 5 risky, shaky **6** chancy, unsafe, unsure **7** ominous **8** insecure,
slippery, ticklish **9** dangerous, hazardous, uncertain **10** precarious, vulnerable **11** threatening, venturesome

perimeter 4 edge **6** border, bounds,
margin **8** confines **9** periphery **10** borderline **13** circumference

period 3 age, end, eon, era **4** halt,
stop, term, time **5** close, epoch, limit
6 finale, finish, season **7** curtain **8** duration, interval **9** cessation, interlude
French: **6** siecle

periodic, periodical 6 cyclic **7** regular, routine **8** frequent, repeated, sea-
sonal **9** recurrent, recurring **12** intermittent

periodical 5 daily, paper **6** annual, review, weekly **7** journal, monthly **8**
bulletin, magazine **9** newspaper, quarterly **10** newsletter **11** publication **12**
newsmagazine

periodically 5 often **9** regularly, routinely **10** frequently, repeatedly **12** occasionally

peripatetic 6 roving **7** migrant, nomadic, roaming, walking **8** rambling,
tramping **9** itinerant, migratory, traveling, wandering **10** ambulating, ambulatory **12** Aristotelian, gallivanting
13 peregrinating

periphery 4 edge **5** bound **6** border **7**
fringes **8** boundary **9** outskirts, perimeter **13** circumference

perish 3 die **5** decay **6** expire, vanish **7**
crumble **8** pass away **9** disappear **10**
come to ruin, wither away **11** be destroyed

perishable 8 fleeting, unstable **9**

ephemeral **10** evanescent, short-lived,
transitory **12** decomposable

perished 4 dead, died **7** expired **8** lifeless **10** passed away

periwinkle 5 Vinca **12** Catharanthus
varieties: **4** Rose **6** Common, Lesser
7 Greater **10** Madagascar

perjury 13 false swearing **14** lying under oath **20** giving false testimony

Perker
character in: **14** Pickwick Papers
author: **7** Dickens

Perkins, Anthony
born: **9** New York NY
roles: **6** Psycho **11** Norman Bates **14**
Catch Twenty-Two **17** Look Homeward Angel **18** Desire Under the
Elms, Friendly Persuasion

perk up 4 lift **5** cheer, rally, renew **6**
buoy up, lift up, revive **7** animate, enliven, gladden **8** brighten, vitalize **9**
stimulate **10** rejuvenate

perky 3 gay **4** pert **5** alert, brisk,
happy, saucy, sunny **6** jaunty, lively **7**
smiling **8** animated, cheerful, spirited
9 sprightly, vivacious **11** free and
easy **12** full of spirit, lighthearted

permanent 3 set **4** perm, wave **6** stable **7** abiding, durable, endless, eternal, lasting, undying **8** constant, enduring, immortal, infinite, unending,
unfading **9** deathless, immutable,
long-lived, perpetual, unfailing **10**
changeless, unyielding **11** everlasting,
long-lasting, never-ending, unalterable
12 imperishable

permeate 4 fill **5** imbue **6** infuse **7**
pervade **8** saturate **9** penetrate **11**
pass through, seep through, soak
through

per mensem 10 by the month

permissible 5 legal, licit **6** lawful **7** allowed, granted **8** licensed **9** allowable, permitted, tolerated **10** admissible, authorized, legitimate, sanctioned
12 unprohibited

permission 5 grant, leave **6** assent,
permit **7** consent, license **8** approval,
sanction **9** agreement, allowance **10**
compliance, concession, indulgence
11 approbation, endorsement **12** acquiescence, dispensation **13** authorization

permissive 3 lax **7** lenient **8** allowing,
granting, tolerant **9** assenting, easygoing, indulgent **10** consenting, forbearing, permitting **11** acquiescent **13** un-
prohibitive **14** unproscriptive

permit 2 OK **3** let **5** allow **6** endure,
suffer **7** agree to, approve, condone,
endorse, let pass, license, warrant **8**
bear with, sanction, tolerate **9** authority, authorize, consent to, put up with
11 give leave to **12** give assent to **13**
authorization
French: **13** laissez passer

permit to leave 4 free **5** let go **6** excuse **7** dismiss, release, set free **8** liberate **9** allow to go, discharge, send
forth

pernicious 5 fatal, toxic **6** deadly, lethal, mortal **7** baneful, harmful, noxious, serious **8** damaging, venomous
9 dangerous, injurious, malignant,
poisonous **10** disastrous **11** deleterious, destructive, detrimental

pernod
type: **8** aperitif
flavor: **5** anise
substitute for: **8** absinthe
with gin: **7** Dubarry
with orange juice: **9** Tiger Tail
with rum: **8** Shanghai
with rye: **3** TNT

peroration 6 sermon, speech, tirade **7**
address, lecture, oration **8** diatribe,
harangue, jeremiad **9** discourse, phi-
lippic **10** filibuster **11** declamation,
exhortation

perpendicular 4 sine **5** erect, plumb,
sheer, steep **7** upright **8** vertical **10**
right angle

perpetrate 2 do **5** enact **6** commit,
pursue **7** execute, inflict, perform, pull
off **8** carry out, transact

perpetration 5 doing **9** committal **10**
commission, committing, performing
11 carrying out, performance

perpetrator 9 performer **11** participant

perpetual 7 abiding, endless, eternal,
lasting **8** constant, enduring, repeated,
unending **9** ceaseless, continual, incessant, permanent, sustained, unceasing **10** continuous **11** everlasting,
never ending, unremitting **12** interminable **13** inexhaustible, uninterrupted

perpetuate 4 save **7** sustain **8** continue, maintain, make last, preserve
10 eternalize **11** immortalize, memorialize

perpetuity 7 all time, forever **8** eternity, infinity **9** end of time **10** permanence **11** endlessness **12** perpetuation, timelessness **13** perdurability,
perennialness

perplex 5 mix up, stump **6** baffle, boggle, muddle, puzzle, rattle **7** confuse,
mystify, nonplus **8** befuddle, bewilder,
confound **9** dumbfound

perplexed 7 anxious, amazed, baffled,
bemused, muddled, puzzled **8** confused, doubtful, involved **9** befuddled,
intricate, mystified **10** astonished, bewildered, nonplussed

perplexing 4 hard, mazy **6** thorny **7**
complex **10** mysterious
riddle: **9** conundrum

perplexity 9 confusion **10** bafflement,
puzzlement **12** bewilderment **13** mystification

perquisite 3 due **4** gift, perk **5** right **6**

reward **7** benefit, present **9** advantage, emolument, privilege **10** honorarium, inducement, recompense **13** fringe benefit

Perrine, Valerie
born: 11 Galveston TX
roles: 5 Lenny **8** Superman **18** Slaughterhouse Five

Perry, Matthew Calbraith
served in: 10 Mexican War **19** War of Eighteen Twelve
rank: 9 commodore
helped establish: 7 Liberia
commander of: 17 US African Squadron
gained treaty with: 5 Japan

Perry, Oliver Hazard
nickname: 14 Hero of Lake Erie
served in: 13 Tripolitan War **19** War of Eighteen-Twelve
battle: 8 Lake Erie
commander of ship: 7 Niagara **8** Lawrence
defeated: 7 British
saying: 31 We have met the enemy and they are ours

Perry, William
nickname: 12 Refrigerator
sport: 8 football
team: 12 Chicago Bears

Perry Como Show, The
regulars: 8 Don Adams **9** Jack Duffy, Paul Lynde **10** Pierre Olaf **11** Kaye Ballard **13** Sandy Stewart **14** Fontane Sisters **17** Ray Charles Singers **18** Louis Da Pron Dancers **19** Peter Gennaro Dancers
announcer: 9 Dick Stark, Ed Herlihy **11** Frank Gallop, Martin Block **12** Durward Kirby
orchestra: 13 Mitchell Ayres
theme: 16 Dream Along with Me

Perry Mason
character: 6 Lt Drum **7** Lt Tragg **9** Paul Drake **10** Lt Anderson **11** Della Street **14** Hamilton Burger
cast: 9 Wesley Lau **10** Ray Collins **11** Barbara Hale, Raymond Burr **13** William Hopper, William Talman **15** Richard Anderson

persecute 3 vex **4** bait **5** abuse, annoy, bully, harry, hound **6** badger, harass, harrow, hector, plague **7** oppress, torment **8** maltreat **9** tyrannize, victimize

Persephone
also: 4 Cora, Kore **10** Perserpina, Proserpine
queen of: 5 Hades
father: 4 Zeus
mother: 7 Demeter
husband: 5 Hades
abducted by: 5 Pluto
ate seeds of: 11 pomegranate
epithet: 11 Carpophorus
corresponds to: 5 Brimo **6** Libera **8** Despoena

Persepolis
capital of: 13 Persian Empire
near modern-day: 10 Shiraz, Iran

Perseus
father: 4 Zeus
mother: 5 Danae
grandfather: 8 Acrisius
wife: 9 Andromeda
son: 6 Mestor, Perses **7** Alcaeus, Heleius **9** Electryon, Sthenelus
daughter: 10 Gorgophone
saved: 9 Andromeda
killed: 6 Gorgon, Medusa

perseverance 8 tenacity **10** doggedness, resolution **11** persistence **12** resoluteness **13** determination, steadfastness

persevere 6 hang on, keep on **7** persist **8** keep at it, plug away, work hard **9** not give up, stick to it **10** be resolute, be resolved, hammer away **11** be obstinate, be steadfast, hang in there

persevering 6 dogged **8** constant, diligent, resolute, sedulous **9** keeping on, steadfast, tenacious **10** determined, persistent, unflagging **11** hardworking, industrious, unremitting

Pershing, John J
nickname: 9 Black Jack
served in: 3 WWI **11** Philippines, World War One **18** Spanish-American War
commander of: 21 Mexican border campaign
trained: 27 American Expeditionary Forces
battle: 10 Kettle Hill **11** San Juan Hill
fought against: 5 Moros **11** Pancho Villa
rank: 16 brigadier general **18** general of the armies
memoirs: 26 My Experiences in the World War
won: 13 Pulitzer Prize (for history)

Persia *see* **4** Iran

Persian Gulf War
caused by: 4 Iraq **13** Saddam Hussein **14** Kuwait invasion
took place in: 4 Iraq **6** Kuwait **10** Middle East **11** Saudi Arabia
leaders:
 Allies: 11 Colin Powell **15** Khalid bin Sultan **18** H Norman Schwarzkopf
 Iraq: 13 Saddam Hussein
operations: 11 Desert Storm **12** Desert Shield
weapons: 4 Scud **5** AWACS **6** Abrams, Apache **7** Bradley, Patriot, Stealth **8** Tomahawk
battle: 6 Khafji **18** mother of all battles

Persian Mythology
god of light/truth: 7 Mithras

Persians, The
author: 9 Aeschylus

character: 6 Atossa, Xerxes **13** Ghost of Darius

persist 4 go on, last, stay **6** endure, hang on, hold on, remain **7** hold out, survive **8** continue, keep at it, not yield **9** not give up, persevere, stand fast, stick to it **10** be resolute **11** be obstinate, be tenacious, hang in there, never say die

persistence 8 tenacity **9** diligence **11** application **12** perseverance **13** determination

persistent 6 dogged **7** abiding, endless, eternal, lasting **8** constant, enduring, obdurate, resolute, stubborn **9** continual, incessant, obstinate, perpetual, steadfast, sustained, tenacious, unceasing, unfailing **10** continuous, determined, persisting, relentless, unshakable, unswerving **11** persevering, unrelenting, unremitting **12** interminable **13** inexhaustible

persnickety 5 fussy **6** choosy **7** finical, finicky **8** picayune **10** fastidious, fuddy-duddy, meticulous, nitpicking, particular, pernickety **11** overprecise, punctilious **13** overdemanding

person 4 body, soul **5** being, human **6** mortal **8** creature **9** earthling **10** human being, individual, living body, living soul

persona 5 being **6** facade **9** character

personable 4 warm **7** affable, amiable, cordial, likable, tactful **8** amicable, charming, friendly, outgoing, pleasant, sociable **9** agreeable **10** attractive, diplomatic **11** complaisant, sympathetic **12** well-disposed, well-mannered

Personae
author: 9 Ezra Pound

personage 3 VIP **5** nabob **6** bigwig **7** big name, big shot, notable **8** big wheel, luminary, somebody **9** celebrity, dignitary **11** heavyweight **12** leading light, public figure **13** high-muck-a-muck

persona grata 8 diplomat **16** acceptable person **34** acceptable diplomatic representative

personal 3 own **5** privy **6** bodily, inward, secret **7** private, special **8** intimate, physical **9** corporeal, exclusive **10** individual, particular, subjective **12** confidential

Personal Anthology, A
author: 15 Jorge Luis Borges

personality 3 ego **4** self **5** charm **6** makeup, nature **8** charisma, identity **9** magnetism **10** affability, amiability **11** disposition, temperament **12** friendliness **13** agreeableness, individuality **15** distinctiveness

persona non grata 15 unwelcome person **18** unacceptable person **33** unwelcome diplomatic representative

Personification of
aging: 4 Elli
air: 4 Amen, Amon **5** Ammon **6** Aether
astronomy: 6 Urania
breath: 4 Amen, Amon **5** Ammon
chaos: 4 Nunu
choral song: 11 Terpsichore
comedy: 6 Thalia
confusion: 5 Chaos
conscience: 5 Aidos
courage: 5 Arete **6** Virtus
dance: 8 Polymnia **10** Polyhymnia **11** Terpsichore
death: 4 Mors **6** Namtar **8** Thanatos
desert: 3 Set **4** Seth
desire: 6 Pothos
divine punishment: 3 Ate **7** Nemesis
east wind: 5 Eurus **9** Volturnus
echo: 4 Echo
emulation: 5 Zelos
familial affection: 6 Pietas
fate: 4 Norn **5** Moira, Moras
fear: 6 Deimos
femininity: 5 Neith
fire: 4 Logi
force: 3 Bia
good faith: 5 Fides
grain blight: 7 Robigus
heaven: 6 Uranus
hostile nature: 8 Fomorian
idyllic poetry: 6 Thalia
liberty: 8 Libertas
longing: 6 Pothos
lotus: 8 Nefertem
meditation: 6 Melete
memory: 5 Mneme, Munin
moon: 4 Luna
nature: 7 Erlking
night: 3 Nox
north wind: 6 Boreas
order: 7 Eunomia
pain: 5 Oizys
past: 3 Urd
peace: 5 Irene
prayer: 5 Litae
present: 8 Verdandi
punishment: 7 Poena, Poine
recklessness: 3 Ate
retribution: 7 Nemesis
revenge: 5 Poena, Poine
Roman nation: 8 Quirinus
sacred music: 8 Polymnia **10** Polyhymnia
sea: 3 Ler, Lir **5** Nammu **6** Pontus **8** Thalassa
sky: 6 Aether, Hathor
soul: 6 Psyche
southeast wind: 5 Eurus **9** Volturnus
south wind: 5 Notus **7** Ninurta
strength: 6 Cratus
sun: 3 Sol
thought: 5 Hugin
tragedy: 9 Melpomene
truth: 7 Alethia
unavailing effort: 5 Ocnus
victory: 4 Nike
wealth: 6 Plutus

west wind: 8 Favonius, Zephyrus
wind: 7 Ninurta
zeal: 5 Zelos
personify 6 embody **7** express **9** exemplify, incarnate, represent, symbolize **11** externalize, incorporate, personalize **12** characterize
personnel 4 crew **5** staff **7** members, workers **8** manpower **9** employees, work force **10** associates

Person to Person
host: 13 Edward R Murrow **18** Charles Collingwood
perspective 4 view **5** scape, scene, vista **7** outlook **8** overview, prospect **9** broad view, viewpoint **12** bird's-eye view
perspicacious 4 keen **5** acute, alert, awake, sharp **6** astute, shrewd **9** clear-eyed, sagacious **10** discerning, perceptive **11** clearheaded, keen-sighted, penetrating, sharp-witted **12** clear-sighted
perspicacity 6 acumen **8** keenness, sagacity **9** acuteness, alertness, sharpness **10** astuteness, perception, shrewdness **11** discernment **14** discrimination
persuadable 7 willing **8** amenable, obliging **9** malleable, tractable **10** open-minded **16** open to suggestion
persuade 3 get **4** coax, lure, move, sway **5** tempt **6** cajole, entice, induce, prompt **7** wheedle, win over **8** convince, inveigle, motivate, talk into **9** influence

Persuasion
author: 10 Jane Austen
character: 7 Mrs Clay **8** Mrs Croft **11** Lady Russell **12** Admiral Croft **25** Captain Frederick Wentworth
  Elliot family: 4 Anne **7** William **9** Elizabeth, Sir Walter
  Musgrove family: 4 Mary **6** Louisa **7** Charles **9** Henrietta
persuasive 6 cogent **7** coaxing, logical, winning **8** alluring, credible, forceful, inviting **9** effective, plausible, seductive **10** believable, compelling, convincing **11** influential
pert 4 flip, spry **5** alert, brash, brisk, fresh, nervy, perky, quick, saucy **6** brassy, brazen, cheeky, lively, nimble **7** chipper **8** flippant, impolite, impudent, insolent **9** audacious, energetic, insulting, sprightly, wide-awake **11** impertinent, smart-alecky **12** discourteous
pertain 2 be **5** apply, touch **6** befall, belong, relate **7** concern, connect

Perth *see Australia*
pertinacious 6 dogged **8** stubborn **9** obstinate, tenacious **10** persistent, unyielding **11** persevering
pertinacity 9 obstinacy **10** mulishness **11** persistence, willfulness **12** contrari-

ness, obdurateness, perverseness, stubbornness **13** determination, inflexibility, intransigence, pigheadedness **14** bullheadedness, intractability
pertinence 9 relevance **11** germaneness **12** appositeness **13** applicability
pertinent 3 apt **4** meet **7** apropos, fitting, germane, related **8** apposite, material, relevant, suitable **9** befitting, concerned, congruent, connected **10** applicable, consistent, to the point
  Latin: 5 ad rem
perturb 5 upset, worry **6** bother **7** disturb, fluster, trouble **8** disquiet, distress **10** discompose, disconcert
perturbation 5 alarm, upset, worry **6** dismay **7** anxiety, concern, turmoil **8** distress **9** agitation, commotion **10** excitement **11** disquietude, trepidation **12** apprehension, discomposure **13** consternation
perturbed 5 upset **7** annoyed, worried **8** agitated, troubled **9** disturbed **12** disconcerted
perturbing 6 vexing **7** irksome **8** annoying **9** vexatious **10** bothersome, irritating, unsettling **11** disquieting, distressing, troublesome **13** disconcerting

Peru
capital/largest city: 4 Lima
  Inca capital: 5 Cuzco
others: 3 Ica **4** Puno **5** Cuzco, Paita, Pisco, Tacna **6** Callao, Talara **7** Huanuco, Iquitos **8** Arequipa, Castilla, Chiclayo, Chimbote, Mollendo, Pucallpa, Trujillo **9** Cajamarca **10** Yurimaguas
school: 8 Trujillo **8** San Marcos
division: 3 Ica **4** Lima, Puno **5** Cusco, Cuzco, Junin, Piura, Tacna **6** Ancash, Loreto, Tumbes
  Inca empire: 13 Tahuantinsuyo
measure: 4 topo **5** galon **7** celemin
monetary unit: 3 sol **5** libra **6** dinero, reseta **7** centavo
weight: 5 libra **7** quintal
island: 6 Chinca **7** Chincha
lake: 8 Titicaca
mountain: 5 Andes **7** El Misti, Huamina **8** Coropuna
highest point: 9 Huascaran
river: 3 Ene, Ica, Ilo **4** Napo, Napu **5** Piura, Rimac **6** Amazon, Oroton, Pampas, Yaguas, Yavari **7** Curaray, Mantaro, Maranon, Pastaza, Tapiche, Ucayali **8** Apurimac, Huallaga, Urubamba **11** Madre de Dios, Paucartambo
sea: 7 Pacific
physical feature:
  current: 6 el nino
  desert: 5 Nazca **7** Atacama, Sechura
  drizzling rain: 8 ilovizna
  fog: 5 garua
  gulf: 9 Guayaquil
  plateau: 7 Tablazo

people: 4 Ande, Boro, Cana, Inca, Inka, Lama, Pano, Peba, Piro, Yutu **5** Campa, Carib, Chana, Colan, Colla, Jwaro, Moche, Nasca, Senci, Yagua, Yunca **6** Atalan, Aymara, Canchi, Chanca, Chanka, Chimer, Cholos, Cocama, Jibaro, Kechua, Omagua, Quiche, Quolla, Setibo, Sipibo **7** Changos, Chincha, Chuncho, Mestizo, Mochica **8** Amahuaca, Criollos, Mayoruma, Quechuia **9** Callawaya **10** Tiahuanaca, Tiatinagua **11** Chumpivilca

   artist: 4 Lazo **7** Montero, Sabogal, Szyszlo **8** Codesido

   author: 4 Vega **5** Palma, Prada **8** Caviedes **10** Mariategui

   explorer: 7 Pizarro

   Inca leader: 7 Huascar **9** Atahualpa **10** Manco Capac

   leader: 5 Balta, Pardo, Prado, Torre **7** Bolivar **8** Castilla, Fujimori **9** Santa Cruz **13** Belaunde Terry **15** Leguiay y Salcedo, Morales Bermudez

language: 6 Aymara **7** English, Quechua, Spanish

religion: 13 Roman Catholic

place:

   bullring: 11 Plaza de Acho

   center of Lima: 12 Plaza de Armas

   church: 10 La Compania

   open market/street: 9 Calle Real

   ruins: 5 Huaco **8** Chan-Chan **9** Cajamarca **11** Machu- Picchu **22** Fortress of Sacsayhuaman

feature:

   animal: 5 llama **6** alpaca, vicuna **7** guanaco

   commune: 6 ayllus

   dance: 5 cueca, kaswa **6** cachua

   farmers: 10 campesinos

   priest: 6 villac

   slums: 9 barriadas

   tree: 8 cinchona

food:

   dish: 3 aji, cuy **7** ceviche **10** anticuchos

   drink: 5 pisco **6** chicha **11** aguardiente

Perugino, Pietro

real name: 14 Pietro Vannucci

also called: 10 Il Perugino **14** Pier della Pieve

born: 5 Italy **15** Citta della Pieve

artwork: 24 The Crucifixion with Saints **26** Delivery of the Keys to St Peter **27** The Giving of the Keys to St Peter **32** Apparition of the Virgin to St Bernard, Christ Delivering the Keys to St Peter

perusal 5 study **6** review **7** reading **8** scanning, scrutiny **10** inspection, runthrough **11** examination, lookthrough **12** scrutinizing **13** contemplation

peruse 3 con **4** read, scan **5** study **6**

search, survey **7** examine, inspect **10** scrutinize

pervade 4 fill **5** imbue **6** infuse **7** suffuse **8** permeate, saturate **9** penetrate **13** spread through **17** diffuse throughout

pervasive 4 rife **7** rampant **8** dominant **9** prevalent **10** ubiquitous **11** omnipresent, predominant

perverse 5 balky **6** dogged, mulish, ornery **7** wayward, willful **8** contrary, obdurate, stubborn **9** obstinate, pigheaded **10** hardheaded, headstrong, inflexible, rebellious **11** disobedient, intractable, wrongheaded

perversion 9 depravity **10** corruption, degeneracy, immorality **11** dissipation, dissolution

pervert 4 warp **5** abuse **6** debase, misuse **7** contort, corrupt, degrade, deprave, distort, falsify, subvert **8** misapply **9** desecrate **12** misrepresent

perverted 5 false **6** faulty, untrue, warped **7** corrupt, debased, deviant, twisted, unsound **8** aberrant, abnormal, degraded, depraved **9** contorted, distorted, erroneous, imperfect, unnatural **10** fallacious, unbalanced **12** misconceived, misconstrued **13** misunderstood

pesky 7 chafing, galling, irksome **8** annoying **9** maddening, obnoxious, offensive, vexatious **10** bothersome, disturbing, nettlesome **11** aggravating, distasteful, infuriating, pestiferous, troublesome **12** disagreeable, exasperating **13** objectionable

pessimism 5 gloom **7** despair **10** gloominess **13** hopelessness **13** gloomy outlook **14** discouragement **15** downheartedness

pessimist 7 kill-joy **8** sourpuss **9** Cassandra, defeatist, gloomy Gus **10** spoilsport, wet blanket **11** crepehanger **13** prophet of doom

pessimistic 6 gloomy **8** hopeless **10** despairing, dispirited **11** discouraged, downhearted

pest 4 bane **5** curse **6** blight, bother **7** scourge **8** nuisance, vexation **9** annoyance **10** irritation **13** pain in the neck

pester 3 irk, nag, vex **4** bait, fret **5** annoy, harry, taunt, worry **6** badger, bother, harass, hector, nettle, plague **7** disturb, provoke, torment, trouble **8** irritate

pesticide 3 DDT **7** biocide **8** fumigant **9** fungicide, germacide, vermicide **11** insecticide

   user: 12 exterminator

pestilence 6 blight, plague **7** disease **8** epidemic

   god of: 4 Irra

pesto sauce

   ingredients: 5 basil **6** garlic **8** olive oil

pet 3 pat **4** baby, dear **6** caress, choice, fondle, stroke **7** beloved, darling, dearest, favored **8** favorite **9** cherished, preferred **10** sweetheart **14** apple of one's eye

pet activity 5 hobby **7** passion **8** interest **10** enthusiasm, hobbyhorse

Petain, Henri Philippe

   rank: 7 general, premier

   nationality: 6 French

   leader of government at: 5 Vichy

   convicted of: 7 treason

Peter 7 apostle

   means: 4 rock

   also called: 5 Simon **6** Cephas

   father: 4 John **5** Jonas

   brother: 6 Andrew

   birthplace: 9 Bethsaida

   hometown: 9 Capernaum

   disciple of: 5 Jesus

   companion: 4 John **5** James

   rebuked: 7 Ananias **8** Sapphira

   secretary: 8 Silvanus

   pertaining to: 7 Petrine

Peter and the Wolf

   composed by: 9 Prokofiev

Peter Grimes

   opera by: 7 Britten

   character: 11 Ellen Orford

Peter Heering, Cherry Heering

   type: 6 brandy **7** liqueur

   origin: 7 Denmark

   flavor: 6 cherry

   color: 3 red

Peter Ibbetson

   author: 15 George Du Maurier

peter out 3 ebb **7** decline, dwindle, fall off, give out **8** diminish

Peter Pan

   author: 11 James Barrie

   character: 4 John, Smee **7** Michael **9** Nurse Nana, Tiger Lily **10** Tinker Bell **11** Captain Hook **12** Wendy Darling

   locale: 14 Never-never Land

petiole 4 stem **5** spine, stalk, stipe **8** peduncle **9** leafstalk

petite 3 wee **4** tiny **5** small **6** little **9** miniature **10** diminutive

petition 3 ask, beg, sue **4** plea, pray, seek, suit, urge **5** press **6** appeal, invoke, orison, prayer **7** apply to, beseech, entreat **8** appeal to, call upon, entreaty, proposal **9** imploring, plead with, request of **10** invocation, supplicate **11** application, beseechment, requisition **12** solicitation, supplication

petitioner 6 suitor **8** claimant **9** solicitor, suppliant **10** supplicant

pet name 8 nickname **9** sobriquet **10** diminutive, endearment

pet phrase 5 maxim, motto **6** saying, slogan **9** catchword

Petre (Lord)

character in: 16 The Rape of the Lock
author: 4 Pope

petrified 4 hard 5 dense, solid, stony 6 frozen 8 hardened, rocklike 9 paralyzed 10 solidified 11 hard as a rock, scared stiff 13 turned to stone

Petrified Forest, The
director: 10 Archie Mayo
based on play by: 14 Robert Sherwood
cast: 9 Dick Foran 10 Bette Davis 12 Leslie Howard 14 Humphrey Bogart (Duke Mantee)
setting: 7 Arizona

Petronius
author of: 9 Satyricon

Petruchio
character in: 19 The Taming of the Shrew
author: 11 Shakespeare

Petticoat Junction
character: 10 Floyd Smoot, Sam Drucker 11 Homer Bedloe, Kate Bradley 12 Charlie Pratt, Dr Janet Craig, Steve Elliott, Wendell Gibbs 14 Betty Jo Bradley, Uncle Joe Carson 15 Billie Jo Bradley, Bobbie Jo Bradley
cast: 9 Frank Cady, Linda Kaye, Mike Minor, Rufe Davis 10 Pat Woodell 11 Charles Lane 12 Bea Benaderet, Byron Foulger, June Lockhart, Lori Saunders 13 Edgar Buchanan, Gunilla Hutton, Jeannine Riley 14 Meredith MacRae, Smiley Burnette
setting: 11 Hooterville 14 Shady Rest Hotel
train: 10 Cannonball

petto 5 chest 6 breast

petty 4 mean 5 minor, small 6 flimsy, paltry, shabby, slight 7 ignoble, trivial 8 niggling, picayune, piddling, trifling 10 ungenerous 11 small-minded, unimportant 12 narrow-minded 13 insignificant 14 inconsiderable 15 inconsequential

petulance 9 poutiness, sulkiness 11 fretfulness, peevishness 12 irritability

petulant 4 sour 5 cross, gruff, huffy, sulky, surly, testy 6 grumpy, sullen, tetchy, touchy 7 bearish, crabbed, fretful, grouchy, peevish, pettish, uncivil 8 snappish 9 crotchety, fractious, irascible, irritable 10 ill-natured, out of sorts, ungracious 11 complaining, contentious, ill-tempered, quarrelsome, thin-skinned 12 cantankerous, faultfinding

Petulia
director: 13 Richard Lester
cast: 10 Arthur Hill, Pippa Scott 12 George C Scott, Joseph Cotten 13 Julie Christie, Shirley Knight 18 Richard Chamberlain
setting: 12 San Francisco

petunia
varieties: 4 Wild 7 Mexican, Seaside

10 Large white 12 Common garden 14 Violet-flowered

peu a peu 14 little by little

peu de chose 14 trifling matter 17 unimportant matter

pew 4 seat 5 bench 6 settle

Peychaud Bitters
type: 8 aperitif
origin: 10 New Orleans

Peyton Place
author: 14 Grace Metalious
character: 9 Rita Jacks (Harrington) 10 Hannah Cord, Steven Cord 12 Matthew Swain 13 Betty Anderson (Harrington Cord Harrington), Elliott Carson, Julie Anderson 14 Dr Michael Rossi, Dr Robert Morton, George Anderson 16 Allison Mackenzie (Harrington), Leslie Harrington, Norman Harrington, Rodney Harrington 18 Constance Mackenzie (Carson)
cast (television): 8 Ed Nelson 9 Kent Smith, Mia Farrow, Ryan O'Neal 10 Tim O'Connor 11 Kasey Rogers, Paul Langton, Ruth Warrick 12 Henry Beckman, James Douglas 13 Dorothy Malone 14 Barbara Parkins, Patricia Morrow, Warner Anderson 19 Christopher Connelly
director (movie): 10 Mark Robson
cast (movie): 9 Hope Lange 10 Lana Turner, Lloyd Nolan 13 Arthur Kennedy
score: 11 Franz Waxman

Phaedo
author: 5 Plato

Phaedra
father: 5 Minos
mother: 8 Pasiphae
sister: 7 Ariadne
husband: 7 Theseus
son: 6 Acamas 8 Demophon
stepson: 10 Hippolytus
loved: 10 Hippolytus
death by: 7 hanging, suicide

Phaenna
origin: 5 Greek 7 Spartan
member of: 6 Graces

Phaethon
father: 6 Helios
mother: 7 Clymene

phalanx 6 column, parade 9 formation 13 ranks and files

Phallus
image of: 9 male organ
symbol of: 9 fertility
carried in: 6 comedy 9 festivals
associated with: 3 Pan 6 Hermes 7 Demeter 8 Dionysus

phantasm 5 ghost, shade, spook 6 mirage, spirit, vision 7 fantasy, figment, incubus, phantom, specter 8 delusion, illusion, succubus 10 apparition

Phantasus
origin: 5 Greek
god of: 6 dreams

phantom 5 dream, ghost 6 mirage, spirit, vision, wraith 7 chimera, specter 8 illusion, phantasm 10 apparition 13 hallucination

Phantom, The
creator: 7 Lee Falk 8 Ray Moore
nickname: 16 The Ghost Who Walks
mask: 5 black
costume: 6 purple

Phantom of the Opera, The
director:
 1925 version: 12 Rupert Julian
 1943 version: 11 Arthur Lubin
cast:
 1925 version: 9 Lon Chaney 11 Mary Philbin, Norman Kerry
 1943 version: 10 Hume Cronyn, Jane Farrar, Nelson Eddy 11 Claude Rains 12 Edgar Barrier 13 Susanna Foster
setting: 10 Paris Opera

Phaon
occupation: 7 boatman
location: 8 Mitylene
given: 5 youth 6 beauty
given by: 9 Aphrodite

pharos 5 light 6 beacon, signal 7 seamark 10 lighthouse, watchtower

phase 4 side, step, view 5 angle, facet, guise, level, slant, stage 6 aspect, degree, period 7 feature 8 attitude, juncture 9 condition, viewpoint 10 appearance 11 development 12 circumstance

pheasant
group of: 4 nest, nide

Phedre, Phaedra
author: 6 Racine
character: 6 Aricia 7 Theseus 10 Hippolytus

phenomenal 5 super 6 unique 7 amazing, unusual 8 singular, superior, uncommon 9 fantastic, marvelous, unheard-of 10 incredible, miraculous, prodigious, remarkable, stupendous, surpassing 11 astonishing, exceptional, outstanding, sensational, spectacular 12 overwhelming, unparalleled 13 extraordinary, unprecedented

phenomenon 5 thing 6 marvel, rarity, wonder 7 episode, miracle 8 incident, occasion 9 actuality, curiosity, exception, happening, nonpareil, sensation 10 fact of life, occurrence, proceeding 11 contingency

phial 4 vial 6 bottle, vessel 9 container

Phidias
born: 6 Athens, Greece
artwork: 4 Zeus 6 Amazon 13 Lemnian Athene (Athena Lemnia) 15 Apollo Parnopios, Athena Parthenos, Athena Promachos

Philadelphia
baseball team: 8 Phillies
basketball team: 13 Seventy-Sixers
bay: 8 Delaware
football team: 5 Stars 6 Eagles

founded/planned by: 4 Penn

hockey team: 6 Flyers

landmark: 6 US Mint **8** City Hall **11** Liberty Bell **12** Christ Church, Congress Hall **13** Franklin Field, Roosevelt Park **14** Betsy Ross House, Carpenter's Hall **15** Gloria Dei Church, Veterans Stadium **16** Independence Hall

means: 19 city of brotherly love

museum: 5 Rodin **15** Fels Planetarium **16** Barnes Foundation **17** Franklin Institute

river: 8 Delaware **10** Schuylkill

university: 4 Penn **6** Drexel, Temple **9** Jefferson, St Joseph's **22** Curtis Institute of Music

Philadelphia Story, The

director: 11 George Cukor

based on play by: 11 Philip Barry

cast: 9 Cary Grant **10** Ruth Hussey **12** James Stewart **16** Katharine Hepburn

Oscar for: 5 actor (Stewart)

remade as: 11 High Society

philanderer 3 rip **4** rake, wolf **5** flirt **6** lecher, tomcat, wanton **7** dallier, Don Juan, gallant, swinger, trifler **8** lothario, lover boy, rakehell **9** adulterer, libertine, womanizer **10** ladykiller **11** woman-chaser

philanthropic, philanthropical 7 liberal **8** generous **9** bounteous **10** almsgiving, beneficent, benevolent, charitable, munificent **11** magnanimous **12** eleemosynary, humanitarian

philanthropist 5 donor, giver **8** dogooder **9** almsgiver **11** contributor **12** humanitarian **13** Good Samaritan

philanthropy 6 bounty **7** charity **8** goodness **10** almsgiving, generosity, liberality **11** beneficence, benevolence, munificence **13** unselfishness **14** charitableness, openhandedness **15** humanitarianism **16** largeheartedness **18** public-spiritedness

Philaster

author: 30 Francis Beaumont and John Fletcher

Philemon

friend: 4 Paul

slave: 8 Onesimus

wife: 6 Baucis

entertained: 4 Hera, Zeus

became: 12 temple priest

Philip

hometown: 9 Bethsaida

disciple of: 5 Jesus

Philippines

named for: 15 Philip II of Spain

capital/largest city: 6 Manila

others: 3 Iba **4** Agoa, Bogo, Cebu, Debu, Naga, Palo **5** Albay, Davao, Gapan, Iriga, Lanao, Laoag, Pasay, Vigan **6** Aparri, Baguio, Cavite, Ilagan, Iloilo, Tarlac **7** Bacolod, Basilan, Calapan, Dagupan, Legaspi **8** Batangas, Caloocan, Cotabato, Tacloban **9** Zamboanga **10** Cabanutuan, Dumaguette, Quezon City

school: 10 Santo Tomas **14** Ateneo de Manila

division: 4 Abra, Cebu **5** Aklan, Albay, Bohol, Capiz, Davao, Lanao, Leyte, Rizal, Samar **6** Agusan, Bataan, Cavite, Iloilo, Laguna, Quezon, Tarlac **7** Isabela, Lepanto, Surigao

measure: 4 loan **5** braza, catty, cavan, chupa, fardo, ganta, picul, punto **6** apatan, balita, lachsa, quinon **7** quilate **8** chinanta

monetary unit: 4 peso **6** conant, peseta **7** centavo

weight: 5 catty, picul **6** lachsa **7** quilate **8** chinanta

island: 4 Cebu, Cuyo, Jolo, Poro, Sulu **5** Batan, Bohol, Leyte, Luzon, Panay, Samar, Ticao **6** Culion, Lubang, Negros **7** Babuyan, Batanes, Bisayan, Masbate, Mindoro, Palawan, Paragua, Polillo, Visoyan **8** Mindanao **10** Corregidor, Marinduque

lake: 4 Taal **5** Lanao

mountain: 3 Iba **4** Mayo, Taal **5** Albay, Askja, Hibok, Mayon, Pulog **6** Pagsan **7** Banahao, Canlaon

highest point: 3 Apo

river: 4 Abra, Agno **5** Magat, Pasig **6** Agusan, Laoang **7** Cagayan **8** Mindanao, Pampanga

sea: 4 Sulu **5** Samar **7** Celebes, Pacific, Visayan **10** Philippine, South China

physical feature:

bay: 6 Manila

falls: 9 Pagsanjan **14** Maria Christina

gulf: 4 Moro **5** Albay, Davao, Leyte, Ragay **8** Lingayen

hot springs: 8 Los Banos

national park: 12 Mayon Volcano

ocean trench: 8 Mindanao

peninsula: 6 Bataan

storm: 6 bagyos **7** monsoon, typhoon

volcano: 8 Pinatubo

people: 3 Ati, Eta, Ita, Tao **4** Aeta, Ifil, Moro, Sulu, Tino **5** Abaca, Aripa, Batak, Batan, Bicol, Bikol, Busao, Lutao, Mundo, Sinay, Tagal, Vicol, Yakan **6** Apayao, Baluga, Bilaan, Biscol, Bontoc, Bontok, Busaos, Ibanag, Ibilao, Ifugao, Igalot, Igorot, Illano, Isinai, Lutayo, Manabo, Manobo, Montes, Sambal, Tagala, Timaua, Timawa, Zambal **7** Bagoboo, Bisayan, Cagayan, Ilocano, Itanega, Malanoa, Mangyan, Naboloi, Negrito, Tagalog, Tirurai, Visayan **8** Arupaata, Babaylan, Bukidono, Filipino, Igorotte, Manguian, Pampanga **9** Arupaatta, Dulangane, Macajambo, Pampangao, Tinguiane **10** Magindanao, Pangasinan **11** Calalangane

author: 5 Rizal

explorer: 7 Legazpe **8** Magellan **10** Villalobos

leader: 5 Ramos **6** Aquino, Marcos, Osmena, Quezon **9** Aguinaldo, Bonifacio, Macapagal, Magsaysay **11** Roxas y Acuna

language: 4 Moro **5** Bicol, Bikol **6** Ibanag **7** Cebuano, English, Ilocano, Spanish, Tagalog, Visayan **8** Filipino, Pilipino **9** Pampangan **10** Samar-Leyte **13** Bamboo-English

religion: 7 animism **9** Aglipayan **10** Protestant **13** Roman Catholic **15** Iglesia ni Kristo

place:

church: 14 Saint Augustine

esplanade: 6 Luneta

fort: 4 Cota, Gota, Kota **5** Lotta **10** Corregidor

president's palace: 10 Malacanang

street: 7 Escolta

US bases: 5 Clark **8** Subic Bay

walled city: 10 Intramuros

feature:

animal: 7 carabao, tamarau, tarsier **9** mouse deer

bird: 7 creeper

clothing: 4 saya **6** camisa **10** balintawak **12** mestiza terno **13** barong tagalog

dance: 9 tinikling

drama: 8 moro-moro

guerrilla fighter: 3 huk

musicians: 12 musikongbuho

naval base: 6 Cavite

song: 8 kundiman

village: 8 barangay

food:

dish: 3 poi **4** baha, sabu, taro **5** balut

drink: 4 beno, vino **5** bubud **6** tampoy **7** pangasi

philistine 5 yahoo **6** savage **7** Babbitt, lowbrow, prosaic **8** ignorant **9** barbarian, bourgeois, unrefined, untutored **10** conformist, uncultured, uneducated, uninformed, unlettered **11** commonplace **12** conventional, uncultivated **13** unenlightened **15** conventionalist **16** anti-intellectual

Philistine city 4 Gath

Philius

epithet of: 4 Zeus

means: 8 friendly

Phillotson, Richard

character in: 14 Jude the Obscure

author: 5 Hardy

Philoctetes

author: 9 Sophocles

character: 8 Heracles, Odysseus **11** Neoptolemus

inherits arms of: 8 Hercules

father: 5 Poeas, Poias

killed: 5 Paris

philodendron

varieties: 5 Dubia, giant **6** common **7** cut-leaf, red-leaf **8** blushing **9** blackgold, heart-leaf, horsehead, spade-

leaf, split-leaf **10** fiddle-leaf, variegated, velvet-leaf **11** leather-leaf

Philomela
　position: 8 princess
　realm: 6 Athens
　father: 7 Pandion
　sister: 6 Procne
　brother-in-law: 6 Tereus
　raped by: 6 Tereus
　transformed into: 7 swallow **11**
　　nightingale

Philomelides
　king of: 6 Lesbos
　defeated by: 8 Odysseus

philosopher/theologian 4 sage **6** sa-
vant **7** thinker, wise man **8** logician,
reasoner **9** theorizer **11** rationalist,
truth seeker **12** dialectician **13** meta-
physician
　Alsatian: 10 Schweitzer
　American: 4 Eddy **5** Dewey, James,
　　Royce, Smith, Young **6** Mather,
　　Peirce **7** Edwards, Niebuhr, Russell,
　　Tillich **8** Williams **9** McPherson **14**
　　Elijah Muhammad
　Austrian: 12 Wittgenstein
　British: 3 Fox **4** Hume, Inge, Knox,
　　More, Owen **5** Bacon, Burke, Locke,
　　Moore **6** Biddle, Cotton, Hobbes,
　　Huxley, Newman, Wesley **7** Ben-
　　tham, Bradley, Carlyle, Cranmer,
　　Russell, Spencer **8** Berkeley, Wycliffe
　　9 Whitehead **13** Thomas a Becket **14**
　　William of Occam
　Chinese: 6 Lao-tzu **9** Confucius
　Christian: 6 Calvin, Luther, Origen, St
　　Paul **7** Abelard **8** St Anselm **9** St Pat-
　　rick **10** Duns Scotus, St Benedict **11**
　　St Augustine **14** William of Occam
　　15 St Thomas Aquinas **16** St Alber-
　　tus Magnus
　Czech: 3 Hus
　Danish: 11 Kierkegaard
　Dutch: 7 Erasmus, Spinoza
　El Salvadorian: 9 Masferrer
　French: 5 Comte **6** Calvin, Pascal,
　　Sartre **7** Abelard, Bergson, Diderot **8**
　　Maritain, Rousseau, Voltaire **9** Des-
　　cartes, Levy-Bruhl, Montaigne **11**
　　Montesquieu
　German: 4 Kant, Marx **5** Buber, He-
　　gel **6** Boehme, Fichte, Herder, Luther
　　7 Husserl, Jaspers, Leibniz **9** Heideg-
　　ger, Nietzsche, Schelling **10** Muhlen-
　　berg **11** Melanchthon **12** Schopen-
　　hauer **13** Thomas a Kempis **14**
　　Schleiermacher
　Greek: 5 Plato **6** St Paul, Thales **8**
　　Socrates **9** Aristotle **10** Anaxagoras,
　　Anaximenes, Heraclitus, Parmenides,
　　Pythagoras **11** Anaximander
　Indian: 6 Buddha **16** Siddharta Gau-
　　tama
　Islamic: 7 al Kindi **8** al-Farabi, Aver-
　　roes, Avicenna **9** al Ghazali **10** Ibn
　　Khaldun
　Italian: 5 Bruno **7** Aquinas, Mazzini
　　10 St Benedict, Zeno of Elea **17** St

Francis of Assisi
　Japanese: 6 Suzuki
　Jewish: 7 Spinoza **10** Maimonides
　Latin: 8 Plotinus **11** St Augustine
　Spanish: 8 Averroes **10** Maimonides
　　13 Ortega y Gasset **16** Ignatius of
　　Loyola
　Swedish: 10 Swedenborg
　Swiss: 7 Zwingli

Philosopher's Pupil, The
　author: 11 Iris Murdoch

philosophic, philosophical 4 calm **5**
quiet, stoic **6** serene **7** erudite,
learned, logical, patient, stoical **8** abstract, composed, rational, resigned,
tranquil **9** impassive, judicious, sagacious, unexcited, unruffled **10** complacent, fatalistic, reasonable, theorizing,
thoughtful **11** imperturbed, theoretical, unemotional **14** self-restrained

philosophy 4 calm, view **5** ideas, logic
6 reason **7** beliefs, opinion, thought **8**
doctrine, fatalism, patience, serenity,
stoicism, thinking **9** basic idea, composure, esthetics, principle, reasoning,
restraint, viewpoint **10** conception,
theorizing **11** complacency, convictions, forbearance, impassivity, metaphysics, rationalism, resignation
　means: 12 love of wisdom
　branch: 6 ethics **8** ontology **10** aes-
　　thetics **11** metaphysics **12** epistemol-
　　ogy
　term: 8 noumenon **9** causality, dialec-
　　tic, solipsism
　school of: 7 Sophism **8** idealism, Mi-
　　lesian, Stoicism **9** Epicurean, panthe-
　　ism, Platonism **10** empiricism, prag-
　　matism, Skepticism **11** rationalism
　　12 Aristotelian, neoplatonism **13**
　　Phenomenology, scholasticism **14** ex-
　　istentialism **17** logical positivism

Phil Silvers Show, The
　character: 6 Fender **7** Col Hall, Hen-
　　shaw **8** Doberman **9** Sgt Ritzik **12**
　　Sgt Joan Hogan **13** Rocco Barbella,
　　Sgt Ernie Bilko
　cast: 8 Joe E Ross, Paul Ford **10** Alan
　　Melvin, Herbie Faye **13** Harvey Lem-
　　beck **15** Elisabeth Fraser, Maurice
　　Gosfield
　setting: 6 Kansas **10** Fort Baxter

phlegmatic 4 calm, cool, dull **6** serene
7 languid, passive, stoical **8** listless,
sluggish, tranquil **9** apathetic, impassive, lethargic, unfeeling **10** nonchalant, spiritless **11** indifferent, insensitive, unconcerned, unemotional,
unexcitable **12** unresponsive **13** imperturbable, unimpassioned **15** undemonstrative

phlox
　varieties: 4 blue, fall, moss, sand,
　　star **6** annual, smooth **7** prickly **8**
　　creeping, drummond, mountain,
　　trailing **9** perennial, sword-leaf,
　　thick-leaf **15** summer perennial

Phnom-Penh
　airport: 10 Pochentong
　also: 8 Pnom Penh
　capital of: 8 Cambodia **9** Kampuchea
　pagoda: 12 Preah Morokot
　river: 6 Mekong **8** Tonle Sap

phobia 5 dread **6** horror, terror **7** bugaboo, bugbear **8** aversion, loathing **12**
apprehension **16** unreasonable fear **19**
overwhelming anxiety
　fear of animals: 9 zoophobia
　fear of birds: 13 ornithophobia
　fear of blushing: 13 erythrophobia
　fear of bridges: 13 gephyrophobia
　fear of cats: 10 gatophobia **12** aelu-
　　rophobia, ailurophobia
　fear of closed/confined spaces: 14
　　claustrophobia
　fear of crowds: 11 ochlophobia
　fear of darkness/the dark of night:
　　11 nyctophobia
　fear of death: 13 thanatophobia
　fear of death/dead bodies: 11 nec-
　　rophobia
　fear of dirt: 10 mysophobia
　fear of disease: 11 pathophobia
　fear of fire: 10 pyrophobia
　fear of flowers: 11 anthophobia
　fear of flying: 10 aerophobia
　fear of germs: 11 mikrophobia
　fear of hair: 12 trichophobia
　fear of heights: 10 acrophobia
　fear of insanity: 13 dementophobia
　fear of lightning: 11 astraphobia
　fear of men: 11 androphobia
　fear of mice: 10 murophobia
　fear of numbers: 12 numerophobia
　fear of open spaces: 11 agoraphobia
　fear of pain: 10 algophobia
　fear of people: 12 anthrophobia
　fear of reptiles: 13 herpetophobia
　fear of snakes: 13 ophidiophobia
　fear of speaking aloud: 11 pho-
　　nophobia
　fear of spiders: 13 arachnophobia
　fear of strangers: 10 xenophobia
　fear of thunder: 12 brontophobia
　fear of the number thirteen: 17 tris-
　　kaidekaphobia
　fear of vehicles/driving: 11 amax-
　　ophobia
　fear of water: 10 aquaphobia **11** hy-
　　drophobia
　fear of women: 10 gynophobia

Phoebe
　member of: 6 Titans
　father: 6 Uranus
　mother: 4 Gaea
　sister: 6 Themis
　daughter: 4 Leto **7** Asteria
　identified with: 4 moon
　corresponds to: 5 Diana **7** Artemis

Phoebus see **6** Apollo

Phoenicia see **7** Lebanon

Phoenician Mythology
　god of agriculture/earth: 5 Dagon
　corresponds to Mesopotamian: 5
　　Dagan

bird: 6 Phenix **7** Phoenix
goddess of fertility/reproduction: 7 Astarte

Phoenissae (The Phoenician Maidens)
author: 9 Euripides
character: 5 Creon **7** Jocasta, Oedipus **8** Adrastus, Antigone, Eteocles, Tiresias **9** Polynices **10** Menoikieus

Phoenix
basketball team: 4 Suns **7** Mercury
capital of: 7 Arizona
event: 5 rodeo
feature: 10 Papago Park **22** Desert Botanical Gardens
football team: 9 Cardinals
hockey team: 7 Coyotes
river: 4 Salt

Phoenix
also: 6 Phenix
origin: 10 Phoenician
form: 4 bird
gift: 11 immortality
king of: 9 Dolopians
father: 7 Amyntor
mother: 8 Cleobule
brother: 6 Cadmus
sister: 6 Europa
foster son: 8 Achilles
ancestor of: 11 Phoenicians

Pholus
form: 7 centaur
guarded: 4 wine
wine a gift from: 8 Dionysus

phonograph 4 hi-fi **5** phono **6** stereo **8** Victrola **9** turntable **10** gramophone **12** record player

phonophobia
fear of: 13 speaking aloud

phony, phoney 4 fake, hoax, mock, sham **5** bogus, false, fraud, trick **6** forged, pseudo, unreal, untrue **7** forgery **8** specious, spurious **9** deceptive, imitation, pretended, synthetic **10** artificial, fraudulent, not genuine **11** counterfeit, make-believe, unauthentic

Phorcys
god of: 3 sea
sister: 4 Ceto
children: 5 Ladon **6** Graiae **7** Echidna, Gorgons **8** Phorcids
harbor in: 6 Ithaca

phosphorus
chemical symbol: 1 P

photograph 3 pic **4** film, snap **5** image, print, shoot, still **6** candid, glossy **7** mugshot, picture, tintype **8** likeness, portrait, snapshot **12** daguerreotype
bath: 5 fixer, toner **7** reducer **9** developer
book: 5 album

photographer
American: 4 Haas, Hine, Penn, Riis, Rose, Tice **5** (Ansel) Adams, Annan, Arbus, Brady, Evans, Hawes, Lange, Lynes, Smith, White **6** Avedon, Coburn, Eakins, Man Ray, Strand, Turner, Weston **7** Burrows, Eastman, Gardner, Jackson, Watkins **8** Bogardus, Davidson, Steichen **9** Muybridge, O'Sullivan, Rothstein, Stieglitz **10** Cunningham, Southworth **11** Bourke-White, Eisenstaedt, Turberville **13** Watson-Schutze
British: 5 Evans, Frith **6** Bailey, Beaton, Fenton, Mayall, Talbot **7** Cameron **8** Brewster, Robinson **9** Rejlander **10** MacPherson
French: 5 Marey, Nadar **6** Baldus, DuCamp, Le Secq, Newton, Niepce **7** Lumiere **8** Daguerre **12** Sabatier-Blot **14** Cartier-Bresson
German: 4 Hoch **5** Ernst **7** Hausman **8** Stelzner **13** Renger-Patzsch
Hungarian: 7 Kertesz **10** Moholy-Nagy
Japanese: 4 Ikko
Scottish: 4 Hill **7** Adamson
Spanish: 7 Picabia

photostat 4 copy **7** replica **9** duplicate, facsimile **12** reproduction

phrase 3 put, say **4** word **5** couch, idiom, maxim, state, utter, voice, words **6** cliche, dictum, impart, remark, saying, truism **7** declare, express, proverb **8** aphorism, banality, locution **9** enunciate, find words, platitude, utterance, verbalize, word group **10** articulate, expression **11** communicate

phraseology 5 style **7** diction, wording **13** choice of words **18** manner of expression

Phrixus
father: 7 Athamas
mother: 7 Nephele
stepmother: 3 Ino
sister: 5 Helle
wife: 9 Chalciope
son: 5 Argus, Melas **8** Phrontis **10** Cytissorus

physical 4 real **5** human, solid **6** actual, animal, bodily, carnal, living **7** fleshly, natural, sensual **8** apparent, concrete, corporal, existent, existing, external, material, palpable, tangible **9** corporeal, essential, of the body **11** substantive

physical checkup 4 exam **8** physical **11** examination **19** physical examination

physical condition 5 shape **7** fitness, stamina **12** constitution

physical disorder 6 malady **7** ailment, disease, illness **8** sickness **9** ill health, infirmity

physical training 3 gym **6** sports **8** exercise **9** athletics, shaping up **10** gymnastics, working out **12** conditioning

physician 2 GP, MD **3** doc **5** medic **6** doctor, medico **7** surgeon **8** sawbones **10** specialist **11** medicine man, pill peddler **13** medical doctor
Alsatian: 10 Schweitzer
American: 4 Long, Rush, Salk **5** Sabin **6** Dooley, Gorgas **7** Huggins, Whipple **8** Williams **9** Blackwell **11** Landsteiner
British: 5 Paget **6** Adrian, Harvey, Jenner, Lister
Canadian: 4 Best **7** Banting
Dutch: 7 Eijkman
French: 7 Charcot
German: 6 Mesmer **7** Fechner, Virchow **10** Blumenbach
Greek: 10 Herophilus **11** Hippocrates **12** Erasistratus
Italian: 6 Malpighi
Russian: 6 Pavlov
Scottish: 4 Lind
South African: 7 Barnard

Physician to Olympian gods 5 Paeon **6** Apollo

physicist
American: 4 Hess, Rabi **5** Bethe, Gamow, Pauli, Yalow **6** Bekesy, Teller, Townes, Watson **7** Feynman, Richter, Seaborg **8** Einstein, Lawrence, Van Allen **9** Michelson **11** Chamberlain, Oppenheimer
Austrian: 7 Doppler, Meitner
British: 4 Born **5** Bragg, Hooke, Joule **6** Kelvin **7** Gilbert, Thomson **8** Chadwick, Rayleigh **9** Cockcroft **10** Rutherford
Danish: 4 Bohr **7** Oersted
Dutch: 6 Zeeman **7** Lorentz
French: 6 Ampere **7** Broglie, Coulomb, Fresnel **8** Foucault **9** Becquerel **11** Joliot-Curie
German: 3 Ohm **5** Hertz, Stark **6** Planck **7** Rontgen, Wegener **8** Humboldt, Roentgen **9** Kirchhoff, Mossbauer **10** Fahrenheit, Fraunhofer
Indian: 5 Raman
Irish: 7 Tyndall **10** Fitzgerald
Italian: 5 Fermi
Russian: 6 Landau **8** Cerenkov, Sakharov
Scottish: 7 Rankine

Physics
author: 9 Aristotle

physiognomy 4 face **5** shape **6** facade, visage **7** contour, outline, profile **8** features **10** silhouette **11** countenance

physiology
founder: 13 William Harvey
study of: 8 function
study of nervous sytem: 15 neurophysiology

pianissimo
music: 8 very soft
abbreviation: 2 pp

pianist 4 Hess **5** Liszt, Watts **6** Busoni, Chopin, Gilels, Serkin **7** Cliburn, Hofmann, Richter **8** Backhaus, Horowitz, Schnabel, Schumann, Thalberg, von Bulow **9** Barenboim, Casadesus, Gieseking **10** Gottschalk, Rubinstein **12** Rachmaninoff

piano
invented by: **10** Cristofori
player piano: **9** Fourneaux
forerunner: **6** spinet **10** clavichord **11** harpsichord
piano
music: **4** soft
abbreviation: **1** p
piazza 5 patio, porch **6** square **7** gallery, portico, veranda
Piazzi, Giuseppe
field: **9** astronomy
nationality: **7** Italian
discovered: **5** Ceres
catalogued: **5** stars
picaresque 6 daring **7** raffish, roguish, waggish **8** devilish, prankish, rascally, scampish **9** foolhardy **10** roistering **13** adventuresome **14** mischief-loving
Picasso, Pablo
born: **5** Spain **6** Malaga
artwork: **4** Dove **6** Guitar, Jester **7** Ma Jolie, Rooster, She-Goat **8** Guernica **9** Bull's Head, Notre Dame **11** Seated Woman, Woman Diving **12** Head of a Woman **13** Seated Bathers **14** Minotauromachy, Mother and Child, Women of Algiers **15** Ambroise Vollard, Man Holding a Lamb, The Charnel-House, The Large Profile, The Three Dancers **16** Nude in an Armchair **17** Girl Before a Mirror, The Glass of Absinth, The Three Musicians **20** Still Life with a Candle **22** Les Demoiselles d'Avignon **23** Portrait of Gertrude Stein
picayune, picayunish 5 dinky, petty, small **6** flimsy, little, measly, paltry, slight **7** trivial **8** niggling, nugatory, piddling, trifling **11** unimportant **13** insignificant **14** inconsiderable **15** inconsequential
Piccini, Nicola (Piccinni, Niccola)
born: **4** Bari **5** Italy
composer of: **5** Didon **6** Roland **11** The Good Girl **15** La buona figliola **18** Iphigenie en Tauride
pick 3 cut **4** crop **5** cream, elect, elite, pluck, prize **6** choice, choose, detach, flower, gather, opt for, select **7** collect, fix upon, harvest, pull off, pull out, the best **9** single out **10** decide upon, favored one, preference, settle upon
picket 4 pale, post **5** fence, go out, guard, hem in, pen in, stake, watch **6** corral, paling, patrol, sentry, shut in, strike, tether, wall in **7** boycott, enclose, hedge in, lookout, striker, upright, walk out **8** blockade, palisade, restrain, restrict, sentinel **9** blockader, boycotter, protester, restraint, stanchion
picketing 5 march **7** protest **8** marching, on strike, striking **10** protesting **12** protest march **13** demonstrating, demonstration

Pickett, George E
served in: **8** Civil War **10** Mexican War
side: **11** Confederate
battle: **10** Gettysburg
famous for: **6** charge
Pickford, Mary
real name: **15** Gladys Mary Smith
nickname: **18** America's Sweetheart
born: **6** Canada **7** Toronto
husband: **16** Douglas Fairbanks **18** Charles Buddy Rogers
roles: **4** Rags **8** Coquette (Oscar) **9** Pollyanna **19** The Taming of the Shrew **21** The Poor Little Rich Girl **23** Rebecca of Sunnybrook Farm
home: **8** Pickfair
memoirs: **17** Sunshine and Shadow
formed: **13** United Artists
partners: **10** D W Griffith **14** Charlie Chaplin **16** Douglas Fairbanks
pickings 4 loot **5** booty **6** scraps, spoils **7** plunder, takings **9** leftovers
pickle 3 fix, jam **4** corn, dill, mess, sour **6** crisis, plight, scrape **7** dilemma, gherkin, mustard **8** cucumber, hot water, quandary **9** emergency, extremity, tight spot **10** difficulty, kosher dill, pretty pass **11** predicament **14** bread-and-butter
pickled 5 drunk **6** soused **8** powdered
pick on 5 annoy, bully **6** harass, jibe at **7** torment **8** browbeat
pick out 3 see **4** espy **6** choose, descry, detect, notice, select **7** discern, make out **8** perceive **12** catch sight of
pickup 4 rise **5** boost, truck **7** advance **9** impromptu **11** improvement **12** acceleration
pick up 3 buy, get **6** gather, lift up, look up, obtain, secure **7** acquire, develop, improve, procure **8** contract, retrieve **9** cultivate, get better
Pickwick Papers
author: **14** Charles Dickens
character: **6** Perker, Tupman, Wardle, Winkle **9** Sam Weller, Snodgrass **10** Mrs Bardell **11** Emily Wardle **12** Alfred Jingle, Rachel Wardle **13** Arabella Allen
picky 5 fussy **6** choosy **7** finicky **10** fastidious, particular **11** persnickety **14** discriminating
Picrochole
character in: **22** Gargantua and Pantagruel
author: **8** Rabelais
picture 3 see **4** copy, draw, film **5** fancy, flick, image, model, movie, paint, photo, study **6** cinema, depict, double, mirror, sketch **7** believe, drawing, essence, etching, feature, imagine, paragon, portray, tintype **8** envision, likeness, painting, snapshot **9** delineate, duplicate, facsimile, portrayal, represent **10** call to mind, carbon copy, conceive of, dead ringer,

embodiment, illustrate, photograph **11** delineation **12** illustration, see in the mind **13** daguerreotype, motion picture, moving picture, spitting image **14** representation **15** exemplification, personification
Picture of Dorian Gray, The
author: **10** Oscar Wilde
character: **9** James Vane, Sibyl Vane **13** Basil Hallward **15** Lord Henry Wotton
picturesque 6 exotic, quaint **7** unusual **8** artistic, charming, colorful, striking **9** beautiful, pictorial **10** attractive **11** distinctive, imaginative, interesting
Picus
origin: **5** Roman **7** Italian
god of: **11** agriculture
father: **6** Saturn
associated with: **10** woodpecker
loved by: **5** Circe
changed into: **10** woodpecker
son: **6** Faunus
piddling 4 puny **5** petty, small **6** flimsy, little, measly, modest, paltry, skimpy, slight **7** trivial **8** picayune, trifling **9** niggardly **11** unimportant **13** insignificant **15** inconsequential
pie 4 tart **6** pastry, quiche **7** cobbler, dessert **8** turnover
liner: **5** crust, shell
top: **7** lattice **8** meringue
piebald 6 motley **7** dappled, flecked, mottled, spotted **8** many-hued, speckled **10** variegated **11** many-colored, varicolored **12** multicolored, particolored
piece 3 bit, cut, fix, pat **4** blob, case, hunk, item, lump, mend, part, play, unit, work **5** chunk, drama, essay, patch, scrap, shard, share, shred, slice, story, study, thing **6** amount, entity, length, member, paring, repair, review, sample, sketch, sliver, swatch **7** article, cutting, example, patch up, portion, restore, section, segment **8** creation, division, fraction, fragment, instance, quantity, specimen **9** component, selection **11** composition
piece de resistance 13 principal dish **14** principal event
piece goods 5 cloth, goods **6** fabric **8** dry goods, material **9** yard goods
piecemeal 9 gradually **10** fragmented, one at a time **14** little by little
piece of the action 3 cut, fee **5** piece **7** portion, rake-off **10** commission, percentage
pied 6 motley **7** checked, dappled, mottled, piebald **8** colorful **9** checkered **10** variegated **11** many-colored **12** parti-colored
pied-a-terre 17 temporary dwelling
literally: **12** foot on ground
Pied Piper
source: **6** German, legend

town: 7 Hamelin
plague: 4 rats
charmed by: 6 piping
led away: 4 rats **8** children
Pied Piper of Hamlin, The
   author: 14 Robert Browning
pier 4 anta, dock, mole, quay, slip **5** jetty, levee, wharf **6** pillar **7** landing, support **10** breakwater
pierce 3 cut **4** hurt, pain, stab **5** drill, lance, prick, spear, spike, stick, sting, wound **6** grieve, impale **7** affront **8** distress, puncture **9** penetrate, perforate **10** cut through, run through
Pierce, Franklin
   nickname: 29 Young Hickory of the Granite Hills
   presidential rank: 10 fourteenth
   party: 8 Democrat
   state represented: 2 NH
   defeated: 4 (John Parker) Hale **5** (Winfield) Scott
   vice president: 4 (William Rufus Devane) King (died in office)
   cabinet:
      state: 5 (William Learned) Marcy
      treasury: 7 (James) Guthrie
      war: 5 (Jefferson) Davis
      attorney general: 7 (Caleb) Cushing
      navy: 6 (James Cochran) Dobbin
      postmaster general: 8 (James) Campbell
      interior: 10 (Robert) McClelland
   born: 14 Hillsborough (Hillsboro) NH
   died/buried: 9 Concord NH
   education:
      academy: 7 Hancock **11** Francestown
      college: 7 Bowdoin
      studied: 3 law
   religion: 12 Episcopalian
   political career: 8 US Senate **16** state legislature **24** US House of Representatives
   civilian career: 6 lawyer
   military service: 6 US Army **10** Mexican War **16** brigadier general
   notable events of lifetime/term:
      Act: 6 Tariff (of 1857)
      bill: 14 Kansas-Nebraska
      civil war in: 6 Kansas
      first US: 10 World's Fair
      Manifesto: 6 Ostend
      Purchase: 7 Gadsden
      treaty of: 8 Kanagawa
   father: 8 Benjamin
   mother: 4 Anna (Kendrick)
   siblings: 5 Henry, Nancy **7** Charles, Harriet **9** Charlotte **12** John Sullivan **16** Benjamin Kendrick
   half sister: 9 Elizabeth
   wife: 4 Jane (Means Appleton)
   children: 8 Benjamin, Franklin **11** Frank Robert
piercing 3 raw **4** keen, loud **5** angry, cruel, sharp **6** biting, bitter, fierce, shrill **7** caustic, cutting, furious, grat-

ing, hurtful, intense, painful, probing **8** strident **9** agonizing, deafening, searching, shrieking, torturous **10** screeching **11** penetrating **12** earsplitting, excruciating **13** ear- shattering
Pierian
   pertains to: 5 Muses
Pierian Spring
   form: 8 fountain
Pierides *see* **5** Muses
Piero della Francesca (Piero dei Franceschi)
   born: 5 Italy **16** Borgo San Sepolcro
   artwork: 12 Duke of Urbino **15** The Resurrection **18** Federigo and His Wife **19** St John the Evangelist **20** Flagellation of Christ **23** The Compassionate Madonna, The Legend of the True Cross, The Old Age and Death of Adam **24** The History of the True Cross **45** The Madonna and Saints with Frederigo da Montefeltro
Piers Plowman
   author: 15 William Langland
Pietas
   personifies: 17 familial affection
piety 7 loyalty, respect **8** devotion, humility **9** godliness, piousness, reverence **10** devoutness **11** dutifulness, religiosity **13** religiousness
pig 3 hog **5** piggy, porky, swine **6** porker **7** glutton, guzzler **8** gourmand **9** chowhound **11** gormandizer
   male: 4 boar
   female: 3 sow
   young: 5 shoat **6** piglet **11** suckling pig
pigeon
   young: 5 squab **8** squeaker
pigeonhole 4 rank, rate, type **5** brand, cubby, group, label, niche **8** category, classify **9** cubbyhole **10** categorize **11** compartment
pigheaded 6 dogged, mulish **7** willful **8** contrary, obdurate, perverse, stubborn **9** insistent, obstinate, unbending **10** bullheaded, inflexible, refractory, unyielding **11** opinionated, wrongheaded
Piglet
   character in: 13 Winnie-the-Pooh
   author: 5 Milne
pigment 3 dye **4** tint **5** color **8** coloring, dyestuff **14** coloring matter
pigmentation 5 color **9** skin color **10** coloration
pigtail 5 braid, plait, queue **8** ponytail
pike 4 bill **5** lance, spear, spike **6** poleax **7** assegai, freeway, halberd, harpoon, highway, javelin, parkway, thruway **8** autobahn, hard road, speedway, toll road, turnpike **10** expressway, interstate, throughway **12** superhighway
   British: 12 King's Highway **13**

Queen's highway
   German: 8 autobahn
piker 5 miser **7** niggard, trifler **8** tightwad **9** skinflint **10** cheapskate, pinchpenny **12** penny pincher
Pilar
   character in: 19 For Whom the Bell Tolls
   author: 9 Hemingway
pilaster 4 pier **6** column, pillar **7** support, upright **8** baluster
pile 3 nap **4** heap, mass, pier, post, shag, warp **5** amass, batch, fluff, grain, hoard, mound, plush, stack, store **6** fleece, gather, piling, pillar **7** collect, pyramid, support, surface, upright **8** assemble, quantity **9** abundance, amassment, profusion, stanchion **10** accumulate, assortment, collection, foundation **11** agglomerate, aggregation, fibrousness **12** accumulation
pile up 4 bank, heap **5** amass, hoard, mound, stack **7** collect **10** accumulate
pile-up 3 jam, mob **4** mass **5** snarl **8** crowding, gridlock **10** bottleneck, congestion **11** obstruction **12** overcrowding
pilfer 3 cop, rob **4** hook, lift **5** boost, filch, heist, pinch, steal, swipe **6** finger, pirate, snitch, thieve **7** purloin **8** shoplift **10** plagiarize
pilferer 5 thief **6** robber **7** burglar **10** shoplifter, sneak thief
pilgrim, Pilgrim 4 haji **5** exile, hadji **6** palmer **7** pioneer, Puritan, settler **8** newcomer, traveler, wanderer, wayfarer **9** foreigner
   father: 5 Alden
   founder: 10 Separatist
   interpreter: 7 Squanto
   leader: 8 Standish
   protector: 7 Templar
   ship: 9 Mayflower, Speedwell
Pilgrim, Billy
   character in: 18 Slaughterhouse Five
   author: 8 Vonnegut
pilgrimage 4 hadj, trek **6** ramble, roving, voyage **7** journey, roaming, sojourn **8** long trip **9** excursion, wandering **13** peregrination
   destination: 5 Mecca **10** Canterbury
Pilgrim's Progress, The
   author: 10 John Bunyan
   character: 7 Despair, Hopeful **8** Apollyon, Faithful **9** Christian, Ignorance **10** Evangelist **14** Worldly Wiseman
pill 3 rob **4** ball, pell **5** bolus **6** bullet, pellet, tablet, pilule **7** capsule **8** medicine **9** cigarette
pillage 3 rob **4** loot, raid, sack **5** booty, rifle, strip **6** fleece, maraud, piracy, ravage, spoils **7** despoil, looting, plunder, robbery **9** filchings **10** plundering

pillager 6 looter, vandal **7** brigand **9** despoiler, plunderer

pillar 3 VIP **4** pile, post, rock **5** shaft, wheel **6** column, piling **7** obelisk, support, upright **8** champion, mainstay, pilaster, somebody **9** colonnade, stanchion

Pillars of Society, The
author: **11** Henrik Ibsen

pillow 3 pad **7** bolster, cushion **8** headrest

pilot 4 lead **5** flyer, guide, steer **6** airman, direct, escort, fly-boy, handle, leader, manage **7** aviator, birdman, conduct, control **8** aeronaut, coxswain, helmsman, navigate, wheelman **9** accompany, sky jockey, steersman

Pilot, The
author: **19** James Fenimore Cooper

Pima (Aatam, Pima Alto)
language family: **10** Uto-Aztekan
location: **7** Arizona
related to: **6** Papago
descendants of: **7** Hohokam

Pima Alto see **4** Pima

pin 4 bind, clip, tine **5** affix, badge, clasp, dowel, medal, prong **6** brooch, fasten, pinion, secure, skewer **8** hold down, hold fast, restrain **10** decoration
type: **3** hat **4** push **5** stick, thole **6** breast, common, diaper, safety **8** straight

pincer 4 claw **5** chela

pinch 3 bit, cop, jam, jot, nab, nip **4** bust, crib, grab, iota, lift, mite, pain, snip, spot **5** catch, cramp, crimp, crush, filch, run in, speck, steal, swipe, trace, trial, tweak **6** arrest, clutch, collar, crisis, misery, ordeal, pickle, plight, snatch, snitch, strait, tittle **7** capture, purloin, squeeze, tighten **8** compress, exigency, hardship **9** apprehend, emergency **10** affliction, difficulty, discomfort **11** predicament

Pinch, Tom
character in: **16** Martin Chuzzlewit
author: **7** Dickens

pinch hitter 5 proxy **7** stand-in **9** alternate **10** substitute

pinchpenny 5 miser **6** frugal, stingy **7** niggard, prudent, thrifty
Dickensian: **7** Scrooge

Pindar
author of: **4** Odes **8** Epinicea

pine 3 die, ebb **4** flag, long, sigh, wilt **5** covet, crave, droop, yearn **6** desire, expire, hanker, weaken, wither **7** decline, dwindle, pant for **8** languish **9** hunger for, waste away **11** have a yen for, thirst after **12** fail in health

pine 5 Pinus
varieties: **3** air, nut, red **4** blue, chir, gray, hoop, Huon, Imou, Jack **5** beach, cedar, Cuban, Emodi, giant, house, Kauri, pitch, Scots, screw, scrub, shore, slash, stone, sugar, white **6** Aleppo, Apache, Bhutan, Bishop, celery, Dammar, digger, ground, Jersey, Korean, limber, Mallee, Norway, Parana, Pinyon, Scotch, spruce, Torrey, Totara, yellow **7** Amboina, Benguet, big-cone, Chilean, Chinese, cluster, Cypress, Formosa, Georgia, Gerard's, hickory, jointed, long-tag, poverty, prickly, prince's, running, Soledad **8** Austrian, Buddhist, cow's-tail, knob-cone, lacebark, Loblolly, longleaf, mahogany, Monterey, mountain, Nepal nut, oldfield, princess, umbrella **9** Brazilian, Calabrian, Chilghoza, Jerusalem, lodgepole, Oyster Bay, shortleaf, white-bark **10** Australian, Bunyabunya, dwarf stone, Macedonian, Moreton Bay, red cypress, Swiss stone, Tenasserim **11** African fern, bristlecone, common screw, Japanese red, Parry pinyon, Port Jackson, thatch screw, twisted-leaf, Veitch screw **12** black cypress, Canary Island, Chinese water, eastern white, frankincense, Italian stone, Mexican stone, Mexican white, two-leaved nut, western white **13** dwarf Siberian, Japanese black, Japanese white, Mexican yellow, New Caledonian, Norfolk Island, Swiss mountain, table mountain **14** Himalayan white, Rottnest Island, southern yellow **15** Mueller's cypress **16** Japanese umbrella, single-leaf pinyon **18** Rough-barked Mexican **19** Rocky Mountain yellow

Pine Tree State
nickname of: **5** Maine

pin hope on 6 bank on **7** count on, long for, wish for **8** aspire to, yearn for **10** anticipate

pink 8 Dianthus
varieties: **3** Sea **4** fire, moss, pine, rose, wild **5** cameo, clove, dairy, grass, marsh, swamp **6** button, ground, indian, Kirtle, maiden **7** cheddar, cottage, cushion, Mullein, rainbow **8** Childing, Deptford, election **11** cluster-head **13** fringed indian, spottle kirtle **16** California indian

pinnacle 3 cap, top **4** acme, apex, peak **5** crest, crown, spire, tower **6** belfry, height, summit, tiptop, vertex, zenith **7** steeple **9** bell tower, campanile

pinochle
also known as: **7** binocle, pinocle **8** penuchle
derived from: **7** bezique
points/game: **11** one thousand
lowest card: **4** nine

pinpoint 3 dot, jot **4** iota, spot **5** speck **6** detail **8** home in on, localize, zero in on **12** characterize

pint
abbreviation of: **2** pt

pinxit 11 he painted it **12** she painted it

pioneer 5 found, start **6** create, father, herald, invent, leader **7** develop, founder **8** colonist, discover, explorer **9** be a leader, developer, establish, harbinger, innovator, precursor **10** antecedent, forerunner, lead the way, pathfinder, show the way **11** establisher, predecessor, trailblazer **12** first settler, frontiersman **13** blaze the trail **14** early immigrant, founding father
Hebrew: **6** halutz **7** chalutz

Pioneers, The
author: **19** James Fenimore Cooper
character: **10** Indian John **11** Judge Temple, Natty Bumppo **13** Oliver Edwards **14** Hiram Doolittle **15** Elizabeth Temple

pious 4 holy **5** godly **6** devout, divine **7** sainted, saintly **8** faithful, reverent, unctuous **9** dedicated, insincere, pietistic, religious, spiritual **10** worshipful **11** reverential **12** hypocritical **13** rationalizing, sanctimonious, self-righteous **14** holier-than-thou

Pip
character in: **17** Great Expectations
author: **7** Dickens

pipe 4 duct, main, peep, sing, tube **5** cheep, chirp, trill, tweet **6** warble **7** conduit, twitter, whistle **8** conveyor **9** conductor **10** play a flute **12** play a bagpipe

Pippa Passes
author: **14** Robert Browning

piquant 3 hot **4** acid, racy **5** peppy, salty, sharp, spicy, tangy, zesty **6** biting, bitter, bright, clever, lively, savory **7** mordant, peppery, pungent, rousing **8** animated, incisive, piercing, spirited, stinging, vigorous **9** sparkling, trenchant **11** interesting, provacative, stimulating **13** scintillating **14** highly seasoned, strong-flavored

pique 3 ire, irk, vex **4** gall, goad, miff, snit, spur, stir **5** annoy, peeve, rouse, spite **6** arouse, excite, grudge, kindle, malice, nettle, offend **7** affront, incense, perturb, provoke, quicken, umbrage **8** disquiet, irritate, vexation **9** annoyance, displease, stimulate **10** discomfort, exasperate, irritation, resentment **11** displeasure, humiliation, ill feelings, indignation **12** exasperation, hurt feelings **13** embarrassment, mortification, put one's back up **14** vindictiveness

piqued 5 angry, riled, vexed **6** galled, miffed, peeved **7** annoyed, aroused, excited, kindled, nettled, stirred **9** affronted, irritated **10** displeased, stimulated

Pirandello, Luigi
  author of: 17 The Old and the Young
  18 Tonight We Improvise 19 The
  Late Mattia Pascal 31 Six Characters
  in Search of an Author

pirate 3 rob 5 steal 6 raider, robber,
  sea dog 7 brigand, corsair, plunder 8
  marauder 9 buccaneer, privateer 10
  freebooter
  flag: 9 blackjack 10 Jolly Roger
  name: 4 Kidd 6 Morgan 7 Lafitte 10
  Blackbeard

Pirate Coast see 18 United Arab Emirates

Pirates of Penzance, The
  author: 9 W S Gilbert
  comic opera by: 18 Gilbert and Sullivan
  character: 4 Kate, Ruth 5 Edith, Mabel 6 Isabel 8 Frederic, Sergeant 10
  Pirate King 14 General Stanley

pis aller 10 last resort 12 last resource

Pisan Cantos
  author: 9 Ezra Pound

Pisanio
  character in: 9 Cymbeline
  author: 11 Shakespeare

Pisces
  symbol: 4 fish
  planet: 7 Jupiter, Neptune
  rules: 7 secrets
  born: 13 February-March

Pisistratus
  tyrant of: 6 Athens
  father: 11 Hippocrates
  son: 7 Hippias 10 Hipparchus

Pissarro, Camille
  born: 8 St Thomas 16 Danish West
  Indies
  artwork: 8 Red Roofs 15 Morning
  Sunlight 21 Lower Norwood Snow
  Scene 28 Peasant Woman with a
  Wheelbarrow

pistol (revolver) 3 gat, gun, rod 4
  colt, iron 5 luger 6 heater, mauser 7
  firearm, sidearm 9 automatic, derringer 20 Saturday night special

pit 3 dip, nut 4 dent, hole, nick, pock,
  scar, seed 5 gouge, gully, match,
  notch, stone 6 cavity, crater, dimple,
  furrow, hollow, indent, kernel, oppose, trough 7 scratch 8 contrast,
  pockmark 9 concavity, juxtapose 10
  depression, set against 11 indentation

Pit, The
  author: 11 Frank Norris

Pit and the Pendulum, The
  author: 13 Edgar Allan Poe

pitch 3 bob, dip, fix, lob, set, shy, top
  4 apex, cant, cast, fall, fire, hurl, jerk,
  jolt, peak, rock, tone, toss 5 angle,
  chuck, crown, erect, fling, grade,
  heave, level, lurch, place, plant, point,
  raise, set up, shake, slant, sling,
  slope, sound, throw 6 degree, height,
  let fly, locate, plunge, propel, settle,
  summit, topple, tumble, zenith 7 bobbing, incline, rocking, station 8 delivery, harmonic, lurching, pinnacle, undulate 9 declivity, establish, oscillate
10 undulation 11 oscillation 12 fall
headlong
  speed of: 9 vibration

pitcher 3 jar, jug 4 ewer 6 carafe 8 decanter 9 container 10 spitballer
  and catcher: 7 battery
  award: 7 Cy Young
  brother duo: 4 Dean 5 Perry 6
  Niekro
  Hall of Famer: 4 Dean, Ford, Wynn 5
  Young 6 Hunter, Koufax, Palmer,
  Willis 7 Carlton, Fingers 8 Drysdale
  9 Newhouser
  left-hander: 8 southpaw
  relief staff: 7 bullpen
  reliever: 7 fireman

pitch in 5 begin 7 share in 8 take part
  9 cooperate, get to work, join hands
  10 act jointly, contribute, get started
  11 collaborate, participate 12 make an
  effort, pull together, work together

pitch into 5 fly at 6 assail, have at 7
  assault, set upon

piteous 3 sad 6 moving, woeful 7 pitiful 8 pathetic, pitiable, poignant,
  touching 9 affecting 10 deplorable 11
  distressing 12 heart-rending 13 heartbreaking

pitfall 4 risk, trap 5 peril, snare 6 ambush, danger, hazard 7 springe 8
  quagmire 9 booby trap, quicksand 14
  stumbling block

pith 4 core, gist, meat 5 heart, point 7
  essence, meaning 12 significance

pithy 5 terse 6 cogent 7 concise 8
  forceful, succinct 9 effective, trenchant 10 expressive, meaningful, to the
  point 12 concentrated

pitiful 3 sad 4 poor 5 sorry 6 abject,
  measly, moving, paltry, shabby 7
  doleful, forlorn, piteous 8 dreadful,
  god- awful, mournful, pathetic, pitiable, poignant, touching, wretched 9
  miserable, plaintive, worthless 10
  abominable, despicable, lamentable
  11 distressing 12 arousing pity, contemptible, heartrending

pitiless 5 cruel 6 brutal 7 inhuman,
  unmoved 8 ruthless, uncaring 9 heartless, merciless, unpitying, unsparing
  untouched 10 implacable, relentless,
  unmerciful 11 cold-blooded, hardhearted, indifferent, insensitive, unrelenting

pittance 4 mite 5 crumb 6 little, trifle
  7 minimum, modicum, smidgen

Pittsburgh
  baseball team: 7 Pirates
  feature: 14 Fort Pitt Museum 15 Buhl
  Planetarium
  football team: 8 Steelers
  formerly: 8 Fort Pitt 12 Fort Duquesne
  hockey team: 8 Penguins
noted for: 5 steel
  river: 4 Ohio 9 Allegheny 11 Monongahela
  university: 8 Duquesne 14 Carnegie-
  Mellon

Pittypat, Aunt
  character in: 15 Gone With the Wind
  author: 8 Mitchell

pituitary
  located in: 5 brain
  known as: 11 master gland

pity 5 mercy, shame 6 lament, lenity,
  regret 7 charity, feel for, weep for 8
  bleed for, clemency, humanity, leniency, sad thing, sympathy 10 compassion, condolence, indulgence, kindliness, tenderness 11 crying shame,
  forbearance, magnanimity 12 feel
  sorry for 13 commiseration

piu
  music: 4 more

pivot 4 axis, axle, hang, rely, spin,
  turn 5 focus, hinge, twirl, wheel,
  whirl 6 center, circle, depend, rotate,
  swivel 7 fulcrum, hinge on, revolve 9
  pirouette

pivotal 5 vital 7 crucial 8 critical, decisive 9 climactic 11 determining

pivotal point 4 axis 12 turning point
  13 crucial moment

pixie, pixy 3 elf 5 fairy 6 sprite 10
  leprechaun

pizazz 5 flair, vigor, style 6 energy,
  spirit 8 vitality

pizzicato
  music: 21 plucked instead of bowed
  abbreviation: 4 pizz

placable 7 lenient 8 flexible, tolerant,
  yielding 9 indulgent, relenting 10 ap-
  peasable, forbearing 12 reconcilable

placard 4 bill, sign 6 notice, poster 8
  bulletin 13 advertisement

placate 4 calm, lull 5 quiet 6 pacify,
  soothe 7 appease, assuage, mollify,
  win over 9 alleviate 10 conciliate,
  propitiate

placatory 9 appeasing, pacifying 10
  mollifying 12 conciliatory 13 accommodative

place 3 fix, job, put, set 4 area, city,
  digs, duty, farm, firm, home, land,
  plot, post, rank, rest, shop, site, spot,
  town, zone 5 abode, affix, array,
  berth, house, lodge, niche, plant,
  point, ranch, space, stand, state, store,
  venue 6 assign, attach, county, harbor, invest, locale, locate, office, region, settle 7 appoint, borough, company, concern, country, deposit,
  install, quarter, shelter, situate, station, village 8 building, business, classify, district, domicile, dwelling, ensconce, find hire, function, identify,
  locality, location, lodgings, position,
  premises, property, province, quarters,
  remember, standing, township, vicin-

ity **9** recognize, residence, situation, territory **10** commission, get a job for, habitation **11** appointment, find work for, whereabouts **12** neighborhood **13** establishment
Latin: 4 situ

Place in the Sun, A
 director: 13 George Stevens
 based on novel by: 15 Theodore Dreiser (An American Tragedy)
 cast: 14 Keefe Brasselle, Shelley Winters **15** Elizabeth Taylor, Montgomery Clift
 Oscar for: 5 score **9** direction **10** screenplay

placement 8 grouping, location **10** assignment, employment **11** arrangement, disposition, positioning

place of residence 4 home **5** abode, house **7** address, lodging **8** domicile, dwelling **9** residence **10** habitation **14** living quarters

place to stand on
 Greek: 6 pou sto

place upright 5 erect, raise **7** stand up

placid 4 calm, mild **5** quiet **6** gentle, poised, serene, smooth **7** pacific, restful **8** composed, peaceful, tranquil **9** collected, unexcited, unruffled **10** untroubled **11** undisturbed, unexcitable **13** imperturbable, self-possessed **15** undemonstrative

plague 3 irk, vex, woe **4** bane, evil, fret, gall, pain, pest **5** agony, chafe, curse, harry, haunt, peeve, worry **6** badger, blight, bother, burden, cancer, harass, misery, nettle **7** afflict, disturb, perturb, scourge, torment, trouble **8** aggrieve, calamity, disquiet, distress, hardship, pandemic **9** embarrass, persecute, suffering **10** affliction, Black Death, pestilence, visitation
French: 5 peste

Plague, The
 author: 11 Albert Camus
 character: 7 Rambert **10** Jean Tarrou **11** Joseph Grand **14** Father Paneloux, Raymond Cottard **15** Dr Bernard R Rieux

plain 4 bald, bare, open **5** blunt, clear, frank, naked, vivid **6** candid, common, direct, homely, honest, modest, simple **7** average, glaring, legible, obscure, obvious, plateau, prairie, sincere, visible **8** apparent, clear-cut, distinct, everyday, explicit, manifest, ordinary, palpable, specific, straight, striking, uncomely, unlovely **9** grassland, outspoken, prominent, tableland, unadorned, undiluted **10** forthright, pronounced, unaffected, unassuming, unhandsome, unreserved, well-marked **11** commonplace, conspicuous, discernible, not striking, open country, outstanding, plain-spoken, unambigu-

ous, undecorated, undisguised, unequivocal, ungarnished, unvarnished, well-defined **12** matter-of- fact, not beautiful, unattractive, unmistakable, unornamented **13** unembellished, unpretentious, without frills **14** comprehensible, understandable **15** straightforward, undistinguished

plainly 6 baldly, openly, simply **7** bluntly, clearly, frankly, visibly, vividly **8** candidly, directly, honestly, markedly, modestly **9** doubtless, obviously **10** apparently, definitely, distinctly, explicitly, manifestly, ordinarily, positively, strikingly, undeniably **11** beyond doubt, discernibly, prominently, undoubtedly **12** unaffectedly, unassumingly, unmistakably, without doubt **13** conspicuously, unambiguously, unequivocably **14** comprehensibly, unquestionably

plainness 10 homeliness, simplicity **12** ordinariness

plainspoken 4 open **5** bluff, blunt, frank, plain **6** candid, direct, honest **7** genuine, sincere **8** explicit, straight **9** open-faced, outspoken, unsparing **10** above board, forthright, point-blank **11** straight-out **15** straightforward

plaint 3 cry, sob **4** beef, moan, wail **5** gripe **6** charge, grouse, grudge, lament, regret, squawk **7** grumble, reproof **8** reproach **9** complaint, grievance, objection **10** accusation, resentment **12** remonstrance

plaintive 3 sad **6** rueful **7** doleful, moaning, piteous, pitiful, tearful **8** dolorous, grievous, mournful, pathetic, wretched **9** lamenting, sorrowful, woebegone **10** lugubrious, melancholy **12** heartrending

plait 5 braid, queue, twine, twist, weave **7** pigtail **10** intertwine

plan 3 aim, map, way **4** form, idea, plot **5** frame, shape **6** design, devise, intend, lay out, map out, method, scheme, sketch **7** diagram, outline, prepare, program, project, propose, purpose **8** block out, conceive, contrive, organize, proposal, strategy, think out **9** blueprint, fabricate, procedure, stratagem **10** conception, suggestion **11** proposition
French: 8 demarche

Planchet
 character in: 18 The Three Musketeers
 author: 5 Dumas (pere)

Planck, Max
 field: 7 physics
 nationality: 6 German
 developed: 13 quantum theory **15** Planck's constant
 awarded: 10 Nobel Prize

plane 3 jet **4** bird, flat **5** level, plumb **6** degree, status **7** regular, station **8** aircraft, airplane, position, standing **9**

condition, elevation
type: 4 jack **5** block

planet, planets 13 celestial body
 first: 7 Mercury
 second: 5 Venus
 third: 5 Earth
  satellite: 4 Moon
 fourth: 4 Mars
  satellite: 6 Deimos, Phobos
  nickname: 9 Red Planet
 fifth: 7 Jupiter
  satellite: 2 Io **6** Europa **8** Amalthea, Callisto, Ganymede
  characteristic: 7 red spot
 sixth: 6 Saturn
  satellite: 4 Rhea **5** Dione, Janus, Mimas, Titan **6** Phoebe, Tethys **7** Iapetus **8** Hyperion **9** Enceladus
  characteristic: 5 rings
 seventh: 6 Uranus
  satellite: 5 Ariel **6** Oberon **7** Miranda, Titania, Umbriel
  color: 9 blue-green
  characteristic: 5 rings
 eighth: 7 Neptune
  satellite: 6 Nereid, Triton
  color: 5 green
 ninth: 5 Pluto
  satellite: 6 Charon
 asteroid/minor planet/planetoid: 4 Eros, Juno **5** Ceres, Vesta **6** Chiron, Hermes, Icarus, Pallas **7** Astraea, Hidalgo

planetary 6 astral **7** earthly **9** celestial **11** terrestrial **12** astronomical

Planet of the Apes
 director: 18 Franklin J Schaffner
 based on novel by: 12 Pierre Boulle
 cast: 9 Kim Hunter **12** Maurice Evans **13** Roddy McDowall **14** Charlton Heston
 script: 10 Rod Serling

plank 4 deal, deck, slab **5** board, shole, stone **8** platform

planned 7 devised, schemed **8** designed, expected, foreseen, intended, prepared **9** mapped out, organized, projected, rehearsed **10** calculated, purposeful, thought out **11** intentional, prearranged, prepared for **12** premeditated

planner 6 author, framer **7** creator, deviser **8** arranger, designer **9** architect, organizer

plant 4 bush, herb, mill, moss, shop, slip, tree, vine, weed, wort, yard **5** algae, flora, fungi, grass, set in, shrub, works **6** flower, foster, infuse, set out **7** factory, foundry, herbage, implant, inspire, instill, scatter, sow seed **8** business, engender, seedling **9** broadcast, cultivate, establish, inculcate, propagate, vegetable **10** transplant, vegetation **13** establishment, sow the seeds of **14** put in the ground

plaster 4 coat, daub, sand **5** grout, smear **6** bedaub, gypsum, lather,

stucco **7** overlay, spackle
mixture of: 4 lime **5** water **6** gypsum

plastered 5 drunk **6** coated, daubed, soused **7** covered, crocked, smeared, swacked **8** mortared, polluted, stuccoed **10** inebriated **11** intoxicated

plastic 4 soft **6** pliant, supple **7** ductile, elastic, pliable **8** flexible, formable, moldable, shapable, yielding **9** malleable, tractable

plate 4 dish **6** saucer **7** helping, platter, portion, serving **10** platterful **11** serving dish

plateau 4 mesa **5** table **6** upland **8** highland **9** tableland

platform 4 dais, goal, plan **5** creed, plank, stage, stand **6** podium, policy, pulpit, tenets **7** program, rostrum

Plath, Sylvia
author of: 5 Ariel **10** The Bell Jar

platinum
chemical symbol: 2 Pt

platitude 3 saw **6** cliche, old saw, truism **7** bromide **8** banality, chestnut **11** commonplace

platitudinous 5 banal, corny, stale, tired, trite, vapid **6** jejune **8** bromidic, ordinary **9** hackneyed **10** pedestrian, unexciting, unoriginal **12** cliche-ridden, conventional **13** unimaginative

Plato
author of: 4 Laws **5** Crito **6** Phaedo **7** Apology, Gorgias, Sophist, Timaeus **8** Philebus, Republic **9** Symposium **10** Parmenides

platoon 4 band, body, crew, team, unit **5** corps, force, group **10** detachment

platter 4 dish, disk, lanx **6** salver **7** record **8** trencher **9** recording

plaudit, plaudits 4 rave **5** cheer, kudos **6** hurrah, huzzah, praise **7** acclaim, bouquet, ovation **8** applause, approval, cheering **10** compliment, hallelujah **11** approbation **12** commendation

plauditory 8 admiring, praising **9** extolling, laudatory, praiseful **12** commendatory **13** complimentary

plausible 5 sound, valid **6** likely **7** logical, tenable **8** credible, feasible, possible, probable, rational, sensible **10** acceptable, believable, convincing, persuasive, reasonable **11** conceivable, justifiable

Plautus
author of: 7 Stichus **8** Mercator **9** Amphitruo, Menaechmi, Pseudolus **10** Amphitryon **14** Miles Gloriosus

play 3 act, fun, toy **4** jest, lark, romp, room, show **5** antic, caper, drama, enact, farce, frisk, revel, space, sport, sweep, swing **6** act out, cavort, comedy, frolic, gambol, leeway, trifle **7** disport, have fun, pageant, perform, skylark, tragedy, vie with **8** pleasure,

take part **9** amusement, diversion, elbowroom, enjoyment, make merry, melodrama, perform on, personify, represent, spectacle **10** recreation **11** impersonate, merrymaking

playboy 4 rake, wolf **5** Romeo, sheik **6** lecher **7** Don Juan, swinger **8** Casanova, hedonist, Lothario, party boy **9** jet-setter, ladies' man, partygoer, womanizer **10** lady-killer, profligate **14** pleasure seeker **15** good-time Charlie

Playboy of the Western World, The
author: 19 John Millington Synge
character: 8 Old Mahon **9** Widow Quin **10** Shawn Keogh **16** Christopher Mahon, Margaret Flaherty (Pegeen)

play down 9 underplay **11** de-emphasize

played out 4 beat **5** all in, spent, weary **6** bushed, done in, pooped **7** drained, wearied, worn out **8** depleted, dog tired, fatigued, tired out, unreeled **9** dead tired, exhausted

player 4 jock, mime **5** actor **6** mummer **7** actress, athlete, trouper **8** gamester, opponent, thespian **9** adversary, contender, performer **10** antagonist, competitor, contestant, team member **11** entertainer, participant

play false 4 dupe **5** trick **6** betray **7** deceive, two-time **10** be disloyal **12** be unfaithful **13** be treacherous

playfellow 3 pal **4** chum **5** buddy **6** friend **8** playmate

playful 6 frisky, impish, lively **7** amusing, coltish, jesting, waggish **8** humorous, mirthful, prankish, sportive **9** fun-loving, sprightly **10** capricious, frolicsome, rollicking **12** lighthearted
French: 8 espiegle

play host 4 host **9** entertain **10** give a party, have guests **13** keep open house

playing field 4 bowl **5** arena **7** diamond, stadium **8** gridiron **10** playground **12** amphitheater

playing piece 3 man **4** disk **5** piece **7** counter

play in water 3 dip **4** swim **6** dabble, paddle, splash

play Judas 6 betray **7** sell out, two-time **9** play false **11** double-cross

playmate 3 pal **4** chum **5** buddy **6** friend **9** playfellow

play of spirit
French: 10 jeu d'esprit

play on words
French: 3 pun **9** jeu de mots

plaything 3 toy **4** dupe **5** patsy, sport **6** bauble, trifle **9** diversion

play truant 3 cut **4** skip **8** be absent **9** play hooky

play with 5 bandy **7** torment, toy with **11** have fun with

playwright 6 author, writer **9** dramatist, scenarist **10** dramatizer, dramaturge, librettist, play doctor **12** dramatic poet, dramaturgist, scriptwriter **13** melodramatist

plea 4 suit **5** alibi **6** appeal, excuse, prayer **7** apology, begging, defense, pretext, request **8** argument, entreaty, petition **10** adjuration, beseeching **11** explanation, extenuation, vindication **12** solicitation, supplication **13** justification

plead 3 ask, beg **6** adjure, enjoin **7** beseech, entreat, implore, request, solicit **8** appeal to, petition **9** importune **10** supplicate

pleader 6 beggar **8** advocate, defender, implorer **9** apologist, beseecher **10** importuner, supplicant

plead with 3 beg **4** pray **6** adjure **7** beseech, implore **10** supplicate

Pleasance, Donald
born: 7 England, Worksop
roles: 12 The Caretaker **14** The Great Escape **16** You Only Live Twice **17** The Eagle Has Landed **24** The Greatest Story Ever Told

pleasant 4 fine, good, mild, nice, soft, warm **6** genial, gentle, lovely, polite **7** affable, amiable, cordial, likable, tactful **8** amicable, charming, cheerful, friendly, inviting, pleasing, sociable **9** agreeable, congenial, enjoyable **10** attractive, felicitous, gratifying, gregarious, satisfying **11** good-humored, good-natured, pleasurable **13** companionable

Pleasant Island see **5** Nauru

pleasantry 4 jape, jest, joke, quip **5** sally **6** bon mot **8** greeting **9** wisecrack, witticism **10** salutation

pleasant-tasting 4 mild **5** sweet, tasty **6** savory **8** luscious **9** delicious, palatable, succulent **10** appetizing, delectable **11** scrumptious **13** mouthwatering

please 3 opt **4** like, suit, want, will, wish **5** amuse, charm, elate, elect **6** choose, desire, divert, prefer, thrill, tickle **7** content, delight, gladden, gratify, satisfy **8** enthrall, entrance **9** enrapture, entertain, fascinate, make happy **10** be inclined **14** give pleasure to
French: 12 s'il vous plait
German: 5 bitte
Spanish: 8 por favor

pleased 4 glad **5** happy, proud **6** elated **8** thrilled **9** delighted, gratified

please reply
French: 4 rsvp **20** repondez s'il vous plait

pleasing 6 genial, polite **7** affable, amiable, amusing, likable, winning **8** charming, cheerful, friendly, inviting,

mannerly 9 agreeable, congenial, diverting, enjoyable 10 attractive, delightful, gladdening, gratifying, satisfying 11 captivating, fascinating, good-humored, good- natured, pleasurable 12 entertaining, well-mannered

pleasing inactivity
Italian: 14 dolce far niente

pleasurable 8 pleasing 9 agreeable, enjoyable 10 delightful

pleasure 3 fun, joy 4 like, will, wish 5 bliss, cheer, mirth 6 choice, desire, gaiety, option 7 delight, elation, rapture 9 amusement, diversion, enjoyment, festivity, happiness, merriment, selection 10 exultation, jubilation, preference, recreation 11 high spirits, inclination 13 entertainment, gratification 15 beer and skittles 16 lightheartedness
goddess of: 8 Voluptas

pleasure-giving 7 amusing 8 pleasing 9 agreeable, enjoyable 10 delightful 11 pleasurable 12 entertaining

Pleasure of His Company, The
author: 19 Cornelia Otis Skinner

pleasure trip 4 tour 5 jaunt 6 outing 8 vacation 9 excursion

pleat 4 fold 5 crimp, frill 6 crease

pleated 6 fluted, folded 7 creased, crimped 10 corrugated

plebeian 3 low 4 base, mean 5 banal 6 coarse, common, vulgar 7 lowborn, lowbrow, popular 8 commoner, everyman, low-class, ordinary 9 bourgeois, common man, unrefined 10 average man, uncultured 11 bourgeoisie, commonplace, proletarian 12 uncultivated

plebs 5 demos 6 masses 7 commons 8 populace 9 commoners, hoi polloi, plebeians 11 bourgeoisie 12 common people

plecoptera
class: 8 hexapoda
phylum: 10 arthropoda
group: 8 stone fly

pledge 3 vow 4 bail, bond, oath, pact, pawn, word 5 swear, troth 6 assert, avowal, surety 7 compact, promise, warrant 8 contract, covenant, guaranty, security, warranty 9 agreement, assurance, guarantee 10 adjuration, collateral

Pleiades
father: 5 Atlas
mother: 7 Pleione
half-sisters: 6 Hyades
names: 4 Maia 6 Merope 7 Alcyone, Celaeno, Electra, Sterope, Taygete
number of daughters: 5 seven

plenary 4 full 6 entire 7 perfect 8 absolute, complete

plenitude 4 glut, heap, mass 5 flood 6 bounty, plenty, wealth 7 quality, surfeit, surplus 8 fullness, plethora, totality 9 abundance, amplitude, profu-

sion, repletion, wholeness 10 cornucopia, entireness, quantities 11 ample supply, copiousness, full measure, sufficiency 12 completeness 14 more than enough

plenteous 6 lavish 7 copious, profuse 8 abundant 9 bountiful, plentiful

plentiful 4 lush 5 ample, large 6 lavish 7 copious, liberal, profuse 8 abundant, generous, infinite, prolific 9 abounding, bounteous, bountiful, plenteous, unsparing, unstinted 11 overflowing 13 inexhaustible

plenty 4 gobs, lots, slew 5 scads 6 luxury, oceans, oodles, riches, wealth, worlds 8 opulence 9 abundance, affluence, good times, great deal, plenitude, profusion, well-being 10 prosperity 11 ample amount, good fortune, sufficiency 12 a full measure
goddess of: 3 Ops

plethora 4 glut 5 flood 6 excess, wealth 7 overage, surfeit, surplus 8 fullness 9 abundance, amplitude, plenitude, profusion 10 oversupply, redundancy, surplusage 11 superfluity 13 overabundance 14 more than enough, superabundance

pliable 5 lithe 6 limber, pliant, supple 7 elastic, plastic, springy, willing 8 flexible, yielding 9 adaptable, compliant, receptive, resilient, tractable 10 manageable, responsive, submissive 11 acquiescent 13 accommodating 14 easily bendable, impressionable

pliancy 8 docility, meekness, yielding 9 passivity 10 compliance, pliability, submission, suppleness 11 flexibility 12 complaisance

pliant 4 meek 6 supple 7 pliable 8 flexible, yielding 9 compliant 10 submissive 11 deferential

pliers
type: 10 fixed-joint 11 combination, needle-nosed, side- cutting 17 offset combination

plight 3 fix, jam 5 pinch, state, trial 6 crisis, muddle, pickle, scrape 7 dilemma, impasse, straits, trouble 8 distress, exigency 9 condition, emergency, extremity, situation 10 difficulty 11 predicament, tribulation, vicissitude 12 circumstance

Plisthenes
brother/half-brother: 8 Menelaus 9 Agamemnon
father: 6 Atreus
mother: 6 Cleola
sister/half-sister: 8 Anaxibia
sister-in-law: 12 Clytemnestra
uncle: 8 Thyestes

plod 4 drag, grub, moil, plug, slog, toil 5 grind, sweat, tramp 6 drudge, lumber, trudge, waddle 7 peg away, shuffle 8 struggle 9 persevere

plodding 4 dull 6 clumsy 8 trudging 9 laborious 10 pedestrian

plot 3 lot, map 4 area, draw, mark, plan, tale, yarn 5 chart, draft, field, patch, space, story, tract 6 action, design, scheme, sketch 7 collude, compute, diagram, outline, section 8 clearing, conspire, contrive, evil plan, intrigue, maneuver 9 blueprint, calculate, determine, incidents, narrative, story line, stratagem 10 conspiracy, secret plan 11 machination

plotting 4 wily 6 artful, crafty 7 cunning 8 scheming 9 conniving, designing 10 intriguing

Plough and the Stars, The
author: 10 Sean O'Casey

plover
group of: 4 wing 12 congregation

plow, plough 3 cut, dig 4 push, till, work 5 break, dig up, drive, forge, press, shove, spade 6 furrow, harrow, loosen, plunge, turn up 7 break up 8 bulldoze 9 cultivate
invented by:
cast iron: 7 Ransome
disc: 5 Hardy

plowable 6 arable 7 friable 8 farmable, tillable 10 cultivable

Plowright, Joan
born: 5 Brigg 7 England
husband: 15 Laurence Olivier
roles: 13 A Taste of Honey 14 The Entertainer

ploy 4 game, ruse, wile 5 trick 6 design, gambit, scheme, tactic 7 gimmick 8 artifice, maneuver, strategy 9 stratagem 10 subterfuge

pluck 4 draw, grab, grit, guts, jerk, pick, sand, yank 5 spunk, valor 6 daring, mettle, pull at, snatch, spirit, uproot 7 bravery, courage, pull off, pull out, resolve 8 boldness, temerity, tenacity 9 extirpate, fortitude 10 doggedness, resolution 11 persistence 12 perseverance 13 determination

pluck out 7 extract, pick out, pull out

plucky 4 bold, game 5 brave, gutsy 6 daring, spunky 7 doughty, valiant 8 fearless, intrepid, spirited, unafraid, valorous 9 audacious, dauntless, undaunted 10 courageous, mettlesome 11 lionhearted, unflinching 12 stouthearted

plug 4 bung, cork 5 close, stuff 6 fill up, stanch, stop up 7 shut off, stopper, stopple

plug up 3 dam 4 clog, plug 5 block, choke, dam up, stuff 6 stop up 7 congest 8 obstruct

plum
varieties: 3 hog 4 Coco, date, Duhr, gage, Java, sand, sloe, wild 5 beach, black, goose, Islay, Jaman, Lansa, Moxie, nanny, Natal, shore, Simon 6 August, Batoko, Canada, Cheney, cherry, common, Damson, ground, Indian, Jambul, Kaffir, Kelsey, Lomboy, Pigeon, Sapote, Sierra, Sisson 7

apricot, Burbank, Cheston, Jambosa, Malabar, Orleans, Pacific, Spanish, Wickson **8** American, Assyrian, Burdekin, European, Hortulan, Jambolan, Japanese, Oklahoma, Prunello, Victoria **9** Allegheny, Chickasaw, Governor's, greengage, marmalade, Myrobalan, wild-goose **10** Madagascar **13** Queensland hog

plumb 4 lead, test, true **5** gauge, level, probe, sheer, sound **6** fathom **7** examine, measure, plummet **8** plumb bob, straight, vertical **9** penetrate

plume 3 pen **4** down **5** egret, pique, preen, pride, prize, quill **7** feather
military: **7** panache

Plumed Serpent, The
author: **10** D H Lawrence

Plummer, Christopher
real name: **28** Arthur Christopher Orme Plummer
born: **6** Canada **7** Toronto
wife: **11** Tammy Grimes **12** Elaine Taylor
roles: **14** Murder by Decree **15** The Sound of Music **18** Baron Georg von Trapp **20** The Man Who Would Be King **25** The Return of the Pink Panther

plummet 4 dive, fall **6** plunge, tumble **8** nosedive **12** fall headlong

plump 4 drop, firm, flop, plop, sink **5** blunt, buxom, obese, plunk, pudgy, solid, spill, stout **6** abrupt, chubby, direct, fleshy, portly, rotund, sprawl, stocky, tumble **7** rounded **8** collapse, outright **9** corpulent

plumpness
French: **10** embonpoint

plunder 3 rob **4** haul, loot, raid, sack, swag, take **5** booty, rifle, prize, strip **6** fleece, maraud, pilfer, ravage, spoils **7** despoil, pillage, ransack, takings **9** filchings **10** pilferings

plunderer 6 looter, vandal **7** brigand **8** pillager **9** despoiler

plunge 3 dip, fly, run **4** bolt, cast, dart, dash, dive, drop, duck, fall, jerk, roll, jump, leap, push, reel, rock, rush, sink, sway, tear, toss **5** douse, drive, heave, lunge, lurch, pitch, press, shoot, speed, surge, swarm, whisk **6** charge, hasten, hurtle, hustle, scurry, sprint, streak, thrust, tumble **7** descend, immerse, scuttle **8** scramble, submerge, submerse **12** fall headlong

plunk 4 pick, thud **5** pluck, plumb, strum, twang **6** dollar **7** exactly **8** squarely **9** precisely

plurality 4 bulk, most **8** majority **13** preponderance

plus 5 added, extra, other, spare **6** useful **7** helpful **9** auxiliary, desirable **10** additional, beneficial **12** advantageous, supplemental **13** supplementary

plush 4 lush, posh, rich **5** fancy, grand, ritzy, swank, thick **6** classy, deluxe, lavish, snazzy, swanky **7** elegant, opulent **8** palatial **9** luxurious, sumptuous **11** extravagant

plushy 4 soft **5** cushy, swank **7** opulent, velvety **9** luxurious, sumptuous

Plutarch
author of: **13** Parallel Lives

Plutarch's Lives
author: **8** Plutarch

Pluto
also: **5** Hades
god of: **10** underworld
corresponds to: **3** Dis **5** Orcus **8** Dis Pater

Pluto
position: **5** ninth
satellite: **6** Charon

plutocrat 5 mogul **6** fat cat, tycoon **9** financier **10** capitalist

plutonic 7 abyssal, igneous **9** cimmerian, intrusive, vulcanian

plutonium
chemical symbol: **2** Pu

Plutus
author: **12** Aristophanes
character: **5** Cario **9** Chremylus **11** Blepsidemus
god of: **6** wealth

Plutus
personifies: **6** wealth
father: **6** Iasion
mother: **7** Demeter

Pluvius
epithet of: **7** Jupiter
realm: **4** rain

ply 3 fly, run **4** leaf, sail, work **5** layer, offer, plait, plate, press, sheet, slice, twist, wield **6** employ, follow, handle, lamina, pursue, sheath, strand, supply **7** besiege, carry on, labor at, operate, stratum, utilize **8** exercise, navigate, practice, put to use, urge upon **9** thickness **10** manipulate

poach 3 rob **4** cook **5** shirr, steal **6** plunge, simmer **7** trample **8** encroach, trespass

pocket 3 bag, get, pit **4** gain, lode, sack, vein **5** pouch, purse, pygmy, small, steal, strip, usurp **6** attain, bantam, cavity, come by, hollow, little, obtain, pilfer, strain, streak **7** chamber, compact, handbag, placket, receive **8** arrogate, envelope, portable **9** miniature **10** diminutive, receptacle **11** appropriate, compartment

Pocket, Herbert
character in: **17** Great Expectations
author: **7** Dickens

pocketbook 3 bag **5** pouch, purse **6** clutch, wallet **7** handbag, satchel **8** moneybag, notecase **9** coin purse **10** money purse **11** shoulder bag
French: **12** porte-monnaie

pocket flask 5 flask **6** bottle **7** canteen

pocket-sized 3 wee **4** tiny **5** dwarf, pygmy, small **6** bantam, little, midget, minute, petite **7** compact **9** miniature **10** diminutive, vest-pocket

poco
music: **6** little

Pocock, Mamie
character in: **14** The Ambassadors
author: **5** James

pod 4 case, hull, husk **5** shell **6** jacket, sheath **8** pericarp, seed case **10** seed vessel

Podgorica
capital of: **10** Montenegro
once called: Titograd

podium 4 dais, foot, wall **5** stipe **7** lectern **8** pedestal, platform **9** footstalk

Poe, Edgar Allan
author of: **6** Ligeia **7** Israfel, To Helen **8** The Bells, The Raven **10** Annabel Lee, The Gold Bug **18** The Purloined Letter **20** The Cask of Amontillado, The Pit and the Pendulum **22** The Masque of the Red Death **24** The Fall of the House of Usher, The Murders in the Rue Morgue **29** The Narrative of Arthur Gordon Pym

Poeas
also: **5** Poias
lit: **11** funeral pyre
pyre of: **8** Hercules
son: **11** Philoctetes

poem 3 lay, ode **4** epic, song **5** elegy, idyll, lyric, rhyme, verse **6** ballad, jingle, sonnet **8** doggerel, limerick, madrigal

Poema del Cid see **6** The Cid

Poems Chiefly in the Scottish Dialect
author: **11** Robert Burns

poet 4 bard **5** maker **6** lyrist, rhymer, singer **7** reciter **8** lyricist, minstrel, verseman **9** balladeer, balladist, poetaster, rhymester, sonneteer, versifier **10** improviser, librettist, songwriter

poetaster 4 bard, poet **6** rhymer, writer **8** poetizer, rimester **9** rhymester, versifier

poetic, poetical 5 lyric **7** lilting, lyrical, melodic, musical **8** metrical, rhythmic, songlike **9** melodious **11** imaginative

Poetics
author: **9** Aristotle

poetizer 4 bard, poet **6** rhymer, writer **8** rhymster **9** poetaster, versifier

poetry 5 poesy, rhyme, verse **13** versification
god of: **4** Odin, Ogma **5** Brage, Bragi, Othin **6** Apollo **7** Phoebus, Pythius **9** Musagetes

Pogo
creator: **9** Walt Kelly
character: **9** Porkypine, Wiley Catt **10** Boll Weevil **12** PT Bridgeport **13**

Deacon Mushrat, Mole MacCarony
alligator: 6 Albert
fox: 11 Seminole Sam
frog: 15 Moonshine Sonata
hound: 18 Beauregard Bugleboy
possum: 4 Pogo
skunk: 16 Ma'm'selle Hepzibah
snake: 7 Snavely
sorcerer: 10 Howland Owl
turtle/pirate captain: 14 Churchy La Femme
place: 15 Okefenokee Swamp

Pohjola
origin: 7 Finnish
identified with: 7 Lapland
location: 12 North Finland

poignant 3 sad **5** sharp **6** biting, moving, rueful, woeful **7** cutting, doleful, piquant, piteous, pitiful, pungent, tearful **8** grievous, pathetic, piercing, pitiable, touching **9** affecting, sorrowful, trenchant **10** lamentable **11** distressing, penetrating **12** heartrending

poilu
slang: 13 French soldier
in: 9 World War I

point 3 aim, end, hit, nib, run, tip, use **4** apex, bend, bode, core, game, gist, goal, item, mark, meat, pike, pith, spur, time, turn, unit **5** argue, cause, guide, heart, imply, level, limit, place, prong, prove, score, sense, slant, spike, stage, steer, tally, train, value **6** aspect, basket, degree, detail, direct, hint at, kernel, marrow, moment, number, object, reason **7** essence, feature, instant, portend, presage, purpose, quality, signify, suggest, testify **8** indicate, intimate, juncture, main idea, manifest, offshoot, position, sharp end **9** condition, extension, intention, objective, outgrowth **10** foreshadow, particular, projection, prominence, promontory **11** demonstrate **12** protuberance

point-blank 5 blunt **6** direct **10** forthright **11** plainspoken

Point Counter Point
author: 12 Aldous Huxley

point d'appui 4 prop, stay **24** point of battle line support

pointed 5 acute, blunt, sharp **6** biting, direct, peaked, pointy **7** cutting, fitting, hinting, telling **8** accurate, incisive, piercing **9** aciculate, acuminate, cuspidate, pertinent, trenchant **10** emphasized, forthright **11** appropriate, conspicuous, insinuating, penetrating

pointer 3 arm, tip **4** hand, hint **5** arrow, guide, stick **6** needle **7** caution, warning **9** indicator **10** admonition, advisement, suggestion **13** piece of advice **14** recommendation
dog breed: 16 German wirehaired **17** German shorthaired **25** wirehaired pointing griffon

pointless 4 dull **5** blunt **6** absurd, futile, obtuse, stupid **7** aimless, invalid, rounded, unedged, useless **8** bootless, worn down **9** fruitless, illogical, senseless, unpointed, worthless **10** irrational, irrelevant, ridiculous, unavailing **11** ineffectual, meaningless, purposeless, unsharpened **12** inapplicable, preposterous, unproductive, unprofitable, unreasonable

point of view 4 side **5** angle, slant **6** aspect **7** outlook **8** attitude **9** viewpoint **10** standpoint **11** frame of mind, perspective

point the way 5 guide, pilot, usher **6** direct **8** indicate, navigate **14** give directions

point to 5 argue, imply **6** denote **7** express **8** indicate

point up 6 stress **9** emphasize, underline **10** accentuate, underscore

Poirot, Hercule
detective created by: 14 Agatha Christie
nationality: 7 Belgian
famed for: 10 moustaches
phrase: 15 little grey cells
played by: 11 David Suchet (PBS Mystery) **12** Peter Sellers

poise 4 calm **5** raise **6** aplomb **7** balance, elevate **8** presence **9** assurance, composure, hold aloft, sangfroid **10** equanimity **11** savoir faire, self-command, self-control **13** self-assurance **14** presence of mind, self-confidence **15** be in equilibrium

poised 7 assured **8** composed **9** confident **10** controlled **11** self-assured **13** self-possessed

poison 4 bane, evil, harm **5** curse, taint, toxin, venom **6** cancer, canker, debase, defile, impair, infect, plague, weaken **7** corrode, corrupt, degrade, disease, outrage, pollute **8** enormity, make sick **9** malignity **10** adulterate, corruption, debilitate, malignancy, pestilence **11** abomination, contaminate

poisonous 5 fatal, toxic **6** deadly, lethal, mortal **7** baneful, noxious **8** venomous, virulent **10** pernicious **11** deleterious **12** pestilential

Poitier, Sidney
born: 7 Miami FL
wife: 13 Joanna Shimkus
roles: 11 Virgil Tibbs **12** A Patch of Blue, For Love of Ivy, Porgy and Bess **13** To Sir with Love **14** The Defiant Ones **15** A Raisin in the Sun **16** Lilies of the Field (Oscar) **17** They Call Me Mr Tibbs **19** In the Heat of the Night, The Blackboard Jungle, Uptown Saturday Night **23** Guess Who's Coming to Dinner?

Pokanoket see **10** Wampanoags

poke 3 dig, hit, jab **4** butt, drag, gore, idle, jolt, prod, push, stab **5** crawl, dally, delay, mosey, nudge, punch, stick, thump **6** dawdle, fiddle, potter, thrust **7** meander, saunter, shamble, shuffle **8** hang back **10** dillydally **12** shilly-shally

poker
derived from: 5 as nas, gilet **6** brelan **7** primero **11** brouillotte
cards/hand: 4 five **5** seven
bets: 4 ante **5** chips
hand: 4 pair **5** flush **8** straight, two pairs **9** full house **10** royal flush **11** four of a kind **12** three of a kind **13** straight flush
term: 4 ante, call, fold **5** check, raise **6** ante up **7** reraise
variation: 4 draw, stud **5** jacks, Omaha **6** hold em, pai gow **8** jackpots **12** five-card draw **13** seven-card stud

poky, pokey 4 dull, jail, slow **5** dowdy, small **6** dreary, shabby, stodgy, stuffy **7** cramped **8** confined, dawdling, dilatory, frumpish **9** puttering **10** monotonous
creature: 5 sloth, snail **6** turtle **8** slowpoke, tortoise

Poland
other name: 6 Polska **17** the land of the plain
capital/largest city: 6 Warsaw
  medieval capital: 6 Cracow, Krakow
others: 3 Lwo **4** Kodz, Kolo, Lida, Lodz, Lvov, Lyck, Nysa, Oels, Pila **5** Brest, Bytom, Chelm, Dukla, Narev, Opole, Posen, Radom, Sroda, Torun, Vilna **6** Danzig, Elblag, Gdansk, Gdynia, Gnesen, Grodno, Kalisz, Kielce, Kracow, Lublin, Poznan, Tarnow, Zabrze **7** Beuthen, Breslau, Chorzow, Garocin, Gliwice, Litousk, Litovsk, Lyublin, Oleztyn, Stettin, Wroclaw **8** Frombork, Gleiwitz, Katowice, Lidzbark, Liegnitz, Oswiecim, Przemysl, Szczecin, Tarnopol **9** Auschwitz, Bialogard, Bialystok, Bydgoszcz, Sosnowiec, Szcezecin, Walbrzych **11** Czestochowa
school: 6 Warsaw **12** Jagiellonian
division: 7 Galicia, Silesia **8** Podlesia, Volhynia **9** Lithuania, Pomerania
measure: 3 cal **4** mila, pret **5** morga, sazen, vloka, wloka **6** cwierc, cwierk, kwarta, lokiec **7** garniec **9** kwarterka
monetary unit: 4 abia **5** dalar, ducat, grosz, marka, zloty **6** fennig, groszy, gulden, halerz, ko rona **8** groschen
weight: 3 lut **4** funt **6** kamian **7** skrupul
island: 5 Wolin
lake: 5 Goplo, Mamry **8** Niegocin, Sniardwy **13** Stettin Lagoon
mountain: 5 Tatra **6** Beskid **7** Pieniny, Sudeten **9** Beshchady, High Tatra, Holy Cross **10** Carpathian
highest point: 4 Rysy
river: 3 Bug, San **4** Alle, Brda, Gwda,

Lyna, Nysa, Oder, Styr **5** Biala, Drana, Dwina, Narev, Narew, Notec, Podra, Seret, Warta, Wista **6** Neisse, Niemen, Nyeman, Pilica, Pripet, Prosna, Styrpa, Wieprz **7** Nemunas, Vistula, Wistoka **8** Dniester
sea: 6 Baltic
physical feature:
   forest: 10 Bialowieza
   gulf: 6 Danzig, Gdansk
   lagoon: 7 Stettin **12** Frischeshaff
   plain: 7 Silesia
   plateau: 6 Lublin
people: 4 Pole, Slav **5** Mazur **8** Silesian
   astronomer: 10 Copernicus
   author: 7 Reymont **8** Zeromski **10** Mickiewicz, Wyspianski **11** Sienkiewicz
   composer: 6 Chopin **10** Paderewski
   dynasty: 5 Piast **7** Jagello
   king: 7 Casimir **8** Augustus
   leader: 5 Kania **6** Gierek **7** Gomulka, Mieszko **8** Boleslaw **9** Pilsudski, Stanislaw **10** Jaruzel ski, Kosciuszko, Lech Walesa
   pope: 10 John Paul II **20** Cardinal Carol Wojtyla
   queen: 7 Jadwiga
   musician: 7 Kiepura **9** Landowska
   scientist: 5 Curie
language: 6 Kaszub, Polish **10** Pomeranian
religion: 13 Roman Catholic
title: 3 pan **4** pani
place:
   castle: 5 Wawel
   church: 6 St John **10** Panna Maria
   monastery: 9 Jasna Gora
   monument: 17 Heroes of the Ghetto
   national park: 5 Ojcow **10** Bialowieza
   palace: 7 Casimir
feature:
   folk dance: 5 polka **7** mazurka **9** krakowiak, polonaise
   union: 10 Solidarity
food:
   dish: 5 bigos **6** pirogi **7** borscht **7** kolduny
   drink: 5 vodka **7** Krupnik
   sausage: 8 kielbasa
   soup: 7 barszca
Polanski, Roman
   director of: 4 Tess **7** Macbeth **9** Chinatown **13** Rosemary's Baby
polar 3 icy **6** arctic, frigid, wintry **7** glacial, ice-cold **8** freezing **9** antarctic **11** nothernmost **12** southernmost
polaroid 6 camera
   invented by: 4 Land
pole 3 rod **4** mast, spar **5** shaft, staff, stick **6** tongue **9** pikestaff
   flax holder: 7 distaff
   pertaining to: 5 nodal
   sacred: 7 Asherah
   Scottish: 5 caber

tribal: 5 totem
vehicular: 4 neap
police, police officer 4 cops, dick, fuzz, tidy **5** clean, guard **6** neaten, patrol, tidy up **7** clean up, control, marshal, officer, protect, sheriff **8** blue coat, flatfoot, gendarme, regulate, spruce up, troopers **9** gendarmes, men in blue, patrolmen **10** traffic cop **11** arm of the law, keep in order **12** constabulary, cop on the beat
   French: 8 gendarme
   Italian: 11 carabiniere
Police Woman
   character: 9 (Det) Joe Styles, (Lt) Paul Marsh **11** (Det) Pete Royster, (Lt) Bill Crowley **12** (Sgt Suzanne) Pepper Martin
   cast: 9 Ed Bernard **11** Val Bisoglio **12** Earl Holliman **14** Angie Dickinson, Charles Dierkop
policy 3 way **4** plan, rule **5** habit, style **6** custom, design, method, scheme, system **7** program, routine, tactics **8** behavior, platform, practice, strategy **9** principle, procedure
polish 3 oil, wax **4** buff, sand **5** class, emend, glaze, gloss, grace, rouge, rub up, shine **6** pumice, refine, smooth **7** burnish, correct, culture, enhance, finesse, improve, perfect, sauvity, touch up, varnish **8** abrasive, courtesy, elegance, round out, urbanity **9** gentility, politesse, sandpaper **10** politeness, refinement **11** cultivation, good manners
polished 4 able, deft, fine, oily **5** oiled, suave, waxed **6** buffed, expert, glassy, glazed, glossy, polite, rubbed, sanded, shined, urbane **7** capable, elegant, genteel, refined, skilled **8** cultured, finished, mannerly, masterly, skillful, smoothed **9** brilliant, burnished, courteous, masterful, practiced, varnished **10** cultivated, profi- cient **11** experienced **12** accomplished
polish off 6 finish **8** complete, get rid of **9** dispose of
polite 4 high **5** civil, elite **6** proper **7** courtly, elegant, gallant, genteel, refined **8** cultured, mannerly, polished, well-bred **9** civilized, courteous, diffident, patrician **10** cultivated, respectful **11** ceremonious, fashionable, gentlemanly, well-behaved **12** well-mannered
politeness 7 decorum **8** courtesy **9** gentility, propriety **10** refinement **11** good manners
Polites
   character in: 7 Odyssey
   brother: 5 Paris **6** Hector
   companion: 8 Odysseus
   father: 5 Priam
   mother: 6 Hecuba
   sister: 9 Cassandra

transformed by: 5 Aeaea, Circe
transformed into: 3 hog, pig **5** swine
politic 4 wily, wise **5** chary, suave **6** artful, astute, shrewd, subtle **7** mindful, prudent, tactful **8** cautious, discreet, scheming **9** designing, expedient, judicious, opportune **10** contriving, diplomatic **11** calculating, circumspect, machinating **13** Machiavellian
political party 3 GOP **4** Tory, Whig **5** Labor **7** faction **9** Communist, Greenback, Socialist **10** Democratic, Republican **11** Know-Nothing
political refugee 2 DP **5** exile **6** emigre **10** expatriate **15** displaced person
politician 8 politico **9** incumbent, statesman **10** campaigner, legislator **12** officeholder, office seeker **13** public servant
politics 10 government, statecraft **11** party policy **13** statesmanship **14** affairs of state
Politics
   author: 9 Aristotle
Politic Would-Be, Lord and Lady
   characters in: 7 Volpone
   author: 6 Jonson
Polixenes
   character in: 14 The Winter's Tale
   author: 11 Shakespeare
Polk, James Knox
   presidential rank: 8 eleventh
   party: 8 Democrat
   state represented: 2 TN
   defeated: 4 (Henry) Clay **6** (James Gillespie) Birney
   vice president: 6 (George Mifflin) Dallas
   cabinet:
     state: 8 (James) Buchanan
     treasury: 6 (Robert John) Walker
     war: 5 (William Learned) Marcy
     attorney general: 5 (John Young) Mason **6** (Isaac) Toucey **8** (Nathan) Clifford
     navy: 5 (John Young) Mason **8** (George) Bancroft
     postmaster general: 7 (Cave) Johnson
   born: 2 NC **17** Mecklenburg County
   died/buried: 2 TN **9** Nashville
   education: 11 prep schools **16** tutored privately
     University: 13 North Carolina
   religion: 9 Methodist
   political career: 16 state legislature **17** Speaker of the House **24** US House of Representatives
     governor of: 9 Tennessee
   civilian career: 6 lawyer
   notable events of lifetime/term:
     boundary dispute: 9 Northwest
     discovery in California of: 4 gold
     Proviso: 6 Wilmot
     treaty of: 16 Guadalupe Hidalgo
     war: 7 Mexican

father: 6 Samuel
mother: 4 Jane
siblings: 7 John Lee **9** Jane Maria, Naomi Tate **10** Lydia Eliza **12** Marshall Tate, Samuel Wilson **14** William Hawkins **15** Franklin Ezekiel, Ophelia Clarissa
wife: 5 Sarah (Childress)
children: 4 none

polka 5 dance **10** round dance **13** Bohemian dance

poll 4 head, vote **5** count, tally **6** census, survey, voting **7** canvass, figures, returns **8** register, sampling **9** interview, nose count **10** count noses, voting list **11** voting place

Pollack, Sydney
director of: 11 Out of Africa (Oscar) **12** The Way We Were **15** Absence of Malice **23** They Shoot Horses Don't They?

Pollock, Jackson
born: 6 Cody WY
artwork: 5 Scent **9** Blue Poles **10** The She-Wolf **11** Convergence **12** Autumn Rhythm **13** Eyes in the Heat **17** Easter and the Totem **20** Guardians of the Secret

pollutant 5 fumes, smoke, waste **7** exhaust **8** emission, impurity

pollute 4 foul, soil **5** dirty, sully **6** befoul, debase, defile **7** deprave, profane **9** desecrate **10** adulterate, make filthy **11** contaminate

polluted 4 foul **5** dirty, drunk **6** impure, soiled **7** corrupt, profane, smashed, unclean **9** poisonous **12** contaminated

pollution 7 fouling, soiling **8** defiling, dirtying, foulness, impurity **9** befouling, pollutant **11** uncleanness **12** adulteration **13** contaminating, contamination

Pollux *see* **15** Castor and Pollux

Pollyanna
director: 10 David Swift
based on story by: 13 Eleanor Porter
cast: 9 Jane Wyman **10** Karl Malden **11** Hayley Mills, Richard Egan

polo
equipment: 6 mallet
period of play: 7 chukker
championship: 10 Camacho Cup **13** Coronation Cup **16** Cup of the Americas

Polonius
character in: 6 Hamlet
author: 11 Shakespeare

Polska *see* **6** Poland

poltergeist 5 ghost **6** spirit
literally: 10 noise-ghost
manifestation: 5 knock, noise, prank

Poltergeist
director: 10 Tobe Hooper
cast: 12 Craig T Nelson **14** Jobeth Williams **16** Beatrice Straight

co-writer/producer: 15 Steven Spielberg

poltroon 6 coward, craven **7** caitiff, chicken, dastard **11** yellow-belly

polygon 10 multiangle **11** plane figure
eight-sided: 7 octagon
equal angled: 6 isogon
five-sided: 8 pentagon
four-sided: 6 square **7** rhombus **8** tetragon **9** rectangle, trapezoid
nine-sided: 7 nonagon
seven-sided: 8 heptagon
six-sided: 7 hexagon
ten-sided: 7 decagon
three-sided: 8 triangle
twelve-sided: 9 dodecagon

Polyhymnia
also: 8 Polymnia
member of: 5 Muses
personifies: 5 dance **11** sacred music
mother: 9 Mnemosyne

polymer 5 dimer, nylon **6** hydrol **7** hexamer **8** oligomer

Polynesia
name means: 11 many islands
cities: 4 Apia **7** Papeete **8** Auckland, Pago Pago **9** Nukualofa
island: 4 Cook, Line **5** Samoa, Tonga **6** Easter, Ellice, Hawaii, Midway, Tahiti, Tubuai, Tuvalu **7** Austral, Maupiti, Phoenix, Society, Tokelau, Tuamotu **8** Pitcairn **9** Marquesas **10** New Zealand **15** French Polynesia
sea: 7 Pacific
people: 3 Ati **5** Maori **6** Kanaka, Nivean, Samoan, Tongan **9** Nesogaean **10** Polynesian
  explorer: 4 Cook **6** Tasman, Wallis **8** Magellan **9** Roggeveen **12** Bougainville
language: 4 Niue, Uvea **5** Maori **6** Samoan, Tongan **7** Austral, Tagalog, Tokelau **8** Hawaiian, Tahitian **9** Marquesan, Tuamatuan **10** Mangarevan
religion: 12 Christianity
place:
  legendary origin: 8 Hawaiiki
feature:
  chief: 5 matai
  clothing: 5 pareu **6** sarong **8** lava-lava
  dance: 4 hula, siva
  dwelling: 4 fale
  family social unit: 4 aiga
  priest: 7 kahunas
  supernatural power: 4 mana
food:
  dish: 3 kai, poi **4** taro **8** palusami
  drink: 3 ava **4** kava, kawa

Polynices
also: 10 Polyneices
father: 7 Oedipus
mother: 7 Jocasta
uncle: 5 Creon
brother: 7 Oedipus **8** Eteocles
sister: 6 Ismene **8** Antigone
killed by: 8 Eteocles

polyp 5 coral, hydra, tumor **6** growth, isopod **7** octopod **10** sea anemone

Polyphemus
form: 7 Cyclops **12** one-eyed giant
father: 6 Elatus **8** Poseidon
mother: 6 Thoosa
joined: 9 Argonauts
killed: 4 Acis
blinded by: 8 Odysseus
loved: 7 Galatea

Polyphides
king of: 6 Sicyon
vocation: 4 seer
protected: 8 Menelaus **9** Agamemnon

polyphony 7 organum **8** faburden **11** fauxbourdon **12** counterpoint

Polypoetes
king of: 10 Thesprotia
father: 6 Apollo **8** Odysseus **9** Pirithous
mother: 6 Phthia **9** Callidice **10** Hippodamia
leader of: 6 Greeks

polysaccharide 6 insulin, starch **7** dextrin **8** galactin, lichenin **9** cellulose **12** carbohydrate

Polyxena
father: 5 Priam
mother: 6 Hecuba
loved by: 8 Achilles

Pomaria *see* **7** Algeria

Pomerania
capital: 7 Stettin
city: 5 Thorn, Torun **6** Anklam
country: 6 Poland **7** Germany
island: 5 Rugen **6** Usedom
province: 7 Pomorze

pommel, pummel 4 beat, hilt, horn, knob, pake **6** finial, strike **9** saddlebow

Pomona
origin: 5 Roman
goddess of: 10 fruit trees

pomp 4 show **5** front, glory, style **7** display **8** ceremony, flourish, grandeur, splendor **9** pageantry, showiness, solemnity, spectacle **10** brilliance **11** affectation, grandiosity, ostentation, pompousness **12** magnificence **14** stately display **15** pretentiousness

pompous 4 vain **5** proud **6** lordly, uppish **7** haughty **8** affected, arrogant, mannered, overdone, puffed-up, snobbish **9** conceited, egotistic, grandiose, imperious **10** blustering, swaggering **11** overbearing, patronizing, pretentious **12** ostentatious, presumptuous, supercilious, vainglorious **13** condescending, high and mighty, self-important

Ponchielli, Amilcare
born: 5 Italy **7** Cremona
composer of: 10 La Gioconda **15** Dance of the Hours

poncho 4 cape **5** cloak, shawl **6** mantle, serape

pond 4 pool, tarn 5 basin 6 lagoon 9 small lake, water hole

ponder 4 muse 5 study 6 wonder 7 examine, reflect 8 cogitate, consider, mull over, ruminate 9 brood over, cerebrate, reflect on, speculate, think over 10 deliberate, meditate on, puzzle over 11 contemplate

ponderous 3 big 4 dull 5 bulky, heavy, hefty, large, wordy 6 boring, bovine, dreary 7 awkward, droning, hulking, labored, lumpish, massive, tedious, weighty 8 cumbrous, enormous, sluggish, unlively, unwieldy 9 corpulent, graceless, lumbering, wearisome 10 burdensome, cumbersome, long-winded, lusterless, monotonous, unexciting, ungraceful 11 heavy-handed

pontiff 4 pope 6 bishop, priest 8 pontifex

pontifical 7 pompous 8 churchly, clerical, dogmatic, priestly 9 apostolic, episcopal, imperious 11 opinionated, overbearing, patronizing, pretentious 13 authoritarian, condescending 14 ecclesiastical

Pontus
   personifies: 3 sea
   father: 2 Ge
   son: 6 Nereus 7 Phorcys

pony 3 nag 4 crib, trot 5 glass, horse, pinto 7 mustang 9 racehorse
   breed: 6 Exmoor 8 Shetland

Pooh See 13 Winnie-the-Pooh

pooh-pooh 5 knock 7 disdain, put down, run down, sneer at 8 belittle 9 disparage

Pooka see 4 Puca

pool 3 pot 4 ally, bank, lake, mere, pond, tarn 5 group, kitty, merge, share, union, unite 6 puddle, splash, stakes 7 combine 8 alliance, fishpond, millpool 9 coalition 10 amalgamate, collective 11 association, consolidate, cooperative 13 confederation

Poole, Grace
   character in: 8 Jane Eyre
   author: 6 Bronte

poop 3 fag 4 bush, deck, do in, tire 7 exhaust, fatigue, wear out 8 enervate

pooped 4 beat 5 all in, spent, tired, weary 6 bushed, done in 7 drained, wearied, worn out 8 fatigued, tired out 9 dead tired, exhausted, played out

poor 3 sad 4 bare, dead, vain, worn 5 broke, empty, needy, sorry 6 barren, fallow, faulty, futile, hard up, in need, in want, meager, paltry, wasted 7 forlorn, sterile, unhappy, unlucky, wanting 8 badly off, bankrupt, beggarly, depleted, desolate, devoid of, grieving, indigent, inferior, pathetic, pitiable, strapped, unworthy, wretched 9 defective, deficient, destitute, exhausted, fruitless, imperfect, infertile, insolvent, in straits, miserable, moneyless, penniless, unfertile, worthless 10 distressed, inadequate, pauperized 11 impecunious, unfortunate 12 impoverished, uncultivable, unproductive, unprofitable 15 poverty-stricken

Poor People
   author: 16 Fyodor Dostoevsky

Poor Richard's Almanack
   author: 16 Benjamin Franklin

Poor White
   author: 16 Sherwood Anderson

pop 4 bang, boom, come, shot, snap, soda 5 arise, blast, burst, crack 6 appear, report 7 explode 8 detonate 9 discharge, explosion, soft drink 10 detonation

pope 3 Leo 4 John, Paul, Pius 5 Peter, Urban 6 Adrian, Eugene, Julius, Martin, Sixtus 7 Clement, Gregory 8 Benedict, Innocent, John Paul, Nicholas 9 Alexander, Callistus
   also: 12 Bishop of Rome 13 Vicar of Christ 14 Primate of Italy, Supreme Pontiff 16 Archbishop of Rome 18 Metropolitan of Rome, Patriarch of the West 25 Servant of the Servants of God
   office: 6 Papacy 7 Holy See 11 Seat of Peter
   elected by: 18 College of Cardinals
   elected in: 8 conclave
   signal that election is concluded: 10 white smoke
   resides: 4 Rome 10 the Vatican 11 Vatican City
   former residence: 13 Lateran Palace
   summer residence: 14 Castel Gondolfo
   papal land holding: 9 patrimony 21 patrimony of Saint Peter
   first pope: 10 Saint Peter
   pope who crowned Charlemagne: 6 Leo III
   pope who excommunicated Luther: 4 Leo X
   pope who authorized Michelangelo to paint Sistine Chapel: 8 Julius II
   "September Pope": 9 John Paul I
   original name of pope:
      Alexander VI: 15 Rodrigo de Borgia
      Callistus III: 15 Alfonso de Borgia
      Clement VII: 14 Giulio de' Medici
      John XXIII: 22 Angelo Giuseppe Roncalli
      John Paul I: 13 Albino Luciani
      John Paul II: 12 Karol Wojtyla 18 Archbishop of Krakow
      Leo X: 16 Giovanni de' Medici
      Pius XI: 12 Achille Ratti
      Pius XII: 35 Eugenio Maria Giuseppe Giovanni Pacelli
   popes of Avignon papacy: 6 Urban V 8 Clement V, John XXII 9 Clement VI, Gregory XI, Nicholas V 10 Innocent VI 11 Benedict XII
   popes during Great Western Schism:
      Avignon: 10 Clement VII 12 Benedict XIII
      Pisa: 9 John XXIII 10 Alexander V
      Rome: 7 Urban VI 10 Boniface IX, Gregory XII 11 Innocent VII
   papal bull/encyclical: 11 Unam sanctam 12 Humanae vitae, Rerum novarum, Vox in excelso 13 Pacem in terris 15 Mater et magistra 19 Populorum progressio 22 Sacerdotalis caelibatus

Pope, Alexander
   author of: 10 The Dunciad 12 An Essay on Man 15 Eloisa to Abelard 16 The Rape of the Lock 18 An Essay on Criticism 20 Epistle to Dr Arbuthnot

Pope, John Russell
   architect of: 17 Jefferson Memorial 20 National Gallery of Art 23 Temple of the Scottish Rite 24 National Archives Building

Popeye
   character in: 9 Sanctuary
   author: 8 Faulkner

Popeye
   cartoonist: 10 Elzie Segar
   character: 5 Bluto, Wimpy 7 Swee' Pea 8 Olive Oyl
   food: 7 spinach

popinjay 3 fop 4 beau 5 dandy 7 coxcomb

poplar 7 Populus 22 Liriodendron tulipifera
   varieties: 4 gray 5 black, downy, tulip, white 6 balsam, Eugene, yellow 8 Car- olina, Lombardy, necklace 10 Queensland 12 Chinese white, silver-leaved 13 Western balsam

poppy 7 Papaver
   varieties: 3 sea 4 blue, bush, corn, snow, tree, wind, wood 5 field, opium, plume, satin, tulip, water, Welsh 6 arctic, desert, horned 7 Asiatic, flaming, Iceland, Mexican, prickly, Shirley, Western 8 Flanders, harebell, Matilija, oriental 9 Celandine 10 California, island tree 12 Mexican tulip 13 yellow Chinese 14 California tree
   drug: 5 opium 6 heroin 8 morphine

poppycock 3 rot 4 bosh, bunk, jive, tosh 5 froth, fudge, hooey, stuff, trash 6 drivel, humbug 7 baloney, blabber, blather, eyewash, fustian, garbage, hogwash, inanity, prattle, rubbish, twaddle 8 falderal, flummery, nonsense, tommyrot, wish-wash 9 absurdity, gibberish, moonshine, rigmarole 10 applesauce, balderdash, flapdoodle, hocus-pocus, mumbo-jumbo, rigamarole 11 abracadabra, jabberwocky 12 fiddlefaddle, gobbledygook

poppy seed
   botanical name: 7 Papaver 11 P somniferum (sleep- bearing poppy)
   color: 4 blue 5 white

origin: 4 Asia **6** Europe
guards against: 9 creditors
use: 5 bread, cakes, rolls **6** sweets **10** vegetables **11** butter sauce

populace 4 folk **6** people, public **7** society **9** citizenry, community **10** population

popular 5 cheap, civic, civil, stock **6** famous, public, social **7** admired, current, general, in favor **8** accepted, approved, communal, familiar, favorite, in demand, national, orthodox **9** community, preferred, prevalent, well-known, well-liked **10** affordable, celebrated, democratic **11** established, fashionable, inexpensive, of the people, sought-after

popularity 4 fame, note **5** favor, glory, kudos, vogue **6** esteem, regard, renown, repute **7** acclaim, fashion **8** approval **9** celebrity, notoriety **10** acceptance, admiration, notability, reputation **11** acclamation

popular opinion
    Latin: 9 vox populi

popular whim 3 fad **4** rage **5** craze, mania **7** passion **11** infatuation

populate 6 occupy, people, settle **7** inhabit

populated 5 urban **7** peopled, settled **8** citified, occupied **9** inhabited

population 4 folk **6** people, public **8** citizens, populace **9** citizenry, habitancy, residents **11** body politic, commonality, inhabitants

populous 5 dense **6** jammed **7** crowded, peopled, teeming **8** swarming, thronged

porcelain 5 china **11** ceramic ware

porch 4 stoa **5** lanai, stoop **7** balcony, narthex, portico, veranda **8** solarium, verandah **9** colonnade, vestibule

pore 4 hole, read, scan **5** probe, study **6** outlet, peruse, ponder, review, search, survey **7** dig into, examine, explore, inspect, orifice **8** aperture, consider **9** delve into

Porfiry
    character in: 18 Crime and Punishment
    author: 10 Dostoevsky

Porgy
    author: 13 DuBose Heyward

Porgy and Bess
    opera by: 14 George Gershwin
    character: 4 Bess **5** Clara, Crown, Porgy **6** Serena **11** Sportin' Life
    setting: 10 Catfish Row

pornographic 4 blue, lewd **5** bawdy, dirty, gross **6** coarse, filthy, smutty, vulgar **7** obscene **8** indecent, off-color, prurient **9** salacious **10** lascivious, licentious

porous 4 lacy **6** spongy **7** riddled **8** cellular, pervious **9** absorbent, permeable, sievelike **10** penetrable **11** honeycombed

porpoise 4 leap **5** whale **6** palach, puffer, seahog **7** cowfish, dolphin, surface **8** cetacean
    genus: 8 Phocaena **9** Delphinus

porridge 4 pobs, samp **5** atole, brose, brout, gruel **6** cereal **7** crowdie, oatmeal, polenta **8** flummery

porringer 4 bowl, dish **6** vessel **9** container **10** receptacle

Porsena, Lars
    nationality: 8 Etruscan
    attacked: 4 Rome
    to reinstate: 7 Tarquin

port 4 dock, pier, quay **5** haven, wharf **6** harbor, refuge **7** dry dock, landing, mooring, seaport, shelter **9** anchorage, harborage **11** destination

port
    type: 4 wine **6** brandy
    origin: 8 Portugal
    variety: 4 ruby **5** tawny **7** vintage
    with brandy: 9 Betsy Ross
    with vermouth: 10 Broken Spur

portable 5 handy, light, small **6** bantam, pocket **7** compact, folding, movable **8** cartable, haulable, liftable **9** ready-to-go **10** convenient, conveyable, manageable, vest-pocket **11** pocket-sized

portal, portals 4 adit, arch, door, gate **5** entry **6** wicket **7** doorway, gateway, portico **8** approach, entrance **9** threshold, vestibule **10** portcullis **11** entranceway

Port-au-Prince
    capital of: 5 Haiti

porte-monnaie 5 purse **10** pocketbook **12** money-carrier

portend 4 bode **5** augur **6** denote, herald, warn of **7** bespeak, betoken, point to, predict, presage, signify, suggest **8** forebode, forecast, foretell, forewarn, prophesy **9** foretoken, prefigure **10** foreshadow

portent 4 omen, sign **5** token **6** augury, boding, threat **7** presage, warning **9** harbinger **10** foreboding **11** forewarning

portentous 6 superb **7** amazing, fateful, ominous, pompous **8** alarming, menacing **9** bombastic, grandiose, prophetic **10** foreboding, incredible, prodigious, remarkable, stupendous, surprising **11** astonishing, exceptional, frightening, pretentious, significant, superlative, threatening **12** inauspicious, intimidating, unpropitious

porter 4 brew **5** stout **6** bearer, coolie, redcap, skycap **7** carrier **8** conveyer **9** conductor

Porter, Katherine Anne
    author of: 11 Ship of Fools **12** Old Mortality **14** Flowering Judas **15** The

Leaning Tower **18** Pale Horse Pale Rider

Porter, William Sidney
    real name of: 6 O Henry

portfolio 4 case, file **5** album **6** binder, folder **7** dossier **8** envelope **9** scrapbook **10** securities

Porthos
    character in: 18 The Three Musketeers
    author: 5 Dumas (pere)

Portia
    character in: 12 Julius Caesar **19** The Merchant of Venice
    author: 11 Shakespeare

portico 4 stoa **5** lanai **6** piazza **7** balcony, veranda, walkway

portion 3 cut, lot, sum **4** dole, doom, fate, luck, part **5** carve, cut up, moira, piece, sever, share, slice, split **6** amount, divide, kismet, parcel, ration, sector **7** break up, deal out, destiny, fortune, helping, measure, section, segment, serving **8** allocate, disperse, division, fraction, fragment, quantity, separate **9** allotment, allowance, demarcate, partition **10** allocation, distribute, percentage

portion out 5 allot **6** ration **7** dole out, mete out, prorate **8** allocate, dispense, divide up **9** apportion, parcel out **10** distribute, measure out

Portland
    basketball team: 12 Trail Blazers
    football team: 8 Breakers
    river: 8 Columbia **10** Willamette
    university: 4 Reed

Port Louis
    capital of: 9 Mauritius

portly 3 big, fat **4** full **5** beefy, burly, heavy, large, obese, plump, pudgy, round, stout, tubby **6** brawny, chubby, fleshy, rotund, stocky **9** corpulent

Portman, John
    architect of: 15 Peachtree Center (Atlanta)

portmanteau 3 bag **4** grip **5** cloak **6** mantle, valise **8** suitcase **9** gladstone

Port Moresby
    capital of: 9 New Guinea

Portnoy's Complaint
    author: 10 Philip Roth

Port of Spain
    capital of: 17 Trinidad and Tobago

Porto-Novo
    capital of: 5 Benin

portrait 5 cameo **6** sketch **7** drawing, picture **8** likeness, painting, vignette **9** depiction **10** impression, photograph **11** description

Portrait of a Lady, The
    author: 10 Henry James
    character: 11 Madame Merle, Pansy Osmond **12** Isabel Archer **13** Gilbert Osmond, Lord Warburton, Ralph

Touchett **14** Caspar Goodwood **18** Henrietta Stackpole

Portrait of the Artist as a Young Man
author: 10 James Joyce
character: 4 Emma **12** Simon Dedalus **14** Stephen Dedalus

portray 3 ape **4** draw, play **5** carve, enact, mimic, model, paint **6** depict, detail, figure, pose as, sketch **7** imitate, narrate, picture **8** describe, set forth, simulate **9** delineate, represent, sculpture **10** illustrate, photograph **11** impersonate **12** characterize

portrayal 7 picture **8** portrait **9** picturing **11** delineation, description **14** representation **16** characterization

ports
god of: **8** Portunus

Portugal
capital/largest city: 6 Lisbon
others: 4 Beja, Faro, Ovar **5** Braga, Evora, Olhao, Porto, Viseu **6** Aveiro, Guarda, Leiria, Oporto, Sintra **7** Algarve, Amadora, Bragama, Cascoes, Coimbra, Covilha, Estoril, Funchal, Granada, Setubal **8** Barreiro, Portimao **9** Lusitania **10** Portalegre **14** Vila Nova de Gaia
Roman city: 10 Portus Cale
school: 5 Minho **6** Aveiro, Lisbon, Oporto **7** Coimbra
division: 3 Goa **4** Tejo, Tete **5** Beira, Evora, Macao, Minho, Timor **6** Azores, Loanda **7** Algarve, Madeira **8** Alemteho, Rebatejo **9** Cape Verde **10** Mozambique **11** Estremadura
Roman district: 9 Lusitania
measure: 2 pe **4** bota, moio, vara **5** almud, fanga, geira, linha, milha **6** almude, covado **7** alquier, ferrado, selamin **8** alqueire
monetary unit: 3 avo, rei **4** peca, real **5** conto, crown, dobra, indio, justo, rupia **6** escudo, macuta, octave, pataca, testad, tostao, vintem **7** angalar, centavo, crusado, miereis, testone **8** equipaga, johannes
weight: 4 onca, once **5** libra, marco **6** arroba **7** arratel **9** excropulo
island: 6 Azores **7** Madeira **8** Terceira
mountain: 4 Acor, Lapa **5** Gerez, Marao, Mousa **6** Bornes, Peneda **7** Larouco **8** Caramulo **9** Caldeirao, Monchique **14** Serra da Estrela
highest point: 11 Pico da Serra
river: 3 Sor, Tua **4** Lima, Mino, Mira, Sado, Seda, Tago, Tajo, Tejo, Vara **5** Douro, Duero, Le goa, Micha, Minho, Sabar, Tagus, Vouga, Zatas **6** Cavado, Chanca, Quarto, Tamega, Zezere **7** Mondego, Selamin, Sorraia **8** Quadiana, Tonelada
ocean: 8 Atlantic
physical feature:
  bay: 7 Setubal
  cape: 4 Roca **7** Mondego **8** Espichel **9** St Vincent

peninsula: 7 Iberian
port: 4 Faro **6** Aveiro, Lisbon, Oporto **7** Leixoes
people: 4 Celt, Moor **7** Iberian **10** Portuguese
  artist: 7 Pereira **9** Goncalves **13** Soares dos Reis
  author: 5 Dinis **6** Camoes, Vieira **7** Garrett, Vicente **9** Deus-Ramos
  explorer: 3 Cam, Cao **4** Dias, Diaz **6** Cabral, Da Gama **7** Almeida **8** Magellan **11** Albuquerque **23** Prince Henry the Navigator
  king: 6 Manuel, Philip, Sancho **7** Alfonso **9** Ferdinand, Sebastian
  leader: 5 Eanes **6** Dombal, Soares **7** Caetano, Carmona, Salazar, Spinola
  queen: 5 Maria **9** Elizabeth
language: 10 Portuguese
religion: 13 Roman Catholic
place:
  church: 5 Jesus **6** Christ **11** Os Jeronimos, Sao Lourenco **12** Old Cathedral **13** Santa Engracia **16** Sao Vicente de Fora
  city square: 15 Praca do Comercio
  dam: 6 Belver, Idanha **13** Castelo do Bode
  fortress-church: 12 Leco do Bailio
  monastery: 8 Alcobaca **12** Hieronymites **20** Santa Maria da Victoria
  monument: 11 Discoveries
  museum: 13 Soares dos Reis
  palace: 6 Cintra
  shrine: 6 Fatima
colony: 5 Macad, Macao
  former colony: 3 Goa **5** Timor **6** Angola **7** Sao Tome **8** Principe, St Thomas **9** Cape Verde **10** Mozambique **12** Guinea Bissau
feature:
  song: 4 fado
food:
  dish: 8 bacalhau, bucellas **10** calcavella **11** carcavellos
  sausage: 8 linguica
  wine: 4 port **7** madeira

Portuguese Guinea *see* **12** Guinea-Bissau

Portuguese West Africa *see* **6** Angola

Portunus
origin: 5 Roman
god of: 5 ports **7** harbors

posada 3 inn **12** halting place

pose 3 air, set **4** cast, mien **5** group, order, state, style **6** line up, stance, submit **7** advance, arrange, bearing, bring up, posture, present, propose, show off, suggest **8** attitude, carriage, position, propound, set forth, throw out **9** mannerism, postulate **10** put forward

Poseidon
also: 9 Asphalius
origin: 5 Greek
god of: 3 sea

caused: 11 earthquakes
father: 6 Cronos
mother: 4 Rhea
brother: 4 Zeus
wife: 10 Amphitrite
lover: 2 Ge **6** Aethra, Medusa, Thoosa **7** Demeter
child: 5 Arion **6** Triton **7** Antaeus, Pegasus, Theseus **8** Chrysaor **10** Polyphemus
symbol: 5 horse **7** trident
epithet: 11 Ennosigaeus, Hippocurius **12** Prosclystius
corresponds to: 7 Neptune

poser 5 facer **6** puzzle **7** problem **8** examiner, stickler

posh 4 chic **5** fancy, ritzy, smart, swell **6** chi-chi, classy, deluxe, lavish, swanky **7** elegant, opulent, refined, stylish **9** high-class, luxurious **11** extravagant

position 3 fix, job, put, set **4** duty, pose, post, role, site **5** array, caste, class, locus, lodge, order, place, stand, state **6** career, charge, ground, locate, office, plight, stance, status **7** arrange, deposit, opinion, outlook, posture, situate, station, vantage **8** attitude, capacity, eminence, function, locality, location, prestige, standing **9** condition, elevation, establish, placement, situation, viewpoint **10** assignment, commission, importance, notability, prominence **11** appointment, consequence, disposition, distinction, frame of mind, point of view

position decided upon
French: 9 parti pris

positive 4 firm, good, real, sure **5** total **6** narrow, useful **7** assured, certain, gainful, helpful **8** absolute, cocksure, complete, decisive, definite, dogmatic, explicit, obdurate, salutary **9** assertive, confident, convinced, effective, immovable, practical, satisfied, veritable **10** applicable, autocratic, beneficial, conclusive, definitive, optimistic, undisputed, undoubting **11** affirmative, cooperative, dead certain, dictatorial, irrefutable, opinionated, overbearing, practicable, progressive, self-assured, serviceable, unequivocal, unqualified **12** confirmatory, constructive, contributory, unchangeable **13** corroborative, thoroughgoing **16** incontrovertible

positively 9 assuredly, certainly, decidedly, literally **10** absolutely, definitely **11** confidently, indubitably **12** emphatically, indisputably, unmistakably, without doubt **13** affirmatively, categorically, unqualifiedly **14** beyond question, unhesitatingly, unquestionably

possess 3 own **4** grab, have, hold **5** boast, enjoy **6** absorb, fixate, obsess, occupy **7** acquire, bedevil, bewitch, command, conquer, consume, control, enchant, overrun **8** dominate, maintain, take over, vanquish **9** fascinate, hypnotize, influence, mesmerize

Possessed, The
author: **16** Fyodor Dostoevsky
character: **5** Marya, Pyotr **6** Shatov **7** Nikolay **16** Varvara Stavrogin **17** Stepan Verhovensky

possession 4 hold **5** asset, poise, title **6** effect, owning **7** command, control, control, custody, tenancy **8** calmness, coolness, dominion, province, resource **9** belonging, composure, occupancy, ownership, placidity, sangfroid, territory **10** equanimity, even temper, occupation, possessing **11** equilibrium, self-control **12** accoutrement, protectorate

possibility 4 hope, odds, risk **6** chance, gamble, hazard **7** promise **8** prospect **9** prospects **10** likelihood **11** contingency, eventuality, feasibility, probability, workability **12** potentiality **14** practicability

possible 8 credible, feasible, workable **9** potential, thinkable **10** achievable, admissible, attainable, cognizable, compatible, contingent, imaginable, manageable, obtainable, reasonable **11** conceivable, performable, practicable **12** hypothetical

possibly 5 at all, maybe **6** mayhap **7** could be, perhaps **8** in any way, normally **9** at the most, perchance **10** by any means, God willing **11** conceivably

post 2 PX **3** fix, job, put, set **4** base, beat, camp, pale, part, pile, pole, role, seat, send, spot, work **5** brace, house, lodge, place, put up, round, shaft, stake **6** advise, column, inform, locate, notify, office, picket, report, settle, splint, tack up **7** apprise, declare, install, mission, publish, quarter, routine, situate, station, support, upright **8** acquaint, announce, capacity, disclose, exchange, fasten up, function, instruct, mainstay, position, proclaim **9** advertise, broadcast, circulate, enlighten, establish, make known, situation **10** assignment, settlement

postdate 6 follow **7** succeed **9** come after

poster 4 bill, sign **6** notice **7** placard **8** bulletin **13** advertisement

posterior 3 bum, can **4** back, butt, prat, rear, rump, seat, tail, tush **5** fanny, stern, tushy **6** behind, bottom, caudal, dorsal, hinder **7** keister **8** backside, buttocks, derriere, hindmost, rearward **9** aftermost

posterity 5 heirs, issue, young **6** family **7** descent, history, lineage, progeny **8** children **9** offspring **10** succession, successors **11** descendants

post hoc, ergo propter hoc 29 after

this therefore because of it
describes: **14** logical fallacy

Posthumus, Leonatus
character in: **9** Cymbeline
author: **11** Shakespeare

Postman Always Rings Twice, The
director: **10** Tay Garnett
based on story by: **10** James M Cain
cast: **10** Hume Cronym, Lana Turner **12** John Garfield **13** Cecil Kellaway

postpone 4 stay **5** defer, delay, table, waive **6** put off, remand, shelve **7** adjourn, lay over, reserve, suspend

postponement 4 stay **5** delay **6** recess **7** tabling **8** abeyance, deferral **9** deferment, extension **10** suspension

postscript 2 ps **5** rider **7** codicil **8** addendum **10** attachment

postulate 5 axiom, guess **6** assume, hazard, submit, theory **7** premise, presume, propose, surmise, theorem **8** put forth, theorize **9** speculate **10** assumption, conjecture, hypothesis, presuppose **11** hypothesize, presumption

posture 3 air, set **4** case, mien, mood, pose, post, tone **5** phase, place, shape, state, tenor **6** aspect, stance, status **7** bearing, contour, station **8** attitude, carriage, position, standing **9** condition, situation **11** predicament **12** circumstance

Postvorta
form: **5** nymph
member of: **7** Camenae
knowledge of: **4** past

posy 5 bloom, motto **6** flower, phrase **7** blossom, bouquet, corsage, garland, nosegay

pot 3 pan **4** ruin **5** crock, kitty **6** vessel **9** container, marijuana **11** rack and ruin
Spanish: **4** olla

potable 3 ale **5** clean, drink, water **6** liquor **8** beverage, quencher **9** drinkable

potage 4 soup **9** thick soup

potassium
chemical symbol: **1** K

potato 16 Solanum tuberosum
varieties: **3** air, yam **4** duck, swan, wild, Zulu **5** Idaho, Irish, Maine, rural, swamp, sweet, white **6** Russet **7** Burbank, epicure, prairie, Telinga
dish: **4** chip **5** baked, salad **6** mashed **8** au gratin **9** lyonnaise, scalloped **11** french fries **12** baked stuffed

Potawatomi
language family: **9** Algonkian **10** Algonquian
location: **4** Ohio **6** Kansas **7** Indiana **8** Illinois, Michigan, Oklahoma **9** Wisconsin
leader: **7** Pontiac
united with: **6** Ojibwa, Ottawa **7** Ojibway

Potemkin

director: **17** Sergei Eisenstein
cast: **14** Vladimir Barsky **16** Alexander Antonov **17** Grigori Alexandrov
famous segment: **11** Odessa Steps

potency 3 vis **5** force, power **6** energy **8** efficacy, strength, virility, vitality

potent 5 solid, tough **6** mighty, strong **7** dynamic **8** forceful, forcible, powerful, vigorous **9** effective, operative **10** compelling, convincing, formidable, impressive, persuasive **11** efficacious, influential **12** overpowering

potentate 4 lord **5** chief, mogul, ruler **6** prince, satrap, sultan **7** emperor, monarch **8** overlord, suzerain **9** chieftain, sovereign

potential 6 covert, hidden, latent **7** dormant, lurking, passive **8** implicit, possible **9** concealed, quiescent, unexerted **10** unapparent, unrealized **11** conceivable, undisclosed, unexpressed

potentiality 7 ability **10** capability **13** possibilities

potentially
Latin: **7** in posse

pother 3 ado **4** fuss, stir, to-do **6** bustle, flurry, hustle, tumult **8** activity **9** agitation, commotion

Pothos
companion of: **9** Aphrodite
personifies: **6** desire **7** longing

potion 4 brew, dram **5** draft, tonic **6** elixir **7** mixture, philter **8** libation, potation **10** concoction

Potlatch people see **8** Kwakiutl

Pot of Gold, The
author: **7** Plautus

Potok, Chaim
author of: **9** The Chosen **10** Wanderings **15** The Book of Lights

potpourri 4 hash, mess, olio, stew **6** jumble, medley, mosaic, motley **7** farrago, goulash, melange, mixture **8** mishmash, pastiche **9** patchwork **10** hodgepodge, miscellany, salmagundi **11** gallimaufry, olla podrida

pottage 4 soup, stew **6** brewis **8** porridge

Potter, Beatrix
author of: **11** (The Tale of) Peter Rabbit **21** The Tailor of Gloucester

Potter, Muff
character in: **9** Tom Sawyer
author: **5** Twain

potter's field 8 boneyard, cemetery **9** graveyard **12** burial ground **13** burying ground

pottery 5 china **8** clayware, crockery **11** ceramic ware, earthenware

pouch 3 bag, kit, sac **4** sack **5** purse **6** pocket, wallet **7** handbag, satchel **8** carryall, ditty bag, reticule, rucksack **9** container **10** pocketbook, receptacle

Poulenc, Francis
born: **5** Paris **6** France
member of: **6** Les Six, The Six

composer of: 9 Les Biches **13** The Carmelites **22** Dialogues des Carmelites

poultice 7 plaster **8** dressing **10** medicament

poultry 3 hen **4** cock, duck, fowl, swan **5** capon, geese, goose, quail **6** grouse, layers, pigeon, turkey **7** chicken, peacock, rooster **8** pheasant **9** partridge **10** guinea fowl
breed: 6 Ancona, Bantam **7** Cornish, Dorking, Leghorn **9** Wyandotte **12** Plymouth Rock **14** Rhode Island Red
disease: 3 pip **4** roup, tick
farm: 7 hennery
house: 4 coop

pounce 4 jump, leap **5** fly at, swoop **6** ambush, dash at, jump at, plunge, snatch, spring **8** downrush, fall upon, surprise

Pounce, Peter
character in: 13 Joseph Andrews
author: 8 Fielding

pound 4 bang, beat, drub, drum, maul **5** clomp, clout, crush, grind, march, paste, smack, stomp, throb, thump, tramp **6** batter, bruise, cudgel, hammer, pummel, strike, thrash, thwack, wallop **7** clobber, crumble, pulsate, thunder, trounce **8** lambaste **9** fustigate, palpitate, pulverize **13** sixteen ounces
abbreviation: 2 lb

Pound, Ezra
author of: 6 Cantos **8** Personae **11** Exultations, Pisan Cantos

pound troy
abbreviation: 3 lb t

pour 3 tap **4** drip, drop, flow, gush, ooze, rain, seep, slop **5** drain, flood, issue, spill, spout **6** decant, deluge, drench, effuse, squirt, stream **7** cascade, draw off, dribble, lade out **15** rain cats and dogs **16** come down in sheets **17** come down in buckets

pourboire 3 tip **8** gratuity
literally: 11 for drinking

pourparler 29 informal preliminary conference
literally: 10 for talking

Poussin, Nicholas
born: 6 France **10** Les Andelys
artwork: 10 The Seasons **14** Birth of Bacchus, St John on Patmos **17** Bacchanalian Revel **18** The Burial of Phocion **19** The Poet's Inspiration **20** The Arcadian Shepherds **23** Landscape with Polyphemus, The Holy Family on the Steps **27** The Adoration of the Golden Calf

pou sto 14 place to stand on, where I may stand **16** base of operations

pout 4 crab, fret, fume, mope, sulk **5** brood, frown, lower, scowl **6** glower
French: 4 moue

poverty 4 lack, need, want **6** dearth, penury **7** beggary, deficit, paucity **8** scarcity, shortage **9** indigence, neediness, pauperism, privation **10** bankruptcy, deficiency, insolvency, meagerness, mendicancy **11** destitution **13** insufficiency, pennilessness **14** impoverishment

poverty-stricken 4 poor **5** broke, needy **8** indigent **9** destitute, penniless **10** down and out

powder 4 dust, talc **5** emery **6** pollen, talcum **7** crumble **9** pulverize
antiseptic: 6 formin **7** aristol
applier: 4 puff
cookery: 4 soda
cosmetic: 5 blush, rouge **7** compact
poisonous: 5 robin

powder-blue 5 azure **6** pastel **7** skyblue **8** pale-blue **9** light-blue, robin's egg

powdery 5 dusty, mealy **6** chalky, floury, grated, ground, milled **7** crushed, pestled **8** shredded **10** comminuted, pulverized, triturated

Powell, Dick
real name: 14 Richard E Powell
born: 14 Mountain View AR
wife: 11 June Allyson **12** Joan Blondell
costar: 10 Ruby Keeler
roles: 7 Mrs Mike **8** Cornered **12** Johnny O'Clock **13** Murder My Sweet **15** Footlight Parade **17** Forty-second Street **32** Gold Diggers of Nineteen Thirty-three

Powell, Jane
real name: 12 Suzanne Burce
born: 10 Portland OR
roles: 5 Irene **12** Royal Wedding **13** A Date with Judy **27** Seven Brides for Seven Brothers

Powell, John
nickname: 4 Boog
sport: 8 baseball
team: 16 Baltimore Orioles

Powell, Michael
codirector: 17 Emeric Pressburger
director of: 11 The Red Shoes **14** Black Narcissus **16** Stairway to Heaven

Powell, SR
creator/artist of: 22 Sheena Queen of the Jungle

Powell, William
born: 12 Pittsburgh PA
wife: 13 Carole Lombard
costar: 8 Myrna Loy
roles: 10 Philo Vance, The Thin Man **11** Nick Charles **12** My Man Godfrey **13** Mister Roberts **14** Life with Father **16** The Great Ziegfeld **22** How to Marry a Millionaire

power 4 gift, sway **5** brawn, force, might, right, ruler, skill, vigor **6** energy, genius, muscle, status, talent **7** faculty, license, operate, potency, quality **8** activate, aptitude, capacity, energize, iron grip, pressure, prestige, property, strength, vitality **9** attribute, authority, endowment, influence, puissance **10** capability, competence
Latin: 3 vis

Power, Tyrone
born: 12 Cincinnati OH
wife: 9 Annabella **14** Linda Christian
roles: 10 Jesse James **12** Blood and Sand **13** The Razor's Edge **14** Nightmare Alley, The Mark of Zorro **15** The Sun Also Rises **18** Captain from Castile

powerful 5 hardy, husky, stout **6** brawny, cogent, mighty, moving, potent, robust, sturdy **7** intense, rousing **8** athletic, emphatic, exciting, forceful, incisive, muscular, stalwart, vigorous **9** effective, energetic, herculean, strapping **10** able-bodied, commanding, invincible

powerhouse 9 strongman **10** power plant **15** generating plant

powerless 4 weak **6** feeble, infirm **7** unarmed **8** crippled, disabled, feckless, helpless, impotent **9** incapable, pregnable, prostrate **10** impuissant, vulnerable, weaponless **11** debilitated, defenseless, immobilized **13** incapacitated

powerlessness 8 debility, weakness **9** impotence, inability, infirmity **10** enervation, feebleness, inadequacy, incapacity **12** helplessness, incapability, inefficiency **13** vulnerability

Power Politics
author: 14 Margaret Atwood

powers that be 9 higher-ups **10** government **11** authorities **13** establishment **14** administration

Powhatan
language family: 9 Algonkian **10** Algonquian
tribe: 11 Confederacy
location: 8 Atlantic, Maryland, Virginia
leader: 8 Powhatan **11** Opechancano **13** Wahunsonacock
member: 10 Pocahontas

powwow 4 meet, talk **5** forum **6** caucus, confer, huddle, parley **7** consult, convene, council, discuss, meeting, palaver **8** assembly, colloquy, conclave, congress **9** discourse, interview **10** colloquium, conference, convention, discussion, round table **12** consultation

Poyser, Martin
character in: 8 Adam Bede
author: 5 Eliot

practicable 6 doable, viable **8** feasible, possible, workable **9** practical **10** achievable, attainable, functional

practical 4 able **5** solid, sound **6** expert, useful, versed **7** skilled, trained, veteran, working **8** seasoned, sensible, skillful **9** efficient, judicious, practiced, pragmatic, qualified, realistic **10**

functional, hardheaded, instructed, proficient, systematic, unromantic **11** down-to-earth, experienced, pragmatical, serviceable, utilitarian **12** accomplished, businesslike, matter-of-fact **13** unsentimental

practical joke 4 jape **5** caper, prank, stunt, trick

practically 6 all but, almost, nearly **8** actually, in effect **9** basically, in the main, just about, virtually **11** essentially **13** fundamentally, substantially

practice 2 do **3** use, way **4** deed, mode, play, rule, ruse, ways, wont **5** apply, dodge, drill, habit, train, trick, usage **6** action, custom, device, effect, follow, manner, method, pursue, ritual, work at **7** conduct, fashion, perform, process, qualify, routine, utilize **8** carry out, engage in, exercise, live up to, maneuver, rehearse, tendency, training **9** execution, operation, perform in, procedure, rehearsal, seasoning, set to work, turn to use **10** discipline, observance, prepare for, repetition **11** application, be engaged in, performance, preparation

practiced 4 able, fine **5** adept **6** adroit, expert **7** capable, drilled, pursued, skilled, trained **8** masterly, polished, seasoned, skillful, worked at **9** competent, engaged in, masterful, qualified, rehearsed **10** cultivated, proficient **11** experienced, prepared for **12** accomplished

practice sorcery 5 charm **7** bewitch, conjure, enchant **9** work magic **10** cast a spell

Practicing History
author: 15 Barbara W Tuchman

practitioner 6 doctor **7** dentist **9** performer **12** professional

pragmatic 5 sober **8** sensible **9** hard-nosed, practical, realistic **10** hardheaded, hard-boiled **11** down-to-earth, utilitarian **12** businesslike, matter-of-fact, unidealistic **13** materialistic, unsentimental

Praia
capital of: 9 Cape Verde

prairie 3 bay **5** llano, pampa, plain **6** camass, meadow, steppe **7** quamash **9** grassland
apple: 9 breadroot
berry: 9 trampillo
chicken: 6 grouse
dog: 6 gopher, marmot
schooner: 12 covered wagon
state: 8 Illinois
wolf: 6 coyote

Prairie, The
author: 19 James Fenimore Cooper
character: 4 Inez **9** Dr Battius, Ellen Wade, Hard-Heart, Paul Hover **10** Esther Bush **11** Abiram White, Ishmael Bush, Natty Bumppo **16** Captain Middleton

Prairie State
nickname of: 8 Illinois

praise 4 laud, tout **5** cheer, exalt, extol, honor **6** esteem, eulogy, hurrah, regard, revere **7** acclaim, applaud, approve, build up, commend, glorify, plaudit, respect, root for, tribute, worship **8** accolade, applause, approval, encomium, eulogize, venerate **9** adoration, celebrate, good words, laudation, panegyric **10** admiration, compliment, panegyrize **11** approbation, compliments, testimonial **12** appreciation, commendation, congratulate **14** congratulation
Hebrew: 6 hallel

praise be to God
Latin: 7 laus Deo

praiseful 8 praising **9** extolling, laudatory **10** plauditory **12** commendatory **13** complimentary

praiseworthiness 5 merit **10** excellence **12** admirability, desirability **14** commendability

praiseworthy 4 fine **6** worthy **8** laudable **9** admirable, estimable, excellent, exemplary **11** commendable, meritorious

pram, praam, prahm 4 boat **5** buggy **6** vessel **7** rowboat **8** carriage, stroller **12** perambulator

prance 4 jump, leap, romp, skip **5** bound, caper, dance, frisk, strut, vault **6** bounce, cavort, frolic, gambol, spring **7** swagger

prank 4 joke, lark **5** antic, caper, spoof, stunt, trick **6** gambol **8** escapade, mischief **9** horseplay **10** shenanigan, tomfoolery

prate 3 gab, yak **4** blab, brag, chat, crow, talk **5** boast **6** babble, gabble, jabber **7** blabber, chatter, prattle, twaddle, twattle

Prathet Thai *see* **8** Thailand

prattle 3 gab, yak **4** blab **5** prate **6** babble, gabble, hot air, jabber **7** blather, chatter, twaddle **8** cackling, chitchat, gabbling **9** gibbering, jabbering

Pravda 15 Soviet newspaper
literally: 5 truth

pray 3 beg, bid, sue **4** urge **5** cry to, plead **7** beseech, entreat, implore, request, solicit **8** call upon, invocate, petition **9** importune **10** supplicate

prayer 6 litany, orison, praise **7** worship **9** adoration **12** thanksgiving **13** glorification

prayerful 4 holy **5** godly, pious **6** devout, solemn **8** reverent **9** pietistic, religious, spiritual **10** worshipful **11** reverential

prayers 4 hope, plea, suit **5** dream **6** appeal **7** request **8** entreaty, petition **10** aspiration, invocation **11** beseechment **12** solicitation, supplication

prayer service 9 devotions **13** prayer meeting **14** worship service

pray for us
Latin: 11 ora pro nobis

pray to 3 beg **5** plead **7** address, entreat, worship **8** call upon, petition, venerate **10** supplicate

preach 4 urge **6** advise, exhort **7** counsel, declare, expound, profess **8** admonish, advocate, homilize, proclaim, stand for **9** discourse, hold forth, preachify, prescribe, pronounce, propagate, sermonize **10** evangelize, promulgate

preacher 5 vicar **6** curate, parson, pastor **8** chaplain, homilist, minister, reverend, sky pilot **9** churchman, clergyman **10** evangelist, prebendary, sermonizer **12** ecclesiastic **13** man of the cloth

preachy 8 didactic, pedantic **10** moralistic, moralizing

prearranged 7 planned **10** calculated, deliberate, purposeful **11** intentional **12** premeditated

pre-Cambrian 5 Azoic **6** Eozoic **7** primary **10** Archeozoic **11** Proterozoic

precarious 5 risky, shaky **6** chancy, unsafe **7** dubious **8** alarming, critical, doubtful, insecure, perilous, sinister, ticklish, unstable, unsteady **9** hazardous, uncertain **10** touch-and-go, unreliable, vulnerable **12** questionable, uncontrolled, undependable **13** problematical

precaution 4 care **7** caution, defense **8** prudence, security, wariness **9** foresight, provision, safeguard **10** protection **11** carefulness, forethought, heedfulness **12** anticipation **14** circumspection

precede 8 antecede, antedate, go before **9** go ahead of **10** come before

precedence, precedency 8 priority **10** importance, preference, prevalence **11** antecedence, preeminence **12** predominance, preexistence

precedent 5 model **7** example, pattern **8** standard **9** criterion, guideline

preceding 5 prior **6** former **7** earlier **8** anterior, previous **9** aforesaid, foregoing **10** antecedent, first-named, precursory **11** preexistent, preliminary **14** abovementioned, aforementioned, first-mentioned

precept 3 law **4** bull, code, rule **5** axiom, canon, edict, maxim, motto, tenet, truth, ukase **6** byword, decree, dictum **7** dictate, mandate, statute **8** standard, teaching **9** ordinance, principle, yard stick **10** regulation **11** commandment, declaration

preceptor 5 coach, tutor **6** mentor **7** advisor, teacher **8** director **9** admonitor, counselor, principal **10** headmaster **12** headmistress

precincts 7 suburbs 8 environs 9 districts, outskirts 10 boundaries 12 subdivisions 15 surrounding area

precious 4 dear, rare 5 fussy, sweet 6 adored, choice, costly, dainty, prissy, prized, valued 7 beloved, darling, finical, finicky, lovable 8 adorable, affected, uncommon, valuable 9 cherished, expensive, exquisite, priceless, treasured 10 fastidious, high-priced, invaluable, meticulous, particular 11 beyond price, inestimable, overrefined, pretentious

precipice 4 crag 5 bluff, cliff, ledge 8 headland, palisade 9 cliff edge, declivity 10 escarpment

precipitate 4 cast, hurl, rash, spur 5 drive, fling, hasty, throw 6 abrupt, hasten, launch, let fly, propel, rushed, speedy, thrust 7 advance, bring on, hurried, quicken, speed up 8 catapult, expedite, headlong, reckless 9 discharge, foolhardy, impetuous, imprudent, impulsive 10 accelerate, incautious 11 thoughtless

precipitation 4 hail, rain, rush, snow 5 haste, sleet 8 rainfall, rashness 9 hastiness 11 impetuously

precipitous 5 hasty, sharp, sheer, steep 6 abrupt 9 impetuous

precis 5 brief 6 apercu, digest, resume, sketch 7 epitome, outline, rundown, summary 8 abstract, synopsis 10 abridgment, compendium 12 condensation 14 recapitulation

precise 4 true 5 exact, fussy, rigid 6 strict 7 careful, express, finicky, literal 8 accurate, clear-cut, definite, distinct, explicit, incisive, specific 9 unbending 10 fastidious, inflexible, meticulous, particular, to the point 11 painstaking, unequivocal

precision 5 rigor 8 accuracy, fidelity 9 attention, exactness 11 factualness, preciseness 12 authenticity, truthfulness 14 meticulousness

preclude 3 bar, dam 4 balk, curb, foil, stop 5 avert, avoid, block, check, debar, deter 6 arrest, hamper, hinder, thwart 7 head off, inhibit, prevent 8 stave off 9 forestall, frustrate 11 nip in the bud

preclusion 9 exclusion, restraint 10 prevention

precocious 3 apt 5 quick, smart 6 bright, clever, gifted, mature 8 advanced 9 brilliant

preconception 4 bias 6 notion 9 fixed idea, prejudice 11 prejudgment, presumption 14 predisposition

precursor 4 mark, omen, sign 5 token, usher 6 herald 7 portent, symptom, warning 8 vanguard 9 harbinger, messenger 10 antecedent, forerunner 11 predecessor

precursory 5 prior 8 anterior, previous

9 precedent 10 antecedent 11 preexistent

predaceous, predacious 9 predatory, rapacious 10 meat-eating 11 carnivorous, flesh-eating

predate 7 precede 8 antecede, antedate, go before

predatory 8 thievish 9 larcenous, marauding, pillaging, piratical, rapacious, raptorial, vulturine 10 plunderous, predacious

predecessor 7 forbear 8 ancestor, forebear, foregoer 10 antecedent, forefather, forerunner

predestination 4 fate 6 kismet 7 destiny, fortune 8 God's will 10 providence 13 inevitability, preordination 16 predetermination

predetermined 5 fated 7 decided, planned 8 destined 10 calculated, deliberate, preplanned 11 intentional, prearranged, predestined 12 foreordained, premeditated

predicament 3 fix, jam 4 bind, mess 5 pinch 6 corner, crisis, pickle, plight, scrape, strait 7 dilemma, trouble 8 hot water, quandary 9 imbroglio, sad plight 10 difficulty, perplexity

predicate 4 base, real, rest, true 5 found, imply 6 affirm, assert 7 commend, connote, declare 8 proclaim

predict 4 omen 5 augur 6 divine 7 betoken, foresee, presage 8 envision, forecast, foretell, prophesy 10 anticipate 13 prognosticate

prediction 6 augury 7 portent 8 forecast, prophecy 10 divination 11 declaration, foretelling, soothsaying 12 announcement, anticipation, proclamation 13 crystal gazing 15 prognostication

predilection 4 bent, bias, love 5 fancy, favor, taste 6 desire, hunger, liking, relish 7 leaning 8 appetite, fondness, penchant, tendency 9 prejudice, proneness 10 attraction, partiality, preference, proclivity, propensity 11 inclination 13 prepossession 14 predisposition

predispose 4 bias, lure, sway, urge 5 tempt 6 entice, induce, prompt, seduce 7 dispose, incline, win over 8 persuade 9 encourage, influence, prejudice

predisposed 3 apt 5 given, prone 8 inclined

predisposition 7 leaning 8 tendency 11 inclination

predominance 7 command, control 8 currency 9 dominance, supremacy 10 ascendancy, importance, prevalence 11 preeminence, superiority 12 universality

predominant 4 main 5 chief, major 6 potent, ruling, strong 7 leading, supreme 8 dominant, forceful, powerful,

reigning, vigorous 9 ascendant, important, paramount, sovereign 11 controlling, influential 13 authoritative

predominate 4 lead 7 prevail 8 dominate

predominating 5 chief 6 ruling 8 dominant, superior 9 principal 10 commanding, prevailing 11 controlling, predominant 13 authoritative

preeminence 9 greatness, supremacy 10 ascendancy, importance, leadership, notability, prominence 11 distinction, superiority 12 predominance

preeminent 4 best 5 famed 6 famous 7 eminent, honored, supreme 8 dominant, foremost, greatest, peerless, renowned, superior 9 matchless, paramount, unequaled, unrivaled 10 celebrated, consummate 11 illustrious, predominant, unsurpassed 12 incomparable, second to none, unparalleled 13 distinguished
French: 13 par excellence

preempt 4 take 5 seize, usurp 8 arrogate, take over 10 commandeer, confiscate 11 appropriate, expropriate

preen 3 pin 4 perk, trim 5 adorn, dress, groom, plume, pride, primp, prink 6 brooch, smooth
wings: 4 whet

preexistent 5 prior 8 anterior, previous 9 precedent 10 antecedent, precursory

preface 4 open 5 begin, proem, start 6 launch 7 prelude 8 commence, foreword, initiate, lead into, overture, preamble, prologue 9 introduce 12 introduction

prefer 3 opt 4 file 5 adopt, elect, exalt, fancy, favor, lodge, offer 6 select, take to, tender 7 dignify, elevate, ennoble, fix upon, pick out, present, proffer, promote 8 graduate, set forth 9 single out

preference 4 bent, bias, pick 5 fancy 6 liking, option 7 leaning 8 favoring, priority 9 advantage, prejudice, proneness, selection, supremacy 10 ascendancy, partiality, precedence, proclivity, propensity 11 first choice, inclination 12 predilection 13 predomination 14 predisposition
French: 4 gout

prefigure 4 hint, type 6 shadow, typify 7 foresee, imagine, presage, suggest 9 adumbrate 10 foreshadow

pregnant 4 full, rich 6 fecund, filled, gravid 7 copious, fertile, fraught, replete, seminal, teeming, weighty 8 forceful, fruitful, prolific 9 abounding, expecting, gestating, important, luxuriant, momentous, plenteous, potential, with child, with young 10 impressive, life-giving, meaningful, parturient, productive, suggestive 11 having a baby, proliferous, provocative, signifi-

cant **12** fructiferous, in a family way
French: 8 enceinte

prehistoric 3 old **7** ancient **10** immemorial
continent: 8 Atlantis
epoch: 6 Eocene **7** Miocene **8** Pliocene **9** Oligocene, Paleocene **11** Pleistocene
era: 8 Cenozoic, Mesozoic **9** Paleozoic **10** Archeozoic **11** Proterozoic
implement: 4 celt **6** eolith
period: 7 Neogene, Permian **8** Cambrian, Devonian, Jurassic, Silurian, Triassic **9** Paleogene **10** Cretaceous, Ordovician, Quaternary
reptile: 8 dinosaur

prehistoric era 6 Ice Age **8** Cenozoic, Jurassic, Mesozoic, Triassic **9** Paleozoic **10** Cenomanian, Cretaceous **11** Precambrian **15** Upper Cretaceous **16** Pleistocene Epoch

prehistoric man see **8** early man

prejudice 3 ill, mar **4** bias, harm, hurt, loss, sway **5** slant, spoil, taint **6** damage, impair, infect, injure, injury, poison **7** bigotry **8** jaundice **9** detriment **10** favoritism, impairment, partiality, predispose, unfairness **11** contaminate, intolerance, prejudgment **12** disadvantage, one-sidedness, predilection **13** preconception **14** discrimination, predisposition

prejudiced 6 biased, unfair, unjust **7** bigoted, slanted **9** arbitrary **10** intolerant **11** close-minded, opinionated **12** narrow-minded

prejudicial 3 bad **6** biased **7** harmful, hurtful **8** damaging, inimical, sinister **9** injurious **11** deleterious, detrimental

prelate 5 abbot **6** bishop, cleric **9** churchman, clergy man **12** ecclesiastic

preliminary 9 prelusive, prelusory **10** initiatory, precursory, prefactory **11** preparative, preparatory **12** introductory

prelude 7 opening, preface **8** overture, preamble, prologue **9** beginning **11** preliminary, preparation **12** introduction

premature 3 raw **5** green, hasty **6** callow, unripe **7** too soon, unready **8** abortive, ill- timed, immature, previous, too early, untimely **9** embryonic, overhasty, unfledged, unhatched, vestigial **10** incomplete, unprepared **11** inopportune, precipitate, rudimentary, undeveloped **12** unseasonable

premeditated 7 planned, plotted, studied, willful **8** intended **9** conscious, contrived, voluntary **10** calculated, considered, deliberate, predevised, purposeful **11** in cold blood, intentional, prearranged, predesigned **13** predetermined **22** with malice aforethought

premeditation 4 plan **6** design **7** purpose **11** calculation, forethought, preplanning **12** deliberation

premier 3 bet **4** head **5** chief, first **6** oldest **7** leading, supreme **8** earliest, foremost **9** principal **13** prime minister

Preminger, Otto
director of: 5 Laura **11** Carmen Jones **16** Anatomy of a Murder

premise 6 theory **8** argument **9** postulate, principle **10** assumption, hypothesis **11** presumption, proposition, supposition **14** presupposition

premises 4 site **8** environs, property, vicinity **9** precincts

premium 4 gain, gift **5** award, bonus, prize **6** bounty, return, reward **7** benefit, payment **8** priority **9** high value, incentive **10** great stock, recompense, reparation **11** overpayment **12** appreciation, compensation, inflated rate, remuneration **13** consideration, encouragement

premonition 4 omen, sign **5** hunch, token **6** augury **7** auspice, feeling, inkling, portent, presage **9** foretoken **10** foreboding, indication, prediction **11** forewarning **12** presentiment

Prendergast, Maurice Brazil
born: 6 Canada **7** St John's **12** Newfoundland
artwork: 6 Dieppe **8** Seashore **11** Picnic Grove **12** The Promenade **16** Ponte della Paglia **17** Along the Boulevard, Four Girls in Meadow **24** Umbrellas in the Rain Venice

Prentice, John
creator/artist of: 8 Rip Kirby

preoccupation 9 immersion, obsession **10** absorption, detachment, dreaminess, employment **11** abstraction, involvement **16** absentmindedness

preoccupied 6 absent, dreamy **8** absorbed, immersed, involved, obsessed **9** engrossed, wrapped up **10** abstracted, distracted **12** absent-minded

preoccupy 6 absorb, arrest, obsess, take up, wrap up **7** engross, immerse **9** fascinate

preparation 8 prudence, readying **9** foresight, preparing, provision, safeguard **10** precaution **11** expectation, forethought **12** anticipation

preparations 5 plans **7** elixirs **8** guidance, measures, mixtures, training, tutelage **9** dressings, education, seasoning, tinctures **11** concoctions, confections **12** arrangements **13** preliminaries, prepared foods, prescriptions **14** qualifications

prepare 3 fix **5** adapt, prime, ready **7** arrange, be ready, provide **8** get ready **9** make ready, rearrange, take steps

prepared 4 done **5** fixed, ready **6** cooked, primed **7** planned **8** arranged, finished **9** made ready, rehearsed **11** provided for

prepayment 6 credit **7** advance **9** allowance **11** downpayment

preponderance, preponderancy 4 bulk, glut, mass **6** excess **7** surfeit, surplus **8** majority, plethora **9** dominance, plurality, profusion **10** domination, lion's share, oversupply, prevalence, redundance **12** predominance **14** superabundance

preponderant 3 key **4** main **5** chief, first, major, prime **7** highest, leading, primary, supreme **8** dominant, foremost, greatest **9** paramount, principal, uppermost **10** prevailing **11** outstanding, predominant

prepossessing 4 nice **7** winsome **8** alluring, charming, engaging, inviting, pleasant, striking **9** beguiling **10** attractive, bewitching, enchanting, entrancing, personable **11** captivating, fascinating, tantalizing

preposterous 5 inane, outre, silly **6** absurd, stupid **7** asinine, bizarre, fatuous, foolish, idiotic **9** imbecilic, laughable, ludicrous **10** irrational, outrageous, ridiculous **11** nonsensical, unthinkable **12** unreasonable

prerequisite 4 need **6** demand **8** demanded, exigency, required **9** called for, condition, de rigueur, essential, mandatory, necessary, necessity, postulate, requisite **10** imperative, sine qua non **11** requirement, stipulation **13** indispensable, qualification

prerogative 3 due **5** claim, grant, right **6** choice, option **7** freedom, liberty, license, warrant **9** advantage, exemption, franchise, privilege **10** birthright

presage 4 bode, omen, osse, sign **5** augur, token **6** augury, herald **7** betoken, portend, portent, predict **8** forecast, foreshow, foretell, indicate **9** foresight **10** foreboding, foreshadow, indication, prediction, prescience, prognostic **11** premonition **12** presentiment

presbyter 5 elder **13** church officer

prescience 7 presage **9** foresight, prevision **13** foreknowledge

prescribe 3 fix, set **4** rule, urge **5** enact, order **6** assign, decree, demand, direct, enjoin, impose, ordain, settle **7** appoint, command, dictate, require, specify **8** advocate, proclaim **9** authorize, establish, institute, legislate, recommend, stipulate

prescribed 3 set **5** fixed **6** thetic **9** formulary

prescript 3 law **4** rule **5** order **7** precept, statute **10** regulation

prescriptive 7 binding **8** demanded, dictated, didactic, required **9** customary, mandatory, requisite **10** compulsory, imperative, obligatory

presence 3 air **4** life, look, mien **5** being, curse, favor, ghost, group, midst **6** aspect, entity, figure, manner, shadow, spirit, vision, wraith **7** bearing, company, eidolon, phantom, specter **8** carriage, charisma, demeanor, features, phantasm, revenant, vitality **9** character, existence **10** apparition, attendance, deportment, expression, lineaments **11** reification, subsistence **12** neighborhood **13** manifestation

presence of mind 6 aplomb **8** calmness, coolness **9** composure, sangfroid **10** equanimity, steadiness **14** self-possession **16** imperturbability

present 2 in **3** fee, now, tip **4** alms, aver, boon, cite, gift, give, here, near, nigh, read, show, tell **5** about, award, frame, grant, offer, state, today **6** accord, allege, assert, at hand, bestow, bounty, call up, chip in, coeval, confer, donate, hand in, impart, legacy, nearby, on hand, recite, relate, render, rooted, submit, summon, supply, tender, turn in **7** advance, bequest, bring on, current, declare, deliver, display, dole out, exhibit, expound, give out, instant, largess, mete out, not away, produce, profess, proffer, propose, provide, recount, vicinal **8** donation, embedded, existent, existing, give away, give over, gratuity, hand over, nowadays, oblation, offering, propound, put forth **9** apprise of, attending, draw forth, endowment, ensconced, hold forth, immediate, implanted, in the room, introduce, make known, not absent, on-the-spot, prevalent, pronounce, surrender, the moment, unremoved **10** asseverate, come up with, contribute, here and now, liberality, perquisite, put forward **11** benefaction, communicate **12** accounted for, bring forward, contemporary, in attendance

presentable 4 chic, so-so **6** decent, modish, not bad, proper **7** stylish **8** becoming, passable, suitable **9** tolerable **10** acceptable, good enough **11** appropriate, fashionable, fit to be seen, respectable

presentation 3 fee, tip **4** boon, gift, show **5** favor, grant, offer **6** bounty **7** advance, display, exhibit, largess, present, proffer **8** bestowal, exposure, gratuity, oblation, offering, overture, proposal **9** unfolding **10** appearance, compliment, disclosure, exhibition, exposition, liberality, production, proffering, submission, unfoldment **11** benefaction, performance, proposition **13** demonstration

Present at the Creation
    author: 11 Dean Acheson

presentiment 7 feeling **10** foreboding **11** forewarning, premonition **12** apprehension

presently 3 now **4** anon, soon **7** shortly **8** directly, in a while, this week, this year **9** at present, currently, forth with **10** any time now, before long, pretty soon **11** after a while, at the moment **12** in a short time
    French: 11 tout a l'heure

preservation 6 saving **7** defense **9** salvation **10** protection **11** maintenance, safekeeping **12** conservation, safeguarding

preservative 4 salt **5** brine, spice **8** marinade **12** formaldehyde

preserve, preserves 3 can, dry, jam **4** corn, cure, park, salt, save, seal **5** guard, haven, jelly, nurse, put up, smoke, sweet **6** comfit, defend, embalm, foster, freeze, pickle, refuge, season, secure, shield **7** care for, compote, mummify, protect, reserve, shelter **8** conserve, insulate, keep safe, maintain, marinate **9** dehydrate, keep sound, marmalade, safeguard, sanctuary, sweetmeat, watch over **10** confection, keep intact, perpetuate **11** refrigerate, reservation

preside 4 boss, host, rule **5** chair, watch **6** direct, govern, manage **7** command, conduct, control, hostess, oversee **8** chairman, overlook, regulate **9** keep order, supervise **10** administer **11** superintend **12** administrate, take the chair

president, President 4 head **5** ruler **8** chairman **12** chief officer, chief of state, first citizen **14** chief executive **16** commander in chief, executive officer, head of government

President of the United States
    first: 16 George Washington
    second: 9 John Adams
    third: 15 Thomas Jefferson
    fourth: 12 James Madison
    fifth: 11 James Monroe
    sixth: 15 John Quincy Adams
    seventh: 13 Andrew Jackson
    eighth: 14 Martin Van Buren
    ninth: 20 William Henry Harrison
    tenth: 9 John Tyler
    eleventh: 11 James K Polk
    twelfth: 13 Zachary Taylor
    thirteenth: 15 Millard Fillmore
    fourteenth: 14 Franklin Pierce
    fifteenth: 13 James Buchanan
    sixteenth: 14 Abraham Lincoln
    seventeenth: 13 Andrew Johnson
    eighteenth: 13 Ulysses S Grant
    nineteenth: 16 Rutherford B Hayes
    twentieth: 14 James A Garfield
    twenty-first: 17 Chester Alan Arthur
    twenty-second: 15 Grover Cleveland
    twenty-third: 16 Benjamin Harrison
    twenty-fourth: 15 Grover Cleveland
    twenty-fifth: 15 William McKinley
    twenty-sixth: 17 Theodore Roosevelt
    twenty-seventh: 17 William Howard Taft

    twenty-eighth: 13 Woodrow Wilson
    twenty-ninth: 14 Warren G Harding
    thirtieth: 14 Calvin Coolidge
    thirty-first: 13 Herbert Hoover
    thirty-second: 18 Franklin D Roosevelt
    thirty-third: 12 Harry S Truman
    thirty-fourth: 17 Dwight D Eisenhower
    thirty-fifth: 12 John F Kennedy
    thirty-sixth: 14 Lyndon B Johnson
    thirty-seventh: 13 Richard M Nixon
    thirty-eighth: 11 Gerald R Ford
    thirty-ninth: 11 (James E) Jimmy Carter (Jr)
    fortieth: 12 Ronald Reagan
    forty-first: 10 George Bush
    forty-second: 11 (William Jefferson) Bill Clinton

President's Analyst, The
    director: 16 Theodore J Flicker
    cast: 8 Will Geer **11** James Coburn **12** Severn Darden **16** Godfrey Cambridge

preside over 5 chair, guide **6** direct, govern, manage **7** conduct **8** dominate **9** supervise **10** administer **11** superintend

Presley, Elvis Aron
    nickname: 7 The King **14** Elvis the Pelvis **15** King of Rock n Roll
    born: 6 Tupelo **11** Mississippi
    wife: 9 Priscilla
    daughter: 9 Lisa Marie
    father: 6 Vernon
    mother: 6 Gladys
    twin brother: 11 Jessie Garon
    manager: 16 Colonel Tom Parker
    home: 9 Graceland
    location: 7 Memphis **9** Tennessee
    song: 8 Hound Dog **10** All Shook Up **11** Don't Be Cruel **12** Love Me Tender **13** Jailhouse Rock **14** Blue Suede Shoes **15** Heartbreak Hotel **17** That's All Right Mama
    film: 7 G I Blues **9** Loving You **10** Blue Hawaii, King Creole **12** Love Me Tender, Viva Las Vegas **13** Jailhouse Rock

press 2 TV **3** beg, bug, dun, hit, hug, jam, mob, pet, tap, tax **4** army, body, cram, duty, heap, herd, host, iron, mash, mill, pack, prod, push, rush **5** beset, bunch, clasp, crowd, crush, drove, exact, flick, force, horde, hound, hurry, media, plead, radio, set on, steam, stuff, surge, swarm **6** appeal, bother, burden, caress, compel, duress, enjoin, exhort, extort, fondle, gather, huddle, legion, mangle, push in, reduce, smooth, strain, stress, throng **7** cluster, collect, depress, embrace, entreat, flatten, implore, newsmen, oppress, snuggle, squeeze, trouble **8** assemble, bear down, bear upon, calender, compress, condense, hot-press, insist on, pressure, printing, push down **9** annoyance, be hard put, constrain, constrict, final form, force down, force from, importune, multitude, reporters **10** compulsion, congregate, newspapers, obligation, supplicate, television, thrust down **11** journalists, periodicals, publication **12** bear down upon, broadcasting, come together, news services, newspapermen **14** Fourth Estate

press down 7 compact, depress **8** push down

press forward 5 drive **6** push on **7** advance **10** forge ahead

press home 6 stress **9** emphasize, underline **10** accentuate, underscore

pressing 5 vital **6** crying, needed, urgent **7** crucial, exigent, needful **8** critical **9** clamoring, demanding, essential, important, insistent, necessary **10** imperative **11** importunate **13** indispensable

pressing necessity 6 crisis **7** urgency **8** exigency **9** emergency

press on 9 move ahead, persevere **10** accelerate, forge ahead **11** move forward

pressure 4 bias, care, load, need, pull, sway, want **5** force, hurry, pinch, power, press, trial **6** burden, demand, strain, stress, weight **7** anxiety, density, gravity, potency, squeeze, straits, tension, trouble, urgency **8** coercion, distress, exigency, interest **9** adversity, grievance, heaviness, influence, necessity **10** affliction, compaction, compulsion, difficulty, oppression

pressure measurement 6 pascal **10** atmosphere

prestige 4 fame, mark, note **5** glory, honor **6** esteem, import, regard, renown, report, repute **7** account, respect **8** eminence **9** authority, celebrity **10** importance, notability, prominence, reputation **11** consequence, distinction, preeminence **12** significance

prestigious 5 famed **6** famous **7** eminent, honored, notable **8** esteemed, renowned **9** acclaimed, important, prominent, reputable, respected, well-known **10** celebrated **11** illustrious, outstanding **13** distinguished

Preston, Robert
real name: 21 Robert Preston Meservey
born: 17 Newton Highlands MA
roles: 4 Mame **9** Semi-Tough **11** The Music Man **12** Junior Bonner **14** Victor Victoria **16** How the West Was Won

presumable 6 likely **8** apparent, probable **10** ostensible

presumably 6 likely **8** probably **9** assumably, doubtless **10** apparently, ostensibly **13** presumptively **14** unquestionably **15** in all likelihood **16** in all probability

presume 4 dare **5** fancy, guess, posit **6** assume, deduce, gather, have it, impose, take it **7** believe, imagine, suppose, surmise, suspect, venture **8** be so bold, conceive, make bold, make free **9** postulate, take leave **11** hypothesize, rely too much, think likely **12** take a liberty

presumed 7 assumed, deduced, posited **8** believed, imagined, supposed, surmised **9** suspected **10** postulated **13** took advantage **15** taken for granted

presumption 3 lip **4** gall **5** brass, cheek, guess, nerve, pride **6** belief, daring **7** egotism, premise, surmise **8** audacity, boldness, chutzpah, rudeness **9** arrogance, flippancy, impudence, insolence, postulate **10** assumption, conjecture, effrontery **11** forwardness, haughtiness, prejudgment, speculation, supposition **12** impertinence **13** preconception **14** presupposition

presumptuous 4 bold **5** brash, cocky, fresh, lofty, nervy, proud **6** brassy, brazen, daring, lordly **7** forward, haughty, pompous **8** arrogant, assuming, snobbish **9** audacious, imperious, shameless **10** disdainful **11** dictatorial, domineering, overbearing, patronizing **12** contemptuous, overfamiliar **13** overconfident

presuppose 6 assume **7** presume, suppose **9** speculate **10** conjecture **11** hypothesize

presupposed 7 assumed **8** presumed, supposed **10** speculated **11** conjectured

presupposition 7 premise **10** assumption **11** postulation, presumption

pretend 4 fake, sham **5** claim, fancy, feign, mimic, put on **6** affect, assume **7** imagine, imitate, playact, purport, suppose **8** simulate **9** dissemble **10** masquerade **11** counterfeit, dissimulate, impersonate, make believe

pretended
French: **9** soi-disant

pretender 5 faker, fraud, phony **8** claimant, imposter

pretense 4 airs, fake, hoax, mask, sham, show **5** cloak, cover, feint, guile, trick, vaunt **6** deceit **7** bluster, bombast, display, pretext **8** boasting, bragging, disguise, trickery **9** deception, false show, imposture, invention, pomposity **10** camouflage, pretension, showing off, subterfuge **11** affectation, counterfeit, fabrication, fanfaronade, make-believe, ostentation **12** affectedness

pretension 4 airs, pomp, show **5** claim, right, title **7** bombast, display **8** ambition, pretense, snobbery **9** hypocrisy, pomposity, showiness **10** aspiration, showing off **11** affectation, os-

tentation **13** grandioseness **14** self-importance **16** ostentatiousness

pretentious 4 airy, smug **5** gaudy, lofty, showy, stagy **6** flashy, florid, garish, ornate, tawdry **7** blown-up, fatuous, pompous, stuck-up **8** affected, assuming, boastful, inflated, overdone, pedantic, puffed-up, snobbish **9** bombastic, flaunting, insincere, presuming, unnatural **10** hoity-toity, theatrical **11** exaggerated, extravagant, overbearing **12** ostentatious, self-praising **13** high-and-mighty, self-important

pretentiousness 4 cant **6** humbug **9** hypocrisy **11** insincerity **17** sanctimoniousness

preternatural 5 eerie, weird **6** arcane, occult **7** bizarre, strange, uncanny **8** esoteric, mystical **9** unearthly, unworldly **10** miraculous, mysterious, superhuman **11** hypernormal, preterhuman, supernormal **12** extramundane, metaphysical, supernatural, supranatural **14** transcendental

pretext 5 basis, bluff, feint **6** excuse, ground **8** pretense **9** semblance **10** pretension, subterfuge **11** vindication

pretty 4 fair **5** bonny **6** comely, dainty, fairly, goodly, lovely, rather **7** shapely, sightly, well-set **8** alluring, charming, delicate, engaging, fetching, graceful, handsome, somewhat, well-made **9** beauteous, beautiful **10** adequately, attractive, moderately, reasonably **11** captivating, good-looking, symmetrical, well-favored

pretty child 4 doll **5** cutie **10** living doll

prevail 3 win **4** rule **5** exist, reign **6** abound, obtain, win out **7** conquer, succeed, triumph **8** have sway, hold sway, overcome **9** be a winner, be current **11** be prevalent, be the victor, carry the day, gain the palm, predominate **12** be victorious, be widespread, preponderate

prevailing 3 set **4** main **5** fixed, usual **6** normal **7** current, general, in style, popular **8** definite, dominant **9** customary, prevalent, principal **10** accustomed, widespread **11** established, predominant **12** conventional, preponderant

prevail over 4 beat **5** outdo **6** defeat **7** eclipse, surpass **8** overcome

prevail upon 4 sway **8** convince, persuade **9** influence

prevalent 4 rife **5** usual **6** common, normal **7** general, popular, rampant **8** abundant, everyday, familiar, frequent, habitual, numerous **9** customary, extensive, pervasive, universal **10** prevailing, ubiquitous, widespread **11** commonplace **12** conventional

prevaricate 3 fib, lie **4** fake **6** palter **7** deceive, distort, falsify, mislead, perjure **8** hoodwink, misstate **9** be evasive, dissemble **10** equivocate, tell a story **11** counterfeit **12** be untruthful, misrepresent

prevarication 3 fib, lie **5** fable **7** fiction, untruth, whopper **9** fairy tale, falsehood, fish story, invention **11** fabrication **12** equivocation **16** cock-and-bull story **17** misrepresentation

prevent 3 bar, dam **4** balk, foil, halt, stop, veto **5** avert, avoid, block, deter **6** arrest, forbid, thwart **7** deflect, draw off, fend off, obviate, rule out, ward off **8** hold back, preclude, prohibit, stave off, turn away **9** forestall, frustrate, intercept, sidetrack, turn aside **10** anticipate, counteract **11** nip in the bud

prevention 6 defeat **8** stoppage **9** avoidance, hindrance, obviation, restraint, thwarting **10** deterrence, inhibition, preclusion **11** elimination, frustration **12** interception **13** forestallment

preview 5 sneak **6** sample, survey **8** futurama **9** foretaste **10** inspection

previous 5 early, prior **6** before, former **7** earlier **8** foregone **9** aforesaid, erstwhile, foregoing, preceding **10** antecedent **14** aforementioned

previously 4 once **6** before **7** earlier, long ago **8** back when, formerly **9** at one time, a while ago, earlier on **10** a while back, heretofore **11** in times past **12** sometime back

Prevost, Abbe
author of: 12 Manon Lescaut

prey 3 eat **4** dupe, food, game, gull, kill **5** patsy, prize, quest **6** devour, infest, pigeon, quarry, sucker, target, victim **7** cat's-paw, consume, fall guy, live off **8** feed upon **9** feast upon **10** fasten upon, fatten upon, parasitize

Priam
king of: 4 Troy
father: 8 Laomedon
brother: 8 Tithonus
wife: 6 Hecuba
son: 5 Paris **6** Hector **9** Polydorus
daughter: 8 Polyxena **9** Cassandra
number of sons: 5 fifty
number of daughters: 5 fifty
killed by: 11 Neoptolemus

Priamid
father: 5 Priam

Priapus
god of: 5 herds **7** gardens **9** fertility, male power **11** procreation
father: 8 Dionysus
mother: 9 Aphrodite
corresponds to: 7 Mutinus

price 3 fee **4** cost, fine, rate **5** value, worth **6** amount, assess, charge, outlay **7** expense, penalty **8** appraise, evaluate, par value **9** face value, list price **10** forfeiture, punishment

Price, Fanny

character in: 13 Mansfield Park
author: 6 Austen

Price, Vincent
born: 9 St Louis MO
wife: 11 Coral Browne **12** Edith Barrett
roles: 6 The Fly **8** The Raven **10** House of Wax **13** Tower of London **15** The House of Usher **20** The Pit and the Pendulum **22** The Masque of the Red Death
expert in: 3 art

Price Is Right, The
host: 9 Bob Barker **10** Bill Cullen

priceless 4 dear, rare **6** costly, prized, valued **8** peerless, precious, valuable **9** cherished, expensive, treasured **10** high-priced, invaluable **11** beyond price **12** incomparable, without price **13** irreplaceable **17** worth a king's ransom

prick 5 stick **6** pierce **8** puncture

prickle 4 barb, itch **5** point, quill, smart, sting, thorn **6** tingle **7** barbule, bristle, spicule

prickly 5 itchy **6** coarse, thorny **8** scratchy, stinging **9** vexatious

pride 3 joy **4** airs, pomp, show **5** honor **6** egoism, parade, vanity **7** comfort, conceit, delight, dignity, display, egotism, swagger **8** pleasure, self-love, smugness **9** arrogance, be proud of, enjoyment, happiness, immodesty, pomposity, vainglory **10** pretension, self-esteem **11** haughtiness, ostentation, self-respect **14** self-importance

Pride and Prejudice
author: 10 Jane Austen
character: 7 Mr Darcy **9** Mr Bingley, Mr Collins, Mr Wickham **14** Charlotte Lucas **15** Caroline Bingley **21** Lady Catherine de Bourgh
  Bennet daughters: 4 Jane, Mary **5** Kitty, Lydia **9** Elizabeth
director: 14 Robert Z Leonard
cast: 10 Mary Boland **11** Edmund Gwenn, Greer Garson, Karen Morley **13** Ann Rutherford, Edna May Oliver **15** Laurence Olivier **16** Maureen O'Sullivan

Pride of the Yankees, The
director: 7 Sam Wood
cast: 8 Babe Ruth **9** Dan Duryea **10** Gary Cooper (Lou Gehrig) **12** Teresa Wright **13** Walter Brennan

priest 5 padre **6** cleric, father **8** minister, preacher **9** churchman **13** man of the cloth

priesthood 5 cloth **6** clergy **8** ministry, the cloth **9** pastorage

Priestley, J B
author of: 9 Bright Day **11** Lost Empires **13** Angel Pavement **17** The Good Companions

Priestley, Joseph
field: 9 chemistry

nationality: 7 British
discovered: 6 oxygen **7** ammonia **13** nitrogen oxide
invented: 11 carbonation

priestly 8 churchly, clerical **10** sacerdotal **14** ecclesiastical

prig 5 bigot, prude **6** pedant **7** puritan **8** bluenose **9** formalist, hypocrite, nitpicker, pretender **10** fuddy-duddy **11** faultfinder **12** bluestocking, precisionist, stuffed shirt **14** attitudinarian

priggish 4 prim, smug **6** stuffy **7** prudish **9** blue-nosed **10** tight-laced **11** puritanical, straitlaced **13** self-righteous, self-satisfied

prim 4 smug, tidy **5** fussy **6** prissy, proper, strict, stuffy **7** haughty, prudish **8** priggish, starched **9** squeamish, unbending **10** fastidious, fuddy-duddy, inflexible, no-nonsense, particular **11** overprecise, puritanical, stiff-necked, straitlaced

prima donna 4 diva, lead, star **6** singer **9** principal
literally: 9 first lady

primarily 6 mainly, mostly **7** chiefly, largely **9** basically, generally, in the main **11** essentially, principally **13** fundamentally, predominantly **14** for the most part **16** first and foremost

primary 3 key **4** main, star **5** basal, basic, chief, first, prime, vital **6** innate, native, oldest, primal, ruling, utmost **7** highest, initial, leading, nascent, natural **8** cardinal, dominant, earliest, greatest, inherent, original, primeval **9** beginning, elemental, essential, important, necessary, primitive, principal, prominent **10** aboriginal, elementary, indigenous, primordial, rudimental **11** fundamental, predominant, preparatory, rudimentary **12** introductory

primary constituent 5 basic **9** basic need, essential, necessity, requisite **10** sine qua non

primate 3 ape, man **5** avahi, indri, lemur, loris, potto **6** aye-aye, baboon, bishop, galago, gibbon, mammal, monkey **7** gorilla, tamarin, tarsier **8** marmoset, simpoona **9** orangutan, tree shrew **10** archbishop, chimpanzee

prime 2 A1 **3** ace, fit **4** best, main, peak, pink **5** adapt, basal, basic, bloom, breed, brief, chief, coach, early, first, groom, guide, lucky, raise, ready, train, tutor, vital **6** adjust, choice, fill in, flower, Grade A, height, heyday, inform, innate, native, oldest, primal, prompt, ruling, school, seemly, select, timely, utmost, zenith **7** educate, fitting, highest, leading, maximal, natural, prepare, primary, quality, supreme, top-hole **8** best days, cardinal, crowning, earliest, get ready, greatest, inherent, instruct, maturity, original, peerless, suitable, superior **9** befitting, elemental, essential, expedient, important, intrinsic, make ready, matchless, necessary, opportune, paramount, preferred, principal, provident, top-drawer, top-flight, unmatched, well-timed **11** superlative, unsurpassed, without peer **12** unparalleled

prime example 5 model **7** classic **8** exemplar **9** archetype

prime mover 6 author **9** initiator, organizer **10** originator
Latin: 12 primum mobile

Prime of Miss Jean Brodie, The
author: 11 Muriel Spark

primer 3 cap **4** book **5** paint **6** manual, reader **8** hornbook, textbook **9** undercoat

primeval 5 early **6** oldest, primal **7** ancient, archaic **8** earliest, original **9** ancestral, legendary, primitive **10** aboriginal, indigenous, primordial **11** fundamental, prehistoric **12** antediluvian, mythological

primitive 4 bare **5** crude, early, first **6** native, simple **7** antique, archaic, artless, ascetic, austere, primary, Spartan **8** backward, earliest, original **9** beginning, unlearned, unrefined, unskilled **10** aboriginal, elementary **11** rudimentary, uncivilized, undeveloped

primordial 5 first **6** primal **7** initial **8** original, primeval **9** beginning, primitive **10** elementary **11** fundamental, prehistoric

primp 5 groom, plume, preen **6** doll up, make up **7** gussy up **8** prettify, spruce up

primrose 7 Primula **15** Primula vulgaris
varieties: 4 baby, cape, star **5** fairy **6** German, poison **7** Chinese, English, evening **8** bird's-eye **9** buttercup **12** beach evening, white evening **13** desert evening **14** Mexican evening

primum mobile 10 prime mover **16** first moving thing

primus inter pares 16 first among equals

prince
Italian: 8 principe
Turkish: 3 beg, bey
Prince
original name: 18 Prince Rogers Nelson
alias: 9 The Artist **30** The Artist Formerly Known as Prince
nickname: 12 Royal Badness
born: 2 MN **11** Minneapolis
recording: 6 For You, Parade, Prince **9** Dirty Mind **10** Purple Rain **11** Controversy, Crystal Ball **20** Around the World in a Day
film: 10 Purple Rain **12** 3 Chains o' Gold **13** Sign o' the Times **14** Graffiti Bridge **18** Under the Cherry Moon

Prince, The
author: 18 Niccolo Machiavelli
Prince and the Pauper, The
author: 9 Mark Twain
character: 4 Hugo **8** Tom Canty **9** John Canty **10** Hugh Hendon **11** Miles Hendon **19** Edward Prince of Wales
Prince Edward Island
abbreviation: 3 PEI
bay: 5 Rollo **6** Egmont **7** Bedeque **8** Cardigan, Malpeque **9** Cascumpec **12** Hillsborough
capital: 13 Charlottetown
gulf: 10 St Lawrence
people: 4 Scot **5** Irish, Scots **6** French **7** English
discoverer: 7 Cartier
province of: 6 Canada
river: 4 Dunk **5** Eliot, Yorke **12** Hillsborough
strait: 14 Northumberland
Prince Igor
also: 9 Kniaz Igor
opera by: 7 Borodin
character: 11 Khan Konchak
contains: 17 Polovetsian dances
princely 3 big **5** noble, royal **8** generous **11** magnificent
prince of darkness 5 Satan **7** Lucifer **8** the Devil **9** Beelzebub
Prince of Peace 5 Jesus **6** Christ
Princess and the Pea, The
author: 21 Hans Christian Andersen
Princess Casamassima
author: 10 Henry James
Princess Daisy
author: 12 Judith Krantz
Princesse de Cleves, La
author: 14 Mme de LaFayette
Princess Flavia
character in: 15 Prisoner of Zenda
author: 4 Hope
Prince Valiant
creator: 12 Harold Foster
character: 5 Ilene **9** Prince Arn **10** King Arthur
wife: 5 Aleta
nickname: 3 Val
principal 4 dean, fund, main, star **5** basic, chief, first, money, prime **6** master **7** capital, leading, primary, supreme **8** cardinal, dominant, foremost, greatest, superior, ultimate **9** essential, paramount, preceptor, prominent **10** capital sum, headmaster, leading man, preeminent **11** fundamental, predominant, protagonist **13** most important
principal constituent 4 base **12** chief feature **14** main ingredient
principal dish of a meal
French: 17 piece de resistance
principal event
French: 17 piece de resistance
principality 5 angel **9** princedom **14** celestial being, heavenly spirit

principally 6 mainly, mostly **7** chiefly, largely **8** above all **9** basically, primarily **10** especially **12** particularly **13** fundamentally, predominantly **14** for the most part **16** first and foremost
principe 6 prince
principle 3 law **4** code, fact, rule, view **5** axiom, basis, canon, credo, creed, dogma, honor, maxim, tenet, truth **6** belief, dictum, ethics, morals, theory, virtue **7** element, formula, honesty, precept, probity, scruple, theorem **8** attitude, doctrine, goodness, morality, position, rudiment, scruples, teaching **9** direction, integrity, rectitude, standards **10** assumption, regulation **11** fundamental, proposition, uprightness
principled 6 honest **7** upright **9** honorable **10** aboveboard, forthright
Pringle, John
real name of: 11 John Gilbert
prink 4 deck, fuss **5** adorn, preen, primp **6** spruce
print 3 die **4** copy, text, type **5** issue, plate, press, stamp, write **7** compose, edition, engrave, etching, gravure, impress, picture, publish, woodcut **10** lithograph, silkscreen **11** letterpress
printing press
invented by:
rotary: 3 Hoe
web: 7 Bullock
prior 6 former **7** earlier **8** anterior, previous **9** aforesaid, erstwhile, foregoing, prefatory **10** antecedent, precursory **11** going before, preexistent, preexisting, preparatory **14** aforementioned
Prioress
character in: 18 The Canterbury Tales
author: 7 Chaucer
priority 7 urgency **9** immediacy, seniority **10** ascendancy, precedence, precedency, preference **11** antecedence, preeminence, superiority
priory 5 abbey **6** friary **7** convent, nunnery **8** cloister **9** hermitage, monastery
Prism, Letitia
character in: 27 The Importance of Being Earnest
author: 5 Wilde
prison 3 can, jug, pen **4** brig, gaol, jail, stir, tank **5** clink, joint, pokey, tower **6** cooler **7** dungeon, slammer **8** bastille, big house **9** calaboose, jailhouse
Prisoner of Zenda
author: 11 Anthony Hope
character: 14 Princess Flavia **17** Lady Rose Burlesdon, Rudolph Rassendyll **18** Antoinette de Mauban, Fritz von Tarlenhein **21** Michael Duke of Strelsau **22** Rudolph King of Ruritania
director: 12 John Cromwell
cast: 9 Mary Astor **10** David Niven **12** C Aubrey Smith, Ronald Colman

(Rudolf Rassendyll) **16** Madeleine Carroll **18** Douglas Fairbanks Jr (Rupert of Hentzau)
setting: 9 Ruritania

prissy 4 prim **5** fussy **6** proper, stuffy **7** finicky, prudish **8** overnice **9** sissified **10** effeminate **11** strait-laced

Prissy
character in: 15 Gone With the Wind
author: 8 Mitchell

pristine 4 pure **8** unmarred, virginal **9** undefiled, unspoiled, unsullied, untouched **10** unpolluted **11** untarnished **14** uncontaminated

Pritchett, V S
author of: 11 Midnight Oil **16** Collected Stories, The Spanish Temper **19** On the Edge of the Cliff

privacy 6 secret **7** privity, retreat, secrecy **8** security, solitude **9** integrity, isolation, seclusion **10** retirement, withdrawal **11** privateness **12** dissociation, solitariness **13** sequestration

private 4 dark **5** fixed, privy **6** buried, closed, covert, hidden, lonely, remote, secret **7** cryptic, express, limited, obscure, special **8** confined, desolate, esoteric, hush-hush, isolated, lonesome, personal, secluded, solitary **9** concealed, exclusive, inviolate, invisible, nonpublic, not public, reclusive **10** classified, indistinct, mysterious, restricted, undercover, under wraps, unofficial, unrevealed **11** clandestine, nonofficial, sequestered, underground, undisclosed **12** confidential, off-the-record, unfrequented

privateer 6 pirate **7** brigand, corsair **9** buccaneer

private eye 4 dick **6** shamus **7** gumshoe **9** detective **12** investigator

Private Life of Henry VIII, The
director: 14 Alexander Korda
cast: 11 Merle Oberon, Robert Donat **12** Binnie Barnes **14** Elsa Lanchester (Anne of Cleves) **15** Charles Laughton (Henry VIII)

Private Life of the Master Race, The
author: 13 Bertold Brecht

Private Lives
author: 10 Noel Coward
character: 10 Elyot Chase, Sibyl Chase **12** Amanda Prynne, Victor Prynne

Private Lives of Elizabeth and Essex, The
director: 13 Michael Curtiz
cast: 10 Bette Davis (Elizabeth I), Errol Flynn (Essex) **11** Donald Crisp **12** Vincent Price **13** Nanette Fabray **17** Olivia de Havilland
also known as: 17 Elizabeth the Queen

privately 7 sub rosa **8** in secret, secretly **9** between us, entre nous, in private **12** in confidence **14** confiden-

tially **15** between you and me **16** between ourselves **17** behind closed doors

privation 4 lack, need, want **5** pinch **6** misery, penury **7** beggary, poverty, straits **8** distress, exigency, hardship **9** indigence, neediness, pauperism **10** bankruptcy, mendicancy **11** destitution **14** impoverishment **15** impecuniousness

privilege 3 due **4** boon **5** allow, favor, grant, honor, power, right, title **6** patent, permit **7** benefit, charter, empower, entitle, freedom, liberty, license **8** pleasure **9** advantage, authority, franchise **10** birthright **11** entitlement, prerogative **12** prerequisite

privileged 4 free **6** exempt, immune **7** allowed, excused, granted, limited, special **8** entitled, licensed **9** empowered, not liable, permitted, warranted **10** authorized, sanctioned **13** unaccountable

prize 3 cup, gem, pip **4** like, lulu **5** award, catch, crown, dandy, honey, honor, jewel, medal, peach, pearl, value **6** admire, esteem, honors, regard, reward, ribbon, trophy **7** cherish, diamond, guerdon, honored, laurels, premium, respect, winning **8** accolade, champion, citation, hold dear, look up to, pure gold, treasure **9** humdinger, medallion **10** appreciate, blue ribbon, decoration, set store by **11** crackerjack, masterpiece

prized 4 dear **8** esteemed, precious **9** cherished, treasured

prizefight 2 go **4** bout **5** match **6** boxing **7** contest **10** fisticuffs

prizefighter 3 pug **5** boxer **7** slugger **8** pugilist **9** flyweight **11** heavyweight, lightweight **12** bantamweight, middleweight, welterweight **13** featherweight **16** light heavyweight

pro 3 for **5** forth **6** before, expert, master **8** favoring **9** authority **11** affirmative
opposite: 3 con **7** amateur

probability 4 odds **6** chance **10** likelihood

probable 6 likely **7** logical, seeming, tenable **8** apparent, assuring, credible, expected, possible, presumed, supposed **9** plausible, promising, thinkable **10** believable, in the cards, ostensible, presumable, reasonable **11** conceivable, encouraging, presumptive

probably 6 likely **10** most likely, presumably, supposedly **11** as like as not **15** in all likelihood

probe 4 hunt, quiz, seek, test **5** query, study, trial **6** pursue, review, search, survey **7** examine, fish for, inquest, inquire, inquiry, inspect, pry into, rummage **8** analysis, look into, question, research **9** penetrate **10** inspec-

tion, scrutinize **11** examination, exploration, interrogate, investigate **13** investigation

probity 5 honor **6** virtue **7** decency, honesty **8** goodness, morality **9** character, integrity, principle **11** uprightness **12** straightness **13** righteousness **14** high-mindedness **15** trustworthiness **16** incorruptibility

problem 5 poser, query **6** puzzle, riddle, unruly **8** question, stubborn **9** conundrum, difficult **10** difficulty **11** intractable **12** disagreement, hard to manage, incorrigible, unmanageable

problematic 7 dubious, unknown **8** doubtful, puzzling **9** difficult, enigmatic, uncertain, unsettled, worrisome **10** perplexing **11** paradoxical, troublesome **12** questionable, undetermined

pro bono publico 16 for the public good

proboscis 4 beak, nose **5** snoot, snout, trunk **6** siphon, sucker, syphon **7** rostrum
monkey: 4 kaha **5** kahua

procedure 2 MO **3** way **4** mode **6** course, manner, method **7** process, routine **8** approach, strategy **9** technique **11** methodology **13** modus operandi

proceed 2 go **3** act **4** come, flow, go on, grow, move, stem, work **5** arise, begin, ensue, issue, start **6** derive, follow, move on, push on, result, set out, spring **7** advance, carry on, emanate, go ahead, operate, press on, succeed **8** be caused, commence, continue, function, progress, take rise **9** be derived, go forward, move ahead, originate, undertake

proceedings 4 case, suit **5** cause, trial **6** doings, events, report **7** account, actions, affairs, lawsuit, matters, minutes, records, returns **8** activity, archives, goings on **9** incidents, memoranda **10** happenings, litigation, operations **11** occurrences **12** transactions

proceeds 3 net **4** gain, gate, pelf, take **5** gross, lucre, money, yield **6** assets, income, profit, reward **7** returns, revenue **8** earnings, pickings, receipts, winnings **9** box office

process 3 can, dry **4** fill, flow, flux, mode, plan, ship, step, writ **5** alter, candy, smoke, treat, usage **6** change, course, freeze, handle, manner, method, motion, policy, scheme, system **7** convert, measure, passage, prepare, project, summons **8** deal with, function, movement, practice, preserve, progress, subpoena **9** dehydrate, dispose of, freeze-dry, procedure, transform, unfolding **10** court order, proceeding

procession 4 file, line, rank **5** array, march, train **6** column, course, parade

7 caravan, cortege, pageant, passage **8** progress, sequence **9** cavalcade, motorcade **10** succession **11** progression

Procheneosaurus
  type: **8** dinosaur **10** ornithopod
  location: **6** Canada
  period: **10** Cretaceous

proclaim 3 cry **4** tell **5** blare, state, voice **6** affirm, assert, blazon, herald, report, reveal **7** call out, declare, divulge, give out, profess, publish, release, sing out, trumpet **8** announce, disclose, set forth **9** advertise, broadcast, circulate, enunciate, hawk about, make known, publicize **10** make public, promulgate

proclamation 5 edict, ukase **6** decree **12** announcement **13** pronouncement

proclivity 3 yen **4** bent, bias **5** taste **6** desire, liking **7** impulse, leaning **8** affinity, appetite, penchant, soft spot, tendency **9** affection, prejudice, proneness **10** partiality, propensity **11** disposition, inclination **12** predilection **14** predisposition

procrastinate 3 lag **5** dally, defer, delay, stall, tarry **6** dawdle, linger, loiter **7** adjourn **8** hang back, hesitate, hold back, kill time, postpone, put on ice **9** temporize, waste time **10** be dilatory, dillydally **11** play for time **12** drag one's feet

procrastinating 4 slow **5** tardy **6** remiss **8** dilatory **9** reluctant **12** footdragging **13** dillydallying

procreate 3 get **4** bear, sire **5** beget, breed, spawn **6** create, father, mother **7** produce **8** conceive, engender, generate, multiply **9** propagate, reproduce **10** bring forth **11** give birth to, proliferate

procreation
  god of: **7** Priapus

procreator 4 sire **6** father **8** begetter

procrustean 7 drastic **8** ruthless **19** conforming at any cost

Procrustes
  also: **5** giant **8** Damastes **9** Polypemon
  seized: **9** travelers
  killed by: **7** Theseus
  tied them to: **3** bed
  made them fit by: **10** stretching **14** cutting off their feet

procure 3 buy, get, win **4** earn, gain, take **5** evoke, seize **6** attain, come by, effect, elicit, gather, incite, induce, obtain, pick up, secure **7** achieve, acquire, receive **8** contrive, purchase **10** accumulate, bring about, commandeer, lay hands on **11** appropriate

procurement 4 gain **7** seizure **8** purchase **10** attainment, purchasing **11** achievement, acquirement, acquisition **12** accumulation **13** appropriation

prod 3 jab, nag **4** flog, goad, lash, move, poke, push, spur, stir, urge,

whip **5** egg on, impel, prick, rouse, shove, speed **6** excite, exhort, incite, needle, prompt, propel, stir up **7** actuate, animate, provoke, quicken **8** motivate, pressure **9** encourage, instigate, stimulate

prodigal 4 lush **5** ample **6** lavish, myriad, wanton **7** copious, profuse, replete, spender, teeming, wastrel **8** abundant, generous, numerous, reckless, swarming, wasteful **9** abounding, bounteous, bountiful, countless, excessive, exuberant, impetuous, luxuriant, plentiful, unthrifty **10** exorbitant, gluttonous, immoderate, inordinate, numberless, profligate, squanderer, thriftless **11** dissipating, extravagant, improvident, innumerable, intemperate, overliberal, precipitate, spendthrift **13** multitudinous

prodigality 10 imprudence, lavishness **12** extravagance, improvidence, overspending, wastefulness

prodigious 3 big **4** huge, rare, vast **5** grand, great, large **6** mighty, unique **7** amazing, immense **8** colossal, enormous, gigantic, renowned, singular, striking, terrific, uncommon, unwonted, wondrous **9** marvelous, monstrous, startling, wonderful **10** astounding, impressive, miraculous, monumental, noteworthy, remarkable, stupendous, surprising, tremendous **11** astonishing, exceptional, farreaching, uncustomary, unthinkable **12** dumbfounding, overwhelming, unimaginable **13** extraordinary, inconceivable, unprecedented

prodigiously 10 enormously, incredibly, remarkably **12** inordinately, tremendously **13** astonishingly, exceptionally, extravagantly, outstandingly, spectacularly **14** overwhelmingly

prodigiousness 6 rarity **8** enormity, hugeness, vastness **10** uniqueness **11** singularity **12** extravagance

prodigy 4 whiz **6** expert, genius, marvel, master, rarity, wizard, wonder **7** stunner, whiz kid **8** rara avis **9** sensation **10** mastermind, phenomenon, wunderkind **11** wonder child

produce 4 bear, form, give, make, show **5** beget, bloom, cause, found, frame, hatch, set up, shape, yield **6** adduce, afford, create, devise, effect, evince, evolve, flower, fruits, greens, invent, reveal, sprout, supply, unmask, unveil **7** achieve, advance, bring in, compose, concoct, develop, display, divulge, exhibit, fashion, furnish, present, provide, staples, turn out, uncover **8** bring off, bring out, conceive, disclose, discover, generate, manifest, set forth **9** bear fruit, construct, fabricate, institute, make plain, originate, procreate, put on view, show forth **10** accomplish, bring

about, come up with, effectuate, foodstuffs, give life to, give rise to, put in force, vegetables **11** bring to pass, give birth to, manufacture, materialize **14** bring into being

Producers, The
  director: **9** Mel Brooks
  cast: **9** Dick Shawn **10** Gene Wilder, Zero Mostel **11** Kenneth Mars

production 4 film, play, show **5** drama, movie **6** cinema, circus, making **7** display, exhibit, musical, showing **8** building, carnival, creation **9** execution, formation, producing, stage show **10** appearance, disclosure, revelation **11** fabrication, fulfillment, manufacture, origination, performance **12** construction, effectuation, introduction, presentation **13** demonstration, entertainment, manifestation, manufacturing, motion picture **15** materialization

productive 4 busy, rich **6** active, fecund, paying, useful **7** causing, copious, dynamic, fertile, gainful, teeming **8** creating, creative, fruitful, prolific, valuable, vigorous, yielding **9** effectual, luxuriant, plenteous, plentiful, producing **10** invaluable, profitable, worthwhile **11** efficacious, moneymaking, proliferous **12** contributing, fructiferous, remunerative

profanation 9 sacrilege **10** defilement **11** desecration

profane 3 lay **4** evil, foul, lewd, mock, vile **5** abuse, bawdy, crude, nasty, scorn, waste **6** coarse, debase, filthy, ill-use, impure, misuse, offend, revile, ribald, sinful, unholy, vulgar, wicked **7** abusive, earthly, godless, impious, obscene, outrage, pervert, pollute, satanic, secular, ungodly, violate, worldly **8** agnostic, diabolic, off-color, temporal, unchaste, undevout, unseemly **9** atheistic, blaspheme, desecrate, hellbound, heretical, misemploy, shameless, unsaintly **10** irreverent, prostitute **11** blasphemous, contaminate, irreligious, terrestrial, unbelieving **12** nonreligious, sacrilegious

profanity 5 filth, oaths **7** cursing, cussing, impiety **8** swearing **9** blasphemy, obscenity, scatology **10** dirty words, execration, expletives, scurrility, swearwords **11** irreverence, obscenities, ungodliness **12** billingsgate **15** four-letter words

profess 3 act, own, say **4** aver, avow, fake, sham, tell **5** admit, claim, feign, offer, put on, state, vouch **6** affirm, allege, assert, assume, depose **7** advance, certify, confess, confirm, contend, declare, embrace, pretend, purport **8** announce, lay claim, maintain, practice, proclaim, propound, simulate **9** believe in, dissemble, enunciate, hold forth **10** asseverate, put forward **11** acknowledge, counterfeit, dissimulate

professed 6 avowed **7** alleged **8** admitted **9** confessed, purported **12** acknowledged, self-declared **14** self-proclaimed

profession 3 job, law, vow **4** line, post, word, work **5** claim, craft, field, trade, troth **6** avowal, career, metier, office, pledge, plight, sphere **7** calling, promise, pursuit, service **8** averment, business, endeavor, industry, medicine, position, practice, teaching, vocation **9** assertion, assurance, guarantee, situation, specialty, statement, testimony **10** allegation, confession, deposition, employment, line of work, occupation, walk of life **11** affirmation, attestation, declaration, undertaking, word of honor **12** announcement, confirmation **13** pronouncement **15** acknowledgement

professional 4 paid **5** adept **6** expert **9** authority, competent, practiced **10** specialist **11** experienced

professionalism 5 savvy, skill **7** know-how **9** expertise **10** expertness

professor 3 don **6** regent **7** adjoint, teacher **8** lecturer **10** instructor **retired: 8** emeritus

Professor, The
author: 15 Charlotte Bronte

professorial 6 teachy **7** bookish, donnish, preachy **8** academic, didactic, pedantic, teachery **11** pedagoguish **13** schoolmarmish **15** schoolmasterish **16** schoolteacherish

Professor's House, The
author: 11 Willa Cather

proffer 5 offer **6** extend, tender **7** advance, hold out, present

proficiency 5 knack, skill **6** acumen **7** ability, know-how **8** aptitude, capacity, deftness, facility **9** adeptness, dexterity, expertise, handiness **10** adroitness, capability, competence **13** qualification **14** accomplishment

proficient 3 apt **4** able, deft, good **5** adept, handy, quick, ready, sharp **6** adroit, clever, expert, gifted **7** capable, skilled, trained **8** masterly, polished, skillful, talented **9** competent, dexterous, effective, efficient, masterful, practiced, qualified, versatile **11** experienced **12** accomplished, professional

profile 4 form, side, tale **5** shape **6** figure, sketch **7** contour, drawing, outline, picture, skyline **8** half face, portrait, side view, vignette **9** biography **10** lineaments, silhouette **11** delineation **13** configuration

Profiles in Courage
author: 12 John F Kennedy

profit 3 pay, use **4** boon, earn, gain, good, help **5** avail, favor, money, serve, value **6** income, return **7** account, benefit, revenue, service, utility, utilize **8** earnings, interest, proceeds, receipts **9** advantage, make money **11** advancement

profitable 6 paying, useful **7** gainful **8** fruitful, salutary, valuable **9** favorable, lucrative, rewarding **10** beneficial, invaluable, productive, well-paying, worthwhile **11** moneymaking, serviceable **12** advantageous, remunerative

profitmaking 8 business **11** moneymaking **13** noncharitable

profits 4 gate, take **5** gains, yield **6** assets, income **7** returns, revenue **8** earnings, receipts

profligacy 10 lavishness **11** dissipation, dissolution, prodigality, unrestraint **12** extravagance, immoderation, improvidence, recklessness, wastefulness **13** excessiveness

profligate 4 evil, fast, rake, roue, wild **5** loose, satyr **6** erotic, lavish, sinful, sinner, wanton, wicked **7** corrupt, immoral, pervert, satyric, wastrel **8** degraded, depraved, prodigal, reckless, wasteful **9** abandoned, debauched, debauchee, dissolute, libertine, reprobate, sybaritic, unbridled, unthrifty, wrongdoer **10** degenerate, dissipated, dissipater, iniquitous, lascivious, licentious **11** extravagant, improvident, promiscuous, spendthrift **12** unprincipled, unrestrained

pro forma 15 according to form, as a matter of form

profound 4 deep, keen, sage, wise **5** acute, sober, utter **6** abject, hearty, moving, severe **7** decided, erudite, extreme, intense, knowing, learned, radical, serious, sincere **8** complete, educated, informed, piercing, positive, thorough **9** heartfelt, out-and-out, recondite, sagacious, scholarly **10** all-knowing, consummate, deep-seated, omniscient, pronounced, reflective, thoughtful **11** enlightened, far-reaching, penetrating **12** intellectual, soul-stirring **13** comprehensive, knowledgeable, philosophical, thoroughgoing

profundity 5 abyss, depth **6** wisdom **8** deepness, sagacity, sapience **9** erudition **11** learnedness, penetration **12** abstractness, abstruseness, profoundness **13** reconditeness, sagaciousness **16** impenetrableness

profuse 4 rich **5** ample, wordy **6** lavish, prolix **7** copious, diffuse, verbose **8** abundant, generous, prodigal, rambling, wasteful **9** bounteous, bountiful, excessive, garrulous, unthrifty **10** digressive, discursive, immoderate, inordinate, long-winded, loquacious, munificent **11** extravagant, improvident, intemperate, spendthrift

profuseness 9 abundance, diffusion, profusion, prolixity, verbosity, wordi-

ness **10** lavishness **11** copiousness, diffuseness

profusion 4 glut **5** waste **6** excess **7** surfeit, surplus **8** plethora **9** abundance, multitude **10** oversupply **11** superfluity **12** extravagance, multiplicity

progenitor 8 ancestor, forebear **10** forefather

progeny 3 kin, son **4** clan, heir, line, race, seed **5** blood, breed, child, heirs, issue, scion, stock, young **6** family **7** kindred, lineage **8** children, offshoot **9** offspring, posterity **10** descendant

prognosticate 7 predict, presage **8** forecast, foretell, prophesy **9** foretoken

prognostication 6 augury **8** forecast, prophecy **10** divination, prediction

prognosticator 4 seer **5** augur **7** prophet **9** predictor **10** forecaster

program 4 bill, book, card, list, plan, show **5** slate **6** agenda, design, docket, expect, intend, line up, notice, series, sketch **7** arrange, outline **8** bulletin, calendar, playbill, register, schedule, syllabus **9** timetable **10** curriculum, production, prospectus **12** presentation

progress 4 gain, grow, rise **5** climb, get on, mount, ripen **6** action, course, grow up, growth, mature, stride **7** advance, develop, headway, improve, proceed, process, success **8** get ahead, increase, movement **9** get better, go forward, move ahead, promotion, unfolding **10** betterment, enrichment, gain ground **11** achievement, advancement, development, enhancement, furtherance, improvement, make headway, make strides

progression 3 run **5** chain, climb, order **6** ascent, course, series, strain, string **7** advance **8** progress, sequence **10** succession **11** advancement, continuance, furtherance **12** continuation **14** continuousness **15** consecutiveness

progressive 7 dynamic, gradual, liberal, ongoing **8** activist, advanced, populist, up-to-date **9** advancing, enlarging, reformist, spreading, traveling **10** ameliorist **11** incremental **12** enterprising

prohibit 3 ban, bar **4** curb, deny, stay, stop, veto **5** block, check, delay, limit **6** enjoin, forbid, hamper, hinder, impede, negate **7** inhibit, obviate, prevent, repress **8** disallow, obstruct, preclude, restrain, restrict, suppress, withhold **9** proscribe

prohibited
German: 8 verboten

prohibition 3 ban **4** veto **5** edict **7** embargo, sanction **10** temperance **11** forbiddance **12** interdiction

prohibitive, prohibitory 9 enjoining, hindering **10** forbidding, inhibitive, injunction, preventative, repressive **11**

disallowing, obstructive, restraining, restrictive, suppressive **12** inadmissible, unacceptable **13** disqualifying **15** circumscriptive

project 3 aim, job **4** cast, emit, fire, goal, plan, send, task, work **5** draft, eject, expel, fling, frame, shoot, throw **6** beetle, design, devise, extend, hurtle, invent, jut out, launch, map out, propel, scheme **7** concoct, outline, propose **8** activity, ambition, bend over, contrive, forecast, overhang, protrude, stand out, stick out, throw out, transmit **9** calculate, discharge, ejaculate, intention, objective, plan ahead **10** assignment **11** extrapolate, undertaking **12** predetermine

projected 6 hurled **7** hurtled, planned **8** extended, forecast, launched, overhung, proposed, stood out, stuck out **9** mapped out, propelled, protruded **10** catapulted **11** conjectural

projectile 4 dart **5** arrow, spear **6** rocket **7** javelin, missile

projecting part 3 arm, ell, leg **4** eave, limb, tail **6** branch, feeler, member **7** antenna **8** tentacle **9** appendage

projection 4 brow, bump, eave **5** bulge, guess, jetty, jutty, ledge, ridge, shelf **8** estimate, forecast, overhang **9** extension, extrusion **10** estimation, prediction, prospectus, protrusion **11** guesstimate **12** protuberance **13** approximation, extrapolation

Prokofiev, Serge
  born: 6 Russia **9** Sontsovka
  composer of: 6 Lt Kije **10** Cinderella, The Gambler **11** War and Peace **13** Scythian Suite, The Fiery Angel **14** Lieutenant Kije, Romeo and Juliet, The Prodigal Son **15** Alexander Nevsky, Peter and the Wolf **17** Classical Symphony **22** The Love for Three Oranges **57** Cantata for the Twentieth Anniversary of the October Revolution

proletarian 6 worker **7** laborer **10** working man

proletariat 5 plebs **6** rabble, the mob **7** populus **8** canaille, laborers, populace **9** commonage, commoners, hoi polloi, the masses **10** commonalty **11** lower orders, rank and file, wage earners **12** lower classes, vulgus mobile, working class **15** the common people **16** the great unwashed

proliferate 4 teem **5** breed, hatch, spawn, swarm **8** increase, multiply **9** procreate, propagate, pullulate **10** regenerate **11** overproduce

prolific 4 lush **6** fecund **7** copious, fertile, profuse **8** abundant, breeding, creative, fruitful, yielding **9** luxuriant **11** germinative, multiplying, procreative, progenitive, proliferous, propagating **12** reproductive

prolix 5 wordy **7** verbose **10** long-winded

prolixity 9 verbosity, wordiness **11** profuseness **14** long- windedness

prologue 7 opening, preface, prelude **8** foreword, overture, preamble **9** beginning **12** introduction

prolong 5 delay **6** extend, retard **7** drag out, draw out, spin out, stretch, sustain **8** continue, elongate, lengthen, maintain, protract **9** attenuate **10** perpetuate

prolongation 5 delay **9** extending, extension **10** drawing out **11** attenuation, dragging out, lengthening, protraction, retardation **12** perpetuation **13** streching out

prolonged 7 lengthy **8** drawn-out, extended **9** continued, long-lived **10** continuing, lengthened, persistent, protracted **11** long-lasting

prom 3 hop **4** ball **5** dance **9** cotillion, promenade

promenade 3 hop **4** ball, prom, walk **5** dance **6** soiree, stroll **9** cotillion

Prometheus
  member of: 6 Titans
  father: 7 Iapetus
  mother: 6 Themis **7** Clymene
  brother: 5 Atlas **10** Epimetheus
  son: 9 Deucalion
  created mankind from: 4 clay
  stole: 4 fire
  punished by: 4 Zeus
  chained to: 4 rock
  released by: 8 Hercules

Prometheus Bound
  author: 9 Aeschylus
  character: 2 Io **3** Bia **6** Hermes, Kratos **7** Oceanus **10** Hephaestus

Prometheus Unbound
  author: 18 Percy Bysshe Shelley
  character: 4 Asia, Ione **5** Earth **7** Jupiter, Mercury, Panthea **8** Hercules **9** Demogoron

prominence 3 tor **4** bump, dune, fame, hill, hump, knob, lump, mark, mesa, name, node, peak, rise, spur **5** bluff, bulge, cliff, crest, honor, jetty, jutty, knoll, knurl, might, mound **6** credit, height, renown, rising, summit, weight **7** dignity, hillock, majesty, process **8** eminence, grandeur, mountain, nobility, outshoot, overhang, pinnacle, prestige, salience, splendor, swelling **9** celebrity, convexity, elevation, extension, extrusion, greatness, influence, notoriety, precipice **10** brilliance, importance, notability, popularity, projection, promontory, protrusion, reputation, tumescence **11** distinction, excrescence, excurvature, preeminence, superiority **12** protuberance, significance

prominent 6 convex, famous **7** bulging, eminent, evident, glaring, honored, jutting, leading, notable, ob-

vious, salient, staring, swollen **8** apparent, definite, excurved, extended, renowned, striking, swelling **9** arresting, important, respected, well-known **10** celebrated, easily seen, jutting out, noticeable, preeminent, projecting, pronounced, protruding, protrusive, remarkable **11** conspicuous, discernible, illustrious, outstanding, prestigious, protuberant **12** recognizable **13** distinguished

promiscuous 3 lax **4** fast, lewd, wild **5** loose, mixed **6** casual, impure, medley, motley, rakish, wanton **7** aimless, chaotic, diverse, immoral, jumbled, mingled, mixed-up, satyric **8** careless, confused, immodest, sweeping, unchaste **9** composite, desultory, dissolute, haphazard, perplexed, scrambled, wholesale **10** commingled, disordered, disorderly, dissipated, intermixed, lascivious, licentious, uncritical, undirected, unvirtuous, variegated **11** disarranged, incontinent, indifferent, intemperate, unselective **12** disorganized, of easy virtue, undiscerning **13** helter-skelter, heterogeneous, miscellaneous **14** indiscriminate

promise 3 vow **4** aver, avow, oath, word **5** agree, augur, imply, swear, troth, vouch **6** assure, avowal, hint of, parole, pledge, plight **7** be bound, betoken, suggest, warrant **8** covenant, indicate, warranty **9** agreement, assurance, guarantee, potential, undertake **11** declaration, stipulation, swear an oath, word of honor

Promised Land 6 Canaan
  nickname of: 10 California **6** Israel

promising 4 rosy **5** happy, lucky **6** bright, rising **7** hopeful **8** assuring, cheerful, cheering **9** advancing, favorable, fortunate, looking up **10** auspicious, of good omen, optimistic, propitious, reassuring **11** encouraging, inspiriting, up-and-coming

promissory note 3 IOU **4** bond, chit **6** pledge **7** promise **9** agreement **10** obligation **11** certificate

promontory 4 cape, hill, ness, spur **5** bluff, cliff, jetty, jutty, point **6** height **8** headland, overhang **9** peninsula, precipice **10** embankment, projection

promote 3 aid **4** abet, ease, help, plug, push **5** raise **6** assist, foster, prefer, refine **7** advance, develop, elevate, enhance, forward, further, support, upgrade, work for **8** advocate, expedite, graduate **9** advertise, cultivate, encourage, publicize

promoter 6 backer **8** advocate, champion **9** proponent, supporter

promotion 4 hype **5** raise **7** advance, fanfare, puffery **8** ballyhoo, boosting, progress **9** elevation, publicity, upgrading **10** preferment **11** advancement, advertising, furtherance **12**

promulgation 13 advertisement, encouragement

promotive 7 helpful **9** conducive **10** beneficial **12** contributive, contributory, instrumental

prompt 3 cue **4** goad, keen, move, prod, push, spur, stir **5** alert, alive, cause, drive, eager, force, impel, press, quick, ready, sharp **6** active, assist, bright, excite, incite, induce, intent, lively, on time, propel, remind, thrust, timely **7** actuate, animate, dispose, help out, incline, inspire, instant, on guard, provoke, zealous **8** activate, inspirit, motivate, occasion, open-eyed, persuade, punctual, vigilant, watchful **9** attentive, determine, efficient, immediate, influence, instigate, observant, open- eared, stimulate, wide-awake **10** on one's toes **12** jog the memory, unhesitating **13** instantaneous

prompting 6 cueing, urging **7** goading **8** egging on **10** motivation **11** exhortation

promptly 3 pat **4** anon, soon, tite **6** pronto **7** quickly, swiftly **10** punctually **11** immediately

promptness 5 haste **8** alacrity, celerity, dispatch **9** quickness, readiness, swiftness **11** punctuality **15** expeditiousness

promulgate 6 foster **7** explain, expound, present, promote, sponsor **8** instruct, set forth **9** elucidate, enunciate, interpret **11** communicate

promulgation 9 fostering, promotion **11** circulation, instruction, sponsorship **12** distribution, presentation, transmission **13** communication **14** interpretation

prone 3 apt **4** flat **5** level **6** liable, likely **7** subject, tending **8** disposed, face-down, inclined **9** prostrate, reclining, recumbent **10** accustomed, habituated, horizontal **11** predisposed, susceptible

proneness 4 bent, bias, turn **7** leaning **8** penchant, tendency **9** prejudice **10** proclivity, propensity **11** inclination **12** predilection **14** predisposition

prong 4 barb, hook, horn, spur, tine **5** point, spike, tooth **6** branch **10** projection

pronoun 2 he, it, me, my, us, we, ye **3** all, any, few, her, his, one, she, thy, who, you **4** hers, mine, ours, some, thee, them, they, that, this, thou, what, whom **5** no one, their, these, thine, those, which, whose, yours **6** anyone, itself, myself, nobody **7** anybody, herself, himself, nothing, someone, whoever **8** somebody, whomever **9** everybody, something, whosoever **10** everything, themselves
French: 2 il, je, tu **3** ils, lui, mes, moi **4** elle, vous

German: 2 er, es, du **3** ich, mir, sie **4** dein, mein, mich, sich
Italian: 2 io, me, mi, ti, tu, vi **3** cio, lei, lui, mio, tei, voi **4** egli, ella, essa, esse, essi, loro
Spanish: 2 el, la, lo, me, mi, tu, yo **4** ella, ello, suyo, tuyo **5** usted

pronounce 3 say **4** emit, form, rule **5** frame, judge, orate, sound, speak, state, utter, voice **6** decree **7** declare, enounce **8** announce, proclaim, vocalize **9** enunciate **10** articulate

pronounced 4 bold **5** broad, clear, plain, vivid **6** patent **7** decided, evident, obvious, visible **8** apparent, clear-cut, definite, distinct, manifest, positive, unhidden **9** arresting **10** noticeable **11** conspicuous, outstanding, undisguised, well-defined **12** recognizable, unmistakable **14** unquestionable

pronouncement 6 decree **11** declaration **12** announcement, proclamation

pronto 3 now **4** asap, fast, stat **5** quick **7** quickly **8** promptly **11** immediately

Pronuba
epithet of: **4** Juno

pronunciamento 5 edict **12** proclamation **13** pronouncement

pronunciation 6 accent **10** inflection **11** enunciation **12** articulation **16** manner of speaking

proof 4 test **5** essay, proof, sheet, trial **6** galley, ordeal **8** scrutiny, weighing **9** probation **10** assessment **11** attestation, examination **12** confirmation, ratification, verification **13** certification, corroboration, documentation **14** substantiation

proofreader's mark 3 cap, rom **4** dele, ital, stet **5** caret, space

prop 3 set **4** lean, rest, stay **5** brace, stand **6** hold up, pillar **7** bolster, shore up, support **8** buttress, mainstay, shoulder, underpin **9** stanchion, supporter, sustainer **13** reinforcement
French: 11 point d'appui

propaganda 6 hoopla **8** ballyhoo **9** party line, promotion, publicity **10** persuasion **11** advertising

propagandist 6 zealot **8** activist, exponent **9** apologist, proponent, publicist **12** spokesperson

propagate 3 air, sow **4** bear, tell **5** beget, breed, hatch, issue, rumor, spawn, spray **6** blazon, herald, impart, notify, preach, purvey, repeat, report, spread **7** bestrew, give out, implant, instill, publish, scatter, trumpet **8** disperse, engender, generate, increase, multiply, proclaim, put forth **9** broadcast, circulate, enunciate, give birth, inculcate, make known, procreate, publicize, reproduce

propagation 6 laying, siring **7** bearing **8** breeding, hatching, issuance, spawning, yielding **9** begetting, diffu-

sion, gestation, pregnancy, spreading **10** dispersion, generation **11** circulation, engendering, giving birth, procreation, publication **12** distribution, reproduction, transmission **13** dissemination

pro patria 14 for one's country

propel 4 cast, goad, hurl, poke, prod, push, send, toss **5** drive, eject, force, heave, impel, pitch, shoot, shove, sling, start **6** launch, thrust **7** project **8** catapult **9** discharge **11** precipitate, set in motion

propeller, screw
invented by: **7** Stevens **8** Ericsson

propensity 4 bent, bias, turn **5** fancy, favor, taste **6** liking **7** leaning **8** affinity, penchant, pleasure, sympathy, tendency, weakness **9** prejudice **10** attraction, partiality, preference, proclivity **11** disposition, inclination **12** predilection **14** predisposition

proper 3 apt, fit, own **4** meet, nice, true **5** per se, right **6** decent, marked, modest, polite, seemly **7** apropos, correct, express, fitting, germane, precise, typical **8** assigned, becoming, decorous, orthodox, peculiar, relevant, specific, suitable **9** befitting, courteous, pertinent **10** acceptable, applicable, individual, particular, respective **11** appropriate, conformable, distinctive **12** conventional **14** characteristic, distinguishing, representative
French: 11 comme il faut

properly 5 aptly, right **7** exactly **8** decently, politely, suitably **9** correctly, perfectly, precisely **10** acceptably, accurately, decorously, tastefully **12** without error **13** appropriately **14** conventionally

property 4 hold, land, mark **5** acres, badge, funds, goods, means, point, stock, title, trait **6** aspect, assets, estate, moneys, realty, wealth **7** acreage, capital, earmark, effects, estates, feature, grounds, quality **8** chattels, holdings, treasure **9** attribute, ownership, resources, territory **10** belongings, real estate **11** investments, peculiarity, possessions, singularity **12** appointments, idiosyncrasy **13** individuality, particularity **14** characteristic, proprietorship

prophecy 6 augury **7** portent **8** forecast **10** divination, prediction, revelation **15** prognostication
god of: 6 Apollo **7** Phoebus, Pythius **9** Musagetes

prophesy 4 warn **5** augur **6** divine **7** forbode, foresee, portend, predict, presage **8** forecast, foretell, forewarn, soothsay **9** apprehend, premonish **13** prognosticate

prophet 4 seer **5** augur, guide, sibyl **6** oracle **7** diviner, palmist, seeress **8** preacher, sorcerer **9** Cassandra, divinator, geomancer, predictor, sorceress **10** evangelist, forecaster, foreteller, prophesier, prophetess, soothsayer **11** clairvoyant, intercessor, interpreter **12** crystal gazer **13** fortune-teller **14** prognosticator

Prophet, major 6 Baruch, Daniel, Elijah, Isaiah **7** Ezekiel **8** Jeremiah

Prophet, minor 3 Gad **4** Amos, Joel **5** Hosea, Jonah, Micah, Nahum **6** Haggai, Nathan **7** Malachi, Obadiah **8** Habakkuk **9** Zechariah, Zephaniah

Prophetess 4 Anna **6** Miriam **7** Deborah **9** Cassandra

prophetic, prophetical 5 vatic **6** mantic **7** fateful, ominous **8** oracular **10** portentous, predictive, presageful

Prophetic Books
author: **12** William Blake

prophylactic 8 hygienic **10** preventive **13** contraceptive

propinquity 7 kinship **8** affinity, nearness, vicinity **9** closeness, proximity **10** similarity

propitiate 4 calm **5** allay **6** pacify, soothe **7** appease, assuage, mollify, placate **10** conciliate **11** accommodate

propitiation 8 soothing **11** appeasement **12** conciliation, pacification

propitious 3 fit **5** bonny, happy, lucky **6** benign, golden **8** suitable **9** agreeable, favorable, fortunate, opportune, promising, well-timed **10** auspicious, beneficial, felicitous **12** advantageous, providential

proponent 6 backer, friend, patron, votary **7** booster **8** advocate, champion, defender, endorser, espouser, exponent, partisan, upholder **9** apologist, spokesman, supporter **10** enthusiast, vindicator **14** representative

proportion 5 ratio **7** balance, harmony **8** evenness, symmetry **9** agreement **11** consistency, correlation, perspective **12** distribution, relationship **14** commensuration, correspondence

proportionate 5 equal **8** balanced **10** comparable, equivalent **12** commensurate **13** commensurable, corresponding

proportions 3 fit, lot **4** area, bulk, form, gear, mass, part, size, span **5** adapt, gauge, grade, match, order, poise, quota, range, ratio, scope, shape, share, width **6** amount, degree, equate, extent, spread, volume **7** balance, breadth, conform, correct, expanse, measure, portion, rectify, segment **8** capacity, division, equalize, fraction, graduate, modulate, regulate **9** amplitude, apportion, greatness, harmonize, magnitude **10** dimensions **12** measurements

proposal 3 bid **4** idea, plan, plot, suit **5** draft, offer **6** appeal, course, design, motion, scheme, sketch, theory **7** out-

line, proffer, program, project **8** overture, prospect **9** stratagem **10** conception, invitation, nomination, prospectus, resolution, suggestion **11** proposition **12** presentation **14** recommendation

propose 3 aim, woo **4** hope, mean, plan, plot **6** aspire, design, expect, intend, scheme, submit, tender **7** advance, present, proffer, purpose, suggest, venture **8** affiance, propound, put forth, set about, set forth **9** determine, have a mind, introduce, recommend, undertake **10** come up with, have in mind, have in view, put forward **11** contemplate **14** pop the question **21** offer for consideration

proposition 4 deal, pass, plan **5** issue, offer, point, topic **6** matter, scheme **7** advance, bargain, solicit, subject **8** contract, proposal, question **9** agreement, assurance, guarantee **10** resolution, suggestion **11** make a pass at, negotiation, stipulation, undertaking **14** recommendation

propound 4 pose **5** boost **6** assert **7** advance, profess, propose **8** put forth, set forth

proprieties 7 decorum, manners **8** protocol **9** amenities, etiquette **10** civilities **11** conventions

proprietor 5 owner **6** holder, master **7** manager **8** landlord **9** landowner, possessor **10** landholder **11** titleholder **12** proprietress

propriety 7 aptness, decorum, dignity, fitness **8** courtesy **9** etiquette, formality, rightness **10** seemliness **11** correctness, good manners, savoir faire **12** becomingness, decorousness, good behavior, suitableness **13** applicability **14** respectability **15** appropriateness

propulsion 6 launch, thrust **9** launching **10** propelling

prop up 5 brace **7** bolster, support **8** buttress

pro rata 12 in proportion

prorate 6 divide **9** apportion **10** distribute

prosaic 3 dry **4** blah, dull, flat **5** prosy, stale, trite, vapid, wordy **6** common, jejune **7** humdrum, tedious **8** ordinary, plebeian, tiresome **9** hackneyed **10** monotonous, pedestrian, spiritless, unpoetical **12** matter-of-fact **13** platitudinous, unimaginative, uninteresting

Prosclystius
epithet of: **8** Poseidon
means: **7** flooder

proscribe 3 ban **4** damn **5** curse, exile **6** banish, forbid, outlaw **7** boycott, censure, condemn **8** denounce, prohibit **9** interdict, repudiate **10** disapprove **12** anathematize **13** excommunicate

proscription 3 ban **7** barring, censure **8** anathema **9** interdict **11** forbid-

dance, prohibition **12** condemnation, denunciation, interdiction **15** excommunication

prose 3 dry **4** dull **5** novel **7** fiction, quality, tedious, writing **8** sequence **9** discourse **10** expression **11** commonplace **13** unimaginative

prosecute 3 sue, try **4** wage **6** direct, go with, handle, indict, manage, pursue **7** arraign, carry on, conduct, execute, go to law, perform, prolong, stick to, sustain **8** continue, deal with, follow up, maintain **9** discharge, persist in **10** administer, put on trial, see through **11** take to court **12** bring to trial **14** bring to justice

prosecution 4 suit **6** action **7** conduct, pursuit **11** performance **14** administration

Proserpina see **10** Persephone

prosit 11 may it do good
used as: **5** toast

prospect, prospects 4 hope, plan, seek, view **5** scene, vista **6** aspect, design, search, vision **7** chances, explore, go after, look for, outlook, picture, promise, scenery **8** ambition, panorama, proposal **9** candidate, foretaste, intention, landscape, work a mine **10** expectancy, likelihood **11** expectation, possibility, probability **12** anticipation **13** contemplation

prospective 4 to be **6** coming, future, in view, likely, to come **7** looming **8** destined, eventual, expected, foreseen, hoped-for, intended, possible **9** about to be, impending, in the wind, looked-for, potential, promising **10** in prospect **11** approaching, forthcoming, threatening

prosper 4 gain **5** get on **6** flower, thrive **7** advance, succeed **8** fare well, flourish, fructify, get ahead, grow rich, increase, make good, progress **9** bear fruit **15** make one's fortune

prosperity 4 ease, gain **6** luxury, plenty, profit, wealth **7** advance, success, welfare **8** good luck, progress **9** abundance, advantage, affluence, blessings, golden age, good times, palmy days, run of luck, well-being **11** advancement, good fortune
god of: **4** Frey **5** Freyr, Niord, Njord **12** Bonus Eventus
goddess of: **5** Salus

Prospero
character in: **10** The Tempest
author: **11** Shakespeare

prosperous 4 fair, good, rich, rosy **5** happy, lucky, sunny **6** bright, golden, timely **7** hopeful, moneyed, opulent, smiling, wealthy, well-off **8** affluent, cheering, pleasing, thriving, well-to-do **9** favorable, fortunate, opportune, promising **10** auspicious, heartening, of good omen, propitious, reassuring, successful **11** comfortable, encouraging, flourishing **12** on easy street

Pross, Miss
character in: **16** A Tale of Two Cities
author: **7** Dickens

prostitute 4 bawd, jade, slut, tart **5** abuse, hussy, lower, spoil, whore **6** chippy, debase, defile, demean, floozy, harlot, hooker, misuse **7** cheapen, corrupt, debauch, degrade, hustler, pervert, profane, sell out, trollop **8** call girl, misapply, strumpet **9** courtesan, desecrate, misdirect, misemploy **12** streetwalker **14** lady of the night

prostrate 4 deck, flat **5** abase, floor, prone, spent **6** fagged, kowtow **7** bow down, flatten, laid out, worn out **8** bowed low, overcome **9** bone weary, crouching, dead tired, exhausted, kneel down, lying flat, overthrow, recumbent **10** beseeching, horizontal **11** on one's knees **12** on bended knee, stretched out, supplicating **13** lying face down **15** fall to one's knees

prostration 3 bow, woe **5** grief **6** misery, sorrow **7** anguish, despair **8** distress, kneeling, weakness **9** abasement, dejection, heartache, impotence, lowliness, paralysis, weariness **10** depression, desolation, enervation, exhaustion, subjection, submission **11** desperation, despondency **12** genuflection, helplessness, wretchedness **13** depth of misery

prosy 4 dull, flat **5** banal, inane **6** stupid **7** humdrum, prosaic, tedious **9** wearisome **11** commonplace **13** uninteresting

protagonist 4 diva, hero, lead, star **7** heroine **9** headliner, principal, superstar, title role **10** leading man, prima donna **11** leading lady **12** danseur noble, jeune premier **13** jeune premiere, main character **14** prima ballerina **16** central character

protect 4 hide, keep, save, tend, veil **5** cover, guard **6** defend, harbor, screen, secure, shield **7** care for, shelter, sustain **8** conserve, maintain, preserve **9** look after, safeguard, watch over **10** take care of

protected 4 safe **5** saved **6** immune, secure **7** guarded, secured **8** anchored, defended, shielded **9** sheltered **10** inviolable **12** invulnerable

protection 3 aid **4** care, keep, wall **5** cover, fence, guard, haven, shade **6** asylum, buffer, charge, harbor, refuge, safety, saving, screen, shield **7** barrier, custody, defense, shelter, support **8** guarding, immunity, preserve, security **9** preserver, safeguard, sanctuary **10** assistance **11** safekeeping **12** championship, conservation, guardianship, preservation

protective 7 careful, heedful **8** fatherly, guarding, maternal, motherly, paternal, sisterly, vigilant, watchful **9** avuncular, brotherly, defensive, shielding **10** preventive, sheltering, solicitous **11** safekeeping **12** big-brotherly, safeguarding

protective covering 4 coat, husk, mail **5** armor, shell **6** shield **7** coating, plating **8** carapace **10** coat of mail **11** suit of armor **12** armor plating

protectorate 6 colony **7** mandate **8** province, dominion **9** satellite, territory **10** dependency, possession, settlement

protege 4 ward **5** pupil **6** charge **7** student, trainee **9** dependent

pro tempore 9 temporary **11** temporarily **15** for the time being

protest 3 vow **4** aver, avow, beef, deny, kick **5** gripe, march, offer, sit-in, speak, state **6** affirm, allege, assert, assure, attest, avouch, cry out, insist, object, oppose, strike **7** boycott, contend, declare, dispute, dissent, hold out, profess, testify **8** announce, complain, demurral, disagree, maintain, propound, put forth, set forth **9** enunciate, objection, picketing, pronounce **10** asseverate, contradict, controvert, disapprove, disclaimer, dissidence, opposition, put forward, resistance **11** beg to differ, deprecation **12** disaffection, disagreement, remonstrance, renunciation **13** contradiction, demonstration, remonstration, take exception **14** discountenance

Protestant 5 Amish **6** Mormon, Quaker, Shaker **7** Baptist, Puritan **8** Anglican, Huguenot, Lutheran **9** Adventist, Calvinist, Methodist, Unitarian **12** Episcopalian, Presbyterian **17** Congregationalist **18** Christian Scientist

protest meeting 5 rally, sit-in **13** demonstration

Proteus
character in: **20** Two Gentlemen of Verona
author: **11** Shakespeare

Proteus
god of: **3** sea
king of: **5** Egypt
father: **7** Oceanus
mother: **6** Tethys
wife: **8** Psamathe
son: **12** Theoclymenus
daughter: **7** Theonoe
gift: **8** prophesy **12** form-changing **13** shape-changing

Prothoenor
leader of: **9** Boeotians

protocol 5 usage **7** customs, decorum, manners **8** good form **9** amenities, etiquette, formality, standards **11** conventions, proprieties **14** code of behavior, court etiquette, diplomatic code **17** dictates of society

prototypal 5 model **7** classic **9** exemplary **10** archetypal, definitive **12** prototypical

prototype 5 model **7** example **8** original **9** archetype

protozoan 4 cell **5** ameba, cilia **6** amoeba **7** euglena **8** flagella, protista **9** eukaryote, pseudopod **10** paramecium, plasmodium **11** microscopic, unicellular **17** nonphotosynthetic

protract 6 extend, keep up **7** drag out, draw out, prolong, spin out **8** lengthen **9** keep going **10** stretch out

protracted 4 long **7** lengthy **8** drawn-out, extended **9** continued, long-lived, prolonged **10** lengthened, persistent **11** long-lasting

protraction 4 stay **7** lasting **9** extension **10** continuing, drawing out **11** continuance, dragging out, persistence **12** perseverance, prolongation

protrude 5 belly, bulge, swell **6** jut out **7** project **8** stand out, stick out **11** push forward

protrusion 4 bump, hump **6** hernia **8** swelling **9** extension **10** projection **12** prolongation, protuberance

protuberance 3 bow **4** bump, hump, knob, knot, lump, node, weal, welt **5** bulge, gnarl, ridge **6** rising **8** swelling **9** convexity, elevation, roundness **10** projection, prominence **11** excrescence, excurvature

protura
class: **8** hexapoda
phylum: **10** arthropoda
characteristic: **5** small **6** minute **7** eyeless **8** wingless

proud 4 fine, smug, vain **5** aloof, cocky, grand, great, happy, lofty, noble **6** august, lordly, snooty, snotty, strict, uppish, uppity **7** bloated, exalted, haughty, high-hat, pleased, pompous, revered, stately, storied, stuck-up, swollen **8** affected, arrogant, assuming, boastful, braggart, bragging, elevated, euphoric, glorious, inflated, insolent, majestic, prideful, puffed up, reserved, snobbish **9** admirable, cherished, conceited, contented, delighted, dignified, flaunting, gratified, honorable, imperious, know-it-all, satisfied, venerable **10** complacent, disdainful, high-minded, intolerant, principled, scrupulous **11** egotistical, independent, magnificent, overbearing, patronizing, punctilious **12** contemptuous, self-praising, supercilious, vainglorious **13** condescending, distinguished, high-and-mighty, self-important, self-satisfied **14** self-respecting, self-sufficient

Proudie, Dr
character in: **16** Barchester Towers
author: **8** Trollope

Proust, Marcel
author of: **23** Remembrance of

Things Past **24** A la Recherche du Temps Perdu

prove 3 try **4** test **5** check, end up, probe **6** affirm, attest, result, try out, uphold, verify, wind up **7** analyze, bear out, certify, confirm, examine, justify, support, sustain, warrant, witness **8** document, evidence, look into, make good, manifest, result in, validate **9** ascertain, establish, eventuate, testify to **11** corroborate, demonstrate **12** authenticate, substantiate

proved 5 known **6** proven, upheld **8** affirmed, attested, borne out, verified **9** certified, confirmed, supported, sustained, warranted, witnessed **10** documented **11** established **12** corroborated, demonstrable **13** authenticated, substantiated

prove false 5 belie **6** refute, reject **7** explode **8** disprove **9** discredit **10** invalidate

proven 5 known **6** proved, upheld **8** accepted, affirmed, attested, borne out, verified **9** certified, confirmed, supported, sustained, warranted, witnessed **10** documented, verifiable **11** established **12** corroborated, demonstrable **13** authenticated, substantiated

provender 3 hay **4** chow, corn, eats, feed, food, grub, oats **5** grain **6** fodder, forage, ration, viands **7** nurture **10** provisions **11** subsistence

proverb 3 mot, saw **5** adage, axiom, maxim, moral, motto **6** byword, cliche, dictum, saying, truism **7** bromide, epigram, precept **8** aphorism, apothegm **9** platitude **11** commonplace **13** accepted truth, popular saying

prove wrong 5 belie **6** expose, refute **7** explode **8** disprove **9** discredit

provide 3 arm, fit, pay **4** give, plan **5** allow, award, cater, equip, grant, offer, state, yield **6** accord, afford, bestow, confer, donate, impart, outfit, render, save up, submit, supply, tender **7** arrange, deliver, furnish, prepare, present, produce, require, specify **8** dispense, get ready **9** make plans, postulate, stipulate **10** accumulate, contribute

provide for 7 care for **8** attend to, wait upon **9** look after **10** minister to, take care of

providence 8 prudence **9** foresight, husbandry, provision **11** forethought **14** circumspection, farsightedness, forehandedness

provident 4 wary **5** chary, ready **6** frugal, saving **7** careful, prudent, thrifty **8** cautious, discreet, equipped, vigilant **9** farseeing, judicious **10** discerning, economical, farsighted, forehanded, foreseeing, thoughtful **11** circumspect, foresighted, precautious **12** parsimonious, well-prepared

province 3 job **4** area, duty, part, role, zone **5** field, place, state **6** canton, charge, county, domain, office, region, sphere **7** section, station **8** business, capacity, function **9** authority, bailiwick, territory **10** assignment, department **11** subdivision **12** jurisdiction **13** scope of duties **14** arrondissement, responsibility

provincial 4 rude **5** crude, gawky, local, rough, rural **6** clumsy, gauche, homely, narrow, oafish, rustic **7** awkward, boorish, bucolic, country, hayseed, insular, loutish **8** cloddish, clownish, down-home, homespun, regional, yokelish **9** backwoods, parochial, small-town, unrefined **10** unpolished **11** clodhopping, countrified, territorial **15** unsophisticated

provision 6 giving **8** donation **9** endowment, providing, supplying **10** furnishing

provisional 6 acting, pro tem **7** interim **9** surrogate, temporary, tentative **10** substitute **11** conditional **12** probationary **15** for the time being

provisions 4 feed, food, term **5** clause, fodder, forage, stores, string, viands **7** article, commons, edibles, proviso **8** eatables, supplies, victuals **9** condition, groceries, provender, readiness, requisite **10** limitation, obligation, precaution, sustenance **11** arrangement, comestibles, forethought, preparation, requirement, reservation, restriction, stipulation, wherewithal **12** anticipation, modification **13** qualification **14** forehandedness, prearrangement

proviso 5 rider **6** clause, string **8** addition **9** amendment, condition **10** limitation **11** requirement, restriction, stipulation **12** modification **13** qualification

provocation 4 goad, spur **5** cause, pique **6** insult, slight **7** affront, offense **8** prodding, stimulus, vexation **9** actuation, annoyance **10** excitation, incitement, irritation, motivation **11** aggravation, fomentation, instigation, stimulation **12** perturbation

provocative 4 sexy **6** vexing **7** irksome **8** alluring, annoying, arousing, exciting, inviting, tempting **9** beguiling, provoking, ravishing, seductive, thrilling, vexatious **10** attractive, bewitching, enchanting, entrancing, intriguing, irritating **11** aggravating, captivating, fascinating, stimulating, tantalizing **12** intoxicating, irresistible

provoke 3 irk, vex **4** fire, gall, move, rile, stir **5** anger, annoy, cause, chafe, evoke, grate, impel, pique, rouse **6** arouse, awaken, compel, create, effect, elicit, enrage, excite, foment, incite, induce, kindle, madden, prompt, put out, stir up **7** actuate, agitate, animate, bring on, incense, inflame, in-

spire, outrage, produce, quicken **8** generate, get to one, irritate, motivate **9** aggravate, call forth, establish, galvanize, infuriate, instigate, stimulate **10** bring about, exasperate, give rise to **11** get one's goat, put in motion **15** try one's patience **16** get under one's skin

prow 3 bow **4** stem **5** front **10** forward end

prowess 4 grit, guts **5** knack, might, nerve, power, skill, spunk, valor, vigor **6** daring, genius, mettle, spirit, talent **7** ability, bravery, courage, faculty, heroism, know-how, stamina **8** aptitude, boldness, strength **9** adeptness, derring-do, endurance, fortitude, gallantry, hardihood **10** competence, expertness **11** intrepidity, proficiency **12** fearlessness, skillfulness **13** dauntlessness **14** accomplishment

prowl 4 hunt, lurk, roam **5** creep, range, skulk, slink, snack, stalk, steal **6** ramble **8** scavenge

prowler 7 burglar **10** peeping Tom **16** suspicious person

proximate 4 near **5** close **6** beside, nearby, next to **8** adjacent, imminent, next-door **11** forthcoming

proximity 7 presence **8** locality, nearness, vicinity **9** closeness **10** contiguity **11** propinquity **12** togetherness

proximo *see* month

proxy 3 sub **4** vote **5** agent **6** ballot, deputy **7** stand-in **9** alternate **10** substitute

prude 4 prig **6** modest **7** puritan **9** hypocrite **10** goody- goody **13** prim and proper

prudence 4 care, tact **6** thrift, wisdom **7** caution, economy **9** austerity, foresight, frugality, parsimony **10** discretion, precaution **11** calculation, thriftiness **14** thoughtfulness

prudent 4 sage, sane, wary, wise **5** chary **6** frugal, saving, shrewd **7** careful, guarded, heedful, politic, sapient, sparing, thrifty **8** cautious, discreet, prepared, rational, sensible, vigilant **9** expedient, judicious, provident, sagacious, wideawake **10** discerning, economical, farsighted, prudential, reflecting, thoughtful **11** circumspect, considerate, foresighted, levelheaded, precautious, well-advised **13** self-possessed

Prud'hon, Pierre-Paul
  born: 5 Cluny **6** France
  artwork: 14 Venus and Adonis **15** The Rape of Psyche **16** Empress Josephine **33** Crime Pursued by Vengeance and Justice **38** Justice and Divine Vengeance Pursuing Crime

prudish 3 shy **4** prim, smug **5** timid **6** demure, modest, prissy, queasy, stuffy **7** finical, mincing, precise, stilted **8** pedantic, priggish, skittish, starched **9**

squeamish, Victorian **10** fastidious, old-maidish, overmodest, particular **11** punctilious, puritanical, straitlaced **13** sanctimonious, self-righteous

prudishness 8 primness **10** prissiness, puritanism **11** overmodesty **12** overdelicacy, priggishness **14** overrefinement

prudish phrase 9 euphemism **10** bowdlerism

prune 3 cut, lop **4** clip, crop, pull, snip, thin, trim **5** shear **6** reduce **7** abridge, clarify, curtail, shorten, thin out **8** condense, simplify **10** abbreviate

prunelle
type: **7** liqueur
origin: **6** France
flavor: **4** plum

pruning 6 digest **8** clipping, snipping, synopsis, trimming **10** shortening **11** abridgement, cutting back, cut-down form **12** abbreviation, condensation

prurient 4 lewd, sexy **6** carnal **7** fleshy, goatish, immoral, lustful, obscene, priapic, satyric **9** lecherous, salacious **10** hot-blooded, lascivious, libidinous, licentious, lubricious, passionate **12** concupiscent

pry 4 butt, nose, peek, peer, poke, tear, work, worm **5** break, crack, delve, force, jimmy, lever, mix in, prize, probe, smoke, sniff, snoop, wrest, wring **6** butt in, ferret, horn in, meddle, search, winkle, wrench **7** explore, extract, inquire, intrude, squeeze **9** interfere, intervene **15** stick one's nose in

prying 4 busy, nosy **7** peering, raising, seeking **8** levering, snooping **9** searching **10** intrusive, meddling **11** inquisitive

Prynne, Hester
character in: **16** The Scarlet Letter
author: **9** Hawthorne

Pryor, Richard
born: **8** Peoria IL
roles: **6** The Wiz **9** Stir Crazy **12** Silver Streak **17** Lady Sings the Blues **19** Uptown Saturday Night

psalm 3 ode **4** hymn, poem, song **5** canon, chant, verse **6** praise **7** cantata, glorify, introit **8** canticle

Psalter 12 Book of Psalms

Psamathe
member of: **6** Nereid
form: **8** princess
husband: **7** Proteus
son: **5** Linus **6** Phocus **12** Theoclymenus
daughter: **7** Theonoe

pseudo 4 fake, mock, sham **5** bogus, false, phony **6** forged **7** feigned **8** spurious **9** pretended, simulated, soidisant **10** fictitious, fraudulent, self-styled **11** counterfeit, make-believe **13** self-described

pseudonym 5 alias **6** anonym **7** pen name **8** cognomen, nickname **9** false name, sobriquet, stage name **11** assumed name **16** professional name
French: **10** nom de plume **11** nom de guerre **12** nom de theatre

pseudonymous 7 assumed **10** fictitious **11** pseudonymic

psocoptera
class: **8** hexapoda
phylum: **10** arthropoda
group: **8** booklice

psyche 2 id **3** ego **4** mind, self, soul **5** anima **6** bowels, make up, spirit **8** superego **10** penetralia **11** personality, unconscious **12** subconscious

Psyche
personifies: **4** soul
loved by: **4** Eros **5** Cupid
persecutor: **5** Venus
immortalized by: **7** Jupiter
daughter: **8** Voluptas

psychic 5 augur **6** medium, mental, mystic, occult, voyant **7** diviner, prophet, voyante **8** cerebral **9** paragnost, sensitive, spiritual **10** soothsayer, telepathic **11** clairvoyant, telekinetic, telepathist **12** extrasensory, intellectual, spiritualist, supernatural, supersensory **13** preternatural

Psycho
director: **15** Alfred Hitchcock
cast: **9** John Gavin, Vera Miles **10** Janet Leigh **12** Martin Balsam **14** Anthony Perkins
score: **15** Bernard Herrmann
feature: **10** Bates Motel **11** shower scene

psychoanalysis 7 therapy **8** analysis **14** physchotherapy

psychoanalyst 6 shrink **7** analyst **12** headshrinker

psychologist/psychiatrist
American: **4** Hall, Hull **5** Dewey, James, Lewin **6** Harlow, Horney, Miller, Rogers, Terman, Tolman, Watson, Witmer **7** Cattell, Chomsky, Erikson, Goddard, Guthrie, Johnson, Masters, Skinner **8** Brothers, Wechsler **9** Thorndike **10** Westheimer
Austrian: **5** Adler, Freud, Reich
British: **5** Ellis **7** Eysenck **9** Titchener
French: **5** Binet
German: **5** Wundt **6** Koffka, Kohler **7** Fechner **9** Helmholtz, Kraepelin **10** Ebbinghaus, Wertheimer **11** Krafft-Ebing
Russian: **6** Pavlov
Swiss: **4** Jung **6** Piaget

psychology 4 head, mind **6** makeup **7** feeling **8** attitude **15** mental processes
problem/illness: **6** phobia **7** obesity, smoking **8** hysteria, neuroses, paranoia, schizoid **9** drug abuse, obsession, psychoses **10** alcoholism, compulsion, depression **11** sociopathic **13** schizophrenia **14** sexual deviance

15 anxiety reaction **17** passive-aggressive
term: **2** id **3** ego **6** libido **7** empathy **8** neuroses, superego **9** catatonic, cognition, psychoses **10** inhibition, repression **11** behaviorism, unconscious **12** conditioning, transference **13** actualization, Rorschach test **14** identification, Oedipus complex **19** operant conditioning **20** behavior modification
type: **6** social **7** Gestalt **8** abnormal, clinical **9** cognitive **10** industrial **11** educational **12** experimental **13** developmental, physiological, psychometrics, psychophysics

psychopomp
conductor of spirits to: **5** Hades **10** otherworld
epithet: **12** psychopompus
epithet of: **6** Charon, Hermes

psychosis 8 dementia, insanity, neurosis, paranoia **9** paranomia, unreality **10** pathomania **12** hallucinosis **13** schizophrenia **14** mental disorder

psychotherapy 7 therapy **8** analysis **14** psychoanalysis

psychotic 3 mad, nut **4** kook, loon **5** crazy, kooky, loony, nutty **6** insane, madman, maniac **7** lunatic **8** demented, deranged **9** disturbed **10** psychopath **12** insane person, psychopathic **15** non compos mentis

Ptah
origin: **8** Egyptian
deity of: **17** universal creation
worshiped at: **7** Memphis

Ptolemy
author of: **8** Almagest **9** Geography

pub 3 bar, inn **5** local **6** bistro, saloon, lounge, tavern **7** bar room, ginmill, rummery, rum shop, taproom **8** alehouse, grogshop, pothouse **9** road house, speakeasy **10** beer parlor **11** public house

pubescent 7 teenage **8** immature, juvenile **10** adolescent

public 3 mob **4** folk, open **5** civic, civil, frank, overt, plain, state, trade **6** buyers, common, in view, masses, nation, patent, people, shared, social **7** evident, exposed, general, in sight, obvious, outward, patrons, popular, society, visible **8** apparent, audience, communal, divulged, everyone, manifest, national, passable, populace, revealed, societal, unbarred, unfenced **9** available, citizenry, clientele, community, disclosed, followers, following, free to all, hoi polloi, multitude, notorious, political, statewide, unabashed, unashamed, unbounded, used by all **10** accessible, attendance, nationwide, not private, observable, population, purchasers, recognized, supporters, unenclosed **11** body politic, bourgeoisie, commonality, conspicuous, countrywide, discernible, perceivable, proletariat, rank and file, unconcealed, undisguised **12** acknowledged, constituency, unobstructed, unrestricted **14** community-owned

publication 4 book, news **5** issue, paper **6** digest, report **7** edition, gazette, journal, tabloid **8** bulletin, magazine, pamphlet **9** broadcast, newspaper **10** periodical **11** circulation, information **12** announcement, notification

public disturbance 4 riot **6** fracas, ruckus, uproar **7** turmoil **9** commotion

public house 3 bar, pub **5** local **6** saloon, tavern **7** gin mill, taproom **8** alehouse **9** roadhouse

publicity 4 hype, plug, puff **5** blurb, flack **7** build-up, puffery, write-up **8** ballyhoo, currency **9** attention, notoriety, promotion **10** propaganda, publicness **11** advertising, circulation, information **12** promulgation, public notice, salesmanship

publicize 4 hype, plug, puff, push, sell **6** herald **7** acclaim, promote **8** announce, ballyhoo, emblazon, proclaim **9** advertise, broadcast, make known, propagate **10** make public, promulgate **11** circularize **12** propagandize

publicly
   Latin: 11 coram populo

public matter
   Latin: 10 res publica

public notice 5 edict, ukase **6** decree **8** bulletin **9** manifesto **12** proclamation **13** pronouncement **14** pronunciamento
   French: 7 affiche

public speaking 7 oratory **9** lecturing **12** speechmaking

public-spirited 8 generous **10** altruistic, benevolent **12** humanitarian

publish 3 air **4** tell, vent **5** issue, print, utter **6** herald, impart, put out, spread **7** declare, diffuse, divulge, give out, placard, promote, release, trumpet **8** announce, bring out, disclose, proclaim **9** advertise, broadcast, circulate, make known, propagate, publicize **10** make public, promulgate, put to press **11** communicate, disseminate

Puca
   also: 5 Pooka
   origin: 5 Irish
   form: 6 spirit
   corresponds to: 4 Puck

Puccini, Giacomo
   born: 5 Italy, Lucca
   composer of: 5 Tosca **8** La Boheme, Turandot **12** Manon Lescaut **14** Gianni Schicchi, Madam Butterfly **15** Madama Butterfly **18** La Fanciulla del West **22** The Girl of the Golden West

puce 3 red **7** dark red **13** purplish-brown

Puck
   also: 15 Robin Goodfellow
   character in: 21 A Midsummer Night's Dream
   author: 11 Shakespeare
   form: 6 spirit
   characteristic: 11 mischievous
   corresponds to: 4 Puca **5** Pooka

pucker 4 fold, tuck **5** pinch, pleat, purse **6** crease, gather, ruffle, rumple, shrink **7** crinkle, crumble, squeeze, wrinkle **8** compress, contract **12** draw together

puckered 6 pursed, rucked, tucked **7** creased, crinkly, pinched, pleated **8** crinkled, gathered, wrinkled **10** compressed, corrugated

puckish 5 elfin **6** impish **7** playful **8** annoying **9** whimsical **11** mischievous

pudding 5 jello **6** junket **7** custard, dessert, tapioca **8** pandowdy **9** charlotte, yorkshire **14** floating island

pudgy, podgy 3 fat **5** buxom, dumpy, obese, plump, squat, stout, tubby **6** chubby, chunky, fleshy, rotund, stocky, stubby **7** paunchy **8** roly-poly, thickset

Pueblo (Cliff Dwellers)
   language family: 4 Tewa, Zuni **6** Queres, Tanoan **10** Shoshonean
   tribe: 4 Hopi, Tiwa, Towa, Tuei **5** Acoma, Kiowa **6** Isleta
   location: 4 Utah **7** Arizona **8** Colorado **9** New Mexico
   noted for: 5 adobe **12** architecture
   spirit: 7 Kachina **8** Katchina

puerile 3 raw **5** green, inane, petty, silly, vapid **6** callow, simple **7** babyish, foolish, trivial **8** childish, immature, juvenile, piddling **9** childlike, frivolous, infantile, senseless, worthless **10** irrational, ridiculous, sophomoric **11** harebrained, nonsensical

Puerto Rico
   name means: 8 rich port
   other name: 9 Borinquen **15** San Juan Bautista
   capital/largest city: 7 San Juan
   others: 5 Cayey, Coamo, Lares, Ponce **6** Caguas, Dorado, Manati, Utuado **7** Arecibo, Bayamon, Fajardo, Guanica, Guayama, Humacao **8** Adjuntas, Cabo Rojo, Mayaguez **9** Aquadilla **11** Santa Isabel
   government: 32 self-governing commonwealth of the U S
   measure: 6 cuerda **10** caballeria
   island: 4 Mona **7** Culebra, Vieques **13** Caja de Muertos **15** Greater Antilles
   lake: 4 Loiza **6** Carite **8** Dos Bocas **9** Caonillas, Guatajaca
   mountain: 4 Toro **5** Cayey **6** Yunque **8** Guilarte, Luquilla **10** Torrecilla **17** Cordillera Central
   highest point: 5 Punta
   river: 5 Camuy, Canas, Loiza, Yauco **6** Anasco, Manati, Tanama **7** Arecibo, Fajardo, La Plata **9** Caonillas
   sea: 8 Atlantic **9** Caribbean
   physical feature:
      bay: 5 Sucia **6** Rincon **8** Boqueron **9** Aquadilla **14** Phosphorescent
      sound: 7 Vieques
   people: 6 gibaro **10** borinqueno
      explorer: 8 Columbus **11** Ponce de Leon
      leader: 10 Munoz Marin
   language: 7 English, Spanish
   religion: 10 Protestant **13** Roman Catholic
   place:
      area of San Juan: 7 Hato Rey **10** Rio Piedras
      beach: 7 Condado
      cathedral: 15 San Juan Bautista
      fortress: 7 El Morro **11** San Jeronimo **12** San Cristobal
      governor's residence: 11 La Fortaleza
      museum: 14 El Museo de Ponce
      reservoir: 5 Loiza
      tomb: 11 Ponce de Leon
   feature:
      bird: 4 rola **7** yeguita
      festival: 6 Casals
      housing development: 14 urbanizaciones
      song: 9 aguinaldo
      strolling musicians: 9 parrandas
      tree: 4 mora **5** yafua, yaray **8** emajagua, guayrote **10** guaranguao
   food:
      dish: 4 sama, sisi **9** moreillas **11** lechon asado
      drink: 3 rum **10** anis-golila

puff 3 bow **4** blow, draw, emit, gasp, hump, node, pant, plug, suck, wisp **5** bloat, blurb, bulge, heave, smoke, swell, whiff **6** blow up, breath, dilate, exhale, expand, extend, flurry, inhale, rising, wheeze **7** bluster, bombast, distend, inflate, puffery, stretch **8** ballyhoo, be winded, dilation, encomium, flattery, flummery, swelling **9** convexity, discharge, elevation, euphemism, extension, inflation, panegyric, publicity, sales talk **10** be inflated, distention, exhalation, overpraise, protrusion, tuberosity **11** be distended, breathe hard, excrescence, excurvature **12** exaggeration, inflammation, protuberance, protuberancy **13** overlaudation **16** overcommendation **17** misrepresentation

puffed 5 baggy **7** bulbous, swollen **9** ballooned

puffed up 4 vain **5** proud, puffy **7** swollen **8** inflated **9** conceited **11** swell-headed **12** vainglorious **13** self-important

puffery 4 hype **7** big talk, bluster, bombast **9** hyperbole **11** braggadocio

puff out 5 bloat, bulge, swell **6** billow, expand **7** balloon, distend, enlarge, inflate

puffy 3 fat 5 round 6 fleshy 7 bloated, bulging, swollen 8 enlarged, expanded, inflamed, inflated, puffed up 9 corpulent, distended

pugilist 3 pug 5 boxer 7 battler, bruiser, fighter 12 prizefighter

pugnacious 7 defiant, hostile, warlike 8 menacing, militant 9 bellicose, combative, fractious 10 aggressive, unfriendly 11 belligerent, contentious, quarrelsome, threatening 12 antagonistic, disputatious 13 argumentative

pugnacity 9 hostility 10 antagonism 12 belligerence 13 combativeness 14 aggressiveness, fighting spirit 15 contentiousness

puissance 5 force, might, power 6 energy 7 potency, prowess 8 strength

pulchritude 6 beauty 8 fairness 9 bonniness, good looks 10 comeliness, loveliness, prettiness 12 gorgeousness, handsomeness 13 beauteousness, exquisiteness 14 attractiveness, personableness

pulchritudinous 4 fair, fine 5 bonny 6 comely, lovely, pretty 8 gorgeous, handsome 9 beauteous, beautiful, ravishing 10 attractive 11 good-looking

Pulitzer
  author: 10 W A Swanberg

Pulitzer Prize
  originator: 14 Joseph Pulitzer
  administered by: 18 Columbia University
  awarded for: 4 play 5 drama, music, novel 6 poetry 7 cartoon, feature, fiction, history, letters 9 biography, criticism, editorial, reporting 10 commentary, journalism, literature, nonfiction 11 photography 13 autobiography

pull 2 go 3 lug, rip, tow, tug 4 drag, draw, grab, haul, jerk, lure, move, rend, rive, tear, yank 5 drive, sever, shake, split, trawl, troll, twist, wrest, wring 6 allure, appeal, detach, dig out, entice, remove, sprain, strain, uproot, wrench 7 attract, draw out, extract, gravity, stretch, weed out 8 withdraw 9 extirpate, influence, magnetism, take in tow 10 allurement, attraction, enticement 11 fascination 14 attractiveness

pull apart 3 rip, tug 4 drag, rend, tear 6 detach, wrench 7 extract 8 separate 9 criticize, disengage 10 disconnect

pull away 5 wrest 7 remove 8 drawback, withdraw

pull back 7 back off, retreat 8 fall back, withdraw

Pullman, George Mortimer
  nationality: 8 American
  developed: 9 (railroad) dining car 11 (railroad) sleeping car

pull off 4 pull 6 commit, effect 7 execute, perform 8 carry out 10 perpetuate 13 participate in

pull on 3 don 5 put on 7 get into

pull one's leg 3 kid 4 fool, hoax 5 tease, trick 7 deceive 9 make fun of

pull out 5 leave 7 draw out, extract 8 withdraw

pull over, pullover 4 cite, stop 5 shirt 6 arrest, jersey, slip on, ticket, t-shirt 7 maillot, sweater 8 slip over

pull together 4 join 5 unite 7 pitch in, share in 8 take part 9 cooperate, join hands 10 act jointly, join forces 11 collaborate, participate

pull to pieces 5 shred 4 rend 6 tear up 7 destroy 9 tear apart

pull up 4 halt, rein, stop, weed 5 check, hoist 6 arrest, uplift, uproot 7 extract, reprove

pulp 4 curd, mash, mush, pith 5 crush, flesh, paste, puree, slush, smash 6 squash, tissue 7 journal 8 magazine 9 masticate

pulsate 4 beat, tick, wave 5 pound, pulse, shake, throb, thump, waver 6 quaver, quiver, shiver 7 flutter, shudder, tremble, vibrate 8 undulate 9 alternate, come and go, oscillate, palpitate 10 ebb and flow 11 reverberate

pulse 4 beat 5 throb, thump 6 quiver, rhythm, stroke 7 cadence, pulsate, shudder, tremble, vibrate 9 oscillate, palpitate, pulsation, vibration 10 recurrence, undulation 11 oscillation, palpitation

pulverize 4 mash, mill 5 crumb, crush, grind, mince, pound 6 powder 7 atomize, crumble 9 comminate, granulate, triturate 12 reduce to dust

pulverized 6 ground, milled 7 crumbed, crushed, pounded 8 atomized, crumbled, crunched, powdered 10 granulated 12 ground to dust

pummel 4 beat, maul 5 pound 6 batter, thrash 7 trounce

pump 4 quiz, shoe, well 5 grill 7 inflate, slipper 8 question 9 draw water

Pump
  constellation of: 6 Antlia

Pump House Gang, The
  author: 8 Tom Wolfe

pumpkin 5 fruit, gourd, melon 6 squash 9 vegetable 12 jack o'lantern

pun
  French: 9 jeu de mots

punch 3 box, hit, jab 4 beat, blow, chop, clip, conk, cuff, pelt, plug, poke, slam, sock, swat 5 baste, clout, knock, paste, pound, smite, thump, whack 6 pummel, strike, stroke, thrust, thwack, wallop 7 clobber 8 haymaker 10 roundhouse

punchy 3 fat 5 dazed 6 stubby 8 confused, forceful 9 befuddled

punctilious 5 exact, fussy, picky, rigid 6 proper, strict 7 correct, finicky, precise 8 exacting, rigorous 9 demanding 10 meticulous, particular, scrupulous 11 painstaking

punctual 5 early, quick, ready 6 on time, prompt, steady, timely 7 instant, not late, regular 8 constant, on the dot 9 immediate, well-timed 10 in good time, seasonable 11 expeditious 13 instantaneous

punctuate 4 lace 5 break 6 pepper 7 scatter 8 separate, sprinkle 9 interrupt 11 intersperse

punctuation mark 4 dash 5 colon, comma, pause, point, slash 6 accent, ending, hyphen, parens, period, quotes 7 bracket 8 ellipsis 9 semicolon 10 apostrophe 11 parenthesis 12 question mark 13 quotation mark 16 exclamation point

puncture 3 cut 4 bite, hole, nick, pink 5 break, prick, stick, sting, wound 6 pierce 7 deflate, let down, opening, rupture 9 knock down, shoot down 10 depreciate 11 perforation

pundit 4 guru, sage 5 guide 6 critic, expert, master, mentor, savant, wizard 7 thinker 9 authority 13 learned person

pungent 3 hot 4 acid, keen, racy, sour, tart 5 acrid, acute, nippy, salty, sharp, smart, spicy, tangy, tasty, witty 6 biting, bitter, clever, savory, snappy, strong 7 acetous, caustic, cutting, mordent, peppery, piquant, pointed 8 incisive, piercing, poignant, smarting, stinging, stirring, vinegary, wounding 9 brilliant, flavorful, invidious, palatable, sarcastic, sparkling, trenchant 10 astringent, flavorsome, keen-witted 11 acrimonious, penetrating, provocative, stimulating, tantalizing 12 sharp-tasting 13 scintillating, sharp-smelling 14 highly flavored, highly seasoned

punish 4 beat, fine, flog, whip 5 avenge, rebuke 7 chasten, correct, reprove 8 admonish, chastise, imprison, penalize, sentence 9 castigate, dress down, retaliate 10 discipline, take to task 11 get even with, take revenge 14 bring to account 15 take vengeance on

punishing 5 harsh, penal 6 brutal, severe 7 abusive 8 scolding 9 torturing 10 chastizing, tormenting 11 castigating

punishment 4 fine 5 price 7 damages, deserts, flaying, forfeit, hanging, payment, penalty, penance, redress 8 flogging, punition, spanking, whipping 10 chastening, correction, crucifying, discipline, reparation 11 castigation, retribution 12 chastisement, penalization

punk 4 hood, lout, poor 5 bully, lousy, rowdy, tough 6 crummy, rotten 7 hoodlum, ruffian 8 hooligan 9 barbarian, roughneck 10 delinquent

Punt see 7 Somalia

Puntarvolo
  character in: **22** Every Man Out of
    His Humour
  author: **6** Jonson
punt e mes
  type: **8** aperitif
  origin: **5** Italy
  flavor: **6** orange
  color: **12** reddish-brown

puny 4 poor, thin, tiny, weak **5** frail,
light, petty, runty, small **6** bantam,
feeble, flimsy, infirm, little, meager,
measly, paltry, sickly, slight, weakly **7**
fragile, shallow, tenuous, trivial **8** delicate, impotent, picayune, piddling,
runtlike, sawed-off, trifling **9** emaciated, miniature, mite- sized, pint-
sized, worthless **10** diminutive, inadequate, picayunish, under sized **11** unimportant **12** insufficient
13 insignificant **14** inconsiderable, underdeveloped

pupa 3 egg **5** larva, nymph **6** cocoon **7**
wiggler **9** chrysalis **14** transformation

pupil 4 coed, tyro **5** tutee **6** novice **7**
learner, scholar, student, trainee **8** beginner, disciple, initiate **9** schoolboy
10 apprentice, schoolgirl **11** probationer **13** undergraduate

puppet 3 toy **4** doll, dupe, pawn, tool
6 flunky, lackey **7** cat's-paw, manikin,
servant **8** creature, henchman, hireling **9** jackstraw, lay figure, underling
10 figurehead, instrument, man of
straw, marionette **11** subordinate

puppeteer 4 sarg **5** (Bil) Baird **8** Gep-
petto **9** Jim Henson **10** Shari Lewis

puppy 3 dog, pet, pup **6** canine

Purcell, Henry
  born: **6** London **7** England
  composer of: **9** Fantasias **10** Bell An-
    them, Dioclesian, King Arthur (The
    British Worthy), The Tempest **12**
    Golden Sonata **13** Dido and Aeneas
    14 The Indian Queen

purchase 3 buy **4** edge, hold **6** buying,
pay for, pick up **7** footing, support,
toehold **8** foothold, leverage **9** advantage, influence **11** acquirement, acquisition

pure 4 full, mere, neat, true **5** basic,
clean, fresh, moral, sheer, stark, utter,
whole **6** chaste, decent, entire, higher,
virgin **7** angelic, ethical, perfect, sincere, sinless, sterile, unmixed, upright
8 absolute, abstract, complete, flawless, germfree, innocent, positive,
purebred, sanitary, spotless, straight,
thorough, unmarred, virginal, virtuous
9 blameless, downright, faultless,
guileless, guiltless, healthful, inviolate,
out-and-out, pedigreed, righteous, unalloyed, undefiled, unmingled, unspoiled, unsullied, untainted, wholesome **10** antiseptic, immaculate,
inviolable, sterilized, uninfected, unmodified, unpolluted **11** conjectural,

disinfected, fundamental, pureblooded, speculative, theoretical, unblemished, uncorrupted, unqualified,
untarnished **12** full-strength, hypothetical, thoroughbred **13** unadulterated,
unimpeachable **14** above suspicion,
uncontaminated

puree 4 bisk, pulp, soup **5** paste **6**
bisque

purely 4 only **5** fully **6** merely, simply,
solely, wholly **7** cleanly, morally, pi-
ously, totally **8** chastely, devoutly, entirely, worthily **9** admirably **10** absolutely, completely, flawlessly, in all
honor, innocently, virginally, virtu-
ously **11** essentially, faultlessly **13** in-
corruptibly

Purgatory, Purgatorio
  part II of: **12** Divine Comedy
  author: **14** Dante Alighieri

purge 4 kill, oust **5** crush, expel **6** banish, emetic, pardon, physic, purify, remove, up- root **7** clean up, cleanse,
cleanup, clyster, dismiss, expiate,
purging, rout out, shake up **8** aperient, atone for, clean out, get rid of,
laxative, sweep out, wash away **9** cathartic, discharge, eliminate, eradicate,
liquidate, purgation, purgative **10** do
away with **11** exterminate **12** obtain
pardon (from), purification **15** obtain
remission (from) **16** obtain absolution
(from) **17** obtain forgiveness

purification 7 baptism **9** cleansing **13**
sterilization

purify 4 boil **5** clear **6** filter **7** clarify,
distill **8** make pure, sanitize **9** disinfect, sterilize **10** chlorinate, pasteurize
13 decontaminate

Purim 11 Feast of Lots
  celebrates: **7** deliverance
  heroine: **6** Esther
  villian: **5** Haman
  month: **4** Adar

Puritani, I
  also: **11** The Puritans
  opera by: **7** Bellini
  character: **14** Oliver Cromwell, Queen
    Henrietta **16** Lord Arthur Talbot

puritanical 4 prim **5** rigid, stiff **6** narrow, prissy, severe, strict, stuffy **7** ascetic, austere, bigoted, prudish, puritan, stilted **8** dogmatic, priggish **9**
bluenosed, fanatical **11** stiff-necked,
straitlaced **13** sanctimonious

Puritan State
  nickname of: **13** Massachusetts

purity 5 honor, piety **6** virtue **7** clarity,
decency, honesty, modesty **8** chastity,
fineness, holiness, lucidity, morality,
pureness, sanctity **9** cleanness, clearness, innocence, integrity, limpidity,
plainness, rectitude, virginity **10** brilliance, chasteness, directness, excellence, immaculacy, simplicity, temperance, uniformity **11** cleanliness,
homogeneity, saintliness, uprightness

12 virtuousness **13** guilelessness,
guiltlessness **14** immaculateness **15**
clear conscience **16** incorruptibility

purlieu 4 area **5** haunt, limit **6** border,
locale, region, resort **7** district, envi-
ron **8** out- skirt **11** surrounding **12**
neighborhood

purloin 3 rob **5** steal **6** pilfer **11** appropriate, make off with

Purloined Letter, The
  author: **13** Edgar Allan Poe

purloiner 5 thief **6** robber **7** burglar **8**
pilferer

purple 4 plum, puce, racy **5** color,
grape, lilac, lurid, mauve, royal **6**
florid, orchid, turgid, violet **7** crimson,
flowery, furious, fuchsia, magenta **8**
amethyst, burgundy, imperial, lavender **9** gastropod

Purple Land see **7** Uruguay

Purple Rose of Cairo, The
  director: **10** Woody Allen
  cast: **9** Mia Farrow **11** Danny Aiello,
    Jeff Daniels

purport 3 aim, end **4** gist **5** claim,
drift, point, sense, tenor, trend **6** allege, burden, design, import, intent,
object, reason **7** bearing, meaning,
profess, purpose **9** intention, objective, rationale, substance **11** implication **12** significance **13** signification

purpose 3 aim **4** goal, hope, mean,
plan, will, wish **5** elect, point, sense **6**
aspire, choose, decide, design, desire,
intend, intent, motive, object, reason,
scheme, target **7** drive at, meaning,
mission, persist, project, propose, resolve, think to **8** ambition, conclude,
endeavor, function, proposal, set
about **9** determine, intention, objective, persevere, rationale, undertake
10 aspiration, motivation, resolution
11 contemplate, disposition, expectation, fixed intent, have a mind to, raison d'etre **13** commit one self, determination

purposeful 7 decided, studied **8** resolute, resolved **9** committed, conscious
10 calculated, considered, deliberate,
determined **11** intentional **12** premeditated, strong-willed

purposefulness 7 purpose, resolve **10**
resolution **11** decidedness **12** decisiveness, resoluteness **13** determination

purposeless 6 random **7** aimless, useless **8** needless, plotless **9** desultory,
driftless, haphazard, irregular, senseless, unplanned **11** meaningless **12**
functionless, undetermined, unprofitable

purposely 8 by design **9** advisedly, expressly, knowingly, on purpose, will-
fully, wittingly **10** designedly, with intent **11** consciously, voluntarily **12**
calculatedly, deliberately **13** intention-
ally

purse 3 bag **4** fold, fund, knit **5** award,

bunch, pinch, pleat, pouch, prize,
stake **6** clutch, coffer, gather, pucker,
wallet **7** handbag, sporran, wrinkle **8**
contract, moneybag, proceeds, treasury, winnings **10** pocketbook **11**
shoulder bag
French: 12 porte-monnaie

purser 6 bursar **7** cashier **9** paymaster
10 cashkeeper

pursue 4 seek **5** aim at, chase, track,
trail **6** aim for, follow, try for **7** be after, carry on, go after, perform **8** aspire to, engage in, labor for, run after
9 race after, strive for **10** chase after,
push toward

pursuer 5 pupil **6** seeker **7** devotee,
student **8** disciple, follower, searcher
10 aficionado

pursuit 4 hunt **5** chase **6** search
7 pastime **8** activity **9** following **10**
occupation

purvey 3 get **4** give, hand **5** cater,
equip, yield **6** obtain, outfit, supply **7**
deliver, furnish, procure, provide

purveyor 4 pimp **6** seller **8** procurer,
provider, supplier

purview 3 ken **4** area **5** field, range,
reach, realm, savvy, scope, sweep **6**
domain, extent **7** compass, horizon,
outlook **8** dominion, overview **9** territory, viewpoint **10** commission, experience **11** mental grasp **13** comprehension, understanding **14**
responsibility

push 2 go **3** dun, ram **4** butt, goad,
jolt, move, plug, prod, spur, sway,
urge, work, worm **5** boost, drive, egg
on, elbow, fight, foray, force, forge,
harry, hound, impel, nudge, press,
rouse, shove, stick, stuff, vigor, wedge
6 arouse, badger, coerce, compel, energy, exhort, harass, heckle, hustle,
incite, induce, inroad, jostle, plunge,
prompt, propel, thrust, wiggle **7** advance, animate, buffalo, inspire, promote, provoke, squeeze **8** ambition,
browbeat, motivate, persuade, shoulder, struggle, vitality **9** advertise, constrain, encourage, importune, incursion, instigate, make known,
publicize, stimulate, strong-arm **10**
get-up-and-go **11** make one's way,
prevail upon, vim and vigor **12** force
one's way, propagandize **13** determination

pushcart 5 wagon **6** barrow **8** handcart **10** handbarrow **11** wheelbarrow

push forward 4 goad, prod, spur **5**
drive, impel, press **9** urge along

Pushkin, Alexander (Aleksandr)
author: 12 Boris Godunov, Eugene
Onegin **16** The Queen of Spades **17**
The Bronze Horseman **19** The Captain's Daughter

push through 6 hasten **7** advance,
forward **8** dispatch, expedite **10** accelerate, facilitate

pushy 8 forceful **9** assertive, insistent
10 aggressive **11** domineering **12**
strong-willed **13** self-assertive

pusillanimous 7 fearful **8** cowardly,
timorous **10** spiritless **11** lily-livered
12 apprehensive, fainthearted, mean-
spirited

pusillanimousness 8 timidity **9** cowardice **12** yellow streak **13** yellow
feather **16** faint heartedness **18** chickenheartedness

puss 3 cat, mug, pan **4** face **5** kitty **6**
feline, kisser, kitten

pussyfoot 5 dodge, evade, hedge,
sneak **6** tiptoe, weasel **8** sidestep **13**
evade the issue **14** beg the question
15 walk on eggshells **16** straddle the
fence

put 3 fix, lay, set **4** cast, pose, rest,
word **5** bring, drive, force, heave, offer, pitch, place, state, throw **6** assign,
employ, impute, phrase, submit **7** ascribe, deposit, express, present, propose **8** position **9** attribute, enunciate
10 articulate

put a damper on 4 cool, dull **7** depress, squelch **10** discourage, dishearten

put an edge on 4 hone, whet **6** excite
7 sharpen **9** stimulate

put an end to 4 halt, stop **5** annul,
quash **6** cancel, finish, repeal, revoke
7 abolish, blot out, rescind, squelch,
wipe out **8** abrogate, demolish, dispatch, stamp out **9** eliminate, eradicate, finish off **10** discourage, do
away with, put a stop to **12** write
finis to

put aside 5 table **6** forget **7** discard,
lay away **10** relinquish

put away 3 eat **4** down, stow **5** stash
6 commit **7** confine, consume **9** drink
down

put back 4 rout **5** delay **6** defeat, demote, impair, reject, return **7** replace,
restore **9** reinstate

put down 4 note, post **5** crush, enter,
knock, quash, quell **6** dispel, enlist,
record, subdue **7** deposit, disdain,
sneer at, squelch **8** belittle, derogate,
laugh off, pooh-pooh, suppress **9** denigrate, disparage, humiliate, write
down **10** depreciate

put forth 5 offer **6** extend, put out **7**
proffer, send out

put forward 4 pose **6** assert **7** advance, profess, propose **8** propound

put in irons 5 chain **6** fetter **7** manacle, shackle **8** handcuff

put in motion 4 move **5** begin, start
6 arouse, launch **8** activate, carry out,
commence, initiate **9** instigate, undertake

put in order 5 array **6** neaten, tidy up
7 arrange **8** organize **10** straighten

put in plain sight 4 show **6** set out **7**
display, exhibit

put in shackles 6 fetter, hobble **7** enchain, enslave, manacle **8** handcuff,
imprison

put into circulation 4 move **5** issue,
print **7** publish **10** pass around

put into effect 6 effect **7** achieve, enforce, execute, fulfill, realize **8** carry
out, complete **10** accomplish, administer, consummate, effectuate, perpetrate **12** carry through

put into words 5 voice **7** express **8**
describe **9** verbalize **10** articulate **11**
communicate

Putnam, Abbie
character in: 18 Desire Under the
Elms
author: 6 O'Neill

put off 5 delay, repel, stall **6** offend,
rebuff, recess **7** adjourn, repulse, set
sail, suspend **8** hold back, launched,
offended, postpone, rebuffed, repelled,
repulsed **9** interrupt **11** discontinue
13 procrastinate

put off guard 4 lull **6** disarm **10**
make unwary

put on 3 don **5** affix **6** attach **7** dress
in, get into, stick on **8** fasten to

put-on 4 hoax, joke **8** pretense **11** affectation

put on guard 4 warn **5** alert **6** advise,
tip off **7** caution **8** forewarn **9** make
ready **10** precaution

put out 3 irk **5** annoy, issue **6** quench,
retire **7** produce, publish **8** irritate **9**
strike out **10** extinguish **11** manufacture **13** leave the shore

put out of order 5 mix up, upset **6**
jumble, mess up, muddle **7** confuse,
scatter **8** disarray, disorder, displace,
put askew, scramble **10** disarrange **11**
disorganize

putrefaction 3 rot **5** decay **7** rotting **8**
spoilage, spoiling **10** rottenness **12** de-
compostion

putrefy 3 rot **4** turn **5** decay, spoil,
taint **6** molder **8** putresce, stagnate **9**
decompose **10** biodegrade **11** deteriorate **12** disintegrate

putrescent 4 foul, rank **5** fetid **6**
smelly **7** rotting **8** decaying, spoiling,
stinking **9** offensive **10** malodorous,
putrefying **11** decomposing

putrid 3 bad **4** foul, rank **5** fetid **6** rancid, rotten, spoiled **7** tainted **8** decaying, polluted, purulent, stinking **9** putrefied **10** putrescent **11** decomposing
12 contaminated, putrefactive

putridity 5 decay, filth, taint **8** foulness, impurity **9** dirtiness, pollution,
purulence, rancidity **10** rottenness **11**
putrescence, uncleanness **13** contamination, decomposition

putsch 6 revolt **8** uprising

putter 4 fool, idle, laze, loaf, loll **5**

dally, drift **6** dawdle, diddle, fiddle, loiter, lounge, piddle, potter, tinker **8** golf club, lallygag **10** dillydally

put to death 4 do in, hang, kill, slay **5** slain **6** done in, hanged, killed, murder, poison, rub out **7** bump off, butcher, execute **8** dispatch, executed, massacre, murdered, poisoned, strangle **9** bumped off, butchered, finish off, massacred, strangled, suffocate **11** assassinate, electrocute, exterminate **12** assassinated, electrocuted, exterminated

put to flight 4 rout, shoo **5** chase **6** dispel **7** cast out, scatter **8** drive off, send away **11** send packing

put together 4 join **5** unite **7** combine **8** assemble

put to shame 6 ashame **7** chagrin, mortify **9** discomfit, embarrass, humiliate

put to sleep 4 lull **5** quiet **6** sedate **8** knock out **9** narcotize **11** anesthetize

put to use 3 use **5** apply **6** employ, engage, occupy **7** exploit, utilize **9** make use of

put under a spell 5 charm **7** bewitch, enchant **8** entrance **9** fascinate, mesmerize, spellbind

put up 3 can **4** hang **5** erect, house, lodge, raise, store **6** billet **7** shelter **8** preserve **11** accommodate **14** furnish room for

put up with 4 bear, take **5** abide, brave, brook, stand **6** endure, suffer **7** stomach, sustain, undergo **8** stand for, submit to, tolerate **9** withstand **11** countenance

Puvis de Chavannes, Pierre Cecile
    born: 5 Lyons **6** France
    artwork: 6 Summer **13** Shepherd's Song **14** Ludus pro patria **16** The Poor Fisher- man **17** Life of St Genevieve, The Inspiring Muses **21** Science Arts and Letters

Puzo, Mario
    author of: 12 The Godfather

puzzle 4 foil, mull **5** brood, stump **6** baffle, enigma, outwit, ponder, riddle, wonder **7** confuse, dilemma, mystery,

mystify, nonplus, perplex, problem **8** bewilder, confound, hoodwink **9** conundrum **10** bafflement, difficulty, perplexity **12** bewilderment, complication **13** mystification

puzzled 6 amazed **7** baffled **8** befogged, confused, troubled **9** astounded, befuddled, mystified, perplexed **10** bewildered, confounded, nonplussed

puzzling 7 elusive **8** baffling **9** confusing, enigmatic **10** mysterious, mystifying, perplexing **11** bewildering, confounding, enigmatical **12** unfathomable **16** hard to understand, incomprehensible

Pyanepsia
    origin: 5 Greek **8** Athenian
    event: 8 festival
    honoring: 6 Apollo **7** harvest

Pygmalion
    author: 17 George Bernard Shaw
    character: 12 Henry Higgins **14** Eliza Doolittle
    basis for: 10 My Fair Lady
    director: 14 Anthony Asquith
    cast: 11 Wendy Hiller (Eliza Doolittle) **12** Leslie Howard (Professor Henry Higgins) **13** Wilfrid Lawson

Pygmalion
    king of: 6 Cyprus
    avocation: 8 sculptor
    statue named: 7 Galatea
    loved: 7 Galatea
    statue changed to: 5 woman
    wife: 7 Galatea
    daughter: 6 Paphos **8** Metharme

pygmy 3 elf, toy, wee **4** mite, runt, tiny **5** dwarf, elfin, short, small **6** bantam, midget, peewee, shrimp **7** manikin **8** dwarfish, half-pint, Tom Thumb **9** miniature, pipsqueak **10** diminutive, homun culus, undersized **11** Lilliputian

Pyncheon family
    character in: 24 The House of the Seven Gables
    members: 6 Phoebe **8** Clifford, Hepzibah **12** Judge Jaffrey
    author: 9 Hawthorne

Pynchon, Thomas
    author of: 1 V **15** Gravity's Rainbow **23** The Crying of Lot Forty-Nine

Pyongyang
    capital of: 10 North Korea

Pyramus
    form: 5 youth
    location: 7 Babylon
    loved: 6 Thisbe
    died at tomb of: 5 Ninus

pyre 8 woodpile
    rite: 7 funeral
    method: 7 burning

Pyrigenes
    epithet of: 8 Dionysus
    means: 10 born of fire

Pyriphlegethon see **10** Phlegethon

pyromaniac 7 firebug **8** arsonist **10** incendiary **11** firestarter

Pyronia
    epithet of: 7 Artemis
    means: 11 fire goddess

pyrope
    species: 6 garnet
    color: 3 red

pyrophobia
    fear of: 4 fire

pyrotechnics 9 fireworks **16** brilliant display **19** dazzling performance

Pyrrhus
    king of: 6 Epirus
    triumphed over: 5 Romans
    result: 11 heavy losses
    phrase: 14 Pyrrhic victory

Pythagoras
    born: 5 Samos
    vocation: 11 philosopher **13** mathematician
    created: 7 theorem
    of: 13 right triangle

Pythia
    priestess of: 6 Apollo
    location: 6 Delphi
    delivered: 7 oracles

Pythias
    friend: 5 Damon

Pythius see **6** Apollo

Qatar

capital/largest city: 4 Doha **7** al-Dawha

others: 3 Juh **5** Wagra **6** Dukhan, Umm-Bab **7** al-Khawr, Musayid, Umm Said

government: 7 emirate

head of state/government: 4 emir

monetary unit: 5 riyal **6** dirham

highest point: 13 Aba al-Bawl Hill

physical feature:

bay: 5 Salwa

cape: 5 Rakan **6** Laffan **8** Ushayriq **9** al-Matbakh

gulf: 7 Bahrain, Persian

people: 4 Arab **6** Pushtu, Yemeni **7** Baluchi, Iranian **9** Pakistani

rulers: 12 Great Britain, Ottoman Turks

sheik/sheikh: 18 Ahmad bin Ali al-Thani **22** Khalifa bin Hamad al-Thani

language: 6 Arabic

religion: 5 Islam

sect: 7 Wahhabi

war: 4 Gulf **11** Desert Storm

QED 21 quod erat demonstrandum

quack 4 fake, sham **5** phony **6** pseudo **9** charlatan, pretender **10** fake doctor, fraudulent **11** counterfeit, quacksalver **15** medical impostor

quackery 5 bluff, guile **6** deceit **7** cunning **9** deception, duplicity **12** charlatanism

Quadrigesima 4 Lent **9** forty days

quaff 4 down, gulp, swig **5** drink, lap up, swill **6** guzzle, imbibe, tipple **7** swallow, toss off **8** belt down, chug-a-lug **11** drink deeply

quagmire 3 bog, fen, fix, jam **4** mess, mire, ooze, quag, sump **5** marsh, pinch, swamp **6** crisis, morass, muddle, pickle, plight, scrape, slough, sludge, strait **7** dilemma **8** hot water, quandary **9** imbroglio, intricacy, quicksand **10** difficulty, perplexity **11** Gordian knot, involvement, predicament **12** entanglement

quail 3 shy **5** cower, quake, shake **6** blanch, flinch, recoil, shrink **7** run away, shudder, tremble **8** fight shy, turn tail **9** lose heart **10** be cowardly, lose spirit, take fright **11** lose courage **12** have cold feet **16** shake in one's boots **17** shiver in one's shoes, show a yellow streak

quail

group of: 4 bevy **5** covey

quaint 3 odd **4** rare **5** droll, queer **6** unique **7** antique, bizarre, curious, strange, unusual **8** charming, fanciful, old-timey, original, peculiar, singular, uncommon **9** eccentric, whimsical **10** antiquated, outlandish **11** out-of-the-way, picturesque **12** old-fashioned **13** extraordinary **14** unconventional

quake 4 wave **5** quail, shake, spasm, throb **6** blanch, quaver, quiver, ripple, shiver, thrill, tremor **7** shudder, tremble **9** trembling **10** earthquake **18** seismic disturbance

Quaker

founder: 9 George Fox

group: 7 friends

pronoun: 4 thee, thou

qualification 4 gift **5** forte, skill **6** talent **7** ability, faculty, fitness, proviso **8** aptitude, bona fide, capacity, property, standard **9** attribute, condition, endowment, exception, exemption, objection, postulate, provision, requisite **10** capability, competency, credential, limitation **11** achievement, arrangement, eligibility, requirement, reservation, restriction, stipulation **12** escape clause, modification, prerequisite, suitableness **13** certification **14** accomplishment

qualified 3 fit **4** able, meet **5** adept, equal **6** expert, fitted, suited, versed **7** capable, guarded, hedging, knowing, limited, skilled, trained **8** eligible, equipped, licensed, reserved, skillful, talented **9** ambiguous, certified, competent, efficient, equivocal, practiced **10** authorized, indefinite, proficient, restricted **11** conditional, efficacious, experienced, provisional **12** accomplished

qualify 3 fit **4** ease **5** abate, adapt, alter, endow, equip, limit, ready, train **6** adjust, enable, ground, modify, narrow, permit, reduce, soften, temper **7** assuage, certify, empower, entitle, license, make fit, prepare **8** describe, diminish, mitigate, moderate, restrain, restrict, sanction **9** authorize, condition, give power, measure up **10** be accepted, be eligible, commission, legitimate **11** accommodate **12** characterize, circumscribe, make eligible

qualifying 9 tempering **10** mitigating **11** eligibility, extenuating, preparatory

quality 4 mark, rank **5** blood, class, grade, merit, trait, value, worth **6** aspect, family, nature **7** caliber, dignity, faculty, feature **8** capacity, eminence, position, property, standing **9** attribute, character **11** disposition, distinction, high station, temperament **12** constitution, social status **13** qualification **14** characteristic

Quality Street

author: 12 James M Barrie

qualm 4 turn **6** nausea **7** scruple, vertigo **9** faintness, giddiness, misgiving **10** dizzy spell, hesitation, queasiness, reluctance, uneasiness **11** compunction, reservation, sick feeling **13** indisposition, unwillingness **14** disinclination **18** twinge of conscience

quandary 3 fix, jam **4** mire **5** pinch **6** crisis, morass, pickle, plight, scrape, strait **7** dilemma, impasse **8** hot water, quagmire **9** imbroglio **10** difficulty **11** involvement, predicament **12** entanglement, kettle of fish

quantities 4 lots, much **5** heaps, loads **7** amounts

quantity 3 sum **4** area, bulk, dose, mass, size **5** quota, share **6** amount, dosage, extent, length, number, volume **7** expanse, measure, portion **8** vastness **9** abundance, aggregate, allotment, amplitude, extension, greatness, magnitude, multitude **10** proportion **11** measurement **13** apportionment

quarantine 7 confine, isolate **9** isolation, segregate, sequester **13** sequestration **15** cordon sanitaire **18** medical segregation

Quare Fellow, The

author: 12 Brendan Behan

quarrel 3 jar, nag, row **4** carp, feud, fuss, spat, tiff **5** argue, brawl, cavil, clash, fight, scrap **6** bicker, differ, strife **7** contend, discord, dispute, dissent, fall out, wrangle **8** argument, be at odds, conflict, squabble **9** altercate, bickering, complaint, find fault, have words, objection **10** contention, difference, dissension, dissidence, falling out **11** controversy **12** disagreement **13** breach of peace, contradiction, misunderstand **14** apple of discord

15 be at logger heads **16** bone of contention, misunderstanding

quarreling 6 strife **7** discord **8** clashing, conflict, disunity, friction **9** bickering, disputing, scrapping, wrangling **10** contention, dissension, dissidence, squabbling **11** discordance **12** disagreement

quarrelsome 7 peevish **8** captious, churlish, contrary, militant, petulant **9** bellicose, combative, fractious, irascible, querulous, truculent **10** pugnacious **11** belligerent, contentious **12** antagonistic, cantankerous, disagreeable, disputatious **13** argumentative

quarry 3 bed, dig, pit **4** game, lode, mine, prey **5** catch, stone **6** source, victim **8** excavate

quart
   abbreviation: 2 qt

quarter, quarters 4 area, part, pity, post, side, spot, zone **5** board, house, lodge, mercy, place, put up, realm, rooms **6** billet, domain, fourth, locale, region, sphere **7** housing, install, lodging, shelter, station, terrain **8** clemency, district, humanity, leniency, locality, location, lodgings, position, precinct, province, sympathy **9** percent, direction, one-fourth, situation, territory **10** compassion, fourth part, indulgence, quadrisect **11** place to live, place to stay, three months **13** quarter dollar, specific place **14** accommodations **15** twenty-five cents

quarterstaff 4 pole **5** staff **6** cudgel

quartz
   varieties: 4 sard **5** agate, topaz **8** amethyst **9** carnelian, tiger's-eye **11** rock crystal

quash 4 ruin, stop, undo, void **5** annul, crush, erase, quell, smash, wreck **6** cancel, delete, dispel, efface, quench, recall, revoke, squash, subdue, vacate **7** blot out, destroy, expunge, nullify, put down, repress, rescind, retract, reverse, squelch **8** abrogate, dissolve, override, overrule, overturn, set aside, suppress **9** devastate, eradicate, extirpate, overthrow, overwhelm, repudiate, strike out **10** annihilate, extinguish, invalidate, obliterate, put an end to **11** countermand, exterminate

quasi 4 near, part, semi **6** almost, ersatz **7** halfway, seeming, virtual **8** apparent, somewhat, so-called **9** imitation, synthetic **10** resembling

Quasimodo
   character in: 23 The Hunchback of Notre Dame
   author: 4 Hugo

Quatermain, Allan
   character in: 17 King Solomon's Mines
   author: 7 Haggard

quaver 4 beat, sway, wave **5** quake, shake, throb, trill, waver **6** falter, quiver, shiver, teeter, totter, tremor, wobble, writhe **7** pulsate, shudder, tremble, tremolo, vibrate, vibrato, wriggle **9** oscillate, trembling, vibration **14** tremulous shake

quay 4 dock, mole, pier **5** basin, jetty, levee, wharf **6** marina **7** landing **10** waterfront

queasy 5 giddy, upset **6** uneasy **7** bilious, sickish **8** nauseous, qualmish, troubled **9** nauseated, sickening, uncertain **10** nauseating **13** uncomfortable **16** sick to the stomach

Quebec
   borders: 7 Ontario **8** Labrador **9** Hudson Bay **12** Newfoundland, United States **13** Atlantic Ocean **16** Gulf of St Lawrence
   cape: 5 Gaspe
   city: 6 Quebec **8** Montreal **10** Chicoutimi, Sherbrooke **13** Trois Rivieres
   highest point: 18 Mont Jacques Cartier
   hockey team: 9 Canadiens, Nordiques
   island: 9 Anticosti
   lake: 5 Gouin **9** Bienville, Eau Claire, Saint Jean **10** Mistassini **11** Manicouagan
   mineral: 4 gold, zinc **6** copper **7** iron ore **8** asbestos **9** limestone
   mountain: 5 Otish **10** Laurentian, Shickshock **11** Appalachian **12** Monteregians
   province of: 6 Canada

Quechua
   tribe: 4 Inca

queen 5 ranee **7** czarina, empress **8** princess **13** female monarch
   French: 5 reine
   German: 7 Konigin
   Latin: 6 regina
   Spanish: 5 reina

queen/empress/princess
   of Egypt: 9 Cleopatra, Nefertari, Nefertiti **10** Hatshepsut, Hetepheres
   of England: 3 Mab **4** Anne, Bess, Jane, Mary **7** Eleanor **8** Boadicea, Victoria **9** Catherine, Charlotte, Elizabeth, Guinevere **10** Bloody Mary, Elizabeth I **11** Elizabeth II, Jane Seymour
   of France: 7 Eugenie **9** Josephine **11** Marie Louise **14** Marie de Medicis **15** Marie Antoinette
   of Italy/Rome: 7 Poppaea **9** Agrippina, Messalina **13** Livia Drusilla
   of Monaco: 8 Caroline **9** Stephanie **10** Grace Kelly
   of the Netherlands: 7 Beatrix, Juliana **10** Wilhelmina
   of Poland: 7 Jadwiga
   of Portugal: 5 Maria **9** Elizabeth
   of Russia: 9 Alexandra, Catherine **17** Catherine the Great
   of Scotland: 4 Mary **13** Saint Margaret **16** Mary Queen of Scots
   of Spain: 8 Isabella **16** Elizabeth Farnese
   of Sweden: 9 Christina
   of Syria: 7 Zenobia
   in folklore: 3 Mab **7** Titania

Queen Christina
   director: 15 Rouben Mamoulian
   cast: 8 Ian Keith **10** Greta Garbo, Lewis Stone **11** John Gilbert **12** C Aubrey Smith

Queen Mab
   author: 18 Percy Bysshe Shelley

Queen of Amazons 9 Hippolyta, Hippolyte

Queen of Hearts
   character in: 28 Alice's Adventures in Wonderland
   author: 7 Carroll

Queen of Heaven 4 Hera, Mary **6** Ishtar **7** Mylitta

Queen of Spades, The
   also: 12 Pikovaya Dama
   opera by: 11 Tchaikovsky
   character: 4 Lisa **6** Herman **8** Countess

Queen of Spades, The
   author: 16 Alexander Pushkin

Queen of the Surf
   nickname of: 14 Esther Williams

Queen's Necklace, The
   author: 14 Alexandre Dumas (pere)
   character: 5 Oliva **13** Count de Charny **15** Cardinal de Rohan, Count Cagliostro, Marie Antoinette **16** Andree de Taverney **18** Philippe de Taverney **21** Jeanne de la Motte Valois

Queequeg
   character in: 8 Moby Dick
   author: 8 Melville

queer 3 gay, odd **4** daft, harm, hurt, rare, ruin **5** crazy, dizzy, droll, faint, fishy, funny, giddy, shady, spoil, weird, woozy, wreck **6** absurd, damage, exotic, impair, injure, quaint, qualmy, queasy, thwart, unique **7** bizarre, comical, curious, disrupt, erratic, reeling, strange, touched, unusual **8** abnormal, bohemian, doubtful, fanciful, freakish, original, peculiar, uncommon, unhinged **9** eccentric, fantastic, grotesque, homosexual, irregular, laughable, ludicrous, unnatural **10** capricious, compromise, farfetched, irrational, outlandish, remarkable, ridiculous, suspicious, unbalanced, unexampled, unorthodox **11** astonishing, exceptional, light-headed, out of the way, slightly ill, vertiginous **12** preposterous, questionable, unparalleled **13** extraordinary, nonconforming, unprecedented **14** unconventional
   French: 5 outre

quell 4 calm, dull, ease, hush, lull, rout, ruin, stay, stem **5** abate, allay, blunt, crush, quash, quiet, still, worst, wreck **6** becalm, deaden, defeat, pacify, quench, reduce, soften, soothe, subdue **7** appease, assuage, compose, conquer, destroy, mollify, put down, scatter, silence, squelch **8** beat down, disperse, mitigate, overcome, palliate, stamp out, suppress, vanquish **9** alleviate, overpower, overthrow, overwhelm, subjugate **10** extinguish **11** tranquilize

quench 4 cool, sate **5** allay, crush, douse, quell, slake **6** dampen, put out, stifle **7** appease, blow out, put down, satiate, satisfy, smother **8** stamp out, suppress **10** annihilate, extinguish

Quentin Durward
  author: **14** Sir Walter Scott
  character: **8** Isabelle **9** Le Balafre **10** Jacqueline **11** King Louis XI **12** Lady Hameline **13** Ludovic Lesley **15** Countess of Croye **16** William de la Marck **18** Hayraddin Maugrabin **20** King Louis the Eleventh **21** Charles Duke of Burgundy **23** Count Philip de Crevecoeur

querulous 4 sour **5** cross, fussy, testy, whiny **6** cranky, touchy **7** crabbed, finical, finicky, fretful, grouchy, peevish, pettish, waspish, whining **8** captious, exacting, petulant, shrewish **9** difficult, grumbling, irascible, irritable, long-faced, obstinate, resentful, splenetic **10** nettlesome **11** complaining, quarrelsome **12** disagreeable, discontented, disputatious, dissatisfied, faultfinding

query 3 ask **4** quiz **5** doubt, issue, quest **6** demand, impugn, search **7** dispute, examine, impeach, inquest, inquiry, inspect, problem, request, suspect **8** distrust, look into, mistrust, question, sound out **9** catechize, challenge, inquire of **10** controvert **11** examination, inquisition, interrogate, investigate, make inquiry **13** interrogation, investigation

quest 4 hunt, seek **6** pursue, search, voyage **7** crusade, journey, mission, pursuit, seeking **9** adventure **10** enterprise, pilgrimage **11** exploration

Quested, Adela
  character in: **15** A Passage to India
  author: **7** Forster

Quest for Fire
  director: **17** Jean-Jacques Annaud
  cast: **10** Ron Perlman **12** Rae Dawn Chong **13** Everett McGill

question 3 ask, rub **4** pump, quiz, test **5** doubt, drill, grill, issue, query **6** impugn, matter, motion, oppose **7** dispute, dubiety, examine, problem, subject, suspect **8** distrust, look into, mistrust, proposal, sound out **9** catechize, challenge, inquire of, misgiving, moot point, objection **10** difficulty, disbelieve **11** controversy, interrogate,

investigate, proposition, uncertainty **12** cross- examine **13** consideration

questionable 4 moot **5** fishy, shady **6** unsure **7** dubious, in doubt, suspect **8** arguable, doubtful, puzzling, unproven **9** ambiguous, confusing, debatable, enigmatic, equivocal, in dispute, uncertain, undecided **10** apocryphal, disputable, indefinite, mysterious, mystifying, perplexing, suspicious **12** hypothetical **13** controversial, problematical

queue 3 row **4** file, line, rank **5** chain, train **6** column, string

quibble 3 nag **4** carp, spar **5** argue, cavil, dodge, fence, fudge, shift **6** bicker, haggle, hassle, nicety, niggle, waffle **7** evasion, nitpick, shuffle **8** artifice, pretense, squabble, subtlety, white lie **9** be evasive, duplicity **10** equivocate, pick a fight, subterfuge **11** distraction **12** equivocation **13** dodge the issue, prevarication

quick 3 apt **4** able, deft, fast, keen, spry **5** acute, adept, agile, alert, brief, brisk, eager, fiery, fleet, hasty, rapid, sharp, smart, swift, testy **6** abrupt, active, adroit, astute, brainy, bright, clever, expert, facile, flying, frisky, lively, nimble, prompt, shrewd, speedy, sudden, touchy, winged **7** hurried, peppery, waspish **8** animated, choleric, headlong, petulant, skillful, snappish, spirited, vigilant, vigorous **9** dexterous, energetic, excitable, impatient, impetuous, impulsive, irascible, irritable, sagacious, splenetic, sprightly, vivacious, whirlwind, wideawake **10** discerning, high-strung, hot-blooded **11** accelerated, expeditious, hot-tempered, intelligent, light-footed, penetrating, precipitate **12** nimblefooted **13** perspicacious, temperamental

quicken 4 fire, goad, move, rush, spur, stir, urge **5** drive, egg on, hurry, impel, pique, press, rouse, speed **6** affect, arouse, excite, hasten, hustle, incite, kindle, propel, revive, vivify **7** actuate, advance, animate, enliven, further, hurry on, inspire, provoke, refresh, sharpen **8** activate, dispatch, energize, enkindle, expedite, inspirit, vitalize **9** galvanize, instigate, stimulate **10** accelerate, invigorate **11** precipitate

quick glance
  French: **9** coup d'oeil

quickly 4 anon, fast, soon **6** keenly, presto, pronto **7** briefly, hastily, rapidly, swiftly **8** promptly, speedily **9** instantly **11** immediately **12** lickety-split

Quickly, Mistress
  character in: **22** The Merry Wives of Windsor
  author: **11** Shakespeare

quickness 5 haste, speed **6** acuity

8 alacrity, celerity, keenness, rapidity **9** acuteness, alertness, dexterity, sharpness **10** cleverness, nimbleness, promptness **15** expeditiousness

quick-tempered 5 cross, testy **6** cranky, shirty, touchy **7** grouchy, peevish, waspish **8** choleric, churlish, shrewish, snappish **9** emotional, excitable, irascible, irritable **10** ill-humored **11** bad-tempered, hot-tempered, quarrelsome **12** cantankerous **13** temperamental

quick-witted 4 keen **5** acute, alert, aware, quick, ready, sharp, smart, witty **6** astute, bright, clever, shrewd **8** incisive **9** brilliant, wide-awake **10** discerning, perceptive **11** clearheaded, intelligent, penetrating **13** perspicacious

quid pro quo 4 swap **5** trade **8** exchange **9** tit for tat **21** something for something

quien sabe? 8 who knows?

quiescence 7 latency **8** dormancy, inaction **10** inactivity

quiescent 6 latent **7** dormant **8** inactive **10** in abeyance

quiet 3 low, mum **4** calm, curb, dull, ease, hush, lull, meek, mild, mute, rest, soft, stay, stop **5** abate, allay, blunt, check, fixed, inert, peace, plain, quell, still **6** arrest, at rest, deaden, docile, dozing, gentle, humble, hushed, lessen, mellow, modest, muffle, pacify, placid, repose, sedate, serene, settle, silent, simple, soften, soothe, stable, steady, stifle, subdue, weaken **7** assuage, clement, comfort, compose, dormant, halcyon, mollify, not busy, pacific, passive, patient, relieve, restful, silence, smother, subdued, suspend, unmoved **8** becalmed, calmness, comatose, composed, decrease, immobile, inactive, mitigate, moderate, muteness, not rough, not showy, palliate, peaceful, quietude, reserved, reticent, retiring, serenity, sleeping, stagnant, taciturn, tranquil **9** alleviate, collected, contented, easygoing, immovable, lethargic, makequiet, noiseless, not bright, peaceable, placidity, quietness, set at ease, soundless, stillness, temperate, unruffled, voiceless **10** coolheaded, gentleness, motionless, phlegmatic, put a stop to, relaxation, slumbering, speechless, stationary, stock-still, unassuming, untroubled **11** discontinue, tranquility, tranquilize, undisturbed, unexcitable, unobtrusive, unperturbed **12** bring to an end, even-tempered, inarticulate, peacefulness, tranquillity **13** at a standstill, dispassionate, imperturbable, noiselessness, soundlessness, unimpassioned, unpretentious **14** unostentatious, unpresumptuous

15 uncommunicative, undemonstrative

quietly 5 coyly **6** calmly, humbly, meekly, mildly, mutely, softly, tamely **8** demurely, modestly, placidly, serenely, silently **9** bashfully, inaudibly, patiently **10** composedly, moderately, peacefully, tranquilly **11** collectedly, contentedly, diffidently, noiselessly, pacifically, soundlessly, temperately, unexcitedly **12** speechlessly, unassumingly, unboastfully **13** unobtrusively, unperturbedly **15** dispassionately, unpretentiously, without ceremony **16** unostentatiously **17** undemonstratively

Quiet Man, The
director: **8** John Ford
author: **13** Liam O'Flaherty
cast: **9** John Wayne **12** Maureen O'Hara **14** Mildred Natwick, Victor McLaglen **15** Barry Fitzgerald
setting: **7** Ireland
score: **11** Victor Young
Oscar for: **8** director

quietness 5 peace, quiet **7** silence **8** softness **9** stillness **12** peacefulness

quietude 4 calm, rest **6** repose **8** easiness **9** composure

quill 3 pen **4** fold, hair, pick, seta, stem, tube **5** pluck, plume, spike, spine, spool **6** bobbin, needle **7** bristle, feather, spindle **9** toothpick

Quilp
character in: **19** The Old Curiosity Shop
author: **7** Dickens

quilt 5 cover **6** spread **7** blanket **8** coverlet **9** bedspread, comforter

Quin, Widow
character in: **24** Playboy of the Western World
author: **5** Synge

Quincy, M. E.
character: **3** Lee **5** Danny, (Sgt) Brill **11** Sam Fujiyama, (Dr) Robert Astin **12** (Lt) Frank Monahan
cast: **9** Robert Ito **10** John S Ragin **11** Jack Klugman, Joseph Roman, Val Bisoglio **12** Garry Walberg **13** Lynette Mettey
setting: **10** Los Angeles **11** Danny's Place

Quinn, Anthony
born: **6** Mexico **9** Chihuahua
wife: **16** Katherine DeMille
roles: **8** La Strada **10** Viva Zapata **11** Lust for Life **13** Zorba the Greek **17** The Guns of Navarone **22** Requiem for a Heavyweight, The Shoes of the Fisherman
autobiography: **14** The Original Sin

Quintana and Friends
author: **16** John Gregory Dunne

quintessence 4 core, gist, pith, soul **5** heart **6** elixir, marrow, nature **7** essence **8** exemplar, quiddity, sum total **9** substance **10** embodiment **12** distillation **15** personification, sum and substance

quip 3 gag, pun **4** barb, gibe, jape, jeer, jest, joke **5** crack, sally, spoof, taunt **6** banter, retort **7** epigram, putdown, riposte, sarcasm **8** badinage, raillery, repartee, wordplay **9** wisecrack, witticism
French: **6** bon mot **14** double entendre

Quirinus
origin: **5** Roman
god of: **3** war
personifies: **11** Roman nation
identified with: **7** Romulus

quirk 4 kink, turn, whim **6** fetish, foible, oddity, vagary, whimsy **7** caprice **8** crotchet, odd fancy **9** mannerism **10** aberration **11** abnormality, affectation, peculiarity, sudden twist **12** eccentricity, idiosyncrasy

quisling 6 puppet **7** traitor **12** collaborator **16** collaborationist

quit 3 end, rid **4** free, stop **5** cease, clear, forgo, leave, let go, waive, yield **6** depart, desist, disown, exempt, forego, give up, reject, resign, retire **7** abandon, disavow, drop out, forsake, take off **8** abdicate, absolved, forswear, renounce, withdraw **9** acquitted, foreswear, leave a job, surrender, terminate **10** discharged, exculpated, exonerated, relinquish **11** discontinue

quite 4 very **5** fully, truly **6** highly, hugely, indeed, in fact, in toto, really, surely, vastly, verily, wholly **7** exactly, in truth, totally, utterly **8** actually, entirely, outright **9** assuredly, certainly, extremely, in reality, outand-out, perfectly, precisely, unusually, veritably **10** absolutely, altogether, completely, enormously, positively, remarkably, throughout **11** exceedingly, excessively **12** considerably **13** exceptionally

Quito
capital of: **7** Ecuador

quiver 3 tic **4** jerk, jolt, jump, pant **5** quake, shake, spasm, throb **6** quaver, shiver, totter, tremor, twitch, wobble **7** flicker, flutter, pulsate, seizure, shudder, tremble, vibrate, wriggle **8** convulse **9** fluctuate, oscillate, palpitate, pulsation, quivering, twitching, vibration **10** convulsion **11** palpitation

Quiverful, Mr
character in: **16** Barchester Towers
author: **8** Trollope

quivering 7 shaking **9** agitating, quavering, shimmying, shivering, trembling, vibrating **10** flittering, fluttering, shuddering, twittering **11** palpitating

qui vive? 12 who goes there?

quixotic 4 wild **6** absurd, dreamy, madcap, poetic **7** utopian **8** fanciful, romantic **9** fantastic, impulsive, visionary, whimsical **10** chimerical, idealistic, ridiculous, starry-eyed **11** impractical, ineffective, sentimental, unrealistic **12** preposterous **13** inefficacious

quiz 3 ask, rib **4** exam, joke, mock, pump, test **5** prank, query, taunt, tease **6** banter **7** examine, inquest, inquiry **8** question, ridicule, sound out **9** catechism, eccentric, inquire of **11** examination, inquisition, interrogate, investigate, questioning **12** crossexamine **13** interrogation, investigation **16** cross-examination

Quiz Kids
host: **8** Joe Kelly **14** Clifton Fadiman

quizzical 3 coy **4** arch **6** joking **7** baffled, curious, mocking, puzzled, teasing **8** derisive, impudent, insolent **9** bantering, inquiring, perplexed, searching **11** inquisitive, questioning

quoad hoc 12 as much as this, to this extent

quod erat demonstrandum 17 which was to be shown **24** which was to be demonstrated
abbreviation: **3** QED

quod erat faciendum 16 which was to be done

quod vide 8 which see
abbreviation: **2** qv

quo jure? 11 by what right?

quo modo 3 how **9** in what way **19** in the same manner that

quondam 4 erst, late, once, past **6** bygone, former **8** formerly, sometime **9** erstwhile

quota 4 part **5** share **6** ration **7** measure, minimum, portion **8** quantity **9** allotment **10** allocation, assignment, percentage, proportion **12** distribution **13** apportionment

quotation 5 quote **7** cutting, excerpt, extract, passage **8** citation, clipping **9** reference, selection **12** illustration

quote 4 cite, name **6** adduce, recall, repeat, retell **7** excerpt, extract, refer to **8** instance **9** exemplify, recollect, reproduce **10** paraphrase

quoted passage 7 excerpt, extract **9** quotation

quotidian 5 daily **6** common **8** everyday, ordinary **11** commonplace

Quo Vadis?
author: **17** Henryk Sienkiewicz
character: **4** Nero **5** Chilo, Lygia, Peter **8** Vinitius **9** Petronius, Tigellius
director: **11** Mervyn LeRoy
cast: **7** Leo Genn **11** Deborah Kerr **12** Peter Ustinov, Robert Taylor
setting: **11** ancient Rome

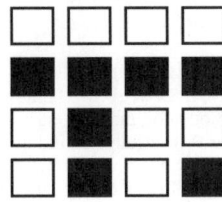

Ra
    also: 2 Re
    origin: 5 Greek 10 Heliopolis
    god of: 3 sun
    also worshipped by: 9 Egyptians

Rabat, Rabbat
    capital of: 7 Morocco

rabbi 6 master, rabbin 7 scholar, teacher 9 clergyman 15 spiritual leader

rabbinical, rabbinic 8 clerical

rabbit 4 cony, hare, jack, lure 5 bunny, coney, lapin 6 novice, rodent 8 beginner 10 cottontail, pacesetter

Rabbit Is Rich
    author: 10 John Updike

Rabbit Redux
    author: 10 John Updike

rabble 3 mob 5 swarm 7 the herd 8 populace, riffraff 9 commoners, hoi polloi, the masses 11 proletariat, rank and file 12 lower classes 15 disorderly crowd 16 the great unwashed
    French: 8 canaille
    German: 17 Lumpenproletariat

Rabelais, Francois
    author of: 22 Gargantua and Pantagruel

rabid 4 wild 6 ardent, crazed, raging 7 berserk, fervent, frantic, violent, zealous 8 deranged, frenzied, maniacal, wild-eyed 9 fanatical 11 hydrophobic 17 foaming at the mouth

race 3 fly, run 4 dart, dash, heat, rush 5 hurry 6 hasten, hustle 7 contest, operate 8 campaign 11 competition

racecourse 4 turf 5 track 6 course 9 racetrack

Rachel
    father: 5 Laban
    husband: 5 Jacob
    sister: 4 Leah
    son: 6 Joseph 8 Benjamin
    slave: 6 Bilhah

Rachmaninov (Rachmaninoff, Rakhmaninov), Sergei
    born: 6 Russia 8 Novgorod
    composer of: 15 Symphonic Dances 16 The Isle of the Dead 19 Second Piano Concerto 26 Rhapsody on a Theme by (of) Paganini

Racine, Jean Baptiste
    author of: 6 Phedre 7 Athalie 8 Berenice 10 Andromache 11 Britannicus

racism 7 bigotry 8 color bar 9 color

line 10 race hatred, racial bias 11 segregation 15 racial prejudice 20 racial discrimination

rack 4 buck, gait, hurt, neck, pace, pain, path 5 agony, cloud, exert, frame, raise, track, trail, worry, wreck, wring 6 canter, holder, strain 7 afflict, agonize, draw off, oppress, stretch, torment, torture 8 distress 9 suffering 10 destruction, excruciate, iron maiden

racked 4 torn 5 paced 6 framed, pained, traced, walked 7 annoyed, tracked, trotted, wronged, worried 8 cantered, suffered, tortured 9 afflicted, anguished, destroyed, oppressed, tormented 10 persecuted

racket 3 din 4 game, line, roar, stir 5 babel 6 clamor, hubbub, rumpus, tumult, uproar 7 clangor, clatter, turmoil 8 business, shouting 9 commotion, loud noise 10 hullabaloo, hurlyburly, occupation, turbulence 11 disturbance, pandemonium 12 caterwauling, vociferation

racketeer 4 hood 5 crook 6 bagman, bandit, extort 7 hoodlum, mafioso, mobster 8 criminal, gangster 12 extortionist

racking 7 painful 9 agonizing, torturous 10 tormenting, unbearable 11 intolerable, unendurable 12 excruciating, insufferable

raconteur 8 fabulist, narrator, romancer 10 anecdotist 11 storyteller 13 teller of tales 14 spinner of yarns

racy 4 keen 5 bawdy, crude, heady, lurid, zesty 6 erotic, lively, ribald, risque, smutty, vulgar 7 buoyant, glowing, obscene, zestful 8 animated, exciting, immodest, indecent, offcolor, prurient, spirited, vigorous 9 energetic, fast-paced, salacious, sparkling 10 suggestive 11 stimulating 12 exhilarating, pornographic

radar
    invented by: 4 Watt 6 Watson

Radcliffe, Mrs Ann
    author of: 10 The Italian 21 The Mysteries of Udolpho

raddle 3 rod 4 reed, scar, twig 5 fence, hedge, rouge, stick, weave 6 branch, ruddle 8 hematite, red ocher, red ochre 10 interweave

radiance, radiancy 3 joy 5 gleam,

gleem, sheen 6 dazzle, luster 7 glitter, rapture, sparkle 8 lambency, splendor 9 animation, happiness 10 brightness, brilliance, brilliancy, effulgence, luminosity, refulgence 11 coruscation, iridescence 12 luminousness, resplendence 13 incandescence
    god of: 5 Baldr 6 Balder, Baldur

radiant 5 aglow, happy, sunny 6 bright, elated, joyous 7 beaming, glowing, pleased, shining 8 blissful, dazzling, ecstatic, flashing, gladsome, gleaming, luminous, lustrous 9 brilliant, delighted, effulgent, overjoyed, rapturous, refulgent, sparkling 10 glittering 12 incandescent 13 scintillating

radiate 4 beam, pour, shed 5 carry 6 spread 7 diffuse, diverge, give off, give out, scatter 8 disperse, emit heat, transmit 9 branch out, circulate, emit light, spread out 11 disseminate

radical 4 rash 5 basic, rebel 6 severe 7 drastic, extreme 8 left-wing, militant 9 extremist, firebrand 10 immoderate, inordinate 11 freethinker, fundamental, precipitate 13 revolutionary 22 antiestablishmentarian

radio
    invented by: 7 Donovan, Fleming, Marconi 8 De Forest, Nicolson 9 Armstrong, Fessenden 12 Alexanderson

radium
    chemical symbol: 2 Ra

radon
    chemical symbol: 2 Rn

raffish 3 low 4 fast, wild 5 cheap, rowdy, showy 6 common, flashy, rakish, tawdry, vulgar 7 boorish 8 rakehell 9 worthless 10 dissipated 12 devil-may-care, disreputable

raft 3 lot 4 mass 5 barge, float 6 plenty 7 carrier, pontoon 8 flatboat, platform, quantity 9 abundance, multitude

Raft, George
    real name: 11 George Ranft
    born: 9 New York NY
    roles: 8 Scarface 11 Johnny Angel 12 Guido Rinaldo 13 Some Like It Hot

rag 3 kid, rib 4 scap, song, tune, twit 5 cloth, taunt, taunt, tease 6 harass 7 torment 8 magazine 9 newspaper 11 ragtime tune 14 worn-out garment

ragamuffin 3 bum 4 hobo, waif

5 gamin, tramp **6** beggar, gamine, hoyden, sloven, urchin, wretch **7** vagrant **8** derelict, vagabond **9** itinerant, ragpicker **10** panhandler, street arab **11** guttersnipe **14** tatterdemalion

rage 3 fad, ire **4** boil, fume, fury, mode, rant, rave, roar **5** craze, furor, mania, pique, storm, vogue, wrath **6** blow up, choler, frenzy, seethe, spleen, temper **7** explode, fashion, ferment, flare up, madness, passion, rampage, umbrage **8** paroxysm, the thing **9** animosity, fulminate, raise cain, throw a fit, vehemence **10** bitterness, excitement, irritation, resentment, the ''in'' thing **11** displeasure, high dudgeon, indignation, the last word **12** current style, le dernier cri, perturbation, violent anger **13** temper tantrum **14** the latest thing **15** fly off the handle, froth at the mouth

ragged 4 rent, torn, worn **5** seedy, tacky **6** beat up, frayed, shabby, shaggy, shoddy **7** patched, run down, worn-out **8** battered, shredded, strained, tattered **9** overtaxed **10** aggravated, threadbare, worn to rags **11** exacerbated

ragging 5 chaff **6** banter **7** kidding, ribbing, teasing **8** chaffing, needling, raillery, taunting, twitting

raging 3 mad **4** wild **5** angry, livid, rabid, rough **6** fierce, raving, stormy **7** fervent, frantic, furious, rampant, violent **8** frenzied, incensed, storming **9** turbulent **10** blustering, ferocious, infuriated **11** tempestuous

Raging Bull
  director: 14 Martin Scorsese
  cast: 8 Joe Pesci **12** Frank Vincent, Robert De Niro (Jake La Motta) **13** Cathy Moriarty
  Oscar for: 5 actor (De Niro)

Ragnarok
  also: 15 Gotterdammerung **17** Twilight of the Gods
  origin: 12 Scandinavian
  event: 11 final battle
  battlefield: 6 Vigrid

ragout 4 hash, stew **7** borscht, goulash **9** fricassee

Ragtime
  author: 10 E L Doctorow

raid 4 bust **5** foray, onset, sally, storm **6** attack, inroad, invade, razzia, sortie **7** assault, round-up **8** invasion **10** pounce upon **14** surprise attack

Raiders of the Lost Ark
  director: 15 Steven Spielberg
  cast: 10 Karen Allen, Wolf Kahler **11** Paul Freeman **12** Harrison Ford
  sequel: 29 Indiana Jones and the Last Crusade **30** Indiana Jones and the Temple of Doom

rail 3 bar **4** rage, rant **5** scold, fence, train **6** blow up, scream, take on **7** barrier, carry on, declaim, inveigh,

railing, railway, the cars **8** banister, railroad **9** fulminate **10** vituperate, vociferate **11** rant and rave **14** foam at the mouth

rail at 5 scold **6** berate **7** chew out **9** castigate **14** inveigh against

railing 3 bar **5** fence, grate, rails **6** fender **7** barrier, parapet, support **8** banister **9** enclosing **10** balustrade

raillery 5 chaff, sport **6** banter, japing, joking, satire **7** fooling, jesting, joshing, kidding, ragging, razzing, ribbing, teasing **8** badinage, chaffing, roasting, twitting **10** lampoonery, persiflage, pleasantry

railroad sleeping car
  French: 8 wagon-lit

railroad station 5 depot **8** terminal, terminus

railway 4 tube **5** track, train **6** cogway, subway **7** cograd, trolley **8** elevated, monorail, railroad **9** streetcar

raiment 4 duds, togs **5** dress **6** attire **7** apparel, clothes, costume, threads **8** clothing, garments **11** habiliments

rain, rains 4 down, drop, mist, pour **5** spate **6** deluge, lavish, shower, squall **7** drizzle, monsoon, torrent **8** downpour, drencher, plethora, rainfall, send down, sprinkle **9** hurricane, rainstorm **10** cloudburst **13** precipitation, thundershower **15** rain cats and dogs **16** come down in sheets **17** come down in buckets
  god of: 4 Thor

Rainbow
  goddess of: 4 Iris

Rainbow, The
  author: 10 D H Lawrence
  character: 10 Anna Lensky **11** Lydia Lensky, Tom Brangwen **12** Will Brangwen **14** Ursula Brangwen **15** Anton Skrebensky

Rainbow Bridge *see* **7** bifrost

raincoat 3 mac **4** mack **6** poncho, ulster **7** oilskin, slicker **8** burberry **9** tarpaulin **10** mackintosh, trenchcoat, waterproof

rainless 3 dry **4** arid, sere **10** desertlike

Rains, Claude
  born: 6 London **7** England
  wife: 11 Isabel Jeans
  roles: 9 Notorious **10** Casablanca, Now Voyager **13** Mr Skeffington **14** Anthony Adverse **15** The Invisible Man **16** Lawrence of Arabia **17** Here Comes Mr Jordan **20** The Phantom of the Opera **23** Mr Smith Goes to Washington **24** The Adventures of Robin Hood

rain shower 6 shower **7** drizzle **8** sprinkle **12** thunderstorm

rainstorm 6 deluge, shower **8** downfall, downpour **10** cloudburst **12** thunderstorm

rainy 3 wet **4** damp **7** drizzly, showery **11** pouring rain **18** raining cats and dogs

raise 3 end **4** grow, hike, lift, rear, spur, urge **5** amass, boost, breed, build, erect, nurse, pique, put up, rouse, set up, spark **6** arouse, awaken, excite, foster, hike up, jack up, kindle, obtain, stir up **7** advance, bring in, bring up, canvass, collect, develop, elevate, inflame, inflate, inspire, nurture, procure, produce, sharpen, solicit **8** increase, summon up **9** construct, cultivate, elevation, promotion, stimulate, terminate **10** make higher, put forward **11** advancement

raise aloft 5 boost, hoist **6** lift up, uplift **7** elevate, upraise

raised 4 bred, grew **5** anted, built, grown **6** anteed, convex, jacked, lifted, reared, roused **7** aroused, erected, exalted, hoisted, honored, incited **8** elevated, embossed, leavened, mustered **9** brought up, collected **10** cultivated **11** resurrected

Raisin in the Sun, A
  director: 12 Daniel Petrie
  based on play by: 17 Lorraine Hansberry
  cast: 7 Ruby Dee **9** Ivan Dixon **10** Diana Sands **13** Claudia McNeil, Sidney Poitier
  setting: 7 Chicago

rake 4 comb, goat, roue **5** rogue, satyr, scour, sport **6** lecher, pepper, rascal **7** Don Juan, playboy, ransack, seducer, swinger **8** Casanova, Lothario, enfilade, prodigal, rakehell **9** debauchee, libertine, womanizer **10** immoralist, profligate, sensualist, voluptuary

rake-off 3 cut, fee **5** piece **10** percentage **16** piece of the action

Rake's Progress, The
  etchings by: 7 Hogarth
  opera by: 10 Stravinsky
  character: 10 Ann Trulove, Nick Shadow **11** Baba the Turk, Mother Goose, Tom Rakewell

rakish 4 airy **6** breezy, dapper, jaunty, sporty **7** dashing, gallant, immoral, lustful **8** cavalier, debonair, depraved, sporting **9** bumptious, debauched, dissolute, lecherous, libertine **10** dissipated, lascivious, profligate, sauntering, swaggering

rally 4 meet, rush **5** score, unite **6** caucus, gather, muster, pick up, powwow, revive **7** catch up, collect, get well, improve, recruit, reunite, revival **8** assemble, assembly, recovery **9** come round, gathering, get better, reconvene **10** assemblage, convalesce, convention, reassemble, recuperate **11** convocation, improvement, mass meeting, pull through, restoration **12**

call together, congregation, recuperation **13** convalescence

ram 3 hit, jam **4** beat, bump, butt, dash, goat, slam **5** crash, drive, force, smash **6** batter, hammer, hurtle, strike, thrust **7** run into

Ram
constellation of: **5** Aries

ramble 3 gad **4** hike, roam, rove, wind **5** amble, drift, range, snake, twist **6** stroll, wander, zigzag **7** meander, saunter, traipse **8** gad about, idle walk **9** gallivant **11** perambulate, peregrinate

rambling 6 prolix, uneven **7** diffuse **10** circuitous, digressive, discursive, disjointed

rambunctious 4 wild **5** noisy, rowdy **6** active, unruly **7** raucous, untamed, violent **9** irascible **10** boisterous, pugnacious **11** quarrelsome **14** uncontrollable

Rameau, Jean-Philippe
born: **5** Dijon **6** France
composer of: **6** Platee **8** Dardanus **13** Les Fetes d'Hebe **14** Castor et Pollux **15** Castor and Pollux **16** Les Indes Galantes, The Indigo Suitors **17** Hippolyte et Aricie **20** La Princesse de Navarre

ramification 3 arm **4** part, spur **5** prong **6** branch **8** division, offshoot **9** branching, outgrowth **10** divergence, separation **11** consequence, subdivision

rampage 4 rage **5** storm **7** run amok, run riot

rampant 4 rife **5** erect **6** raging **8** epidemic, pandemic **9** prevalent, unchecked, universal **10** on hind legs, standing up, widespread **12** ungovernable, unrestrained **14** uncontrollable

rampart 7 barrier, bastion, bulwark, parapet **9** barricade, earthwork **10** breastwork **13** defensive wall, fortification **14** protective wall

Ramsay, William
field: **9** chemistry
nationality: **7** British
discovered: **4** neon **5** argon (in air) **6** helium **7** krypton
awarded: **10** Nobel Prize

ramshackle 5 shaky **6** flimsy, shabby **7** rickety, run-down **8** decrepit, unstable, unsteady **9** crumbling, tottering **10** tumbledown **11** dilapidated **13** deteriorating

Ramtil see **5** Niger

ranch 4 farm **5** range **6** grange, spread **7** acreage, station **8** hacienda **10** plantation

rancher 6 cowboy, farmer, gaucho **7** cowhand, cowpoke **8** herdsman, sheepman, stockman **9** cattleman **10** cowpuncher

rancid 3 old **4** foul, gamy, high, rank **6** putrid, strong **8** mephitic, stinking **10** malodorous

rancor 4 hate **5** spite **6** animus, enmity, hatred, malice, spleen **7** ill will **8** acrimony **9** animosity, antipathy, hostility **10** antagonism, bitterness, ill feeling, resentment **11** malevolence **12** spitefulness

rancorous 5 nasty **6** bitter **7** hostile **8** churlish, spiteful, vengeful, venomous **9** splenetic **10** ill-natured **11** acrimonious **12** antagonistic

Rand, Ayn
author of: **6** Anthem **13** Atlas Shrugged **15** The Fountainhead **17** Romantic Manifesto
philosophy: **11** objectivism

Randall, Tony
real name: **16** Leonard Rosenberg
born: **7** Tulsa OK
wife: **13** Heather Harlan
roles: **9** Mr Peepers **10** Felix Unger, Pillow Talk **12** Harvey Weskit, The Odd Couple **13** Fatal Instinct, The Mating Game **20** The Seven Faces of Dr Lao **22** Hitler's SS: Portrait in Evil

random 5 stray **6** casual, chance **7** aimless, offhand **9** haphazard, hit-or-miss, unplanned **10** accidental, fortuitous, occasional, undesigned, unexpected, unintended **12** adventitious **13** unintentional **14** unpremeditated

range 3 run **4** roam, rove **5** field, gamut, limit, orbit, reach, ridge, scope **6** bounds, domain, extend, massif, plains, radius, sierra, sphere, wander **7** explore, pasture, purview, stretch, variety **8** province **9** selection **11** grazing land **16** chain of mountains

Rangoon
capital of: **5** Burma **7** Myanmar
former name: **5** Dagon **6** Yangon
landmark: **10** Sule Pagoda **15** Shwe Dagon Pagoda
name means: **11** end of strife
river: **7** Rangoon
square: **12** Independence

rangy 4 tall **5** broad, lanky **9** expansive, extensive

rank 3 row **4** bald, file, foul, line, lush, rate, sort, tall, type, wild **5** class, crass, dense, grade, gross, level, nasty, order, sheer, stale, stand, total, utter **6** arrant, coarse, column, estate, filthy, jungly, lavish, rancid, status **7** come out, echelon, glaring, profuse, quality, rampart **8** absolute, complete, flagrant, position, standing, tropical **9** atrocious, be classed, come first, downright, have place, luxuriant, monstrous, overgrown **10** outrageous, scurrilous **11** highgrowing, ill smelling, unmitigated **12** over abundant **14** classification, social standing, strong smelling

rank and file 6 troops **17** enlisted personnel, general membership

Rankine, William John Macquorn
field: **7** physics
nationality: **8** Scottish
devised: **12** Rankine Cycle, Rankine Scale **26** Fahrenheit temperature scale
author of: **22** Manual of the Steam Engine

rankle 4 gall, rile **5** chafe, gripe, pique **6** fester **8** irritate **10** not sit well

ransack 3 gut **4** comb, loot, raid, rake, sack **5** rifle, scour, strip **6** ravage, search **7** despoil, pillage, plunder **8** lay waste **9** devastate, vandalize **14** rummage through, turn upside down

ransom 3 buy **4** free, save **5** atone, price **6** redeem, rescue **7** deliver, expiate, reclaim, recover, release **8** liberate, retrieve **10** liberation, redemption

Ransom, John Crowe
member of: **12** the Fugitives
author of: **14** I'll Take My Stand **16** Captain Carpenter **30** Bells for John Whiteside's Daughter

rant 4 fume, rage, rave, yell **5** orate, scold, spout, storm **6** bellow **7** bluster, bombast, bravado, explode **8** harangue **11** declamation **12** exaggeration

rap 3 jaw, pan, tap **4** bang, chat, drum, talk **5** blame, knock, roast, speak, thump **6** dump on **7** clobber **8** converse **9** criticize **10** come down on **11** communicate **14** responsibility, shoot the breeze

rapacious 6 greedy **7** looting, wolfish **8** covetous, grasping, ravenous, thievish **9** marauding, mercenary, pillaging, predatory, voracious **10** avaricious, insatiable, plundering, ransacking

rapacity 5 greed **7** avarice **10** greediness **12** covetousness, graspingness **13** mercenariness

Rape of Lucrece
author: **18** William Shakespeare
character: **7** Tarquin **9** Collatine

Rape of the Lock, The
author: **13** Alexander Pope
character: **5** Ariel **7** Belinda, Umbriel **9** Lord Petre **10** Thalestris

Raphael 9 archangel

Raphael
real name: **14** Raffaello Santi **15** Raffaello Sanzio
born: **5** Italy **6** Urbino
artwork: **7** Disputa **8** Julius II **10** Entombment **14** Sistine Madonna **17** The School of Athens, The Virgin and Child **18** Madonna di Casa Tempi, The Transfiguration **19** The Triumph of Galatea **21** Baldassare Castiglione **22** The Marriage of the Virgin **24** The Expulsion of Heliodorus **28** The Madonna and Child with St John (La Belle Jardiniere)

architect of: 11 Villa Madama (Rome) **16** Pandolfini Palace (Florence) **22** Vidoni-Caffarelli Palace (Rome)

rapid 4 fast **5** brisk, fleet, hasty, quick, swift **6** active, flying, prompt, speedy **7** express, hurried, instant, rushing **8** agitated, feverish **9** galloping, unchecked **11** accelerated, expeditious, precipitate

rapidity 5 haste, speed **8** celerity, velocity **9** fleetness, quickness, swiftness **10** promptness

rapidly 4 fast **5** apace **7** briskly, hastily, quickly, swiftly **8** pell-mell, speedily **9** hurriedly, like a shot, overnight **10** in high gear **11** at full speed **13** expeditiously, helter-skelter

rapids 5 chute **7** current **10** white water

rapport 3 tie **4** link **10** connection, fellowship **11** affiliation, camaraderie **12** relationship **13** understanding **17** interrelationship

rapprochement 6 accord **7** detente, entente **9** agreement **10** adjustment, compromise, settlement **11** appeasement, arrangement **12** conciliation, pacification **13** accommodation, harmonization, reconcilement, understanding **14** reconciliation **16** mutual concession

rapscallion 5 knave, rogue, scamp **6** rascal **7** low-life, villain **8** scalawag **9** scoundrel **10** blackguard, ne'er-do-well, rascallion **14** good-for-nothing

rapt 6 dreamy, enrapt, intent **7** bemused, charmed **8** absorbed, ecstatic **9** attentive, bewitched, delighted, enchanted, engrossed, entranced, rapturous **10** captivated, enraptured, enthralled, fascinated, interested, moonstruck, spellbound **11** transported

rapture 3 joy **5** bliss **6** thrill **7** delight, ecstasy, elation **8** euphoria, felicity **9** beatitude

rapturous 4 rapt **8** beatific, blissful, ecstatic **10** enraptured, enthralled

rare 3 few **6** scarce, unique **7** unusual **8** uncommon **10** hard to find, infrequent **11** exceptional, seldom found **16** few and far between

rarefied 4 thin **6** dilute, purify, rarify, reduce, refine, subtle **7** inflate **8** diminish **9** attenuate, extenuate

rarely 6 hardly, seldom **8** not often **10** hardly ever, uncommonly **12** infrequently, scarcely ever **15** once in a blue moon, on rare occasions **17** once in a great while

raring 4 agog, avid, keen **5** eager **8** desirous **9** impatient **12** enthusiastic

rarity 6 oddity **7** anomaly **8** scarcity **11** unusualness **12** uncommonness **14** remarkableness

rascal 3 cad, imp **4** rake **5** devil, knave, rogue, scamp **7** villain **8** rakehell, scalawag **9** prankster, reprobate, scoundrel, trickster **10** blackguard, delinquent **11** rapscallion

rash 5 brash, hasty **6** abrupt **7** foolish **8** careless, headlong, heedless, reckless **9** foolhardy, impetuous, imprudent, impulsive, premature, unadvised, unchecked **10** incautious, indiscreet, ungoverned, unthinking **11** adventurous, harebrained, injudicious, precipitate, thoughtless **12** devil-may-care, uncontrolled **13** irresponsible

rashness 8 audacity, boldness **9** riskiness **12** heedlessness, indiscretion, recklessness **13** foolhardiness, impulsiveness **15** precipitousness, thoughtlessness

Rashomon
 author: 18 Ryunosuke Akutagawa
 director: 13 Akira Kurosawa

Raskolnikov
 character in: 18 Crime and Punishment
 author: 10 Dostoevsky

rasp 3 irk, nag, rub, vex **4** file **5** chafe, grate, worry **6** abrade, scrape, wheeze **7** grating, scraper, scratch **8** abrasive, irritate **9** huskiness **10** hoarseness

raspberry 11 Rubus idaeus
 varieties: 3 red **4** hill **5** black, dwarf **6** Mysore, purple **8** European **9** flowering, Mauritius **11** American red **13** Rocky Mountain **15** Purple-flowering **22** Rocky Mountain flowering
 brandy: 9 Framboise

rasping 5 harsh, raspy, rough **6** hoarse **7** chafing, grating, nagging **8** abrading, scraping, worrying **9** offensive **10** irritating

Rasselas
 author: 13 Samuel Johnson
 character: 5 Imlac **6** Pekuah **7** Nekayah
 Rasselas's title: 17 Prince of Abyssinia

rat 3 cad, cur **4** fink, heel **5** churl, knave, louse **6** betray, rascal, rotter, squeal, vermin **7** bounder, villain **8** informer, inform on **9** scoundrel **10** blackguard **11** stool pigeon

rate 3 fee **4** cost, deem, dues, levy, pace, rank, toll **5** class, count, price, speed, tempo **6** charge, figure, look on, regard, tariff **7** expense, measure **8** classify **10** assessment

rate highly 5 prize, value **6** admire, esteem **7** cherish, respect **8** treasure

Rathbone, Basil
 real name: 25 Philip St John Basil Rathbone
 born: 11 South Africa **12** Johannesburg
 roles: 6 Tybalt **7** Karenin **10** Dawn Patrol **11** Mr Murdstone **12** Anna Karenina **14** Romeo and Juliet, Sher-

lock Holmes, The Mark of Zorro **16** A Tale of Two Cities, David Copperfield **20** The Last Days of Pompeii **24** The Adventures of Robin Hood **25** The Hound of the Baskervilles

rather 4 a bit, very **5** quite **6** fairly, kind of, pretty, sort of **8** slightly, somewhat **10** moderately, more or less, relatively **13** comparatively

rathskeller 6 saloon **8** beer hall
 vessel: 4 Toby **5** stein **6** seidel **7** tankard **8** pilsener, schooner

ratification 2 OK **4** okay **7** consent **8** approval, sanction **10** validation **11** affirmation, endorsement **12** confirmation **13** authorization, corroboration **14** seal of approval

ratify 2 OK **4** okay **6** affirm, uphold **7** agree to, approve, certify, confirm, endorse, support **8** accede to, make good, sanction, validate **9** authorize, consent to, make valid **11** acknowledge **12** authenticate

rating 4 mark, rank **5** class, grade, ratio, value **6** degree, rebuke, sailor, seaman **7** ranking **8** standing **9** appraisal **10** assessment, evaluation, percentage **14** classification

ratio 8 equation **10** proportion **11** arrangement **12** distribution **13** apportionment, fixed relation **15** proportionality **17** interrelationship **20** proportional relation

ration, rations 3 due **4** dole, food **5** allot **6** stores **7** measure, mete out **8** allocate **9** allotment, apportion, food share, provender, provision **10** provisions **13** apportionment

rational 4 sage, sane, wise **5** lucid, solid, sound **6** normal **7** logical **8** all there, balanced, credible, feasible **9** advisable, judicious, plausible, sagacious **10** reasonable **11** clearheaded, responsible **12** composmentis **13** perspicacious **15** in one's right mind

rationale 5 basis, logic **6** excuse, reason **7** grounds **9** reasoning **10** key concept, philosophy **11** explanation, foundations **16** underlying reason

rationalize 6 excuse **7** explain, justify **8** palliate **9** whitewash **10** account for **11** explain away **13** put a gloss upon **14** make excuses for **16** make allowance for

ratite 3 em(e)u, moa **4** kiwi, rhea **7** ostrich **9** cassowary

rattan 4 cane, lash, palm, whip **5** thong **6** switch, wicker

Ratti, Achille 10 Pope Pius XI

rattle 3 gab, jar **4** faze **5** clang, clank, clink, prate, shake, throw, upset **6** bounce, flurry, jangle **7** agitate, blather, chatter, clatter, confuse, disturb, fluster, maunder, nonplus, perturb **8** bewilder, clacking, distract **9** discomfit **10** discompose, disconcert **11** roll loosely

rattlebrained 4 dumb **5** silly **6** stupid **7** asinine, doltish, foolish, idiotic, moronic, witless **9** brainless, imbecilic **10** fool-headed, half-witted **11** hare-brained, lamebrained

rattled 5 fazed, upset **7** annoyed **9** disturbed, flustered, perturbed, thrown off **10** distracted **11** discomposed **12** disconcerted

rattle on 3 gab **4** blab **5** prate, run on **6** babble, gabble **7** blabber, chatter, prattle **16** run off at the mouth

ratty 4 poor, worn **5** angry, cross, nasty, testy **6** cranky, shabby, touchy **7** tangled, unkempt **8** wretched **9** irascible, motheaten **11** dilapidated

raucous 4 loud **5** harsh, raspy, rough **6** hoarse, shrill **7** blaring, grating, jarring **8** grinding, jangling, piercing, strident **9** dissonant **10** discordant, stertorous **11** cacophonous **12** ear-splitting, inharmonious

raunchy 4 lewd **5** dirty, gross **6** coarse, smutty, vulgar **8** off-color

Rauschenberg, Robert
  born: 12 Port Arthur TX
  artwork: 3 Bed **5** Barge **7** Jammers **8** Monogram **11** Retroactive

ravage 3 gut **4** loot, raid, rape, raze, ruin, sack **5** strip, waste, wreck **6** maraud **7** despoil, destroy, overrun, pillage, plunder, ransack, shatter **8** demolish, desolate, lay waste, spoliate **9** devastate **10** lay in ruins

rave 3 wax **4** fume, go on, gush, rage, rant **5** be mad, kudos, storm **6** babble, bubble, ramble **7** be angry, bluster, carry on, explode, flare up, run amok, sputter, thunder **8** flattery **9** be furious, expatiate, go on and on, good press, laudatory **10** effervesce, high praise, rhapsodize **11** blow one's top, compliments

ravel 4 undo **6** unknit **7** unravel, untwine, untwist

Ravel, Maurice
  born: 6 France **7** Ciboure
  composer of: 6 Bolero **7** La Valse, Mirrors **8** Jeux d'eau **11** Fountains **11** Mother Goose, Sheherazade **14** Daphnis et Chloe **15** Gaspard de la Nuit, L'Heure Espagnole **17** Rapsodie Espagnole, The Tomb of Couperin **20** Pavane for a Dead Infant **21** Don Quichotte a Dulcinee **22** L'Enfant et les Sortileges, Pavane for a Dead Princess **27** Pavane pour une infante de funte, Valses nobles et sentimentales

raven 3 jet **4** crow, dark, inky, rook **5** black, ebony, sable **6** devour **9** coal-black

Raven, The
  author: 13 Edgar Allan Poe
  woman 6 Lenore
  refrain: 9 nevermore

ravenous 6 greedy, hungry **7** piggish,
starved **8** covetous, famished, grasping, ravening, starving **9** insatiate, predatory, rapacious, voracious **10** avaricious, gluttonous, insatiable

ravine 3 gap **4** pass, rift, wadi **5** abyss, break, chasm, cleft, crack, gorge, gulch, gully, split **6** arroyo, breach, canyon, clough, divide, valley **7** fissure **8** crevasse

raving 3 mad **4** wild **6** insane **7** ranting **8** frenzied **9** delirious

ravish 4 rape **5** abuse, charm, cheer **6** defile, snatch, tickle **7** delight, enchant, gladden, outrage, overjoy, violate **8** deflower, enthrall, entrance, knock out **9** captivate, enrapture, fascinate, transport

ravishing 8 alluring, charming, gorgeous, smashing, splendid, striking **9** beautiful **10** bewitching, delightful, enchanting, entrancing **11** captivating, fascinating, sensational

raw 4 bare, cold, damp, rare **5** basic, bleak, crude, frank, fresh, green, harsh, plain, rough, young **6** biting, bitter, brutal, callow, chilly, rookie, unripe **7** cutting, natural, nipping, numbing, unbaked, untried **8** blustery, freezing, ignorant, immature, inexpert, piercing, pinching, uncooked, untaught, untested **9** inclement, underdone, undrilled, unfledged, unrefined, unskilled, untrained, windswept **10** amateurish, unprepared, unseasoned **11** not finished, undercooked, undeveloped, unexercised, uninitiated, unpracticed, unprocessed, unvarnished **13** inexperienced, undisciplined, unembellished **15** not manufactured

rawboned 4 lean **5** gaunt, lanky, spare **7** angular

Rawdon, Captain
  character in: 10 Bleak House
  author: 7 Dickens

Rawhide
  character: 5 Mushy **8** Gil Favor, Ian Cabot, Wishbone **9** Jim Quince, Pete Nolan **10** Rowdy Yates **11** Joe Scarlett, Solomon King **13** Clay Forrester **14** Hey Soos Patines
  cast: 10 Sheb Wooley **11** Charles Gray, David Watson, Eric Fleming, Robert Cabal, Rocky Shahan, Steve Raines **12** James Murdock, Paul Brinegar **13** Clint Eastwood **16** Raymond St Jacques

Rawlings, Marjorie Kinnan
  author of: 11 The Yearling

rawness 3 nip **4** bite **5** chill **8** rudeness **9** crudeness, greenness, roughness, sharpness, vulgarity **10** chilliness **12** inexperience

ray 3 arm **4** beam, fish, line **5** gleam, light, manta, shaft, shine, skate, trace **6** branch, streak, stream, stripe **7** radiate **8** particle, plowfish, radiance **9** emanation, radiation

Ray, Man
  born: 14 Philadelphia PA
  artwork: 4 Gift (Le Cadeau) **7** Manikin **9** The Lovers **13** Observing Time **45** The Rope Dancer Accompanies Herself with Her Shadows

Rayleigh, John William Strutt
  field: 7 physics
  nationality: 7 British
  discovered: 5 argon
  awarded: 10 Nobel Prize

rayon
  invented by: 4 Swan

raze 4 fell, ruin **5** level, smash, wreck **6** reduce, remove, topple **7** destroy, flatten, wipe out **8** demolish, pull down, tear down **9** break down, dismantle, knock down **10** obliterate

razor
  invented by: 6 Schick **8** Gillette

Razorback State
  nickname of: 8 Arkansas

Re see **2** Ra

reach 3 get, hit **4** find, go to, grab, make, move **5** climb, enter, get to, grasp, seize, touch **6** attain, clutch, come to, extend, grab at, land at, secure, spread **7** contact, stretch **8** amount to, approach, arrive at **9** get hold of, set foot in **10** get as far as, outstretch, stretch out

reachable 6 at hand **8** possible **10** accessible, achievable, attainable, obtainable, procurable

reach the top 6 arrive **7** prosper, succeed **8** make good **13** hit the big time

react 4 work **6** answer, behave, resist, return **7** respond **11** reverberate

reaction 5 reply **6** answer, reflex **8** backlash, response **11** restoration **13** counteraction **14** chemical change **17** counterrevolution, right-wing comeback

reactionary 7 diehard **8** mossback, rightist **9** right-wing **10** regressive **11** right-winger **12** reversionary **17** ultraconservative **20** counterrevolutionary

react to 5 reply **6** answer **7** respond **11** acknowledge

read 2 go **3** say **4** note, scan, show **5** study, utter **6** adduce, peruse, recite **7** analyze, deliver, discern, explain, present **8** construe, decipher, indicate, perceive, pore over **9** apprehend, interpret, translate **10** comprehend, glance over, understand **11** extrapolate

Read, Piers Paul
  author of: 5 Alive **9** Polonaise **10** Monk Dawson, The Junkers, The Upstart **18** Professor's Daughter

Reade, Charles
  author of: 13 Peg Woffington **23** The Cloister and the Hearth

readily 6 at once, easily, freely, pronto **7** quickly **8** in no time, promptly, smoothly, speedily **9** expressly, hands down, instantly, willingly **10** graciously **11** immediately, straightway **12** effortlessly, ungrudgingly

readiness 8 alacrity, dispatch **9** alertness **10** promptness **12** preparedness

read the riot act 5 chide, scold **6** berate, rebuke **7** censure, chasten, correct, lecture, reprove **8** admonish **9** dress down, reprimand **10** take to task

ready 3 apt, fit, set **4** deft, keen, ripe, up to **5** acute, alert, eager, equip, handy, on tap, prone, sharp **6** adroit, all set, artful, astute, at hand, bright, clever, expert, facile, fit out, liable, mature, on hand, primed, prompt, shrewd, speedy **7** cunning, equal to, prepare, present, tending, willing **8** disposed, inclined, masterly, punctual, skillful **9** attentive, dexterous, fitted out, furnished, ingenious, in harness, versatile, wide-awake **10** accessible, discerning, perceptive, put in order **11** acquisitive, expeditious, predisposed, quick-witted, resourceful, serviceable

ready for use 5 handy, on tap **6** at hand, on hand **9** available **10** accessible, convenient **11** at one's elbow **14** at one's disposal

ready-made 10 off-the-rack **11** prêt-à-porter, ready-to-wear, store-bought

ready money 4 cash **8** currency **10** cash on hand

ready to go 5 peppy **9** full of pep **10** raring to go **17** full of vim and vigor **24** bright-eyed and bushy-tailed

Reagan, Ronald Wilson
  nickname: 5 Dutch **6** Ronnie
  presidential rank: 8 fortieth
  party:
    current: 10 Republican
    former: 10 Democratic
  state represented: 2 CA
  defeated: 6 (James Earl) Carter (Jr) **7** (Walter Frederick "Fritz") Mondale **8** (John Bayard) Anderson
  vice president: 4 (George Herbert Walker) Bush
  cabinet:
    state: 4 (Alexander M) Haig (Jr) **6** (George P) Shultz
    treasury: 5 (Donald T) Regan
    defense: 10 (Caspar W) Weinberger
    attorney general: 5 (William French) Smith
    interior: 4 (James) Watt **5** (William P) Clark
    agriculture: 5 (John R) Block
    commerce: 8 (Malcolm) Baldrige
    labor: 7 (Raymond J) Donovan
    health and human services: 7 (Margaret M) Heckler **9** (Richard S) Schweiker

    education: 4 (Terrel H) Bell
    HUD: 6 (Samuel R) Pierce (Jr)
    transportation: 4 (Elizabeth H) Dole **5** (Andrew L) Lewis (Jr)
    energy: 5 (Donald P) Hodel **7** (James B) Edwards
  born: 9 Tampico IL
  college: 6 Eureka
  religion: 17 Disciples of Christ
  interests: 2 TV **5** track **6** movies **8** football **9** chops wood **10** basketball, jelly beans **13** weightlifting **15** horseback riding
  vacation spot: 14 Rancho del Cielo (Santa Barbara CA)
  dog: 5 Lucky
  author: 18 Where Is the Rest of Me?
  political career:
    governor of: 10 California
  civilian career: 5 actor **17** radio sportscaster
    host: 15 Death Valley Days **22** General Electric Theater
    president of: 17 Screen Actors Guild
    roles: 8 King's Row **10** Brother Rat **13** John Loves Mary, The Hasty Heart **15** Bedtime for Bonzo **19** The Voice of the Turtle **20** Cattle Queen of Montana **21** The Girl from Jones Beach **22** Knute Rockne All American
  military service: 6 US Army **7** captain **10** World War II
  notable events of lifetime/term:
    approval of: 10 MX missiles
    assassination attempt on: 6 Reagan **14** Pope John Paul II
    attempted assassination on Reagan by: 15 John W Hinckley Jr
    bombing of: 5 Libya
    hostages freed in: 4 Iran
    invasion of: 7 Grenada
    marines sent to: 7 Lebanon
    nuclear disaster at: 9 Chernobyl
    Russians shot down: 14 Korean airliner
    scandal: 8 Irangate
  father: 10 John Edward
    nickname: 4 Jack
  mother: 5 Nelle (Wilson)
  siblings: 4 (John) Neil
  wife: 4 Jane (Wyman) **5** Nancy (Davis)
    Nancy Davis born: 18 Anne Frances Robbins
  children: 6 Ronald **7** Maureen, Michael (adopted) **8** Patricia
    Patricia also actress known as: 10 Patti Davis
  first lady:
    program: 9 Drug abuse, Just Say No **12** Alcohol abuse **18** Foster Grandparents

real 4 pure, true **5** solid, valid **6** actual, honest **7** certain, factual, genuine, sincere **8** absolute, bona fide, positive, rightful, tangible, truthful **9** authentic,

unalloyed, unfeigned, veracious, veritable **10** legitimate, unaffected **11** not affected, substantial, substantive, unvarnished **12** well-grounded **13** unadulterated **14** unquestionable

realistic 4 real **7** genuine, graphic, natural, precise **8** faithful, lifelike, truthful **9** authentic, depictive, objective, pragmatic **10** true-to-life **11** descriptive, down-to-earth **12** naturalistic **16** representational

reality 4 fact **5** truth **6** verity **9** actuality **11** materiality, tangibility **12** corporeality **14** substantiality **17** physical existence

realization 7 success **8** grasping **10** attainment, perception **11** achievement, culmination, fulfillment **12** appreciation, consummation **13** comprehension, understanding **14** accomplishment

realize 2 do **3** get, net **4** gain **5** clear, grasp **6** absorb, attain, fathom, gather, profit **7** achieve, acquire, cognize, discern, execute, fulfill, imagine, make out, perform, produce **8** carry out, complete, conceive, make good, perceive **9** actualize, apprehend, discharge, make money, penetrate, recognize **10** accomplish, appreciate, bring about, comprehend, consummate, effectuate, understand **11** bring to pass **12** carry through

realized 3 got **6** gained, netted, proved, proven **7** cleared, grasped, made out, saw into **8** absorbed, accepted, effected, executed, existing, fathomed, gathered, imagined, made good, profited **9** completed, conceived, discerned, fulfilled, perceived, performed **10** actualized, penetrated, recognized, understood **11** appreciated, apprehended, consummated, established **12** accomplished, comprehended

really 5 truly **6** indeed, in fact, surely, verily **8** actually **9** certainly, genuinely, literally, veritably **10** absolutely, positively, truthfully **13** categorically **14** unquestionably

realm 4 land **5** field, orbit, state **6** domain, empire, nation, region, sphere **7** country, demesne, kingdom **8** dominion, monarchy, province **11** royal domain

real McCoy, the 4 real **7** genuine **9** authentic **12** the real thing

Realpolitik 10 expediency **13** power politics

reap 3 get, win **4** earn, gain **5** glean, score **6** derive, gather, obtain, profit, secure, take in **7** acquire, bring in, harvest, procure, realize

rear 3 aft, end **4** back, heel **5** after, nurse, raise, stern, train **6** dorsal, foster **7** bring up, care for, cherish, develop, educate, nurture, postern, tail end **8** back part, hind part, hindmost **9** aftermost, after part, at the back, cultivate, in the back, posterior

Rear Window
    director: 15 Alfred Hitchcock
    based on story by: 15 Cornell Woolrich
    cast: 10 Grace Kelly **11** Raymond Burr **12** James Stewart, Thelma Ritter, Wendell Corey

reason 3 wit **4** head **5** cause, logic, sense, solve **6** acumen, brains, figure, motive, sanity **7** grounds, insight **8** lucidity, occasion **9** awareness, faculties, intellect, normality, rationale, reasoning **10** perception **11** common sense, discernment, exhortation, explanation, penetration, rationality **12** apprehension, intelligence, perspicacity, think through **13** argumentation, comprehension, justification, mental balance, understanding **15** clearheadedness

reasonable 4 fair, just, sage, sane, wise **5** sound **6** likely, proper **7** fitting, knowing, lenient, logical, natural, patient, prudent **8** credible, moderate, possible, probable, rational, sensible, suitable, thinking **9** equitable, impartial, judicious, objective, plausible, temperate, tolerable **10** admissible, coolheaded, legitimate, not extreme, reflective, thoughtful **11** circumspect, intelligent, justifiable, levelheaded, not unlikely, of good sense, predictable, well-founded **12** not excessive, well-grounded **13** understanding **14** understandable **15** of sound judgment

reasonableness 5 logic **6** sanity, wisdom **8** fairness, prudence **9** good sense **10** moderation **11** credibility, objectivity, rationality **12** good judgment, impartiality, intelligence **13** judiciousness **14** circumspection, thoughtfulness **15** clearheadedness

reasonably 6 almost, fairly **8** passably, somewhat **10** moderately, more or less **13** approximately

reasoning 5 basis, logic **6** ground **7** thought **8** analysis, argument, thinking **9** deduction, inference, rationale **10** cogitation, reflection **11** penetration **13** ratiocination **14** interpretation

reason out 8 mull over **10** deliberate **12** think through

reassure 5 cheer **6** buoy up, uplift **7** bolster, comfort **8** inspirit **9** encourage **13** inspire hope in

reassured 6 buoyed **9** bolstered, comforted, heartened **10** emboldened, encouraged, inspirited

reassuring 7 hopeful **10** auspicious, comforting, heartening **11** encouraging

Reb 2 Mr **5** Rabbi **6** Mister

rebate 6 refund **8** discount **9** abatement

Rebecca
    author: 15 Daphne du Maurier
    character: 10 Jack Favell, Mrs Danvers (Danny) **12** Frank Crawley **13** Colonel Julyan, Maxim de Winter
    house: 9 Manderley
    director: 15 Alfred Hitchcock
    cast: 10 Nigel Bruce **12** Joan Fontaine **13** George Sanders **14** Judith Anderson (Mrs Danvers) **15** Laurence Olivier (Maxim de Winter)
    Oscar for: 7 picture

Rebecca
    character in: 7 Ivanhoe
    author: 5 Scott

Rebecca *see* **7** Rebekah

Rebecca of Sunnybrook Farm
    author: 17 Kate Douglas Wiggin
    character: 4 Cobb **8** Adam Ladd **11** Aunt Miranda **14** Rebecca Randall **15** Emma Jane Perkins

Rebekah
    also: 7 Rebecca
    father: 7 Bethuel
    husband: 5 Isaac
    brother: 5 Laban
    son: 4 Esau **5** Isaac, Jacob

rebel 3 shy **4** riot **5** avoid, quail, react, wince **6** flinch, mutiny, recoil, revolt, rise up, shrink **7** seceder, traitor, upstart **8** deserter, maverick, resister, turncoat **9** anarchist, dissenter, insurgent **10** iconoclast, malcontent, separatist **12** secessionist **13** nonconformist, revolutionary, revolutionist **15** insurrectionist

rebellion 6 mutiny, putsch, revolt **8** defiance, sedition, upheaval, uprising **9** coup d'etat **10** insurgency, revolution **12** insurrection

rebellious 6 unruly **7** defiant **8** contrary, mutinous, up in arms **9** alienated, fractious, insurgent, seditious, truculent, turbulent **10** disorderly, pugnacious, refractory **11** disobedient, intractable, quarrelsome **12** contumacious, recalcitrant, ungovernable, unmanageable **13** insubordinate, revolutionary **14** uncontrollable **15** insurrectionary

rebelliousness 8 defiance **9** rebellion **12** disobedience

Rebel Without a Cause
    director: 11 Nicholas Ray
    cast: 8 Sal Mineo **9** James Dean, Jim Backus **11** Natalie Wood

Rebirth
    god of: 4 Gwyn

rebound 3 bob **6** bounce, recoil, reecho **7** flounce **8** recovery, ricochet **10** spring back

rebounding 7 rubbery, springy **9** resilient **11** ricocheting **12** bouncing back

rebuff 4 deny, snub **5** check, repel, spurn **6** ignore, put off, refuse, reject, slight **7** decline, put-down, refusal, repulse **8** turn down **9** disregard, rejec-

tion **10** putting off **12** cold shoulder **13** slap in the face **15** keep at a distance

rebuke 5 blame, chide, scold, score **6** berate **7** censure, chew out, chiding, lecture, reproof, reprove, upbraid **8** admonish, berating, call down, reproach, reproval, scolding **9** dress down, reprimand **10** admonition, chewing out, take to task, upbraiding **11** castigation, disapproval **12** admonishment, dressing down, remonstrance, reprehension, take down a peg **13** find fault with, tongue-lashing **15** remonstrate with

rebuttal 5 reply **6** answer, denial, retort **7** defense, riposte **8** disproof, negation, response **9** disproval, rejoinder **10** refutation **11** confutation **12** counterreply, disagreement, surrejoinder **13** contradiction **15** counterargument

recalcitrant 5 balky **6** mulish, unruly **7** willful **8** contrary, stubborn **9** obstinate, pigheaded, unwilling **10** bullheaded, headstrong, refractory **11** disobedient, intractable **12** unsubmissive

recall 5 place **6** memory, revive **8** call back, remember **9** reanimate, recognize, recollect **10** reactivate, remobilize **11** reinstitute, remembrance **12** recollection **17** ability to remember

recant 4 deny **5** unsay **6** abjure, disown, recall, renege, repeal, revoke **7** disavow, rescind, retract **8** disclaim, forswear, renounce, take back, withdraw **9** foreswear, repudiate **10** apostatize **12** eat one's words **14** change one's mind

recantation 6 denial **9** disavowal **10** refutation, retraction, revocation **11** repudiation **12** renunciation

recapitulate 5 recap, sum up **6** relate, repeat, reword **7** recount, restate **8** rephrase **9** epitomize, reiterate, summarize **15** repeat in essence

recapture 6 retake **7** reprise **15** experience again

recede 3 ebb **5** abate **6** back up, go back, retire **7** regress, retreat, subside **10** retrogress

receipt 7 arrival, release, voucher **9** admission, discharge, receiving, reception **10** acceptance, admittance, possession, recipience **11** acquisition, transferral

receipts 3 pay **4** gain, gate, take **5** share, split, wages **6** income, recipe, return **7** formula, payment, profits, returns, revenue **8** earnings, proceeds **9** emolument **10** net profits **12** remuneration **13** reimbursement

receive 3 get **4** meet **5** admit, greet, put up **6** accept, come by, obtain, regard, secure, suffer, take in **7** acquire, adjudge, approve, be given, react to, sustain, undergo, welcome **8** meet with, submit to **9** encounter, entertain **10** experience **11** accommodate

receive willingly 6 accept **10** take gladly **16** accept with thanks **18** accept with open arms

receive with favor 6 praise **7** approve **10** appreciate

receive with open arms 6 invite **7** embrace, welcome **13** accept eagerly **19** roll out the red carpet

recent 3 new **4** late **5** fresh, novel **6** modern **8** up-to-date **9** latter-day **12** contemporary **13** up-to-the-minute

receptacle 3 bag, bin, box, can, jar **4** file, tray **6** basket, bottle, hamper, holder, hopper, vessel **7** carrier **8** receiver **9** container **10** depository, repository **11** compartment

reception 2 do **4** fete **5** party **6** affair, soiree **7** welcome **8** greeting **11** recognition **15** social gathering

receptive 8 amenable, friendly **10** accessible, hospitable, interested, open-minded, responsive **11** susceptible **12** approachable **17** favorably disposed

recess 3 bay, gap **4** bend, cell, cove, fold, gulf, lull, nook, pass, rest, slot **5** break, cleft, gorge, inlet, letup, niche, pause **6** alcove, corner, harbor, hiatus, hollow **7** holiday, interim, respite, time out **8** interval, vacation **9** interlude **10** pigeonhole **11** coffee break, indentation **12** intermission **14** breathing spell

recessed 4 sunk **6** paused, sunken **7** delayed **8** deferred, extended, indented **9** adjourned, dissolved, postponed, prolonged, withdrawn **10** terminated
church wall: 5 ambry
wall: 6 alcove

recesses 6 depths **10** inmost part, penetralia

recession 10 depression **11** recessional **16** economic downturn

recherche 4 rare **5** prize **6** choice, exotic, scarce, select, unique **7** special, unusual **8** original, superior, uncommon, valuable **9** different, priceless **10** one of a kind **11** exceptional

recipe 2 Rx **4** cure, rule **5** axiom **6** elixir, remedy **7** formula, receipt **12** instructions, prescription

recipient 4 heir **5** donee, taker **6** getter **7** legatee **8** accepter, acquirer, obtainer, receiver **9** presentee **11** beneficiary

reciprocal 6 common, linked, mutual, shared **8** returned **9** bilateral, exchanged, one for one **10** equivalent **11** give-and-take **12** interchanged, interrelated **13** complementary, corresponding, given in return **14** interdependent **15** interchangeable

reciprocate 4 feel **6** return **7** requite, respond **9** retaliate **10** make return **11**

act likewise, give and take, interchange **12** give in return **19** return the compliment

reciprocity 8 exchange **11** give and take, interchange

recital 4 talk **6** report **7** concert, telling **8** delivery, reciting **9** discourse, narration, narrative, rendition **10** recitation **11** description, particulars, performance **12** dissertation, oral exercise **13** public reading **14** graphic account, recapitulation

recite 4 tell **5** quote, speak **6** relate, repeat **7** declaim, deliver, narrate, perform, recount **10** say by heart **11** communicate

reckless 4 rash, wild **5** giddy, hasty **6** daring, fickle, madcap, unwary **7** flighty, foolish, unaware **8** careless, cavalier, heedless, mindless, unsteady, volatile **9** daredevil, desperate, foolhardy, imprudent, impulsive, negligent, oblivious, unheeding, unmindful **10** incautious, indiscreet, insensible, neglectful, regardless, unthinking, unwatchful **11** harebrained, inattentive, precipitate, thoughtless, unconcerned **12** devil-may-care, unsolicitous **13** inconsiderate, irresponsible, uncircumspect **14** scatterbrained

recklessly 4 fast **5** blind **6** rashly, wildly **7** hastily **8** headlong **9** headfirst **10** carelessly, heedlessly **11** audaciously, desperately, impetuously, impulsively **12** unmindfully **13** irresponsibly, unconcernedly

recklessness 7 abandon **8** rashness **9** disregard, unconcern **10** imprudence, profligacy **11** impetuosity **12** heedlessness, immoderation **13** foolhardiness **15** thoughtlessness **16** irresponsibility

reckon 3 add **4** bank, cope, deal, deem, plan, rank, rate **5** add up, class, count, fancy, guess, judge, tally, think, total, value **6** assess, decide, esteem, expect, figure, handle, regard **7** account, adjudge, balance, bargain, compute, imagine, presume, suppose, surmise **8** appraise, consider, estimate **9** calculate, determine, speculate

reckoning 3 tab **4** bill, doom **5** count, tally, total **6** adding, charge **7** account **8** estimate, judgment **9** appraisal, summation **10** estimation, evaluation **11** calculation, computation **13** final judgment **19** settling of an account

reclaim 6 reform, rescue **7** correct, recover, rectify, restore

reclame 9 notoriety, publicity

recline 4 lean, loll, rest **6** lounge, repose, sprawl **7** lie back, lie down **12** take one's ease

reclining 7 lolling, resting **8** lounging, reposing **9** lying down, recumbent

recluse 3 nun **4** monk **5** crank, loner **6** hermit, hidden, secret **7** ascetic, eremite, erratic, oddball **8** cenobite,

crackpot **9** eccentric **10** cloistered **11** sequestered **13** nonconformist

recognition 6 notice **9** discovery **10** acceptance, validation **13** comprehension, understanding **14** acknowledgment, identification **19** diplomatic relations

recognizable 5 clear, plain **8** distinct **10** detectable **11** discernable, perceivable, perceptible **12** identifiable, intelligible **13** ascertainable **14** comprehensible, understandable **15** distinguishable

recognizance 4 bond **6** pledge **10** obligation **11** recognition **15** acknowledgement

recognize 3 see **4** know, spot **5** admit, place, sight **7** discern, make out, pick out, realize, respect, yield to **8** identify, submit to **9** be aware of, concede to **10** appreciate, comprehend, understand **11** acknowledge **14** give the floor to

recognized 5 known **8** accepted, admitted, approved, familiar, realized **9** customary **10** accredited **11** traditional **12** acknowledged, conventional

recoil 4 fail, kick **5** blink, cower, demur, quail, shirk, start, wince **6** blench, cringe, falter, flinch, revolt **7** fly back, rebound, retreat **8** draw back, hang back, jump back **9** bound back **10** shrink back, spring back

recoil at 4 hate **5** abhor **6** detest, eschew, loathe **7** despise **9** abominate, shudder at **10** shrink from **12** be revolted by **14** view with horror **18** feel aversion toward

recoiling 7 wincing **9** flinching **10** rebounding **11** drawing back **13** shrinking back, springing back

recollect 5 place **6** recall **8** remember **10** call to mind

recollection 4 mind **6** memoir, memory, recall, record **11** remembrance **12** reminiscence **13** retrospection
French: 8 souvenir

recommend 4 urge **5** favor, order **6** advise **7** counsel, endorse, propose, suggest **8** advocate, vouch for **9** encourage, prescribe **10** put forward **11** speak well of

recommendable 9 advisable, favorable **10** worthwhile

recommendation 4 plug **6** behest, praise **8** approval, good word **9** reference **11** endorsement **12** commendation

recompense 3 pay **5** repay **6** return, reward **7** payment **9** reimburse, repayment **10** compensate, remunerate, reparation **12** compensation, remuneration **15** indemnification

reconcile 5 fix up **6** adjust, make up, resign, settle, square **7** correct, patch up, rectify, reunite, win over **8** persuade **9** harmonize **10** conciliate, propitiate **11** set straight

reconcile oneself 6 submit **9** acquiesce **13** resign oneself

reconciliation 8 fixing up, making up, settling, squaring **10** adjustment, correction, patching up, rectifying **11** resignation, winning over **12** conciliation **13** justification, rectification **15** setting straight

recondite 4 deep **6** arcane, hidden **7** obscure **8** abstruse, esoteric **9** concealed **10** mysterious **16** incomprehensible

reconnaissance 6 survey **7** viewing **8** scouting, scrutiny **10** inspection **11** exploration, observation **12** surveillance **13** investigation **14** reconnoitering

reconnoiter 4 look **5** probe, scout **6** patrol, picket, survey **7** examine **8** remember, traverse

reconsider 5 amend **6** modify, ponder, review, revise **7** correct, rethink, sleep on **8** mull over, reassess **9** reexamine, think over **10** reevaluate **13** think better of **15** think twice about

reconstitute 7 restore **9** recompose **10** add water to **11** reconstruct

reconstruct 7 rebuild **8** make over, recreate **10** reassemble **11** reestablish **12** reconstitute

record 3 log **4** copy, file, list, memo, note, post, show, tape **5** admit, enter **6** annals, career, docket, enroll, report **7** account, archive, catalog, conduct, history, jot down, jotting, journal **8** document, indicate, register, take down **9** chronicle, introduce, write down **10** adventures, background, memorandum, transcribe **11** experiences, make an entry, performance, proceedings **12** unbeaten mark **14** top performance
French: 11 compte rendu

record, phonograph 2 EP, LP **5** vinyl **7** platter
invented by: 4 Bell **6** Edison **7** Tainter **8** Berliner **10** Goldenmark

recount 4 tell **6** detail, recite, relate **7** explain, narrate **8** describe **9** count over

recoup 5 atone **6** redeem, regain **7** recover, replace **8** make good, retrieve **9** make up for, reacquire **13** make amends for

recourse 6 choice, option, resort **11** alternative, other choice

recover 4 heal, mend **5** rally **6** offset, pick up, recoup, redeem, regain, retake, revive **7** balance, get back, get well, improve, reclaim, restore, win back **8** make good, retrieve, revivify **9** make up for, reacquire, recapture, reconquer, repossess **10** come around, compensate, convalesce, recuperate, rejuvenate **11** pull through, resuscitate

recovery 4 cure **5** rally **6** recoup, rescue, upturn **7** revival, salvage **8** comeback **9** retrieval **10** betterment, regainment **11** improvement, reclamation, reformation, restoration **12** recuperation **13** business cycle, convalescence

recreancy 8 apostasy **9** cowardice, desertion **10** cravenness, disloyalty, infidelity **13** faithlessness, pusillanimity **14** unfaithfulness

recreant 6 coward, craven, yellow **8** apostate, cowardly, deserter, disloyal, renegade **9** undutiful **10** unfaithful **11** lily-livered **12** dishonorable **13** pusillanimous, yellow-bellied

recreation 4 play **5** hobby, sport **7** pastime **9** amusement, avocation, diversion **10** relaxation **13** entertainment **15** leisure activity

recrimination 5 blame **6** charge **10** accusation **13** countercharge

recruit 4 hire **5** raise, renew **6** employ, enlist, enroll, muster, novice, recoup, revive, rookie **7** draftee, provide, recover, restore **8** beginner, newcomer **9** conscript **10** recuperate

rectangle 3 box **6** oblong, square **7** polygon **10** quadrangle **13** parallelogram, quadrilateral

rectangular 4 long **6** square **7** boxlike **11** right-angled **12** quadrangular **13** quadrilateral

rectification 6 fixing, reform **7** redress **8** righting, squaring **9** remedying, repairing **10** adjustment, correction, regulation **12** setting right **15** putting straight, putting to rights **16** straightening out

rectify 3 fix **4** cure, mend **5** amend, emend, focus, right **6** adjust, attune, reform, remedy, repair, revise, square **7** correct, redress **8** put right, regulate, set right **9** make right **10** straighten

rectitude 5 honor **7** decency, probity **8** morality **9** integrity, principle **11** uprightness **12** virtuousness **13** righteousness **14** high-mindedness **15** trustworthiness **16** incorruptibility **17** irreproachability

rector 6 cleric, parson, pastor, priest **8** minister, preacher **9** churchman, clergyman **12** ecclesiastic

recumbent 4 flat **5** prone **6** supine **7** leaning **8** couchant **9** lying down, prostrate, reclining **10** horizontal **12** stretched out

recuperate 4 heal, mend **7** get well, improve, recover **8** come back **9** get better **10** come around, convalesce **11** be on the mend, pull through **14** return to health **16** regain one's health

recuperation 8 recovery **11** restoration **13** convalescence

recuperative 11 restorative **15** health-restoring

recur 6 repeat, resume, return **7** persist **8** come back, continue, reappear **9** come again **10** occur again

recurrence 5 cycle, round **6** repeat, return **7** relapse, renewal, reprise, routine **8** iterance, rotation **10** continuity, repetition **11** periodicity **12** reappearance

recurrent 7 regular **8** frequent, periodic **9** recurring, repeating **10** repetitive **11** reappearing **12** intermittent **14** appearing again

red 4 pink, rose, rosy, ruby, wine **5** aglow, coral, flame, ruddy **6** auburn, cherry, florid, maroon **7** burning, crimson, flaming, flushed, glowing, scarlet **8** blooming, blushing, cardinal, inflamed, reddened, rubicund **9** rubescent, vermilion **12** blood-colored

Red and the Black, The (Le Rouge et le Noir)
author: 8 Stendhal
character: 6 Fouque **8** M de Renal **11** Julien Sorel **16** Mathilde de la Mole

Red Badge of Courage, The
author: 12 Stephen Crane
character: 6 Wilson **10** Jim Conklin **12** Henry Fleming

red-blooded 5 lusty, peppy, vital **6** ardent, robust, strong, sturdy **7** dynamic, intense **8** forceful, powerful, spirited, vigorous **9** energetic **10** hot-blooded, passionate

Red Branch
origin: 5 Irish
warriors of: 9 Conchobar

Redburn
author: 14 Herman Melville

red-cheeked 4 rosy **5** ruddy **6** robust **8** blushing **12** apple-cheeked

Red Cross Knight
character in: 15 The Faerie Queene
author: 7 Spenser

redden 4 burn, glow **5** blush, color, flame, flush **9** go crimson **12** become florid

reddish 4 rosy, ruby **5** ruddy, rufus **6** flushy, rufous **7** roseate **8** rubicund

reddish-brown 4 rust **5** henna **6** auburn, copper, russet, sienna **8** chestnut, cinnamon

Red Earth People *see* **3** Fox

redeem 4 keep, save **5** cover **6** defray, ransom, recoup, reform, regain, rescue, settle **7** buy back, convert, fulfill, reclaim, recover, satisfy **8** atone for, make good, retrieve **9** discharge, make up for, repossess **10** evangelize, repurchase

redeemed 5 saved **7** claimed, rescued **8** made good, ransomed, reformed **9** atoned for, delivered, fulfilled, recovered **10** carried out, regenerate **11** repossessed

redemption 6 excuse, pardon, ransom, reform, rescue **7** salvage **8** recovery **9** amendment, atonement, exemption, expiation, salvation **10** conversion **11** deliverance, reformation

Redford, Robert
  real name: 20 Charles Robert Redford
  born: 13 Santa Monica CA
  roles: 8 The Sting **10** The Natural **11** Legal Eagles **12** The Candidate, The Way We Were **13** Downhill Racer **14** The Great Gatsby **15** Jeremiah Johnson **17** Barefoot in the Park **19** All the President's Men **20** Three Days of the Condor **29** Butch Cassidy and the Sundance Kid
  director: 8 Quiz Show **14** Ordinary People (Oscar) **17** The Horse Whisperer **19** A River Runs Through It

Redgrave, Corin
  born: 6 London **7** England
  sisters: 4 Lynn **7** Vanessa
  roles: 8 The Magus **17** A Man for All Seasons **20** In the Name of the Father **23** Four Weddings and a Funeral

Redgrave, Lynn
  born: 6 London **7** England
  father: 18 Sir Michael Redgrave
  sister: 15 Vanessa Redgrave
  roles: 10 Georgy Girl, Howard's End **13** The Bostonians **14** The Happy Hooker **26** Whatever Happened to Baby Jane
  author of: 7 Vanessa **16** Pussies and Tigers

Redgrave, Sir Michael
  born: 7 Bristol, England
  daughter: 4 Lynn **7** Vanessa
  roles: 11 Dan Peggotty **15** The Lady Vanishes **16** David Copperfield **22** Mourning Becomes Electra **27** The Importance of Being Earnest

Redgrave, Vanessa
  born: 6 London **7** England
  father: 18 Sir Michael Redgrave
  sister: 12 Lynn Redgrave
  husband: 14 Tony Richardson
  roles: 5 Julia, Yanks **6** Agatha, Blow-Up, Morgan **7** Camelot, Isadora **9** Guinevere **16** Mary Queen of Scots **17** The Lady from the Sea

red-hot 5 aglow, fiery **6** heated, raging **7** blazing, burning, glowing, intense **12** all-consuming

red-letter 5 happy, lucky **6** banner **10** auspicious, felicitous

redness 4 glow **5** blush, flush **8** rosiness **9** ruddiness **10** floridness

redolence 5 aroma, savor **7** bouquet **9** fragrance, good smell **12** pleasant odor

redolent 5 balmy, spicy **6** savory, smelly **7** mindful, odorous, reeking, scented **8** aromatic, fragrant, perfumed, stinking **9** evocative, odiferous

10 expressive, indicative, suggestive **11** odoriferous, reminiscent **13** sweet-smelling

Redon, Odilon
  born: 6 France **8** Bordeaux
  artwork: 10 In the Dream, The Cyclops **11** Le Vieil Ange **13** Flowers of Evil **15** Violette Heymann

redouble 7 augment, magnify **8** heighten, multiply **9** intensify

redoubtable 7 awesome **8** alarming, imposing **10** formidable **11** illustrious **12** awe-inspiring

redound 4 lead, tend **5** cause, surge **6** abound **7** conduce, incline **8** overflow **10** contribute **11** reverberate

redress 4 ease **5** amend, right **6** amends, reform, relief, remedy **7** correct, payment, rectify, relieve **8** easement, set right **9** make up for **10** recompense, reparation **11** restitution **12** compensation, satisfaction **13** compensate for, rectification **15** indemnification **16** make retribution for

Red River
  director: 11 Howard Hawks
  cast: 9 Joanne Dru, John Wayne **11** John Ireland **13** Walter Brennan **15** Montgomery Clift

Reds
  director: 12 Warren Beatty
  cast: 11 Diane Keaton (Louise Bryant), Paul Sorvino **12** Warren Beatty (John Reed) **13** Jack Nicholson, Jerzy Kosinski **14** Edward Herrmann **16** Maureen Stapleton
  Oscar for: 8 director **17** supporting actress (Stapleton)

Red Shoes, The
  author: 21 Hans Christian Andersen
  director: 13 Michael Powell **17** Emeric Pressburger
  cast: 12 Marius Goring, Moira Shearer **13** Anton Walbrook **14** Robert Helpmann

Red Skelton Show, The
  character: 8 Gertrude **10** Heathcliff **13** Mean Widdle Kid **14** San Fernando Red, Sheriff Deadeye, Willie Lump-Lump **16** Bolivar Shagnasty **17** Cauliflower McPugg **18** Clem Kadiddlehopper **20** Freddie the Freeloader
  saying: 7 I dood it
  closing line: 8 God bless

Red Sky at Morning
  author: 15 Richard Bradford

reduce 3 cut **4** bust, curb, diet, dull, ease, thin **5** abate, blunt, break, check, force, lower, slash, water **6** damage, demote, dilute, lessen, retard, soften, temper, weaken **7** assuage, atrophy, cripple, cut down, leave in **8** diminish, discount, enfeeble, mark down, minimize, mitigate, moderate, modulate, slim down, slow down, tone down, trim down **9** bring down, checkmate, undermine **10** debilitate,

devitalize, slenderize **11** lower in rank **12** incapacitate

reduced form 6 digest **7** summary **9** short form **11** abridgement, contraction **12** abbreviation, condensation

reduce speed 4 slow **5** brake **6** rein in **8** slow down **10** decelerate

reduce to nothing 5 erase **7** abolish, destroy, wipe out **8** lay waste **9** eradicate, liquidate **10** annihilate **11** exterminate

reductio ad absurdum 22 reduction to an absurdity

reduction 3 cut **5** break **8** decrease, discount **9** abatement, lessening **10** concession **11** abridgement, subtraction

reduction to an absurdity
  Latin: 18 reductio ad absurdum

redundancy 6 excess **7** surplus **8** verbiage **9** tautology **10** repetition **11** diffuseness, superfluity **13** overabundance **14** circumlocution, repetitiveness

redundant 5 extra **6** excess **7** surplus **10** pleonastic **11** dispensable, inessential, overflowing, repetitious, superfluous, unnecessary **12** tautological **13** superabundant

redwood 19 Adenanthera pavonina, Sequoia sempervirens
  varieties: 4 dawn **5** coast, giant **7** Madeira

reed
  varieties: 3 bur **4** vine **5** Burma, giant **6** common **14** Mauritania vine

reed 9 six cubits

Reed, Sir Carol
  director of: 6 Oliver (Oscar) **11** The Third Man

Reed, Walter S
  field: 12 bacteriology
  discovered cause of: 11 yellow fever

reef 3 bar **4** bank, flat, spit **5** shelf, shoal **7** sandbar, shallow

reek 4 fume **5** smell, smoke, steam, stink **6** stench **7** give off **9** effluvium, emanation

reel 4 rock, roll, spin, sway **5** lurch, pitch, swirl, waver, whirl **6** rotate, teeter, totter, wobble **7** revolve, stagger, stumble

reeling 5 dizzy, giddy, shaky **6** whirly **8** spinning, unsteady **10** staggering **11** vertiginous

Reese, Harold
  nickname: 6 Pee Wee
  sport: 8 baseball
  position: 9 shortstop
  team: 15 Brooklyn Dodgers

Reeve
  character in: 18 The Canterbury Tales
  author: 7 Chaucer

Reeve, Christopher
  born: 9 New York NY
  author of: 7 Still Me

roles: 8 Superman **9** Deathtrap **13** The Bostonians **15** Remains of the Day, Somewhere in Time **18** Village of the Damned

refer 2 go **4** cite, send, turn **6** advert, allude, direct, submit **7** consult, deliver, mention **8** hand over, transfer, transmit **9** pass along

referee 5 judge **6** decree, settle, umpire **7** arbiter, mediate **8** judgment, mediator, moderate **9** arbitrate, determine, intercede, intervene, moderator, pronounce **10** adjudicate, arbitrator **11** adjudicator, intercessor **12** intermediary

reference 4 hint **7** inkling, mention **8** allusion, good word, innuendo **10** deposition, intimation, suggestion **11** affirmation, credentials, endorsement, implication, testimonial **13** certification **14** recommendation

reference book 5 atlas, bible **6** manual **9** guidebook **10** dictionary **12** encyclopedia

refine 6 filter, purify, strain **7** cleanse, develop, improve, perfect, process **9** cultivate

refined 5 clean, suave **6** gentle, polite, urbane **7** courtly, elegant, genteel **8** cleansed, cultured, delicate, finished, graceful, ladylike, mannerly, polished, purified, well-bred **9** civilized, clarified, courteous **10** cultivated, fastidious **11** gentlemanly **14** discriminating

refinement 5 grace **6** finish, nicety, polish, step up **7** advance, culture, dignity, finesse, suavity **8** breeding, civility, cleaning, courtesy, delicacy, elegance, fineness, revision, urbanity **9** amendment, cleansing, gentility, propriety **10** betterment, filtration, gentleness, politeness **11** advancement, cultivation, development, discernment, enhancement, good manners, improvement, progression, savoir faire, step forward **12** amelioration, distillation, graciousness, purification, tastefulness **13** courteousness, rectification **14** discrimination, fastidiousness

refitting 8 adapting **10** adaptation, remodeling **11** reequipping, resupplying

reflect 4 cast, copy, muse, show, undo **5** image, study, think, throw **6** betray, evince, expose, mirror, ponder, reason, return, reveal **7** condemn, display, exhibit, express, imitate, present, rebound, uncover **8** cogitate, consider, disclose, give back, indicate, manifest, meditate, mull over, register, ruminate, send back, set forth **9** bring upon, cerebrate, dwell upon, represent, reproduce, speculate, throw back, undermine **10** deliberate **11** concentrate, contemplate, demonstrate

reflection 4 blot, idea, slur, view **5** image, study **6** insult, musing, notion

7 opinion, reproof, thought **8** reproach, thinking **9** attention, pondering, sentiment **10** cogitation, conviction, derogation, impression, imputation, meditation, rumination **11** cerebration, insinuation, mirror image, pensiveness **12** deliberation **13** concentration, consideration, disparagement

French: 6 pensee

reflective 7 pensive **8** thinking **9** judicious, pondering **10** meditative, ruminative, thoughtful **11** speculative **13** contemplative

reform 4 mend **5** amend, atone, emend **6** better, remedy, repair, repent, revise **7** convert, correct, improve, rebuild, rectify, remodel, restore **8** progress **9** amendment **10** correction **12** mend one's ways, rehabilitate **13** rectification **16** set straight again, turn over a new leaf

reformation 6 change, reform **9** amendment, reforming **10** alteration, conversion **11** improvement **12** modification **14** reorganization

refractory 5 balky **6** mulish, unruly **7** restive, wayward, willful **8** contrary, stubborn **9** fractious, obstinate, pigheaded **10** rebellious **11** disobedient, intractable **12** unmanageable

refrain 5 avoid, forgo **6** desist, eschew, forego, refuse, resist **7** abstain, forbear, hold off **8** leave off, renounce **11** curb oneself, keep oneself **12** stay one's hand **15** restrain oneself

refrain from 5 avoid, forgo **6** desist, eschew, forego **7** abstain, forbear **8** leave off, renounce

refresh 3 jog **4** prod **5** brace, renew, rouse **6** arouse, awaken, prompt, revive, stir up, vivify **7** cool off, freshen, quicken, recruit, restore **8** activate, energize, recreate **9** reanimate, stimulate **10** invigorate, rejuvenate, strengthen

refreshed 7 revived **8** animated, restored, vivified **9** enlivened, freshened **11** invigorated

refreshing 7 bracing **11** revivifying **12** invigorating **13** strengthening **15** thirst-quenching

refreshment 4 bite, eats **5** drink, snack **6** bracer **7** potable **8** beverage, cocktail, pick-me-up, potation **9** appetizer, drinkable, refresher **10** recreation, relaxation **11** hors d'oeuvre, nourishment, restoration, restorative **12** food and drink, invigoration, rejuvenation **14** reinvigoration, thirst quencher

refrigerate 4 cool **5** chill **6** freeze **7** congeal **8** keep cold, keep cool, put on ice **9** keep on ice

Refrigerator, The
nickname of: **12** William Perry

refuge 4 home **5** haven **6** asylum, har-

bor, resort **7** hideout, retreat, shelter **8** safehold **9** anchorage, harborage, sanctuary **10** protection **12** port in a storm **14** help in distress, place of shelter

refugee 2 DP **5** exile **6** bolter, eloper, emigre **7** escapee, evacuee, runaway **8** emigrant, fugitive **9** absconder **10** expatriate **15** displaced person

refulgent 6 bright, lucent **7** glowing, lambent, radiant, shining **8** luminous, relucent **9** brilliant

refund 5 remit, repay **6** rebate, return **7** pay back **9** reimburse, repayment **10** recompense, remittance, remunerate **12** amount repaid **13** give back money, reimbursement **18** make restitution for **19** make compensation for

refurbish 4 mend, redo **5** clean, fix up, renew **6** repair, tidy up **7** freshen, improve, remodel, restore **8** overhaul, renovate, spruce up **11** recondition

refusal 2 no **3** nay **4** veto **6** denial **7** regrets **8** turndown **9** declining, rejection **10** nonconsent **11** declination, disapproval **13** nonacceptance, noncompliance, unwillingness

refuse 2 no **4** deny, junk, veto **5** spurn, trash, waste **6** forbid, litter, reject **7** decline, garbage, rubbish, say no to **8** disallow, prohibit, turn down, withhold

refuse pile 4 dump **6** midden **11** rubbish heap

refuse to submit 4 defy **5** rebel **6** resist **7** disobey, hold out, violate **10** transgress **12** fail to comply

refutation 4 veto **6** denial **7** counter **8** negation, rebuttal **9** disavowal **11** confutation, repudiation **12** invalidation **13** contradiction

refutatory 8 contrary, opposing **10** discrepant **11** conflicting, disagreeing **12** antithetical, inconsistent **13** contradictory **14** countervailing, irreconcilable

refute 4 deny **5** rebut **6** answer **7** confute, counter **8** disprove **9** challenge **10** contradict, invalidate **12** give the lie to

regain 6 recoup, redeem, retake **7** get back, reclaim, recover, win back **8** gain anew, get again, retrieve **9** recapture, repossess

regal 5 grand, noble, proud, royal **6** august, kingly, lordly **7** queenly, stately **8** imposing, kinglike, majestic, princely, splendid **9** queenlike **10** princelike **11** magnificent **13** splendiferous

regale 3 ply **4** fete **5** amuse, feast **6** divert, please **7** banquet, delight, lionize **8** enthrall **9** entertain **10** serve nobly **11** wine and dine **15** feed sumptuously

Regan

character in: 8 King Lear
author: 11 Shakespeare

regard 3 eye, see 4 care, heed, hold, mind, note, rate, scan, view 5 judge, point, think, value, watch 6 accept, admire, aspect, behold, detail, esteem, follow, gaze at, look at, matter, notice, reckon, survey, take in 7 account, believe, concern, put down, respect, set down, subject, thought 8 consider, estimate, listen to, look upon, look up to, note well, relation 9 attention, hearken to, reference 10 admiration, connection, estimation, meditation, reflection, scrutinize 11 contemplate, observation, think well of 12 appreciation 13 cast the eyes on, consideration, think highly of 14 pay attention to

regardful 5 civil 6 polite 7 mindful 8 reverent 9 courteous, observant 10 respectful 11 deferential, reverential

regard highly 6 admire, esteem 7 respect 10 appreciate

regarding 4 in re 5 about, anent 7 apropos 10 concerning, respecting

regardless 6 anyhow, anyway 10 for all that 11 nonetheless 12 nevertheless 15 notwithstanding 19 in spite of everything

regard with repugnance 4 hate 5 abhor 6 detest, loathe 7 despise 8 execrate 9 abominate, can't stand, shudder at 10 recoil from, shrink from 11 can't stomach 12 be revolted by 13 be nauseated by, find repulsive 18 feel aversion toward

regard with suspicion 5 doubt 7 suspect 8 distrust, mistrust, question

regenerate 5 renew 6 redeem, reform, revive, uplift 7 restore 8 inspirit, reawaken, retrieve, revivify 9 enlighten, resurrect 10 rejuvenate 11 resuscitate 12 generate anew 13 give new life to, make a new man of

regent 4 king 5 queen, ruler 8 governor 9 protecter, protector

regime 4 rule 5 power, reign 7 command, control, dynasty 8 dominion 9 direction 10 government, leadership, management 12 jurisdiction 14 administration

regimen 4 diet, rule 6 system 10 government

regimentation 5 order, rigor 6 method, system 7 control, regimen 9 orthodoxy 10 discipline, regulation, uniformity 12 rigorousness 13 methodization 19 doctrinaire approach

Regin
origin: 12 Scandinavian
mentioned in: 8 Volsunga
brother: 6 Fafnir
raised: 6 Sigurd

region 4 area, land, zone 5 field, range, realm, space, tract 6 domain, sphere 7 country, expanse 8 district, locality, province, vicinity 9 territory 12 neighborhood

regional 5 areal, local, zonal 7 dialect 10 locational, provincial 11 territorial 12 geographical

register 3 log 4 dial, mark, roll, show 5 diary, gauge, meter, range, scale 6 betray, enlist, enroll, heater, ledger, record, sign up 7 betoken, check in, compass, counter, daybook, exhibit, express, logbook, point to, portray, set down 8 disclose, heat duct, heat vent, indicate, manifest, note down, radiator, recorder, registry, take down 9 indicator, write down 10 calculator, heat outlet, hot-air vent, record book 12 put in writing

regnat populus 16 let the people rule
motto of: 8 Arkansas

regress 3 ebb 4 back, exit, fall 6 go back, recede, return, revert 7 relapse, retreat, reverse 8 fall back, pass back, withdraw 9 backslide 10 lose ground, retrogress 11 deteriorate 12 move backward

regressive 8 backward 9 declining, worsening 10 retrograde 13 retrogressive

regret 3 rue, woe 4 moan 5 grief, mourn, qualm 6 bemoan, bewail, lament, repent, sorrow, twinge 7 anguish, apology, deplore, eat crow, remorse, scruple 8 be rueful, grieve at, weep over 9 apologies, grievance, heartache, rue the day 10 be sorry for, contrition, repentance, ruefulness 11 be ashamed of, compunction, lamentation, reservation 12 be remorseful, eat humble pie, eat one's words, self-reproach 13 feel sorrow for, regretfulness, second thought 14 disappointment, feel remorse for, remorsefulness 15 dissatisfaction 16 feel distress over, pang of conscience, self-condemnation

regretful 6 rueful 8 contrite 9 sorrowful 10 apologetic, remorseful 15 self-reproachful

regrettable 6 woeful 7 unhappy 8 grievous, pitiable 10 calamitous, deplorable, lamentable 11 unfortunate

regular 3 set 4 even, fine, real 5 daily, fixed, plain, usual 6 common, normal, proper, smooth, steady, trusty 7 classic, correct, genuine, habitue, natural, typical, uniform 8 absolute, accepted, complete, constant, everyday, faithful, familiar, frequent, habitual, loyalist, ordinary, orthodox, periodic, stalwart, standard, thorough, true blue 9 customary, recurrent, recurring, unvarying 10 consistent, dependable, invariable, periodical, unchanging 11 commonplace, down-to-earth, established, old reliable, symmetrical, undeviating 12 well-balanced 16 well-proportioned

regulate 3 fix 5 guide 6 adjust, direct, govern, handle, manage 7 balance, control, monitor, oversee, rectify 8 moderate, modulate, organize 9 supervise 10 regularize 11 superintend

regulation 4 rule 5 edict, order 6 decree 7 command, control, dictate, statute 8 handling 9 adjusting, direction, ordinance 10 adjustment 11 commandment 13 standing order

regulator 5 guide 7 manager 8 director, governor, overseer 9 moderator, modulator 10 adjustment, supervisor 14 superintendent 15 adjusting device

regurgitate 4 barf 5 vomit 7 throw up 8 disgorge

rehabilitate 3 fix 4 save 6 redeem, remake 7 restore, salvage 8 make over, readjust, renovate 9 reeducate, refurbish, reinstate 11 recondition, reconstruct, resocialize, set straight 13 straighten out 16 restore to society

rehash 6 repeat, retell, reword 7 restate 8 rephrase 9 iteration, rechauffe

rehearsal 5 drill, recap 6 tryout 7 hearing, reading, test run 8 audition, exercise, practice, trial run 9 polishing 10 perfecting, repetition, run-through 11 preparation, reiteration, walk-through 14 recapitulation

rehearse 5 drill, ready, train 6 go over, polish, recite, relate, repeat, retell 7 narrate, prepare, recount 8 practice 9 reiterate 10 run through 13 read one's lines 14 give a recital of, study one's lines

rehoboam 18 oversize wine bottle

Rehoboth
founder: 6 Nimrod

Reich, Charles
author of: 20 The Greening of America

Reichsfuhrer 11 Reich leader
chief of: 8 SS troops

reign 4 rule 6 govern, regime, regnum, tenure 7 command 8 dominion, hold sway, regnancy, tutelage 9 dominance, influence 10 government, incumbency 11 sovereignty, supervision 12 wear the crown 13 hold authority 14 have royal power, sit on the throne 15 occupy the throne 17 exercise authority 19 exercise sovereignty
Hindu: 3 raj

reign over 4 rule 6 govern 7 command, control 8 dominate

reimburse 5 pay up, remit, repay 6 rebate, refund 7 pay back 8 square up 9 indemnify 10 compensate, recompense, remunerate 15 make restitution

reimbursement 6 refund 9 indemnity, repayment 12 compensation, remuneration

rein, reins 4 curb, hold 5 check, limit, watch 6 bridle 7 control, harness 8 hold back, restrict, suppress **9** restraint **11** keep an eye on

Reiner, Carl
  born: **7** Bronx NY
  son: **9** Rob Reiner
  roles: **15** Your Show of Shows **21** It's a Mad Mad Mad Mad World
  created: **15** Dick Van Dyke Show
  director: **5** Oh God **7** The Jerk **8** The Comic **11** Where's Poppa?
  novel: **13** Enter Laughing

Reiner, Rob
  father: **10** Carl Reiner
  roles: **8** Meathead **10** Mike Stivik **14** All in the Family
  director of: **6** Misery **9** Stand By Me **11** A Few Good Men **15** This Is Spinal Tap **16** The Princess Bride **17** When Harry Met Sally

reinforce 4 prop **5** steel **7** bolster, brace up, fortify, support **8** buttress **10** strengthen **12** make stronger

reinforcement 4 stay **5** brace, strut **7** bracing, support **10** assistance **11** buttressing **13** strengthening

reinstate 5 renew **6** revive **7** readmit, restore **11** reestablish, reinstitute, reintroduce

reinstatement 7 renewal, revival **11** restoration **13** reinstitution **14** reintroduction **15** reestablishment

reiterate 5 resay **6** hammer, rehash, repeat, retell, reword, stress **7** iterate, reprise, restate **8** rephrase **11** pound away at **12** recapitulate **13** go over and over

reject 4 deny **5** repel, spurn **6** rebuff, refuse **7** castoff, decline, discard, disdain, dismiss, flotsam, repulse, say no to **8** castaway, disallow, shrug off, turn down, turn from **9** repudiate

rejected 6 denied, dumped, jilted **7** cast off, outcast, refused, spurned, unloved **8** disowned, forsaken, lovelorn **9** abandoned, discarded, disproved **10** unaccepted, repudiated **11** invalidated

rejection 6 rebuff **7** disdain, refusal **8** scorning, spurning **9** declining, dismissal, rebuffing, rejecting, ruling out

rejoice 5 exult, glory, revel **6** be glad **7** be happy, delight **8** be elated, jubilate **9** be pleased, celebrate, make merry **10** exhilarate, sing for joy **11** be delighted, be overjoyed **13** be transported

rejoice in 5 eat up, enjoy, savor **6** relish **7** revel in **9** delight in **13** be pleased with, get a kick out of **14** take pleasure in

rejoicing 5 mirth **6** gaiety **7** delight, ecstasy, elation, jollity, jubilee, revelry, triumph **8** cheering, gladness, pleasure, reveling **9** festivity, good cheer, happiness, jubilance, merriment **10** exultation, joyfulness, jubilation, liveliness **11** celebration, merrymaking

rejoin 6 answer, retort **7** respond

rejoinder 5 reply **6** answer, retort, return **7** riposte **8** backtalk, comeback, rebuttal, repartee, response **10** refutation **11** surrebuttal **12** counterblast, remonstrance, surrejoinder **13** countercharge **16** counterstatement

rejuvenate 6 revive **7** restore **8** revivify **9** reanimate **10** revitalize **12** reinvigorate **14** put new life into **17** make youthful again

relapse 4 fall **5** lapse **6** revert, worsen **7** decline, regress, reverse **8** fall back, sink back, slip back, turn back **9** backslide, reversion, worsening **10** degenerate, recurrence, regression, retrogress **11** backsliding, falling back **13** deterioration, retrogression **15** return to illness, turn for the worse

relate 3 say **4** link, tell **5** apply, refer, speak, state, utter **6** attach, belong, convey, detail, impart, recite, report, reveal **7** concern, connect, divulge, narrate, pertain, recount **8** describe, disclose **9** appertain, associate, feel close, make known **10** be relevant **11** communicate, have rapport **12** be responsive, interact well, recapitulate **13** be sympathetic, have reference, particularize **15** feel empathy with, give an account of

related 3 kin **4** akin, said, told **7** kindred, recited **8** narrated, reported **9** recounted **15** of the same family

related by blood 3 kin **4** akin **7** kindred **14** consanguineous, of the same stock **21** having a common ancestor

relation 3 kin, tie **4** bond, link **5** tie-in **6** regard, report **7** account, bearing, concern, kinsman, recital, telling, version **8** relative **9** narrating, narration, narrative, reference, relevance, retelling **10** connection, pertinence, recitation **11** affiliation, application, association, correlation, description **13** applicability, communication **17** interrelationship

relationship 3 kin **5** blood, union **6** affair **7** kindred, kinship, liaison, sibship, society **8** affinity, alliance **10** connection **11** affiliation, association, correlation **13** consanguinity

relative 3 kin **4** clan, kith **5** blood, folks, tribe **6** allied, cousin, family, people **7** cognate, germane, kinfolk, kinsman, related **8** relation, relevant **9** connected, dependent, kinswoman, pertinent, referable **10** affiliated, applicable, associated, comparable, connection, connective, correlated, kith and kin, pertaining, relational, respective **11** appropriate, comparative, correlative, not absolute **12** interrelated **13** flesh and blood **14** interconnected

relax 4 bend, calm, ease, idle, laze, loaf, rest **5** let up, slack **6** be idle, be lazy, ease up, loosen, soften, soothe, unbend, unwind **7** cool off, holiday,

make lax, slacken, take ten **8** decrease, loosen up, take five, vacation **9** lie around **10** take it easy **12** enjoy oneself **13** make less tense **14** make less severe, make less strict

relaxation 3 fun **5** games, hobby, sport **6** repose **7** bending, leisure, pastime **8** pleasure **9** abatement, amusement, avocation, diversion, enjoyment, loosening, remission **10** recreation, slackening **11** refreshment **12** rest from work **13** entertainment

relaxed 3 lax **4** calm, cool, easy, slow, soft **5** loose, slack **6** at ease, casual, gentle, remiss **7** flaccid, lenient **8** informal, laid back, unstrict **9** easygoing, leisurely, negligent, nerveless, unnervous **10** unstrained **11** free and easy, thoughtless
  French: **6** degage

relaxed manner 4 ease **5** poise **6** aplomb **9** composure **10** confidence **11** naturalness **12** unconstraint **14** unaffectedness

relay 3 leg **4** race, tour **5** shift **6** length **8** transfer, transmit **9** conductor, regulator, satellite **10** retransmit
  cylinder: **5** baton
  part: **8** armature, receiver **11** transmitter **13** electromagnet
  race: **6** medley **10** track event

release 4 free **5** let go, loose, untie **6** detach, let out, unbind **7** freeing, present, relieve, set free, unloose **8** liberate, set loose, unfasten **9** circulate, discharge, disengage, dismissal, extricate, letting go, releasing **10** distribute, liberating, liberation **11** circulation, communicate, extrication, publication, setting free **12** distribution, emancipation, set at liberty, setting loose

relegate 3 bar **5** eject, expel **6** assign, banish, charge, commit, demote, reject **7** cast out, consign, discard, dismiss, exclude, keep out, shut out **8** delegate **9** ostracize

relent 4 bend, melt **5** let up, relax, yield **6** give in, soften, unbend, weaken **7** give way **8** have pity **10** be merciful, capitulate, come around **11** give quarter, grow lenient **12** become milder **14** grow less severe

relentless 4 hard **5** harsh, rigid, stern, stiff **6** severe **7** adamant **8** pitiless, rigorous, ruthless **9** merciless **10** implacable, inexorable, inflexible, unyielding **11** remorseless, undeviating, unrelenting **14** uncompromising

relevance 7 aptness, fitness, meaning **9** propriety **10** pertinence **11** materiality, relatedness, suitability **12** significance **13** applicability **15** appropriateness

relevant 3 apt, fit **6** allied, suited, tied in **7** apropos, bearing, cognate, fitting, germane, related **8** apposite, material, suitable **9** connected, intrinsic, pertinent, referring **10** applicable, associated, concerning, to the point **11** appropriate, significant **12** on the subject, to the purpose

reliable 4 true **5** solid, sound **6** trusty **8** faithful **9** unfailing **10** dependable **11** responsible, trustworthy **12** tried and true **13** conscientious

reliance 5 faith, trust **6** belief, credit **8** credence **9** assurance **10** confidence, dependence

relic 5 scrap, token, trace **7** antique, memento, records, remnant, vestige **8** artifact, fragment, heirloom, keepsake, reminder, souvenir **11** remembrance

relief 4 balm, cure, dole, rest **5** break, cheer **6** remedy **7** anodyne, elation, panacea, respite, welfare **8** antidote, easement, lenitive **9** abatement, reduction **10** mitigation, palliation, palliative **11** alleviation, assuagement, peace of mind **12** amelioration **13** encouragement **16** public assistance **17** welfare assistance
Italian: 7 rilievo

relieve 3 aid **4** calm, ease, free, help, mark **5** abate, allay, cheer, spell **6** assist, let out, pacify, remove, set off, solace, soothe, subdue, succor, temper **7** appease, assuage, break up, comfort, console, lighten, mollify, release, replace, support, take out **8** contrast, mitigate, palliate, reassure **9** alleviate, encourage, interrupt, punctuate **12** free from fear

relieved 5 freed **6** calmed, exempt **7** cheered, excused, solaced **8** consoled **9** comforted, reassured **10** encouraged

religion 4 cult, sect **5** canon, creed, dogma, faith, piety **6** belief, church, homage **7** worship **8** devotion, theology **9** adoration, godliness, reverence **10** devoutness, persuasion, veneration **11** affiliation, belief in God **12** belief in gods, denomination, spirituality **13** system of faith **15** system of worship

religionist 8 believer

religiosity 5 piety **8** devotion **10** fanaticism **15** religious fervor

religious 3 nun **4** holy, monk **5** exact, friar, godly, rigid **6** ardent, devout, divine, priest, sacred **7** devoted, staunch **8** constant, faithful, unerring **9** spiritual, steadfast **10** devotional, fastidious, God-fearing, meticulous, scrupulous, unswerving **11** punctilious, theological, undeviating **12** wholehearted **13** conscientious **14** denominational **15** spiritual-minded

religious belief 5 canon, credo, creed, dogma, tenet **8** doctrine

religious fervor 5 piety **7** ecstasy **8** holiness **9** godliness **10** devoutness **12** religiosity, spirituality

religious group 4 sect **12** denomination

religious orders
Christian: 6 Jesuit **7** Cluniac, Templar **8** Capuchin, Theatine, Trappist, Ursuline **9** Carmelite, Dominican **10** Carthusian, Cistercian, Franciscan **11** Augustinian, Benedictine, Camaldolite **16** Sisters of Charity **20** Order of the Visitation
non-Christian: 4 Sufi **7** Jainism **8** Dasanami

relinquish 4 cede, deny, drop, quit, shed **5** forgo, leave, let go, waive, yield **6** forego, give up, resign, vacate **7** abandon, cast off, discard, dismiss, forbear, forsake, release **8** abdicate, break off, disclaim, hand over, lay aside, put aside, renounce, sign away **9** deliver up, repudiate, surrender

relinquishable 9 forgoable **10** expendable, foregoable **11** dispensable **12** renounceable

relinquished 5 ceded, let go **6** gave up **7** forgone, given up, yielded **8** cast away, foregone, forsaken **9** abandoned, given away, renounced **10** left behind

relinquishment 7 cession **8** giving up, yielding **9** letting go, rejection, surrender **10** abnegation **11** repudiation **12** renunciation

relish 3 dig **4** like, love, tang, want, wish, zest **5** enjoy, fancy, gusto, savor, spice, taste **6** accent, desire, dote on, flavor, liking, palate **7** delight, longing, stomach **8** appetite, fondness, groove on, penchant, piquancy, pleasure **9** condiment, delight in, enjoyment, hankering, rejoice in **10** appreciate, ebullience, enthusiasm, exuberance, partiality, propensity **11** luxuriate in **12** appreciation, be crazy about, predilection, satisfaction **13** gratification
type: 4 beef, corn **5** sweet **7** chutney **6** pickle, tomato **10** chili sauce, piccalilli **11** horseradish

reluctance 10 hesitation **13** unwillingness **14** disinclination

reluctant 3 shy **4** slow **5** loath **6** averse **7** laggard **8** hesitant **9** diffident, unwilling **10** indisposed **11** disinclined

rely 3 bet **4** bank, lean, rest **5** count, swear, trust **6** credit, depend, reckon **7** believe **10** feel sure of **11** be dependent **12** give credence

remain 4 go on, last, stay, wait **5** abide, stand **6** be left, endure, hang on, hold up, linger **7** not move, not stir, persist, prevail, stay put, subsist, survive **8** continue, stand pat **10** be left over, stay behind

remainder 4 rest **5** waste **6** excess, refuse **7** balance, overage, remains, remnant, residue, surplus, wastage **8** leavings, residual, residuum **9**

leftovers, scourings **10** surplusage **11** superfluity

remains 4 body **5** stiff **6** corpse, scraps **7** cadaver **8** dead body **9** leftovers

remark 3 say, see **4** espy, mark, mind, note, view, word **6** behold, look at, notice, regard, survey **7** comment, mention, observe, pay heed **8** perceive **9** attention **10** commentary, give heed to, make note of, reflection, take note of **11** contemplate, observation **12** fix the mind on, say in passing, take notice of **13** consideration **14** pay attention to

remarkable 6 signal **7** notable, unusual **8** singular, striking **9** memorable **10** impressive, noteworthy, phenomenal **11** conspicuous, exceptional, outstanding **13** distinguished, extraordinary, unforgettable

Remarque, Erich Maria
author of: 25 All Quiet on the Western Front

Rembrandt (Harmensz) van Rijn
born: 6 Leiden, Leyden **14** The Netherlands
artwork: 6 Balaam **9** Bathsheba **13** The Night Watch (The Sortie of the Company of Captain Banning Cocq) **14** The Jewish Bride **15** Old Woman Reading, The Bridal Couple **19** The Blinding of Samson **20** Christ Healing the Sick **21** The Stoning of St Stephen **22** Man with the Golden Helmet, Self-Portrait with Saskia, The Descent from the Cross **24** The Anatomy Lesson of Dr Tulp, The Syndics of the Cloth Hall **36** Aristotle Contemplating the Bust of Homer

remedial 7 healing, helpful, mending **8** curative, salutary, sanative **10** beneficial, corrective **11** meliorative, reformative, restorative, therapeutic **12** advantageous, correctional, prophylactic

remedy 3 aid, fix **4** calm, cure, ease, heal, help, mend **5** amend, amend, right **6** relief, repair, soothe **7** assuage, correct, cure-all, improve, mollify, nostrum, panacea, rectify, redress, relieve, restore **8** make easy, medicine, mitigate, palliate, regulate, set right **9** alleviate, make sound, treatment **10** ameliorate, assistance, corrective, make better, medicament, medication, preventive **13** rectification **15** restore to health

remember 3 tip **6** recall, reward **9** not forget, recognize, recollect **10** appreciate, bear in mind, call to mind, have in mind, keep in mind, take care of, take note of **11** bring to mind **12** bear in memory

remember that thou must die
Latin: 11 memento mori

remembrance 5 favor, relic, token **6** memory, recall **7** memento **8** keepsake, memorial, reminder, souvenir **9** nostalgia **11** recognition, remembering **12** recognizance, recollection, reminiscence **13** commemoration

Remembrance of Things Past
author: **12** Marcel Proust

Remembrance Rock
author: **12** Carl Sandburg

Remick, Lee
born: **8** Quincy MA
roles: **16** Anatomy of a Murder, The Long Hot Summer **18** Days of Wine and Roses

remind 9 put in mind, suggest to **11** bring back to, bring to mind, put in memory **16** awaken memories of

reminder of death
Latin: **11** memento mori

Remington, Frederic Sackrider
born: **8** Canton NY
artwork: **12** Bronco Buster **23** Roping Horses in the Corral **32** Cavalry Charge on the Southern Plains

reminisce 4 mull, muse **6** ponder **7** reflect **8** hark back, look back, remember **9** recollect, think back **12** tell old tales **16** exchange memories, swap remembrances

reminiscent 9 nostalgic, remindful, similar to **11** analogous to, remembering **12** recollecting **13** retrospective

remiss 3 lax **4** idle, lazy, slow **5** loose, slack **6** sloppy **7** laggard, loafing **8** careless, derelict, dilatory, inactive, indolent, slipshod, slothful, uncaring **9** do-nothing, forgetful, negligent, oblivious, shiftless, undutiful, unmindful **10** delinquent, neglectful, unthinking, unwatchful **11** inattentive, indifferent, thoughtless

remission 4 cure **5** lapse, pause **6** hiatus, pardon **7** respite, retreat **8** decrease **9** abatement, acquittal, cessation, reduction, shrinkage **10** absolution, diminution, hesitation, moderation, modulation, subsidence **11** exoneration, forgiveness, vindication

remit 3 pay **4** free, send, ship **5** clear, let go, relax, slack **6** excuse, let out, pardon, reduce **7** absolve, forgive, forward, release, set free, slacken **8** decrease, diminish, dispatch, liberate, make good, moderate, overlook, pass over, transmit **9** discharge, reimburse **10** compensate **11** put to rights **13** send in payment

remnant 3 bit **5** piece, relic, scrap, shred, token, trace **7** discard, remains, residue, vestige **8** fragment, leavings, leftover, monument, residuum, survival **9** remainder **11** odds and ends

remodel 4 redo **5** adapt, alter, fix up **6** change, modify **7** convert, reshape **8** overhaul, renovate **9** refashion, transform **11** recondition

remodeling 6 change **10** alteration,

conversion **12** modification **13** transmutation **14** transformation

remonstrance 6 rebuke **7** censure **8** reproach, scolding **9** criticism, reprimand **10** admonition

remonstrate 5 argue, chide, demur, scold **6** differ, object, rebuke **7** censure, chasten, contend, dispute, dissent, protest, reprove, upbraid **8** admonish, complain, reproach **9** criticize **10** take to task **11** expostulate **13** call to account

remorse 3 rue **4** pang **5** grief, guilt, qualm **6** regret, sorrow **7** anguish **9** penitence **10** contrition, repentance, ruefulness **11** compunction, lamentation, self-reproof **12** self-reproach **13** regretfulness **14** second thoughts

remorseful 8 contrite, penitent **9** chastened, regretful, repentant, sorrowful **10** apologetic **13** grief-stricken **18** conscience-stricken

remote 3 far **4** slim **5** alien, alone, aloof, faint, quiet **6** exotic, far-off, lonely, meager, slight **7** distant, dubious, faraway, foreign, removed, strange **8** detached, doubtful, isolated, secluded, separate, set apart, solitary, unlikely **9** withdrawn **10** far-removed, segregated **11** God-forsaken, implausible, out of the way, sequestered, standoffish

removal 6 moving, ouster **7** doffing **8** deletion, ejection **9** discharge, dismissal, expulsion, taking off, taking out **10** amputation, carting off, cutting away, dislodging, evacuation, lopping off **11** carrying off, chopping off, elimination, transferral **12** cancellation, displacement **14** transportation **15** transplantation

remove 4 doff, drop, fire, move, oust, quit **5** eject, erase, expel, leave, shift **6** cancel, change, cut off, delete, depart, go away, lop off, retire, unseat, vacate **7** blot out, boot out, cart off, chop off, cut away, dismiss, extract, kick out, retreat, take off, take out, wipe out **8** amputate, carry off, dislodge, displace, evacuate, get rid of, sweep out, take away, transfer, withdraw **9** discharge, eliminate, take leave, transport **10** make an exit, transplant

removed 3 off **4** away, took **5** alone, aloof, apart **6** remote **7** distant, faraway **8** abstract, detached, isolated, reticent, secluded **9** alienated, separate, unrelated, withdrawn **10** segregated, unsociable **11** interspaced, standoffish

remove from office 4 oust **6** depose, unseat **9** discharge

remunerate 3 pay **5** award, grant, repay **6** reward **7** requite, satisfy **9** indemnify, reimburse, vouchsafe **10**

compensate, recompense **15** make restitution

remuneration 7 payment **9** repayment **10** recompense, reparation **12** compensation **13** reimbursement **15** indemnification

Remus
father: **4** Mars
mother: **4** Ilia **9** Rea Silvia **10** Rhea Silvia
twin brother: **7** Romulus
raised by: **7** she-wolf

renaissance 7 rebirth, renewal, revival **10** rekindling, renascence, resurgence **11** reawakening, reemergence, restoration **12** regeneration, rejuvenation, resurrection, risorgimento **14** revitalization, revivification **15** reestablishment

rend 3 cut, rip **4** hurt, pain, rive, sear, tear **5** break, crack, sever, split, wound **6** cleave, divide, pierce, sunder **7** afflict, rupture, shatter **8** dissever, fracture, lacerate, polarize, splinter **12** disintegrate, fall to pieces **15** break into pieces

render 2 do **4** cede, give, make, play **5** allot, grant, remit, yield **6** accord, donate, give up, supply, tender **7** deal out, dole out, execute, hand out, pay back, perform, present, requite **8** construe, dispense, fork over, hand over, pay as due, shell out, turn over **9** cause to be, interpret, surrender, translate **10** relinquish **12** give in return, make requital **13** cause to become, make available, make payment of

render impotent 6 defuse, weaken **7** disable, unnerve **8** paralyze **9** undermine **10** devitalize, emasculate

render inoperable 6 damage, impair **7** cripple, disable **12** incapacitate

render null and void 4 void **5** annul **6** cancel, repeal, revoke **7** abolish, nullify, rescind, retract, reverse **8** abrogate, dissolve **10** invalidate

rendezvous 4 date **5** focus, haunt, mecca, tryst **6** gather, muster **7** retreat **8** assemble **9** encounter, tete-a-tete **10** engagement, focal point **11** appointment, assignation, get together **12** meeting place, watering hole **14** gathering place, stamping ground **15** agreement to meet **17** meet by appointment **18** prearranged meeting

rendition 7 edition, reading, version **9** depiction, portrayal, rendering **11** arrangement, performance, translation **14** interpretation

rend the air 3 cry **4** bawl, howl, wail **6** clamor, scream, shriek, squeal **7** screech **9** caterwaul

Renee Mauperin
author: **24** Edmond and Jules de Goncourt

renegade 5 rebel **6** outlaw **7** heretic,

runaway, slacker, traitor **8** apostate, betrayer, defector, deserter, forsaker, fugitive, mutineer, mutinous, quisling, recreant, turncoat **9** dissenter, insurgent **10** backslider, traitorous, treasonist, unfaithful

renege 7 back out, fink out, pull out **8** back down, fall back, withdraw **9** repudiate, weasel out **11** get cold feet **12** turn one's back **13** break a promise, break one's word **16** go back on one's word

renew 4 save **6** extend, pick up, redeem, resume, retain, revive **7** prolong, refresh, restore, salvage **8** continue, maintain **9** make sound, reinstate, sign again **10** begin again, offer again, regenerate, rejuvenate, revitalize **11** reestablish, take up again **12** reinvigorate **16** put back into shape

renewal 7 revival **9** extension **10** redemption **11** restoration **12** regeneration **13** reinstatement **14** revitalization

Renoir, Pierre-Auguste
   born: **6** France **7** Limoges
   artwork: **4** Lise **6** La Loge **10** The Bathers **12** Margot Berard, The Umbrellas **14** La Grenouillere **19** Le Moulin de la Galette **28** Mme Charpentier and Her Children, The Luncheon of the Boating Party

renounce 4 cede, deny, quit **5** forgo, waive **6** abjure, disown, eschew, forego, give up, recant, reject, resign **7** abandon, cast off, disavow, discard, dismiss **8** abdicate, abnegate, abrogate, disclaim, forswear, lay aside, part with, put aside, turn from, write off **9** cast aside, foreswear, repudiate **10** relinquish **13** give up claim to **15** wash one's hands of

renovate 3 fix **4** mend **6** remake, repair, revamp **7** improve, remodel, restore **8** make over **9** modernize, refurbish **10** redecorate

renown 4 fame, mark, note **6** repute, status **7** acclaim **8** eminence **9** celebrity, notoriety **10** popularity, prominence, reputation **11** distinction

renowned 5 famed, noted **6** famous **7** eminent, notable, popular **9** acclaimed, prominent, well-known **10** celebrated, noteworthy **11** outstanding **13** distinguished

rent 3 fee, gap, let, rip **4** dues, gash, hire, hole, rift, slit, tear **5** break, chasm, chink, cleft, crack, lease, split **6** breach, hiatus, rental, schism, tatter, wrench **7** charter, fissure, opening, payment, rent out, rupture **8** cleavage, crevasse, division, fracture **11** buy the use of **12** sell the use of

rente 6 income **7** revenue **12** annual income

rentier 21 one who has a fixed income

renunciation 6 denial **7** refusal **8** for-going, spurning **9** disavowal, eschewing, foregoing, rejection, repulsion **10** abjuration, renouncing **11** abandonment, disclaiming, forswearing, repudiation **12** foreswearing **14** relinquishment

Renwick, James, Jr
   architect of: **8** Main Hall (Vassar College) **11** Grace Church (NYC) **15** Corcoran Gallery (now Renwick Gallery, Washington, DC) **19** St Patrick's Cathedral (NYC) **22** Smithsonian Institution (Washington DC)
   style: **13** Gothic Revival

reopen 7 restart **9** begin anew, reconvene, start anew **10** recommence, reinitiate **11** reestablish, reinstitute **12** reinaugurate

repair 2 go **3** fix **4** mend, move **5** amend, emend, patch, renew, shape, state **6** fixing, remedy, remove, retire **7** correct, mending, patch up, rebuild, rectify, redress, restore **8** make good, overhaul, patching, set right, withdraw **9** condition, make up for, refurbish, repairing **10** rebuilding **11** recondition **12** refurbishing **14** reconditioning

reparation 6 amends, return **7** damages, redress **8** requital **9** quittance **10** recompense **11** restitution **12** compensation, satisfaction **13** peace offering

repartee 6 banter, bon mot **7** riposte **8** badinage, chit chat, word play **10** persiflage, witty reply **11** witty retort **12** pleasantries **14** snappy comeback

repast 4 food, meal **5** board, feast, snack, table **6** spread **7** banquet **8** victuals **9** provision **11** nourishment, refreshment

repay 5 match **6** refund, return, reward **7** pay back, requite **9** get back at, indemnify, pay in kind, reimburse **10** recompense, remunerate **11** get even with, reciprocate **12** make requital **14** give in exchange, make a return for **15** make restitution, make retribution **19** return the compliment

repayment 10 paying back, recompense **12** compensation **13** reimbursement **17** making restitution

repeal 4 void **5** annul **6** cancel, revoke **7** abolish, nullify, rescind, voiding **8** abrogate, set aside **9** abolition, annulment **10** abrogation, invalidate, revocation **11** termination **12** cancellation, invalidation **13** nullification **18** declare null and void

repeat 4 echo, redo, tell **5** mimic, quote, rerun **6** pass on, recite, relate, retell **7** imitate, recount, restate, retread, say over **8** say again **9** duplicate, reiterate, reproduce **10** repetition **11** duplication, reiteration **12** perform again

repeated exercises 4 rote **5** drill **8** practice, training

repel 4 foil, rout **5** check **6** dispel, offend, oppose, put off, rebuff, resist, revolt, sicken **7** deflect, disgust, fend off, forfend, hold off, keep off, keep out, repulse, scatter, turn off, ward off **8** alienate, beat back, disperse, nauseate, push back, stave off, throw off **9** chase away, drive away, drive back, force back, frustrate, keep at bay, withstand

repellent 5 proof **9** abhorrent, loathsome, offensive, repelling, repugnant, repulsive, resisting, revolting, sickening **10** disgusting, nauseating **11** distasteful, impermeable

repent 3 rue **6** bemoan, bewail, lament, regret, repine **7** deplore **8** mea culpa, weep over **9** be ashamed **10** be contrite, be penitent **11** be regretful, feel remorse

repentance 5 grief, guilt **6** regret, sorrow **7** remorse **9** penitence **10** contrition **11** compunction **12** self-reproach **16** self-condemnation **17** pangs of conscience

repercussion 4 echo **6** effect, result **8** backlash, reaction **10** concussion, side effect **11** aftereffect, consequence **13** reverberation **15** boomerang effect

repetition 6 repeat **9** iteration, retelling **11** reiteration, restatement **14** recapitulation

repetitious 5 wordy **6** prolix **8** repeated **9** redundant **10** repetitive

Repin, Ilya Efimovich
   born: **6** Russia **8** Chugeyev
   artwork: **15** The Volga Boatmen **18** Zaporozhye Cossacks **19** They Did Not Expect Him **26** Ivan the Terrible Kills His Son

replace 5 spell **6** return **7** put back, restore, succeed **8** supplant **9** supersede

replaceable 10 disposable, expendable **11** dispensable

replenish 5 renew **6** refill, reload **7** refresh, reorder, replace, restock, restore

replenished 7 renewed **8** refilled, replaced, restored **9** restocked

replenishment 7 renewal **9** refilling **10** restocking **11** replacement, restoration

replete 4 full **5** sated **6** gorged, loaded **7** crammed, fraught, stuffed, teeming **8** brimming, satiated **9** abounding, jam-packed, surfeited **11** well-stocked

repletion 4 glut **6** excess **7** surfeit, surplus **9** abundance, plenitude, profusion, satiation **11** sufficiency

replica 4 copy **5** model **6** double **8** likeness **9** duplicate, facsimile, imitation **12** reproduction

reply 5 react **6** answer, rejoin, retort **7** counter, respond **8** reaction, response **9** rejoinder **14** acknowledgment

reply if you please
   French: 4 rsvp **20** repondez s'il vous plait

reply to 6 answer **7** counter, react to **8** retort to **9** respond to **11** acknowledge

repondez s'il vous plait 11 please reply **16** reply if you please
   abbreviation: 4 rsvp

report 4 bang, boom, note, talk, tell, word **5** crack, noise, rumor, sound, state, story **6** appear, detail, expose, gossip, recite, record, relate, reveal, show up, tell on **7** account, article, check in, divulge, hearsay, message, missive, recount, summary, version, write-up **8** announce, denounce, describe, disclose, dispatch, relation **9** discharge, narration **10** communique, detonation, memorandum **11** communicate, description, information
   French: 11 compte rendu

reporter 7 newshen, newsman **8** newshawk **9** anchorman, announcer, columnist, newshound, newswoman **10** journalist, newscaster **11** commentator **12** newspaperman **13** correspondent **14** newspaperwoman

repose 3 lie **4** calm, ease, rest **5** quiet, relax **6** be calm, settle **7** leisure, recline, respite **8** quietude **10** inactivity, quiescence, relaxation **11** tranquility **12** peacefulness, tranquillity

repository 5 depot **8** magazine **9** warehouse **10** storehouse

reprehend 5 decry **7** censure, condemn, reprove **8** denounce, reproach **9** criticize **10** disapprove

reprehensible 3 bad **4** base, evil, foul, vile **6** guilty, wicked **7** heinous, ignoble **8** blamable, culpable, infamous, shameful, unworthy **9** nefarious **10** censurable, despicable, villainous **11** blameworthy, condemnable, disgraceful, inexcusable, opprobrious **12** unpardonable **13** objectionable, unjustifiable

reprehension 6 rebuke **7** censure, reproof **8** reproach **9** criticism **11** disapproval **12** condemnation, denunciation **14** disapprobation

represent 2 be **4** mean, show **5** enact, equal, state **6** denote, depict, pose as, sketch, typify **7** betoken, express, outline, picture, portray, present, serve as **8** appear as, describe, indicate, stand for **9** delineate, designate, symbolize **10** illustrate **11** emblematize, impersonate **12** characterize

representation 5 image **6** effigy, emblem, symbol **7** epitome, essence, picture **8** likeness **9** depiction, portrayal **10** embodiment **12** illustration **15** exemplification **16** characterization

representative 2 MP **3** rep **5** agent, envoy, proxy **6** deputy, varied **7** deputed, elected, proctor, typical **8** balanced, delegate, elective, emissary,

symbolic **9** delegated, exemplary, spokesman, surrogate, typifying **10** delegatory, democratic, denotative, emblematic, legislator, mouthpiece, republican, substitute, symbolical **11** assemblyman, congressman, delineative, descriptive **12** exemplifying, illustrative **13** assemblywoman, congresswoman **14** characteristic, crosssectional

repress 4 curb, hide, mask, veil **5** box up, check, cloak, cover, crush, pen up, quash, quell **6** hold in, muffle, shut up, squash, stifle, subdue **7** conceal, control, inhibit, put down, silence, smother, squelch **8** bottle up, hold back, keep down, restrain, strangle, suppress

repression 8 muffling **9** holding in, restraint, retention **10** inhibition, throttling **11** concealment, holding back, suppression

reprieve 4 lull, stay **5** delay, pause **6** pardon, parole **7** amnesty, respite **8** breather **9** remission **10** moratorium, suspension **11** adjournment **12** postponement **14** breathing spell

reprimand 4 trim **5** chide, scold **6** berate, rail at, rebuff, rebuke, revile **7** censure, chew out, chiding, lecture, obloquy, tell off, upbraid **8** admonish, berating, chastise, denounce, reproach, reproval, scolding, take down, trimming **9** castigate, criticism, criticize, disparage, dispraise, dress down, reprehend, reprobate **10** admonition, chewing out, opprobrium, take to task, upbraiding **11** castigation **12** admonishment, denunciation, dressing down, remonstrance **13** disparagement **16** rap on the knuckles

reprisal 7 redress, revenge **8** requital **9** tit for tat, vengeance **11** counterblow, retaliation, retribution **13** counterattack **16** counteroffensive
   Latin: 10 quid pro quo

reproach 4 blot, slur, spot **5** blame, chide, scold, shame, stain, taint **6** charge, insult, malign, rail at, rebuke, revile, stigma, tirade, vilify **7** asperse, blemish, censure, condemn, offense, reproof, reprove, scandal, tarnish, upbraid **8** admonish, denounce, diatribe, disgrace, dishonor, scolding **9** castigate, criticism, criticize, discredit, disparage, indignity, reprimand **10** stigmatize, take to task, tongue-lash, upbraiding **11** degradation, humiliation **12** remonstrance **13** call to account, embarrassment

reprobate 3 bad, low **4** base, evil, rake, roue, vile **5** scamp **6** pariah, rascal, rotter, sinner, wanton, wicked **7** corrupt, outcast **8** castaway, depraved, derelict, evildoer, prodigal, rakehell **9** abandoned, dissolute, miscreant, shameless, wrongdoer **10**

black sheep, degenerate, immoralist, profligate, voluptuary **11** rapscallion, untouchable **12** incorrigible, transgressor, wicked person

reproduce 4 copy, redo, sire **5** beget, breed, match, spawn **6** mirror, repeat, re-echo **7** imitate, reflect **8** generate, multiply **9** duplicate, procreate, propagate, replicate, represent **11** counterfeit, proliferate

reproduction 4 copy **7** replica **8** breeding, likeness **9** duplicate, facsimile, imitation **10** carbon copy, generation, simulation **11** procreation, propagation **13** progeneration, proliferation **14** multiplication, representation
   goddess of: 7 Astarte

reproductive system
   component: 5 penis **6** testes, uterus, vagina **7** ovaries

reproof 5 blame **6** rebuke **7** censure, chiding **8** reproach, scolding **9** criticism, reprimand **10** admonition **12** condemnation, dressing-down, remonstrance

reprovable 7 at fault **8** blamable, culpable **10** censurable **11** blameworthy **12** reproachable

reprove 5 chide, scold **6** rebuke **7** censure, chasten **8** admonish, reproach **9** castigate, reprimand

reptile 3 asp, eft **4** newt, teju **5** agama, anole, gecko, skink, snake, viper **6** dragon, iguana, lizard, mugger, turtle **7** crawler, creeper, serpent, tuatara **8** basilisk, dinosaur, groveler, terrapin, tortoise **9** alligator, chameleon, crocodile, pterosaur **10** salamander, vertebrate **11** Gila monster, pterodactyl

republic 9 democracy
   Latin: 10 res publica

Republic
   author: 5 Plato

Republican Party
   also called: 3 GOP **13** Grand Old Party
   president belonging to: 4 Bush, Ford, Taft **5** Grant, Hayes, Nixon **6** Arthur, Hoover, Reagan **7** Harding, Lincoln, (Andrew) Johnson **8** Coolidge, Garfield, Harrison, McKinley **9** (Theodore) Roosevelt **10** Eisenhower
   symbol: 8 elephant

Republic of China *see* **6** Taiwan

repudiate 4 deny, void **5** annul **6** cancel, desert, disown, reject, repeal, revoke **7** abandon, abolish, cast off, disavow, discard, forsake, nullify, protest, rescind, retract, reverse **8** abrogate, disclaim, dissolve, renounce

repudiation 6 denial **9** disavowal, rejection **10** abrogation, disclaimer, retraction

repugnance 4 hate **5** odium **6** hatred **7** disgust **8** aversion, loathing **9** antipathy, revulsion **10** abhorrence **11** abomination, detestation

repugnant 4 foul, vile **5** nasty **6** odious **7** adverse, counter, hateful, opposed **8** contrary, unsavory **9** abhorrent, loathsome, obnoxious, offensive, repellent, repulsive, revolting, sickening **10** abominable, detestable, disgusting, nauseating, unpleasant **11** distasteful, uncongenial, undesirable, unpalatable **12** antipathetic, disagreeable, insufferable, unacceptable, unappetizing **13** objectionable

repulse 4 shun **5** avoid, repel, spurn **6** ignore, rebuff, refuse, reject **7** refusal **8** shunning, spurning **9** rejection

repulsion 6 hatred **7** disgust, dislike **8** aversion, distaste, loathing **9** antipathy **10** abhorrence, repugnance **11** abomination, detestation **13** indisposition **14** disinclination

repulsive 4 vile **5** nasty **6** odious **7** hateful **9** abhorrent, loathsome, obnoxious, offensive, repellent, repugnant, revolting **10** abominable, detestable, disgusting, nauseating **11** distasteful **12** disagreeable **13** objectionable

repulsiveness 8 ugliness **13** loathsomeness, offensiveness **14** disgustingness, unpleasantness **16** disagreeableness

reputable 7 honored **8** esteemed, reliable **9** respected **10** creditable **11** respectable, trustworthy

reputation 4 name **7** stature **8** standing

repute 3 say **4** deem, fame, hold, view **5** judge, think **6** esteem, reckon, regard, renown **7** account, believe, suppose **8** consider, estimate, standing **9** celebrity, notoriety **10** prominence **14** respectability

request 3 ask **4** seek **6** ask for, bid for, desire, sue for **7** call for, entreat, solicit **8** petition **9** importune **11** application **12** solicitation

requiem 5 dirge **6** lament **8** threnody

requiescat in pace 11 rest in peace **16** may he rest in peace **17** may she rest in peace

require 3 bid **4** lack, miss, need, want **5** crave, imply, order **6** charge, compel, desire, direct, enjoin, entail, oblige **7** command, dictate **9** constrain **11** necessitate

required 6 forced, needed **7** obliged **9** compelled, essential, necessary **10** compulsory, imperative, obligatory

requirement 4 must **8** standard **9** criterion, essential, guideline, requisite **12** prerequisite **13** specification
Latin: 10 sine qua non **11** desideratum

requisite 4 must, need **6** needed **8** required **9** essential, mandatory, necessary, necessity **10** compulsory, imperative, obligatory **11** requirement **12** prerequisite **13** indispensable

Latin: 10 sine qua non **11** desideratum

requisition 4 form **7** request **11** application

requital 7 redress **9** repayment **11** retaliation **12** compensation **15** indemnification

rescind 4 void **5** annul, quash **6** cancel, recall, repeal, revoke **7** abolish, discard, nullify, retract, reverse **8** abrogate, dissolve, override, overrule **10** invalidate **11** countermand **12** counterorder

rescinding 6 recall **7** voiding **8** recision **9** abolition **10** abrogation, retraction, revocation **11** abolishment, dissolution **12** cancellation, invalidation **13** nullification

rescue 4 save **6** ransom, saving **7** deliver, freeing, recover, release, salvage **8** liberate, recovery **9** extricate **10** liberation **11** deliverance, extrication

research 5 probe, study **7** delving, inquiry **8** analysis, scrutiny **10** inspection **11** examination, exploration, fact-finding, investigate, scholarship **13** investigation

resemblance 7 analogy **8** affinity, likeness, parallel **10** congruence, similarity, similitude **14** correspondence

resemble 5 favor **6** be like **8** be akin to, look like, parallel **9** take after

resent 7 dislike

resentful 5 angry **6** bitter **7** annoyed **8** grudging, offended, provoked **10** displeased **12** dissatisfied

resentfulness 5 anger, spite **10** bitterness **15** dissatisfaction

resentment 3 ire **4** huff **5** anger, pique, spite **6** animus, malice, rancor **7** dudgeon, ill will, offense, umbrage **8** acerbity, acrimony, asperity, jealousy, soreness, sourness **9** animosity, crossness **10** bitterness, irritation **11** displeasure, indignation **12** irritability, vengefulness **14** vindictiveness

reservation 4 date **5** doubt **7** booking, proviso, scruple, strings **8** preserve **9** condition, hesitancy, provision **10** encampment, reluctance, settlement **11** appointment, compunction, stipulation, uncertainty **12** installation **13** accommodation, establishment, qualification **14** prearrangement

reserve 4 book, hold, keep, save **5** amass, delay, extra, hoard, lay up, spare, stock, table **6** backup, engage, retain, shelve, unused **7** husband, nest egg, savings **8** conserve, keep back, postpone, preserve, salt away, schedule, withhold **9** aloofness, reticence, stockpile **10** additional, prearrange

reserved 5 aloof, taken **6** booked, formal **7** distant, engaged **8** bespoken, retained, reticent, strained, unsocial **9**
inhibited, spoken for **10** restrained, unsociable **11** ceremonious, constrained, standoffish **12** unresponsive **15** uncommunicative, undemonstrative

reservoir 4 fund, pool, tank, well **5** basin, fount, hoard, stock, store **6** supply **7** backlog, cistern **8** millpond **9** container, stockpile **10** depository, receptacle, repository **12** accumulation

res gestae 5 deeds **10** things done **15** accomplishments

reshape 4 redo **5** adapt, alter, block **6** change, modify, reform, remold, rework **7** convert, reframe, remodel **9** refashion, transform

reside 3 lie **4** live, rest, room **5** dwell, exist, lodge **6** belong, occupy **7** inhabit, sojourn **8** domicile

residence 3 pad **4** digs, flat, home, room, stay **5** abode, house, place **7** address, lodging, sojourn **8** domicile, dwelling, quarters **9** apartment, homestead, household **10** habitation
French: 10 pied a terre

resident 5 local **6** lodger, tenant **7** citizen, denizen, dweller **8** occupant, townsman **9** sojourner **10** inhabitant **11** housekeeper

residual 5 extra **7** abiding, lasting, surplus **8** enduring, leftover **9** lingering, remaining **10** continuing **13** supplementary

residue 4 rest **5** dregs **6** scraps **7** balance, remains, remnant **8** leavings **9** remainder

resign 4 quit **5** leave **6** give up, submit **8** abdicate, disclaim, renounce **9** reconcile **10** relinquish

resignation 8 fatalism, patience, quitting, stoicism **9** departure **10** equanimity, retirement, submission, withdrawal **11** passiveness **12** acquiescence **13** nonresistance **14** submissiveness

resign oneself 5 yield **6** submit **9** acquiesce

resilience 6 recoil **7** rebound **8** buoyancy **10** elasticity **11** flexibility **12** adaptability **13** changeability, nonuniformity **16** lightheartedness

resilient 5 hardy **6** supple **7** buoyant, elastic, rubbery, springy **8** flexible **9** adaptable, expansive, resistant, tenacious **10** rebounding, responsive **13** irrepressible

resin 3 gum, lac, tar **5** amber, copal, elemi, epoxy, jalap, myrrh, pitch, rosin **6** balsam, guaiac, mastic **7** galipot, lacquer, shellac

resist 4 balk, foil, stem, stop **5** fight, repel **6** baffle, combat, oppose, refuse, reject, thwart **7** contest, counter, weather **8** beat back, turn down **9** frustrate, withstand **10** counteract

resistance 6 mutiny, rebuff **7** refusal **8**

defiance, struggle **9** obstinacy, rebellion, rejection **10** contention, insurgency, opposition **11** obstruction **12** insurrection **13** intransigence, noncompliance, recalcitrance

resolute 5 stern **6** dogged, steady **7** earnest, staunch, zealous **8** decisive, diligent, intrepid, stubborn, untiring, vigorous **9** assiduous, obstinate, purposive, steadfast, tenacious, unbending **10** deliberate, determined, inflexible, persistent, relentless, unflagging, unswerving, unwavering, unyielding **11** industrious, persevering, undeviating, unfaltering, unflinching **12** pertinacious, strong-minded, strong-willed **13** indefatigable **14** uncompromising

resoluteness 7 purpose, resolve **8** decision, tenacity **11** decidedness, persistence **12** decisiveness, perseverance **13** determination, steadfastness **14** purposefulness

resolution 3 aim **4** goal, plan, zeal **6** design, energy, intent, mettle, motion, object, spirit **7** promise, purpose, resolve **8** ambition, proposal, solution, tenacity **9** constancy, intention, objective, resolving, stability **10** resilience, steadiness **11** earnestness, persistence **12** perseverance, resoluteness **13** determination, steadfastness **14** aggressiveness **16** indefatigability

resolve 4 plan **6** answer, decide, design, intend, set out, settle, vote on **7** adjudge, clear up, explain, purpose **8** decision **9** determine, elucidate **10** commitment, resolution **12** resoluteness **13** determination **14** make up one's mind

resonant 4 full, rich **7** booming, orotund, ringing, vibrant **8** sonorous **9** bellowing **10** resounding, stentorian, thunderous **11** reverberant

resort 3 use **4** hope **5** apply, avail **6** chance, employ, take up **7** utilize **8** exercise, recourse **9** expedient

resound 4 echo, peal, ring **5** clang **6** re-echo **7** vibrate **11** reverberate **14** tintinnabulate

resounding 7 echoing, ringing **9** re-echoing **10** thundering, thunderous **13** reverberating

resource 8 recourse **9** expedient **11** wherewithal

resourceful 4 able **5** ready, sharp, smart **6** adroit, artful, bright, shrewd **7** capable, cunning **8** creative, original, skillful, talented **9** competent, effectual, ingenious, inventive **10** innovative, proficient **11** imaginative **12** enterprising

resourcefulness 9 ingenuity **10** creativity, enterprise **13** inventiveness

resources 5 funds, means, money **6** assets, income **7** capital, effects, revenue **10** belongings, collateral **11** possessions, wherewithal

respect 5 honor, point, sense **6** detail, esteem, matter, notice, praise, regard **7** bearing, feature, viewing **8** approval, courtesy, relation **9** affection, attention, deference, laudation, reference, relevance, reverence **10** admiration, connection, particular, veneration **11** point of view, recognition **12** appreciation, circumstance **13** consideration

respectability 7 decency, decorum **9** gentility, propriety **11** correctness, genteelness

respectable 4 fair **5** ample, civil, noble **6** decent, honest, polite, proper, worthy **7** correct, courtly, passing, refined, upright **8** becoming, decorous, moderate, polished **9** admirable, dignified, estimable, honorable, reputable **10** aboveboard, admissible, sufficient **11** presentable **12** considerable, praiseworthy, satisfactory

respected 6 valued, worthy **7** admired, honored, revered **8** esteemed **9** admirable, venerated

respectful 5 civil **6** formal, genial, polite **7** amiable, winning **8** admiring, decorous, gracious, mannerly, obliging, reverent **9** attentive, courteous, regardful **10** personable, solicitous **11** ceremonious, deferential, reverential **13** accommodating

respects 4 heed, obey **5** honor, prize, value **6** admire, esteem, fealty, follow, regard, revere **7** abide by, cherish, defer to, observe, regards, tribute **8** adhere to, consider, venerate **9** greetings **10** appreciate, understand **11** acknowledge, compliments **12** remembrances **13** consideration

Respighi, Ottorino
  born: 5 Italy **7** Bologna
  composer of: 8 La Fiamma, The Birds **14** The Pines of Rome **18** The Fountains of Rome **19** La Boutique Fantasque, The Fantastic Toyshop **27** Ancient Airs and Dances for Lute

respiration 9 breathing

respiratory system
  component: 4 lung, nose **6** larynx **7** pharynx, trachea **8** voice box, windpipe **9** bronchius, diaphragm
  action: 9 breathing

respire 7 breathe

respite 4 lull **5** break, delay, letup, pause **6** recess **8** reprieve **9** extension **12** intermission

resplendence 6 dazzle, luster **7** glitter **8** lambency, radiance **10** brilliance, luminosity, refulgence **12** circumstance, magnificence

resplendent 6 bright **7** beaming, blazing, glowing, lambent, radiant **8** dazzling, gleaming, luminous, lustrous, splendid **9** brilliant, refulgent, sparkling **10** glittering **11** coruscating

respond 5 react, reply **6** answer, rejoin

7 speak up **9** recognize **11** acknowledge

respond to 6 answer **7** act upon, react to, reply to **8** thank for **11** acknowledge

response 5 reply **6** answer, retort, return **7** riposte **8** comeback, feedback, reaction, rebuttal **9** rejoinder **10** impression **13** countercharge **14** acknowledgment **16** counterstatement

responsibility 4 duty, task **5** blame, order, trust **6** burden, charge **8** function **9** liability **10** obligation **11** culpability, reliability **13** answerability, dependability **14** accountability **15** trustworthiness

responsible 5 adult, of age **6** guilty, liable, mature **7** at fault, capable **8** culpable, reliable **9** demanding, executive, important **10** answerable, creditable, dependable **11** accountable, challenging, trustworthy **13** conscientious **14** administrative

responsive 5 alive, awake, sharp **8** reactive **9** receptive, sensitive **11** retaliative, retaliatory, susceptible, sympathetic **13** compassionate, understanding **14** impressionable

responsiveness 6 action **7** concern **8** interest **9** attention, awareness **11** sensitivity **13** understanding

res publica 8 republic, the state **12** commonwealth, public matter

rest 2 be **3** end, lay, lie, nap, set **4** base, ease, halt, hang, keep, laze, lean, loaf, loll, lull, prop, rely, stay, stop **5** break, death, exist, hinge, let up, pause, peace, place, quiet, relax, sleep, stand **6** demise, depend, holder, lounge, others, recess, remain, repose, reside, scraps, siesta, snooze, trivet **7** balance, be based, be found, be quiet, decease, deposit, holiday, leisure, lie down, recline, remains, remnant, residue, respite, set down, slumber, support **8** breather, platform, vacation **9** cessation, departure, leftovers, remainder, stillness **10** complement, quiet spell, relaxation, standstill, suspension **11** hibernation, take time out **12** intermission, interruption **13** take a breather
  Latin: 8 residuum

restaurant 5 diner **6** eatery **7** beanery, tearoom **9** cafeteria, chophouse, grillroom, hashhouse, luncheon **11** coffeehouse **12** luncheonette
  French: 4 cafe **6** bistro **9** brasserie
  German: 11 rathskeller

restful 4 calm **5** quiet **6** placid, serene **7** pacific, relaxed **8** peaceful, soothing, tranquil **10** unagitated **11** comfortable, undisturbed

restfulness 4 ease **5** quiet **6** repose **8** serenity, softness **10** relaxation **11** tranquility **12** tranquillity

rest in peace
Latin: **16** requiescat in pace

restitution 6 amends **7** redress, replevy **8** replevin, requital, restoral **9** atonement, indemnity, repayment **10** recompense, reparation **11** restoration **12** compensation, remuneration, satisfaction **13** reimbursement, reinstatement **15** indemnification

restive 5 balky **6** mulish, ornery, unruly **7** fidgety, wayward, willful **8** contrary, stubborn **9** fractious, pigheaded **10** rebellious, refractory **11** disobedient, intractable **12** recalcitrant, unmanageable

restless 5 awake, jumpy **6** fitful, uneasy **7** anxious, fidgety, fretful, jittery, nervous, on the go, unquiet, wakeful, worried **8** agitated **9** excitable, impatient, incessant, insomniac, on the move, sleepless, transient, unsettled **10** disquieted, highstrung **11** hyperactive **13** uncomfortable

restoration 7 revival **8** recovery **12** recuperation **13** convalescence, reinstatement **14** rehabilitation, reintroduction, reinvigoration **15** reestablishment

restorative 5 tonic **6** elixir **7** bracing, healing **8** curative **10** beneficial, energizing, fortifying **11** revivifying **12** invigorating, revitalizing **13** strengthening

restore 3 fix **4** cure, dose, heal, mend **5** rally, renew, treat **6** do over, recoup, remedy, repair, rescue, return, revive **7** convert, get back, patch up, put back, rebuild, reclaim, recover, refresh, remodel, retouch, touch up **8** energize, give back, make over, make well, medicate, renovate, retrieve, revivify, recreate **9** reanimate, refurbish, reinstall, reinstate, stimulate **10** exhilarate, revitalize, strengthen **11** recondition, reconstruct, reestablish, reinstitute, resuscitate **12** rehabilitate, reinvigorate

restored 4 kept **5** saved **7** revived **8** replaced **9** conserved, pressured **11** replenished **13** rehabilitated

restrain 3 gag **4** bind, curb, hold, stop **5** check, leash, limit **6** arrest, bridle, fetter, muzzle, pinion, temper, tether **7** chasten, contain, curtail, harness, inhibit, prevent, shackle, trammel **8** handicap, hold back, restrict, suppress, withhold

restrained 4 cool **5** aloof **6** curbed **7** checked, distant **8** held back, reined in, reserved **10** controlled, unfriendly

restraint 4 curb **5** check **7** control **10** limitation

restrict 4 curb, hold **5** check, cramp, crimp, hem in, limit **6** hamper, impede, narrow, thwart **7** confine, inhibit, prevent, squelch **8** hold back,

obstruct, straiten, suppress **9** constrain, frustrate **12** circumscribe

restricted 7 cramped, limited **8** confined, hampered, held back **9** exclusive **10** suppressed **13** circumscribed

restriction 4 rule **7** control, curbing, proviso **9** condition, provision **10** limitation, regulation **11** requirement, reservation, stipulation **13** consideration, qualification

restrictive 8 limiting **9** confining, exclusive **12** constraining

result 4 stem **5** arise, end up, ensue, fruit, issue, owe to **6** derive, effect, happen, pan out, report, sequel, spring, upshot, wind up **7** finding, opinion, outcome, product, turn out, verdict **8** decision, judgment, reaction, solution **9** aftermath, culminate, eventuate, originate, outgrowth **10** resolution **11** aftereffect, consequence, development, eventuality **13** determination

resume 2 CV **3** bio **4** go on **5** brief **6** digest **7** epitome, proceed, summary **8** abstract, continue, reembark, synopsis **9** biography, summation **10** abridgment, recommence **11** reestablish **12** condensation
Latin: **15** curriculum vitae
French: **6** precis

resumption 11 recommenced, restoration **12** continuation

resurgam 15 I shall rise again

resurgence 6 return **7** rebirth, renewal, revival **10** renascence **11** reemergence, renaissance **12** rejuvenation **13** recrudescence

ret 4 soak **6** dampen

retailer 5 store **6** dealer, seller, trader **8** merchant, provider, supplier **9** tradesman **10** wholesaler **11** distributor, storekeeper, tradeswoman **12** merchandiser
French: **9** vivandier **10** vivandiere

retain 4 hold, keep **5** grasp **6** absorb, recall **7** possess **8** hang on to, hold on to, maintain, memorize, remember **9** recollect

retainer 7 servant **8** employee **9** attendant

retainership 4 hire **6** employ **7** service **10** employment

retaliate 5 repay **6** avenge, pay off, return **7** counter, pay back, requite, revenge **11** reciprocate

retaliation 6 talion **7** deserts, revenge **8** reprisal, requital **9** vengeance **10** recompense **11** comeuppance, eye for an eye, interchange, just deserts, lex talionis, retribution **12** compensation **13** reciprocation **14** tooth for a tooth

retard 4 clog, drag **5** block, brake, check, delay **6** arrest, baffle, detain, fetter, hamper, hinder, hold up, impede, slow up **7** draw out, inhibit,

prevent, prolong, slacken **8** hold back, obstruct, slow down **10** decelerate

retarded 4 dull, slow **6** simple **7** idiotic, moronic, unsound **8** backward, disabled **9** imbecilic, mongoloid, subnormal **10** slow-witted **11** handicapped **12** simpleminded

reticent 3 shy **5** quiet **6** closed, silent **7** subdued **8** reserved, retiring, taciturn **9** diffident, withdrawn **10** restrained **11** tight-lipped **12** closemouthed **15** uncommunicative

retinue 5 court, staff, suite, train **6** convoy **9** courtiers, employees, entourage, followers, following, personnel, retainers **10** associates, attendance, attendants

retire 6 depart, go away, remove, resign, resort, secede, turn in **7** drop out, retreat **8** abdicate, flake out, withdraw

retired
French: **8** ci-devant

retiring 3 shy **4** meek **5** quiet, timid **6** demure, humble, modest **7** bashful **8** reserved, reticent, sheepish, timorous, unsocial **9** diffident, shrinking, withdrawn **10** unassuming **11** unassertive **12** self-effacing **13** inconspicuous, unpretentious **15** uncommunicative

retort 3 say **4** quip **5** rebut, reply **6** answer, rejoin, return **7** counter, respond, riposte **8** fire back, rebuttal **9** rejoinder

retract 4 deny **6** abjure, disown, draw in, recall, recant, recede, recoil, reel in, repeal, revoke **7** disavow, rescind, retreat, reverse **8** abnegate, abrogate, disclaim, draw back, forswear, peel back, pull back, renounce, take back, withdraw **9** foreswear, repudiate

retraction 6 recall **8** recision **9** disavowal **10** disclaimer, refutation, withdrawal

retreat 2 go **3** den **4** bolt, flee, port **5** haunt, haven, leave **6** asylum, depart, escape, flight, harbor, recoil, refuge, resort, retire, shrink **7** abscond, getaway, privacy, sanctum, shelter, shy away **8** back away, draw back, fall back, hideaway, move back, solitude, turn tail, withdraw **9** departure, isolation, reclusion, sanctuary, seclusion **10** evacuation, immurement, retirement, withdrawal **11** hibernation, rustication

retrench 5 slash **6** reduce, scrape, scrimp **7** curtail, cut back, cut down **8** conserve, cut costs **9** economize **15** tighten one's belt

retribution 6 amends, return, reward **7** justice, nemesis, penalty, redress, revenge **8** reprisal, requital **9** vengeance **10** punishment, recompense, reparation **11** just deserts, restitution, retaliation, vindication **12** satisfaction **13** reciprocation, recrimination

retrieve 4 snag **5** fetch **6** ransom, recoup, redeem, regain, rescue **7** get back, reclaim, recover, salvage **9** recapture, repossess

retriever

    dog breed: 5 Irish **6** golden, Gordon **7** English **8** Labrador **10** flat-coated **11** curly-coated **13** Chesapeake Bay

retrograde 5 worse **6** worsen **7** inverse, retreat, reverse **8** backward **10** regressive **13** retrogressive

retrogress 6 worsen **9** backslide

retrogression 7 decline, setback **9** worsening **11** backsliding

retrogressive 8 backward **9** declining, worsening **11** backsliding

retrospect 6 review **9** flashback, hindsight **11** remembrance **12** afterthought, reminiscence **15** reconsideration

return 3 net **4** earn, gain **5** gross, recur, repay, yield **6** advent, come to, go back, income, profit, render, reseat, reward **7** arrival, benefit, produce, provide, put back, requite, restore, revenue **8** announce, come back, earnings, give back, hand down, interest, proceeds, reappear, recovery, restoral, send back **9** advantage, reinstall, reinstate, retrieval, reversion **10** homecoming, recurrence **11** reciprocate, reestablish, restoration **12** compensation, reappearance **13** reinstatement **15** reestablishment

Return of the Native

    author: 11 Thomas Hardy

    character: 11 Diggory Venn, Eustacia Vye **12** Damon Wildeve **13** Clym Yeobright **17** Thomasin Yeobright

Reuben

    father: 5 Jacob

    mother: 4 Leah

    brother: 3 Dan, Gad **4** Levi **5** Asher, Judah **6** Joseph, Simeon **7** Zebulun **8** Benjamin, Issachar, Naphtali

    sister: 5 Dinah

    descendant of: 9 Reubenite

Reuben sandwich

    ingredient: 3 rye **8** dressing **10** corned beef, sauerkraut **11** Swiss cheese

reunite 5 rewed **7** remarry **9** reconcile

reveal 4 bare, show **6** betray, expose, impart, let out, unfold, unmask, unveil **7** display, divulge, exhibit, give out, lay bare, publish, uncover, unearth **8** disclose, evidence, manifest, point out

revealed 4 open **5** clear, known **7** evident, obvious **8** manifest

revel 4 romp **5** caper, enjoy **6** bask in, frolic, gambol, relish **7** carouse, delight, indulge, rejoice, roister, skylark **8** wallow in **9** celebrate

revelation 6 expose, vision **7** shocker **8** exposure, prophecy **9** admission, bombshell, discovery, eyeopener, unveiling **10** apocalypse, confession, disclosure, divulgence **11** divulgation, divulgement

revelatory 10 expressive **11** informative **13** communicative

reveler 6 barfly, ranter, player **7** drinker **8** bacchant, carouser, drunkard **9** roisterer, rollicker, skylarker **10** merrymaker

revelry 5 spree **7** jollity **8** carnival, carousal, festival, jamboree **9** high jinks, merriment, rejoicing **10** exultation, roistering **11** celebrating, celebration, merrymaking **12** conviviality **13** jollification **14** boisterousness

    god of: 5 Comus

revenge 5 repay **7** pay back, requite **8** reprisal, requital **9** repayment, retaliate, vengeance, vindicate **10** recompense **11** eye for an eye, reciprocate, retaliation, retribution **12** satisfaction

revenue 3 pay **4** take **5** gains, wages, yield **6** income, profit, return, salary **7** annuity, pension, subsidy **8** earnings, interest, pickings, proceeds, receipts **9** allowance, emolument **12** compensation, remuneration

revenue, annual

    French: 5 rente

reverberate 4 boom, echo, ring **5** carry **6** rumble **7** resound, thunder, vibrate

reverberation 4 boom, echo **6** rumble **7** ringing, thunder **8** rumbling **9** vibration **10** resounding, thundering

revere 5 honor **6** esteem **7** defer to, respect **8** venerate

revered 6 adored **7** admired, honored **9** estimable, respected, venerated, worshiped **10** worshipped

reverence 3 awe **4** fear **5** honor, piety **6** esteem, homage, regard **7** respect, worship **8** devotion **9** adoration, deference **10** admiration, devoutness, observance, veneration **11** prostration, religiosity **12** genuflection

reverent 4 pure **5** pious **6** devout, humble, solemn **7** adoring, awesome, devoted **8** faithful **9** religious, spiritual **10** respectful, worshipful

reverential 4 awed **10** respectful, worshipful **11** deferential

reverie 5 dream, fancy **6** musing **7** fantasy **8** daydream **9** dreamland, quixotism **10** brown study, meditation **12** extravagance **13** woolgathering **14** fantasticality

reverse 4 back, rear, tail, undo, void **5** annul, upend, upset **6** cancel, change, defeat, invert, mishap, negate, recall, recant, repeal, revoke, unmake, upturn **7** counter, failure, nullify, rescind, retract, setback, trouble **8** abrogate, backward, contrary, converse, hardship, inverted, opposite, override, overrule, set aside, turn over, withdraw **9** adversity, mischance, posterior, transpose **10** antithesis, invalidate, misfortune **11** countermand, counterpart, frustration **14** disappointment

revert 5 lapse **6** go back, repeat, return **7** regress, relapse **9** backslide **10** recidivate, retrogress

review 4 show **5** study, sum up **6** notice, parade, rehash, survey **7** analyze, journal, retrace, run over **8** critique, evaluate, hash over, magazine, reassess, report on, scrutiny **9** criticism, criticize, reexamine, reiterate, summarize **10** commentary, evaluation, exhibition, exposition, procession, reconsider, reevaluate, reflection, scrutinize **11** examination **12** presentation, reassessment, recapitulate, reevaluation **13** demonstration, retrospection **14** recapitulation **15** reconsideration

    French: 11 compte rendu

revile 4 slur **5** abuse, curse, scold, scorn **6** berate, defame, deride, malign, rebuke, vilify **7** bawl out, chew out, slander, upbraid **8** belittle, denounce, execrate, reproach, sail into **9** blaspheme, castigate, denigrate, disparage **10** vituperate

reviler 6 critic, curser **8** vilifier **9** backbiter, slanderer **10** blasphemer

revise 4 edit, redo **5** alter, amend, emend, fix up **6** change, doctor, modify, recast, redact, revamp, review, update **7** correct, rectify, rewrite **8** emendate, overhaul

revision 6 change **7** edition **9** amendment, recension **10** alteration, correction, emendation **11** improvement **12** modification

revival 7 renewal **11** restoration **13** reinstatement, reinstitution, resuscitation

revive 5 dig up, renew **6** drag up, repeat **7** freshen, refresh, restage **8** reawaken **9** reanimate, reproduce, resurrect **11** resuscitate

revived 7 renewed **8** animated, repeated, restaged **9** enlivened, freshened, refreshed **10** reanimated, reawakened, reproduced **11** invigorated, resurrected **12** resuscitated

revocation 6 repeal **8** recision **9** abolition, annulment **10** abrogation, retraction **11** abolishment, elimination, repudiation **12** cancellation **13** nullification

revoke 4 void **5** annul, erase, quash **6** abjure, cancel, negate, recall, repeal, vacate **7** abolish, dismiss, expunge, nullify, rescind, retract, reverse **8** abrogate, call back, disallow, disclaim, override, overrule, renounce, set aside, take back, withdraw **9** repudiate **10** invalidate **11** countermand

revolt 4 coup, rise **5** rebel, repel,

shock **6** appall, mutiny, offend, rise up, sicken **7** disgust, dissent, horrify, repulse **8** disorder, distress, nauseate, sedition, uprising **9** rebellion **10** insurgency, opposition, **12** factiousness, insurrection
German: 6 Putsch

revolting 4 foul, grim, vile **5** nasty **6** horrid, odious **7** hateful, noisome, noxious **8** dreadful, horrible, horrific, shocking, stinking **9** abhorrent, appalling, frightful, invidious, loathsome, obnoxious, offensive, repellent, repugnant, repulsive, sickening **10** abominable, disgusting, malodorous, nauseating **11** distasteful **12** disagreeable **13** objectionable

revolution 6 mutiny, revolt, rising **8** circling, gyration, rotation, uprising **9** rebellion **12** insurrection **14** circumrotation, circumvolution
French: 4 coup **9** coup d'etat
German: 6 Putsch

revolutionary 7 radical **8** mutinous **9** extremist, insurgent, seditious **10** dissenting, rebellious, subversive **13** superadvanced, unprecedented **15** insurrectionary

revolve 4 spin, turn **5** twist, wheel **6** circle, gyrate, rotate **12** circumrotate

revolver 3 gat, gun, rod **4** colt **6** pistol, weapon **7** firearm, handgun, rotator, sidearm **10** six-shooter **20** Saturday night special

revulsion 8 aversion, distaste, loathing **10** abhorrence, repugnance **11** detestation

reward 3 due **5** bonus, prize, repay, wages **6** bounty **7** deserts, guerdon, payment, premium, requite **9** reckoning **10** compensate, recompense, remunerate **12** compensation, remuneration **13** consideration
Latin: 10 quid pro quo

rewarding 8 pleasant, valuable **9** enjoyable **10** delightful, gratifying, satisfying **11** pleasurable

rework 4 redo **5** adapt, alter **6** modify **7** remodel, reshape **9** refashion, transform

rex 4 king

Reykjavik
capital of: 7 Iceland

Reynolds, Burt
born: 10 Waycross GA
wife: 9 Judy Carne **12** Loni Anderson
roles: 4 Bean **6** Shamus **9** Dan August, Semi-Tough, The Player **10** Striptease **11** Cop-and-a-half, Deliverance **12** Boogie Nights **14** The Longest Yard **18** Smokey and the Bandit

Reynolds, Debbie
real name: 19 Mary Frances Reynolds
born: 8 El Paso TX
husband: 11 Eddie Fisher
roles: 13 The Singing Nun, The Tender Trap **15** Singin' in the Rain **19** Tammy and the Bachelor **23** The Unsinkable Molly Brown

Reynolds, Sir Joshua
born: 7 England **8** Plympton
artwork: 14 Lord Heathfield, Miss Jane Bowles **15** Commodore Keppel **18** Mrs Francis Beckford **21** Mrs Abington as Miss Prue **25** Mrs Siddons as the Tragic Muse **38** Lady Sarah Bunbury Sacrificing to the Graces

Rhadamanthus, Rhadamanthys
father: 4 Zeus
mother: 6 Europa
brother: 5 Minos **6** Aeacus **8** Sarpedon
became a judge in: 5 Hades

rhapsodic 6 elated **7** beaming, excited **8** blissful, ecstatic, thrilled **9** delirious, overjoyed, rapturous **11** exhilarated, transported

Rhea
member of: 6 Titans
father: 6 Uranus
mother: 4 Gaea
brother: 6 Cronos, Cronus, Kronos
husband: 6 Cronos, Cronus, Kronos
son: 4 Zeus **5** Hades **8** Poseidon
daughter: 4 Hera **6** Hestia **7** Demeter
called: 10 Magna Mater
corresponds to: 3 Ops **5** Cybele **9** Dindymene **10** Berecyntia
epithet: 6 Antaea

Rhea Silvia
form: 12 vestal virgin
lover: 4 Mars
son: 5 Remus **7** Romulus

Rheingold *see* **Ring des Nibelungen, Der**

Rhesus
owned: 6 horses
horses captured by: 8 Diomedes, Odysseus

rhetoric 4 bunk, wind **5** hokum, hooey **6** bunkum, hot air **7** fustian, oratory **8** euphuism **9** discourse, elocution, eloquence, hyperbole **10** hocus-pocus **11** flamboyance **13** magniloquence **14** grandiloquence

Rhetoric
author: 9 Aristotle

rhetorical 5 showy, windy **6** florid, ornate, purple, verbal **7** aureate, flowery **8** eloquent, inflated **9** bombastic, grandiose, highflown, stylistic **10** decorative, discursive, euphuistic, expressive, flamboyant, linguistic, oratorical, ornamental **11** disputative, embellished, extravagant **12** disputatious, elocutionary, magniloquent **13** argumentative, grandiloquent

Rhoda
character: 8 Gary Levy **9** Joe Gerard **12** Benny Goodwin **14** Ida Morgenstern, Sally Gallagher **17** Brenda Morgenstern, Martin Morgenstern **22** Rhoda Morgenstern Gerard
cast: 9 Anne Meara, David Groh, Ron

Silver **11** Julie Kavner, Nancy Walker **12** Harold J Gould, Ray Buktenica **13** Valerie Harper

Rhode Island
abbreviation: 2 RI
nickname: 11 Little Rhody
capital/largest city: 10 Providence
others: 7 Bristol, Newport **8** Cranston, Kingston, Westerly **9** Pawtucket, Wakefield **10** Woonsocket
college: 5 Brown **6** Bryant **8** Pembroke **10** Barrington, Providence **11** Salve Regina **13** Mount St Joseph, Roger Williams **15** Johnson and Wales, Naval War College
feature: 7 Newport
tribe: 7 Niantic **9** Wampanoag **12** Narragansett
people: 8 Puritans **12** George M Cohan **13** Gilbert Stuart, Matthew C Perry, Roger Williams **15** Ambrose Burnside, Nathanael Greene **17** Oliver Hazard Perry
island: 5 Block, Rhode **8** Prudence **9** Aquidneck, Conanicut
lake: 8 Scituate
pond: 7 Wordens **8** Stafford, Watchaug
land rank: 8 fiftieth
mountain: 10 Durfee Hill
    highest point: 12 Jerimoth Hill
physical feature:
    bay: 12 Narragansett
    sea: 8 Atlantic
    sound: 11 Block Island
river: 7 Seekonk **8** Pawtuxet **9** Pawcatuck, Pawtucket, Potowomut **10** Blackstone, Providence
state admission: 10 thirteenth
state bird: 14 Rhode Island Red
state flower: 6 violet
state motto: 4 Hope
state song: 11 Rhode Island
state tree: 8 red maple

Rhodesia *see* **8** Zimbabwe

rhodium
chemical symbol: 2 Rh

rhododendron
varieties: 4 tree **5** Bluet **6** Indian, Yunnan **7** catawba, fringed, Lapland, silvery, Smirnow **8** Carolina, Chapman's, Fortune's, Fujiyama, piedmont **9** Caucasian, honey-bell, West Coast **11** leather-leaf **12** willow-leaved

rhodolite
species: 6 garnet

rhubarb 5 Rheum **16** Rheum rhabarbarum
varieties: 4 wild **5** monk's **6** garden, Sikkim **7** spinach **8** mountain

rhyme 3 pun **4** poem, rune, song **5** chime, clink, meter, poesy, verse **6** jingle, poetry, rhythm **7** measure, poetize, versify **8** assonate, doggerel **10** consonance **12** alliteration
game: 6 crambo

rhymer, rhymester 4 bard, poet **6** writer **8** minstrel, poetizer **9** poetaster, versifier **10** troubadour

Rhys, Jean
  author of: 7 Quartet **15** Voyage in the Dark, Wide Sargasso Sea

rhythm 4 beat, lilt, time **5** meter, pulse, swing, throb **6** accent, number, stress **7** cadence, measure **8** emphasis, movement **9** pulsation **10** recurrence **11** fluctuation, syncopation **12** accentuation

riant 3 gay **4** airy **5** jolly, merry **6** blithe, bright, jocund, jovial **7** smiling **8** cheer- ful, laughing, mirthful

rib 3 kid, rag **4** bait, bone, josh **5** chaff, costa, jolly, tease

ribald 4 lewd, racy, rude **5** bawdy, crude, gross **6** coarse, earthy, rakish, risque, vulgar, wanton **7** raffish, uncouth **8** improper, indecent, off-color, prurient, shocking **9** salacious, unrefined **10** lascivious, libidinous, licentious, suggestive

ribbon 3 bow, ray **4** band, sash **5** award, braid, prize, reins, strip **6** cordon, riband **7** binding, rosette **8** memorial, streamer **10** decoration

rice 5 Oryza **11** Oryza sativa
  varieties: 4 wild **6** Indian, pampas **7** basmati **8** mountain **9** Tennessee **10** annual wild
  dish: 5 grits, pilaf, pilau **7** pudding, risotto **8** porridge **9** jambalaya
  liquor: 4 sake

Rice, Anne
  lives: 10 New Orleans
  character: 6 Lestat **7** vampire
  author of: 11 Cry to Heaven **16** The Vampire Lestat **19** The Queen of the Damned **23** Interview with the Vampire

Rice, Elmer
  author of: 11 Street Scene **16** The Adding Machine

rich 4 dark, deep, fine, lush **5** flush, heavy, loamy, sweet, vivid **6** bright, costly, fecund, lavish, mellow **7** fertile, filling, intense, moneyed, opulent, wealthy, well-off **8** abundant, affluent, fruitful, in clover, precious, prodigal, resonant, sonorous, splendid, valuable, well-to-do **9** abounding, estimable, expensive, luxuriant, luxurious, priceless, sumptuous **10** euphonious, productive, propertied, prosperous **11** mellifluous **12** on easy street

Richard, Maurice
  nickname: 6 Rocket
  sport: 6 hockey
  position: 7 forward
  team: 17 Montreal Canadiens

Richard Cory
  author: 22 Edwin Arlington Robinson

Richard Diamond, Private Detective
  character: 3 Sam **6** Lt Kile **9** Lt Mc-

Gough **10** Karen Wells
  cast: 10 Russ Conway **11** Barbara Bain, Regis Toomey **12** David Janssen **13** Roxanne Brooks **14** Mary Tyler Moore
  viewers saw only Sam's: 4 legs

Richard I 11 Coeur de Lion, Lion-Hearted
  father: 7 Henry II
  mother: 7 Eleanor (of Aquitaine)
  brother: 4 John

Richard II
  author: 18 William Shakespeare
  character: 11 John of Gaunt **13** Edmund Langley, Thomas Mowbray **16** Henry Bolingbroke **20** Earl of Northumberland
  Duke of: 4 York **7** Aumerle, Norfolk **8** Hereford **9** Lancaster

Richard III
  author: 18 William Shakespeare
  character: 6 George **7** Richard **8** Edward IV, Lady Anne **10** Henry Tudor (Earl of Richmond) **11** Lord Stanley **12** Lord Hastings **13** Queen Margaret **14** Queen Elizabeth **15** Edward the Fourth **17** Sir William Catesby **19** Edward Prince of Wales
  Duke of: 4 York **8** Clarence **10** Buckingham, Gloucester

Richardson, Joely
  parents: 14 Tony Richardson **15** Vanessa Redgrave
  sister: 7 Natasha
  roles: 12 Event Horizon **13** 101 Dalmatians **14** Shining Through **17** Drowning By Numbers

Richardson, Henry Hobson
  architect of: 9 Sever Hall (Harvard) **11** Grace Church (West Medford MA) **13** Trinity Church (Boston) **23** State Asylum for the Insane (Buffalo NY) **27** Marshall Field Wholesale Store (Chicago)

Richardson, Natasha
  parents: 14 Tony Richardson **15** Vanessa Redgrave
  sister: 5 Joely
  roles: 11 Patty Hearst **12** The Handmaid's Tale **23** Every Picture Tells a Story

Richardson, Samuel
  author of: 6 Pamela (or Virtue Rewarded) **8** Clarissa (Harlowe) **19** Sir Charles Grandison

Richardson, Sir Ralph
  born: 7 England **10** Cheltenham
  roles: 6 Exodus **10** Oscar Wilde, Richard III, The Heiress **11** A Doll's House **12** Anna Karenina **13** Doctor Zhivago **15** Richard the Third **20** Little Lord Fauntleroy **24** Long Day's Journey into Night **26** Greystoke The Legend of Tarzan

Richardson, Tony
  wife: 15 Vanessa Redgrave
  daughter: 5 Joely **7** Natasha

  director of: 7 Blue Sky **8** Tom Jones (Oscar) **14** The Entertainer **15** Look Back in Anger **36** The Loneliness of the Long Distance Runner

riches 4 pelf **5** lucre, means **6** assets, mammon, wealth **7** fortune **8** opulence, treasure **9** resources **10** prosperity **11** possessions

richness 6 wealth **8** fullness, lushness, opulence **9** amplitude, intensity **10** lavishness, mellowness **12** completeness **13** luxuriousness

Richter, Charles Francis
  field: 10 geophysics, seismology
  developed: 12 Richter scale **24** measurement of earthquakes

rickety 4 weak **5** frail, shaky **6** feeble, flimsy, infirm, wasted, weakly, wobbly **7** fragile **8** decrepit, unsteady, withered **9** tottering **10** brokendown, tumbledown **11** debilitated, dilapidated, weakjointed **12** deteriorated

rid 4 free **5** clear, purge **6** remove **8** disabuse, liberate, unburden **9** disburden, eliminate **11** disencumber

Ridd, John
  character in: 10 Lorna Doone
  author: 9 Blackmore

riddance 6 ouster, relief **7** freeing, removal **8** ejection **9** clearance, expulsion **11** deliverance, dislodgment

riddle 5 poser, rebus **6** enigma, puzzle, secret **7** mystery, problem, puzzler, stumper **9** conundrum

ride 4 move **5** annoy, carry, drive, harry, hound **6** badger, handle, harass, hector, manage, needle, travel **7** control, journey, support **8** progress **9** transport

rider 5 affix **6** suffix **7** adjunct, codicil **8** addendum, addition, appendix **9** amendment, appendage **10** attachment, supplement

ridge 3 bar, rib, rim **4** bank, fret, hill, hump, rise, wale, weal, welt **5** bluff, crest, crimp, knoll, mound, spine **6** ripple **7** crinkle, hillock, wrinkle **10** promontory **11** corrugation

ridicule 3 guy, rib **4** gibe, jeer, josh, mock, razz, ride, twit **5** mimic, scorn, taunt, tease **6** deride, gibe at, parody **7** lampoon, laugh at, mockery, ribbing, sarcasm, scoff at, sneer at, snicker, teasing **8** belittle, derision, sneering, travesty **9** aspersion, burlesque, disparage, humiliate, make fun of, poke fun at **10** caricature, derogation, lampoonery **13** disparagement
  god of: 5 Momos, Momus

ridiculous 3 odd **5** crazy, droll, funny, inane, nutty, queer, silly **6** absurd, screwy **7** amusing, asinine, bizarre, comical, fatuous, foolish, idiotic **8** farcical **9** fantastic, frivolous, grotesque, laughable, ludicrous, screwball, senseless **10** hysterical, incredible, irrational, outlandish **11** astonishing, nonsensical **12** preposterous, unreasonable

Rienzi
author: **18** Edward Bulwer-Lytton
composer: **6** Wagner

Riesling, Paul
character in: **7** Babbitt
author: **5** Lewis

rife 5 close, dense, solid, thick **6** common, packed **7** crowded, general, studded, teeming **8** epidemic, pandemic, populous, swarming **9** chockfull, extensive, plumbfull, prevalent, universal **10** prevailing, widespread **11** predominant

riffraff 3 mob **4** herd, scum **5** crowd, dregs, trash **6** masses, proles, rabble, vermin **9** peasantry **10** commonalty **11** proletariat
French: **8** canaille

rifle 3 rob **4** loot, sack **6** ravage **7** despoil, pillage, plunder, ransack **8** spoliate **10** burglarize

rifle, repeating
invented by: **7** Spencer

Rifleman, The
character: **10** Lou Mallory, Mark McCain **11** Lucas McCain **14** Miss Milly Scott **20** Marshal Micah Torrance
cast: **7** Paul Fix **10** Joan Taylor **12** Chuck Connors **13** Patricia Blair **14** Johnny Crawford
setting: **9** New Mexico, North Fork

rift 3 cut, gap **4** gash, gulf, rent, slit **5** abyss, break, chasm, chink, cleft, crack, fault, gorge, gulch, gully, split **6** breach, cranny, ravine **7** breakup, crevice, fissure, quarrel, rupture **8** aperture, crevasse, division, fracture **12** disagreement **16** misunderstanding

rig 4 gear **5** equip **6** fit out, outfit **8** carriage **9** apparatus, equipment, machinery

Riga *see* **Latvia**

Rigaud
character in: **12** Little Dorrit
author: **7** Dickens

Rigg, Diana
born: **7** England **9** Doncaster
title: **4** Dame
roles: **6** Helena **8** Emma Peel **10** Bleak House **11** Lady Dedlock, The Avengers **12** Julius Caesar **21** A Midsummer Night's Dream **26** On Her Majesty's Secret Service

right 2 OK **3** due **4** deed, fair, good, just, meet, nice, real, sane, true, well **5** amend, emend, exact, grant, honor, ideal, legal, licit, moral, power, solve, sound, valid **6** actual, at once, decent, honest, lawful, morals, normal, proper, remedy, seemly, square, virtue **7** certain, correct, ethical, exactly, factual, fitting, freedom, genuine, liberty, license, perfect, precise, probity, redress, regular, standup, warrant **8** accurate, becoming, clear-cut, definite,

directly, goodness, morality, promptly, properly, rational, sanction, straight, suitable, suitably, truthful, virtuous **9** allowable, authentic, authority, correctly, desirable, equitable, exemplary, favorable, favorably, honorable, integrity, nobleness, opportune, ownership, perfectly, precisely, presently, privilege, propriety, rectitude, veracious, veridical, vindicate **10** aboveboard, accurately, admissible, completely, convenient, infallible, legitimate, permission, preferable, reasonable, recompense, scrupulous, undisputed, unmistaken **11** inheritance, immediately, irrefutable, prerogative, punctilious **12** advantageous, jurisdiction, satisfactory **13** appropriately, authorization, incontestable, justification, unimpeachable **14** proprietorship, satisfactorily, unquestionable
Latin: **3** jus

right beside 6 next to **8** abutting, adjacent, touching

righteous 4 fair, good, holy, just **5** godly, moral, pious **6** chaste, devout, honest **7** ethical **8** elevated, innocent, reverent, virtuous **9** blameless, equitable, honorable, incorrupt, religious, spiritual, unsullied

righteousness
goddess of: **4** Maat

righteous person
Hebrew: **6** zaddik

rightful 3 due **4** just, true **5** legal, valid **6** lawful, proper **7** allowed, condign, correct, fitting, merited **8** deserved **9** deserving, equitable **10** authorized, designated, legitimate, prescribed, sanctioned **11** appropriate, inalienable **14** constitutional

right hand 4 aide, ally **6** helper **7** partner **8** adjutant **9** assistant
French: **10** aide-de-camp

right of blood
Latin: **12** jus sanguinis

right of soil/land
Latin: **7** jus soli

Right People, The
author: **17** Stephen Birmingham

right side up 7 upright **10** on one's feet

Right Stuff, The
director: **13** Philip Kaufman
author: **8** Tom Wolfe
cast: **8** Ed Harris **10** Sam Shepard
Oscar for: **5** score

right-wing 7 old-line **10** nonliberal **11** reactionary **12** conservative **14** nonprogressive

right-winger 8 rightist **11** reactionary **12** conservative

rigid 3 set **4** firm, hard, taut **5** fixed, harsh, sharp, stern, stiff, tense **6** formal, severe, strict, strong, wooden **7** austere **8** exacting, obdurate, rigorous, stubborn, unpliant **9** inelastic, strin-

gent, unbending **10** inflexible, unyielding **11** puritanical, unrelenting **14** uncompromising

Rigoletto
opera by: **5** Verdi
character: **5** Gilda **9** Maddalena **11** Sparafucile **12** Duke of Mantua **15** Countess Ceprano **16** Count of Monterone

rigorous 5 exact, harsh, stern, tough **6** severe, strict, trying **7** austere, correct, precise **8** accurate, exacting **9** demanding, stringent **10** meticulous, scrupulous **11** challenging, punctilious

rig out 4 garb **5** array, dress **6** attire, clothe

rile 3 irk, vex **4** gall, miff, roil **5** anger, annoy, chafe, gripe, peeve, pique **6** bother, enrage, nettle, offend, plague **7** incense, inflame, provoke **8** irritate **9** aggravate, infuriate

Riley, James Whitcomb
called: **11** Hoosier poet
author of: **18** Little Orphant Annie **25** When the Frost Is on the Punkin

rilievo 6 relief

Rilke, Rainer Maria
author of: **11** Book of Hours **12** Duino Elegies, Life and Songs **13** Divine Elegies **16** Sonnets to Orpheus **19** Letters to a Young Poet

rill 5 brook, cleft, creek **6** furrow, groove, runnel, stream **7** channel, rivulet **9** streamlet

rim 3 lip **4** edge, side **5** brink, ledge, verge **6** border, margin **9** outer edge

Rimbaud, Arthur
born: **6** France
author of: **12** Le Bateau Ivre **13** A Season in Hell **14** The Drunken Boat **16** Les Illuminations **17** Sonnet of the Vowels

rime 3 ice **4** hoar **5** chink, cleft, crack, crust, frost **7** crevice, fissure **9** hoarfrost

Rime of the Ancient Mariner, The
author: **21** Samuel Taylor Coleridge
character: **6** Hermit **9** Albatross **12** Wedding Guest **14** Ancient Mariner

Rimsky-Korsakov, Nikolai (Nicholas)
born: **6** Russia **8** Novgorod
member of: **7** The Five
composer of: **5** Mlada, Sadko **6** Kitezh **10** Night in May, Snow Maiden, Tzar Saltan **11** Sheherazade **12** Christmas Eve, Scheherazade **16** Spanish Capriccio, The Golden Cockerel **21** Russian Easter Overture **29** Russian Easter Festival Overture

rind 4 bark, hull, husk, peel, skin **5** crust, shell **6** cortex, fringe **7** epicarp, surface **8** exterior
pork: **9** crackling

ring 4 aura, band, bloc, buzz, call,

echo, gang, hoop, loop, peal, toll, tone **5** cabal, chime, clang, knell, party, sound **6** cartel, circle, cordon, herald, jangle, jingle, league, signal, strike, summon, tinkle **7** besiege, circuit, combine, enclose, quality, resound, seal off, vibrate **8** announce, blockade, encircle, proclaim, striking, surround **9** broadcast, encompass, perimeter, resonance, syndicate, ting-a-ling, vibration **10** federation **11** reverberate **12** circumscribe **13** circumference, reverberation **14** tintinnabulate **16** tintinnabulation

Ring and the Book, The
  author: 14 Robert Browning
Ring des Nibelungen, Der
  also: 12 The Ring Cycle **20** The Ring of the Nibelung(s)
  opera by: 6 Wagner
  part one: 12 Das Rheingold, The Rhine Gold
  part two: 10 Die Walkure **11** The Valkyrie
  part three: 9 Siegfried
  part four: 15 Gotterdammerung **17** Twilight of the Gods
  character: 4 Erda, Mime **5** Freia, Hagen, Wotan **6** Fafner, Fasolt **7** Gunther, Gutrune, Hunding **8** Alberich, Siegmund **9** Siegfried, Sieglinde, Valkyries **10** Brunnhilde
ringleader 5 chief **6** master **10** mastermind
ringlet 4 curl **6** circle
ring-shaped 5 round **8** circular
Rin Tin Tin, The Adventures of
  character: 5 Rusty, (Cpl) Boone **9** (Sgt) Biff O'Hara **10** (Lt) Rip Masters
  cast: 8 Lee Aaker **9** Joe Sawyer **10** James Brown, Rand Brooks
Rio Bravo
  director: 11 Howard Hawks
  cast: 8 Ward Bond **9** John Wayne **10** Dean Martin **11** Ricky Nelson **13** Walter Brennan **14** Angie Dickinson
Rio de Janeiro
  airport: 6 Galeao
  architect: 5 Costa, Reidy **8** Niemeyer
  area: 4 Caju, Lapa **6** Catete, Gamboa, Gloria, Grajau, Tijuca **7** Catumbi, Ipanema **8** Botafogo **10** Copacabana, Vila Isabel **12** Sao Cristovao
  bay: 8 Botafogo, Jurujuba **9** Guanabara
  bridge: 11 Costa e Silva
  celebration: 8 Carnival **9** Mardi Gras
  discovered by: 6 Coelho
  former capital of: 6 Brazil
  island: 10 Governador
  lake: 16 Rodrigo de Freitas
  landmark: 10 Candelaria **14** Mount Corcovado **15** Maracana Stadium **17** Sugarloaf Mountain
    statue of: 17 Christ the Redeemer
  means: 14 river of January
  ocean: 8 Atlantic

  people: 8 Cariocas
  replaced as capital by: 8 Brasilia
  slums: 7 favelas
  suburb: 7 Niteroi
riot 4 rage **5** act up, arise, melee, rebel **6** fracas, mutiny, resist, revolt, rumpus, strife, tumult, uproar **7** rampage, run amok, trouble, turmoil **8** disorder, outburst, uprising, violence **9** commotion, confusion, rebellion **10** Donnybrook, turbulence **11** lawlessness, pandemonium **12** insurrection
rioting 6 tumult, uproar **7** turmoil **8** disorder, outbreak, violence **9** commotion **11** disturbance
riotous 4 loud, wild **5** arroar, noisy, randy **6** stormy, unruly, wanton **7** bacchic, rampant, violent **8** bacchian **9** debauched, dissolute, insurgent, plentiful, tumultuous, turbulent **10** boisterous, dissipated, licentious, rebellious **11** intemperate, overcopious **12** unrestrained **13** superabundant **15** insurrectionary
  party: 4 orgy
rip 3 cut, gap **4** rend, rent, rift, rive, slit, tear **5** burst, sever, shred, slash, split **6** cleave **7** fissure, rupture **8** cleavage, cut apart, fracture, incision, tear open **10** laceration
ripe 3 due, fit **4** come **5** ideal, ready **6** mature, mellow, primed, timely **7** perfect **8** complete, finished, seasoned **9** maturated **10** consummate **12** accomplished
ripen 3 age **4** grow **5** bloom, fruit **6** flower, mature, mellow **7** develop
Rip Kirby
  creator: 11 Alex Raymond **12** John Prentice
Ripley, Robert L
  author of: 14 Believe It or Not
Rip Van Winkle
  author: 16 Washington Irving
rise 4 bank, defy, dune, face, gain, go up, grow, hill, lift, meet, soar **5** climb, get up, knoll, march, mount, rebel, ridge, spire, stand, surge, swell, tower **6** ascend, growth, mutiny, resist, revolt, rocket, strike, thrive **7** advance, balloon, burgeon, disobey, elevate, headway, improve, prosper, stand up, succeed, upswing **8** addition, flourish, increase, progress **9** expansion, extension **10** embankment **11** advancement, enlargement
Rise and Fall of the Third Reich, The
  author: 14 William L Shirer
Rise of Silas Lapham, The
  author: 18 William Dean Howells
  character: 5 Irene **8** Mr Rogers, Penelope, Tom Corey **9** Mrs Lapham
risible 4 rich **5** comic, droll, funny, merry, silly, witty **6** absurd, jocose, jovial **7** amusing, comical, jocular **8** farcical, humorous, mirthful **9** face-

tious, laughable, ludicrous, whimsical **10** ridiculous **11** nonsensical
rising sun
  god of: 5 Janus
risk 4 dare **5** peril **6** chance, danger, gamble, hazard **7** imperil, venture **8** endanger, jeopardy **9** speculate **10** jeopardize **11** imperilment, speculation, uncertainty **12** endangerment
risky 6 chancy, daring, unsafe **8** insecure, perilous, ticklish **9** dangerous, daredevil, haphazard, hazardous, hit or miss, uncertain **10** precarious **11** adventurous, unprotected, venturesome
risque 4 blue, lewd, racy **5** bawdy, dirty, gross, spicy **6** coarse, daring, ribald, smutty, vulgar **7** immoral, obscene **8** immodest, improper, indecent, off-color **9** offensive, salacious **10** indecorous, indelicate, lascivious, licentious, suggestive **12** pornographic
rite 6 ritual **7** liturgy, service **8** ceremony **9** formality, solemnity **10** ceremonial, observance
rite of passage 6 ritual **7** baptism **8** ceremony, marriage **10** bar mitzvah, bat mitzvah, initiation **11** christening **12** confirmation
Rites of Passage
  author: 14 William Golding
Ritt, Martin
  director of: 3 Hud **7** Sounder **8** Norma Rae, The Front **26** The Spy Who Came in From the Cold
Ritter, John
  born: 9 Burbank CA
  father: 9 Tex Ritter
  roles: 9 Hooperman **11** Americathon, Jack Tripper **13** Three's Company **14** Captain Avenger
Ritter, Thelma
  born: 10 Brooklyn NY
  roles: 10 Pillow Talk, Rear Window, The Misfits **11** All About Eve **15** The Mating Season **17** Birdman of Alcatraz **18** With a Song in My Heart **19** A Letter to Three Wives, Pickup on South Street **21** The Proud and the Profane **27** Miracle on Thirty-Fourth Street
ritual 4 rite **7** service **8** ceremony **10** observance
ritual bathing place
  Jewish Orthodox: 6 mikvah
ritualistic 6 formal, solemn **10** ceremonial **11** ceremonious
ritualize 7 observe **9** celebrate, solemnize **13** ceremonialize
ritzy 4 chic, posh, tony **5** sharp, swank **6** classy, snazzy, spiffy **7** elegant, stylish **9** high-class, high-toned, luxurious, sumptuous
rival 3 foe **5** enemy, equal, excel, fight, match, outdo, touch **6** strive **7** eclipse, surpass **8** approach, oppo-

nent, opposing, outshine **9** adversary, competing, contender, disputant **10** antagonist, competitor, contending, contestant

Rivals, The
author: **23** Richard Brinsley Sheridan
character: **8** Bob Acres **9** Faulkland **11** Mrs Malaprop **13** Julia Melville, Lydia Languish **17** Sir Lucius O'Trigger **18** Sir Anthony Absolute **19** Captain Jack Absolute (Ensign Beverley)

rive 4 rend **5** crack, split **6** cleave, detach, divide, sunder **7** shatter **8** fracture

riven 4 rent, torn **5** split **7** cleaved, cracked **8** sundered **9** fractured, shattered

River, The
director: **10** Jean Renoir
based on novel by: **11** Rumer Godden
cast: **5** Radha **13** Adrienne Corri, Arthur Shields, Nora Swinburne **15** Patricia Walters
setting: **5** India **6** Bengal

Rivera, Diego
born: **6** Mexico **10** Guanajuato
artwork: **5** Sleep **8** Creation **11** Mother Earth **14** The Fecund Earth **15** Detroit Industry **18** Man at the Crossroads **21** Carnival of Mexican Life **23** Life in Pre-Hispanic Mexico

river mouth 5 delta, firth **7** estuary

rivers
god of: **6** Peneus, Simois **7** Inachus

Rivers, Reba
character in: **9** Sanctuary
author: **8** Faulkner

rivet 3 fix, pin **6** absorb, clinch, engage, fasten, occupy **7** engross **8** fastener **9** fascinate

Rivieres du Sud see **6** Guinea

rivulet 3 run **4** rill **5** brook, creek **6** stream **9** streamlet

Riyadh
capital of: **11** Saudi Arabia

Rizzuto, Phil
nickname: **7** Scooter
position: **9** shortstop
sport: **8** baseball
team: **14** New York Yankees

road 3 via, way **4** lane, path **5** byway, route, trail **6** avenue, street **7** freeway, highway, parkway **8** turnpike **9** boulevard **10** expressway, throughway **12** thoroughfare

Road Not Taken, The
author: **11** Robert Frost

roads
god of: **6** Hermes

road safety
god of: **6** Sancus **10** Semo Sancus

Road to Gandolfo, The
author: **12** Robert Ludlum

roam 3 gad **4** rove **5** drift, jaunt,

prowl, range, stray, tramp **6** ramble, stroll, travel, wander **7** meander, traipse **8** divagate **9** gallivant **11** peregrinate

roan 5 horse **7** grayish, reddish, tannish **8** blackish, brownish

Roan Stallion
author: **15** Robinson Jeffers

roar 3 bay, cry, din **4** bawl, boom, howl, roll, yell **5** blare, growl, grunt, noise, shout, snort **6** bellow, clamor, guffaw, outcry, racket, rumble, scream, shriek **7** bluster, resound, thunder **8** outburst **10** vociferate

roast 3 pan **4** bake **6** berate **7** scourge **8** barbecue **9** criticize

rob 4 bilk, lift, loot, raid, sack, skin **5** cheat, filch, heist, rifle, seize, steal **6** burgle, fleece, forage, hold up, pilfer, thieve **7** despoil, pillage, plunder, purloin, ransack, stick up, swindle **8** carry off, embezzle **9** bamboozle **10** burglarize **11** appropriate

Robards, Jason
born: **9** Chicago IL
wife: **12** Lauren Bacall
roles: **5** Julia **7** Isadora **9** Dick Diver **10** Ben Bradlee **11** Jamie Tyrone **12** Hour of the Gun **15** A Thousand Clowns, Dashiell Hammett, Melvin and Howard, The Disenchanted **17** Tender Is the Night **19** All the President's Men **24** Long Day's Journey into Night

Robbe-Grillet, Alain
author of: **8** Jealousy **9** The Voyeur **10** The Erasers **14** In the Labyrinth **19** Last Year at Marienbad

robber 4 yegg **5** crook, thief **6** bandit, con man, outlaw, pirate, raider **7** brigand, burglar, forager, rustler, sharper **8** Barabbas, marauder, swindler **9** buccaneer, despoiler, embezzler, larcenist, plunderer **10** highwayman, pickpocket

Robbins, Harold
author of: **8** The Betsy **13** The Inheritors **14** Dreams Die First, The Adventurers **16** The Carpetbaggers **17** The Dream Merchants **18** Never Love a Stranger **20** A Stone for Danny Fisher **21** Seventy-Nine Park Avenue

Robbins, Jerome
choreographer of: **8** Les Noces **9** Fancy Free, Interplay
director of: **13** West Side Story (with Robert Wise, Oscar)

robe 4 gown **5** dress, habit, smock **6** duster **7** costume, garment **8** bathrobe, vestment **9** housecoat
French: **8** negligee
Japanese: **6** kimono

Robe, The
author: **13** Lloyd C Douglas

robe-de-chambre 12 dressing-gown

Robert Kennedy and His Times
author: **20** Arthur M Schlesinger Jr

Roberts, Kenneth
author of: **16** Northwest Passage

Roberts, Rachel
born: **5** Wales **8** Llanelly
husband: **11** Rex Harrison
roles: **8** Foul Play **10** Oh Lucky Man **16** This Sporting Life **24** Murder on the Orient Express **29** Saturday Night and Sunday Morning

Robertson, Cliff
real name: **23** Clifford Parker Robertson
born: **9** La Jolla CA
wife: **11** Dina Merrill
roles: **5** PT-109 **6** Charly (Oscar) **9** Obsession **11** Falcon Crest

Robertson, Oscar
nickname: **7** The Big O
sport: **10** basketball
position: **5** guard
team: **14** Milwaukee Bucks **16** Cincinnati Royals

Robeson, Paul
born: **11** Princeton NJ
roles: **7** Othello **8** Show Boat **11** Brutus Jones **15** The Emperor Jones **17** King Solomon's Mines **22** All God's Chillun Got Wings

Robin Hood's Adventures
author: **7** unknown
character: **9** Friar Tuck **10** Little John **11** Will Scarlet **14** Band of Merry Men **18** Sir Richard of the Lea **19** Sheriff of Nottingham

robin's-egg-blue 4 aqua **5** azure **7** sky-blue **8** cerulean **9** light blue **10** aquamarine, powder-blue

Robinson, Edward G
real name: **18** Emmanuel Goldenberg
born: **7** Romania **9** Bucharest
roles: **8** Key Largo **12** Little Caesar, Rico Bandello **13** Scarlet Street **15** Double Indemnity, Flesh and Fantasy **16** House of Strangers **19** The Woman in the Window **20** A Dispatch from Reuters **21** Dr Ehrlich's Magic Bullet

Robinson, Edwin Arlington
author of: **6** Merlin **8** Amaranth, Tristram **10** King Jasper **11** Richard Cory **12** Captain Craig **13** Miniver Cheevy, Mr Flood's Party

Robinson, Jackie
sport: **8** baseball
team: **15** Brooklyn Dodgers
first black in: **12** major leagues

Robinson, Sugar Ray
real name: **19** Walker Smith Robinson
sport: **6** boxing
class: **12** middleweight, welterweight

Robinson Crusoe
author: **11** Daniel Defoe
character: **6** Friday

Rob Roy

author: **14** Sir Walter Scott

character: **11** Diana Vernon **18** Sir Frederick Vernon **23** Rob Roy MacGregor Campbell

   Osbaldistone family: **5** Frank **7** William **9** Rashleigh **13** Sir Hildebrand

robust 3 fit **4** firm, hale, well, wiry **5** hardy, husky, lusty, sound, stout, tough **6** active, brawny, hearty, mighty, potent, rugged, sinewy, strong, sturdy, virile **7** healthy, staunch **8** athletic, forceful, muscular, powerful, stalwart, vigorous **9** energetic, healthful, strapping, wholesome **10** able-bodied **12** in fine fettle

French: **8** puissant

robustness 5 vigor **8** strength **10** good health, ruggedness, sturdiness **11** healthiness

Roche, Kevin

architect of: **13** Oakland Museum (CA) **14** Fine Arts Center (U of MA), Ford Foundation (NYC) **17** Knights of Columbus (New Haven CT) **21** One United Nations Plaza (NYC) **24** Union Carbide Headquarters (Danbury CT) **31** Power Center for the Performing Arts (U of Michigan)

Rochester

football team: **8** Panthers

Rochester, Edward

character in: **8** Jane Eyre

author: **6** Bronte

rock 3 bob, jar **4** crag, reef, roll, stun, sway, toss **5** cliff, flint, pitch, quake, shake, stone, swing, upset **6** gravel, marble, pebble, totter, wobble **7** agitate, bobbing, boulder, disturb, shaking **8** convulse, flounder, undulate, wobbling **9** limestone, oscillate, tottering **10** convulsion, undulation

rock & rye

type: **7** liqueur

flavor: **6** citrus

ingredient: **3** rye **9** rock candy

rock crystal

species: **6** quartz

color: **9** colorless

Rocket

nickname of: **14** Maurice Richard

rocket engine

invented by: **7** Goddard

Rockford Files, The

character: **10** John Cooper **11** Angel Martin, Jim Rockford **12** (Det) Dennis Becker **13** Beth Davenport, (Joseph) Rocky Rockford

cast: **9** Bo Hopkins, Joe Santos, Noah Beery **11** James Garner **14** Stuart Margolin **15** Gretchen Corbett

rock of Tarik see **9** Gibraltar

Rockwell, Norman

born: **9** New York NY

artwork:

   covers: **19** Saturday Evening Post

   mural: **15** Freedom of Speech

Rocky

director: **13** John G Avildsen

cast: **9** Burt Young **10** Talia Shire **11** Thayer David **12** Carl Weathers **15** Burgess Meredith **17** Sylvester Stallone (Rocky Balboa, the Italian Stallion)

setting: **12** Philadelphia

Oscar for: **7** editing, picture **8** director

sequel: **7** Rocky II, Rocky IV **8** Rocky III, Rocky Two **9** Rocky Four **10** Rocky Three

rod 4 cane, lash, mace, pale, pole, wand, whip **5** baton, birch, crook, staff, stake, stick **6** cudgel, rattan, switch **7** penalty, scepter, scourge **8** caduceus **9** stanchion **10** alpenstock, punishment **11** retribution **12** swagger stick

rod, Aaron's see **9** Aaron's rod

rodent 4 cavy, vole **5** coypu, gundi, hutia, mouse **6** agouti, beaver, cururo, gerbil, gopher, jerboa, nutria **7** blesmol, cane rat, hamster, lemming, mole-rat, rock rat **8** capybara, chipmunk, dormouse, pacarana, sewellel, spiny rat, squirrel, tucu-tuco, viscacha **9** chozchori, false paca, porcupine, woodchuck **10** chinchilla, prairie dog, springhare **11** kangaroo rat, pocket mouse, viscacha rat **13** kangaroo mouse **16** Speke's pectinator

Roderick Hudson

author: **10** Henry James

Roderick Random

author: **14** Tobias Smollett

character: **5** Strap **8** Narcissa **10** Tom Bowling **12** Miss Williams

Rodin, (Francois) Auguste Rene

born: **5** Paris **6** France

artwork: **7** The Kiss **10** Head of Iris, The Thinker, Victor Hugo, Walking Man **14** John the Baptist, The Age of Bronze, The Gates of Hell **16** Monument to Balzac **19** The Burghers of Calais **23** The Man with the Broken Nose

rodomontade 4 rant **5** boast **6** hot air **7** blather, bluster, bombast, fustian **8** bragging, folderol, nonsense, rhetoric **10** balderdash, doubletalk **11** braggadocio **12** boastfulness

roe 3 doe, elk, hen **4** buck, deer, eggs, fawn, fish, hart, hind, milt **5** spawn, sperm **6** caviar **8** fish eggs

of lobster: **5** coral

Roentgen, Rontgen, Wilhelm Konrad

field: **7** physics

nationality: **6** German

discovered: **5** X-rays

awarded: **10** Nobel Prize

Roethke, Theodore

author of: **9** Open House, The Waking **11** The Far Field **15** Straw for the Fire, Words for the Wind

Rogers, Ginger

real name: **23** Virginia Katherine McMath

born: **14** Independence MO

husband: **8** Lew Ayres **15** Jacques Bergerac, William Marshall

partner: **11** Fred Astaire

roles: **6** Top Hat **9** Stage Door **10** Hello Dolly, Kitty Foyle (Oscar) **12** Shall We Dance? **14** The Gay Divorcee **15** Flying Down to Rio, Tom Dick and Harry **17** Forty-Second Street **19** The Major and the Minor **21** The Barkleys of Broadway **30** The Story of Vernon and Irene Castle

Rogers, James Gamble

architect of: **22** Northwestern University (Chicago) **33** Columbia-Presbyterian Medical Center (NYC)

Rogers, Roy

real name: **11** Leonard Slye

born: **12** Cincinnati OH

wife: **9** Dale Evans

sidekick: **10** Gabby Hayes

singing group: **17** Sons of the Pioneers

horse: **7** Trigger

roles: **10** Apache Rose **11** Song of Texas **12** My Pal Trigger **13** Song of Arizona, Son of Paleface **17** Heart of the Rockies, Under Western Stars **18** Billy the Kid Returns **19** Tumbling Tumbleweeds **20** The Yellow Rose of Texas **22** Springtime in the Sierras

rogue 3 cur **5** devil, fraud, knave, scamp **6** bad man, rascal, rotter, varlet, wretch **7** bounder, hellion, villain **8** deceiver, evildoer, scalawag **9** miscreant, reprobate, scoundrel **10** blackguard, malefactor, mountebank, scapegrace **11** rapscallion **13** mischiefmaker **14** good-for-nothing **15** snake in the grass

Rogue Herries

author: **11** Hugh Walpole

roguish 3 sly **4** arch **5** saucy **8** devilish, rascally **11** mischievous

roil 3 irk, vex **4** mill, rile, stir **5** annoy, muddy **6** ruffle, seethe **7** agitate, disturb, perturb, provoke, turmoil **8** irritate **9** aggravate **10** exasperate

role 3 job **4** duty, part, pose, post, task, work **5** chore, guise **7** posture, service **8** capacity, function **9** character, portrayal **13** assignment **13** impersonation **14** representation **15** personification **16** characterization

Latin: **7** persona

roll 4 boom, coil, curl, echo, flip, flow, furl, knot, list, loop, reel, roar, rock, spin, sway, toss, tube, turn, wind **5** coast, crack, lurch, pitch, sound, spool, surge, swell, swing, swirl, throw, twirl, twist, wheel, whirl **6** billow, gyrate, muster, roster, rotate, rumble, scroll, tumble **7** booming, catalog, entwine, resound, revolve, rocking, thunder, tossing, turning **8** cylinder, drumbeat, drumming, rumbling, schedule, tumbling, undulate **9** inventory **10** undulation **11** reverberate **13** reverberation **15** turn over and over

Rolland, Romain
  author of: **14** Jean-Christophe **16** The Soul Enchanted

rollicking 3 gay **5** happy, jolly, merry, sunny **6** bright, hearty, jocund, jovial, joyous, lively **7** gleeful, jocular, playful, romping **8** cheerful, mirthful, spirited **9** exuberant, gamboling, sparkling, sprightly **10** frolicking, frolicsome, hysterical, rip-roaring **12** lighthearted

Rolvaag, Ole Edvart
  author of: **15** Peder Victorious, Their Father's God **16** Giants in the Earth

roly-poly 3 fat **5** obese, plump, pudgy, round **6** chubby, rotund **9** corpulent

roman 5 novel **17** metrical narrative

Roman Catholic church
  council/synod: **4** Pisa **5** Basel, Trent **6** Nicaea, Vienne, Whitby **7** Ephesus, Pistoia, Sardica **9** Chalcedon, Constance **12** First Vatican **13** Fourth Lateran, Second Vatican **14** Constantinople **15** Ferrara-Florence
  official Vatican yearbook: **18** Annuario Pontificio
  first Christian emperor: **11** Constantine
  gifts of territory/sovereignty to papacy: **15** Donation of Pepin **21** Donation of Constantine

romance 4 bosh, call, pull **5** amour, idyll, novel **6** affair, allure **7** fantasy, fiction **8** illusion **9** courtship, exoticism, fairy tale, fish story, invention, love story, melodrama, moonshine, tall story **10** attachment, concoction, flirtation, love affair **11** fabrication, fascination, imagination **12** exaggeration, relationship, self-delusion **13** flight of fancy, tender passion **16** affair of the heart

Romance language see **5** Latin

Romances sans paroles
  author: **12** Paul Verlaine

Romancing the Stone
  director: **14** Robert Zemeckis
  cast: **11** Danny De Vito **14** Kathleen Turner, Michael Douglas
  sequel: **17** The Jewel of the Nile

Roman Holiday
  director: **12** William Wyler
  cast: **11** Eddie Albert, Gregory Peck **13** Audrey Hepburn
  Oscar for: **7** actress (Hepburn)

Romania
  other name: **7** Rumania
  capital/largest city: **9** Bucharest
  others: **4** Aiud, Arad, Cluj, Deva, Iasi **5** Bacau, Balta, Cerna, Jassy, Neamt, Sibiu, Turnu, Yassy **6** Braila, Brasov, Brasso, Eforie, Galatz, Galeti, Lupeni, Mamaia, Oradea, Sighet **7** Bendery, Craiova, Focsani, Giurgiu, Ploesti, Severin **8** Bloiesti, Cernavti, Chisinau, Irongate, Kishenef, Satu-Mare, Temesvar **9** Constanta, Kolozsvar, Timisoara **10** Czernowitz **11** Klausenburg
  school: **4** Cuza
  division: **4** Alba, Iasi **5** Banat, Bihor, Jassy **6** Ardeal **7** Dobruja **8** Bucovina, Bukovina, Dobrogea, Moldavia, Walachia **9** Maramures **10** Bessarabia **12** Transylvania
    Roman province: **5** Dacia
  measure: **7** faltche
  monetary unit: **3** ban, lei, leu, lev, ley **4** bani **5** uncia **6** triens
  lake: **5** Sinoe **6** Snagov
  mountain: **5** Banat, Bihor **6** Codrul, Rodnei **7** Apuseni, Balkans, Caliman, Fagaras **8** Pietrosu **9** Moldavian **10** Carpathian, Moldoveanu **17** Transylvanian Alps
  highest point: **11** Moldoveanul
  river: **3** Alt, Jui, Olt **4** Prut **5** Aluta, Arges, Buzdu, Moros, Mures, Oltul, Schyl, Siret, Somes, Timis, Vedea **6** Crasna, Danube **7** Argesul **8** Bistrita, Ialomita, Iniester **9** Dimbovita, Jiul Mures
  sea: **5** Black
  physical feature:
    canal: **4** Bega
    forest: **6** Snagov **7** Baneasa
    gorge: **8** Iron Gate
    peninsula: **6** Balkan
    plain: **5** Banat **9** Moldavian, Walachian **13** Prahova Valley
    plateau: **7** Dobruja
    wind: **6** crivat
  people: **6** Dacian **8** Romanian, Rumanian
    artist: **8** Brancusi
    author: **7** Ionesco
    composer: **6** Enesco
    leader: **6** Carol I **7** Michael, Iliescu **8** Ioan Cuza **9** Ceausescu **12** Gheorghiu-Dej, Ion Antonescu
  language: **6** French, Magyar **7** Russian **8** Romanian, Rumanian **9** Hungarian
  religion: **7** Judaism **8** Lutheran **9** Calvinism, Unitarian **10** Protestant **13** Roman Catholic **16** Romanian Orthodox
  place:
    castle: **4** Bran **7** Huniady
    church: **5** Golia **9** Mihaivoda **10** Cretulescu, Patriarchy **11** Curtea Veche, Stavropdeos, Trei Ierarhi
    monastery: **5** Humor **6** Arbore **7** Voronet **8** Sucerita **9** Moldovita
    museum: **11** Peles Castle
    palace: **9** mogosoaia
    park: **7** Baneasa
    resort: **5** Venus **6** Eforie, Mamaia, Neptun **7** Jupiter **10** Costinesti
  feature:
    community gathering: **9** sezatoare
    game: **4** oina
    food:
      dish: **6** ciorba **7** mititei, sarmala **8** mamaliga **11** imam bayildi
      plum brandy: **5** tuica

Roman measure 2 as **5** cubit, libra **6** pondus **7** stadium

Roman Mythology
  collective name for gods: **6** Superi
  goddess of anguish: **8** Angerona
  goddess of agriculture: **5** Ceres **6** Dea Dia, Vacuna **13** Acca Laurentia
    Ceres corresponds to Greek: **7** Demeter
  goddess of the arts: **7** Minerva
    corresponds to Greek: **6** Athena
  goddess of baking: **6** Fornax
  goddess of chastity: **5** Fauna **7** Bona Dea
  goddess of childbirth: **5** Parca **6** Lucina, Matuta, Parcae **11** Mater Matuta
  goddess of the dawn: **6** Aurora, Matuta **11** Mater Matuta
    Aurora corresponds to Greek: **3** Eos
  goddess of destiny: **5** Parca **6** Parcae
  goddess of discord: **9** Discordia
  goddess of door hinges: **6** Cardea
  goddess of the earth: **6** Tellus
    corresponds to Greek: **4** Gaea
  goddess of the family: **6** Cardea
  goddess of fertility: **5** Fauna **6** Libera, Tellus **7** Bona Dea
    Libera corresponds to Greek: **10** Persephone
    Tellus corresponds to Greek: **4** Gaea
  goddess of flowers: **5** Flora
  goddess of fortune: **7** Fortuna
    corresponds to Greek: **5** Tyche
  goddess of fruit trees: **6** Pomona
  goddess of gardens: **5** Venus
    corresponds to Greek: **9** Aphrodite
  goddess of grain/protectress against grain blight: **6** Robigo
  goddess of harbors: **6** Matuta **11** Mater Matuta
  goddess of harmony: **9** Concordia
  goddess of the hearth: **4** Caca **5** Salus, Vesta
    Salus corresponds to Greek: **6** Hygeia
  goddess of heaven: **4** Juno
    corresponds to Greek: **4** Hera
  goddess of hunting: **5** Diana
    corresponds to Greek: **6** Phoebe **7** Artemis
  goddess of longevity: **11** Anna Perenna
  goddess of love: **5** Venus
    corresponds to Greek: **9** Aphrodite
  goddess of marriage: **4** Juno **6** Tellus
    corresponds to Greek: **4** Gaea, Hera
  goddess of marshes: **6** Marica **9** Dea

Marica
goddess of the moon: 5 Diana
   corresponds to Greek: 6 Phoebe **7** Artemis
goddess of peace: 3 Pax **9** Concordia
   Pax corresponds to Greek: 5 Irene
goddess of pleasure: 8 Voluptas
goddess of plenty: 3 Ops **10** Magna Mater
goddess of prosperity: 5 Salus
   corresponds to Greek: 6 Hygeia
goddess of the sea: 6 Matuta **11** Mater Matuta
goddess of sleeping infants: 6 Cunina
goddess of the spring: 5 Venus
   corresponds to Greek: 9 Aphrodite
goddess of storms: 11 Tempestates
goddess of victory: 8 Victoria
   corresponds to Greek: 4 Nike
goddess of vineyards: 6 Libera
   corresponds to Greek: 10 Persephone
goddess of war: 7 Bellona
   corresponds to Greek: 5 Enyon
goddess of wine: 6 Libera
   corresponds to Greek: 10 Persephone
goddess of wisdom: 7 Minerva
   corresponds to Greek: 6 Athena
god of agriculture: 5 Picus **6** Saturn **7** Eventus **12** Bonus Eventus
   corresponds to Greek: 6 Cronos, Cronus, Kronos
god of beginnings: 5 Janus
god of boundaries: 8 Terminus
god of commerce: 7 Mercury
   corresponds to Greek: 6 Hermes
god of the dead: 7 Veiovis
god of doorways: 5 Janus
god of drinking/revelry: 5 Comus
god of eloquence: 7 Mercury
   corresponds to Greek: 6 Hermes
god of farm boundaries: 8 Silvanus, Sylvanus
god of fertility: 7 Mutinus, Priapus **8** Lupercus, Picumnus
god of fire/metalworking: 6 Vulcan
   corresponds to Greek: 10 Hephaestus, Hephaistos
god of forest: 7 Virbius
god of gardens: 9 Vertumnus
god of good counsel: 3 Ops **6** Consus
god of grain/protector against grain blight: 7 Robigus
god of healing: 11 Aesculapius
   corresponds to Greek: 9 Asclepius
god of heavens: 4 Jove **7** Jupiter
   corresponds to Greek: 4 Zeus
god of herds: 8 Silvanus, Sylvanus
god of horse racing: 3 Ops **6** Consus
god of hospitality: 6 Sancus **10** Dius Fidius, Semo Sancus
god of the house: 8 Silvanus, Sylvanus
god of hunting: 7 Virbius
god of international affairs: 6 Sancus **10** Dius Fidius, Semo Sancus
god of landmarks: 8 Terminus
god of light: 6 Apollo
god of love: 4 Amor **5** Cupid
   corresponds to Greek: 4 Eros
god of luck: 7 Eventus **12** Bonus Eventus
god of medicine: 11 Aesculapius
   corresponds to Greek: 9 Asclepius
god of music: 6 Apollo
god of oaths: 6 Sancus **10** Dius Fidius, Semo Sancus
god of orchards: 9 Vertumnus
god of ports/harbors: 8 Portunus
god of prosperity: 7 Eventus **12** Bonus Eventus
god of the rising sun: 5 Janus
god of science: 7 Mercury
   corresponds to Greek: 6 Hermes
god of sea: 7 Neptune
   corresponds to Greek: 8 Poseidon
god of seasons: 9 Vertumnus
god of the setting sun: 5 Janus
god of sleep: 6 Somnus
   corresponds to Greek: 6 Hypnos, Hypnus
god of springs: 4 Fons
gods of sulphur springs (twins): 6 Palici
god of the sun: 3 Sol
   corresponds to Greek: 6 Helios **8** Hyperion
god of thievery: 7 Mercury
   corresponds to Greek: 6 Hermes
god of thunder: 7 Taranis
god of thunderstorms: 8 Summanus
god of the Tiber: 9 Tiberinus
god of uncultivated land: 8 Silvanus, Sylvanus
god of underworld: 3 Dis **5** Orcus **8** Dis Pater
   corresponds to Greek: 5 Pluto
god of war: 4 Mars **6** Mamers, Mavors **8** Quirinus
   corresponds to Greek: 4 Ares
god of weather: 4 Jove **7** Jupiter
god of weddings: 8 Talassio
   corresponds to Greek: 5 Hymen **9** Hymenaeus
god of the woods: 6 Faunus **8** Silvanus, Sylvanus
household gods: 5 lares **7** penates
nymphs/deities with gift of prophecy: 7 Camenae
   names: 6 Egeria **8** Carmenta **9** Antevorta, Postvorta
   correspond to Greek: 5 Muses
protectress of childbirth: 8 Carmenta
protectress of cows/oxen: 6 Bubona
protector of flocks/shepherds: 5 Pales
protectress of military age men: 8 Juventas
   corresponds to Greek: 4 Hebe
protectress of women: 5 Diana
   corresponds to Greek: 6 Phoebe **7** Artemis
protectress of women/marriage: 4

Juno
queen of heaven: 4 Juno
   corresponds to Greek: 4 Hera, Here
staff of Mercury: 8 Caduceus
troublesome ghosts: 7 lemures
romantic 4 fond **5** mushy, soppy **6** ardent, dreamy, loving, tender, unreal **7** amorous, devoted, fervent, flighty, idyllic, utopian **8** enamored, fanciful, quixotic **9** fantastic, idealized, imaginary, sensitive, visionary, whimsical **10** idealistic, improbable, passionate **11** extravagant, impassioned, impractical, rhapsodical, sentimental, unrealistic, warmhearted **12** melodramatic, preposterous
Romantic Comedians, The
   author: 12 Ellen Glasgow
romanticize 8 idealize **9** embroider
Romantic Manifesto
   author: 7 Ayn Rand
Romany Rye, The
   author: 17 George Henry Borrow
Rome, ancient
   emperor: 4 Nero, Otho **5** Galba, Nerva, Titus **6** Trajan **7** Hadrian **8** Augustus, Caligula, Claudius, Commodus, Domitian, Tiberius **9** Caracalla, Vespasian, Vitellius **10** Diocletian **11** Constantine, Lucius Verus **13** Antoninus Pius **14** Marcus Aurelius
   emperor's bodyguard: 15 Praetorian Guard
   first citizen title: 8 princeps
   first triumvirate: 6 Caesar, Pompey **7** Crassus
   foe: 4 Gaul **5** Spain **6** Cimbri **7** Perseus, Philip V, Pyrrhus, Teutons **8** Carthage, Hannibal, Iberians, Jugurtha, Samnites, Tarentum, Umbrians **9** Etruscans, Macedonia, Seleucids **11** Latin League **12** Antiochus III **13** Achaean League, Hamilcar Barca
   general: 5 Sulla **6** Brutus, Marius, Pompey **7** Crassus **8** Octavian **10** Flamininus, Mark Antony **12** Julius Caesar **14** Caesar Augustus **20** Quintus Fabius Maximus, Scipio Africanus Major, Scipio Africanus Minor
   king: 12 Ancus Marcius **13** Numa Pompilius **16** Sextus Tarquinius **17** Tarquinius Priscus (Tarquin the Elder) **18** Tarquinius Superbus (Tarquin the Proud)
   reformer: 8 Gracchus
   republican ruler: 6 consul **7** senator, tribune **8** plebeian **9** optimates, patrician, populares **10** magistrate
   Roman peace: 9 Pax Romana
   second triumvirate: 6 Antony **7** Lepidus **8** Octavian (Caesar Augustus)
Rome, Roma
   airport: 8 Ciampino **15** Leonardo da Vinci
   area: 9 Cinecitta (Cinema City) **10** Trastevere **11** Vatican City

capital of: 5 Italy **6** Latium **11** Papal States, Roman Empire

church: 8 St Peter's **11** San Giovanni **18** Santa Maria Maggiore **19** San Paolo Fuori le Mura

Italian: 4 Roma

landmark: 5 Forum **7** Capitol **8** Pantheon **9** catacombs, Colosseum **12** Palazzo Doria **13** Circus Maximus, Lateran Palace, Sistine Chapel, Vatican Palace, Villa Borghese **14** Palazzo Corsini, Villa Farnesina **16** Baths of Caracalla, Castel Sant'Angelo, Palazzo Barberini **17** Arch of Constantine **19** Saint Peter's Basilica

legendary founders: 5 Remus **6** Aeneas **7** Romulus

nickname: 11 Eternal City

mountain: 8 Apennine

museum: 5 Doria **7** Colonna, Corsini, Vatican **8** Borghese, National **10** Capitoline

river: 5 Tiber

school: 33 Conservatorio di Musica Santa Cecilia

sea: 10 Tyrrhenian

seven hills: 7 Caelian, Viminal **8** Aventine, Palatine, Quirinal **9** Esquiline **10** Capitoline

square/piazza: 6 Popolo, Spagna **7** Colonna, Venezia **9** Quirinale **11** Campidoglio

state within: 11 Vatican City

street: 9 Appian Way, Emmanuele **11** Via del Corso **13** Corso Vittorio

subway: 13 Metropolitana

Romeo 4 beau **5** lover, sheik, swain, wooer **7** Don Juan, gallant **8** Casanova, cavalier, Lothario **9** boyfriend, Lochinvar

French: 8 paramour

Latin: 9 inamorato

Romeo and Juliet
author: 18 William Shakespeare
character: 5 Nurse, Paris **6** Tybalt **8** Benvolio, Mercutio **13** Friar Laurence
  family: 7 Capulet **8** Montague
setting: 6 Verona

Romeo and Juliet
director:
  1936 version: 11 George Cukor
  1968 version: 16 Franco Zeffirelli
based on play by: 18 William Shakespeare
cast:
  1936 version: 12 Leslie Howard, Norma Shearer **13** Basil Rathbone, Edna May Oliver, John Barrymore
  1968 version: 9 Milo O'Shea **11** John McEnery, Michael York **14** Leonard Whiting
Olivia Hussey **14** Leonard Whiting
score: 8 Nino Rota

Romeo and Juliet
symphony by: 7 Berlioz
opera by: 6 Gounod
orchestral piece by: 11 Tchaikovsky
ballet by: 9 Prokofiev

Romney, George
born: 7 England **15** Dalton-in-Furness
artwork: 5 Circe **9** Joan of Arc **11** Mrs Robinson, Sensibility **12** Mrs Davenport, Saint Cecilia **19** Mrs Cardwardine and Son **22** The Death of General Wolfe **24** The Levenson-Gower Children **26** Sir Christopher and Lady Sykes

Romola
author: 11 George Eliot
character: 5 Bardo, Tessa **10** Tito Melema **15** Baldasarre Calvo

romp 3 hop **4** skip **5** caper, cut up, frisk, sport **6** frolic, gambol **7** disport, rollick

Romulus
father: 4 Mars
mother: 4 Ilia **9** Rea Silvia **10** Rhea Silvia
twin brother: 5 Remus
raised by: 7 she-wolf **9** Faustulus **12** Acca Larentia
first king of: 4 Rome
founder of: 4 Rome

Romus
father: 6 Aeneas **8** Ascanius
possible founder of: 4 Rome

Roncalli, Angelo Giuseppe 13 Pope John XXIII **22** Pope John the Twenty-Third

Ronsard, Pierre de
author of: 17 Sonnets pour Helene
member of: 7 Pleiade

roofing 4 tile, turf **5** slate, terne **6** thatch **7** asphalt, ceiling, pantile, shingle **8** housetop

Roof of the World see **5** Tibet

rook 3 gyp **4** bilk, crow, dupe, gull **5** cheat, cozen, raven, trick **6** castle, fleece **7** deceive, defraud, swindle **8** chessman **9** bamboozle, victimize

rookie 4 tyro **6** novice **7** beginner **9** fledgling, greenhorn **10** apprentice, tenderfoot

Rookies, The
character: 9 Jill Danko, (Officer) Mike Danko **10** (Lt) Eddie Ryker, (Officer) Chris Owens **12** (Officer) Terry Webster, (Officer) Willie Gillis
cast: 11 Kate Jackson, Sam Melville **14** Bruce Fairbairn, Michael Ontkean **16** Gerald S O'Loughlin **18** Georg Stanford Brown

room 4 area **5** range, scope, space **6** chance, extent, leeway, margin, volume **7** chamber, cubicle, expanse, lodging **9** allowance, provision, territory **11** compartment
French: 5 salle
Spanish: 4 sala

Room at the Top
director: 11 Jack Clayton
based on novel by: 10 John Braine
cast: 12 Heather Sears **14** Laurence Harvey, Simone Signoret **16** Hermione Baddeley

Oscar for: 7 actress (Signoret)
sequel: 11 Man at the Top **12** Life at the Top

Room 222
character: 6 Bernie **9** Pete Dixon **11** Liz McIntyre **12** Alice Johnson **14** Seymour Kaufman
cast: 11 Lloyd Haynes **13** David Jolliffe **14** Denise Nicholas, Karen Valentine **18** Michael Constantine
school: 15 Walt Whitman High

roomy 3 big **4** huge, long, vast, wide **5** ample, broad, large **7** immense, lengthy, sizable **8** generous, spacious **9** boundless, capacious, expansive, extensive, unlimited **10** commodious

Rooney, Mickey
real name: 9 Joe Yule Jr
born: 10 Brooklyn NY
wife: 10 Ava Gardner **13** Martha Vickers
co-star: 11 Judy Garland
roles: 4 Puck **8** Boys' Town **9** Andy Hardy **11** Sugar Babies **13** Mickey McGuire **14** Baby Face Nelson, National Velvet, The Human Comedy **21** A Midsummer Night's Dream **30** The Adventures of Huckleberry Finn

Roosevelt, Franklin Delano
presidential rank: 12 thirty-second
party: 10 Democratic
state represented: 2 NY
defeated: 5 (Jacob Sechler) Coxey, (John W) Aiken, (Thomas Edmund) Dewey, (William) Lemke **6** (Alfred Mossman) Landon, (Claude A) Watson, (David Leigh) Colvin, (Herbert Clark) Hoover, (Norman) Thomas, (Roger Ward) Babson, (William David) Upshaw, (William Hope) Harvey, (William Zebulon) Foster **7** (Earl Russell) Browder, (Wendell Lewis) Willkie **8** (Edward A) Teichert, (Verne L) Reynolds
vice president: 6 (Harry S) Truman, (John Nance) Garner **7** (Henry Agard) Wallace
cabinet:
  state: 4 (Cordell) Hull **10** (Edward Reilly) Stettinius (Jr)
  treasury: 6 (William Hartman) Woodin **10** (Henry) Morgenthau (Jr)
  war: 4 (George Henry) Dern **7** (Henry Lewis) Stimson **8** (Harry Hines) Woodring
  attorney general: 6 (Francis) Biddle, (Frank) Murphy **7** (Robert Houghwout) Jackson **8** (Homer Stille) Cummings
  navy: 4 (Frank) Knox **6** (Charles) Edison **7** (Claude Augustus) Swanson **9** (James Vincent) Forrestal
  postmaster general: 6 (Frank Comerford) Walker, (James Aloysius) Farley
  interior: 5 (Harold LeClaire) Ickes
  agriculture: 7 (Claude Raymond)

Wickard, (Henry Agard) Wallace
commerce: 5 (Daniel Calhoun) Roper, (Jesse Holman) Jones **7** (Henry Agard) Wallace, (Henry Lloyd) Hopkins
labor: 7 (Frances) Perkins (Wilson)
born: 10 Hyde Park NY
died: 13 Warm Springs GA **16** Little White House
buried: 10 Hyde Park NY
education:
  prep school: 6 Groton
  university: 7 Harvard
  law school: 8 Columbia
religion: 12 Episcopalian
interests: 3 art **6** polo **6** tennis, travel **7** fishing, hunting **8** shooting
vacation spot: 13 Warm Springs GA **16** Campobello Island (Canada)
dog: 4 Fala
author: 27 The Happy Warrior: Alfred E Smith
political career: 12 state senator
  assistant secretary of: 4 Navy
  governor of: 7 New York
civilian career: 6 lawyer **11** bank officer
notable events of lifetime/term: 4 D-Day, WWII **7** New Deal **10** atomic bomb, Depression, World War II **11** World War Two **13** United Nations **15** Atlantic Charter
  act: 9 Lend-Lease
  attack on: 11 Pearl Harbor
  conference: 5 Cairo, Yalta **7** Arcadia, Crimean, Teheran
  scandal: 11 Tammany Hall
quote: 24 A day that will live in infamy **31** Meet every day's troubles as they come **36** The only thing we have to fear is fear itself **50** This generation of Americans has a rendezvous with destiny **53** I pledge you I pledge myself to a new deal for the American people
father: 5 James
mother: 4 Sara (Delano)
siblings:
  half-brother: 5 James
wife: 7 (Anna) Eleanor (Roosevelt)
children: 5 James **7** Elliott **11** Anna Eleanor **13** John Aspinwell **14** Franklin Delano
first lady:
  author: 7 On My Own **13** This I Remember, This Is My Story **34** The Autobiography of Eleanor Roosevelt
  chairwoman: 25 UN Commission on Human Rights
  codirector: 23 Office of Civilian Defense
  member: 35 Democratic National Campaign Committee
  newspaper column: 5 My Day
  US delegate to: 2 UN
Roosevelt, Theodore
  nickname: 5 Teddy

presidential rank: 11 twenty-sixth
party: 10 Republican
state represented: 2 NY
succeeded: 8 McKinley
defeated (second term): 4 (Eugene Victor) Debs **6** (Alton Brooks) Parker, (Thomas Edward) Watson **7** (Austin) Holcomb, (Silas Comfort) Swallow **8** (Charles Hunter) Corregan
vice president: 4 none (1st term) **9** (Charles Warren) Fairbanks
cabinet:
  state: 3 (John Milton) Hay **4** (Elihu) Root **5** (Robert) Bacon
  treasury: 4 (Leslie Mortier) Shaw, (Lyman Judson) Gage **9** (George Bruce) Cortelyou
  war: 4 (Elihu) Root, (William Howard) Taft **6** (Luke Edward) Wright
  attorney general: 4 (Philander Chase) Knox **5** (William Henry) Moody **9** (Charles Joseph) Bonaparte
  navy: 4 (John Davis) Long **5** (William Henry) Moody **6** (Paul) Morton **7** (Victor Howard) Metcalf **8** (Truman Handy) Newberry **9** (Charles Joseph) Bonaparte
  postmaster general: 5 (Charles Emory) Smith, (George von Lengerke) Meyer, (Henry Clay) Payne, (Robert John) Wynne **9** (George Bruce) Cortelyou
  interior: 8 (James Rudolph) Garfield **9** (Ethan Allen) Hitchcock
  agriculture: 6 (James) Wilson
  commerce and labor: 6 (Oscar Solomon) Straus **7** (Victor Howard) Metcalf **9** (George Bruce) Cortelyou
born: 13 New York City NY
died/buried: 2 NY **9** Oyster Bay **10** Long Island
education:
  university: 7 Harvard
  law school: 8 Columbia (did not graduate)
religion: 13 Dutch Reformed
interests: 7 hunting (African game), writing **9** exploring (South America) **14** natural history
author: 11 Rough Riders **14** Oliver Cromwell **16** Gouverneur Morris, Thomas Hart Benton **17** African Game Trails, The New Nationalism **19** The Winning of the West **20** Letters to His Children **21** America and the World War **24** The Foes of Our Own Household **25** Fear God and Take Your Own Part **27** A Booklover's Holiday in the Open, Ranch Life and the Hunting Trail, The Naval War of Eighteen-Twelve **28** Hero Tales from American History **29** Through the Brazilian Wilderness **33** Life Histories of African Game Animals

political career: 13 Vice President **15** NY State Assembly **24** US Civil Service Commission
  assistant secretary: 4 Navy
  governor of: 7 New York
  organized party: 9 Bull Moose **11** Progressive
civilian career: 6 author **7** rancher **14** public lecturer
military service: 15 NY National Guard **18** Spanish- American War
  organized cavalry regiment: 11 Rough Riders
  led charge up: 11 San Juan Hill
notable events of lifetime/term: 5 Panic (of 1907) **10** Square Deal **15** Nobel Peace Prize **22** San Francisco earthquake
  Act: 11 Reclamation **14** Meat Inspection **15** Hepburn Railroad, Pure Food and Drug
  bureau of: 12 Corporations **28** Immigration and Naturalization
  first flight by: 14 Wright Brothers
  revolution: 6 Panama
  treaty: 13 Hay-Pauncefote **15** Hay-Bunau-Varilla
quotes: 25 Hasten forward quickly there **28** Speak softly and carry a big stick
father: 8 Theodore
mother: 6 Martha (Bulloch)
siblings: 4 Anna **7** Corinne, Elliott
wife: 5 Alice (Hathaway Lee), Edith (Kermit Carow)
children: 6 Kermit **7** Quentin **8** Alice Lee, Theodore **10** Ethel Carow **16** Archibald Bulloch

rooster
  young: 8 cockerel

root 3 fix, set **4** back, base, bind, bulb, clap, hail, nail, rise, stem **5** basis, boost, cheer, fount, radix, start, stick, tubes **6** bottom, fasten, ground, motive, origin, reason, second, source, spring **7** acclaim, applaud, bolster, cheer on, pull for, radicle, support **8** fountain, occasion, shout for **9** beginning, encourage, establish, inception, rationale **10** derivation, foundation, mainspring **11** fundamental **12** commencement, fountainhead

Root, John Wellborn
  partner: 14 Daniel H Burnham
  architect of: 10 The Rookery **12** Hotel Statler (Washington DC), Montauk Block **13** Hotel Tamanaco (Caracas) **17** Monadnock Building, Palmolive Building (Chicago) **19** Rand-McNally Building

root for 5 boost **6** urge on **7** cheer on, pull for

root out 5 dig up **6** remove **7** extract, pull out, uncover, unearth **8** discover **9** extirpate, ferret out **12** bring to light

Roots
  author: 9 Alex Haley
  character: 3 Tom **4** Ames, Bell, Noah

5 Binta, Fanta, Grill, Irene, Kizzy, Lewis, Mingo, Omoro **6** Justin, Martha, Ordell **7** Fiddler, Gardner, Nyo Boto **8** Kintango, Mathilda, Mrs Moore, Tom Moore **9** Evan Brent, Missy Anne **10** Brima Cesay, Capt Davies, Carrington, Jemmy Brent, Kadi Touray, Kunta Kinte, Sam Bennett, Sister Sara **11** Mrs Reynolds, Squire James **12** John Reynolds **13** Chicken George **14** Sir Eric Russell, Stephen Bennett **15** Ol' George Johnson, Third Mate Slater **17** Dr William Reynolds

cast: 8 Burl Ives, John Amos, Ren Woods **9** Ben Vereen, Brad Davis, Moses Gunn, O J Simpson, Vic Morrow **10** Billy Hicks, Ian McShane, John Schuck, Lynne Moody, Olivia Cole, Paul Shenar, Ralph Waite, Robert Reed **11** Beverly Todd, Cicely Tyson, Doug McClure, Edward Asner, Gary Collins, Harry Rhodes, Lane Binkley, LeVar Burton, Lorne Greene, Maya Angelou, Sandy Duncan **12** Carolyn Jones, Chuck Connors, Leslie Uggams, Lloyd Bridges **13** Louis Gosset Jr, Madge Sinclair, William Watson **14** George Hamilton, Lynda Day George, Macdonald Carey **15** Lillian Randolph, Scatman Crothers, Thalmus Rasulala **16** Raymond St Jacques, Richard Roundtree **18** Georg Stanford Brown **20** Lawrence Hilton-Jacobs

rope 3 gad, guy, tie, tow **4** bind, cord, fast, guss, hemp, line, lure, snag, trap, wire, yarn **5** cable, catch, chord, lasso, noose, riata, shank, strap, twine **6** corral, entice, hawser, lariat, seduce, string, tether **7** bobstay, cordage, halyard, lanyard, lashing, painter **8** dragline, restrain

fiber: 5 sisal

Rosaline
character in: 16 Love's Labour's Lost
author: 11 Shakespeare

rose 4 Rosa
varieties: 3 bog, dog, sun, tea, wax **4** baby, gold, moss, musk, rock, rush, sand, wood **5** briar, brier, China, fairy, field, malva, Ophir, pygmy, swamp **6** Alpine, Burnet, copper, cotton, damask, desert, French, ground, Karroo, Lenten, mallow, Nootka, Scotch, velvet **7** baby sun, Banksia, Bourbon, cabbage, cluster, Guelder, Manetti, pasture, prairie, rambler **8** Burgundy, Champney, Cherokee, chestnut, cinnamon, climbing, Japanese, Memorial, mountain, Noisette **9** Christmas, evergreen, hybrid tea, McCartney, Polyantha, Remontant, Turkestan **10** California, Chinquapin, shaggy-rock, underwater **11** confederate, giant velvet, hairy alpine **12** green Mexican, Hawaiian wood, Seven-sisters,

white Mexican **13** Himalayan musk, Hybrid Bourbon, Persian yellow, Stuart's desert **15** hybrid perpetual **16** York-and-Lancaster

Rose, Pete (Peter Edward)
nickname: 13 Charlie Hustle
sport: 8 baseball
position: 7 baseman **8** outfield
team: 14 Cincinnati Reds **20** Philadelphia Phillies
scandal: 8 gambling

Roseanne
former name: 4 Barr **6** Arnold
husband: 3 Tom **6** Thomas
television:
  show: 8 Roseanne
  husband: 3 Dan
  children: 2 DJ **5** Becky **7** Darlene
  sister: Jackie
  town: Lanford

Rosedale, Mr
character in: 15 The House of Mirth
author: 7 Wharton

Rosemary's Baby
director: 13 Roman Polanski
based on novel by: 8 Ira Levin
cast: 9 Mia Farrow **10** Ruth Gordon **14** John Cassavetes, Sidney Blackmer
Oscar for: 17 supporting actress (Gordon)

Rosenberg, Stuart
director of: 12 Cool Hand Luke

Rosenbloom, Maxie
nickname: 12 Slapsie Maxie
sport: 6 boxing
class: 16 light heavyweight

Rosencrantz
character in: 6 Hamlet
author: 11 Shakespeare

Rosenkavalier, Der
also: 18 The Knight of the Rose
opera by: 7 (Richard) Strauss
character: 6 Sophie **8** Octavian **9** Baron Ochs **11** Marschallin (Princess von Werderberg)

Rose of Sharon
character in: 16 The Grapes of Wrath
author: 9 Steinbeck

Rose Tattoo, The
director: 10 Daniel Mann
based on play by: 17 Tennessee Williams
cast: 11 Anna Magnani **13** Burt Lancaster
Oscar for: 7 actress (Magnani)

rosiness 5 bloom, blush, flush **7** redness **8** pinkness

Ross, Barney
real name: 14 Barnet Rosofsky
sport: 6 boxing
class: 12 welterweight

Ross, Herbert
director of: 14 The Goodbye Girl **15** The Turning Point

Ross, Katharine
born: 12 Los Angeles CA
aunt: 16 Katharine Hepburn

roles: 9 The Colbys **11** The Graduate **13** Stepford Wives **29** Butch Cassidy and the Sundance Kid

Rossellini, Roberto
director of: 6 Paisan **8** Open City **9** Stromboli **10** The Miracle **15** Germany Year Zero
wife: 13 Ingrid Bergman
daughter: 8 Isabella

Rossen, Robert
director of: 11 Body and Soul **14** All the King's Men

Rossetti, Dante Gabriel
author of: 17 The Blessed Damozel
born: 6 London **7** England
group: 14 Pre-Raphaelites
artwork: 12 Beata Beatrix **15** The Annunciation **17** Ecce Ancilla Domini

Rossini, Gioacchino Antonio
born: 5 Italy **6** Pesaro
composer of: 5 Moise **6** Otello **8** Tancredi **10** Le Comte Ory, Semiramide **11** William Tell **12** Mose in Egitto **13** Guillaume Tell, La Cenerentola **15** Barber of Seville **20** Il Barbiere di Siviglia **22** La Cambiale di Matrimonio

Rossner, Judith
author of: 11 Attachments **14** Ordinary People **19** Looking for Mr Goodbar

Rostand, Edmond
author of: 7 L'Aiglon **10** Chantecler **12** The Romancers **16** Cyrano de Bergerac

roster 4 list, roll **5** cadre, panel, slate **6** agenda, docket, muster, record **7** catalog, listing, posting **8** register, schedule **9** catalogue, directory

rostrum 4 dais **5** stage, stand, stump **6** podium, pulpit **7** lectern, soapbox **8** platform

rosy 4 pink **5** ruddy **6** bright, florid **7** flushed, glowing, hopeful, reddish **8** blooming, blushing, cheerful, cheering, flushing, inflamed, rubicund **9** confident, favorable, promising, reddening, rubescent **10** auspicious, felicitous, optimistic, propitious, reassuring **11** encouraging, high-colored, inspiriting **13** full of promise

Roszak, Theodore
born: 6 Poland, Poznan
artwork: 5 Raven, Surge **7** Anguish **9** Chrysalis, Scavenger, Sea Quarry **11** Sea Sentinel **12** Amorphic Form, Thorn Blossom **18** Specter of Kitty Hawk **20** The Whaler of Nantucket **27** Recollections of the Southwest

rot 3 mar **4** bosh, bull, bunk, harm, hurt, warp **5** decay, go bad, spoil, stain, taint, trash **6** damage, debase, defile, drivel, impair, infect, injure, jabber, molder, poison **7** blather, corrupt, crumble, deprave, inanity, pervert, pollute, putrefy, rubbish, twaddle **8** flummery, folderol, nonsense, putresce **9** absurdity, decompose, gibberish, moonshine, poppycock, purulence, putridity **10** balderdash, corruption, degenerate, deteriorate, putrescence **12** disintegrate, fiddle-faddle, gobbledygook, putrefaction **13** contamination, decomposition, deterioration **14** disintegration **16** stuff and nonsense

rotate 4 eddy, reel, roll, spin, turn **5** pivot, swirl, twirl, twist, wheel, whirl **6** change, circle, gyrate, swivel **7** revolve **9** alternate, circulate, pirouette **11** interchange

Roth, Philip
> **author of: 8** The Facts **15** Goodbye Columbus **16** The Anatomy Lesson, Zuckerman Unbound **17** Portnoy's Complaint

Rothko, Mark
> **born: 6** Dvinsk, Latvia, Russia **16** Daugavpils Latvia
> **artwork: 5** Light **12** Central Green, Earth and Blue **14** Four Darks in Red

rotten 3 bad **4** base, foul, rank **5** dirty, fetid, nasty, reeky, venal **6** filthy, putrid, rancid, scurvy **7** corrupt, crooked, decayed, devious, immoral, tainted, very bad, vicious **8** criminal, decaying, indecent, purulent, two-faced **9** deceitful, dishonest, dissolute, faithless, insincere, mercenary, moldering, putrefied, worm-eaten **10** decomposed, iniquitous, putrescent, scurrilous, unpleasant, villainous **11** decomposing, disgraceful, treacherous **12** contemptible, dishonorable, unforgivable, unscrupulous **13** double-dealing, untrustworthy

rotter 3 cad, cur, rat **4** heel **5** knave, louse, rogue **6** no-good, rascal **7** bounder, caitiff, villain **9** scoundrel

rotund 3 fat **5** obese, ovate, ovoid, plump, pudgy, round, stout, tubby **6** chubby, curved, fleshy, portly **7** bulbous, lumpish, rounded **8** circular, globular **9** corpulent, egg-shaped, spherical **10** potbellied **11** full-fleshed

Rouault, Georges
> **born: 5** Paris **6** France
> **artwork: 3** Mr X **5** Clown **8** Le Chahut, Miserere, Twilight **9** The Mirror **10** The Old King **11** Fleurs du mal, The Holy Face **12** Head of a Clown **13** Little Olympia **14** The Three Judges **19** Small Family of Clowns **22** Christ Mocked by Soldiers **26** Les Reincarnations du Pere Ubu **28** The Child Jesus among the Doctors

roue 3 cad, rip **4** rake, wolf **6** lecher, wanton **7** bounder, dallier, Don Juan, playboy, seducer, trifler **8** Casanova, debauche, Lothario, rakehell **9** libertine, womanizer **10** profligate **11** philanderer, skirt-chaser

Rouget de Lisle 17 French army officer

composer of: 14 La Marseillaise

rough 3 raw **4** beat, hard, rude, wild **5** bluff, blunt, bumpy, crude, cruel, draft, green, gruff, harsh, hasty, husky, quick, raspy, rocky, scaly, sharp, surly, tough, vague **6** abrupt, beat on, broken, brutal, callow, choppy, clumsy, coarse, craggy, crusty, gauche, hoarse, jagged, knotty, ragged, raging, roiled, rugged, savage, severe, stormy, thrash, turbid, uneven, vulgar **7** austere, awkward, bearish, boorish, brusque, chapped, coarsen, drastic, extreme, general, gnarled, grating, ill-bred, inexact, jarring, loutish, outline, rasping, raucous, scraggy, sketchy, stubbly, uncouth, unlevel, untamed, violent **8** agitated, churlish, rigorous, scabrous, scratchy, strident, ungentle, unsmooth **9** brutalize, difficult, ferocious, imperfect, imprecise, inelegant, irregular, manhandle, sketch out, stringent, turbulent, uncourtly, unfeeling, ungenteel, unmusical, unrefined **10** discordant, incomplete, indelicate, push around, tumultuous, unfinished, ungracious, unmannerly, unpleasant, unpolished **11** approximate, cacophonous, ill-mannered, preliminary, rudimentary, tempestuous, unluxurious **12** inharmonious **13** inconsiderate, uncomfortable, ungentlemanly

rough going 8 struggle **10** difficulty **11** arduousness **13** laboriousness

Roughing It
> **author: 9** Mark Twain
> **character: 12** Brigham Young, Hank Erickson **16** Slade the Terrible

rough it 4 camp **7** camp out

roughneck 4 hood, lout, punk **5** bully, rowdy, tough **6** vandal **7** hoodlum, ruffian **8** hooligan **9** barbarian **10** delinquent

roughness 7 crudity **8** acrimony, aviation, pungency, violence **9** gruffness, harshness, vulgarity **10** coarseness, inelegance, unevenness, unkindness **11** raucousness **12** irregularity, unsmoothness, unrefinement **13** undevelopment

Rough Riders *see* Roosevelt, Theodore

rough sketch 5 draft **7** cartoon, outline

rough-textured 5 harsh **6** coarse, nubbly, shaggy, tweedy **7** bristly, prickly **8** scratchy **9** bristling **10** sandpapery

round 3 fat **4** full, oval **5** cycle, obese, orbed, ovate, ovoid, plump, pudgy, stout, total, tubby, whole **6** chubby, circle, curved, entire, fluent, intact, portly, rotund, series, smooth **7** flowing, globoid, perfect, rounded **8** circular, complete, globular, resonant, sonorous, spheroid, thorough, unbroken

9 corpulent, egg-shaped, spherical, undivided **10** ball-shaped, elliptical, harmonious, pear-shaped, procession, succession **11** cylindrical, full-fleshed, mellifluent, progression

roundabout 5 wordy **6** random, zigzag **7** devious, erratic, oblique, sinuous, winding **8** indirect, rambling, tortuous, twisting **9** desultory **10** circuitous, discursive, meandering, serpentine **12** labyrinthine **14** circumlocutory

roundaboutness 9 wandering **10** digression, meandering **11** indirection **14** circuitousness, circumlocution

rounded 6 convex **7** curving **11** protuberant

rounding out 10 developing **12** augmentation **13** amplification

rounding-out 10 complement, completion, perfecting **12** consummation

rounds 4 beat **5** route, skirt, watch **7** circuit

roundup 6 muster, resume **7** meeting, summary **8** assembly **9** gathering **11** convocation

round up 6 gather, muster, summon **7** collect, convene, convoke, marshal **8** assemble **10** accumulate **12** call together

rouse 4 call, goad, move, prod, spur, stir, wake **5** arise, awake, get up, pique, rally, waken **6** awaken, excite, foment, kindle, incite, stir up, summon, turn on, wake up **7** animate, inflame, inspire, provoke, shake up **8** activate **9** galvanize, instigate, stimulate

roused 2 up **5** astir, awake **7** excited, incited, kindled, rallied, shook up **8** awakened, inflamed, inspired, out of bed, shaken up **9** stirred up **10** up and about

rousing 5 brisk, peppy **6** active, lively **8** animated, exciting, stirring, vigorous **9** awakening, inspiring **10** energizing, refreshing, remarkable **11** provocative, stimulating **12** exhilarating, intoxicating **13** extraordinary

Rousseau, Henri Julien Felix
> **nickname: 10** Le Douanier
> **born: 5** Laval **6** France
> **artwork: 3** War **8** The Dream **12** Child on Rocks, The Waterfall **13** The Hungry Lion **15** Carnival Evening, The Snake Charmer **16** Bouquet of Flowers, The Sleeping Gypsy **17** The Poet and his Muse

Rousseau, Jean Jacques
> **author of: 5** Emile **11** Confessions **17** La Nouvelle Heloise, The Social Contract

Rousseau, (Pierre Etienne) Theodore
> **born: 5** Paris **6** France
> **artwork: 7** Evening **12** After the Rain **15** Edge of the Forest, Under the

Birches **18** Descent of the Cattle, Oak Trees at Apremont **19** The Marsh in the Landes **20** The Valley of Tiffauges **21** Meadow Bordered by Trees

roust 4 bust **5** rouse **6** arrest, hassle **7** capture, seizure **12** apprehension

rout 4 beat, drub, lick, ruin, trim **5** chaos, cream, crush, panic, quell, repel, worst **6** defeat, subdue, thrash **7** beating, clobber, conquer, licking, repulse, scatter **8** drive off, drubbing, lambaste, overcome, vanquish **9** chase away, drive away, overpower, overthrow **11** put to flight **15** disorganization **18** throw into confusion

route 3 run **4** beat, pass, path, road, ship, tack **5** remit, round, track **6** artery, course, detour, direct **7** circuit, highway, parkway, passage, roadway **8** dispatch, transmit, turnpike **9** boulevard, itinerary **10** throughway **12** thoroughfare

Route 66
character: 8 Linc Case **9** Tod Stiles **10** Buz Murdock
cast: 12 Glenn Corbett, Martin Milner **13** George Maharis
car: 8 Corvette

routine 4 dull **5** order, usual **6** boring, custom, method, normal, system **7** formula, regular, tedious, typical **8** habitual, ordinary, periodic, practice **9** customary, operation, technique **11** arrangement, predictable **12** conventional, run-of-the-mill **13** unexceptional

rove 4 roam **5** drift, prowl, range **6** ramble, stroll, travel, wander **7** meander, traipse **9** gallivant

roving 6 errant **7** aimless, gadding, migrant, nomadic, roaming, vagrant **8** errantry, rambling, restless **9** desultory, itinerant, traveling, uncertain, wandering **10** changeable, discursive, meandering, inconstant **11** peripatetic **14** discursiveness

row 4 file, line, rank, spat, tier, tiff **5** brawl, chain, melee, queue, range, scrap, set-to, train, words **6** column, fracas, scrape, series, string **7** echelon, quarrel, wrangle **8** argument, disorder, sequence, squabble **9** imbroglio, wrangling **10** difference, succession **11** altercation, contretemps

rowboat 3 gig **4** bark, dory **5** barge, canoe, dingy, scull, shell, skiff **6** barque, caique, dinghy, wherry
seat: 4 taft

rowdy 6 unruly **7** lawless, raffish **9** roughneck **10** boisterous, disorderly **11** mischievous **12** obstreperous

Rowena, Lady
character in: 7 Ivanhoe
author: 5 Scott

rowing
athlete: 10 James Dietz **14** Anthony Johnson

Rowlands, Gena
real name: 23 Virginia Cathryn Rowlands
born: 9 Cambria WI
husband: 14 John Cassavetes
roles: 5 Faces **12** Opening Night **23** A Woman Under the Influence

Roxana
subtitle: 20 The Fortunate Mistress
author: 11 Daniel Defoe

Roxane see Cyrano de Bergerac

royal 5 grand, regal **6** august, lavish, superb **7** stately **8** imposing, majestic, splendid **9** monarchal, sovereign **10** munificent **11** fit for a king, magnificent, resplendent

royalty 4 sway **7** command, majesty **8** dominion, hegemony, kingship, regality **9** queenship, supremacy **11** divine right, sovereignty

Royaume de Belgique see **7** Belgium

Roy Rogers Show, The
regular: 8 Pat Brady **9** Dale Evans
theme: 16 Happy Trails to You
horse: 7 Trigger
dog: 6 Bullet
jeep: 10 Nellybelle
ranch: 10 Double R Bar

Ruanda see **6** Rwanda

rub 4 buff, swab, wipe **5** annoy, braze, catch, chafe, clean, hitch, knead, pinch, scour, scrub, smear, thing, touch, trick **6** abrade, finger, handle, polish, secret, smooth, spread, strait, stroke **7** burnish, dilemma, massage, problem, rubdown, setback, slather, trouble **8** handling, hardship, kneading, obstacle, stroking **10** difficulty, impediment, manipulate **12** manipulation

Rubaiyat of Omar Khayyam, The
author: 11 Omar Khayyam
translator: 16 Edward FitzGerald

rubber, vulcanized
invented by: 8 Goodyear

rubber plant 13 Ficus elastica
varieties: 4 baby **5** dwarf **7** Chinese **8** American, creeping, Japanese **9** mistletoe **11** small-leaved **16** broad-leaved India

rubberstamp 6 affirm **7** approve, endorse

rubber tree 10 Schefflera
varieties: 4 Para **5** India **8** Castilla **11** West African

rubbery 5 tough **6** supple **7** elastic **8** flexible **9** resilient **11** stretchable

rubbing 7 chafing **8** abrading, scraping **12** manipulation

rubbish 3 rot **4** bosh, junk **5** dross, offal, trash, waste **6** babble, debris, drivel, idiocy, jetsam, litter, refuse, rubble **7** blather, garbage, inanity, twaddle **8** folderol, nonsense **9** gibberish, rigmarole, silliness **10** balderdash, flapdoodle, rigamarole

rubbish heap 4 dump **6** midden **10** refuse pile

rubble 4 junk, rock **5** brash, chalk, stent, stone, talus, trash **6** debris, refuse **7** rubbish **8** nonsense **9** fragments **11** foolishness

rube 3 oaf **4** boor, clod, hick **5** yokel **6** rustic **7** bumpkin, hayseed, peasant **10** clodhopper

Rube Goldberg 10 cartoonist
known for: 23 complicated contraptions

rub elbows 3 mix **4** club **6** hobnob, mingle **7** consort, hang out **9** associate **10** fraternize

Rubens, Peter Paul
born: 6 Siegen **10** Westphalia
artwork: 8 Lion Hunt **10** The Rainbow **15** The Garden of Love **17** Laocoon and his Sons **18** Battle of the Amazons **20** The Raising of the Cross **21** Landscape with Het Steen **22** The Descent from the Cross **23** Altarpiece of St Aldefonso **26** The Adoration of the Shepherds **27** Marchesa Brigida Spinola-Doria, Mystic Marriage of St Catherine **29** Rape of the Daughters of Leucippus **34** Helene Fourment with Two of her Children

rubicund 3 red **4** rosy **5** ruddy **6** florid **7** flushed, reddish

rubidium
chemical symbol: 2 Rb

rub out 4 do in, kill, slay **5** erase **6** efface, murder **7** bump off, destroy, execute, expunge **8** massacre **10** obliterate, put to death **11** assassinate, exterminate

ruby
species: 8 corundum
source: 5 Burma, India, Mogok **7** Bangkok, Kashmir **8** Sri Lanka, Thailand
kind: 4 star
color: 3 red

ruckus 3 row **4** fray, to-do **5** brawl, broil, clash, fight, melee **6** battle, fracas, rumpus, uproar **7** scuffle **9** imbroglio **10** donnybrook, free-for-all **11** embroilment

ruddy 3 red **4** rosy **6** florid **7** flushed, reddish, roseate, scarlet **8** blushing, rubicund, sanguine **11** rosy-cheeked

rude 3 raw **4** wild **5** blunt, crude, fresh, green, gross, gruff, rough, saucy, sulky, surly **6** abrupt, callow, clumsy, coarse, crusty, gauche, homely, rugged, rustic, sullen, uneven, vulgar **7** abusive, artless, awkward, boorish, brusque, brutish, ill-bred, loutish, profane, scraggy, uncivil, uncouth **8** churlish, homebred, ignorant, impolite, impudent, indecent, insolent, slapdash, untaught **9** inelegant, insulting, makeshift, primitive, roughhewn, uncourtly, ungallant, unlearned, unrefined, untrained, untutored **10** illiterate, indecorous, indelicate, peremptory, provincial, uncultured, uneducated, ungraceful, ungracious, unladylike, unmannerly, unpolished **11** bad-mannered, countrified, impertinent, uncivilized, uncourteous, undignified **12** discourteous, roughly built **13** disrespectful, inconsiderate, ungentlemanly

rudeness 9 bluntness, impudence, insolence, sauciness **10** bad manners, coarseness, disrespect, incivility **11** boorishness, discourtesy **12** impertinence, impoliteness **14** ungraciousness **17** inconsiderateness

rudimentary 5 basic **6** simple **7** initial, primary **8** immature **9** elemental, formative, imperfect, premature, primitive, vestigial **10** elementary, incomplete, prototypal **11** undeveloped

rudiments 6 basics **7** essence **8** elements **9** beginning **10** principles **12** fundamentals

Rudkus, Jurgis and Antanas
characters in: 9 The Jungle
author: 8 Sinclair

Rudolph, Paul
architect of: 16 Jewett Arts Center (Wellesley College) **24** Government Services Center (Boston) **28** School of Architecture Building (Yale)

rue 4 Ruta
varieties: 4 bush, lady, wall **5** goat's **6** common, meadow **10** tall meadow **11** early meadow **12** Alpine meadow

rue 5 mourn **6** bemoan, lament, regret, repent, repine **7** deplore

rueful 3 sad **5** sorry **6** woeful **7** doleful **8** contrite, mournful, dolorous, penitent, repining **9** depressed, plaintive, regretful, sorrowful, sorrowing **10** deplorable, lamentable, melancholy, remorseful, unpleasant

ruff 9 sandpiper
female: 3 ree

ruffian 4 hood, thug **5** brute, bully, crook, knave, rogue, rough, rowdy, tough **6** mugger **7** hoodlum, villain **8** gangster, hooligan **9** cutthroat, roisterer, roughneck, scoundrel **10** blackguard

ruffle 4 fold, muss, wave **5** frill, plait, pleat, ruche, upset **6** edging, excite, muss up, pucker, rimple, ripple, rumple **7** agitate, confuse, crinkle, disturb, flounce, perturb, roughen, trouble, wrinkle **8** dishevel, disorder, disquiet, furbelow, unsettle **9** aggravate, agitation, commotion, corrugate **10** disarrange, discompose, disconcert **11** disturbance

ruffled 5 upset, vexed **7** annoyed, frilled, nettled, pleated **8** agitated, flounced, troubled **9** nonplused, unsettled **10** nonplussed

ruffle one's feathers 3 vex **5** anger, annoy, pique **6** enrage, madden, nettle **7** incense, outrage, provoke **9** displease, infuriate

Rugg
character in: 12 Little Dorrit
author: 7 Dickens

rugged 4 hale, hard, rude, wiry, worn **5** bumpy, hardy, harsh, husky, lined, rocky, rough, stern, tough **6** brawny, coarse, craggy, jagged, ridged, robust, severe, sinewy, sturdy, taxing, trying, uneven, virile **7** arduous, cragged, onerous, scraggy, uncouth **8** athletic, furrowed, muscular, stalwart, vigorous, wrinkled **9** difficult, graceless, irregular, laborious, masculine, roughhewn, strenuous, unrefined, weathered **12** uncultivated **13** weather-beaten

Ruggles of Red Gap
director: 10 Leo McCarey
cast: 9 ZaSu Pitts **10** Mary Boland **14** Charlie Ruggles **15** Charles Laughton
remade as: 10 Fancy Pants

ruin, ruins 3 gut, pot **4** doom, fall, fell, harm, raze, seed **5** break, crush, decay, level, quash, quell, shell, spoil, upset, wreck **6** beggar, defeat, ravage, squash **7** destroy, failure, remains, shatter, undoing **8** bankrupt, demolish, downfall, lay waste, make poor, overturn, remnants, wreckage **9** breakdown, devastate, disrepair, overthrow, pauperize **10** impoverish **11** destruction, devastation, dissolution **14** disintegration

ruination 4 ruin **5** wreck **6** fiasco **7** trouble **8** disaster **9** adversity, cataclysm **11** destruction, devastation **12** misadventure

ruinous 4 dire **5** fatal **6** deadly **7** adverse, baneful **8** damaging, ravaging **10** calamitous, disastrous, pernicious **11** cataclysmic, deleterious, destructive, devastating **12** catastrophic

Ruisdael, Jacob (Jakob) van
born: 7 Haarlem **14** The Netherlands
uncle: 18 Salomon van Ruysdael
artwork: 5 Dunes **12** The Waterfall **13** View of Haarlem **14** Bentheim Castle **15** Winter Landscape **17** The Jewish Cemetery **28** View on the Amstel near Amsterdam

rule 3 law, run **4** find, form, head, lead, sway **5** adage, axiom, canon, guide, judge, maxim, model, order, reign **6** custom, decide, decree, direct, empire, govern, manage, method, policy, regime, settle, system **7** adjudge, command, control, declare, formula, precept, prevail, resolve, routine **8** conclude, doctrine, dominate, domineer, dominion, pass upon, practice, regnancy, regulate, standard **9** authority, criterion, determine, direction, establish, guideline, influence, ordinance, precedent, principle,

pronounce, supremacy **10** adjudicate, administer, convention, domination, government, leadership, regulation, suzerainty **11** predominate, preside over, sovereignty **12** jurisdiction, prescription **14** administration
type: 5 bench **7** folding **9** steel tape
constellation of: 5 Norma

rule out 4 omit **6** delete, except **7** exclude **9** eliminate

ruler 4 boss, czar, emir, head, khan, king, lord, shah, tsar, tzar **5** chief, judge, queen, rajah, sheik **6** dynast, leader, prince, satrap, shogun, sultan **7** arbiter, emperor, manager, measure, monarch, pharaoh, referee, viceroy **8** chairman, director, governor, suzerain **9** chieftain, commander, potentate, president, sovereign, yardstick **10** controller, supervisor **11** coordinator, crowned head, head of state, tape measure **12** straightedge **13** administrator

rules of conduct 6 ethics **9** moral code **10** principles **12** code of ethics

Rules of the Game
director: 10 Jean Renoir
cast: 10 Jean Renoir, Mila Parely, Nora Gregor **11** Marcel Dalio

ruling 6 decree **7** regnant **8** decision, dominant, reigning **9** enactment, governing, prescript **10** commanding, widespread **11** controlling, predominant **13** authoritative, predominating

ruling class 11 aristocracy **13** Establishment

Ruling Class, The
director: 10 Peter Medak
cast: 10 Arthur Lowe **11** Alastair Sim, Peter O'Toole **12** Harry Andrews

rum
drink: 4 Bolo, Grog **6** Mojito **7** Gauguin **8** Daiquiri, Navy Grog, Pina Fria **9** Borinquen, Hurricane **10** Pina Colada **12** Boston Cooler **13** Planter's Punch **14** Fish House Punch **15** Bacardi Cocktail **18** Barbados Rum Swizzle
ingredient: 8 molasses **9** sugar cane
origin: 10 West Indies
type: 4 dark **5** light
with apple brandy: 6 Bolero **8** Apple Pie
with apricot brandy: 11 Apricot Lady
with black coffee: 9 Black Rose
with bouillon: 6 Creole
with bourbon: 14 Artillery Punch
with brandy: 15 Quaker's Cocktail
with Cointreau: 8 Acapulco **10** Casa Blanca **11** Beachcomber **12** Blue Hawaiian
with cola: 9 Cuba Libre
with creme de cacao: 6 Panama
with curacao: 6 Mai-Tai **8** Blue Lady **12** Blue Hawaiian
with Dubonnet: 3 BVD **10** Bushranger

with Galliano: 9 Bossa Nova
with gin: 3 BVD
with guava: 8 Ocho Rios
with kahlua: 10 Black Maria
with milk: 6 Rum Cow **11** Tom-and-Jerry
with Pernod: 8 Shanghai
with sloe gin: 11 Shark's Tooth
with Tia Maria: 10 Black Maria
with vermouth: 6 Bolero **8** Apple Pie **10** Black Devil **11** Shark's Tooth

rumble 4 bang, boom, clap, roar, roll **7** booming, resound, thunder **8** drumming **9** resonance **11** reverberate **13** reverberation

Rumford, Benjamin Thomson
invented: 10 photometer **11** calorimeter

Rumina
protectress of: 14 nursing mothers

ruminant 3 cow, elk, yak **4** deer, oxen **5** bison, camel, llama, moose, sheep **6** alpaca, cattle, vicuna **7** buffalo, giraffe, pensive **8** antelope **10** chevrotain, meditative, thoughtful **13** contemplative

ruminate 4 mull, muse **5** brood, study, think, weigh **6** ponder **7** reflect **8** cogitate, consider, meditate, mull over **9** speculate, think over **10** deliberate, think about **11** contemplate

ruminating 6 musing **7** pensive **8** thinking **10** meditating, meditative, reflecting, reflective, thoughtful **11** chewing over, mulling over, speculative **13** contemplating, contemplative, introspective

rumination 5 study **6** musing **7** mulling, reverie, thought **8** brooding, thinking **9** pondering **10** cogitation, meditation, reflection **11** speculation **12** deliberation **13** consideration, contemplation **15** reconsideration

rummage 4 root **5** probe **7** examine, explore, ransack **10** disarrange, poke around **11** look through

rummy 3 sot **4** lush, soak **5** drunk, souse, toper **6** barfly, boozer **7** tippler **8** card game, drunkard **9** alcoholic **11** dipsomaniac
also known as: 3 gin, rum **4** rhum **5** romme **8** gin rummy
derived from: 8 conquien

rumor 4 talk **5** story **6** babble, gossip, report **7** hearsay, whisper **8** innuendo, intimate **9** circulate, insinuate **11** insinuation, scuttlebutt, supposition

rump 4 rear, seat **5** croup, stern **6** behind, bottom, breech, dorsum **7** rear end **8** backside, buttocks, derriere, haunches **9** posterior **12** hindquarters

Rumpelstiltskin
origin: 8 Germanic
form: 5 dwarf
spun: 4 flax
made: 4 gold

rumple 4 fold, muss **5** crimp, crush **6**

crease, pucker, rimple, ruffle, tousle **7** crinkle, crumple, wrinkle **8** dishevel, disorder **9** corrugate **10** disarrange

rumpus 3 ado, row **4** fray, fuss, stir, to-do **5** brawl, melee, noise **6** affray, fracas, hubbub, pother, racket, ruckus, tumult, uproar **7** rhubarb, scuffle, tempest **8** brouhaha, upheaval **9** agitation, commotion, confusion, imbroglio **10** hullabaloo **11** disturbance, embroilment

run 2 be, go **3** fly, get, hie, jog, pen, ply **4** bolt, boss, cost, dart, dash, defy, flee, flow, go by, head, kind, last, meet, melt, pass, pour, push, race, roll, rush, sort, tear, tour, trip, trot, type, vary **5** bleed, bound, class, court, drift, drive, genre, glide, hurry, impel, incur, issue, leave, pilot, print, speed, spell, split, stand, surge, total, while **6** become, canter, course, decamp, direct, elapse, endure, escape, extend, gallop, hasten, hustle, invite, ladder, manage, motion, move on, outing, period, pierce, propel, scurry, series, sprint, streak, stream, thrust, vanish, voyage, wander **7** abscond, add up to, advance, bring on, compete, current, display, freedom, get past, journey, liquefy, meander, operate, oversee, passage, proceed, publish, running, scamper, stretch, take off, vamoose **8** amount to, campaign, continue, dissolve, duration, evanesce, maneuver, meet with, navigate, progress, scramble, separate, tendency **9** direction, disappear, enclosure, encounter, excursion, go quickly, lose color, penetrate, skedaddle, supervise **10** coordinate, pilgrimage **11** continuance **12** beat a retreat, continuation, perpetuation
baseball: 5 point, score, tally **17** circuit of the bases

run aground 7 founder **8** collapse

runaround 4 slip **5** dodge **6** bypass **7** evasion **8** shunning, sidestep **9** avoidance **11** elusiveness, evasiveness **12** equivocation

run around 7 consort, hang out **9** associate, pal around **10** fraternize

runaway 4 pure **6** bolter **7** escapee, perfect, refugee **8** absolute, complete, deserter, fugitive **9** out-and-out, unalloyed **10** skedaddler **11** unmitigated, unqualified

run away 3 fly **4** flee **5** elope **6** decamp, escape, run off **7** abscond, make off **8** sneak off **10** fly the coop, make a break, take flight **12** make a getaway

rundown 5 brief **6** digest, precis, resume, review, sketch **7** outline, summary **8** abstract, synopsis **12** capitulation, condensation

run-down 5 frail, seedy, tacky, tired, weary **6** ailing, beat-up, feeble,

shabby, sickly **7** rickety, worn out **8** fatigued, tattered **9** crumbling, exhausted **10** broken-down, tumbledown **11** dilapidated **12** deteriorated

run down 4 scan **5** knock **6** slight **7** detract, put down, run over **8** belittle, derogate, ridicule **9** denigrate, deprecate, discredit, disparage, downgrade, enumerate, underrate **10** depreciate, undervalue

run-in 5 brush, set-to **6** battle, fracas **7** scuffle **8** skirmish **9** encounter **10** engagement

run into 4 meet **8** flow into **9** encounter **10** chance upon, meet up with **11** collide with

run off 3 fly **4** flee **5** elope **6** escape **7** abscond, make off, runaway **9** steal away **10** take flight **15** head for the hills

run off at the mouth 3 gab **5** prate **6** babble, gabble **8** rattle on **11** talk too much

run off with 5 seize **6** abduct, kidnap **7** bear off **8** carry off **9** elope with **11** abscond with, make off with

run-of-the-mill 4 dull, so-so **5** banal, stock, usual **6** common, modest **7** average, humdrum, mundane, routine, typical **8** everyday, mediocre, middling, ordinary, passable, standard **10** second-rate **11** commonplace, indifferent, nondescript **12** unimpressive **13** unimaginative **15** undistinguished

runt 3 elf **4** chit **5** dwarf, pygmy **6** midget, peewee, shrimp **8** half-pint, Tom Thumb **11** Lilliputian
Latin: 10 homunculus

run through 5 spend, waste **6** expend, pierce **7** deplete, exhaust **8** rehearse, squander

runty 5 short **6** bantam **7** dwarfed, squatty, stunted **9** pint-sized

Runyon, Damon
author of: 12 Guys and Dolls **16** Blue Plate Special

rupture 3 pop **4** part, rent, rift, snap **5** break, burst, clash, cleft, crack, split **6** breach, divide, schism, sunder **7** discord, disrupt, fissure **8** breaking, bursting, cleavage, dissever, disunion, disunite, fracture, friction, puncture **9** severance **10** dissension, falling out, separation **12** disagreement

R U R
author: 10 Karel Capek **22** Rossum's Universal Robots

rural 4 hick **6** rustic **7** bucolic, country **8** pastoral **10** provincial **11** countrified

rural area 6 sticks **7** boonies, country **8** farmland **9** backwater, backwoods, boondocks **10** hinterland **11** countryside

ruse 4 hoax **5** blind, dodge, feint, shift, trick **6** deceit, device, scheme **8** artifice, maneuver **9** deception, stratagem

10 subterfuge **11** contrivance, machination

rush 3 hie, run **4** dart, dash, goad, leap, push, race, spur, tear, urge, whip **5** drive, haste, hurry, press, speed, storm **6** charge, hasten, hustle, plunge, scurry, sprint, urgent **7** scamper, urgency **8** dispatch, expedite, pressure, scramble **9** emergency **10** accelerate **11** top priority

rush 6 Juncus
  varieties: 3 bog **4** salt, soft, wood **5** spike **6** grassy **8** scouring **9** field wood, flowering **10** common wood, least spike **11** chair-maker's, greater wood, Japanese-mat **12** slender spike **13** dwarf scouring **14** common scouring **18** variegated scouring

Rush, Benjamin
  field: 8 medicine
  established first: 21 free medical dispensary
  signer of: 25 Declaration of Independence

rush light 3 dip **5** torch **6** candle, tallow

Rushworth
  character in: 13 Mansfield Park
  author: 6 Austen

Ruskin, John
  author of: 13 Fors Clavigera **14** Modern Painters **17** The Stones of Venice **27** The Seven Lamps of Architecture

Russell, Bertrand
  author of: 19 Why I Am Not a Christian **20** Principia Mathematica (with Alfred North)

Russell, Jane
  real name: 29 Ernestine Jane Geraldine Russell
  born: 9 Bemidji MN
  discovered by: 12 Howard Hughes
  roles: 4 Waco **9** The Outlaw **13** The French Line **22** Gentlemen Prefer Blondes, The Revolt of Mamie Stover

Russell, Rosalind
  born: 11 Waterbury CT
  roles: 5 Gypsy **6** Picnic **8** The Women **9** Hired Wife **10** Auntie Mame **11** Sister Kenny **13** His Girl Friday **14** My Sister Eileen **22** Mourning Becomes Electra

russet 5 apple, umber **6** auburn, copper **10** terra-cotta **11** rust-colored **12** reddish-brown

Russia (includes constituent republics of the former USSR)
  other name: 17 Russian Federation
  former name: 4 USSR **11** Soviet Union **31** Union of Soviet Socialist Republics
  member of: 3 CIS **31** Commonwealth of Independent States
  capital/largest city: 6 Moscow
  others: 4 Baku, Eisk, Kiev, Okha, Omsk, Poti, Riga **5** Anapa, Batum, Gorki, Gorky, Memel, Minsk, Sochi, Vilna, Yeisk **6** Batumi, Erevan, Frunze, Odessa, Rostov, Samara, Tiflis **7** Alma-Ata, Derbent, Donetsk, Kharkov, Liepaja, Petsamo, Pivonia, Saratov, Tallinn, Tbilisi, Yerevan **8** Dushanbe, Kishinev, Murmansk, Pechenga, Taganrog, Tashkent **9** Ashkhabad, Astrakhan, Balaklava, Kronstadt, Kuibyshev, Leningrad, Nikolayev, Petrograd, Ulyanovsk, Volgograd, Yaroslavl **10** Kronshtadt, Sevastopol, Stalingrad, Sverdlovsk **11** Chelyabinsk, Kaliningrad, Makhachkala, Novorossisk, Novosibirsk, Vladivostok **12** St Petersburg, Vladisvostok **14** Dnepropetrovsk
  division/country: 6 Latvia **7** Armenia, Belarus, Estonia, Georgia, Moldova, Siberia, Ukraine **8** Moldavia **9** Kirghizia, Lithuania, Turkmenia **10** Azerbaijan, Belorussia, Kazakhstan, Kyrgyzstan, Tajikistan, Uzbekistan **12** Tadzhikistan, Turkmenistan
    former: 4 Kiev **8** Novgorod
  government:
    legislature: 4 Duma, Rada **7** Zemstvo **8** Congress
  measure: 3 fut, lof **4** duim, fass, loof, pood, quar, stof **5** duime, foute, korec, korek, ligne, osmin, pajak, stoff, stoof, vedro, verst **6** charka, liniya, osmina, paletz, sagene, stekar, tchast, tsarki, versta, verste **7** archine, arsheen, botchka, chkalik, garnetz, verchoc, verchok **8** boutylka, chetvert, krouchka, kroushka **9** chetverik **10** dessiatine **11** polugarnetz
  monetary unit: 5 altin, bisti, copec, denga, grosh, kopek, ruble, shaur **6** abassi, copeck, grivna, kopeck, piatak, rouble **7** poltina, valiuta **8** auksinas, deneshka, imperial, polushka **9** poltinnik **10** altininink, chervonets
  weight: 3 lof, lot **4** dola, funt, lana, last, loof, loth, once, pood, poud **5** dolia
  island: 5 Kuril **7** Hiiumaa, Karagin, Shantar, Vaygach, Wrangel **8** Kolguyev, Saaremaa, Sakhalin **9** Andreanof **12** Novaya Zemlya **13** Komandorskiye **14** Franz Josef Land, Novosibirskiye **15** Severnaya Zemlya
  lake: 3 Seg **4** Aral, Azov, Kola, Sego, Topo, Vigo **5** Chany, Elton, Erara, Ilmen, Lacha, Onega, Pskov, Vozhe **6** Baikal, Byeloe, Ladoga, Peipus, Selety, Taymyr, Tengiz, Zaysan **8** Balkhash **10** Caspian Sea
  mountain: 5 Altai, Lenin, Sayan, Urals **6** Anadyr, Elbrus, Koryak, Pamirs, Pobedy **7** Belukha, Crimean, Khibiny, Stanovi, Zhiguli **8** Caucasus, Dzhughur, Stanavoi, Tien Shan **9** Kopet Dagh, Narodnaya, Pamir-Alai, Yablonovy **10** Carpathian **11** Sikhote-Alin, Verkhoyansk
  highest point: 9 Communism

  river: 3 Don, Ili **4** Amur, Lena, Neva, Ural **5** Dvina, Kuban, Neman, Volga **6** Kolyma, Moskva **7** Dnieper, Pechora, Yenisei **8** Amu Darya, Dniester, Ob-Irtysh, Syr Darya **9** Indigirka
  sea: 4 Aral, Azov, Kara **5** Black, Japan, White **6** Arctic, Baltic, Bering, Laptev **7** Barents, Caspian, Chukchi, Okhotsk, Pacific
  physical feature:
    gulf: 4 Azov **5** Mezen **9** Kara-Bogaz, Shelikhov
    peninsula: 4 Kola **5** Yamal **6** Crimea, Taymyr **7** Chukchi, Karelia **9** Kamchatka **10** Mangyshlak
    strait: 5 Tatar **6** Bering **8** Bosporus **11** Dardanelles
  people: 3 Jew **4** Slav **5** Ersar, Kulak, Tatar, Uzbec **6** Kazakh, Soviet, Velika **7** Chukchi, Cossack, Kirghiz, Latvian, Russian, Tadzhik, Turkmen **8** Armenian, Estonian, Georgian, Siberian **9** Moldavian, Ukrainian **10** Lithuanian **11** Azerbaijani, Belorussian
    actor: 12 Stanislavsky
    author: 5 Gogol **7** Nabokov, Pushkin, Tolstoy **8** Turgenev **9** Ehrenburg, Pasternak, Sholokhov **10** Dostoevsky **12** Solzhenitsyn
    composer: 6 Glinka **7** Borodin **9** Prokofiev **10** Mussorgsky, Stravinsky **11** Tchaikovsky **12** Rachmaninoff, Shostakovich **14** Rimsky-Korsakov
    cosmonaut: 11 Yuri Gagarin
    czar/tsar/tzar: 4 Ivan, Paul **5** Peter **6** Alexis **7** Michael **8** Nicholas **9** Alexander **12** Boris Godunov
    dancer: 7 Nureyev, Pavlova **8** Danilova, Nijinsky **11** Baryshnikov
    dynasty: 7 Romanov
    early people: 3 Hun **4** Goth **5** Tatar **6** Khazar, Mongol, Tartar **8** Norsemen, Scythian **9** Cimmerian, Sarmatian, Varangian
    empress: 9 Alexandra, Catherine
    hereditary noble: 5 boyar
    leader: 5 Beria, Lenin **6** Stalin, Suslov **7** Gromyko, Kosygin, Molotov, Trotsky, Yeltsin **8** Andropov, Brezhnev, Bukharin, Bulganin, Kerensky, Malenkov, Podgorny **9** Chernenko, Gorbachev **10** Khrushchev
    monk: 8 Rasputin
    prince: 4 Oleg **5** Rurik **8** Vladimir
    revolutionary: 9 bolshevik **10** Decembrist
    ruler: 5 Tatar **6** Mongol **8** Batu Khan
    scientist: 6 Pavlov **9** Mendeleev **11** Tsiolkovsky
  language: 5 Evenk, Tatar, Uzbek **6** Buriat, Kalmyk, Kazakh **7** Finnish, Kirghiz, Latvian, Russian, Tadzhik, Turkmen **8** Armenian, Estonian, Georgian, Ossetian **9** Moldavian,

Ukrainian **10** Lithuanian **11** Belorussian
  alphabet: 8 cyrillic
religion: 5 Islam **7** Judaism **8** Buddhism, Lutheran **10** Protestant **13** Roman Catholic **15** Russian Orthodox **16** Armenian Orthodox, Georgian Orthodox
place: 7 Kremlin **9** Red Square
  art gallery: 9 Tretyakov
  castle: 8 Starosty
  cathedral: 5 Sobor **7** Zagorsk **8** St Basils
  cemetery: 11 Piskarevsky
  museum: 9 Hermitage **12** Petrodvorets **18** Cathedral of St Isaac
  palace: 6 Winter
  park: 5 Gorky
  ruins: 7 Bukhara **10** Echmiadzin **15** Gediminas Castle
  prison: 8 Lubyanka
  street: 11 Kreshchatik **14** Nevski Prospekt
  theater: 7 Bolshoi
feature:
  collective farm: 7 kolkhoz
  country house: 5 dacha
  dance: 4 kolo **5** gopac, hopak, saber **6** cossac, trepak **7** cosaque, ziganka **8** kozachok **9** tzazatski
  dance company: 5 Kirov **7** Bolshoi
  labor camp: 5 gulag
  musical instrument: 9 balalaika
  secret police: 3 KGB, MGB **4** NKVD, OGPU **5** Cheka
  state farm: 7 sovkhoz
food:
  caviar: 13 ikra zernistia
  cereal: 5 kasha
  sour cream: 7 smetana
  dessert: 8 vareniki
  dish: 4 plov **5** pirau **6** pelemo **8** osetrina, shashlyk **16** kotleta po kievski
  drink: 4 kvas **5** kvass, vodka **6** chacha, kumiss
  filled pastries: 8 piroshki, pirozhki
  soup: 5 shchi **6** borshch **7** borscht, borsh

Russian village commune 3 mir

rust 3 rot **5** decay, stain **6** auburn, blight, russet **7** corrode, crumble, decline, oxidize **9** corrosion, oxidation **11** deteriorate **12** reddish-brown **13** reddish-yellow

rust-colored 5 henna **6** auburn, russet **8** cinnamon **12** reddish-brown

rustic 4 rube, rude **5** crude, plain, rough, rural, yokel **6** coarse, gauche, simple **7** awkward, boorish, bucolic, bumpkin, country, hayseed, loutish, peasant, uncouth **8** agrarian, churlish, cloddish, pastoral **9** inelegant, unrefined **10** clodhopper, countryman, provincial, uncultured, unpolished **11**
countrified **13** country person **15** unsophisticated

rustle 3 rub **4** hiss, stir **5** swish, whish **6** riffle

rustler 5 thief **6** bandit, outlaw **7** brigand **9** desperado

rusty 5 moldy, stiff **6** rotten, rusted **7** reddish, tainted **8** corroded, sluggish **11** rust-colored **13** out of practice

rut 3 cut **4** mark **5** ditch, habit, score, tread **6** furrow, groove, gutter, hollow, trench, trough **7** channel, depress, dig into, pattern **8** monotony **9** deep track **10** depression **11** dull routine

Ruth
  husband: 4 Boaz **6** Mahlon
  son: 4 Obed
  father-in-law: 9 Elimelech
  mother-in-law: 5 Naomi
  brother-in-law: 7 Chilion

Ruth, George Herman
  nickname: 4 Babe **12** Sultan of Swat
  sport: 8 baseball
  position: 8 outfield
  team: 14 New York Yankees

Rutherford, Dame Margaret
  born: 6 London **7** England
  roles: 7 The VIPs **10** Jane Marple **12** Blithe Spirit **27** The Importance of Being Earnest

Rutherford, Ernest
  field: 7 physics
  nationality: 7 British
  discovered: 6 proton **13** atomic nucleus, beta radiation **14** alpha radiation, gamma radiation
  awarded: 10 Nobel Prize

ruthless 5 cruel, harsh **6** brutal, deadly, savage **7** bestial, brutish, callous, inhuman, vicious **8** pitiless **9** barbarous, ferocious, heartless, merciless, murderous, unfeeling, unpitying, unsparing **10** relentless, sanguinary, unmerciful **11** cold-blooded, hardhearted, remorseless, unforgiving, unrelenting **12** bloodthirsty

ruthlessness 7 cruelty **9** barbarity, brutality, harshness **10** inhumanity, savageness **11** viciousness

Ruysdael, Salomon van
  born: 7 Naarden **14** The Netherlands
  nephew: 16 Jacob van Ruisdael
  artwork: 9 River Bank **10** River Scene **14** River Landscape **18** River with Ferry Boat

Rwanda
  other name: 6 Ruanda
  capital/largest city: 6 Kigali
  others: 6 Biumba, Butare, Kibuye, Nyanza **7** Astrida, Gisenyi, Kibungu **8** Cyangugu **9** Ruhengeri
  division:
    colonial: 12 Ruanda-Urundi
monetary unit: 5 franc **7** centime
lake: 4 Kivu **5** Ihema **6** Bufera, Bulera, Mohasi **7** Rugwero, Ruhnodo **8** Mugesera, Tshohoha
mountain: 7 Mitumba, Virunga **8** Muhavura
highest point: 9 Karisimbi
river: 6 Kagera, Ruzizi **7** Akagera **8** Akanyaru **9** Luvironza **10** Nyawarongo
physical feature:
  forest: 7 Nyungwe
  valley: 11 Western Rift
people: 3 Twa **4** Hutu **5** Batwa, Pygmy, Tutsi **6** Bahutu, Watusi **7** Batutsi
  explorer: 5 Speke **6** Gotzen
  leader: 9 Kayibanda **11** Habyarimana
language: 6 French **7** Swahili **11** Kinyarwanda
religion: 7 animism **13** Roman Catholic
place:
  game reserve: 6 Gabiro
  park: 6 Albert, Kagera **16** Virunga Volcanoes
feature:
  clothing: 5 pagne
  king: 5 mwami

Ryan, Cornelius
  author of: 13 A Bridge Too Far, The Last Battle, The Longest Day

Ryan, Robert
  born: 9 Chicago IL
  roles: 6 Caught **8** The Set-Up **9** Billy Budd, Crossfire **12** Clash by Night, The Wild Bunch **13** Act of Violence, The Longest Day **14** About Mrs Leslie, God's Little Acre **17** Bad Day at Black Rock **18** The Woman on the Beach

Ryder, Albert Pinkham
  born: 12 New Bedford MA
  artwork: 12 The Race Track (Death on a Pale Horse) **15** Toilers of the Sea **27** Siegfried and the Rhine Maidens

rye 6 Secale
  varieties: 4 wild **5** giant **6** common **8** Aral wild, blue wild **9** Altai wild, giant wild, Volga wild **10** Canada wild **11** Chinese wild, Russian wild **12** Siberian wild, Virginia wild
  type: 6 liquor **7** whiskey
  origin: 7 Ireland **8** Scotland
  ingredient: 10 mash grains
  drink: 9 Cablegram **11** John Collins, Whiskey Sour
  with Cointreau: 10 Temptation
  with Pernod: 3 TNT
  with vermouth: 8 Brooklyn **9** Algonquin

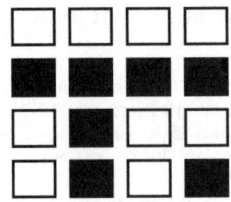

Saarinen, Eero
  father: 5 Eliel
  architect of: 11 St Louis Arch 20 Gateway to the West Arch (St Louis) 26 Trans World Airlines Terminal (NYC) 28 General Motors Technical Center (Warren MI) 39 Columbia Broadcasting Company Headquarters (NYC)
  style: 13 International

Saarinen, Eliel
  son: 4 Eero
  architect of: 16 Cranbrook Academy (Bloomfield Hills MI) 18 Kleinhaus Music Hall (Buffalo) 19 Tanglewood Music Shed (MA) 20 Christ Lutheran Church (Minneapolis MN), First Christian Church (Columbus IN)

Saba see 5 Sheba

Sabbath 8 Lord's Day 9 day of rest

Sabbatical: A Romance
  author: 9 John Barth

saber, sabre 3 cut 4 kill, stab 5 blade, sword, wound 6 cutlas, rapier, strike 7 cutlass, soldier 8 scimitar 10 broadsword

Sabin, Albert Bruce
  field: 8 medicine
  developed: 16 oral polio vaccine

sable 3 fur, jet 4 dark, inky 5 black, ebony, raven

sabotage 3 sap 6 retard 7 cripple, destroy, disable, disrupt, subvert 8 paralyze 9 undermine, vandalize 10 subversion 12 incapacitate

sabra 11 Israeli-born 14 native of Israel

Sabra
  type: 7 liqueur
  origin: 6 Israel
  flavor: 6 orange 9 chocolate

Sac see 4 Sauk

saccharine 5 gooey, mushy, soppy, sweet 6 sugary, syrupy 7 candied, cloying, honeyed, maudlin, mawkish, sugared 9 offensive, oversweet, revolting, sickening 10 disgusting, nauseating 11 sentimental

sacerdotal 5 papal 8 clerical, pastoral, priestly 9 apostolic, canonical, episcopal 10 pontifical 11 ministerial 12 hierarchical 14 ecclesiastical

Sachs, Hans 13 Meistersinger

sack 3 bag, rob 4 loot, pack, raid 5 pouch, spoil, store, waste 6 duffel, maraud, rapine, ravage, tear up 7 de-spoil, pillage, plunder, ransack 8 spoliate 9 depredate, duffel bag, gunnysack, haversack, marauding 10 plundering, ravishment 11 depredation, devastation 12 despoliation

sackbut 18 medieval instrument
  resembles: 8 trombone

sacrament 3 vow 4 rite 5 troth 6 pledge, plight, ritual 7 liturgy, promise, service 8 ceremony, contract, covenant 9 solemnity 10 ceremonial, obligation, observance 11 affirmation 12 ministration

sacramental 4 holy 6 ritual 7 blessed 10 ceremonial, liturgical

Sacraments, Seven 7 Baptism, Penance 9 Eucharist, Last Rites, Matrimony 10 Holy Orders 12 Confirmation 13 Holy Communion 14 Extreme Unction, Reconciliation 18 Anointing of the Sick

sacred 4 holy 6 church 7 blessed, revered 8 Biblical, hallowed, hieratic 9 religious, venerable 10 sanctified, scriptural 11 consecrated 14 ecclesiastical

Sacred and Profane Love Machine, The
  author: 11 Iris Murdoch

Sacred writings 5 Bible 11 Bibliotheca

sacrifice 4 cede, loss 5 forgo, waive 6 forego, give up, homage 7 cession, forfeit, offer up 8 immolate, oblation, offering, renounce 9 surrender 10 concession, immolation, lustration, relinquish 12 renunciation 14 relinquishment

sacrilege 3 sin 7 impiety, mockery, outrage 8 iniquity 9 blasphemy, profanity, violation 10 irreligion, sinfulness, wickedness 11 desecration, impiousness, irreverence, profanation, profaneness

sacrilegious 7 impious, profane 10 irreverent 11 blasphemous, irreligious

sacrosanct 4 holy 5 godly 6 divine, solemn 8 hallowed, heavenly 9 celestial, inviolate, religious, spiritual 10 inviolable, unexamined 11 consecrated 12 unquestioned

sacrum
  bone of: 11 base of spine

sad 3 low 4 blue, grim, hard, hurt 5 grave 6 dismal, solemn, taxing, tragic, trying, woeful 7 adverse, crushed, doleful, forlorn, grieved, joyless, maudlin, pitiful, serious, unhappy 8 dejected, desolate, downcast, grievous, mournful, pathetic, touching, troubled, wretched 9 cheerless, depressed, difficult, miserable, sorrowful 10 calamitous, chapfallen, despairing, despondent, dispirited, distressed, lachrymose, lamentable, melancholy 11 crestfallen, distressing, pessimistic, troublesome, unfortunate 12 disconsolate, heartrending, heavyhearted, inconsolable 13 brokenhearted, griefstricken, heartbreaking 14 down in the dumps, down in the mouth
  French: 6 triste

Sadat, Anwar el-
  president of: 5 Egypt
  awarded: 15 Nobel Peace Prize
  author of: 18 In Search of Identity

sadden 4 damp, dash 5 crush 6 burden, deject, grieve, sorrow, subdue 7 depress 8 aggrieve, dispirit 10 discourage, dishearten

saddle with 9 stick with 10 burden with 12 encumber with 18 make responsible for

Sade, Marquis de
  author of: 7 Justine 8 Juliette 14 120 Days of Sodom 26 The Philosopher in the Bedroom

sadistic 6 brutal 7 vicious 8 fiendish, perverse 9 perverted 12 bloodthirsty

sadness
  French: 9 tristesse

sad poem 5 elegy 6 lament

Sad Sack
  creator: 11 George Baker

Saehrimnir
  origin: 12 Scandinavian
  form: 4 boar
  served in: 8 Valhalla
  feat: 12 regeneration

safe 4 firm, sure, wary 5 sound, vault, whole 6 intact, modest, secure, stable, steady, unhurt 7 certain, guarded, prudent 8 cautious, defended, discreet, harmless, reliable, unbroken, unharmed 9 innocuous, protected, undamaged, unexposed, unscathed 10 dependable, protecting 11 circumspect, impregnable, out of danger, trustworthy, unscratched 12 conservative, invulnerable, noncommittal

safeguard 4 ward **5** armor, charm **6** amulet, buffer, defend, harbor, screen, secure, shield **7** bulwark, defense, fortify, protect, shelter **8** conserve, garrison, preserve, security, talisman **10** precaution, protection

safekeeping 4 care **6** charge **7** custody **8** security **9** husbandry **10** protection **12** conservation, guardianship, preservation

Safety Net, The
author: **12** Heinrich Boll

saffron
botanical name: **13** Crocus sativus
also called: **6** Krokus
Moorish: **6** Zafran
of all spices most: **6** costly
color: **6** orange, yellow **12** yellow-orange
used as: **8** coloring, cosmetic, medicine **9** fabric dye
origin: **5** Egypt, Syria **8** Holy Land **9** Palestine
use: **4** rice **5** bread, rolls

sag 3 bow, dip **4** drop, fail, flag, flap, flop, keel, lean, list, sink, sway, tilt, tire **5** droop, pitch, slump, weary **6** billow, plunge, settle, weaken **7** decline, descend, give way **8** diminish

saga 4 epic, myth, tale, yarn **6** legend **7** history, romance **9** adventure, chronicle, narrative
French: **11** roman-fleuve

sagacious 4 foxy, wise **5** acute, canny, sharp, smart, sound **6** astute, brainy, clever, shrewd **7** cunning, knowing, prudent, sapient, tactful **8** discreet, rational, sensible **9** judicious, practical **10** diplomatic, discerning, perceptive **11** calculating, intelligent **13** perspicacious **14** discriminating

sagacity 6 acumen, brains, smarts, wisdom **8** sapience **9** canniness, smartness **10** astuteness, braininess, cleverness, shrewdness **11** discernment **12** intelligence, perspicacity **13** judiciousness **14** discrimination

Sagan, Carl
author of: **6** Cosmos **7** Contact **16** The Dragons of Eden

Sagan, Francoise
real name: **16** Francoise Quoirez
author of: **13** A Certain Smile **15** Aimez-vous Brahms **16** Bonjour Tristesse

sage 4 guru, wise **5** sound **6** astute, pundit, savant, shrewd **7** egghead, knowing, prudent, sapient, scholar, wise man **8** mandarin, sensible **11** intelligent, philosopher
French: **6** savant
Latin: **5** magus, solon

sage 6 Salvia **12** S officinalis
varieties: **3** bog **4** baby, blue, gray, rose, sand, wood **5** black, lilac, Texas, white **6** autumn, common, desert, garden, purple, silver, yellow **7** bladder, gentian, scarlet, Spanish, thistle, Vervain **8** creeping, gray ball, mealy-cup, rose-leaf **9** Bethlehem, Jerusalem **11** Mexican bush **16** pineapple-scented
means: **6** to heal, to save
strengthens: **6** memory, wisdom **8** prudence
makes men: **8** immortal
origin: **7** Albania **10** Yugoslavia **13** Mediterranean
use: **4** pork **6** breads, cheese **7** chicken, poultry, seafood **8** stuffing

Sage of Concord
nickname of: **17** Ralph Waldo Emerson

Sagittarius
symbol: **6** archer **7** centaur
planet: **7** Jupiter
rules: **10** philosophy **15** higher education
born: **8** November, December

Sagittary
form: **7** centaur
carried: **3** bow

said 5 above, quoth **6** quoted, spoken, stated **7** related, uttered **8** repeated

Saigon
capital of: **7** Vietnam
now: **13** Ho Chi Minh City

sail 3 fly **4** boat, scud, skim, soar **5** drift, float, glide, steam **6** course, cruise, voyage **8** navigate **9** excursion

sailboat 4 saic, yawl **5** craft, ketch, sloop, yacht **6** vessel **7** sunfish **8** schooner **9** catamaran
part: **4** boom, mast **6** canvas **7** rigging **9** mainsheet

sailcloth 4 duck **6** canvas

Sailing to Byzantium
author: **7** W B Yeats

sailor 3 gob, tar **4** salt **6** sea dog, seaman **7** mariner, voyager **8** deckhand, seafarer **9** navigator, yachtsman
terms: **3** yaw **4** ahoy, alee, conn, draw, fast, furl, heel, list, luff, moor, scud, tack, trim, wake **5** avast, belay, heave, hoist, lie to, pilot, pitch, weigh **6** aweigh **8** aweather, put about

sailors
patron saint: **4** Elmo

Sails (of Argo)
constellation of: **4** Vela

saint 6 martyr
Buddhist: **5** arhat **11** bodhisattva
Chinese: **8** immortal
Islamic: **3** pir
lives of the saints: **8** menology **9** hagiology **11** hagiography **13** acta sanctorum
process of becoming: **12** canonization
relic box: **6** chasse
remains: **5** relic
symbol: **4** halo

Saint, Eva Marie
born: **8** Newark NJ
roles: **6** Exodus **15** On the Waterfront **16** North by Northwest

saint, patron
acolytes: **13** John Berchmans
actors: **8** Genesius
artists: **4** Luke
astronomers: **7** Dominic
athletes: **9** Sebastian
authors: **14** Francis de Sales
aviators: **15** Our Lady of Loreto **16** Therese of Lisieux **17** Joseph of Cupertino
bakers: **8** Nicholas **18** Elizabeth of Hungary
bankers: **7** Matthew
barbers: **5** Louis **6** Cosmas, Damian
barren women: **9** Felicitas **14** Anthony of Padua
beggars/cripples: **5** Giles
blind: **6** Odilia **7** Raphael
bodily ills: **16** Our Lady of Lourdes
boy scouts: **6** George
brides: **14** Nicholas of Myra
builders: **13** Vincent Ferrer
butchers: **4** Luke **7** Hadrian **14** Anthony of Egypt
carpenters: **6** Joseph
cancer patients: **9** Peregrine
children: **10** Santa Claus **14** Nicholas of Myra
comedians: **5** Vitus
cooks: **6** Martha **8** Lawrence
deaf: **14** Francis de Sales
dying: **6** Joseph **7** Barbara
emigrants: **14** Frances Cabrini
England: **6** George
eye sufferers: **4** Lucy
falsely accused: **15** Raymond Nonnatus
farmers: **6** George **7** Isidore
fishermen: **5** Peter **6** Andrew
foreign missions: **13** Francis Xavier **16** Therese of Lisieux
foundlings: **13** Holy Innocents
France: **5** Denis
gardeners: **6** Fiacre, Phocas **7** Adelard, Dorothy, Tryphon
heart patients: **9** John of God
hospitals: **9** John of God **12** Jude Thaddeus **16** Camillus de Lellis
housewives: **4** Anne
hunters: **6** Hubert **10** Eustachius
invalids: **4** Roch
Ireland: **7** Patrick
Italy: **7** Anthony
laborers: **5** James **7** Isidore **9** John Bosco
lawyers: **3** Ivo **4** Ives **8** Genesius **10** Thomas More
librarians: **6** Jerome
lovers: **9** Valentine
mariners: **4** Elmo **7** Michael **19** Nicholas of Tolentino
mentally ill: **6** Dympna
merchants: **14** Nicholas of Myra **15** Francis of Assisi
metalworkers: **7** Eligius

miners: 7 Barbara
mothers: 6 Monica
musicians: 7 Cecilia, Dunstan **15** Gregory the Great
Norway: 4 Olaf, Olav
nurses: 6 Agatha **7** Alexius, Raphael **9** John of God **16** Camillus de Lellis
painters: 4 Luke
philosophers: 6 Justin **21** Catherine of Alexandria
physicians: 4 Luke **6** Cosmas, Damian **7** Raphael **9** Pantaleon
pilgrims: 5 James **7** Alexius
poets: 5 David **7** Cecilia
policemen: 7 Michael
poor souls: 19 Nicholas of Tolentino
postal workers: 7 Gabriel
priests: 19 Jean-Baptiste Vianney
printers: 8 Genesius **9** John of God **16** Augustine of Hippo
prisoners: 6 Dismas **7** Barbara **13** Joseph Cafasso
rheumatism: 15 James the Greater
sailors: 4 Elmo **7** Brendan, Erasmus, Eulalia **8** Cuthbert, Nicholas **11** Christopher **13** Peter Gonzales
scholars: 6 Brigid
scientists: 6 Albert
Scotland: 6 Andrew
sculptors: 6 Claude
seamen: 4 Elmo **14** Francis of Paolo
sick: 7 Michael **9** John of God **16** Camillus de Lellis
singers: 7 Cecilia, Gregory
skiers: 7 Bernard
shoemakers: 7 Crispin
soldiers: 6 George **7** Hadrian **8** Ignatius **9** Joan of Arc, Sebastian **13** Martin of Tours
Spain: 5 James **8** Santiago
students: 13 Thomas Aquinas **21** Catherine of Alexandria
surgeons: 6 Cosmas, Damian
tailors: 9 Homobonus
tax collectors: 7 Matthew
teachers: 15 Gregory the Great **21** Catherine of Alexandria, Jean Baptiste de la Salle
theologians: 9 Augustine **16** Alphonsus Liguori
throat sufferers: 6 Blaise
travelers: 7 Raphael **11** Christopher **14** Anthony of Padua, Nicholas of Myra
Wales: 5 David
winegrowers: 7 Vincent
workingmen: 6 Joseph
writers: 14 Francis de Sales
youth: 13 John Berchmans **15** Aloysius Gonzaga, Gabriel Possenti
Saint, The
author: 15 Leslie Charteris
character: 12 Simon Templar **26** Inspector Claude Eustace Teal
cast: 10 Roger Moore
Saint Anthony's fire 6 herpes **8** ergotism, shingles **10** erysipelas
Saint Elmo's fire 5 flame, hermo **6**

castor, corona, furole, helena **9** corposant **12** luminescence
Saint Esprit 9 Holy Ghost **10** Holy Spirit
Saint-Exupery, Antoine de
author of: 11 Night Flight **12** Southern Mail **15** The Little Prince **16** Wind Sand and Stars
Saint Francis
born: 6 Assisi
called: 9 Poverello
Saint-Gaudens, Augustus
born: 6 Dublin **7** Ireland
artwork: 7 Puritan **13** Mrs Henry Adams (Grief) **14** General Sherman **15** Admiral Farragut **16** President Lincoln
Saint Jack
author: 11 Paul Theroux
Saint Joan
author: 17 George Bernard Shaw
Saint John's bread 5 carob
Saint John's wort 5 amber **6** tutsan **7** ascyrum, cammock **9** androseme, hypericum, rosin-rose **10** broombrush **11** Aaron's-beard
saintliness 6 purity **8** goodness, holiness **9** beatitude, godliness **11** blessedness **12** spirituality
Saint Lucia, St Lucia
capital: 8 Castries
highest point: 5 Gimie
island group: 8 Windward **14** Lesser Antilles
language: 6 patois
location: 9 Caribbean
saintly 4 good, holy **5** godly, moral, pious **6** devout **7** angelic, blessed, exalted, sinless, upright **8** beatific, faithful, reverent, virtuous **9** believing, religious, righteous, spiritual **10** benevolent
Saint Paul
born: 6 Tarsus
companion: 4 Luke
epistle: 5 Titus **6** Romans **7** Hebrews, Timothy **8** Philemon **9** Ephesians, Galatians **10** Colossians **11** Corinthians, Philippians **13** Thessalonians
Saint Paul's Cathedral (London)
architect: 4 Wren
Saint Peter
called: 4 Rock **5** Simon **6** Cephas
brother: 6 Andrew
Saint-Saens, (Charles) Camille
born: 5 Paris **6** France
composer of: 12 Danse Macabre **14** Samson et Dalila **16** Samson and Delilah **18** La Jeunesse d'Hercule **20** Carnival of the Animals
Saints' lives
writer of: 12 hagiographer
Saint Vincent, St Vincent
capital: 9 Kingstown
highest point: 9 Soufriere
Indian: 5 Carib **6** Arawak

island group: 8 Windward **14** Lesser Antilles
islands: 10 Grenadines
language: 6 patois
location: 9 Caribbean
volcano: 9 Soufriere
Saint Vitus' dance 6 chorea
sake 3 end **4** care, gain, good **5** cause **6** behalf, object, profit, regard **7** account, benefit, concern, purpose, respect, welfare **8** interest **9** advantage **11** enhancement **13** consideration
sake
type: 4 wine **6** spirit
origin: 5 Japan
ingredient: 4 rice
Sakharov, Andrei Dimitrievich
field: 7 physics
nationality: 7 Russian
researched: 14 nuclear fission
defended: 12 civil liberty
exiled to: 5 Gorky
awarded: 10 Nobel Prize
Saki
real name: 7 H H Munro
author of: 8 Reginald **20** Beasts and Super-Beasts **21** The Chronicles of Clovis **23** The Unbearable Bassington
salaam 3 bow **6** homage **9** obeisance
Salacia
partner of: 7 Neptune
salacious 4 lewd, sexy **7** lustful, obscene **8** indecent **9** lecherous **10** lascivious, libidinous **12** pornographic
salad days 5 prime, youth **6** heyday **9** flowering
salamander 3 eft **4** newt **5** giant, siren, tiger **6** lizard, red eft **7** axolotl, urodela **8** congo eel, mudpuppy **9** amphibian, fire-eater, proteidae **10** hellbender, necturidae **14** red-spotted newt
Salamis
father: 6 Asopus
mother: 6 Metope
son: 8 Cychreus
Salammbo
author: 15 Gustave Flaubert
character: 5 Matho **8** Hamilcar, Spendius **9** Narr Havas
setting: 8 Carthage
salary 3 pay **5** wages **6** income **7** stipend **8** earnings **9** allowance, emolument **10** recompense **12** remuneration
sale 3 cut **7** auction, bargain, selling, special **8** discount, exchange, markdown, transfer **9** reduction
Salem
suburb of: 6 Boston
old site of: 11 witch trials
salesperson 5 agent, clerk **6** vendor **8** huckster
salient 6 arrant, marked **7** glaring, notable, obvious **8** flagrant, manifest, palpable, striking **9** egregious, important, prominent **10** noteworthy, no-

ticeable, pronounced, protruding, remarkable **11** conspicuous,
outstanding, substantial **12** considerable

Salii
also: **6** Salian
form: **7** priests
priests of: **4** Mars
guarded: **7** ancilia **13** sacred shields

saline 4 salt **5** briny, salty **8** brackish

Salinger, J D 7 recluse
author of: **11** Nine Stories **14** Franny
and Zooey **18** The Catcher in the
Rye
character: **4** Esme

Salisbury
capital of: **8** Zimbabwe

Salisbury, Harrison E
author of: **16** American in Russia **19**
A Journey for Our Times, Black
Night White Snow

Salish (Flatheads)
language family: **8** Salishan
location: **5** Idaho **6** Oregon **7** Montana **10** Washington **15** British Columbia

Salk, Jonas Edward
field: **8** medicine
developed: **12** (inactivated) polio
vaccine

salle a manger 10 dining room
literally: **13** hall for eating

sallow 3 wan **4** gray, pale **5** ashen,
livid **6** anemic, pallid, sickly, yellow **7**
bilious **9** jaundiced, washed-out, yellowish

sallowness 6 pallor **7** wanness **8** paleness **10** sickliness **11** biliousness **13**
colorlessness, yellowishness

Sallust
author of: **9** Histories **13** War of Jugurtha **20** Conspiracy of Catiline

sally 3 mot **4** flow, pour, quip, raid,
trip **5** erupt, foray, surge **6** attack,
banter, charge, outing, retort, sortie,
spring, thrust **7** debouch, journey **8**
badinage, repartee **9** excursion, wisecrack, witticism **10** expedition **13**
counterattack

Salmacis
form: **5** nymph
loved: **14** Hermaphroditus
joined with: **14** Hermaphroditus
became: **13** hermaphrodite **14** bisexual person

Salmagundi
author: **16** Washington Irving

salmon 4 fish, king **5** cohoe **6** silver
7 chinook, Pacific, quinnat, sockeye,
spawner **8** Atlantic, humpback
enclosure: **4** yair
female: **4** raun **6** baggit
genus: **12** Oncorhynchus
hatchling: **4** pink **6** alevin
male: **3** gib **4** buck, cock
post-spawning: **4** kelt **7** shedder

pre-spawning: **7** gilling, girling
young: **4** parr **7** essling

Salome
father: **11** Herod Philip
mother: **8** Herodias
husband: **7** Zebedee
opera by: **7** (Richard) Strauss
character: **5** Herod (the Tetrarch)
8 Herodias, Jokanaan (John the Baptist) **9** Narraboth

salon 4 hall **7** gallery **11** drawing room
13 establishment

saloon 3 bar, inn, pub **6** bistro, tavern
7 barroom, ginmill, taproom **8** alehouse **9** roadhouse, speakeasy

salt 3 wit **4** best, corn, cure, pick, save
5 brine, briny, cream, elect, humor,
savor, smack, souse, spice **6** choice,
flavor, pickle, saline, season, select **8**
brackish, marinate, piquancy, pungency **9** seasoning **12** quintessence

Salten, Felix
author of: **5** Bambi

saltwater 3 sea **5** brine, ocean

salty 4 racy **5** briny, funny, spicy,
terse, witty **6** corned, ribald, risque,
saline **7** pungent, zestful **8** brackish,
improper

salubrious 7 bracing, healthy **9** healthful, wholesome **10** beneficial, lifegiv-
ing **11** therapeutic **12** invigorating

salubriousness 11 healthiness **13**
healthfulness, wholesomeness

Salus
origin: **5** Roman
goddess of: **6** health **10** prosperity
corresponds to: **6** Hygeia

salutary 4 good **5** tonic **6** useful **7**
healing, healthy **8** curative, sanitary **9**
healthful, wholesome **10** beneficial,
profitable **12** advantageous

salutation 3 bow **5** hello, howdy,
toast **6** curtsy **7** address, welcome **8**
greeting **9** reception
Hawaiian: **5** aloha
Italian: **4** ciao
Latin: **3** ave

salute 3 ave **4** hail, kiss **5** bow to,
cheer, greet, honor, nod to, salvo **6**
accost, homage, praise, wave to **7** address, applaud, respect, welcome **8**
accolade, applause, greeting **9** laudation, reverence **11** acclamation, recognition **12** congratulate

Salvador
author: **10** Joan Didion

salvage 4 junk, save **5** scrap **6** debris,
rescue **7** recover, remains, restore **8**
recovery, retrieve **9** retrieval **11** reclamation **12** rehabilitate

salvation 4 rock **5** grace **6** rescue, saving **8** election, lifeline, mainstay, recovery, survival **9** retrieval **10** protection, redemption **11** deliverance,
reclamation **12** preservation

salve 4 aloe, balm, calm, ease, hail **5**

hello **6** lessen, lotion, pacify, reduce,
soothe, temper **7** anodyne, assuage,
mollify, relieve, unguent **8** dressing,
liniment, mitigate, moderate, ointment
9 alleviate, emollient, greetings **11** alleviative

salver 4 bowl, dish, tray **6** waiter **7**
coaster

salvia 4 herb, mint, sage **5** shrub **8**
mejorana **9** artemisia

salvo 5 burst **6** volley **7** barrage, battery **8** shelling **9** cannonade, fusillade
11 bombardment

sambuca
type: **7** liqueur
origin: **5** Italy
flavor: **5** anise **10** elderberry

same 4 like, twin, very **5** alike, equal **6**
on a par **7** similar, uniform **8** parallel
9 identical, unchanged **10** consistent,
equivalent, invariable **13** corresponding

same as previously given
Latin: **4** idem

sameness 6 parity **8** equality, evenness, likeness, monotony **10** similarity, uniformity **11** homogeneity **14** ho-
mogenousness

Samoa
capital:
American Samoa: 8 Pago Pago
Western Samoa: 4 Apia
studied by: **13** Margaret Mead
cities: **6** Utulei **7** Palauli **8** Fagatogo
division: **12** Western Samoa **13** American Samoa
monetary unit: **4** tala
island: **3** Ofu, Tau **4** Rose **5** Aunuu,
Manua, Namua, Upolu **6** Manono,
Nuulua, Savaii, Swains **7** Apolima,
Nuutele, Olosega, Tutuila **8** Nuusafee
mountain: **4** Vaea **5** Alava **6** Savaii **7**
Matafao **9** Rainmaker
highest point: **4** Fito **8** Silisili
sea: **12** South Pacific
physical feature:
bay: **5** Afono, Leone **6** Fagasa,
Falefa, Safata **7** Lafanga, Masefau,
Matautu **8** Massacre, Salealua **9**
Saluofata
people: **6** Samoan **10** Polynesian
explorer: **9** Roggeveen **12** Bougainville
language: **6** Samoan **7** English
religion: **6** Mormon **8** Methodist **13**
Roman Catholic **15** Latter Day Saints
19 Seventh-Day Adventist **26** Congregational Christianity
feature:
bird: **3** iao **4** lulu, lupe **6** manuao,
manuma, maomao **7** manuali **8**
manusina, manutagi
chief: **5** matai
chief's daughter: **5** taupo
cloth: **4** para, tapa
clothing: **5** pareu **8** lavalava, puletasi

dance: 4 siva
dwelling: 4 fale
food:
drink: 3 ava
Samoyed
language family: 6 Uralic
spoken in: 7 Siberia
sample 3 try **4** test **5** model, taste **7** dip into, examine, example, pattern, portion, segment **8** instance, paradigm, specimen **10** experience **12** cross section, illustration **14** representative **15** exemplification
Samson 11 Hebrew judge
father: 6 Manoah
feature: 4 hair **8** strength
weapon: 7 jawbone
mistress/betrayer: 7 Delilah
hometown: 5 Zorah
fate: 7 blinded
brought down: 4 Gaza
Samson Agonistes
author: 10 John Milton
Samuel 11 Hebrew judge
father: 7 Elkanah
mother: 6 Hannah
hometown: 5 Ramah
anointed: 4 Saul **5** David
Sana, Sanaa
capital of: 10 North Yemen
San Antonio
basketball team: 5 Spurs
football team: 11 Gunslingers
landmark: 8 The Alamo **9** River Walk
sanctification 8 blessing **9** hallowing **12** consecration
Hebrew: 7 Kiddush
sanctified 4 holy **6** sacred **7** blessed **8** hallowed **11** consecrated
sanctify 5 bless, exalt **6** anoint, hallow, purify, uphold **7** absolve, beatify, cleanse **8** dedicate, enshrine, make holy **10** consecrate, legitimate, legitimize **12** legitimatize
sanctimonious 6 solemn **7** canting, pompous, preachy **8** unctuous **9** overblown, pietistic **11** pharisaical, pretentious **14** holier-than-thou
sanctimoniousness 4 cant, sham **6** humbug **9** hypocrisy **11** insincerity **15** pretentiousness
sanction 5 allow, favor, leave **6** accept, assent, permit, ratify **7** agree to, approve, consent, endorse, liberty, license, penalty, support **8** approval, coercion, pressure **9** authority, authorize **10** legitimate, permission **11** countenance, endorsement **12** commendation, confirmation, ratification **13** authorization
sanctuary 4 park **5** cover, haven **6** asylum, chapel, church, refuge, safety, shrine, temple **7** reserve, retreat, shelter **8** preserve **10** protection
Sanctuary
author: 15 William Faulkner

character: 5 Tommy **6** Popeye **9** Ruby Lamar **10** Lee Goodwin, Reba Rivers **11** Temple Drake **12** Gowan Stevens, Horace Benbow
sanctum sanctorum 12 holy of holies
sanctus 4 holy
Sancus
also: 10 Semo Sancus
origin: 5 Roman
god of: 5 oaths **10** road safety **11** hospitality **20** international affairs
corresponds to: 8 Hercules **10** Dius Fidius
sand 4 grit, guts **5** pluck, spunk **6** mettle **7** bravery, courage, resolve **8** backbone **9** fortitude **10** resolution **12** resoluteness
Sand, George
real name: 14 Aurore Dudevant
protege: 6 Chopin
author of: 5 Lelia **7** Indiana **8** Consuelo **9** Valentine **13** Story of My Life **14** The Country Waif, The Haunted Pool **17** Fanchon the Cricket **18** Les Maitres Sonneurs **23** The Countess of Rudolstadt
sandal 4 clog, flat, shoe, zori **5** scuff, thong **6** loafer **7** slipper **8** flipflop, huarache, moccasin, overshoe **10** espadrille
sandalwood 5 Algum, Almug
sandbank 4 dune, reef **5** shelf, shoal **7** shallow
sandbar 4 bank, flat, reef, spit **5** shelf, shoal **7** shallow
Sandbox, The
author: 11 Edward Albee
Sandburg, Carl
author of: 3 Fog **7** Chicago **12** Harvest Poems **13** Smoke and Steel **14** Abraham Lincoln, The Cornhuskers **15** Remembrance Rock
Sanders, George
born: 6 Russia **12** St Petersburg
wife: 10 Benita Hume, Magda Gabor **11** Zsa Zsa Gabor
roles: 6 The Fan **7** Ivanhoe, Rebecca **8** The Saint **9** The Falcon **11** All About Eve **12** Forever Amber, The Gay Falcon **18** The Moon and Sixpence **20** Foreign Correspondent **22** The Picture of Dorian Gray **24** The House of the Seven Gables
autobiography: 25 Memoirs of a Professional Cad
San Diego
airport: 14 Lindbergh Field
area: 7 La Jolla, Old Town **8** Coronado **9** Point Loma **10** Balboa Park, Mission Bay **13** Mission Valley **14** Gaslamp Quarter
baseball team: 6 Padres
football team: 8 Chargers
founder: 13 Junipero Serra
landmark: 11 San Diego Zoo **14** Wild Animal Park **30** Scripps Institute of Oceanography

sandpiper 3 ree **4** bird, ruff **5** reeve, stint, wader **6** common, oxbird, plover **7** fiddler, haybird, spotted, tipbird **8** graybird, sandpeep, shadbird **10** beachrobin
Sands of Iwo Jima
director: 9 Allan Dwan
cast: 8 John Agar **9** Adele Mara, John Wayne **13** Forrest Tucker
sandwich 3 BLT, sub **4** club, deli, hero **5** hogie **6** burger, hoagie, insert **7** grinder, western **8** laminate **9** interpose, submarine **10** lamination **11** combination
sane 5 lucid, sober **7** logical **8** all there, balanced, credible, rational, sensible **9** judicious, plausible, sagacious **10** farsighted, reasonable **11** clearheaded, responsible
Latin: 12 compos mentis
Sanford and Son
character: 5 Bubba **6** Melvin **10** Aunt Esther **11** Donna Harris, Fred Sanford, Grady Wilson, Rollo Larson **12** Julio Fuentes, Officer Smith (Smitty) **13** Lamont Sanford
cast: 8 Redd Foxx **9** Don Bexley **11** Hal Williams, LaWanda Page, Slappy White, Whitman Mayo **12** Demond Wilson, Lynn Hamilton **13** Gregory Sierra **15** Nathaniel Taylor
San Francisco
baseball team: 6 Giants
bay: 12 San Francisco
county: 5 Marin **8** San Mateo **12** San Francisco
football team: 11 Forty-Niners
known as: 12 City by the Bay **19** City by the Golden Gate
landmark: 8 Alcatraz **16** Golden Gate Bridge
noted for: 8 cable car **9** earthquake (1906) **26** crookedest street in the world
street/section: 6 Market **7** Lombard, Nob Hill **8** Presidio **9** Chinatown **10** Montgomery **11** Embarcadero, Russian Hill
sangaree, sangria
flavor: 5 fruit, spice
sangfroid 5 poise **6** aplomb **7** balance **8** coolness **9** composure **10** confidence, equanimity **11** tranquility **12** tranquillity **16** imperturbability
sanguine 3 red **4** rosy **5** happy, ruddy, sunny **6** bright, elated, florid **7** buoyant, crimson, flushed, glowing, hopeful, reddish, scarlet **8** blooming, cheerful, inflamed, rubicund **9** confident **10** optimistic **12** lighthearted
Sanhedrin 7 council
sanitarium, sanitorium 8 hospital **11** institution
French: 13 maison de sante
sanitary 5 clean **7** aseptic, healthy, sterile **8** germ-free, hygienic **9** healthful, wholesome **10** salubrious, steri-

lized, uninfected, unpolluted **11** disinfected **12** prophylactic

sanitorium *see* **10** sanitarium

sanity 5 sense **6** reason **8** lucidity, saneness **9** coherence, normality **11** rationality **12** sensibleness **14** reasonableness **15** clearheadedness

San Jose
   capital of: **9** Costa Rica

San Juan
   capital of: **10** Puerto Rico

San Juan Bautista *see* **10** Puerto Rico

San Marino
   capital/largest city: **9** San Marino
   enclave in: **5** Italy
   others: **10** Serravalle **13** Borgo Maggiore
   division: **8** Castelli
   government:
      legislature: **22** Great and General Council
   monetary unit: **4** lira, lire **9** centesimi
   mountain: **9** Apennines
   highest point: **6** Titano
   people: **7** Italian **11** San Marinese
      founder: **7** Marinus
   language: **7** Italian
   religion: **13** Roman Catholic
   place: **13** Valloni Palace **17** Palazzo del Governo **19** Basilica of San Marino
   church: **5** Pieve **9** St Francis

San Salvador
   capital of: **10** El Salvador

sans doute 12 without doubt

Sansovino, Andrea
   real name: **14** Andrea Contucci
   born: **5** Italy **14** Monte San Savino
   artwork: **15** Baptism of Christ **20** Virgin Child and St Anne

Sansovino, Il
   real name: **11** Jacopo Tatti
   born: **5** Italy **7** Caprese
   artwork: **4** Mars **7** Bacchus, Logetta, Neptune **10** Old Library **15** Madonna del Parto **16** St John the Baptist

sans pareil 12 without equal

sans peur et sans reproche 29 without fear and without reproach

sans souci 8 carefree **11** without care

Santa Cruz de Tenerife
   capital of: **13** Canary Islands

Santayana, George
   author of: **14** The Last Puritan **16** The Realms of Being, The Sense of Beauty **24** Skepticism and Animal Faith

Santiago
   capital of: **5** Chile

Santiago
   character in: **18** The Old Man and the Sea
   author: **9** Hemingway

Santo Domingo
   capital of: **17** Dominican Republic

Santo Domingo *see* **5** Haiti

Sao Tome
   capital of: **18** Sao Tome and Principe

Sao Tome and Principe
   capital/largest city: **7** Sao Tome
   others: **8** Trindade **11** Porto Alegre **12** Santo Antonio
   monetary unit: **5** dobra **6** escudo **7** centavo
   highest point: **7** Sao Tome
   sea: **8** Atlantic
   physical feature:
      bay: **11** Ana de Chaves
      gulf: **6** Guinea
   people: **7** African **10** Portuguese **11** Cape Verdean
      explorer: **7** Escobar **8** Santarem
   language: **10** Portuguese
   religion: **7** animism **13** Roman Catholic **19** Seventh Day Adventist **21** Evangelical Protestant

sap 3 rob, tax **4** ruin, wear **5** bleed, drain **6** impair, reduce, weaken **7** afflict, cripple, deplete, destroy, disable, exhaust, subvert **8** enervate, enfeeble **9** devastate, undermine **10** debilitate, devitalize

sapient 4 wise **7** knowing **8** profound **9** sagacious **10** discerning, perceptive **11** intelligent **12** knowledgeable

sap one's energy 3 fag **4** bush, poop, tire **5** drain, weary **6** tucker, weaken **7** deplete, exhaust, fatigue, wash out **8** enervate, enfeeble **10** debilitate, devitalize

Sapphira
   husband: **7** Ananias
   lied to: **5** Peter

sapphire 3 gem **4** blue **5** azure, jewel **6** indigo
   species: **8** corundum
   source: **5** Burma, Mogok **6** Ceylon **7** Kashmir **8** Sri Lanka, Thailand **9** Australia
   kind: **4** star

Sappho
   author: **14** Alphonse Daudet

Sarah, Sarai
   father: **5** Asher
   former name: **5** Sarai
   husband: **7** Abraham
   son: **5** Isaac
   slave: **5** Hagar
   burial place: **9** Machpelah

sarcasm 3 rub **4** gibe, jeer, jest **5** irony, scorn, sneer, taunt **7** mockery **8** contempt, derision, ridicule, scoffing **13** disparagement

sarcastic 5 acerb **6** biting, bitter, ironic **7** caustic, cutting, mocking, mordant **8** derisive, piercing, sardonic, scornful, sneering, stinging, taunting **11** disparaging **12** contemptuous

sarcoma 5 tumor **6** cancer, growth **8** neoplasm **10** malignancy

sarcophagus 4 pall **6** coffin

sard
   species: **6** quartz

sardine 4 bang, cram, fish, lile, lour, pack **5** crowd **7** alewife, anchovy, herring **8** pilchard

Sardinia
   other name: **8** Sardegna
   capital: **8** Cagliari
   cities: **4** Bono, Bosa **5** Nuoro, Olbia **7** Alghero, Bonorva, Sassari, Thatari **8** Iglesias, Oristano **11** Porto Torres
   division: **5** Nuoro **7** Arborea, Gallura, Sassari **8** Cagliari, Logudoro
   government: **13** region of Italy
   monetary unit: **7** carline
   island: **7** Caprera **8** Tavolara **9** Maddalena
   lake: **6** Omodeo
   mountain: **4** Rasu **5** Ferry, Linas **7** Gallura, Limbara **8** Marghine, Serpeddi, Vittoria **11** Gennargentu
   river: **5** Mannu, Tirso **6** Lascia **8** Coghinas **10** Flumendosa
   sea: **13** Mediterranean
   physical feature:
      gulf: **6** Orosei, Palmas **7** Asinara **8** Cagliari, Oristano
      plain: **7** Sassari **9** Campidano
      strait: **9** Bonifacio
   people:
      king: **12** Charles Felix **13** Charles Albert **14** Victor Emmanuel
      leader: **6** Cavour
      ruler: **4** Pisa **5** Genoa, Spain **7** Austria, Vandals **9** Byzantium, Phoenicia **12** House of Savoy
   language: **7** Italian
   religion: **13** Roman Catholic
   feature:
      towers: **7** nuraghi
   food:
      cheese: **6** romano **8** pecorino

Sardius 8 gemstone

sardonic 6 biting **7** caustic, cynical, jeering, mocking, mordant, satiric **8** derisive, scornful, sneering, taunting **9** sarcastic **11** disparaging **12** contemptuous

sardonyx 8 gemstone

Sargent, John Singer
   born: **5** Italy **8** Florence
   artwork: **6** Madam X (Madame Gautreau) **7** El Jaleo **17** The Wyndham Sisters **20** Robert Louis Stevenson **21** Carnation Lily Lily Rose **22** Daughters of Edward D Boit **24** Oyster Gatherers of Cancale

Sargon
   captured: **5** Accad
   successor: **11** Sennacherib

Saroyan, William
   author of: **12** My Name Is Aram **14** The Human Comedy **17** The Time of Your Life **22** My Heart's in the Highlands

Sarton, May
   author of: **5** Anger **11** Kinds of Love

17 Plant Dreaming Deep **20** Faithful Are the Wounds **33** Mrs Stevens Hears the Mermaids Singing

Sartor Resartus
   author: **13** Thomas Carlyle

Sartre, Jean-Paul
   author of: **6** Nausea, No Exit **8** The Words **17** The Roads to Freedom **19** Being and Nothingness
   philosophy: **14** Existentialism
   quote: **17** Hell is other people

sash 3 tie **4** band, belt **5** frame, scarf, strip **6** casing, corset, girdle, ribbon, window **7** baldric **8** casement **9** doorframe, waistband **10** cummerbund **11** windowframe
   Japanese: **3** obi
   pulley weight: **5** mouse
   window: **5** chess

sashay 4 move, skip **5** glide, mince **6** chasse, travel

sashimi 7 raw fish **12** Japanese dish

Saskatchewan 5 river **8** province
   boundary: **7** Alberta, Montana **8** Manitoba **11** North Dakota **12** Old Northwest **20** Northwest Territories
   capital: **6** Regina
   city: **8** Moose Jaw **9** Saskatoon **12** Prince Albert, Swift Current
   country: **6** Canada
   Indian: **4** Cree **9** Chipewyan **10** Assiniboin
   lake: **8** Reindeer **9** Athabasca, Wollaston
   mountain: **7** Cypress, Pasquia **9** Porcupine **14** Missouri Coteau
   river: **9** Churchill, Frenchman
   river mouth: **12** Lake Winnipeg

Sassoon, Siegfried
   author of: **26** The Memoirs of a Fox-Hunting Man **26** The Memoirs of George Sherston **29** The Memoirs of an Infantry Officer

sassy 4 bark, bold, flip, rude, tree **5** brash, fresh, saucy **6** mouthy, snippy **7** forward **8** impolite, impudent, insolent **12** discourteous **13** disrespectful

Satan 6 Belial, Moloch **7** Lucifer, Old Nick **8** Apollyon, the Devil **9** Beelzebub **10** Old Scratch, the Evil One, the Tempter **11** fallen angel **12** the Foul Fiend **13** the Old Serpent **14** Mephistopheles **19** the Prince of Darkness

satanic 3 bad **4** evil, vile **5** cruel **6** wicked **7** demonic, heinous, hellish, inhuman, vicious **8** devilish, fiendish, infamous, infernal, sadistic **9** malicious, malignant **10** demoniacal, diabolical, malevolent

satchel, Satchel 3 bag **4** case, grip, sack **5** purse **6** valise **7** handbag **8** reticule, suitcase **9** carpetbag, Gladstone, schoolbag
   pitcher, Hall of Famer: **5** Paige

sate 4 cloy, fill, glut **5** gorge, stuff **7** surfeit

satellite 4 moon **5** crony, toady **6** me-nial, puppet, vassal **7** servant **8** disciple, follower, hanger-on, parasite, retainer **9** assistant, attendant, companion, sycophant, tributary, underling

satellite state 6 colony **8** dominion **10** possession **12** protectorate

satiate 4 bore, cloy, fill, glut, jade **5** slake, stuff, weary **6** overdo, quench, sicken **7** content, disgust, gratify, suffice, surfeit **8** nauseate, overfill, saturate

Satie, Erik
   born: **6** France **8** Honfleur
   composer of: **6** Parade **13** Pieces froides **16** The Three Gymnasts **19** Limp Preludes for a Dog **20** Pieces en forme de poire **23** Pieces in the Shape of a Pear

satiny 4 fine **5** shiny, silky **6** smooth

satire 5 irony **6** banter, parody, send up **7** lampoon, mockery, sarcasm, takeoff **8** acrimony, derision, raillery, ridicule, travesty **9** burlesque **10** caricature, persiflage

satirical 5 comic **6** biting, bitter **7** caustic, mocking, mordant **8** derisive, humorous, ironical, sardonic, scornful, sneering **9** malicious, sarcastic

satirize 4 mock **6** parody **7** lampoon **9** burlesque **10** caricature

satisfaction 5 pride **6** amends **7** comfort, content, damages, deserts, justice, payment, redress **8** pleasure, requital **9** answering, atonement, happiness, quittance, reckoning, repayment **10** correction, recompense, remittance, settlement **11** contentment, fulfillment, restitution **12** compensation, remuneration **13** gratification, rectification, reimbursement

satisfactory 2 OK **4** okay **8** adequate, all right, passable, suitable **9** competent **10** acceptable, sufficient

satisfied 5 happy **7** content, pleased **9** gratified **10** complacent **11** comfortable

satisfy 3 pay **4** fill, meet **5** annul, clear, remit, repay, serve, slake **6** answer, assure, pacify, pay off, please, quench, remove, settle **7** appease, content, delight, fulfill, gratify, mollify, requite, suffice **8** convince, persuade, reassure **9** discharge, reimburse **10** compensate, recompense

satisfying 8 pleasant, pleasing **9** agreeable, enjoyable, rewarding **10** delightful, fulfilling, gratifying **11** pleasurable

satori
   term in: **3** Zen
   means: **13** enlightenment

saturate 4 fill **5** cover, douse, imbue, souse **6** drench, infuse **7** immerse, pervade, suffuse **8** permeate, submerge **10** impregnate, infiltrate

saturated 3 wet **4** full **5** drunk, soggy, soppy **6** soaked, sodden **8** bursting

Saturday
   day of: **15** Biblical Sabbath
   French: **6** samedi
   from: **8** Saturnus
   German: **7** samstag
   heavenly body: **6** Saturn
   Italian: **6** sabato
   observance: **33** Jewish Sabbath **20** Seventh Day Adventists
   Spanish: **6** sabado

Saturday Night Fever
   director: **10** John Badham
   cast: **11** Barry Miller **12** John Travolta **15** Karen Lynn Gorney
   setting: **8** Brooklyn
   score: **7** Bee Gees
   sequel: **12** Staying Alive

Saturday Night Live, NBC's
   regular: **9** Mike Myers **10** Bill Murray, Chevy Chase, Dana Carvey, Dan Aykroyd, Jane Curtin **11** Eddie Murphy, Gilda Radner, John Belushi **13** Garrett Morris, Laraine Newman
   group: **27** Not Ready For Prime Time Players
   bits: **4** Bees **7** Samurai **9** Coneheads **10** Church Lady **13** Blues Brothers, Weekend Update **16** Pathological Liar **18** Rosanne Rosanna-Dana

Saturn
   origin: **5** Roman
   god of: **11** agriculture
   consort of: **3** Ops
   son: **5** Picus
   corresponds to: **6** Cronos, Cronus, Kronos

Saturn
   position: **5** sixth
   satellite: **4** Rhea **5** Dione, Janus, Mimas, Titan **6** Phoebe, Tethys **7** Iapetus **8** Hyperion **9** Enceladus
   characteristic: **5** rings

saturnalia, Saturnalia 4 orgy **5** revel, spree **7** carouse, debauch, revelry **8** carousal **9** bacchanal **10** debauchery
   origin: **5** Roman
   event: **8** festival
   honoring: **6** Saturn **13** sowing of crops

saturnine 4 dour, glum, grim **5** grave, staid, stern, sulky **6** gloomy, moping, morose, solemn, somber, sullen **7** austere, serious **8** dejected, downcast, reserved, sardonic, taciturn **9** apathetic, cheerless, withdrawn **11** downhearted **15** uncommunicative

satyr
   form: **4** faun **5** deity
   location: **8** woodland
   part: **3** man **4** goat
   attendant of: **7** Bacchus
   known for: **7** lechery

Satyricon
   author: **9** Petronius

character: 4 Gito **8** Ascyltus, Eumolpus **9** Encolpius **10** Trimalchio

sauce 3 dip **4** sass **5** booze, gravy, salsa **6** fillip, flavor **7** alcohol **8** dressing, pertness **9** condiment, flippancy **12** impertinence
basil: 5 pesto
fish: 4 alec
hot: 7 Tabasco
Indian: 5 curry
salty: 3 soy

saucy 4 bold, pert, rude, trim **5** brash, cocky, fresh, natty, smart **6** brazen, cheeky, jaunty, lively, spruce **7** forward **8** flippant, impolite, impudent, insolent **9** audacious, barefaced, unabashed **11** impertinent, smart-alecky **12** discourteous **13** disrespectful

Saudi Arabia
capital/largest city: 6 Riyadh
others: 4 Abha, Hail, Taif **5** Hofuf, Hufuf, Jedda, Jidda, Yanbu, Yenbo **6** Anaiza, Dammam, Jiddah, Jubail **7** Alhofuf, Buraido, Dhahran **9** Ras Tanura
holy city: 5 Mecca **6** Medina
school: 5 Islam **13** King Abd al-Aziz **19** Imam Muhammad bin Saud **20** Petroleum and Minerals
division: 4 Asir, Nejd **5** Hejaz **6** El Hasa
government: 8 monarchy
head of state/government: 4 king
monetary unit: 5 girsh, gursh, pound, riyal
weight: 3 oke
mountain: 6 Tuwayq
highlands: 4 Asir **5** Hejaz
highest point: 5 Razih **10** Jebal Sawda
sea: 3 Red
physical feature:
desert: 3 Red **5** Dahna, Nafud, Nefud, Nufud **6** al-Dahy, Dahana **10** Rub al Khali
gulf: 5 Aqaba **7** Persian
peninsula: 7 Arabian
plain: 6 Tihama
plateau: 4 Nejd
people: 4 Arab **7** Bedouin
king: 4 Fahd, Saud **6** Faisal, Khalid **7** Ibn Saud **9** Abdul Aziz
religious leader: 8 Mohammed, Muhammad
language: 6 Arabic
religion: 5 Islam
sect: 5 Sunni **6** Shiite **7** Wahhabi
place:
shrine: 5 Kaaba **10** Black Stone
feature:
annual pilgrimage: 4 hadj, hajj
clothing: 3 aba **4** agal **5** thobe **6** ghutra
kingdom: 5 Hejaz **7** Minaean, Ottoman, Sabaean **9** Himyarite
laws of Islam: 6 sharia
village school: 6 kuttab

war: 4 Gulf **11** Desert Storm **12** Desert Shield

Sauguet, Henri
born: 6 France **8** Bordeaux
composer of: 6 La Nuit **10** Les Forains, Les Mirages

Sauk, Sac
family: 9 Algonkian **10** Algonquian
tribe: 3 Fox, Sac **8** Kickapoo
location: 4 Iowa, Ohio **6** Kansas **7** Indiana **8** Illinois, Michigan, Oklahoma **9** Wisconsin
leader: 9 Blackhawk
related to: 8 Kickapoo **9** Mesquakie **11** Potawatomie
involved in: 12 Black Hawk War

Saul
king of: 4 Edom **6** Israel
father: 4 Kish
daughter: 5 Merab **6** Michal
son: 7 Abinoam **8** Jonathan **10** Ishbosheth
anointed by: 6 Samuel
hometown: 6 Gibeah **8** Rehoboth
successor: 5 David

Saunders, Allen
creator/artist of: 9 Mary Worth

saunter 4 roam **5** amble, mosey, stray **6** loiter, ramble, stroll, wander **7** meander, traipse **8** straggle **9** promenade

sausage 5 frank, gigot, wurst **6** hotdog, salami, weenie, wiener **7** baloney, bologna **8** kielbasa **9** bratwurst, pepperoni **10** liverwurst **11** frankfurter
British: 6 banger

sauve qui peut 4 rout **8** stampede **18** every man for himself **23** let him save himself who can

savage 4 boor, wild **5** brute, cruel, feral, fiend, harsh, rough, yahoo **6** animal, bloody, brutal, fierce, maniac, native, rugged, unkind **7** brutish, hoodlum, ruffian, untamed, violent **8** barbaric, hooligan, pitiless, ruthless, sadistic **9** aborigine, barbarian, barbarous, ferocious, merciless, murderous, primitive **10** aboriginal, heathenish, relentless, uncultured, unmerciful **11** uncivilized **12** uncultivated **14** undomesticated

savagery 7 cruelty **8** ferocity **9** barbarism, barbarity, brutality **10** fierceness, inhumanity **12** pitilessness, ruthlessness

savanna, savannah 5 campo, plain **9** grassland

savant 6 genius **7** scholar **13** learned person

save 3 but **4** bank, free, help, hold, keep **5** amass, guard, hoard, lay by, lay up, put by, spare, stock, store **6** defend, except, garner, heap up, redeem, rescue, shield **7** deliver, deposit, husband, protect, put away, recover, reserve, salvage **8** conserve,

preserve, retrench, withhold **9** economize, safeguard **10** accumulate

save up 5 amass, hoard **7** collect, put away **8** salt away, sock away **10** accumulate **12** squirrel away

saving 5 close, tight **6** frugal, stingy **7** careful, miserly, prudent, sparing, thrifty **8** markdown, stinting **9** illiberal, niggardly, provident, redeeming, restoring **10** economical, reclaiming, redemptory, reparative **12** compensating, conservative

savings 3 IRA **5** hoard **7** nest egg, reserve

savior 5 freer **7** rescuer **8** champion, defender, guardian, redeemer **9** deliverer, liberator, preserver, protecter, protector, salvation **11** emancipator

Savior 5 Jesus **6** Christ **8** Redeemer **10** the Messiah **11** Jesus Christ, the Son of God **13** Prince of Peace

Savior anointed 5 Jesus

savoir-faire 4 tact **5** poise **6** aplomb, polish **7** finesse, know-how, suavity **8** presence, urbanity **9** assurance, composure **10** adroitness, discretion, smoothness **11** worldliness **12** complaisance, graciousness **14** self-possession

savoir-vivre 16 knowing how to live **19** knowledge of the world

savor 3 try **4** aura, gist, like, odor, soul, tang, zest **5** aroma, enjoy, scent, smack, smell, spice, taste, trait **6** flavor, nature, relish, sample, season, spirit **7** essence, quality **8** piquancy, property, pungency **9** character, fragrance, substance **10** appreciate, experience **11** peculiarity **13** particularity **14** characteristic

savory 5 tangy, tasty, yummy **6** honest **7** odorous, piquant, pungent **8** alluring, aromatic, charming, edifying, fragrant, luscious, tasteful **9** delicious, flavorous, palatable, reputable, toothsome **10** appetizing, attractive, delectable **11** inoffensive, respectable, scrumptious **13** mouth-watering

savory
botanical name: 8 Satureia, S montana **10** S hortensis
origin: 13 Mediterranean
varieties: 6 summer, winter
use: 4 eggs, meat **5** beans, salad **6** sauces **8** dressing **11** chicken soup

savvy 5 catch, get it **7** know-how **10** comprehend, understand **13** understanding

saw 3 cut **4** tool **5** adage, maxim, slash **6** saying **7** proverb **8** aphorism
type: 3 jig, rip **4** back, band, hack **5** miter **6** coping **7** keyhole **8** circular, crosscut

sawfly
varieties: 4 stem, wood **5** cedar **6** pergid **7** conifer **8** horntail **11** web spinning

saxophone
  type: **4** alto **5** tenor
say 2 do **4** hint, hold, read, tell, vote, word **5** bruit, claim, guess, imply, judge, mouth, rumor, speak, state, utter, voice **6** allege, assert, assume, chance, convey, phrase, reason, recite, remark, render, repeat, report, reveal, spread **7** comment, contend, declare, deliver, divulge, express, imagine, mention, perform, suggest, suppose, surmise **8** announce, disclose, intimate, maintain, rehearse, vocalize **9** circulate, franchise, insinuate, pronounce, verbalize **10** articulate, conjecture **11** communicate

Sayers, Dorothy L
  author of: **9** Whose Body **12** Strong Poison **14** Have His Carcase, The Nine Tailors, Unnatural Death **15** Clouds of Witness, Five Red Herrings **16** Busman's Honeymoon **19** Murder Must Advertise **30** Unpleasantness at the Bellona Club
  character: **6** Bunter **11** Harriet Vane **15** Lord Peter Wimsey

Say Hey Kid
  nickname of: **10** Willie Mays
saying 3 saw **5** adage, maxim, moral, motto **6** byword, dictum, truism **7** epigram, precept, proverb **8** aphorism, apothegm **10** expression

Sayonara
  director: **11** Joshua Logan
  author: **13** James Michener
  cast: **9** Miiko Taka **10** Red Buttons **11** James Garner, Martha Scott **12** Marlon Brando, Miyoshi Umeki **16** Ricardo Montalban
  score: **12** Irving Berlin
  Oscar for: **15** supporting actor (Buttons) **17** supporting actress (Umeki)

scabrous 5 dirty, rough, scaly **7** immoral, leprous **8** indecent, off-color **9** salacious **10** suggestive **12** pornographic
scalding 3 hot **5** harsh **7** boiling, caustic **8** seething, steaming **9** sarcastic
scale, scales 3 key, set **4** chip, film, husk, peel, rise, rule, skin **5** crust, flake, layer, mount, order, plate, range, ratio, scour, shave, shell, weigh **6** adjust, ascend, goupen, ladder, lamina, octave, rub off, scrape, series, spread **7** balance, chip off, clamber, climb up, coating, lamella, measure **8** escalade, membrane, register, regulate, spectrum, surmount **9** continuum, gradation, solfeggio **10** delaminate, graduation, proportion **11** calibration, progression **14** classification
scale down 4 trim **6** reduce **7** abridge, curtail, shorten **8** compress, condense, decrease, diminish, downsize, moderate **10** abbreviate
scale insects

varieties: 3 lac, pit, wax **5** giant **6** ensign **7** armored **8** mealybug, tortoise **12** ground pearls
scale note 2 do, fa, la, mi, re, so, ti **3** sol
  Guido's: **3** ela
scamp 3 imp, rip **5** cut-up, knave, rogue, tease **6** rascal, rotter **7** bounder, villain **8** blighter, scalawag **9** miscreant, prankster, scoundrel **10** scapegrace **11** rapscallion **13** mischiefmaker
scamper 3 fly, run, zip **4** dart, dash, flit, race, romp, rush, scud **5** frisk, hurry, scoot **6** frolic, gambol, hasten, scurry, sprint **7** scuttle **9** skedaddle **21** running about playfully
scan 4 skim **5** check, probe, scour, study, sweep **6** peruse, search, size up, survey **7** analyze, examine, explore, inspect **10** scrutinize
scandal 4 blot **5** abuse, libel, odium, shame, stain **6** expose, smirch, stigma **7** calumny, obloquy, outrage, slander **8** disgrace, dishonor, ignominy **9** aspersion, discredit, disesteem, sensation **10** debasement, detraction, opprobrium, revilement **12** vituperation **13** disparagement, embarrassment
scandalize 5 shock **6** appall, defame, insult, offend **7** horrify, outrage **10** calumniate
scandalmonger 6 gossip **8** busybody **10** talebearer, tattletale
scandalous 8 libelous, shameful, shocking **9** gossiping, offensive **10** defamatory, outrageous, scurrilous, slanderous **11** disgraceful **12** disreputable **13** reprehensible
Scandinavia 6 Norway, Sweden **7** Denmark, Faeroes, Iceland
Scandinavian (Norse)
  language family: **12** Indo-European
  branch: **8** Germanic
  group: **15** Western Germanic
  language: **6** Danish **7** Faroese, Swedish **9** Icelandic, Norwegian
scant 3 cut **4** bare **5** limit, short, small, stint **6** in need, meager, paltry, reduce, sparse **7** limited **8** exiguous, hold back **9** deficient **10** inadequate, incomplete **12** insufficient
scantiness 10 deficiency, inadequacy, meagerness, skimpiness **13** insufficiency
scanty 4 thin **5** short, small **6** meager, modest, paltry, skimpy, sparse **7** slender, stunted **9** deficient **10** inadequate, undersized **12** insufficient
scapegoat, Scapegoat 4 butt, dupe, gull **5** patsy **6** Azazel, victim **7** fall guy **11** whipping boy **13** laughingstock
scapolite
  source: **5** Burma, Mogok

scapula
  bone of: **13** shoulder blade
scar 3 cut, pit **4** dent, flaw, gash, hurt, mark, pock, seam **5** brand, wound **6** affect, bruise, damage, deface, defect, impair, mangle **7** blemish, scratch **8** cicatrix, lacerate, mutilate **9** disfigure, influence
Scaramouch(e) 6 coward, rascal **8** braggart, poltroon
scarce 4 rare **6** scanty, sparse **7** unusual, wanting **8** uncommon **9** deficient
scarcely 4 just **6** at most, barely, hardly **7** but just, faintly **8** slightly
scarcity 4 lack, want **5** stint **6** dearth, rarity **7** fewness, paucity **8** rareness, shortage, sparsity, thinness **10** deficiency, scantiness, sparseness **12** uncommonness **13** insufficiency
scare 4 turn **5** alarm, daunt, panic, shake, shock, start **6** harrow, shiver **7** horrify, jitters, startle, terrify **8** disquiet, frighten **9** terrorize **10** disconcert, dishearten, intimidate **11** nervousness, palpitation **13** consternation
scarecrow 6 effigy **8** straw man
Scarecrow
  character in: **13** The Wizard of Oz
  author: **4** Baum
scared 5 shaky, timid, upset **6** afraid **7** alarmed, fearful, nervous, spooked **8** startled, timorous **9** diffident, terrified, tremulous **10** frightened **12** apprehensive, fainthearted **13** panic-stricken
scarf 3 boa **4** sash, veil, wrap **5** ascot, shawl, stole **6** choker, cravat, tippet **7** foulard, muffler, overlay **8** babushka, bandanna, mantilla **11** neckerchief
Scarface
  director: **11** Howard Hawks
  cast: **8** Paul Muni **9** Ann Dvorak **10** George Raft **12** Boris Karloff
scarify 3 cut **6** incise, loosen **7** break up, scratch **8** lacerate **9** cultivate
Scarlatti, Alessandro
  born: **6** Sicily **7** Palermo
  composer of: **11** Stabat Mater **17** Mitridate Eupatore, The Triumph of Honor **18** Il Trionfo dell Onore **23** Gli equivoci nel sembiante
Scarlatti, Domenico
  born: **5** Italy **6** Naples
  composer of: **7** Sonatas **9** Cat's Fugue, Essercizi **18** Le Donne di Buon Umore **20** The Good-Humored Ladies **23** Ottavia risituita al trono
scarlet 3 red **6** cherry, claret **7** carmine **8** cardinal
Scarlet Letter, The
  author: **18** Nathaniel Hawthorne
  character: **5** Pearl **12** Hester Prynne **16** Arthur Dimmesdale **18** Roger Chillingworth
Scarlett see Gone With the Wind
scary 3 bad **5** awful, hairy **6** creepy **7**

fearful 8 alarming, menacing, shocking **9** difficult **10** disturbing, terrifying **11** frightening, goosepimply, hairraising, threatening **12** discomfiting

scat 3 off, out **4** away, shoo **5** be off, leave, scram **6** beat it, be gone, depart, get out, go away **7** get lost, vamoose

scathing 4 keen, tart **5** sharp **6** biting, brutal, savage **7** caustic, cutting, hostile, mordant, pointed, searing **8** incisive, stinging, virulent **9** ferocious, rancorous, scorching, trenchant, vitriolic, withering **10** lacerating **11** acrimonious, excoriating

scatter 3 sow **4** cast, flee, rout **5** strew, throw **6** dispel **8** disperse, sprinkle **9** broadcast, circulate, dissipate **10** distribute **11** disseminate

scatterbrained 4 rash, wild, zany **5** crazy, dizzy, giddy, nutty, silly **6** madcap, stupid **7** flighty, foolish **8** careless, heedless, reckless, unstable, unsteady **9** foolhardy, forgetful, frivolous, imprudent **11** birdbrained, empty-headed, harebrained **12** absentminded, muddleheaded **13** irresponsible

scattered 6 random, spotty **7** diffuse **9** irregular **10** infrequent, occasional

scattering 6 sowing **7** casting **8** strewing **9** dispersal **10** dispersing, sprinkling **12** broadcasting, distribution **13** dissemination

scavenger 5 hyena **6** magpie **7** vulture **8** salvager **9** collector

scenario 4 book, idea, plan **6** scheme **7** concept, outline, summary **8** abstract, game plan, synopsis, teleplay **10** conception, manuscript, screenplay **French: 6** precis

scene 3 act **4** fuss, part, show, site, spot, to-do, view **5** place, sight, vista **6** locale, region, survey, vision **7** display, episode, picture, scenery, setting **8** backdrop, division, locality, location, panorama, position, prospect, sequence **9** commotion, spectacle **10** background **11** whereabouts

scenery 4 sets, view **5** vista **7** terrain **9** backdrops, landscape, spectacle **11** backgrounds

Scenes from a Marriage
  director: 13 Ingmar Bergman
  cast: 10 Liv Ullmann **13** Bibi Andersson **15** Erland Josephson

scent 4 odor, path, wake, wind **5** aroma, smell, sniff, spoor, trace, track, trail **6** course, detect, inhale **7** bouquet, breathe, discern, essence, perfume, pursuit, suspect **9** aromatize, fragrance, get wind of, recognize **11** distinguish

scented 5 spicy **7** odorous, piquant, pungent **8** aromatic, fragrant, perfumed **9** odiferous **13** sweet-smelling

Schaffner, Franklin

  director of: 6 Patton (Oscar) **15** Planet of the Apes

schedule 3 fix **4** book, list, plan, roll **5** fit in, slate, table **6** agenda **7** appoint, program, put down, set down **8** calendar **9** inventory, timetable

Scheele, Karl Wilhelm
  field: 9 chemistry
  nationality: 7 Swedish
  discovered: 6 oxygen **8** chlorine **9** glycerine

Scheider, Roy
  born: 8 Orange NJ
  roles: 4 Jaws **11** All That Jazz, Blue Thunder, The Seven-Ups **14** Fifty-two Pickup **19** The French Connection

Schell, Maria
  real name: 15 Margarete Schell
  born: 6 Vienna **7** Austria
  brother: 16 Maximilian Schell
  roles: 8 Cimarron, Gervaise **11** End of Desire, White Nights **13** The Last Bridge **20** The Brothers Karamazov

Schell, Maximilian
  born: 6 Vienna **7** Austria
  sister: 11 Maria Schell
  roles: 5 Julia **13** The Young Lions **19** Judgment at Nuremberg (Oscar) **21** The Man in the Glass Booth

scheme 3 map, way **4** plan, plot, ruse **5** cabal, chart, frame, means, shift, study **6** course, design, device, devise, layout, method, policy, sketch, system **7** complot, concoct, connive, drawing, network, outline, program, project, tactics **8** conspire, contrive, grouping, intrigue, maneuver, organize, strategy **9** machinate, procedure, stratagem **10** connivance, conspiracy **11** arrangement, contrivance, delineation, disposition, machination **12** organization

scheming 3 sly **4** arch, wily **6** artful, crafty, shrewd, tricky **7** cunning **8** slippery **9** conniving, designing, insidious **10** contriving, intriguing **11** calculating **13** Machiavellian

Schiller, (Johann) Friedrich von
  author of: 8 Ode to Joy **9** Don Carlos **11** Maria Stuart, William Tell **17** The Bride of Messina **18** The Maiden of Orleans

schism 5 break, split **8** division **10** separation **14** disassociation

Schlegel family
  characters in: 10 Howards End
  members: 5 Helen **8** Margaret, Theobald
  author: 7 Forster

schlepp 3 lug **4** cart, haul, tote **5** carry **6** convey **9** transport

Schlesinger, Arthur M, Jr
  author of: 13 A Thousand Days **15** The Age of Jackson **21** The Imperial Presidency **24** Robert Kennedy and His Times

Schlesinger, John

  director of: 7 Darling **14** Midnight Cowboy (Oscar) **22** The Falcon and the Snowman

Schlesinger, Leon
  creator/artist of: 9 Bugs Bunny

schmaltz 4 corn **14** sentimentalism, sentimentality

Schmeling, Max (Maxmillian Adolph Otto Siegfried)
  nickname: 10 Black Uhlan
  sport: 6 boxing
  class: 11 heavyweight

Schneider, Romy
  real name: 20 Rosemarie Albach-Retty
  born: 6 Vienna **7** Austria
  roles: 8 The Trial **11** The Cardinal **16** Boccaccio Seventy

Schoenberg, Arnold
  born: 6 Vienna **7** Austria
  composer of: 9 Erwartung **11** De Profundis, Expectation, Gurrelieder **12** The Lucky Hand **13** Moses and Aaron, Ode to Napoleon **14** Verklarte Nacht **16** Die Glucklich Hand, Resplendent Night **17** Transfigured Night **19** A Survivor from Warsaw, Pelleas and Melisande **26** The Book of the Hanging Gardens

Schoenius
  father: 7 Athamas
  mother: 8 Themisto
  wife: 7 Clymene
  daughter: 8 Atalanta

scholar 4 coed, sage **5** brain, grind, pupil **6** pundit, savant **7** egghead, learner, student, studier, wise man **8** bookworm, humanist, mandarin **9** collegian, schoolboy **10** schoolgirl **11** matriculant **12** intellectual **13** undergraduate

scholarly 6 humane **7** erudite, learned, liberal **8** academic, educated, informed, lettered, literate, well-read **12** intellectual

scholarship 5 grant **7** stipend **8** learning **9** education, endowment, erudition **12** intelligence, thoroughness **13** enlightenment

scholastic 8 academic, pedantic **9** pedagogic **11** educational **12** professorial **13** instructional

school 3 ism **4** view **5** bunch, crowd, faith, order, style, teach, train **6** belief, lyceum, method, system, theory **7** academy, college, educate, faction, thought **8** doctrine, instruct, seminary **9** institute **10** persuasion, university **12** denomination, kindergarten

schoolbook 3 abc **4** text **5** atlas **6** manual, primer, reader **7** grammar, lessons, speller

School for Scandal, The
  author: 23 Richard Brinsley Sheridan
  character: 5 Maria **6** Rowley **10** Lady Teazle **13** Joseph Surface, Lady

Sneerwell **14** Charles Surface, Sir Peter Teazle **16** Sir Oliver Surface

School for Wives, The
author: 7 Moliere
character: 5 Agnes **6** Horace, Oronte **7** Enrique **8** Arnolphe **9** Chrysalde

schooling 5 drill **8** drilling, training **9** education **11** instruction, preparation **14** indoctrination

schoolmaster 4 head **5** tutor **7** dominie, pedagog, scholar, teacher **9** pedagogue, principal, professor **10** headmaster, instructor **12** disciplinarian
fish: 7 snapper
genus: 8 Lutianus
species: 6 apodus

Schubert, Franz Peter
born: 6 Vienna **7** Austria
composer of: 6 Little (symphony), Tragic (symphony No 4) **8** Sad Waltz **9** Rosamunde **11** Winterreise **12** Trout Quintet **13** Mourning Waltz **17** Die Schone Mullerin **18** Unfinished Symphony (No 8) **24** Death and the Maiden Quartet, Symphony of Heavenly Length

Schulz, Charles
creator/artist of: 7 Peanuts

Schuman, William
born: 9 New York NY
composer of: 8 Undertow **9** Credendum **14** The Mighty Casey **16** American Festival **18** New England Triptych

Schumann, Robert Alexander
born: 7 Germany, Zwickau
composer of: 6 Myrten, Spring (symphony No 1) **7** Rhenish (symphony No 3) **8** Arabeske, Carnival **9** Papillons **10** Novelettes **11** Blumenstuck, Butterflies, Nachtstucke, Nightpieces, Novelletten **12** Bunte Blatter, Dichterliebe, Flower Pieces, Kinderscenen, Kreisleriana, Motley Leaves **14** Fantasiestucke **16** David's Band Dances, Symphonic Studies **18** Davidsbundlertanze **19** Frauenliebe und Leben

Schwann, Theodor
field: 7 biology
nationality: 6 German
established: 10 cell theory

Schwarzenegger, Arnold
roles: 5 Twins **7** Red Heat **8** Commando, Predator, Red Sonja, True Lies **11** Total Recall **13** The Terminator **15** Kindergarten Cop **17** Conan the Barbarian, Conan the Destroyer
wife: 12 Maria Shriver

Schweitzer, Albert
field: 8 medicine
worked in: 5 Gabon **6** Africa
founded: 17 Lambarene Hospital
awarded: 15 Nobel Peace Prize

Schwitters, Kurt
born: 7 Germany **8** Hannover
artwork: 7 Merzbau
collages called: 10 Merzbilden

science 3 art **5** skill **6** method **7** finesse **8** aptitude, facility **9** technique **10** discipline **11** acquirement
god of: 7 Mercury

scintilla 3 dot, jot **4** atom, iota **5** shred, spark, speck, trace **7** glimmer **10** smithereen

scintillate 4 joke, snap **5** amuse, charm, flash, gleam, glint, shine, spark **7** glimmer, glisten, glitter, shimmer, sparkle, twinkle **9** coruscate **10** effervesce

scintillating 5 witty **6** bright, lively **8** animated, charming, dazzling **9** brilliant, ebullient, exuberant, sparkling **10** glittering **11** stimulating **12** effervescent

scion 3 son **4** heir, seed **5** child, issue **7** heiress, progeny **8** daughter, offshoot **9** offspring, posterity, successor **10** descendant **11** progeniture

scissors 5 snips **6** blades, cutter, shears **7** clipper, snipper, trimmer
French: 8 secateur

scoff 4 jeer, mock, razz **5** flout, knock, taunt **6** deride, rail at, revile **7** condemn, laugh at, put down, run down **8** belittle, ridicule

Scofield, Paul
real name: 13 David Scofield
born: 7 England **14** Hurstpierpoint
roles: 8 King Lear **13** Sir Thomas More **17** A Man for All Seasons (Oscar)

scold 3 nag **5** chide, shrew **6** berate, carp at, nagger, rail at, rebuke, virago **7** censure, reprove, upbraid **9** castigate, criticize, dress down, reprehend, reprimand, termagant **10** complainer
Yiddish: 6 kvetch

scolding 7 chiding, reproof **8** berating, rebuking **9** reprimand, talking-to **10** admonition, upbraiding **11** castigation **12** admonishment **13** tongue-lashing

sconce 7 bracket **11** candlestick **12** candleholder

scoop 4 bail, beat **5** clean, clear, gouge, ladle, spoon **6** burrow, dig out, dipper, hollow, shovel, trowel **7** dish out, lade out, lift out **8** excavate

scoop out 3 dig **5** gouge **8** excavate

scoot 3 run **4** dash, rush **6** scurry, sprint

Scooter
nickname of: 11 Phil Rizzuto

scope 3 aim **4** area, goal, rein, room, span, vent **5** field, force, grasp, range, reach **6** bounds, effect, margin, motive, spread, vision **7** bearing, compass, freedom, liberty, purpose, stretch **8** ambition, confines, latitude **9** extension, influence, intention **10** competence **11** application, destination **13** determination

scorch 3 dry **4** char, sear **5** parch, singe **6** dry out, scathe, wither **7** blacken **8** discolor **9** dehydrate

score, scores 3 cut, mar, run, tab, win **4** bill, debt, gain, gash, goal, lots, make, mark, nick, slit **5** amass, count, facts, grade, hosts, judge, notch, point, slash, tally, truth **6** basket, charge, damage, deface, droves, groove, grudge, masses, pile up, strike, swarms, twenty **7** account, achieve, arrange, legions, reality, scratch, throngs **8** evaluate, incision, register **9** grievance **10** amount owed, difference, multitudes, obligation **11** orchestrate

scoria 4 slag **5** dross **6** cinder, refuse

scorn 5 spurn **6** ignore, rebuff, refuse, reject, slight **7** condemn, despise, disdain, mockery, repulse, sarcasm **8** contempt, derision, ridicule, scoffing, spit upon **9** arrogance, contumely, disregard, ostracize **10** look down on, opprobrium **11** haughtiness

scorned 7 derided, refused **8** despised, rebuffed, rejected, repulsed **9** disdained **10** deprecated, disparaged

scornful 6 lordly **7** cynical **8** arrogant, derisive, insolent, sardonic, scoffing, sneering **9** sarcastic **10** disdainful, ridiculing **11** disparaging **12** contemptuous, supercilious

Scorpio, Scorpius
symbol: 8 scorpion
planet: 4 Mars **5** Pluto
rules: 5 death **7** passion
born: 7 October **8** November

Scorpion 4 whip **7** scourge
constellation of: 8 Scorpius

Scorsese, Martin
director of: 6 Casino, Kundun **8** Cape Fear **9** Good Fellas **10** After Hours, Raging Bull, Taxi Driver **11** Mean Streets **12** The Last Waltz **14** Mad Dog and Glory **25** The Last Temptation of Christ

scotch 4 foil, kill, stop **5** crush, quash **6** thwart **7** destroy **8** confound, obstruct, sabotage, suppress **9** undermine **11** nip in the bud

scotch
type: 6 whisky **7** whiskey **10** singlemalt
origin: 8 Scotland
ingredient: 12 cereal grains
drink: 10 Scotch Mist **14** Highland Cooler
with amaretto: 9 Godfather
with cherry brandy: 12 Blood and Sand
with Drambuie: 9 Rusty Nail
with gin: 12 Barbary Coast
with vermouth: 6 Rob Roy **8** Affinity **10** Bobby Burns
brands: 5 J and B **7** Dewars **10** White Horse **11** Chivas Regal, Wild Grouse **12** Johnny Walker

Scotia
poetic: 8 Scotland

Scotland
Roman name: 9 Caledonia
capital: 9 Edinburgh
symbol: 7 thistle
poetic: 6 Scotia
largest city: 7 Glasgow
  others: 3 Ayr **4** Duns, Oban **5** Alloa, Banff, Brora, Burgh, Cupar, Ellon, Leith, Perth, Salen, Troon **6** Dundee, Girvan, Hawick **7** Airdrie, Alloway, Dunkeld, Falkirk, Frunock, Mallaig, Paisley, Renfrew **8** Aberdeen, Dumfries, Greenock, Hamilton, Kirkwall, Rothesay, Stirling **9** Clydebank, Dumbarton, Greenlock, Inverness, Kirkcaldy, Peter head, St Andrews **10** Coatbridge, Kilmarnock, Motherwell **11** Dunfermline, Grangemouth
school: 7 Glasgow **8** Aberdeen **9** Edinburgh **12** Saint Andrew's
division: 3 Ayr **4** Bute, Fife, Ross **5** Angus, Banff, Moray, Nairn, Perth **6** Argyll, Lanark, Orkney **7** Berwick, Kinross, Lothian, Peebles, Renfrew, Selkirk, Wigtown **8** Aberdeen, Ayrshire, Cromarty, Dumfries, Roxburgh, Shetland, Stirling **9** Buteshire, Caithness, Dumbarton **10** Kincardine, Midlothian, Sutherland **11** Clackmannan, Kincudbight **12** Renfrewshire **13** Stirlingshire
  kingdom: 8 Dalriada **11** Northumbria, Strathclyde
government: 13 United Kingdom
measure: 3 cop **4** boll, cran, fall, mile, peck, pint, rood, rope, span **5** crane, lippy **6** audlet, davach, firlot, lippie, noggin **7** chalder, choppin **8** mutchkin, stimpart, stimpert **9** particate, shaftment, shathmont
monetary unit: 3 ecu **4** demy, doit, lion, mark, rial, ryal **5** bodle, broad, groat, plack, rider, turne **6** bawbee, folles **7** unicorn **8** atchison, hardhead **9** halfpenny **11** bonnetpiece
weight: 4 boll, drop **5** trone **6** bushel
island: 3 Rum **4** Aran, Bute, Eigg, Fair, Inch, Iona, Jura, Lona, Muck, Mull, Rhum, Skye **5** Arran, Barra, Islay, Lewis **6** Harris, Orkney, Staffa **7** St Kilda **8** Berneray, Cumbraes, Hebrides, Shetland **9** North Uist, South Uist
lake/loch: 3 Awe, Dee, Lin, Tay **4** Earn, Fyne, Gair, Gare, Linn, Ness, Oich, Ryan, Sloy **5** Duich, Leven, Lochy, Lough, Morar, Maree, Nevis **6** Laggan, Linnhe, Lomond **7** Katrine, Rannoch, St Mary's
mountain: 4 Hope **5** Attow, Dearg, Nevis, Tinto, Wyvis **7** Cheviot, Macdhui, Merrick **8** Grampian **9** Ben Lomond, Cairngorm, Highlands, Trossachs
  hills: 5 Ochil **6** Calton, Sidlaw **7** Cheviot
highest point: 8 Ben Nevis
river: 3 Ayr, Dee, Don, Esk, Tay **4** Doon, Glen, Nith, Norn, Spey **5** Afton, Annan, Clyde, Forth, Garry, North, Tweed, Ythan **6** Affric, Teviot, Tummel **7** Deveron **8** Findhorn
sea: 5 Irish, North **8** Atlantic, Hebrides
physical feature:
  bay: 5 Scapa
  canal: 10 Caledonian
  channel: 5 Minch, North
  firth: 3 Tay **4** Kyle, Lorn **5** Clyde, Forth, Lorne, Moray **6** Linnhe, Solway **7** Comarty, Dornoch **8** Pentland
  glen: 8 Glen More **9** Great Glen
  hillside: 4 brae
  moor: 7 Rannoch
  valley: 8 Trossach
people: 4 Gael, Pict, Scot **5** Norse
  artist: 7 Raeburn
  author: 5 Burns, Scott **6** Barrie, Cronin, Dunbar **7** Barbour, Douglas **8** Henryson **9** Stevenson **10** Conan-Doyle, MacDiarmid, Macpherson
  economist: 5 Smith
  historian: 7 Carlyle
  inventor: 4 Bell
  king: 5 David, James **6** Duncan **7** Kenneth, Macbeth, Malcolm, Stuarts, William **9** Alexander **14** Robert the Bruce
  landowner: 5 laird
  philosopher: 4 Hume
  prime minister: 9 Macdonald, MacMillan **11** Douglas-Home
  prince: 19 Bonnie Prince Charlie
  queen: 4 Mary **13** Saint Margaret
  religious leader: 8 John Knox
  scientist: 7 Fleming
  patronymic: 3 Mac
  patron saint: 6 Andrew
language: 4 Erse **6** Celtic, Gaelic, Keltic, Lallan **7** English, Lalland
religion: 12 Episcopalian, Presbyterian **13** Roman Catholic
place:
  abbey: 5 Kelso **7** Melrose **8** Dryburgh, Jedburgh
  castle: 8 Stirling **9** Edinburgh **11** Eilean Donan
  church/kirk: 7 St Giles **11** St Cuthbert's
  coronation site: 12 Stone of Scone
  royal residence: 8 Balmoral
  Scott's home: 10 Abbotsford
  street: 7 Prince's **9** Royal Mile **11** Sauchiehall
feature:
  bird: 3 bae, cae **4** hern, muir, smeu **6** grouse, smeuth, snabby **7** jackdaw **8** throstle **9** swinepipe
  clothing: 3 tam **4** kilt **6** tartan **7** filibeg **12** Harris tweeds **13** Shetland knits **15** Fair Isle sweater
  dance: 3 bob **4** reel **7** walloch **9** ecossaise **10** petronella **11** strathsprey **12** gilliecallum **13** Highland fling
  game: 4 golf **12** caber tossing
  holiday: 8 Hogmanay
  monster: 6 Nessie **8** Loch Ness
  musical instrument: 7 bagpipe
  symbol: 7 thistle
  food:
    bread: 5 scone
    cheese: 7 crowdie
    dish: 6 haggis **12** finnan haddie **15** kippered herring
    drink: 12 Scotch whisky
    soup: 11 cock-a-leekie
  football team: 6 Oilers

Scott, George C
born: 6 Wise VA
wife: 14 Trish Van Devere **15** Colleen Dewhurst
roles: 4 Rage **6** Patton (Oscar, refused) **8** Jane Eyre **16** The New Centurions **18** The Day of the Dolphin

Scott, Sir Walter
author of: 6 Rob Roy **7** Ivanhoe, Marmion **8** The Abbot, Waverley **10** Kenilworth **11** The Talisman **12** Guy Mannering, Old Mortality, The Antiquary **14** Quentin Durward **16** The Lady of the Lake **20** The Bride of Lammermoor, The Heart of Midlothian **23** The Lay of the Last Minstrel

Scottish Mythology
spirit/horse: 6 kelpie

scoundrel 3 cad, cur **5** crook, knave, rogue, scamp, thief **6** rascal, rotter, varlet, weasel **7** bounder, ruffian, sharper, varmint, villain **8** scalawag, swindler, turncoat **9** miscreant, trickster **10** blackguard, copperhead, mountebank, ne'er-do-well **11** fourflusher, rapscallion **12** carpetbagger

scoundrelly 3 low **4** mean **7** debased **8** rascally **10** degenerate, despicable, villainous **12** contemptible, disreputable **13** reprehensible

Scoundrel Time
author: 14 Lillian Hellman

scour 4 buff, comb, rake, scan **5** scrub, shine **6** abrade, polish, scrape **7** burnish, cleanse, ransack, rummage **8** brighten, traverse

scourge 3 rod **4** bane, beat, cane, flog, lash, whip **5** birch, blast, curse, flail, strap **6** punish, smeuth, thrash **7** censure, chasten **8** chastise, scorpion, vexation **9** castigate, excoriate **10** affliction, discipline, flagellate **11** troublement **13** cat-o'-nine-tails

scout 3 spy **4** case **5** guide, pilot **6** escort, spy out, survey **7** lookout, observe **8** outrider, point man, vanguard **9** recruiter **11** reconnoiter **13** reconnoiterer

scowl 4 pout **5** frown, glare, lower **6** glower **7** grimace

scrabble 3 paw **4** claw, rake **5** climb **6** drudge, jostle, scrape, scrawl **7** clamber, grapple, scratch **8** struggle

scram 3 out **4** scat, shoo **5** be off, leave **6** beat it, begone, depart, get out, go away **7** get lost, vamoose **10** make tracks

scramble 3 run, vie **4** race, rush **5** clash, fight, mix up, scrap, upset **6** battle, combat, engage, garble, jostle, jumble, mess up, scurry, strive, tussle **7** collide, confuse, disturb, scatter, scuffle, shuffle **8** disorder, struggle, unsettle **9** scrimmage **10** disarrange, free-for-all **11** competition, disorganize

scramble up 5 climb, mount, scale **7** clamber

scrap 3 bit, dab, jot, row **4** atom, drop, iota, junk, spat **5** brawl, crumb, fight, grain, melee, speck, trace, trash **6** fracas, morsel, refuse, ruckus, sliver **7** abandon, glimmer, minimum, modicum, quarrel, snippet **8** brouhaha, fraction, fragment, jettison, molecule, particle, squabble **10** free-for-all, smattering, sprinkling

scrapbook 5 album **9** portfolio **11** memorabilia, miscellanea

scrape 3 dig **4** buff, gash, mark, rasp, save, skin **5** amass, clean, fight, glean, gouge, grate, graze, grind, plane, run-in, score, scour, scuff, stint **6** abrade, bruise, forage, gather, groove, obtain, pick up, plight, scrimp, secure, smooth, tussle **7** acquire, burnish, dilemma, procure, rub hard, scratch, scuffle, straits **8** abrasion **9** economize, tight spot **10** difficulty **11** predicament **13** confrontation

scratch 3 cut, mar, rub **4** claw, etch, gash, nick, omit, rasp **5** dig at, erase, grate, graze, grind, score **6** cancel, delete, incise, remove, rub out, scrape, scrawl, streak, strike **7** blemish, blot out, exclude, expunge, rule out **8** abrasion, cross out, lacerate, scribble, withdraw **9** eliminate **10** laceration

scratchy 4 rough **6** coarse **7** bristly, prickly **9** irritated **10** irritating

scrawl 4 draw **5** write **6** doodle **7** scratch, writing **8** scrabble, scribble, squiggle **10** penmanship **11** handwriting

scrawniness 8 lankness, leanness, slimness, thinness **10** skinniness, slightness **11** slenderness

scrawny 4 bony, lank, lean, puny **5** drawn, gaunt, lanky, runty, spare **6** sinewy, skinny, wasted **7** angular, scraggy, spindly, stunted **8** rawboned, skeletal **9** emaciated, fleshless **10** attenuated, undersized **11** underweight

screak 4 rasp **5** grate, grind **6** shriek, squeak **7** screech

scream 4 howl, loud, roar, wail, yell,

yelp, yowl **5** shout, whine **6** bellow, cry out, holler, outcry, shriek, squawk, squeal **7** screech **11** lamentation

screech 3 cry **4** howl, rasp **6** screak, scream, shriek **9** caterwaul

screen 3 see, web **4** cull, mask, mesh, rate, show, sift, sort, veil, view **5** class, cloak, cover, eject, films, grade, grate, group, guard, order, shade, sieve **6** buffer, cinema, defend, filter, mantle, movies, secure, shield, shroud, sifter, size up, strain, winnow **7** arrange, conceal, curtain, defense, discard, lattice, present, preview, project, protect, secrete, shelter, shutter, weed out **8** colander, coverage, evaluate, jalousie, separate, strainer, withhold **9** eliminate, partition, safeguard **10** protection **11** concealment

screw 4 bolt, join, knot, turn, warp **5** clamp, exact, force, gnarl, rivet, twist, wrest, wring **6** adjust, attach, deform, driver, extort, fasten, garble, wrench **7** contort, distort, pervert, squeeze, tighten **8** fastener, misshape **9** propeller

screwball 3 nut **4** kook **5** flake, freak **6** looney **7** lunatic **8** crackpot **9** character, eccentric

screwdriver
type: 6 rachet **11** spiral-drive **12** Phillips-head

screwy 3 odd **4** daft **5** batty, dotty, flaky, funny, kinky, kooky, nutty, queer, wacky, weird **6** weirdo **7** oddball **8** peculiar **9** eccentric **10** unbalanced

Scriabin, Aleksandr (Scriabine, Skryabin)
born: 6 Moscow, Russia
composer of: 7 Mystery **10** Prometheus **12** Vers la flamme **13** Poem of Ecstasy, The Divine Poem, The Poem of Fire

scribble 4 tear **5** squib **6** doodle, scrawl **7** scratch **8** squiggle **9** pull apart
fiber: 4 wool
procedure: 7 carding

scribe, Scribe 3 cut **4** mark, tool **5** clerk, score **6** author, copier, penman, writer **7** copyist, teacher **8** recorder **9** archivist, scrivener, secretary **10** amanuensis, translator **12** newspaperman, stenographer **13** calligraphist
Biblical: 4 Ezra **6** Esdras
French dramatist: 8 Augustin
Palestinian: 5 sofer **6** sopher

scribe of gods 5 Thoth

scrimp 4 save **5** hoard, pinch, skimp, stint **8** begrudge **9** besparing **12** pinch pennies

scrimping 6 frugal **7** sparing **10** economical **11** economizing **12** cheeseparing **15** pinching pennies

scrip 5 paper **8** document **11** certificate

scripsit 7 he wrote **8** she wrote

script 4 book, hand **5** lines, score **6** dialog **7** cursive **8** dialogue, libretto, longhand, scenario **10** manuscript, penmanship **11** calligraphy, chirography, handwriting

Scriptures, the 5 Bible **6** the Law, oracle **8** holy writ, the Bible, the Torah **10** the Gospels **11** The Good Book **12** New Testament, Old Testament, the Word of God **13** the Pentateuch, the Septuagint **14** sacred writings see also **5** Bible

scroll of the Torah
Hebrew: 11 Sepher Torah

Scrooge, Ebenezer
character in: 15 A Christmas Carol
author: 7 Dickens

scrub 4 swab **5** brush, scour **8** scouring **9** brushwood, scrubbing

scrubby 4 base **6** brushy **7** stunted **8** inferior **10** undersized

scrumptious 5 juicy, tasty **6** savory, tender **8** luscious, pleasant, pleasing **9** agreeable, delicious, enjoyable, flavorful, succulent, toothsome **10** appetizing, delectable, delightful, flavorsome **13** mouth-watering

scruple 3 shy **4** care, halt **5** demur, pause, qualm, waver **6** blench, ethics, falter **7** anxiety, concern, refrain **8** hesitate **9** fluctuate, misgiving, principle **10** conscience, hesitation **11** compunction, fearfulness, uncertainty **12** apprehension, doubtfulness, protestation **13** squeamishness **17** conscientiousness

Scruples
author: 12 Judith Krantz

scrupulous 5 exact **6** honest **7** careful, dutiful, precise, upright **8** cautious, exacting, sedulous **9** honorable **10** deliberate, fastidious, meticulous, principled **11** painstaking, punctilious **13** conscientious

scrupulousness 4 care **5** pains **9** exactness **14** meticulousness **17** conscientiousness

scrutinize 4 scan **5** probe, study **6** peruse, search, survey **7** explore, inspect, observe **11** investigate

scrutiny 5 study, watch **7** inquiry, perusal **9** attention **10** inspection **11** examination **12** surveillance **13** investigation

scuffle 3 row **4** spar **5** brawl, clash, fight, melee, scrap **6** fracas, jostle, rumpus, tussle **8** squabble, struggle **9** commotion, imbroglio **10** donnybrook, free-for-all

sculpsit 10 he carved it **11** she carved it **12** he engraved it **13** she engraved it **14** he sculptured it **15** she sculptured it

sculptor 6 artist, carver, caster, imager, molder **7** marbler, modeler **8**

chiseler, engraver
constellation: 19 Apparatus Sculptoris
French: 5 Rodin
Greek: 7 Phidias **10** Praxiteles
Irish-American: 12 Saint-Gaudens
Italian: 7 Cellini **12** Michelangelo
tool: 6 chisel, graver **7** spatula **9** ebauchoir

sculpture 3 cut **4** bust, cast, head, work **5** cameo, carve, erode, model, mould **6** chisel, relief, statue **7** carving, erosion, faience **8** intaglio, statuary **9** cloissone, medallion, statuette
medium: 4 clay **5** china, stone **6** bronze, enamel, marble **7** ceramic **9** porcelain **10** terra cotta **11** earthenware

scum 4 film, slag **5** crust, dregs, dross, trash **6** rabble, refuse **7** deposit, rubbish, surface **8** riffraff

scurrility 5 abuse **8** rudeness **9** indecency, obscenity, profanity **13** offensiveness, salaciousness

scurrilous 3 low **5** gross **6** coarse, vulgar **7** obscene **8** churlish, derisive, indecent, reviling **9** insulting, offensive, shameless **10** derogatory, detracting, indelicate, slanderous **11** disparaging, foulmouthed **12** contemptuous

scurry 3 hie **4** race, rush, skim **5** haste, hurry, scoot, speed **6** bustle, hasten, hustle, spring **7** rushing, scamper, scuttle **8** hurrying, scooting, scramble **9** confusion, dispersal **10** scattering

scurvy 3 low **4** base, mean, vile **6** shabby **7** ignoble **9** worthless **10** despicable **12** contemptible, dishonorable

scuttle 4 sink **5** abort, hurry, scrap, speed, wreck **6** hasten, scurry **7** destroy, discard, scamper **8** dispatch, scramble

scuttlebutt 4 talk **5** rumor **6** gossip **7** hearsay, prattle, scandal **8** chitchat

Scylaceus
origin: 6 Lycian
ally of: 7 Trojans
death by: 7 stoning

Scylla
form: 5 nymph **7** monster
location: 3 sea **16** Straits of Messina **20** Whirlpool of Charybdis
father: 7 Phorcys
mother: 6 Hecate
loved by: 8 Poseidon
rival: 10 Amphitrite

Scyphius
first: 5 horse
created by: 8 Poseidon

sea 3 bay, ton **4** deep, gulf, host, lake, leap, lots, main, mass, slew, wave **5** bight, flock, flood, ocean, scads, spate, surge, swarm, swell, waves **6** legion, roller, scores, waters **7** breaker **9** abundance, multitude, profusion
French: 3 mer
god of: 5 Aegir, Memir **6** Nereus, Tri-

ton **7** Glaucus, Neptune, Phorcys, Proteus **8** Poseidon **9** Asphalius
goddess of: 3 Ino, Ran **6** Graeae, Graiae, Matuta **8** Dictynna, Menannan **9** Leucothea **10** Amphitrite

Sea, the Sea, The
author: 11 Iris Murdoch

Sea Around Us, The
author: 13 Rachel L Carson

seaboard 5 coast **9** shoreline

Seaborg, Glen Theodore
field: 7 physics
worked with: 14 actinide series **19** transuranic elements
headed: 3 AEC **22** Atomic Energy Commission
awarded: 10 Nobel Prize

seacoast 5 beach, coast, shore **7** seaside **8** littoral **9** coastland, coastline, shoreline, waterside
French: 4 cote
Italian: 4 lido **7** riviera

seafarers 4 tars **5** salts **7** sailors, seadogs **8** mariners

Seagull, The
author: 12 Anton Chekhov
character: 5 Masha **6** Polina **10** Pyotr Sorin **11** Yevgeny Dorn **12** Ilya Shamraev, Irina Arkadin **13** Boris Trigorin, Nina Zaretchyn **16** Semyon Medvedenko **17** Konstantin Treplev

Seah 15 Biblical measure

Sea Hawk, The
director: 13 Michael Curtiz
cast: 10 Errol Flynn **11** Claude Rains, Donald Crisp **14** Brenda Marshall
score: 21 Erich Wolfgang Korngold

seal 2 OK **3** dam, fix **4** cork, lock, mark, plug, shut, stop **5** brand, close, stamp **6** accept, affirm, emblem, fasten, figure, ratify, secure, settle, shut up, signet, stop up, symbol, verify **7** approve, certify, confirm, endorse, imprint **8** colophon, conclude, fastener, hallmark, insignia, sanction, validate **9** determine, establish, trademark **10** impression **12** authenticate
Latin: 10 imprimatur

seal
young: 3 pup
group of: 3 pod

sea lion
young: 3 pup

seam 3 gap **4** line, lode, mark, scar, vein **5** break, chink, cleft, crack, joint, layer, notch **6** breach, furrow, incise, suture **7** crevice, fissure, joining, opening, rupture, stratum, wrinkle **8** junction, juncture **9** interface

seaman 3 gob, tar **4** hand, mate, salt **5** bosun, middy **6** lubber, merman, sailor, sea dog **7** mariner **9** boatswain **10** bluejacket, midshipman

seamark 5 light **6** beacon, pharos, signal **10** lighthouse, watchtower

sea monster 6 dragon **9** Leviathan

seamstress 10 dressmaker
French: 9 midinette **10** couturiere

seamy 3 raw **4** dark **5** dirty, nasty, rough **6** coarse, sordid **7** squalid, unclean **10** unpleasant **11** unwholesome **12** disagreeable

Sea of Grass, The
author: 13 Conrad Richter

sear 4 burn, char, scar **5** blast, singe, steel **6** harden, scorch **7** blister **9** cauterize **10** caseharden

search 4 comb, drag, fish, hunt, look, seek, sift **5** check, frisk, probe, quest, rifle, scour, snoop, study **6** survey, tracer **7** dragnet, examine, explore, inquiry, inspect, pry into, pursuit, ransack, rummage **8** overhaul, scrutiny **10** inspection, scrutinize **11** examination, exploration **13** investigation

Search, The
director: 13 Fred Zinnemann
cast: 9 Ivan Jandl **13** Aline MacMahon **14** Jarmila Novotna **15** Montgomery Clift
setting: 6 Berlin

Searchers, The
director: 8 John Ford
cast: 8 Ward Bond **9** John Wayne, Vera Miles **11** Natalie Wood **13** Jeffrey Hunter

searching 4 dour, keen, nosy **5** sharp **6** prying, shrewd, snoopy **7** curious, groping **8** exacting, piercing, rigorous, thorough **9** observant, quizzical, unsparing **11** inquisitive, penetrating **13** investigative

Seascape
author: 11 Edward Albee

seashore 5 beach, coast

seasick 3 ill **5** barfy, dizzy, faint, giddy, woozy **6** queasy **8** qualmish, vomitous **9** nauseated, squeamish **11** vertiginous

seasickness
French: 8 mal de mer

seaside 5 beach, coast, shore **9** shoreline

season 3 age, dry **4** fall, lace, tame, term **5** adapt, color, drill, inure, prime, ripen, shape, spell, spice, stage, train **6** accent, autumn, finish, flavor, inform, leaven, mature, mellow, period, refine, soften, spring, summer, temper, winter **7** enhance, enliven, prepare, quarter, stretch **8** accustom, duration, heighten, interval, ornament, practice **9** condition, cultivate, embellish **10** discipline

seasoned 6 herbed, inured, salted, spiced **7** veteran **8** flavored, hardened, peppered **9** competent, qualified **10** acclimated, accustomed, habituated **11** experienced **12** familiarized

seasoning 4 dill, herb, mace, sage, salt, zest **5** aging, basil, clove, gusto, onion, spice, thyme **6** drying, garlic, ginger, nutmeg, pepper, relish **7** oregano, paprika, parsley **8** allspice, cinnamon, marjoram, practice, ripening, rosemary, training **9** condiment, flavoring **10** maturation **11** orientation, preparation **15** familiarization

seasons
  god of: 9 Vertumnus
  goddess of: 5 Horae, Hours

seat 3 box, hub **4** axis, core, home, rump, site, sofa **5** abode, bench, chair, couch, croup, divan, fanny, heart, house, locus, place **6** behind, bottom, center, locale, settle **7** address, capital, cushion, habitat, housing, nucleus, rear end, situate **8** backside, buttocks, derriere, domicile, dwelling, haunches, location, quarters **9** posterior, residence **10** incumbency, membership **12** hindquarters

seat of justice 5 bench, court **8** tribunal **9** judiciary **10** courthouse

Seattle
  baseball team: 8 Mariners
  basketball team: 11 Supersonics
  bay: 7 Elliott
  football team: 8 Seahawks
  lake: 10 Washington
  landmark: 11 Space Needle
  site of: 10 World's Fair
  sound: 5 Puget

Sea Wolf, The
  author: 10 Jack London

Sebastian
  character in: 12 Twelfth Night
  author: 11 Shakespeare

Seberg, Jean
  born: 14 Marshalltown IA
  husband: 10 Romain Gary
  roles: 6 Lilith **7** Airport **9** Saint Joan **10** Breathless **16** Bonjour Tristesse

Secchi, Angelo
  field: 9 astronomy
  nationality: 7 Italian
  classified: 5 stars

secede 4 quit **5** leave **6** resign, retire **7** forsake **8** withdraw **12** disaffiliate

secession 10 separation, withdrawal **14** disaffiliation

seclude 4 hide **6** retire **7** isolate **8** separate **9** sequester **10** dissociate

secluded 6 covert, cut off, lonely, remote, shut in **7** private **8** closeted, confined, isolated, shut away, solitary **9** reclusive, sheltered, unvisited, withdrawn **10** cloistered **11** out-of-the-way, sequestered **12** unfrequented

seclusion 5 exile **6** asylum, hiding **7** retreat **8** cloister, hideaway, solitude **9** hermitage, isolation, reclusion, sanctuary **10** quarantine, retirement, withdrawal **11** concealment **13** sequestration

second 3 aid **4** abet, back, help, wink **5** agent, favor, flash, jiffy, other, proxy, trice **6** assist, back up, deputy, fill-in, helper, minute, moment, up-

hold **7** advance, another, endorse, further, instant, one more, outdone, promote, stand by, stand-in, support **8** advocate, delegate, exceeded, inferior **9** alternate, assistant, attendant, encourage, surpassed, twinkling **10** additional, lieutenant, substitute, understudy **11** alternating, subordinate **14** representative
  abbreviation: 1 s **3** sec

secondary 5 lower, minor, other **6** backup, lesser **7** smaller **8** inferior, mediocre, middling **9** alternate, ancillary, auxiliary, following, resultant **10** consequent, subsequent, subsidiary **11** subordinate

second childhood 6 dotage **8** senility

secondhand 4 used **8** indirect **10** derivative, hand me down

second-in-command 6 deputy **8** adjutant **9** assistant **10** lieutenant **13** vice president

second-rate 3 bad **4** poor, so-so **5** cheap, tacky **6** shabby **7** average **8** everyday, inferior, mediocre, middling **9** imperfect **10** inadequate, outclassed, pedestrian **11** commonplace, substandard **15** undistinguished

Second Sex, The
  author: 16 Simone de Beauvoir

second-story man 5 thief **6** robber **7** burglar **9** cracksman **10** cat burglar

second string 4 subs **5** bench **11** substitutes

second team 5 bench **11** substitutes

secrecy 6 hiding **7** mystery, privacy, private, silence, stealth **8** muteness, solitude **9** closeness, seclusion **10** covertness **11** concealment, furtiveness **13** sequestration **15** clandestineness, confidentiality, underhandedness **17** surreptitiousness **19** uncommunicativeness

secret 3 key, mum **4** dark **6** arcane, covert, enigma, hidden, mystic, occult, puzzle, recipe, unseen **7** formula, furtive, mystery, private, unknown **8** discreet, esoteric, hush-hush, secluded, stealthy **9** concealed, disguised, invisible, secretive **10** confidence, mysterious, undercover, unrevealed **11** camouflaged, clandestine, undisclosed, unpublished **12** confidential, unrevealable **13** surreptitious

Secret Agent
  character: 9 John Drake
  cast: 15 Patrick McGoohan
  theme: 14 Secret Agent Man

secretary 4 aide, desk **5** clerk **6** scribe **7** officer **8** recorder **10** amanuensis **12** stenographer
  French: 10 escritoire

secret council 8 conclave

secrete 4 hide, veil **5** cache, cloak, cover, stash **6** screen, shroud **7** conceal, curtain **8** disguise

secretive 3 mum, sly **4** mute **6** covert, silent **7** cryptic, evasive, furtive, laconic, private **8** discreet, reserved, reticent, stealthy, taciturn **9** enigmatic, withdrawn **10** mysterious **11** tight-lipped, underhanded, unrevealing **13** surreptitious **15** uncommunicative

secretiveness 7 mystery, stealth **9** reticence **11** furtiveness **14** inscrutability, mysteriousness **19** uncommunicativeness

Secret Life of Walter Mitty, The
  author: 12 James Thurber
  cast: 10 Danny Kaye

sect 4 camp, cult **7** faction **8** division **10** persuasion **11** affiliation **12** denomination

sectarian 6 narrow **7** limited **8** clannish **9** exclusive, parochial **10** provincial, restricted

section 4 area, part, side, unit, ward, zone **5** piece, range, share, slice **6** region, sample, sphere **7** chapter, cutting, measure, passage, portion, segment, terrain **8** district, division, province, specimen, vicinity **9** allotment, increment, territory **10** department, proportion **11** installment **12** neighborhood

sector 4 area, zone **7** theater **8** district

secular 3 lay **4** laic **6** carnal **7** earthly, fleshly, mundane, profane, sensual, worldly **8** material, temporal **9** nonsacred **11** nonclerical **12** nonreligious, nonspiritual **17** nonecclesiastical

secundum 11 according to

secure 3 get, set **4** bind, easy, safe, sure **5** fixed, tight **6** at ease, defend, ensure, fasten, immune, insure, obtain **7** acquire, assured, certain, protect, shelter, tie down **8** absolute, carefree, composed, defended, definite, in the bag, positive, surefire **9** confident, guarantee, protected, reassured, safeguard, sheltered **10** guaranteed **11** impregnable **12** invulnerable, unassailable, unattackable, unthreatened

securities 5 bonds, title **6** stocks **12** certificates

security 4 bond, care, hope, keep **5** faith, trust **6** guards, pledge, police, safety, surety, troops **7** defense, deposit, promise, support **8** reliance, sureness, warranty **9** assurance, certainty, guarantee **10** collateral, confidence, conviction, protection, safeguards **11** maintenance, safekeeping **12** absoluteness, decisiveness, definiteness, positiveness, preservation

sedate 4 calm, cool **5** grave, quiet, sober, staid, still **6** poised, serene, solemn, steady **7** serious, subdued **8** composed, decorous, reserved, unexcited, unruffled **10** cool-headed **11** level-headed **13** imperturbable **15** undemonstrative

sedateness 7 decorum, dignity, gravity, reserve 8 calmness 9 composure, soberness, solemnity 11 impassivity, seriousness

sedative 6 easing, opiate 7 anodyne, calming 8 allaying, lenitive, narcotic, relaxing, soothing 9 analgesic, assuasive, calmative, composing, mitigator, soporific 10 comforting, palliative 11 alleviative 12 tranquilizer 13 tranquilizing

sedentary 5 fixed, inert, still 6 seated 7 resting, sitting 8 inactive, unmoving 9 quiescent 10 stationary, unstirring

sedge 4 reed 5 grass 10 marsh grass

sediment 4 lees, scum, slag 5 dregs, dross, waste 6 debris, sludge 7 grounds, remains, residue 8 leavings 9 settlings

sedition 6 mutiny, revolt 7 treason 8 defiance, uprising 9 rebellion 10 disloyalty, insurgency, subversion, unruliness 11 lawlessness 12 disobedience, insurrection 14 rebelliousness, subversiveness

Sedley, Amelia and Joseph
  characters in: 10 Vanity Fair
  author: 9 Thackeray

seduce 4 lure, ruin 5 abuse, charm, tempt 6 allure, defile, entice, ravish 7 attract, conquer, corrupt, debauch, deprave, pervert, violate, win over 8 deflower, disgrace, dishonor, persuade 9 captivate

seducer 3 cad 4 wolf 5 letch, Romeo 7 defiler, Don Juan, playboy 8 Casanova, Lothario, lover-boy, ravisher, violater 9 corrupter, debaucher, womanizer 10 deflowerer 11 philanderer 12 heartbreaker
  French: 4 roue

seductive 4 sexy 8 alluring, charming, enticing, tempting 9 beguiling, disarming 10 attractive, bewitching, come-hither, enchanting, voluptuous 11 captivating, provocative

seductress 4 vamp 5 siren 7 charmer, Jezebel, Lorelei, mantrap 9 temptress 11 adventuress, enchantress
  French: 7 cocotte 11 femme fatale

sedulous 6 dogged 8 diligent, thorough 9 assiduous, steadfast 10 determined, persistent 11 industrious, painstaking, persevering 13 conscientious, indefatigable

sedulousness 4 zeal 8 industry, tenacity 9 assiduity, diligence 11 persistence 12 perseverance

see 3 dig, eye, spy, woo 4 date, espy, know, meet, mind, spot, view 5 court, grasp, sight, visit, watch 6 attend, behold, descry, escort, fathom, notice, regard, survey 7 consult, discern, glimpse, observe, picture, realize, receive, undergo, witness 8 conceive, consider, discover, envision, meditate, perceive, register, ruminate 9 accom-

pany, apprehend, ascertain, determine, encounter, entertain, interview, recognize, visualize 10 appreciate, comprehend, experience, understand 11 contemplate, distinguish
  Latin: 4 vide

see above
  Latin: 9 vide supra

see after
  Latin: 8 vide post

see before
  Latin: 8 vide ante

see below
  Latin: 9 vide infra

seed 3 pit, sow 4 germ 5 basis, grain, heirs, issue, ovule, plant, stone 6 embryo, origin, source 7 progeny 8 children 9 beginning, offspring, posterity 11 descendants

seedy 4 worn 5 dingy, faded, lousy, mangy, ratty, spent, tacky 6 scuffy, shabby 7 haggard, sickish, squalid 8 slovenly 10 threadbare 11 debilitated

see fit 5 deign 6 choose, please

seek 4 try 4 hunt 5 court, essay, trace 6 demand, invite, pursue 7 attempt, examine, explore, inspect, request, solicit, venture 8 endeavor 9 undertake 10 scrutinize 11 investigate

seek out 4 find 6 pursue 7 embrace, look for, solicit

seem 4 look 6 appear

seeming 7 evident, obvious, surface 8 apparent, presumed, putative, supposed 10 ostensible 11 superficial

seemly 3 due 5 right 6 decent, polite, proper 7 correct, fitting, prudent, refined 8 becoming, decorous, suitable, tasteful, well-bred 9 befitting, courteous 10 acceptable, felicitous 11 appropriate 12 conventional
  French: 11 comme il faut

seep 4 drip, leak, ooze, soak 7 diffuse, dribble, suffuse, trickle 8 permeate 9 penetrate

seepage 4 ooze 5 flour, issue 7 leakage, outflow 9 discharge, dribbling, secretion, trickling

seer 4 sage 5 augur 6 medium, oracle 7 diviner, prophet, psychic 8 conjurer, sorcerer 9 sorceress, stargazer 10 astrologer, soothsayer 11 clairvoyant, necromancer 13 fortuneteller 14 prognosticator

seesaw 5 waver 6 teeter 9 alternate, fluctuate, up-and-down, vacillate 12 teeter-totter

seethe 4 boil, brew, cook, fume, rage, rant, rave, roil, stew 5 churn, storm 6 blow up, bubble, simmer 7 bluster, smolder

seething 3 mad 7 boiling 8 agitated, bubbling, frenzied 10 distraught

see through 3 get 6 detect, effect, finish 7 achieve, execute, perform 8 carry out, complete, conclude 9 catch

onto, figure out, penetrate 10 comprehend, understand

Segal, Erich
  author of: 9 Love Story 12 Oliver's Story 16 Man Woman and Child

Segal, George
  born: 9 New York NY
  roles: 11 Blume in Love, Where's Poppa? 13 A Touch of Class 18 Fun with Dick and Jane 25 Who's Afraid of Virginia Woolf?

segment 3 leg 4 part 5 cut up, piece, stage 6 cleave 7 disjoin, portion, section, split up 8 disunite, division, separate 9 increment 11 installment

segmented 5 cut up 7 split up 9 sectioned, separated

segregate 6 cut off, detach, divide 7 divorce, isolate, seclude, sort out 8 disunite, insulate, separate 9 sequester 10 disconnect, quarantine

seine 3 net 4 drag, fish 5 trawl 7 dragnet

Seinfeld
  Network: 3 NBC
  cast: 11 Wayne Knight (Newman) 13 Jerry Seinfeld (Jerry) 14 Jason Alexander (George) 15 Michael Richards (Kramer) 17 Julia Louis-Dreyfus (Elaine)
  characters: 6 Newman 11 Elaine Benes, Cosmo Kramer 13 Jerry Seinfeld 14 George Costanza
  episodes/themes: 8 Man Hands, Soup Nazi 9 Marble Rye 10 The Contest 11 Junior Mints 12 masturbation, yada-yada-yada 16 Master of My Domain

seism 5 quake, shock 6 tremor 8 temblor, upheaval 10 earthquake

seize 3 bag, nab 4 grab, read 5 catch, glean, grasp, pinch, pluck, usurp 6 arrest, clutch, collar, gather, snatch 7 capture, embrace, impound, possess, utilize 8 arrogate 9 apprehend, overpower, overwhelm 10 commandeer, comprehend, confiscate, understand 11 appropriate

seize the day
  Latin: 9 carpe diem

seizure 3 fit 5 onset, spell, throe 6 access, arrest, attack, crisis, stroke, taking 7 capture, episode 8 grasping, paroxysm 9 abduction, snatching 10 convulsion, kidnapping, possession, usurpation, visitation 11 impressment 12 apprehension, confiscation 13 appropriation, commandeering

Sekhmet
  origin: 8 Egyptian
  goddess of: 4 evil

seldom 6 rarely 8 scarcely 10 uncommonly 12 infrequently, occasionally, sporadically

select 3 tap 4 A-one, pick, posh 5 elect, elite, fancy 6 choice, choose, chosen, opt for, picked, prefer 8 four-star, superior, top-notch **9** exclusive, first-rate, preferred **10** first-class, privileged

selection 4 pick **5** range **6** choice, medley, option **7** program, variety **8** choosing, decision **9** potpourri **10** collection, miscellany, preference

selective 5 fussy, picky **6** choosy **7** careful, finicky **8** cautious **10** discerning, fastidious, meticulous, particular **14** discriminating

Selene
    goddess of: 4 moon
    father: 8 Hyperion
    mother: 5 Theia
    brother: 6 Helios
    sister: 3 Eos
    loved: 8 Endymion
    daughter: 5 Herse **6** Pandia
    corresponds to: 5 Diana **7** Artemis

self 3 ego **6** person, psyche **8** identity **10** individual **11** homogeneity, personality
    inner: 5 anima **6** animus
    Universal: 5 Atman

self-abnegation 7 modesty **8** humility **10** diffidence **11** bashfulness

self-absorbed 4 vain **8** egoistic **9** egotistic **10** egocentric **11** egotistical **12** narcissistic

self-absorption 6 egoism, vanity **7** conceit **11** egocentrism, selfishness **16** self-centeredness

self-admiration 6 vanity **7** conceit, egotism **8** smugness **9** immodesty, vainglory

self-assertive 4 bold **7** dynamic **8** forceful **9** ambitious, confident **10** aggressive

self-assuming 4 vain **8** arrogant, egoistic **9** conceited **10** egoistical **11** egotistical

self-assurance 6 aplomb **9** brashness **12** cocksureness
    French: 9 sangfroid

self-assured 5 brash, cocky **8** cocksure **9** confident

self-centered 4 vain **8** egoistic, immodest **9** conceited, egotistic **10** egocentric **11** egotistical, swellheaded **12** narcissistic

self-centeredness 6 egoism, vanity **7** conceit **10** narcissism **11** egocentrism

self-composure 5 poise **6** aplomb **8** calmness **10** equanimity

self-confidence 5 nerve, pluck **6** mettle, spirit **8** boldness, gameness **9** cockiness **10** resolution **12** cocksureness

self-conscious 7 awkward **8** affected **9** chagrined, ill at ease, unnatural **11** discomposed, embarrassed **12** disconcerted

self-consciousness 7 modesty, reserve, shyness **8** timidity **9** abashment, hesitancy, reticence **10** con-

straint, demureness, diffidence **11** bashfulness, fearfulness **12** apprehension, sheepishness

self-control 5 poise **6** aplomb **8** firmness, patience, sobriety **9** composure, soberness, soundness, stability, willpower **10** temperance **11** forbearance **14** cool-headedness, unexcitability **15** levelheadedness **16** imperturbability
    French: 9 sangfroid **11** savoir faire

self-critical 6 humble, modest **9** diffident **13** perfectionist

self-criticism 7 modesty **8** humility **10** diffidence **13** perfectionism

self-deception 7 fantasy **8** delusion, illusion **13** hallucination

self-declared 5 sworn **6** avowed **8** admitted **9** confessed, professed **12** acknowledged

self-denial 8 eschewal **10** abnegation, abstention, abstinence, continence **11** forbearance **12** renunciation **14** abstemiousness

self-deprecation
    also: 16 self-depreciation **7** modesty **8** humility, meekness **10** humbleness

self-doubt 11 uncertainty

self-effacement 7 modesty, shyness **8** humility, meekness **10** diffidence **11** bashfulness

self-esteem 5 pride **10** confidence

self-evident 5 plain **6** patent **7** glaring, obvious **8** apparent, distinct, explicit, manifest, palpable **10** unarguable, undeniable **11** unambiguous, unequivocal **12** unmistakable **16** incontrovertible

self-explanatory 5 clear, lucid, plain **7** obvious **8** manifest **12** intelligible **15** straightforward

self-governing 4 free **9** sovereign **10** autonomous **11** independent

self-government 8 autonomy, home rule **11** sovereignty **12** independence

self-gratifying 11 intemperate

self-importance 6 egoism, vanity **8** smugness **9** arrogance, immodesty, pomposity, vainglory **11** egocentrism

self-important 4 smug, vain **7** pompous **8** egoistic, immodest **10** egocentric **11** egotistical **12** vainglorious

self-indulgence 12 extravagance, incontinence, intemperance

self-indulgent 9 libertine, sybaritic **10** hedonistic, voluptuous **11** extravagant, incontinent, intemperate

selfish 4 mean **5** tight, venal **6** greedy, stingy **7** miserly **8** covetous, egoistic, grasping, grudging **9** egotistic, illiberal, mercenary, rapacious **10** avaricious, egocentric, ungenerous **11** egotistical **12** parsimonious, uncharitable

self-love 6 egoism, vanity **7** conceit, egotism **9** vainglory **10** narcissism **11** complacency, egocentrism, haughtiness **13** conceitedness **15** swellhead-

edness
    French: 11 amour propre

self-possessed 4 calm, cool **6** poised **7** assured, courtly, refined **8** balanced, composed, polished, resolute **9** collected, confident **12** aristocratic **13** distinguished

self-possession 5 poise **6** aplomb **7** dignity **8** calmness, coolness **9** composure **10** confidence, equanimity, steadiness **16** imperturbability
    French: 9 sangfroid

self-praise 6 vanity **7** conceit, egotism **8** bragging, smugness **9** arrogance, immodesty, vainglory **12** boastfulness
    Italian: 11 braggadocio

self-propelling 9 automatic

self-questioning 10 uneasiness **13** soul-searching

self-reliance 8 sureness **9** assurance **12** independence

Self-Reliance
    author: 17 Ralph Waldo Emerson

self-reliant 5 hardy **6** plucky **7** assured **8** resolute, spirited **10** mettlesome **11** independent **12** enterprising

self-reproachful 8 contrite **9** regretful **10** apologetic, remorseful

self-respecting 5 proud **7** upright **8** decorous **9** dignified, honorable **10** upstanding **11** circumspect **13** distinguished

self-restraint 9 willpower **10** continence **11** forbearance

self-righteous 4 smug **5** pious **7** pompous **9** insincere, pietistic **10** complacent, moralizing **11** pharisaical, pretentious **12** hypocritical, mealymouthed **13** sanctimonious **14** holier-than-thou

self-sacrificing 6 heroic **7** gallant **9** unselfish **10** altruistic, martyrlike

self-satisfaction 5 pride **6** vanity **8** smugness **11** complacency

self-satisfied 4 smug, vain **8** cocksure, priggish **9** overproud **10** complacent **11** egotistical **12** narcissistic, vainglorious **13** overconfident

self-secure 4 smug **7** content **9** contented **10** complacent

self-seeking 6 greedy **8** covetous

self-styled
    French: 9 soi-disant

self-willed 8 obdurate, stubborn **9** obstinate, pigheaded **10** headstrong, refractory **11** intractable **12** ungovernable, unmanageable

sell 4 dump, hawk, vend **6** barter, betray, deal in, enlist, handle, market, peddle, unload **7** deceive, trade in, win over **8** convince, dispense

Selleck, Tom
    roles: 8 Lassiter, Magnum PI **12** Thomas Magnum **15** High Road to China **16** Three Men and A Baby

seller 6 dealer, jobber, monger, trader, vendor **7** peddler **8** merchant, retailer, salesman **9** middleman, salesgirl, saleslady, tradesman **10** saleswoman, shopkeeper, wholesaler **11** salesperson, storekeeper

Sellers, Peter
  real name: 19 Richard Henry Sellers
  born: 7 England **8** Southsea
  wife: 11 Britt Ekland
  roles: 10 Being There **12** Casino Royale **13** Dr Strangelove, Murder by Death **14** A Shot in the Dark, The Pink Panther **16** What's New Pussycat? **17** Inspector Clouseau **18** The Mouse that Roared **21** The World of Henry Orient

Selli
  priests of: 4 Zeus

sell out 6 betray **11** double-cross

semblance 3 air **4** cast, copy, look, show **5** image **6** aspect **7** bearing, replica **8** likeness, pretense **9** duplicate, facsimile **10** simulacrum **11** counterpart **12** reproduction **14** representation
  French: 4 mien

Semele
  also: 6 Thyone
  father: 6 Cadmus
  mother: 8 Harmonia
  loved by: 4 Zeus
  son: 8 Dionysus
  sister: 3 Ino **5** Agave **7** Autonoe

seminal 7 primary **8** creative, fruitful, germinal, original **9** formative **10** generative, productive **11** germinative, originating

Seminole
  language family: 9 Muskogean
  tribe: 8 Cow Creek, Mikasaki
  location: 6 Mexico **7** Florida, Georgia **10** Everglades
  leader: 7 Osceola, Wild Cat **10** Coacoochie

Semiramis
  queen of: 7 Assyria
  husband: 5 Ninus
  founder of: 7 Babylon

Semitic
  language family: 11 Afro-Asiatic **13** Hamito-Semitic
  eastern branch: 8 Akkadian, Assyrian **10** Babylonian
  western branch: 4 Geez **5** Tigre **6** Arabic, Gurage, Harari, Hebrew, Minean, Sabean, Syriac **7** Amharic, Aramaic, Argobba, Moabite **8** Ethiopic, Tigrinya, Ugaritic **9** Canaanite **10** Himyaritic, Phoenician, Qatabanian
  southwest branch: 6 Minean, Sabean **7** Amharic **10** Himyaritic, Qatabanian **11** North Arabic **19** South Arabic-Ethiopic

Semo Sancus *see* **6** Sancus

senatus consultum 17 Roman senate decree

send 4 cast, emit, head, hurl, lead, show, toss **5** drive, fling, guide, refer, relay, shoot, throw **6** convey, direct, launch, propel **7** conduct, deliver, forward, give off, project **8** dispatch, transmit **9** broadcast, cause to go, discharge **11** disseminate

send away 4 oust, rout, shoo **5** chase, evict

send forth 4 emit, gush **5** erupt, expel, issue, let go **7** dismiss, release **8** disgorge, dispatch **9** discharge

send off 4 post **7** forward **8** dispatch, disperse, transmit

send out 4 beam, emit **8** dispatch, transmit **9** discharge

send packing 3 axe, can **4** fire, oust, rout, sack, shoo **5** evict **6** bounce **7** cast out, dismiss

send to Coventry 3 cut **5** eject, expel **6** banish, ignore **7** cast out, exclude **9** ostracize

Seneca
  language family: 9 Iroquoian
  location: 7 New York **15** Canandaigua Lake
  leader: 9 John Abeel, John O'Bail **11** Cornplanter
  member: 19 League of the Iroquois

Senegal
  capital/largest city: 5 Dakar
  others: 5 Bakel, Matam, Thies **7** Bignona, Kaolack, Kaollak **8** Diourbel, Kedougou, Linguere, Rufisque **10** Saint-Louis, Ziguinchor **11** Richard-Toll, Tambacounda
  division: 7 Sudanic **8** Sahelian **9** Casamance
    empire: 4 Mali **5** Jolof **6** Tekrur
  monetary unit: 5 franc **7** centime
  island: 5 Goree
  lake: 6 Guiers
  mountain: 6 Gounou
  highest point: 12 Fouta Djallon
  river: 4 Sine **6** Faleme, Gambia, Saloum **7** Senegal **9** Casamance
  sea: 8 Atlantic
  physical feature:
    desert: 5 Ferlo
    peninsula: 9 Cape Verde
  people: 4 Lebu, Peul, Soce **5** Diola, Dyola, Foula, Laobe, Peulh, Serer, Wolof **6** Fulani, Serere **7** Bambara, Malinke, Tukuler, Tukulor **8** Mandingo
    leader: 7 Senghor
  language: 5 Wolof **6** French
  religion: 5 Islam **7** animism **13** Roman Catholic
  feature:
    musical instrument: 4 kora
    tree: 6 acacia, baobab **7** juniper, oil palm **10** raffia palm

Senhor, Senhora 2 sr **3** man, sra **5** madam (Portuguese)

senile 6 doting, infirm **7** foolish **8** decrepit **9** doddering, senescent **13** superannuated

senior, Senior 4 head, over **5** above, chief, doyen, elder, older **6** better **7** veteran **8** superior

seniority 6 tenure **9** longevity **10** precedence
  French: 4 pere

senor 2 Mr **3** don **5** title **6** mister **8** Spaniard

senora 3 Mrs, sra **4** lady, wife **5** madam, woman **8** mistress

senorita 4 lass, miss
  abbreviation: 4 srta

senorita 6 wrasse
  genus: 8 Oxyjulis
  species: 11 californica

sensation 3 hit **4** stir, to-do **6** thrill, uproar **7** feeling, scandal **9** agitation, awareness, commotion, detection **10** impression, perception

sensational 5 cheap, lurid **6** superb **8** dramatic, exciting, galvanic, shocking, striking **9** emotional, excellent, thrilling **10** electrical, scandalous **11** exaggerated, exceptional, extravagant, outstanding, spectacular **12** meretricious **13** extraordinary **14** heartthrobbing

sensationalism 7 scandal **9** luridness, melodrama **13** grandstanding **15** blood and thunder **16** yellow journalism

sense 3 see, use **4** aura, espy, feel, good, mind, note **5** grasp, guess, point, sight, smell, taste, touch, value, worth **6** descry, detect, divine, reason, regard, take in, wisdom **7** benefit, discern, faculty, feeling, hearing, meaning, purpose, realize, suspect **8** efficacy, function, judgment, perceive, sagacity **9** apprehend, awareness, intuition, recognize **10** atmosphere, comprehend, definition, denotation, impression, understand **11** connotation, premonition, realization, recognition **12** appreciation, intelligence, perspicacity, practicality, presentiment **13** consciousness, signification, understanding **14** reasonableness

Sense and Sensibility
  author: 10 Jane Austen
  character: 10 Lucy Steele **13** Edward Ferrars, Robert Ferrars **14** Colonel Brandon, John Willoughby **16** Sir John Middleton
    Dashwood family: 4 John **5** Fanny **6** Elinor **8** Marianne

senseless 4 dumb, idle, numb **5** crazy, inane, nutty, silly **6** stupid, unwise **7** aimless, foolish, stunned, useless, witless **8** comatose, deadened **9** brainless, foolhardy, illogical, insensate, pointless **10** groundless, ill-advised, insensible, irrational, ridiculous **11** harebrained, meaningless, purposeless, unconscious **12** unreasonable **13** irresponsible

sense of duty 15 moral obligation **21** sense of responsibility

sensibilities 8 feelings, sore spot, thin skin **12** Achilles' heel **14** susceptibility

sensibility 7 feeling **10** perception **11** temperament **14** responsiveness

sensible 4 just, sage, sane, wise **5** aware, plain, sound **7** evident, knowing, logical, obvious, prudent, visible **8** apparent, apprised, credible, discreet, informed, palpable, possible, rational, tangible **9** cognitive, cognizant, conscious, judicious, plausible, sagacious **10** detectable, discerning, farsighted, noticeable, perceiving, perceptive, reasonable, responsive, thoughtful **11** discernible, enlightened, intelligent, perceptible, susceptible **13** perspicacious **14** discriminating

sensitive 4 fine, keen, sore **5** acute, exact **6** tender, touchy **7** painful, precise **8** accurate, delicate, faithful, sentient **10** perceptive, responsive **11** susceptible, thin-skinned **14** impressionable

sensitiveness 8 delicacy **10** touchiness

sensual 4 lewd, sexy **6** carnal, earthy, erotic **7** fleshly, lustful **9** lecherous **10** hedonistic, licentious, voluptuous

sensualist 8 hedonist, sybarite **9** libertine **10** voluptuary

sensuous 9 delicious, exquisite **10** delightful

sententious 7 orotund, pompous, preachy, stilted **8** didactic, pedantic **9** grandiose, high-flown, pietistic **10** judgmental, moralistic **13** sanctimonious

sentient 5 aware **7** alert to, alive to, awake to, mindful **8** sensible **9** conscious

sentiment, sentiments 4 idea **5** heart **6** notion **7** emotion, feeling, opinion, romance, thought **8** attitude **9** nostalgia, viewpoint **10** tenderness **11** romanticism **12** emotionalism **15** softheartedness

sentimental 5 mushy, weepy **7** maudlin, mawkish, tearful **8** pathetic, romantic **9** emotional, nostalgic **10** lachrymose **12** melodramatic, romanticized

Sentimental Education, A
   author: 15 Gustave Flaubert
   character: 6 Arnoux **9** Dambreuse, Rosanette **11** Des Lauriers, Louise Roque **14** Frederic Moreau

sentimentalism 4 corn, mush **5** slush **6** bathos, pathos **8** schmaltz **9** mushiness, soppiness **10** maudlinism, slushiness **11** mawkishness

sentimentality 4 mush **5** heart **6** bathos, pathos **10** sloppiness **11** mawk-

ishness, temperament **12** emotionalism
   Yiddish: 6 kitsch

Sentimental Journey, A
   author: 14 Laurence Sterne
   character: 5 Maria **6** Yorick **7** La Fleur

sentinel 4 ward **5** guard, scout, watch **6** patrol, picket, ranger **7** lookout **8** guardian, watchman **9** guardsman

sentry 5 guard, watch **7** lookout, vedette, vidette **8** sentinel, watchman
   greeting: 4 halt

Seoul
   capital of: 10 South Korea

separate 3 cut **4** cull, fork, part, sift **5** break, crack, sever, split **6** bisect, detach, divide, ramify, remove, single, spread, sunder **7** crumble, disjoin, diverge, diverse, divorce, isolate, radiate **8** detached, discrete, distinct, disunite **9** bifurcate, break away, come apart, different, disunited, partition, segregate, subdivide **10** autonomous, disconnect, dissimilar, divaricate, individual **11** distinguish, independent

separated 6 cut off **7** severed **8** detached **10** disengaged **12** disconnected, disentangled

separate from 5 apart, leave

separately 5 apart **6** singly **7** asunder **9** severally **12** individually

Separate Tables
   director: 11 Delbert Mann
   based on play by: 15 Terence Rattigan
   cast: 10 David Niven **11** Deborah Kerr, Wendy Hiller **12** Rita Hayworth **13** Burt Lancaster
   Oscar for: 5 actor (Niven) **17** supporting actress (Hiller)

separation 3 gap **4** fork **5** break, space, split **6** breach, divide, schism **7** divider, divorce, good-bye, opening, parting, removal, sorting **8** boundary, distance, disunion, division, farewell, interval **9** branching, isolation, partition, severance **10** detachment, divergence **11** bifurcation, disjunction, segregation **12** estrangement **13** disconnection, disengagement **14** disassociation

Sepharvite god 10 Anammelech **11** Adrammelech

Sepher Torah 16 scroll of the Torah
   literally: 9 book of law

September
   characteristic: 11 harvest moon
   event: 14 aurora borealis, Northern lights **15** autumnal equinox
   flower: 5 aster **12** morning glory
   French: 9 Septembre
   gem: 8 sapphire **12** star sapphire
   German: 9 September
   holiday: 8 Labor Day (1st Monday) **10** Michaelmas (29) **15** Grandparents' Day

   Italian: 9 Settembre
   number of days: 6 thirty
   origin of name: 6 septum (Latin meaning seven)
   place in year:
     Gregorian: 5 ninth
     Roman: 7 seventh
   Spanish: 10 Septiembre
   Zodiac sign: 5 Libra, Virgo

septentrional 6 arctic **8** northern **11** hyperborean

Septuagint
   abbreviation: 3 LXX
   author: 10 the Seventy

sepulcher 4 tomb **5** crypt, grave, vault **7** ossuary **8** cenotaph **9** mausoleum, reliquary **10** necropolis

sepulchral 6 hollow **7** charnel **8** funereal, mournful, tomblike **10** lugubrious

sequel 3 end **6** finish, result, upshot **7** outcome, product **8** addendum, epilogue, follow-up, offshoot **9** aftermath, corollary, outgrowth **10** conclusion, postscript **11** consequence, culmination **12** continuation
   French: 10 denouement

sequence 3 run **4** flow **5** chain, cycle, order, round, train **6** course, parade, series, string **7** routine **8** schedule **9** cavalcade **10** procession, succession **11** arrangement, progression **14** successiveness **15** consecutiveness

sequester 6 banish, lock up, retire **7** confine, isolate, seclude **8** separate, withdraw **9** segregate **10** quarantine

sequestered 8 closeted, confined, isolated, secluded **9** insulated, sheltered, withdrawn **10** cloistered **11** dissociated

sequin 4 coin, disk **5** ducat **7** spangle **8** ornament
   French: 9 paillette

seraglio 3 oda **5** harem, serai **6** zenana **9** gynaeceum

serape 4 cape **5** shawl **6** mantle, poncho

seraph 5 angel

seraphic 7 angelic **8** beatific, ethereal, heavenly **9** celestial

Seraphim 6 angels

Serapis
   origin: 5 Greek **8** Egyptian
   form: 5 deity
   combination of: 4 Apis, Hapi **6** Osiris

Serbia see **10** Yugoslavia

sere 3 dry **4** arid **6** barren **7** parched, wizened **8** droughty, scorched, withered **9** shriveled, unwatered, waterless **10** dehydrated, desiccated **12** dehumidified, moistureless

serene 4 calm, cool, fair **5** clear, quiet, still **6** bright, limpid, placid, poised, sedate, smooth **7** halcyon **8** composed, peaceful, pellucid, tranquil **9** dignified, unruffled **10** nonchalant, unobscured, untroubled **11** undisturbed, unexcitable, unperturbed **13** unimpassioned

serenity 7 dignity **8** calmness, coolness, quietude **9** composure, placidity **10** equanimity, quiescence **11** complacence, nonchalance, tranquility **12** peacefulness, tranquillity **13** collectedness
French: 9 sangfroid

serf 6 cotter, thrall, vassal **7** bondman, peasant, villein

serfdom 4 yoke **6** thrall **7** bondage, slavery **9** servitude, thralldom, vassalage **11** enslavement, subjugation

Sergeant York
director: 11 Howard Hawks
cast: 10 Gary Cooper, Joan Leslie **12** George Tobias **13** Walter Brennan
Oscar for: 5 actor (Cooper)

Sergestus
origin: 6 Trojan
companion to: 6 Aeneas

serial 7 regular **9** continued, piecemeal, recurring **10** continuous, sequential, successive **11** consecutive, incremental

series 3 set **5** chain, cycle, group, order **6** course, number, parade, string **8** sequence **10** procession, succession **11** progression

serious 3 bad, sad **4** grim **5** grave, heavy, sober, staid **6** rueful, sedate, severe, solemn, somber **7** crucial, decided, earnest, fateful, harmful, pensive, sincere, weighty **8** alarming, critical, dejected, downcast, frowning, perilous, resolute, resolved **9** crippling, dangerous, important, momentous, saturnine **10** determined, portentous, purposeful, thoughtful **13** consequential **14** incapacitating

seriousness 7 gravity **8** severity **9** sincerity, soberness, solemnity **10** importance **11** earnestness

sermon 6 homily, rebuke, tirade **7** lecture, reproof **8** diatribe, harangue **9** preaching **10** admonition, preachment **11** exhortation

serpent, Serpent 3 asp **5** cheat, devil, rogue, Satan, snake, viper **7** reptile, traitor **8** deceiver **9** trickster
constellation of: 7 Serpens

Serpent Holder
constellation of: 9 Ophiuchus

serpentine 4 mazy **6** spiral, zigzag **7** coiling, crooked, devious, sinuous, snaking, winding **8** flexuous, tortuous, twisting **10** circuitous, convoluted, meandering, round about, undulating **12** labyrinthine

Serpico
director: 11 Sidney Lumet
based on story by: 9 Peter Maas
cast: 8 Al Pacino **9** Jack Kehoe **12** John Randolph
setting: 11 New York City

serrate 5 notch **6** jagged, pinked, ridged **7** dentate, grooved, notched, toothed **10** sawtoothed

serration 5 notch, ridge, teeth, tooth **8** notching, sawtooth

servant 3 man **4** cook, girl, help, maid **5** valet **6** butler, flunky, helper, lackey, menial, minion, slavey **7** footman **8** domestic, employee, factotum, henchman, hired man, retainer, scullion **9** attendant, chauffeur, hired girl, hired help, man Friday, underling **10** girl Friday **11** housekeeper

serve 2 do **3** act, aid **4** help, pass, suit, tend, work **5** avail, spend, treat **6** assist, attend, be used, do duty, oblige, supply, wait on **7** content, deliver, further, perform, present, promote, satisfy, suffice, work for **8** carry out, complete, function, hand over, minister **9** officiate **11** fill the bill

service, services 3 aid, use **4** help, mend, rite **5** avail, labor **6** adjust, agency, bureau, effort, employ, profit, repair, ritual, system **7** benefit, support, utility, waiting **8** ceremony, facility, maintain, military **9** advantage, provision, treatment **10** assistance, attendance, ceremonial, department, employment, observance, usefulness **11** celebration, convenience, maintenance **12** ministration **13** accommodation

serviceable 5 tough **6** rugged, strong, sturdy, usable, useful **7** durable, lasting **8** workable **9** effective, operative, practical **10** functional **11** utilitarian

serviceman 6 marine, sailor **7** soldier **9** repairman

servile 4 oily **6** abject, humble, menial **7** fawning, in bonds, slavish **8** cringing, scraping, toadying, unctuous **9** groveling, truckling **10** obsequious, submissive **11** bootlicking, subservient, sycophantic

serving 6 acting **7** dishful, helping, portion, waiting **8** plateful **9** assisting, attending, sufficing **11** ministering

serving counter 3 bar **6** buffet **9** sideboard

servitude 5 bonds **6** chains **7** bondage, fetters, serfdom, slavery **8** shackles **9** thralldom, vassalage **10** oppression **11** enslavement, subjugation **12** enthrallment, imprisonment

Servius Tullius
also: 7 Tullius
king of: 4 Rome
daughter: 6 Tullia
son-in-law: 7 Tarquin
killed by: 6 Tullia **7** Tarquin

sesame
also called: 10 benne seeds
botanical name: 14 Sesamum indicum
fairy tale: 10 "open sesame" **25** Ali Baba and the Forty Thieves

high in: 7 protein
former/mythical use: 3 oil **8** medicine **10** opens locks **11** lighting oil **16** discovers secrets **21** discovers secret places
use: 5 bread **6** salads **10** casseroles
use like: 8 nutmeats **11** chopped nuts

Sesame Street
character: 4 Bert, Elmo **5** Ernie, Herry, Oscar **6** Snuffy **7** Barkley, Big Bird, Muppets **8** the Count **12** Telly Monster **13** Cookie Monster **15** Mr Snuffleupagus

Sesostris
king of: 5 Egypt

session 4 bout, term **5** round, synod **6** course, period **7** meeting, quarter, sitting **8** assembly, conclave, semester **10** conference, convention

set 3 cut, fit, fix, gel, kit, lay, put, sic **4** club, drop, firm, line, make, plop, post, rate, sink, stud, suit **5** adapt, align, array, banal, bunch, crowd, embed, fixed, group, imbed, order, place, plunk, ready, rigid, scene, stale, stiff, stock, style, trite, usual **6** adjust, assess, assign, attach, common, confer, create, decree, frozen, harden, line up, locale, locate, ordain, outfit, studio **7** arrange, bearing, complex, congeal, decided, faction, install, jellify, machine, prepare, profile, regular, release, routine, scenery, service, setting, situate, station, thicken, unleash **8** arranged, assembly, backdrop, carriage, definite, estimate, everyday, familiar, firmness, habitual, hardened, location, ornament, position, prepared, regulate, rigidity, solidify, stubborn **9** apparatus, calibrate, customary, determine, establish, hackneyed, immovable, obstinate, prescribe, represent, steadfast **10** accustomed, assortment, collection, inflexible **11** anticipated, commonplace, consolidate, established, prearranged **12** conventional
French: 6 clique **7** coterie

Set
also: 4 Seth
origin: 8 Egyptian
form: 6 animal
personifies: 6 desert
brother: 6 Osiris
killed: 6 Osiris

set about 5 begin **6** assume **9** undertake **10** surrounded

set against 8 alienate, estrange

set apart 5 allot **6** detach, divide **7** earmark, isolate **8** allocate, separate **9** apportion, segregate **11** appropriate

set aside 4 kill **5** allot, annul **6** abjure, cancel, repeal, revoke **7** abandon, abolish, call off, destroy, discard, earmark, nullify, put away, rescind, retract, reverse **8** abrogate, allocate, override, overturn **9** designate, repudiate **10** invalidate **11** discontinue

set at ease 5 cheer **6** please **7** appease, comfort, content, gratify

set at liberty 4 free **5** let go **6** parole **7** manumit, release, unchain **8** liberate, unfetter **9** unshackle **10** emancipate

setback 4 flop, loss, snag **5** hitch, slump **6** defeat, mishap, rebuff **7** failure, relapse, reverse, undoing **8** reversal **9** adversity, mischance, worsening **10** misfortune, regression **13** retrogression **14** disappointment

set down 6 record **7** deposit

set forth 2 go **5** be off, leave **6** assert, avouch, depart **7** advance **8** advocate, propound **10** sally forth

set free 5 let go, loose, untie **6** acquit, loosen, pardon, parole, unbind, uncage, unlock **7** deliver, release **8** liberate, unfetter **9** discharge, disengage, extricate **10** emancipate

Seth *see* **3** Set

Seth
   means: 12 compensation
   father: 4 Adam
   mother: 3 Eve
   son: 4 Enos

set in 5 arise, ensue, occur **6** arrive

set in motion 5 begin, start **6** launch **8** initiate **9** instigate, originate **10** inaugurate

set in order 4 rank, sort **5** align **6** line up **7** arrange, marshal **8** classify, organize **9** methodize **11** systematize

set of beliefs 5 credo, creed, dogma, ethos **6** ethnic, tenets **8** doctrine **10** philosophy, principles **11** convictions

set off 6 depart **7** explode, go forth **8** detonate, start out **10** sally forth

set on fire 4 burn **5** light **6** ignite, kindle

set out 4 pose **5** array, begin, be off, place, range **6** deploy, embark, intend **7** arrange, display **9** undertake

set right 7 correct **8** disabuse

set store by 5 prize, value **6** esteem **7** respect **8** treasure

set straight 5 edify **6** advise, inform **7** educate **8** disabuse **9** enlighten

settee 4 seat, sofa **5** bench

setting 5 scene **6** fixing, locale **7** jelling **8** aligning, ambiance, locating, location, mounting **9** adjusting, arranging, decreeing, hardening, ordaining **10** congealing, regulating, thickening **11** arrangement, determining, environment, prescribing, solidifying **12** establishing, surroundings
   French: 6 milieu **11** mise-en-scene

setting sun
   god of: 5 Janus

settle 3 fix, pay, sag **4** calm, drop, land, sink **5** agree, allay, clear, droop,

light, lodge, perch, quiet **6** alight, choose, decide, locate, move to, pacify, people, soothe **7** arrange, clarify, clear up, compose, inhabit, rectify, resolve, satisfy, sit down, situate **8** colonize, make good, populate, take root **9** determine, discharge, establish, reconcile **11** precipitate

settled 4 sure **7** certain, decided

settlement 3 sum **4** camp, post **6** amount, colony, hamlet **7** bequest, outpost, payment, village **8** clearing, peopling **9** clearance, discharge **10** adjustment, colonizing, encampment, resolution **11** acquittance, arrangement, liquidation **12** amortization, colonization, compensation, satisfaction **14** reconciliation

settler 7 pioneer **8** colonist, squatter **9** colonizer, immigrant **11** homesteader **12** frontiersman

settle upon 6 bestow **7** consign **8** bequeath

settlings 4 lees **5** dregs **7** deposit, grounds, remains, residue **8** leavings

set-to 4 spat **5** brush, clash, run-in **6** battle, fracas **7** dispute, quarrel, scuffle **8** argument, skirmish, squabble **10** engagement, falling out **12** disagreement **13** confrontation
   French: 11 contretemps

setup 4 plan **6** scheme, system **8** practice **9** apparatus **11** arrangement **12** organization

set up 3 rig **5** erect, found **7** arrange, install **8** construct, establish, institute **10** inaugurate, prearrange

set upon 3 mug **5** beset, fly at **6** assail, attack **7** besiege, lunge at **9** pitch into

Seurat, Georges Pierre
   born: 5 Paris **6** France
   artwork: 9 The Chahut, The Circus, The Models, The Parade, The Uproar **10** The Bathers **12** Le Grand Jatte, The Yoked Cart **19** Une Baignade Asnieres **23** A Bathing Scene at Asnieres, The Bec du Hoc at Grand champ **40** Sunday Afternoon on the Island of La Grand Jatte

Seuss, Dr
   real name: 19 Theodore Seuss Geisel
   author of: 12 If I Ran the Zoo **14** The Cat in the Hat **15** Green Eggs and Ham, Horton Hears a Who, If I Ran the Circus **19** Horton Hatches the Egg **23** Mister Brown Can Moo Can You? **26** Thidwick The Big-Hearted Moose, How the Grinch Stole Christmas

Seve
   nickname of: 20 Severiano Ballesteros

Seven Against Thebes
   author: 9 Aeschylus
   character: 6 Ismene **8** Antigone, Eteocles **9** Polynices **11** Theban Women

seven heroes: 6 Tydeus **8** Adrastus, Capaneus **9** Polynices **10** Amphiaraus, Hippomedon **13** Parthenopaeus

Seven Beauties
   director: 14 Lina Wertmuller
   cast: 11 Fernando Rey **13** Shirley Stoler **17** Giancarlo Giannini

Seven Brides for Seven Brothers
   director: 12 Stanley Donen
   cast: 9 Tammy Rall **10** Howard Keel, Jane Powell **11** Julie Newmar (Newmeyer), Russ Tamblyn **12** Jeff Richards **14** Virginia Gibson
   score: 11 Saul Chaplin **12** Johnny Mercer
   choreography: 11 Michael Kidd

Seven Pillars of Wisdom
   author: 10 T E Lawrence

Seven Samurai
   director: 13 Akira Kurosawa
   cast: 11 Yoshio Inaba **13** Toshiro Mifune **14** Takashi Shimura
   remade as: 19 The Magnificent Seven

seven seas 6 Arctic, Indian **9** Antarctic **12** North Pacific, South Pacific **13** North Atlantic, South Atlantic

Seven Sisters colleges 5 Smith **6** Vassar **7** Barnard **8** Bryn Mawr **9** Radcliffe, Wellesley **12** Mount Holyoke

Seventeen
   author: 15 Booth Tarkington
   character: 7 Genesis **9** Miss Pratt, Mrs Baxter **10** Jane Baxter, May Parcher **21** William Sylvanus Baxter

Seventh Seal, The
   director: 13 Ingmar Bergman
   cast: 9 Nils Poppe **11** Max von Sydow **13** Bibi Andersson **17** Gunnar Bjornstrand

Seventy-seven Sunset Strip
   character: 6 J R Hale, Kookie (Gerald Lloyd Kookson III), Roscoe **7** Suzanne **11** Jeff Spencer, Rex Randolph **12** Stuart Bailey
   cast: 9 Edd Byrnes **10** Louis Quinn, Roger Smith **11** Richard Long, Robert Logan **14** Jacqueline Beer **16** Efrem Zimbalist Jr
   Kookie's sayings: 10 a dark seven **12** the ginchiest **13** piling up the Z's **14** lend me your comb **15** play like a pigeon **17** headache grapplers **22** keep the eyeballs rolling

seven wonders of the ancient world 8 pyramids (Egypt) **12** Olympian Zeus (sculpted by Phidias) **15** Temple of Artemis (at Ephesus) **16** Colossus of Rhodes **22** Lighthouse (Pharos) at Alexandria **23** hanging gardens of Babylon (of Semiramis) **24** Mausoleum at Halicarnassus

Seven Year Itch, The
   director: 11 Billy Wilder
   cast: 8 Tom Ewell **10** Sonny Tufts **11** Evelyn Keyes, Victor Moore **13** Mari-

lyn Monroe
setting: 11 New York City

sever 3 saw **4** part, rend, rive, tear **5** slice, split **6** bisect, cleave, cut off, lop off **7** disjoin, rupture, split up **8** amputate, break off, cut in two, dissolve, disunite, separate, truncate **9** dismember, terminate **10** disconnect **11** discontinue

several 3 own **4** a few, some **6** divers, single, sundry **7** certain, diverse, express, private, special **8** assorted, distinct, peculiar, personal, separate, specific **9** different, exclusive **10** individual, particular, respective **11** distinctive, independent

severe 4 cold, dour, grim, wild **5** cruel, grave, harsh, plain, rough, sober, stern, stiff **6** biting, bitter, brutal, chaste, fierce, fuming, raging, savage, sedate, simple, somber, strict, taxing **7** austere, cutting, drastic, extreme, furious, intense, painful, serious, uniform, violent **8** piercing, rigorous, ruthless, stinging, vigorous **9** dangerous, demanding, difficult, draconian, merciless, saturnine, turbulent, unadorned, unsparing **10** forbidding, restrained, tumultuous **11** distressing, undecorated, unrelenting **12** conservative

severed 6 cut off **8** detached **9** uncoupled, unhitched **10** unfastened **11** unconnected **12** disconnected

Severini, Gino
born: 5 Italy **7** Cortona
artwork: 9 Harlequin **15** The Armored Train **25** Dancer Sea and Vase of Flowers **32** Dynamic Hieroglyph of the Bal Tabarin

severity 5 rigor **7** cruelty **8** acrimony, violence **9** austerity, gruffness, harshness, sternness **10** asceticism, difficulty, strictness, stringency **11** seriousness **12** grievousness

Seville
former name: 8 Hispalis
landmark: 7 Alcazar, Giralda
plain: 9 Andalusia
river: 12 Guadalquivir
ruler: 5 Moors **6** Romans **7** Vandals **8** Abbasids, Almohads, Iberians **9** Visigoths **10** Almoravids
Spanish: 7 Sevilla

sew 3 hem **4** mend, seam, tack **5** unite **6** fasten, ground, stitch, suture **10** run aground
loosely: 5 baste

sewage 5 waste **6** efflux, refuse **8** effluent **9** effluence

Seward, Dr
character in: 7 Dracula
author: 6 Stoker

sewing machine
invented by: 4 Howe

sex 4 Eros, love **6** coitus, gender, libido **7** coition **8** maleness **10** copulation,

femaleness, femininity, generation, lovemaking **11** masculinity, procreation **12** reproduction

Sexton, Anne
author of: 15 All My Pretty Ones **22** To Bedlam and Part Way Back **23** The Awful Rowing Toward God

sexual 6 coital, erotic **7** amatory, genital, marital, sensual **8** conjugal, intimate, venereal **10** copulatory, generative, libidinous **11** procreative **12** reproductive

sexually stimulating 3 hot **4** sexy **6** erotic, risque **9** salacious **10** suggestive **12** pornographic

sexy 4 lewd **5** bawdy **6** erotic **8** prurient **9** seductive **10** come-hither, coquettish, suggestive, voluptuous **11** flirtatious, provocative

Seychelles
capital/largest city: 8 Victoria
monetary unit: 4 cent **5** rupee
island: 4 Mahe **7** Aldabra, La Digue, Praslin **8** Farquhar **9** Desroches **10** Silhouette
highest point: 16 Morne Seychellois
sea: 6 Indian
people: 5 Asian **6** Creole, French, Indian **7** African, Chinese
  leader: 4 Rene **7** Mancham
language: 6 Creole, French **7** English
religion: 8 Anglican **13** Roman Catholic

sforzando
music: 12 sudden accent

Shabbas 7 Sabbath

shabby 3 low **4** mean, poor, torn, worn **5** cheap, dirty, mangy, raggy, ratty, seedy, sorry, tatty, tight **6** frayed, meager, ragged, sordid, unfair **7** ignoble, rundown, scruffy **8** beggarly, decaying, inferior, slovenly, unworthy, wretched **9** illiberal, miserable, neglected **10** ramshackle, threadbare, tumbledown, ungenerous **11** dilapidated **12** contemptible, deteriorated, dishonorable, impoverished

shabby bar 4 dive **5** joint **7** gin mill **9** honky-tonk

shack 3 hut **5** cabin **6** lean-to, shanty

shackle 3 bar, tie **4** balk, bind, cuff, curb, foil, rein **5** block, bonds, chain, check, cramp, cuffs, deter, irons, limit, stall **6** chains, fetter, hamper, hinder, hobble, hogtie, impede, pinion, retard, secure, tether, thwart **7** inhibit, manacle, prevent **8** encumber, handcuff, restrict **9** forestall, frustrate, hamstring, handcuffs **12** circumscribe

shackled 7 chained, in irons **8** in chains, manacled **10** handcuffed

shadchan, schatchen 10 matchmaker **14** marriage broker

Shaddai 3 God

shade 3 bit, dim, hue, jot **4** atom, cast, hint, hood, iota, tint, tone, veil, whit

5 blind, color, drape, tinge, touch, trace **6** awning, canopy, darken, screen, shadow, shield **7** curtain, modicum, shadows, shutter **8** darkness, particle, semidark **9** scintilla **10** suggestion
French: 7 soupcon
form: 6 spirit
location: 5 Hades

shadow, shadows 3 bit, dog **4** blot, hint, tail **5** cloud, ghost, hound, shade, smear, stain, stalk, taint, tinge, touch, trace, track, trail **6** blight, follow, pursue, smirch, smudge, threat **7** blemish, specter, whisper **8** penumbra **10** reflection, silhouette, suggestion

Shadow of a Doubt
director: 15 Alfred Hitchcock
cast: 10 Hume Cronyn **12** Joseph Cotten, Teresa Wright **14** Macdonald Carey **16** Patricia Collinge
remade as: 16 Step Down to Terror

Shadows on the Rock
author: 11 Willa Cather

shadowy 3 dim **5** shady **6** gloomy, unreal **7** obscure **8** illusory **9** tenebrous **10** indistinct **13** insubstantial

Shadrach
former name: 8 Hananiah
friend: 6 Daniel
companion: 7 Meshach **8** Abednego

shady 5 fishy **7** crooked, devious, dubious, shadowy **9** dishonest, unethical **10** suspicious **11** underhanded **12** disreputable, questionable **13** untrustworthy

shady dealings 5 fraud, graft **7** bribery **10** corruption, dishonesty

shaft 3 cut, pit, ray **4** barb, beam, dart, duct, flue, gibe, hilt, stem, vent, well **5** abyss, arrow, chasm, gleam, lance, patch, pylon, quill, shank, spear, spire, stalk, tower, trunk **6** cavity, column, funnel, handle, insult, pillar, streak, stream **7** affront, chimney, conduit, minaret, obelisk, spindle, steeple **8** brickbat, monolith, pilaster **9** aspersion **10** excavation

shaggy 5 bushy, downy, fuzzy, hairy, nappy, piled, wooly **6** tufted, woolly **7** bearded, hirsute, shagged, unshorn **9** whiskered **11** bewhiskered

shah 4 king **5** ruler **7** emperor, monarch **8** autocrat **9** sovereign

Shahaptian
tribe: 6 Numipu **8** Nez Perce

Shahn, Ben
born: 6 Kaunas **9** Lithuania
artwork: 5 Epoch **8** Handball **12** Seurat's Lunch, The Physicist **16** Pacific Land scape **18** Willis Avenue Bridge **28** The Passion of Sacco and Vanzetti

shake 3 jar, jog, mix **4** jerk, jolt, move, stir, stun, sway, wave **5** elude, quake, swing, touch **6** affect, bounce, jiggle, joggle, jostle, jounce, quaver, quiver, rattle, ruffle, shimmy, shiver, slough, totter, twitch, wobble **7** agitate, disturb, flicker, flutter, perturb, quaking, shudder, stagger, startle, tremble, unnerve, vibrate **8** brandish, disquiet, distress, flourish, frighten, throw off, unsettle, unstring **9** quivering, shivering, trembling **10** discompose, flickering, fluttering

shakedown 6 extort, payoff, search, tryout **7** testing **8** thorough **9** blackmail, extortion, hush money

Shakespeare, William
  also: 10 bard of Avon **12** immortal bard
  author of: 6 Hamlet, Henry V **7** Henry IV, Henry VI, Macbeth, Othello, Sonnets **8** King John, King Lear, Pericles (Prince of Tyre) **9** Cymbeline, Henry VIII, Richard II **10** Coriolanus, Richard III, The Tempest **11** As You Like It **12** Julius Caesar, Twelfth Night **13** Rape of Lucrece, Timon of Athens **14** Romeo and Juliet, The Winter's Tale, Venus and Adonis **15** Titus Andronicus **16** Love's Labour's Lost **17** Measure for Measure, The Comedy of Errors **18** Antony and Cleopatra, Troilus and Cressida **19** Much Ado About Nothing, The Merchant of Venice, The Taming of the Shrew **20** All's Well That Ends Well **21** A Midsummer Night's Dream **22** The Merry Wives of Windsor **23** The Two Gentlemen of Verona
  birthplace: 15 Stratford-on-Avon
  theater: 4 Swan **5** Globe
  wife: 12 Anne Hathaway

shakeup 5 purge **7** cleanup **8** turnover **10** clean sweep **11** realignment **13** rearrangement, redisposition, restructuring **14** redistribution, reorganization

shake up 3 mix **4** stir **5** churn **7** agitate, disturb

shakiness 6 tremor **10** insecurity **11** instability, uncertainty **12** unsteadiness

shaky 4 weak **5** frail, jumpy **6** flimsy, unsafe, unsure, wobbly **7** dubious, fidgety, fragile, halting, jittery, nervous, teetery **8** hesitant, insecure, unstable, unsteady, wavering **9** faltering, hazardous, quivering, teetering, tottering, trembling, tremulous, uncertain, undecided **10** inconstant, irresolute, precarious, unreliable, unresolved **11** vacillating **12** undependable

shallow 5 shoal **6** frothy, slight **7** surface, trivial **8** knee-deep, skin-deep, trifling **9** frivolous **11** meaningless, superficial, unimportant **13** insubstantial **15** inconsequential

shalom 5 hello, peace **7** goodbye

shalom aleichem 10 peace to you

sham 3 act **4** copy, fake **5** bogus, false, feign, fraud, phony, put on, trick **6** affect, assume, forged **7** feigned, forgery, imitate, pretend **8** pretense, simulate, spurious **9** imitation, pretended, simulated, synthetic **10** artificial, fraudulent **11** counterfeit, makebelieve

Shamash
  origin: 8 Akkadian
  god of: 3 sun

shamble, shambles 4 limp **5** hitch, lurch, stall **6** hobble **7** shuffle **8** butchery **14** slaughterhouse

shame 5 guilt, odium **6** humble, stigma **7** chagrin, mortify, remorse, scandal **8** contempt, disgrace, dishonor, ignominy **9** disrepute, embarrass, humiliate **10** debasement, disrespect **11** degradation, humiliation, self-disgust **12** unworthiness **13** embarrassment, mortification **14** disappointment

shamed be the one who thinks evil of it
  Latin: 20 honi soit qui mal y pense

shamefaced 5 sorry **7** abashed, crushed, humbled, put-down **8** blushing, sheepish **9** chagrined, disgraced, mortified **10** humiliated, remorseful **11** embarrassed

shameful 3 low **4** base, mean, vile **6** odious **7** heinous, ignoble **8** shocking, unworthy **9** dastardly, degrading **10** deplorable, despicable, inglorious, iniquitous, outrageous, villainous **11** disgraceful, ignominious, opprobrious **12** contemptible, dishonorable **13** reprehensible

shameless 4 pert **5** brash, saucy **6** brazen, wanton **7** forward, immoral **8** degraded, flagrant, immodest, impudent, indecent **9** abandoned, audacious, barefaced, boldfaced, dissolute, unabashed **10** indecorous, unblushing, unreserved **11** disgraceful **12** dishonorable

shamelessness 4 gall **5** brass, cheek **8** audacity **10** brazenness, effrontery **11** forwardness, presumption

shamus 3 tec **7** gumshoe **9** detective **10** private eye **12** investigator

Shane
  director: 13 George Stevens
  cast: 8 Alan Ladd **9** Van Heflin **10** Jean Arthur, Jack Palance **12** Elisha Cook Jr **13** Edgar Buchanan **14** Brandon de Wilde

Shanghai
  area: 23 International Settlement
  landmark: 13 Long Hua Temple **17** People's Opera House **28** Shanghai Industrial Exhibition
  river: 6 Wusung **7** Huang-P'u, Yangtze

Shangri-La see **5** Nepal

shanty 3 hut **5** cabin, hovel, shack **6** lean-to

shape 4 form, make, mold, trim **5** array, build, frame, guide, model, order **6** create, fettle, figure, health **7** contour, develop, fashion, outline, profile **8** physique **9** condition, construct, determine **10** silhouette **12** conformation **13** configuration

shapeless 5 baggy **8** formless **9** amorphous, irregular

shapely 3 fit **4** neat, trim **6** comely, gainly **11** symmetrical

shaper 9 architect, innovator **10** instigator, prime mover

Shapley, Howard
  field: 9 astronomy
  studied: 6 galaxy

Shardik
  author: 12 Richard Adams

share 3 cut **4** dole, part **5** allot, cut up, quota, split **6** ration **7** deal out, divvy up, mete out, percent, portion **8** allocate **9** allotment, allowance, apportion **10** percentage **13** apportionment

shared 5 joint **6** common, public **7** general **8** communal **10** collective

share one's sorrow 7 condole **10** sympathize **11** commiserate

Sharif, Omar
  real name: 15 Michael Shalhoub
  born: 5 Egypt **10** Alexandria
  roles: 3 Che **9** Dr Zhivago, Funny Girl, Funny Lady **11** Genghis Khan **12** Nick Arnstein **16** Lawrence of Arabia
  expert on: 6 bridge

shark 3 ace **4** fish **5** cheat **6** expert, usurer, wizard **8** predator **9** trickster **12** extortionist

sharp 3 sly **4** acid, curt, fine, foxy, high, keen, sour, tart, wily **5** acrid, acute, alert, angry, awake, blunt, clear, cruel, edged, gruff, harsh, nippy, piked, quick, rapid, salty, sheer, spiny, steep **6** abrupt, artful, astute, barbed, biting, bitter, clever, crafty, crusty, fierce, keenly, marked, pointy, severe, shrewd, shrill, strong, sudden, thorny, tricky, unkind **7** acutely, alertly, angular, bearish, bristly, brusque, caustic, closely, crabbed, cunning, cutting, drastic, exactly, extreme, galling, intense, nipping, piquant, pointed, prickly, quickly, raucous, toothed, violent **8** abruptly, distinct, on the dot, piercing, promptly, scathing, serrated, spiteful, stinging, strident, suddenly, venomous, vertical, vigilant, vinegary **9** conniving, deceptive, excessive, on the nose, precisely, rancorous, unethical, vitriolic **10** contriving, discerning, immoderate, inordinate, perceptive, punctually **11** attentively, calculating, on the button, penetrating, precipitous **12** unprincipled, unscrupulous **13** precipitously
  French: 5 juste
  Spanish: 7 en punto

Sharp, Becky
  character in: **10** Vanity Fair
  author: **9** Thackeray

sharp-cornered 6 jagged **7** angular

sharp dresser 3 fop **4** dude **5** dandy
  12 Beau Brummell, clotheshorse, fashion plate

sharpen 4 edge, hone, whet **5** grind, strop

sharply pointed 4 keen **5** acute **6** spiked **7** tapered **8** piercing **10** rapierlike **11** needle-nosed

sharpness 3 nip, wit **4** edge, tang **6** acuity, acumen **7** acidity, insight **8** acerbity, acridity, acrimony, keenness, pungency, saliency, tartness **9** acuteness, alertness, quickness **10** causticity, craftiness **12** perspicacity

sharp pain 4 pang, stab **5** cramp **6** twinge

sharpshooter
  French: **10** tirailleur

sharp-sighted 5 acute **6** shrewd **8** piercing **9** far-seeing **10** discerning, perceptive **11** penetrating **13** perspicacious

sharp-witted 4 keen **5** acute, alert, canny, quick, smart **6** astute, brainy, clever

Shatner, William
  born: **6** Canada **8** Montreal
  roles: **8** Star Trek, T J Hooker **17** Captain James T Kirk

shatter 4 rive, ruin **5** break, burst, crack, crash, crush, quash, smash, split, spoil, upset, wreck **6** squash, sunder, topple **7** crumble, destroy, explode, scuttle **8** demolish, fracture, overturn, splinter **9** devastate, pulverize

shattered 6 broken, dashed **7** crushed, smashed **8** crumbled, decrepit **9** flustered **10** demolished, fragmented, splintered, tumbledown **11** crestfallen, demoralized **13** disillusioned, disintegrated

shave 3 cut, lop, mow **4** clip, crop, dock, pare, skin, snip, trim **5** brush, graze, prune, shear **6** barber, cut off, fleece, glance, scrape **7** scissor

Shaw, George Bernard
  author of: **7** Candida **8** Pygmalion, Saint Joan **12** Major Barbara **13** Arms and the Man **14** Man and Superman **15** Heartbreak House **16** Back to Methuselah **17** The Devil's Disciple, The Doctor's Dilemma **18** Caesar and Cleopatra **19** Androcles and the Lion **20** Mrs Warren's Profession
  member of: **13** Fabian Society

Shaw, Irwin
  author of: **12** Top of the Hill **13** The Young Lions **14** Beggarman Thief, Rich Man Poor Man

Shaw, Robert
  born: **7** England **12** Westhoughton
  wife: **7** Mary Ure
  roles: **4** Jaws **7** The Deep **8** The Sting **12** Swashbuckler **13** The Caretakers **17** A Man for All Seasons **20** Force Ten from Navarone **28** The Taking of Pelham One-Two-Three
  author of: **14** The Hiding Place **21** The Man in the Glass Booth

Shawabti
  origin: **8** Egyptian
  form: **8** figurine
  where used: **6** burial

shawl 4 wrap **5** scarf **6** mantle **7** paisley **10** fascinator
  Mexican: **6** serape
  Spanish: **8** mantilla

Shawnee
  language family: **9** Algonkian **10** Algonquian
  location: **4** Ohio **6** Kansas **8** Missouri, Oklahoma **9** Tennessee **12** Pennsylvania **13** South Carolina
  leader: **8** Tecumseh **11** Tenskwatawa
  related to: **8** Delaware

She
  author: **13** H Rider Haggard
  character: **6** Ayesha

shear 3 cut, lop **4** clip, crop, snip, trim **5** prune, shave **6** fleece, remove **7** deprive, relieve, scissor

Shearer, Norma
  born: **6** Canada **8** Montreal
  husband: **14** Irving Thalberg
  roles: **8** The Women **9** A Free Soul **11** The Divorcee (Oscar) **14** Romeo and Juliet, Their Own Desire **15** Marie Antoinette **26** The Barretts of Wimpole Street

shears 5 clips, trims **6** prunes **7** pruners **8** clippers, scissors, trimmers

sheath 3 pod **4** case, coat, skin **6** casing, jacket **7** capsule, coating, wrapper **8** covering, envelope, membrane, scabbard, slipcase, wrapping **9** container **10** receptacle

sheathing 6 casing, siding **8** covering

Sheba
  also: **4** Saba
  visited: **7** Solomon
  father: **6** Bichri, Joktan, Raamah **7** Jokshan
  grandfather: **4** Cush **7** Keturah
  people of: **7** Sabeans

Shebat 19 eleventh Hebrew month

she carved it
  Latin: **8** sculpsit

shed 3 hut **4** cast, doff, drop, emit, molt **5** exude, hovel, shack, spill, strew, throw **6** lean-to, shanty, shower, slough, spread **7** cast off, discard, let fall, let flow, radiate, scatter **8** disperse, lose hair, toolshed **9** broadcast, discharge, tool house **10** distribute **11** disseminate, outbuilding

she died
  Latin: **5** obiit

shed light on 7 clarify, explain **9** elucidate, explicate, make clear, make plain **10** illuminate

She Done Him Wrong
  director: **13** Lowell Sherman
  cast: **7** Mae West (Diamond Lil) **9** Cary Grant, Noah Beery **13** Gilbert Roland

shed tears 3 cry, sob **4** bawl, weep **6** boohoo **7** blubber

Sheehy, Gail
  author of: **8** Passages **14** The Pathfinders

Sheeler, Charles
  born: **14** Philadelphia PA
  artwork: **9** Landscape, Upper Deck **11** Incantation **12** City Interior, Rolling Power **15** Bucks County Barn, River Rouge Plant **31** American Landscape Nineteen Thirty

sheen 4 glow **5** glaze, gleam, glint, gloss, shine **6** luster, patina, polish **7** burnish, glister, glitter, shimmer **8** radiance **9** shininess **10** brightness, brilliance, effulgence, glossiness, luminosity, refulgence **12** luminousness, resplendence

Sheen, Martin
  real name: **12** Ramon Estevez
  born: **8** Dayton OH
  son: **12** Charlie Sheen **13** Emilio Estevez
  roles: **5** Spawn **8** Badlands **12** The Believers **13** Apocalypse Now **14** Catch Twenty-two **18** The Subject Was Roses **20** The American President **27** The Execution of Private Slovik

Sheena, Queen of the Jungle
  creator: **8** SR Powell **13** W Morgan Thomas
  character: **3** Bob **4** Chim

she engraved it
  Latin: **8** sculpsit

sheep
  breed: **5** Iraqi **6** Hirrik, Merino, Panama, Romney, Somali **7** Cheviot, Karakul, Lincoln, Suffolk, Targhee **8** Columbia, Cotswold, Tatarian **9** Montadale, Romeldale, Southdown **10** Corriedale, Dorset Down, Dorset Horn, Shropshire, Sikkim Bera **11** Rambouillet **13** Hampshire Down **15** Border Leicester
  female: **3** ewe
  family: **7** Bovidae
  genus: **4** Ovis
  group of: **5** drove, flock **6** cosset
  meat: **4** lamb **6** mutton
  oil from: **7** lanolin
  wild: **5** urial **6** argali **7** bighorn, mouflon
  young: **4** lamb **7** lambkin **8** yearling

sheepish 3 shy **4** meek **5** timid **6** docile, guilty, humble **7** abashed, ashamed, bashful, fearful, hangdog, passive, servile **8** blushing, obedient, obeisant, timorous, yielding **9** chagrined, chastened, diffident, mortified, shrinking, tractable **10** shamefaced, submissive **11** embarrassed, subservient, unassertive, unresisting

sheepishness 7 chagrin **8** docility, meekness **10** diffidence **11** bashfulness **12** tractability **13** embarrassment **14** submissiveness **15** unassertiveness

Sheep Well, The
also: **13** Fuente Ovejuna
author: **10** Lope de Vega

sheer 4 fine, pure, thin **5** bluff, filmy, gauzy, plumb, sharp, steep, total, utter **6** abrupt **7** perfect, unmixed **8** absolute, complete, gossamer, vertical **9** out and out, unalloyed, unbounded, unlimited **10** consummate, diaphanous **11** precipitous, transparent, unmitigated, unqualified **12** unrestrained **13** perpendicular, unadulterated, unconditional

sheet 3 top **4** coat, film, leaf, pane, slab **5** layer, panel, piece, plate **6** sheath, square **7** blanket, coating, overlay **8** bed sheet, covering, membrane **9** rectangle

shegetz 12 non-Jewish boy, non-Jewish man

Sheldon, Sidney
author of: **9** Bloodline **12** Rage of Angels, The Naked Face **15** If Tomorrow Comes **20** A Stranger in the Mirror **22** The Other Side of Midnight

shelf 4 bank, prop, reef, slab **5** ledge, shoal **6** mantel, mantle **7** bedrock, bracket, stratum **9** supporter **11** mantelpiece, mantlepiece

shell 3 pod **4** bomb, case, hulk, hull, husk, shot **5** pound, round, shuck **6** bullet, fire on, pepper, rocket **7** barrage, bombard, grenade, missile **8** carapace, skeleton **9** cartridge, framework **10** projectile

shellac 4 beat, drub, lick, whip **7** clobber, lacquer, trounce, varnish

Shelley, Mary Wollstonecraft
father: **13** William Godwin
husband: **18** Percy Bysshe Shelley
author of: **12** Frankenstein

Shelley, Percy Bysshe
author of: **7** Adonais, Alastor **8** Queen Mab, The Cenci **10** To a Skylark **16** A Defence of Poetry, Ode to the West Wind **17** Prometheus Unbound

shellfish 4 clam, crab **5** prawn **6** cockle, mussel, oyster, shrimp **7** abalone, lobster, mollusk, scallop **8** barnacle, crawfish, crayfish **9** trunkfish **10** crustacean **13** softshell crab
spawn: **4** spat

shell out 3 pay **6** expend **8** allocate, disburse, dispense **10** contribute

shelter 5 cover, guard, haven, house, lodge **6** asylum, defend, harbor, refuge, safety, shield, take in **7** care for, housing, lodging, protect **8** quarters, security **9** safeguard, sanctuary **10** protection

Sheltered Life
author: **12** Ellen Glasgow

shelve 5 defer, table **6** put off **7** suspend **8** lay aside, postpone, put aside, put on ice, set aside **10** pigeonhole

Shem
father: **4** Noah
brother: **3** Ham **7** Japheth
son: **8** Arphazed
descendant of: **6** Semite

shenanigans 5 sport **6** antics, capers, hijinx, pranks, stunts, tricks **8** deviltry, mischief, nonsense **9** highjinks, horseplay, silliness **10** buffoonery, tomfoolery **11** roguishness **12** monkeyshines, sportiveness **14** monkey business **15** mischievousness

she painted it
Latin: **6** pinxit

shepherd 4 herd, lead, show, tend **5** guard, guide, pilot **6** direct, escort, herder, keeper, patron, shield **7** protect, shelter **8** champion, defender, guardian, herdsman, provider **9** custodian, protector, safeguard **10** benefactor

Shepherdess and the Sweep, The
author: **21** Hans Christian Andersen

shepherds
god of: **3** Pan **6** Tammuz

sherbet 3 ade, ice **6** sorbet **7** dessert

Shere Khan
character in: **14** The Jungle Books
author: **7** Kipling

Sheridan, Ann
real name: **16** Clara Lou Sheridan
nickname: **9** Oomph Girl
born: **8** Denton TX
husband: **10** Scott McKay **11** George Brent **12** Edward Norris
roles: **8** King's Row **11** Silver River **12** Nora Prentiss **16** Wings for the Eagle **20** Angels with Dirty Faces

Sheridan, Philip H
served in: **8** Civil War **10** Indian Wars
side: **5** Union
commander of: **19** Army of the Shenandoah
rank: **22** general in chief of US army
battle: **9** Five Forks **10** Cedar Creek, Winchester **11** Chattanooga, Chickamauga, Fisher's Hill **12** Sayler's Creek **18** Wilderness Campaign

Sheridan, Richard Brinsley
author of: **9** The Critic, The Duenna, The Rivals **18** A Trip to Scarborough **19** The School for Scandal

sheriff 7 officer **9** constable
men: **5** posse

Sheriff of Nottingham
character in: **9** Robin Hood

Sherman, William Tecumseh
nickname: **4** Cump
served in: **8** Civil War **10** Mexican War
side: **5** Union
battle: **6** Shiloh **7** Atlanta, Bull Run **8** Savannah **9** Vicksburg **11** Chattanooga **15** Kenesaw Mountain
fought against: **8** Johnston
rank: **20** general in chief of army
famous for: **13** march to the sea (Georgia)
established: **29** Command and General Staff College
saying: **9** War is hell

sherry
type: **4** wine **6** brandy
origin: **5** Jeres, Spain, Xerez
varieties: **4** fino (dry) **5** cream **7** amoroso (sweet), oloroso (medium dry) **10** Manzanilla **11** Amontillado
drink: **6** Adonis, Bamboo **9** Andalusia
with gin: **11** Renaissance
with vermouth: **6** Brazil

Sherwood, Robert E
author of: **13** Idiot's Delight **15** Reunion in Vienna **18** The Petrified Forest **19** Roosevelt and Hopkins, There Shall Be No Night **20** Abe Lincoln in Illinois
screenplay: **22** The Best Years of Our Lives

she sculptured it
Latin: **8** sculpsit

she speaks
Latin: **8** loquitur

She Stoops to Conquer
author: **15** Oliver Goldsmith
character: **6** Marlow **8** Hastings **10** Sir Charles **11** Tony Lumpkin **12** Mr Hardcastle **13** Mrs Hardcastle **14** Kate Hardcastle **16** Constance Neville

she wrote (it)
Latin: **8** scripsit

shibah, shivah 14 mourning period
literally: **9** seven days

shibboleth 6 byword, saying, slogan **8** apothegm **9** catchword

Shibboleth 17 Gileadite password

shield 4 keep, star **5** aegis, badge, cover, guard, house, shade **6** buffer, button, emblem, ensign, fender, harbor, screen, secure **7** buckler, defense, protect, shelter **8** insignia, keep safe, preserve **9** medallion, protecter, protector, safeguard **10** escutcheon, protection

Shield (of Sobieski)
constellation of: **6** Scutum

shielded 6 hidden **7** guarded **9** concealed, protected, sheltered

Shields, Brooke
real name: **20** Christa Brooke Shields
born: **9** New York NY
roles: **10** Pretty Baby **11** Endless Love **13** The Blue Lagoon, Suddenly Susan
husband: **11** Andre Agassi

shift 2 go 4 move, slip, vary, veer 5 hitch, stint 6 change, swerve, switch 7 chemise, turning, veering 8 exchange, straight, transfer 9 deviation, transpose, variation 10 alteration, assignment, reposition 11 alternating, fluctuation, interchange 12 modification
French: 8 camisole

shiftless 3 lax 4 idle, lazy 8 careless, inactive, indolent, slothful 10 ne'er-do-well 13 lackadaisical 14 good-for-nothing 15 unconscientious

shifty 4 foxy, wily 6 crafty, sneaky, tricky 7 cunning, evasive 8 scheming, slippery 9 conniving, deceitful, dishonest 10 contriving, unreliable 11 maneuvering, treacherous 13 untrustworthy

Shikasta
author: 12 Doris Lessing

shiksa 14 non-Jewish woman

shillelagh 4 club 5 stick 6 cudgel 9 truncheon

shilly-shally 5 stall, waver 6 dawdle, dither, falter, seesaw 8 hesitate 9 fluctuate, hem and haw, oscillate, vacillate

shilly-shallying 8 dawdling, wavering 9 uncertain, undecided 10 indecision, indecisive, irresolute 11 vacillation

Shimazaki Toson
author of: 5 Hakai 20 The Broken Commandment

shimmer 4 beam, glow 5 blink, dance, flash, gleam, quake, shine, waver 6 quiver, shiver 7 flicker, flutter, glisten, sparkle, tremble, twinkle, vibrate 8 blinking 9 coruscate 11 scintillate 12 phosphoresce

shindig 3 hop 4 ball, bash, prom 5 dance, party 6 affair, shindy 7 blowout, revelry 9 barn dance, festivity, record hop 10 masked ball, the dansant
French: 4 fete, gala 6 soiree 9 bal masque 10 bal costume

shine 3 wax 4 beam, buff, glow 5 blink, flash, glare, gleam, glint, gloss, light, rub up, sheen 6 dazzle, luster, polish, waxing 7 buffing, burnish, flicker, glimmer, glisten, glister, glitter, radiate, shimmer, sparkle, twinkle 8 brighten, radiance 9 coruscate, irradiate, polishing 10 brightness, brilliance, burnishing, luminosity 11 scintillate 12 illumination, luminousness 13 incandescence

shininess 5 gleam, glint, gloss, sheen 6 luster, polish 7 shimmer

shining 5 aglow 6 glossy 7 glowing, radiant 8 gleaming, luminous, lustrous 9 brilliant, effulgent 11 illustrious 12 incandescent

Shining, The
author: 11 Stephen King

shiny 6 bright, glossy 7 glaring, glowing, radiant 8 gleaming, luminous, lustrous, polished 9 brilliant, burnished, effulgent, sparkling 10 glistening, glittering, shimmering 12 incandescent 13 scintillating

ship 4 crew, send 5 craft, liner, route, tramp, yacht 6 packet, tanker, vessel 7 carrier, cruiser, forward, steamer 8 dispatch 9 destroyer, freighter, steamship, transport 10 ocean liner

Ship of Fools
author: 19 Katherine Anne Porter
director: 13 Stanley Kramer
cast: 9 Jose Greco, Lee Marvin 10 Jose Ferrer 11 George Segal, Oscar Werner, Vivien Leigh 14 Simone Signoret 15 Elizabeth Ashley

shipshape 4 neat, snug, taut, tidy, trip, trim 5 tight 6 spruce 7 orderly

Shirer, William L
author of: 28 The Collapse of the Third Republic 29 The Rise and Fall of the Third Reich

shirk 4 duck, shun 5 avoid, dodge, elude, evade 6 escape, eschew, ignore 7 goof off, neglect 8 malinger, sidestep 9 goldbrick

shirker 5 piker 6 dodger, evader, loafer, rotter, truant 7 deserter, quitter, slacker 9 goldbrick 10 backslider, malingerer

Shirley Temple
ingredient: 9 ginger ale, grenadine
also called: 9 Roy Rogers

shirr 5 crimp, smock 6 gather, pucker 8 bake eggs

shirt 3 top 4 sark 5 frock, waist 6 blouse, bodice 10 underwaist

shirty 5 angry, irked, testy, vexed 7 annoyed 9 irritated 11 disgruntled

Shittimwood 12 Biblical tree

shiver 5 quake, shake 6 quaver, shimmy 7 shudder, tremble

shivers 3 bit 5 piece, shard 6 sliver 8 fragment

shivery 3 icy, raw 4 cold, cool 5 brisk, chill, crisp, nippy 6 arctic, biting, bitter, chilly, frigid, frosty, wintry 7 quaking, trembly 8 chilling 9 quivering 11 penetrating

shoal 3 bar 4 bank, flat 5 crowd, shelf 6 school 7 sand bar, shallow 8 sand bank

shock 3 jar, mat, mop 4 blow, bush, cock, crop, daze, jolt, mane, mass, pile, rick, rock, stun, turn 5 scare, shake, sheaf, stack, start, upset 6 appall, bundle, dismay, impact, offend, revolt, thatch, trauma 7 astound, disgust, disturb, horrify, outrage, perturb, stagger, startle, stupefy 8 astonish, bowl over, disquiet, distress, paralyze, surprise, unsettle 9 collision, overwhelm 10 concussion, discompose,

disconcert 11 disturbance 13 consternation

shocking 4 foul 5 awful 6 grisly, horrid, odious 7 ghastly, hideous, jarring, jolting 8 gruesome, horrible, indecent, terrible, wretched 9 abhorrent, appalling, frightful, monstrous, offensive, repellent, repugnant, revolting, startling, upsetting 10 abominable, astounding, detestable, disgusting, disturbing, horrifying, outrageous, perturbing, scandalous, staggering, stupefying, surprising, unsettling 11 astonishing, disgraceful, disquieting 12 insufferable, overwhelming 13 disconcerting, reprehensible

shoddy 3 low 4 base, mean, poor 5 dirty, nasty, tacky 6 shabby, sloppy, stingy 7 low-down, miserly 8 careless, inferior, slipshod 9 haphazard, negligent, niggardly 10 second-rate, ungenerous 11 inefficient 12 contemptible 13 inconsiderate, reprehensible

shoe
French: 9 chaussure

shoemaker 7 cobbler 9 bootmaker

Shoemaker's Holiday, The
author: 12 Thomas Dekker

Shoes of the Fisherman, The
author: 11 Morris L West

Shogun
author: 12 James Clavell

Sholokhov, Mikhail
author of: 19 And Quiet Flows the Don 21 The Virgin Soul Upturned

shoo 3 out 4 away, oust, rout, scat 5 be off, chase, leave, scram 6 beat it, be gone, depart, get out, go away 7 cast out, get lost, vamoose

shoot 3 bud, fly, hit 4 bolt, cast, dart, dash, drop, fell, fire, hurl, jump, kill, leap, nick, pelt, plug, race, rain, rush, stem, tear, toss, twig, wing 5 eject, fling, go off, hurry, shell, sling, speed, spray, sprig, spurt, sweep, throw, waste 6 charge, launch, let fly, pepper, propel, riddle, shower, spring, sprout 7 bombard, explode, pick off, tendril 8 catapult, detonate, open fire 9 discharge

Shootist, The
director: 9 Don Siegal
cast: 9 John Wayne, Ron Howard 10 Hugh O'Brien 11 Harry Morgan, Sheree North 12 James Stewart, Lauren Bacall, Richard Boone 13 John Carradine 15 Scatman Crothers

Shoot the Piano Player
director: 16 Francois Truffaut
cast: 11 Marie Dubois 12 Nicole Berger 14 Michele Mercier 15 Charles Aznavour
setting: 5 Paris

shop 3 buy 4 hunt, look, mart, mill 5 plant, store, works 6 browse, market, studio 7 factory 8 emporium, purchase, workshop 9 patronize 10 win-

dowshop **13** establishment
French: 7 atelier **8** boutique

shopkeeper 6 dealer, monger, trader, vendor **8** merchant, purveyor, retailer **9** tradesman

shopworn 5 banal, corny, faded, stale, tired, trite, vapid **6** jejune **10** threadbare

shore 4 bank, hold, land, prop **5** beach, brace, brink, coast **6** hold up, margin, strand **7** bolster, bulwark, seaside, support, sustain **8** buttress, mainstay, seaboard, seacoast, underpin **9** reinforce, riverbank, waterside **10** strengthen
Latin: 10 terra firma

shorebird 3 auk **4** rail, sora **5** snipe, stilt, wader **6** avocet, curlew, plover, puffin **7** lapwing **8** woodcock **9** guillemot, sandpiper **13** oyster catcher

shore up 4 prop **5** brace **6** prop up **7** bolster, support **8** buttress **9** reinforce

short 3 low **4** curt, lean, slim, thin **5** brief, cross, elfin, fleet, gruff, hasty, pygmy, quick, runty, scant, sharp, small, squat, terse, testy, tight **6** abrupt, bantam, little, meager, scanty, scarce, skimpy, slight, sparse, stubby **7** brusque, compact, concise, cursory, lacking, limited, not long, not tall, slender, stunted, summary, wanting **8** abridged, abruptly, dwarfish, fleeting, impolite, snappish, succinct, suddenly, unawares **9** condensed, curtailed, deficient, impatient, momentary, niggardly, pint-sized, truncated **10** by surprise, diminutive, short-lived **11** abbreviated, ill-tempered, Lilliputian, pocket-sized **12** insufficient **13** precipitously **14** without warning

shortage 4 lack, want **6** dearth **7** deficit **8** leanness, scarcity, sparsity **9** shortfall **10** deficiency, inadequacy, scantiness, sparseness **13** insufficiency

shortcoming 4 flaw **5** fault **6** defect, foible **7** blemish, failing, failure, frailty **8** drawback, handicap, weakness **10** deficiency, inadequacy **12** imperfection

shorten 3 cut **4** clip, pare, trim **5** prune, shave, shear **6** lessen, reduce **7** abridge, curtail, cut down **8** condense, contract, cut short, decrease, diminish **10** abbreviate

shortening 3 fat, oil **4** lard, oleo **6** butter, digest **7** cutting, summary **8** abstract, synopsis, trimming **9** hemming up, margarine, reduction **11** abridgement, compression, contraction, curtailment **12** abbreviation, condensation

short form 6 digest, precis **7** summary **8** abstract, synopsis **11** abridgement, contraction **12** abbreviation, condensation

Short Happy Life of Francis Ma-

comber, The
author: 15 Ernest Hemingway

short journey 5 jaunt **6** outing **7** day trip **9** excursion

short-lived 5 brief **7** passing **8** fleeting **9** ephemeral, momentary, temporary, transient **10** evanescent, transitory, unenduring **11** impermanent **24** here today and gone tomorrow

shortly 4 anon, soon **7** by and by **8** directly, in a trice, promptly **9** forthwith, presently **10** before long **11** immediately

short narrative 5 essay, story **6** sketch **8** anecdote **10** short story

shortsighted 4 rash **6** myopic **7** foolish **8** careless, heedless, purblind, reckless, weak-eyed **9** amblyopic, imprudent **10** ill-advised, incautious, unthinking **11** improvident, injudicious, nearsighted, thoughtless **12** undiscerning **13** uncircumspect

short-tempered 4 curt **5** cross, huffy, sharp, testy **6** abrupt, cranky, crusty, grumpy, shirty, touchy **7** bearish, grouchy, peevish, waspish **8** choleric, snappish **9** irascible, irritable, splenetic **10** ill-humored, out of sorts, short-fused **11** hot-tempered, ill-tempered **12** cantankerous

Shosha
author: 19 Isaac Bashevis Singer

Shoshone (Snake)
language family: 10 Shoshonean
location: 4 Utah **5** Idaho **6** Nevada **7** Wyoming
translator: 9 Sacagawea

Shoshonean
tribe: 4 Hopi, Moki **5** Snake **6** Hopitu, Paiute **7** Bannock **8** Comanche, Shoshoni

Shostakovich, Dmitri (Dimitri)
born: 6 Russia **12** St Petersburg
composer of: 7 The Nose **9** Leningrad (symphony No 7) **11** May the First **12** The Golden Age **17** Katerina Ismailova **19** Lady Macbeth of Mzensk

shot 2 go **3** hit, try **4** dose, move, play, toss **5** balls, blast, crack, drive, essay, guess, salvo, slugs, throw **6** beat-up, archer, bowman, chance, report, ruined, shabby, stroke, volley **7** attempt, bullets, gunfire, shooter, surmise, worn-out **8** decrepit, marksman, rifleman **9** discharge, explosion, fusillade, injection **10** ammunition, conjecture, detonation **11** dilapidated, projectiles **12** falling apart, sharpshooter

shot in the arm 4 lift **5** boost **6** uplift **8** stimulus **13** encouragement

shot in the dark 5 guess **6** notion, theory **9** guesswork, suspicion **10** assumption, conjecture, hypothesis

shoulder 3 rim **4** bank, bear, brow, bump, edge, push, side, take **5** brink, carry, crest, elbow, lunge, shove,

skirt, verge **6** assume, border, jostle, margin, take on, thrust, uphold **7** scapula, support, sustain **8** clavicle **9** undertake

shoulder blade 7 scapula **8** omoplate **9** bladebone

shout 3 cry **4** bawl, call, hoot, howl, roar, yell, yelp **5** burst, cheer, hollo, whoop **6** bellow, chorus, clamor, cry out, holler, hurrah, huzzah, outcry, scream, shriek **7** call out, exclaim, screech, thunder **8** outburst **9** hue and cry **10** hullabaloo

shout down 3 boo **4** hiss **6** hoot at, revile **7** catcall, condemn **8** denounce, drown out

shove 4 bump, butt, jolt, prod, push **5** boost, crowd, drive, elbow, force, impel, nudge **6** joggle, jostle, propel, thrust **8** shoulder

show 4 bare, bill, fair, give, lead, mark, play, pomp, pose, sham, sign **5** argue, coach, drama, endow, favor, front, grant, guide, movie, opera, prove, teach, token, tutor, usher **6** appear, attest, ballet, bestow, comedy, direct, effect, evince, expose, hint at, impart, inform, lavish, reveal, school, tender, unveil **7** bear out, bespeak, certify, conduct, confirm, display, exhibit, explain, lay bare, musical, picture, pretext, proffer, program, suggest, uncover **8** ceremony, delusion, disclose, dispense, evidence, illusion, indicate, instruct, intimate, manifest, operetta, point out, pretense, vaunting **9** establish, make clear, make known, represent, spectacle **10** appearance, disclosure, distribute, exhibition, exposition, expression, impression, indication, pretension, production, revelation **11** affectation, attestation, corroborate, counterfeit, demonstrate, performance, testimonial **12** bring to light, substantiate **13** demonstration, entertainment, manifestation, motion picture

Show Boat
author: 10 Edna Ferber

showcase 7 cabinet, counter, display, exhibit, vitrine

showdown 3 war **6** battle, climax, combat, crisis **7** face-off **8** clashing, conflict **9** collision, encounter **13** confrontation

shower 3 wet **4** fall, pour, rain, rush **5** flood, salvo, spray, surge **6** deluge, lavish, splash, stream, volley, wealth **7** barrage, bombard, drizzle, torrent **8** downpour, plethora, sprinkle **9** profusion **10** cloudburst, inundation **11** bombardment

showiness 5 eclat **7** glitter **8** splendor **9** jazziness **10** flashiness **11** ostentation **14** grandiloquence

Show-me State
nickname of: 8 Missouri

show-off 6 egoist **7** boaster, egotist, windbag **8** braggart, fanfaron, flaunter, strutter **9** extrovert, swaggerer **11** braggadocio **13** cock of the walk, exhibitionist **14** life of the party

showpiece 3 gem **5** jewel, pearl, pride, prize **6** rarity, wonder **7** classic, paragon **8** treasure **10** masterwork **11** chef d'oeuvre, masterpiece, prizewinner **17** piece de resistance

show up 4 come **5** outdo **6** appear, arrive, attend, crop up, expose, loom up, reveal, turn up **9** be present **11** come to light, make a fool of **12** come into view **13** become visible

showy 4 loud **5** gaudy, vivid **6** flashy, florid, garish, ornate **7** pompous **8** colorful, gorgeous, imposing, splendid, striking **9** brilliant **11** magnificent, pretentious **12** ostentatious

shred 3 bit, ion, jot, rag **4** atom, band, hair, iota, spot, whit **5** grain, piece, scrap, speck, strip, trace **6** morsel, ribbon, sliver, tatter **7** snippet **8** fragment, molecule, particle **9** scintilla

shrew 3 hag, nag **5** harpy, scold, vixen, yenta **6** kvetch, virago **7** shewolf **8** battle-ax, fishwife, harridan, spitfire **9** termagant, Xanthippe

shrewd 3 sly **4** foxy, keen, wily, wise **5** acute, cagey, canny, quick, sharp, slick, smart **6** artful, astute, clever, crafty, shifty, smooth, tricky **7** careful, cunning, knowing, probing, prudent **8** cautious, piercing, scheming, sensible, slippery **9** designing, farseeing, sagacious **10** contriving, discerning, farsighted, perceptive **11** calculating, circumspect, intelligent, penetrating, quick-witted, self-serving, sharp-witted **12** disingenuous **13** Machiavellian, perspicacious

shrewdness 6 acumen **7** cunning, slyness **8** foxiness, keenness, wiliness **9** acuteness, cageyness, sharpness, slickness, smartness **10** artfulness, astuteness, cleverness, craftiness, smoothness, trickiness **11** carefulness, discernment **12** slipperiness **16** disingenuousness

shriek 3 cry **4** call, hoot, howl, peal, yell, yelp **5** shout, whoop **6** cry out, holler, out-cry, scream, squawk, squeak, squeal **7** screech

shrift 7 penance **9** atonement, expiation **10** confession

shrill 4 high, loud **6** piping **7** blaring, raucous **8** piercing, strident **9** clamorous **10** screeching **11** high-pitched, penetrating

shrimp 5 prawn **6** scampi **8** cocktail

shrine 5 altar **6** chapel, church, temple **7** sanctum **8** monument **9** sanctuary

shrink 3 ebb, shy **4** balk, duck, wane **5** cower, demur, dry up, quail, stick, wince **6** blench, bridle, cringe, flinch, lessen, pucker, recoil, reduce, refuse,

retire **7** curtail, decline, deflate, dwindle, retreat, shorten, shrivel, shudder **8** compress, condense, contract, decrease, diminish, draw back, hang back, make less, withdraw **9** constrict **11** make smaller **12** draw together **13** become smaller

shrink from 4 hate, shun **5** abhor, evade **6** balk at, detest, eschew, loathe, resist **7** despise **8** recoil at **9** abominate, shudder at **12** be revolted by **13** find repulsive

shrinking 3 shy **5** timid **6** ebbing, waning **7** bashful **8** reticent, retiring, timorous **9** declining, dwindling **10** decreasing, shriveling **11** contraction, diminishing

shrive 6 pardon **7** absolve, forgive

shrivel 5 dry up, parch, wizen **6** pucker, scorch, shrink, wither **7** wrinkle

Shropshire Lad, A
 author: 9 A E Housman

shroud 4 hide, pall, veil, wrap **5** cloak, cloud, cover, sheet **6** clothe, mantle, screen, swathe **7** blanket, conceal, envelop **8** covering **9** cerecloth, cerements **11** burial cloth **12** graveclothes, winding sheet

shrub 4 bush **5** brush **8** beverage **10** fruit drink

shrubbery 4 bush **5** brush **6** bushes, shrubs **9** brushwood **10** underbrush **11** undergrowth

shuck 4 husk, peel, shed **5** chaff, shell, strip

shudder 4 jerk, pang **5** quake, shake, spasm, throb **6** quaver, quiver, shimmy, shiver, tremor, twitch **7** flutter, tremble **8** paroxysm **9** pulsation, trembling **10** convulsion

shudder at 4 hate **5** abhor **6** detest, loathe **8** recoil at **9** abominate, can't stand **10** recoil from, shrink from

shuffle 3 mix **4** drag, gimp, limp, step **5** scuff, slide **6** clumsy, jumble, scrape **7** shamble **8** scramble **9** rearrange **10** disarrange **11** interchange

shul, schul 9 synagogue

shun 5 avoid, dodge, elude, evade, forgo **6** eschew, forego, ignore, refuse, reject **7** boycott, disdain **10** circumvent, fight shy of, shrink from **11** keep clear of, shy away from **12** have no part of, keep away from, steer clear of, turn away from

shut 3 box **4** cage, coop, draw, fold, lock, snap **5** clasp, close, drawn, latch **6** closed, closet, corral, draw to, fasten, intern, locked, lock in, secure **7** confine, drawn to, enclose, fence in, impound, latched, secured **8** cloister, closed up, fastened, imprison **9** barricade, constrain **11** incarcerate

shut down 4 halt, stop **5** cease **7** sus-

pend **9** close down, interrupt **11** discontinue

Shute, Nevil
 author of: 10 On the Beach

shut in 4 cage **5** caged, pen in **6** coop up, encage, lock up **7** confine, encaged, enclose **8** confined, cooped up, enclosed, locked up, restrain, restrict **10** restrained, restricted

shut one's eyes to 5 allow **6** ignore, wink at **8** overlook **9** connive in, disregard **11** pay no heed to **14** turn one's back on

shut out 3 bar **5** debar **6** defeat **7** exclude **8** obstruct, prohibit

shutter 5 blind, close, shade **6** screen **7** curtain

shut the door on 3 ban, bar **6** forbid, refuse, reject **7** exclude, keep out, shut out **8** prohibit

shut up 4 cage, coop, hush, lock, pent **5** close, pen in **6** immure **7** be quiet, confine, silence **8** imprison **11** incarcerate

shy 4 balk, meek, wary **5** chary, cower, dodge, leery, minus, scant, short, timid, under, wince **6** blench, demure, flinch, in need, modest, shrink, swerve **7** anxious, bashful, careful, fearful, lacking, needing, nervous, wanting **8** cautious, draw back, jump back, reserved, reticent, skittish, timorous **9** deficient, diffident, shrinking, tremulous **10** suspicious **11** distrustful **12** apprehensive **13** self-conscious

shy away from 4 duck, shun **5** avoid, dodge, spurn **6** balk at, refuse, reject **10** shrink from **12** steer clear of

Shylock
 character in: 19 The Merchant of Venice
 author: 11 Shakespeare

shyness 8 meekness, timidity **9** reticence **10** diffidence, insecurity **11** bashfulness **12** sheepishness, timorousness **14** self-effacement **15** unassertiveness

shyster 5 rogue **6** lawyer **8** attorney **10** mouthpiece **11** pettifogger **15** ambulance chaser

si 3 yes

Siam see **8** Thailand

Sibelius, Jean
 born: 7 Finland **10** Tavastehus
 composer of: 6 En Saga **7** Karelia, Legends, Tapiola, The Band **8** Kalevala **9** Finlandia **10** The Tempest **12** The Oceanides, Voces Intimae **14** Ride and Sunrise

Siberia 8 disfavor **10** punishment **14** undesirability
 city: 4 Omsk **5** Chita, Tomsk **6** Kurgan **7** Irkutsk, Yakutsk
 conqueror: 9 Timafeyev **11** Genghis Khan
 continent: 4 Asia

gulf: 2 Ob
inhabitant: 4 Yaku 5 Sagai, Tatar 6 Tartar 7 Yukagir 8 prisoner 17 political prisoner
mountain range: 4 Ural 5 Altai, Altay
river: 2 Ob 3 Ket, Ili, Taz 4 Amga, Amur, Lena, Onon 5 Ishim, Tobol 6 Olekma
sea: 4 Kara 6 Laptev 7 Okhotsk
sibling 6 sister 7 brother
problem: 7 rivalry
sibyl 4 seer 5 augur 6 oracle 7 diviner 9 predictor, sorceress 10 forecaster, prophetess, soothsayer 13 fortune teller 14 prognosticator

Sibyls
form: 10 prophetess
inspired by: 5 deity 6 Apollo
names: 6 Libyan 7 Cumaean 10 Erythraean
prophecies: 14 Sibylline Books

sic 2 so 4 thus

Sicilian Vespers, The
also: 20 Les Vepres Siciliennes
opera by: 5 Verdi
character: 5 Elena 6 Arrigo 7 Procida 8 Monforte

Sicily
other name: 7 Sicilia 9 Trinacria, Triquetra
capital/largest city: 7 Palermo
others: 3 Aci 4 Enna, Noto 6 Ragusa 7 Augusta, Catania, Marsala, Messina, Trapani 8 Syracuse 10 Montelepre
division: 4 Enna 6 Ragusa 7 Catania, Messina, Palermo, Trapani 8 Siracusa, Syracuse 9 Agrigento 13 Caltanissetta
government: 13 region of Italy
measure: 5 salma 7 caffiso
monetary unit: 5 litra, oncia, uncia 6 carlin 7 carline, oncetta
island: 5 Egadi 6 Lipari, Ustica 7 Pelagie 11 Pantelleria
lake: 7 Pergusa 8 Camarina
mountain: 4 Erei, Moro, Sori 5 Atlas, Erici, Hybla, Iblei, Ibrei 7 Nebrodi, Vulcano 9 Apennines, Le Madonie, Stromboli 10 Peloritani
highest point: 4 Etna 5 Aetna
river: 4 Acis 5 Salso, Torto 6 Belice, Simeto 7 Mazzaro, Platani
sea: 6 Ionian 10 Tyrrhenian 13 Mediterranean
physical feature:
  cape: 4 Boeo, Faro 7 Lilibeo, Passaro, Passero, Pelorus
  gulf: 4 Noto 7 Catania
  strait: 7 Messina
  wind: 7 sirocco
people: 5 Elymi, Sican, Sicel 6 Sicani, Siculi
  author: 9 Lampedusa 10 Pirandello
  composer: 7 Bellini
  king: 4 Eryx 5 Bomba, Henry, Peter, Roger 7 Charles, Cocalus,

Leontes 9 Ferdinand, Frederick
ruler: 4 Rome 5 Arabs, Goths, Spain 6 Greeks 7 Germans, Normans, Vandals, Vikings 8 Carthage, Saracens 9 Aragonese, Byzantium, Egyptians, Phoenicia 15 Holy Roman Empire
language: 7 Italian
religion: 13 Roman Catholic
place:
  cathedral: 8 Monreale
  resort: 4 Enna 8 Taormina
  ruins: 14 Villa Imperiale 15 Temple of Concord 18 Valley of the Temples
feature:
  brigands: 5 Mafia
  evening stroll: 11 passeggiata

sick 3 ill 4 weak 5 frail, tired, weary 6 ailing, infirm, laid up, poorly, queasy, sickly, uneasy, unwell 7 crushed, grieved, invalid, unsound 8 delicate, stricken, troubled, wretched 9 afflicted, bored with, disturbed, miserable, nauseated, perturbed, suffering, unhealthy 10 disquieted, distressed, indisposed 11 discomposed, heartbroken 15 under the weather

sicken 5 repel, shock, upset 6 offend, revolt 7 disgust, horrify, make ill, repulse 8 nauseate 14 turn the stomach

sickening 4 foul, vile 5 nasty 7 noisome 8 horrible, unsavory 9 abhorrent, loathsome, offensive, repellent, repugnant, repulsive, revolting 10 disgusting, nauseating 11 distasteful

sickly 3 ill, wan 4 drab, flat, lame, pale, sick, weak 5 ashen, faint, frail, silly 6 ailing, feeble, flimsy, guilty, infirm, leaden, peaked, poorly, sneaky, torpid, unwell 7 insipid, invalid, unsound 8 delicate, smirking 9 afflicted, apathetic, bloodless, simpering, unhealthy 10 cadaverous, lackluster, namby-pamby, snickering, spiritless, uninspired, wishy-washy 11 ineffective 12 unconvincing 13 self-conscious

sickness 6 malady, nausea 7 ailment, disease, illness 8 debility, disorder, vomiting 9 complaint, frailness, ill health, infirmity 10 affliction, disability, invalidism, poor health, queasiness 11 unsoundness 12 qualmishness 13 indisposition

sic passim 12 so throughout

sic semper tyrannis 19 thus always to tyrants
  motto of: 8 Virginia

sic transit gloria mundi 33 thus passes away the glory of this world

Siddhartha
author: 12 Hermann Hesse
story of: 6 Buddha

siddur 16 Jewish prayer book
literally: 5 order

side 3 hem, rim 4 area, body, brim,

edge, half, hand, part, sect, team, view 5 angle, bound, cause, facet, flank, group, house, light, limit, minor, party, phase, skirt, slant, stand, stock 6 allied, aspect, behalf, belief, border, circle, clique, fringe, lesser, margin, region, sector, strain 7 askance, coterie, faction, lateral, lineage, oblique, opinion, postern, quarter, related, section, segment, surface 8 alliance, attitude, boundary, division, indirect, marginal, position, skirting 9 accessory, bloodline, coalition, on one side, perimeter, periphery, secondary, territory, viewpoint 10 collateral, contingent, federation, incidental, standpoint, subsidiary 11 affiliation, association, unimportant 13 insignificant

Side
origin: 5 Irish
form: 7 fairies
owner: 14 Tuatha De Danann

sideboard 6 buffet 8 credenza

side by side 7 abreast 8 abutting, together 9 adjoining 11 cheek by jowl, in proximity
Latin: 9 pari passu

Side Effects
author: 10 Woody Allen

sidekick 3 pal 4 aide 5 buddy 6 deputy, friend 9 assistant 10 lieutenant

sideline 5 bench, hobby 8 boundary 9 avocation 14 put out of action

sidestep 4 duck 5 avert, avoid, dodge, elude, evade, skirt 6 bypass, escape 10 circumvent, fight shy of 12 steer clear of

sidestepping 7 dodging, ducking, eluding, evasion 8 skirting 9 avoidance 13 circumvention

sidewalk 4 curb 8 footpath, pavement 9 promenade

sideways, sideway 6 aslant 7 askance, lateral, oblique 8 crabwise, edgeways, edgewise, sidelong, sideward, sidewise 9 cross wise, laterally, obliquely, to the side 11 from one side

side with 5 agree 7 stand by, stick by, support 8 champion 12 take one's part

sidle 4 cant, edge, skew, veer 10 lateralize

Sidney, Sir Philip
author of: 7 Arcadia 15 Defence of Poesie, Defence of Poetry 18 Apologie for Poetrie, Astrophel and Stella

Sidney, Sylvia
real name: 11 Sophia Kosow
born: 7 Bronx NY
husband: 11 Luther Adler 12 Bennett A Cerf
roles: 4 Fury 7 Dead End 11 Street Scene 13 Les Miserables 15 Madame Butterfly 17 An American Tragedy 24 Summer Wishes Winter Dreams

Sidrophel
  character in: **8** Hudibras
  author: **6** Butler
siecle 3 age **6** period **7** century
Siegel, Jerry
  creator/artist of: **8** Superman
Siegfried
  origin: **8** Germanic
  mentioned in: **14** Nibelungenlied
  father: **7** Sigmund
  mother: **9** Sieglinde
  wife: **9** Kriemhild
  killed by: **5** Hagen
  same as: **6** Sigurd
  killed: **6** Fafnir
  won for Gunther: **10** Brunnhilde
  stole: **9** Tarnkappe
Sieg Heil 13 hail to victory
  salute used by: **5** Nazis
Sieglinde
  origin: **8** Germanic
  mentioned in: **14** Nibelungenlied
  husband: **7** Sigmund
  son: **9** Siegfried
Sienkiewicz, Henryk
  author of: **8** Quo Vadis?
Sierra Leone
  name means: **12** lion mountain
  other name: **9** Gold Coast **10** Grain Coast, Ivory Coast
  capital/largest city: **8** Freetown
  others: **2** Bo **5** Hepel, Kissi, Lungi, Pepel **6** Bonthe, Kenema, Makeni, Shenge, Sulima
  school: **6** Njaia U **9** Fourah Bay
  measure: **4** load **6** kettle
  monetary unit: **4** cent **5** leone
  island: **4** York **6** Banana, Turtle **7** Sherbro
  mountain: **4** Loma **10** Tingi Hills
  highest point: **9** Bintimani
  river: **3** Moa **4** Jong, Mano, Meli, Ribi, Sewa, Taia **5** Bagbe, Mongo, Morro, Rokel **6** Mabole, Rokkel, Scarcy, Waanje **13** Great Scarcies **14** Little Scarcies
  sea: **8** Atlantic
  physical feature:
    bay: **5** Yawri **7** Sherbro
    cape: **8** Shilling **11** Sierra Leone
    peninsula: **7** Turners **11** Sierra Leone
    wind: **9** harmattan
  people: **3** Vai **4** Kono, Loko, Susu **5** Bulom, Kissi, Limba, Mende, Mendi, Temne **6** Creole, Fulani, Syrian **7** Gallina, Koranko, Kuranko, Sherbro, Yalunka **8** Lebanese, Mandingo
    explorer: **6** Cintra
    leader: **6** Margai **7** Stevens
  language: **4** Krio **5** Limba, Mende, Mendi, Temne **6** Creole **7** English
  religion: **5** Islam **7** animism **12** Christianity
  place:
    wharf: **10** King Jimmys
  feature:

    cloth: **5** garra
  clothing: **5** lappa **6** caftan
  secret society: **4** poro
  food:
    dish: **4** fufu **7** cassava
    sauce: **7** palaver
siesta 3 nap **4** rest **5** break, sleep **6** cat nap, snooze **10** forty winks
sieve 4 sift **6** filter, riddle, screen, sorter, strain **7** tattler **8** colander, strainer **9** separator **12** blabbermouth
sift 4 sort **5** drift, probe, study **6** filter, review, screen, search, winnow **7** analyze, inspect, scatter, sort out **8** separate **10** scrutinize **11** distinguish, investigate **12** discriminate
Siggeir
  origin: **12** Scandinavian
  king of: **5** Goths
  wife: **5** Signy
  causes death of: **7** Volsung
sigh 3 sob **4** hiss, long, moan, pine, weep **5** brood, groan, mourn, whine, yearn **6** grieve, lament, sorrow
sight 3 ken, see, spy **4** bead, espy, gaze, spot, view **5** image, scene, vista **6** behold, seeing, survey, vision **7** display, exhibit, eyeshot, glimpse, observe, pageant, scenery, viewing **8** eyesight, perceive, prospect, scrutiny **9** peepsight, sighthole, spectacle **10** appearance, visibility
sighted 3 saw **4** seen **6** seeing **8** not blind, observed
sightless 5 blind **8** unseeing **9** unsighted
sightly 4 fair **6** lovely, pretty **8** handsome, pleasing **9** appealing, beautiful **10** attractive
Sigmund
  origin: **8** Germanic **12** Scandinavian
  mentioned in: **8** Volsunga **14** Nibelungenlied
  king of: **11** Netherlands
  father: **7** Volsung
  mother: **4** Liod, Ljod **5** Hliod
  wife: **7** Hiordis, Hjordis **8** Borghild **9** Sieglinde
  sister: **5** Signy
  lover: **5** Signy
  son: **6** Sigurd **9** Siegfried, Sinfiotli
sign 3 nod **4** clue, hint, mark, note, omen, wave **5** badge, brand, index, stamp, token, trait **6** emblem, ensign, figure, herald, motion, signal, symbol **7** earmark, endorse, feature, gesture, go-ahead, placard, portent, presage, symptom, warning **8** evidence, forecast, inscribe, neon sign, road sign, signpost **9** autograph, billboard, guidepost, harbinger, indicator, nameplate, trademark **10** indication, intimation, prognostic, suggestion, underwrite **11** forewarning **13** manifestation **14** characteristic *see also* **6** zodiac
signal 3 cue, nod **4** sign **6** beckon, famous, motion, unique **7** command,

eminent, gesture, guiding, honored, notable, warning **8** high sign, password, pointing, renowned, singular, striking **9** arresting, directing, direction, important, indicator, memorable, momentous, prominent, watchword **10** commanding, impressive, indicating, indication, noteworthy, one of-a-kind, remarkable **11** conspicuous, distinctive, exceptional, illustrious, outstanding, significant **12** considerable **13** consequential, distinguished, extraordinary, unforgettable
significance 3 aim **4** note **5** drift, force, merit, sense, value, worth **6** import, intent, moment, object, virtue, weight **7** concern, gravity, meaning, portent, purpose **8** eminence, interest, priority **9** authority, direction, influence, intention, relevance **10** excellence, importance, notability, prominence **11** consequence, distinction, implication
significant 4 main **5** chief, grave, great, major, prime, vital **6** cogent, signal **7** eminent, knowing, notable, serious, telling, weighty **8** critical, distinct, eloquent, eventful, material, pregnant, symbolic **9** important, momentous, paramount, principal, prominent **10** emblematic, expressive, indicative, meaningful, noteworthy, portentous, remarkable, suggestive **11** exceptional, influential, outstanding, substantial, symptomatic **12** considerable **13** consequential, demonstrative **14** representative
signify 4 mean, omen, show, tell **5** argue, augur, imply **6** convey, denote, evince, herald, hint at, import, reveal, typify **7** bespeak, betoken, connote, declare, exhibit, express, portend, predict, presage, promise, suggest **8** announce, disclose, evidence, forebode, foretell, indicate, intimate, manifest, proclaim, set forth, stand for **9** be a sign of, designate, represent, symbolize **10** foreshadow **11** communicate, demonstrate
signing up 7 joining **9** enlisting, enrolling **10** enlistment, enrollment **11** registering **12** registration **13** matriculating, matriculation
Sign of Four, The
  author: **19** Sir Arthur Conan Doyle
  character: **11** Mary Morstan **12** Dr John Watson **13** Jonathan Small **14** Sherlock Holmes, Thaddeus Sholto
Signoret, Simone
  real name: **32** Simone-Henriette-Charlotte Kaminker
  born: **7** Germany **9** Wiesbaden
  husband: **11** Yves Montand **12** Yves Allegret
  roles: **10** Madame Rosa **11** Ship of Fools **12** Room at the Top (Oscar) **14** Is Paris Burning?

autobiography: 27 Nostalgia Isn't What It Used to Be

sign up 4 join **6** enlist, enroll, join up **8** register **9** volunteer **11** matriculate

Sigurd
origin: 12 Scandinavian
mentioned in: 8 Volsunga
father: 7 Sigmund
mother: 7 Hiordis, Hjordis
wife: 6 Gudrun, Kudrun **7** Guthrun
killed: 6 Fafnir
acquired treasure of: 8 Andavari
won for Gunnar: 8 Brynhild

Sigyn
origin: 12 Scandinavian
husband: 4 Loki

Sikes, Bill
character in: 11 Oliver Twist
author: 7 Dickens

Sikkim
capital/largest city: 7 Gangtok
others: 6 Dikchu, Lachen, Namchi, Rangpo, Rumtek **7** Lachung **9** Chungtang
government: 12 state of India
mountain: 7 Dongkya, Donkhya **9** Himalayas, Singalili **10** Darjeeling **12** Kanchenjunga
river: 5 Tista **6** Ranjit **9** Lachen Chu **10** Lachung Chu
physical feature:
　mountain pass: 6 Natu La **7** Jelep La
　storm: 7 monsoon
people: 4 Rong **5** Bhote **6** Bhotia, Bhutia, Indian, Lepcha **7** Tibetan **8** Nepalese **9** Mongoloid
　king: 7 chogyal
religion: 5 Hindu **7** Lamaism **15** Tibetan Buddhism

Sikorsky, Igor
nationality: 7 Russian **8** American
invented: 10 helicopter

Silas Marner
author: 11 George Eliot
profession: 6 weaver
character: 5 Eppie **11** Dunstan Cass, Godfrey Cass **13** Aaron Winthrop, Nancy Lammeter

silence 3 gag **4** calm, curb, halt, hush, kill, rout, stop **5** allay, check, crush, peace, quash, quell, quiet, still **6** banish, deaden, defeat, muffle, muzzle, repose, squash, stifle, subdue **7** conquer, nullify, put down, quieten, repress, reserve, squelch **8** choke off, dumbness, muteness, overcome, serenity, suppress, vanquish **9** lay to rest, placidity, quietness, reticence, stillness, tongue-tie **10** extinguish, placidness, put an end to, strike dumb **11** taciturnity, tranquility **12** tranquillity **13** noiselessness, secretiveness, soundlessness **14** speechlessness **16** closemouthedness **19** uncommunicativeness

silent 3 mum **4** calm, dumb, idle, mute **5** inert, muted, quiet, still, tacit **6** covert, hidden, hushed, placid, serene, unsaid **7** dormant, implied, muffled **8** discreet, implicit, inactive, inferred, lifeless, peaceful, reserved, reticent, taciturn, tranquil, unspoken, wordless **9** concealed, intimated, noiseless, quiescent, secretive, soundless, suggested, unsounded, unwritten **10** insinuated, mysterious, speechless, tongue-tied, undeclared, understood, unrevealed, unstirring, untalked-of **11** close-lipped, tight-lipped, unexpressed, unmentioned, unpublished, untalkative, unvocalized **12** closemouthed, unpronounced **15** uncommunicative

Silent Spring
author: 13 Rachel L Carson

Silenus
god of: 6 forest
oldest: 5 satyr
father: 3 Pan **6** Hermes
foster father of: 8 Dionysus
teacher of: 8 Dionysus
companion of: 8 Dionysus
sons: 6 Sileni

silicon
chemical symbol: 2 Si

silk
fabric: 4 crin **5** crepe, ninon, satin, surah, tulle **6** faille, pongee, sendal, tussah **7** chiffon, foulard, organza, raw silk, taffeta **8** organzie, paduasoy **10** peau de soie **12** crepe de chine
lining: 7 sarsnet **8** sarcenet
measure: 6 denier
raw silk: 5 grege **6** greige **8** marabout
source: 6 cocoon **9** silkworms
waste: 4 noil **5** floss
watered: 5 moire
yarn/thread: 4 tram **5** floss

silk-stocking 6 uptown **8** highborn, highbred, wellborn **9** patrician **10** upper-class **11** blue-blooded **12** aristocratic

Silk Stockings
director: 15 Rouben Mamoulian
cast: 10 Janis Paige, Peter Lorre **11** Cyd Charisse, Fred Astaire
setting: 5 Paris
score: 10 Cole Porter
remake of: 9 Ninotchka

silky 4 fine, soft **6** satiny, smooth **11** fine-grained

silliness 5 folly **6** drivel, idiocy **7** inanity **9** absurdity, asininity, frivolity **10** buffoonery, tomfoolery **11** foolishness **13** pointlessness **14** playing the fool, ridiculousness

Sillitoe, Alan
author of: 10 Her Victory **29** Saturday Night and Sunday Morning **36** The Loneliness of the Long-Distance Runner

silly 3 mad **4** dumb **5** crazy, giddy, inane **6** absurd, frothy, insane, stupid,

unwary, unwise **7** aimless, asinine, fatuous, foolish, idiotic, shallow, witless **8** childish, farcical **9** brainless, foolhardy, frivolous, laughable, ludicrous, pointless, senseless **10** illadvised, irrational, ridiculous **11** empty-headed, harebrained, meaningless, nonsensical, purposeless **12** muddleheaded, preposterous, simpleminded, unreasonable **13** inappropriate, irresponsible, muddlebrained, rattlebrained **14** featherbrained **15** inconsequential

Silmarillion, The
author: 10 J R R Tolkien

silo 3 pit **5** tower
storage of: 6 fodder **7** missile

Silone, Ignazio
real name: 17 Secondo Tranquilli
author of: 9 Fontamara **12** Bread and Wine **26** The Story of a Humble Christian

Silvanus
also: 8 Sylvanus
god of: 5 herds, house, woods **12** farm boundary **16** uncultivated land

silver 5 coins, plate **6** argent, change **7** jewelry **8** argentum, platinum **9** argentine **10** silverware
chemical symbol: 2 Ag

Silver
horse of: 10 Lone Ranger

Silver, Long John
character in: 14 Treasure Island
author: 9 Stevenson

Silver, Mattie
character in: 10 Ethan Frome
author: 7 Wharton

Silvers, Phil
real name: 17 Philip Silversmith
born: 10 Brooklyn NY
roles: 9 Top Banana **13** Sergeant Bilko **15** High Button Shoes **22** A Guide for the Married Man **37** A Funny Thing Happened on the Way to the Forum
autobiography: 14 The Laugh Is on Me

s'il vous plait 6 please **11** if you please

Simenon, Georges
author of: 8 The Train **12** Act of Passion **14** The Little Saint **15** Maigret's Memoirs **28** The Strange Case of Peter the Lett
character: 21 Inspector Jules Maigret

Simeon
father: 5 Jacob
mother: 4 Leah
brother: 3 Dan, Gad **4** Levi **5** Asher, Judah **6** Joseph, Reuben **7** Zebulun **8** Benjamin, Issachar, Naphtali
sister: 5 Dinah
canticle: 12 nunc dimittis
descendant of: 9 Simeonite

similar 4 akin, like, twin **5** close **6** allied **7** cognate, kindred **8** agreeing, matching, parallel **9** analogous, duplicate **10** comparable, equivalent, resembling **11** approximate, correlative, much the same, nearly alike **13** correspondent, corresponding

similarity 7 harmony, kinship, oneness **8** affinity, likeness, nearness, sameness **9** agreement, closeness, congruity, semblance **10** congruence, similitude **11** concordance, conformance, equivalence, parallelism, reciprocity, resemblance **13** comparability **14** conformability, correspondence

similarly 4 thus **5** alike **7** equally **8** likewise **11** furthermore, identically **15** correspondingly

similitude 7 analogy **8** likeness, sameness **10** similarity **11** parallelism, resemblance

simmer 4 boil, burn, foam, fume, stew **5** chafe, smart **6** bubble, burble, gurgle, seethe, sizzle

simmer down 7 cool off **8** calm down **14** collect oneself, compose oneself

Simmons, Jean
    born: 6 London **7** England
    husband: 13 Richard Brooks **14** Stewart Granger
    roles: 4 Trio **6** Hamlet **7** Desiree, Ophelia, The Robe **9** Spartacus, Young Bess **11** Elmer Gantry **12** Guys and Dolls **14** The Happy Ending **17** Great Expectations **19** Androcles and the Lion

Simon
    also known as: 5 Peter
    son: 13 Judas Iscariot
    disciple of: 5 Jesus

Simon, Neil
    author of: 10 Chapter Two, Plaza Suite **11** Biloxi Blues **12** The Odd Couple **15** The Sunshine Boys **16** Come Blow Your Horn **17** Barefoot in the Park **21** Last of the Red Hot Lovers **25** The Prisoner of Second Avenue

Simon & Simon
    character: 7 AJ Simon **9** Rick Simon **12** Cecilia Simon **13** Downtown Brown
    cast: 7 Tim Reid **10** Mary Carver **13** Gerald McRaney, Jameson Parker
    setting: 8 San Diego

Simon Boccanegra
    opera by: 5 Verdi
    setting: 5 Genoa
    character: 5 Maria, Paolo **6** Andrea, Fiesco, Pietro **14** Amelia Grimaldi, Gabriele Adorno

Simon Legree 8 overseer **11** slavedriver
    in: 14 Uncle Tom's Cabin

Simonov, Konstantin
    author of: 13 Days and Nights

Simon Templar *see* Saint, The

simpatico 7 likable **9** agreeable, congenial, gemutlich

simper 5 smirk **6** giggle, tee-hee, titter **7** snicker, snigger

simple 4 bare, dull, dumb, easy, open, slow, soft, true **5** basic, blunt, dense, frank, green, homey, naive, naked, plain, quiet, sheer, stark, thick **6** callow, candid, common, direct, honest, modest, obtuse, rustic, stupid **7** artless, foolish, natural, sincere **8** absolute, innocent, not fancy, ordinary, peaceful, straight, workaday **9** downright, elemental, guileless, ingenuous, out-and-out, unadorned, unfeigned, untrimmed, unworldly **10** elementary, manageable, not complex, unaffected, uninvolved **11** commonplace, fundamental, plain-spoken, rudimentary, thick-witted, undecorated, unvarnished **12** not difficult, not elaborate, uncompounded **13** inexperienced, uncomplicated, unembellished, unpretentious **15** straightforward, unsophisticated

simple house 3 cot, hut **5** shack **6** chalet **7** cottage **8** bungalow

simpleminded 4 dull, dumb, slow **5** dense, silly, thick **6** stupid **7** asinine, fatuous, foolish, idiotic, moronic, witless **8** retarded **9** brainless, dim-witted, imbecilic **10** dull-witted, half-witted **11** empty-headed, harebrained, lamebrained **12** feeble-minded

simpleton 3 ass, oaf **4** dolt, dope, fool, hick, jerk, rube **5** booby, dummy, dunce, goose, idiot, ninny, stupe **6** donkey, rustic **7** dullard, jackass **8** dumbbell, imbecile, numskull **9** blockhead, greenhorn, ignoramus, numbskull **10** nincompoop

simplicity 6 candor, purity **7** clarity, honesty, naivete **8** easiness, openness, serenity **9** austerity, clearness, innocence, plainness, restraint, sincerity **10** directness **11** artlessness, cleanliness, naturalness, obviousness **12** truthfulness **13** guilelessness, unworldliness **19** straightforwardness

simply 7 clearly, lucidly, plainly, starkly **8** directly, modestly **9** naturally **10** explicitly **11** ingenuously **12** intelligibly, unaffectedly **15** uncomplicatedly, unpretentiously **17** straightforwardly

Simpson, O J (Orenthal James)
    nickname: 5 Juice
    sport: 8 football
    position: 11 running back
    team: 10 USC Trojans **12** Buffalo Bills **23** San Francisco Forty-Niners
    film: 11 The Naked Gun

Simpsons, The
    creator: 12 Matt Groening
    roles: 3 Apu, Moe **4** Bart, Lisa, Otto **5** Homer, Marge **6** Barney **7** Mr Burns **8** Smithers **11** Chief Wiggum **12** Mrs. Karbappel

simulate 3 act, ape **4** copy, fake, play, pose, sham **5** feign, mimic, put on **6** affect, assume, invent **7** imitate, play-act, pretend **9** dissemble, fabricate **11** counterfeit, make believe

simulated 4 fake, sham **5** phony **6** forged **7** manmade, pretend **9** imitation, synthetic **10** artificial, fabricated **11** counterfeit, make-believe

simultaneous 6 coeval **10** coexistent, coexisting, coincident, concurrent, synchronal, synchronic **11** concomitant, synchronous **12** accompanying, contemporary **15** contemporaneous

sin 3 err **4** evil, fall, slip, vice **5** crime, error, lapse, shame, stray, wrong **6** breach, do evil, offend **7** do wrong, misdeed, offense, scandal **8** disgrace, evil deed, iniquity, trespass, villainy **9** violation **10** infraction, transgress, wrongdoing **13** transgression

Sin
    origin: 8 Akkadian
    god of: 4 moon

Sinatra, Frank
    real name: 20 Francis Albert Sinatra
    nickname: 8 The Voice **11** Old Blue Eyes **18** Chairman of the Board
    born: 9 Hoboken NJ
    wife: 9 Mia Farrow **10** Ava Gardner
    daughter: 12 Nancy Sinatra
    son: 14 Frank Sinatra Jr
    leader of: 7 Rat Pack
    roles: 8 Tony Rome **12** Angelo Maggio, Guys and Dolls, The Detective **14** The Joker Is Wild **17** The First Deadly Sin **18** From Here to Eternity **22** The Man with the Golden Arm

Sinbad the Sailor
    character in: 27 Arabian Nights' Entertainments

since 2 as **3** ago, for, yet **4** ergo, from **5** after, hence, later **6** thence, whence **7** because, whereas **8** in as much **9** therefore **10** afterwards **11** accordingly, considering **12** subsequently
    archaic: 4 sith
    prefix: 3 cis
    Scottish: 4 syne

sincere 4 real **5** frank **6** candid, honest **7** artless, earnest, genuine, natural, serious **8** truthful **9** authentic, guileless, heartfelt, ingenuous, unfeigned **10** forthright, unaffected **11** in good faith, undeceitful **12** wholehearted **15** straightforward

sincerely 5 truly **6** really **8** honestly **9** earnestly, genuinely, seriously **10** truthfully **14** wholeheartedly

sincerity 6 candor **7** honesty, probity **8** openness **9** frankness, good faith **11** artlessness, earnestness, genuineness, seriousness **12** truthfulness **13** guilelessness, ingenuousness **14** forthrightness, unaffectedness **16** wholeheartedness **19** straightforwardness

Sinclair, Upton
    author of: 9 The Jungle, World's End

12 Dragon's Teeth
character: 9 Lanny Budd

Sindhi
language family: 12 Indo-European
branch: 11 Indo-Iranian
group: 5 Indic
spoken in: 13 Northern India

sine die 17 without fixing a day (for future action or a future meeting)
literally: 13 without the day

sine prole 14 without progeny **16** without offspring

sine qua non 15 without which not **18** something essential **22** indispensable condition

sinew, sinews 4 grit, thew **5** fiber, nerve, power, vigor **6** muscle, tendon **7** stamina **8** ligament, strength, virility, vitality **10** resilience, strengthen

sinewy 4 wiry **5** beefy, nervy, thewy, tough **6** brawny, robust, strong **7** fibrose, stringy **8** muscular, powerful, vigorous

sinful 3 bad **4** evil, vile **5** wrong **6** errant, unholy, wicked **7** corrupt, heinous, immoral, impious, ungodly, wayward **8** criminal, depraved, shameful **9** miscreant **10** degenerate, despicable, iniquitous, profligate, villainous **11** disgraceful, irreligious, unrighteous

sing 3 hum **4** lilt, pipe **5** carol, chant, chirp, croon, trill, tweet **6** intone, warble **7** chir rup, whistle **8** melodize

Sing Along with Mitch
regulars: 10 Diana Trask **11** Mitch Miller **12** Leslie Uggams, Louise O'Brien, Sandy Stewart **13** Gloria Lambert, Sing Along Gang, Sing Along Kids

Singapore
other name: 8 Singa Pur
name means: 13 city of the lion
capital/largest city: 9 Singapore
others: 4 Tuas **6** Changi, Jurong **7** Nee Soon **8** Paya Lebar, Woodlands **10** Bukit Timah, Queenstown **12** Bukit Panjang **15** Toa Payoh New Town
  medieval town: 7 Temasek
school: 7 Nanyang **8** National **9** Singapore
monetary unit: 4 cent **6** dollar
island: 4 Ubin **5** Brani, Bukum, Pesek **7** Semakau **8** Merlimau, Southern **10** Ayer Chawan, Ayer Merbau **11** Blakang Mati, Tekong Besar **12** Tekong Kechil
mountain: 6 Mandai **7** Panjang
highest point: 10 Bukit Timah
river: 6 Jurong, Sungei **7** Kallang, Seletar **9** Singapore
sea: 6 Indian **10** South China
physical feature:
  harbor: 6 Keppel **9** Serangoon
  strait: 6 Johore, Pandan **8** Sembilan **9** Singapore

people: 5 Malay **6** Indian **7** Chinese **9** Malaysian, Pakistani, Sri Lankan
  founder: 7 Raffles
  leader: 10 Lee Kwan Yew
language: 5 Malay, Tamil **7** Chinese, English **8** Mandarin
religion: 4 Sikh **5** Hindu, Islam **6** Taoism **8** Buddhism **12** Christianity, Confucianism
place:
  amusement park: 8 New World **10** Great World, Happy World
  aquarium: 8 Van Kleef
  cathedral: 9 St Andrews
  gardens: 7 Botanic
  hall: 16 Victoria Memorial
  industrial park: 6 Jurong
  mosque: 6 Sultan
  park: 6 Farber **7** Merlion **12** Raffles Place
  street: 16 Raffles Boulevard
  temple: 17 One Thousand Lights
feature:
  boat: 4 junk **6** sampan
  clothing: 4 sari

singe 4 burn, char, sear **5** brand **6** scorch

singer 4 alto, bard, bass, diva, lark **5** tenor **6** canary **7** crooner, soprano **8** baritone, minstrel, songbird, songster, vocalist **9** chanteuse, chantress, contralto **10** cantatrice, songstress, troubadour **11** nightingale **12** countertenor, mezzo-soprano

Singer, Isaac Bashevis
author of: 6 Shosha **7** Old Love **8** The Manor **9** The Estate **13** Gimpel the Fool **15** The Family Moskat **16** In My Father's Court **24** The Spinoza of Market Street

singing group 4 trio **5** choir, nonet, octet **6** chorus, sextet **7** quartet, quintet **8** glee club **13** choral society **17** barbershop quartet

Singin' in the Rain
director: 9 Gene Kelly **12** Stanley Donen
cast: 9 Gene Kelly, Jean Hagen **11** Cyd Charisse **13** Donald O'Connor **14** Debbie Reynolds
song: 11 Make 'em Laugh

single 3 one **4** lone, sole **5** unwed **6** maiden **7** only one **8** bachelor, singular, solitary, spinster, wifeless **9** unmarried **10** individual, spouseless **11** husbandless

single file 8 one by one **10** Indian file, one at a time **13** in a single line **16** one behind another

single-handedly 5 alone **7** unaided **9** by oneself, on one's own **10** unassisted **11** without help

single-minded 4 firm **6** dogged **7** devoted, intense, staunch, zealous **8** resolved, tireless, untiring **9** dedicated, steadfast, tenacious **10** determined, inflexible, persistent, relentless, un-

swerving, unwavering **11** persevering, unflinching

singleness 12 bachelorhood, spinsterhood **14** unmarried state **17** single blessedness

single out 4 pick, take **6** choose, opt for, select **7** call out, extract, fix upon, pick out **8** decide on, set apart, settle on **11** distinguish

sing the praises of 4 hail, laud, tout **5** boost, cheer, exalt, extol, honor **6** praise **7** acclaim, applaud, approve, commend **8** eulogize **9** celebrate **10** compliment

singular 3 odd **4** rare **5** queer **6** choice, quaint, select, unique **7** bizarre, curious, strange, unusual **8** aberrant, abnormal, atypical, freakish, peculiar, peerless, superior, uncommon, unwonted **9** anomalous, different, eccentric, fantastic, marvelous, matchless, unequaled, unnatural, wonderful **10** noteworthy, outlandish, prodigious, remarkable, surpassing, unfamiliar **11** exceptional, uncustomary **12** unparalleled **13** extraordinary, unaccountable, unprecedented **14** unconventional **16** out-of-the-ordinary

Sinhalese
language family: 12 Indo-European
branch: 11 Indo-Iranian
group: 5 Indic
spoken in: 6 Ceylon **8** Sri Lanka

sinister 4 dark, dire, evil, foul, rank, vile **5** black **6** cursed, malign, wicked **7** adverse, fearful, hellish, ominous, unlucky **8** accursed, alarming, damnable, devilish, infernal, menacing, rascally **9** dismaying, insidious, malignant **10** despicable, detestable, diabolical, disturbing, malevolent, perfidious, villainous **11** disquieting, frightening, threatening, treacherous, unfavorable, unpromising **12** blackhearted, inauspicious, unpropitious **13** Machiavellian, reprehensible

sink 3 dig, dip, ebb, lay, sag, set **4** bore, bowl, bury, drop, fall, seep, slip, soak, tilt, wane **5** basin, drill, drive, droop, drown, gouge, lower, slant, slope, slump, stoop, yield **6** engulf, go down, lessen, plunge, reduce, shrink, worsen **7** decline, descend, give way, go to pot, go under, put down, regress, subside, succumb **8** diminish, excavate, languish, lavatory, scoop out, submerge, submerse, washbowl **9** hollow out, wash basin **10** degenerate, depreciate, go downhill, retrogress **11** deteriorate, go to the dogs

sinless 4 good, holy, pure **6** chaste **7** upright **8** innocent, spotless, virtuous **9** reputable, righteous

sinner 8 apostate, evildoer, offender **9** miscreant, misfeasor, reprobate, wrongdoer **10** backslider, malefactor, malfeasant, recidivist, trespasser **12** transgressor

Sinon
pretended to be: **13** Greek deserter
told Trojans of: **11** Trojan Horse

Sino-Tibetan
language branch: **7** Sinitic **12** Tibeto-Burman
includes: **4** Naga **5** Karen **7** Burmese, Chinese **8** Kuki-Chin, Mandarin

Sins, Seven 4 envy, lust **5** anger, pride, sloth **8** gluttony **12** covetousness

sinuosity 10 slinkiness **11** convolution, sinuousness **12** tortuousness

sinuous 6 curved, folded, volute, zig-zag **7** bending, coiling, curving, twisted, winding **8** indirect, mazelike, rambling, tortuous, twisting **9** wandering **10** circuitous, convoluted, meandering, roundabout, serpentine, undulating **12** labyrinthine

sinuousness 9 sinuosity **10** slinkiness **11** convolution **12** tortuousness

Siouan
tribe: **4** Crow, Iowa **5** Ioway, Omaha, Osage, Sioux **6** Dakota, Mandan **7** Hidatsa **8** Minitari, Wazhazhe **10** Assiniboin, Gros Ventre **11** Assiniboine

Sioux *see* **6** Dakota

Sioux State
nickname of: **11** North Dakota

sip 3 lap, nip, sup **4** dram, drop **5** drink, savor, taste **6** sample **7** soupcon, swallow **10** thimbleful

siphon 4 tube **5** drain **7** draw off

siphonaptera
class: **8** hexapoda
phylum: **10** arthropoda
group: **4** flea

Sippar residents 11 Sepharvites

Siqueiros, David Alfaro
born: **6** Mexico **9** Chihuahua
artwork: **12** New Democracy **13** Echo of a Scream **14** Trial of Fascism **15** Ascent of Culture, Burial of a Worker **16** Towards the Cosmos **17** Death to the Invader **18** Polyforum Siqueiros **22** March of Humanity on Earth **24** Cuauhtemoc Against the Myth

sir *see* **6** *mister*

sire 4 king, lord **5** beget, breed **6** create, father **7** creator **9** originate **10** originator, progenitor

siren, Siren 4 horn, vamp **5** alarm, nymph, witch **6** sexpot **7** charmer, whistle **8** deceiver, sea nymph **9** temptress **10** seductress **11** enchantress **13** warning signal **15** bewitching woman
French: **11** femme fatale
form: **5** nymph
location: **3** sea
lured sailors by: **7** singing

Sir Gawain and the Green Knight
author: **7** unknown
character: **10** King Arthur **22** Sir Bernlak de Hautdesert
horse: **9** Gringalet

Sirian Experiments, The
author: **12** Doris Lessing

sissified 6 prissy **7** unmanly **8** womanish **10** effeminate

sissy 6 coward **8** weakling **9** fraidy-cat **10** scaredy-cat

sister 3 nun, kin, sib **5** nurse **6** female **7** sibling **8** feminist, relation, relative
nautically: **6** secure **10** strengthen
society: **8** sorority

Sister Carrie
author: **15** Theodore Dreiser
character: **11** G W Hurstwood **12** Carrie Meeber **13** Charles Drouet

Sister Woman
character in: **16** Cat on a Hot Tin Roof
author: **8** Williams

Sisyphean 4 hard **5** tough **6** uphill **7** arduous, onerous **8** toilsome **9** demanding, difficult, strenuous, wearisome **10** exhausting

Sisyphus
king of: **7** Corinth
father: **6** Aeolus
mother: **7** Enarete
brother: **9** Salmoneus
wife: **6** Merope
son: **5** Almus **7** Glaucus **8** Ornytion **10** Thersander
founded: **6** Ephyra **7** Corinth
rolled: **11** stone uphill

sit 3 lie **4** loll, meet, mind, rest, rule, stay **5** abide, chair, nurse, perch, reign, roost, squat, stand, teach, watch **6** attend, endure, gather, govern, linger, remain, reside, settle, sprawl **7** baby-sit, care for, convene, preside **8** assemble, be placed, be seated, chaperon **9** have a seat, officiate **10** deliberate **11** be in session

site 4 area, post, spot, zone **5** field, locus, place, point, scene **6** ground, locale, region, sector **7** section, setting, station **8** district, locality, location, position, province **9** territory **11** whereabouts

sit in judgment 5 judge **6** decide, settle **7** adjudge, mediate **9** arbitrate, reconcile **10** adjudicate **12** bring to terms

situ 5 place

situate 3 put, set **4** post **5** build, house, lodge, place, plant, stand **6** billet, locate, settle **7** install, station **8** ensconce, position **9** construct, establish

situation 3 fix, job **4** case, duty, post, role, seat, site, spot, work **5** berth, place, state **6** locale, office, plight, status **7** dilemma, posture, station **8** capacity, function, locality, location, position, quandary **9** condition **10** assignment, livelihood **11** predicament **13** circumstances **14** state of affairs

sit upon 5 brood, cover, hatch **8** incubate

Sivan 16 third Hebrew month

Six Characters in Search of an Author
author: **15** Luigi Pirandello

six cubits 4 reed

Six Million Dollar Man
character: **11** Dr Rudy Wells, (Col) Steve Austin **12** Oscar Goldman
cast: **9** Lee Majors **13** Martin E Brooks **15** Alan Oppenheimer, Richard Anderson
spinoff: **11** Bionic Woman

Sixty Minutes
correspondent: **9** Dan Rather, Ed Bradley **10** Andy Rooney, Steve Kroft **11** Diane Sawyer, Leslie Stahl, Mike Wallace, Morley Safer **13** Harry Reasoner

sizable 5 ample, broad, large, roomy **7** immense **8** spacious **9** capacious, good-sized

size 3 sum **4** area, bulk, mass, sort **5** array, grade, group, scope, total **6** amount, extent, spread, volume **7** arrange, bigness, content, expanse, stretch **8** capacity, classify, quantity, totality **9** aggregate, amplitude, greatness, largeness, magnitude **10** dimensions **11** measurement, proportions

sizzle 3 fry **4** hiss, spit **7** crackle, frizzle, hissing, sputter **8** splutter **10** sputtering

skate 3 nag, ray **4** skid, skim, slip **5** blade, coast, glide, horse, slide **6** rotter
female: **4** maid
genus: **4** Raja
mark: **4** cusp

skein 4 coil, hank, reel, yarn **5** twist **6** tangle, thread **9** filaments, twistings
members: **4** fowl **5** ducks, flock, geese **6** flyers

skeletal 4 bony, thin **5** gaunt **6** wasted **9** emaciated **10** cadaverous

skeleton 4 hulk **5** bones, frame, shell **9** framework
purpose: **7** support **8** protects **9** framework

Skelton, Red
real name: **21** Richard Bernard Skelton
born: **11** Vincennes IN
roles: **7** I Dood It **8** Ship Ahoy **12** Panama Hattie **16** Neptune's Daughter **17** The Fuller Brush Man **18** Clem Kadiddlehopper, Whistling in the Dark **20** Freddie the Freeloader

skeptic, sceptic 7 atheist, doubter, scoffer **8** agnostic **10** questioner, unbeliever **14** doubting Thomas

skeptical, sceptical 6 unsure **7** cynical, dubious **8** doubtful, doubting, scoffing **9** uncertain **11** incredulous, questioning, unbelieving, unconvinced **12** disbelieving **13** hypercritical

skepticism 5 doubt **7** dubiety **8** distrust, mistrust, unbelief **9** disbelief, suspicion **11** agnosticism, incredulity **12** doubtfulness **13** faithlessness

sketch 3 map **4** draw, plot, skit **5** chart, draft, graph, scene **6** depict, digest, precis, satire **7** drawing, lampoon, mark out, outline, picture, portray, summary, takeoff **8** abstract, rough out, synopsis, vignette **9** blueprint, burlesque, delineate, short play, summarize **11** preliminary **16** characterization

Sketch Book, The
   author: **16** Washington Irving

sketchy 4 bare, hazy **5** brief, crude, light, rough, short, vague **6** meager, skimpy, slight **7** cursory, outline, shallow, slender **9** essential, rough-hewn, unrefined **10** incomplete, undetailed, unfinished, unpolished **11** preliminary, preparatory, provisional, superficial

skewed 5 slued **6** veered, warped **7** oblique, sheered, slanted, swerved, twisted **9** distorted

skewer 3 pin, rod **4** spit, stab **5** truss **6** pierce, skiver **7** impale **9** brochette **10** run through

skid 3 ski **4** drag, dray, skim, skip, sled, slip **5** coast, glide, skate, slide **6** runner, sledge **7** skitter **8** glissade, platform, sideslip

Skidbladnir
   origin: **12** Scandinavian
   ship of: **4** Frey **5** Freyr
   feature: **11** collapsible

Skidmore, Owings, and Merrill
   partners: **13** John Merrill Sr, Louis Skidmore **15** Nathaniel Owings
   architects of: **10** Lever House (NYC) **11** AEC town site (Oak Ridge TN) **13** Banque Lambert (Brussels) **16** John Hancock Tower (Chicago) **17** Terrace Plaza Hotel (Cincinnati), US Air Force Academy (CO) **18** Mauna Kea Beach Hotel (Kamuela HI) **19** Istanbul Hilton Hotel (Turkey) **23** Beinecke Rare Book Library (Yale) **26** Chase Manhattan Bank Building (NYC) **33** American Republic Insurance Building (Des Moines IA)
      world's tallest building: **10** Sears Tower (Chicago)

skiff 4 boat **6** dinghy **7** rowboat

skiing
   athlete: **9** Phil Mahre **11** Bill Johnson, Cindy Nelson **13** Gustavo Thoeni, Robert Cochran **14** Marilyn Cochran, Martha Rockwell **15** Debbie Armstrong, Ingemar Stenmark, Jean Claude Killy **16** Michael Gallagher **17** Barbara Ann Cochran **20** Annemarie Proell Moser

skill 4 gift **5** craft, knack **6** acumen, tal-

ent **7** ability, cunning, faculty, know-how, mastery, prowess **8** artistry, capacity, deftness, facility **9** adeptness, dexterity, expertise, handiness, ingenuity **10** adroitness, cleverness, competence, experience, expertness **11** proficiency **12** skillfulness **13** inventiveness

skilled 6 adroit, expert **7** trained **8** skillful **9** competent, masterful, practiced **10** proficient **12** accomplished

skilled worker 7 artisan **9** craftsman **10** technician **15** master craftsman

skillful 3 apt **4** able, deft, keen **5** adept, handy, sharp, slick **6** adroit, clever, expert, facile, gifted **7** capable, cunning, skilled, trained, veteran **8** masterly, talented **9** competent, dexterous, ingenious, masterful, practiced, qualified **10** proficient, well-versed **11** experienced **12** accomplished, professional

skim 3 fly **4** flip, ream, sail, scan, scud, skid, skip **5** coast, float, glide, skate, sweep **6** bounce, scrape **7** dip into **8** glissade **10** glance over **11** leaf through, move lightly **12** thumb through

skimp 5 pinch, stint **6** scrimp, slight **8** be frugal, be stingy, hold back, withhold **9** economize **11** cut expenses, scrape along

Skimpole, Harold
   character in: **10** Bleak House
   author: **7** Dickens

skimpy 5 close, scant, small, spare, tight **6** frugal, meager, modest, scanty, slight, sparse, stingy **7** miserly, scrimpy, sparing, wanting **8** exiguous, grudging, smallish, stinting **9** illiberal, niggardly, penurious, scrimping **10** inadequate, incomplete, too thrifty **11** close fisted, tightfisted **12** insufficient, parsimonious **13** pennypinching **14** inconsiderable

skin 3 fur, pod **4** bark, case, coat, flay, hide, hull, husk, peel, pelt, rind **5** shell **6** abrade, casing, fleece, jacket, scrape, sheath **7** lay bare **9** epidermis **10** complexion, integument **12** body covering, outer coating
   outer layer: **9** epidermis
   contains: **3** fat **4** hair, pore, root **5** nerve **6** vessel **8** oil gland **10** sweat gland
   body's largest: **5** organ
   sense of: **4** cold, heat, pain **5** touch **8** pressure, tickling

skinflint 5 miser **7** hoarder, niggard, scrooge **8** tightwad **10** pinchpenny **12** penny pincher

Skinner, Cornelia Otis
   author of: **23** The Pleasure of His Company (with Samuel Taylor) **24** Our Hearts Were Young and Gay (with Emily Kimbrough)

skinny 4 lank, lean, thin, wiry **5** gaunt,

gawky, lanky, spare **6** slight **7** angular, scraggy, scrawny, slender, spindly **8** gangling, rawboned, shrunken, skeletal **9** emaciated

Skin of Our Teeth, The
   author: **14** Thornton Wilder

skip 3 bob, cut, hop **4** flee, flit, jump, leap, miss, omit, romp, shun, trip **5** bound, caper, dodge, elude, evade **6** bounce, escape, eschew, gambol, ignore, prance, spring **7** abscond, make off, neglect **8** leap over, leave out, overlook, pass over **9** disappear, disregard, do without, play hooky, skedaddle **10** fly the coop **12** be absent from

skirmish 4 fray, tilt **5** brush, clash, joust, run-in, scrap, set-to **6** action, affray, battle, fracas, tussle **7** scuffle **8** struggle **9** encounter, firefight, scrimmage **10** engagement

skirt 3 hem, rim **4** edge, gird, kilt, maxi, mini, ring, shun **5** avoid, evade, flank, hem in, verge **6** border, bounds, circle, dirndl, fringe, girdle, margin **7** enclose, envelop **8** boundary, encircle, go around, lie along **9** crinoline, outer area, perimeter, periphery **10** circumvent, fight shy of **12** circumscribe, detour around

skittish 3 shy **4** wary **5** chary, jumpy, leery, shaky, timid **6** fitful, unsure **7** bashful, fearful, fidgety, flighty, guarded, jittery, nervous, restive **8** cautious, restless, unstable, unsteady, volatile **9** demurring, excitable, impulsive, mercurial, reluctant **10** suspicious **11** distrustful

skittles
   equipment: **4** pins **6** cheese
   also called: **5** closh **6** cloddy **8** roly-poly **10** Dutch bowls
   tabletop version: **15** Enfield skittles

Skrymir
   also: **10** Utgardloki
   origin: **12** Scandinavian
   form: **5** giant
   took to Jotunheim: **4** Loki, Thor **7** Thialfi

Skuld 4 Norn
   origin: **12** Scandinavian
   form: **5** dwarf
   personifies: **6** future
   developed from: **5** Urdar
   companions: **3** Urd **8** Verdandi

skulduggery, skullduggery 7 knavery **8** trickery **9** chicanery, deception **10** dirty trick **12** pettifoggery

skulk 4 hide, lurk **5** cower, creep, prowl, slink, sneak **9** pussyfoot

skull
   contains: **5** brain

Skull place 7 Calvary **8** Golgotha

sky 5 space **9** firmament **10** atmosphere, outer space, the heavens **12** arch of heaven

goddess of: 3 Fri, Nut **5** Frigg, Frija **6** Frigga

sky blue 5 azure **8** cerulean, pale blue **9** clear blue, light blue

Sky King
character: 5 Penny **7** Clipper
cast: 10 Kirby Grant **11** Ron Haggerty **13** Gloria Winters
ranch: 11 Flying Crown
plane: 8 Songbird

skylarking 6 sport **6** antics **7** hijinks, romping **10** frolicking

skypilot 5 padre, rabbi **6** cleric, parson, priest **8** chaplain, minister **9** clergyman

skyward 2 up **6** upward **8** to the sky **10** heavenward **12** to the heavens

slab 3 wad **4** hunk, slat **5** block, board, chunk, plank, slice, wedge **10** thick slice

slack 3 lax **4** dull, easy, free, lazy, limp, slow, soft **5** baggy, loose, quiet, relax **6** easily, flabby, freely, limply, loosen, pliant, remiss, slowly, untied **7** flaccid, let up on, loosely, not busy, not firm, not taut, offhand, relaxed, slacken **8** careless, dilatory, flexible, heedless, inactive, indolent, listless, not tight, slapdash, slipshod, slothful, sluggish **9** leisurely, lethargic, negligent, slow-paced, unmindful, untighten **10** neglectful, nonchalant, permissive, slow-moving, sluggishly, unexacting, unfastened, unthinking **11** inattentive, indifferent, thoughtless, unconcerned, undemanding

slacken 4 curb, ease, flag, free, slow **5** abate, check, let go, let up, limit, loose, relax, slack **6** arrest, go limp, lessen, loosen, reduce, retard, soften, temper, weaken **7** dwindle, inhibit, release **8** decrease, diminish, keep back, mitigate, moderate, restrain, slow down, taper off **9** untighten

slacker 5 idler **6** dodger, loafer, truant **7** dallier, dawdler, goof-off, laggard, quitter, shirker **9** do-nothing, goldbrick **10** malingerer **14** good-fornothing, procrastinator

slag 5 dross **6** cinder, scoria **8** clinkers

slake 4 calm, cool, curb, ease, hush, sate **5** allay, quell, quiet, still **6** modify, quench, soothe, subdue, temper **7** appease, assuage, compose, gratify, mollify, relieve, satiate, satisfy **8** decrease, mitigate, moderate **9** alleviate **11** tranquilize **14** take the edge off

slake off 4 wane **5** abate **6** lessen, reduce, weaken **7** decline, subside **8** diminish, fade away, slack off

slam 3 hit **4** bang, bump, slap **5** crash, smack, smash, throw

slammer 3 jug, pen **4** jail, stir **5** clink **6** cooler, lockup, prison **8** big house, hoosegow **9** calaboose, jailhouse **12** penitentiary

Slammin' Sammy
nickname of: 8 Sam Snead

slander 4 soil **5** libel, smear, sully **6** defame, malign, revile, vilify **7** calumny **8** besmirch **9** falsehood **10** defamation, distortion **12** vilification **14** false statement **17** misrepresentation

Slaney, Mary *see* **10** Mary Decker

slang 4 cant, jive **5** argot, idiom, lingo **6** jargon **7** dialect

slant 4 bias, lean, list, rake, tilt, view **5** angle, color, pitch, slope **7** distort, incline, leaning **8** attitude **9** prejudice, viewpoint

slanted 4 awry **6** biased, tilted **7** colored, crooked, leaning, pitched, sloping **8** inclined **9** on an angle, on the bias **10** prejudiced

slanting 4 bias **5** alean, atilt **7** oblique, sloping **8** diagonal, glancing, inclined **10** distorting

slap 3 cut, hit **4** blow, clap, cuff, snub, swat **5** smack, whack **6** insult, rebuff, strike, wallop **9** rejection

slapdash 6 casual, sloppy **8** careless, slipshod, slovenly **9** haphazard

Slapsie Maxie
nickname of: 15 Maxie Rosenbloom

slash 3 cut, rip **4** drop, gash, mark, pare, rend, rent, slit, tear **5** lower, slice **6** reduce, stroke **8** decrease, lacerate, lowering **9** reduction **10** laceration

slate 4 list **6** ballot, tablet, ticket **10** blackboard, chalkboard

slattern 4 drab, slob, slut **5** bitch, frump **6** harlot, sloven **7** trollop

slatternly 6 frowsy, frumpy, sloppy, untidy **7** unkempt **8** slipshod, slovenly

slaughter 4 kill, slay **6** pogrom **7** butcher, destroy, killing, wipe out **8** decimate, massacre **9** bloodbath **10** annihilate, butchering, mass murder **11** exterminate

Slaughterhouse Five
author: 12 Kurt Vonnegut
character: 12 Billy Pilgrim
setting: 7 Dresden

Slav 4 Pole, Serb, Sorb, Wend **5** Croat, Czech **6** Bulgar, Slovak **7** Russian, Serbian, Slovene, Sorbian **8** Bohemian, Croatian, Moravian **9** Bulgarian, Ruthenian, Slavonian, Slovadian, Ukrainian

slave 4 prey, serf, toil **6** addict, drudge, menial, thrall, toiler, vassal, victim **7** chattel, plodder **8** bondsman **9** workhorse **11** bond servant

slaver 5 drool **6** drivel **7** slobber

slavery 4 toil **5** grind, labor, sweat **6** strain **7** bondage, serfdom, travail **8** drudgery, struggle **9** captivity, treadmill, vassalage **11** enslavement, impressment, subjugation **12** enthrallment

Slavic
language family: 12 Indo-European
group: 11 Balto-Slavic
subgroup: 12 Old Bulgarian **13** Eastern Slavic, Western Slavic **14** Southern Slavic **15** Old Church Slavic

slavish 5 exact **6** strict **7** literal, servile **9** imitative, slavelike **10** derivative, obsequious, submissive, unoriginal **11** subservient **13** unimaginative

slay 4 do in, kill **6** murder **7** destroy, execute **8** massacre **9** slaughter **10** annihilate

slayer 6 hit man, killer **7** butcher **8** assassin, murderer **11** executioner **12** exterminator

slaying 6 murder **7** killing **8** homicide **9** execution

sleazy 5 cheap, tacky **6** flimsy, shabby, shoddy, trashy, vulgar **7** schlock **13** insubstantial

sleek 4 oily **5** shiny, silky, slick, suave **6** glossy, satiny, smooth **7** fawning, velvety **8** lustrous, unctuous **12** ingratiating

sleep 3 nap **4** doze, rest **5** death, peace **6** repose, snooze **7** slumber
god of: 6 Hypnos, Hypnus, Somnus

sleeping 6 asleep, dozing **7** dormant, napping, resting **8** snoozing **9** quiescent, somnolent **13** hibernating **19** in the arms of Morpheus

Sleeping Beauty, The
composer: 11 Tchaikovsky

sleeping car (railroad)
invented by: 7 Pullman

sleeping infants
goddess of: 6 Cunina

sleeping place 3 bed, cot **4** bunk **5** berth **6** pallet **7** bedroom **9** dormitory **10** bedchamber

sleepless 5 alert **7** wakeful **8** restless, watchful **9** insomniac, wide awake **11** industrious

sleeplessness 8 insomnia **9** alertness, attention **11** wakefulness **12** restlessness

sleep lightly 3 nap, nod **4** doze **6** catnap, snooze **15** catch forty winks

sleepy 4 dull **5** quiet, tired, weary **6** drowsy **8** fatigued, inactive **9** exhausted

sleigh 4 dray, sled **6** cutter, sledge, troika **8** transport

Sleipnir
origin: 12 Scandinavian
horse of: 4 Odin **5** Othin
legs: 5 eight

slender 4 lean, poor, slim, thin, weak **5** faint, scant, small, spare **6** feeble, little, meager, narrow, remote, skinny, slight **7** willowy **8** delicate

Slender
character in: 22 The Merry Wives of Windsor
author: 11 Shakespeare

Sleuth
director: 17 Joseph L Mankiewicz
based on play by: 14 Anthony Shaffer
cast: 12 Michael Caine **15** Laurence Olivier

slew 3 lot, ton **4** gang, heap, load, lots, peck, pile, raft **5** batch, did in **6** killed **8** murdered **12** assassinated

Slezak, Walter
born: 6 Vienna **7** Austria
father: 9 Leo Slezak
roles: 5 Fanny **8** Lifeboat **11** Dr Coppelius

slice 3 cut **4** pare **5** carve, piece, sever, shave **6** cut off, divide **7** portion, section, segment, whittle **8** separate **9** dismember

slick 3 sly **4** coat, film, foxy, oily, scum, waxy, wily **5** sharp, shiny, sleek **6** clever, glassy, glossy, greasy, satiny, smooth, tricky **7** coating, cunning **8** slippery **10** make glossy **11** fast-talking **13** smooth-talking

slicker 8 raincoat **9** sou'wester **10** mackintosh, waterproof

slide 4 fall, pass, ramp, skid, slip, veer **5** chute, coast, glide, lapse, slope **7** slither **8** sideslip **11** diapositive **12** transparency

slide by 4 go by **5** lapse **6** elapse, roll by, slip by **7** glide by **8** slip away

slight 3 cut **4** lean, slap, slim, snub, thin, tiny **5** frail, small, spare **6** insult, little, modest, rebuff **7** fragile, limited, slender **8** moderate **10** incivility, negligible, restricted **11** unimportant **13** imperceptible, inappreciable, infinitesimal

slight amount 3 bit **4** dash, drop **5** pinch, touch, trace **6** little **7** smidgen, smidgin, soupcon **8** smidgeon **9** little bit **10** smattering

slightly 6 feebly, rarely **8** meagerly, scantily, scarcely, somewhat **10** negligibly **13** superficially **15** insignificantly

slim 4 lean, thin **5** faint, small **6** meager, remote, skinny, slight, svelte **7** distant, slender, thready, willowy **10** negligible

slime 3 mud **4** mire, muck, ooze **6** sludge

slimy 4 foul, vile **5** gummy, mucky, nasty **6** creepy, putrid, sticky **7** viscous **9** glutinous, loathsome, obnoxious, offensive, repulsive

sling 3 net **4** cast **5** fling, throw **9** slingshot **10** arm support

Slingin' Sammy
nickname of: 10 Sammy Baugh

slingshot 5 sling **8** catapult

slink 4 slip **5** creep, prowl, skulk, sneak, steal **6** tiptoe

slip 3 put **4** dock, drop, fail, fall, leak, pass, sink, skid **5** berth, error, glide, lapse, scrap, shoot, shred, slide, sneak, sprig, steal, strip **6** escape, sprout, ticket, worsen **7** blunder, chemise, cutting, decline, faux pas, receipt, sapling, voucher **9** petticoat, stripling, youngling, youngster **10** be revealed, get clear of, imprudence, underdress **12** indiscretion

slip away 4 go by **5** lapse **6** elapse, escape **7** run away, slide by **8** creep off **9** tiptoe off

slip by 4 go by, pass **5** lapse **6** elapse, pass by, roll by **7** glide by, slide by

slip of the tongue, a
Latin: 13 lapsus linguae

slipper 4 mule, shoe **5** scuff **6** sandal

slippery 4 foxy, oily, waxy, wily **5** slick, soapy **6** crafty, glassy, greasy, shifty, smooth, sneaky, tricky **7** devious **9** deceitful **10** contriving, unreliable **11** treacherous **13** untrustworthy

slipshod 3 lax **5** loose, messy **6** casual, sloppy, untidy **7** offhand **8** careless, slovenly **11** thoughtless

slip-up 4 flub, goof **5** botch, error, gaffe, lapse **6** boo-boo, bungle, foul-up, mess-up, miscue **7** blooper, blunder, clinker, faux pas, mistake, screw-up **9** oversight

slit 3 cut **4** gash **5** crack, slash **7** crevice, fissure **8** incision

slither 5 glide, slide **25** move with a side-to-side motion

sliver 5 crumb, shred, slice, snick **6** morsel **8** splinter

slivovitz
type: 6 brandy **7** liqueur
origin: 10 Yugoslavia
flavor: 4 plum

Sloan, John F
born: 11 Lock Haven PA
artwork: 12 McSorley's Bar **14** Wake of the Ferry **18** Hairdresser's Window **25** Backyards Greenwich Village

slob 6 sloven **8** slattern

slobber 4 slop **5** drool **6** drivel, slaver **7** dribble, sputter **8** salivate, splutter

sloe gin
type: 7 liqueur
flavor: 9 sloe berry **15** blackthorn berry
drink: 11 Sloe Gin Fizz
with bourbon: 9 Black Hawk
with rum: 11 Shark's Tooth
with vermouth: 10 Blackthorn

slogan 5 motto **6** byword **9** battle cry, catchword, watchword

sloop 4 boat, brig, ship **5** smack **8** sailboat, schooner

slop 3 mud **4** mire, muck, ooze **5** filth, slosh, slush, spill, swash, swill, waste **6** refuse, sludge, splash **7** garbage, spatter **8** splatter

Slop, Dr
character in: 14 Tristram Shandy
author: 6 Sterne

slope 3 tip **4** bank, bend, lean, tilt **5** angle, pitch, slant **7** descent, incline **9** downgrade **11** inclination

sloping 5 alean, steep **6** aslant **7** leaning, oblique, tilting **8** diagonal, inclined, on a slant, slanting **9** slantways **11** declivitous

sloppiness 5 chaos, mix-up, upset **6** jumble **7** clutter **8** disarray, disorder, shambles **9** messiness **10** disharmony, untidiness **12** dishevelment **14** disarrangement **15** disorganization

sloppy 3 wet **5** dirty, messy, muddy **6** marshy, sloshy, slushy, sodden, soiled, swampy, untidy, watery **7** unclean **10** disorderly

sloppy person 4 slob **6** sloven

slosh 3 lap **4** drop, mire, stir **5** slush, spill, swash **6** splash **8** flounder

slot 3 gap **4** slit **5** crack, niche, notch
machine: 14 one-armed bandit

sloth 6 phlegm, torpor **7** languor **8** idleness, laziness, lethargy **9** indolence, lassitude, torpidity **12** listlessness, sluggishness **13** do-nothingness, shiftlessness

slothful 3 lax **4** idle, lazy **5** inert **6** drowsy, otiose, supine, torpid **8** indolent, listless, sluggish **9** do-nothing, lethargic, negligent, shiftless **10** sluggardly **11** unambitious

slouch 4 bend **5** droop, hunch, idler, slump, stoop **6** loafer **7** laggard, shirker, slacker **8** sluggard **9** goldbrick, lazybones

Slovakia
formerly part of: 14 Czechoslovakia
capital/largest city: 10 Bratislava
others: 6 Kosice
head of state: 9 president
government: 8 republic
monetary unit: 5 crown **6** koruna
mountain: 7 Sudetes **8** Low Tatra **9** High Tatra, Slovak Ore **10** Carpathian, Nizke Tatry **11** Visoke Tatry **15** White Carpathian
river: 2 Uh **3** Vah **4** Hron **5** Nitra, Slana **6** Danube, Hornad, Ondava, Poprad **7** Laborec **8** Latorica
people: 5 Czech **6** Slavik, Slovak **9** Hungarian
language: 6 Slavik, Slovak
religion: 9 Christian **13** Roman Catholic

Slovenia
capital/largest city: 9 Ljubljana
others: 5 Celje, Koper, Kranj **7** Maribor
head of state: 9 president
government: 8 republic
monetary unit: 5 tolar
river: 4 Sava **5** Drava
sea: 8 Adriatic
people: 8 Slovenes
language: 7 Slovene
religion: 13 Roman Catholic

slovenly 5 dirty, dowdy, messy **6**

frowzy, sloppy, untidy **7** unclean, un-kempt **8** careless, slapdash, slipshod **10** disorderly, slatternly **11** indifferent, unconcerned

slow 3 dim, off **4** curb, dull, dumb, flag, late, long **5** brake, check, dense, heavy, loath, quiet **6** averse, boring, falter, hinder, hold up, impede, ob-tuse, retard, stupid, torpid **7** belated, delayed, laggard, lumpish, not busy, overdue, tedious, unhasty **8** back-ward, cautious, dawdling, dilatory, dragging, drawn out, extended, hesi-tant, inactive, obstruct, sluggish, tarry-ing **9** dim-witted, leisurely, lingering, ponderous, prolonged, reluctant, snail-like, unhurried **10** behind time, decel-erate, deliberate, dull-witted, indis-posed, protracted, unexciting, unpunc-tual

slowdown 4 curb, flag **5** brake, delay, letup, slump **6** ease-up, falter, hinder, impede, lessen, retard, slow-up **7** de-cline, fall off, letdown, setback, slow-ing, subside **8** diminish, downturn, flagging **9** grind down **10** decelerate, slackening, stagnation **11** reduce speed, retardation **12** deceleration

slow-moving 4 poky **5** pokey **6** idling **8** crawling, creeping, dawdling, slug-gish **9** leisurely, snaillike **10** turtlelike **12** tortoiselike
  creature: 4 slug **5** loris, sloth, snail **6** turtle **8** tortoise

slowness 6 tedium **8** dullness **9** tor-pidity **10** snail's pace **12** backward-ness, sluggishness

slow-paced 4 easy **7** gradual, laggard **8** sluggish **9** leisurely, lethargic, un-hurried **10** deliberate

slowpoke 4 slug **5** idler, snail **7** dal-lier, dawdler, laggard, lie-abed, plod-der **8** lingerer, slugabed, tortoise **9** saunterer, straggler **11** foot-dragger

slow to learn 4 dull **5** dense, inapt **6** stupid **8** retarded **10** slow-witted

slow up 4 stem **5** delay **6** detain, hin-der, impede, retard **8** slow down

slow-witted 4 dull **5** dense **7** doltish, idiotic, moronic **8** backward, retarded **9** imbecilic

sludge 3 mud **4** mire, muck, ooze, slop **5** dregs, slime, slush **8** sediment

slug 3 bat, hit **4** bash, belt, sock **5** baste, clout, pound, punch, smite, thump, whack, whale **6** batter, strike, wallop **7** clobber **8** lambaste

sluggard 4 lazy **5** drone, idler, sloth, snail **6** loafer, truant, turtle **7** daw-dler, laggard **8** loiterer, slothful, slow-poke, tortoise **9** do-nothing, lazybones **11** couch potato **12** lounge lizard **13** stick-in-the-mud

sluggish 4 lazy, slow **5** inert **6** torpid **7** languid **8** inactive, indolent, lifeless, listless, slothful **9** leisurely, lethargic,

soporific, unhurried **10** phlegmatic, protracted, spiritless

sluggishness 6 torpor **7** inertia **8** leth-argy, slowness **9** lassitude **10** inactiv-ity **12** listlessness

slum
  Portuguese: 6 favela

slumber 3 nap **4** doze **5** sleep **6** snooze **8** vegetate **9** hibernate **10** be inactive, lie dormant

slump 3 dip, sag **4** drop, fall, slip **5** droop, lapse **6** plunge, slouch, tumble **7** decline, give way, reverse, setback **8** collapse

slur 3 cut, dig **4** mark, skip, spot **5** smear, stain, sully, taint **6** defame, ig-nore, insult, malign, mumble, mutter, slight **7** affront, blacken, blemish, let pass **8** mumbling, overlook, pass over **9** disregard, gloss over, muttering **11** run together

slush 4 slop **6** bathos **9** soppiness **11** mawkishness, melting snow **14** senti-mentalism, sentimentality

slushiness 5 slush **10** sponginess **11** mawkishness **14** sentimentalism, sen-timentality

slut 4 doxy, jade **5** bimbo, frump, hussy, tramp, wench, whore **6** floozy, harlot, sloven, wanton **7** jezebel, trol-lop **8** slattern, strumpet **10** prostitute

sly 4 foxy, wily **6** artful, covert, crafty, secret, shrewd, sneaky, tricky **7** cun-ning, furtive, playful, private **8** stealthy **9** conniving **11** dissembling, mischievous **12** confidential

Slye, Leonard
  real name of: 9 Roy Rogers

slyness 5 craft **7** cunning, stealth **8** archness, foxiness, subtlety, wiliness **10** artfulness, craftiness, shrewdness, trickiness **11** furtiveness **15** under-handedness

smack 3 bit, hit, rap **4** blow, buss, clap, cuff, dash, hint, kiss, slap **5** sa-vor, smell, smite, spank, taste, tinge, touch, trace, whack **6** buffet, flavor **7** suggest

small 4 mean, tiny, weak **5** faint, mi-nor, petty, scant **6** feeble, lesser, little, meager, modest, narrow, petite, slight **7** bigoted, fragile, ignoble, trivial **8** not great, trifling **10** diminutive, pro-vincial, undersized **11** of no account, opinionated, superficial, unimportant **13** insignificant **15** inconsequential

Small, Lennie
  character in: 12 Of Mice and Men
  author: 9 Steinbeck

small details
  Latin: 8 minutiae

smaller 4 less **5** lower **6** lesser, tinier **7** dinkier, littler, pettier, reduced, shorter **8** inferior

smallest 5 least **6** lowest **7** tiniest **8** dinkiest, pettiest, shortest **9** slightest

Small House at Allington, The
  author: 15 Anthony Trollope

small intestine
  part of: 15 digestive system
  lined with: 5 villi

small-minded 4 mean **5** petty **6** nar-row **7** bigoted **9** parochial **10** preju-diced **12** mean-spirited

smallness 8 meanness, tininess **9** pet-tiness **10** meagerness, triviality **12** dwarfishness **14** insignificance **18** in-consequentiality

small piece 3 bit, dab **4** chip, drop, snip **5** crumb, grain, piece, pinch, scrap, shred, speck **6** dollop, morsel **7** granule, smidgen, smidgin **8** fragment, particle, smidgeon

small quantity 3 bit, dab, few **5** touch **7** smidgen, smidgin, soupcon **8** smidgeon **9** little bit

small round window
  French: 11 oeil-de-boeuf

small spot 3 dab, dot **5** fleck, speck

small talk 6 banter, gossip **7** chatter, prattle **8** chitchat, idle talk, repartee **9** bavardage, prattling **12** tittle-tattle

smart 4 ache, burn, chic, hurt, keen, neat, trim **5** brash, brisk, quick, sassy, sharp, sting, wince, witty **6** astute, blench, brainy, bright, clever, flinch, modish, shrewd, suffer **7** elegant, styl-ish **8** feel pain, vigorous **9** be painful, energetic **10** smart-aleck **11** fashiona-ble, intelligent

smart aleck 6 smarty **7** show-off, windbag, wiseass, wise guy **8** blow-hard, braggart, saucebox, wiseacre **9** know-it-all **11** smarty-pants **12** grand stander **13** exhibitionist

smarten up 7 dress up, improve **8** beautify, spruce up

smartness 6 acumen, wisdom **8** keen-ness, sagacity **9** acuteness **10** astute-ness, cleverness, perception, shrewd-ness **12** intelligence, perspicacity

smash 3 hit **4** bang, bash, beat, blow **5** break, clout, crack, crash, crush **6** batter, strike, winner **7** clobber, crack-up, destroy, shatter, success, tri-umph **8** accident, demolish, splinter **9** collision, sensation **12** disintegrate

smash against 4 beat, lash **5** crash, pound, smite **6** batter, buffet **7** break on

smashed 5 drunk **6** soused, wasted, zapped, zonked **7** crashed, crushed **8** squashed **9** plastered, shattered **10** in-ebriated **11** intoxicated **17** under the influence **20** three sheets to the wind

smashing 5 great, super **6** superb **8** fabulous, terrific **9** fantastic, marvel-ous, wonderful **10** stupendous **11** magnificent, sensational **13** extraordi-nary

smashup 5 crash, wreck **7** crackup **8** accident **9** collision **12** fender bender

smattering 3 bit, dab 4 dash, drop 5 scrap 7 smidgen, smidgin, snippet 8 smidgeon 10 sprinkling

smear 3 mar, rub 4 blur, coat, daub, soil 5 cover, lay on, libel, stain 6 blotch, injure, malign, smirch, smudge, spread, streak 7 blacken, blemish, degrade, slander, splotch, tarnish 8 besmirch, besmudge 9 denigrate 10 accusation, obliterate

smell 4 feel, nose, odor, reek 5 aroma, fetor, scent, sense, sniff, stink 6 detect, stench 7 bouquet, perfume, suspect 8 perceive 9 emanation, fragrance, get wind of

smelly 4 rank 5 fetid 6 putrid 7 noisome, odorous, reeking 8 stinking 10 malodorous

Smerdyakov
    character in: 20 The Brothers Karamazov
    author: 10 Dostoevsky

Smetana, Bedrich
    born: 7 Bohemia 8 Litomysl 11 Leitomischl 14 Czechoslovakia
    composer of: 7 Ma Vlast 9 My Country 10 From My Life 11 Czech Dances 12 The Two Widows 16 The Bartered Bride

smidgen, smidgin, smidgeon 3 bit, dab 4 mite, snip 5 crumb, pinch, scrap, shred, speck, trace 6 dollop, morsel

Smike
    character in: 16 Nicholas Nickleby
    author: 7 Dickens

smile 4 beam, grin 5 favor, shine, smirk 6 simper

Smiles of a Summer Night
    director: 13 Ingmar Bergman
    cast: 11 Eva Dahlbeck 13 Ulla Jacobsson 15 Margit Carlquist 16 Harriet Andersson
    remade as: 17 A Little Night Music

Smiley's People
    author: 11 John Le Carre

Smintheus
    epithet of: 6 Apollo

smirch 4 blot, mark, soil, spot 5 dirty, smear, stain, sully, taint 6 blotch, damage, smudge, stigma 7 begrime, blacken, blemish, slander, tarnish 8 besmirch, besmudge, dishonor 9 discredit

smirk 4 grin, leer 5 sneer 6 simper 7 grimace

Smirke, Sir Robert
    architect of: 12 King's College (U of London) 13 British Museum (London) 19 Covent Garden Theater (London)
    style: 12 Greek Revival

smite 3 hit 4 swat 5 knock, smack, whack 6 enamor, strike, wallop 7 clobber

Smith, Adam
    author of: 18 The Wealth of Nations

Smith, Al
    creator/artist of: 11 Mutt and Jeff

Smith, Betty
    author of: 20 A Tree Grows in Brooklyn

Smith, Charles Aaron
    nickname: 5 Bubba
    sport: 8 football
    team: 14 Baltimore Colts

Smith, David
    born: 8 Decatur IN
    artwork: 3 Zig 4 Cubi 6 Oculus 8 Agricola, Main View, Sentinel, Star Cage 9 Australia, Royal Bird, Tank Totem 10 The Banquet 12 Detroit Queen 15 Lectern Sentinel 17 Medals for Dishonor 20 Hudson River Landscape 23 Song of an Irish Blacksmith

Smith, Harriet
    character in: 4 Emma
    author: 6 Austen

Smith, Lillian
    author: 12 Strange Fruit

Smith, Maggie
    born: 6 Ilford 7 England
    husband: 14 Robert Stephens
    roles: 7 Othello 15 California Suite, The Pumpkin Eater 17 Travels with My Aunt 24 The Prime of Miss Jean Brodie (Oscar)

Smith, Winston
    character in: 18 Nineteen Eighty-Four
    author: 6 Orwell

smithereen 3 bit 4 atom 5 crumb, shard 8 fragment, particle 9 scintilla

Smithson, James
    field: 9 chemistry
    nationality: 7 British
    discovered: 11 smithsonite 13 zinc carbonite
    funded: 22 Smithsonian Institution

smitten 8 enamored 9 bewitched 10 enraptured, infatuated

smoke 4 draw, fume, pipe, puff, reek, suck 5 cigar, fumes 6 billow, inhale 7 light up, smolder 9 cigarette, have a drag

Smoke
    author: 12 Ivan Turgenev
    character: 5 Irina 7 Potugin 13 Tanya Shestoff 16 General Ratmiroff, Grigory Litvinoff 18 Kapitolina Shestoff

smoke screen 4 ruse 5 cover, dodge, front 6 screen 7 deception 10 camouflage, subterfuge

smoky 5 dingy, grimy, sooty 6 fuming, smudgy 7 reeking 10 smoldering

smolder 4 burn, fume, rage 5 smoke 6 seethe

Smollett, Tobias George
    author of: 14 (The Expedition of) Humphry Clinker, Roderick Random 15 Peregrine Pickle

smooch 3 pet 4 buss, kiss, neck 5 smack, spoon 7 make out

smooth 4 calm, ease, easy, even, flat, glib, help, mild, open, pave 5 allay, level, silky, sleek, suave 6 facile, mellow, placid, polish, refine, serene, soften, soothe, steady 7 appease, assuage, flatten, mollify, orderly, perfect, prepare, velvety 8 civilize, composed, make even, mitigate, peaceful, pleasant 9 collected, cultivate, easygoing, make level 10 facilitate, flattering, harmonious, methodical, uneventful 11 well-ordered 12 ingratiating 13 self-possessed, well-regulated

smoothness 8 evenness, fineness, flatness 9 silkiness, sleekness

smooth the feathers 4 calm 6 pacify, soothe 7 appease, assuage, mollify, placate 10 conciliate

smooth-tongued 4 glib 5 suave 6 fluent 8 unctuous 10 flattering 11 fast-talking 12 hypocritical, ingratiating

smother 4 hide, mask, wrap 5 choke, quash, snuff 6 deaden, quench, shower 7 conceal 8 keep down, strangle, suppress, surround 9 choke back, envelop in, suffocate 10 asphyxiate, extinguish

Smothers Brothers Comedy Hour, The
    regulars: 10 Don Novello, Pat Paulsen 11 Bob Einstein, Leigh French, Steve Martin, Tom Smothers 12 Betty Aberlin, Dick Smothers, John Hartford, Nino Senporty, Spencer Quinn 13 Mason Williams 14 Jennifer Warren, Sally Struthers 16 Anita Kerr Singers 17 Jimmy Joyce Singers 18 Louis DaPron Dancers 19 Marty Paich Orchestra 20 Denny Vaughn Orchestra, Ron Poindexter Dancers 21 Nelson Riddle Orchestra

smudge 4 blot, mark, soil, spot 5 dirty, smear, stain 6 smutch

smudgy 5 dirty, messy 6 filthy, grubby, smeary 7 sullied 8 befouled, unwashed 9 besmeared

smug 8 superior, virtuous 10 complacent 13 self-righteous, self-satisfied

smuggle 5 sneak 15 export illegally, import illegally

smuggled goods 10 contraband 14 illegal exports, illegal imports 18 prohibited articles

smuggler 6 runner 9 gunrunner, rumrunner 10 bootlegger 13 contrabandist

smugness 7 egotism 9 immodesty 11 superiority 12 virtuousness 16 self-satisfaction 17 self-righteousness

smut 4 dirt, porn, soot 5 filth, grime 6 smudge 9 obscenity, scatology 11 pornography

smutty 4 lewd 5 dirty, grimy, sooty 6

filthy, soiled, vulgar **7** obscene **8** indecent **12** pornographic

Smyrna *see* **6** Myrrha

Smythe, Reginald
  creator/artist of: 8 Andy Capp

snack 3 eat, tea **4** bite, nosh **5** munch **6** nibble, tidbit **7** take tea **8** lap lunch, munchies, nibblies, pick-me-up, snackies **9** collation, crunchies, elevenses **10** finger food, light lunch **11** cassecroute, coffee break, light repast, refreshment

snag 3 bar, rip **4** grab, stub, tear **5** block, catch, hitch, stump **7** barrier **8** obstacle **9** hindrance **10** difficulty, impediment, projection, protrusion **11** encumbrance, obstruction **14** stumbling block

snail
  French: 8 escargot

snake 5 sneak, viper **7** reptile, serpent, traitor **8** ophidian **9** reptilian
  combining form: 4 ophi **5** ophio, ophis **6** herpes **7** herpeto
  expert: 13 herpetologist
  fear of: 13 herpetophobia
  genus: 7 Ophidia
  kind: 3 asp, boa, sea **4** file, habu, wart, whip **5** aboma, adder, cobra, coral, krait, mamba, tiger, viper **6** bongar, elapid, garter, gopher, python, taipan **7** rattler, sunbeam **8** anaconda, cerastes, moccasin, pit viper, ringhals **9** boomslang, colubrina, mole viper, puff adder **10** black mamba, bushmaster, copperhead, fer-de-lance, sidewinder **11** cottonmouth, diamond back, Gaboon viper, rattlesnake **12** slender blind **13** elephant-trunk, water moccasin **14** boa constrictor
  shedding: 7 ecdysis **8** moulting
  skin: 6 exuvia
  snake killer: 8 mongoose

Snake *see* **8** Shoshone

Snake, the
  nickname of: 10 Ken Stabler

Snake Pit, The
  author: 12 Mary Jane Ward, Sigrid Undset

snap 3 nip, pop **4** bark, bite, grab, lock, yelp **5** break, catch, cinch, clasp, click, close, crack, growl, hasty, latch, quick, snarl, spell **6** breeze, period, secure, snatch, sudden **8** careless, fastener, fracture **9** impulsive **11** thoughtless

snapdragon 11 Antirrhinum
  varieties: 4 wild **5** dwarf **6** common, garden, lesser **7** spurred **8** withered

snappish 4 edgy **5** cross, huffy, surly, testy **6** crabby, cranky, shirty, touchy **7** grouchy, huffish, peevish, waspish **8** captious, petulant **9** irascible, irritable, querulous **10** ill-humored, ill-natured, out of sorts **11** hot-tempered

12 cantankerous **13** quick-tempered, short-tempered

snappy 4 fast, tony **5** hasty, quick, rapid, ritzy, sharp, smart, swank, swift, swish **6** classy, dapper, jaunty, speedy, spiffy **7** stylish **12** lickety-split

snare 3 net **4** bait, hook, lure, ruse, trap **5** catch, decoy, noose, seize, trick **6** entrap **7** capture, ensnare, pitfall **9** deception **12** entanglement

snarl 3 mat **4** bark, clog, kink, knot, mess, snap **5** chaos, growl, ravel, twist **6** hinder, impede, jumble, muddle, tangle **7** confuse, lash out **8** disorder, entangle **9** confusion

snatch 3 bit, nab **4** grab, part, pull, take **5** catch, grasp, piece, pluck, seize, wrest **7** snippet **8** fragment

Snead, Sam
  nickname: 12 Slammin' Sammy
  sport: 4 golf
  won: 7 Masters

sneak 3 sly **4** slip **5** creep, knave, rogue, scamp, steal **6** lurker, rascal, secret, spirit **7** bounder, furtive, skulker, slinker, smuggle **8** scalawag, surprise **9** miscreant, scoundrel, secretive, underhand **11** rapscallion **13** surreptitious

sneak attack 4 raid **6** ambush **7** assault **9** ambuscade, incursion

sneakers
  brands: 4 Avia, Fila, Keds, Nike, Puma **5** Asics **6** Adidas, Reebok **7** Saucony **10** New Balance

sneak off 5 elope **6** decamp **7** abscond **9** steal away

sneaky 3 sly **4** mean **7** devious, furtive, vicious **9** malicious, secretive, underhand **10** traitorous **11** treacherous

sneer 4 jeer, leer, mock **5** scoff, scorn, smirk **6** deride, rebuff **7** disdain **8** belittle, ridicule

sneer at 5 knock, scorn **6** deride, malign **7** disdain, put down, run down **8** pooh-pooh **16** cast aspersions on

Sneerwell, Lady
  character in: 19 The School for Scandal
  author: 8 Sheridan

snicker 5 snort **6** cackle, giggle, simper, titter **7** snigger

snide 5 nasty **7** mocking **8** scoffing **9** malicious, sarcastic **11** insinuating **12** contemptuous

Snider, Edwin
  nickname: 4 Duke
  sport: 8 baseball
  position: 7 fielder
  team: 15 Brooklyn Dodgers

sniff 4 jeer, mock, odor **5** aroma, scoff, smell, snort, snuff, whiff **6** snivel **7** disdain, sniffle, snuffle **9** disparage

snip 3 bit, bob, cut, lop **4** brat, clip, crop, punk, snap, trim **5** clack, click,

piece, prune, scrap, shear, twerp **6** sample, shrimp, swatch **7** cutting **8** fragment

snippy 4 curt, rude **5** sassy, saucy, short **6** cheeky, snotty **7** brusque **8** flippant, impudent, insolent, snippety **11** ill- mannered, impertinent, smartalecky

snivel 3 cry **5** sniff, whine **6** boohoo **7** sniffle **8** complain

sniveler 6 coward, whiner **7** crybaby **10** complainer

snob 7 elitist **13** social climber

snobbish 4 vain **6** snooty, snotty **7** haughty, high-hat, stuck-up **8** arrogant, superior **10** disdainful **11** overbearing, patronizing, pretentious **13** condescending

Snodgrass
  character in: 14 Pickwick Papers
  author: 7 Dickens

snoop 3 pry **7** meddler, Paul Pry **8** busybody **10** Nosy Parker **12** eavesdropper

Snoopy 6 beagle
  brother: 5 Spike
  creator: 6 Schulz
  friend: 9 Woodstock
  master: 12 Charlie Brown

snooze 3 nap **4** doze **5** sleep **6** catnap, drowse, siesta **7** slumber **10** forty winks

Snopes family
  characters in: 9 The Hamlet
  members: 2 Ab **4** Flem, Mink **5** Isaac
  author: 8 Faulkner

snort 4 blow, gasp, huff, jeer, pant, puff, rage **5** blast, grunt, scoff, sneer, storm

snout 3 neb **4** beak, bill, nose **5** snoot, spout **6** muzzle, nozzle **9** proboscis

Snow, C P (Charles Percy Snow, Lord Snow)
  author of: 9 The New Men **10** Last Things, The Masters **14** A Coat of Varnish **16** Corridors of Power **20** Strangers and Brothers

snowfall 4 firn, neve **6** flurry **8** blizzard
  Scottish: 6 onding

Snow Leopard, The
  author: 16 Peter Matthiessen

Snow Queen, The
  author: 21 Hans Christian Andersen

Snows of Kilimanjaro, The
  author: 15 Ernest Hemingway

snow-white 4 pure **6** snowy **9** lilywhite, pure white **11** white as snow

Snow White and the Seven Dwarfs
  character: 3 Doc **5** Dopey, Happy, Queen **6** Grumpy, Sleepy, Sneezy, mirror **7** Bashful **14** Prince Charming

snowy 4 pure **5** white **7** nievous **8** pristine, spotless **9** blizzardy

snub 3 cut **5** blunt, check, scorn, short

dain **9** retrousse **11** repudiation **12** cold shoulder **16** turn up one's nose at **19** give the cold shoulder

snuff 5 scent, smell, sniff, whiff **7** sniffle, snuffle

snuff out 5 crush **8** suppress **10** extinguish, put an end to

snug 4 cozy, neat, safe **5** close, tight **6** secure **7** compact **8** tranquil **9** sheltered, skin-tight **11** comfortable **12** close-fitting, tight-fitting **13** well-organized

snuggle 3 hug **4** nest **6** cuddle, curl up, enfold, nestle, nuzzle

so
Latin: 3 sic

soak 3 wet **4** seep **5** bathe, enter, steep **6** absorb, drench, sink in, take in, take up **7** immerse, pervade **8** permeate, saturate **9** penetrate

soaked 5 soggy **6** sodden, soused **7** sopping **8** drenched **9** saturated **11** waterlogged, wringing wet

soak up 4 blot **6** absorb, take up **8** sponge up

soak up warmth 4 bask **11** warm oneself **12** toast oneself

Soames Forsyte
character in: 14 The Forsyte Saga
author: 10 Galsworthy

Soap
character: 5 Major **6** Benson **9** Billy Tate **10** Eunice Tate **11** Chester Tate, Corrine Tate, Danny Dallas, Jessica Tate, Jodie Dallas **12** Burt Campbell **18** Mary Dallas Campbell
cast: 7 Ted Wass **9** Jimmy Baio **11** Diana Canova **12** Billy Crystal, Cathryn Damon, Jennifer Salt, Robert Mandan **14** Arthur Peterson **15** Richard Mulligan, Robert Guillaume **16** Katherine Helmond

soar 3 fly **4** rise, wing **5** climb, float, glide, mount, tower **8** take wing

soave
music: 6 gentle

sob 3 cry **4** howl, wail, weep **6** lament, plaint, snivel **7** blubber, whimper

so be it 4 amen **7** let it be **9** let it be so

sober 3 dry, sad **4** cool, drab, dull, grim, sane **5** grave, sound, staid **6** dreary, sedate, solemn, somber, steady **7** joyless, prudent, serious, subdued **8** moderate, not drunk, rational **9** judicious, realistic, sorrowful, temperate **10** abstemious **11** levelheaded **13** dispassionate

So Big
author: 10 Edna Ferber

sobriety 10 abstention, abstinence, continence, temperance **13** nonindulgence **14** abstemiousness

sobriquet 7 epithet, pet name **8** nickname **11** appellation

so-called
French: 9 soi-disant

soccer
athlete: 4 Pele **11** Johan Cruyff
players/team: 6 eleven
position: 6 goalie **7** forward **8** fullback, halfback **10** goalkeeper
championship: 8 World Cup **11** European Cup, National Cup **13** Cup Winner's Cup
violation: 5 hands **7** hacking, offside **11** obstructing
gaining control of ball: 4 trap

sociable 6 social **7** affable, cordial **8** friendly, gracious, outgoing **9** agreeable, congenial, convivial **10** gregarious, neighborly **11** extroverted **13** companionable

social 2 in **5** smart **7** stylish **8** friendly, pleasant, sociable **9** agreeable **10** gregarious, neighborly **11** cooperative, fashionable **14** interdependent

Social Contract, The
author: 19 Jean-Jacques Rousseau

social order
goddess of: 4 Hour **5** Horae

society 4 body, club **5** elite, group **6** circle, gentry, league **7** mankind **8** alliance, humanity, nobility **9** community, humankind **10** blue bloods **11** aristocracy, association, high society, social order **12** organization **14** the four hundred **16** the general public

sociologist
American: 4 Mead, Park, Ward **5** Coser, Gerth, Mills, Small, Wirth **6** Bendix, Cooley, Merton, Speier, Sumner, Thomas **7** Parsons, Sorokin **8** Eberhard **10** Lazarsfeld
British: 4 Webb **8** Hobhouse, Mannheim **12** Carr-Saunders
Danish: 6 Geiger
French: 4 Aron **5** Comte **8** Durkheim, Gurvitch **9** Friedmann
German: 5 Konig, Weber, Wiese **6** Simmel **8** Habermas, Luckmann **10** Dahrendorf, Horkheimer
Hungarian: 6 Lukacs **8** Mannheim
Israeli: 5 Buber **10** Eisenstadt
Norwegian: 6 Aubert **7** Galtung
Swedish: 8 Carlsson

sociopathic 9 alienated **10** antisocial, rebellious

sock 3 box, hit, sox **4** belt, blow, slap **5** punch, smack, smash **6** strike, wallop **7** clobber **8** knee sock **9** ankle sock **13** short stocking

Socrates
born: 6 Athens
taught using: 5 irony **6** method
disciple: 5 Plato **8** Xenophon
wife: 9 Xanthippe
death potion: 7 hemlock

sod 4 soil, turf **5** divot, earth, grass, sward **10** greensward

soda 3 pop **4** base, cola **5** tonic **6** bicarb, sodium **7** barilla, seltzer **8** beverage, root beer **9** ginger ale, soft drink **11** bicarbonate **12** sarsaparilla
ash: 6 alkali
in faro: 9 first card
maker: 4 jerk

sodden 4 dull **5** heavy, lumpy, mushy, pasty, soggy, soppy **6** doughy, soaked **7** sopping **8** besotted, drenched, dripping, listless **9** saturated **10** wet through **14** expressionless

Soddy, Frederick
field: 9 chemistry
nationality: 7 British
discovered: 8 isotopes
worked with: 13 William Ramsay **16** Ernest Rutherford
awarded: 10 Nobel Prize

sodium
chemical symbol: 2 Na

Sodom
destroyed with: 5 Admah **6** Zeboim **8** Gomorrah

sofa 5 couch, divan **6** canape, lounge, settee **8** love seat **9** davenport **12** chesterfield

Sofia
Roman name: 12 Ulpia Serdica
Byzantine name: 9 Traditsa
capital of: 8 Bulgaria
landmark: 13 Buyuk Dzhamiya **16** Saint Sofia Church **17** Saint George Church **24** Alexander Nevsky Cathedral **32** Cyril and Methodius National Library

soft 4 easy, kind, mild, pale, weak **5** downy, faint, furry, muted, quiet, silky, sleek **6** feeble, gentle, hushed, pliant, satiny, shaded, silken, smooth, supple, tender **7** lenient, not hard, pitying, pliable, restful, subdued, velvety **8** delicate, not sharp, shadowed, tolerant, tranquil, twilight **9** malleable, not strong **10** harmonious **11** sentimental, sympathetic **12** easily molded, low intensity **13** compassionate, pleasantly low **16** easily penetrated **19** having a breathy sound **21** requiring little effort **25** incapable of great endurance

soften 5 lower **6** lessen, subdue, temper **7** cushion, mollify **8** make soft, mitigate, moderate, palliate, tone down, turn down **10** ameliorate, make softer

softhearted 4 kind, soft, warm **6** benign, gentle, humane, kindly, tender **8** generous **9** forgiving, indulgent **10** benevolent **11** considerate, kindhearted, sympathetic, warmhearted **13** compassionate, tenderhearted

softly 6 easily, gently, mildly, weakly **7** quietly

softness 8 mildness **9** downiness, silkiness **10** fluffiness, gentleness, smoothness, tenderness **11** tranquility **12** tranquillity

soft soap 7 blarney **8** cajolery, flattery **10** persuasion

sogginess 7 wetness **8** dampness **9** mushiness **10** soddenness

soggy 5 heavy, mushy, pasty, soppy **6** doughy, soaked, sodden **7** sopping **8** drenched, dripping **9** saturated

Sogliardo
  character in: 22 Every Man out of His Humour
  author: 6 Jonson

Soglow, Otto
  creator/artist of: 13 The Little King

soi-disant 8 so-called **9** pretended **10** self-styled **18** calling oneself thus

soigne, soignee 4 chic, neat, tidy **5** sleek, smart **6** classy, modish **7** elegant **11** well-groomed

soil 4 dirt, foul, land, loam, ruin, soot, spot **5** dirty, earth, grime, humus, muddy, smear, stain, sully **6** debase, defile, ground, region, smudge **7** blacken, country, tarnish **8** disgrace

soiled 5 dirty, grimy, messy **6** filthy, grubby, smudgy **7** muddied, sullied, unclean **8** begrimed, unwashed **9** besmeared

soiree 4 ball, prom **5** dance, party **9** cotillion, promenade

sojourn 4 stay **5** abide, pause, visit **6** stay at **7** holiday, layover **8** stay over, stopover, vacation

sojourner 6 lodger, tenant **7** pilgrim, tourist, visitor **8** traveler **9** transient, weekender **10** daytripper, vacationer

Sol
  origin: 5 Roman
  form: 3 god
  personifies: 3 sun
  corresponds to: 6 Helios **7** Mithras **8** Hyperion

sola, solus 5 alone **9** by oneself

solace 4 calm **5** cheer **6** soothe **7** assuage, comfort, console **8** reassure **10** help in need **11** consolation, reassurance **18** relief in affliction

solder 4 fuse, join, weld **5** braze, stick

soldier 2 GI **3** PFC **5** GI Joe, major **6** worker, zealot **7** captain, colonel, dogface, general, private, servant, trooper, veteran, warrior **8** corporal, follower, partisan, sergeant **10** lieutenant, serviceman, specialist **11** enlisted man, military man **14** militant leader **16** brigadier general

Soldier of Orange
  director: 13 Paul Verhoeven
  based on novel by: 13 Erik Hazelhoff
  cast: 10 Peter Faber **11** Derek De Lint, Eddy Habbema, Rutger Hauer **12** Jeroen Krabbe **15** Susan Penhaligon
  setting: 14 The Netherlands

Soldier's Embrace, A
  author: 14 Nadine Gordimer

soldiery 4 army **6** legion, troops **7** legions, militia **8** military, soldiers **11** fighting men

sole 4 lone, only **6** single **8** solitary **9** exclusive

solely 5 alone **6** merely, purely, singly **8** uniquely **11** exclusively **14** singlehandedly

solemn 4 dark, drab, grim, holy **5** grave, sober, staid **6** formal, gloomy, sacred, sedate, somber **7** earnest, serious, sincere **8** absolute **9** dignified, religious, spiritual, steadfast **10** ceremonial, depressing, determined **11** ceremonious **12** awe-inspiring

solemnity 3 awe **7** dignity **8** ceremony **9** formality, reverence **11** seriousness **12** circumstance

solemnize 4 mark **5** honor **6** hallow **7** observe **9** celebrate **10** consecrate **11** commemorate

solicit 3 ask **4** seek **5** plead **7** entreat, request **9** appeal for, importune

solicitation 6 appeal **7** request **8** entreaty **11** importuning

solicitor 6 beggar, lawyer **7** counsel **8** salesman **10** supplicant

solicitous 4 avid, keen **5** eager **6** ardent, intent **7** anxious, intense, longing, mindful, zealous **8** desirous **9** attentive, concerned, regardful **10** thoughtful **12** enthusiastic

solicitude 4 care, zeal **5** worry **7** anxiety, avidity, concern **9** attention **10** enthusiasm, inquietude, uneasiness **11** disquietude, fearfulness, overconcern **12** apprehension

solid 4 firm, hard, pure, real **5** dense, massy, sober, sound, tough **6** rugged, stable, steady, strong, sturdy **7** durable, genuine, lasting, unmixed **8** complete, concrete, constant, rational, reliable, sensible, tangible, thorough, unbroken **9** not hollow, unalloyed, unanimous, undivided, well-built **10** continuous, dependable, solidified **11** impermeable, levelheaded, substantial, trustworthy **13** impenetrable, uninterrupted **15** well-constructed

solidarity 5 union, unity **7** harmony **9** closeness **11** cooperation, unification

solidify 3 fix, gel, set **4** cake, jell **6** cement, harden **7** congeal, stiffen, thicken **9** coagulate **11** crystallize **12** agglomerate

soliloquy 9 monologue **10** solo speech

Solinus
  character in: 17 The Comedy of Errors
  author: 11 Shakespeare

solitariness 8 solitude **9** aloneness, seclusion **13** reclusiveness

solitary 4 lone **6** hidden, lonely, remote, single **8** desolate, isolated, lonesome, secluded **9** concealed **10** cloistered **11** out-of-the-way, uninhabited **13** companionless

solitude 9 aloneness, isolation, seclu-

sion, wasteland **10** desolation, loneliness, remoteness, wilderness

solo 5 alone **8** solitary **9** by oneself **10** unattended **12** singlehanded **13** unaccompanied
  operatic: 4 aria

solo dance
  ballet: 7 pas seul

Solomon
  father: 5 David
  mother: 9 Bathsheba
  wife: 6 Naamah
  son: 8 Rehoboam
  brother: 5 Amnon **7** Absalom, Chileab **8** Adonijah
  sister: 5 Tamar
  visitor: 5 Sheba
  wrote: 8 Proverbs **12** Ecclesiastes **13** Song of Solomon
  built: 6 temple

Solomon Islands
  capital/largest city: 7 Honiara
  others: 4 Auki, Bina, Gizo, Luti **5** Kieta, Munda **6** Tulagi **7** Yandina **8** Kira Kira **9** Tangarare **10** Sasamungga
  head of state: 14 British monarch **15** governor-general
  member of: 14 Spearhead Group
  monetary unit: 4 cent **6** dollar
  island: 4 Buka, Gizo, Savo **5** Ndeni, Ulawa **6** Tulagi **7** Malaita, Rennell, Solomon, Vangunu **8** Choiseul, Sikaiana, Vanikoro **9** Santa Cruz **10** New Georgia, Ontong Java **11** Guadalcanal, Santa Isabel **12** Bougainville, San Cristobal
  mountain: 5 Balbi
  highest point: 11 Popomanasiu
  ocean: 7 Pacific
  physical feature:
    gulf: 4 Huon, Kula
    sound: 10 New Georgia
    strait: 13 Indispensable
  people: 7 Chinese **8** European **10** Melanesian, Polynesian
    explorer: 14 Mendana de Neyra
    leader: 8 Mamaloni **9** Kenilorea
  language: 7 English **13** Pidgin English **16** Melanesian pidgin
  religion: 8 Anglican **13** Roman Catholic

so long
  Spanish: 12 hasta la vista

solution 3 key **5** blend **6** answer, cipher **7** mixture, solving **8** emulsion **9** resolving **10** resolution, suspension, unraveling **11** explanation

solve 7 resolve, unravel, work out **8** decipher, unriddle, untangle **9** figure out **10** find the key **13** find the answer

solvent 7 diluent, soluble **9** dilutable **10** dissoluble, dissolvent **11** dissolvable **16** financially sound

Solymi

origin: 9 Asia Minor
occupation: 8 warriors

Solzhenitsyn, Aleksandr
author of: 13 The Cancer Ward **14** The First Circle **19** The Gulag Archipelago **22** August Nineteen-Fourteen **31** One Day in the Life of Ivan Denisovich

Somalia
other name: 4 Punt **10** Somaliland **12** Horn of Africa
capital/largest city: 9 Mogadishu **10** Mogadiscio
others: 5 Burao, Merca **6** Mereka **7** Berbera, Galkayu, Kismayu **8** Belet Uen, Hargeisa **9** Chisimaio
division: 6 Hawiya **9** Mijirtein **10** Midjertein
  colonial: 17 British Somaliland, Italian Somaliland
measure: 3 top **4** caba **5** chela, darat, tabla **6** cubito **8** parsalah
monetary unit: 4 besa **6** somalo **8** shilling **9** centesimi
weight: 8 parsalah
mountain: 5 Guban **11** Migiurtinia, Ogo Highland
highest point: 7 Surud Ad
river: 4 Juba **5** Daror, Nogal **9** Nugaaleed **11** Webi Shebeli **13** Webi Shabeelle
sea: 6 Indian
physical feature:
  bay: 5 Negro
  cape: 9 Guardafui
  desert: 4 Aror
  gulf: 4 Aden
  plateau: 3 Ogo **4** Haud
people: 3 Sab **4** Asha **5** Galla **6** Hawiya, Isbaak, Somali **7** Danakil, Hamitic, Marehan, Samaale, Shuhali **8** Rahanwin
  leader: 9 Siad Barre **12** Ali Shermarke
language: 6 Arabic, Somali **7** English, Italian
religion: 5 Islam
feature:
  boat: 4 dhow
  cloth: 7 banadir
  clothing: 4 futa, toga **6** sarong
  tree: 6 acacia, baobab **7** incense

Somaliland *see* **7** Somalia

somber 4 dark, drab, gray, grim **5** grave, sober **6** dreary, gloomy, solemn **7** serious **8** funereal, mournful, toneless **9** cheerless **10** depressing, melancholy

Some Like It Hot
  director: 11 Billy Wilder
  cast: 9 Joe E Brown, Pat O'Brien **10** George Raft, Jack Lemmon, Tony Curtis **13** Marilyn Monroe

Somers Islands *see* **7** Bermuda

something essential
  Latin: 10 sine qua non

something for something
  Latin: 10 quid pro quo

Something Happened
  author: 12 Joseph Heller

sometime 4 late, once **5** later **6** former **7** quondam **8** formerly, previous **9** erstwhile **10** occasional

sometimes 7 at times **10** now and then, on occasion **12** occasionally, once in a while

somewhat 6 fairly, kind of, partly, sort of **8** passably **9** tolerably **10** moderately, more or less, reasonably **13** approximately

somnolent 4 dozy, dull **5** dopey **6** drowsy, groggy, sleepy, torpid **7** languid, nodding, out of it, yawning **8** hypnotic, sluggish **9** half-awake, lethargic, sopoforic **10** half-asleep, slumberous **11** heavy-lidded **13** semiconscious

Somnus
  origin: 5 Roman
  god of: 5 sleep
  mother: 3 Nyx
  brother: 4 Mors
  corresponds to: 6 Hypnos, Hypnus

son
  French: 4 fils

sone
  unit of: 8 loudness

song 4 call, poem, tune **5** ditty, lyric, verse **6** ballad, melody, number, piping
  French: 7 chanson

songbird 4 chat, lark, wren **5** robin, veery, vireo **6** canary, singer, thrush **7** warbler **11** nightingale

Song of Bernadette, The
  author: 11 Franz Werfel
  character: 13 Dean Peyramale **18** Sister Marie Therese **19** Bernadette Soubirous
  director: 9 Henry King
  cast: 8 Lee J Cobb **12** Vincent Price, William Eythe **13** Jennifer Jones **15** Charles Bickford
  Oscar for: 7 actress (Jones)

Song of Hiawatha *see* **8** Hiawatha

Song of Roland, The *see* **15** Chanson de Roland

Song of Solomon
  author: 12 Toni Morrison

Song of Solomon
  bride: 9 Shulamite

Song of Songs, The
  author: 16 Hermann Sudermann

Song of the Lark, The
  author: 11 Willa Cather

Songs of Experience
  author: 12 William Blake

Songs of Innocence
  author: 12 William Blake

Sonnets from the Portuguese
  author: 24 Elizabeth Barrett Browning

Sonnets to Orpheus
  author: 16 Rainer Maria Rilke

Sonny
  nickname of: 13 Charles Liston

Son of the Morning
  author: 15 Joyce Carol Oates

sonorous 4 deep, rich **6** florid **7** ringing, vibrant **8** eloquent, resonant **9** full-toned, grandiose **10** flamboyant, impressive, resounding **13** reverberating

Sons and Lovers
  author: 10 D H Lawrence
  character: 10 Clara Dawes **11** Baxter Dawes **13** Miriam Leivers
    Morel family: 4 Paul **5** Annie **6** Arthur, Walter **7** William **8** Gertrude

Sons of thunder 4 John **5** James
  also: 9 Boanerges

Soo
  canals at: 13 Sault Ste. Marie

soon 4 anon **6** pronto **7** betimes, by and by, early on, ere long, quickly, shortly **8** directly **9** any minute, forthwith, instantly, presently, right away **10** before long **12** without delay **14** in a little while

sooner 6 before, in time **7** earlier **9** before now, in advance **10** beforehand **11** ahead of time

sooner or later 6 one day **7** finally, someday **8** in the end, sometime **10** eventually, ultimately **17** in the course of time, sometime or another

Sooner State
  nickname of: 8 Oklahoma

soot 4 dirt, smut **5** crock, grime **6** carbon, smudge, smutch **7** residue **9** lampblack

soothe 4 calm, ease **6** lessen, pacify **7** appease, comfort, console, mollify, placate, relieve **8** mitigate, moderate **9** alleviate **11** tranquilize

soothing 4 mild **7** calming, healing, salving **9** appeasing, consoling, emollient, pacifying, placating **10** comforting, mitigating **13** tranquilizing

soothsayer 4 seer **5** sibyl **7** diviner, prophet **10** forecaster **13** fortune-teller

soothsaying 6 augury **8** divining, prophecy **10** divination, predicting, prediction **11** foretelling, prophesying

sooty 4 inky **5** black, dingy, dirty, grimy **6** smudgy, smutty **9** coal-black

sop 3 dip, tip, wet **4** dunk, soak **5** bribe **6** absorb, drench, payoff, payola, take up **8** gratuity, saturate **9** baksheesh, become wet, hush money

Sophie's Choice
  author: 13 William Styron

Sophisms
  author: 9 Aristotle

sophisticate 8 civilize **11** cosmopolite, disillusion, make worldly **12** cosmopolitan

sophisticated 6 subtle **7** complex,

studied, worldly **8** advanced, cultured, highbrow, mannered, precious, seasoned **9** difficult **10** artificial, cultivated **11** complicated, experienced, worldly-wise **12** cosmopolitan, intellectual

sophistry 6 deceit **7** fallacy **8** subtlety **9** casuistry, chicanery, deception **10** distortion **12** speciousness

Sophocles
　　author of: 4 Ajax **7** Electra, Oedipus **8** Antigone **10** Oedipus Rex, Trachiniae **11** Philoctetes **16** Oedipus at Colonus **18** The Trachinian Women

sophomoric 6 callow **7** foolish, puerile **8** childish, immature, juvenile **9** infantile **10** adolescent **12** schoolboyish

soporific 4 lazy **5** balmy, heavy **6** drowsy, sleepy **8** hypnotic, sedative, sluggish **9** lethargic, somnolent **10** slumberous **11** somniferous **12** sleep-inducer **13** sleep-inducing

soppiness 4 corn, mush **5** slush **6** bathos **7** wetness **9** mushiness **10** slushiness **11** mawkishness **14** sentimentalism, sentimentality

sopping 3 wet **5** soggy, soppy **6** soaked, sodden **8** drenched, dripping **9** saturated **10** bedraggled, soaking wet

sorcerer 5 witch **6** shaman, wizard **7** warlock **8** magician **11** medicine man

sorceress 5 siren, witch **11** enchantress

sorcery 8 witchery, wizardry **9** shamanism **10** black magic, necromancy, witchcraft **11** enchantment

Sordello
　　author: 14 Robert Browning

sordid 3 low **4** base, rank, vile **5** dirty, gross **6** filthy, putrid, rotten, vulgar, wicked **7** corrupt, ignoble, squalid, unclean **8** degraded, depraved **9** debauched **12** disreputable

Sordido
　　character in: 22 Every Man out of His Humour
　　author: 6 Jonson

sordino, con
　　music: 11 with the mute

sore 4 hurt **5** acute, angry, great, harsh, irked, sharp, upset, wound **6** aching, pained, severe, tender **7** bruised, extreme, grieved, hurting, painful **8** agonized, critical, grievous, smarting, sorespot, wounding **9** agonizing, desperate, indignant, irritated, sensitive **10** distressed, unbearable **11** distressing **12** inflammation

So Red the Rose
　　author: 10 Stark Young

Sorel, Julien
　　character in: 17 The Red and the Black
　　author: 8 Stendhal

sorely 5 badly **7** greatly **8** severely **9** extremely **10** critically **11** desperately

soreness 4 ache, pain **10** discomfort, irritation, tenderness

sorrel 3 bay **4** herb, roan, weed **5** brown, plant, Rumex **8** chestnut **12** reddish-brown
　　varieties: 3 red **4** dock, tree, wood **5** lady's, sheep **6** common, French, garden, Indian **7** redwood **8** Jamaican, mountain **10** violet wood **12** European wood

Sorrel, Hetty
　　character in: 8 Adam Bede
　　author: 5 Eliot

sorrow 3 woe **4** loss, weep **5** be sad, mourn, trial **6** grieve, lament **7** despair, sadness, travail, trouble **8** disaster, hardship **10** affliction, bad fortune, misfortune **11** catastrophe, unhappiness
　　French: 9 tristesse

sorrowful 3 sad **6** woeful **7** unhappy **8** affected, grieving, mournful **9** lamenting

Sorrows of Young Werther, The
　　author: 6 Goethe
　　character: 6 Albert **9** Charlotte (Lotte)

sorry 3 sad **6** woeful **7** grieved, pitiful, unhappy **8** contrite, pathetic, pitiable, wretched **9** miserable, regretful, repentant, sorrowful **10** deplorable, melancholy, remorseful, ridiculous **11** crestfallen **13** brokenhearted

sort 4 kind, list, make, sift, type **5** brand, class, grade, group, index, order **6** divide, person **7** arrange, catalog, species, variety **8** classify, organize, separate, take from **9** segregate **10** categorize, individual **11** systematize **14** classification

sortie 4 rush **5** onset **6** attack, charge **7** assault **8** storming **9** onslaught

sortilege 6 augury **7** auspice, sorcery **10** divination, witchcraft

sorting 8 dividing, grouping **9** arranging **10** organizing **11** classifying **12** categorizing

so-so 4 blah, fair **5** ho-hum **6** casual, modest **7** average, humdrum **8** adequate, bearable, mediocre, middling, ordinary, passable **9** tolerable **10** second-rate **11** commonplace, indifferent **12** run-of-the-mill **13** unexceptional **15** undistinguished

sot 4 lush, soak **5** drunk, rummy, souse, toper **8** drunkard, rumhound **9** alcoholic, inebriate **11** dipsomaniac

Soter
　　epithet of: 4 Zeus
　　means: 6 savior

Sothern, Ann
　　real name: 13 Harriette Lake
　　born: 12 Valley City ND
　　husband: 10 Roger Pryor **14** Robert Sterling

roles: 6 Maisie **8** Cry Havoc **10** Lady Be Good **16** Private Secretary **19** A Letter to Three Wives

so throughout
　　Latin: 9 sic passim

sotto voce
　　music: 11 in a low voice **13** in an undertone, under the voice

sought 6 hunted **7** pursued, quested **9** attempted, looked for **10** endeavored

soul 5 being, force **6** person, spirit **7** essence **8** creature, vitality **9** inner core **10** embodiment, individual, vital force **11** inspiration **12** quintessence

soul-searching 10 discontent, insecurity, uneasiness **15** dissatisfaction, self-questioning

soul-stirring 7 rousing **8** electric, exciting, stirring **9** inspiring, thrilling **11** galvanizing

sound 3 fit **4** deep, firm, good, seem, tone, wise **5** drift, hardy, noise, range, sober, solid, tenor, utter, voice **6** intact, robust, severe, signal, stable, strong, sturdy **7** durable, earshot, healthy, lasting, perfect, solvent **8** announce, rational, reliable, sensible, thorough, unmarred **9** come off as, competent, enunciate, pronounce, undamaged, well-built **10** articulate, dependable, make a noise, reasonable, suggestion, untroubled **11** implication, penetrating, responsible, substantial **13** thoroughgoing **15** hearing distance, well-constructed

Sound and the Fury, The
　　author: 15 William Faulkner
　　character: 6 Dilsey **17** Sydney Herbert Head
　　　　Compson family: 5 Jason **7** Candace (Caddy), Quentin **8** Benjamin (Benjy)

Sounder
　　director: 10 Martin Ritt
　　cast: 8 Taj Mahal **10** Kevin Hooks **11** Cicely Tyson **12** Paul Winfield **13** Carmen Mathews
　　sequel: 13 Sounder Part II

sound measure 7 decibel

sound mind in a sound body
　　Latin: 21 mens sana in cor pore sano

soundness of mind 6 reason, sanity **9** normality **12** mental health

Sound of Music, The
　　director: 10 Robert Wise
　　cast: 9 Peggy Wood **12** Julie Andrews (Maria Von Trapp) **13** Eleanor Parker **18** Christopher Plummer
　　setting: 7 Austria
　　score: 21 Rodgers and Hammerstein
　　Oscar for: 7 picture **8** director
　　song: 5 Maria **8** Do-Re-Mi **9** Edelweiss **16** My Favorite Things

sound out 3 ask **8** approach **15** make a proposal to, make overtures to, put out feelers to

soup

clear: 5 broth 8 bouillon, consomme

server: 6 tureen

spoon: 5 ladle

thick: 5 cream, gumbo 6 bisque, potage 7 chowder 10 minestrone

soupcon 3 bit, dab, jot, tad 4 clue, dash, drop, hint 5 pinch, shade, taint, taste, tinge, touch, trace, whiff 6 little, trifle 7 smidgen, smidgin, vestige 8 smidgeon 9 little bit, suspicion 10 smattering, sprinkling, suggestion 12 slight amount

Soupy Sales

character: 9 White Fang 10 Black Tooth 13 Herman the Flea, Hippy the Hippo, Pookie the Lion, Willie the Worm 14 Marilyn Monwolf

sour 3 bad 4 acid, dour, keen, tart, turn 5 nasty, sharp, spoil, surly, tangy, testy 6 crabby, cranky, curdle, rancid, sullen, turned 7 acerbic, bilious, crabbed, curdled, ferment, grouchy, peevish, spoiled, turn off, uncivil, waspish 8 alienate, choleric, embitter, jaundice, petulant, unsavory, vinegary 9 acidulous, clabbered, fermented, irritable, jaundiced, offensive, prejudice, repugnant 10 astringent, ill-dispose, ill-humored, unpleasant 11 bad-tempered, distasteful, ill-tempered 12 disagreeable

sourball 4 crab 5 crank, grump 6 grouch 9 hard candy 10 curmudgeon

source 4 font, head, root 5 basis, cause, fount 6 author, father, origin, rising, spring 8 begetter, fountain 9 authority, beginning, headwater 10 antecedent, derivation, foundation, prime mover, wellspring

source and origin

Latin: 11 fons et origo

Sourdough State

nickname of: 6 Alaska

sourness 7 acidity, vinegar 8 acerbity, acrimony, ill humor, pungency, tartness 9 acridness, greenness 10 bitterness

sourpuss 4 bear, crab 5 crank, grump 6 griper, grouch 7 grouser, killjoy 8 grumbler, sorehead 10 bellyacher, complainer, crosspatch, curmudgeon, spoilsport

Sousa, John Philip

born: 12 Washington DC

composer of: 9 El Capitan 14 Washington Post 25 The Stars and Stripes Forever

souse 3 dip, sot 4 duck, dunk, lush, soak 5 douse, drunk, rummy, steep, toper 6 barfly, boozer, drench, pickle 7 immerse, tippler 8 drunkard, inundate, marinate, saturate, submerge 9 alcoholic, inebriate 11 dipsomaniac

soused 5 drunk 6 dunked, potted, zapped, zonked 7 pickled, sloshed, smashed 8 immersed 9 plastered 10 inebriated 11 intoxicated 17 under the influence 20 three sheets to the wind

South Africa

capital: 8 Cape Town, Pretoria 12 Bloemfontein

largest city: 12 Johannesburg

others: 3 Aus 4 Mara, Stad 6 Benoni, Bononi, Braker, Durban, Garies, Severn, Soweto, Umtata, Untata 7 Brakpan, Kokstad 8 Kaapstad, Mafeking, Modjadji 9 Germiston, Kimberley 10 East London, Oudtshoorn 11 Krugersdorp, Vereeniging 13 Port Elizabeth 16 Pietermaritzburg

school: 5 Natal 8 Capetown 13 Witwatersrand 15 Orange Free State

division: 5 Natal 8 Backveld 9 Transvaal 10 Basutoland 12 Cape Province 14 Cape of Good Hope 15 Orange Free State

independent homelands: 5 Venda 6 Ciskei 8 Transkei 10 bantustans 14 Bophuthatswana

goverment:

legislature: 4 Raad

measure: 4 vara

monetary unit: 4 cent, pond, rand 5 pound 6 florin 7 daalder 9 krugerrand

mountain: 3 Aux, Kop 5 Table 7 Kathkin 9 Stormberg 10 Devil's Peak, Sneeuwberg 11 Drakensberg 12 Giant's Castle 13 Witwatersrand 14 Mont-aux-Sources 15 Great Escarpment

highest point: 8 Injasuti

river: 3 Hex 4 Vaal 5 Nosob 6 Modder, Molopo, Orange, Tugela 7 Caledon, Kurumam, Limpopo 8 Olifants 9 Crocodile, Great Fish

ocean: 6 Indian 8 Atlantic

physical feature:

bay: 5 Algoa, False, Table 6 Mossel, Walvis 7 Walfish 8 Richard's, Saldanha 11 Saint Helena

cape: 7 Agulhas 8 Good Hope

current: 8 Benguela

desert: 5 Namib 8 Kalahari

plateau: 6 Karroo

region: 8 Highveld, Zululand 9 Kaffraria 11 Great Karroo 12 Little Karroo

people: 3 San 4 Boer, Yosa, Zulu 5 Asian, Bantu, Namas, Nguni, Pondo, Sotho, Swazi, Tembu, Venda, Xhosa 6 Damara, Kaffir 7 African, British, Bushmen, English, Swahili 8 Bechuana, Khoikhoi 9 Afrikaner, Hottentot

author: 5 Paton 7 Luthuli 8 Gordimer

civil rights advocate: 6 Gandhi

explorer: 8 Riebeeck

leader: 4 Biko, Tutu 5 Botha, Malan, Smuts, Tomba 6 Kruger, Rhodes 7 de Klerk, Hertzog, Mandela, Vorster 8 Verwoerd 9 Buthelezi, Pretorius

language: 4 Taal, Zulu 5 Bantu, Hindi, Nguni, Sotho, Swazi, Tamil, Venda, Xhosa 6 Telegu, Thonga 7 English, Khoisan, Ndebele, Sesotho 8 Bujarati, Fanakalo 9 Afrikaans

religion: 5 Hindu, Islam 7 animism, Judaism 8 Anglican 9 Methodist 12 Episcopalian, Presbyterian 13 Dutch Reformed, Roman Catholic

place:

Cecil Rhodes' estate: 11 Groote Shuur

game reserve: 5 Mkuze 6 Kruger 8 Hluhluwe

monument: 11 Voortrekker

feature:

bird: 4 taha

bride price: 6 lobolo

flower: 5 coral 6 clivia, protea 7 cowslip, fuchsia 9 phygelius 10 lachenalia

oganization: 3 ANC 7 Inkatha 23 African National Congress

segregation: 9 apartheid

tree: 7 assagai 9 jacaranda

food:

corn: 6 mealie

drink: 9 sundowner

meat: 7 biltong 8 sosaties 9 boerewors

South America

bird: 5 macaw 7 seriema, tinamou 8 caracara

cape: 4 Horn

country: 4 Peru 5 Chile 6 Brazil, Guyana 7 Bolivia, Ecuador, Surinam, Uruguay 8 Colombia, Paraguay 9 Argentina, Venezuela 12 French Guiana

desert: 7 Atacama

explorer: 16 Francisco Pizarro 18 Pedro Alvares Cabral

hero: 12 Simon Bolivar 15 Jose de San Martin 16 Bernardo O'Higgins 18 Antonio Jose de Sucre

highest mountain: 9 Aconcagua

islands: 8 Falkland 9 Galapagos

lake: 8 Titicaca 9 Maracaibo

mountain range: 5 Andes

native: 2 Ge 3 Ona 4 Inca 5 Carib, Mayan 7 Quechua 10 Araucanian

plain: 5 llano, pampa

region: 9 Patagonia

river: 3 Apa 5 Plata 6 Amazon 7 Orinoco

South Carolina

abbreviation: 2 SC

nickname: 7 Calinky 8 Palmetto

capital/largest city: 8 Columbia

others: 5 Aiken, Greer, Union 6 Belton, Camden, Cheraw, Conway, Dillon, Seneca, Sumter 7 Bamberg, Laurens, Manning 8 Beaufort, Florence, Newberry, Rock Hill, Walhalla 9 Greenwood 10 Charleston, Greenville, Orangeburg 11 Spartanburg

college: 5 Allen, Coker 6 Furman, Lander 7 Claffin, Clemson, Erskine, Wofford 8 Benedict, Bob Jones, Columbia, Winthrop **13** Francis Marion **15** Citadel Military

explorer: 6 Ayllon, Ribaut

feature:
  beach: 6 Myrtle
  dam: 6 Saluda
  fort: 6 Sumter
  gardens: 7 Cypress
  tribe: 5 Pedee, Sewee **6** Cusabo, Santee, Waxhaw, Yamasi **7** Catawba, Shawnee, Sugeree, Wateree **8** Congaree
  people: 11 James Byrnes **12** Althea Gibson, John C Calhoun **13** Bernard Baruch, Francis Marion **14** Dizzy Gillespie
  island: 3 Sea **6** Parris **10** Hilton Head
  lake: 6 Marion, Murray **7** Catawba, Wateree **8** Hartwell, Moultrie **9** Clark Hill
  land rank: 8 fortieth
  mountain: 5 Kings **6** Little **9** Blue Ridge, Sassafras
  physical feature:
    bay: 8 Carolina
    plateau: 8 Piedmont
  president: 13 Andrew Jackson
  river: 5 Broad **6** Edisto, Pee Dee, Saluda, Santee **7** Ashepoo **8** Savannah
  state admission: 6 eighth
  state bird: 12 Carolina wren
  state flower: 13 yellow jasmine **17** Carolina jessamine
  state motto: 18 While I Breathe I Hope **26** Prepared in Mind and Resources
  state song: 8 Carolina
  state tree: 8 palmetto

South Dakota
  abbreviation: 2 SD **4** S Dak
  nickname: 6 Coyote **8** Blizzard, Sunshine
  capital: 6 Pierre
  largest city: 10 Sioux Falls
  others: 4 Lead, Leap **5** Huron **6** Custer, Eureka, Lemmon, Miller, Winner **7** Sturgis, Webster, Yankton **8** Aberdeen, Deadwood, Sisseton **9** Brookings, Rapid City **10** Vermillion
  college: 5 Huron **7** Yankton **9** Augustana **10** Mount Marty, Sioux Falls **14** Dakota Wesleyan
  explorer: 8 Varennes **13** Lewis and Clark
  feature: 8 Deadwood
    battlefield: 11 Wounded Knee
    dam: 4 Oahe
    mine: 9 Homestake
    monument: 13 Mount Rushmore
    national park: 8 Badlands, Wind Cave
    tribe: 5 Brule, Sioux **6** Dakota, Sutaio **8** Cheyenne
  people: 10 Crazy Horse **11** Sitting Bull **14** George McGovern, Hubert Humphrey
  lake: 4 Oahe **5** Sharp **8** Big Stone,

Traverse **11** Francis Case **13** Lewis and Clark
  land rank: 9 sixteenth
  mountain: 4 Bear **5** Sheep, Table **6** Crook's, Moreau
    highest point: 6 Harney
    hills: 5 Black **7** Prairie
  physical feature:
    butte: 7 Thunder **9** Deer's Ears **10** Castle Rock
    cave: 5 Jewel
    river: 3 Bad **5** Grand, James, White **6** Moreau **8** Big Sioux, Cheyenne, Missouri **10** Vermillion
  state admission: 8 fortieth **11** thirty-ninth (with North Dakota)
  state bird: 18 ring-necked pheasant
  state flower: 12 pasqueflower
  state animal: 6 coyote
  state motto: 21 Under God the People Rule
  state song: 15 Hail South Dakota
  state tree: 11 white spruce **16** Black Hills spruce

southeast wind
  associated with: 5 Eurus **9** Volturnus

Southern Comfort
  type: 7 liqueur
  origin: 10 New Orleans
  flavor: 5 peach
  base: 7 bourbon
  drink: 13 Scarlett O'Hara **15** Plantation Punch
  with bourbon: 14 Blended Comfort

Southern Cross
  constellation of: 4 Crux

Southern Crown
  constellation of: 15 Corona Australis

Southerner, The
  director: 10 Jean Renoir
  cast: 10 Betty Field **11** Beu lah Bondi **12** Zachary Scott **13** Bunny Sunshine

Southern Fish
  constellation of: 15 Piscis Austrinus

Southern Fly
  constellation of: 5 Musca

Southern Rhodesia *see* **8** Zimbabwe

Southern Slavic
  language family: 12 Indo-European
  group: 11 Balto-Slavic
  branch: 6 Slavic
  language: 7 Slovene **9** Bulgarian **10** Macedonian **13** Serbo-Croatian

Southern Triangle
  constellation of: 18 Triangulum Australe

South Korea *see* **5** Korea
South Vietnam *see* **7** Vietnam
South West Africa *see* **7** Namibia
south wind
  associated with: 5 Notus

South Wind
  author: 13 Norman Douglas
South Yemen *see* **5** Yemen
souvenir 4 scar **5** relic, token **6** em-

blem, memory, trophy **7** memento **8** keepsake, reminder **11** remembrance

sovereign 4 czar, free, king, lord, main, tsar **5** chief, major, prime, queen, regal, royal **6** kingly, potent, prince, ruling, utmost **7** emperor, highest, leading, monarch, queenly, supreme **8** absolute, autocrat, dominant, foremost, imperial, overlord, powerful, princely, reigning **9** chieftain, governing, paramount, potentate, prepotent, principal, uppermost **10** autonomous, self-ruling **11** all-powerful, crowned head, independent, monarchical **12** supreme ruler **13** self-directing, self-governing

sovereignty 4 sway **5** crown, power **6** throne **7** command, control, freedom, primacy, scepter **8** autonomy, dominion, home rule, kingship, lordship, self-rule **9** authority, suprem acy **10** ascendancy **11** paramountcy **12** independence, jurisdiction, predominance **14** self-government **17** self-determination

Soviet Union *see* **6** Russia

sow 4 cast, seed **5** lodge, plant, set in, strew **6** inject, spread **7** implant, instill, scatter **8** disperse, sprinkle **9** broadcast, establish, introduce **11** disseminate

space 3 gap, sky **4** area, part, rank, room, seat, span, spot, term, time **5** berth, blank, break, chasm, ether, field, order, place, range, reach, scope, sweep, swing, width **6** hiatus, lacuna, line up, margin, period, set out, spread **7** arrange, breadth, compass, expanse, mark out, the void **8** distance, duration, infinity, interval, latitude, omission, organize, schedule, separate **9** amplitude, emptiness, keep apart, territory **10** distribute, interspace, interstice, outer space, separation, the heavens **11** nothingness, reservation, the universe **12** interruption, the firmament **13** accommodation

Space
  author: 13 James Michener

spacecraft 4 ship **6** rocket **7** orbiter, shuttle **9** satellite **10** rocketship

space flight
  US mission: 6 Apollo, Gemini, Skylab **7** Mercury
  US rocket: 5 Atlas, Titan **6** Saturn **8** Redstone
  US space shuttle: 8 Columbia **9** Discovery **10** Challenger
  Soviet mission: 5 Soyuz **6** Salyut, Vostok **7** Voskhod
  Soviet astronaut:
    first man in space: 11 Yuri Gagarin
    first woman in space: 19 Valentina Tereshkova
    first space walk by: 13 Aleksei Leonov

American astronaut: 9 John Glenn, John Young **11** Alan Shepard, Edward White, Edwin Aldrin, Frank Borman, James Lovell **12** Roger Chaffee, Wally (Walter) Schirra **13** Charles Conrad, L Gordon Cooper, Virgil (Gus) Grissom **14** Scott Carpenter, Thomas Stafford

  first man on moon: 13 Neil Armstrong

  Challenger seven: 12 Michael Smith, Ronald McNair **13** Francis Scobee, Gregory Jarvis, Judith Resnick **14** Ellison Onizuka **16** Christa McAuliffe

Spacek, Sissy
  real name: 19 Mary Elizabeth Spacek
  born: 9 Quitman TX
  roles: 6 Carrie **7** Missing **8** Badlands, The River **10** Raggedy Man **16** Crimes of the Heart **18** Coal Miner's Daughter (Oscar)

spacious 4 vast, wide **5** ample, broad, large, roomy **7** immense, sizable **8** enormous **9** capacious, expansive, extensive, uncrowded **10** commodious

spaciousness 9 amplitude, largeness, roominess **13** capaciousness **14** commodiousness

Spade, Sam
  character in: 16 The Maltese Falcon
  author: 7 Hammett

Spain
  other name: 6 Iberia **8** Hispania
  capital/largest city: 6 Madrid
  others: 4 Adra, Aspe, Baza, Elda, Horo, Irun, Jaen, Leon, Noya, Olot, Reus, Rota, Sama, Vigo **5** Baena, Bejar, Cadiz, Cieza, Cueta, Ecija, Eibar, Elche, Gades, Gadir, Gijon, Ibiza, Jerez, Jodar, Liego, Lorca, Oliva, Palma, Palos, Ronda, Siero, Ubeda, Xeres, Yecla, Zafra **6** Abdera, Aviles, Azuaga, Bilbao, Burgos, Coruna, Duenca, Gandia, Gerona, Getafe, Guadix, Hellin, Huelva, Huesca, Jativa, Lerida, Lucena, Malaga, Mataro, Merida, Murcia, Orense, Oviedo, Termel, Toledo, Utrera, Zamora **7** Almeria, Badajos, Cordoba, Daimiel, Granada, Jumilla, Linares, Logrono, Manresa, Segovia, Sevilla, Seville, Tarrasa, Vitoria **8** Alicante, Badalona, Figueras, Pamplona, Sabadell, Santiago, Torrente, Valencia, Zaragoza **9** Barcelona, Las Palmas, Saragossa
  school: 6 Ciudad, Madrid
  division: 4 Jaen, Leon, Lugo **5** Alava, Avila, Cadiz, Soria **6** Basque, Burgos, Coruna, Cuenca, Gerona, Huelva, Huesca, Lerida, Madrid, Malaga, Murcia, Orense, Oviedo, Teruel, Toledo, Zamora **7** Almeria, Caceres, Cordoba, Granada, Logrono, Navarra, Segovia, Sevilla, Vizcaya, Zadajoz **8** Albacete, Alicante, Baleares, Palencia, Valencia, Zaragoza **9** Cata-

lonia
  kingdom: 4 Leon **6** Aragon **7** Castile, Galicia, Granada, Navarre **8** Asturias **9** al-Andalus, Catalonia **12** Spanish March
  government: 8 monarchy
  legislature: 6 Cortes
  head of state: 4 king
  measure: 3 pie **4** codo, dedo, paso, vara **5** braza, cahiz, carga, legua, medio, palmo, sesma **6** cordel, cuarta, fanega, racion, yugada **7** azumbre, celemin, estadel, pulgada **8** fanegada
  monetary unit: 3 cob **4** duro **5** dobla **6** cuarto, dinero, escudo, peseta **7** alfonso, centimo, pistole **8** doubloon
  weight: 4 onza **5** frail, libra, marco, tomin **6** arroba, dinero, dracma **7** arienzo, quilate, quintal **8** tonelada
  island: 5 Ceuta, Ibiza, Iviza, Palma **6** Canary, Gomera, Hierro **7** Alboran, Majorca, Melilla, Minorca **8** Balearic, Mallorca, Tagomago, Tenerife **9** Lanzarote **13** Fuerteventura
  lake: 4 lago **8** Albufera
  mountain: 4 Gata **5** Aneto, Rouch **6** Cuenca, Estats, Europa, Gredos, Magina, Morena, Nethou, Nevada, Teleno, Toledo **7** Alcaraz, Banuelo, Catalan, Cerredo, Demanda, Iberian, La Sagra, Moncayo, Perdido **8** Almanzor, Asturias, Galician, Maladeta, Monegros, Montseny, Penalara, Pyrenees **10** Albarracin, Cantabrian, Guadarrama, Torrecilla
  highest point: 5 Teide **8** Mulhacen
  river: 3 Sil, Ter **4** Cega, Ebro, Esla, Lima, Mino, Muga, Tajo, Ulla **5** Adaja, Cinca, Douro, Duero, Genil, Jalon, Jucar, Navia, Odiel, Riaza, Segie, Tagus, Tinto, Turia **6** Alagon, Aragon, Eresma, Huerva, Jarama, Orbigo, Segura, Torote **7** Almeria, Almonte, Arlanza, Barbate, Cabriel, Gallego, Henares, Mijares, Perales **8** Duration, Guadiana **12** Guadalquivir
  sea: 8 Atlantic, Balearic **13** Mediterranean
  physical feature:
    bay: 5 Bahia **6** Biscay
    cape: 9 Trafalgar
    gulf: 5 Cadiz **8** San Jorge, Valencia
    peninsula: 7 Iberian
    plateau: 7 meseta
    strait: 9 Gibraltar
  people: 5 Diego, Gente, Latin **6** Basque, Espana **7** Catalan, Espanol, Iberian **8** Galician, Gallegos, Maragato
    architect: 5 Gaudi
    artist: 4 Dali, Goya, Gris, Miro **6** Ribera **7** El Greco, Murillo, Picasso **8** Zurbaran **9** Velazquez
    author: 4 Cela, Vega **5** Barea, Cueva, Rojas **6** Aleman, Alonso, Azorin, Baroja, Castro, Encina, Felipe, Ibanez, Miguel **7** Alarcon,

Becquer, Cernuda, Ercilla, Gongora, Guillen, Jimenez, Machado, Unamuno **8** Montalvo, Zorrilla **9** Benavente, Cervantes, Goytisola **10** Aleixandre, Espronceda, Lope de Vega, Pardo Bazan **11** Garcia Lorca **12** Lopez de Ayala **13** Tirso de Molina **17** Calderon de la Barca
    cellist: 6 Casals
    composer: 7 Albeniz **8** Granados, Victoria **13** Manuel de Falla
    converted Moslem: 7 morisco
    dynasty: 7 Almohad, Umayyad **9** Almoravid
    explorer: 6 Balboa, Cortes **7** Pizarro **8** Columbus
    Jesuit founder: 14 Ignatius Loyola
    king: 6 Pelayo, Philip, Ramiro, Sancho, Witiza **7** Alfonso, Charles **8** al-Mansur, Reccared, Roderick **9** Ferdinand, Leovigild **10** Juan Carlos **11** Abd al-Rahman, Reccosvinth
    leader: 4 Prim **5** Godoy **6** Franco **7** Canovas **11** Calvo Sotelo **13** Primo de Rivera **14** Suarez-Gonzalez
    queen: 8 Isabella **16** Elizabeth Farnese
    ruler: 4 Rome **5** Celts, Moors **6** Greece **7** Almeria, Vandals **8** Carthage **9** Phoenicia, Visigoths
    scholar: 8 Averroes
    singer: 7 Domingo **8** Iglesias
    warrior: 14 El Cid Campeador
  language: 6 Basque **7** Catalan, Spanish **8** Balearic, Galician **9** Castilian, Valencian
  expressions: 5 adios **10** buenos dias **11** que sera sera **12** hasta la vista
  religion: 7 Judaism **10** Protestant **13** Roman Catholic
  place:
    aqueduct: 7 Segovia
    bridge: 7 Cordoba
    castle: 7 Alcazar **12** Santa Barbara
    cathedral bell tower: 7 Giralda
    center of Madrid: 12 Puerto del Sol
    church/cathedral: 4 Leon **6** Burgos, Gerona, Toledo **7** Seville **9** Barcelona, San Isidro **10** Santa Maria **14** Sagrada Familia
    fountain: 6 Cibele
    library: 8 Columbus
    minaret: 7 Seville
    mosque: 11 Great Mosque **19** Santo Cristo de la Cruz
    museum: 5 Prado **15** Museo de Pinturas
    palace: 7 Granada, Naranco **8** Alhambra, Escorial **9** Real Mayor
    park: 6 Retiro
    resort: 8 Marbella **10** Costa Brava **12** Torremolinos
    shrine: 32 Saint James at Santiago de Compostela
    street: 7 Ramblas **13** Paseo del Prado **16** Plaza de la Cibeles **19**

Paseo de la Castellana
  synagogue: 10 El Transito
  theater: 6 Merida
  wall paintings/caves: 8 Altamira
possession: 5 Ceuta **6** Melill
feature:
  bar: 6 tascas
  dance: 5 tango **8** fandango, flamenco
  estate: 10 latifundia
  matador's suit: 12 traje de luces
  political party: 7 Falange
food:
  dish: 6 cocido, paella **8** zarzuela
  soup: 8 gazpacho

span 4 arch, area, last, term, wing **5**
cover, cross, range, reach, scope,
spell, sweep, vault **6** bridge, endure,
extent, length, period **7** archway,
breadth, measure, stretch, survive,
trestle **8** distance, duration, interval **9**
extension, reach over, territory **10**
bridge over, dimensions **11**
proportions, reach across, stretch over
12 extend across

spangle 4 star **5** bedew **6** sequin **7**
glisten, glitter, shimmer, twinkle **9** bugle bead, coruscate, paillette

spaniel
  dog breed: 5 field **6** cocker, Sussex **7**
  clumber, Tibetan **8** Brittany **10** Irish
  water **13** American water, English
  cocker, Welsh springer **15** English
  springer **19** Cavalier King Charles

Spanish (language, person) 7 espanol

Spanish Guinea *see* **16** Equatorial
Guinea

Spanish Sahara *see* **13** Western Sahara

Spanish Tragedy, The
  author: 9 Thomas Kyd
  character: 7 Horatio, Lorenzo, Villupo
  9 Alexandro, Balthazar, Hieronimo
  10 Bel-Imperia **16** Ghost of Don Andrea

spank 3 hit, tan **4** beat, belt, blow,
cane, flog, hide, lick, slap, whip,
whop **5** birch, strap, whale **6** paddle,
strike, switch, thrash, wallop **8** paddling **10** flagellate

spanking 4 very **5** brisk, fresh **7** beating **8** paddling, whipping **9** extremely,
thrashing **10** punishment **12** chastisement

spanking new 5 fresh **6** unused **8**
brand new **9** untouched

spar 4 boom, mast, pole **5** argue, fight,
sprit **6** bicker **7** dispute, quarrel,
wrangle **8** crossbar **10** crosspiece

spare 3 odd **4** bony, cede, free, give,
keep, lank, lean, save, thin **5** amass,
extra, forgo, gaunt, grant, guard,
hoard, lanky, lay up, limit, pinch,
rangy, scant, stint, weedy **6** acquit, afford, defend, donate, excess, exempt,
forego, let off, meager, not use, par-

don, scanty, shield, skimpy, skinny,
slight, unused **7** forgive, haggard, husband, let go of, protect, release, relieve, reserve, scraggy, scrawny, shelter, skimp on, slender, surplus **8**
conserve, hold back, leftover, liberate,
part with, reprieve, set aside, skeletal,
withhold **9** auxiliary, emaciated, exonerate, fleshless, safeguard, show
mercy **10** additional, extraneous, relinquish, substitute, unconsumed **11**
economize on, have mercy on, superfluous, unnecessary, use frugally **12**
be merciful to, dispense with, supplemental **13** supernumerary, supplementary

spared 5 freed **6** exempt, immune **7**
excused **8** absolved, excepted, relieved

sparing 4 near **5** close, scant **6** frugal,
meager, saving, scanty, stingy **7** careful, miserly, thrifty **8** grudging, stinting **9** niggardly, penurious **10** economical, ungenerous **11** closefisted,
tightfisted **12** parsimonious

spark 3 bit, jot **4** atom, beam, fire,
iota, life **5** brand, ember, flash, gleam,
pique, trace **6** arouse, excite, incite,
spirit **7** flicker, glimmer, glitter, inspire, provoke, sparkle **8** vitality **9** animation, instigate, stimulate **10** get-up-
and-go

Spark, Muriel
  author of: 11 Memento Mori **14** The
  Driver's Seat, The Only Problem **17**
  The Mandelbaum Gate, Territorial
  Rights **19** Loitering with Intent **21** A
  Far Cry from Kensington **24** The
  Prime of Miss Jean Brodie

sparkle 3 pep, pop, vim **4** dash, elan,
fizz, foam, glow, life **5** be gay, brand,
cheer, ember, flash, froth, gleam,
glint, light, shine, verve **6** bubble,
dazzle, fizzle, gaiety, spirit **7** be witty,
flicker, glimmer, glisten, glitter, jollity,
rejoice, shimmer, twinkle **8** radiance,
vitality, vivacity **9** alertness, animation, briskness, coruscate, quickness
10 be cheerful, brilliance, ebullience,
effervesce, effulgence, exuberance,
liveliness, luminosity **11** be vivacious,
scintillate **12** cheerfulness, exhilaration, luminousness **13** effervescence,
scintillation

sparkling 5 fizzy **6** bubbly **7** fizzing,
twinkly **8** bubbling, dazzling, glittery
9 twinkling **10** glistening, glittering **11**
coruscating **12** effervescent **13** scintillating

Sparky Lyle
  nickname of: 16 Albert Walter Lyle

sparse 3 few **4** thin **5** scant, spare **6**
meager, scanty, scarce, skimpy,
spotty, strewn **7** diffuse **8** exiguous,
sporadic **9** dispersed, scattered,
spaced-out, uncrowded **10** infrequent
16 few and far between

sparseness 7 paucity **8** sparsity, thinness **10** meagerness, scantiness

Sparsit, Mrs
  character in: 9 Hard Times
  author: 7 Dickens

Spartacus
  director: 14 Stanley Kubrick
  cast: 8 Nina Foch **9** John Gavin **10**
  Tony Curtis **11** Jean Simmons, Kirk
  Douglas **12** Peter Ustinov **15** Charles
  Laughton, Laurence Olivier
  setting: 4 Rome
  score: 9 Alex North

spartan 4 hard **5** plain, stark, stern,
stiff **6** frugal, severe, simple, strict **7**
ascetic, austere **8** exacting, rigorous **9**
stringent **10** abstemious, inexorable,
inflexible, restrained, restricted **11** disciplined, self-denying **15** self-
disciplined

Sparti
  occupation: 8 warriors

spasm 3 fit, tic **4** grip, jerk, pang **5**
burst, cramp, crick, flash, onset, spell,
spurt, start, storm, throe **6** access, attack, frenzy, twitch **7** seizure, shudder, tempest **8** eruption, paroxysm **9**
explosion **10** convulsion

spasmodic 6 fitful **7** erratic, flighty **8**
fleeting, periodic, sporadic **9** desultory, irregular, mercurial, transient **10**
capricious, inconstant, occasional **12**
intermittent **13** discontinuous

spat 4 tiff **5** argue, fight, scrap, set-to **6**
bicker, differ **7** contend, dispute, dissent, quarrel, wrangle **8** disagree,
squabble **10** difference **11** altercation
12 disagreement **16** misunderstanding

spatter 4 slop, soil, spot **5** fleck, plash,
spray, spurt, stain, swash **6** mottle,
shower, splash **7** speckle, stipple **8**
splatter, sprinkle

spawn 4 eggs, seed, teem **5** beget,
breed, brood, fruit, yield **7** lay eggs,
produce, product **8** engender, generate, multiply **9** offspring, propagate,
reproduce **10** bring forth, give rise to
11 deposit eggs, give birth to, proliferate

speak 3 air, say **4** call, chat, deal, talk,
tell **5** imply, orate, refer, shout,
sound, state, treat, voice **6** advise,
confer, convey, cry out, dilate, impart,
mumble, murmur, mutter, preach, recite, relate, remark, report, reveal **7**
bespeak, comment, consult, declaim,
declare, discuss, divulge, expound, express, lecture, mention, suggest, whisper **8** announce, converse, disclose,
harangue, indicate, proclaim, vocalize
9 discourse, enunciate, expatiate, hold
forth, make known, pronounce, sermonize **10** articulate **11** communicate,
give a speech

speakeasy 3 bar **6** saloon, tavern **7**
gin mill **14** cocktail lounge

speaker 5 voice **6** orator, reader, talker

7 reciter **8** advocate, lecturer, preacher **9** declaimer, spokesman **10** discourser, monologist, mouthpiece, sermonizer **11** rhetorician, speechmaker, spokeswoman **13** valedictorian

speak highly of 4 laud **5** exalt, extol **6** praise **7** commend **8** eulogize **10** compliment **16** sing the praises of

speak ill of 4 slur **5** curse, knock, libel **6** defame, insult, malign, vilify **7** slander **8** bad-mouth **9** criticize, denigrate, discredit, disparage **13** find fault with **14** inveigh against

speak loudly 3 cry **4** bawl, call, hail, roar, yell **5** shout **6** bellow, clamor, cry out, halloo, holler **7** call out, speak up

speak of 7 mention, refer to **8** allude to **9** talk about, touch upon

speak to 6 talk to **7** address, lecture

speak together 3 gab, jaw, rap **4** chat, chin, talk **6** confer **7** chatter, palaver **8** chitchat, converse **10** chew the fat, chew the rag **11** communicate, confabulate

speak well of 4 laud **5** boost, extol **6** praise **7** acclaim, approve, commend, flatter, root for **8** eulogize **9** sweet talk **10** compliment, stick up for **13** speak highly of **16** sing the praises of **17** put in a good word for

spear 4 bolt, dart, gaff, gore, pike, spit, stab **5** lance, prick, shaft, spike, stick **6** impale, pierce **7** harpoon, javelin **8** puncture, transfix **9** penetrate **10** run through

spearhead 4 iron, lead **5** begin, found, start **6** launch, leader **7** creator, develop, founder, pioneer **8** begetter, conceive, initiate **9** establish, initiator, institute, originate, spokesman **10** inaugurate, instituter, prime mover **11** establisher, inaugurator, spokeswoman **12** avant-gardist

special 4 fast, good, rare **5** close, great, novel **6** ardent, proper, select, signal, unique **7** bargain, certain, devoted, endemic, feature, staunch, typical, unusual **8** distinct, especial, intimate, peculiar, personal, sale item, singular, specific, uncommon **9** headliner, high point, highlight, important, momentous, specialty, steadfast **10** attraction, individual, noteworthy, particular, remarkable **11** distinctive, exceptional, outstanding, specialized **12** extravaganza **13** distinguished, extraordinary **14** representative, unconventional **16** out of the ordinary **17** piece de resistance

specialist 4 buff **5** adept, maven **6** expert, master **9** authority **10** past master **11** connoisseur

specialization 5 focus, forte, major **6** metier **8** province **10** speciality **13** concentration

specialize 5 adapt, focus, major **6** pursue **10** narrow down **11** concentrate

specialty 4 bent, mark, turn **5** badge, focus, forte, hobby, major, stamp **6** genius, talent **7** earmark, faculty, feature, pursuit, special **8** aptitude **9** endowment, trademark **10** competence, profession **11** claim to fame, distinction

species 4 form, kind, make, sort, type **5** breed, class, genre, group, order **6** kidney, nature, stripe **7** variety **8** category, division **11** designation, subdivision **14** classification

specific 5 exact, fixed **6** minute, stated, unique **7** bounded, certain, endemic, limited, pointed, precise, special, typical **8** clear-cut, concrete, confined, definite, detailed, especial, peculiar, personal, relevant, singular, tied-down **9** intrinsic, pertinent, specified **10** individual, particular, pinned-down, restricted **11** categorical, determinate, distinctive, unequivocal **13** circumscribed **14** characteristic

specification 6 detail **7** clarity **9** condition, precision, substance **11** enumeration, itemization, requirement, stipulation **12** concreteness **13** particularity, qualification **17** particularization

specifics 4 cure, fact, item **5** datum **6** detail, physic **10** medication, particular **12** circumstance

specify 4 cite, name **5** order **6** adduce, define, denote, detail **7** call for, focus on, itemize **8** describe, indicate, set forth **9** designate, enumerate, stipulate **13** particularize

specimen 4 case, type **5** model **6** sample **7** example **8** exemplar, instance **9** prototype **14** representative **15** exemplification

specious 5 false **6** faulty, tricky, untrue **7** dubious, in valid, unsound **8** slippery, spurious **9** casuistic, deceptive, illogical, incorrect, unfounded **10** fallacious, inaccurate, misleading **11** sophistical **12** questionable **15** unsubstantiated

speck 3 bit, dot, jot, pin **4** drop, hair, iota, mark, mite, mote, spot, whit **5** fleck, grain, pinch, trace **6** shadow, trifle **7** glimmer, modicum, speckle **8** farthing, flyspeck, particle **9** scintilla

speckled 4 pied **6** dotted **7** flecked, spotted, studded **8** freckled, peppered **9** sprinkled

spectacle 5 scene, sight **6** marvel, parade, rarity, wonder **7** display, exhibit, pageant **9** curiosity, rare sight **10** exhibition, exposition, phenomenon, production **12** extravaganza, presentation **13** demonstration

spectacles 6 lenses, shades **7** glasses **8** bifocals, pince-nez **10** eyeglasses

spectacular 4 gala, rich **5** grand, showy **6** daring **7** jeweled, opulent, stately **8** dramatic, fabulous, glorious, gorgeous, splendid, striking **9** daredevil, elaborate, marvelous, spectacle, sumptuous, thrilling **10** astounding, bespangled, eye-filling, impressive, theatrical **11** ceremonious, hairraising, magnificent, sensational **12** extravaganza, overwhelming **16** ostentatious show **19** elaborate production

spectator 3 fan **5** house **6** viewer **7** gallery, witness **8** audience, beholder, kibitzer, observer, onlooker **9** bystander, sightseer **10** aficionado, eyewitness **11** afficionado, theatergoer **12** rubbernecker

Spectator, The
  author: **13** Joseph Addison, Richard Steele

specter 5 demon, ghost, ghoul, shade, spook **6** spirit, sprite, vision, wraith **7** banshee, fantasy, phantom **8** phantasm, presence, revenant **9** hobgoblin **10** apparition

spectral 4 airy **5** eerie, weird **6** creepy, spooky, unreal **7** ghastly, ghostly, phantom, shadowy, uncanny **8** ethereal, gossamer, vaporous **9** unearthly **10** chimerical, phantasmal, wraithlike **11** incorporeal **12** otherworldly, supernatural **13** insubstantial

speculate 4 muse **5** brood, dream, fancy, guess, study, think, wager **6** chance, gamble, hazard, ponder, reason, wonder **7** imagine, reflect, suppose, surmise, venture **8** cogitate, consider, meditate, ruminate, theorize **10** conjecture, deliberate, excogitate, play a hunch **11** contemplate, hypothesize, take a chance **13** play the market

speculation 4 risk **7** venture **8** gambling **9** guesswork **10** conjecture, estimation **11** supposition

speculative 4 iffy **5** dicey, risky **6** chancy **8** academic **11** conjectural, theoretical **12** experimental, hypothetical **13** suppositional

speculator 7 gambler, plunger **8** investor, operator, theorist **10** adventurer, arbitrager **11** arbitrageur

speech 4 talk **5** idiom, lingo, slang, voice **6** appeal, gossip, homily, jargon, sermon, tirade, tongue **7** address, chatter, comment, dialect, diction, lecture, oration, palaver, prattle, remarks, talking **8** chitchat, colloquy, converse, dialogue, diatribe, harangue, language, parlance, rhetoric, speaking **9** discourse, elocution, monologue, soliloquy, statement, utterance **10** discussion, expression, recitation, salutation **11** declamation, declaration, enunciation, exhortation, observation, valedictory **12** articulation, conversation, dissertation, vocalization **13** colloquialism, confabulation, pronounce-ment, pronunciation, verbalization

speechless 3 mum 4 dumb, mute 6 silent 7 aphonic 8 wordless 9 stupefied 10 tongue-tied

speed 3 aid, hie, run, zip 4 dart, dash, help, race, rate, rush, tear, zoom 5 boost, favor, gun it, haste, hurry, impel, speed, tempo 6 assist, barrel, gallop, hasten, hurtle, hustle, pick up, plunge, propel, scurry, step up 7 advance, further, hurry up, promote, quicken, tear off 8 alacrity, celerity, dispatch, expedite, high tail, make time, momentum, rapidity, step on it, velocity 9 bowl along, briskness, fleetness, give a lift, hastiness, make haste, move along, quickness, rapidness, swiftness 10 accelerate, expedition, get a move on, go hell-bent, lose no time, promptness, spurt ahead 11 push forward 12 acceleration 13 burn up the road

speedily 4 fast 5 apace, quick 6 pronto 7 hastily, rapidly, swiftly 8 in no time, promptly 9 post haste, right away, summarily 11 on the double 12 lickety-split

speed up 4 rush 5 hurry 6 hasten, step up 7 hop to it, quicken 8 expedite, multiply, step on it 9 encourage, intensify 10 accelerate, facilitate, get a move on 12 step on the gas

speedy 4 fast 5 brisk, early, fleet, hasty, quick, rapid, ready, swift 6 abrupt, lively, sudden 7 express, hurried, running, summary 8 headlong 9 quick-fire, rapid-fire 10 not delayed 11 precipitate

Spelaites
epithet of: 6 Hermes
means: 9 of the cave

spell 2 go 3 bit, hex 4 bout, free, lull, mean, omen, snap, term, time, tour, turn, wave 5 augur, break, charm, hitch, imply, magic, pause, round, stint, trick, while 6 allure, course, denote, herald, hoodoo, make up, period, recess, tenure, typify, voodoo 7 bespeak, betoken, connote, glamour, portend, presage, promise, purport, rapture, release, relieve, respite, signify, sorcery, stretch, suggest 8 amount to, cover for, duration, forebode, forecast, foretell, indicate, interval, stand for, witchery 9 form a word, influence, interlude, represent, symbolize 10 assignment, invocation, mumbo jumbo, open-sesame 11 abracadabra, bewitchment, enchantment, fascination, incantation, pinch-hit for, take over for 12 magic formula

spellbind 5 charm 7 bewitch, enchant 8 enthrall, entrance, intrigue, transfix 9 enrapture, fascinate, hypnotize, mesmerize, transport

spellbound 4 rapt 5 agape 7 charmed 8 wordless 9 awestruck, bewitched, enchanted, entranced, possessed 10 breathless, dumbstruck, enraptured, enthralled, fascinated, hypnotized, mesmerized, speechless, tongue-tied, transfixed 11 openmouthed, transported

Spellbound
director: 15 Alfred Hitchcock
cast: 9 John Emery 11 Gregory Peck, Leo G Carroll 13 Ingrid Bergman 14 Michael Chekhov
score: 11 Miklos Rosza
Oscar for: 5 score
dream sequences by: 12 Salvador Dali

spell out 6 define, detail 7 clarify, clear up, explain, expound, specify 8 describe 9 delineate, designate, elucidate, explicate, interpret, make plain 10 illustrate

Spemann, Hans
field: 7 zoology
nationality: 6 German
worked in: 20 embryonic development
awarded: 10 Nobel Prize

Spencer, Sir Stanley
born: 7 Cookham, England 9 Berkshire
artwork: 22 Resurrection of Soldiers, The Resurrection Cookham 31 Christ Preaching at Cookham Regatta 43 Double Nude Portrait the Artist and his Second Wife

spend 3 pay, use 4 dole, fill, give, pass 5 drain, empty, use up, waste 6 devote, employ, expend, invest, occupy, outlay, pay out, take up 7 burn out, consume, deplete, destroy, exhaust, fork out, scatter, wear out 8 allocate, disburse, dispense, shell out, squander 9 dissipate, while away 10 impoverish

spendable 9 available 10 expendable 13 discretionary

spend foolishly 5 waste 8 misspend, squander 9 dissipate, throw away 11 fritter away

spendthrift 6 lavish, waster 7 wastrel 8 prodigal, spend-all, wasteful 10 big spender, profligate, squanderer 11 extravagant, improvident 12 overgenerous

Spengler, Oswald
author of: 19 The Decline of the West

Spenlow, Dora
character in: 16 David Copperfield
author: 7 Dickens

Spenser, Edmund
author of: 8 Amoretti 12 Epithalamion 15 The Faerie Queene 22 The Shephearde's Calendar

spent 4 beat, done, weak 5 faint, weary 6 bushed, done in, used up 7 laid low, wearied, worn out 8 drooping, fatigued, tired out 9 enfeebled, exhausted, fagged out, played out, powerless, prostrate 11 debilitated, ready to drop 12 strengthless 14 on one's last legs

Sperry, Elmer Ambrose
invented: 11 gyrocompass 22 airplane automatic pilot

spew 5 eject, expel, heave, vomit 6 cast up 7 spit out 8 disgorge, throw out 11 regurgitate

spew up 4 spew 5 eject, expel, spout, vomit 6 cast up 7 cough up, throw up 8 disgorge 11 regurgitate

sphere 3 orb 4 area, ball, beat, pale 5 globe, orbit, range, realm, scope 6 domain 7 compass, globule 8 province, spheroid 9 bailiwick, round body, territory 10 experience

spherical 5 orbic, round 6 global, rotund 7 globate, globose, orbical 8 globular 9 orbicular 11 globe-shaped
nearly: 8 obrotund

spheroid 3 orb 4 ball 5 globe 6 sphere 7 globule

spherule 4 ball, bead, drop 6 pellet 7 droplet, globule

Sphinx
form: 7 monster
bust of: 5 woman
body of: 4 lion
father: 6 Typhon 7 Orthrus
mother: 7 Echidna 8 Chimaera
proposed: 7 riddles
location: 4 Giza 6 Thebes
answered by: 7 Oedipus

spice 3 zip 4 herb, kick, snap, tang, zest 5 savor 6 accent, flavor, relish, stacte 7 pizzazz 8 piquancy, pungency 9 condiment, flavoring, seasoning 10 excitement

spicule 4 barb 5 point, spine 7 prickle

spicy 3 hot 4 keen, racy 5 acute, bawdy, fiery, nippy, pithy, salty, sharp, tangy, witty, zippy 6 clever, ribald, risque, snappy, strong 7 gingery, peppery, piquant, pungent 8 aromatic, improper, incisive, indecent, off-color, piercing, redolent, spirited 9 sparkling, trenchant 10 indelicate, scandalous, suggestive 11 provocative 12 questionable 13 scintillating

spider
black widow marking: 9 hourglass
class: 9 Arachnida
combining form: 6 arachn 7 arachno
family: 7 Attidae 9 Drassidae 10 Citigradae, Pisauridae
famous: 9 Charlotte
fear of: 13 arachnophobia
kind: 4 crab, wolf 5 taint 7 jumping 8 trap-door 9 orb weaver, solpugida, tarantula 10 black widow 13 daddy longlegs
mythology: 7 Arachne
nest: 5 nidus
order: 7 Araneae
part: 4 claw, coxa 5 femur, tibia 6

tarsus **7** abdomen, mammula, patella, pedicel, scopula **9** chelicera, protarsis, spinneret **10** pedipalpus, trochanter **11** calamistrum **13** cephalothorax
study of: 10 araneology **11** arachnology
young: 11 spiderlings
Spielberg, Steven
wife: 11 Kate Capshaw
former wife: 9 Amy Irving
company: 13 Dreamworks SKG
director of: 4 Jaws **7** Amistad **11** Poltergeist **12** Jurassic Park, The Lost World **14** Schindler's List (Oscar), The Color Purple **19** Raiders of the Lost Ark **21** ET The Extra Terrestrial **29** Close Encounters of the Third Kind, Indiana Jones and the Last Crusade **30** Indiana Jones and the Temple of Doom
spike 3 peg, pin **4** barb, nail, spur, tine **5** briar, point, prong, rivet, spine, stake, thorn **6** needle, skewer **7** bramble, bristle, hobnail **8** spikelet
spill 3 run **4** blab, drip, drop, dump, fall, flow, shed, slop, tell, toss **5** slosh, throw, waste **6** reveal, splash **7** let flow, pour out **8** disclose, overflow, overturn
Spillane, Mickey
real name: 13 Frank Morrison
author of: 8 I the Jury **12** Kiss Me Deadly **14** The Girl Hunters **15** The Death Dealers
character: 10 Mike Hammer
spin 4 roll, tell, turn **5** swirl, twirl, wheel, whirl **6** gyrate, invent, relate, render, rotate, unfold **7** concoct, narrate, recount, revolve **8** rotation, spinning **9** fabricate, pirouette
spinach 3 rot **4** bull, bunk **5** hokum, hooey, stuff **6** bunkum, hot air, humbug **7** baloney, blather, hogwash, potherb **8** claptrap, nonsense, tommyrot **9** poppycock, vegetable **10** applesauce **11** foolishness **16** stuff and nonsense
spinach 16 Spinacia oleracea
varieties: 4 wild **5** Cuban **6** Indian **7** Malabar **8** mountain **10** New Zealand **11** round-seeded **13** prickly-seeded
spinal column 4 back **5** spine **8** backbone
spindly 4 puny **5** frail, leggy **6** skinny **7** scraggy **8** skeletal
spine 4 barb, horn, spur **5** briar, point, prong, quill, spike, thorn **6** needle **7** bramble, bristle, prickle **8** backbone **9** vertebrae **12** spinal column
spinel
source: 5 Burma, Mogok
color: 3 red **5** mauve
spineless 4 weak **5** timid **7** fearful **8** cowardly, cowering, cringing, timorous, wavering **10** indecisive, irresolute, spiritless, weak-willed **11** lily-

livered, vacillating **12** fainthearted **13** pusillanimous **14** chickenhearted
spinelessness 8 timidity, weakness **9** cowardice **10** indecision **11** fearfulness **12** cowardliness, irresolution **13** pusillanimity
spine-tingling 7 rousing **8** exciting **9** thrilling **11** hair-raising, sensational **12** breathtaking, electrifying
spinning jenny
invented by: 10 Hargreaves
spinoff 5 issue **6** result **7** ad junct, outcome **8** offshoot **9** byproduct, outgrowth **10** descendant, side effect, supplement **11** aftereffect, consequence
spin out 4 skid **7** draw out **8** lengthen **9** attenuate
spinster 6 virgin **7** old maid **14** unmarried woman
spinsterhood 8 celibacy **9** virginity **11** old maidhood
spiral 4 coil, curl, gyre **5** helix, screw, whirl, whorl **6** coiled, curled **7** helical, ringlet, spiroid, whorled, winding **8** curlicue, twisting **9** corkscrew **11** screw-shaped
Spiral Staircase, The
director: 13 Robert Siodmak
based on story by: 14 Ethel Lina White (Some Must Watch)
cast: 9 Kent Smith **11** George Brent **13** Rhonda Fleming **14** Dorothy McGuire, Ethel Barrymore
spire 3 cap, tip **4** apex, cone, peak **5** crest, point, shaft, tower **6** belfry, summit, turret, vertex **7** minaret, obelisk, steeple **8** pinnacle **9** bell tower, campanile
spirit 3 elf **4** mind, soul, urge, will **5** fairy, ghost, ghoul, heart, shade, spook **6** animus, dybbuk, goblin, psyche, sprite, wraith **7** banshee, bugaboo, bugbear, impulse, phantom, resolve, specter **8** phantasm, presence **9** hobgoblin, intellect **10** apparition, motivation, resolution
German: 5 Geist
spirited 4 bold **5** fiery, nervy **6** frisky, lively, plucky **8** fearless, intrepid **10** courageous, mettlesome
spiritless 4 dull, limp, tame **6** abject **8** cowardly, lifeless, listless **9** apathetic, spineless **10** unanimated, worldweary **11** passionless
spirit of the time
German: 9 Zeitgeist
spirits 3 aim, vim **4** bond, elan, fire, gist, glow, grit, guts, mood, sand, tone, vein, zeal, zest **5** ardor, drive, humor, pluck, sense, spunk, tenor, valor, verve, vigor **6** daring, effect, elixir, energy, fervor, intent, liquor, mettle, morale, stripe, temper, warmth **7** alcohol, avidity, bravery, courage, essence, extract, feeling, loyalty,

meaning, purport, purpose, sparkle **8** attitude, audacity, backbone, boldness, devotion, emotions, feelings, tincture, vitality, vivacity **9** animation, eagerness, fortitude, intention, sentiment, stoutness, substance **10** allegiance, attachment, enterprise, enthusiasm, liveliness **11** disposition, doughtiness, staunchness **12** fearlessness, significance **13** dauntlessness, sprightliness **16** stoutheartedness **17** alcoholic solution
spiritual 4 holy **5** godly, inner, moral, pious **6** divine, mental **7** blessed, churchy, ghostly, phantom, psychic **8** cerebral, hallowed, heavenly, platonic, priestly, spectral, supernal **9** celestial, Christian, innermost, of the soul, religious, unearthly, unfleshly, unworldly **10** devotional, immaterial, intangible, sacrosanct, sanctified **11** consecrated, incorporeal **12** metaphysical, otherworldly, supernatural **13** insubstantial, psychological **14** ecclesiastical
spirituality 5 piety **8** devotion, holiness **9** godliness, reverence **10** devoutness
spirituous 4 hard **6** strong **9** alcoholic, distilled **12** intoxicating
spit 3 bar, pop, rod **4** foam, hiss, reef, spew **5** atoll, drool, eject, fling, froth, shoal, throw **6** saliva, shower, shriek, skewer, slaver, sputum **7** dribble, scatter, slobber, spatter, spittle, sputter **8** headland, sandbank, turnspit **9** brochette, peninsula **10** promontory **11** expectorate
spite 3 irk, vex **4** gall, hate, hurt, pain **5** annoy, odium, sting, venom, wound **6** animus, enmity, grudge, harass, hatred, injure, malice, misuse, nettle, put out, rancor **7** ill will, mortify, provoke **8** bad blood, ill-treat, irritate, loathing, meanness **9** animosity, antipathy, hostility, humiliate, malignity, nastiness, vengeance **10** bitterness, resentment **11** detestation, malevolence **12** vengefulness **13** maliciousness, slap in the face **14** revengefulness, vindictiveness
spiteful 4 evil **5** nasty **6** bitter, malign, wicked **7** caustic, envious, hateful, hostile, vicious **8** grudging, vengeful, venomous **9** malicious, merciless, rancorous, resentful, sarcastic, splenetic **10** ill-natured, malevolent, vindictive **11** acrimonious, unforgiving **12** antagonistic
spitting image (spit and image) 4 copy, mate, twin **6** double **9** duplicate **15** perfect likeness
splash 3 ado, hit **4** cast, dash, daub, soil, stir, toss, wash **5** bathe, break, fling, plash, slosh, smack, smear, stain, strew, surge, swash **6** batter, blazon, buffet, effect, impact, paddle, plunge, shower, spread, streak, strike,

uproar, wallow, welter **7** bestrew, scatter, spatter, splotch **8** besmirch, discolor, disperse, splatter, sprinkle **9** bespatter, broadcast, commotion, sensation **10** spattering **11** splattering

splashy 5 jazzy, showy **6** flashy **10** glittering **11** spectacular **12** ostentatious

splatter 4 dash **6** splash **7** spatter

splay 4 awry **5** askew, broad **6** aslant, clumsy, extend, tilted, warped **7** awkward, crooked, fanlike, slanted, sloping, turn out **8** inclined, slanting **9** distorted, fan-shaped, irregular, outspread, spread out **10** stretch out

spleen 4 bile, gall **5** anger, spite, venom **6** animus, enmity, hatred, malice, rancor **7** ill will **8** acrimony, ill humor, vexation **9** animosity, bad temper, hostility **10** bitterness, resentment **11** malevolence, peevishness **12** irritability, spitefulness

splendid 4 fine, high, rare, rich **5** grand, lofty, noble, regal, royal **6** august, costly, ornate, superb **7** elegant, eminent, exalted, stately **8** dazzling, elevated, flashing, gleaming, glorious, gorgeous, imposing, majestic, palatial, peerless, terrific **9** admirable, beautiful, brilliant, effulgent, estimable, excellent, marvelous, sumptuous, wonderful **10** glittering, preeminent, remarkable, surpassing **11** exceptional, illustrious, magnificent, outstanding, resplendent, splendorous **12** transcendent **13** distinguished, splendiferous

Splendid Splinter
nickname of: 11 Ted Williams

splendor 4 fire, pomp **5** gleam, glory, light, sheen, shine **6** beauty, dazzle, luster, renown **7** burnish, glitter **8** grandeur, nobility, opulence, radiance **9** intensity, sublimity **10** augustness, brilliance, effulgence, irradiance, luminosity **11** preeminence, stateliness **12** gorgeousness, luminousness, magnificence, resplendence **13** incandescence

Splendor in the Grass
director: 9 Elia Kazan
based on story by: 11 William Inge
cast: 9 Pat Hingle **11** Natalie Wood **12** Sean Garrison, Warren Beatty **14** Audrey Christie

splenetic 5 cross, nasty, surly, testy **6** cranky, malign **7** bilious, hostile, peevish **8** choleric, spiteful, venomous **9** irascible, rancorous **11** acrimonious, ill-tempered **12** cantankerous, disagreeable

splice 3 wed **4** join, knit **5** graft, merge, plait, unite **7** connect **8** dovetail **9** interlace **10** intertwine, interweave **12** interconnect

splinter 4 chip **5** smash, split **6** needle, shiver, sliver **7** break up, crumble, explode, shatter **8** fly apart, frac-

ture, fragment **9** pulverize **12** disintegrate

split 3 hew **4** deal, dole, dual, mete, part, rent, rift, rive, snap, tear, torn **5** allot, break, burst, cleft, crack, halve, mixed, riven, sever, share **6** bisect, breach, broken, cleave, differ, divide, ripped, schism, shiver, sunder, varied **7** be riven, cracked, diverge, divided, divorce, divvy up, fissure, give way, opening, portion, quarrel, rupture, severed, twofold **8** alienate, allocate, cleavage, disagree, dispense, disperse, dissever, disunion, disunite, division, fracture, ruptured, splinter **9** apportion, fractured, parcel out, partition, segmented, segregate, separated, set at odds, subdivide, undecided **10** alienation, ambivalent, break apart, difference, dissension, dissevered, distribute, divergence, falling out, separation, splintered **11** come between, part company, tear asunder **12** disagreement, estrangement

split off 7 deviate, diverge **8** separate **9** draw apart

split the difference 5 agree **6** settle **9** make a deal **10** compromise **11** come to terms, meet halfway **14** strike a bargain

splitting off 9 diverging **10** separating **12** drawing apart

splitting up 8 dividing **9** divorcing **10** breaking up, separating **11** subdividing **12** partitioning

splotch 4 blot, daub, mark, spot **5** smear, stain **6** blotch, smudge **13** discoloration

splurge 5 binge, spree **6** bender **8** live it up **10** indulgence, showing off **12** showy display **13** be extravagant, shoot the works **14** indulge oneself, self-indulgence **22** throw caution to the winds

splutter 4 hiss, spew, spit **5** burst, spray **6** gibber, jabber, mumble, seethe **7** bluster, slobber, spatter, sputter, stammer, stumble, stutter **9** hem and haw **11** expectorate

spoil 3 mar, rot **4** baby, flaw, harm, mold, ruin, sour, turn **5** addle, botch, decay, go bad, humor, taint **6** blight, bungle, coddle, damage, deface, foul up, impair, injure, mess up, mildew, muddle, pamper **7** blemish, destroy, disrupt, putrefy **8** mutilate **9** decompose, disfigure **11** deteriorate, mollycoddle, overgratify, overindulge

spoiled 3 bad, off **6** putrid, rotten, ruined **7** coddled, corrupt, decayed, gone bad, went bad **8** indulged, overripe, pampered **9** putrefied **10** decomposed, frustrated **12** deteriorated **15** rotten to the core

spoiler 6 vandal **8** underdog **9** deflector

spoils 4 haul, loot, swag, take **5** booty

6 bounty, prizes, quarry **7** plunder, profits **8** benefits, comforts, pickings **9** amenities, patronage **11** perquisites **12** acquisitions

spoilsport 4 drag **10** wet blanket **11** party-pooper

spoken 4 oral, said **5** parol **6** verbal, voiced **7** uttered **9** expressed **10** pronounced **11** articulated

spokesman 5 agent, PR man, proxy **6** backer, deputy **7** speaker **8** delegate, promoter **9** middleman, proponent, supporter, surrogate **10** mouthpiece, negotiator, press agent **11** protagonist

sponge 3 bum, dry, mop, rub **4** blot, swab, wash **5** cadge, clean, leech, mooch, towel **6** borrow, live on **7** cleanse, moisten **8** freeload, impose on, scrounge **9** panhandle

sponger 5 leech **6** cadger, sponge **7** moocher **8** barnacle, borrower, deadbeat **9** scrounger **10** freeloader **11** bloodsucker

sponsor 4 back **5** angel, set up **6** backer, patron, uphold **7** finance, promote, support **8** advocate, champion, defender, financer, guardian, partisan, promoter, start out, upholder, vouch for, warranty **9** guarantee, financier, guarantor, proponent, protecter, protector, supporter **10** advertiser, stand up for, underwrite

sponsorship 5 aegis **7** support **8** advocacy, auspices **9** patronage **12** championship

spontaneity 7 freedom **11** impetuosity, naturalness **12** unconstraint **13** impulsiveness, offhandedness **18** extemporaneousness

spontaneous 4 free **5** ad lib **7** natural, offhand, willing **8** unbidden **9** automatic, extempore, impetuous, impromptu, impulsive, ingenuous, unplanned, unstudied, voluntary **10** gratuitous, improvised, off the cuff, unprompted **11** independent, instinctive, uncontrived **12** unhesitating **13** unconstrained **14** extemporaneous, unpremeditated

spoof 3 kid **4** joke, josh, twit **6** parody, satire, sendup **7** joshing, kidding, lampoon, mockery, ribbing, takeoff **8** satirize, travesty **9** burlesque, take off on **10** caricature

spook 5 alarm, bogey, ghost, haunt, scare, shade **6** goblin, shadow, spirit **7** disturb, phantom, specter, startle, terrify, unnerve **8** disquiet, frighten, unsettle **9** hobgoblin, terrorize **10** apparition, intimidate

spooky 5 eerie, jumpy, scary, weird **6** creepy **7** ghostly, nervous **8** skittish **10** mysterious

sporadic 3 few **4** rare, thin **6** fitful, meager, random, scarce, sparse, spotty **8** isolated, periodic, uncommon **9** haphazard, irregular, scattered,

spasmodic 10 infrequent, now and then, occasional **11** fragmentary **12** intermittent, widely spaced **13** discontinuous **16** few and far between

sport 3 fun, toy **4** bear, butt, game, goat, jest, joke, lark, play, romp, trip **5** abuse, caper, carry, chaff, dally, frisk, hobby, mirth, revel **6** antics, cavort, frolic, gaiety, gambol, misuse, monkey, take in, trifle **7** buffoon, contest, display, disport, exhibit, gambler, jesting, jollity, kidding, mockery, rollick, show off, skylark **8** badinage, derision, fair game, flourish, hilarity, illtreat, raillery, ridicule, scoffing, trifling **9** amusement, athletics, daredevil, diversion, festivity, joviality, make merry, play games, scapegoat **10** persiflage, pleasantry, recreation, relaxation, skylarking **11** competition, distraction, merrymaking **12** depreciation **13** entertainment, laughingstock **14** divertissement

sporting house 4 stew **5** house **6** bagnio, bordel **7** brothel **8** bordello, cathouse **10** bawdy house, fancy house, whorehouse **14** house of ill fame **16** house of ill repute **19** house of prostitution

sportive 6 blithe, frisky **7** playful **8** animated **10** frolicsome

sportsman 6 hunter **9** fisherman

Sportsman's Notebook, A
    author: **12** Ivan Turgenev

sporty 6 casual, flashy, jaunty **8** informal

spot 3 dot, fix, see, spy **4** area, bind, blot, daub, espy, flaw, mark, part, seat, site, slur, soil **5** brand, fleck, grime, locus, patch, place, point, smear, space, speck, stain, sully, taint, tract **6** blotch, defect, detect, locale, locate, plight, region, sector, smirch, smudge, splash, stigma **7** blemish, dilemma, discern, light on, pick out, quarter, section, spatter, speckle, splotch, station **8** discolor, discover, disgrace, district, flyspeck, locality, location, position, premises, reproach, sprinkle **9** aspersion, discredit, recognize, situation, territory **10** difficulty, imputation **11** predicament **12** bad situation, neighborhood **13** discoloration

spotless 4 pure **5** clean, snowy **7** perfect, shining **8** flawless, gleaming, pristine, unflawed, unmarred, unsoiled **9** faultless, stainless, unspotted, unstained, unsullied, untainted **10** immaculate, impeccable **11** unblemished, untarnished **14** irreproachable **15** unexceptionable

spotted 3 saw **6** dotted, espied, soiled **7** dappled, located, mottled, stained **8** detected, speckled **9** blemished, discerned, spattered **10** discovered **13** caught sight of

spotty 6 fitful, pimply, random, une-ven **7** blotchy, dappled, erratic, flecked, mottled, spotted **8** episodic, freckled, splotchy, sporadic, unsteady, variable, wavering **9** broken out, desultory, irregular, spasmodic, uncertain **10** capricious, inconstant, unreliable, variegated **11** full of spots **12** disorganized, intermittent, undependable, unmethodical, unsystematic

spouse 4 mate, wife **7** consort, husband, partner **8** helpmate **10** better half

spout 3 jet, lip **4** beak, flow, go on, gush, nose, pipe, rant, spew, tube, vent, well **5** eject, erupt, expel, exude, issue, mouth, shoot, snout, spray, spurt, surge, vomit **6** nozzle, outlet, sluice, squirt, stream, trough **7** bluster, carry on, channel, conduit, pour out **8** disgorge, fountain, harangue **9** discharge, hold forth **10** waterspout **11** pontificate **12** emit forcibly **14** speak pompously

sprawl 4 flop, lean, loll, wind **5** slump **6** branch, extend, lounge, slouch **7** gush out, meander, recline **8** languish, reach out, straggle **9** spread out **10** stretch out **11** spread-eagle

spray 4 coat, mist, posy, twig **5** bough, burst, shoot, sprig, treat, vapor **6** dampen, nozzle, shower, splash, switch, volley **7** atomize, barrage, blossom, bouquet, drizzle, moisten, nosegay, scatter, spatter, sprayer, syringe **8** atomizer, disperse, droplets, moisture, sprinkle **9** discharge, fusillade, sprinkler, vaporizer

spread 3 air, lay **4** area, cast, coat, open, pave, shed, span, vent **5** apply, bruit, cloak, cover, feast, field, issue, range, reach, scope, smear, spray, story, strew, sweep, table, tract, width **6** bedaub, beshed, blazon, extend, extent, herald, length, notice, repeat, report, unfold, unfurl **7** account, advance, article, banquet, besmear, bestrew, breadth, circuit, compass, declare, diffuse, divulge, expanse, overlay, overrun, pervade, plaster, publish, radiate, scatter, spatter, stretch, suffuse, trumpet, untwine, write-up **8** announce, coverage, disperse, distance, increase, permeate, proclaim, sprinkle **9** broadcast, circulate, diffusion, expansion, extension, make known, penetrate, pervasion, propagate, publicize, radiation, spreading, suffusion, ventilate **10** dispersion, distribute, make public, permeation, promulgate, stretch out **11** communicate, disseminate, noise abroad, proliferate **13** amplification, dissemination, proliferation

spread out 5 broad, widen **6** expand, extend **7** broaden, diffuse, enlarge, radiate, stretch **8** expanded, extended, open wide **9** dispersed, outspread, scattered **10** distribute, unhampered

11 unconfirmed **12** unrestricted **14** unconcentrated

spree 4 bout, orgy, toot **5** binge, drunk, fling, revel **6** bender **7** carouse, debauch, revelry, splurge, wassail **8** carousal **9** bacchanal **10** saturnalia

sprightliness 8 buoyancy, spryness, vivacity **9** animation, briskness **10** breeziness, liveliness **16** lightheartedness

sprightly 3 gay **4** keen, spry **5** agile, alive, brisk, jolly, merry **6** active, blithe, breezy, cheery, jaunty, jovial, lively, nimble **7** buoyant, chipper, dashing, dynamic, playful **8** animated, cheerful, spirited, sportive **9** energetic, vivacious **10** blithesome, frolicsome **12** lighthearted

spring 3 hop, jet, pop, spa **4** come, dart, flow, gush, jump, kick, leap, loom, pool, pour, rise, rush, stem, well **5** arise, baths, begin, bound, caper, ensue, fount, issue, lunge, shoot, spout, spurt, start, surge, vault **6** appear, bounce, derive, gambol, recoil, reflex, result, sprout, stream **7** burgeon, crop out, descend, emanate, proceed, release, shoot up, start up, stretch, trigger **8** buoyancy, commence, fountain, mushroom **9** come forth, entrechat, germinate, originate, saltation, waterhole **10** break forth, burst forth, elasticity, resiliency **11** flexibility
    goddess of: **4** Hebe **5** Venus

spring back 6 bounce, recoil **7** rebound **8** ricochet

spring flowers
    goddess of: **6** Thallo

springlike 4 mild, soft, warm **5** balmy

springs
    god of: **4** Fons **6** Palici
    goddess of: **4** Idun **5** Idura, Ithun **6** Ithunn

spring up 4 grow, rise **5** arise, occur, pop up **6** crop up, emerge, happen, sprout **9** originate **10** burst forth

springy 6 bouncy, spongy, supple **7** elastic **9** resilient **10** rebounding

sprinkle 4 dash, dust, rain **5** spray, strew, water **6** powder, shower, splash, spread, squirt **7** bestrew, diffuse, drizzle, moisten, scatter, spatter **8** splatter

sprinkling 4 dash, drop, hint **5** pinch, touch **7** droplet, minimum, modicum, soupcon **8** sprinkle **10** smattering

sprint 3 run **4** dart, dash, kick, race, rush, tear, whiz **5** burst, shoot, spurt, whisk **7** scamper

sprit 3 bar **4** spar **8** crossbar **10** crosspiece

sprite 3 elf **5** fairy, pixie **10** leprechaun

sprout 3 bud, wax **4** grow **5** bloom, shoot, sprig **6** come up, flower,

721

squash

spread, thrive **7** blossom, burgeon **8** multiply, offshoot, put forth, spring up **9** germinate, outgrowth

spruce 4 chic, neat, tidy, trim **5** kempt, natty, sharp, smart **6** dapper **7** conifer, elegant **9** evergreen, shipshape **11** well-groomed **12** spick-and-span
French: 6 soigne

spruce 5 Picea
varieties: 3 bog, cat, red **4** blue **5** black, Hondo, Sitka, snake, white, Yeddo **6** double, Norway **7** Alberta, big-cone, Finnish, hemlock **8** Colorado, Sakhalin, Siberian **9** Himalayan, tiger-tail **10** Black Hills **12** Colorado blue, Japanese bush

spry 4 deft, hale **5** agile, brisk, quick **6** active, frisky, hearty, jaunty, lively, nimble, supple **7** buoyant, chipper, playful **8** animated, spirited, sportive, vigorous **9** energetic, sprightly, vivacious **11** lightfooted

spunk 4 fire, grit, guts, salt, sand **5** heart, nerve, pluck **6** daring, ginger, mettle, pepper, spirit **7** bravery, courage **8** backbone, boldness, gumption **10** feistiness

spur 3 arm, leg **4** fork, goad, prod, whet, whip, wing **5** prick **6** branch, feeder, fillip, hasten, motive, siding **7** impetus, impulse **8** excitant, stimulus **9** boot spike, encourage, incentive, stimulant, stimulate, tributary **10** incitement, inducement **11** instigation, provocation, stimulation **13** encouragement

spurge 9 Euphorbia **11** Pachysandra
varieties: 5 caper, leafy, melon **6** ipecac, myrtle, tramp's **7** cypress, mottled, seaside, slipper **8** fiddler's, Japanese **9** Allegheny, flowering **10** Indian tree

spurious 4 fake, mock, sham **5** bogus, false, phony **6** faulty, forged, hollow **7** feigned, unsound **8** specious **9** imitation, simulated **10** fallacious, fraudulent, not genuine **11** counterfeit, make-believe, unauthentic **12** illegitimate

spurn 4 mock, snub **5** flout, repel, scorn **6** rebuff, refuse, reject, slight **7** condemn, decline, disdain, dismiss, repulse, scoff at, sneer at **8** turn down **9** cast aside, disparage, repudiate **12** coldshoulder, look down upon **16** turn up one's nose at

spur-of-the-moment 5 ad-lib **7** offhand **9** extempore, impromptu **10** improvised, unprepared **11** extemporary, spontaneous, unrehearsed **14** extemporaneous, unpremeditated

spurt 3 jet **4** dart, dash, emit, flow, gush, gust, rush, tear, whiz **5** burst, flash, issue, lunge, scoot, shoot, speed, spout, spray, surge **6** access, spring, sprint, squirt, stream **7** pour out **8** disgorge, ejection, eruption,

fountain, outbreak, outburst **9** discharge, explosion, spring out **10** outpouring

spy 3 pry, see **4** find, peep, spot, view **5** scout, sight, snoop **6** behold, descry, detect, notice, shadow **7** discern, glimpse, make out, observe **8** discover, informer, Mata Hari, perceive, saboteur **9** keep watch, operative, recognize **11** reconnoiter, secret agent **12** catch sight of **13** undercover man, watch secretly **14** espionage agent, fifth columnist **16** agent provocateur **17** intelligence agent
famous: 4 Abel, Hale **5** Andre, Caleb, Pitts **6** Arnold, Dulles, Philby, Powers, Smiley **8** Mata Hari **9** James Bond, Nicholson, Philbrick, Pinkerton, Rosenberg

Spy, The
author: 19 James Fenimore Cooper

Spy Who Came In from the Cold, The
director: 10 Martin Ritt
based on novel by: 11 John LeCarre
cast: 11 Claire Bloom, Oskar Werner **12** Peter Van Eyck **13** Richard Burton

Spy Who Loved Me, The
author: 10 Ian Fleming
director: 12 Lewis Gilbert
cast: 10 Bernard Lee (M), Roger Moore (James Bond) **11** Barbara Bach, Curt Jurgens (Stromberg), Richard Kiel (Jaws)

squabble 3 row, war **4** spat, tiff **5** argue, brawl, clash, fight, run-in, scrap, set-to, words **6** battle, bicker, differ **7** contend, contest, dispute, quarrel, wrangle **8** argument **9** have words, lock horns **10** bandy words, contention, difference, dissension **11** altercation, controversy **12** disagreement

squadron 5 fleet **6** armada **8** flotilla **9** naval unit **10** escadrille **11** cavalry unit **12** military unit

squalid 4 foul, mean **5** dirty, nasty **6** abject, filthy, horrid, rotten, shabby, sloppy, sordid **7** decayed, reeking, run-down, unclean **8** battered, degraded, slovenly, wretched **9** miserable **10** broken-down, disheveled, ramshackle, slatternly, tumbledown **11** dilapidated **12** deteriorated

squalor 4 dirt **5** filth **6** misery **7** neglect, poverty **8** foulness, meanness, ugliness **9** dinginess, dirtiness, nastiness, seediness **10** abjectness, grubbiness, sordidness **11** squalidness, uncleanness **12** wretchedness **13** uncleanliness

squander 4 blow **5** spend, waste **6** lavish, misuse **7** consume, deplete, exhaust **8** misspend **9** dissipate, throw away **10** run through **11** fritter away **14** spend like water

squanderer 6 waster **7** wastrel **8**

prodigal **10** dissipater, profligate **11** spendthrift

squandering 7 wasting **8** prodigal, wasteful **9** imprudent **10** profligate **11** dissipating, extravagant, improvident, spendthrift **12** overspending, throwing away **14** frittering away **17** spending like water

square 3 box, fit **4** even, fogy, heal, hick, jerk, jibe, just, mend, park, prig **5** agree, align, blend, block, close, equal, green, match, place, plane, plaza, prude, tally **6** accord, adjust, candid, circus, cohere, common, concur, even up, fall in, honest, pay off, settle, smooth **7** arrange, balance, clear up, compose, conform, even out, flatten, mediate, patch up, rectify, resolve **8** block out, cornball, make even, quadrate, set right, settle up, truthful **9** arbitrate, discharge, equitable, harmonize, liquidate, make level, reconcile **10** clodhopper, correspond, quadrangle, straighten **11** marketplace **12** apple knocker, conservative **13** quadrilateral, stick-in-the- mud **15** straightforward
type: 1 T **3** try **11** combination

Square
character in: 8 Tom Jones
author: 8 Fielding

Square
constellation of: 5 Norma

square centimeter
abbreviation: 4 sq cm

square decimeter
abbreviation: 4 sq dm

square dekameter
abbreviation: 5 sq dam

square foot
abbreviation: 4 sq ft

square hectometer
abbreviation: 4 sq hm

square inch
abbreviation: 4 sq in

square kilometer
abbreviation: 4 sq km

square meter
abbreviation: 3 sq m

square mile
abbreviation: 4 sq mi

square millimeter
abbreviation: 4 sq mm

square rod
abbreviation: 4 sq rd

square yard
abbreviation: 4 sq yd

squash 3 jam **4** cram, mash, pulp **5** crowd, crush, level, quash, quell, smash, upset **6** dispel, squish **7** compact, destroy, flatten, put down, ram down, repress, squeeze, squelch, trample **8** compress, suppress **9** dissipate, overthrow, prostrate, undermine **10** annihilate, obliterate **11** concentrate

squash 9 Cucurbita
  varieties: 4 bush 5 acorn 6 autumn, banana, summer, turban, winter 7 Hubbard, scallop 8 pattypan, zucchini 9 cocozelle, crookneck 12 Boston marrow 13 sweet dumpling 15 Canada crookneck, summer crookneck, winter crookneck

squat 5 cower, dumpy, dwell, kneel, pudgy 6 chunky, cringe, crouch, encamp, hunker, lie low, locate, move in, shrink, square, stocky, stubby, stumpy 8 thickset

squawk 5 blare, croak, gripe 6 scream, squall 7 grumble, protest, screech 8 complain

squeak 3 cry 4 peep, yelp 5 cheep, chirp, creak, grate 6 shriek, shrill, squeal 7 screech

squeal 3 cry 4 bawl, blab, fink, peep, sing, wail, yell, yelp 5 cheep, whine 6 inform, scream, shriek, shrill, squeak 7 screech

squealer 3 pig, rat 4 fink 6 canary, piglet, snitch 7 stoolie, tattler, traitor 8 informer 10 tattletale 11 stool pigeon 12 blabbermouth

squeamish 3 coy 4 prim, sick 5 fussy 6 demure, modest, proper, queasy 7 finical, finicky, mincing, prudish, sickish 8 delicate, nauseous, priggish, qualmish 9 finicking 10 fastidious 11 puritanical, straitlaced 13 sanctimonious

Squeers, Wackford
  character in: 16 Nicholas Nickleby
  author: 7 Dickens

squeeze 3 hug, jam, pry, ram 4 butt, cram, edge, grip, hold, pack, push 5 clasp, cramp, crowd, drive, elbow, grasp, press, shove, stuff, wedge, wrest, wring 6 clutch, coerce, compel, defile, elicit, extort, jostle, thrust, wrench 7 compact, draw out, embrace, extract, passage, pull out, tear out 8 compress, crowding, crushing, force out, pinching, press out, pressure, shoulder, withdraw 9 extricate, narrowing, stricture 10 bottleneck 11 compression, concentrate, consolidate 12 constriction

squelch 4 hush 5 abort, crush, quash, quell, quiet, smash 6 retort, squash 7 put down, riposte, silence 8 silencer, suppress

squire 4 date, take 5 court 6 attend, escort 7 consort, gallant, planter 8 cavalier, chaperon 9 accompany, attendant, boyfriend, chauffeur, companion, landowner 14 lord of the manor 16 country gentleman

Squire
  character in: 18 The Canterbury Tales
  author: 7 Chaucer

squirm 4 bend, jerk, toss, turn 5 pitch, shift, smart, sweat, twist, wince 6 blench, fidget, flinch, shrink, twitch, wiggle, writhe 7 agonize, contort, wriggle 8 flounder

squirt 3 jet 4 dash, gush, punk, runt 5 piker, shoot, spout, spray, spurt 6 shower, splash, stream 7 spatter 8 sprinkle 9 discharge, pipsqueak 10 besprinkle

Sri Lanka
  other name: 6 Ceylon 8 Serendib 9 Taprobane
  capital/largest city: 7 Colombo
    ancient capital: 11 Polonnaruwa 12 Anuradhapura
  others: 3 Uva 5 Galle, Kandy 6 Jaffna, Mannar, Matale, Matara 7 Badulla, Kegalle, Negombo 8 Kalutara, Mankulem, Moratuwa, Puttalam 9 Ratnapura 10 Batticaloa, Mullaitivu 11 Ambalangoda, Trincomalee
  division: 8 Dambulla, Sri Lanka 9 Taprobane
  measure: 4 para, seer 5 parah 6 amunam, parrah
  monetary unit: 4 cent 5 rupee
  island: 5 Delft 6 Mannar 8 Sri Lanka
  mountain: 5 Pedro 7 Sri Pada 9 Adam's Peak
  highest point: 14 Pidurutalagala
  river: 4 Kala 6 Deduru, Gal Ova 8 Aruvi Aru 9 Deburu Ova 11 Kelani Ganga 13 Mahaweli Ganga
  sea: 6 Indian
  physical feature:
    bay: 6 Bengal 8 Koddiyar
    falls: 8 Lazapana
    gulf: 6 Mannar
    peninsula: 6 Jaffna
    plateau: 6 Hatton
    strait: 4 Palk
  people: 5 Malay, Tamil, Vedda 6 Veddah, Weddah 7 Burgher, Mahinda, Malabar 8 Eurasian 9 Cingalese, Dravidian, Sinhalese 10 Singhalese
    leader: 11 Jayawardene 12 Bandaranaike
    ruler: 5 Dutch 7 British, Chinese 10 Portuguese
  language: 4 Pali 5 Tamil 7 English 9 Sinhalese
  religion: 5 Hindu, Islam 8 Buddhism
  place:
    fortress: 8 Sigiriya
    gardens: 8 Hakgalle 10 Peradiniya
    national park: 6 Ruhuna 8 Wilpattu
    temple: 5 Tooth 6 Gal Oya 7 Kelanya 8 Runaweli 9 Ruanvelli 10 Dankahlaka 12 Asokharamaya
  feature:
    animal: 5 loris 12 wild elephant
    clothing: 4 sari 5 camba 6 sarong 7 cambaya 8 sherwani
    dancer: 7 Kandyan
    drama: 5 kolam 7 nadagam
    festival: 8 Perahera
    shrine: 6 dagoba
    tree: 4 doon, hora, palu, tala 5 domba, ebony 7 talipot 8 halmilla, ironwood 9 satinwood 11 allaeanthus 12 shimohabodhi

SS-GB
  author: 11 Len Deighton
SS troops, chief of 12 Reichsfuhrer

stab 2 go 3 cut, jab, try 4 ache, bite, gash, gore, hurt, pain, pang, pass, shot, spit 5 essay, gouge, knife, lance, lunge, prick, qualm, slash, spear, spike, stick, sting, trial, wound 6 cleave, dagger, effort, impale, pierce, shiver, stroke, thrill, thrust, twinge 7 attempt, bayonet 8 endeavor, lacerate, transfix 10 laceration, run through

stability 5 poise 6 aplomb, fixity 7 balance 8 evenness, firmness, security, solidity 9 constancy, fixedness, solidness, soundness 10 continuity, durability, permanence, stableness, steadiness, sturdiness 11 abidingness, equilibrium, reliability 13 steadfastness 14 changelessness 16 unchangeableness

stabilize 7 balance 8 hold firm, make firm 10 hold steady, make steady

stabilizer 7 balance, ballast 8 additive 9 equipoise, gyroscope 10 ballasting 12 airplane part 14 counterbalance

stable 4 barn, byre, even, firm, mews, safe, true 5 fixed, loyal, solid, sound 6 moored, secure, steady, sturdy 7 abiding, durable, staunch, uniform 8 anchored, constant, cowhouse, cowshed, enduring, faithful, reliable, resolute, stalwart 9 immovable, steadfast 10 dependable, persisting, stationary, unchanging, unwavering 11 established, unfaltering 12 indissoluble, unchangeable

Stabler, Ken
  nickname: 8 the Snake
  sport: 8 football
  position: 11 quarterback
  team: 13 Houston Oilers 14 Oakland Raiders

staccato
  music: 12 disconnected 16 each note separate

stack 4 bank, flue, heap, load, lump, mass, pile, rick 5 amass, batch, bunch, clump, hoard, mound, sheaf 6 bundle, funnel, gather 7 chimney 8 assemble, mountain 9 amassment 10 accumulate 11 aggregation 12 accumulation

Stack, Robert
  born: 12 Los Angeles CA
  roles: 9 Eliot Ness 13 Name of the Game 15 The Untouchables 16 Written on the Wind 19 The High and the Mighty 24 The Bullfighter and the Lady

Stackpole, Henrietta
  character in: 18 The Portrait of a Lady
  author: 5 James

Stacte 5 spice

stadium 4 bowl, park 5 arena, field, stade 6 circus 8 ballpark, coliseum 9 palaestra 10 hippodrome 12 amphitheater

Stael, Madame de
  author of: 7 Corinne 8 Delphine 9 On Germany 35 The Influence of Literature upon Society

staff 3 bat, man, rod 4 cane, crew, help, pole, team, tend, wand, work 5 cadre, force, group, stave, stick 6 crutch, cudgel, manage 7 retinue, scepter, service, support 8 advisors, bludgeon, flagpole 9 billy club, employees, flagstaff, personnel 10 alpenstock, assistants, shillelagh 12 walking stick

staff member 4 aide 6 worker 8 employee

stage 3 act 4 dais, play, spot, step 5 arena, drama, grade, level, phase, put on, sight, stump 6 acting, locale, period, podium, pulpit 7 perform, present, produce, rostrum, setting, show biz, soapbox, theater 8 bearings, locality, location, position, scaffold 9 dramatize, the boards

Stagecoach
  director: 8 John Ford
  cast: 9 John Wayne 10 Andy Devine 11 Louise Platt 12 Claire Trevor 13 John Carradine 14 George Bancroft, Thomas Mitchell
  Oscar for: 15 supporting actor (Mitchell)

stagecraft 5 drama 7 theater 9 theatrics 10 dramaturgy 11 thespianism 12 dramatic arts

Stage Door
  author: 10 Edna Ferber 14 George S Kaufman
  director: 13 Gregory La Cava
  cast: 11 Andrea Leeds, Gail Patrick 12 Ginger Rogers 13 Adolphe Menjou 16 Katharine Hepburn

stage setting
  French: 11 mise en scene

stagger 3 jar 4 jolt, reel, stun, sway 5 amaze, lurch, shake, shock, waver 6 hobble, totter, wobble 7 astound, blunder, nonplus, overlap, shamble, startle, stumble, stupefy 8 astonish, bewilder, bowl over, confound, flounder, unsettle 9 alternate, dumbfound, give a turn, overwhelm, spread out 10 disconcert, knock silly, strike dumb 11 cause to reel, cause to sway, consternate, flabbergast, take in turns 12 make unsteady 15 throw off balance

staggering 7 amazing 8 shocking, stunning 9 startling 10 astounding 11 astonishing 12 breathtaking

stagnant 4 dead, dull, foul, lazy, slow 5 close, inert, quiet, slimy, stale, still 6 filthy, leaden, putrid, static, supine, torpid 7 dormant, dronish, languid, tainted 8 inactive, lifeless, listless, polluted, sluggish, standing 9 lethargic, ponderous, putrefied, quiescent 10 monotonous, motionless, not flowing, not running, stationary, unstirring, vegetative 13 uncirculating

stagnate 7 go to pot, lie idle, putrefy 8 go to seed, lie still, vegetate 10 stand still 11 cease to flow, deteriorate, stop growing 14 become inactive, become polluted, become sluggish

stagy 5 phony 8 affected, mannered 9 unnatural 10 artificial, factitious, theatrical

staid 5 grave, quiet, sober, stiff 6 decent, demure, proper, sedate, seemly, solemn, somber 7 earnest, prudish, serious, settled, subdued 8 decorous, priggish, reserved 9 dignified 10 complacent 15 undemonstrative

stain 3 dye, mar 4 blot, daub, flaw, foul, mark, ruin, slur, soil, spot, tint 5 brand, color, dirty, grime, libel, patch, shame, smear, speck, spoil, sully, taint 6 befoul, blotch, debase, defile, impair, malign, smirch, smudge, stigma, vilify 7 blacken, blemish, pigment, slander, splotch, subvert, tarnish 8 besmirch, coloring, discolor, disgrace, dishonor, dyestuff, tincture 9 denigrate, discredit, disparage, undermine 10 imputation, stigmatize 13 discoloration

stainless 5 clean, moral 6 chaste, decent 8 spotless, unsoiled 9 exemplary, unspotted, unsullied, untainted 11 unblemished

Stairway to Heaven
  director: 13 Michael Powell 17 Emeric Pressburger
  cast: 9 Kim Hunter 10 David Niven 12 Roger Livesey 13 Raymond Massey
  original title: 21 A Matter of Life and Death

stake 3 bar, bet, peg, pot, rod 4 ante, back, grab, haul, lash, loot, moor, pale, pawn, pile, play, pole, post, prop, risk, stay, take 5 booty, brace, hitch, kitty, prize, purse, share, spike, stand, stick, treat, wager 6 chance, column, define, fasten, fetter, hazard, hold up, marker, picket, pillar, reward, secure, spoils, tether 7 delimit, finance, jackpot, mark off, mark out, outline, peg down, returns, sponsor, support, trammel, venture 8 interest, make fast, pickings, standard, winnings 9 delineate, demarcate, speculate, subsidize 10 investment, jeopardize, underwrite 11 involvement, speculation

Stalag 17
  director: 11 Billy Wilder
  cast: 9 Don Taylor 11 Peter Graves 12 Neville Brand 13 Harvey Lem-beck, Otto Preminger, Richard Erdman, Robert Strauss, William Holden
  Oscar for: 5 actor (Holden)

stale 4 dull, flat 5 banal, close, fusty, musty, trite, vapid 6 common 7 humdrum, insipid, prosaic, tedious, worn-out 8 mediocre, not fresh, ordinary, stagnant, unvaried 9 hackneyed, savorless, tasteless 10 monotonous, pedestrian, threadbare 11 commonplace 13 unimaginative, uninteresting

stalemate 3 tie 4 draw, halt 7 dead end, impasse 8 blockage, cul-de-sac, dead heat, deadlock, standoff 10 standstill

stalk 4 hunt, lurk, stem 5 haunt, march, prowl, shaft, spire, stamp, steal, stomp, strut, track, tramp, trunk 6 column, menance, stride 7 pedicel, pervade, swagger 8 hang over, threaten 9 creep up on, go through, sneak up on

stall 3 box, pen 4 cell, coop, halt, shed, shop, stop 5 block, booth, check, delay, kiosk, stand 6 arcade, arrest, hobble, impede, pull up, put off 7 bed down, confine, cubicle, disable, trammel 8 obstruct, paralyze, postpone 9 be evasive, interrupt, stop short, temporize 10 equivocate 11 compartment, play for time, stop running 12 incapacitate 13 orchestra seat

Stallone, Sylvester
  born: 9 New York NY
  nickname: 3 Sly
  roles: 4 FIST 5 Rambo, Rocky (Oscar) 7 Copland 10 First Blood, Judge Dredd, Rhinestone 11 Cliffhanger 18 The Lords of Flatbush

stalwart 4 bold, firm, hale 5 beefy, brave, hardy, hefty, husky, manly, sound 6 brawny, gritty, heroic, mighty, plucky, robust, rugged, spunky, stable, strong, sturdy 7 gallant, staunch, valiant 8 constant, intrepid, muscular, powerful, resolute, valorous, vigorous 9 steadfast, strapping, unbending, undaunted 10 able-bodied, courageous, persistent, unflagging, unshakable, unswerving, unwavering, unyielding 11 indomitable, lionhearted, undeviating, unfaltering, unflinching, unshrinking 12 intransigent, stouthearted, strong-willed 14 uncompromising

stamina 4 pith 5 vigor 6 energy 8 vitality 9 endurance, hardiness, stoutness 10 ruggedness, sturdiness 12 perseverance, staying power

stammer 6 falter, fumble, mumble 7 sputter, stumble, stutter 8 splutter 9 hem and haw

stamp
  block: 4 pane
  collecting: 9 philately
  first: 10 Penny Black
    issued by: 12 Great Britain

inscribed with: 8 One Penny
picture of: 13 Queen Victoria
first-day hand stamper: 6 cachet
hole measurer: 16 perforation gauge
mounting paper: 5 hinge
not perforated: 11 imperforate
paper design: 9 watermark
rolls: 4 coil
tear holes: 12 perforations
tear slit: 8 roulette
unseparated group: 5 block
used mark: 8 postmark **12** cancellation

stamp, stamp out 2 OK **3** die, tag **4** cast, kind, make, mark, mint, mold, seal, sort, type **5** brand, breed, clump, crush, erase, genre, label, march, order, print, pound, punch, quash, smash, stalk, stomp, strut, thump, tramp **6** banish, betray, emblem, expose, matrix, nature, put out, reveal, rub out, signet, step on, strain, stride, trudge **7** abolish, blot out, display, engrave, exhibit, impress, imprint, put down, squelch, trample, variety, voucher **8** get rid of, hallmark, identify, inscribe, intaglio, manifest, suppress, typecast **9** character, eliminate, engraving, eradicate, personify, signature, trademark **10** annihilate, do away with, extinguish, imprimatur, stigmatize, validation **11** attestation, certificate, demonstrate, distinguish, endorsement, exterminate, **12** characterize, official mark, ratification **13** certification **14** authentication, characteristic, identification

stampede 4 bolt, dash, flee, race, rout, rush **5** chaos, flood, panic **6** engulf **7** overrun, retreat, scatter **8** inundate **10** take flight **11** crowd around, pandemonium **12** beat a retreat
French: 12 sauve qui peut

stanchion 4 post, prop, stay **5** brace, strut **7** support, upright

stand 2 be **3** put, set **4** draw, face, hold, last, move, rank, rear, rest, rise, stay, step, take, tent **5** abide, argue, booth, brook, erect, exist, get up, hoist, honor, kiosk, mount, place, put up, raise, shift, stall, treat **6** bear up, effort, endure, obtain, pay for, policy, remain, remove, stance, suffer, uphold **7** carry on, commend, counter, defense, endorse, finance, hold out, opinion, persist, posture, prevail, provide, stick up, stomach, support, survive, sustain, undergo, weather **8** advocate, be placed, champion, continue, pavilion, position, sanction, submit to, tolerate **9** be located, be present, be upright, persevere, put up with, sentiment, undertake, viewpoint **10** resistance, set upright **11** be permanent, countenance, disposition, point of view **13** remain in force, take a position

Stand, The
author: 11 Stephen King

standard 3 leg **4** base, flag, foot, jack, post **5** basic, canon, guide, ideal, stock, usual **6** banner, column, common, ensign, normal, pillar **7** measure, pennant, regular, support, typical, upright **8** accepted, ordinary, streamer **9** criterion, customary, guideline, principle, prototype, stanchion, universal, yardstick **10** foundation, touchstone **11** requirement **13** specification

stand behind 4 back **7** endorse, support **8** champion, vouch for **9** recommend

standby 6 backup **9** alternate, available **10** substitute, understudy **11** old reliable **12** tried-and-true

stand by 4 keep **5** cling **6** adhere, be true, defend, hold to, keep to **7** be loyal, stick by **8** cleave to, maintain **10** be constant, be faithful, stick up for

stand fast 4 hold **6** resist **8** stand pat

stand for 4 bear **5** abide, favor, stand **6** embody **7** signify **8** advocate, submit to, tolerate **9** personify, put up with, represent, symbolize

stand-in 3 sub **5** agent, proxy **6** backup, deputy, double, fill-in, second **9** alternate, assistant, surrogate **10** substitute, understudy **11** pinch hitter, replacement

standing 3 age **4** life, rank, term, time **5** erect, fixed, grade, inert, order, place, still **6** at rest, static, status, tenure **7** dormant, footing, lasting, station, upended, upright **8** duration, inactive, position, stagnant, vertical **9** immovable, permanent, perpetual, quiescent, renewable **10** continuing, importance, motionless, reputation, stationary, unstirring **11** continuance **13** perpendicular

standoff 7 impasse **8** deadlock

standoffish 4 cool **5** aloof **6** formal, remote **7** distant, haughty **8** detached, reserved, solitary, taciturn **9** reclusive, withdrawn **10** antisocial, restrained, unfriendly, unsociable **12** inaccessible, misanthropic, unresponsive **14** unapproachable **15** uncommunicative, uncompanionable

standpoint 4 side **5** angle, slant **6** aspect **9** viewpoint **11** point of view

standstill 3 end **4** halt, stop **5** pause **6** hiatus **7** dead end, impasse **8** abeyance, deadlock, dead stop, full stop **9** breakdown, cessation, stalemate **10** suspension **11** termination **14** discontinuance

stand up for 4 back **5** boost **6** defend **7** further, promote, support **8** advocate, champion

stand up to 4 defy, face **5** brave **6** resist **8** confront **9** challenge

Stant, Charlotte
character in: 13 The Golden Bowl
author: 5 James

Stan the Man
nickname of: 10 Stan Musial

Stanton, Adam
character in: 14 All the King's Men
author: 6 Warren

Stanwyck, Barbara
real name: 11 Ruby Stevens
born: 10 Brooklyn NY
husband: 8 Frank Fay **12** Robert Taylor
roles: 9 Big Valley, The Colbys **10** Ball of Fire, The Lady Eve **11** Meet John Doe **12** Stella Dallas **15** Double Indemnity **16** Sorry Wrong Number **20** Cattle Queen of Montana **22** Christmas in Connecticut

staple 3 key **4** main **5** basic, chief, major, prime, vital **6** leader **7** feature, primary, product **8** resource, vendible **9** commodity, essential, necessary **11** fundamental, raw material **13** indispensable

Stapleton, Jean
real name: 12 Jeanne Murray
born: 9 New York NY
roles: 7 Dingbat **11** Edith Bunker **14** All in the Family

Stapleton, Maureen
born: 6 Troy NY
roles: 7 Airport **9** Interiors **12** Lonelyhearts **13** The Rose Tattoo **18** A View from the Bridge

star, stars 3 god, sun, VIP **4** diva, fate, hero, idol, lead, lion, name **5** comet, excel, giant, great, omens, shine **6** big wig, do well, galaxy, meteor, nebula, planet **7** destiny, feature, fortune, goddess, heroine, notable, soloist, starlet, succeed, top draw **8** asteroid, cynosure, eminence, immortal, luminary, mainstay, Milky Way, portents, showcase, stand out, virtuoso **9** celebrity, headliner, meteoroid, principal, satellite, top banana **10** prima donna **11** All-American, drawing card, play the lead, protagonist **12** famous person, gain approval, heavenly body **13** celestial body, constellation **14** main attraction, predestination, prima ballerina
brightest: 6 Sirius
brightness measure: 9 magnitude **10** luminosity
color: 3 red **4** blue **5** black, white **6** orange, yellow
distance measure: 6 parsec **9** light year
double star: 6 binary
exploding star: 4 nova **9** supernova
French: 6 etoile
name: 4 Mira, Ross, Vega, Wolf **5** Cygni, Deneb, Rigel, Spica **6** Altair, Luyten, Pollux **7** Antares, Canopus, Capella, Lalande, Polaris, Procyon,

Regulus, Tau Ceti **8** Achernar, Arcturus, Barnard's, Lacaille, Pleiades **9** Aldebaran, Fomalhaut **10** Beta Crucis, Betelgeuse **11** Delta Cephei, Epsilon Indi, Groombridge **12** Beta Centauri **14** Epsilon Eridani
nearest: 13 Alpha Centauri
position/motion: 7 azimuth **8** parallax **11** declination
type: 5 dwarf, giant **6** pulsar **7** cluster, neutron **8** variable **9** black hole, collapsed

Starbuck
character in: 8 Moby Dick
author: 8 Melville

starch 5 vigor **6** sizing **8** backbone, gumption **10** stiffening

starched 5 crisp, sized, stiff **7** starchy **9** stiffened

starchy 5 rigid, stiff **6** formal, proper **7** correct **10** meticulous

stare 3 eye **4** gape, gawk, gaze, ogle, peep, peer **5** glare, lower, watch **6** gaping, glower, goggle, ogling, regard **7** staring **8** once-over, scrutiny **9** fixed look **10** inspection, rubberneck

stare at 3 eye **4** ogle **5** watch **6** behold, gaze at, look at, regard **7** inspect, observe **10** scrutinize **11** contemplate

Star Is Born, A
director:
1937 version: 14 William Wellman
1954 version: 11 George Cukor
1976 version: 12 Frank Pierson
cast:
1937 version: 11 Janet Gaynor **13** Adolphe Menjou, Frederic March
1954 version: 10 Jack Carson, James Mason **11** Judy Garland **15** Charles Bickford
1976 version: 9 Gary Busey **11** Oliver Clark **15** Barbra Streisand **17** Kris Kristofferson
Oscar for:
1937 version: 5 story
song:
1954 version: 17 The Man That Got Away

stark 4 bare, bold, cold, grim, pure **5** bleak, blunt, clean, empty, fully, gross, harsh, naked, plain, plumb, quite, sheer, total, utter **6** arrant, barren, chaste, patent, severe, simple, vacant, wholly **7** austere, evident, forlorn, glaring, obvious, staring, utterly **8** absolute, complete, deserted, desolate, entirely, flagrant, forsaken, outright, palpable **9** abandoned, downright, out-and-out, unadorned, unalloyed, veritable **10** absolutely, altogether, completely, consummate **11** conspicuous, unmitigated **12** unmistakable

Stark, Johannes
field: 7 physics
nationality: 6 German

described: 11 Stark Effect **14** dispersed light
awarded: 10 Nobel Prize

Stark, Willie
character in: 14 All the King's Men
author: 6 Warren

starlet 7 actress, ingenue **9** bit player, pinup girl

Starsky and Hutch
character: 5 Hutch (Ken Hutchinson) **7** (Dave) Starsky **9** Huggy Bear **11** (Capt) Harold Dobey
cast: 9 David Soul **13** Antonio Fargas **14** Bernie Hamilton **17** Paul Michael Glaser
car: 10 Ford Torino

start 3 aid, shy **4** dawn, drop, edge, form, gush, jerk, jolt, jump, lead, leap, odds, rush, turn **5** beget, begin, birth, blink, bound, eject, erupt, evict, flush, forge, found, issue, leave, leg up, onset, rouse, set up, shoot, spasm, spurt, wince **6** blench, broach, chance, create, depart, embark, emerge, fall to, father, flinch, ignite, kindle, launch, origin, outset, pop out, propel, recoil, set off, set out, spring, take up, twitch **7** advance, backing, disturb, genesis, make off, opening, push off, scatter, set sail, support, take off, turn out, usher in **8** advocacy, commence, creation, dis place, embark on, engender, generate, get going, initiate, organize, priority, set about, set going, touch off **9** advantage, beginning, establish, fabricate, first step, inception, institute, introduce, originate, propagate, undertake, venture on **10** assistance, break forth, bring about, buckle down, burst forth, give rise to, inaugurate, initiation, plunge into, sally forth, venture out **11** break ground, put in motion, set in action **12** commencement, inauguration, introduction **14** set in operation

starting point 5 onset, start **8** zero hour **9** beginning
Latin: 12 terminus a quo

startle 3 jar **4** faze **5** alarm, scare, shake, shock, upset **7** perturb, unnerve **8** disquiet, frighten, surprise, unsettle **9** give a turn **10** discompose, disconcert, intimidate

Star Trek
character: 4 Sulu **5** Uhura **6** Scotty (Engineer Montgomery Scott), (Ensign Pavel) Chekov **7** Mr Spock **10** (Captain) James T Kirk, (Yeoman) Janice Rand **12** (Dr) Leonard McCoy **15** (Nurse) Christine Chapel
cast: 11 George Takei, James Doohan **12** Leonard Nimoy, Majel Barrett, Walter Koenig **13** DeForest Kelly **14** William Shatner **15** Grace Lee Whitney, Nichelle Nichols
ship: 10 (USS) Enterprise
aliens: 8 Klingons, Romulans

Spock's planet: 6 Vulcan
pet: 7 tribble

starve 3 yen **4** burn, deny, fast, gasp, long, lust, pine **5** crave, raven, yearn **6** aspire, cut off, famish, hunger, refuse, thirst **7** deprive **8** be hungry, go hungry, languish

Star Wars
director: 11 George Lucas
cast: 10 Kenny Baker, Mark Hamill (Luke Skywalker) **12** Alec Guinness, Carrie Fisher (Princess Leia), Harrison Ford (Han Solo), Peter Cushing **14** Anthony Daniels
voice of Darth Vader: 14 James Earl Jones
score: 12 John Williams
Oscar for: 5 score
sequel: 15 Return of the Jedi **20** The Empire Strikes Back

stasimon 9 choral ode
literally: 8 standing

state 3 put **4** form, land, mind, mode, mood, pass, pomp **5** guise, offer, phase, realm, shape, stage **6** aspect, luxury, morale, nation, people, plight, recite, relate, report, ritual, status **7** comfort, country, declare, explain, expound, express, kingdom, narrate, posture, present, recount, spirits **8** attitude, ceremony, describe, dominion, monarchy, official, position, propound, republic, set forth **9** condition, elucidate, formality, full dress, high style, situation, structure **10** ceremonial, government **11** body politic, frame of mind, predicament, state of mind **12** commonwealth, constitution, governmental, principality **13** circumstances

state abbreviations
Alabama: 2 AL **3** Ala
Alaska: 2 AK **4** Alas
Arizona: 2 AZ **4** Ariz
Arkansas: 2 AR **3** Ark
California: 2 CA **3** Cal **5** Calif
Colorado: 2 CO **4** Colo
Connecticut: 2 CT **4** Conn
Delaware: 2 DE **3** Del
Florida: 2 FL **3** Fla
Georgia: 2 GA
Hawaii: 2 HI
Idaho: 2 ID **3** Ida
Illinois: 2 IL **3** Ill
Indiana: 2 IN **3** Ind
Iowa: 2 IA
Kansas: 2 KS **4** Kans
Kentucky: 2 KY
Louisiana: 2 LA
Maine: 2 ME
Maryland: 2 MD
Massachusetts: 2 MA **4** Mass
Michigan: 2 MI **4** Mich
Minnesota: 2 MN **4** Minn
Mississippi: 2 MS **4** Miss
Missouri: 2 MO
Montana: 2 MT
Nebraska: 2 NE **4** Nebr

Nevada: 2 NV **3** Nev
New Hampshire: 2 NH
New Jersey: 2 NJ
New Mexico: 2 NM **4** N Mex
New York: 2 NY
North Carolina: 2 NC **4** N Car
North Dakota: 2 ND **4** N Dak
Ohio: 2 OH
Oklahoma: 2 OK **4** Okla
Oregon: 2 OR **4** Oreg
Pennsylvania: 2 PA **4** Penn **5** Penna
Rhode Island: 2 RI
South Carolina: 2 SC
South Dakota: 2 SD **4** S Dak
Tennessee: 2 TN **4** Tenn
Texas: 2 TX **3** Tex
Utah: 2 UT
Vermont: 2 VT
Virginia: 2 VA
Washington: 2 WA **4** Wash
West Virginia: 2 WV **3** W Va
Wisconsin: 2 WI **3** Wis
Wyoming: 2 WY **3** Wyo
state admittance
first: 8 Delaware
second: 12 Pennsylvania
third: 9 New Jersey
fourth: 7 Georgia
fifth: 11 Connecticut
sixth: 13 Massachusetts
seventh: 8 Maryland
eighth: 13 South Carolina
ninth: 12 New Hampshire
tenth: 8 Virginia
eleventh: 7 New York
twelfth: 13 North Carolina
thirteenth: 11 Rhode Island
fourteenth: 7 Vermont
fifteenth: 8 Kentucky
sixteenth: 9 Tennessee
seventeenth: 4 Ohio
eighteenth: 9 Louisiana
nineteenth: 7 Indiana
twentieth: 11 Mississippi
twenty-first: 8 Illinois
twenty-second: 7 Alabama
twenty-third: 5 Maine
twenty-fourth: 8 Missouri
twenty-fifth: 8 Arkansas
twenty-sixth: 8 Michigan
twenty-seventh: 7 Florida
twenty-eighth: 5 Texas
twenty-ninth: 4 Iowa
thirtieth: 9 Wisconsin
thirty-first: 10 California
thirty-second: 9 Minnesota
thirty-third: 6 Oregon
thirty-fourth: 6 Kansas
thirty-fifth: 12 West Virginia
thirty-sixth: 6 Nevada
thirty-seventh: 8 Nebraska
thirty-eighth: 8 Colorado
thirty-ninth/fortieth: 11 North Dakota, South Dakota
forty-first: 7 Montana
forty-second: 10 Washington
forty-third: 5 Idaho
forty-fourth: 7 Wyoming

forty-fifth: 4 Utah
forty-sixth: 8 Oklahoma
forty-seventh: 9 New Mexico
forty-eighth: 7 Arizona
forty-ninth: 6 Alaska
fiftieth: 6 Hawaii
state capitals
Alabama: 10 Montgomery
Alaska: 6 Juneau
Arizona: 7 Phoenix
Arkansas: 10 Little Rock
California: 10 Sacramento
Colorado: 6 Denver
Connecticut: 8 Hartford
Delaware: 5 Dover
Florida: 11 Tallahassee
Georgia: 7 Atlanta
Hawaii: 8 Honolulu
Idaho: 5 Boise
Illinois: 11 Springfield
Indiana: 12 Indianapolis
Iowa: 9 Des Moines
Kansas: 6 Topeka
Kentucky: 9 Frankfort
Louisiana: 10 Baton Rouge
Maine: 7 Augusta
Maryland: 9 Annapolis
Massachusetts: 6 Boston
Michigan: 7 Lansing
Minnesota: 6 St Paul
Mississippi: 7 Jackson
Missouri: 13 Jefferson City
Montana: 6 Helena
Nebraska: 7 Lincoln
Nevada: 10 Carson City
New Hampshire: 7 Concord
New Jersey: 7 Trenton
New Mexico: 7 Santa Fe
New York: 6 Albany
North Carolina: 7 Raleigh
North Dakota: 8 Bismarck
Ohio: 8 Columbus
Oklahoma: 12 Oklahoma City
Oregon: 5 Salem
Pennsylvania: 10 Harrisburg
Rhode Island: 10 Providence
South Carolina: 8 Columbia
South Dakota: 6 Pierre
Tennessee: 9 Nashville
Texas: 6 Austin
Utah: 12 Salt Lake City
Vermont: 10 Montpelier
Virginia: 8 Richmond
Washington: 7 Olympia
West Virginia: 10 Charleston
Wisconsin: 7 Madison
Wyoming: 8 Cheyenne
State Fair
author: 9 Phil Stong
movie composers: 7 Rodgers **11** Hammerstein
state in detail 7 explain, expound **8** describe, spell out **9** explicate **16** give a full account
stateliness 7 dignity, majesty **10** augustness
stately 5 grand, lofty, noble, proud, regal, royal **6** august, formal, lordly **7**

awesome, elegant, eminent **8** glorious, imperial, imposing, majestic **9** dignified, grandiose **10** ceremonial, impressive **11** magnificent
statement 3 tab **4** bill **5** check, claim, count, tally **6** avowal, charge, record, remark, report, speech **7** account, comment, invoice, mention, recital **8** relation, sentence **9** assertion, manifesto, reckoning, testimony, utterance, valuation **10** accounting, allegation, communique, exposition, profession, recitation **11** declaration, delineation, explanation, observation **12** announcement, balance sheet **13** pronouncement, specification
state of affairs 5 state **6** status **9** condition, situation **13** circumstances
State of the Union
director: 10 Frank Capra
cast: 10 Van Johnson **12** Spencer Tracy **13** Adolphe Menjou **14** Angela Lansbury **16** Katharine Hepburn
stateroom 5 cabin **8** quarters **11** compartment
statesman 8 diplomat **15** political leader
statesmanship 9 diplomacy **19** political leadership
static 5 fixed, inert, still **8** immobile, inactive, stagnant, unmoving **9** crackling, suspended **10** changeless, motionless, stationary, unchanging **12** interference
station 4 post, rank, site, spot, stop **5** caste, class, depot, grade, level, place **6** assign, degree, locate, sphere, status **7** footing, install **8** ensconce, facility, location, position, prestige, terminal, terminus **9** condition, firehouse, placement **10** dispensary, guardhouse, importance **11** emplacement, whistlestop **12** headquarters
stationary 4 even, firm **5** fixed, inert **6** intact, moored, stable, steady **7** riveted, uniform **8** constant, immobile, standing **9** dead-still, immovable, immutable, unchanged, unvarying **10** motionless, stock-still, transfixed **11** not changing, undeviating **12** unchangeable **13** standing still
Statius
author of: 6 Silvae **10** The Thebaid **12** The Achilleid
statue 8 monument **9** sculpture **14** representation
statuesque 5 regal **7** stately **8** majestic **9** dignified
stature 4 rank, size **5** place **6** height, regard **8** eminence, position, prestige, standing, tallness **9** elevation **10** importance, prominence, reputation **11** distinction
status 4 rank **5** caste, class, grade, place, state **6** degree **7** caliber, footing, station **8** eminence, position,

prestige, standing **9** condition, situation **10** estimation **11** distinction

statute 3 law **7** precept **9** prescript

statute law
Latin: **10** lex scripta

staunch, stanch 3 dam **4** firm, stem, true **5** check, loyal, solid, sound, stout **6** impede, rugged, steady, strong, sturdy **7** contain, zealous **8** constant, faithful, hold back, obstruct, resolute, stalwart **9** steadfast, well-built **10** watertight **11** substantial

stave off 7 beat off, fend off, keep off, ward off **9** keep at bay

stay 3 aim, guy, rib, rod **4** bunk, curb, foil, halt, live, pole, prop, rest, room, stem, stop **5** abide, block, brace, check, delay, dwell, lodge, quell, shore, stick, tarry, visit **6** endure, keep in, linger, rein in, remain, reside, splint, stifle, thwart **7** carry on, hold out, holiday, last out, persist, sojourn, support, ward off **8** abeyance, buttress, continue, hold back, mainstay, postpone, reprieve, restrain, standard, stopover, suppress, vacation, withhold **9** deferment, frustrate, persevere, staunchion **10** hang around, see through, suspension **12** postponement, reinforcement

stay put 4 stay **6** remain **8** stand pat

St Clare, Eva
character in: **14** Uncle Tom's Cabin
author: **5** Stowe

steadfast 4 keen, rapt **5** fixed **6** direct, intent, steady **8** resolute **9** attentive, obstinate, tenacious, undaunted **10** deep-rooted, deep-seated, inflexible, unchanging, unflagging, unwavering, unyielding **11** indomitable, persevering, unalterable, undeviating, unfaltering, unflinching **12** intransigent, single-minded, unchangeable, undistracted **14** uncompromising

steadfastness 8 tenacity **10** resolution **11** persistence **12** perseverance, resoluteness **13** determination

Steadfast Tin Soldier, The
author: **21** Hans Christian Andersen

steadiness 4 care **5** poise **6** aplomb **8** calmness, coolness, evenness, firmness **9** composure, sangfroid, stability **10** equanimity, resolution **11** carefulness, persistence, self-control, tranquility **12** resoluteness, tranquillity **13** dependability, steadfastness **14** presence of mind, self-possession **16** imperturbability

steady 4 even, firm, sure **5** sober **6** secure, stable **7** balance, careful, devoted, regular, serious, staunch **8** constant, faithful, frequent, habitual, hold fast, reliable, resolute, unending, untiring **9** ceaseless, confirmed, dedicated, immovable, incessant, stabilize, steadfast, tenacious, unceasing **10** continuing, continuous, coolheaded,

deliberate, dependable, methodical, persistent, unflagging, unwavering **11** levelheaded, persevering, substantial, undeviating, unfaltering, unremitting **12** single-minded **13** conscientious

steal 3 buy, cop **4** copy, crib, flit, flow, lift, slip, take **5** creep, drift, filch, glide, pinch, skulk, slide, slink, sneak, swipe, usurp **6** borrow, elapse, escape, extort, filter, pilfer, pocket, rip off, snatch, snitch, thieve **7** bargain, defraud, diffuse, good buy, imitate, purloin, swindle **8** abstract, embezzle, good deal, liberate **10** burglarize, plagiarize **11** abscond with, appropriate, make off with **14** misappropriate

steal away 3 fly **4** bolt, flee, skip **5** elope **6** escape **7** get away, make off, slip out **8** creep off, slip away, sneak off **9** break free, tiptoe out **10** break loose, fly the coop **12** make a getaway

stealth 7 secrecy, slyness **10** covertness, sneakiness, subterfuge **11** furtiveness **12** stealthiness **13** secretiveness **15** unobtrusiveness **17** surreptitiousness

stealthy 3 sly **5** shady **6** covert, shifty, sneaky **7** devious, furtive **8** slippery, sneaking **9** secretive, underhand **11** clandestine, underhanded **12** huggermugger **13** surreptitious

steamboat
invented by: **6** Fulton **9** Symington

steamed up 5 angry, het up, irate **6** raging **7** enraged, furious, riled up **8** heated up, inflamed **10** infuriated **12** mad as a wet hen **14** hot and bothered **17** hot under the collar

steamer 4 boat, clam, ship **5** liner, trunk **10** paddleboat **11** side-wheeler **12** stern-wheeler **13** paddle-wheeler

steel 4 dirk, foil, gird **5** blade, brace, knife, nerve, saber, sword **6** dagger, rapier **7** bayonet, cutlass, fortify, machete **8** falchion, scimitar **10** broadsword
process invented by: **8** Bessemer

Steele, Sir Richard
pseudonym: **16** Isaac Bickerstaff
author of: **9** The Tatler (with Joseph Addison) **10** The Funeral **12** The Spectator (with Joseph Addison) **13** The Lying Lover **16** The Tender Husband **18** The Conscious Lovers

steely 4 hard **5** stony **6** flinty **9** heartless, unfeeling **10** forbidding **11** coldhearted

Steen, Jan
born: **6** Leiden, Leyden **14** The Netherlands
artwork: **7** Cabaret **11** The Egg Dance **12** Merry Company **14** Garden of the Inn **15** The Doctor's Visit, The Rhetoricians **16** The Morning Toilet **17** The Skittle Players **18** The World

Topsy-Turvy, Young Woman Dressing

Steenburgen, Mary
roles: **10** Cross Creek **12** Dead of Winter **13** Time After Time **22** Attic: Hiding of Anne Frank

steep 4 brew, bury, fill, soak **5** imbue, sharp, sheer, souse **6** abrupt, drench, engulf, infuse, plunge **7** immerse, pervade, suffuse **8** marinate, saturate, submerge **10** impregnate **11** precipitous

steeple 5 spire, tower **6** belfry **9** campanile

steer 3 aim, lay, run **4** bear, head, lead, make, sail **5** coach, guide, pilot **6** direct, govern, manage **7** conduct, proceed **8** navigate **9** supervise

steer clear of 4 shun **5** avert, avoid, dodge, evade, forgo, skirt **6** escape, eschew, forego **8** sidestep **9** keep shy of **11** abstain from, refrain from **16** give a wide berth to

Steerforth
character in: **16** David Copperfield
author: **7** Dickens

Steffens, Lincoln
author of: **19** The Shame of the Cities

Steiger, Rod
real name: **20** Rodney Stephen Steiger
born: **13** Westhampton NY
wife: **11** Claire Bloom
roles: **8** Waterloo **13** The Longest Day, The Pawnbroker, W C Fields and Me **15** On the Waterfront **19** In the Heat of the Night (Oscar)

Stein, Clarence S
architect of: **13** Temple Emanu-El (NYC)

Stein, Gertrude
author of: **10** Three Lives **13** Tender Buttons **20** The Making of Americans **27** Autobiography of Alice B Toklas
coined phrase: **14** lost generation

Steinbeck, John
author of: **8** The Pearl **10** Cannery Row, East of Eden, The Red Pony **12** Of Mice and Men, Tortilla Flat **15** In Dubious Battle **16** The Grapes of Wrath **18** Travels with Charley **24** The Winter of Our Discontent

Steinmetz, Charles P
field: **11** engineering
developed: **2** AC **18** alternating current

Stella, Frank
born: **8** Malden MA
artwork: **4** Jill **5** Itata **14** Jasper's Dilemma **15** Guadalupe Island

Stella, Joseph
born: **5** Italy **6** Naples
artwork: **8** Full Moon (Barbados) **9** Sunflower, The Bridge **14** Brooklyn Bridge **16** Pittsburgh Winter **18** New

York Interpreted **28** Battle of the Lights Coney Island

Stella Dallas
director: **9** King Vidor
cast: **9** John Boles **11** Anne Shirley **12** Barbara O'Neil **15** Barbara Stanwyck

stellar 6 astral, starry **7** leading **8** starring **9** brilliant, celestial, principal **11** outstanding

stem 3 dam **4** buck, cane, come, curb, grow, halt, rise, stay, stop **5** arise, block, check, deter, ensue, issue, quell, shank, shoot, speak, spire, stalk, stall, stock, trunk **6** arrest, derive, hinder, impede, oppose, resist, result, retard, spring, stanch, thwart **7** counter, pedicel, petiole, prevent, proceed, tendril **8** hold back, obstruct, peduncle, restrain, surmount **9** leafstalk, originate, withstand

stem from 5 arise, begin, start **6** derive **9** originate

stench 4 odor, reek **5** fetor, stink **8** bad smell **9** fetidness

Stendhal (Henri Marie Beyle)
author of: **17** The Red and the Black **18** Memoirs of an Egotist **22** The Charterhouse of Parma

Stengel, Charles Dillon
nickname: **5** Casey
sport: **8** baseball
position: **7** manager
team: **11** New York Mets **14** New York Yankees **15** Brooklyn Dodgers

Stentor
vocation: **6** herald
characteristic: **10** loud-voiced
voice as loud as: **8** fifty men

step 3 act **4** clip, gait, move, pace, rank, rung, span, walk **5** notch, phase, point, riser, stage, stair, strut, track, tramp, tread **6** action, degree, hobble, period, remove, stride **7** footing, measure, process, shamble, shuffle, swagger, trample **8** footfall, foothold, maneuver, purchase **9** footprint, gradation, procedure **10** proceeding

step down 4 quit **5** leave **6** resign, retire

Stephens, James
author of: **7** Deirdre **14** The Crock of Gold **21** The Charwoman's Daughter

Stephenson, George and Robert
nationality: **7** English
developed: **15** steam locomotive

Steppenwolf
author: **12** Hermann Hesse
character: **5** Maria, Pablo **7** Hermine **11** Harry Haller

Steps
author: **13** Jerzy Kosinski

step up 4 spur **6** come up **7** quicken, speed up **8** approach, escalate, expedite, increase **9** intensify **10** accelerate

stereotype 4 type **6** cliche **7** formula

8 typecast **10** categorize, pigeonhole **13** preconception

stereotyped 5 stale, trite **9** hackneyed **11** commonplace **13** unimaginative

sterile 4 bare, pure, vain **5** empty **6** barren, fallow, futile **7** aseptic, useless **8** abortive, bootless, impotent, infecund, sanitary **9** childless, fruitless, infertile, worthless **10** antiseptic, profitless, sterilized, unavailing, unfruitful, uninfected **11** disinfected, ineffective, ineffectual, unrewarding **12** unproductive, unprofitable **13** free from germs **14** uncontaminated

sterilize 6 purify **9** autoclave, disinfect **13** decontaminate

sterling 4 pure, true **5** noble **6** silver, superb, worthy **7** genuine, perfect **8** flawless, superior **9** admirable, estimable, first-rate, honorable **10** invaluable **11** meritorious, superlative

stern 4 cold, grim, hard **5** cruel, grave, harsh, rigid, sharp, stiff **6** brutal, gloomy, severe, somber, strict, unkind **7** austere, serious **8** coercive, despotic, frowning, pitiless, rigorous, ruthless, ungentle **9** reproving, stringent, unfeeling **10** forbidding, implacable, ironfisted, ironhanded, tyrannical, unmerciful **11** admonishing, coldblooded, reproachful **12** unreasonable **13** unsympathetic **14** unapproachable

Sterne, Laurence
author of: **14** Tristram Shandy **19** A Sentimental Journey
character: **9** Uncle Toby **12** Parson Yorick, Walter Shandy

sternum
bone of: **6** breast

Steve Canyon
creator: **12** Milton Caniff
character: **7** Cheetah **9** Madam Lynx **10** Doe Redwood, Miss Mizzou **11** Savannah Gay **13** Copper Calhoun **14** Herself Muldoon **17** Princess Sun Flower
  wife: **6** Summer
  ward/cousin: **12** Poteet Canyon
  Summer's son: **13** Leigh ton Olson

Stevens, George
director of: **5** Giant (Oscar), Shane **8** Gunga Din **9** Swing Time **13** I Remember Mama, Penny Serenade **14** A Place in the Sun (Oscar), Woman of the Year **16** The Talk of the Town **19** The Diary of Anne Frank

Stevens, Gowan
character in: **9** Sanctuary
author: **8** Faulkner

Stevens, James
author of: **10** Paul Bunyan

Stevens, Wallace
author of: **7** The Rock **9** Harmonium **13** Sunday Morning **17** Transport to Summer **23** Peter Quince at the Clavier, The Idea of Order at Key West, The Man with the Blue Guitar

Stevenson, Robert
director of: **8** Jane Eyre **10** Back Street **11** Mary Poppins

Stevenson, Robert Louis
author of: **9** Kidnapped **13** The Black Arrow **14** Treasure Island **18** Travels with a Donkey **21** A Child's Garden of Verses, Doctor Jekyll and Mr Hyde, The Master of Ballantrae

St Evremond, Marquis
character in: **16** A Tale of Two Cities
author: **7** Dickens

stew 4 fret, fume, fuss **5** chafe, gripe, steep, tizzy, worry **6** grouse, ragout, seethe, simmer **7** agonize, fluster, flutter, grumble, mixture **10** miscellany

steward 5 agent, proxy **6** deputy, factor, waiter **7** bailiff, manager, trustee **8** executor, overseer **10** controller, supervisor **11** comptroller **13** administrator **14** representative, ship's attendant **15** flight attendant

Stewart, James
born: **9** Indiana PA
roles: **4** Rope **6** Harvey **7** Vertigo **10** Rear Window, Shenandoah **11** Elwood P Dowd **14** Cheyenne Autumn **16** Anatomy of a Murder, Destry Rides Again, The Stratton Story **17** Bell Book and Candle, It's a Wonderful Life **18** It's a Wonderful World, The Spirit of St Louis **19** The Glenn Miller Story **20** The Philadelphia Story (Oscar), You Can't Take It with You **22** The Greatest Show on Earth **23** Mr Smith Goes to Washington

Stewart, Mary
real name: **22** Florence Rainbow Stewart
author of: **11** Crystal Cave **14** The Hollow Hills **15** The Moon-Spinners **16** My Brother Michael, The Gabriel Hounds **18** Airs Above the Ground, The Last Enchantment

St George's
capital of: **7** Grenada

stick 3 bar, bat, cue, dig, fix, jab, pin, put, rod, set **4** balk, bind, cane, club, curb, fuse, glue, hold, join, last, mire, nail, pink, poke, pole, seal, snag, stab, stop, tack, twig, wand, weld **5** abide, affix, baton, billy, block, catch, check, fagot, leave, lodge, paste, place, plant, prick, punch, shift, snarl, spear, spike, staff, stall, stake, stand, stave, stump **6** adhere, attach, boggle, branch, burden, cement, cudgel, detain, endure, fasten, hamper, hinder, hog-tie, impede, insert, pierce, puzzle, scotch, skewer, stymie, switch, thrust, thwart **7** confuse, crosier, inhibit, perplex, shackle, trammel **8** bewilder, bludgeon, caduceus, continue, obstruct, puncture **9** checkmate, constrain, perforate, truncheon, victimize **10** immobilize, shillelagh

stick fast 4 hold **5** cling, stick **6** adhere, cleave

stickler 3 bug, nut **5** crank, poser **6** enigma, purist, puzzle, riddle, zealot **7** devotee, dilemma, fanatic, mystery, stumper **8** martinet **10** enthusiast, monomaniac

sticks 4 skis **5** bonds, glues, twigs **6** pastes, Podunk **7** adheres, boonies, catches, cements, country **8** kindling **9** backwoods, boondocks, golf clubs, provinces **10** hicksville, hinterland **11** countryside, hinterlands

stick together 4 bind, fuse, glue, hold, join **5** cling, stick, unite **6** cement, cohere

stick-to-itiveness 8 tenacity **9** endurance **10** resolution **11** persistence **12** perseverance, resoluteness **13** determination, tenaciousness

stickum 3 gum **4** glue **5** paste **6** cement **8** adhesive, mucilage **12** rubber cement

stick up for 5 boost **6** defend **7** root for **11** speak well of **17** put in a good word for

stick with 4 stay **5** abide **6** keep at **7** stand by **9** accompany, persevere

sticky 3 wet **4** damp, dank **5** gluey, gooey, gummy, humid, moist, muggy, pasty, tacky **6** clammy, clingy, steamy, sultry, viscid **7** viscous **8** adherent, adhesive, clinging, cohesive, sticking **9** glutinous, tenacious **10** gelatinous **12** mucilaginous

stiff 4 body, cold, cool, firm, grim, hard, high, iron, keen, prim, sore, taut **5** aloof, awful, brave, brisk, crisp, cruel, dense, fixed, gusty, harsh, heavy, rigid, sharp, smart, solid, steep, stern, tense, thick, tight, tough, undue **6** bitter, brutal, chilly, clumsy, corpse, dogged, forced, formal, raging, severe, steady, steely, strong, uneasy, viscid, wooden **7** austere, awkward, cadaver, clotted, decided, distant, drastic, extreme, fearful, intense, jellied, labored, precise, remains, settled, starchy, stately, staunch, steeled, stilted, uptight, valiant, violent, viscous **8** affected, constant, dead body, exacting, forceful, grievous, mannered, pitiless, pounding, powerful, resolute, resolved, rigorous, ruthless, spanking, stubborn, ungainly, unlimber, unshaken, vigorous **9** difficult, draconian, excessive, graceless, inelastic, inelegant, laborious, merciless, obstinate, resistant, steadfast, stringent, tenacious, unnatural **10** artificial, courageous, determined, exorbitant, formidable, gelatinous, immoderate, inflexible, inordinate, persistent, solidified, unswerving, unyielding **11** ceremonious, constrained, extravagant, indomitable, straitlaced, unfaltering, unflinching, unwarranted **12**

strong-willed, unreasonable **14** uncompromising

stiff-necked 6 mulish **7** will ful **8** contrary, obdurate, stubborn **9** obstinate, pigheaded, unbending **10** bullheaded, refractory, self-willed, unshakable, unyielding **11** intractable **12** intransigent, pertinacious

stiffness 7 tension **8** firmness, rigidity **9** aloofness, formality, tenseness, tightness **10** constraint **11** starchiness

stifle 3 gag **4** curb **5** check, choke **6** muffle, subdue **7** garrote, inhibit, repress, smother, squelch, swelter **8** keep back, restrain, strangle, suppress, throttle **9** suffocate **10** asphyxiate

stifling 3 hot **6** stuffy **7** airless **10** overheated

stigma 4 blot, flaw, mark, scar **5** brand, odium, shame, stain, taint **6** smirch, smudge **7** blemish, tarnish **8** disgrace, dishonor **11** mark of shame **12** besmirchment

stigmatize 5 brand, smear **6** debase, defame, smirch **7** villify **9** discredit, disparage

still 4 calm, hush **5** inert, quiet **6** at rest, hushed, pacify, settle, silent **7** appease, as suage, gratify, put down, repress, silence, turn off **8** immobile, overcome, restrain, suppress, unmoving **9** noiseless, soundless **10** motionless, put an end to, stationary, unstirring

stillness 4 calm, hush **5** quiet **6** repose **7** silence **8** calmness, inaction, quietude **9** composure **10** immobility, inactivity, quiescence **11** tranquility **12** tranquillity

Stillness at Appomattox, A
author: 11 Bruce Catton

stilted 4 cold, prim **5** rigid, stiff **6** forced, formal, stuffy, wooden **7** awkward, labored, pompous, starchy, studied, uptight **8** mannered, priggish, starched **9** graceless, unnatural **10** artificial **11** ceremonious, constrained

Stilwell, Joseph W
nickname: 10 Vinegar Joe
served in: 3 WWI **4** WWII
chief of staff for: 13 Chiang Kai-shek
driven out of: 5 Burma

stimulant 5 tonic, upper **6** bracer **8** excitant **9** energizer

stimulate 3 fan **4** spur, stir, wake **5** alert, rouse **6** arouse, awaken, excite, incite, prompt, vivify **7** actuate, animate, inflame, inspire, quicken, sharpen **8** activate, enkindle, initiate, inspirit

stimulating 5 tonic **7** piquing **8** arousing, exciting, spurring, stirring, whetting **9** animating, provoking **10** energizing, refreshing **11** interesting, provocative

stimulus 4 goad, spur, whet **5** tonic **6** bracer, fillip, motive **7** impetus **8** excitant **9** activator, energizer, incentive, quickener, stimulant **10** incitement, inducement **11** provocation **13** encouragement

sting 3 cut, nip, rub, vex **4** ache, barb, bite, blow, burn, fire, gall, gnaw, goad, grip, hurt, itch, lash, move, pain, prod, rack, rasp, rile, sore, spur, stab, whip **5** anger, chafe, cross, egg on, grate, impel, pinch, pique, prick, shake, shock, smart, venom, wince, wound **6** arouse, awaken, excite, harrow, incite, insult, kindle, madden, nettle, offend, pierce, prompt, propel, stir up, tingle, twinge **7** actuate, agonize, disturb, incense, inflame, prickle, provoke, quicken, scourge, stinger, torment, torture **8** irritate, motivate, vexation **9** infuriate, instigate, penetrate **10** affliction, irritation

Sting, The
director: 13 George Roy Hill
cast: 10 Paul Newman, Ray Walston, Robert Shaw **13** Eileen Brennan, Robert Redford **14** Charles Durning
score: 11 Scott Joplin
Oscar for: 7 picture **8** director

stinginess 6 penury **9** parsimony **11** miserliness **13** niggardliness, penny-pinching **15** tight-fistedness

stinging 4 acid **5** harsh, sharp **6** biting, bitter **7** burning, caustic, cutting, pungent **8** piercing **9** sarcastic, satirical **10** astringent

stingy 4 lean, mean, thin **5** close, scant, small, tight **6** frugal, meager, modest, paltry, scanty, skimpy, sparse **7** miserly, scrimpy, slender, sparing **8** piddling, stinting **9** illiberal, niggardly, penurious **10** inadequate, ungenerous **11** closefisted, tightfisted **12** cheeseparing, insufficient, parsimonious **13** penny-pinching

stink 4 odor, reek **5** fetor **6** stench **8** bad smell **17** smell to high heaven

stint 3 job **4** curb, duty, part, save, task, term, turn **5** check, chore, limit, quota, shift **6** reduce, scrimp **8** hold back, restrain, restrict, withhold **9** constrain, cut down on, economize **10** assignment, engagement **12** circumscribe, pinch pennies

stipend 5 grant, wages **6** income, salary **7** pension **8** fixed pay **9** allowance, emolument **10** honorarium, recompense **11** scholarship **12** compensation, remuneration

stipulate 4 cite, name **5** agree, allow, grant, state **6** assure, insure, pledge **7** promise, provide, specify, warrant **8** indicate, set forth **9** designate, guarantee

stipulation 4 term **7** proviso **9** condition **10** limitation **11** requirement, restriction

stipulative 7 limited 9 qualified, tentative 10 contingent, restricted 11 conditional, provisional 16 with reservations

stir 3 act, mix 4 beat, fire, goad, jolt, move, prod, rush, spur, to-do, whip 5 blend, rouse, shake, sough, start 6 arouse, awaken, bustle, commix, excite, flurry, hasten, hustle, kindle, mingle, mixing, moving, pother, quiver, rustle, shiver, tumult, twitch, uproar, vivify, work up 7 agitate, animate, enflame, flutter, inspire, provoke, quicken, scamper 8 energize, inspirit, intermix, mingling, movement, prodding, rustling, scramble, stirring 9 agitation, commingle, commotion, electrify, stimulate 10 get a move on, step lively 11 set in motion 12 exert oneself, make an effort

stirred up 5 riled, upset 7 aroused, excited, kindled, ruffled 8 agitated, inflamed 9 disturbed 10 stimulated

stirring 5 astir, awake 6 moving 7 rousing 8 electric, exalting, exciting, in motion, spirited 9 inspiring, thrilling 10 up and about 11 galvanizing, stimulating 12 electrifying

stir up 5 upset 6 arouse, awaken, excite, kindle, ruffle 7 agitate, disturb 9 call forth, stimulate 10 antagonize

stir vigorously 3 mix 4 beat, whip 7 agitate

stitch 3 bit, jot, sew 4 ache, iota, kink, mend, pain, pang, seam, tack 5 baste, cramp, crick, piece, scrap, shoot, shred 6 suture, tingle, twinge, twitch 7 article, garment 8 particle 9 embroider 12 charley horse

St John's
    capital of: 17 Antigua and Barbuda
St Louis
    baseball team: 9 Cardinals
    football team: 9 Cardinals
    founded by: 13 Pierre Laclede
    hockey team: 5 Blues
    landmark: 11 Gateway Arch
    newspaper: 12 Post-Dispatch
    river: 11 Mississippi
    site of: 10 Exposition (1904)
    university: 10 Washington

stock 4 butt, clan, form, fund, haft, herd, hold, kind, line, pull, race, root, type 5 array, basic, birth, blood, breed, broth, cache, caste, equip, goods, grasp, hoard, house, offer, shaft, store, tribe, wares 6 cattle, family, fit out, formal, handle, origin, people, shares, source, staple, strain, supply 7 appoint, capital, descent, dynasty, furnish, lineage, provide, regular, reserve, routine 8 accoutre, ancestry, bouillon, heredity, pedigree, pro forma, quantity, standard 9 forebears, genealogy, inventory, livestock, ownership, parentage, provision, reservoir, selection 10 assortment, background,

extraction, family tree, investment 11 merchandise, nationality, progeniture 12 accumulation 13 capital shares

Stockhausen, Karlheinz
    born: 7 Germany, Modrath
    composer of: 5 Cycle, Tempi 6 Groups, Hymnen, Mantra, Zyklus 7 Anthems, Gruppen, Momente 8 Attuning, Gold Dust, Kontakte, Stimmung 9 Goldstaub, Zeitmasze 10 Procession, Prozession 12 Kontrapunkte 13 Klavierstucke 16 From the Seven Days 17 Aus den Sieben Tagen

Stockholm
    nickname: 16 Venice of the North
    capital of: 6 Sweden
    sea: 6 Baltic
    lake: 7 Malaren
    section: 8 Norrmalm 9 Sodermalm 11 Gamla Staden
    landmark: 7 Skansen 8 City Hall 11 Great Church
    site of: 10 Nobel Prize

stockpile 5 cache, hoard, stock, store 10 accumulate

stocky 5 dumpy, husky, pudgy, solid, squat, stout 6 blocky, chunky, stubby, stumpy, sturdy 8 thickset

stodgy 4 dull, flat 5 dated, heavy, lumpy, passe, staid, thick 6 boring, clumsy, dreary, narrow, prolix, stuffy 7 humdrum, pompous, prosaic, serious, starchy, tedious 8 lifeless, pedantic, tiresome 9 laborious, lumbering, wearisome 10 antiquated, inflexible, monotonous 12 indigestible, old-fashioned 13 uninteresting

stoic 4 calm 8 detached, fatalist, quietist, tranquil 9 impassive, unruffled 11 philosophic 12 dispassionate, imperturbable, unimpassioned

stoicism 8 fatalism 9 fortitude 11 impassivity, tranquility 12 tranquillity 16 imperturbability

Stoker, Bram
    author of: 7 Dracula

stole 3 fur 4 cape, robe, took, wrap 5 crept, orary, scarf 6 swiped 7 filched, pinched, sneaked, tiptoed 8 mantilla, pilfered, snatched, vestment 9 embezzled, purloined

stolen 3 hot 5 taken 6 swiped 7 filched, pinched 8 pilfered, snatched 9 embezzled, ill-gotten, purloined

stolid 4 dull 5 dense 6 bovine, obtuse 7 lumpish 8 sluggish 9 apathetic, impassive, lethargic 10 phlegmatic 11 insensitive, unemotional

stolidity 6 apathy 8 lethargy 9 inertness 11 impassivity 12 sluggishness

stomach 3 maw, pot 4 bear, bent, bias, craw, crop, guts, mind, take 5 abide, belly, brook, fancy, humor, stand, taste, tummy 6 desire, endure, hunger, liking, middle, paunch, relish, retain, suffer, temper, thirst 7 abdo-

men, gizzard, leaning, midriff, swallow 8 affinity, appetite, bear with, keenness, overlook, pass over, pleasure, potbelly, sympathy, tolerate 9 put up with 10 attraction, midsection, partiality, proclivity, propensity 11 breadbasket, countenance, disposition, inclination 12 predilection

stone 3 gem, nut, pip, pit 4 rock, seed 5 bijou, jewel 6 kernel, pebble 9 brilliant 10 throw rocks

Stone, Edward Durell
    architect of: 9 US Embassy 17 Museum of Modern Art 33 Kennedy Center for the Performing Arts

Stone, Irving
    author of: 9 The Origin 11 Lust for Life 12 Those Who Love 17 Sailor on Horseback, The President's Lady 19 Adversary in the House 21 The Agony and the Ecstasy

Stone, Oliver
    born: 9 New York NY
    profession: 6 writer 8 director
    films: 3 JFK 5 Nixon, U-Turn 7 Platoon (Oscar) 10 Wall Street 12 Patriot Games 14 Heaven and Earth 15 Midnight Express 18 Natural Born Killers 21 Born on the Fourth of July

stonefly
    varieties: 5 giant, green 6 spring, winter 8 perlodid 9 roachlike 11 green-winged 12 rolled-winged

Stone of Scone
    location: 8 Scotland
    purpose: 12 crowning king
    moved to: 16 Westminster Abbey

stoneware 5 china 7 ceramic, pottery 8 crockery

stony 3 icy 4 cold 5 blank, bumpy, chill, rocky, rough, stern 6 coarse, craggy, flinty, frigid, jagged, marble, pebbly, rugged, severe, steely, stolid, uneven 7 austere, callous, granite, lithoid, stoical 8 concrete, deadened, gravelly, hardened, indurate, obdurate, ossified, pitiless, rocklike, soulless, uncaring 9 bloodless, heartless, merciless, petrified, unfeeling, untouched 10 ada mantine, forbidding, fossilized, hard-boiled, inexorable, insensible, unaffected, unyielding

stool 5 bench 7 cricket, has sock, ottoman

stool pigeon 3 rat, spy 4 fink 5 decoy, patsy 6 snitch 7 peacher, stoolie, tattler 8 informer, squealer 10 talebearer, tattletale

stoop 3 bow, sag 4 bend, fall, sink 5 deign, droop, porch, slump, steps, yield 6 resort, slouch, submit 7 concede, descend, succumb 8 doorstep 9 acquiesce 10 condescend 11 entranceway 19 round-shoulderedness

stooped 4 bent 5 bowed 7 deigned, hunched 9 contorted 12 condescended

stop 3 ban, bar, end **4** curb, fill, halt, hold, idle, plug, quit, rest, seal, stay, stem, wait **5** abide, block, brake, break, caulk, cease, check, close, depot, deter, dwell, lapse, lodge, pause, put up, spell, stall, stand, tarry, visit **6** alight, arrest, cut off, desist, draw up, expire, falter, finish, hamper, hiatus, hinder, pull up, recess, rein in, repose, run out, stanch, stop up, thwart **7** close up, halting, layover, occlude, prevent, respite, sojourn, station, suspend **8** abeyance, break off, conclude, cut short, hold back, intermit, interval, leave off, obstruct, pass away, peter out, postpone, preclude, restrain, suppress, surcease, terminal, terminus, wind down **9** cessation, frustrate, interlude, stand fast, terminate **10** desistance, drop anchor, put an end to, standstill, suspension **11** come to a halt, come to an end, destination, discontinue, prohibition, termination **12** intermission, interruption **17** come to a standstill **18** bring to a standstill

stopgap 7 stand-by **9** contrived, emergency, expedient, impromptu, makeshift, temporary, tentative **10** improvised, substitute **11** provisional
Latin: 5 ad hoc **6** pro tem

stop in 4 call **5** visit **6** drop in, look in

stop off 4 call **5** visit **6** drop in, look in, stop by

stoppage 4 halt **5** check, tieup **6** arrest **7** barrier, embargo, staying **8** blockage, checking, clogging, gridlock, obstacle **9** checkmate, hindrance, restraint, stricture **10** disruption, impediment **11** curtailment, obstruction **12** interruption

Stoppard, Tom
    author of: 10 Travesties **33** Rosencrantz and Guildenstern Are Dead

stopper 3 lid **4** bung, cock, cork, plug **5** spile

Stopping by Woods on a Snowy Evening
    author: 11 Robert Frost

Stop the Music
    host: 9 Bert Parks
    orchestra: 11 Harry Salter
    vocalist: 9 June Valli **11** Jaye P Morgan, Jimmy Blaine **12** Marion Morgan **13** Betty Ann Grove, Estelle Loring

stop up 3 jam **4** clog **5** block, choke **8** obstruct

store 3 lot **4** fund, hold, host, keep, mart, pack, pile, save, shop **5** amass, array, cache, faith, hoard, lay by, lay in, lay up, stash, stock, trust, value, wares **6** credit, esteem, gather, heap up, legion, market, plenty, regard, riches, scores, supply, volume, wealth **7** deposit, effects, husband, put away, reserve, satiety **8** emporium, lay

aside, overflow, plethora, quantity, reliance, richness, salt away, sock away, stow away **9** abundance, inventory, multitude, profusion, provision, reservoir, stockpile **10** accumulate, confidence, cornucopia, dependence, estimation, exuberance, luxuriance **11** copiousness, full measure, prodigality, supermarket **12** accumulation **13** establishment

storehouse 4 bank, silo **5** depot, vault **7** arsenal, granary **8** elevator, magazine, treasury **9** stockroom, warehouse **10** depository, repository

storied 4 epic **6** fabled **8** fabulous **9** legendary

Stories and Texts for Nothing
    author: 13 Samuel Beckett

storm 3 ado, row **4** blow, fume, fuss, gale, rage, rant, rave, roar, rush, stir, tear, to-do **5** burst, furor, snarl, stalk, stamp, stomp, tramp **6** assail, attack, charge, clamor, deluge, flurry, hubbub, pother, ruckus, squall, strike, tumult, uproar **7** assault, besiege, bluster, carry on, cyclone, rampage, tempest, tornado, torrent, turmoil, twister, typhoon **8** blizzard, brouhaha, downpour, eruption, fall upon, outbreak, outburst, upheaval **9** agitation, commotion, explosion, fulminate, hurricane, raise hell **10** cloudburst, hullabaloo **11** blow one's top, disturbance **12** blow one's cool, vent one's rage

storm and stress
    German: 13 Sturm und Drang
    name of 18th century: 16 literary movement

storm troopers
    German: 14 Sturmabteilung

stormy 4 foul, wild **5** rainy, rough, snowy, windy **6** raging, rugged **7** howling, roaring, squally, violent **8** blustery **9** inclement, turbulent **10** blustering **11** tempestuous

story 3 fib, lie **4** news, plot, tale, word, yarn **5** alibi, fable, piece **6** excuse, legend, report, sketch **7** account, article, parable, romance, tidings, version **8** allegory, anecdote, argument, dispatch, news item, white lie **9** falsehood, narrative, statement, testimony **10** allegation **11** fabrication, information **13** prevarication

Story of a Bad Boy, The
    author: 19 Thomas Bailey Aldrich

Story of G I Joe, The
    director: 14 William Wellman
    cast: 13 Freddie Steele, Robert Mitchum **15** Burgess Meredith (Ernie Pyle)

Story of Louis Pasteur, The
    director: 15 William Dieterle
    cast: 8 Paul Muni (Pasteur) **11** Anita Louise **19** Josephine Hutchinson
    Oscar for: 5 actor (Muni)

stout 3 big, fat, fit **4** able, bold, firm,

true **5** brave, bulky, burly, hardy, heavy, hefty, husky, large, obese, plump, pudgy, round, solid, tough, tubby **6** brawny, chubby, daring, fleshy, heroic, mighty, plucky, portly, robust, rotund, rugged, spunky, steady, stocky, strong, sturdy **7** doughty, gallant, staunch, valiant **8** athletic, constant, enduring, faithful, fearless, intrepid, leathery, muscular, resolute, resolved, stalwart, thickset, untiring, valorous, vigorous **9** confident, corpulent, dauntless, steadfast, strapping **10** able-bodied, courageous, determined, inflexible, unshakable, unswerving, unwavering **11** indomitable, lionhearted, unfaltering, unflinching, unshrinking

Stout, Rex
    author of: 10 Fer-de-Lance **12** Too Many Cooks **16** If Death Ever Slept
    character: 5 Fritz **9** Nero Wolfe **13** Archie Goodwin

stouthearted 4 bold **5** brave, gutsy, hardy **6** heroic, plucky, spunky **7** valiant **8** fearless, intrepid, resolute, spirited, stalwart, unafraid, valorous **9** dauntless, undaunted **10** courageous **11** indomitable, lionhearted, unblenching, unflinching

stoutheartedness 4 grit, guts, sand **5** nerve, pluck, spunk, valor **6** daring, mettle **7** bravery, courage **8** boldness **12** fearlessness **13** dauntlessness

stoutness
    French: 10 embonpoint

stow 3 jam, put, set **4** cram, load, pack, tuck **5** cache, crowd, place, stash, store, stuff, wedge **7** deposit, squeeze **8** ensconce, salt away

Stowe, Harriet Beecher
    author of: 4 Dred **12** Oldtown Folks **14** Uncle Tom's Cabin

Strachey, Lytton
    author of: 13 Queen Victoria **17** Elizabeth and Essex, Eminent Victorians
    member of: 15 Bloomsbury Group

strafe 7 bombard **8** fire upon **10** machine-gun

straggle 4 rove **5** drift, stray **6** sprawl, wander **7** deviate, meander **8** divagate

straight 4 even, neat, tidy, true **5** clear, frank, right, solid, sound **6** candid, direct, evenly, honest, square, unbent **7** aligned, erectly, in order, orderly, upright **8** accurate, adjusted, arranged, directly, on a level, reliable, squarely, truthful, unbroken **9** ceaseless, forthwith, incessant, instantly, not curved, shipshape, sorted out, sustained, veracious **10** aboveboard, continuous, forthright, four-square, methodical, persistent, straightly, successive, unrelieved, unswerving, unwavering **11** consecutive, coordinated, immediately, trustworthy, undeviating **13** uninterrupted

straighten 4 tidy 5 align 6 adjust, neaten, unbend 7 even out 8 level out, square up 9 put in line 10 put in order, stand erect

straightening 7 tidying 9 adjusting, alignment, evening up, unbending 10 evening out 11 leveling out 13 putting in line 14 putting in order

straighten out 6 unbend 7 realign 8 redirect 10 discipline

straighten up 4 tidy 5 align, clean, order 6 neaten, tidy up 7 arrange, stand up 8 organize

straightforward 4 open 5 blunt, frank 6 candid, direct, honest, square 7 ethical, upright 8 straight 9 guileless, honorable 10 aboveboard, creditable, forthright, scrupulous 11 plainspoken, trustworthy

straightforwardness 6 candor 7 honesty 12 truthfulness 14 forthrightness

straight from the shoulder 4 open 5 frank 6 candid, direct, openly 7 bluntly, frankly, sincere 8 candidly, directly 9 downright

straightness 7 honesty 8 evenness 10 directness 11 uprightness

strain 3 air, tax, tug 4 kind, line, pull, sift, song, sort, toil, tune, type, vein 5 blood, breed, drain, force, grain, grind, group, heave, labor, people, press, sieve, streak, stock, trait, twist 6 burden, drudge, effort, extend, family, filter, genius, injure, injury, melody, overdo, purify, refine, screen, sprain, stress, weaken, winnow, wrench 7 descent, distend, exhaust, fatigue, lineage, overtax, species, stretch, tension, tighten, try hard, variety, wear out 8 ancestry, bear down, elongate, exertion, hardship, heredity, make taut, overwork, pressure, protract, struggle, tendency 9 draw tight, make tense, overexert, parentage 10 buckle down, derivation, extraction, overburden 11 disposition, huff and puff, inclination 12 do double duty, drive oneself, exert oneself 14 predisposition, work like a horse, work like a slave

strained 5 tense 6 touchy 8 volatile 9 explosive 10 precarious

strait 7 channel, narrows, passage

straitened 5 broke, needy 6 hard-up 7 pinched 8 bank rupt, indigent, strapped, wiped-out 9 destitute, penniless, penurious 10 distressed, pauperized, restricted 11 embarrassed 12 impoverished 15 poverty-stricken

Strait Is the Gate
author: 9 Andre Gide

straitlaced 4 prim 5 rigid, stiff 6 formal, narrow, proper, severe, strict 7 austere, prudish, uptight 8 reserved 9 inhibited 11 puritanical 14 overscrupulous 15 undemonstrative

straits 3 fix 4 hole 6 pickle, plight 8 distress 9 extremity 10 difficulty 11 predicament 13 embarrassment

strand 4 bank, cord, lock, rope 5 beach, braid, coast, fiber, leave, shore, tress, twist 6 desert, ground, maroon, string, thread 8 filament, necklace, seacoast, seashore 9 component, go aground, riverside, shipwreck 10 ingredient, run aground 15 leave high and dry, leave in the lurch

stranded 5 stuck 6 ashore 7 aground, beached 8 grounded 9 foundered 11 shipwrecked 14 left high and dry, left in the lurch

strange 3 new, odd 4 lost 5 alien, queer 6 uneasy, unused 7 awkward, bizarre, curious, erratic, foreign, unknown, unusual 8 aberrant, abnormal, freakish, peculiar, singular, uncommon 9 alienated, anomalous, eccentric, estranged, fantastic, ill at ease, irregular, unnatural 10 bewildered, farfetched, out of place, outlandish, unexplored, unfamiliar 11 discomposed, disoriented, out-of-the-way 12 unaccustomed, undiscovered, unhabituated 13 extraordinary, unaccountable, uncomfortable 14 unconventional

Strange Fruit
author: 12 Lillian Smith

Strange Interlude
author: 12 Eugene O'Neill

strangeness 7 anomaly, oddness 9 queerness 10 aberration 11 abnormality, peculiarity 12 eccentricity, idiosyncrasy, irregularity, unconformity 13 nonconformity

stranger 5 alien 8 newcomer, outsider 9 auslander, foreigner, immigrant, outlander

Stranger, The
author: 11 Albert Camus

Strangers on a Train
director: 15 Alfred Hitchcock
cast: 9 Ruth Roman 11 Leo G Carroll, Marion Lorne 12 Robert Walker 13 Farley Granger 17 Patricia Hitchcock
remade as: 20 Once You Kiss a Stranger

strange to say
Latin: 13 mirabile dictu

strangle 3 gag 4 stop 5 burke, check, choke, crush, quell 6 muzzle, stifle 7 garrote, put down, repress, smother, squelch 8 choke off, snuff out, suppress, throttle 9 suffocate 10 asphyxiate, extinguish

strangulate 8 choke off, compress, strangle 9 constrict

strap 3 tie 4 band, beat, belt, bind, cord, flog, lash, whip 5 flail, leash, thong, truss 6 tether, thrash 7 scourge

strapped 8 bankrupt, wiped out 9 insolvent, penniless 12 impoverished, without funds

strapping 5 burly, hardy, husky, stout 6 brawny, robust, strong, sturdy 8 muscular, powerful, stalwart

stratagem 4 game, plan, plot, ploy, ruse, wile 5 blind, dodge, feint, trick 6 deceit, device, scheme, tactic 8 artifice, intrigue, maneuver, trickery 9 deception 10 subterfuge 11 contrivance, machination

strategic 3 key 4 wary 5 vital 6 clever 7 careful, crucial, cunning, guarded, planned, politic, prudent, turning 8 cautious, critical, decisive, military, tactical, vigilant 9 important, momentous, principal 10 calculated, deliberate, diplomatic 11 significant 13 consequential, precautionary

strategy 4 game 5 craft, wiles 6 policy, scheme 7 cunning, devices, tactics 8 artifice, art of war, game plan, plotting 9 war policy 10 artfulness, craftiness 11 grand design, machination, maneuvering 12 military plan 15 military science

stratosphere 3 sky 5 ozone 7 heavens 8 upper air 12 high altitude 14 wild blue yonder

stratum 4 band, belt, seam, zone 5 layer

Strauss, Johann (the Elder)
composer of: 13 Radetzky March

Strauss, Johann (the Younger)
composer of: 6 The Bat 13 Die Fledermaus, The Gipsy Baron 16 Der Zigeunerbaron
waltz: 12 Emperor Waltz 13 The Blue Danube 23 Tales from the Vienna Woods

Strauss, Joseph
composer of: 17 Music of the Spheres 27 The Village Swallows in Austria

Strauss, Levi
make of: 5 jeans 9 dungarees

Strauss, Richard
born: 6 Munich 7 Germany
composer of: 6 Salome 7 Don Juan, Elektra 8 Arabella 9 Capriccio 10 Don Quixote 14 Ein Heldenleben 15 Ariadne auf Naxos 16 Der Rosenkavalier, Domestic Symphony, Till Eulenspiegel 19 Die Frau ohne Schatten 20 Die Aegyptische Helena, Thus Spake Zarathustra 21 Also Sprach Zarathustra 23 Death and Transfiguration

Stravinsky, Igor Feodorovich
born: 6 Russia 11 Oranienbaum
composer of: 4 Agon 6 Threni 7 Orpheus 8 The Flood 9 Card Party, Fireworks 10 Oedipus Rex, Petrouchka, Petruschka, Pulcinella 11 Jeu de Cartes, The Firebird 13 Dumbarton Oaks, Psalm Symphony 14 The Nightingale 15 Abraham and Isaac, The Rite of Spring 16 Requiem

Canticles, The Rake's Progress **18** Le Sacre du Printemps

straw 3 hay **4** tube **5** chaff **7** pipette

strawberry 8 Fragaria
varieties: 4 mock **5** beach **6** barren, Dunlap, garden, Indian **7** sow-teat **8** Klondike, Rosacean, Virginia, woodland
liqueur: 13 creme de fraise

Straw Dogs
director: 12 Sam Peckinpah
cast: 9 T P McKenna **11** Susan George **12** Peter Vaughan **13** Dustin Hoffman

straw man 6 effigy **9** scapegoat, scarecrow

stray 4 lost, roam, rove, waif **5** drift **6** random, wander **7** digress, drifter **8** go astray, sepa rate, set apart, straggle, straying, vagabond, wanderer **9** itinerant, misplaced, scat tered, straggler **10** lost animal, lost person **11** lose one's way

straying 5 lapse **8** drifting, rambling **9** departure, deviation, wandering **10** abberation, digression, divergence

streak 3 bar, bed, fly **4** band, blot, blur, cast, dart, dash, daub, line, lode, race, rush, seam, tear, vein, whiz, zoom **5** layer, level, plane, smear, speed, strip, touch **6** blotch, hurtle, smirch, smudge, strain, stripe **7** portion, splotch, stratum

stream 3 jet, run **4** blow, file, flow, flux, gush, pour, race, rill, rush, teem, tide, waft, wave **5** brook, burst, creek, float, flood, issue, river, shoot, spate, spill, spout, spurt, surge **6** abound, branch, course, deluge, extend, feeder, onrush, sluice **7** current, flutter, freshet, rivulet, torrent **8** effusion, fountain, overflow **9** profusion, tributary **11** watercourse

streamer 4 flag **6** banner, burgee **7** pennant

streamlet 3 run **4** rill **5** brook, creek **7** rivulet

streamlined 4 racy **5** clean, sleek **7** compact **8** up-to-date **9** organized **10** futuristic, modernized, simplified **11** aerodynamic

stream of abuse 6 tirade **8** diatribe, harangue **9** contumely, invective **12** vituperation

Streep, Meryl
real name: 16 Mary Louise Streep
born: 14 Basking Ridge NJ
roles: 8 Ironweed, Silkwood **11** Out of Africa **13** Falling in Love, Sophie's Choice (Oscar), The Deer Hunter **14** Before and After, Kramer vs Kramer **20** Postcards from the Edge, The House of the Spirits **25** The Bridges of Madison County, The French Lieutenant's Woman

street 3 way **4** lane, mews, road **5** alley, block, route **6** avenue **7** highway, roadway, terrace, thruway **8** turnpike **9** boulevard **10** expressway **12** thoroughfare

Streetcar Named Desire, A
author: 17 Tennessee Williams
director: 9 Elia Kazan
cast: 9 Kim Hunter (Stella Dubois Kowalski) **10** Karl Malden **11** Vivien Leigh (Blanche Dubois) **12** Marlon Brando (Stanley Kowalski)
setting: 10 New Orleans
score: 9 Alex North
Oscar for: 7 actress (Leigh) **15** supporting actor (Malden) **17** supporting actress (Hunter)

Streets of San Francisco, The
character: 9 (Det Lt) Mike Stone **10** (Inspector) Dan Robbins **11** (Inspector) Steve Keller
cast: 10 Karl Malden **12** Richard Hatch **14** Michael Douglas

strega
type: 7 liqueur
origin: 5 Italy
flavor: 6 spices **10** orange peel
with brandy: 10 Strega Flip

Streisand, Barbra
real name: 20 Barbara Joan Streisand
born: 10 Brooklyn NY
husband: 11 Elliot Gould
roles: 5 Yentl **9** Funny Girl (Oscar), Funny Lady **10** Fanny Brice, Hello Dolly, What's Up Doc? **11** A Star Is Born **12** The Main Event, The Way We Were **13** The Prince of Tides **20** The Mirror Has Two Faces
recordings: 10 The Concert **11** A Star Is Born **23** The Barbra Streisand Album

strength 4 beef, grit, kick, pith, sand, size **5** brawn, force, forte, might, pluck, power, sinew, spice, vigor **6** anchor, mettle, number, purity, spirit, succor, virtue **7** bravery, muscles, potency, stamina, support **8** backbone, buttress, efficacy, firmness, mainstay, security, solidity, tenacity, vitality **9** endurance, fortitude, hardiness, intensity, lustiness, puissance, stoutness, toughness, viability **10** robustness, sturdiness, sustenance **13** concentration, effectiveness **16** stoutheartedness
Latin: 3 vis

strengthen 4 prop **5** brace, renew, steel **6** harden **7** build up, enhance, fortify, improve, restore, shore up, support, sustain **8** buttress **9** reinforce

strength of character 4 grit, guts **5** pluck, spunk **6** mettle **7** resolve **8** backbone **9** fortitude **10** resolution **12** resoluteness **13** steadfastness

strenuous 4 hard **5** eager **6** active, ardent, dogged, taxing, uphill **7** arduous, dynamic, earnest, intense, zealous **8** animated, diligent, sedulous, spirited, untiring, vigorous **9** assiduous, difficult, energetic, laborious,

punishing **10** exhausting, on one's toes **11** hardworking, industrious, painstaking **12** enterprising **13** indefatigable

stress 4 beat, mark **5** force, value, worth **6** accent, affirm, assert, burden, moment, repeat, strain, weight **7** anxiety, concern, feature, gravity, meaning, sawdust, tension, urgency **8** emphasis, pressure **9** emphasize, necessity, underline **10** accentuate, importance, insist upon, oppression, prominence, underscore **11** consequence, seriousness **12** accentuation, significance **13** consideration

stretch 4 span, term, tire **5** cover, reach, spell, stint, tract, while, widen **6** burden, deepen, expand, extend, period, sprawl, spread, spring, strain **7** distend, draw out, expanse, fatigue, lie over, over tax, pull out **8** distance, draw taut, duration, elongate, interval, lengthen, overtask, over work, protract, put forth, reach out, tautness, traverse **9** be elastic, draw tight, make tense, make tight, overexert **10** elasticity, exaggerate, overburden, overcharge, overstrain, push too far, resiliency **11** carry too far **12** be expandable, be extendable **14** push to the limit

stretchable 7 elastic, rubbery **8** flexible **9** resilient

stretching 9 extending, extension **10** drawing out, elongation **11** attenuation, enlargement, lengthening, protraction **12** prolongation **13** amplification

stretching out 8 outreach **9** expansion, extending, extension **10** elongation **11** attenuation, lengthening **12** prolongation

stretch out 6 expand, extend **7** amplify, augment, draw out **8** elongate, lengthen, protract

Strether
character in: 14 The Ambassadors
author: 10 Henry James

strew 3 sow **6** litter **7** scatter **8** disperse **9** broadcast **11** disseminate

stricken 3 ill **4** hurt, sick **7** injured, smitten, wounded **8** blighted, diseased **9** afflicted, taken sick **13** incapacitated

strict 4 nice **5** exact, rigid, stern **6** severe **7** austere, perfect **8** absolute, complete, exacting, rigorous, unerring **9** stringent **10** fastidious, inflexible, meticulous, scrupulous, unyielding **13** authoritarian, conscientious **14** uncompromising

strictly required
French: 9 de rigueur

stride 4 gait, lope, pace, step **5** march, stalk **7** advance, headway **8** long step, progress **11** advancement, improvement **13** take long steps

strident 5 harsh **6** shrill **7** grating, jarring, rasping, raucous **8** clashing, grinding, jangling, piercing, twanging **9** dissonant **10** discordant, screeching **11** cacophonous, high-pitched

Striebel, John H
creator/artist of: **10** Dixie Dugan

strife 6 unrest **7** discord, trouble, turmoil, warfare **8** conflict, disquiet, fighting, struggle, upheaval, violence **10** contention, convulsion, disharmony, dissension **11** altercation, disturbance

Strife
author: **14** John Galsworthy

strike 3 bat, box, hit, run, tap **4** bang, beat, belt, bump, clap, clip, club, come, cuff, drub, find, flog, lash, make, meet, pelt, ring, slam, slap, slug, sock, toll, whip, wipe **5** chime, clout, erase, flail, knell, knock, light, pound, punch, reach, smash, smite, sound, thump, tie-up, whack, whale **6** affect, arrive, assail, attack, batter, buffet, cancel, chance, charge, cudgel, delete, effect, fold up, hammer, pommel, remove, seem to, thrash, wallop **7** achieve, arrange, assault, boycott, impress, occur to, protest, put away, ram into, run into, scourge, scratch, stumble, unearth, walk out **8** appear to, bump into, come upon, cross out, dawn upon, discover, fall upon, lambaste, pull down, take down **9** burst upon, devastate, eliminate, encounter, eradicate, knock into, take apart **10** come across, flagellate, meet head-on **11** beat against, collide with, dash against **12** labor dispute, work stoppage

strike a bargain 5 agree **6** settle **9** make a deal **10** compromise **11** come to terms, meet halfway **18** split the difference **20** reach an understanding

strike back 7 counter, get even, hit back, pay back, riposte **9** fight back, retaliate **13** counterattack

strike dumb 4 daze, stun **5** amaze, shock **7** astound, stagger, stupefy **8** astonish, dumfound **9** dumbfound, electrify **11** flabbergast

strike noisily 4 bang, beat, clap, slam **5** thump

strike out 6 delete, fan out, set off, set out **7** take out **10** sally forth

strike sharply 3 rap **4** slap **5** crack

striking 6 marked **7** notable **9** prominent **10** astounding, impressive, noteworthy, noticeable, remarkable, surprising **11** conspicuous, outstanding **13** extraordinary

Strindberg, August
author of: **9** Miss Julie, The Father **10** A Dream Play **12** The Creditors **14** The Ghost Sonata **15** The Dance of Death

string 3 row **4** cord, file, line, rope **5** chain, queue, train, twine **6** column,

extend, parade, series, spread, strand, thread **7** binding, stretch **8** necklace, sequence **10** procession, succession

stringent 5 close, harsh, spare, stern, stiff, tight **6** cogent, frugal, severe, strict **7** sparing **8** exacting, forceful, rigorous **9** demanding, effectual, unbending **10** inflexible, unyielding **14** uncompromising

strip 3 rob **4** band, flay, loot, peel, raid, sack, skin, slip, tear **5** field, flake, rifle, shave **6** denude, divest, length, ravage, remove, ribbon, stripe, unwrap **7** deprive, despoil, disrobe, draw off, lay bare, measure, plunder, pull off, ransack, uncover, undrape, undress **8** airstrip, desolate, lay waste, spoliate, unclothe **9** steal from **11** disencumber

stripe 3 bar **4** band, line, tape **5** braid, strip, swath **6** ribbon, streak **7** chevron **8** insignia **9** striation

stripling 3 boy, lad **5** minor, youth **8** teenager, young man **9** schoolboy, youngster **10** adolescent

stripped 4 bare, nude **5** naked **6** peeled, unclad **7** denuded, exposed, unrobed **8** disrobed, divested **9** unclothed, uncovered, undressed

strive 3 vie **4** push **5** essay, fight, labor **6** battle, strain **7** contend, try hard **8** endeavor, struggle **9** take pains, undertake **10** do one's best **12** apply oneself, do one's utmost, exert oneself, spare no pains **15** work like a Trojan **18** move heaven and earth **20** leave no stone unturned

striving 4 toil **5** exert, labor **6** effort, strain **7** toiling, travail **8** exertion, struggle **9** straining **10** struggling

stroke 3 bat, hit, pat, pet, tap **4** blow, chop, coup, deed, feat, poke, slap, sock, swat **5** brush, chime, fluke, punch, whack **6** caress, chance, wallop **7** massage, ringing, seizure, tolling **8** accident, apoplexy, flourish, movement, sounding, striking **11** achievement, coincidence, piece of luck, transaction **15** brain hemorrhage

stroll 4 tour, turn, walk **5** amble, mosey **6** ramble, wander **7** meander, saunter **9** poke along, promenade **14** constitutional

stroller 4 pram **5** buggy **6** ambler, walker **7** rambler **8** carriage **9** itinerant, pushchair, saunterer **10** promenader **12** perambulator

strong 3 hot **4** able, bold, deep, keen, tart **5** burly, clear, close, fiery, hardy, nippy, sharp, solid, sound, stout, tangy, tough, vivid **6** ardent, biting, brawny, bright, cogent, fervid, fierce, gritty, hearty, mighty, moving, plucky, potent, robust, savory, severe, sinewy, sturdy **7** buoyant, capable, devoted, earnest, fervent, healthy, intense, piquant, pungent, skilled, violent, zeal-

ous **8** animated, athletic, definite, diligent, distinct, emphatic, faithful, forceful, muscular, powerful, puissant, sedulous, spirited, stalwart, tireless, vehement, vigorous **9** assiduous, competent, confirmed, effective, energetic, herculean, resilient, tenacious, undiluted **10** compelling, convincing, courageous, deep-seated, persistent, proficient **11** impassioned, persevering, resourceful **12** advantageous, concentrated, highly spiced, high-spirited, unmistakable **13** indefatigable, well-qualified **14** highly flavored, highly seasoned
Spanish: **5** macho

Strong
character in: **7** Erewhon
author: **6** Butler

strong-arm 3 cow **5** bully, force **6** coerce, compel **8** browbeat, threaten **10** intimidate

strong feeling 4 fear, hate, heat, love, zeal **5** anger, ardor **6** fervor, sorrow, warmth **7** despair, emotion, passion, sadness **8** jealousy **9** happiness, vehemence **12** satisfaction

stronghold 4 fort, hold, home, keep **6** bunker, center, locale, refuge **7** bastion, bulwark, citadel, rampart, redoubt **8** fastness, fortress, safehold, stockade **10** battlement, blockhouse **13** fortification

strongly committed 4 true **5** loyal **6** ardent **7** devoted, staunch, zealous **8** adhering, faithful **9** dedicated, steadfast **10** passionate, unwavering

strong point 5 forte **6** anchor **8** mainstay, strength

strong-willed 5 pushy **8** forceful, positive **9** assertive **10** aggressive **11** domineering, self-assured **13** self-assertive

structural support 3 bar **4** beam, prop, stud **5** brace, joist **6** girder, rafter, timber **7** trestle **12** underpinning

structure 4 form, plan **6** design, makeup **7** arrange, edifice, pattern **8** assemble, building, conceive, organize **9** construct, formation **11** arrangement, composition, put together **12** conformation, construction, organization **13** configuration

struggle 3 vie, war **4** duel, feud, pull, push, spar, tilt **5** argue, brawl, brush, clash, fight, grind, joust, labor, match, scrap, trial **6** action, battle, combat, differ, effort, engage, jostle, oppose, resist, strain, stress, strife, strive, tussle **7** compete, contend, contest, grapple, quarrel, scuffle **8** conflict, endeavor, exertion, long haul, skirmish, work hard **9** encounter, lock horns, take pains **10** engagement **11** altercation, cross swords **15** work like a Trojan **18** move heaven and earth **20** leave no stone unturned

strut 4 sail 6 parade, sashay 7 peacock, swagger 9 promenade

Struthiomimus
type: 8 dinosaur, theropod
known as: 15 ostrich dinosaur
period: 10 Cretaceous
characteristic: 9 toothless

Stryver
character in: 16 A Tale of Two Cities
author: 7 Dickens

Stuart, Gilbert
born: 15 North Kingston RI
artwork: 16 George Washington

Stuart, J E B
served in: 8 Civil War
side: 11 Confederate
commander of: 7 cavalry
battle: 7 Bull Run 8 Antietam 10 Gettysburg 14 Fredericksburg 16 Chancellorsville 18 Peninsular campaign

Stuart Little
author: 7 E B White

stub 3 end 4 bump, butt, dock, tail 5 crush, knock, snuff, stump 6 fag end, scrape 7 receipt, remains, tamp out, voucher 10 extinguish, torn ticket 11 counterfoil

stubble 5 beard 6 stumps 8 bristles, whiskers 9 cut stalks 16 five-o'clock shadow

stubborn 6 dogged, mulish, strong, sturdy 7 willful 8 forceful, obdurate, perverse, resolute 9 concerted, immovable, obstinate, pigheaded, resistant, tenacious, unbending, unmovable 10 bullheaded, headstrong, inflexible, persistent, purposeful, refractory, self-willed, unshakable, unyielding 11 indomitable, intractable, opinionated, uncompliant 12 hard to handle, recalcitrant, ungovernable, wholehearted

stubbornness 10 mulishness, obstinancy, resistance 11 willfulness 13 intransigence, pigheadedness

stubby 5 dumpy, pudgy, squab, squat, tubby 6 chubby, chunky, stocky, stodgy, stumpy 7 squatty 8 thickset

Stubtoe State
nickname of: 7 Montana

stuck 3 dug, put 4 held 5 bound, fixed, fused, glued, mired, poked 6 balked, curbed, jabbed, joined, nailed, pasted, pinned, placed, sealed, spiked, tacked, thrust, welded 7 adhered, affixed, boggled, impeded, planted, pricked, punched, saddled, snarled, speared, stabbed, stalled, stumped, stymied 8 attached, burdened, cemented, fastened, inserted 9 punctured 10 obstructed, perforated 11 immobilized

stuck-up 4 vain 5 cocky 6 snooty, uppish, uppity 7 haughty, high-hat 8 arrogant, snobbish 9 bigheaded, conceited 10 disdainful, egocentric, hoity-toity 11 overbearing, swellheaded 13 self-important, self-satisfied

stud 3 dot 4 beam, buck, dude, sire 5

board, rivet 6 button 7 upright 8 fastener, macho man, nailhead

student 4 coed 5 pupil 6 reader 7 analyst, learner, scholar, watcher 8 disciple, examiner, follower, observer, reviewer 9 collegian, schoolboy, spectator 10 schoolgirl 11 commentator, interpreter, matriculant 13 undergraduate

studied 8 measured 10 calculated, deliberate, purposeful 11 intentional 12 premeditated

studious 6 brainy, intent 7 bookish, earnest, erudite 8 academic, cerebral, diligent, literate, well-read 9 laborious, scholarly 10 determined, purposeful, scholastic 11 painstaking 12 intellectual

Studs Lonigan
series includes: 11 Judgment Day 12 Young Lonigan 29 The Young Manhood of Studs Lonigan
author: 13 James T Farrell

study 3 den 4 cram, read 5 grind, probe 6 office, peruse, review, search, studio, survey 7 examine, explore, inquiry, library, observe, reading 8 analysis, consider, learning, pore over, read up on, research, scrutiny 9 delve into, education 10 glance over, inspection, scrutinize 11 examination, exploration, hit the books, inquire into, instruction, investigate, read closely, reading room, scholarship 13 consideration, investigation, school oneself, search through

Study in Scarlet, A
author: 19 Sir Arthur Conan Doyle
character: 12 Dr John Watson 13 Jefferson Hope, Tobias Gregson 14 Sherlock Holmes 17 Inspector Lestrade

Study of History, A
author: 14 Arnold J Toynbee

stuff 3 act, bit, jam, pad, wad 4 best, bosh, bunk, cram, fill, gear, heap, load, pack, pile, sate, stow 5 cache, crowd, gorge, hokum, hooey, stash, store, thing, trash, wedge 6 burden, fill up, humbug, matter, staple, tackle, things, thrust, tricks, utmost 7 effects, essence, hogwash, overeat, rubbish, satiate, spinach, twaddle 8 darndest, falderal, material, nonsense 9 component, empty talk, substance 10 balderdash, belongings, gluttonize, ingredient, make a pig of 11 constituent, foolishness, overindulge, performance, possessions, raw material 12 quintessence 13 paraphernalia

stuff-and-nonsense 3 rot 4 bosh, bull, bunk 5 hokum, hooey, trash 6 bunkum, drivel, humbug 7 baloney, hogwash, spinach, twaddle 8 buncombe, claptrap, nonsense, tommyrot 9 poppycock 10 applesauce, balder-

dash, tomfoolery 11 foolishness 12 fiddlesticks 13 horsefeathers

stuffed 4 full 6 filled, jammed, loaded, packed, rammed, wadded 7 crammed, crushed, replete 8 overfull, satiated, squeezed 10 sandwiched

stuff in 4 cram, pack 6 devour 8 bolt down, compress, gobble up, wolf down

stuffing 5 farce 7 filling, packing, padding, wadding 8 dressing 9 forcemeat

stuffy 4 cold, smug 5 close, fusty, heavy, muggy, musty, staid 6 stodgy, sultry 7 airless, pompous 8 reserved, stagnant, stifling 9 clogged-up, congested, high-flown, stopped-up, stuffed-up 10 old-fogyish, oppressive, sweltering 11 pretentious, straitlaced, suffocating 12 supercilious, unventilated 13 ill-ventilated, self-satisfied, stale-smelling

stultify 4 balk 6 hinder, impair, impede, thwart 7 cripple, inhibit, nullify, vitiate 8 suppress 9 frustrate, hamstring 11 make useless

stumble 3 hit 4 fall, reel, roll, sway, trip 5 botch, lurch, pitch, spill 6 bungle, falter, happen, hash up, hobble, mess up, slip up, sprawl, topple, totter 7 blunder, misstep, shamble, stagger 8 flounder 10 take a spill 12 come by chance, make mistakes, pitch forward

stumble upon 4 find 7 learn of 8 come upon, discover 10 chance upon, happen upon 14 find by accident

stumbling block 3 bar, rub 4 snag 5 block, catch, hitch 6 hamper, hurdle 7 barrier, problem 8 drawback, obstacle 9 detriment, hindrance 10 difficulty, impediment 11 obstruction 12 complication, interference

stump 3 end 4 butt, foil, stub, thud 5 befog, clomp, clonk, clump, clunk, stamp, stomp, tramp 6 baffle, nubbin, stymie 7 confuse, mystify, nonplus, perplex 8 bewilder, confound, dumfound, footfall, stomping, tramping 9 bamboozle, dumbfound

stun 4 daze, numb 5 amaze, shock 7 astound, stagger, startle, stupefy 8 astonish, dumfound 9 dumbfound 11 flabbergast

stunner 4 doll 5 beaut, Venus 6 beauty, eyeful 8 knockout 9 dreamboat 10 good-looker

stunning 6 dazing, lovely 7 amazing, numbing 8 shocking, striking 9 beautiful, exquisite, startling 10 astounding, staggering, stupefying 11 astonishing, dumfounding 12 dumbfounding, electrifying 14 flabbergasting

stunt 3 act 4 curb, feat 5 abort, check, cramp, dwarf, limit, stint, trick 6 impede, number, stifle **7** curtail, delimit **8** restrain, restrict, suppress

stunted 5 dumpy, runty **6** bantam **7** dwarfed, squatty, wizened **9** pint-sized **13** foreshortened

Stunt Man, The
   director: 11 Richard Rush
   cast: 9 Alex Rocco **11** Peter O'Toole (Eli Cross) **13** Allen Goorwitz, Sharon Farrell **14** Barbara Hershey, Steve Railsback

stupefaction 5 shock **8** numbness, surprise **9** amazement **12** astonishment

stupefied 5 dazed **6** amazed **7** shocked, stunned **8** benumbed **10** dumbstruck, dumfounded **11** dumbfounded **13** flabbergasted, thunderstruck

stupefy 4 daze, stun **5** amaze, shock **7** astound, nonplus, stagger **8** astonish, confound, dumfound, surprise **9** dumbfound, overwhelm **11** flabbergast

stupefying 8 shocking, stunning **11** dumfounding **12** dumbfounding, electrifying, overwhelming **14** flabbergasting

stupendous 3 big **4** huge, vast **5** giant, great, jumbo **6** mighty **7** amazing, immense, mammoth, massive, titanic, unusual **8** colossal, enormous, fabulous, gigantic, imposing, stunning, terrific **9** cyclopean, herculean, marvelous, monstrous, very great, very large, wonderful **10** astounding, gargantuan, incredible, monumental, phenomenal, prodigious, remarkable, surprising, tremendous, unexpected **11** astonishing, elephantine **13** extraordinary

stupid 4 dull, dumb **5** dense, inane, inept, silly **6** absurd, oafish, obtuse, simple, unwise **7** aimless, asinine, boorish, doltish, fatuous, foolish, idiotic, moronic, witless **8** backward, childish, heedless, mistaken, reckless, tactless **9** brainless, cretinous, dimwitted, duncelike, foolhardy, ill-judged, imbecilic, imprudent, pointless, senseless **10** half-witted, ill-advised, indiscreet, irrelevant, weak-minded **11** empty-headed, meaningless, nonsensical, purposeless, thoughtless **12** absentminded, muddleheaded, preposterous, simpleminded, slow-learning, unreasonable **13** ill-considered, inappropriate, irresponsible, rattlebrained, unintelligent

stupor 4 daze **5** faint **6** apathy, torpor **7** inertia **8** blackout, lethargy, numbness **9** inertness **10** somnolence **12** stupefaction **13** insensibility

sturdy 4 able, firm **5** brave, burly, gutsy, hardy, heavy, solid, sound, stout, tough **6** daring, dogged, gritty, heroic, mighty, plucky, robust, rug-

ged, secure, sinewy, spunky, strong **7** defiant, doughty, durable, gallant, lasting, valiant **8** enduring, fearless, forceful, intrepid, muscular, powerful, resolute, spirited, stalwart, stubborn, vigorous, well-made **9** dauntless, strapping, unabashed, undaunted, well-built **10** courageous, determined, invincible **11** indomitable, substantial, unshrinking **12** high-spirited, stouthearted **15** well-constructed

Sturges, John
   director of: 14 The Great Escape **19** The Magnificent Seven

Sturges, Preston
   director of: 10 The Lady Eve **16** Sullivan's Travels **17** The Palm Beach Story, Unfaithfully Yours **21** Hail the Conquering Hero **24** The Miracle of Morgan's Creek

Sturmabteilung 13 storm troopers

Sturm und Drang 22 German literary movement (18th century)
   literally: 14 storm and stress

stygian 3 dim **4** dark **5** black, murky **6** dreary, gloomy, somber **7** hellish **8** funereal, infernal, starless **9** tenebrous, unlighted

style 3 fad **4** call, elan, kind, mode, name, pomp, rage, sort, type **5** charm, class, craze, favor, flair, grace, model, taste, trend, vogue **6** design, luxury, manner, polish **7** arrange, comfort, fashion, pattern **8** currency, elegance **9** affluence, designate **10** smoothness **11** savoir faire
   French: 4 gout

stylish 3 hip, new **4** chic **5** natty, smart, swank **6** dapper, latest, modern, modish, with-it **7** a la mode, elegant, in vogue, voguish **8** up-to-date **9** in fashion **11** fashionable **13** sophisticated, up-to-the-minute

stymie 4 balk **5** block, check, stump **6** baffle, hinder, puzzle, thwart **7** confuse, mystify **8** confound, obstruct **9** frustrate

Styracosaurus
   type: 8 dinosaur **10** ceratopsid
   location: 12 North America
   period: 10 Cretaceous
   characteristic: 6 horned

Styron, William
   author of: 12 The Long March **13** Sophie's Choice **15** Darkness Visible **17** Lie Down in Darkness **18** Set This House on Fire **25** The Confessions of Nat Turner

Styx
   form: 5 river
   location: 5 Hades **10** underworld
   father: 7 Oceanus
   ferryman: 6 Charon

suave 6 silken, smooth, urbane **7** affable, elegant, politic **8** charming, gracious, mannerly, polished, unctuous **9**

civilized **10** diplomatic, flattering **12** ingratiating **13** smooth-tongued

sub 5 below, proxy, under **6** backup, deputy, second **7** beneath, standby, stand-in **9** alternate, submarine, surrogate **10** substitute, understudy **11** pinch-hitter

subaltern 4 aide **6** helper **9** assistant **10** lieutenant **11** subordinate

subconscious 3 dim **7** dawning **9** intuitive **10** subliminal **11** instinctive

subdivide 6 divide **7** split up **8** separate **9** partition

subdivision 3 arm **4** wing **6** branch **7** chapter, section **8** offshoot **11** development **12** neighborhood

subdue 3 bow **4** calm, curb, down, drub, ease, foil, mute, rout, trim, whip **5** allay, break, check, crush, floor, quell, salve, smash, still **6** deaden, defeat, master, mellow, muffle, reduce, soften, soothe, temper, thrash **7** appease, assuage, conquer, mollify, oppress, overrun, put down, relieve, slacken, subject, trample **8** mitigate, moderate, overcome, palliate, surmount, tone down, vanquish **9** meliorate, overpower, overwhelm, quiet down, soft-pedal, subjugate **10** ameliorate **11** triumph over **12** tranquillize

subdued 4 dull **5** cowed, muted, quiet **7** abashed, crushed, humbled, muffled, quelled **8** deadened, overcame **10** humiliated, indistinct, lackluster **11** intimidated, overpowered

subduer 6 victor, winner **9** conqueror, overcomer **10** subjugator, vanquisher **11** intimidator

subject 4 bare, case, gist, open, pith, text **5** field, issue, liege, motif, prone, study, theme, topic **6** affair, expose, liable, matter, submit, thesis, vassal **7** bound by, citizen, concern, exposed, lay open **8** business, disposed, follower, obedient, question **9** dependent, subjected, substance **10** answerable, discipline, in danger of, make liable, put through, vulnerable **11** stipulatory, subordinate, subservient, susceptible

subjection 11 subjugation **12** subservience **13** regimentation, subordination

subjective 5 inner **6** biased **7** partial **8** partisan, personal **9** emotional **10** individual, prejudiced **12** nonobjective

subjoin 5 add on, affix, annex **6** append, attach, tack on

subjugate 4 tame **5** crush, quell **6** subdue **7** conquer, put down **8** dominate, suppress, vanquish **10** over master

subjugation 6 chains, thrall **7** bondage, slavery **9** dominance, mastering, servitude, thralldom **10** conquering, domination **11** enslavement, vanquishing

subjugator 6 master, victor 7 subduer 9 conqueror, dominator 10 vanquisher 11 slavemaster

sublimate 4 turn 5 exalt, shift 6 divert, purify 7 channel, convert, elevate, ennoble 8 redirect, transfer 9 transform, transmute 12 spiritualize

sublime 4 high 5 grand, great, lofty, noble 6 superb 7 exalted, stately 8 elevated, imposing, majestic, splendid, terrific, very good 9 estimable, excellent, marvelous, wonderful 12 awe-inspiring, praiseworthy

submarine
  invented by: 7 Holland
  even keel: 4 Lake
  torpedo: 8 Bushnell

submerge 4 dive, sink 5 douse, drown, flood, souse 6 deluge, engulf, go down, plunge 7 go under, immerse 8 inundate, pour over, submerse

submerse 5 drown 6 engulf 7 immerse 8 inundate, submerge

submersion 7 sinking 8 drowning 9 immersion 10 inundation 11 submergence

submission 8 giving in, meekness, tameness, yielding 9 handing in, obedience, passivity, surrender, tendering 10 compliance, remittance, submitting 11 passiveness 12 acquiescence, capitulation, presentation, subservience, tractability 13 nonresistance 14 submissiveness

submissive 4 meek, mild 6 docile, humble, pliant 7 dutiful, fawning, passive, servile, slavish 8 crawling, obedient, toadying, yielding 9 compliant, malleable, tractable, truckling 10 obsequious 11 acquiescent, bootlicking, complaisant, deferential, subservient, unassertive 12 capitulating, ingratiating, nonresisting 13 accommodating

submissiveness 8 docility, meekness 9 passivity 10 compliance 11 resignation 12 complaisance, tractability

submit 3 bow 4 bend, cede 5 agree, argue, claim, defer, kneel, offer, stoop, yield 6 accede, assert, commit, comply, give in, give up, resort, tender 7 contend, hold out, present, proffer, propose, succumb, suggest 8 back down, put forth 9 acquiesce, surrender, volunteer 10 capitulate, put forward 12 knuckle under

submit an offer 3 bid 6 tender 7 proffer, propose

submit to 4 bear, take 5 abide, brave, brook, stand 6 endure, suffer 7 stomach, undergo 8 stand for, tolerate 9 put up with

subnormal 3 bad, low 5 seedy, sorry 6 crummy, dismal, shabby, sleazy, subpar 7 abysmal 8 below par, inferior, mediocre, wretched 9 defective, deficient 10 inadequate, second-rate 11 below normal, substandard 12 insufficient

subordinate 4 help 5 lower 6 junior, lackey, lesser, menial, worker 7 servant, subject 8 hireling, inferior 9 ancillary, assistant, attendant, auxiliary, dependent, of low rank, outranked, secondary, subaltern, underling 10 subsidiary 11 subservient

subordination 10 subjection 11 inferiority, subjugation 12 subservience 13 regimentation

suborn 5 bribe 6 buy off, pay off

sub rosa 8 covertly, in secret, on the sly, secretly 9 in private, privately 12 off-the-record 14 confidentially 15 behind-the-scenes 17 behind closed doors

subscribe 4 help, sign 6 assent, chip in, donate 7 consent, endorse, support 8 hold with 9 undersign 10 contribute

subsequent 4 next 7 ensuing 9 following, proximate 10 consequent, succeeding, successive

subsequently 2 so 5 after, later, since 9 afterward, following 10 succeeding 12 consequently

subservient 6 docile, menial 7 fawning, servile, slavish, subject 8 cringing, toadying, truckling 9 accessory, ancillary, auxiliary, prostrate 10 obsequious, subsidiary 11 bootlicking, subordinate, sycophantic 12 contributory, ingratiating

subside 3 ebb, sag 4 calm, drop, ease, sink, wane 5 abate, let up 6 cave in, lessen, recede, settle, shrink 7 descend, dwindle 8 decrease, diminish, level off, melt away, moderate

subsidence 5 letup 6 easing, ebbing, waning 7 calming 9 abatement, dwindling, lessening, recession, shrinking 10 decreasing, inactivity, moderation 12 diminishment

subsidiary 5 extra, lower, minor 6 branch, junior, lesser 7 adjunct 8 addition, division, inferior 9 accessory, affiliate, auxiliary, secondary 10 additional, supplement 11 subordinate 12 supplemental 13 supplementary

subsidy 3 aid 4 gift 5 award, grant 7 backing, support 9 allotment, provision 10 fellowship, grant-in-aid, honorarium, subvention 11 scholarship, sponsorship 13 appropriation, assistantship

subsist 4 live 5 exist 7 survive 9 stay alive 11 feed oneself, support life 12 make ends meet 23 keep body and soul together

subsistence 6 living, upkeep 7 support 8 survival 10 livelihood, sustenance 11 maintenance, nourishment

substance 4 body, core, germ, gist, pith, soul 5 force, heart, means, money, sense, stuff 6 burden, import, intent, marrow, matter, riches, thrust, wealth 7 element, essence, keynote, purport, reality 8 backbone, material, property, solidity 9 actuality, affluence, basic idea, main point 10 ingredient 11 connotation, constituent, corporality 12 corporeality, quintessence 13 corporealness

substandard 3 bad 4 poor 5 awful, lousy 6 crummy, shoddy 8 below par, inferior, terrible 9 imperfect 10 second-rate 11 second-class 12 below average

substantial 3 big 4 firm, full 5 ample, bulky, large, massy, solid, sound 7 massive, sizable 8 abundant 9 plenteous, plentiful 10 monumental 12 considerable

substantiate 5 prove 6 verify 7 confirm, support, sustain 11 corroborate, demonstrate 12 authenticate

substantiated 6 proved, proven 7 factual 8 verified 9 supported 11 well-founded 12 corroborated, demonstrated, well-grounded 13 authenticated

substantiation 5 proof 8 evidence 11 affirmation 12 verification 13 corroboration, demonstration, documentation 14 authentication

substitute 3 act 6 backup, change, ersatz, fill in, switch 7 standby, stand in, stopgap 8 deputize, exchange, pinch-hit, take over 9 alternate, makeshift, surrogate, temporary 10 understudy 11 alternative, pinch hitter, replacement

substitution 5 shift 6 change, switch 8 exchange, swapping 9 variation 10 alteration 11 replacement

substructure 4 base 6 ground 10 foundation, groundwork 12 underpinning

subsume 5 cover 6 assume, deduce 7 explain, include, involve 8 consider 13 subcategorize

subterfuge 4 ruse, sham, wile 5 blind, dodge, guile, shift, trick 6 scheme 7 evasion 8 artifice, intrigue, pretense, scheming 9 casuistry, chicanery, deception, duplicity, imposture, sophistry, stratagem 10 camouflage, sneakiness 11 deviousness, evasiveness, game-playing, machination, make-believe, smoke screen

subtle, subtile 3 sly 4 cagy, deft, fine, foxy, keen, wily 5 light, quick, sharp, slick 6 artful, astute, clever, crafty, expert, shifty, shrewd, tricky 7 cunning, devious, elusive, refined 8 delicate, indirect, masterly, skillful 9 deceptive, designing, ingenious, underhand 10 discerning 11 understated 13 perspicacious, sophisticated 14 discriminating

Subtle

character in: 12 The Alchemist
author: 6 Jonson

subtleties 7 nuances **10** fine points **11** refinements **12** distinctions

subtract 6 deduct, detach, lessen, reduce, remove **8** decrease, diminish, take away, withdraw

subtraction 7 removal **8** decrease **9** deduction, lessening, reduction **10** diminution, taking away, withdrawal **11** diminishing

suburbs 8 environs, vicinity **9** outskirts, periphery, precincts

sub verbo 12 under the word **15** under the heading

subversion 4 fall, ruin **6** defeat, mutiny **8** disorder, sabotage **9** overthrow, rebellion **10** corruption, disruption **11** destruction

subversive 7 traitor **8** quisling **9** insurgent, seditious **10** incendiary, traitorous, treasonous **11** seditionary **12** collaborator **13** revolutionary **14** fifth columnist **15** insurrectionary **16** collaborationist

subvert 3 mar **4** ruin, undo **5** smash, spoil, upset, wreck **6** defile, poison, ravage **7** despoil, destroy, disrupt, shatter **8** demolish, overturn **9** devastate, overthrow, undermine **11** contaminate

sub voce 21 under the specified word
literally: 13 under the voice

subway 2 El **4** tube **5** metro, train **11** underground
New York City line: 3 BMT, IND, IRT
San Francisco: 4 BART

succeed 3 hit, win **5** avail, catch, click **6** accede, do well, follow, move up **7** inherit, prevail, prosper, replace, triumph **8** make a hit, make good, supplant, take over **9** bear fruit, strike oil

succeed at 2 do **6** attain **7** execute, fulfill, perform, realize **8** carry out **9** make a go of **10** accomplish

succeeding 5 later **6** coming, future **7** ensuing **8** oncoming **9** following, impending, posterior **10** consequent, subsequent, successive

succeed to 6 follow **7** inherit **15** ascend the throne

succes d'estime 15 critical success

success 3 hit **4** fame **5** smash **7** triumph, victory **8** conquest **9** affluence **10** ascendancy, attainment, prosperity **11** achievement, advancement, fulfillment, good fortune

successful 4 rich **6** proven **7** perfect, wealthy, well-off **8** achieved, affluent, complete, fruitful, thriving **9** effective **10** prosperous, triumphant **11** efficacious, flourishing **12** accomplished, acknowledged

successful completion 7 success, victory, winning **9** execution **10** making good **11** achievement, culmina-

tion, fulfillment, realization **12** consummation **14** accomplishment

succession 3 run **5** chain, cycle, round, train **6** course, series **8** sequence **9** accession **10** assumption, procession, stepping-up, taking over **11** inheritance, progression

successive 7 ensuing **10** continuous, succeeding **11** consecutive

successor 4 heir **5** donee **7** devisee, heiress, heritor, legatee **8** follower, parcener **9** heritress, joint heir **10** coparcener, substitute **11** beneficiary, replacement, reversioner **12** heir apparent

succinct 4 neat **5** brief, crisp, pithy, short, terse, tight **6** direct, gnomic **7** clipped, compact, concise, summary **9** condensed **10** aphoristic, to the point **12** epigrammatic

succinctness 7 brevity **9** crispness, terseness **11** compactness, conciseness **12** condensation

succor 3 aid **4** help **5** nurse **6** assist, back up, relief, shield, wait on **7** comfort, nurture, protect, relieve, support, sustain **8** befriend **10** assistance, minister to, sustenance, take care of **11** helping hand, lend a hand to, maintenance **13** accommodation

succulent 5 juicy **6** fleshy **9** toothsome **10** appetizing

succumb 3 die **5** yield **6** accede, expire, give in, submit **7** defer to, give way, go under **8** pass away **9** surrender **10** capitulate, comply with **12** fall victim to

such as
Latin: 2 eg **13** exempli gratia

such is life
French: 9 c'est la vie

sucker 3 sap **4** boob, butt, dupe, fool, goat, gull, jerk, mark **5** chump, patsy **6** pigeon, victim **7** cat's-paw, fall guy **8** easy mark, fair game, pushover **9** schlemiel, soft touch **11** sitting duck

Sucker State
nickname of: 8 Illinois

suck up 6 absorb, soak up **7** drink in **8** sponge up **9** swallow up

Sucre
legal capital of: 7 Bolivia

Sudan
capital/largest city: 8 Khartoum
others: 3 Waw, Yei **4** Juba **5** Kosti, Meroe, Nyala, Obeid, Opari, Segon **6** Atbara, Suakin **7** Aluboyd, Elobeid, Geneina, Kassala, Malakal **8** Elfasher, Omdurman **9** al-Ubayyid, Elgeneina, Port Sudan, Wad Medani
division: 7 Jonglei **9** Upper Nile **12** Bahr el Ghazal **16** Eastern Equatoria, Western Equatoria
   ancient kingdom: 4 Alwa, Funj, Kush **7** Maqurra
measure: 2 ud

monetary unit: 5 pound **8** piastres
weight: 5 habba
lake: 2 No **4** Chad, Toad **6** Nasser
mountain: 4 Nuba **7** Imatong **9** Dongotona **10** Jabal Marra, Jebel Marra **18** Ethiopian Highlands
highest point: 7 Kinyeti
river: 4 Nile **5** Sobat **6** Atbara **8** Blue Nile **9** White Nile **10** Bahr el-Arab **11** Bahr el-Jebel **12** Bahr el-Ghazal
sea: 3 Red
physical feature:
   desert: 6 Libyan, Nubian
   gum forest: 8 Kordofan
   plain: 6 Gezira
   sandstorm: 6 haboob
   plateau: 8 Kordufan
   swamp: 4 Sudd
people: 3 Bor, Dor, Fur **4** Arab, Bari, Beri, Bobo, Daza, Egba, Fula, Golo, Nuba, Nuer, Poul, Sere **5** Anuak, Bongo, Dinka, Fulah, Hausa, Joluo, Junje, Mosgu, Mossi, Negro, Tibbu, Volta **6** Acholi, Azande, Gurusi, Hamite, Lotuho, Makari, Nilote, Nubian, Senufo, Surhai, Tuareg **7** Balante, Baqqara, Gubayna, Jaaliin, Nilotes, Shilluk, Songhai, Songhay, Songhoi, Sourhai **8** Kababish, Mandingo, Menkiera **9** Sarakille **10** Gurmantshi, Shaiquiyya
   leader: 5 Mahdi **9** al-Nimeiry **10** Mehemet Ali **22** Jaafar Mohammed al-Nemery
language: 2 Ga **3** Efe, Ewe, Ibo, Kru, Vak, Vei **4** Efik, Mole, Tshi **6** Arabic, Nubian, Yoruba **7** English **8** Mandango, Mandingo **9** Ta Bedawie
religion: 5 Islam **7** animism **12** Christianity
place:
   canal: 7 Jonglei
   dam: 6 Sennar **8** Roseires **10** Jebel Aulia
   temple: 4 Lion
   tomb: 5 Mahdi
feature:
   boat: 6 murkab
food: 4 dura **5** dukhn, kisra

Sudanese Republic see **4** Mali

sudden 4 rash **5** hasty, quick, rapid **6** abrupt, speedy **7** instant **9** immediate, impetuous **10** surprising, unexpected, unforeseen **11** precipitate, unlooked-for **13** instantaneous, unanticipated, unforeseeable

suddenly 7 quickly **8** abruptly, in no time **9** all at once, instantly, on the spot **11** in an instant **12** all of a sudden, unexpectedly **13** at short notice **14** without warning **21** in the twinkling of an eye

sudden movement 4 dart, jolt **5** flash, spurt

sudden noise 3 pop **4** bang, clap, slam **5** burst, crash **6** report **9** explosion

Sudermann, Hermann

sumac

author of: 5 Honor **8** Dame Care **14** The Song of Songs

suds 3 ale **4** beer, brew, foam **5** draft, froth, lager **10** malt liquor

sue 3 beg **4** pray **5** plead **6** appeal **7** beseech, entreat, implore **8** petition **9** importune **10** supplicate

Sue, Eugene (Marie-Joseph)
author of: 15 The Wandering Jew **19** The Mysteries of Paris

suffer 4 ache, bear, hurt, pine **5** stand **6** endure, grieve, lament **7** agonize, despair, drop off, fall off, stomach, sustain, undergo **8** bear with, feel pain, tolerate **9** go through, put up with, withstand **10** be impaired **11** deteriorate

suffer for 6 pay for **8** atone for **9** answer for

suffering 3 woe **4** ache, care, hurt, pain, pang **5** agony, dolor, grief, throe, trial **6** misery, sorrow, twinge **7** anguish, anxiety, torment, torture, travail **8** distress, soreness **9** heartache **10** affliction, discomfort, heavy heart, irritation **11** tribulation

suffice 2 do **4** last, meet, pass **5** avail, get by, serve **6** answer, make do **7** fulfill, qualify, satisfy

sufficiency 6 enough, plenty **7** surfeit **8** adequacy **9** abundance, ampleness, profusion

sufficient 5 ample **6** enough, plenty **7** copious, minimal **8** abundant, adequate **9** plenteous, plentiful **11** up to the mark **12** satisfactory

suffocate 3 gag **5** choke **6** quench, stifle **7** garrote, smother **8** snuff out, strangle, throttle **10** asphyxiate, extinguish

suffuse 4 fill, soak **5** cover, steep **6** infuse **7** diffuse, overrun, pervade **8** overflow, permeate, saturate **9** transfuse **10** impregnate, infiltrate, overspread

Sugar State
nickname of: 9 Louisiana

sugary 5 mushy, sweet **6** syrupy **7** cloying, fulsome, gushing, honeyed, mawkish **8** cajoling, unctuous **10** flattering, saccharine

suggest 3 bid **4** move, urge **5** imply, posit **6** advise, hint at, submit **7** advance, counsel, propose **8** advocate, indicate, intimate, propound **9** give a clue, recommend **16** lead one to believe

suggested 6 hinted **7** implied, oblique **8** implicit, indirect, possible, proposed

suggestion 3 dab, tip **4** dash, hint, tint **5** grain, shade, taste, tinge, touch, trace **6** advice, urging **7** counsel, feeling, pointer, soupcon **9** prompting, suspicion **10** intimation, sprinkling **11** exhortation **14** recommendation

suggestive 4 lewd, racy **5** bawdy,

loose **6** risque, sexual, wanton **8** allusive, improper, indecent, off-color, prurient, unseemly **9** evocative, remindful, seductive, shameless **10** expressive, indelicate, licentious **11** provocative, reminiscent, stimulating

sui generis 6 unique **10** one of a kind

sui juris 14 of one's own right

suit 3 fit **4** duds, garb, plea, togs **5** befit, court, getup, habit, match **6** appeal, attire, become, beseem, follow, livery, oblige, outfit, please, prayer, wooing **7** apparel, begging, clothes, content, costume, delight, gladden, gratify, raiment, satisfy, uniform **8** clothing, entreaty, jell with, make glad, petition **9** addresses, agree with, conform to, courtship, do one good, overtures, tally with, trappings **10** accord with, attentions, comply with, fall in with, habiliment, lovemaking, square with **11** accommodate, go along with **12** be becoming to, blandishment, correspond to, dovetail with, solicitation, supplication **13** accoutrements, be agreeable to, harmonize with **14** be acceptable to, be convenient to **15** be appropriate to **16** be appropriate for

suitable 3 apt, fit **4** meet **5** right **6** proper, seemly, worthy **7** apropos, fitting, germane **8** adequate, becoming, relevant **9** befitting, congruous, cut out for, pertinent, qualified **10** applicable, seasonable **11** appropriate **12** commensurate

suitcase 3 bag **4** grip **6** valise **7** satchel **8** knapsack, rucksack **9** duffel bag, gladstone, two-suiter **11** portmanteau **12** overnight bag, traveling bag

suite 3 set **4** flat **5** chain, court, group, rooms, round **6** convoy, series **7** company, cortege, retinue **8** servants **9** apartment, followers, following **10** attendants **11** progression

suited 3 fit **7** adapted, attired, clothed, dressed, good for, matched **8** adjusted, agreeing, becoming **9** agreeable **10** appropriate, harmonizing

suit of armor 4 mail **5** armor **9** chain mail **10** coat of mail

suitor 4 beau, love **5** flame, lover, swain, wooer **6** fellow **7** admirer, gallant **8** young man **9** boyfriend **10** sweetheart

sulfur
chemical symbol: 1 S

sulk 4 crab, fret, fume, mope, pout **5** brood, chafe, frown, grump, scowl **6** glower, grouch **7** grumble **8** be in a pet, be miffed, be put out, be sullen, look glum **9** be in a huff **11** be resentful **12** be out of humor

sulky 6 morose, sullen **7** pouting **8** petulant

sullen 4 blue, dark, glum, grim, sore,

sour **5** cross, heavy, moody, sulky, surly **6** crabby, dismal, dreary, gloomy, grumpy, morose, somber, touchy **7** crabbed, doleful, forlorn, grouchy, peevish **8** brooding, desolate, dolorous, funereal, mournful, petulant, scowling **9** cheerless, glowering, resentful, saturnine, splenetic, unamiable **10** depressing, foreboding, ill-humored, ill-natured, melancholy, out of humor, out of sorts, unsociable **11** ill-tempered **13** temperamental
French: 8 farouche

sullied 5 dirty **6** impure, soiled **7** defiled, stained, unclean **9** tarnished

Sullivan, John L (Lawrence)
nickname: 15 Boston Strong Boy
sport: 6 boxing
class: 11 heavyweight
fought: 12 bareknuckled

Sullivan, Louis H
architect of: 16 Guaranty (now Prudential) Building (Buffalo NY) **18** Auditorium Building (Chicago), Wainwright Building (St Louis MO) **21** Carson Pirie Scott Store (Chicago), Stock Exchange Building (Chicago), Merchants' National Bank (Grinnell, IA), National Farmers' Bank (Owatonna, MN)
principle: 21 "form follows function"
student: 16 Frank Lloyd Wright

Sullivan, Pat
creator/artist of: 11 Felix the Cat

Sullivan's Travels
director: 14 Preston Sturges
cast: 10 Joel McCrea **12** Veronica Lake **13** Robert Warwick **15** William Demarest

sully 4 ruin, soil, spot **5** dirty, spoil, stain **6** befoul, defame, defile, smudge **7** begrime, besmear, blemish, corrupt, pollute, tarnish **8** disgrace, dishonor **10** adulterate **11** contaminate

Sully, Thomas
born: 7 England **10** Horncastle
artwork: 13 Queen Victoria **23** The Passage of the Delaware **28** Colonel Thomas Handasyd Perkins **29** Washington Crossing the Delaware

sultan 4 king **5** ruler **7** emperor, monarch **9** sovereign

sultana 5 grape **6** raisin **7** empress **11** sultan's wife

sultry 3 hot **4** sexy **5** close, humid, muggy **6** erotic, stuffy, sweaty **7** sensual **8** stifling **10** oppressive, sweltering, voluptuous **11** provocative, suffocating

sum 4 cash, coin, jack **5** bread, bucks, dough, funds, score, tally, whole **6** amount, moolah **7** lettuce, measure **8** currency, entirety, quantity, sum total, totality **9** aggregate, summation

sumac 4 Rhus
varieties: 5 dwarf, lemon, scrub, sugar, swamp **6** desert, laurel, poi-

son, smooth, velvet **7** scarlet, shining, tanner's, tobacco, wing-rib **8** fragrant, lemonade, Sicilian, staghorn, Venetian **9** elm-leaved, evergreen, Virginian **11** small-leaved **12** sweet-scented

sum and substance 4 core, crux, gist, guts, meat **5** heart **7** essence **10** brass tacks **11** nitty-gritty

Sumatra
  chevrotain: 4 napu
  city: 5 Medan **6** Padang **9** Palembang
  country: 9 Indonesia
  crop: 3 tea **6** coffee, rubber
  currency: 6 rupiah
  empire: 9 Srivijaya
  highest point: 10 Mt Kerintji
  inhabitant: 5 Batak, Malay **11** Minangkabau
  mountain range: 7 Barisan
  river: 4 Musi, Siak **6** Asahan
  squirrel shrew: 4 tana
  strait: 5 Sunda **7** Malacca

Sumerian Mythology *see* **19** Babylonian Mythology

summa cum laude 17 with highest praise

summarily 6 at once **7** quickly **8** directly, promptly, speedily **9** forthwith, on the spot **11** arbitrarily, immediately, straightway **12** straightaway, with dispatch, without delay **13** at short notice, precipitately

summarize 5 sum up **6** digest **7** abridge, outline **8** abstract, compress, condense **9** capsulize, epitomize, synopsize **10** abbreviate **11** concentrate **12** recapitulate

summary 4 curt **5** brief, hasty, rapid, short, terse, token **6** apercu, digest, precis, resume, sketch, sudden, survey **7** concise, cursory, epitome, hurried, rundown **8** abridged, abstract, analysis, succinct, syllabus, synopsis **9** breakdown, condensed **10** abridgment, peremptory **11** perfunctory **12** abbreviation, condensation, short version **13** instantaneous

Summa Theologiae
  author: 13 Thomas Aquinas

summation 5 total **6** review **7** summary **8** addition **9** reckoning **19** concluding statement

Summer and Smoke
  author: 17 Tennessee Williams
  director: 14 Peter Glenville
  cast: 9 Una Merkel **10** Rita Moreno **12** Earl Holliman **13** Geraldine Page **14** Laurence Harvey

summerhouse 5 arbor, cabin, kiosk **6** cabana, gazebo, pagoda **7** cottage

Summerson, Esther
  character in: 10 Bleak House
  author: 7 Dickens

Summertime
  director: 9 David Lean
  based on story by: 14 Arthur Lau-

rents (The Time of the Cuckoo)
  cast: 10 Isa Miranda **13** Darren McGavin, Rossano Brazzi **16** Katharine Hepburn
  setting: 6 Venice

summery 3 hot **4** warm **5** balmy, close, humid, muggy, sunny **6** stuffy, sultry, torrid, vernal **8** aestival, roasting, stifling, sunshiny **9** scorching, temperate **10** oppressive, summerlike

summit 3 tip, top **4** acme, apex, peak **5** crest, crown **6** apogee, climax, height, vertex, zenith **8** pinnacle **11** culmination **12** highest point **13** crowning point

summon 4 call **5** rouse **6** beckon, call on, draw on, gather, invoke, muster, strain **7** call for, call out, command, send for **8** activate, subpoena **9** call forth **12** call together

summons 4 call **8** citation, subpoena **12** notification

summon up 4 stir **5** evoke **6** arouse, excite **7** collect, marshal, provoke **8** assemble **9** call forth, stimulate

summum bonum 9 chief good **11** highest good

sumptuous 4 dear, posh, rich **5** grand, plush, regal **6** costly, deluxe, lavish, superb **7** elegant **8** splendid **9** elaborate, expensive, luxurious **10** exorbitant, munificent **11** extravagant, magnificent, spectacular

sumptuousness 4 luxe **6** luxury **8** elegance, grandeur, richness, splendor **12** magnificence **13** expensiveness, luxuriousness

sum total 6 amount **8** totality **9** aggregate **11** final result

sum up 3 add **5** tally, total, tot up **6** reckon **7** compute, count up **9** calculate, enumerate, summarize

sun
  god of: 2 Ra, Re **3** Sol, Utu **5** Horus **6** Apollo, Helios **7** Shamesh **8** Hyperion

Sun Also Rises, The
  author: 15 Ernest Hemingway
  character: 10 Bill Gorton, Jake Barnes, Robert Cohn **11** Pedro Romero **15** Lady Brett Ashley, Michael (Mike) Campbell

sunbathe 3 tan **4** bask **12** soak up the sun **13** catch some rays

Sunday
  means: 11 day of the sun
  heavenly body: 3 sun
  day of: 4 rest **7** worship **8** blue laws
  observance: 16 Christian Sabbath
  French: 8 dimanche
  Italian: 8 domenica
  Spanish: 7 domingo
  German: 8 sonntag

Sunday best 6 finery **8** glad rags **11** fine clothes **16** best bib and tucker

sunder 4 rend, rive **5** crack, sever **6**

cleave, divide **8** separate **9** tear apart **10** break in two **11** break in half

sundown 4 dusk **6** sunset **7** evening **8** eventide, twilight **9** nightfall

Sundowners, The
  director: 13 Fred Zinnemann
  cast: 11 Deborah Kerr, Dina Merrill, Glynis Johns **12** Peter Ustinov **13** Robert Mitchum
  setting: 9 Australia

sundry 4 many **5** mixed **6** divers, motley, myriad, varied **7** diverse, several, various **8** assorted, manifold, numerous **9** different **12** multifarious **13** heterogeneous, miscellaneous

sun-filled 4 fair **5** clear, sunny **6** bright, cheery **8** cheerful **9** cloudless

sunfish 5 dwarf, perch, pigmy, sunny **6** redear **7** lepomis, longear, teleost **8** bluegill, sailboat **9** blackband **10** Sacramento **11** bluespotted, centrarchid, pumpkinseed, yellowbelly

sunflower 10 Helianthus **12** Balsamorhiza
  varieties: 4 ashy **5** giant, showy, stiff, swamp **6** common, desert, Oregon **7** dark-eye, Mexican **8** thin-leaf **10** Maximilian **12** cucumber-leaf

Sunflower State
  nickname of: 6 Kansas

sunless 4 dark, dull, gray, hazy **5** bleak, foggy, misty, murky, rainy **6** cloudy, dismal, dreary, gloomy, leaden, somber **8** overcast **9** cheerless **10** depressing

sunny 4 fair, fine **5** clear, happy, jolly, merry **6** blithe, breezy, bright, cheery, genial, jovial, joyful, joyous, sunlit **7** affable, amiable, buoyant, shining, smiling **8** cheerful, sunshiny **9** brilliant, cloudless, sparkling, unclouded **10** optimistic **12** lighthearted

sunrise 4 dawn **5** sunup **6** aurora **7** dawning **8** cockcrow, daybreak, daylight **10** break of day, crepuscule, newborn day **15** dawn's early light **16** rosy-fingered dawn

sunset 4 dusk **7** sundown **8** blue hour, eventide, gloaming, twilight **9** nightfall **10** close of day, crepuscule

Sunset Boulevard
  director: 11 Billy Wilder
  cast: 8 Jack Webb **9** Fred Clark **11** Hedda Hopper **12** Buster Keaton **13** Cecil B DeMille, Gloria Swanson (Norma Desmond), William Holden **16** Erich von Stroheim

Sunset State
  nickname of: 6 Oregon

sunshade 3 hat **5** visor **6** awning **7** parasol, roundel **8** sombrero, umbrella

Sunshine State
  nickname of: 7 Florida **9** New Mexico

sunstone
  species: 8 feldspar

suntan 3 tan **5** brown **6** bronze **7** sunburn

suo jure 14 in one's own right

suo loco 14 in one's own place **19** in one's rightful place

Suomen Tasavalta *see* **7** Finland

Suomi *see* **7** Finland

sup 3 eat, sip **4** dine, feed **5** drink, feast, supra **6** absorb, supper, supply **7** consume **8** superior **10** supplement **11** superlative **13** supplementary

super 4 A-one, fine **5** grand, great, prime, prize, swell **6** grade-A, superb, tip-top **7** capital **8** peerless, superior, terrific, top-notch **9** excellent, fantastic, first-rate, marvelous, matchless, non pareil, superfine, wonderful **10** first-class, tremendous, unexcelled, world-class **11** outstanding, superlative **12** incomparable **13** extraordinary

superabound 4 teem **5** swarm **6** thrive **7** burgeon **8** be rich in, flourish, overflow

superabundance 4 glut, riot **5** flood, spate **6** deluge, excess, plenty **7** surfeit, surplus **8** overdose, overflow, pleonasm, plethora **9** avalanche **10** inundation, oversupply, redundance **11** superfluity **12** extravagance **13** overabundance **14** more than enough **French: 19** embarras de richesses

superabundant 4 lush **6** lavish **7** copious, profuse, teeming **8** swarming, thriving **9** exuberant, luxuriant **10** burgeoning **11** flourishing, overflowing

superb 4 A-one, rare, rich **5** elect, grand, regal **6** choice, costly, deluxe, golden, lordly, select, tip-top **7** elegant, stately **8** gorgeous, imposing, laudable, majestic, peerless, precious, princely, splendid, top-notch, very fine **9** admirable, excellent, expensive, exquisite, first-rate, luxurious, marvelous, matchless, priceless, sumptuous, top-drawer **10** first-class **11** crackerjack, magnificent **12** breathtaking, praiseworthy **15** of the first water

Super Bowl
1967:
  winner: **15** Green Bay Packers
  loser: **16** Kansas City Chiefs
  site: **8** Coliseum **10** Los Angeles
1968:
  winner: **15** Green Bay Packers
  loser: **14** Oakland Raiders
  site: **5** Miami **10** Orange Bowl
1969:
  winner: **11** New York Jets
  loser: **14** Baltimore Colts
  site: **5** Miami **10** Orange Bowl
1970:
  winner: **16** Kansas City Chiefs
  loser: **16** Minnesota Vikings
  site: **10** New Orleans **13** Tulane Stadium
1971:
  winner: **14** Baltimore Colts
  loser: **13** Dallas Cowboys
  site: **5** Miami **10** Orange Bowl
1972:
  winner: **13** Dallas Cowboys
  loser: **13** Miami Dolphins
  site: **10** New Orleans **13** Tulane Stadium
1973:
  winner: **13** Miami Dolphins
  loser: **18** Washington Redskins
  site: **8** Coliseum **10** Los Angeles
1974:
  winner: **13** Miami Dolphins
  loser: **16** Minnesota Vikings
  site: **7** Houston **11** Rice Stadium
1975:
  winner: **18** Pittsburgh Steelers
  loser: **16** Minnesota Vikings
  site: **10** New Orleans **13** Tulane Stadium
1976:
  winner: **18** Pittsburgh Steelers
  loser: **13** Dallas Cowboys
  site: **5** Miami **10** Orange Bowl
1977:
  winner: **14** Oakland Raiders
  loser: **16** Minnesota Vikings
  site: **8** Pasadena, Rose Bowl
1978:
  winner: **13** Dallas Cowboys
  loser: **13** Denver Broncos
  site: **9** Superdome **10** New Orleans
1979:
  winner: **18** Pittsburgh Steelers
  loser: **13** Dallas Cowboys
  site: **5** Miami **10** Orange Bowl
1980:
  winner: **18** Pittsburgh Steelers
  loser: **14** Los Angeles Rams
  site: **8** Pasadena, Rose Bowl
1981:
  winner: **14** Oakland Raiders
  loser: **18** Philadelphia Eagles
  site: **9** Superdome **10** New Orleans
1982:
  winner: **23** San Francisco Forty-Niners
  loser: **17** Cincinnati Bengals
  site: **7** Pontiac **10** Silverdome
1983:
  winner: **18** Washington Redskins
  loser: **13** Miami Dolphins
  site: **8** Pasadena, Rose Bowl
1984:
  winner: **17** Los Angeles Raiders
  loser: **18** Washington Redskins
  site: **12** Tampa Stadium
1985:
  winner: **23** San Francisco Forty-Niners
  loser: **13** Miami Dolphins
  site: **8** Palo Alto **15** Stanford Stadium
1986:
  winner: **12** Chicago Bears
  loser: **18** New England Patriots
  site: **9** Superdome **10** New Orleans
1987:
  winner: **13** New York Giants
  loser: **13** Denver Broncos
  site: **8** Pasadena, Rose Bowl
1988:
  winner: **18** Washington Redskins
  loser: **13** Denver Broncos
  site: **8** San Diego **17** Jack Murphy Stadium
1989:
  winner: **23** San Francisco Forty-Niners
  loser: **17** Cincinnati Bengals
  site: **5** Miami **16** Joe Robbie Stadium
1990:
  winner: **23** San Francisco Forty-Niners
  loser: **13** Denver Broncos
  site: **9** Superdome **10** New Orleans
1991:
  winner: **13** New York Giants
  loser: **12** Buffalo Bills
  site: **5** Tampa **12** Tampa Stadium
1992:
  winner: **18** Washington Redskins
  loser: **12** Buffalo Bills
  site: **9** Metrodome **11** Minneapolis
1993:
  winner: **13** Dallas Cowboys
  loser: **12** Buffalo Bills
  site: **8** Pasadena, Rose Bowl
1994:
  winner: **13** Dallas Cowboys
  loser: **12** Buffalo Bills
  site: **7** Atlanta **11** Georgia Dome
1995:
  winner: **23** San Francisco Forty-Niners
  loser: **16** San Diego Chargers
  site: **5** Miami **9** Joe Robbie
1996:
  winner: **13** Dallas Cowboys
  loser: **18** Pittsburgh Steelers
  site: **5** Tempe **8** Sun Devil
1997:
  winner: **15** Green Bay Packers
  loser: **18** New England Patriots
  site: **9** Superdome **10** New Orleans
1998:
  winner: **13** Denver Broncos
  loser: **15** Green Bay Packers
  site: **8** San Diego
1999:
  winner: **13** Denver Broncos
  loser: **14** Atlanta Falcons
  site: **5** Miami **9** Pro Player

supercilious 5 proud **6** lordly, snooty, uppity **7** haughty, pompous, stuck-up **8** arrogant, prideful, snobbish **10** disdainful **11** egotistical, magisterial, overbearing, patronizing **12** vainglorious **13** condescending, high-and-mighty, self-important

superciliousness 4 airs **7** hauteur **8** snobbery **9** arrogance, pomposity **10** lordliness, snootiness **11** haughtiness **12** snobbishness **14** disdainfulness

superficial 4 slim **5** faint, outer, silly, trite **6** flimsy, hollow, myopic, slight **7** cursory, minimal, nodding, partial, passing, shallow, summary, surface **8** exterior, mindless, skin-deep **9** desultory, frivolous **10** incomplete **11** empty-headed, perfunctory **12** lacking depth, narrow-minded, on the surface

superficiality 6 myopia **9** frivolity **11** cursoriness, shallowness **13** desultoriness **16** narrow-mindedness, shortsightedness

superfine 4 A-one **6** choice, grade-A, superb, tip-top **8** superior, top-notch **9** excellent, extra fine, first-rate **10** first-class **11** outstanding, overrefined, superlative **13** extraordinary

superfluity 3 fat **5** extra, frill **6** excess, luxury **7** greater, surfeit, surplus **8** overflow, overmuch, plethora **11** gingerbread **12** extravagance **13** embellishment **14** superabundance

superfluous 5 extra, spare **6** excess **7** surplus **8** needless **9** excessive, redundant **10** extraneous, gratuitous, pleonastic **11** inessential, unnecessary **12** nonessential, overgenerous **13** superabundant, supernumerary **14** supererogatory

superhuman 4 epic **5** great **6** divine, heroic **7** godlike, supreme **8** superior **9** herculean, unearthly **10** miraculous, omnipotent **12** otherworldly, supermundane, supernatural, supranatural, transcendent **13** preternatural

superintend 3 run **4** boss **6** direct, govern, manage **7** oversee **9** supervise, watch over **10** administer **12** administrate, have charge of

superintendence 6 charge **7** bossing, running **9** direction, governing **10** leadership, management, overseeing **12** jurisdiction **14** administration

superintendent 4 boss, head **5** chief **6** warden **7** foreman, headman, manager, proctor, steward **8** director, guardian, overseer **9** custodian **10** supervisor

superior 4 boss, fine **5** chief **6** better, choice, deluxe, leader, lordly, senior **7** greater, haughty, notable **8** arrogant, foremost, higher-up, peerless, snobbish **9** commander, excellent, first-rate, imperious, matchless, nonpareil, unrivaled **10** inimitable, noteworthy, preeminent, supervisor **11** exceptional, illustrious, patronizing **12** incomparable, more advanced, vainglorious **13** condescending, distinguished, high-and-mighty **French: 13** par excellence

superlative 4 best **5** crack, prime **6** expert **7** supreme **8** foremost, greatest, peerless, superior **9** exquisite, first-rate, matchless, nonpareil, paramount, unequaled, unmatched, unrivaled **10** consummate, preeminent,

surpassing **11** magnificent, unsurpassed **12** incomparable, transcendent, unparalleled **15** of the first water **17** of the highest order

superman
  German: **10** Ubermensch

Superman
  artist: **11** Jerry Siegel
  creator: **10** Joe Shuster
  character: **4** Lara **5** Jor-el, Kal-el **8** Eben Kent, Lois Lane, Sy Horton **9** Clark Kent **10** Jimmy Olsen, Martha Kent, Perry White **22** Inspector Bill Henderson **23** Professor JJ Pepperwinkle
  place: **7** Krypton **10** Metropolis, Smallville **14** telephone booth
  nickname: **10** Man of Steel
  director: **13** Richard Donner
  cast: **9** Glenn Ford, Ned Beatty **11** Gene Hackman **12** Jackie Cooper, Margot Kidder (Lois Lane), Marlon Brando **14** Valerie Perrine **16** Christopher Reeve

supernatural 6 mystic, occult **7** psychic **9** spiritual, unearthly **10** miraculous, paranormal **12** otherworldly, supranatural **13** preternatural, superphysical **14** transcendental

superpatriotism 8 jingoism **10** chauvinism **11** nationalism

supersede 7 discard, replace, succeed **8** displace, set aside, supplant

supervise 4 boss, head **5** guide **6** direct, govern, handle, manage, survey **7** conduct, control, oversee **8** regulate **9** look after, watch over **10** administer **11** preside over, superintend **12** have charge of

supervision 6 orders **7** control **8** guidance **9** direction **10** governance, government, management, regulation **12** surveillance **15** superintendence

supervisor 4 boss, head **5** chief **7** foreman, manager, steward **8** director, overseer **9** commander **13** administrator **14** superintendent

supper club 4 cafe **6** bistro **7** cabaret **9** nightclub, night spot

supplant 6 depose **7** replace **8** displace **9** supersede **14** take the place of

supple 5 lithe **6** limber, pliant **7** elastic, lissome, plastic, pliable **8** amenable, bendable, flexible, graceful, yielding **9** adaptable, compliant, malleable, tractable **10** submissive **11** acquiescent, complaisant, coordinated

supplement 5 add to, annex, extra, rider **6** extend, insert **7** adjunct, augment, codicil, section **8** addendum, addition, appendix, increase **9** added part, corollary, extension **10** attachment, complement, postscript **12** augmentation

supplementary 5 added, extra **6** backup **7** added on, reserve **8** appended, attached, expanded, extended

9 ancillary, auxiliary, enlarging, secondary **10** additional, amplifying, augmenting **11** subordinate **13** complementary

suppliant 5 asker **6** beggar, cadger, seeker, suitor **7** almsman **8** claimant **9** almswoman, appellant, beseecher, entreater, mendicant **10** petitioner, supplicant **11** supplicator

Suppliants, The
  author: **9** Aeschylus
  character: **6** Danaus **8** Pelasgus **19** Fifty Sons of Aegyptus **20** Fifty Maiden Daughters

Suppliants, The
  author: **9** Euripides
  character: **6** Aethra, Evadne **7** Theseus **8** Adrastus

supplicate 3 ask, beg **4** pray **5** plead **6** ask for **7** entreat **8** appeal to, call upon, petition

supplication 3 cry **4** plea, suit **6** appeal, orison, prayer **7** bumming, cadging, request **8** entreaty, mooching, petition **10** invocation **11** application, beseechment, imploration, imprecation, panhandling **12** solicitation

supplies 4 gear **5** goods, items **8** material **9** equipment, foodstuff, trappings **10** provisions **13** accoutrements

supply 4 fund, give **5** cache, equip, grant, quota, stock, store, yield **6** bestow, outfit, render **7** deal out, deliver, furnish, present, provide, reserve **9** providing, provision, reservoir **10** allocation, come up with, contribute, furnishing **12** provisioning

support 3 aid **4** base, bear, help, hold, keep, lift, pile, post, prop, stay **5** abide, boost, brace, brook, carry, favor, means, shore, stand **6** assist, back up, bear up, clinch, column, defend, endure, foster, hold up, pay for, pillar, ratify, second, succor, suffer, uphold, upkeep, verify **7** backing, bear out, bolster, comfort, confirm, defense, endorse, espouse, finance, further, keeping, nurture, shore up, sustain, warrant **8** abutment, accredit, advocacy, advocate, buttress, champion, espousal, maintain, pedestal, pilaster, sanction, strength, tolerate, vouch for **9** establish, guarantee, patronage, patronize, promotion, put up with, reinforce, stanchion, subsidize **10** assistance, livelihood, provide for, stand up for, stick up for, strengthen, sustenance, underwrite **11** buttressing, consolation, corroborate, countenance, furtherance, go along with, involvement, maintenance, subsistence **12** substantiate, underpinning **13** encouragement

supportable 9 endurable **10** defensible, verifiable **11** sustainable **12** demonstrable, maintainable

supporter 4 ally **6** backer, helper, patron **8** adherent, advocate, champion, defender, disciple, follower, partisan, upholder **10** benefactor, well-wisher **11** sympathizer

supposable 8 credible **9** thinkable **10** believable, imaginable **11** conceivable, perceivable

suppose 5 fancy, guess, judge, posit **6** assume, divine, gather, reckon **7** believe, imagine, presume, surmise, suspect **8** conceive, consider **9** predicate **11** hypothesize **14** take for granted

supposed 5 given **7** alleged, assumed **8** probable, putative **9** imaginary **11** conjectural, speculative, theoretical **12** hypothetical

supposition 4 idea, view **5** given, guess **6** belief, notion, theory, thesis **7** opinion, surmise **9** guesswork, postulate, suspicion **10** assumption, conjecture, hypothesis **11** predication, presumption, proposition, speculation

suppress 4 bury, curb, hide **5** check, crush, quash, quell, still **6** keep in, muffle, quench, squash, stifle, subdue **7** conceal, control, cover up, inhibit, put down, repress, silence, smother, squelch **8** hold back, keep back, overcome, restrain, restrict, snuff out, withhold **9** overpower **10** extinguish, keep secret, put an end to **11** hold in leash, keep private **12** put a damper on **13** put under wraps

suppressant 4 curb **5** brake **7** control **9** restraint

suppressed feelings 7 reserve **9** restraint **10** constraint, diffidence

supremacy 5 power **7** mastery, primacy **10** ascendancy, domination, precedence **11** omnipotence, paramountcy, preeminence, sovereignty, superiority **13** transcendency

supreme 4 tops **5** chief, first, prime **6** ruling **7** extreme, highest, leading, perfect, topmost **8** absolute, dominant, foremost, peerless **9** matchless, nonpareil, paramount, principal, sovereign, unequaled, unlimited, unmatched, unrivaled, uppermost **10** commanding, consummate, unexcelled **11** all-powerful, superlative, unqualified, unsurpassed **12** front-ranking, immeasurable, incomparable, second to none, unparalleled

Supreme Court
  Chief Justices: 3 Jay (John) **4** Taft (William Howard) **5** Chase (Salmon), Stone (Harlan Fiske), Taney (Roger Brooke), Waite (Morrison), White (Edward) **6** Burger (Warren), Fuller (Melville), Hughes (Charles Evans), Vinson (Frederick), Warren (Earl) **8** Marshall (John), Rutledge (John) **9** Ellsworth (Oliver), Rehnquist (William)
  Associate Justices: 5 Black (Hugo), Story (Joseph), White (Byron) **6**
Breyer (Stephen), Fortas (Abe), Holmes (Oliver Wendell), Powell (Lewis), Scalia (Antonin), Souter (David), Thomas (Clarence) **7** Brennan (William), Cardozo (Benjamin), Douglas (William O), Kennedy (Anthony), O'Connor (Sandra Day), Stevens (John), Stewart (Potter) **8** Blackmun (Harry), Brandeis (Louis), Ginsburg (Ruth Bader), Goldberg (Arthur), Marshall (Thurgood) **11** Frankfurter (Felix)
  Cases: 15 Marbury v Madison **17** Gideon v Wainwright **18** McCulloch v Maryland **20** Griswold v Connecticut
    abortion: 8 Roe v Wade
    antitrust: 8 E C Knight **11** Standard Oil **15** Swift and Company **22** American Tobacco Company
    civil rights: 9 Bakke Case **15** Plessy v Ferguson **30** Brown v Board of Education of Topeka
    Japanese internment: 22 Korematsu v United States **24** Hirabayashi v United States
    rights of accused: 15 Miranda v Arizona **17** Escobedo v Illinois
    slavery: 13 Dred Scott Case **14** Scott v Sandford

surcease 4 quit, rest, stop **5** abate, cease, pause **7** die away, respite **8** conclude, leave off **11** come to an end, discontinue **17** come to a standstill

surcharge 3 tax **4** levy **6** excise, impost

surcingle 4 band, belt **5** girth **6** girdle **8** cincture

sure 4 fast, firm, true **5** solid, sound **6** stable, steady **7** assured, certain **8** accurate, fail-safe, faithful, flawless, positive, reliable, surefire, unerring **9** confident, convinced, unfailing **10** dependable, infallible, undoubting **11** trustworthy **12** never-failing

sure bet 4 fact **5** cinch **7** reality **9** actuality, certainty, sure thing **13** inevitability **14** inescapability

surely 7 no doubt **8** of course, to be sure **9** assuredly, certainly, doubtless **10** by all means, definitely, for certain, infallibly, positively **11** come what may, indubitably, undoubtedly, without fail **12** emphatically, without doubt **14** unquestionably

sureness 6 surety **9** assurance, certainty, certitude **10** confidence **11** assuredness **12** positiveness **13** self-assurance **14** conclusiveness, self-confidence, self-possession

sure thing 4 fact **5** cinch **7** reality, sure bet **9** actuality, certainty **13** inevitability **14** inescapability

surety 4 bail, bond **8** sureness **9** certainty, certitude, guarantee **10** confidence **12** positiveness

surface 3 top **4** coat, face, skin **5**
crust, shell **6** facade, finish, veneer **7** coating, outside **8** covering, exterior **11** superficies

Surface family
  characters in: 19 The School for Scandal
  member: 6 Joseph **7** Charles **9** Sir Oliver
  author: 8 Sheridan

surfeit 4 cloy, glut, sate **5** gorge, stuff **6** excess **7** satiate, satisfy, surplus **8** overmuch, plethora **9** plenitude, profusion, repletion, satiation **10** oversupply, surplusage **11** exorbitance, overindulge, prodigality, superfluity **12** extravagance **13** overabundance **14** more than enough, superabundance **15** supersaturation

surfeited 4 full **5** sated **6** gorged **7** glutted, replete, stuffed **8** overfull, satiated **9** satisfied

surge 4 rush, wave **5** flood, swell **7** torrent

Suriname
  other name: 7 Surinam **11** Dutch Guiana
  capital/largest city: 10 Paramaribo
  others: 6 Albina **7** Totness **9** Groningen **10** Brokopondo, Onverwacht **13** Nieuw Nickerie **14** Nieuw Amsterdam
  measure: 7 ketting
  monetary unit: 4 cent **7** guilder
  lake: 14 Van Blommestein
  mountain: 4 Emma **6** Kayser, Oranje **10** Tumuc-Humac, Wilhelmina **13** Eilerts Il Haan, Van Ach Van Wyck **15** Guiana Highlands
  highest point: 10 Julianatop
  river: 6 Maroni **7** Surinam **8** Nickerie, Suriname **9** Coppename **10** Courantijn, Courantyne, Tapanahoni
  ocean: 8 Atlantic
  physical feature:
    falls: 7 Kaieteur
  people: 4 Boni, Bush, Trio **5** Djuka, Dutch **6** Creole, Wayana **7** African, Chinese **10** Amerindian, Boschneger, West Indian **11** Asian Indian
    settler: 22 Lord Willoughby of Parham
  language: 5 Carib, Dutch, Hindi **6** Arawak **7** English **8** Javanese, Taki-Taki **10** Hindustani **11** Sranan Tongo **12** Sranang Tongo
  religion: 5 Hindu, Islam **10** Protestant **13** Roman Catholic
  feature:
    canoe: 6 corial
    clothing: 4 sari **5** dhoti **6** kamisa, sarong **10** kotomissie
    hat: 3 fez
    hut: 5 benab
    scarf: 9 selendong
    tree: 4 dali, lana, mora **5** dalli, genip, icica **7** acuyari, quassia **9** bethabara

food:
　drink: 7 paiwari

surliness 8 ill humor, rudeness **9** bad temper **11** discourtesy, grouchiness **12** irascibility

surly 4 rude, sour **5** cross, gruff, harsh, testy **6** abrupt, crusty, grumpy, sullen, touchy **7** bearish, crabbed, grouchy, hostile, peevish, uncivil, waspish **8** choleric, churlish, insolent, petulant, snappish, snarling **9** irascible, splenetic, unamiable **10** ill-humored, ill-natured, unfriendly **11** bad-tempered **12** discourteous

surmise 4 deem, idea **5** guess, infer, judge, opine, posit, think **6** belief, notion **7** believe, imagine, opinion, presume, suppose, suspect, thought **8** conclude, consider, theorize **9** suspicion **10** assumption, conjecture, hypothesis, presuppose **11** hypothesize, presumption, speculation, supposition **13** shot in the dark

surmount 3 top **4** best **5** clear, climb, scale, worst **6** defeat, master **7** conquer, get over **8** overcome, vanquish **11** prevail over, triumph over **14** get the better of

surpass 3 top **4** beat, best **5** excel, outdo **6** exceed, outrun **7** eclipse **8** go beyond, outclass, outshine, outstrip, override **9** rise above, transcend **10** overshadow **11** go one better, leave behind, outdistance, triumph over **12** be better than, be superior to **13** have it all over

surplus 4 glut **5** extra **6** excess **7** overage, surfeit **8** leftover, overflow, plethora, residual **10** oversupply, surplusage **11** superfluity, superfluous **14** overproduction

surprise 4 stun **5** amaze, shock **6** ambush, wonder **7** astound, nonplus, set upon, stagger, startle, stupefy **8** astonish, confound, discover, dumfound, fall upon **9** amazement, bombshell, burst in on, dumbfound, take aback **10** defy belief, pounce upon, revelation, wonderment **11** flabbergast, incredulity **12** astonishment, take unawares **13** boggle the mind

surprise attack
　French: 10 coup de main

surrender 4 cede **5** forgo, let go, waive, yield **6** accede, forego, give up, render, submit, vacate **7** abandon, concede, forsake **8** delivery, forgoing, give over, giving up, hand over, part with, renounce, turn over, yielding **9** deliver up, foregoing **10** capitulate, relinquish, submission **11** lay down arms **12** capitulation, renunciation **14** relinquishment **15** throw in the towel **16** show the white flag

surreptitious 6 covert, hidden, secret, veiled **7** furtive **8** hush-hush, stealthy **9** concealed, secretive **10** undercover

surrogate 6 acting, deputy **7** interim, stand-in **9** temporary **10** substitute **11** provisional

surround 4 belt, ring **5** hedge, hem in **6** circle, enfold, engird, girdle, shut in **7** close in, compass, enclose, envelop, fence in, hedge in **8** encircle **9** encompass **12** circumscribe

surrounding area 7 suburbs **8** environs, vicinity **9** outskirts, precincts

surroundings 5 scene **6** milieu **7** habitat, setting **8** ambience, environs **10** atmosphere, conditions **11** environment **13** circumstances
　French: 11 mise en scene

surveillance 5 vigil, watch **8** scrutiny, trailing **11** observation **13** eavesdropping

survey 4 plot, poll, scan **5** gauge, graph, plumb, probe, scout, study **6** fathom, review **7** canvass, delimit, examine, inspect, measure, observe **8** analysis, block out, consider, look over, overview **10** scrutinize **11** contemplate, reconnoiter **12** pass in review **13** investigation

survival 5 relic **6** living **7** atavism, vestige **8** hangover **9** carry-over, throwback **11** subsistence **12** continuation, keeping alive

survive 4 last **5** abide, exist **6** endure, hang on, live on **7** hold out, outlast, outlive, persist, prevail, subsist **8** be extant, continue **9** keep alive **11** live through

surviving 6 extant **7** abiding, lasting **8** enduring, existent, existing, living on **9** hanging on, outliving, to be found **10** continuing, holding out, outlasting, persistent, persisting, subsisting **11** in existence **13** living through

Susann, Jacqueline
　author of: 14 The Love Machine **15** Once Is Not Enough **16** Valley of the Dolls

Susanna
　husband: 6 Joakim
　accused of: 8 adultery
　saved by: 6 Daniel

susceptible 4 open **5** prone **7** alive to, subject **8** liable to, sensible **9** sensitive **10** disposed to, responsive, vulnerable **11** conducive to, receptive to, sensitive to, sympathetic

suspect 5 doubt, fancy, guess, judge, opine, posit, think **7** believe, imagine, presume, suppose, surmise **8** distrust, misdoubt, mistrust, question, theorize **9** speculate **10** conjecture **11** hypothesize, wonder about **14** alleged culprit, be suspicious of **19** have one's doubts about

suspend 4 halt, hang, quit, stay, stop **5** cease, check, defer, delay, sling, swing, table **6** append, arrest, dangle, put off, shelve **7** reserve **8** break off, cut short, leave off, postpone, with-

hold **9** interrupt, stop short **10** put an end to **11** discontinue **12** bring to a stop **18** bring to a standstill

suspenders 6 braces, straps **7** gallows, garters, hangers **8** elastics, galluses **10** supporters

suspense 7 anxiety, tension **8** edginess **9** curiosity **10** indecision **11** expectation, incertitude, uncertainty **12** anticipation **15** indetermination

suspenseful 7 anxious **8** dramatic, exciting **9** climactic, uncertain

suspension 4 stay **5** pause **6** hiatus, recess **7** tabling **8** abeyance, deferral **12** postponement **14** discontinuance

suspicion 4 idea **5** guess, hunch **6** notion **7** feeling, surmise **8** distrust, mistrust **10** conjecture, hypothesis **11** supposition

Suspicion
　director: 15 Alfred Hitchcock
　cast: 9 Cary Grant **10** Nigel Bruce **12** Joan Fontaine **13** Dame May Whitty **15** Cedric Hardwicke
　Oscar for: 7 actress (Fontaine)

suspicious 4 wary **5** shady **7** dubious, suspect **8** doubtful, doubting, slippery **9** ambiguous **10** untrusting **11** distrustful, incredulous, mistrustful, open to doubt **12** disbelieving, questionable **13** untrustworthy

sustain 4 bear, feed, prop **5** abide, brave, brook, stand **6** bear up, endure, hold up, keep up, suffer, uphold **7** nourish, nurture, prolong, support, undergo **8** maintain, protract, tolerate, underpin **9** keep alive, withstand **10** experience **12** carry on under **14** hold out against

sustenance 4 food, gear **5** bread, means **6** living **7** aliment, support **9** provender **10** provisions **11** maintenance, nourishment, subsistence
　heaven-sent: 5 manna

sustineo alas 16 I sustain the wings
　motto of: 10 US Air Force

Sutherland, Donald
　born: 6 Canada, St John **12** New Brunswick
　roles: 4 MASH **5** Klute **13** Hawkeye Pierce **14** Eye of the Needle, Ordinary People **16** Fellini's Casanova **17** The Eagle Has Landed **26** Invasion of the Body Snatchers

Sutpen, Colonel Thomas
　character in: 14 Absalom Absalom
　author: 8 Faulkner

Suva
　capital of: 4 Fiji

Suzanne
　character in: 19 The Marriage of Figaro
　author: 12 Beaumarchais

svelte 4 fine, lean, neat, slim, thin, trim **5** lithe, spare **7** elegant, lissome, shapely, slender, willowy **8** graceful **9** sylphlike

Svengali
   character in: 6 Trilby
   author: 9 Du Maurier
Sverige *see* **6** Sweden
swab 3 dab, mop **4** daub, lout, wipe **5** clean, cloth, patch, scrub **6** cotton, sponge **7** cleanse **8** specimen
   brand name: 4 Q-tip
swagger 5 strut, sweep **6** parade, sashay, stride **7** saunter **11** swashbuckle
swaggerer 6 gascon **7** boaster, bragger **8** blowhard, braggart, strutter **11** braggadocio
swain 4 beau **6** fellow, suitor **7** admirer, gallant **8** cavalier, young man **9** boyfriend **10** sweetheart
swallow 3 bit, nip, sip **4** down, gulp, swig **5** drink, quaff, swill, taste **6** credit, devour, gobble, guzzle, hold in, imbibe, ingest, tipple **7** believe, fall for, repress **8** gulp down, hold back, keep back, mouthful, suppress, withhold
swallow up 5 drown, eat up, swamp **6** absorb, engulf **7** consume, envelop **8** inundate **9** overwhelm **10** assimilate
swallow words 6 mumble, mutter
swamp 3 bog, fen **4** fill, mire, moor, ooze, quag, sink, slew, slue **5** bayou, beset, flood, marsh, swale **6** deluge, engulf, morass, slough **7** besiege, bottoms, envelop **8** inundate, quagmire, submerge, wash over **9** everglade, marshland, overwhelm, snow under, swallow up
swamped 7 deluged, flooded, glutted, overrun **9** inundated **11** overwhelmed
Swan
   constellation of: 6 Cygnus
swan
   young: 6 cygnet
   group of: 4 bevy
swank 4 airs **5** ritzy **6** la-di-da, snooty, swanky **9** high-class, top-drawer **11** pretensions, pretentious **12** affectations, ostentatious **15** pretentiousness **16** superciliousness
swanky 4 chic, posh, rich **5** fancy, grand, jazzy, plush, ritzy, sharp, showy, smart, swank **6** flashy, snazzy, spiffy, sporty **7** dashing, elegant, splashy, stylish **9** sumptuous **11** fashionable
Swan Lake
   composer: 11 Tchaikovsky
Swanson, Gloria
   real name: 25 Gloria Josephine Mae Swenson
   born: 9 Chicago IL
   husband: 12 Wallace Beery
   roles: 13 Sadie Thompson, The Trespasser **15** Sunset Boulevard
swap 5 trade **6** barter, dicker, switch **7** bargain **8** exchange **11** give and take

sward 3 sod **4** lawn, rind, skin, turf **5** grass
swarm 4 herd, host, mass, rush, teem **5** cloud, crowd, drove, flock, horde, press, surge **6** abound, legion, myriad, stream, throng **7** cluster, overrun **8** stampede **9** multitude
swarthy 4 dark **5** dusky, swart, tawny **6** brunet **8** brunette **11** dark-skinned **12** brown-colored, brown-skinned, olive-skinned **14** dark-complected **16** dark-complexioned
swashbuckler 9 buccaneer, daredevil **10** adventurer
swashbuckling 4 bold **7** dashing **8** boasting **9** audacious, daredevil
swat 3 hit, tap **4** bash, belt, slam, slap, slug, sock **5** clout, knock, smack, smite, whack **6** buffet, strike, thwack, wallop **7** clobber
swathe 4 bind, wrap **5** cloak, cover **6** encase, enfold, enwrap **7** envelop, sheathe, swaddle
sway 4 bend, grip, hold, lead, list, move, reel, rock, roll, rule, spur, vary, wave **5** alter, clout, impel, power, reign, rouse, shift, swing, waver **6** change, domain, incite, induce, prompt, swerve, totter, waving, wobble **7** command, control, dispose, mastery, stagger, swaying **8** hesitate, iron hand, motivate, persuade, swinging, to-and-fro, undulate **9** authority, direction, encourage, fluctuate, influence, oscillate, pendulate, pulsation, stimulate, vacillate **10** domination, government, predispose, suzerainty, undulation **11** fluctuation, oscillation **12** back and forth, dictatorship, jurisdiction, manipulation

Swaziland
   capital/largest city: 7 Mbabane
   others: 5 Bunya, Hluti, Mpaka, Nsoko, Stegi **6** Gollel, Mhlume **7** Big Bend, Lobamba, Manzini **8** Havelock, Malkerns **9** Geodgegun, Hlatikulu, Mankaiana, Mankayana, Nhlangano, Pigg's Peak, Rocklands
   government: 22 constitutional monarchy
   head of state: 4 king
   monetary unit: 4 rand **9** lilangeni
   mountain: 8 Highveld **11** Drakensberg
   highest point: 7 Emlembe
   river: 5 Usutu **6** Komati, Lomati **8** Mhlatuze, Ngwavuma, Umbeluzi, Umbuluzi
   physical feature:
      forest: 5 Usutu
      plateau: 7 Lebombo, Lubombo
   people: 5 Asian, Bantu, Swazi **11** Eurafricans
      king: 3 Kbe **5** Nyama **6** Mswati **7** Sobhuza
      prince: 6 Sozisa
   language: 5 Ngumi **7** English, Siswati

9 Afrikaans **10** Portuguese
   religion: 7 animism **10** Protestant **13** Roman Catholic
   feature:
      bride payment: 6 lobolo
      god: 14 Mkhulumngcandi
      ritual dance: 7 Incwala
swear 3 vow **4** aver, avow, cuss **5** curse, vouch **6** adjure, assert, attest, pledge **7** certify, promise, warrant **9** blaspheme **10** take an oath, utter oaths **11** bear witness
swear by 7 believe, count on **9** believe in **10** put faith in
sweat 4 ooze, toil **5** exude, worry **6** effort **7** agonize **8** drudgery, hard work, perspire **9** exudation **12** perspiration
sweaty 3 wet **6** clammy, sticky **10** perspiring
Sweden
   other name: 7 Sverige
   capital/largest city: 9 Stockholm
   others: 4 Lund, Umea **5** Boden, Boras, Edane, Falun, Gavle, Lulea, Malmo, Pitea, Visby **6** Arvika, Kiruna, Orebro **7** Uppsala **8** Goteborg, Jokkmokk, Vasteras **9** Jonkoping, Linkoping, Sundsvall **10** Eskilstuna, Gottenburg, Norrkoping, Skelleftea **11** Halsingborg
   school: 4 Lund **7** Uppsala **8** Goteborg **9** Stockholm
   division: 3 Lan **4** Laen **5** Skane **6** Kalmar, Orebro **7** Dalarna, Gotland, Lapland **8** Alvsborg, Blekinge, Elfsborg, Gotaland, Jamtland, Malmohus, Norrland, Svealand
   government: 22 constitutional monarchy
      legislature: 7 Riksdag
   head of state: 4 king
   measure: 3 aln, fot, ref **4** alar, amar, famn, kapp, last, stop **5** carat, foder, kanna, linje, nymil, spann **6** fathom, jumfru **7** oxhuvud, tunland **8** fjarding, koltunna, tunnland
   monetary unit: 3 ore **5** krona, krone **7** carolin **8** skilling **9** rigsdaler
   weight: 3 ass, lod **4** last, mark, sten **5** carat **6** nylast **7** centner, lispund **8** skalpund, skeppund **9** shippound
   island: 5 Oland **7** Gotland
   lake: 4 Ster **5** Asnen, Malar, Silja, Vaner **6** Vanern, Vetter, Wenner **7** Hielmar, Malaren, Vattern **8** Dalalven **9** Hjalmaren
   mountain: 4 Sarv **5** Ammar **6** Helags, Kjolen, Ovniks, Sarjek **7** Kjollen
   highest point: 5 Kebne **10** Kebnekaise
   river: 3 Dal **4** Gota, Klar, Lule, Pite, Umea **5** Indal, Kalix, Lulea, Pitea, Ranea, Torne **6** Lainio, Muonio **7** Ljusnan **8** Angerman
   sea: 6 Baltic **8** Atlantic
   physical feature:
      canal: 4 Gota
      gulf: 7 Bothnia

sound: 6 Kalmar
strait: 7 Oresund **8** Kattegat **9** Skagerrak
people: 4 Lapp **5** Norse, Swede **6** Viking
  actress: 9 Liv Ullman **10** Greta Garbo **13** Ingrid Bergman
  astronomer: 7 Celsius **8** Angstrom
  author: 8 Lagerlof **10** Lagerkvist, Strindberg
  diplomat: 12 Hammarskjold
  director: 13 Ingmar Bergman **14** Arne Sucksdorff
  inventor: 5 Nobel
  king: 4 Vosa, Wasa **5** Oscar **6** Gustav **8** Gustavus **10** Carl Gustav **12** Gustav Adolph **13** Charles Gustav **22** Jean Baptiste Bernadotte
  philosopher/scientist: 10 Swedenborg
  queen: 9 Christina
  scientist: 8 Linnaeus
language: 4 Lapp **7** Swedish
religion: 19 Evangelical Lutheran
place:
  castle: 9 Gripsholm
  center of Stockholm: 11 Gamla Staden
  park: 7 Skansen **12** Millesgarden
  theater: 18 Drottningholm Court
  walled city: 5 Visby
food: 11 smorgasbord
  cheese: 7 fontina **8** jarlberg **9** jarlsberg
  dish: 10 kottbullar
  drink: 5 glogg **7** aquavit

Swedish Punch
  type: 7 liqueur
  origin: 6 Sweden
  base: 3 rum
  with gin: 5 Biffy
  with vermouth: 9 Grand Slam

Sweeney Among the Nightingales
  author: 7 T S Eliot

sweep 3 arc, fly **4** dart, dash, race, rush, scud, tear, zoom **5** hurry, spell, swing, swish, swoop, whisk **6** charge, gather, scurry, stroke **7** stretch **8** distance

sweeping 5 broad **7** blanket, radical **9** extensive, out-and-out, wholesale **10** exhaustive, large-scale, widespread **11** far-reaching, wide-ranging **12** all-inclusive **13** comprehensive, thoroughgoing

sweepings 4 dirt, dust **6** refuse

sweep off one's feet 7 enchant **8** bedazzle **9** captivate, overpower, overwhelm

sweet 4 dear, kind, nice **5** candy, fresh **6** dulcet, mellow, smooth, sugary **7** amiable, cloying, darling, dessert, lovable, nonsalt, not salt, tuneful **8** fragrant, pleasant, pleasing **9** agreeable, melodious, sweetmeat, wholesome **10** attractive, confection, euphonious, saccharine **11** good-natured, melliflu-

ous, silver-toned, sympathetic **12** nonfermented

Sweet Bird of Youth
  director: 13 Richard Brooks
  based on play by: 17 Tennessee Williams
  cast: 8 Ed Begley **10** Paul Newman **13** Geraldine Page, Shirley Knight **17** Madeleine Sherwood
  Oscar for: 15 supporting actor (Begley)

sweetheart 4 beau, dear, love **5** flame, honey, lover, swain **6** fiance, old man, steady, suitor **7** beloved, darling, fiancee, old lady **8** ladylove, mistress, true love **9** boyfriend, inamorata, valentine **10** girlfriend, lady friend **15** gentleman friend
  French: 6 cherie

sweet life
  Italian: 9 dolce vita

Sweet Mama Stringbean
  nickname of: 11 Ethel Waters

sweetmeats 5 candy **6** sweets **7** bonbons **10** sugar candy **11** confections **13** confectionery

sweet-natured 5 sweet **6** benign, gentle, kindly **7** likable, lovable **8** pleasant **13** compassionate

sweetness
  French: 7 douceur

sweet roll 3 bun **6** Danish **7** cruller **8** doughnut **10** coffee cake **11** cinnamon bun

sweets 5 candy **7** goodies **8** desserts **10** sugar candy, sweetmeats **11** confections **13** confectionery

sweet-scented 8 aromatic, fragrant, perfumed, redolent

sweet-smelling 5 spicy **7** scented **8** aromatic, fragrant, perfumed, redolent **9** odiferous

sweet talk 6 cajole, praise **7** blarney, flatter **8** cajolery, flattery, soft soap **10** compliment **11** endearments, loving words **13** blandishments **14** fond utterances

Sweetwater
  nickname of: 16 Nathaniel Clifton

sweet words 7 blarney **8** flattery, soft soap **9** sweet talk **12** honeyed words

swell 3 fop, wax **4** A-one, fine, good, grow, okay, puff, rise, wave **5** bloat, bulge, dandy, great, heave, mount, super, surge, throb, widen **6** billow, blow up, comber, expand, extend, fatten, puff up **7** amplify, breaker, burgeon, distend, inflate, stretch, thicken **8** fabulous, heighten, increase, lengthen, splendid, terrific **9** excellent, first-rate, intensify, marvelous, spread out **10** delightful, first-class, tremendous, undulation **11** pleasurable **12** clotheshorse, fashion plate, smart dresser

swell-headed 8 egoistic, puffed up **9**

conceited **10** egoistical **11** egotistical **12** vainglorious **13** self-important

swelling 4 bump, lump **5** bulge, swell **8** dilation **9** puffiness **10** distension **11** enlargement **12** protuberance

swell out 5 bloat, bulge **6** billow, expand **7** distend, inflate, puff out

swelter 3 fry **4** boil, cook **5** be hot, broil, sweat **8** languish, perspire

sweltering 3 hot **5** humid, muggy **6** sultry, torrid **7** burning **8** sweating **10** oppressive, perspiring

sweltry 3 hot **4** dank **5** humid, muggy **6** baking, clammy, steamy, sticky, sultry, torrid **7** boiling **8** broiling, roasting, sizzling, stifling **9** scorching **10** blistering **11** suffocating

Swept Away
  subtitle: 38 by an unusual destiny in the blue sea of August
  director: 14 Lina Wertmuller
  cast: 16 Mariangela Melato **17** Giancarlo Giannini

swerve 3 shy, yaw **4** tack, turn, veer **5** avert, dodge, sheer, shift, stray **6** careen, change **7** deviate, digress, diverge **9** turn aside

swift 4 fast **5** brisk, fleet, hasty, quick, rapid **6** abrupt, flying, prompt, speedy **8** headlong **9** immediate **11** expeditious, precipitate

Swift, Jonathan
  author of: 11 A Tale of a Tub **15** A Modest Proposal **16** Battle of the Books, Gulliver's Travels
  fictional places: 6 Laputa **8** Lilliput **11** Brobdingnag
  character: 6 Yahoos **10** Houyhnhnms **14** Lemuel Gulliver

swiftness 5 haste, speed **8** alacrity, celerity, dispatch, rapidity **9** quickness

swill 4 mash, slop, swig **5** quaff, waste **6** guzzle, refuse, scraps, soak up, tipple **7** garbage **8** chugalug, gulp down

swimming
  athlete: 9 Diana Nyad, John Naber, Mark Spitz **10** Dawn Fraser, Kim Linehan, Linda Jezek **11** Claudia Kolb, Debbie Meyer, John Hencken **12** Brian Goodell, Bruce Furniss, Greg Louganis, John Kinsella **13** Jim Montgomery, Kornelia Ender, Michael Burton, Tracy Caulkens **14** Charles Hickcox, Duke Kahanamoku, Esther Williams, Gertrude Ederle **15** Cynthia Woodhead **16** Shirley Babashoff **17** Johnny Weissmuller

Swinburne, Algernon Charles
  author of: 16 Hymn to Perserpine **17** Atalanta in Calydon **18** Songs Before Sunrise

swindle 2 do **3** con, gyp **4** bilk, dupe, gull, hoax, rook **5** cheat, cozen, fraud, mulct, steal, trick **6** delude, fleece, racket, rip-off **7** con game, deceive, defraud **8** embezzle, hoodwink **9**

bamboozle, defalcate **12** embezzlement **14** confidence game

swindler 3 gyp **5** cheat, crook, faker,
fraud **6** con man **7** sharper **8** chiseler,
deceiver **9** charlatan, embezzler **10**
mountebank **12** rip-off artist

swine 3 cad, cur, rat **4** pigs **5** beast,
brute **6** animal
   group of: 5 drift **7** sounder

Swineherd, The
   author: 21 Hans Christian Andersen

swing 4 drop, hang, loop, move, rein,
rock, sway, turn **5** pivot, rally, scope,
sweep, whirl **6** dangle, decide, handle, manage, rotate, seesaw, stroke,
wangle **7** compass, extract, freedom,
inveigh, liberty, license, listing, pull
off, rocking, rolling, suspend, swaying
8 maneuver, pitching, undulate **9** determine, influence, oscillate **10** accomplish, manipulate **11** be suspended,
oscillation

Swing Time
   director: 13 George Stevens
   cast: 9 Eric Blore **11** Fred Astaire,
      Victor Moore **12** Betty Furness, Gin-
      ger Rogers **14** Helen Broderick
   score: 10 Jerome Kern **13** Dorothy
      Fields
   Oscar for: 4 song
   song: 12 A Fine Romance **14** Pick
      Yourself Up **20** The Way You Look
      Tonight

swirl 4 bowl, eddy, reel, roll, spin,
swim, turn **5** churn, twirl, twist,
wheel, whirl **6** gyrate, rotate **7** revolve

Swiss Family Robinson
   director: 10 Ken Annakin
   cast: 9 John Mills **10** Janet Munro **14**
      Dorothy McGuire, James MacArthur,
      Sessue Hayakawa
   author: 16 Johann Rudolf Wyss
   character: 13 Emily Montrose
      Robinson family: 4 Jack **5** Fritz **6**
         Ernest **7** Francis

switch 3 box, rod, tan **4** cane, jerk,
lash, move, whip **5** birch, lever, shift,
shunt, stick, swing, trade, whisk **6**
button, change, handle **8** exchange **9**
sidetrack **11** alternation

Switzerland
   also: 6 Suisse (French) **7** Schweiz
      (German) **8** Helvetia (Latin)
   capital: 4 Bern(e)
   largest city: 6 Zurich
   others: 3 Zug **4** Bale, Bern, Biel, Brig,
      Chur, Nyon, Sion, Thun **5** Basel,
      Basle, Berne, Coire, Surat, Vevey **6**
      Geneva, Geneve, Glarus, Lugano,
      Sarnen, Schwyz **7** Altdorf, Fyzabad,
      Herisau, Locarno, Lucerne, Luzerne,
      Zermatt **8** Lausanne, Montreux, St
      Moritz **9** Neuchatel, Solothurn **10**
      Bellinzona, Interlaken, Winterthur **12**
      Schaffhausen
   school: 4 Bern **5** Basel **8** Catholic,

Lausanne **28** Federal Institute of
Technology
   division: 3 Uri, Zug **4** Bern, Chur,
      Nyon, Vaud **5** Aarau, Basel, Basle,
      Berne, Sankt, Waadt **6** Aargau, can-
      ton, Gallen, Geneva, Geneve, Glaris,
      Glarus, Luzern, Obwald, Schwyz, St
      Gall, Tessin, Ticino, Valais, Wallis,
      Zurich **7** Atldorf, Grisons, Lucerne,
      Nidwald, Thurgau **8** Fribourg, Ob-
      walden, St Gallen **9** Appenzell, Neu-
      chatel, Neuenberg, Solothurn **10**
      Graubunden **11** Unterwalden **12**
      Schaffhausen
   measure: 3 imi, pot **4** aune, fuss,
      muid, pied, zoll **5** lieue, linie, maass,
      pouce, staab, toise **6** perche, strich **7**
      klafter, viertel **9** quarteron **10** hol-
      zlafter **11** holzklafter
   monetary unit: 5 franc, rappe **6** hal-
      lar, rappen **7** centime, duplone **8**
      baetzner
   weight: 4 fund **5** pfund **7** centner,
      quintal **12** zugthierlast
   lake: 3 Uri, Zug **4** Biel, Thon, Thun **5**
      Ageri, Leman, Morat **6** Bienne, Bri-
      enz, Geneva, Lugano, Sarnen, Wal-
      len, Zurich **7** Hallwil, Lucerne, Lung-
      ern **8** Maggiore, Viervald **9** Bielersee,
      Constance, Neuchatel, Sarnersee,
      Thunersee
   mountain: 3 Dom **4** Alps, Jura, Rigi,
      Rosa, Todi **5** Adula, Blanc, Cenis,
      Eiger, Genis, Karpf, Righi **6** Linard,
      Pizela, Sentis **7** Bernina, Beverin,
      Grimsel, Pilatus, Rotondo **8** Balm-
      horn, Jungfrau **9** Weisshorn **10**
      Diablerets, Matterhorn, St Gotthard,
      Wetterhorn **11** Burgenstock **12** Du-
      fourspitze **13** Rheinwaldhorn **14** Fin-
      steraarhorn
      mountain pass: 5 Cenis, Furka,
         Gemmi **6** Albula, Kinzig, Maloja,
         Usteri **7** Bernina, Brenner, Grim-
         sel, Simplon, Splugen **8** Lotschen
         10 St Gotthard
   highest point: 12 Dufourspitze
   river: 2 Po **3** Aar, Inn **4** Aare, Arve,
      Thur, Toss **5** Broye, Doubs, Linth,
      Reuss, Rhine, Rhone, Saane **6** Lim-
      mat, Maggia, Safane, Sarine, Ticino
      8 Engadine, Pratigau
   physical feature:
      glacier: 5 Rhone
      plateau: 5 Swiss
   people: 5 Swiss
      artist: 4 Klee
      author: 5 Hesse, Spyri **6** Keller **8**
         Gotthelf, Rousseau **10** Durrenmatt
      educational reformer: 10 Pesta-
         lozzi
      hero: 4 Tell
      psychologist: 4 Jung **6** Piaget
      religious leader: 6 Calvin
         7 Zwingli
      scientist: 9 Bernoulli
   language: 5 Ladin **6** French, German
      7 Italian **8** Romansch **14**

Switzerdeutsch
   religion: 9 Calvinism **10** Protestant
      13 Roman Catholic
   place:
      castle: 7 Chillon
      fountain: 7 Jet d'Eau
      playhouse: 6 Zurich
      resort: 5 Arosa, Davos **6** Gstaad **7**
         Zermatt **8** St Moritz **9** Schwagalp
         10 Interlaken
      street: 14 Bahnhofstrasse
      tower: 5 Clock
   feature:
      animal: 4 ibex **7** chamois
      flower: 9 edelweiss
      pageant: 9 Alpenfest
   food:
      cheese: 6 bagnes, sbrinz **7** Gruyere
         10 Emmentaler **11** Appenzeller
      dish: 5 rosti **6** fondue **8** raclette **11**
         grisons beef **14** bundnerfleisch
      drink: 11 cheri-suisse **14** marmot-
         chocolat

Swiveller, Dick
   character in: 19 The Old Curiosity
      Shop
   author: 7 Dickens

swollen 5 puffy **7** bloated, bulging,
swelled **8** inflated, puffed-up **9** distended

swoon 5 faint **8** collapse, keel over **13**
fall prostrate **17** become unconscious

swoop 5 dive, drop, rush **5** pitch,
sweep **6** plunge, pounce, spring **7** descend, plummet **8** nose-dive, swoop-
ing **9** sweep down **12** rush headlong

sword 4 epee, foil **5** blade, saber, steel
6 rapier **7** cutlass **8** scimitar **10**
broadsword

sybarite 8 hedonist **10** sensualist, voluptuary

sybaritic 4 rich **6** lavish **7** sensual **9**
dissolute, epicurean, luxurious **10** dissipated, hedonistic, voluptuous **12**
luxury-loving, pleasure-bent **13** self-
indulgent **14** pleasure-loving **15** pleasure-seeking

sycamore 8 Platanus **18** Acer pseudo-
platanus
   varieties: 7 eastern **8** Egyptian

sycophant 4 tool **5** slave, toady **6**
fawner, flunky, jackal, lackey, puppet,
stooge, yes-man **7** cat's-paw **8** hanger-on, parasite, truckler **9** brown-nose,
flatterer **10** bootlicker **11** lickspittle,
rubber stamp **13** apple-polisher

Sydney
   bay: 5 Walsh **11** Rushcutter's **13**
      Woolloomooloo
   capital of: 13 New South Wales
   cove: 4 Farm
   founder: 7 Phillip
   harbor: 7 Darling **11** Port Jackson
   island: 4 Goat **6** Garden
   landmark: 10 Opera House **11** Wyn-
      yard Park **13** Harbour Bridge **14**
      Fitzroy Gardens **15** Mitchell Library

16 Australian Museum, Hyde Park Barracks, Saint James Church **18** Rushcutter's Bay Park **21** Royal Botanical Gardens
river: **10** Parramatta
university: **9** Macquarie **13** New South Wales

sylvan 5 bushy, leafy, woody **6** wooded, woodsy **8** arcadian, forested, timbered, woodland **9** luxuriant, overgrown **10** forestlike

Sylvanus see **8** Silvanus

Sylvia
character in: **20** Two Gentlemen of Verona
author: **11** Shakespeare

symbol 4 mark, sign **5** badge, token **6** emblem, figure, signal **10** indication **14** representation **15** exemplification

symbolize 4 mean **5** imply **6** denote, embody, symbol **7** betoken, connote, express, signify **8** stand for **9** emblemize, exemplify, personify, represent, signalize **10** allegorize **11** emblematize

symmetrical 7 orderly, regular **8** balanced **9** congruent **12** well-balanced **16** well-proportioned

symmetry 4 form **5** order **7** balance, harmony **9** congruity **10** conformity, regularity **11** equilibrium, orderliness, parallelism, shapeliness **15** proportionality

sympathetic 6 benign, humane, kindly **7** feeling, pitying **8** friendly, merciful **9** agreeable, approving, benignant, sensitive **10** benevolent, comforting **11** soft-hearted, warm-hearted **12** sympathizing, well-disposed **13** commiserative, compassionate, tenderhearted, understanding

sympathize 4 back, pity, side **5** agree, favor **7** approve, feel for, go along, support **8** sanction **9** empathize **10** appreciate, be in accord, be sorry for **11** condole with, have pity for, stand behind

sympathy 4 pity **5** amity, favor, grief **6** accord, regard, sorrow **7** concern, concert, concord, empathy, feeling, harmony, rapport, support **8** advocacy, affinity, approval, sanction **9** agreement, communion, patronage, unanimity **10** compassion, consonance, fellowship, friendship, tenderness **11** well-wishing **12** congeniality, partisanship **13** commiseration, fellow feeling, understanding

Symplegades
form: **5** rocks
location: **8** Bosporus **9** Euxine Sea
characteristic: **8** clashing, dark-blue

symposium 5 forum, synod **6** debate, parley, powwow **7** meeting **8** colloquy, congress **10** conference, discussion, round table **12** deliberation **15** panel discussion

Symposium
author: **5** Plato
character: **7** Agathon **8** Phaedrus, Socrates **9** Pausanias **10** Alcibiades **11** Aristodemus **12** Aristophanes

symptom 4 mark, sign **5** token **6** signal **7** earmark, warning **8** evidence, giveaway **10** indication **15** prognostication

synagogue
Yiddish: **4** shul **5** schul

synchronal 11 concomitant, synchronous **12** contemporary, simultaneous

synchronous 10 synchronal **11** concomitant **12** contemporary, simultaneous

syndicalist 5 rebel **9** anarchist, insurgent **13** revolutionary

syndicate 5 group, trust, union **6** cartel, league, merger **7** combine **8** alliance **9** coalition **10** consortium, federation **11** association

Synge, John Millington
author of: **14** Riders to the Sea **19** Deirdre of the Sorrows **20** In the Shadow of the Glen **27** The Playboy of the Western World

synod 4 diet **13** governing body **15** advisory council **21** ecclesiastical council

synonym 8 analogue **10** equivalent **11** another name

synonymous 4 like, same **5** alike, equal **7** coequal **10** equivalent

synopsis 5 brief **6** apercu, digest, precis, resume **7** epitome, outline, rundown, summary **8** abstract, argument **11** abridgement

synopsize 6 digest **7** abridge, outline **8** abstract, condense **9** summarize

Synoptist 12 Gospel writer

synthesize 3 mix **4** fuse **5** blend **7** combine **8** compound **10** amalgamate

synthetic 4 fake, sham **5** phony **6** ersatz **7** man-made **9** unnatural **10** artificial **11** counterfeit **12** manufactured

Syria
other name: **4** Aram
capital/largest city: **8** Damascus
others: **4** Hama, Homs, Nawa **5** Busra, Calno, Derra, Emesa, Halab, Hamah, Idlib, Jerud, Raqqa **6** Aleppo, Calneh, Dumeir, Fajami, Tadmor, Ugarit **7** Antioch, Latakia, Palmyra **8** Seleucia **9** Ghabaghib
school: **6** Aleppo, Syrian **11** Arab Academy
measure: **5** makuk **6** garava
monetary unit: **4** lira **5** pound **6** talent **7** piaster
weight: **4** cola **5** artal, ratel **6** talent
lake: **5** Merom **7** Djeboid **8** Tiberias
mountain: **6** Carmel **7** Alawite, Libanus **10** Nusairiyya **11** Anti-Lebanon
highest point: **6** Hermon
river: **3** Asi **6** Balikh, Barada, Jordan, Khabur, Yarmuk **7** Orontes **9** Asi

Knabur, Euphrates
sea: **13** Mediterranean
physical feature:
desert: **5** Hamad **6** Hauran, Syrian
heights: **5** Golan
people: **4** Arab, Kurd, Turk **5** Alawi, Aptal, Druse, Druze **6** Afshar, Aissor, Aushar, Avshar, Awshar **7** Amorite, Ansarie, Bedouin, Nosaris, Saracen, Shemite **8** Ansarieh, Armenian **9** Ansariyah **10** Circassian **12** Khachaturian
king: **5** Rezin **6** Faisal, Hazael **8** Benhadad **9** Antiochus
leader: **10** T E Lawrence **12** Hafiz al-Assad **16** Lawrence of Arabia
queen: **7** Zenobia
ruler: **4** Rome **5** Arabs **6** France, Greeks, Persia **7** Mongols **8** Abbasids **9** Mamelukes, Phoenicia, Seleucids **11** Seljuk Turks **12** Ottoman Turks
language: **6** Arabic, French, Syriac **7** Aramaic, English, Kurdish, Turkish **8** Armenian
religion: **5** Druze, Islam **7** Alawite **12** Christianity **13** Greek Orthodox **23** Eastern Rite Christianity
place:
dam: **5** Tabqa **9** Euphrates
ruins: **7** Palmyra
square: **7** Martyrs'
feature:
animal: **9** dromedary
clothing: **3** aba **4** abah **7** abayyah **8** kafiyyah
marketplace: **4** souk
tent: **8** bayt shar
village common: **6** maidan

Syrinx
form: **5** nymph
location: **8** mountain
transformed into: **4** reed
transformed by: **3** Pan
made into: **7** panpipe
pipes called: **6** syrinx

system 4 body, unit **5** setup **6** method, scheme, theory **7** program, regimen, routine **8** organism **9** procedure, structure **10** hypothesis **11** arrangement **12** constitution, organization **13** modus operandi **15** mode of operation

systematic 4 neat, tidy **7** ordered, orderly, planned, precise, regular **8** constant **9** organized **10** methodical **12** businesslike, systematized **13** well-organized, well-regulated

systematization 5 order **8** ordering **9** gradation **10** organizing **11** arrangement **12** categorizing, codification, organization **13** methodization **14** categorization, classification

systematize 5 order **7** arrange **8** classify, organize **9** methodize

systematized 7 ordered **8** arranged, codified **9** organized **10** classified, methodized, systematic

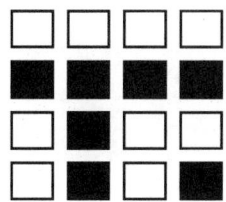

tab 3 lip **4** bill, cost, flap, loop **5** check, PC key, price, strip, tally **6** tongue **7** eyehole **10** projection

tabard 4 cape, coat **5** cloak, tunic

Tabard Inn
   starting point in: 18 The Canterbury Tales

tabernacle 6 church, temple **14** house of worship

Tabeth 16 tenth Hebrew month

Tabitha
   also called: 6 Dorcas
   revived by: 5 Peter
   hometown: 5 Joppa

table 4 fare, list, roll **5** board, chart, index **6** record, roster, shelve, spread **7** catalog **8** lay aside, postpone, put aside, register, schedule, syllabus, synopsis **9** inventory **10** tabulation

Table
   constellation of: 5 Mensa

tableau 4 view **5** scene **7** pageant, picture, setting **8** grouping **9** depiction, spectacle, still life **11** arrangement, delineation **12** illustration **13** picturization

tableau vivant 13 living picture

tablespoon
   abbreviation: 3 tbs **4** tbsp

tablet 3 pad **4** leaf **5** bolus, panel, sheet, wafer **6** pellet, plaque, troche **7** lozenge, memo pad, surface **8** flat cake, thin slab **9** tablature **10** pad of paper, writing pad

tableware 5 china **6** dishes, plates **7** cutlery, utensils **9** chinaware, glassware **10** dinnerware, silverware **14** cups and saucers

taboo, tabu 3 ban **4** no-no **6** banned **8** anathema, outlawed, verboten **9** forbidden, social ban **10** in bad taste, prohibited, proscribed **11** disapproved, prohibition, unthinkable **12** interdiction, proscription, religious ban, unacceptable **13** unmentionable

tabulate 4 file, list, rank, rate, sort **5** chart, grade, group, index, order, range **6** codify **7** arrange, catalog, compute, diagram, sort out **8** classify, organize **9** methodize **10** categorize, make a table **11** systematize

tace
   music: 6 silent

tacit 7 assumed, implied **8** implicit, inferred, unspoken, unstated, wordless **10** undeclared, understood **11** unexpressed **15** taken for granted

taciturn 5 aloof, quiet **6** silent **7** laconic **8** reserved, reticent **9** secretive **11** tight-lipped **12** close-mouthed **15** uncommunicative

tack 3 add, peg, pin, way **4** clap, nail, slap, veer **5** affix, sheer, shift, spike, thole **6** append, attach, change, fasten, method, swerve, switch, zigzag **7** go about **8** approach, tholepin **9** short nail **12** change course **14** course of action

tackle 3 try **4** gear, lift **5** assay, begin, crane, hoist, jenny, throw, tools, winch **6** accept, assume, attack, take on, take up **7** attempt, capstan, derrick, embrace, go about, halyard, rigging **8** endeavor, engage in, material, set about, windlass **9** apparatus, enter upon, equipment, trappings, undertake **10** appliances, embark upon, implements **11** instruments **12** appointments **13** accoutrements, paraphernalia

tack on 3 add **5** annex **6** adjoin, append, attach **7** stick on, subjoin **8** fasten to

tacky 5 dowdy, gluey, gooey, gucky, gummy, messy, ratty, seedy, tatty **6** grubby, shabby, shoddy, sloppy, sticky, untidy, viscid **7** stringy, unkempt, viscous **8** adhesive, frazzled, slipshod, slovenly **10** disordered

tact 7 finesse, suavity **8** delicacy **9** diplomacy, suaveness **10** discretion **11** savoir faire, sensibility **13** consideration **14** circumspection
   French: 11 savoir-faire

tactful 5 suave **6** polite, smooth, subtle **7** politic **8** decorous, delicate, discreet, mannerly **9** sensitive **10** diplomatic, thoughtful **11** considerate

tactic 3 way **4** line, plan, tack **6** method, policy, scheme **8** approach **9** stratagem **14** course of action

tactics 9 maneuvers **18** battle arrangements, military operations

tactless 4 curt, rude **5** blunt, brash, rough **6** abrupt, clumsy, gauche, stupid **7** boorish **8** impolite **9** hamhanded, impolitic, imprudent, untactful **10** blundering, indelicate, indiscreet **11** insensitive, thoughtless **12** undiplomatic **13** ill-considered, inconsiderate
   French: 6 gauche

tactlessness 8 curtness **9** bluntness, gaucherie **10** abruptness, clumsiness, indelicacy **13** insensitivity, tastelessness

taedium vitae 5 ennui **12** tedium of life **22** feeling life is wearisome

Taft, William Howard
   presidential rank: 13 twenty-seventh
   party: 10 Republican
   state represented: 2 OH
   defeated: 4 (Eugene Victor) Debs **5** (William Jennings) Bryan **6** (Daniel Braxton) Turney, (Eugene Wilder) Chafin, (Thomas Edward) Watson, (Thomas Louis) Hisgen **8** (August) Gillhaus
   vice president: 7 (James Schoolcraft) Sherman
   cabinet:
      state: 4 (Philander Chase) Knox
      treasury: 8 (Franklin) MacVeagh
      war: 7 (Henry Lewis) Stimson **9** (Jacob McGavock) Dickinson
      attorney general: 10 (George Woodward) Wickersham
      navy: 5 (George von Lengerke) Meyer
      postmaster general: 9 (Frank Harris) Hitchcock
      interior: 6 (Walter Lowrie) Fisher **9** (Richard Achilles) Ballinger
      agriculture: 6 (James) Wilson
      commerce and labor: 5 (Charles) Nagel
   born: 12 Cincinnati OH
   died: 12 Washington DC
   buried: 25 Arlington National Cemetery
   education:
      university: 4 Yale
      law school: 10 Cincinnati
   religion: 9 Unitarian
   interests: 4 golf
   author: 22 Four Aspects of Civic Duty **23** The United States and Peace **30** Our Chief Magistrate and His Powers **33** The Anti-Trust Act and the Supreme Court **65** The Presidency: Its Duties Its Powers Its Opportunities and Its Limitation
   political career: 18 US Solicitor General
      judge: 19 Federal Circuit Court
      president of: 21 Philippines

Commission
civil governor of: 11 Philippines
secretary of: 3 War
US Supreme Court: 12 Chief Justice
civilian career:
  law professor: 4 Yale
  president: 22 American Bar Association
notable events of lifetime/term: 19 Postal Savings System
  Act: 10 Webb-Kenyon **11** Mann-Elkinst **12** Payne-Aldrich
  sinking of: 7 Titanic
father: 8 Alphonso
mother: 6 Louisa (Maria Torrey)
siblings: 5 Fanny **11** Henry Waters **12** Horace Dutton **15** Samuel Davenport
  half-brothers: 11 Peter Rawson **13** Charles Phelps
wife: 5 Helen (Herron)
  nickname: 6 Nellie
children: 11 Helen Herron **13** Charles Phelps **14** Robert Alphonso
first lady:
  author: 24 Recollections of Full Years

tag 3 add, dog, tab **4** card, heel, mark, name, slip, stub, tail, term **5** add on, affix, annex, hound, label, title, trail **6** append, attach, attend, fasten, follow, handle, join to, marker, shadow, tack on, ticket **7** earmark, moniker, pendant **8** cognomen, identify, nickname **9** accompany, appendage, sobriquet

Tahiti
artist: 7 Gauguin
author: 9 Stevenson
capital: 7 Papeete
formerly: 8 Otaheite
island group: 7 Society
isthmus: 7 Taravao
ocean: 7 Pacific
volcano: 5 Roniu **7** Orohena

tail 3 dog **4** butt, seat **5** fanny, stalk, track, trail **6** follow, shadow **7** back end, rear end **8** buttocks

tail end, tail-end 4 back, butt, rear, rump, tail **6** caudal **7** hind end, rear end **8** backside, buttocks, last part **9** posterior

tailor 3 fit, sew **4** make, redo **5** adapt, alter, build, shape **6** change, create, design, devise, modify **7** convert, fashion, produce **8** clothier, costumer **9** construct, couturier, fabricate, transform **10** dressmaker, seamstress

taint 3 mar, rot **4** blot, flaw, ruin, soil, spot, turn **5** dirty, fault, go bad, smear, spoil, stain, sully **6** damage, debase, defect, defile, smudge, stigma **7** blemish, putrefy, tarnish **8** besmirch **12** imperfection

tainted 5 dirty **6** impure, rotten **7** spoiled, stained, unclean **9** blemished, tarnished **10** besmirched

Taipei
capital of: 6 Taiwan
Taiwan
name means: 11 terraced bay
other name: 7 Formosa **11** Ilha Formosa **15** Republic of China
capital/largest city: 6 Taipei
others: 4 Suao **5** Shoka, Takao **6** Tainan **7** Chilung, Hualien, Keelong, Keelung, Taoyuan **8** Fengshan, Kaohiung, Taichung **9** Kaohsiung
school: 7 Soochow, Tunghai **14** National Taiwan
monetary unit: 4 yuan **6** dollar
island: 5 Matsu **6** Lan Hsu, Penghu, Quemoy, Taiwan **7** Hungtou, Huoshao **10** Pescadores
mountain: 5 Tatun **6** Tzukao **7** Taitung **15** Chungyang Shanmo
highest point: 6 Yu Shan **8** Morrison **10** Sinkao Shan **11** Hsin-Kao Shan
river: 5 Wuchi **6** Tachia **7** Choshui, Hualien, Tanshui
sea: 7 Pacific **9** East China **10** Philippine, South China
physical feature:
  cape: 7 Olwanpi
  channel: 5 Bashi
  gorge: 6 Taroko
  storm: 7 monsoon, typhoon
  strait: 6 Taiwan **7** Formosa
people: 4 Yami **5** Hakka, Hoklo **7** Chinese, Malayan **9** Fukienese, Taiwanese **10** Indonesian, Polynesian **12** Kwangtungese
  goddess: 5 Matsu
  leader: 7 Koxinga **9** Sun Yat-sen **10** Yen Chia-Kan **13** Chiang Kai-shek **14** Cheng Cheng-Kung, Chiang Ching-kuo
language: 4 Amon, Amoy **5** Hakka, Kuo Yu **6** Minnan **9** Taiwanese **15** Mandarin Chinese
religion: 6 Taoism **7** animism **8** Buddhism **12** Christianity, Confucianism
place:
  museum: 14 National Palace
  square: 12 Presidential
feature:
  festival: 5 Ghost
  political party: 10 Kuomintang
food:
  feast: 6 pai-pai

Tajikistan
other name: 12 Tadzhikistan
capital/largest city: 8 Dushanbe
head of state: 9 president
government: 8 republic
monetary unit: 5 ruble
mountain: 13 Communism Peak
people: 5 Tajik, Uzbek **7** Tadzhik
language: 7 Tadzhik
religion: 11 Sunni Muslim
Taj Mahal 4 tomb **9** mausoleum
location: 4 Agra **5** India
built by: 9 Shah, Jahan
for: 4 wife

take 3 buy, get, lug, nab, net, see, use

4 bear, bilk, deem, draw, feel, gain, grab, grip, haul, have, heed, hire, hold, know, lead, loot, mark, mind, move, need, obey, read, rent, sack, tote, work **5** bring, brook, carry, catch, cheat, claim, clasp, filch, grasp, gross, guide, infer, lease, seize, stand, steal, use up, usher, usurp **6** accept, assume, attain, clutch, convey, deduce, deduct, demand, derive, divest, employ, endure, escort, fleece, follow, look on, obtain, pilfer, pocket, profit, regard, remove, secure, snatch, suffer **7** acquire, agree to, believe, call for, capture, conduct, consume, deliver, make out, observe, pillage, plunder, purloin, receive, require, respect, stomach, succeed, suppose, undergo **8** accede to, assent to, conceive, conclude, consider, listen to, perceive, proceeds, purchase, shoulder, submit to, subtract, take away, tolerate, transfer **9** ascertain, be ruled by, consent to, deprive of, eliminate, get hold of, interpret, lay hold of, put up with, respond to, transport, undertake **10** commandeer, comply with, comprehend, confiscate, experience, lay hands on, take effect, understand **11** appropriate, begin to work, go along with, necessitate **13** help oneself to **14** avail oneself of, misappropriate

take aback 5 amaze **7** astound **8** astonish, surprise **9** overwhelm

take a crack at 3 try **5** essay **6** hazard, tackle, take on **7** attempt, venture **9** have a go at, undertake **11** make a stab at

take advantage of 3 use **5** avail **7** exploit, utilize **10** profit from

take after 4 copy, echo **6** follow, repeat **7** imitate **8** resemble, simulate **9** duplicate, reproduce

take apart 7 destroy **8** demolish **9** dismantle, knock down **11** disassemble

take a powder 4 blow, exit **5** go out, leave, scram, split **6** cut out, depart, escape **8** withdraw

take away 5 seize **6** lessen, reduce **7** abridge, bear off, curtail, detract **8** carry off, decrease, subtract **9** deprive of **11** make off with

take a whack at 3 try **5** essay **6** hazard, tackle **7** attempt, venture **8** give a try **9** have a go at **10** give a whirl **12** take a crack at

take back 6 abjure, recall, recant, renege **7** disavow, retract, reverse **8** forswear, withdraw

take captive 3 bag **4** snag, take, trap **5** catch, seize, snare **7** capture, ensnare **9** apprehend, lay hold of **12** take prisoner

take care 6 beware, be wary **9** be careful **10** be cautious **17** look before you leap

take care of 4 tend **6** assume **7** nurture **8** attend to, shoulder **10** minister to

take exception 5 demur **6** object, resent **11** look askance

take flight 3 fly **4** flee **6** escape, run off **7** abscond, fly away, run away, run free, take off **9** make a dash **10** fly the coop **12** make a getaway

take for granted 6 assume **10** undervalue

take heed 4 mind **6** beware **7** look out **8** take care, watch out **11** take warning

take hold 4 bite, grab, grip **5** grasp **6** clutch **7** catch on

take in stride 12 not skip a beat **13** be unperturbed

take into custody 3 bag, nab **4** book, bust, hold **5** catch, pinch, seize **6** arrest, collar, detain, secure **7** capture **9** apprehend **12** take prisoner

take into service 4 hire **6** employ, engage, retain, secure, take on

take issue 5 demur **6** differ **8** disagree **12** be at variance, stand opposed

take no notice of 6 ignore **9** disregard **11** pay no heed to **15** fail to recognize **16** pay no attention to **17** fail to acknowledge

take notice
Latin: **8** nota bene

take notice of 3 see **4** heed, mark, note **6** call on, regard **7** observe **8** call upon **9** recognize **10** get a load of **11** acknowledge **14** pay attention to

take nourishment 3 eat **4** feed **10** break bread **14** take sustenance

takeoff 5 spoof **6** parody, satire **7** lampoon **9** burlesque **10** caricature

take off 4 doff, lift **5** leave **6** decamp, depart, detach, remove **7** lift off, peel off, run away **8** strip off **14** leave the ground

take off guard 5 catch **8** surprise **14** take by surprise

take on 4 bear, hire **6** accept, assume, engage **8** shoulder **9** undertake

take one's breath away 4 daze, stun **6** shock **7** stupefy **8** astonish, dumfound **9** dumbfound, electrify **11** flabbergast **15** make one's eyes pop

take out 4 date **5** court **6** delete, escort, remove **7** extract, isolate **8** abstract, separate, take home, withdraw **9** strike out

take over 4 take **5** seize **6** assume, take on, take up **8** shoulder **10** commandeer, confiscate **11** appropriate, expropriate, gain control

take pains 6 strive **7** attempt, try hard **8** endeavor, go all out **10** do one's best **11** give one's all **12** make an effort **15** knock oneself out **16** give one's best shot

take pleasure in 4 like, love **5** adore,

eat up, enjoy, fancy, savor **6** dote on, relish, relish **7** revel in **9** rejoice in **10** appreciate **13** be pleased with, get a kick out of

take possession of 5 claim **10** confiscate **11** appropriate, expropriate

take prisoner 3 bag, nab **4** book, bust **5** catch, pinch, seize **6** arrest, collar **7** capture **9** apprehend **11** take captive **15** take into custody

take sick 3 ail **6** sicken **8** collapse **9** become ill **10** be stricken

take stock of 5 audit, check **6** assess, review, survey **7** examine, inspect **8** look over **9** inventory

take sustenance 3 eat **4** feed **10** break bread **15** take nourishment

take the cake 5 excel **7** beat all, surpass **12** beat the devil, win hands down

take the edge off 6 lessen, pacify, soothe, temper **7** appease, assuage, lighten, mollify **8** tone down

take the first step 5 begin, start **6** launch, set out **8** commence, embark on, initiate **9** undertake **10** inaugurate

take the place of 7 replace **8** displace, supplant **9** supersede

take to be 4 deem, hold **5** count, judge, think **6** assume, regard, view as **7** account, believe **8** consider **10** look upon as

take to heart 4 heed, mind **6** attend **8** consider **9** hearken to **13** give thought to **14** pay attention to

take to one's heels 3 fly **4** flee **6** escape **7** get away, run away **10** fly the coop, make a break, take flight **12** make a getaway **15** head for the hills

take to task 5 chide, scold **6** accuse, berate, charge, rail at, rebuke **7** bawl out, censure, chasten, chew out, reprove, upbraid **8** admonish, chastise, reproach **9** castigate, criticize, dress down, reprimand **10** tongue-lash **11** remonstrate **13** call to account

take turns 5 share **6** rotate **9** alternate

take under one's wing 6 assist, defend **7** protect **8** befriend **9** look after

take unfair advantage of 5 abuse **6** misuse **7** exploit

take up 4 lift **6** absorb, accept, assume, occupy, pick up, resume, soak up, suck up **7** discuss, drink in **8** consider, continue, sponge up, talk over **9** cultivate, swallow up

taking a siesta 6 dozing **7** napping **8** snoozing **10** taking a nap **18** catching forty winks

takings 4 loot **5** booty **6** spoils **7** plunder **8** pickings

Talaria
form: **7** sandals
owner: **6** Hermes **7** Mercury
characteristic: **6** winged

tale 3 fib, lie **4** epic, myth, saga, yarn

5 fable, novel, rumor, story **6** legend, report **7** account, fiction, hearsay, recital, romance, scandal, untruth **8** anecdote **9** falsehood, fish story, narration, narrative, tall story **10** short story **11** fabrication, scuttlebutt **12** tittle-tattle **13** falsification, piece of gossip **16** cock-and-bull story

talebearer 6 gossip **7** blabber, reciter, tattler **8** busybody, informer, reporter, telltale **10** newsmonger, tattletale **11** storyteller **12** blabbermouth **13** scandalmonger

talent 4 bent, gift, turn **5** flair, forte, knack, skill **6** genius **7** faculty **8** aptitude, capacity, facility, strength **9** endowment **10** capability **11** proficiency

Talent 14 Biblical weight

talented 4 able **5** adept **6** expert, gifted **7** born for, capable, endowed, skilled **8** artistic, polished **9** brilliant, competent **10** proficient **11** well-endowed **12** accomplished

Tale of a Tub, A
author: **9** Ben Jonson **13** Jonathan Swift

Tale of Genji
author: **19** Lady Murasaki Shikibu

Tale of Two Cities, A
author: **14** Charles Dickens
character: **7** Gaspard, Stryver **9** Dr Manette, Miss Pross **11** Jarvis Lorry, John Barstad **12** Lucie Manette, Sydney Carton **13** Charles Darnay, Jerry Cruncher, Madame Defarge **18** Marquis St Evremonde
director: **10** Jack Conway
cast: **12** Blanche Yurka, Isabel Jewell, Reginald Owen, Ronald Colman (Sydney Carton) **13** Basil Rathbone, Edna May Oliver **14** Elizabeth Allan
setting: **16** French Revolution

Tales Before Midnight
author: **19** Stephen Vincent Benet

Talese, Gay
author of: **14** Honor Thy Father **16** Thy Neighbor's Wife

Tales of a Fourth Grade Nothing
author: **9** Judy Blume

Tales of a Wayside Inn
author: **24** Henry Wadsworth Longfellow

Tales of Hoffmann, The
also: **18** Les Contes d'Hoffmann
opera by: **9** Offenbach
character: **6** Stella **7** Antonia, Olympia **9** Dr Miracle, Giulietta **11** E T A Hoffmann **14** mechanical doll

Tales of Manhattan
author: **16** Louis Auchincloss

talisman 4 tiki **5** charm **6** amulet, fetish, grigri **10** lucky piece

Talisman, The
author: **14** Sir Walter Scott
character: **7** Conrade, El Hakim **10** Sir Kenneth **15** Queen Berengaria

19 Theodorick of Engaddi **20** Lady Edith Plantagenet **21** Richard the Lion-Hearted **31** Grand Master of the Knights Templars

talk 3 gab, jaw, rap, say **4** cant, chat, word **5** argot, idiom, lingo, noise, prate, rumor, slang, speak, state, utter **6** babble, bunkum, confab, confer, gossip, hot air, intone, jargon, parley, patois, powwow, preach, report, sermon, speech, take up, tirade **7** address, blarney, blather, chatter, consult, declare, deliver, dialect, discuss, express, hearsay, lecture, oration, palaver, prattle, twaddle **8** chitchat, colloquy, converse, dialogue, harangue, language, proclaim, rattle on, verbiage **9** discourse, enunciate, negotiate, pronounce, tete-a-tete, utterance **10** bandy words, conference, discussion, rap session, recitation, speak about **11** declamation, exhortation, pontificate, scuttlebutt **12** blatherskite, consultation, conversation, tittle-tattle **13** confabulation

talkative 5 gabby, talky, windy, wordy **6** babbly, chatty, prolix **7** gossipy, verbose, voluble **8** effusive **9** garrulous **10** long-winded, loquacious

talk big 4 brag, crow **5** boast, vaunt **13** puff oneself up **15** blow one's own horn **19** pat oneself on the back

talk down to 9 patronize **10** condescend

talker 6 gabber, gossip, magpie, orator **7** babbler, speaker, windbag **8** lecturer, prattler **9** chatterer, converser **10** chatterbox, mouthpiece **11** rumormonger, speechifier, speechmaker **12** blatherskite, spokesperson **13** scandalmonger **17** conversationalist

talk nonsense 6 babble, drivel, ramble

Talk of the Town, The
director: **13** George Stevens
cast: **9** Cary Grant **10** Jean Arthur **12** Ronald Colman **13** Edgar Buchanan, Glenda Farrell

talk out of 4 balk **6** thwart **8** dissuade **10** discourage

talk over 6 confer, review **7** consult, discuss, hash out

Talk-show hosts 5 Leeza **7** Jay Leno, Geraldo **8** Cristina **9** Ricki Lake **10** Jenny Jones **11** Phil Donahue, Conan O'Brian, Arsenio Hall, Maury Povich **12** Johnny Carson, Oprah Winfrey **13** Rosie O'Donnell, Jerry Springer **14** David Letterman, Montel Williams, Regis & Kathy Lee **17** Sally Jessy Raphael

talk to 7 address, lecture, speak to **12** converse with

talk together 4 talk **6** confer **7** discuss **8** converse **9** discourse

tall 3 big **4** high **5** lanky, lofty, rangy **6** absurd **7** soaring, stringy **8** elevated,

gangling, towering **10** incredible, long-limbed **11** embellished, exaggerated, implausible **12** preposterous, unbelievable **13** hard to believe, hard to swallow

tallow 3 fat, tip **5** taper **6** bougie, candle, cierge **9** rushlight

Tall State
nickname of: **8** Illinois

tall story 3 fib, lie **4** yarn **5** fable **7** fiction, untruth, whopper **9** fairy tale, falsehood, fish story, invention **11** fabrication **16** cock-and-bull story

tally 3 add, sum **4** jibe, list, mark, poll, post **5** agree, count, match, score, sum up, total **6** accord, census, concur, muster, reckon, record, square **7** catalog, compute, conform **8** coincide, mark down, register, scorepad, tabulate **9** calculate, harmonize, reckoning, scorecard **10** correspond **11** enumeration

talon 4 claw, nail, spur

Talos
form: **5** youth **7** monster
calling: **8** inventor
made of: **5** brass **6** bronze
made by: **10** Hephaestus
guarded: **5** Crete
destroyed by: **5** Medea
uncle: **8** Daedalus
killed by: **8** Daedalus
because of: **8** jealousy

talus
bone of: **5** ankle
connected to: **5** tibia **6** fibula

Tamar
father: **5** David
mother: **6** Maacah
husband: **2** Er **4** Onan **5** Judah, Uriah
brother: **5** Amnon **7** Absalom, Chileab, Solomon **8** Adonijah
son: **5** Zarah **6** Pharez
daughter: **8** Maachiah
father-in-law: **5** Judah

Tamburlaine the Great
author: **18** Christopher Marlowe
character: **6** Cosroe **7** Mycetes, Orcanes **8** Bajazeth **9** Callepine, Techelles, Zenocrate **10** Theridamas, Usumcasane

tame 4 curb, damp, dull, flat, meek, mild, rein **5** break, check, quiet, timid, train **6** boring, bridle, broken, docile, gentle, govern, manage, master, placid, pliant, serene, subdue **7** conquer, control, pliable, prosaic, repress, subdued, tedious **8** amenable, domestic, dominate, lifeless, overcome, regulate, restrain, suppress, timorous, tranquil **9** tractable **10** make docile, submissive, unexciting **11** complaisant, domesticate, unresisting **12** domesticated **13** uninteresting

tameness 8 docility **9** placidity **10** gentleness, insipidity **12** complai-

sance, tractability **13** domestication **14** submissiveness

Taming of the Shrew, The
author: **18** William Shakespeare
character: **6** Bianca, Gremio, Tranio **8** Baptista, Lucentio **9** Hortensio, Katharina, Petruchio, Vincentio
director: **16** Franco Zeffirelli
cast: **11** Michael York, Natasha Pyne **13** Richard Burton (Petruchio) **14** Michael Hordern **15** Elizabeth Taylor (Katharina), Vernon Dobtcheff
score: **8** Nino Rota

Tammuz
origin: **8** Sumerian
god of: **9** shepherds
Hebrew month: **6** fourth

Tam O'Shanter
author: **11** Robert Burns

Tampa Bay
football team: **7** Bandits **10** Buccaneers
baseball team: **9** Devil Rays

tamper 3 mix **4** muck **6** butt in, fiddle, horn in, meddle, tinker **7** intrude, obtrude **9** interfere, intervene **10** fool around, mess around **12** monkey around

tamper with 5 alter **6** change, doctor **7** falsify

tan 4 roan **5** beige, brown, khaki, sandy, tawny **6** bronze, sorrel, suntan **7** bronzed **8** brownish, cinnamon, sunburnt **9** sunburned, suntanned **10** light brown **11** yellow-brown

Tanah Airkita *see* **9** Indonesia

Tan, Amy
author of: **14** The Joy Luck Club **18** The Kitchen God's Wife **22** The Hundred Secret Senses

Tananarive, Antananarivo
capital of: **10** Madagascar

Tanaquil
origin: **5** Roman
form: **5** queen
husband: **7** Tarquin **17** Tarquinius Priscus

Tandy, Jessica
born: **6** London **7** England
husband: **10** Hume Cronyn **11** Jack Hawkins
roles: **8** The Birds **10** The Gin Game **12** Forever Amber **16** Driving Miss Daisy (Oscar) **21** A Streetcar Named Desire

tang 3 bit **4** bite, hint, odor, reek **5** aroma, punch, savor, scent, smack, smell, sting, tinge, touch, trace **6** flavor **8** acridity, piquancy, pungency, tartness **9** acridness, sharpness, spiciness **10** suggestion

Tange, Kenzo
architect of: **11** Press Center (Kofu) **16** Shizuoka Building (Tokyo) **19** Olympic Sports Stadia (Tokyo) **24** Kagawa Prefecture Offices (Takama-

tsu) **30** Imabara Municipal Office Building

tangibility 11 materiality, palpability **12** touchability

tangible 4 real **5** solid **6** actual **7** obvious **8** clear-cut, concrete, manifest, material, palpable, physical, positive **9** corporeal, touchable **10** verifiable **11** indubitable, substantial

tangle 3 fix, net, web **4** knot, maze, mesh, muss **5** ravel, skein, snarl, twist **6** jumble, jungle, ruffle, rumple, tousle **7** impasse, network **8** dishevel, disorder **9** labyrinth **10** disarrange

tangled 6 knotty **7** chaotic, complex, jumbled, mixed-up, snarled **11** complicated, intertwined

Tanguy, Yves
  born: 5 Paris **6** France
  artwork: 4 Fear **17** Mama Papa is Wounded, Untitled Landscape **18** Rose of the Four Winds **20** Slowly Toward the North **22** Four O'Clock in Summer Hope, Indefinite Divisibility **23** Multiplication of the Arcs **25** Extinction of Useless Lights

tank 3 vat **6** boiler **7** cistern **8** aquarium, fish tank **9** container, reservoir **10** armored car, receptacle **11** storage tank

Tannhauser and the Tournament of Song at Wartburg
  opera by: 6 Wagner
  also: 41 Tannhauser und der Sangerkrieg auf dem Wartburg
  character: 5 Venus **7** Wolfram **9** Elizabeth

Tanoan
  tribe: 4 Tuei **5** Kiowa **6** Isleta

tantalize 4 bait **5** charm, taunt, tease, tempt **6** entice, lead on **7** bewitch, provoke, torment **8** intrigue **9** captivate, fascinate, titillate **15** whet the appetite **18** make one's mouth water

tantalizing 7 teasing **8** inviting, tempting **9** appealing, leading on **10** intriguing **11** fascinating

Tantalus
  king of: 4 Pisa **7** Phrygia
  father: 8 Thyestes
  wife: 12 Clytemnestra
  son: 6 Pelops
  daughter: 5 Niobe
  punishment in Hades: 6 hunger, thirst

tantamount 4 like **5** equal **9** analogous **10** comparable, equivalent, on a par with **12** commensurate **13** commensurable

tantrum 3 fit **5** storm **7** flare-up, rampage **8** outburst, paroxysm **9** explosion **12** fit of passion **13** burst of temper, conniption fit

Tanzania
  other name: 12 isle of cloves
  capital/largest city: 11 Dar es Salaam
    new capital: 6 Dodoma

others: 4 Wete, **5** Kilwa, Lindi, Moshi, Tanga, Ujiji **6** Arusha, Kigoma, Mwadui, Mwanza, Tabora **7** Korogwe, Mtawara **8** Morogoro, Zanzibar **12** Kwasemangube, Zanzibar Town
  division: 8 Zanzibar **17** union of Tanganyika
  monetary unit: 4 cent **8** shilling
  weight: 8 farsalah
  island: 5 Mafia, Pemba **6** Latham **8** Zanzibar
  lake: 5 Eyasi, Nyasa, Rukwa **6** Malawi, Natron, Nyassa **7** Manyara **8** Victoria **10** Tanganyika
  mountain: 4 Kibo, Mero **8** Usambara
  highest point: 11 Kilimanjaro
  river: 4 Lupa, Ruvu, Wami **5** Ruaha **6** Kagera, Luwegu, Mbaesa, Rufiji, Rungwa, Ruvuma **7** Nkululu, Pangani **8** Mbenkuru **11** Mbarangandu
  sea: 6 Indian
  physical feature:
    crater: 10 Ngorongoro
    gorge: 7 Olduvai
    national park: 9 Serengeti
    plains: 9 Serengeti
    steppe: 5 Masai **8** Iwembere
    valley: 9 Great Rift
  people: 2 Ha **4** Arab, Gogo, Goma, Haya, Hehe **5** Asian, Bantu, Masai **6** Arusha, Chagga, Sukuma, Wagogo, Wagoma **7** African, Makonde, Sambara, Sandawe, Shirazi, Swahili, Wabunga, Zongora **8** Nyakyusa, Nyamwezi
    early man: 13 zinjanthropus
    explorer: 6 Da Gama **7** Rebmann **11** Livingstone
    leader: 5 Sayid **6** Karume **7** Nyerere **16** Sultan of Zanzibar
  language: 5 Bantu **6** Arabic **7** English, Khoisan, Nilotic, Swahili **8** Cushitic, Gujarati
  religion: 5 Islam **7** animism **12** Christianity
  feature:
    animal: 6 dik-dik
    cattle barn: 4 byre
    clothing: 4 sari **6** bui bui
    fly: 6 tsetse
    holiday: 8 Saba Saba
    homestead: 8 manyatta
  food:
    dish: 5 ugali

Tao Te Ching
  author: 6 Lao-tzu

Taotieh
  origin: 7 Chinese
  form: 6 animal

tap 3 pat, rap, use **4** cock, drum, peck, thud **5** spout, touch, valve **6** broach, employ, faucet, hammer, spigot, stroke, uncork, unplug **7** draw off, exploit, utilize **8** draw upon, stopcock **9** put to work, unstopper

taper 3 dip, wax **4** wick **5** light **6** candle, cierge, narrow **8** decrease **9** nar-

rowing **10** diminution **12** come to a point

taper off 4 wane **5** abate **6** weaken **7** slacken, subside **8** decrease, diminish, fade away, slack off

tapestry 3 rug **5** arras, tapis **6** Bruges, fabric, mosaic **7** Gobelin, hanging, montage, weaving **8** Aubusson **12** wallcovering

Tapley, Mark
  character in: 16 Martin Chuzzlewit
  author: 7 Dickens

Tappertit, Simon
  character in: 12 Barnaby Rudge
  author: 7 Dickens

Taprobane *see* **8** Sri Lanka

taproom 3 bar, pub **6** lounge, saloon, tavern **8** alehouse **11** bar and grill, public house **14** cocktail lounge

Taras Bulba
  author: 12 Nikolai Gogol
  character: 5 Ostap **6** Andrii, Yankel **26** Daughter of the Polish Waiwode

Tarascans, Tarascos
  location: 6 Mexico **9** Michoacan **14** Central America
  leader: 8 Zincicha **9** Tangaxoan, Tariacuri

Tarawa
  capital of: 8 Kiribati

Tar Baby
  author: 12 Toni Morrison

Tarchetius
  king of: 9 Alba Longa

tardy 4 late, slow **5** slack **6** remiss **7** belated, languid, overdue **8** crawling, creeping, dilatory, slowpoke, sluggish **9** leisurely, not on time, reluctant, slow-paced, snail-like **10** behindhand, behind time, unpunctual **14** slow as molasses **15** procrastinating

tare 12 Biblical weed **15** weight deduction

target 3 aim, end **4** butt, dupe, goal, goat, gull, mark, plan, prey **5** patsy **6** design, intent, object, pigeon, victim **7** purpose **8** ambition **9** intention, objective **13** laughingstock

Targitaus
  father: 4 Zeus
  first inhabitant of: 7 Scythia

Tar Heel State
  nickname of: 13 North Carolina

tariff 3 fee **4** cost, duty, fare, levy, rate, rent **5** price **6** charge, excise, impost **7** expense **8** input tax **9** excise tax, export tax **10** assessment, commission, freightage

Tarkington, Booth
  author of: 6 Penrod **9** Seventeen **10** Alice Adams **13** Kate Fennigate **14** The Man from Home **17** Monsieur Beaucaire **19** The World Does Not Move **23** The Magnificent Ambersons

Tarleton, Stuart and Brent

characters in: 15 Gone With the Wind
author: 8 Mitchell

tarnish 3 dim **4** blot, dull, foul, soil, spot **5** dirty, erode, stain, sully, taint **6** befoul, darken, defame, defile, smirch, vilify **7** blacken, blemish, corrode, degrade, oxidize **8** besmirch, discolor, disgrace, dishonor **9** denigrate, discredit **10** lose luster, stigmatize **17** drag through the mud

tarnished 5 dirty **6** soiled **7** stained, sullied **8** oxidized **10** discolored

Tarnkappe
origin: 8 Germanic
mentioned in: 14 Nibelungenlied
form: 5 cloak
gives wearer: 8 strength **12** invisibility
stolen by: 9 Siegfried
stolen from: 8 Niblungs **9** Nibelungs

tarot
Italian: 6 naibes **7** attutti **8** tarocchi
German: 5 tarok
French: 5 tarau, tarot
cards/deck: 12 seventy-eight
division: 11 major arcana, minor arcana **12** lesser arcana **13** greater arcana
suit: 3 cup **4** coin, wand **5** baton, money, sword **6** cudgel **8** pentacle
face card: 4 king, page **5** knave, queen, valet **6** knight
major arcana: 4 Fool, Moon **5** Death **7** Justice **8** Judgment **9** Hanged Man **14** Wheel of Fortune

tarpaulin 4 tarp **6** canvas **9** dropcloth **15** waterproof cover

Tarpeia
form: 12 vestal virgin
father: 15 Spurius Tarpeius
betrayed: 4 Rome
betrayed to: 7 Sabines
killed by: 7 Sabines

Tarquin
king of: 4 Rome
origin: 8 Etruscan
also called: 17 Tarquinius Priscus **18** Tarquinius Superbus
wife: 8 Tanaquil

tarragon
botanical name: 20 Artemisia dracunculus
means: 6 dragon **12** little dragon
Arab: 7 tarkhum
French: 8 estragon
origin: 7 Siberia
used as: 8 purifier
flavor: 8 licorice
use: 4 fish **5** salad, sauce **10** mayonnaise **14** Bearnaise sauce

tarry 3 lag **4** bide, rest, stay, wait **5** abide, dally, delay, pause, stall **6** dawdle, linger, put off, remain **7** be tardy **8** hang back, postpone, stave off, take time **9** temporize **10** hang

around **13** cool one's heels, procrastinate

tarsal
bone of: 5 ankle

tart 3 pie **4** acid, sour **5** acerb, acrid, sharp, spicy, tangy **6** acetic, barbed, biting, bitter, crusty **7** caustic, cutting, piquant, pungent, sourish **8** vinegary **10** astringent **11** pastry shell

tartan
fabric: 6 woolen
pattern: 5 plaid
identifies: 4 clan
in: 8 Scotland **9** Highlands
skirt: 4 kilt
trousers: 5 trews

Tartarean *see* **8** infernal

Tartarin of Tarascon
author: 14 Alphonse Daudet

Tartarus
form: 5 abyss
below: 5 Hades
imprisoned: 6 Titans

tartness 7 acidity, sarcasm **8** acerbity **9** sharpness **11** astringency

Tartuffe
author: 7 Moliere
character: 5 Damis, Orgon **6** Dorine, Elmire, Valere **7** Cleante, Mariane **14** Madame Pernelle

Tarzan
author: 18 Edgar Rice Burroughs
character: 3 Boy **4** Jane **7** Cheetah
Tarzan also called: 15 Lord of Greystoke, Lord of the Jungle
comic strip creator: 9 Hal Foster **12** Burme Hogarth
played by: 6 Ron Ely **9** Lex Barker **11** Elmo Lincoln **12** Buster Crabbe **17** Johnny Weissmuller

task 3 job **4** duty, work **5** chore, labor, stint **6** charge, errand **7** mission **8** business **10** assignment **11** undertaking **14** responsibility

Task, The
author: 13 William Cowper

taskmaster 4 boss **6** despot, master, tyrant **7** foreman, headman, manager **8** director, martinet, overseer, stickler **10** supervisor **11** Simon Legree, slave driver **14** disciplinarian, superintendent

Tasmania
bay: 5 Storm **6** Oyster
capital: 6 Hobart
city: 10 Launceston
country: 9 Australia
formerly: 14 Van Diemen's Land
island: 4 Echo **6** Sorell
mountain: 4 Ossa **6** Cradle
river: 3 Esk
strait: 4 Bass
birthplace of: 10 Errol Flynn

Tasso, Torquato
author of: 6 Aminta **7** Rinaldo **18** Jerusalem Delivered

taste 3 bit, nip, sip, try, yen **4** bent, bite, feel, meet, tang, test, whim **5** crumb, enjoy, fancy, savor, smack **6** desire, flavor, hunger, liking, morsel, relish, sample, thirst **7** craving, decorum, discern, forkful, insight, leaning, longing, savor of, smack of, swallow, undergo **8** appetite, delicacy, fondness, judgment, mouthful, penchant, piquancy, spoonful, yearning **9** encounter, hankering, partake of, propriety **10** experience, partiality, propensity, take a sip of **11** correctness, discernment, disposition, inclination, take a bite of **12** eat a little of, predilection **14** discrimination, drink a little of
French: 4 gout

tasteful 7 elegant, refined **8** artistic, becoming, cultured, esthetic, handsome, suitable **9** beautiful, exquisite **10** attractive, well-chosen

tasteless 3 low **4** flat, mild, rude, weak **5** bland, cheap, crass, crude, gaudy, gross, tacky **6** coarse, common, flashy, garish, ribald, watery **7** insipid, uncouth **8** improper, indecent, unseemly **9** inelegant, offensive, unrefined **10** disgusting, flavorless, indecorous, indelicate, uncultured, unesthetic, unflavored, unsuitable **11** distasteful, insensitive

tastemakers 7 leaders **10** avant-garde, innovators **12** stylesetters, trendsetters

tasty 3 hot **5** spicy, tangy, yummy **6** savory **7** piquant, zestful **8** luscious **9** delicious, flavorful, palatable, toothsome **10** appetizing, delectable, flavorsome **11** good-tasting, scrumptious **12** full-flavored, well-seasoned

Tatar, Mr
character in: 22 The Mystery of Edwin Drood
author: 7 Dickens

Tatius
also: 5 Titus
co-ruler with: 7 Romulus

Tatler, The
author: 13 Joseph Addison, Richard Steele

tattered 4 torn **6** broken, ragged, ripped, shabby, shaggy **10** disheveled **11** dilapidated

tatters 4 rags **6** shreds **7** patches

tattle 3 rat **4** blab **5** prate **6** gabble, gossip, snitch, squeal, tell on **7** blather, chatter, hearsay, prattle, twaddle **8** inform on **9** loose talk **11** mudslinging **12** tittle-tattle **13** tongue-wagging

tattletale 3 rat **4** fink **5** sneak **6** gossip, snitch **7** ratfink, stoolie, tattler **8** betrayer, busybody, informer, squealer, telltale **8** informer **10** newsmonger, talebearer **11** rumormonger, stool pigeon **12** blabbermouth, troublemaker **13** scandalmonger

Tatum, Edward Lawrie
  field: **8** genetics **12** biochemistry
  discovered: **19** gene characteristics
  awarded: **10** Nobel Prize

taunt 3 guy, rag **4** gibe, jeer, jive,
  mock, slur, twit **5** scoff, sneer, tease **6**
  deride, harass, insult, jeer at **7** provoke, ragging, sneer at, snigger, torment **8** chaffing, derision, ridicule **9**
  make fun of, poke fun at, snigger at
  10 harassment, make game of, tormenting **11** provocation

Taura
  form: **3** cow
  attribute: **6** sacred

taurobolium
  rite of: **7** baptism

Taurog, Norman
  director of: **6** Skippy (Oscar) **8** Boys
  Town

Taurus
  symbol: **4** bull
  planet: **5** Venus
  rules: **5** money **9** resources
  born: **3** May **5** April

taut 4 neat, snug, tidy, trig, trim **5**
  rigid, smart, tense, tight **6** spruce **7**
  orderly **8** not loose, not slack **9** shipshape, unbending, unrelaxed **10**
  drawn tight, inflexible, no-nonsense
  11 under strain **12** businesslike **13**
  well-regulated **15** well-disciplined

tavern 3 bar, pub **4** dive **6** bistro, saloon **7** barroom, gin mill, taproom **8**
  alehouse, drinkery, grogshop **9** beer
  joint, brasserie, honky-tonk, roadhouse **10** restaurant **11** public house
  12 watering hole **14** cocktail lounge
  French: **7** auberge
  German: **8** Brauhaus

tawdry 4 loud **5** cheap, crass, gaudy,
  showy, tacky **6** flashy, garish, tinsel,
  vulgar **7** raffish **8** gimcrack **9** inelegant, obtrusive, tasteless **10** flamboyant **11** conspicuous, pretentious **12**
  meretricious, ostentatious

tawny 3 tan **4** fawn **5** beige, dusky, olive, sandy **6** bronze **7** swarthy **8**
  brownish **10** light brown **14** yellowish-brown

tax 3 sap, try **4** duty, lade, levy, load,
  tire, toll **5** drain, weigh **6** assess, burden, charge, custom, excise, impost,
  saddle, strain, tariff, weight **7** deplete,
  exhaust, stretch, wear out **8** exertion,
  overwork **10** assessment, obligation,
  overburden
  kind: **4** city **5** sales, state **6** county,
  excise, income, luxury **8** property
  11 inheritance **12** excess profit

Taxi
  character: **9** John Burns, Tony Banta
  10 Alex Rieger **11** Elaine Nardo,
  Latka Gravas **12** Bobby Wheeler,
  Louie De Palma
  cast: **9** Carol Kane, Tony Danza **10**
  Judd Hirsch **11** Andy Kaufman,
  Danny DeVito, Jeff Conaway
  12 Marilu Henner **13** Randall Carver
  company: **11** Sunshine Cab

taxicab 4 hack **6** jitney **7** droshky,
  hackney **8** hired car, rickshaw **10** automobile **11** jinrickshaw

Taxi Driver
  director: **14** Martin Scorsese
  cast: **10** Peter Boyle **11** Jodie Foster
  12 Albert Brooks, Harvey Keitel, Robert De Niro **13** Leonard Harris **14**
  Cybill Shepherd
  setting: **11** New York City
  score: **15** Bernard Herrmann
  script: **12** Paul Schrader

taxon 5 class, genus, order **6** family,
  phylum **7** kingdom, species

taxonomy
  study of: **17** structure contrast **19**
  structure comparison

Taylor, Elizabeth
  born: **6** London **7** England
  husband: **8** Mike Todd **10** John
  Warner **11** Eddie Fisher, Nicky Hilton **13** Richard Burton **14** Michael
  Wilding
  roles: **5** Giant **7** Ivanhoe **9** Cleopatra
  11 Little Women **12** The Sandpiper
  14 A Place in the Sun, National Velvet, Raintree County **16** Butterfield
  Eight (Oscar), Cat on a Hot Tin Roof,
  Father of the Bride **18** Suddenly Last
  Summer **19** The Taming of the
  Shrew **25** Who's Afraid of Virginia
  Woolf (Oscar)

Taylor, Robert
  real name: **22** Spangler Arlington
  Brugh
  wife: **12** Ursula Thiess **15** Barbara
  Stanwyck
  roles: **7** Camille, Ivanhoe **8** Quo Vadis
  11 Billy the Kid **14** Waterloo Bridge
  20 Magnificent Obsession

Taylor, Zachary
  nickname: **16** Old Rough and Ready
  presidential rank: **7** twelfth
  party: **4** Whig
  state represented: **2** LA
  defeated: **4** (Lewis) Cass **8** (Martin)
  Van Buren
  vice president: **8** (Millard) Fillmore
  cabinet:
    state: **7** (John Middleton) Clayton
    treasury: **8** (William Morris) Mere-
    dith
    war: **8** (George Walker) Crawford
    attorney general: **7** (Reverdy)
    Johnson
    navy: **7** (William Ballard) Preston
    postmaster general: **8** (Jacob) Col-
    lamer
    interior: **5** (Thomas) Ewing
  born: **12** Montebello VA **12** Orange
  County
  died: **12** Washington DC
  buried: **12** Louisville KY
  education: **9** no college **16** privately
  tutored
  religion: **12** Episcopalian
  political career: **21** none prior to
  presidency
  civilian career: **7** planter, soldier
  military service: **6** US Army **12** major
  general
    War: **7** Mexican **9** Black Hawk **19**
    War of Eighteen-Twelve **14** Sec-
    ond Seminole
  notable events of lifetime/
  presidency:
    treaty: **13** Clayton-Bulwer
  father: **7** Richard
  mother: **5** Sarah (Dabney Strother)
  siblings: **6** George **7** Hancock **11**
  Sarah Bailey **12** Elizabeth Lee, Emily
  Richard **13** Joseph Pannill **21** William Dabney Strother
  wife: **8** Margaret (Mackall Smith)
  children: **7** Richard **9** Sarah Knox **10**
  Ann Mackall **13** Margaret Smith,
  Mary Elizabeth, Octavia Panill

Tchad see **4** Chad

**Tchaikovsky, Peter (Piotr Ilyich
Chaikovsky)**
  born: **6** Russia **8** Votkinsk
  composer of: **7** Manfred, Mazeppa **8**
  Iolanthe, Pathetic (symphony No 6),
  Swan Lake **9** Joan of Arc **10** Nut-
  cracker **12** Eugene Onegin, Winter
  Dreams **14** Italian Caprice, Romeo
  and Juliet, The Enchantress **16** The
  Queen of Spades **17** Francesca da
  Rimini, The Sleeping Beauty **22**
  Eighteen-Twelve Overture

tea 16 Camellia sinensis
  varieties: **4** chai **5** Assam, Bohea,
  China, green, pekoe, Yerba **6** Ceylon,
  Oolong, Oswego, Tisane **7** African,
  Arabian, cambric, crystal, Lapsang,
  Mexican, redroot, Spanish **8** bergamot, camomile, Earl Grey, Labrador,
  mountain, Paraguay, Siberian, Sou-
  chong, Woodruff **9** gunpowder,
  lemon balm, New Jersey, sassafras
  10 Darjeeling, Philippine **11** Appalachian, Orange Pekoe **14** Irish breakfast **16** English breakfast

teach 5 coach, drill, edify, prime, tutor
  6 inform, school **7** educate, implant,
  prepare **8** exercise, instruct **9** enlighten, inculcate **10** discipline **12** indoctrinate

Teach
  character in: **21** The Master of Ballantrae
  author: **9** Stevenson

teacher 3 don **5** coach, tutor **6** master,
  mentor **7** maestro, trainer **8** educator
  9 preceptor, professor **10** instructor,
  schoolmarm **12** schoolmaster **13**
  schoolteacher **14** schoolmistress

teaching 5 dogma, tenet **6** belief **7**
  nurture, precept **8** doctrine, pedagogy,
  training, tutelage, tutoring **9** education, principle, schooling **10** convic-

tion, philosophy **11** inculcation, instructing, instruction, preparation **14** indoctrination

tea dance
> French: **10** the dansant

teal
> group of: **5** ducks
> color: **4** blue **5** green

team 3 rig, set **4** ally, band, crew, five, gang, join, nine, pair, side, unit, yoke **5** force, group, merge, party, squad, staff, unify, unite **6** circle, clique, couple, eleven, league, tandem **7** combine, company, coterie, faction **8** alliance, federate **9** coalition, cooperate **10** amalgamate, federation, sports team, yoked group **11** association, consolidate, get together, incorporate **12** band together, join together **13** confederation

teammate 4 ally **7** partner **8** coplayer, coworker **9** associate, colleague, co-partner **11** confederate **12** collaborator

team spirit 10 group pride, solidarity **13** esprit de corps

team up 4 ally **5** unite **9** cooperate **10** join forces **11** collaborate

tear 3 fly, gap, hie, rip, run **4** bolt, dart, dash, grab, hole, mist, pull, race, rend, rent, rift, rive, rush, scud, slit, snag, swim, whiz, yank **5** abuse, break, crack, fault, pluck, scoot, seize, sever, shoot, shred, speed, split, spurt, sweep, whisk **6** breach, cleave, damage, divide, gallop, hasten, hustle, injury, plunge, ravage, scurry, snatch, sprint, sunder, wrench **7** disrupt, fissure, hard use, opening, rupture, scamper, scuttle **8** disunite, teardrop, scramble, splinter **9** come apart, hotfoot it, pull apart, skedaddle **10** impairment, make tracks **11** destruction **12** pull to pieces

tear down 4 raze **5** level, smash, wreck **7** destroy, flatten **8** demolish **9** dismantle, take apart

tearful 5 teary, weepy **6** crying **7** bawling, crushed, sobbing, wailing, weeping **8** mournful **9** lamenting, sniveling **10** blubbering, lachrymose, whimpering **11** heartbroken **12** inconsolable **13** brokenhearted

tear off 5 sever **6** detach, rip off **7** pull off **8** break off, separate **10** wrench away

Teasdale, Sara
> author of: **8** Love Song **11** Helen of Troy **13** Dark of the Moon **14** Flame and Shadow, Rivers to the Sea, Strange Victory

tease 3 guy, irk, nag, rag, vex **4** bait, gall, gibe, goad, haze, jeer, josh, mock, pest, rile, twit **5** annoy, chafe, harry, mimic, pique, scoff, sneer, taunt, worry **6** bad- ger, bother, harass, hazing, heckle, hector, mocker,

needle, pester, plague, teaser **7** bedevil, chafing, laugh at, needler, provoke, razzing, snigger, taunter, torment, worrier **8** derision, heckling, irritate, needling, ridicule **9** aggravate, make fun of, mimicking, persecute, tantalize, tormentor **10** harassment, tantalizer **11** persecution

teaspoon
> abbreviation: **3** tsp

Teazle, Sir Peter and Lady
> characters in: **19** The School for Scandal
> author: **8** Sheridan

technical 5 trade **10** mechanical, vocational **11** complicated, nonacademic **13** technological

technique 3 art, way **4** form **5** craft, knack, style **6** manner, method, system **7** formula, know-how **8** approach, facility **9** procedure **10** adroitness, expertness, technology **11** proficiency **12** skillfulness

tedious 3 dry **4** drab, dull, long, slow **5** vapid **6** boring, dismal, dreary, jejune, tiring **7** humdrum, insipid, irksome, onerous, prosaic **8** drawn-out, lifeless, tiresome, wearying **9** fatiguing, laborious, wearisome **10** burdensome, exhausting, monotonous, oppressive, unexciting **13** time-consuming, unimaginative, uninteresting

tediousness 5 ennui **7** boredom **8** dullness, monotony

tedium 3 rut **5** ennui **7** boredom **8** drabness, dullness, monotony, sameness **10** dreariness **11** routineness **12** tiresomeness

tedium of life
> Latin: **12** taedium vitae

teem 4 brim, gush **5** swarm **6** abound **8** be full of, overflow **9** be overrun **15** burst at the seams

teeming 4 full **7** crowded **8** swarming **9** abounding, bounteous **11** overflowing

teeny-weeny 3 wee **4** tiny **5** dwarf **6** little, minute, petite **9** miniature, minuscule **10** diminutive, pocket-size **11** lilliputian, microscopic, pocket-sized

teeter 4 reel, sway **5** lurch, waver **6** seesaw, totter, wobble **7** stagger **8** hesitate **9** vacillate

teetotaler 3 dry **9** abstainer **10** nondrinker **14** prohibitionist

Tegucigalpa
> capital of: **8** Honduras

Tegyrius
> king of: **6** Thrace

Tehani
> character in: **17** Mutiny on the Bounty
> authors: **4** Hall **8** Nordhoff

Tehran, Teheran
> capital of: **4** Iran

landmark: **10** Melaat Park **12** Marble Palace, Marmar Palace **14** Azadai Monument, Gulestan Palace, Saadabad Palace **15** Freedom Monument, Hosseineh Mosque, Shahyad Monument **23** Center for Islamic Studies
> means: **9** warm place
> mountain: **6** Elburz **8** Demavend
> ruler: **8** Khomeini **23** Muhammad Reza Shah Pahlavi

Telamon
> king of: **7** Salamis
> member of: **9** Argonauts
> father: **6** Aeacus
> mother: **6** Endeis
> brother: **6** Peleus
> half-brother: **6** Phocus
> wife: **6** Glauce **7** Eriboea
> son: **4** Ajax **6** Teucer
> friend: **8** Hercules

Telegonus
> father: **7** Proteus **8** Odysseus
> mother: **5** Circe
> wife: **2** Io **8** Penelope
> killed: **8** Odysseus
> killed by: **8** Hercules

telegraph
> invented by: **5** Morse, Woods **6** Edison **7** Marconi

Telemachus
> father: **8** Odysseus
> mother: **8** Penelope
> son: **7** Latinus

Telemann, Georg Philipp
> born: **7** Germany **9** Magdeburg
> composer of: **9** Fantasias **10** Times of Day **12** Don Quichotte **14** Die Tageszeiten, Musique de Table

Telemus
> vocation: **4** seer
> father: **7** Eurymus
> warned: **10** Polyphemus

telepathy 3 ESP **10** sixth sense **11** second sight **12** clairvoyance **19** spirit communication, thought transference **22** extrasensory perception

telephone
> invented by: **4** Bell
> type: **3** cell, pay, TDD **6** mobile, rotary **8** cellular, portable, princess, wireless **9** extension, touch-tone **10** push-button

Telephone, The
> opera by: **7** Menotti

telescope
> invented by: **7** Galileo **10** Lippershey
> astronomical: **6** Kepler

telesterion
> form: **8** building
> purpose: **8** religion **11** celebration

television
> invented by: **5** Baird **8** Zworykin **10** Farnsworth

tell 3 ask, bid, own, say, see **4** blab **5** bruit, count, order, speak, spout, state, utter, weigh, write **6** advise, babble, betray, blazon, depict, detail, direct, figure, impart, inform, number, recite, reckon, relate, report, reveal, sketch, unfold **7** apprise, command, compute, confess, declare, discern, divulge, express, find out, mention, narrate, portray, predict, publish, recount, request **8** acquaint, count off, describe, disclose, estimate, forecast, foretell, identify, instruct, perceive, register, set forth **9** apprehend, ascertain, broadcast, calculate, chronicle, enumerate, enunciate, influence, make known, pronounce, recognize **10** take effect **11** communicate, distinguish **12** discriminate **17** breathe a word about

Teller, Edward
field: **7** physics
developed: **8** atom bomb **12** hydrogen bomb

telling 5 solid, valid **6** cogent, potent **7** decided, weighty **8** decisive, definite, forceful, material, positive, powerful, striking **9** effective, effectual, important, momentous, trenchant **10** conclusive, definitive, impressive **11** efficacious, influential, significant **13** consequential

telltale 6 gossip **7** tattler **8** busybody, giveaway, informer, squealer **9** affirming, betraying, divulging, revealing, verifying **10** confirming, disclosing, newsbearer, talebearer, tattletale **11** informative **12** blabbermouth, enlightening **13** scandalmonger

Tellus
called: **10** Terra Mater
origin: **5** Roman
goddess of: **5** earth **8** marriage **9** fertility **11** agriculture
corresponds to: **4** Gaea

temerity 4 gall **5** brass, cheek, nerve **8** audacity, boldness, chutzpah, rashness **9** brashness, freshness, impudence, insolence, pushiness, sauciness **10** brazenness, effrontery **11** forwardness **12** impertinence, indiscretion **13** foolhardiness, intrusiveness

Temin, Howard Martin
field: **8** genetics, oncology
discovered: **20** reverse transcriptase
awarded: **10** Nobel Prize

temper 3 ire **4** bile, calm, fury, gall, mood, rage **5** allay, anger, humor, pique, quiet, still, wrath **6** animus, anneal, choler, dander, harden, pacify, soften, soothe, spleen **7** appease, balance, compose, dudgeon, emotion, ferment, passion, toughen, umbrage **8** acrimony, bad humor, calmness, mitigate, moderate, palliate, vexation **9** annoyance, composure, huffiness **10** irritation, strengthen **11** displeasure, disposition, equilibrium, frame of mind, indignation, peevishness, tranquilize **12** churlishness, irascibility, irritability

temperament 4 bent, cast, mood,

soul, tone **5** humor, tenor **6** makeup, nature, spirit, temper **7** leaning, quality **8** tendency **9** character **10** complexion **11** disposition, frame of mind, personality

temperamental 5 fiery, moody **6** fickle **7** erratic, peppery, willful **8** unstable, volatile **9** emotional, excitable, explosive, hotheaded, mercurial, sensitive, turbulent **10** capricious, headstrong, high-strung, hysterical, mettlesome, passionate, unreliable **11** tempestuous, thin-skinned **12** undependable **13** unpredictable

temperance 8 prudence, sobriety **9** restraint **10** abstention, abstinence, discretion, moderation, self-denial **11** forbearance, prohibition, self-control, teetotalism **14** abstemiousness, self-discipline

temperate 4 calm, cool, even, mild, sane, soft, warm **5** balmy, sober, sunny **6** gen- tle, mellow, sedate, steady **7** clement, patient, sparing **8** composed, moderate, pleasant, rational, tranquil **9** collected, easygoing, unruffled **10** coolheaded, reasonable **11** levelheaded **13** dispassionate, self-possessed, unextravagant, unimpassioned **14** self-controlled, self-restrained

temperature measurement 6 degree, Kelvin **7** Celsius **10** Fahrenheit

tempest 5 chaos, furor, storm **6** hubbub, tumult, uproar **8** brouhaha, outbreak, upheaval **9** agitation, cataclysm, commotion **10** hurly-burly, turbulence **11** disturbance

Tempest, The
author: **18** William Shakespeare
character: **5** Ariel **6** Alonso **7** Antonio, Caliban, Gonzalo, Miranda **8** Prospero **9** Ferdinand, Sebastian

Tempestates
origin: **5** Roman
goddesses of: **6** storms

tempestuous 3 hot **5** fiery **6** raging, stormy **7** excited, frantic, furious, violent **8** agitated, feverish, frenzied **9** emotional, explosive, turbulent, wrought-up **10** hysterical, passionate, tumultuous **11** impassioned, overwrought

Templar, Simon
character in: **8** The Saint
author: **9** Charteris

temple 4 fane, kirk **6** chapel, church, mosque, pagoda, priory, shrine **7** convent **8** basilica, pantheon **9** cathedral, joss house, monastery, sanctuary, synagogue **10** house of God, tabernacle **12** meeting house

Temple, Shirley
married name: **18** Shirley Temple Black
born: **13** Santa Monica CA
roles: **5** Heidi **10** Bright Eyes **15** Wee

Willie Winkie **16** Little Miss Marker, The Little Colonel, The Littlest Rebel **18** Poor Little Rich Girl **21** Susannah of the Mounties **23** Rebecca of Sunnybrook Farm

tempo 4 clip, gait, pace, rate, time **5** meter, speed **6** pacing, stride, timing **8** momentum, velocity

tempo giusto
music: **10** strict time

temporal 3 lay **5** civil **6** mortal **7** mundane, passing, profane, secular, worldly **8** day-to-day, fleeting, fugitive **9** ephemeral, temporary, transient **10** evanescent, noneternal **11** impermanent, nonclerical **12** nonspiritual **17** nonecclesiastical

temporary, temporarily 5 brief, fleet **7** interim, passing, stopgap **8** fleeting, fugitive **9** ephemeral, momentary, provisory, transient **10** evanescent, short-lived, transitory **11** impermanent, provisional **13** flash-in-the-pan
Latin: **10** pro tempore

temporary dwelling
French: **10** pied-a-terre

temporize 5 delay, hedge, stall, tarry, waver **8** hang back, maneuver **9** hem and haw, vacillate **10** equivocate **11** play for time **12** drag one's feet, tergiversate **13** procrastinate

tempt 3 try, woo **4** bait, draw, goad, lure, pull, risk **5** charm, decoy, prick, rouse **6** allure, arouse, entice, incite, invite, seduce **7** attract, bewitch, provoke **8** appeal to, intrigue, inveigle **9** captivate, tantalize **12** put to the test **13** take one's fancy **14** fly in the face of **15** whet the appetite

temptation 4 bait, draw, lure, pull, urge **5** charm, snare, spell **8** stimulus, tempting **9** incentive, seduction **10** allurement, attraction, enticement, incitement, inducement **11** captivation, fascination, provocation

tempter 5 Satan **7** enticer, seducer **8** the Devil

temptress 4 vamp **5** Circe, flirt, siren **7** charmer, Delilah, Jezebel, Lorelei, vampire **8** coquette **9** odalisque, sorceress **10** seductress **11** enchantress, femme fatale

tempus fugit 9 time flies

Ten (10)
director: **12** Blake Edwards
cast: **7** Bo Derek **11** Dudley Moore **12** Julie Andrews

tenable 6 viable **8** arguable, rational, sensible, workable **9** excusable **10** condonable, defendable, defensible, vindicable **11** justifiable, warrantable **12** maintainable

tenacious 3 set **4** fast, firm, hard, iron **6** dogged, mulish **7** adamant, staunch **8** clinging, constant, obdurate, resolute, stalwart, stubborn **9** immovable, obstinate, pigheaded, steadfast, unbending **10** determined, inexorable, inflexible, persistent, relentless, unswerving, unwavering, unyielding **11** persevering, undeviating, unfaltering, unremitting **12** intransigent, unchangeable **14** uncompromising

tenaciousness 8 tenacity **9** endurance **10** resolution **11** persistence **12** perseverance, resoluteness **13** determination **16** stick-to-itiveness

tenacity 8 strength **9** toughness **10** resolution **11** persistence **12** cohesiveness, perseverance, resoluteness **13** determination, tenaciousness **16** stick-to-itiveness

tenant 6 lessee, lodger, renter, roomer **7** boarder, denizen, dweller **8** occupant, resident **10** inhabitant **11** householder, leaseholder, paying guest

Tenant of Wildfell Hall, The
  author: 10 Anne Bronte

Tenants, The
  author: 14 Bernard Malamud

Ten Commandments
  also: 9 Decalogue
  given to: 5 Moses
  where given: 10 Mount Sinai
  inscribed on: 12 stone tablets
  first: 32 Thou shalt have no other Gods before me
  second: 37 Thou shalt not bow down before graven images
  third: 44 Thou shalt not take the name of the Lord thy God in vain
  fourth: 34 Remember the Sabbath Day and keep it holy
  fifth: 26 Honor thy father and thy mother
  sixth: 16 Thou shalt not kill
  seventh: 26 Thou shalt not commit adultery
  eighth: 17 Thou shalt not steal
  ninth: 46 Thou shalt not bear false witness against thy neighbor
  tenth: 17 Thou shalt not covet

Ten Commandments, The
  director: 13 Cecil B DeMille
  cast: 8 Nina Foch **9** John Derek **10** Anne Baxter, Debra Paget, Yul Brynner **11** Martha Scott **12** Vincent Price **13** John Carradine, Yvonne De Carlo **14** Charlton Heston (Moses), Judith Anderson **15** Cedric Hardwicke, Edward G Robinson

tend 3 aim **4** bear, head, lead, lean, mind, move **5** be apt, guide, nurse, point, watch **6** extend, foster, manage, wait on **7** care for, nurture **8** attend to, be liable, be likely **9** bid fair to, gravitate, look after, supervise, watch over **10** minister to, predispose, take care of **11** keep an eye on

tendency 3 aim, set **4** bent **5** drift, drive, habit, trend **6** course **7** heading, impulse, leaning, turning **8** penchant **9** direction, proneness, readiness **10** proclivity, propensity **11** disposition, gravitation, inclination **14** predisposition

tender 3 raw **4** fond, give, good, kind, soft, sore, weak **5** frail, green, place, young **6** aching, benign, callow, caring, dainty, extend, feeble, gentle, hand in, loving, prefer, submit, weakly **7** advance, fragile, hold out, painful, present, proffer, propose, suggest, swollen **8** delicate, generous, immature, inflamed, juvenile, merciful, propound, underage, youthful **9** lay before, sensitive, volunteer **10** benevolent, put forward, thoughtful, vulnerable **11** considerate, sentimental, softhearted, sympathetic, warmhearted **12** affectionate **13** compassionate, inexperienced, understanding **14** impressionable **15** unsophisticated

tenderfoot 4 tyro **6** novice, rookie **8** beginner, neophyte **9** fledgling, greenhorn **10** apprentice

tenderhearted 4 mild **6** benign, gentle, humane **8** generous, merciful **10** altruistic, benevolent, responsive, thoughtful **11** considerate, kindhearted, softhearted, sympathetic, warmhearted **13** compassionate, understanding

tenderheartedness 4 pity **5** heart **7** empathy **8** sympathy **10** compassion

tendering 6 giving **8** offering **9** advancing, extending, proposing **10** holding out, preferring, proffering, submitting, suggesting **11** propounding **12** volunteering

Tender Is the Night
  author: 16 F Scott Fitzgerald
  character: 8 Abe North **9** Dick Diver **11** Nicole Diver, Tommy Barban **12** Rosemary Hoyt

tenderness 4 love **6** aching, warmth **7** rawness **8** delicacy, fondness, goodness, humanity, kindness, mildness, smarting, softness, soreness, sympathy **9** affection **10** compassion, gentleness, humaneness, kindliness, lovingness **11** beneficence, benevolence, painfulness, sensitivity **12** mercifulness **14** loving kindness

tendon 4 cord **5** sinew
  connects: 4 bone **6** muscle

tendril 4 coil, curl **5** crook, shoot, sprig, twist **6** winder **7** climber, ringlet

tenebrous 3 dim **4** dark **5** murky **6** gloomy **7** obscure, shadowy **8** darkened, obscured **13** unilluminated

tenet 4 rule, view **5** canon, credo, creed, dogma, maxim **6** belief, thesis **7** opinion **8** doctrine, ideology, position, teaching **9** principle **10** conviction, persuasion

Tennessee
  abbreviation: 2 TN **4** Tenn
  nickname: 7 Big Bend **9** Volunteer **11** Old Franklin
  capital: 9 Nashville
  largest city: 7 Memphis
  others: 5 Alcoa, Paris **6** Camden, Sparta **7** Bristol, Dickson, Pulaski **8** Franklin, Gallatin, Oak Ridge **9** Cedar Hill, Cleveland, Inglewood, Kingsport, Knoxville, Lexington **10** Greenbrier, Morristown, Old Hickory **11** Chattanooga, Clarksville, Springfield **12** Fayetteville, Murfreesboro **14** Hendersonville
  college: 4 Fisk, Lane **5** Bryan, Siena **6** Bethel **7** Belmont, Lambuth, Lemoyne **8** Milligan, Tusculum **10** Vanderbilt **12** Southwestern **13** David Lipscomb **14** Meharry Medical **17** Tennessee Wesleyan
  feature: 12 The Hermitage
  dam: 6 Norris, Wilson **7** Douglas
  fort: 5 Henry **8** Donalson, Nashboro
  national park: 6 Shiloh **13** Cumberland Gap **19** Great Smoky Mountains (with North Carolina)
  national parkway: 12 Natchez Trace
  tribe: 7 Shawnee **8** Cherokee **9** Chickasaw
  people: 7 Sequoya **8** John Bell **9** James Agee **10** Grace Moore **11** Bessie Smith, Cordell Hull **12** Davy Crockett **18** Carey Estes Kefauver **23** Alvin Cullum "Sergeant" York **32** Ernest Jennings "Tennessee Ernie" Ford
  explorer: 6 Arthur, De Soto **7** Jolliet, La Salle, Needham **9** Marquette
  lake: 7 Douglas **8** Barkeley, Cherokee, Reelfoot, Watts Bar **10** Center Hill **11** Chickamauga
  land rank: 12 thirty-fourth
  mountain: 5 Guyot **7** Lookout, Smokies **9** Blue Ridge **10** Cumberland, Great Smoky
  highest point: 13 Clingman's Dome
  physical feature:
  basin: 9 Nashville
  highlands: 11 Appalachian
  plain: 7 Coastal
  plateau: 10 Cumberland
  president: 10 James K Polk **13** Andrew Jackson, Andrew Johnson
  river: 3 Elk **4** Duck **5** Caney, Obion, Stone **6** Clinch **7** Hatchie, Holston **8** Hiwassee **9** Tennessee **10** Cumberland **11** French Broad, Mississippi **15** Little Tennessee
  state admission: 9 sixteenth
  state bird: 11 mockingbird
  state flower: 4 flag, iris **6** maypop **13** passion flower
  state motto: 16 America at Its Best **22** Agriculture and Commerce
  state song: 11 My Tennessee **17** The Tennessee Waltz **19** My Homeland

Tennessee 26 When It's Iris Time in Tennessee
state tree: 11 tulip poplar **12** yellow poplar

tennis
athlete: 8 Don Budge, Jan Kodes, Rod Laver, Tom Okker **9** Bjorn Borg, Ivan Lendl, Stan Smith **10** Arthur Ashe, Bill Tilden, Jack Kramer, Maria Bueno, Pam Shriver, Roy Emerson, Steffi Graf **11** Alice Marble, Andre Agassi, Boris Becker, Edward Dibbs, Ilie Nastase, John McEnroe, Ken Rosewall, Monica Seles, Pete Sampras, Tracy Austin **12** Althea Gibson, Darren Cahill, Francois Durr, Jimmy Connors, John Newcombe, Mats Wilander, Roscoe Tanner, Virginia Wade **13** Dennis Ralston, Harold Solomon, Manuel Orantes, Manuel Santana, Martina Hingis, Martin Riessen, Wendy Turnbull **14** Brian Gottfried, Guillermo Vilas, Hana Mandlikova, Pancho Gonzalez, Rosemary Casals **15** Charles Pasarell, Chris Evert Lloyd, Maureen Connolly, Richard Stockton, Vitas Gerulaitis **17** Donald Schollander, Nancy Richey Gunter **18** Margaret Smith Court, Martina Navratilova **20** Helen Wills Moody Roark **21** Billie Jean Moffitt King, Evonne Goolagong Cawley
cup: 5 Davis

Tennyson, Alfred, Lord
author of: 4 Maud **7** Mariana, Ulysses **10** Enoch Arden, In Memoriam (A H H) **12** Locksley Hall, Morte d'Arthur **16** The Lady of Shalott **18** The Idylls of the King **26** The Charge of the Light Brigade

tenor 4 gist **5** drift, sense, trend **6** course, import, intent, nature, object **7** content, essence, meaning, purport, purpose **8** argument, tendency **9** direction, intention, substance **11** connotation, implication **12** significance

tense 4 taut **5** brace, drawn, rigid, shaky, stiff, tight **6** braced, draw up, on edge, uneasy **7** anxious, excited, fearful, fidgety, jittery, nervous, restive, stiffen, uptight **8** agitated, make taut, restless, strained, timorous **9** tighten up, tremulous, wrought-up **10** high-strung, inflexible, unyielding **12** apprehensive

tension 5 dread **6** spring, strain, stress **7** anxiety, pulling, tugging **8** bad vibes, exertion, pressure, rigidity, tautness, traction **9** hostility, misgiving, stiffness, straining, tightness **10** stretching **11** fearfulness, nervousness, restiveness, trepidation **12** apprehension, elastic force, perturbation **13** bad vibrations, combativeness

tent 3 pup **4** care, hard **5** gauze, probe, tepee **6** bigtop, canvas, search, teepee, wigwam **7** shelter **8** pavilion **10** tabernacle

tentacle 3 arm **6** feeler **9** appendage
tentative 4 iffy **5** trial **6** acting **8** not final, proposed **9** ad interim, temporary, undecided, unsettled **10** contingent, indefinite, not settled **11** conditional, probational, provisional, speculative, unconfirmed **12** experimental, probationary **15** subject to change **18** under consideration
tentative procedure 4 test **5** flier, trail **6** feeler, tryout **7** venture **10** experiment **12** trial balloon
tenuous 4 slim, thin, weak **5** frail, shaky **6** flimsy, paltry, slight **7** fragile, shallow, slender **8** delicate, gossamer **9** uncertain **10** indefinite **11** halfhearted, unsupported **12** unconvincing **13** unsubstantial
tenure 4 rule, term, time **5** reign **7** tenancy **9** occupancy, retention **10** incumbency, occupation, permanency, possession **11** entitlement, job security **14** administration
tepee, teepee 4 chum, tent **5** lodge **6** wigwam **7** wickiup
tepid 4 cool, mild **7** languid, warmish **8** lukewarm, moderate **9** apathetic, impassive, temperate **10** nonchalant, phlegmatic **11** halfhearted, indifferent, unemotional **13** lackadaisical **14** unenthusiastic

tequila
type: 6 spirit
origin: 6 Mexico
made from: 5 agave **6** maguey
used with: 4 lime, salt **5** lemon
drink: 7 Chapala **8** El Diablo
with creme de cacao: 8 Toreador
with kahlua: 9 Brave Bull
with orange juice: 7 Sunrise
with Tia Maria: 9 Brave Bull
with triple sec: 9 Margarita

Teraphim
origin: 6 Hebrew
form: 4 idol

Ter Borch, Gerard
born: 6 Zwolle **14** The Netherlands
artwork: 8 Flea Hunt **10** The Concert **14** Peace of Munster **21** The Parental Admonition

Terbrugghen, Hendrick
born: 8 Deventer **14** The Netherlands
artwork: 14 The Flute Player **19** Liberation of St Peter **21** The Calling of St Matthew

Tereshkova, Valentina
first: 12 woman in space
terete 7 tapered **11** cylindrical
tergal 4 back **6** dorsal

Terkel, Studs
author of: 4 Race **7** Working **9** Hard Times **10** "The Good War" **14** American Dreams

term, terms 3 age, dub, era, tag **4** call, cite, item, name, span, time, word **5** catch, cycle, epoch, idiom,

reign, spell, stage, state, style, while **6** clause, course, detail, period, phrase, status, string **7** dynasty, footing, proviso **8** duration, interval, position, standing **9** condition, designate, provision, relations, requisite **10** expression, span of time **11** appellation, designation, requirement, stipulation **12** characterize, circumstance, prerequisite **14** administration

termagant 3 nag **4** fury **5** scold, shrew, vixen **6** ogress, virago **7** hellcat, hellion, she-wolf, tigress **8** battle-ax, fishwife, harridan, spitfire **9** Xanthippe

Termagant
character in: 21 medieval morality plays

terminal 3 end **4** last **5** depot, fatal, final, stand **6** deadly, lethal, mortal **7** station **8** terminus **10** concluding

terminate 3 end **4** stop **5** cease, close, lapse **6** expire, finish, run out, wind up **8** complete, conclude **11** come to an end, discontinue **12** bring to an end

termination 3 end **4** halt **5** close, finis, lapse **6** ending, finale, finish, windup **7** closing **8** stoppage **9** cessation **10** completion, concluding, conclusion, expiration **15** discontinuation

terminus 3 end **4** stop **5** depot, limit **6** ending **7** extreme, station **8** boundary, last stop, terminal **9** extremity **10** conclusion

Terminus
origin: 5 Roman
god of: 9 landmarks **10** boundaries

terminus ad quem 10 end to which, final limit **11** ending point
terminus a quo 9 beginning **12** end from which **13** starting point

termite
variety: 6 desert **7** dry wood **8** damp wood **10** powderpost, rotten wood **11** soldierless **12** subterranean

Terms of Endearment
director: 12 James L Brooks
based on novel by: 13 Larry McMurtry
cast: 11 Debra Winger **13** Jack Nicholson **15** Shirley MacLaine
Oscar for: 7 actress (MacLaine), picture **8** director **15** supporting actor (Nicholson)

Terpsichore
member of: 5 Muses
personifies: 7 dancing **10** choral song

Terra
goddess of: 5 Earth
Greek: 4 Gaea
mother: 5 Chaos
offspring: 6 Pontus, Titans, Uranus **7** Erinyes, Oceanus **8** Cyclopes **9** mountains **13** Hecatonchires

terrace 4 roof **5** level, patio, plane, porch **6** street **7** balcony, plateau **9**

esplanade, promenade **10** embankment

Terraced Bay *see* **6** Taiwan

terra-cotta 4 clay **6** russet **8** brownish **12** reddish-brown **14** brownish-orange

terrain 4 area, zone **5** tract **6** ground, milieu, region **7** setting **8** district **9** territory **10** topography **11** countryside, environment **12** surroundings

terra incognita 11 unknown land **14** unexplored land, unknown subject **16** unknown territory

terrapin 3 box **4** emyd, emys **6** slider, turpin, turtle **8** tortoise **11** diamond back
family: 8 Emydidae
female: 6 heifer
male: 4 bull

terrestrial 4 land **6** earth's, global, ground **7** earthly, mundane, worldly **8** riparian **10** earthbound

terrible 3 bad **4** dire, huge **5** awful, great, harsh, rough, scary **6** brutal, fierce, horrid, odious, severe, strong **7** beastly, extreme, fearful, ghastly, hateful, heinous, hideous, intense **8** alarming, dreadful, enormous, fearsome, horrible, shocking, terrific **9** appalling, excessive, harrowing, monstrous, obnoxious, offensive, repulsive, revolting, upsetting **10** disturbing, formidable, horrifying, immoderate, inordinate, terrifying, tremendous, unpleasant **11** distasteful, distressing, frightening, intolerable **12** insufferable **13** objectionable

terrier
dog breed: 3 fox **4** bull, Skye **5** Cairn, Irish, Welsh **6** border, Boston **7** Norfolk, Tibetan, wire fox **8** Airedale, Lakeland, Scottish, Sealyham **9** Kerry Blue **10** Australian, Bedlington, Manchester **13** Dandie Dinmont **17** soft-coated wheaten, Staffordshire bull, West Highland white **18** miniature schnauzer **21** American Staffordshire

terrific 3 fab **4** fine, good, huge **5** awful, great, harsh, marvy, scary, super **6** bang-up, fierce, severe, superb **7** extreme, fearful, intense, sensash **8** alarming, dreadful, enormous, fabulous, fearsome, smashing, splendid, terrible **9** excellent, excessive, fantastic, harrowing, marvelous, monstrous, upsetting, wonderful **10** disturbing, horrifying, immoderate, inordinate, remarkable, stupendous, superduper, terrifying, tremendous **11** distressing, exceptional, frightening, sensational **13** extraordinary **14** out of this world

terrified 6 afraid, scared **7** alarmed, panicky **9** petrified **10** frightened **11** scared stiff **13** panic-stricken **14** terror-stricken **17** frightened to death

terrify 3 cow **5** abash, alarm, daunt, panic, scare, unman, upset **6** appall,

dismay **7** agitate, disturb, horrify, overawe, petrify **8** disquiet, frighten **10** intimidate **17** make one's skin crawl **20** make one's blood run cold **22** make one's hair stand on end

terrifying 5 awful, dread **7** fearful **8** alarming, dreadful **9** frightful **11** frightening, hair-raising

territory 4 area, land, pale, zone **5** clime, realm, state, tract **6** bounds, colony, domain, empire, limits, locale, nation, region, sector **7** acreage, kingdom, mandate, terrain **8** confines, district, dominion, province **9** bailiwick **10** dependency **11** countryside **12** commonwealth, principality, protectorate

terror 3 awe **4** fear **5** alarm, dread, panic **6** dismay, fright, horror **7** anxiety **8** affright, disquiet **9** agitation **11** disquietude, trepidation **12** apprehension, perturbation **13** consternation **16** fear and trembling

terrorize 3 cow **5** abash, force **6** menace **7** browbeat, bulldoze, threaten **10** intimidate

terror-stricken 6 afraid, scared **7** alarmed, panicky **9** horrified, petrified, terrified **11** scared green, scared stiff **13** panic-stricken, scared to death

Terry and the Pirates
creator: 12 Milton Caniff
character: 7 Pat Ryan **8** Terry Lee **10** Dragon Lady

terse 4 curt, neat **5** brief, clear, crisp, pithy, short **6** abrupt **7** clipped, compact, concise, laconic, pointed, summary **8** clearcut, incisive, succinct **9** axiomatic, condensed, trenchant **10** compressed **11** unambiguous **12** epigrammatic **18** brief and to the point

terseness 7 brevity **8** curtness **9** crispness **10** abruptness **11** compactness, conciseness **12** succinctness

Tesman family
characters in: 11 Hedda Gabler
members: 5 Hedda **6** George **7** Juliana
author: 5 Ibsen

Tess (of the D'Urbervilles)
author: 11 Thomas Hardy
director: 13 Roman Polanski
cast: 8 John Bett **10** Peter Firth, Tom Chadbon **14** Rosemary Martin **15** Nastassia Kinski (Tess)

test 4 exam, quiz **5** check, final, flyer, probe, proof, prove, trial **6** dry run, feeler, try out, verify **7** analyze, confirm, examine, midterm **8** analysis, validate **9** catechism **11** corroborate, examination, investigate, questioning **12** confirmation, substantiate, verification **13** comprehensive, corroboration, investigation, questionnaire

Testament 5 Bible **7** the Book **10** Scriptures **12** New Testament, Old Testament

testament 6 legacy **7** bequest **10** settlement

tester 6 canopy **8** examiner **10** questioner

testify 4 show **5** prove, swear **6** affirm, attest, evince **7** declare, signify **8** evidence, indicate, manifest **11** bear witness, demonstrate **12** give evidence

testimonial 5 medal **6** ribbon, trophy **7** tribute **8** citation, memorial, monument **9** affidavit, reference **10** deposition **11** certificate, endorsement **12** commendation **14** recommendation

testimony 5 proof **6** avowal **7** witness **8** averment, evidence **9** affidavit, statement **10** deposition, indication, profession **11** affirmation, attestation, endorsement **12** confirmation, verification **13** certification, corroboration, demonstration, documentation, manifestation **14** acknowledgment

testy 5 cross, moody **6** crabby, cranky, crusty, filthy, grumpy, snappy, sullen, touchy **7** fretful, peevish, waspish **8** captious, caviling, choleric, churlish, perverse, petulant, snappish, snarling **9** fractious, impatient, irascible, irritable, splenetic **10** ill-humored **11** acrimonious, contentious **12** cantankerous, faultfinding, sharp-tongued **13** quick-tempered, temperamental

tete-a-tete 4 chat, talk **6** parley **9** interview **12** conversation **13** confabulation

tether 3 tie **4** cord, rein, rope **5** chain, leash **6** fasten, halter, hobble, secure

Tethys
member of: 6 Titans
father: 6 Uranus
mother: 4 Gaea
husband: 7 Oceanus
mother of: 8 Oceanids **9** river gods
daughters: 13 three thousand
foster child: 4 Hera

Tetragrammaton
consonants in: 10 name for God **4** JHVH, IHVH, JHWH, YHVH, YHWH

Teutonic 5 Dutch **6** German, Gothic, Nordic **7** British, English **8** Germanic **12** Scandinavian
alphabet character: 4 rune
demon: 3 alp
goddess of death: 3 Hel, Ran
goddess of peace: 7 Nerthus
god of peace: 6 Balder
god of thunder: 4 Thor
god of war: 3 Tiu, Tyr
god of wisdom: 4 Odin

Teutonic Mythology *see* **17** Germanic Mythology

Texas
abbreviation: 2 TX **3** Tex
nickname: 8 Lone Star
capital: 6 Austin
largest city: 7 Houston
others: 4 Gail, Rice, Vega, Waco **5** Bryan, Marfa, Ozona, Pampa, Tyler,

Wiley **6** Baylor, Borger, Dallas, Denton, El Paso, Kileen, Laredo, Odessa, Quanah, Sonora **7** Abilene, Denison, Lubbock **8** Amarillo, Beaumont, Floydada **9** Fort Worth, Galveston **10** San Antonio **13** Corpus Christi
college: 3 SMU, TCU **4** Rice **5** Lamar, Wiley **6** Austin, Baylor **7** St Mary's, Trinity **10** Texas A and M **12** Southwestern **14** Texas Christian **16** Abilene Christian **17** Southern Methodist
feature:
  fort: 5 Alamo
  national park: 7 Big Bend **18** Guadalupe Mountains
  national seashore: 11 Padre Island
  state park: 10 San Jacinto
tribe: 4 Adar, Waco **5** Caddo, Lipan **6** Apache, Biloxi, Jumano, Kichai, Shuman, Tejano **7** Alabama, Hasinai, Tonkawa **8** Comanche, Querecho **9** Coushatta, Karankawa
people: 10 James S Hogg **12** Edward M House, Thomas C Clark **13** John B Connally, Samuel Houston **14** Chester W Nimitz, Mirabeau B Lamar, Samuel T Rayburn, Stephen F Austin, William B Travis **15** John Nance Garner, Thomas T Connally **19** Katherine Anne Porter
  explorer: 4 Vaca **7** La Salle
island: 5 Padre
lake: 6 Falcon, Sabine, Texoma **7** Amistad
river: 3 Red **5** Pecos **6** Brazos, Neches, Nueces, Sabine **7** Trinity **8** Colorado **9** Rio Grande **10** San Jacinto
land rank: 12 second
physical feature:
  bay: 13 Corpus Christi
  port: 7 Houston **9** Galveston **13** Corpus Christi
president: 14 Lyndon B Johnson **17** Dwight D Eisenhower
  Republic of Texas: 10 Sam Houston
state admission: 12 twenty-eighth
state bird: 11 mockingbird
state flower: 10 bluebonnet, yellow rose
state motto: 10 Friendship
state song: 13 Texas Our Texas
state tree: 5 pecan
baseball team: 7 Rangers
text 5 motif, theme, topic, verse, words **6** manual, primer, sermon, thesis **7** content, passage, subject, wording **8** argument, sentence, textbook, workbook **9** paragraph, quotation **10** schoolbook **13** subject matter
textile 4 yarn **5** cloth, fiber **6** fabric **8** filament, material **9** yard goods **10** piece goods
texture 3 nap **4** feel, look **5** grain, touch, weave **6** makeup **7** quality, surface **8** fineness **9** character, structure **10** coarseness **11** composition
Tey, Josephine

real name: 19 Elizabeth MacKintosh
author of: 10 Brat Farrar **15** Miss Pym Disposes, The Singing Sands **17** The Daughter of Time **19** A Shilling for Candles
character: 9 Alan Grant
Thackeray, William Makepeace
author of: 9 Pendennis **10** Vanity Fair **11** Barry Lyndon, Henry Esmond, The Newcomes **13** The Virginians
Thaddeus of Arimathea see **5** Judas
Thai-Austronesian
language branch: 9 Thai-Kadai **12** Austronesian
includes: 5 Batak, Malay **6** Fijian, Samoan **7** Tagalog **8** Hawaiian, Javanese **15** Bahasa Indonesia
spoken in: 4 Fiji, Java **5** China, Samoa **6** Hawaii, Taiwan **7** Sumatra **9** Indonesia, Polynesia **10** Madagascar **11** Philippines **12** Easter Island
Thailand
name means: 13 land of the free
other name: 4 Siam **11** Prathet Thai
capital/largest city: 6 Bankok **7** Bangkok
  old capital: 8 Thonburi **9** Ayutthaya
others: 4 Ubon **5** Puket **6** Nakhon, Ranong **7** Ayudhya, Ayuthea, Lampang, Lamphur, Lopburi, Rahaeng, Singora, Songkla **8** Khonkaen, Kiangmai, Songkhla, Sukhotai, Thonburi **9** Ayutthaya, Chiangmai, Chiengmai **10** Ratchasima **11** Phitsanulok **14** Ubonratchthani
kingdom: 5 Funan **6** Khymer **8** Thonburi **9** Ayutthaya, Chiang Mai, Dvaravati, Sukhothai **12** Subarnabhumi
school: 9 Thammasat **13** Chulalongkorn
head of state: 4 king
measure: 2 wa **3** can, ken, niv, rai, sat, sok, wah **4** cohi, keup, niou, tang **5** kwien, leeng, sesti, vouah **6** kabiet, kanahn **7** chaimeu **8** changawn **9** anukabiet
monetary unit: 2 at **3** att **4** baht **5** cutty, fuang **6** pynung, salung **11** bullet money
weight: 3 bat, hap, pay, sen, sok **4** baht, haph, kati, klam **5** catty, chang, fuang, picul, pilul, tical **6** fluang, graini, salung, **7** tamlung
island: 2 Ko **3** Kut, Tao **4** Chan, Rawi **5** Chang, Lanta, Samui, Thalu **6** Libong, Phuket **7** Phangan, Terutao
lake: 9 Nong Lahan
mountain: 5 Dawna, Khieo **6** Phanom **8** Dang Raek, Kao Prawa, Maelamun **9** Khao Luang **11** Bilauktaung
highest point: 8 Inthanon **11** Doi Inthanon
river: 3 Chi, Mun, Nan, Yom **4** Ping **5** Menam **6** Mekong, Meping **7** Sal-

ween **10** Chaophraya
sea: 7 Andaman
physical feature:
  gulf: 4 Siam **8** Thailand
  isthmus: 3 Kra
  pass: 12 Three Pagodas
  peninsula: 5 Malay
  plateau: 5 Korat **6** Khorat
people: 3 Lao, Mon **4** Lawa, Shan, Thai **5** Malay **6** Indian, Khymer **7** Chinese, Siamese **9** Cambodian **10** Vietnamese
  king: 4 Rama **7** Chakkri, Mongkut **10** Chao Phraya **12** Prahjadhipok **13** Chulalongkorn **17** Bhumibol Adulyadej
  leader: 9 Phraruang **12** Kukrit-Pramoj
language: 3 Lao, Tai **4** Ahom, Shan, Thai **5** Kadai, Malay **7** Bangkok, Chinese, English **9** Krung Thep
religion: 5 Islam **8** Buddhism **12** Christianity, Confucianism **17** Theravada Buddhism
place:
  dam: 8 Bhumibol
  palace: 5 Grand
  ruins: 7 Ayuthia **9** Ayutthaya
  street: 7 Yawarai
  temple: 4 Dawn **7** Trimitr **10** Wat Phra Keo **11** Royal Chapel **13** Emerald Buddha
feature:
  canal: 5 klong
  clothing: 6 panung, sarong **12** saffron robes
  festival: 12 Surin Round Up
  houseboat: 6 sampan
  temple: 3 wat
  tree: 4 teak
food:
  fruit: 5 camut **6** durian, litchi, pomelo **8** rambutan **10** mangosteen
Thais
author: 13 Anatole France
character: 8 Athanael
composer: 8 Massenet
Thalassa
personifies: 3 sea
thalassic 6 marine **7** aquatic, deep-sea, neritic, oceanic, pelagic
Thales
field: 11 mathematics
nationality: 5 Greek
discovered: 18 geometry principles
predicted: 11 sun's eclipse
Thalestris
character in: 16 The Rape of the Lock
author: 4 Pope
Thalia
member of: 5 Muses **6** Graces
personifies: 6 comedy **13** idyllic poetry
lover: 4 Zeus
killed by: 5 Erato
Thallo

member of: 5 Horae
goddess of: 13 spring flowers

Thamyris
    vocation: 4 poet **8** musician
    father: 9 Philammon
    mother: 7 Argiope
    punished for: 9 arrogance
    punished by: 5 Muses
    punishment: 7 maiming **8** blinding

thanatophobia
    fear of: 5 death

Thanatos
    personifies: 5 death

thank 5 bless **12** be grateful to **13** be much obliged **18** express gratitude to

thankful 7 obliged **8** beholden, grateful **10** indebted to **12** appreciative, full of thanks **16** feeling gratitude **22** expressing appreciation

thankfulness 6 thanks **9** gratitude **12** appreciation, gratefulness

thankless 4 vain **7** ingrate, useless **8** bootless, caviling, critical, heedless **9** fruitless, unmindful, unwelcome **10** profitless, ungracious, ungrateful, uninviting, unpleasant, unrewarded, unthankful **11** distasteful, thoughtless, undesirable, unrewarding **12** disagreeable, faultfinding **13** inconsiderate, unappreciated **14** unacknowledged, unappreciative

thanks 5 grace **8** blessing **9** gratitude **11** benediction **12** appreciation, gratefulness

thanks be to God
    Latin: 10 Deo gratias

thanksgiving 6 thanks **8** blessing

Thanksgiving
    started by: 8 Bradford, Pilgrims
    traditional food: 4 corn, yams **6** turkey **10** pumpkin pie **13** sweet potatoes **14** cranberry sauce
    symbol: 9 ear of corn **12** horn of plenty

thank you
    French: 5 merci
    German: 5 danke
    Spanish: 7 gracias
    Italian: 6 grazie
    Japanese: 4 domo

Thank You, Jeeves
    author: 11 P G Wodehouse

thank you very much
    French: 9 merci bien **13** merci beaucoup
    German: 10 danke schon
    Japanese: 11 domo arigato
    Spanish: 13 muchas gracias

That Certain Feeling
    author: 12 Kingsley Amis

Thatcher, Becky
    character in: 9 Tom Sawyer
    author: 5 Twain

Thatcher, Judge
    character in: 15 (The Adventures of)

Huckleberry Finn
    author: 5 Twain

That Girl
    character: 8 Ann Marie, Lou Marie **10** Helen Marie, Ruth Bauman **11** Jerry Bauman **12** Don Hollinger, Judy Bessemer **14** Dr Leon Bessemer
    cast: 9 Lew Parker **10** Ted Bessell **11** Alice Borden, Bonnie Scott, Marlo Thomas **12** Bernie Kopell **13** Dabney Coleman **14** Carolyn Daniels, Rosemary DeCamp

that is
    Latin: 2 ie **5** id est

that is to say
    Latin: 3 viz **9** videlicet

that's life
    French: 9 c'est la vie

thaw 4 melt, warm **5** relax **6** soften, unbend, warm up **7** liquefy, melting, thawing **8** dissolve **11** break the ice

Thea
    companion of: 7 Artemis
    ravished by: 6 Aeolus
    changed into: 4 mare
        mare named: 6 Euippe

Theale, Milly
    character in: 17 The Wings of the Dove
    author: 5 James

theater 4 site **5** arena, drama, house, movie, odeum, place, scene, stage **6** cinema, lyceum **7** gallery, setting **8** assembly, audience, coliseum **9** colosseum, music hall, playhouse **10** assemblage, auditorium, movie house, spectators **11** histrionics, lecture hall, theatricals **12** amphitheater, show business

theatrical 4 film **5** hammy, movie, showy, stage, stagy **6** flashy **7** fustian, show-biz, stilted **8** affected, dramatic, mannered, thespian **9** grandiose, unnatural **10** artificial, histrionic **11** exaggerated, extravagant, pretentious, spectacular **12** magniloquent, ostentatious, show-business **13** entertainment, grandiloquent **14** larger-than-life

theatrical trick
    French: 13 coup de theatre

Thebaid
    author: 7 Statius
    character: 4 Atys **5** Creon **6** Ismene, Tydeus **7** Jocasta, Theseus **8** Antigone, Capaneus, Eteocles, Opheltes, Tiresias **9** Menoeceus, Polynices **10** Amphiaraus, Hippomedon, Melanippus

the bottle 5 booze, drink, sauce **6** liquor **7** alcohol **8** demon rum

the dansant 8 tea dance

thee therefore
    Latin: 8 te igitur

theft 5 fraud **7** larceny, looting, robbery **8** burglary, filching, rustling,

stealing, thievery **9** hijacking, pilfering, swindling **10** purloining **11** shoplifting **12** embezzlement
    god of: 6 Hermes **7** Mercury

Theia
    also: 4 Thia
    member of: 6 Titans
    father: 6 Uranus
    mother: 4 Gaea
    brother: 8 Hyperion
    mother of: 8 Cercopes
    son: 6 Helios
    daughter: 3 Eos **6** Selene

the life of the land is maintained by righteousness
    Hawaiian: 52 ua mau ke ea o ka aina i ka pono
    motto of: 6 Hawaii

Them
    author: 15 Joyce Carol Oates

theme 3 air **4** song, text, tune **5** essay, focus, motif, point, topic, tract **6** melody, report, review, strain, thesis **7** keynote, premise, subject **8** argument, critique, question, treatise **9** discourse, leitmotif, monograph **10** commentary **11** composition, proposition **12** dissertation

Then Again, Maybe I Won't
    author: 9 Judy Blume

thence 6 whence **9** from there, therefore **11** accordingly, in due course **13** from that place

the next world 6 Heaven **8** eternity, paradise **12** the hereafter **14** the world to come

the norm 7 the mean, the rule **9** the median **10** the average **14** the common thing

the Occident 7 the West **20** the western hemisphere

theologian *see* **22** philosopher/ theologian

theological 4 holy **6** sacred **8** Biblical, dogmatic **9** apostolic, canonical, doctrinal, religious, spiritual **10** scriptural **14** ecclesiastical

theology 5 dogma **8** divinity, doctrine, religion

Theophane
    bore: 3 ram
    fleece of ram: 6 golden

theoretical 8 abstract, academic, putative **11** conjectural, postulatory, speculative **12** hypothetical, nonpractical **13** suppositional

theorize 5 infer, posit, think **6** assume **7** imagine, presume, propose, suppose, surmise **8** propound **9** formulate, postulate, predicate, speculate **10** conjecture **11** hypothecate, hypothesize

theory 3 law **4** idea, view **5** guess **6** belief, notion, thesis **7** concept, opinion, science, surmise, thought **8** doctrine, ideology, judgment **9** deduction, postulate, principle **10** conclusion, conjecture, hypothesis, persuasion, philosophy **11** presumption, speculation, supposition

therapeutic, therapeutical 7 healing **8** curative, remedial, salutary, sanative **11** restorative **12** ameliorative

therapy 7 healing **9** treatment **14** rehabilitation

thereafter 5 later **9** after that, afterward **10** afterwards, from then on **11** thenceforth **12** subsequently **14** from that time on

therefore 2 so **4** ergo, thus **5** hence **11** accordingly **12** consequently, on that ground **13** for that reason, in consequence, on that account **14** for which reason

there is no disputing about tastes
Latin: **27** de gustibus non est disputandum

there it is
French: **5** voila

Therese Raquin
author: **9** Emile Zola
character: **7** Camille, Laurent

There Shall Be No Night
author: **15** Robert E Sherwood

thereupon 4 then **6** at once **7** thereon **8** directly, suddenly, upon that **9** forthwith, in a moment, upon which **11** immediately **12** straightaway, without delay

thermometer
invented by: **7** Galileo, Reaumur
mercury: **10** Fahrenheit

Thero
nurse of: **4** Ares

theropod
type of: **8** dinosaur
member: **10** Allosaurus, Antrodemus **11** Coelophysis, Gorgosaurus **13** Albertosaurus, Compsognathus, Struthiomimus, Tyrannosaurus

Theroux, Paul
author of: **9** Saint Jack **16** The Mosquito Coast **20** Riding the Iron Rooster **21** The Great Railway Bazaar **23** The Old Patagonian Express

Thersites
mentioned in: **5** Iliad
origin: **5** Greek
characteristics: **4** ugly **8** deformed **11** quarrelsome
accused Agamemnon of: **5** greed
accused Achilles of: **9** cowardice
fought in: **9** Trojan War
killed by: **8** Achilles

the same as 4 like **7** equal to **9** a match for **12** comparable to, equivalent to, tantamount to **16** commensurate with

thesaurus 8 synonymy **10** word finder **11** synonymicon **12** word treasury **13** synonym finder **17** synonym dictionary **18** semantic dictionary

Thescelosaurus
type: **8** dinosaur **10** ornithopod
location: **6** Canada **12** United States
period: **10** Cretaceous

These Three
director: **12** William Wyler
based on play by: **14** Lillian Hellman (The Children's Hour)
cast: **10** Alma Kruger, Joel McCrea **11** Merle Oberon **13** Miriam Hopkins **15** Bonita Granville, Catherine Doucet

Theseus
king of: **6** Athens
father: **6** Aegeus **8** Poseidon
mother: **6** Aethra
wife: **7** Phaedra
consort: **9** Hippolyta
lover: **7** Ariadne
son: **6** Acamas **8** Demophon **10** Hippolytus, Melanippus
helmsman: **10** Nausithous
killed: **5** Sinis **6** Sciron **8** Minotaur **10** Cretan bull, Procrustes

thesis 5 essay, paper, tract **6** notion, theory **7** article, concept, surmise **8** argument, critique, proposal, treatise **9** discourse, monograph, postulate, term paper **10** commentary, conjecture, hypothesis **11** composition, proposition, speculation, supposition **12** disquisition, dissertation

Thesmia
epithet of: **7** Demeter
means: **12** goddess of law

Thesmophorus
epithet of: **7** Demeter
means: **8** lawgiver

thespian 3 ham **4** star **5** actor, extra **6** co-star, player, walk-on **7** actress, ingenue, trouper **8** juvenile **9** bit-player, guest star, performer, tragedian **10** leading man **11** leading lady, stage player

Thespis 9 Greek poet
originator of: **12** Greek tragedy

Thessalus
king of: **8** Thessaly
father: **5** Jason **8** Hercules
mother: **5** Medea **9** Chalciope

the state
Latin: **10** res publica

Thetis
member of: **7** Nereids
husband: **7** Peleus
sister: **8** Eurynome
son: **8** Achilles

the very words
Latin: **14** ipsissima verba

the world over 10 every place, everywhere, far and wide, near and far **11** in all places

They Shoot Horses, Don't They?
director: **13** Sydney Pollack
cast: **8** Gig Young **9** Bruce Dern, Jane Fonda **10** Red Buttons **12** Susannah York **13** Bonnie Bedelia **15** Michael Sarrazin

Oscar for: **15** supporting actor (Young)

They Won't Forget
director: **11** Mervyn LeRoy
cast: **10** Lana Turner, Otto Kruger **11** Allyn Joslyn, Claude Rains **12** Elisha Cook Jr **13** Gloria Dickson

thiasus
also: **7** thiasos
group worshipping: **11** patron deity
followers of: **8** Dionysus
followers called: **6** satyrs **7** maenads

thick 3 big, fat **4** deep, dull, dumb, slow, wide **5** broad, bulky, close, dense, fuzzy, great, heavy, husky, piled, solid **6** chummy, heaped, hoarse, lavish, obtuse, packed, strong, stupid, viscid, wooden **7** blurred, clotted, compact, copious, crowded, decided, devoted, doltish, extreme, intense, liberal, muffled, profuse, teeming, throaty, viscous **8** abundant, familiar, friendly, generous, guttural, intimate, profound, sisterly, swarming **9** brotherly, condensed, fatheaded, glutinous, plenteous, unstinted **10** coagulated, dull-witted, gelatinous, indistinct, munificent, pronounced, slow-witted **11** inseparable, overflowing **12** concentrated, impenetrable, inarticulate

thicken 3 set **4** cake, clot, jell **5** muddy **6** darken, deepen, muddle **7** compact, congeal, jellify **8** condense **9** coagulate, intensify **10** gelatinize

thicket 4 bush, wood **5** brake, brush, copse, grove, scrub **6** bushes, covert, forest, shrubs **7** bracken **9** shrubbery **10** underbrush **11** undergrowth

thickheaded 4 dull, dumb, slow **5** blank, dense, dopey, thick **6** obtuse, stupid **8** ignorant **9** dim-witted, fatheaded **10** boneheaded, dull-witted, half-witted, slow-witted **11** blockheaded, thick-witted **12** dunderheaded, thick-skulled **13** chuckleheaded, knuckleheaded

thickset 5 bulky, close, dense, dumpy, husky, solid, squat, stout, tubby **6** chunky, packed, stocky, stubby, stumpy, sturdy **8** close-set, heavyset, roly-poly

thickskinned 4 hard **5** horny, tough **6** inured **7** callous **8** calloused, hardened **9** unfeeling, unmovable **10** impervious, insensible **11** insensitive, unconcerned **13** imperturbable, unsusceptible **14** pachydermatous

thick-skulled 4 dull **5** dense **6** stupid **11** thickheaded **12** dunderheaded

thick-witted 4 dull, slow **5** dense **6** stupid **7** idiotic, moronic **9** dim-witted, imbecilic **11** thickheaded **12** dunderheaded, simple-minded

thief 5 crook **6** bandit, mugger, robber **7** burglar, filcher, rustler **8** hijacker, pilferer, swindler **9** defrauder, embezzler, holdup man, larcenist, purloiner, racketeer **10** highwayman, pickpocket, shoplifter **12** housebreaker, kleptomaniac **13** confidence man, pursesnatcher **14** second-story man

Thief of Bagdad, The
director: 9 Tim Whelan **12** Ludwig Berger **13** Michael Powell
cast: 4 Sabu **9** Rex Ingram **10** John Justin, June Duprez **11** Conrad Veidt

Thieves' Carnival
also: 15 Le Bal des Voleurs
author: 11 Jean Anouilh

thievish 3 sly **6** sneaky **7** furtive **8** stealthy, thieving **9** dishonest, larcenous, secretive, thieflike **13** light-fingered, surreptitious **14** sticky-fingered

thigh 3 ham, leg **4** hock **5** femur, flank, ilium **6** gammon
pain: 8 meralgia

Thimbu, Thimphu
capital of: 6 Bhutan

thin 4 fine, lank, lean, slim, weak **5** faint, gaunt, lanky, prune, runny, scant, sheer, spare, water **6** dilute, feeble, narrow, not fat, reduce, skinny, slight, sparse, watery **7** curtail, diluted, fragile, scrawny, slender, spindly **8** delicate, diminish, finespun **9** emaciated, water down **10** inadequate, threadlike **11** transparent **12** insufficient **13** unsubstantial

thin-blooded 3 wan **4** pale, weak **6** anemic, sickly

thing, things 3 act **4** deed, feat, gear, item **5** event, gizmo, goods, point **6** action, affair, aspect, detail, dingus, entity, gadget, matter, object, person **7** article, clothes, concern, effects, feature, thought **8** business, clothing, creature, movables **9** doohickey, equipment, happening, statement **10** belongings, human being, occurrence, particular, proceeding **11** eventuality, living being, possessions, thingamabob, thingamajig, transaction **12** circumstance **13** paraphernalia

Thing
legislative body of: 11 Scandinavia

thing already done
French: 12 fait accompli

thingamajig 5 gizmo **6** doodad, gadget **11** contraption, contrivance, thingamabob **15** whatchamacallit

thing of no value
Latin: 5 nihil

things done
Latin: 9 res gestae

think 4 deem, mean, plan **5** brood, fancy, guess, judge **6** design, expect, intend, ponder, reason, recall, reckon **7** believe, dwell on, imagine, presume, propose, purpose, reflect, suppose, surmise **8** cogitate, conceive, conclude, contrive, meditate, mull

over, remember, ruminate **9** recollect, speculate **10** anticipate, deliberate, have in mind, keep in mind **11** contemplate, use one's mind, use one's wits **13** rack one's brain

thinkable 8 knowable **10** imaginable **11** conceivable, perceivable

think about 4 mull **6** debate, ponder **7** reflect **8** consider, mull over **10** deliberate

think alike 5 agree **11** be of one mind, see eye to eye

thinker 4 sage **6** savant, wizard **7** egghead, scholar **9** intellect **10** mastermind **11** mental giant, philosopher **13** metaphysician

Thinker, The
by: 5 Rodin

think fit 4 deem **5** deign, stoop **7** consent **10** condescend

think highly of 5 favor, honor, value **6** admire, esteem, revere **7** approve, respect **8** look up to, venerate **10** set store by

think ill of 4 hate **5** decry **6** detest **7** condemn, deplore, despise, dislike **8** object to **9** abominate, disparage, frown upon **10** disapprove **13** look askance at **14** discountenance **15** take exception to **16** find unacceptable, view with disfavor

thinking 4 view **5** smart, stand, study **6** belief, bright **7** concept, surmise, thought **8** cultured, educated, judgment, position, rational, studious **9** brainwork, deduction, inference, reasoning **10** conclusion, cultivated, impression, meditation, meditative, reflection, reflective, rumination, thoughtful **11** intelligent, speculation **12** deliberation **13** consideration, contemplation, contemplative, philosophical, sophisticated, using one's head **15** paying attention

Thinking Reed, The
author: 15 Dame Rebecca West

think over 5 study, weigh **8** cogitate, consider, mull over **11** reflect upon **12** deliberate on

think through 5 weigh **6** ponder **7** analyze **8** appraise, consider, evaluate

think up 5 frame, hatch **6** create, invent **7** concoct, dream up **8** conceive, contrive

think well of 4 like **6** admire **8** look up to **10** appreciate

Thin Man, The
author: 15 Dashiell Hammett
character: 4 Asta (pet terrier) **7** Morelli **11** Nick Charles, Nora Charles **13** Arthur Nunheim, Mimi Jorgensen **15** Herbert Macaulay **18** Christian Jorgensen
  Wynant family: 5 Clyde **7** Dorothy, Gilbert
director: 11 W S Van Dyke II

cast: 4 Asta **8** Myrna Loy (Nora Charles) **13** William Powell (Nick Charles)
thin man is: 6 victim
sequel (film): 14 Another Thin Man **15** After the Thin Man **16** Song of the Thin Man **18** The Thin Man Goes Home

Thin Mountain Air, The
author: 10 Paul Horgan

thin out 5 prune **6** dilute, reduce, weaken **7** weed out **9** water down **10** adulterate

thinskinned 5 cross, huffy, sulky, testy **6** grumpy, sullen, touchy **7** crabbed, peevish **8** petulant, snappish **9** irascible, irritable, sensitive, squeamish **11** ill-tempered, quarrelsome, susceptible **12** cantankerous **13** oversensitive **14** hypersensitive

third estate
French: 9 tiers etat

Third Man, The
director: 9 Carol Reed
based on story by: 12 Graham Greene
cast: 10 Alida Valli **11** Orson Welles (Harry Lime) **12** Joseph Cotten, Trevor Howard **16** Wilfrid Hyde-White
setting: 6 Vienna

Third Wave, The
author: 12 Alvin Toffler

thirst 3 yen **4** itch, lust, pant **5** ardor, covet, crave, yearn **6** desire, fervor, hunger, relish **7** craving, passion, stomach **8** appetite, keenness, voracity, yearning **9** hanker for, hankering **11** thirstiness

thirsty 3 dry **4** avid **5** eager **7** parched **9** thirsting

Thirteen O'Clock
author: 19 Stephen Vincent Benet

Thirty-Nine Steps, The (The 39 Steps)
author: 10 John Buchan
director: 15 Alfred Hitchcock
cast: 11 Robert Donat **13** Godfrey Tearle, Lucie Mannheim, Peggy Ashcroft **16** Madeleine Carroll

This Above All
author: 10 Eric Knight

Thisbe
loved: 7 Pyramus
location: 7 Babylon
death by: 7 suicide
death at tomb of: 5 Ninus

this is
Latin: 6 hoc est

This Is Your Life
host: 12 Ralph Edwards
announcer: 9 Bob Warren

thistle 7 Cirsium
varieties: 3 Oat **4** Bull, Holy, Milk, Star **5** Glove, Plume, White **6** Canada, Cotton, Golden, Scotch, Silver

7 Blessed, St Mary's **8** Fishbone, Mountain, Plumless **9** Argentine, Thornless **10** Great globe, Small globe **11** Mountain sow **14** Acanthus-leaved
emblem of: **8** Scotland

Thomas 7 apostle
means: **4** twin
also called: **7** Didymus, Doubter **8** Doubting

Thomas, Ambroise
born: **4** Metz **6** France
composer of: **6** Mignon

Thomas, Danny
real name: **16** Amos Muzyad Jacobs
born: **11** Deerfield MI
daughter: **11** Marlo Thomas
roles: **13** The Jazz Singer **16** Make Room for Daddy **19** I'll See You in My Dreams

Thomas, Dylan
author of: **8** Fern Hill **13** Under Milk Wood **23** A Child's Christmas in Wales

Thomas, George H
nickname: **20** The Rock of Chickamauga
served in: **8** Civil War **10** Mexican War
side: **5** Union
commander of: **19** Army of the Cumberland
battle: **9** Nashville **11** Chattanooga, Chickamauga

Thomas, Marlo
real name: **14** Margaret Thomas
born: **9** Detroit MI
father: **11** Danny Thomas
husband: **11** Phil Donahue
roles: **8** That Girl

Thomas, W Morgan
creator/artist of: **22** Sheena Queen of the Jungle

Thomas a Kempis
author of: **20** The Imitation of Christ

Thomson, Joseph John
field: **7** physics
nationality: **7** British
discovered: **8** electron
awarded: **10** Nobel Prize

Thomson, Thomas John
born: **6** Canada **9** Claremont
artwork: **9** Spring Ice **11** The Jack Pine **12** Northern Lake **13** Northern River

Thomson, Virgil
born: **12** Kansas City MO
composer of: **9** Portraits **16** The Mother of Us All **21** Four Saints in Three Acts

thong 4 band **5** strap, strip **6** sandal **7** binding **8** swimsuit **9** underwear

Thor
origin: **12** Scandinavian
god of: **4** rain **7** farming, thunder
rode: **7** chariot
chariot pulled by: **5** goats

wielded: **6** hammer **7** Miolnir
father: **4** Odin **5** Othin

thorax 5 chest, trunk **6** breast, cavity **8** forebody

Thoreau, Henry David
author of: **6** Walden (Life in the Woods) **17** Civil Disobedience

thorium
chemical symbol: **2** Th

thorn 2 th **4** rune

thorn 3 woe **4** bane, barb, care, gall, spur **5** cross, curse, spike, spine, sting **6** plague **7** prickle, scourge, torment, trouble **8** nuisance, vexation **9** annoyance, sore point **10** affliction, bitter pill, infliction, irritation

thorn 9 Crataegus
varieties: **3** Box **4** Lily, Pear **5** Camel, Hedge, White **6** Christ, Karroo, Mysore, Sallow, Sickle, Winter **7** Thirsty **8** Cockspur, Egyptian, Kangaroo, Quick-set **9** Jerusalem, Paper-bark **10** Washington **11** Crucifixion **13** Yellow-fruited

Thornbirds, The
author: **17** Colleen McCullough

Thornburg, Betty June
real name of: **11** Betty Hutton

Thornfield
house in: **8** Jane Eyre
author: **6** Bronte

Thornhill, Squire
character in: **19** The Vicar of Wakefield
author: **9** Goldsmith

thorn in the side 4 bane **7** torment **9** annoyance **10** irritation

thorny 4 dire, hard **5** spiny, tough **6** barbed, spiked, sticky, trying **7** arduous, brambly, complex, crucial, irksome, prickly **8** annoying, critical, involved, ticklish **9** bristling, dangerous, difficult, vexatious **10** formidable, nettlesome, perplexing **11** complicated, troublesome

thorough 4 full, pure **5** sheer, total, utter **6** entire **7** careful, perfect, uniform **8** absolute, complete, of a piece **9** downright, out-and-out **10** consistent, definitive, exhaustive, meticulous **11** painstaking, unmitigated, unqualified **12** all-embracing, all-inclusive

thoroughbred 7 unmixed **8** purebred **9** blueblood, pedigreed, racehorse **10** aristocrat **11** full-blooded, pureblooded **12** silkstocking

thoroughfare 4 road **6** avenue, street **7** freeway, highway, parkway, roadway, thruway **8** main road, turnpike **9** boulevard, concourse **10** expressway, interstate **12** superhighway **13** through street

thoroughgoing 5 utter **6** arrant **7** extreme **8** outright **9** confirmed, notorious, out-and-out **11** undisguised, unmitigated

thoroughly 5 fully **7** totally, utterly **8** entirely **9** carefully, downright, out-and-out, perfectly, uniformly **10** absolutely, completely, throughout **11** inclusively **12** consistently, exhaustively, meticulously **13** in all respects **15** from top to bottom **17** through and through **18** from beginning to end

Thorpe, Isabella
character in: **15** Northanger Abbey
author: **6** Austen

Thorpe, Jim (James Francis)
sport: **8** football **13** track and field
won: **8** Olympics
named: **11** All-American

Thorvaldsen, Albert Bertel
born: **7** Denmark **10** Copenhagen
artwork: **4** Hope **9** Lord Byron **14** Cupid and Psyche **16** The Lion of Lucerne **22** Cupid and the Three Graces **24** Jason with the Golden Fleece

Thoth
origin: **8** Egyptian
god of: **5** magic **6** wisdom **8** learning
scribe of: **4** gods
inventor of: **6** letter **7** numbers
corresponds to: **6** Hermes
head of: **3** dog **4** ibis

though 3 tho, yet **4** even, that **5** still **6** albeit, even if **7** granted **8** although, granting **9** admitting **12** nevertheless **15** notwithstanding

thought 3 aim, end **4** goal, idea, plan, view **5** credo, dogma, fancy, tenet **6** belief, caring, design, intent, musing, notion, object, regard, scheme **7** concept, concern, opinion, purpose, reverie, surmise **8** doctrine, judgment, kindness, thinking **9** attention, intention, objective, sentiment **10** brown study, cogitation, conception, conclusion, meditation, reflection, rumination **11** expectation, imagination, speculation, supposition **12** anticipation, deliberation **13** consideration, contemplation, introspection
French: **6** pensee

thoughtful 4 kind **6** caring, loving, musing **7** pensive, probing, serious, wistful **8** thinking **9** attentive **10** meditative, neighborly, reflective, solicitous **11** considerate, kindhearted **13** contemplative, introspective

thoughtfulness 7 probing, thought **8** kindness, thinking **10** meditation, reflection **11** questioning **13** attentiveness, consideration, contemplation **14** solicitousness **15** kindheartedness

thoughtless 4 dumb, rash, rude **5** silly **6** stupid, unkind **7** foolish **8** careless, heedless, impolite, reckless **9** imprudent **10** ill-advised, indiscreet, neglectful, unthinking **11** harebrained, improvident, inadvertent, inattentive, insensitive **12** absent-minded, unreflecting **13** ill-considered, inconsiderate, rattlebrained **14** scatterbrained

thoughtlessness 7 neglect **8** rashness, rudeness **9** oversight, unconcern **10** imprudence, negligence, unkindness **11** inattention **12** carelessness, heedlessness, impoliteness, recklessness **13** insensitivity **15** inattentiveness **16** absentmindedness

Thousand Clowns, A
  director: **7** Fred Coe
  based on play by: **11** Herb Gardner
  cast: **11** Barry Gordon **12** Jason Robards, Martin Balsam **13** Barbara Harris
  setting: **11** New York City
  Oscar for: **15** supporting actor (Balsam)

Thousand Days, A
  author: **20** Arthur M Schlesinger Jr

thou too
  Latin: **8** tu quoque

thrall 4 serf **5** slave **6** chains **7** bondage, serfdom, servant, slavery **9** servitude **11** enslavement, subjugation

thralldom 6 chains **7** bondage, serfdom, slavery **9** servitude **11** enslavement, subjugation

thrash 4 beat, cane, drub, flog, jerk, lash, maul, toss, whip **5** birch, flail, heave, solve, spank, strap **6** jiggle, joggle, plunge, pommel, squirm, switch, thresh, tumble, wiggle, writhe **7** flounce, resolve, scourge, trounce **8** argue out, lambaste **9** thresh out **10** flagellate

threadbare 4 dull, worn **5** banal, stale, stock, tacky, trite **6** boring, frayed, jejune, ragged, shabby **7** cliched, humdrum, napless, prosaic, raveled, routine, worn-out **8** bromidic, everyday, pileworn **9** hackneyed, well-known **11** commonplace, stereotyped **12** conventional, overfamiliar **15** the worse for wear

threads 4 duds, togs **6** attire **7** apparel, clothes, strands, strings **8** clothing, garments **9** filaments

threat 4 omen, risk **5** peril **6** danger, hazard, menace **7** ill omen, portent, warning **8** jeopardy **10** foreboding **11** commination, premonition **12** intimidation

threaten 3 cow **4** warn **6** impend, menace **7** imperil **8** endanger, forewarn, hang over **9** terrorize **10** be imminent, intimidate, jeopardize

threatening 4 grim **7** baleful, ominous, warning **8** alarming, imminent, menacing, sinister **9** ill-omened, impending **10** forbidding, foreboding **11** approaching, forewarning, terrorizing **12** inauspicious, intimidating, unpropitious

three
  French: **5** trois

Three-Cornered Hat, The
  author: **21** Pedro Antonio de Alarcon

Three Faces of Eve, The
  director: **15** Nunnally Johnson
  cast: **8** Lee J Cobb **9** Nancy Kulp **10** David Wayne **12** Vince Edwards **14** Joanne Woodward
    narration by: **13** Alistair Cooke
  Oscar for: **7** actress (Woodward)

Three Lives
  includes: **9** Melanctha **11** The Good Anna **13** The Gentle Lena
  author: **13** Gertrude Stein

Three Men in a Boat
  author: **13** Jerome K Jerome

Three Musketeers, The
  author: **14** Alexandre Dumas (pere)
  director: **13** Richard Lester
  character: **5** Athos **6** Aramis **7** Porthos **8** Planchet **9** D'Artagnan **12** Lady de Winter **17** Cardinal Richelieu **18** Constance Bonacieux
  cast: **10** Oliver Reed **11** Faye Dunaway (Milady), Michael York (D'Artagnan), Raquel Welch **12** Frank Findlay **14** Charlton Heston, Christopher Lee **16** Geraldine Chaplin **18** Richard Chamberlain
  sequel: **17** The Four Musketeers

Threepenny Opera, The
  author: **6** Brecht
  composer: **5** Weill
  based on: **15** The Beggar's Opera
  by: **7** John Gay
  song: **11** Mack the Knife

three R's 6 'riting **7** reading **9** 'rithmatic

Three's Company
  character: **5** Larry **9** Janet Wood **10** Helen Roper **11** Chrissy Snow, Jack Tripper **12** Stanley Roper
  cast: **10** John Ritter, Norman Fell **11** Joyce DeWitt **12** Audra Lindley, Richard Kline **13** Suzanne Somers

Three Sisters
  director: **10** John Sichel **15** Laurence Olivier
  author: **12** Anton Chekhov
  character: **13** Fyodor Kuligin **14** Baron Tusenbach, Vassily Solyony **17** Alexandr Vershinin
    Prozorov family: **4** Olga **5** Irina, Masha **6** Andrey **7** Natasha
  cast: **9** Alan Bates **11** Derek Jacobi, Jeanne Watts **13** Joan Plowright, Louise Purnell **15** Laurence Olivier

Three Soldiers
  author: **13** John Dos Passos

threnody 5 dirge, elegy **6** lament **7** requiem

threshold 4 dawn, door, edge, sill **5** brink, limen, onset, start, verge **6** portal **7** doorway, gateway, opening, prelude **8** doorsill, entrance **9** beginning, groundsel, inception **10** groundsill **11** entranceway **12** commencement **13** starting point

thrift 7 economy **8** prudence **9** frugality, husbandry, parsimony **10** moderation **11** sparingness, thriftiness **14** reasonableness **15** closefistedness **16** parsimoniousness

thriftiness 5 tight **6** thrift **7** economy **8** prudence **9** frugality, parsimony **13** penny-pinching **15** closefistedness, tightfistedness **16** parsimoniousness

thriftless 6 lavish **8** feckless, prodigal, wasteful **11** extravagant, improvident

thrifty 6 frugal, saving, stingy **7** sparing **9** niggardly, penny-wise **10** economical **11** closefisted, economizing, tightfisted **12** parsimonious **13** penny-pinching

thrill 4 fire, glow, kick, stir **5** flush, rouse, throb **6** arouse, excite, quiver, tickle, tingle, tremor **7** delight, impress, inspire, tremble **9** adventure, electrify, enrapture, galvanize, stimulate, transport **12** satisfaction

thrilled 4 agog **7** excited **9** delighted, overjoyed **11** transported

thrilling 7 awesome **8** engaging, exciting, riveting, stirring **9** absorbing, exquisite **10** delightful **11** fascinating, pleasurable, provocative, sensational, tantalizing, titillating **12** electrifying

thrip
  variety: **6** banded **10** tube tailed **11** heterothrip, merothripid

thrive 3 wax **4** boom **5** bloom, get on **6** fatten **7** burgeon, prosper, succeed **8** flourish, get ahead, grow rich

thriving 4 busy, lush, rank, rich **7** wealthy, well-off **8** blooming, in clover, vigorous, well-to-do **9** flowering, luxuriant **10** blossoming, prospering, prosperous, succeeding, successful **11** flourishing

throat 3 maw **4** craw, gula, neck **5** gorge **6** gullet **7** chamber, jugulum, passage, pharynx
  lozenge: **6** pastil
  nautical: **3** jaw **4** jaws, nock
  part: **6** fauces, larynx, tonsil **7** glottis, trachea
  pertaining to: **5** gular
  seizing: **4** knot **5** hitch **12** cuckold's knot
  swelling: **6** goiter

throaty 3 dry, low **4** base, deep **5** gruff, husky, thick **6** hoarse **7** cracked, grating, rasping **8** croaking, guttural, resonant, sonorous **9** full-toned

throb 4 beat, jerk, pant **5** heave, pulse, shake **6** quiver, tremor, twitch **7** beating, flutter, pulsate, shaking, tremble, vibrate **9** palpitate, pulsation, quivering, throbbing, trembling, vibration **10** fluttering **11** oscillation, palpitation **13** reverberation

throes 5 agony, chaos, pangs **6** ordeal, spasms, tumult **7** anguish, turmoil **8** disorder, paroxysm, upheaval **9** confusion, paroxysms **10** convulsion, disruption

thrombus 4 clot **9** blood clot **11** coagulation

throng 3 jam **4** army, cram, herd, host, mass, mill, pack, rush **5** bunch, crowd, crush, flock, flood, horde, press, surge, swarm **6** deluge, gather, huddle, stream **7** cluster, collect **8** assemble, converge **9** multitude **10** assemblage, congregate

thronged 4 full **6** jammed, mobbed, packed **7** crammed, crowded, flocked, swarmed, teeming **8** swarming **9** congested, jampacked **11** overflowing

throttle 3 gag, gas **4** stop **5** block, burke, check, choke **6** stifle **7** garrote, seal off, shut off, silence, smother **8** choke off, gas pedal, strangle **9** fuel lever, fuel valve **11** strangulate

through, thru 4 done, past **5** ended **6** direct **7** express **8** finished, from A to Z, to the end **9** all the way, completed, concluded **10** terminated **12** long-distance **15** from first to last **18** from beginning to end **20** from one end to the other

through and through 5 total **6** wholly **7** totally, utterly **8** complete **10** completely, thoroughly **15** from top to bottom **18** from beginning to end **20** from one end to the other

through my fault
   Latin: **8** mea culpa

throughout 7 all over **10** all the time, everywhere **11** in every part **16** all the way through **18** from beginning to end

Through the Looking Glass
   sequel to: **28** Alice's Adventures in Wonderland
   author: **12** Lewis Carroll
   character: **4** Gnat, Lion **5** Alice, Dinah **7** Red King, Unicorn **8** Red Queen **9** Red Knight, White King **10** Tweedledee, Tweedledum, White Queen **11** Black Kitten, White Kitten, White Knight **12** Humpty Dumpty

throw 3 lob, pit, put, shy **4** cast, hurl, shot, toss **5** chuck, fling, floor, heave, impel, pitch, place, put in, put on, sling **6** hurtle, launch, let fly, propel, unseat **7** project **8** delivery **9** knock down, put around

throw away 7 cast off, discard **8** get rid of

throw down 5 let go **8** drop hard, hurl down, toss down **9** fling down

throw into disorder 5 upset **7** agitate, disrupt **10** disarrange

throw off 4 emit, gush **5** exude **7** abandon, cast off, mislead **8** get rid of, shake off, shrug off **9** cast aside, discharge, give forth, pour forth

throw off the scent 7 confuse, mis-

lead **8** confound **19** throw out a red herring

throw out 4 beam, emit, oust **5** eject, evict, expel, exude **6** banish, bounce, remove **7** discard, dismiss, toss out **8** get rid of, jettison **9** cast aside, throw away

throw overboard 4 dump **7** cast off, discard **8** jettison, toss over

throw suspicion upon 11 cast doubt on **17** bring into question

throw up 4 barf, spew **5** eject, expel, spout, vomit **6** cast up, spew up **7** cough up **8** disgorge **9** discharge **11** regurgitate

thrust 3 jab, jam, ram **4** butt, pass, poke, prod, push, raid, stab **5** boost, drive, foray, force, impel, lunge, press, sally, shove, swipe **6** attack, charge, pierce, plunge, propel, sortie, strike, stroke **7** assault, impetus, impulse, riposte **8** momentum **9** incursion **10** aggression

thrust aside 4 dump **6** shelve **7** discard **8** get rid of, throw off, throw out **9** cast aside, dispose of, throw away

thrust at 6 assail, attack **7** lunge at **8** strike at

thrust out 4 spew, spit **5** eject, expel, vomit **6** extend, propel **7** protrude

Thucydides
   author of: **28** History of the Peloponnesian War

thud 4 bang **5** clunk, knock, smack, thump

thug 4 hood **6** bandit, gunman, hit man, killer, mugger, robber **7** hoodlum, mobster, ruffian **8** assassin, gangster, murderer **9** cutthroat

thumb 5 hitch **6** finger, handle **9** hitchhike **10** catch a ride, hitch a ride **11** flip through, leaf through

Thumbelina
   author: **21** Hans Christian Andersen

thumbnail 5 brief, short **7** compact, concise

thump 3 hit, jab, rap **4** bang, beat, clip, cuff, poke, slam, slap, swat, thud **5** clout, clunk, knock, pound, punch, smack, whack **6** batter, bounce, buffet, pommel, strike, thwack **8** collapse, lambaste

thunder 4 boom, clap, echo, peal, roar, roll **5** crack, crash **6** rumble **7** explode, resound **8** rumbling **9** discharge, explosion **11** reverberate, thunderbolt, thunderclap
   god of: **4** Thor **5** Donar **7** Taranis

thunderbolt 4 dart **5** flash, shaft **6** stroke

Thunderstorms, god of 8 Summanus

thunderstruck 4 agog, awed **5** agape **6** aghast, amazed **8** confused, overcome **9** astounded, awestruck, perplexed, surprised **10** astonished, be-

wildered **11** dumbfounded **13** flabbergasted

Thunder-ten-Tronckh
   character in: **7** Candide
   author: **8** Voltaire

Thurber, James
   author of: **12** The New Yorker **14** Is Sex Necessary (with E B White), The Catbird Seat **16** The Owl in the Attic **18** My Life and Hard Times, The Thurber Carnival **26** The Secret Life of Walter Mitty

Thurber Carnival, The
   author: **12** James Thurber

Thurio
   character in: **20** Two Gentlemen of Verona
   author: **11** Shakespeare

Thursday
   French: **5** jeudi
   from: **4** Thor
   German: **10** donnerstag
   heavenly body: **4** Jove **7** Jupiter
   Italian: **7** giovedi
   Latin: **9** Dies Jovis
   observance: **12** Holy Thursday, Thanksgiving **13** Corpus Christi **14** Maundy Thursday **17** Ascension Thursday
   Scandinavian: **7** torsdag
   Spanish: **6** jueves

thus 2 so **4** ergo **5** hence **6** like so **8** like this **9** as follows, in this way, therefore, wherefore **11** accordingly **12** consequently, in this manner **13** for this reason
   Latin: **3** sic

thus always to tyrants
   Latin: **17** sic semper tyrannis
   motto of: **8** Virginia

thus passes away the glory of this world
   Latin: **21** sic transit gloria mundi

Thus Spake Zarathustra
   also: **21** Also Sprach Zarathustra
   author: **18** Friedrich Nietzsche

thwack 3 box, hit, rap **4** bang, blow, slam, slap **5** baste, clout, knock, smack, thump, whack **6** buffet, paddle, strike, wallop

Thwackum
   character in: **8** Tom Jones
   author: **8** Fielding

thwart 3 bar **4** balk, foil, stop **5** check, cross **6** baffle, hinder, oppose **7** inhibit, prevent, ward off **8** obstruct, stave off **9** frustrate **10** contravene

Thyestean banquet
   meal of: **10** human flesh

Thyestes
   author: **6** Seneca

Thyestes
   father: **6** Pelops
   mother: **10** Hippodamia
   brother: **6** Atreus
   half-brother: **10** Chrysippus

sister-in-law: 6 Aerope
son: 9 Aegisthus
daughter: 7 Pelopia
Thyiad *see* **9** bacchante
Thymbraeus
  father: 7 Laocoon
thyme
  botanical name: 6 Thymus **9** T vulgaris
  varieties: 4 Wild **5** Basil, Lemon, Water **6** Common, Garden, Golden **7** Caraway, Spanish
  symbol of: 8 activity
  attracts: 4 bees
  conjures: 9 fairy folk
  use: 4 fish **7** poultry **8** stuffing **10** Creole food **21** New England clam chowder
Thyrus
  staff of: 8 Dionysus
  tipped with: 8 pine cone
  twined with: 3 ivy **5** vines
thysanoptera
  class: 8 hexapoda
  phylum: 10 arthropoda
  group: 5 thrip
thysanura
  class: 8 hexapoda
  phylum: 10 arthropoda
  group: 8 firebrat **10** silverfish **11** bristletail
Tia Maria
  type: 6 brandy **7** liqueur
  origin: 7 Jamaica
  flavor: 6 coffee
  with rum: 10 Black Maria
  with tequila: 9 Brave Bull
  with vodka: 12 Black Russian
tiara 4 band **5** crown, miter **6** diadem **7** coronet **8** frontlet, ornament **9** headdress
Tibet
  other name: 3 Bod **4** Bhot **5** Tobet **8** Hsitsang **10** Land of Snow **14** Roof of the World
  capital: 5 Lassa, Lhasa
  city: 3 Noh **5** Karak **6** Chamdo, Gartok **7** Changtu, Totling **8** Gyangtse, Jihkatse, Shigatse **9** Chiangtzu
  government: 23 autonomous region of China
  monetary unit: 5 tanga
  lake: 3 Aru, Bam, Bun, Nam **4** Mema, Tosu **5** Jagok, Tabia **6** Dagtse, Garhur, Kashun, Nam Iso, Seling, Tangra, Yamdok **7** Kyaring, Teriman, Tsaring, Zilling **8** Jiggitai **9** Tengrinor **11** Manasarowar
  mountain: 5 Kamet, Sajum **6** Kailas, Kunlun **7** Bandala **8** Himalaya **9** Karakoram
  highest point: 7 Everest
  river: 3 Nak, Nau, Sak **4** Song **5** Hwang, Indus **6** Mekong, Sutlej, Yellow **7** Hwang Ho, Matsang, Melsang, Salween, Tsangpo, Yangtze **11** Brahmaputra

physical feature:
  plain: 4 Kham **9** Chang Tang
  valley: 7 Tsangpo
people: 5 Asian, Balti, Bodpa, Drupa **6** Bhotia, Champa, Drokpa, Khamba, Khambu, Panaka, Sherpa, Tangut **7** Bhotiya, Bhutani, Gyarung, Taghlik, Tibetan **9** Mongoloid
  patron god: 14 Avalokitesvara
  ruler: 4 Yuan **6** Mongol **9** dalai lama **13** Songtsan Gampo
language: 5 Balti **6** Ladkhi **7** Bhutani, Bodskad **8** Sanskrit **9** Bhutanese
religion: 5 Bonko **7** Lamaism
place:
  Indian border: 11 McMahon Line
  palace: 7 Potalaf
  temple: 7 Jokhang **10** Tashi Lumpo **11** Tashi Lhunpo
feature:
  animal: 3 dzo, yak **5** kiang **7** mastiff **8** musk deer **10** giant panda
  clothing: 5 chuba
  dance: 4 cham **9** achelhamo
  dog: 9 lhasa apso
  leader: 9 dalai lama
  legend: 4 yeti **17** abominable snowman
  monastery: 8 lamasery
  monk: 4 lama
food:
  dish: 6 tsamba, tsampa
  drink: 5 chang
tibia
  bone of: 4 shin
tic 5 spasm **6** twitch **12** facial twitch **13** tic douloureux **19** trigemi nal neuralgia
tick 3 dot, tap **4** beat, line, list, mark, nick, note **5** blaze, check, clack, click, enter, notch, swing, throb **6** record, slight, stroke **7** scratch, vibrate **8** mark down, register, ticktock **9** checkmark, chronicle, oscillate, pulsation, vibration
ticket 3 tag **4** card, mark, pass, slip, stub **5** label, slate **6** ballot, coupon, marker, roster **7** sticker, voucher **14** list of nominees, traffic summons
  type: 4 trip **7** parking, traffic **9** admission
  free: 11 Annie Oakley
tickle 4 itch **5** amuse, cheer, prick, sting, throb **6** divert, please, regale, stroke, thrill, tingle, twitch **7** delight, enchant, enliven, gladden, gratify, prickle, rejoice **8** enthrall, entrance **9** captivate, fascinate, titillate **12** scratchiness **15** do one's heart good
ticklish 4 hard **5** itchy, tough **6** knotty, thorny, tickly, touchy, tricky **7** awkward, prickly **8** critical, delicate, scratchy, tingling **9** difficult, intricate, sensitive, uncertain **11** complicated
tidal basin 3 bay **5** inlet, sound **6** lagoon **7** estuary **11** arm of the sea

tidbit 3 bit **4** item **5** treat **6** morsel **8** delicacy, mouthful **9** choice bit
tide 4 flow, neap, wave **5** drift, state **7** current **8** movement, tendency, undertow **9** direction **10** ebb and flow, wax and wane **11** rise and fall
tidings 4 news, word **6** advice, notice, report **8** good word **11** declaration, information **12** announcement, intelligence, notification
tidy 4 neat, trig, trim **5** ample, array, clean **6** goodly, neaten, tidy up **7** arrange, careful, clean up, orderly, precise, regular, sizable **8** neaten up, spotless, spruce up **9** organized, regulated, shipshape **10** immaculate, methodical, meticulous, put in order, straighten, systematic **11** substantial **12** businesslike, considerable, straighten up **15** in apple-pie order
tidy up 5 clean **6** neaten **9** freshen up **10** put in order, straighten
tie 3 rod **4** ally, band, beam, belt, bind, bond, cord, draw, duty, join, knot, lash, line, link, rope, sash, yoke **5** brace, ca- ble, cinch, limit, marry, match, truss, unite **6** attach, bow tie, clinch, couple, cravat, engage, fasten, girdle, hamper, hinder, ribbon, secure, string, tether **7** confine, connect, kinship, necktie, support **8** affinity, cincture, dead heat, make a bow, make fast, relation, restrain, restrict, tied vote **9** constrain, crossbeam, fastening **10** allegiance, connection, cummerbund, obligation **11** affiliation, come out even **12** relationship **13** connecting rod **15** divide the honors
Tiepolo, Giovanni Battista (Giambattista)
  born: 5 Italy **6** Venice
  artwork: 10 Kaisersaal (salon) **11** Treppenhaus (staircase) **14** The Crucifixion **16** Ronaldo and Armida **20** Madonna of Mount Carmel **21** The Communion of St Lucia, The Triumph of Aphrodite **24** St Thekla and the Pestilence **28** Apotheosis of Francesco Barbaro **28** The Worship of the Bronze Serpent
tier 3 row **4** bank, file, line, rank, step **5** layer, level, range, story **7** stratum **14** stratification
Tierney, Gene
  born: 10 Brooklyn NY
  husband: 11 Oleg Cassini
  roles: 5 Laura **10** Belle Starr **11** Tobacco Road **13** A Bell for Adano **16** Leave Her to Heaven **18** The Ghost and Mrs Muir
tiers etat 11 third estate
  in French politics: 7 commons
tie-up 3 jam **4** snag **5** block, hitch, snarl **6** slow-up **7** failure **8** blockage, gridlock, stop page **9** breakdown **10** bottleneck, disruption **11** malfunction **13** embouteillage

tie up 3 tie **4** bind, gird, lash, rope **5** hitch, snarl, strap, truss **6** engage, fasten, hinder, impede, occupy, secure, tangle **8** entangle

tiff 4 huff, miff, rage, snit, spat **5** clash, run-in, scrap, tizzy, words **6** hassle **7** dispute, quarrel, rhubarb, wrangle **8** argument, ill humor, squabble **10** difference **11** altercation **12** disagreement **16** misunderstanding

tiger 3 cat **6** cougar, jaguar **7** fighter, wildcat
   young: 5 whelp

Tiger Joy
   author: 19 Stephen Vincent Benet

tiger's-eye
   species: 6 quartz

Tigger
   character in: 13 Winnie-the-Pooh
   author: 5 Milne

tight 4 busy, firm, full, hard, high, snug, taut **5** blind, close, dense, drunk, exact, happy, harsh, lit up, rigid, scant, solid, stern, stiff, tense, tipsy, tough **6** firmly, frugal, gorged, hard-up, jammed, juiced, loaded, scarce, secure, severe, skimpy, sloppy, soused, stewed, stingy, stoned, strict, trying, zonked **7** austere, closely, com- pact, crammed, crowded, drunken, miserly, onerous, pickled, pie-eyed, smashed, solidly, sparing, stuffed **8** grudging, rigorous, securely, too small **9** deficient, difficult, illiberal, jam-packed, niggardly, penurious, plastered, skintight, stringent, worrisome **10** burdensome, compressed, glassy-eyed, impassable, inadequate, inebriated, inflexible, in one's cups, nip-and-tuck, nose-to-nose, tyrannical, ungenerous, unyielding **11** closefisted, constricted, dictatorial, impermeable, intoxicated, troublesome, well-matched **12** close-fitting, impenetrable, insufficient, parsimonious **13** closely fitted, feeling no pain **14** fitting closely, uncompromising **20** three sheets to the wind

tighten 5 pinch **6** anchor, fasten, narrow, secure **7** squeeze **8** contract, make fast, make taut **9** constrict **14** take up the slack

tighten one's belt 4 save **5** skimp, stint **6** scrimp **8** conserve, cut costs **9** economize **11** cut expenses **12** pinch pennies

tightfisted 5 cheap, mingy, tight **6** greedy, stingy **7** miserly **9** illiberal, niggardly, penurious **10** avaricious **11** closefisted **12** cheeseparing, parsimonious **13** penny-pinching

tightfistedness 6 penury **9** parsimony **10** stinginess **11** miserliness **13** niggardliness, penny-pinching

tight-fitting 4 snug **5** tight **8** too small **9** skintight **11** constricted **12** constricting **15** like a second skin

tight-laced 4 prim **6** prissy, stuffy **7** prudish **8** priggish **9** inhibited, repressed, Victorian **11** puritanical, standoffish, straitlaced **13** self-righteous

tight-lipped 3 mum **4** curt **5** brief, quiet, short, terse **8** discreet, reserved, reticent, taciturn **10** unsociable **11** untalkative **12** close-mouthed **15** uncommunicative

tightly packed 5 dense **6** jammed **7** compact, crammed, stuffed **10** compressed **12** concentrated

tightwad 5 miser, piker **7** niggard, Scrooge **9** lickpenny, skinflint **10** cheapskate, pinchpenny **12** money-grubber

Tiki
   Polynesian: 8 first man **6** amulet

till 3 sow **4** even, farm, plow, seed, tray, unto up to **6** before, coffer, drawer, harrow, plough **7** as far as, develop, prepare **8** moneybox, treasury **9** cultivate **12** cash register
   geological: 5 drift

tillable 6 arable **8** farmable, plowable **10** cultivable

tillage 7 farming, plowing **11** agriculture, cultivation

Till Eulenspiegel
   also: 16 Tyll Eulenspiegel
   origin: 8 Germanic
   means: 14 practical joker

Tillie the Toiler
   creator: 12 Russ Westover
   character: 3 Mac **7** Mr Chase

Tilney, Henry
   character in: 15 Northanger Abbey
   author: 6 Austen

tilt 3 row, tip **4** cant, lean, list, rake, spar, tiff **5** brawl, fence, fight, grade, joust, pitch, slant, slope **6** affray, battle, combat, oppose **7** contest, dispute, incline, quarrel **8** argument, skirmish, squabble **9** encounter **10** tournament **11** altercation

Timaeus
   author: 5 Plato

Timandra
   father: 9 Tyndareus
   mother: 4 Leda
   brother: 6 Castor, Pollux
   sister: 5 Helen **12** Clytemnestra
   husband: 7 Echemus, Phyleus
   son: 5 Meges
   cursed by: 9 Aphrodite

timber 4 bush, logs, wood **5** copse, trees, woods **6** boards, forest, lumber **7** thicket

timberland 5 woods **6** forest, sticks **8** woodland

timbre 4 tone **5** pitch **9** resonance

time, times 3 age, day, eon, era **4** beat, days, hour, term, week, year **5** clock, cycle, epoch, event, match, month, phase, spell, stage, tempo,

while, years **6** adjust, chance, decade, moment, period, rhythm, season **7** century, episode, freedom, instant, liberty, measure, stretch **8** duration, incident, interval, occasion **10** experience, generation **11** opportunity, synchronize

time flies
   Latin: 11 tempus fugit

time-honored 6 common, normal **7** regular, revered **8** accepted, standard **9** customary, respected, universal

timeless 7 abiding, durable, endless, eternal, lasting, undying **8** enduring, immortal, infinite, unending **9** boundless, ceaseless, deathless, immutable, incessant, permanent, perpetual **10** continuous, persistent **11** everlasting, never-ending **12** interminable, unchangeable **13** never-stopping **14** indestructible

timely 6 prompt **8** punctual **9** opportune, well-timed **10** convenient, felicitous, seasonable **12** providential

Time Machine, The
   author: 7 H G Wells
   character: 4 Eloi **5** Weena **8** Morlocks **12** Time Traveler

Time of Your Life, The
   author: 14 William Saroyan
   director: 8 H C Potter
   cast: 8 Ward Bond **11** James Cagney, Wayne Morris **12** Jeanne Cagney **13** William Bendix **17** Broderick Crawford

timepiece 5 clock, watch **8** horologe **11** chronometer

Time Remembered
   author: 11 Jean Anouilh

Timerman, Jacobo
   author of: 38 Prisoner Without a Name Cell Without a Number

timesaving 5 quick **6** speedy **9** efficient **11** expeditious

time without end 7 forever **8** eternity, infinity

timeworn 3 old **4** aged, worn **5** dated, hoary, passe, stale, trite **6** age-old, beat-up, old-hat, shabby **7** ancient, antique **8** battered, dog-eared, obsolete, overused **9** hackneyed, out of date, venerable, weathered **10** antiquated **12** antediluvian

timid 3 coy, shy **6** afraid, humble, modest, scared **7** bashful, fearful **8** cowardly, retiring, sheepish, timorous **9** diffident, shrinking, spineless, weak-kneed **10** unassuming **12** apprehensive, fainthearted **13** pusillanimous

timidity 7 modesty, shyness **8** cold feet, humility **9** cowardice, timidness **10** diffidence **11** bashfulness, fearfulness, trepidation **12** sheepishness, timorousness **13** spinelessness **16** faint-heartedness

timidness 7 shyness **8** meekness, timidity **10** diffidence, insecurity **11** bashfulness **12** timorousness **14** submissiveness **15** unassertiveness **16** faintheartedness

Timon of Athens
   author: **18** William Shakespeare
   character: **6** Lucius **7** Flavius **8** Lucullus **9** Apemantus, Ventidius **10** Alcibiades, Sempronius

Timor
   capital: **4** Dili
   country: **8** Portugal **9** Indonesia
   islands: **5** Sunda **11** Lesser Sunda
   strait: **5** Ombai

timorous 3 shy **4** meek **5** timid **6** afraid **7** anxious, bashful, fearful **8** retiring **9** shrinking **10** submissive **12** fainthearted

timorousness 7 shyness **8** cold feet, meekness, timidity **9** cowardice **11** fearfulness, trepidation **16** faintheartedness

Timothy
   mother: **6** Eunice
   grandmother: **4** Lois
   companion: **4** Paul **8** Silvanus

tin
   chemical symbol: **2** Sn

tincture 6 elixir **7** essence, extract, spirits **8** solution **11** concentrate

Tinder Box, The
   author: **21** Hans Christian Andersen

Tin Drum, The
   author: **11** Gunter Grass
   director: **17** Volker Schlondorff
   character: **14** Oskar Matzerath
   cast: **10** Mario Adorf **12** David Bennent (Oskar) **13** Angela Winkler **16** Daniel Olbrychski **17** Katharina Tahlbach
   Oscar for: **11** foreign film

tine 3 die, tip **4** barb, lose, tyne **5** point, prong, spike **6** bodkin, branch, perish, skewer **7** destroy, forfeit

tinge 3 dye **4** cast, dash, hint, lace, tint, tone, vein **5** color, imbue, shade, smack, stain, taste, touch, trace **6** flavor, infuse, nuance, season **7** instill, soupcon **9** suspicion

tingle 5 sting, throb **6** thrill, tickle, tremor **7** flutter, prickle **9** prickling, pulsation **11** palpitation

Tinker, Tailor, Soldier, Spy
   author: **11** John Le Carre

Tinker Bell
   character in: **8** Peter Pan
   author: **6** Barrie

tinkle 4 ding, peal, ping, ring **5** chime, chink, clank, clink, plink **6** jingle **9** ting-a-ling

tin lizzie 3 car **4** auto, heap **5** motor **6** jalopy, wheels **7** flivver, machine, vehicle **8** motorcar **10** automobile **12** motor vehicle

Tin Man, Tin Woodsman

character in: **13** The Wizard of Oz
   author: **4** Baum

tinsel 4 sham, show **5** gloss **6** sequin **7** glitter, spangle **8** pretense **9** gaudiness **10** camouflage, decoration, masquerade **11** affectation, false colors, make-believe, ostentation

tint 3 dye, hue **4** hint, tone, wash **5** color, frost, shade, stain, tinge, touch, trace **6** nuance **7** pigment **8** coloring, tincture **10** suggestion

Tintern Abbey
   author: **17** William Wordsworth

tintinnabulate 4 peal, ring, toll **5** chime, clang, knell, sound **6** jingle, tinkle

tintinnabulation 4 gong, peal, ring, toll **5** chime, knell **6** jingle **7** clangor, pealing, ringing **8** clanging, ding-dong, jingling, tinkling **11** peal of bells

Tintoretto, Jacopo
   real name: **13** Jacopo Robusti
   born: **5** Italy **6** Venice
   artwork: **8** Paradise **13** The Last Supper **14** The Crucifixion **16** The Road to Calvary **17** Bacchus and Ariadne **18** Apotheosis of St Roch, The Flight into Egypt **20** Susannah and the Elders **21** The Temptation of Christ **26** St Mark Frees a Christian Slave **27** The Finding of the Body of St Mark **32** The Miracle of St Mark Rescuing a Slave

tiny 3 wee **5** pygmy, runty, small, teeny **6** bantam, little, midget, minute, petite **8** dwarfish **9** itsy-bitsy, miniature, minuscule, pint-sized **10** diminutive, teeny-weeny, undersized **11** Lilliputian, microscopic, pocket-sized **12** teensy-weensy

Tiny Alice
   author: **11** Edward Albee

Tiny Tim
   character in: **15** A Christmas Carol
   author: **7** Dickens

tip 3 cap, pat, tap, top **4** acme, apex, barb, brow, cant, clue, head, hint, hook, lean, list, peak, rake, tilt **5** crest, crown, pitch, point, prong, slant, slope, spike, upend, upset **6** advice, reward, stroke, summit, tip-off, topple, upturn, vertex, zenith **7** capsize, incline, leaning, lowdown, pointer, sharpen, tilting, tipping, warning **8** gratuity, over turn, pinnacle, slanting **9** baksheesh, lagniappe **10** admonition, inside dope, perquisite, suggestion, turn turtle **11** forewarning **13** word to the wise
   French: **7** douceur

tipcart 4 cart **8** dumpcart, pushcart

Tiphys
   member of: **9** Argonauts
   occupation: **9** steersman

tip off 3 tip **4** warn **5** alert **6** caveat **7** caution, warning **8** forewarn **11** forewarning

tip over 5 upend, upset **7** capsize **8** flip over, keel over, overturn, turn over **10** turn turtle

Tippett, Michael Kemp
   born: **6** London **7** England
   composer of: **9** King Priam **13** The Knot Garden **15** A Child of Our Time **20** The Midsummer Marriage **22** The Vision of St Augustine **32** Concerto for Double String Orchestra

tipple 5 drink, quaff **6** guzzle, imbibe, liquor **8** beverage

tippler 3 sot **4** lush, soak, wino **5** drunk, rummy, souse, toper **6** bibber, boozer, sponge **7** guzzler, imbiber, swiller, tosspot **8** drunkard **9** alcoholic, inebriate **10** booze hound **11** dipsomaniac

tipsy 4 high **5** awash, blind, drunk, happy, lit-up, stiff, tight **6** juiced, loaded, sloppy, sodden, soused, stewed, stoned **7** drunken, pickled, pie-eyed, smashed **9** inebriate, plastered **10** glassy-eyed, inebriated, in one's cups **11** intoxicated **12** half seas over **13** feeling no pain **20** three sheets to the wind

tip-top 4 A-one **5** elite, super **7** supreme **8** very fine **10** consummate **11** exceptional, superlative **13** extraordinary

tirade 5 curse **6** screed **7** lecture **8** diatribe, harangue, jeremiad, scolding **9** invective, reprimand **11** castigation, fulmination **12** condemnation, denunciation, dressing-down, vilification, vituperation

tirailleur 10 skirmisher **12** sharpshooter

Tirane, Tirana
   capital of: **7** Albania

tire 3 fag, irk **4** bore **5** annoy, weary **6** bother, tucker **7** disgust, exhaust, fatigue, wear out **8** be sick of **10** make sleepy **11** be fed up with **12** lose interest, lose patience

tire
   invented by: **6** Dunlop **7** Thomson

tired 4 beat **5** all in, weary **6** bushed, drowsy, fagged, pooped, sleepy **7** wearied, worn out **8** dog-tired, fatigued, tuckered **9** enervated, exhausted, played out

tireless 6 steady **7** devoted, staunch **8** constant, faithful, resolute, untiring **9** steadfast, unceasing, unwearied **10** determined, unflagging, unswerving **11** hard-working, industrious, nevertiring, persevering, unfaltering, unremitting **13** indefatigable

Tiresias
   also: **9** Teiresias
   vocation: **4** seer **7** prophet
   father: **6** Everes
   mother: **8** Chariclo
   grandfather: **6** Udaeus
   home: **6** Thebes

struck: **5** blind
character in: **7** Odyssey **10** Oedipus Rex
characteristic: **9** blind seer

tiresome 4 drab, dull, hard **6** boring, deadly, dismal, tiring, trying, vexing **7** arduous, fagging, humdrum, irksome, tedious, wearing **8** annoying, wearying **9** difficult, fatiguing, laborious, wearisome **10** bothersome, exhausting, monotonous **13** uninteresting

Tishri 18 seventh Hebrew month

Tisiphone
member of: **6** Furies

'Tis Pity She's a Whore
author: **8** John Ford
character: **6** Donado, Florio, Putana **7** Soranzo, Vasques **8** Bergetto, Giovanni, Grimaldi **9** Annabella, Hippolita **11** Richardetto **16** Friar Bonaventura

tissue
kind: **4** bone, skin **5** nerve **6** muscle

titan 5 giant, great, mogul **7** magnate

Titan
race of: **4** gods
father: **6** Uranus
mother: **2** Ge **4** Gaea
names: **5** Coeus, Crius **6** Cronus **7** Iapetus, Oceanus **8** Hyperion
sisters: **8** Titaness
  names of sisters: **4** Rhea **5** Theia **6** Phoebe, Tethys, Themis **9** Mnemosyne

Titan, The
sequel to: **12** The Financier
author: **15** Theodore Dreiser
character: **13** Peter Laughlin **15** Berenice Fleming, Stephanie Platow **16** Aileen Cowperwood **23** Frank Algernon Cowperwood

Titan, the see **6** Helios

Titaness see **5** Titan

Titania
character in: **21** A Midsummer Night's Dream
author: **11** Shakespeare

titanic 4 huge, vast **5** giant, great, stout **6** mighty, strong **7** immense, mammoth **8** colossal, enormous, gigantic, whopping **9** herculean, humongous, monstrous **10** gargantuan, monumental, prodigious, stupendous

titanium
chemical symbol: **2** Ti

tit for tat 8 exchange **10** quid pro quo **13** an eye for an eye

Titian
real name: **15** Tiziano Vecellio
born: **5** Italy **13** Pieve di Cadore
artwork: **5** Pieta **12** The Bacchanal, Tribute Money **13** Noli Me Tangere **15** Diana and Actaeon, The Rape of Europa **16** The Pesaro Madonna, The Venus of Urbino **17** Bacchus and Ariadne, The Death of Actaeon, The

Girl in a Fur Wrap, The Three Ages of Man **18** Charles V at Muhlberg, The Adrian Bacchanal, The Young Englishman **19** Francis I Roi de France **20** Sacred and Profane Love **21** Venus and the Lute Player **23** The Madonna of the Cherries **24** Pope Paul III and his Nephews, The Assumption of the Virgin

titillate 5 charm, rouse, tease, tempt **6** allure, arouse, excite, seduce, tickle, turn on **7** attract, provoke **8** entrance **9** captivate, fascinate, stimulate **15** whet the appetite

titillating 8 alluring, exciting, tempting **9** seductive **10** suggestive **11** provocative

title 3 dub **4** deed, name, rank, term **5** claim, crown, grade, label, place, right **6** status, tenure **7** entitle, epithet, station **8** christen, nobility, position **9** condition, designate, ownership **10** legal right, lordly rank, noble birth, possession **11** appellation, designation **12** championship

titled 5 named, noble, regal, royal **6** called, lordly **7** courtly **8** entitled **10** designated **11** blue-blooded **12** aristocratic

Titograd 9 Podgorica
capital of: **10** Montenegro

titter 5 chirp, smirk **6** cackle, giggle, simper, teehee **7** chuckle, snicker, snigger

tittle 3 bit, dot, jot **4** atom, iota, mite **5** speck **8** particle

Tittle, Y A (Yelberton Abraham)
sport: **8** football
position: **11** quarterback
team: **13** New York Giants **14** Baltimore Colts **23** San Francisco Forty-Niners

titular 7 known as, nominal **8** so-called **10** in name only, ostensible **11** in title only

Titus
surname: **6** Justus
hometown: **7** Corinth
companion: **4** Paul

Titus see **6** Tatius

Titus Andronicus
author: **18** William Shakespeare
character: **5** Aaron **6** Chiron, Marcus, Tamora **7** Alarbus, Lavinia **9** Bassianus, Demetrius **10** Saturninus

Tiu
Germanic god of: **3** sky, war
Norse: **3** Tyr
eponym of: **7** Tuesday

tizzy 4 snit **6** dither, swivet **7** dudgeon **8** tailspin
British: **8** sixpence

Tjaden
character in: **25** All Quiet on the Western Front
author: **8** Remarque

to 2 ad, on **3** for **4** into, near, unto, upon, with **5** about, until **6** at hand, closed, toward **7** against, forward **8** together **10** concerning, included in **11** contained in
prefix: **2** ac, ad
Scottish: **3** tae

toad
group of: **4** knot

toady 4 fawn **6** fawner, flunky, stooge, yes-man **8** hanger-on, kowtow to, parasite, truckler **9** flatterer, sycophant **10** bootlicker, curry favor **11** apple-polish, lickspittle **13** apple-polisher, backscratcher

To Althea, From Prison
author: **15** Richard Lovelace

to a man 3 all **8** every one **9** one and all **10** completely **12** to the last man

To a Skylark
author: **18** Percy Bysshe Shelley

toast 3 dry **4** heat, warm **5** brown, grill, honor **6** salute, warm up **9** celebrate **10** compliment **11** commemorate **12** browned bread, clink glasses **15** drink one's health

tobacco
varieties: **4** tree, wild **6** Indian **7** jasmine, Turkish **9** broadleaf, flowering, Nicotiana **12** long-flowered **16** Nicotiana rustica, Nicotiana tabacum

Tobacco Road
author: **15** Erskine Caldwell
character: **3** Ada **4** Dude **5** Pearl **6** Bessie **8** Ellie May **9** Lov Bensey **12** Jeeter Lester

To Be or Not To Be
director: **13** Ernst Lubitsch
cast: **9** Jack Benny **11** Robert Stack **12** Lionel Atwill **13** Carole Lombard, Felix Bressart
setting: **6** Poland

To Catch a Thief
director: **15** Alfred Hitchcock
cast: **9** Cary Grant **10** Grace Kelly **12** John Williams **17** Jessie Royce Landis
setting: **13** French Riviera

Tocqueville, Alexis de
author of: **18** Democracy in America

tocsin 4 bell **5** alarm **7** warning

today 3 now **7** this day, this era **8** nowadays, this time **9** in this era, on this day, this epoch **10** the present **11** in this epoch, modern times **13** in modern times, the present age, the present day **15** in this day and age

Todd, Richard
real name: **27** Richard Andrew Palethorpe-Todd
born: **6** Dublin **7** Ireland
roles: **13** The Hasty Heart, The Longest Day **14** The Virgin Queen **15** A Man Called Peter

toddle 6 waddle, wobble **14** take short steps, walk unsteadily

toddler 3 tot **4** babe, baby, tyke **5** child **6** infant **9** little one

to-do 3 ado **4** fuss, stir **5** furor, noise **6** bustle, flurry, hubbub, hustle, pother, racket, ruckus, rumpus, tumult, uproar **7** turmoil **8** activity **9** agitation, commotion **10** excitement, hullabaloo, hurly-burly **11** disturbance

Toe, The
  nickname of: **8** Lou Groza

to err is human
  Latin: **16** errare humanum est

toff 3 nob **4** beau **5** dandy, swell **10** young blood

Toffler, Alvin
  author of: **11** Future Shock **12** The Third Wave

toga 4 aba **4** garb, gown, robe **6** trabea **7** garment **12** outergarment
  virilis: **9** white robe **11** manhood robe

Togo
  other name: **14** French Togoland
  capital/largest city: **4** Lome
  others: **5** Badon, Kpeme **6** Anecho, Ansoho, Blitta, Klonto, Nuatja, Palime, Sokode **7** Bassari, Dopango, Pagonda **8** Atakpame, Tabligbo **10** Niamtougou
  school: **5** Benin **6** Mawull
  monetary unit: **5** franc **7** centime
  mountain: **4** Togo **7** Atakora, Koronga
  highest point: **7** Baumann
  river: **3** Oti **4** Anie, Haho, Mono, Ogou
  sea: **8** Atlantic
  physical feature:
    bight: **5** Benin
    gulf: **6** Guinea
    plain: **4** Mono
  people: **3** Ana, Ewe, Twi **4** Mina **5** Hausa **6** Akposa, Kabrai **7** Bassari, Cabrais, Kabrais, Ouatchi **8** Konkomba, Kotokoli, Lotokoli
    leader: **7** Eyadema **15** Sylvanus Olympio **16** Nicolas Grunitzky
  language: **3** Ana, Ewe, Twi **4** Mina **5** Hausa **6** French, Kabrai, Kabrie **7** Bassari, Dagomba, Ouatchi **8** Kotokoli, Lotocoli
  religion: **5** Islam **7** animism **12** Christianity

togs 4 duds **6** attire, outfit **7** apparel, clothes, threads **8** clothing, garments

To Have and Have Not
  director: **11** Howard Hawks
  based on novel by: **15** Ernest Hemingway
  cast: **12** Dolores Moran, Lauren Bacall **13** Walter Brennan **14** Humphrey Bogart **15** Hoagy Carmichael
  remade as: **13** The Gunrunners **16** The Breaking Point

To His Coy Mistress
  author: **13** Andrew Marvell

toil 4 grub, moil, work **5** grind, labor, pains, slave, sweat **6** drudge, effort **7**

travail **8** drudgery, exertion, hardship, hard work, industry, struggle, work hard **11** application, elbow grease **12** apply oneself, exert oneself **14** work like a horse

toiler 4 peon, serf, swot **5** navvy, prole, slave **6** drudge, flunky, menial, slavey, worker **7** grubber, laborer, servant, slogger **9** workhorse **10** wage earner **11** galley slave

toilet 2 WC **3** can, loo **4** john **5** privy **7** commode, latrine **8** facility, lavatory, men's room, outhouse, rest room, washroom **10** ladies' room **11** convenience, water closet

toilet water 5 scent **7** cologne, essence, perfume **9** fragrance

toilsome 4 hard **5** tough **6** tiring, uphill **7** arduous, onerous, tedious **8** wearying **9** difficult, effortful, fatiguing, herculean, laborious, strenuous, wearisome **10** burdensome, exhausting **12** backbreaking

To Jerusalem and Back
  author: **10** Saul Bellow

token 4 mark, sign **5** index, proof **6** jetton, symbol **7** for show, memento, minimal, nodding, nominal, passing **8** evidence, keepsake, reminder, souvenir, symbolic **9** vestigial **10** expression, indication **11** perfunctory, remembrance, superficial, testimonial **13** manifestation

To Kill a Mockingbird
  director: **14** Robert Mulligan
  based on novel by: **9** Harper Lee
  cast: **9** John Megna **10** Mary Badham **11** Gregory Peck **12** Philip Alford
  Oscar for: **5** actor (Peck)

Tokyo
  airport: **6** Haneda
  capital of: **5** Japan
  district: **5** Ginza **6** Keihin **7** Chiyoda **8** Yokohama **10** Marunouchi **18** Tama New Town Project
  former name: **3** Edo
  island: **6** Honshu
  landmark: **8** Ueno Park **11** Meiji Shrine **12** National Diet **14** Imperial Palace, Kitanomaru Park **19** Komazawa Olympic Park
  means: **14** Eastern capital

tolerable 4 fair, so-so **7** allowed, average **8** abidable, accepted, adequate, bearable, mediocre, middling, ordinary, passable **9** allowable, endurable, innocuous, permitted **10** acceptable, admissible, fairly good, sufferable **11** commonplace, indifferent, permissible **12** run-of-the-mill **14** fair-to-middling

tolerance 7 charity **8** fairness, goodwill, patience, sympathy **9** endurance **10** compassion, sufferance **11** forbearance **13** brotherly love, fair treatment, fellow feeling, power to endure **15** lack of prejudice

tolerant 4 easy, fair, soft **7** lenient, li-

beral, patient, sparing **8** moderate **9** easygoing, forgiving, indulgent, unbigoted **10** charitable, forbearing, permissive **11** broad-minded, kindhearted, softhearted, sympathetic **12** unprejudiced **13** compassionate, uncomplaining, understanding

tolerate 3 let **4** bear, take **5** abide, admit, allow, brook, stand **7** endure, permit, suffer, wink at **7** indulge, stomach, undergo **8** be easy on, be soft on, sanction, submit to **9** consent to, put up with, recognize, vouchsafe

To Let
  author: **14** John Galsworthy

to life
  Hebrew: **7** lehayim **8** lechayim

Tolkien, J R R
  author of: **9** The Hobbit **15** The Silmarillion **17** The Lord of the Rings
  creature: **3** ent orc
  fictional setting: **11** Middle Earth

toll 3 fee, tax **4** duty, levy, loss **6** charge, impost, tariff **7** payment, penalty, tribute, undoing **8** exaction **9** depletion, sacrifice **10** assessment, disruption, extinction **11** destruction **12** annihilation **13** extermination

Tolstoy, Leo
  author of: **11** War and Peace **12** Anna Karenina, Resurrection **17** The Kreutzer Sonata **18** Death of Ivan Ilyitch

Toltec
  city: **4** Tula
  preceded: **5** Aztec
  tribe: **4** Itza

To Lucasta, Going to the Wars
  author: **15** Richard Lovelace

tom 3 cat **6** tomcat **10** male turkey

tomato 12 Lycopersicon **24** Lycopersicon lycopersicum
  varieties: **4** Husk, Pear, Tree **6** Cherry **7** Currant **10** Gooseberry, Strawberry **11** Mexican husk
  soup: **8** gazpacho
  sauce: **6** catsup **7** ketchup

tomb 5 crypt, grave, vault **8** monument **9** mausoleum, sepulcher **11** burial place **12** resting place **13** burial chamber

tomboy 3 meg **4** girl, romp **5** rowdy **6** female, gamine, hoiden, hoyden, tomrig **8** strumpet

Tom Brown's School Days
  author: **12** Thomas Hughes

tombs
  god of: **6** Anubis

tomcat 3 cat, tom **9** womanizer

tomfoolery 4 play **6** antics **8** drollery, nonsense **9** high jinks, horseplay, silliness **10** goofing off, skylarking **11** foolishness **12** lollygagging, monkeyshines, prankishness **13** fooling around, messing around, playing around

tooth

Tom Jones
also: 29 The History of Tom Jones Foundling
author: 13 Henry Fielding
character: 6 Square **7** Bridget, Western **8** Mrs Honor, Thwackum **9** Mrs Miller, Partridge **11** Black George, Nightingale **12** Master Blifil **13** Lady Bellaston, Sophia Western **15** Squire Allworthy
director: 14 Tony Richardson
cast: 11 Joyce Redman **12** Albert Finney, Diane Cilento, Hugh Griffith, Susannah York **14** Dame Edith Evans
score: 11 John Addison
Oscar for: 5 score **7** picture **9** direction **10** screenplay

Tomlin, Lily
real name: 14 Mary Jean Tomlin
born: 9 Detroit MI
roles: 7 Laugh-In **8** Edith Ann **9** Ernestine, Nashville, The Player **11** The Late Show **14** Moment By Moment **20** Flirting with Disaster **27** The Incredible Shrinking Woman

tommyrot 3 rot **4** bosh, bull, bunk, crap, tosh **5** bilge, hokum, hooey, trash **6** bunkum, drivel, humbug **7** baloney, hogwash, spinach, rubbish, twaddle **8** buncombe, claptrap, folderol, malarkey, nonsense **9** poppycock **10** applesauce, balderdash, tomfoolery **11** foolishness **12** bullfeathers, fiddle-faddle **13** horsefeathers **16** stuff-and-nonsense

tomorrow 9 the future, the morrow **11** in the future **12** in days to come **16** the day after today **17** the next generation
Spanish: 6 manana

Tom Sawyer
author: 9 Mark Twain
character: 8 Huck (Huckleberry) Finn, Injun Joe **9** Aunt Polly, Joe Harper **10** Muff Potter **13** Becky Thatcher

Tom Thumb the Great
author: 13 Henry Fielding

ton
abbreviation: 1 t

tone 3 hue **4** cast, lilt, mood, note, tint **5** color, pitch, shade, sound, style, tenor, tinge **6** accent, chroma, firm up, manner, soften, spirit, stress, subdue, temper **7** cadence, quality **8** attitude, harmonic, make firm, moderate, modulate, overtone, tonality **10** inflection, intonation, make supple, modulation

Tone, Franchot
real name: 27 Stanislas Pascal Franchot Tone
born: 14 Niagara Falls NY
wife: 11 Jean Wallace **12** Joan Crawford **13** Barbara Payton **15** Dolores Dorn-Heft
roles: 10 Uncle Vanya **11** Phantom

Lady **13** Three Comrades **16** Advise and Consent **17** Five Graves to Cairo, Mutiny on the Bounty **23** The Lives of a Bengal Lancer

tone up 7 make fit, shape up **9** condition **10** put in shape

Tonga
other name: 15 Friendly Islands
capital/largest city: 9 Nukualofa
others: 3 Mua, Pea **6** Neiafu **7** Haakame, Kolonga, Kolovai **8** Fuaamotu
division: 5 Vavau **6** Haapai **9** Tongatapu
government: 8 monarchy
head of state: 4 king
monetary unit: 6 paanga, seniti
island: 3 Eua, Kao, Ono **4** Kotu **5** Tofua, Vavau **6** Haapai, Lifuke, Nomuka **7** Otu Tolu **9** Tongatapu
highest point: 3 Kao
sea: 7 Pacific
people: 10 Polynesian
  explorer: 4 Cook **5** Bligh **6** Tasman
  king: 11 George Tupou **14** Taufaahau Tupou
  missionary: 12 Shirley Baker
  queen: 6 Salote
language: 6 Tongan **7** English
religion: 9 Methodist **12** Christianity **25** Wesleyan Free Church of Tonga
feature:
  fabric: 4 tapa
  spiritual king: 8 tui tonga

tongue 3 lap **4** flap, lick, spit **5** point, shaft **6** lingua, patois, speech **7** dialect, lingula **8** language **10** promontory, vernacular, vocabulary **13** organ of speech, power of speech, style of speech
tastes: 4 salt, sour **5** sweet **6** bitter

tongue-lash 5 scold **6** berate, rail at, rebuke **7** bawl out, chew out, reprove, upbraid **8** reproach **9** castigate, reprimand **10** take to task

tongue-lashing 6 rebuke **7** censure, chiding, reproof **8** reproach, scolding **9** reprimand **10** bawling-out, chewing-out, upbraiding **11** castigation, reprobation **12** dressing-down, remonstrance

tonic 6 bracer, pickup **7** keynote **8** pick-me-up **9** analeptic, refresher, stimulant **10** invigorant **11** restorative

Tono-Bungay
author: 7 H G Wells

tonsure 3 cut **4** trim **8** bald spot **11** shaven patch

too
French: 4 trop

tool 4 dupe, pawn **5** agent, means **6** device, medium, puppet, stooge **7** cat's-paw, machine, utensil, vehicle **8** hireling **9** apparatus, appliance, implement, mechanism **10** instrument **11** contrivance, wherewithal **12** intermediary **15** instrumentality

carpenter's: 3 adz, awl, bit, peg, saw **4** adze, nail, rasp, vise **5** auger, brace, edger, gouge, knife, lathe, plane, ruler, screw **6** bodkin, chisel, gimlet, hammer, pliers, router, sander **7** bradawl, scraper **9** hand drill, try square **11** screwdriver
cutting/shaping: 2 ax **3** adz, axe, saw **4** adze, burr, file, froe, frow, rasp **5** burin, croze, gouge, knife, plane, razor, shave, wedge **6** chisel, sander, shears, trepan **7** hatchet, scraper **8** scissors
drilling/boring: 3 awl, bit, zax **4** pick **5** chuck, drill **6** gimlet, wimble **7** bradawl **11** countersink
farmer's: 2 ax **3** axe, hoe **4** plow, rake **5** spade **6** cradle, harrow, pickax, plough, scythe, seeder, shovel, sickle, tiller, trowel **7** hayfork **9** plowshare **10** cultivator
gripping/turning: 6 pliers, wrench **11** screwdriver
holding: 4 vise **5** clamp
measuring: 4 rule **5** gauge, level **6** square **7** caliper **8** dividers **10** micrometer
mechanic's: 3 awl, zax **4** burr, file, vise **5** bevel, lathe **6** bodkin, pliers **7** bradawl, crowbar **8** calipers **9** jackscrew **11** screwdriver **12** monkey wrench
pounding/striking: 4 maul **5** punch, wedge **6** hammer, mallet

too little 4 lack **6** dearth, scanty, scarce **7** paucity **8** scarcity, shortage **9** deficient, not enough, scantness **10** deficiency, inadequacy, inadequate **12** insufficient **13** insufficiency

too many
French: 6 de trop

too much 4 glut **5** flood **6** excess **7** profuse, surfeit, surplus **8** fullness, overflow, plethora **9** avalanche, excessive, profusion, repletion **10** inundation, oversupply **12** overabundant **13** overabundance **14** superabundance
French: 4 trop

Toonerville Folks
creator: 11 Fontaine Fox
character: 7 skipper **13** Aunt Eppie Hogg **15** Little Scorpions, Powerful Katrina, Suitcase Simpson **20** Mickey Himself McGuire **22** Terrible Tempered Mr Bang
rode on: 7 trolley

to one side 4 over **5** aloof, apart, aside **6** aslant **14** on the sidelines

to one's liking 7 fitting **8** pleasant, pleasing, suitable **9** agreeable **10** acceptable, gratifying **11** appropriate, to one's taste **12** satisfactory

toot 4 blow, honk **5** binge, blare, blast, spree **6** bender **7** trumpet **8** wingding

tooth 3 cog, nib **4** barb, cusp, fang, spur, tang, tine, tusk **5** molar, point, spike, thorn **6** canine, cuspid **7**

grinder, incisor **8** bicuspid, sprocket **9** serration

toothed 6 fanged, tusked **7** dentate, notched, serrate, virgate

toothsome 6 savory **8** luscious **9** delicious, palatable **10** appetizing

Toots
character in: **12** Dombey and Son
author: **7** Dickens

top 3 cap, lid, van **4** acme, apex, best, brow, cork, fore, head, lead, peak **5** chief, cover, crest, crown, excel, front, noted, outdo, upper **6** better, exceed, famous, summit, tiptop, vertex, zenith **7** eclipse, eminent, highest, notable, put over, stopper, surpass, topmost **8** complete, fore most, greatest, outshine, outstrip, pinnacle, renowned **9** paramount, principal, put a top on, transcend, uppermost, upper part **10** celebrated, first place, overshadow, preeminent

topaz
color: **4** blue **5** brown **6** yellow
source: **5** Japan **6** Brazil, Mexico, Saxony **13** Ural Mountains **18** Cairngorm Mountains
month: **8** November

Topaz
director: **9** Hitchcock
book by: **4** Uris

Topaze
author: **12** Marcel Pagnol

topaz quartz
species: **6** quartz
color: **4** blue, pink **5** brown, green **6** sherry

toper 3 sot **4** lush, soak **5** drunk **6** boozer **7** tippler **8** drunkard **9** alcoholic **11** dispomaniac

Top Hat
director: **12** Mark Sandrich
cast: **9** Eric Blore **11** Fred Astaire **12** Ginger Rogers **14** Helen Broderick **19** Edward Everett Horton
score: **12** Irving Berlin
song: **12** Cheek to Cheek **22** Top Hat White Tie and Tails

topic 4 text **5** theme **6** thesis **7** keynote, subject

topical 5 local **6** timely **7** current, limited **9** localized, parochial **10** particular, restricted **12** contemporary

Topkapi
director: **11** Jules Dassin
cast: **12** Peter Ustinov, Robert Morley **14** Melina Mercouri **16** Maximilian Schell
book by: **6** Ambler
setting: **8** Istanbul
Oscar for: **15** supporting actor (Ustinov)

topknot 4 comb, tuft **5** crest **9** cockscomb, headdress, headpiece

topmost 3 top **4** head **5** chief **7** highest, leading, supreme **8** foremost **9**

paramount, principal, uppermost **10** preeminent

topnotch 3 ace **4** best **5** prime **6** choice, finest, tip-top **7** supreme **8** superior, very fine **9** excellent, first-rate, nonpareil, unequaled, unrivaled **10** preeminent **11** outstanding, unsurpassed **12** incomparable, unparalleled

top of the head 4 dome, pate **5** crown **6** noggin, noodle

Topper
director: **13** Norman Z McLeod
based on novel by: **11** Thorne Smith
cast: **9** Cary Grant **11** Alan Mowbray, Billie Burke, Hedda Hopper, Roland Young **16** Constance Bennett
sequel: **13** Topper Returns **16** Topper Takes a Trip

topple 4 fall **5** crush, quash, quell, smash, upset **6** defeat, sprawl, tumble **7** abolish, shatter, tip over **8** fall over, over come, overturn, turn over, vanquish **9** bring down, overpower, overthrow **12** pitch forward

tops 4 aces, A-one, fine **5** great, prime, super, swell **6** choice, grade-A, superb, tip-top **7** capital **8** peerless, sterling, superior, terrific, top-notch **9** excellent, first-rate, marvelous, matchless, superfine, wonderful **10** first-class, inimitable, out-of-sight, tremendous **11** outstanding, superlative **12** incomparable **13** extraordinary

top-secret 5 privy **7** private **8** eyesonly, hush-hush **12** confidential

topsoil 4 dirt, loam **5** earth

Topsy
character in: **14** Uncle Tom's Cabin
author: **5** Stowe

topsy-turvy 5 messy **6** untidy **7** chaotic **8** confused, inverted, reversed **9** confusing, inside out **10** disorderly, upside down **11** disarranged, wrong side up **12** disorganized

Torah 10 law of Moses

torch 5 brand **7** cresset **8** arsonist, flambeau **9** firebrand **9** set fire to **10** flashlight

torment 3 nag, vex **4** bane, pain, rack **5** agony, annoy, curse, worry **6** harass, harrow, misery, pester, plague **7** afflict, agonize, anguish, despair, scourge, torture, trouble **8** distress, irritate **9** annoyance, persecute, suffering **10** irritation

tormenter 5 bully, tease **6** despot, tyrant **7** coercer **9** oppressor **10** browbeater **11** intimidator

tormenting 7 painful, racking **9** agonizing, torturous **10** unbearable **11** unendurable **12** excruciating, insufferable

torn 4 rent, slit **5** split **6** ragged, ripped **8** ruptured, shredded **9** unraveled

tornado 4 wind **5** storm **6** funnel, squall, vortex **7** cyclone, twister, ty-

phoon **8** outburst **9** hurricane, whirlwind, windstorm **10** waterspout **12** thunderstorm
belt: **7** Midwest
cloud: **4** tuba

torn apart 4 rent **6** ripped **7** asunder **8** in pieces, in shreds, shredded

toro 4 bull

Toronto
baseball team: **8** Blue Jays
bay: **6** Humber
football team: **9** Argonauts
former name: **4** York
harbor: **5** Inner
hockey team: **10** Maple Leafs
lake: **7** Ontario
landmark: **7** CN Tower **12** Ontario Place, O'Keefe Centre **13** Dufferin Grove **14** Dominion Centre **15** Roy Thompson Hall **16** Maple Leaf Stadium, St Lawrence Centre **17** Commerce Court West **18** Royal Ontario Museum **20** Nathan Phillips Square
park: **7** Chorley, Stanley, Trinity **8** Winthrow **9** Cedarvale **12** Center Island **16** Winston Churchill
street: **5** Yonge
university: **4** York

torpedo 4 sink **5** wreck **7** destroy, missile, scuttle **9** explosive **10** projectile

torpedo (marine)
invented by: **6** Fulton

torpid 4 dull, lazy **5** inert **6** drowsy, sleepy **7** dormant, languid, passive **8** inactive, indolent, listless, sluggish **9** apathetic, lethargic, somnolent **10** half asleep, languorous, slow-moving, spiritless **12** slow-thinking **13** lackadaisical

torpor, torpidity 6 apathy **7** inertia, languor **8** dullness, laziness, lethargy **9** indolence, lassitude **10** drowsiness, inactivity, sleepiness, somnolence **11** languidness, passiveness **12** listlessness, sluggishness

torrent 4 gush, rain, rush **5** burst, flood, salvo **6** deluge, rapids, stream, volley **7** barrage, cascade, Niagara **8** cataract, downpour, effusion, eruption, outburst **9** discharge, heavy rain, rapid flow, waterfall **10** cloudburst, outpouring, white water

Torrey, John
field: **6** botany
developed: **16** botanical library

Torricelli, Evangelista
nationality: **7** Italian
discovered concept leading to development of: **9** barometer

torrid 3 hot **4** sexy **5** fiery **6** ardent, erotic, fervid, heated, sexual, sultry **7** amorous, boiling, burning, excited, fervent, intense, lustful **8** broiling, desirous, parching, sizzling, spirited, tropical, vehement **9** hot and dry,

scorching 10 passionate, sweltering **11** hot and heavy, impassioned

torte 4 cake **7** dessert **9** layer cake

tortilla 7 tostada **8** corncake **11** Mexican cake
  griddle: 5 comal

Tortilla Flat
  author: 13 John Steinbeck

tortuous 4 bent **5** snaky **6** spiral, zigzag **7** crooked, devious, sinuous, turning, winding, wriggly **8** indirect, involved, twisting, wrongful **9** ambiguous **10** circuitous, convoluted, meandering, roundabout, serpentine **11** complicated **12** full of curves, hard to follow, labyrinthine

tortuousness 9 sinuosity **11** indirection, sinuousness **12** convolutions **14** circuitousness

torture 4 pain, rack **5** abuse, agony, prick, smite, trial, wring **6** harrow, ordeal **7** anguish, cruelty, torment **8** distress, maltreat, mistreat **9** brutality, suffering **10** infliction, punishment **11** tribulation **12** put to the rack

torturous 5 cruel **7** galling, irksome, painful, racking **8** annoying **9** agonizing, anguished, harrowing, miserable, tormented, torturing **10** anguishing, distressed, tormenting, unpleasant **11** distressful, distressing **12** disagreeable, excruciating

tory 8 loyalist, royalist **12** conservative

Tosca
  opera by: 7 Puccini
  character: 7 Scarpia **9** Angelotti **11** Floria Tosca **16** Mario Cavaradossi

To Sir With Love
  director: 12 James Clavell
  cast: 4 Lulu **10** Judy Geeson **11** Suzy Kendall **13** Sidney Poitier **16** Christian Roberts
  setting: 6 London

toss 3 lob **4** cast, flip, hurl, jerk, rock, roll, sway **5** churn, fling, heave, pitch, shake, sling, throw **6** joggle, let fly, propel, tumble, wiggle, writhe **7** agitate, flounce, wriggle **8** flourish, undulate **9** oscillate

toss about 4 roil **5** bandy **6** jostle, jounce

toss back and forth 5 bandy **8** exchange

total 3 add, sum **4** full **5** add up, gross, sheer, solid, sum up, utter, whole **6** entire, figure, reckon, tote up **7** add up to, compute, perfect, total up **8** absolute, combined, complete, entirety, figure up, integral, outright, sum total, sweeping, thorough, totality **9** aggregate, calculate, down right, out-and-out, unlimited, wholesale **10** full amount, undisputed, unmodified **11** unqualified, whole amount **13** comprehensive, unconditional

totaling 8 addition, coming to **9** reckoning **10** adding up to

totalitarian 7 fascist **8** despotic **9** fascistic, tyrannous **10** autocratic, tyrannical **11** dictatorial **12** undemocratic **16** unrepresentative

totally 7 solidly, utterly **8** entirely **9** downright, out-and-out, perfectly **10** absolutely, completely, thoroughly, throughout **15** unconditionally **18** from beginning to end **20** without qualification

tote 3 lug **4** bear, cart, drag, haul, move, pack, pull **5** carry, fetch **6** convey **7** schlepp **9** transport

to the city and the world
  Latin: 10 urbi et orbi
  form of address used on: 10 papal bulls

to the four winds 7 all over **10** everywhere, far and wide **26** to the four corners of the world

to the letter 5 exact, right **7** correct, precise **8** accurate, explicit, specific **9** on the nose

To the Lighthouse
  author: 13 Virginia Woolf
  character: 4 Prue **5** James **7** Camilla **8** Mr Ramsey **9** Mr Tansley, Mrs Ramsey **11** Lily Briscoe **12** Mr Carmichael

to the point 6 direct **7** apropos, germane **8** explicit, relevant **9** pertinent **12** to the purpose

to the rear 3 aft **4** back **5** abaft **6** astern, behind **8** backward, rearward **9** backwards, sternward **10** to the stern **14** toward the stern

to the stern 6 astern, behind **8** rearward **9** sternward **10** to the stern

to the word
  Latin: 8 ad verbum

to this extent
  Latin: 8 quoad hoc

Toto
  dog in: 13 The Wizard of Oz
  author: 4 Baum

totter 4 reel, rock, sway **5** lurch, shake, waver **6** falter, teeter, waddle, wobble **7** shuffle, stagger, stumble **9** oscillate, vacillate

tottering 5 shaky **6** wobbly **7** rickety, shaking **8** insecure, topheavy, unstable, unsteady, wobbling **9** doddering, quivering, trembling **10** ramshackle, staggering

Toucan
  constellation of: 6 Tucana

touch 3 art, bit, paw, pet, rub, use **4** abut, cite, dash, feel, fire, form, gift, hand, hint, join, meet, melt, move, note, stir, sway, tint, work **5** equal, flair, match, pinch, rival, rouse, skill, smack, speck, style, taste, thumb, tinge, trace, unite **6** adjoin, affect, arouse, border, broach, caress, excite,

finger, finish, fondle, handle, hint at, manner, method, pawing, polish, sadden, soften, strike, stroke, thrill **7** concern, consume, contact, feeling, finesse, impress, inflame, inspire, mastery, mention, quality, refer to, soupcon, surface, texture, utilize **8** allude to, artistry, bear upon, come near, come up to, converge, deal with, deftness, fineness, fondling, handling, inspirit, resort to, thumbing **9** awareness, direction, electrify, fingering, influence, palpation, pertain to, suspicion, technique **10** adroitness, intimation, manipulate, perception, sprinkling, suggestion, virtuosity **11** be in contact, compare with, familiarity, guiding hand, realization **12** acquaintance, manipulation **13** communication, comprehension, understanding

touched 3 mad **4** daft, felt, nuts **5** crazy, moved, nutty **6** insane, joined **7** abutted, cracked, handled **8** demented, deranged, unhinged **10** unbalanced **12** mad as a hatter **13** off one's rocker, out of one's head **14** off one's trolley **15** mad as a March hare

Touchett, Ralph
  character in: 18 The Portrait of a Lady
  author: 5 James

touching 3 sad **6** moving, tender **7** pitiful **8** dramatic, pathetic, poignant, stirring **9** affecting, emotional, heartfelt, saddening, sorrowful **11** distressing, sentimental **12** heartrending **13** heartbreaking

touch me not
  Latin: 13 noli me tangere

Touch of Evil
  director: 11 Orson Welles
  cast: 10 Janet Leigh, Ray Collins **11** Joanna Moore, Orson Welles, Zsa Zsa Gabor **12** Akim Tamiroff, Dennis Weaver **13** Joseph Calleia **14** Charlton Heston
    cameo: 15 Marlene Dietrich **19** Mercedes McCambridge

touch off 5 shoot **6** set off **7** explode, fire off, trigger **8** activate, detonate **9** discharge

touch on 4 pose **6** broach, submit **7** advance, bring up, mention, propose, suggest **9** introduce

touchstone 4 norm, rule **5** basis, gauge, guide, model, proof **7** example, measure, pattern **8** standard **9** benchmark, criterion, guideline, precedent, principle, yardstick

Touchstone
  character in: 11 As You Like It
  author: 11 Shakespeare

touch upon 7 apply to, concern, mention, refer to **8** allude to, bear upon, relate to **9** appertain

touchy 5 cross, huffy, surly, testy **6**

bitter, crabby, grumpy **7** awkward, fragile, grouchy, peevish, waspish **8** captious, critical, delicate, petulant, snappish, ticklish **9** concerned, difficult, irascible, irritable, querulous, resentful, sensitive **10** precarious **11** thinskinned **12** cantankerous **13** quick-tempered

tough 4 cold, firm, hard, hood, lout, mean, punk, wily **5** bully, cagey, canny, cruel, hardy, rigid, rough, rowdy, solid, stern **6** brutal, crafty, dogged, knotty, mulish, rugged, savage, strict, strong, sturdy, thorny, trying **7** adamant, arduous, callous, complex, durable, hoodlum, inhuman, irksome, lasting, onerous, ruffian, vicious **8** baffling, barbaric, enduring, exacting, grievous, hooligan, involved, leathery, obdurate, perverse, pitiless, puzzling, ruthless, stubborn, ticklish, toilsome **9** barbarian, confusing, difficult, enigmatic, heartless, heavy-duty, intricate, laborious, obstinate, pigheaded, resistant, roughneck, strenuous, unbending, unfeeling **10** bullheaded, delinquent, exhausting, formidable, hardheaded, inflexible, perplexing, unyielding **11** bewildering, calculating, cold-blooded, complicated, hardhearted, hard-to-solve, infrangible, insensitive, troublesome **12** bloodthirsty, impenetrable **13** unsympathetic **14** uncompromising

toughen 4 firm **5** inure, steel **6** firm up, harden, season, temper **7** fortify, stiffen **8** accustom **9** acclimate, habituate **10** discipline, strengthen **11** acclimatize

Toulouse-Lautrec, Henri Marie Raymond de
born: **4** Albi **6** France **8** Albigois
artwork: **7** Friends **13** The Inspection **16** At the Moulin Rouge **24** Au Salon de la Rue des Moulins **27** Jane Avril at the Jardin de Paris **29** Cirque Fernando The Equestrienne **29** In the Parlor at the Rue des Moulins **29** The English Girl at Le Star Le Havre **30** La Goulue Entering the Moulin Rouge

toupee 3 rug, wig **6** carpet, peruke **7** periwig **9** hairpiece

tour 4 trek, trip **5** jaunt, visit **6** junket, safari, travel, voyage **7** inspect, journey **8** sightsee **9** excursion, itinerary

tourist 7 pilgrim, tripper, voyager **8** traveler, vagabond, wanderer, wayfarer **9** journeyer, sightseer **10** rubberneck **12** excursionist, globetrotter

tourmaline
color: **3** red **4** blue, pink **5** green

tournament 4 game **5** event, match **7** contest, rivalry, tourney **11** competition

tourney 4 game **5** event, joust, match

7 contest, rivalry **10** tournament **11** competition

tousled 5 messy **6** mussed, untidy **7** rumpled, tangled, unkempt **8** mussed-up, uncombed **10** disheveled, disordered

tout 4 plug, push **5** boost, exalt, extol, vaunt **6** praise, talk up **7** acclaim, commend, glorify, promote, tipster **8** ballyhoo, eulogize, give a tip **9** advertise, brag about, celebrate, publicize, recommend **10** aggrandize, noise about

tout a fait 8 entirely
literally: **12** wholly to fact

tout a l'heure 7 just now **8** very soon **9** presently **14** just a moment ago
literally: **15** wholly to the hour

tout de suite 6 at once **11** immediately
literally: **19** wholly consecutively

tout ensemble 11 all together

tout le monde 8 everyone **9** everybody **13** the whole world

tovarich 7 comrade

tow 3 lug **4** drag, draw, haul, lift, pull **5** hoist, trail

toward the end
Latin: **5** ad fin

toward the front 5 ahead **6** before **7** forward **9** to the fore **13** in the vanguard **14** in the forefront

toward the rear 4 back **6** astern **8** backward, rearward **9** sternward

toward the stern 6 astern **8** rearward **9** sternward **10** to the stern

tower 4 keep, loom, rock, soar **5** mount, outdo, spire, surge **6** ascend, belfry, castle, column, exceed, pillar, refuge, turret **7** bulwark, eclipse, minaret, obelisk, overtop, shoot up, steeple, surpass **8** mainstay, outclass, outshine, overhang, rise high **9** bell tower, rise above, transcend **10** foundation, overshadow, skyscraper, stronghold, wellspring **12** fountainhead

towering 4 high, tall **5** lofty **6** alpine **7** soaring, sublime, supreme **8** dominant, foremost, mounting, peerless, snowclad, superior **9** ascending, matchless, paramount, principal, unequaled, unmatched, unrivaled **10** cloud-swept, preeminent, surpassing, unexcelled **11** cloud-capped, overhanging **12** incomparable, second to none, transcendent, unparalleled **13** extraordinary

Tower of London, The
author: **24** William Harrison Ainsworth

tower over 5 dwarf **7** surpass **8** dominate **9** rise above

Townes, Charles Hard
field: **7** physics

invented: **5** maser
awarded: **10** Nobel Prize

town hall
German: **7** Rathaus

town house 8 row house **10** brownstone, pied-a-terre **13** city residence

township 4 town **7** village **11** subdivision **12** municipality

toxic 5 fatal **6** deadly, lethal, mortal **7** noxious **8** poisoned, venomous **9** poisonous, unhealthy **10** pernicious

toxin 4 bane **5** venom **6** poison **8** pathogen

toy 4 play, tiny, yoyo **5** dally, pygmy, sport **6** bantam, bauble, fiddle, gadget, gewgaw, little, midget, trifle **7** dwarfed, for play, stunted, trinket **8** gimcrack **9** miniature, plaything, small-size **10** diminutive, small-scale **11** Lilliputian

Toy Bulldog
nickname of: **12** Mickey Walker

Toynbee, Arnold
author of: **15** A Study of History

to your health
French: **11** a votre sante

toy with 8 play with **9** flirt with **10** trifle with **16** amuse oneself with

trace 3 bit, jot, map **4** draw, drop, find, hint, hunt, iota, mark, seek, sign **5** dig up, relic, shade, tinge, token, touch, track, trail **6** depict, flavor, trifle **7** diagram, hunt for, look for, mark out, nose out, outline, remains, uncover, unearth, vestige **8** describe, discover, draw over, evidence **9** delineate, ferret out, footprint, light upon, little bit, search for, suspicion, track down **10** come across, indication, suggestion **11** small amount

trace to 6 credit **7** ascribe **8** charge to **9** attribute

Trachiniae
author: **9** Sophocles
characters: **4** Iole **6** Hyllus, Nessus **8** Deianira, Heracles

track 3 way **4** mark, path, rail, sign, tack **5** dirty, route, scent, spoor, trail **6** course, follow **9** footprint, guide rail

track and field
athlete: **7** Jim Ryun, Ray Ewry **8** Al Oerter, Lee Evans, Zola Budd **9** Ben Jonson, Bob Beamon, Carl Lewis, Henry Rono, Jim Thorpe **10** Bob Mathias, Bob Seagren, Edwin Moses, Grete Waitz, James Hines, Jesse Owens, John Carlos, Lasse Viren, Mac Wilkins, Paavo Nurmi, Peter Snell, Steve Ovett, Wyomia Tyus **11** Bill Rodgers, Bruce Jenner, Marty Liouri, David Wottle, Dick Fosbury, Doug Padilla, Emil Zatopek, Joni Huntley, Ralph Boston, Randy Matson, Tommie Smith **12** Dwight Stones, Frank Shorter, Harvey Glance, Jay Silvester,

Kathy Hammond, Maren Seidler, Rafer Johnson, Sebastian Coe, Willie B White, Wilma Rudolph **13** Allan Feurbach, Arnie Robinson, Janice Merrill, Kathy McMillan, Kipchoge Keino, Rodney Milburn, Ronny Ray Smith, Rosalyn Bryant, William Toomey **14** Alberto Salazar, Francie Larrieu, Roger Bannister **15** Martha Rae Watson, Renaldo Nehemiah, Willie Davenport **16** Madeleine Manning, Mary Decker Slaney, Richard Wohlhuter, Steve Prefontaine **17** Alberto Juantoreno **18** Jackie Joyner-Kersee, Stephanie Hightower **21** Babe Didrikson Zaharias **22** Florence Griffith-Joyner

tract 3 lot **4** area, plot, zone **5** essay **6** parcel, region **7** booklet, expanse, leaflet, quarter, stretch **8** brochure, district, pamphlet, treatise **9** monograph, territory **12** disquisition

tractable 4 tame **6** docile **8** amenable, obedient, yielding **9** compliant, teachable, trainable **10** governable, manageable, submissive **12** controllable, easy to manage **13** easy to control

tractate 8 treatise **9** discourse, monograph **12** disquisition, dissertation

Tracy, Spencer
  born: 11 Milwaukee WI
  costar: 16 Katharine Hepburn
  roles: 7 Desk Set **8** Adam's Rib, Boys Town (Oscar) **10** Pat and Mike **12** San Francisco, Tortilla Flat **13** The Last Hurrah **14** Cass Timberlane, Inherit the Wind, Woman of the Year **15** State of the Union **16** Father of the Bride, Keeper of the Flame **17** Bad Day at Black Rock **18** Captains Courageous (Oscar), The Old Man and the Sea **19** Judgment at Nuremberg **23** Guess Who's Coming to Dinner

Traddles
  character in: 16 David Copperfield
  author: 7 Dickens

trade 3 buy **4** deal, line, shop, swap **5** craft **6** barter, buyers **7** calling, patrons, pursuit **8** business, commerce, exchange, shoppers, vocation **9** clientele, customers, patronize **10** buy and sell, do business, employment, handicraft, line of work, occupation, profession **12** transactions **13** merchandising **16** business dealings, buying and selling

trade commodity 5 goods, wares

trademark 6 emblem **7** feature **8** property **9** specialty **11** peculiarity **14** characteristic

trade off 4 swap **5** trade **6** barter **8** exchange

trader 6 dealer, monger, seller **7** drummer **8** merchant, retailer **10** shopkeeper, trafficker, wholesaler **11** sales-person, storekeeper **12** merchandiser, tradesperson **14** businessperson

tradesman 6 dealer, seller **8** merchant, retailer **9** craftsman **10** shopkeeper **11** storekeeper

tradition 4 lore, myth, saga, tale **5** habit, usage **6** custom, legend **8** folklore, practice **10** convention **12** superstition

traditional 3 old **5** fixed, usual **7** typical **8** habitual, historic **9** ancestral, customary **10** accustomed, inveterate **11** established **12** acknowledged, conventional

traduce 5 abuse, libel, smear, sully **6** defame, malign, vilify **7** run down, slander **8** backbite, bad-mouth, besmirch **9** deprecate, disparage **10** calumniate

traffic 4 cars, deal **5** buses, ships, trade **6** barter, doings, planes, riders, trains, trucks **7** bootleg, contact, freight, smuggle **8** business, commerce, dealings, exchange, tourists, voyagers **9** commuters, relations, smuggling, travelers **10** buy and sell, enterprise, passengers **11** bootlegging, intercourse, pedestrians, proceedings **12** transactions, vacationists **13** excursionists

tragedy 3 woe **4** blow **5** grief **6** misery, sorrow **7** anguish, setback **8** accident, calamity, disaster, reversal, sad thing **9** heartache **10** affliction, heartbreak **11** catastrophe

tragic 3 sad **4** dire **5** awful, fatal **6** deadly, dreary, woeful **7** piteous, pitiful, ruinous, serious, unhappy **8** dramatic, dreadful, grievous, horrible, mournful, pathetic, pitiable, shocking, terrible **9** appalling, frightful **10** calamitous, deplorable, disastrous, lamentable **11** destructive, devastating, unfortunate **12** catastrophic **13** heartbreaking

trail 3 dog, tow, way **4** drag, draw, fall, flow, hunt, mark, path, poke, sign, tail **5** float, hound, scent, spoor, trace, track **6** be down, course, dangle, dawdle, follow, lessen, shrink, stream **7** dwindle, pathway, subside **8** decrease, diminish, footpath, grow weak, hand down, peter out, taper off **9** drag along, grow faint, grow small, lag behind **10** bridle path, drag behind, footprints, move slowly **11** beaten track **14** bring up the rear

trailblazers 7 leaders **8** pioneers **10** avant-garde, innovators **11** forerunners, originators, tastemakers **12** trendsetters

train 2 el **3** aim, set **4** line **5** break, chain, drill, focus, level, point, queue, sight, teach, trail, tutor **6** column, direct, escort, school, series, subway **7** caravan, cortege, educate, prepare, retinue **8** elevated, exercise, instruct, practice, rehearse, sequence **9** afterpart, appendage, entourage, followers **10** attendants, discipline, get in shape, procession, succession **11** bring to bear, domesticate, progression **12** continuation

Train, The
  director: 17 John Frankenheimer
  cast: 10 Albert Remy **11** Michel Simon **12** Jeanne Moreau, Paul Scofield **13** Burt Lancaster

trained 4 able **6** expert, master **7** capable, skilled **8** schooled, seasoned **9** competent, qualified **11** experienced **12** accomplished

trainee 4 boot **5** cadet **6** rookie **7** private, rookie, student **9** greenhorn **10** apprentice

trainer 5 coach, tutor **7** teacher **16** athletic director

training 5 drill **8** coaching, drilling, practice, teaching **9** education, schooling **10** discipline **11** preparation **14** apprenticeship, indoctrination

traipse 3 gad **4** roam, walk **5** range, tramp, tread **6** stroll, trapes, wander **7** meander, saunter **8** gadabout **9** gallivant

trait 4 mark **5** quirk **7** earmark, feature, quality **8** hallmark **9** attribute, mannerism **11** peculiarity **12** idiosyncracy **14** characteristic

traitor 3 rat **5** Judas, rebel **6** ratter **7** ratfink, serpent **8** apostate, betrayer, deceiver, deserter, mutineer, quisling, renegade, turncoat **9** hypocrite **11** false friend **12** double-dealer **13** double-crosser, revolutionary **14** fifth columnist **15** snake in the grass **20** wolf in sheep's clothing

traitorous 5 false **7** corrupt **8** disloyal, renegade **9** betraying, faithless **10** perfidious, treasonous, unfaithful **11** treacherous

tramp 3 bum **4** hike, hobo, roam, rove, slog, trek, walk **5** march, prowl, stamp, stomp **6** ramble, trudge, wander **7** floater, meander, traipse, trample, vagrant **8** derelict **9** gallivant, itinerant **10** panhandler **11** perambulate, peregrinate **15** knight-of-the-road

trample 5 crush, stamp, stomp **6** squash **7** flatten, run over **14** grind under foot **15** step heavily upon

trance 4 coma, daze **5** dream, spell **6** stupor, vision **7** reverie **8** daydream, hypnosis **9** pipe dream **10** absorption, brown study **11** abstraction **12** sleepwalking **13** concentration, preoccupation, woolgathering

tranquil 4 calm, cool, mild **5** quiet, still **6** gentle, placid, serene **7** halcyon, restful **8** composed, peaceful **9** unexcited, unruffled **11** undisturbed, unperturbed **13** self-possessed

tranquility 4 calm, hush **5** peace, quiet **6** repose **7** concord, harmony **8**

quietude, serenity **9** composure, placidity, stillness **11** restfulness **12** peacefulness

tranquilize 4 calm, drug, lull **5** allay, quiet, relax, still **6** becalm, pacify, sedate, settle, soothe **7** appease, assuage **9** alleviate

transact 2 do **5** exact **6** handle, manage, settle **7** achieve, carry on, conduct, execute, perform **8** carry out, exercise **9** discharge **10** accomplish, take care of **12** carry through

transaction 4 deal **6** affair **7** bargain, dealing, venture **8** exchange **9** operation **10** enterprise, settlement **11** negotiation **15** business dealing, piece of business

transcend 5 excel, outdo **6** exceed **7** eclipse, outrank, surpass **8** go beyond, outrival, outshine, outstrip, overleap, overstep, surmount **9** rise above **10** overshadow **11** outdistance

transcendence 5 merit **8** eminence **9** exceeding, greatness **10** exaltation, excellence, surpassing **11** distinction, preeminence, superiority

transcendental 5 great **6** mental **7** supreme, unusual **8** elevated, peerless, superior, uncommon **9** exceeding, intuitive, matchless, spiritual, unequaled, unrivaled **10** surpassing **11** unsurpassed **12** incomparable, metaphysical **13** extraordinary

transfer 4 cede, deed, move, send **5** bring, carry, shift **6** change, convey, moving, remove **7** consign, deeding, removal, sending **8** bringing, carrying, hand over, make over, relegate, relocate, shifting, shipment, transmit, turn over **9** conveying, transport **10** delivering, relegation, relocating, relocation **11** consignment, transmittal **12** transporting **14** transportation

transferable 8 catching **10** contagious, infectious **12** communicable **13** transmissible, transmittable

transferal 8 delivery, transfer **10** giving over **11** handing over, transmittal **12** transmission

transference 5 shift **6** change **7** passage, removal **9** transport **11** transmittal **12** dislodgement, displacement, transmission **13** transmittance

transfiguration 10 conversion **13** metamorphosis, transmutation **14** transformation

transfigure 6 change **9** transform **12** metamorphose

transfix 3 pin **4** hold, stab, stun **5** rivet, spear, spike, stick **6** absorb, impale, pierce, skewer **7** astound, bewitch, enchant, engross, fix fast, terrify **8** astonish, hold rapt, intrigue **9** captivate, fascinate, hypnotize, mesmerize, penetrate, spellbind **10** run through

transform 4 turn **5** alter **6** change, recast, remold **7** convert, remodel **8** make over **9** refurbish, transmute **11** reconstruct, transfigure **12** metamorphose, transmogrify

transformation 6 change **9** restyling **10** alteration, conversion, remodeling **13** metamorphosis, transmutation **15** transfiguration

transgress 3 err, sin **4** slip **5** break, cross, fault, lapse, wrong **6** exceed, impose, offend **7** digress, infract, violate **8** infringe, trespass

transgression 3 sin **5** crime, error, lapse, wrong **6** breach **7** misdeed, offense **8** evil deed, iniquity, trespass **9** violation **10** immorality, infraction, wrongdoing **11** lawbreaking **12** encroachment, infringement, overstepping **13** contravention

transgressor 5 felon **6** sinner **7** culprit **8** criminal, evildoer, offender, violator **9** miscreant, wrongdoer **10** lawbreaker, malefactor, trespasser

transience 7 brevity **11** evanescence **12** ephemerality, impermanence

transient 5 brief **7** passing **8** fleeting, soon past, temporal **9** ephemeral, momentary, short-term, temporary **10** evanescent, perishable, short-lived, transitory, unenduring **11** impermanent **14** passing through **24** here today and gone tomorrow

transistor
  invented by: 7 Bardeen **8** Brattain, Shockley

transition 4 jump, leap **6** change **7** passage, passing **8** shifting **9** gradation, variation **10** alteration, changeover, conversion, graduation **11** progression **13** transmutation **14** transformation

transitory 5 brief **7** passing **8** fleeting, fugitive **9** ephemeral, temporary, transient **10** evanescent, not lasting, short-lived, unenduring **11** impermanent **24** here today and gone tomorrow

translate 4 turn **5** alter, apply **6** change, decode, recast, render, reword **7** clarify, convert, explain **8** decipher, rephrase, simplify, spell out **9** elucidate, interpret, make clear, transform, transmute **10** paraphrase

translucence 7 clarity **8** lucidity **10** luminosity **12** transparency **16** semitransparency

translucent 8 pellucid **10** semiopaque, translucid **15** semitransparent

transmissible 8 catching **10** contagious, infectious **12** communicable, transferable **13** transmittable

transmission 4 note **7** message, passage, passing, sending **8** delivery, dispatch, transfer **9** broadcast **10** conveyance, forwarding, remittance **11** handing over, transmittal **12** transference, transferring **13** communication **14** transportation

transmit 4 send, ship **5** carry, issue, relay, remit **6** convey, pass on, spread **7** deliver, forward **8** dispatch, televise, transfer **9** broadcast **11** communicate, disseminate

transmittable 8 catching **10** contagious, infectious **12** communicable, transferable

transmittal 7 sending **8** delivery, transfer **10** giving over, transferal **11** handing over **12** transmission

transmutation 6 change **10** conversion **13** metamorphosis **14** transformation **15** transfiguration

transmute 5 alter **6** change **7** convert **9** transform **12** metamorphose

transparency 6 purity **7** clarity **8** lucidity **9** clearness, sheerness **11** obviousness **14** diaphanousness

transparent 4 thin **5** clear, gauzy, lucid, plain, sheer **6** glassy, limpid, patent **7** evident, obvious, visible **8** apparent, clear-cut, distinct, explicit, manifest, palpable, peekaboo, pellucid **10** diaphanous, see-through **11** perceptible, self-evident, translucent, unambiguous, unequivocal **12** crystal-clear, unmistakable

transpire 5 arise, occur **6** appear, befall, chance, crop up, evolve, happen, turn up **7** come out, leak out **9** be met with, eventuate, take place **10** be revealed, come to pass, make public **11** become known, be disclosed, come to light, show its face

transplant 5 graft, repot, shift **7** replant **8** displace, relocate, resettle, transfer **9** transport, transpose

transport 3 bus, lug **4** bear, cart, lift, move, send, ship, take, tote **5** bring, carry, charm, fetch, train, truck **6** convey, moving, remove, thrill **7** bearing, bewitch, carting, delight, deliver, enchant, freight, removal, sending, vehicle **8** airplane, carrying, delivery, dispatch, enthrall, entrance, shipment, shipping, transfer, transmit, trucking **9** captivate, cargo ship, carry away, conveying, electrify, enrapture, freighter, overpower **10** cargo plane, conveyance **12** freight train

transportation 7 cartage, haulage, portage, removal, transit **8** delivery, dispatch, movement, shipment **9** transport **10** conveyance, transferal **12** transference, transmission **13** transmittance

transported 5 moved **6** lifted **7** charmed **8** ecstatic, thrilled, uplifted **9** bewitched, entranced **10** captivated, enthralled **11** carried away, electrified **13** beside oneself

transverse 5 cross **6** across **7** athwart, oblique, transom **8** crossbar, crossing, diagonal, traverse **9** crosswise **10** crosspiece, horizontal

transversely 9 crossways, crosswise, laterally

Transylvania
    region of: 7 Romania
    city: 4 Cluj
    fictional home of: 7 Dracula

trap 3 net, pit **4** lure, ploy, ruse, seal, stop, wile **5** catch, feint, snare, trick **6** ambush, device, enmesh, entrap, lock in **7** ensnare, pitfall, springe **8** artifice, entangle, hold back, hunt down, maneuver **9** booby trap, stratagem **11** machination **16** compartmentalize

trappings 4 garb, gear **5** array, dress **6** attire, outfit, things **7** apparel, clothes, costume, effects, raiment, vesture **8** adjuncts, clothing, fittings **9** ornaments, trimmings **10** adornments, habiliment, investment **11** decorations **13** accoutrements, paraphernalia **14** embellishments

trash 3 rot **4** bums, crap, junk, scum **5** dregs, dross, tripe, waste **6** debris, drivel, idlers, litter, refuse, rubble, tramps **7** garbage, hogwash, loafers, residue, rubbish, twaddle **8** castoffs, leavings, nonsense, riffraff **9** poppycock, sweepings **10** balderdash **11** foolishness, ne'er-do-wells, odds and ends **15** good-for-nothings, unsavory element

trashy 4 vile **5** cheap, inane, junky, tacky **6** flashy, flimsy **7** rubbish, trivial, useless **8** riff-raff, trumpery, wasteful **9** worthless **13** insignificant

trauma 4 hurt **5** shock, wound **6** injury, stress

travail 4 pain, toil **5** labor, worry **6** strain, stress **7** anguish **8** delivery, distress, drudgery, exertion, hard work, hardship **9** suffering **10** birth pains, childbirth, labor pains **11** parturition **12** accouchement

travel 2 go **4** be on, move, roam, rove, sail, tour, trek, wend **5** cross, drive, range, visit **6** cruise, junket, voyage, wander **7** journey, proceed **8** pass over, progress, sightsee, traverse **9** globetrot, hitchhike, take a trip **11** pass through, press onward

traveler 5 gypsy, nomad, rover **7** drummer, migrant, pilgrim, tourist, trekker, tripper, voyager **8** vagabond, wanderer, wayfarer **9** itinerant, journeyer, sightseer **10** vacationer **12** excursionist, globetrotter

Traveller Without Luggage
    author: 11 Jean Anouilh

Travels With a Donkey
    author: 20 Robert Louis Stevenson
    donkey: 9 Modestine

Travels With My Aunt
    author: 12 Graham Greene

travel through 2 do **5** cover, cross,

visit **8** traverse **9** negotiate **11** pass through

traverse 4 span **5** cross **6** bridge, travel **8** go across, move over, overpass **9** cross over, cut across, intersect, move along, negotiate, reach over **10** extend over, run through, travel over **11** move through, pass through, reach across

travesty 4 sham **5** farce, spoof **6** parody, satire **7** lampoon, mockery, takeoff **8** disgrace **9** burlesque **10** caricature, distortion, perversion **17** misrepresentation

Traviata, La
    also: 9 The Misled **23** The Woman Who Was Led Astray
    opera by: 5 Verdi
    based on a story by: 14 Alexandre Dumas (fils)
        called: 7 Camille **17** La Dame aux Camelias
    character: 8 Violetta **14** Alfredo Germont

Travolta, John
    born: 11 Englewood NJ
    roles: 6 Carrie, Grease **7** Face/Off, Mad City **9** Get Shorty **10** Tony Manero **11** Pulp Fiction, Urban Cowboy **12** She's So Lovely, Staying Alive **13** Primary Colors **14** Moment By Moment **15** Vinnie Barbarino **17** Welcome Back Kotter **18** Saturday Night Fever

trawl 3 net **4** drag, fish, haul, line **5** seine, troll **6** dredge **7** dragnet

Treacher, Arthur
    real name: 11 Arthur Veary
    born: 7 England **8** Brighton
    roles: 11 Mary Poppins **14** National Velvet, Thank You Jeeves **16** David Copperfield **20** Magnificent Obsession

treacherous 5 false, risky **6** tricky, unsafe, untrue **7** devious **8** disloyal, perilous, two-faced **9** dangerous, deceitful, deceptive, faithless, hazardous **10** misleading, perfidious, precarious, traitorous, treasonous, unfaithful **12** falsehearted **13** untrustworthy

treachery 5 guile **6** deceit **7** perfidy, treason **8** apostasy, betrayal, trickery **9** deception, duplicity, falseness **10** disloyalty, infidelity **11** double cross **13** breach of faith, deceitfulness, double-dealing, faithlessness **15** underhandedness **17** untrustworthiness

tread 4 gait, hike, pace, roam, rove, step, walk **5** prowl, range, stamp, stomp, tramp **6** step on, stride, stroll, trudge, walk on **7** trample **8** footfall, footstep

treason 6 mutiny, revolt **7** perfidy **8** apostasy, betrayal, sedition **9** duplicity, rebellion, treachery **10** conspiracy, disloyalty, insurgence, revolution, sub-

version **11** lese majesty **12** insurrection

treasonable 9 faithless, seditious **10** perfidious, subversive, traitorous **11** treacherous

treasure 3 gem **4** gold **5** hoard, jewel, prize, store, value **6** esteem, jewels, regard, revere, riches, silver **7** cherish, deposit, paragon **8** bank upon, dote upon, gold mine, hold dear **11** pride and joy **14** apple of one's eye **17** pearl of great price

treasure chest 3 box **4** case **5** chest, trunk **6** coffer

treasured 4 dear **5** loved **6** adored, valued **7** beloved **8** precious **9** cherished

Treasure Island
    author: 20 Robert Louis Stevenson
    character: 7 Ben Gunn **8** Smollett **9** Dr Livesey **10** Jim Hawkins **14** Long John Silver **15** Squire Trelawney
    director:
        1934 version: 13 Victor Fleming
        1950 version: 11 Byron Haskin
    based on novel by: 20 Robert Louis Stevenson
    cast:
        1934 version: 10 Lewis Stone **12** Jackie Cooper (Jim Hawkins), Wallace Beery (Long John Silver) **15** Lionel Barrymore
        1950 version: 11 Basil Sydney **12** Robert Newton (Long John Silver) **13** Bobby Driscoll (Jim Hawkins) **16** Walter Fitzgerald

Treasure of the Sierra Madre, The
    director: 10 John Huston
    cast: 7 Tim Holt **12** Bruce Bennett, Walter Huston **13** Alfonso Bedoya, Barton MacLane **14** Humphrey Bogart
    Oscar for: 8 director **10** screenplay **15** supporting actor (Huston)

treasurer 6 banker, bursar, purser, teller **7** auditor, cashier **9** financier **10** accountant, bookkeeper, cash-keeper, controller **16** financial officer **17** minister of finance **22** secretary of the treasury **24** Chancellor of the Exchequer

Treasure State
    nickname of: 7 Montana

treasury 4 bank, safe, till **5** funds, purse, vault **6** coffer **8** money box **9** anthology, exchequer, strongbox, thesaurus **10** collection, compendium, depository, repository, storehouse **11** bank account, compilation

treasury note 4 bill **8** bank note **9** greenback **12** currency note **17** silver certificate

treat 3 joy **4** blow, coat, give **5** apply, cover, favor, grant, imbue, stand **6** attend, divert, doctor, handle, manage, remedy, spring, thrill **7** comfort, delight, discuss, patch up, take out **8** consider, deal with, look upon, medicate, pleasure, relate to **9** act toward, small gift, try to cure, try to heal **10** impregnate, minister to, speak about, write about **12** prescribe for, satisfaction **13** gratification

treat as inferior 7 disdain **9** patronize **12** condescend to **18** look down one's nose at **19** discriminate against

treatise 4 text **5** essay, study, tract **6** manual, memoir, report, thesis **8** textbook, tractate **9** discourse, monograph **12** dissertation

treatment 3 way **4** cure **6** course, remedy **7** conduct, process, regimen, therapy **8** antidote, approach, handling, treating **9** doctoring, operation, procedure **10** management, medication **11** application, medical care **12** manipulation

treaty 4 deal, pact **6** accord **7** bargain, compact, entente **8** covenant **9** concordat **13** understanding **15** formal agreement **22** international agreement

tree 3 ash, elm, fir, oak **4** bush, palm, pine, wood **5** beech, birch, chase, maple, plane, plant, scrub, staff, stake, stick **6** corner, cudgel, redbud, spruce, timber, willow **7** gallows, lineage, live oak, sapling **8** ancestry, chestnut, hardwood, mahogany, pedigree, seedling **9** ailanthus, evergreen **10** cottonwood, eucalyptus

Tree Grows in Brooklyn, A
  author: **10** Betty Smith
  character:
    Nolan family: **5** Katie **6** Neeley **7** Francie, Johnnie
  director: **9** Elia Kazan
  cast: **9** James Dunn **10** Lloyd Nolan **12** Joan Blondell **14** Dorothy McGuire, Peggy Ann Garner
  Oscar for: **7** special (Garner) **15** supporting actor (Dunn)

treeless 4 bald, bare **6** barren **7** denuded **8** unwooded **10** unforested

Treeplanters State
  nickname of: **8** Nebraska

tref 9 not kosher

trek 4 hike, plod, roam, rove, sail, slog, trip **5** jaunt, march, range, tramp **6** junket, outing, travel, trudge, voyage, wander **7** journey, odyssey, passage **8** traverse **9** excursion, migration **10** expedition, pilgrimage **11** peregrinate **13** peregrination

trellis 5 arbor, bower, cross, frame, grill, trail **6** gazebo, screen **7** lattice, network, pergola **8** espalier **10** interweave **11** summerhouse

tremble 5 quail, quake, shake, waver **6** quaver, quiver, shiver **7** flutter, pulsate, shudder **9** palpitate

trembling 5 shaky **7** quaking, shaking **8** unsteady **9** doddering, quavering,

quivering, shivering **10** shuddering **11** palpitating

tremblor 5 quake, seism, shock **6** tremor **8** upheaval **10** earthquake

tremendous 4 fine, huge, vast **5** giant, great, major **7** amazing, awesome, immense, mammoth, sizable, titanic, unusual **8** colossal, enormous, fabulous, gigantic, terrific, towering, uncommon **9** excellent, fantastic, first-rate, humongous, important, marvelous, monstrous, wonderful **10** formidable, gargantuan, incredible, noteworthy, stupendous **11** elephantine, exceptional **12** considerable **13** consequential, extraordinary

tremolo
  music: **9** trembling, vibrating **30** rapid reiteration of a single pitch

tremor 3 jar **4** jolt **5** quake, shake, shock, spasm, throb, waver **6** quiver, shiver **7** flutter, shaking, shudder, tremble **8** paroxysm **9** pulsation, quavering, quivering, shivering, trembling, vibration **10** convulsion **11** palpitation

tremulous 5 jumpy, shaky, timid **6** wobbly **7** aquiver, excited, fearful, jittery, keyed-up, nervous, panicky, quaking **8** aflutter, agitated, atremble, hesitant, restless, wavering, worked-up **9** faltering, impatient, quivering, trembling, uncertain **10** irresolute, stimulated **13** on tenterhooks, panic-stricken

trench 3 cut, rut **4** scar **5** canal, ditch, drain, fosse, slash, slice **6** dugout, furrow, gutter, trough **7** channel, wrinkle **8** aqueduct **9** earthwork **10** depression

trenchant 4 acid, keen, tart **5** crisp **6** bitter **7** acerbic, caustic, concise, mordant, probing **8** clear-cut, distinct, incisive, scathing **9** sarcastic, scorching **10** razor-sharp **11** acrimonious, penetrating, well-defined

trend 4 bent, flow, mode **5** drift, style **7** fashion, impulse, leaning **8** movement, tendency **9** direction **10** proclivity, propensity **11** inclination

trendsetters 7 leaders **8** trendies, vanguard **10** avant-garde, innovators **11** pacesetters, tastemakers **12** advance guard, stylesetters, trailblazers

trendy 2 in **4** chic, tony **5** swank **6** modern, modish, with-it **7** current, faddish, popular, stylish, voguish **8** up-to-date **10** all the rage **11** fashionable **13** up-to-the-minute

Trenor, Gus and Judy
  characters in: **15** The House of Mirth
  author: **7** Wharton

Trent, Little Nell
  character in: **19** The Old Curiosity Shop
  author: **7** Dickens

trepidation 4 fear **5** alarm, dread,

panic, worry **7** anxiety, jitters **8** cold feet, disquiet **10** uneasiness **11** butterflies, disquietude, jitteriness, nervousness **12** apprehension **13** consternation

trespass 3 sin **5** error, wrong **6** invade **7** impinge, intrude, misdeed, offense **8** encroach, infringe, iniquity, invasion **9** evildoing, intrusion, violation **10** immorality, infraction, misconduct, wrongdoing **11** delinquency, misbehavior **12** encroachment, infringement, overstepping **13** transgression, unlawful entry, wrongful entry

tress 4 curl, hair, lock, mane **5** braid, plait **6** strand **7** ringlet, wimpler **8** spitcurl

trestle 4 beam **5** board, brace, frame, table **6** timber **9** framework

trial 2 go **3** try, woe **4** care, pain, shot, test **5** agony, essay, flyer, whirl, worry **6** burden, effort, misery, ordeal, trying, tryout **7** anguish, attempt, bad luck, hearing, testing, test run, torment, trouble, venture **8** accident, distress, endeavor, hardship, vexation **9** adversity, court case, heartache, suffering **10** affliction, litigation, misfortune **11** cross to bear **12** misadventure, wretchedness

Trial, The
  author: **10** Franz Kafka
  character: **4** Leni **7** Joseph K **9** Titorelli **11** The Advocate

trial and error 10 experiment **13** investigation **15** experimentation **20** process of elimination

tribe *see* **11** ethnic group

Tribes of Israel *see* **6** Israel

tribulation 3 woe **4** care, pain **5** agony, grief, trial, worry **6** misery, ordeal, sorrow **7** anguish, bad luck, torment, trouble **8** distress, hardship, vexation **9** adversity, heartache, suffering **10** affliction, ill fortune, misfortune **11** unhappiness **12** wretchedness

Tribulation Wholesome
  character in: **12** The Alchemist
  author: **6** Jonson

tribunal 3 bar **5** bench, court, forum **6** judges **9** authority, judiciary **10** ruling body **11** judge's bench, judge's chair **14** seat of judgment

tributary 6 branch, feeder, source, stream **7** helping, subject **8** affluent **9** ancillary, auxiliary, confluent, secondary **10** subjugated, subsidiary **11** subordinate **12** contributing, contributory

tribute 3 tax **4** duty, levy, toll **5** bribe, honor, kudos **6** esteem, eulogy, excise, impost, payoff, praise, ransom **7** payment, respect **8** accolade, encomium, memorial **9** extolling, gratitude, laudation, panegyric **10** assessment, blood money, compliment, settlement **11** recognition, testimonial **12** commendation, pound of flesh **13**

consideration, peace offering **14** acknowledgment

trice 3 sec **4** jiff, wink **5** blink, flash, jiffy, shake **6** minute, moment, second **7** instant **9** coup d'oeil, twinkling **11** split second

trichophobia
fear of: **4** hair

trichoptera
class: **8** hexapoda
phylum: **10** arthropoda
group: **3** fly **6** caddis

trick 3 art, gag **4** bait, dupe, feat, gift, gull, have, hoax, joke, ploy, ruse, trap, wile **5** antic, blind, bluff, caper, cheat, dodge, feint, fraud, knack, prank, put-on, skill, stunt **6** deceit, device, number, outfox, outwit, resort, secret, take in **7** deceive, gimmick, know-how, mislead, swindle **8** artifice, deftness, flimflam, hoodwink, maneuver **9** bamboozle, chicanery, deception, dexterity, imposture, sophistry, stratagem, technique **10** adroitness, hocus-pocus, manipulate, subterfuge **11** contrivance, machination, outmaneuver **13** practical joke, sleight of hand **16** prestidigitation

trickery 5 guile **6** bunkum, deceit **8** artifice, flimflam, pretense, quackery, wiliness **9** chicanery, deception, duplicity, imposture, rascality, stratagem **10** artfulness, craftiness, hocus-pocus, shiftiness **11** crookedness, deviousness **12** charlatanism, skullduggery, slipperiness **13** deceitfulness

trickiness 6 deceit **7** cunning, slyness **8** trickery **9** duplicity **10** craftiness **15** underhandedness

trickle 4 drip, leak, ooze, seep **5** exude **7** dribble, seepage **9** percolate

trickster 5 cheat, joker **6** dodger, rascal **8** deceiver, impostor, sleeveen **9** prankster

tricky 3 sly **4** foxy, wily **5** risky **6** artful, crafty, shifty, unsafe **7** cunning, devious **8** rascally, slippery, unstable **9** dangerous, deceptive, difficult, hazardous **10** touch-and-go, unreliable **11** complicated, underhanded **12** hard to handle, undependable **13** temperamental, unpredictable

trident
form: **5** spear
number of prongs: **5** three
scepter of: **7** Neptune **8** Poseidon

trifle 3 bit, dab, jot, nip, toy **4** dash, drop, idle, iota, mite, play **5** crumb, dally, pinch, scrap, speck, tinge, touch, trace **6** bauble, dawdle, gewgaw, linger, little, morsel, sliver **7** modicum, nothing, trinket **8** fragment, gimcrack, kill time **9** bagatelle, plaything, waste time **10** dillydally, knickknack, sprinkling, triviality **11** deal lightly, small matter **12** amuse oneself, treat lightly **13** small quantity

trifler 5 flirt, idler **6** coquet **7** dabbler, dallier **8** coquette **10** dilettante

trifling 4 puny **5** petty, small, sorry, token **6** paltry, slight **7** nominal, trivial **8** beggarly, niggling, nugatory, picayune, piddling **9** worthless **10** negligible **11** unimportant **13** beneath notice, inappreciable, insignificant **14** inconsiderable **15** inconsequential

trifling circumstances
Latin: **8** minutiae

trifling matter
French: **10** peu de chose

trigger 5 shoot **6** set off **7** fire off **8** activate, detonate, touch off **9** discharge

trikerion 11 candelabrum, candlestick **12** candleholder

Trilby
author: **15** George du Maurier
character: **5** Gecko, Sandy, Taffy **8** Svengali **12** Little Billee **14** Trilby O'Ferrall

trill
music: **7** shaking, tremolo **9** quavering

trim 3 cut, fit, lop **4** clip, crop, deck, form, lean, pare, slim, thin **5** adorn, array, lithe, prune, shape, shave, shear, shift, sleek, state **6** adjust, bedeck, border, change, fettle, kilter, limber, paring, piping, supple, svelte **7** arrange, balance, bedizen, compact, cutting, fitness, furbish, garnish, lissome, pruning, shapely, slender, willowy **8** athletic, beautify, clipping, cropping, decorate, equalize, ornament, shearing, trick out, trimming **9** adornment, condition, embellish, embroider, shipshape **10** decoration, distribute **11** streamlined **13** embellishment, ornamentation

Trim, Corporal
character in: **14** Tristram Shandy
author: **6** Sterne

trimming 4 trim **5** frill **7** cutting, pruning, slicing **8** clipping **9** adornment **10** decoration, shortening, truncation **11** abridgement, contraction, curtailment **12** abbreviation **13** embellishment

Trinacria see **6** Sicily

Trinidad and Tobago
capital/largest city: **11** Port of Spain
others: **4** Debe, Toco **5** Arima **6** Canaan, Coryal, Labrea **7** San Juan, Siparia **8** Rio Claro, Tunapuna **10** Roxborough **11** San Fernando, Scarborough **12** Princess Town, Sangre Grande **14** Charlotteville
school: **6** Fatima **7** St Mary's **11** Queen's Royal
head of state: **14** British monarch **15** governor general
monetary unit: **4** cent **6** dollar
island: **12** Chacachacare, Little Tobago **14** Bird of Paradise

lake: **5** Pitch
mountain:
hills: **7** Trinity **10** Montserrat **12** Three Sisters
highest point: **5** Aripo
river: **6** Caroni **7** Ortoire **8** Oropuche, Trinidad
sea: **8** Atlantic **9** Caribbean
physical feature:
bay: **5** Cocos, Guapo **6** Matura, Mayaro
channel: **12** Dragon's Mouth **13** Serpent's Mouth
gulf: **5** Paria
point: **5** Radix **6** Arenal, Galera **7** Chupara, Galeota **8** Columbus
people: **5** Irish **6** French, Syrian **7** African, Chinese, English, Spanish **8** European, Lebanese **10** East Indian, Portuguese, Venezuelan **11** Asian Indian **13** Latin American
explorer: **8** Columbus
leader: **8** Williams
language: **6** French **7** Chinese, English, Spanish **10** Portuguese **12** French Patois
religion: **5** Hindu, Islam **8** Anglican **10** Protestant **12** Christianity **13** Roman Catholic
place:
asphalt lake: **9** Pitch Lake
mansions: **16** Magnificent Seven
park: **18** Queen's Park Savannah
feature:
bird: **7** oilbird **8** cocorico
clothing: **4** sari **5** dhoti
dance: **6** Dragon, Shango
festival: **6** Hosein, Lights
fish: **5** guppy
music: **7** calypso, goombay
tree: **4** mora
food:
drink: **16** Angostura Bitters

Trinity
author: **8** Leon Uris

trinket 3 toy **5** bijou, charm, jewel **6** bauble, gewgaw, notion, trifle **8** gimcrack, ornament **9** bagatelle, plaything **10** knickknack

trip 3 bob, err **4** flip, flub, fool, muff, pull, skip, slip, tour, trek, undo **5** caper, catch, dance, fluff, foray, jaunt, outdo, throw, upset **6** bungle, cruise, frolic, gambol, junket, outfox, outing, prance, safari, set off, slip up, voyage **7** blunder, commute, confuse, flounce, journey, misstep, release, scamper, stumble **8** activate, fall over, flounder, hoodwink, throw off **9** excursion **10** disconcert, expedition, pilgrimage **11** step lightly

Triple Crown 7 Belmont **9** Preakness **13** Kentucky Derby
winner: **5** Omaha **7** Assault **8** Affirmed, Citation **9** Sir Barton, Whirlaway **10** Count Fleet, Gallant Fox, War Admiral **11** Seattle Slew, Secretariat

Triple Sec *see* **9** Cointreau

Tripoli
capital of: **5** Libya

Triptolemos, Triptolemus
favorite of: **7** Demeter
inventor of: **4** plow **5** wheel
patron of: **11** agriculture

Triquetra *see* **6** Sicily

triskaidekaphobia
fear of: **14** number thirteen

Trismegistus *see* **5** Thoth

Tristan and Isolde
also: **16** Tristan und Isolde
opera by: **6** Wagner
character: **5** Melot **8** Brangane, Kurwenal **18** King Mark of Cornwall

triste 3 sad **10** melancholy

tristesse 6 sorrow **7** sadness **10** melancholy

Tristram
author: **22** Edwin Arlington Robinson
character in: **16** Arthurian romance

Tristram Shandy
author: **14** Laurence Sterne
character: **6** Dr Slop **8** Mr Yorick **10** Toby Shandy **11** Widow Wadman **12** Corporal Trim, Walter Shandy

trite 5 banal, silly, stale **6** common **7** cliched, humdrum, routine, shallow, worn-out **8** bromidic, everyday, ordinary, overdone, shopworn **9** frivolous, hackneyed **10** pedestrian, threadbare **11** commonplace, oft-repeated, stereotyped, unimportant **12** run-of-the-mill **13** platitudinous

Tritogeneia *see* **6** Athena

Triton
god of: **3** sea
father: **8** Poseidon
mother: **10** Amphitrite
shape: **6** merman
trumpet: **10** conch-shell

triumph 3 hit, win **4** best, coup **5** smash **6** subdue **7** conquer, mastery, prevail, succeed, success, surpass, victory **8** conquest, overcome, smash hit, vanquish **9** overwhelm **10** ascendancy, attainment, gain the day **11** achievement, superiority **12** come out on top, take the prize **14** accomplishment, get the better of

triumphal 5 proud **6** joyous **8** exultant **9** ascendant, rewarding **10** fulfilling, gratifying, successful, triumphant, victorious **11** spectacular

triumphant 6 elated, joyful **7** winning **8** exultant, jubilant **9** rejoicing **10** conquering, first-place, successful, victorious **11** celebrating **12** prizewinning

Triumph of Death, The
author: **17** Gabriele D'Annunzio

trivia
Latin: **8** minutiae

trivial 4 idle, puny, slim **5** banal, petty, small, trite **6** common, flimsy, little,

meager, paltry, slight, two-bit **7** foolish **8** beggarly, everyday, niggling, nugatory, ordinary, picayune, piddling, trifling **9** rinky-dink, worthless **10** incidental, pedestrian **11** commonplace, meaningless, unessential, unimportant **13** inappreciable, insignificant, of little value **14** inconsiderable **15** inconsequential

triviality 5 frill **6** trifle **9** frivolity **10** paltriness **12** nonessential, unimportance **14** insignificance **18** inconsequentiality

troglodyte 5 brute **6** hermit **9** barbarian **11** cave dweller

Troilus
father: **5** Priam
mother: **6** Hecuba

Troilus and Cressida
author: **18** William Shakespeare
character: **4** Ajax **5** Priam **6** Hector **7** Ulysses **8** Achilles, Diomedes, Pandarus **9** Agamemnon

Troilus and Criseyde
author: **15** Geoffrey Chaucer
character: **8** Diomedes, Pandarus

trois 5 three

Trojan Horse
made of: **4** wood
made by: **7** Epeiosk
contained in: **8** Odysseus, warriors

Trojans, The
also: **10** Les Troyens
opera by: **7** Berlioz
part one: **14** La Prise de Troie **16** The Capture of Troy
part two: **19** Les Troyens a Carthage **20** The Trojans in Carthage
character: **4** Dido **6** Aeneas, Hector

Trojan War
length: **8** ten years
combatants: **6** Greeks **7** Trojans
cause: **5** Helen, Paris **14** Apple of Discord

Trojan Women, The
author: **9** Euripides
character: **5** Helen **6** Hecuba **8** Astyanax, Menelaus, Odysseus, Polyxena **9** Agamemnon, Cassandra **10** Andromache, Talthybius **11** Neoptolemus

troll 3 imp **4** ogre **5** dwarf, gnome **6** goblin
origin: **12** Scandinavian
form: **12** supernatural
inhabits: **10** subterrain

trollop 4 doxy, slut **5** bitch, doxie, frump, hussy, trull, whore **6** floozy, harlot, wanton **7** baggage **8** slattern, strumpet **10** prostitute

Trollope, Anthony
author of: **9** Orley Farm, The Warden **15** The Way We Live Now **16** Barchester Towers, Framley Parsonage
character: **11** Phineas Finn

troop, troops 4 army, band, file, gang, herd, step, unit **5** bunch,

crowd, crush, drove, flock, horde, march, press, swarm, tramp **6** parade, stride, throng, trudge **7** cavalry, company, militia **8** infantry, soldiers, soldiery, troopers **9** aggregate, gathering **10** armed force, assemblage **11** cavalry unit, fighting men, police force **12** congregation **13** military force

trop 3 too **7** too many, too much

Trophonius
vocation: **7** builder
father: **7** Erginus
brother: **8** Agamedes
god of: **5** earth
killed: **8** Agamedes
became: **6** oracle
oracle called: **14** Zeus Trophonius

trophy 4 palm **5** award, booty, honor, kudos, medal, prize, relic, spoil **6** wreath **7** laurels, memento **8** citation, souvenir **9** loving cup **10** blue ribbon **11** testimonial

tropical 5 muggy **6** sultry, torrid **8** stifling **10** sweltering **11** hot and humid

troppo, non
music: **10** not too much

Tros
king of: **4** Troy
father: **12** Erichthonius
mother: **8** Astyoche
wife: **10** Callirrhoe
son: **4** Ilus **8** Ganymede **9** Assaracus

trot 3 jog **9** go briskly **11** step quickly, walk smartly

troth 8 fidelity **9** betrothal **10** affiancing, engagement **12** faithfulness

Trotwood, Betsey
character in: **16** David Copperfield
author: **7** Dickens

trouble 3 fix, row, vex, woe **4** blow, care, fuss, heed, mess, pain, pass, snag, work **5** agony, annoy, grief, harry, labor, pains, pinch, think, trial, upset, worry **6** affect, attend, badger, bother, burden, crisis, defect, dismay, effort, grieve, harass, misery, ordeal, pester, pickle, plague, pother, put out, scrape, sorrow, strain, strait, stress, strife, unrest **7** afflict, agitate, ailment, attempt, concern, depress, dilemma, discord, disturb, ferment, ill wind, oppress, perturb, reverse, setback, torment **8** disaster, disorder, disquiet, distress, disunity, exertion, hardship, hot water, quandary, rainy day, struggle, take time, unsettle, vexation **9** adversity, agitation, annoyance, attention, breakdown, challenge, commotion, deep water, hard times, suffering **10** affliction, convulsion, difficulty, disability, discommode, discompose, disconcert, discontent, dissension, irritation, make uneasy, misfortune, opposition **11** competition, disturbance, embroilment, instability, malfunction, predicament, tribulation **12** entanglement, exert oneself

13 inconvenience, make the effort **14** discontentment **15** dissatisfaction

troubled 5 upset **7** worried **8** bothered, careworn **9** disturbed, perturbed **10** distressed **12** heavyhearted

troublemaker 6 gossip **7** inciter **8** agitator, fomenter, provoker **9** miscreant **10** incendiary, instigator **11** rumormonger, scaremonger **12** rabble-rouser **13** mischief-maker, scandalmonger **16** agent provocateur

troublesome 4 hard **5** heavy, pesky, tough **6** cursed, knotty, taxing, thorny, tiring, trying, vexing **7** arduous, irksome, onerous, tedious **8** annoying, tiresome, unwieldy **9** demanding, difficult, fatiguing, harassing, herculean, laborious, wearisome, worrisome **10** bothersome, burdensome, cumbersome, disturbing, irritating, oppressive, tormenting, unpleasant **11** disobedient, distressing **12** disagreeable, exasperating, inconvenient, uncontrolled **13** undisciplined

troublesomeness 5 trial **10** difficulty **11** arduousness **13** inconvenience, laboriousness, vexatiousness, worrisomeness **14** bothersomeness

Trouble with Harry, The
director: **15** Alfred Hitchcock
cast: **11** Edmund Gwenn **12** John Forsythe **14** Mildred Dunnock, Mildred Natwick **15** Shirley MacLaine

troubling 6 vexing **8** worrying **9** worrisome **10** bothersome, disturbing, unsettling

trough 4 duct, moat, race, tray **5** canal, ditch, flume, gorge, gully **6** furrow, hollow, ravine, trench **7** channel **8** aqueduct **10** depression

trounce 4 beat, drub, lick, trim, whip **5** cream, skunk **6** humble **7** clobber **8** vanquish **9** overpower, overwhelm **10** take care of **11** carry the day **14** get the better of

troupe 4 band, cast **5** group, troop **6** actors **7** company, players **10** performers **11** road company

trouper 5 actor **7** actress **8** thespian **9** performer **13** touring player **15** repertory player

trousers 5 jeans, pants **6** chinos, slacks **7** drawers **8** breeches, britches, jodhpurs, knickers, overalls **9** dungarees **10** pantaloons **11** bellbottoms **12** pedal pushers **14** knickerbockers

Trovatore, Il
also: **13** The Troubadour
opera by: **5** Verdi
character: **7** Azucena, Leonora, Manrico **11** Count di Luna

Troy
abducted queen: **5** Helen
archaeologist: **6** Blegen **8** Dorpfeld **10** Schliemann
defender: **5** Eneas **6** Aeneas

Greek name: **5** Ilion
hero: **6** Hector
king: **5** Priam
Latin name: **5** Ilium
modern name: **9** Hissarlik
mountain: **3** Ida
neighboring city in NY: **6** Albany **10** Watervliet
river: **6** Hudson
city in: **7** Alabama, New York **8** Michigan
story: **5** Iliad **7** Odyssey
surrounding region: **5** Troad, Troas

Troy, Sergeant
character in: **22** Far From the Madding Crowd
author: **5** Hardy

truancy 3 cut **7** absence **11** absenteeism, nonpresence **12** playing hooky **13** nonappearance, nonattendance **14** cutting classes, skipping school

truant 4 gone **5** idler **6** absent, dodger, evader, loafer, no show **7** drifter, goof-off, missing, not here, shirker, slacker, vagrant **8** absentee, deserter, layabout **9** goldbrick **10** delinquent, malingerer, nonpresent, not present **11** boondoggler, hooky-player **12** nonattendant, playing hooky

truce 4 halt, lull, rest, stay, stop **5** break, pause **7** respite **9** armistice, cease-fire **12** interruption **14** breathing spell, discontinuance **23** suspension of hostilities

Trucial Oman, Trucial States see **18** United Arab Emirates

truck 3 rig, van **5** lorry **15** eighteen-wheeler
type: **5** panel **6** pickup **7** trailer **8** delivery

truckle 3 bow **4** fawn **5** court, defer, yield **6** grovel, pander, submit **7** flatter **8** bootlick, butter up, suck up to **9** shine up to **10** curry favor, take orders **11** apple-polish, fall all over **12** knuckle under **17** ingratiate oneself

truculence 8 defiance, ill humor **9** hostility, ill temper, pugnacity, surliness **10** fierceness **11** bellicosity **12** belligerence, churlishness **14** aggressiveness

truculent 4 rude, sour **5** cross, nasty, sulky, surly **6** fierce, touchy **7** defiant, hostile, peevish **8** churlish, insolent, petulant, snappish, snarling **9** bellicose **10** aggressive, ill-humored, ill-natured, pugnacious, ungracious **11** bad-tempered, belligerent, ill-tempered

Trudeau, Garry
creator/artist of: **10** Doonesbury

Trudeau Pierre
home: **6** Canada
office: **13** prime minister

trudge 4 drag, limp, plod **5** clump, march, tramp **6** hobble, lumber **7** shamble

true 4 even, firm, full, just, pure, real **5**

exact, legal, loyal, right, usual, valid **6** actual, lawful, normal, proper, steady, strict, trusty **7** correct, devoted, factual, genuine, literal, precise, regular, staunch, typical **8** absolute, accurate, bona fide, constant, faithful, official, positive, reliable, rightful, true-blue, truthful **9** authentic, simon-pure, steadfast **10** dependable, legitimate, unswerving, unwavering **11** trustworthy **14** unquestionable

true being 4 core, soul **6** nature, psyche, spirit **7** essence

True Grit
director: **13** Henry Hathaway
based on novel by: **13** Charles Portis
cast: **8** Kim Darby **9** John Wayne **11** Jeremy Slate **12** Glen Campbell, Robert Duvall **14** Strother Martin
Oscar for: **5** actor (Wayne)

Truffaut, Francois
director of: **11** Day for Night, Jules and Jim **19** Shoot the Piano Player, The Four Hundred Blows

truism 3 saw **5** adage, axiom **6** cliche, dictum, saying **9** platitude

truly 6 indeed, in fact, really, surely, verily **7** exactly, in truth, no doubt **8** actually, honestly, to be sure **9** assuredly, certainly, correctly, factually, genuinely, literally, precisely, sincerely **10** absolutely, accurately, definitely, faithfully, positively, truthfully, upon my word **11** beyond doubt, in actuality, indubitably, so help me God **12** indisputably **13** incontestably, unequivocally **14** beyond question, unquestionably **15** all kidding aside, without question

Truman, Harry S
nickname: **15** Give Em Hell Harry
presidential rank: **11** thirty-third
party: **10** Democratic
state represented: **8** Missouri
succeeded upon death of: **9** Roosevelt
defeated: **5** (Farrell) Dobbs, (Thomas Edmund) Dewey **6** (Claude A) Watson, (Norman) Thomas **7** (Henry Agard) Wallace **8** (Edward A) Teichert, (James Strom) Thurmond
vice president: **7** (Alben William) Barkley
cabinet:
  state: **6** (James Francis) Byrnes **7** (Dean Gooderham) Acheson **8** (George Catlett) Marshall **10** (Edward Reilly) Stettinius (Jr)
  treasury: **6** (Frederick Moore) Vinson, (John Wesley) Snyder **10** (Henry) Morgenthau (Jr)
  war: **6** (Kenneth Claiborne) Royall **7** (Henry Lewis) Stimson **9** (Robert Porter) Patterson
  defense: **6** (Robert Abercrombie) Lovett **7** (Louis Arthur) Johnson **8** (George Catlett) Marshall **9** (James Vincent) Forrestal

attorney general: 5 (Thomas Campbell) Clark **6** (Francis) Biddle **7** (James Howard) McGrath **9** (James Patrick) McGranery
navy: 9 (James Vincent) Forrestal
postmaster general: 6 (Frank Comerford) Walker **8** (Robert Emmet) Hannegan **9** (Jesse Monroe) Donaldson
interior: 4 (Julius Albert) Krug **5** (Harold LeClaire) Ickes **7** (Oscar Littleton) Chapman
agriculture: 7 (Charles Franklin) Brannan, (Claude Raymond) Wickard **8** (Clinton Presba) Anderson
commerce: 6 (Charles) Sawyer **7** (Henry Agard) Wallace **8** (William Averell) Harriman
labor: 5 (Maurice Joseph) Tobin **7** (Frances), Perkins (Wilson) **13** (Lewis Baxter) Schwellenbach
born: 2 MO **5** Lamar **8** Missouri
died: 2 MO **8** Missouri **10** Kansas City
buried: 2 MO **8** Missouri **12** Independence
education:
  law school: 21 Kansas City School of Law (did not graduate)
religion: 7 Baptist
interests: 5 piano **7** history
vacation spot: 2 FL **7** Florida, Key West
author: 14 Year of Decision **19** Years of Trial and Hope
political career: 8 US Senate **13** Vice President
  presiding judge of: 13 Jackson County
civilian career: 6 farmer
  owned: 9 men's store **12** haberdashery
military service: 5 major **9** World War I **15** MO National Guard **18** Army Reserve colonel
notable events of lifetime/term: 4 NATO **5** V-E Day **8** Fair Deal **9** Korean War **17** iron-curtain speech **20** assassination attempt **31** North Atlantic Treaty Organization
  act: 11 Taft-Hartley **12** Bretton-Woods
  airlift to: 6 Berlin
  conference: 7 Potsdam
  dropping of first: 5 A-bomb **8** atom bomb
  plan: 8 Marshall **9** Point Four
  signing of: 9 UN charter
  Treaty of: 12 Rio de Janeiro
  trial of: 9 Alger Hiss
father: 12 John Anderson
mother: 6 Martha (Ellen Young)
siblings: 8 Mary Jane **10** John Vivian
wife: 9 Elizabeth (Virginia Wallace)
  nickname: 4 Bess
children: 12 Mary Margaret
Trumbull, John
  born: 9 Lebanon CT

artwork: 21 The Battle of Bunker Hill **26** The Resignation of Washington **28** The Declaration of Independence **29** The Surrender of General Burgoyne **32** The Capture of the Hessians at Trenton **38** The Surrender of Lord Cornwallis at Yorktown **46** The Death of General Montgomery in the Attack of Quebec, The Death of General Warren at the Battle of Bunker Hill
trumpery 5 showy, trash **6** deceit, trashy, trivia **7** rubbish, twaddle, useless **8** frippery, nonsense, trifling **9** deception, worthless **11** nonsensical
trumpet 4 honk, horn **5** blare, bugle **6** cornet **7** clarion **8** proclaim **10** hearing aid
Trumpet of the Swan, The
  author: 7 E B White
trump up 4 fake **6** invent, make up **7** concoct, falsify **9** fabricate
truncate 3 bob, lop, nip **4** clip, crop, dock, snub, trim **5** prune **7** abridge, curtail, shorten **8** amputate, condense, cut short **10** abbreviate
truncheon 3 bat **4** club **5** baton, billy, stick **6** cudgel **8** bludgeon **9** billyclub
trunker 3 box, die **4** body, bole, dado, line, main **5** chief, pants, shaft, snout, stock, torso **6** coffer, engine, locker, shut up, thorax **7** baggage, close in
truss 3 tie **4** beam, bind, prop, stay **5** brace, hitch, shore, strap, tie up **6** bind up, fasten, girder, pinion, secure **7** confine, support **8** make fast **9** constrict, framework, stanchion **12** underpinning
trust 4 care, duty, hope **5** faith, hands **6** accept, assume, belief, charge, credit, expect, look to, rely on **7** believe, count on, custody, keeping, presume, swear by **8** credence, feel sure, reliance, sureness **9** certainty, certitude, count upon **10** anticipate, confidence, conviction, depend upon, obligation, protection **11** assuredness, contemplate, have faith in, safekeeping, subscribe to, take on faith, take stock in **12** guardianship **14** give credence to, responsibility, take for granted
trusted 6 trusty **8** reliable **9** unfailing **10** dependable **11** trustworthy
trustee 8 guardian **9** caretaker, custodian, protector
trusteeship 4 care **6** charge **7** custody **10** protection **11** safekeeping **12** guardianship
trusting 8 gullible, trustful **9** believing, credulous **12** unsuspicious
trustworthy 4 true **5** loyal **6** honest **7** ethical, trusted, upright **8** faithful, reliable, true-blue **9** honorable, steadfast **10** aboveboard, dependable, scrupulous **11** responsible **12** tried and true

13 incorruptible, unimpeachable **14** high-principled
trusty 7 trusted **8** reliable **9** unfailing **10** dependable **11** trustworthy
trusty companion 3 pal **5** buddy, crony **6** friend **8** intimate, sidekick **9** confidant **10** bosom buddy, confidante
truth 3 law **4** fact **5** facts **6** verity **7** reality **8** accuracy, fidelity, trueness, veracity **9** actuality, exactness, integrity **11** reliability **12** authenticity, faithfulness, truthfulness **15** proven principle, trustworthiness
  Russian: 6 Pravda
  also name of: 9 newspaper
  god of: 7 Mithras
truth conquers all things
  Latin: 18 vincit omnia veritas
truthful 4 open, true **5** exact, frank **6** candid, honest **7** artless, correct, factual, precise, sincere **8** accurate, faithful, reliable **9** authentic, guileless, veracious **10** aboveboard, meticulous, scrupulous **11** trustworthy, undeceitful, unvarnished **13** unadulterated **15** straightforward
truthfulness 6 candor **7** honesty **8** veracity
Truth or Consequences
  host: 10 Jack Bailey, Steve Dunne **12** Ralph Edwards
try 2 go **3** aim, use **4** risk, seek, shot, test, turn **5** crack, essay, fling, prove, trial, whack **6** effort, sample, strain, strive, tackle **7** adjudge, attempt, venture **8** endeavor **9** have a go at, partake of, undertake **10** adjudicate, deliberate, put to a test **11** opportunity **12** have a fling at, make an effort, take a crack at
trying 4 hard **5** pesky, tough **6** taxing, vexing **7** arduous, irksome, onerous, tedious **8** tiresome **9** difficult, fatiguing, harrowing, wearisome **10** bothersome, burdensome, exhausting, irritating **11** aggravating, distressing, troublesome **12** exasperating
tryout 4 test **5** trial **7** hearing **8** audition **10** experiment
try out 3 fry **6** render **7** compete **8** audition **9** give a test **11** performance
tryst 4 date **7** meeting, vis-a-vis **9** tete-a-tete **10** engagement, rendezvous **11** appointment, assignation
try the patience of 5 annoy **7** provoke **8** irritate **10** exasperate
try to equal 5 rival **7** compete, emulate
Tuatha De Danann 4 gods
  origin: 5 Irish
  mother: 4 Danu
tub 3 keg, kit, pot, tun, vat **4** bath, boat, butt, cask, ship, tank, tram, wash **5** barge, bathe, fatso, fatty, keeve, tramp **6** barrel, bucket, firkin, ore car, vessel **7** cistern, tankard **8**

cauldron, slow boat **9** container, freighter

tube 4 duct, hose, pipe **7** conduit **8** cylinder

tuber 3 anu, yam **4** beet, bulb, corm, eddo, root, taro **5** jalop, shoot **6** potato, turnip **8** rutabaga, swelling **11** enlargement

Tuchman, Barbara W
  author of: 14 A Distant Mirror, The First Salute **15** The Guns of August, The March of Folly **17** Practicing History

tuck 3 put **4** cram **5** pleat, shove, stick, stuff **6** enwrap, gather, insert, pucker, roll up, ruffle, shroud, swathe, thrust **7** crinkle, swaddle

tucker 3 fag **4** bush, poop, tire **5** weary **7** exhaust, fatigue

tuckered out 5 all in, tired, weary **6** bushed, done in, pooped **8** fatigued **9** exhausted, fagged out

Tudor
  dynasty of: 7 England
  rulers: 8 Henry VII **9** Henry VIII **8** Edward VI **5** Mary I **10** Elizabeth I

Tudor, Antony
  choreographer of: 11 Lilac Garden **12** Pillar of Fire

tuebor 11 I will defend

Tuei *see* **6** Isleta

Tuesday
  from: 3 Tiw
  heavenly body: 4 Mars
  French: 5 mardi
  Italian: 7 martedi
  Spanish: 6 martes
  German: 8 dienstag

tuft 4 wisp **5** batch, brush, bunch, clump, crest, plume, sheaf **6** bundle, tassel **7** cluster, topknot

tug 3 lug, tow **4** drag, draw, haul, jerk, pull, yank **6** wrench **7** wrestle

tulip 6 Tulipa
  varieties: 4 lady, star **5** globe **7** Turkish **9** butterfly, guinea-hen, waterlily **10** Sierra star **11** golden globe, purple globe **16** common late garden **17** common early garden

Tulkinghorn
  character in: 10 Bleak House
  author: 7 Dickens

Tullia
  father: 14 Servius Tullius
  husband: 7 Tarquin

Tullius *see* **14** Servius Tullius

Tulsa
  football team: 7 Outlaws

tumble 3 mix **4** dive, drop, fall, flip, roll, toss **5** whirl **6** bounce, jumble, plunge, stir up, topple **7** descend, shuffle, stumble **9** cartwheel **10** somersault

tumbledown 5 shaky **7** rickety, rundown **8** decaying, decrepit, unstable **9** crumbling, tottering **10** broken-down,

jerry-built, ramshackle **11** dilapidated, falling-down **14** disintegrating

tumbler 3 cog, dog **5** drier, glass, lever **6** goblet, vessel **7** acrobat, athlete, gymnast, juggler **12** somersaulter

tumbrel 4 cart **5** wagon **7** tipcart **8** dumpcart

tumbril
  French: 7 fourgon

tumid 5 puffy **6** turgid **7** bloated, bulging, dilated, pompous, swollen **8** enlarged, expanded, inflated **9** bombastic, distended, edematous, tumescent **11** protuberant **12** magniloquent **13** grandiloquent

tummy 3 gut **5** belly **6** paunch, tumtum **7** abdomen, midriff, stomach **9** bay window **11** breadbasket

tumor 3 wen **4** cyst, lump, wart **5** pride **6** cancer, growth **7** bombast, sarcoma **8** hematoma, neoplasm, swelling, tubercle **9** carcinoma, papilloma, pomposity **11** tumefaction

tumult 3 ado, din **6** bedlam, bustle, clamor, hubbub, racket, uproar **7** turmoil **8** disorder, upheaval **9** agitation, commotion, confusion **10** excitement, hullabaloo **11** disturbance, pandemonium

tumultuous 4 loud **5** noisy, rough, rowdy **6** stormy, unruly **7** chaotic, furious, lawless, raucous, riotous, violent **8** agitated, confused **9** clamorous, disturbed, turbulent **10** boisterous, disorderly, uproarious **11** tempestuous

tun 3 keg, tub, vat **4** butt, cast, drum **6** barrel **8** hogshead

tune 3 air **4** aria, line, song, step **5** adjust, ditty, motif, pitch, theme **6** accord, adjust, melody, number, strain, unison **7** concert, concord, harmony **9** agreement **10** conformity

tuneful 6 catchy, dulcet **7** lyrical, musical **9** melodious

tungsten
  chemical symbol: 1 W

tunic 4 robe **5** cloak **6** jacket, mantle, poncho, tabard **7** garment, surcoat

Tunica
  tribe: 10 Chitimacha

Tunis
  capital of: 7 Tunisia

Tunisia
  other name: 8 Carthage **9** Ifriqiyah
  capital/largest city: 5 Tunis
  others: 4 Beja, Sfax, Susa **5** Gabes, Gofsa **6** Djerba, Mateur, Nabeul, Remada, Sousse, Tozeur **7** Bizerte, Kairwan **8** Carthage, Jendouba, Kairouan, Monastir, Tebourba, Zaghouan **9** Grombalia **10** Ferryville
  empire: 8 Carthage **13** Barbary States
  school: 5 Tunis **16** Pasteur Institute
  measure: 3 saa **4** saah **5** cafiz **6** mettar **8** milerole
  monetary unit: 5 dinar **6** dollar **7**

millime
  weight: 3 saa **4** rotl **5** artal, ratel, uckia
  island: 6 Djerba, Galite
  lake: 6 Achkel, Djerid **7** Bizerte
  mountain: 5 Atlas **6** Mrhila **7** Tebessa **8** High Tell, Zaghouan **12** Northern Tell **17** Dorsale Tunisienne
  highest point: 6 Chambi
  river: 8 Medjerda, Mellegue
  sea: 13 Mediterranean
  physical feature:
    cape: 3 Bon **5** Blanc **8** Rasaddar
    desert: 6 Sahara
    gulf: 5 Gabes, Tunis **8** Hammamet
    oasis: 5 Gabes, Gafsa, Nefta **6** Djerba, Tozeur **9** El Oudiane **13** El Hamma Djerid
    plains: 5 Sahel
    salt lake: 11 Chott Djerid, Shatt Djerid
    valley: 8 Medjerda
    wind: 5 chile **6** chilli **7** sirocco
  people: 3 Jew **4** Arab **6** Berber
    artist: 5 Gorgi, Turki
    dynasty: 6 Hafsid **7** Fatimid **8** Aghlabid, Almohade **10** Husseinite
    leader: 6 Ben Ali **9** Bourguiba
  language: 6 Arabic, Berber, French
  religion: 5 Islam **7** Judaism **12** Christianity
  place:
    center of Tunis: 13 Place d'Afrique
    mosque: 5 Great **7** Zitouna
    museum: 5 Bardo, Kouba **6** Sousse
    palace: 14 Dar Ben Abdallah
    ruins: 8 Carthage
    street: 14 Habib Bourguiba
  feature:
    cap: 7 chechia
    clothing: 5 jebba **7** safasri **9** babbouche
    market: 4 souk
  food:
    dish: 7 mesfouf **8** couscous
    drink: 4 iban **5** legmi
    fruit: 12 deglet en nour

Tunney, Gene
  real name: 17 James Joseph Tunney
  nickname: 14 Fighting Marine
  sport: 6 boxing
  class: 11 heavyweight

Tuonela
  also: 6 Manala
  origin: 7 Finnish
  name of: 10 afterworld
  form: 6 island
  lacked: 3 sun **4** moon

Tupman
  character in: 14 Pickwick Papers
  author: 7 Dickens

tu quoque 7 thou too

Turandot
  opera by: 7 Puccini
  character: 3 Liu **4** Pang, Ping, Pong **5** Calaf, Timur **8** Turandot (Princess of China)

turbid 5 muddy, murky **6** cloudy,

opaque, roiled **7** clouded, unclear **8** agitated **9** disturbed, stirred up, unsettled

turbulence 4 fury **6** frenzy, hubbub, tumult, unrest, uproar **7** ferment, rioting, torrent, turmoil **8** disorder, violence **9** agitation, commotion **10** excitement, unruliness **11** disturbance

turbulent 5 rowdy **6** fierce, raging, stormy, unruly **7** chaotic, furious, riotous, violent **8** agitated, restless **9** clamorous, disturbed **10** blustering, boisterous, disorderly, tumultuous, uproarious **11** tempestuous

tureen 4 bowl, dish **9** casserole, container **10** receptacle

turf 3 sod **4** area, peat, plot, soil **5** divot, grass, haunt, sward, track **7** verdure **9** racetrack, territory **10** greensward

Turgenev, Ivan
　author of: 5 Smoke **9** First Love **10** Virgin Soil **14** Fathers and Sons **18** A Month in the Country **19** A Sportsman's Notebook, A Sportsman's Sketches, The Torrents of Spring

turgid 5 puffy, showy **6** florid, ornate **7** flowery, pompous, swollen **8** inflated, puffed up **9** bombastic, grandiose, overblown **10** hyperbolic

Turkey
　capital: 6 Angora, Ankara
　largest city: 8 Istanbul
　others: 4 Enos, Troy, Urfa **5** Adana, Bursa, Izmir, Konya, Maras, Siirt, Sivas **6** Aintab, Edessa, Edirne, Elaziz, Marash, Samsun, Smyrna **7** Antakya, Antioch, Erzurum, Kayseri, MMersin, Scutari, Trabzon, Uskudar **8** Stamboul **9** Byzantium, Eskisehir, Gaziantep **10** Adrianople **14** Constantinople
　school: 6 Aegean, Ankara **8** Istanbul
　division: 4 Pera, Sert **5** Siirt, Troad **6** Angora, Eyalet, Thrace **7** Anadolu, Beyoglu, Cilicia **8** Anatolia **9** Asia Minor, Kurdistan
　measure: 3 dra, oka, pik **4** draa, khat, kile, zira **5** berri, kileh, zirai **6** arshin, chinik, fortin, halebi **7** nocktat
　monetary unit: 4 lira, para **5** akcha, asper, kurus, pound, rebia **6** akcheh, zequin **7** aetilik, beshlik, piaster **8** medjidie
　weight: 3 oka, oke **4** aqui, dram, rotl **5** artal, cheke, kerat, obolu, ratel **6** batman, dirhem, kantar, maunch, miskal **7** drachma, quintal, yusdrum
　island: 6 Cyprus, Kibris
　lake: 3 Tuz, Van **7** Egridir **8** Beysehir
　mountain: 2 Ak **3** Ala **4** Alai, Dagh, Kara **5** Hasan, Hinis, Honaz, Murat, Murit **6** Ala Dag, Bingol, Bolgar, Pontic, Suphan, Taurus **7** Aladagh, Erciyas **8** Karacali **10** Kackar Dagi
　highest point: 6 Ararat
　river: 4 Aras, Kura **5** Araks, Dicle, Firat, Gediz, Goksu, Halys, Irmak, Kizil, Mesta, Murat, Sarus **6** Araxes, Ceyhan, Seihun, Seyhan, Seylan, Tigris **7** Kurucay, Muradsu, Orontes, Sakarya **8** Granicus, Macestus, Maeander, Menderes **9** Euphrates **13** Buyukmenderes
　sea: 4 Aral **5** Black **6** Aegean **7** Marmara **13** Mediterranean
　physical feature:
　　cape: 4 Baba, Ince **5** Bafra **6** Anamur, Helles, Hinzir **7** Karatas, Kerempe
　　gulf: 3 Cos **5** Izmir **7** Antalya
　　inlet: 10 Golden Horn
　　peninsula: 9 Anatolian, Gallipoli
　　plateau: 9 Anatolian
　　strait: 8 Bosporus **9** Bosphorus **11** Dardanelles
　people: 4 Arab, Kurd, Turk **6** Seljuk
　　king: 8 Mausolus
　　leader: 5 Inonu, Osman **6** Ecevit **7** Demirel **8** Menderes, Suleiman **12** Kemal Ataturk
　　poet: 5 Homer
　language: 6 Arabic **7** Kurdish, Turkish
　religion: 5 Islam **7** Judaism **12** Christianity **13** Greek Orthodox, Roman Catholic
　place:
　　bridge: 6 Galata
　　dam: 9 Gokcekaya
　　mosque: 4 Blue, Yeni **8** Selimiye **11** Hagia Sophia, Sultan Ahmed
　　museum: 7 Topkapi
　　ruins: 4 Troy **7** Ephesus **8** Pergamum
　　tomb: 12 Kemal Ataturk
　feature:
　　cap: 3 fez **6** calpac **7** calpack
　　clothing: 6 caftan, dolman, jelick **7** yashrak **8** charshaf, maharmah, shakseer
　　goat hair: 6 mohair
　　grill: 6 mangal
　　harem: 5 serai **8** seraglio
　　musical instrument: 5 canum, kanum **6** canoon, johnie, kussir, zither **8** crescent, jingling
　　pipe: 10 meerschaum
　food:
　　dish: 5 halva, pilaw **10** doner kebab, shish kebab
　　drink: 4 boza, raki **5** airan, pasha, rakee **6** mastic
　　pastry: 7 baklava
　　turkey: 4 hind

Turkic
　language family: 6 Altaic
　group: 5 Kazak, Nogai, Uigur, Uzbek, Yakut **7** Chuvash, Kirghiz **8** Turkoman **10** Karakalpak **11** Azerbaijani **14** Osmanli Turkish

Turkmenistan
　capital/largest city: 9 Ashkhabad
　head of state: 9 president
　government: 8 republic
　monetary unit: 5 ruble
　river: 8 Amu Darya
　sea: 7 Caspian
　physical feature: 13 Kara Kum Desert
　people: 7 Turkmen **10** Turkmenian
　language: 6 Turkic **10** West Turkic
　religion: 11 Sunni Muslim
　feature: 9 Altyn Depe

turmeric
　botanical name: 12 Curcuma longa
　also called: 7 tumeric **13** Crocus indicus, Indian saffron
　family: 6 ginger
　color: 6 yellow
　used as: 3 dye **6** amulet **8** cosmetic, medicine
　origin: 4 Asia **9** Caribbean, East India
　charm against: 5 ghost **10** tree spirit

turmoil 4 mess **5** chaos **6** tumult, uproar **7** ferment **8** disorder **9** agitation, commotion, confusion **10** convulsion **11** disturbance, pandemonium
　French: 14 bouleversement

turn 2 do, go **3** act, arc, lie, put **4** bend, coil, come, deed, flex, hang, look, loop, make, rest, ride, roll, send, shot, sour, spin, time, veer, walk, wing **5** alter, apply, crack, curve, drive, eject, fling, hinge, pivot, round, scare, shift, shock, spell, spoil, start, stint, swing, throw, twist, whack, wheel, whirl **6** action, become, chance, change, curdle, depend, direct, effort, fright, gyrate, invert, period, reside, rotate, sprain, stroll, swerve, swivel, wrench, zigzag **7** acidify, attempt, convert, deliver, execute, ferment, perform, reverse, revolve, service, winding **8** gyration, overturn, roll over, rotation, surprise **9** cause to go, deviation, discharge, transform **10** accomplish, alteration, revolution

turn a deaf ear to 6 ignore, slight **9** disregard

turn aside 5 avert **6** divert **7** deflect, deviate **8** turn away

turn away 5 avert **6** give up **8** alienate, estrange, send away **9** turn aside **12** turn one's back

turnback 4 fold, quit, tack **5** repel **6** defect, desert, return, revert **7** forsake, regress, relapse, repulse, retrace, retreat, reverse **9** backslide

turncoat 5 Judas **6** bolter **7** traitor **8** apostate, betrayer, defector, deserter, quisling, renegade **12** double-dealer

turn down 5 spurn **6** refuse, reject **14** lower the volume, refuse to accept

Turner, Joseph Mallord William
　born: 6 London **7** England
　artwork: 12 The Shipwreck, The Slave Ship, Tintern Abbey **17** Dawn After the Wreck **20** Dido Building Carthage **22** Venice S Giorgio Maggiore **24** The Sun of Venice Going to Sea **25** The Thames near Walton

Bridge, Ulysses Deriding Polyphemus **30** Burning of the Houses of Parliament **32** Snowstorm Hannibal Crossing the Alps **32** The Falls of the Rhine at Schaffhausen **34** The Bay of Baiae with Apollo and the Sibyl **37** Fighting Temeraire Tugged to her Last Berth **47** The Parting of Hero and Leander from the Greek of Musaeus **50** The Shipwreck Fishing Boats Endeavoring to Rescue the Crew

Turner, Kathleen
roles: **8** Body Heat **9** Serial Mom **12** Prizzi's Honor **13** The Real Blonde, War of the Roses **17** Romancing the Stone, The Jewel of the Nile **18** Peggy Sue Got Married

Turner, Lana
real name: **29** Julia Jean Mildred Frances Turner
nickname: **11** Sweater Girl
born: **9** Wallace ID
discovered at: **16** Schwab's Drugstore
husband: **9** Artie Shaw, Lex Barker **10** Bob Topping **12** Stephen Crane
roles: **7** Madame X **11** Peyton Place **15** By Love Possessed, Imitation of Life **26** The Postman Always Rings Twice

turning 4 bend **5** curve **7** bending, curving, winding **8** pivoting, rotating, spinning, twisting, whirling **9** revolving, swiveling

turnip 12 Brassica rapa
group: **8** Rapifera
varieties: **6** Indian **7** Italian, Swedish **8** rutabaga, seven-top

turn off 4 bore, exit **5** douse, leave, repel **6** revolt, sicken **7** disgust, repulse **8** alienate, turn away **9** switch off **10** deactivate

turn of phrase 5 idiom **8** locution, phrasing **10** expression **11** phraseology

Turn of the Screw, The
author: **10** Henry James
character: **5** Flora, Miles **7** Mr Quint **8** Mrs Grose **10** Miss Jessel **12** The Governess

turn on 5 start, tempt **6** allure, attack, entice, excite **7** actuate, attract **8** activate, energize, interest, switch on

turn one's stomach 6 revolt, sicken **7** disgust **8** nauseate

turnout 5 crowd **6** output, throng **8** assembly, audience **9** gathering **10** assemblage, production

turn out 4 garb, oust **5** array, dress, eject, end up, evict, exile, expel **6** appear, attend, attire, banish, clothe, evolve, fit out, invest, rig out, show up, unfold **7** cast out, come out, costume, develop, kick out **8** drive out, send away **9** switch off **11** come to light

turn over 4 flip **5** upset **6** bestow, ro-

tate **7** deliver **8** flipflop, give over, hand over, overturn **9** surrender **10** relinquish, somersault

turn pale 4 fade **6** blanch, whiten **7** lighten

turn tail 4 flee **7** retreat, run away **8** back away **12** beat a retreat

turn to account 7 exploit, utilize **8** profit by, put to use **9** make use of **12** capitalize on

turn topsy turvy 5 upset **7** capsize, confuse, tip over **8** flip-flop, overturn, put askew **10** disarrange, turn turtle **11** disorganize

turn turtle 5 upset **7** capsize, tip over **8** flip over, keel over, overturn, turn over **14** turn upside down

turn up 4 come **6** appear, arrive, crop up, drop in, emerge, loom up, show up **7** develop, surface **11** come to light

Turpentine State
nickname of: **13** North Carolina

turpitude 4 evil, vice **8** baseness, lewdness, vileness **9** depravity **10** corruption, debauchery, defilement, degeneracy, immorality, perversion, sinfulness, wickedness, wrongdoing **13** dissoluteness **14** licentiousness

turquoise 4 aqua **5** stone **7** mineral, sky-blue **10** aquamarine **12** greenish-blue, Prussian-blue
source: **12** United States

turret 5 tower **6** belfry, cupola, garret, gazebo, louver, terret **7** minaret, rotator, steeple **8** gunhouse, gunmount **9** belvedere, pepperbox **10** watchtower
tool: **5** lathe

turtle 3 box **4** musk, wood **6** slider **7** painted, reptile, snapper, spotted **8** slowpoke, terrapin, tortoise **10** turtledove **11** leatherback
dorsal shell: **8** carapace
nautical: **5** upset **6** pocket **7** capsize **8** overturn
order: **8** Chelonia
ventral shell: **8** plastron
young: **7** turtlet

Turveydrop
character in: **10** Bleak House
author: **7** Dickens

tussle 4 fray **5** brawl, fight, melee, scrap, set-to **6** battle, fracas **7** grapple, scuffle, wrestle **8** conflict, struggle **10** donnybrook, free-for-all **11** altercation

tussock 4 hair, tuft **5** brush, bunch, clump, grass, sedge **7** bulrush, cluster, thicket **8** feathers

tutelage 8 coaching, guidance, teaching, training, tutoring **9** direction, education, schooling **10** discipline **11** inculcation, instruction, supervision, trusteeship **12** guardianship **14** indoctrination

tutor 4 guru **5** coach, drill, teach **6** master, mentor, school **7** prepare,

teacher **8** instruct **10** instructor **11** give lessons

tutorial 5 class **8** didactic, edifying **11** educational, instructive **12** prescriptive

tutti
music: **3** all **18** all players together, all singers together

Tuvalu
other name: **13** Ellice Islands, Lagoon Islands
capital: **8** Funafuti
head of state: **14** British monarch **15** governor general
monetary unit: **4** cent **6** dollar
island: **3** Nui **6** Niutao **7** Nanumea, Vaitupu **8** Funafuti **9** Nanumanga, Niulakita, Nukufetau **10** Nukulaelae
highest point: **5** Nuwak
sea: **7** Pacific
people: **6** Samoan **10** Polynesian
leader: **5** Lauti
language: **6** Samoan **7** English **8** Tuvaluan **10** Polynesian
religion: **10** Protestant **12** Tuvalu Church

twaddle 3 rot **4** bosh, bunk **5** trash, tripe **6** babble, drivel, gabble, jabber, piffle **7** chatter, prattle, rubbish **8** claptrap, idle talk, nonsense, tommyrot **9** jabbering, silly talk **10** balderdash **16** stuff-and-nonsense

Twain, Mark
real name: **13** Samuel Clemens
author of: **9** Tom Sawyer **10** Roughing It **12** A Tramp Abroad, The Gilded Age **15** (Adventures of) Huckleberry Finn **18** The Innocents Abroad **20** Life on the Mississippi **21** The Mysterious Stranger, The Prince and the Pauper **29** The Man That Corrupted Hadleyburg **36** A Connecticut Yankee in King Arthur's Court **41** The Celebrated Jumping Frog of Calaveras County

twang 9 resonance, vibration **10** nasal sound **13** reverberation

Tweedledee
character in: **22** Through the Looking Glass
author: **7** Carroll

Tweedledum
character in: **22** Through the Looking Glass
author: **7** Carroll

tweet 4 peep **5** cheep, chirp **7** chirrup, chitter, twitter

Twelfth Night
author: **18** William Shakespeare
character: **5** Feste, Maria, Viola (Cesario) **6** Olivia, Orsino **7** Antonio **8** Malvolio **9** Sebastian **12** Sir Toby Belch **18** Sir Andrew Aguecheek

Twelve Angry Men
director: **11** Sidney Lumet
cast: **8** Ed Begley, Lee J Cobb **10** E G Marshall, Henry Fonda, Jack Warden

11 Jack Klugman, John Fiedler **12** Martin Balsam

Twelve O'Clock High
director: **9** Henry King
cast: **10** Dean Jagger **11** Gary Merrill, Gregory Peck, Hugh Marlowe **15** Millard Mitchell
Oscar for: **15** supporting actor (Jagger)

Twentieth Century
director: **11** Howard Hawks
based on play by: **8** Ben Hecht **16** Charles MacArthur
cast: **11** Roscoe Karns **13** Carole Lombard, John Barrymore **14** Walter Connolly

Twentieth Century, The
narrator: **14** Walter Cronkite
twenty-one *see* **9** blackjack

Twenty Questions
host: **10** Bill Slater, Jay Jackson
panelist: **11** Herb Polesie **12** Bobby McGuire **13** Johnnie McPhee **14** Dickie Harrison, Florence Rinard **15** Fred Van De Venter

Twenty Thousand Leagues Under the Sea
author: **10** Jules Verne
character: **7** Conseil, Ned Land **11** Captain Nemo **22** Professor Pierre Aronnax
submarine: **8** Nautilus

Twenty Years After
author: **14** Alexandre Dumas (pere)

Twice-Told Tales
author: **18** Nathaniel Hawthorne

Twightwee *see* **5** Miami

twilight 3 ebb, eve **4** dusk **6** sunset **7** decline, evening, sundown **8** eventide, gloaming, moonrise **9** half-light, last phase, nightfall **14** edge of darkness

Twilight of the Gods 8 Ragnarok
German: **15** Gotterdammerung

Twilight Zone, The
host: **10** Rod Serling

twin 4 dual, like **5** alike **6** double, paired **7** matched, twofold **9** duplicate, identical

Twin 6 Thomas

twine 4 coil, cord, rope, wind **5** braid, cable, plait, twist, weave **6** string, thread **7** binding, entwine **9** interlace **10** intertwine

twinge 4 pain, pang, stab **5** cramp, spasm, throb **6** stitch, tingle, twitch

twinkle 4 glow **5** blaze, flare, flash, gleam, shine **7** flicker, glimmer, glisten, shimmer, sparkle **11** scintillate

Twinkleton, Miss
character in: **22** The Mystery of Edwin Drood
author: **7** Dickens

Twins
constellation of: **6** Gemini

twirl 4 spin **5** pivot, twine, wheel, whirl **6** gyrate, rotate **7** revolve **9** pirouette

twist 3 arc, way **4** bend, coil, curl, idea, kink, knot, pull, roll, spin, turn, veer, wind, wrap, yank **5** curve, pivot, ravel, slant, snake, swing, twine, whirl, wrest **6** change, method, notion, rotate, spiral, sprain, swerve, swivel, system, tangle, wrench, zigzag **7** contort, distort, entwine, meander **8** approach, rotation, surprise **9** corkscrew, interlace, treatment **10** intertwine, involution **11** convolution, development

twisted 4 bent **6** warped **7** crooked, gnarled **8** deformed **9** contorted, distorted, misshapen

twisting 7 crooked, curving, turning **9** contorted, revolving, spiraling, swiveling

twist out of shape 4 warp **6** deform **7** contort, distort

twitch 3 tic **4** jerk **5** shake, spasm, throb **6** quaver, quiver, squirm, tremor, wiggle, writhe **7** tremble **8** paroxysm **10** convulsion

twitter 4 fuss, peep, stew **5** cheep, chirp, tizzy, tweet, whirl **6** bustle, flurry, pother, uproar, warble **7** chatter, chirrup, ferment, fluster, flutter **8** chirping **10** turbulence **11** chirruping

two-faced 5 false **7** devious **8** slippery **9** deceitful, deceptive, dishonest, insincere **10** perfidious **11** dissembling, double-faced, duplicitous, forktongued, treacherous, underhanded **12** dishonorable, disingenuous, falsehearted, hypocritical **13** doubledealing, untrustworthy

twofold 4 dual **6** double **7** two-part

Two Gentlemen of Verona, The
author: **18** William Shakespeare
character: **5** Julia **6** Silvia, Thurio **7** Proteus **9** Valentine **11** Duke of Milan

Two Lands, The *see* **5** Egypt

two of a kind 4 pair **5** twins **6** couple **7** doublet

two-part 4 dual, twin **6** double, paired **9** bipartite

twosome 3 duo **4** pair **5** brace **6** couple

2001: A Space Odyssey
author: **13** Arthur C Clarke
director: **14** Stanley Kubrick
character: **4** Dave **5** Steve
computer: **3** HAL
cast: **3** HAL **10** Keir Dullea **12** Gary Lockwood **16** William Sylvester
song: **20** Thus Spake Zarathustra (Richard Strauss)
sequel: **24** Two Thousand Ten: Odyssey Two

two-time 6 betray **10** be disloyal **11** double-cross **12** be unfaithful **13** be treacherous, play false with **14** break faith with

two-timing 5 false **6** tricky **7** perfidy **8** bad faith, betrayal, disloyal, trickery **9** deceiving, deception, duplicity, falseness, treachery **10** disloyalty, perfidious **11** double-cross, duplicitous, treacherous **13** breach of faith, double-dealing, faithlessness **14** doublecrossing

two-wheeler 4 bike **5** cycle **7** bicycle

Two Years Before the Mast
author: **18** Richard Henry Dana Jr

Tybalt
character in: **14** Romeo and Juliet
author: **11** Shakespeare

Tyche
origin: **5** Greek
goddess of: **7** fortune
corresponds to: **7** Fortuna

tycoon 4 boss **5** mogul, nabob **6** big gun, bigwig **7** big shot, magnate **8** big wheel **9** potentate **12** entrepreneur **13** industrialist **17** captain of industry

tyke 3 kid, tad, tot **5** child **6** shaver, squirt, wee one **9** little one

Tyler, John
presidential rank: **5** tenth
party: **4** Whig **20** Democratic-Republican
state represented: **2** VA **8** Virginia
defeated: **5** no-one
succeeded upon death of: **8** Harrison
vice president: **4** none
cabinet:
state: **6** (Abel Parker) Upshur **7** (Daniel) Webster, (John C) Calhoun
treasury: **4** (George Mortimer) Bibb **5** (Thomas) Ewing **7** (John Canfield) Spencer, (Walter) Forward
war: **4** (John) Bell **7** (John Canfield) Spencer, (William) Wilkins
attorney general: **6** (Hugh Swinton) Legare, (John) Nelson **10** (John Jordan) Crittenden
navy: **5** (John Young) Mason **6** (Abel Parker) Upshur, (George Edmund) Badger, (Thomas Walker) Gilmer
postmaster general: **7** (Francis) Granger **9** (Charles Anderson) Wickliffe
born: **2** VA **8** Greenway, Virginia **17** Charles City County
died/buried: **2** VA **8** Richmond, Virginia
education: **14** William and Mary
religion: **12** Episcopalian
vacation spot: **2** VA **7** Hampton **8** Virginia
political career: **8** US Senate **12** State Council **13** vice president **24** US House of Representatives
delegate to: **13** State Assembly
governor of: **8** Virginia

civilian career: 6 farmer, lawyer
military service: 19 War of Eighteen Twelve
notable events of lifetime/term:
  act: 6 Tariff (of 1842)
  annexation of: 5 Texas
  treaty: 16 Webster-Ashburton
father: 4 John
mother: 4 Mary (Marott Armistead)
siblings: 7 William **8** Wat Henry **10** Maria Henry **12** Anne Contesse **14** Christina Booth **15** Martha Jefferson **18** Elizabeth Armistead
wife: 5 Julia (Gardiner) **7** Letitia (Christian)
children: 4 John, Mary **5** Alice, Julia, Pearl **6** Robert **7** Lachlan, Letitia **8** Tazewell **9** Elizabeth **12** Anne Contesse, Lyon Gardiner **13** David Gardiner, John Alexander **16** Robert FitzWalter

Tyll Eulenspiegel *see* **16** Till Eulenspiegel

Tyndall, John
  field: 7 physics
  nationality: 5 Irish
  studied diffusion of: 5 light

Tyndareus
  wife: 4 Leda
  daughter: 6 Phoebe **8** Philonoe, Timandra **12** Clytemnestra

Tyndaridae *see* **15** Castor and Pollux

type 4 font, kind, race, sort **5** brand, class, genus, group, model, order, print **6** design, family, phylum, sample **7** pattern, species, variety **8** category, division, specimen, typeface **9** archetype, prototype **10** typography

type, movable
  invented by: 9 Gutenberg

Typee
  author: 14 Herman Melville
  character: 3 Tom (Melville) **4** Toby **6** Marnoo, Mehevi **7** Fayaway **8** Kory-Kory

typewriter

invented by: 5 Soule **6** Sholes **7** Glidden

Typhoeus
  form: 7 monster
  father: 8 Tartarus
  mother: 2 Ge
  number of heads: 10 one hundred

typhoon 4 gale, gust, wind **5** storm **7** cyclone, tempest, tornado, twister **9** hurricane, whirlwind

Typhoon
  author: 12 Joseph Conrad

typical 5 model, stock, usual **6** normal **7** average, regular **8** ordinary, orthodox, standard **9** exemplary, in keeping **10** individual, prototypal, true to type **11** distinctive, in character **12** conventional, to be expected **14** characteristic, representative

typify 5 sum up **6** embody **7** betoken, connote, pass for **8** instance, stand for **9** epitomize, exemplify, incarnate, personify, represent **10** illustrate **12** characterize

typography measure 2 em, en **4** pica **5** point

Tyr
  origin: 12 Scandinavian
  god of: 7 victory
  father: 4 Odin **5** Othin
  mother: 3 Fri **5** Frigg, Frija **6** Frigga
  killed by: 4 Garm

tyrannical 7 fascist **8** despotic **9** imperious **10** oppressive **11** dictatorial, domineering **13** authoritarian

tyrannize 7 oppress **8** domineer, overlord **10** slave drive

tyrannized 9 exploited, oppressed **11** downtrodden, subservient **12** harshly ruled

Tyrannosaurus
  type: 8 dinosaur, theropod
  location: 7 Montana **12** North America
  period: 10 Cretaceous

tyrannous 8 despotic **9** imperious **10**

iron-handed, oppressive, repressive, tyrannical

tyranny 7 cruelty, fascism **8** coercion, iron fist, iron hand, iron rule, severity **9** despotism, harshness **10** domination, oppression, repression **11** persecution **12** dictatorship **13** reign of terror **15** totalitarianism

tyrant 5 bully **6** despot **8** dictator, martinet **10** persecutor, taskmaster **11** cruel master, slave driver

Tyre
  king of: 5 Hiram

tyro 6 intern, novice, rookie **7** learner, recruit, trainee **8** beginner, initiate, neophyte, newcomer **9** greenhorn **10** apprentice, tenderfoot

Tyro
  father: 9 Salmoneus
  loved by: 8 Cretheus, Poseidon
  son: 5 Aeson **6** Neleus, Pelias
  grandson: 5 Jason **6** Nestor

Tyrrheus
  occupation: 8 shepherd

Tyson, Cicely
  born: 9 New York NY
  roles: 5 Roots **7** Sounder **33** The Autobiography of Miss Jane Pittman

Tyson, Mike
  original name: 7 Michael
  nickname: 8 Iron Mike
  born: 2 NY **8** Brooklyn **17** Bedford-Stuyvesant
  wife: 11 Robin Givens
  manager: 9 Cus D'Amato **10** Bill Cayton **11** Jimmy Jacobs
  trainer: 12 Angelo Dundee
  promoter: 7 Don King
  boxing title: 3 IBF, WBA, WBC **11** heavyweight
  defeated: 6 Holmes, Spinks, Thomas, Tillis, Tucker **7** Berbick
  defeated by: 7 Douglas (Buster)
  convicted of: 4 rape

tzimmes 4 fuss **6** uproar **10** hullabaloo
  literally: 4 stew **9** mixed dish

Ubangi-Shari *see* **22** Central African Republic

Ubermensch 8 superman

ubiquitous 7 allover **9** pervading, pervasive, prevalent, universal, worldwide **10** everywhere, widespread **11** everpresent, omnipresent **12** all-pervading

ubiquitously 10 everywhere **11** extensively

ubi supra 19 where mentioned above

Ucalegon
   counselor to: 5 Priam

Uccello, Paolo
   real name: 11 Paolo di Dono
   born: 5 Italy **8** Florence
   artwork: 8 The Flood **12** The Night Hunt **15** Sir John Hawkwood **18** The Rout (Battle) of San Romano **20** St George and the Dragon

Udall, Nicholas
   author of: 19 Ralph Roister Doister

Uganda
   capital/largest city: 7 Kampala
   others: 4 Arua, Gulu, Lira **5** Atiak, Jinja, Mbale, Mengo **6** Kasese, Kiboga, Kitgum, Masaka, Moroto, Pajule, Soroti, Tororo **7** Entebbe, Kachung, Kilembe, Mbarara, Mombasa **8** Kyenjojo **11** Port Masindi
   school: 8 Makerere
   division: 4 Toro **6** Ankole, Busoga **7** Buganda, Bunyoro
   monetary unit: 4 cent **8** shilling
   island: 4 Sese
   lake: 5 Kioga, Kyoga **6** Albert, Edward, George **8** Victoria
   mountain: 4 Oboa **5** Elgon **7** Virunga **9** Mufumbiro, Ruwenzori **18** Mountains of the Moon
   highest point: 10 Margherita
   river: 4 Aswa, Kafu **5** Pager **7** Katonga **9** White Nile **10** Albert Nile **12** Victoria Nile
   physical feature:
     falls: 5 Owens **8** Kabalega **9** Murchison
     plateau: 6 Ankole **11** East African
     valley: 9 Great Rift
   people: 4 Alur, Gisu, Soga, Teso **5** Ateso, Bantu, Chiga, Ganda, Langi, Lango, Nkole, Pygmy **6** Acholi, Ankole, Bagisu, Bakega, Basiga, Batoro **7** Baganda, Banyoro, Bunyoro, Hamitic, Lugbara, Nilotic, Sudanic **9** Nyoro-Toro **10** Banyankole,

Karamojong
   explorer: 5 Baker, Speke **7** Stanley
   king: 6 Mutesa, Mwanga **8** Kabarega
   leader: 5 Obote **6** Mutesa **7** Omukama **11** Idi Amin Dada
   language: 5 Ateso, Ganda **7** English, Luganda, Swahili
   religion: 5 Islam **7** animism **8** Anglican **10** Protestant **13** Roman Catholic
   place:
     airport: 7 Entebbe
     dam: 10 Owens Falls
     national park: 6 Kidepo **14** Murchison Falls, Queen Elizabeth
   feature:
     clothing: 7 busuuti
     council of chiefs: 6 lukiko
     dance group: 17 Heart Beat of Africa
     king: 6 kabaka
   food:
     drink: 6 waragi

ugliness 8 ill-favor **9** grossness **10** homeliness **11** hideousness, monstrosity **12** unseemliness **13** frightfulness, grotesqueness, monstrousness, repulsiveness, unsightliness **14** unpleasantness **16** unattractiveness

ugly 4 foul, mean, vile **5** nasty **6** homely, horrid, odious **7** hideous, hostile, ominous **8** dreadful, horrible, menacing, unseemly **9** abhorrent, dangerous, difficult, frightful, grotesque, monstrous, obnoxious, offensive, repellent, repugnant, repulsive, sickening, unsightly **10** abominable, disgusting

ugly as sin 7 hideous **9** frightful, grotesque, monstrous, repulsive

Ugly Duckling, The
   author: 21 Hans Christian Andersen

ukase 4 fiat **5** edict, order **6** decree, dictum, ruling **7** command, mandate, statute **9** directive, manifesto, ordinance **10** injunction **12** proclamation **13** pronouncement

Ukraine
   capital/largest city: 4 Kiev
   others: 4 Lviv (Lvov), **6** Odessa **7** Donetsk, Kharkov, Lugansk (Voroshilovgrad) **8** Mariupol (Zhdanov) **9** Krivoi Rog, Zaporozhe **14** Dnepropetrovsk
   head of state: 9 president
   government: 8 republic

   monetary unit: 6 grivna **10** karbovanet
   mountain: 7 Crimean **10** Carpathian
   river: 3 Bug **6** Donets **7** Dnieper
   sea: 5 Black
   people: 7 Russian **9** Ukrainian
   language: 9 Ukrainian
   religion: 17 Ukrainian Catholic, Ukrainian Orthodox
   feature: 25 Askaniya Nova Nature Reserve

Ulan Bator
   capital of: 8 Mongolia

ulcer 4 sore **6** canker

Uller
   also: 4 Ullr
   origin: 8 Teutonic
   god of: 12 winter sports
   stepfather: 4 Thor

Ullmann, Liv
   born: 5 Japan, Tokyo
   nationality: 9 Norwegian
   roles: 7 Persona **10** Face to Face **11** Forty Carats, Lost Horizon **12** The Emigrants **16** Cries and Whispers **19** Scenes from a Marriage

ulna
   bone of: 8 lower arm
   neighbor: 6 radius

ulterior 6 covert, hidden, secret **7** selfish **9** concealed **10** undivulged, unrevealed **11** self-serving, undisclosed, unexpressed **13** opportunistic

ultimate 3 end **4** acme, apex, last, peak **5** final **6** height, utmost **7** extreme, maximum, supreme **8** crowning, eventual, greatest, terminal **9** at the peak, high point, last straw, long-range, resulting **10** conclusive, definitive
   French: 7 dernier

Ultima Thule 12 far-off region **15** uttermost degree

Ultor
   epithet of: 7 Jupiter
   means: 7 avenger

ultra 7 extreme **9** excessive, extremist

ultramodern 8 advanced, brand-new **10** avant-garde, newfangled **13** in the vanguard, up-to-the-minute

ulu 5 knife
   used by: 11 Eskimo women

ululate 4 hoot, howl, wail **6** lament

Ulysses
   author: 10 James Joyce

character: 10 Molly Bloom **12** Blazes Boylan, Buck Mulligan, Leopold Bloom **14** Stephen Dedalus

Ulysses *see* **8** Odysseus

umber 5 brown **7** pigment **9** dark-brown **14** yellowish-brown

umbilicus 5 navel **11** belly button

umbrage 5 pique, shade **6** leaves, shadow **7** foliage, offense, outrage **10** resentment

umbrella 6 brolly **7** parasol **11** bumbershoot

Umbrellas of Cherbourg, The
director: 11 Jacques Demy
cast: 10 Anne Vernon **15** Nino Castelnuovo **16** Catharine Deneuve
score: 13 Michel Legrand

Umbrian
language family: 12 Indo-European
branch: 6 Italic

umpire 5 judge **7** arbiter, mediate, referee **8** mediator, moderate **9** arbitrate, go-between, moderator **10** adjudicate, arbitrator, negotiator **11** adjudicator, intercessor

umpteen 4 many, slew **5** loads (of)

Una
character in: 15 The Faerie Queene
author: 7 Spenser

unabbreviated 5 uncut **8** complete, undocked, unpruned **9** uncropped, unreduced, unsnipped, untrimmed **10** full-length, unabridged **11** uncondensed, uncurtailed, unshortened **12** uncompressed, unexpurgated

unable 5 unfit **6** cannot **8** helpless, impotent **9** incapable **10** inadequate, unequipped **11** incompetent, unqualified
to tell pitch: 8 tone deaf

unabridged 5 uncut **6** entire, intact **8** complete **10** full-length **11** uncondensed

unacceptable 8 below par, improper, unseemly, unworthy **9** deficient, out of line, unwelcome **10** disallowed, inadequate, unsuitable **11** displeasing, intolerable **12** inadmissible, not allowable, not up to snuff **13** insupportable **14** unsatisfactory **15** not up to standard

unacceptableness 8 disfavor, disgrace, ignominy **18** unsatisfactoriness

unaccommodating 4 rude **8** churlish **9** difficult, unhelpful **10** inflexible, intolerant, unyielding **11** disobliging **13** inconsiderate

unaccompanied 4 lone, solo **5** alone, apart **6** single, singly **8** isolated, lonesome, separate, solitary **9** a cappella, by oneself **10** unattended, unescorted **12** all by oneself **13** companionless

unaccountable 3 odd **4** free **5** clear, queer, weird **6** exempt, immune **7** bizarre, curious, excused, strange, unusual **8** baffling, innocent, peculiar **9** blameless, not liable, unheard-of

10 inculpable, intriguing, mysterious, surprising **11** astonishing, unexplained **12** inexplicable, unfathomable **13** extraordinary, not answerable **14** not responsible **16** incomprehensible

unaccustomed 3 new, odd **4** rare, wild **5** green, new to, novel, queer **6** quaint, unique, unused **7** amazing, bizarre, curious, foreign, not used, strange, ungiven, untried, unusual **8** original, peculiar, singular, uncommon **9** fantastic, startling, unheard-of **10** remarkable, surprising, unfamiliar, unversed in **11** astonishing, out-of-the-way, unpracticed **12** unacquainted, unhabituated, unimaginable **13** extraordinary, inexperienced **14** unfamiliar with **16** out of the ordinary

unacknowledged 9 anonymous **10** unanswered **11** disregarded **12** unidentified, unrecognized

unadorned 4 bald, bare **5** naked, plain, stark **6** simple **7** austere **11** undecorated **12** unornamented **13** unembellished **15** straightforward

unadulterated 4 pure, true **5** clear, uncut **7** genuine **9** unalloyed, untainted **14** untampered-with

unadventurous 5 chary, timid **7** careful **8** cautious, hesitant **11** circumspect

unadvisable 5 silly **6** stupid, unwise **8** unseemly **9** imprudent **11** inadvisable, inexpedient, injudicious, undesirable **15** disadvantageous

unaesthetic 9 tasteless **10** inartistic **11** insensitive **16** undiscriminating

unaffected 4 open **5** frank, naive, plain **6** candid, direct, honest, simple **7** genuine, natural, sincere, unmoved **8** innocent **9** childlike, guileless, ingenuous, unfeeling, unstirred, untouched, unworldly, wholesome **10** impervious, unbothered, unreserved **11** indifferent, insensitive, openhearted, plain-spoken, unconcerned, undesigning, undisturbed **12** unresponsive **13** unsympathetic **15** straightforward, unsophisticated

unaffectedness 4 ease **11** naturalness **12** unconstraint

unafraid 4 bold **5** brave **6** daring, heroic, plucky **7** valiant **8** fearless, intrepid, stalwart, valorous **9** audacious, daredevil, dauntless **10** courageous **11** indomitable, lionhearted, venturesome **12** stouthearted **13** adventuresome

unaggressive 3 shy **4** meek **5** timid **7** passive **8** peaceful, timorous **9** peaceable, shrinking **11** unambitious **14** unenterprising

unagitated 4 calm **6** gentle, placid, serene **8** composed, tranquil **9** collected, unexcited, unruffled **10** untroubled **11** undisturbed, unperturbed **13** self-possessed

unalloyed 4 pure **7** unmixed **11** unqualified **13** unadulterated

unalterable 5 fixed, rigid **6** stable **8** constant **9** immutable, indelible, obstinate, permanent, perennial **10** inflexible, persistent **11** irrevocable **12** indissoluble, unchangeable **13** irretrievable

unambitious 4 easy, lazy **6** humble, modest, simple **8** slothful **10** unaspiring **12** unaggressive **14** unenterprising

unamiable 4 sour **5** cross, surly, testy **6** sullen **7** grouchy, hostile, peevish **8** churlish **9** irascible **10** ill-humored, unfriendly, unpleasant, unsociable **11** bad-tempered, uncongenial **12** disagreeable

unamorous 4 cold, cool **6** frigid **8** unloving **11** passionless

unanimated 4 dull, flat, limp **5** inert, vapid **7** insipid **8** lifeless **10** insentient **11** unconscious

unanimity 6 accord **7** concord, harmony **9** agreement, consensus **11** concordance, concurrence **17** meeting of the minds

unanimous 6 allied, united **9** accordant, consonant, of one mind **10** harmonious, like-minded

unannounced 6 secret, sudden **8** surprise, withheld **10** suppressed, unheralded **11** undisclosed, unlooked for, unpublished **12** unadvertised **13** unanticipated

unanticipated 6 sudden **8** surprise **10** unexpected, unforeseen, unheralded **11** unannounced, unlooked-for, unpredicted

unappealing 10 disgusting, uninviting, unpleasant **11** displeasing **12** disagreeable, unappetizing, unattractive

unappetizing 6 horrid **7** insipid **10** bad-tasting, disgusting, uninviting **11** unpalatable **12** disagreeable

unapproachable 4 cold, cool **5** aloof **6** remote, unique **7** austere, awesome, distant, supreme **8** foremost, peerless, superior **9** matchless, nonpareil, unequaled, unrivaled **10** forbidding, inimitable, preeminent **11** beyond reach, stand-offish, unreachable **12** inaccessible, incomparable, intimidating, second to none, unattainable, unparalleled **13** beyond compare

unasked 6 wanton **8** unbidden, unsought, unwanted **9** uninvited, unwelcome **10** gratuitous **11** uncalled-for, undesirable, unrequested, unsolicited

unassertive 3 shy **5** timid **6** humble, modest **7** bashful **8** sheepish **9** diffident, shrinking

unassertiveness 7 modesty, shyness **8** docility, timidity **9** timidness **10** diffidence, humbleness **11** bashfulness **12** sheepishness

unassuming 5 muted, plain **6** homely, modest, simple **7** natural **9** easygoing

11 unassertive, unobtrusive **13** unpretentious **14** unostentatious

unattached 5 apart, split **6** single **8** detached, separate **9** separated **11** unconnected **12** disconnected

unattractive 4 dull, ugly **5** plain **6** homely **8** frumpish **11** unappealing, undesirable **12** unappetizing

unauthentic 4 fake, mock, sham **5** bogus, false, phony **6** untrue **7** dubious **8** doubtful **9** imitation, synthetic **10** fraudulent **11** counterfeit **12** questionable

unauthenticated 8 disputed **10** apocryphal, unverified **15** unsubstantiated

unauthorized 6 banned, covert **7** furtive **8** outlawed, unlawful **9** concealed, unallowed, underhand **10** prohibited, unapproved, unofficial **11** clandestine, uncertified, unpermitted, unwarranted **12** unaccredited, unsanctioned **13** under-the-table

unavailable 5 taken **6** scarce **7** lacking, married **9** not at hand **10** nonpresent **11** nonexistent

unavailing 4 idle, vain, weak **5** empty, inept **6** futile, no good **7** invalid, useless **8** bootless, impotent **9** fruitless, worthless **11** ineffective, ineffectual **12** unproductive, unsuccessful

unavoidable 4 sure **5** fated, fixed **7** certain **9** necessary, requisite **10** compulsory, imperative, inevitable, obligatory **11** inescapable **13** unpreventable **14** uncontrollable

unaware 8 heedless, ignorant, unwarned **9** in the dark, unalerted, unknowing, unmindful **10** unapprised **11** incognizant, unconscious **12** off one's guard, unacquainted, unsuspecting **13** unenlightened

unawares 8 abruptly, by chance, suddenly **9** by mistake **10** by accident, by surprise, mistakenly **11** unknowingly, unwittingly **12** accidentally, out of nowhere, unexpectedly, unthinkingly **13** inadvertently, involuntarily, unconsciously **14** without warning **15** unintentionally **16** like a thunderbolt **20** like a bolt from the blue, like a thief in the night

unbalanced 3 mad **4** daft, loco **5** batty, nutty, wacky **6** crazed, uneven, warped **7** bonkers, cracked, leaning, unequal, unglued, unsound **8** demented, deranged, lopsided, unhinged, unpoised, unstable, unsteady **9** disturbed, illogical, psychotic, unsettled **10** irrational, unadjusted **11** not all there **12** psychopathic

unbearable 11 intolerable, unendurable, unthinkable **12** inadmissible, insufferable, unacceptable **13** insupportable

unbecoming 4 ugly **6** homely, vulgar **8** improper, unfitted, unseemly,

unsuited **9** offensive, tasteless, unsightly **10** indecorous, unsuitable **11** unappealing, unbefitting **12** unattractive **13** inappropriate

unbelief 5 doubt **7** dubiety **9** disbelief **10** skepticism **11** incredulity **12** doubtfulness

unbelievable 5 false **6** absurd, insane **7** amazing, asinine, idiotic **10** astounding, farfetched, incredible, irrational, remarkable, ridiculous **11** astonishing **12** preposterous, unimaginable, unreasonable **13** hard to swallow

unbeliever 7 atheist, heathen infidel, skeptic **8** apostate **10** godless one **11** disbeliever, nonbeliever

unbelieving 7 dubious **8** doubting **9** quizzical, skeptical **10** suspicious **11** distrustful, incredulous, questioning, unconvinced **12** disbelieving, nonbelieving

unbend 5 relax **6** relent, unflex **10** straighten **12** straighten up **13** straighten out

unbending 4 firm **5** rigid, stiff, tough **6** severe, strict **8** stubborn **9** obstinate **10** inflexible, stone-faced, unyielding **11** hard as nails **14** uncompromising

unbent 5 erect **7** relaxed, unbowed, upright, yielded **8** relented, straight, uncurved, unflexed **9** unstooped **12** straightened

unbiased 4 fair, just **7** liberal, neutral **8** detached, tolerant **9** impartial, unbigoted **10** fair-minded, open-minded, undogmatic **11** broad-minded **12** uninfluenced, unprejudiced **13** disinterested, dispassionate

unbigoted 8 tolerant, unbiased **10** open-minded **11** broad-minded **12** unprejudiced

unbind 4 free, undo **5** loose, untie **6** detach, loosen, ungird **7** deliver, release, undress **8** let loose, unfasten

unblamable 5 clear **8** innocent **9** blameless, guiltless, not guilty **10** inculpable, not at fault **14** not responsible

unblemished 4 pure **7** perfect **8** flawless, spotless, unmarred, unsoiled **9** unsullied **10** immaculate, unvitiated **11** white as snow **13** unadulterated **14** uncontaminated **15** clean as a whistle

unblock 4 free, open **5** unbar, unjam **6** unclog, unstop

unborn 5 fetal, later **6** coming, future, to come **7** in utero **9** embryonic **10** subsequent, succeeding **11** prospective

unbosom oneself 7 confess, confide, lay bare **15** unburden oneself

unbound 4 free **5** freed, loose **6** loosed, untied **8** detached, let loose,

loosened, released **10** unconfined, unfastened **12** unrestrained

unbounded 8 absolute **9** boundless, unbridled, unlimited **12** uncontrolled, unrestrained, unrestricted **13** unconditional, unconstrained

unbreakable 5 tough **6** strong

unbroken 5 whole **6** entire, intact **7** endless **8** complete **9** ceaseless, continual, incessant, uncracked, undivided, unsmashed **10** continuous, sequential, successive, unruptured **11** consecutive, progressive, unremitting, unshattered **12** undiminished **13** uninterrupted

unbuckle 4 undo **6** loosen **7** release, unhitch, unstrap **8** uncouple, unfasten

unburden 4 free **6** reveal **7** confess, confide, relieve, unbosom **8** disclose **9** disburden **10** unencumber **11** disencumber **15** get off one's chest **18** get out of one's system

unbusinesslike 6 casual, sloppy **8** informal **11** impractical, inefficient

uncalculated 9 unplanned **10** accidental, unintended **11** inadvertent **14** unpremeditated

uncalled-for 6 wanton **7** unasked **8** needless, unneeded, unsought, unwanted **9** redundant, uninvited **10** gratuitous, unprompted **11** unjustified, unnecessary, unsolicited **12** nonessential **14** supererogatory

uncanny 5 eerie, weird **6** spooky **7** curious, strange **8** inspired **9** fantastic, intuitive, marvelous, unearthly, unheard-of, unnatural **10** incredible, mysterious, prodigious, remarkable, unexampled **11** astonishing, exceptional **12** unbelievable, unimaginable **13** extraordinary, uncomfortable

uncanonical 12 unauthorized, unscriptural

Uncas
 character in: 20 The Last of the Mohicans
 author: 6 Cooper

unceasing 7 endless, eternal **8** constant **9** continual, incessant, perpetual, sustained **10** continuous, persistent, without end

uncelebrated 6 unsung **7** obscure, unknown **9** anonymous **14** uncommemorated

unceremonious 4 curt, rude **5** hasty, rough **6** abrupt **7** brusque **8** informal **11** precipitate

uncertain 4 hazy **6** fitful, unsure **7** dubious, erratic, not sure, obscure, unclear **8** doubtful, hesitant, nebulous, not fixed, variable, wavering **9** debatable, undecided, unsettled **10** disputable, indefinite, indistinct, in question, irresolute, unresolved, up in the air **11** conjectural, fluctuating, not definite, speculative, unconfirmed, vacillating

12 not confident, questionable, undetermined **13** indeterminate, unpredictable

uncertainty 4 odds, risk **5** doubt **6** chance, gamble **8** quandary **9** ambiguity, confusion, hesitancy, vagueness **10** hesitation, indecision, perplexity, unsureness **11** ambivalence, vacillation **12** equivocation, irresolution, shilly-shally **14** indefiniteness

unchain 4 free **7** release, set free **8** liberate, unfetter **9** unshackle

unchangeable 5 rigid **6** stable **7** uniform **8** stubborn **9** immutable, obstinate, permanent **10** inflexible, invariable **11** unalterable **12** intransigent

unchanging 4 fast, firm **5** fixed **6** stable, static **7** abiding, durable, lasting **8** constant **9** immutable, permanent, steadfast **10** monotonous **11** everlasting **12** indissoluble

unchaperoned 10 unattended, unescorted **12** unsupervised **13** unaccompanied

uncharacteristic 8 atypical **12** out of keeping **16** unrepresentative

uncharitable 5 tight **6** stingy, unkind **7** miserly **9** illiberal, niggardly, unfeeling **10** unfriendly, ungenerous, ungracious **11** closefisted, insensitive, tightfisted **12** parsimonious **13** unsympathetic **15** uncompassionate

unchaste 4 lewd **5** loose **6** erotic, impure **7** corrupt, immoral **8** immodest **9** abandoned, debauched **10** dishonored

unchecked 4 free **5** loose **6** unruly **7** liberal, rampant **8** reinless, unreined **9** out of hand, unbridled, unmuzzled **10** unhindered **12** out of control, unrestrained, unsuppressed

uncial 6 script
 form: 5 large, round
 used in: 5 Greek, Latin

unciform 10 hook-shaped

uncivil 4 curt, rude **5** blunt, surly **6** abrupt, gauche **7** boorish, brusque **8** impolite **10** ungracious **11** ill-mannered **12** disagreeable, discourteous

uncivilized 4 rude **6** savage, vulgar **7** boorish, brutish, ill-bred, uncouth, untamed **8** barbaric, churlish **9** barbarous, obnoxious, ungenteel **10** uncultured, unpolished **12** uncultivated

unclad 4 bare, nude **5** naked **7** exposed, unrobed **8** disrobed, in the raw, starkers, stripped **9** in the nude, unclothed, uncovered, undressed **10** stark-naked **15** in the altogether

unclean 4 evil, foul, tref, vile **5** dirty, dusty, grimy, messy, muddy, sooty **6** filthy, impure, soiled **7** defiled, immoral, obscene, smutted, stained **8** polluted, unchaste **9** blemished **10** besmirched

unclear 3 dim **4** hazy **5** blear, faint, foggy, fuzzy, misty, vague **6** bleary, cloudy, vapory **7** clouded, obscure, shadowy **8** shrouded, vaporous **9** ambiguous, uncertain **10** indefinite, indistinct

Uncle Remus
 author: 18 Joel Chandler Harris
Uncle Sam
 personification of: 7 America
Uncle Tom's Cabin
 author: 19 Harriet Beecher Stowe
 character: 5 Eliza, Topsy **10** Eva St Clare **11** Simon Legree
Uncle Vanya
 author: 12 Anton Chekhov
 character: 6 Marina **12** Mihail Astrov **13** Ivan Voynitsky (Uncle Vanya) **14** Marya Voynitsky **15** Sonya Andreyevna **16** Yelena Andreyevna **19** Alexandr Serebryakov

unclose 4 open **6** reveal, unclog, unfold, unshut, unstop, unwrap **7** unblock
 poetic: 3 ope

unclothed 4 bare, nude **5** naked **6** unclad **7** exposed, unrobed **8** stripped **9** in the nude, uncovered, undressed

unclouded 5 clear, light, sunny **6** bright, serene **10** unobscured

uncollected 4 owed **5** owing, upset **6** shaken **8** agitated, troubled **9** disturbed, perturbed **11** discomposed, outstanding

uncolored 4 bald, bare, true **5** plain, stark **6** simple **9** unadorned **11** unvarnished **12** unelaborated **13** unembellished **15** straightforward

uncombed 5 messy **6** blowsy, frowzy, matted, mussed, untidy **7** ruffled, rumpled, snarled, tangled, tousled, unkempt **11** disarranged

uncomfortable 4 edgy **5** tense, upset **6** on edge, uneasy **7** awkward, keyed up, nervous, painful **8** confused, strained, troubled **9** ill at ease **10** bothersome, disquieted, irritating, out of place **11** discomfit, discomposed, distressful **13** on tenterhooks

uncommitted 9 unpledged **11** undedicated

uncommon 4 rare **5** novel **6** scarce, unique **7** bizarre, curious, notable, supreme, unusual **8** peculiar, peerless, superior **9** matchless, unmatched **10** infrequent, remarkable, unexcelled, unfamiliar **11** exceptional, outstanding, superlative **12** incomparable, unparalleled **13** extraordinary **14** unconventional **15** once in a lifetime **16** few and far between

uncommunicative 3 mum, shy **4** dumb, mute **5** quiet **6** silent **8** reserved, reticent, retiring, taciturn **9** secretive, withdrawn **10** speechless, tongue-tied, unsociable **11** untalkative **12** close-mouthed, inexpressive

uncomplicated 4 easy **5** clear, plain **6** simple **10** uninvolved

uncomplimentary 8 critical, derisive, negative **9** insulting **10** unadmiring **11** disparaging **12** disapproving, unflattering

uncompromising 4 firm **5** rigid, stiff **6** strict **8** exacting, hardline, obdurate **9** immovable, unbending, unvarying **10** inexorable, inflexible, scrupulous, unyielding **11** unrelenting

unconcealed 4 bald, bare, open **5** overt **6** in view **7** exposed, in sight, obvious, visible **8** apparent, manifest, revealed **9** uncovered **11** discernible, perceivable, perceptible **12** in plain sight, out in the open

unconcentrated 4 weak **7** diffuse, diluted, thinned **9** dispersed, scattered, spread out **11** watered down

unconcern 10 dispassion **11** insouciance, nonchalance **12** indifference

unconcerned 4 cold **5** aloof **6** serene **7** distant, unaware, unmoved **8** composed, uncaring **9** apathetic, oblivious, unfeeling, unmindful **10** impervious, nonchalant, uninvolved, untroubled **11** indifferent, insensitive, passionless, unperturbed **12** unresponsive **13** unsympathetic

unconditional 5 utter **6** entire **8** absolute, complete, outright **9** downright, unlimited **10** conclusive **11** categorical, unqualified **12** unrestricted **13** thoroughgoing

unconfident 3 shy **5** timid **7** bashful **8** reticent, retiring, timorous **9** diffident, shrinking, uncertain

unconfirmed 7 dubious **8** unproved **10** unapproved, unverified **11** unvalidated **12** questionable **14** uncorroborated **15** unsubstantiated

unconformity 7 anomaly **9** deviation **10** aberration, divergence **11** abnormality, peculiarity **12** eccentricity, idiosyncrasy, irregularity **13** nonconformity

uncongenial 9 ill-suited, unamiable **10** dissimilar, unfriendly, unpleasant **12** disagreeable, incompatible **13** unsympathetic

unconnected 7 severed **8** detached, discrete, separate **9** uncoupled, unhitched, unrelated **12** disconnected

unconquerable 6 innate **9** ingrained **10** inveterate, invincible, unbeatable **12** impenetrable, invulnerable, undefeatable **14** insurmountable, unvanquishable

unconscionable 7 extreme **9** excessive **10** immoderate, inordinate, outrageous **11** inexcusable, unjustified, unwarranted **12** indefensible, preposterous, unforgivable, unpardonable, unreasonable **13** unjustifiable

unconscious 3 out **6** latent **7** in a

coma, out cold **8** comatose, in a faint **9** insensate, senseless, unknowing, unmindful **10** suppressed, unrealized **11** incognizant **12** unsuspecting **14** dead to the world

unconstitutional 7 illegal **8** unlawful **12** unauthorized

unconstrained 4 bold, easy **7** natural, relaxed **8** unforced **9** abandoned **10** unaffected **11** spontaneous, uninhibited
French: **6** degage

unconstraint 4 ease **7** abandon **8** boldness, free will, openness **9** frankness **11** naturalness, spontaneity

uncontrollable 6 unruly **7** wayward **12** ungovernable, unmanageable

uncontrolled 4 free, wild **8** absolute **9** abandoned, unlimited **10** ungoverned **12** unrestrained

unconventional 3 odd **4** rare **5** crazy, kinky, nutty, queer, wacky, weird **6** far-out, quaint, unique **7** bizarre, curious, offbeat, strange, unusual **8** aberrant, atypical, bohemian, freakish, original, peculiar, singular, uncommon **9** different, eccentric, fantastic, irregular **10** newfangled, outlandish, unorthodox **11** exceptional **12** unaccustomed **13** extraordinary, idiosyncratic, nonconforming, nonconformist **15** individualistic

unconvinced 7 dubious **8** doubtful **9** skeptical, uncertain, unsettled

unconvincing 5 false, fishy **7** dubious, suspect **10** suspicious **11** implausible **12** questionable, unbelievable

uncooked
French: **9** au naturel

uncooperative 6 ornery **7** selfish **8** perverse, stubborn **9** difficult, unhelpful, unwilling **11** intractable **12** intransigent

uncoordinated 6 clumsy **7** awkward **8** ungainly **9** graceless

uncouple 4 undo **6** detach, loosen, unhook **7** release, unhitch **8** unbuckle

uncoupled 8 detached, loosened **9** separated, unhitched **10** disengaged **11** unconnected **12** disconnected

uncourageous 5 timid **8** cowardly, timorous **9** dastardly, shrinking **13** pusillanimous

uncourtly 7 ill-bred, uncivil, uncouth **9** ungallant **10** ill- behaved, ungracious, unmannerly **11** uncourteous **12** discourteous **13** ungentlemanly

uncouth 4 rude **5** crass, crude, gross, rough **6** callow, coarse **7** boorish, brutish, ill-bred, loutish, uncivil **8** barbaric, churlish, impolite **9** unrefined **10** indelicate, uncultured, unmannerly **11** ill-mannered, uncivilized **12** uncultivated

uncover 4 bare, undo **5** dig up, strip **6** denude, dig out, expose, reveal,

unmask, unveil, unwrap **7** disrobe, lay bare, uncloak, undrape, undress, unearth **8** disclose, unclothe **9** make known, unsheathe **11** make visible **12** bring to light

uncovered 4 bare **5** bared, dug up, naked **7** exposed, noticed **8** detected, revealed **9** disclosed, made known **10** discovered **13** brought to view **14** brought to light

uncovering 8 exposure **9** divulging, unmasking **10** disclosure, divulgence, laying open, revelation **15** bringing to light **20** bringing out in the open

uncritical 4 dull, dumb **6** casual, obtuse, stupid **7** inexact, offhand, shallow **8** careless, ignorant, slipshod **9** imprecise, untutored **10** inaccurate, uneducated, unschooled, unthinking **11** perfunctory, superficial **12** unreflecting **16** undiscriminating

unctuous 4 oily, smug **6** smarmy **7** fawning, honeyed, servile **8** slippery, too suave **9** pietistic, too smooth **10** flattering, obsequious **11** sycophantic **12** honey- tongued, ingratiating **13** sanctimonious, self-righteous

uncultivated 3 raw **4** wild **7** uncouth **8** unfarmed, unplowed, untilled **9** unrefined **10** unimproved **11** undeveloped

uncultivated land
god of: **8** Silvanus, Sylvanus

uncultured 5 crass **6** coarse, common, vulgar **7** low-bred **9** inelegant, unrefined **10** unpolished **12** uncultivated

uncustomary 4 rare **6** unique **7** amazing, unusual **8** singular, uncommon, unwonted **9** unheard-of **10** incredible, unexpected **11** astonishing, exceptional **12** unaccustomed, unbelievable **13** extraordinary, unanticipated

undaunted 5 brave **6** gritty, heroic, plucky **7** unfazed, valiant **8** fearless, intrepid, resolute, stalwart, valorous **9** not put off **10** courageous, undismayed **11** indomitable, unflinching, unperturbed, unshrinking **12** stouthearted **13** undiscouraged

undeceive 8 disabuse **10** disenchant **11** disenthrall, disillusion **12** open one's eyes **13** break the spell **15** burst one's bubble **19** bring one down to earth **20** shatter one's illusions

undecided 4 open **5** vague **6** unsure **7** dubious, pending **8** not final, wavering **9** tentative, uncertain, unsettled **10** indecisive, indefinite, in abeyance, in a dilemma, irresolute, of two minds, open-minded, unresolved, up in the air **11** fluctuating, vacillating **12** undetermined, unformulated **16** hemming and hawing **17** blowing hot and cold **20** going around in circles

undecorated 4 bare **5** blank, plain, stark **6** simple **7** austere **9** unadorned **13** unembellished

undedicated 11 indifferent, uncommitted

undefiled 4 pure **5** clean **6** chaste, intact, virgin **7** natural **8** innocent, spotless **9** stainless, unsullied **10** unpolluted

undemanding 4 easy **6** low-key, simple **7** patient, relaxed **9** easygoing **10** submissive **12** easy to please, laissez-faire **14** live-and-let-live

undemonstrative 3 shy **4** cold **5** aloof **7** distant, stoical **8** reserved **9** impassive **11** unemotional **12** inexpressive, unresponsive **14** self-controlled

undeniable 4 sure **6** patent, proven **7** certain, obvious **8** decisive, manifest **10** conclusive **11** established, indubitable, irrefutable **12** beyond a doubt, demonstrable, indisputable **13** incontestable **14** unquestionable **16** incontrovertible

undeniably 6 surely **9** certainly **10** decisively, definitely **11** irrefutably **12** conclusively, demonstrably, indisputably **13** incontestably **14** beyond question, unquestionably **16** incontrovertibly

undependable 6 fickle **7** erratic, flighty **8** unstable, variable, wavering **10** capricious, changeable, inconstant, unreliable **13** irresponsible, unpredictable, untrustworthy

under 3 sub **5** below, lower, neath, short **7** beneath, sedated **8** inferior, less than **9** because of **11** subordinate, unconscious

undercover 3 sly **6** covert, hidden, secret **7** furtive, sub rosa **8** hush-hush, stealthy **9** concealed, disguised, incognito **10** unrevealed **11** clandestine, undisclosed **12** confidential **13** surreptitious
French: **8** a couvert

undercurrent 4 aura, hint, mood **5** sense, tinge, vibes **7** quality, riptide **8** undertow **9** undertone **10** atmosphere, intimation, suggestion, vibrations **12** crosscurrent

undercut 9 discredit, undermine, undersell **10** compromise

underestimate 7 dismiss, put down **8** belittle, minimize, misjudge **9** deprecate, discredit, disparage, disregard, sell short, underrate, undersell **10** depreciate, undervalue **11** detract from **12** miscalculate

undergarment 3 bra **4** BVDs, slip **5** pants, shift, teddy, thong **6** boxers, corset, girdle, shorts **7** chemise, panties **8** bloomers, camisole, knickers, lingerie, skivvies **9** brassiere, petticoat, union suit **12** jockey shorts

undergo 5 brave, stand **6** endure, suffer **7** sustain, weather **8** submit to **9** encounter, go through, withstand **10** experience

undergraduate 4 coed, soph 5 frosh, plebe 6 junior, senior 7 scholar, student 8 freshman 9 sophomore, undegreed 10 degreeless, nondegreed 13 underclassman, upperclassman

underground 6 buried, covert, secret 7 sub-rosa 10 undercover 11 belowground, clandestine 12 subterranean 13 surreptitious 15 below the surface

underground chamber 4 tomb 5 crypt, vault 6 cellar 8 catacomb 9 sepulcher

underhand, underhanded 6 covert, crafty, sneaky, tricky 7 corrupt, crooked, cunning, devious, evasive, furtive, illegal 8 sneaking, stealthy 9 conniving, dishonest, unethical 10 fraudulent 12 unprincipled, unscrupulous 13 surreptitious

underhandedness 5 guile 6 deceit 7 slyness 8 trickery 9 chicanery, deception, duplicity 10 sneakiness, trickiness 13 secretiveness

underline 6 accent, stress 7 dwell on, point up 9 emphasize, press home 10 accentuate, underscore 15 bring into relief

underling 4 serf 6 flunky, lackey, menial, minion, thrall, vassal 7 servant, subject 8 employee, hireling, inferior 9 attendant, hired hand 11 subordinate

underlying 5 basic 6 covert 7 beneath, radical 8 implicit 9 elemental, essential 10 subtending 11 fundamental

undermine 4 foil, ruin 5 erode 6 injure, riddle, scotch, thwart, weaken 7 cripple, destroy, subvert, torpedo 8 sabotage 9 eat away at, frustrate, hamstring 10 neutralize 11 burrow under, tunnel under

underneath 5 below, lower 6 bottom, hidden 9 disguised, subject to 14 misrepresented

undernourished 8 starving, underfed 12 malnourished

under obligation 5 bound 6 liable 7 obliged 8 beholden, indebted 9 obligated 10 answerable, in one's debt 11 accountable, responsible

underpart 4 sole 5 belly, tails 6 bottom 9 lower side, underside

underpin 4 bear 7 bolster, support 10 strengthen 12 substantiate

underpinning 4 base 5 basic 6 ground 7 support 9 essential 10 foundation, groundwork 11 fundamental 12 substructure

underplay 8 play down 11 deemphasize

underprivileged 4 poor 5 needy 6 in need 7 hapless, unlucky 8 badly-off, deprived, ill-fated, indigent 9 destitute, penniless, penurious 10 illstarred, pauperized 11 handicapped,

unfortunate 12 impoverished 13 disadvantaged 22 in adverse circumstances

underrate 6 slight 8 belittle, derogate, minimize 9 denigrate, deprecate, disparage 10 depreciate, undervalue 13 underestimate

underscore 4 mark 6 accent, deepen, play up, stress 7 feature, point up 8 heighten 9 emphasize, intensify, press home, underline 10 accentuate 15 draw attention to

underscoring 6 stress 8 emphasis 11 underlining

underside 4 back, sole 5 belly, tails 6 bottom 7 reverse 9 lower side, underpart

undersized 4 tiny 5 elfin, short, small 6 little, petite, slight 7 stunted 8 dwarfish 10 diminutive 11 lilliputian

underskirt 4 slip 7 pannier 9 crinoline, hoopskirt, petticoat

understand 3 dig, get, see 4 hear, know, read, take 5 grasp, learn 6 absorb, accept, assume, can see, fathom, gather, take it 7 be aware, discern, make out, presume, realize 8 conclude, perceive 9 apprehend, interpret, recognize 10 appreciate, comprehend, take to mean 14 sympathize with, take for granted

understandable 8 apparent 12 recognizable, unmistakable 14 comprehensible

understanding 4 pact 5 grasp 7 empathy, insight, knowing 8 sympathy, tolerant 9 agreement, awareness, intuition, knowledge, sensitive 10 cognizance, compassion, compromise, discerning, perception, perceptive, responsive 11 concordance, sensitivity, sympathetic 12 appreciation, appreciative, apprehension 13 compassionate, comprehension 17 meeting of the minds

understate 8 minimize 11 deemphasize

understated 9 minimized 10 restrained 12 conservative, deemphasized

understatement 7 litotes 10 minimizing 20 conservative estimate

understudy 3 sub 6 backup, double, fill-in, relief 7 stand-by, stand-in 9 alternate, surrogate 10 substitute 11 pinch hitter, replacement

undertake 3 try 5 begin, essay, start 6 assume, strive, tackle, take on 7 attempt 8 commence, embark on, endeavor, set about, shoulder 9 agree to do, enter upon 11 promise to do 13 get involved in

undertaking 3 job 4 task 6 effort 7 concern, project, pursuit, venture 8 endeavor 10 commitment, enterprise

Under the Greenwood Tree author: 11 Thomas Hardy

under the influence 5 drunk 6 sodden, soused, wasted, zapped, zonked 7 smashed 8 besotted 9 plastered 10 inebriated 11 intoxicated 20 three sheets to the wind

under the weather 3 bad, ill 4 sick 6 ailing, sickly, unwell 9 unhealthy 10 indisposed

undertone 4 aura, hint, mood 5 scent, sense, tinge, trace 6 flavor, mumble, murmur, nuance 7 feeling, inkling, low tone, quality, whisper 8 coloring 10 atmosphere, intimation, suggestion 11 connotation, implication 12 subdued voice, undercurrent

undervalue 6 slight 8 belittle, derogate 9 discredit, disparage, underrate 10 depreciate 13 underestimate

underwear 3 bra 4 BVDs, slip 5 pants, teddy, thong 6 boxers, briefs, corset, girdle, shorts 7 chemise, panties 8 bloomers, camisole, knickers, lingerie, skivvies 9 brassiere, petticoat, union suit 12 jockey shorts, smallclothes 14 unmentionables

underweight 4 bony, lank 5 gaunt, lanky 6 skinny 7 scrawny, spindly 8 skeletal, underfed 9 emaciated 12 skin-and-bones 13 hollow-cheeked 14 spindle-shanked, undernourished

underworld 4 Hell 5 Hades, limbo 6 the mob 8 mobsters, the Mafia 9 criminals, gangsters, purgatory 10 Cosa Nostra 11 shades below 12 the syndicate 13 bottomless pit, nether regions 14 organized crime 15 criminal element, infernal regions 16 abode of the damned
    god of: 3 Dis 5 Hades, Orcus, Pluto 8 Dis Pater

under wraps 6 hidden, secret 9 concealed 10 suppressed, under cover

underwrite 3 aid 4 back 7 approve, endorse, finance, sponsor, support, warrant 8 invest in, sanction, validate 9 guarantee, subsidize 11 countersign

underwriter 5 angel 6 backer, patron 7 sponsor 8 investor 9 financier, guarantor

undeserving 3 bad 8 inferior, unworthy

undesirable 5 unfit 8 disliked, improper, unbidden, unsavory, unseemly, unwanted, unworthy 9 offensive, unpopular 10 unbecoming, uninviting, unsuitable, unwelcomed 11 distasteful, unbefitting, unwishedfor 12 disagreeable, inadmissible, unacceptable, unattractive 13 inappropriate, objectionable 14 unsatisfactory

undetectable 12 unnoticeable, unobservable 13 imperceptible, unsubstantial

undetermined 6 chance 7 unfixed, unknown 8 unproved, unproven

9 uncertain, undecided **10** indefinite, irresolute **13** indeterminate, unascertained

undeveloped 3 raw **5** crude, green **6** callow, unripe **8** immature, inchoate, unformed **9** embryonic, half-baked **10** unfinished **11** rudimentary, unexploited **12** uncultivated

undignified 3 low **7** boorish **8** improper, shameful, unseemly, unworthy **9** degrading, inelegant, tasteless, unrefined **10** beneath one, indecorous, indelicate, in bad taste, unbecoming, unladylike, unsuitable **11** unbefitting **13** discreditable, inappropriate, ungentlemanly **18** beneath one's dignity Latin: **8** infra dig **15** infra dignitatem

undiluted 4 neat, pure **5** sheer **7** unmixed **8** straight **11** unfortified **12** full-strength **13** unadulterated

Undine
   form: **6** spirit
   location: **5** water
   sex: **6** female

undiscerning 11 insensitive **12** unperceptive **14** indiscriminate

undisciplined 4 wild **6** fickle, fitful **7** erratic, wayward, willful **8** unsteady, untaught **9** mercurial, untrained, untutored **10** capricious, changeable, inconstant, uneducated, unfinished, unreliable, unschooled **11** unpracticed **12** obstreperous, uncontrolled, undependable, unrestrained **13** unpredictable

undisclosed 6 hidden, secret **7** private **9** concealed **10** unrevealed **12** confidential

undisguised 4 open **5** clear, utter **7** evident, obvious **8** complete, distinct, manifest, unhidden **9** out-and-out **10** plain as day, pronounced, unreserved **11** unconcealed **12** unmistakable, wholehearted **13** thoroughgoing **24** plain as the nose on one's face

undismayed 7 uncowed **8** unafraid, unscared **9** confident, unabashed, unalarmed, undaunted **12** unfrightened **13** undiscouraged, unintimidated

undisputed 4 sure **7** certain, granted **8** accepted **9** undoubted **10** conclusive, undeniable **11** beyond doubt, indubitable, irrefutable, past dispute, uncontested **12** acknowledged, indisputable, unchallenged, unquestioned **13** a matter of fact, incontestable **14** beyond question, freely admitted, unquestionable **15** without question **16** incontrovertible

undistinguished 5 plain, usual **6** common **7** prosaic **8** everyday, mediocre, ordinary **10** pedestrian, unexciting **11** commonplace **12** run-of-the-mill, unremarkable **13** unexceptional **18** nothing to rave about

undistracted 4 calm **6** serene, stolid

7 unfazed **9** impassive, unruffled **10** untroubled **11** undisturbed

undisturbed 4 calm, cool **5** quiet **6** placid, serene, steady **7** equable, unmoved **8** composed, peaceful, tranquil **9** collected, inviolate, unexcited, unruffled, untouched **10** of solitude, unagitated, unbothered, untroubled **11** left in order, unperturbed **13** imperturbable, self-possessed, uninterrupted

undivided 5 solid, whole **6** entire, united **7** unified, unsplit **8** complete **9** of one mind, unanimous **10** not divided, unstinting **12** wholehearted

undo 3 end **4** free, open, ruin, void **5** annul, erase, loose, quash, untie **6** cancel, defeat, loosen, offset, repair, unbind, unfold, unhook, unknot, unlace, unlock, unwrap **7** destroy, nullify, rectify, reverse, subvert, unchain, unravel, wipe out **8** demolish, overturn, unbutton, unfasten **9** disengage, eliminate, make up for, undermine **10** counteract, invalidate, neutralize **11** disentangle **13** compensate for **14** counterbalance

undogmatic 7 liberal **8** flexible, tolerant **10** open-minded **11** broad-minded

undoing 4 doom, jinx, ruin **5** upset **6** defeat **7** erasure, nemesis **8** collapse, downfall, negation, reversal, weakness **9** annulment, breakdown, overthrow, ruination, thwarting, wiping out **11** cause of ruin, destruction **12** Achilles' heel, cancellation, invalidation **13** counteraction, nullification **14** neutralization

undomesticated 4 wild **5** feral **6** ferine, savage **7** untamed **8** barbaric **9** barbarous **11** uncivilized

undone 6 ruined **9** come apart, destroyed **10** incomplete, unfastened **12** not completed

undoubted 4 sure **5** utter **7** certain **8** absolute, complete, definite, positive **11** indubitable, unequivocal **12** indisputable **13** unimpeachable **14** unquestionable

undoubtedly 6 surely **7** no doubt **9** assuredly, certainly, decidedly, doubtless **10** absolutely, definitely, positively, undeniably **11** indubitably **12** beyond a doubt, unmistakably, without doubt **13** unequivocally **14** beyond question, unquestionably **15** without question

undress 5 strip **6** nudity **7** disrobe, uncover, undrape **8** disarray, unclothe **9** nakedness **10** dishabille **18** take off one's clothes

undressed 4 bare, nude **5** naked **6** unclad **7** denuded, exposed, unrobed **8** disrobed, stripped, undraped **9** unclothed, uncovered

Undset, Sigrid
   author of: **6** The Axe **20** Kristin Lavransdatter, The Master of Hestviken

undue 6 unmeet **8** impolite, improper, needless, overmuch, too great, unseemly, unworthy **9** excessive, tasteless **10** ill-advised, indiscreet, in bad taste, inordinate, not fitting, unbecoming, unsuitable **11** superfluous, uncalled-for, unjustified, unnecessary, unwarranted **13** inappropriate, objectionable

undulate 4 coil **5** slink, weave **9** fluctuate **11** rise and fall

undulating 4 wavy **5** bumpy **6** uneven

undulation 7 coiling **8** slinking, twisting **10** contortion **11** convolution **16** rising and falling

undutiful 6 remiss **8** disloyal **11** disobedient

undying 6 steady **7** abiding, endless, eternal, lasting **8** constant, enduring, immortal, unending, unfading, untiring **9** continual, deathless, incessant, perennial, permanent, perpetual, unceasing **10** continuing **11** everlasting, never-ending, unfaltering, unrelenting, unremitting **12** imperishable, neverfailing, undiminished **13** uninterrupted **14** indestructible

unearth 4 find, show **5** dig up **6** dig out, exhume, expose, reveal **7** display, divulge, exhibit, root out, uncover **8** disclose, discover, disinter, dredge up, excavate **9** disentomb, ferret out **10** come across, come up with **12** bring to light

unearthly 5 awful, eerie, weird **6** absurd **7** extreme, ghostly, phantom, strange, uncanny, ungodly, unusual **8** abnormal, ethereal, spectral, terrible **10** horrendous, unpleasant **11** disembodied, incorporeal, unspeakable **12** disagreeable, extramundane, supernatural **13** extraordinary, preternatural

unease 5 worry **7** tension **8** disquiet **9** misgiving **10** discomfort, uneasiness **11** disquietude **12** apprehension

uneasiness 5 dread **6** dismay **7** anxiety **9** agitation, misgiving **10** discomfort, foreboding **11** disquietude, distraction, nervousness **12** apprehension, discomfiture, discomposure, perturbation **16** apprehensiveness

uneasy 4 edgy **5** nervy, tense, upset **6** on edge, queasy, unsure **7** awkward, irksome, nervous, uptight, worried **8** strained, troubled, worrying **9** disturbed, ill at ease, perturbed, upsetting **10** bothersome, disquieted, disturbing, unpleasant **11** constrained, disquieting **12** apprehensive **13** uncomfortable

uneatable 8 inedible **11** not fit to eat

uneconomical 4 dear **6** costly **8** wasteful **9** expensive **10** exorbitant, high-priced, immoderate, overpriced **11** extravagant **12** unreasonable

uneducated 8 ignorant, untaught 9 unlearned, untrained, untutored 10 illiterate, uncultured, unlettered, unschooled 12 uncultivated, uninstructed 13 unenlightened

unelaborated 4 bald, bare 5 plain, stark 6 simple 9 essential, unadorned, uncolored 11 fundamental, unvarnished 13 unembellished 15 straightforward

unembellished 4 bald, bare 5 naked, plain, stark 7 austere 9 unadorned 11 undecorated 12 unornamented

unemotional 4 cold, cool 6 formal, remote 7 distant 8 lukewarm, reserved 9 apathetic, impassive, unfeeling 11 indifferent, passionless, unconcerned 12 unresponsive 15 undemonstrative

unemployed 4 axed, idle 5 fired 6 canned, sacked, unused 7 bounced, jobless, laid-off 8 workless 9 at leisure, at liberty, booted-out, dismissed, on the dole, on welfare, out of a job, out of work 10 discharged, unoccupied 11 pink-slipped

unencumbered 4 free 6 vacant 7 unladen 8 expedite 10 unburdened, unhindered 13 unhandicapped

unending 6 steady 7 endless, eternal, lasting 8 constant, enduring 9 continual, incessant, perennial, permanent, perpetual, unceasing 10 continuous, unwavering 11 everlasting, neverending, unremitting 12 undiminished 13 uninterrupted

unendurable 7 racking 9 agonizing, torturous 10 tormenting, unbearable 11 intolerable 12 excruciating, insufferable

unenlightened 8 ignorant 9 in the dark, unlearned 10 uneducated, uninformed 11 uninitiated 12 uninstructed

unenterprising 4 lazy 11 unambitious 12 unaggressive

unenthusiastic 8 lukewarm 10 unspirited 11 halfhearted, indifferent 13 unimpassioned

unequal 6 biased, uneven, unfair, unjust, unlike 7 bigoted, partial 9 different, disparate, unmatched 10 dissimilar, not uniform, prejudiced 11 inequitable

unequaled 7 supreme 8 peerless 9 matchless, paramount, unmatched, unrivaled 10 consummate, unexcelled 11 ne plus ultra, unsurpassed 12 incomparable, second to none, unapproached, unparalleled 13 beyond compare 16 beyond comparison

unequivocable 4 bald 5 utter 8 outright 9 out-and-out 11 categorical, unqualified

unequivocal 5 clear, final 7 certain 8 absolute, clear-cut, decisive, definite, emphatic 11 unambiguous 12 indisputable 13 incontestable 16 incontrovertible

unequivocally 7 clearly 9 certainly, downright 10 completely, decisively, definitely, thoroughly 12 emphatically, indisputably, unmistakably 13 incontestably 14 unquestionably, wholeheartedly 16 incontrovertibly

unerring 4 sure 7 certain, precise 8 constant, faithful, reliable 9 faultless, unfailing 10 infallible, unchanging

unessential 8 nonvital 9 accessory, extrinsic 10 disposable, expendable 11 dispensable, superfluous, unimportant, unnecessary 12 nonessential

unethical 5 dirty, shady, wrong 6 shoddy, unfair 7 devious 8 unworthy 9 dishonest, underhand 10 unladylike 12 dishonorable, disreputable, questionable, unprincipled 13 ungentlemanly 14 unconscionable

uneven 4 awry, bent 5 bumpy, lumpy, rough 6 angled, coarse, craggy, curved, jagged, tilted, unfair, unjust, unlike 7 crooked, not flat, slanted, sloping, unequal 8 lopsided, not level, not plumb, one-sided, unsmooth 9 different, disparate 10 dissimilar, ill-matched, unbalanced

unevenness 7 oddness 9 bumpiness, lumpiness, roughness 10 jaggedness, ruggedness 11 crookedness 12 irregularity 14 changeableness

uneventful 4 dull 5 quiet, usual 6 boring 7 average, humdrum, prosaic, routine, tedious 8 ordinary, standard, tiresome 10 monotonous 11 commonplace 12 conventional 13 insignificant, unexceptional, uninteresting

unexcelled 7 supreme 8 flawless, peerless, superior, unbeaten 9 faultless, matchless, unequaled, unmatched, unrivaled 10 consummate 11 unsurpassed 12 incomparable, second to none, transcendent, unapproached, unparalleled 13 beyond compare

unexceptional 5 usual 6 normal 7 mundane, typical 8 ordinary, standard 9 customary 12 conventional, run of the mill

unexcited 4 calm, cool 6 placid, serene 7 unmoved 8 composed, detached 9 collected, unruffled 11 undisturbed, unemotional 13 dispassionate, unimpassioned

unexciting 4 dull, flat 5 vapid 6 boring 7 insipid 10 lackluster

unexpected 6 sudden 9 startling, unplanned 10 accidental, surprising, undesigned, unforeseen, unintended 11 astonishing, unlooked-for, unpredicted 12 out of the blue 13 unanticipated, unintentional

unextinguished 5 alive 10 unquenched 12 still burning
unfaded 5 fresh 6 bright 8 undimmed 10 unwithered

unfailing 4 true 5 loyal 6 steady 7 endless 8 constant, enduring, faithful, reliable 9 continual 10 continuous, dependable, infallible, unchanging, unwavering 12 never-failing 13 inexhaustible

unfair 4 foul 5 dirty 6 biased, unjust 7 corrupt, crooked, partial, unequal 8 not right, onesided, partisan 9 dishonest, underhand, unethical 10 not cricket, prejudiced 11 inequitable 12 dishonorable, unprincipled, unreasonable, unscrupulous 14 unconscionable

unfaithful 5 false 6 faulty, untrue 7 inexact 8 disloyal, unchaste 9 deceitful, distorted, erroneous, faithless, imperfect 10 adulterous, inaccurate, inconstant, perfidious 11 not accurate, treacherous 12 falsehearted 13 untrustworthy

Unfaithfully Yours
director: 14 Preston Sturges
cast: 10 Rudy Vallee 11 Rex Harrison 12 Edgar Kennedy, Linda Darnell 15 Barbara Lawrence

unfaithfulness 7 falsity, perfidy 9 falseness, treachery 10 disloyalty, fickleness, infidelity 11 inconstancy 13 faithlessness 14 perfidiousness

unfaltering 4 firm, sure 6 steady 8 enduring, resolute 9 obstinate, steadfast, unfailing 10 dependable, persistent, unflagging, unswerving, unwavering 11 persevering, undeviating 12 never-failing, wholehearted

unfamiliar 3 new 5 novel 6 exotic, unique 7 curious, foreign, strange, unknown, unusual 9 different 10 ignorant of, unversed in 11 a stranger to, little known, out-of-the-way, unexposed to, uninitiated, unskilled in 12 not well- known, unacquainted, unconversant 13 not acquainted, unpracticed in 14 unaccustomed to 15 inexperienced in, uninformed about 18 unenlightened about

unfamiliarity 9 ignorance 11 strangeness 12 inexperience 15 lack of knowledge

unfashionable 5 dated, dowdy, passe 6 frumpy, old-hat 8 outmoded 9 out-of-date, unstylish 12 old-fashioned

unfasten 4 undo 5 unpin, untie 6 detach, unbind, unbolt, unhook, unlace, unlash, unlink, unlock 7 unclose, unhitch, unlatch, unstick 8 unbutton, uncouple

unfastened 5 apart, undid 6 undone, untied 7 severed, unlaced, unstuck 8 detached, unhooked 9 unbuckled, uncoupled, unhitched 11 unconnected 12 disconnected

unfathomable 4 deep, vast 6 arcane, remote, subtle 7 complex, extreme, obscure 8 abstract, abstruse, esoteric, profound, puzzling **9** enigmatic **10** bottomless, perplexing **16** hard to understand, incomprehensible

unfavorable 3 bad **4** poor **7** adverse, unhappy **8** unsuited, untimely **9** ill-suited **10** ill-favored, regretable **11** inopportune, regrettable, unfortunate, unpromising **12** inauspicious, inconvenient, infelicitous, unpropitious, unseasonable **15** disadvantageous

unfeasible 10 impossible, infeasible, unsuitable, unworkable **11** impractical **12** unachievable **13** impracticable

unfeeling 4 cold **5** cruel **9** heartless **11** hardhearted, insensitive **13** unsympathetic

unfeigned 4 real, true **7** genuine, sincere **10** unaffected

unfetter 4 free **7** release, set free, unchain **8** liberate **9** unshackle

unfilled 4 open **5** blank, empty **6** hollow, vacant **7** drained **9** available **10** unoccupied

unfinished 5 crude, rough **6** undone **7** lacking, sketchy, wanting **8** immature **9** deficient, imperfect, unnatural, unpainted, unrefined, unstained **10** incomplete, unexecuted, unpolished **11** uncompleted, unfulfilled, unlacquered, unvarnished

unfit 4 sick, weak **5** frail **6** infirm, not fit, sickly **7** not up to, unequal, unready, unsound, useless **8** delicate, disabled, unsuited **9** incapable, not suited, unhealthy, unskilled, untrained **10** inadequate, ineligible, not equal to, unequipped, unprepared, unsuitable **11** debilitated, ill-equipped, incompetent, ineffective, inefficient, not designed, unqualified **12** ill-contrived, not cut out for **13** inappropriate, incapacitated

unflagging 4 firm **5** fixed **6** steady **7** staunch **8** constant, enduring, resolute, tireless, unshaken, untiring **9** steadfast, tenacious, undaunted **10** determined, persistent, relentless, undrooping, unswerving, unwavering, unyielding **11** indomitable, persevering, undeviating, unfaltering, unremitting **13** indefatigable **14** uncompromising

unflappable 4 calm, cool **6** placid, serene **8** composed **9** collected **10** cool-headed **11** unexcitable **13** imperturbable, self-possessed

unflinching 4 firm, game **6** gritty, plucky, steady, strong **7** staunch **8** fearless, resolute, stalwart, unshaken **9** steadfast, tenacious, unabashed, undaunted **10** persistent, unswerving, unwavering, unyielding **11** indomitable, unfaltering, unshrinking **12** unhesitating

unfold 4 bare, show, tell **6** open up, reveal, unfurl, unroll, unveil, unwrap **7** divulge, explain, expound, lay open,

open out, present, recount, uncover **8** describe, disclose, set forth **9** elucidate, explicate, make known, spread out **10** stretch out

unfolding 4 rise **5** birth, start **9** beginning, evolution, inception, unfurling **10** revelation **11** development

unforced 4 easy **5** frank **6** candid, casual **7** natural, relaxed **8** informal **9** easygoing **10** unaffected **13** unconstrained

unforeseen 6 abrupt, sudden **8** surprise **9** unplanned **10** accidental, surprising, unexpected, unintended **11** unlooked-for, unpredicted **12** out of the blue **13** unanticipated

unforeseen danger 7 pitfall **8** exigency **9** emergency **11** contingency

unforgettable 7 notable **8** eventful, exciting **9** important, memorable, thrilling **10** noteworthy **11** significant

unfortunate 5 sorry **6** cursed, jinxed, woeful **7** hapless, unblest, unhappy, unlucky **8** ill-fated, ill-timed, luckless, untimely, wretched **10** disastrous, ill-advised, ill-starred **11** inopportune, regrettable, unfavorable **12** inauspicious, infelicitous, unpropitious, unprosperous, unsuccessful

unfounded 4 idle **5** false **6** untrue **8** baseless, spurious **9** erroneous **10** fabricated, groundless

unfrequented 5 empty **6** lonely **7** remote, uncouth **8** isolated, solitary **9** unvisited **11** out-of-the-way **16** off the beaten path

unfriendly 4 cold **5** aloof **6** at odds, chilly **7** distant, haughty, hostile, warlike **8** inimical, snobbish **9** on the outs, reclusive, withdrawn **10** ungracious, unsociable **11** belligerent, contentious, quarrelsome, uncongenial **12** antagonistic, disagreeable, disputatious, inhospitable **13** at loggerheads, at sword's point, unsympathetic

unfruitful 4 vain **6** barren, fallow, futile **7** useless, worn- out **8** infecund **9** fruitless **10** unavailing **11** purposeless, unrewarding **12** impoverished, unproductive, unprofitable **14** unremunerative

unfulfilled 8 thwarted **10** frustrated, unrealized **11** unsatisfied
French: 6 manque

unfurl 4 open **6** expand, spread, unfold, unroll **7** develop, roll out **8** shake out **9** spread out

ungainly 5 stiff **6** clumsy, klutzy **7** awkward **9** lumbering, maladroit **10** ungraceful **13** uncoordinated

ungallant 4 rude **7** boorish, uncivil, uncouth **8** impolite **9** uncourtly **10** ill-behaved, ungracious, unmannerly **11** ill-mannered, uncourteous **12** discourteous **13** ungentlemanly

ungenerous 4 mean, near **5** close,

cruel, petty, small, venal **6** greedy, shabby, sordid, stingy **7** miserly, selfish, sparing **8** churlish, covetous, cowardly, grudging **9** illiberal, mercenary, niggardly, penurious, rapacious **10** avaricious **11** small-minded **12** narrow-minded, parsimonious, uncharitable

ungifted 8 mediocre **9** unskilled **10** amateurish, unskillful, untalented **14** unaccomplished

unglue 6 unseal **7** peel off, unstick **9** pull apart

ungodly 4 base, vile **5** awful **6** rotten, sinful, wicked **7** corrupt, ghastly, godless, heinous, immoral, impious **8** depraved, dreadful, terrible **9** dissolute **10** degenerate, horrendous, iniquitous, outrageous, villainous **11** blasphemous **12** dishonorable, unreasonable

ungovernable 6 unruly **7** defiant, froward, naughty, wayward **8** contrary, mutinous, perverse, stubborn **9** fractious, obstinate **10** disorderly, rebellious, refractory **11** disobedient, intractable **12** noncompliant, recalcitrant, unmanageable, unsubmissive

ungraceful 5 inept **6** clumsy **7** awkward **9** inelegant

ungracious 4 rude **5** bluff, blunt, gruff, harsh, short **6** abrupt, coarse, crusty, vulgar **7** boorish, brusque, loutish, uncivil, uncouth **8** churlish, grudging, impolite **9** uncourtly, ungallant **10** ill-behaved, unladylike, unmannerly **11** bad-mannered, ill-mannered, impertinent, uncourteous **12** disagreeable, discourteous, inhospitable **13** disrespectful, ungentlemanly

unguarded 6 unwary **8** careless, tactless, too frank **9** imprudent, unmindful, unwatched **10** incautious, indiscreet, undefended **11** defenseless, unpatrolled, unprotected **12** undiplomatic, unrestrained **13** ill- considered, uncircumspect

unguent 4 balm **5** cream, salve **6** lotion **8** ointment **9** emollient

ungula 4 hoof, nail

ungulate 2 ox **3** cow, gnu, hog, pig, yak **4** boar, calf, deer, goat, ibex **5** camel, daman, horse, llama, tapir **6** hoofed, vicuna **7** buffalo, caribou, giraffe, peccary **8** antelope, elephant, hooflike, ruminant **9** dromedary **10** hartebeest, rhinoceros, wildebeest **12** hippopotamus

unhampered 4 free **8** expedite **9** unimpeded **10** unconfined **11** unencumbered, unrestrained, unrestricted

unhandy 5 inept **6** clumsy, gauche, klutzy **7** awkward **8** bumbling, fumbling, inexpert, unwieldy **9** all thumbs, ham-handed, maladroit, unskilled **10** cumbersome, unskillful

11 inefficient **12** inconvenient, unmanageable **14** butterfingered

unhappiness 3 woe **5** grief **6** misery, sorrow **7** anguish, sadness **8** distress **9** heartache

unhappy 3 bad, sad **4** blue, poor **5** inapt, sorry **6** gloomy, somber, unwise **7** adverse, awkward, doleful, foolish, forlorn, hapless, joyless, unlucky **8** dejected, downcast, luckless, unseemly **9** depressed, imprudent, long-faced, sorrowful, woebegone **10** despondent, dispirited, ill-advised, melancholy, unbecoming, unsuitable **11** crestfallen, injudicious, regrettable, unbefitting, unfortunate **12** heavy-hearted, infelicitous, unsuccessful **13** inappropriate **14** down in the mouth

unharmed 5 whole **6** unhurt **9** uninjured, unscathed, untouched **10** in one piece, unaffected **14** with a whole skin

unhealthy 3 bad **4** sick, weak **6** ailing, feeble, infirm, morbid, poorly, sickly, unwell **7** harmful, hurtful, invalid, not well, noxious, unsound **8** depraved, diseased, negative, perilous **9** dangerous, degrading, hazardous **10** corrupting, indisposed, morally bad **11** destructive, detrimental, undesirable, unhealthful, unwholesome **12** demoralizing, in poor health, insalubrious **13** contaminating

unheard-of 3 odd **4** rare **6** unique **7** amazing, curious, unknown, unusual **8** freakish, original, singular, uncommon **9** irregular, matchless **10** incredible, outlandish, outrageous, phenomenal, unexpected **11** exceptional **12** incomparable, preposterous, unbelievable, unparalleled, unreasonable **13** extraordinary, inconceivable, unprecedented

unheated 3 icy **4** cold **6** chilly, drafty, frosty **7** ice-cold **8** unwarmed

unheeding 7 ignored **8** mindless **12** disregarding

unhelpful 7 of no use, useless **8** in the way **9** hindering **11** disobliging **13** inconsiderate, uncooperative

unheralded 6 unsung **10** unexpected, unforeseen **11** unacclaimed, unannounced, unlooked-for **12** unproclaimed, unpublicized, unrecognized **13** unanticipated

unhesitating 5 eager, quick, ready **6** direct, prompt **9** immediate **10** unreserved **11** unflinching **12** wholehearted, without delay **13** instantaneous **18** without reservation

unhinge 6 detach **7** disrupt **8** separate, unsettle **9** disengage, dislocate, disorient, unbalance **10** disconnect **13** disarticulate

unhitch 6 detach **8** separate, uncouple, unfasten **9** disengage **10** disconnect

unhitched 8 detached **9** uncoupled **10** unfastened **12** disconnected

unholy 4 base, evil, vile **5** awful **6** rotten, sinful, wicked **7** corrupt, heinous, immoral, ungodly **8** depraved, dreadful, shocking **9** dishonest **10** horrendous, iniquitous, outrageous, villainous **12** dishonorable, unreasonable

Unholy Loves
   author: 15 Joyce Carol Oates

unhurried 4 easy, slow **7** gradual **9** leisurely **10** deliberate, slow-moving

unicorn
   form: 5 horse
   feature: 4 horn
   symbolizes: 6 purity **8** chastity
   constellation of: 9 Monoceros

unidentified 5 vague **7** unknown, unnamed **8** nameless **9** anonymous, unlabeled **11** unspecified **12** undesignated, unrecognized

unification 5 union, unity **6** fusion, merger **7** uniting **8** alliance, junction **9** coalition, combining **11** coalescence, combination, confederacy **12** amalgamation **13** confederation, consolidating, consolidation, incorporation

uniform 4 even, garb **5** alike, array, at one, dress, equal, habit **6** attire, in line, in step, livery **7** apparel, costume, regalia, regular, similar, the same **8** agreeing, constant, in accord, of a piece, unvaried, vestment **9** consonant, identical, of one mind, unaltered, unvarying **10** conforming, consistent, harmonious, unchanging **11** regimentals, undeviating

uniformity 8 equality, monotony, sameness **10** consonance **11** consistency, equivalency, homogeneity **15** standardization

unify 3 wed **4** ally, fuse, join **5** blend, merge, unite **6** couple, link up **7** combine **8** coalesce, federate **10** amalgamate **11** confederate, consolidate, form into one, incorporate **12** lump together **13** bring together

unilluminated 3 dim **4** dark **5** murky, unlit **6** gloomy **7** obscure **8** darkened **9** lightless, unlighted

unimaginable 10 incredible **12** unbelievable **13** inconceivable **16** incomprehensible

unimaginative 4 dull **5** stale, stock, trite, usual, vapid **6** dreary **7** cliched, humdrum, prosaic, routine, tedious **8** everyday, mediocre, ordinary **9** hackneyed **10** pedestrian, uncreative, unexciting, uninspired, unoriginal, unromantic **11** commonplace, predictable **12** run-of-the-mill, unremarkable **13** uninteresting

unimpaired 4 good **5** clear, sound **6** intact, unhurt **8** unbroken, unharmed **9** uninjured, unscathed, unspoiled **10** undeformed

unimpassioned 4 calm, cool **6** placid,

serene, stolid **7** unmoved **8** detached, unloving **9** apathetic, impassive, objective, unexcited **11** indifferent, unemotional **13** dispassionate

unimpeachable 4 pure **5** clean, solid **7** perfect **8** reliable, spotless, unmarred **9** blameless, faultless, inviolate, stainless, undefiled, untainted **10** immaculate, impeccable, inculpable, infallible **11** trustworthy, unblemished **12** unassailable **13** above reproach, totally honest **14** beyond question, irreproachable, unquestionable **15** beyond criticism, unchallengeable

unimportant 5 minor **6** lesser, meager, paltry, slight **7** trivial **8** inferior, mediocre, not vital, nugatory, piddling, trifling **10** immaterial, irrelevant, low-ranking, negligible, of no moment, second-rate **11** subordinate **12** nonessential, not important **13** insignificant **14** inconsiderable **15** inconsequential, of no consequence

uninformed 6 unread **7** unaware **8** ignorant **9** in the dark, not with it, unadvised, unknowing, unlearned **10** uneducated, unschooled **12** unconversant, uninstructed **13** unenlightened

uninhabited 5 empty **6** vacant **8** deserted, forsaken **9** abandoned, unlived in, unpeopled, unsettled **10** unoccupied, untenanted **11** unpopulated

uninhibited 4 fast, free, open, rash **5** frank **6** candid, daring, madcap, not shy, unwary **8** careless, heedless, immodest, reckless, uncurbed, unreined **9** abandoned, impetuous, impulsive, outspoken, unbridled, unchecked, unguarded, unimpeded, unstopped **10** capricious, flamboyant, forthright, headstrong, incautious, indiscreet, unhampered, unhindered, unreserved **11** instinctive, plainspoken, spontaneous **12** free-spirited, uncontrolled, unobstructed, unrestrained, unrestricted **13** unconstrained **15** straightforward, unself-conscious

uninjured 5 whole **6** intact, unhurt **8** unharmed **9** unscathed, untouched **10** in one piece **14** with a whole skin

uninspired 4 dull **5** stale, stock, trite, vapid **7** cliched, humdrum, prosaic, unmoved **8** ordinary **9** hackneyed, unexcited, unstirred, untouched **10** pedestrian, unaffected, unexciting, unoriginal **11** commonplace, indifferent, predictable, unemotional, unimpressed **12** run-of-the-mill, uninfluenced, unstimulated **13** unimaginative, uninteresting

uninspiring 4 dull **5** bland, stale **6** boring **7** insipid, prosaic **10** lackluster **13** uninteresting

uninstructive 6 barren **9** unhelpful **10** unedifying **12** unproductive **13** uninformative

unintelligent 4 dull, dumb, slow

5 blank, dense, dopey, thick **6** obtuse, stupid **7** asinine, doltish, idiotic, moronic **8** retarded **9** cretinous, dim-witted, imbecilic **10** dull-witted, half-witted, slow-witted **11** blockheaded, thickheaded **12** simpleminded

unintelligible 8 baffling, puzzling **9** confusing, illegible, insoluble **10** incoherent, perplexing **11** meaningless **12** impenetrable, inarticulate, unfathomable **14** undecipherable **16** incomprehensible

unintentional 9 unplanned, unwitting **10** accidental, fortuitous, undesigned, unintended, unthinking **11** inadvertent, involuntary, unconscious **14** unpremeditated

uninterested 5 aloof, blase **6** remote **8** heedless, listless, uncaring **9** apathetic, incurious, unmindful **10** above it all, uninvolved **11** indifferent, unconcerned **13** unimpressible

uninteresting 3 dry **4** drab, dull **5** trite, vapid **6** boring, dreary, jejune **7** humdrum, insipid, prosaic, tedious **8** lifeless, ordinary, tiresome, unmoving **9** colorless, wearisome **10** monotonous, pedestrian, uneventful **11** uninspiring **12** unsatisfying **13** insignificant

uninterrupted 8 unbroken **9** ceaseless, continual, incessant **10** continuous **11** unremitting

uninviting 8 annoying **9** offensive **10** unalluring, unpleasant, untempting **11** displeasing, distasteful, unappealing, undesirable, unwelcoming **12** disagreeable, unappetizing, unattractive

uninvolved 4 easy **5** clear **6** simple **7** neutral, obvious, outside **8** detached **9** impartial **10** unaffected **13** disinterested, dispassionate, uncomplicated

union 5 blend, guild, unity **6** fusion, league, merger **7** amalgam, joining, mixture, oneness, uniting, wedding **8** alliance, marriage, unifying **9** synthesis **10** federation, fraternity **11** affiliation, association, combination, corporation, partnership, unification **12** amalgamation **13** confederation, consolidation
    type: 5 craft, labor, trade

Union of Soviet Socialist Republics
    abbr: 4 CCCP, USSR
    see **Russia**

unique 8 by itself, peerless, singular **9** matchless, nonpareil, unequaled, unmatched, unrivaled **10** inimitable, one of a kind, surpassing, unexampled, unexcelled **11** distinctive, unsurpassed **12** incomparable, unapproached, unparalleled

unit 4 part **5** group, whole **6** entity, member **7** element, measure, package, section, segment **8** category, division, quantity **9** component **10** detachment **11** constituent, measurement **12** denomination

Unitas, Johnny
    nickname: 7 Johnny U
    sport: 8 football
    position: 11 quarterback
    team: 14 Baltimore Colts

unite 4 ally, fuse, join, pool **5** blend, merge, unify **6** couple **7** combine **8** coalesce, federate, lock arms, organize **10** amalgamate, homogenize, join forces **11** confederate, consolidate, incorporate **12** join together, lump together **13** stand together

united 3 one **5** fused **6** allied, joined, merged, pooled **7** blended, coupled, leagued, unified **8** combined **9** federated, of one mind, unanimous **10** collective **11** amalgamated, in agreement **12** consolidated, incorporated **14** joined together, lumped together

United Arab Emirates
    other name: 11 Pirate Coast, Trucial Oman **13** Trucial States
    capital/largest city: 8 Abu Dhabi
    others: 5 Ajman, Dubai, Kalba, Tarif **6** Sharja **7** Fujaira **11** Ras al Khaima **12** Umm al Qaiwain
    division: 5 Ajman, Dibai, Dubai **6** Sharja **7** Fujaira, Sharjah **8** Abu Dhabi, Fujairah **11** Ras al Khaima, Umm al Qaiwan **12** Ral al Khaimah, Umm al-Qaiwain
    monetary unit: 3 fil **6** dirham
    highest point: 5 Hafit
    physical feature:
        desert: 10 Rub al Khali
        gulf: 4 Oman **7** Persian
        oasis: 7 Buraimi **9** Al Buraymi
        peninsula: 7 Arabian
    people: 4 Arab **6** Indian **7** African, Iranian **9** Pakistani **10** South Asian
        leader: 22 Zaid Bin Sultan al-Nahayan
    language: 5 Farsi **6** Arabic **7** English, Persian
    religion: 5 Islam
    war: 4 Gulf **11** Desert Storm

United Arab Republic 3 UAR
    onetime union of: 5 Egypt, Syria

United Kingdom
    union of: 12 Great Britain **15** Northern Ireland

United States
    capital: 12 Washington DC
    largest city: 11 New York City
    others: 4 Nome **5** Miami **6** Boston, Dallas, El Paso **7** Chicago, Detroit, Houston, Memphis, Phoenix, San Jose, Seattle **8** Columbus, Honolulu, San Diego **9** Anchorage, Baltimore, Cleveland, Milwaukee **10** Los Angeles, New Orleans, San Antonio **12** Indianapolis, Jacksonville, Philadelphia, Salt Lake City, San Francisco
    school: 3 MIT **4** Penn, Yale **5** Brown **6** Baylor, Drexel, Vassar **7** Amherst, Colgate, Cornell, Fordham, Harvard, Oberlin **8** Bryn Mawr, Columbia, Stanford, Wesleyan **9** Dartmouth, Princeton, Radcliffe **10** Bennington **12** Johns Hopkins, Mount Holyoke
    division: 4 Iowa, Ohio, Utah **5** Idaho, Maine, Texas **6** Alaska, Hawaii, Kansas, Nevada, Oregon **7** Alabama, Arizona, Florida, Georgia, Indiana, Montana, New York, Vermont, Wyoming **8** Arkansas, Colorado, Delaware, Illinois, Kentucky, Maryland, Michigan, Missouri, Nebraska, Oklahoma, Virginia **9** Louisiana, Minnesota, New Jersey, New Mexico, Tennessee, Wisconsin **10** California, Puerto Rico, Washington **11** Connecticut, Mississippi, North Dakota, Rhode Island, South Dakota **12** New Hampshire, Pennsylvania, West Virginia **13** Massachusetts, North Carolina, South Carolina **18** District of Columbia
    island: 4 Guam, Long, Maui, Oahu **5** Block, Ellis, Kauai, Lanai, Umnak **6** Hawaii, Kodiak, Niihau, Unimak, Virgin **7** Baranof, Key West, Long Key, Molokai, Nunivak, Sanibel **8** Aleutian, Hawaiian, Key Largo, Shumagin, Unalaska **9** Atka Amlia, Canal Zone, Chichagof, Kahoolawe, Nantucket, Snipe Keys **10** Islamorada, Oyster Keys, Puerto Rico, St. Lawrence **11** Longboat Key **12** Santa Barbara **13** American Samoa, Marquesas Keys, Prince of Wales, Santa Catalina, Summerland Key **15** Martha's Vineyard **16** Cantout Enderbury **26** Trust Territory of the Pacific
    lake: 4 Erie, Mead **5** Huron, Tahoe **6** Cayuga, Finger, George, Itasca, Oneida, Seneca **7** Iliamma, Ontario **8** Michigan, Superior **9** Champlain, Great Salt, Salton Sea, Teshekpuk, Winnebago **10** Okeechobee **11** Yellowstone **13** Pontchartrain, Wallenpaupack, Winnipesaukee **14** Lake of the Woods
    mountain: 4 Hood **5** Coast, Green, Kenai, Ozark, Rocky, White **6** Alaska, Brooks, DeLong, Elbert, Helena, Mesabi, Pocono, Shasta **7** Cascade, Chugach, Foraker, Harvard, Kilauea, Massive, Olympic, Olympus, Rainier, St Elias, Whitney **8** Catskill, Davidson, Endicott, Katahdin, Mauna Loa, Mitchell, Ouachita, St Helens, Wrangell **9** Allegheny, Blue Ridge, Kuskokwim, North Peak, Pikes Peak **10** Black Hills, Blanca Peak, Grand Teton, Washington, Williamson **11** Appalachian, Santa Monica **12** Sierra Nevada **14** Berkshire Hills
    highest point: 6 Denali **8** McKinley
    river: 3 New, Red **4** Gila, Iowa, Milk, Ohio, Rock **5** Black, Cedar, Coosa, Flint, Grand, Green, James, Neuse, Osage, Pearl, Pecos, Snake, White, Yukon **6** Brazos, Hudson, Neches,

Neosho, Nueces, Owybee, Pee Dee, Platte, Powder, Sabine, Salmon, Wabash **7** Alabama, Big Horn, John Day, Klamath, Potomac, Roanoke, San Juan, St Johns, Trinity **8** Arkansas, Big Black, Canadian, Cheyenne, Cimarron, Colorado, Columbia, Delaware, Humboldt, Illinois, Kentucky, Kootenay, Missouri, Niabrana, Ouachita, Savannah **9** Allegheny, Deschutes, Des Moines, Minnesota, Rio Grande, Smoky Hill, St Francis, Tennessee, Tombigbee, Wisconsin **10** Cumberland, Republican, Sacramento, San Joaquin, St Lawrence, Tallapoosa **11** Connecticut, Mississippi, North Platte, South Platte, Susquehanna, Yellowstone **12** Tallahatchie **14** Little Colorado, Little Missouri

sea: 6 Arctic, Bering **7** Pacific **8** Atlantic, Beaufort

physical feature:
  bay: 5 Tampa **7** Bristol, Prudhoe **8** Biscayne, Monterey **9** Apalachee **10** Chesapeake **12** San Francisco
  desert: 4 Gila **6** Mojave **7** Painted **8** Colorado, Vizcaino **9** Black Rock **11** Death Valley
  falls: 7 Niagara
  gulf: 6 Alaska, Mexico **10** California
  plain: 5 Great
  plateau: 8 Colorado, Piedmont **10** Cumberland **11** Appalachian
  strait: 6 Bering **7** Florida

people:
  architect: 4 Root **5** Davis **6** Upjohn, Wright **7** Burnham, Downing, Furness, Gilbert, Gropius, Latrobe **8** Bogardus, Holabird, Sullivan **9** Bullfinch, Jefferson **10** Richardson **14** Mies van der Rohe
  artist: 5 Henri, Homer, Leutz, Moses, Peale, Wyeth **6** Copley, Durand, Millet, Rothko, Stuart **7** Audubon, Cassatt, O'Keeffe, Pollock, Sargent **8** Whistler
  author: 3 Poe **4** Grey, Inge, Loos, Luce, West, Wouk **5** Aiken, Albee, Beach, Benet, Crane, Eliot, Frost, Guest, Harte, Hecht, James, Lewis, Oates, Odets, O'Hara, Paine, Pound, Stowe, Twain, Vidal, Welty, Wolfe, Wylie **6** Bellow, Bierce, Bryant, Cabell, Capote, Cather, Cooper, Cullen, Ferber, Holmes, Hughes, Irving, Kilmer, Lanier, London, Lowell, Mather, Millay, Miller, Norris, O'Neill, Porter, Styron, Updike, Wilder **7** Angelou, Baldwin, Clemens, Costain, Dreiser, Emerson, Gallico, Hammett, Hellman, Howells, Jeffers, Kerouac, Lardner, Malamud, Nabokov, Roethke, Stevens, Thoreau, Webster, Wharton, Whitman **8** Anderson, Bradbury, Caldwell, Cummings, Faulkner, Macleish, McCarthy, Melville, Michener, Mitchell, Morrison, Rawlings, Robinson, Sandburg, Schwartz, Sherwood, Sinclair, Teasdale, Whittier, Williams **9** Burroughs, Dickinson, Dos Passos, Hawthorne, Hemingway, McCullers, Steinbeck **10** Fitzgerald, Longfellow, Tarkington

composer: 4 Ives, Kern **5** Cohan, Loewe, Sousa **6** Berlin, Foster, Joplin, Lerner, Porter **7** Copland, Gilbert, Rodgers **8** Gershwin, Sullivan **9** Bernstein **11** Hammerstein

explorer: 4 Byrd, Pike **5** Boone, Cabot, Clark, Lewis, Perry **6** Hudson, Joliet **7** Jolliet **8** Columbus **9** Marquette **10** Eric the Red

leader: 3 Jay **4** Clay, King, Penn **5** Bryan, Davis, Henry, Paine **6** Revere, Sumner **7** Stevens, Webster **8** Franklin, Humphrey **9** Goldwater

military leader: 3 Lee **4** Pike **5** Clark, Gates, Grant, Meade, Tyler **6** Austin, Custer, Marion, Patton **7** Bradley, Houston, Jackson, Sherman **8** Marshall, Pershing **9** MacArthur, Roosevelt, Stillwell **10** Eisenhower, Vandenburg, Washington **11** Schwarzkopf

president: 4 Bush, Ford, Polk, Taft **5** Adams, Grant, Hayes, Nixon, Tyler **6** Arthur, Carter, Hoover, Monroe, Pierce, Reagan, Taylor, Truman, Wilson **7** Clinton, Harding, Jackson, Johnson, Kennedy, Lincoln, Madison **8** Buchanan, Coolidge, Fillmore, Garfield, Hamilton, Harrison, McKinley, Van Buren **9** Cleveland, Jefferson, Roosevelt **10** Eisenhower, Washington

sculptor: 4 Rush **6** Calder, French, Rogers **7** Borglum **9** Greenough, Remington **12** Saint-Gaudens

language: 7 English, Spanish

religion: 5 Amish **6** Mormon **7** Baptist, Judaism, Shakers **8** Lutheran **9** Methodist **10** Protestant **11** Pentacostal **12** Episcopalian, Presbyterian **13** Roman Catholic **14** Church of Christ, Congregational **15** Eastern Orthodox, Latter Day Saints **19** Seventh Day Adventist

place:
  national park: 4 Zion **5** Platt **6** Acadia **7** Big Bend, Glacier, Olympic, Redwood, Sequoia **8** Wind Cave, Yosemite **9** Haleakala, Mesa Verde, Multnomah **10** Crater Lake, Everglades, Grand Teton, Hot Springs, Isle Royale, Shenandoah **11** Bryce Canyon, Canyonlands, Grand Canyon, Kings Canyon, Mammoth Cave, Yellowstone **12** Mount Rainier **13** Mount McKinley, Virgin Islands **14** Lassen Volcanic, Rocky Mountains **15** Carlsbad Caverns, Petrified Forest **19** Great Smoky Mountains

possession: 4 Guam **10** Puerto Rico **13** American Samoa, Virgin Islands **14** Mariana Islands **15** Caroline Islands, Marshall Islands

feature:
  colony: 7 Roanoke **8** Plymouth **9** Jamestown **11** Rhode Island **12** New Amsterdam, New Hampshire **14** New Netherlands **16** Massachusetts Bay
  festival: 9 Mardi Gras
  national symbol: 9 bald eagle
  tree: 7 redwood, sequoia

unity 5 peace, union **6** accord, entity, fusion, league, merger **7** concord, harmony, joining, oneness, rapport **8** alliance, goodwill **9** synthesis, unanimity, wholeness **10** federation, fellowship, friendship **11** affiliation, association, cooperation, partnership, unification **12** amalgamation, amicableness **13** compatibility, confederation, consolidation, understanding **14** likemindedness

universal 7 general **9** worldwide **10** ubiquitous, widespread **11** omnipresent **12** affecting all, all-embracing, all-inclusive **13** international

Universal creator
  Egyptian: 4 Ptah

universality 8 currency **10** prevalence **12** predominance **17** comprehensiveness

universe
  god of: 6 Amen Ra, Amon Ra

university 6 campus, school **7** academy, college **11** institution
  English: 6 Oxford **9** Cambridge
  Cambridge: 7 Harvard
  former: 9 alma mater
  French: 8 Sorbonne
  Hanover: 9 Dartmouth
  lecturer: 9 prelector
  New Haven: 4 Yale
  New Jersey: 9 Princeton
  New York: 8 Columbia
  Providence: 5 Brown
  session: 4 term **7** seminar **8** semester
  Wit: 4 Lyly, Nash **5** Peele **6** Greene

unjust 6 biased, unfair, warped **7** partial **8** one-sided, partisan, wrongful **9** unmerited **10** prejudiced, unbalanced, undeserved **11** inequitable, unjustified, unwarranted

unjustifiable 11 inexcusable **12** indefensible

unjustly 7 falsely, wrongly **8** unfairly **10** wrongfully **11** dishonestly, faithlessly, inequitably **12** undeservedly

unkempt 5 messy **6** sloppy, untidy **7** rumpled, tousled **8** mussed-up, slovenly, uncombed **9** ungroomed **10** disheveled, disordered **11** disarranged

unkind 4 mean **5** nasty **7** abusive **8** uncaring **9** malicious, unfeeling

10 unfriendly, ungenerous, ungracious **11** insensitive, thoughtless **12** inhospitable, uncharitable **13** inconsiderate, unsympathetic

unknot 5 untie **7** unsnarl **8** untangle **11** disentangle

unknowable 12 inaccessible **13** inconceivable

unknown 7 obscure, unnamed **8** nameless **9** anonymous, unheard-of **10** unrenowned **12** uncelebrated, undesignated, undetermined, undiscovered, unidentified

unknown authors
   abbr.: **4** anon
   author of: **4** Edda (elder) **7** Beowulf **8** Everyman, King Horn, Stasimon **10** Cinderella **11** Poema del Cid **12** Panchatantra, Vercelli Book, Volsunga Saga **14** Gesta Romanorum, Sibylline Books **15** Chanson de Roland, The Forty Thieves, The Song of Roland **16** Grettir the Strong **17** The Nibelungenlied **20** Aucassin and Nicolette, Robin Hood's Adventures **23** The Dream of the Red Chamber, The Thousand and One Nights **26** Sir Gawain and the Green Knight **29** Collection of Ten Thousand Leaves **29** The Arabian Nights' Entertainment

unladylike 4 rude **6** coarse, common, vulgar **7** ill-bred, uncouth **8** impolite **10** unmannerly **12** discourteous

unlawful 7 illegal, illegit, illicit, lawless **8** criminal **9** forbidden **10** prohibited, unlicensed, unofficial **12** unauthorized **13** against the law **16** unconstitutional

unlawful act 5 crime **6** felony **10** wrongdoing **11** lawbreaking, malfeasance, misdemeanor

unleash 4 free **5** let go **7** release, set free **8** let loose, liberate **12** give free rein

unlettered 8 ignorant, untaught **9** unlearned, untutored **10** illiterate, uneducated, unschooled **11** unscholarly

unlighted 3 dim **4** dark **5** murky, unlit **6** gloomy **7** stygian, sunless **8** moonless **9** lightless **13** unilluminated

unlikable, unlikeable 7 hateful **9** offensive, unlovable **10** hard to like, unloveable, unpleasant **11** displeasing, unappealing **12** disagreeable

unlike 7 diverse, unalike, unequal **9** different, disparate **10** dissimilar

unlikelihood 12 doubtfulness, unlikeliness **13** improbability

unlikely 8 hopeless **10** improbable **11** unpromising **12** questionable, unbelievable, unpropitious **19** scarcely conceivable

unlikeness 8 contrast, variance **9** disparity, variation **10** difference, divergence **13** dissimilarity, dissimilitude

unlimited 4 huge, vast **5** total **7** endless, immense **8** absolute, complete, infinite **9** boundless, limitless, unbounded, unchecked **11** unqualified **12** immeasurable, totalitarian, uncontrolled, unrestrained, unrestricted **13** comprehensive, inexhaustible, unconstrained **15** all- encompassing

unload 4 dump **7** off-load **8** get rid of, unburden **9** dispose of **10** unencumber

unlooked for 6 sudden **7** unasked **8** surprise **10** unexpected, unforeseen, unheralded **11** unannounced, uncalled for, unpredicted, unsolicited **13** serendipitous, unanticipated

unlovable, unloveable 7 hateful **9** unlikable **10** hard to like, unlikeable, unpleasant **11** displeasing, unappealing **12** disagreeable

unloving 4 cold, cool **6** frigid **11** indifferent, passionless **13** unimpassioned

unlucky 6 cursed, jinxed **7** hapless, unhappy **8** ill-fated, luckless, untoward **9** ill-omened **10** ill-starred **11** star- crossed, unfortunate **12** inauspicious, misfortunate

unman 7 unnerve **8** castrate **10** discourage, emasculate

unmanageable 5 balky, bulky **6** mulish, unruly **7** awkward, unhandy, wayward, willful **8** ungainly, unwieldy **9** fractious, pigheaded **10** cumbersome, rebellious, refractory **11** disobedient, intractable, troublesome **12** incorrigible **14** uncontrollable

unmanly 5 timid **6** yellow **8** cowardly, sissyish, womanish **9** sissified, weak-kneed **10** effeminate **11** lily-livered, unmasculine, weakhearted **12** fainthearted **13** pusillanimous **14** chickenhearted

unmannerly 5 crude, gross, surly **6** coarse **7** boorish, ill- bred, loutish, uncivil, uncouth **8** impolite **10** ungracious, unladylike **11** ill-mannered **12** badly behaved, discourteous **13** ungentlemanly

unmarked 5 clean, clear **9** undamaged, undefaced, unnoticed **10** unobserved **11** unblemished **15** undistinguished

unmarried 4 free **5** unwed **6** maiden, single **7** old maid, widowed **8** bachelor, divorced, spinster, unwedded, virginal, wifeless **9** available, fancy free **10** spouseless, unattached **11** husbandless **21** footloose and fancy-free

unmarried girl
   French: **10** jeune fille
   German: **8** fraulein
   Spanish: **8** senorita

Unmarried Woman, An
   director: **12** Paul Mazursky
   cast: **9** Alan Bates **11** Cliff Gorman **13** Jill Clayburgh, Michael Murphy

unmask 4 bare, show **6** betray, expose, reveal, unveil **7** lay open,

uncover 8 disclose, discover **12** bring to light

unmasking 6 baring **8** betrayal, exposure **9** discovery, unveiling **10** disclosure, laying open, revelation, uncovering **15** bringing to light

unmatched 6 unlike **7** diverse, supreme, unequal **8** peerless, variable **9** differing, disparate, matchless, unequaled **10** dissimilar **12** second to none, unparalleled **13** beyond compare

unmerciful 4 cold, evil **5** cruel, harsh **6** brutal, severe, unkind **7** brutish, extreme, inhuman **8** inhumane, pitiless, ruthless **9** excessive, heartless, inclement, merciless, unfeeling, unpitying, unsparing **10** malevolent, relentless **11** hardhearted **14** unconscionable

unmindful 3 lax **6** remiss **7** unaware **8** careless, derelict, heedless **9** forgetful, negligent, oblivious, unheeding **11** thoughtless, unconscious

unmistakable 5 clear, plain **6** patent **7** evident, glaring, obvious **8** apparent, distinct, manifest, palpable **9** prominent **10** pronounced, undeniable **11** conspicuous, unequivocal **12** indisputable **14** unquestionable

unmistakably 7 clearly, plainly **8** palpably, patently **9** certainly, decidedly, downright, evidently, glaringly, obviously **10** definitely, distinctly, manifestly, positively, thoroughly, undeniably **11** prominently **12** indisputably **13** conspicuously, unequivocally **14** unquestionably **17** beyond all question

unmitigated 6 arrant **8** absolute, unabated, unbroken **9** downright, out-and-out **10** persistent, unrelieved **11** unqualified **12** unalleviated **13** uninterrupted

unmixed 4 neat, pure **5** sheer **6** simple **8** straight **9** unalloyed, unblended, undiluted, unmingled **13** unadulterated

unmoved 4 calm, cold, firm **5** aloof **6** dogged **7** devoted, staunch **8** resolute, resolved, uncaring, unshaken **9** dedicated, obstinate, steadfast, unfeeling, unpitying, unstirred, untouched **10** determined, inflexible, not shifted, persistent, relentless, unaffected, unswerving, unwavering **11** indifferent, unconcerned, undeviating, undisturbed, unfaltering **12** stonyhearted, uninterested, unresponsive **14** uncompromising

unmoving 4 dead, dull **5** fixed, inert, still **6** boring, serene **8** immobile **9** powerless **10** motionless, stationary **11** emotionless **13** at a standstill

unnamed 8 nameless, unsigned **9** anonymous, incognito **10** innominate, uncredited, unreported, unrevealed **11** undisclosed, unspecified **12** pseudonymous, undesignated, undiscovered, unidentified **14** unacknowledged

unnatural 4 fake **5** phony, put-on **6** forced **7** assumed, stilted, studied, unusual **8** aberrant, abnormal, affected, freakish, mannered, peculiar **9** anomalous, contrived **10** artificial, theatrical **13** self-conscious

unnecessary 5 extra **6** excess **7** surplus **8** needless, overmuch **9** auxiliary, excessive **10** expendable, gratuitous, unrequired **11** dispensable, superfluous, uncalled- for, unessential **13** supplementary

unnerve 5 daunt, scare, upset **7** agitate, unhinge **8** frighten, unsettle **10** intimidate

unnerving 5 scary **8** daunting **9** upsetting **10** enervating, unsettling **11** frightening

unnoticeable 3 dim **5** faint **6** hidden **7** obscure **9** concealed **10** indistinct, unassuming, unemphatic, unobserved **11** unobtrusive **12** undetectable **13** imperceptible, inconspicuous, insignificant, undiscernible **14** unostentatious

unnoticed 6 unfelt, unseen **7** unheard, unnoted **8** unheeded, untasted **10** not smelled, overlooked, unobserved **11** disregarded, unperceived **12** undiscovered

unobservant 4 dull **5** blind **8** unseeing **9** unmindful **11** incognizant

unobstructed 4 fair, free, open **5** clear **8** apparent **9** unimpeded **10** unhampered, unhindered **11** unprevented

unobtainable 9 hard to get **10** impossible, out of reach, out of touch **11** unavailable, unreachable **12** improcurable, inaccessible

unobtrusive 3 shy **6** humble, modest **7** bashful **8** reserved, reticent, retiring **9** diffident **10** unassuming **11** unassertive **13** inconspicuous, unpretentious **14** unostentatious

unoccupied 4 idle **5** empty **6** vacant **8** unfilled **9** abandoned, unengaged **10** untenanted **11** uninhabited

unofficial 8 informal **12** unauthorized

unorganized 5 loose **6** casual, random **7** aimless, chaotic **8** confused **9** haphazard, orderless, unordered **10** disjointed, unarranged, undirected **11** harum-scarum **12** unclassified, unsystematic **13** helter-skelter **14** unsystematized

unornamented 4 bald, bare **5** blank, naked, plain, stark **6** simple **7** austere **9** unadorned **11** undecorated **13** unembellished

unorthodox 7 erratic **9** eccentric, irregular **14** unconventional

unostentatious 3 shy **5** plain, quiet **6** humble, modest, simple **9** unadorned, unaffected **10** unassuming **11** con-

strained **13** inconspicuous, unpretentious **14** unpresumptuous

unpaid 3 due **4** owed **5** owing **9** in arrears **11** outstanding

unpaid debt 5 debit **7** arrears **9** liability **10** balance due, obligation **12** indebtedness

unpalatable 5 nasty **8** inedible, unsavory **9** repellent, repulsive **10** badtasting, unpleasant **11** displeasing, distasteful **12** disagreeable, unappetizing **13** hard to swallow

unparalleled 4 best, rare **5** alone, crack, elect **6** unique **8** gilt-edge, peerless, singular **9** matchless, superfine, unequaled, unmatched, unrivaled **10** crackajack, inimitable, unimitated **11** unsurpassed **12** unapproached **13** unprecedented **15** of the first water

unperceptive 5 blind **9** unfeeling **11** insensitive, unobservant **12** imperceptive, imperciptient **13** unsympathetic

unperturbed 4 calm, cool **6** poised **8** composed, tranquil **9** collected, unexcited, unruffled **10** coolheaded, nonchalant, unagitated, undismayed, untroubled **11** levelheaded, undisturbed **13** unimpassioned

unplanned 9 impromptu **10** accidental, fortuitous, improvised, unexpected, unforeseen **11** spontaneous **12** uncalculated **13** unintentional **14** extemporaneous, unpremeditated **15** spur-of-the-moment

unpleasant 5 nasty, pesky **7** irksome, noisome **8** annoying, churlish **9** obnoxious, offensive, repugnant, repulsive, unlikable, vexatious **10** illhumored, ill-natured **11** displeasing, distasteful **12** disagreeable, unattractive **13** objectionable

unpleasantness 8 ugliness **9** ill nature, nastiness **12** churlishness **13** obnoxiousness, offensiveness, repulsiveness **15** distastefulness **16** disagreeableness, unattractiveness

unpointed 4 dull **5** blunt **6** dulled **11** unsharpened

unpolished 3 raw **5** gawky, inept, rough **6** cloudy, clumsy **7** amateur, awkward, unwaxed **8** inexpert, unbuffed, unglazed, unshined **9** inelegant, unrefined, unskilled **10** uncultured, unfinished, unskillful **11** unburnished, unpracticed **12** uncultivated **13** inexperienced **14** unaccomplished **15** unsophisticated

unpopular 7 snubbed **8** disliked, rebuffed, rejected, slighted, unwanted **9** disdained, neglected, unwelcome **10** unaccepted **11** disapproved, undesirable **12** looked down on, unacceptable

unpopulated 5 rural **9** backwoods, unpeopled, unsettled

unprecedented 5 novel **6** unique **9** unheard-of **10** unexampled **11** excep-

tional **12** unparalleled **13** extraordinary **15** hitherto unknown

unpredictable 6 fitful **7** erratic **8** fanciful, unstable, variable **9** arbitrary, eccentric, impulsive, mercurial, uncertain, whimsical **10** capricious, changeable, inconstant

unprejudiced 4 fair, just **8** unbiased, unswayed **9** impartial, objective, unbigoted **10** even-handed, fair-minded, open-minded, undogmatic **11** broadminded **12** uninfluenced **13** disinterested

unpremeditated 5 ad-lib **9** impetuous, impromptu, impulsive, unplanned **10** accidental, improvised, unintended **11** involuntary, spontaneous **12** uncalculated, unthought-out **13** unintentional **14** extemporaneous **15** spur-of-the-moment

unprepared 5 ad-lib **7** offhand, unready **8** off guard **9** extempore, impromptu **10** flat-footed, improvised **11** spontaneous, unrehearsed **14** extemporaneous **15** spur-of-the-moment

unprepossessing 4 grim **5** seedy **10** ill-favored, ill- looking **12** unattractive

unpressed 5 baggy **6** mussed, sloppy **7** creased, rumpled **8** unironed, wrinkled **9** shapeless, uncreased

unpretentious 5 plain **6** homely, humble, modest, simple **10** unassuming, unimposing **11** unelaborate, unobtrusive **14** unostentatious

unprincipled 6 amoral **12** unscrupulous **14** conscienceless, unconscionable

unproductive 4 poor **6** barren **7** sterile, useless **8** bootless **9** infertile **10** unfruitful, unyielding **11** ineffective, ineffectual, inefficient **12** unprofitable

unprofessional 6 shoddy, sloppy **7** amateur **8** bungling, careless **9** negligent, unethical **10** amateurish **11** incompetent, inefficient, unpracticed **12** unprincipled **13** inexperienced, undisciplined, unworkmanlike **14** unbusinesslike

unprofitable 4 vain **7** useless **8** bootless **11** ineffective, ineffectual

unprogressive 7 diehard **8** backward, standpat, stubborn **9** benighted, rightwing **11** reactionary, reactionist **12** conservative **17** ultraconservative

unprolific 6 barren **7** sterile **9** infertile, unfertile **10** nonbearing **12** unproductive

unpromising 5 bleak **9** ill-omened **10** forbidding **11** unfavorable **12** inauspicious, unpropitious

unpropitious 7 adverse **8** contrary **9** unfitting **10** unsuitable **11** unfavorable **12** antagonistic, inauspicious, infelicitous

unprotected 4 open **5** naked **6** unsafe **7** exposed, unarmed **8** helpless, insecure, perilous **9** dangerous, hazardous, unguarded **10** undefended, vulnerable **11** defenseless

unproven 7 in doubt **8** arguable, doubtful **10** indefinite, in question, up in the air **11** open to doubt, unconfirmed **12** experimental, inconclusive, questionable **13** unestablished **14** open to question

unpunctual 4 late **5** tardy **7** belated **10** behindhand, behindtime

unqualified 5 total, unfit, utter **8** absolute, complete, inexpert, positive, thorough, unsuited **9** downright, out-and-out, unskilled, untrained **10** consummate, undisputed, uneducated, unprepared, unschooled **11** ill-equipped, incompetent **13** inexperienced, unconditional

unquenched 8 unslaked **11** unsatisfied **14** unextinguished

unquestionable 4 sure **5** clear, plain **6** proven **7** certain, evident, obvious, perfect **8** definite, flawless **9** blameless, errorless, faultless **10** impeccable, undeniable **11** beyond doubt, irrefutable, self-evident, unequivocal **12** indisputable, uncensurable **13** uncontestable, unimpeachable **14** irreproachable

unquestionably 6 surely **7** totally **9** certainly, doubtless **10** absolutely, completely, definitely, positively, unarguably **12** conclusively, indisputably, without doubt **13** unequivocally

unravel 4 undo **5** feaze, solve **6** unfold, unfurl, unknit **7** clear up, resolve **8** decipher, separate, untangle **9** pull apart **10** disinvolve **11** disentangle

unreachable 10 impossible, out of touch **11** out of the way, unavailable, unrealistic **12** inaccessible, unobtainable **14** unapproachable

unreal 4 airy **5** dream **6** dreamy **7** ghostly, not real, phantom, shadowy **8** ethereal, illusive, illusory, imagined, spectral **9** dreamlike, fantastic, imaginary, legendary **10** chimerical, fictitious, idealistic, intangible **11** nonexistent **13** insubstantial **16** phantasmagorical

unrealistic 4 wild **5** crazy, silly **6** absurd **7** asinine, foolish **8** crackpot, delusory, fanciful **9** illogical **10** idealistic, improbable, infeasible, starry-eyed **11** impractical **12** unreasonable

unrealized 8 thwarted **10** frustrated, incomplete **11** nonexistent, unfulfilled, unsatisfied **14** unaccomplished

unreasonable 5 undue **6** absurd, biased, mulish, unfair **7** bigoted **8** obdurate, stubborn, too great **9** excessive, fanatical, illogical, obstinate, pigheaded, senseless, unbending **10** bullheaded, exorbitant, far-fetched, headstrong, immoderate, inflexible, inordinate, irrational, prejudiced, un-

yielding **11** extravagant, intractable, nonsensical, opinionated, uncalled-for, unwarranted **12** closed-minded, preposterous, ungovernable, unmanageable **13** unjustifiable

unreasoning 8 careless, heedless **9** impulsive **10** irrational, unthinking **11** thoughtless **13** unintelligent

unrecognizable 9 disguised, incognito **10** in disguise **11** camouflaged **14** unidentifiable

unrecognized 6 unsung **7** cryptic, unknown **9** incognito, unnoticed

unrefined 3 raw **5** crude, rough **6** coarse, vulgar **7** boorish, low-bred **9** inelegant

unrehearsed 7 offhand **8** informal **9** extempore, impromptu, impulsive, unplanned, unstudied **10** improvised, off-the-cuff, unprepared **11** extemporary, spontaneous **14** extemporaneous, unpremeditated **15** improvisational, spur-of-the-moment **19** off the top of one's head

unrelated 6 not kin, unlike **7** foreign **8** unallied **10** dissimilar, extraneous, irrelevant, non-germane **11** unconnected **12** inapplicable, incompatible, unassociated **13** inappropriate

unrelenting 5 rigid **6** steady **7** adamant, endless **8** constant, unabated, unbroken **9** ceaseless, incessant, tenacious, unbending **10** implacable, inexorable, inflexible, relentless, unrelieved, unswerving, unwavering, unyielding **11** undeviating, unremitting **14** uncompromising

unreliable 4 fake **5** false, phony **6** fickle **8** fallible, mistaken, unstable **9** deceitful, erroneous, uncertain **10** capricious, changeable, inaccurate, inconstant **12** questionable, undependable **13** irresponsible, untrustworthy

unremarkable 5 usual **6** common **7** average **8** everyday, mediocre, ordinary **11** commonplace **12** unimpressive, unsurprising **13** insignificant, unexceptional **15** undistinguished

unremitting 6 dogged **8** constant, tireless, untiring **9** ceaseless, continual, incessant, unceasing **10** continuous, persistent **11** persevering

unrepentant 7 callous **8** hardened, obdurate, unatoned **9** unashamed **10** uncontrite, unexpiated **11** remorseless **12** incorrigible, unregenerate

unrepressed 4 free, open **7** liberal **8** effusive, outgoing **9** expansive, exuberant **11** extroverted, uninhibited **12** unrestrained

unreserved 4 full, open **5** frank **6** entire **11** unqualified **12** wholehearted

unresolved 4 moot **5** vague **7** pending **8** doubtful, unsolved **9** tentative, uncertain, undecided, unsettled **10** disputable, unanswered **11** contestable, speculative **12** questionable, undeter-

mined **13** problematical, unascertained

unresponsive 4 cold, cool, dull, limp **5** inert **6** frigid **7** passive **8** lifeless **9** apathetic, unfeeling **11** cold-blooded, inattentive, indifferent, unemotional **13** dispassionate, unsympathetic

unresponsiveness 6 apathy **7** inertia **9** lassitude, passivity **11** inattention, passiveness **12** indifference

unrest 5 chaos **6** tumult **7** anarchy, discord, ferment, protest, turmoil **8** disorder, disquiet, upheaval **9** agitation, rebellion **10** discontent, turbulence **12** restlessness **15** dissatisfaction

unrestrained 8 uncurbed **9** abandoned, boundless, excessive, unbridled, unchecked, unlimited **10** immoderate, inordinate, unfettered, ungoverned, unhampered, unhindered, unreserved **11** extravagant, intemperate, uninhibited, unrepressed **12** uncontrolled, unrestricted, unsuppressed **13** irrepressible

unrestraint 6 excess **7** abandon **9** uncontrol **10** unruliness **12** extravagance, immoderation, recklessness **13** excessiveness, impulsiveness

unrestricted 8 absolute, complete **9** out-and-out, unbounded, unlimited **11** unqualified **12** unrestrained **13** unconditional

unrigid 3 lax **4** easy, limp, soft **5** loose **6** giving, limber, mobile, pliant, supple **7** elastic, lenient, plastic, pliable **8** flexible, informal, merciful, tolerant, yielding **9** indulgent, malleable **11** conformable

unrigorous 4 easy **5** loose, slack **6** casual, sloppy **7** inexact **8** careless, slapdash **9** imprecise

unripe 5 green **8** immature **10** unseasoned **11** undeveloped **14** underdeveloped

unrivaled 8 superior, topnotch **9** unequaled **10** undisputed **11** unsurpassed

unroll 6 reveal, uncoil, unfold, unfurl, unwind **7** display, lay open, play out **9** spread out

unruffled 4 calm, cool, even, mild **5** quiet, still **6** placid, serene, smooth **8** composed, tranquil **9** collected **10** coolheaded, nonchalant, unagitated, untroubled **11** undisturbed, unperturbed **13** self-possessed

unruly 4 wild **5** rowdy **7** restive, wayward, willful **8** contrary, perverse **9** fractious, unbridled **10** boisterous, disorderly, headstrong, refractory **11** disobedient, intractable **12** obstreperous, ungovernable, unmanageable **13** undisciplined **14** uncontrollable

unsafe 5 risky **7** exposed **8** insecure, perilous **9** dangerous, hazardous, unguarded **10** undefended, unreliable, vulnerable **11** defenseless, treacherous, unprotected **13** untrustworthy

unsatisfactory 4 poor **5** inept, unfit **8** below par, inferior, unworthy **9** deficient **10** inadequate, ineligible, unsuitable **12** inadmissible, unacceptable **13** inappropriate

unsavory 3 bad **4** flat, foul **5** nasty **7** insipid, tainted **9** tasteless **10** bad-tasting, nauseating, unpleasant **11** distasteful, unpalatable **12** disagreeable, unappetizing

unscathed 5 sound, whole **6** entire, intact, unhurt **7** perfect **8** unharmed **9** uninjured, untouched **10** unimpaired **11** unscratched **13** all in one piece

unscholarly 8 ignorant **9** unlearned **10** illiterate, uneducated, uninformed **11** ill-informed **13** unintelligent

unschooled 3 raw **5** green **6** callow **8** ignorant, untaught **9** unlearned **10** illiterate, uneducated, uninformed, unlettered, unseasoned **11** uninitiated **13** inexperienced

unscrupulous 5 sharp **6** amoral **7** crooked, devious, immoral **9** unethical **12** dishonorable, unprincipled

unseasonable 6 too hot **7** too cold, too warm **8** abnormal, untimely

unseasoned 3 raw **5** bland, green, plain **6** callow **7** untried **8** immature **13** inexperienced

unseeing 5 blind **7** unaware **9** oblivious, sightless **11** unobservant

unseemly 4 rude **5** crude, gross **6** coarse, vulgar **7** boorish, loutish **8** churlish, improper, indecent, unworthy **9** incorrect, offensive, tasteless **10** indecorous, indelicate, out of place, unbecoming, unladylike, unsuitable **11** distasteful, ill-mannered, unbefitting, undignified **12** discourteous, disreputable **13** discreditable, inappropriate, reprehensible, ungentlemanly

unselfconscious 7 artless **10** unaffected **13** unpretentious

unselfish 7 liberal **8** generous, handsome, princely, selfless **10** altruistic, benevolent, big-hearted, charitable, open-handed **11** considerate, magnanimous, magnificent **12** humanitarian **13** philanthropic **15** self-sacrificing

unserviceable 7 useless **8** unusable

unsettle 5 upset **6** bother, rattle, ruffle **7** agitate, confuse, disturb, fluster, perturb, trouble, unhinge **8** bewilder, confound, disorder **9** unbalance **10** disconcert **13** throw off guard

unsettled 5 fazed **7** anxious, nervous, ruffled **8** agitated, confused, doubtful **9** disturbed, nonplused, perturbed, undecided **10** disquieted, distracted, nonplussed, up in the air **11** discomfited **12** disconcerted **16** at sixes and sevens

unshackle 4 free **7** release, set free, unchain **8** liberate, unfetter

unshakable 4 fast **6** stable **7** abiding, staunch **8** constant, enduring **9** dauntless, permanent, steadfast, unruffled **10** changeless, inflexible, unsinkable, unwavering **11** levelheaded, unflappable **13** imperturbable

unshaken 4 calm, cool **6** poised, serene, stable **7** staunch, unmoved **8** composed, constant, resolved **9** steadfast, tenacious, undaunted, unexcited, unruffled **10** controlled, determined, inflexible, relentless, unaffected, unswerving, untroubled, unwavering **11** levelheaded, undeviating, undisturbed, unemotional, unfaltering, unflinching, unperturbed **13** self-possessed **14** uncompromising

unshapely 5 baggy **9** amorphous, shapeless

unshaven 5 hairy **7** bearded, bristly, hirsute, stubbly, unkempt **9** whiskered **11** bewhiskered

unsheathe 4 bare **6** expose **7** pull out **8** withdraw

unsightly 4 ugly **6** horrid, odious **7** hideous u **9** obnoxious, offensive, repellent, repulsive, revolting, sickening **11** distasteful **12** unattractive

unsigned 9 anonymous **13** bearing no name

unskilled 5 green, inept **7** untried **9** untrained **10** amateurish, apprentice **11** incompetent, unqualified **13** inexperienced

unskillful 5 inept **6** clumsy, unable **7** awkward **8** inexpert **9** incapable, maladroit, untrained **10** amateurish **11** incompetent, ineffective, unpracticed **13** inexperienced

unsmiling 3 sad **4** glum, grim **5** grave **6** dismal **7** austere, joyless, serious **9** cheerless, grim-faced

unsociable 7 haughty **9** withdrawn **10** antisocial, unfriendly, ungracious **11** introverted **14** unapproachable

unsoiled 4 pure **5** clean, fresh, white **6** chaste **8** innocent, pristine, spotless **9** unstained, unsullied **10** immaculate **11** unblemished, untarnished

unsolicited 4 free **8** unforced, unsought, unwanted **9** undesired, uninvited, unwelcome, voluntary **10** gratuitous, unasked for **11** spontaneous, unnecessary, unrequested, unwished for, volunteered

unsophisticated 4 open **5** green, naive **6** candid **7** artless, natural **8** homespun, innocent, trusting **9** ingenuous, unstudied, unworldly **10** unaffected, unassuming **11** uncontrived **13** undissembling, unpretentious **15** straightforward

unsound 3 mad, off **4** weak **5** risky, shaky, unfit, wrong **6** absurd, ailing,

faulty, feeble, flawed, infirm, insane, marred, sickly, unsafe **7** foolish, invalid, rickety, tottery **8** confused, crippled, decrepit, deranged, diseased, drooping, impaired, insecure, not solid, not valid, perilous, specious, spurious, unhinged, unstable, unsteady **9** blemished, dangerous, defective, erroneous, hazardous, illogical, imperfect, incorrect, senseless, uncertain, unfounded, unhealthy, unsettled, untenable **10** disordered, fallacious, groundless, irrational, precarious, unbalanced, unreliable **11** languishing, mentally ill **12** in poor health **13** off one's rocker, unsubstantial

unsoundness 7 frailty **8** delicacy, weakness **9** fragility, frailness, shakiness **11** decrepitude, derangement, instability **12** unsteadiness

unsparing 4 full **6** giving, lavish **7** copious, liberal, profuse **8** abundant, generous **9** bountiful, plenteous, plentiful, unlimited **10** big-hearted, munificent, ungrudging, unstinting **11** extravagant, magnanimous, unqualified **13** unconditional

unspeakable 4 huge, vast **5** awful, great **6** odious **7** fearful, immense **8** enormous, shocking **9** abhorrent, frightful, loathsome, monstrous, repellent, repulsive, revolting, sickening, unheard-of **10** abominable, disgusting, incredible, nauseating, prodigious **11** astonishing, unutterable **12** overwhelming, unimaginable **13** extraordinary, inconceivable, inexpressible, undescribable

unspecified 5 vague **7** general, unnamed **9** undefined, unsettled **10** indefinite **11** unannounced, unindicated, unmentioned **12** undesignated, undetermined, unpublicized, unstipulated

unspoiled 4 open **7** artless, natural, perfect **8** pristine, spotless, trusting, unharmed, unmarred **9** preserved, undamaged, unscarred, unspotted, unstudied, unworldly **10** unaffected, unassuming, unimpaired, unpampered **11** unblemished, uncorrupted **13** unpretentious **15** unself-conscious, unsophisticated

unspoken 5 tacit **6** silent **7** implied **8** implicit **9** ineffable, not voiced, unuttered **10** understood **11** unexpressed

unspotted 5 clean **8** spotless, unsoiled **9** undefiled, unstained, unsullied **11** unblemished

unstable 4 weak **5** frail, shaky, tippy **6** fickle, fitful, flimsy, wobbly **7** erratic, fragile, rickety **8** changing, insecure, shifting, unsteady, volatile **9** emotional, mercurial, tottering **10** capricious, changeable, fly-by-night, irrational **11** fluctuating, vacillating **12** inconsistent **13** irresponsible, unpredictable, unsubstantial

unstained 5 clean 8 spotless 9 unspotted, unsullied, untainted 11 unblemished, uncorrupted

unsteady 6 fickle, wobbly 7 rickety 8 doubtful, unstable 10 unreliable 12 questionable, undependable 13 untrustworthy

unstinting 11 unqualified 12 enthusiastic, unrestrained, wholehearted

unstooped 5 erect 6 unbent 7 upright 8 straight, vertical

unstudied 4 glib 6 casual 7 artless, natural 8 informal, unforced, unversed 9 guileless, unuttered 10 unaffected 11 spontaneous 12 uncalculated

unsubmissive 6 unruly 7 defiant, froward, naughty, wayward 8 contrary, mutinous, perverse, stubborn 9 fractious, insurgent, obstinate, seditious, undutiful 10 disorderly, rebellious, refractory, unyielding 11 disobedient, intractable 12 noncompliant, recalcitrant, ungovernable, unmanageable 13 insubordinate

unsubstantial 4 airy, weak 5 filmy 6 feeble, flimsy 7 unsound 8 ethereal, fanciful, illusory 9 idealized, imaginary 10 jerrybuilt 11 lightweight 12 undetectable 13 imperceptible 17 indistinguishable

unsubstantiated 8 disputed 10 unverified 15 unauthenticated

unsuccessful 4 poor, vain 6 foiled, futile, hard up 7 baffled, hapless, unlucky, useless 8 abortive, badly off, luckless, strapped, thwarted 9 fruitless, moneyless, penniless 10 illstarred, profitless, unavailing, unfruitful 11 ineffectual, unfortunate 12 unproductive, unprofitable, unprosperous 14 unremunerative

unsuitability 9 unfitness, wrongness 11 impropriety, uselessness 12 unseemliness 13 inconsistency 15 incompatibility, unacceptability 17 inappropriateness

unsuitable 5 inapt, unfit 7 unhappy, useless 8 improper, unseemly 9 unfitting, worthless 10 inadequate, indecorous, out of place, unbecoming, unsuitable 11 incongruous, unbefitting 12 inadmissible, incompatible, inconsistent, infelicitous, out of keeping, unacceptable 13 inappropriate

unsuited 5 inapt, wrong 9 unfitting 10 out of place 13 inappropriate

unsullied 5 clean 8 spotless, unsoiled 9 undefiled, uninjured, untainted 10 unpolluted 11 unblackened, unblemished, uncorrupted, untarnished 14 uncontaminated

unsupportable 6 faulty 9 unfounded, untenable 12 indefensible

unsure 3 shy 5 timid 7 bashful 8 hesitant, insecure, reserved 9 unassured, uncertain, undecided 11 in a quan-

dary, unconfi- dent, unconvinced 12 self-doubting 15 self-distrustful

unsurpassed 4 best 7 highest, supreme 8 greatest, peerless, superior 9 matchless, nonpareil, paramount, unequaled, unmatched, unrivaled 10 consummate, unexcelled 11 exceptional 12 incomparable, transcendent, unparalleled

unsuspecting 5 naive 6 unwary 7 unaware 8 gullible, off guard, trusting 9 believing, credulous 12 overtrustful, unsuspicious 13 overcredulous

unsuspicious 5 naive 8 gullible, trustful, trusting 9 credulous 12 unsuspecting 13 unquestioning

unswerving 4 firm 6 steady, strong 7 devoted, staunch 8 faithful, resolute, resolved, unshaken, untiring 9 dedicated, steadfast, undaunted 10 determined, inflexible, unflagging, unwavering, unyielding 11 undeviating, unfaltering, unflinching, unremitting 12 single-minded 14 uncompromising

unsympathetic 7 callous 8 pitiless, uncaring 9 heartless, repellent, repugnant, unfeeling, unlikable 10 hardboiled, unlikeable, unmerciful, unpleasant 11 coldhearted, displeasing, hardhearted, indifferent, uncongenial 12 antipathetic, unattractive 15 uncompassionate

unsystematic 6 sloppy 7 chaotic, jumbled, muddled 8 confused 9 haphazard, unplanned 10 disordered, disorderly 12 disorganized, unmethodical

untainted 4 pure 5 clear 9 unsullied 11 uncorrupted 13 unadulterated

untalented 5 inept 8 mediocre, ungifted 9 unskilled 10 amateurish, unskillful 14 unaccomplished

untamed 4 wild 5 feral 6 savage 9 unsubdued 11 uncivilized 12 uncultivated

untangle 5 solve 7 clear up, unravel, unsnarl, untwist 9 extricate 11 disentangle 13 straighten out

untarnished 6 bright 7 perfect, shining 8 flawless, polished, spotless, unsoiled 9 faultless, undefiled, unstained, unsullied, untainted 10 immaculate, impeccable, undisputed, unoxidized 11 unblackened, unblemished 12 unbesmirched 13 unimpeachable

untaught 6 unread 7 natural 8 ignorant 9 untutored 10 illiterate, uneducated, unlettered, unschooled 11 spontaneous 12 uninstructed

untenable 4 weak 6 faulty, flawed 7 invalid, unsound 8 baseless, specious, spurious 9 debatable, erroneous, illogical 10 fallacious, groundless, unreliable 11 contestable 12 indefensible, questionable 13 insupportable, unjustifiable, unsustainable 14 unmaintainable

unthinkable 11 unwarranted 12 unimaginable 13 inconceivable, insupportable, unjustifiable 16 incomprehensible, out of the question

unthinking 7 witless 8 careless, heedless, mindless, tactless 9 imprudent, negligent, senseless 11 inadvertent, insensitive, thoughtless 12 undiplomatic 13 inconsiderate, uncircumspect

untidiness 5 chaos, mix-up, upset 6 jumble 7 clutter 8 disarray, disorder, scramble, shambles 9 confusion, messiness 10 sloppiness 12 dishevelment 14 disarrangement 15 disorganization

untidy 5 dowdy, messy 6 frowsy, mussed, sloppy 7 chaotic, rumpled, tousled, unkempt 8 careless, confused, littered, mussed up, slipshod, slovenly 9 cluttered 10 bedraggled, disarrayed, disheveled, disorderly, slatternly, topsy-turvy 12 unmethodical 13 helter-skelter

untie 4 free, undo 5 loose 6 loosen, unbind, unlace 7 unchain, unstrap 8 make free, unfasten 11 disentangle

untilled 6 fallow 8 unplowed 12 uncultivated

until we meet again
  French: 5 adieu 8 au revoir
  German: 14 auf Wiedersehen
  Hawaiian: 5 aloha
  Italian: 4 ciao 5 addio 11 arrivederci
  Japanese: 8 sayonara
  Spanish: 5 adios

untimely 5 inapt 7 unhappy 8 illtimed, mistimed, unseemly 9 imprudent, premature, unfitting 10 illadvised, malapropos, out of place, unbecoming, unexpected, unsuitable 11 inopportune, unbefitting, unfortunate 12 inconvenient, infelicitous 13 inappropriate

untiring 5 fresh 6 steady 7 devoted, earnest, patient, staunch, zealous 8 constant, diligent, resolute, sedulous, tireless 9 assiduous, dedicated, steadfast, tenacious, unceasing, unwearied 10 determined, persistent, relentless, unflagging 11 never tiring, persevering, unfaltering, unremitting 12 wholehearted 13 indefatigable

untold 6 myriad, secret, unsaid 7 endless, private, unknown 8 hushed up, infinite, numerous, unspoken, withheld 9 concealed, countless, limitless, unbounded, uncounted, unrelated 10 numberless, suppressed, unnumbered, unreported, unrevealed 11 innumerable, undisclosed, unexpressed, unpublished 12 immeasurable, incalculable, undetermined

Untouchables, The
  character: 7 Rossman 9 Eliot Ness, Lee Hobson 10 Cam Allison, Frank Nitti 11 Enrico Rossi 14 Martin Flaherty 18 William Youngfellow

cast: 10 Jerry Paris **11** Bruce Gordon, Paul Picerni, Robert Stack, Steve London **13** Abel Fernandez, Anthony George, Nick Georgiade
narrator: 14 Walter Winchell

untouched 3 new **4** pure **5** alone **6** intact, virgin **8** pristine, unharmed **9** uninjured **10** unaffected, unmolested

untoward 5 amiss **6** unruly **7** adverse **8** contrary **9** difficult **11** unfavorable **12** inauspicious, unpropitious

untrainable 6 unruly **11** intractable, unteachable **12** ungovernable

untrained 3 raw **5** green **7** untried **9** unskilled **11** unqualified **13** inexperienced

untried 3 raw **5** green **6** callow **8** immature, untested **10** unseasoned **13** inexperienced

untroubled 4 calm **6** placid, serene **7** halcyon, relaxed **8** carefree, careless, peaceful, tranquil **9** easygoing, unworried **10** unbothered **11** free-and-easy, undisturbed, unperturbed **12** happy-go-lucky, lighthearted

untrue 4 fake, sham **5** false **6** made up **7** not true **8** disloyal, spurious, unchaste **9** dishonest, erroneous, faithless, falsified, incorrect, unfounded **10** adulterous, fallacious, fictitious, fraudulent, groundless, inaccurate, inconstant, perfidious, unfaithful, untruthful **11** promiscuous, treacherous **12** meretricious **13** double-dealing

untrustworthy 5 false **6** fickle, shifty, untrue **7** corrupt, crooked, devious **8** disloyal, fallible, slippery, two-faced **9** corrupted, deceitful, dishonest, faithless, insincere, uncertain, unethical **10** capricious, inconstant, perfidious, unfaithful, unreliable, untruthful **11** treacherous **12** dishonorable, disreputable, questionable, undependable, unprincipled, unscrupulous **13** irresponsible **15** unauthenticated

untruth 3 fib, lie **4** hoax, tale, yarn **5** fable, story **6** canard, humbug **8** flimflam **9** deception, falsehood, fish story, invention **11** fabrication **12** equivocation **13** falsification, prevarication **16** cock-and-bull story **17** misrepresentation

untruthful 5 false, lying **8** specious, spurious **9** deceptive, dishonest **10** fraudulent, mendacious

untutored 5 naive **6** native, unread **8** ignorant, untaught **10** illiterate, uneducated, unlettered, unschooled **12** uninstructed **15** unsophisticated

untypical 3 odd **4** rare **5** alien **7** bizarre, deviant, strange, unusual **8** aberrant, abnormal, atypical, uncommon **9** anomalous, irregular, unnatural **10** unfamiliar **16** unrepresentative

unused 3 new **7** strange, untried **8** left over, not given, pristine, unopened **9** remaining, untouched **10** unemployed **12** unaccustomed, unacquainted, unhabituated

unusual 4 rare **5** novel **6** unique **7** curious, offbeat, strange **8** atypical, peculiar, singular, uncommon **9** unequaled, unheard-of, unmatched, untypical **10** noteworthy, one of a kind, phenomenal, remarkable, surprising, unfamiliar **11** exceptional **12** incomparable, unparalleled **13** extraordinary, unprecedented **16** out of the ordinary

unvaried 4 even **5** fixed **6** steady **7** regular, uniform **8** all alike, constant **9** identical, unchanged **10** all the same, invariable, monotonous, unchanging **11** homogeneous, unalterable, undeviating

unvarnished 3 raw **4** bald, bare **5** blunt, crude, frank, naked, plain, stark **6** candid, direct, honest, simple **7** sincere **8** straight **9** unadorned, uncolored **10** unfinished **11** fundamental, undisguised **13** unembellished **15** straightforward **23** straight-from-the-shoulder

unvarying 4 even **6** steady **7** regular, uniform **8** constant **10** unwavering

unveil 4 bare **6** reveal **7** divulge, publish, uncloak, uncover **8** announce, disclose **9** broadcast, make known, unsheathe **12** bring to light

unveiled 5 bared **8** divulged, laid bare, revealed **9** announced, broadcast, disclosed, made known, published, uncovered **14** brought to light

unveiling 4 show **5** array **7** display, exhibit, showing **10** exhibition, exposition **13** demonstration

unverified 7 alleged, rumored **8** disputed **15** unauthenticated, unsubstantiated

unwarranted 7 illegal **8** culpable, unlawful **9** arbitrary, unfounded **10** censurable, groundless, unapproved **11** inexcusable, uncalled-for, unjustified **12** indefensible, unauthorized, unreasonable, unsanctioned

unwary 4 rash **5** hasty **7** unalert **8** careless, headlong, heedless, reckless **9** imprudent, unguarded **10** incautious, indiscreet, unwatchful **11** precipitate **12** disregardful **13** uncircumspect

unwashed 4 foul **5** dirty, grimy, muddy **6** filthy, grubby, smudgy, soiled **7** unclean **8** begrimed

unwasteful 6 frugal **7** thrifty **9** effective, effectual, efficient **10** productive

unwavering 4 firm **6** steady, strong **7** staunch **8** faithful, resolute, unshaken, untiring **9** dedicated, steadfast, tenacious **10** determined, persistent, unflagging, unswerving **11** persevering, undeviating, unfaltering, unflinching,

unremitting 12 single-minded **14** uncompromising

unwelcome 7 outcast **8** excluded, rejected, unwanted **9** thankless, uninvited, unpopular **10** uncared for, unpleasant, unrequired **11** displeasing, distasteful, undesirable, unessential, unnecessary, unwished **12** disagreeable, unacceptable

unwell 3 ill, low **4** sick **5** frail **6** ailing, infirm, laid up, poorly, queasy, sickly **7** run-down **8** delicate, qualmish **10** indisposed **11** off one's feed **15** under the weather

unwholesome 3 bad **4** evil, foul **5** toxic **6** deadly, filthy, sinful, wicked **7** baneful, harmful, hurtful, immoral, noxious, ruinous **8** depraved, venomous **9** corrupted, dangerous, degrading, poisonous, polluting, unhealthy **10** corrupting, pernicious **11** deleterious, detrimental, undesirable, unhealthful **12** demoralizing, dishonorable, insalubrious, unnourishing **13** contaminating

unwieldy 5 bulky, heavy **6** clumsy **7** awkward, weighty **8** not handy **10** burdensome, cumbersome **12** hard to handle, incommodious, inconvenient **13** uncomfortable

unwilled 6 reflex **9** automatic **11** involuntary, unconscious **12** uncontrolled **13** nonvolitional

unwilling 5 loath **6** averse **7** against, opposed **9** demurring, reluctant, resistant **10** dissenting, indisposed, undesirous **11** disinclined **12** not in the mood, recalcitrant **14** unenthusiastic

unwillingness 8 aversion **10** opposition, reluctance, resistance **13** indisposition **14** disinclination

unwise 4 dumb **5** crazy, silly **6** stupid **7** foolish, unsound **8** reckless **9** foolhardy, imprudent, senseless **10** ill-advised **11** improvident, inadvisable, injudicious **12** shortsighted, unreasonable **13** irresponsible, unintelligent

unwitting 7 unaware, unmeant **9** unknowing, unplanned **10** accidental, undesigned, unexpected, unthinking **11** inadvertent, involuntary **12** unconsenting **13** unintentional **14** unpremeditated

unwonted 4 rare **7** unusual **8** atypical, uncommon **10** infrequent, remarkable, unexpected, unfamiliar **11** exceptional **12** unaccustomed **13** extraordinary

unworkmanlike 6 clumsy, sloppy **11** inefficient

unworldly 4 holy, pure **5** godly, green, moral, naive, pious **6** callow, devout, divine, sacred, solemn **7** ethical **8** ethereal, heavenly, innocent, trusting **9** aesthetic, celestial, religious, spiritual, unearthly **10** idealistic, immaterial, provincial **12** intellectual, metaphysical, overtrusting **13** inexperienced, philosophical **14** transcendental **15** unsophisticated

unworried 4 calm **6** serene **7** relaxed **8** carefree, composed, peaceful, tranquil **9** easygoing, unruffled **10** untroubled

unworthy 5 unfit **7** ignoble **8** improper, shameful, unseemly **9** degrading, unethical **10** unbecoming, unsuitable **11** unbefitting **12** dishonorable, disreputable, unacceptable **13** discreditable, inappropriate, objectionable

unwrap 4 open **6** loosen, unbind **7** uncover

unwrinkled 4 even, flat **6** ironed, smooth **7** unlined **8** smoothed **9** uncreased, unrumpled

unwritten 4 oral **5** tacit, vocal **7** assumed, implied **8** implicit, inferred, unstated **9** customary **10** spoken only, understood, unrecorded **11** traditional, unexpressed **12** unformulated, unregistered **13** by word of mouth

unwritten law
Latin: **13** lex non scripta

unyielding 4 firm, hard **5** rigid, stiff, stony, tough **6** wooden **8** resolute, rocklike, stubborn **9** obstinate, steadfast, unbending, unpliable **10** determined, inexorable, inflexible, persistent, unswerving, unwavering **11** undeviating **14** uncompromising

up 4 atop, lift, over, rear **5** about, above, aloft, along, aside, astir, at bat, built, close, equal, erect, raise **6** apiece, ascend, higher, lifted **7** abreast, batting, forward, promote, skyward, through **8** advanced, cheerful, increase, out of bed, overhead, standing, together, windward **9** northward **10** optimistic **11** constructed

up and about 5 afoot, astir **6** active, mobile, roused **7** walking **8** out of bed **10** ambulatory, on one's feet

up-and-down 6 fitful, seesaw, uneven **7** bobbing **8** jouncing, wavering **11** alternating, fluctuating, vacillating

upbraid 5 scold **6** berate, rebuke, revile **7** bawl out, censure, chew out, reprove **8** admonish, chastise, denounce, reproach **9** castigate, dress down, reprimand **10** tongue-lash

upbringing 7 rearing **8** breeding, training **10** background

upcoming 6 coming, nearby **7** looming, nearing, pending **8** imminent **9** impending, momentary **11** approaching, drawing nigh, forthcoming, in the offing, prospective

update 5 amend, emend, renew **6** recast, revamp, revise, rework **7** restore, touch up, upgrade **8** overhaul, renovate **9** refurbish **10** rejuvenate, reorganize, streamline

up for grabs 4 open **9** available

upgrade 5 raise, slope **6** ascent, better **7** advance, dignify, elevate, incline, inflate, promote **8** gradient

upheaval 5 flood, quake **6** blowup, tumult **7** turmoil **8** disorder, upthrust **9** cataclysm, explosion, tidal wave **10** disruption, earthquake, revolution **11** catastrophe, disturbance

uphill 4 hard **5** tough **6** rising, taxing, tiring, upward **7** arduous, onerous **8** toilsome, wearying **9** ascending, difficult, fatiguing, strenuous, wearisome **10** burdensome, enervating, exhausting **12** backbreaking

uphill work 8 struggle, tough job **10** difficulty, rough going **11** arduousness **12** hard sledding **13** laboriousness

uphold 4 bear, prop **5** brace, carry, raise, shore **6** defend, hold up, prop up **7** approve, bolster, confirm, elevate, endorse, protect, shore up, support, sustain **8** advocate, buttress, champion, maintain, preserve, underpin **9** encourage **10** stand up for, underbrace **11** acknowledge, corroborate

upholder 7 devotee **8** adherent, advocate, defender, partisan **9** supporter

up in the clouds 6 elated, joyful, joyous **8** ecstatic, euphoric **9** exuberant, rapturous **11** on cloud nine **15** in seventh heaven

Upis
goddess of: **10** childbirth

Upjohn, Richard
architect of: **13** Trinity Church (NYC)
style: **13** Gothic Revival

upkeep 4 keep **6** living **7** support **8** expenses, overhead **10** management, sustenance **11** maintenance, subsistence **12** conservation, preservation

upland 4 high, rise **5** ridge **6** height **7** plateau **8** eminence, highland **9** elevation, high place, high point **10** prominence

uplift 5 edify, raise **6** better, refine **7** advance, bracing, elevate, improve, inspire, lifting, shoring, support, upgrade **8** civilize, propping **9** cultivate, elevation **10** betterment, bolstering, enrichment, refinement **11** advancement, buttressing, cultivation, edification, enhancement, improvement **12** underpinning

uplifting 9 elevating, elevation, improving, inspiring **11** improvement **12** enlightening **13** enlightenment, inspirational

upon 2 at, on **4** atop **5** about **6** toward **7** against, thereon **9** by means of, thereupon **10** after which, thereafter

upper 3 top **4** high **5** major **6** higher, inland **7** eminent, greater, topmost **8** elevated, northern, superior **9** important

upper-case letter 7 capital **9** majuscule **13** capital letter

upper class 5 elite **6** gentry, uptown **7** (high) society **8** highborn, highbred, wellborn **9** beau monde, haut monde, high-class, patrician, top drawer **10** upper crust **11** aristocracy, blue-blooded **12** aristocratic, silk-stocking **14** creme de la creme, to the manor born **15** to the manner born

upper crust 5 elite **6** gentry **7** (high) society **9** beau monde, haut monde, top drawer **10** upper class **11** aristocracy **14** creme de la creme

upper hand 4 edge, sway **5** power **7** command, control, mastery **8** whip hand **9** advantage, authority, supremacy **10** domination **12** predominance

upper house 6 Senate **12** House of Lords

uppermost, upmost 3 top **4** main **5** chief, first, major, prime **7** highest, leading, primary, supreme, topmost **8** crowning, dominant, foremost, greatest, loftiest **9** essential, paramount, principal **10** preeminent **11** predominant **12** transcendent **13** most important

Upper Volta
other name **11** Burkina Faso (Fasso)
capital/largest city: **11** Ouagadougou
others: **4** Kaya **7** Banfora **9** Koudougou **10** Ouahigouya
division: **7** Yatenga **9** Tenkodogo **11** Fada Ngourma
monetary unit: **5** franc **7** centime
mountain: **4** Tema
highest point: **8** Nakourou **10** Tenakourou, Tenekourou
river: **5** Komoe **6** Mekrou, Sourou **8** Pendjari, Red Volta **10** Black Volta, White Volta
physical feature:
  plateau: **5** Sahel **7** Sikasso, Voltaic
  wind: **9** harmattan
people: **4** Bobo, Lobi, Samo **5** Bella, Bissa, Dyula, Fulbe, Hausa, Mande, Marka, Mossi, Puehl **6** Fulani, Senufo, Tuareg **7** Grunshi, Voltaic, Yatenga **8** Mandingo **9** Gourounsi **15** Bunsansi Gambaga
  French governor: **7** Hesling
  god: **4** Wuro **5** Tenga
  king: **4** Naba **5** Mogho
  leader: **5** Oubri, Zerbo **7** Yameogo **8** Lamizana **9** Mogho Naba
language: **4** Bobo, Lobi, More, Samo **5** Dyula, Mande, Mossi **6** French
religion: **5** Islam **7** animism **12** Christianity
place:
  game reserve: **11** Arlyand Pama
feature:
  animal: **5** hyena **6** duiker, jackal **7** gazelle, warthog **10** hartebeest
  tree: **4** shea **6** acacia, baobab, karite, locust

upright 3 rib 4 fair, good, just, pale, pier, pile, pole, post, prop 5 erect, moral, shaft, stake, strut 6 column, honest, picket, pillar 7 ethical, support, upended 8 reliable, standard, vertical 9 honorable, righteous, stanchion 10 aboveboard, high-minded, principled, standing-up, upstanding 11 trustworthy 12 on the up-and-up 13 perpendicular

uprightness 5 honor 7 dignity, honesty 8 morality 9 integrity 13 righteousness 15 trustworthiness

uprising 4 riot 6 mutiny, revolt 8 outbreak 9 rebellion 10 insurgence, revolution 12 insurrection

uproar 3 ado 4 stir, to-do 5 furor 6 clamor, tumult 7 turmoil 9 agitation, commotion 11 disturbance, pandemonium 16 state of confusion

uproarious 4 loud, wild 5 noisy 6 raging, stormy 7 furious, intense, riotous 9 clamorous, hilarious, turbulent, very funny 10 boisterous, disorderly, hysterical, tumultuous 11 tempestuous 13 sidesplitting

uproot 6 banish 7 abolish, cast out, destroy, root out, wipe out 8 dislodge, displace, force out 9 eliminate, extirpate 10 annihilate, do away with 11 exterminate

upset 3 ire, irk, mad, vex 4 beat 5 anger, annoy, crush, irked, messy, mix up, pique, quash, smash, upend, vexed, worry 6 bother, cancel, change, defeat, enrage, grieve, invert, jumble, muddle, mussed, rattle, thrash, untidy 7 agitate, angered, annoyed, capsize, chaotic, confuse, conquer, disturb, enraged, fluster, furious, grieved, incense, jumbled, mixed-up, perturb, reverse, tip over, trouble, trounce, unnerve, upended, worried 8 agitated, bothered, capsized, confused, demolish, disorder, distress, incensed, inverted, overcome, overturn, slovenly, troubled, turn over, unnerved, upturned, vanquish 9 discomfit, disturbed, infuriate, overpower, overthrow, overwhelm, perturbed 10 discompose, disconcert, disheveled, disordered, disorderly, disquieted, distressed, hysterical, overturned, tipped over, topple over, topsy-turvy, turned over, upside-down 11 disarranged, disorganize, overwrought, wrong side up 12 disorganized 13 make miserable 14 turn topsy-turvy

upsetting
French: 14 bouleversement

upshot 3 end 6 effect, payoff, result, sequel 7 outcome 8 offshoot 9 aftermath, outgrowth 10 conclusion 11 aftereffect, consequence, culmination, eventuality 16 final development

upside down 7 chaotic 8 reversed 10 disorderly 11 topsy turvey 12 bottomside up 16 at sixes and sevens

upstairs 2 up 11 above stairs, second floor

upstanding 4 good, tall, true 5 erect, moral, on end 6 honest 7 ethical, upright 8 straight, truthful, vertical, virtuous 9 honorable, righteous 11 trustworthy 13 incorruptible, perpendicular

upstart 4 snip, snob, snub 6 nobody 7 bounder, parvenu 8 mushroom 9 conceited, newly-rich 10 adventurer 12 nouveau riche 13 self-assertive

upsurge 4 gain, push, rise 5 spurt 6 pickup, thrust, upturn 7 advance, upswing 8 increase 11 improvement

upswing 4 rise 6 pickup 7 upsurge 11 improvement, upward trend

uptight 5 tense 7 anxious, fearful, nervous, worried, wound up 8 insecure, neurotic, troubled 9 unbending 10 unyielding 12 apprehensive

up-to-date 2 in 3 new 5 today 6 modern, modish, timely, trendy, with-it 7 current, stylish 9 in fashion 12 contemporary 13 up-to-the-minute
French: 9 au courant

upturn 4 gain, push 6 thrust 7 advance, upsurge 8 increase 9 expansion 11 improvement

upward 4 high, more 5 above, aloft 7 skyward 9 ascending, uppermost

upward movement 4 rise 5 climb 6 ascent, rising, upturn 7 scaling, takeoff 8 climbing, mounting 9 ascension

upward trend 4 rise 5 boost 6 pickup 7 advance, upsurge, upswing 8 increase 11 improvement

uraeus
figure of: 3 asp 5 cobra
on: 9 headdress
of: 7 pharoah

Uralic
language branch: 7 Samoyed 10 Finno-Ugric

Urania
member of: 5 Muses
personifies: 9 astronomy

uranium
chemical symbol: 1 U

Uranus
mother: 4 Gaea
wife: 4 Gaea
father of: 6 Giants, Titans 8 Cyclopes 10 Titanesses 13 Hecatonchires
castrated by: 6 Cronos, Cronus Kronos

Uranus
position: 7 seventh
satellite: 5 Ariel 6 Oberon 7 Miranda, Titania, Umbriel
color: 9 blue-green
characteristic: 5 rings

Urartu *see* 7 Armenia

urban 4 city, town 5 civic 8 citified 9 municipal 11 worldly- wise 12 cosmopolitan, metropolitan 13 sophisticated

urban area 3 urb 4 city 9 inner city 10 metropolis 11 megalopolis 16 metropolitan area

urbane 5 civil, suave 6 polite, smooth 7 courtly, elegant, gallant, genteel, politic, refined, tactful 8 debonair, gracious, mannerly, polished, wellbred 9 civilized, courteous 10 chivalrous, cultivated, diplomatic 11 gentlemanly 12 cosmopolitan, wellmannered 13 sophisticated

urchin 3 boy, imp, lad 4 brat, waif 5 gamin, stray, whelp, youth 6 gamine, laddie 8 young pup 9 stripling, young punk, youngster 10 young rogue, young tough 11 guttersnipe

Urd 4 Norn
origin: 12 Scandinavian
form: 8 giantess
personifies: 4 past
developed from: 5 Urdar
companion: 5 Skuld 8 Verdandi

Urey, Harold Clayton
field: 9 chemistry
isolated: 9 deuterium
awarded: 10 Nobel prize

urge 3 yen 4 back, coax, goad, itch, poke, prod, push, spur, sway, wish 5 drive, egg on, fancy, force, press, prick, speed 6 advise, desire, exhort, hasten, hunger, motive, reason, thirst 7 beseech, counsel, craving, dictate, entreat, implore, impulse, longing, passion, push for, quicken, request, solicit, suggest 8 advocate, appeal to, argue for, champion, convince, persuade, petition, pressure, stimulus, yearning 9 hankering, importune, incentive, plead with, prescribe, prompting, recommend 10 accelerate, inducement, motivation, supplicate 11 prevail upon, provocation

urgency 4 need, urge, want 5 press 6 stress 8 exigency, pressure 9 necessity 10 importance, insistence 11 persistence 14 imperativeness 15 importunateness

urgent 5 grave 6 ardent 7 crucial, earnest, fervent, intense, serious, weighty, zealous 8 critical, pleading, pressing, required, spirited 9 demanding, essential, heartfelt, important, insistent, momentous, necessary 10 beseeching, compelling, compulsory, imperative, obligatory, passionate 12 wholehearted 13 indispensable

urge on 4 push 5 boost 7 cheer on, pull for, root for

urging 7 bidding, counsel, goading 8 egging on 9 prompting 11 exhortation

Uri 6 canton
in: 11 Switzerland
home of: 11 William Tell

Uriah
father: 7 Shemiah

wife: 9 Bathsheba
served: 5 David

urinary system
  component: 6 kidney, ureter **7** bladder, urethra
  rids body of: 5 salts, waste, water **8** minerals

Uris, Leon
  author of: 5 Topaz **6** Exodus **7** Trinity **9** Battle Cry **10** Armageddon

urn 3 jar, pig **4** ewer, kist, tomb, vase **5** grave, steen **6** teapot **7** samovar **9** coffeepot
  botanical: 7 capsule **11** spore-bearer
  in keno: 5 goose

Ursa Major 9 Great Bear
  contains: 9 Big Dipper

Ursa Minor 10 Little Bear
  contains: 7 Polaris **12** Little Dipper

Uruguay
  other name: 10 Purple Land
  capital/largest city: 10 Montevideo
  others: 4 Fray, Melo **5** Minas, Rocha, Salto **6** Bentos, Rivera **7** Artigas, Colonia, Dolores, Durazno, Florida, San Jose **8** Mercedes, Paysandu, Trinidad **9** Maldonado **10** Las Piedras, Santa Lucia, Tacuarembo **12** Treinta y Tres **13** San Jose de Mayo
  measure: 4 vara **6** cuadra, suerte
  monetary unit: 4 peso **9** centesimo, centisimo
  weight: 7 quintal
  island: 5 Lobos
  lake: 5 Merin, Mirim **18** Embalse del Rio Negro
  mountain: 6 Animas **10** Grand Hills **14** Cuchilla Grande
  highest point: 15 Mirador Nacional
  river: 4 Malo **5** Mirim, Negro, Plata **6** Parana, Ulimar **7** Cuareim, Queguay, Uruguay **8** Yaguaron **9** Cebollati **10** Tacuarembo
  sea: 8 Atlantic
  physical feature:
    estuary: 5 Plata
  people: 4 Yaro **5** Swiss **6** Indian **7** Italian, mestizo, Russian, Spanish **8** Charruas
    artist: 6 Figari
    author: 4 Rodo **5** Reyes **6** Onetti **7** Sanchez **9** San Martin **10** Ibarbourou
    leader: 5 Oribe **6** Rivera **7** Artigas **9** Lavelleja **10** Bordaberry **14** Batlle y Ordonez
  language: 7 Italian, Spanish
  religion: 13 Roman Catholic
  place:
    resort: 12 Punta del Este
    square: 13 Independencia
  feature:
    animal: 4 puma **6** jaguar **8** capybara **9** armadillo
    bird: 4 rhea **5** nandu **7** hornero, ostrich
    cattle ranch: 8 estancia
    cowboy: 6 gaucho
  dance: 5 tango **7** milonga
  festival: 8 Carnival **13** Semana Criolla
  lasso: 10 boleadoras
  metal straw: 8 bombilla
  music: 9 candomble
  musical drama: 7 tablado
  ruling class: 10 Patriciado
  food:
    barbecue: 5 asado
    dish: 7 puchero **9** churrasco **13** asado con cuero
    drink: 4 mate

U S A
  author: 13 John Dos Passos
  character: 10 Ben Compton, Mary French **11** Joe Williams **12** Margo Dowling **13** Fainy McCreary (Mac), Janey Williams **14** J Ward Morehouse **15** Charley Anderson, Eleanor Stoddard, Eveline Hutchins **18** Anne Elizabeth Trent **22** Richard Ellsworth Savage

usable 5 handy **6** useful **9** adaptable **10** functional **11** serviceable

usage 3 use **4** care, mode **5** habit **6** custom, manner, method, system **7** control **8** good form, habitude, handling, practice **9** etiquette, operation, tradition, treatment **10** convention, employment, management **12** manipulation

use 3 aid, ply, sap **4** good, help, work **5** apply, avail, drain, exert, spend, treat, usage, value, waste, wield, worth **6** devour, employ, expend, handle, profit **7** benefit, consume, deplete, exhaust, exploit, operate, service, utilize **8** deal with, exercise, function, handling, profit by, put to use, resort to, squander **9** act toward, advantage, dissipate, enjoyment, make use of, operation, swallow up, throw away **10** employment, manipulate, run through, usefulness **11** application, convenience, fritter away, utilization **12** behave toward, capitalize on **13** make the most of **14** serviceability

used 3 old **5** eaten, spent **7** applied, treated **8** actuated, consumed, depleted, employed, occupied, operated, utilized **9** customary, exercised, exhausted, exploited, practiced **10** accustomed, habituated, secondhand **11** implemented, manipulated

used up 4 beat, shot **5** all in, spent **6** wasted **7** worn out **8** depleted, tired out **9** exhausted

useful 5 handy, utile **7** helpful **8** valuable **9** effective, practical, rewarding **10** beneficial, convenient, functional, profitable, time-saving, worthwhile **11** serviceable, utilitarian **12** advantageous

usefulness 5 avail, value, worth **6** profit **7** benefit, purpose, utility **9** advantage **11** convenience, helpfulness, suitability **12** adaptability, practicality **13** effectiveness **14** serviceability

useless 4 vain **6** futile **7** of no use **8** bootless, unusable **9** fruitless, unhelpful, worthless **10** inadequate, profitless, unavailing **11** incompetent, ineffectual, inefficient **12** unproductive **13** impracticable, inefficacious, nonfunctional, unserviceable

uselessness 6 vanity **8** futility, idleness **9** inutility **10** inefficacy **13** fruitlessness, worthlessness

Uses of Enchantment, The
  author: 15 Bruno Bettelheim

use sparingly 4 save **5** hoard, stint **6** scrimp **7** cut back, dole out **8** conserve, not waste, preserve

use to advantage 7 exploit **8** profit by **12** capitalize on **13** turn to account

use up 5 drain, spend **6** expend, finish **7** consume, deplete, exhaust **9** dissipate **10** run through

Ushant
  author: 11 Conrad Aiken

usher 4 lead, show **5** guide, steer **6** attend, convoy, direct, escort, herald, launch, leader, porter, ring in, squire **7** conduct, precede, preface **8** announce, director, proclaim **9** conductor, introduce **10** doorkeeper, gatekeeper, inaugurate

Usnech see **6** Usnach

USSR see **6** Russia

Ustinov, Peter
  born: 6 London **7** England
  roles: 7 Topkapi **8** Quo Vadis? **9** Billy Budd, Spartacus **12** We're No Angels

usual 5 stock, trite **6** common, normal, wonted **7** popular, regular, routine, typical **8** expected, familiar, habitual, ordinary, orthodox, standard **9** customary, hackneyed **10** accustomed, prescribed, threadbare **11** commonplace, established, oft-repeated, traditional **12** conventional, run-of-the-mill **15** well-established

usurer 9 loan shark **11** money lender

usurp 4 grab **5** steal **7** preempt **8** arrogate **10** commandeer **11** appropriate **12** encroach upon, infringe upon

usurpation 6 taking **7** seizure **8** grabbing, stealing **10** arrogation, preemption **13** appropriation

Utah
  abbreviation: 2 UT
  nickname: 6 Mormon **7** Beehive
  capital/largest city: 12 Salt Lake City
  others: 3 Roy **4** Moab, Orem **5** Delta, Heber, Kanab, Logan, Magna, Manti, Nepli, Ogden, Price, Provo **6** Beaver, Eureka, Kearns, Layton, Murray, Tooele, Vernal **7** Bingham **8** American **9** Bountiful **11** Brigham City
  college: 5 Weber **11** Westminster **12** Brigham Young

feature:
bridge: 7 Rainbow
dam: 6 Hoover **10** Glen Canyon
gorge: 7 Flaming
national historic site: 11 Golden
Spike
national monument: 8 Dinosaur
14 Natural Bridges
national park: 4 Zion **6** Arches **11**
Bryce Canyon, Canyonlands, Capital Reef
reef: 7 Capital
tribe: 3 Ute **5** Piute, Uinta(h), Yampa
6 Navajo, Paiute **7** Gosiute **8** Paviotso, Shoshoni
people: 7 Mormons **10** Maude Adams
11 Karl G Maeser **12** Brigham Young
13 John M Browning **15** Latter-Day
Saints **16** George Sutherland **19** Daniel Cowan Jackling
explorer: 9 Dominguez, Escalante
lake: 4 Mead, Swan, Utah **6** Powell,
Sevier **9** Great Salt
land rank: 8 eleventh
mountain: 4 Lena, Lion, Waas **5** Cedar, Henry, Hogup, Peale, Rocky,
Trail, Uinta **6** Frisco, Navajo,
Swasey, Wahwah **7** Granite, Griffin,
Hawkins, Pennell, Terrace, Wasatch
8 Linnaeus **9** Confusion
highest point: 9 Kings Peak
physical feature:
basin: 5 Great
canyon: 4 Echo
desert: 6 Sevier
plateau: 7 Wasatch **8** Colorado,
Tavaputs
river: 4 Bear **5** Grand, Green, Weber
6 Jordan, Sevier, Virgin **7** San Juan
8 Colorado
basketball team: 4 Jazz **6** Starzz
state admission: 10 forty-fifth
state bird: 7 seagull
state flower: 8 sego lily
state motto: 8 Industry
state song: 14 Utah We Love Thee
state tree: 10 blue spruce
utensils 4 gear **5** tools **6** outfit, silver,

tackle **8** flatware **9** apparatus **10** implements, silverware **11** instruments
13 paraphernalia
utilitarian 5 handy **6** usable, useful **8**
sensible, valuable, workable **9** effective, efficient, practical, pragmatic **10**
beneficial, convenient, functional,
profitable **11** serviceable **12** advantageous
utility 3 aid, gas, use **4** help **5** avail,
extra **6** backup **7** benefit, reserve,
service **8** function **9** accessory, advantage, alternate, auxiliary, secondary,
surrogate, telephone **10** additional,
substitute, usefulness **11** convenience,
electricity **12** availability, supplemental **13** public service **14** serviceability
utilization 3 use **10** employment **11**
application **12** exploitation
utilize 3 use **6** employ **7** exploit **8**
profit by, put to use, resort to **9** make
use of **12** capitalize on **13** bring into
play, make the most of, turn to account **14** avail oneself of, have recourse to, put into service **15** take advantage of
utmost, uttermost 4 acme, best,
main, peak, tops **5** chief, first, major,
prime **6** tiptop, zenith **7** capital, highest, leading, maximum, primary, supreme, the most **8** cardinal, foremost,
greatest, last word, ultimate **9** paramount, principal, sovereign **10** preeminent **11** predominant
Uto-Aztecan (Nahuatl)
tribe: 4 Pima **5** Aatam, Aztec, Nahua
6 Mexica, Papago **8** Pima Alto
utopia 4 Eden **6** heaven **7** Erewhon **8**
paradise **9** ideal life, Shangri-la **12**
perfect bliss, perfect place **13** seventh
heaven
utopian 9 visionary **10** idealistic, unfeasible, unworkable **11** unrealistic **12**
otherworldly, unattainable, unrealizable **13** impractical, insubstantial,
unfulfillable
Utrillo, Maurice

born: 5 Paris **6** France
mother: 14 Suzanne Valadon
artwork: 16 The Church at Deuil, The
Church of Blevy **17** Church at St Hilaire **19** La Petite Communiante **22**
Sacre Coeur de Montmartre
ut supra 7 as above
utter 3 say **4** emit, pure, talk, tell, yell
5 sheer, shout, speak, state, total,
voice **6** entire, mutter, reveal **7** declare, deliver, divulge, exclaim, express, perfect, whisper **8** absolute,
complete, disclose, outright, proclaim,
thorough, vocalize **9** downright, enunciate, out-and-out, pronounce, unchecked **10** articulate, unmodified,
unrelieved **11** categorical, unequivocal, unmitigated, unqualified
utterance 4 talk, word **6** answer, remark, speech **7** opinion **9** discourse,
statement **10** expression **11** declaration, exclamation **12** articulation,
proclamation, vocalization **13** pronouncement, verbalization
utterly 4 just **5** fully **6** wholly **7** totally
8 entirely, outright **9** downright,
extremely, perfectly **10** absolutely,
completely, thoroughly **14** to the nth
degree
uttermost 6 utmost **7** extreme, maximum, supreme **9** outermost, sovereign
12 extreme limit
uxorious
doting on: 8 one's wife
from Latin: 4 uxor, wife
Uzbekistan
capital/largest city: 8 Tashkent
others: 9 Samarkand
head of state: 9 president
government: 8 republic
monetary unit: 5 ruble
river: 8 Amu Darya, Syr Darya
sea: 4 Aral
people: 5 Uzbek
language: 5 Uzbek
religion: 5 Islam **11** Sunni Muslim
Uzi 10 Israeli gun, machine gun

vacancy 3 gap **4** hole, void **5** abode, place **6** breach, cavity, hollow **7** crevice, fissure, housing, lodging, opening **9** emptiness, situation **10** empty space, vacantness **11** room for rent **12** house for rent

vacant 4 dull, free, idle, open **5** aloof, blank, blase, clear, empty, vapid **6** unused, wooden **7** deadpan, for rent, leisure, vacuous **8** deserted, detached, for lease, forsaken, not in use, unfilled **9** abandoned, apathetic, incurious, oblivious, poker-face, unengaged **10** tenantless, unemployed, unoccupied, untenanted **11** indifferent, unconcerned, unfurnished, uninhabited **12** unencumbered **14** expressionless **15** uncomprehending

vacate 4 quit **5** empty, leave **6** give up, resign **8** abdicate, evacuate, hand over **9** surrender **10** depart from, relinquish

vacate the throne 4 cede, flee, quit **5** yield **6** give up, resign, retire **7** abandon **8** abdicate **10** relinquish

vacation 4 rest **5** leave, R and R **6** recess **7** holiday **8** furlough, holidays **10** sabbatical **12** intermission **13** take a vacation **14** leave of absence **17** rest-and-recreation
   French: 8 vacances

vaccine 5 serum **8** antitoxin
   inventor: 4 Salk **5** Sabin **6** Jenner **7** Pasteur

vacillate 4 reel, rock, roll, sway, toss **5** pitch, shift, waver **6** falter, teeter, totter, wobble **7** flutter, vibrate **8** hesitate **9** fluctuate, hem and haw, oscillate **12** shilly-shally **14** blow hot and cold

vacillating 7 swaying **8** wavering **9** diffident, uncertain, vibrating **10** hesitating, irresolute, on the fence **11** fluctuating, uncertainty **12** irresolution **15** shilly-shallying

vacillation 7 swaying **8** wavering **9** faltering, vibration **10** indecision **11** fluctuation, uncertainty **12** irresolution **15** shilly-shallying

Vacuna
   origin: 6 Sabine
   goddess of: 11 agriculture

vacuous 4 dull, idle, void **5** blank, empty, inane, silly **6** stupid, vacant **7** fatuous, foolish **8** indolent, unfilled **9** senseless **11** empty-headed, purposeless

Vaduz
   capital of: 13 Liechtenstein

vae victis 18 woe to the vanquished

vagabond 4 hobo **5** gypsy, nomad, rover, tramp **6** roamer, roving **7** drifter, floater, migrant, nomadic, rambler, roaming, vagrant **8** bohemian, carefree, homeless, rambling, wanderer, wayfarer **9** footloose, itinerant, transient, traveling, wandering, wayfaring **10** journeying **11** beachcomber

Vagabond Lover
   nickname of: 10 Rudy Vallee

vagary 4 kink, whim **5** fancy, humor, quirk **6** notion, oddity, whimsy **7** caprice, fantasy, impulse **8** crotchet, daydream **10** brainstorm, erraticism **11** peculiarity **12** eccentricity, idiosyncrasy, passing fancy

vagrant 3 bum **4** hobo **5** nomad, rover, tramp **6** beggar, loafer, roamer, roving **7** floater, migrant, nomadic, roaming **8** homeless, rambling, vagabond, wanderer **9** itinerant, transient, wandering **10** panhandler **11** peripatetic **15** knight-of-the-road

vague 4 hazy **5** fuzzy, loose **6** casual, random, unsure **7** general, unclear **8** confused, nebulous **9** imprecise, uncertain, unsettled **10** ill-defined, indefinite, inexplicit, undetailed, unspecific **11** not definite, unspecified **12** undetermined

vaguely 5 dimly **6** hazily **7** loosely **8** dreamily, slightly, vacantly **9** obscurely, sketchily **10** nebulously **11** ambiguously **12** indistinctly

vagueness 8 haziness **9** ambiguity, confusion, fuzziness **11** uncertainty **13** lack of clarity **14** indefiniteness

vain 4 idle **5** cocky, proud, silly **6** futile **7** foolish, pompous, stuck-up, useless **8** arrogant, boastful, bootless, dandyish, egoistic, nugatory, puffed-up, trifling **9** conceited, egotistic, fruitless, pointless, worthless **10** disdainful, profitless, swaggering, unavailing **11** egotistical, ineffective, ineffectual, superficial, time-wasting **12** self-admiring, supercilious, unprofitable, unsuccessful, vainglorious **13** self-important, self-satisfied

Vainamoinen
   origin: 7 Finnish
   hero of: 8 Kalevala
   form: 8 magician
   opposes: 5 Louhi **11** Joukahainen

vainglorious 5 cocky **7** haughty, pompous, stuck-up **8** affected, arrogant, boastful, bragging, insolent **9** conceited **10** egoistical, pretentious, swaggering **11** egotistical, swell-headed **12** narcissistic, supercilious **13** full of oneself, self-important

vainglory 6 vanity **7** conceit, swagger **9** cockiness **10** pretension **11** braggadocio **14** self-importance **16** overbearing pride

vale 6 good-by **8** farewell

valedictory 4 last **5** final **7** parting **8** farewell, terminal, ultimate **9** departing **10** conclusive **11** leavetaking **14** farewell speech **19** commencement address

Valentine
   character in: 20 Two Gentlemen of Verona
   author: 11 Shakespeare

Valentino, Rudolph
   real name: 16 Rodolfo (Alfonzo Raffaele Pierre Philibert) Guglielmi
   born: 5 Italy **12** Castellaneta
   wife: 9 Jean Acker **14** Natasha Rambova
   roles: 8 The Sheik **12** Blood and Sand **16** The Son of the Sheik **17** Monsieur Beaucaire **30** The Four Horsemen of the Apocalypse

valerian 9 Valeriana
   varieties: 3 red **5** Greek **6** common **7** African **8** American **11** long-spurred

Valery, Paul
   author of: 7 Cahiers, Charmes **12** The Young Fate **13** Le Jeune Parque **16** Sketch of a Serpent **20** The Graveyard by the Sea

Valhalla
   origin: 8 Teutonic
   hall of: 4 Odin **5** Othin

valiant 4 bold **5** brave, noble **6** daring, heroic **7** gallant **8** fearless, intrepid, knightly, resolute, stalwart, unafraid, valorous **9** audacious, dauntless, undaunted **10** chivalrous, courageous **11** lionhearted, unflinching **12** bold-spirited, great-hearted, stouthearted

valid 4 good **5** legal, licit, sound

6 lawful, proper, strong 7 fitting, genuine, logical, weighty 8 accurate, decisive, forceful, official, powerful, suitable, truthful 9 authentic, effective, legalized, realistic 10 acceptable, applicable, compelling, convincing, legitimate 11 substantial, well- founded 12 well-grounded 13 authoritative, being in effect 14 constitutional, legally binding

validate 5 enact, prove, stamp 6 ratify, verify 7 certify, confirm, sustain, warrant, witness 8 legalize, sanction 9 authorize, make legal, make valid 10 make lawful 11 corroborate, countersign 12 authenticate, make official, substantiate

validation 8 sanction 12 confirmation, legalization, ratification 13 authorization, certification

validity 5 force, logic, power, right 6 weight 7 grounds, potency 8 accuracy, legality, strength 9 authority, soundness, substance 10 legal force, legitimacy, properness 11 suitability 12 authenticity, truthfulness 13 acceptability, applicability, effectiveness 14 conclusiveness, convincingness

valise 3 bag 4 grip 7 handbag, luggage, satchel 8 suitcase 9 briefcase, Gladstone 11 portmanteau

Valjean, Jean
character in: 13 Les Miserables
author: 4 Hugo

Valkyrie
origin: 8 Teutonic
home: 8 Valhalla
attendant of: 4 Odin 5 Othin
queen: 8 Brunhild, Brynhild 10 Brunnhilde

Vallee, Rudy
real name: 17 Hubert Prior Vallee
nickname: 16 The Vagabond Lover
born: 13 Island Point VT
played: 9 saxophone
wife: 9 Jane Greer
roles: 16 The Vagabond Lover 17 The Palm Beach Story, Unfaithfully Yours 41 How to Succeed in Business Without Really Trying

Valletta
capital of: 5 Malta

valley 3 cut, dip, gap 4 dale, dell, glen, vale 5 basin, chasm, glade, gorge, gulch, gully 6 bottom, canyon, divide, hollow, ravine 8 water gap

Valley Forge
author: 15 Maxwell Anderson

Valley of Horses, The
author: 9 Jean M Auel

Valley of the Dolls
author: 16 Jacqueline Susann

valor 4 grit, guts 5 nerve, pluck, spunk 6 daring, mettle 7 bravery, courage, heroism 8 boldness, chivalry 9 fortitude, gallantry 11 intrepidity 12 fearlessness 13 dauntlessness

valorous 4 bold 5 brave, gutsy 6 heroic, plucky 7 valiant 8 fearless, intrepid, stalwart, unafraid 9 dauntless 10 courageous 11 indomitable, lionhearted 12 stouthearted

valse 5 waltz

valuable 4 dear, good 6 costly, prized, useful, valued 7 admired, helpful 8 esteemed, fruitful, precious 9 expensive, important, priceless, respected, treasured 10 beneficial, high-priced, invaluable, profitable, worthwhile 11 serviceable, significant, utilitarian 12 advantageous

valuation 9 appraisal 10 assessment, evaluation 14 estimated value

value, values 3 use 4 cost, help, rate 5 assay, count, judge, merit, price, prize, rules, weigh, worth 6 admire, amount, assess, charge, esteem, ideals, profit, reckon, revere, size up 7 beliefs, benefit, cherish, compute, customs, respect, service, utility 8 appraise, evaluate, prestige, treasure 9 advantage, appraisal, greatness, moral code, practices, standards 10 admiration, appreciate, assessment, estimation, excellence, importance, set store by, usefulness 11 conventions, market price, superiority 12 code of ethics, institutions, significance

valued 6 prized 7 revered 8 esteemed 9 cherished, respected, treasured 11 appreciated 14 highly regarded

valueless 7 trivial, useless 9 worthless 11 of no account, unimportant 13 insignificant 14 good for nothing 15 inconsequential

vamoose 3 out 4 away, scat, shoo 5 be off, leave, scram 6 beat it, begone, depart, get out, go away 7 get lost

vamp 5 siren 9 temptress 10 seductress 11 enchantress, femme fatale 12 introduction

Vamp
nickname of: 9 Theda Bara

vampire 3 bat 7 Dracula 11 bloodsucker

van 4 cart, dray, head 5 lorry, scout, truck, wagon 6 camper, picket 7 trailer 8 sentinel, vanguard 9 first line, forefront, front rank 10 avantgarde, large truck 12 advance guard, covered truck 13 front of an army 16 foremost division
french: 7 fourgon

Van, Bobby
real name: 10 Robert King
born: 9 New York NY
roles: 10 Kiss Me Kate, On Your Toes 11 No No Nanette 12 It's Only Money, The Ladies' Man 13 Small Town Girl 23 The Affairs of Dobie Gillis

van Alen, William
architect of: 16 Chrysler Building (NYC)

Van Allen, James Alfred
field: 7 physics
invented: 18 radio proximity fuse
discovered: 22 Van Allen radiation belts

Van Buren, Martin
nicknames: 9 The Red Fox 17 The Little Magician 18 The Careful Dutchman
presidential rank: 6 eighth
party: 8 Democrat
state represented: 7 New York
defeated: 5 (Hugh Lawson) White 6 (William Person) Mangum 7 (Daniel) Webster 8 (William Henry) Harrison
vice president: 7 (Richard Mentor) Johnson
cabinet:
  state: 7 (John) Forsyth
  treasury: 8 (Levi) Woodbury
  war: 8 (Joel Roberts) Poinsett
  attorney general: 6 (Benjamin Franklin) Butler, (Felix) Grundy, (Henry Dilworth) Gilpin
  navy: 8 (James Kirke) Paulding 9 (Mahlon) Dickerson
  postmaster general: 5 (John Milton) Niles 7 (Amos) Kendall
born/died/buried: 12 Kinderhook NY
education:
  Academy: 10 Kinderhook
  college: 4 none
  studied: 3 law
religion: 13 Dutch Reformed
vacation:
  toured: 6 Europe (1853-1855)
author: 64 Inquiry into the Origin and Course of Political Parties in the United States
political career: 8 US Senate 11 state Senate 13 vice presi dent 20 state Attorney General
  governor of: 7 New York
  secretary of: 5 State
  minister: 12 Great Britain
civilian career: lawyer
notable events of lifetime/term: 5 Panic (of 1837)
  treaty: 16 Webster-Ashburton
  war: 9 Aroostook
father: 7 Abraham
mother: 5 Maria (Hoes Van Alen)
siblings: 6 Derike, Hannah 7 Abraham 8 Lawrence
wife: 6 Hannah (Hoes)
children: 4 John 6 Martin 7 Abraham 13 Smith Thompson

Vance, Vivian
real name: 11 Vivian Jones
born: 12 Cherryvale KS
roles: 9 I Love Lucy 10 Ethel Mertz

Vancouver
hockey team: 7 Canucks

vandal 6 looter, raider 7 ravager, wrecker 8 marauder, pillager, saboteur 9 barbarian, despoiler, destroyer, plunderer 10 demolisher

vandalism 6 damage **10** de facement **11** destruction **17** malicious mischief

vandalize 3 mar **5** trash, wreck **6** damage, deface **7** despoil, destroy

Vanderlyn, John
born: Kingston NY
artwork: **14** Ariadne on Naxos **20** The Death of Jane McCrea **28** Marius Amid the Ruins of Carthage **31** Ariadne Asleep on the Island of Naxos

Van Dyck, Sir Anthony
born: **7** Antwerp **8** Flanders
artwork: **8** Charles I (in Hunting Dress) **11** Iconography **18** Madonna of the Rosary **19** Blessed Herman Joseph, Cardinal Bentiroglio **20** Ecstasy of St Augustine **21** Marchesa Elena Grimaldi

Van Dyke, Dick
born: **12** West Plains MO
roles: **11** Mary Poppins **12** Bye Bye Birdie **15** Diagnosis Murder, Dick Van Dyke Show
brother: **5** Jerry
son: **5** Barry

Vane, Sutton
author of: **12** Outward Bound

Vanessa
author: **11** Hugh Walpole

Van Gogh, Vincent
born: **12** GrootZundert **14** The Netherlands
artwork: **10** Pere Tanguy **11** Cafe at Night, L'Arle sienne **13** The Olive Grove **14** The Starry Night **15** The Potato Eaters **16** The Bridge at Arles **18** Portrait of Dr Gachet, The Chair and the Pipe **22** Cornfield with Cypresses

vanguard 3 van **7** leaders **8** forerank **9** first line, forefront, front line, front rank, spearhead **10** avant-garde, in novators, leadership, modernists **11** pacesetters, tastemakers **12** advance guard, trailblazers, trendsetters

Van Helsing, Dr
character in: **7** Dracula
author: **6** Stoker

vanish 3 die, end **5** cease **6** die out, expire, perish **7** die away **8** dissolve, fade away, melt away, pass away **9** disappear, evaporate, terminate **13** dematerialize **15** become invisible

vanished 4 dead, gone, lost **7** defunct, died out, extinct **11** disappeared

vanishing 9 dying out **10** ex tinction, fading away **11** passing away **12** disappearing **13** disappearance **15** dematerializing

vanitas vanitatum 16 vanity of vanities

vanity 4 sham **5** folly, pride **6** mirage **7** compact, conceit, egotism, falsity, inanity **8** de lusion, futility, idleness, self- love **9** emptiness, powder box, vainglory, vanity bag **10** hollowness, narcissism, self-praise, vanity case **11** makeup table, mirror table, self-conceit, uselessness **13** dressing table, fruitlessness, worthlessness **14** self-admiration, superficiality

Vanity Fair
author: **25** William Makepeace Thackeray
character: **10** Becky Sharp **11** Miss Crawley **12** Amelia Sedley, Joseph (Jos) Sedley **13** George Osborne, Rawdon Crawley **14** Sir Pitt Crawley **20** Captain William Dobbin

vanity of vanities
Latin: **16** vanitas vanitatum

vanquish 4 beat, best, drub, lick, rout **5** crush **6** defeat, master, subdue, thrash **7** conquer **8** overcome **9** overpower, overthrow, overwhelm, subjugate **11** triumph over

vanquisher 6 master, victor, winner **7** subduer **8** champion **9** conqueror **10** subjugator

vanquishment 6 defeat **7** mastery, triumph, victory, winning **8** conquest **10** conquering, overcoming

Van Slyke, Helen
author of: **10** No Love Lost **15** A Necessary Woman, The Heart Listens **18** Always Is Not Forever

Van Tassel, Katrina
character in: **23** The Legend of Sleepy Hollow
author: **6** Irving

Vanuatu
other name: **11** New Hebrides
capital/largest city: **4** Vila
others: **5** Santo **6** Forari **10** Luganville
school: **7** Malapoa
monetary unit: **5** franc **7** centime
island: **3** Api, Epi **4** Aoba, Gaua, Malo, Tana, Vate **5** Banks, Efate, Maewo, Santo, Tanna **6** Ambrym, Mabrim, Torres **8** Anei tyum, Malekula **9** Erromanga, Pentecost, Vanua Lava **13** Espiritu Santo
mountain: **6** Lopevi
highest point: **11** Tabwemasana
sea: **7** Pacific
people: **8** European **10** Melanesian, Polynesian **11** Micronesian
  explorer: **4** Cook **7** Queiros
  leader: **4** Lini
language: **6** French **7** Bislama, English **16** Melanesian Pidgin
religion: **7** animism **8** Anglican, John Frum **10** Protestant **12** Presbyterian **13** Roman Catholic
feature:
  cult: **5** cargo

vapid 4 dull, flat, lame, tame **5** bland, empty, stale **7** insipid **8** lifeless **9** colorless, pointless **10** flavorless, wishy-washy **11** meaningless, uninspiring **12** unsatisfying **13** characterless

vapor 3 dew, fog **4** haze, mist, smog **5** fumes, smoke, steam **6** miasma **8** moisture

vaporize 5 dry up **7** distill **8** condense, melt away **9** dissipate, evaporate

Varden, Gabriel/Dolly
character in: **12** Barnaby Rudge
author: **7** Dickens

Vargas Llosa, Mario
author of: **13** The Green House **16** The Time of the Hero **26** Conversation in the Cathedral **27** Aunt Julia and the Scriptwriter **34** Captain Pantoja and the Special Service

variable 6 fickle, fitful, uneven, unlike **7** diverse, mutable **8** changing, shifting, unstable, wavering **9** alterable, different, spasmodic, unsettled **10** capricious, changeable, inconstant, indefinite **11** fluctuating

variance 4 odds **6** change **7** dispute, quarrel **9** deviation, disparity **10** contention, difference, dissension, divergence, unlikeness **11** discrepancy, incongruity **12** disagreement, modification **13** dissimilarity, inconsistency

variant 7 altered, derived, take off **8** modified **9** departure, different, divergent, variation **10** alteration **11** transformed **12** modification **14** transformation

variation 6 change **7** variant, variety **8** mutation, variance **9** departure, deviation, diversity **10** aberration, alteration, difference, divergency, innovation **11** discrepancy **12** disagreement, modification **13** metamorphosis **14** transformation

varicolored 6 calico, motley, tartan **7** dappled, flecked, marbled, mottled, piebald **9** multi-hued **10** iridescent, opalescent, variegated **11** rainbowlike, technicolor **12** multicolored, particolored **13** polychromatic

varied 5 mixed **6** motley, sundry **7** diverse, various **8** assorted **9** different **10** variegated **11** diversified **13** heterogeneous, miscellaneous

variegated 4 pied **6** motley **7** checked, dappled, mottled, piebald **9** checkered **12** parti-colored

variety 4 hash, kind, race, sort, type **5** brand, breed, class, genre, genus, group, stock, tribe **6** change, family, jumble, medley, motley, strain **7** melange, mixture, species **8** category, division, pastiche **9** diversity, patchwork, variation **10** assortment, collection, difference, hodgepodge, innovation, miscellany, subspecies **11** subdivision **12** denomination, multiplicity, unconformity **13** dissimilarity, heterogeneity, nonuniformity **14** classification, omnium-gatherum **15** diversification

various 3 few **4** many, some **5** other **6** divers, myriad, sundry, varied

7 diverse, several **8** assorted, manifold, numerous **9** countless, different **10** dissimilar **11** innumerable **12** multifarious **13** miscellaneous, multitudinous

varlet 3 cur **6** rascal, wretch **7** villain **9** scoundrel **10** blackguard

Varner, Will
character in: **9** The Hamlet
author: **8** Faulkner

varnish 4 gilt **5** adorn, cover, gloss, stain **6** excuse, soften **7** conceal, lacquer **8** disguise, mitigate **9** embellish, gloss over **10** smooth over

vary 4 veer **5** alter, shift **6** change, depart, differ, modify **7** deviate, dissent, diverge **8** be unlike, contrast, disagree **9** alternate, disaccord, diversify, fluctuate

vase 3 jar, jug, pot, urn **5** crock, diota **8** canister **9** container **10** jardiniere

Vashti
husband: **9** Ahasuerus
replaced by: **6** Esther

vassal 4 serf **5** helot, liege, slave **6** tenant, thrall **7** bondman, servant, subject, villein **8** retainer **9** bondslave, bondwoman, dependent **11** subordinate

vassalage 4 yoke **7** bondage, serfdom, slavery **9** servitude **11** enslavement

vast 4 huge, wide **5** great, jumbo **7** endless, immense, titanic, very big **8** colossal, enormous, far-flung, gigantic, infinite, spacious **9** boundless, capacious, extensive, limitless, monstrous, unbounded, unlimited, very large **10** monumental, prodigious, stupendous, tremendous, voluminous, widespread **11** far-reaching, measureless, significant, substantial **12** immeasurable, interminable

vastness 7 bigness **8** enormity, hugeness **9** immensity, largeness **12** enormousness

Vatican City 10 papal state
enclave in: **4** Rome
includes: **7** Vatican **13** Sistine Chapel **16** St. Peter's Basilica
retreat: **14** Castel Gandolfo
statue: **7** Laocoon

Vaughan Williams, Ralph
born: **7** Britain **10** Down Ampney
composer of: **3** Job **8** The Wasps **9** Flos Campi **10** Antarctica (symphony No 7), **11** Old King Cole **12** A Sea Symphony **13** Hugh the Drover, On Wenlock Edge, Sir John in Love, Songs of Travel **14** Riders to the Sea, The House of Life, The Sons of Light **15** A London Symphony, The Poisoned Kiss **16** The Lark Ascending **17** A Pastoral Symphony **18** Five Tudor Portraits, Sinfonia Antartica **19** The Pilgrim's Progress **22** Toward the Unknown Region

Vaughn, Robert

born: **9** New York NY
roles: **7** Bullitt **12** Napoleon Solo **15** The Man from UNCLE **19** The Magnificent Seven **22** The Young Philadelphians

vault 4 arch, dome, jump, leap, safe, tomb **5** bound, clear, crypt **6** arcade, cupola, hurdle, spring **7** ossuary **8** catacomb, jump over, leapfrog, leap over, wall safe **9** mausoleum, polevault, sepulcher, strongbox **10** arched roof, spring over, strongroom **13** arched ceiling, burial chamber

vaunt 5 strut **6** brag of, flaunt **7** exult in, show off, swagger **9** crow about, gasconade, gloat over **10** boast about

vaunted 7 exalted, praised **11** gloated over, overpraised **12** boasted about

veer 3 yaw **4** jibe, tack, turn **5** curve, dodge, drift, shift, wheel **6** swerve, zigzag **7** go about **9** come round, turn aside **15** change direction

Vegas
character: **5** Angie **6** Binzer **8** Beatrice, Dan Tanna **10** Bernie Roth **11** (Sgt) Bella Archer
cast: **10** Tony Curtis **11** Judy Landers, Robert Urich **12** Naomi Stevens, Phyllis Davis **13** Bart Braverman

vegetable 3 pea **4** bean, beet, corn **6** carrot, greens, legume, squash, turnip **7** cabbage, lettuce, parsnip, produce, spinach **8** broccoli, eggplant, lima bean, rutabaga, zucchini **10** string bean **11** cauliflower

vegetarian 5 vegan **8** meatless **9** herbivore **11** herbivorous

vegetation 5 flora, grass, sloth, weeds **6** leaves, plants, torpor **7** foliage, herbage, languor, loafing, verdure **8** dormancy, idleness, lethargy **9** flowerage, indolence, plant life, shrubbery **10** inactivity **11** hibernation, languidness, rustication **12** sluggishness
god of: **6** Dumuzi

vehemence 4 heat, zeal **5** ardor **6** fervor, warmth **7** passion **9** intensity

vehement 3 hot **4** wild **5** eager, fiery, rabid **6** ardent, fervid, fierce, heated, stormy **7** earnest, excited, fanatic, fervent, furious, intense, violent, zealous **8** agitated, forceful, frenzied, vigorous **9** emotional, fanatical, hotheaded **10** passionate **11** impassioned, tempestuous **12** enthusiastic

vehemently 5 hotly **6** wildly **7** eagerly **8** ardently, fiercely, strongly **9** earnestly, excitedly, fervently, furiously, intensely, violently, zealously **10** vigorously **11** emotionally, fanatically **12** passionately **13** tempestuously **16** enthusiastically

vehicle 3 bus, car **4** tool **5** agent, means, organ, plane, train, truck **6** agency, device, medium **7** bicycle **9** mechanism **10** automobile, conveyance, instrument, motorcycle, rocket

ship **12** intermediary **14** transportation

veil 3 dim **4** hide, mask **5** cloak, cloud, cover **6** enwrap, mantle, screen, shroud **7** blanket, conceal, curtain, envelop, obscure **8** covering **10** camouflage

veiled 3 dim **5** murky **6** draped, hidden **7** muffled **8** obscured, shrouded **9** concealed, covered up, disguised, enveloped, enwrapped **11** camouflaged

veiling 3 net **4** mesh **8** cloaking, covering **9** obscurity **10** concealing

vein 3 rib, web **4** bent, hint, line, lode, mark, mood, seam, tone **5** fleck, layer, stria, style, touch **6** furrow, manner, marble, nature, strain, streak, stripe, temper, thread **7** stra turn **8** tendency **9** capillary, character **10** complexion, propensity **11** blood vessel, disposition, inclination, temperament **12** predilection **14** predisposition

Velazquez (Velasquez), Diego Rodriguez de Silvay
born: **5** Spain **7** Seville
artwork: **8** Philip IV **10** Las Meninas **13** Luis de Gongora, Pope Innocent X, Venus and Cupid **14** Cardinal Borgia **17** Don Gaspar de Guzman, Isabella of Bourbon **18** Adoration of the Magi, The Tapestry Weavers **19** The Infanta Margarita, The Surrender of Breda **20** Infanta Maria Theresia **21** An Old Woman Cooking Eggs **22** Portrait of a Court Jester, Portrait of Juan de Pareja **23** The Immaculate Conception **30** Prince Balthasar Carlos at the Hunt

veloce
music: **4** fast

velocity 4 pace **5** haste, speed **8** alacrity, celerity, rapidity **9** fleetness, quickness, swiftness **10** expedition, speediness

venal 5 shady **6** greedy **7** corrupt, crooked, selfish **8** bribable, covetous, grasping **9** dishonest, mercenary, rapacious **10** avaricious **11** corruptible **12** unprincipled, unscrupulous **13** money-grubbing

venality 7 avarice **10** corruption **11** bribe-taking **13** mercenariness, money-grubbing

vend 4 hawk, sell **5** trade **6** barter, deal in, market, peddle, retail **7** auction, trade in **8** huckster **11** merchandise

Vendetta, La
author: **14** Honore de Balzac

vendor, vender 6 dealer, hawker, monger, seller, trader **7** peddler **8** huckster, merchant, purveyor, retailer, salesman, supplier **9** tradesman **10** wholesaler **12** merchandiser **13** street peddler

veneer 4 coat, mask, show 5 front, layer 6 casing, facade, facing, jacket, sheath 7 coating, overlay, wrapper 8 covering, envelope, pretense 10 outer layer

venerable 3 old 4 aged 5 hoary 6 august 7 admired, ancient, elderly, honored, revered 8 esteemed 9 respected, venerated 11 patriarchal, white-haired

venerate 5 adore, extol, honor 6 admire, esteem, hallow, revere 7 cherish, glorify, idolize, respect, worship 8 look up to 9 reverence 11 pay homage to

venerated 4 holy 5 loved 6 adored, sacred 7 honored, revered 8 hallowed 9 respected 10 reverenced, worshipped 12 paid homage to

veneration 3 awe 5 honor 6 esteem, homage, wonder 7 respect, worship 8 devotion 9 adoration, adulation, reverence 10 admiration, exaltation 11 idolization 13 glorification

venereal 6 carnal, sexual 7 genital

Venezuela
 name means: 12 little Venice
 capital/largest city: 7 Caracas
 others: 4 Aroa, Coro 6 Atures, Cumana, Merida 7 Barinas, Barines, Cabello, Guaware, Maracay, Maturin 8 Asuncion, Carupano, La Guaira, La Gyayra, Tacupita, Valencia 9 Barcelona, Maracaibo, Tacarigua 12 Barquisimeto, Puerto La Cruz, San Cristobal 13 Ciudad Bolivar, Puerto Cabello 18 Santo Tome de Guayana
 division: 4 Lara 5 Apure, Sucre, Zulia 6 Aragua, Falcon, Merida 7 Barinas, Bolivar, Cojedes, Guarico, Monagas, Tachira, Yaracuy 8 Carabobo, Trujillo
 measure: 5 galon 6 fanega 7 estadel
 monetary unit: 4 peso 5 medio 6 fuerte 7 bolivar, centimo 8 morocota 10 venezolano
 weight: 3 bag 5 libra
 island: 4 Aves 7 Cubagua, Tortuga 9 La Orchila, Los Roques, Margarita 11 Los Hermanos 12 La Blanquilla
 lake: 9 Maracaibo, Tacarigua
 mountain: 3 Pao 4 Pava, Yair 5 Andes, Duida, Icutu 6 Concha, Cuneva, Merida, Parima, Sierra, Yumari 7 Imutaca, Masaiti, Roraima 8 Gurupira 9 Pacaraima 10 Auyan-Tepui 11 Turimiquire 18 Cordillera del Norte
 highest point: 7 Bolivar
 river: 3 Oro, Pao 4 Meta 5 Apure, Caura, Negro, Suata, Tigre, Unare, Zulia 6 Amazon, Arauca, Caroni, Cuyuni 7 Guanare, Guanipa, Guarico, Orinoco, Oritueo, Paragua, Suapure, Vichada, Yuruari 8 Guaviare, Manapire, Ventuari 9 Cuchivero 10 Casiquiare, Portuguesa
 sea: 8 Atlantic 9 Caribbean
 physical feature:

 falls: 5 Angel
 gulf: 5 Paria 6 Triste 9 Venezuela
 highlands: 6 Guiana 7 Guayana, Segovia
 plains: 6 Llanos
 people: 4 Bare, Pume 5 Bello, Carib, pardo, zambo 6 Arawak, Creole, Timote 7 Charoya, Guahibo, Kaliana, mestizo, mulatto, Otomaca, Timotex 8 Caquetio, Guarauno, Matilone 11 Maquiritare
  artist: 7 Marisol
  author: 5 Bello 8 Gallegos 13 Diaz-Rodriguez
  explorer: 8 Columbus
  god: 5 Tsuma
  leader: 4 Paez 5 Gomez, Leoni 6 Castro 7 Bolivar, Miranda 10 Betancourt 12 Guzman Blanco 14 Herrera Campins
 language: 4 Pume 7 Spanish
 religion: 5 Islam 7 Judaism 10 Protestant 13 Roman Catholic
 feature:
  animal: 4 puma 5 sloth 6 jaguar, ocelot 7 manatee, peccary 8 anteater, capybara 9 armadillo
  cowboy: 7 llanero
  dance: 6 joropo 16 diablos danzantes
  folk entertainment: 10 burriquita
  musical instrument: 6 cuatro 7 maracas
  street performance: 8 parranda
 food:
  black beans: 8 caraotas
  bread: 5 arepa
  dish: 7 hallaca 8 cachapos, pabellon
  soup/stew: 8 sancocho

vengeance 7 revenge 8 avenging, reprisal, requital 11 malevolence, retaliation, retribution 12 ruthlessness 13 an eye for an eye, implacability 14 revengefulness, vindictiveness 15 a tooth for a tooth

veni, vidi, vici 19 I came I saw I conquered
 author: 12 Julius Caesar

venial 5 minor 6 slight 7 trivial 9 allowable, excusable 10 defensible, forgivable, not serious, pardonable 11 justifiable, unimportant, warrantable

Venice
 art exhibition: 8 Biennale
 artist: 7 Bellini, Codussi 8 Fabriano, Longhena, Mantegna, Palladio, Scamozzi, Veronese 9 Canaletto, Carpaccio, Giorgione, Sansovino 10 Tintoretto
 capital of: 6 Veneto 15 Venezia province
 church: 18 San Giorgio Maggiore, Santa Maria dei Frari 19 Santi Giovanni e Paolo
 Italian: 7 Venezia
 landmark: 6 Ca' d'Oro 9 Campanile 10 Grand Canal 11 Doge's Palace

 13 Bridge of Sighs 15 Libreria Vecchia 16 Palazzo Rezzonico, Saint Mark's Church 20 Accademia di Belle Arti 21 Palazzo dei Procuratori 22 Scuola Grande di San Rocco 23 Palazzo Vendramin-Calergi
 port: 8 Marghera
 resort: 9 Lido Beach
 sea: 8 Adriatic
 small canal: 3 rii
 tomb: 5 Titan
 traveler: 9 Marco Polo

Venn, Diggory
 character in: 17 Return of the Native
 author: 5 Hardy

venom 3 ire 4 gall, hate 5 anger, spite, toxin, virus 6 choler, enmity, grudge, hatred, malice, poison, rancor, spleen 7 ill will 8 acrimony, savagery 9 animosity, barbarity, brutality, hostility 10 bitterness, resentment 11 malevolence 12 spitefulness 13 maliciousness, rancorousness

venomous 5 cruel, fatal, toxic 6 bitter, brutal, deadly, lethal, malign, savage 7 abusive, caustic, hostile, noxious, vicious 8 spiteful, virulent 9 malicious, malignant, poisonous, rancorous, resentful 10 malevolent 11 illdisposed 12 bloodthirsty

vent 3 air, tap 4 bare, drip, emit, flue, gush, hole, ooze, pipe 5 exude, spout, utter, voice 6 effuse, escape, faucet, let out, outlet, reveal, spigot 7 air hole, chimney, debouch, declare, divulge, express, opening, orifice, release 8 aperture, disclose, exposure, venthole 9 discharge, let escape, pour forth, utterance 10 disclosure, expression, revelation, smoke stack, ventilator 11 communicate, declaration

ventilate 3 air, sow 5 voice 6 aerate, air out, report, review, spread 7 analyze, declare, discuss, dissent, divulge, examine, express 9 broadcast, circulate, comment on, criticize, oxygenate, publicize, talk about 10 bandy about 11 disseminate, noise abroad

ventilator 3 fan 4 flue 7 aera tor 10 exhaust fan, smoke stack 14 air conditioner

venture 2 go 3 bet, try 4 dare, risk 5 flyer, offer, wager 6 chance, gamble, hazard, plunge, submit, tender, travel 7 advance, attempt, hold out, presume, proffer, project 8 endeavor, make bold 9 adventure, risk going, strive for, undertake, volunteer 10 enterprise, put forward, take a flyer 11 speculation, uncertainty, undertaking

venturesome, adventuresome 4 bold, rash 5 risky 6 daring, tricky, unsafe, unsure 7 dubious 8 doubtful, insecure, perilous, reckless, ticklish 9 ambitious, audacious, dangerous, daredevil, energetic, foolhardy, hazardous, impetuous, impulsive, uncertain **10** aggressive, precarious **11** adventurous, speculative **12** enterprising, questionable

venturesomeness 6 daring **8** audacity, boldness **9** derring-do **11** impetuosity **12** recklessness

Venus
origin: **5** Roman **7** Italian
goddess of: **4** love **6** beauty, spring **7** gardens
son: **6** Aeneas
grandson: **6** Iulus
epithet: **7** Erycina **8** Gene trix **10** Erticordia
also see Aphrodite

Venus and Adonis
author: **18** William Shakespeare

veracious 4 true **6** honest **7** sincere **8** accurate, faithful, truthful **10** scrupulous **11** punctilious

veracity 5 truth **6** candor, verity **7** honesty, probity **8** accu racy, openness **9** exactness, frankness, integrity, sincerity **10** exactitude **11** correctness **12** truthfulness **13** guileless ness, ingenuousness **14** verisimilitude

Vera-Ellen
real name: **13** Vera-Ellen Rohe
born: **12** Cincinnati OH
roles: **9** On the Town **14** White Christmas

veranda
Hawaiian: **5** lanai

verbal 4 oral, said **5** vocal **6** spoken, voiced **7** in words, of verbs, of words, uttered **9** expressed, unwritten

verbal exchange 6 dialog **8** dialogue **10** discussion **12** conversation

verbalize 5 speak, utter, voice **7** express **10** articulate **12** put into words

verbal thrust 3 dig **4** gibe, jeer **5** taunt **13** cutting remark

verbatim 5 exact **7** exactly, literal, precise **8** accurate, faith ful **9** literally, literatim, precisely **10** accurately, faithfully **11** to the letter, word for word **15** chapter and verse, letter for letter
Latin: **14** ipsissima verba

verbatim et literatim 21 in exactly the same words **29** word for word and letter for letter

verbena
varieties: **4** moss, rose, sand **5** clump, lemon, shrub **7** red sand **8** pink sand **9** beach sand **10** desert sand, Mojave sand, yellow sand **12** common garden

verbiage 9 logorrhea, loquacity, prolixity, verbosity, wordiness **10** volubility **11** verboseness **12** effusiveness **14** circumlocution, grandiloquence, longwindedness

verbose 5 gabby, wordy **6** prolix **7** voluble **8** effusive **9** garrulous, talka-

tive **10** longwinded, loquacious **13** grandiloquent **14** circumlocutory

verbosity 9 diffusion, prolixity, talkiness, wordiness **11** diffuseness **13** talkativeness **14** long-windedness

verboten 9 forbidden **10** prohibited

Verdandi 4 Norn
origin: **12** Scandinavian
form: **3** elf
personifies: **7** present
developed from: **5** Urdar
companions: **3** Urd **5** Skuld

verdant 4 lush **5** green, leafy, shady, turfy **6** grassy **7** meadowy **8** blooming, thriving **9** luxuriant **10** burgeoning, springlike **11** flourishing

Verdi, Giuseppe
born: **5** Italy **7** Busseto
composer of: **4** Aida **6** Otello **7** Macbeth, Nabucco, Othello **8** Falstaff **9** Don Carlos, Il Corsaro, Rigoletto, The Misled **10** La Traviata **11** Il Trovatore **13** The Troubadour **14** Manzoni Requiem **15** Simon Boccanegra

verdict 6 answer, decree, ruling **7** finding, opinion **8** decision, judgment, sentence **9** valuation **10** assessment, estimation **11** arbitrament, arbitration **12** adjudication **13** determination

Vere, Captain
character in: **9** Billy Budd
author: **8** Melville

Vereen, Ben
born: **7** Miami FL
roles: **5** Roots **6** Pippin **13** Chicken George **20** Jesus Christ Superstar

verge 3 end, hem, lip, rim **4** brim, edge **5** bound, brink, ledge, limit, skirt **6** be near, border, flange, fringe, margin **7** confine, extreme **8** approach, boundary, frontier, terminus **9** threshold **11** approximate **12** be on the brink

verge upon 4 abut **5** flank **6** adjoin, border **8** be next to **10** neighbor on

Vergil, Virgil
author of: **6** Aeneid **8** Bucolics, Eclogues, Georgics

verification 5 proof **7** support **9** guarantee **10** validation **12** confirmation **13** accreditation, certification, corroboration, documentation **14** authentication, substantiation

verify 5 prove **7** certify, confirm, support, sustain, witness **8** accredit, attest to, document, validate, vouch for **9** establish, guarantee, testify to **11** corroborate **12** authenticate, substantiate

verily 4 amen **5** truly **6** really **9** certainly, yes indeed **10** positively

veritable 4 real, true **5** utter, valid **6** actual **7** genuine, literal **8** absolute, bona fide, complete, positive, true-blue **9** authentic **13** incontestable, unimpeachable **14** unquestionable **17** through-and-through

Verlaine, Paul
author of: **6** Wisdom **7** Sagesse **8** Langueur **17** Songs Without Words **19** Romances sans Paroles

Vermeer, Jan
born: **5** Delft **7** Holland
artwork: **11** View of Delft **12** The Lace Maker, The Procuress **13** Drinking Scene **14** A Street in Delft, The Head of a Girl **15** Alle gory of Faith, Girl with a Red Hat **16** The Artist's Studio **18** Girl Reading a Letter, Girl with a Wine-glass **19** A Girl Asleep at a Table, A Painter in his Studio **20** A Woman Weighing Pearls **22** Maidservant Pouring Milk **23** Young Woman with a Water Jug **24** A Soldier and a Laughing Girl **31** Christ in the House of Mary and Martha

vermilion 3 red **7** scarlet **8** cinnabar **9** bright red **15** mercuric sulfide

vermin 4 ants, lice, mice, owls, rats **5** crows, fleas, foxes, pests **6** snakes, wolves **7** bed bugs, coyotes, roaches, spiders, weasels **8** termites, varmints **9** water bugs **10** centipedes, silverfish **11** birds of prey **18** pestiferous insects

Vermont
abbreviation: **2** VT
nickname: **13** Green Mountain **20** Four-Season Recreation
capital: **10** Montpelier
largest city: **10** Burlington
others: **5** Barre, Stowe **7** Grafton, Newfane, Newport, Rutland **8** St Albans, Winooski **9** Bountiful, Vergennes **10** Bennington **11** Brattleboro
college: **7** Goddard, Norwich, Trinity, Windham **8** Marlboro **10** Bennington, Middlebury, St Michaels
feature:
  covered bridge: **5** Scott
  house: **15** Old Constitution
  monument: **6** Battle
people: **9** John Deere, John Dewey **10** Ethan Allen **12** Brigham Young **13** Warren R Austin **15** Stephen A Douglas
lake: **7** Caspian, Dunmore, Seymour **8** Bomoseen **9** Champlain **10** Willoughby **12** Memphremagog
land rank: **10** forty-third
mountain: **5** Green, White **7** Bromley, Hogback, Taconic **8** Prospect, Stratton
  highest point: **9** Mansfield
physical feature:
  uplands: **10** New England
  valley: **9** Champlain
president: **14** Calvin Coolidge, Chester A Arthur
river: **4** West **5** Otter, White **7** Saxtons **8** Lamoille, Nulhegan, Winooski **10** Missisquoi **11** Connecticut
state admission: **10** fourteenth
state bird: **12** hermit thrush
state animal: **11** Morgan horse
state flower: **9** red clover

state motto: 15 Freedom and Unity
state song: 11 Hail Vermont
state tree: 10 sugar maple

vermouth
type: 4 wine **6** brandy **8** aperitif
origin: 5 Italy **6** France
varieties: 3 dry **5** sweet
drink: 9 Boomerang **11** Bittersweet
with bourbon: 9 Allegheny
with brandy: 3 BVD
with Dubonnet: 3 BVD
gin: 5 Bijou, Bronx, Tango **6** Caruso **7** Bermuda, Caberet, Martini **10** Bloodhound
with rum: 6 Bolero **8** Apple Pie **10** Black Devil **11** Shark's Tooth
with rye: 8 Brooklyn **9** Algonquin
with scotch: 8 Affinity **10** Bobby Burns
with sherry: 6 Bamboo, Brazil
with sloe gin: 10 Blackthorn
with vodka: 8 Kangaroo **9** Corkscrew
with whiskey: 9 Manhattan

vernacular 4 cant **5** idiom, lingo, slang **6** jargon, patois **7** dialect **8** parlance, shoptalk **9** the vulgar **12** common speech, native tongue **13** natural speech **14** informal speech, native language

vernal 3 new **5** fresh, green **6** spring **8** youthful **10** springlike

Verne, Jules
author of: 19 Five Weeks in a Balloon **21** From the Earth to the Moon **26** Around the World in Eighty Days **32** Twenty Thousand Leagues Under the Sea
character: 11 Captain Nemo, Phineas Fogg **12** Passepartout

Veronese, Paolo (Cagliari)
born: 5 Italy **6** Verona
artwork: 12 Book of Esther **13** The Last Supper **14** Supper at Emmaus **15** The Rape of Europa, Triumph of Venice **17** Mary with the Saints, The Finding of Moses, The Marriage at Cana, Wisdom and Strength **19** Martyrdom of St George, The Choice of Hercules **21** Esther before Ahasuerus **22** Feast at the House of Simon **24** Mars and Venus United in Love, The Feast in the House of Levi, The Temptation of St Anthony **31** Jesus and the Centurion of Capernaum **32** The Family of Darius before Alexander

Verrocchio, Andrea del
real name: 31 Andrea di Michele di Francesco Cione
born: 5 Italy **8** Florence
artwork: 5 David **15** Boy with a Dolphin **17** Christ and St Thomas **18** The Baptism of Christ **19** Bartolommeo Colleoni **23** Christ and Doubting Thomas **25** Beheading of John the Baptist

versatile 3 apt **4** able **5** handy

6 adroit, clever, expert, gifted **7** protean **8** talented **9** adaptable, all-around, ingenious, many-sided **10** proficient **11** many-skilled, resourceful **12** accomplished, multifaceted

verse 4 poem **5** meter, rhyme, stave **6** jingle, poetry, stanza **7** measure, strophe

versed 4 able **5** adept **6** expert, taught **7** erudite, learned, skilled, tutored **8** lettered, schooled, skillful, well-read **9** competent, practiced, scholarly **10** at home with, instructed, proficient **11** enlightened, experienced **12** accomplished, familiar with, well-informed **14** acquainted with, conversant with

versifier 4 bard **6** rhymer, writer **8** minstrel, poetizer, poetling, rhymster **9** poetaster, rhymester **10** rhymesmith, troubadour, versemaker, versesmith **11** versemonger **12** balladmonger

version 4 side **5** story **6** report **7** account **9** depiction, rendering **10** adaptation, paraphrase, re-creation **11** description, re statement, translation **14** interpretation

vers libre 9 free verse

vertebral column
bone of: 5 spine **8** backbone

vertex 3 cap, tip **4** apex, peak **5** crown **6** summit, zenith **8** pinnacle **12** highest point **13** crowning point

vertical 5 plumb, sheer **7** up right **12** ninety-degree **13** perpendicular

vertiginous 5 dizzy, giddy, shaky **6** whirly **7** reeling **11** lightheaded

vertigo 7 reeling **8** fainting **9** dizziness, giddiness **12** unsteadiness **15** lightheadedness

Vertigo
director: 15 Alfred Hitchcock
cast: 8 Kim Novak **12** James Stewart **16** Barbara Bel Geddes
setting: 12 San Francisco
score: 15 Bernard Herrmann

verve 3 vim, zip **4** dash, elan, fire, zeal **5** ardor, drive, force, gusto, punch, vigor **6** energy, fervor, relish, spirit, warmth **7** abandon, feeling, passion, rapture, sparkle **8** vitality, vivacity **9** animation, eagerness, vehemence **10** enthusiasm, liveliness

Verver, Maggie
character in: 13 The Golden Bowl
author: 5 James

very 4 bare, mere, most, much, pure **5** exact, extra, plain, quite, sheer, truly **6** deeply, highly, hugely, mighty, really, simple, vastly **7** awfully, exactly, fitting, greatly, notably, perfect, precise, totally **8** actually, entirely, markedly, specific, suitable, terribly **9** assuredly, certainly, decidedly, eminently, essential, extremely, immensely, intensely, necessary, obviously, perfectly, precisely, unusually,

veritably **10** abnormally, absolutely, abundantly, completely, defi nitely, especially, particular, profoundly, remarkably, strikingly, thoroughly, uncommonly, undeniably **11** appropriate, exceedingly, excessively **12** emphatically, surpassingly, tremendously **13** exceptionally, significantly **14** unquestionably

very best
French: 14 creme de la creme

Very Easy Death, A
author: 16 Simone de Beauvoir

very great 4 huge **6** severe **7** extreme, intense, mammoth, titanic **8** colossal, enormous, gigantic **9** excessive, monstrous **10** gargantuan, immoderate, inordinate, prodigious **11** magnificent, spectacular **14** Brobdingnagian

very nearly 6 almost **7** close to **9** just about **10** more or less, not far from **13** approximately

very old 4 aged **6** primal **7** ancient, antique, archaic **8** primeval **10** antiquated, primordial **11** prehistoric **12** antediluvian

very soon
French: 11 tout a l'heure

vessel 3 cup, jar, jug, keg, mug, pot, tub, vat **4** boat, bowl, butt, cask, dish, duct, scow, ship, tube, vase, vein **5** barge, craft, crock, flask, glass, liner, plate, yacht **6** artery, barrel, beaker, carafe, flagon, goblet, packet, tanker, whaler **7** caldron, collier, cruiser, platter, tankard, trawler, tugboat, tumbler, utensil **8** decanter, paquebot, sailboat **9** capillary, container, ferry boat, freighter, houseboat, steamboat, steamship **10** ocean liner, receptacle

vest 3 rig **4** garb, robe **5** array, drape, dress **6** attire, clothe, enwrap, fit out, jacket, jerkin **7** apparel, deck out, doublet, envelop **8** accouter **9** waistcoat

Vesta
origin: 5 Roman
goddess of: 6 hearth
festival: 8 Vestalia
corresponds to: 4 Caca **6** Hestia

vestal 4 pure **6** chaste, maiden, simple, virgin **8** maidenly, virginal, virtuous **9** pure woman, undefiled, unmarried, unworldly **10** immaculate **15** unsophisticated

vested 5 fixed **7** settled **8** absolute, complete **9** permanent **10** guaranteed **11** established, inalienable **12** indisputable **14** unquestionable

vestibule 4 hall **5** entry, foyer, lobby **6** lounge **7** hallway, passage **8** anteroom, corridor **10** passageway **11** antecham ber, entrance way, waiting room **12** entrance hall

vestige 4 sign **5** relic, token, trace

6 record 7 memento, remnant 8 evidence, souvenir

vestment 3 alb 4 garb, gear 5 amice, dress 6 livery, outfit 7 apparel, clothes, costume, raiment, regalia, uniform 8 clothing 9 trappings 13 accoutrements

vesture 4 robe 5 robes 7 apparel, clothes, garment, raiment 8 clothing, garments 9 vestments

vetch 5 Vicia
varieties: 3 cow 4 bard, bird, milk 5 crown, hairy, Sitka 6 bitter, common, kidney, purple, smooth, spring, tufted, winter 8 Narbonne 9 horseshoe, Hungarian, woolly-pod 12 large Russian

veteran 3 vet 6 expert, master 7 old hand 8 old-timer, seasoned 9 ex-soldier 10 campaigner, old soldier, war veteran 11 experienced 12 ex-serviceman 13 long- practiced

veto 4 deny, void 6 denial, enjoin, forbid, negate, reject 7 nullify, prevent, refusal 8 disallow, prohibit, turn down 9 rejection 10 prevention 11 disallowing, prohibition 12 disallowance 16 turn thumbs down on

vex 3 bug, irk 4 fret, gall, miff, pain, rile 5 anger, annoy, chafe, harry, pique, upset, worry 6 badger, bother, grieve, harass, hassle, nettle, pester, plague, ruffle 7 chagrin, disturb, provoke, torment, trouble 8 distress, irritate 9 displease 10 exasperate 18 ruffle one's feathers

vexation 5 pique, trial 6 hassle 7 torment 8 headache, nuisance 9 annoyance 10 affliction, harassment, irritation 11 aggravation 13 pain in the neck

vexatious 5 pesky 6 thorny, vexing 8 annoying, nettling 9 badgering, harassing, hectoring, provoking, troubling, worrisome 10 bothersome, irritating 11 disquieting, pestiferous, troublesome

vexed 5 irked, riled, testy 6 galled, miffed, piqued 7 annoyed, nettled, peevish 8 provoked 9 irritated 11 disgruntled, exasperated

viable 6 usable 8 feasible, workable 9 adaptable, practical 10 applicable 11 practicable

viaduct 4 ramp, span 8 overpass

vial 5 ampul, flask, phial 7 ampoule

via media 10 a middle way

viands 4 cate, diet, eats, fare, food 7 cuisine, edibles, vittles 8 victuals 9 provender 10 foodstuffs, provisions

vibrancy 4 fire 5 ardor 7 elation 8 vitality, vivacity 9 animation 10 enthusiasm 11 high spirits

vibrant 4 deep, loud 5 alive, eager, vital, vivid 6 ardent, bright, florid, lively 7 fervent, glowing, intense,

orotund, pealing, pulsing, radiant, ringing 8 animated, bell-like, colorful, forceful, luminous, lustrous, resonant, sonorous, spirited, vehement 9 brilliant, deep-toned, energetic, quivering, thrilling, throbbing, vibrating, vivacious 10 fluttering, glittering, resounding, shimmering 11 full of vigor, resplendent, reverber ant 12 electrifying, enthusiastic

vibrate 4 beat, sway 5 quake, swing, throb, waver 6 quaver, quiver, ripple, wobble 7 flut ter, pulsate, tremble 8 undulate 9 oscillate, palpitate, pendulate 11 reverberate

vibration 5 quake 6 quiver, tremor 7 quaking 9 quivering, throbbing, trembling

vicar 6 cleric, parson, pastor 8 preacher 9 churchman, clergyman 12 ecclesiastic

vicarious 6 mental 7 by proxy 8 imagined, indirect 9 imaginary, surrogate 10 empathetic, fantasized, secondhand 11 at one remove, sympathetic

Vicar of Wakefield, The
author: 15 Oliver Goldsmith
character: 6 George, Olivia, Sophia 7 Deborah 10 Dr Primrose, Mr Burchill 14 Arabella Wilmot 15 Squire Thornhill 19 Sir William Thornhill

vice 4 flaw 5 fault 6 defect 7 blemish, failing, frailty 8 iniquity, weakness 9 depravity, weak point 10 corruption, debauchery, degeneracy, profligacy, wantonness, wickedness 11 shortcoming 12 imperfection 14 licentiousness

vice president
resigned: 10 Spiro Agnew 12 John C Calhoun
accused of treason: 9 Aaron Burr 17 John C Breckinridge
youngest elected: 17 John C Breckinridge
elected by Senate: 14 Richard Johnson
elected but did not serve: 11 William King
rejected nomination: 11 Frank Lowden, Silas Wright
lived longest: 15 John Nance Garner
succeeded to presidency: 9 John Tyler 10 Gerald Ford 12 Harry S Truman 13 Andrew Johnson 14 Calvin Coolidge, Chester A Arthur, Lyndon B Johnson 15 Millard Fillmore 17 Theodore Roosevelt

vice versa 9 in reverse 10 conversely 12 contrariwise 16 the other way round 18 in the opposite order

vicinity 4 area 6 region 8 environs, locality, vicinage 9 adjoining, precincts, proximity 11 environment, propinquity 12 neighborhood, surroundings

vicious 3 bad 4 base, evil, foul, mean, vile, wild 5 awful, cruel, gross, nasty, surly 6 brutal, fierce, horrid, savage,

sullen, wicked 7 hateful, heinous, hellish, immoral, inhuman, untamed, violent 8 churlish, depraved, fiendish, libelous, shocking, spiteful, terrible, venomous 9 abhorrent, atrocious, barbarous, dangerous, ferocious, invidious, malicious, monstrous, nefarious, offensive, predatory, rancorous 10 abominable, defamatory, diabolical, ill-humored, ill-natured, malevolent, pernicious, slanderous, villainous, vindictive 11 acrimonious, ill-tempered, treacherous 12 bloodthirsty

viciousness 4 evil 6 malice 7 cruelty 8 ferocity, savagery, villainy, violence 9 barbarity, brutality, ill nature 10 fierceness, wickedness 11 heinousness

vicissitude 6 change 8 mutation 9 variation 10 difficulty, mutability, succession 11 fluctuation

Vicomte of Bragelonne, The
author: 14 Alexandre Dumas (pere)

victim 4 butt, dead, dupe, gull, mark, pawn, prey, tool 5 patsy 6 pigeon, quarry, sucker, target 7 injured, wounded 8 casualty, fatality, innocent 9 scapegoat

victimize 3 con 4 dupe, gull, hoax 5 bully, cheat, cozen 6 betray, delude 7 deceive, defraud 8 hoodwink 9 bamboozle

victor 6 winner 8 champion, medalist 9 conqueror 10 vanquisher 11 prizewinner

Victoria, Queen
realm: 13 British Empire
House of: 7 Hanover
Prince Consort: 6 Albert
son; successor: 9 Edward VII

Victoria
capital of: 8 Hong Kong 10 Seychelles

Victoria
origin: 5 Roman
goddess of: 7 victory
corresponds to: 4 Nike

Victorian 4 prim, smug 6 narrow, proper, stuffy 7 insular, prudish 8 priggish 9 pietistic 10 tight-laced 11 puritanical, straitlaced 12 conventional, hypocritical 13 sanctimonious

victorious 7 winning 8 champion 10 conquering, successful, triumphant 11 vanquishing 12 championship, prizewinning

Victor Victoria
director: 12 Blake Edwards
cast: 10 Alex Karras 11 James Garner 12 Julie Andrews 13 Robert Preston 14 John Rhys-Davies 15 Lesley Ann Warren
setting: 5 Paris

victory 7 laurels, success, the palm, triumph 8 conquest, the prize 9 supremacy 10 ascendancy 11 superiority
god of: 3 Tyr
goddess of: 4 Nike 8 Victoria

Victory
  author: 12 Joseph Conrad
  character: 4 Lena, Wang **5** Jonas, Pedro **8** Davidson **9** Axel Heyst, Schomberg **13** Martin Ricardo

victuals 4 chow, diet, eats, fare, feed, food, grub, meat **5** meals **6** fodder, forage, repast, stores, viands **7** cooking, cuisine, edibles, rations, vittles **8** supplies **9** groceries, provender **10** foodstuffs, provisions **11** comestibles, nourishment, refreshment

Vidal, Gore
  author of: 4 Burr **5** Kalki **6** Julian **8** Creation **16** Myra Breckinridge **18** Eighteen Seventy-Six, The Judgment of Paris **19** Visit to a Small Planet

Vidar
  origin: 12 Scandinavian
  father: 4 Odin **5** Othin
  killed: 6 Fenrir, Fenris

vide 3 see

vide ante 9 see before

vide infra 8 see below

videlicet 6 namely **11** that is to say
  abbreviation: 3 viz

vide post 8 see after **10** see further

vide supra 8 see above

vide ut supra 10 see as above **16** see as stated above

Vidor, King
  director of: 8 The Crowd **12** Stella Dallas, The Big Parade **16** Northwest Passage

vie 4 life **5** fight **6** strive **7** compete, contend, contest **8** be a rival, struggle, tilt with **9** challenge

Vienna
  airport: 9 Schwechat
  area: 11 Innere Stadt
  capital of: 7 Austria
  early name: 4 Wena **9** Vindobono
  German: 4 Wien
  landmark: 6 Prater **7** Hofburg **10** Stadtsoper **13** Saint Stephen's **15** Albertina Museum, Belvedere Palace **16** Historical Museum, Schonbrunn Palace
  river: 6 Danube
  ruler: 8 Hapsburg
  street: 11 Ringstrasse

Vientiane, Viengchan
  capital of: 4 Laos

vi et armis 20 with force and with arms

Vietnam
  other name: 5 Annam **15** French Indochina
  capital: 5 Hanoi **6** Saigon
  largest city: 6 Saigon **13** Ho Chi Minh City
  others: 3 Hue, Ron **4** Ngai, Vinh **5** Dalat, Hoa Da, Hoian **6** Annhon, Cholon, Danang, Hongay **7** Bacninh, Cam Ranh, Caobang, Donghoi, Hoabinh, Namdinh, Quinhon, Songoan, Tayninh, Viettri, Vinhloi **8** Binhdinh, Haiphong, Nhatrang, Panthiet, Phan Rang, Quangtri, Quangyen, Thanhhoa, Vinhlong **9** Haiphoang, Longxuyen **11** Dienbienphu
  school: 3 Hue **5** Hanoi **9** Ho Chi Minh
  division: 5 Annam, North, South **6** Tonkin **11** Cochin China
  measure: 4 gang, phan, thon
  monetary unit: 2 xu **4** dong **7** piaster
  weight: 3 can, yet **4** uyen
  mountain: 6 Badinh, Badink **7** Nindhoa, Ninhhoa **8** Fansipan, Knontran, Ngoklinh, Ngoolink, Tchepone, Tclepore **18** Annamese Cordillera
  highest point: 8 Fan Si Pan
  river: 2 Bo, Ca, Da, Lo, Ma **3** Chu, Gam, Koi, Red **4** Chay **5** Nhiha **6** Mekong **7** Dongnai
  sea: 10 South China
  physical feature:
    delta: 6 Mekong **8** Red River
    gulf: 4 Siam **6** Tonkin **7** Tonking **8** Thailand
    peninsula: 11 Indochinese
  people: 3 Hoa, Man, Meo, Tai, Tay **4** Cham, Kinh, Nung, Thai **5** Khmer, Malay, Muong **7** Chinese **8** Annamese, Annamite **9** Cambodian **10** montagnard, Vietnamese
    leader: 5 Le Loi **8** Le Duc Tho **9** Ho Chi Minh **11** Ngo Dinh Diem, Pham Van Doug **14** Nguyen Van Thieu
  language: 3 Yue **4** Cham **5** Khmer, Rhade **6** French **7** Chinese, English **9** Cantonese **10** Vietnamese
  religion: 6 Cao Dai, Hoa Hao, Taoism **7** animism **8** Buddhism **12** Christianity, Confucianism **13** Roman Catholic
  place:
    ruins: 10 Nguyen tomb
  feature:
    army: 4 ARVN **5** COSVN **8** Communsi, Viet Cong, Viet Minh
    clothing: 5 ao dai
    new year: 3 Tet

view 3 eye, ken, see **4** gaze, look, note, peek, peep, scan **5** judge, scene, sight, study, vista, watch **6** behold, belief, gaze at, glance, look at, notion, regard, survey, take in, theory, vision **7** diorama, examine, explore, feeling, glimpse, inspect, observe, opinion, outlook, picture, scenery, thought, witness **8** attitude, consider, glance at, judgment, panorama, perceive, pore over, prospect **9** landscape, sentiment, spectacle **10** conception, conviction, scrutinize, think about **11** contemplate, perspective

view as 4 deem, hold **5** count, judge, think **6** regard **7** account, believe **8** consider, take to be **10** look upon as

viewpoint 4 bias, side **5** angle, slant **6** aspect, belief **7** feeling, opinion **8** attitude, position **9** sentiment **10** conviction, standpoint **11** orientation, perspective **12** vantage point **16** frame of reference

view with disfavor 7 condemn, dislike **8** object to **9** frown upon **10** disapprove, think ill of **13** look askance at, regard as wrong **14** discountenance **15** take exception to

view with horror 5 abhor **6** eschew **8** sicken at **9** abominate, shudder at **10** recoil from, shrink from

vif
  music: 6 lively

vigilance 4 care, heed **7** caution, concern **8** prudence **9** alertness, attention **10** precaution **11** carefulness, forethought, guardedness, heedfulness **12** cautiousness, watchfulness **14** circumspection

vigilant 4 wary **5** alert, chary **7** careful, guarded, heedful, on guard, prudent **8** cautious, watchful **9** attentive, observant, wide-awake **10** on one's toes, on the alert **11** circumspect, on one's guard **12** on the lookout, on the qui vive

vigor 3 pep, vim, zip **4** dash, elan, fire, zeal **5** ardor, drive, force, might, power, verve **6** energy, fervor, spirit **7** passion, stamina **8** haleness, strength, vitality, vivacity **9** animation, hardiness, intensity, vehemence **10** enthusiasm, liveliness, robustness **11** earnestness **12** forcefulness

vigorous 4 bold, hale **5** hardy, lusty, vital **6** active, ardent, brawny, lively, mighty, robust, strong, sturdy, virile **7** dynamic, intense, vibrant **8** forceful, muscular, powerful, spirited **9** assertive, energetic **10** aggressive

vigorously 4 hard **7** briskly, lustily **8** actively, cogently, forcibly, robustly, strongly, sturdily **9** with force **10** forcefully, powerfully **11** strenuously **13** energetically

Vigrid
  origin: 12 Scandinavian
  final battlefield of: 4 gods

Viking, viking 4 Dane **6** pirate **7** mariner **8** Norseman, Northman, searover **9** plunderer **12** Scandinavian
  boat: 8 long ship
  burial: 9 ship grave
  chieftain: 4 jarl
  exploration: 5 Italy, Spain **6** France, Russia **7** England, Germany, Iceland, Ireland, Vinland **9** Greenland
  famous: 4 Eric **8** Eirikson, Ericsson **10** Eric the Red **11** Leif Ericson
  governing council: 4 Ting **5** Thing **8** Folkmoot
  legend: 4 Edda, saga
  origin: 6 Norway, Sweden **7** Denmark, Finland
  warrior: 7 beserk **9** berserker
  writing: 4 rune

Vila
capital of: 7 Vanuatu

vile 3 bad, low **4** base, evil, foul, lewd, mean, ugly **5** aw ful, gross, nasty **6** coarse, filthy, odious, sinful, smutty, sordid, vulgar, wicked **7** beastly, hateful, heinous, ignoble, immoral, obscene, vicious **8** depraved, shameful, shocking, wretched **9** abhorrent, degrading, execrable, invidious, loathsome, nefarious, obnoxious, offensive, perverted, repellent, repugnant, repulsive, revolting, salacious **10** abominable, degenerate, despicable, detestable, disgusting, iniquitous, unpleasant, villainous **11** disgraceful, foul mouthed, humiliating **12** contemptible **13** objectionable

Vile Bodies
author: 11 Evelyn Waugh

vileness 4 evil **8** foulness, iniquity, villainy **9** depravity, nastiness **10** immorality, odiousness **11** degradation, heinousness, viciousness **12** wretchedness **13** offensiveness

Vili
origin: 12 Scandinavian
brother: 4 Odin **5** Othin

vilification 5 libel **7** calumny, slander **10** defamation **13** disparagement

vilifier 5 scold **6** carper, critic **7** reviler **9** backbiter

vilify 5 abuse **6** defame, revile **7** slander **8** bad-mouth, dis honor **9** criticize, disparage **14** inveigh against

vilifying 7 abusive **8** libelous **9** malignant **10** calumnious, defamatory, slanderous

villa, Villa 5 aldea, dacha **6** castle, Pancho **7** chateau, mansion **9** residence **13** coun try estate

village 4 burg **6** hamlet, suburb **8** hick town **9** smalltown **11** whistlestop **12** municipality

Village, A
author: 10 Sholem Asch

villain 3 cad, cur, rat **5** knave, louse, rogue **6** rascal, rotter, varlet **7** caitiff, stinker **8** evil doer, scalawag **9** miscreant, scoundrel **10** blackguard, malefactor **11** rapscallion **12** transgressor, wicked person **15** snake in the grass

villainous 4 base, evil, foul, vile **6** wicked **7** caddish, heinous **8** horrible, infamous **9** monstrous, nefarious **10** abominable, despicable, detestable, maleficent **12** blackguardly **13** reprehensible

villainy 4 evil **8** vileness **9** depravity, rascality **10** wickedness **11** viciousness, maleficence

Villa-Lobos, Heitor
born: 6 Brazil **12** Rio de Janeiro
composer of: 6 Choros **20** Bachianas Brasileiras

Villefort

character in: 21 The Count of Monte Cristo
author: 5 Dumas (pere)

villein 4 carl, esne, serf **5** ceorl, churl, slave **6** drudge **7** bondman, peasant **9** bondwoman

Villette
author: 15 Charlotte Bronte

Villon, Francois
author of: 9 The Legacy **16** Le grand testament, Le petit testament
quote: 25 Mais ou sont les neiges d'antan **31** But where are the snows of yesteryear

Villuppo
character in: 17 The Spanish Tragedy
author: 3 Kyd

vim 2 go **3** pep, zip **4** dash, fire, snap, zeal **5** ardor, drive, force, might, power, punch, verve, vigor **6** energy, fervor, spirit **7** passion, potency **8** strength, vitality, vivacity **9** animation, intensity, vehemence **10** enthusiasm, liveliness

vin, vino 4 wine

Vincentio
character in: 17 Measure for Measure
author: 11 Shakespeare

vincit omnia veritas 16 truth conquers all **22** truth conquers all things

vindicate 4 free **5** clear **6** acquit, assert, defend, excuse, uphold **7** absolve, bear out, bolster, justify, support **8** advocate, champion, maintain **9** discharge, exculpate, exonerate **11** corroborate **12** substantiate

vindication 6 excuse **7** apology, defense **11** explanation **13** justification

vindictive 6 bitter, malign **8** avenging, punitive, spiteful, vengeful **9** malicious **10** malevolent, revengeful **11** retaliative, retaliatory, unforgiving

vinegarish 4 acid, sour, tart **5** harsh **6** acidic, biting **7** acerbic, pungent **9** acidulous **10** astringent

vin ordinaire 12 ordinary wine **20** inexpensive table wine

vintage 3 era, old **4** aged, date, fine, rare **5** epoch, great, prime, prize **6** choice, period **7** ancient, antique **8** sterling, superior **9** excellent, out-of-date, wonderful **11** outstanding **12** old-fashioned

Viola (Cesario)
character in: 12 Twelfth Night
author: 11 Shakespeare

violate 4 rape **5** abuse, break **6** defile, invade, ravish **7** disobey, outrage, profane **8** dishonor, infringe, trespass **9** blaspheme, desecrate, disregard, trample on **10** contravene, transgress **12** encroach upon

violation 5 abuse **6** breach **8** trespass **9** sacrilege **10** defilement, infraction **11** desecration, dishonoring **12** en-

croachment, infringement **13** contravention, nonobservance, transgression

violence 4 fury, rage **5** force, might, power **6** impact **7** out rage **8** ferocity, savagery, severity **9** brutality, intensity, onslaught **10** bestiality, fierceness **11** desecration, profanation **13** ferociousness, physical force **16** bloodthirstiness

violent 3 hot **4** wild **5** cruel, fiery **6** brutal, fierce, insane, raging, savage, severe, strong, unruly **7** berserk, furious, intense, rampant **8** maniacal, vehement **9** explosive, ferocious, hotheaded, murderous, unbridled **10** passionate **11** full of force, intractable, tempestuous **12** ungovernable **14** uncontrollable

Violent Bear It Away, The
author: 15 Flannery O'Connor

Violent Land, The
author: 10 Jorge Amado

violet 5 Viola
varieties: 3 dog, red **4** bush, pale, pine, rock, tree, wood **5** coast, cream, dame's, false, flame, green, marsh, pansy, sweet, water **6** Alaska, alpine, Canada, garden, German, horned, plains, stream **7** African, English, Mexican, Olympic, Persian, redwood, scarlet, striped, two-eyed **8** bird-foot, crowfoot, dogtooth, florist's, hook-spur, Labrador, larkspur, Missouri, trailing **9** early blue, evergreen, ivy-leaved, marsh blue, sage brush, tall white **10** Australian, great basin, Philippine, sweet white, western dog, woolly blue, yellow wood **11** Alpine marsh, American dog, arrow-leaved, Confederate, downy yellow, early yellow, lance-leaved, long-spurred, northern bog, strap-leaved **12** eastern water, great-spurred, kidney-leaved, northern blue, smooth yellow **13** common African, Halberd-leaved, northern downy, northern white, purple prairie, southern coast, white dog-tooth, yellow prairie **14** primrose-leaved, triangle-leaved **16** California golden, large-leaved white **17** round-leaved yellow, western sweet white **18** western round-leaved

violin family
instruments: 3 kit **5** cello, rebec, viola **7** baryton **8** bass viol, lyra viol, violetta **10** hurdy-gurdy **11** viola d'a more, violoncello **12** tromba marina, viola pomposa **13** lira da braccio **14** violino piccolo **15** hardanger fiddle

viper 3 asp, boa **5** adder, krait **9** puff adder **10** copperhead, fer-de-lance **11** rattlesnake
group of: 4 nest

Viper's Tangle, The
author: 15 Francois Mauriac

virago 3 nag **4** fury **5** harpy, scold,

shrew, vixen **6** dragon, gorgon **7** she-wolf **8** battle-ax, fishwife, harridan **9** termagant, Xanthippe

Virbius
  origin: **5** Roman
  god of: **6** forest **7** hunting

Virchow, Rudolf
  field: **8** medicine **9** pathology
  nationality: **6** German
  completed formulation of: **10** cell theory

Virgil *see* **8** Vergil

virgin 4 girl, lass, maid, Mary, pure **6** chaste, damsel, maiden, unused **7** unmixed **8** pristine **9** unalloyed, undefiled, unsullied, untouched **10** unpolluted **13** unadulterated **14** uncontaminated
  constellation of: **5** Virgo

Virgin *see* **4** Mary

Virginia
  abbreviation: **2** VA
  nickname: **11** Old Dominion
  capital: **8** Richmond
  largest city: **7** Norfolk
  others: **5** Galax, Luray, Salem **6** Marion **7** Bedford, Bristol, Emporia, Fairfax, Pulaski, Roanoke **8** Danville, Hopewell, Manassas, Staunton, St Albans, Tazewell, Yorktown **9** Arlington, Lexington, Lynchburg **10** Alexandria, Appomattox, Petersburg, Portsmouth, Waynesboro, Winchester **11** Newport News **12** Hampton Roads, Martinsville, Williamsburg **13** Virginia Beach **14** Fredericksburg **15** Charlottesville
  college: **3** Lee **7** Hampton, Madison, Radford **8** Longwood, Richmond **10** Washington **11** Mary Baldwin, Old Dominion **13** Randolph Macon **14** Averett Hollins, Mary Washington, William and Mary
  feature:
    battle site: **7** Bull Run **8** Fair Oaks, Manassas, Richmond, Yorktown **10** Petersburg, Seven Pines, Wilderness **12** Spotsylvania **14** Fredericksburg **16** Chancellorsville
    dam: **4** Kerr
    historical site: **10** Monticello **11** Mount Vernon **12** Williamsburg **13** Stratford Hall
    national monument: **26** George Washington Birthplace
    national park: **10** Shenandoah **26** Colonial National Historical
    tribe: **6** Saponi, Tutelo **7** Monacan **8** Manahoac, Meherrin, Nottaway, Pamunkey, Powhatan **9** Matchotic **10** Appomuttoc
    people: **9** Henry Clay, John Rolfe, John Smith **10** Robert E Lee, Walter Reed **11** George Mason **12** John Marshall, Patrick Henry **13** Samuel Houston **14** Cyrus McCormick **15** Meriwether Lewis **17** Booker T Washington, Richard Evelyn Bird

18 Light-Horse Harry (Henry) Lee
  lake: **4** Kerr **5** Smith
  land rank: **11** thirty-sixth
  mountain: **5** Cedar **6** Clinch, Elliot **8** Baldknob **9** Allegheny, Blueridge
    highest point: **6** Rogers
  physical feature:
    bay: **10** Chesapeake
    bridge: **7** Natural
    caverns: **5** Luray
    port: **7** Norfolk **8** Richmond **10** Portsmouth **11** Newport News
    tunnel: **7** Natural
    valley: **10** Shenandoah
  president: **9** John Tyler **11** James Monroe **12** James Madison **13** Woodrow Wilson, Zachary Taylor **15** Thomas Jefferson **16** George Washington **20** William Henry Harrison
  river: **3** Dan **4** York **5** James **7** Potomac, Rapidan, Roanoke **10** Appomattox, Shenandoah **12** Rappahannock
  state admission: **5** tenth
  state bird: **8** cardinal
  state flower: **16** flowering dogwood
  state motto: **17** Thus Ever To Tyrants
  state song: **24** Carry Me Back to Old Virginia
  state tree: **7** dogwood

Virginian, The
  author: **10** Owen Wister
  character: **5** Betsy, Randy, Steve **6** Shorty **7** Trampas **9** Molly Wood **10** Judge (Henry) Garth
  cast: **8** Lee J Cobb **10** Gary Clarke, James Drury, Pippa Scott, Randy Boone **11** Doug McClure **12** Roberta Shore
  setting: **11** Shiloh Ranch **16** Wyoming Territory

Virginians, The
  author: **25** William Makepeace Thackeray

Virgin Mary
  ingredient: **11** tomato juice

Virgin Soil
  author: **12** Ivan Turgenev

Virgo
  symbol: **6** virgin
  planet: **7** Mercury
  rules: **7** service
  zodiac: **5** sixth
  born: **6** August **9** September

virile 4 bold **5** brave, hardy, husky, lusty, macho, manly **6** brawny, heroic, manful, mighty, potent, robust, strong **7** valiant **8** fearless, forceful, muscular, powerful, resolute, stalwart, vigorous **9** audacious, masculine, masterful, strapping, undaunted **10** courageous **12** stouthearted

virtual 5 tacit **7** implied **8** implicit, indirect **9** essential, practical **11** substantial

virtually 8 in effect **9** in essence **11** essentially, in substance, practically

13 substantially **14** for the most part **23** for all practical purposes, to all intents and purposes

virtue 5 honor, value **6** purity, reward **7** benefit, decency, honesty, modesty, probity **8** chastity, goodness, morality, strength **9** advantage, good point, innocence, integrity, principle, rectitude, virginity **11** strong point, uprightness

virtuosity 7 mastery **8** artistry, wizardry **14** accomplishment

virtuoso 4 whiz **6** expert, genius, master, wizard **7** artiste, prodigy **10** master hand

virtuous 4 good, just, pure **5** moral **6** chaste, decent, modest **7** ethical, upright **8** innocent, laudable, virginal **9** continent, exemplary, honorable, righteous, unsullied **11** commendable, meritorious **12** praiseworthy **14** high-principled

virtuous person
  Hebrew: **6** zaddik

Virtus
  personifies: **7** courage

virtute et armis 15 by virtue and arms
  motto of: **11** Mississippi

virulent 5 toxic **6** bitter, deadly, lethal, malign **7** harmful, hostile, hurtful, noxious, vicious **8** spiteful, venomous **9** injurious, malicious, poisonous, rancorous, resentful, unhealthy **10** malevolent, pernicious **11** acrimonious, deleterious

virus 3 bug **4** germ **7** microbe **11** computer bug **13** microorganism

vis 5 force, power **8** strength

visage 3 air **4** face, look, mien **5** image **6** aspect **7** profile **8** demeanor, features **9** semblance **10** appearance **11** countenance, physiognomy

vis-a-vis 8 eye to eye, together **9** in company, privately, tete-a-tete **10** face-to-face, side by side **11** as opposed to **12** in contrast to **14** as compared with, confidentially **19** as distinguished from

viscera 4 guts **6** bowels **7** innards, insides **8** entrails **10** intestines

visceral 3 gut **5** crude **6** earthy **11** instinctive

viscous 5 gluey, gooey, gummy, slimy, tacky, thick **6** sticky, syrupy, viscid **9** glutinous

Vishnu
  in trinity of: **4** Siva **5** Shiva **6** Brahma
  religion: **8** Hinduism
  called: **9** Preserver
  avatar: **7** Krishna

visibility 7 ceiling, clarity, horizon **10** definition, prominence **11** range of view **12** distinctness **14** perceptibility **15** conspicuousness, discernibleness

visible 4 open **5** clear, plain **6** in view,

marked, patent **7** blatant, evident, glaring, in focus, in sight, obvious, pointed, salient, seeable **8** apparent, distinct, manifest, palpable, revealed **9** prominent **10** noticeable, observable, pronounced **11** conspicuous, discernible, inescapable, perceivable, perceptible, well-defined **12** unmistakable

vision 4 idea **5** dream, fancy, ghost, sight **6** notion **7** concept, fantasy, phantom, specter **8** daydream, eyesight, illusion **9** foresight **10** apparition, conception, perception, revelation **11** discernment, imagination **15** materialization

visionary 4 seer **6** dreamy, unreal, zealot **7** dreamer, fanatic, fancied, utopian **8** delusive, fanciful, idealist, illusory, romantic, theorist **9** imaginary, unfounded **10** chimerical, daydreamer, idealistic, starry-eyed **11** imaginative, impractical **13** insubstantial

Vision of Judgement, The
author: **9** Lord Byron

visit 4 call, stay **5** haunt, smite **6** affect, assail, attack, befall, call on, punish **7** afflict, assault, go to see, sojourn **8** drop in on, frequent, happen to, look in on, stay with **9** sojourn at **10** be a guest of

Visit, The
author: **19** Friedrich Durrenmatt

visitant 5 alien **7** arrival, visitor

visitor 5 guest **6** caller **7** company, tourist, tripper, voyager **8** traveler **9** journeyer, sightseer, sojourner, transient **10** houseguest, vacationer

vista 4 view **5** scene **6** vision **7** outlook, picture, scenery **8** panorama, prospect **9** landscape **11** perspective

visual 5 optic **6** ocular **7** optical, seeable, visible **9** for the eye **10** noticeable, observable, ophthalmic **11** perceptible

visualize 5 fancy, image **7** dream of, foresee, imagine, picture **8** envision **10** conceive of, daydream of **16** see in the mind's eye

vita 3 bio **6** resume **9** biography **13** autobiography **15** curriculum vitae

vital 4 life, live **5** alive, basic, chief, quick **6** lively, living, urgent, viable **7** animate, crucial, dynamic, primary, serious, vibrant **8** animated, cardinal, critical, existing, forceful, foremost, material, pressing, spirited, vigorous **9** breathing, energetic, essential, important, necessary, paramount, requisite, vivifying **11** fundamental, significant **13** indispensable

vitality 3 pep, vim, zip **4** zeal, zest **5** verve, vigor **6** energy **8** dynamism, strength, vivacity **9** animation, life force **10** ebullience, enthusiasm, exuberance, liveliness **13** animal spirits

vitalize 6 excite, vivify **7** animate, quicken **8** activate, energize **9** stimu-

late **10** invigorate, strengthen **11** bring to life

vital part 9 essential, necessity, requisite **10** key element, sine qua non **11** requirement

Vital Parts
author: **12** Thomas Berger

vital principle 5 blood **6** source **9** lifeblood **10** sine qua non

vitals 5 belly **6** bowels **10** intestines **11** vital organs **14** liver and lights

Vita Nuova
author: **14** Dante Alighieri

vitiate 3 mar **4** thin, undo, void **5** spoil, taint **6** blight, cancel, debase, defile, dilute, impair, infect, injure, poison, weaken **7** abolish, corrupt, pervert, pollute **8** sabotage **9** discredit, undermine **10** adulterate, depreciate, invalidate, make faulty, obliterate **11** contaminate

vitriolic 4 acid **5** acerb, nasty, sharp **6** biting **7** abusive, acerbic, caustic, cutting **8** sardonic, scathing **9** sarcastic, satirical, withering **11** acrimonious **13** hypercritical

vituperate 5 abuse **6** carp at, defame, malign, rail at, rebuke, revile, vilify **7** censure **9** castigate **10** speak ill of **14** inveigh against

vituperation 5 abuse, blame, scorn **6** insult, rebuke, tirade **7** censure, obloquy, slander **8** acrimony, scolding **9** invective **10** defamation, revilement, scurrility **11** castigation, deprecation **12** calumniation, denunciation, faultfinding, vilification **13** tongue-lashing

vituperative 5 harsh **7** abusive **8** scornful **9** insulting, maligning, vilifying **10** censorious, defamatory, scurrilous, slanderous **11** acrimonious, deprecatory

vivace
music: **5** quick **9** vivacious

vivacious 3 gay **5** jolly, merry, sunny, vital **6** active, bright, bubbly, cheery, genial, lively **7** buoyant **8** animated, bubbling, cheerful, spirited **9** convivial, ebullient, sparkling, sprightly **10** frolicsome, full of life **12** effervescent, lighthearted

vivacity 3 zip **4** dash, elan **5** gaity, verve, vigor **6** energy, spirit **8** buoyancy, vitality **9** animation **10** ebullience, liveliness **13** effervescence

Vivaldi, Antonio
born: **5** Italy **6** Venice
composer of: **10** Gloria Mass **14** L'Estro Armonico, The Four Seasons **16** Judith Triumphant **17** Juditha Triumphans, Le Quattro Stagioni **19** Harmonic Inspiration

viva voce 5 aloud **6** orally

Viva Zapata!
director: **9** Elia Kazan
cast: **10** Jean Peters **12** Anthony

Quinn, Marlon Brando
Oscar for: **15** supporting actor (Quinn)
script: **13** John Steinbeck

vive 8 long live (whomever)
opposite: **4** a bas

vive valeque 15 live and keep well

Vivian
also: **16** The Lady of the Lake
character in: **16** Arthurian romance
lover: **6** Merlin

Vivian Grey
author: **16** Benjamin Disraeli

vivid 3 gay **4** deep, loud, rich **5** clear, shiny, showy **6** bright, florid, garish, lively, moving, strong **7** glowing, graphic, in tense, radiant, shining **8** colorful, definite, distinct, dramatic, emphatic, forceful, lifelike, luminous, lustrous, powerful, stirring, striking, true-life, vigorous **9** brilliant, effulgent, energetic, marvelous, memorable, pictorial, realistic **10** astounding, expressive, impressive, remarkable **11** astonishing, conspicuous, descriptive, inescapable, luminescent, picturesque, resplendent **12** unmistakable **13** extraordinary

vividness 9 intensity **10** brightness, brilliance

vivified 7 revived **8** animated, awakened **9** enlivened, quickened, vitalized **11** invigorated

vivify 6 revive, wake up **7** animate, enliven, quicken **8** vitalize **10** invigorate

vixen 4 fury **5** scold, shrew, witch **6** virago **8** fishwife, harridan, spitfire **9** female fox, termagant

Vladimir
character in: **15** Waiting for Godot
author: **7** Beckett

Vlaminck, Maurice de
born: **5** Paris **6** France
artwork: **8** Red Trees, The Storm **15** Hamlet in the Snow, Winter Landscape **17** The Bridge at Chatou **18** Picnic in the Country, Street at Marly-le-Roi **21** Landscape with Red Trees

vocabulary 4 cant **5** argot, idiom, lingo, slang, style **6** jargon, patois, speech, tongue **7** dialect, lexicon **8** language, glossary, phrasing **9** word stock **10** vernacular **11** phraseology, terminology

vocal 4 open, oral, sung **5** blunt, frank, lyric **6** candid, choral, direct, spoken, voiced **7** uttered, voluble **8** operatic, viva-voce **9** outspoken, vocalized **10** forthright, of the voice **11** articulated, plainspoken

vocalize 3 air, say **4** sing, vent **5** speak, utter **7** express **9** ventilate **10** articulate **12** put into words

vocation 3 job **4** line, post, role, task

5 berth, field, stint, trade **6** career, estate, metier **7** calling, pursuit, station **8** business, lifework **9** situation **10** assignment, employment, line of work, occupation, profession

vocational 3 job **5** trade **6** career **9** technical **11** specialized **12** occupational

vociferate 4 howl, yell, yelp **5** shout, shout **6** bellow, clamor, cry out, holler, shriek, squeal **7** bluster, call out, exclaim, screech **9** ejaculate **11** make a racket **12** raise a rumpus

vociferation 3 cry **4** howl, yell, yelp **5** noise, shout **6** bellow, clamor, outcry, shriek, squeal, uproar **7** screech **11** ejaculation, exclamation

vociferous 4 loud **5** noisy, vocal **6** shrill **7** blatant **8** piercing, shouting, strident, vehement **9** clamorous, outspoken **10** boisterous, loud-voiced, uproarious **11** importunate

vodka
origin: **6** Poland, Russia
drink: **10** Moscow Mule **12** Cosmopolitan
with amaretto: **9** Godmother
with bouillon: **8** Bullshot
with cider: **15** Brewster Special
with Cognac: **7** Cossack
with cranberry juice: **10** Cape Codder
with creme de cacao: **7** Barbara **9** Ninotchka **11** Russian Bear **12** Velvet Hammer, White Russian
with curacao: **8** Aqueduct
with Galliano: **16** Harvey Wallbanger
with gin: **15** Russian Cocktail
with kahlua or Tia Maria: **12** Black Russian
with kirsch: **12** Volga Boatman
with orange juice: **11** screwdriver
with tomato juice: **10** Bloody Mary
with vermouth: **8** Kangaroo **9** Corkscrew

vogue 3 fad **4** mode, rage **5** craze, style, trend **6** custom **7** fashion **8** currency, practice, the thing **10** acceptance, popularity **11** the last word **12** popular favor **14** the latest thing **15** prevailing taste

voguish 4 chic **5** smart **6** modish **7** faddish, stylish **11** fashionable

voice 3 air, say **4** alto, bass, part, role, tone, vent, vote, will, wish **5** speak, state, tenor, utter **6** choice, desire, option, reveal, singer, speech **7** declare, divulge, express, opinion, singers, soprano **8** announce, baritone, delivery, disclose, proclaim, vocalize **9** contralto, enunciate, pronounce, ventilate **10** articulate, intonation, modulation, prefer ence, vocal sound **11** communicate **12** articulation, mezzo-soprano **13** participation, power of speech

voiceless 3 mum **4** deaf, mute, surd **6** silent **7** anaudia, aphonic, spirate

voice of the people
Latin: **9** vox populi

void 4 bare, emit, free, null, pass **5** annul, blank, clear, drain, eject, empty, purge **6** barren, cancel, devoid, recant, repeal, revoke, vacant, vacuum **7** abolish, drained, emptied, exhaust, invalid, lacking, nullify, pour out, rescind, reverse, vacuity, wanting **8** depleted, evacuate, nugatory, renounce, throw out, destitute, discharge, emptiness, exhausted, repudiate **10** empty space, invalidate, not in force **11** countermand, inoperative

voidance 7 voiding **8** ejection, emission **9** discharge, expulsion

Voight, Jon
born: **9** Yonkers NY
roles: **7** Joe Buck **8** The Champ **10** Coming Home (Oscar) **11** Deliverance **13** The Odessa File **14** Catch Twenty-Two, Midnight Cowboy

voila 3 see **4** look **9** there it is

volatile 4 rash, wild **5** brash, giddy, moody **6** fickle, fitful **7** erratic, flighty, gaseous **8** eruptive, reckless, unstable, unsteady, vaporous, variable **9** explosive, frivolous, mercurial, spasmodic, unsettled **10** capricious, changeable, evaporable, inconstant, irresolute, vaporizing **12** undependable **13** temperamental, unpredictable

volition 4 will **6** choice, option **8** choosing, decision, free will **10** discretion, resolution **13** determination

volley 5 burst, salvo **6** shower **7** barrage **8** outbreak, outburst **9** broadside, discharge, fusillade **10** outpouring

Volpone (The Fox)
author: **9** Ben Jonson
character: **5** Celia, Mosca **7** Bonario, Corvino, Voltore **9** Corbaccio, Peregrine **18** Lady Politic Would-Be, Lord Politic Would-Be

Volsung
origin: **12** Scandinavian
mentioned in: **8** Volsunga
grandfather: **4** Odin **5** Othin
son: **7** Sigmund
daughter: **5** Signy

Volsunga
origin: **9** Icelandic **12** Scandinavian
form: **4** saga
time: **17** thirteenth century
subject: **8** Volsungs

Volta, Alessandro, Count
nationality: **7** Italian
invented: **15** electric battery
discovered: **10** methane gas

Voltaic
also: **3** Gur
language family: **16** Niger-Kordofanian
group: **10** Niger-Congo
includes: **5** Mossi

Voltaire, Francois
real name: **19** Francois Marie Arouet

author of: **5** Zadig, Zaire **6** Alzire, Merope **7** Candide, L'Ingenu, Mahomet **11** The Henriade **16** The Maid of Orleans **23** Philosophical Dictionary
member of: **11** Philosophes

Volturnus
origin: **5** Roman
personifies: **4** wind **8** east wind **13** southeast wind

voluble 4 glib **5** wordy **6** chatty, fluent **7** twining **8** effusive, flippant, rotating, twisting **9** garrulous, talkative **10** loquacious

volume 4 book, bulk, heap, mass, size, tome **5** folio, sound, tract **6** amount, extent, quarto **7** measure **8** capacity, loudness, quantity, treatise, vastness **9** abundance, aggregate, magnitude, monograph **10** dimensions

voluminous 5 ample, large **7** copious, massive, sizable **8** abundant **9** extensive

Volund see **7** Wayland

voluntary 6 willed **8** free-will, intended, optional, unforced **10** deliberate **11** intentional, volunteered **13** discretionary, noncompulsory

volunteer 5 offer **6** extend, tender, unpaid **7** advance, present, proffer, recruit **8** enlistee **9** voluntary **10** put forward **11** step forward **12** unpaid worker **13** charityworker

Volunteer State
nickname of: **9** Tennessee

Voluptas
origin: **5** Roman
goddess of: **8** pleasure

voluptuary 4 rake, roue **7** epicure, gourmet, seducer **8** gourmand, hedonist, sybarite **9** bon vivant, debauchee, high liver, libertine, womanizer **10** gastronome, sensualist **14** pleasure seeker

voluptuous 4 soft **6** carnal, erotic, sexual, smooth, wanton **7** fleshly, lustful, sensual **8** sensuous **9** debauched, dissolute, luxurious, sybaritic **10** dissipated, hedonistic, lascivious, licentious, profligate **13** self-indulgent **14** pleasure-loving **15** pleasure-seeking

vomit 4 barf, emit, puke **5** eject, expel, heave, retch **7** bring up, throw up, upchuck **8** disgorge **9** discharge, spew forth **10** belch forth **11** regurgitate **15** toss one's cookies

Vonnegut, Kurt, Jr
author of: **8** Jailbird **9** Slapstick **10** Cat's Cradle, Palm Sunday **11** Player Piano **18** Slaughterhouse Five **20** Breakfast of Champions **22** Happy Birthday Wanda June

Von Sternberg, Josef
director of: **12** The Blue Angel

Von Sydow, Max

real name: 18 Carl Adolph von Sydow

born: 4 Lund **6** Sweden

roles: 12 The Emigrants **14** The Seventh Seal **15** The Virgin Spring **16** Wild Strawberries **24** The Greatest Story Ever Told

voracious 6 greedy **7** hoggish **8** edacious, ravenous **10** gluttonous, insatiable, omnivorous

vortex 4 eddy **7** cyclone, twister **9** maelstrom, whirlpool, whirlwind

votary 3 fan **4** buff **6** zealot **7** admirer, devotee, fanatic, habitue **8** adherent, champion, disciple, follower, partisan **10** aficionado, enthusiast **11** afficionado

vote 3 say **4** poll **5** voice **6** ballot, choice, option, ticket **8** approval, decision, election, judgment, suffrage **9** franchise, selection **10** plebiscite, preference, referendum **11** cast a ballot **13** determination

vouch 4 back **6** affirm, attest, back up, uphold, verify **7** certify, confirm, endorse, support, sustain, swear to, warrant, witness **8** attest to, maintain **9** guarantee **11** corroborate **12** authenticate

voucher 4 chip, chit **5** check, proof **6** surety, ticket **7** receipt, warrant **8** warranty **9** affidavit, debenture **10** credential **11** certificate **12** verification **14** authentication

vouchsafe 4 give **5** allow, deign,

favor, grant **6** bestow, convey, tender **7** concede **10** condescend

vow 4 oath, word **5** swear, troth, vouch **6** affirm, assert, assure, parole, pledge, plight, stress **7** declare, promise, resolve **8** contract **9** emphasize **11** word of honor **13** solemn promise

vox populi 14 popular opinion **16** voice of the people

voyage 4 sail **6** cruise **7** passage **8** crossing, navigate **9** ocean trip **10** sea journey

Voyage of the Beagle, The

author: 13 Charles Darwin

voyager 5 rover **7** cruiser, pilgrim, rambler, tourist **8** traveler, wayfarer **9** jet-setter, journeyer, sightseer **10** adventurer **12** excursionist, globe-trotter, peregrinator **13** world traveler

Voyage to the Bottom of the Sea

character: 6 Doctor **8** Kowalsky, Stu Riley, (Cdr/Capt) Lee Crane **9** Patterson **10** (Lt Cdr) Chip Morton **11** (Chief Petty Officer) Curley Jones **12** Chief Sharkey **14** (Adm) Harriman Nelson

cast: 9 Allan Hunt, Del Monroe **10** Henry Kulky, Paul Trinka **11** Richard Bull, Terry Becker **12** David Hedison **13** Robert Dowdell **15** Richard Basehart

submarine: 7 Seaview

explorer: 7 Sea Crab

mini-sub: 10 Flying Fish

Vronsky, Count Alexei

character in: 12 Anna Karenina

author: 7 Tolstoy

Vulcan

origin: 5 Roman

god of: 4 fire **12** metalworking

epithet: 8 Mulciber

corresponds to: 10 Hephaestus, Hephaistos

vulgar 3 low **4** base, rude **5** crude, dirty, gross, rough **6** coarse, common, filthy, ribald, risque, smutty **7** boorish, ill-bred, lowbrow, obscene, uncouth **8** impolite, indecent, off-color, ordinary, plebeian **9** offensive, tasteless, unrefined **10** suggestive **11** ill-mannered, proletarian **12** pornographic, uncultivated

vulgarian 3 oaf **4** boor, lout **5** brute, yahoo **7** Babbitt **9** ignoramus **10** philistine **16** anti-intellectual

vulgarity 8 bad taste, rudeness **9** crudeness, grossness, indecency, indecorum, obscenity **10** coarseness, ill manners, indelicacy, smuttiness **11** boorishness, pornography **12** impoliteness **13** tastelessness

vulnerable 4 weak **7** exposed **8** helpless, insecure **9** sensitive, unguarded **10** easily hurt, undefended **11** defenseless, susceptible, thin-skinned, unprotected

Vye, Eustacia

character in: 17 Return of the Native

author: 5 Hardy

wacky, whacky 3 odd **4** nuts **5** crazy, kooky **6** cuckoo, insane, kookie **7** cracked, foolish, touched **9** eccentric, senseless **10** irrational **12** crackbrained

wad 3 bat, pad **4** cram, head, heap, lump, mass, tuft **5** money, stuff **6** bundle, riches, stop up **7** fortune **8** bankroll, plumbago

waddle 3 wag **4** sway **6** hobble, toddle, totter, wobble

wade 4 ford, plod, plow, toil, trek **5** labor **6** drudge, trudge **9** walk in mud **11** walk in water

wafer 4 chip **5** candy, flake **6** cookie **7** cracker **15** unleavened bread

waft 4 blow, puff **5** drift, float

wag 3 bob, wit **4** card, move, stir, wave **5** clown, droll, flick, joker, shake **6** jester, jiggle, switch, twitch, waggle, wiggle, wigwag **7** buffoon, farceur, flicker, flutter **8** comedian, humorist, jokester **9** oscillate **11** wisecracker **14** life of the party

wage 3 fee, pay **6** income, salary **7** carry on, conduct, payment, revenue, stipend **8** earnings, engage in, maintain, practice **9** emolument, undertake **10** recompense **12** compensation, remuneration

wage earner 6 worker **8** employee **9** job holder **12** hourly worker

wager 3 bet, pot **4** ante, pool, risk **5** fancy, guess, stake **6** assume, gamble, hazard **7** imagine, jackpot, presume, suppose, surmise, venture **8** make a bet, theorize **9** speculate **10** conjecture, take a flyer **11** speculation, try one's luck **12** tempt fortune **15** hazard an opinion

wages 3 bet, fee, pay **4** gage, hire **6** fights, reward, return, salary **7** engages, payment, stipend **8** conducts, earnings **9** emolument **10** prosecutes, recompense **12** remuneration

wage war 5 fight **6** combat **7** contend, make war **8** do battle **12** march against

waggery 5 chaff **6** banter, riding **7** joshing, kidding, ragging, ribbing **8** chaffing, drollery, raillery, twitting **French: 8** badinage

waggish 5 droll, funny **7** comical, puckish **8** humorous

waggle 4 wave **5** wield **8** brandish

Wagner, Honus
    real name: 15 John Peter Wagner
    nickname: 14 Flying Dutchman
    sport: 8 baseball
    position: 9 shortstop
    team: 17 Pittsburgh Pirates

Wagner, Richard
    born: 7 Germany, Leipzig
    composer of: 5 Faust **6** Rienzi **7** Die Feen **8** Parsifal **9** Lohengrin **10** Tannhauser, The Fairies **14** Siegfried Idyll **16** The Mastersingers, Tristan and Isolde, Wesendonck Lieder **17** The Flying Dutchman **20** Der Ring des Nibelungen, The Ring of the Nibelungs **27** Die Meistersinger von Nurnberg
        the Ring Cycle Part 1: 12 Das Rheingold, The Rhine Gold
        the Ring Cycle Part 2: 10 Die Walkure **11** The Valkyrie
        the Ring Cycle Part 3: 9 Siegfried
        the Ring Cycle Part 4: 15 Gotterdammerung **17** Twilight of the Gods

Wagner, Robert
    born: 9 Detroit MI
    wife: 11 Natalie Wood
    roles: 6 Switch **10** Hart to Hart **13** It Takes a Thief, Prince Valiant, The Longest Day **24** All the Fine Young Cannibals

wagon 3 car, van **4** cart, dray, tram, wain **5** coach, lorry, tonga, truck **7** caisson **10** automobile, battleship
    covered: 15 prairie schooner
    maker: 10 wainwright
    police: 10 Black Maria
    Russian: 6 telega
    sideless: 6 rolley
    track: 3 rut

Wagon Train
    character: 9 Bill Hawks **11** Barnaby West, Cooper Smith, Duke Shannon **14** Charlie Wooster, Major Seth Adams **15** Christopher Hale, Flint McCullough
    cast: 8 Ward Bond **11** Scott Miller, Terry Wilson **12** Frank McGrath, John McIntire, Michael Burns, Robert Fuller, Robert Horton

waif 5 gamin, stray **6** gamine, urchin **7** mudlark **9** foundling **10** ragamuffin, street arab **11** guttersnipe **13** homeless child **14** tatterdemalion

wail 3 cry **4** bawl, howl, keen, moan,

roar, weep, yell **5** groan, shout, whine **6** bellow, bemoan, bewail, cry out, lament, outcry, plaint **7** keening, moaning, wailing **9** caterwaul **10** rend the air **11** lamentation

waist 3 top **5** shirt **6** blouse, bodice, middle **7** midriff **9** mid-region, waistband, waistline **10** middle part, midsection, shirtwaist

waistband 4 belt, sash **5** cinch **6** girdle

waistcoat 4 vest **5** benjy **6** jacket, jerkin, veskit, vestee, weskit **7** singlet **French:** gilet

wait 4 halt, stay, stop **5** dally, delay, pause, tarry **6** linger, put off **7** suspend **8** postpone, stopover **9** deferment **10** suspension **11** continuance **12** postponement

wait for 6 expect **10** anticipate

Waiting for Godot
    author: 13 Samuel Beckett
    character: 8 Estragon, Vladimir

wait on 5 serve **6** assist, attend

waive 4 stay **5** defer, forgo, let go, table, yield **6** give up, not use, put off, shelve **7** forbear, lay over **8** disclaim, forswear, postpone, renounce **9** surrender

waiver 9 dismissal **10** abdication, disclaimer **11** abandonment **12** renunciation **14** relinquishment

wake 4 fire, path, stir, wash **5** rally, rouse, trail, train, vigil **6** arouse, course, excite, kindle, revive **7** enliven, provoke, quicken **8** backwash **9** galvanize, stimulate **11** resuscitate

wakeful 4 wary **5** alert, astir **7** careful, heedful **8** cautious, restless, vigilant, watchful **9** insomniac, observant, sleepless **10** unsleeping **11** circumspect

wake up 4 rise **5** arise **6** vivify **7** animate, enliven **8** vitalize **9** stimulate

Walcott, Joe
    real name: 18 Arnold Raymond Cream
    nickname: 9 Jersey Joe
    sport: 6 boxing
    class: 11 heavyweight

Walden, or Life in the Woods
    author: 17 Henry David Thoreau

Wales
    other name: 5 Cymru **7** Cambria
    part of: 13 United Kingdom

title of British heir apparent: 13 Prince of Wales
capital: 7 Cardiff
cities: 4 Rhyl, Ross **5** Flint, Towyn **6** Amlwch, Bangor, Brecon, Sidney **7** Cwmbran, Herford, Newport, Rhondda, Swansea **8** Aberdare, Caerleon, Holyhead, Pembroke **9** Fishguard, Glamorgan **10** Caernarvon, Caerphilly, Carmarthen **11** Aberystwyth **12** Milford Haven **13** Kidderminster, Merthyr-Tydfil
division: 5 Clwyd, Dyfed, Flint, Gwent, Powys **6** Radnor **7** Denbigh, Gwynedd **8** Anglesey, Cardigan, Monmouth, Pembroke **9** Brecknoch, Glamorgan, Merioneth **10** Caernarvon, Carmarthen, Montgomery
emblem: 4 leek
government: 29 constituent part of Great Britain
measure: 5 cover **7** cantred, crannoc, listred
island: 4 Mona **5** Caldy **8** Anglesey, Holyhead
lake: 4 Bala **6** Vyrnwy
mountain: 6 Berwyn **8** Cambrian **9** Prescelly **13** Brecon Beacons
highest point: 7 Snowdon
river: 3 Dee, Usk, Wye **4** Alun, Taff, Tawe, Teme, Towy **5** Clwyd, Conwy, Dovey, Neath, Teifi **6** Conway, Severn, Vyrnwy
sea: 5 Irish **8** Atlantic
physical feature:
  bay: 7 Swansea **8** Cardigan, Tremadoc, Tremadog
  channel: 7 Bristol **9** St George's
  hills: 7 Malvern
  peninsula: 5 Lleyn
  strait: 5 Menai
  valley: 7 Rhondda
people: 4 Celt, Kelt **5** Cymry, Kymry, Welsh **7** Brython, Silures, Taffies **8** Awabokal, Cambrian **9** Siluridan
  actor: 6 Burton **8** Williams **13** Richard Burton, Emlyn Williams
  artist: 4 John
  author: 3 Map **5** Jones, Lewis, Mapes, Parry **6** Machan, Thrale **9** Llewellyn **11** Dylan Thomas **14** Dafydd ap Gwylym
  god: 3 Deu, Dew **4** Bran, Gwyn **5** Dylan **7** Gwydion
  leader: 5 Bevan **6** Rhodri **8** Hywel Dwa **11** Cadwallader **12** Bishop Morgan **13** Owen Glendower **16** David Lloyd George **18** Llewelyn ap Gruffydd
language: 5 Welsh **6** Celtic, Cymric, Keltic, Kymric **7** Cymraeg, English
religion: 8 Anglican **9** Methodist **10** Protestant **12** Presbyterian
place:
  bridge: 6 Severn
  castle: 6 Conway **7** Harlech **9** Beaumaris **10** Caernarvon, Caerphilly **11** Aberystwyth

feature:
  festival: 10 Eisteddfod
  stories: 10 Mabinogion
food:
  dish: 8 flummery
Walesa, Lech
  born: 6 Poland
  leader of: 10 Solidarity
  voted: 7 premier
wander aimlessly 5 amble, stray **6** ramble, stroll **7** meander, saunter
wandering 5 lapse **8** rambling, straying **9** deviation **10** aberration, digressive, discursive, maundering, meandering, roundabout **11** abnormality **12** idiosyncrasy **13** nonconformity **14** circumlocutory
Wandering Jew, The
  author: 9 Eugene Sue
Wanderings
  author: 10 Chaim Potok
wane 3 ebb **4** fade, sink **5** abate, droop, waste **6** ebbing, fading, lessen, weaken, wither **7** abating, decline, dwindle, subside **8** decrease, diminish, fade away **9** dwindling, lessening, recession, subsiding, weakening, withering
wangle 4 worm **5** trick **6** jockey, scheme **7** finagle, wheedle **8** engineer, intrigue, maneuver **9** machinate **10** manipulate
wanness 6 pallor **8** grayness, paleness **9** ashenness **10** sallowness, sickliness **13** colorlessness
want 4 hunt, lack, need, seek, wish **5** covet, crave, fancy **6** dearth, demand, desire, hunger, penury **7** be needy, craving, hope for, long for, paucity, pine for, poverty, require, wish for **8** scarcity, shortage, yearn for, yearning **9** indigence, necessity, pauperism, privation, requisite **10** deficiency, insolvency **11** destitution, requirement **13** impecuniosity, insufficiency, pennilessness **14** impoverishment
Wanted: Dead or Alive
  character: 11 Josh Randall
  cast: 12 Steve McQueen
  job: 12 bounty hunter
  gun: 8 Mare's Leg
wanting 5 short **6** absent **7** lacking, missing **9** defective, deficient, imperfect **10** inadequate **11** substandard **12** insufficient
wanton 4 bawd, fast, jade, lewd, rake, roue, slut, tart **5** gross, hussy, loose, satyr, whore **6** chippy, harlot, lecher **7** bestial, immoral, lustful, obscene, seducer, trollop, willful **8** careless, heedless, mindless, needless, strumpet, sybarite, unchaste **9** abandoned, adulterer, concubine, debauched, debauchee, dissolute, lecherous, libertine, malicious, senseless, womanizer **10** deliberate, fornicator, groundless, licentious, malevolent, profligate,

prostitute, sensualist, unprovoked, voluptuary **11** fornicatrix, promiscuous, unjustified, whoremaster **13** inconsiderate, irresponsible
wapiti 3 elk **4** deer **11** American elk
  female: 3 cow
  literally: 9 white rump
  male: 4 bull
  species: 16 Cervus canadensis
Wapshot Chronicle
  author: 11 John Cheever
war 5 clash, fight **6** attack, battle, combat, invade **7** contend **8** conflict, fighting, struggle **10** opposition **11** hostilities
  god of: 4 Ares, Odin **5** Othin **8** Quirinus
  goddess of: 4 Enyo **6** Athena, Athene, Inanna, Ishtar, Pallas, Saitis **7** Bellona, Mylitta **11** Tritogeneia **12** Pallas Athena **18** Alalcomenean Athena
War and Peace
  author: 10 Leo Tolstoy
  character: 7 Kutuzov **8** Napoleon **13** Natasha Rostov, Nikolay Rostov, Pierre Bezuhov **14** Anatole Kuragin **15** Andrey Bolkonsky **19** Ellen Kuragin Bezuhov **22** Princess Marya Bolkonsky
War and Remembrance
  author: 10 Herman Wouk
warble 4 lump, purl, sing **5** carol, larva, trill, tumor, yodel **6** growth, quaver, ripple **7** twitter, vibrate, whistle
war cry 6 slogan **8** Geronimo
ward 4 zone **5** avert, block, repel **6** charge, thwart **7** beat off, fend off, prevent, quarter **8** pavilion, precinct, stave off, turn away **9** dependent, forestall
  French: 7 protege
warden 5 guard **6** keeper, ranger, sentry **7** curator, manager **8** guardian, watchman **9** protector **14** superintendent
Warden, The
  author: 15 Anthony Trollope
ward off 5 avert **7** prevent
wardrobe 4 togs **5** chest **6** attire, closet, outfit **7** apparel, clothes **8** clothing, garments **10** cedar chest **12** clothespress
  French: 6 bureau **7** armoire, commode **10** chiffonier **11** habillement
wares 4 line **5** stock **7** staples **8** supplies **9** inventory **11** commodities, merchandise
warfare 5 fight **6** battle, combat **8** conflict, fighting **11** hostilities
Warhol, Andy
  born: 14 Philadelphia PA
  artwork: 9 Brillo Box, Liz Taylor **13** Marilyn Monroe **16** Campbell's Soup

Can **20** Green Coca-Cola Bottles
protegee: 12 Edie Sedgwick

wariness 7 caution **9** alertness, suspicion, vigilance **11** carefulness, guardedness, heedfulness **12** watchfulness **14** circumspection

warlike 7 hostile, martial, valiant **8** inimical, militant, military **9** bellicose, combative **10** unfriendly **11** belligerent, contentious, threatening
Indian: 8 Arapahoe

warlike attitude 9 hostility, pugnacity **11** bellicosity **12** belligerence, belligerency **13** combativeness **14** aggressiveness

warm 3 hot **4** cook, heat, kind, melt, thaw **5** cheer, happy, sunny, tepid, vivid **6** bright, heated, heat up, joyful, joyous, kindly, lively, loving, simmer, tender **7** affable, cordial, earnest, fervent, glowing, intense **8** animated, cheerful, friendly, gracious, outgoing, pleasant, spirited, vehement, vigorous **9** brilliant **10** passionate **11** kindhearted, sympathetic **12** affectionate, enthusiastic **13** compassionate, tenderhearted

warmhearted 4 kind **6** genial, kindly, loving **7** cordial **10** solicitous **11** sympathetic **12** affectionate **13** compassionate

warm-hued 3 red **4** rosy **5** ruddy, vivid **6** golden, orange, yellow **7** crimson, roseate, scarlet **8** blushing

warmish 5 tepid **7** cooling

warm oneself 4 bask **12** soak up warmth, toast oneself

warmth 3 joy **4** fire, heat, zeal **5** ardor, cheer, verve, vigor **6** fervor, spirit **7** hotness, passion **8** kindness, sympathy **9** animation, happiness, intensity, vehemence **10** affability, compassion, cordiality, enthusiasm, excitement, joyfulness, kindliness, liveliness, lovingness, tenderness **11** earnestness **12** cheerfulness, friendliness, graciousness **15** kindheartedness **17** tenderheartedness

warn 5 alert **6** advise, inform, notify, signal **7** apprise, caution, counsel **8** admonish

warning 4 hint, omen, sign **5** alarm, token **6** advice, notice, signal **7** portent, presage **8** apprisal **9** foretoken **10** intimation **12** notification

War of the Worlds, The
author: 7 H G Wells
invasion by: 8 Martians

war of words 7 dispute, quarrel **8** argument **11** altercation, controversy **12** disagreement

warp 4 bend, bent, bias **5** quirk, twist **6** debase, deform, infect **7** contort, corrupt, distort, leaning, mislead, pervert **8** misguide, misshape, tendency **9** prejudice, proneness **10** contortion, distortion, partiality, proclivity,

propensity **11** deformation, disposition, inclination **14** predisposition

warrant 3 vow **4** aver, avow **5** swear **6** affirm, assert, assure, attest, permit, pledge **7** certify, declare, justify, license, promise **9** authorize, guarantee **10** asseverate, permission **13** authorization

warranty 6 pledge **9** agreement **11** certificate

Warren, Robert Penn
author of: 5 Flood **7** Audubon **8** Promises **10** Now and Then **12** Incarnations **14** All the King's Men **18** World Enough and Time
member of: 12 the Fugitives

warring 7 hostile **8** battling, clashing, fighting, opposing **9** combatant **10** contending **11** belligerent, conflicting, contentious

warrior 7 fighter, soldier, veteran **9** combatant, man-at-arms **10** campaigner **11** legionnaire

Warsaw
area: 11 Stare Miasto
capital of: 6 Poland
landmark: 14 Kazimierzowski **25** Palace of Culture and Science
Polish: 8 Warszawa
river: 7 Vistula
square: 5 Rynek

warship 5 Maine, U-boat **6** corvet **7** Alabama, cruiser, frigate, gunboat, Monitor **8** Bismarck, corvette, Graf Spee, ironclad, man-of-war **9** destroyer, ironsides, Merrimack, submarine **11** dreadnought, torpedo boat **12** Constitution, Old Ironsides **13** Constellation **15** aircraft carrier **16** superdreadnought
fleet: 6 armada
part: 6 turret
plating: 5 armor

War Within and Without
author: 19 Anne Morrow Lindbergh

wary 5 alert **7** careful, guarded, heedful, mindful, prudent, wakeful **8** cautious, discreet, vigilant, watchful **10** suspicious **11** circumspect

wash 3 mop, rub, wet **4** bath, lave, soak, swab, wipe **5** bathe, clean, float, flood, rinse, scour, scrub **6** drench, shower, sponge **7** cleanse, immerse, launder, laundry, moisten, mopping, shampoo **8** ablution, cleaning, inundate, irrigate, lavation, scouring **9** cleansing **10** laundering

washbasin 3 tub **4** bowl **5** laver **6** lavabo **8** lavatory

washed out 4 drab, dull, pale **5** dingy, faded, white **6** dreary, grayed **8** bleached **9** colorless

washed up, washed-up 4 lost, shot **6** bathed, broken, ruined, undone **7** done for, preened, through **8** bankrupt, done with, fatigued, finished, scrubbed **9** played out, showered

washing 6 laving **7** bathing, laundry, purging, rinsing, soaking **8** cleaning, scouring **9** ablutions, drenching, scrubbing, showering **10** laundering, shampooing

Washington
abbreviation: 2 WA **4** Wash
nickname: 7 Chinook **9** Evergreen
capital: 7 Olympia
largest city: 7 Seattle
others: 4 Omak **5** Pasco **6** Renton, Tacoma, Yakima **7** Ephrata, Everett, Hoquiam, Othello, Pullman, Spokane **8** Aberdeen, Bellevue, Longview, Puyallup, Richland **9** Anacortes, Bremerton, Kennewick, Vancouver, Wenatchee **10** Bellingham, Burlington, Walla Walla **11** Port Angeles
college: 7 Gonzaga, Seattle, Whitman **9** Evergreen, Whitworth **10** Puget Sound **14** Seattle Pacific **15** Pacific Lutheran
feature:
  dam: 10 Bonneville, **11** Grand Coulee
  fort: 5 Lewis
  national park: 7 Olympic **12** Mount Rainier **13** North Cascades
tribe: 3 Hoh **5** Lummi, Makah, Twana **6** Cayuse, Samish, Skagit, Yakima **7** Chinook, Clallam, Clatsop, Cowlitz, Dwamish, Nooksak, Palouse, Quaitso, Sanpoil, Spokane, Squaxon, Tulalip **8** Chehalis, Chimakum, Colville, Nespelim, Nez Perce, Okanagon, Pishquow, Puyallup, Quileute, Quinault, Sahaptin, Salishan, Sinkiuse **9** Nisqually, Quinaielt, Semiahmoo, Skokomish, Swinomish **10** Senijextee, Shoalwater **11** Shahaptaine
people: 7 Seattle **10** Bing Crosby **11** Hank Ketcham **12** Elisha P Ferry **13** Marcus Whitman **15** William O Douglas **19** Isaac Ingalls Stevens
explorer: 4 Cook, Gray **6** Heceta **9** Vancouver **13** Lewis and Clark
lake: 4 Soap **5** Moses, Union **6** Chelan, Ozette **7** Cle Elum, Cushman, Kachess **8** Crescent, Quinault **9** Keechelus, Wenatchee **10** Washington
land rank: 9 twentieth
mountain: 4 Blue, Jack, Tunk **5** Adams, Baker, Lemei, Logan, Moses, Sloan **6** Kettle, Quartz, Simcoe, Stuart **7** Shuksan **8** Cascades, Olympics, St Helens **11** Kettle River
highest point: 7 Rainier
physical feature:
  falls: 10 Snoqualmie
  port: 6 Tacoma **7** Everett, Seattle **10** Bellingham
  sound: 5 Puget **7** Rosario
river: 5 Snake, White **6** Yakima **7** Spokane **8** Columbia, Quinault **9** Snohomish **10** Snoqualmie **11** Pend Oreille
state admission: 11 forty-second

state bird: 15 willow goldfinch
state fish: 14 steelhead trout
state flower: 17 coast rhododendron **19** western rhododendron
state motto: 7 By and By (Alki)
state song: 16 Washington My Home
state tree: 14 western hemlock
Washington, George
  nickname: 18 Father of His Country
  presidential rank: 5 first
  party: 10 Federalist
  state represented: 2 VA
  elected: 11 unanimously
  vice president: 5 (John) Adams
  cabinet:
    state: 9 (Thomas) Jefferson
    treasury: 8 (Alexander) Hamilton
    war: 4 (Henry) Knox **7** (James) McHenry **9** (Timothy) Pickering
    attorney general: 3 (Charles) Lee **8** (Edmund Jennings) Randolph, (William) Bradford
  born: 2 VA **9** Wakefield **18** Westmoreland County
  died/buried: 11 Mount Vernon
  religion: 12 Episcopalian
  interests: 7 fishing, hunting, theater **17** scientific farming
  vacation: 11 Mount Vernon
  author: 33 The Journal of Major George Washington
  political career: 9 president **16** House of Burgesses **24** First Continental Congress **25** Second Continental Congress
    signed: 12 Constitution
  civilian career: 6 farmer **8** surveyor
  military service:
    war: 13 Revolutionary **15** French and Indian
  notable events of lifetime/term: 18 American Revolution
    crossed: 13 Delaware River
    rebellion: 7 Whiskey
    winter at: 11 Valley Forge
  father: 9 Augustine
  mother: 4 Mary (Ball)
  siblings: 5 Betty **6** Samuel **7** Charles, Mildred **13** John Augustine
    half-brother: 6 Butler **8** Lawrence **9** Augustine
    half-sister: 4 Jane
  wife: 6 Martha (Dandridge Custis)
  children:
    stepchildren: 15 John Parke Custis **17** Martha Parke Custis
Washington DC
  airport: 6 Dulles **8** National
  basketball team: 7 Mystics, Wizards
  capital of: 12 United States
  designed by: 7 L'Enfant
  football team: 8 Redskins
  hockey team: 8 Capitals
  landmark: 4 Mall **7** Capitol, Ellipse **8** Pentagon **10** White House **11** National Zoo **12** Ford's Theatre, Franklin Park, Supreme Court **13** Lafayette Park, Rock Creek Park **14** Farragut

Square, Reflecting Pool, Watergate Hotel **15** Lincoln Memorial, McPherson Square **16** National Archives **17** Jefferson Memorial, Library of Congress, National Arboretum **18** Washington Monument **21** Frederick Douglass Home, Robert F Kennedy Stadium **22** Smithsonian Institution **23** National Sculpture Garden **25** Arlington National Cemetery **33** Kennedy Center for the Performing Arts
  museum: 5 Freer **7** Renwick **8** Corcoran **9** Hirshhorn **10** African Art **11** Smithsonian **13** Dumbarton Oaks **15** National Gallery **17** Folger Shakespeare **18** Phillips Collection **23** National Portrait Gallery
  river: 7 Potomac **9** Rock Creek
  street/avenue: 4 Ohio **7** New York, Potomac **12** Constitution, Independence, Pennsylvania **13** Massachusetts
  university: 6 Howard **8** American, Catholic **10** Georgetown **11** George Mason **16** George Washington
Washington Square
  author: 10 Henry James
wash one's hands of 4 deny, quit **6** give up **7** abandon, decline, disavow, forsake **8** abnegate, cast away, disclaim, forswear, renounce **9** repudiate **10** relinquish
washout 6 fiasco, fizzle **7** failure, letdown **8** disaster **14** disappointment
wash out 4 fade, fail **6** bleach **7** deplete, fatigue **8** enervate, enfeeble **10** debilitate, devitalize
wasp 5 vespa **6** vespid
  variety: 5 paper **6** cuckoo, ensign, hornet, potter, spider **12** yellow jacket
waspish 5 huffy, testy **6** crabby, cranky, ornery, shirty **7** bearish, fretful, peevish, pettish **8** petulant, snappish **9** crotchety, fractious, irascible, irritable, querulous **12** cantankerous
Wasps, The
  author: 12 Aristophanes
  character: 10 Bdelycleon, Philocleon
  dog: 5 Labes
wassail 5 drink, punch, revel, toast **6** liquor, tipple **7** carouse, revelry **8** beverage, carousal
waste 3 die, ebb, rob **4** fade, loot, melt, rape, raze, ruin, sack, sink, void, wane **5** abate, crush, decay, drain, dregs, droop, empty, offal, smash, spoil, strip, trash, wreck **6** barren, burn up, debris, devour, litter, misuse, ravage, razing, refuse, scraps, steppe, tundra, weaken, wither **7** crumble, decline, deplete, despoil, destroy, dwindle, exhaust, garbage, looting, pillage, plunder, rubbish, shatter, subside **8** badlands, decrease, demolish, diminish, leavings, misapply, misspend, needless, prey upon, remnants, squander, wrecking **9** devastate, dis-

appear, dissipate, emptiness, evaporate, excrement, leftovers, misemploy, ruination, sweepings **10** demolition, plundering, remainders, wilderness **11** destruction, devastation, dissipation, expenditure, fritter away, prodigality, squandering **12** despoliation, extravagance **14** misapplication
waste away 4 fail, rust **7** corrode, decline, eat into
wasted 5 spent **6** used-up **7** ravaged **9** emaciated, exhausted **12** unproductive
wasteful 8 prodigal **9** unthrifty **10** thriftless **11** extravagant, improvident, spendthrift, squandering **12** uneconomical
wastefulness 10 imprudence, lavishness **11** prodigality, squandering **12** extravagance, improvidence
wasteland 6 desert
Waste Land, The
  author: 7 T S Eliot
  editor: 9 Ezra Pound
waste time 5 dally **6** dawdle, loiter **10** dillydally
watch 3 eye, see **4** heed, look, mark, mind, note, ogle, save, tend **5** alert, guard, scout, stare **6** attend, be wary, gaze at, guards, look at, look on, notice, patrol, peep at, peer at, picket, regard, sentry, survey, tend to **7** be chary, care for, examine, lookout, observe, oversee, protect, stare at **8** pore over, preserve, sentinel, sentries, take heed **9** attention, patrolman, vigilance **10** observance, scrutinize **11** contemplate, observation, superintend, supervision **15** superintendence
watch fire 6 beacon
  kinds: 4 bale **6** signal
watchful 4 wary **5** alert, aware, canny, chary **6** shrewd **7** careful, guarded, heedful, mindful, prudent **8** cautious, open-eyed, vigilant **9** attentive, observant **11** circumspect
watchfulness 4 care, heed **9** attention, diligence, vigilance **13** attentiveness
watchman 5 guard, scout **6** patrol, picket, sentry **7** lookout **8** sentinel **9** patrolman
Watch on the Rhine
  director: 13 Herman Shumlin
  based on play by: 14 Lillian Hellman
  cast: 9 Paul Lukas **10** Bette Davis **19** Geraldine Fitzgerald
  Oscar for: 5 actor (Lukas)
watch over 5 guard **6** attend **7** oversee, protect **11** superintend
watchtower 6 beacon, pharos, signal **7** seamark **8** landmark **10** lighthouse
watchword 5 motto **6** byword, slogan
water 3 cut, dip, sea, wet **4** damp, lake, pond, pool, soak, tear, thin **5** douse, flood, H two O, ocean, river, souse **6** dampen, deluge, dilute,

drench, lagoon, splash, stream **7** immerse, moisten **8** inundate, irrigate, sprinkle, submerge **10** adulterate
goddess of: 4 Enki

Water Carrier (Water Bearer)
constellation of: **8** Aquarius

watercolor
French: **9** aquarelle

watercourse 5 canal, river **6** strait **7** channel, conduit, narrows, passage **8** aqueduct

water down 3 cut **6** censor, dilute, weaken **7** thin out **9** expurgate **10** adulterate

watered down 4 weak **6** dilute **7** diluted **8** weakened **11** adulterated

waterfall 7 cascade, Niagara **8** cataract

waterfront 4 dock, mole, pier, quay **5** basin, jetty, levee, wharf **6** marina **7** landing

waterless 3 dry **4** arid, sere **6** barren **7** parched, thirsty **10** desertlike

Waterloo Bridge
director: **11** Mervyn LeRoy
cast: **11** Vivien Leigh **12** Lucile Watson, Robert Taylor **13** Virginia Field
remade as: **4** Gaby

Water Monster (Sea Serpent)
constellation of: **5** Hydra

water of life
Latin: **9** aqua vitae

Waters, Ethel
nickname: **19** Sweet Mama Stringbean
born: **9** Chester PA
roles: **5** Pinky **6** Beulah **21** The Member of the Wedding

Watership Down
author: **12** Richard Adams

Water Snake
constellation of: **6** Hydrus

watertight 9 nonporous **10** impervious **11** impermeable

waterway 5 canal, inlet, river, route **6** gutter, strait, strake, stream **7** channel

Water Wonderland
nickname of: **8** Michigan

watery 3 wet **4** damp, thin, weak **5** fluid, moist, teary **6** liquid, rheumy **7** aqueous, diluted, tearful, tearing **11** adulterated

Watling, Belle
character in: **15** Gone With the Wind
author: **8** Mitchell

Watt, James
nationality: **8** Scottish
developed: **11** steam engine **12** piston engine

Watteau, Jean Antoine
born: **6** France **12** Valenciennes
artwork: **6** Gilles **8** Mezzetin **9** La Finette **10** La Toilette **12** Joys of Living, L'indifferent **13** La Gamme d'Amour **16** Company in the Park, La Lecon de Musique **18** Enseigne de

Gersaint, Gersaint's Signboard, La Comedie Francaise, La Concert de Famille **20** Le Dejeuner en plein air, L'assemblee dans un parc **21** Harlequin and Columbine **23** Embarquement pour Cythere, Italian and French Theater, Jupiter Surprises Antiope, Les Amusements Champetres **24** Conversation in the Open Air, The Embarkation for Cythera

wattle 6 Acacia
varieties: **5** black, broom, cedar, glory, green, hairy, oven's, Sally, swamp **6** frosty, golden, mudgee, orange, silver, sticky **7** bramble, buffalo, coastal, prickly, weeping, Wyalong **8** blue-leaf, cinna- mon, graceful, screw-pod, sunshine **9** redleaved **10** golden-rain, needle-bush **11** Cootamundra, Mount Morgan, Wallangarra **12** Sydney golden **14** Peppermint-tree **16** Queensland silver

Watts, Sir George Frederic
born: **6** London **7** England
artwork: **4** Hope **14** Physical Energy **17** Paolo and Francesca **19** Anastasio degl'Onesti **45** Caractacus Led in Triumph Through the Streets of Rome **54** Alfred Inciting his Subjects to Prevent the Landing of the Danes

Waugh, Evelyn
author of: **9** Men at Arms **10** Vile Bodies **11** The Loved One **13** Black Mischief, Edmund Campion **14** A Handful of Dust, Decline and Fall **15** A Little Learning **19** Brideshead Revisited **20** Officers and Gentlemen **22** Unconditional Surrender

wave 4 coil, curl, file, flap, line, rank, rise, roll, rush, sway, tier **5** curve, flood, pulse, shake, surge, swell, swing, train, twirl, wield **6** billow, column, comber, deluge, motion, quiver, ripple, roller, signal, spiral, string **7** breaker, flutter, gesture, pulsate, tremble, vibrate, winding **8** brandish, flourish, increase, undulate, whitecap **9** advancing, oscillate, pulsation, vibration **10** salutation, undulation **11** gesticulate, heightening **13** gesticulation

wave at 4 hail **6** signal **7** gesture

wave on 6 beckon, signal **7** gesture **11** gesticulate

waver 4 flap, reel, sway, vary **5** pause, shake, swing, weave **6** careen, change, falter, quiver, totter, wobble **7** flutter, stagger, tremble **8** hesitate, undulate **9** fluctuate, vacillate **10** dillydally **12** shilly-shally

wavering 8 hesitant, waffling **9** undecided **10** hesitating, indecisive, irresolute **11** vacillating

Waverley
author: **14** Sir Walter Scott
character: **12** Flora MacIvor **14** Don-

ald Bean Lean, Edward Waverley **15** Rose Bradwardine **16** Baron Bradwardine **17** Evan Dhu MacCombich **24** Fergus MacIvor Vich Ian Vohr **25** Prince Charles Edward Stuart

wavy 4 onde, unde **5** curly **6** coiled, curved **7** rolling, sinuous, winding **8** mazelike, rippling, tortuous **10** meandering, serpentine, undulating **11** curvilinear **12** labyrinthine

wax 4 grow **5** swell, widen **6** become, blow up, dilate, expand, extend, thrive **7** balloon, develop, enlarge, fill out, inflate, puff out **8** increase

way 3 far, off **4** area, form, lane, pass, path, road, room, wont **5** habit, means, route, space, trail, usage **6** course, custom, far off, manner, method, nature, region, system **7** conduct, passage, pathway, process **8** behavior, distance, practice, remotely, vicinity **9** direction, procedure, technique **12** neighborhood

wayfarer 8 traveler, wanderer **9** sojourner

Wayfaring Stranger
nickname of: **8** Burl Ives

way in 4 door, gate **5** entry **6** access, portal **7** doorway, gateway, ingress **8** approach, entrance

Wayland
also: **6** Volund **7** Wieland
origin: **8** European
king of: **5** elves

waylay 4 lure **5** decoy **6** ambush, assail, attack, entrap **7** assault, ensnare, set upon **8** inveigle

Wayne, Anthony
nickname: **10** Mad Anthony
served in: **10** Indian Wars **16** Revolutionary War
captured: **10** Stony Point
battle: **10** Brandywine, Germantown **13** Fallen Timbers

Wayne, David
real name: **13** Wayne McMeekan
born: **14** Traverse City MI
roles: **6** Sakini **8** Adam's Rib **12** The Front Page **13** Mister Roberts, Tonight We Sing **15** Huckleberry Finn **16** Portrait of Jennie **26** The Teahouse of the August Moon

Wayne, John
real name: **21** Marion Michael Morrison
nickname: **4** Duke
born: **11** Winterset IA
roles: **5** Hondo **6** Chisum **8** Ringo Kid, Rio Bravo, The Alamo, True Grit (Oscar) **9** McLintock, Rio Grande **10** Stagecoach **11** The Quiet Man, The Shootist **12** The Searchers **14** Rooster Cogburn, The Green Berets **16** How the West Was Won **17** The Sands of Iwo Jima **27** The Man Who Shot Liberty Valance

Way of All Flesh, The

author: 12 Samuel Butler
character: 9 Mr Overton
  Pontifex family: 5 Ellen **6** Althea, Ernest, George **8** Theobald **9** Christina

Way of the World, The
  author: 15 William Congreve
  character: 6 Foible **7** Fainall, Witwoud **8** Mirabell, Waitwell **10** Mrs Fainall, Mrs Marwood **12** Lady Wishfort, Mrs Millamant **17** Sir Wilfull Witwoud

way of thinking 7 beliefs **9** principle **10** conviction **11** persuasions

way out 4 exit **6** egress, escape, outlet

Ways of Escape
  author: 12 Graham Greene

wayward 5 balky **6** fickle, fitful, mulish, unruly **7** erratic, restive, willful **8** contrary, perverse, stubborn, variable **9** mercurial, obstinate, whimsical **10** capricious, changeable, headstrong, inconstant, rebellious, refractory, self-willed **11** disobedient, fluctuating, intractable, troublesome **12** inconsistent, incorrigible, recalcitrant, undependable, ungovernable, unmanageable **13** insubordinate

Wazhazhe *see* **5** Osage

weak 4 lame, poor, puny, soft, thin **5** faint, frail, shaky, spent **6** feeble, flimsy, unsafe, wasted, watery **7** brittle, diluted, exposed, fragile, insipid, lacking, unmanly **8** cowardly, delicate, helpless, timorous, unsteady, wide open **9** breakable, enervated, exhausted, frangible, powerless, spineless, tasteless, unguarded, untenable **10** assailable, effeminate, irresolute, namby-pamby, vulnerable, wishy-washy **11** adulterated, debilitated, defenseless, ineffective, ineffectual, inefficient, unprotected, unsupported **12** unconvincing **13** inefficacious, unsubstantial, untrustworthy **14** unsatisfactory

weaken 3 sap **4** fade, fail, flag, thin, wane **5** abate, droop, lower, unman, waste **6** dilute, expose, impair, lessen, soften **7** cripple, dwindle, exhaust, thin out **8** diminish, enervate, mitigate, moderate **9** undermine **10** devitalize, emasculate

weakened 5 frail **6** dilute, faulty, flawed, watery **7** diluted **8** delicate, disabled **9** enfeebled **10** undermined **11** adulterated, debilitated, watered down

weakling 4 twit, wimp **5** mouse, sissy **6** coward **7** chicken, milksop **9** cream puff, jellyfish **10** namby-pamby, pantywaist **11** milquetoast, mollycoddle

weak-minded 4 daft, dull **7** foolish **8** backward, mindless **10** irresolute **11** addleheaded, vacillating **12** feebleminded, muddleheaded, thick-skulled

weakness 4 bent, bias **5** fault **6** defect, hunger, thirst **7** failing, frailty, leaning, passion **8** appetite, debility, fondness, lameness, penchant, tendency **9** prejudice, proneness, shakiness **10** deficiency, feebleness, flimsiness, proclivity, propensity **11** inclination **12** debilitation, imperfection, unsteadiness **13** vulnerability **14** susceptibility **15** ineffectiveness **16** unconvincingness, unsubstantiality **17** untrustworthiness

weak point 4 flaw **5** break, crack, fault **6** defect **10** deficiency **11** shortcoming **12** Achilles heel

weak position 8 handicap **12** disadvantage

weak-willed 8 hesitant, wavering **10** hesitating, indecisive, irresolute

wealth 4 fund, mine **5** goods, means, money, store **6** assets, bounty, estate, luxury, mammon, riches **7** capital, fortune **8** chattels, fullness, opulence, property, richness **9** abundance, affluence, amplitude, plenitude, profusion, resources **10** easy street, prosperity **11** copiousness **12** independence **13** luxuriousness

wealthy 4 rich **5** flush **6** loaded **7** moneyed, well-off **8** affluent, well-to-do **9** well-fixed **10** prosperous, well- heeled

weapon 3 arm **5** guard, means **6** attack, resort **7** bulwark, defense, measure, offense **8** armament, resource, security **9** offensive, safeguard **10** protection **14** countermeasure

weaponry 4 arms, guns **8** armament, materiel, ordnance

wear 3 don, tax, use **4** duds, fray, last, tire, togs, wrap **5** drain, erode, put on, shred, weary **6** abrade, attire, damage, endure, injury, shroud, slip on, swathe **7** apparel, clothes, corrode, dress in, eat away, exhaust, fatigue, frazzle, rub away, service, swaddle, utility **8** clothing, costumes, garments, overwork, wash away **9** disrepair **10** employment, overburden **11** application, consumption, utilization **12** dilapidation **13** deterioration **14** disintegration

wear away 4 rust **5** erase, erode **7** corrode, eat into

weariness
  French: 5 ennui

wearing apparel 4 duds, garb, rags, togs, wear **5** dress **6** attire, finery **7** clothes, costume, raiment, regalia, threads **8** clothing, ensemble, garments, wardrobe
  French: 11 habillement

wearing away 7 erosion **8** abrasion, friction, grinding, scraping **9** corrosion

wearing down 6 tiring **7** eroding, erosion **8** abrasion, friction, grinding, scraping **10** overcoming

wearisome 4 dull **6** boring, dreary, tiring, trying **7** arduous, irksome, tedious **8** annoying, tiresome, toilsome **9** fatiguing, laborious, vexatious **10** bothersome, burdensome, exhausting, irritating, monotonous, oppressive

wear out 4 tire **7** exhaust, fatigue **8** enervate, enfeeble **10** debilitate

weary 3 fag **4** beat, dull, tire **5** all in, blase, bored, fed up, jaded, spent, tired **6** boring, bushed, done in, drowsy, pooped, sleepy, tiring, tucker **7** annoyed, drained, exhaust, fatigue, humdrum, overtax, play out, routine, tedious, tire out, worn-out **8** dog tired, fatigued, overwork, tiresome **9** disgusted, exhausted, fatiguing, impatient, soporific, wearisome **10** dispirited, exhausting, monotonous, overburden **11** somniferous **12** discontented, dissatisfied

weather 3 dry, tan **4** face, rust **5** brave, clime, stand **6** bleach, season **7** climate, oxidize, toughen **8** confront, windward **9** withstand **11** temperature
  god of: 4 Jove **7** Jupiter

weather line 6 isobar

weave 4 fuse, join, knit, lace, link, loom, meld, wind **5** blend, braid, curve, plait, snake, twist, unify, unite **6** mingle, writhe, zigzag **7** combine, entwine, meander, texture **9** interlace **10** crisscross, intertwine **11** incorporate

Weaver, Earl
  nickname: 15 Earl of Baltimore
  sport: 8 baseball
  position: 7 manager
  team: 16 Baltimore Orioles

Weaver, Dennis
  born: 8 Joplin MO
  roles: 7 Chester, McCloud **8** Gunsmoke **9** Gentle Ben **13** Kentucky Jones

Weaver, Sigourney
  born: 12 Los Angeles CA
  roles: 5 Alien **6** Aliens **10** Eyewitness **12** Ghostbusters **17** Gorillas in the Mist **26** The Year of Living Dangerously

web 3 net **4** maze, mesh, trap **5** snare **6** screen, tangle, tissue **7** complex, netting, network **8** gossamer **9** labyrinth, screening

Web and the Rock, The
  author: 11 Thomas Wolfe
  character: 10 Esther Jack **12** George Webber

Webb, Jack
  born: 13 Santa Monica CA
  wife: 11 Julie London
  roles: 6 The Men **7** Dragnet **9** Joe Friday **15** Sunset Boulevard

Webber, George
  character in: 16 The Web and the Rock **18** You Can't Go Home Again
  author: 5 Wolfe

Webb family

characters in: 7 Our Town
member: 5 Emily, Wally
author: 6 Wilder

Weber, Karl Maria Friedrich Ernst von
born: 6 Lubeck **7** Germany
composer of: 6 Oberon **9** Euryanthe **13** Der Freischutz **20** Invitation to the Dance

Weber, Max
born: 6 Russia **9** Bialystok
artwork: 11 The Geranium **17** Chinese Restaurant **18** Adoration of the Moon

Webfoot State
nickname of: 6 Oregon

Webster
character: 6 George **7** Webster **9** Katherine
cast: 10 Alex Karras, Susan Clark **13** Emmanuel Lewis

Webster, John
author of: 13 The White Devil **17** The Duchess of Malfi

we cannot
Latin: 11 non possumus

we command
Latin: 8 mandamus

wed 3 tie **4** bind, fuse, link, mate, meld **5** blend, hitch, marry, merge, unify, unite, weave **6** attach, commit, couple, devote, pledge, splice **7** combine, espouse, make one, win over **8** dedicate **11** incorporate

wedded 4 tied **5** bound, fused **6** joined, linked, melded, merged, united **7** blended, devoted, marital, married, pledged, unified **9** committed, connected **12** incorporated

wedding 8 marriage, nuptials

wedding anniversaries
first: 5 clock, paper
second: 5 china **6** cotton
third: 5 glass **7** crystal, leather
fourth: 4 silk **5** linen **20** electrical appliances
fifth: 4 wood **10** silverware
sixth: 4 iron, wood
seventh: 4 wool **6** copper **8** desk sets **16** pen and pencil sets
eighth: 4 lace **6** bronze, linens
ninth: 5 china **7** leather, pottery
tenth: 3 tin **8** aluminum **14** diamond jewelry
eleventh: 5 steel **11** accessories **14** fashion jewelry
twelfth: 4 silk **6** pearls **11** colored gems
thirteenth: 4 furs, lace **8** textiles
fourteenth: 5 ivory **11** gold jewelry
fifteenth: 7 crystal, watches
twentieth: 5 china **8** platinum
twenty-fifth: 6 silver **21** sterling silver jubilee
thirtieth: 5 pearl **7** diamond
thirty-fifth: 4 jade **5** coral
fortieth: 4 ruby
forty-fifth: 8 sapphire
fiftieth: 4 gold **13** golden jubilee
fifty-fifth: 7 emerald
sixtieth: 7 diamond

weddings
god of: 8 Talassio

wedge 3 jam, ram **4** cram, pack, rend, rive **5** chock, chunk, crowd, force, press, split, stuff **6** cleave **7** squeeze

wedlock 8 marriage **9** matrimony

Wednesday
Dutch: 8 woensdag
French: 8 mercredi
German: 8 mittwoch
heavenly body: 7 Mercury
Italian: 9 mercoledi
name comes from: 4 Odin **5** Woden
observance: 12 Ash Wednesday
Spanish: 9 miercoles
Swedish: 6 onsdag

wee 4 tiny **5** dwarf, scant, teeny **6** little, minute, petite, scanty **9** itty-bitty, miniature, minuscule **10** diminutive, teeny-weeny, undersized **11** Lilliputian, microscopic

weed 3 bur, hoe, nag, pot **4** burr, butt, cull, dock, hemp, rake **5** cigar, joint, vetch **6** darnel, harrow, pull up, root up, uproot **7** tobacco **8** nuisance, plantain, purslane, toadflax **9** cigarette, crabgrass, cultivate, dandelion, eliminate, extirpate, marijuana **12** mourning band

weed out 6 banish **7** abolish, discard **8** get rid of, throw out **9** eliminate

Weena
character in: 14 The Time Machine
author: 5 Wells

weeny 3 wee **4** tiny **5** frank, small, teeny **6** hotdog, little, teensy, wiener **11** frankfurter

weep 3 cry, orp, sob **4** bawl, bend, drip, leak, lerm, ooze, shed, tear, wail **5** exude, mourn **6** bewail, boohoo, lament, shower **7** blubber, lapwing, whimper **8** sweating **9** exudation
genus: 8 Vanellus

weep over 5 mourn **6** bemoan, bewail, lament

weevil
variety: 4 boll, rice

Wegener, Alfred L
field: 10 geophysics **11** meteorology
nationality: 6 German
theory of: 16 continental drift

Wegg
character in: 15 Our Mutual Friend
author: 7 Dickens

weigh 4 lift **5** count, hoist, raise, scale **6** burden, charge, ponder, regard **7** balance, compare, measure **8** consider, encumber, evaluate, ruminate **11** contemplate **12** counterbalance

weigh anchor 4 sail **7** cast off, set sail, ship out

weigh down 4 load **6** anchor, burden **7** oppress **8** encumber, obligate, overload

weight 3 tax **4** heft, load, mass **5** value **6** burden, import, saddle, strain, stress **7** ballast, concern, oppress, tonnage, urgency **8** emphasis, encumber, poundage, pressure **9** heaviness, influence, magnitude **10** importance **11** consequence **12** significance **13** consideration, ponderousness

weight, unit of
of Afghanistan: 3 pau, paw, ser, sir
of Algeria: 4 rotl
of Argentina: 4 last **5** grano, libra **7** quintal **8** tonelada
of Austria: 4 marc, saum, unze **5** denat, karch, pfund, stein **6** centner, pfennig **8** vierling **9** quantchen
of Belgium: 4 last **5** carat, livre, pound **6** charge **7** chariot **9** esterling
of Bolivia: 5 libra, marco
of Borneo: 4 para **6** chapah
of Brazil: 3 bag **4** onca, onza **5** libra **6** arroba, oitava **7** arratel, quilate, quintal **8** tonelada
of Bulgaria: 3 oka, oke **5** tovar
of Cambodia: 4 mace, tael
of Chile: 5 grano, libra **7** quintal
of China: 3 fan, fen, hao, kin, ssu, tan, yin **4** chee, chin, dong, shih, tael, tsin **5** catty, chien, picul, tchin, tsien **6** kungli **7** haikwan, kungfen, kungssu, kungtun **8** kungchin **9** candareen **10** kupingtael
of Colombia: 3 bag **4** saco **5** carga, libra **7** quilate, quintal
of Costa Rica: 3 bag **4** caja **5** libra
of Cuba: 5 libra **6** tercio
of Ecuador: 5 libra
of Egypt: 3 kat, ket, oka, oke **4** dera, heml, khar, okia, rotl **5** artal, artel, deben, kerat, minae, minas, okieh, pound, ratel, uckia **6** hamlah, kantar **7** drachma, quintal
of El Salvador: 3 bag **4** caja **5** libra
of England: 3 bag, kip, tod, ton **4** keel, last, mast, maun **5** barge, fagot, grain, maund, pound, score, stand, stone, truss **6** bushel, cental, fangot, firkin, fother, fotmal, pocket **7** quarter, quintal, sarpler
of Estonia: 4 lood, nael, puud
of Ethiopia: 3 pek **4** kasm, natr, oket, rotl **5** alada, artal, mocha, neter, ratel, wakea **6** wogiet **8** farasula **9** mutagalla
of France: 3 sol **4** gros, kilo, marc, once **5** carat, livre, pound, tonne, uckia **6** gramme, passir **7** tonneau **8** esterlin **9** esterling
of Greece: 3 mna, oka, oke **4** mina, obol **5** litra, livre, maneh, pound **6** diobol, dramme, kantar, obolos, obolus, stater, talent **7** chalcon, chalque, drachma **8** diobolon, talanton
of Guatemala: 4 caja **5** libra
of Guinea: 4 akey, piso, uzan **5** benda, seron **6** quinto **8** aguirage

of Hungary: 7 vamfont **8** vammazsa
of Iceland: 4 pund **5** pound, tunna **6** smjors
of India: 3 mod, pai, ser, vis **4** dhan, drum, hoen, kona, myat, pala, pank, pice, raik, ruay, tael, tali, tank, tola, wang, yava **5** adpad, bahar, hubba, masha, maund, tical **6** abucco, karsha **8** mangelin
of Indonesia: 5 catty, ounce, thail **6** soekoe
of Iran: 3 ser **4** dram, dung, rotl, sang, seer **5** abbas, artel, maund, pinar, ratel **6** dirhem, gandum, karwar, miscal, nakhod, nimman **7** abbassi **8** tcheirek
of Italy: 5 carat, libra, oncia, pound **6** carato, denaro, libbra, ottava
of Japan: 2 mo **3** fun, kin, kon, rin, shi **4** kati, kwan, niyo **5** carat, catty, momme, picul **6** kwamme **8** hiyakkin
of Java: 4 amat, pond, tali **5** pound **6** soekel
of Korea: 3 won
of Latvia: 9 liespfund
of Libya: 3 pik, saa **4** kele **5** teman, uckia **6** gorraf, misura **7** mattaro, termino **8** kharouba
of Malaysia: 4 chee, mace, tael, wang **7** tampang
of Mexico: 3 bag **4** onza **5** carga, libra, marco **6** adarme, arroba, ochava, tercio **7** quintal
of Mongolia: 3 lan
of Morocco: 4 rotl **5** artal, artel, gerbe, ratel **6** dirhem, kintar **7** quintal
of Myanmar: 2 ta **3** can, mat, moo, pai, vis **4** binh, dong, kyat, ruay, viss **5** bahar, behar, candy, tical, ticul **6** abucco **7** peiktha
of the Netherlands: 3 ons **4** last, lood, pond **5** bahar, grein **6** korrel **7** wichtje **8** esterlin
of Nicaragua: 3 bag **4** caha, caja **8** tonelada
of Norway: 3 lod **4** mark, pund **9** skaalpund **10** bismerpund
of Pakistan: 4 seer, tola **5** maund
of Paraguay: 7 quintal
of Peru: 5 libra **7** quintal
of the Philippines: 5 catty, fardo, picul, punto **6** lachsa **7** quilate **8** chinanta
of Poland: 3 lut **4** funt **5** uncya **6** kamian **7** centner, skrupul
of Portugal: 4 grao, onca, once **5** libra, marco **6** arroba, oitava **7** arratel, quintal **9** excropulo
of Russia: 3 lof, lot **4** dola, funt, lana, last, loof, loth, once, pood, poud **5** dolia
of Saudi Arabia: 3 oke
of Scotland: 4 boll, drop **5** trone **6** bushel
of Somalia: 8 parsalah
of Spain: 4 onza **5** frail, grano, libra,

marco, tomin **6** adarme, arroba, dinero, dracma, ochava **7** arienzo, quilate, quintal **8** caracter, tonelada
of Sudan: 5 habba
of Sweden: 3 ass, lod, ort **4** last, mark, sten **5** carat **6** nylast **7** centner, lispund **8** skalpund, skeppund **9** shippound
of Switzerland: 4 fund **5** pfund **7** centner, quintal **12** zugthierlast
of Syria: 4 cola, rotl **5** artal, artel, ratel **6** talent
of Tanzania: 8 farsalah
of Thailand: 3 bat, hap, pai, pay, sen, sok **4** baht, haph, kati, klam, klom **5** catty, chang, coyan, fuang, picul, pilul, tical **6** fluang, graini, salung, sompay **7** tamlung
of Tunisia: 3 saa **4** rotl **5** artal, artel, ratel, uckia **6** kantar
of Turkey: 3 oka, oke **4** aqui, dram, kile, rotl **5** artal, artel, cheke, kerat, obolu, ratel **6** batman, dirhem, kantar, maunch, miskal **7** drachma, quintal, yusdrum
of Uruguay: 7 quintal
of Venezuela: 3 bag **5** libra
of Vietnam: 3 can, yet **4** uyen
of Yugoslavia: 3 oka **5** dramm, tovar, wagon **7** satlijk
weightlessness 8 buoyancy **9** lightness **11** zero gravity
weighty 5 grave, heavy, hefty, vital **6** solemn, taxing, trying, urgent **7** arduous, crucial, earnest, massive, onerous, serious **8** critical, crushing, cumbrous, pressing **9** difficult, essential, important, ponderous **10** burdensome, cumbersome, oppressive **11** significant, substantial, troublesome **12** considerable **13** consequential
Weill, Kurt
  born: 6 Dessau **7** Germany
  composer of: 8 Happy End **13** Lady in the Dark **15** Down in the Valley **18** The Lindbergh Flight, The Threepenny Opera **19** Die Dreigroschenoper **31** Rise and Fall of the City of Mahagonny **32** Aufstieg und Fall der Stadt Mahagonny
Weir, Peter
  director of: 7 Witness **9** Gallipoli **11** The Last Wave **26** The Year of Living Dangerously
weird 3 odd **4** wild **5** crazy, eerie, kooky, nutty, queer **6** far-out, mystic, spooky **7** bizarre, curious, ghostly, magical, strange, unusual **8** abnormal, freakish, peculiar **9** eccentric, grotesque, irregular, unearthly, unnatural **10** mysterious, outlandish, phantasmal, unorthodox **12** supernatural **14** unconventional
weirdo 3 nut **4** kook **5** flake, freak **6** looney **7** lunatic, oddball **8** crackpot, original **9** character, eccentric, screwball **10** one-of-a-kind

Weird sisters 5 Fates, Norns
Weisenfreund, Muni
  real name of: 8 Paul Muni
Weismuller, Johnny
  real name: 20 Peter John Weissmuller
  born: 9 Windbar PA
  Olympic sport: 8 swimming
  Olympic gold medals: 4 five
  wife: 9 Lupe Velez
  roles: 6 Tarzan **9** Jungle Jim
Weiss, Peter
  author of: 10 Marat/Sade **14** Vanishing Point
welcome 4 meet **5** admit, greet **6** at home, salute, wanted **7** embrace, receive, usher in, winning **8** accepted, admitted, charming, engaging, enticing, greeting, inviting, pleasant, pleasing **9** agreeable, entertain, reception **10** delightful, gratifying, salutation **11** comfortable
Weld, Tuesday
  real name: 12 Susan Ker Weld
  born: 9 New York NY
  husband: 11 Dudley Moore
  roles: 12 I Walk the Line **14** Play It as It Lays **16** The Cincinnati Kid, Wild in the Country **19** Looking for Mr Goodbar
welfare 4 good **6** health, profit, relief **7** benefit, success, the dole **9** advantage, happiness
well 3 jet, run **4** flow, fund, good, gush, hale, mine, ooze, pool, pour, rise **5** amply, fount, fully, issue, lucky, right, shaft, sound, spout, spurt, store, surge **6** easily, fairly, hearty, justly, kindly, nicely, proper, robust, source, spring, stream, strong, warmly **7** chipper, fitting, healthy, readily, rightly **8** famously, fountain, laudably, properly, suitably, very much, vigorous **9** agreeably, capitally, carefully, correctly, favorable, favorably, fortunate, promising, quite well **10** abundantly, acceptably, adequately, auspicious, completely, familiarly, felicitous, intimately, personally, prosperous, splendidly, successful, thoroughly **11** approvingly, commendably **12** advantageous, auspiciously, considerably, propitiously, satisfactory, successfully, sufficiently **13** substantially **14** advantageously, satisfactorily **15** sympathetically **16** enthusiastically
    hole drilled in ground for: 3 gas, oil **5** water
well-adjusted 6 normal, secure **8** sensible
Welland, May
  character in: 17 The Age of Innocence
  author: 7 Wharton
well-behaved 6 polite, sedate **8** decorous

well-being 4 ease, good, luck, weal **6** health, profit **7** benefit, comfort, fortune, success, welfare **8** felicity, good luck **9** advantage, affluence, happiness **10** prosperity

wellborn 8 highbred **9** patrician **10** upper-class **12** aristocratic, silk-stocking

Wellbred
character in: **19** Every Man in His Humour
author: **6** Jonson

well-bred 5 civil, suave **6** polite, urbane **7** elegant, gallant, genteel, refined **8** cultured, ladylike, mannerly, polished **9** civilized, courteous **10** cultivated **11** gentlemanly **13** sophisticated

well-chosen 3 apt **4** fine **5** prize **6** choice, seemly, select **7** apropos, correct, fitting, special **8** superior **9** excellent **11** appropriate

well-considered 7 careful, prudent **8** cautious **10** thoughtful **11** circumspect

well-coordinated 6 smooth **8** graceful **9** dexterous **10** effortless

well-defined 5 clear, plain **8** clear-cut, definite, distinct, palpable **10** pronounced

well-dressed 4 chic **5** natty, smart **6** dapper **11** fashionable

well-educated 7 erudite, learned **8** cultured, literate **9** scholarly **10** cultivated **13** knowledgeable

Weller, Sam
character in: **14** Pickwick Papers
author: **7** Dickens

Welles, Orson
real name: **17** George Orson Welles
born: **9** Kenosha WI
wife: **9** Paola Mori **12** Rita Hayworth
formed: **14** Mercury Theatre
radio show: **14** War of the Worlds
roles: **8** Jane Eyre **11** Citizen Kane, The Third Man, Touch of Evil
director of: **7** Macbeth, Othello **8** Falstaff **11** Citizen Kane, The Stranger, Touch of Evil **23** The Magnificent Ambersons

well-favored 4 fair **5** bonny **6** comely, pretty **7** sightly, winsome **8** fetching, handsome **9** beautiful **10** attractive **11** good looking

well-fed 5 hefty, plump, stout **6** portly, rotund **9** corpulent

well-fixed 4 rich **7** moneyed, wealthy **8** affluent **10** prosperous

well-founded 7 factual **9** supported **12** corroborated **13** substantiated

well-groomed 4 neat, tidy **5** natty **6** spruce **10** impeccable

well-grounded 5 valid **7** factual **8** reliable **9** supported **10** undeniable, undisputed, unshakable **11** irrefutable **12** corroborated, indisputable **13** in-

contestable, substantiated **16** incontrovertible

well-heeled 4 rich **7** moneyed, wealthy **8** affluent **10** in the chips, in the money, prosperous

Wellington
capital of: **10** New Zealand

Wellington, Duke of
also: **15** Arthur Wellesley
nickname: **6** Hookey **12** The Great Duke
nationality: **7** British
served in: **5** India **14** Napoleonic Wars
battle: **6** Assaye **7** Vitoria **8** Talavera, Waterloo **9** Salamanca
served as: **13** prime minister
memoirs: **20** Wellington Dispatches

well-kept 4 heat, neat, tidy **7** orderly **9** organized **10** systematic **11** disciplined, uncluttered

well-known 4 open **5** famed, noted **6** common, famous **7** big-time, eminent, evident, leading, obvious, popular **8** familiar, infamous, renowned **9** important, notorious, prominent **10** celebrated, scandalous, understood **11** established, illustrious, outstanding

well-lighted 5 lit up **6** ablaze, bright **11** illuminated

well-made 4 fine **7** perfect **8** executed, flawless **9** faultless **11** beautifully

Wellman, William
director of: **5** Wings **9** Beau Geste **11** A Star Is Born **13** Nothing Sacred **15** The Story of GI Joe **16** The Ox-Bow Incident

well-mannered 6 polite **7** genteel, refined **8** cultured, decorous, ladylike, polished **9** courteous, dignified **10** cultivated **11** gentlemanly

well-matched 5 close **10** nip-and-tuck

well-off 4 rich **5** flush **6** loaded **7** moneyed, wealthy **8** affluent **10** prosperous **11** comfortable

well-padded 5 plump, stout **6** chubby, fleshy, portly, rotund **9** corpulent

well-proportioned 7 classic, elegant, shapely **8** graceful **11** symmetrical

well-read 7 erudite, learned **8** cultured, literate **9** scholarly **10** cultivated

well-reasoned 4 wise **10** perceptive, thoughtful **11** intelligent

well-rehearsed 6 smooth **7** planned **8** prepared **9** practiced

Wells, H G (Herbert George)
author of: **5** Kipps **10** Tono-Bungay **11** Ann Veronica **14** The Time Machine **15** The Invisible Man **16** Outline of History **17** Love and Mr Lewisham, The War of the Worlds **19** The History of Mr Polly **22** The Shape of Things to Come **23** Mr Britling Sees It Through

wellspring 4 font **6** origin, source **9** beginning **10** birthplace **12** fountainhead

well-stocked 4 full **11** overflowing

well-suited 6 proper **7** correct, fitting **8** suitable **9** congenial, congruous **10** compatible, harmonious **11** appropriate

well-to-do 4 rich **7** moneyed, wealthy **8** affluent **10** in the chips, in the money, prosperous

well up 4 boil, rise **6** bubble **7** surface

well-ventilated 4 airy **5** windy **6** breezy, drafty

well-versed 7 knowing **9** qualified **10** conversant **11** experienced **13** knowledgeable
French: **9** au courant

well-wisher 6 friend **8** advocate, champion **9** supported

Welsh Mythology
goddess: **3** Don
goddess of fire/fertility/agriculture/ household/wisdom: **6** Brigit
king: **4** Bran, Llud, Ludd, Nudd
magician: **5** Lloyd
paradise: **5** Annwn **6** Annfwn
prince: **5** Pwyll **7** Kilwich
princess: **5** Olwen
romantic tales: **10** Mabinogian

welt 4 bump, lump, mark, wale, weal **6** bruise, streak, stripe **8** swelling **9** contusion

Weltanschauung 25 manner of looking at the world

Weltansicht 9 world view

Weltschmerz 6 sorrow **9** world pain **10** melancholy **20** sentimental pessimism

Welty, Eudora
author of: **12** Delta Wedding, Golden Apples **13** Losing Battles **14** The Ponder Heart **15** A Sweet Devouring **19** The Robber Bridegroom **20** The Optimist's Daughter

wench 4 doxy, girl, lass, maid, slut **5** whore **6** damsel, lassie, maiden **8** strumpet **10** prostitute

Wend 4 Slav, Sorb
in: **7** Germany

wend 4 make **5** hie to

went 3 ran **4** flew, left **5** faded, got on **6** flew by, lapsed, passed **7** elapsed, sallied **8** departed, filed off, passed by, took wing, vanished **9** proceeded, took leave **10** shuffled on, took flight **11** disappeared, forged ahead **12** sallied forth **13** pressed onward

Wentworth, Captain Frederick
character in: **10** Persuasion
author: **6** Austen

Werfel, Franz
author of: **9** Mirror Man **19** Forty Days of Musa Dagh, The Song of Bernadette

Werle, Gregers

character in: 11 The Wild Duck
author: 5 Ibsen

Werner, Oskar
real name: 24 Oskar Josef Bschliess-mayer
born: 6 Vienna **7** Austria
roles: 11 Jules and Jim, Ship of Fools **17** Voyage of the Damned **22** Fahrenheit Four Fifty One, The Shoes of the Fisherman **26** The Spy Who Came in from the Cold

Wertmuller, Lina
director of: 9 Swept Away (by an unusual destiny in the blue sea of August) **13** Seven Beauties

Wescott, Glenway
author of: 14 The Grandmother, The Pilgrim Hawk **16** The Apple of the Eye **17** Apartment in Athens

Wessex
fictional place created by: 5 Hardy

West, Benjamin
born: 13 Springfield PA
artwork: 17 Death on a Pale Horse **19** Death of General Wolfe **22** Saul and the Witch of Endor

West, Dame Rebecca
real name: 28 Cicily Isabel Fairfield Andrews
author of: 8 The Judge **11** Harriet Hume **13** Birds Fall Down **15** The Thinking Reed **19** The Strange Necessity **20** The Fountain Overflows **21** The Return of the Soldier **22** Black Lamb and Grey Falcon

West, Jessamyn
author of: 11 Leafy Rivers **13** A Matter of Time **18** Except for Me and Thee **21** The Friendly Persuasion **22** The Massacre at Fall Creek

West, Mae
born: 10 Brooklyn NY
roles: 3 Sex **8** Sextette **9** I'm No Angel **10** Diamond Lil **13** Klondike Annie **14** Go West Young Man **15** Night After Night, She Done Him Wrong **16** Myra Breckinridge **17** My Little Chickadee
autobiography: 28 Goodness Had Nothing To Do With It
quote: 18 Beulah peel me a grape **22** Come up and see me sometime

West, Morris L
author of: 7 Proteus **9** Harlequin **13** The Salamander **14** The Clowns of God **15** The Tower of Babel **17** The Devil's Advocate **22** The Shoes of the Fisherman

West, Nathanael
author of: 12 A Cool Million **16** Miss Lonelyhearts **17** The Day of the Locust

Westcott, Edward Noyes
author of: 10 David Harum

Westenra, Lucy
character in: 7 Dracula
author: 6 Stoker

Western, Sophia
character in: 8 Tom Jones
author: 8 Fielding

Western Sahara
other name: 13 Spanish Sahara
capital: 6 Al Aiun **7** El Aaiun
city: 3 Zug **5** Daora, Smara **6** Aargub, Dakhla, Tichla **9** Asqueimat, Bir Gandus **10** Bir Enzaran **12** Guelta Zemmur
government: 33 disputed territory claimed by Morocco
river: 7 Uad Atui **8** Uad Assag **13** Saguia el Hamra
sea: 8 Atlantic
physical feature:
  cape: 6 Barbas **7** Bojador
  desert: 6 Sahara
  wind: 5 leste **6** gibleh
people: 4 Arab **6** Berber
language: 16 Hassaniyya Arabic
religion: 5 Islam
feature:
  political group: 14 Polisario Front

Western Samoa
other name: 17 Navigator's Islands
capital/largest city: 4 Apia
others: 6 Safotu, Sataua **7** Faleolo, Palauli, Poutasi, Tuasivi **8** Fagamalo, Falelima, Lufilufi **9** Falealupo, Mulifanua **10** Samalaeulu, Satupaitea
monetary unit: 4 sene, tala
island: 5 Upolu **6** Manono, Savaii **7** Apolima
mountain: 4 Fito, Vaea
highest point: 13 Mauga Silisili
sea: 7 Pacific
physical feature:
  bay: 4 Asau, Salu **6** Safata **7** Lafanga, Matautu **8** Fangaloa, Salealua **9** Saluofata
  strait: 7 Apolima
people: 6 Samoan **10** Melanesian, Polynesian
  author: 20 Robert Louis Stevenson (Tusitala, Teller of Tales)
  explorer: 6 Wilkes **9** Roggeveen **12** Bougainville
language: 6 Samoan **7** English
religion: 9 Methodist **10** Protestant **13** Roman Catholic **14** Congregational
place:
  observatory: 4 Apia
  tomb: 9 Stevenson
feature:
  chief: 5 matai
  clothing: 5 pareu **8** lavalava, puletasi
  dance: 4 siva
  daughter of chief: 5 taupo
  house: 4 fale
food:
  dish: 8 palusami
  drink: 3 ava

Western Star
author: 19 Stephen Vincent Benet

Westhus, Haie

character in: 25 All Quiet on the Western Front
author: 8 Remarque

West Indies 11 archipelago
Associated States: 7 Antigua, Grenada, St Lucia **8** Anguilla, Dominica **12** St Kitts-Nevis
bird: 4 tody **6** mucaro
channel: 7 Jamaica **9** Old Bahama
component: 4 Cuba **5** Haiti **6** Tobago **7** Bahamas, Jamaica **8** Barbados, Trinidad **10** Hispaniola, Puerto Rico **13** Virgin Islands **14** Leeward Islands, Lesser Antilles **15** Greater Antilles, Windward Islands **17** Dominican Republic
crop: 6 coffee **9** sugarcane
fish: 4 pega **5** pelon
formerly: 10 federation
fruit: 5 papaw **6** pawpaw **7** genipap
islands: 5 Turks **6** Caicos, Cayman, Virgin **7** Bahamas, Leeward **8** Windward
kale: 7 malanga
lizard: 6 arbalo
music: 7 calypso
passage: 4 Mona **8** Windward
rodent: 5 hutia
sea: 9 Caribbean
shark: 4 gata
sorcery: 3 obi **5** obeah
tree: 5 genip **6** aralie
tribesman: 5 Carib **6** Arawak **7** Ciboney
vessel: 6 droger, drogher
volcano: 5 Pelee

Westinghouse, George
nationality: 8 American
invented: 8 air brake **12** railroad frog **20** railroad signal system

Westlake, Donald E
author of: 8 Bank Shot **10** The Hot Rock **13** Dancing Aztecs **15** Brothers Keepers
  as Richard Stark: 9 The Hunter **10** The Seventh
  as Tucker Coe: 19 Murder Among Children

Westover, Russ
creator/artist of: 15 Tillie the Toiler

West Side Story
director: 10 Robert Wise **13** Jerome Robbins
cast: 10 Rita Moreno **11** Natalie Wood, Russ Tamblyn **13** Richard Beymer **14** George Chakiris
score: 15 Stephen Sondheim **16** Leonard Bernstein
Oscar for: 7 picture **8** director **15** supporting actor (Chakiris) **17** supporting actress (Moreno)

West Virginia
abbreviation: 2 WV **3** W Va
nickname: 8 Mountain **9** Panhandle
capital: 10 Charleston
largest city: 10 Huntington
others: 5 Logan **6** Elkins, Keyser, Ripley, Vienna, Weston **7** Beckley,

Grafton, Spencer, Weirton **8** Fairmont, Wheeling **10** Clarksburg **11** Moundsville, Parkersburg
college: 5 Salem **7** Bethany, Concord **8** Marshall, Wheeling **9** Bluefield **10** Charleston **14** Davis and Elkins **16** Alderson Broaddus **20** West Virginia Wesleyan
feature:
   historical site: 12 Harper's Ferry
   national road: 10 Cumberland
tribe: 7 Moneton
people: 9 Pearl Buck **14** Arthur I Boreman **19** Walter Philip Reuther **24** Thomas "Stonewall" Jackson
   explorer: 12 Morgan Morgan
island: 14 Blennerhassett
lake: 4 Lynn
land rank: 10 forty-first
mountain:
   highest point: 10 Spruce Knob
physical feature:
   cavern: 6 Seneca
   plateau: 9 Allegheny
   rock: 6 Seneca
   spring: 8 Berkeley **12** White Sulphur
river: 3 Elk **4** Ohio **6** Gauley **7** Kanawha, Potomac, Tug Fork **8** Big Sandy, Guyandot **11** Monongahela
state admission: 11 Thirty-fifth
state bird: 8 cardinal
state fish: 10 brook trout
state flower: 11 great laurel **15** big rhododendron **17** great rhododendron
state motto: 25 Mountaineers Are Always Free
state song: 17 West Virginia Hills **20** This Is My West Virginia **27** West Virginia My Home Sweet Home
state tree: 10 sugar maple
Westward Ho!
   author: 15 Charles Kingsley
west wind
   associated with: 8 Favonius, Zephyrus
wet 3 dip **4** damp, dank, rain, soak **5** humid, moist, rainy, soggy, steep, storm, water **6** clammy, dampen, drench, liquid, shower, soaked, sodden, splash, stormy, watery **7** immerse, moisten, showery, soaking, sopping, squishy, wetness **8** dampened, dampness, dankness, drenched, dripping, inundate, irrigate, moisture, sprinkle, submerge **9** exudation, liquified, moistness, rainstorm **10** clamminess **11** waterlogged **12** condensation **13** precipitation
wet blanket 4 drag **6** damper **10** spoilsport **11** party-pooper
wet down 5 spray **6** dampen **7** moisten **8** sprinkle
wettish 4 damp **5** moist **6** clammy
we who are about to die salute thee

Latin: 19 morituri te salutamus
said by: 15 Roman gladiators
said to: 13 Roman emperors
whack 2 go **3** box, hit, rap, try **4** bang, belt, blow, cuff, slam, slap, slug, sock, stab, turn **5** baste, clout, crack, knock, pound, punch, smack, smite, thump, trial **6** strike, wallop **7** attempt, venture **8** endeavor
whale 4 beat, cane, drub, flog, orca, whip **6** baleen, thrash **9** bastinado
   constellation of: 5 Cetus
   group of: 3 gam, pod
   swallowed: 5 Jonah
   Melville: 8 Moby Dick
whammy 3 hex **4** jinx **5** curse **7** evil eye **9** evil spell
wharf 3 key **4** dock, pier, quai, quay, slip **5** jetty **6** marina **7** landing **10** breakwater
Wharton, Edith
   author of: 10 Ethan Frome, The Old Maid **15** The House of Mirth **17** The Age of Innocence **21** The Custom of the Country
Whatever Happened to Baby Jane?
   director: 13 Robert Aldrich
   cast: 10 Bette Davis **11** Victor Buono **12** Joan Crawford **15** Marjorie Bennett
What Every Woman Knows
   author: 12 James M Barrie
   character: 9 John Shand **15** Charles Venables **18** Comtesse de la Briere, Lady Sybil Tenterden
      Wylie family: 5 Alick, David, James **6** Maggie
what it takes 5 knack, skill **7** ability, know-how, mastery **9** expertise **10** capability, competence, expertness **11** proficiency **13** the right stuff
What Mrs McGillicuddy Saw!
   author: 14 Agatha Christie
What Price Glory?
   author: 15 Maxwell Anderson
What's Happening!!
   character: 5 Rerun **6** Dwayne **7** Shirley **9** Dee Thomas, (Mama) Mrs Thomas **11** Roger (Raj) Thomas
   cast: 9 Fred Berry, Mabel King **12** Ernest Thomas **13** Haywood Nelson **15** Danielle Spencer, Shirley Hemphill
What's My Line?
   host: 8 John Daly
   panelist: 8 Hal Block **9** Fred Allen **10** Steve Allen **11** Bennett Cerf **13** Arlene Francis **15** Louis Untermeyer **16** Dorothy Kilgallen
wheat 8 Triticum
   varieties: 4 club, rice **5** durum, dwarf, India, river **6** Alaska, common, German, Polish, starch **7** English, poulard **8** hedgehog **10** one-grained, two-grained **13** Mediterranean

   product: 4 bran **5** bread, flour, pasta **6** cereal **8** macaroni **9** spaghetti
Wheat State
   nickname of: 6 Kansas
wheedle 4 coax, lure **5** charm **6** cajole, entice, induce **7** beguile, flatter **8** butter up, inveigle, persuade, soft soap
wheel 4 disk, drum, hoop, ring, roll, spin **5** pivot, round, swirl, twirl, whirl **6** caster, circle, gilgal, gyrate, roller, rotate, swivel **7** revolve **9** pirouette
Wheel of Fortune
   host: 8 Pat Sajak
   assistant: 10 Vanna White
wheels 3 car **4** auto, heap **5** motor **6** jalopy **7** flivver, vehicle **8** motorcar **9** tin lizzie **10** automobile
wheeze 4 gasp, hiss, pant, puff **7** panting, whistle
whelp 3 boy, cub, kid, lad, pup **4** brat **5** child, puppy, youth **6** urchin **9** stripling, youngster **14** whippersnapper
whence 9 from where **10** antecedent **14** from what source
Where Eagles Dare
   director: 12 Brian G Hutton
   based on novel by: 15 Alistair MacLean
   cast: 7 Mary Ure **12** Robert Beatty **13** Clint Eastwood, Patrick Wymark, Richard Burton **14** Michael Hordern
wherefore 2 so **3** why **7** because **13** for what reason
where I may stand
   Greek: 6 pou sto
where mentioned above
   Latin: 8 ubi supra
whereupon 8 upon what **10** after which **14** upon which point
wherewithal 4 cash **5** funds, means **6** assets **7** capital **9** financing, resources
whet 4 edge, hone, stir **5** grind, pique, strop, tempt **6** allure, arouse, awaken, entice, excite, induce, kindle **7** animate, provoke, quicken, sharpen **9** stimulate **11** put an edge on
whether willing or not
   Latin: 12 nolens volens
which see
   Latin: 2 qv **8** quod vide
which was to be demonstrated
   Latin: 3 QED **21** quod erat demonstrandum
which was to be done
   Latin: 17 quod erat faciendum
which was to be shown
   Latin: 3 QED **21** quod erat demonstrandum
whiff 4 hint, odor, puff **5** aroma, draft, scent, smell, sniff, trace **6** breath, breeze, zephyr **7** bouquet
   French: 7 soupcon
Whig Party

president belonging to: 5 Tyler **6** Taylor **8** Fillmore, Harrison

while 2 as **3** yet **4** idle, till, time, when **5** until **6** during, effort, whilst **7** filling, interim, trouble, whereas **8** although, occasion

whim 4 urge **5** fancy, quirk **6** notion, vagary **7** caprice, conceit, impulse **8** crotchet **11** inspiration **12** eccentricity

whimper 3 sob **4** pule **5** whine **6** snivel **7** blubber, sniffle, sobbing **9** cry softly, sniveling **11** sob brokenly **16** whine plaintively

whimsical 5 droll **6** fickle, fitful, quaint **7** amusing, erratic, waggish **8** fanciful, notional, quixotic **9** eccentric **10** capricious, changeable, chimerical **12** inconsistent

whimsy, whimsey 4 bent, wish **5** fancy, humor, prank, quirk **6** notion, vagary **7** caprice, fantasy **8** escapade, drollery **11** make-believe

whine 3 cry, sob **4** fret, mewl, moan, wail **6** grouse, murmur, mutter, snivel **7** grumble, whimper **8** complain **9** complaint **11** gripe meekly **12** plaintive cry **14** cry plaintively

whip 3 rod **4** beat, cane, drub, flap, flog, jerk, jolt, lash, lick, maul, rout **5** birch, flick, spank, strap, thong, whisk **6** rattan, snatch, switch **7** cowhide, rawhide, scourge, trounce **8** birch rod, vanquish **9** horsewhip, toss about **10** blacksnake, flagellate **13** cat-o'-nine-tails, defeat soundly, move violently **14** beat decisively, beat into a froth

Whip 8 scorpion

whip hand 4 sway **5** power **7** control, mastery **9** advantage, authority, dominance, supremacy, upper hand **10** ascendancy, domination

whipped 5 caned, waled **6** beaten, darted, flayed, frothy, lashed, roused **7** flogged, frothed, incited, revived, spanked, subdued, swished, whisked **8** defeated, overlaid, punished, scourged, switched **9** chastised **10** vanquished

whir 3 hum **4** buzz, purr **5** drone **7** whisper

whirl 2 go **3** try **4** reel, spin, stab, turn **5** crack, fling, pivot, swirl, trial, twirl, whack, wheel **6** circle, dither, flurry, gyrate, rotate **7** attempt, revolve, turning **8** circling, gyration, pivoting, rotation, spinning, swirling, twirling, wheeling **9** feel dizzy, feel giddy, pirouette, revolving, turn round **10** dizzy round, rapid round, revolution **12** merry-go-round **17** state of excitement **18** dizzying succession

whirlpool 4 eddy **5** swirl, whirl **6** vortex **9** maelstrom **15** whirling current

whirlwind 4 rash **5** hasty, quick, rapid, short, swift **7** cyclone, tornado, twister **8** headlong **9** breakneck, impetuous, impulsive **10** waterspout

whirly 5 dizzy, giddy, shaky **7** reeling **8** spinning **11** vertiginous

whisk 3 fly, zip **4** beat, bolt, dart, dash, race, rush, tear, whip, whiz **5** bound, brush, flick, hurry, scoot, shoot, speed, spurt, sweep **6** hasten, scurry, spring, sprint
type: 4 wire **6** French **8** omelette

whiskbroom 5 brush

whiskered 5 bushy, hairy **6** shaggy **7** bearded, bristly, hirsute **8** unshaven **11** bewhiskered, mustachioed

whiskers 3 awn **5** beard **7** stubble **8** bristles

whiskey, whisky 3 gin, rum, rye **4** corn, shot **5** booze, hooch, Irish, juice, vodka **6** liquor, red eye, rotgut, Scotch **7** alcohol, aquavit, blended, bourbon, spirits **8** eau-de-vie **9** aquavitae, firewater, moonshine, unblended **10** sneaky pete, usquebaugh **11** mountain dew **14** John Barleycorn, white lightning
type: 3 rye **6** Scotch **7** bourbon
drink: 8 hot toddy **14** Klondike Cooler
with beer: 11 Boilermaker
with Benedictine: 10 Frisco Sour
with Cointreau: 16 Canadian Cocktail
with vermouth: 9 Manhattan

whisper 3 hum **4** blab, buzz, hint, purr, sigh, tell **5** blurt, bruit, drone, rumor **6** gossip, murmur, mutter, reveal, rustle **7** breathe, confide, divulge, inkling **8** disclose, innuendo, intimate **9** undertone **10** suggestion **11** insinuation

whist
derived from: 8 triomphe
descendant: 6 bridge
number of players: 4 four
six tricks: 4 book

Whistle
author: 10 James Jones

Whistler, James Abbott McNeill
born: 8 Lowell MA
artwork: 6 Etudes **9** Harmonies, Nocturnes **10** Rosa Corder **12** Arrangements, The White Girl **13** Thomas Carlyle **15** Cicely Alexander, Wapping-on-Thames **24** Venetian Palaces Nocturnes **28** Arrangement in Grey and Black No 1 (The Artist's Mother) **29** Chelsea Nocturne in Blue and Green **31** Princess of the Land of the Porcelain **35** Falling Rocket Nocturne in Black and Gold **37** Cremorne Lights Nocturne in Blue and Silver

whistle-stop 5 stump **8** campaign **11** electioneer

whit 3 dab, dot, jot **4** chip, dash, drop, iota, mite, snip **5** crumb, grain, pinch, speck **6** morsel, tittle, trifle **7** modicum, smidgen **8** fragment, particle, splinter **9** scintilla

white 3 wan **4** ashy, fair, gray, pale, pure **5** ashen, blond, clean, filmy, hoary, ivory, milky, pasty, pearl, smoky, snowy **6** benign, chalky, chaste, cloudy, frosty, leaden, pallid, pearly, sallow, silver **7** ghostly, silvery **8** blanched, bleached, grizzled, harmless, innocent, spotless, virtuous **9** alabaster, bloodless, Caucasian, colorless, stainless, undefiled, unspotted, unstained, unsullied **10** cadaverous, immaculate **11** translucent, unblemished, unmalicious

White, E B (Elwyn Brooks)
author of: 11 One Man's Meat **12** Stuart Little **13** Charlotte's Web **14** Is Sex Necessary? (with James Thurber) **19** The Trumpet of the Swan
column: 13 Talk of the Town

White, Stanford see **17** Mead McKim and White

White, T H (Terence Hanbury)
author of: 15 The Book of Merlyn **16** The Ill-Made Knight **17** The Witch in the Wood **18** The Candle in the Wind, The Sword in the Stone **20** The Once and Future King

White Album
author: 10 Joan Didion

White Company, The
author: 19 Sir Arthur Conan Doyle

White Heat
director: 10 Raoul Walsh
cast: 11 James Cagney **12** Edmond O'Brien, Virginia Mayo **16** Margaret Wycherly

White-Jacket
author: 14 Herman Melville

whiten 4 pale **5** clean, frost **6** blanch, bleach, silver **7** lighten

whiteness 6 pallor **7** wanness **8** paleness **9** snowiness **10** sallowness **13** colorlessness

White Nights
director: 14 Taylor Hackford
cast: 12 Gregory Hines **18** Mikhail Baryshnikov
choreographer: 10 Twyla Tharp

White Rabbit
character in: 28 Alice's Adventures in Wonderland
author: 7 Carroll

whitewash 6 excuse **7** absolve, cover up, justify **8** downplay, minimize, play down **9** calcimine, exonerate, vindicate
paint made by mixing: 12 lime and water

Whitewater
author: 10 Paul Horgan

whitish 4 buff, pale **6** chalky, creamy **7** grayish

Whitman, Bert
creator/artist of: 14 The Green Hornet

Whitman, Walt
author of: 12 Song of Myself **13** Leaves of Grass **18** Oh Captain My

Captain **33** When Lilacs Last in the Dooryard Bloom'd

Whitmore, James
born: **13** White Plains NY
roles: **4** Them **5** Bully **8** Oklahoma **9** Battlecry **10** Will Rogers **11** Black Like Me **12** Battleground, Harry S Truman, Tora Tora Tora **15** Command Decision, Give 'em Hell Harry **19** The Next Voice You Hear

Whitney, Eli
nationality: **8** American
invented: **9** cotton gin
pioneered use of: **14** mass production

Whittier, John Greenleaf
author of: **9** Snow-Bound **10** Maud Muller **14** The Barefoot Boy **16** Barbara Frietchie

whittle 3 cut **4** clip, pare **5** carve, shave, slash **7** curtail, shorten **8** decrease

whiz 3 fly, hum, zip **4** bolt, buzz, dart, dash, hiss, race, rush, scud, tear, whir, zoom **5** adept, drone, scoot, shark, shoot, speed, spurt, sweep, swish, whine, whisk **6** expert, genius, hasten, master, scurry, sizzle, sprint, wizard **7** prodigy, scuttle, whistle **11** crackerjack

who goes there?
French: **7** qui vive

who knows?
Spanish: **9** quien sabe

whole 4 body, bulk, full, hale, unit, well **5** sound, total, uncut **6** entire, intact, robust, system **7** essence, healthy, perfect **8** complete, ensemble, entirety, totality, unbroken, unharmed, vigorous **9** aggregate, undivided, uninjured **10** assemblage, unabridged **12** completeness, quintessence, undiminished

wholehearted 4 true **7** earnest, serious, sincere, zealous **8** complete, emphatic **9** unfeigned **10** unreserved, unstinting **12** enthusiastic

wholesome 4 hale, nice, pure, well **5** clean, fresh, hardy, moral, sound **6** decent, honest, worthy **7** chipper, dutiful, ethical, healthy, upright **8** blooming, hygienic, innocent, sanitary, vigorous, virtuous **9** exemplary, healthful, honorable, uplifting **10** nourishing, nutritious, principled **11** meritorious, responsible **12** invigorating **13** strengthening

whole world, the
French: **11** tout le monde

wholly 5 fully, quite **7** totally, utterly **8** as a whole, entirely **9** perfectly **10** altogether, completely, thoroughly
Latin: **6** in toto

whoop 3 cry **4** hoot, howl, roar, yell **5** cheer, hollo, shout **6** bellow, cry out, holler, hurrah, outcry, scream, shriek **7** screech **9** hue and cry

whopper 3 fib, lie **6** big one **7** fiction **9** falsehood, fish story, tall story **16** cock-and-bull story

whopping 4 huge **5** giant, large **8** thumping, whacking, whapping **10** incredible **13** extraordinary

whore 3 pro **4** bawd, doxy, jade, slut, tart **5** hussy, tramp **6** chippy, harlot, hooker, prosty, wanton **7** demirep, hustler, trollop **8** call girl, mistress, strumpet **9** concubine **10** prostitute **12** streetwalker
French: **9** courtesan **12** demimondaine

whorl 4 coil, curl, roll **5** helix **6** circle, spiral **9** corkscrew **11** convolution

Who's Afraid of Virginia Woolf?
author: **11** Edward Albee
director: **11** Mike Nichols
cast: **11** George Segal, Sandy Dennis **13** Richard Burton **15** Elizabeth Taylor
Oscar for: **7** actress (Taylor) **17** supporting actress (Dennis)

Who Said That?
host: **8** John Daly **11** Robert Trout **13** Walter Kiernan
panelist: **9** Bill Henry **12** Bob Considine, H V Kaltenborn, June Lockhart **14** John Mason Brown, Morey Amsterdam **17** John Cameron Swayze

Who's on First?
comedy routine by: **6** Abbott **8** Costello
first base: **3** who
second base: **4** what
third base: **9** I don't know
shortstop: **9** I don't care
catcher: **5** today
pitcher: **8** tomorrow
left field: **3** why
center field: **7** because

Who's on First?
author: **17** William F Buckley Jr

wicked 3 bad, low **4** base, evil, foul, vile **5** acute, awful, gross, rowdy **6** cursed, fierce, impish, raging, severe, sinful **7** corrupt, extreme, fearful, galling, heinous, hellish, immoral, intense, knavish, naughty, painful, rampant, Satanic, serious, vicious **8** depraved, devilish, dreadful, fiendish, infamous, rascally, shameful **9** atrocious, malicious, monstrous, nefarious **10** abominable, bothersome, degenerate, iniquitous, malevolent, scandalous, villainous **11** disgraceful, mischievous, troublesome **12** blackhearted, dishonorable, incorrigible **13** reprehensible

wickedness 4 evil **6** infamy **8** baseness, foulness, iniquity, vileness **9** depravity, malignity **10** immorality, sinfulness **11** malevolence **13** maliciousness, nefariousness

Wicked Witch of the West

character in: **13** The Wizard of Oz
author: **4** Baum

Wickfield, Agnes
character in: **16** David Copperfield
author: **7** Dickens

Wickford Point
author: **13** John P Marquand

Wickham, Mr
character in: **17** Pride and Prejudice
author: **6** Austen

wide 4 vast **5** ample, broad, fully, great, large, roomy **7** dilated, immense **8** expanded, extended, spacious **9** boundless, capacious, distended, extensive, outspread **10** commodious, completely

wide-awake 2 up **5** alert, aware, quick **8** vigilant, watchful **9** attentive, insomniac, observant, sleepless

widely 3 far **5** broad **6** abroad **7** broadly, greatly, largely **10** by and large, far and near **11** extensively

widely known 5 famed, noted **6** common **7** popular **8** familiar **9** universal, worldwide

widen 6 expand, extend, spread **7** broaden, enlarge, stretch

widened 7 swelled, swollen **8** enlarged, expanded, extended **9** broadened, distended, stretched

wide open 4 ajar, vast **5** agape **6** gaping **7** exposed, yawning **8** extended, unfenced **9** cavernous, expansive, outspread, unbounded **12** outstretched, unobstructed

wide open spaces 7 boonies, country **9** boondocks **11** countryside, hinterlands

wide-ranging 5 broad **7** immense **8** sweeping **9** extensive, universal, unlimited **10** exhaustive **11** diversified, far-reaching **12** encyclopedic **13** comprehensive

Wide Sargasso Sea
author: **8** Jean Rhys

widespread 5 broad **9** extensive, outspread, pervasive, worldwide **10** nationwide **11** far-reaching

Widmark, Richard
born: **9** Sunrise MN
roles: **4** Coma **7** Madigan **8** The Alamo **11** Kiss of Death **12** The Long Ships **16** Halls of Montezuma, How the West Was Won **19** Judgment at Nuremberg

Widow Douglas
character in: **15** (The Adventures of) Huckleberry Finn
author: **5** Twain

wie geht's 9 how are you?

wield 3 ply, use **4** wave **5** apply, exert, swing **6** employ, handle, manage **7** display, utilize **8** brandish, exercise, flourish **10** manipulate

wife 3 rib **4** mate **5** bride, squaw, woman **6** missus, spouse **7** consort,

old lady 8 helpmate, helpmeet **9** companion
French: 5 femme
German: 4 frau

Wife of Bath
character in: **18** The Canterbury Tales
author: **7** Chaucer

Wifey
author: **9** Judy Blume

wig 3 rug **4** fall **6** carpet, peruke, switch, topper, toupee, wiglet **7** periwig **9** hairpiece

Wiggin, Kate Douglas
author of: **23** Rebecca of Sunnybrook Farm

wiggle 3 wag **4** jerk **5** shake, twist **6** quiver, squirm, twitch, writhe **7** flutter **8** writhing **9** squirming

wigwam, Wigwam 3 hut **4** tent, tipi **5** hogan, lodge, tepee **6** teepee **7** weekwam, wickiup **11** Tammany Hall

Wilcox family
characters in: **10** Howard's End
members: **4** Paul, Ruth **5** Henry **7** Charles
author: **7** Forster

wild, wilds, the wild 3 mad **4** bush, rash **5** bleak, feral, giddy, madly, nutty, rabid, rough, waste **6** choppy, crazed, fierce, insane, madcap, raging, raving, rugged, savage, unruly, wooded **7** berserk, bizarre, flighty, frantic, furious, howling, lawless, natural, untamed, violent **8** barbaric, blustery, demented, desolate, fanciful, forested, frenzied, insanely, maniacal, reckless, unbroken, unhinged **9** abandoned, fanatical, fantastic, ferocious, furiously, illogical, lawlessly, naturally, overgrown, primitive, rampantly, screwball, turbulent, violently, wasteland **10** disorderly, maniacally, uninformed **11** harebrained, impractical, tempestuous, uncivilized, uninhabited **12** uncultivated, ungovernable, unrestrained **13** rattlebrained, undisciplined **14** undomesticated

wild animal 5 beast, brute

Wild Ass's Skin
author: **14** Honore de Balzac

Wild Bunch, The
director: **12** Sam Peckinpah
cast: **10** Ben Johnson, Robert Ryan **11** Warren Oates **12** Edmond O'Brien **13** William Holden **14** Ernest Borgnine

wildcat 3 cat **4** lynx **6** ocelot

Wild Duck, The
author: **11** Henrik Ibsen
character: **5** Werle **8** Old Ekdal **9** Gina Ekdal **12** Gregers Werle, Hjalmar Ekdal **13** Hedvig Relling

Wilde, Cornel
real name: **19** Cornelius Louis Wilde
born: **9** New York NY
wife: **11** Jean Wallace
roles: **9** Maracaibo **11** Omar Khayyam

12 Forever Amber, The Naked Prey **15** A Song to Remember **21** A Thousand and One Nights **22** The Greatest Show on Earth

Wilde, Oscar
author of: **6** Salome **17** The Critic as Artist **18** Lady Windermere's Fan **22** The Ballad of Reading Gaol, The Picture of Dorian Gray **27** The Importance of Being Earnest

Wilder, Billy
director of: **11** One Two Three **12** The Apartment (Oscar) **13** Some Like It Hot **14** The Lost Weekend (Oscar) **15** Double Indemnity, Stalag Seventeen, Sunset Boulevard **16** The Seven Year Itch **18** Love in the Afternoon **24** Witness for the Prosecution

Wilder, Gene
real name: **14** Jerry Silberman
born: **11** Milwaukee WI
roles: **12** Silver Streak, The Producers **14** Blazing Saddles, Bonnie and Clyde **17** Young Frankenstein **22** The World's Greatest Lover **27** Start the Revolution Without Me **43** The Adventures of Sherlock Holmes' Smarter Brother

Wilder, Laura Ingalls
author of: **26** The Little House on the Prairie

Wilder, Thornton
author of: **7** Our Town **9** The Cabala **13** The Matchmaker **14** The Ides of March **16** The Woman of Andros **17** The Skin of Our Teeth **20** Heaven's My Destination **21** The Bridge of San Luis Rey

wilderness 4 bush **5** waste **6** barren, desert, forest, plains, tundra **7** barrens **8** badlands, wasteland **9** mountains

Wildeve, Damon
character in: **17** Return of the Native
author: **5** Hardy

Wild Is the River
author: **14** Louis Bromfield

Wild Kingdom
host/narrator: **9** Jim Fowler, Stan Brock **13** Marlin Perkins

Wild One, The
director: **12** Laslo Benedek
cast: **9** Lee Marvin **10** Mary Murphy **12** Marlon Brando

Wild Strawberries
director: **13** Ingmar Bergman
cast: **12** Ingrid Thulin **13** Bibi Andersson **14** Victor Sjostrom **17** Gunnar Bjornstrand

Wild Wild West
character: **10** James T West **13** Artemus Gordon
cast: **10** Ross Martin **12** Robert Conrad
traveled by: **5** train

wile, wiles 4 coax, lure, ploy, ruse, trap **5** charm, guile **6** cajole, entice, gambit, seduce **7** cunning **8** artifice,

maneuver, persuade, subtlety, trickery **9** chicanery, expedient, stratagem **10** artfulness, craftiness, subterfuge **11** contrivance, machination

Wilfer, Bella
character in: **15** Our Mutual Friend
author: **7** Dickens

Wilhelm, Kate
author of: **10** City of Cain, Fault Lines **11** The Planners **14** The Infinity Box **16** The Clewiston Test **19** More Bitter than Death **26** Where Late the Sweet Birds Sang

Wilhelm Meister
author: **6** Goethe

Wilhelm Tell
also: **11** William Tell
author: **17** Johann von Schiller

wiliness 5 guile **7** cunning, slyness **8** artifice, foxiness, scheming, trickery **10** artfulness, craftiness **11** machination

Wilkes family
characters in: **15** Gone With the Wind
members: **4** John **5** Honey, India **6** Ashley **15** Melanie Hamilton
author: **8** Mitchell

will 4 want, wish **5** endow **6** bestow, confer, desire **7** craving, feeling, longing, resolve, wish for **8** attitude, bequeath, pleasure, yearning **9** hankering, testament **10** conviction, preference, resolution **11** disposition, inclination **12** resoluteness **13** determination

Willard, Frank
creator/artist of: **11** Moon Mullins

Willet, John
character in: **12** Barnaby Rudge
author: **7** Dickens

willful 6 mulish, unruly **7** planned, studied **8** designed, intended, obdurate, perverse, stubborn **9** obstinate, pigheaded **10** bullheaded, deliberate, determined, headstrong, inflexible, persistent, purposeful, unyielding **11** intentional, intractable **12** contemplated, premeditated, ungovernable **13** undisciplined **14** uncompromising

Williams, Esther
nickname: **13** Mermaid Tycoon **14** Queen of the Surf **17** Hollywood's Mermaid
born: **12** Los Angeles CA
husband: **13** Fernando Lamas
roles: **13** Bathing Beauty **15** Jupiter's Darling, Ziegfeld Follies **16** Dangerous When Wet, Neptune's Daughter **20** Million Dollar Mermaid

Williams, Janey
character in: **3** USA
author: **9** Dos Passos

Williams, Robin
born: **9** Chicago IL
roles: **6** Popeye **12** Mork and Mindy **15** Good Will Hunting (Oscar)

18 Good Morning Vietnam **23** The World According to Garp

Williams, Ted
nickname: **6** the Kid **16** Splendid Splinter
sport: **8** baseball
position: **8** outfield
team: **12** Boston Red Sox

Williams, Tennessee
author of: **10** Camino Real **13** The Rose Tattoo **14** Summer and Smoke **16** Cat on a Hot Tin Roof, Night of the Iguana, Sweet Bird of Youth **17** Orpheus Descending, The Glass Menagerie **18** Small Craft Warnings, Suddenly Last Summer **21** A Streetcar Named Desire **24** The Roman Spring of Mrs Stone

Williams, William Carlos
author of: **7** Tempers **8** Paterson **9** White Mule **11** Al Que Quiere **20** Pictures from Brueghel

William Tell
also: **13** Guillaume Tell
opera by: **7** Rossini
character: **6** Arnold **7** Gessler

William the Conqueror
also: **17** William of Normandy **21** William I King of England
fought against: **8** Harold II
battle: **8** Hastings
succeeded by: **6** Henry I **9** William II

Willie and Joe
creator: **11** Bill Mauldin

willing 4 game **5** ready **7** content **8** amenable **9** agreeable, compliant, not averse **10** responsive

willingly 4 gain, lief, soon **6** freely, gladly, liefly **7** eagerly, happily, readily **8** by choice **10** cheerfully, graciously **11** voluntarily **12** with pleasure

willingness 4 zeal **8** alacrity **9** eagerness, readiness **10** enthusiasm **11** inclination

Willoughby, John
character in: **19** Sense and Sensibility
author: **6** Austen

willow 5 Salix
varieties: **3** bay, red **4** bush, goat, gray, seep **5** black, crack, false, Niobe, Pekin, pussy, silky, water, white **6** Arctic, arroyo, basket, desert, golden, laurel, puzzle, woolly, yellow **7** brittle, prairie, sandbar, scouler, shining, weeping **8** creeping, florist's, polished, Virginia **9** bay-leaved, bearberry, flowering, sprouting **10** cricket- bat, dragon-claw, large pussy, small pussy **11** green-scaled, heart-leaved, peach-leaved, Port Jackson **13** halberd-leaved **16** Wisconsin weeping

willowy 5 lithe **6** limber, pliant, supple, svelte **7** lissome **8** flexible **9** sylphlike

Wills, Chill

born: **12** Seagoville TX
group: **26** Chill Wills and the Avalon Boys
voice of: **21** Francis the Talking Mule
roles: **5** Giant **8** The Alamo **10** Way Out West **11** The Yearling **15** Meet Me in St Louis

Wills, Garry
author of: **14** Nixon Agonistes, Reagan's America **16** Inventing America

Will Scarlet
character in: **9** Robin Hood

willy-nilly 8 perforce **10** helplessly, inevitably **11** inescapably, unavoidably **12** compulsively, irresistibly **14** uncontrollably
Latin: **12** nolens volens

Wilmer
character in: **16** The Maltese Falcon
author: **7** Hammett

Wilson, Edmund
author of: **11** Axel's Castle **19** To the Finland Station

Wilson, Myrtle
character in: **14** The Great Gatsby
author: **10** Fitzgerald

Wilson, Sloan
author of: **26** The Man in the Gray Flannel Suit

Wilson, Woodrow
name at birth: **19** Thomas Woodrow Wilson
nickname: **5** Tommy
presidential rank: **12** twenty-eighth
party: **10** Democratic
state represented: **2** NJ
defeated: **4** (Eugene Victor) Debs, (William Howard) Taft **5** (James Franklin) Hanly **6** (Allen Louis) Benson, (Arthur Edward) Reimer, (Charles Evans) Hughes, (Eugene Wilder) Chafin **9** (Theodore) Roosevelt
vice president: **8** (Thomas Riley) Marshall
cabinet:
  state: **5** (Bainbridge) Colby, (William Jennings) Bryan **7** (Robert) Lansing
  treasury: **5** (Carter) Glass **6** (William Gibbs) McAdoo **7** (David Franklin) Houston
  war: **5** (Newton Diehl) Baker **8** (Lindley Miller) Garrison
  attorney general: **6** (Alexander Mitchell) Palmer **7** (Thomas Watt) Gregory **10** (James Clark) McReynolds
  navy: **7** (Josephus) Daniels
  postmaster general: **8** (Albert Sidney) Burleson
  interior: **4** (Franklin Knight) Lane **5** (John Barton) Payne
  agriculture: **7** (David Franklin) Houston **8** (Edwin Thomas) Meredith
  commerce: **8** (William Cox) Red-

field **9** (Joshua Willis) Alexander
  labor: **6** (William Bauchop) Wilson
born: **2** VA **8** Staunton
died/buried: **2** DC **10** Washington
education:
  college: **8** Davidson **18** College of New Jersey (later known as Princeton U)
  law School: **20** University of Virginia
  university: **12** Johns Hopkins
religion: **12** Presbyterian
author: **8** The State **16** George Washington **18** Division and Reunion **27** A History of the American People **28** More Literature and Other Essays **34** An Old Master and Other Political Essays **41** President Wilson's Case for the League of Nations **47** Congressional Government: A Study in American Politics
political career:
  governor of: **9** New Jersey
civilian career: **6** lawyer
  professor of history: **15** Bryn Mawr College **18** Wesleyan University
  professor of jurisprudence: **9** Princeton
  president of: **9** Princeton
notable events of lifetime/term: **14** Fourteen Points **15** League of Nations
  Act: **7** Adamson **8** Sedition **9** Espionage **10** Child Labor **11** Liberty Loan, Panama Canal **14** Federal Reserve **15** Federal Farm Loan **16** Clayton Antitrust, Selective Service **22** Federal Trade Commission
  conference: **3** ABC **10** Paris Peace
  18th Amendment: **11** Prohibition
  program: **10** New Freedom
  sinking of: **9** Lusitania
  Treaty: **10** Versailles
  won: **15** Nobel Peace Prize
quote: **34** The world must be made safe for democracy
father: **13** Joseph Ruggles
mother: **5** Janet (Woodrow)
siblings: **13** Joseph Ruggles **14** Annie Josephson **16** Marion Williamson
wife: **5** Edith (Bolling Galt), Ellen (Louise Axson)
children: **13** Jessie Woodrow **15** Eleanor Randolph, Margaret Woodrow

wilt 3 die, ebb, sag **4** fade, flag, sink, wane **5** droop **6** recede, weaken, wither **7** decline, dwindle, shrivel, subside **8** decrease, diminish, languish **10** degenerate **11** deteriorate

Wilt the Stilt
nickname of: **15** Wilt Chamberlain

wily 3 sly **4** foxy **5** alert, sharp **6** artful, crafty, shifty, shrewd, tricky **7** crooked, cunning, devious **8** guileful, scheming **9** deceitful, deceptive, designing, underhand **10** intriguing **11** calculating, treacherous

Wimbledon
  suburb of: 6 London
  site of: 16 tennis tournament
  court surface: 5 grass
win 3 bag, get, net **4** earn, gain, sway
  6 attain, induce, master, obtain, pick
  up, secure **7** achieve, acquire, collect,
  conquer, convert, prevail, procure,
  realize, receive, success, triumph, victory **8** conquest, convince, overcome,
  persuade, vanquish **9** influence
  10 accomplish
win acceptance 9 establish **10** ingratiate
wince 5 cower, quail **6** cringe, flinch,
  recoil, shrink **7** grimace, shudder **8**
  cowering, cringing, draw back, quail-
  ing **9** shrinking
wind 3 air, lap **4** bend, blow, clue,
  coil, curl, fold, gale, gust, hint, loop,
  news, puff, roll **5** blast, bluff, curve,
  draft, scent, smell, snake, twine, twirl,
  twist, whiff **6** breath, breeze, hot air,
  ramble, report, wander, zephyr, zigzag **7** bluster, bombast, cyclone, entwine, inkling, meander, sinuate, tempest, tidings, tornado, twaddle,
  twister, typhoon, whisper **8** boasting,
  idle talk **9** aerophone, hurricane,
  knowledge, whirlwind **10** intimation,
  suggestion **11** braggadocio, fanfaronade, information **12** intelligence
  god of: 5 Eurus, Niord, Njord, Notus
  6 Aquilo, Auster, Boreas **8** Favonius,
  Zephyrus
  father: 8 Astraeus
  mother: 3 Eos
windfall 7 bonanza
Windhoek
  capital of: 7 Namibia
Wind in the Willows, The
  author: 14 Kenneth Grahame
  character: 4 Mole, Toad **6** Badger **8**
  Water Rat
windless 4 calm **5** still **8** stifling
window 3 bay **5** oriel **6** dormer **7**
  opening, orifice, transom **8** aperture,
  casement, porthole, skylight
Winds of War, The
  author: 10 Herman Wouk
windstorm 4 gale **6** squall **7** cyclone,
  tempest, tornado, twister, typhoon **9**
  hurricane, whirlwind
windswept 4 bare **5** bleak **6** barren **8**
  desolate **13** weatherbeaten
windup 3 end **5** close **6** ending, finish
  10 completion, conclusion, expiration
  11 termination
wind up 3 end **4** halt, stop **5** cease,
  close **6** finish, settle **8** complete, conclude **9** terminate
windy 5 blowy, empty, gabby, gusty,
  wordy **6** breezy **7** verbose **8** blustery,
  rambling **9** bombastic, garrulous, talkative **10** loquacious, meandering,
  rhetorical **13** grandiloquent

wine
  French: 3 vin
  Italian: 4 vino
  god of: 7 Bacchus
  goddess of: 6 Libera
wine-colored 6 claret **8** burgundy,
  cardinal
winemaking
  god of: 9 Aristaeus
Winesburg, Ohio
  author: 16 Sherwood Anderson
Winfrey, Oprah
  born: 12 Kosciusko MS
  host of: 19 The Oprah Winfrey Show
  author of: 17 Make the Connection
  20 Oprah An Autobiography **21** In
  the Kitchen with Rosie
  Roles: 7 Beloved **14** The Color Purple
  23 The Women of Brewster Place
wing 3 ala, fly, set **4** band, clip, flap,
  knot, nick, soar, zoom **5** annex,
  graze, group **6** circle, clique, pennon,
  pinion **7** adjunct, aileron, coterie, faction, section, segment **8** addition, cou-
  lisse **9** appendage, extension
  10 fraternity
Winged Horse
  constellation of: 7 Pegasus
Winger, Debra
  husband: 13 Timothy Hutton
  roles: 10 Black Widow, Cannery Row
  11 Urban Cowboy **17** Terms of
  Endearment **22** An Officer and a
  Gentleman
Wingert, Dick
  creator/artist of: 6 Hubert
Wingfield family
  characters in: 17 The Glass Menagerie
  member: 3 Tom **5** Laura **6** Amanda
  author: 8 Williams
Wings
  director: 15 William A Wellman
  cast: 8 Clara Bow **10** Gary Cooper **12**
  Richard Arlen **18** Charles Buddy
  Rogers
  Oscar for: 7 picture
Wings of the Dove, The
  author: 10 Henry James
  character: 8 Kate Croy, Lord Mark **9**
  Mrs Lowder **11** Milly Theale **12** Mrs
  Stringham **13** Merton Densher, Sir
  Luke Strett
wink at 6 ignore **7** condone, let pass **8**
  overlook **9** disregard
Winkle
  character in: 14 Pickwick Papers
  author: 7 Dickens
winner 5 champ **6** master, victor **8**
  champion **9** conqueror **10** vanquisher
Winnie-the-Pooh
  author: 7 A A Milne
  character: 3 Owl **5** Kanga **6** Eeyore,
  Piglet, Rabbit, Tigger **7** Baby Roo **16**
  Christopher Robin
winning 7 amiable **8** charming, engag-

ing, pleasing **9** appealing, beguiling,
  disarming **10** attractive, bewitching,
  entrancing **11** captivating **12** ingratiating, irresistible
Winnipeg
  hockey team: 3 Jets
win over 4 beat, best **5** charm **6** defeat, seduce **7** convert **8** overcome,
  vanquish **9** captivate, overpower
winsome 5 sweet **6** comely **7** amiable,
  likable, lovable **8** charming, cheerful,
  engaging, pleasing **9** agreeable, appealing, endearing **10** attractive,
  bewitching, delightful
Winter, Lady de
  character in: 18 The Three
  Musketeers
  author: 5 Dumas (pere)
Winter, Maxim de
  character in: 7 Rebecca
  author: 9 Du Maurier
Winterbourne
  character in: 11 Daisy Miller
  author: 5 James
Winter of Our Discontent, The
  author: 13 John Steinbeck
Winters, Shelley
  real name: 14 Shirley Schrift
  born: 9 St Louis IL
  husband: 13 Tony Franciosa
  15 Vittorio Gassman
  roles: 11 A Double Life **12** A Patch of
  Blue **14** A Place in the Sun **16** A
  House Is Not a Home **19** The Diary
  of Anne Frank **20** The Poseidon
  Adventure
Winterset
  author: 15 Maxwell Anderson
winter sports
  god of: 4 Ullr **5** Uller
Winter's Tale, The
  author: 18 William Shakespeare
  character: 7 Camillo, Leontes,
  Paulina, Perdita **8** Florizel, Hermione
  9 Autolycus, Polixenes
Winter Wonderland
  nickname of: 8 Michigan
wintry 3 icy, raw **4** cold **5** bleak,
  chilly, harsh, polar, snowy, stark **6**
  arctic, chilly, dreary, frigid, frosty,
  frozen, gloomy, stormy **7** glacial **8** Siberian **9** cheerless
wipe 3 dry, mop, rub **4** swab **5** apply,
  brush, clean, erase, rub on, scour,
  scrub, swipe, towel **6** banish, remove,
  rub off, sponge, stroke
wiped out 5 broke **6** failed, ruined **8**
  bankrupt, indigent, strapped **9** destitute, insolvent, penniless **12** impoverished
wipe out 4 ruin **5** erase **7** abolish, destroy, eclipse **8** bankrupt **9** devastate,
  eliminate, eradicate, extirpate, liquidate **10** annihilate, obliterate **11** exterminate
wiping out 7 erasing **9** eclipsing, ex-

punging **10** abolishing, destroying **11** eliminating, eradicating **12** annihilating, obliterating

wire 5 cable **8** filament, telegram **9** cablegram, telegraph

wiry 4 lean **5** agile, kinky, lanky, spare, stiff **6** limber, pliant, sinewy **7** brittle

Wisconsin
abbreviation: 2 WI **3** Wis
nickname: 6 Badger
capital: 7 Madison
largest city: 9 Milwaukee
others: 5 Ripon **6** Antigo, Beloit, Cudahy, Neenag, Racine, Wausau **7** Ashland, Baraboo, Bloomer, Kenosha, Menasha, Oshkosh, Portage, Shawano **8** Appleton, Boscobel, Green Bay, Lacrosse, Superior, Waukesha **9** Eau Claire, Fond du Lac, Sheboygan, Shorewood, Wauwatosa, West Allis **10** Brookfield, Janesville **12** Steven's Point
college: 5 Ripon **6** Beloit **7** Alverno, Carroll, Viterbo **8** Carthage, Lawrence **9** Marquette, Northland
feature:
  fort: 6 Howard **8** Crawford **9** Winnebago
  national lakeshore: 14 Apostle Islands
tribe: 3 Fox, Sac **4** Sauk **5** Huron **6** Oneida, Ottawa **8** Chippewa, Kickapoo **9** Winnebago **10** Potawatomi
people: 11 Orson Welles **12** Fredric March, Harry Houdini, Spencer Tracy **13** Hamlin Garland **14** Joseph McCarthy, Georgia O'Keeffe, Thornton Wilder **16** Frank Lloyd Wright **17** Robert M LaFollette
  explorer: 6 Joliet **7** Allouez, Nicolet **8** Radisson **9** Marquette **12** Groseilliers
island: 8 Madeline
lake: 6 Geneva, Poygan **7** Kenosha, Mendota, Wissota **8** Michigan, Superior **9** Winnebago
land rank: 11 twenty-sixth
mountain: 7 Baraboo **9** Sugarbush **10** Blue Mounds
  highest point: 9 Timm's Hill
physical feature:
  glacial hills: 13 Kettle Moraine
  rock formations: 8 The Dells
river: 3 Fox **4** Wolf **7** St Croix **8** Chippewa **9** Black Rock, Wisconsin **11** Mississippi
state admission: 9 thirtieth
state bird: 5 robin
state fish: 11 muskellunge
state flower: 5 pansy **6** violet **10** wood violet
state motto: 7 Forward
state song: 11 On Wisconsin
state tree: 10 sugar maple
wisdom 6 brains **8** sagacity **9** teachings **10** philosophy, principles, profundity **11** discernment, penetra-

tion **12** apperception, intelligence **13** comprehension, judiciousness, understanding
god of: 2 Ea **4** Enki, Odin **5** Othin, Thoth
goddess of: 6 Athena, Athene, Brigit, Pallas, Saitis **7** Minerva **11** Tritogeneia **12** Pallas Athena **18** Alalcomenean Athena

wise 3 way **4** sage **6** manner **7** knowing, respect, sapient **8** profound **9** judicious, sagacious **10** discerning, perceptive **11** intelligent **13** knowledgeable, perspicacious, understanding

Wise, Robert
director of: 11 I Want to Live **13** West Side Story (with Jerome Robbins, Oscar) **15** The Sound of Music (Oscar)

wiseacre 4 fool, sage **5** idiot **7** tomfool **9** know-it-all, simpleton **10** smart aleck

Wise Blood
author: 15 Flannery O'Connor

wisecrack 4 jest, joke, quip **5** flash, sally **8** cut jokes **9** witticism **11** smart saying

Wise men *see* **4** Magi

wise up 5 edify **6** advise, in form **7** apprise **9** enlighten, make aware

wish 3 yen **4** hope, long, love, pine, want, whim, will **5** crave, yearn **6** aspire, desire, hunger, thirst **7** command, craving, leaning, longing, request **8** ambition, appetite, fondness, penchant, yearning **10** aspiration, partiality **11** inclination **12** predilection

wishes 11 compliments **13** felicitations **15** congratulations

wish for 4 want **5** covet, crave **6** desire

Wishfort, Lady
character in: 16 The Way of the World
author: 8 Congreve

wishful 4 avid **5** eager **6** keen on, pining **7** anxious, craving, hopeful, longing, wanting, wistful **8** aspiring, bent upon, desirous, fanciful, yearning **9** ambitious, expectant

wish well 10 felicitate **12** congratulate

wishy-washy 4 blah, dull, weak **5** inane, vapid, wimpy **6** jejune **7** insipid **8** wavering **10** indecisive, irresolute **11** ineffective, ineffectual, vacillating **12** equivocating, noncommittal **14** tergiversating **15** shilly-shallying

wisp 4 lock, tuft **5** bunch, shred, torch, twist **6** bundle, rumple **8** fragment **10** whisk broom **11** ignis fatuus **13** friar's lantern

wispy 4 thin **5** frail **6** slight **8** fleeting, nebulous

wistaria, wisteria

varieties: 4 pink, wild **5** silky, water **7** Chinese **8** Japanese **9** Rhodesian

Wister, Owen
author of: 12 The Virginian

wistful 3 sad **6** musing, pining **7** craving, doleful, forlorn, longing, pensive **8** desirous, mournful, yearning **9** hankering, sorrowful, woebegone **10** meditative, melancholy, reflective **12** disconsolate **13** contemplative, introspective

wit 3 wag **4** gags **5** comic, humor, joker, jokes, quips, sense **6** acumen, banter, brains, jester, joking, levity, wisdom **7** cunning, funster, gagster, insight, punster, sparkle, waggery **8** comedian, drollery, humorist, jokester, judgment, raillery, sagacity, satirist, vivacity **9** funniness, intellect **10** astuteness, brightness, cleverness, jocularity, perception, shrewdness, witticisms **11** discernment, penetration, wisecracker **12** intelligence, perspicacity **13** comprehension, epigrammatist, sagaciousness, understanding
French: 8 badinage **9** bel-esprit **10** persiflage

witch 3 hag **4** fury **5** crone, scold, shrew, vixen **6** beldam, ogress, virago **7** seeress **8** battle-ax, harridan **9** sorceress, temptress, termagant **10** prophetess **11** enchantress

witchcraft 5 obeah **6** hoodoo, voodoo **7** sorcery **8** black art, witchery, wizardry **9** diabolism, fetishism, voodooism **10** black magic, divination, necromancy **11** conjuration, enchantment

with
French: 4 avec, chez

with a grain of salt
Latin: 13 cum grano salis

with a lawsuit pending
Latin: 12 pendente lite

with authority
Latin: 10 ex cathedra

withdraw 2 go **5** leave, split **6** depart, go away, recall, recant, remove, retire **7** extract, rescind, retract, retreat, take off, vamoose **9** disappear, unsheathe

withdrawal 4 exit **6** egress **7** leaving, retreat **9** departure **10** retirement, retraction **14** discontinuance

withdrawn 3 shy **5** quiet **8** reserved, retiring, unsocial **9** reclusive **10** unfriendly **11** introverted **15** uncommunicative

wither 4 fade, wilt **5** abash, blast, droop, dry up, shame **7** cut down, mortify, shrivel **9** dehydrate, desiccate, humiliate

withered 3 dry **4** arid, sere **5** dried, faded **6** shrunk, wilted **7** decayed, dried up, drooped, stunned, wizened **9** petrified, shriveled **10** languished

withering 6 biting **7** caustic **8** scathing **9** shrinkage, shrinking, wrinkling

10 shriveling **11** contracting, contraction, devastating

with few words
  Latin: **12** paucis verbis

with force and with arms
  Latin: **9** vi et armis

with great praise
  Latin: **13** magna cum laude

withheld 4 kept **7** checked, forbore, refused, starved **8** kept back **9** boycotted, refrained

with highest praise
  Latin: **13** summa cum laude

withhold 4 hide, keep **6** hush up, retain **7** conceal, cover up **8** suppress

withhold from 4 deny **6** refuse

within 2 on **4** into **5** inner **6** during, inside **7** indoors **8** inwardly
  combining form: **3** eso **4** endo
  prefix: **5** intra

within an inch of 4 near **6** all but, almost, nearly

with-it 7 current **8** up-to-date
  French: **9** au courant

with one's own two hands 7 oneself, unaided **10** unassisted

without 4 save **5** minus **6** beyond, except, unless **7** lacking, nowhere, outside, wanting **8** exterior, external, free from, outdoors **9** excepting **10** externally
  appointment: **7** sine die
  care: **8** sine cure
  charge: **4** free **6** gratis **8** sine cure
  combining form: **4** ecto
  doubt: **9** sine dubio
  feet: **4** apod **6** apodal
  French: **4** sans
  horns: **7** acerous
  Latin: **4** sine
  law: **8** anarchic
  light: **7** aphotic
  life: **5** amort **9** inanimate
  luster: **3** mat **5** matte
  offspring: **9** sine prole
  prefix: **2** in
  roads: **7** invious
  saddles: **8** asellate, bareback
  subcalyx leaves: **9** bractless
  teeth: **5** morne **8** edentate
  this: **7** sine hoc
  tongue, teeth, or claws: **5** morne
  which not: **10** sine qua non
  wings: **7** apteral **8** apterous

without a doubt 6 surely **8** of course **9** certainly **10** absolutely, positively **11** indubitably **12** indisputably **14** unquestionably

without basis 7 unsound **9** unfounded **10** groundless, ungrounded **11** unjustified, unsupported **15** unsubstantiated

without care
  French: **9** sans souci

without charge 4 free **10** gratuitous,

on the house **13** complimentary
  Latin: **6** gratis

without doubt
  French: **9** sans doute

without end 7 endless, eternal, forever **8** immortal, infinite, timeless, unending **9** ceaseless, continual, endlessly, eternally, perpetual **10** immortally, infinitely, timelessly, unendingly **11** ceaselessly, continually, everlasting, never-ending **13** everlastingly **14** lasting forever

without equal
  French: **10** sans pareil

without error 4 true **5** exact, right **7** correct, perfect, precise, sinless **8** accurate, truthful, unerring **9** faultless **10** infallible

without exception 5 never **6** always, wholly **8** entirely **10** absolutely, completely, invariably, positively

without fear and without reproach
  French: **22** sans peur et sans reproche

Without Feathers
  author: **10** Woody Allen

without funds 5 broke **6** ruined **8** bankrupt, indigent, strapped, wiped out **9** destitute, flat broke, insolvent, penniless **10** stone broke **12** impoverished

without light 3 dim **4** dark **5** black, dusky, murky, shady **6** opaque **7** obscure, shadowy, stygian, sunless

without limit
  Latin: **11** ad infinitum

without limitation 6 wholly **7** totally, utterly **8** entirely **9** endlessly **10** absolutely, completely, definitely, positively, thoroughly **11** boundlessly **13** unequivocally **15** unconditionally
  French: **12** carte blanche

without notice 5 ad-lib **9** impromptu **10** improvised **11** extemporary **14** extemporaneous
  Latin: **9** extempore

without offspring, without progeny
  Latin: **9** sine prole

without the day
  Latin: **7** sine die

without which not
  Latin: **10** sine qua non

with praise
  Latin: **8** cum laude

withstand 4 bear, defy **5** brave **6** endure, resist, suffer **7** weather **8** confront, cope with, tolerate

witless 3 mad **5** crazy **6** insane, stupid **7** fatuous, foolish, unaware **9** slaphappy

witness 3 see **4** mark, note, sign, view **5** proof **6** attend, behold, look on, notice, verify **7** bear out, certify, confirm, endorse, initial, observe **8** attester, attest to, beholder, deponent,

document, evidence, looker-on, observer, onlooker, perceive, validate, vouch for **9** establish, spectator, testifier, testimony **10** validation **11** corroborate, countersign **12** authenticate, confirmation, substantiate, verification **13** corroboration, documentation **14** authentication, substantiation

Witness for the Prosecution
  director: **11** Billy Wilder
  based on play by: **14** Agatha Christie
  cast: **11** Tyrone Power **14** Elsa Lanchester **15** Charles Laughton, Marlene Dietrich

wits 4 mind **6** sanity **9** composure **14** coolheadedness

witticism 4 jest, joke, quip **5** sally **7** epigram
  French: **6** bon mot **10** jeu d'esprit

witty 5 comic, droll, funny **6** bright, clever, jocose **7** amusing, jocular, waggish **8** humorous, mirthful **9** brilliant, sparkling, whimsical **11** quick-witted **13** scintillating

witty saying 4 jest, quip **6** bon mot **7** epigram **9** witticism **13** clever comment

Witwoud, Sir Wilfull
  character in: **16** The Way of the World
  author: **8** Congreve

wizard 4 sage, seer, whiz **5** adept, shark **6** expert, genius, oracle **7** diviner, prodigy, wise man **8** conjurer, magician, sorcerer, virtuoso **9** enchanter **10** soothsayer **11** clairvoyant, necromancer

Wizard of Id, The
  creator: **10** Johnny Hart **11** Brant Parker
  character: **4** King **5** Spook **6** jester, Rodney, Tyrant

Wizard of Oz, The
  director: **13** Victor Fleming
  author: **10** L Frank Baum
  cast: **4** Toto **8** Bert Lahr (Zeke, Cowardly Lion) **9** Jack Haley (Hickory, Tin Woodsman), Ray Bolger (Hunk, Scarecrow) **11** Billie Burke (Good Witch of the North), Frank Morgan (wizard), Judy Garland (Dorothy Gale) **13** Clara Blandick **15** Charley Grapewin **16** Margaret Hamilton (Almira Gulch, Wicked Witch of the West), The Singer Midgets (Munchkins)
  other roles: **6** Aunt Em **10** Uncle Henry
  score: **9** E Y Harburg **11** Harold Arlen
  remade as: **6** The Wiz
  place: **6** Kansas **8** Land of Oz **11** Emerald City
  Dorothy wore: **8** red shoes

wizened 3 dry **5** dried **7** dried up **8** shrunken, withered, wrinkled **9** shriveled

WKRP in Cincinnati

character: 10 Andy Travis, Herb Tarlek, Les Nessman **12** Venus Flytrap **13** Arthur Carlson, Dr Johnny Fever **14** Bailey Quarters **15** Jennifer Marlowe

cast: 7 Tim Reid **9** Gary Sandy **10** Gordon Jump **11** Frank Bonner, Jan Smithers **12** Loni Anderson **14** Howard Hesseman, Richard Sanders

wobble 4 reel, sway **5** quake, shake, waver **6** shimmy, teeter, totter **7** quaking, shaking, stagger, swaying **8** wavering **9** shimmying, teetering, tottering **12** unsteadiness

wobbly, Wobbly 5 loose, shaky **7** doubtful **8** hesitant, insecure, unstable, unsteady, wavering **9** quavering, trembling **11** vacillating
union: 17 Industrial Workers

Wodehouse, P G (Pelham Grenville)
author of: 8 Full Moon **14** Thank You Jeeves **15** The Mating Season
character: 6 Jeeves, Psmith **13** Bertie Wooster

Woden
origin: 10 Anglo-Saxon
chief of: 4 gods

woe 5 agony, gloom, grief, trial, worry **6** misery, sorrow **7** anguish, anxiety, despair, torment, torture, trouble **8** calamity, distress **9** adversity, dejection, heartache, suffering **10** affliction, depression, melancholy, misfortune **11** tribulation **12** wretchedness

woebegone 3 sad **4** glum **6** gloomy **7** doleful, forlorn **8** dejected, funereal, mournful, tortured, troubled, wretched **9** agonizing, anguished, miserable, sorrowful, suffering **10** distressed

woeful 3 bad, sad **5** awful, cruel **6** tragic **7** doleful, painful, unhappy **8** crushing, dreadful, grievous, hopeless, horrible, terrible, unlikely, wretched **9** agonizing, appalling, miserable, sorrowful **10** calamitous, deplorable, depressing, disastrous, lamentable **11** distressing, unpromising **12** catastrophic, heartrending **13** disheartening, heartbreaking

woe to the vanquished
Latin: 9 vae victis

Wofford, Chloe Anthony
real name of: 12 Toni Morrison

Wojtyla, Karol
real name of: 14 Pope John Paul II **18** Archbishop of Krakow

wolf 4 bolt, gulp **5** scarf **6** devour, gobble **7** consume
constellation of: 5 Lupus
group of: 4 pack

Wolf, The
author: 11 Frank Norris

Wolfe, Nero see Stout, Rex

Wolfe, Thomas
author of: 14 The Hills Beyond **16** The Web and the Rock **17** Look Homeward Angel, Of Time and the River **18** You Can't Go Home Again
character: 10 Eugene Gant **12** George Webber

Wolfe, Tom
author of: 11 Radical Chic **13** The Right Stuff **14** The Painted Word **16** The Pump House Gang **21** From Bauhaus to Our House **23** The Bonfire of the Vanities **24** Mau-mauing the Flak Catchers **26** The Electric Kool-Aid Acid Test **43** The Kandy Kolored Tangerine Flake Streamline Baby

Wollstonecraft, Mary
husband: 13 William Godwin
daughter: 25 Mary Wollstonecraft Shelley
author of: 30 A Vindication of the Rights of Women

Wolverine State
nickname of: 8 Michigan

woman 4 girl, lady, maid, wife **5** flame, lover **6** damsel, maiden, matron **7** beloved, darling, dowager, females, fiancee, sweetie **8** ladylove, mistress **9** charwoman, concubine **10** girlfriend, hand maiden, sweetheart, sweetie pie **11** chambermaid, housekeeper, maidservant
French: 5 femme **8** paramour
Latin: 9 inamorata

Woman, first 3 Eve **5** Embla **7** Pandora

Woman in White, A
author: 13 Wilkie Collins

womanish 7 unmanly **8** feminine, ladylike **9** sissified **10** effeminate

womanlike 8 feminine **10** effeminate

womanly 8 feminine, matronly

Woman of Substance, A
author: 21 Barbara Taylor Bradford

Woman of the Year
director: 13 George Stevens
cast: 10 Fay Bainter **12** Reginald Owen, Spencer Tracy **16** Katharine Hepburn

Woman's Life, A
author: 15 Guy de Maupassant

Women, The
director: 11 George Cukor
based on play by: 15 Clare Boothe Luce
cast: 11 Hedda Hopper **12** Joan Crawford, Joan Fontaine, Marjorie Main, Norma Shearer **15** Paulette Goddard, Rosalind Russell
remade as: 14 The Opposite Sex

Women in Love
director: 10 Ken Russell
based on novel by: 10 DH Lawrence
character: 11 Gerald Crich **12** Rupert Birkin **14** Gudrun Brangwen, Ursula Brangwen
cast: 9 Alan Bates **10** Oliver Reed **11** Eleanor Bron **12** Jennie Linden **13** Glenda Jackson
Oscar for: 7 actress (Jackson)

wonder 3 awe **4** gape **5** sight, stare **6** marvel, ponder, rarity **7** miracle **8** cogitate, meditate, question **9** amazement, spectacle, speculate **10** conjecture, phenomenon **11** fascination **12** astonishment, stupefaction

wonder child
German: 10 wunderkind

wonderful 4 fine, good **5** great, super **6** divine, superb, tiptop, unique **7** amazing, capital **8** fabulous, singular, smashing, striking, terrific **9** admirable, excellent, fantastic, marvelous **10** astounding, incredible, miraculous, phenomenal, staggering, surprising **11** astonishing, crackerjack, fascinating, magnificent, sensational, spectacular **13** extraordinary

Wonderland State
nickname of: 5 Maine

wonderstruck 4 agog **6** amazed **8** thrilled **9** astounded, stupefied **10** astonished, enthralled, spellbound **11** dumbfounded **13** flabbergasted

Wonder Woman
character: 9 (Corp) Etta Candy **11** Diana Prince, Joe Atkinson, (Maj) Steve Trevor **13** Gen Blankenship
cast: 11 Lynda Carter **12** Lyle Waggoner **13** Beatrice Colen, Normann Burton **14** Richard Eastham

wont 3 apt, use **4** used, vain **5** habit, haunt, usage **6** custom, desire **8** accustom, inclined, practice **10** accustomed

wonted 3 apt **5** prone **6** likely **7** given to **10** accustomed, habituated

woo 3 sue **5** chase, court **6** cajole, pursue **7** address, entreat, solicit **8** petition **9** importune

wood 3 log **4** bush **5** brake, brush, copse, grove **6** boards, forest, lumber, planks, siding, timber **7** thicket **8** firewood, kindling **9** clapboard, wallboard **10** timberland

Wood, Grant
born: 9 Anamosa IA
artwork: 12 Spring in Town **13** Stone City Iowa **14** American Gothic **15** Woman with Plants **16** Parson Weems' Fable **18** Dinner for Threshers, John B Turner Pioneer **21** Daughters of Revolution

Wood, John, Sr
architect of: 6 Circus (Bath)

Wood, Natalie
real name: 13 Natasha Gurdin
born: 14 San Francisco CA
husband: 12 Robert Wagner
roles: 5 Gypsy **10** Brainstorm **12** The Great Race, The Searchers **13** West Side Story **17** Inside Daisy Clover **18** Rebel Without a Cause, Splendor in the Grass **19** Sex and the Single Girl **23** This Property Is Condemned **25**

Love with the Proper Stranger **27** Miracle on Thirty- fourth Street

wooded 5 treed **8** forested

wooden 4 dull **5** frame, rigid, stiff **6** clumsy, vacant **7** awkward, deadpan **8** lifeless, ungainly **9** impassive, unbending **10** inflexible, ungraceful **11** unemotional **14** expressionless

Woodhouse, Emma
character in: **4** Emma
author: **6** Austen

woodland 5 copse, grove, treed **6** forest **7** coppice, thicket **8** forested

wood of life
Latin: **11** lignum vitae

woods
god of: **8** Silvanus, Sylvanus

Woods, Sara
real name: **13** Sara Bowen-Judd
author of: **11** Done to Death **12** My Life Is Done **13** Yet She Must Die **15** A Show of Violence, Knives Have Edges **16** And Shame the Devil **17** The Third Encounter, Trusted Like the Fox **18** Bloody Instructions
character: **15** Anthony Maitland

Woodstock
also called: **11** The Cavalier
author: **14** Sir Walter Scott

Woodstock
director: **15** Michael Wadleigh
cast: **6** The Who **7** Santana **8** Joan Baez **9** Joe Cocker **12** Richie Havens **13** John Sebastian, Ten Years After **17** Jefferson Airplane **19** Crosby Stills and Nash **20** Country Joe and the Fish, Sly and the Family Stone
Oscar for: **11** documentary

Woodward, Bob
author of: **4** Veil **19** All the President's Men (with Carl Bernstein)

Woodward, Joanne
born: **13** Thomasville GA
husband: **10** Paul Newman
roles: **12** A Fine Madness, Rachel Rachel **15** Three Faces of Eve (Oscar) **16** The Long Hot Summer **43** The Effect of Gamma Rays on Man-in-the-Moon Marigolds

woodwind instrument 4 oboe **5** flute **7** bassoon, piccolo **8** clarinet **9** bass flute **10** cor anglais **12** bass clarinet **13** double bassoon

wooer 4 beau, love **5** flame, lover, swain **6** adorer, suitor **7** admirer, courter **8** para mour **10** sweetheart

wool
fabric: **4** felt **5** crepe, llama, serge, tweed, twill **6** alpaca, angora, boucle, covert, faille, melton, vicuna, woolen **7** challis, doeskin, Donegal, worsted **8** cashmere, homespun, shetland **9** Astrakhan, camelhair, gabardine, sharkskin **10** hopsacking **11** Harris tweed, herringbone

Woolf, Virginia

author of: **7** Orlando **8** The Waves, The Years **10** Jacob's Room **11** Mrs Dalloway **14** A Room of One's Own **15** To the Lighthouse
member of: **15** Bloomsbury Group

wool-gather 8 daydream, muse idly

woolly, wooly 5 downy, furry, fuzzy, hairy, sheep, vague **6** fleecy, lanate, lanose **7** blurred, muddled, unclear **8** confused, floccose, peronate **10** flocculent, indistinct **12** disorganized

woozy 4 hazy **5** dizzy, faint, foggy, fuzzy, giddy, shaky **6** punchy **7** muddled **9** befuddled **11** light-headed

word, words 3 vow **4** chat, dirt, news, poop, term **5** edict, order, rumor, set-to, voice **6** advice, avowal, decree, gossip, letter, notice, phrase, pledge, remark, report, ruling, signal **7** command, comment, dictate, dispute, explain, express, hearsay, lowdown, mandate, message, promise, quarrel, summons, tidings **8** argument, audience, bulletin, chitchat, colloquy, decision, describe, dialogue, dispatch, locution, telegram **9** assertion, assurance, bickering, direction, discourse, interview, sobriquet, ultimatum, utterance, wrangling **10** articulate, communique, conference, contention, discussion, expression **11** altercation, appellation, declaration, designation, information, scuttlebutt **12** consultation, intelligence, tittletattle **13** communication, pronouncement
French: **9** tete-a-tete

word for word and letter for letter
Latin: **19** verbatim et literatim

wordiness 9 diffusion, prolixity, verbosity **11** diffuseness, profuseness

wording 8 language, phrasing **11** phraseology

wordless 4 dumb, mute **5** tacit **6** silent **8** implicit, taciturn **10** speechless **11** unexpressed

word of honor 3 vow **4** oath **6** pledge **9** assurance

word play 6 banter **7** jesting, kidding
French: **8** badinage, repartee

Words, The
author: **14** Jean-Paul Sartre

Wordsworth, William
author of: **7** Michael **9** Ode to Duty **10** The Prelude **12** Tintern Abbey **14** Lyrical Ballads (with Coleridge) **16** The Ruined Cottage **24** Intimations of Immortality **25** Resolution and Independence
home: **11** Dove Cottage

wordy 5 windy **6** prolix, turgid **7** fustian, gushing, verbose **8** effusive, mumbling **9** bombastic, garrulous, redundant, talkative **10** discursive, loquacious, rhetorical, roundabout **12** tautological **13** grandiloquent

work, works 2 do, go **3** act, job, run, win **4** book, deed, duty, feat, form, gain, line, make, mill, mold, move, shop, song, task, toil, yard **5** beget, cause, chore, craft, enact, labor, opera, piece, plant, shape, slave, solve, sweat, trade **6** drudge, effect, effort, office, output **7** achieve, calling, drawing, execute, exploit, factory, fashion, foundry, innards, insides, operate, perform, produce, product, pursuit, succeed, trouble **8** building, business, concerto, contents, creation, drudgery, endeavor, engender, exertion, function, industry, maneuver, painting, progress, symphony, transmit, vocation **9** originate, sculpture, structure **10** assignment, employment, enterprise, manipulate, occupation, production, profession **11** achievement, composition, performance, transaction
Latin: **4** opus **5** opera
French: **6** metier

work, artistic or literary
French: **6** oeuvre

workaday 5 plain **6** common **7** humdrum, prosaic, routine **8** ordinary **10** unexciting **11** commonplace

work at 3 try **5** essay **6** tackle **7** attempt **8** endeavor

workbench 5 board, table **7** counter

work conquers all
Latin: **16** labor omnia vincit
motto of: **8** Oklahoma

worker 4 doer, hand **5** grind **6** drudge, toiler **7** artisan, hustler, laborer, plodder **8** achiever, employee, producer **9** craftsman, performer **11** breadwinner, eager beaver, proletarian

work for 6 assist **7** support **8** champion

working 3 job **4** duty, toil **5** labor, tasks **6** action, chores, fluent, usable, useful **8** business, drudgery, employed, exertion, industry, laboring **9** effective, operation, operative, practical **10** employment, occupation, profession **11** assignments, functioning, performance

Working
author: **11** Studs Terkel

working-class 5 labor **8** plebian **10** blue-collar **11** proletarian

working class 4 Non-U **9** commoners, common man **10** lower class **11** blue collars, proletariat
Greek: **9** hoi polloi

workmanlike 5 adept **8** skillful **9** efficient **10** productive

workmanship 5 skill **9** handcraft, handiwork, technique **10** handicraft **11** manufacture **12** construction

work out 5 solve, train **6** figure, reckon **7** compute, resolve **8** exercise, practice **9** ascertain, calculate, determine

Works and Days
author: 6 Hesiod

work saver 9 appliance 11 convenience

work-saving 4 easy 6 simple 9 efficient

worktable 4 desk 5 bench, board, table 7 counter

work together 5 unite 7 pitch in, share in 8 take part 9 cooperate 11 collaborate, participate

work toward 3 try 4 seek 6 aim for 7 attempt 8 aspire to, endeavor, reach for

work up 4 goad, urge 5 upset 6 excite 7 agitate, ferment, provoke

work with 5 coach, drill, teach, train 6 assist 8 exercise, instruct 9 cooperate 11 collaborate

world 3 age, era, orb 4 gobs, lots, star 5 class, Earth, epoch, globe, group, heaps, realm, times 6 domain, nature, oodles, people, period, planet, sphere, system 7 mankind, society 8 creation, division, duration, everyone, humanity, industry, universe 9 everybody, humankind, macrocosm 10 profession
Latin: 6 cosmos
Russian: 3 mir

World According to Garp, The
author: 10 John Irving
director: 13 George Roy Hill
cast: 10 Glenn Close, Hume Cronyn 11 John Lithgow 12 Jessica Tandy, Mary Beth Hurt 13 Robin Williams

World Enough and Time
author: 16 Robert Penn Warren

worldly 5 blase 6 astute, shrewd, urbane 7 callous, earthly, fleshly, knowing, mundane, profane, secular 8 material, physical, temporal 9 corporeal, mercenary 11 experienced, terrestrial 12 cosmopolitan 13 sophisticated

world pain
German: 11 Weltschmerz

world view
German: 11 Weltansicht

world-weary 5 blase, bored, jaded 9 unexcited

worldwide 4 rife 6 global 8 catholic, ecumenic, globular, planetal, sweeping 9 universal

worm 4 edge, inch 5 crawl, creep, steal 6 writhe 7 wriggle 9 penetrate 10 infiltrate
kinds: 4 inch, tape 5 angle, earth

worn 4 weak 5 dingy, drawn, faded, seedy, spent, tired, weary 6 frayed, shabby, wasted 7 abraded, haggard, pinched, rickety, wearied 8 battered, decrepit, dog-tired, drooping, fatigued 9 enfeebled, exhausted 10 threadbare, tumbledown 11 debilitated, dilapidated

worn-out 4 dead, shot 5 spent, tired 6 beat-up, effete, shabby, used-up 7

run-down 9 exhausted 10 threadbare 11 dilapidated 12 deteriorated

worn thin 9 motheaten 10 threadbare 11 dilapidated

worried 6 afraid, scared 7 anxious, fearful 9 concerned 10 distressed 12 apprehensive

worrisome 5 fussy, pesty 6 trying, uneasy, vexing 7 anxious, fretful, irksome 8 annoying 10 bothersome, despairing, disturbing, irritating, tormenting 11 aggravating, troublesome 12 apprehensive

worry 3 vex, woe 4 care, fret, stew 5 agony, beset, dread, grief, harry, upset 6 badger, bother, dismay, harass, hector, misery, pester, plague 7 agitate, agonize, anguish, anxiety, bugaboo, concern, despair, disturb, perturb, problem, torment, trouble 8 distress, vexation 9 misgiving, persecute 10 difficulty, uneasiness 12 apprehension 13 consternation

worsen 4 fail, slip 5 erode, lapse, slide 7 decline 10 degenerate, retrogress 11 deteriorate 12 disintegrate

worsening 7 setback 9 inflaming 10 increasing, regressing, regression 11 aggravating, heightening 12 exacerbating, intensifying 13 retrogressing, retrogression

worship 5 adore, exalt, extol 6 admire, esteem, praise, pray to, revere 7 adulate, glorify, idolize, lionize 8 dote upon, venerate 9 adoration, reverence 10 exaltation, veneration 11 devotionals

worshipful 5 pious 6 devout 8 reverent

worshiping 7 adoring 8 exalting 9 adoration, adulation, adulating, idolizing, reverence 10 exaltation, glorifying, magnifying, venerating, veneration 11 idolization 13 glorification, magnification

worst 3 bad 4 beat, best, rout 5 floor, outdo 6 defeat, lowest, outwit 7 conquer, poorest, triumph 8 inferior, overcome, vanquish 9 discomfit 10 overmaster, unpleasant

worth 3 use 4 cost, good 5 merit, price, value 6 assets, estate, wealth 7 benefit, effects, utility 8 holdings 9 appraisal, resources, valuation 10 importance, usefulness 11 consequence, possessions

worth having 8 valuable 9 desirable

Worthing, Jack
character in: 27 The Importance of Being Earnest
author: 5 Wilde

worthless 6 futile, paltry 7 trivial, useless 8 bootless, piddling, unusable 9 fruitless, meritless, pointless 10 unavailing 11 ineffectual, undeserving, unimportant 12 meretricious, unpro-

ductive 13 insignificant 14 good-for-nothing

worthless objects 4 junk 5 trash 7 garbage, rubbish 8 discards 11 odds and ends

worthwhile 4 good 6 usable, useful 8 valuable 9 rewarding 10 beneficial, profitable

worthy 3 fit, VIP 4 good, name 5 moral, noble 6 bigwig, decent, honest, leader, proper 7 big shot, ethical, fitting, notable, upright 8 big wheel, great man, immortal, laudable, luminary, official, reliable, suitable, virtuous 9 admirable, befitting, deserving, dignitary, estimable, excellent, honorable, personage, reputable 10 creditable 11 appropriate, commendable, meritorious, respectable

worthy of imitation 5 model 9 emulative, exemplary

Wotan
origin: 8 Germanic
chief of: 4 gods
corresponds to: 4 Odin 5 Othin

Wouk, Herman
author of: 13 The Winds of War 14 The Caine Mutiny 17 War and Remembrance 19 Marjorie Morningstar
character: 12 Captain Queeg

wound 3 cut 4 gash, harm, hurt, pain, slit, tear 5 slash, sting 6 bruise, damage, grieve, injure, injury, lesion, offend, pierce, trauma 7 anguish, mortify, torment 8 distress, lacerate, vexation 9 contusion 10 affliction, irritation, laceration 11 provocation

wounded 3 cut 4 hurt 6 mauled 7 damaged, injured, pierced, stabbed 8 impaired, ruptured, stricken 11 traumatized

wrack 4 kelp, ruin 5 ruins, trash 6 clouds, refuse 7 destroy, seaweed, torment 8 downfall, eelgrass, wreckage 9 cloud rack 11 destruction, storm clouds

wraith 5 ghost, shade, spook 6 spirit 7 phantom, specter 8 phantasm 10 apparition 15 materialization
Irish: 7 banshee
German: 12 doppelganger
French: 8 revenant

wrangle 4 tiff 5 argue, brawl 6 bicker 7 dispute, quarrel 8 squabble

wrangling 6 strife 7 arguing, discord 8 clashing, friction 9 bickering 10 contention 11 quarrelling

wrap 4 bind, cape, coat, fold, gird, hide, mask, veil, wind 5 cloak, cover, scarf, shawl, stole 6 bundle, clothe, encase, enfold, girdle, jacket, mantle, shroud, swathe 7 conceal, en close, envelop, sweater 8 surround

wrapper, wrapping paper 4 case 6 casing, jacket, sheath 8 covering, envelope, slipcase 9 container

wrapping 6 caping, hiding **7** veiling **8** cerement, bundling, swathing **9** embracing, packaging, shrouding **10** engrossing, enswathing, enveloping **11** enshrouding, surrounding

wrap up 3 end **4** pack **6** finish, wind up **7** engross, envelop, involve, package **8** bundle up, complete, conclude **9** polish off **11** dress warmly

wrath 3 ire **4** bile, fury, gall, rage **5** anger **6** animus, choler, rancor, spleen **8** vexation **9** animosity, hostility **10** irritation, resentment **11** displeasure, indignation **13** irritableness

wrathful 3 mad **5** angry, irate **6** bitter, raging **7** furious **8** incensed, virulent

wreak 4 vent, work **5** visit **7** execute, indulge, inflict, unleash

wreak vengeance 6 avenge **7** get even, revenge **9** retaliate

wreath 5 crown **6** diadem, laurel **7** chaplet, coronet, festoon, garland
Hawaiian: 3 lei

wreathe 4 bend, coil, wind **5** curve, twist **7** entwine, envelop **8** encircle **10** intertwine, interweave

wreck 3 end **4** mess, raze, ruin **5** break, crash, death, level, ruins, smash, total, up set **6** finish, ravage, wretch **7** breakup, crack-up, destroy, shatter, undoing **8** demolish, derelict **9** devastate, over throw **10** disruption **11** destruction, devastation, dissolution **12** annihilation

wreckage 4 ruin **5** ruins **6** jet sam **7** flotsam, remains **8** shambles **11** destruction

Wren, P C
author of: 9 Beau Geste

wrench 3 rip **4** jerk, pull, tear, warp **5** force, twist, wrest, wring **6** sprain, strain **7** distort, pervert **12** misrepresent
type: 6 monkey, socket **7** spanner

wrest 3 get, rip **4** earn, gain, grab, jerk, make, pull, take, tear **5** force, glean, twist, wring **6** attain, obtain, secure, wrench **7** achieve, extract, squeeze

wrestle 4 toil **5** labor **6** battle, strive, tussle **7** contend, grapple, scuffle **8** struggle **10** struggling

wrestling
athlete: 8 Dan Gable

wretch 3 cur, pig, rat **4** hobo, waif, worm **5** knave, louse, rogue, swine, tramp **6** misfit, rascal, rotter, varlet **7** castoff, outcast, stinker, villain **8** derelict, scalawag, sufferer, vagabond **9** scoundrel **10** blackguard **11** unfortunate

wretched 3 low **4** base, mean, vile **5** awful, lousy, sorry **6** abject, gloomy, rotten, shabby, sleazy **7** crushed, doleful, forlorn, hapless, pitiful, scruffy, unhappy, worried **8** dejected,

downcast, dreadful, hopeless, inferior, pathetic, pitiable, terrible **9** cheerless, depressed, miserable, nig gardly, sorrowful, woebegone, worthless **10** abominable, despairing, despicable, despondent, melancholy **11** crestfallen, unfortunate **12** contemptible, disconsolate, disheartened, inconsolable **13** brokenhearted

wretchedness 4 pain **6** misery, sorrow **7** despair, torment, trouble **8** distress, hardship **9** adversity **10** affliction, melancholy, misfortune **11** un happiness **12** hopelessness

wriggle 5 twist **6** squirm, wangle, writhe **7** meander

Wright, Frank Lloyd
architect of: 8 Taliesin (Spring Green WI) **10** Robie House (Chicago) **11** Martin House (Buffalo NY), Unity Church (Oak Park IL) **12** Fallingwater (Kaufmann House Bear Run PA), Taliesin West (near Phoenix AZ) **13** Imperial Hotel (To kyo) **16** Guggenheim Museum (NYC) **22** Marin County Civic Center (CA) **35** Larkin Company Administration Building (Buffalo NY) **45** S C Johnson and Son Wax Company Administration Center (Racine WI)
style: 6 Modern **7** Organic, Prairie

Wright, Orville and Wilbur
invented: 8 airplane
first plane: 6 Flyer I **9** Kitty Hawk

Wright, Richard
author of: 8 Black Boy **9** Native Son **17** Uncle Tom's Children

wring 4 hurt, pain, rend, stab **5** choke, force, press, twist, wrest **6** coerce, grieve, pierce, sadden, wrench **7** agonize, extract, squeeze, torture **8** compress, distress

wrinkle 4 fold, idea **5** crimp, fancy, pleat, slant, trick **6** crease, device, furrow, gather, notion, pucker, rimple, rumple **7** crumple, gimmick **9** crow's-feet, viewpoint **11** corrugation

wrinkled 3 old **4** aged **5** lined **6** folded, ridged, rucked, rugate, rugose, rugous, seamed **7** creased, crimped, rimpled, rippled, ruckled, rumpled **8** crimpled, furrowed, puckered **9** shriveled

writ 10 court order **11** sealed order **14** mandatory order

write 3 pen **4** copy, show **5** draft **6** author, draw up, record, scrawl **7** compose, dash off, jot down, make out, produce, set down, turn out **8** inscribe, scribble **10** transcribe

write down 3 jot **4** note, post **5** enter **6** record

write in full 5 add to **6** expand, extend, pad out **7** amplify, augment, stretch **9** expatiate

write out 6 expand, extend **7** amplify, enlarge, stretch **8** lengthen

writer 4 hack, poet **6** author, critic, penman, scribe **7** copyist **8** essayist, novelist, reporter, reviewer, scrawler **9** columnist, dramatist, scribbler **10** journalist, librettist, playwright, songwriter **11** penny-a-liner **12** calligrapher, newspaperman **13** correspondent **14** newspaperwoman
French: 11 litterateur

write to 7 address **8** send word **9** drop a line, send a card, send a note **10** correspond **11** send a letter

write-up 4 item **5** piece, story **7** article

write up 5 cover **6** report

writhe 4 jerk **5** flail **6** squirm, thrash, thresh, wiggle **7** contort, wriggle

writing 4 book, play, poem, tome, work **5** diary, essay, novel, print, story **6** column, letter, report, script, volume **7** article, copying, journal, penning **8** critique, document, drafting, libretto, longhand **9** authoring, composing, editorial, recording **10** inscribing, manuscript, penmanship **11** calligraphy, composition, publication **12** transcribing
Latin: 4 opus

writings
Hebrew: 7 Ketubim

written agreement 6 treaty **7** compact **8** contract

written law
Latin: 10 lex scripta

written-out form 9 extension **12** augmentation **13** amplification

wrong 3 bad, sin **4** awry, bilk, evil, harm, hurt, ruin, vice **5** abuse, amiss, cheat, crime, false, inapt, kaput, unfit **6** faulty, fleece, injure, injury, ruined, sinful, unfair, unjust, untrue, wicked **7** crooked, defraud, illegal, illicit, immoral, inexact, inverse, misdeed, offense, reverse, swindle, unhappy, unsound **8** criminal, dishonor, evil deed, ill-treat, immodest, improper, iniquity, maltreat, mistaken, mistreat, opposite, trespass, unlawful, unseemly, villain **9** dishonest, erroneous, felonious, illogical, incorrect, injustice, unethical, unfitting **10** dishonesty, fallacious, illegality, immorality, inaccurate, indecorous, indelicate, iniquitous, malapropos, mistakenly, sinfulness, unbecoming, unfairness, unsuitable, wickedness, wrongdoing **11** blameworthy, erroneously, incongruous, incorrectly, inexcusable, unbefitting, undesirable, unwarranted **12** dishonorable, inaccurately, infelicitous, unlawfulness **13** inappropriate, reprehensible, transgression, unjustifiable **15** unrighteousness

wrongdoer 5 crook, felon, knave, rogue **6** rascal, sinner **7** culprit, misdoer, villain **8** evildoer, offender **9** miscreant, scoundrel **10** blackguard, delinquent, lawbreaker, malefactor,

wrongdoing (cont.)

trespasser **11** perpetrator **12** transgressor

wrongdoing 3 sin **4** evil, vice **5** crime **8** misdeeds **10** misconduct **11** delinquency, malfeasance, misbehavior

wrongful 3 bad **6** unfair, unjust **7** illegal **8** criminal, unlawful **10** iniquitous, inequitable **12** illegitimate
act: 4 tort
dispossession: 6 ouster

wrongheaded 3 wry **8** perverse, stubborn **9** misguided

wrong side out 9 backwards **10** topsy-turvy

wrought 4 made **6** beaten, formed, worked **7** crafted **8** hammered **9** fashioned **11** constructed, handcrafted

wrought-up 7 excited **8** agitated **9** emotional **10** hysterical

wry 3 dry **5** askew, droll **6** bitter, ironic, warped **7** amusing, caustic, crooked, cynical, satiric, twisted **8** perverse, sardonic **9** contorted, distorted, sarcastic

Wunderkind 11 wonder child **12** child prodigy

Wurster, William
architect of: 13 Cowell College (UC Berkeley) **17** Ghirardelli Square (San Francisco CA)

Wuthering Heights
character: 9 Ellen Dean **10** Heathcliff, Mr Lockwood **11** Edgar Linton **14** Isabella Linton **15** Catherine Linton, Frances Earnshaw, Hareton Earnshaw, Hindley Earnshaw **16** Linton Heathcliff **17** Catherine Earnshaw
director: 12 William Wyler
author: 11 Emily Bronte
cast: 10 David Niven **11** Donald Crisp, Flora Robson, Leo G Carroll, Merle Oberon (Cathy) **15** Laurence Olivier (Heathcliff) **19** Geraldine Fitzgerald

Wyatt, James
architect of: 8 Pantheon (London) **9** Lee Priory (Kent) **10** Stoke Poges (Buckinghamshire) **13** Fonthill Abbey (Wiltshire) **14** Dodington House Gloucestershire) **15** Heveningham Hall (Suffolk) **16** Sandleford Priory (Berkshire)
style: 13 Gothic Revival

Wyatt, Jane
born: 9 Campgaw NJ

roles: 9 Boomerang **11** Lost Horizon **15** Father Knows Best **17** Great Expectations **19** Gentleman's Agreement **21** None But the Lonely Heart

Wyatt Earp, The Life and Legend of
character: 10 Morgan Earp, Virgil Earp **11** Ben Thompson, Doc Holliday **12** Bat Masterson, Bill Thompson **13** Old Man Clanton
cast: 9 Hal Baylor **10** Denver Pyle, Dirk London, Hugh O'Brien **12** John Anderson **13** Douglas Fowley **14** Trevor Bardette **20** Mason Alan Dinehart III
setting: 8 OK Corral **9** Dodge City, Ellsworth, Tombstone
Wyatt's pistols: 15 Buntline Special

Wyeth, Andrew Newell
born: 2 PA **10** Chadds Ford
father: 7 N C Wyeth
artwork: 9 Grape Wine, River Cove **12** Nick and Jamie **14** Christina Olson, Distant Thunder **15** Christina's World **22** Winter Nineteen Forty-six

Wyler, William
director of: 6 Ben Hur (Oscar) **7** Jezebel **9** Dodsworth, Funny Girl, The Letter **10** Mrs Miniver (Oscar), The Heiress, These Three **12** Roman Holiday **14** The Little Foxes **15** Counsellor-at-Law **16** Wuthering Heights **18** Friendly Persuasion **22** The Best Years of Our Lives (Oscar)

Wylie, Philip
author of: 13 Opus Twenty-one **19** A Generation of Vipers

Wyman, Jane
real name: 14 Sarah Jane Fulks
born: 10 St Joseph MO
husband: 12 Ronald Reagan
daughter: 13 Maureen Reagan
son: 13 Michael Reagan
roles: 5 So Big **9** Pollyanna **11** Falcon Crest, The Blue Veil, The Yearling **13** Johnny Belinda (Oscar) **14** Angela Channing, The Lost Weekend **17** The Glass Menagerie **20** Magnificent Obsession

Wyndham, John
real name: 16 John Beynon Harris
author of: 14 The Kraken Wakes **15** Consider Her Ways **17** The Midwich Cuckoos, Trouble with Lichen **19** The Day of the Triffids

Wyoming

abbreviation: 2 WY **3** Wyo
nickname: 8 Equality
capital: 8 Cheyenne
largest city: 6 Casper
others: 4 Cody, Lusk **7** Bighorn, Buffalo, Laramie, Rawlins, Worland **8** Gillette, Greybull, Kemmerer, Riverton, Sheridan, Sundance **11** Rock Springs
feature:
  center: 11 Buffalo Bill
  dam: 8 Shoshone
  fort: 7 Laramie
  historical preserve: 11 Fort Bridger
  national grassland: 11 Tunder Basin
  national monument: 11 Devil's Tower, Fossil Butte
  national park: 10 Grand Teton **11** Yellowstone
  reservoir: 12 Flaming Gorge
tribe: 4 Crow **5** Kiowa, Sioux **7** Arapaho, Bannock **8** Cheyenne
people: 11 Buffalo Bill **14** Jackson Pollock **16** Nellie Tayloe Ross **18** Francis Emroy Warren
  explorer: 6 Colter, Stuart **7** Bridger **10** Bonneville
lake: 7 Jackson **11** Yellowstone
land rank: 5 ninth
mountain: 3 Elk **5** Cloud, Moran **6** Absaro, Hoback, Tetons **7** Bighorn, Fremont, Laramie, Rockies **8** Atlantic, Sheridan **9** Wind River **10** Black Hills **11** Rattlesnake
  highest point: 11 Gannett Peak
physical feature: 11 Jackson Hole
  basin: 7 Wyoming
  cave: 8 Shoshone
  hot springs: 11 Thermopolis
  plains: 5 Great
river: 4 Bear, Wind **5** Green, Snake **6** Platte, Powder, Tongue **7** Bighorn **8** Cheyenne, Shoshone **10** Sweetwater **11** Yellowstone **12** Belle Fourche
state admission: 11 forty-fourth
state bird: 17 western meadowlark
state flower: 10 painted cup **16** Indian paintbrush
state motto: 11 Equal Rights
state song: 7 Wyoming
state tree: 10 cottonwood

Wyss, Johann Rudolf
author of: 22 The Swiss Family Robinson
  inspired by: 14 Robinson Crusoe

Xanthippe, Xantippe **3** hag **4** fury **5** scold, shrew, vixen **6** dragon, virago **7** scolder **8** spitfire **9** termagant
husband: 8 Socrates

Xanthus and Balius
horses of: 8 Achilles
trait: 8 immortal

Xenia
epithet of: 6 Athena
means: 10 hospitable

xeno- 6 prefix **7** foreign, strange

Xenoclea
form: 9 priestess

xenon
chemical symbol: 2 Xe

xenophobia
fear of: 9 strangers

xerox 4 copy

Xerxes see **9** Ahasuerus

X-Files
Creator: 11 Chris Carter
director: 11 Chris Carter
characters: 3 Mr. X (Steven Williams) **9** Fox Mulder (David Duchovny) **10** Alex Krycek (Nick Lea), Dana Scully (Gillian Anderson), Deep Throat (Jerry Hardin) **13** Walter Skinner (Mitch Pileggi) **19** Cigarette-Smoking Man (William B. Davis)

x-ray 9 radiogram **10** radiograph **13** roentgenogram **14** roentgenograph

X-ray tube
invented by: 8 Coolidge

yacht 4 boat, race, sail, ship, yawl **5** ketch, sloop **6** cruise, cutter **7** catboat **8** schooner
race: 11 America's Cup

yachting
athlete: 9 Ted Turner **11** Lowell North

yahoo 4 lout **5** brute, yokel **7** lowbrow **9** barbarian, ignoramus, vulgarian

Yahoos
fictional people in: 16 Gulliver's Travels
author: 5 Swift

Yahweh 3 God **4** Lord **5** Jahve, Jahwe, Yahve **6** Author, I am I am, Jahveh **7** Creator, Eternal, Jehovah **8** Absolute, Almighty, Infinite
component: 2 he **3** yod, vav
pronunciation: 6 Adonai, Elohim **9** forbidden
transliteration: 4 YHVH

Yale, Linus, Jr

invented: 12 cylinder lock **27** dial-operated combination lock

Yalta
in: 7 Ukraine
conference participant: 6 Stalin **9** Churchill, Roosevelt

yam 9 Dioscorea **14** Ipomoea batatas
varieties: 4 wild **5** Negro, water, white **6** Attoto, potato, yellow **7** Chinese **11** sweet potato

Yamasaki, Minoru
architect of: 14 St Louis Airport (MO) **16** World Trade Center (NYC) **21** Woodrow Wilson Building (Princeton NJ)

yammer 3 cry **4** carp, harp, howl, wail, yell **5** whine **7** grumble, whimper **8** complain

yank 3 tug **4** jerk, pull **5** pluck, wrest **6** snatch, wrench **7** draw out, extract, pull out

Yankee, Yank 2 GI **5** teddy **6** gringo **8** American, doughboy **10** Northerner
Spanish: 6 yanqui

Yankee Doodle Dandy
director: 13 Michael Curtiz
cast: 10 Joan Leslie **11** James Cagney (George M Cohan) **12** Irene Manning, Walter Huston
Oscar for: 5 actor (Cagney)

yanqui 6 Yankee **9** US citizen

Yaounde
capital of: 8 Cameroon

yap 3 yip **4** blab, gush, rave, talk, yawp, yelp **5** scold **6** babble, gabble, gossip, jabber, rave on, tattle **7** blather, chatter, lecture, palaver, prattle **8** complain, converse

Yaqui
language family: 6 Cahita
location: 6 Mexico, Sonora **7** Arizona

yard 4 lawn **5** close, court **6** garden **7** confine, grounds, pasture **8** compound **9** enclosure, three feet
abbreviation: 2 yd

yardbird 3 con **5** felon **7** convict **8** prisoner

yard goods 5 cloth **6** fabric **8** material, textiles

Yard of Sun
author: 14 Christopher Fry

yardstick 4 rule **7** measure **8** standard **9** criterion

Yaren District
capital of: 5 Nauru

yarn 4 tale **5** story **7** account **8** anecdote **9** adventure, narrative **10** experience

Yastrzemski, Carl
nickname: 3 Yaz
sport: 8 baseball
team: 12 Boston Red Sox

Yates, Peter
director of: 7 Bullitt **12** Breaking Away

yawn 3 gap **4** bore, gape **5** chasm **8** open wide, oscitate

yawp 4 roar, yelp **5** noise **6** clamor, squawk, yammer

Yaz
nickname of: 15 Carl Yastrzemski

Yazoo
author: 12 Willie Morris

year, years 3 age, era **4** time **5** cycle, epoch **6** period
abbreviation: 2 yr

Yearling, The
director: 13 Clarence Brown
author: 22 Marjorie Kinnan Rawlings
cast: 9 Jane Wyman **10** Chill Wills **11** Gregory Peck **14** Claude Jarman Jr
character: 9 Ora Baxter **10** Jody Baxter **11** Oliver Hutto, Penny Baxter **12** Grandma Hutto **14** Twink Weatherby **19** Fodder-Wing Forrester

yearn 4 ache, long, pine, sigh, want, wish **5** crave **6** hanker, hunger, thirst **8** languish

yearning 3 yen **4** ache, want, wish **5** fancy **6** desire, hunger, thirst **7** craving, longing, passion **9** hankering **10** aspiration **11** inclination

Year of Living Dangerously, The
director: 9 Peter Weir
cast: 9 Linda Hunt (Billy Kwan), Mel Gibson **15** Sigourney Weaver
setting: 7 Jakarta
Oscar for: 17 supporting actress (Hunt)

year of wonders
Latin: 14 annus mirabilis

Yeats, William Butler
author of: 7 A Vision **8** The Tower **9** Last Poems **14** Leda and the Swan **15** The Winding Stair **18** Sailing to Byzantium **19** Among School Children, The Wild Swans at Coole **21** Easter Nineteen Sixteen **22** The Lake Isle of Innisfree **29** An Irish Airman Foresees His Death

yegg 6 bomber 9 cracksman 11 safe-cracker

yell 3 boo, cry 4 bawl, hoot, howl, roar, yowl 5 cheer, hollo, shout, whoop 6 bellow, clamor, cry out, holler, hurrah, huzzah, outcry, scream, shriek, squall, squeal 7 screech

yellow 4 gold 5 blond, lemon, ocher 6 afraid, canary, craven, flaxen 7 chicken, fearful, saffron 8 cowardly, timorous 10 frightened 12 apprehensive, fainthearted 13 pusillanimous 14 chickenhearted

yellow-belly 6 coward 7 caitiff, chicken, dastard 8 poltroon

Yellowhammer State
  nickname of: 7 Alabama

yellowish 4 buff 5 blond, cream 6 blonde, creamy, flaxen

Yellow Kid, The
  creator: 10 R F Outcault
  trademark: 10 nightshirt
  place: 5 slums 11 Hogan's Alley
  coined term: 16 yellow journalism
  first: 10 comic strip

yelp 3 yap, yip 4 bark, howl 5 shout 6 clamor, holler, scream, shriek, squeal 7 screech

Yemen, North
  other name: 4 Sana
  capital/largest city: 4 Sana 5 Sanaa
  others: 4 Moka, Taiz 5 Dahhi, Damar, Jibla, Mocha, Mukha, Taizz, Umram 7 Hodeida, Hudayda
  monetary unit: 4 fils, rial 5 riyal
  island: 5 Zugar 6 Hanish
  highest point: 6 Shuayb
  river: 5 Abrad, Zabid 6 al-Jawf, Surdud
  sea: 3 Red
  physical feature:
    desert: 10 Rub al Khali
    gulf: 4 Aden
    lowlands: 6 Tihama
    peninsula: 7 Arabian
    strait: 11 Bab el Mandeb
  people: 4 Arab 5 Zaidi 6 Shafai, Yemeni 8 Yemenite
    leader: 16 Ali Abdallah Saleh 19 Abd al-Aziz Abd al-Ghani
  language: 6 Arabic
  religion: 5 Islam
  place:
    ruins: 5 Marib
  feature:
    dagger: 7 jambiya
    king: 4 imam
    kingdom: 4 Saba 5 Sheba 11 Arabia Felix
    tree: 3 fig 5 carob, mango, myrrh
  food:
    coffee: 5 mocha

Yemen, South
  capital: 4 Aden 14 Madinat al-Shaab
  largest city: 4 Aden
  others: 5 Ahwar, Shihr, Tarim 6 Balhaf, Damqut, Seiyun, Shabwa,

Shibam, Zamakh 7 Mukalla
  monetary unit: 4 fils 5 dinar
  island: 5 Perim 7 Kamaran, Socotra
  mountain: 7 Djehaff
  highest point: 6 Thamir
  river: 4 Bana 6 Tibban 7 Masilah 9 Hadramaut
  sea: 6 Indian 7 Arabian
  physical feature:
    desert: 10 Rub al Khali 12 Empty Quarter
    gulf: 4 Aden
    peninsula: 7 Arabian
    valley: 9 Hadramawt
  people: 4 Arab
  language: 6 Arabic
  religion: 5 Islam
  feature:
    animal: 4 ibex, oryx
    clothing: 4 futa

yen 4 ache, long, pine, sigh, want, wish 5 crave, fancy, yearn 6 aching, desire, hanker, hunger, relish, thirst 7 craving, longing, passion 8 appetite, languish, yearning 9 hankering 10 aspiration 11 inclination

yenta 3 hen 6 gossip 8 busybody 12 blabbermouth

Yentl
  director: 15 Barbra Streisand
  based on story by: 19 Isaac Bashevis Singer
  cast: 13 Mandy Patinkin 15 Barbra Streisand

Yeobright, Thomasin and Clym
  characters in: 17 Return of the Native
  author: 5 Hardy

yeoman 4 chap, exon 5 churl, clerk, swain 6 farmer, fellow 7 granger, plowman, servant 8 graycoat, retainer 9 beefeater 10 freeholder 12 petty officer

Yerby, Frank
  author of: 8 Fair Oaks 10 Health Card 11 Griffin's Way 12 Pride's Castle 16 The Foxes of Harrow 21 Hail the Conquering Hero

yes 3 aye, yea 4 amen, okay, true 5 truly 6 assent, indeed, it is so, just so, really, so be it, surely, verily 7 consent, exactly, granted, no doubt 8 approval, of course, to be sure 9 agreement, assuredly, certainly, doubtless, precisely 10 acceptance, positively 11 affirmation, undoubtedly 12 acquiescence, emphatically 13 affirmatively, authorization
  French: 3 oui
  German: 2 ja
  Spanish: 2 si

yesterday 7 the past 10 bygone days, days of yore, olden times, time gone by 11 former times 13 the recent past 14 the good old days 17 the day before today 22 on the day preceding today

yet 3 but 4 also, even, then, up to

5 again, still, while, until 6 no less, though 7 besides, earlier, even now, further, however, thus far 8 although, hitherto, moreover 9 presently 10 eventually, ultimately 12 nevertheless 15 notwithstanding

yew 5 Taxus
  varieties: 4 plum 5 Irish 6 golden 7 Chinese, English, Florida, Western 8 American, Japanese, Southern 11 Chinese plum, Plum-fruited 12 Japanese plum, Prince Albert 14 Harrington plum

Yggdrasil
  also: 9 Iggdrasil
  origin: 12 Scandinavian
  kind of tree: 12 evergreen ash
  roots: 5 three
  binds: 6 Asgard 7 Midgard 8 Niflheim 10 Mithgarthr

yield 3 pay, sag 4 bear, crop, earn, gain, give 5 beget, break, burst, defer, droop, forgo, grant, spawn, split, waive 6 accede, cave in, give in, give up, kowtow, ren- der, return, submit, supply 7 bow down, concede, forbear, furnish, give way, harvest, pay ment, premium, produce, product, provide, revenue, succumb, truckle 8 collapse, cry uncle, earnings, generate, interest, proceeds, renounce 9 acquiesce, gleanings, procreate, surrender 10 capitulate, relinquish

yielding 3 lax 4 soft 6 ceding, spongy 7 sagging 8 flexible, obedient 9 compliant 11 complaisant 13 accommodating

Yigdal 22 Jewish liturgical prayer
  literally: 12 becomes great

Yizkor 33 Jewish service to commemorate the dead
  literally: 9 be mindful

Ymir
  origin: 12 Scandinavian
  progenitor of: 6 giants
  earth made from: 5 flesh
  water made from: 5 blood
  heavens made from: 5 skull

yoga, yogi 5 Hindu 6 mystic 7 ascetic

Yogi Bear
  creator: 12 Hanna-Barbera
  character: 6 BooBoo
  setting: 14 Jellystone Park

yoke 3 tax 4 bond, join, link, load, pair, span, team 5 brace, clasp, hitch, trial, unite 6 at tach, burden, collar, couple, fasten, strain, weight 7 bondage, coupler, harness, serfdom, slavery 8 distress, pressure, troubles 9 servitude, thralldom, vassalage 10 oppression 11 enslavement, tribulation

yokel 4 clod, hick, rube 7 bumpkin, hayseed, peasant, plowboy 10 clodhopper, provincial

yolk 6 yellow

yonder 3 yon 5 there 6 far-off 7 faraway, farther, thither

Yorick
skull in: **6** Hamlet
author: **11** Shakespeare
Yorick, Mr
character in: **14** Tristram Shandy
author: **6** Sterne
York, Michael
born: **6** Fulmer **7** England
roles: **6** Tybalt **7** Cabaret **11** Lost Horizon **14** Four Musketeers, Romeo and Juliet, The Forsyte Saga **15** Three Musketeers **19** The Island of Dr Moreau **24** The Last Remake of Beau Geste
York, Susannah
real name: **23** Susannah Yolande Fletcher
born: **6** London **7** England
roles: **5** Freud **6** Images **8** Jane Eyre, Tom Jones **12** The Awakening
author of: **18** In Search of Unicorns
Yossarian
character in: **14** Catch Twenty-two
author: **6** Heller
You Asked for It
host: **8** Art Baker **9** Jack Smith
You Bet Your Life
host: **11** Groucho Marx
announcer: **14** George Fenneman
You Can't Go Home Again
author: **11** Thomas Wolfe
character: **10** Esther Jack **11** Lloyd McHarg **12** George Webber **13** Else von Kohler **14** Foxhall Edwards
You Can't Take It With You
author: **8** Moss Hart **14** George S Kaufman
director: **10** Frank Capra
cast: **10** Jean Arthur, Mischa Auer **12** Edward Arnold, James Stewart **15** Lionel Barrymore
Oscar for: **7** picture **8** director
young 3 cub, pup **4** baby, kids **5** child, issue, minor, whelp **6** boyish, callow, junior, kitten, youths **7** budding, girlish, growing, progeny, puerile, teenage **8** childish, children, immature, juvenile, underage, youthful **9** beardless, infantile, juveniles, offspring, teenagers **10** adolescent, descendant, sophomoric, youngsters **11** adolescents, undeveloped **13** inexperienced
god of: **7** Angus Og
goddess of: **4** Hebe
Young, Chic
creator/artist of: **7** Blondie
Young, Denton True
nickname: **2** Cy **7** Cyclone
sport: **8** baseball
position: **7** pitcher
team: **12** Boston Braves, Boston Red Sox **16** Cleveland Indians, St Louis Cardinals
Young, Loretta
real name: **13** Gretchen Young
husband: **12** Grant Withers
roles: **13** Cause for Alarm **14** The

Bishop's Wife **15** Come to the Stable **18** The Farmer's Daughter (Oscar) **20** Rachel and the Stranger
Young, Robert
born: **9** Chicago IL
roles: **10** Relentless **11** H M Pulham Esq **13** Marcus Welby M D **15** Father Knows Best **16** Strange Interlude
Young Adventure
author: **19** Stephen Vincent Benet
Young Frankenstein
director: **9** Mel Brooks
cast: **8** Teri Garr **10** Gene Wilder, Peter Boyle **11** Gene Hackman **12** Madeline Kahn, Marty Feldman **14** Cloris Leachman
score: **10** John Morris
young girl
French: **10** jeune fille
young lady
German: **8** fraulein
Young Lonigan
author: **13** James T Farrell
Young Manhood of Studs Lonigan
author: **13** James T Farrell
youngster 3 boy, kid, tot **4** baby, girl **5** child, minor, youth **7** progeny **8** juvenile, teenager **9** fledgling, offspring **10** adolescent
young Turks 6 rebels **8** radicals, upstarts **9** activists **10** insurgents **15** revolutionaries
young woman
French: **10** demoiselle
you're welcome
German: **5** bitte
Your Show of Shows
regular: **9** Bill Hayes, Jerry Ross, Sid Caesar **10** Carl Reiner **11** Imogene Coca **12** Howard Morris, Nellie Fisher **13** James Starbuck, Robert Merrill **16** Marguerite Piazza
youth 3 boy, kid, lad **4** kids **5** bloom, child, minor, prime, teens **6** heyday **7** boyhood **8** children, girlhood, juvenile, minority, teenager **9** childhood, fledgling, juveniles, schoolboy, stripling, teenagers, youngster **10** adolescent, pubescence, youngsters **11** adolescence, adolescents
youthful 5 fresh, young **6** boyish, callow **7** girlish, puerile, teenage **8** childish, immature, juvenile **10** adolescent, sophomoric **12** enthusiastic, light hearted **13** inexperienced
yowl 3 bay, cry **4** bawl, roar, wail, yelp **5** shout, whine **6** bellow, holler, scream, shriek, squeal **7** screech **9** caterwaul
Ypres
in: **7** Belgium
WWI: **10** battle site
yuan
currency of: **5** China
yucca 5 agave

varieties: **4** blue **6** banana **9** San Angelo, spineless **11** twisted-leaf
Yugoslavia
other name: **8** Dalmatia **34** Kingdom of the Serbs Croats and Slovenes
capital/largest city: **7** Beograd **8** Belgrade
others: **3** Nis **4** Pola, Pula, Savo, Zara **5** Agram, Bosna, Budva, Fiume, Kotor, Pirot, Rieka, Rtanj, Senta, Split, Tuzla, Uskub, Zadar **6** Bitola, Bitolj, Ca Haro, Maglaj, Morava, Mostar, Osijek, Prilep, Ragusa, Rijeka, Skopje, Trogir, Visoko, Zagreb **7** Cetinje, Laibach, Maribor, Novisad, Skoplje, Spalato **8** Monastir, Pristina, Sarajevo, Subotica, Titograd **9** Banja Luka, Dubrovnik, Ljubljana, Podgorica, Smederevo
divisioin/former division: **6** Bosnia, Serbia **7** Croatia **8** Crna Gora, Slovenia **9** Macedonia, Vojvodina, Voyvodina **10** Montenegro **11** Hercegovina, Herzegovina **14** Kosovo-Metohija
measure: **3** oka, rif **4** akov, ralo **5** donum, khvat, lanaz, plaze, stopa **6** motyka, ralico **9** danoranja
monetary unit: **4** para **5** dinar
weight: **3** oka **5** dramm, tovar, wagon **7** satljik
island: **3** Rab **4** Arbe, Brac, Cres, Hvar, Pago **5** Mljet, Solta, Susac, Susak **7** Korcula
lake: **4** Bled **5** Ohrid **6** Prespa **7** Ochrida, Scutari
mountain: **5** Karst **6** Balkan **7** Rhodope **8** Crna Gora, Durmitor **9** Sar-Pindus **10** Karawanken
Alps: **6** Carnic, Julian **7** Dinaric **9** Slovenian **16** Northern Albanian
highest point: **7** Triglav
river: **3** Una **4** Drim, Drin, Ibar, Krka, Kupa, Sava, Tisa **5** Anube, Bosna, Cazma, Drava, Drina, Raska, Tamis, Timok, Tisza, Vrbas **6** Danube, Morava, Vardar, Velika **7** Neretva **9** Vojvodina
sea: **8** Adriatic
physical feature:
bay: **5** Kotor
cave: **8** Postojna
channel: **7** Narento
gulf: **5** Kotor **7** Kvarner, Trieste
hot springs: **16** Krapinske Toplice
peninsula: **6** Balkan **7** Istrian
people: **4** Serb, Slav **5** Croat **7** Slovene **8** Albanian **10** Macedonian **11** Montenegrin
author: **6** Andric, Djilas, Krleza **7** Dedijer
leader: **4** Tito **5** Dusan, Pasic **6** Djilas **7** Nemanja **9** Milosevic, Obrenovic **13** Mikhailovitch
ruler: **5** Peter **9** Hapsburgs **12** Ottoman Turks
sculptor: **9** Mestrovic
language: **7** Bosnian, Slovene **8** Alba-

nian, Croatian **9** Hungarian, Slovenian **10** Macedonian **11** Montenegrin **13** Herzegovinian, Serbo-Croatian

alphabet: 5 Latin **8** Cyrillic
religion: 5 Islam **13** Roman Catholic **15** Eastern Orthodox, Serbian Orthodox

place:
  amphitheater: 4 Pula
  bridge: 9 Stari Most
  fortress: 10 Kalemedgan
  monastery: 8 Sopocani
  mosque: 6 Begova **15** Bajrakli Dzamija
  ruins: 14 Hadrian's Palace
  square: 8 Republic

feature:
  coffee house: 7 kafanas
  fields: 5 polje
  military governor: 7 vojvodi
  musical instrument: 5 gusla
  poems: 5 pesme
  slippers: 6 opanki

food:
  dessert: 4 pita
  drink: 5 rakia **6** rakija **7** maraska **9** slivovitz **10** sljivovice **13** Turkish coffee
  meat: 7 shaslik **9** cevapcici **10** culbastija
  soup: 6 corbas

Yuit *see* **6** Eskimo

Yukon Territory
  border: 6 Alaska **15** British Columbia, Selwyn Mountains **18** Mackenzie Mountains
  capital: 10 Whitehorse
  country: 6 Canada
  event: 8 gold rush (1897)
  Indian: 4 Dene **6** Eskimo **7** Kutchin **8** Loucheux **9** Athabasca
  lake: 6 Kluane **9** Great Bear
  mineral: 4 gold **6** silver
  mountain: 3 Joy **5** Logan **6** Harper **7** Kennedy **8** Campbell
  region: 8 Klondike
  river: 5 Pelly **9** Porcupine
  sea: 8 Beaufort
  town: 4 Elsa, Faro, Mayo, Snag **5** Rocky **6** Dawson **8** Franklin, Wernecke **9** Mackenzie

yule 4 Noel **9** Christmas

Yule, Joe, Jr
  real name of: 12 Mickey Rooney

Yuman
  tribe: 6 Mohave, Mojave **8** Hualapai

Zachariah
  father: 4 Babi, Elam **9** Barachias
  wife: 9 Elizabeth
  son: 3 Abi **14** John the Baptist
  succeeded: 8 Jeroboam
  visitor: 7 Gabriel

zaddik 14 virtuous person **15** righteous person

Zadkine, Ossip
  born: 6 Russia **8** Smolensk
  artwork: 4 Stag **6** Christ **7** Orpheus

9 Musicians **10** The Prophet **13** Woman with a Fan **14** Mother and Child **16** The Destroyed City

Zadok
  father: 5 Baana, Immer **6** Ahitub
  son: 7 Shallum
  daughter: 7 Jerusha
  served: 5 David

zaftig 5 buxom, plump **6** bosomy

Zagreus
  form: 5 child, deity
  father: 4 Zeus
  mother: 6 Semele **10** Persephone

Zaire
  other name: 5 Congo **12** Belgian Congo **13** Congo-Kinshasa **17** Congo-Leopoldville
  capital/largest city: 8 Kinshasa
  others: 4 Baya, Boma, Lebo **5** Aketi, Ilebo **6** Banana, Kamina, Kasaji, Kikwit, Matadi, Sandoa **7** Butembo, Kananga, Kolwezi **8** Bakwanga, Yangambi **9** Kisangani **10** Lubumbashi, Luluabourg, Mutshatsha **12** Port-Francqui, Stanleyville **14** Elisabethville
  school: 5 Zaire **8** Lovanium
  division: 4 Kivu **5** Kasai, Shaba **7** Equator, Katanga **8** Oriental
  monetary unit: 5 zaire **6** makuta
  lake: 4 Kivu **5** Mweru, Tumba **6** Albert, Edward, Upemba **9** Mai-Ndombe **10** Tanganyika
  mountain: 7 Crystal, Mitumba, Virunga **9** Ruwenzori **10** Nyaragongo **18** Mountains of the Moon
  highest point: 10 Margherita
  river: 4 Ruki, Uele **5** Congo, Dengu, Ibina, Kasai, Lindi, Zaire **6** Likati, Lomami, Lukuga, Ubangi **7** Aruwimi, Lualaba, Lulonga
  sea: 8 Atlantic
  physical feature:
    falls: 4 Kivu **6** Tshopo **7** Stanley
    forest: 5 Ituri
    valley: 9 Great Rift
  people: 4 Kuba, Luba, Yaka **5** Bantu, Bashi, Bemba, Kongo, Lulue, Lunda, Mongo, Pygmy **6** Azande, Baluba, Watusi **7** Bakongo, Nilotes, Tshokwe **8** European, Mangbetu, Sudanese
    explorer: 3 Cao **7** Stanley
    leader: 6 Mobutu (Sese Seko) **7** Lumumba, Tshombe **8** Kasavubu
    ruler: 7 Belgium, Leopold
  language: 5 Bantu **6** French **7** Chiluba, Kikongo, Lingala, Swahili **8** Sudanese, Tshiluba
  religion: 5 Islam **7** animism, Kimbang **10** Protestant **13** Roman Catholic
  place:
    dam: 4 Inga **9** Le Marinee **10** Del Commune
    national park: 6 Albert, Upemba **7** Garamba
  feature:
    animal: 5 hyena, okapi **7** giraffe,

gorilla **10** rhinoceros
    fish: 11 electric eel

Zambia
  other name: 16 Northern Rhodesia
  capital/largest city: 6 Lusaka
  others: 4 Kafu **5** Choma, Isoka, Kabwe, Kitwe, Mansa, Mbala, Mongu, Mpika, Mumba, Ndola **6** Mwenda **7** Chipata, Luapula, Mankoya **8** Balovale, Chingola, Luanshya, Mazabuka, Mufulira, Mulobezi **11** Livingstone
  division: 7 Puapula **10** Copperbelt **11** Barotseland
  monetary unit: 5 ngwee **6** kwacha
  lake: 5 Mweru **6** Kariba **9** Bangweulu **10** Tanganyika
  mountain: 8 Muchinga
  highest point: 12 Mafinga Hills
  river: 5 Congo, Kafue **7** Luangwa, Luapula, Zambezi **8** Chambezi **9** Chambeshi
  physical feature:
    cave: 5 Nsalu **14** Chifabwa Stream
    falls: 7 Kalambo **8** Victoria
    gorge: 6 Kariba
    plateau: 7 Zambian
    swamp: 7 Lukanga **9** Bangweulu **12** Mweru Wantipa
    valley: 8 Chambezi **9** Great Rift
  people: 4 Lozi **5** Bantu, Bemba, Ngoni, Tonga
    developer: 6 Rhodes
    explorer: 11 Livingstone
    hero: 11 Chitimukulu
    leader: 6 Kaunda
  language: 4 Lozi **5** Bemba, Lunda, Tonga **6** Luvale, Nyanja **7** English **9** Afrikaans
  religion: 5 Hindu, Islam **7** animism **10** Protestant **13** Roman Catholic
  place:
    botanical garden: 10 Munda Wanga
    dam: 5 Kafue **6** Kariba
    game reserve: 6 Valley
    library: 20 Hammerskjold Memorial
    museum: 11 Livingstone
    national park: 5 Kafue, Sumbu **12** South Luangwa
  feature:
    canoe: 10 nalikwanda
    king: 7 litunga
    king's aide: 5 sungu, twite **8** inabanza
    taxi: 6 zamcab

zany 3 nut **4** wild **5** balmy, batty, booby, buffo, clown, comic, crazy, cutup, daffy, dizzy, goofy, inane, nutty, silly, wacky **6** jester, nitwit, screwy, weirdo **7** buffoon, half-wit, lunatic **8** bonehead, clownish, imbecile, lunkhead, numskull **9** blockhead, eccentric, harlequin, ludicrous, pantaloon, simpleton, slapstick **10** nincompoop, noodlehead, outlandish **11** nonsensical person
  French: 7 farceur

Zapotec

language family: 5 Otomi **6** mixtec

location: 6 Mexico, Oaxaca

zapped 5 drunk **6** killed, soused, wasted, zonked **7** smashed **9** destroyed, plastered **10** inebriated **11** annihilated, intoxicated

zeal 4 fire, zest **5** ardor, gusto, verve, vigor **6** fervor, relish **7** passion **8** devotion, industry **9** animation, eagerness, intensity, vehemence **10** enthusiasm, fanaticism, fierceness, intentness **11** earnestness

zealot 3 fan, nut **4** buff **5** bigot, crank **6** pusher **7** devotee, fanatic, hustler **8** believer, champion, crackpot, go-getter, livewire, partisan **9** extremist **10** enthusiast

zealous 5 eager, rabid **6** ardent, fervid, fierce, gung ho, raging, raving **7** devoted, earnest, fanatic, fervent, intense **8** animated, vehement, vigorous **10** passionate **11** impassioned, industrious **12** enthusiastic

Zebedee

wife: 6 Salome

son: 4 John **5** James

Zeboim

destroyed with: 5 Admah, Sodom **8** Gomorrah

Zebulun

father: 5 Jacob

mother: 4 Leah

brother: 3 Dan, Gad **4** Levi **5** Asher, Judah **6** Joseph, Reuben, Simeon **8** Benjamin, Issachar, Naphtali

sister: 5 Dinah

descendant of: 10 Zebulunite

Zechariah

father: 5 Bebai, Hosah **6** Jehiel, Pashur **7** Isshiah **8** Jehoiada, Jonathan **9** Berechiah **11** Jeberechiah, Meshelemiah

grandfather: 4 Iddo

mother: 6 Merari

son: 8 Jahaziel

daughter: 6 Abijah

Zeffirelli, Franco

director of: 14 Romeo and Juliet **19** The Taming of the Shrew **20** Brother Sun Sister Moon

Zeitgeist 18 the spirit of the time

Zelos

origin: 5 Greek

personifies: 4 zeal **9** emulation

father: 11 Titan Palles

mother: 4 Styx

brother: 3 Bia **6** Cratus

sister: 4 Nike

Zemeckis, Robert

director of: 15 Back to the Future **17** Romancing the Stone

zenith 4 acme, apex, best, peak **6** apogee, climax, summit, vertex **7** maximum **8** pinnacle **11** culmination

Zenobia (Zeena)

character in: 10 Ethan Frome

author: 7 Wharton

zephyr 8 west wind **9** puff of air **10** gentle wind **11** breath of air, light breeze

Zephyrus

personifies: 8 west wind

father: 8 Astraeus

mother: 3 Eos

loved: 10 Hyacinthus

son: 6 Balius **7** Xanthus

Zeppelin, Ferdinand Graf von

nationality: 6 German

invented: 9 dirigible **21** rigid dirigible airship

famous ship: 10 Hindenberg

zero 2 no **3** nil, zip **5** aught, nadir, zilch **6** cipher, naught **7** nothing **8** goose egg **11** nonexistent, nothingness

zero hour 5 onset, start **7** liftoff **9** beginning **12** commencement

zest 3 joy, zip **4** salt, tang, zeal, zing **5** gusto, savor, spice, taste, verve **6** flavor, relish, thrill **7** delight, passion **8** appetite, piquancy, pleasure **9** eagerness, flavoring, seasoning **10** enthusiasm, excitement **12** exhilaration, satisfaction

zestful 6 active, lively **7** dynamic, vibrant **8** animated, spirited, vigorous **9** vivacious **12** invigorating

zesty 5 spicy, tangy **7** piquant

Zeus

also: 7 Cenaean **9** Atabyriam, Ithomatas **10** Anchesmius **11** Panomphaeus **12** Cithaeronian

birthplace: 5 Crete

brother: 5 Hades **8** Poseidon

corresponds to: 4 Amen, Amon, Jove **5** Ammon **6** Amen Ra, Amon Ra **7** Jupiter

daughter: 4 Hebe **6** Athene **10** Eileithyia, Persephone

epithet: 5 Areus, Arius, Sotor **6** Aqueus, Nemean, Philus **7** Alastor, Apemius, Ctesius, Lycaeus, Polieus, Stenius **8** Agoraeus, Aphesius, Apomyius, Catharius, Chthonius, Coccygius, Hecalesius, Lecheates, Mechaneus **10** Cataebates, Coryphaeus, Homagyrius, Laphystius, Meilichius **11** Eleutherius **12** Panhellenius

father: 6 Cronus

form: 5 deity

god of: 7 heavens

lover: 4 Leto **7** Demeter

mother: 4 Rhea

position: 7 supreme

sister: 4 Hera **6** Hestia **7** Demeter

son: 4 Ares **6** Apollo, Hermes

wife: 4 Hera **5** Metis

zigzag 4 awry, tack **6** angles, forked, jagged **7** chevron, crankle, crooked, notched, sinuous, stagger **8** crotched, serrated, sideling, traverse **9** bifurcate **10** circuitous, deflection

Zilpah

slave of: 4 Leah

concubine of: 5 Jacob

son: 3 Gad **5** Asher

Zimbabwe

other name: 8 Rhodesia **16** Southern Rhodesia

capital/largest city: 6 Harare **9** Salisbury

others: 5 Gwelo, Gweru **6** Kariba, KweKwe, Mutare, QueQue, Umtali **7** Gatooma, Rusambo, Selukwe, Shabani **8** Bulawayo, Zimbabwe **10** Beitbridge

monetary unit: 4 cent **6** dollar

lake: 4 Kyle **6** Kariba

mountain: 5 Vumba **6** Manica **7** Inyanga **11** Chimanimani, Matopo Hills

highest point: 9 Inyangani

river: 4 Sabi, Save **5** Lundi **6** Shashi **7** Limpopo, Umniati, Zambezi

physical feature:

falls: 8 Victoria

grassland: 4 veld

plateau: 8 Highveld **11** Mashonaland

people: 3 Ila **4** Sena **5** Asian, Bantu, Bemba, Sotho, Tongo, White **6** Indian **7** Barotse, Chinese, English, Mashoma, Mashona, Ndebele **8** Coloured, Japanese, Matabele **9** Afrikaner **10** Balokwakwa

developer: 6 Rhodes

explorer: 11 Livingstone

king: 9 Lobengula, Mzilikaze

leader: 5 Nkomo **6** Mugabe **7** Sithole **8** Muzorewa **9** Ian D Smith

language: 3 Ila **5** Bantu, Shona **7** English, Ndebele

religion: 7 animism **8** Anglican **12** Christianity, Presbyterian **13** Dutch Reformed, Roman Catholic

place:

dam: 6 Kariba

national park: 6 Hwange, Wankie **7** Matopos **9** Inyan gani **13** Victoria Falls

ruins: 5 Khami **6** Temple **8** Zimbabwe **9** Acropolis **13** Valley of Ruins

feature:

cattle pen: 5 kraal

game: 5 tsoro **7** mandani

hut: 4 kaia

kingdom: 5 Rozwi **10** Monomotapa

tree: 4 teak **6** baobab, mopani

Zimbalist, Efrem, Jr

born: 9 New York NY

father: 14 Efrem Zimbalist

mother: 9 Alma Gluck

daughter: 18 Stephanie Zimbalist

roles: 3 FBI **13** Wait Until Dark **15** By Love Possessed **16** The Chapman Report **23** Seventy-seven Sunset Strip

zinc

chemical symbol: 2 Zn

zing 3 pep, vim, zap, zip **4** dash, snap, tang, whiz, zest **5** gusto, speed, vigor, whine **6** energy, spirit **7** liven up

8 satirize, vitality **9** animation, criticize **10** enthusiasm, liveliness

zingara, zingaro 5 gypsy

Zinnemann, Fred
  director of: 5 Julia **8** High Noon, Oklahoma **9** The Search **12** The Nun's Story **13** The Sundowners **17** A Man for All Seasons (Oscar) **18** From Here to Eternity (Oscar)

Zion 6 utopia **9** city of God **11** City of David **13** ancient Israel
  hill in: 9 Jerusalem
  built on the hill: 6 Temple

zip 3 fly, nil, pep, run, vim **4** buzz, dart, dash, hiss, life, nada, rush, zero, zest **5** aught, close, drive, force, gusto, hurry, power, punch, speed, verve, vigor, whine, zilch **6** cipher, energy, impact, naught, spirit, streak **7** nothing, whistle **8** goose egg, strength, vitality, vivacity **9** animation, intensity **10** enthusiasm, exuberance, liveliness **13** effervescence

zipper
  invented by: 6 Judson

Zipporah
  father: 5 Reuel **6** Jethro
  husband: 5 Moses
  son: 7 Eliezer, Gershom

zircon
  source: 5 Burma **6** Ceylon **8** Cambodia, Sri Lanka **9** Kampuchea

zirconium
  chemical symbol: 2 Zr

zloty
  currency of: 6 Poland

zodiac 4 belt, zone **5** stars **7** circuit
  fire sign: 3 Leo **5** Aries **11** Sagittarius
  earth sign: 5 Virgo **6** Taurus **9** Capricorn
  air sign: 5 Libra **6** Gemini **8** Aquarius
  water: 6 Cancer, Pisces **7** Scorpio
  division: 4 sign **5** decan **6** trigon
  number of houses: 6 twelve
  falling between two signs: 4 cusp

Zola, Emile
  author of: 4 Nana **7** The Soil **8** Germinal **10** L'Assommoir **11** The Downfall, The Dram Shop **13** Therese Raquin **14** The Human Animal **20** The Experimental Novel

zone 4 area, belt, ward **5** tract **6** region, sector **7** quarter, section, terrain **8** district, locality, location, precinct **9** territory

zonked 5 drunk **6** soused, wasted, zapped **7** smashed **9** plastered **10** inebriated **11** intoxicated

zoo 8 vivarium **9** menagerie

zoom 3 fly, zip **4** buzz, race, rise, soar **5** climb, flash, shoot, speed **6** ascend, rocket, streak **7** advance, take off **9** skyrocket

zoophobia
  fear of: 7 animals

Zophar
  friend: 3 Job **5** Elihu **6** Bildad **7** Eliphaz

Zorba the Greek
  director: 17 Michael Cacoyannis
  based on the story by: 11 Kazantzakis
  cast: 9 Alan Bates **11** Irene Pappas, Lila Kedrova **12** Anthony Quinn
  score: 16 Mikis Theodorakis
  Oscar for: 17 supporting actress (Kedrova)

zori 14 Japanese sandal

zucchini 5 gourd **6** squash **12** summer squash

Zuckerman Unbound
  author: 10 Philip Roth

Zurich
  festival: 12 Sechselanten
  landmark: 8 Rietberg **9** Kunsthaus **15** CG Jung Institute **17** Centre Le Corbusier, Fraumunster Kirche **21** Grossmunster Cathedral
  religious figure: 7 Zwingli **9** Bullinger
  river: 6 Limmat
  Roman name: 7 Turicum

Zweig, Arnold
  author of: 7 Claudia **24** The Case of Sergeant Grischa